修文县志

（1978—2010）

修文县地方志编纂委员会　编纂

（上 卷）

方志出版社
Publishing House of Local Records

图书在版编目(CIP)数据

修文县志.1978—2010 / 修文县地方志编纂委员会编. —北京：方志出版社，2018. 9

ISBN 978－7－5144－3298－5

Ⅰ. ①修… Ⅱ. ①修… Ⅲ. ①修文县－地方志－1978－2010 Ⅳ. ①K297. 34

中国版本图书馆CIP数据核字(2018)第224455号

修文县志(1978-2010)

编　　者：修文县地方志编纂委员会

责任编辑：黄　彦

出 版 人：冀祥德

出 版 者：方志出版社

地址　北京市朝阳区潘家园东里9号(国家方志馆4层)

邮编　100021

网址　http://www.fzph.org

发　　行：方志出版社发行中心

电话　(010) 67110500

经　　销：各地新华书店

印　　刷：深圳市新联美术印刷有限公司

开　　本：889×1194　　1/16

印　　张：100

字　　数：2748千字

版　　次：2018年9月第1版　　2018年9月第1次印刷

印　　数：0001—4000册

ISBN　978－7－5144－3298－5　　定价：1288.00元

修文县地方志编纂委员会

第一届（2003 年 10 月至 2006 年 4 月）

主任委员　魏明禄

副主任委员　石　洪　李玉轩　殷建中　王成林　王世利

委　　员　史瑞林　肖　飞　夏芝奎　李祖炎　陈德芳　韩虞梅　韩虞军　李继彬　陈太明　董　浩　范光森　谌　勇　唐金文　葛正敏

顾　　问　陈福桐　史继忠　罗再麟　张桂江　王亚平　何静梧　郑荣晴

第二届（2006 年 4 月至 2008 年 8 月）

主任委员　魏明禄

副主任委员　石　洪　李玉轩　殷建中　王成林　王世利

委　　员　庹朝金　刘桂均　邓龙江　夏芝奎　李祖炎　陈德芳　胡春贵　韩虞梅　李继彬　朱永彬　范光森　谌　勇　王帮椿　席毅龙

顾　　问　陈福桐　史继忠　罗再麟　张桂江　王亚平　何静梧　郑荣晴

第五届（2017 年 5 月至 2018 年 10 月）

《修文县志》（1978—2010）编辑部

主　　编　李祖炎

副 主 编　夏芝奎　胡光胤

初期编辑　李祖炎　夏芝奎　胡光胤　李元明　杨德俊　古学明　李成举　贾　文　王作伦　陈新国　蒋科文　周世经　李朝鼎　朱　屏　陈君生　林明礼　傅启刚　李明祥　刘子弘　汤远声　贾长远　罗国通　路登荣　刘耀辉　陈家贵

成书编辑　李祖炎　夏芝奎　胡光胤　陈新国　周世经　李朝鼎　罗国通　陈家贵　李成举　李召锋　罗四锡

封面装潢及电子书签设计　胡光胤

图片设计　夏芝奎　王江江

图片提供　县属各单位部门

特邀摄影　周尚明　余　岚

航模摄影　王江江

编　　排　夏芝奎　胡光胤　王江江

校　　对　李祖炎　夏芝奎　胡光胤　陈新国　周世经　李朝鼎　罗国通　陈家贵　李成举　李召锋　罗四锡

总 编 务　胡光胤

编　　务　金志军　路登荣　杨德俊　余　漫　古学明　贾　文　陈春兰　李成举　李召锋　姚华芳　罗四锡　王江江　徐彩云

审　稿

初　审	蒋志伦	佘　龙	王成林	陈雄标	何发兵
	娄　果	文清武	王　劼	胡祥碧	李继彬
	杨　杏	孙庆英	陈国邦	黄玉勤	江之浩
	罗　林	胡晓明			
复　审	邓忠元	陈起荣	韦俊帆	曾一凇	
终　审	归　然	梁贵钢	范同寿	周声浩	钟　莉
	陆　震	车秀琴			
专家审稿	张英聘	史继忠	魏明禄	肖先志	韩章训
	伍启林	龚力新	聂步兴	王学斌	李祖运
	王海光				
县情审查	谭荣先	林志云	王清义	李小龙	

审图号：图黔 A（2018）01 号　　二〇一八年八月

修文县政区图

比例尺 1:205 000

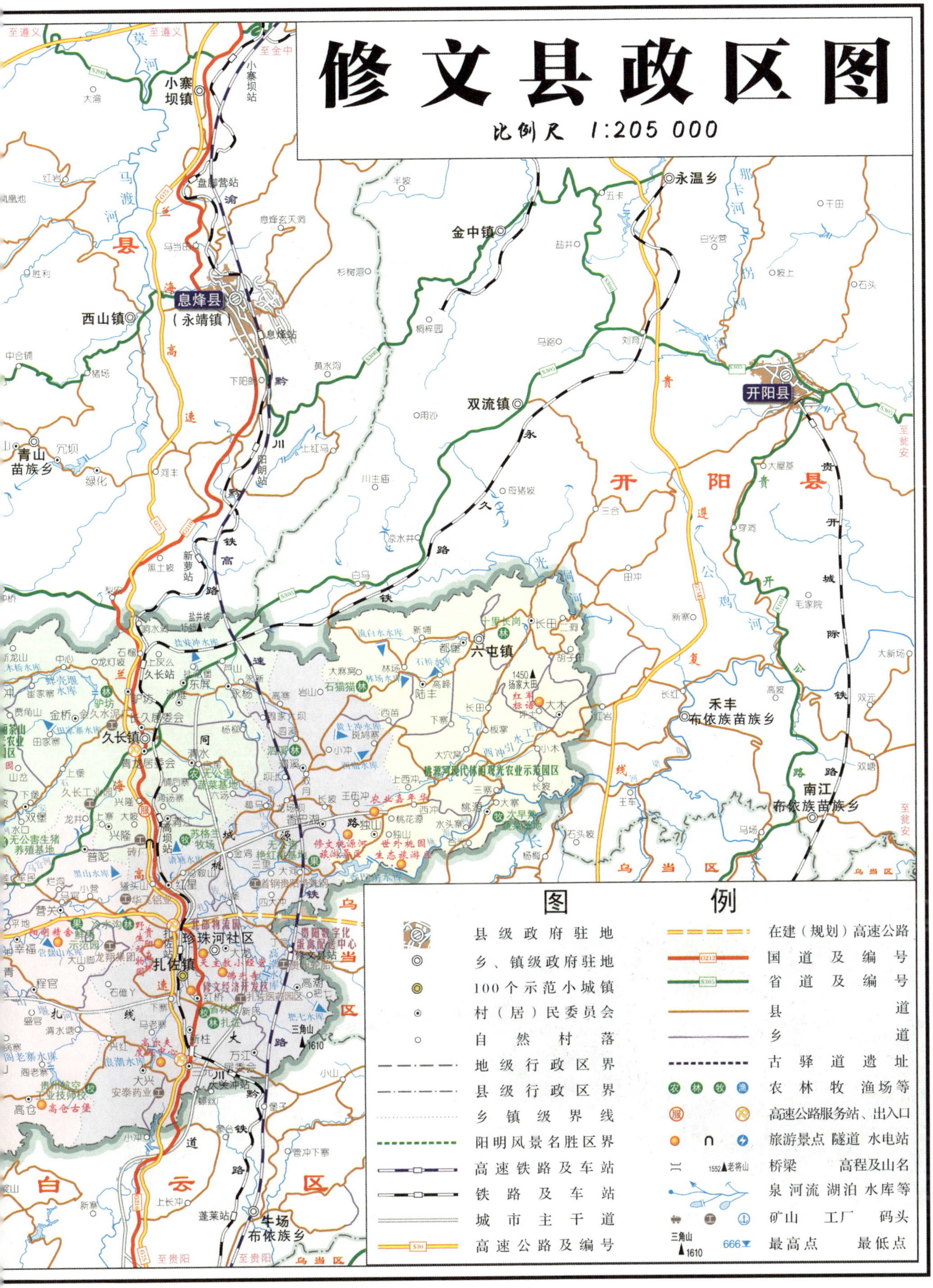

王学圣地

修文古名“龙场”，明代著名哲学家、教育家王阳明于此悟道讲学，创立“知行合一”的心学体系。

阳明心学发源于此，远播海内外，龙场被誉为“王学圣地”。

王阳明研读《易经》处—玩易窝

阳明洞。该洞原系龙岗山东洞，是王阳明草创龙冈书院授徒讲学之处

王文成公祠

君子亭

王阳明与龙冈书院弟子陈宗鲁、汤伯元、叶子苍群雕青铜铸像（1999年塑造）

王阳明纪念馆(1999年10月落成)

1999 年中国·贵阳（修文）第一届国际阳明文化节

2002 年中国·贵阳（修文）第二届国际阳明文化节

2005 年中国·贵阳（修文）第三届国际阳明文化节

2009 年中国·贵阳（修文）第四届国际阳明文化节

秀美修文

修文地处黔中，系山多地少的喀斯特地貌，天造地设形成若干奇特的洞穴和峭壁，又有长江流域乌江水系的多条河流流经境内与群山紧紧相连，构成的自然景观琳琅满目。改革开放后山门大开，迎来众多商家合力打造，使景观美不胜收。“装点此关山，今朝更好看”，“秀美修文”的誉称遍及神州大地。

六广河峡谷风光

桃源河—银丝挂碧玉

苏格兰牧场

森林野生动物园

岩鹰湖

六广河净瓶峰

桃源河漂流

高尔夫度假中心球场

1998 年的县城

2010 年的县城

1980 年的县城

1996 年的县城

县城新貌

阳明大道

东片区夜景

文城逸都

生态家园

河滨花园一景

1960 年落成的县委办公楼，2010 年仍在此办公

1960 年落成的县政府办公楼，2010 年仍在此办公

1988 年落成的县人大、县政协办公楼，2010 年仍在此办公

2003年12月23日上午，修文县第二轮修志启动仪式在县城文广楼会议室举行。次日起对全县各乡（镇）、各部门修志人员进行为期3天的修志业务培训。图为分管修志工作的县委副书记王成林（前排右七）与授课老师、参训学员合影

2017年2月14日，《修文县志》（1978—2010）志稿终审会议在县政府会议中心召开，志稿通过终审。图为参加终审人员（前排左起）陆震、钟莉、梁贵钢、史继忠、归然、邓忠元、范同寿、周声浩、陈起荣（三排左三）、车秀琴（三排右二）和县分管领导（二排左四起）王劼、文清武、李继彬、杨杏与县志正副主编和全体成书编辑、编务人员合影

序　一

修文，乃位居黔中名扬海内外的文化之乡。从元代至元年间开始行政建置至今已经走过700多年起伏跌宕的历程。其间，得益于明代思想家、教育家王阳明谪居龙场悟道讲学赋予的深厚文化底蕴和具有山水相依相谐生态资源绝佳的自然环境，从而取得了“王学圣地，秀美修文”的地域名片。1949年11月修文解放，旋即建立中共修文县委作为坚强的政治领导，同时建立修文县人民政府带领全县人民有效地实施民主建设和进行经济建设、文化建设，使社会面貌发生了深刻的变化。进入社会主义建设新时期，历届县委、县政府团结一致，在改革开放总方针的指引下，奋发图强，锐意进取，把全县的政治、经济、文化和社会建设推进到最为生动、最为辉煌的境地，跻身全省经济强县之列，成为贵州高原一颗熠熠生辉的明珠。这些历史信息使我们感到先辈们创业付出的艰辛，其经验教训着实弥足珍贵。我们当责无旁贷地采取编纂志书的方法将数百年修文的沧桑巨变载进史册，以备后来者育人和资政。

从20世纪80年代开始，县委、县政府就将《修文县志》的编修纳入议事日程，构建起党委领导、政府主持、志办实施、社会参与和专家编纂的修志格局，落实领导、机构、队伍和经费“四到位”，为志书的编纂营造出良好的工作环境和社会氛围。经过13载的努力，完成了论述707年人民群众改造社会、征服自然的斗争史实的通志。接着马不停蹄地转向编纂全面反映改革开放历史时期的续志。又耗时15年经过全体编辑呕心沥血，辛勤耕耘，三改篇目，七修其稿，终于做成这部时代特色鲜明、地方特点凸显和可读、可信、可用的权威官书。与此同时，还实现了全县乡（镇）志书出版全覆盖，又付梓问世30部部门志、校志和村志。这是社会各界通力合作的结果，也是全县人民智慧的结晶。

修志问道，以启未来。如若这部续修的《修文县志》论述的改革开放所走之道能使读者深刻地体味到其间的深邃内涵，能够增强广大干部和群众继续开拓进取的信心和力量，我们当感欣慰。

编修地方志是一项只有起点、没有终点的文化建设工程，是存史、育人和资政的伟大事业，我们将一如既往地把修志工作抓细、抓好和抓扎实，忠实地记述好具有中国特色的社会主义事业的新篇章，让改革开放的雄壮史诗耀眼后世，激励前行。

中共修文县委书记 薛玉伦

修文县人民政府县长 余稀

二〇一七年二月十八日

序　二

《修文县志》（1978—2010）（以下简称《修志》）经过15年的努力终于成书。《修志》以翔实的资料记述了修文县改革开放33年的发展变化。这33年是修文历史上“伟大的一瞬”，在政治、经济、文化、社会各方面取得的成就，超过了以往的几十年、几百年、几千年，看了《综述》、《全县国民经济和社会发展主要数据》和图片，令人无比欣喜。这是个历史性变革的时代，一日千里，瞬息万变，若不把变革的历史进程如实地记录下来，后人很难深刻认识改革开放的伟大意义。

这部志书以改革开放为主线贯穿各个方面。“改革开放”绝不是一句空洞的政治术语，而是这一时期历史变革的基本动因，是历史发展的伟大转折，从“以阶级斗争为纲”转向“以经济建设为中心”。在政治建设中，首先写政治体制改革，并从民主政治建设、行政管理体制改革、机构改革、司法制度改革、干部人事制度改革5个方面展开记述，反映了新时期的政治面貌。经过拨乱反正，进一步确立了中国共产党的领导地位，恢复被“文化大革命”中断的人民代表大会制度，设立了“多党合作，民主协商”的政协，建立建全了社会主义法治，为改革开放提供了基本保障。人民公社束缚了生产力的发展，经济建设首先从农村经济体制改革开始，《修志》围绕这一主题，从土地经营制度改革、农产品流通体制改革、税费改革及农业经济结构变革几方面展开记述，全面、真实地反映了这一时期农业的发展变化。拿商业来说，在计划经济时期，条块分割，商业、农村供销合作社、粮食、物资自成一体，统购统销，计划供应，经济体制改革后，市场放开，商业繁荣，设体制改革，市场、行业经营、行业服务等节十分恰当。工业设体制改革、行业结构、工业产业园区建设、企业管理4节，恰如其份地反映了新时期工业的发展变化。总之，没有改革开放，就没有新的发展变化，把改革开放具体到各个方面，是《修志》的最大特色。

方志体例“因事发凡”，不可能一成不变，要根据时代发展设置篇、章、节、目。《修志》将全书分为地理篇、政治建设篇、经济建设篇、文化建设篇、社会建设篇及人物六个部分，是方志体例的一大创新，充分表现了“以经济建设为中心”的时代特点。“建设”是这一时期的主题，用“建设”立篇有高度的概括性，并附合“横分门类，纵写历史”的修志传统。说志书标题不能用动词只是一家之言，事实上在志书中已经使用“城乡建设”、“生态建设”、“水利建设”、“资源开发”、“旅游发展” 之类的标题，用“建设”做篇名是顺理成章的事。“建设”恰好是事物发展的动态表现，社会在进步，自然也在变化，没有凝固不变的东西。

《修志》突出了地方特色，浓墨重彩地写“阳明文化”，用“一产稳县，二产强县，三产活县”提出修文县委、县政府的战略决策，用企业简介突出工业发展状况，以“下硐猕猴桃”、“王官延晚番茄”、“折溪金秋梨”、“六屯半夏”等种植业基地反映修文县的农业特色，以“六桶林下养鸡”、“石安生猪养殖”、“好1多乳品”、“扎佐兰地蛋鸡”等反映养殖业的新成就。在志书中用了许多“专记”，把一些典型而又不便在正文中展开的事物记入“专记”，使读者了解事情的真相和细节，既保存了珍贵史料又使正文简明扼要。

《修志》是修文县改革开放33年的真实记录，体例多有创新，对存史、育人、资政有重要意义，是一部成功的志书。

史继忠

（本序作者系贵州省文史研究馆原副馆长、贵州省志原副总纂）

二〇一七年三月十六日

凡　例

一、指导思想

本志以马克思列宁主义、毛泽东思想、邓小平理论、“三个代表”重要思想、科学发展观、习近平新时代中国特色社会主义思想为指导，坚持辩证唯物主义和历史唯物主义的立场、观点和方法，实事求是地记述修文县改革开放和政治、经济、文化、社会建设的巨大成就和基本经验，为社会主义现代化建设服务。

二、内容

全书以中共十一届三中全会以来各项方针政策的实施为主线，突出记述以改革助推经济社会发展的重大的历史性突破，融时代性、地方性为一体。

三、时限

上限起于1978年，下限止于2010年。

四、体式

采用章节与条目结合，章节记述史实的发展概貌，视需要置条目命名“专记”作点的深入，使面和点有机契合，相得益彰。

全志以志体为主，兼用述、记、传、图、表、录和索引。为增强直观效应，根据文字记述所需配以统计图和照片，体现图文并茂。

五、篇目

使用大篇结构。全书除总述、大事记、经济社会发展数据和附录不列入篇的序列外，设地理篇、政治建设篇、经济建设篇、文化建设篇、社会建设篇和人物6篇分别记述各自的发展情况。篇下置39章、180节、133个专记和随文图、照1088幅。

六、文体

综述以叙为主，叙议结合。其余为记叙文体，基本是据事记述，寓理于事。若史实清楚且有定论者。

除引文外，一律使用语体文记述。

目录和综述之后配以英语译文。

七、资料

数据资料主要使用县统计局公布的法定统计数据，统计局缺者则用有关部门提供的数据。

史实资料一是在县档案馆和县直部门、乡（镇）档案室所藏档案和志书中摘抄；二是在电子档案提取；三是向知情人索取。所用资料一般不注明出处。

八、数字

具有科学计量和统计意义的数值一律使用阿拉伯数字。

除表列数据外，文字记述使用整数，遇小数即用四舍五入法处理。数据除人口外，上5至8位的以“万”为单位，上9位及其以上的以“亿”为单位。反映比例、速度、结构的数据取原始数据计算，小数点后最多只取两位，不用无意义的“0”补位。

分数、百分数、千分数使用阿拉伯数字。

九、计量

除耕地用亩、里程用公里、重量用公斤或吨外，其余均用中华人民共和国法定计量单位。上1000公斤及其以上的计量单位用“吨”。

十、纪年

清代及其以前的纪年和夏历使用汉字，民国纪年、公元纪年、世纪年代和公历使用阿拉伯数字。公元纪年省写“公元”2字，括注内省写“公元”和“年”字。

十一、地名

一般使用现行标准地名。使用原地名之处，第一次出现时注以今名。

十二、注释

主要用括注，括注不了的用页末注。专用名词简称在首次出现时加注，其后用简称。

十三、称谓

人物直书其名，不加褒贬之词。官阶、职务置于姓名之前。

十四、入志作品

文学、书法、美术、摄影、篆刻、音乐一为县籍人的创作，一为外籍人以修文的事或人作题材的撰著。

十五、人物

立传者主要是贡献突出和社会影响大的已故人物。有重大贡献的在世人物用“简介”或在有关篇章以事系人方法加以记述。副县级及其以上的干部、中高级职称的科技工作者和获地市级及其以上表彰的劳动模范、先进工作者分别以一览表或名录加以记载。立传人物和简介人物分别按卒年先后和生年先后次序排列。

对危害社会治安的犯罪分子，择其个别首恶者记入，排列在人物传记之末，并以空行标志正面人物与反面人物的区别。

十六、附录

附载内容一是时限内产生的要文和佐证史实的材料；二是2011至2017年发生的大事、要事和县委、县人大、县政府、县政协领导班子成员、副县级及其以上干部名录、中高级职称的科技工作者；三是首轮新县志勘误。

十七、索引

汉字条目按首字笔画从少到多和起笔笔形横、竖、撇、点、折排列，阿拉伯数字按从小到大顺序排列。目录未载条目可在索引中查找。

目　　录

地　理　篇

政治建设篇

经济建设篇

文化建设篇

社会建设篇

人 物

附　　录

综　　述

修文县位于贵州省中部，享有“王学圣地，秀美修文”的美誉。县境东倚开阳，南界白云，西望黔西，北连息烽，东南与乌当相连，西南与清镇接壤，西北与金沙毗邻，为山多平地少的地貌特征和东高西低的地势走向。山川秀丽，气候温和，土质良好，资源丰富，交通畅达，人民勤劳。是省城贵阳的北大门，为入渝进川的必经之道，又是贵阳果蔬蛋禽的主产区和农副土特产的集散地。县城龙场镇是全县政治、经济、文化中心，距贵阳市行政中心金阳27公里。1996年实施市管县体制，修文划归贵阳市管辖。2010年，全县辖4镇6乡217个行政村和10个社区居民委员会，户籍人口30.59万人，土地面积1075.7平方公里。

从1978年中国跨入改革开放和社会主义现代化建设新时期，到2010年完成国民经济和社会发展“十一五”计划，已经历33个年头。此间，中共修文县委和县人民政府带领全县各族人民全面拨乱反正，停止使用“以阶级斗争为纲”的口号，实现以经济建设为中心的工作重点转移，开拓进取，艰苦奋斗，迎来了政治安定、经济发展、文化繁荣、社会稳定、人民生活蒸蒸日上的喜人局面，各项建设事业取得令人瞩目的成就。

改革开放以来，县委、县政府坚持和完善社会主义民主政治，建设社会主义政治文明，积极推进政治体制改革。从1980年起，县委遵照党中央统一部署，按照实事求是、有错必纠的原则，从平反“文化大革命”中的冤假错案入手，全面地落实党的干部政策，解决历史上的遗留问题。经过3年工作，使60名蒙受冤屈的干部重新走上工作岗位及其受株连的亲属得以解脱，积极投身于社会主义现代化建设事业。

1981年，根据《中华人民共和国地方各级人民代表大会和地方各级人民政府组织法》规定，恢复了中断长达15年的人民代表大会制度，在县人大七届一次会议上选举产生县人民代表大会的常设机构常务委员会和县人民政府、县人民法院、县人民检察院的领导人，并复建县人民政府取代县革命委员会。1983年，贯彻落实中国共产党与各民主党派和无党派人士“长期共存，互相监督”“肝胆相照，荣辱与共”的方针，建立政治协商会议修文县委员会。1984年，按照《中华人民共和国宪法》规定，在全县32乡（镇）建立乡（镇）人民政府，正式行使政府管理职能。建立乡（镇）人民政府的同时，按照《中华人民共和国村民委员会组织法》和《中华人民共和国居民委员会组织法》，在县辖所有行政村和街道分别建立村民委员会和居民委员会取代原建的生产大队革命委员会和街道革命委员会，村委会和居委会下建村民小组和居民小组，实行城乡居民自我教育、自我管理、自我服务、自我监督。

为了加强法治建设，从健全政法机构切入，1978年恢复重建县人民检察院，1980年建立县司法局，局设法律顾问处，后改为律师事务所，运用法律手段维护公共利益和公民的合法权益。为保障经济建设顺利进行和人民生命财产安全，从1983年开始，在全县范围内开展严厉打击危害社会治安的刑事犯罪分子的斗争，惩治和震慑了违法犯罪分子，使社会治安得到根本好转。为保持社会长治久安，在县委、县政府领导下，组织公安、检察、法院、司法行政部门和群众团体以及县直相关部门参加，普遍建立社会治安综合治理组织，结合村委会和居委会的组织建设，整顿全县治安保卫委员会，依靠社会力量，加强治安管理和安全防范工作，保持了社会稳定。

1985年，县委遵照《中共中央关于整党的决定》部署，在全县419个党组织和5311名党员中进行整党，解决党内思想、作风和组织不纯的问题。通过整党，多数党员受到一次深刻的党性教育，93.6%的党员经过评议、审查予以登记。2000年，县委根据中共中央《关于在县级以上党政领导班子、领导干部中深入开展以“讲学习、讲政治、讲正气”为主要内容的党风教育的意见》，在县委、人大、政府、政协、纪检、法院、检察院、公安局的领导班子和领导干部中，在县委组织部、宣传部的班子成员中开展“三讲”教育活动。教育活动采取学习提高、自我剖析、开展批评、认真整改的方法进行。通过教育，使52名领导干部经受一次党内民主生活的锻炼，自己所领导的工作得到明显改进。2001年，县委遵照中共中央关于在农村开展“三个代表”（中国共产党始终代表中国先进生产力的发展要求、代表中国先进文化的前进方向、代表中国最广大人民的根本利益）重要思想学习教育活动的部署，用480天时间在全县10乡（镇）、90个县直部门和229个村（居）委会的4682名干部中分3批开展学教活动。学教活动分为学习培训、对照检查、整改提高3个阶段进行。通过学教活动，广大基层干部的思想作风和工作作风明显改进，从而推动农村经济的发展和农民生活的改善，收到了“干部受教育，农民得实惠”的效果。2005年，县委遵照中共中央《关于在全党开展的实践“三个代表”重要思想为主要内容的保持共产党员先进性教育活动的意见》，用545天时间在全县467个党组织和8225名党员中分3批开展保持共产党员先进性教育活动。“保先”活动分成学习培训、分析评议、整改提高3个阶段进行。通过“保先”活动，在党的先进性建设和执政能力建设方面取得明显成效，得到社会各界的好评。

修文的经济建设，在改革开放总方针的指引下，县委、县政府制定“一产稳县，二产强县，三产活县”的战略决策，带领干部群众攻坚克难，大干快上，使全县经济面貌发生巨大变化。以2010年的实绩与1978年相比，地区生产总值从3580万元增至46.18亿元，按1990年不变价计算，年均递增11.44%，人均量从149元增至1.51万元，增长100.3倍；财政总收入从188.9万元增至5.44亿元，年均递增19.36%，人均量从7.8元增至1777.8元，增长226.9倍。巨大变化还体现在地区生产总值的构成上，1980年第一产业、第二产业、第三产业的构成为45.04：34.3：20.66，到2010年改变为17.13：37.05：45.82。经贵州省建设经济强县领导小组考核，于2008年纳入全省经济强县行列。

农业发展从20世纪80年代起，以农村经济体制改革为抓手，普遍实行家庭联产承包责任制，极大地调动农民的生产积极性，在责任地里精耕细作，依靠科技兴农，使粮食产量1983年突破5万吨大关，人均268公斤，解决了指望多年未曾解决的吃饭问题。进入90年代，主要是组织农村富余劳动力向非农业领域转移，并实行土地承包经营权流转，围绕市场导向，以“果、菜、畜、药”为支柱，着力调整产业结构，实行规模经营。按照“一乡一品，一村一业”的规划，采取“公司+协会+农户”的运作方式，打造出“下硐猕猴桃”“折溪金秋梨”“王官延晚番茄”“大堡萝卜”“大河艳红桃”“郭田酥李”“桃源柑橘”“久长青菜”“六屯半夏”等种植基地和“六桶林下养鸡”“石安生猪育肥”“小箐优良牛肉”“清水‘好1多’乳品”“扎佐兰地蛋鸡”等养殖基地。以基地成龙头，带动众多农民投入果蔬种植和禽畜养殖，在资金筹措、劳力务工、技术指导、产品经销等方面均给予支持和帮助，促使家家从

事种和养，户户产品进市场。基地拉长了产业链，农民跨上了拾金路，一改若干年只靠种粮糊口的单一产业格局为今天多业并举的商品生产格局。被誉为“维C王中王”的猕猴桃，从试种百亩发展到规范化种植3.7万亩，果农从50多户增为3000余户。修文猕猴桃因其品质好，有批量、竞成为享誉省内外的一张名片。2010年，全县农业总产值达到13.14亿元，比1978年的2111万元增长61.24倍；农民人均纯收入在1978年的基础增长35.54倍。基地星罗棋布，产量不断攀升，产品琳琅满目。

工业生产在80年代初期，实行国营、集体、个体一起上，鼓励县办工业、社队工业、私营工业与中央和省驻县工业齐肩并进，共同发展。至1982年，全县工业总产值达4481万元，比1978年的2614万元增长71.42%。1984年，县委、县政府提出大办乡镇工业，实行乡（镇）办、村办、乡（镇）村联办、联户办、户办“五个轮子一起转”，使乡镇工业在县域工业经济中占了“半壁河山”。至1990年，全县乡镇工业企业发展到1593家，从业者达1.11万人，企业总收入6206万元，分别比1978年的223家、2668人和309万元增长6.14倍、3.16倍和19.08倍。乡镇工业产值占全县工业总产值的66.92%。1991年，启动对县属国营工业企业的改革，实施政企分开和党委领导下的厂长负责制，分离企业的资产权和经营权，变国营企业为国有企业，将利润分成上交改为税费缴纳，实行工人劳动与工资报酬挂钩，端掉“企业吃国家大锅饭，工人吃企业大锅饭”的“铁饭碗”；与此同时，随着民营经济的发展，以农村集体组织和农民投资为主的乡镇工业也逐步转为民营企业。到2000年，国营工业改制收官，民营工业迅猛发展，全县工业总产值翻过10亿元大关，其中民营工业独占鳌头。2001年，县委、县政府下决心淘汰能耗高、污染大的“傻、大、黑、粗”企业，内引外联招商引资，以“企业低门槛入驻，地款用税收补齐”的“安泰模式”陆续引进15家医药企业，建起1座现代化的修文医药产业园区，被称为“修文经济的引擎”。继后，按照贵州省政府构建贵阳至遵义产业带的规划，沿着贵（阳）遵（义）、贵（阳）毕（节）高等级公路修文段发力建设“一区三园”（修文工业园区，龙场工业园、扎佐工业园、久长工业园）和“十里工业走廊”（龙场镇程官至扎佐镇三元），以“布局集中、产业集聚、资源集约、配套完善”的综合优势和“言行一致，开明开放”的修文精神，引进首钢·贵阳特殊钢厂、贵州轮胎厂、金久水泥厂、华飞氧化铝厂和中（美）陶石油支撑剂公司、贵阳天成热陶瓷有限公司、贵州天龙摩擦材料有限公司、贵州龙翔能源集团有限公司凸轮轴厂、贵州高新盛远玻璃钢锚杆有限公司、贵州怡丰日化公司、贵州好一多乳业有限公司、贵州贵酒公司等51家耗能低、排污好、效益增的现代化企业落户园区，形成以医药、食品、新材料、新建材、精密铸件、机械加工等行业构成的新型工业循环经济区。到2010年，全县工业总产值达56.09亿元，比1978年的2614万元增长213.58倍，年均递增18.27%，工业增加值在全县生产总值中占27.84%。工业生产从此进入黄金时期，走上以高新外向型为支撑的发展之路。

旅游业是新时期修文的新兴产业。1984年，县委、县政府提出“旅游搭台，经济唱戏”的发展思路，启动开发坐落在县境北端藏有13个洞口、66个洞厅和千姿百态自然景观的地下溶洞多缤洞和贵州高原喀斯特绿色石林的代表大石石林，后因资金不济和交通制约而搁浅。1996年，抓住贵遵和贵毕高等级公路修建取道县境的契机，重整旗鼓，借鸡生蛋，以招商引资的举措聚力开发旅游。山门打开，香港英皇有限公司和广东揭阳金华实业有限公司捷足先登，踩点在贵遵、贵毕高等级公路交汇处的扎佐浪潮湖边，占地3015亩，建起国内唯一的高原森林球场和全国最凉爽的康体休闲避暑胜地——贵阳高尔夫度假中心。该中心搭起修文与外界经济、文化交流的桥梁，每年有数以万计的海内外宾朋到此挥杆绿茵，以球会友。继高尔夫度假中心落户后，各地客商接踵而至：贵州公路工程建设总公司踩点六广河开发中国西部最典型的喀斯特地貌七峡景观；云南民营企业家张彦军看好扎佐林场荆棘丛生的千亩散林地，建起

国内唯一的高原森林型的野生动物园，并获得国家旅游局批准为AAAA级景区；重庆民营企业家张元亮发现藏在深闺的桃源河，创建出中国首家航程9.5公里的魔幻漂流；贵阳市人民防空战备办公室选择在蚌壳堰湖岸的半岛上建起“平战结合人口疏散基地”珍珠岛避暑中心；海南投资商冷静看准坐落在久长镇清江村的千亩草原，营造出独具异国风情的苏格兰牧场；贵州黔中绿色石林生态旅游开发有限公司选择贵州高原石林的拔萃者“大石石林”，按照国家AAAA级旅游景区标准进行开发……在引资开发自然景点的同时重点打造人文景观，将明代哲学家、教育家王阳明谪居龙场悟道的中国第一哲理山洞阳明洞拓展建成文化主题公园，将王阳明栖身研读《易经》的玩易窝、亲自掩埋并撰《瘗旅文》哀悼过境吏目及其子仆的三人坟和游览吟诗赞叹的天生桥、六广河畔等遗迹予以修复保护，供海内外游人拜谒览胜和文化交流。此外，还建起月月有花香、季季有果品的全国农业旅游示范点谷堡花果之乡和8个乡村旅游点、7个万亩生态农业观光园，形成一个以康体休闲旅游、文化旅游和生态旅游为支撑的旅游体系，使修文成为“爽爽贵阳”的后花园和人们心向往的地方。2010年，全县接待游客388.6万人次，旅游收入达19.95亿元。

旅游业的兴起为商业贸易、交通运输、邮电通信拓展了市场，为农产品外销带来商机。随着高尔夫度假中心落成开业，贵阳高尔夫旅行社首家开业，实现了旅行社零的突破。接着，中国旅行社、海外旅行社和原野旅行社在县城设立办事处，百事通旅行社和宝中旅行社设立营业点，多彩旅行社设立修文分社，分别接待旅游团体和为县内游客代办出境通行证和出国护照。矗立在县城中心的腾晖酒店和建珍珠岛避暑中心的三星级宾馆，倚景点而建的黔龙酒家、春华酒家、龙场驿食府、御品轩酒楼、一合山庄、潮水山庄、扎佐“快活林”、桃源食府、六广河畔竹楼宾馆，以及分布在各地的70多个“农家乐”接待点，都以集吃、住、玩为一体的经营模式热情地接待中外嘉宾和旅游者。集铁路、公路、水路为一体构建的交通运输网络已经形成。川黔铁路过境列车改内燃机车为电力机车，大大地缩短了时空距离和减轻碳气排放。东抵开阳、南进贵阳、西达昆明、北至重庆的连线高等级公路和南来北往的210国道皆为柏油路面。自六广河码头至乌江渡电站74公里的航道全程开通。县至乡（镇）的公路均是渣油浇灌，至行政村实现“村村通”。已推出以文化、科普、康乐休闲、生态观光、特色饮食为主题的一日、二日、三日游的10条旅游线路，可供游人畅达心向往的景区、景点。坐落在县城小桥河边取名“新都口岸”的二级汽车客运站，开设线路36条，拥有客车150辆，日发车350班次，日均发送旅客5000人次。建在乡（镇）的扎佐三级客车站和久长、六广、六桶、乌栗、洒坪、小箐车站都承担着派车载客安全到达目的地的重任。采用预应力钢混桁式组合建成一孔跨百米的六广河大桥，在险峻的山岭中凸显雄姿，结束了千百年被天堑隔断修文、黔西两县交通的历史，揭开了两地物资交流和发展经济的新篇章。建于县城中心的私营经济一条街落成，与先建的人民路并列，逢中穿过翠屏大道，构成一个繁荣的商业区。与此同时，扎佐、久长、六广、六桶、谷堡、小箐、洒坪、六屯、大石等地农贸市场相继建成。继后，具有卸载、转运、发送功能的现代化物流园落地贵阳北端卫星城扎佐，创建起北部物资集散旱码头，更加合理地布局全县的商业网络。全县经营生产和销售的商户达4500多家，其中不乏四川、湖南、湖北、浙江等地外商入境经销。个体店铺、农贸综合市场、农家店、超级市场、商品展销……比比皆是，商品美不胜收，应有尽有。配送中心、电子商务也跻入商品大流通领域，金融市场、劳务市场、中介市场、房地产市场相继出现，邮政快递、通信、互联网络陆续应市，形成了完善的市场体系，使生产、生活供给更加优裕。更令人惊讶的是每年数十万吨产量迭出的金秋梨进入贵阳、延晚番茄进入广州，猕猴桃进入北京、上海、南宁、深圳、长春、哈尔滨……产品上市，市民青睐，供不应求。2010年，包括旅游、商贸、交通

运输、邮政通信在内的经营总收入达42.66亿元，比1997年的1.79亿元增长22.8倍。

在“科教兴县”的战略思想指导下，县委、县政府把教育置于优先发展的地位，着力进行教育体制改革，健全学校基础设施，改善办学条件，加强对学校的领导，积极推进教育普及，建立起学前教育、义务教育、普高教育、职业教育、成人教育一体化的教育体系，形成学校、家庭、社会“三结合”的教育格局。通过国家检查验收实现了“两基”（基本普及九年义务教育，基本扫除青壮年文盲）目标，各级学校为上一级学校不断输送数以万计的合格新生和为各项建设事业培养了众多德才兼备的专业人才，涌现出一批“坚守三尺讲台，辛勤育人成才”的教育工作者。2010年，全县有幼儿园13所，入园幼儿4082人，是1978年的20.4倍；有小学52所，学生1.83万人，入学率达99.63%；有初级中学19所，在校学生1.39万人，入学率为106.9%；有高级中学5所，在校学生4447人，比1978年增长1.64倍；有特殊教育学校1所，在校“三残”（盲目、聋哑、弱智）儿童125人，入学率达90.79%；有职业教育培训中心1所，在册学生105人。全县公办教职工2422人，比1978年增加1.73倍。进入贵阳市“五好学校”行列的修文中学，2010年814名高中毕业生高考应试，上线一本院校70名，二本院校239名，高考教学质量“入出口”评估总分全市排名第二，经贵州省教育厅评估验收入围省级示范性高中。已有校龄17年并颇具规模的民办景阳中学，创办至今已为大中专学校输送新生2000多名。

与教育联动发展的文化事业通过体制改革，实行政事分开和政企分开，打破了由国家垄断运营的格局，书店、网吧、茶室、棋牌、台球、歌舞厅、电子游戏室、音像制品销售店等文化场所破茧而出，个体经营户达52家，从业者131人，构成了新的文化市场，促进了文化事业的发展繁荣。1999年和2008年，广播和电视分别实现“村村通”。以“四德”（社会公德、职业道德、家庭美德、个人品德）教育为主要内容的精神文明创建活动在全县广泛开展，突出了活动的内涵，使人们的思想得到净化，涌现出一批助人为乐、见义勇为、诚实守信、敬业奉献、孝老爱亲的道德模范荣登“修文好人榜”，孕育出一批文明村镇、文明社区和爱心家庭、五好文明家庭、少生快富文明家庭、绿色环保家庭、书香人家，分别受到贵阳市五好文明家庭协调小组和贵阳市精神文明建设指导委员会表彰。龙场镇城北村被中央精神文明建设委员会授予“全国孝亲敬老模范村”称号和六广镇沙坡村村民殷华利获“全国孝亲敬老之星”称号，成为平凡之中见伟大的典型，让人见贤思齐，发挥了道德模范的榜样作用。群众性的文化艺术活动呈现出百花盛开、姹紫嫣红的繁荣景象。以宣传“双为”方向、“双百”方针和展示文艺工作者创作成果为宗旨的《栖霞文艺》13年刊龄不衰。国画家郝承德从天命初度到耄耋之年一直笔耕不辍，出版画集2册，集山水、花鸟画百余幅行世。具有书艺学养的青年书法家朱俊首以其作品参加全国书法新人新作展，一举荣获中国“梵净山杯”全国书法篆刻大赛金奖和“金海杯”贵州省第四届行草书大展金奖，并遴选出37幅精品成册《朱俊首书法作品集》付梓。擅长摄影的余岚、周尚明不断深入改革开放第一线摄制出热情讴歌人民群众精神风貌的作品。被誉为“新世纪多产作家”的肖江虹，3年创作各类小说12篇，容量100万字，其中的中篇小说《百鸟朝凤》发表在全国大型文学期刊《当代》后，又被全国第一流文学刊物《中篇小说选刊》《北京文学》和被《新华文摘》选载，还被中国作家协会创联部编入《2009年中篇小说精选》，全国著名导演吴天明又以《百鸟朝凤》为蓝本编成电影剧本并制作成影片在海内外公开上映。于是被称为“中国70后有影响的作家”，进京接受中国作家协会主席铁凝亲手颁发的奖励，并跨进中国作协行列，又担任贵州省作协常务理事和贵阳市作协主席。音乐、舞蹈、戏剧多为群众自编自演，自娱自乐，从丰富多彩的文化活动中享受美好的精神文化生活。坚守文化工作岗位30年的张禧年为歌词谱曲百余首。被列为非物质文化遗产的下堡苗族舞蹈和六广花灯一直得到保护传承。苗族舞蹈系列芦笙舞、花棍舞、板凳舞、斗牛舞还亮相日本，在东京等地演出14场，深得日本友人赞许。集乐、舞、游戏为一体并富有民族特色和地方特色的原生态歌舞《红苞谷》走进中央电视台“舞蹈世界”栏目，面向全国播放，赢得观众好评。以展示家庭才艺为内容的胡林一家3口登上中央电视台“神舟大舞台”，使观众既分享了户主胡林握笔挥就“留有山河秀，侗家情意浓”的书艺秀，又共享了妻子高唱《美丽的侗乡》和女儿表演侗家舞的演艺美，家庭魅力着实令人陶醉。图书撰著出版方兴未艾，经贵州省新闻出版局批准出版社出版和内资出版各类图书86种。民国《修文县志》经过整理点校得以保护，新编《修文县志》（1283—1990）公开出版即获国家新闻出版署优秀图书奖和贵阳市第四次哲学社会科学优秀科研成果一等奖、贵州省第五次哲学社会科学科研优秀成果三等奖。依托阳明文化的独特优势，以媒体推介、导游览胜、接待谒拜、著书立说、学者论道、书画展览、文艺表演和举办文化节等多种活动载体传承和弘扬王阳明“致良知”之说和践行“知行合一”的阳明精神，以活动引导人们崇德向善。从1999到2009年，11年举办阳明文化节4届，每届文化节均有百余海内外的“王学”研究专家、学者和数以万计的干部、群众云集阳明洞，或祭拜，或游览，或观看文艺演出，或参加高端论坛，通过办节助推了阳明文化的传播，提升了修文的知名度。以增强群众体质为目的的体育事业蓬勃发展，作为县城形象标志的县体育馆建起后，相继有大石少数民族运动体育场和乡村各类球场、城镇社区健身房500多个建成。群众性的体育锻炼和健身活动在全县普及，运动水平不断提高。至2010年，修文籍运动员获得国际单项比赛和国家级、省级、市级金牌61枚。运动员罗文代表国家队参加A级拳击赛，一路击败印度、韩国、俄罗斯和中国台北4名选手，夺得比赛桂冠。民间武术爱好者组队赴香港参加国际武术节，获太极拳集体项目冠军。文武学校两次组队参加贵州省武术比赛均摘金牌。在贵州省第二届残疾人运动会上，许嘉和赵小丽分别获得乒乓球女子单打和女子44公斤级卧举冠军。在贵阳市第五届少数民族传统体育运动会上，射弩项目金奖被修文代表团摘取。科技工作坚持为经济建设服务，在全县形成科技兴农、科技兴工的格局，促使传统农业向现代农业转化，传统产业企业向高新技术产业转轨，一批农业科技重点攻关项目得以扶持，一批以高新技术产业研发、生产为主的企业落地修文，一批科研人员的发明创造得到企业首肯和认可，一批科研成果经过评审获得奖励。县科学技术局与贵州大学合作申报《修文县“六广河”牌猕猴桃产业化关键技术开发与应用》项目得到贵州省科学技术厅的农业科技重点攻关项目扶持资金25万元。入驻扎佐的外商独资企业中国陶粒（贵州）有限公司生产出口高强度的石油压裂支撑剂，规划3年达到6万吨、产值1.5亿元的规模。扎佐电影院下岗职工陈志明办起个体汽车修理场，一边修车，一边构想，发明了汽车刹车专用控制器获得国家专利证书，并送澳大利亚世界博览会参展荣获金奖，紧接着又发明汽车电子脉冲节能器仍获国家专利证，并获日内瓦专利成果博览会金奖和伦敦国际专利技术博览会金奖。奖项公布后，奥地利一家电子公司与陈志明合作在贵阳开设中外合资公司，陈志明担任副董事长兼总工程师，年产节能器10万只，70%的产品销往西欧。至2010年，全县科研成果获国家级奖1项、省级奖23项、市级奖31项。由工程师李家平担纲设计，以土法建造、质量坚固、造型美观、拦水有效著称的“岩鹰山水库石拱坝设计施工”荣获国家级科技成果奖。

经济增长与社会建设奠定了物质基础，使城乡居民住有所居、劳有所得、病有所医、老有所养的民生得以改善。从1996年起，实施“城乡一体化”和“生态建设”的战略部署，在抓城镇基础设施建设的同时，着力农村的茅草房改造。一改县城旧貌的“九三”工程（1条双轨大道、1个休闲广场、1座体育馆、1座办公楼、1所九年制学校、1个居民小区、1个服务中心、1条河道、1座桥梁和3条联网市街）告竣后，新都口岸、文城逸都、翰林花园、明河花园、龙岗花园、利尔上河城和星河银座大厦、腾晖花园

小区等一批商住房拔地而起，其中住房1.15万套，使万户居民陆续住进款式别致的新居。扎佐等集镇的居民住宅也不断更新。举全县之力攻克的农村“茅改”工程，仅4年时间使1.16万户村民换成砖混结构的房舍。到2010年，城镇和农村居民人均住房面积分别达到33平方米和31平方米，居住水平明显提高，居住环境也随之改观。经济文化建设的拓展为劳动就业广开了门路，果、菜、畜、药规模生产产品入市，民营企业快速攀升，个体工商户注册营运……多渠道为劳动者搭建起就业平台，就业结构得以改善，自主择业政策放开，使98%以上具有劳动能力的城乡居民有业可就，劳动所得得以保护，一批创业者脱颖而出，“零就业”家庭化为乌有。关系群众身体健康的医疗卫生事业从制度改革破题，2005年起实施完整的“离休干部享受公费医疗、城镇职工纳入医疗保险、农民参加新型农村合作医疗”的就医制度，健全了全民医保体系。到2010年，100%的离休干部和97%的城乡居民有了医疗保障。全县还健全了县、乡（镇）、村三级医疗网络，县有医院，乡（镇）有卫生院，村有卫生室，医务工作者共776人，每千人均有病床2张，一条“有病就医，医之得当”的医疗保障之路基本铺就。城乡居民养老制度逐步健全，老龄服务事业日臻完善。县老龄委员会、离退休干部管理局、老年人活动中心、老年公寓相继建立，机关事业单位离退休职工基本养老金按月发放，企业退休人员纳入社会保障，城乡居民参加基本养老保险，年满80周岁以上的老人还按月领取老龄生活补贴。到2010年，全县享有城市低保1904户3839人，享有农村低保5154户1.13万人，达到“应保尽保”的要求，实现了城乡贫困人口社会保障全覆盖。

经济社会发展带来人民生活的改善，建设成果使群众共享。2010年，城镇居民人均可支配收入达1.58万元，比1996年的3480元增长3.53倍，年均递增11.39%；农民人均纯收入达5152元，比1978年141元增长35.54倍，年均递增11.9%。按照国际通用评价居民富裕程度的恩格尔系数衡量，2010年用于食品消费的支出占家庭生活消费总支出的比例，城镇居民为36.58%达富裕水平，农村居民为43.61%达小康水平。高档耐用消费品进入平民百姓家，城镇居民固定电话和移动电话普及率分别达到71部/百户和210部/百户，家用汽车3.33辆/百户，电脑50台/百户；农村居民固定电话0.17部/百户，移动电话0.45部/百户，生活用车0.01台/百户。新三件洗衣机、电视机、电冰箱普遍取代旧三件单车、手表、缝纫机。一幅住得宽敞、吃讲营养、穿的时尚、用取高档、出行用车的小康生活壮景展现在修文城乡，见证了人民生活的提高有赖于经济社会的发展，也是经济社会发展的必然归宿。

综观新时期修文的建设历程，成就辉煌。但前进的道路上还存在一定的困难和问题：城乡、区域经济社会发展不平衡，居民收入有差距，部分低收入群众的生活需要救助；农业基础比较薄弱，工业科技含量较低，产业结构不尽合理；节能减排力度不够，生态建设尚须努力；道德失范、诚信缺失现象时有发生，社会治安综合治理有待加强；部分党员干部理想信念动摇，作风不正，工作浮飘，形式主义、官僚主义、拜金主义突出，奢侈浪费严重，消极腐败多发，群众对此极不满意。

回顾过去，修文人民为取得的累累硕果而骄傲；展望未来，修文儿女倍感任重而道远。面对全面建成小康战略和实现现代化的宏伟目标，全县人民将继续在县委、县政府的带领下，坚定不移地贯彻落实中共中央、国务院的战略决策，不忘初心，肩负重担，承前启后，再铸辉煌。

小康昭示未来，修文的明天必将更加美好！

Review

Xiuwen County is located in the central part of Guizhou Province and enjoys the reputation of "The holy land of Wang Xue, heavenly Xiuwen". The county borders on Kaiyang in the east, Baiyun in the south, Qianxi in the west, Xifeng in the north, Wudang in the southeast, Qingzhen in the southwest and Jinsha in the northwest. It is mountainous and the terrain is high in the east and low in the west. The mountains and rivers are beautiful, the climate is mild, the soil is good, the resources are abundant, the traffic is smooth, and the people are hardworking. It is the northern gate of Guiyang, the provincial capital. It is the only way to enter Sichuan and is the main producing area of Guiyang fruit and vegetable poultry and the distribution center of agricultural and sideline products. The county town Longchang Town is the political, economic and cultural center of the county, 27 kilometers away from the administrative center of Guiyang City. In 1996, the municipal administration system was implemented, and Xiuwen was placed under the jurisdiction of Guiyang City. In 2010, the county governed 4 towns, 6 townships, 217 administrative villages and 10 community residents committees, with a registered population of 305,900 and a land area of 1075.7 square kilometers.

From 1978, China entered the new era of reform, opening up, and socialist modernization, and completed the 11th Five-Year Plan for national economic and social development in 2010. It has gone through 33 years. During this period, the Chinese Communist Party's Xiuwen County Party Committee and the County People's Government led the people of all ethnic groups in the county to comprehensively bring order out of chaos, stop using the slogan "Taking class struggle as the key link", and realize the shift of work focus on economic construction, pioneering and enterprising, arduous struggle, and ushered in Political stability, economic development, cultural prosperity, social stability, and the gratifying situation of the people´s livelihood have made remarkable achievements in various construction projects.

Since the reform and opening up, the county party committee and county government have upheld and improved socialist democratic politics, built socialist political civilization, and actively promoted political system reform. Since 1980, the county party committee has followed the principle of seeking truth from facts and correcting mistakes in accordance with the principle of seeking truth from facts and correcting mistakes. Starting from rebelling against the false and false cases in the "Cultural Revolution," comprehensively implementing the party´s cadre policies and resolving the remaining problems in history. After three years of work, 60 grievous cadres have returned to work and their relatives have been relieved, and they are actively involved in the cause of socialist modernization.

In 1981, according to the "Organization of the People´s Congress of the People´s Republic of China and the Organizational Law of Local People´s Governments", the system of people´s congresses that had been interrupted for

15 years was resumed, and the people of the county were elected at the first meeting of the Seventh National People´s Congress. The Standing Committee of the Standing Committee of the Congress and the leaders of the County People´s Government, the County People´s Court, and the County People´s Procuratorate, and the County People´s Government to replace the County Revolutionary Committee. In 1983, the CPC implemented the policy of "long-term coexistence and mutual supervision" with the democratic parties and non-party members, and established the Political Consultative Conference Xiuwen County Committee. In 1984, in accordance with the Constitution of the People´s Republic of China, the township (town) people´s government was established in 32 townships (towns) of the county, and the government management functions were formally exercised. While establishing the township (town) people´s government, in accordance with the "Organization Law of the Villagers´ Committee of the People´s Republic of China" and the "Organization Law of the People´s Republic of China Residents´ Committee", village committees and residents´ committees are established in all administrative villages and streets under the county to replace the original ones. The production brigade revolutionary committee and the street revolutionary committee, the village committee and the neighborhood committee will build village groups and resident groups to implement self-education, self-management, self-service and self-monitoring of urban and rural residents.In order to strengthen the rule of law, from the establishment of a sound political and legal institution, the county people´s procuratorate was restored and rebuilt in 1978. The county judicial bureau was established in 1980. The bureau established a legal advisory office and later became a law firm, using legal means to safeguard the public interest and the legitimate rights and interests of citizens. . In order to ensure the smooth progress of economic construction and the safety of people´s lives and property, since 1983, the county has launched a series of crackdowns on cracking down on criminals who endanger public security, punishing and deterring criminals, and making social security fundamentally better. In order to maintain long-term stability in the society, under the leadership of the county party committee and county government, the public security, procuratorial, court, judicial administrative departments and mass organizations, as well as the relevant departments of the county, will be organized to participate in the establishment of a comprehensive social security management organization, combined with the organization of the village committee and the neighborhood committee. Reorganize the county´s public security committee, relying on social forces, strengthen public security management and security prevention, and maintain social stability.

In 1985, the county party committee followed the "Decision of the Central Committee of the Communist Party of China on the Party´s decision" and deployed the party in 419 party organizations and 5,311 party members in the county to solve the problem of the party´s ideological, work style and organizational impureness. Through the whole party, most party members received a profound party education, and 93.6% of the party members were registered and reviewed for registration. In 2000, according to the CPC Central Committee´s "Opinions on Party Style Education with the main content of "learning, politics, and righteousness" in the party and government leading bodies and leading cadres at or above the county level, in the county party committee, the National People´s Congress, Among the leading bodies and leading cadres of the government, CPPCC, discipline inspection, courts, procuratorates and public security bureaus, the "three stresses" education activities were carried out among the members of the organization department of the county party committee and the propaganda department. Educational activities are carried out by means of learning improvement, self-analysis, criticism, and serious rectification. Through education, 52 leading cadres have undergone a life of democratic life within the party, and their work has been significantly improved.In 2001, the county party committee followed the CPC Central Committee´s important educational activities on the important thinking of the "three represents" in the rural areas (the Chinese Communist Party always represents the development requirements of China´s advanced productive forces, represents the direction of China´s advanced culture, and represents the fundamental interests of the overwhelming majority of the Chinese people). The deployment took 480 days to carry out academic activities in 3 batches of 4,682 cadres in 10 townships (towns), 90 county departments and 229 village (residential) committees. The learning and learning activities are divided into three stages: learning training, control inspection, and improvement. Through the activities of learning and teaching, the ideological style and work style of the grassroots cadres have been significantly improved, thus promoting the development of the rural economy and the improvement of the peasant life, and receiving the effect of "cadre education, farmers benefit". In 2005, the county party committee complied with the Central Committee of the Communist Party of China on the implementation of the "three represents" important thinking in the practice of the whole party as the main content of the education activities to maintain the advanced nature of party members," 545 days in the county 467 party organizations and 8225 The party members were divided into three batches to carry out educational activities to maintain the advanced nature of party members. The "Baoxian" activities are divided into three stages: learning training, analysis and evaluation, and improvement. Through the "guarantee first" activities, the party has achieved remarkable results in the construction of the party´s advanced nature and the building of its ability to govern, and has been well received by the community.

Under the guidance of the general policy of reform and opening up, the county party committee and the county government formulated the strategic decision of "one production stable county, two production strong county, and three production live county", leading the cadres and the masses to overcome difficulties and make great efforts. This has brought about tremendous changes in the economic outlook of the county. Compared with 1978, the regional GDP increased from 35.8 million yuan to 4.618 billion yuan. According to the 1990 constant price, the average annual increase was 11.44%, and the per capita amount increased from 149 yuan to 1.51 million yuan. 100.3 times; the total fiscal revenue increased from 1.889 million yuan to 544 million yuan, an average annual increase of 19.36%, and the per capita amount increased from 7.8 yuan to 1777.8 yuan, an increase of 226.9 times. The huge changes are also reflected in the composition of the regional GDP. In 1980, the composition of the primary, secondary and tertiary industries was 45.04:34.3:20.66, and by 2010 it was changed to 17.13:37.05:45.82. In 2008, it was included in the ranks of the province´s economically strong counties.

Since the 1980s, agricultural development has taken the reform of the rural economic system as the starting point, and the household contract responsibility system has been widely implemented, which has greatly mobilized the enthusiasm of farmers for production, intensively cultivated in responsible areas, and relied on science and technology to promote agriculture and make grain output 1983. Breaking through the 50,000-ton mark in the year, the average per capita is 268 kilograms, which solves the problem of eating that is expected to be solved for many years. In the 1990s, it mainly organized the transfer of rural surplus labor to the non-agricultural sector, and implemented the transfer of land contractual management rights. Focusing on market orientation, the company focused on "fruit, vegetables, livestock and medicine" and adjusted its industrial structure and implemented scale operations. In ac-

cordance with the planning of "one town, one product, one village and one industry", the operation mode of "company + association + farmer" was adopted to create "Xiadong kiwifruit" "Zhexi Jinqiu pear" "Wang Guanyan late tomato" "Dalbao radish" Daheyan Red Peach" "Guo Tian Crispy pear" "Taoyuan Citrus" "Jiuchang Vegetable" "Liutun Pinellia" and other planting bases and "six barrels of chicken under the forest" "Shi´an pig fattening" "Xiaojing fine beef" "Qingshui "Hao 1 duo ´milk" "Zazo Landi laying hens" and other breeding bases.Taking the base into a leading position, many farmers are encouraged to invest in fruit and vegetable cultivation and poultry breeding. They provide support and assistance in fund raising, labor and labor, technical guidance, and product distribution, so as to encourage families to cultivate and raise household products into the market. The base has lengthened the industrial chain, and the peasants have stepped up the golden road. They have changed the single industry pattern that only relies on grain and food for several years to become the commodity production pattern of many industries today. The kiwifruit, which is known as the "King of the King of Vitamin C", has grown from a trial of 100 mu to a standardized planting of 37,000 mu, and the number of fruit farmers has increased from more than 50 to more than 3, 000. Due to its good quality, Xiuwen kiwifruit has become a business card in the province and abroad. In 2010, the county´s total agricultural output value reached 1.314 billion yuan, an increase of 61.24 times compared with 21.81 million yuan in 1978; the per capita net income of farmers increased by 35.54 times in 1978. The base is dotted, and the output is constantly rising, and the products are dazzling.

In the early 1980s, industrial production was carried out by state-run, collective, and individual. Encourage county-run industry, social industry, and private industry to go hand in hand with the central and provincial industries in the county to develop together. By 1982, the county´s total industrial output value reached 44.81 million yuan, an increase of 71.42% over the 26,14 million yuan in 1978. In 1984, the county party committee and the county government proposed to set up a township and township industry, and implemented the township (town) office, the village office, the township (town) village joint office, the joint household office, and the household office to "turn five wheels together" to make the township industry in the county. The industrial economy accounts for "half of the river". By 1990, the county´s township industrial enterprises had grown to 1,593, with 11,100 employees, and the total enterprise income was 62.06 million yuan, which was 6.14 times, 3.16 times and 19.08 more than the 223, 2,668 and 3.09 million yuan in 1978. Times. The industrial output value of township and township accounts for 66.92% of the total industrial output value of the county. In 1991, the reform of state-owned industrial enterprises in the county was initiated, the separation of government and enterprises and the responsibility of the factory manager under the leadership of the party committee were implemented, the assets and management rights of the enterprises were separated, and the state-owned enterprises were changed into state-owned enterprises. Taxes and fees are paid, and workers' labor is linked to wages and wages. The "iron rice bowl" where "enterprise eats national cauldron rice and workers eat enterprise big pot rice" is eliminated. At the same time, with the development of private economy, rural collective organizations and farmers' investment are The main township industry has gradually turned into a private enterprise.By the year 2000, the state-owned industrial restructuring ended, private industry developed rapidly, and the county´s total industrial output value exceeded 1 billion yuan, of which private industry dominated. In 2001, the county party committee and the county government made up their minds to eliminate the "stupid, big, black, and rough" enterprises with high energy consumption and high pollution, and cited the foreign investment in attracting foreign investment, with "the low threshold for enterprises to enter, and the land payment with tax revenue". The "Antai Model" has successively introduced 15 pharmaceutical companies and built a modern Xiuwen Pharmaceutical Industrial Park, which is known as the "engine of Xiuwen Economy".Following the construction of the Guiyang-Zunyi Industrial Belt in accordance with the planning of the Guiyang Provincial Government, the construction of the "One District, Three Parks" along the high-grade highways of Gui (Yang) and Gui (Yang) The park, Longchang Industrial Park, Zhazuo Industrial Park, Jiuchang Industrial Park) and "Shili Industrial Corridor" (Sanyuan, Guanchang to Zhazuo Town, Longchang Town), with "concentration of layout, industrial agglomeration, resource intensive, perfect supporting "Comprehensive advantages and the spirit of "explaining words and deeds, opening up and opening up", introducing Shougang • Guiyang Special Steel Plant, Guizhou Tire Factory, Jinjiu Cement Factory, Huafei Alumina Plant and China (US) Pottery Petroleum Proppant Company, Guiyang Tiancheng Thermal Ceramics Co., Ltd., Guizhou Tianlong Friction Material Co., Ltd., Guizhou Longxiang Energy Group Co., Ltd. Camshaft Factory, Guizhou Gaoxin Shengyuan FRP Anchor Co., Ltd., Guizhou Yifeng Daily Chemical Co., Ltd., Guizhou "Good 1" Dairy Co., Ltd. 51 modern enterprises such as Guizhou Guijiu Co., Ltd., which have low energy consumption, good sewage discharge and increased efficiency, settled in the park, forming medicine, food, new materials, new building materials, precision castings and machines. Processing industries constitute a new industrial recycling economic zone. By 2010, the county's total industrial output value reached 5.609 billion yuan, an increase of 213.58 times compared with 26.14 million yuan in 1978, an average annual increase of 18.27%, and industrial added value accounted for 27.84% of the county's total GDP. Industrial production has since entered a golden age and embarked on a development path supported by high-tech export-oriented.

Tourism is an emerging industry in the new era of revision. In 1984, the county party committee and the county government proposed the development idea of "tourism and economic singing" and started to develop the underground caves in the northern end of the county with 13 holes, 66 caves and various natural landscapes. The large stone forest of the karst green stone forest was stranded due to lack of funds and traffic constraints. In 1996, we seized the opportunity of constructing the county roads of Guizun and Guibi high-grade roads, regrouped, borrowed chicken eggs, and concentrated on developing tourism with the initiative of attracting investment. The Shanmen opened, Hong Kong Emperor Co., Ltd. and Guangdong Jieyang Jinhua Industrial Co., Ltd. took the lead and stepped on the Zhazi wave lake at the intersection of Guizun and Guibi high-grade highways. It occupies an area of 3015 mu and builds the only plateau forest stadium and the whole country. The coolest recreational and summer resort - Guiyang Golf Resort. The center sets up a bridge between Xiuwen and the outside world for economic and cultural exchanges. Every year, tens of thousands of friends from home and abroad come here to make a swing and join the ball. After the establishment of the golf resort center, merchants from all over the world came one after another: Guizhou Highway Engineering Construction Corporation stepped on the Liuguang River to develop the most typical karst landform in the western part of China; the private entrepreneur Zhang Yanjun of Yunnan Province is optimistic about the thorns of Zhazuolin Woodland, built the only high-altitude forest-type safari park in China, and was approved by the National Tourism Administration as an AAAA-level scenic spot; Chongqing private entrepreneur Zhang Yuanliang discovered the hidden Taoyuan River in the deep, creating the first 9.5-kilometer magic drift in China; The Guiyang People's Air Defense Readiness Office chose to build a Pearl Island Summer Resort on the pen-

insula on the shore of the Qihu Lake. The Hainan investors calmly look at the thousands of acres of grassland located in Qingjiang Village of Jiuchang Town to create a The exotic Scottish pasture; Guizhou Suizhong Green Stone Forest Eco-tourism Development Co., Ltd. selects the "Dashi Stone Forest", the excavator of the Guizhou Plateau Stone Forest, and develops according to the national AAAA-level tourist scenic spot standards...Focusing on the creation of natural landscapes while attracting investment, the Chinese philosopher and educator Wang Yangming's first philosophical cave Yangmingdong was built into a cultural theme park, and Wang Yangming's study of Yijing was carried out. Wo, personally buried and wrote "Yi Lv Wen" mourning the three-way graves of the transit and its servants and the ruins of the Tiansheng Bridge and the Liuguang River, which are admired by the poems, for the restoration and protection of tourists and tourists at home and abroad. In addition, it has also built a national agricultural tourism demonstration site with moon and moon, fruit and fruit in the season, and eight rural tourist spots and seven 10,000 mu ecological agriculture sightseeing parks to form a leisure and tourism. Cultural tourism and eco-tourism are the supporting tourism system, making Xiuwen the back garden of "Shuang Shuang Guiyang" and the place that people yearn for. In 2010, the county received 3.886 million tourists and the tourism revenue reached 1.995 billion yuan.

The rise of tourism has expanded the market for commercial trade, transportation, post and telecommunications, and brought business opportunities for the export of agricultural products. With the opening of the Golf Resort Center, Guiyang Golf Travel Agency was the first to open, achieving a zero breakthrough in travel agencies. Then, China Travel Service, Overseas Travel Agency and Wilderness Travel Agency set up offices in the county, and the Known Travel Agency and Baozhong Travel Service set up business offices. The colorful travel agency set up a repair and text branch to receive travel groups and expatriate passes and passports for the county. The three-star hotel of the Tenghui Hotel and the Jianzhu Island Summer Center, which stands in the center of the county, is built by the Xiaolong Restaurant, Chunhua Restaurant, Longchang Restaurant, Yupinxuan Restaurant, Yihe Villa, Chaoshui Villa. Zhazuo "Happy Forest", Taoyuan Restaurant, Liuguang Riverside Zhulou Hotel, and more than 70 "farmhouse" reception points distributed around the country, all of them are warmly receiving Chinese and foreign business modes with food, accommodation and play as one. Guests and tourists. A transportation network integrating railways, highways and waterways has been formed.The change of the cross-border trains of Sichuan-Chongqing Railway to diesel locomotives has greatly shortened the space-time distance and reduced carbon emissions. The high-grade highways connecting Kaiyang, Nanjin Guiyang, Xida Kunming, and Chongqing to the north and the 210 national highways to the north and south are all tarmac. The 74-kilometer waterway from the Liuguanghe Wharf to the Wujiangdu Power Station was opened. The roads from county to township (town) are all slag-watered, and the villages are connected to the administrative village. It has launched 10 tourist routes on the day, 2nd and 3rd days with the theme of culture, popular science, recreation, eco-tourism and special diets, which can be used by tourists to enjoy the scenic spots and attractions. It is located in the second-class automobile passenger station named "Xindu Port" on the Xiaoqiao River in the county. It has 36 lines, 150 passenger cars, 350 daily trains, and 5,000 passengers per day. The Zhasuo three-class passenger station and the Jiuchang, Liuguang, Liubu, Wuli, Shuiping and Xiaoyu stations built in the township (town) are responsible for the safety of the vehicle passengers. The pre-stressed steel-mixed combination is used to build a Liuguanghe Bridge with a hole spanning 100 meters. It highlights the majestic appearance in the steep mountains. It has ended the history of the traffic of Xiuwen and the two counties in the west of the country for thousands of years. A new chapter in the exchange of materials and the development of the economy.The private economic street built in the center of the county is completed, juxtaposed with the first-built Renmin Road, and crosses Tsui Ping Avenue to form a prosperous business district. At the same time, the farmers′ markets in Zhazuo, Jiuchang, Liuguang, Liubu, Gubao, Xiaoyu, Sheping, Liuyi and Dashi were built. Following this, the modern logistics park with functions of unloading, transshipment and transmission has landed in the satellite city of Zhazuo in the north of Guiyang, creating a distribution center for the northern materials and more rational distribution of the county′s commercial network. There are more than 4,500 merchants operating and selling in the county, including foreign companies in Sichuan, Hunan, Hubei, and Zhejiang. Individual shops, farmer′s comprehensive markets, farmhouses, supermarkets, merchandise exhibitions, etc. are everywhere, and the products are beautiful and have everything. Distribution centers and e-commerce have also entered the field of large commodity circulation. Financial markets, labor markets, intermediary markets, and real estate markets have emerged one after another. Postal express delivery, communication, and Internet have emerged in succession, forming a sound market system to enable production and living supply. More plentiful. What is even more surprising is that the annual output of hundreds of thousands of tons of Jinqiu pears has entered Guiyang and the late tomato has entered Guangzhou. Kiwifruit has entered Beijing, Shanghai, Nanning, Shenzhen, Changchun and Harbin. The products are on the market and are favored by the public. In 2010, the total operating income including tourism, commerce, transportation, postal communication reached 4.266 billion yuan, 22.8 times higher than the 179 million yuan in 1997.

Under the guidance of the strategic thinking of “revitalizing the county through science and education”, the county party committee and the county government placed education in a priority position, focused on reforming the education system, improving school infrastructure, improving school conditions, strengthening leadership over schools, and actively promoting education. Establish an education system that integrates pre-school education, compulsory education, general education, vocational education, and adult education, and forms an educational pattern of “three integrations” between schools, families, and society. Through the national inspection and acceptance, the goal of “two basics” (basic universal nine-year compulsory education and basic elimination of illiteracy among young and middle-aged adults) has been achieved. Schools at all levels have continuously sent tens of thousands of qualified freshmen to the higher-level schools and trained for various construction projects. A large number of professionals with both ability and political integrity have emerged as a group of educators who "stick to the three-foot platform and work hard to become talented people."In 2010, there were 13 kindergartens in the county, 4082 children in kindergartens, 20.4 times in 1978; 52 primary schools with 18,300 students, enrollment rate of 99.63%; 19 junior high schools with 13,900 students The enrollment rate is 106.9%; there are 5 high schools, 4447 students, which is 1.64 times higher than that in 1978; there is a special education school, and there are “three disabled” (blind, deaf, mentally handicapped) children 125. The enrollment rate is 90.79%; there are 1 vocational education and training center and 105 registered students. There were 2,422 public faculty members in the county, an increase of 1.73 times over 1978. In the Xiuwen Middle School of Guiyang City′s “Five Good Schools”, in 2010, 814 high school graduates took the college entrance examination, 70 on-line colleges, 239 colleges and universities, and the quality of college entrance examinations was “exported”. Second, the provincial education demonstration high

school was assessed by the Guizhou Provincial Department of Education. The privately- run Jingyang Middle School, which has a school age of 17 years and has a large scale, has already sent more than 2,000 new students to colleges and universities.

Through the institutional reform, the cultural undertakings linked to the development of education have separated the separation of government and enterprises, breaking the pattern of monopoly operations by the state, bookstores, Internet cafes, tea rooms, chess and cards, billiards, dance halls, electronic game rooms, audio-visual products sales shops, etc. Cultural places broke out, with 52 self-employed households and 131 practitioners, which constitute a new cultural market and promote the development and prosperity of cultural undertakings. In 1999 and 2008, radio and television were respectively implemented as “village villages”. The spiritual civilization creation activities with the "four virtues" (social morality, professional ethics, family virtues, personal morality) as the main content have been widely carried out in the county, highlighting the connotation of activities, purifying people´s ideas, and emerging a batch of The moral model of helping others, being brave, being honest and trustworthy, dedication, dedication, and filial piety is honored as a list of "cultivating good people", and has nurtured a group of civilized villages, civilized communities and loving families, five good civilized families, and less prosperous and fast-rich civilizations. The family, the green family and the scholarly family were commended by the Guiyang Wuhao Civilized Family Coordination Group and the Guiyang Spiritual Civilization Construction Steering Committee.Chengbei Village of Longchang Town was awarded the title of “National Filial Piety and Retirement Model Village” by the Central Spiritual Civilization Construction Committee and Yin Huali, a villager of Shapo Village in Liuguang Town, was awarded the title of “National Filial Piety and Respect for the Elderly” and became a typical example of greatness in ordinary times. Let people see the good and the good, play a role model role model. The mass cultural and artistic activities presented a flourishing scene of blooming flowers and colorful flowers. The 13-year publication of Qixia Art and Literature, which aims to promote the "double-oriented" direction, the "double-hundred" policy, and the achievements of the literary and art workers, is not bad. The Chinese painter Hao Chengde has been writing and painting since the beginning of his life. He has published 2 volumes of paintings and collected hundreds of landscapes and flowers and birds. Zhu Jun, a young calligrapher with a book-education, participated in the National Calligraphy Newcomer´s New Works Exhibition with his works, and won the Gold Medal of the “Fanjingshan Cup” National Calligraphy Engraving Competition in China and the Gold Medal of the “Guihai Cup” in the 4th Cursive Exhibition of Guizhou Province. And selected 37 pieces of fine book "Zhu Jun´s first calligraphy works collection". Yu Yu and Zhou Shangming, who are good at photography, continue to deepen the first line of reform and opening up to produce works that enthusiastically sing the people´s spiritual outlook.Xiao Jianghong, known as the "promising writer of the new century", created 12 novels of various novels in 3 years, with a capacity of 1 million words. Among them, the novella "Hundred Birds and Phoenix" was published in the national large-scale literary journal "Contemporary". The first-class literary journal of the country, "Selected Journal of Novella", "Beijing Literature" and selected by "Xinhua Digest", was also included in the "Selection of Novella in 2009" by the China Writers Association, and the famous national director Wu Tianming The film script was compiled based on "Hundred Birds and Phoenix" and produced into a film for public release at home and abroad. So he was called "China´s post-70s influential writer" and went to Beijing to accept the awards handed by Tie Ning, chairman of the Chinese Writers Association, and entered the ranks of the Chinese Writers Association. He also served as the executive director of the Guizhou Provincial Writers Association and the chairman of the Guiyang Municipal Writers Association. Music, dance, and drama are mostly self-produced by the masses, self-entertainment, and enjoy a beautiful spiritual and cultural life from rich and colorful cultural activities. Zhang Shuinian, who has been adhering to the 30-year history of cultural work, has composed more than 100 songs. The Xiabao Miao dance and the Liuguang Lantern, which are listed as intangible cultural heritage, have been protected and passed down. The Miao dance series of reed dance, flower stick dance, bench dance, and bullfighting dance also appeared in Japan, and performed 14 performances in Tokyo and other places, which won the praise of the Japanese people. The original ecological song and dance "Hung Ho Valley", which integrates music, dance and games, is rich in national characteristics and local characteristics. It enters the "Dance World" section of CCTV and is broadcasted nationwide to win the audience´s praise.The Hulin family, who showed the talents of the family, boarded the CCTV "Shenzhou Grand Stage", which enabled the audience to share the book show of Hu Lin's pen and the "Leave a Mountain River Show and a Strong Family". I also shared the performance of the wife singing "Beautiful Shuxiang" and her daughter performing the dance of the family. The charm of the family is really intoxicating. The book authoring publication is in the ascendant. It has been approved by the Guizhou Provincial Press and Publication Bureau to publish and domestically publish 86 kinds of books. The "Xiuwen County" of the Republic of China was protected by the arrangement of the school. The newly-edited "Xiuwen County" (1283-1990) was publicly published and won the first prize of the National Press and Publication Administration Excellent Book Award and the fourth scientific and social science outstanding scientific research achievement of Guiyang. The third prize of the fifth outstanding achievement in philosophy and social science research in Guizhou Province. Relying on the unique advantages of Yangming culture, the media will promote and promote Wang Yangming's "conscience" by media promotion, tour and tour, reception, worship, scholars, scholars, paintings, cultural performances and cultural festivals. The theory and practice of the spirit of "the combination of knowing and doing" Yang Ming, to guide people to respect the good.From 1999 to 2009, 11 years of Yangming Cultural Festival was held in 11 years. Each cultural festival has more than 100 research experts and scholars from Wang Xue at home and abroad, and tens of thousands of cadres and people gathered in Yangmingdong, or Worship, or visit, or watch cultural performances, or participate in high-end forums, through the festival to promote the spread of Yangming culture, enhance the popularity of Xiuwen. The sports industry with the purpose of enhancing the masses of the people flourished. After the establishment of the county gymnasium as the image of the county, there were more than 500 gymnastics stadiums in Dashi and various gymnasiums and gymnasiums in urban communities. Mass physical exercise and fitness activities are popularized throughout the county, and the level of exercise continues to increase. By 2010, Xiuwen athletes won international single competitions and 61 national, provincial and municipal gold medals.Athlete Rowan represented the national team in the A-level boxing match and defeated four players from India, South Korea, Russia and Chinese Taipei all the way to win the championship. Folk martial arts enthusiasts teamed up to participate in the International Wushu Festival in Hong Kong and won the Taijiquan collective project champion. Wenwu School teamed up twice to participate in the Guizhou Province martial arts competition to pick gold medals. In the second disabled sports meeting in Guizhou Province, Xu Jia and Zhao Xiaoli won the women´s singles table tennis and the women´s 44 kg class. At the 5th National Minority Traditional Sports

Games in Guiyang, the gold medal of the shooting project was taken by the delegation of the revised text. Science and technology work insists on serving the economic construction, forming a pattern of science and technology, agriculture and science and technology in the county, promoting the transformation of traditional agriculture into modern agriculture, turning traditional industrial enterprises into high-tech industries, and supporting a number of key agricultural science and technology projects. The research and creation of a group of scientific research personnel has been approved and recognized by enterprises with high-tech industry research and development and production. A batch of scientific research results have been evaluated and rewarded.The County Science and Technology Bureau cooperated with Guizhou University to declare the "Key Technology Development and Application of the "Six-Guanghe" Brand Kiwifruit Industrialization in Xiuwen County". The project supported by the Ministry of Science and Technology of Guizhou Province supported the agricultural science and technology key project support fund of 250,000 yuan. China's ceramsite (Guizhou) Co., Ltd., a wholly foreign-owned enterprise located in Zazo, produces high-strength petroleum fracturing proppant, which is planned to reach 60,000 tons and output value of 150 million yuan in three years. Chen Zhiming, a laid-off worker at Zazo Cinema, set up an individual auto repair shop. While renovating the car, he conceived and invented the special controller for the car brakes and obtained the national patent certificate. He also won the gold medal at the Australia World Expo, and then invented the car electronic pulse energy saver. He still obtained the national patent certificate and won the Gold Award of the Geneva Patent Achievement Expo and the Gold Prize of the London International Patent Technology Fair. After the award was announced, an Austrian electronics company cooperated with Chen Zhiming to open a Sino-foreign joint venture in Guiyang. Chen Zhiming served as the vice chairman and chief engineer, with an annual output of 100,000 energy-saving devices, 70% of which were sold to Western Europe. By 2010, the county's scientific research achievements won 1 national award, 23 provincial awards, and 31 municipal awards. Designed by engineer Li Jiaping, the "Yanyingshan Reservoir Stone Arch Dam Design and Construction", which is built with the soil method, is of high quality, beautiful appearance and effective water blocking, won the national scientific and technological achievement award.

Economic growth and social construction have laid a material foundation for urban and rural residents to live and work, to have medical care, to be old, and to improve people's livelihood. Since 1996, the strategic deployment of "urban-rural integration" and "ecological construction" has been implemented. While building urban infrastructure, we have focused on the transformation of thatched houses in rural areas. The "Jiusan" project (1 double-track avenue, 1 leisure plaza, 1 gymnasium, 1 office building, 1 nine-year school, 1 residential area, 1 service center, 1 After the river, a bridge and three connected city streets, Xindu Port, Wencheng Yidu, Hanlin Garden, Minghe Garden, Longgang Garden, Lier Shanghe City, Xinghe Ginza Building, Tenghui Garden Community, etc. Up to the ground, the housing of 11,500 sets, so that 10,000 households continue to live in a unique style of new home. The residential buildings in the market towns such as Zazo are also constantly updated. In the rural "Maochang" project, which was conquered by the county, only 166,000 villagers were replaced with brick-and-mortar buildings in only 4 years. By 2010, the per capita housing area of urban and rural residents will reach 33 square meters and 31 square meters, respectively, and the living level will be significantly improved, and the living environment will also change.The expansion of economic and cultural construction has opened the way for labor and employment. Fruit, vegetable, livestock, and medicine-scale production products have entered the market, private enterprises have risen rapidly, and individual industrial and commercial households have registered and operated... Multi-channels have established employment platforms for workers, and the employment structure has been able to Improvement and self-employment policy have been liberalized, so that more than 98% of the urban and rural residents with working ability can do business, the labor income can be protected, and a group of entrepreneurs stand out, and the "zero employment" family is gone. The medical and health undertakings that are related to the health of the masses have been broken from institutional reforms. Since 2005, the complete medical system for "retired cadres enjoying public medical care, urban workers have been included in medical insurance, and farmers participating in new rural cooperative medical care" has been implemented, and the universal medical insurance system has been improved. By 2010, 100% of retired cadres and 97% of urban and rural residents have medical security. The county has also improved the county, township (town) and village level three medical networks. There are hospitals in the county, health centers in townships (towns), health clinics in the villages, and 776 medical workers. There are 2 beds for every thousand people. A road to medical insurance that is "disease for medical treatment and medical treatment is appropriate" is basically paved.The pension system for urban and rural residents has gradually improved, and the service industry for the elderly has been improving day by day. The county aging committee, the retired cadre administration, the elderly activity center, and the senior apartment have been established one after another. The basic pension for retired employees of government agencies and institutions is paid monthly. Corporate retirees are included in social security, and urban and rural residents participate in basic old-age insurance. Older people over the age of 10 also receive monthly old-age living allowances. By 2010, the county enjoys 1,904 households with 3,839 people in urban subsistence allowances, and enjoys 5,154 households with 11,300 people in rural subsistence allowances, meeting the requirements of "guarantee insurance" and realizing the full coverage of social security for urban and rural poor.

Economic and social development has brought about the improvement of people´s lives, and the fruits of construction have been shared by the masses. In 2010, the per capita disposable income of urban residents reached 15, 800 yuan, an increase of 3.53 times over the 3480 yuan in 1996, an average annual increase of 11.39%; the per capita net income of farmers reached 5,152 yuan, an increase of 35.54 times compared with 141 yuan in 1978, an average annual increase. 11.9%. According to the internationally evaluated Engel coefficient of the wealth of residents, the expenditure on food consumption in 2010 accounted for the proportion of total household consumption expenditure, urban residents were 36.58%, and rural residents were 43.61%. High-end and durable consumer goods have entered the homes of civilians. The penetration rate of fixed-line telephones and mobile phones for urban residents has reached 71/100 households and 210 units/100 households respectively. Household cars have 3.33 vehicles/100 households, and computers have 50/100 households; rural residents have fixed telephone numbers. 0.17/100 households, 0.45 mobile phones/100 households, and 0.01 household vehicles/100 households. The new three-piece washing machine, TV set and refrigerator generally replace the old three bicycles, watches and sewing machines. A well-off living, eating nutrition, wearing fashion, using high-end, traveling cars, showing the well-being of life in Xiuwen Township, witnessed the improvement of people´s life depends on the development of economy and society, and also the inevitable economic and social development. Home.

Looking at the construction process of the revision of the text in the new era, the achievements are brilliant.

However, there are still certain difficulties and problems on the road ahead: urban and rural areas, regional economic and social development are unbalanced, residents have income gaps, and some low–income people need help; the agricultural foundation is relatively weak, the industrial science and technology content is low, and the industrial structure is not As far as is reasonable; energy conservation and emission reduction are not enough, ecological construction still needs to work hard; moral misconduct, lack of integrity occurs from time to time, comprehensive social security management needs to be strengthened; some party members and cadres have unswerving ideals and beliefs, work style is not correct, work is floating, formalism, bureaucracy Doctrine and money worship are prominent, extravagance and waste are serious, and negative corruption is frequent. The masses are extremely dissatisfied with this.

Looking back on the past, the people of Xiuwen are proud of the fruits they have achieved; looking forward to the future, Xiuwen's children feel a long way to go. Facing the grand goal of building a well–off strategy and realizing modernization, the people of the county will continue to implement the strategic decisions of the CPC Central Committee and the State Council under the leadership of the county party committee and the county government, and do not forget the initial heart, shoulder the burden, inherit the past and start, and then cast brilliant.

Xiaokang shows the future, the future of Xiuwen will be even better!

全县国民经济和社会发展主要数据
(1978—2010)

2010年行政区划、土地面积、人口及人口密度

乡镇名称	行政区划(个)			土地面积(平方公里)	公安户籍人口(人)			人口密度(人/平方公里)
	村民委员会	村民小组	社区居委会		总人口	农业人口	非农业人口	
全县合计	217	1414	10	1075.70	305917	263842	40430	284.4
龙场镇	36	219	4	174.86	73515	50744	22605	420.4
扎佐镇	25	140	3	139.48	41887	31122	10324	300.3
久长镇	22	167	1	117.51	35109	32079	2746	298.8
六广镇	24	145	1	94.10	29358	27838	1275	312.0
谷堡乡	19	129	—	121.10	25872	25274	501	213.6
六屯乡	13	76	—	77.95	16767	16235	462	215.1
小箐乡	17	139	1	103.90	23727	22753	825	228.4
洒坪乡	18	134	—	85.70	17200	16778	418	200.7
大石乡	15	78	—	51.10	13638	13222	406	266.9
六桶乡	28	187	—	110.00	28844	27797	868	262.2

注：总人口中含虽常住，但无法明确是农业或是非农业的人口在内

1978—2010年公安年报：户数、人口及人口“三率”一览表

年份	户数(户)	总人口(人)	按性别分		按农业、非农业分		人口“三率”(‰)		
			男	女	农业人口	非农业人口	出生率	死亡率	自增率
1978	46624	240976	123455	117521	181886	59090	22.84	5.50	17.88
1979	46841	243224	124625	118599	197120	46104	21.73	5.46	16.23
1980	47311	245397	125488	119909	199394	46003	20.33	4.97	14.87
1981	47798	249589	127797	121792	203028	46561	19.54	5.14	14.57
1982	17970	251720	129319	122401	206170	45550	20.10	7.08	15.96
1983	49242	251329	128655	122674	207706	43623	16.65	3.67	9.57

续表

年份	户数(户)	总人口(人)	按性别分		按农业、非农业分		人口“三率”(‰)		
			男	女	农业人口	非农业人口	出生率	死亡率	自增率
1984	48172	250424	128197	122227	209661	40763	17.82	5.38	11.45
1985	50141	251651	128045	123606	211519	40132	13.93	5.93	7.55
1986	51419	252783	129383	123400	213379	39404	14.34	5.95	8.41
1987	52362	252022	129333	122689	215734	36288	16.54	5.73	10.57
1988	55307	260168	132460	127708	224055	36113	12.92	5.36	7.19
1989	56850	259330	132570	126760	225862	33468	13.04	3.86	7.68
1990	58587	265579	136075	129504	231638	33941	12.01	5.53	8.15
1991	59460	267839	137605	130234	233719	34120	13.57	5.29	8.03
1992	59365	268850	137549	131301	237967	30883	17.93	6.07	12.64
1993	60781	272466	139567	132899	240604	31862	16.61	6.44	10.54
1994	61878	275735	151125	134610	241462	34273	17.80	5.76	11.36
1995	63175	282713	144667	138046	246785	35928	18.79	7.76	13.03
1996	64528	283770	143848	139922	245004	38766	21.15	7.58	13.57
1997	65720	278507	141632	136875	244839	33668	15.05	4.92	10.11
1998	68394	280127	143029	137098	247405	32722	27.69	8.48	19.22
1999	68238	283482	144604	138878	250313	33169	19.05	5.99	13.06
2000	69004	289516	147610	141906	253394	36122	32.77	8.75	24.02
2001	71734	289983	148411	141572	253704	36279	9.74	5.10	4.64
2002	71391	290528	149154	141374	253090	37438	10.00	4.70	5.30
2003	72823	288166	147319	140847	251295	36871	7.48	4.47	3.01
2004	75784	283917	145677	138240	245213	38704	12.77	13.08	-0.40
2005	77991	283939	145694	138245	244363	39150	12.35	7.07	5.28
2006	79871	286268	147983	138285	246712	39305	11.19	3.20	7.99
2007	81447	288912	148888	140024	249566	39277	14.08	4.65	9.43
2008	84196	292692	150845	141847	251608	39782	14.12	5.50	8.71
2009	87329	296616	152960	143656	253656	40115	14.26	6.74	7.52
2010	88584	305917	158411	147506	263842	40430	37.76	6.37	31.39

注：1.人口“六普”工作中，为过去未申报户口的人员（主要是超生）补办户口，显得2010年人口出生率和自增率反常偏高。据计划生育部门统计，2010年人口出生率为13.22‰，人口自然增长率为8.76‰。

2.2008—2010年总人口中包含常住但又未落户的人口，故与农业人口和非农业人口之和的数据不一致

1978—2010年生产总值及构成（当年价）一览表

年份	生产总值(万元)				构成(%)			
	合计	一产增加值	二产增加值	三产增加值	生产总值	一产所占比重	二产所占比重	三产所占比重
1978	3580	1379	1490	711	100.00	38.52	41.62	19.86
1979	3670	1475	1400	795	100.00	40.19	38.15	21.66
1980	4318	1945	1481	892	100.00	45.04	34.30	20.66
1981	4846	2177	1657	1012	100.00	44.93	34.19	20.88
1982	5455	2436	1854	1165	100.00	44.66	33.99	21.35
1983	6650	3051	2323	1276	100.00	45.88	34.93	19.19
1984	8888	4933	2606	1349	100.00	55.50	29.32	15.18
1985	10222	4111	4044	2067	100.00	40.22	39.56	20.22
1986	10394	4547	3651	2196	100.00	43.75	35.12	21.13
1987	12765	6327	3204	3234	100.00	49.57	25.10	25.33
1988	16325	9712	2938	3675	100.00	59.49	18.00	22.51
1989	19561	10725	5414	3422	100.00	54.83	27.68	17.49
1990	19725	8204	7689	3832	100.00	41.59	38.98	19.43
1991	21717	10032	7334	4351	100.00	46.19	33.77	20.04
1992	20953	8480	7469	5004	100.00	40.47	35.65	23.88
1993	30877	11901	12774	6202	100.00	38.54	41.37	20.09
1994	40133	16228	16568	7337	100.00	40.44	41.28	18.28
1995	45895	19491	18227	8177	100.00	42.87	39.71	17.82
1996	64906	28214	25261	11431	100.00	43.47	38.92	17.61
1997	74956	30217	29248	15491	100.00	40.31	39.02	20.67
1998	81722	32054	31031	18637	100.00	39.23	37.97	22.80
1999	88295	33181	34170	20944	100.00	37.58	38.70	23.72
2000	93104	34973	23255	34876	100.00	37.56	24.98	37.46
2001	108162	36404	35452	36306	100.00	33.66	32.78	33.56
2002	121807	38045	39019	44743	100.00	31.24	32.03	36.73
2003	140238	40939	44581	54718	100.00	29.19	31.79	39.02
2004	162800	44200	53800	64800	100.00	27.15	33.05	39.80
2005	200071	49162	76609	74300	100.00	24.57	38.29	37.14
2006	236575	54422	91066	91087	100.00	23.01	38.49	38.50
2007	296599	59755	125635	111209	100.00	20.15	42.36	37.49
2008	356325	65192	150535	140598	100.00	18.29	42.25	39.46
2009	392646	70200	172567	149879	100.00	17.88	43.95	38.17
2010	461839	79100	171130	211609	100.00	17.13	37.05	45.82

1978—2010年工业总产值（当年价）一览表

计量单位：万元

年份	全部工业总产值	县级及县以下工业总产值	其中：规模以上（营业收入在500万元以上的）企业			
			合计	国有经济	集体经济	私营及其他
1978	2614	1093	—	—	—	—
1979	2618	1020	—	—	—	—
1980	1991	1697	—	—	—	—
1981	3226	1810	—	—	—	—
1982	4481	2403	—	—	—	—
1983	4361	1786	—	—	—	—
1984	5150	3175	—	—	—	—
1985	7486	3469	—	—	—	—
1986	7587	3613	—	—	—	—
1987	7230	3023	—	—	—	—
1988	9893	6803	—	—	—	—
1989	12060	8189	—	—	—	—
1990	16499	9274	—	—	—	—
1991	16778	8790	—	—	—	—
1992	15436	9951	—	—	—	—
1993	27260	18073	—	—	—	—
1994	40681	25444	—	—	—	—
1995	40053	23843	—	—	—	—
1996	59281	47306	—	—	—	—
1997	66596	55316	—	—	—	—
1998	78293	77196	12279	671	3643	7965
1999	88442	86601	9824	1082	2546	6196
2000	101354	99297	9654	644	1546	7464
2001	109965	108902	29303	714	4556	24033
2002	129836	128731	28553	857	2878	24818
2003	155630	153380	37399	3352	—	34047
2004	108867	107392	70649	12190	—	58459
2005	192516	177451	148053	30924	—	117129
2006	233487	233488	189771	39402	—	150369
2007	312415	312415	269314	65217	—	204097
2008	392393	392393	341336	71893	—	269443
2009	435717	435717	401511	77521	—	323990
2010	560900	560900	512360	83546	—	428814

1978—2010年县及县以下主要工业产品产量表

年份	原煤（万吨）	水泥（万吨）	砖（万块）	饮料酒（吨）	皮鞋（万双）	生铁（吨）	铁矿石（万吨）	生铝矾土（万吨）
1978	39.52	0.27	2952	379	0.60	—	0.95	
1979	23.13	0.52	3200	330	0.65	—	0.30	2.90
1980	29.24	0.37	646	295	1.15	—	3.60	1.97
1981	27.61	0.89	758	390	1.69	—	7.80	2.30
1982	25.86	1.10	1179	382	2.14	—	5.20	2.20
1983	22.17	1.94	976	488	2.56	—	5.90	2.90
1984	33.56	2.38	2400	797	2.80	—	7.70	3.50
1985	34.80	2.42	4563	1255	4.63	—	5.33	2.20
1986	35.45	2.64	6295	2415	4.25	1000	1.00	2.20
1987	33.55	3.80	7269	1154	4.65	2009	0.50	2.19
1988	31.57	4.21	6185	1888	8.89	3211	2.20	2.21
1989	35.88	5.32	5636	1324	2.84	4050	1.70	2.27
1990	34.03	4.29	5614	1937	0.90	5569	1.36	19.71
1991	29.10	4.56	3842	2368	1.27	5600	1.44	16.70
1992	31.94	6.17	4220	2171	3.26	5300	5.86	14.65
1993	49.92	5.88	6163	1907	5.19	6571	6.31	14.19
1994	59.00	9.76	6761	2253	13.82	28923	19.27	32.81
1995	62.00	12.94	5727	2974	3.16	30576	21.23	31.72
1996	106.82	20.79	8610	4370	6.15	47100	29.95	54.31
1997	83.17	30.77	8007	4440	16.84	53100	37.99	54.75
1998	78.39	39.90	9695	8484	20.20	53000	64.12	51.80
1999	33.50	41.30	11213	7516	23.40	60500	43.93	65.00
2000	27.05	60.10	10342	9705	25.20	58200	51.22	70.30
2001	24.50	64.20	11070	18824	22.10	66500	55.15	76.00
2002	69.00	64.47	8968	19310	24.30	52000	50.52	74.00
2003	65.70	72.29	11777	2051	20.80	73850	20.77	60.00
2004	82.60	86.96	18522	2168	20.10	130000	25.32	41.20
2005	77.50	43.00	19470	1842	19.00	79300	19.00	47.00
2006	96.76	51.00	21668	4956	15.00	100000	31.00	55.00
2007	105.60	68.80	13979	2264	6.50	125300	24.00	23.00
2008	106.30	88.00	10205	3054	6.85	89000	17.00	25.60
2009	159.45	118.00	12990	18850	6.00	80000	3.00	22.00
2010	167.00	211.00	14150	9280	2.10	122000	9.00	33.00

1978—2010年县及县以下主要工业产品产量表

年份	熟铝矾土（万吨）	发电量（万度）	供电量（万度）	自来水供应（万吨）	乙醛（吨）	中成药（吨）	成药片剂（万片）	耐火材料制品（万吨）
1978	—	1.00	—	—	—	—	—	—
1979	—	4.10	—	—	—	—	—	—
1980	0.99	45.00	—	—	—	—	—	—
1981	—	22.00	—	—	—	—	—	—
1982	—	45.00	—	—	—	—	—	—
1983	—	31.00	—	—	—	—	—	—
1984	—	119.50	—	—	—	—	—	—
1985	—	130.00	—	—	—	—	—	—
1986	2.19	136.00	—	35.00	—	—	—	—
1987	8.50	138.00	—	—	—	—	—	—
1988	—	187.00	—	—	—	—	—	—
1989	—	185.00	—	51.00	—	—	—	—
1990	13.02	150.20	—	55.00	—	—	—	—
1991	7.82	135.60	—	66.00	—	—	—	—
1992	7.80	154.00	—	68.00	—	—	—	—
1993	5.50	149.00	—	67.00	—	—	—	—
1994	6.08	147.00	—	75.00	—	—	—	—
1995	7.68	260.00	—	104.00	—	—	—	—
1996	22.48	167.00	—	96.00	—	—	—	—
1997	17.87	158.00	—	125.00	—	—	—	—
1998	19.60	153.00	15678	141.00	—	—	—	—
1999	19.80	236.00	16211	161.00	—	14.70	—	—
2000	23.00	222.00	16676	190.00	—	16.80	—	—
2001	27.00	108.00	19850	199.00	3727.00	160.90	—	—
2002	28.20	108.00	21825	214.20	2352.70	164.20	—	—
2003	28.90	113.00	20818	219.90	14612.60	166.90	—	—
2004	26.60	121.00	29355	228.30	12179.50	321.40	—	—
2005	30.00	49270.00	40194	290.00	5856.70	770.10	31772.00	3.13
2006	36.00	98462.00	46313	368.00	3374.00	1101.00	33276.00	2.87
2007	31.60	193574.00	67731	235.00	6189.00	2117.00	33556.00	2.94
2008	25.00	224248.00	64528	281.00	2509.00	2238.00	33781.00	4.50
2009	23.00	207110.00	62576	297.00	7577.00	1933.00	—	3.60
2010	31.00	130067.00	82446	349.00	8797.00	2642.00	—	8.40

1978—2010年农业总产值及构成表（当年价）

计量单位：万元

年份	农业总产值	其中：					各业占农业总产值比重(%)					
		农业产值	林业产值	牧业产值	渔业产值	农林牧渔服务业产值	合计	农业产值	林业产值	牧业产值	渔业产值	农林牧渔服务业产值
1978	2111	1585	63	462	1	—	100.00	75.08	2.98	21.89	0.05	—
1979	2585	2110	54	420	1	—	100.00	81.62	2.09	16.25	0.04	—
1980	2449	1940	59	448	2	—	100.00	79.22	2.41	18.29	0.08	—
1981	3260	2553	56	648	3	—	100.00	78.31	1.72	19.88	0.09	—
1982	4312	3369	93	847	3	—	100.00	78.13	2.16	19.64	0.07	—
1983	4092	3078	159	851	4	—	100.00	75.22	3.88	20.80	0.10	—
1984	5314	3863	124	1310	17	—	100.00	72.70	2.33	24.65	0.32	—
1985	5380	3461	147	1738	34	—	100.00	64.33	2.73	32.31	0.63	—
1986	5800	3713	128	1918	41	—	100.00	64.02	2.20	33.07	0.71	—
1987	6847	4506	153	2166	22	—	100.00	65.81	2.24	31.63	0.32	—
1988	12270	7435	330	4458	47	—	100.00	60.60	2.69	36.33	0.38	—
1989	13789	8921	242	4590	36	—	100.00	64.69	1.76	33.29	0.26	—
1990	11203	7326	397	3440	40	—	100.00	65.39	3.54	30.71	0.36	—
1991	13478	9291	337	3813	37	—	100.00	68.94	2.50	28.29	0.27	—
1992	11747	7281	498	3928	40	—	100.00	61.83	4.24	33.44	0.34	—
1993	15583	9583	710	5242	48	—	100.00	61.49	4.56	33.64	0.31	—
1994	22009	13844	500	7598	67	—	100.00	62.90	2.27	34.52	0.31	—
1995	28753	17366	503	10774	110	—	100.00	60.40	1.75	37.47	0.38	—
1996	42317	27835	702	13582	198	—	100.00	65.78	1.66	32.09	0.47	—
1997	45394	28834	762	15582	216	—	100.00	63.52	4.68	34.33	0.47	—
1998	46543	28533	951	16791	268	—	100.00	61.30	2.04	36.08	0.58	—
1999	44887	26971	1226	16422	268	—	100.00	60.09	2.73	36.58	0.60	—
2000	45669	28519	1038	15829	283	—	100.00	62.45	2.27	34.66	0.62	—
2001	50343	27952	1077	20737	577	—	100.00	55.52	2.14	41.19	1.15	—
2002	53605	28748	1375	22866	616	—	100.00	53.63	2.56	42.66	1.15	—
2003	59152	33748	1115	23090	574	625	100.00	57.05	1.88	39.04	0.97	1.06
2004	68757	37894	1085	28809	768	201	100.00	55.11	1.58	41.90	1.12	0.29
2005	76264	41951	943	32337	832	201	100.00	55.01	1.24	42.40	1.09	0.26
2006	84229	46809	759	35507	921	233	100.00	55.57	0.90	42.16	1.09	0.28
2007	86740	56463	624	28630	780	243	100.00	65.09	0.01	33.01	0.01	0.00
2008	101423	67563	706	32130	742	282	100.00	66.61	0.70	31.68	0.73	0.28
2009	111319	78845	678	30711	782	303	100.00	70.83	0.61	27.59	0.70	0.27
2010	131404	95222	752	34098	982	350	100.00	72.46	0.57	25.95	0.75	0.27

注：从2003年起执行新行业分类标准，将“农林牧渔服务业”产值从三产调至一产

1978—2010年年末耕地、人均面积、农作物总播面及复种指数表

计量单位：亩

年份	耕地面积			人均耕地		农作物播种总面积	复种指数(%)
	合计	田	土	以总人口计算	以农业人口计算		
1978	277803	99829	178874	1.16	1.53	464432	166.64
1979	276150	99165	176985	1.14	1.40	446880	161.83
1980	276073	99118	197655	1.13	1.38	423031	153.23
1981	275501	99109	176329	1.10	1.36	409505	147.64
1982	275790	98740	177050	1.10	1.34	421719	152.91
1983	275779	98751	177028	1.10	1.33	411400	149.18
1984	274773	98498	176275	1.10	1.31	417557	151.96
1985	274521	98459	176062	1.09	1.30	412744	150.35
1986	274133	98384	175749	1.08	1.28	425599	155.25
1987	275032	98290	176742	1.09	1.27	472033	171.83
1988	274805	98275	176530	1.06	1.23	498251	181.32
1989	274346	98277	176069	1.06	1.21	508905	185.50
1990	274331	98260	176071	1.03	1.18	522501	190.46
1991	273864	98170	175694	1.02	1.17	546074	199.40
1992	273933	98197	175736	1.02	1.15	536083	195.70
1993	272675	97548	175127	1.00	1.13	536662	196.81
1994	270663	96814	173849	0.98	1.12	550257	203.30
1995	269680	96150	173530	0.95	1.09	546032	202.47
1996	268650	95985	172665	0.95	1.10	561600	209.05
1997	268650	95985	172665	0.96	1.10	575055	214.05
1998	266385	95280	171105	0.95	1.08	552825	207.53
1999	264930	94485	170445	0.93	1.06	549465	207.40
2000	264345	94305	170040	0.91	1.04	547320	207.05
2001	262845	94305	168540	0.91	1.04	537390	204.45
2002	262770	94305	168465	0.90	1.04	573315	218.18
2003	262770	94305	168465	0.86	0.98	592590	225.52
2004	262020	94305	167715	0.85	0.99	594255	226.80
2005	262020	94305	167715	0.85	0.98	623415	237.93
2006	262020	94305	167715	0.84	0.98	628350	239.81
2007	262005	94185	167820	0.84	0.97	610515	233.02
2008	262005	94185	167820	0.83	0.97	657105	250.80
2009	262005	94185	167820	0.83	0.97	677865	258.72
2010	262005	94185	167820	0.83	0.96	722220	275.65

注：“人均耕地”为便于可比，2009年和2010年也全部换算为“常住一年及以上”口径的人口计算

1978—2010年农业物耗及生产条件的主要指标表

年份	农村用电量(万度)	农机总动力(千瓦)	化肥施用量(吨)		农用塑料薄膜用量(吨)	农药使用量(吨)	有效灌溉面积	
			合计	其中氮肥			合计(亩)	占总耕地%
1978	432	5429	5574	2510	—	—	69598	24.97
1979	259	15267	6994	3490	—	—	57280	20.74
1980	327	16059	4745	2975	—	—	57180	20.71
1981	239	14654	7005	4498	—	—	69598	25.26
1982	321	18049	6010	2846	—	—	64598	23.42
1983	836	21667	7195	3170	—	—	56999	20.67
1984	560	20470	7493	3680	—	—	59736	21.74
1985	449	22323	12028	5951	—	—	59854	21.80
1986	329	23846	9105	3967	—	—	58159	21.22
1987	288	24616	8998	3644	—	—	85535	31.10
1988	366	24642	8159	3708	—	—	85398	31.08
1989	498	26694	8705	4049	—	—	53357	19.45
1990	393	26470	11337	4969	—	—	85050	31.00
1991	396	25778	14497	5154	—	—	77775	28.40
1992	—	25885	13736	5811	—	—	83025	30.31
1993	415	39636	13453	5337	—	—	67650	24.81
1994	478	30652	13292	5403	—	—	86100	31.81
1995	590	36715	18188	6772	—	—	88950	32.98
1996	—	52155	11426	4672	—	—	90110	33.54
1997	—	58613	11531	4730	—	—	92450	34.41
1998	660	63713	16542	6431	—	—	96450	36.21
1999	802	65320	16245	6817	—	—	95805	36.16
2000	780	81501	19979	7830	151	39	98250	37.17
2001	925	88769	19815	7004	159	66	98250	37.38
2002	1188	93339	19702	7313	150	56	98445	37.46
2003	1208	98962	18945	7099	157	48	98610	37.53
2004	1272	101238	18733	6816	161	47	99855	38.11
2005	1301	115290	18050	6561	167	44	100455	38.34
2006	2485	137456	18770	6952	157	41	101250	38.64
2007	2525	159175	19093	6997	157	42	101655	38.80
2008	2561	166782	19450	6842	156	45	68995	26.33
2009	2620	168798	19448	6795	158	40	74085	28.28
2010	2561	175925	19437	6785	171	36	74085	28.28

1978—2010年主要农产品产量表（一）

计量单位：吨

年份	粮食总产	油菜籽产量	烤烟产量	蔬菜产量	干鲜果产量		茶叶产量
					水果	干果	
1978	52970	565	904	7200	446	8	8
1979	49004	908	1243	4700	425	8	16
1980	49200	1613	431	6800	485	10	14
1981	33790	3500	1630	7500	586	12	11
1982	42422	6517	3021	1180	1007	5	19
1983	55630	3150	1525	11000	566	8	21
1984	59076	3076	3695	9000	389	7	14
1985	39002	1386	4468	11200	332	5	24
1986	45107	2988	2839	11900	577	6	12
1987	46432	4492	2605	14800	631	9	14
1988	44762	397	4814	23400	603	14	21
1989	53296	3282	4823	31200	4207	3	13
1990	40569	4992	3213	22600	647	6	18
1991	60570	6962	3932	29800	706	8	16
1992	50447	4355	4305	60300	580	5	18
1993	65861	3537	4823	60300	1125	9	29
1994	66024	2183	2778	74700	706	28	24
1995	67600	4164	2955	67200	904	16	33
1996	72321	5062	4982	76700	583	11	49
1997	76777	6491	5911	33900	974	14	52
1998	82216	6098	3194	36800	1817	26	54
1999	84528	7406	2884	42322	2747	36	51
2000	88904	9039	2814	57480	2547	35	49
2001	83554	6772	1667	71788	8396	36	36
2002	60285	7235	1614	89314	9603	39	38
2003	84865	7309	2138	93985	10414	44	36
2004	91186	8095	1977	107425	12007	68	40
2005	97677	8855	2329	118710	13337	72	41
2006	93126	8947	2105	146132	16246	84	41
2007	98183	7130	2058	154365	19002	93	42
2008	103219	7306	2284	213025	20613	106	43
2009	106378	7624	1418	242416	22515	101	54
2010	104336	6305	3821	272108	24637	108	55

注：“干果”指核桃和板栗

1978—2010年主要农产品产量表（二）

年份	大牲畜(头)		生猪(头)		肉类总产量(吨)	禽蛋产量(吨)	水产品产量(吨)
	年末存栏	年内出栏	年末存栏	年内出栏			
1978	25315	—	67906	—	1542	171	5
1979	25127	—	73335	31059	1680	184	4
1980	25832	—	74706	33380	2421	218	20
1981	28213	—	61537	33592	2476	365	21
1982	29353	—	64415	35862	2901	452	19
1983	30496	—	64848	35696	2867	459	28
1984	32397	—	75130	39658	3353	710	55
1985	33751	—	83235	52980	4569	441	93
1986	35262	—	80636	51007	4540	61	82
1987	37763	—	80677	41772	4481	462	44
1988	37841	—	81113	44802	5562	399	59
1989	38066	—	80711	47165	5754	308	39
1990	39958	—	84204	47409	5134	303	35
1991	40941	—	83604	51528	5670	302	47
1992	42614	—	81538	56000	6085	289	52
1993	43342	4617	89390	62643	7320	383	60
1994	46522	4248	95250	6592	8168	530	72
1995	48835	5302	100638	76289	9227	598	110
1996	50674	5398	117631	90469	11229	606	179
1997	51047	9495	122973	99036	12568	630	200
1998	55221	13195	137841	117536	14189	768	249
1999	55400	12551	148451	131500	15708	820	266
2000	57469	13113	157128	142336	17040	1039	303
2001	58256	14049	181866	182866	21521	1775	713
2002	62186	15170	188127	201394	23740	2907	763
2003	64124	15595	194333	210767	24602	3106	770
2004	68129	16998	209216	238813	27420	3419	848
2005	72807	22103	218551	261653	30354	3665	919
2006	72709	24708	228457	285028	32661	3904	956
2007	39868	12342	82498	132006	14780	2577	600
2008	41978	12455	88628	141421	15860	2792	618
2009	43003	13228	92731	152508	17103	2949	651
2010	47288	13973	96765	159144	17192	3155	658

注：为与全国第二次农业普查成果相衔接，2007年养殖业产量指标在原统计数据的基础上作了修正

1978—2010年乡镇企业基本情况表

年份	企业数（个）	从业人员（人）	现价总产值（万元）	营业收入（万元）	实交税金（万元）	工资总额（万元）	纯利润（万元）
1978	498	4391	477	477	3	54	116
1979	386	6203	743	485	8	62	134
1980	220	4026	628	552	21	172	164
1981	177	3667	1467	561	26	124	74
1982	227	4867	1210	771	33	102	116
1983	253	5871	1087	986	58	190	183
1984	2106	11722	2787	2258	77	245	512
1985	1585	6651	3341	2399	32	310	91
1986	3069	14388	4341	3841	43	310	240
1987	3267	14808	5004	4324	153	341	636
1988	3646	16251	7185	6584	206	652	861
1989	4343	17364	8224	7463	386	538	990
1990	4537	17355	9258	8169	370	678	1026
1991	4440	15196	9061	9061	217	2335	950
1992	4699	16541	11321	10414	385	2296	999
1993	5417	20925	19454	21321	582	3495	2459
1994	6740	21969	30108	28229	1040	4070	3675
1995	5092	18730	39147	44383	1309	6948	5188
1996	7892	22898	81934	77602	1509	8606	6200
1997	7949	24665	87827	120888	1747	9360	7200
1998	7992	25738	138026	157937	2114	10972	8747
1999	2490	4982	164437	189955	2376	11372	14858
2000	2656	5274	193512	224231	2673	11514	16004
2001	2076	4295	231381	268882	3003	12446	21253
2002	8061	28666	279683	314728	3373	15554	26396
2003	8104	29065	280180	316074	4181	20316	18251
2004	6498	22746	258395	283158	4848	15377	18763
2005	6298	23954	253164	267541	6682	18096	26402
2006	6521	25369	295410	300842	9176	20945	23429
2007	332	13379	282189	258332	15681	17845	23694
2008	6450	30507	423562	411242	22119	31152	34003
2009	6378	33353	561438	517649	24695	38658	45866
2010	6482	33005	696695	640194	26456	43696	46580

注：2007年“企业数”为符合四个条件的企业个数

1978—2010年全社会固定资产投资完成情况表

计量单位：万元

年份	全社会固定资产完成额	50万元以上项目投资				50万元以下项目投资	房地产开发投资	农村集体	农村个人	城镇工矿区私人建房	个体私营	跨地区项目
		合计	基本建设	更新改造	其他投资							
1978	213	213	213	—	—	—	—	—	—	—	—	—
1979	211	211	211	—	—	—	—	—	—	—	—	—
1980	126	126	116	10	—	—	—	—	—	—	—	—
1981	253	253	59	194	—	—	—	—	—	—	—	—
1982	304	304	128	176	—	—	—	—	—	—	—	—
1983	631	592	181	411	—	39	—	—	—	—	—	—
1984	444	444	210	182	52	—	—	—	—	—	—	—
1985	1326	1326	328	998	—	—	—	—	—	—	—	—
1986	364	364	128	236	—	—	—	—	—	—	—	—
1987	402	402	114	288	—	—	—	—	—	—	—	—
1988	858	858	263	595	—	—	—	—	—	—	—	—
1989	682	682	597	85	—	—	—	—	—	—	—	—
1990	645	645	645	—	—	—	—	—	—	—	—	—
1991	766	766	433	333	—	—	—	—	—	—	—	—
1992	636	636	200	436	—	—	—	—	—	—	—	—
1993	759	759	639	120	—	—	—	—	—	—	—	—
1994	1698	1698	779	919	—	—	—	—	—	—	—	—
1995	4616	4616	2376	2240	—	—	—	—	—	—	—	—
1996	5021	5021	4371	650	—	—	—	—	—	—	—	—
1997	27729	27729	27729	—	—	—	—	—	—	—	—	—
1998	6280	6280	6280	—	—	—	—	—	—	—	—	—
1999	14230	6831	6831	—	—	—	—	5881	—	1518	—	—
2000	31343	21542	20542	1000	—	—	2242	2872	2009	1720	958	—
2001	59350	45701	42627	3074	—	—	1029	3100	2100	2658	4762	—
2002	60704	43774	31493	12281	—	—	3029	5200	5500	450	2751	—
2003	85427	55659	36290	18699	670	—	656	9965	9866	1619	7012	650
2004	122766	98414	69354	28832	288	—	2097	—	9962	2195	—	10098
2005	170060	142950	90631	39556	12763	897	2362	—	14832	9019	—	—
2006	180000	88486	30963	49163	8360	978	501	—	23568	—	—	66467
2007	250060	137844	43040	56000	38804	14349	2750	—	25678	—	—	69439
2008	274548	174269	42440	94415	37414	32150	22769	—	31256	—	—	14104
2009	373900	215621	69258	98025	48338	35426	41487	—	32547	—	—	48819
2010	510800	351591	35701	292319	23571	54312	42017	—	20154	—	—	42726

1978—2010年社会消费品零售总额表

计量单位：万元

年份	合计	其中			各经济类型所占比重(%)		
		国有经济	集体经济	个体及其他	国有经济	集体经济	个体及其他
1978	2472.00	1219.00	1253.00	—	49.31	50.69	—
1979	2449.00	1208.00	1241.00	—	49.33	50.67	—
1980	2566.00	2208.00	350.00	8.00	86.06	13.64	0.31
1981	3016.20	1489.90	1338.90	187.40	49.40	44.39	6.21
1982	3175.40	1293.30	1554.70	327.40	40.73	48.96	10.31
1983	3503.30	1531.70	1418.70	552.90	43.72	40.50	15.78
1984	4120.50	1817.10	1311.70	991.70	44.10	31.83	24.07
1985	4781.40	1989.80	1599.00	1192.60	41.62	33.44	24.94
1986	4953.90	1764.90	1826.70	1362.30	35.63	36.87	27.50
1987	5757.10	2217.90	2003.50	1535.70	38.52	34.80	26.68
1988	6090.80	2198.10	2198.90	1693.80	36.09	36.10	27.81
1989	6751.90	2316.10	2365.00	2069.80	34.31	35.03	30.66
1990	6794.00	2125.00	2129.00	2540.00	31.28	31.34	37.38
1991	7211.00	2132.00	2332.00	2747.00	29.57	32.34	38.01
1992	7450.00	2383.00	2222.00	2848.00	31.99	29.82	38.19
1993	8261.00	3544.00	1353.00	3364.00	42.90	16.38	40.72
1994	9355.00	3898.00	1682.00	3775.00	41.67	17.98	40.35
1995	12084.00	4940.00	2082.00	5062.00	40.88	17.23	41.89
1996	13897.00	5672.00	2351.00	5874.00	40.81	16.92	42.27
1997	15982.00	6108.00	3040.00	6834.00	38.22	19.02	42.76
1998	17590.00	4991.00	3373.00	9226.00	28.37	19.18	52.45
1999	19007.00	其中:城镇8971.00万元，占47.20%,乡村10036.00万元,占52.80%					
2000	20555.00	其中:城镇9688.00万元，占41.73%,乡村10867.00万元,占52.87%					
2001	23227.00	其中:城镇10851.00万元,占46.72%,乡村12376.00万元,占53.28%					
2002	26479.00	其中:城镇12262.00万元,占46.31%,乡村14217.00万元,占53.69%					
2003	30186.00	其中:城镇12691.00万元,占42.04%,乡村17495.00万元,占57.96%					
2004	35139.00	其中:城镇14773.00万元,占42.04%,乡村20366.00万元,占57.96%					
2005	41617.00	其中:城镇17589.00万元,占42.26%,乡村24028.00万元,占57.74%					
2006	48285.00	其中:城镇20407.00万元,占42.26%,乡村27878.00万元,占57.74%					
2007	57935.00	其中:城镇24747.00万元,占42.72%,乡村33188.00万元,占57.28%					
2008	72137.10	其中:城镇30843.90万元,占42.76%,乡村41293.20万元,占57.24%					
2009	86565.00	其中:城镇36905.00万元,占42.63%,乡村49660.00万元,占57.37%					
2010	101300.00	其中:城镇40616.00万元,占40.09%,乡村60684.00万元,占59.91%					

注：1999年起，因统计指标调整，只反映城镇和乡村实现值，无不同经济成分的数据

1978—2010年公路运输及邮政、电信业务总量表

年份	客货汽车拥有量(辆)	公路运输量		邮电业务总量(万元)		
		客运量(万人次)	货运量(万吨)	合计	邮政业务总量	电信业务总量
1978	28	—	29.30	19.10	—	—
1979	30	—	41.30	19.60	—	—
1980	50	—	38.10	17.10	—	—
1981	85	—	35.00	26.10	—	—
1982	105	—	26.10	26.20	—	—
1983	120	—	33.50	27.20	—	—
1984	158	—	22.10	29.60	—	—
1985	203	61.40	28.30	32.40	—	—
1986	361	69.10	30.20	33.70	—	—
1987	361	120.70	75.50	36.60	—	—
1988	385	145.50	87.90	40.40	—	—
1989	395	126.20	67.40	48.80	—	—
1990	457	138.70	66.10	86.20	—	—
1991	407	133.40	57.20	97.30	—	—
1992	472	122.40	93.60	111.30	—	—
1993	481	154.90	108.80	141.20	—	—
1994	565	161.60	149.80	219.80	—	—
1995	671	192.00	178.00	325.30	—	—
1996	720	197.00	161.00	478.30	—	—
1997	769	215.40	240.30	814.00	—	—
1998	842	202.00	192.00	1955.00	207.00	1748.00
1999	1137	206.00	210.00	1138.00	256.00	882.00
2000	1262	325.00	330.00	1361.00	244.00	1117.00
2001	1345	360.00	353.00	1401.00	296.00	1105.00
2002	1452	376.00	401.00	2984.50	254.50	2730.00
2003	1612	384.00	432.00	3344.20	295.00	3049.00
2004	1953	425.00	269.00	3836.80	253.00	3583.80
2005	2012	483.00	303.00	5131.00	261.00	4870.00
2006	1338	301.00	359.00	5468.50	344.50	5124.00
2007	1499	308.00	373.00	8470.00	420.00	8050.00
2008	1664	400.00	410.00	11728.00	526.00	11202.00
2009	1751	490.00	455.00	13895.00	534.00	13361.00
2010	2117	528.00	510.00	14767.00	750.00	14017.00

注：2008年“客运量”和“货运量”为统计测算数

1978—2010年财政收入一览表

计量单位：万元

年份	（一）财政总收入	其中：						（二）上级财政补助收入
		县级财政收入	其中：				上级财政收入	
			农业税收入	工商税收入	国有企业收入	其他收入		
1978	188.90	188.90	55.88	182.34	-52.13	2.81	—	325.60
1979	230.56	230.56	53.00	199.73	-22.89	0.72	—	313.40
1980	188.26	188.26	52.80	169.75	-38.27	3.98	—	313.40
1981	295.53	295.53	49.76	296.68	-54.25	3.34	—	482.20
1982	635.01	635.01	51.92	579.76	1.33	2.00	—	372.20
1983	795.96	795.96	84.72	673.17	33.83	4.24	—	470.30
1984	968.93	968.93	84.09	856.19	22.96	5.69	—	387.30
1985	962.57	962.57	58.89	856.00	37.32	10.36	—	260.00
1986	864.92	864.92	85.20	742.90	16.40	20.42	—	347.06
1987	993.02	993.02	105.34	842.20	21.80	23.68	—	310.70
1988	1351.77	1351.77	119.85	1148.40	33.80	49.72	—	350.45
1989	1615.46	1615.46	159.17	1351.46	40.10	64.73	—	398.86
1990	1415.90	1415.90	119.99	1230.65	16.60	48.66	—	432.70
1991	1644.46	1644.46	123.28	1391.08	46.40	83.70	—	583.80
1992	1849.38	1849.38	187.05	1444.10	121.30	96.93	—	531.60
1993	2270.01	2270.01	230.99	1880.37	74.20	84.45	—	611.60
1994	2228.20	2228.20	614.50	961.10	278.50	374.10	—	1345.30
1995	2203.10	2203.10	680.00	939.10	75.80	508.20	—	1136.40
1996	4006.30	2541.20	1013.40	1018.50	47.00	462.30	1465.10	2339.20
1997	5660.73	3147.56	1195.05	1460.29	-12.84	505.06	2513.17	1917.10
1998	6566.28	3741.16	1114.29	1845.84	29.26	751.77	2825.12	2481.00
1999	7174.73	4269.19	823.00	2506.00	—	940.19	2905.54	4150.00
2000	8003.09	4853.75	895.74	2393.00	-25.00	1590.01	3149.34	4531.00
2001	9202.95	5635.00	611.00	3051.00	—	1973.00	3567.95	8712.00
2002	11746.00	7086.00	855.00	3695.00	—	2536.00	4660.00	10108.00
2003	13214.00	8592.00	848.00	4331.00	—	3413.00	4622.00	11549.00
2004	17122.51	10399.00	753.00	5999.00	309.00	3647.00	6723.51	14919.00
2005	21382.49	12828.00	530.00	8257.00	49.00	3722.00	8554.49	17157.00
2006	28580.47	14553.00	610.00	8506.00	124.00	5313.00	14027.47	22492.00
2007	32453.53	15791.37	税收收入：11051.00		非税收入：4740.37		16662.16	28154.00
2008	43062.37	19091.14	税收收入：13324.39		非税收入：5766.75		23971.23	44024.00
2009	44065.37	23028.00	税收收入：15445.37		非税收入：7582.63		21037.37	32839.00
2010	54386.79	27960.08	税收收入：19634.57		非税收入：8325.51		26426.71	41679.00

注：财政收入包含基金收入在内

1978—2010年财政支出一览表

计量单位：万元

年份	一、预算支出	其中				二、上解支出
		农业类支出	教科文卫支出	行政管理支出	基本建设及城市维护支出	
1978	492.78	163.09	145.30	73.15	15.00	88.10
1979	527.66	176.64	174.61	82.89	1.00	24.30
1980	517.91	141.22	197.37	91.26	—	
1981	564.40	158.48	223.06	95.34	—	59.20
1982	717.87	133.47	281.19	148.16	—	287.40
1983	937.83	228.42	349.14	162.56	10.00	291.80
1984	1154.38	152.57	445.76	197.34	113.00	312.90
1985	1013.91	113.25	462.19	224.80	13.06	167.50
1986	1133.05	122.80	505.80	234.23	24.71	85.70
1987	1199.50	132.70	465.95	277.93	40.30	76.50
1988	1517.94	158.74	581.27	299.15	61.57	223.10
1989	1779.26	213.49	619.20	302.41	114.61	246.80
1990	1732.29	206.11	666.18	335.55	113.51	213.70
1991	1964.50	239.90	720.70	321.30	72.80	315.50
1992	2614.49	347.89	887.80	450.10	140.50	174.50
1993	2800.20	470.40	976.80	525.70	32.90	187.00
1994	3794.10	466.10	1289.40	638.80	109.30	91.90
1995	4246.40	456.90	1471.40	765.10	49.00	89.00
1996	4742.10	731.00	1701.20	1043.00	41.90	140.00
1997	4636.40	845.00	1408.00	928.00	57.60	192.20
1998	6097.00	1214.00	2391.00	1185.00	88.00	215.80
1999	6268.00	772.00	2591.00	1401.00	183.00	165.00
2000	7023.00	874.00	3515.00	1175.00	154.00	123.00
2001	9848.00	1110.00	4478.00	1766.00	271.00	121.00
2002	13830.00	1253.00	5586.00	2420.00	700.00	164.00
2003	15746.00	1536.00	6717.00	2684.00	234.00	185.00
2004	18628.00	1753.00	7705.00	3283.00	531.00	162.00
2005	22193.00	2606.00	8888.00	4463.00	418.00	215.00
2006	27941.00	2511.00	11085.00	5471.00	1137.00	330.00
2007	41828.00	5965.00	15017.00	8628.00	1274.00	330.00
2008	54959.00	9331.00	19154.00	10258.00	2005.00	392.00
2009	72619.00	12394.00	21819.00	13337.00	1495.00	320.00
2010	89801.00	18831.00	28084.00	14779.00	1318.00	378.00

1978—2010年金融机构年末存、贷款余额及现金收支情况表

计量单位：万元

年份	存贷款余额			现金收支	
	存款		贷款	收入	支出
	合计	其中:城乡居民存款			
1978	1044	155	1680	2117	2631
1979	978	211	1759	2362	3028
1980	1500	350	1330	2100	2800
1981	1688	415	1568	3421	4418
1982	1793	545	1705	3806	5284
1983	1765	665	1262	4043	5512
1984	2872	887	1712	4881	7142
1985	3969	1410	4254	6254	8468
1986	4097	1787	6886	6352	8720
1987	5390	2412	8351	8025	10635
1988	6358	2494	5960	10045	13863
1989	6487	3135	9556	9117	13988
1990	8165	4090	11109	9268	14553
1991	9398	5019	11248	11133	17494
1992	13970	7388	15017	14775	20581
1993	16379	7856	16075	28938	35096
1994	19709	12375	20439	27257	35222
1995	27287	17314	27019	35785	49159
1996	34372	22638	30664	60169	72196
1997	35826	34884	35633	58528	72531
1998	42155	28992	38073	86025	101972
1999	47581	30708	46050	100900	120231
2000	55021	33886	47279	117925	134594
2001	64136	38384	50792	143852	156905
2002	73773	41486	52402	170503	186996
2003	78506	46730	46636	214173	224138
2004	103680	43356	57864	279211	301451
2005	117621	67686	69524	614764	660433
2006	154119	80413	109660	681981	767300
2007	180433	94613	131193	882735	893881
2008	218207	96123	111345	931699	957593
2009	235656	131112	147681	818951	841055
2010	277261	157075	193055	990697	1022224

1978—2010年学校数量，教职工及在校学生人数表

年份	中学(含农中、职中)			小学(含特校)		
	学校数(所)	教职工人数(人)	在校学生数(人)	学校数(所)	教职工人数(人)	在校学生数(人)
1978	8	361	9412	213	1646	42995
1979	17	521	12276	222	2092	44302
1980	20	244	14745	216	2130	44486
1981	22	289	13368	207	2369	44320
1982	21	313	12234	201	2180	41857
1983	24	353	12238	200	2272	43851
1984	25	383	11447	198	2282	44114
1985	10	455	11970	197	2319	44809
1986	21	457	12488	192	2448	45282
1987	26	472	11098	184	2363	42915
1988	20	506	10733	194	2255	41927
1989	14	814	9421	181	2033	41373
1990	23	795	8973	174	1933	39603
1991	23	670	8864	194	1928	37719
1992	22	704	9956	170	1977	36230
1993	22	729	9059	168	1980	32842
1994	22	774	9229	158	2067	33662
1995	26	782	9287	158	2082	37700
1996	23	742	9225	180	2173	38832
1997	24	820	9869	159	2242	39977
1998	22	999	10662	183	2402	37407
1999	23	999	13613	150	2265	38152
2000	23	1051	16247	124	2281	36517
2001	23	1149	18389	116	2151	33788
2002	24	859	12719	113	1536	30939
2003	25	1286	17767	113	2154	29076
2004	28	1029	21020	74	1934	28459
2005	28	1225	19955	72	1751	26833
2006	28	1183	18170	70	1603	26395
2007	27	1028	16959	68	1489	24708
2008	23	1030	17091	64	1498	22565
2009	24	973	17656	73	1424	20277
2010	23	972	18346	70	1349	18570

1978—2010年卫生机构、病床及人员配备情况表

年份	机构（个）	病床（张）	总人数（人）	其中:技术人员(人)							
				合计	医生				护师护士	其他
					小计	中医师	西医师	医士		
1978	42	133	349	188	111	16	47	48	22	55
1979	41	135	—	200	—	—	—	—	—	—
1980	42	180	—	211	—	—	—	—	—	—
1981	44	180	440	240	96	20	50	26	35	109
1982	45	182	496	272	101	26	53	22	53	118
1983	44	194	—	278	—	—	—	—	—	—
1984	44	194	530	280	113	25	53	35	52	115
1985	42	213	507	307	114	23	53	38	46	147
1986	51	317	560	417	141	23	64	54	70	206
1987	51	245	570	531	—	—	—	—	—	—
1988	51	255	530	530	—	—	—	—	—	—
1989	53	336	499	496	156	14	82	60	93	247
1990	53	374	574	487	146	15	76	55	91	250
1991	57	368	596	499	172	14	78	80	78	249
1992	24	402	651	571	181	13	75	93	91	299
1993	57	368	596	499	163	14	78	71	82	254
1994	57	368	596	499	163	14	78	71	82	254
1995	27	460	704	605	202	21	108	73	148	255
1996	24	460	628	543	205	22	114	69	141	197
1997	24	394	629	536	207	21	114	72	124	205
1998	24	349	629	544	195	22	102	71	137	212
1999	25	329	640	539	142	—	—	—	170	227
2000	25	329	640	549	132	—	—	—	158	259
2001	22	349	642	550	125	14	67	44	164	261
2002	18	310	504	418	144	14	74	56	171	103
2003	18	333	487	411	160	17	79	64	177	74
2004	17	341	451	398	212	21	116	75	186	—
2005	20	475	596	504	268	34	149	85	194	42
2006	18	479	556	474	243	27	129	87	179	52
2007	18	496	569	486	250	28	132	90	183	53
2008	40	464	709	603	—	—		—	—	—
2009	39	547	768	664	296	168		128	214	154
2010	29	583	776	616	336	213		123	123	157

注：2008年卫生机构的“人员配备”只有总数，无具体分类数据

1978—2010年年末职工人数与工资总额表

年份	职工人数（人）				工资总额（万元）			
	合计	全民所有制单位	城镇集体单位	其他单位	合计	全民所有制单位	城镇集体单位	其他单位
1978	19260	15531	3729	—	11180.00	1025.00	93.00	—
1979	19253	15690	3563	—	1209.00	1077.00	132.00	—
1980	18003	15645	2358	—	1381.00	1253.00	128.00	—
1981	19689	16768	1921	—	1457.00	1352.00	105.00	—
1982	18237	16521	1716	—	1473.00	1363.00	110.00	—
1983	9387	7444	1943	—	651.00	519.00	132.00	—
1984	9887	7141	2746	—	1023.80	574.20	449.60	—
1985	10047	8213	1834	—	886.10	770.20	115.90	—
1986	10363	8711	1652	—	1097.50	976.00	121.50	—
1987	10772	8730	2042	—	1113.50	963.00	150.50	—
1988	10582	8631	1951	—	1229.00	1070.50	158.50	—
1989	10830	8790	2040	—	1374.70	1201.00	173.70	—
1990	10937	9032	1905	—	1557.00	1335.00	222.00	—
1991	10736	8830	1906	—	1618.00	1395.00	223.00	—
1992	10363	8856	1507	—	1918.00	1712.00	206.00	—
1993	10327	8858	1469	—	2261.00	2015.00	246.00	—
1994	8917	7838	1079	—	2773.00	2528.00	245.00	—
1995	8944	8472	472	—	3262.00	3147.00	115.00	—
1996	8353	7722	631	—	3647.00	3463.00	184.00	—
1997	8423	8071	352	—	4060.00	3914.00	146.00	—
1998	8162	7424	738	11	4343.00	4013.00	325.00	5.00
1999	7009	6557	317	135	4835.00	4596.00	168.00	71.00
2000	7323	6624	460	239	5779.70	5377.50	271.30	130.90
2001	8298	7600	401	297	8198.30	7750.50	354.10	93.70
2002	8402	7280	456	666	8643.80	7740.90	469.40	433.50
2003	9910	8046	577	1287	11588.30	9927.20	570.70	1090.40
2004	11985	7619	302	4064	14552.50	10710.60	691.70	3150.20
2005	12512	8096	300	4116	16992.60	12683.60	301.00	4008.00
2006	13000	7685	406	4909	19951.10	15199.20	305.10	4446.80
2007	13906	7413	549	5944	26489.20	19574.30	595.40	6319.50
2008	13680	7207	500	5973	32803.50	21075.00	715.40	11013.10
2009	13717	7504	534	5679	35563.90	23942.60	834.00	10787.30
2010	14231	8065	579	5587	43859.10	27874.00	2419.30	13565.80

注：1982年（含1982年）前，职工人数和工资总额包括水电九局在内；1998年起，职工人数和工资总额只计在岗职工

1978—2010年农民、城镇居民、职工年收入及城乡居民储蓄表

计量单位：元

年份	农民人均年纯收入	城镇居民年人均可支配收入	职工年人均工资收入	其中			城乡居民人均储蓄存款
				全民所有制职工	城镇集体所有制职工	其他职工	
1978	141	—	580.50	660.00	249.40	—	6
1979	155	—	628.00	686.40	370.50	—	9
1980	178	—	767.10	800.90	54.80	—	14
1981	180	—	779.60	806.30	546.60	—	17
1982	221	—	807.70	825.00	641.00	—	22
1983	250	—	693.50	679.20	679.40	—	26
1984	303	—	1035.50	804.10	1637.30	—	35
1985	305	—	882.00	937.80	632.10	—	56
1986	310	—	1059.10	1120.40	735.50	—	71
1987	372	—	1033.70	1103.10	737.00	—	96
1988	471	—	1161.40	1240.36	812.40	—	86
1989	506	—	1269.30	1366.30	851.50	—	121
1990	538	—	1423.60	1478.10	1165.40	—	154
1991	551	—	1507.10	1579.80	1170.00	—	187
1992	581	—	1850.80	1933.20	1367.00	—	275
1993	639	—	2189.40	2274.80	1674.60	—	288
1994	879	—	3109.80	3255.30	2270.60	—	449
1995	1194	—	3647.10	3714.60	2436.40	—	612
1996	1459	3480	4366.10	4484.60	2916.00	—	798
1997	1608	3908	4820.10	4849.50	4147.70	—	893
1998	1673	4082	5314.90	5405.40	4403.80	4545.50	1035
1999	1746	4524	6891.00	7009.30	5299.70	5259.30	1083
2000	1808	5110	7911.00	8118.00	6102.00	5519.00	1132
2001	1906	5526	10146.00	10283.00	8765.00	6741.00	1268
2002	2028	5899	11017.00	11185.00	10294.00	9243.00	1366
2003	2158	6461	11813.00	12356.00	9891.00	9094.00	1536
2004	2390	7394	12431.00	13487.00	12030.00	8970.00	1740
2005	2702	8503	14750.00	16498.00	9934.00	9945.00	2193
2006	2968	9729	15828.00	18665.00	10316.00	10687.00	2591
2007	3535	11591	20764.00	25208.00	14522.00	13972.00	3031
2008	4178	12796	23979.00	29249.00	14308.00	18438.00	3056
2009	4620	14200	26472.00	32168.00	16194.00	19721.00	4152
2010	5152	15756	31176.00	34934.00	42222.00	24594.00	4952

注：1.2000年起“职工年均工资收入”是以在岗职工人数计算的

2.从2010年起，农村信用联社纳入城镇集体单位报表，其人数和工资总额占集体单位比重较高

2000—2010年农村居民小康综合评价表（实绩）

指　标	评价标准		权数	有关指标各年实绩										
	温饱值	小康值		2000年	2001年	2002年	2003年	2004年	2005年	2006年	2007年	2008年	2009年	2010年
1.人均纯收入	600元	2500元	30.0	1808.8	1906.0	2028.0	2158.0	2390.0	2702.0	2968.0	3535.0	4188.0	4620.0	5152.0
2.基尼系数	20.0%	35.0%	5.0	29.0	29.0	29.0	26.0	25.0	25.0	25.0	25.0	26.0	27.0	27.6
3.恩格尔系数	60.0%	50.0%	6.0	59.0	57.0	56.0	52.0	52.0	51.8	51.7	51.5	51.3	51.1	50.1
4.蛋白质摄入	47克/日·人	75克/日·人	9.0	69.0	58.0	56.0	53.0	55.0	55.0	55.0	56.0	58.0	62.0	63.0
5.衣着消费支出	27元/人	70元/人	3.0	56.0	62.0	68.0	66.0	68.0	75.0	78.0	157.0	204.0	212.0	287.0
6.钢木结构住房比重	43.0%	80.0%	7.0	53.0	32.0	62.0	43.0	64.0	65.0	69.0	71.0	73.0	74.0	74.0
7.电视机普及率	1台/百户	70台/百户	6.0	46.0	54.0	54.0	52.0	54.0	56.0	57.0	57.0	61.0	68.0	68.0
8.服务消费支出比重	2.0%	10.0%	6.0	7.0	7.0	6.2	6.6	6.7	6.7	6.7	6.7	6.7	6.7	6.7
9.人口平均预期寿命	68岁	70岁	4.0	69.0	70.0	70.0	69.0	69.0	69.0	69.0	69.0	69.0	69.0	69.0
10.劳动力平均受教育程度	6年	8年	5.0	6.8	7.0	7.0	6.8	6.8	6.8	6.8	6.8	6.8	6.8	6.8
11.已通公路行政村比重	50.0%	86.0%	3.0	100.0	100.0	100.0	100.0	100.0	100.0	100.0	100.0	100.0	100.0	100.0
12.安全卫生水普及率	50.0%	90.0%	3.0	60.0	62.0	62.0	62.0	63.0	63.0	63.0	63.0	68.0	68.0	74.0
13.用电户比重	50.0%	95.0%	3.0	99.0	99.0	99.0	99.0	99.0	99.0	99.0	99.0	99.0	99.0	100.0
14.已通电话行政村比重	50.0%	70.0%	2.0	50.0	53.0	67.0	67.0	69.0	81.0	81.0	81.0	81.0	88.0	74.0
15.享受社会五保人口比重	50.0%	90.0%	4.0	80.0	100.0	100.0	100.0	100.0	100.0	100.0	100.0	100.0	100.0	100.0
16.万人刑事案件立案件数	5件	20件	4.0	20.0	16.0	17.0	32.0	29.0	24.0	24.0	25.0	29.0	47.0	52.0
17.小康户所占比重	—	70.0%												
合　　计	—	—	100.0											

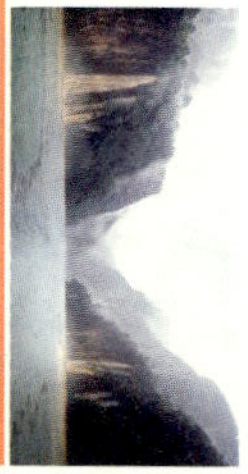

2000年——2010年农村居民小康综合评价表（量化评分）

指　标	评价标准		权数	各年最终评价分数(分)										
	温饱值	小康值		2000年	2001年	2002年	2003年	2004年	2005年	2006年	2007年	2008年	2009年	2010年
1.人均纯收入	600元	2500元	30.0	19.07	22.5	22.56	24.60	28.26	30.00	30.00	30.00	30.00	30.00	30.00
2.基尼系数	20.0%	35.0%	5.0	3.00	3.00	3.00	2.00	1.67	1.67	1.67	1.67	2.00	2.33	2.53
3.恩格尔系数	60.0%	50.0%	6.0	0.60	1.80	2.40	4.80	4.80	4.92	4.98	5.10	5.22	5.34	5.94
4.蛋白质摄入	47克/日·人	75克/日·人	9.0	7.07	3.54	2.89	1.93	2.57	2.57	2.57	2.89	3.54	4.82	5.14
5.衣着消费支出	27元/人	70元/人	3.0	2.02	0.20	2.86	2.72	2.86	3.35	3.56	3.56	1.42	1.53	3.00
6.钢木结构住房比重	43.0%	80.0%	7.0	1.89	2.84	3.59	3.78	3.97	4.16	4.92	5.30	5.68	5.86	5.86
7.电视机普及率	1台/百户	70台/百户	6.0	3.91	4.61	4.61	4.43	4.61	4.78	4.87	4.87	5.22	5.83	5.83
8.服务消费支出比重	2.0%	10.0%	6.0	3.75	3.75	3.15	3.15	3.53	3.53	3.53	3.53	3.53	3.53	3.53
9.人口平均预期寿命	68岁	70岁	4.0	2.00	4.00	4.00	2.00	2.00	2.00	2.00	2.00	2.00	2.00	2.00
10.劳动力平均受教育程度	6年	8年	5.0	2.00	2.50	2.50	2.00	2.00	2.00	2.00	2.00	2.00	2.30	2.00
11.已通公路行政村比重	50.0%	86.0%	3.0	3.00	3.00	3.00	3.00	3.00	3.00	3.00	3.00	3.00	3.00	3.00
12.安全卫生水普及率	50.0%	90.0%	3.0	0.75	0.90	0.90	0.90	0.98	0.98	0.98	0.98	1.35	1.38	1.38
13.用电户比重	50.0%	95.0%	3.0	3.00	3.00	3.00	3.00	3.00	3.00	3.00	3.00	3.00	3.00	3.00
14.已通电话行政村比重	50.0%	70.0%	2.0	0.00	0.30	1.70	1.70	1.90	2.00	2.00	2.00	2.00	2.00	2.00
15.享受社会五保人口比重	50.0%	90.0%	4.0	3.00	4.00	4.00	4.00	4.00	4.00	4.00	4.00	4.00	4.00	4.00
16.万人刑事案件立案件数	5件	20件	4.0	4.00	2.93	3.20	4.00	4.00	4.00	4.00	4.00	4.00	4.00	4.00
17.小康户所占比重	—	70.0%												
合　　计	—	—	100.0	59.06	60.99	67.35	68.01	73.15	75.96	77.08	77.90	77.96	80.62	83.21

修文县1978至2010年国民经济和社会发展主要指标统计图

地方生产总值及年均递增速度

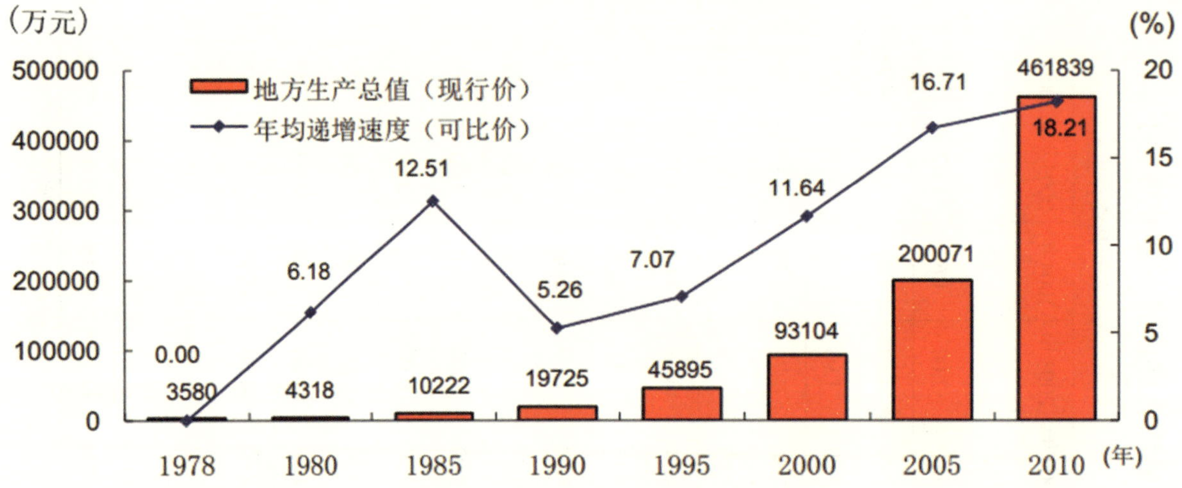

注：期内最高值为461839万元（2010年），最低值为3580万元（1978年）

地方生产总值产业构成变化走势（当年价）

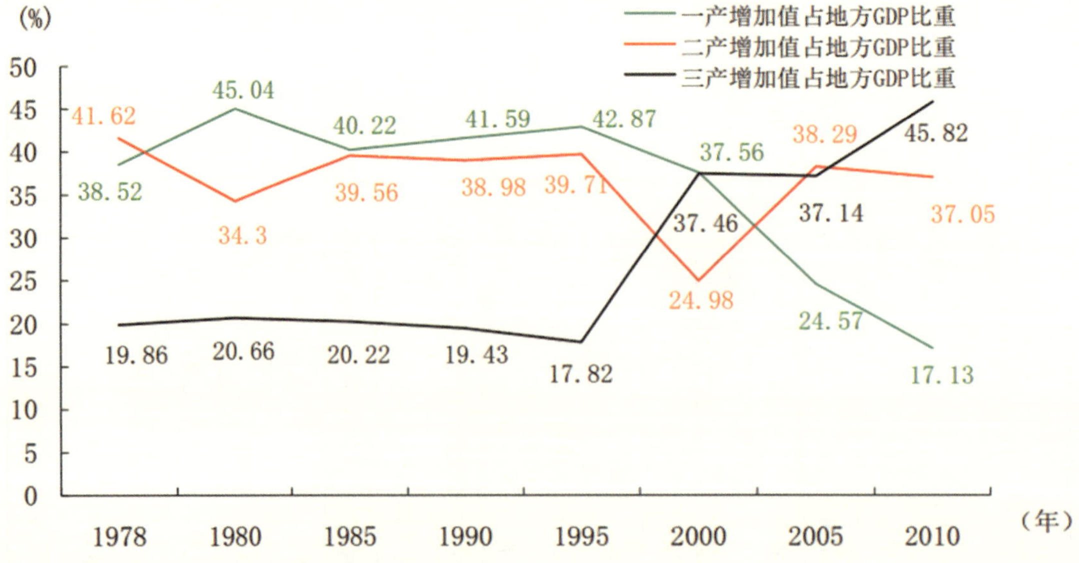

注：“地方GDP”为地方生产总值

农业总产值及年均递增速度

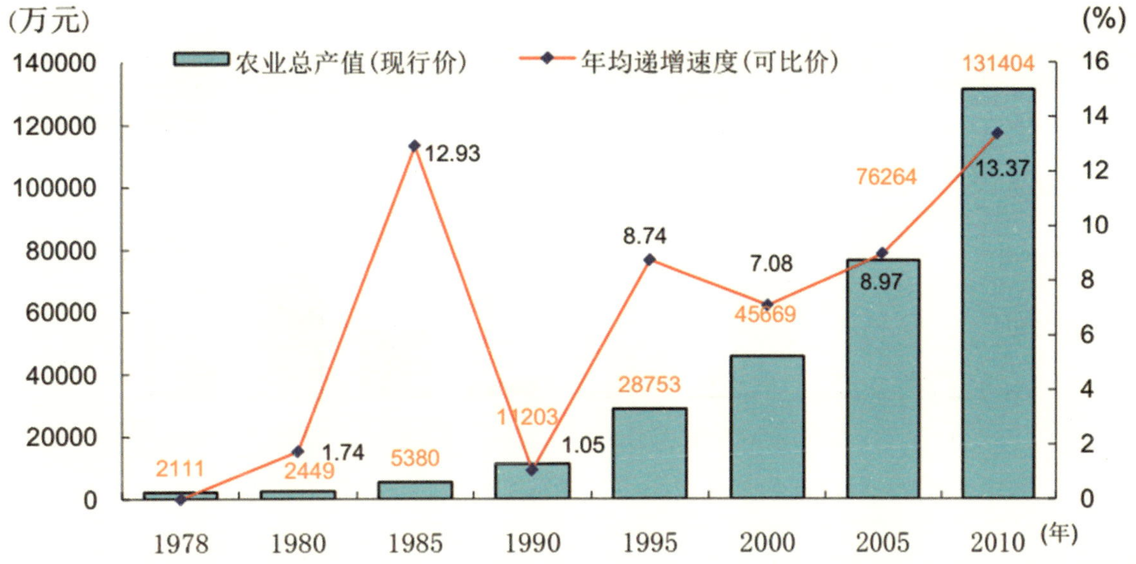

注：期内最高值为 131404 万元（2010 年），最低值为 2111 万元（1978 年）

1978 年和 2010 年农业总产值对照图

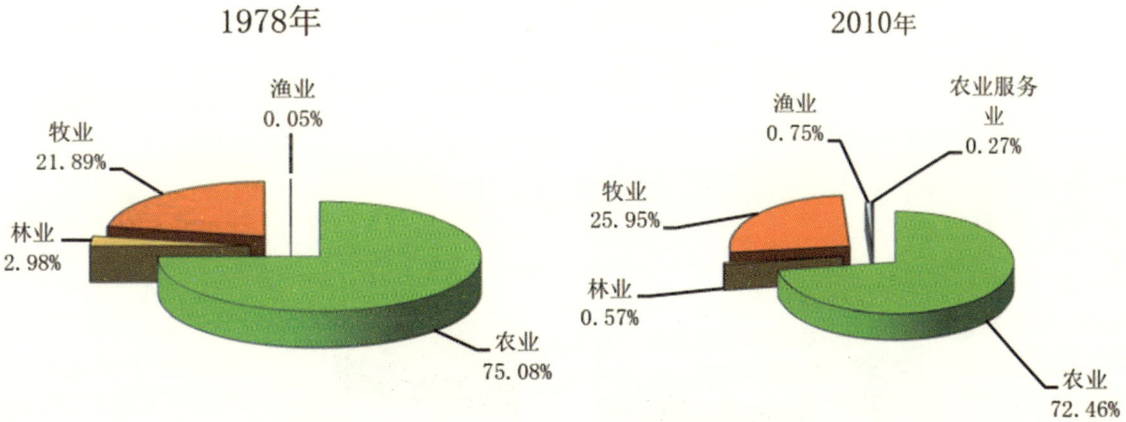

工业总产值及年均递增速度

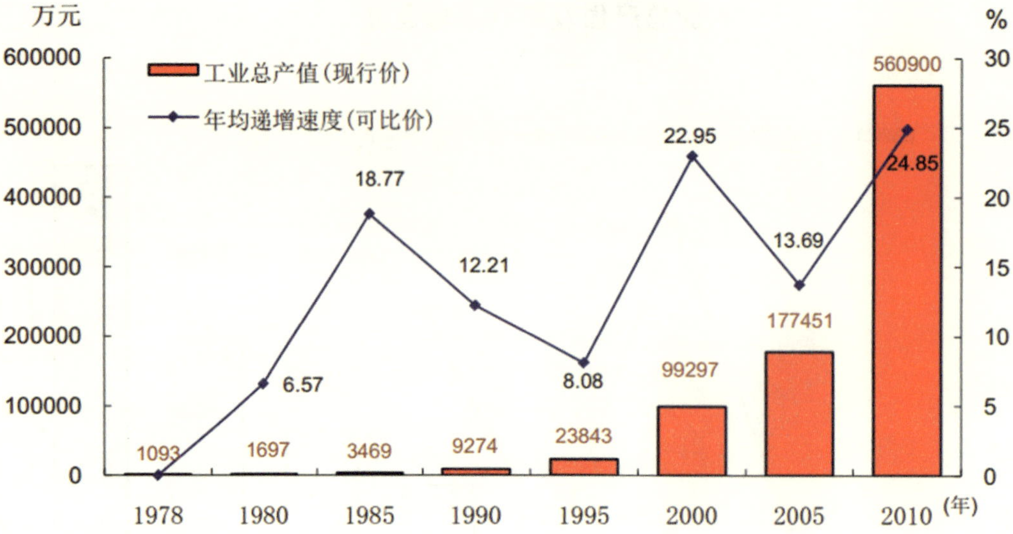

注：期内最高值为560900万元（2010年），最低值为1020万元（1979年）

工业总产值的构成（现行价）

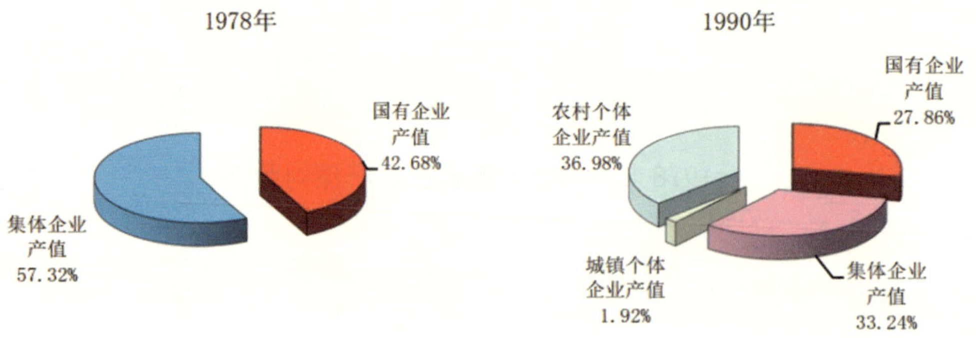

2010年（规模以上）

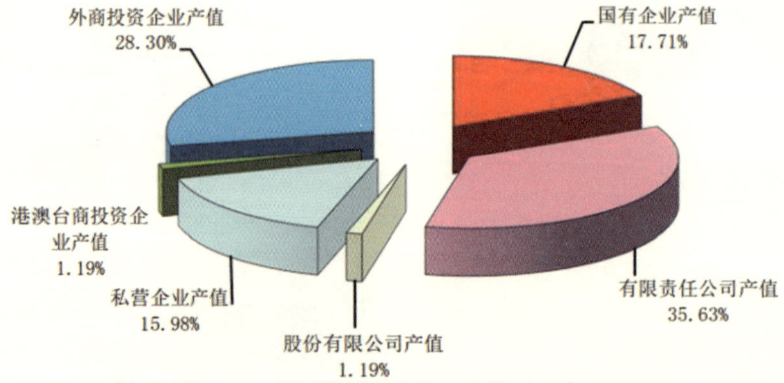

粮食总产量及定基发展速度

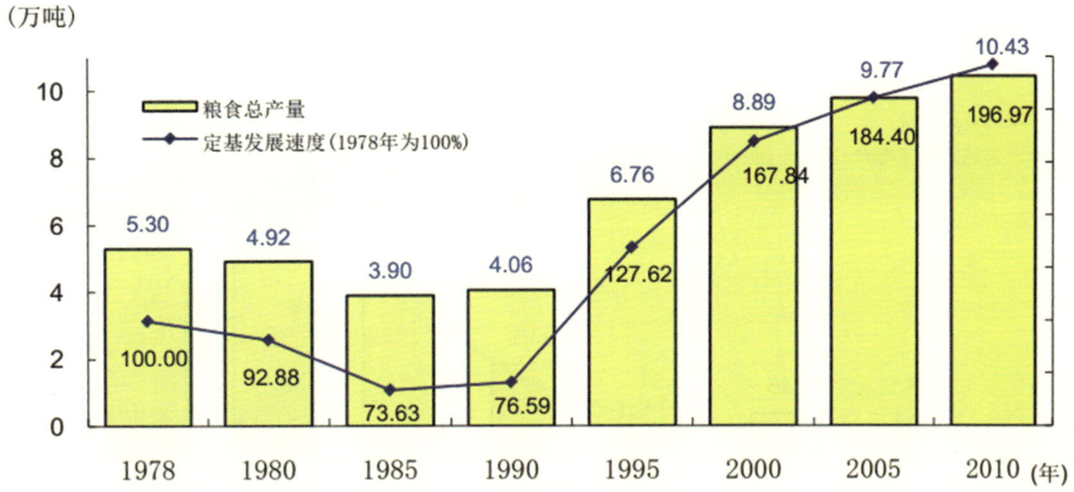

注：期内最高值为 104336 吨（2010 年），最低值为 33789 吨（1981 年）

油菜籽产量

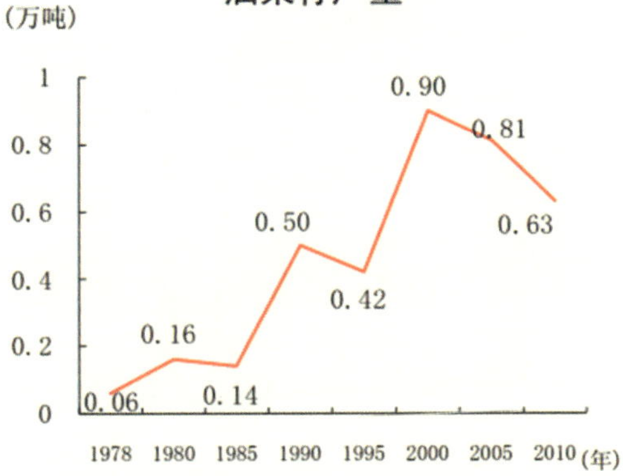

注：期内最高值为 8947 吨（2006 年），
最低值为 565 吨（1978 年）

烤烟产量

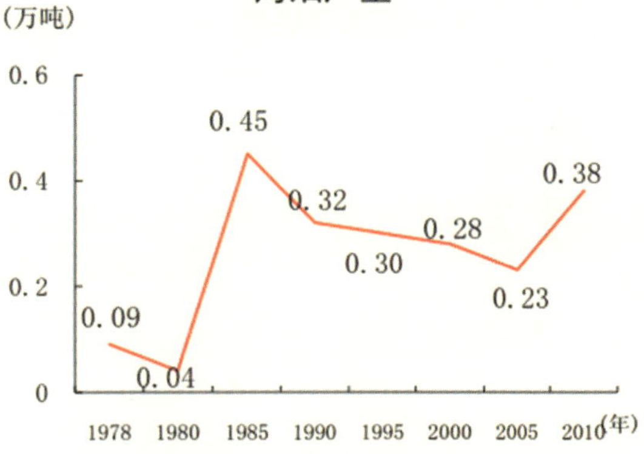

注：期内最高值为 5911 吨（1997 年），
最低值为 431 吨（1980 年）

蔬菜产量

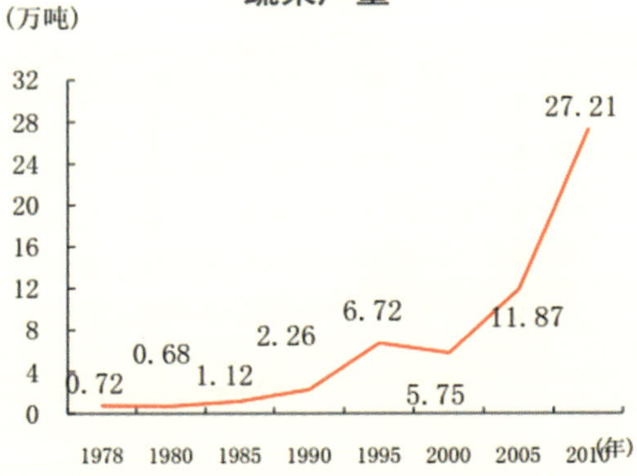

注：期内最高值为 272108 吨（2010 年），
最低值为 1180 吨（1982 年）

水果产量

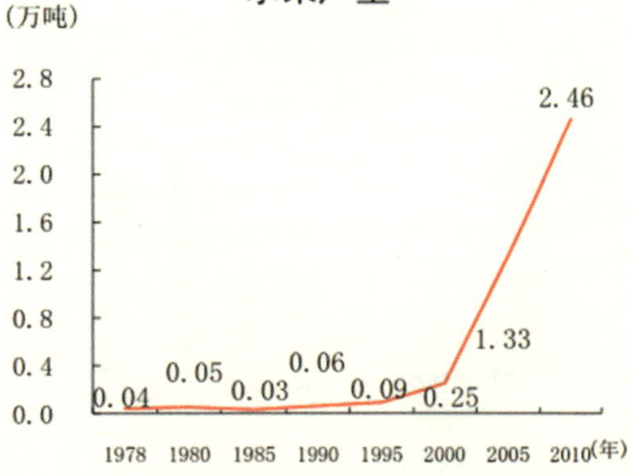

注：期内最高值为 24637 吨（2010 年），
最低值为 332 吨（1985 年）

肉类总产量及定基发展速度

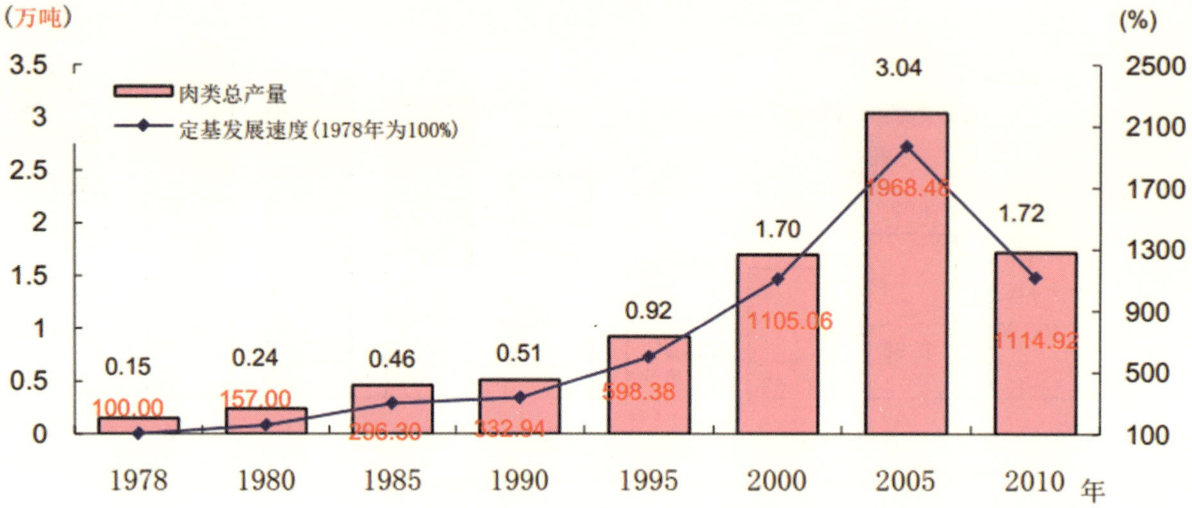

注：期内最高值为 32661 吨（2006 年），最低值为 1542 吨（1978 年）

生猪年末存栏数

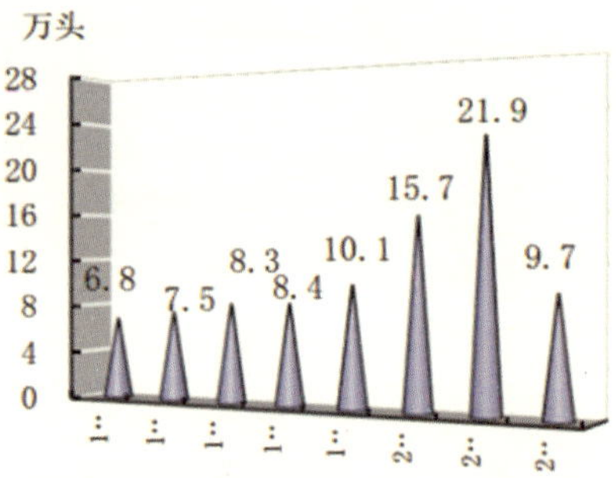

注：期内最高值为 241466 头（2007 年），
最低值为 61537 头（1981 年）

大牲畜年末存栏数

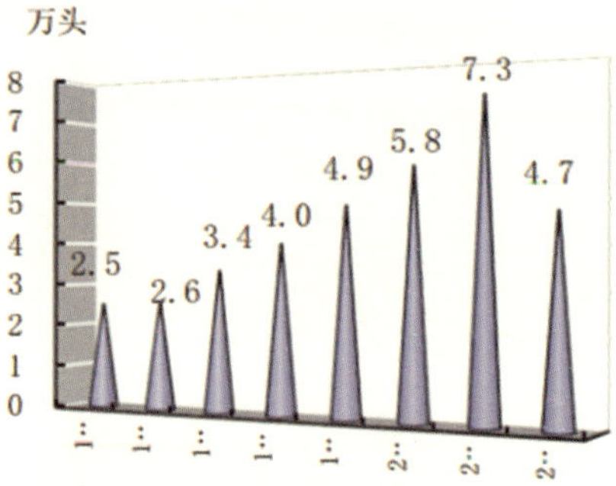

注：期内最高值为 72709 头（2006 年），
最低值为 25127 头（1979 年）

禽蛋产量

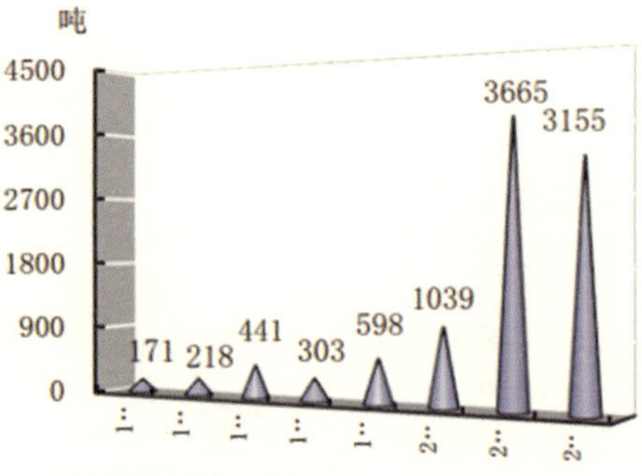

注：期内最高值为 3904 吨（2006 年），
最低值为 171 吨（1978 年）

水产品产量

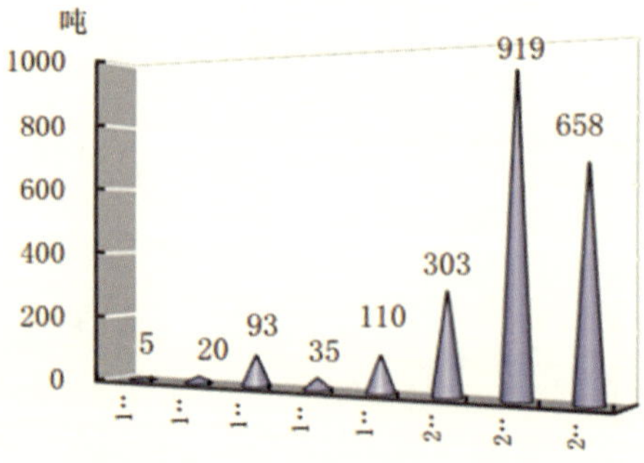

注：期内最高值为 956 吨（2006 年），
最低值为 4 吨（1978 年）

代表性年份养殖业主要产品产量

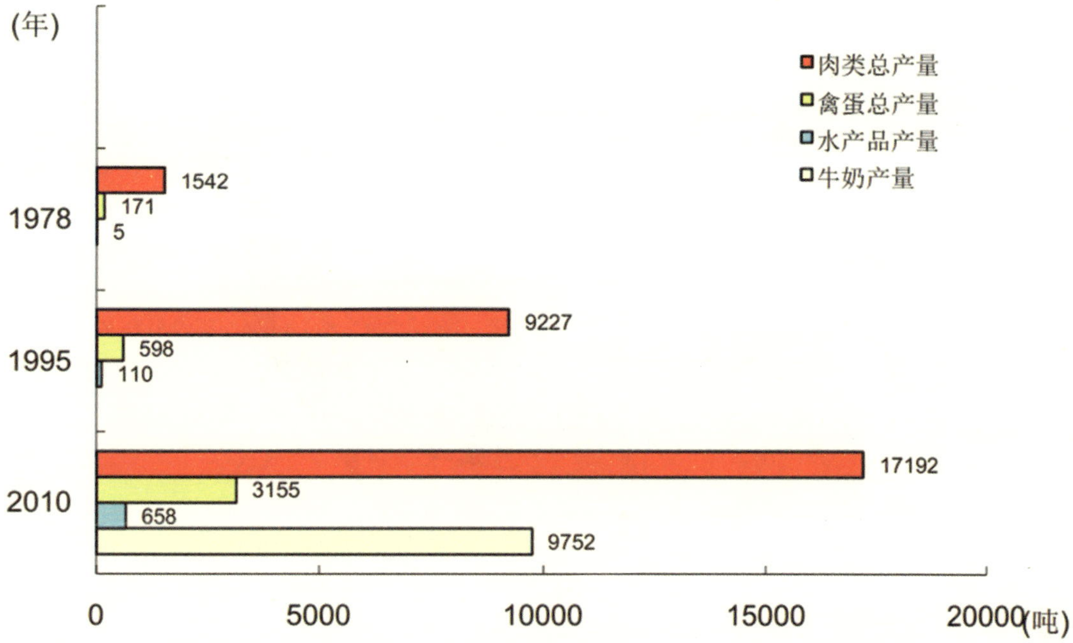

乡镇企业发展情况

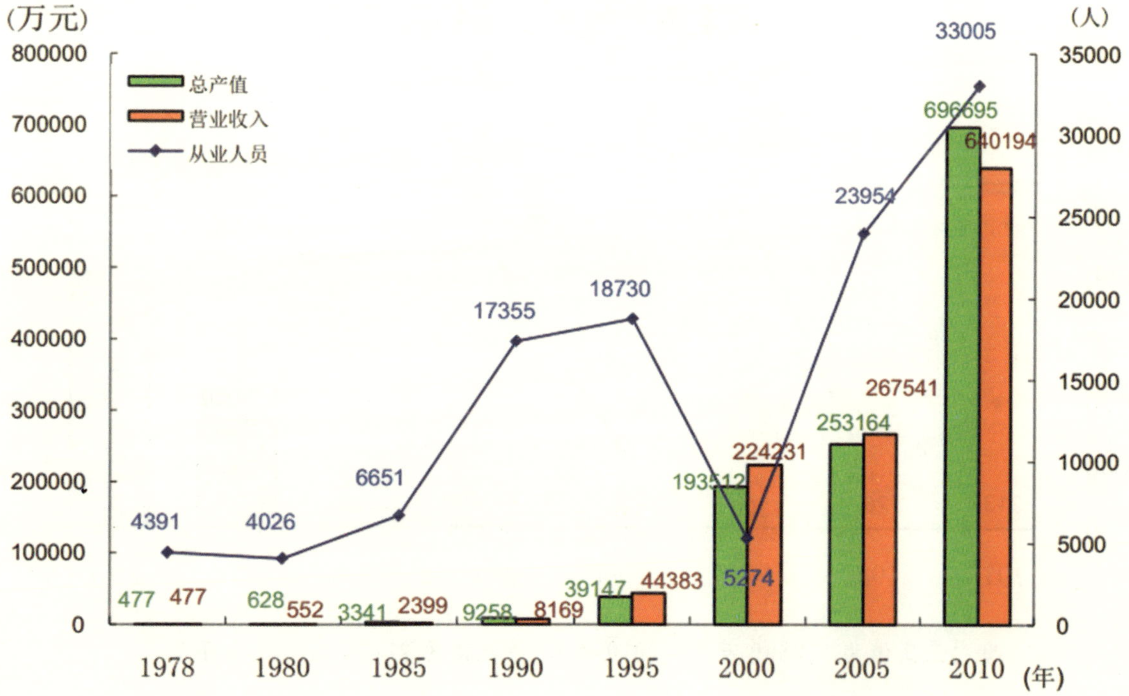

地方财政收入与支出情况

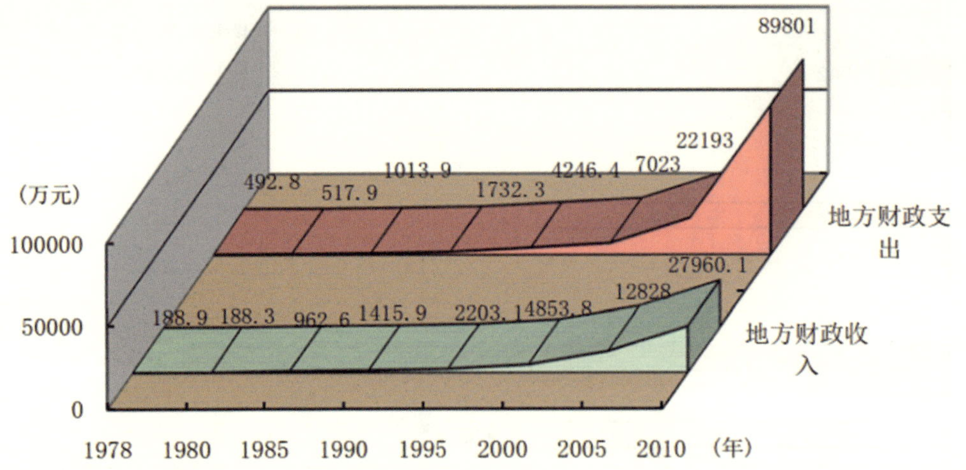

注1：地方财政收入期内最高值为27960.1万元（2010年），最低值为188.3万元（1980年）

注2：地方财政支出期内最高值为89801.0万元（2010年），最低值为492.8万元（1978年）

全社会固定资产投资及年均递增速度

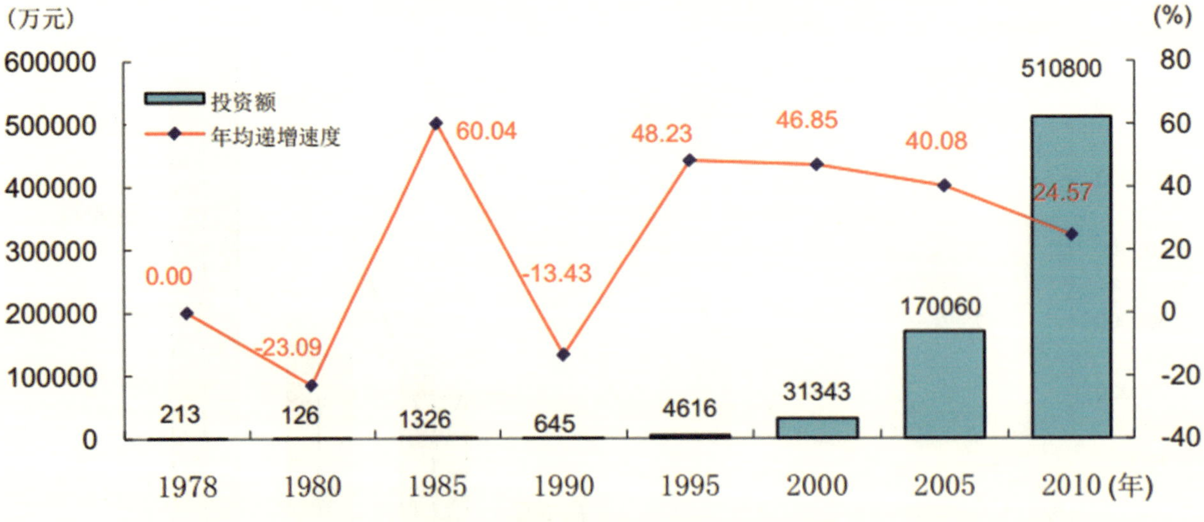

注：期内最高值为510800万元（2010年），最低值为211万元（1979年）

社会消费品零售总额及年均递增速度

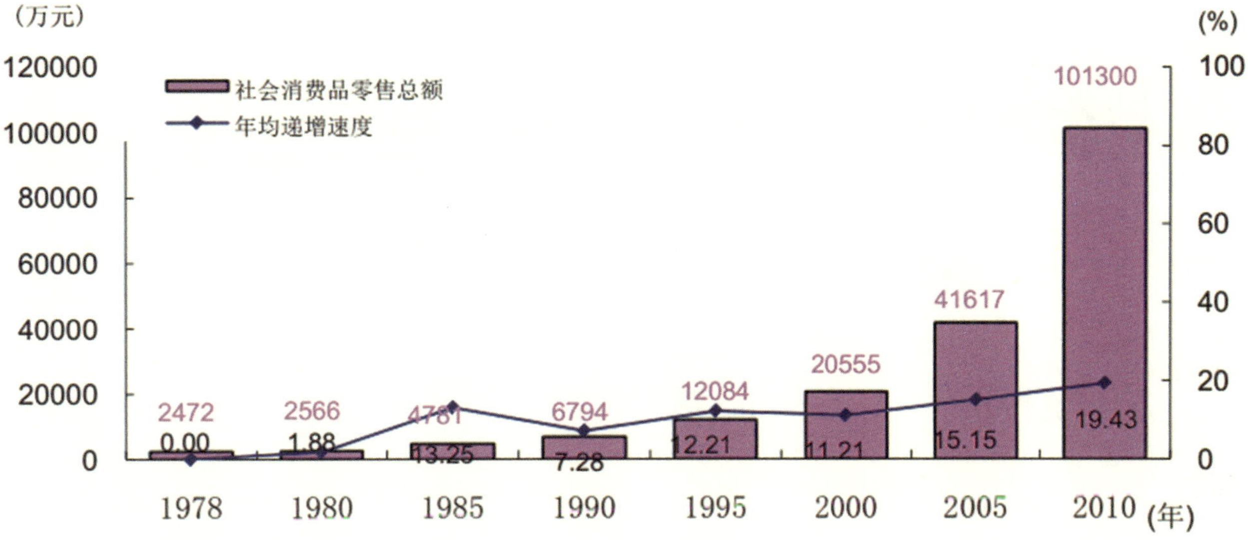

注：期内最高值为101300万元（2010年），最低值为2449万元（1979年）

小学数量、教职工及在校学生数

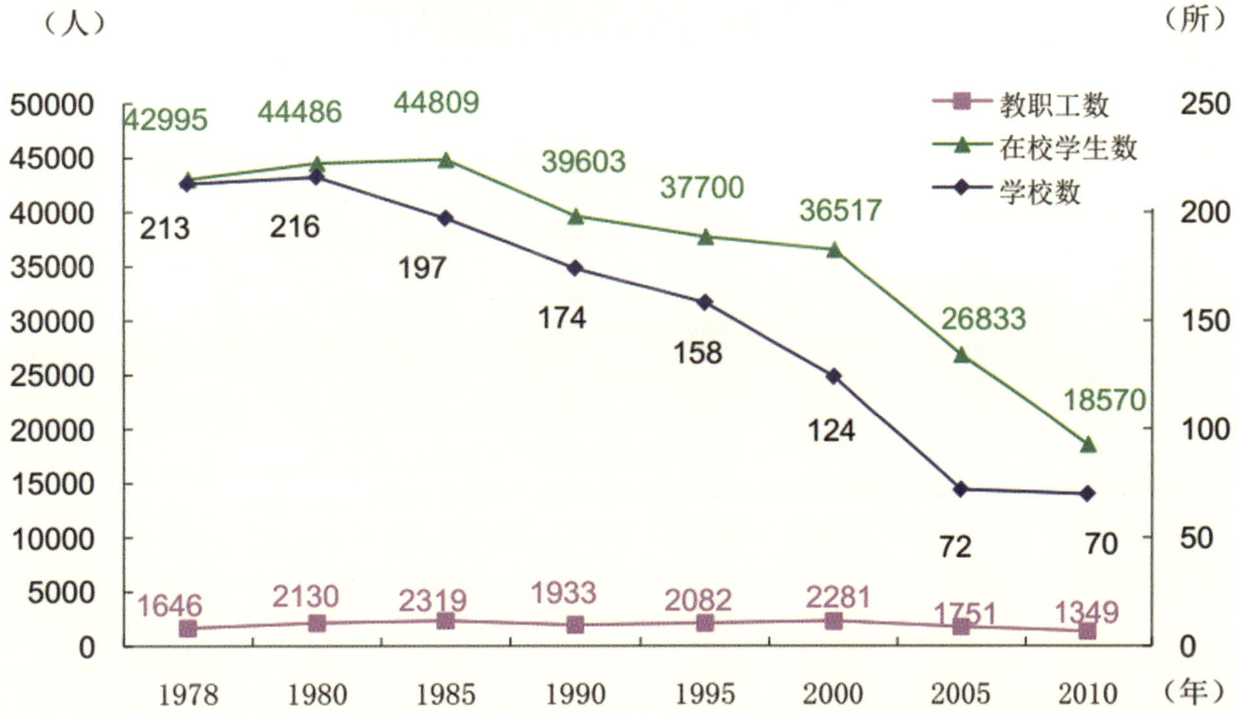

中学数量、教职工及在校学生数

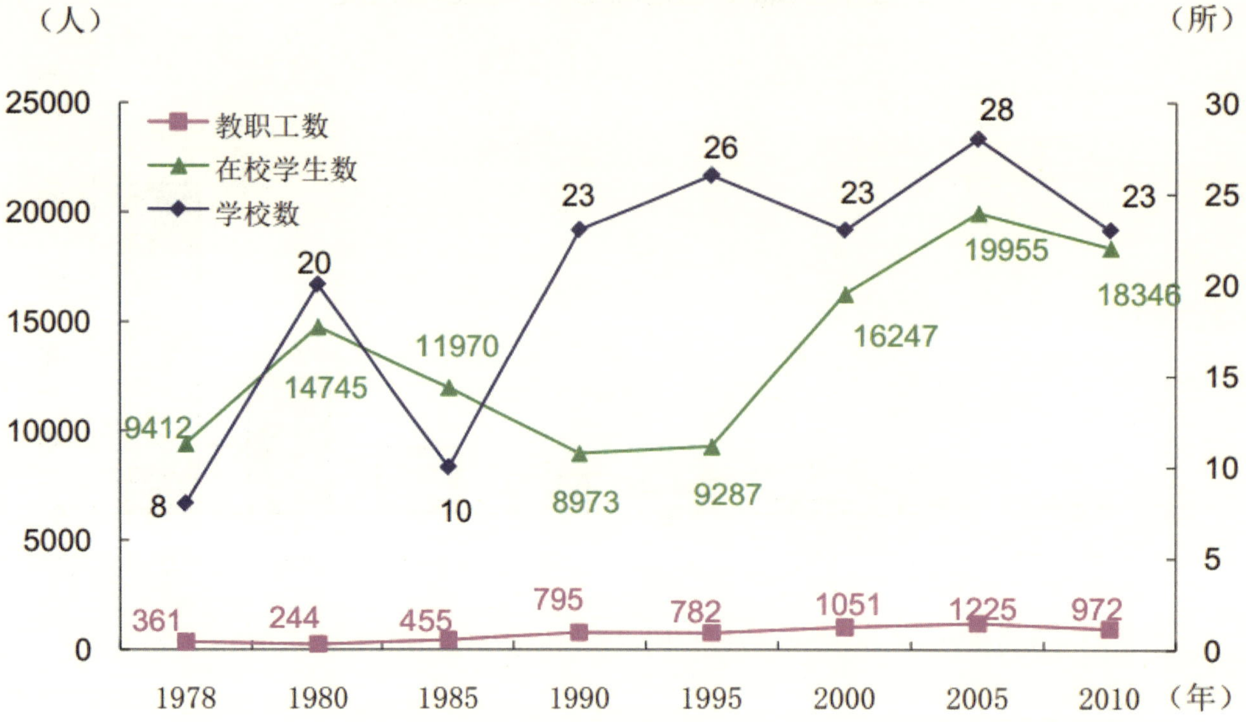

卫生机构、病床及医疗技术人员

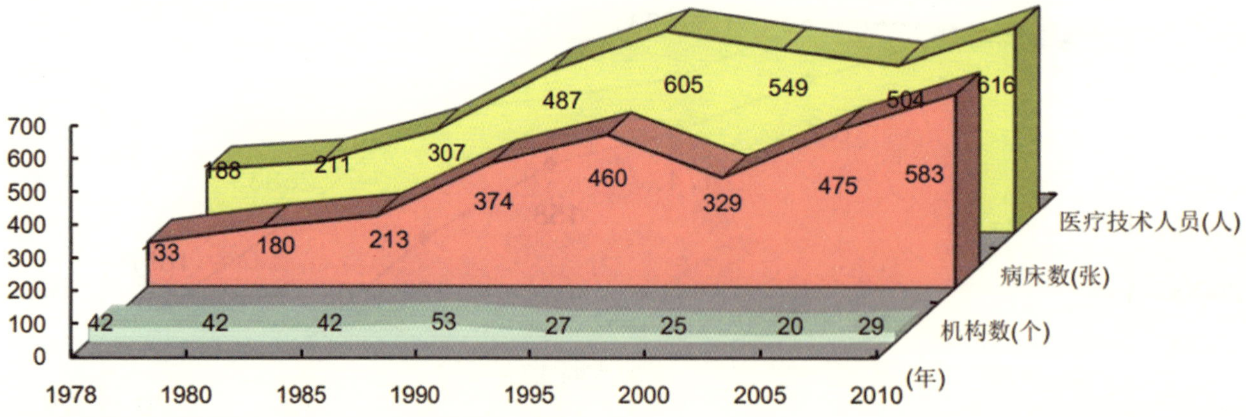

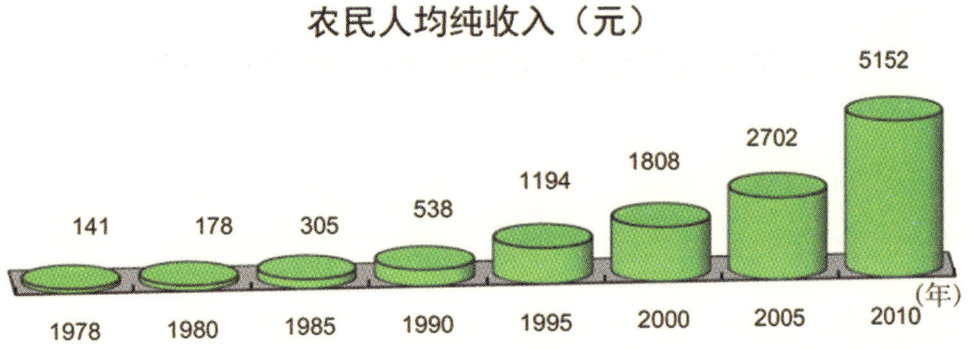
农民人均纯收入（元）
141
178
305
538
1194
1808
2702
5152
1978
1980
1985
1990
1995
2000
2005
2010
(年)

城镇居民年人均可支配收入（元）
3480
4082
5110
5899
7394
9729
12796
15756
1996
1998
2000
2002
2004
2006
2008
2010

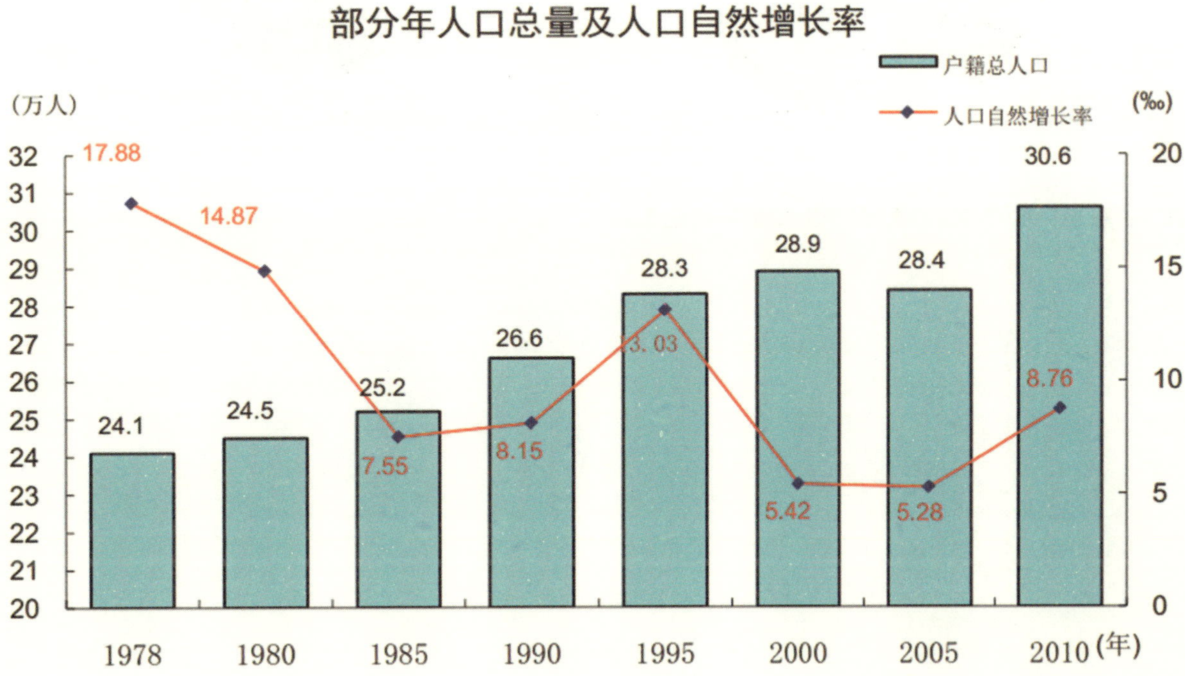
部分年人口总量及人口自然增长率
户籍总人口
人口自然增长率
(万人)
(‰)
32
31
30
29
28
27
26
25
24
23
22
21
20
20
15
10
5
0
17.88
14.87
7.55
8.15
13.03
5.42
5.28
8.76
24.1
24.5
25.2
26.6
28.3
28.9
28.4
30.6
1978
1980
1985
1990
1995
2000
2005
2010
(年)

四次人口普查6岁及以上人口的文化结构

第三次人口普查(1982年)

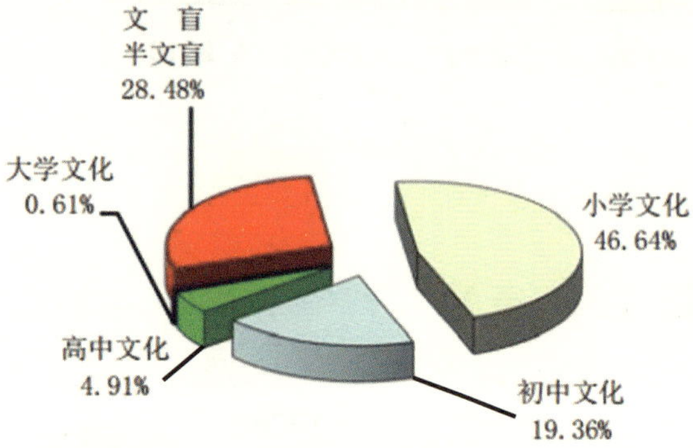

第四次人口普查(1990年)

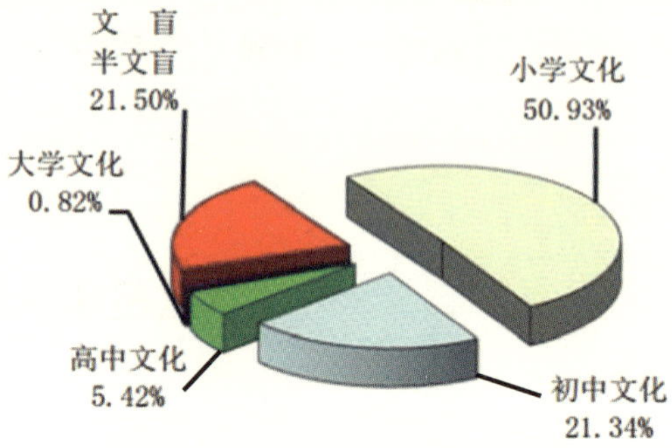

第五次人口普查(2000年)

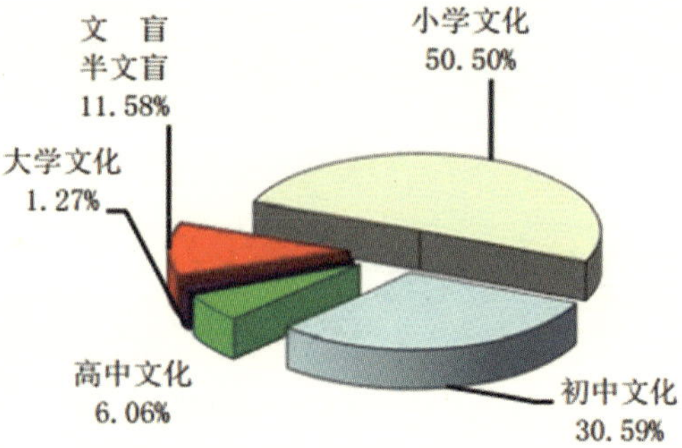

第六次人口普查(2010年)

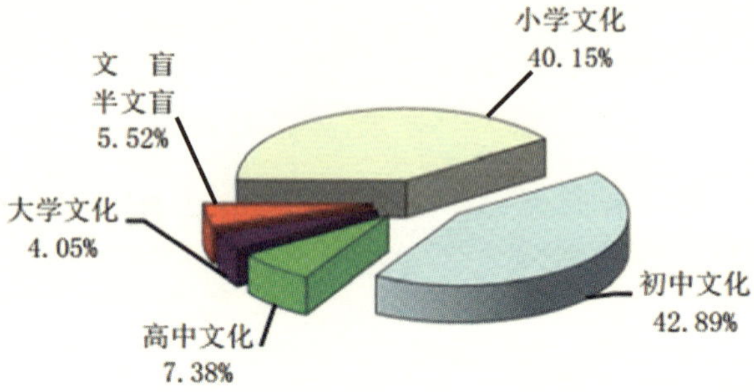

注:“高中”含中专,“大学”含大专及研究生

大 事 记

1978

1月26日　县委、县革委召开全县劳动模范和先进生产者（工作者）大会，授予农业学大寨、工业学大庆和财贸双学（学大庆、学大寨）运动中涌现出的27个先进单位和377个先进集体奖旗，颁发322个先进个人奖状。

3月13日　县委下达《关于大力发展社队企业的意见》，号召在全县掀起大办社队企业的群众运动。

16日　县委召开会议部署进一步开展批判“江青反革命集团”和打击刑事犯罪、打击经济犯罪的“一批双打”运动。至9月27日，全县揭发出经济犯罪万元以上的3人，千元以上至万元的23人，共贪污现金5.7万元，粮票3.4万公斤，物资折款5517元。

6月12—14日　县委召开落实干部政策工作会议，提出对“文化大革命”中被列入审查对象的干部进行复查。12月8日，印发《关于加紧落实干部政策的意见》，要求复查纠正“四清”和“文化大革命”中被错处理的案件。月底，成立县委落实政策办公室，抽调专人办公，复查反右派、“反右倾”“四清”“文化大革命”等“四个时期”和“五个方面”（反右派、“反右倾”“四清”“文化大革命”、因刘少奇案被牵连）以及其他历史上遗留问题的案件。1981年将落实政策办合并信访科，按照中共十一届三中全会的方针，平反冤、假、错案，解决大批历史遗留问题。

10月　县委常委召开会议学习讨论实践是检验真理的唯一标准，要求各级党委认真开展关于真理标准问题的学习和讨论。

11月　花椰公社黄银生产队借土地给社员种植夏收作物，翌年全队夏粮比上年增长24%，开创全县实行农业生产责任制的先河。

1979

2月13日　县委召开五级干部会议，传达贯彻中共十一届三中全会精神。与会人员学习讨论关于实践是检验真理的唯一标准问题，批判“两个凡是”（凡是毛主席作出的决策，我们都坚决拥护；凡是毛主席的指示，我们都始终不渝地遵循），讨论停止使用“以阶级斗争为纲”的口号，并充分讨论了把工作重点转移到社会主义现代化建设上来和加快农业发展的问题。

是月 县委责成公安部门对“四类分子”评审摘帽。3月，评审摘帽工作结束。

3月 县人民检察院恢复。

4月5日 《修文县计划生育办法》颁布，要求做到“晚、稀、少”，奖励每对夫妇只生一个孩子，提倡晚婚。

5月 县委召开三级干部会议，传达贯彻中央工作会议提出对国民经济实行“调整、改革、整顿、提高”的方针，重点讨论集中主要精力把农业搞上去的问题。

9月 县委召开三级干部会议，传达贯彻省委《关于放宽农业政策的指示》，并制发《全县试行包产到组联产计酬的意见》，决定放宽农业政策，改善经营管理，加快发展农业。

12月15日 久长区妇联主任陈国芳、城关镇沙溪生产大队妇女主任黄桂芬和清让公社妇女干部夏国芬被评为“全国三八红旗手”，受全国妇联表彰。

1980

4月 县委召开党员干部会议，组织学习中纪委发布的《关于党内政治生活的若干准则》，要求各级党组织特别是各级领导干部要自觉地、严格地遵守《准则》规定，切实搞好党风。

6月16日 县委、县革委作出决定，凡集体有宜林荒山的生产队，可就近划给每户社员3至5亩自留山植树造林，并由县革委发给林权使用证。

19日 县境发生地震，受震地区在宝寨公社顺江、海马、复兴大队，震级为二级，曾三次发生地下轰鸣，房屋家具抖动，沿河石山出现断裂。12月17日，地震又在原公社发生，震情与上次相似，波及7个生产大队。

是月 县委、县革委召开计划生育工作会议，进一步强调提倡一对夫妇只生一个孩子，严格控制第二胎，坚决刹住第三胎，把人口出生率降下来。

是月 县选举委员会成立，开展县、社（镇）两级选举工作，改间接选举为直接选举，改等额选举为差额选举。11月正式选举社（镇）人民代表和县人民代表。12月，各社（镇）先后召开人民代表大会，选举社管会和镇人民政府成员。1981年1月召开县人民代表大会，选举人大常委和县人民政府领导成员后，选举工作告竣。

9月13日 县革委下达《关于普及全县小学五年制教育的意见》，计划分3批施行。至1986年，全县实现普及小学五年制教育。

22—25日 县科学技术协会首次代表大会召开，正式成立县科协组织。大会号召全县科技人员同心同德，鼓足干劲，为实现科学技术现代化而奋斗。

10月6日 县革委决定设立县粮油议购议销公司，允许粮油进入市场自由买卖。

12月1日 县科技干部技术职称评定委员会成立，开始进行各系列技术干部职称考核评定工作。

1981

1月11—16日 县第七届人民代表大会第一次会议召开。会议选举产生县人大常务委员会组成人员和

县长、副县长，并设立人大常委办事机构。从此，县人大常委会为县人民代表大会的常设机构。同时撤销县革命委员会，正式恢复县人民政府建制。

26日 全县恢复久长区和久长、清水、金桥3个公社及扎佐镇建制，调为5区、2镇、30个公社。

5月14日 县委为1966年“八卅”烤火事件中的受害者平反昭雪，为无辜入狱的原中共城关镇委员会书记周克昌平反，安排工作。

6月23日 县委组织47人的工作队，以阳早公社为试点，开展稳定山林权、划定自留山、确定责任制的林业“三定”工作。

7月21日 县政府发布《修文县矿藏资源开采管理试行条例》。

8月3—9日 县委召开扩大会议，传达学习中国共产党十一届六中全会通过的《关于建国以来党的若干历史问题的决议》和贵州省委四届七次扩大会议精神。

9月15—17日 县委召开第一次统战工作会议，学习讨论新时期统战工作的重要意义、任务和基本政策。

1982

1月7—10日 县委、县政府召开劳动致富“冒尖户”代表大会，与会代表103人交流致富经验。

2月11日 经县人大常委会第七届第五次会议通过的《城镇建设管理暂行规定》开始实施。

是月 水电部副部长李鹏到红枫电厂红林电站考察。

3月 全县开展第一个以“五讲四美”（讲文明、讲礼貌、讲卫生、讲秩序、讲道德，心灵美、语言美、行为美、环境美）为内容的“文明礼貌月”活动。

6月23日 贵州省农民业余教育现场会在修文召开，与会代表参观了小箐乡杉林生产队农民夜校。推广该校把学习文化科学知识与农业生产相结合，带领农民走科学致富道路的经验。

7月1日 以零时为标准时间，全县进行第三次人口普查，总人口为257024人。

8月26—30日 中共修文县第四次代表大会召开。

9月2—5日 县第七届人民代表大会第二次会议召开。

12月25日 县委制定《修文县经济建设奋斗目标方案》，实行从单一种植变为多种经营，从自然经济变为发展商品生产，从主要为本地服务变为为城市服务。

是年 红枫电厂三级至六级电站的电力税由清镇县改向修文县交纳，全年向修文缴税234万元。

1983

3月2日 县政府发出通知，就“文化大革命”期间改名的26个大队予以复名、更名和重新命名。

17—22日 中国人民政治协商会议县第一届委员会第一次会议召开，选举产生县政协首届常务委员会，自此置政协常设办事机构。

18—21日 县第七届人民代表大会第三次会议召开。

31日 贵州省委组织部就1949年修文“二一六”武装暴动的结论予以批复，认定暴动属于有组织、有计划、有准备的进步性武装暴动，对其成员按暴动性质落实政策。

是月 县委、县政府部署开展第二个“文明礼貌月”活动。活动内容除“五讲四美”外，还加上“三热爱”（热爱祖国、热爱社会主义、热爱中国共产党）。活动以治理“脏、乱、差”为重点，开展“三优一学”（优美环境、优良秩序、优质服务，学习雷锋）活动。

5月9日 县委和县政府批转商业局《关于全面推行经营承包责任制的报告》，以改革为动力，推动企业整顿，解决吃“大锅饭”和平均主义问题，将责、权、利结合起来，兼顾国家、企业、职工、生产者和消费者的利益。

8月17日 县委在县电影院召开职工群众大会，贯彻中共中央《关于严厉打击刑事犯罪活动的决定》，正式宣布“严打”开始，并部署公安、检察和司法部门联合行动，打好第一战役第一仗。

9月18日 县人民法院在县城体育馆召开万人宣判大会，首批判处在“严打”斗争中捕获的杀人、抢劫、强奸、流氓和拐卖儿童妇女等犯罪分子7人的死刑，立即执行。

11月6日 县委、县政府印发《关于从重从快严厉打击经济领域中严重犯罪活动的工作意见》，加大力度查处经济犯罪案件。至年底，全县计查处经济案件77起，退赔赃款7.3万元，补税38.6万元，处以罚金1.5万元。

是月 红六军团卫生连原连长、中国人民解放军总后勤部副政委李真重游长征时战斗过的扎佐，在县委题书毛泽东《七律·长征》留念。

12月15—16日 修文、开阳两县联合调查组对两县相邻边界实地踏勘，并签订两县境界调查修正协议书。

20日 县首次个体劳动者协会会员代表大会召开。

1984

1月17日 贵州省科学院山地资源研究所洞穴考察组，对位于修文、息烽两县交界处的躲兵洞（休息洞、多缤洞）进行考察。

2月27—3月2日 中国人民政治协商会议县第一届委员会第二次会议召开。

28—31日 县第七届人民代表大会第四次会议召开。

3月1日 县人大七届四次会议通过《关于开发回水石林、花榔多缤洞旅游区》提案的决议。6月8日，成立县旅游开发工程指挥部，县财政投资20万元修筑从大石至回水石林和火石丫口至花榔多缤洞的公路。

4月27日 省政府批准成立以贵阳市为中心的贵阳副食品经营协作区，修文被列为协作区的县。

30日 县委结束县级党政机关二级机构改革，全县53个局以上机构配备正、副职干部107人，平均年龄43.4岁，比原班子降低5.4岁。

是月 县委、县政府贯彻中共中央、国务院《关于实行政社分开建立乡政府的通知》，开始进行政社分设工作，至年底，公社、生产大队、生产队分别改为乡（镇）、村、村民小组。

是月 县委、县政府召开三级干部会议，贯彻贵州省委、省政府《关于发展专业户、重点户若干政策问题的规定》，放手发展各行各业的“两户”。

5月 城关镇升格为区级镇。

6月 改桃源乡和大石乡为布依族乡。

7月3日 县政府决定分期拨款50万元改建烈士陵园为革命公墓，8月动工，至1986年，第一期工程告竣。

是月 县组织人事部门开始采取“几不要”(不要户口、不要人事档案、不要组织手续、不要口粮关系等)手段招聘知识分子。至年底，全县有12名中学教师到贵阳、六盘水市等地应聘，有3名科技人员流向外地。修文亦向外地招进知识分子28人。

9月 改久长乡为久长镇，改六广乡为六广镇。至此，全县共有5个区 、1个区级镇、28个乡和3个乡级镇。

是月 中央顾问委员会委员、红六军团十六师原师长、中国人民解放军海军副司令员周球保（周仁杰）重游长征时战斗过的扎佐，留下回忆录《奔袭贵阳北部重镇——扎佐》。

11月6—10日 县第八届人民代表大会第一次会议召开。

1985

1月 县委、县政府召开三级干部会议，传达学习中共中央《关于经济体制改革的决定》和《关于进一步活跃农村经济的十条政策》，讨论进一步改革农村经济管理体制，放宽统购政策，扩大市场调节，搞活农村经济等事项。

县公费医疗管理委员会成立，下设办公室，启动公费医疗制度改革。

4月25日 县委、县政府规定全县企事业单位开始实行经济承包责任制，行政单位实行岗位责任制，两种责任制均实行经济效益、社会效益与奖金挂钩的奖惩办法。

5月18日 修文县地方志编纂委员会及办公室正式成立，着手《修文县志》的编修。1989年3月建立县志编辑部，开始县志总纂。

7月12日 县委遵照中共中央《关于整党的决定》，开始对党的作风和组织进行全面整顿。全县参加整党的党员共5311人，分3批进行。至1987年5月，整党全部结束。

是月 县委决定建立核查组，在进行整党的同时，对“文化大革命”中追随林彪、江青反革命集团造反起家、帮派思想严重和打砸抢分子等“三种人”进行清理核查。

9月10日 县委和县政府召开解放后第一个教师节庆祝大会，表彰一批优秀教师和先进教育工作者。

16—18日 县第八届人民代表大会第二次会议召开。

10月26—27日 贵州省委书记胡锦涛莅县视察，听取县委、县政府工作汇报后重点考察马家桥乡的乡镇企业。

11月19日 县委书记刘清德因严重失职使妻王忠兰和子刘智诈骗公款经商造成巨大损失问题，被安顺地委免去中共修文县委常委和县委书记职务。1987年7月25日，经安顺地委会议讨论决定，给予撤销县委书记职务处分。

1986

3月25—30日 中国人民政治协商会议县第一届委员会第三次会议召开。

26—30日 县第八届人民代表大会第三次会议召开。

5月5日 县政府颁发《土地管理暂行规定》。

30日 中国人民解放军修文县人民武装部由军队转为地方建制，改称修文县人民武装部。

8月 贵州省委副书记丁廷模一行3人莅县检查村级整党。

9月 中国人民解放军第二野战军军事政治大学第五分校原副政委兼修文县委书记、军事科学院副院长姜思毅重游修文故地，并与在县的原军大五分校学员座谈。

10月1日 县地面卫星接收站建成，开始试播。

11月 经省、地教育部门组织验收，认定修文县为实现普及初等教育县和实现基本扫除文盲县。

12月2—6日 安顺地区地方志编纂工作现场会在县召开，县志办公室推出12部部门志稿交大会评审。

1987

4月2—4日 县第八届人民代表大会第四次会议召开。

6月27—30日 中共修文县第五次代表大会召开。

8月24—28日 中国人民政治协商会议县第二届委员会第一次会议召开。

25—29日 县第九届人民代表大会第一次会议召开。

9月22日 县政府下达《关于加快推行法定计量单位工作进程的通知》，从10月1日起，全面使用法定计量单位。肉油类市场以铝制公斤秤代替木杆市斤秤。

28日 在贵州省商业（供销）、粮食、劳改系统“雪水杯”酒类大奖赛中，修文酒厂生产的阳明大曲获金奖，蜜源花粉酒获银奖，刺梨花粉酒和马家桥乡桂花树酒厂生产的黔井窖酒获铜奖。

10月4日 县三角山水泥厂产品经贵州省建材局初审，后经12月29日国家建材局复审合格，获“甲秀牌”水泥生产许可证。1989年12月，其产品425＃普硅水泥获贵州省人民政府颁发的“优质产品证书”。

12月7日 县财政拨款35万元铺设县城羊落井至阳明洞供水管道，1988年3月竣工投入使用，使市民用水的供需矛盾有所缓解。

1988

1月7日 县政府在全县张贴保护森林资源的布告，加强林政管理，坚决制止乱砍滥伐。

4月6—9日 中国人民政治协商会议县第二届委员会第二次会议召开。

7—9日 县第九届人民代表大会第二次会议召开。

7月8日 乌栗乡下洞联户合作农场正式成立，入场农户开发非耕地种植果树和营造速生丰产林，开

创了贵州省农业组建股份制经济实体的先河。

21日 县政府以小箐乡郭田村试点实施《中华人民共和国村民委员会组织法》，1989年3月全面铺开，7月10日起全县施行。

8月15日 县政府发布《征收耕地占用税布告》，将全县32个乡（镇）划分为3类确定税额。

10月 县委、县政府召开三级干部会议，传达贯彻中共十三届三中全会和中央工作会议精神，讨论治理经济环境，整顿经济秩序，全面深化改革工作。部署清理整顿公司，开展双增双节（增产节约、增收节支）活动。

1989

3月27—31日 中国人民政治协商会议县第二届委员会第三次会议召开。

28—31日 县第九届人民代表大会第三次会议召开。

4月23日 贵州省政府批准乌栗乡为安顺地区农业经济综合发展规划试点乡，属全省10个试点乡之一。

27日 县委召开常委会议学习《人民日报》社论《必须旗帜鲜明的反对动乱》。

9月1日 县政府发布居民身份证使用和检查的通告，5日起施行。

23日 县政府主持召开职工大会，热烈欢送被评为全国劳动模范的红旗煤矿工人宋均成赴京参加中华人民共和国建立四十周年庆祝活动。

12月1日 县政府颁布《水资源管理暂行规定》。

是月 县消费者协会成立。次年2月，首次消协会员代表大会召开，选举产生首届消协理事会，受理消费者投诉案件。

1990

4月23—27日 中国人民政治协商会议县第三届委员会第一次会议召开。

24—28日 县第十届人民代表大会第一次会议召开。

6月18日 宝寨乡干部张福华因嫉恨乡党委副书记、乡长焦兴佑被提拔，便唆使表弟方正祥抱炸药包将焦家房顶炸穿，木床炸毁，女儿被炸成重伤。经司法机关审理认定为故意杀人罪，判处张福华死刑立即执行，判处方正祥死刑缓期2年执行。

21日 全县开展第十一届亚运会集资活动，至9月21日，共集款19万元。

7月1日 以零时为标准时间，全县进行第四次人口普查，总人口为266694人。12月，县人口普查办公室编印出《修文县第四次人口普查手工汇总资料初步分析》。

8月 县委、县政府召开三级干部会议，贯彻贵州省委、省政府《关于进一步搞好扶贫开发工作的决定》，要求落实脱贫致富规划，积极发展种养业，用好扶贫资金，抓紧“温饱工程”，打好扶贫攻坚战。

9月8日 修文县文学艺术界联合会首次代表大会召开，正式成立县文学艺术界联合会。

18—22日 中共修文县第六次代表大会召开。

是月 农业因旱灾造成严重损失。自6月中旬起至9月未下透雨，全县有7万多人和8000余头大牲畜饮水发生困难，秋收结果，粮食比上年歉收1273万公斤，减产24%。

12月7—8日 修文县残疾人联合会首次会员代表大会召开，选举残联第一届主席团和执行委员会，正式建立县残疾人联合会。

1991

3月23日 县政府投资48万元扩建县城自来水工程，1992年年底工程完工。

24—29日 中国人民政治协商会议县第三届委员会第二次会议召开。

26—29日 县第十届人民代表大会第二次会议召开。

是月 县综合农业区划编写组编制的《修文县综合农业区划》被列为贵州省农业区划丛书正式出版发行。

7月29日 县委、县政府召开邮电管理部门负责人和工程技术人员办公会议，决定建设程控电话。工程概算投资410万元。1992年1月开始兴建，因程控交换机供货推迟，故暂用日本X-23自动交换机。全县更换、新装话机439户，8月22日凌晨正式投入使用。

9月30日 川黔铁路高坝车站正式启用，仅贵阳、遵义往来短途客运停靠，日上下旅客30人左右。

11月6日 县建立建镇并乡撤区领导小组抓建并撤工作，将全县6区(镇)31乡（镇）撤并为4镇6乡，以体现“小政府，大服务”的特点，次年2月完成。

27日 县委、县政府发出通知，先从领导机关入手推行丧葬改革，职工去世不成立治丧机构，不设立悼念场所，不搞遗体告别仪式，不开追悼会，从简治丧，严禁大操大办和搞封建迷信活动。

12月2日 修文县红十字会成立，下设办公室于卫生局内。

1992

2月 县委全会扩大会议召开，学习中共中央印发的中发〔1992〕2号文件（邓小平视察南方重要谈话），讨论解放思想，清除“左”的障碍，加快步伐发展经济问题。

3月25—29日 中国人民政治协商会议县第三届委员会第三次会议召开。

26—29日 县第十届人民代表大会第三次会议召开。

4月 修文籍运动员徐刚参加在蒙古首都乌兰巴托举办的中国、蒙古、俄罗斯3国国际举重邀请赛，荣获78公斤级举重金牌。

5月11日 省交通厅下达《关于六广河大桥项目建设书的批复》，桥命名贵州六广河大桥，桥长248米，桥式为预应力桁式组合拱桥，引道6公里，单跨150米，桥面宽10米，设计荷载汽—20，挂—100，投资668万元，由毕节地区、安顺地区各承担25%，省交通厅补助50%。

30日 金沙、开阳、息烽、修文4县公安局长、刑侦队长联席会议在修文召开，共商侦破抢劫庙宇案件。会后组织专案组，1个月内破获以王忠亮、叶有才为首的12名犯罪团伙作案43起，抢劫现金和财物价值共2万余元，经安顺中级人民法院12月27日审理，判处6人死刑，其余6人分别判处3—15年的有期徒刑。

是月 县广播电视局筹建县城有线电视工程，6月开工，7月试播，安装工程前期1100户于9月底告竣，后期1000户年底完成，可收视7套节目。1998年1月，县有线电视中心与贵阳市有线电视台通过光缆联网，使收视节目增为29套，收视户达3800户。

7月16日 全县贯彻落实县委、县政府《关于实行计划生育合同管理的意见》，开始实行计划生育合同管理。

8月14日 县公安局开始办理“蓝皮户口”，即农村户口转城镇户口，规定办理1个蓝皮户口交费4000元，办1个粮食供应证交费500元，1个月共办理“农转非”405人后停办。

是月 在贵州省第八届运动会上，修文县运动员罗文获青少年男子拳击57公斤级金牌，刘文华获青少年男子52公斤级举重金牌，谌宏丽获青少年女子皮划艇金牌。

是月 罗文参加全国“风华杯”拳击邀请赛，获57公斤级第一名。

10月 县委召开扩大会议，学习中共中央总书记江泽民在中共十四大所作题为《加快改革开放和现代化建设步伐，夺取有中国特色社会主义事业的更大胜利》的报告，讨论社会主义市场经济和加快建设步伐问题。

11月12日 修文县第十届人民代表大会第四次会议召开。

29日 修（文）六（广）公路柿花树处发生1起特大恶性交通事故。王官小学校长、个体运输户彭江涛违反交通安全法规，雇请无客车驾驶证照的拖拉机驾驶员吴维均驾驶03—06244号客车从六桶开往县城，车行至柿花树，翻入85米深的悬岩底，当即死亡23人，重伤8人，轻伤1人。事故发生后，省、地、县有关领导立即赶往现场组织抢救和处理善后事宜，遇难者由亲人领回，每人发给3000元丧葬费。12月4日，县委、县政府在事故地点召开700余人的全县交通安全教育现场会，并立“血字碑”昭示后人吸取血的教训。

12月25日 县委、县政府作出《关于分流行政机关事业单位人员的决定》，规定除学校、医院和按规定不能经商办企业的单位外，其余属县财政拨款的党政机关、事业单位和群众团体，可采取单位集体转公司、单位经办经济实体、个人从事生产经营活动和自愿留职停薪等形式，实行人员分流，其比例为6/10留任，4/10分流离岗。

1993

1月16日 于县城南面洗脚塘举行过境公路竣工典礼。

3月30日 跨越六广河连接修文、黔西两县的六广河大桥举行开工典礼。历经两年半连续施工，于1996年10月10日建成通车。

4月1—3日 中共修文县第七次代表大会召开。

6—10日 中国人民政治协商会议县第四届委员会第一次会议召开。

7—10日 县第十一届人民代表大会第一次会议召开。

5月24日 县政府批准成立由退休教师史作经、杜声太等筹办的解放后第一所私立中学——华驿初级中学。8月18日开学，共有教职工11人，设1个初中班，招生36人。办学资金来源于收取学生学杂费，实行以教养学。

是月 为隆重纪念毛泽东诞辰100周年，由县委宣传部牵头，组织文化局、党史办、团县委和文联等10个单位主办全县性的纪念活动。12月底，纪念活动结束。

9月28日 县邮电局从上海贝尔公司购进的S－1240程控交换机在县城正式开通启用，原X－23自动交换机退出。

是月 贵（阳）遵（义）高等级公路开工，取道筑北重镇扎佐，县境里程23公里，1997年11月29日全线竣工投入使用。

11月6日 县委决定恢复已经停刊34年的《修文报》，27日成立修文报社，12月4日出版复刊号第1期（总第99期）。版面为4开4版，半月刊出1期。

是年 全县实行住房制度改革，采取售、租、建综合的配套方式，先后制发《修文县城镇住房制度改革实施方案》和13个配套办法。

1994

1月9日 邮电部批准修文县程控电话于1994年1月9日零时进入全国长途自动网，区号为08637。

3月21—24日 中国人民政治协商会议县第四届委员会第二次会议召开。

22—25日 县十一届人民代表大会第二次会议召开。

4月 修文县商会挂牌，与县工商联合会合署办公。

5月20日 县人民法院以修民破字1号民事裁定书裁定，正式宣告资不抵债的县酒厂破产。

6月3日 县委发出通知，要求县级班子和有关单位对照中纪委和中组部关于领导干部廉洁自律规定，开好民主生活会，认真执行中共中央、国务院《关于反腐败斗争近期抓好几项工作的决定》，迅速刹住不正之风，切实搞好廉政建设。

7月26日 中国工农红军第六军团原军团长、中顾委常委、全国政协副主席、中华炎黄文化研究会执行会会长萧克经扎佐抵县城，重游58年前指挥过战斗的扎佐。同行的有中国人民解放军第二野战军军事政治大学第五分校原副政委兼修文县委书记、军事科学院副院长姜思毅中将。

8月 国家行政机关、事业单位工资套改兑现，从1993年10月起计发，全县5500名职工（含离退休干部）人人增加工资，月人均增资135.5元（包括交通费、洗理费和报刊费）。

23日 县政府在久长镇芦山小学召开非耕地使用权拍卖现场会，当日成交21宗面积1129.5亩，每亩单价最低45元，最高145元。同日在扎佐镇拍卖公房，当日成交金额33万元。成功拍卖非耕地和拍卖公房在全县尚属首例，也是安顺地区的第一家。

9月16日 实施税务体制改革，分设修文县国家税务局和修文县地方税务局，原修文县税务局同日撤销。

11月15日 县人民法院〔1994〕修民破字第5号裁定书裁定：修文酒厂至宣布破产之日，共欠国家税款241.2万元，评估老酒厂固定资产房66.5万元和设备11.8万元抵缴部分税款。

17日 《修文县志》审稿会议召开，历时3天，与会的省、地、县有关领导、专家、知情者和兄弟县方志界同仁106人，对长达165万字的志稿作了充分肯定，并提出修改意见1294条。

23日 县委根据中共中央组织部和贵州省委指示，印发《关于加强农村基层组织建设试点工作的实

施意见》，提出“四个一”的要求，即：配备一个坚强的领导班子，选好一个支部书记，找准一条好的致富路子，制定一套切实的工作制度和乡规民约。确定谷堡乡为试点开展工作。

1995

1月28日　县政府发布关于拍卖修文县酒厂有关事宜的通告。地方税务局代表熊永忠（甲方）与个体经营户赵俊文（乙方）签订协议，将县酒厂东门车间固定资产折款60万元，一次转给乙方；乙方在1998年1月30日前分4期付清款额并按劳动法保证安排酒厂50名以内工人再就业。

30日　在北京龙潭公园举行第九届“龙潭杯”全国优秀民间花会大赛上，唯一代表贵州省参赛的修文芦笙舞《庆丰收》获二等奖，队名刻在龙潭公园的大理石碑上。中共修文县委获组织奖，演员邓开林、陶明琼获个人表演奖。

3月　贵州省政府以〔1995〕黔府发10号文件批准修文阳明风景名胜区为省级风景名胜区。

21—24日　中国人民政治协商会议县第四届委员会第三次会议召开。

22—24日　县第十一届人民代表大会第三次会议召开。

4月28日　福（州）杭（州）、贵（阳）、成（都）光缆通信工程修文段正式动工。

5月　经国务院批准，修文县被列为对外国人开放县。

29日　县酒厂破产清算组与贵州港澳保健药品有限公司签订酒厂房地产、附属配套设备买卖协议，成交额为500万元。

6月16日　县阳明学研究会在阳明洞宾阳堂正式成立。

28日　县委、县政府在洒坪乡召开群众大会，授予因抢救落水儿童而献身的洒坪中学学生魏先志“舍己救人好少年”光荣称号，并登门慰问魏先志的父母。团县委追认魏先志为共青团员，《修文报》和《贵州日报》均作了报道。

8月　山西省“锅炉大王”梁文海投资1102万元在久长镇大坝原烽光厂址兴建环海金属镁厂，设计能力年产金属镁1000吨。该企业属全国光彩事业东西部合作示范项目。1996年11月建成，1997年8月试产，后因产品价格下跌和后续资金跟不上，并负银行债款400万元，即行停产。

9月14日　扎佐坝子被列为国家“九五”重点工程磷铵项目选址比较点，县成立25人组成的磷铵项目选址协调领导小组。

10月21日　22岁的修文籍青年罗文参加95北京国际A级拳击赛，一举击败俄罗斯和韩国对手，夺得60公斤级冠军。

30日　六广河大桥合龙，总工期共2年零7个月。

1996

1月1日　遵照国务院1995年7月21日69号文批示，修文县划归贵阳市管辖。

18—19日　县第十一届人民代表大会第四次会议召开。

2月13日　县红十字会血站于县医院住院部成立。

3月6—7日 中共修文县委七届四次全委会议召开，讨论国民经济和社会发展规划。

18—21日 中国人民政治协商会议县第四届委员会第四次会议召开。

19—21日 县第十一届人民代表大会第五次会议召开。

26日 根据中共中央、中央军委关于人武部收归军队建制的决定，将贵州省修文县人民武装部改为中国人民解放军贵州省修文县人民武装部。

29日 县城高层建筑——修文电力大楼动工。整个建筑面积3890平方米，楼高39米，共9层，装有电梯。耗资345万元。1997年7月1日竣工投入使用。是为县内最高层的房舍建筑。

5月27日 贵阳市高尔夫度假中心在扎佐镇三元村举行开工典礼。该工程坐落于扎佐浪潮水库湖畔，占地3000亩，总投资10亿元。分为南、北两座18洞72杆国际高标准高尔夫球场，并附有高级酒店、别墅、娱乐、健身、购物、餐饮、医疗等配套设施。1997年5月28日，南半场的9个球洞正式开放。

6月1日 县城移动电话站开始运行，该站建在察院坡山顶，建筑面积151平方米。

15日 县第一所希望小学——大山日光小学在扎佐镇大山村落成。

是月 在贵阳市旅游评审会上，修文县被评为“一个旅游区，二条旅游线”，即：阳明文化旅游区；贵阳—阳明洞—三潮水—三人坟—天生桥峡谷—贵阳和贵阳—六广河峡谷—息烽温泉—贵阳旅游线。

7月2日 县境遭遇暴雨袭击，县城降雨315.3毫米，雨量最小的六桶为87.1毫米。据气象资料所载，这是71年来未遇到过的降雨量。3日，雨量也是194.6毫米。暴雨造成水灾，全县农作物受灾8.57万亩，其中绝收占5%，直接经济损失2267万元。

10月18日 久长镇下堡村苗族芦笙歌舞队组成贵州省修文县苗族艺术团与北京风雷京剧团联合组成由文化部批准的“中国艺术团”，应日中艺术文化交流协会邀请赴日本演出，在日本东京等地共演14场，观众达1.5万人次，完成演出计划后于11月20日返县。

12月1日 贵州省基本农田建设现场会在洒坪乡召开。

16日 县农业银行开通全国农行系统电子汇兑。

20日 全县实现村村通电。

是月 县委书记罗筑云调任贵阳市南明区委书记，贵阳市委副秘书长黄乃铸接任县委书记。

1997

2月20日 邓小平逝世，县委当即发出《关于认真搞好悼念邓小平同志活动的通知》，升国旗的机关部门自行下半旗志哀，全县各单位纷纷组织学习中共中央、全国人大常委会、国务院、全国政协、中央军委《告全党全军全国各族人民书》。25日上午，各地、各单位群众就地聚集在电视机前，收看北京追悼大会实况。

3月1日 县委组织县级班子领导成员学习中共中央总书记江泽民在邓小平追悼会上所致悼词，缅怀邓小平的丰功伟绩和崇高风范。

18—21日 中国人民政治协商会议县第四届委员会第五次会议召开。

19—21日 县第十一届人民代表大会第六次会议召开。

5月1日 县政府出台殡葬管理实施办法，规定除小箐、洒坪、六广、大石、六桶、六屯等偏僻乡

（镇）外，其余乡（镇）人口死亡，一律火化。

7月1日　上午9时，县城万余群众齐集在体育场新建升旗台前举行庆祝党的生日和迎接香港回归升旗仪式。

是月　中国农业发展银行修文支行正式建立，主要经营属农业政策性金融业务，是为全县唯一的国家政策性的银行。

8月　扎佐中学教师江洪滨发明的“三等分圆弧曲线规”获国际金奖。

9月12日　县领导和各部门干部集中收视中国共产党第十五次全国代表大会现场直播。

16日　县委中心学习组认真学习中共中央总书记江泽民在中共十五大所作题为《高举邓小平理论伟大旗帜，把建设有中国特色社会主义事业全面推向二十一世纪》的报告，并结合实际进行讨论。

27日　97修文板栗节拉开序幕。经贸洽谈签订7项意向协议书，引资1.3亿元；推销猕猴桃2.5万公斤，板栗0.75万公斤，销售金额达35万元。

是月　县政府批准恢复三潮水知非寺，为广大佛教信徒提供从事佛教活动的场所。

10月20日　修文籍拳击运动员罗文获全国第八届运动会60公斤级拳击比赛金牌，县委书记黄乃铸和副书记卢永康亲临罗文家中向家人祝贺。

28日　县第十一届人民代表大会第七次会议召开。

11月　县自来水公司羊落井新水厂通过验收合格，正式启用，日供水量5000吨。

12月25日　县委、县政府根据“抓大放小”的改制方针，决定将红旗煤矿有偿转让给原煤矿矿长应锡文，由县政府计经贸局代表转让方与受让方应锡文正式签订转让合约。

1998

3月23—27日　中国人民政治协商会议县第五届委员会第一次会议召开。

24—28日　县第十二届人民代表大会第一次会议召开。

4月8—10日　中共修文县第八次代表大会召开。

5月5日　全县延长农村土地承包工作启动。

6月23日　曾获全国八运会60公斤级拳击比赛金牌的修文县城人罗文被选为中国共产主义青年团第十四届中央委员会候补委员。

24—25日　县委、县政府召开稳定和完善农村土地承包关系培训会议，明确从1994年起计算，耕地承包期再延长50年，非耕地资源开发承包使用期再延长60年。要求立即着手调查登记、签订合同、完善承包手续等工作，整个工作于1998年8月底完成。

30日　中国人民解放军第二野战军军事政治大学第五分校原副政委兼修文县委书记、军事科学院副院长姜思毅中将重游48年前曾经战斗过的扎佐、马家桥等地。

11月22日　根据群众举报，县工商局夜间在久长火车站路口拦截一辆从遵义方向驶往贵阳的货车，查扣标值12万元的假茅台酒60件，经化验实为假酒。嗣后，工商局对货主处以3万元罚款，对承运假酒的驾驶员罚款600元。

12月18日　县委召开纪念中共十一届三中全会20周年座谈会，畅谈改革开放和现代化建设取得的巨大成就。

19日　召开县委常委扩大会议，审定县政府提出的1999年城镇基础设施建设项目“九三”工程(兴建综合体育馆，兴建文化广播电视大楼，建设绿色人民广场，整治修文河小桥至北门段，拓宽东门桥，建设社会服务中心，建设阳明大道，修建安居工程迎春小区，建立一所九年一贯制学校和修筑翠屏东路、河滨大道中段、迎春中路)，并即启动实施。

1999

1月23日　贵阳市市长孙国强到城关镇红峰村陈灯宝和薛佳两位小朋友家里，将500元现金交到他们手中，并将一件新衣服和书包、文具等送给陈灯宝，勉励他好好学习。孙国强还表示将资助小灯宝完成小学6年的学业。

28日　贵阳市副市长杨哲慧率市民政、卫生、红十字会、皮防所等单位负责人到六桶乡何田村硝厂医院慰问麻风病患者，送去4000元慰问金和棉被、猪肉、日杂用品等慰问品。

2月28日　应中华全国总工会邀请，日本工会总联合会高级代表团先遣团一行3人到县阳明洞参观访问。

3月5日　县纪律检查委员会第二次全体会议召开。会议总结1998年度全县党风廉政建设和反腐败斗争，同时研究部署1999年全县党风廉政建设和反腐败工作。

11日　贵州省委常委、贵阳市委书记庹文升率市直有关部门负责人到县检查春耕备耕情况，并视察贵州天地人实业有限公司养殖基地、久长镇石安村生猪分户养殖、城关镇马家桥猕猴桃苗圃基地以及顺通公司万头香猪养殖基地、乌栗猕猴桃种植基地。

23日　由县委书记黄乃铸和副书记王真霖领队，10乡（镇）党委书记、县农办、县委政研室负责人参加的考察团前往赤水市和仁怀县、湄潭县，对常规农业、城镇建设、农村税费改革进行为期5天的考察和学习。

29日　由贵州省国土厅、贵阳市国土局和县直有关部门领导、专家联合组成的评审验收组，对扎佐等9个乡（镇）土地利用总体规划进行评审验收。

29—31日　中国人民政治协商会议县第五届委员会第二次会议召开。

30—4月2日　县第十二届人民代表大会第二次会议召开。

4月2日　县国有资产管理委员会、国有资产投资经营有限责任公司挂牌成立。

23日　贵州省农业综合开发宣传工作会在县城召开，全省9个地州（市）及41个农业综合开发项目县的代表莅会。会议传达全国农业综合开发宣传工作会议精神，总结交流宣传工作经验，分析农业综合开发宣传工作的新形势、新任务，并部署1999年的宣传工作。

5月9日　县社会各界集会，强烈抗议以美国为首的北约袭击我驻南使馆的侵略行径。

6月11—17日　国家林业局人工造林实绩核查组教授高级工程师蔡时钧、工程师张罗恩到县检查1998年人工造林任务落实情况。

18日　全县农村电网改造启动。改造工程由贵州省电力公司和贵阳市北供电局投资3700万元，由县供电局具体负责规划、设计和施工。改造后的农村电网实行电价、发票、抄表、核算、考核“五统一”

和电价、电量、电费“三公开”。

7月14日 贵阳市北供电局在六屯乡都堡村举行农网35千伏工程启动暨六屯变电站开工典礼。六屯变电站的开工系贵州全省农村电网改造工作中建设35千伏变电站的首家，它标志着修文农村电网改造工程进入全面实施阶段。

8月2日 中国人民解放军贵阳陆军预备役工兵团在县成立。

9月28日 新编《修文县志》首发式在县政府礼堂举行，来自省、市及兄弟市县、外专州方志部门领导、专家，曾担任过修文县党政领导的老同志，时任县委、县人大常委会、县政府、县政协领导，县直部门、乡（镇）领导，县志编修期间的历届编委、编辑200余人参加首发式。

10月6日 县综合体育馆开馆。该馆占地21亩，建筑面积5700平方米，置有座位2292个（含主席台座位60个），置有贵宾馆、裁判员休息室、办公室及卫生间等设施。全部工程耗时9个月，总投资1199.4万元。

14日 中国·贵阳（修文）’99国际阳明文化节投资贸易洽谈会在县体育馆举行，当天签约投资项目13个，投资金额近3亿元。

15日 中国贵阳’99阳明文化节在贵阳百花剧院举行闭幕式，贵阳市京剧团在闭幕式上演出京剧《龙冈悟道》。

28日 由日本民间慈善组织“水月会”捐资修建的六广镇中松小学竣工并投入使用。

11月18日 国土资源部规划管理司副司长殷卫平一行到县对土地利用总体规划编制工作进行调研和核查。县土地利用总体规划编制工作自1997年3月启动，1998年3月全面完成县和10乡（镇）两级土地利用总体规划，同年12月通过省级验收。

2000

1月18—19日 全县2000年工作会议在县政府礼堂召开。会议全面总结1999年度工作，部署2000年各项工作。

2月22—24日 中国人民政治协商会议县第五届委员会第三次会议召开。

23—25日 县第十二届人民代表大会第三次会议召开。

28日 县领导干部“三讲”（讲学习，讲政治，讲正气）教育会议在县政府礼堂召开，贵阳市委常委、市政法委书记林连华，省委“三讲”教育巡视组组长陈德安出席并讲话。自此，县领导干部“三讲”教育进入第一阶段。

3月3日 全县农村工作会议召开。会议提出2000年农业和农村经济发展要求，大力推进农业和农村经济结构战略性调整，全面提高农业和农村经济的效益，增加农民收入。

22日 全省第一家县级用电营业自动化系统在县内建成并通过省级验收。

29日 中外合作贵阳黔豪冶金有限发展公司向贵州雅筑园艺有限公司投资4500万元生产竹荪、花卉，签约仪式在扎佐镇竹荪、花卉基地举行。

4月5日 以张汉夫为组长的中央“三讲”教育检查组，在贵阳市委书记王晓东的陪同下到县检查“三讲”教育开展情况。

14日　实施西部大开发战略动员会在县体育馆召开，会议标志着修文已吹响西部大开发的号角。

15日　最高人民检察院检察长韩杼滨一行到县调研。

18—19日　由中共中央组织部组织的检查组在组长孙祖梅的带领下莅县就《党政领导干部选拔任用工作暂行条例》贯彻执行情况进行检查。

5月25日　贵州省实施丰收计划项目培训会在县举行。培训会明确当年全省农业丰收计划项目在县境实施水稻轻型栽培技术7万亩。

29日　贵阳市人民满意的公务员巡回报告团到县作报告。

6月12日　《修文报》主编陈新国的短篇小说集《野山》荣获贵阳市人民政府颁发的金筑文艺奖。

16日　县人民法院与贵州省民族学院建立实习基地举行仪式，标志着县人民法院与高等院校之间在改革、调研、人才培养等方面的交流与合作迈出新的一步。

30日　县委召开纪念中国共产党建党79周年大会。

7月14日　2000年“贵阳杯”全国业余高尔夫球公开赛在扎佐贵阳高尔夫度假中心落下帷幕。四川高尔夫球协会杨军以总成绩243杆摘取男子组桂冠，广东省中山市长江高尔夫球协会的马燕嫦以总成绩241杆夺取女子组冠军。

21日　全省迎接新世纪青少年运动会羽毛球比赛在县体育馆落下帷幕。

26日　县委召开八届五次全会。会议审议通过《县委、县政府关于加强人口与计划生育工作，严格控制人口过快增长的决定》和《县委、县政府关于改善投资环境，扩大招商引资的决定》。

9月14日　县招商引资领导小组办公室正式挂牌。

22日　由张竹梧带领的中央“三讲”教育检查组莅县检查整改工作，要求进一步加强学习，落实整改，把“三个代表”重要思想贯彻到全体干部和群众中去，加快经济和社会发展。

28日　县“一控双达标”（污染物总量控制；工业污染源要达到国家或地方规定的污染物排放标准，空气和地面水按功能区达到国家规定的环境质量标准）工作接受省、市有关部门检查。通过检查组检查，“一控双达标”指标达到有关标准，如期完成全县工业污染源达标排放工作，率先在全省通过检查验收。

10月16日　县政府邀请贵州大学、贵州农学院和省农业综合开发、财政等单位的专家参加论证会，对县编制的《国家农业综合开发科技推广示范项目—贵州省修文县高科技农业示范建设规划》进行论证。该项目通过专家论证。

11月1日　以零时为标准时间，全县进行第五次人口普查，总人口为262039人。

10日　县教育“两基”（基本普及九年义务教育、基本扫除青壮年文盲）工作通过省政府评估验收。

28日　贵州省农业厅授予“六广河”牌猕猴桃为贵州省优质农产品称号，并颁发证书。

12月14日　国家环保局评估中心研究员毛永久、梁学功、王家骥及中国农业大学教授费先斌在贵州省和贵阳市环保局环境工程评估中心、环境监测中心及索风营电站筹建处专家陪同下，到拟建的索风营电站坝址考察环境保护和水土保持工作。

22日　县政府2000年第十二次常务扩大会议召开，讨论全县国民经济和社会发展“十五”计划纲要和2001年为民要办的实事。

2001

1月18—19日 全县2001年工作会议在县政府礼堂召开。会议全面总结2000年的工作，部署2001年各项任务。

2月9日 贵州省政府科技工作创先考评验收专家组对县科技创先工作采取听、看、查、议、问等方式进行综合考评，最后一致同意通过省级验收。

11日 台湾旅行社经理协会赴贵州旅游线路考察团一行20人在国家旅游局和省、市旅游部门负责人以及县领导陪同下到阳明洞、高尔夫度假中心考察旅游线路。

20—22日 中国人民政治协商会议县第五届委员会第四次会议召开。

21—23日 县第十二届人民代表大会第四次会议召开。

26日 县委召开“三个代表”（中国共产党要始终代表中国先进生产力的发展要求、代表中国先进文化的前进方向、代表中国最广大人民的根本利益）重要思想学习教育动员会，开始在县级领导干部中进行为期3个月的学习教育活动。

3月27—28日 县委召开农村税费改革工作培训会，启动全县农村税费改革。

5月18日 修文黔鑫磷化工有限责任公司挂牌开业。该公司是一家外商投资公司，经过5个月的紧张筹建，已建成年产3000吨85%磷酸、1000吨磷酸二氢钾、1000吨磷酸二氢铵和1000吨磷酸二氢钙的磷酸及磷酸盐系列产品生产线。

6月5日 县8个小康村道路硬化工程通过市级验收，4000村民走上“小康路”。

12日 县委召开第二批“三个代表”重要思想学习教育活动动员大会，开始在部门领导干部中开展学习教育活动，到9月29日，召开总结大会，活动结束。

29日 《中国共产党修文县组织史资料》《修文县政军统群组织史资料》正式出版。

8月3日 由贵阳市纪委主办和市委组织部、宣传部、政法委协办的“黔灵峰谷—党风廉政建设和反腐败斗争巡礼展”在县体育馆开展。展览以图文并茂的形式和丰富翔实的内容全面回顾了中共十五大后贵阳市党风廉政建设和反腐败斗争的历程。

是月 全国政协副主席万国权到阳明洞考察，县政协主席王清义和县委副书记胡晓刚陪同。

11月9日 县委召开村级“三个代表”重要思想学习教育活动工作会议，全面部署全县村级“学教”工作，12日全面铺开，历时两个月，到2002年1月中旬结束。

12月5日 县农业科技园区建设启动，县政府召开会议对园区建设进行专题部署。

11日 贵州省第二届农民电影节贵阳分会场开幕式在县体育馆举行。

2002

1月10日 贵阳市“136”工程竹园总规评审会在县内召开，由杭州蓝天园林设计院编制的《贵阳市修文县竹文化园（阳明园）规划方案》通过评审。

22—23日 全县2002年工作会议在县政府礼堂召开。会议高举邓小平理论伟大旗帜，以中共中央总书记江泽民“七一”重要讲话和“三个代表”重要思想为指导，全面贯彻落实中央和省、市有关会议精神，结合全县实际，总结2001年的工作，部署2002年各项任务。

3月1日 县委召开八届七次全委（扩大）会议，选举出席贵阳市党代表大会的代表。

4—6日 中国人民政治协商会议县第五届委员会第五次会议召开。

5—7日 县第十二届人民代表大会第五次会议召开。

26日 国家农业综合开发科技综合示范园项目评估小组组长王永权一行5人在省、市农发部门领导陪同下莅县对2002年申报的无公害优质产品“粮—猪—沼—果”四位一体项目进行实地考察。

4月10日 县政府举行医保培训工作会，启动全县城镇职工医疗保险制度改革。

5月21日 《人民日报》、中央人民广播电台、《经济日报》等新闻媒体组成的中央新闻采访团一行到县就“茅改”工程进行专题采访。

6月5—6日 贵阳市少数民族运动会大象拔河项目比赛在县体育馆举行，由县体育部门组织参赛的选手在比赛中取得60公斤级第一名。

20日 县委召开农村“三个代表”重要思想学习教育活动总结会议，全面回顾从2001年2月在县农村开展“学教”活动后的基本情况，并对扩大学教活动成果，推动深入整改，建立并启动学习实践“三个代表”重要思想常抓不懈工作机制，明确要求进一步做好全县农业、农村工作。

26日 贵阳市首家无害化处理可燃性废弃物裂解项目在龙场镇马关村铁合金厂建成，并试运行成功。

7月10日 全县首家企业武装部——供电局武装部正式挂牌成立。

26日 位于六广河段的国家西电东送重点项目乌江索风营水电站正式开工。2006年6月6日 索风营电站最后一台3号机组发电投入商业运行，标志着贵州首批国家西电东送工程项目全部建成。

8月3日 贵州省委常委、组织部部长刘也强到县就学习贯彻《党政领导干部选拔任用工作条例》进行调研。

23日 全省“扶残助学·春晖行动”在县特殊教育学校启动。贵阳市政府市长孙国强和县领导以及省、市残疾人联合会、市教育局负责人参加启动仪式并向贫困残疾儿童捐款。

9月20日 2002中国·贵阳（修文）阳明文化节新闻发布会在贵阳举行。

10月1日 县对外形象的标志性建筑—“王学圣地”牌坊竣工。牌坊位于阳明大道接贵（阳）毕（节）高等级公路路口，高17.1米，宽28米，属仿古建筑。由浙江省璜店古典建筑设计院设计，工程总投资87万元。

18日 2002中国·贵阳（修文）国际阳明文化节在县体育馆开幕，19日在六广河畔翠竹楼闭幕。

第二届“泛鹰杯”高尔夫球公开赛在扎佐贵阳高尔夫度假中心落下帷幕，北京选手高磊夺冠。

11月4—5日 县第十二届人民代表大会第六次会议召开。

29日 修文三中举行落成（授牌）座谈会。三中始建于1999年，总投资362万元。

12月12日 县委召开八届八次全体（扩大）会议，学习贯彻党的十六大和贵州省委九届二次全体（扩大）会议、贵阳市委七届八次全体（扩大）会议精神。

2003

1月9日 全县2003年工作会议在县政府礼堂召开。会议以邓小平理论和“三个代表”重要思想为指导，全面贯彻落实中共十六大和中央、全省、全市经济工作会议精神，总结2002年工作，对2003年工作进行部署。

19日 由贵州省委宣传部和贵阳市委宣传部主办，县委宣传部等单位参加的贵阳市2003年“百城万店无假货”活动在县城拉开帷幕，50余车货真价实的年货送到农民朋友家门口。

3月6—8日 中共修文县第九次代表大会召开。

18—21日 中国人民政治协商会议县第六届委员会第一次会议召开。

19—22日 县第十三届人民代表大会第一次会议召开。

21日 央视《走遍中国——贵阳》阳明文化专题在县开机拍摄。

4月1日 扎佐医药园被农业部正式命名为“全国乡镇企业科技园区”。

3日 中国贵航集团贵阳云天航空工贸有限公司整体移交县人民政府，签约仪式在贵阳贵龙饭店举行。

7日 县委转发《中共贵州省委关于认真开展学习郑培民同志活动的通知》，要求全县党员干部特别是领导干部要认真开展学习郑培民活动。

22日 县委召开非典型肺炎防治工作紧急会议，部署全县的防治工作。5月12日，县委、县政府在防治“非典”工作会议上与10乡（镇）和县直部门签订防治“非典”责任书，强化责任，层层落实，誓阻“非典”于县门之外。16日，首批由市直单位抽调的75名机关干部分13个组奔赴县内各乡（镇）进村入户宣传防治“非典”的相关知识。

6月3日 共青团贵州省委和贵州省计生委在贵阳召开“计生好帮手，爱心传万家”计生志愿者工作新闻发布会，修文被列为“贵州省计生志愿者工作”唯一的省级试点县。

25—27日 县委中心学习组学习中共中央和贵州省委、贵阳市委关于在全党掀起学习贯彻“三个代表”重要思想新高潮的指示精神和《“三个代表”重要思想学习纲要》。

是月 县远程教育网络正式开通，标志着全县党员干部教育培训步入现代化轨道。

30日 科技部委托省科技部门组织的专家组对修文争创国家级科技进步先进县工作进行考核。专家组通过观看专题片，查阅资料，实地考察，一致通过修文2001—2002年国家级科技进步先进县的考核。

7月13日 参加贵阳市第一期农村党支部书记培训班的103名学员到谷堡乡参观考察，学习折溪村、红星村的产业结构调整和支书“双带”（村党支部书记带头致富和带领群众共同致富）典型事例。

23日 县司法机关在县城召开公捕大会，对龙场镇阳明村阻碍国家机关工作人员依法执行任务，非法拘禁，伤害他人，打砸县人民政府和县人民法院的犯罪嫌疑人进行公捕。

8月7日 县委召开九届二次全体扩大会议，传达贯彻贵州省委九届三次、贵阳市委七届十次全体扩大会议精神，总结上半年工作，安排下半年任务。以掀起学习“三个代表”重要思想新高潮为总揽，统一思想，激发斗志，全力以赴抓好后5个月的工作，确保完成全年各项目标任务。

26日 索风营水电站施工区移民搬迁安置工作省级验收会在县召开，经过专家评审，索风营水电站修文县施工区移民安置工作通过省级验收。

9月4日 贵阳陆军预备役工兵团舟桥四连在六广旅游公司挂牌成立。

9日 扎佐高潮水厂建成供水。高潮水厂总投资800万元，日供水5000吨。

19日 一部全面反映修文改革开放重大成果的大型航拍电视片《王学圣地》开机仪式在阳明园举行。

26日 中韩合作贵州修文造林示范项目执行协议签字仪式在贵阳举行。项目涉及六广、大石、小箐、洒坪4个乡（镇），总投资1654万元，其中韩国政府无偿援助100万美元。

10月22日 全县已安装卫星接收天线358套，电视入户2000户，收取匹配资金30万元，发出转换器1080个，提前38天全面完成“自然村通”的各项工作。

28日 首届贵州名特优农产品展销会在贵阳五里冲农副产品批发市场揭幕，修文县组织的24个（种）农产品参加展出，其中3个被评为“首届贵州名特优农产品展销会名牌农产品”，签约项目7个，涉及金额1.25亿元。

11月20日 县医药行业首家民营科研机构——国光民间医药研究所在县城洗脚塘挂牌成立。

26日 县委中心学习组召开会议，传达学习贵阳市委七届十一次全会和中共中央、贵州省委有关文件精神，并就抓好全县2004年的各项工作进行部署。

是月 县内部分街道居民委员会调整并冠以“社区”称谓，计有龙场镇6个居民委员会调整并命名为龙岗、栖凤、宾阳、虎山4个社区居民委员会；扎佐镇第一、第二居民委员会分别命名为襄阳、景阳2个社区居民委员会；久长镇久长居民委员会命名为长久社区居民委员会；六广镇六广居民委员会命名为松江社区居民委员会；小箐乡小箐居民委员会命名为小箐社区居民委员会。

2004

1月16—17日 县委九届三次全体（扩大）会议召开，贯彻落实中共十六届三中全会、中央经济工作会议、贵州省委九届四次全会、全省经济工作会议和贵阳市委七届十一次全会精神，总结2003年工作和部署2004年任务。

2月10—12日 中国人民政治协商会议县第六届委员会第二次会议召开。

11—13日 县第十三届人民代表大会第二次会议召开。

3月4—8日 韩国国际协力团韩中造林事务所安国荣博士率领韩方造林专家组莅县检查中韩合作造林示范项目执行情况。通过实地检查，一致认为修文实施的造林项目质量高、效果好，要求严格按照双方签署《项目执行协议》抓好各项措施的落实。

17日 贵阳全市茅草房改造工程捐款暨奠基仪式在洒坪乡小坝村举行，13家参建单位共捐款200万元，帮助500户贫困户茅改。

31日 县委中心学习组组织县级领导班子集中观看反腐警示片《绝路》，并学习《中国共产党纪律处分条例》《中国共产党党内监督条例（试行）》和中共中央、国务院关于促进农民增加收入若干政策的意见。

7月1日 县委召开大会，纪念中国共产党建党83周年，表彰在各条战线上涌现出来的先进党组织、优秀共产党员和优秀党务工作者。

14日 贵州省计生志愿者工作现场会在县召开，省内各地州市团委书记、各县团委书记和志愿者代表共180人参加会议。

29日 全县农村劳动力家政服务员初级培训班在小箐乡远程教育接收站举行开班仪式。

9月3日 县委九届四次全体（扩大）会议召开。会议总结4年间全县实施西部大开发战略的成果。并对贯彻落实贵阳市委、市政府《关于进一步推进西部大开发战略的实施意见》作具体部署。

10月11日 贵阳森林野生动物园总体规划评审会在扎佐林场会议室举行，与会专家通过认真评审，一致同意通过总规，并要求设计单位按照专家组提出的要求进行修改后上报审批。18日，投资8000多万元的全国首家森林公园——贵阳森林野生动物园正式在扎佐林场破土动工。野生动物园建设用地为扎佐林场所属的国有山林，总面积3099亩。

11月18日 县委、县政府在扎佐医药园区内的贵州科开医药股份有限公司举行授奖仪式，向全县招商引资企业中第一纳税大户——贵州科开医药股份有限公司兑现奖励“奥迪”轿车一辆，并授予该公司重点纳税企业先进单位称号。

12月20日 截至当日下午17时，县财政总收入完成1.67亿元。其中地方财政收入完成1.02亿元，首次突破亿元大关。

2005

1月21日 县委九届五次全委（扩大）会议举行。会议落实中央经济工作会议、贵州省委九届六次全会和全省经济工作会议、贵阳市委七届十三次全会精神，以科学发展观为统领，听取和讨论《中共修文县委2005年工作要点》，总结2004年的经济工作，对做好2005年经济工作进行全面部署。

2月10日 中共中央总书记、国家主席胡锦涛在贵州省委书记钱运录等领导的陪同下视察六广河索风营电站的建设情况，并慰问施工的全体职工。

3月4日 由共青团贵州省委发起并组织实施的“春晖行动”在县内启动。

7—9日 中国人民政治协商会议县第六届委员会第三次会议召开。

8—10日 县十三届人民代表大会第三次会议召开。

4月8日 贵阳·修文第二届梨花节开幕式在谷堡乡折溪村梨花湖畔举行。

5月22日 由贵州省和贵阳市科技部门组织的“科技以人为本，全面建设小康”为主题的2005年科技活动周“三下乡”（文化下乡、科技下乡、卫生下乡）活动在县城启动。

8月10日 县委九届六次全体扩大会议召开，学习贵州省委九届七次、贵阳市委七届十四次全委扩大会议精神，坚持以科学发展观统揽，部署全县人口资源环境工作和建立健全教育、制度、监督并重的惩治预防腐败体系工作。

30日 中国·贵阳（修文）第三届国际阳明文化节新闻发布会在省城贵阳举行。来自中央驻筑新闻媒体、境外驻筑新闻媒体和省、市新闻单位的数十名新闻记者参加发布会。

是月 扎佐镇增建万江社区居民委员会，将原万江机电公司和药业园区、兴红厂区整合为万江社区居民委员会，纳入社会化管理。

9月19日 中国·贵阳（修文）第三届国际阳明文化节在阳明文化主题公园广场开幕，来自美、日、韩等13个国家和地区的省内外百余名专家学者出席开幕式。

10月14日　县委召开常委会议，学习贯彻贵阳市委严格《干部任用条例》选拔任用干部会议精神。

27日　县委邀请中国项目管理研究委员会副秘书长揭津荣女士为全县领导干部开展现代项目管理——全球管理新趋势专题知识讲座。

11月21日　教育部计财司副司长崔帮焱率相关人员到县检查农村中、小学校实施“三小”（小伙房、小基地、小厕所）工程的相关情况，并就进一步做好“三小”工程与学校教育工作的结合提出建议和意见。

12月7日　县委、县政府召开县、乡（镇）领导干部会，对全县启动新型农村合作医疗工作进行部署。

2006

1月19日　中国·贵阳（修文）第三届国际阳明文化节总结表彰大会在文广大楼举行，一批在阳明文化节活动中做出成绩的单位和个人受到县委、县政府表彰。

2月24日　金黔在线网站评选“最吸引外国人的贵州旅游景点”揭幕，阳明洞获117.32万张票，在25个参评景点中得票数名列首位。

28—3月2日　中国人民政治协商会议县第六届委员会第四次会议召开。

3月1—3日　县第十三届人民代表大会第四次会议召开。

18日　中央编办监督检查司副司长李世春率队的乡镇机构改革调研组到县调研乡镇机构改革试点工作情况。

5月16日　贵州省委巡视组二组组长曾康带队莅县，对县委2000年起贯彻落实科学发展观，执行党的路线、方针、政策和贵州省委的指示决议，贯彻民主集中制，落实党风廉政建设责任制和勤政廉政，选拔任用干部，处理改革发展稳定等工作开展情况进行巡视。

24日　由修文县与贵阳日报社联合举办的“游王学圣地·看野生动物·品乡村风情”贵阳日报读者自驾游活动启动，200名游客到县观光旅游，推介王学圣地旅游品牌。

25日　根据《国务院关于核定并公布第六批全国重点文物保护单位的通知》，阳明洞作为全国513个古建筑之一被列入全国重点文物保护单位。

8月28日　县委、县政府在阳明洞举行全国文物保护单位授牌暨保护标志碑揭幕仪式。

29日　在施秉县召开的贵州省地方志协会第三次会员代表大会暨学术年会上，修文县地方志编辑部主编李祖炎被聘为贵州省地方志协会顾问。

9月8日　县电视台举办建台十周年暨贵阳电视台修文记者站挂牌庆典活动。

13日　在贵阳市第四届群众文艺调演闭幕式暨颁奖晚会上，修文县选送的舞蹈《红苞谷》荣获一等奖，舞蹈《孔雀飞来》《高原女人》《杜鹃花开》分别荣获二、三等奖。

25—27日　中共修文县第十次代表大会召开。

10月27日　全县第一届中小学艺术节活动在县城举行。

11月20—22日　中国人民政治协商会议修文县第七届委员会第一次会议召开。

21—23日　县第十四届人民代表大会第一次会议召开。

12月31日　县委召开十届三次全体会议，选举产生县出席中共十七大和贵州省第十次党代会代表候选人。

2007

1月8日　2006年“奥林匹克”中华儿女书画大奖赛揭晓，扎佐叮铛幼儿园取得好成绩，12名小朋友获奖。

24日　修文阳明诗社正式成立并举行授牌仪式，标志着县对优秀传统文化的传承和发展进入一个新的时期。

27日　县猕猴桃项目通过国标验收。

2月10日　在全省“双拥”（拥军优属、拥政爱民）模范县（城）命名大会上，修文县被贵州省委、省政府、省军区授予全省双拥模范县称号。

3月1日　国家农业综合开发办公室专家莅县检查土地治理工作。

8日　第二届贵州省“千万妇女健身展示活动大赛”在省体育馆拉开序幕，县选送的舞蹈“红包谷”代表县妇联参加开幕式文艺演出。

20—22日　中国人民政治协商会议县第七届委员会第二次会议召开。

21—23日　县第十四届人民代表大会第二次会议召开。

4月17日　贵阳市教育局对全市2006年教学质量优异的学校进行表彰，修文中学再次获奖。自2003年起，修文中学已连续3年荣获贵阳市普通高中学校“入口出口”学科成绩评估一等奖。

5月4—5日　由日本学者矢畸胜彦及浙江等地7名专家组成的王阳明学术研究考察团莅县，考察阳明文化研究及文物保护。

14日　共青团中央书记处书记王晓到县检查“春晖行动”开展情况。王晓在了解县“春晖行动”工作开展情况后，深入到久长镇永兴村实地查看“春晖行动”工作展板及叶辛春晖小学远程教育教室、图书室运行情况，并参观叶辛插队当知青的旧居。

6月9日　贵阳（修文）首届漂流节暨桃源河魔幻漂流大赛在桃源河举行。

21日　德国的生态旅游专家Vloker Kienast（中文名字叫傅宜楷）到县考察生态旅游。

22日　原中宣部副部长龚心瀚、原国务院特派稽查员刘吉到县考察阳明文化资源的开发与保护情况。

7月27日　县纪委、县委组织部组织县级班子领导及各乡（镇）、各部门正科级领导干部赴全省反腐倡廉警示教育基地——贵州省大洞口监狱开展“现身说法”警示教育活动。

8月1日　在中央召开的庆祝中国人民解放军建军八十周年暨全军英模代表大会上，县委书记魏明禄荣获“全国爱国拥军模范”称号。

13日　国务院新闻办网络新闻管理局副局长彭波到县考察。

17日　县政府召开专题会议，部署北京奥运会火炬接力贵阳境内传递修文县火炬手的选拔工作。会议要求全县上下充分认识奥运火炬手选拔工作的重要性，以求真务实的精神抓好选拔工作，从而圆满完成光荣任务。

24日　全县完成2.87万座广播电视卫星转星调整工作，占任务2.82万座的101.69%。通过接收新的卫星信号，使广播电视用户能收到34套以上信号质量好的电视节目。

9月4日　由贵阳市委宣传部、市纪委及市妇联组织的“迎奥运、讲文明、树新风，贵阳市读书学习在万家——林城学习型家庭事迹”巡回报告团到县举行报告会。

10月10—11日　贵州省地方志学术研讨会在久长镇珍珠岛举行，省志办主任彭钢出席会议，县委书记魏明禄到会致辞。

27—28日　卫生部国外贷款办高级项目官员王晓华率卫生部卫IX项目专家组莅县检查实施世行贷款卫IX项目妇幼卫生子项目完成情况。

11月14日　国家烟草专卖局组织验收组莅县验收2006年烟叶基础设施建设，对县“烟水配套”工程给予高度评价和充分肯定。

12月3—5日　由贵阳市委台湾工作办公室、市人民政府台湾事务办公室主办的贵阳“中国台湾问题图片展览”在县城开展。图片展以“一个中国，和平发展”为主题，分为前言、台湾是中国不可分割的一部分、中国政府解决台湾问题的方针政策、两岸关系现状与发展、两岸对话和谈判、国际共识、贵阳与台湾、结语等8个方面的内容。

5日　县政府开通“整脏治乱”县长热线，热线开通的当天接到100余个热线电话和10余封电子邮件。

14日　全国政协常委、民革中央副主席、北京大学经济学教授厉以宁带领台湾阳明大学荣誉教授、前任校长张心湜，台湾阳明大学教授陈维熊及台湾大学教授、北大光华学院名誉董事尹衍梁等一行莅县考察阳明文化资源开发利用与保护情况。

19日　中国医药集团公司董事长刘存周率队到县考察，并就如何立足优势，优化配置，开拓企业前景，扩大市场占有率，做大做强医药产业等问题进行交流。

21日　美国哈佛大学教授、燕京学院院长杜维明莅临阳明洞、玩易窝考察阳明文化，在阳明洞接受贵州电视台论道栏目组记者专访。

2008

1月13日　县境普遍降温，温度为-1.7℃，随后气温继续下降，到2月7日降至-5.9℃，后虽有回升，但也仅到-3.6℃，直至2月14日才予回暖。气温下降带来若干年未遇的严重凝冻灾害，其特点一是范围广，涉及全县10乡（镇）的217个行政村；二是强度大，平均气温低于有气象记载以来的最低值；三是时间长，整个低温凝冻持续42天；四是损失重，给交通运输、电力传输、通信设施、工农业生产和群众生活造成影响，直接经济损失达2亿多元。

是日　香港文汇报以《王阳明学说500年不老——小洞天悟出大道理，龙场山野宣教心学》为主题报道阳明文化。

2月2日　县委召开县级班子联席会议，传达学习中央政治局常委、中央书记处书记习近平在贵州视察抗灾救灾工作时的重要讲话，进一步部署赈灾救灾和灾后重建工作。12日，县委召开常委扩大会议传达市委扩大会议精神，研究部署灾后重建事宜，强调要千方百计抓重建，尽心竭力保民生，确保“抗凝

冻、保民生”工作取得最后胜利。

3月11—13日 中国人民政治协商会议县第七届委员会第三次会议召开。

12—14日 县第十四届人民代表大会第三次会议召开。

25日 监察部驻水利部监察局副局长陈庚寅率水利部视察组到县视察高潮水库除险加固工程实施情况。

4月30日 1000多名机关干部和街道居民、学校师生在体育馆参加“迎奥运倒计时100天全民健身与奥运同行”活动。

是月 县委书记魏明禄因组织领导全县抗凝救灾工作成绩突出被贵州省委、省政府记一等功。

5月6日 香港慈恩基金会在扎佐中学开展捐资助学活动，全校50名优秀贫困高中生每人获得400元助学金。

7日 县委召开2008年宣传思想暨“整脏治乱”工作推进会，进一步贯彻落实中央、省、市宣传思想工作会议精神，总结2007年全县宣传思想和“整脏治乱”工作，部署2008年宣传思想和“整脏治乱”任务。

14日 县委举行支援四川汶川地震灾区捐赠启动仪式，全县机关职工、群众、学生踊跃捐款，将爱心和问候带给灾区人民。23日，县委组织召开常委会议，所有参会人员向党组织交纳特殊党费，积极支持灾区抗震救灾工作。

18日 首期经济适用住房和廉租房工程开工仪式在县城阳明大道举行。

6月11日 由国家安监总局监管二司副司长陈列率队的国家安全生产百日督查组到县检查百日安全生产工作开展情况。

7月24日 在2008中国·贵阳避暑季之第四届医药博览会暨中国民族医药论坛上，全县产品推介、招商引资获得丰厚回报，共引进项目5个，签约资金3.5亿元。

8月1日 县委召开全县领导干部大会，宣布贵阳市委对县委主要领导变动的决定：县委书记魏明禄他调，遗缺由县委副书记、县长石洪递补，蒋志伦接任县委副书记并提名为县长候选人。

16日 2008“多彩贵州”歌唱大赛贵阳赛区决赛进行最后一场比赛，修文选手王靖绮以一首《山里女人喊太阳》获贵阳赛区民族唱法职业组第二名，成功晋级决赛。

31日 “要爽到贵阳”网络媒体暨外国记者中国避暑之都体验游大型活动采访团到县采访，县委书记石洪致欢迎辞并接受《中国日报》外国记者专访。

是月 经贵州省建设经济领导小组考察，将修文县纳入全省第三批经济强县。

9月4日 贵州省委政研室巡视员和省经济强县建设工作领导小组领导莅县调研经济强县建设工作，对修文县被列入全省第三轮经济强县建设表示祝贺。

10月17日 阳明文化主题公园广场顺利通过验收，该工程总投资170万元，建设规模7911平方米。

28日 扎佐医药产业园区被农业部评审为第三批全国农产品加工示范基地。

30—31日 贵阳市区、县（市）政协工作研讨会在县城召开，来自10区县（市）的政协主席、副主席、秘书长围绕新时期如何履行政协职能，服务大局，推进生态文明城市建设进行探讨。

11月29日 贵阳森林野生动物园通过国家旅游局评审组评定，认定其园为国家级AAAA级景区。

30日 省委副书记、省长林树森到县考察阳明文化资源与保护情况。

12月12日 首钢集团总公司党委书记、董事长朱继民在县领导及贵钢负责人陪同下到贵钢搬迁拟选址的扎佐镇小堡村考察，并就该地的土地利用、水源供给等相关工作进行详细了解。

2009

1月5日 全县“心系民生解民困，情暖民心化民忧”——2009年修文温暖行动启动仪式在体育馆举行。县委、县政府向2085户城市低保户发放41.7万元温暖行动购物卡，户均受益200元。

17日 县人大常委会召开十四届十七次会议，任命蒋志伦为县政府副县长并代理县长，同时补选为贵阳市第十二届人民代表大会代表。

19日 县委召开第十届委员会第七次全体（扩大）会议，全面贯彻落实中共十七届三中全会、贵州省委十届四次全会、贵阳市委八届六次全会和中央、省、市经济工作会议精神。会议总结2008年的工作，部署2009年全县的工作任务。

2月5日 县委、县政府召开筹备举办2009中国·贵阳避暑季开幕式、中国·贵阳（修文）第四届国际阳明文化节和贵阳市第三届旅游发展大会专题会议，部署相关工作。5月5日 以“避暑·生态·产业”为主题的大型旅游文化活动——2009年中国·贵阳避暑季活动暨中国·贵阳（修文）第四届国际阳明文化节开幕式在阳明文化主题公园广场举行。同日上午，贵阳市第三届旅游产业发展大会在扎佐贵阳野生动物园广场召开。

3月3日 首钢贵阳特殊钢有限公司新特材料循环经济项目进厂主通道开工建设，标志着贵钢100万吨特殊钢异地技改项目正式进入实质性实施阶段。

10—12日 中国人民政治协商会议县第七届委员会第四次会议召开。

11—13日 县第十四届人民代表大会第四次会议召开。

4月19日 由县委、县政府组织创编的第一张旅游风光歌曲专辑——《爽爽贵阳·秀美修文》音视频合成完毕。歌曲专辑由贵州音像文化出版社正式出版发行。

7日 “春晖家园”揭牌暨贵州省少年夏令营基地授牌仪式在久长镇永兴村砂锅寨举行。

26日 博鳌亚洲论坛秘书长龙永图与著名文化学者、厦门大学教授易中天做客“中国避暑之都·爽爽的贵阳·阳明高端电视论坛”在阳明洞前畅谈“一个城市的文化记忆”。

6月25日 贵阳电视台通联工作会暨《回眸——辉煌贵阳30年》好稿评析会在县城召开，修文电视台报送的《家乡的变化我是见证者》等4篇获二等奖。

27日 贵阳（修文）第二届漂流节暨2009桃源河魔幻漂流大赛在桃源河景区举行。

7月17日 贵阳市2009年青少年跆拳道锦标赛在市体育中学训练馆举行，县文武学校在比赛中夺取竞技组个人12金、6银、3铜的好成绩，并分获区县市团体及道馆学校团体两个总分第二。

24日 2009“拓达杯”中国（贵州）德国（汉堡）乒乓球对抗赛在县体育馆举行。

8月2日 在贵阳举行的“2009十大影响力风景名胜区”和“2009十大魅力旅游景区”评选活动颁奖典礼暨景区图片展，修文阳明旅游景区获得“2009十大魅力旅游景区”称号。

4日 县文化部门选送的原生态舞蹈作品《牛角舞》在贵阳大剧院参加“中天城投”杯2009多彩贵州舞蹈大赛贵阳赛区民族民间舞原生态舞专项决赛获得二等奖第三名的好成绩。该作品将代表贵阳角逐全

省“多彩贵州”舞台。

8日　被列为2009中国·贵阳（修文）第四届国际阳明文化节系列活动之一的“六广河杯”大力士比赛开幕式在六广河畔举行。

28日　广东百强民企EMBA班学员一行10人到县考察投资环境，考察组一行先后参观县医药园区、宇丰熔料厂和谷堡乡全国农业旅游示范点。

9月8日　由贵阳市纪委、贵阳市监察局和贵阳市文联主办的“风清气正·庆祖国60华诞贵阳市反腐倡廉书法、美术作品展”在贵阳美术馆开展，修文有6件作品入选参展。

19日　贵州省首家县级特种设备培训中心在盛鑫工程机械公司成立并开班培训作业人员，来自县内外的80余名特种设备从业人员参加培训。

26日　修文中学举行建校七十周年庆典，在校师生、历届校友、社会各界群众共3000余人参加庆典活动。

29日　县残联组织7名残疾人选手参加贵阳市第三届残疾人技能比赛，陈希敏取得钩针编织第一名。

10月7日　县城综合管网改造工程在位于迎春路以北路口正式启动。该工程由县财政投入4500万元资金，对阳明大道、人民路、迎春路等13条主次干道和流经城内的高涧河、小桥河、大寨河3条河段进行改造，改造项目包括净水、河水分流和电力、电信管网埋藏。

14日　人民日报社原社长、中华全国新闻协会名誉主席邵华泽在县领导陪同下考察阳明文化资源的开发和保护。

11月2日　全县首批廉租住房入住仪式在县城思源路举行。首批建成的廉租住房共33套，平均面积为45.2平方米，按照每平方米每月1元的标准收取租金。入住者系龙场镇的33户“双困户”（低保户、住房困难户）优先迁入，占全镇住房困难205户的16.1%。

9日　修文县被列入贵州省村级农家综合服务站建设的试点县。

11日　县政协七届十二次常委会议召开。

24日　县实验小学被教育部授予基础教育改革综合实践活动研究与实验重点研究项目“全国先进实验学校”称号。该校选送教师论文5篇和课堂实录3节课参加评比，其中3篇获一等奖。

28日　县人民政府与贵州同济堂制药有限公司在县城腾晖酒店举行由公司投资20亿元在修文打造包括食品加工、酿酒、保健、物流、配送等在内的产业园区的签约仪式。

12月31日　落户久长镇金桥村的金久水泥厂生产线成功点火。该生产线设计规模为日产4000吨新型干法回转窑熟料水泥，投产后年产值可达4.5亿元。

2010

1月18日　县政府与中国太平洋建设集团公司成功签署引进建设县城至扎佐城市主要干道的协议。该项目采取BT方式实施，总投资3亿元，路宽40米，全长约11公里，全部按城市一级主干道标准建设，起点从县医院路口起、终点至扎佐医药产业园路口。

2月9日　县人大常委会第十四届二十五次会议召开。

3月1日　县城“白改黑”工程启动。该工程投资1500万元，规模6.7万平方米，涉及人民路、翠屏路、阳明东路、迎春路、河滨路、长征路、龙山路、宾阳路、文成路10条路段。4月5日，通过施工队伍45天的奋战，工程全部告竣。

4日 县人大常委会第十四届二十六次会议召开。

16—18日 中国人民政治协商会议县第七届委员会第五次会议召开。

17—19日 县第十四届人民代表大会第五次会议召开。

3月 县文化信息资源共享工程县级支中心正式投入使用。该工程于2009年3月开始建设，总投资68万元，中心建在县文广局二楼大厅，设电子阅览室、控制室、多媒体室、中心管理办公室。

4月25日 首届"茅台杯"小说选刊年度小说排行榜大奖颁奖典礼在北京国际饭店举行，县青年作家肖江虹发表在《当代》2009年第二期的中篇小说《百鸟朝凤》榜上有名。

5月18日 县委举行公推竞岗大会，有16位干部参加竞岗陈述，竞岗者从德、能、勤、绩、廉以及履职工作思路和措施作陈述。县委依据推荐结果按照干部任用选拔条例有关规定对参加竞岗的干部进行评价，最终产生拟任干部人选。

6月2日 县委召开乡（镇）党委书记公开推荐大会，民主推荐龙场镇党委书记竞岗人选。会议采取实名方式，从参加报名的9名领导干部中推荐5名参加第二轮推荐，最终左军、付坤、包本志、李晓阳、袁莉入围作为竞岗候选人。

26日 上海华飞投资集团氢氧化铝项目一期投产暨二期动工典礼在龙场镇小营村举行。华飞集团有限公司投资10亿元建设的年产20万吨氢氧化铝项目，于2006年动工兴建。

30日 海马大桥在六桶乡海马村开工。大桥起于金沙县化觉乡柏坪村跨越乌江接海马至六桶公路。桥梁全长249.5米，桥面宽11.5米，汽车设计荷载为公路1级，设计基准期100年。项目总投资4500万元。

7月8日 县委宣传部与贵阳人民广播电台签署战略合作协议签约仪式。

18日 中国作协副主席、上海市文联副主席叶辛赴久长镇永兴村考察生态农业建设及春辉小学使用情况。

20日 由省委组织部巡视员冷春芳率队的省委组织部检查一组对县2008年后开展整治用人上不正之风工作和学习贯彻四项监督制度工作进行专项检查。检查将覆盖有用人权的地区和单位，时间持续到2011年6月底。

23日 2010"多彩贵州·爽爽贵阳"第九届全国城市国际标准舞锦标赛在县体育馆举行，来自遵义、重庆、成都、安顺、铜仁、凯里等地区的30多支队伍参赛。

29日 2010年生态文明贵阳会议企业家高尔夫联谊赛在扎佐高尔夫球场举行。联谊赛由20国集团研究中心秘书长、博鳌亚洲论坛原秘书长、原经贸部副部长龙永图，贵阳市政协主席陈石，蒙牛集团董事会主席牛根生和县长蒋志伦共同开杆。

27日 县委宣传部与法制生活报社宣传报道合作签约仪式举行，《法制生活报》修文工作站正式成立。按照约定，从27日起到2011年9月，《法制生活报》每月1次集中推出修文新闻。县委宣传部在适当时候选派通讯员到法制生活报社挂职锻炼。

9月30日 县政府召开第八届村（居）民委员会换届选举工作会议，对全县第八届村（居）民委员会换届选举工作进行部署。

10月11日 县众弗小额贷款有限公司成立。该公司系县第一家经省信委批复开业的小额贷款公司，

注册资本2000万元，享有独立经营权，独立承担法律责任。

11月1日 以零时为标准时间，全县进行第六次人口普查，总人口为248026人。

12日 利尔公司按照《中华人民共和国人民防空法》规定修建的县首家人防地下室——翰林花园人防地下室通过市人防办验收。可容纳1000余人防空避险。

29日 县工业园区建设开发办公室举行成立暨挂牌（揭牌）仪式，正式成立县工业园区开发办公室。

12月17日 在中国计划生育协会第七次全国会员代表大会暨先进表彰会上，龙场镇放马坪村计生协会被表彰为2010年全国计划生育协会“先进单位”。

19日 贵州贵酒年产万吨麸曲酱香型白酒生产线异地技改项目一期投料下沙暨二期启动、贵州诺亚精工铸造公司年产20万套精密铸件等投资总额逾10亿元的7个工业项目同时开工。

21日 新版《今日看修文》在贵阳新闻荟萃频道正式播出，改版后的《今日看修文》由原来的每周3期改为每周5期，播出内容由《今日要闻》《今日视点》《今日快报》3个板块组成。观众可通过数字电话201频道收看《今日看修文》。

27日 六广河景区二期工程阳明古渡开工建设，项目计划总投资3.3亿元，分3批实施，首批投入6130万元。

31日 据县统计局年终汇报资料称：2010年全县生产总值达46.18亿元，比上年的39.27增加17.6%；财政总收入5.43亿元，比上年4.47亿元增加21.4%，其中县级财政收入达2.8亿元；农民人均纯收入为5152元，城镇居民人均可支配收入达1.58万元。

地　理　篇

修文县位于云贵高原东部、贵州省中部，地处北纬26°45′~27°12′、东经106°21′~106°53′之间，总面积1075.7平方公里。1978年隶属安顺地区，1996年划归贵阳市管辖。县城驻地龙场镇，位于县境南部，距省会贵阳38公里，距市行政中心金阳27公里。全县共置有龙场、扎佐、久长、六广4个镇和谷堡、六屯、小箐、洒坪、大石、六桶6个乡，辖217个行政村、10个社区、1434个村民组。县系多民族杂居县，2010年总人口30.59万人，有28个民族，其中汉族人口占91.89%。千人以上少数民族中苗族人口最多，有1.11万人，其次布依族0.54万人，彝族0.19万人。

地势东高西低，海拔一般在1200—1400米之间，最高海拔1610米，最低海拔760米，平均海拔1270米，县城海拔1240米。地貌类型属黔中丘陵区，除西部及西北部以峡谷、峰丛、洼地为主外，其余中、东部地区主要以丘陵盆地和中山槽谷为主。气候属北亚热带季风湿润气候，冬暖夏凉，年平均气温13.8℃，年平均降水量为1114.5毫米，年平均无霜期267天左右。

县境河流属长江流域乌江水系，平均河网密度248.8米/平方公里，年水资源总量为6.64亿立方米，水能资源技术可开发总量为914.57兆瓦，已建成河口、修文、窄巷口、红林、红岩和索风营6个水力发电站，开发798.5兆瓦，占可开发总量的87.31%。矿产资源主要有原煤、铝土、赤铁、硫铁、重晶石、磷、硅、汞、高岭土、耐火黏土、溶剂灰岩、水泥灰岩等，其中铝土矿总储量7700万吨以上，赤铁矿储量2200万吨以上，原煤储量3亿吨以上。旅游资源有享誉国内外的阳明文化遗迹阳明洞、玩易窝、三人坟和历史遗迹蜈蚣桥、高仓古堡、石安古寨、乌栗索桥等；自然景观主要有六广7峡42景、回水石林、高枧石仓、多缤洞、天生桥、猫跳河峡谷风光、两蓬岩兰花谷和扎佐林场等。已开发成功的旅游项目主要有野生动物园、桃源河漂流、六广河谷风光、苏格兰风情牧场等。县境冬暖夏凉的宜人气候、青山绿水的生态环境、丰富的人文景观和自然景观，是国内外少有的避暑越冬胜地，故被世人称之为“王学圣地，秀美修文”。

第一章　政　　区

1978年，修文县隶属安顺地区，总面积为1071平方公里，设有5个区（含直隶属于县的久长公社），辖2个镇、27个公社，206个大队，1028个生产队。1983年，生产大队增为217个，生产队减为1668个，有12个居民段。1984年4月政社分设，公社改建为乡，复建乡（镇）政权，乡（镇）辖村民委员会（居民委员会），村下建村民小组。全县建立5个区，辖2个镇和30个乡、217个村民委员会和12个居民委员会、1403个村民小组。1992年2月，撤区并乡建镇，将全县政区调整为10个乡（镇），217个行政村、12个居民段，1434个村民组。1996年1月，改属贵阳市管辖。2002年，经与周边区、市、县勘界议定后，县境总面积增为1075.7平方公里。至2010年年底，共置有10个乡（镇）、217个行政村、10个社区居民委员会、1414个村民组。

第一节 境 域

由于历史上勘界工作粗疏，导致修文县与挨邻的县（区、市）边界线不准确，造成全县土地总面积1071平方公里与实际情况不符。1997年1月，根据贵州省政府关于开展勘界工作的要求成立县勘界工作领导小组会同周边县（区、市）临地踏勘修文与各县（区、市）接壤的界线。到2000年先后分别与息烽县、开阳县、乌当区、白云区、清镇市、黔西县和金沙县签订《联合勘定行政区域界线协议书》，并将有关文件、资料和标有实际边界的比例尺地图上报省政府，同时报送省测绘局备案。联合勘界过程中，确定了清镇—黔西—修文3县（市）、清镇—白云—修文3县（市、区）、开阳—乌当—修文3县（区）、金沙—黔西—修文3县和息烽—开阳—修文3县的交点位置和边界走向，并在修文、息烽2县交点，修文、开阳、息烽3县交点，修文、白云、乌当3县（区）交点上竖立起永久性界桩。联合勘界工作结束后，经省测绘局按新的边界重新计算各县（市、区）土地面积并进行平衡后，从2002年起，修文土地总面积更正为1075.7平方公里。据此，全县疆域东西长51.8公里，南北宽48.5公里，边界总长261.27公里。

一、北部和东部边界线

（一）修文与息烽

由西向东先呈西北向东南走向，行约30公里后转东走向，全长66.87公里。北起金沙、息烽、修文3县交会点的242425232524号界点，向东南离开河道上行300米，转南偏西南上行至陡崖顶部，又转东偏东北沿陡崖边缘行800米，再转向偏东南行至980米高程点。从980米高程点，界线往南上行至小山顶后，界线跨越沟谷行至青龙山鞍部处，转向偏东南沿沟谷下行650米至木林沟河道中，又转南偏西南沿木林沟河道中心线逆流上行300米，再转向西南行至835米高程点。从835米高程点起，界线往南行450米，转向西南行300米，又往南行1500米，再转向东南行850米，继转东偏东南界线离开木林沟河道沿沟谷上行200米后，沿山脊上行至1148米山顶。从山顶起，界线向东偏东北沿山脊下行过小路后，又上至山脊行600米，转向东北又沿山脊下行过小路后，上至山顶，再下行至凹地行600米，继转东偏东北沿山脊上行至山脊后，下行至小路行300米，再转东偏东南沿山脊上行经1191米山顶边缘行至山腰1160米高程点。从1160米高程点起，界线南偏东南沿山腰上行至小山顶后，又沿山脊下行至小路，向西行200米，往南界线上行至山脊后，转向西南沿山脊上行120米后，又沿山脊下行至大车路。再上行至山脊行500米，向西沿山脊上行至1209米山顶后，又转向西南下行400米至小路，再上行至老房子处山顶，再转向东南沿山脊下行至1171.1米高程点。从1171.1米高程点起，界线向西南上行至山顶后，又下行至老白头村民组东侧150米处1087.5米高程点，转南偏东南行300米，又转向东南沿山脊行500米后，向东上行至鞍部1178米高程点，再转向东南沿山脊行

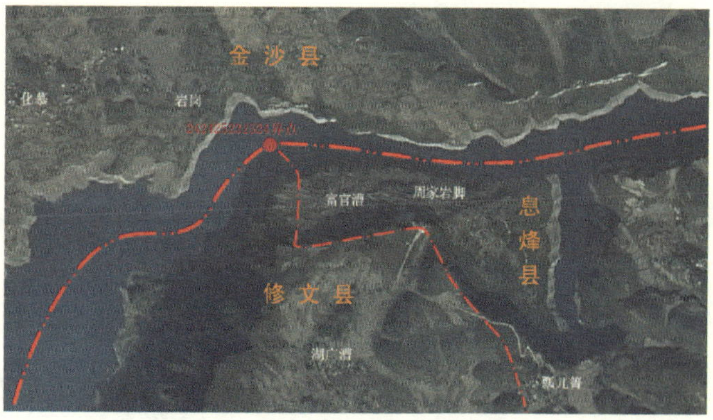

修息金界点

至鞍部1107米高程点。从1107米高程点起，界线南偏西南沿山脊上行跨越两个山顶后，又沿山脊下行经躲兵洞（多缤洞）大洞口至出水洞洞口处，界线向东方向呈圆弧沿沟谷上行至1138.5米高程点，又转向西南沿山脊行300米至山顶，往南跨沟谷200米后再转东偏东北沿山脊行至1135米高程点。从1135米高程点起，界线向东南沿山脊上行200米，转南偏西上行300米，东沿山脊经1191米，向东沿山脊经1191米山顶行650米至大落树居民点西侧山脊上，又转东偏东南沿山脊行350米，再转东偏东北沿山脊上行至天生桥西侧1106米山顶。从山顶起，界线向东沿山脊下行至天生桥后，转南偏东南沿大麻窝与中寨村民组之间山脊穿行1400米至珍珠井东侧350米处鞍部，又转东偏东北行200米，再转东偏东南沿山脊行至棋山坡山顶(高程为1430米)。从山顶起，界线南偏西南上行至1441米山顶后，转西偏西南沿山脊上行至棋山坡山顶(三角点，高程为1444.1米)，再沿山脊下行至鞍部后，又上行至1444.9米山顶，又转西偏西南沿山脊行900米，界线由南转向西经1453米山顶行至1441米山顶。从山顶起，界线向东南下行100米后，转向西南沿山脊行350米至小山顶，又转向东南下行400米至山嘴，往南跨沟谷、山脊行700米，再转向西南下行至小路边1230米高程点。从1230米高程点起，界线南偏东南沿沟谷下行至落水洞陡崖顶部，向东沿陡崖边缘行150米，转南偏东南沿山脊上行至1256米山顶，又转向东南行200米，再转东偏东南沿小路行300米至联江村北侧岔路口1320米高程点。从1320米高程点起，界线南偏东南穿行居民点上行至山顶后，又下行到小路，再沿沟谷上行至1305米山顶，转向西南沿山脊上行400米，又转南偏东南行300米，向东沿山脊行200米至山顶边缘，再转向东南上行经鞍部行200米至苗寨东侧250米处山脊1310米高程点。界线继向东偏东南沿山脊上行途经（高程1359米）山顶、大箐坡（高程1373米）山顶至格老寨西南侧鞍部后，向东行至（高程1359米）山顶，转东偏东南跨越山脊经汤家大坡（高程1400米）山顶至灯龙坡（高程1371米）山顶后，下行至汪家坡山顶西侧250米处小路，又转南偏西南上行至山顶后，又下行至山脊上1300米高程点。再转向西北沿山腰行至1301米高程点。界线继向西南沿山腰下行过大车路后，又沿沟谷上行500米至山顶，再沿山脊下行至建筑屯居民点西侧山脊上1320来高程点，转西偏西南沿山脊上行500米至小山顶后，又转东偏东南沿山脊经1442米山顶行至（高程1437.7米）山顶，再转向东南沿山脊下行过小路后，又上行至（高程1396.3米）山顶。界线继向东行至（高程1410米）山顶后，转向东南跨越山脊、山顶行1750米至西牛口东侧250米处沟谷中，向东沿山脊上行至（高程1319米）山顶，又转南偏东南行250米，又向东沿山脊上行450米至山顶西侧，再转北偏东北沿山脊行至安坡(高程1384米)山顶后，又沿山脊下行至山嘴处凹地1300米高程点。界线继向东下行至坝龙居民点北侧1230米高程点，转东偏东南上行经山顶后，再沿山脊上行至1339.5米山顶。又转南偏西南上行至白岩凹(高程1429米)山顶，再转向东南行至1433米山顶。从山顶起，界线向东北沿山脊上行至火金山(高程1502米)山顶。从山顶起，界线东偏东南沿山脊、山顶行1250米至（高程1478.6米）山顶，转向东南沿山脊上行600米至山顶，向东下行至沟谷，又沿山脊上行至（高程1531米）山顶后，再沿山脊行200米，又转北偏东北沿山脊下行至小路后，又上行田家革家坝东侧（高程1490.5米）山顶，再转东偏东南沿山脊下行至鞍部后，又上行至山顶，再沿山脊下行至山嘴1405米高程点。从1405米高程点起，界线东偏东北沿山脊下行过大车路后，又上行100米至山脊，转北偏东北行至1456.3米山顶，界线由东北方向转向东呈圆弧沿山腰上行至1488.2米，又转向东北沿山脊上行至鸡冠山1496米高程点后，沿山脊下行至岔路口东侧20米处，向东沿小路行250米，往南沿沟谷上行经畜牧场东侧山脚行400米后，界线由西南转向南沿小路行至鞍部1442.1米高程点。界线继向东偏东南上行至（高程1498米）山顶后，又沿山脊下行100米，转向东南沿山脊下行至鞍部后，又上行至水沟行750米，向东上行至1504米山顶后，又下行150米，又转向东北沿山脊下地行经水库边缘过堤坝后，界线沿沟谷边缘下行250米，再转向西北行至1363米高程点，最后界线北偏东北行至位于梨安哨东南侧过境公路边的2523252401号界桩点止这段界线长59.87公里。

2523252401号界桩点为单立双白型石质界桩。位于息烽县永靖镇梨安村与修文县久场镇石榴村连界处。在磁方位角46度34分，距离182米处为一堤坝头（高程为1349米）；磁方位角178度49分，距离420米处为一山头（高程为1418米）；磁方位角231度19分，距离317米处为一山头（高程为1463.8米），界桩点埋设在核定边界线北偏西北40米处息烽县境。

210国道旁修息界桩

从2523252401号界桩起，界线过公路后北偏东北行50米，向东沿山脊下行250米，转北偏东北跨山脊行300米至小山顶，又转北偏西北沿山腰行200米，再转东偏东北行300米至响水河村民组北侧铁路边路堑顶部。从路堑顶部起，界线向东南上行500米，转向东北沿山脊行200米至山顶，向东下坡过小路后，又上行100米至山脊，又转向东南沿山脊上行至（高程1427米）山顶后，沿山脊下行至交叉路口北侧50米处，向东沿山脊上行至盐井坡山顶(三角点，高程1545.7米)，又沿山脊下行至鞍部小路，再转向东北沿山脊上行至（高程1503米）山顶后，向北沿山脊下行至1500米高程点，界线再向东沿山脊下地行经鞍部行250米，转中东南沿山谷下行至小路，又上行至鞍部，又转东偏东北沿山脊上行550米，再转东偏东南界线下行至公路上，最后界线至位于毛稗冲西南侧过境公路边小山顶的开阳、息烽、修文县3县边界交会点252225232524号界桩点，这段界线长7公里。

（二）修文与开阳

先西东走向，继转北南向,再回转为东西向。西起252225232524号界桩，东至011225222524号界点止，全长32.72公里。

252225232524号界桩点为石质界桩，位于开阳县双流镇桐心村、息烽县永靖镇安马村和修文县久长镇芦山村之间，在磁方位角123度19分，距离162米处为一山头；磁方位角183度49分，距离280米处为一（高程1418.6米）山头；磁方位角318度34分,距离470米处为一山头(高程为1352.2米)，界桩埋设在核定点位西偏西南侧60米处息烽县境。边界线向东下至公路后，沿山脊上行200米，往南上行至高程1467米山顶，转向东南沿山脊下行过大车路后，又沿山脊上行600米至山顶，再转南偏西南跨越山顶行300米，又再转向西南界线呈圆弧沿山脊上行至高程1437.8米山顶。从山顶起，界线向东下行过小路后，又沿山脊上行至高程1495米山顶，转向东南行200米，又转南偏东南沿山脊经高程1515米山顶行400米，向东行200米，再转向东北沿山脊上行至山顶后，又沿山脊下行至苗寨北侧大车路高程1450米点。由此起，界线向东上行250米至山顶，转南偏东南沿山脊下行200米，又转东偏东南沿山脊行500米，朝北行100米，再转北偏西北沿山脊上行至1475米高程点。界线继北偏东北行100米至山顶，转北偏西北沿山脊下行过大车路后，又上行150米至山脊，再转北偏东北沿山脊下行又至大车路后，又再转向东北沿山脊行

200米至山顶，折转向北偏西北下行至山脊上1480米高程点。界线再向东北下行至鞍部后，又沿山脊上行300米，向东界线上行至山顶，再沿山下行至鞍部，又再上行至高程1465米山顶。界线折转向东北下行过小路后，转向东沿山脊上行至山顶，继沿山脊下行900米至小溪，转东偏东南上行300米，再向东沿山腰行300米至小路，转东偏东南界线呈圆弧，行至高程1435米山顶。从山顶起，界线向东下行至鞍部后，又上至山脊上行200米，朝北沿山脊上行100米至山顶，转东偏东北沿山脊下行至高程1402米山顶，向东沿山脊下行至小路后，继沿山脊上行至高程1401.6米山顶，转向北偏东北沿山脊下行400米至小路，转向东沿沟谷上行250米，至山脊顶上，再转东偏东北沿山脊行至1300米高程点。界线继向北偏东北沿山脊行150米，转东偏东南行250米，又转北偏东北行200米，再转向东南沿山脊下行过鞍部后，又上行至1397米高程点。界线再向东偏东北下行150米，转北偏东北沿脊上行350米，又转东偏东南下行过鞍部后，继沿山脊行至高程1428米山顶，再转东偏东北沿山脊下行至聂家湾北侧1412米高程点。界线继向北偏东北沿山脊下行450米，转向东北下行至小路后，又上行300米至山脊，再转向东偏东南下行至小路后上行300米越过山脊下行至小路，又上行50米至山腰，再转北偏东北沿山腰上行至鞍部北侧1365米高程点。界线继向东跨沟谷行200米至山脊上，转向西南上行200米，折向东北70米，往南沿山腰行200米，转向东偏东北沿山脊下行150米，又折向西南上行150米，再往南沿山腰行150米后，界线向东沿山脊行至高程1281.7米小山顶。界线继向东北沿山脊下行650米至光洞河中，再向东沿光洞河河道中心线下行150米，转向东南行150米，折向北偏东北行150米，再向东行150米后，界线由南转向西行300米，再转东偏东南行至闵家寨西侧河道中1143米高程点。界线继向南偏西南沿河道中心线下行300米，再转南偏东南行900米，向东行至河坝处落水洞入口，转向东南过洞顶上行至鞍部后，又下行至沟谷底，再上行500米至山脊行，继往南上行400米至山脊上，再转西偏西南沿山脊上行至1310米高程点。界线继向西南沿山脊上行250米，转南偏东南上行300米，又转南偏西南行500米，再转向西南上行至高程1405米山顶。从山顶起，界线向南偏西南下行150米，向东沿山脊行150米，转向东南下行200米至沟谷，又转东偏东北上行200米，再转向东南沿山腰行至山脊上1350.2米高程点。界线继往南沿山脊下行至鞍部后，又上行200米至山顶，转向西南沿山脊下行250米，往南沿山脊、跨沟谷行至1203.2米高程点，又转向西南沿山腰行350米，转向南上行经鞍部行250米至山脊上，再转向西南上至山顶后，又沿山脊下行至1225米高程点。界线继向西偏西南下至沟谷后，沿山脊上行至小山顶，再下行至沟谷，又再沿山脊上行至山脊行750米，转南偏东南跨越百花山村民组西侧山脊、山顶行950米，又转东偏东南沿山腰行600米至山脊上，再转向东南沿山脊下行至长滩河中967.2米高程点。界线继向西偏西北沿长滩河河道中心线逆流上行300米，转向西南行150米，又转南偏东南行250米，最后界线向西南行700米至长滩河中心线与支流冷水河中心线交会的011225222524号界点。此界点位于开阳县禾丰布依族苗族乡王车村与乌当区新场乡杨梅村和修文县六屯乡小木村之间。

修开息界桩

二、南部边界线

(一) 修文与白云

界线呈西东走向，西起011325022524号界点，东接011201132524号界桩，全长40.05公里。

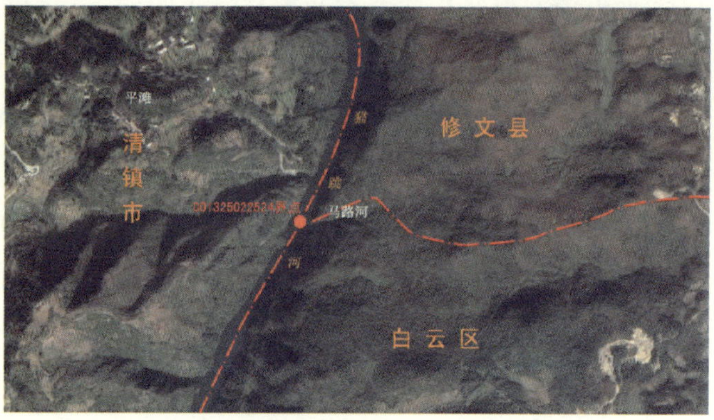

修清白界点

011325022524号界点为白云、清镇、修文3区(县、市)边界交会点，位于白云区麦架乡摆茅村、清镇市麦格苗族布依族乡谷当拜村和修文县龙场镇杨寨村之间猫跳河主航道中心线。由此向东边界线离开河道向东偏东北沿山脊上行470米，转南偏东南下行穿过凹地上行350米至山脊，向东沿山脊上行至高程1354米山顶，又转向东北沿山脊行850米，再向东沿山脊、沟谷下行600米，转向东北沿沟谷上行至小中哨村民组西侧山腰1320米高程点。界线继向东南沿小中哨村民组西南侧山脊下行150米，转向西行200米，往南下行过小溪行至摆茅村西北侧沟谷中，折转向北沿小溪上行400米后，向东偏东北行150米，又转东偏东南上行400米，继往南沿山脊上至山顶，再沿山脊下行至公路。从公路起，界线沿沟谷上行至高程1434.2米山顶，转北偏东北跨沟谷行至高程1490米山顶后，沿山脊下行至沟谷小路上，又转东偏东北上行400米至小山顶，再转向东南沿山脊上行至高程1539.2米山顶。从山顶起，界线向北偏东北沿山脊上行500米，转东偏东南行250米，又转向东北经高程1594米山顶行550米，再转向西北行至鞍部1562米高程点。界线继向东偏东北沿山脊下行经高程1602米山顶西侧边缘行1000米，转北偏西北行200米至山脊上，又转向东北下行沿沟谷绕行至1510米高程点。再 向东沿山脊下行200米，转北偏西北下行过凹地行经1475米高程点。界线继向东北行500米至山脊上，向东下行至公路后，穿行小山坝铝厂上至乌龙寺处山脊上，转向东南行400米，又转向西南行250米至鞍部，再转北偏东北沿山脊下行至1470米高程点。界线继向北偏西北下行200米，折向东北行370米至1450米高程点。界线向南偏东南沿沟谷上行350米，转向东北沿山脊行250米，又转向东南沿沟谷上行300米至小山顶，再转北偏东北下行至1475米高程点。界线继向东行200米后沿山脊下行150米，折转向西行150米，又折向东北行至豆腐田西侧小路上，转向西南行150米，又转向西北上行跨越山顶行至响鼓坡山顶(高程1489米)。界线继向东北沿山脊下行350米，转东偏东南下行过小路后，又上行经鞍部沿山脊上行至1510米高程点，再转向东南行至鞍部，往南行400米、转东南行至大车路东侧1441米高程点。界线呈圆弧继续向东北行200米，转向东南沿沟谷上行250米，向东上至鞍部后，又沿沟谷下行至1480米高程点，再转北偏东北下行250米，向东上行至鞍部后，又下行至高程1509米山顶南侧小路上，再转向东北沿沟谷、小路下行至1425米高程点。界线继向东上行650米至小冲村民组西南侧150米处山脊上，往南行100米，转东偏东南下行500米至大车路，又转北偏东北沿

朱官坡修文与白云界点

沙田水库边缘行200米，再转向西北行150米至1312米高程点。界线继向东偏东南行200米，朝北行450米，转南偏东南行200米，又转东偏东北行250米，再转向西南行400米，往南行至1313.8米高程点。界线继向东沿沟谷上行越过公路行至高程1370米山顶，转东偏东北跨过公路上行500米，又转北偏东北沿山脊边缘行至1481米山顶西侧，朝北下行至1420米高程点。界线沿山腰向东偏东北行350米，向东呈圆弧又沿山腰行至1420米高程点，转向西北下行150米，又转向东北下行至沟谷后，界线折向东南沿山腰转东北方向绕行至1415米高程点。界线继向北偏东北沿山脊经1469米高程点上行400米，转向东北沿山脊下行350米，又转向西南上行至鞍部，向东沿山腰行700米至小山顶，再由北偏西北下行150米后，折向东偏东南行至1420米高程点。界线再向北偏东北沿沟谷下行250米，向东沿山脚绕行至铁路边，过铁路后，转向东北上行至大车路，又转东偏东北过凹地后沿山脊上行至小山顶，再转北偏东北下行经过小路后沿沟谷上行400米至高程1543米山顶西侧鞍部。从鞍部起，界线向东偏东北行300米，转向东南沿山脊下行250米，又转向东北沿山脊上行至高程1557米山顶后，跨过沟谷、山脊行至大山村民组西北侧1800米处岔路口的乌当、白云、修文3区(县)边界线交会点011201132524号界桩点。011201132524号界桩为单立三面型石质界桩，竖立在乌当区新场乡大坝村、白云区牛场布依族乡小山村和修文县扎佐镇把七村之间。

（二）修文与乌当

先南北走向后西东走向，西起011201132524号界桩，东至011225222524号界点，全长31.78公里。

011201132524号界桩点为单立三面型石质界桩。位于乌当区新场乡达古村、白云区牛场布依族乡尖山村和修文县扎佐镇把七村之间。由此起，边界线向东北上行100米至山脊后，又沿沟谷下行300米，朝北沿沟谷下行300米转向东北下行200米至王潮水库（把七水库）边缘，向东沿水库边缘行150米，又转向东北行100米，再转向西偏西北行至1356米高程点。界线朝北经过山脊后，又下行400米至1400米高程点，转向西北行150米，折向东偏东南沿沟谷上行350米，又转北偏东北上行至山顶后，向东下行100米，再转北偏西北沿山脊、跨沟谷行至1400米高程点。界线继向西下行至小路后，

修乌白界点

转向西北沿松山仪表厂西南侧山腰行450米，向西下行至沟谷行150米，朝北沿沟谷下行250米，又向西再沿山脚行250米，转向西北行150米，再向西上行经鞍部后，又下行至沟谷行200米，又转向西北经鞍部下至沟谷行300米，再朝北沿沟谷下行450米至小路边1327米高程点。界线东偏东北行200米至公路，折向东沿公路南侧行450米，转向东北过公路后，界线穿行稻田至小溪行250米，向东上行150米至山脊，朝北沿山腰下行200米，又转向东北行至大车路，再转北偏西北顺大车路行300米至岔路口1338米高程点。界线继续向西北沿大车路行800米，又向西行850米至毛狗洞村民组小桥头，转向西北沿小溪西南侧行150米，转西偏西南沿沟谷上行200米；再转南偏西南呈圆弧沿小路行300米至李家井北侧1300米高程点。界线再向西沿稻田边缘行200米，折向东南行150米，转向西北行400米至公路边，又转东偏东北

沿小路行100米，折向北偏西北沿山脊上行300米至小路，再转北偏东北沿小路行至1335米高程点。界线继向东偏东北沿山脊下行至鞍部小路上后，又上行300米至山脊。转向东北沿沟谷下行350米，又转东偏东南行200米至小溪，再转东偏东北沿小溪东南侧岸边行至1261米高程点。界线向东偏东南呈圆弧上行至山脊后，又沿山腰行至鞍部西侧边缘，再沿山脊下行至1310米高程点，向东沿山脚行150米，折向西北行80米，转北偏东北行150米，又转东偏东南沿山脊边缘上行350米，向北经鞍部上行至山脊，转向西北沿山腰行150米，再转北偏东北沿山脊下行至小分田西侧鞍部小路，继续上行至山顶，又沿山腰行至1300米高程点。界线向东越过山脊下至沟谷行120米，转东偏东南沿沟谷上行经鞍部行300米，又转北偏西北上行又经鞍部行至1268.7米高程点，再转向东南沿沟谷上行至1310米高程点。界线继向东沿沟谷上至山脊行300米，转北偏东北沿山脊上行150米至山顶，又向东沿山脊下行至1402米高程注记点北侧线50米处山脊，又转东偏东北沿山脊、跨沟谷行550米至山顶，再转北偏东北下250米至山腰1300米高程点。界线向东下行200米至小溪，转向东南界线沿小溪中心线顺流行300米，又向东行250米，转东偏东南行1100米，又转北偏东北行400米，再转向东北行至1160米高程点。界线北偏东北行500米，转向东北行400米，又转东偏东北行200米后，界线离开河道向东南沿山脊上行400米，向东经鞍部小路行150米，再转东偏东北沿山脊上行至1340米高程山顶。从山顶起，界线向东沿山脊经1376米山顶行750米，转北偏东北沿山脊下行650米，又转东偏东北跨沟谷行300米至山脊，再转北偏东北沿山脊下行至1200米高程点。界线向东沿山脊上行300米，转向东北行350米，又转东偏东南行300米后，界线沿1313米高程山顶南侧山腰下行至沟谷小路，再转西偏西南沿小路边缘行至1095米高程点。界线向西偏西北沿沟谷上行250米折向东偏东南沿山脊下行150米，界线呈东南方向绕小弯后行至小路，向东下行至支流河，沿支流河中心线顺自然河道走向行450米，又转北偏东北行300米，再转向西北行250米后，界线离开河道上行至小路上1100米高程点。界线向东北沿山腰行150米，转东偏东南下行至支流河中，再沿支流河中心线向东偏东北行150米，转北行200米，又北偏西北行250米至大河边村民组南侧岔河口，再转北偏东北沿长滩河中心线顺流行至1011.1米高程点。界线东偏东南行350米，转北偏东北行250米，向东行100米，又转南偏东南行150米，再向东行至位于大田坎村民组西侧支流冷水河中心线与长滩河中心线交会处的乌当、开阳、修文3区(县)边界线交会点011225222524号界点。此界点为乌当、开阳、修文3区(县)边界线交会点，位于乌当区新场乡杨梅村，开阳县禾丰布依族苗族乡王车村，修文县六屯乡小木村之间。

三、西部边界线

（一）修文与金沙

以鸭池河（修文县境段称六广河）中心线为界，呈北南偏西走向，从242425232524号界点起，向西南逆六广河上至242324242524号界点。全长12.94公里。

242425232524号界点为金沙、息烽、修文3县交会点，位于金沙县化觉乡下坝村、息烽县九庄镇柏茂村、修文县六桶乡黄金村处六广河主航道3县边界线交会处（见图1-1-1-2-1）。界线由此起向西南逆流而上，经678米高程点至望香台人渡后，转

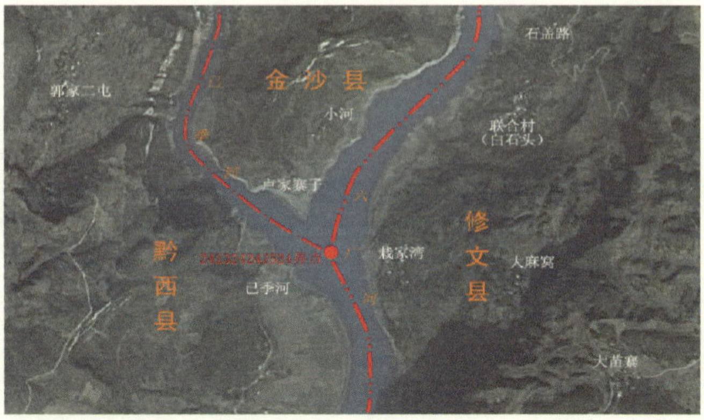

修黔金界点

向南经化觉乡顺江村、二屯岩至杨家湾河道转弯处690米高程点，界线转向西至海马村人渡后，又转西南至支流河交会处695米高程点。再转南偏西南经六桶乡顺江村、化觉乡下坝村、大白滩人渡至联河村栽家湾西面已季河中心线与六广河中心线相交的黔西、金沙、修文3交点242324242524号界点。

（二） 修文与黔西

以鸭池河（六广河）中心线为界，呈北南走向。从242324242524号界点起，先向东南后向西南逆六广河上至鸭池河与猫跳河交汇处三叉河的242325022524号界点，全长29.49公里。

242324242524号界点为黔西、金沙、修文3县交会点，位于黔西县泰来乡荆江村、金沙县化觉乡下坝村、修文县六桶乡联河村已季河中心线与鸭池河中心线交会处。界线由此起以六广河河道中心线为界，向南偏东南逆流行500米至田坝东侧河道转弯处，转南偏西南行350米，向南行400米，又转南偏西南经荆江村至730米高程点。再向南偏东南经六桶河人渡至黑塘沟支流与六广河交会处，转东南行1000米，又转南偏东南行300米至六桶乡和大石布依族乡的乡界线与边界线相交处，再转南偏西南经陈家沟村人渡、竹坪村西侧至750米高程点。再向南偏东南至龚家寨人渡后前行200米，转东偏东南行1100米，又转南偏东南经花地行900米，向南行155米，再转东南经大石布依族乡大屯村与素朴镇屯江村东侧之间河道转弯处755米高程点。再向南偏东南至罗家寨人渡后，转东南行600米，向东行1200米至1075米高程注记点北面260米河道转弯处，又转向东南行330米，再往南至和尚大坡西侧河道转弯处765米高程点。从765米高程点起，界线西偏西南经高坎子、方家坝至河道中770米高程点，往南行500米，转向西南经五显台村至六广大桥，此段界线长17.57公里。

六广大桥两端各竖有一面石质界桩，西北端为24232524001A号，东南端为24232524001B号。

边界线继续逆河道中心线呈西偏西南经六广镇西面行2300米至擦耳岩（1122米高程）西偏西南300米河道转弯处，向西行450米，转西偏西南行650米，又经大坪子、冯家湾人渡至木龙西面河道中750米高程点，再转西南方向行650米至龙泉村东侧支流河与河道中心线交会处。从两河道交会处起，界线向南偏西南逆流上至砂坡村西侧河道中766米高程点处，继续逆流行350米转西南方向经马路河村767米高程点至龙洞岭岗东南侧河道中768米高程点，往南经李家大寨人渡至位于三岔河处猫跳河中心线与鸭池河中心线相交的黔西、清镇、修文三交点242325022524号界点，这段界线长11.96公里。修文与黔西段界线全长29.49公里。

修黔边界

（三）修文与清镇

呈北南走向，从242325022524号界点起，南至011325022524号界点，全线均以河流为界线，全长47.42公里。

242325022524号界点为黔西、清镇、修文3县交会点，位于黔西县素朴镇马路河村、清镇县暗流乡矿山村、修文县六广镇合营村处鸭池河中心线与猫跳河中心线的交会处。边界沿猫跳河中心线向东偏东南逆流上行650米,转向东南行400米，又转东偏东南行750米，再转南偏东南行850米，经小岩头村民组东偏东北侧河道中785米高程点。再向东偏东南沿河道逆流上行1050米，转向东南行650米，往南途经801米高程点、黄草坪村民组至800米高程点后，又转南偏西南行550米，再转南偏东南逆流上行途经贾家寨、河口寨村民组之间行经828米高程点至830米高程点。再向东偏东南行300米，转向东南行1100米，又转南偏西南上行至红岩电站堤坝后，前行300米，再转南偏东南逆行至小红岩村民组东偏东北侧河弯道处835米高程点。再向东行400米，转向东北行500米，又转北偏北经840米高程点行800米,再转东偏东北逆流上行至猫洞河与猫跳河交汇的三岔河转弯道处850米高程点。界线折转向东南行650米，转东偏东北行250米，又转向东南行450米，往南行300米后，再转向西南逆流上行1900米经喇洒河村民组东侧河弯道处865米高程点。界线再向南偏西南逆流上500米，转向西南行700米后又向南行1000米后，再转南偏东南行经886米高程点。界线向南偏西南经双山村民组东侧铁索桥行950米，转向东南沿途经河边村民组行1100米，往南行250米后，又转西偏西南行400米再转南偏西南途经大塘村与三岔沟村民组之间行经890米高程点。界线往南逆流上行350米，转西偏西南行400米后，又往南行400米，转向东南行400米，向东行至岩脚村民组西南侧索桥，再转向东南行经河边村民组东北侧河道中955米高程点。界线向东逆流上行1600米，转南偏东南行350米后又转向东南行350米，再转东偏东北行经1020米高程点。界线向北偏东北逆流上行至公路桥后，前行350米至小桥，转东偏东北行950米后，向东行500米，又转东偏东南行850米至窄巷口电站处河道中,再转东偏东北经堤坝，前行300米经猫冲南侧河道中1085米高程点。界线向东穿行吊桥后行250米至两河道中心线交汇处，转东偏东南行500米，向东行350米，又转东偏东北行1100米经1082米高程点，再转北偏东北行经马鞍山东南侧河道中1086米高程点。界线向东行300米，转向东南行1250米，向东行至修文电站西侧岔河口后，又转向东南行300米，往南行200米，再转向西南经电站、过境桥至吊桥。从吊桥起，界线继续沿猫跳河中心线 向西逆流上行150米，转向西南行300米，又转南偏东南行700米后，界线由西南转向西行400米，再转向西南呈圆弧，行至蜂窝塘村民组东偏东南侧1126米高程点。从1126米高程点起，界线往南行400米，转向东南行500米，又转南偏西南经龙坝麻窝人渡行1700米，再转南偏东南又经人渡行1000米，最后界线南偏西南行至位于平滩村民组东侧猫跳河中的011325022524号界点。此界点为白云区、清镇市、修文县边界线交会点，位于白云区麦架乡摆茅村、清镇市麦格苗族布依族乡谷荡稗村和修文县龙场镇杨寨村之间。

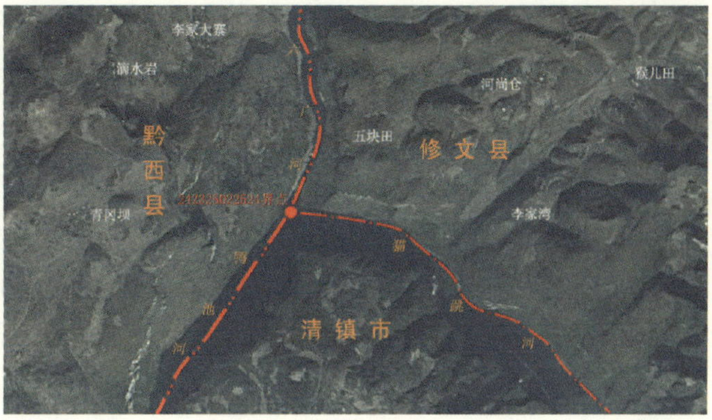

修清黔界点

修清黔三岔河

第二节　政区沿革

1978年，全县置城关、扎佐、小箐、六广4个区和县直属久长公社，辖王官、程官、马家桥、阳早、场坝、谷堡、乌栗、扎佐、三元、清让、六屯、桃源、小箐、崇恩、小坝、洒坪、中寨、六广、德政、广田、大石、回水、花梆、六桶、凉井、宝寨26个公社和城关镇，206个生产大队、1110个生产队。1981年1月，撤县直属久长公社，复置久长区，原直属久长公社分置为久长、清水、金桥、石安4个公社；扎佐公社析出扎佐集镇部分恢复扎佐镇建制。全县计有5个区，辖2个镇、30个公社，215个大队，1739个生产队。1983年，生产大队增为217个，生产队减为1668个，并有12个居民段。

1984年4月，政社分设，公社均改建为乡，复建乡（镇）政权，乡（镇）辖村民委员会和居民委员会，村下建村民小组。全县建立5个区，辖2个镇和30个乡、217个村民委员会和12个居民委员会、1403个村民小组。5月，城关镇升格为区级镇；6月，桃源、大石布依族乡改为布依族乡。1985年9月，久长、六广2乡改为区辖镇。至此，全县行政区划调整为5个区和1个区级镇，辖28个乡(其中有2个布依族乡)和3个镇、217个村和12个居民段、1434个村民组。

1991年11月启动撤区并乡建镇工作，次年2月完成，将全县5区32乡(镇)撤并建为城关、扎佐、久长、六广4个镇和谷堡、六屯、小箐、洒坪、大石、六桶6个乡，体现“小政府，大服务”的特点。

城关镇辖原城关镇、王官乡、程官乡、阳早乡和马家桥乡等地的36个村民委员会219个村民组，7个居民委员会12个居民组，面积181平方公里，人口57964人。镇人民政府县城驻南门口。

扎佐镇辖原扎佐镇、三元乡、清让乡和扎佐乡的25个村委会138个村民组，2个居委会8个居民组，面积125平方公里，人口42413人。镇人民政府驻扎佐。

久长镇辖原久长镇、清水乡、金桥乡和石安乡等地的22个村委会167个村民组和1个居委会，面积115平方公里，人口27908人。镇人民政府驻久长。

六广镇辖原六广镇、广田乡全部和德政乡部分（平营、前丰、团山、元庆、金山和岩脚6个村委会），共24个村委会144个村民组，1个居委会，面积93平方公里，人口26428人。镇人民政府驻六广。

谷堡乡辖原谷堡乡、乌栗乡和场坝乡的19个村委会134个村民组，面积120平方公里，人口22780人。乡人民政府驻谷堡。

六屯乡辖原六屯乡和桃源布依族乡的13个村委会75个村民组，面积88平方公里，人口14801人。乡人民政府驻格都堡。

小箐乡辖原小箐乡、崇恩乡和小坝乡的17个村委会144个村民组，1个居委会，面积104平方公里，人口20951人。乡人民政府驻小箐。

洒坪乡辖原洒坪乡和中寨乡的18个村委会136个村民组，面积86平方公里，人口15947人。乡人民政府驻小坝。

大石布依族乡辖原大石布依族乡全部和回水乡的回水、天桥、沙坝、红岩4个村委会以及德政乡的联江、联合2个村委会。共15个村委会77个村民组，面积50平方公里，人口12314人。乡人民政府驻大石板。

六桶乡辖原六桶乡、凉井乡、宝寨乡、花椰乡全部和回水乡的石板、平山2个村委会。共28个村委会185个村民组，面积109平方公里，人口26333人。乡人民政府驻六桶坝。

全县有10个乡（镇），217个行政村，12个居民段，1434个村民组。1999年9月，城关镇复名为龙场镇。2003年11月，全县将居民段改置社区居民委员会，龙场镇于老城区和新城区置龙岗、栖凤、宾阳、虎山4个社区居民委会；六广、小箐、久长镇分别将原来的居民段改为社区居民委员会，其中六广居民段命名为松江社区居民委员会，久长居民段命名为长久社区居民委员会；扎佐镇原2个居民段改建为景阳和襄阳2个社区居民委员会，2005年8月增设万江社区居民委员会。至2010年底，全县有10乡（镇），217个行政村、10个社区和1414个村民组。

2010年县辖乡（镇）村及社区一览表

表1—01—01

乡(镇)	政府驻地	辖　村	社　区
龙场镇	县　城	新春　沙溪　阳明　新水　城南　城北　王官　建新　新寨　木厂 干坝　马口　茶田　杨寨　中哨　中哨坝　白莲　马官　小营　普陀　军 民　幸福　新生　平地　程官　青龙　大地　高仓　水塘 小山　阳早　红旗　红峰　花桥　放马坪　三潮水	龙岗社区 栖凤社区 宾阳社区 虎山社区
扎佐镇	扎　佐	新庄　前进　中营　桥头　大园　猪头山　马鞍山　金鸡塘 小堡　三里　大河　丁官　大堡　龙王　喻家街　把七　三元 大山　石竹　新民　兴红　双月　泗溪　长坡　葛马	景阳社区 襄阳社区 万江社区
久长镇	久　长	久长　兴隆　沙雁　兴民　芦山　上寨　清水　白窑　清江　杨柳 永新　金桥　驴坊　石榴　栋青　中心　石安　茶山　上堡　下堡 山岔　新田	长久社区
六广镇	六　广	六广　滨江　中心　新河　广利　广城　中坪　沙坡　合兴　兴义 新中　合营　广山　松山　青龙　四寨　龙窝　中山　平营　前丰 团山　元庆　金山　岩脚	松江社区
谷堡乡	谷　堡	谷堡　富裕　新堰　平寨　折溪　大塘　下硐　大寨　长冲　红焰 尖山　上花　水口　下花　大堰　红星　绿水　平滩　哨上	
六屯乡	格都堡	都堡　高峰　新堡　安全　全心　星中　长田　大寨　三寨　小木 大木　西冲　独山	
小箐乡	小　箐	小箐　郭田　大坝　杉林　大兴　凤凰　崇恩　尖山　龙塘　万兴 新场　大林　小坝　紫江　全兴　青中　宝山	小箐社区
洒坪乡	小　坝	小坝　青山　中明　新乐　蜈蚣桥　高寨　五老山　青杠林　轿子山 阳桥　上坝　五江　硐口　麻窝　蛇场　东庄　北庄　上寨	
大石布依族乡	大　石	大石　大屯　大寨　高枧　高山　红岩　回水　联丰　联合　联江 沙坝　天桥　新光　岩湾　竹坪	
六桶乡	六桶坝	盐井　石头　大兴　金星　河银　花椰　来鹤　石板　坪山　六桶 凤联　春江　官寨　木林　何田　下坝　复兴　榨土　保坪　大新 海马　顺江　联合　山宝　长新　凉井　团兴　黄金	

第三节　乡（镇）

1978年，县以下沿袭原有建制为区、公社（镇）、生产大队、生产小队，从区到大队均有革命委员会管理，县辖城关、扎佐、小箐、六广4个区和直属县的久长大公社，区下辖27个公社、1个镇。1980年5月取消革命委员会，复建区公所，公社复建管理委员会。1981年1月，调整行政区划，增设久长区，原久长公社分为久长、清水、金桥、石安4个公社；5月增设扎佐镇，全县有5个区，辖2个镇、30个公社。1984年4月实行政社分设，公社均改建为乡，复建乡（镇）政权。5月，城关镇升格为区级镇；6月，桃源乡和大石布依族乡改为布依族乡。1985年9月，久长、六广2乡改为区辖镇。至此，全县行政区划调整为5个区和1个区级镇，下辖28个乡（其中有2个布依族乡）和3个镇。1992年实施撤区建镇并乡的行政建制后，全县10乡（镇）紧紧围绕经济建设这个中心，开拓进取，奋力争先，使乡（镇）的经济面貌出现了前所未有的变化，揭开了经济建设的历史新篇章。

一、龙场镇

1999年废止“城关镇”镇名，恢复原名龙场镇。因明代大儒王阳明在龙场悟道讲学，其心学思想中外传承不衰，故有“文化名镇”之美誉。镇境位于县的中南部，地跨东经106°32′~106°41′，北纬26°45′~26°54′。镇东邻扎佐镇，西连谷堡乡，南与白云区毗邻，北与小箐乡接壤。南北长14公里，东西宽13.2公里，土地面积174.43平方公里，耕地面积3.99万亩。地势东南和西北部较高，中部和西南部较低。一般海拔1200至1300米，最高峰在中哨坝村的箐坡海拔1571米，最低点修文河与猫跳河的交汇处海拔1118米。属北亚热带季性风湿润气候，年平均气温13.2°C，日照1315小时，降水量1205毫米，无霜期266天。镇政府驻县城，城区面积5.2平方公里，历为修文县政治、经济、文化中心。镇中心距省城贵阳38公里，距贵阳市行政中心金阳27公里。

镇境原属城关区，1978年区辖城关镇和乌栗、谷堡、场坝等公社。1984年4月公社改设为乡，城关镇升格为区级镇。1992年撤区并乡建镇，将原城关镇和王官、马家桥、程官、阳早乡合并建成新城关镇。1999年9月29日复名龙场镇。2010年，全镇辖36个行政村和4个社区，219个村民组，总人口73515人，其中农业人口50744人，人口密度420人/平方公里，居住着汉、苗、满、回、彝、布依等民族，其中汉族人口68186人，占94.59%。全镇有中学5所、小学26所，2004年通过省级“普九”“普实”验收。2010年有在校中、小学学生6376人，适龄儿童入学率达99.5%。

境内矿产资源主要有原煤、铝矾土、铁矿石等。原煤储量1000万吨，发热量6500—8000大卡/千克；铝矾土储量5800万吨，含铝量56%—68%；铁矿已探明储量690万吨，含铁量40%—60%。此外还有耐火黏土、白云石、大理石等。水资源富足，水质优良。城区自来水日供水能力3000吨，已探明的地下水含水层遍布全镇各村。过境的猫跳河属乌江水系，建有装机容量2万千瓦的水电站1座。猫跳河谷水清谷险，峡深景幽。境内河流主要有小桥河、穿山堰河和路家河等汇成的修文河，流域面积232.6平方公里，多年平均流量5.4立方米/秒，年径流量1.7亿立方米，下游河口建一水电站，装机容量1500千瓦。有阁老寨小（Ⅰ）型和王官、营盘山、黑山小（Ⅱ）型水库，总库容298万立方米。农作物一年两熟，出产水

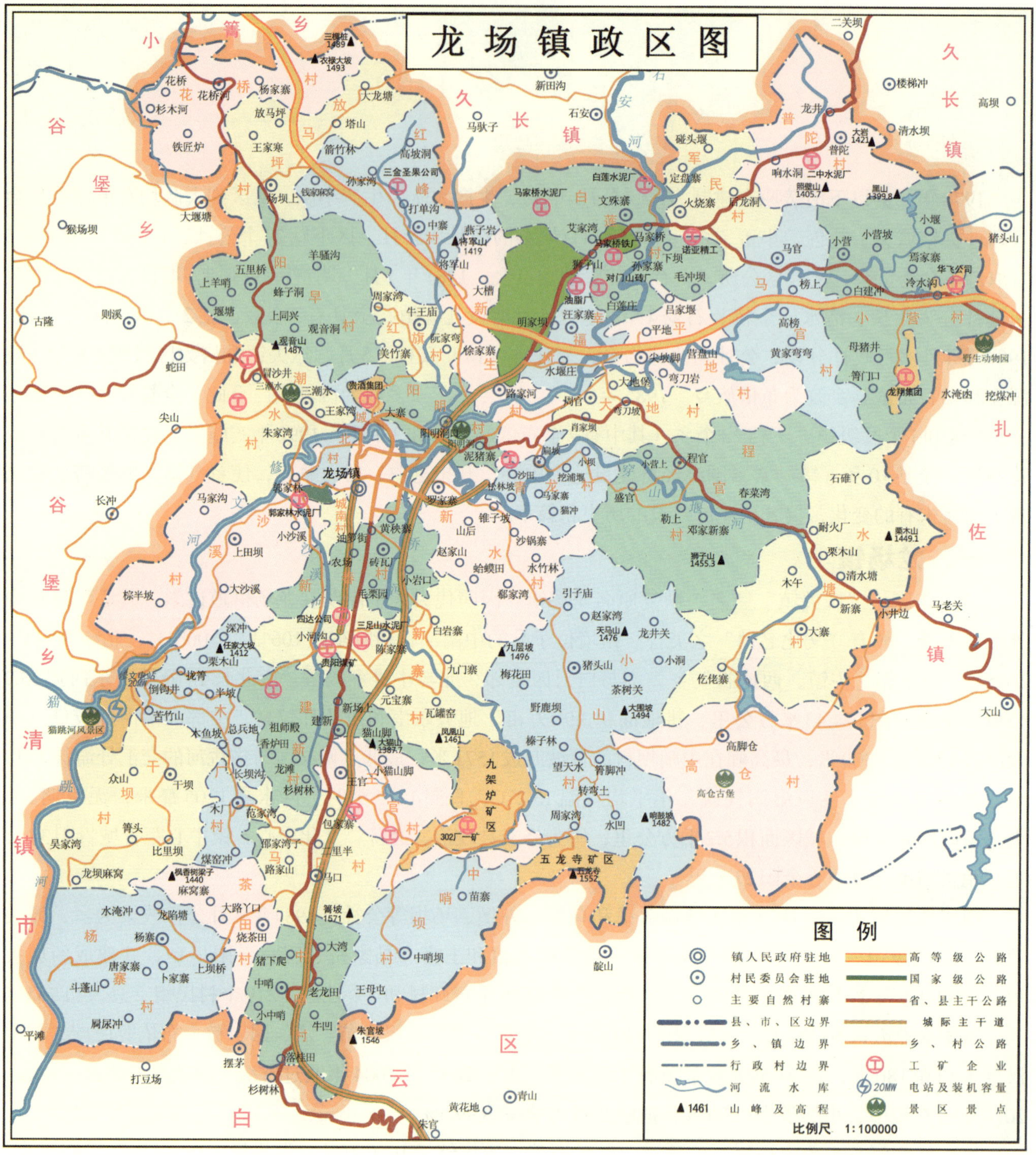

稻、玉米、小麦、马铃薯（洋芋）和油菜等。果类主要有梨、桃、李、杏、猕猴桃等，其中王官梨久负盛名。

1998年，全镇实现村村通公路。粑（粑坳）修（文）公路（S107）和修（文）开（阳）公路（S305）自南向北纵贯境内，贵（阳）毕（节）高等级公路（G321）横贯镇境东西，县城经小箐至六广公路（X184）公路、马家桥至扎佐公路（X156）、王官至贵铝一矿公路、小河沟至三级电站公路和阳明洞经高尔夫度假中心至210国道等纵横镇境，连接全镇36个村。境内开通国内、国际程控电话网，汉、数兼

容移动电话均投入使用。全境为国家电网覆盖。

镇境人文资源阳明洞风景名胜区被列为省级风景名胜区。明代思想家王阳明谪居3年传道的阳明洞被列为国家级文物保护单位；有王阳明研读《易经》并被中外学者尊为阳明心学“耶路撒冷”的玩易窝；有每日数潮数落的间歇名泉三潮水，凸显出丰富的文化底蕴。

村村建有文化室开展远程教育和丰富多彩的文娱活动。2005年，已实现有线电视村村通。镇有卫生院，村有卫生室，在基本普及医疗卫生的基础上实施新型农村合作医疗，参合率达90%以上。

经济建设以农业为基础，以发展工业为重点，依靠科技，面向市场，外引内联，努力培育社会主义市场体系，大力开发矿产资源和非耕地资源。特别是调整农业产业结构后，农、林、牧、渔、果、蔬全面发展。全镇工业已形成以建材、采矿、矿产品加工、冶炼为主，运输业、建筑业同时发展的格局。

镇的规模居全县10乡（镇）之首。“撤并建”后，镇党委、政府在抓经济工作中思路清晰，措施得当，从而取得显著成效。农业总产值由1992年的0.24亿元发展至2010年的2.4亿元，年均递增达13.7%；粮食总产由1.16万吨增长至1.98万吨，年均递增2.99%；乡镇企业总产值由1993年的0.93亿元发展至22.73亿元，年均递增20.68%。2010年，上述3项指标的绝对数分别占全县总量的18.23%、18.96%和32.63%，前两项排位第一，乡镇企业总产值处第二位。此外，2010年油菜籽1374吨，蔬菜5.84万吨，水果4189吨，肉类总产2542吨，分别占全县总产的21.79%、21.47%、17%和14.79%，除水果名列第三位之外，其余的也居10乡（镇）之首。不但农业为全县产出大镇，而工业也有快速发展。2010年全镇工业总产值达17.92亿元，仅位居扎佐镇之后，占10乡（镇）总量的31.94%，占全镇工农业总产值的88.21%，人均工农业总产达2.76万元。2010年全镇3.01万从业人员中，从事非农产业的0.93万人，占30.97%。随着生产的发展，导致乡（镇）财政收入大幅增长，由1992年的300.64万元和人均52元发展至2010年的2953万元和人均402元，分别增长8.82倍和7.73倍。农民人均纯收入1998年为1752元，到2010年达7015元，分别比全县平均数高出4.72%和36.16%，综合反映了全镇经济发展使农民得到了巨大实惠。

二、扎佐镇

位于县境东部，历为筑北重镇。因气候宜人和入驻众多医药企业，故有“林城氧吧”和“黔中药谷”之称。镇境地跨北纬26°50′~26°57′，东经106°41′~106°47′。东与六屯乡及乌当区友邻，南与白云区沙文镇和牛场乡相连，西与龙场镇小营村和马官村毗连，北与久长镇接壤。南北长20公里，东西宽7.9公里，土地面积128.71平方公里，耕地面积2.33万亩。地势南、西、北3面较高，中、东部较低，一般海拔1300米—1430米之间，最高点南部三角山主峰海拔1610米。气候属亚热带季风湿润气候，年平均气温12.9℃，日照1300小时，降水量1229.8毫米，无霜期269天。镇政府驻地扎佐，为省城北面的卫星城，距县城14公里，距省城贵阳38公里，距贵阳市行政中心金阳20公里。

镇境原属扎佐区，1978年区辖扎佐、三元、清让、六屯和桃源5个公社，1981年增设扎佐镇，1984年4月公社改设为乡。1992年撤区并乡建镇，将原扎佐镇和三元乡、清让乡合并建成新扎佐镇。2010年，全镇辖25个行政村和3个社区，140个村民组，总人口41887人，其中农业人口31563人，人口密度300人/平方公里。居民有汉、苗、满、回、彝、布依等民族，其中汉族占90%以上。有贵州省林校、航空高等技工学校、扎佐中学、景阳中学和14所小学及幼儿园，2010年有在校中、小学学生6051人。2005年建成投入使用的贵阳市第一人民医院扎佐分院，完善的设备和优质的服务使全镇和周边群众的身体健康得以保障。

境内资源矿藏主要有煤、硫铁矿、重晶石、铝矾土和铁矿等。其中原煤储量1000万吨以上，发热量在6500至8000大卡/千克之间。农业盛产水稻、玉米、马铃薯、萝卜等。城镇居民多从事商业，商户千家云集。水资源充足，水质优良。镇区自来水日供水能力2000吨。境内河流有可供工业用水的鱼梁河、葛马河2条，年径流量5.7亿立方米。有高潮、浪潮、把七、西苗和黄土冲等5座小二型以上水库，蓄水量274万立方米。森林覆盖面积达40%。

镇境区位优势明显，交通便捷。川黔铁路、210国道和贵（阳）遵（义）高等级公路南北纵贯镇境；贵（阳）毕（节）高等级公路与贵遵高等级公路在扎佐交汇。至县城仅需15分钟车程，至贵阳也只30分钟车程。扎佐至马家桥、扎佐三元至修文阳明洞、扎佐三元至牛场落刀井、扎佐至乌当区新场乡、扎佐至六屯、扎佐至久长等公路辐射周边乡镇。镇内已修筑村际公路21条，总里程100公里。1998年实现村村通公路。国家大电网覆盖全镇；开通国内、国际程控电话网，汉、数兼容移动电话均投入使用，通信网络遍布镇区各个村寨。

镇以农业为基础，工业为重点，三产为支撑。2000年开始，规划占地4.3平方公里落地扎佐的修文医药产业园，采取“安泰模式”引进了安泰、德昌祥、绿太阳、光正、天方等17家药业入驻。2006年，园区经省政府批准为省级开发区，并报国家发改委备案，命名“贵州修文医药产业园区”。全国唯一的高原森林球场—高尔夫休闲度假中心建在浪潮水库的青山绿水之间。贵阳森林野生动物园于2006年“五一”向游客开放。2009—2010年又先后引进首都钢铁公司贵阳特殊钢厂和贵州轮胎厂两家大型企业落户扎佐。建成有万亩无公害萝卜基地和蔬菜、艳红桃、金秋梨、中药材等各具特色的果蔬、药材生产基地；引进 “兰地公司”20万只蛋鸡养殖项目、“好1多”日处理200吨鲜奶加工基地和“龙山乳业”1200头奶牛养殖基地等落户境内。以地方特色“扎佐蹄膀”为名菜的饮食服务业快速发展，建成以“桃源食府”为龙头的饮食娱乐城，改建长500米的林场饮食一条街，建设占地1500余亩的大型物流中心。

镇地处于省会贵阳北大门，全省交通大动脉纵贯全境，有极好的区位优势。“撤、并、建”后的新党委、政府在县委、县政府领导下，抢抓机遇，将区位优势转化为经济优势，将经济工作推上新的台阶，成就令人瞩目。在农业生产方面，针对人均耕地少（2010年农业人口人均耕地仅0.74亩，为全县最低数）的不利因素，着力在耕作制度改革上狠下功夫，使复种指数由1992年的189.83%位居10乡（镇）第六跃升至2010年的348.59%居10乡（镇）之首，大大提升了有限耕地的利用率。与此同时，加大农业实用技术推广应用的力度，农作物单位面积产量普遍位列前茅。2010年粮食总产1.15万吨，在10乡（镇）中排位由1992年的第三位降至第四位，但仍占全县粮食总产量的11.01%，农业人口人均产粮364公斤。紧盯贵阳大市场的需求，狠抓蔬菜、水果和养殖业的发展。2010年产出蔬菜5.54万吨和水果4354吨，肉类总产达1835吨，禽蛋1183吨，使扎佐成为贵阳重要的菜、果、肉、禽、蛋、奶的生产基地。与1992年相比，农、畜产品在10乡（镇）中的排位变化很大：蔬菜产量由第三位升至第二位，水果产量由第十位升至第二位，肉类总产由第二位降至第六位，禽蛋产量由第二位升至第一位。2010年全县禽蛋总产有37.5%产自扎佐镇。在农业人口中人均产蛋37.5公斤，比全县平均数高出22.5公斤。农业总产值1992年为1490万元，农业人口人均465元，分别位居10乡（镇）的第三位和第六位，2010年发展至1.82亿元，农业人口人均5769元，排序均改写为第二位。最为突出的是2010年全镇工业总产值达22.95亿元，占10乡（镇）全部工业总产值的40.91%，人均5.48万元，各列前茅，雄居榜首。工业的迅猛发展，使全镇工农业

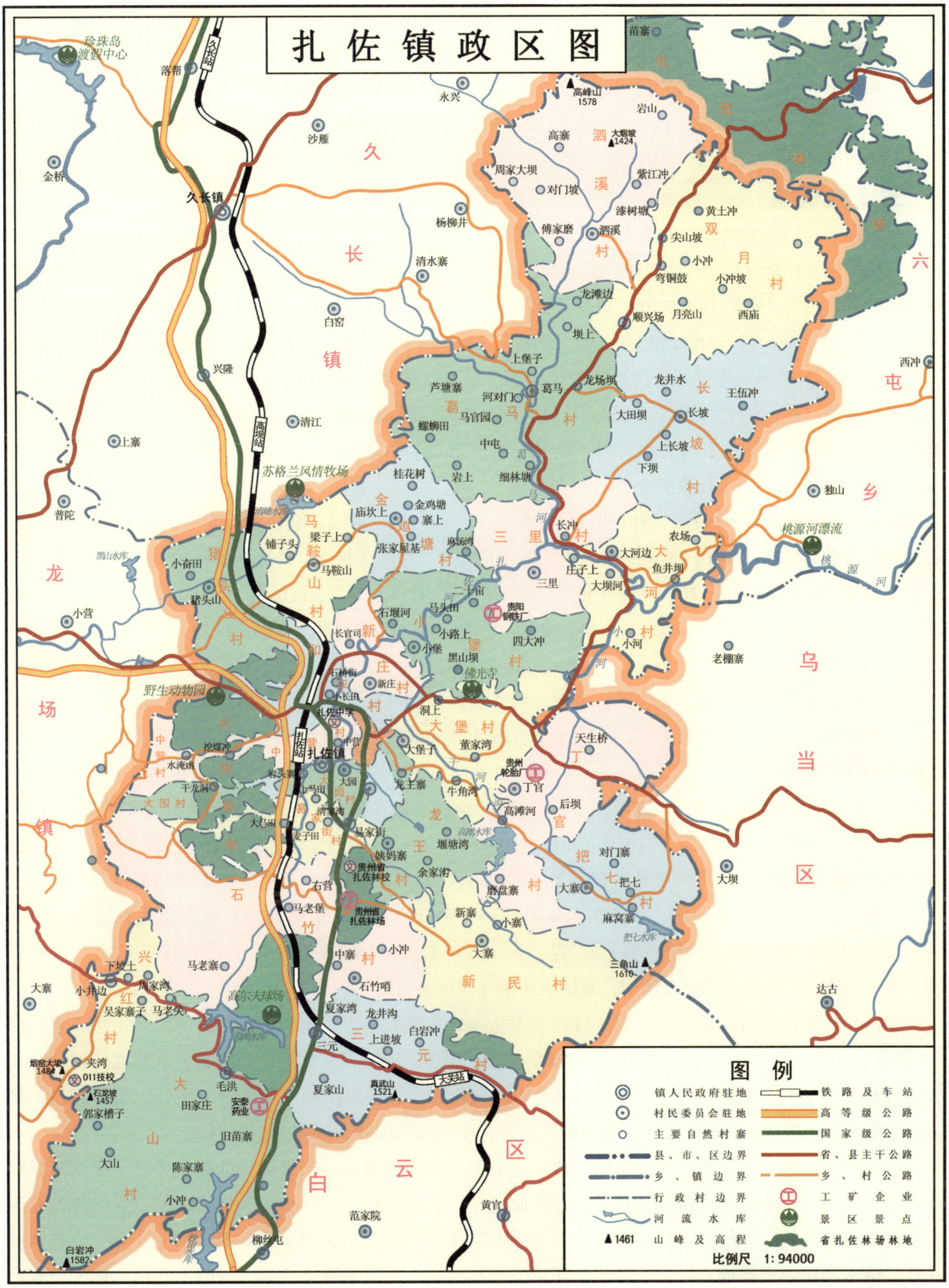

扎佐镇政区图
久长站
高坝站
扎佐站
大关站
珍珠岛渡假中心
落帮
苗寨
高峰山 1578
永兴
岩山
高寨
大烟坡 1424
沙雁
金桥
久长镇
周家大坝
紫江冲
对门坡
漆树塘
黄土冲
杨柳井
傅家磨
泗溪
尖山坡
清水寨
小冲
弯铜鼓
小冲坡
龙滩边
白窑
顺兴场
月亮山
西庙
坝上
兴隆
上堡子
芦塘寨
葛马
龙场坝
龙井水
西冲
河对门
王伍冲
马官园
大田坝
长坡
清江
螺蛳田
上寨
中屯
上长坡
苏格兰风情牧场
下坝
桂花树
岩上
细林塘
金鸡塘
独山
普陀
庙坎上
寨上
长冲
桃源河漂流
铺子头
梁子上
农场
张家屋基
麻饭湾
大河边
小奋田
马鞍山
庄子上
鱼井坝
鹦山水库
二十亩
三里
大坝河
猪头山
小营
马头田
贵阳钢铁厂
石堰河
长官司
小路上
四大冲
小河
小堡
黑山坝
老棚寨
石桥街
佛光寺
新庄
小长田
扎佐中学
洞上
野生动物园
大堡子
董家湾
天生桥
挖煤冲
中营
扎佐镇
水淹凼
岩头寨
大园
龙主寨
贵州轮胎厂
丁官
干龙洞
七马田
牛角湾
清塘湾
高滩河
后坝
大马田
易家街
堰塘湾
麦子田
对门寨
姨妈寨
高潮水库
大坝
贵州省扎佐林校
余家沟
把七
右营
大寨
马老堡
磨盘寨
贵州省扎佐林场
新寨
麻窝寨
小寨
把七水库
小冲
大寨
三角山 1610
中寨
下坡上
马老寨
石竹哨
达古
大寨
小井边
周家湾
吴家寨子
马老关
高尔夫球场
夏家湾
龙井沟
白岩冲
上进坡
三元
烟窑大坡 1484
夹湾
011技校
石龙坡 1457
毛洪
真武山 1521
夏家山
郭家槽子
田家庄
安泰企业
旧苗寨
大山
陈家寨
小冲
黄官
范家院
白岩冲 1582
柳丝屯
久长镇
泗溪村
双月村
葛马村
长坡村
金鸡塘村
马鞍山村
猪头山村
三里村
大河村
小堡村
新庄村
大堡村
丁官村
中营村
大园村
易街村
龙王村
把七村
石竹村
兴红村
三元村
新民村
大山村
扎佐林场
六屯乡
乌当区
龙场镇
白云区
图例
镇人民政府驻地
村民委员会驻地
主要自然村寨
县、市、区边界
乡、镇边界
行政村边界
河流水库
▲1461 山峰及高程
铁路及车站
高等级公路
国家级公路
省、县主干公路
乡、村公路
工矿企业
景区景点
省扎佐林场林地
比例尺 1:94000

总产值达到24.77亿元，其中工业总产值占92.65%，农业总产值占7.35%，践行了县委、县政府提出“工业强县”的战略目标并取得了显著的成效。2010年全镇财政收入2466万元，在1992年315.93万元的基础上增长6.81倍，人均数由1992年建镇时的74元升至2010年的589元，增长6.96倍，与1992年一样，均列10乡（镇）的第一位，但财政收入绝对数由1992年的第一位降至第二位，被龙场镇超越。农民人均纯收入由1998年的1734元上升至2010年的6625元，排名由10乡（镇）第三位升至第二位。

三、久长镇

久长原名狗场，地处黔中腹地，位于县境东北部，介于修文、开阳、息烽3县交界处，古有“鸡鸣三县”之说。镇境地跨北纬26°.80′~26°.83′，东经106°25′~106°32′。镇境东及东南面与扎佐镇接壤，西南与龙场镇毗邻，西与小箐乡相连，北与息烽县永靖镇交界，东北与开阳县双流镇睦邻。东西长12公里，南北宽9.5公里，土地面积118.42平方公里。2010年耕地面积3.2万亩。地势西、北高，东、南低，一般海拔1300—1400米之间，为全县平均海拔最高乡镇，最高点西北部断龙山主峰海拔1573.2米。气候属北亚热带季风湿润气候，年平均气温13.2℃，日照1254.9小时，降水量1180毫米，无霜期258天。鉴于暑季气温低于贵阳市中心区，故有“爽爽贵阳，最爽久长”之说。镇政府驻地久长街上，距县城15公里，距省城贵阳45公里，距贵阳市行政中心金阳30公里。

镇境原为县直属久长公社，1981年改设为久长区，辖久长、清水、金桥和石安4个公社。1984年4月公社改设为乡。1985年9月，久长乡改为久长镇。1992年2月撤久长区，将原久长镇、清水乡、金桥乡和石安乡合并建成新久长镇。2010年，全镇辖22个村和1个社区、167个村民组，总人口35109人，其中农业人口32079人,人口密度298人/平方公里。全镇有中学1所、小学11所、幼儿园1所，在校中、小学学生3913人。

境内矿产资源主要有煤、硫铁矿、铁矿、磷矿、硅矿和石灰岩等。农业盛产水稻、玉米、小麦、油菜、马铃薯和烤烟等。水资源充足，水质优良。镇区自来水日供水能力1000吨。境内河流有可供工业用水的石安河和葛马河。有蚌壳堰小（Ⅰ）型和盐井冲、孟冲、田家寨 和烂木桥小（Ⅱ）型水库，总库容642万立方米，兴利库容472万立方米，水域面积800亩。全镇有林地6.26万亩，森林覆盖率达35.3%。

镇境交通便捷。川黔铁路、210国道和贵（阳）遵（义）高速公路南北纵贯全境，修文至开阳的305省道与上述道路在久长交汇。至县城仅需20分钟车程，至贵阳35分钟车程。久长至马家桥、久长至葛马、久长至高枧、久长至阳早、久长至息烽石硐和开阳双流等公路辐射周边乡镇。镇内有村际公路31条，总里程80公里。1999年实现村村通公路。全镇处于国家大电网覆盖之下；开通国内、国际程控电话网，汉、数兼容移动电话均投入使用，通信网络遍布镇区各村寨。

2010年，镇内建有久长镇卫生院，村建有卫生室，主要服务于全镇和周边群众的医疗卫生。永兴村（砂锅寨）知青文化遗址，作家叶辛曾在此插队劳动7年多。有知青文化遗址及非物质文化遗产的“叶辛故居”被誉为“知青文园”。有已列为国家非物质文化遗产进行保护的芦笙歌舞表演，以质朴高昂的舞风、多姿多彩的服饰、鲜见的古艺古物享誉海内外，多次参加国际、国内大型演出。

改革开放以来，镇党委、镇政府按照“农业稳镇，工业强镇，三产兴镇”的战略思路，加快镇域经济建设。农业农村经济结构调整紧紧围绕“农业增产、农民增收、农村稳定”为目标，以各类种养业为重点，以土地流转、“企业+基地+农户”“基地+协会+农户”等形式发展农业。建成“好1多”奶牛养殖基地、清水肉兔养殖基地、石安三元杂交仔猪生产基地、沙雁破季豌豆基地、兴隆莲花白基地、上寨反

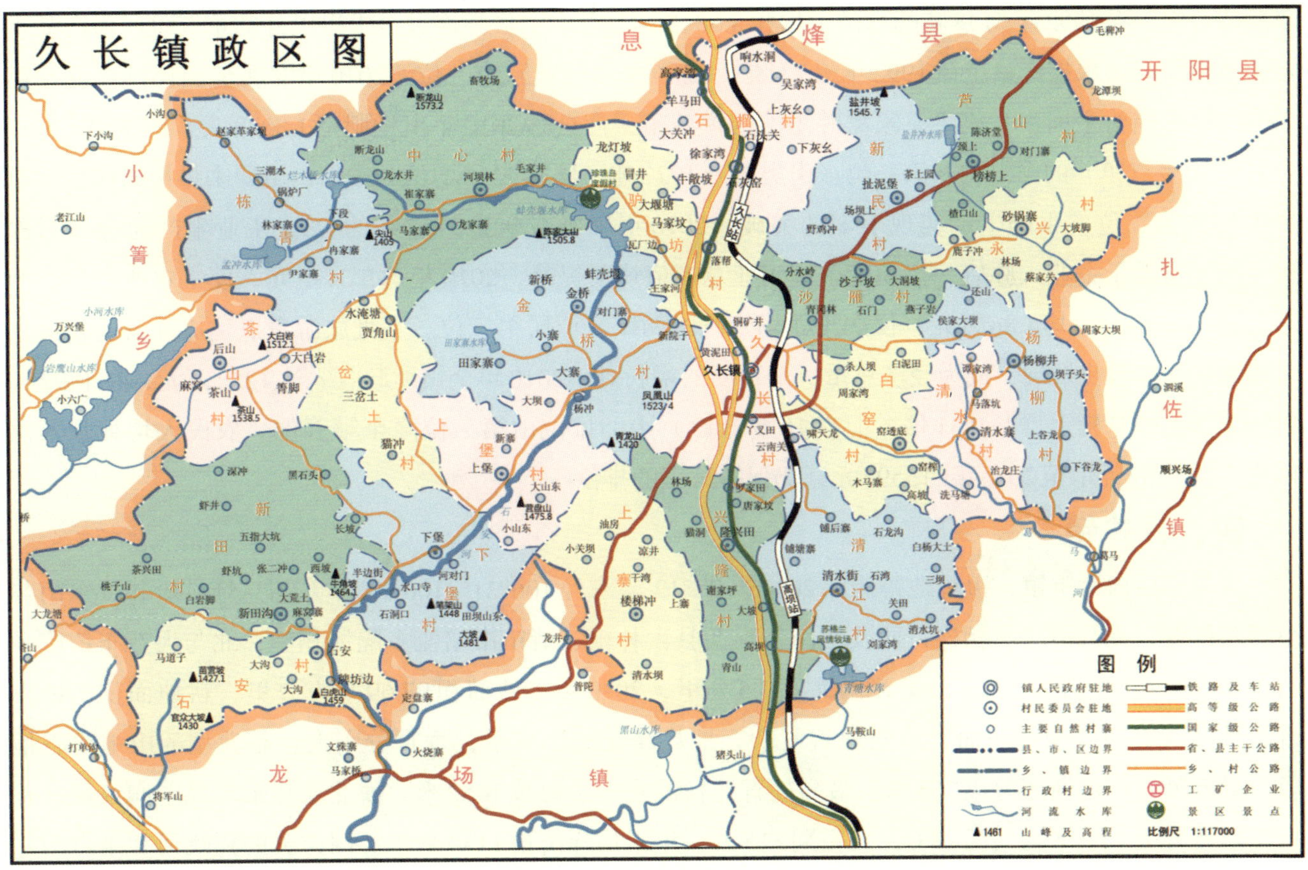

季节白菜基地、顺兴苑园艺公司苗木种植基地和果树种植基地等。工业发展依托资源优势，按照“工业特色镇”的定位，在着力提升建材、冶炼等传统产业的基础上调整工业发展布局，积极营造招商环境，大力培育新型工业经济，形成投资凹地和产业集群，新引进华宏公司、三阳公司、川黔饲料厂等企业。同时重点建设“四园区一走廊”（二官坝清洁能源生产工业园区、清水塘食品工业园区、峰光建材工业园区、新民高能耗工业园区，久长至开阳和久长至息烽磷化工走廊），打造化工、加工、材料三大支柱产业。第三产业按照“以旅游为龙头带动发展”思路，充分发挥区位、交通、资源优势，建成珍珠岛休闲度假中心，苏格兰风情牧场等。

镇境地势平缓，田、土耕地各半，发展农业生产的基础条件较好，以工业为主的乡镇企业起步较早，发展也比较快。至1992年“撤、并、建”时，与龙场、扎佐两镇农业总产值共计5419万元，乡镇企业总产值6349万元，粮食总产2.7万吨，乡（镇）级财政收入737.98万元，分别占全县总数的46.13%、40.7%、53.45%和59.45%，被称为全县经济发展的“金三角”。新建的镇党委和镇政府狠抓经济建设，确立“以农业为基础，以工业为重点”的指导思想，大力破解制约第三产业发展的“瓶颈”，使镇域经济走上协调发展之路。农业生产以种植、养殖业为重点，拉动农业总产值稳步增长，由1992年的1554万元增至2010年的1.47亿元，年均递增13.32%，位列前茅。粮食总产由1992年的6866吨增至2010年的1.36万吨，在10乡（镇）中由第三位升至第二位，粮食作物平均亩产354.4公斤，仅次于龙场镇，高出全县平均水平61.3公斤，农业人口人均产粮424.4公斤。烤烟原来一直是全镇农业的主打产品，1992年为571吨，占全县总产的13.26%，在国家限产政策下种植面积逐渐压缩，至2010年全部停种，对农民收入影响很大。镇党委、政府及时引导农民扩大蔬菜、水果种植面积，疏通销售渠道促使农民增收。2010年蔬菜总产3.44万吨，在1992年5148吨的基础上增长5.68倍，不仅主销贵阳连远至千里以外的重庆也成为产品重要的销售流向。水果产量全镇1992年仅23吨，位居10乡（镇）第九位，2010年发展至1416吨，升至第三位。以生猪为主肉牛、奶牛、家禽并重的规模养殖，使全镇2010年出栏肥猪1.82万头，肉牛1912头，分别居10乡（镇）的第二位和第一位。肉类总产1927吨，比1992年增长1.76倍，由原来排位第四上升至2010年的第二位。牛奶生产实现了零的突破，2010年产奶占全县9752吨的1/3。工业生产通过外引内联，特别是骨干企业入驻后，拉动了全镇工业总产值快速提升，2010年达5.04亿元，使工农业总产值的比重达77.36%，人均1.86万元，仅次于龙场、扎佐两镇，位居第三位。一批旅游景点建成并营运，促进全镇第三产业较快发展，成为经济总量一个重要的增长点。2010年全镇财政收入达1252万元，在1992年121.41万元的基础上增长9.31倍，但在10乡（镇）中的排位由第三位降至第五位。农民人均纯收入由1998年的1752元增至2010年的5597元，仍保持第三的排位。

四、六广镇

历为县境西北重镇，镇境地跨北纬26°45′~27°12′，东经106°21′~106°34′。东与息烽县毗邻，东南与小箐乡接壤，南与洒坪乡相连，西及西南与黔西县素朴镇、清镇市暗流乡隔河相望，北与大石布依族乡山水相依。境域东西长22.4公里，南北宽7.5公里，2010年土地面积97.69平方公里，耕地面积2.89万亩。镇境地处河谷地带东面，地质地貌复杂，地势高低起伏不平，垂直分布大，是典型的山地河谷地形，最低处六广河河床海拔755米，最高处青龙村的将军山海拔1452米。属北亚热带季风湿润气候，垂直气候差异大。年平均气温18℃，无霜期315天，年平均降雨量1134毫米。因秀美的猫跳河和雄奇的六广河流经镇境,沿河两岸峡谷风光秀丽,素有“山水名镇”的美誉。镇政府驻地六广，距县城37.5公里，距省城贵阳80公里，距贵阳市行政中心金阳70公里。

镇境原属六广区，1978年区辖六广、广田、德政、大石、回水、花椰、六桶、凉井和宝寨9个公社。1984年4月公社改设为乡，1985年9月六广公社改为六广镇。1992年，撤区并乡建镇，将原六广镇、广田乡和德政乡的平营、前丰、团山、元庆、金山、岩脚6个村合并建成新六广镇。2010年，全镇辖24个行政村和1个社区，145个村民组，总人口29358人，其中农业人口27838人。全镇有中学1所、小学11所、幼儿园1所，在校中、小学学生3913人。镇建有六广镇卫生院，村建有卫生室，主要服务于全镇和周边群众的医疗卫生。

镇境处于修文、黔西两县的交通枢纽地带，水陆交通十分便捷。乌江经县境段称六广河，是连接贵阳与遵义的主要水上通道。国道321复线及贵阳至金沙公路穿越全境。2001年开通贵（阳）毕（节）高等级公路，六广成为贵州入滇进川至渝的主要通道之一。1999年实现全镇村村通公路。

地下矿产主要有煤、铁、汞、重晶石等，其中以煤炭储量最大，已探明达1亿吨。森林覆盖面积4696余亩。经济林木有油桐、漆树等。六广柑橘闻名县内外。“六广面条”采用传统工艺精制而成，煮不黏汤，软脆爽口，香味独特；六广苞谷酒有百年历史，远近闻名，入口甘洌，回味悠长；六广河鲶鱼营养丰富，肉质细嫩、入口香醇，为游客的必尝佳品。

镇内旅游资源。有秀美的猫跳河和雄奇的六广河大峡谷，有亚洲第二高桥—六广河特大桥，有绿色环保与科技观光型电站—索风营水电站，有神奇的古佛洞寺贾家洞。流经镇境的六广河和猫跳河，沿岸风光旖旎，景色迷人。为纪念明代奢香开龙场九驿，六广河又名为“奢香湖”。奢香湖从白马滩起至姊妹

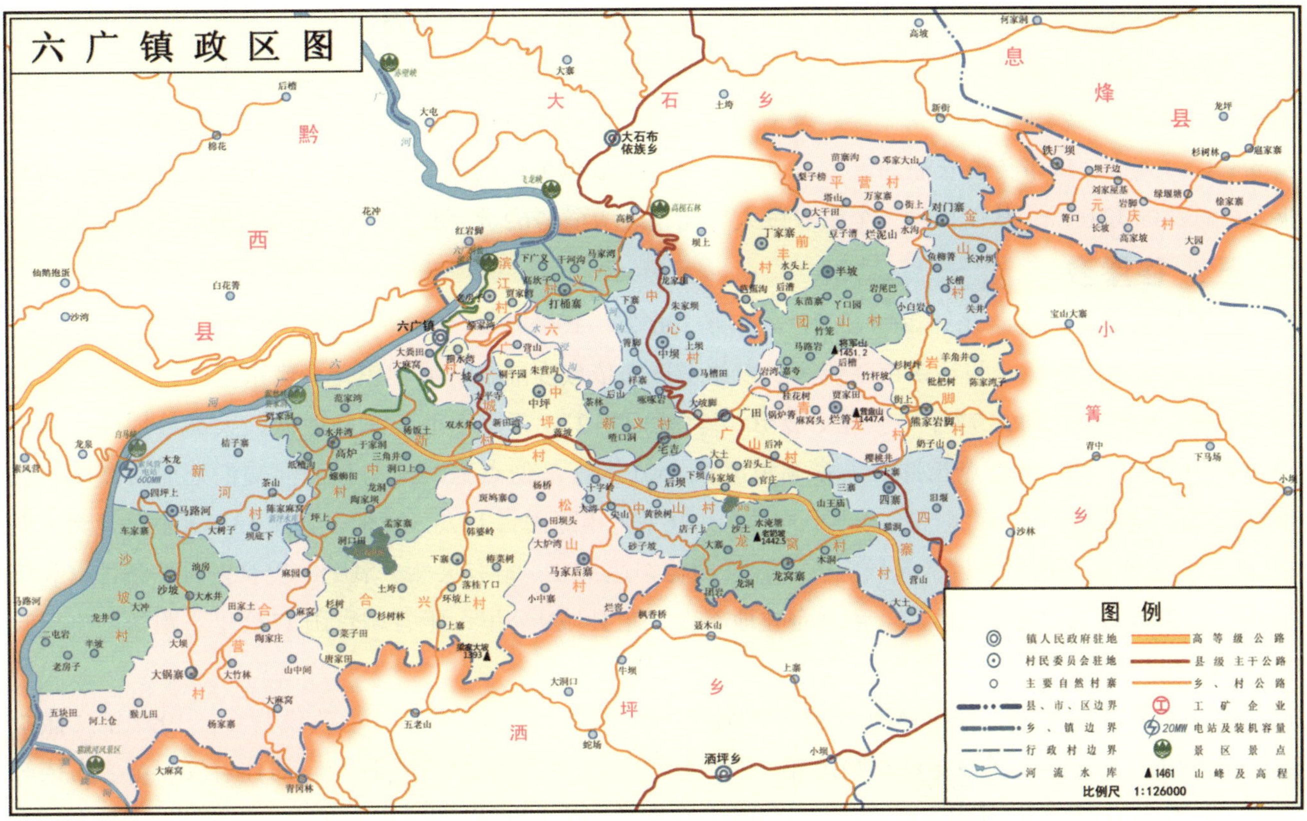

峰，水路长40余公里，全湖容山、水、洞、瀑为一体，春夏秋冬景色变化迥异，共7峡42景。明代大儒王阳明游六广河时曾发出“遍行奇胜才经此，江上无劳羡九华”的赞叹。神奇幽邃的猫跳河，两岸植被林荫茂密，人迹稀少，自然生态保存完好。

2001年，国家投资30亿元在六广河兴建装机容量为3×20万千瓦的索风营电站3台机组于2006年6月并网发电，当年发电量达9.5亿千瓦时；成功改制的白水电站装机容量640千瓦。12家煤矿年生产能力达40万吨，以煤电为主的能源基地初步形成。六广河旅游景区有各类旅游船只50多艘，餐馆10余家，日接待游客量达千余人。

镇的规模是全县4个建制镇中最小的镇。境内干旱缺水，土多田少，农业生产条件较差。1992年建镇时，农业总产值1202万元，粮食总产量4141吨，分别占全县总数的10.23%和8.21%。农业人口人均产粮仅164公斤，有40%的农民口粮不能自给。全镇政收入66.16万元，占全县乡（镇）级财政收入的5.33%。1993以煤炭开采为主的乡镇企业总产值1023万元，占全县乡镇企业产值的5.26%。从整体看，全镇经济发展水平是较为滞后的。1998年农民人均纯收入1473元，仅为全县平均数1673的88.05%。镇党委、政府立足全镇实际，集中精力抓经济建设，在确保农业稳步发展的基础上，大力发展第二、第三产业，从而取得较好的成效。2010年，全镇工农业总产值达3.31亿元，其中工业、农业总产值为2.15亿元、1.16亿元，分别占工农业总产值的比重为64.88%、35.12%。农业总产值在1992年的基础上增长8.67倍。粮食总产1.05万吨，农业人口人均产粮377公斤，分别在1992年的基础上增长1.54倍和1.3倍，农民口粮自给有余，为发展养殖业奠定了基础，使畜牧业产值在农业总产值中的比重达28.96%，高出全县3.01个百分点。2010年全镇共出栏肥猪1.71万头，大牲畜1681头，分别居10乡（镇）的第四位和第二位，肉类总产1895吨，居第三位，在1982年852吨的基础上增长1.33培，农业人口人均产肉68公斤。由于六广河峡谷风光旅游项目知名度的提升，贵（阳）毕（节）高等级公路的贯通，带动了第三产业的发展，成为乡（镇）级财政收入新的增长点。2010年全镇财政收入1791万元，仅次于龙场、扎佐两镇，位居第三。为了增加农民收入，镇党委、政府引导大批农村剩余劳动力向非农领域转移，2010年农村从业人员1.81万人中，从事传统农业的仅占42.28%，从事非农领域的劳动力中，外出打工的达5018人，占从业人员总数的32.05%，从而拉动了全镇农民人均纯收入增至4762元，位居10乡（镇）第五位。

五、谷堡乡

位于县境西南，地跨北纬26°47′~27°，东经106°25′~106°35′。东与龙场镇水土相连，北与洒坪乡、小箐乡一衣带水，西、南与清镇市暗流乡、麦格苗族布依族乡隔猫跳河相望。乡境东西长15公里，南北宽13公里，土地面积122.77平方公里，2010年耕地面积2.47万亩。地势东高西低，大部分地区在海拔1000—1300米之间，最高点长冲村吴家高坡海拔1501米，最低点猫跳河与猫洞河交汇处地面高度海拔850米。属亚热带季风性湿润气候，年平均气温13.6℃，年降雨量1179.5毫米，日照1336.8小时，无霜期265天，冬无严寒，夏无酷暑，气候宜人。森林覆盖率达50%，素有天然“氧吧”美誉。自然条件有利于花果生长,世人誉为“花果之乡”。乡政府驻地谷堡，距县城9公里，距省城贵阳47公里，距贵阳市行政中心金阳36公里。

乡境原隶属城关区，分属乌栗、谷堡和场坝3个公社。1984年4月公社改设为乡。1992年“撤并建”，将原3乡合并建成新谷堡乡。2010年，全乡辖19个行政村，130个村民组。居住着汉、苗、布依等民族，总人口25872人，其中农业人口25274人。有小学5所，初中2所，有在校中、小学学生808人。乡建有谷堡卫生院，村建有卫生室，主要服务于全乡和周边群众的医疗卫生。

境内矿藏主要有煤、铝矾土、铁矿、硫铁矿、重晶石等。其中原煤储量6657万吨，发热量在6500至8000大卡/千克之间；铝矿藏量790万吨，平均铝含量64.53%；铁矿储量8074万吨，平均品位37.6%。农业盛产水稻、玉米、马铃薯、小麦、油菜、蚕豆和豌豆等。果类盛产猕猴桃、金秋梨、水蜜桃、酥李和板栗等。水资源充足，水质优良。过境河流猫跳河年径流量17亿立方米；境内河流平寨河，年径流量0.19亿立方米。有小（Ⅰ）型烂沟和小（Ⅱ）型古隆、许家田坝3座水库，总蓄水量221万立方米。

1999年，全乡实现村村通公路。已经油化的修（文）乌（栗）公路(X190)自东向西横贯全境，猫跳河三、四、五级电站专用公路连通乡境南部各村。由主干公路辐射各村的公路有：三潮水经长冲至大丫口公路，蛇田经场坝、哨上、下花、上花至谷堡，谷堡经梨花湖、猴坝、大堰塘至放马坪，箐口经改城至大寨，谷堡经尖山至平寨，水口至大塘，水口至绿水等乡村公路连通乡境各村寨。另有水口经红枫电厂五级电站过猫跳河可至清镇卫城。国家大电网覆盖全乡；已开通国内、国际程控电话网，汉、数兼容移动电话均投入使用，通信网络遍布全乡各村寨。

旅游资源有一代哲人王阳明著《瘗旅文》悲述的“一吏一子一仆”瘴毙客乡的省级文物保护单位“三人坟”，有明代贵州宣慰使奢香建“龙场九驿”开辟的古驿道，有王阳明慨叹“移放长江还济险”的天生桥自然风景，有神秘的猫跳河（古称“滴澄河”）峡谷风光，有全国农业旅游示范点金秋梨园—古隆等。

从20世纪90年代起，乡党委、乡政府带领谷堡人民狠抓农业产业结构调整，利用本地良好的自然环境和气候优势，大力发展果蔬种植。走市场农业、观光农业兴乡富民之路，取得可喜成绩。至2006年，已建成猕猴桃、金秋梨为龙头产品的3.85万亩经果园，红星猕猴桃、古隆金秋梨闻名省内外，“花果之

乡”享誉全省。特色蔬菜基地也基本建成，沿猫跳河流域建成早毛豆、早辣椒、早糯玉米等次早蔬菜基地，规模已达2000余亩。

谷堡原是一个以种植业为主体的传统农业乡。1992年种植业产值1118万元，占全乡农业总产值的比重76.39%，居全县10乡（镇）之巅，结构极为单一。1993年乡镇企业总产值1354万元，虽占全县9.52%，位居第五，但主要是靠开采铝矾土及生产部分熟铝矾土而实现的，附加值比较低。1992年全乡财政收入仅54.62万元，位列10乡（镇）第九，人均不足23元。粮食总产5035吨，农业人口人均219公斤。后来凭借20世纪80年代开发非耕地资源，以猕猴桃和金秋梨为主的水果种植有了一定基础，但1992年的水果产量也只93吨，位列六广镇之后。1998年全乡农民人均纯收入1520元，也低于全县平均值1673元的9.15%。新的乡党委、乡政府组建后认真分析乡情，在发展以农业为主的经济工作中走出老套路，对农业产业结构不断探索，闯出了一条发展特色农业的路子，初步实现了农业增效、农民增收的既定目标，使乡域经济面貌得到很大改观。2010年，全乡实现工农业总产值3.65亿元，其中工业总产值

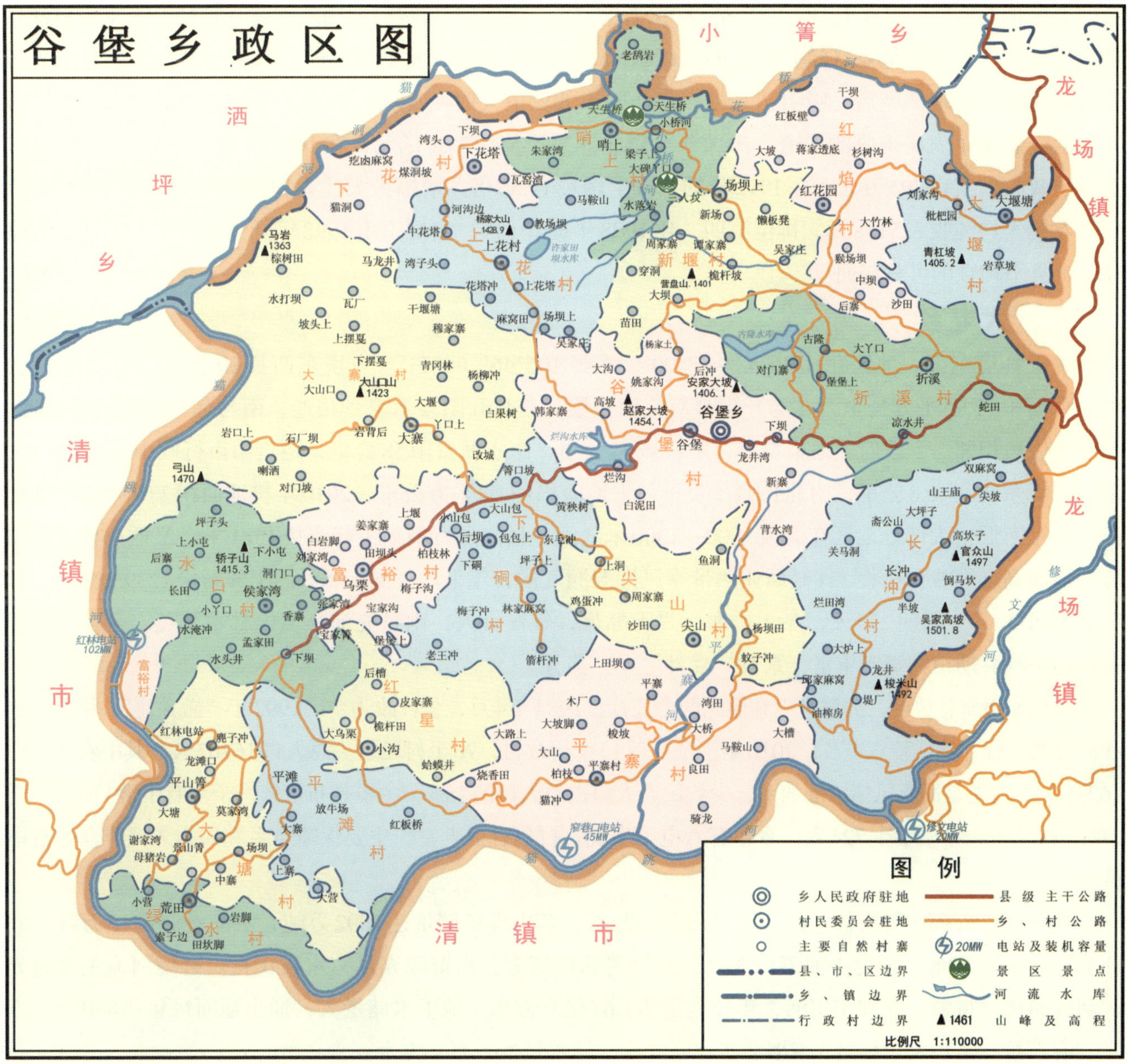

2.31亿元，占63.34%，农业总产值1.34亿元，占36.66%。农业人口人均农业总产值5285元，比1992年的485元增长9.9倍。通过兴办不同规模的养殖场，生猪年末存栏1.03万头和大牲畜存栏6200头，分别居乡（镇）的第四位和第一位；农业户均出栏生猪2.51头和大牲畜1头，创本乡历史新高，也分别名列全县第四和第一。奶牛饲养为养殖业增添了新的内容。家禽饲养年内农业人口人均产禽肉6公斤，禽蛋6.2公斤。使畜牧业产值在农业总产值中的比重由1992年的18.69%上升至24.01%。粮食总产8897吨，农业人口人均产粮352公斤，比1992年的219公斤增长60.73%。根据2005年农业部门对全县逐村调查统计，谷堡乡各类水果种植面积达3.85万亩，占全县水果种植总面积的48.86%，其中猕猴桃和金秋梨分别占全县的61.39%和53.26%，凸显出谷堡“人无我有，人有我优”的农业种植特色。2010年全乡水果总产8666吨，占全总产量2.46万吨的35.17%，农业人口人均产水果358公斤，荣登全县10乡（镇）榜首。乡党委、乡政府还利用猫跳河河谷低热地带的有利条件大力发展早熟蔬菜供应市场，成为农业种植的又一特色。2010年全乡种植蔬菜1.67万亩，占农作物种植总面积的28.15%，产蔬菜2.13万吨，在1992年3744吨基础上增长4.69倍，农业人口人均产菜880公斤。还有利用露天和塑料大棚从事花卉种植及人工培植盆景供应市场，这也是其他乡（镇）罕见的。以果园、花卉种植园、盆景培植园、水库和良好生态环境为载体的观光农业初现端倪后，吸引越来越多身居闹市的城里人前往赏玩，带动了为数不少的“农家乐”应运而生，新添了农民增收的渠道。2010年乡镇企业总产值达3.69亿元，在10乡（镇）的排位仍居第四。全乡财政收入实现795万元，在1992年的基础上增长13.56倍，增幅很大，人均307元，居乡（镇）第六位。农民人均纯收入5158元，排位第四，比1998年提升1档。出现了由1998年低于全县平均数转变为略高于全县平均数的可喜局面。

六、六屯乡

位于县境东部。地跨北纬26°53′~27°00′，东经106°46′~06°53′。乡境东西长10公里，南北宽12公里，总面积77.95平方公里。北与开阳县双流镇接壤，东与开阳县禾丰乡相连，南与乌当区新场乡毗连，西与扎佐镇相邻。乡政府驻地格都堡，距县城32公里，距省城贵阳58公里，距贵阳市行政中心金阳38公里。乡境东西宽10.8公里，南北长11.5公里，土地面积83.08平方公里，2010年耕地面积2.07万亩。地势西北高东南低，大部分地区在海拔1000—1300米之间，最高点石猫猫主峰海拔1581米，最低点桃源河出境处地面高度海拔950米。气候属亚热带季风性湿润气候，年平均气温13.5℃，年降雨量1239.3毫米，日照1350小时，无霜期275天，冬无严寒，夏无酷暑，气候宜人，雨量充沛。境内林木繁茂，全乡森林覆盖率达48%，动植物资源丰富，素有“森林之乡”美誉。

乡境原隶属扎佐区，分属六屯和桃源两个公社。1984年4月，公社改为乡。1992年“撤并建”，将原六屯和桃源两乡合并建成新六屯乡。2010年，全乡辖13个行政村，76个村民组。总人口16767人，其中农业人口16235人。六屯是民族风情浓郁的乡，少数民族人口占总人口的28%，主要是布依族。全乡有中学1所、小学7所，在校中、小学学生724人。乡建有六屯卫生院，村建有卫生室，主要保障全乡和周边人民群众的身体健康。

境内矿产资源主要有煤、硅、重晶石和石灰石，其中煤矿储量达2092万吨，重晶石储量13万吨。农业盛产水稻、玉米、小麦、油菜、大豆、马铃薯和烤烟等。水资源充足，水质优良。过境河流主要有光洞河、鱼梁（桃源）河和车田河，年径流量达1.67亿立方米。地下水储量大，涌出地面每年达880万立方米。有石桥、流白水、林场3座小（Ⅱ）型水库，储水量80.9万立方米。

1999年全乡实现村村通公路。主干道扎（佐）六（屯）公路由西向东横贯乡境，往东延伸可通开阳县城。次干道由扎六公路三里大河处分道，经独山、西冲、长田至星中接六屯至开阳主干道。由两条干道辐射出的各条乡村公路形成县、乡、村三级公路纵横交错网络，连通乡内各村及周边乡镇。全乡通车总里程86公里，平均每平方公里有公路1公里。国家大电网覆盖全乡；1999年开通国内、国际程控电话网，汉、数兼容移动电话均投入使用，移动电话信号覆盖整个乡境。

桃源河在乡境内流程10余公里，两岸奇峰峭壁，林木荫翳，植被良好。从桃子湾到三道响水，长5公里大峡谷风景特佳。集幽谷、青山、流水、洞穴、泉瀑、古生物化石群等景观于一体，山青水绿，植被茂密，鸟语花香，空气清新，涧流湍急，蜿蜒绵延。落差38米的三道响水梯级大瀑布，终年涛声悦耳。还有珍珠滩、犀牛潭、玉女裙瀑布等著名景观。紧邻桃源河的独山、西冲两个布依山寨，村民纯朴勤劳、热情好客。1935年，中央红军长征入乡境，过疙蔸堡（今格都堡）经大木、桃源取道开阳小田坝

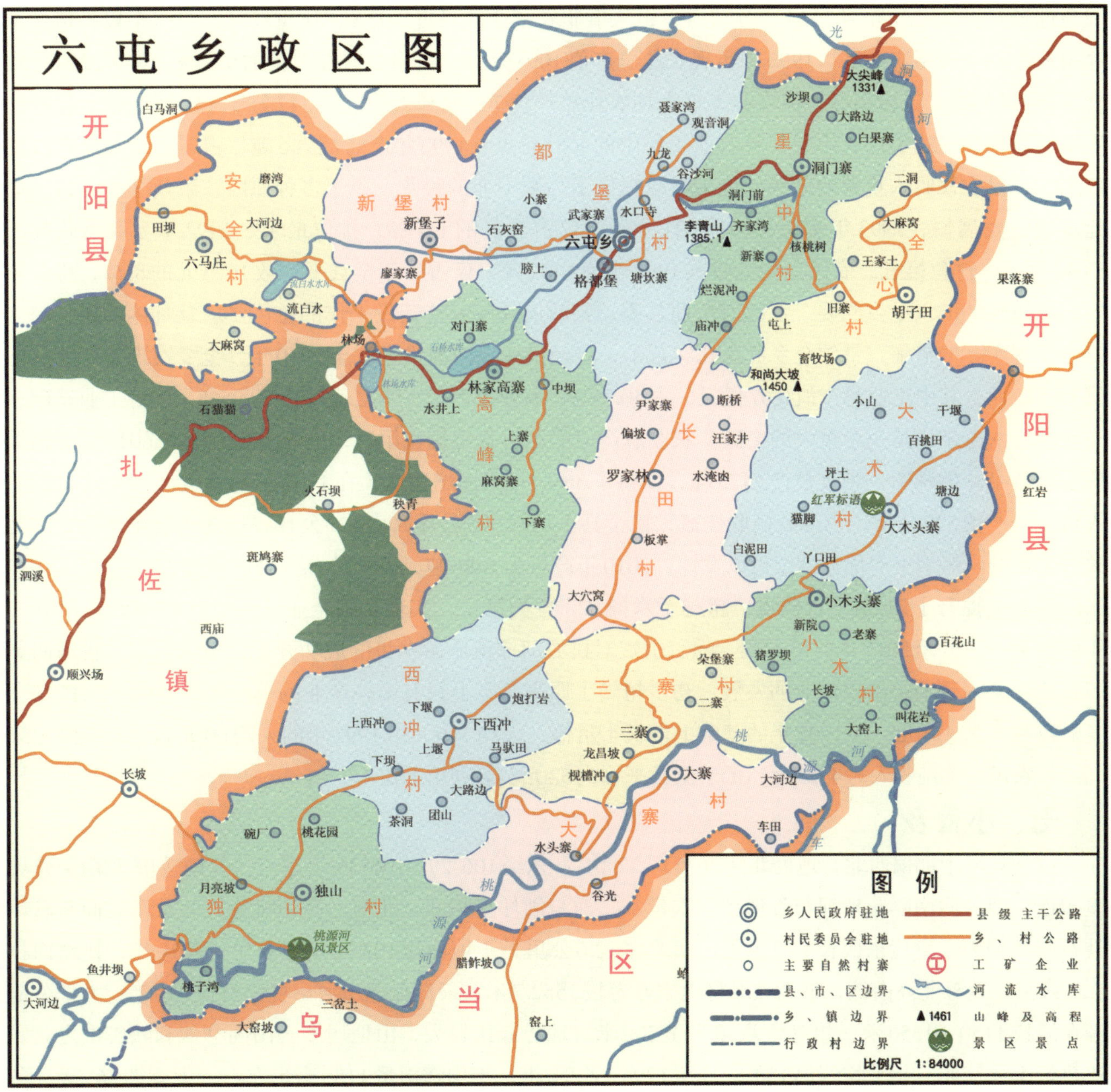

出境。部队在乡境长田、大木、桃源等地宿营，惩恶除霸，开仓济贫，播下革命的火种。朱德总司令率军委纵队一部进驻净慈寺，红五军团在大木布依寨书写“红军是干人的军队”至今保存完好，成为珍贵的革命文物。

从20世纪90年代起，乡党委、乡政府带领六屯人民，狠抓农业产业结构调整，利用丰富的自然资源发展乡域经济。引进神州漂流公司落户独山村桃源河，投资1600万元开发旅游业，建成集漂流、观光、会议接待、餐饮住宿为一体的桃源河漂流景区，是度假、休闲、探险的绝佳之所；号海科技公司择址西冲村发展早熟无公害蔬菜，建成蔬菜基地4000亩；兴达、鼎业、昊天等企业在星中、长田、大木、小木等村发展采掘业。

乡的规模较小，土地总面积和总人口仅在大石布依族乡之前，居第九位。耕地中水田面积较大，占全乡总耕地的42.26%，2010年农业人口人均耕地1.28亩，远在全县平均数不足1亩之上，发展农业的基础条件较好。1992年全乡7154个劳动力中，从事非农产业的只占8.02%，比重较低，是一个以种植业和养殖业为主的典型农业乡。1992年实现农业总产值1097万元，占全县农业总值的9.34%，位列第六，粮食总产4981吨，位居第五，但农业人口人均农业总产值765元和人均产粮347公斤，又居榜首。以量大质优而著称的烤烟生产，不失全乡农业生产中的又一亮点。1992年产烤烟746吨，占全县烤烟总产量的17.33%，是农民收入重要的来源，也为财政提供了为数不菲的税收。由于多种原因，致使全乡乡镇企业起步晚、发展慢，1993年实现总产值321万元，仅占全县的1.65%，排位最末。1992年乡级财政收入88.44万元，排位第五。农民人均纯收入1998年为1422元，仅占当年全县平均数1673元的85%，排位第七。新组建的的六屯乡党委、乡政府按照县委、县政府关于经济建设工作的总体要求及具体部署，制订符合客观实际的措施，带领全乡群众扎实苦干，将经济建设向前推进。至2010年，全乡实现工农业总产值1.65亿元，其中工业总产值0.67亿元，占40.75%，农业总产值0.98亿元，占59.25%，这对工业基础相当薄弱的六屯来说是一个重大的突破。农业总产值的绝对数虽排位第八，但农业人口人均6019元，仍保持了全县第一的殊荣。粮食总产8475吨，保持了3%的年均递增速度，在1992年基础增长70.15%。农业人口人均产粮522公斤，仍继续摘取桂冠，比全县平均数395公斤高出127公斤，这在全县乡（镇）中是独占鳌头的。烤烟生产优势继续得以发挥，2010年产量为1486吨，占全县总产的份额达38.89%，在1992年的基础上提升了21.56个百分点，超越了六桶乡，位列第一。实现乡镇企业总产值8040万元，由1992年倒数第一，升至2010年的第七位。随着引资对桃源河漂流旅游项目的成功开发，境内六屯、桃源两集镇日渐繁荣，带动了第三产业的发展，初步扭转了原来基本上只有第一产业的单一经济结构。2010年全乡财政收入529万元，在1992年的基础上增长4.98倍，人均316元由1992年的人均60元名列第三降至第九位。农民人均纯收入为4323元，低于全县平均5152元，名列第七位。

七、小箐乡

位于县境中部偏西北，地处北纬26°53′~27°01′、东经106°29′~106°36′，东与久长镇接壤,东南与龙场镇相连，南及西南隔花桥河与谷堡乡一衣带水，西与洒坪乡相邻，北与六广镇毗连，北及东北面与息烽县石硐乡相邻。乡境东西长13.2公里，南北宽12.6公里，土地面积103.38平方公里，2010年，耕地面积2.25万亩。地势北高南低，最高点老将山主峰海拔1552.7米，最低点郭田河出境处海拔920米，大部分地区在海拔1150—1350米，相对高差50米至200米，地势起伏较大，山地居多，山间盆地和峡谷次之。属亚热带季风气候，年平均气温13℃，日照1296.5小时/年，年均降雨量1185毫米左右，无霜期269天。冬

无严寒，夏无酷暑，气候宜人，雨量充沛。乡政府驻小箐街上，距县城17公里，距省城贵阳55公里，距贵阳市行政中心金阳44公里。

乡境原隶属六广区，分属小箐、崇恩和马场3个公社。1984年4月公社改设为乡。1992年“撤并建”，将原3个乡合并建成新小箐乡。至2010年，全乡辖17个行政村和1个社区，139个村民组。居住有汉、苗、彝等民族，总人口23727人，其中农业人口22753人。全乡有中学1所、小学8所，在校中、小学学生805人。乡建有小箐卫生院，村建有卫生室，主要保障全镇和周边人民群众身体健康。

乡境森林面积5.78万亩，森林覆盖率达41%。其中，用材林3.5万亩，经济林0.95万亩，灌木林1.33万亩。已探明蕴藏有煤、铁、硅、页岩、石灰石、硫铁矿、大理石和耐火黏土等，尤以新场村煤的储量大，野鹿大坡石灰石品质好，崇恩、尖山页岩和耐火黏土多。农业主产水稻、玉米、小麦、马铃薯、油菜籽和烤烟等。果类盛产酥李，全乡种植面积达6000亩，年产李子200万公斤，产值200万元。其中郭田酥李被创为品牌，果大核小、色艳味美，入口酥脆甜香，深受消费者的青睐。境内河流主要有花桥河、郭田河和小沟河，总长16公里，流域面积32平方公里。1972年建成的岩鹰山水库，库容1755万立方米，润泽全乡，为工农业发展提供优异条件。另有小（Ⅱ）型水库1座，山塘24座，蓄水25.12万立方米；农用电灌站19座，装机容量514千瓦。岩鹰湖山水相连，坝隧结合，林木葱绿，碧波荡漾。湖西南侧有清初开辟的四面坡大道，有建于清康熙十九年（1680）的觉先桥，有林荫遮日、溪水长流、多级瀑布、百鸟群集的兰花岩峡谷，是避暑旅游的理想之地。

1999年，全乡实现村村通公路。修（文）六（广）公路和2001年建成的贵（阳）毕（节）高等级公路由东南入乡地西北出乡境。2004年硬化的久（长）大（石）公路跨越乡西北15公里，2005年硬化的崇（恩）栋（青）公路将修六公路和久大公路连接。乡村公路19条总长78公里，纵横交错，四通八达。1998至2002年实施农村电网改造后，100%的村、组，99.8%的农户用上可靠的网络供电。2006年，所有村、组通电话，移动、联通网络覆盖全乡。

改革开放后，乡的经济建设速度加快。1992年，实现农业总产值786万元。从1993年起，调整产业结构，培育社会主义市场经济体系，加紧交通、通信基础设施建设，推动经济快速发展。2000年实现农业总产值3278万元。生态养殖、花卉种植、延晚番茄等一批产业应运而生，酥李成为乡村经济的重要品牌，以夏家沟为主的生态旅游初步形成。冶炼和建材工业初见端倪，为实施工业强乡战略奠定了基础。

乡境矿产资源较少，乡镇企业发展滞后。1992年全乡从业者1.04万人中，从事农林、牧、渔业的占96.32%，在全县10乡（镇）中比重最高。至1993年全乡乡镇企业总产值仅557万元，占全县总产值的2.86%，是一个地道的农业乡。1992年实现农业总产值933万元，农业人口人均445元，绝对数和人均数都名列10乡（镇）中的第七位。粮食总产2913吨，农业人口人均产粮139公斤，口粮不能自给。当年收获烤烟314吨、油菜籽627吨，出栏肥猪5024头，分别占全县总数的7.29%、14.4%和9.01%，饲养家禽和所产禽蛋是农民收入的重要来源。乡级财政收入55.94万元，人均27元，而财政支出竟为63.28万元，入不敷出。1998年农民人均收入1309元，名列10乡（镇）的第九位。面对如此乡情，乡党委、乡政府首先从加大科技投入，大力发展粮食生产，解决农民吃饭问题入手，从1992年起实现粮食总产8年连续增产，跃升至2000年的5436吨，农业人口人均产粮256公斤，一举解决了长期困扰全局的农民吃饭问题。与此同时，加大农村产业结构调整力度，发展第二、第三产业，为富余劳动力创造就业机会和培植税源。在农业内部，利用农民粮食自给有余的物质基础，把发展规模养殖作为主攻方向，并把发展水果、蔬菜生产作为农民增收的重要措施来抓，故取得了预期的成效。2010年全乡实现工农业总产值1.23亿元，其中工业总产值0.21亿元占17.05%，农业总产值1.02亿元占82.95%。这在原来基础上向前迈出了可喜的一步。以猕猴桃、梨子和酥李为主的果树种植面积达7463亩，居全县第三，粮食总产7139吨，比1992年增长1.45倍，年均递增5.11%，高出全县平均4.12%的发展速度。农业人口人均产粮374公斤，产烤烟261吨，产油菜籽393吨。农民户均出栏肥猪3.03头，居全县首位。大牲畜出栏5400万头，仅次于谷堡乡，名列第二。农民人均产猪、牛、羊、禽、兔肉76.3公斤，名列第三。全乡财政收入1526万元，跃升至全县第四，人均财政收入643元，名列前茅。农民人均纯收入4176元，在1998年基础上以年均10.15%的速度递增。

八、洒坪乡

位于县境西北部，地处北纬26°51′~26°57′，东经106°22′~106°29′，东与小箐乡接壤，南与谷堡乡毗邻，西及西北隔猫跳河与清镇市暗流乡对峙，北及东北面与六广镇相连。乡境东西长11.6公里，南北宽9.3公里，土地面积85.33平方公里，2010年耕地面积1.83万亩。地势向西南倾斜，北高西低。最高点五老山海拔1468.2米，最低点阳桥村花地河海拔782米，大部分地区海拔在950至1250米之间，相对高差50至200米之间，地势起伏较大，呈典型的喀斯特地貌特征。气候属亚热带季风气候，冬无严寒，夏无酷暑，雨热同期，气候温和。年平均气温13℃，日照1212.1小时，平均降雨量1185毫米左右，无霜期269天。乡政府驻小坝村小坝，距县城25公里，距省城贵阳63公里，距贵阳市行政中心金阳52公里。

乡境原隶属小箐区，分属洒坪和中寨两个公社。1984年4月公社改设为乡。1992年2月撤区并乡，洒坪乡和中寨乡合并建成新洒坪乡。2010年，全乡辖18个行政村134个村民组。居民主要是汉、苗、彝等民族，总人口17200人，其中农业人口16778人。全乡有中学1所、小学9所，在校中、小学学生689人。乡建有洒坪卫生院，村建有卫生室，主要保障全乡和周边群众的身体健康。

矿藏主要有铝土矿、硫铁矿、煤矿、铁矿。其中煤炭最为丰富。已探明原煤储量1亿吨，主要分布在阳桥、五江、青杠林、洞口、麻窝、上坝等村，尤以上坝枫香桥梁子和阳桥一带的煤质最佳；铝土矿储量3000万吨，三氧化二铝含量高达75%；硫铁矿储量超过2000万吨，含铁量在60%以上。过境河主要是猫跳河，属乌江水系，流经乡境总长23.5公里，流域面积85平方公里，建有装机容量3万千瓦的水电站1座。猫跳河河谷水清谷险，峡深景幽。境内河流猫洞河，流经乡境长8公里，多年平均流量2.2平方米/秒。两条河流沿岸藏有若干奇峰异石和波平河滩尚待开发，有望建成生态科普乐园。农作物一年两熟，出产水稻、玉米、高粱、小麦、洋芋、油菜和烤烟等。果类主要有李、桃、杏、梨、柑橘、猕猴桃、核桃、板栗等。其中蜈蚣桥蜜李享有盛名，果大核小、酥脆甜香。

1999年，全乡实现村村通公路，以小箐至轿子山公路（X188）主干道为主轴，由主轴辐射出四连线有小坝经上寨至上坝村级公路，青山经蛇场、硐口、五老山至青杠林村级公路，小坝经新乐至蜈蚣桥村级公路，中明经北庄、高寨至青杠林村级公路。“一轴四连线”为骨架的交通网络遍布18个行政村，全乡通公路里程达124公里。1999年开通国内、国际程控电话网，汉、数兼容移动电话均投入使用，移动电话信号覆盖整个乡境。2002年实施农村电网改造后，国家大电网覆盖全乡。

著名历史文物古迹有建于明成化五年（1469）贵阳通往毕节古驿道上素有“十桥之冠”美誉的蜈蚣桥凌驾于猫洞河之上，历经500多年的河水侵蚀及数百次山洪冲击，桥身至今仍雄姿依然。1982年贵州省人民政府将其列为省级重点文物保护单位。

实行改革开放后，乡党委、乡政府坚持以农业产业结构调整为主线，围绕“三种三养”（种植大蒜、大葱、生姜，养殖生猪、肉牛、肉兔）发展思路，着力打造“菜、畜、果、烟”四大特色产业，使农业出现新跨越。2006年，全乡以大蒜为主的特色蔬菜种植面积达6000亩，畜牧业产值2886万元，占农业总产值的51.57%，以“蜜李”为主的特色水果产量达1600吨，营造优质烤烟基地2000亩。建成年产30万吨和15万吨煤矿各1家。

乡境土多田少，是人口密度最低的一个乡。缺水是影响人们正常生产和生活主要的不利因素。境内蕴藏着量大质优的原煤、铝矾土和铁矿资源，助推了以采掘业为主的乡镇企业的发展。1993年实现总产值689万元，位居全县10乡（镇）第六。1992年全乡粮食总产2003吨，只占全县的第九位，农业人口人均产粮125公斤，占第八位，产烤烟260吨、产油菜籽168吨和肉类总产412吨，排位均挂末。实现农业总产值641万元，农业和畜牧业产值分别占51.79%和43.99%，但结构单一。全乡财政收入37.35万元，排位第十，人均财政收入22元，全县最低，财政收支逆差9.9万元。1998年，农民人均纯收入1410元，仅为全县平均数的84.28%，是全县农村贫困户较为集中的乡（镇）之一。在县委、县政府的领导下，乡党委、乡政府紧密依靠群众，制定切合实际的发展策略和奋斗目标，扎实苦干，终于将全乡的经济工作向前推进。1993年起，全乡粮食总产从3456吨发展至2000年的4441吨，取得7年连续增产的好成绩，农业人口人均产粮287公斤，农民要求最紧迫需要解决的吃饭问题得以解决。乡党委和乡政府将进一步发展乡镇企业，大力发展养殖业，种植烤烟、油菜、蔬菜和引导剩余劳动力外出打工作为增加农民收入的主要措施来抓。2010年全乡实现工农业业总产值1.39亿元，其中工业总产值4500万元，占32.19%，农业总产值9400万元，占67.81%。粮食总产6279吨，农业人口人均产粮374公斤，分别在1992年的基础上增长2.13倍和1.99倍。烤烟、油菜籽增长至365吨 和269吨，特别引人瞩目的是肉类总产1424吨，绝对数虽处于第八位，但农业人口人均产肉84.9公斤是全县最高的一个乡。水果产量1124吨，农业人口人均产67公斤，也是较为突出的。全乡财政收入680万元，排位第八，但人均395元，又位列第五。全乡当年从业者7583人中，在本地和外地从事非农领域务工的占57.23%。农民年纯收入人均4176元，虽在1998年基础上增长1.96倍，但排名仍靠末处于第八位。

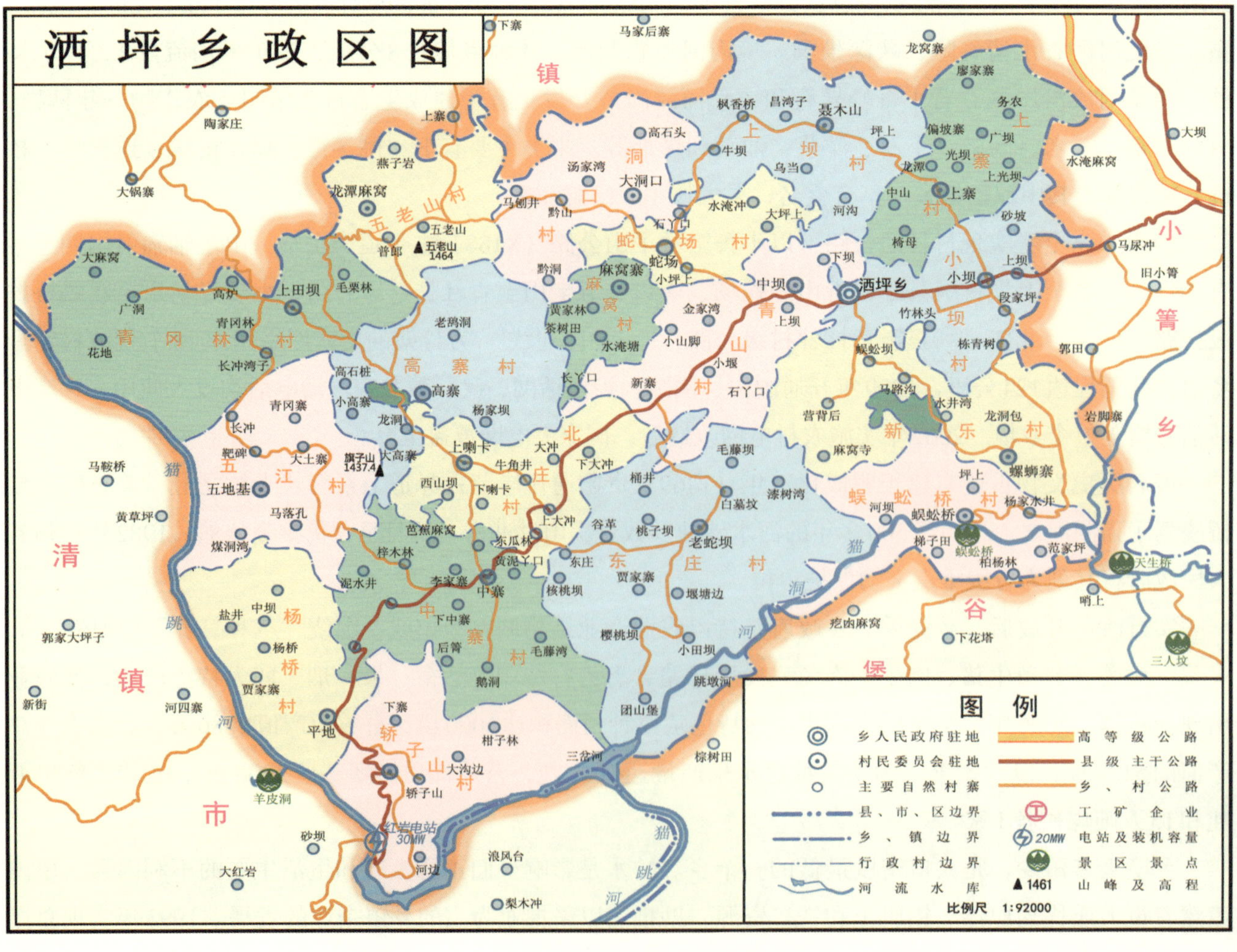

九、大石布依族乡

位于县境西北部，地处北纬26°59′~27°04′，东经106°25′~106°32′。乡境东与息烽县石硐乡毗邻，南与六广镇相连，西隔六广河与黔西县相望，北与六桶乡接壤。乡境南北长10.5公里，东西宽8.3公里，土地面积51.14平方公里，2010年耕地面积1.54万亩。乡境地势向西南倾斜，北高西低。一般地区海拔高度从760米至1350米呈梯形分布，最高点高山村牛项包山海拔1435.5米，最低点竹坪村西侧六广河中河床海拔753米。相对高差在50米至200米之间，地势起伏较大，呈典型的喀斯特地貌特征，因境内有天造地设的回水、高枧两座绿色石林以及其间一座座形态各异的石峰，故有“神奇大石”之称。属亚热带季风气候，冬无严寒，夏无酷暑，雨热同期，气候温和。年平均气温在13℃至15℃，年降雨量1000毫米左右,日照1215小时，无霜期266天。乡政府驻地大石板，距县城39公里，距省城贵阳77公里，距贵阳市行政中心金阳66公里。

乡境原隶属六广区，分属大石公社、回水公社和德政公社的一部分。1984年4月公社改设为乡。1992年“撤并建”，将原大石、回水两乡和德政乡的部分合并建成新大石布依族乡。2010年，全乡辖15个行政村，78个村民组，总人口13638人，其中农业人口13222人。主要居住有汉、布依、苗、彝等民族，其中少数民族3812人，占27.95%，是全县唯一的少数民族乡。全乡有中学1所、小学4所，在校中、小学学生510人。乡建有大石卫生院和各村建有卫生室，主要保障全乡和周边人民群众的身体健康。

境内矿藏主要有煤、硫铁矿、大理石、石灰石等，已探明煤的储量1000万吨以上，硫铁矿储量500万吨以上，大理石储量100万吨以上。农作物一年两熟，出产玉米、水稻、小麦、茶叶等，经济作物以烤烟、油菜为主；果类主要有李、桃、杏、梨、柑橘、猕猴桃、核桃、板栗等。水资源有过境河流六广河年径流量70.03亿立方米，因河谷深切，山高水低，难以利用；有大煤厂小（Ⅱ）型水库1座，蓄水量22万立方米；境内人畜饮水多系开采地下水资源。旅游资源较为丰富，可供开发的有高枧石林、回水石林和大屯民族风情等。其中，高枧石林被誉为“拟态动物园”，回水石林素有“贵州绿色石林”之称。大屯民族风情村位于风光优美的六广河畔，一面临江，三面环绕悬崖峭壁，布依风情浓郁，犹如世外桃源。大石布依人喜爱唱歌，每年“三月三”“六月六”是布依族传统民歌节，还有“正月十四歌会”“开场（乡场赶集）赛歌”“斗鸟赛歌”“赶表”“爬六月坡”等歌节和歌会。

1999年，全乡实现村村通公路。广田至海马孔（X186）公路自南向北纵贯乡境，由主干公路辐射出的乡村公路有高枧至久长的久高路、木踏石至大屯、大石至高山竹坪、上大坝经红岩至六桶乡火石丫、丫口田经联江村至息烽县何家洞和回水至沙坝等公路，构成乡境交通网络，连通全乡村村寨寨。2000年开通国内、国际程控电话网，汉、数兼容移动电话均投入使用，移动电话信号覆盖整个乡境；2002年实施农村电网改造后，国家大电网覆盖全乡。

改革开放后，大石布依族乡党委、乡政府率领全乡各族人民，利用丰富的自然资源，以发展旅游为“龙头”，优化环境搞好服务，进一步挖掘民族民间文化，推动一、二、三产业齐头并进。

大石是全县规模最小、农业生产条件较差、基础薄弱、农村贫困发生率最高的一个乡。1992年全乡农业总产值454万元，粮食总产1350吨，烤烟225吨，油菜籽205吨，肉类总产290吨，乡镇企业总产值356万元，全乡财政收入89.25万元，农民人均纯收入1025元，主要指标在10乡（镇）中都居后。粮食不能自给，农民收入水平低，农村贫困面大是最基本的乡情。乡党委、乡政府始终以“脱贫致富奔小康”宏伟目标总揽全局，以“团结务实，乘势争先”的修文精神带领全乡各族群众集中精力，扎实苦干，推进经济建设。将国家先后投入巨额的扶贫专项基金，大小数百个扶贫项目的实施作为工作重点，使全乡各族群众生产、生活条件逐步得以改善。“造血式”的扶贫方式帮助贫困群众解决发展生产在资金、物资和技术方面的困难，致使全乡发展速度明显加快。引导剩余劳动力向非农领域转移，在本地或外地从业也作为农民增收的一项措施来抓。至2010年，全乡实现工农业总产值1.57亿元，其中工业总产值0.85亿元，占54.25%，农业总产值0.72亿元，占45.75%。人均工农业总产值1.15万元，仅位列全县4镇和谷堡乡之后，位居第六。农业总产值为1992年的15.81倍，其增速荣登榜首。粮食总产4617吨，在1992年基础上年递增达7.11%，农业人口人均产粮352公斤，实现了自给有余的目标，在1992年人均产粮仅有99公斤的基础上增长2.56倍。产烤烟286吨，在6个种植烤烟乡中处第三位。肉产量1114吨，农业人口人均产肉84.3公斤，跃升至第二位。全乡财政收入523万元居第十位，但人均财政收入67元又仅次于扎佐镇，居第二位，这是来之不易的骄人战绩。农民人均纯收入3308元，仍处第十位。众多贫困人口脱贫步伐明显加快。

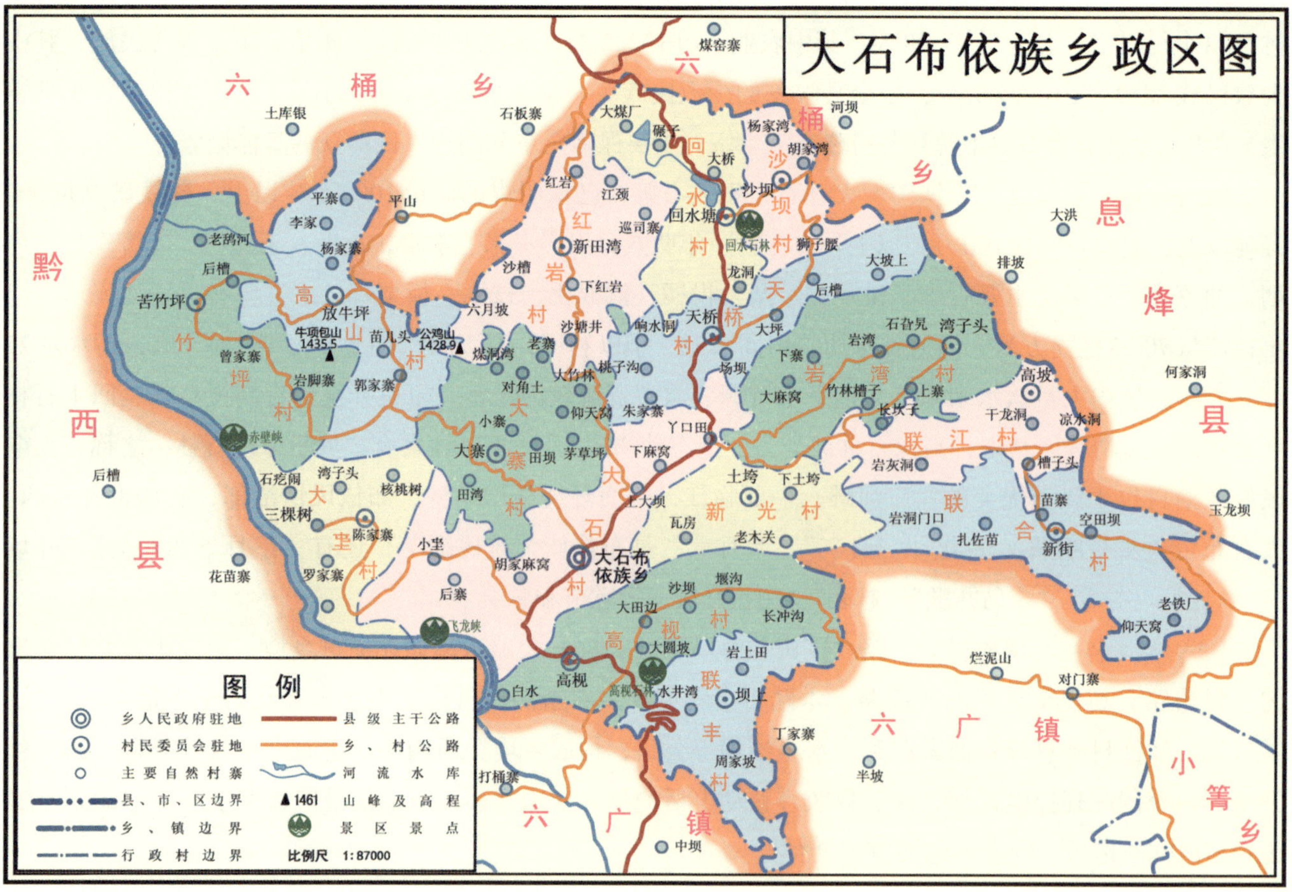

大石布依族乡政区图

十、六桶乡

位于县境西北六广河东岸，系县辖最边远乡，地处北纬27°03′~27°12′，东经106°23′~106°30′。东面与息烽县九庄镇毗邻，南与大石布依族乡接壤，西及北面与黔西、金沙两县隔六广河相望。乡境南北长15.6公里，东西宽11.4公里，土地面积111.75平方公里，2010年耕地面积3.64万亩。乡境地势南面高，东、西、北三面低，一般地区海拔高度在1000—1200米之间，最高点坪山村公鸡山海拔1428.9米，最低点黄金村周家堰六广河出境处河床海拔666米。境内山地分布广，喀斯特地貌明显，地下溶洞分布多。属

亚热带季风气候，冬无严寒，夏无酷暑，雨热同期，气候温和。年平均气温在12.8℃至14.5℃之间，年降雨量1000毫米左右,日照1215小时，无霜期266天。乡政府驻地盐井村坪上，是修文、息烽、金沙、黔西四县的延边贸易中心，距县城龙场50公里，距省城贵阳88公里，距贵阳市行政中心金阳77公里。

乡境原隶属六广区，分属六桶、花椒、凉井和宝寨4个公社，1984年4月公社改设为乡。1992年“撤并建”，将4个乡和回水乡的石板、坪山两村合并建成新六桶乡。2010年，辖28个行政村，187个村民组。有汉、布依、彝等13个民族，总人口28844人，其中农业人口27797人。全乡有中学1所和小学12所，在校中、小学学生2357人。乡建有六桶卫生院，村建有卫生室，主要保障全乡和周边人民群众的身体健康。

境内矿藏主要有煤、汞、铁、锰和硫铁矿等，已探明煤的储量1000万吨以上。农作物一年两熟，出产玉米、水稻、小麦、茶叶等，经济作物以烤烟、油菜为主；果类主要有李、桃、杏、梨、柑橘、猕猴桃、核桃、板栗等。水资源有过境河流六广河年径流量13.6亿立方米，由于河谷深切，山高水低，难以利用；有金星小（Ⅱ）型水库1座，蓄水量13.5万立方米。生态多样性保持较为完好，森林覆盖率达30%以上。山地分布广，喀斯特地貌明显，形成众多溶洞，主要有多缤洞、老硝洞、关牛洞、天宝洞、何家洞等，其中多缤洞是国内目前发现的较长洞穴之一，已勘测长达21.4公里，是世界一流的喀斯特洞穴艺术宝库，地下岩溶地貌被专家称为“天下奇观”。

1999年，全乡已实现村村通公路。修文至海马孔（X186）公路自南向北纵贯乡境，火石丫至息烽九庄（X194）公路自南向东横贯东南乡境，构成乡内两大主干道路。由两大主干道辐射出的乡村公路主要有六桶至黄金村湖广漕、六桶至春江村刘家沟、六桶至九庄、六桶至官寨、六桶至下坝村土库银、六桶至何田村班家寨、柿花树至大兴田大麻窝、宝宝寨至联合村和火石丫至花椒、来鹤、河银等公路，构成乡境四通八达的交通网络。2000年，电信公司、移动公司、联通公司相继在六桶开展业务，有线、无线通信网络覆盖全乡。2002年经过农村电网改造，全乡实现了规范、安全的电网供电。

乡里文化开发较早，乌江河畔海马村的土法造纸，被列入修文县第一批非物质文化遗产。黄金村苗族蜡染、纺织、刺绣等手工技艺精湛，是不可多得的民族民间文化瑰宝。

改革开放后，六桶乡以集镇建设为重点，以产业结构调整为主线，以发展畜牧业为突破口，以增加农民收入为目标。大力调整农业结构，围绕“烟、畜、菜、果、药”五大产业，优化农业内部结构，引进资金，壮大特色经济规模，促进农民增收。目前，已建成一批以土鸡、肉牛、柑橘、次早熟蔬菜等为代表的特色农产品生产基地。

六桶原来一直是一个以种、养殖业为主的传统农业乡。由于生产水平低下，除烤烟、油菜籽和部分畜禽产品能提供给社会外，整体看商品生产率较差，属全县经济欠发达的乡（镇）之一。“撤、并、建”的1992年，全乡实现农业总产值876万元，虽排位第八，但农业人口人均产值仅331元，处于倒数第一位。粮食总产2944吨，排位第七，农业人口人均产粮111公斤，只略高于大石乡，处第九位，农民口粮还有较大缺口。产油菜籽474吨，名列全县第四。作为拳头产品的烤烟当年产955吨，占全县总产的22.18%，排位全县第一。肉类总产407吨、虽处于第八位，但农业人口人均产肉15公斤，比全县平均数23公斤还少8公斤。乡镇企业总产值423万元，只占全县的1.98%。全乡财政收入133.69万元，排第三位，人均财政收入44人，排第六位。1998年农民人均纯收入1605元，但也低于全县平均数1673元。新的乡党委、乡政府通过调研，发现全乡虽有制约经济发展的不利因素，但也有许多有利条件，他们决定扬长避短，充分利用人均耕地较多和乡政府所在地新集镇建成后成为黔西、金沙、息烽和修文4县重要物资集散地的有利条件，大力调整产业结构，狠抓粮食生产，推动第二、第三产业发展。在扶贫攻坚战中管好用好专项资金，认真抓好扶贫项目的逐一实施广开门路解决好剩余劳动力的就业问题，使全乡较为后进的经济形势日益向好。2010年全乡实现工农业总产值1.5亿元，工业和农业总产值分别为0.22亿元和1.28亿元，占工农业总产值的比重分别为14.66%和85.34%，其中农业总产值人均4608元，由1992年10乡（镇）的第十位升至第七位。在狠抓生猪、肉牛、家禽饲养的同时，还发展奶牛、肉鸽、肉兔生产、

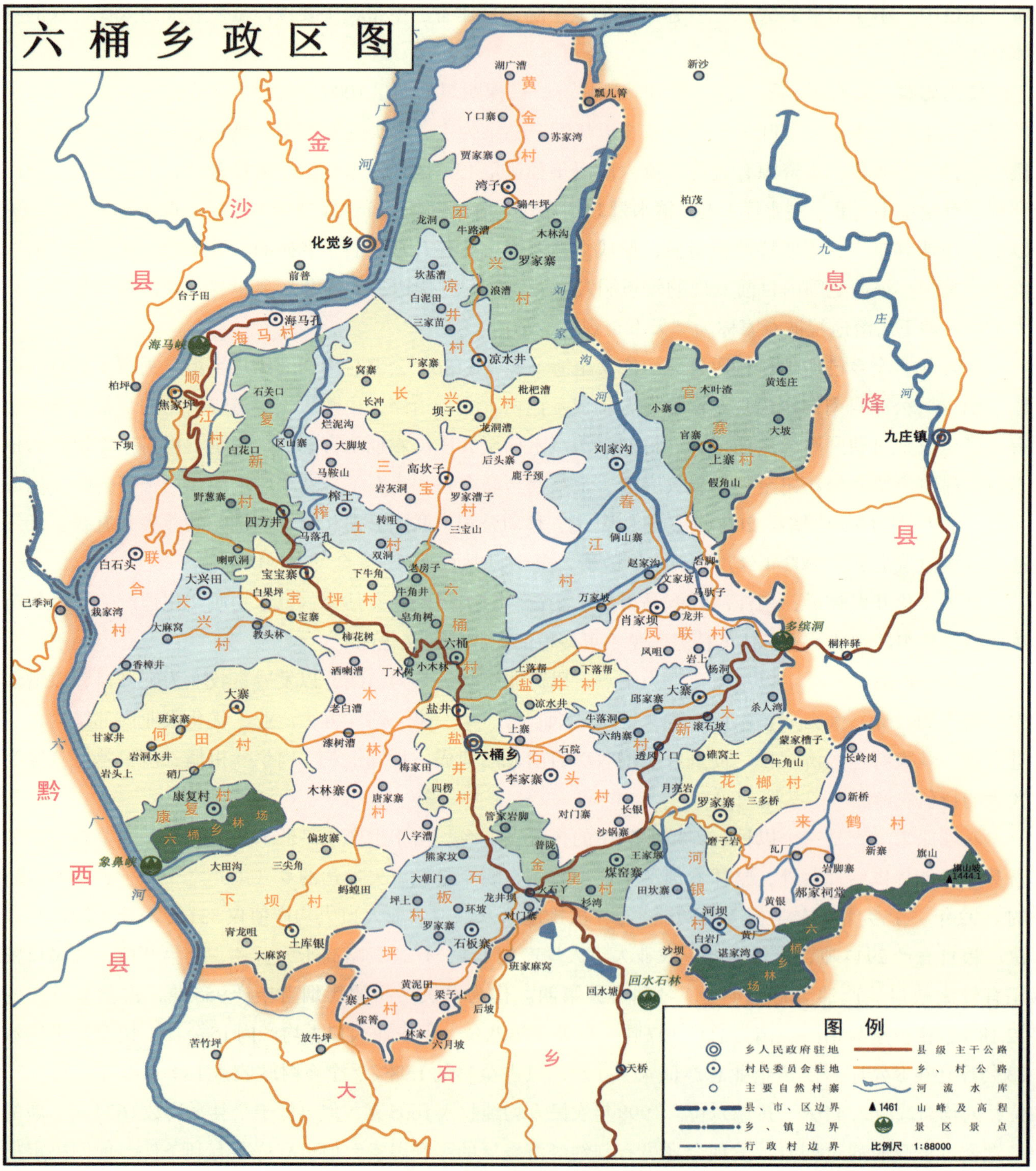

使畜牧业产值达3712万元，在1992年266万元的基础上增长12.95倍，在农业总产值中占28.98%。粮食总产1.35万吨，其中夏粮比重高达35.69%，排位全县第一。农业人口人均产粮486公斤，仅次于六屯乡，升位第二。生产烤烟1285吨，占全县总产的33.63%。产油菜籽1247吨，占19.78%，产猪、牛、羊、兔、禽肉1846吨，名列第四。乡级财政收入711万元，处第7位。农民人均纯收入4716元，在1992年基础上增长1.94倍。

第四节　行政村和社区

一、行政村

王官村　位于龙场镇南面，东邻贵州铝厂一矿，南接中哨坝村和马口村，西面和北面与建新村接壤。境内主要有王官、大路边和唐家猫山等自然村寨。村委会驻王官寨上，距龙场镇政府5公里。辖7个村民组，2010年有村民332户1175人。

村境地形东高西低，东部多山、西部为较平坦的王官田坝，土地面积3.57平方公里。有耕地911亩，其中水田609亩，旱地302亩。农作物主要有水稻、玉米、油菜、小麦、马铃薯、番茄（西红柿）等。其中番茄种植较有规模，是县内延晚番茄种植基地中心。

王官延晚番茄

矿产资源主要有铝矾土、铁矿、重晶石等。驻村企业主要有贵州铝厂一矿和童家桥铁厂、磨料厂、砂厂和商砼厂等。

村内有小（Ⅱ）型水库1座，兴利库容61.5万立方米；另有童家桥山塘和小冲山塘。主干渠从王官水库起流经王官至大路边，总长2.5公里。

省道粑（粑坳）修（文）公路由村境东部经过，于蒋家龙滩分道经童家桥撒金坡可至贵铝一矿、小山、五龙寺、中哨坝等地；另一条从新场上经过唐家猫山、王官水库大坝至童家桥公路。3条公路形成1个“△”形，构成村内交通网。

建新村　位于龙场镇南面，东南邻王官村，南连马口村，西接木厂村，北和东北与新寨村接壤。境内主要有新场上、猫山脚、祖师店、龙潭、杉树林、香炉田、大麻窝等自然村寨。村委会驻新场上，距龙场镇政府3公里。下辖12个村民组，2010年有村民528户1952人。

村境地形西部多山、东部为平地，土地面积3.85平方公里，有耕地1400亩，其中水田738亩，旱地662亩。农作物主要有水稻、玉米、油菜、小麦、番茄、马铃薯等。水稻为主要农产品，产区分布在门口田坝、下干坝、小麻窝（牛吃水）、祖师店和杉树林田坝。有名的王官梨产于新场上。

建新村境内的王官糖梨

农业灌溉主要靠王官水库和瓦罐窑河之水。主干渠有从王官水库经王官至新场上、至祖师店、至杉树林和金龙水库瓦罐窑至新场上等，总长约7公里。

矿产资源主要有煤炭、铝矾土、铁矿、重晶石等。驻村企业有大麻窝铁厂、兴林耐火厂、三脚山砂厂等。

省道粑（粑坳）修（文）公路自南向北纵贯村境，为境内主干线，并于两侧分出有王官经杉树林至香炉田、王官至祖师店、新场上至祖师店、新场上至王官水库、新场上经小麻窝至大麻窝、新场上至猫山脚和新场上经小河沟至大麻窝等乡村公路。此外通往村内各大田坝均有水泥机耕道。

马口村 位于龙场镇南面，东邻中哨坝村，南接中哨村，西连茶田村、干坝村，北抵建新村、王官村。境内主要有马口、祠堂湾子、路家山、包家寨等自然村寨。村委会驻马口，距龙场镇政府5公里。下辖5个村民组，2010年有村民347户1238人。

村境地形东、西两面多山，南北纵向较平坦。土地面积3.89平方公里，有耕地1320亩，其中水田550亩，旱地770亩。农作物主要有水稻、玉米、油菜、小麦、番茄、马铃薯等。蔬菜种植面积较大，品种有晚番茄、辣椒、大葱等。

省道粑（粑坳）修（文）公路自南向北纵贯村境，成为境内主干线，并于村南分一岔道乡村公路通往茶田村和杨寨村。

中哨村 位于龙场镇南面，东靠中哨坝村，南邻白云区麦架乡摆茅村，西连茶田村，北接马口村。境内主要有中哨、大湾、老龙田、落桂田、猪下巴等自然村寨。村委会驻中哨，距龙场镇政府9公里。下辖5个村民组，2010年有村民248户948人。

村境地形东高西低，山地相间，土地总面积3.4平方公里，有耕地918亩，其中水田438亩，旱地480亩。农作物主要有水稻、玉米、油菜、小麦、番茄、马铃薯等。经济作物种植面积约400亩，年产晚番茄50万公斤。全村水利多为山间自流灌溉，有灌渠全长12公里。

境内有完全小学1所。省道（107）粑（粑坳）修（文）公路自南向北穿境而过，村民多居住在公路两侧。

中哨坝村 位于龙场镇南部，东、南两面邻白云区麦架乡青山村，西连中哨村、马口村，北接王官村和贵州铝厂一矿。境内主要有中哨坝、苗寨、龙塘沟、熊家沟、王母屯等自然村寨。村委会驻中哨坝，距龙场镇政府10公里。下辖3个村民组，2010年有村民112户435人。

小山坝露天采矿

村境地形多山，是龙场镇海拔最高的村，平均海拔在1300米以上。土地面积5.68平方公里，有耕地536亩，其中水田143亩，旱地393亩。农作物主要有玉米、水稻、油菜、小麦、番茄、马铃薯等。矿产资源主要有铝矾土、铁矿、重晶石等。有乡村公路1条由中哨坝经大营坡至王官村接省道粑（粑坳）修（文）公路。

杨寨村 位于龙场镇西南面，东接茶田村，南与白云区麦架乡摆茅村毗邻，西隔猫跳河与清镇市麦格乡谷荡拜村相望，北抵干坝村。境内主要有杨家寨（杨寨）、上坝桥、卜家寨、唐家寨、下坝、屙尿冲、斗篷山、水淹冲等自然村寨。村委会驻杨家寨，距龙场镇政府10公里。下辖4个村民组，2010年有村民227户1042人。

村境地形多山，土地面积6.69平方公里，有耕地1277亩，其中水田389亩，旱地888亩。农作物主要有水稻、玉米、油菜、小麦、番茄、马铃薯等。

矿产资源主要有煤、铝矾土、铁矿等。农业灌溉有从杨寨河上游建石坝拦河水筑1000米长的防渗沟进行灌溉。有乡村公路1条由杨寨经茶田村至马口村接省道（107）粑（粑坳）修（文）公路。

茶田村 位于龙场镇西南面，东邻中哨村，南抵白云区麦架乡摆茅村，西连杨寨村，北接木厂村和马口村。境内主要有烧茶田、烂坝、大路丫口、麻窝寨等自然村寨。村委会驻烧茶田，距龙场镇政府7公里。下辖3个村民组，2010年有村民109户427人。

村境地形多山，西高东低，田少土多。土地面积2.29平方公里，有耕地459亩，其中水田112亩，旱地347亩。农作物主要有玉米、水稻、油菜、小麦、番茄、马铃薯等。水利工程有1997年建岩脚田提水站1座，1999年建茶田下湾提水站1座，全村有灌渠6公里。交通有马口至杨寨乡村公路穿境而过。

干坝村 位于龙场镇西南面，东邻茶田村，南接杨寨村，西隔猫跳河与清镇市麦格乡大谷佐村相望，北抵三级（修文）电站和木厂村。境内主要有干坝、比例坝、龙坝麻窝、箐头、众山、石门坎等自然村寨。村委会驻干坝，距龙场镇政府6公里。下辖5个村民组，2010年有村民186户776人。

村境地形多山，历来缺水，田少土多，故称“干坝”。土地面积6.17平方公里，有耕地1349亩，其中水田216亩，旱地1133亩。农作物主要有玉米、水稻、油菜、小麦、马铃薯、番茄、红薯等。2002年修建1条从西南向东北走向的人畜引水工程，解决了全村人畜引水问题。村内乡村公路连接可通各组，南与茶田、杨寨村相连，北与三级电站、木厂村相通。

猫跳河人行铁索桥

木厂村 位于龙场镇南面，东邻建新村、马口村，南抵茶田村，西南连干坝村，北接沙溪村。境内主要有田坝、陇箐、大麻窝、生冲、栗木山、半坡、下坝、苦竹山、箐头、木厂、倒沟井等自然村寨。村委会驻田坝，距龙场镇政府5公里。下辖5个村民组，2010年有村民211户695人。

村境地形多山、缺水。土地面积5.24平方公里，有耕地774亩，其中水田261亩，旱地513亩。农作物主要有玉米、水稻、油菜、小麦、马铃薯、红薯、番茄等。小河沟至三级电站公路从由东北向西南穿境而过，与村境内乡村公路连接可通各组。

新寨村 位于龙场镇东南面，东邻小山村，南抵建新村和贵州铝厂一矿，西连沙溪村，北接新春村和新水村。境内主要有陈家寨、白岩寨、元宝寨、瓦罐窑、小河沟、磅称房、九门寨、小沟等自然村寨。村委会驻陈家寨，距龙场镇政府2.5公里。下辖13个村民组，2010年有村民681户2171人。

村境地形东西两面多山，大部分地区较平坦，土地面积6.7平方公里，有耕地2144亩，其中水田1306亩，旱地838亩。农作物主要有水稻、玉米、油菜、小麦、番茄、马铃薯等。矿产资源主要有煤、铁矿和重晶石等。驻村企业主要有贵阳煤矿和三角山水泥厂。省道粑（粑坳）修（文）公路自南向北纵贯村境，为境内主干道，并于两侧分出有三角山往东经元宝寨至瓦罐窑和三角山往西经小河沟至猫跳河三、四、五级电站公路。通往村内各组和各大田坝均修通串户路和水泥机耕道。

新春村　位于龙场镇南面、县城南面，地处城乡接合部，东邻新水村，南接新寨村，西连沙溪村，北抵县城龙场和城南村。境内主要有砖瓦厂、小岩口、毛栗园、玩易窝、油萝街、黄秧寨、吴家湾等自然村寨。村委会驻吴家湾，距龙场镇政府1公里。下辖6个村民组，2010年有村民705户2456人。

村境地形大部分地区较为平坦，土地面积2.64平方公里，有耕地1383亩，其中水田899亩，旱地484亩。农作物主要有水稻、玉米、油菜、小麦、番茄、马铃薯等。矿产资源主要有煤和重晶石等，驻村企业主要有四达公司耐火厂和星原燃气厂等。省道粑（粑坳）修（文）公路自南向北纵贯村境，为境内主干道，并于两侧分出通往村内各组和各大田坝串户路和水泥机耕道。名胜古迹有明代哲学家王阳明读经悟道之处“玩易窝”，属省级文物保护单位。

新水村　位于龙场镇东面，东邻青龙村、程官村，南接小山村、新寨村，西连新春村、城南村，北抵阳明村、新生村。境内主要有罗家寨、山后、锥子坡、沙锅寨、水竹林、奚家湾、赵家山和蛤蟆田等自然村寨。村委会驻罗家寨，距龙场镇政府1公里。下辖6个村民组，2010年有村民705户2014人。

村境地形地势较缓，东高西低。土地面积4.49平方公里，有耕地1579亩，其中水田1101亩，旱地478亩。农作物主要有水稻、玉米、油菜、小麦、番茄、马铃薯等。矿产资源主要有铝矾土、铁矿、重晶石等。县城翠屏东路直达罗家寨，村境主干公路西接县城，东可通小山、高仓等村。穿山堰河流经村境，农田大部分属自流灌溉，境内有奚家湾堰塘1座，提水站3座，装机容量77千瓦。

2000年的新水村村貌

小山村　位于龙场镇东南面，东邻水塘村、高仓村，南抵贵铝一矿和白云区沙文乡靛山村，西连新寨村，北接新水村、程官村。境内主要有猪头山、砂坝、引子苗、大湾沟、龙井湾、茶树湾、水凹、赵家湾、野鹿坝、转弯土、梅花田、新寨、望天水、榛子林、五龙寺等自然村寨。村委会驻猪头山，距龙场镇政府5公里。下辖8个村民组，2010年有村民389户1332人。

村境地形东部多山、西部较平缓，土地面积11平方公里，有耕地1425亩，其中水田940亩，旱地485

亩。农作物主要有水稻、玉米、油菜、小麦、番茄、马铃薯等。矿产资源主要有铝矾土、铁矿、重晶石等。村内企业，多为民营采矿和煅烧。乡村公路横贯东西，东至高仓村，可通302厂一矿和1028厂；西经新水村可通县城。水利设施有山塘8座，采用提水灌溉，有灌渠3000米，防渗渠3000米。

高仓村 位于龙场镇东南面，东邻扎佐镇大山村，南抵白云区沙文乡龊山村，西连小山村，北接水塘村。境内主要有高脚仓等自然村寨。村委会驻高脚仓寨上，距龙场镇政府7公里。下辖3个村民组，2010年有村民146户593人。高仓村属民族村，村民全属苗族，主要是王、刘二姓。名胜古迹有“高仓古堡”，属省级文物保护单位。

高仓谷堡

村境地形多山，东高西低。土地面积7.21平方公里，有耕地593亩，其中水田296亩，旱地297亩。建有阁老寨水库1座，属小二型水库。农作物主要有水稻、玉米等。矿产资源主要有铝矾土、铁矿、重晶石等。村境企业主要是铝矿开采和煅烧。村内乡村公路纵贯村境，南通302厂一矿至王官接107省道，北通1028厂和水塘村，西可经小山村、新水村至县城。

水塘村 位于龙场镇东面，东邻扎佐镇石竹村、兴红村，南连龙镇高仓村，西接小山村、程官村，北抵大地村、马官村。境内主要有大寨、清水塘、木午、新寨 、栗木山等自然村寨。村委会驻大寨，距龙场镇政府7公里。下辖5个村民组，2010年有村民435户1425人。

村境地形东部多山，西部较为平缓，土地面积9.71平方公里，有耕地1710亩，其中水田939亩，旱地771亩。农作物主要有水稻、玉米、油菜、小麦、番茄、马铃薯等。

矿产资源主要有铝矾土、铁矿等。驻村企业主要有金兴水泥厂、棕刚玉厂、矿粉厂和1028厂4家企业。主干公路经1028厂横贯东西，西连县城，东接210国道。村境水资源丰富，穿山堰河发源于村境内东南，蜿蜒向西北流经村境，稻田多为自流水灌溉，在大寨大堰边、兴寨新桥分别建有50千瓦提水站，在三车碾建有30千瓦提水站，引水渠4250米。

程官村 位于龙场镇东面，东邻水塘村，南接小山村，西连新水村、青龙村，北抵大地村、平地村、马官村。境内主要有程官、小营上、邓家新寨、勒上、盛官等自然村寨。村委会驻程官，距龙场镇政府5公里。下辖4个村民组，2010年有村民526户1844人。

村境地形较为平缓，土地面积8.24平方公里，有耕地1967亩，其中水田1205亩，旱地762亩。农作物主要有水稻、玉米、油菜、小麦、番茄、马铃薯等。矿产资源主要有铝矾土、铁矿、重晶石等。内村企业主要有村办煅烧窑和私营耐火厂。穿山堰河由东南清水塘村流入，自东向西经村境流往青龙村境，农田多为自流灌溉，沿河另设有头堰、吉家堰，提灌站3座，装机110千瓦，主干沟渠10公里。经1028厂连通县城与210国道的县级公路由西向东横贯村境。

青龙村 位于龙场镇东面，东邻程官村，南接新水村，西连新生村，北抵大地村。境内主要有扁坡、沙田、挖浦堰、马家寨、小坝、羊场坝等自然村寨。村委会驻扁坡，距龙场镇政府3公里。下辖6个村民组，2010年有村民232户1014人。

村境地形较平缓，属河流冲积平地，土地面积2.07平方公里，有耕地999亩，其中水田841亩，旱地158亩。农作物主要有水稻、玉米、油菜、小麦、番茄、马铃薯等。穿山堰河由东面程官村流入，向西南经村境流进新水村境，农田多为自流灌溉，沿河另设有提灌站2座，装机47千瓦，主干沟渠8公里。经1028厂连通县城与210国道的县级公路由西向东横贯村境。驻村企业有落户羊场坝一带的3家冶炼铁厂。

阳明村 位于县城东北面，东邻新生村，南接新水村，西南靠县城龙场，西连城北村，北抵红旗村。境内主要有阳明新村、泥猪寨、黄家湾、东门大寨、黄家土、小冲湾、君子土等自然村寨。村委会驻阳明大道南段，距龙场镇政府1.5公里。下辖6个村民组，2010年有村民476户1746人。

阳明新村

村境地形较为平缓，土地面积1.81平方公里，有耕地513亩，其中水田364亩，旱地149亩。农作物主要有水稻、玉米、油菜、小麦、番茄、马铃薯等。修文河自东北向西南流经村境，农田多筑堰引河水自流灌溉。沿河还设有提灌站3座，灌溉较高处农田。村境紧邻县城，宽36米双向四车道的阳明大道自西南向东北纵贯村境，南连城区，北接贵（阳）毕（节）高等级公路。境内有享誉中外的阳明洞，为明代著名哲学家、教育家王阳明悟道讲学之地，属国家重点文物保护单位。

新生村 位于龙场镇北面，东邻大地村，南接青龙村，西连阳明村、红旗村，北抵红峰村，北部土地与马家桥部队农场南北纵向平行。境内主要有路家河、高家新寨、黄家湾、郭家寨、黄家庄、徐家寨、大槽等自然村寨。村委会驻路家河，距龙场镇政府2.5公里。下辖5个村民组，2010年有村民480户1920人。

村境地形较平缓，属河流冲积平地，土地面积3.12平方公里，有耕地1060亩，其中水田610亩，旱地450亩。农作物主要有水稻、玉米、油菜等。修文河（此段称路家河）自东北向西南流经村境，沿河筑有断桥堰、尖角堰、碾子堰，引河水自流灌溉农田。另设有提灌站4座，抽水灌溉较高处农田。贵（阳）毕（节）高等级公路横跨村境北部，阳明大道自西南向东北纵贯村境，通往村内各组和各大田坝均修通进村公路和水泥机耕道。

大地村 位于龙场镇东北面，东邻平地村，南接程官村、青龙村，西连新生村，北抵幸福村。境内主要有周官、肖家坝、大地堡、弯刀坡等自然村寨。村委会驻周官寨上，距龙场镇政府4公里。下辖5个村民组，2010年有村民370户1406人。

村境地形较平缓，北、西、南3面邻水，东南面稍高。北面有马官河由东北入境，向西与马家桥河汇合后称路家河，西面路家河为大地村与幸福村的界河，南面穿山堰河掠边而过。村境大部分地区属河流冲积平地。土地面积2.62平方公里，有耕地1038亩，其中水田874亩，旱地164亩。农作物主要有水稻、玉米、油菜等。村内农灌主要引洗马堰、弯刀堰河水自流灌溉。村境公路主干道向西连通县城，向东经1028厂接210国道。

幸福村 位于龙场镇东北面，东邻平地村，南接大地村、新生村，西连马家桥部队农场，北抵白莲村。境内主要有汪家寨、明家坝、水堰庄、周家寨、龙头坡等自然村寨。村委会驻汪家寨，距龙场镇政府4公里。下辖8个村民组，2010年有村民392户1472人。

村境地形较平缓，东部多水田，西部多旱地。土地面积1.51平方公里，有耕地805亩，其中水田736亩，旱地69亩。农作物主要有水稻、玉米、油菜马铃薯等。修文河（此段称马家桥河）从村东边缘流过，农田主要靠提河水灌溉，沿河建有电力提水站2座。全村沟渠相连，灌渠长4800米。公路主要有305省道顺村西而过，南接阳明大道可通县城，北至久长接210国道。贵（阳）毕（节）高等级公路由东向西横贯村境。进村公路和机耕道四通八达。驻村企业主要是矿粉厂和砖厂。

平地村 位于龙场镇东北面，东邻马官村，南接大地村、程官村，西连幸福村，北抵白莲村。境内主要有平地、尖山脚、白杨树、湾子头、弯刀岩、营盘山、大堰、吕家堰等自然村寨。村委会驻尖坡脚，距龙场镇政府5公里。下辖6个村民组，2010年有村民317户1230人。

村境地形东部稍高，西部多为河流冲积平地。马官河由东北向西南穿境而过，马家桥河自北向南掠过西部边境，营盘山水库位于村东，农田大多为自流灌溉。土地面积3.5平方公里，有耕地449亩，其中水田322亩，旱地127亩。农作物主要有水稻、玉米、油菜、马铃薯等。贵（阳）毕（节）高等级公路由东向西横贯村境。进村公路和机耕道四通八达。村境企业有砖厂、水泥厂各1家。村内著名山峰营盘山，山势不高，因古代山顶设过军营而得名，山后东北面建有一水库名“营盘山水库”，水库东面建有一仿古江浙风格山庄，取名“阳明精舍”，系深圳行政学院教授蒋庆所建并于此研究儒学及阳明文化。

平地村苗族刺绣

白莲村 位于龙场镇北面，东邻马官村，南接平地村、幸福村，西连马家桥部队农场和新生村，北抵久长镇石安村。境内主要有马家桥、孙家寨、狮子山、白泥庄、艾家湾、文书寨、姚家寨、下坝等自然村寨。村委会驻马家桥小街上，距龙场镇政府6公里。下辖6个村民组，2010年有村民583户2480人。

白莲水泥厂

村境地形西部较高多山、中部较低、东部隆起但较为平缓。修文河的上游石安河由村北入境，自北向南流经村境中部。土地面积5.29平方公里，有耕地1473亩，其中水田1053亩，旱地420亩。农作物主要有水稻、玉米、油菜、马铃薯等。农田主要靠抽河水灌溉，沿河有抽水站4个，总功力110千瓦，全村沟渠相连。驻村企业主要有马家桥水泥厂、白莲水泥厂、生铁冶炼厂、杨家弯砖厂、艾家弯水泥预制件厂等18家企业。主干公路有305省道由南向北穿过村境中部，南接阳明大道可通县城，北至久长接210国道。村境西部往南至新生村一带，抗日战争时期辟为军事驻地，直至20世纪80年代才改为贵州省军区农场。

军民村　位于龙场镇东北面，东连普陀村、马官村，南接白莲村，西邻久长镇石安村，北抵下堡村。境内主要有火烧寨、后龙洞、大园、定盘寨、孔龙坝、碰头堰等自然村寨。村委会驻火烧寨，距龙场镇政府7公里。下辖4个村民组，2010年有村民334户1106人。

村境地形北部多山较高、中部由东向西为河谷地带，地势较平坦多水田，南部为低矮山丘，土地面积2.93平方公里，有耕地899亩，其中水田623亩，旱地276亩。农作物主要有水稻、玉米、油菜、马铃薯等。境内小河由西北普陀村流入，称“小桥河”，由东向西流经村境中部，于村西与石安河汇合后称“马家桥河”。小桥河上筑有黄家堰、陈家堰、老破堰等河堰，引河水自流灌溉村内半数以上农田；1971年建39千瓦提水站1座，可灌田200余亩。公路有305省道由南向东北纵贯村境东南部，往西南通县城，往东北达久长，另有修（文）扎（佐）公路于村境东南由305省道分路通往扎佐。

马官村　位于龙场镇东北面，东邻小营村，南接平地村，西连白莲村，北抵军民村、普陀村。境内主要有马官、烂沟、高塝、下堰等自然村寨。村委会驻马官，距龙场镇政府8公里。下辖5个村民组，2010年有村民474户1641人。

村境地形北部较高多山、中部和南部较为平缓，土地面积5.05平方公里，有耕地1167亩，其中水田839亩，旱地328亩。农作物主要有水稻、玉米、油菜、马铃薯等。村内河流马官河由东北向西南流经村境，农田主要靠筑堰引流灌溉和电力提灌。建有提灌站3个，总功率达153千瓦。村内矿产资源硅砂是建筑优质材料。驻村企业主要有马官砖厂、铁合金厂和耐火材料厂等9家。村内主干公路南有贵（阳）毕（节）高等级公路、北有马（家桥）扎（佐）公路，两条公路由东向西平行横贯村境。

马官高塝种植的猕猴桃

小营村　位于龙场镇东北面，东邻扎佐镇猪头山、中营、大园村，南抵龙场镇程官村，西连马官村，北接普陀村和久长镇上寨村。境内主要有小营、小营坡、大寨、小堰、团坡、瓦窑寨、白箭冲、后寨、美珠井、箐门口、石碓丫等自然村寨。村委会驻小营，距龙场镇政府9公里。下辖7个村民组，2010年有村民601户2178人。

村境地形北部较高多山，中部和南部较为平缓，土地面积8.08平方公里，有耕地1824亩，其中水田1517亩，旱地307亩。农作物主要有水稻、玉米、油菜、马铃薯等。村内筑有金沟、黑山、老虎洞3座水库，有可供灌溉的沟渠4公里。全村建提水站2个，分别配有17千瓦、30千瓦抽水机，可灌稻田410亩。贵（阳）毕（节）高等级公路横穿第三、四、五村民组，修（文）扎（佐）公路经过一、二、五组，乡村公路通各村寨。驻村企业有华飞公司氧化铝厂和龙翔公司轴承厂、利尔水泥厂等7家。

普陀村　位于龙场镇东北面，东邻久长镇上寨村，南连龙场镇小营村、马官村，西连军民村，北抵久长镇下堡村。境内主要有普陀、大水塘、响水洞、龙井、付家湾等自然村寨。村委会驻普陀寨上，距

龙场镇政府12公里。下辖5个村民组，2010年有村民363户1396人。

村境地形西北和东南部较高多山，东北经中部向西南逐步倾斜较为平缓。土地面积4.56平方公里，有耕地1161亩，其中水田804亩，旱地357亩。农作物主要有水稻、玉米、油菜、马铃薯等。村内小河发源于村西北部，向西南流入军民村境。全村有300多亩农田可引河水自流灌溉，另于龙井和响水洞各有1座37千瓦提水站提水灌田。村内主干公路305省道由西南向东北贯穿全村各组，西南通县城，东北达久长接210国道。村境自然资源主要有煤和山砂。企业以建材为主，有二中水泥厂、普陀砖厂和联合砂石厂等。其中普陀联合砂石厂的7个砂场，所产白砂为优质建筑浆砌用砂，销往修文、白云和息烽等地。

普陀村的普陀寨

城南村　位于县城南面。村境东邻新水村，南接新春村，西连沙溪村，北靠县城。村民主要居住在县域南面和东面。村委会驻人民南路，距龙场镇政府0.5公里。下辖7个村民组，2010年有村民672户2272人。

村境地形大部分较平坦，土地面积约1.13平方公里。1990年起，县城逐步向东片区发展，村域大部分地区变为城区，2010年，全村仅有耕地153亩，其中水田20亩，旱地133亩。农作物主要以种植蔬菜为主，20世纪50—90年代，全村耕地多为供应城镇居民蔬菜的主要种植基地。县城东片区开发后，耕地面积随之减少，以种植蔬菜为主的多数居民弃农改行经营工贸，因此人们称为“城中村”。

城北村　位于县城北面，东邻阳明村，南靠县城，西接潮水村，北抵红旗村、阳早村。村民主要居住在县城北部。村委会驻县城人民北路，距龙场镇政府1公里。下辖4个村民组，2010年有村民475户1804人。

村境地形西部高、东部低，土地面积0.03平方公里。1990年起，县城向外拓展,逐步朝东片区延伸，致村境东部拓展为城区，2010年，全村仅有耕地86亩，其中水田57亩，旱地29亩。农作物主要有水稻、玉米、蔬菜等。20世纪90年代起，土地渐被征用，面积随之减少，村民大部分转向工商贸易。

沙溪村　位于龙场镇西面，东邻城南村和新春村，南接新寨村和木厂村，西抵谷堡乡长冲村，北连潮水村。境内主要有上坝田、马家沟、小沙溪、郭家林、大沙溪、棕半坡、大冲等自然村寨。村委会驻上田坝，距龙场镇政府3公里。下辖5个村民组，2010年有村民215户1261人。

村境地形多山，东、西两面两列山脉南北纵向排列，两山之间修文河（此段又称蛮子河或沙溪河）自北向南纵贯村境。土地面积6.9平方公里，有耕地1276亩，其中水田566亩，旱地710亩。农

流经沙溪村境的修文河

作物主要有水稻、玉米、油菜、马铃薯等。农田主要靠筑堰引水和电力提灌，另有山塘1座，灌渠总长10公里。村内公路北接县城至郭家林，南接猫跳河三级至四级电站。2000年起，村民由农耕为主转为蔬菜种植和养殖，所产蔬菜主要供应县城，年出栏生猪2000余头、肉鸡3000余只。

潮水村 位于龙场镇西面，东邻城北村，南连沙溪村，西抵谷堡乡折溪村，北接阳早村。境内主要有三潮水、王家湾、白腊寨、朱家湾、双麻窝、冒沙井、尖坡等自然村寨。村委会驻三潮水，距龙场镇政府3公里。下辖5个村民组，2010年有村民332户1046人。

潮水村因三潮水而得名

村境地形东、西、北3面较高多山，南部较低，东西两山之间由西北向东南逐步倾斜。土地面积4.55平方公里，有耕地504亩，其中水田239亩，旱地265亩。农作物主要有水稻、玉米、油菜、马铃薯等。修文至六广公路（X184）自东南向西北穿境而过，又一条公路于冒沙井分道向西至乌栗。村内水资源丰富，修文河自东向西流过南部边沿，北部和中部有冒沙井、小龙潭等水源。村建有提灌站1个，大型抽水站2个，供居民和企业用水。村内名胜有三潮水和知非寺，属省级文物保护单位。

阳早村 位于龙场镇西北面，东连红旗村，南接潮水村，西邻谷堡乡折溪村、大堰村，北抵放马坪村、红峰村。境内主要有五里桥、下寨、上羊哨、堰塘冲、上同兴、蜂子洞、大坪上、观音洞、陈家寨、砂锅滩等自然村寨。村委会驻五里桥，距龙场镇政府6公里。下辖7个村民组，2010年有村民442户1385人。土地面积5.81平方公里，有耕地1331亩，其中水田711亩，旱地620亩。农作物主要有水稻、玉米、油菜、马铃薯等。

村境地形东南部和北部较高多山、东部至西部地势较低，由东至西有一条小河沟筑堰自流灌溉农田300余亩，其余稻田靠提水灌溉。修文至六广县级公路（X184)）自南向北穿境而过，为村境主干道，乡村公路及机耕道联通村内各自然村寨。

红旗村 位于龙场镇西北面，东邻新生村，南接阳明村，西连阳早村，北抵红峰村。境内主要有美竹寨、阮家寨、牛王庙、余家冲、彭家湾、周家寨、三棵树、桅杆坡等自然村寨。村委会驻牛王庙，距龙场镇政府6公里。下辖7个村民组，2010年有村民221户971人。土地面积1.85平方公里，有耕地760亩，其中水田627亩，旱地133亩。农作物主要有水稻、玉米、油菜、马铃薯等。

耸立在红旗村的将军山

村境地形西部较高多山、东部较低。村内有3座山塘和由西北向东南有2条小河，农田大多靠自流灌溉。村内乡村公路及机耕道联通各自然村寨。

红峰村 位于龙场镇西北面，东邻新生村，南接红旗村、阳早村，西连放马坪村，北抵花桥村，东北与久长镇石安村毗邻。境内主要有将军山、铜钱沟、中寨、五大块、燕子岩、高坡洞、孙家寨等自然

村寨。村委会驻中寨，距龙场镇政府7公里。下辖5个村民组，2010年有村民306户1196人。土地面积5.41平方公里，有耕地1064亩，其中水田552亩，旱地512亩。农作物主要有水稻、玉米、油菜、马铃薯等。

村境地形西部和北部较高多山、东部较低。村内有灯草坝堰塘和由西北流向东南的两条小河，农田大多靠自流灌溉。贵（阳）毕（节）高等级公路由东南向西北穿境而过，村内主干公路向东南经红旗村接阳明大道，西北可达放马坪村接修（文）六（广）公路。

放马坪村 位于龙场镇西北面，东连红峰村，南接阳早村，西与谷堡乡大堰村毗邻，北抵花桥村。境内主要有放马坪、场坝上、钱家麻窝、孙家寨、王家寨、塔山、熊家寨、大龙塘、大山脚、龙家田、陈家麻窝等自然村寨。村委会驻放马坪，距龙场镇政府7公里。下辖6个村民组，2010年有村民185户732人。

土地面积4.34平方公里，有耕地725亩，其中水田274亩，旱地451亩。农作物主要有水稻、玉米、油菜、马铃薯等。

村境地形相对较高多山，东部稍低，较缺水，田少土多，农田主要靠抽水灌溉。修（文）六（广）公路自南向北纵贯村境西部，另一条乡村公路自东向西横穿村境，贵（阳）毕（节）高等级公路自南向北穿境而过。

花桥村 位于龙场镇西北角，东邻久长镇石安村，南接龙场镇放马坪村，西连谷堡乡大堰村，北抵小箐乡崇恩村。境内主要有和尚洞、花桥、铁匠炉、杉木河、龙井、杨家寨等自然村寨。村委会驻龙井，距龙场镇政府9公里。下辖7个村民组，2010年有村民190户768人，其中苗族250人。

土地面积4.16平方公里，有耕地650亩，其中水田240亩，旱地410亩。农作物主要有水稻、玉米、油菜、马铃薯等。

村境地形东南高、西北低。修（文）六（广）公路自南向北纵贯村境西部，贵（阳）毕（节）高等级公路自南向北穿越村境东部。

花桥村境的花桥

泗溪村 位于扎佐镇北面，东接双月村黄土冲，西连久长镇杨柳村，南靠葛马村五组，北邻开阳县双流镇。村委会驻泗溪，距扎佐镇政府11公里。下辖13个村民组，有泗溪、高寨、紫江冲、岩山、苗寨、周家大坝和漆树塘7个自然村寨。2010年有村民377户1805人，其中苗族24人。全村土地面积4.13平方公里，耕地1628亩,其中水田952亩,旱地676亩。主要农作物有水稻、玉米、马铃薯、油菜、烤烟、萝卜等。

泗溪寨

境内有山王庙至高寨组1.6公里和泗溪至大坝组1.1公里大道2条，机耕道3条。主要矿藏有煤、硅，硅矿含硅量达98%。林地2600亩，主要林产品有杉、桦山松、马尾松等。水利设施主要有大石板堰、高外冲山塘、大塘水库及双洞其、花鱼坑 、吊井 、老虎洞4座提灌站。主干渠4条，总长8.5公里。人畜饮水工程有紫江冲沙井饮水工程和漆树塘蓄水池。

双月村 位于扎佐镇北面，东接六屯乡长田村，西连葛马村和泗溪村，南靠长坡村，北邻贵州省扎佐林场六屯林区。村委会驻顺兴场，距扎佐镇政府8公里。下辖7个村民组。主要有顺兴场、月亮山、小冲坡、西庙、小冲、弯铜鼓、尖山坡、斑鸠寨和黄土冲9个自然村寨。2010年有村民446户 1689人，其中苗族30人。

全村土地面积8.48平方公里，耕地1531亩，其中水田778亩，旱地753亩。主要农作物有水稻、玉米、洋芋、油菜、烤烟、蔬菜等。矿藏有煤，分布在西庙、斑鸠寨、黄土冲一带。森林覆盖面积2200亩，主要林产品有杉、桦山松、马尾松等。有县道扎（佐）六（屯）公路从境内通过。各组均有乡村公路连接，主干道有1组至5组4公里与扎六公路相连。水利设施主要有西庙水库、黄土冲水库、清让饮水工程等。

葛马村 位于扎佐镇东北面，东接长坡村大田坝，西连久长镇清水村洗马塘，南靠三里村，北邻泗溪村、双月村。村委会驻龙场坝，距扎佐镇政府7公里。下辖10个村民组，主要有葛马、河对门、马官园、芦塘寨、细林塘、中屯、岩上、螺蛳田、杨家寨、上堡子、龙场坝、坝上、傅家磨和龙滩边等自然村寨。2010年有村民576户 2137人，其中苗族30人。土地面积8.9平方公里，耕地1917亩,其中水田1165亩，旱地752亩，农作物主要有水稻、玉米、烤烟、油菜、马铃薯等。有林木2314亩。

葛马寨

矿藏有煤，主要分布在八组、九组、细林塘、中屯等地。水利设施主要有杨家寨、芦塘、野猫山、付家磨4座提灌站，并有锅底潭、付家磨、中屯、岩上、细林塘5处饮水工程。有县道扎（佐）六（屯）公路从农场坝通过经六屯到开阳，乡村公路联通村内各组。

长坡村 位于扎佐镇东北面，东接六屯乡独山村、高峰村，南连扎佐大河村，西靠金鸡村及葛马村龙场坝，北邻双月村。村委会驻下长坡，距扎佐镇政府10公里。下辖6个村民组，主要有下长坡、上长坡、下坝、王伍冲、龙井水、大田坝和水路坝等自然村寨。2010年有村民246户 1035人。有土地面积6.86平方公里，耕地1082亩，其中水田664亩，旱地418亩。农作物主要有水稻、玉米、马铃薯、油菜、烤烟、萝卜等。

村内主干公路东至独山村和西冲村接扎（佐）桃（源）公路，西至葛马村龙场坝接扎（佐）六（屯）公路。各组间均有乡村公路联通。主要矿藏重晶石分布在王五冲，含硫酸钡97%，储量1万吨。森林覆盖面积3050亩，林产品有杉、松。经果林750亩，主要产猕猴桃、金秋梨、艳红桃。水利设施有龙井溪流、龙井沟水碓边堰、长滩河堰和下长坡龙洞饮水工程等。主干渠有杨家寨至大田坝和后洞至下坝两条，总长7公里。

大河村 位于扎佐镇东面，东接六屯乡独山村，南靠乌当区新场乡尖坡村，西连三里村，北邻长坡村。有大坝河、庄子上、鱼井坝和小河等自然村寨。村委会驻大坝河，距扎佐镇政府6.5公里。下辖4个村民组。2010年有村民172户659人，其中苗族148人。土地面积3.98平方公里，耕地773亩，其中水田440亩，旱地333亩。主要农作物有水稻、玉米、马铃薯、油菜、萝卜、折耳根、辣椒等。

大河村农家乐及艳红桃

扎（佐）至桃（源）公路3.5公里经过村境，全村各组均通乡村公路，其中主干道2条，一条为扎六公路至小河2公里，另一条为扎六公路至大坝河1.5公里，均与扎桃公路相接。矿产资源有煤，储量30万吨。有林地2808亩，主要品种是松和杉。经果林2300亩，主要品种有艳红桃、葡萄、金秋梨、板栗、李子等。水利设施有大河堰、鱼井坝堰，大河一组、三组提灌站和引水主干渠4条，总长10.5公里。

三里村 位于扎佐镇东面，东接大河村，南靠小堡村，西接金鸡村，北邻葛马村细林塘。村委会驻三里，距扎佐镇政府3.5公里。下辖5个村民组，主要有三里、长冲2个自然村寨。2010年有村民236户870人，其中苗族101人，占总人口的11.6%。土地面积4.02平方公里，有耕地775亩，其中水田480亩，旱地295亩。主要农作物有水稻、玉米、马铃薯、油菜、蔬菜等。

主要矿藏有煤，分布在对门坡、长冲一带。全村有林地1500亩，品种以松木为主；有经果林150亩，均为梨树。水利设施主要有三里拦河堰、大桥提灌站、三家湾提灌站和看牛坡饮水工程。主干渠由细里塘至河关塘,总长2.5公里。

小堡村 位于扎佐镇东北面，东接三里村，南靠大堡村， 西连新庄村，北邻金鸡村。村委会驻小堡子，距扎佐镇政府4公里。下辖9个村民组。主要有小堡子、石堰河、二十亩、黑山坝和四大冲等自然村寨。2010年有村民479户1888人。土地面积4.74平方公里，耕地1239亩，其中水田919亩，旱地320亩。主要农作物有水稻、玉米、马铃薯、油菜、蔬菜、折耳根等。

县道扎（佐）六（屯）公路黑山坝至回头山段1.5公里从村境黑山坝通过，全村各组均通乡村公路。主干道2.5公里由新庄村经小堡村至扎六公路。主要矿产品有煤，分布在挖煤冲至二十亩。有森林面积1000亩，品种以松木为主；有经果林300亩，均为梨树。水利设施主要有拦河堰3处和马潮田提灌站、二十亩提灌站。全村主干渠3条，共5.5公里。黑山坝饮水工程建有供水池蓄水80立方米，解决全村人畜饮用。

金鸡村 位于扎佐镇北面，东接三里村，南靠小堡村， 西连马鞍村，北邻久长镇清江村。有金鸡塘、庙坎脚、对门寨和桂花树4个自然村寨。村委会驻金鸡塘，距扎佐镇政府5公里。下辖2个村民组，2010年有村民119户533人。土地面积2.88平方公里，有耕地539亩，其中水田374亩，旱地165亩。主要农作物有水稻、玉米、马铃薯、油菜、萝卜等。

金鸡塘大寨

主要公路有经小堡石堰河、新庄接210国道5公里，金鸡至马鞍接210国道3公里，村内各组均通公路。矿藏有煤，主要分布在大湾一带。有林地1100亩，经果林80亩，其中金秋梨50亩、猕猴桃30亩。水利设施主要有花园坑堰和赵家冲山塘、周文冲山塘、张家湾山塘以及花园坑提灌站、龙洞提灌站等。

马鞍山村　位于扎佐镇正北面，北邻久长镇清江村，东北和东南接金鸡塘村、新庄村，南连和平村，西靠猪头山村。主要有马鞍山、堡子头和梁子上等自然村寨。村委会驻马鞍山，距扎佐镇政府4公里。下辖3个村民组，2010年有村民146户627人。土地面积2.37平方公里，耕地541亩，其中水田452亩，旱地89亩。主要农作物有水稻、玉米、油菜、马铃薯、蔬菜等。

村境近邻210国道、川黔铁路、贵（阳）遵（义）高等级公路。全村各组均通乡村公路。古代川黔驿道过村境，今路段保存较为完好。主要矿产资源有原煤。有林地1050亩，树种有杉和马尾松、华山松。另有经果林300亩，品种有金秋梨、艳红桃、板栗等。

猪头山村　位于扎佐镇西北面，东接马鞍山村，南靠和平村小长田，西连龙场镇小营村，北邻久长镇兴隆村。主要有猪头山、小畲田等自然村寨，村委会驻猪头山，距扎佐镇政府3.5公里。下辖4个村民组，2010年有村民180户768人。土地面积3.05平方公里，有耕地492亩，其中水田349亩，旱地143亩。主要农作物有水稻、玉米、马铃薯、油菜、萝卜、蔬菜等。2002年建猪头村生猪养殖示范基地，养殖生猪300头，并带动家禽养殖，养鸡1万多只。

210国道有2公里从猪头山寨内通过，川黔铁路有2.3公里直穿村境，全村各组均通公路。村有林地920亩，主要品种有马尾松和杉。水利设施主要有大水地提灌站、大水地山塘和倒流水山塘等。

桥头村　位于扎佐镇中部，东接龙王村姨妈寨，南靠易家街，西连大园村，北邻和平村。下辖桥头街、小场口等3个村民小组。村委会驻桥头街，距扎佐镇政府0.5公里。2010年有村民327户1102人。土地面积0.31平方公里,有耕地416亩，其中水田245亩，旱地171亩。主要农作物有水稻、萝卜、蔬菜等，是扎佐镇蔬菜种植大村之一。

桥头村交通便利，210国道有2公里南北纵贯村境，全村各组通公路。水利设施主要有堰塘湾拦河堰和杨柳井提灌站，主渠道2条总长4公里。

桥头村石拱桥

新庄村　位于扎佐镇中部扎佐街东北面，东接小堡村，南靠大堡村，西连和平村，北邻金鸡村。村委会驻新庄，距扎佐镇政府2公里。下辖3个村民组,村民主要居住在新庄寨内。2010年有村民317户1160人。土地面积1.74平方公里，有耕地717亩，其中水田561亩，旱地156亩。主要农作物有水稻、玉米、油菜、萝卜、蔬菜等。村民除农耕外，多从事养殖业，部分外出务工和经商。

村主干道由南向北连接210国道经三岔路至石堰河，2009年新修贵钢大道由西向东横贯村境。矿产资源有煤，主要分布在大石堰、小冲岩。有林地170亩。水利设施主要有新庄堰、小石堰、大石堰、杉树湾提灌站等。主渠道1条由红卫桥经新庄至小堡村，总长2.5公里。

中营村　位于扎佐镇东北面，东接和平村和襄阳社区，南靠大园村，西连龙场镇小营村，北邻和平村。有中营上、西门桥、红卫桥等自然村寨，村委会驻中营上，距扎佐镇政府0.5公里。下辖1个村民

组，2010年有村民220户802人。土地面积1.87平方公里，有耕地224亩，其中水田197亩，旱地27亩。主要农作物有水稻、玉米、油菜、白菜、萝卜等。村内人均耕地仅有0.28亩，村民多从事农产品加工业或进企业务工和从事三产服务业等。

村境地处交通要道，贵（阳）遵（义）、贵（阳）毕（节）高等级公路经过村境；川黔铁路扎佐火车站坐落境内，火车站至铁路桥1.5公里铁路穿境而过。中营处于扎佐街区西段,道路四通八达,襄阳大道从村境通过；中营大街经襄阳大道至扎佐火车站1公里改造成中营步行街；串寨路一条由扎佐重晶石粉厂至西门桥，另一条公路由林家坡至水淹凼。水利设施主要有鱼梁河洋藿堰、鱼梁河下堰、敬家塘山塘、洋藿堰提灌站等。灌溉主干渠方家堰至洋藿堰,长4公里。矿产资源有煤，主要分布在黄花地，储量20余万吨；另有铝土矿分布在黄坟一带，储量10万吨。有林地1500亩，其中国有林场1000亩、集体林场500亩。境内工矿企业主要有林东矿务局贵阳煤矿扎佐工区、修文矿粉厂、警民矿粉厂、扎佐重晶石粉厂、林东矿务局扎佐站台、渝鑫水泥制造有限公司、兴达仓储责任有限公司、盛源公司、林海公司等。

和平村 位于扎佐镇东北面，东接大堡村、龙王村和桥头村，南靠中营村和襄阳社区，西连中营村和龙场镇小营村，北邻猪头山村和新庄村。有沙银厂、石桥街、小长田、扎佐桥头、北门、皂角树和黑神庙等自然村寨，村委会驻沙银厂，距扎佐镇政府1公里。下辖7个村民组，2010年有村民391户1613人。土地面积2.47平方公里，耕地300亩，其中水田259亩，旱地41亩。农作物主要有水稻、玉米、油菜、蔬菜等。村耕地较少，村民多从事蔬菜种植和农产品加工或进企业务工、经商和经营服务业。

村境交通区位优势明显，地处扎佐街北部,210国道穿境近2公里与襄阳大道、扎（佐）六（屯）公路相连，贵（阳）遵（义）与贵（阳）毕（节）高等级公路在此交汇，川黔铁路穿境而过。道路四通八达，小道有扎佐中学桥头至石桥街水井、小长田变电站至铁路边、小长田变电站至石桥街等。水利设施主要有石桥边提灌站和石桥街饮水工程。

大堡村 位于扎佐镇东南面，东接丁官村，南靠丁官村高滩河，西连龙王寨，北邻和平村、小堡村。有大堡子、牛角湾、董家湾和洞上等自然村寨。村委会驻大堡子，距扎佐镇政府2公里。下辖6个村民组，2010年有村民493户1801人。土地面积3.32平方公里，耕地1389亩，其中水田1070亩，旱地319亩。农作物主要有水稻、玉米、油菜、萝卜、蔬菜等。大堡子白萝卜远近闻名。农业产业结构调整后大堡村既是扎佐万亩无公害优质萝卜基地主产区，也是外销蔬菜种植主产区。村民以种植萝卜等蔬菜为主，部分劳动力从事工商业和外出务工。

大堡村白萝卜

村境交通便利，距210国道0.5公里，距川黔铁路2公里，距贵（阳）遵（义）、贵（阳）毕（节）高等级公路2.2公里，县道扎（佐）六（屯）公路1公里从村境通过。全村各组均通公路，主要有丁官村至电台门与扎六公路相接，民办景阳中学交叉口经丁官高滩河至把七。矿产资源有重晶石，多分布在大堡子旱地内及贺家山一带。有用材林地500亩，梨树林150亩。水利设施主要有三叉堰、蔡家堰。主干渠有

2条，一条称东沟，长4.5公里；一条称西沟，长4公里。扎佐镇四门洞佛光寺位于大堡村洞上。

龙王村 位于扎佐镇东南面，东接丁官村，南靠新民村，西连喻家街村，北邻大堡村。主要有龙王寨、姨妈寨、余家沟等自然村寨。村委会驻龙王寨，距扎佐镇政府1公里。下辖3个村民组。2010年有村民342户1121人。土地面积3.12平方公里，耕地1120亩，其中水田800亩，旱地320亩。主要农作物有水稻、玉米、油菜、马铃薯、白萝卜等。所产白萝卜个大、皮薄、清脆、甘甜，远近闻名。

村境紧邻公路210国道，一条乡村公路贯穿全村各组。境内地下水资源丰富，几处古井均为扎佐珍珠河源头，其中余家沟龙井日出水量达2400立方米，堰塘湾水库库容3万立方米。95%以上的水田可自流灌溉。

丁官村 位于扎佐镇东南面，东接把七村和乌当区新场乡下坝村，南靠新民村大寨，西连大堡村、龙王村，北邻新场乡尖坡村。主要有天生桥、丁官、后坝、高滩河、磨盘寨等自然村寨。村委会驻丁官寨上，距扎佐镇政府4.5公里。下辖8个村民组，2010年有村民349户1462人。土地面积5.86平方公里，耕地1396亩，其中水田996亩，旱地400亩。主要农作物有水稻、玉米、油菜、蔬菜等。村民多以种植蔬菜为主，外出务工为辅。

村民淘洗折耳根运往市场

扎佐至乌当区新场乡原航空工业部属371厂专用线公路5公里从村境通过，全村各组均通公路。村有林地650亩，建丁官村梨树种植基地，主要品种为糖梨和金秋梨。水利设施主要有高潮水库和高滩河提灌站、丁官提灌站等。

把七村 位于扎佐镇东南面，东接乌当区新场乡，南靠新民村，西连龙王村，北邻丁官村。主要有把七大寨 、对门寨、麻窝寨自然村寨。村委会驻把七大寨，距扎佐镇政府7公里。下辖5个村民组，2010年有村民209户802人。土地面积4.21平方公里，耕地695亩，其中水田487亩，旱地208亩。农作物主要有水稻、玉米、油菜、蔬菜、折耳根等。

村距县道扎（佐）六（屯）公路5公里，距210国道7公里。扎佐经乌当区新场往羊昌镇到乌当公路从境内通过。一条小道由高潮水库穿大寨、麻窝坡与至贵航集团501厂专用线相接，全长4.5公里；对门寨有1条长2公里的小道通往501厂区。矿产资源主要有硫铁矿。有林地1580亩，另有经果林617亩。水利设施主要有把七水库、牛滚凼山塘、尖坡山塘、张家井提灌站；主干渠有把七水库至丁官后坝水渠，总长4.5公里。

喻家街村 位于扎佐镇中心南面，东接龙王村，南靠石竹村，西连贵州省扎佐林场煤湾林区，北邻大园村、桥头村。主要有喻家街、清家湾、麦子田、上马寨、大马田、卖酒坡等自然村寨。村委会驻喻家街，距扎佐镇政府1公里。下辖5个村民组，2010年有村民234户980人。土地面积2.49平方公里，耕地323亩，其中水田259亩，旱地64亩。主要农作物有水稻、玉米、油菜、蔬菜等。耕地人均3.3分地，村民除农业生产外，有的还从事粮食加工、百货销售、饮食服务、机械运输、机械加工和外出务工等。

境内交通便利，210国道穿境而过，并与襄阳大道交汇于此；川黔铁路、贵（阳）遵（义）高等级公路近邻村境。全村各组均通公路。资源主要有煤，有林地500余亩，其中集体林场319亩。水利设施主要

有喻家街堰、黎家碾房堰、方家堰、尖山口堰、方家堰提灌站等。

大园村 位于扎佐镇西南面，东接桥头村，南靠喻家街村，西连贵州省扎佐林场煤湾林区，北邻襄阳社区和中营村。主要有大园头、银鸡坡、干龙洞和岩头寨等自然村寨。村委会驻桥头街，距扎佐镇政府0.5公里。下辖4个村民组，2010年有村民321户1149人。土地面积2.28平方公里，耕地428亩，其中水田368亩，旱地60亩。农作物主要有水稻、玉米、油菜、蔬菜等。人多地少，村民多兼营农产品加工或进企业务工和经商等。

村地处扎佐镇街区，交通便利，东有川黔公路210国道，西有川黔铁路、贵（阳）遵（义）高等级公路，扎佐火车站坐落在岩头寨西，襄阳大道穿境而过。矿产资源主要有煤、硫铁矿，煤多分布在甘龙洞、豺狗冲、冒沙井一带，属有烟煤；硫铁矿多分布在羊圈坑、唐子坡一带，属鸡窝矿。另有林地210亩，主要林产品有杉、松。水利设施主要有方家堰、珍珠河堰坎、撑腰岩提灌站、大石岩提灌站、岩头寨饮水工程等，主干渠有方家鄢、珍珠河、包包边3条引水渠，全长2300米。驻村企业主要有机制水泥砖厂和大园农贸市场。驻村单位主要有扎佐第二小学和扎佐镇卫生院住院部。

石竹村 位于扎佐镇南面，东接龙王村，南靠三元村，西连兴红村，北邻大园村、喻家街村、中营村、桥头村。主要有石竹哨、小冲、中坡、马老堡、右营、下寨、转山丘、青冈林、马老寨等自然村寨，村委会驻石竹哨，距扎佐镇政府3公里。下辖8个村民组，2010年有村民462户1969人，其中布依族403人。土地面积9.72平方公里，耕地1640亩，其中水田1181亩，旱地459亩。主要农作物有水稻、玉米、油菜、蔬菜等。

村境交通区位优势明显，210国道穿境而过，近邻川黔铁路和贵（阳）遵（义）高等级公路。贵州省扎佐林场、航空工业部万江厂、扎佐医药园区及部分医药企业专用线公路纵横与210国道相连，各自然村寨、村民组之间的公路均贯通与210国道和专用线公路。矿产资源有煤和铝土矿，煤主要分布在大麻窝、土地塘一带；铝土矿主要分布于白岩丫口。有林地4000亩，其中集体林场3000亩，主要林产品有马尾松、华山松、杉等。水利设施主要有八鸡堰、岩头堰、洗马堰、中槽水库、龙井提灌站、渴望提灌站、龙井饮水工程等。主干渠1条总长3500米。

石竹村快活林餐饮一条街

大山村 位于扎佐镇南面，东南接白云区扁山村、范家堰村，西连龙场镇高仓村，北邻三元村、石竹村。主要有毛洪、小冲、陈家寨、大山、旧苗寨、郭家槽子、田家庄、石板哨等自然村寨。村委会驻毛洪，距扎佐镇政府8公里。下辖8个村民组，2010年有村民434户1620人。其中苗族、布依族205人。土地面积11.24平方公里，耕地1280亩，其中水田835亩，旱地445亩。主要农作物有水稻、玉米、油菜、蔬菜等。

村境交通便利，210国道、贵（阳）遵（义）高等级公路和川黔铁路穿境而过，贵州省扎佐林场、航空工业部万江厂、扎佐医药园区及部分医药企业专用线公路纵横与210国道相连，各自然村寨、村民组之间的公路均与210国道和专用线公路相接。矿产资源有煤，有林地2000亩，非耕地3000亩。

新民村　位于扎佐镇南面，东接把七村大寨、丁官村磨盘寨，南靠白云区尖山村，西连三元村龙井沟、石竹村小冲，北邻龙王村余家沟。主要有大寨 、新寨、小寨、高寨坝等自然村寨。村委会驻大寨，距扎佐镇政府5公里。下辖4个村民组，2010年有村民157户721人，其中苗族、布依族658人。土地面积6.36平方公里，耕地568亩，其中水田494亩，旱地74亩。主要农作物有水稻、玉米、油菜、蔬菜等。

公路210国道从境内通过3公里，全村各组均通公路。有林地1650亩，其中国有林场1000亩。树种主要有马尾松、华山松、杉等。

三元村　位于扎佐镇南面，东接白云区流场乡落刀井，南靠白云区蒙台村范家园， 西连大山村和石竹村，北邻石竹村和新民村。主要有新街、老街、田坝头、夏家湾、对门寨、上进坡、龙井沟等自然村寨。村委会驻三元新街，距扎佐镇政府5公里。下辖9个村民组，2010年有村民455户1873人。土地面积5.84平方公里，耕地460亩，其中水田390亩，旱地70亩。主要农作物有水稻、玉米、油菜、蔬菜等。

三元村

驻村企业有贵阳高尔夫度假中心、大兴饲料厂、富源饲料厂、银星磨料厂、鑫益能石油支撑剂厂、中泰商砼和自立耐火材料厂等。村民除部分农耕外，大多数进厂务工。

公路210国道、川黔铁路和贵（阳）遵（义）高等级公路穿境而过，全村各组均通公路。矿产资源主要是原煤。有林地1100余亩，树种主要是马尾松、华山松、杉等。

兴红村　位于扎佐镇西南面，东接三元村老街，南靠大山村毛洪，西连龙场镇水塘村新寨，北邻石竹村马老寨。主要有小井边、下坡土、周家湾、吴家寨、夹湾、马老关等自然村寨。村委会驻小井边，距扎佐镇政府8公里。下辖1个村民组，2010年有村民94户402人。土地面积2.5平方公里，有耕地189亩，其中水田76亩，旱地113亩。主要农作物有水稻、玉米、油菜、蔬菜等。

村境近邻210国道、川黔铁路、贵（阳）遵（义）高等级公路，距离2至3公里，阳明洞至三元公路横贯村境，全村各组均通乡村公路。主要矿产资源有原煤。有林地1975亩，树种有马尾松、华山松、杉。另有经果林480亩，品种有金秋梨、艳红桃、板栗等。

久长村　位于久长镇中部，东接沙雁村和白窑村，南抵清江村、兴隆村和上寨村，西邻金桥村、北连驴坊村。主要有久长街和丫叉田、铜矿井、云南关等自然村寨。村委会驻久长街上。下辖11个村民组，2010年有村民371户1661人。土地面积4.19平方公里，有耕地639亩，其中水田312亩，旱地327亩。村内盛产玉米、马铃薯。村有林地973亩，其中经果林312亩。境内矿产以石灰石居多，为水泥厂和村民建筑提供原料。其次是煤，主要分布在烟灯坡至猴子岩大坡一带。久长村为久长镇政治、

川黔铁路旁的久长集镇

经济、文化中心，幼儿园和久长中心小学位于久长镇南街，久长中学位于久长龙山脚下。

水利设施主要有铜矿井饮水工程和位于金桥对门寨田坝中的久长人畜饮水工程，2003年3月，经改造后将久长人畜饮水工程改为“久长水厂”。并有田冲湾、周家大田、学校、金鸡山和湾子山塘。

村境地处修文、开阳、息烽三县的交通咽喉地带，素有“鸡鸣三县”之称。古代川贵驿道由此经过，今210国道、贵（阳）遵（义）高等级公路、川黔铁路、305省道在此交汇，村内各组均通公路。

沙雁村 位于久长镇东面，东与永兴村和杨柳村接壤，南接白窑村，西邻久长村，北与新民村相邻。有青杠林、分水岭、沙子坡、燕子窝、石门等自然村寨。村委会驻沙子坡，距久长镇政府2公里。下辖6个村民组，2010年有村民283户1178人。

村境地形北高南低，属低山丘陵盆地地貌。土地面积3.27平方公里，有耕地1542亩，其中水田712亩，旱地830亩。农作物主要有水稻、玉米、马铃薯，油菜，蔬菜等。有林地969亩，其中森林地47亩，灌木林922亩。果园11.7亩，其中猕猴桃7.1亩。有305省道穿境而过，各组均有乡村公路与道路相连。有蚌壳堰水库配套工程和支渠，通往白窑村白泥田的倒虹管、杨柳冲至燕子窝支渠和青石林至石门支渠总长3.8公里，有效灌溉面积400余亩。位于沙子坡的沙雁人畜饮水工程解决附近村寨人畜饮水和上百亩田的灌溉以及久长变电站的生活用水。驻村企业有捷克人办的贵阳富捷化工有限公司，主要生产黄磷，毗邻沙子坡有久长变电站；还有贵州华祥矿产有限责任公司，主要生产矿粉、磷肥，年产量3万吨。

新民村 位于久长镇东北面，南接沙雁村，西连驴坊村和石榴村，北与息烽县安马村以盐井峰为界，东与芦山村和永兴村毗邻。有扯泥堡、颈上、茶上园、野鸡冲、场坝上、黄土园、山背后等自然村寨，村委会驻扯泥堡，距久长镇政府4公里。下辖9个村民组，2010年有村民266户1209人，其中少数民族29户128人。土地面积4.72平方公里，有耕地1434亩，其中水田928亩，旱地506亩。村域经济以农业为主，主要农作物有水稻、玉米、油菜、马铃薯、萝卜、土烟、辣椒等。特产土烟叶梢长，叶片厚，色泽好，味纯、劲足，远销省内外；马铃薯产量高，个头大，色泽好，所产淀粉含量高；萝卜易种高产，个大皮薄，不空心，味甘甜，水分足，制成萝卜干，风味独特，远销省内外。

村内有林地1615亩，其中经果林157.2亩，以猕猴桃为主。矿产主要有煤、硅、磷和汞，煤主要分布在石人山南麓后林、大洼、新田一带及刘家大坡；硅矿主要分布于石人山、仰天窝；磷矿主要分布在盐井坡；汞矿主要集于盐井坡南麓坡脚。水利设施主要有盐井冲水库、野绿田水库、小塘弯山塘和野鸡冲龙洞湾提水站。各类干渠沟渠总长10公里。村境交通便利，接210国道的久（长）铜（仁）路，由西向东从山背后、场坝上、扯泥堡、茶上园4个自然村寨横贯村境。驻村工矿企业主要有坐落在上坡树的黄磷厂，位于上坡树东麓的久长变电站，野鸡冲背后石人山南麓的三阳冶炼厂，石人山的微波站和地震监测站。

芦山村陈济堂水井

芦山村 位于久长镇东北面，东接开阳双流镇同心村，南与永兴村相连，西靠新民村，北连息烽县永靖镇安马村。村东北为修文、息烽、开阳三县边界交汇处。有膀膀上、楂口山、对门坡、龙潭坝、陈济堂等自然村寨。村委会驻膀膀上，距久长镇政府5公里。下辖9个村民组，2010年有村民245户1138人。土地面积4.59平方公里，有耕地1160亩，其中水田800亩，旱地360亩。农作物以产水稻为主，玉米、马铃薯、油菜为辅。水田较为集中，旱地分散，是久长镇主要的水稻产区之一。

村境交通方便，305省道横贯全村，总长3公里，另有接省道的马蹄关至龙滩坝乡村马路。

水利设施主要有盐井冲水库、大龙洞提灌站和3处人畜饮水工程。主干渠2条共2000米，有效灌溉面积800亩。

永兴村 位于久长镇东北面，东接开阳县双流镇同心村，南连杨柳村，北与芦山村相邻，西与沙雁村接壤。有沙锅寨、鹿子冲、大坡脚、对门寨、林场等自然村寨。村委会驻沙锅寨，距久长镇政府5.5公里。下辖3个村民组，2010年有村民273户1265人。土地面积4.32平方公里，有耕地1508亩，其中水田786亩，旱地722亩。经济主要以农业为主，农作物主要有水稻、玉米、豆类、马铃薯、油菜籽、辣椒等。特产有土烟、折耳根、萝卜，其中白萝卜个大皮薄，脆嫩甘甜，产量高，年产量7.5万公斤以上，远近闻名。

永兴村叶辛春晖小学

永兴村是现代著名作家叶辛在“文化大革命”时期上山下乡落户的地方，其代表作《蹉跎岁月》在此成稿。村内兴建有以“叶辛”命名的春晖小学。

矿产资源主要有硅、煤、硫铁矿，其中硅矿主要分布在云盘山一带，煤和硫铁矿主要分布在野狗坡、捆柴坝、土地庙、猫山、老夫田、高外冲等地。有森林2042亩，其中自然林234亩，人工林1808亩，林木主要以松、杉为主。水利设施主要有老夫田山塘、鸡笼田山塘，鹿子冲提灌站；主干渠有蚌壳堰水利工程入境道涵管、盐井冲水库水利工程入境干渠、龙洞大坡自流灌溉沟渠、青坑提灌站水利工程入境沟渠等。村境主干道路横贯东西，东达六屯乡，西通久长。乡村公路南通杨柳村，北达芦山村、新民村，东北进入开阳县双流镇罗家坝，东南连接扎佐镇泗溪高寨。

清水村 位于久长镇东南面，东靠杨柳村，南与清江村和扎佐镇葛马村毗邻，西北与白窑村接壤。主要有清水寨、马落坑、后冲湾、洗马塘、治农庄5个自然村寨，村委会驻清水寨，距久长镇政府4公里。下辖10个村民组，2010年有村民296户1329人。土地面积3.53平方公里，有耕地1496亩，其中水田808亩，旱地688亩。还有可待开发荒山600余亩。

清水村民养殖的奶牛

村境地势北高南低，四面多山，中间坝子属低山丘陵盆地。农作物主要有水稻、玉米、豆类、油菜、马铃薯、萝卜、辣椒和牧草等，其中特别盛产马铃薯、萝卜和辣椒。有林地2600亩，主要林木有杉、柏、马尾松等。

村境交通便利，久长至葛马的公路纵贯村境，清水寨经马落坑至杨柳村乡村公路畅通。水利设施主要有洗马塘、回头山、官山脚、龙坑等处提灌站和四方井人畜饮水工程。主干渠一条，总长3000米。

2003年入驻的"好1多"奶牛场，饲养奶牛600头，村办奶牛场饲养奶牛200余头，两场年产鲜奶4800吨。2007年在三湾子兴建1个规模20万羽蛋鸡养殖场，产品主销贵阳市场。

白窑村 位于久长镇东南面，东邻清水村、杨柳村，南接清江村，西靠久长村，北连沙雁村。有木马寨（木把寨），告榨（窨鲊）、高坡、窑透底（窑下寨）、啸天龙、杀人坝（达人坝）、白泥田、周家湾等自然村寨。村民委员会驻窑透底，距久长镇政府3公里。下辖12个村民组，2010年有村民401户1370人。土地面积4.37平方公里，有耕地1454亩，其中水田933亩，旱地521亩。农作物主产水稻、玉米、马铃薯等。农副特产有青菜、辣椒、白菜、莲花白、破季豌豆、萝卜等。年产青菜20万公斤，远销贵阳。

久（长）清（水）公路自西北起经啸天龙、窑透底穿境而过，村内各组均通公路。村水利设施完善，建有木马寨山塘和周家湾、窨榨提水站，由蚌壳堰水库和清水村马落坑引水渠均通村境。

杨柳村 位于久长镇东面，东接扎佐镇葛马村付家磨，南与葛马村相邻，北与永兴村接壤，西与清水村、白窑村毗邻。有上谷龙、下谷龙、藏溪洞、杨柳井、侯家大坝、环山等自然村寨。村委会驻杨柳井，距久长镇政府5公里。下辖6个村民组，2010年有村民294户1297人。土地面积4.34平方公里，有耕地1306亩，其中水田765亩，旱地541亩。农作物主要有水稻、玉米、马铃薯、蔬菜。盛产蔬菜，以谷龙大蒜驰名。

杨柳村种植的蔬菜

全村有林地1500亩，其中森林地280亩，灌木林地1216亩。经果林763亩，以猕猴桃为主。村内有优质石灰岩，为各种石材的好料，藏量数万立方米，有部分村民开采做石碑出售。水利设施主要有中塘水库、上中塘山塘、廖家塘、清坑提灌站、下谷龙提灌站、鬼门关提灌站、消洞提灌站、龙滩提灌站和清坑人畜饮水工程。主干渠有侯家大坝排洪大沟、清坑水利配套沟渠、消洞配套沟渠等。境内地下泉水主要有清坑、鬼门关、消洞、龙滩4处，均属一个地下流域，泉水清澈透明，水质较好，冬暖夏凉。道路有久长至侯家大坝公路、清水村马落坑至杨柳井公路、牛老壳至上谷龙公路一至六组主干道路。

清江村 位于久长镇南面，有民谣称村境分界线为"三坡一岩云南关，老仡寨抵麻窝山，外加一块罗盘田，锁定东西北与南"。即大山坡、大关坡东麓为清水村、葛马村，盐井坡、黑打岩之南属马鞍村、金鸡村，云南关，老仡寨抵麻窝山以北归久长村、白窑村管辖，西面以罗盘田与兴隆村交界。辖有清水街、蒲塘寨、铺后寨、川洞湾、石湾、石龙沟、三坝、关田、刘家湾等自然村寨。村委会

清江村500多年树龄的大杉树

驻清水街，距久长镇政府4公里。下辖12个村民组，2010年有村民580户2137人。土地面积6.2平方公里，有耕地2919亩，其中水田1792亩，旱地1127亩。林地405亩，其中有林地364亩，灌木林地41亩。有果园64.9亩，其中猕猴桃14.9亩。农作物主要有水稻、玉米、豆类、烤烟、马铃薯、萝卜等。

水利设施有清塘水库、石龙沟山塘、恶丫叉山塘。主干渠渔久大沟，总长7500米，境内长300米，于石龙沟建三级提水站。全村提灌设施有大龙滩、大杉树、石湾、山坝、消水坑、蒲塘寨等6个站，总装机容量137.5千瓦。村境地处黔中要冲，古代川贵驿道、大道由此经过。今近邻川黔铁路、210国道和贵（阳）遵（义）高等级公路，各组间乡村车道均与210国道相通。2006年欧洲风情园苏格兰牧场于落户村境，拥有400亩森林及300亩牧场草地，属休闲度假景区，2009年9月开始营运。

兴隆村　位于久长镇南面。东接清江村、白窑村，南与扎佐镇马鞍村、猪头山村相邻，西与上寨村接壤，北邻久长村。有隆兴田、谢家坪、青山、林场、罗家田、猫洞、唐家坟、大坡、高坝等自然村寨。村委会驻隆兴田，距镇久长镇政府2.5公里。下辖9个村民组，2010年有村民430户1882人。土地面积6.03平方公里，有耕地1700亩，其中水田777亩，旱地923亩。农作物主要有水稻、玉米、马铃薯等。

全村有林地2308亩，其中果园1230亩，以猕猴桃、金秋梨、葡萄为主。水利设施主要有青山山塘、寨门口山塘、小关山塘、罗家田山塘、鱼广田山塘和高坝提灌站、大坡提灌站、鱼广田提灌站。主干渠有罗家田山塘配套沟渠和大坡提灌站配套沟渠，总长500米。贵（阳）遵（义）高等级公路、210国道和川黔铁路自南向北纵贯村境，全村有8个村民组近邻210国道，交通条件十分优越。驻村企业主要有高坝砖厂、柠檬酸厂、雅馨花卉公司和与久长、上寨村交界处的贵遵水泥厂等。

上寨村　位于久长镇南面，东接兴隆村，南靠龙场镇小营村，西连龙场镇普陀村，北邻上堡村、下堡村。有楼梯冲、上寨、油房、凉井、清水坝、小官坝等自然村寨。村委会驻楼梯冲，距久长镇政府4公里。下辖7个村民组，2010年有村民278户1355人。土地面积5.45平方公里，有耕地1498亩，其中水田661亩，旱地837亩。农作物以水稻、玉米、油菜、马铃薯为主。

村内清水坝一带营造有果园1200余亩，种植猕猴桃、梨、李子等。境内石灰石质优、量大，是贵遵水泥厂原材料供给地。村境东邻210国道，西部二关坝一带有305省道经过一、二组。村内乡村车道联通各个自然村寨。水利设施有周家冲山塘、干弯山塘、姜家湾山塘、大青岗山塘、唐湾山塘，其中干弯山塘灌溉面积最大，常年有地下水注入塘中。全村有5个提水站，4个人饮抽水站，渠系长8000米。驻村企业主要有位于久长、兴隆、上寨三村交界处的贵遵水泥厂（奇峰工贸有限公司），年产水泥10万吨；华宏公司，年产铁合金20万吨；许启光耐火材料厂，主要生产耐火材料。

金桥村　位于久长镇中部，东连驴坊村和久长村，南接上堡村，北与中心村接壤，西与山岔村毗邻。有新桥、对门寨、蚌壳堰、新院子、田家寨、小寨、大寨等自然村寨。村委会驻对门寨，距久长镇政府2公里。下辖9个村民组，2010年有村民614户2824人。地形北高南低，地貌多低山丘陵。主要以石安河上游河道流域两岸坝子及小寨、田家寨山地坝子为村寨聚居地。土地面积9.24平方公里，有耕地2242亩，其中水田1222亩，旱地1020亩。农作物主要有水稻、玉米、马铃薯、油菜、蔬菜等，盛产马铃薯，全村经济以蔬菜种植为主。

村境矿藏主要有煤、硫铁矿，分布于青龙山南麓窑子上和陈家大山一带。有林地面积6305亩。村境地下水资源丰富，主要有三岔田地下泉、大寨月亮井泉，水利设施有蚌壳堰水库、田家寨水库、火烤山山塘、小冲山塘、大鹅田山塘和田家寨库内提灌站、田家寨提灌站、潘家坡提灌站、蚌壳堰槽沟提灌

站、山岔田人畜饮水工程、鸡心石人畜饮水工程等。有蚌壳堰水库水利配套工程主干渠1条，田家寨水库配套工程沟渠2条。公路东接210国道，南有经上堡、石安至马家桥接修（文）开（阳）公路，乡村道路均已连通村内各组。驻村企业主要有金久水泥厂。村民自办企业有杨冲采石场、村林场等。

驴坊村 位于久长镇北面，东与沙雁村、新民村相连，南与久长村相接，西抵金桥村、中心村，北与石榴村交界。有落邦、王家河、大堰、龙灯坡、冒井、瓦厂边等自然村寨。村委会驻落邦长坡预制厂旁，距久长镇政府2公里。下辖5个村民组，2010年有村民358户1841人。土地面积4.13平方公里，有耕地1319亩，其中水田708亩，旱地611亩。农作物主要有稻谷、玉米、马铃薯、油菜等。

驴坊村肉兔养殖

矿产有硅，主要分布在项家朝、龙灯坡、照壁山、金盆穴等地。有林地1800多亩，树种以杉、松为主。其中，长坡林场700亩，老虎冲林场200亩，马槽湾林场幼林300亩，经果林603亩，其余系待开发的灌木林。村境处于黔中要冲，古代川贵驿道、大道经此，今川黔铁路、210国道、贵（阳）遵（义）高等级公路自南向北穿境而过，久长至大石高枧公路从村西穿向村东，是去珍珠岛度假村的必经之道，由此往西可分别通往大石高枧和小箐。水利设施主要有大冲坝山塘和后甫坝山塘，引水沟渠总长1.15万米。驻村企业有久长水泥厂和村办预制厂。

石榴村 位于久长镇北面，东连新民村，南接驴坊村，西抵中心村，北邻息烽县黎安村。有石灰窑、上灰幺、下灰幺、吴家湾、响水洞、羊马田、大关冲、徐家湾、石头关、牛敞坡、高家湾等自然村寨。村委会驻石灰窑，距久长镇政府4公里。下辖9个村民组，2010年有村民325户1311人。土地面积5.41平方公里，有耕地1294亩，其中旱地713亩，水田581亩。农作物主要有玉米、水稻、马铃薯等。

矿产资源主要是煤炭，分布在大关冲一带。有林地315亩，树种以杉、松为主。

村境地处黔中要冲，古代川贵驿道、大道由此经过，今川黔铁路、210国道、贵（阳）遵（义）高等级公路自南向北穿境。通往村内各组车道均与210国道连通。川黔铁路2号隧道坐落村境，长360米。地势北高南低，一条河穿过坝子入驴坊村。另一溪流从羊马田至响水河入息烽境，常年流水不断。水利设施主要有中路坝山塘、轿子山山塘、关冲山塘和大坡提灌站、石头关提灌站、梅家田提灌站、响水河提灌站。驻村单位和企业有久长火车站、修文县国家粮食储备库、贵州省石油公司沥青供应站、中义牧业有限公司、徐州国华公司等。

中心村 位于久长镇西北面，东连驴坊村、南接金桥村、西抵栋青村、北邻息烽县南冲桥村。有毛家井、河坝林、沙坝、龙家寨 、马家寨、崔家寨、断龙山等自然村寨。村委会驻沙坝孟冲，距久长镇政府5.5公里。下辖7个村民组，2010年有村民269户1225人。土地面积8.37平方公里，有耕地1258亩，其中水田411亩，旱地847亩。主要农作物有玉米、水稻、马铃薯等。

村境属高山丘陵河槽地貌，海拔1380米至1574米，河槽中间有1条溪流，发源于栋青村，直入村内蚌壳堰水库。有林地5914亩，多以松、杉、杂木为主，其中经果林470亩。矿产资源有硅和煤，硅矿分布在平子上、陈家湾、芹菜麻窝、贾角山一带；煤蕴藏在八湾一带。村境交通便利，久长至大石高枧、至小箐的公路由东向西横贯村境，各自然村寨间均有乡村公路连接。水利设施主要有蚌壳堰水库、烂木桥水库，有断龙山、毛家寨、沙坝和毛家井4座提灌站，主干渠有断龙山、毛家井2处。驻村企业有珍珠岛旅游度假中心和在枧槽坡兴建的久兴肉牛养殖场。

栋青村　位于久长镇西北面，东与中心村相邻，南接山岔村、茶山村，西接小箐乡万兴村、全兴村，北抵息烽县石硐乡猫场村。有林家寨、赵家革家坝、下段、尹家寨、冉家寨等自然村寨。村委会驻下段，距久长镇政府8公里。下辖4个村民组，2010年有村民340户，1478人。土地面积6.87平方公里，有耕地1389亩，其中水田577亩，旱地812亩。主要农作物有水稻、玉米、马铃薯、蔬菜等，其中盛产马铃薯。

栋青村莲藕种植

矿产主要有煤、铁、硅等，分布在赵家坝（小箐坪）一带。有林地4405亩，其中林地1971亩，未成林造林地1946亩，灌木林地485亩，果园3亩。有小溪流1条，由西向东经尹家寨、林家寨过田坝中心流入中心村。溪流上游是孟冲水库，村西有烂木桥水库，村南有尹家寨山塘。孟冲水库配套沟渠2条：一条经尹家寨至尖山，长1.5公里；一条至林家寨，长1公里。另有栋青提灌站、烂木桥提灌站及村的人畜饮水工程。境内公路从中心通往赵家坝公路长3公里，从中心至大石高枧和中心经岩鹰山至小箐路路段均已修通。

茶山村　位于久长镇西面，东接山岔村一、二组，南与兴田村四组相邻，西与小箐乡大林村一、二、三组和新场村龙滩接壤，北与栋青村相连。有大白岩、龙孔、后山、麻窝、茶山5个自然村寨。村委会驻后山，距久长镇政府11公里。下辖4个村民组，2010年有村民141户，636人，其中苗族8户36人。土地面积3.58平方公里，有耕地643亩，其中水田259亩，旱地384亩。还有可开发非耕地150余亩。农作物主要有水稻、玉米、马铃薯、油菜等。

矿产资源有铝、煤、石灰石、硅石等。地下水资源丰富，但水位低，自流灌溉面积较少。1972年岩鹰山水库配套工程实施，建50千瓦的水利提灌站一座，基本解决了稻田用水问题。提灌干渠3000米，自流干渠2000米。村距公路210国道10公里，距川黔铁路12公里，乡村公路连接5个自然村寨。

山岔村　位于久长镇西北面，东接金桥村，南与上堡村、下堡村、兴田村相邻，西与茶山村接壤，北邻中心村。有猫冲、山岔土、贾角山等自然村寨，村委会驻猫冲，距久长镇政府7.5公里。下辖3个村民组，2010年有村民91户379人，其中苗族27户120人。土地面积4.05平方公里，有耕地面积472亩，其中水田180亩，旱地292亩。农作物主要有水稻、玉米、马铃薯等。

山岔村养殖的的绿壳蛋鸡

村境森林覆盖面较广，有森林1900亩，其中经果林220亩。矿藏主要有煤和硅，煤分布在猫冲一带，硅分布在山岔、贾角山一带。乡村公路联通村内各个自然村寨，南可到石安寨、马家桥，东可通金桥、久长。地下水资源丰富，水田多属自流灌溉。有2处人畜饮水工程，保障全村人畜饮用。村副业主要以养殖绿壳蛋鸡为主，并注册为“岔沟通”品牌绿壳鸡蛋。

兴田村 位于久长镇西南面，东接下堡村，南抵石安村，西靠龙场镇放马坪和小箐乡新场村，北邻茶山村。有新田沟、白岩脚、桃子山、麻窝寨、黑石头、虾井、茶兴田、五指大坑、西坡、深冲、长坡等自然村寨。村委会驻兴田沟，距久长镇政府11公里。下辖6个村民小组，2010年有村民272户1080人，其中苗族52户，212人；彝族8户，35人。土地面积10.04平方公里，有耕地1220亩，其中水田350亩，旱地870亩。农作物主要有水稻、玉米、油菜、马铃薯等。

有林地7500亩，其中1100余亩种植经果猕猴桃，森林覆盖率达45%。矿产资源有煤炭和硅矿。煤主要分布在一、三、六组，硅矿分布在四组。全村6个组均通乡村公路。兴田沟黄堰河总长1200米，注入石安河。龙潭沟主干渠总长1200米、灌溉面积200余亩。

上堡村 位于久长镇西南面，东连上寨村，西抵山岔村，北接金桥村，南与下堡村相邻。有下堡、新寨、大坝、杨冲、大山东、小山东等自然村寨。村委会驻上堡（原名“老鸹堡”），距久长镇政府5公里。下辖8个村民组，2010年有村民318户1367人，其中苗族24户92人。土地面积4.71平方公里，有耕地1423亩，其中水田666亩，旱地757亩。农作物主要有玉米、水稻、马铃薯、油菜籽，烟草等，特产土烟。有林地1358亩，经果林783亩，其中猕猴桃230亩。矿产资源主要是煤，分布在村西挖煤冲一带。煤层厚4米余，质优，颇有开采价值。

村境地形山谷河流自东北向西南平行排列，东面五朵莲花山似一道高高屏风一字排开，石安河顺山间谷槽向南缓缓流淌，形成狭长河谷地貌，南北长3公里，东西宽2.5公里。农田依靠自流灌溉和机电提灌，石安河村境段筑有大桥堰、朱家堰、高天坝堰和建有新寨提灌站、上堡提灌站。有挖煤冲山塘、塘边山塘。干渠有老虎坡上沟、老虎坡下沟、猫冲万家门前至挖煤冲，土石沟、猫冲口至刺梨山脚土沟等，总长1.32万米。村内公路自东北向西南顺山脉走向纵贯全境，北行经大桥、鸡心石到落邦接210国道，往南经下堡、石安、马家桥可达修文。

下堡村 位于久长镇西南面，东连龙场镇普陀村，南与军民村相邻，西抵久长镇石安村、兴田村，北接上堡村和三岔村。有下堡、田坝山东、石硐口、半边街、河对门、水口寺等自然村寨。村委会驻下堡，距久长镇政府7公里。下辖7个村民组，2010年有村民408户1438人，其中苗族135户530人。土地面积5.63平方公里，有耕地1797亩，其中水田834亩，旱地963亩。农作物主要有水稻、玉米、马铃薯、油菜籽、烟草等。是久长镇水稻、油菜籽主产区。有林地2959亩，经果林240亩，其中猕猴桃243亩。矿产资源主要有煤，分布在村西小麻坑一带。煤层厚2米余，质优，尚未开采。

下堡村芦笙歌舞

村境地形山谷河流自东北向西南平行排列，村东五朵莲花山山脉与村西大西坡山山脉东西对峙，两山脉间石安河自北向南纵贯村境。田野阡陌纵横，自流灌溉面积达70%。石安河上筑有大桥堰、官坝堰、小坝堰、麻子河堰、长堰，还有山东山塘、小坝堰提灌站等，干渠总长6.5千米。公路自东北向西南顺山脉走向纵贯全境，上行经上堡、大桥、鸡心石到落邦接210国道，下行过石安至马家桥接修（文）开（阳）公路。

下堡系苗族同胞聚居地，民族风情浓郁，非物质文化凸显，是贵阳市“斗牛舞”的传承地，“芦笙舞”曾东渡日本，在东京等地频繁演出。乡土苗族诗人王占一经常以诗作歌颂中国共产党领导各族人民走向新时代创建的幸福生活，已集诗歌2000余首。

石安村 位于久长镇西南面，东邻上堡村和龙场镇军民村，南接龙场镇白莲村，西与龙场镇红峰村毗连，北抵久长镇兴田村。有石安寨、马道子、牌坊边、上大沟和下大沟等自然村寨。村委会驻石安寨，距久长镇政府9公里。下辖10个村民组，2010年有村民276户1276人。土地面积5.38平方公里，有耕地988亩，其中水田442亩，旱地546亩。农作物主要有水稻、玉米、马铃薯和豆类等。

村境地形西北高东南低，石安河自东北上堡流来，到石安寨后折向东南向马家桥流去。河上置有双沟坝堰、石安提灌站、大坝提灌站等水利设施，配套沟渠2.7公里；另有自流灌溉沟渠6条，总长7000米，自流灌溉面积达50%。

境内有森林面积3436亩，其中林地2034亩，灌木林地1402亩。建有果园354.3亩，其中猕猴桃33.8亩。村境煤资源丰富，煤质好，煤层最高厚达5米，主要分布在大沟，硫铁矿亦分布于大沟。经济特色是酿酒，石安白酒远近闻名，全村酿酒作房32家，年产量达100多万公斤。酿酒业带动生猪饲养发展，年出栏生猪1.2万头。公路纵横村境，东北经下堡、上堡村入金桥村境接210国道，东南行至马家桥与修（文）开（阳）路相连往西经新田村可达龙场镇放马坪村接修（文）六（广）公路。

石安村烤酒养猪产业

六广村 位于六广镇北面，系镇政府所在地，南与广城村相连，东南与中坪村接壤，东与中心村和东北与广义村、西北与滨江村相邻，西南与黔西隔六广河相望。村民居住点有六广街和大粪田、大麻窝、营山、后山、上南江、下南江等自然村寨。村委会驻六广街后山马路边。下辖松江、营山、上南江、下南江和合群5个村民组，2010年有村民615户1709人。土地面积3.46平方公里，有耕地1453亩，其中水田132亩，旱地1321亩。

六广花灯

全村处于六广河右岸大滑坡地带，地形南高北低，矿产以煤为主。村境交通便利，公路主干道除修（文）六（广）路（X184）外，西有六广河旅游专用线，东有六（广）高（枧）公路。农作物主要有水稻、玉米、马铃薯和豆类等；果类有柑橘、樱桃、杨梅、板栗、金秋梨、石榴、艳红桃等。松江组盛产柑橘，有柑橘园200多亩。松江观光园地处松江境内贵（阳）毕（节）公路出口旁，占地100多亩，种有蔬菜和果树，为次早熟蔬菜的生产基

地。驻村企业主要有营山煤矿和松韵山庄。村境还有六广中学置于松江组贵（阳）毕（节）公路进场路旁；大田医院坐落在合群组，是六广镇最大的卫生医疗机构；位于六广下街松江社区办公室背后的六广卫生院亦是六广镇重要的医疗部门。

滨江村 位于乌江上游六广码头东岸，西面和西北面与黔西县古胜村隔六广河相望，东面与广义村接壤，南面与六广村相邻。村境有老房子、方家坝、贾家湾、黄水湾、颜家湾等自然村寨。村委会驻老房子，距六广镇政府2公里。下辖4个村民组，2010年有村民325户1037人。土地面积1.20平方公里，有耕地351亩，其中水田305亩，旱地46亩。农作物以水稻为主，盛产柑橘。

村境水陆交通方便，水路朔六广河上行至贾家洞，顺流下达乌江电站，横渡至五显台；陆路六广河旅游专用线纵贯村境，为村内公路主干线。驻村企业主要是六广河旅游公司。

游客纷至沓来的滨江码头

广义村 位于六广镇中部，南邻六广村合群组，西连滨江村，隔六广河与黔西县古胜村相望，东靠中心村，北接大石布依族乡高枧村。村境属于山地梯形，全村处在一个大斜坡上。有打桶寨、干河沟、马家湾、高坎子、下广义等自然村寨，村委会驻打桶寨，距六广镇政府2公里。下辖5个村民组，2010年有村民403户1227人。土地面积2.11平方公里，有耕地935亩，其中水田475亩，旱地460亩，旱地中有370亩是经果林。

村内矿产主要是煤，大桥沟煤矿坐落在村上河沟边东南面，年产原煤3万吨。水利设施有山塘1个，提灌站1个，沟渠8条共5500米。农作物主要有水稻、玉米、马铃薯及豆类等，果类盛产柑橘。高（枧）六（广）公路由西向东贯穿村境3公里。另有乡村道路3条，全长1公里，联通村内各组。

中心村 位于六广镇中部，东与大石布依族乡联丰村毗邻，南与广山村和新义村相接，西与广义村和六广村营山组接壤，北与大石布依族乡高枧村相连。有朱家坝、中坝、下寨、龙家田、马家湾、水口寺、瓦房寨、啄啄岩、马槽田、阿祥寨、箐脚、后山等自然村寨。村委会驻地朱家坝，距镇政府4公里。下辖8个村民组，2010年有村民572户1797人。土地面积4.37平方公里，有耕地1690亩，其中水田244亩，旱地1446亩。

村境属于山地，由南至北呈坡地梯形，除南面和西面有梯形稻田外，其余均为旱地。东北部有集体人造针叶林林场1个，种有松树、杉树等，西北部有1条由东南至西北长4公里的小溪沟，经广义村注入六广河。境内富藏煤炭资源，是六广镇的主要产煤区，已探明原煤储量约800万吨，有6家煤炭企业在村境开采。经济以农业为主，主要农作物有玉米、小麦、水稻、马铃薯等，经济作物有烤烟、油菜等。修文至六桶公路（X184）县道自南向北横贯村境，全村8个组基本实现组组通公路。

新河村 位于六广镇西南面，东接新中村，南邻合营村，西南靠沙坡村，西北隔河与黔西县索风村相望。有马路河、桔子寨、木拢、茶山、大树子、坝底下、四坪上、陈家麻窝等自然村寨，村委会驻马路河，距六广镇政府7公里。下辖7个村民组，2010年有村民314户1086人。土地面积6.01平方公里，有耕地1190亩，其中水田208亩，旱地982亩。

村域经济以农业为主，农作物种植主要有玉米、大豆、小麦、烤烟、水稻等。农村产业调整后种植有300亩经果林，并养殖生猪，形成林、粮、家庭养殖同步发展。

六广至沙坡、合营公路经过村境3公里，成为村内主干公路，每日有4趟客车经过。串组路连通村内各自然村寨。

新义村 位于六广镇中部，南邻中山村，西靠中坪村，北接六广村和中心村，东连广山村。有马路边、十字岭、叉口洞、宅吉、高坎子、茶林、大岩头等自然村寨。村委会驻马路边，距六广镇政府5公里。下辖4个村民小组，2010年有村民269户865人，其中苗族8人。土地面积1.77平方公里，有耕地733亩，其中水田238亩，旱地495亩。有森林402亩。农作物主产玉米和稻谷。

村境煤炭资源丰富，叉口洞煤矿地处叉口洞寨。驻村企业有砂厂和4家砖厂。公路（X184）县道经过村境3公里，另有乡村公路4公里联通村内各组。

中坪村 位于六广镇中部，南邻中山村、松山村，西连广城村、新中村，北依六广村，东接新义村。有中坪、颈坡、桐子园、朱营沟、新田湾等自然村寨。村委会驻上中坪与下中坪连接处的中坪小学旁，距六广镇政府3公里。下辖5个村民组，2010年有村民273户870人。土地面积2.59平方公里，大部分耕地为坡地，面积984亩，其中水田185亩，旱地799亩。有林地264亩。经济以农业为主，兼营养殖业。

村境有丰富的煤炭资源，储藏量在20万吨以上，硫铁矿资源储量1万吨。贵（阳）毕（毕）高等级公路和公路（X184）县道横贯村境，并有村级公路3.5公里联通村内各组。

村内有两棵桂花古树，其中一棵胸径95厘米，高4.5米，已有百年树龄；另一棵胸径85厘米，高3.5米，树龄已有80多年。

广城村 位于六广镇中部，东与中坪村接壤，南与新中村相邻，西北和六广村相连，是六广街的南大门。有广城、大元头、太平寺、姚家坪等自然村寨。村委会驻广城，距六广镇政府3公里。下辖上广城、中广城、下广城3个村民组，2010年有村民158户539人。土地面积0.88平方公里，有耕地485亩，其中水田131亩，旱地354亩，还有可开发非耕地100余亩。

经济以农业为主，农作物主要有水稻、玉米、小麦、油菜籽，盛产蔬菜。驻村企业有下广城养猪场、刘家湾养牛场和下广城水泥砖厂。公路（X184）县道纵贯村境2公里，并有姚家坪至煤水坝便道1公里。

广城村生产的六广面条

新中村 位于六广镇西南面，东连中坪村，东南邻松山村，南与合兴村接壤，西与新河村连接，北面隔六广河与黔西古胜村相望。有西门坡、高炉、三角井、双水井、洞口上、杉林、龙洞、陶家湾、孟家寨、坪上、螺丝田、子江、大坪子等自然村寨。村委会驻高炉，距六广镇政府2公里。下辖10个村民组，2010年有村民357户1184人，其中苗、彝少数民族89人。土地面积7.33平方公里，有耕地1868亩，其中水田157亩，旱地1711亩。主要分布在坪上、孟家寨、螺丝田、子江等地。农作物有小麦、油菜、

蔬菜、玉米等；经果林有板栗、石榴、杨梅等。矿产资源主要有滑石粉、铁矿、煤矿，集中分布在坪上、螺丝田、子江、西门坡等地。

村境新坪水库始建于1976年，蓄水20万立方米，配套工程有混凝土沟渠1条，全长5000米，为新中、六广、广城等村的590多亩水田提供农田灌溉。

贵（阳）毕（节）高等级公路经村境段长2公里，新中至合营乡村公路全长4公里。名胜古迹有著名的贾家洞古佛寺，坐落在村西佛洞山。

新中村白花桃

合兴村 位于六广镇南面，南及东南邻洒坪乡五老山村和洞口村，西与合营村、新河村接壤，东北靠松山村，北与新中村相连。有下寨、椿菜树、上寨、环坡上、土垮、唐家田、杉树林、韩婆岭等自然村寨。村委会驻下寨，距六广镇政府5公里。下辖4个村民小组，2010年有村民255户867人，其中苗族3户14人。土地面积6.9平方公里，有耕地973亩，其中水田151亩，旱地822亩。农作物主要有玉米、水稻、小麦，马铃薯。森林覆盖面积约1000亩（含退耕还林500亩）。土特产主要有板栗，人工种植板栗约250亩。合兴林场面积300亩，木材主要有松树、杉树。矿产资源主要有铁矿、铝矿、硅矿等。有村内公路1条，由下寨至上寨村级公路长3公里。村际公路1条，由合营村至村内双山组，长4公里。

合兴村板栗

合营村 位于六广镇西南面，东抵合兴村、南邻洒坪乡青杠林村，西靠沙坡村，北连新河村。有大锅寨、堡堡田坝、芦稿冲、大坝、大竹林、陶家庄、麻圆7个自然村寨，村委会驻大锅寨，距六广镇政府10公里。下辖7个村民组，2010年有村民536户1836人，其中苗族41户198人。土地面积10.72平方公里，耕地1677亩，其中水田385亩，旱地1292亩。50%以上是望天水田。

矿产资源有铁、铝、煤、汞、锌、锰、硫铁和重晶石等。森林面积1000亩，以松、岩青杠、山白杨为主。老河田坝1500亩非耕地适宜发展种植中药材和养殖业。经济以农业为主，农作物主要有玉米、大豆、小麦、烤烟、水稻等。农村产业结构调整后已发展种植并挂果400亩梨子。水利设施有山塘4个，其中麻圆塘能蓄水500立方米，灌溉面积50亩。主干渠有大干沟渠500米。大戈寨至大坝公路1.5公里，广营（六广至合营）路3公里。

沙坡村 位于六广镇西南面，东、南与合营相连，北邻新河村，西面与黔西县马路河村隔六广河相望。有沙坡、大冲、龙井、油房4个自然村寨。村委会驻沙坡，距六广镇政府10公里。下辖6个村民组，2010年有村民195户725人，其中苗族155人。土地面积5.69平方公里，有耕地1021亩，其中水田68亩，旱地953亩。经济以农业为主，农作物主要有玉米、大豆、烤烟、小麦等。

农村产业结构调整后已发展有700多亩经果林，形成林、粮、畜结合的产业结构管理。村办企业有沙坡砂厂和砖厂。村际公路1条纵贯村境，长9.5公里，北连新中村，南达合营村。

青龙村　位于六广镇东南面，东邻团山村，南接岩脚村，西靠广山村，北连中心村。有岩湾、烂箐、樱桃井、贾家田、竹竿坡、后槽、桂花树、麻窝头、锅炉箐9个自然村寨。村委会驻岩湾，距六广镇政府10公里。下辖3个村民组，2010年有村民211户689人。土地面积3.26平方公里，有耕地998亩，全为旱地。有森林1000亩，可开发非耕地1000亩，农作物主要有玉米、马铃薯。

岩鹰山水库主干渠经过村境，长400米，宽60厘米，深1米，基本解决全村人畜饮水难困难。广田至德政的乡村公路经过村境，长0.5公里。另有岩湾至贾家田的乡村公路，长1公里。

广山村　位于六广镇东面，东连四寨村，南邻中山村，西接新义村和中心村，北靠青龙村。有广田、马家坡、大土、岩头上、官庄、后冲、大坡脚等自然村寨。村委会驻广田街上，距六广镇政府8公里。下辖7个村民小组，2010年有村民352户1221人。土地面积2.9平方公里，有耕地1292亩，其中水田184亩，旱地1108亩。村境地形为丘陵山区，海拔1100米，气候温和。农作物有玉米、水稻、大豆、小麦、烤烟等。村内企业有民营小型酒厂1个，水泥砖厂2个。

村境地处要冲，为六广镇的东大门，公路（X184）县道纵贯通村境4公里，贵（阳）毕（节）高等级公路横跨村境2公里。由于地理条件优越，交通便利，经营运输业为村民主要经济来源。

修文至六广、六桶的公路分道处

中山村　位于六广镇东南面，东邻广山村，东南与龙窝村和洒坪乡相邻，南接松山村，西靠中坪村，北连新义村。有十字岭、大湾、尖山、砂子坡、黄杨树、马家坡、后坝、下坝、店子上9个自然村寨。村委会驻后坝，距六广镇政府8公里。下辖7个村民组，2010年有村民372户1184人。土地面积3.14平方公里，有耕地1395亩，其中水田383亩，旱地1012亩。

经济以农业为主，农作物主要有玉米、大豆、小麦、烤烟、水稻等。岩鹰山水库灌溉支渠“红樱渠”通水后在村境段渠长2500米，流经三、五、六3个组，可灌面积增至60%。村境交通便利，贵（阳）毕（节）高等级公路横贯村境东西，公路（X184）县道由北向南掠村东面。

四寨村　位于六广镇东南面，东与小箐乡杉林村相接，南与小箐乡大坝村接壤，西靠龙窝村，北邻岩脚、青龙、广山三村。村委会驻猫洞，距六广镇政府11公里。下辖8个村民组，有上寨、三寨、四寨、敖家寨、旧堰、猫洞、李家寨、草鞋丫、大土9个自然村寨。2010年有村民280户902人。土地面积3. 8平方公里，有耕地1081亩，其中旱地990亩，水田91亩。农作物主要有玉米、油菜、小麦、马铃薯。岩鹰山水库主干渠贯穿二、三、四、五组，长2000米。

公路（X184）县道纵贯全村3公里。贵（阳）毕（节）高等级公路横穿六、七、八组，长1.5公里。村级公路经六组进村，穿越七、八组与（X184）县道连接，各组之间公路全部连通。

松山村　位于六广镇南面，东接龙窝村，南连洒坪乡上坝村和洞口村，西南与合兴村毗邻，北与中坪村接壤。有小中寨、烂窖、马家后寨、老虎洞、斑鸠寨、韩堰坎6个自然村寨。村委会驻马家后寨，距六广镇政府8公里。下辖11个村民组，2010年有村民337户1145人。

村境地形为丘陵山区，是典型的喀斯特地貌地区，土地面积5.27平方公里，有耕地1347亩，其中水田186亩，旱地1161亩。矿产资源主要有煤和铁。农作物主要有玉米、水稻、大豆、小麦、烤烟等。有两条长为1500米的岩鹰山水库支渠引水灌溉。公路有大湾至斑鸠寨和十字岭至小中寨两条，共长8公里。

龙窝村 位于六广镇南面，东邻四寨村，南接洒坪乡上寨村和上坝村，西靠中山村，北与广山村毗邻。有龙窝寨、砂土、大寨、团岩、龙洞、水淹塘、山王庙、木洞等8个自然村寨。村委会驻龙窝寨，距六广镇政府12公里。下辖7个村民组，2010年有村民450户1579人。土地面积4.52平方公里，有耕地1293亩，其中水田403亩，旱地890亩。农作物主要有玉米、水稻、大豆、小麦、马铃薯、大蒜和烤烟等，其中盛产大蒜和马铃薯。

矿产资源主要是煤，分布在龙洞、团岩、大寨等地。贵（阳）毕（节）公路经水淹塘。龙窝一组、二组、四组、五组有乡村公路在四寨连接（X184）县道。四组到中山村、五组到广山村通乡村公路。从修（文）六（广）公路岩鹰山水库干渠六号隧洞起有乡村公路通至沙土。全村公路共长11公里。

前丰村 位于六广镇东面，东与坪营村和团山村相邻，西北接大石布依族乡联丰村，南连广山村和青龙村。有丁家寨、水头上、芭蕉沟和后槽4个自然村寨。村委会驻丁家寨，距六广政府约6公里。下辖4个村民组，2010年有村民243户842人。土地面积1.8平方公里，有耕地970亩，其中水田135亩，旱地835亩。农作物主要有玉米、小麦和马铃薯。村内盛产生漆。

乡村公路通达各组，其中至大石布依族乡联丰村公路5公里，广田至元庆公路经村境2公里。

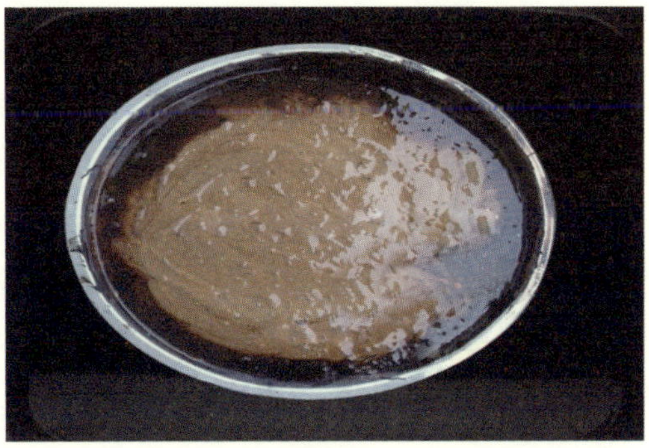

前丰生漆

团山村 位于六广镇东面，东邻金山村，南接青龙村和岩脚村，西与前丰村接壤，北连坪营村。有岩尾巴、半坡、丫口园、筑陇、东苗寨、马落岩6个自然村寨。村委会驻半坡，距六广镇政府10公里。下辖6个村民组，2010年有村民234户825人。土地面积3.33平方公里，有耕地1180亩，其中水田60亩，旱地1120亩。有森林190亩。农作物主要有油菜、玉米、大豆、土豆、小麦等。

村境煤炭资源丰富，其中嘉夸煤炭煤质最佳，享有盛名，已大量开采。村内乡村公路往南4公里可连接（X184）县道。

岩脚村 位于六广镇东面，东与小箐乡保山村接壤，东南与小箐乡杉林村相邻，南接四寨村、西靠青龙村，北连金山村。有岩脚街上、奶子山、朝门口、仡佬坟、羊角井、杉树坪、小白岩7个自然村寨。村委会驻岩脚寨，距六广镇政府10公里。下辖4个村民小组，2010年有村民271户971人。土地面积3.51平方公里，有耕地1219亩，其中水田91亩，旱地1128。有林地2021亩。经济以农业为主，兼以养殖。农作物主要有水稻、玉米、小麦、油菜籽和烤烟等。养殖业以猪、牛养殖为主。岩鹰山水库渠系贯穿村境，人畜饮水工程可覆盖全村。

岩脚村民养殖的商品兔

进村公路连通村内各组，全长10公里，往南于四寨村的三寨与（X184）县道连通。

金山村 位于六广镇东面，西邻坪营村，南靠岩脚村，东与小箐乡宝山村相连，东北与元庆村接壤，北隔何家大坡与大石布依族乡联合村相邻。有对门寨、长冲坝、关井、郑家寨、小白岩5个自然村寨。村委会驻堡堡上，距六广镇政府12公里。下辖5个村民组，2010年有村民372户1104人。土地面积3.45平方公里，有耕地1411亩，其中水田192亩，主要集中在关井、长冲坝一带，旱地1219亩。村境地形四周高中间低，中部为山间盆地，称作“坝子”。经济主要以农业为主，农作物主要有玉米、水稻、马铃薯等。

久（长）高（枧）公路由东向西贯穿村境，另有乡村公路与团山、坪营、元庆及小箐乡宝山村相连，村内组组通公路。

元庆村 位于六广镇东面，东、北两面与息烽县石硐乡接壤，南靠小箐乡宝山村，西邻大石布依族乡联合村，西南与金山村相连。有铁厂坝、坝子边、刘家屋基、岩脚、绿堰塘、徐家寨、大园、高家坡、箐口、长坡等10个自然村寨。村委会驻铁厂坝，距六广镇政府14公里。下辖4个村民组，2010年有村民382户1342人。土地面积5.9平方公里，有耕地1038亩，其中水田474亩，旱地564亩。可开发的非耕地资源有587亩。森林面积830亩。经济以农业为主，农作物主要有玉米、小麦、水稻、马铃薯。

有山塘4个，灌渠长5000米。乡村公路连通村内各组，共计11.7公里，西南可通金山村接久（长）高（枧）公路，西北可达大石布依族乡联江村连接大石至息烽石硐的公路。

坪营村 位于六广镇东面，东邻金山村，南连团山村，西接前丰村和大石布依族乡高枧村，北靠大石布依族乡联合村。有烂泥山、水沟、邓家大山、豆子槽、梨子塝、塔山、万家寨、苗寨沟、大干田9个自然村寨。村委会驻烂泥山，距六广镇政府9公里。下辖5个村民组，2010年有村民380户1266人。土地面积3.78平方公里，有耕地面积1470亩，其中水田194亩，旱地1276亩。经济以传统农业为主，粮食作物主要有玉米、马铃薯，经济作物有油菜、烤烟等。

有水库1座，库容量1.5万立方米，主干渠长1000米，可灌溉农田110亩。矿产资源有煤炭、汞矿、铀矿、硫铁矿和冰洲石等。久长至大石高枧的县道自东向西横贯村境2公里，乡村公路联通村内各组。

谷堡村 位于谷堡乡中部，东邻折溪村和长冲村，南接尖山村，西连下硐村和大寨村，北抵上花村和新场村。属汉、苗杂居地区，境内有谷堡、背水湾、新寨、干田坳、陈家弯、白泥田、龙井湾、下坝、杨家土、姚家沟、烂沟、高坡、韩家寨等自然村寨。村委会驻谷堡，挨邻谷堡乡政府。下辖9个村民组，2010年有村民388户，1431人，其中苗族179人。土地面积10.28平方公里，有耕地1410亩，其中水田455亩，旱地955亩。经济以传统农业为主，农作物主要有水稻、玉米、小麦、油菜、马铃薯等。

冒乌公路从谷堡村穿境而过

村境矿藏有铝矾土、铁和煤。有森林面积700亩，树种主要是松、杉、柏杨等。县城至乌栗县道由东向西横穿村境，村内公路连接各自然村寨，并与修（文）乌（栗）公路贯通。水利设施有烂沟水库，库容124.7万立方米，水域面积0.5平方公里，适宜养鱼。库水灌溉下硐、富裕、红星、水口等村耕地6000亩。驻村企业主要有新泉水厂、龙岗耐火材料厂、隰苑山庄、顺通养殖场、生物甲肥厂、三茗公司、白泥田矿山等。

折溪村 位于谷堡乡境东面，东与龙场镇阳早村和潮水村毗邻，南连长冲村，西接谷堡村，北抵新堰村、红焰村和大堰村。境内有折溪、古隆、对门寨、上寨、堡堡上、蛇田、凉水井、大丫口等自然村寨。村委驻凉水井，距谷堡乡政府3公里。下辖11个村民组，2010年有村民395户1581人。全村土地面积8.44平方公里，有耕地1509亩，其中水田814亩，旱地695亩。农作物主要有水稻、玉米、小麦、油菜、马铃薯等。

折溪村金秋梨

矿藏有铁和铝矾土。林地面积7342亩，其中金秋梨3235亩，猕猴桃1386亩。村以金秋梨、猕猴桃的质优味美被誉为贵阳市的“水果第一村”，古隆一带已成为全县万亩梨园中心。

修文至乌栗公路横穿折溪村蛇田、凉水井等自然村寨。蛇田至花塔公路贯穿蛇田、折溪、古隆等村寨。谷堡经万亩梨园至放马坪公路横贯村境，各自然村寨有公路与这两条主干公路相连。村内有古隆小（Ⅱ）型水库，库容70万立方米，水库周边山青水绿，梨树满园，故有“梨花湖”美称。

长冲村 位于谷堡乡东南面，东连龙场镇潮水村和沙溪村，南与清镇市麦格乡大谷佐隔猫跳河相望，西接平寨村和尖山村，北抵谷堡村和折溪村。境内有长冲、半坡、倒马坎、高石坎、上长冲、斋公山等自然村寨。村委会驻长冲，距谷堡乡政府5公里。下辖5个村民组，2010年有村民184户855人，其中少数民族41户174人。

村境地形南北山峦起伏，东西长6公里，南北宽3公里，中间形成一个东西长6公里、南北宽0.5公里的大谷槽，世称“十里长冲”。土地面积10.01平方公里，有耕地945亩，其中水田233亩，旱地712亩。农作物主要有水稻、玉米、油菜、马铃薯、烟草等。

境内蕴藏丰富的铝、铁等矿。有烂田湾水库，库容2000立方米。主干公路有从龙场镇潮水村至平寨村大垭口，由东往西贯穿村境7公里。驻村企业有营销股份矿业有限公司、牛洞矿山、大槽矿山、刘学卿铝矿。

尖山村 位于谷堡乡南面，东邻长冲村，南连平寨村，西接下硐村，北抵谷堡村。境内有上洞、鱼洞、尖山、杨坝等自然村寨。村委会驻尖山，距谷堡乡政府3公里，辖3个村民组。2010年，有村民196户973人。

村境地形山高沟深，溶洞众多，为典型的喀斯特岩溶地貌。土地面积5.46平方公里，有耕地1022亩，其中旱地622亩，水田400亩。农作物以水稻、玉米为主。

村内富藏铝、铁、煤等矿。有枧槽沟和芦稿塘山塘。在尖山、杨坝各建有一个电力提灌站。村内公路连通各个自然村寨，从箭竹沟至上洞3公里，马道子至谷堡4公里，上洞袁家寨至马道子1.5公里，谷堡至平寨穿过鱼洞和杨坝，再由杨坝分道至尖山的1.5公里。

平寨村　位于谷堡乡境西南面，东接长冲村，北连尖山村，西靠红星村、下硐村和平滩村，南与清镇市麦格乡大谷佐村隔猫跳河相望。境内有猫冲、木厂、七龙、良田、柏枝、梭坡、平寨等自然村寨。村委会驻猫冲，距谷堡乡政府8公里。下辖9个村民组，2010年有村民457户2074人，其中苗族152人。

村境地形北高南低，群山林立，沟谷纵横。土地面积10.63平方公里，有耕地1818亩，其中水田698亩，旱地1120亩。农作物主要有水稻、玉米、小麦、油菜、马铃薯等。有大山、陈家湾、莫家湾、三道沟和平寨山塘。主干渠有洪家堰大沟，经过杨坝、大桥、良田、七龙，全长4000米，灌溉面积350亩。

境内富藏铁和铝矿。森林覆盖率达40%，主要木材为松木。另有可开发的非耕地600亩。植有经果林2170亩，其中猕猴桃1800亩，杨梅250亩，柑橘70亩，桃梨50亩。

猫跳河梯级电站专用公路经过大槽、良田、七龙、柏枝、木厂，系村的主干公路，往西经水口寺、红林电站过猫跳河去清镇卫城，往东南经修文电站至小河沟与粑（粑坳）修（文）公路建设连接。另有连接主干公路的平寨经良田公路、梭坡至猫冲公路和木厂经柏枝公路构成村内的交通网络。

驻村企业主要有木厂矿山、竹林矿山、大槽矿山、窄巷口电站。有集贸市场一个，星期五为场期。

下硐村　位于谷堡乡境西面，东邻谷堡村和尖山村，南接平寨村和红星村，西连富裕村，北与大寨村毗邻。境内有后坝、黄杨树、上寨、柴山、麦子冲、张家寨、马家寨、烂沟、箭杆冲、老王冲、箐口坡等自然村寨。村委会驻后坝，距谷堡乡政府5公里。下辖6个村民组，2010年有村民205户875人。

境内多山多溶洞，属典型的喀斯特岩溶地貌。土地面积5.74平方公里，有耕地1131亩，其中水田225亩，旱地906亩。农作物主要有水稻、玉米、小麦、油菜、马铃薯、烟草等。矿藏主要有铝、铁等矿。

1988年成立下硐联户农场，董事长马怀麟，场长马一忠，技术队长马道静，全场技术队员163人。1989年种下桃子220亩，猕猴桃1400亩，枇杷380亩，相继挂果见效。下硐村开先河，最早成为全县猕猴桃种植重点村。

下硐村种植的猕猴桃

冒沙井至乌栗（X190）县道有1公里路段经过村境。箐口坡至箭杆冲乡村公路贯穿村境南北，分道连通各个自然村寨。1989年在黄杨树建防雹点，2004年建成下硐气象观测站，每天3次向县气象局报告数据。

富裕村　位于谷堡乡中西部，东邻下硐村，南连红星村，西接水口寺村，北抵大寨村。境内有上堰、姜家寨、张家堡、乌栗街上、保家箐、保家沟、白岩角、后水井等自然村寨。村委会驻乌栗街上，距谷堡乡政府7公里。下辖11个村民组，2010年有村民415户1680人，其中苗族19户64人。

村境地势东北高，西南低，南北为山，中为平川，东西长2公里，南北宽1公里，土地面积4.77

富裕村村口

平方公里，有耕地1000亩，其中水田520亩，旱地480亩。经济以农业为主，主要农作物有水稻、玉米、小麦、油菜、马铃薯等。

修文至乌栗县道由东向西横贯村境，并向西延伸至水口寺，经红林电站，过猫跳河与清镇市卫城镇连接。村内公路连接各自然村寨，并与（X190）县道贯通。

乌栗街上置邮政负责谷堡乡西片区8个村的投递、汇兑、报刊发行等。

民间文艺主要是乌栗花灯，属太平灯类，灯堂设在姜家寨。乌栗人爱好体育，擅长篮球，篮球队多次与其他乡镇比赛取得较好名次，属县内一级球队。

红星村 位于谷堡乡西南角，东邻平寨村，南连平滩村，西接水口村，北抵富裕村和下硐村。境内有小沟、桅杆田、皮家寨、大乌栗、蛤蟆井、后槽等自然村寨。村委会驻小沟，距谷堡乡政府10公里。下辖5个村民组，2010年有村民188户802人，其中苗族67户204人。

红星村猕猴桃园

村境地形多山，土地面积3.69平方公里，有耕地953亩，其中水田214亩，旱地739亩。农作物主要有水稻、玉米等。有森林650亩，树种以马尾松为主。非耕地资源开发1900亩，主产板栗、猕猴桃。红星猕猴桃为黔中名产，远近闻名。

猫跳河梯级电站专用线窄巷口电站至红林电站公路从村境穿过。6公里乡道连通全村各个自然村寨。

水口村 位于谷堡乡西面，东邻富裕村和红星村，南连大塘村，西达猫跳河与清镇市卫城镇双山村和栽江村隔河相望，北抵大寨村。境内有水口寺、下坝、魏家寨、杨家寨、胡家寨、邓家寨、王家寨、张家寨、枧上、洞门口、刘家弯、后寨、小垭口、长田等自然村寨。村委会驻下坝，距谷堡乡政府8公里。下辖5个村民组，2010年有村民275户1161人，其中苗族27户110人。土地面积6.85平方公里，有耕地1302亩，其中水田560亩，旱地742亩。农作物主要有水稻、玉米等。全村灌溉主要靠烂沟水库东来之水。

矿藏资源主要有铝矾土矿和铁矿。村内公路主要有（X190）县道穿过下坝组，各个自然村寨之间均通村道。水口寺石雕艺术远近闻名，主要雕刻园林石材和墓碑、墓石等。

平滩村 位于谷堡乡西南面，东隔猫跳河峡谷红板桥河段与清镇市麦格乡龙窝村相望，南接绿水村，西连大塘村，北抵水口村，东北与红星村毗邻。有平滩、大寨、上寨、放牛场等自然村寨。村委会驻平滩新村，距谷堡乡政府10公里。下辖6个村民组，2010年有村民342户1132人，其中少数民族34户110人。土地面积5.33平方公里，有耕地938亩，其中水田323亩，旱地615亩。农作物主要有水稻、玉米。有林地1600亩，其中成材林200亩，灌木荒山1400亩。

境内蕴藏丰富的煤炭资源，驻村企业有杉树麻窝平滩煤厂和挖蕨坡天字煤厂。水利灌溉主要靠烂沟水库干渠经乌栗引入大沟，灌溉全村耕地。村主干公路由东电站专用公路原水电九局三处分道，经槽子土至龙家弯子和大场坝进村，向西一直延伸到绿水村，全长2.5公里。至各自然村寨公路均与主干公路相连。

大塘村 位于谷堡乡境西南面，东接平滩村，南连绿水村，北抵水口村，西隔猫跳河与清镇市卫城镇大土村毗邻。境内有平山箐、麂子冲、龙滩口、冷家寨、郭家寨、莫家湾、谢家湾、下寨、场坝上、中寨、母猪岩等自然村寨。村委会驻平山箐，距谷堡乡政府10公里。下辖9个村民组，2010年有村民614户2458人，其中少数民族61户262人。

村境地形东南高，西北低，平均海拔900米为谷堡乡海拔最低村。土地面积5.82平方公里，有耕地2093亩，其中水田908亩，旱地1185亩。主要农作物有水稻、玉米、小麦、油菜、马铃薯等，还有成片的花卉种植。

大塘村大棚花卉种植

村地富藏煤炭资源。退耕还林种植楠竹1000余亩，早熟蔬菜200亩。筑有蓑衣塘、绿水筲箕塘、圆塘和谢家湾小山塘。建有老虎洞、猫跳河两处提水站。主干渠有烂沟水库经平滩、青山组至绿水大沟，由水口村经平滩村、场坝上至绿水大沟，由老虎洞经龙滩、莫家湾、大塘至下寨的下大沟。村内主干公路两条，上一条由原水电九局三处起，经莫家湾至中寨；下一条由三处起，经龙滩口、平山箐、下寨通往绿水村小营。驻村企业有红枫发电厂五级电站和与绿水村交界处的贵阳市宏河矿业煤厂。

绿水村 位于谷堡乡境西南角，北接平滩村和大塘村，东、南、西3面与清镇市麦格乡龙窝村、和平村隔猫跳河相望。境内有张家寨、邹家寨、田坎脚、广冲寨、岩根脚、荒田、山后、小营上等自然村寨。村委会驻荒田，距谷堡乡政府15公里。下辖5个村民组，2010年有村民244户844人，其中苗族39户136人。

村境地形是一个东北高、西南低的大斜坡。土地面积2.57平方公里，有耕地865亩，其中水田338亩，旱地527亩。农作物主要有水稻、玉米等。有森林面积480亩，树种多为马尾松。

境内蕴藏丰富煤矿，2002年建贵州宏河煤厂落地在与大塘村交界的大营上。农业灌溉有烂沟水库配套工程上大沟通到大营上，另有董家寨山塘和槽子田山塘。村主干公路由电站专用公路原水电九局三处分道，经平滩村一直延伸到绿水村的荒田，4米宽乡村道路连通8个自然村寨。位于猫跳河边岩脚索桥横跨在猫跳河上，为古代两岸过渡的交通工具，1936年红军二、六军团长征由此经过，今遗址尚存，属省级重点文物保护单位。

大寨村 位于谷堡乡境西南面，北抵下花村，东连上花村和谷堡村，南接下硐村、富裕村和水口村，西以猫跳河与清镇市卫城镇栽江村和梨木冲村隔河相望，西北与洒坪乡东庄村毗邻。境内有改城、大寨、小田坝、哪洒、摆嘎、马龙井、干堰塘、穆家寨、杨柳井等自然村寨。村委会驻大寨，距谷堡乡政府6公里。下辖9个村民组，2010年有村民427户1761人，其中少数民族128户342人。

村境山多地少，土地面积14.74平方公里，有耕地1883亩，其中水田1063亩，旱地820亩。农作物主要有水稻、玉米、油菜、马铃薯、烟草等。村境有8口山塘，水田主要靠山塘蓄水自流灌溉。村地有森林2500亩，树种主要为马尾松。2010年，各自然村寨均通乡村公路。

上花村 位于谷堡乡北面，东邻新堰村，南连谷堡村的韩家寨，西接大寨村，北抵下花村和哨上村。有中花塔、上花塔、吴家庄等自然村寨。村委会驻上花塔，距谷堡乡政府6公里。下辖6村民组，

2010年有村民217户889人，其中彝族4户14人。

村境多山，南高北低。土地面积5.28平方公里，有耕地1480亩，其中水田493亩，旱地987亩，农作物主要有水稻、玉米。有可开发荒地5000亩，经果林1200亩，栽有金秋梨、猕猴桃等。村内有许家田坝小（Ⅱ）型水库1座，山塘4口。上花村主干公路1条7.5公里，往南至谷堡村韩家寨连通（X190）县道，往北经下花村、哨上村接天生桥旅游公路。

上花塔村貌

下花村　位于谷堡乡西北面，东邻哨上村，东南接上花村，南抵大寨村，北与洒坪乡蜈蚣桥村毗邻。境内有下花塔、湾头、猫硐、下坝等自然村寨。村委会驻下坝，距谷堡乡政府8公里。下辖4个村民组，2010年有村民135户603人。

村境地形东南高、西北低，土地面积3.94平方公里，有耕地650亩，其中旱地400亩，水田250亩。农作物以水稻、玉米为主。

境内有下花山塘、大水井山塘和猫硐山塘，为村内主要灌溉水源。谷堡到下花的谷花公路从东南进入，绕经村境贯穿各自然村寨至东北接哨上村蛇（田）花（塔）公路。

哨上村　位于谷堡乡北面，东邻红焰村，南连新堰村和上花村，西接下花村，北面与洒坪乡蜈蚣桥村和小箐乡龙塘村隔猫洞河、花桥河相望。有朱家湾、哨上、小桥、梁子、大碑丫口、水落岩、老鸹岩等自然村寨。村委会驻小桥，距谷堡乡政府6公里。下辖7个村民组，2010年有村民190户788人，其中少数民族26户103人。村地形山高坡陡，沟谷纵横。土地面积4.17平方公里，有耕地880亩，其中水田280亩，旱地600亩。农作物主要有水稻、玉米等。

（X190）县道从蛇田分路至花塔公路穿过全村，各个自然村寨均通进组公路。全村有山塘4个，主要沟渠3条，倒虹管3道。著名的天生桥峡谷风景区坐落在村境哨上与老鸹岩之间，距县城11公里。

哨上村天生桥景观

新堰村　位于谷堡乡北面，东邻红焰村，南连折溪村和谷堡村，西接上花村，北抵哨上村。境内有吴家庄、桅杆坡、苗田、大坝、猫坡、周家寨、谭家寨、场坝上、懒板凳等自然村寨。村委会驻场坝上，距谷堡乡政府4.5公里。下辖6个村民组，2010年有村民275户1067人。

村地属低山丘陵地带，土地面积5.16平方公里，有耕地1400亩，其中水田627亩，旱地773亩。主要农作物是水稻、玉米、油菜籽，还有烤烟、金秋梨、猕猴桃等。金秋梨种植1140亩，猕猴桃种植400亩。有用材林2100亩，木材以松树为主。

蛇田至花塔公路纵贯境内吴家庄、谭家寨、场坝上等村寨；另一条公路从万亩梨园（贯穿谷堡、古隆、新堰）分道经过吴家庄、大坝、苗田入谷堡村接（X190）县道。耕地主要靠山塘自流灌溉，有枧槽沟、新堰、马槽田、龙洞、大堰、小堰、懒板凳等堰塘。

新堰村属小乌栗民居

红焰村 位于谷堡乡东面，东与大堰村相连，南接折溪村，西邻新堰村，北与小箐乡尖山村隔花桥河相望。境内有大坡、杉树林、干坝、大竹林、红花园、后寨、中坝等自然村寨。村委会驻后寨，距谷堡乡政府6公里。下辖7个村民组，2010年有村民217户878人，其中苗族（青苗）33户113人。

村境多山，山高沟深。土地面积5.97平方公里，有耕地1383亩，其中水田623亩，旱地760亩。农作物主要有水稻、玉米、油菜、马铃薯、烟草等。

森林面积2137亩，主要是马尾松。种植有金秋梨800亩。村境有杉树沟、后寨张家堰、大坡毛家堰、干坝小堰和4口山塘，均系地势低洼长年积水形成。修建有红花园提灌站和人畜饮水工程。主干渠拦山沟从大竹林燕家岩洞至王家门口。蛇田至花塔公路穿后寨而过，后寨至杉树沟修有4米宽3公里长的机耕道，2003年修通杉树沟至大雁村接修（文）六（广）公路。

大堰村 位于谷堡乡东北面，东邻龙场镇放马坪村和阳早村，南连折溪村，西接红焰村，北抵龙场镇花桥村。境内有大堰塘、枇杷园、刘家湾、沙田、岩草坡等自然村寨。村委会驻大堰塘，距谷堡乡政府8公里。下辖5个村民组，2010年有村民202户762人。村地属低山丘陵区，土地面积3.92平方公里，有耕地873亩，其中水田420亩，旱地453亩。农作物主要有水稻、玉米等。森林面积340亩，树种主要是马尾松。

村境有山塘5个，灌溉面积450亩。修文至六广的（X190）县道从大堰村东掠边而过。在县道7公里处有乡村公路由东向西横贯村境，往西与蛇田至花塔公路连接，继往西通梨花湖和谷堡等地。

都堡村 位于六屯乡北面，为六屯乡政府驻地，村境东连星中村，南接长田村，西抵高峰和新埔村，北与开阳县双流镇情久村毗邻。境内有格都堡、九龙、水口寺、塘坎寨、塝上、武家寨、小寨、石灰窑等自然村寨。村委会驻格都堡中心组，紧挨六屯乡政府。下辖13个村民组，2010年有村民538户2497人，其中少数民族28户79人。

六屯茶场

村地属低山丘陵盆地区，西南高，东北低。土地面积9.3平方公里，有耕地3550亩，其中水田

1850亩，旱地1700亩。有林地4639亩，种植经济林木800余亩，主要有桃、李、梨、猕猴桃和茶叶等。矿藏有硅和重晶石。可开发的非耕地近1000亩。农作物主要有水稻、玉米、油菜、豆类、烟草、马铃薯等。特产主要是茶叶。

2003年，引资建成200亩半夏规范种植基地，并成功引进私营企业投资新建都堡村低压电器开关厂。

水利设施有大滩凹、苍甫塘、雹打山、观音洞和九龙山等山塘；有石桥大沟、武家寨引水渠2条，干渠总长1.3万米；公用机灌4站5台37.5千瓦。

扎（佐）六（屯）公路横贯村境，东经星中村入开阳县禾丰乡，西经高峰、双月、三里接210国道。村内乡村公路、串寨路通连各自然村寨。

高峰村 位于六屯乡西北面，东连都堡村和长田村，南接西冲村和大寨村，北抵新堡村，西隔扎佐林场石猫猫分场与扎佐镇双月村毗邻。境内有林家高寨、下寨、麻窝寨、上寨、秧箐、火石坝、水井上、中坝、对门坡等自然村寨。村委会驻林家高寨，距六屯乡政府2.5公里。下辖7个村民组，2010年有村民344户1452人，其中少数民族17户33人。

村境地势属低山丘陵区，西南高，东北低。土地面积8.14平方公里，有耕地1830亩，其中水田880亩，旱地950亩。有林地2500亩，经果林500余亩，主要产梨、猕猴桃等。还有可开发的非耕地近850亩。

农作物主要有水稻、玉米、油菜、豆类、烟草、马铃薯等。有林场、石桥和流白水3座小（Ⅱ）型水库。有下寨、上寨卧底冲、中坝3口山塘。公用机灌设施4台90千瓦，主要干渠有林场水库至上寨大沟7000米，林场水库至对门坡3000米，下寨大沟1000米。

主要矿藏有硅和煤等。

扎（佐）六（屯）公路横贯村境，东经都堡村、星中村入开阳县禾丰乡境；西经扎佐镇双月、三里接210国道。村内有高峰至下寨、高峰至火石坝、大寨至对门坡3条乡村公路，总长11公里。

新堡村 位于六屯乡西北面，东连都堡村，南接高峰村，西抵安全村，北邻开阳双流镇情久村。境内主要有新堡子和廖家寨2个自然村寨，村委会驻新堡子古回龙寺旧址，距六屯乡政府3公里。下辖3个村民组，2010年有村民246户826人，其中少数民族13户19人。

村地属低山丘陵区，西南高，东北低。土地面积3.45平方公里，有耕地859亩，其中水田473亩，旱地386亩。农作物主要有水稻、玉米、油菜、豆类、烟草等。有林地1700亩，可开发的非耕地100亩。

筑有山王庙山塘1口，库容0.6万立方米，灌面积40亩，有公用机灌设施1台7.5千瓦，主要干渠有流白水水库引水渠8000米。

境内有林场至新堡、新堡至都堡、流白水至花椒园、流白水至对门寨等乡村公路和村寨间串寨路，通车里程总长3.5公里。

安全村 位于六屯乡西北角，东连新堡村，南隔扎佐林场石猫猫分场与扎佐镇泗溪村、双月村毗邻，西北面抵开阳县双流镇六坪村和白马村。境内有六马庄、大麻窝、流白水、大河边、磨湾、田坝、石猫猫等自然村寨。村委会驻六马庄寨上，距六屯乡政府7公里。下辖6个村民组，2010年有村民239户1048人。村地属低山丘陵区，西南高东北低。土地面积5.54平方公里，有耕地1389亩，其中水田826亩，旱地563亩。有林地3561亩，其中经果种植156亩，主要产梨、桃、李等。矿产资源有硅和铁，但储量不大。另有可开发非耕地1000亩。农作物主要有水稻、玉米、油菜、豆类、烟草。境内有流白水小

（Ⅱ）型水库1座，有简上、大麻窝、何家水、六马庄山塘4口。主干渠有洞门前、跟斗坡、杨家林、龙滩、武家田、杨家岩6条，总长1.1万米。

境内乡村公路四通八达，主要有砂石路林场至曹家丫口、雷家丫口至寨上、分水关至寨上、桂家丫口至大河边、梅家湾至王家湾、石猫猫至大麻窝等6条，总长11公里。

全心村 位于六屯乡东北面，东南连大木村，西南接长田村，西抵星中村，东面与开阳县禾丰乡红竹村毗邻。境内有胡子田、二洞、大麻窝、王家土、屯上、畜牧场旧寨等自然村寨。村委会驻胡子田，距六屯乡政府6公里。下辖5个村民组，2010年有村民140户498人。地属低山丘陵区，西南高，东北低。土地面积5.01平方公里，有耕地826亩，其中水田146亩，旱地680亩。另有林地4284亩，可开发的非耕地800亩。矿产资源有硅和重晶石。经济以农业为主，农作物主要有水稻、玉米、油菜、豆类和烟草等。全村发展经果林种植300余亩，主要有桃、葡萄、梨、猕猴桃等，中药材有天麻、杜仲等。水利设施有人畜饮用兼机灌设施2台，装机容量15千瓦。

村境公路主要有二硐寨上串寨路硬化2公里、六（屯）香（火岩）公路穿境4公里、青山至胡子田1公里、青山至屯上1公里、六香公路出口至王家土1公里、吴家丫口至果圃场2公里。

星中村 位于乡境东北面，东连全心村，南接长田村，西抵都堡村，北与开阳县双流镇田村毗邻。境内主要有洞门前、沙坝、白果寨、大路齐家湾、核桃树、新寨、烂泥冲、庙边、洞门寨等自然村寨。村委会驻大路边，距六屯乡政府3公里。下辖5个村民组，2010年有村民322户1258人，其中少数民族20户54人。村地属低山丘陵区，西南高，东北低，土地面积6.36平方公里。有耕地1430亩，其中水田800亩，旱地630亩。有林地1508亩，矿产资源主要有重晶石。

村域经济以农业为主，农作物主要有水稻、玉米、油菜、豆类、烟草等。村境主要干渠道有擦耳岩引水渠6000米，擦耳岩排洪渠4800米，对门前引水渠3000米。

村境公路主要有六香公路3公里、星中至长田6公里、大路边至光渡河2公里。

长田村 位于六屯乡中部，东连大木村，南接西冲村，西抵高峰村，北邻星中村。境内主要有罗家林、断桥、水淹凼、尹家寨、偏坡、板掌、大穴窝、汪家寨等自然村寨。村委会驻罗家林，距六屯乡政府7.5公里。下辖7个村民组，2010年有村民332户1369人，其中少数民族23户43人。

村地属低山丘陵区，西南高，东北低，土地面积6.8平方公里，有耕地1570亩，其中水田253亩，旱地1317亩。另有林地2001亩，可开发的非耕地近1500亩。矿产资源有硅、煤和重晶石等。

经济以农业为主，农作物有水稻、玉米、油菜、豆类、烟草等。境内筑有家林山塘1口，容量1.2万立方米，灌溉面积70亩。主干渠有板掌大沟3500米，尹家寨引水渠3000米，罗家林引水渠3500米。

村境公路主要有星中至长田4公里、尹家寨至水淹凼1.5公里、板掌至张家坡0.8公里。

大寨村 位于乡境东南面，东连开阳县禾丰乡，南接乌当区新场乡，西抵西冲村，北邻长田村。境内有大寨、水头寨、谷光、车田等自然村寨。村委会驻大寨，距六屯乡政府12公里。下辖5个村民组，2010年有村民336户1241人。村地属低山丘陵河谷地带，西南高，东北低。土地面积5.79平方公里，有耕地1807亩，其中水田634亩，旱地1173亩，土壤富含硒，有利开发优质蔬菜。有林地4008亩。

经济以农业为主，农作物主要有水稻、玉米、油菜、豆类、烟草等。全村发展经济果树林种植1100亩，主要有柑橘、桃、李、猕猴桃等。已发展无公害蔬菜种植300余亩。村境地处河谷地带，水利资源丰富，筑有拦河坝3道，主要干渠有岩脚田引水渠1500米，菜田坝引水渠5000米。

村境公路主要有大路边至水头寨5.5公里，三寨至水头寨4.8公里，大寨至尧上9公里，大寨桥头至土地关6公里。

三寨村 位于六屯乡东南面，东连小木村，南接大寨村，西抵西冲村，北靠长田村。境内有桃源三寨、桃源二寨、朵堡寨、龙昌坡、枧槽冲等自然村寨。村委会驻桃源三寨，距六屯乡政府11公里。下辖中元、和平、明星、龙昌坡、流江、新生、沿江7个村民组，2010年有村民435户1673人，其中少数民族46人。村地属低山丘陵区河谷地带，西北高，东北低。土地面积6.04平方公里，有耕地1773亩，其中水田788亩，旱地985亩，土壤富含硒，所产大米远近闻名。有林地1290亩，可开发非耕地900亩。已种植经果林300余亩，主要有柑橘、李、梨、猕猴桃等。矿资源有硅、重晶石。

桃源三寨

经济以农业为主，主要农作物有水稻、玉米、油菜、豆类、烟草等。因地处河谷地带，土壤富硒，有利于开发优质蔬菜，已发展蔬菜种植50余亩。鱼梁河（桃源河）穿境而过。境内有大水塘山塘1口。主干渠有关沟引水渠3000米，枧槽冲引水渠2000米，西冲水库引水渠3500米，流白水引水渠4000米，堰塘沟引水渠1500米。

公路主要有炮打岩至三寨3公里，场坝至水头寨2公里。串寨路有和尚林至寨上1.5公里，冯家门口至周家门口0.5公里，和尚林至明星组0.5公里，场坝至大寨0.5公里，二寨至医院1.5公里，二寨庙上至和尚林0.5公里。

小木村 位于六屯乡境东南面，东与开阳县禾丰乡白花村和王车村毗邻，南以长滩河与乌当区新场乡杨梅村隔河相望，西南抵大寨村，西连三寨村，北接大木村。境内有小木头寨、田坝、大窑上、长坡、猪罗坝等自然村寨。村委会驻小木头寨，距六屯乡政府12公里。下辖4个村民组，2010年有村民162户667人，其中少数民族125户464人。村地属低山丘陵区，西南高，东北低。土地面积4.32平方公里，有耕地908亩，其中水田338亩，旱地570亩。有林地3268亩，其中经果林600余亩，品种主要是桃、李、梨、猕猴桃、柑橘、柿子等。矿藏主要有硅。

经济以农业为主，农作物有水稻、玉米、油菜、豆类、烟草等。村内农田主要靠自流灌溉，主干渠有田坝引水渠3000米，阳关冲引水渠1000米。

小木村无核柿子

村境公路主要有蜂糖坡至长坡3公里，牛背上至田坝0.5公里，牛背上至老寨0.5公里。

大木村 位于六屯乡东南面，东与开阳县禾丰乡红竹和白花村毗邻，南连小木村，西抵长田村，北接全心村。境内有大木头寨、干堰、小山、百桃田、塘边、平土、猫脚、白泥田、丫口田等自然村寨。村委会驻大木头寨，距六屯乡政府14.5公里。下辖6个村民组，2010年有村民210户764人，其中布依族136户502人。红军长征时经过大木头寨留下“红军是干人的军队”等标语至今保存完好。

村地属低山丘陵区，西北高，东南低。土地面积7.78平方公里，有耕地1110亩，其中水田430亩，旱地680亩。村有林地5133亩，可开发的非耕地400亩。有经果林460余亩，种有桃、李、梨、猕猴桃、柿子、银杏等。矿藏资源有硅、硝、铁、重晶石、大理石等。

主要农作物有水稻、玉米、油菜、豆类、烟草等。农田主要靠自流灌溉，干渠有田坝引水渠3000米，阳关冲引水渠1000米，龙洞引水渠1000米。建有电力提灌站1座，装机容量30千瓦。

公路主要有大木至全心4公里，大木至香火岩5公里，大木至开阳县长红村5公里，大木至开阳县马头村4公里，大木至小木2公里，大木至猫脚1.5公里，大木至干堰4公里。

西冲村 位于六屯乡西南面，东接大寨村和三寨村，南抵独山村，西与扎佐镇双月村和长坡村毗邻，北连高峰村和长田村。有上西冲、下西冲、上堰、下堰、大路边、马驮田、团山、茶洞等自然村寨。村委会驻下西冲，距六屯乡政府10公里。下辖5个村民组，2010年有村民265户975人，其中布依族164户523人。村内布依民俗风情浓郁，可开发田园观光旅游。村地属低山丘陵区，西南高，东北低。土地面积6.68平方公里，有耕地1430亩，其中水田738亩，旱地692亩。有林地2994亩。可开发的非耕地近50亩。农作物主要有水稻、玉米、油菜、豆类、烤烟、叶子烟等。有经果林70余亩，种有桃、李、梨、猕猴桃、椪柑等。村内建有二元杂交母猪繁殖基地，已发展到养殖能繁母猪100头的规模。水利设施有大路边山塘1口，库容3万立方米，灌溉面积150亩；机灌设施1台17千瓦；主干渠有三岔河沟渠4500米，西冲大沟5000米。

西冲村布依风情—客人进村喝拦路酒

村境公路主要有独山至炮打岩3公里，炮打岩至下西冲1公里，上西冲至大路边0.5公里，蚂蚁坟至马驮田0.5公里。

独山村 位于六屯乡西南面，北连西冲村，东接大寨村，南以桃源河南岸山脉与乌当区新场乡尖坡村为界，西与扎佐镇长坡村和大河村毗邻。境内有独山、桃花园、碗厂、桃子湾、下坝等自然村寨。村委会驻独山，距六屯乡政府13公里。下辖4个村民组，2010年有村民247户918人，其中少数民族600人。地形属低山丘陵区，西南高，东北低。土地面积7.87平方公里，有耕地1360亩，其中水田720亩，旱地640亩。有林地3105亩。农作物主要有水稻、玉米、油菜、豆类和烟草等。水利设施有漆树井山塘，库容0.5万立方米，灌溉面积46亩。主干渠有后洞水库大沟，渠长8000米。机灌设施3站，总装机容量165.5千瓦。

独山布依风情村寨

全村布依民俗风情浓郁，水利资源丰富，自然风光秀丽，可开发田园观光旅游和民族风情游。已开发香巴房小水电站和桃源河漂流。

村境公路有独山至碗厂1公里，桃子湾至桃花园4公里，桃花园至长坡4公里，另有串寨道路3

公里。

小箐村 位于小箐乡境中西部，东接崇恩村，南连龙塘村，西南抵郭田村，西北邻洒坪乡小坝村，北靠大坝村和大兴村。有小箐街和旧小箐、后田坝、石朝门、马屎冲、小红岩、撮箕田、大桥沟等自然村寨，村委会驻小箐街上。下辖9个村民组，2010年有村民500户1849人，其中苗族8户35人，彝族9户89人。

村境地形东北高，西南低，土地面积5.26平方公里，有耕地1042亩，其中水田240亩，旱地802亩。

农作物主产水稻、玉米。果品酥李年产30万公斤销往修文、贵阳。境内的岩鹰山水库小箐支渠，东起大兴村4号隧洞绕捆牛大坡山脚经石朝门、旧小箐至西南郭田村，全长6250米。

交通有贵（阳）毕（毕）高等级公路由村东至西穿越村境2公里，设有小箐收费站于小箐街南。修（文）六（广）公路由村东至村西穿越村境2公里，沿公路建有小箐街道。由小箐至郭田公路长5公里，过境3公里。小（箐）中（寨）公路由村西至中寨，过境2公里。

村南大桥沟小流域下两蓬岩峡谷是可开发的旅游景点，位于村东南1公里，上接凤凰村下半沟，下连郭田村花鱼洞，全长3公里，峡谷深300米，宽100至200米，海拔980米左右。河水长年不断，两岸四季常青。上游有清代开辟的四面坡大道和觉先桥，下游有锅圈岩、兰花岩、龙潭瀑布、花鱼洞等景观。

小箐兰花岩幽潭梯级瀑布

小箐乡党政机关驻小箐街上，小箐中学、小学、卫生院、计划生育服务站均建在小箐村境内。

郭田村 位于小箐乡西南面，东接龙塘村，南靠谷堡乡哨上村和洒坪乡蜈蚣桥村，西抵洒坪乡新乐村，北邻大坝村和小箐村。有郭田、水沟、岩脚寨、大麻窝、红岩麻窝和青杠林等自然村寨。村委会驻郭田老包山，距小箐乡政府4.5公里。下辖4个村民组，2010年有村民166户667人，其中苗族9户33人。

村境地形东北高西南低，土地面积3.11平方公里，有耕地606亩，其中水田226亩，旱地380亩。农作物主产水稻、玉米。特产郭田酥李，果大核小，肉质酥脆，年产量约40万公斤，远销修文、贵阳等地。

天生桥水利工程郭田支渠建于1973年，渠长2000米。

由小箐街至郭田的乡村公路，连接村内4个村民组及主要自然村寨。

大坝村 位于小箐乡西面，东接大兴村，南靠小箐村和郭田村，西抵洒坪乡小坝村和上寨村，北邻六广镇四寨村和小箐杉林村。有大坝、大丫口、虾蚂冲、下坝、龙洞、龙塘湾、砂湾、田湾、水淹麻窝、杨柳冲、杨家麻窝等自然村寨。村委会驻大坝，距小箐乡政府2公里。下辖6个村民组，2010年有村民336户1201人。

村境地势东高西低，土地面积4.73平方公里，有耕地1168亩，其中水田475亩，旱地693亩。农作物主产水稻、玉米。田湾水库，蓄水0.7万立方米。岩鹰山水库洒坪支渠穿越村境，东起羊子丫口，西至马落坑，全长2000米，灌溉稻田400亩。

贵（阳）毕（节）高等级公路由东至西穿越4个村民组3公里。修（文）六（广）公路由东至西穿越

5个村民组，小（箐）中（寨）公路由村东南至西南穿越大丫口村民组，3条公路于龙洞大桥交汇。

2003年启动大坝异地搬迁工程，在龙洞大桥北侧的修（文）六（广）公路两侧修建搬迁房32户。

杉林村 位于小箐乡西面，东接大兴村，南靠大坝村，西抵六广镇四寨村，北邻青中村。境内有中坝、上寨、堰塘、官地上、杉树林、大水井、白花坝等自然村寨。村委会驻杉树林，距小箐乡政府4公里。下辖7个村民组，2010年有村民251户1073人，其中苗族29户110人，多居住在大水井村民组。土地面积3.96平方公里，有耕地1300亩，其中水田568亩，旱地732亩。

农作物主产水稻、玉米、烤烟等。岩鹰山水库主干渠由村东至村西，居高临下，穿过村境4公里，灌溉全村稻田，干渠上建有大水井倒洪管一座，全长230米，过水2.7升/秒。

乡村公路有小箐至宝山公路由南向北经过村境3公里，另有官地上经革佬坟至熊家岩脚1公里。

大兴村 位于小箐乡境西北面，东接凤凰村，南靠小箐村，西抵杉林村，北邻大坝村和青中村。有尹家寨、偏坡寨、柿花树、永兴、白果、大兴田、中间、茨蓬、塝上、石坎和猴子山等自然村寨，村委会驻偏坡寨，距小箐乡政府7.57公里。下辖9个村民组，2010年有村民386户1546人。

全村土地面积6.14平方公里，有耕地1651亩，其中水田672亩，旱地979亩。农作物主产水稻、玉米、烤烟等。岩鹰山水库主干渠由村东尹家寨至村西的郭家丫口，境内长5000米，灌溉全村稻田。

贵（阳）毕（节）高等级公路经过村境1公里。村主干公路由柿花树经永兴、白果至小坝村，过境长4.5公里。各村民组和主要村寨间均通乡村公路。

凤凰村 位于小箐乡中部，东接万兴村，南靠崇恩村，西抵小箐村和大兴村，北邻小坝村。有烧炭窑、白岩脚、大山、大碑、青龙、上半沟、下半沟等自然村寨。村委会驻烧炭窑，距小箐乡政府4公里。下辖7个村民组，2010年有村民225户907人。

村地东高西低，土地面积5.86平方公里，有耕地530亩，其中水田231亩，旱地299亩。有森林3045亩，水土保持良好，森林中还生长有三类保护树种铁尖杉。农作物主要有水稻、玉米等。特产红皮萝卜（胭脂萝卜），皮薄个大，年产量10万公斤，远销修文、贵阳等地。

岩鹰山水库石坝库区位于村的东面，水库干渠东起二号隧洞，西至干冲出村境至六广，过境长4000米。

修（文）六（广）公路南进西出贯穿5个村民组。贵（阳）毕（节）高等级公路东进西出穿越村境3公里，建有下半沟和白岩脚大桥。各村民组和主要村寨间均通乡村公路。

崇恩村 位于小箐乡境南面，东接新场村，南靠龙场镇花桥村，西抵尖山村和龙塘村，北邻小箐村、凤凰村和万兴村。有坡背寨、余家湾、杨家寨、仓上、银山、卡子坡、车家湾、苗坝、大丫口、红星、红卫、西家湾、水浸塘、杨泗河、桂家湾、桂下坝等自然村寨。村委会驻仓上，距小箐乡政府9公里。下辖17个村民组，2010年有村民581户2680人，其中彝族8户41人，苗族1户5人。

村地东高西低，土地面积12.16平方公里，有耕地2424亩，其中水田1151亩，旱地1273亩。农作物主要有水稻、玉米、马铃薯等。建有余家湾蔬菜基地500亩，产品销往修文市场。岩鹰山水库崇恩支渠，东起岩鹰山水库土坝，经新场、崇恩两村西至尖山村黄泥田，全长7350米。

矿藏有煤和大理石，其中煤蓄量约2000万吨。

修（文）六（广）公路从花桥入村，经桂下坝、杨家寨、仓上、余家湾、苗坝、车家湾出村境至六广，穿越村境4.5公里。贵（阳）毕（节）高等级公路从杨泗河入村经西家湾、杨家寨、余家湾、苗坝出境至毕节，穿越村境3.5公里。2004年修筑崇（恩）栋（青）公路，由苗坝接修（文）六（广）公路经大

丫口出村至久长镇栋青村，穿越村境2公里。3条公路在苗坝交汇，17个村民组和主要村寨均通公路。

尖山村 位于小箐乡南面，东南接龙场镇花桥村，南靠谷堡乡红焰村，西抵龙塘村，东、北邻崇恩村。有坝上、杜家寨、三家庙、黄泥田、尖山和马路边等自然村寨。村委会驻黄泥田，距小箐乡政府11公里。下辖3个村民组，2010年有村民216户930人。

村境地势东高西低，土地面积4.32平方公里，有耕地896亩，其中水田414亩，旱地482亩。有2220亩森林覆盖山头空地，村内蓄存有大量黄泥黏土和约10万立方米页岩，适宜生产页岩红砖。

尖山村种植的折耳根

农作物主产水稻、玉米、马铃薯等。所产大米质地优良，味香，黏性好。特产折耳根，年产约5万公斤，销往修文、贵阳等地。岩鹰山水库崇恩支渠和龙塘支渠在村内各长3000米，灌溉300亩水田。花桥河由小青山入村至鲤鱼塘出村，长约2000米。

村距修（文）六（广）公路3公里，主干公路自崇恩桥修六路公道通黄泥田，连接3个村民组及主要村寨。

龙塘村 位于小箐乡西南面，东接尖山村，南靠谷堡乡红焰村和哨上村，西抵郭田村，北邻小箐村。有关庆、打铁沟、关田坝、大寨、大朝门、小洞口、后山、水落洞等自然村寨。村委会驻大寨，距小箐乡政府13公里。下辖8个村民组，2010年有村民244户1158人，其中彝族2户10人。

村地东高西低，土地面积6.47平方公里，有耕地1517亩，其中水田374亩，旱地1143亩。有3700亩森林覆盖山头空地，植被和水土保持良好。地下矿产有铀，另有白云石蓄量约1万立方米，红土蓄量约8000立方米。

农作物主产水稻、玉米。特产酥李，果质酥脆，口感相宜，千亩酥李、桃子遍布各自然村寨，年产80万公斤，主要销往修文、贵阳等地。建有鲤鱼塘电灌站，装机容量100千瓦，93米扬程，灌溉面积300亩。

龙塘村距修（文）六（广）公路5公里，村内主干公路由花桥通往大寨，10公里村道连接8个村民组和主要自然村寨。

万兴村万兴湖

万兴村 位于小箐乡东面，东接久长镇栋青村，南靠大林村和新场村，西抵崇恩村和凤凰村，北邻小坝村、全兴村和息烽县泉福村。有万兴堡、革家坝、蒋家田、老将山、龙洞湾、关口田、田坝等自然村寨。村委会驻龙洞湾，距小箐乡政府7公里。下辖6个村民组，200年有村民214户932人，其中苗族2户8人。

村地东高西低，平均海拔1380米，最高峰老将山顶峰海拔1552.7米。土地面积7.45平方公里，有耕地907亩，其中水田294亩，旱地613亩。有4500亩森林覆盖山头荒地，植被良好。矿藏有硅、煤、铁、大理石等待开采，其中煤蓄量50万吨，大理石蓄量300万立方米。

农作物主产水稻、玉米、马铃薯等。特产马铃薯个大粉多，销往贵阳、修文等市场。县内 第一大水库—岩鹰山水库坐落村境，石坝库区位于岩鹰山西侧，通过岩鹰山地下溶洞与万兴库区连为一体，库容蓄水930万立方米。另有小河水库位于村东，库容16.3万立方米，有效灌溉300亩。

修（文）六（广）公路由崇恩至紫江公路和水库指挥部经水库石坝至凤凰村公路，过境长2公里。2004年又修通经栋青村至久长镇公路，过境长2公里。分支村道连通村内各村民组和主要自然村寨。

新场村 位于小箐乡东面，东接久长镇茶山村，南靠久长镇兴田村和龙场镇放马坪村，西抵崇恩村和凤凰村，北邻万兴村和大林村。有新村、新场上、小六广、麻窝寨、偏坡寨、六岔路、下坝、王五桥、大冲、蚂蝗田、大九寨和六广坡等自然村寨。村委会驻新村，距小箐乡政府9公里。下辖8个村民组，2010年有村民338户，1310人，其中苗族162户650人，主要居住在麻窝寨、偏坡寨、下坝和大九寨。

村境地势东高西低，平均海拔1330米，土地面积约6.22平方公里，有耕地1050亩，其中水田475亩，旱地575亩。农作物主产水稻、玉米、马铃薯。岩鹰山水库土坝库区，位于村境的小六广，库区蓄水825万立方米。崇恩支渠东起土坝经新场村、崇恩村至尖山村黄泥田，全长7350米，村境段长3000米。

矿藏蓄量有煤2000万吨，硫铁矿2000万吨，枣红大理石100万立方米，石灰石3万立方米，还有铀、钛、水晶石、高岭土等。有2340亩森林覆盖山头空地。

修（文）六（广）公路由崇恩村苗坝分道达4公里的乡村公路，连通村属8个村民组和主要自然村寨，2004年又修通经栋青村至久长镇公路。

大林村 位于小箐乡东面，东接久长镇栋青村，南靠久长镇茶山村，西抵新场村，北邻万兴村，有上寨、小河、雷神坡、后寨、大林寨、水井湾等自然村寨。村委会驻大林寨，距小箐乡政府13公里。下辖4个村民组，2010年有村民86户483人。岩鹰山水库土坝库区居中，把一、二组和三、四组切成南、北两面。全村土地面积3.19平方公里，有耕地407亩，其中水田80亩，旱地327亩。农作物主产水稻、玉米。有138亩森林覆盖山头空地。岩鹰山水库土坝库区上游在村境内。另有小河水库位于村西北与万兴交界的小河，库容16.3万立方米，有效灌溉300亩。

地下矿藏有煤、硅等，煤储量200万吨，硅100万吨。

村距修（文）六（广）公路8公里，崇恩至栋青县级公路和新场新村经土坝至上寨围库公路和乡村公路连通村内各组。

小坝村 位于小箐乡东北面，东接万兴村，南靠凤凰村，西抵大兴村和青中村，北邻紫江村和全兴村。有栋青、小坝街、小寨坡、兰家冲、龙家冲、宋大寨、关田、大湾、石旮旯、罗大寨、玉皇阁等自然村寨。村委会驻小坝街，距小箐乡政府7公里。下辖10个村民组，2010年有村民450户1695人，其中苗族18户71人。村地东高西低，土地面积7.7平方公里，有耕地2584亩，其中水田632亩，旱地1952亩。森林覆盖面积2500亩。农作物主产水稻、玉米、马铃薯。岩鹰山水库马场支渠，由大兴尹家寨至紫江大屋基和村内罗大寨长1.13万米，经马槽冲建有铸铁倒虹管1座长196米，经马鞍山建水泥倒虹管1座长514米。

小坝村距修（文）六（广）公路6公里，由大兴柿花村民组经永兴至栋青坝的乡村公路入村境，连接10个村民组。久（长）大（石）公路穿过村境3公里。

2002年11月恢复小坝街集市贸易，每逢星期二赶场。

紫江村 位于小箐乡北面，东接全兴村，南靠小坝村，西抵青中村，北邻宝山村和息烽县石硐乡小山村和老街村。有胡家土、马场坝（一）、马场坝（二）、紫江田、谷龙、岩湾、上坝、下坝、老鸦坪、后山、大屋基、犀牛口等自然村寨。村委会驻马场坝，距小箐乡政府8.5公里。下辖12个村民组，2010年有村民356户1559人，其中苗族113户450人，主要居住在老鸦坪、犀牛口、后山等地。土地面积7.26平方公里，有耕地1923亩，其中水田372亩，旱地1551亩。森林覆盖面积2200亩。农作物主产水稻、玉米、烤烟、马铃薯等。岩鹰山水库马场支渠，由尹家寨主干渠引水，全长1.13万米，过村境4000米。

有久（长）大（石）公路由村东至村西穿越村境4公里，分支公路连接各村民组和部分村寨。

全兴村 位于小箐乡东北面，东接久长镇栋青村，南靠万兴村和小坝村，西抵紫江村，北邻息烽县石硐乡泉湖村。有苗寨、田坝、后丘田、庙坎、牌坊边、小沟、烂泥冲、凌家湾、中坝、下坝等自然村寨。村委会驻牌坊边，距小箐乡政府12公里。下辖10个村民组，2010年有村民263户1375人，其中苗族29户118人。土地面积6.44平方公里，有耕地1651亩，其中水田527亩，旱地1124亩。森林覆盖面积2370亩。农作物有水稻、玉米、小麦、油菜、马铃薯和烤烟等。

村委会所在地距修（文）六（广）公路10公里，有由修六公路从柿花树经小坝至全兴和全兴通息烽县石硐乡泉湖村公路及乡村道路连通10个村民组及主要村寨。久（长）高（枧）公路经过村境3公里。

青中村 位于小箐乡北面，东接紫江村，南靠大兴村，西抵杉林村和六广镇四寨村，北邻宝山村。有新屋基、肖老田、红房子、王家田、老房子、营盘山、芦茅寨、水淹塘、仡佬坟等自然村寨。村委会驻肖老田，距小箐乡政府5公里。下辖8个村民组，2010年有村民340户1585人，其中苗族7户26人。土地面积4.02平方公里。有耕地961亩，其中水田152亩，旱地809亩。森林覆盖面积2800亩。农作物主产水稻、玉米、马铃薯，还有花菜番茄等。岩鹰山水库宝山支渠由高粱井经青中至宝山，境内长3000米。

村距修（文）六（广）公路5公里，分道的乡村公路由大坝经杉林进入村境至肖老田，向东延伸2.5公里与久（长）高（枧）公路在马场坝汇合，各村民组及主要村寨均通公路。

青中村延晚蕃茄

宝山村 位于小箐乡西北面，东接紫江村，南靠青中村，西抵六广镇岩脚村和团山村，北邻大石布依族乡元庆村。有新寨、长坡、后山、田湾、前明、茶树、龙山、上寨、大寨、高坡等自然村寨。村委会驻大寨，距小箐乡政府10公里。下辖10个村民组，2010年有村民331户1492人，其中苗、彝少数民族51户198人。土地面积7.66平方公里，有耕地1975亩，其中水田376亩，旱地1599亩。森林面积2300亩。农作物主产水稻、玉米。岩鹰山水库宝山支渠由大兴村高粱井经青中村入境，长6600米。

乡村公路由大兴村柿花树起经小坝、紫江进入村境连接10个村民组。其中小坝至宝山为久（长）高

（枧）公路段。

小坝村 位于洒坪乡东面，系乡政府驻地，东邻小箐乡大坝村、小箐村和郭田村，南接新乐村，西连青山村，北抵上寨村。境内主要有小坝、沙坡、山背后、栋青坝、竹林头、中坝、上坝、下坝、水井湾、龙洞等自然村寨。村委会驻小坝，距洒坪乡政府2公里。下辖7个村民组，2010年有村民336户1201人。村境属丘陵地带，呈喀斯特地貌。土地面积4.04平方公里，有耕地850亩，其中水田210亩，旱地640亩。农作物主要有水稻、玉米、小麦、马铃薯、油菜、蔬菜和烤烟。蔬菜种植比重较大，养鹅、养牛也较突出。驻村企业有采石场2个，养殖基地3家。

小坝村新农村全景

小箐至红枫电厂六级电站公路自东向西横贯村境，东接修（文）六（广）公路，西可跨猫跳河进清镇市至卫城镇连通省道贵（阳）毕（节）公路。乡级公路南可通蜈蚣桥，北可至六广镇中山村接修六公路。

青山村 位于洒坪乡中部，东邻小坝村和新乐村，南连东庄村，西接北庄村和麻窝村，北抵蛇场村和上坝村。境内有中坝、上坝、下坝、新寨、小山脚、金家湾、小堰和石丫口等自然村寨。村委会驻中坝，距洒坪乡政府1公里。下辖7村民组，2010年有村民457户1642人。土地面积4.85平方公里，有耕地1247亩，其中水田460亩，旱地787亩。农作物主产水稻、玉米、小麦、马铃薯、油菜和烤烟。村内企业有青山砖瓦厂，主要生产红砖。养殖业饲养中华竹鼠为村特色产业。

青山村600亩标准化蔬菜基地

小箐至红枫六级电站公路自东向西横贯村境。另有青山经蛇场、洞口至五老山和青山经麻窝村至高寨2条村际公路。

中明村 位于洒坪乡西南面，东邻东庄村，南连轿子山村，西接阳桥村和五江村，北抵北庄村。境内有中寨、下中寨、黄泥丫口、毛藤湾、后箐、三岔河、芭蕉麻窝、龙洞、泥水井、梓木林、高坡、长冲、偏坡寨等自然村寨。村委会驻中寨，距洒坪乡政府8公里。下辖11个村民组，2010年有村民257户919人。土地面积5.86平方公里，有耕地面积为1826亩，其中水田230亩，旱地1596亩。有林地2200亩。农作物主产水稻、玉米、小麦、马铃薯、油菜和烤烟。特产大蒜，年产3万公斤。

小箐至红枫电厂六级电站公路自东向西横贯村境，往东经青山、小坝至小箐接修（文）六（广）公路，往西经轿子山至六级电站。另有中寨分别至北庄、至五江、至杨桥等村的乡村公路。

新乐村 位于洒坪乡东南面，东邻小箐乡郭田村，南连谷堡乡哨上村和洒坪乡蜈蚣桥村，西接东庄村和青山村，北抵小坝村。境内有螺蛳寨、营背后、蜈蚣坝、马路沟、水井湾、麻窝寺等自然村寨。村委会驻螺蛳寨，距洒坪乡政府3公里。下辖8个村民组，2010年有村民283户1009人。土地面积5.39平方公里，有耕地1970亩，其中水田220亩，旱地1750亩。有林地4400亩，水土保持良好。农作物主产水稻、玉米、小麦、马铃薯、油菜和烤烟。特产酥李年产量约15万公斤，多销往修文、贵阳等地。

境内主干道有小坝至蜈蚣桥乡级公路，北接小坝，南过蜈蚣桥至谷堡乡，另有村级公路自螺蛳寨往东经郭田至小箐接修（文）六（广）公路。天生桥引水工程由太阳坪分出的蜈蚣桥支渠、郭田支渠和小坝支渠，灌溉全村稻田。

蜈蚣桥村 位于洒坪乡东南面，东邻谷堡乡哨上村，南连下花村，西接东庄村，北抵新乐村。境内有蜈蚣桥、坪上、杨家水井、梯子田、范家坪、白杨林、河坝等自然村寨。村委会驻蜈蚣桥，距洒坪乡政府7.5公里。下辖5个村民组，2010年有村民215户758人。土地面积4.24平方公里，有耕地面积920亩，其中水田270亩，旱地650亩。农作物主产水稻、玉米、小麦、马铃薯、油菜和烤烟。特产“蜈蚣桥蜜李”和“蜈蚣桥豆腐”远近闻名。

蜈蚣桥蜜李

明朝初年奢香开龙场九驿，村境为驿道必经之处，明中期修建蜈蚣桥，村寨因而得名。驿道和蜈蚣桥遗址今尚存。境内主干道公路有小坝至蜈蚣桥乡级公路，北接小坝，中经新乐村螺蛳寨，至蜈蚣桥后，南过蜈蚣桥可入谷堡乡境。

高寨村 位于洒坪乡西面，东邻麻窝村，南连北庄村，西接五江村和青杠林村，北抵五老山村和洞口村。有高寨、老鸹洞、大高寨、龙洞、小高寨、杨家坝和高石桩等自然村寨。村委会驻高寨，距洒坪乡政府6公里。下辖5个村民组，2010年有村民179户637人。土地面积5.14平方公里，有耕地1040亩，其中水田152亩，旱地888亩。农作物主产水稻、玉米、小麦、马铃薯、油菜和烤烟。矿藏有煤、铁、铝等。有林地2710亩覆盖山头空地，植被及水土保持良好。水利设施主要有弥纳井、水井湾和杨家坝3座山塘。

境内有3条村际公路，往东经麻窝村至青山接小箐至红枫电厂六级电站县级公路，往南经北庄可至中寨，往西可至五江、青杠林等地。

五老山村 位于洒坪乡西北面，东邻洞口村，南连高寨村，西接青杠林村和六广镇合营村，北抵合兴村。境内有龙潭麻窝、燕子岩、五老山、普郎等自然村寨。村委会驻龙潭麻窝，距洒坪乡政府8公里。下辖4个村民组，2010年有村民132户471人。土地面积3.41平方公里，有耕地1170亩，其中水田167亩，旱地1003亩。农作物主产水稻、玉米、小麦、马铃薯、油菜和烤烟。水利设施主要有三岔土、磨石湾、梁子山和瓦厂堡4座山塘。

矿产资源有铁、铝、硅、煤和硫铁矿，其中铁和煤储量丰富。

主干公路有东经洞口村和蛇场村至青山村接小箐至六级电站公路，南经青杠林村至中寨，西经六广镇合营村至六广，北经六广镇合兴村接修（文）六（广）公路。

青杠林村 位于洒坪乡西北部，东邻五老山村和高寨村，南连五江村，西以猫跳河为界与清镇市暗流乡矿山村隔河相望，北抵六广镇合营村。境内有上田坝、花地、青杠林、毛栗林、长冲湾子、大麻窝、广洞、高炉等自然村寨。村委会驻上田坝，距洒坪乡政府11公里。下辖4个村民组，2010年有村民195户659人，其中苗族10户41人。土地面积6.76平方公里，有耕地720亩，其中水田250亩，旱地470亩。农作物主产水稻、玉米、小麦、马铃薯、油菜和烤烟。特产野生杨梅。5500亩森林覆盖山头空地，植被和水土保持良好。水利设施有贾家堰山塘1座。矿藏有铝、铁、煤和硫铁矿。

村内主干公路中寨至青杠林6公里。另有由小（箐）中（寨）公路青山双坟经蛇场、洞口、毛栗林入村境和中寨经五江长冲入村境至上坝田2条公路。

轿子山村 位于洒坪乡西南面，东邻东庄村和中明村，北抵中明村，西接杨桥村，西南和南面以猫跳河为界与清镇市暗流乡栗木冲村隔河相望。境内有河边、轿子山、下寨、柑子林等自然村寨。村委会驻河边，距洒坪乡政府8公里。下辖3个村民组，2010年有村民103户，346人。土地面积5.68平方公里，有耕地365亩，多属旱地。农作物主产玉米，年产量约11万公斤。特产柑橘和李子，年产量约20万公斤。水利设施有堰沟山塘1个。

轿子山村因轿子山而得名

小箐至红枫电厂六级电站公路自北向南经过村境，成为村内公路主干线。另有1条往东经团山坝到东庄的村际公路。猫跳河由东庄三岔河入境至虎山注入乌江过村境段4公里。1968年，在猫跳河上建红岩水电站，拦河大坝关闸蓄水后形成红岩湖，两岸绿树成荫，野生动物随处可见，清澈的湖水相衬奇山异石，壮丽多彩。

阳桥村 位于洒坪乡西面，东邻中明村和轿子山村，北抵五江村，西、南以猫跳河为界与清镇市暗流乡洋桥村隔河相望。境内有杨桥、平地、贾家寨、后坝、中坝、盐井等自然村寨。村委会驻平地，距洒坪乡政府11公里。下辖5个村民组，2010年有村民191户698人。土地面积4.2平方公里，有耕地823亩，其中水田125亩，旱地698亩。有2400亩各类林木覆盖山头空地。农作物主产水稻、玉米，水稻年产量约5万公斤，玉米年产量约21万公斤。矿藏有煤和硫铁。

石家洞钟乳石

村境地势东高西低，喀斯特地貌特征明显，多石山溶洞。主要有石家洞，位于大坪子，与阳皮洞隔猫跳河对峙。洞高40米，宽30米，深60米，洞内钟乳石发育丰富。民国年间有人在洞内熬硝，洞口筑有防御工事。高洞位于平地，洞高30米，宽20米至50米，长2公里，洞内有石柱、石笋、石山和暗流。

村内主干公路由小（箐）中（寨）公路平地至阳桥公路，全长4公里。

上坝村 位于洒坪乡北面，东邻上寨村，南连青山村，西接蛇场村和洞口村，北抵六广镇松山村和龙窝村。境内有栗木山、牛坝、枫香桥坪上、昌湾子、乌当、长冲坪上、河沟等自然村寨。村委会驻聂木山，距洒坪乡政府7公里。下辖15个村民组，2010年有村民452户1665人。土地面积4.88平方公里，有耕地1623亩，其中水田401亩，旱地1222亩。农作物主产水稻、玉米、小麦、马铃薯、油菜和烤烟。矿藏主要有煤，驻村企业栗木山煤矿，年采原煤3万吨。

村内主干公路往东经上寨至小坝接小箐至红枫电厂六级电站4公里，往西分别可通六广镇中山和松山等地。

五江村 位于洒坪乡西面，东邻高寨村和北庄村，南连中明村和杨桥村，北抵青杠林村，西以猫跳河为界与清镇市暗流乡矿山村隔河相望。境内有五基地、靶碑、长冲、煤洞湾、青杠寨、大土寨、马落孔等自然村寨。村委会驻五基地，距洒坪乡政府12公里。下辖7个村民组，2010年有村民175户646人。土地面积4.79平方公里，有耕地880亩，其中水田120亩，旱地760亩。农作物有水稻、玉米、小麦、马铃薯、油菜和烤烟等。矿产资源有煤、铁、硫铁矿等。

村内主要有2条主干公路，一条自五基地往东经龙洞至中寨，另一条自五基地绕经高寨、北庄、中寨、杨桥又再回到五基地，形成一个环形公路连通途经各村。

猫跳河边小仓山，有一圆形石柱高100米，直径50米，石柱左侧有一溶洞，名为官家洞，洞中有泉水流出注入猫跳河。

硐口村 位于洒坪乡北面，东邻上坝村和蛇场村，南连青山村和麻窝村，西接高寨村和五老山村，北抵六广镇合兴村和松山村。有大洞口、石丫口、汤家湾、高石头、马刨井、黔山、黔洞等自然村寨。村委会驻大洞口，距洒坪乡政府6公里。下辖4个村民组，2010年有村民128户638人。土地面积3.85平方公里，有耕地1137亩，其中水田161亩，旱地976亩。农作物主产水稻、玉米、小麦、马铃薯、油菜和烤烟。矿产资源有铁和煤，分布全村。

境内主干公路由大洞口往东经蛇场至青山接小箐至红枫电厂六级电站公路，往西经五老山至六广镇合兴村接六广镇公路网。

麻窝村 位于洒坪乡中部偏北，东邻青山村，南连北庄村，西接高寨村，北抵洞口村和蛇场村。有麻窝寨、黄家林、茶树林、长丫口、水淹塘等自然村寨。村委会驻麻窝寨，距洒坪乡政府6公里。下辖5个村民组，2010年有村民192户691人。土地面积1.6平方公里，有耕地1246亩，其中水田76亩，旱地1170亩。农作物主产水稻、玉米、小麦、马铃薯、油菜和烤烟。矿产资源主要有铁和煤。

境内主干公路由蛇场岩脚入村境经方家丫口至徐家丫口去高寨，另一条由青山村金家湾入村经水淹塘至徐家丫口去高寨。

蛇场村 位于洒坪乡北面，东邻上寨村和小坝村，南连青山村，西接麻窝村和硐口村，北抵上坝村。有蛇场、水淹冲、大坪上、小坪上等自然村寨。村委会驻蛇场，距洒坪乡政府6公里。下辖10个村民组，2010年有村民226户798人，其中彝族5户20人。土地面积2.21平方公里，有耕地987亩，其中水田287亩，旱地700亩。农作物主产水稻、玉米、小麦、马铃薯、油菜和烤烟。水利设施有大堰坡山塘1座，库容6万立方米；电力提灌站1个，配套沟渠2条共3000米。

蛇场村烤烟基地

境内主干公路东连青山接小箐至六级电站公路，西通高寨、洞口、五老山等村。

东庄村 位于洒坪乡南面，东连新乐村和蜈蚣桥村，西接中明村，北抵北庄村和青山村，南与谷堡乡大寨村毗邻。境内有老蛇坝、谷革、樱桃坝、核桃坝、团山堡、小田坝、跳墩河、堰塘边、贾家寨、桃子坝、桶井、旧寨、白磨坟、漆树湾等自然村寨。村委会驻老蛇坝，距洒坪乡政府6公里。下辖7个村民组，2010年有村民272户967人。土地面积10.14平方公里，有耕地1158亩，其中水田105亩，旱地1053亩。农作物主产水稻、玉米、小麦、马铃薯、油菜和烤烟。

境内横跨东西公路东达蜈蚣桥，西至红枫电厂六级电站公路和北庄。纵贯南北公路北经旧寨、营背后至洒坪，南经堰塘边、团山坝至轿子山。

村内有一岩洞名书房洞，位于村西。民国年间方必成、路锡山在洞内分别设馆开办私塾，收学生20至30人，故此得名。解放初期，村农协会常在洞内召开群众大会。继后又在洞内开办东庄耕读小学，1963年耕读小学从洞内迁至距洞300米的校舍。

北庄村 位于洒坪乡西面，东邻东庄村，南连中民村，西接高寨村西面，北抵高寨村东部和麻窝村、青山村。境内有上那卡、下那卡、大冲、冬瓜林、牛角井、西山坝等自然村寨。村委会驻上那卡，距洒坪乡政府6公里。下辖4个村民组，2010年有村民225户805人，其中苗族2户11人。

全村土地面积4.05亩，有耕地736亩，其中水田66亩，旱地670亩。农作物主产水稻、玉米、小麦、马铃薯、油菜和烤烟。特产梨和花椒。水利设施主要有堰塘湾和烂田湾两座山塘。

境内主要公路由那卡向东3公里于黄泥丫口接小（箐）中（寨）公路，向南3公里抵中寨，向西北可通高寨、青枫林等地。

上寨村 位于洒坪乡东北面，东邻小箐乡大坝村，南连洒坪乡小坝村，西接青山村和上坝村，北抵六广镇龙窝村和四寨村。境内有上寨、云峰廖家寨、上光坝、光坝、中山、以母、务农、偏坡寨、龙潭等自然村寨。村委会驻上寨，距洒坪乡政府2公里。下辖15个村民组，2010年有村民413户1485人。土地面积3.91平方公里，有耕地1310亩，其中水田330亩，旱地980亩。农作物主产水稻、玉米、小麦、马铃薯、油菜和烤烟。特产牛腿南瓜，个大、味美、产量高。小坝至六广镇中山村公路穿过村境，经上寨、梨木山至枫香桥。东南至小坝接小箐至红枫电厂六级电站公路，西北经上坝通六广镇中山、松山等地。

上寨村牛腿瓜

大石村 位于大石布依族乡西南面，系乡政府驻地，东邻新光村和高枧村，西连大屯村，北抵大寨村，西南角以猫跳河为界与黔西县素朴镇花冲村隔河相望。境内有大石板、上大坝、小屯、对门寨、木踏石、街上、坡脚、丫口田等自然村寨。村委会驻大石板。下辖7个村民组，2010年有村民402户1688人，其中布依族等少数民族204户669人。土地面积5.41平方公里，有耕地1688亩，其中水田126亩，旱地1562亩。农作物主要有水稻、玉米、小麦、马铃薯等。水利设施主干渠有大干田至民义长2000米，窖化洞至大干田长100米，何家湾至沙坝长160米。

矿产主要是页岩，建有年产15万块页岩砖厂1个。

有广（田）六（桶）公路自南向北穿境而过。村际道路主要有木踏石通往大屯公路和大石通往大寨公路。

大屯村 位于大石布依族乡西面，东接大石村，西、南两面邻六广河与黔西县素朴镇花苗村隔河相望，北靠高山村和竹坪村。境内有茶山堡、罗家寨、陈家寨、湾子头、石格闹等自然村寨。村委会驻茶山堡，距大石布依族乡政府5.5公里。下辖3个村民组，2010年有村民211户713人，其中布依族191户639人。村境地形东、南、北3面环山，西面临六广河，海拔950米左右，为典型的盆地气候。土地面积2.99平方公里，有耕地870亩，其中水田335亩，旱地535亩。农作物主要有水稻、玉米、蚕豆、黄瓜、棒豆等。二道水至大屯引水工程，主干渠长4000米，配套支渠4300米，灌溉面积360亩，节水灌溉面积550亩，并解决一、二组人畜饮用水。

大屯村村貌

大屯村以往只有1条小路从手爬岩到大石，2005年修通从六广河边经村内各自然村寨出马路坡至木踏石接修文至六桶公路5公里。水路六广河上溯六广，顺达乌江。

大寨村 位于大石布依族乡中部，东邻天桥村，南连大石村，西接高山村和大屯村，北抵红岩村。境内有大寨 、对角土、大竹林、茅草坪、煤洞湾、老寨、仰天窝、田坝、小寨、田湾等自然村寨。村委会驻大寨，距大石布依族乡政府2公里。下辖7个村民组，2001年有村民211户1075人，其中布依族204户1025人。土地面积3.39平方公里，有耕地1306亩，其中旱地1013亩，水田293亩。农作物主产水稻、玉米、小麦、洋芋等。矿产资源主要有煤，储量丰富。

境内交通较为便利，主干公路有从大石至高山村公路穿境而过，村内各组及主要村寨均可通车。

高山村 位于大石布依族乡西北面，东邻红岩村和大寨村，南连大屯村，西接竹坪村，北抵六桶乡下坝村和坪山村。境内有放牛坪、平寨、苗儿头、郭家寨、杨家寨、李家等自然村寨。村委会驻放牛坪，距大石布依族乡政府5.6公里。下辖6个村民组，2010年有村民240户899人，其中布依族和苗族120户464人。土地面积3.93平方公里，有耕地1534亩，其中水田8亩，旱地1526亩。农作物主产玉米、马铃薯和烤烟。

村内公路往东南经大寨至大石接广（田）六（桶）公路，往西通竹坪，往北经六桶乡下坝、木林通六桶，往东北经六桶乡平山至石板接广六公路。

竹坪村 位于大石布依族乡西北角，东接高山村，南连大屯村，西与黔西县素朴镇李家寨村隔六广河相望，北连六桶乡下坝村。境内有苦竹坪、曾家寨、岩脚寨、老鸹河、后漕等自然村寨。村委会驻苦竹坪，距大石布依族乡政府6.5公里。下辖4个村民组，2010年有村民156户554人，其中布依族、苗族共98户321人。土地面积4.62平方公里，有耕地1277亩，其中水田31亩，旱地1246亩。农作物主产玉米、小麦、马铃薯和烤烟等。

乡村公路有大石经大寨、放牛坪至苦竹坪、老鸹河，基本连通村内各自然村寨。

红岩村 位于大石布依族乡北面，东邻回水村和天桥村，南连大寨村，西接高山村和六桶乡坪山村，北抵石板村。境内有新田湾、巡司寨、江颈、红岩、沙槽、六月坡、沙塘井等自然村寨。村委会驻红岩街上，距大石布依族乡政府3.2公里。下辖7个村民组，2010年有村民198户803人，其中布依族等少数民族114户368人。土地面积3.85平方公里，有耕地1069.3亩，其中水田174亩，旱地895.3亩。有300亩马尾松林分布在老县道两侧。农作物主产水稻、玉米、马铃薯等。有江颈、新田湾2个山塘，库容1.5万立方米；主干渠2条，总长3500余米，灌面110亩。矿产资源主要有煤、硫铁和汞等。

原有的广（田）六（桶）公路有3.8公里自南向北纵贯村境，南接大石，北至六桶乡火石丫新的广（田）六（桶）公路。

回水村 位于大石布依族乡东北面，东邻沙坝村，南连天桥村，西接红岩村，北抵六桶乡石板村和金星村。有回水塘、大煤厂、大桥、碾子、龙洞等自然村寨。村委会驻回水街上，距大石布依族乡政府4公里。下辖7个村民组，2010年有村民255户1122人，其中布依族等少数民族10户20人。土地面积2.92平方公里，耕地805亩，其中水田280亩，旱地525亩。农作物主产水稻、玉米、油菜等。水利设施有大煤厂水库，库容20万立方米，主干渠3.7公里，灌溉面积500亩。另有林场、回水2个山塘，库容1.9万立方米，浇灌面积220亩。有提灌站1个，浇灌周边田地200亩。矿产资源主要有煤、汞、硫铁矿。200亩马尾松林环绕自然村寨。

（X186）县道自南向北纵贯村境，串组公路连通村内各自然村寨。著名的回水石林位于村境东部，占地1000亩，石林中植被完好，被誉为贵州最具代表性的绿色石林。因其处于原生状态，显得格外灵秀清新，幽美淡雅，有一种朴素的天然美，具有较高的开发价值。玉竹寺位于回水湖畔，原名观音寺，已有100多年历史，今称观音峰。

回水村前回水塘

沙坝村 位于大石布依族乡东北面，东邻息烽县石硐乡大洪村，南连天桥村，西接回水村，北抵六桶乡河银村。境内有沙坝、杨家湾、新坝、胡家湾、狮子丫等自然村寨。村委会驻沙坝，距大石布依族乡政府6公里。下辖5个村民组，2010年有村民103户486人，其中少数民族7户28人。土地面积1.49平方公里，有耕地567亩，其中水田30亩，旱地537亩。农作物主产玉米、小麦、油菜。有783亩松树林环绕各自然村寨。

村内主干公路西至回水接广（田）六（桶）公路，东至六桶乡河银。另一条公路自沙坝往东南经后槽转向西至天桥接广六公路。

沙坝村桃园

天桥村 位于大石布依族乡的东北面，东邻息烽县石硐乡大洪村，南连岩湾村和大石村，西接大寨村和红岩村，北抵回水村。境内有天桥、响水洞、桃子沟、场坝、大坪、后槽、朱家寨、大坡上等自然

村寨。村委会驻天桥，距大石布依族乡政府3公里。下辖5个村民组，2010年有村民183户690人，其中少数民族19户51人。土地面积3.05平方公里，有耕地760亩，其中水田120亩，旱地640亩。矿产资源有煤、硫铁矿、高岭土等。有1465亩松树林环绕自然村寨。

农作物主产水稻、玉米、小麦、马铃薯等。种植牧草960亩，饲养肉牛和能繁母牛134头，种植猕猴桃108亩，退耕还林（用材林）238亩。境内地下伏流于响水洞处流出，洞前筑一大坝储水，引水干渠2条，各长4500米，除供桃子沟组农田灌溉用水外，还供大石街上居民生活用水和大石村上大坝组耕地灌溉。

广（田）六（桶）公路自南向北纵贯村境1.5公里。村际公路起自天桥、东经后槽通沙坝村，西通红岩村。

岩湾村 位于大石布依族乡东北面，东邻息烽县石硐乡大洪村，南连联江村和新光村，西接大石村，北抵天桥村。境内有湾子头、岩头上、大麻窝、竹林槽子、岩湾、下寨、石旮旯、上寨、海螺山、长坎子等自然村寨。村委会驻下寨，距大石布依族乡政府5公里。下辖4个村民组，2010年有村民245户，929人，其中少数民族60户，190人。土地面积4.23平方公里，有耕地1260亩，其中水田85亩，旱地1175亩。农作物主产玉米、水稻、小麦、烤烟和花生等。岩湾引水工程筑有水坝一座，引水主干渠4800米。

境内有公路2条，一条往南通联江接丫口田至息烽石硐公路，另一条往西接丫口田接广（田）六（桶）公路。串组路和机耕道10公里连通村内各自然村寨。

新光村 位于大石布依族乡东面，东邻联江村和联合村，南连高枧村和六广镇平营村，西接大石村，北抵岩湾村。境内有土垮、下土垮、瓦房、老木关等自然村寨，村委会驻土垮，距大石布依族乡政府2.5公里。下辖3个村民组，2010年有村民127户545人，其中少数民族10户29人。地势西、南高，东、北低，境内多山，呈典型的喀斯特地貌特征。土地面积2.31平方公里，有耕地699亩，其中水田5亩，旱地694亩。有林地面积700亩。农作物主产玉米、马铃薯等。

村主干公路横贯村境，西至大石接广（田）六（桶）公路，东经扎佐苗通六广镇元庆村铁厂坝。

联江村 位于大石布依族乡东面，东邻息烽县石硐乡何家洞村，南接联合村，西连新光村，北抵岩湾村。境内有高坡、槽子头、岩灰洞、干龙洞、凉水洞等自然村寨。村委会驻高坡，距大石布依族乡政府6公里。下辖5个村民组，2010年有村民154户554人，其中少数民族15户35人。土地面积2.47平方公里，有耕地853亩，其中水田65亩，旱地788亩。农作物主产玉米、水稻、马铃薯、大豆和烤烟，是全乡相对连片优质烤烟基地之一。

境内主干公路西至丫口田接广（田）六（桶）公路，东通息烽县何家洞、石硐等地。村际公路北通岩湾、河银，南通联合、元庆。

联合村 位于大石布依族乡东南面，东南抵六广镇元庆村，南连六广镇平营村，西接大石布依族乡新光村，北靠联江村，东北与息烽县石硐乡何家洞村毗邻。有新街、苗寨、扎佐苗、仰天窝、老铁厂、岩洞门口、空田坝等自然村寨。村委会驻新街，距大石布依族乡乡政府8公里。下辖5个村民组，2010年有村民171户699人，其中少数民族81户225人。土地面积4.16平方公里，有耕地1077亩，其中水田207亩，旱地870亩。农作物主产玉米、水稻、马铃薯等。水利设施有苗寨山塘，库容量1.3万立方米，主干渠2000米，浇灌周边田地近80亩。有5.5千瓦提水站1个，主要解决三组、四组人畜饮水。矿产主要有煤和硫铁矿。

乡村公路连接扎佐苗、新街、仰天窝3个村寨，东达六广镇元庆村，西通新光、大石接广（田）六（桶）公路。

高枧村 位于大石布依族乡南面，东邻六广镇平营村，西连大石村，南接联丰村和六广镇广义村，北抵新光村。有高枧、木塔石、大田边、沙坝、民义、大秧土、堰沟、大干田、长冲沟和白水等自然村寨。村委会驻高枧，距大石布依族乡政府3公里。下辖7个村民组，2010年有村民259户940人，其中少数民族20户35人。土地面积3.9平方公里，有耕地980亩，其中水田180亩，旱地800亩。农作物主产玉米、水稻、小麦、油菜等。矿产资源以煤为主。有私营企业何家湾煤矿、沙坝煤矿和落地木踏石的宏达采石场。

高枧石仓

广（田）六（桶）公路由南至西北穿村而过，久（长）高（枧）公路往东经德政可通往久长接210国道。村内串组公路连通各自然村寨。有大干田引水主干渠2000米，灌溉面积120亩。

著名的高枧石林位于村境南面，是修文县重要的风景名胜之一。景点占地400余亩，内有奇峰异石密布，石沟石硐纵横，并以森林植被完好著称。四季绿树成荫，奇石形态丰富多姿，素有“拟态动物园”之美誉。

联丰村 位于大石布依族乡东南面，东邻六广镇前丰村，西、南连六广镇中心村，北接大石布依族乡高枧村。境内有坝上、水井湾、周家坡、岩上田等自然村寨。村委会驻水井湾，距大石布依族乡政府4公里。下辖3个村民组，2010年有村民320户1054人。土地总面积2.42平方公里，有耕地961亩，其中水田332亩，旱地629亩。

农作物主产水稻、玉米、小麦等。水利设施有山塘2座，其中巴蕉沟山塘库容量7000立方米，灌溉农田70亩；水井湾山塘库容量0.79万立方米，灌溉20亩。另有提水站1个，装机容量18千瓦，安装供水管道700米，扬程120米。

矿产资源以煤为主。驻村企业主要有坝上宏达煤厂，年产煤6万吨。

广（田）六（桶）公路2公里沿村西而过，串组公路全部修通。

盐井村 位于六桶乡中部，系六桶乡政府驻地，东邻石头村，西连木林村，南接石板村，北抵六桶村。境内有盐井、上落邦、下落邦、四楞、凉水井等自然村寨，村委会驻盐井。下辖4个村民组，2010年有村民235户，2283人。土地面积2.44平方公里，有耕地1616亩，其中水田85亩，旱地1531亩。另有可开发非耕地253亩。农作物主产玉米、大豆、小麦、马铃薯和烤烟、油菜。村地土质适宜烤烟、油菜生长，烤烟、油菜是村的经济支柱

盐井村千亩优质烤烟生产基地

产业，年产烤烟9万公斤，油菜5万公斤。

1995年6月，六桶乡政府从六桶老街迁驻盐井后，辟有颇具规模的集市贸易，命名为六桶坝农贸市场，因地处黔西、金沙、息烽、修文交界点，是四县边境居民交易的集中场所，每到场天，商贾云集，集市繁荣。

修文至六桶公路自南向北纵贯村境，南可通修文，北可达海马孔渡口。另有往东通石头村、大兴村和往西通木林村、何田村的两条乡村公路，境内各长1公里。

石头村 位于六桶乡南面，东邻大新村和花椰村，南连金星村，西接盐井村，北抵六桶村及盐井村东北面。境内有李家寨、谢家寨、新街、石院、上寨、沙锅寨等自然村寨。村委会驻李家寨，距六桶乡政府2公里。下辖10个村民组，2010年有村民328户1509人，其中少数民族208户836人。土地面积3.37平方公里，有耕地1329亩，其中水田615亩，旱地714亩。农作物主产玉米、水稻、小麦、大豆、烤烟、油菜等。矿产资源主要是煤。手工业主要是烧制砂锅。

水利设施有山塘3座，其中文家坡山塘库容7000立方米，灌田60亩；三叉窝山塘库容6000立方米，灌田40亩；箭竹林山塘库容3000立方米，灌田30亩。干渠除山塘引水渠4条全长2000米外，金星水库至村境的3000米主干渠和1000米沟渠，成为石头村的主要灌溉渠道。

火石丫至九庄的公路由西向东掠南边村境而过，东可达息烽县城，西可通六桶和修文等地。

大新村 位于六桶乡东面，东邻息烽县九庄镇同心村，南连六桶乡花椰村，西接石头村和盐井村，北抵凤联村。境内有大寨、杨洞、邱家寨、六纳寨、尖坡、滚石坡、透风丫口、马鞍山、高炉、杀人湾等自然村寨。村委会驻大寨，距六桶乡政府3公里。下辖8个村民组，2010年有村民306户1382人。土地面积4.11平方公里，有耕地1542亩，其中水田342亩，旱地1200亩。农作物主产玉米、水稻、小麦等。经济作物以烤烟、油菜为主。水利设施有山塘2座，其中邱家寨山塘库容2000立方米，灌田20亩，尖坡山塘库容1.2万立方米，灌田40亩。村境煤矿资源较为丰富。

村的地形西北高东南低，东部和南部多山，呈典型的喀斯特地貌特征，地下溶洞发育丰富。著名的多缤洞位于大新村与息烽县九庄镇桐枝驿村交界的凤凰山下，洞内自然景观千姿百态，被专家称为“天下奇观”，具有较高的旅游开发价值。

火石丫至九庄的公路由西南向东北纵贯村境，东可通息烽县城，西可通六桶、修文等地。

多缤洞内的钟乳石

金星村 位于六桶乡南面，东邻花椰村和河银村，南接大石布依族乡回水村，西连石板村，北抵石头村。境内有煤窑寨、普陇、火石丫、堰塘、杨家麻窝、杉湾、王家堰、管家岩脚等自然村寨。村委会驻煤窑寨，距六桶乡政府5公里。下辖5个村民组，2010年有村民149户768人，其中少数民族40户155人。土地面积2.25平方公里，有耕地709亩，其中水田335亩，旱地374亩。

村境地形西北高东南低，多山，自然植被较好，森林覆盖率达40%以上，其中人工造林500多亩，天然林2000多亩。农作物主产玉米、水稻、小麦等。经济作物以烤烟、油菜为主。金星水库属小（Ⅱ）型水库，面积0.65平方公里，库容119万立方米。主渠道长1500米，支渠道3条总长7600米。共灌溉金星、花榔、石头、大新4个村的农田650亩。

火石丫至九庄的公路由西向东掠北边村境而过，东可达息烽县城，西可通六桶、修文等地。

河银村 位于六桶乡东南面，东邻来鹤村，南连六桶乡林场和大石布依族乡回水村，西接金星村，北抵花榔村。境内有河坝、田坎寨、白岩厂、谌家湾、黄厂、高家湾等自然村寨。村委会驻河坝，距六桶乡政府9公里。下辖7个村民组，2010年有村民217户1186人，其中少数民族175人。土地面积2.6平方公里，有耕地1636亩，其中水田446亩，旱地1190亩。农作物主产玉米、水稻、小麦、烤烟、油菜等。村内筑有谌家湾、豆腐湾山塘2座，蓄水8000立方米，灌田55亩。主干水渠两条，总长1100米。

河银村境小白岩

矿产资源主要有煤、汞和硫铁矿。明万历至清道光年间，熊百万家和伍满公家在村里开采汞矿冶炼水银，人称“白岩厂”，规模较大。后因山体垮塌，汞矿开采逐渐消失，今仅存遗址。20世纪80至90年代曾零星开采硫铁矿和煤炭。

村内各组均有村级公路通向火石丫至九庄。

花榔村 位于六桶乡东南面，东邻来鹤村，南连河银村，西接金星村和石头村，北抵大新村，东北边境与息烽县九庄镇桐枝驿村接壤。境内有花榔、罗家寨、蒙家槽子、碓窝土、岩湾、大坪、老鹰岩、牛角土等自然村寨。村委会驻花榔，距六桶乡政府7公里。下辖10个村民组，2010年有村民261户1298人，其中少数民族75户285人。土地面积3.59平方公里，有耕地1383亩，其中水田429亩，旱地954亩。农作物主产玉米、水稻、小麦、油菜、花生等。村办有林场1个，面积150亩。

村境地势西北和东南高，中间低，有得天独厚的灌溉资源，上有合银村田园水系，金星村煤幺寨水库的溪流和水渠在村境清水沟相聚，穿过花榔田坝，于孟家槽子进入落水洞，形成伏流。水系全长5000米，灌溉农田650多亩。另有牛角土、中心、大坪、豆腐湾4个山塘，总库容1.9万立方米，渠道5条，总长2100米，灌溉农田100余亩。

火石丫至九庄的公路由西向东掠北边村境而过，东可通息烽县城，西可达六桶、修文等地。

来鹤村 位于六桶乡东南面，东邻息烽县九庄镇桐梓坡村，南连六桶乡林场，西接河银村，北抵花榔村和息烽县九庄镇桐枝驿村。境内主要有郝家祠堂、黄银、猫冲、大水井、瓦厂、长岭岗、大麻窝、新桥、岩脚寨、旗山、新寨、珍珠井、洞口河等自然村寨。村委会驻郝家祠堂，距六桶乡政府10公里。下辖16个村民组，2010年有村民352户1749人。土地面积5.89平方公里，有耕地2329亩，其中水田805亩，旱地1524亩。农作物主要有玉米、水稻、小麦和油菜等。境内有歧山、新银等村办林场，村南有六桶乡林场，全村森林覆盖率达83%。水利资源丰富，西面有猫冲、大龙洞两条溪流交汇，东面有洞口河、珍珠井水源，汇成来鹤水系，贯穿来鹤田坝，穿过天生桥再流经息烽地界后形成多缤洞伏流。可灌溉农田500余亩。另有南京、岩脚、来鹤3个山塘，总蓄水2.8立方米，主干渠5条，总长2200米，灌溉农田120余亩。

村境蕴藏有丰富的煤矿和硫铁矿，20世纪90年代有零星开采。

村内有1条4公里的主干公路通往花榔，各组间的村级公路均与主干公路连接。

石板村 位于六桶乡南面，东邻金星村和大石布依族乡的回水村、红岩村，南连坪山村，西接下坝村和木林村，北抵盐井村。境内有石板寨、熊家坟、大朝门、坪上、环坡、罗家寨、对门寨、龙井坝等自然村寨。村委会驻石板寨，距六桶乡政府3.5公里。下辖9个村民组，2010年有村民271户984人，其中少数民族8户35人。土地面积3.44平方公里，有耕地1824亩，其中水田287亩，旱地1537亩。农作物主产玉米、水稻、大豆、小麦、马铃薯、烤烟和油菜等。有烂冲湾、苗寨沟山塘2个，库容2万立方米，灌溉农田130亩。

修（文）六（桶）公路自南向北经过石板村东部边沿，火石丫至炮台村级公路环绕全村，连通各自然村寨。

坪山村 位于六桶乡最南面，东邻大石布依族乡红岩村，南面和西面连接高山村，北抵下坝村。境内有寨上、梁子上、黄泥田、雀箐、林家等自然村寨。村委会驻寨上，距六桶乡政府4.5公里。下辖6个村民组，2010年有村民127户529人，其中少数民族15户47人。土地面积2.69平方公里，有耕地1022亩，其中水田50亩，旱地972亩。有天然草场1000亩，适宜发展养殖业和畜牧业。农作物主要有玉米、大豆、小麦、马铃薯、烤烟和油菜。

从石板村火石丫沿山筑有1条村级公路，长3.5公里，为村内主干道，串组路和串户路全长5公里，与通往各自然村寨的公路相连。2001年，开通六桶至平山客车。

六桶村 位于六桶乡中部，东邻春江村，南连盐井村，西接木林村和宝坪村，北抵榨土村和三宝村。境内有六桶坝、小木林、丁木树、牛角井、老房子、皂角树等自然村寨。村委会驻六桶坝，距六桶乡政府1.5公里。下辖7个村民组，2010年有村民235户1114人，其中少数民族5户15人。六桶坝是原来集市所在地，人口居住比较集中。土地面积3.46平方公里，有耕地1361亩，其中水田61亩，旱地1300亩。农作物主产玉米、大豆、小麦、烤烟、油菜、马铃薯等。

六桶老场坝

村境为六桶乡连接各村的交通枢纽，北达黄金村，东可通息烽九庄，西可至凉井、宝寨和海马孔，南有修文至六桶县道可抵县城和省城。

凤联村 位于六桶乡东面，东邻息烽县九庄镇三合村，南连大新村，西接盐井村，北抵春江村和官寨村。境内有肖家坝、老白头、岩脚、沙塘井、岩上、龙井、文家坝、马垛子等自然村寨。村委会驻肖家坝，距六桶乡政府5公里。下辖8个村民组，2010年有村民296户1231人，其中少数民族6户24人。村境地形西高东低向九庄方向倾斜，土地面积3.21平方公里，有耕地1099亩，其中水田374亩，旱地724亩。农作物主产玉米、水稻、小麦、油菜等。水源有沙塘井、龙井、樱桃井等古井，泉水既供全村人畜饮用，又可灌溉村内农田。另有多缤洞至木林沟河流1条，建有芭蕉沟提水站，不仅供村内灌溉和村民饮用，又解决盐井、六桶新老集镇居民用水。

境内蕴藏有煤矿资源，为有利于水土保持，暂无开采。

六桶至官寨公路自西向东穿过村境中部，成为村的主干道。

春江村 位于六桶乡东面，东邻官寨村，南连凤联村和盐井村，西接六桶村和三宝村，北抵长新村。境内有刘家沟、碾子、俩山寨、赵家沟、万家坡等自然村寨。村委会驻碾子，距六桶乡政府4.5公里。下辖11个村民组，2010年有村民228户1141人。土地面积6.58平方公里，有耕地1301亩，其中水田304亩，旱地997亩。

村境气候温和，水源丰富，是六桶乡玉米和水稻的主产区。经济作物以油菜为主。刘家沟经村境段筑有6道河堰和水渠3条，饮水灌溉凤联、春江两村500余亩稻田。另有俩山寨山塘蓄水1000余立方米，灌溉农田10余亩。

2005年，修通六桶老街通往春江各组的村级公路，基本解决了村民的交通运输问题。

官寨村 位于六桶乡东北面，北面和东面邻息烽县九庄镇上坝村和大槽村，南连凤联村，西接春江村和长新村。境内有官寨、黄莲庄、木叶渣、小寨、大坡、上寨、贾角山等自然村寨。村委会驻小寨组，距六桶乡政府6公里。下辖7个村民组，2010年有村民271户，1112人。土地面积4.39平方公里，有耕地1533亩，其中水田59亩，旱地1474亩。农作物主产玉米、小麦、洋芋、烤烟、油菜等。其中，烤烟生产是村的支柱产业。

官寨村烤烟生产基地

主干公路往西经凤联于六桶坝与186县道相连，村内村级公路连通各村民组，营运客车每天1班通往官寨。

木林村 位于六桶乡中部，东邻六桶村和盐井村，南连石板村和下坝村，西接何田村，北抵大新村和宝坪村。境内有木林寨、唐家寨、八字漕、苗寨、漆树漕、洒拉漕、堰塘、桐子漕和皮坡等自然村寨。村委会驻木林寨，距六桶乡政府2公里。下辖5个村民组，2010年有村民216户1068人。土地面积5.58平方公里，有耕地1803亩，其中水田134亩，旱地1669亩。农作物主产玉米、大豆、小麦、烤烟、油菜等。

六桶至康复村公路经堰塘、漆树漕为主干路横贯村境，并筑有堰塘至木林寨、蒋坡至洒拉漕、八字槽至下坝等村公路连通村内各自然村寨。

何田村 位于六桶乡西面，东邻木林村，南连康复村，北抵大兴村，西隔六广河与黔西县太来乡凉台村相望。境内有大寨、何家田、后坝、后槽、班家寨、岩头上、硝厂、神树丫口等自然村寨。村委会驻大寨，距六桶乡政府5公里。下辖8个村民组，2010年有村民225户1119人，其中苗、彝、布依少数民族35户115人。土地面积7.41平方公里，有耕地1764亩，其中水田39亩，旱地1725亩。农作物主产玉米、大豆、小麦、烤烟、油菜等。

1958年县民政局在硝厂建麻风病医院收治麻风病人。1966年修通麻风病院至六桶公路，成为村的交通主干线。20世纪90年代，兴修村级公路连通主干线通到后坝、大寨、班家寨、岩头等自然村寨。水路六广河上通六广，下至乌江电站。

下坝村　位于六桶乡西南面，北接何田村和木林村，东连石板村，南与大石布依族乡高山村和竹坪村毗邻，西以六广河与黔西县太来乡大寨村隔河相望。境内有土库营、坟坝、下坝、三尖角、后漕、偏坡寨、刘家湾子、大麻窝、青龙嘴、半坡、青龙山、蚂蝗田等自然村寨。村委会驻下坝刘家湾子，距六桶乡政府5公里。下辖8个村民组，2010年有村民214户1061人，其中苗、彝、布依少数民族16户77人。土地面积5.67平方公里，有耕地1778亩，其中水田88亩，旱地1690亩。农作物主产玉米、大豆、小麦、油菜、烤烟、马铃薯等。有山塘1个，蓄水量6000立方米，灌溉农田20亩。

村内主干公路自下坝往东北经木林至六桶，另一条往东至盐井村四楞接修文至六桶公路。

复兴村　位于六桶乡西北面，东邻榨土村，南连宝坪村和大兴村，西接联江村和顺江村，北抵海马村。境内有四方井、喇叭洞、胡家寨、白花口、大寨、新寨、野葱寨、白岩上等自然村寨。村委会驻四方井，距六桶乡政府5公里。下辖6个村民组，2010年有村民283户1024人，其中少数民族8户50人。土地面积4.44平方公里，有耕地1614亩，其中水田146亩，旱地1468亩，水田主要分布在水源较丰富的复兴组和野冲组。农作物主产玉米、水稻、小麦、烤烟和油菜等。筑有野葱寨山塘1个，蓄水2000立方米，主干渠1000米，灌溉农田100余亩。

保坪至顺江、保坪至联合两条过境公路经过村境，并与村级公路连通分别至百花和野葱寨。

榨土村　位于六桶乡西北面，东邻长兴村和三宝村，南连六桶村和宝坪村，西接复兴村，北抵海马村。境内有榨土、区山寨、双洞、马落孔、杨家沟等自然村寨。村委会驻榨土，距六桶乡政府4公里。下辖4个村民组，2010年有村民127户722人。土地面积2.66平方公里，有耕地1054亩，其中水田115亩，旱地939亩。农作物主产玉米、水稻、小麦、大豆、烤烟、油菜和马铃薯等。村内筑有山塘1个，蓄水量3500立方米，灌溉农田30余亩。

境内有榨土至万家槽、马落孔至四方井、青山至四方井3条村级公路，基本连通村内各自然村寨。

宝坪村　位于六桶乡中部偏向西北面，东邻六桶村，南连木林村，西接大兴村，北抵复兴村和榨土村。境内有宝宝寨、龙家坝、白果坪、柿花树、下牛角等自然村寨。村委会驻保保寨，距六桶乡政府5公里。下辖5个村民组，2010年有村民185户824人。土地面积3.21平方公里，有耕地1223亩，其中水田101亩，旱地1122亩。农作物主产玉米、水稻、小麦、大豆、烤烟、油菜和马铃薯等。村内白果坪建有宏兴肉牛养殖基地，草场160亩，年出栏肉牛300余头。

六桶至海马孔县级公路从村境中部经过，另有柿花树至白果坪、牛角井至下牛角村级公路，连通村内各自然村寨。

大兴村　位于六桶乡西北面，东邻保坪村，南连何田村，西接联合村，北抵复兴村。境内有大兴田、麻窝田、教林头、大苗寨、仰天窝、梯子岩等自然村寨。村委会驻麻窝田，距六桶乡政府5公里。下辖4个村民组，2010年有村民164户679人，其中彝族4户17人。土地面积3.37平方公里，有耕地1116亩，其中水田96亩，旱地1020亩。有林地面积600亩。农作物主产玉米、水稻、小麦、烤烟、油菜、花生和马铃薯等。

村内主干公路至宝坪村柿花树与六桶至海马孔公路相连。另一条由主干公路从教林头分道至大苗寨。

海马村　位于六桶乡西北面，东邻榨土村，南接复新村和顺江村，西北临六广河与金沙县化觉乡凉水井村和下坝村隔河相望。境内有海马孔、石关口、杨柳湾等自然村寨。村委会驻海马孔，距六桶乡政府12公里。下辖2个村民组。20世纪80年代修建乌江电站，因水淹迁出村民56户258人。2010年有村民

89户314人。土地面积1.55平方公里，修建乌江电站淹没海马村旱地290亩，水田118亩，荒山300亩。2010年村有耕地190亩，其中水田22亩，旱地168亩。农作物主产玉米、水稻、小麦、油菜、柑橘。

境内矿产资源主要有煤矿、铁矿、锰矿等。手工造纸在海马发展历史比较悠久，清代嘉庆年间（1796—1820），海马村任姓村民开始以构皮为原料，制造白纸，供给周围居民书写或从事祭奠活动之用。其造纸工艺已被列为县首批非物质文化遗产名录。

海马村手工造纸

村境地处修文、金沙两县交通咽喉地带，正在修建的海马大桥连通两岸。修文至六桶县级公路向北延伸至海马渡口。航运上达六广，下至乌江电站，货运客运络绎不绝。

顺江村　位于六桶乡西北面，东、南邻复新村，北抵海马村，西与金沙县化觉乡下坝村隔六广河对峙。境内有焦家坪、半坡、锈水田等自然村寨。村委会驻焦家坪，距六桶乡政府10公里。下辖3个村民组，2010年有村民123户617人。土地面积1.37平方公里，有耕地509亩，其中水田87亩，旱地422亩。农作物主产玉米、水稻、小麦、油菜、柑橘等。村水利灌溉得天独厚，从何家洞数十米高的悬崖上有飞瀑流水，为村农田灌溉主要水源，筑有1条800米长主干渠，保障全村农田及人畜饮用水。

境内矿产资源主要有煤、铁、锰等。

顺江村紧靠海马村，六桶至海马县道经过村境，另辟有从河边渡口至宝寨、至中寨的村级公路。航运上抵六广，下达乌江电站。

联合村　位于六桶乡西面，东邻大兴村，南接何田村，北抵复兴村，西隔六广河与黔西县太来乡凉台村和金沙县化觉乡下坝村隔河相望。境内有白石头、水沟、栽家湾、大麻窝等自然村寨。村委会驻白石头，距六桶乡政府10公里。下辖5个村民组，2010年有村民96户535人。土地面积2.9平方公里，有耕地503亩，其中水田57亩，旱地446亩。农作物主产玉米、水稻、小麦、油菜、柑橘等。水源主要靠顺江村何家洞牛鼻子眼洞中流出的终年不竭的泉水，筑有引水渠3000米，供全村农灌和人畜饮用。

境内蕴藏有煤、铁等矿资源。

村际公路主要有白石头往东北经喇叭洞至复兴村连通六桶至海马孔公路，另1条往北连通顺江村。

三宝村　位于六桶乡中部偏北，紧靠六桶村北面，东邻春江村，西接榨土村，北抵长新村。境内有高坎子、三宝山（原名纱帽山）、雷家湾、湾子、后头寨、大苗寨、烂泥沟、大坡脚、马鞍山、岩灰洞、罗家漕子等自然村寨。村委会驻高坎子，距六桶乡政府4公里。下辖9个村民组，2010年有村民235户1203人，其中彝族4户17人。土地面积5.71平方公里，有耕地1533亩，其中水田79亩，旱地1454亩。农作物主产玉米、大豆、小麦、马铃薯、烤烟、油菜等。筑有山塘3个，其中在三宝山2个，龙井湾1个，总库容3万立方米，可灌农田200亩。村内企业有养鸡场1个，年出栏肉鸡约5万只。兴宏养殖场在村境内置有分场，养殖母牛100余头，年繁殖牛犊60头左右。

六桶至黄金公路自南向北纵贯村境，分出的村级公路还有从榨土至马鞍山、大坡脚，三宝山至雷家弯、弯子后头寨和后槽。

长新村 位于六桶乡北面，东邻官寨村和春江村，南连三宝村，西接榨土村和海马村，北抵凉井村和团兴村，东北角与息烽县九庄镇上坝村以木林沟为界。境内有坝子、长冲、丁家漕、窝寨、龙洞漕、大寨、马道子、枇杷漕等自然村寨。村委会驻长冲，距六桶乡政府5公里。下辖6个村民组，2010年有村民182户994人。土地面积5.17平方公里，有耕地1304亩，其中水田14亩，旱地1290亩。农作物主产玉米、大豆、小麦、马铃薯、油菜、烤烟等。

六桶至黄金的县级公路自南向北经过村境，于境内向西分出至窝寨子、丁家漕和向东分出至枇杷漕，连通村内各自然村寨。

凉井村 位于六桶乡北面，北面和东面邻团兴村，南连长新村，西接海马村并与金沙县化觉乡隔六广河相望。境内有凉水井、三家苗、白泥土等自然村寨。村委会驻凉水井，距六桶乡政府6公里。下辖4个村民组，2010年有村民131户622人，其中少数民族10户37人。土地面积2.37平方公里，有耕地660亩，其中水田16亩，旱地644亩。农作物主产玉米、大豆、小麦、马铃薯、烤烟、油菜等。

六桶至黄金的县级公路自南向北经过村境中部，为境内主干公路，另又分出凉井至白泥土、凉井至砍基槽村级公路，连通村内各自然村寨。

六（桶）黄（金）公路从凉井村穿境而过

团兴村 位于六桶乡北面，东与息烽县九庄镇柏茂村毗邻，南连长新村和凉井村，北抵黄金村，西隔六广河与金沙县化觉乡相望。境内有罗家寨、木林沟、龙洞、浪漕、下坝、大水井等自然村寨。村委会驻罗家寨，距六桶乡政府9公里。下辖6个村民组，2010年有村民196户741人，其中苗、彝少数民族32户109人。土地面积4.31平方公里，有耕地1354亩，其中水田33亩，旱地1321亩。

农作物主产玉米、大豆、小麦、洋芋、烤烟、油菜等。筑有龙洞山塘1个，蓄水5000立方米，可灌溉农田40亩。

六桶至黄金的县级公路自南向北穿过村境中部，为境内主干公路，另又分出至麻窝、罗家寨、祠堂、龙洞、下坝、木林沟的村级公路。

黄金村 位于六桶乡最北边，地处县境西北角，东与息烽县九庄镇柏茂村毗邻，南接团兴村，西隔六广河与金沙县化觉乡相望。境内有湾子、白果树、麻窝、丫口寨、漆树湾、骗牛坪、苏家湾、湖广漕等自然村寨。村委会驻湾子，距六桶乡政府12公里。下辖5个村民组，2010年有村民186户706人，其中苗族26户66人。土地面积5.57平方公里，有耕地面积1276亩，其中水田4亩，旱地1272亩。农作物主产玉米、大豆、小麦、马铃薯、烤烟、油菜等。村境内水源较为缺乏，村民靠雨季蓄

黄金村苗族刺绣

积雨水，修建蓄水池5个，基本解决大部分人家的人畜用水问题。

20世纪80年代，修文至六桶县级公路往北延伸经三宝、长新、凉井、团兴至黄金村，成为村境主干公路，90年代又修通至各村民组的村级公路，并开通黄金至修文的客运。

村境内苗族刺绣技艺精湛，被列为县级非物质文化遗产名录。

二、社区

龙岗社区　位于县城西北面，2003年11月设置。东以人民北路为界连宾阳社区，南以翠屏西路为界接翠屏社区，西邻沙溪村，北抵潮水村。社区内主要街道有民主中路、民主北路、阳明西路、文化路、龙井巷、学宫巷、王家巷、温家坡等。社区办事处驻阳明西路，距龙场镇政府1公里。

社区内有温家坡、修中宿舍、龙岗花园、粮贸花园等居民小区。分为龙岗花园、学宫巷、翠屏西路、龙岗路、中山路1至3、秀水路、沙溪水泥厂红旗煤厂、温家巷王家巷温家坡、实小路、文化路1至3、阳明西路1至2、人民北路、粮贸花园共18个居民组。2010年有常住人口2830户7930人。

公共设施有龙岗广场，建筑面积1.44万平方米，是市民休闲娱乐的好地方。县级机关单位有县政府、信访局、民族宗教局、物价局、药品监督局、国税局等。企事业单位有修文中学、修文二中、实验小学、县医院住院部、百货公司、蔬菜公司、粮食局仓库、春华酒家等。

栖凤社区　位于县城西南面，2003年11月设置。东以人民中路为界连接虎山居委会，北以翠屏西路为界紧挨龙岗居委会，南邻新春村，西抵沙溪村。社区办事处驻民主路，距龙场镇政府0.5公里。

社区内主要街道有人民南路、民主路、龙岗路、翠屏西路和栖凤路。有油萝街廉租房区、世纪园小区、民主路左1至2、民主路右1至5、龙场、一矿、栖凤路左1至2、栖凤路右1至2、人民南路1至5、翠屏路1至3、沙溪巷、三角山1至2、油萝街等27个居民小组。2010年有常住人口1973户4695人。

驻社区机关单位有县政府、公安局、供销社、信访局、政法委、发改局、群众工作中心和龙场镇政府等；驻社区企事业单位主要有邮政局、电信局、烟草专卖局、盐业公司、第二实验小学、黔龙酒楼等。

宾阳社区　位于县城东北面，2003年11月设置。东连新水村，南以翠屏中路、翠屏东路为界邻虎山社区，西以人民北路为界接龙岗社区，北抵阳明村，占地面积0.76平方公里。社区办事处驻文成路，距龙场镇政府1公里。

社区内主要有人民北路、迎春路、宾阳路、朝阳路、阳明东路、河滨大道、阳明大道、文成路、良知路、永安巷等街道；有紫荆花园、华兴花园、千禧花园、欣兴花园、邮政花园、翰林花园、河滨花园、明河花园、阳光家园、利尔上河城、静园等25个居民小区。分为人民北路、迎春路、翠屏东路、农贸市场、永安巷、良知路、宾阳路、文成路、朝阳路、河滨大道、阳明大道、阳明东路一、阳明东路共13个居民组。2010年，有常住人口4105户9345人。公共设施有县体育馆、青少年活动中心、农贸市场等。

建在宾阳社区的机关办公楼和居民住房

驻社区县级机关单位有工商局、地方税务局、粮食局、农业办公室、教育局、旅游文体广播电视局、科技局、科学技术协会、新闻信

息中心、文学艺术界联合会、工商业联合会、民政局、离退局、老龄委工作办公室、技术质量监督局、法院、检察院、计划生育局、残疾人联合会等。企事业单位有县信用联社、财产保险公司、商业银行、农业发展银行、移动公司、联通公司、合力超市、大昌隆超市、自来水公司、修文三中、县实验幼儿园、县医院、百信医院等。

虎山社区 位于县城东南面，2003年11月设置。东邻新水村、南抵新春村、北以翠屏中路、翠屏东路为界连宾阳社区，西以人民南路为界接翠屏社区。社区办事处驻长征路，距龙场镇政府1公里。

社区主要有人民路、翠屏东路、长征路、虎山路、玩易路、黄秧巷等街道；有虎山小区、玩易花园、翠园、县委宿舍、人行宿舍、供电局宿舍、迎春家园、物资公司宿舍、烟草公司宿舍等居民小区。分为翠屏路1组至12组、县委路1组至8组、虎山路1组至6组、人民南路1组至5组、新客车站1组至4组共35个居民小组。2010年，全社区有常住人口2745户6713人。

社区内公共设施有客车站、新都广场、县委健身场等。县级机关单位有县委、人大、政协、人武部、档案局、乡镇企业局、审计局、财政局、国土资源局、人力资源和社会保障局、水利局、交通局、供电局、卫生局、气象局和龙场镇公安派出所、县交警队等。企事业单位有中医院、龙泉酒楼、黔龙酒家、人民银行、农业银行、人寿保险公司等。

景阳社区 位于扎佐城北面，1981年建扎佐镇第二居民委员会，2003年改建成景阳社区居民委员会，办公室设在古驿路27号，距扎佐镇政府2公里。区境东西宽1.2公里，南北长1.5公里。2010年有居民1104户3058人。辖区主要有前进北路、中山北路、古驿路、新东路、红卫路、四清路、革命路等街道；有盛世铭都、政府宿舍、烟叶站宿舍、农业服务中心宿舍等居民小区。辖有6个居民段，3个居民小组。

驻社区单位主要有扎佐中学、扎佐幼儿园、扎佐第一小学和农业服务中心等。公共设施主要有社区广场。名胜古迹有景阳书院、西门桥和天主教大经堂等。

襄阳社区 位于扎佐城南部，1981年建扎佐镇第一居民委员会，2003年改建成襄阳社区居民委员会，办公室设在中山北路场坝上，距扎佐镇政府1.5公里，辖区东西宽1.2公里，南北长1.5公里。2010年有居民1201户3328人，其中少数民族13户28人。主要有中山南路、前进南路、襄阳南路、腾飞路、景阳园路和大园路等街道；有珍珠铭园、珍珠新园、明兴佳园、紫竹园、安居工程和珍珠河新城等居民小区。共分6个居民小组。

社区内置有紫竹园广场和扎佐客车站等公共设施和两个农贸市场。驻社区单位有扎佐镇政府、文化服务中心、社保所、土管所、计生站、景阳派出所、交警队、国税分局、地税分局、法庭、财政所、工商所、司法所、村建所、安监站和扎佐卫生院等。驻社区企业主要有盐业公司、检车场、供销社和邮政、电信、农行、信用社营业所。教育单位有扎佐第二小学和民办景阳中学、叮叮当幼儿园等。

万江社区 位于扎佐镇南面石竹、新民两村境域，2005年8月建立，社区办公室设在原万江机电厂内，距扎佐镇政府3公里。社区境域东西宽2.5公里，南北长1公里。居民包括原万江机电公司、医药园区和兴红厂区的非农业人口，分为万江、林场和林校3个居民小组。2010年有居民1354户3750人，其中少数民族27户58人。

公共设施主要有万江社区养老服务中心、万江广场、林场花园广场、林校园林式校园、林场医院、餐饮一条街等。驻社区企业主要有环球塑钢厂、宏达塑钢厂、长运公司、金汇彩印厂、林场食苑、桃源食府等企业。著名的黔中药谷—修文医药产业园位于辖区内，驻有德昌祥、光正、长生、绿太阳、天方、和仁堂、恒和、浩诚、维康、科福、喜儿康、安泰、科开、华德斯、金格等医药食品企业。文教卫生单位有贵州省扎佐林业学校（含贵州师范大学分院）、林场医院。

驰名的快活林饮食一条街位于210国道上，其特色菜肴“扎佐蹄膀”肥而不腻，味香可口，深受食者青睐。

万江社区一隅

长久社区 位于久长镇境中部久长街上，1990年3月建久长镇居民委员会，2003年11月改建成长久社区居民委员会，属久长镇管辖，为避免与镇名、村名重复，故命名“长久社区”。社区办公室驻久长街，距久长镇政府0.5公里。有川黔路、修开路、龙山路、朝阳路和老街巷路等街道。分为久长街上1至4组和驴坊组、兴隆组共6个居民组。2010年有居民1273户2678人，其中少数民族27户86人。

2001年，建成龙山大道，形成以朝阳路，黔川公路（210国道）上重要的商贸集镇。逢场天，沿街头摆摊设点，上市万余人。丫叉田饮食一条街，方便了川黔路上南来北往的旅客及周围居民，生意兴隆。

久长镇政府驻地在社区境内，建有机关办公楼、精神文明活动中心大楼各1幢，建筑面积1850平方米。另驻有久长派出所、财政所、林业站、医院、农技站、计生站等镇属机关、事业单位。社区内还置有久长中学、久长小学及幼儿园等教育机构。

松江社区 1988年，建六广镇六广居民管理委员会，管理六广合群路、团结路、南江路、松江大道、环城路、毓秀路和凤凰路等街道非农业人口，居委会驻南江路4号，距六广镇政府0.5公里。2003年11月改建成社区，取名“松江社区居民委员会”。辖区东与六广村合群组相连，南靠六广村上南江组，西与六广下南江组相邻，北与滨江村接壤。东西宽0.62公里，南北长1.5公里。辖上街、下街、后街和镇机关4个居民组。2010年有常住居民407户749人。居民多以经商为业，在六广街上设店营业。另有在外办企业和从政、从教靠工薪收入生活的住户。特产的六广面条、白酒和臭豆腐远近闻名。

松江社区为六广镇政治、经济、文化中心，驻社区机关单位有六广镇政府、工商分局、地税所、公安派出所和法庭等；文教卫生部门有六广中学、六广小学和六广卫生院；驻社区企业有移动公司、邮政电信、信用合作社等营业部。公共设施有健身体育场、驿韵休闲广场和两个农贸市场。

小箐社区 1982年建立小箐居民委员会，管理小箐街上街道非农业人口，辖区东面和北面接大兴村，南靠小箐村，西抵大坝村。2003年11月改建成小箐社区居民委员会，办公室驻小箐街上，距小箐乡政府0.5公里。下辖4个居民段，2010年有居民366户929人，其中少数民族13户25人。社区境域东西长0.9公里，南北宽0.4公里。主要街道有消极洞至大丫口为迎宾路，老街口北至油脂仓库为太平路，老街口南至小箐小学为兰谷路，农贸市场口至小箐中学为石景路。

小箐乡党、政机关驻小箐社区，是全乡政治、经济、文化中心。社区内设有中学1所，小学1所，卫生院1所，通信基站3座。社区供水、供电和信息网络俱全。2001年建成的贵（阳）毕（毕）高等级公路，在小箐街口设立收费站。

第二章 环 境

县境位于云贵高原东部。地势东高西低，除西部六广河、猫跳河沿岸河谷深切外，大部分地区较平缓，海拔一般在1200—1400米之间，最高海拔1610米，最低海拔760米，平均海拔1270米，县城海拔1240米。地貌类型属黔中丘陵区，西部边缘属猫跳河、六广河河谷深切地带主要以峡谷为主，东部以中山槽谷为主，中部以丘陵盆地为主，中北部及南部以中山峰丛为主，西部和西北部以峰丛洼地为主。县境河流属长江流域乌江水系，有大小河流31条，其中流域面积在20平方公里以上河流12条，县内河总长300.5公里，平均河网密度279.3米/平方公里。

气候温暖湿润，属北亚热带季风湿润气候，划为黔中湿润温和区，其特点为：春秋两季长，夏冬两季短，夏无酷暑，冬无严寒。累年平均气温13.3℃~15℃间，年均降水量为1179.5毫米，常年无霜期269天左右。全年多以多云天气为主，日照偏少，历年年平均日照为1307.5小时。常见不利气候主要有暴雨、冰雹、干旱、倒春寒、秋季绵雨、霜冻、凝冻等，不时影响农业生产。

20世纪80年代，乡镇企业迅猛发展，工业废水、废弃物和废气对环境污染日趋严重。从90年代初开始，政府逐步加强对环境污染治理，一方面对高污染企业采取关、停、并、转等措施进行治理整顿；另一方面引进一批低能耗、低污染企业发展工业经济；同时加强生态建设，先后完成坡改梯、长防林、贵阳市二环林带建设和中韩合作造林工程。至2010年，全县林木覆盖率达40.3%，县境大部分地区山青水秀，生态环境好。

第一节 自然环境

一、地质 地貌

（一）地质

县境在大地构造上处于扬子地台黔桂地台黔北古陆（黔中隆起）南坡，属黔中分区，自下古生代奥陶纪至上古生代泥盆纪期间，地壳升出海面，遭受剥蚀，因而缺失奥陶系、志留系、泥盆系、侏罗系、第三系地层；石炭系地层也只在南部出现。第四系新构造运动上升，但堆积物分布零星，且厚度不大，大部分地层沉积厚度比相邻地区小，无火成岩和变质岩出露。出露的地层主要有震旦系、寒武系、石炭系、二叠系、三迭叠、白垩系和第四系。

出露地层分布一览表

表1—02—01

地 层	出 露 地		矿 藏
	乡（镇）	村	
震旦系	久长镇	芦山村马蹄关一带	只有上统的灯影组，含磷矿，但品位低，开采价值不大
寒武系	扎佐镇	葛马 长坡 大河 大堡 丁官 把七 马鞍山 龙王 喻家街 新民 三元 石竹	有下统的牛蹄塘组、明心寺组、金顶山组、清虚洞组；中统的高台组、石冷水组；上中统的娄山关群。其表面浮土中还有残留的铁矿石，品位高低不一
	六广镇	合营 合兴	
	久长镇	山岔 栋青 中心 石榴 清江	
	六屯乡	都堡 新堡 安全 高峰 大寨 三寨 小木 西冲 独山	
	龙场镇	程官 水塘 高仓 小山 新水 王官 中哨坝 中哨 干坝 沙溪 潮水 小营	
	谷堡乡	长冲 折溪 大寨	
	小箐乡	全新 小坝 凤凰 万兴	
	洒坪乡	五老山 青杠林	
石炭系	龙场镇	小山 水塘 高仓 干坝	蕴藏有铝矾土、耐火黏土和赤铁矿，与铝矾土伴生有镓、铌、钽、钛、锆等稀有元素
	谷堡乡	长冲 尖山 大寨	
	洒坪乡	五老山	
二叠系	各乡镇均有		出露较广，赋生煤、硫铁矿和汞矿。其中煤资源分布面广，储量大
三叠系	全县皆有		出露广泛，赋生白云岩与石灰岩，储量大
白垩系	龙场镇	小营 马关 普陀	只有上统扎佐群，呈砖红、紫红色砾岩，含砾岩屑石英砂岩夹粘土岩
	小箐乡	崇恩 小箐	
第四系	各乡镇均有		堆积物零星，厚度小

（二）地貌

1. 地貌特征

县境地处云贵高原东部，地表总趋势为东高西低，除西部六广河、猫跳河沿岸河谷深切外，大部分地区比较平缓，海拔1200米至1400米地带比重大，面积为718.25平方公里，占全县总面积的66.77%，海拔1400米以上有110.47平方公里，占10.27%，海拔1200米以下有246.98平方公里，占22.96%。全县平均海拔1270.4米，最高点扎佐东南三角山主峰海拔1610米，最低点六广河周家堰出境处正常水位海拔760米，相差850米，一般高差50米至200米，县城海拔1240米。

境内石灰岩、白云岩和白云质灰岩等碳酸盐岩溶分布广，其面积占全县总面积的74.95%。在温暖湿

润的气候条件下，这类岩层的地表发育成石沟、石芽、峰林、峰丛、峡谷、盲谷、旱谷、洼地、漏斗，落水洞、天生桥等。在地下还发育成钟乳石，石笋、石柱、溶洞、伏流等形态各异的岩溶地貌。据1979年3月，县人防办公室对溶洞的普查，全县有溶洞230个，洞多且深，洞景千姿百态，适宜旅游开发。

2. 地貌类型

1984年调查，县境地貌类型属黔中丘陵区，类型多样，除西部边缘河谷切割较深外，相对高度多在150米以内。主要地貌组合为：东部以中山槽谷为主，中部以丘陵盆地为主，中北部和南部以中山峰丛为主，西部和西北部以峰丛洼地为主，西部边缘以峡谷为主。

山地 各乡镇均有，相对高度在100米以上，山势连绵，喀斯特地貌特征明显，面积459.67平方公里，占全县总面积42.92%。

丘陵 各乡镇均有，相对高度一般在100米以下，地势起伏，坡度和缓，面积369.92平方公里，占全县总面积34.54%。西部多岩溶丘陵，主要为石灰岩，面积约占全县总面积的60%-70%，喀斯特地貌发育典型，峰林广布，地面崎岖，风景异常优美。中东部除岩溶丘陵外，尚有土山丘陵，面积约占全县总面积30%-40%，易于农耕和造林。

盆地 俗称坝子，三面或四面环山，主要集中在中、东部地区，面积129.27平方公里，占全县面积12.07%，400亩以上的坝子有55个，其中大于5000亩的2个，1000—4999亩的12个，500亩至999亩的10个，400亩至499亩的28个。

峡谷坡地 主要集中在谷堡、小箐、洒坪和六广等乡（镇），面积112.14平方公里，占全县面积的10.47%。

南部低山丘陵盆地区

3.山脉山峰

山脉 县境地处黔北古陆（黔中隆起）南坡，属苗岭山脉北缘。山脉除牛巷包山山脉外大多源起息烽南山（海拔1749.6米）、西山(海拔1622米)，主要山脉呈北东至南西成群展布。

山峰 全县有海拔1500米以上山峰89座，主要集中3大片区，北部小箐、久长有40座，如大山、老江山、贾角山、盐井坡等；东部扎佐、六屯一带有19座，如高峰山及附近的山峰；南部龙场东南和扎佐南部一带有30座。境内山峰大多相对高度在200米以内，坡度亦不太陡峭。

二、河流水系

县境河流属长江流域乌江水系。自久长北部经扎佐至南部三元一线分水岭以西的河流汇入乌江或经猫跳河汇入乌江；以东的河流经鱼梁河注入清水江再汇入乌江。全县有大小河流31条，其中流域面积在20平方公里以上的12条。县内河流总长300.5公里，河网密度279.3米/平方公里。

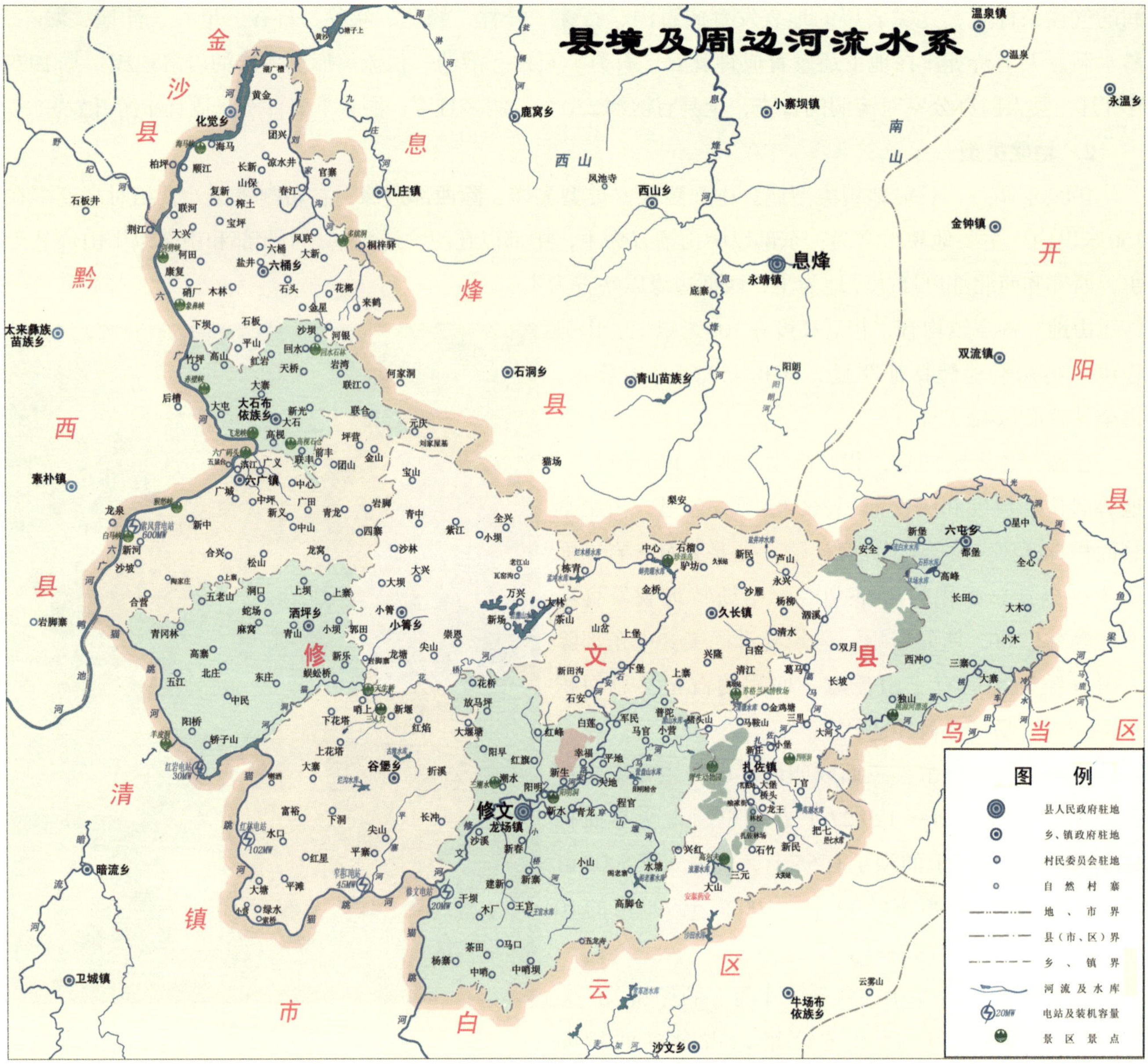

（一）过境河流

乌江　古称延江，亦称黔江。发源于威宁县香炉山，流经县境段称“六广河”，为修文、黔西、金沙3县之界河。在县内流经六广、大石、六桶乡3乡镇，长43.7公里。出境前流域面积2.45万平方公里，年平均流量350立方米/秒，年径流量133.6亿立方米，因河谷深切，田高水低，难于灌溉。水能资源丰富，国家统一开发。1980年，六广渡至乌江渡电站通航，其中县境通航里程41公里，为泛舟游览六广河峡谷风光、捕捞鱼类和水上台阶运输提供了方便。2005年又在六广河白马峡开发建成索风营电站，从电站大坝至猫跳河六级电站又增加了通航里程15公里。

猫跳河　旧名滴澄河，是乌江的一级支流。发源于安顺旧州长山，流经平坝、清镇、贵阳进入县境西部，是修文县和清镇市的界河。河源头海拔高程1400米，汇入乌江河口高程为768米。河流总长181公里。县内经红枫电厂建三、四、五、六级电站，在六广镇三岔河处汇入乌江，县境段河长49.65公里，

流域面积3260.9平方公里，多年平均流量55.9立方米/秒，年径流量17.73亿立方米。河流两岸陡峭，河床低洼，落差较大，水深流急。省沿河建成的6个水电站，有4个在县境内。筑坝引水虽对提高水位、调节水量有很大的作用，但河谷深切，除水能发电和发展旅游外其余利用难度较大。

六广河

猫跳河

光洞河　属乌江三级支流，发源于息烽县境，经开阳流入修文东部边境，为开阳县与修文县的界河，境内河长3.8公里后，于六屯乡河坝潜入地下出境，再进入开阳县境，汇入鱼梁河。伏流前流域面积119.4平方公里，多年平均流量1.01立方米/秒，年径流量0.32亿立方米。

车田河　属乌江三级支流，由贵阳市乌当区流入县东南边境，经2.5公里后汇入鱼梁河。流域面积48.11平方公里，多年平均流量0.68立方米/秒，年径流量0.21亿立方米。

（二）县内河流

修文河　系猫跳河支流，下游原名蛮子河，属乌江二级支流。发源于久长镇栋青村，流经石安、马家桥、县城、沙溪等地，于河口电站汇入猫跳河，源头海拔1352米，汇入猫跳河口高程1100米，流域面积228.2平方公里。主河道长37公里。河口多年平均流量4.25立方米/秒，年径流量1.35亿立方米。源头建有孟冲水库，支流有马官河、穿山堰河、瓦罐窑河、小沙溪河。

马官河　属乌江三级支流，发源于扎佐镇马鞍山村背篼湾，源头高程1320米。源头建有清塘水库。河流由东向西，于堡子头进入伏流，至新寨出露，过猪头山，下游有黑山水库水从右岸汇入，经小营和马官，左岸有云盘山水库水汇入，再经大地堡汇入修文河。河流长13.4公里，流域面积25.9平方公里，多年平均流量0.44立方米/秒，流入修文河口高程1246米，年径流量0.14亿立方米。

穿山堰河　属乌江三级支流，发源于龙场镇高仓村破屋，源头高程1319米。河流由南向北流经木午即转向西，流经邓家新寨、程官、罗家寨，于县城东门外曲尺桥处与瓦罐窑河相汇后，经长征桥流入修文河。河长17.9公里，流域面积69.2平方公里。多年平均流量1.17立方米/秒，年径流量0.37亿立方米。河流沿途设有拦河堰灌溉两岸稻田。

瓦罐窑河　又名白岩寨河，县城河段称小桥河。属乌江四级支流。发源于王官村龙塘沟木阁箐，海拔1358米。由南向北流经瓦罐窑、白岩寨至毛栗园，左岸有陶家龙潭水流汇入，再经吴家湾、黄秧寨于曲尺桥处汇入穿山堰河，全长9公里，流域面积21.3平方公里，河口高程1239米，多年平均流量0.3立方米/秒。上游建有瓦罐窑引水工程，下游两岸均为稻田，便于筑堰引流灌溉。

桃源河

桃源河 属乌江二级支流，亦名扎佐河、三元河、于襄河、鱼梁河。发源于扎佐镇三元村龙井沟，源头高程1350米。河流由南向北流经浪潮水库、马老寨，至扎佐珍珠河从右岸汇入，至小堡高滩河从右岸汇入，至三里葛马河从左岸汇入后河流转向东，流经鱼井坝、桃子湾，过香巴房水库、三道响水，至桃源大寨东下游右岸有车田河汇入，在小木村洞洞塘进入开阳县境。境内河长29.1公里，出境前流域面积375.9平方公里，境内部分流域面积138.8平方公里。河流洪枯水位变化约4米，鱼井坝河段最枯流量0.2立方米/秒。多年平均流量每秒6.5立方米，年径流量2.14亿立方米。

葛马河 属乌江三级支流，发源于久长镇盐井冲，源头高程1353米。河流由北向南，经砂锅寨至泗溪，右岸有一支流由久长上灰腰流来，经扯泥堡、杨柳井进入清水，于藏溪洞入洞形成伏流，至付家磨出露，往下游汇入葛马河。流至葛马寨，右岸有一支流汇入，至三里桥汇入桃源河。河长11.8公里，河口高程1263米，流域面积64平方公里，多年平均流量1.17立方米/秒，年径流量0.38亿立方米。

平寨河 系乌江二级支流，发源于谷堡乡红焰村后寨东南面，源头高程1330米。河流由北向南，经折溪、新寨、鱼洞、杨坝田、平寨，于猫冲汇入猫跳河。河长12.1公里，流域面积34.6平方公里，河口高程1082米。多年平均流量0.59立方米/秒，年径流量0.19亿立方米。

猫洞河 属乌江二级支流，发源于久长镇茶山村大白岩下龙孔，源头高程1358米。河流由东向西，上段称花桥河，经岩鹰山水库土坝流经西家湾、花桥、鲤鱼塘、天生桥。到天生桥下游与郭田河汇集。郭田河发源于小箐乡凤凰村老箐沟，流过万兴堡经石坝库区、车家湾、大桥沟，到天生桥下游与花桥河汇集后称猫洞河，再经蜈蚣桥、白龙洞、团山坝，于轿子山村东缘三岔河处汇入猫跳河。主流长27.3公里，流域面积135.8平方公里，河口高程849米，多年平均流量2.7立方米/秒，年径流量0.85亿立方米。

刘家沟河 属乌江一级支流，发源于六桶乡银河村白岩厂。源头高程1240米，河流由南向北，经花椰田坝，至大兴村孔家大山南麓孟家槽子入洞形成伏流。于杨洞出露地表，流程2公里后，发源于六桶坝的支流在刘家寨附近从左岸汇入，经刘家沟田坝、大林沟，于黄金村流入息烽县境，注入乌江。出境前流域面积162.1平方公里，其中境内流域面积52.2平方公里，境内河长13.92公里，入乌江河口高程760米。多年平均流量每秒1.08立方米，年径流量0.34亿立方米。

三、气候

修文地处黔中腹地，大部分地区属北亚热带季风湿润气候，也有部分属中亚热带气候。整体上，季风交替明显、四季分明、多云寡照、雨量充沛，光热水同季；夏无酷暑，冬无严寒，气候温和，舒适宜人，十分有利于农业生产的发展。

（一）热量

县城累年（1963—2010年，下同）平均气温13.8℃。1963—1997年年平均气温13.64℃，而1998—2010年年均气温14.19℃，较前35年年均数高出0.55℃，显现了年均气温缓慢提升的变化趋势。受海拔高

度、纬度和地貌等因素的影响，各地气温体现出明显的地域差异。2010年除龙场镇（镇政府地处县域）外，其余9乡（镇）政府所在地的气温都不尽一致，六广镇16.3℃为最高，久长镇13.5℃为最低。同一地点的年均气温波动不大，县城平均气温在1963—2010年的48年中，最高的14.6℃（2008年）和最低12.8℃（1984年）之间差距仅1.8℃，但在同年各月份间的差距却较为悬殊。2008年7月平均气温22.4℃，而1月平均气温为0.9℃，两月之间相差达21.5℃，其余年月份之间差距在17℃—21.4℃范围内。同年极端最高和最低气温更为悬殊。2002年极端最高气温32.9℃，而极端最低气温为－3.8℃，两者相差36.7℃。其余年份均在30℃以上。日气温最高和最低的较差一般在9℃左右，但每年2月日较差最大，有相当罕见、日较差达24.1℃的记录。正值主要农作物水稻、玉米和烤烟生长期的4—9月，也是全县每年月均气温最高的时段。

县城1998—2010年月平均气温值表

表1—02—02　　　　单位：℃

全年	1月	2月	3月	4月	5月	6月	7月	8月	9月	10月	11月	12月
14.2	3.6	6.4	10.1	14.9	18.4	21.4	22.8	21.2	19.2	15.0	11.4	5.6

县城≥0℃平均积温为4926.1℃，平均初日为1月30日，终日为12月26日，持续期332天；≥5℃的平均积温4599.1℃，平均初日为3月8日，终日为12月2日，持续期270天；≥10℃平均积温4091.5℃，平均初日4月4日，终日11月8日，持续期220天；≥15℃的平均积湿3018℃，平均初日为5月6日，终日为10月1日，持续期148天；≥20℃的平均积温为1423.1℃，初日为6月25日，终日为8月28日，持续期64天。积温条件完全能满足水稻扬花、灌浆，玉米孕穗、授粉，烤烟叶片干物质积累对热量的要求。

积温高低受多因素的制约，地域差异较为明显，除县城外，各代表点的具体资料如下表：

各代表点积温情况表

表1—02—03

指　标		久长	六广	大屯
≥5℃	初　日	10/3	26/2	19/2
	终　日	28/11	18/12	2/11
	持续期（天）	264	296	318
	积温值（℃）	4392.4	5102.3	5639.9
≥10℃	初日	5/4	24/3	19/3
	终日	4/11	16/11	25/11
	持续期（天）	214	238	252
	积温值（℃）	3899.8	4551.5	5027.8
≥15℃	初日	20/5	5/3	20/4
	终日	27/9	8/10	18/10
	持续期（天）	131	159	182
	积温值（℃）	2852.5	3408.7	4011.8

续表

指标		久长	六广	大屯
≥20℃	初日	2/7	8/6	21/5
	终日	23/8	9/9	22/9
	持续期（天）	53	94	125
	积温值（℃）	1152.5	2135.7	2424.3

县城累年平均无霜期为267天。地势对无霜期影响大，海拔每增高100米，无霜期约缩短11天。在地势较高地区秋初春末易出现霜冻、对农作物造成危害。

（二）降水

县域年降水量多在1000毫米—1250毫米之间，县城1978—2010年年均降水1129.9毫米。降水在地域上呈规律性的变化：由东至西，年降水量递减。在年度间降水量变化幅度较大。县城1978年—2010年的33年中，年降水在1000毫米以下的有5年（1981年、1989年、1998年、2006年和2009年）；年降水在1000毫米—1100毫米的有11年（1983年、1985年、1986年、1990年、1993年、1994年、2001年、2003年、2004年、2005年和2010年）；年降水在1100毫米—1200毫米的有6年（1982年、1987年、1988年、1991年、1992年和1995年）；年降水在1200毫米—1300毫米的有5年（1978年、1979年、1999年、2002年和2008年）；年降水在1300毫米—1400毫米的有4年（1980年、1984年、2000年和2007年）；年降水在1400毫米以上的有2年（1996年和1997年）。时段内2009年降水876.9毫米为最少，仅为最多1996年1444毫米的60.73%。这两年降水量净差567.1毫米。在月际之间降水量也是不均衡的。全县一般都在每年4月进入雨季，10月下旬结束。4—9月是降水量为集中的时段，占全年降水量的78.3%。

1978—2010年平均降水量月际分配表

表1—02—04

月份	全年	1月	2月	3月	4月	5月	6月	7月	8月	9月	10月	11月	12月
降水量（毫米）	1129.9	24.8	25.3	36.0	89.6	161.2	203.6	201.9	123.0	105.4	93.2	45.0	20.9
占全年比重（%）	100.00	2.19	2.24	3.19	7.93	14.27	18.02	17.87	10.88	9.33	8.25	3.98	1.85

在地域上，降水不均的特点表现较为突出，2000年—2010年的11年中，年均降水量以多少为序的情况是：龙场镇1218.6毫米，扎佐镇1160.3毫米，六桶乡1113.9毫米，六屯乡1105.3毫米，谷堡乡1083.8毫米，小箐乡1034.4毫米，久长镇1029毫米，洒坪乡1014.6毫米，大石乡913.3毫米，六广镇846.3毫米。六广镇降水量只为龙场镇的69.45%。

1978—2010年四季降水变化大。春季（3—5月）占25.38%，夏季（6—8月）占46.77%，秋季（9—10月）占17.58%，冬季（11月至次年2月）占10.27%。

（三）日照

县域纬度较低，但因云量和雨天较多，日照时数较少，在全国属低值区，致使太阳辐射量也较少。累年平均日照时数为1296.4小时，平均每天只有3.6小时。一般以每年12月至次年2月为寡照期，而6—8

月日照偏多。在年际间日照时数波动较大，1978—2010年中：日照时数最短的是1997年（990.5小时），在1000—1100小时的有3年，在1100—1200小时的有7年，在1200—1300小时的有6年，在1300—1400小时的有9年，在1400—1500小时的有2年，1978年日照长达1613.2小时为最高，最低的1997日照时数仅占它的61.4%。常年4—9月，集中了全年日照时数的66.97%，很适秋收作物的生长发育。地势，特别是受山体遮蔽和阳坡阴坡的不同，日照时间长短也不相同；地势平坦开阔地区的日照时数高于地势起伏变化大的山区。据此，城关、扎佐地区多年日照时间平均值在1300小时以上，而小箐、六广地区日照年平均值在1300小时以下。全县日照百分率多在25%—30%之间，但7—9月各地日照百分率均在30%以上。

全县各代表点太阳辐射量为35.5—37.3万焦耳/平方厘米。扎佐镇最高，为37.3万焦耳/平方厘米，乌栗只有33.7万焦耳/平方厘米。县城太阳辐射量绝大多数年份达36.9万焦耳以上/平方厘米，其中能为农作物利用，进行光合作用的生理辐射量为18.08万焦耳/平方厘米，占太阳辐射量的48.97%。与日照一样，太阳辐射量在年际之间变化也较大。在一年中，太阳辐射量最低值为1月，只有1.5万焦耳—1.6万焦耳/平方厘米，7月为最高，达4.5—4.9万焦耳/平方厘米。

（四）风

全县累年平均气压为875.2百帕，在年际之间变化幅度极小。1978—2010年最高为1995年的876.3百帕，最低为2000年的874.7百帕，两者差距仅1.6百帕。累年月均以11月最高，为880.3百帕，7月为最低、为868.9百帕，两者差距也仅11.4百帕。

因县处季风区，一年中各方位的风均可出现，但盛行风向又较明显：上年10月至次年4月主要是东北风，5—9月又主要是南风或偏南风。

县域内风力一般较弱，风速不大。月平均风速在2.2—3.2米/秒之间。但寒潮入侵时的北风，夏季的偏南风和发生强对流天气的瞬间强风，为时虽短，但风力强劲，可达5—6级（8—13.8米/秒）。县气象部门2007年3月3日13时17分记录了一次强风，瞬间风速达15.1米/秒。

（五）主要天气现象出现的频率

1963—2010年每年出现主要天气现象的频率分别是（天/年）；降雨249.3，降雪14.6，下冰雹1.5，雾20.4，轻雾107.5，露155.7，霜15.2，雨凇12.6，积雪4.7，结冰26.3，大风3.5。

（六）气候灾害

县内常见气候灾害有：暴雨、冰雹、干旱、倒春寒、秋季绵雨、霜冻、凝冻等。

暴雨 单日降雨量50毫米以上天气每年均有发生，多在一年中的4月—10月之间，尤以5月—7月最多。一般暴雨每年3次左右，雨量＞150毫升以上的暴雨10年一遇，雨量在100毫升左右暴雨3-4年一遇，主要集中在县境东部和南部地区。1996年7月2日—4日，境内遭受百年不遇的暴雨袭击，其中2日23时—3日11时的11小时为特大暴雨时限，降雨量达168.7毫米。3天降雨194.6毫米，突破了修文最大降雨165.2毫米的历史纪录。全县农作物受灾面积8.57万亩，重灾和绝收占一半。房屋、畜圈、烤房倒塌1635间，直接经济损失2267万元。还有13处较大山体滑坡。

冰雹 一年四季均有出现，4至5月较多。冰雹总是伴着大风和雷雨，破坏性很大，常给农业生产造成严重损失。冰雹有较强的地域性，河谷地带和四面环山的槽谷、盆地发生较多，六广金山、小箐小坝、洒坪中明等地较集中，历年受灾较重。次为六桶乡中东部、大石布依族乡东部、小箐乡东部、谷堡乡中西部、龙场镇中南部、扎佐镇中南部和久长镇中部等地。1995年5月1日21时—23时，暴风、大雨和冰雹齐袭境内，最大局部风速20米/秒左右，1小时内降雨量30毫米至40毫米之间，受灾面涉及6个乡(镇)，触电死亡3人，伤8人，农业经济损失达1400万元。

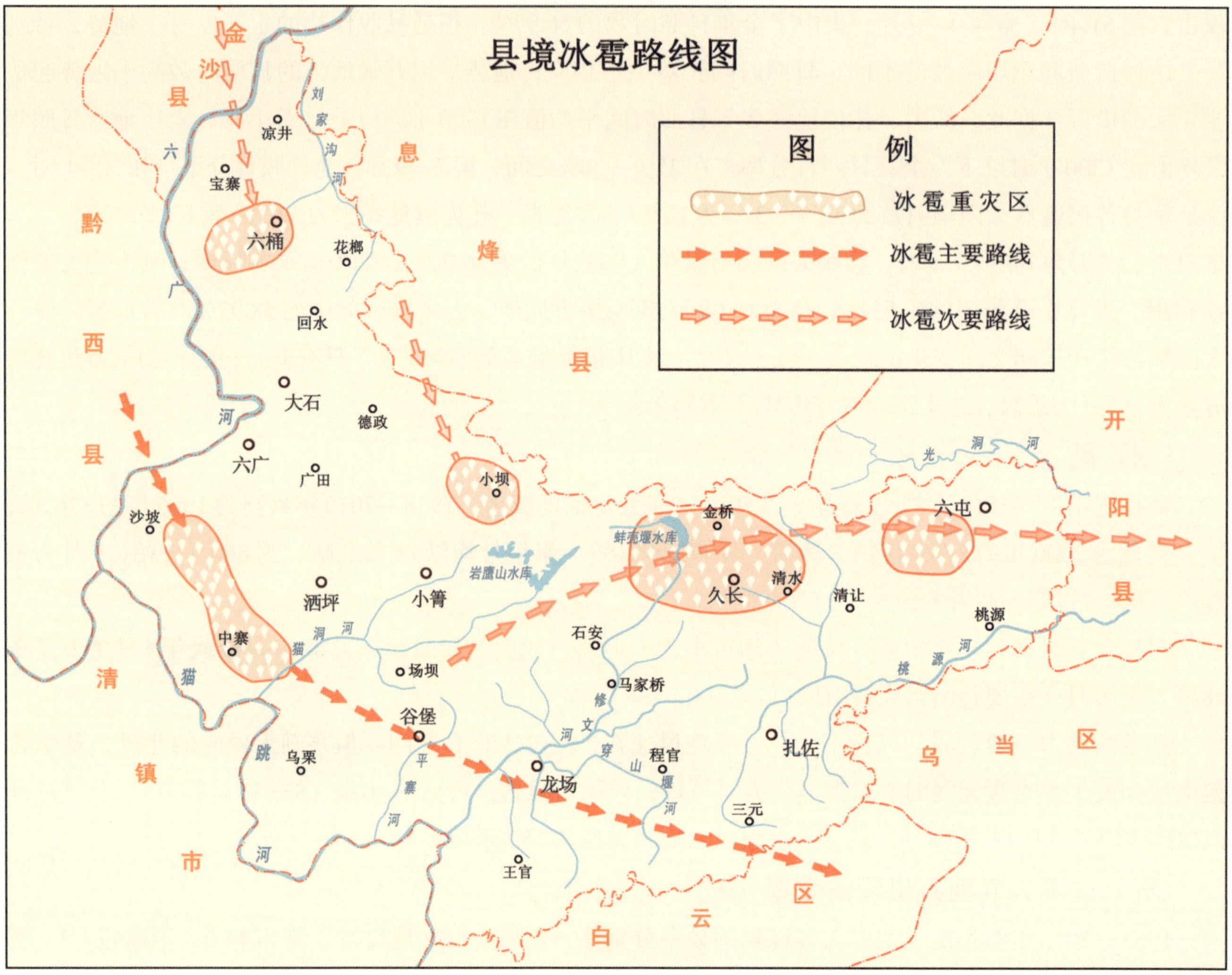

1990年起开展人工防雹，2000年后，防雹设施逐步完善，降雹次数减少，灾害损失减少。1990年至2010年，冰雹次数由以前的年均1.5次减少到年均不到1次。

干旱 一年四季均可发生，出现最多的是春旱和夏旱。春旱发生在一年中的3至5月，夏旱发生在6至8月。1980年到2010年，全县发生旱灾20次，其中春旱发生的频率较高达到旱灾的94%，重大的夏旱持续时间长达30余天。1990年6月中旬至9月未降透雨，全县7万多人和8000多头大牲畜发生饮水困难，全县粮食比上年减产24%。2003年7月11日—8月31日持续干旱52天，全县水库干涸4座，农业经济损失483万元。2009年出现夏秋连旱天气，8月12日—9月15日连续35天干旱。2010年降水量比历年偏少156.5毫米，夏秋冬旱情持续，导致山塘水库蓄水不足，部分水源枯竭，造成1.221万人，6.953万头大牲畜饮水困难，农业生产亦受严重影响。

倒春寒 俗称“反春”，每年3月至4月易出现连续3天气温低于12℃的阴雨天气，严重时易成灾。初春至清明，有时出现0℃以下气温天气，冻坏农作物。3月下旬至4月中旬的倒春寒，易引起烂种烂秧，不仅造成种子损失，而且贻误播种季节，导致8月中旬不能安全齐穗，易受秋风危害，导致减产。1996年3

至4月，持续出现倒春寒天气38天，平均气温仅7.4℃，4月3日最低温为0.5℃，为县境30年一遇最长时间的低温天气。2001年4月10至12日，出现一次低温阴雨，由于大部地区采用地膜育苗技术，故未造成大的损失，仅六桶乡500亩玉米，300亩水稻秧苗和100亩烤烟苗部分受损。

秋风绵雨 每年8月至10月易出现秋风绵雨天气。在8月底至9月初水稻扬花期间连续3天出现日均温低于20℃天气，影响水稻扬花授粉，导致空壳率增加的气候叫“秋风”。9月至10月，正值秋收，若遇多天秋风绵雨，不利水稻、玉米等粮食作物收获和收藏，并会出现发芽、霉变等问题，导致粮食减产。2002年8月9日至18日，连续10天低温阴雨，正处于水稻抽穗扬花授粉期，致使9.41万亩水稻减产。

霜冻 晚秋10月下旬至次年初春3月下旬，约为166天，年均霜冻期96天。年均霜日9天左右，在晴朗无风，气温降至0℃以下的夜晚和凌晨易发生。在丘陵、谷地、盆地，霜冻强度大，持续时间长。俗话说：“雪压高山，霜打平地。”

凝冻 冬末春初，常在境内东部地势较高的久长镇、扎佐镇、龙场镇和六屯乡部分地区出现。1978年至2010年，凝冻发生的年份逐渐减少，但发生的年份中天数则持续长、气温低。1984年1月6日发生凝冻一直持续到2月7日，长达23天；2000年1月16日—31日，最低气温达到-5.9℃；2001年1月发生2次，最低气温降到-5℃；2008年1月12日—2月22日，出现特重级凝冻天气长达42天，最低气温降到-5.9℃，出现百年不遇的凝冻灾害。

专记：2008年年初的凝冻灾害

元旦刚过不久，从1月13日起，全县开始遭遇凝冻天气，当天最低气温降至-1.7℃，接下来数天连续下降，27日降至最低点-5.9℃。28日至2月2日回升到-3.6℃，之后继续回升，至2月6日，大部分地区凝冻灾害基本结束，少数地势较高处持续到2月14日。此次凝冻灾害之重、破坏之大、时间之长史属罕见。这期间，雪凝交织，冰封大地，道路中断；山间林木不堪重负拦腰折断或成片倒伏；电线上的冰块十倍于导线大小，重力将电杆拉断或成列拉倒，电线断裂，供电设施受到严重损坏；水管冻结，供水匮缺，城乡居民生产生活受到严重影响。

全县农作物受灾19.89万亩，绝收7.83万亩；因灾死亡大牲畜190头、生猪2719头、家禽6.49万羽、家兔1.9万只；林木倒伏、折断5.4万立方米，苗木损失214.5万株；农村房屋受损328户(其中倒塌50户)，圈舍受损645间；受损串户路63公里、沼气池4735口、机耕道37.4公里、人饮工程333处、管道218.39公里、水表2.18万块；受损提灌站146站，渠道167.27公里、小山塘32处、小水池939口。直接经济损失1.28亿元。企业全部停产，直接经济损失1.04亿元（其中规模以上工业企业直接经济损失7650万元），产值减少3.1亿元,税金减少2508万元。交通道路路面损毁221.5公里、路基12处，桥（涵）损坏8座，直接经济损失7610.15万元；通信杆路受损403棵，变压器9台，电缆17.2皮公里，光缆10.77皮公里，直接经济损失201.61万元；旅游基础设施受损，景区关闭，直接经济损失235万

2008年凝冻灾害

元。供电设施停电线路102条、断杆1382根、断线126处，停运变电站4个，变压器损坏21台，停电影响4万户20万人，直接经济损失3000万元。城镇供水有3个水厂部分设备损坏，受损供水管网19.5万米，水表8563支，供水及其他市政设施直接经济损失655万元。全县直接经济损失总达2.4亿元。

造成凝冻灾害的原因，根据气象部门和有关专家研究分析是频繁南下的北方冷空气受到云贵高原的阻挡，在贵州西部与云南东部之间的上空形成了天气学上有名的“昆明准静止锋”控制着贵州的中部和西部。当冷空气南下遇到了暖湿气流后就使地面气温骤然降到零度以下，从而导致落下的雨滴冻结成类似玻璃形状的冰块。而因凝冻带来供电网络、供水水管、交通通信的损坏是基础设施薄弱，抗灾能力不强，经不起凝冻灾害考验的结果。

面对严重灾害，县委、县政府作出“凝冻在持续，灾情在加重，干部要下去，措施要得力”的救灾举措，充分发挥各级党组织和广大党员的战斗堡垒和先锋模范作用，团结和带领广大人民群众积极投入到抗灾救灾、恢复生产和灾后重建等“保民生”工作中去。从凝冻发生灾害开始，每天都有1500多名县、乡干部参加抗灾救灾，组织群众抢修供电、供水、通信和道路运输设施，发放款物慰问群众。由于县委、县政府带领全县人民努力奋战，使群众生活需求得到有效保障，干群思想稳定，市场物价平稳，物资储备供应正常，到2月14日，抗凝冻工作基本结束，全县工作重心由抗灾救灾转移到灾后重建上来。

第二节　环境污染

1978年前，县境“三废”（废水、废气和固体废弃物）污染较少。20世纪80年代，工业和乡镇企业迅猛发展，矿业开采遍地开花，大量铝矿煅烧，环境受到污染。尤其是乡镇企业兴起，重经济，轻环保，布局不合理，破坏植被；生产工艺和企业管理落后，能源消耗高，污染物排放量大，又无“三废”治理设施，废水、废气直接排放，影响土壤有机质的转化；土壤中钙、镁、磷、钾等盐基被淋溶，土壤酸化和瘠化，大气中污染物浓度超过作物生长发育的阀值；有毒有害物质增多，酸雨污染严重；工业粉尘黏附在农作物上，影响生长发育，导致污染纠纷。农业生产化肥施用量增加，有机质减少，致土壤板结；烂施农药，不仅治不了病、虫害，反而伤害鸟类和益虫。到1990年，林木覆盖率仅15.4%，自然环境稀释和自净能力减弱，珍稀动植物濒临绝迹，生态环境趋于恶化。据县环保局统计：全县主要污染源77个，“三废”排放量占全县排污总量的85%。其中，驻县中央厂矿13个，县属企业12个，乡镇企业52个。企业里有电镀车间5个，锅炉50台、115.5蒸吨，工业炉窑115座。酒厂8个，水泥厂和砖瓦厂15个，黑色和有色金属冶炼2个，百张病床以上的医院2个。此外，还有141个小煤窑分布在县内。按区域等标污染负前排列，首为城关区，其次扎佐区，第三久长区。小箐和六广污染较轻。污染最严重的有马家桥、水塘、程官等地。县城周围聚集贵阳煤矿、三角山水泥厂、庆文机械厂、红旗煤矿、县酒厂等企业，工业污染和生活污染居全县之首。90年代，县域经济进一步发展，工业“三废”排放量增大；城镇扩展，基础设施建设增加；人口密集，建筑废弃物、生活废水、垃圾排放剧增，使自然环境受到严重影响。据贵阳市环境监测站对县城空气质量监测，1996至1998年城区空气已中度污染达到警戒水平，修文

河水质超过4类水质标准。据2005年污染源普查统计，全县有污染源1022个，其中工业污染232个，养殖业25个，医疗机构236个，服务行业302个，放射源3个，实验室、化验室59个，电磁辐射94个，五金加工28个。污染源主要集中在工矿企业密集的龙场镇、扎佐镇、久长镇和谷堡乡；驻有煤炭开采企业的六广、洒坪、大石、六桶等乡（镇）煤矿废水污染也较严重，仅小箐、六屯两乡污染较轻。2007年11月，县政府针对环境污染问题成立以环境保护局为主的环境污染普查领导小组，拟制《修文县环境污染源普查工作手册》，对全县污染源进行普查，发现有1022个污染源头，其中工业企业232个，占总污染源22.7%；养殖业58个，占5.68%；医疗单位236个，占23.1%；服务业302个，占29.54%；放射源13个，占1.27%；实验化验室59个，占5.77%；电磁辐射源94个，占9.2%；五金加工修理点28个，占2.74%。2008年普查，工业污染源有287处，生活污染源271处，农业污染源695处，共1253处。截至2010年，环保局共接到各类环境污染纠纷投诉263起。

一、废水污染

县境水的污染源主要是城镇生活废水和煤炭生产产生的矿井废水，并未经处理直接排入河道或农田。龙场、六广、大石、洒坪、扎佐等乡镇，由于煤窑废水的污染，使部分农田无法耕种，给当地群众生产和生活带来严重影响。县境长度大于10公里的河流有12条，库容在110万立方米至1755万立方米的水库有6座，除修文河、扎佐河受到不同程度的污染外，其余10条河流和水库水质较好。县城生活饮用水于1997年达到了饮用水标准。2005年10月，对修文河水质监测，新长征桥和水厂北两断面仅是大肠菌群超标，水文站断面溶解氧、氨氮、总磷等均值超标，大肠菌群超23倍，主要原因是河水受生活废水污染，达不到地面水Ⅲ类水质标准。饮用水源监测点水厂，仅溶解氧略微超标外，其余项目均未超标，表明该水源尚未受到污染。2005年环保局统计，重点企业废水排放41.58万吨，排放达标量32.2万吨，达标率77.44%。废水中化学需氧量为4.13吨。县城每天有4000余吨生活废水未经处理排入修文河。

河道污染

生活用水　据县环保局统计，2005年全县重点企业排放污水41.58万吨，达标排放量32.2万吨，达标排放率为77.44%，废水中化学需氧量4.13吨，分别排入全县各饮水源头附近。县城生活污水排放4000吨，县发热病医院废水直接排入饮水源上游的小桥河翠屏桥段。扎佐镇居民生活废水排入于襄河和珍珠河段，使流经镇区的珍珠河成为一条浊流，杂质漂浮，臭气熏天，地下泉水变质。久长镇居民生活废水排入白窑村至清水村水源上游，造成饮水源污染。2006年，全县166个片区饮水源均出现不同程度的异常状况。其中岩鹰山水库集中饮用水源检测发现水库承包养鱼，人工投放牛粪、鸡粪、尿素、复合肥，以微生物大量繁殖作为鱼饵料，致水体富营养化，细菌数超标，库水质变成黑色，直接影响小箐片区5万人的饮水安全。

2010年，贵阳市环境检测中心报告，县城水功能区水质，五日化学需氧量为7.0毫升／升，粪便大肠菌群≥24万个／升，超标量≥正常饮用水质的23倍，溶解氧检测值4.2毫克／升，超标100%。农村分散饮水源受到采掘、冶炼、养殖的废渣、废水排放影响，水环境受到污染。其中主要有扎佐镇丁官奶牛养殖场污染和平村饮水源，久长镇清水奶牛场污染清水村和白窑村饮水源，小箐栋青坝奶牛场污染栋青坝饮水源，贵铝公司详勘打井污染扎佐兴红村饮水源，三角山水泥厂和四达矿产煅烧厂污染陶家龙潭饮用水源。

生产用水 20世纪80年代末，全县乡镇工业企业发展到228家。2000年起民营、外资工业企业相继落户县境，企业投入生产后废物排放量猛增，到2007年工业企业废水万元GDP企业排放强度为1.36吨/万元，化学需氧量万元GDP排放强度为0.000003吨/万元，工业二氧化硫万元GDP排放强度为0.00185吨/万元，使农田水环境受到严重影响。2008年，全县166个片区水源都有不同程度的异常现象，直接影响灌溉农田的水质。

到2010年，工业企业排放污染水环境的情况继续发生，曾出现龙场镇新春村与四达公司铝矾土煅烧，阳明村与鼎鑫冶炼、新生村与华航冶炼、王官村与腾达矿粉加工和金阳洗矿、白莲村与宏华水泥厂、普陀村与建源水泥厂、沙溪村与鸿鑫水泥厂、白莲村与诺亚矿产、久长镇上寨村与华宏冶炼、小箐乡尖山村与创试冶炼、扎佐镇兴红村与中国陶粒和吉隆单宁化工、龙王村与德昌祥和光正药业、中营村与林东矿务局扎佐火车站台和谷堡乡谷堡村与群胜废旧加工厂等因排放污染农田水环境的纠纷。虽经环保部门协调解决，补偿农民，增设治理设备，勒令停产整顿，但只是治标不治本，致污染难以根除。

专记：兴红村饮水源水质异常找到了原因

2008年2月5日，扎佐镇兴红村饮水源出现异常现象，当即引起县环保局的重视，先后几次派环保工作人员对饮水现场检测，寻找水的污染源。经反复查找，没有发现任何污染源头。赓续请来水文地质专家到现场踏勘，仍无结果。

3月4日，环保局敦请贵阳市科协、环保、地质、地理、生态和化工专家一行7人直奔兴红村，原环境调查常规分析水质异常系地下水污染的原因：一是地下水系自然发生变化；二是地面塌陷，溶蚀矿物质渗透；三是矿产勘探施工影响。但专家组认为，结论应当产生于调查情况之后，而不是在它之前。于是，提出以贵州铝厂小山坝钻探影响水环境作为调查的重点，对水源水、沉积物、底泥和小山坝钻探的岩心、钻探使用的循环水、护壁剂等取样检测，并增加水环境的三氧化铝、二氧化硅、硫酸根和硫的指标监测。环保局按照专家的意见，与贵阳市环境检测中心站和贵州省地质化学研究所取得联系，请求协助调查。

3月13日，在缜密调查的基础上取得大量数据由专家会诊，市科协专家技术委员会论证，确认兴红村饮水源水质异常的原因是中国铝业公司贵州分公司委托贵州省冶金地质五队在小山坝铝矿区进行详勘，采用钻孔打穿矿层后遇到岩溶，导致钻机循环水和所带的沉砂、岩粉进入地下水岩溶系统，使水源水质发生异常。县环保局针对污染的原因，采取治理措施，不久水质恢复正常。

二、废气污染

县境空气环境污染为燃烧物产生的二氧化硫、烟尘所致。其中主要是以冶炼、煅烧、水泥生产和机动车辆排放的废气和粉尘，其次是城镇生活用煤、饮食服务用煤和锅炉用煤等散布烟尘和灰渣。

从20世纪90年代中期到2005年，龙场镇自王官经县城到马家桥长12公里公路沿线和城北修（文）

六（广）公路旁潮水村建起冶炼、煅烧、水泥、制砖企业17家。其中冶炼6家，焦炭3家，铝矾土煅烧2家，水泥生产4家，砖厂2家，排放出来的烟尘、粉尘包围着5平方公里居住着5万人口的县城。马家桥的几家水泥厂、冶炼厂和砖厂废气排放使大气中有害物质剧增，酸雨污染农田，严重影响人的身体健康，出现该片区多年征兵入伍体检的合格率为零。尤其是县城南面距城区2公里的三角山水泥厂和四达公司铝矾土煅烧厂两大污染严重的企业正处于城南风口上，5个高耸的烟囱排放的粉尘随风飘扬在城池中心地段，导致县城烟尘弥漫，市民苦不堪言。扎佐镇周边4个水泥厂、4个矿粉厂和10多家锅炉用户排放的烟尘和粉尘，使镇区牛马染患氟骨病，仅和平村就有10余头耕牛因污染患病。

据县环保局2005年统计，全县重点工业企业废气排放量13.84亿标立方米，其中燃料燃烧产生排放3.23亿标立方米，工艺过程排放10.61亿标立方米。可吸入微颗粒物年日均值0.078毫克／立方米，二氧化硫排放量1628.19吨，达标排放量847.65吨，达标率只有50.37%；烟尘排放量946吨，达标排放445.32吨，达标率仅有47.74%；粉尘排放7061.8吨，达标排放6059.06吨，达标排放率85.8%。另有未经严格检测统计的县城饮食服务业燃煤用户70家，洗浴服务燃煤锅炉5家以及县医院医疗废弃物焚烧对空气的污染。至2010年，县城仍有焚烧垃圾池的垃圾污染空气之事，最突出的是龙岗花园旁学宫巷垃圾池，每星期发生焚烧垃圾一两次，余火余烟不断，黑色刺鼻的烟尘漫布巷里，使150户居民直接受害。

马家桥水泥厂排放出口粉尘

四达公司铝矿煅烧厂烟尘污染

三、废弃物污染

据1985年环境污染源统计，全县城镇永久性和临时性的渣场、垃圾池固体废弃物堆积存量达58.1万吨，占地面积1.01万平方米。1998年固体废弃物堆积存量升为73.77万吨，占地面积4.31万平方米，3年间废弃物堆积存量增加27%，占地面积增加3.26倍。

2005年环保部门统计，全县工业生产固体废弃物量达13.64万吨，其中危险性废弃物为106吨。到2008年，工业固体废弃物量达65.89万吨，比2005年增加52.25万吨。仅扎佐镇的小水泥厂、矿粉加工厂、小煤窑的废渣和煤矸石堆积就达万吨，占地70余亩。有的废渣被雨水冲刷进入农田，使土质严重板结，土壤颗粒结构遭到破坏，导致粮食大幅度减产。

除城镇固定的垃圾场外，地处城乡接合部的乡村道路边建筑材料废弃物和生活垃圾也大量堆积。仅龙场镇沙溪村的小沙溪桥边建筑垃圾、生活垃圾堆积于河道两旁，北门桥河边修（文）六（广）公路旁垃圾沿河岸乱倒。谷堡乡折溪村余家田兰花坡垃圾场，积存20万立方米露天固体垃圾，严重污染环境，影响群众身体健康。

专记：难以维系的兰花坡垃圾场

1999年，由于县城扩展，人口集聚，生活垃圾增加，单靠原建在城乡接合部的垃圾场远不能容纳每天产生的生活垃圾。于是，选址在距县城5.5公里的谷堡乡折溪村兰花坡一凹地作为县城垃圾填埋场，场区占地7.32亩，可容垃圾2.5万立方米，预计可堆放垃圾期为10年。

2005年，县城人口增至5万多人，日产生活垃圾80吨。然兰花坡的垃圾已堆山积海，散堆在场内，又没有填埋处理，纯属一个露天垃圾场。每到夏季蚊蝇四处孳生，异味四散，臭气熏天。县环卫站的垃圾中转车无法驶入垃圾场内，每次驶到场边，汽车引擎盖和挡风玻璃就苍蝇密布，周边村民生活在这人为的脏乱差环境里简直不堪言状。尽管县城管委联合龙场镇医院组成灭菌消杀队，用石灰和化学药剂“奋斗纳”“敌敌畏”杀灭，对填埋场附近10余户村民住宅环境使用药物消杀，但终未根治。5月4日，县长办公会议研究县城管委提交的《关于兰花坡垃圾场造成公害的情况反映》，决定投入资金150万元扩建兰花坡垃圾场，但因场内垃圾堆积如山，需另择地建场，致扩建搁浅。不得已只得跨县将垃圾运至毗邻白云区境比例坝垃圾场处理。至此，兰花坡垃圾场才停止使用。

谷堡乡折溪村兰花坡垃圾场2010年改为建筑垃圾倒土场

四、噪声污染

县境噪声污染主要出现在城区交通干道、建筑工地、商铺经营和娱乐场所。1998年和1999年，经贵阳市环境监测站对县城布点监测，声环境质量均达城市区域环境噪声指标。继后随着县城和扎佐镇的城市建设施工量、市民生活量和交通车流量的增加，噪声污染一直呈上升趋势。

2005年，监测县城环境区噪声等效声级为52.8分贝，达到城市区域噪声标准（GB3096—93）二级。其中主要是生活噪声的比重大，占噪声比重的77.1%，形成局部声环境污染。等效应级噪声最大为建筑施工达62.1分贝，其次是交通干道为57.1分贝，再次是生活噪声为51.8分贝。

2007年，区域环境噪声平均值52.5分贝，达到城市区域环境噪声标准二级，交通干道噪声平均值69分贝，达到城市区域环境噪声标准四类。2008年，区域环境噪声平均值52.8分贝，达到城市区域环境噪声标准二级，交通干线噪声平均值64.2分贝，达到城市区域环境噪声标准四类。但时段性、小区域内噪声环境污染日趋增加，噪声严重超标。

至2010年，虽对城区建筑、交通、娱乐场所的噪声污染源进行控制，但噪声仍短时性、间断性发生，甚至污染分贝大大超标。最突出的是街道经营门面开业庆典锣鼓喧天，商业经营招揽喇叭高声叫卖，乔迁新居、婚丧嫁娶鞭炮声震耳，市民意见较大。

第三节　生态建设

20世纪80年代，大力发展乡镇企业，环境污染尚未引起重视。90年代初开始，贯彻《中华人民共和国环境保护法(试行)》，按照国家产业政策进行工业产业结构调整，规划工业布局。驻县中央厂矿陆续迁出县境，铝矿煅烧企业因市场饱和销售不畅自然解体，贵阳煤矿因资源枯竭闭坑，县属国营企业因经营不善而倒闭。与此同时，狠抓节能减排，查封6家生产工艺落后、设备属国家规定的淘汰产品的冶炼企业，关井压产、限制高灰高硫煤生产，炸封、取缔上百家无证非法开采的小煤窑。进入21世纪，引进一批无烟企业，建立扎佐医药园区。规划兴红厂至羊肠坝十里工业长廊。推动绿色发展，加强生态建设、先后完成坡改梯、长防林、贵阳市二环林带建设和启动中韩合作造林工程。2009年，县进一步加大环境治理的力度，投资1.85亿元对环境污染进行治理。其中投入5129.4万元用于县城污水处理、燃气排放、集中供热、园林绿化、垃圾处理等项目工程；投入1.23亿元用于工业污染治理，并建立企业基本建设项目、技术改造项目、区域或自然资源开发项目在防治环境污染和生态破坏的设施，必须与主体工程同时设计、同时施工、同时投产使用的制度，简称“三同时”制度；投入1000多万元用于污染治理设施运行和管理，同时建立完善环境监测、信息、监察、科技、宣传和教育等系统。至2010年，环境治理卓见成效，全县森林覆盖率达到40.3%，生态环境大为改观。

一、城镇环境治理

治理河道　1990年，县钓鱼协会向县政府和城关镇政府呈送书面要求义务管理长征桥至郭家林长3000米的修文河，并由镇政府、县水资源办公室、县环卫局和渔政管理站联合发出保护河道的通告。县人大代表杨忠华向县人大、县政府提交治理修文河的建议，并组织筹集民间资金万余元，揭开修文河治理的帷幕。

1999年，县城实施基础设施“九三”工程，将治理修文河列为“九三”工程项目之一，对修文河道全面整治，包括城区内的小桥河段、修文河段、阳明河段、团鱼湾河段和东门河段，2008年又治理高涧河段。治理采取河道清淤、筑拦河坝、河岸筑堤、修建护坡，营造沿岸20米宽的绿化带，并由县人大、县政府制定法规，严禁经营和建筑占用河道。经治理后河道水位提高，使河流静水面宽从10米增加到20米至30米，治理的河道总长达2200米，出现河水清澈、河岸碧绿的景观，为市民提供了晨练、休闲、散步、垂钓之处。

取直后的团鱼湾河道

1996年，对人口集聚的扎佐镇于襄河的珍珠河段进行首期治理工程，清除河道废弃漂浮物和污泥，修筑河堤，改造整治河道长800米。2003年，进行二期治理，从大石岩到红卫桥长680米河段清淤筑堤，建石混河堤高5米，拦截城镇居民生活污水，使一条水深只有30厘米—50厘米的浊流变成20米宽的珍珠河。

控制燃煤 1997年，县城管委、环保局联合强制取缔县城人民南路燃煤炉经营，向市民推介石油液化气炉灶，关停县城周边冶炼炉窑6家，改造2吨以下燃煤蒸汽锅炉27台，取缔沿街面饮食店的露天明火煤灶270家，使全城饮食经营门面和饮食夜市全都使用液化燃气。当年城区饮食业使用液化气率为60%。2005年12月，贵阳市环境监测站对县城区域空气质量监测结果：可吸入微粒物年日均值为0.078毫克/立方米，达国家二级标准；二氧化硫年日均值为0.036毫克/立方米，优于国家二级标准；二氧化氮年日均值0.026毫克/立方米，优于国家一级标准。到2008年年底，经过长达10年的燃煤使用控制，主城区空气质量达到二级标准以上的天数308天，创下历史最高水平。2010年，将县城和扎佐镇的经营性燃煤2个蒸吨以下设施全部取缔，并促成腾晖酒楼水会洗浴改为空气热源装置。创建阳明大道“无油烟示范一条街”和宾阳社区为“绿化示范区”。是年城区二氧化硫年日平均值为0.05毫克／立方米，优于国家标准。

保护饮水源 2001年2月，治理县城羊落井水厂处团鱼湾河段，改修文河段河水取直道流入东门河。开挖宽30米、长140米的人工河道，修筑河堤、围墙将羊落井与修文河、公路和居民点隔离。

2009年，建立羊落井、陶家龙潭两个水厂水源1级保护区，禁止羊落井周边民用住宅建筑通向水源地的排水沟，对羊落井团鱼湾死水塘进行回填，将与饮水源连通的洞穴进行封堵，避免修文河水渗入。同时对水源点采用彩钢瓦封闭，避免粉尘污染，严禁在水源地保护区内新建项目。修建县城区污水处理厂，切断居民生活污水直接排入饮水源河道。

控制噪声 1999年，县政府下达禁止在县城内燃放鞭炮通告。自县城实施基础设施“九三”工程建设起到2010年，对城区建筑工地噪声加以控制，每天晚10点钟停止作业。每逢学生中、高考期间，县环保局和城管委联合执法，根据《贵阳市建设工地施工管理规定》和《贵阳市环境噪声污染防治规定》，对全城所有建筑施工工地和娱乐场所下达《关于加强中、高考期间噪声污染监督管理的通知》，禁止每年5月30日至6月20日，施工队和娱乐场所每日22:00至次日上午8:00的生产、经营活动。

处理垃圾 1997年开始，开展创建文明卫生县城活动，县城大街小巷、院落、居民小区、机关单位修建起半封闭垃圾池348处，全封闭垃圾池5处，垃圾中转站1座，将全城生活垃圾运至谷堡乡折溪村兰花坡垃圾场。

2007年，当县城扩展，人口增加，生活垃圾量增大时，新建阳明路、虎山路两个垃圾中转站，将县城生活垃圾2万吨/年全部运往贵阳市白云区比例坝垃圾场进行无害化处理，处理率为100%。并对县医院医疗垃圾焚烧炉进行整治改造，控制污染。到2010年，县城所有医疗单位的医疗废弃物全部由贵阳市医疗废弃物回收专用车定期收回，集中处理。

县城虎山路垃圾转运站

二、农村生态建设

建设“四改一气” 1997年，县政府组织成立农村能源环保办公室，开发利用人畜粪便、杂草和废弃农作物密封发酵产生清洁、环保的可燃性沼气供作农村燃料和照明能源。把农村环境保护和能源开发结合起来，既改变农民生活环境，又控制燃煤用量节约能源。以农户改厨、改厕、改圈为基础改造农户生活环境开发沼气能源取代燃煤，称为“三改一气”。到2005年，全县“三改一气”建沼气池3000套。

2006年，为促进城乡一体化建设，在“三改一气”基础上增加农村村寨道路改造，修建进村公路和串户路，把“三改一气”扩展为“四改一气”，拓宽农村环境治理范围。2007年，全县“四改一气”工程建成5000套，利用沼肥种粮4.5万亩、种菜2.5万亩、种玉米示范地2000亩、种果树1100亩，使农业生产和农民生活环境面貌焕然一新。至2010年，农村“四改一气”遍布全县，生态建设取得成效。在“四改一气”推动下涌现出龙场镇中哨村、白莲村，谷堡乡折溪村，六屯乡独山村，大石布依族乡大屯村，久长镇上寨村等16个环境优美的新型村寨。

乡（镇）领导检查“四气一改”中沼气池的修建

开发低碳经济 2010年，县环保局针对分布在农村的奶牛场、饲养基地排放牲畜粪便污染农村饮用水源和粮田的问题，以开发低碳经济建设工程为试点，在六屯乡石猫猫奶牛场、扎佐镇龙山乳业基地、谷堡乡大旺养殖场、久长镇“好1多”奶牛基地、百民鸿养殖场、六桶乡盛鑫兔业和六屯乡西冲肉牛基地进行大型的沼气能源建设，既治理了养殖业污染，又扩展了农村肥料来源和生活能源，减少二氧化碳排放。

治理集中饮水 2007年县环保局对集中饮水的久长镇蚌壳堰水库、扎佐镇双月水库、小箐乡岩鹰山水库肥水养鱼进行水质监测，为治理水环境，防止污染，严禁承包水库养鱼者投放家畜家禽粪便和化学肥料。对水库周边的矿山采掘、冶炼加工企业签订环境管理目标责任书，严格执行持证排污，依法征收排污费以进行排污总量控制。定期取样检测，对超标排放影响环境，造成污染的企业下达限期整改通知，违者停业。

整治裸露矿山 2000年，县环保局和乡镇企业局组织对裸露废弃矿点进行复耕复林。2003年，龙场镇建新村、杨寨村因小煤窑煤锈水污染环境，裸露矿址水土流失毁坏农田，村民自发调整产业结构，炸封小煤窑28处，恢复耕地，植树造林。2004年，贵铝一矿职工义务投劳，在矿区的废料场植树造林500亩，以复垦复林进行综合治理。

2005年12月，省、市、县矿山环境整治检察组到谷堡乡顺达小屯矿山和龙场镇祖师殿矿山实地检查，为遏制矿山环境恶化，帮助矿山落实整治措施，作出裸露矿点复垦复林规划。2007年11月，县国土资源局，环保局为加强裸露矿山、砂石场的整治，开展宣传贯彻省环保局黔环通〔2007〕86号《关于落实科学发展观、切实加强矿山资源开发环境保护、构建和谐矿山的通知》活动，并制定对龙场镇杨寨村上坝桥废旧矿处理和恢复环境原貌规划。

2010年，全县开展以龙场镇小山村、杨寨村，扎佐镇三元村为主的矿山废弃地治理，复林植树1500亩。因管护不到位致复林植树成活率较低，多见树坑不见林，裸露矿山污染仍然严重，全县矿山废弃地尚有4900亩急需整治。

专记：建新村自愿炸封污染煤窑

20世纪80年代后期，龙场镇建新村西部小麻窝片区无证小煤窑采煤泛滥，屡禁不止，煤矸石堆积，煤锈水乱流，使周边环境受到严重破坏。到2003年，地处牛吃水和下干坝一带的500多亩稻田受到重度污染，致粮食大幅度减产，村民深受其害，遭此厄运叫苦不迭。镇长罗万伦急村民之所急，对十多年非法无证煤窑取缔又反弹的情况进行深入调查，采煤的人说：“黑洞洞（煤窑）好找钱，既不上税又不交钱（管理费），是我们发家致富的一条财路。”而村民们则抱怨因煤锈水污染给自己造成的损失说：“等哪天不挖煤了，不受黄汤汤（煤锈水）影响（污染），责任地的谷子（水稻）才有望收割。”

罗万伦根据群众的想法和认识，结合小煤窑污染农田的状况，反复向大家宣讲国家的富民政策，讲解农村经济发展长远之计和环境保护的重要性。分析了是挖煤挣钱重要还是保护生态环境重要，使大家懂得“破坏环境就是犯罪”的道理，为了保护好大家赖以生存的良田好土造福于子孙后代，必须立即停止非法采用小煤窑挖煤挣钱的行为。镇领导语重心长的宣讲使大家明白了道理，受到了教育。村民刘军洪说：“多年来我们受到小煤窑污染的危害，种庄稼无保障，粮食年年欠收，有的连基本口粮都成问题，还不如炸掉黑洞，种粮植树。”刘军洪的意见得到多数村民赞同，纷纷表示改变发展经济、增加收入的思路，调整农村产业结构，封闭煤窑，复垦复林。

是年8月7日，村民自发组织起来，到小麻窝煤窑区拆除挖煤设备，先用农用运输车将设备和废弃的运煤车转出矿山。随即燃炮炸封煤窑，阵阵爆破声响起，20多口小煤窑全被炸掉。至此，建新村结束十多年无证开挖小煤窑历史，大家表示决心在镇党委、镇政府的领导下，改方式，调结构，谋发展。小煤窑污染环境得到根治，良田和青山绿水地将会通过生态文明建设再现。

第三章　自然资源

1978年，全县土地总面积1071平方公里，其中有耕地面积27.87万亩，农业人口人均耕地1.53亩。2002年，经与周边区、市、县行政边界区域重新勘察定界，核定县境实有土地面积为1075. 7平方公里。之后大量陡坡耕地退耕还林还草，大批非耕地资源得到有效开发。2010年，虽然全县耕地面积减少到26.2万亩，农业人均耕地仅0.99亩，但农业产值却比1978年增长20多倍。

县境水资源平水年水资源总量为6.644亿立方米，其中地表径流为5.153亿立方米，地下径流1.491亿立方米。另有乌江、光洞河和车田河等过境河流流经县境东西两面边境，多年平均客水总量151.86亿立方米。全县建有小（Ⅰ）型水库7座和小（Ⅱ）型水库21座，水库总蓄水量3726.5万立方米。水质大部分地表水超标，不能直接饮用，而地下水水质经理化检测基本达标并能满足人们生活用水要求。境内水能蕴藏量丰富，全县水能资源技术可开发总量为914.57兆瓦，已开发798.5兆瓦，占可开发总量的87.31%。

境内矿产资源丰富，种类繁多，有煤、铝土、重晶石、硫铁、赤铁、磷、汞等矿和铌、镓、钽、锆、钛等稀有金属矿，还有高岭土、熔剂灰岩、溶剂白云岩、耐火黏土、硅沙、水泥用灰岩、石灰石、黏土和山砂等。其中煤、铝土矿藏量较大，具有重要的工业开采价值，已探明煤储量3亿多吨，铝土矿储量7700多万吨。至2010年，铝土矿已开采2400万吨，尚存5300万吨；煤在探明储量中已采0.5亿吨，尚存储量2.5亿吨。

改革开放30多年，生态建设取得显著成效。全县森林覆盖率从1981年的15.4%提高到2010年的40.3%。县境生物资源种类繁多，除黔中常规物种外，具有地方特色物种中植物资源主要有猕猴桃、金秋梨、酥李、银杏、杜仲、苦丁茶、老鹰茶等。农村产业结构调整后龙场镇延晚番茄、扎佐镇大白萝卜、久长镇青菜、六屯辣椒、谷堡乡的猕猴桃和金秋梨、小箐乡郭田酥李等久负盛名；动物资源中有国家二类保护动物穿山甲、大鲵、熊猴、红腹角雉，三类保护动物小灵猫，县地特产六广鲶鱼蜚声黔省内外。

县境山川秀美，江河壮丽，拥有丰富自然景观资源，主要有“江上无劳羡九华”的六广七峡四十二景，有两岸峡壁陡峭、青山绿水的猫跳河峡谷风光，有被称为“人间仙境”“黔中福地”桃源河峡谷，有千姿百态、五彩缤纷国内外少有的喀斯特地貌石灰岩溶洞“多缤洞”，有国内少有的回水和高枧绿色石林，有“移放长江还济险”的天生桥，有山青水秀的小箐两蓬岩兰花谷，有号称“黔中茫茫林海”的扎佐林场等。至2010年已开发较为成功的旅游项目主要有扎佐野生动物园、桃源河魔幻漂流、六广河峡谷观光、久长苏格兰风情牧场等。

第一节　土地资源

1978年，全县土地总面积1071平方公里。1997—2002年，经县国土资源局、县民政局与毗邻县、区对全县行政边界再次勘察，核定全县实有土地面积为1075. 7平方公里(折合161.36万亩)。按2010年第六次人口普查248926人计，人均占有6.5亩,为全国人均土地13.96亩的46.56%，为贵州省人均土地9.3亩的69.89%。

一、土地利用

经过20世纪80年代初开展的农业自然资源调查和农业区划工作，摸清了全县土地利用状况。全县土地总面积为1071平方公里，折合160.65万亩，其中农业用地占土地总面积的86.57%，而垦殖指数（耕地面积占土地总面积的比重）竟达44.81%。进入21世纪，县国土资源管理部门将土地利用现状列入经常性的工作进行动态监测。随着各项建设事业的发展和对农业内部产业结构进行调整，至2010年。全县土地利用现状发生了较大变化，总的情况是：农业用地有所增加，但垦殖指数下降，用地内部结构趋于合理，各项建设用地呈增长态势，未被利用土地的比重有较为明显的下降。

（一）农业用地

1984年全县农业用地139.07万亩，占土地总面积的86.57%，2010年为149.13万亩，占土地总面积的92.43%，在1984年基础上增加10.06万亩。

耕地　1984年占地范围71.99万亩（净耕地52.6万亩），耕地占地范围为土地总面积的44.81%，占农业用地面积的51.76%。至2010年，耕地占地范围70.86万亩（净耕地64.44万亩），耕地占地范围占土地总面积的43.92%，占农业用地面积的47.52%。与1984年调查情况相比，耕地占地范围有所减少，但净耕地面积反而增加。这是由于计算田、土坎占耕地占地范围的比重不一致所造成。

园地　专指成片的果园、茶园。1984年全县园地仅有0.17万亩。占土地总面积的0.11%，占农业用地面积的0.13%。在不断实施农村产业结构调整过程中，利用修文毗邻省会贵阳和交通便捷的优势，大力发展水果生产并取得显著成效。至2010年，园地面积上升至3.06万亩，在1984年的基础上增长16.5倍，占土地总面积的比重提升至1.9%，占农业用地的比重为2.14%。

林地　1984年调查为33.81万亩，占土地总面积的21.04%，占农业用地的24.31%。退耕还林、工程造林和封山育林等措施，使林业用地明显增大。至2010年达66.78万亩，占土地总面积的41.39%，在1984年基础上增长近1倍，占农业用地的46.79%。

草地　全县原有草地面积较大，但多为荒草地，利用率较低。1984年调查共有31.52万亩，另有疏林草地1.59万亩，合计为33.11万亩，占土地总面积的20.61%，占农业用地的23.8%。由于林业用地范围拓展，致草地面积大幅度减少，至2010年，全县草地面积仅为8.43万亩，占土地总面积的比重降至5.22%，占农业用地的比重降至5.91%

（二）建设用地

经过1984年调查全县土地利用现状和后来国土资源部门对利用现状进行动态监测，除农业用地外，

土地利用类型的指标设置与统计范围不尽一致，给直接进行对比分析带来困难。2010年全县各类建设用地8.16万亩，占土地总面积的5.06%，其中城乡居民点用地4.23万亩，工矿用地1.92万亩，交通用地1.88万亩，风景名胜及特殊用地0.11万亩，水工建筑用地0.02万亩，分别占土地总面积的2.62%、1.19%、1.17%、0.07%和0.01%。建设用地中，增长最多的是交通建设用地，2005年全县城乡共为1.31万亩，2010年已达到1.88万亩。

（三）其他用地

1984年其他用地为12.51万亩，占土地总面积的7.79%。2010年降为4.06万亩，占土地总面积的2.52%，原因是对非耕地资源开发利用的结果，使1984年8.83万亩未利用土地减至2010年的近2万亩（主要是裸岩和裸地）。2010年的其他用地中，水域面积为1.97万亩（河流0.96万亩，水库0.51万亩，山塘0.2万亩，沟渠0.3万亩），占土地总面积的1.22%。

二、土壤

（一）土壤类型

1984年土壤普查，全县土壤有7个土类，19个亚类，62个土属，347个土种。计122.95万亩，占全县面积的76.53%。县境土壤肥力一般较高，大部分呈中性和微酸性反应，耕层含有机质3%以上土壤占78.5%，全氮含量0.15%以上占87.2%。其类型有黄壤、棕壤、草甸土、石灰土、紫色土、潮土、水稻土。

1984年全县各土壤类型及分布一览表

表1—03—01

土　种	亚　类	面　积（万亩）	占普查比例	集中分布地	宜种植物
黄　壤	1.典型黄壤 2.粗骨黄壤 3.灰化黄壤 4.深洗黄壤	62.77	51.05%	六屯、桃源、清让、三元、马家桥、王官、阳早、六广、回水	土壤肥力较低，只宜种植松、杉、油茶、茶叶等
黄棕壤	1.黄棕壤 2.山地粗骨黄棕壤	0.72	0.59%	六屯、久长、石安、崇恩、王官	土壤肥力虽高，但海拔高气温低，宜发展林木和牧草
石灰土	1.黄色石灰土 2.黑色石灰土 3.棕色石灰土	40.05	32.58%	六广、大石、洒坪、小箐、谷堡	宜种植香樟、棕、漆、油桐、杜仲、玉米、小麦、油菜等
紫色土	1.钙质紫色土 2.中性紫色土 3.酸性紫色土	3.80	3.09%	扎佐、马家桥、谷堡、崇恩、回水、宝寨	适宜种植多种农作物及林木
潮　土	1.湖土	0.06	0.05%	县域内河流沿岸	宜种植水稻、玉米、小麦、油菜和蔬菜等
草甸土	1.山地灌木丛、草甸土	0.47	0.38%	六屯乡和尚坡、王官、中哨	不宜垦殖，只宜作天然牧场和涵养水源。
水稻土	1.渗育型 2.漂洗型 3.潴育型 4.潜育型 5.脱水型	15.07	12.26%	城关镇、马家桥、王官、程官、阳早、谷堡、场坝、乌栗扎佐、三元、清让、桃源、六屯、清水、久长、金桥、石安、崇恩。	宜种植水稻、玉米、小麦、油菜和蔬菜等

（二）土壤质量

1984年全县土地普查，境内土壤耕层含有机质3%以上的土壤占78.5%，全氮含量在0.15%以上的占87.2%。按照国家统一的八级评定标准，对水稻土、旱作土和自然土进行综合评价。

1. 水稻土质量等级

以排灌条件、土壤肥力、土壤质地、产量水平、隆碍层次等指标，分为一等至四等。

一等水稻土，面积3.09万亩，占20.51%。主要分布在村寨附近和盆地，地势平坦，有灌溉设施，耕作历史长，熟化程度高，土层厚，保水保肥，耕性良好，亩产水稻500公斤以上，可以实行粮、油和绿肥轮作。

二等水稻土，面积7.17万亩，占47.57%。分布在一等水稻土上缘，一年两熟，亩产水稻400公斤左右。

三等水稻土，面积3.64万亩，占24.12%。所处地势较高，多为一年一熟，亩产水稻300公斤左右。

四等水稻土，面积1.17万亩，占7.78%。多为冷、烂、锈、毒田及处于高塝地段望天水田，亩产水稻200公斤以下。

2. 旱作土质量等级

根据坡度、侵蚀程度、土层厚度、土壤质地、养分状况、熟制、障碍因子和产量水平等指标，分为一等至五等。

一等土，面积1.9万亩，占5.05%。分布在村寨附近或坡脚地段，耕作历史长，熟化程度高，地势平坦、耕层厚、耕性好，有团粒结构，养分含量高，适种性广，一年两熟或三熟，亩产玉米400公斤以上。如大土泥土、柴油砂土、小黄泥土、无油黄沙土，油黄泥黏土等。

二等土，面积9.89万亩，占26.35%。多分布在村寨附近，多为缓坡土或梯土，耕层较厚，表土疏松，结构良好，养分较高，适种性广，一年两熟，亩产玉米300公斤至400公斤。如大泥土、黑油沙土、紫泥土等。

三等土，面积13.38万亩，占35.64%。坡度较大，耕作条件较差，水土流失中等。土层深浅不一，活土层薄，养分含量中等，耕作性不良，适种性差。可一年两熟，亩产玉米200公斤至300公斤，如黄泥土、黄沙土、白大泥土、黑沙土等。

四等土，面积9.61万亩，占25.61%。坡度大，一般在25度至35度之间。土层薄，养分含量低，耕作条件差，土壤侵蚀严重，亩产玉米100公斤至200公斤。

五等土，面积2.76万亩，占7.35%。坡度大于35度，水土流失严重，耕作粗放，产量很低，亩产玉米100公斤以下。如寡黄泥土、死黄泥土等。

3. 自然土质量等级

按其坡度、土体厚度、土壤质地、植被状况，侵蚀情况等分别评为四至八等。

四、五等自然土，面积分别为2.26万亩、1.01万亩，分别占3.21%、14.29%。土壤多为黄壤、硅质黄壤、硅铝黄镶、硅铁质黄壤等。多分布在海拔1400米以下盆地边缘的缓丘上和坡度15度以下的丘陵下部，土层较深厚，表层厚15厘米以上。土中有机质和氮、钾养分较多，但缺磷，基本无裸岩。

六、七等自然土，面积分别为28万亩、23.72万亩，分别占39.8%、33.72%。土壤多为硅质黄壤、硅铁质黄壤、硅铝质黄壤、厚层黄色石灰土，中性紫色土、酸性紫色土、钙质紫色土、黑色石灰土等。分布在坡度15度至35度的丘陵中、上部，一般裸岩在50%以下。土层较厚，表层为10厘米至5厘米。土层中有机质和氮素较多，土壤质地和结构较好，石砾含量少。

八等自然土，面积6.31万亩，占8.98%，土壤多为裸岩较多的黄色石灰土，裸岩占50%以上，坡度在35度以上，水土泥失严重，土层浅薄，表层厚不足10厘米，土壤质地和结构均差。

第二节　水资源

一、水资源总量

县境水资源主要源于大气降水，平水年水资源总量为6.644亿立方米，其中地表径流为5.153亿立方米，地下径流1.491亿立方米。枯水年水资源总量3.728亿立方米，其中地表径流2.9亿立方米，地下径流0.828亿立方米。此外，还有乌江过境客水80.2亿立方米，光洞河、车田河客水0.64亿立方米。

（一）地表水

全县地表水多年平均年径流总量5.153亿立方米。丰水年达6.76亿立方米，枯水年为4.1亿立方米，特枯年为2.9亿立方米。各乡镇因地理环境不同，降水量和地表水各有差异，总趋势为东部多、西部少，径流深和径流量亦是东多西少。从东部海拔高地区向西部海拔低地区下泄，西部地表水天然储水能力较低，中部、南部年径流值高，西北部年径流值低。地表水资源量最大是龙场镇，为1.09亿立方米，占全县地表水资源量的18%，最小是大石布依族乡0.262亿立方米，占4.3%。不同频率年份径流量相差很大，多水年为特枯年的2.3倍，枯水年和特枯年因缺水往往造成干旱，干旱的程度西部重于东部。径流的年内分配极不均匀，5—9月占全年总量的70%，且集中在少数几次洪水，而洪水又是暴涨暴落，峰量大，历时短。头年10月至次年4月，径流量不多，致部分小溪有断流现象。

全县流域面积在20平方公里以上的主、支干河流有13条，境内河有修文河、马官河、穿山堰河、小桥河、桃源河、葛马河、平寨河、猫洞河和刘家河，流域面积共计826.7平方公里；过境河流有乌江、猫跳河、光洞河和车田河出境前流域面积共计2.79万平方公里。

全县建有小（Ⅰ）型水库7座，小（Ⅱ）型水库21座，总蓄水量3931.7万立方米。其中岩鹰山水库集雨面积达14.5平方公里，容水1755万立方米，是县境西北部地区主要水源地。

岩鹰山水库

（二）地下水

县境地下水主要分为岩溶型、松散岩型和山区基岩裂隙型3种。岩溶型地下水主要分布在碳酸盐类岩层地区，出露面积占全县总面积的74.9%，水量较丰富，多以伏流或井泉形式流出地表，利用价值较大，是境内主要的地下水；松散岩类地下水，分布于县内非岩溶地区，渗透能力较弱；山区基岩裂隙型地下水，水量虽不大，但分布较广，对人畜饮水作用较大。地下水多为雨水补给，其径流量随降水量变化，变幅较地表水小、滞后，水量较稳定，受污染的程度较地表水小，出露高程较低。据1979年9月中国人民解放军00932部队和1981年3—4月修文县水电局对全县排出地表的地下水进行测量，用井泉统计汇总法估算，县内平水年地下水径流量为1.491亿立方米，枯水年为0.8亿立方米。全县共有地下水出露点（泉水点）134处，多年平均流量6.83立方米／秒，流量在100升／秒以上的有9处，10—100升／秒有33处，小于10升／秒有92处。其中龙场镇和扎佐镇三元村地下水资源丰富，径流模数分别为6.5升／秒·平方公里和6.2升／秒·平方公里。

（三）客水

县境客水主要存在于边界河段，包括乌江、猫跳河、光洞河、车田河4条河流，多年平均客水总量151.86亿立方米。其中乌江客水量最大达133.6亿立方米，其次为猫跳河17.73亿立方米。西部客水河流河谷深切，两岸陡峭，水流湍急，势能落差大，有利于水电事业发展，农业灌溉得益较少。

过境河流水资源一览表

表1—03—02

河　流	流域面积（平方公里）	年径流量（亿立方米）	境内及其它流量（亿立方米）	入境客水流量（亿立方米）
乌　江	24451	133.6	19.32	114.28
猫跳河	3261	17.73	3.36	14.37
光洞河	119.4	0.32	0.16	0.16
车田河	62.69	0.21	0.1	0.11
合　计	—	151.86	22.94	128.92

二、水质

（一）地表水水质

2006年，根据生活饮用水质标准按照分级评价法在猫跳河、猫洞河、穿山堰河、修文河、鱼梁河5条河流和古隆、烂沟、白溪、阁老寨、岩鹰山、蚌壳堰、高潮、浪潮、香巴房、煤幺、新坪11个水库设立水质监测评价点，对61公里的河段中水质监测评价为：Ⅲ类水质占15.6%，Ⅳ类水质占33.6%，Ⅴ类水质占22.6%，劣Ⅴ类水质占28.2%。水质超标物有总氮、大肠杆菌、总磷。其中猫跳河上游至修文河段受白云区生活污水污染，4个监测点大肠菌群全部超标，超标最大数是合格值的24倍。

经过对浪潮、高潮、阁老寨、煤幺、新坪、香巴房、岩鹰山、蚌壳堰折溪等主要水库水质监测认定，超标物有总氮、硫化物，其中，岩鹰山、蚌壳堰水库因肥水养鱼，使水体营养化，微生物细菌数超标。

（二）地下水水质

全县城镇集中饮用地下水源主要有龙场镇大龙井、羊落井、陶家龙潭，扎佐镇大园井、右营井、久长镇三岔井，六广镇白水，谷堡乡龙井湾，六屯乡龙冒井，小箐乡兰花岩井，洒坪乡天生桥水渠，大石布依族乡叫化洞井，六桶乡芭蕉沟井。2006年，在以上13个水源设置监测点，监测水质矿化度，总硬度、氨氮、酸碱度、硫酸盐及总大肠菌群。经监测地下水PH值（酸碱度）在7.5~8.5之间，矿化度浓度均值467毫克/升，总硬度均值281.8毫克/升。其余项目超标不大，能满足生活用水要求。

2010年县境主要人饮供水点水质情况及级别评价表

表1—03—03

供水点	酸碱度（PH）	总硬度（毫克/升）	氨氮（毫克/升）	大肠杆菌（个/100毫升）	铁（毫克/升）	锰（毫克/升）	级别评价
县城城南水厂	7.14	328.0	0.04	0	<0.3	<0.1	Ⅱ
县城羊落井水厂	7.36	292.0	0.06	0	<0.3	<0.1	Ⅱ
红旗村人饮工程	7.53	258.0	0.05	5	<0.3	<0.1	Ⅱ
沙溪村人饮工程	7.68	266.0	0.05	3	<0.3	<0.1	Ⅱ
通源扎佐分公司	7.26	214.0	0.05	0	<0.3	<0.1	Ⅱ
扎佐普泉水厂	7.81	283.0	0.05	0	<0.3	<0.1	Ⅲ
久长金桥人饮工程	7.52	272.2	0.06	12	<0.3	<0.1	Ⅱ
谷堡集镇饮水工程	7.66	166.8	0.06	0	<0.3	<0.1	Ⅱ
六屯集镇饮水工程	7.68	318.0	0.05	8	<0.3	<0.1	Ⅱ
小箐岩鹰山水厂	7.31	258.2	0.06	0	<0.3	<0.1	Ⅲ
洒坪五老山人饮	7.01	338.3	0.04	0	<0.3	<0.1	Ⅰ
六广龙窝村人饮	7.24	218.2	0.08	0	<0.3	<0.1	Ⅱ
大石回水村人饮工程	7.44	206.2	0.09	0	<0.3	<0.1	Ⅱ
六桶集镇饮水工程	7.72	166.1	0.07	8	<0.3	<0.1	Ⅱ

三、水能资源

县境部分河流穿过高山峡谷，流域长，落差大，水能蕴藏量丰富。全县水能资源技术可开发总量为914.57兆瓦。已开发猫跳河、修文河的5站共计198.5兆瓦。流域面积在20平方公里以下的溪流、地下河流等水能资源理论蕴藏量为25.8兆瓦，可开发量为7.73兆瓦。1988年前,曾先后修建有县地方小水电站14座。至1990年，有9个站因设备老化、管理不善及自然灾害侵蚀等原因导致运行后不久即停产下马。2000年，实施农村电网改造，因小水电站产能低和设备落后，仅保留六广白水电站，其余全部停运。保留下来的白水电站装机容量320千瓦，保证出力172.6千瓦，年发电量30.77万千瓦时。2005年，贵州省乌江流域开发有限责任公司在六广河建成索风营水电站，为县境水电开发史上规模最大的电站，总库容量2.012亿立方米，装机容量600兆瓦，年发电量20.11亿千瓦时。

第三节　矿产资源

境内矿产资源丰富，种类繁多，已探明金属矿藏有铝土矿、铁矿、汞矿、铌矿、镓矿、钽矿、锆矿、钛矿等。非金属矿有煤、重晶石、硫铁矿、磷矿、高岭土、熔剂灰岩、溶剂白云岩、耐火黏土、硅沙、水泥用灰岩、石灰石、黏土和山砂等。全县共查明各类矿床20处，具有工业生产储量的矿藏铝土矿、煤、硫铁、石灰石、重晶石、白云岩、赤铁、耐火黏土、砖用黏土和页岩等已广泛开采利用，尤其是20世纪80年代中期到2000年以矿产资源为生产对象的采掘、冶炼、建材工业企业在全县形成迅猛发展趋势。

一、矿藏勘察

1978年前，西南地质局534地质勘探队曾对县内小山坝铝土矿蕴藏量进行普查。贵州省地矿局105和117地质队在县境内的铁矿石中发现菱铁、赤铁和褐铁。查明大石、六桶、小箐、清让等乡分布汞矿；小山坝、干坝的溶剂灰岩、三角山的溶剂白云岩；扎佐马鞍山、六广大麻窝、扎佐西米三处的高岭土矿，以及小山坝铝土中发现伴生的金属矿铌钽、锰铌、锰钽、钛、锆和镓，其中镓的储量达636.1万吨。并在大石布依族乡回水塘至狮子丫一带泥土中发现微型金矿，引来成都黄金部队深入到回水、花椤、红岩等地寻找金矿。80年代中期，贵州省地质局105地质队、贵州省冶金地质5队在清水塘、天马山勘明铝土矿；在马家桥、久长勘明砖用黏土、页岩矿；在普陀毛栗山勘明硅酸盐砖用砂岩矿。90年代，贵州省有色地勘局一总队在干坝勘明铝土矿共生耐火黏土矿储量197.7万吨；贵州省化工地质队在回水、花椤探明硫铁矿，其中C级储量75.5万吨，D级388万吨，E级1362万吨，品位含全硫8.4%至20.47%，且矿藏厚度稳定，覆盖层薄，易于露天开采。

2000年，贵州省地质科学研究所，探明石龙坡矿区阁老寨铝土矿；省地矿局117地质队，省有色地勘局一总队、省冶金地质队分别对全县10多种矿藏再次勘察，又探明斗篷山、长冲、干坝、箭杆冲铝土矿区。是年县国土资源局为县境内丰富的铝土矿资源编制《修文县铝土矿资源开发与勘察专项规划》，加强铝土矿的开发和保护。

矿藏资源分布表

表1—03—04

名　称	主要分布地区	已探明储量（万吨）	特性及品位
铝土矿	主要分布地龙场、谷堡和扎佐等乡镇	7709.	含三氧化二铝40.7%至80%，平均含量68%
煤	全县各乡镇均有	12000	发热量在27214焦耳/克至36425焦耳/克之间
重晶石	龙场镇三角山、程关、马家桥，扎佐镇双月，六广镇大锅寨	22.04	含$BaSO_4$在95%至98%

续表

名　称	主要分布地区	已探明储量（万吨）	特性及品位
赤铁矿	龙场镇高仓、小山、干坝、杨寨，谷堡乡乌栗、下洞、长冲、尖山，洒坪乡五老山	2276.72	含铁40%至60%，易于露天开采
硫铁矿又名黄铁矿	各乡镇均有。其中六桶乡来鹤村、河银村，大石乡的沙坝村矿区储量达500万吨	759.87	含全硫8.4%至20.47%
耐火黏土	主要分布在龙场镇小山坝、清水塘、干坝、斗篷山、天马山和中哨坝等地	2800	其耐火度达1666℃至1790℃，可以坑采和露采
石灰岩	全县各乡镇均有分布	储量极大	含CaO54.4%左右，是理想的水泥原料
磷矿	主要分布在久长镇与开阳县接壤的305省道旁的芦山、马蹄关一带	43.8	厚度0.2米至0.77米，含五氧化二磷在10.01%至33.07%，品级为2至3级
大理石	分布在小箐乡的偏坡寨、崇恩、新场、万兴一带	5000万立方米	崇恩、偏坡寨储量5000万方，万兴3000万方，新场100万方。颜色有桃红、墨晶、白玉等
硅矿	主要分布在龙场、扎佐、久长、六屯和谷堡等乡镇	300	一般含二氧化硅51.7%至86.98%，龙场镇干坝石门坎的硅矿达95.2%
汞矿	分布在六桶乡宝坪村、河银村和大石乡红岩村、回水村	—	含氧化汞0.01%至0.18%
稀有金属矿	一般与铝土矿伴生，主要有镓、铌、铂、锆、钛等	—	其中镓的矿石储量4281万吨，金属量1880吨，居全省之冠

二、主要矿藏

（一）铝土矿

县境铝土矿蕴藏量丰富，其中龙场镇小山坝九架炉铝土矿区，探明储量5500万吨。矿区矿藏质地之优，储量之大闻名于世，与清镇市一起共同占有全省总储量的78%。

1988年，贵州省地质科学研究所组织铝土矿勘察组，对蕴藏在龙场镇程官村石龙坡铝土矿进行勘察，认为石龙坡是寻找超大型隐伏铝土矿最理想、最有利地区。在东临川黔铁路及川黔公路，西邻贵州铝厂小山坝矿区，南靠贵州铝厂的面积20余平方公里范围内进行系统的地质调查和实测，勘明勘察范围内含矿岩系105条，分析鉴定岩矿200余件，对铝土矿的成矿条件、环境、机理取得突破性认识，确认石龙坡勘察区铝土矿是其周边北邻清水塘，西靠天马山和小山坝，南接斗篷山，东南紧连杨味湾铝土矿的延伸部分。预测铝土矿蕴藏量达5000万吨，属超大型隐伏铝土矿床。

2001年年初，贵州省地质科学研究所再次对石龙坡已知的铝土矿进行更深入的地质调查，经对石龙坡阁老寨钻探验证，证实在196.8米深处的铝土矿矿层厚0.64米，含矿岩系厚7.73米，为勘采铝土矿提供了科学依据。

是年3月19日，贵州省地质局有色一总队在县矿管部门的协调配合下，对石龙坡阁老寨甘龙洞矿段进行试采开钻，顺利完成钻探试采。5月25日，由贵州省综艺物资有限公司承担甘龙洞矿点铝土矿工业化勘探。经过钻探分析，可建年产20万吨的铝土矿开采矿山，开采250年。按照2000年铝土矿市场价80元/吨计算，年产值可达1600万元，为修文开发建设氧化铝厂、磨料厂、炼铝厂提供资源保障。

2002年勘探资料统计，全县铝土矿储量达7709.52万吨。截至2010年，铝土矿已开采2381.63万吨。

已探明县境铝土矿矿床储量与等级一览表

表1—03—05

矿　山	储量（万吨）	等　级	备　注
	合计：7709.52		
小山坝	2037.6	A+B+C+D	已勘探开发
斗篷山	1138.46	B+C+D	勘探
长　冲	791.75	B+C+D	勘探
干　坝	838.04	B+C+D	勘探
清水塘	253.39	D	勘探
天马山	579.87	D	普查
大豆厂	855.6	C+D	勘探
乌　栗	378.76	D	详勘
上　洞	138.31	C	普查、勘探
箭杆冲	500	B+C+D	勘探
五老山	197.74		普查

（二）煤矿

县境煤矿分布较广，各乡镇均有分部，探明全县保有储量1.2亿吨，远景储量3.5亿吨。其产区主要在六广镇的六广、广田、德政、中心，大石布依族乡的联丰、回水，六桶乡的花椒，小箐的崇恩，洒坪乡的洒坪、中寨，龙场镇的阳早、杨寨、马家桥，扎佐镇的三元、扎佐、清让，久长镇的金桥、石安。尤以六广嘉夸山至洒坪枫香桥梁子一带的煤质最佳。

煤种有烟煤和无烟煤两种，发热量在27214焦耳/克~36425焦耳/克之间，可作生活用煤和工业用煤。无烟煤产于龙场镇、小箐乡、洒坪乡、六广镇、六桶乡，一般4~7层可采2层，烟煤（瘦煤）产于久长镇、扎佐镇、六屯乡有7层可采2层。

开采矿点主要分布：六广镇嘉夸、后坝、大岩头和蒋坡四矿，煤层厚1.8米~2.2米，地质储量3989.4万吨，保有储量3590万吨；龙场镇小河沟、茶田煤矿A+B+C级保有储量172.7万吨，D级142.2万吨；扎佐镇的挖煤冲、石堰河矿点和扎佐普查区，保有储量A+B+C级1035.6万吨，D级储量6887万吨。截至2010年，全县煤炭在探明储量中已采5000万吨。

（三）铁矿

境内铁矿主要是赤铁矿，除六屯乡外其余各乡镇均有分布，蕴藏量2276.72万吨，部分赤铁矿多与铝矿伴生，处于铝土矿下部铁矿系中，呈小透镜及结核状，水文地质简单，多宜露采，易手选，含铁40%~60%。其中小山坝铝土矿区赤铁矿c级储量达337.9万吨。截至2010年，全县铁矿已采68万吨。

（四）重晶石

境内重晶石矿已探明储量1200万吨，矿体多存于第四系浮土中，属残坡积砂矿床，呈透镜状。可以露天开采，品质优良，易手选，一般含硫酸钡（$BaSO_4$）95%—98%。主要分布在龙场、扎佐、六广和六屯等乡镇的三足山、马家桥、程官、长坡、大锅寨、长田、长麻窝和全心8个矿区。其中六屯乡星中村的长麻窝和六广镇合营村的大锅寨两个矿区矿点面积最大，各长1500米，宽100米—300米，厚0.2米—3.5米。截至2010年，重晶石已开采18万吨。

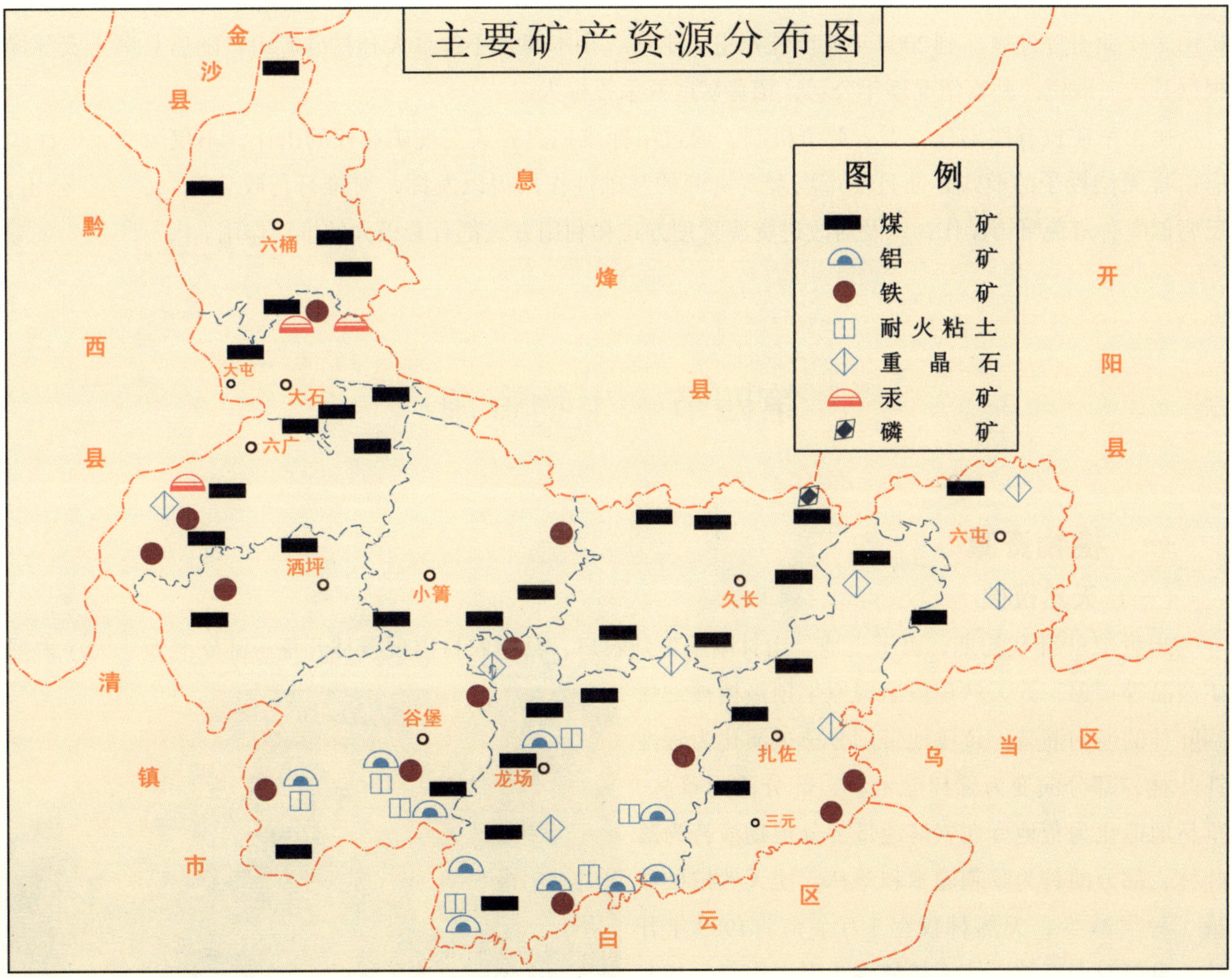

专记：矿山采矿权有偿出让纪实

2001年，县国土资源局为加强矿山采矿权的管理，以保护采矿人的合法权益和国家利益，促进矿产业发展，决定对矿山采矿权进行有偿出让，公开招标拍卖。拍卖采取优惠付款政策分期付款，解决竞标方的暂时困难，鼓励投资者把有限的资金首先用于开发，加快矿产业的发展。是年5月，分别拍卖矿山采矿权3宗。8日，谷堡乡大洞煤矿，由王家烈以13万元投标获得开采权，付款方式为交首付款3万元，其余10万元每年交1万元，10年交清；18日，扎佐镇双月村斑鸠寨煤矿，由贵阳修文振海贸易有限责任公司以40万元投标获得开采权，付款方式先交预付款5万元，申报后动工建井时交付5万元，余款30万元在5年内交清；29日，双月村斑鸠寨另一处煤矿，由白云区沙文乡企业公司以40万元取得采矿权，其付款方式仍按照振海贸易公司优惠对待。

2002年11月25日，县国土资源局发布矿山开采权拍卖公告，决定出让久长镇金桥村大荒坡，上寨村迁马山，扎佐镇老鹰岩，六广镇六广村大坪子和大石山，龙场镇沙溪村老鸭坡等处石灰矿开采权。同时公布各矿山的矿种、面积、储量、可采深度、开发要求和投标事宜。经过招标拍卖成交4宗，成交金额12.7万元。拍卖由县公证处现场公证后，获标者取得县国土资源局颁发的开采权证。

2003年8月，县国土资源局在《修文报》上分期登载矿山探矿权、采矿权的招投标出让管理办法，使矿山采矿业有序发展。到2004年又出让六屯大木寨、小木寨，小箐乡大林村硅矿山，随后县国土资源局根据县内矿藏资源勘察情况逐年公示，招募矿产开采投标人。

矿山采矿权有偿出让，引入竞争机制。通过招标或拍卖方式实现矿业权的出让，不仅改变了以往政府审批无偿授予的模式，而且使市场配置资源的基础性作用得以发挥，对推行行政公开、公平、公正，反腐倡廉、避免暗箱操作，以及对改进资源管理方式和利用方式都有着极大的推动作用。

第四节　生物资源

一、植物资源

（一）天然植被

20世纪80年代初期，由于土地、山林刚承包到农户，县内农村出现毁林开荒、乱砍滥伐、无序采掘矿产品等现象，致天然植被出现原生顶极植被常绿阔叶林的逆向演替。黄壤地带部分植被演化为暖性针叶林，部分演变为稀树灌木丛，部分沦为草丛，草丛地退化为荒地。在岩溶地带部分植物演替为落叶林，部分演替为藤刺灌木和草丛，使天然植被数量、种类减少，天然林仅存3万余亩。1989年开始，重新封山育林，使天然林逐步得以恢复。1999年，经贵州省重点生态工程森林资源调查，全县有林地面积61.29万亩，占土地总面积的38%，森林覆盖率为30.5%。其中，有林地35.41万亩，疏林地28.34万亩，灌木林13.81万亩，幼林地2.02万亩，

天然植被

经果林32.95万亩，苗圃301.5亩。从2003年起到2010年，加大植树造林的力度，完成中韩造林1.95万亩，退耕还林7.91万亩，贵阳市二环林带造林县境部分3.40万亩，使全县有林地增加到48.67万亩。同期，天然林恢复至7万亩,全县森林覆盖率提高到40.3%。

阔叶林 县境海拔1200米以下黄壤地段均有分布，共31科64种好钙树。山地下部有山茶科、杜鹃科植物，在山地上部有山毛榉、樟树、油桐、女贞、泡桐、梓木、枫香、青杠以及混杂其间的光皮桦树。

针叶林 境内有针叶林3科21种，主要树种有松树、杉树和柏树，其中松树以马尾松为主。针叶林中以山地分层，顶部多为针叶，中部间有小乔木和灌木，下部为稀疏草地。

灌木林 阔叶林和针叶林山地中部地段以及岩溶地带间有灌木林，藤、刺植物混杂其间，全县灌木林地达12.91万亩，占林地面积27.86%。

竹林 境内天然竹林零星分布，不成片，竹种主要有金竹、刺竹、绵竹、水竹、黑竹、箭竹、棕竹、苦竹和毛竹等。

牧草 县境成片天然牧草面积在100亩以上的有61片，不成片草地分散在林地底层地面。成片牧草面积呈逐年减少趋势。据2005年统计，全县牧草4.54万亩。禾本科主要草种有：毛草（丝毛、斑毛），箭杆草、铃当草、蓑衣草、马耳草、白花草、猪尾草、毛针草、狗尾草、熟地草、鱼鳅草、节芒草、露水草、爬地草、过江草等。其它科属的主要有三叶草、野花生、野豌豆以及蕨类草本植物。

菌类 在酸性土壤林地、草地中，夏秋季节天气湿热、多雨时，常生长菌类植物，主要有：芝麻菌、黄丝菌、奶浆菌、松包菌、鸡枞菌、青堂菌、刷把菌、石灰菌、青杠菌、毛草菌、紫花菌、核桃菌、青草菌、土冻菌以及木耳（地木耳、树木耳和石木耳）。

野生蔬菜 野菜为非人工种植的蔬菜，营养丰富、美味可口，成为绿色食品家族中的重要一员，不仅含人体所必需的蛋白质、脂肪、碳水化合物、维生素、矿物质等营养成分，而且植物纤维更为丰富，有的野菜维生素、矿物质含量比栽种的蔬菜高几倍甚至几十倍。而且大多数野菜生长于山林之中，未受到现代工业和农药化肥的污染，尤为珍贵。以往野菜仅为遇灾荒时作充饥之用，而今成为人们餐桌上的新宠。野菜还是防病治病的良药：荠菜能清肝明目、中和脾胃、止血降压，马齿菜能清热解毒、凉血止血，苦葱能防动脉硬化，刺嫩芽补肾益精等。县境野生菜品种主要有香椿、漆树巅、刺老包（刺嫩芽）、刺楸颠、钓干麻、竹笋、鱼腥草（折耳根）、马齿苋、苦葱、小蓟（马刺盖）、苦菜、枸杞芽（狗地芽）、荠菜（鸡脚菜）、剪刀菜、灰灰菜、水芹菜、姨妈菜、小禾麻、虎杖苔、蕨苔、纡头鸡（薇菜）、柴胡、何首乌颠、泡参、桔梗、车前草、蒲公英、野山药、百合、鹅儿肠、老鹳筋、薄荷、景菜（土人参）、栀子花等。

野果

草莓类有栽秧泡、薅秧泡、白地母（有一种红色类似称为老蛇泡儿，有毒不能吃）、鸡屎泡、老鹳泡、蚕桑泡（桑葚）、马桑泡（有微毒不宜多吃）。

水果类有洋桃（猕猴桃）、酸梅李、野杏子、野梨子、毛桃子、野樱桃、野枇杷、野葡萄、拐枣、毛栗、丝栗、板栗、青杠子。

棘果类有红刺母（火棘）、刺梨、山楂、羊奶奶（羊奶果）、八月瓜、蜂糖罐、地瓜。

珍稀植物 县境天然珍稀树种有国家Ⅱ级保护树杜仲、银杏、鹅掌楸，Ⅲ级保护树翠柏、厚朴、红豆树、桢楠、铁肩杉。受国家保护古树在200至250年的有15株，251年以上的有12株。其中在251至

300年杉树2株，朴树1株。401年至500年柏树2株（2004年枯死1株），榔树1株。500年以上朴树1株，榔树1株。

1999年全县森林资源调查一览表

表1—03—06

乡　镇	覆盖率%	有林地		灌木林地	
		面积（亩）	覆盖率（%）	面积（亩）	覆盖率（%）
全县合计	30.5	354100.5	21.95	138106.5	8.56
龙场镇	23.43	45825	17.47	15630	5.96
扎佐镇	24.07	34723.5	23.24	1291.5	0.83
久长镇	29.55	42799.5	24.66	8499	4.9
六广镇	31.69	23604	16.72	21124.5	14.97
大石乡	29.55	14082	18.37	8565	11.17
谷堡乡	40.77	48692	26.8	25366.5	13.96
六桶乡	26.15	19606.5	11.88	23548.5	14.27
六屯乡	35.85	36913.5	31.57	5002.5	4.28
洒坪乡	28.59	17296.5	13.64	19212	14.95
小箐乡	31.21	38769	24.88	9876	6.33
扎佐林场	57	31791	57	—	—

（二）人工造林

用材林防护林　全县有省级林场、乡镇林场和防护林工程46.59万亩。主要种植松树、柏树、杉树、檀木和竹类等。在城镇地带种植的绿化树种有香樟、玉兰、梧桐、雪松、滇柏、白皮松、丁香、海棠、银杉、水杉、秃杉、台湾杉、垂柳以及园林风景植物女贞、继木、黄秧等。

经济林木　从20世纪80年代初开发建设经果园到2010年全县相继开发果园、茶园、桑园、苗圃、中药材和花卉盆景园，共植经济园林植被10万亩。果树类主要有柑橘、板栗、葡萄、梨子、桃子、猕猴桃、酥李、布朗李、核桃、杨梅、苹果、石榴、柿子、山楂、拐枣、樱桃、花红、枇杷等。竹类主要有楠竹、斑竹、金竹、刺竹、绵竹、水竹、黑竹、箭干竹、棕竹、苦竹和毛竹等。食用、药材类主要有桑葚、苦丁茶、茶叶、老鹰茶、花椒、银杏、杜仲、黄柏、厚朴等。

（三）农作物

县境禾谷类植物品种有水稻109个，小麦21个，大麦5个，燕麦1个，玉米21个，高粱2个，粟2个，薯10个；豆类植物品种有大豆24个，绿豆2个，蚕豆2个，豌豆3个，菜豆19个，杂豆5个；油科类植物品种有油菜13个，花生3个，向日葵3个，以及芝麻、蓖麻、酥籽等；蔬菜类植物品种更加丰富，常见品种达60余种。

水稻　品种主要分为本地品种和引进品种两大类，本地品种主要有红粘、白粘、麻粘、竹丫粘、乌脚粘、晚谷、高粱糯、樱桃糯等。其特点是植株高，易倒伏，亩产一般200公斤至450公斤，最高可达

500公斤，大米适口性好。本地品种大米较为有名的是六屯乡桃源米和龙场镇青龙村的沙田米。引进品种主要先有珍珠矮、广场矮、矮子粘、川大粳、农育1744、西农175等，1990年后，全县普遍引进种植优质、高产水稻威优48、77，金优207、431，岗优12、22、77，汕优63、64，金桂99，二优838，两优636等品种。其特点是植株矮，不易倒伏，亩产一般400公斤至800公斤，最高可达1000公斤，大米适口性较一般，不及本地品种。引进品种由于产量高和易于耕作，逐步替代了原有的本地品种，进入21世纪，本地水稻品种全被淘汰。2010年，全县种植水稻9.01万亩，全为引进品种。

玉米 俗称“苞谷”，本地品种主要有大白玉米、大黄玉米、小黄玉米、小刺玉米、白糯玉米和黄糯玉米等，其特点是植株高，亩产一般100公斤至250公斤，最高可达300公斤。20世纪80年代，逐渐引进种植杂交玉米，其品种主要是省内优质黔单2、4、5号，其次是中单2号。随后又引进外地优质玉米高油115、安单136、京丰2号、郧单1号、三七单交、兴玉1号、兴单4号等。其特点是植株矮，亩产一般300公斤至600公斤，最高可达700公斤，杂交玉米适口性较本地玉米差，主要用于畜禽养殖。2010年，全县种植玉米10.85万亩，多为引进品种。

小麦 共有21个品种，其中本地品种6个，引进品种15个。1978年，种植面积为6.5万亩。种植的品种分两个阶段，1980年至1999年种植贵农10号、黔荣、贵花5号、绵阳26号等。进入21世纪，主要种植绵阳系列和川农系列小麦。全县小麦种植逐年减少趋势较为突出，2005年种植减少到4.7万亩，2010年减至3.14万亩。

马铃薯 20世纪80年代初期、中期种植米拉、红豆沙、威宁河坝洋芋。80年代后期种脱毒马铃薯3号。90年代引进东北、六枝、威宁洋芋，有六引95-1、中薯费乌瑞它、威宁1、2、3号等品种。到2010年全县种植面积达8.56万亩。

油菜 油菜品种13个，其中本地品种6个，引进品种7个。1979年，全县从种油菜养田和食用出发种植北京型油菜，面积4.1万亩。1982年为发展油料作物，种植面积扩展到6.7万亩，占全县农作物面积33.9%，到2000年一直保持在6万亩左右。其品种为低芥酸、低硫化葡萄糖甙油菜杂选1号，贵杂2、5号，黔西12、17、18号，绵油11号，油研7号等。2010年，全县种植面积8.11万亩。

烤烟 1979年，全县种烤烟1.2万亩。20世纪80年代后期烤烟烟叶销售成为县的重要经济收入，到1988年，已发展到4.5万亩。其品种早先有红花大金元、春雷3号，到1990年后普遍种植高秆多叶新品种G—140、Nc—82、G—28。1991年达5.1万亩。2005年执行国家烟草压缩种植面积政策，以后每年一直稳定在2万亩左右。2010年，全县种烟面积为2.53万亩。

蔬菜 县内蔬菜品种多到近100种，常见60余种。随着人口城镇化率提升和人们饮食结构调整变化，蔬菜种植面积和品种逐年增加。2007年，县委、县政府将蔬菜种植列入县支柱产业培育，开发大宗蔬菜生产基地12万亩。主要种植基地及品种有：久长青菜、豌豆，扎佐地萝卜、大白萝卜、折耳根，六屯辣椒，洒坪大葱，谷堡大蒜，小箐白菜、花菜，龙场西红柿等。2010年，全县种植蔬菜22.77万亩。

专记：中哨村规模种植晚番茄带动邻村

龙场镇中哨村位于县境南部，贵阳市白云区至修文的107省道旁，距县城8公里，距贵阳市区30公里。1998年还是全县贫困村之一。为了改变村贫困落后状况，村党支部根据村的耕地土质和交通便利的有利条件，提出种玉米改为种番茄，在党支委和村委会带领下，发动村里近100户村民种植番茄70亩，当年每亩平均收入700元，比种玉米收入增加1倍。村民得到实惠后，第二年番茄种植增加到120户，面积达200亩。

2003年，村民抓住省农业厅实施夏秋反季节蔬菜种植项目机遇，把番茄种植春种夏收改为夏种秋收，种植延晚番茄500亩。并把产品直接销往贵阳市。随后又开辟两广、重庆夏秋蔬菜市场，省内外蔬菜采购商纷纷在中哨设立进货点。是年每亩平均收入达3000元。2004年，为有利于管理和运输，把山地种植番茄转向公路沿线大坝种植，由粗放种植向大规模、集约型、产业化发展，成为全县番茄种植专业村。是年种植面积增至900余亩。

点燃一盏灯，照亮一大片，到2005年，中哨番茄带动镇内马口、王官、建新、茶田、杨寨、新寨、新春、新水、新生、幸福、平地、小营、马官等村普遍种植，使全县番茄种植面积达到5500亩。

二、动物资源

（一）野生动物

县境有野生动物鱼类14种，两栖类13种，鸟类30余种，哺乳类18种，无脊椎动物40余种。其中有国家二类保护动物穿山甲、大鲵、熊猴、红腹角雉，三类保护动物小灵猫。20世纪80年代将修文河北门桥至沙溪辟为大鲵保护区，将谷堡、洒坪、六广的猫跳河、六广河辟为红腹锦鸡、穿山甲、苍鹰保护区。到2000年，使大鲵数增至100余尾，红腹锦鸡达150只，猕猴7群300余只。2005年，落户扎佐境内的贵阳森林野生动物园，有两栖类、哺乳类、鱼类、鸟类野生动物200多种，5000多头（只）。

1. 脊椎动物

（1）鱼纲

鲤形目　有鲤鱼、草鱼、鲢鱼、鳙鱼、青鱼、鲳鱼、鲂鱼、鲫鱼、红尾鱼、鲈鱼、鲦鱼（分尖嘴白鲦、跷嘴白鲦和马口白鲦）、银鱼、小黄鱼（爬地花鱼）、餐鱼（麻杆餐、谷桩鱼）、花鱼等。

鲶形目　有鲶鱼、长吻鮠（角角鱼，亦称江团）、黄颡鱼（黄蜡丁）等，其中六广鲶鱼为修文特产。

合鳃鱼目　有鳝鱼（黄鳝）。

六广鲶鱼

（2）爬行纲

龟鳖目　有龟、鳖、鼋（绿团鱼）。

鳞甲目　有穿山甲。

有鳞目　有蜥蜴（四脚蛇）、乌梢蛇、菜花蛇、水蛇、赤链蛇、黄颔蛇（黄喉蛇）、白花蛇、金环蛇、银环蛇、粹蛇、青蛇、青竹标、蓝蛇。

（3）两栖纲

无尾目　有青蛙、蛤蟆、蟾蜍、石蛙（石蚌）、树蛙。其中蟾蜍已有人工饲养。

有尾目　有大鲵（娃娃鱼），已有人工饲养。

毒蛇“青竹标”

(4) 鸟纲

雁形目 有野鸭、大雁、鸳鸯、潜鸭、潜鸟、凫。

鹳形目 有老鹳（饿老鹳）、白鹭（鹭鸶）、鹬等。

鹤形目 有白鹤、秧鸡。

鸡形目 有野鸡、锦鸡、竹鸡（箐鸡）、白鹇、鹧鸪等。

鸮形目 有猫头鹰。

鹃形目 有杜鹃（主要为四声杜鹃和大杜鹃两种，前者叫声“薅早包谷”，俗称阳雀，后者叫声“苞谷”，俗称苞谷雀）。

红腹锦鸡

雀形目 有乌鸦、喜鹊、麻雀、黄豆雀、画眉、白颊噪鹛（土画眉）、八哥、鹩哥、翡翠鸟、翠鸟、黄莺、云雀、棕噪鹛（唱歌郎）、白鹡鸰（点水雀）、山雀、柳莺（胡豆雀）、戴胜鸟等。

鸽形目 有鹁鸪（斑鸠）。

隼形目 有隼、鹞（铁鹞子）、鸢（岩闹鹰）等。

20世纪90年代，县花鸟协会成立，出现前所未有的喂鸟热，画眉、八哥、黄豆雀、竹鸡、黄莺、唱歌郎等成为爱鸟者的饲养对象。

(5) 哺乳纲

灵长目 有猕猴。

食肉目 有山猫、小灵猫、黄鼬（黄鼠狼）、狐狸、獾、果子狸（酸枣狗），另虎、豹、豺、狼等野兽在境内已绝迹，仅野生动物园有饲养。

啮齿目 有老鼠（耗子）、山鼠（山耗子）、田鼠（水耗子）、松鼠（貂老鼠）

兔形目 有野兔。

猬形目 有豪猪、刺猬。

2. 无脊椎动物

无脊椎动物包括无脊椎爬行动物和昆虫。

(1) 环节动物

单向蚓目 有黑、油、红、花四种蚯蚓。

蛭纲颚蛭目 有黑、花两种水蛭。

(2) 节肢动物

蜘蛛目 有网蜘蛛、洞蜘蛛、地毛蜘蛛、水蜘蛛、花蜘蛛、小绿蜘蛛等。

十足目 有河虾、小龙虾（马虾）、河蟹等。

蜈蚣目 蜈蚣。

蚰蜒目 蚰蜒（草鞋虫）、马陆（千足虫）。

(3) 软体动物

主要有田螺、蜗牛、河蚌。

（4）昆虫

蜻蜓目 有蜻蜓、红蜻蜓、黄蜻蜓、蓝蜻蜓、绿蜻蜓、黑蜻蜓等。

膜翅目 有蜂（蜜蜂、马蜂、黄蜂、狗屎蜂）和蚂蚁（大黑蚁、小黑蚁、大红蚁、小红蚁、白蚁、臭蚁）等。

双翅目 有蚊、蝇、蠓、蚋、虻等。

鳞翅目 有蛾、蝶两类。

半翅目 有蝉、椿象（打屁虫）、蚜虫、臭虫等。

螳螂目 有螳螂，主要有绿、褐两种。

直翅目 有蝗虫、蟋蟀、蚱蜢、螽斯（蚱啦子）、蝼蛄（土狗儿）。

蜚蠊目 有蟑螂、地鳖虫。

同翅目 有介壳虫、五倍子芽虫等。

鞘翅目 有金龟子、天牛、瓢虫、屎壳郎（推屎爬）、步甲虫、叶甲虫、象鼻虫、虎甲虫、吉丁甲虫及菜蚤等。

脉翅目 有草蛉、粉蛉、蚁蛉、褐蛉、螳蛉等

寄螨目 有蜱虫。

虱目 有人体虱、头虱、阴虱和兽虱等。

蚤目 有跳蚤。

（二）家畜家禽

1. 家畜

猪 20世纪80年代初期，以饲养本地乌栗黑毛猪为主。80年代后期推广杂交猪，引进“二元”公猪，繁殖“三元”猪。2005年统计全县饲养杂交猪18.7万头。品种有苏白、长白、巴克、约克、杜洛克、巴克夏、荣昌猪和香猪。2010年全县生猪出栏15.91万头，存栏9.68万头。

牛 20世纪80年代，农户饲养本地水牛、黄牛，全为劳役耕牛，共存栏2万头。进入90年代，牛从单纯耕地向肉、役兼用的商品牛转变。2000年开始专门饲养肉牛和奶牛，引进国内秦川母牛、泥黑水牛、关岭黄牛以及国外西门塔尔、利木赞、安格斯、摩拉、殷华利、夏洛来、爱沙尼亚和荷兰奶牛。2010年，全县牛出栏1.25万头，存栏4.24万头。

马 20世纪80年代初，马、骡饲养主要用于马车驮运劳役，共计4835匹。主要是大青马、枣红马和灰骡。90年代随乡镇运输发展，马的数量达到7300余匹。2000年，乡村普遍使用农用运输机动车，马车逐步退出运输。到2005年，马、骡数量减少到6971匹，2010年减至4903匹。

羊 20世纪80年代初，全县饲养山羊417只，分散在石安、中寨、六广、大石、凉井等山地乡村。1996年至2003年退耕还林还草，恢复森林、草地，促进黑山羊饲养。到2005年发展到2.5万只。除本地山羊、白花山羊外还引进北方绵羊、威宁黑山羊、赫章山羊。2010年全县羊存栏1.13万只。

兔 20世纪80至90年代农村有少量养殖。进入21世纪，兔肉作为保健食品进入饮食消费市场，推动家兔饲养。引进安哥拉兔、日本大耳兔、长毛兔、齐卡兔以及比利时、新西兰、加利福利亚巨型肉兔。2005年发展到1.8万只。到2010年肉兔保持有1万余只。

2. 家禽

鸡 本地鸡属黔中类型，成年母鸡体重1.5公斤至2公斤，公鸡2公斤至2.5公斤。20世纪80年代引进鸡种主要有来杭鸡、九斤黄（贵农黄）、澳洲黑、芦风花鸡等，多与本地鸡杂交，逐步退化。90年代，主要引进肉用型鸡较多，其中品种有星斯鸡、红育鸡、火鸡、红布罗、艾维因、伏巴特、罗斯鸡、伊利莎、铁脚麻鸡以及湖南闵中麻鸡、广西三黄鸡等。2000年，县内建肉蛋鸡饲养场，农村养鸡专业户利用山林饲养林鸡，到2010年肉鸡出栏198.5万只，存栏73.7万只。

鸭、鹅 1980年，在农村河流、水库、山塘养鸭1.9万只和鹅5000只。1990年鸭、鹅达2.5万只。2000年，久长镇、六广镇诞生鸭鹅饲养专业户，鸭鹅饲养数量大增，到2010年存栏27.4万只。主要有北京鸭、狄高鸭、江西麻鸭、北京鹅、狮头鹅。

鸽 1984年，县信鸽协会成立，开始饲养信鸽。2000年，县城龙岗花园饲养广场鸽。2003年，引进肉鸽饲养，鸽子成为营养调剂食品，使鸽饲养迅速发展，在六广、六桶等地出现肉鸽饲养专业户。到2005年，全县饲养肉鸽达2500只，至2010年一直保持在2000只左右。

第五节　自然景观

县境山川秀丽，六广河7峡42景具有三峡之雄奇，漓江之秀美的特色；多缤洞66个大小洞厅连珠似的延绵14公里，可谓五彩缤纷；猫跳河梯级电站具有较高的现代科普价值；高枧、回水石林是贵州绿色石林的代表；松柏参天，百鸟群集的扎佐林场，被誉为林城氧吧。至2010年，除六广河、桃源河、兰花湖和扎佐林场部分开发外，其余大部分自然景观尚待开发和利用。

一、河湖景观

（一）河流峡谷风光

全县有流域面积在20平方公里以上的河流12条，其中大于100平方公里5条，即乌江（六广河）、猫跳河、猫洞河、鱼梁河（桃源河）、修文河。均属长江流域乌江水系，为雨源型河流。特点是自然风光优美、水域面积宽广、生态植被良好和峡谷景观旖旎，具有较高的旅游开发价值。

六广河 乌江中游流经县境段称六广河，为修文与黔西、金沙三县的界河。1977年乌江电站大坝建成后，河面形成回水70余公里长的巨大人工湖。从上游白马滩起至下游姊妹峰，水路长40余公里，拥有7峡42景。全河段融山、水、洞、瀑、林于一体。明哲学家、教育家王阳明曾以“遍行奇胜才经此，江上无劳羡九华”的诗句赞美其峡谷风光。2000年，六广河旅游公司开始对六广河旅游资源进行开发。

六广河峡谷一景

猫跳河　猫跳河旧名滴澄河，是乌江南岸的一条支流，发源于安顺旧州长山，流经县境西部，于修文、清镇、黔西3县交界的三岔河处与鸭池河汇合注入乌江，全长181公里，落差549.6米。县境段为猫跳河下游，长49.7公里，谷深流急，水力资源丰富。早在20世纪50年代至70年代，建成了坝型各异的6个梯级水电站，其中县境内的三、四、五、六级4座电站坝型独特，风格各异，设计新颖精巧而闻名全国，被誉为“中国水电坝型博物馆”。猫跳河两岸多为深峡陡壁，山清水秀，景观异趣纷呈，蕴含着丰富的旅游文化资源，其中有名的“石老人”位于五级电站拦河坝右侧山崖上。

猫跳河风光

修文河　为猫跳河支流，属乌江二级支流。发源于久长镇栋青村，流经石安、马家桥、县城、沙溪等地，于河口电站汇入猫跳河。源头海拔1352米，汇入猫跳河处海拔1118米。流域面积228.2平方公里，主河道长37公里。修文河上游山、水、林、田相辉映，中游一派田园风光，下游称作“蛮子河”，落差逐渐加大，两岸山清水秀，景色迷人。其中沙溪段可开发漂流旅游，修文电站大坝以下段河谷深切，两岸藤蔓密布，河床上巨石光洁如玉。

桃源河　属乌江二级支流，是县东部干流，上游称扎佐河，流经扎佐三里与葛马河汇集后流经原桃源乡东部边境称桃源河。往东流过桃源田坝，经开阳县注入乌江一级支流清水河。桃源河峡谷，两岸峰峦叠翠，怪石嶙峋，山花烂漫，飞瀑直下，素有“人间仙境”“黔中福地”之称。境内河长29.1公里，境内流域面积375.9平方公里，多年平均流量6.8立方米/秒。桃源河景区段河流长12公里，从香巴房至三道响水5公里河段落差大，水流湍急，2001年开始，已作为景区一期项目漂流开发；2010年，三道响水以下至桃源大寨段，列为二期项目开发，其景点有银滩瀑布、九重天大瀑布、金雕迎客等。

猫洞河　属乌江二级支流，发源于久长镇茶山村大白岩下龙孔，河流上段称花桥河，流经天生桥到下游与郭田河汇合。郭田河发源于小箐乡凤凰村老箐沟，流经两棚岩到天生桥下游与花桥河汇集后称猫洞河，再经蜈蚣桥于轿子山村东缘三岔河处汇入猫跳河。主流长27.3公里，流域面积135.8平方公里。河流流经景区主要有天生桥、两棚岩及蜈蚣桥景区。

（二）湖泊风光

1978年，境内已建成蓄水工程254处，其中小Ⅰ型水库7座，小Ⅱ型水库21座，为全县的工农业生产和人畜饮用提供了良好水源保障，同时也为旅游事业发展创造了良好条件，其中兰花湖（蚌壳堰湖）、浪潮湖及清塘湖于1996年起相继开发为珍珠岛度假中心、高尔夫度假中心、苏格兰牧场度假村等休闲度假旅游区。至2010年，尚有岩鹰山湖、阁老寨湖、逍遥湖和高潮湖4个小Ⅰ型水库和21座小Ⅱ型水库尚待开发。

岩鹰山湖　位于县城北面13公里的小箐乡新场村、万兴村境内，距县城14公里。因水库紧靠岩鹰山，故名“岩鹰山水库”，1971年动工建设，又名“七一水库”。总库容1750万立方米，为县境内最大的人工湖，由岩鹰山、万兴、小六广3个湖区通过地下溶洞及人工隧洞相连而成。3个湖区各具特色，或宽广浩渺，或碧荡漾，或幽静迷人，竞相媲美。

兰花湖 位于久长镇金桥村境内，原名蚌壳堰水库，距县城18公里。是20世纪70年代中期修建的人工湖，其源头有河坝林溪水和孟冲、烂木桥两座湖水注入，水量充足，水位稳定。库容500万立方米，水域面积800亩，为境内第二大人工湖。湖内水域宽阔，水质纯净，郁郁葱葱的千亩森林怀抱着波光粼粼的湖面，四周山青林翠，环境优美。1999年，贵阳市人防战备办公室投资对湖中一半岛进行开发，并命名为“珍珠岛度假中心”。2003年5月，中心一期项目建成运营。2005年，中心继续投资建设二期工程。至2010年，中心对外接待游客9万人次，主要以会议、聚会、度假、避暑、休闲的客人为主。

珍珠岛风光

桃花湖 位于六屯乡独山村境内桃源河上，距县城23公里。系1978年始建，1985年9月竣工的人工湖，总库容138万立方米，原设计主要功能是水力发电，称“香粑房电站”，装机容量320千瓦，主要解决扎佐镇及六屯乡部分村民的用电问题。农村电网改造后，2002年由桃源河峡谷景区对电站职工进行一次性补偿安置，之后电站发电仅供景区自用。桃花湖曲折蜿蜒于山野之间，湖面平静，四周林木苍翠，倒影成趣。

浪潮湖 位于县东部的扎佐镇三元村境，距县城13公里。地处乌江水系扎佐河上游，1957年始建，1959年竣工，总库容245万立方米的人工湖。浪潮湖处于省级景阳森林公园内，湖面被苍翠碧绿的森林植被环绕，蜿蜒狭长。湖尾由两条支流汇集而成。湖面波光粼粼，水鸟群集，湖岸垂柳依依，清风习习，环境十分幽静。1996年，湖区已开发为贵阳高尔夫度假中心配套水域。

逍遥湖 位于县西北面的谷堡乡谷堡村境，距县城12公里。1976年始建，1978年竣工，总库容135万立方米的人工湖。逍遥湖原名烂沟水库，因其三面环山，四周被郁郁葱葱的峰峦环绕，湖面平静，水质清澈，泛舟水面，有逍遥自在之感而得名“逍遥湖”。湖面犹如明镜，群山倒影湖中，其境自然悠闲，可谓人间仙境。湖坝下约500米处有一天然溶洞，洞口高近20米，宽30米，进深约600米，为一座天生桥洞。洞内大厅，面积近千平方米，可容数百人。

逍遥湖

阁老寨湖 位于县东南面的龙场镇高仓村境，距县城8公里，地处乌江水系修文河支流的穿山堰河上游，始建于1958年，1959年竣工，总库容114万立方米。湖中水质清澈透明，湖面宽广浩渺，四周青山环抱，植被葱茏，湖面常见鸳鸯戏水，白鹭群集。湖下游左面山体下有一泉水，名“鱼洞泉”，泉水如桶径不断涌出，水质清澈见底，可见鱼虾游弋，其味清甜。阁老寨湖也叫“高仓湖”，因其湖尾有一苗族村寨，名为高脚仓。寨后的营盘山上保留有苗族古堡遗址“高仓古堡”，为少数民族军事遗迹。

高潮湖 位于县东部扎佐镇丁关村境，距县城20公里。地处扎佐河上游支流。1956年始建，1959年竣工，总库容达112万立方米。湖区所处地势较高，山势平缓，视野开阔。湖岸多有开阔的空地，野草成毯，山花点缀。远处劲松苍翠，近处垂柳依依。湖尾的山坡上有千亩梨园，可赏花观景，可品果采梨。湖下游是万亩无公害蔬菜基地，一年四季都有不同品种的新鲜蔬菜应市。

二、岩溶景观

（一）石林

境内有两处石林资源，均位于县西北部大石布依族乡境内。两座石林被称作“南北双雄”，由回水石林和高枧石林两部分组成，内有自然景观11处，其中：一级景观1处，二级景观6处，三级景观4处。

回水石林 位于大石布依族乡回水村境，距县城44公里，距省城贵阳83公里。景区包括石林、石笋、兰蛇和回水四个部分，总面积4平方公里。石林位于回水东南面斜坡上，面积0.67平方公里。按石林形态可划分为天生桥林、剑林、迷宫林、蟒林、鲸屏林和纸洞林等6片。石林石柱一般高10米至20米，最高可达30米。整个景区怪石嶙峋，姿态万千，神奇险峻，景色奇观，引人入胜。石林中植被生长较好，林中有石，石上有树，多数石笋上生长天然常绿植物，还有古藤缠绕，故有“绿色石林”之称。

回水石林

高枧石仓 位于大石布依族乡高枧村境，景区面积2.4平方公里。距贵（阳）毕（节）高等级公路仅10公里，距修文县城36公里，距省城贵阳74公里。景点面积0.27平方公里，内中奇峰异石密布，石沟石硐纵横，森林植被完好，四季藤蔓密布、绿树成荫。景观由石牙、溶沟、石硐等组成，尤以石牙多而集中，故称“高枧石仓”，意为储存奇石的仓库。奇石形态丰富多姿，几乎无石不成景，具有“绿、奇、幽、迷、趣、怪”等特点。有鸟兽聚会、无言石门、相拥千年、鸳鸯石侣、美发仙子、横空出世等6处景观。其中“夫妻吻”“骆驼石”“卧狮石”“一线天”等景观栩栩如生，素有“拟态动物园”之称。

（二）溶洞

县境大部地区属卡斯特地貌，碳酸盐类岩层分布广泛，岩溶地貌发育丰富，形成众多溶洞，各乡镇均有分布。据统计，全县溶洞有230多个。以地下溶洞为主，规模较大，景观奇特。极具旅游价值的溶洞主要有多缤洞、天生桥、二洞、熬硝洞等。

多缤洞 位于六桶乡大兴村与息烽县九庄镇桐枝驿村交界的凤凰山下，距县城56公里。清代以及民国年间，兵匪为患，百姓借洞藏匿，称“躲兵洞”，又称“休息洞”。1984年1月，贵州省科学院探测考察此洞，见洞景千姿百态，五彩缤纷，遂谐音称“多缤洞”。已探测部分洞长达21.4公里，堪称“亚洲地下长廊”，主要由六支水洞和七支陆洞组成，多洞一体，多洞互通，五层洞道层叠交织，洞中有水，水上有滩，滩下有瀑。洞中水陆并存，曲径通幽。洞厅大小皆备，厅厅有景，各不相同，是旅游、探险、科研的理想之地。多缤洞洞穴系统是世界一流的喀斯特洞穴艺术宝库，地下岩溶地貌博物馆，被专家称为“天下奇观”。

天生桥 位于修文县城西北12.5公里的谷堡乡哨上村哨上组，南有“三人坟”，北有蜈蚣桥，在古驿道上三景毗连相望。桥系横跨两山间一条隆起的山脊，因花桥河伏流长期冲刷侵蚀，致岩石塌落而形

成。流水从山脊下穿过，犹如一座天然石桥。桥高20余米，长约30米，桥洞高10余米，宽约7米，洞深约14米。桥面山脊，长满四季常绿灌木，一条小路从桥面经过。桥下深谷，层岩跌宕，下游500米范围落差约200米，形成多级瀑布群。出桥第一级瀑布，河水绕石而下，如蛟龙出洞，跌落成瀑，激起无数浪花，隐于桥下深谷，瀑高30多米，如白练当空。从下游仰视桥洞，犹似青天白云间露出一透明天窗，瀑流从天窗倾泻而下，十分壮观。下游河道无泥沙细石，惟石屿、石巇相错落，如盘如砥，似禽似兽。水流转向北去1里许注入深谷黑龙潭（又称老黑潭），形成高40米、宽25米的黑龙潭瀑布，水流一泻而下，飞花四溅，涛声如雷，尤以暴雨过后，河水猛涨时更为壮观。明代思想家王阳明在其《过天生桥》诗中发出赞叹："移放长江还济险，可怜虚却万山中。"

六屯二洞 位于六屯乡境内的全兴村与开阳县交界处，距县城38公里，离开阳香火岩景区2公里。因有一大一小两洞相邻的天然溶洞、河水相连，当地人称之为"二洞"。大洞洞长500余米，宽约20米，洞高30米；小洞位于下游，洞长约2公里。河水从二洞中穿过，形成伏流。此段河流为修文和开阳两界河，左岸为开阳县地，山势险峻，树木葱茏；右岸属修文县地，坡缓谷深，林幽洞静。出洞口与其右侧山体间有一峡谷，山泉从谷内流出，清澈透明，甘甜可口，经洞口进入河流。右侧山体有一瀑布从半山飞流而下，与山石、树木冲击，悬瀑飞溅，犹如珠帘叠翠，蔚为壮观。洞内阴森，怪石嶙峋，水声隆隆，没有道路通行，但可涉水而过。1998年，贵州省公路公司对景区进行开发，修建游览步道，在洞顶建接待中心和停车场等，后因公司人事调整和资金不济停工。

熬硝洞 位于小箐乡紫江村境，原名为"助国洞"，又叫"罗汉洞"，因民国年间在洞内熬硝得名"熬硝洞"。洞长5公里，洞口高15米，宽40余米，坐北向南。洞口形成占地800平方米的大厅，右壁有民国14年石刻2块，今尚存当地富豪廖世祯等人捐资在洞口大厅筑墙、修门、建庙等遗址。沿洞口进入洞内，有8个大厅，各厅面积为200平方米—600平方米不等。厅内有形似石钟、石笋、石鼓、石锣、石菩萨等大大小小的钟乳石，形态各异，蔚为壮观。

三、森林谷地景观

兰花谷 位于小箐乡小箐村至郭田村境，距县城16公里，距贵（阳）毕（节）高等级公路小箐出口0.5公里处。兰花峡谷又名两蓬岩，长约3公里，郭田河（又名大桥沟）从峡谷中经过，谷内生长有惠兰、春兰、四季兰等多种野生兰花，春天进入谷内，兰香沁脾，故名"兰花谷"。谷身狭长，两岸山高坡陡，悬崖峭壁，树木葱郁，空气清新，凉风习习，水雾飘拂。峡谷上游入口处有一座单孔石拱桥横跨于大桥沟两山之间，桥高约4米，长10米，宽3米。桥建于清康熙十九年（1680），名为"觉先桥"，原为小箐乡至县城的交通要道。

小箐兰花谷

扎佐林场 位于扎佐镇境，始建于1958年，隶属贵州省林业厅，是以营造杉木、华山松、马尾松等为主的用材林基地。1992年经省计委、建委、财政厅、林业厅批准，扎佐林场由造林林场转为经营林场，经营面积7.73万亩。2001年5月贵州省林业厅将扎佐林场的台墩坝、三元、冷水沟和珍珠井四个分场的经营范围划为省级森林公园，开展森林旅游，总面积2.36万亩,占扎佐林场经营面积的30.5%。森林植被类型主要有以华山松和马尾松为主的针叶林，以桦木、杨树、槐树为主的阔叶林，以华山松、马尾松、杉木、柳杉、水杉和桦木、杨树、栎类、刺槐、梓木、檫木为主的针阔混交林和以华山松、马尾松为主的针叶混交林。此外，有国家一级保护植物珙桐、银杉，国家二级保护植物鹅掌楸和珍贵树种银杏、福建柏、杜仲等。药用植物113种，观赏植物95种，可供食用的野菜类65种。野生动物资源常见的有59种，其中鸟类30种，兽类12种，爬行类10种，两栖类7种。扎佐林场是贵阳市环城防护绿化带的重要组成部分，场内植物种类繁多，森林茂密，林海茫茫，林下草地翠绿如茵，地势平缓，以优美且色彩丰富的针阔混交林景观、针叶林景观和针叶混交林景观以及通透如茵的森林草地景观为特色，集山、水、林、草、古迹于一体，凸显“山缓水秀、林茂草茵”景观和幽、秀、野、旷特色。森林内除有大量森林资源外，还分布有天然溶洞、石林、泉水、溪流、湖泊等自然景物。园内林幽谷静，空气清新，负氧离子含量高，是休闲度假、避暑吸氧、康体健身的好去处。

第四章　人　口

1978年，由于计划生育工作的开展，全县人口自然增长率回落至17.88‰，年末总人口为240976人。1980年党中央将人口计划生育列入基本国策后，县委、县政府为使人口增长与自然资源和环境协调一致，有效地遏制了人口的过快增长，缓解了人口过快增长给经济社会发展带来的压力，人口素质也逐步得以提高。

第一节　人口总量

全县人口状况的掌握，有公安、统计和人口计划生育3个职能部门，其中公安部门的人口数据与户籍管理紧密联系在一起。

1978年年末，全县总人口240976人，到2010年增至305917人，比1978年净增64941人，增长26.95%，33年间年均增长2019.4人，年均递增0.75%。1978—2010年，全县总人口数量较上年减少的有1983年、1984年、1987年、1989年、1997年、2003年和2004年。其中，农业人口较上年减少的有1996年、1997年、2002年、2003年、2004年和2005年；非农业人口较上年减少的有1979年、1980年、1982年、1983年、1984年、1985年、1986年、1987年、1988年、1989年、1992年、1997年、1998年、2003年和2007年。尽管年度之间人口数量有所波动，但呈现人口不断增长是总的趋势。

人口增长最主要的原因是自然增长。1978—2010年，全县累计出生131837人，年均出生3995.1人，出生率为14.71‰；全县累计死亡59691人，年均1808.8人，死亡率为6.66‰；全县累计自然增长82146人，年均2489.3人，自然增长率为9.16‰。在此期间，远远高于年平均值，出生人口、死亡人口和自然增长人口特别反常的情况是：出生人口在5000人以上的有6年，分别是1998年7759人，1996年5990人，1978年5453人，1982年5288人，1979年5261人，1995年5246人；死亡人口在2000人以上有3年，分别是1998年2374人，1996年2146人，2005年2008人；自然增长人口在4000人及以上的有3年，即1988年5385人，1978年4268人，1982年4000人。出生人口和自然增长人口反常偏大的年份与计划生育工作的松紧直接相关。

人口增长的另一个原因是机械增减。鉴于修文毗邻省会贵阳，交通方便和发展经济空间较大，吸引一些中央、省、市属的企、事业单位入驻，导致全县人口总量增加。到1982年6月底就有11个入驻县境的企、事业单位，人口33404人，占当时全县总人口的13%。之后，又有105地质队、林东煤校和省林校在境内落户。经过外地单位入驻增加人口后，又出现单位迁出，致人口减少。截至1990年，承担修建窄巷口、红林、红岩电站的水电九局完成任务后，就有1.5万余人的职工和家属陆续迁出县境。20世纪90年代，航空航天工业部属的华文、烽光、庆文、万江厂和304职工医院以及贵州省105地质队又先后迁出县境，使全县总人口机械减少万余人，导致一些年份全县总人口、特别是非农业人口数量的极大波动。以1978—2010年全县人口自然增长率平均为9.16‰计算，到2010年全县总人口应为322622人，并非实际的305917人，近2万人的差额，主要系入驻县境的企、事业单位外迁的机械因素所造成。至于零星因结婚、就业、工作调动等原因的迁入或迁出，整体上是基本平衡的，对全县人口总量的影响不大。

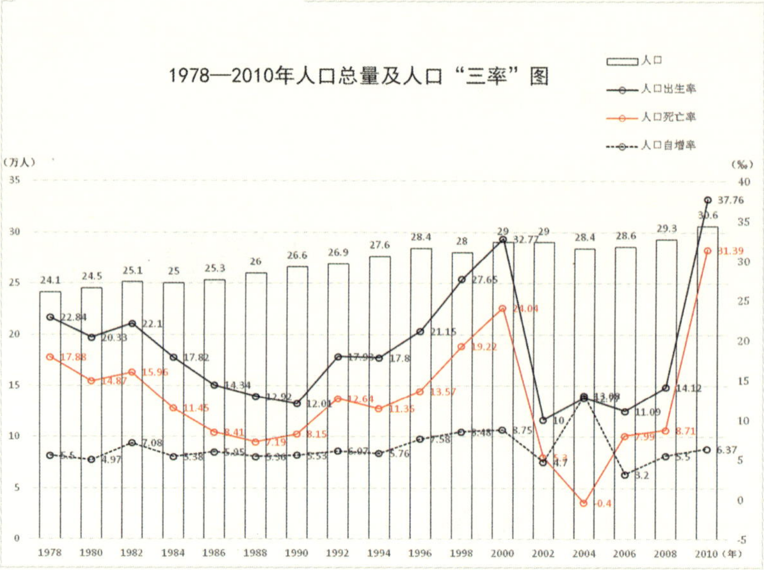

1978—2010年的33年间，随着人口总量增加，农业和非农业人口的数量及占总人口的比重变化也很大。

1978-2010年总人口及农业、非农业人口的数量与比重一览表

表1—04—01

年份	总人口(人)	农业人口		非农业人口	
		数量(人)	占总人口比重(%)	数量(人)	占总人口比重(%)
1978	240976	181886	75.48	59090	24.52
1979	243224	197120	81.04	46104	18.96
1980	245397	199394	81.25	46003	18.75
1981	249589	203028	81.34	46561	18.66
1982	251720	206170	81.90	45550	18.10
1983	251329	207706	82.64	43623	17.36
1984	250424	209661	83.72	40763	16.28
1985	251651	211519	84.05	40132	15.95
1986	252783	213379	84.41	39404	15.59
1987	252022	215734	85.60	36288	14.40
1988	260168	224055	86.12	36113	13.88

续表

年份	总人口(人)	农业人口		非农业人口	
		数量(人)	占总人口比重(%)	数量(人)	占总人口比重(%)
1989	259330	225862	87.09	33468	12.91
1990	265579	231638	87.22	33941	12.78
1991	267839	233719	87.26	34120	12.74
1992	268850	237967	88.51	30883	11.49
1993	272466	240604	88.31	31862	11.69
1994	275735	241462	87.57	34273	12.43
1995	282713	246785	87.29	35928	12.71
1996	283770	245004	86.34	38766	13.66
1997	278507	244839	87.91	33668	12.09
1998	280127	247405	88.32	32722	11.68
1999	283482	250313	88.30	33169	11.70
2000	289516	253394	87.52	36122	12.48
2001	289983	253704	87.49	36279	12.51
2002	290528	253090	87.11	37438	12.89
2003	288166	252295	87.55	35871	12.45
2004	283917	245213	86.37	38704	13.63
2005	283939	244789	86.21	39150	13.79
2006	286268	246712	86.18	39556	13.82
2007	288912	249685	86.42	39227	13.58
2008	292692	252910	86.41	39782	13.59
2009	296616	256501	86.48	40115	13.52
2010	305917	265487	86.82	40430	13.18

进入20世纪80年代后，全县非农业人口比重略呈上升趋势，其中原因：一是中级职称及以上知识分子，全民所有制企业中特殊工种（主要是井下作业）职工，领导干部和民办教师转为公办教师，他们属农业户口的配偶及16岁以下未成年子女；农业户口考入大学、中专的学生；农业户口现役军人提干后的投靠家属；落户小城镇投资、购房的农民；全民所有制企、事业单位聘用的农民工；国家建设征地造成农民失去土地等政策性的“农转非”等，使非农业人口数量增加。二是1992年以筹集城镇建设资金为由办理“蓝皮户口”，将全县400余名原属农业户口的农民转为非农业户口。

公安部门每年提供的人口统计年报，虽为掌握人口状况提供一定的资料，但涉及范围不广，指标不细，在很大程度上影响对这些资料使用。遵照国务院的统一部署，县政府于1982年、1990年、2000年和

2010年，分别开展了第三次、第四次、第五次和第六次人口普查。由于每次普查都组织了强有力的领导班子，并抽调相当力量统一培训后到各区、乡（镇）帮助工作，再加上广泛深入的社会动员，又有由国家统一制定的工作方案和表格，所以取得翔实的资料，既印证常规人口统计数据的质量，又全面、系统地反映全县人口的状况。

第三次至第六次人口普查的标准时间及人口总量表

表1—04—02

次　序	普查标准时间	总人口（人）	与上次普查相比	
			增减人数（人）	增减百分比（%）
第三次	1982年7月1日零时	257024	增125188	增94.96
第四次	1990年7月1日零时	266694	增9670	增3.76
第五次	2000年11月1日零时	262039	减4655	减1.75
第六次	2010年11月1日零时	248926	减13113	减5.00

注：全县第二次人口普查的总人口为131836人。

各次人口普查总人口数据与相应年份公安部门常规统计数据不一致。特别是第五次和第六次人口普查数据相当悬殊，其中原因：一是“时点”上的不一致。公安部门是每年12月31日24时的数据，而第三次、第四次人口普查是1982年和1990年7月1日零时的数据，第五次和第六次普查又分别是2000年和2010年11月1日零时的数据。二是“口径”上的不一致。公安部门常规统计的人口，基本上是户籍人口。只要在辖区内拥有户籍，当年又是没有迁出或注销户口的，都属统计对象。20世纪70年代实行计划生育起，一些地方为了应对考核，不给超生婴儿上户口，而出现一些没有户口的“黑人”，导致人口统计数据不实。1990年第四次人口普查前，县政府专门行文在全县范围开展户口整顿工作，强调既要保护基层干部抓计划生育工作的积极性，又要按照国务院要求补登以往漏报和瞒报超生人口的户籍，从而解决了超生婴儿无法纳入人口统计范围问题，保证了第四次人口普查数据的质量。而第五次和第六次人口普查，是按每次普查标准时间“常住”这个口径进行人口登记的。普查的人口数量等于在户口登记地居住的常住人口加上户籍虽不在本地，但在本地居住已有一定时间（第五次人口普查规定为一年及一年以上，第六次人口普查又规定为半年及半年以上）的人口。按此规定，户籍虽在本地而普查时人已外出一年及一年以上或半年及半年以上的，就不列入户籍所在地的普查对象，而是参加其流入居住地的普查登记，从而反映出在普查标准时间人口在地域分布上的真实状况。尽管全县总人口整体上是增长的，但出现2010年第六次人口普查总人口248926人，比2000年第五次普查时的262039人少13113人的反常现象。其原因：一是对常住人口在时间规定上的不一致。第五次普查是“一年及一年以上”，第六次普查时改为“半年及半年以上”。二是随着改革开放的深入推进，外出务工、经商、读书、学习、投靠亲友等原因，流入城市者逐渐增多，人口流动性不断增大，且流出人口数量大于流入的人口。据第六次人口普查，全县流出半年及半年以上的有90397人，其中流到省内60754人（男29490人，女31264人），流到省外29643人（男15531人，女14112人），非本地户籍从省内外流入县境有关乡镇并已居住半年及半年以上的

40611人，流出人口比流入人口多49786人。此次普查总人口248926人中，有208315人拥有修文户籍，加上虽拥有本县户籍，因流出而未参加本县人口普查登记的90397人，合计298712人，与公安部门截至2010年10月31日（与第六次人口普查标准时间11月1日零时相吻合）全县常规统计人口300806人比较，相差2094人，差率为0.7%。

第二节　人口分布

一、地域分布

1978年，全县有城关、扎佐、小箐、六广4区，城关镇（隶属城关区）和27个人民公社（其中久长公社直隶于县）。当年全县总人口240976人，区级单位人口的地域分布情况是：城关区88166人，占全县总人口的36.59%（其中城关镇35860人，占全县总人口的14.88%，占城关区总人口的40.67%）；扎佐区50290人，占全县总人口的20.89%；久长公社19255人，占全县总人口的7.99%；小箐区29026人，占全县总人口的12.04%；六广区54239人，占全县总人口的22.51%。继后，全县行政区划几经变动，直至1992年撤区、并乡、建镇，将当时的6区（镇）、31乡（镇）撤并为城关镇、扎佐镇、久长镇、六广镇和谷堡乡、六屯乡、小箐乡、洒坪乡、大石布依族乡、六桶乡，使4镇6乡的行政建制得以稳定。2010年年末，全县公安部门常规统计的总人口为305917人，其中龙场镇73515人，占24.03%；扎佐镇41887人，占13.69%；久长镇35109人，占11.48%；六广镇29358人，占9.6%；谷堡乡25872人，占8.46%；六屯乡16767人，占5.48%；小箐乡23727人，占7.75%；洒坪乡17200人，占5.62%；大石布依族乡13638人，占4.46%；六桶乡28844人，占9.43%。

二、城乡分布

1982年第三次人口普查，总人口中只分别记载了农业人口和非农业人口，难以反映人口的城乡分布。从1990年第四次人口普查起增加了城乡分布内容。

第四次至第六次人口普查人口的城乡分布及比重表

表1—04—03

次　序	总人口（人）			占总人口的比重（%）	
	合　计	城镇人口	乡村人口	城镇人口	乡村人口
第四次人口普查（1990年）	266694	38979	227715	14.62	85.38
第五次人口普查（2000年）	262039	55251	206788	21.09	78.91
第六次人口普查（2010年）	248926	72813	176113	29.25	70.75

随着经济社会的发展，全县城镇化率※呈上升趋势。2010年较1990年和2000年分别上升14.63和8.16

※城镇化率又称城市化率。即城镇（城市）人口占总人口的比重。

个百分点。前10年年均上升0.647个百分点，后10年年均上升0.816个百分点。其原因：一是人口的流动性增大。2010年第六次人口普查，全县户籍总人口300806人中，流出（半年以上）本乡（镇）的为90397人，占30.05%，其中主要是农村中的富余劳动力流向城镇就业或生活，与2000年第五次人口普查的数据相比，上升3.99个百分点。二是户籍在外乡（镇）、在外县、在外省的37701人又在县境内城镇常住，纳入了本县人口普查登记范围。中心集镇的龙场和扎佐，就分别流入14679人和5540人。此外，还有一部分农村人口在城镇购买或修建住房成为城镇居民，也是拉动全县城镇化率提升的原因。

由于城镇基础设施水平与经济社会发展不相适应，支撑城镇化的产业基础不牢，城镇管理体制滞后，从而制约了全县城镇化率进一步提升。2010年，全国城镇化率达49.68%，全省达33.81%，贵阳市达68.16%，与其相比，修文均有较大差距。就是与贵阳市所辖10个区（县、市）相比，无论是2010年的实际水平，或是2010年与2000年和1990年比较的提升幅度修文都较滞后。

贵阳市各区（县、市）城镇化水平发展对比表

表1—04—04

单位名称	1990年人口“四普”		2000年人口“五普”		2010年人口“六普”		城镇化率升降百分点	
	总人口（人）	城镇化率（%）	总人口（人）	城镇化率（%）	总人口（人）	城镇化率（%）	2010年与2000年比较	2010年与1990年比较
贵阳市	2960996	43.91	3718449	36.20	4322611	68.13	升 24.97	升 17.36
南明区	472849	100.00	687804	100.00	829326	95.66	降 4.34	降 4.34
云岩区	458552	100.00	698988	100.00	956906	97.31	降 2.69	降 2.69
花溪区	265452	16.11	337177	39.49	358981	43.71	升 4.22	升 27.60
乌当区	243840	20.52	319619	32.23	376971	55.80	升 23_57	升 35.28
白云区	143730	51.98	187695	69.25	264496	76.05	升 6.80	升 24.07
小河区	80286	65.17	142987	98.99	248070	96.07	降 2.92	升 30.90
开阳县	372109	9.85	389252	22.39	358248	30.93	升 8.54	升 21.04
息烽县	223353	10.02	221583	19.71	212897	28.90	升 9.19	升 18.88
修文县	266694	14.62	262039	21.09	248926	29.25	升 8.16	升 14.63
清镇市	434131	11.53	471305	41.22	467790	35.93	降 5.29	升 24.40

三、人口密度

1978年，全县总人口240976人，按土地总面积1075.7平方公里计算，人口密度为224人/平方公里。至2010年，全县常住一年及一年以上的人口为317200人，人口密度上升至294.9人/平方公里，在1978年基础上平均每平方公里增加70.9人。

“撤并建”后，1991—2010年期间，全县人口密度平均每平方公里增加45.9人。扎佐镇、洒坪乡、六桶乡、谷堡乡、六屯乡、小箐乡、大石布依族乡和六广镇低于全县增加的平均值，而龙场镇和久长镇的人口密度2010年分别达438.8人/平方公里和295人/平方公里，分别比1991年增加107.3人和57.5人，大大

高于全县在此期间增长的平均值。2010年人口密度最高的龙场镇（438.8人/平方公里）为最低洒坪乡（209.8人/平方公里）的2.09倍。

各乡（镇）1991年和2010年的人口密度表

表1—04—05

乡镇名称	土地面积（平方公里）	总人口(人)		人口密度(人/平方公里)		2010年比1991年增加（人/平方公里）
		1991年	2010年	1991年	2010年	
全县合计或平均	1075.70	267839	317200	249.0	294.9	45.9
龙场镇	174. 86	57964	76720	331.5	438.8	107. 3
扎佐镇	139.48	42413	44736	304.1	320. 7	16.6
久长镇	117. 51	27908	34667	237.5	295.0	57. 5
六广镇	94. 10	26428	30321	280.9	322.2	41. 3
谷堡乡	121.10	22780	26817	188.1	221.4	33. 3
六屯乡	77.95	14801	17451	189.9	223.9	34.0
小箐乡	103.90	20951	24640	201.6	237.2	35.6
洒坪乡	85. 70	15947	17984	186.1	209.8	23. 7
大石乡	51. 10	12314	14189	241.0	277.7	36. 7
六桶乡	110.00	26333	29675	239.4	269.8	30.4

第三节　人口构成

一、性别构成

1978年总人口240976人中，男性123455人，占51.23%，女性117521人，占48.77%，人口性别比（女性=100）为105.05，基本属于98至105的正常范围。分区域的情况：城关、扎佐、小箐和六广区性别比属正常，久长公社基本正常。但城关区的城关镇性别比高出正常范围上限105的14.14个点，其原因主要是全民所有制和集体所有制单位职工大量集中于县城，然而家庭又不一定居住在城关镇，而职工队伍的现状又是男性大大地超过女性人数。1978—2010年的33年中，性别比超过正常值105这个上限的有16年，其余年份处于正常范围内偏高状况。情况比较突出的是，从2006年起性别比持续突破106，其中2006年和2010年分别高达107.01和107.39。

1978年区级单位人口性别构成表

表1—04—06

单位名称	人口（人）		性比重（%）		性别比（女=100）
	男	女	男	女	
全 县	123455	117521	51.23	48.77	105.05
城关区	26222	26084	50.13	49.87	100.53
扎佐区	25526	24764	50.76	49.24	103.08
久长公社	9881	9374	51.32	48.68	105.41
小箐区	14560	14466	50.16	49.84	100.65
六广区	27749	26490	51.16	48.84	104.75

2010年第六次人口普查标准时间显示，全县户籍总人口300806人，男性154090人、占51.23%，女性146716人、占48.77%，性别比105.03，超出正常范围。各乡（镇）的情况：龙场镇、扎佐镇、久长镇和谷堡乡人口性别比属正常，其余6个乡（镇）偏高，其中大石、洒坪和六桶乡比较突出，分别达115.36、117.53和117.57。

第六次人口普查乡（镇）户籍人口性别构成表

表1—04—07

乡（镇）名称	人口（人）		性比重（%）		性别比（女=100）
	男	女	男	女	
全县	154090	146716	51.23	48.77	105.03
龙场镇	36950	37629	49.54	50.46	98.20
扎佐镇	19667	19568	50.13	49.87	100.51
久长镇	16803	16618	50.28	49.72	101.11
六广镇	15165	13944	52.10	47.90	108.76
谷堡乡	13113	12648	50.90	49.10	103.68
六屯乡	8604	8107	51.49	48.51	106.13
小箐乡	12211	11226	52.10	47.90	108.77
洒坪乡	9117	7757	54.03	45.97	117.53
大石乡	7082	6139	53.57	46.43	115.36
六桶乡	15378	13080	54.04	45.96	117.57

从计划生育主管部门提供的1996—2010年出生婴儿的性别资料看，充分反映出生婴儿性别比偏高是导致全县总人口性别比偏高的重要原因。15年中，只有1996年和1997年出生婴儿的性别比在正常范围内，其余年份均普遍偏高，犹以2005年最为典型，高达120.24，这实质上是“重男轻女”陈旧观念在生育问题上的反映。

1996—2010年出生人口的性别构成表

表1—04—08

年份	出生人口(人)		性比重(%)		性别比(女=100)
	男	女	男	女	
1996	1527	1466	51.02	48. 98	104. 16
1997	2029	1996	50.41	49. 59	101.65
1998	1321	1203	52.34	47. 66	109.81
1999	1527	1305	53.92	46. 08	117.01
2000	1703	1488	53. 35	46.65	114.37
2001	1734	1478	53.99	46.01	117.32
2002	1481	1299	53.27	46.73	114.01
2003	1339	1195	52.84	47. 16	112.05
2004	1239	1068	53.71	46.29	116.01
2005	1313	1092	54.59	45.41	120. 24
2006	1393	1188	53.97	46.03	117. 26
2007	1434	1242	53.59	46.41	115.46
2008	1495	1356	52.44	47.56	110.25
2009	1777	1670	51.55	48.45	106.41
2010	2033	1932	51.27	48.73	105.23

二、年龄构成

第三次至第六次人口普查，人口的年龄构成是分年龄组体现的。各年龄组人数及占总人口的比重变化较大。

第三次至第六次人口普查各年龄组人数及所占比重表

表1—04—09

年龄组	各年龄组人口数(人)				各年龄组人口占总人口比重(%)			
	第三次	第四次	第五次	第六次	第三次	第四次	第五次	第六次
总计	257024	266694	262039	248926	100.00	100.00	100. 00	100. 00
0—4岁	29240	32714	20007	17132	11.38	12.27	7.64	6. 88
5—9岁	39496	26035	23113	12859	15.37	9. 76	8. 82	5. 17
10—14岁	38608	30464	32643	19623	15.02	11.42	12.46	7. 88
15—19岁	30255	34878	20992	19809	11. 77	13.07	8.01	7.96
20—24岁	16449	29698	20273	20092	6. 40	11. 14	7. 74	8.07
25—29岁	19690	19675	25948	16391	7. 66	7. 38	9. 90	6.58

续表

年龄组	各年龄组人口数(人)				各年龄组人口占总人口比重(%)			
	第三次	第四次	第五次	第六次	第三次	第四次	第五次	第六次
30—34岁	16078	15190	25145	19026	6.25	5.70	9.60	7.64
35—39岁	15019	16950	18518	24376	5.84	6.36	7.07	9.79
40—44岁	12679	13614	13316	23727	4.93	5.10	5.08	9.53
45—49岁	10506	11413	15891	17327	4.09	4.28	6.07	6.96
50—54岁	8152	10251	12222	12373	3.17	3.84	4.66	4.97
55—59岁	5576	8380	9863	14506	2.17	3.14	3.76	5.83
60—64岁	4878	6061	8447	10535	1.90	2.27	3.22	4.23
65—69岁	4516	4305	6821	8060	1.76	1.61	2.60	3.24
70—74岁	3326	3238	4384	6074	1.29	1.21	1.67	2.44
75—79岁	1797	2408	2480	4211	0.70	0.90	0.95	1.69
80—84岁	584	1081	1345	1920	0.23	0.41	0.51	0.77
85—89岁	147	294	492	663	0.06	0.11	0.19	0.27
90—94岁	19	40	116	178		0.02	0.04	0.07
95—99岁	9	4	21	42				0.02
100岁及以上		1	2	2				

(一)年龄类型

用国际通用人口年龄类型划分标准与全县第三次至第六次人口普查相关数据进行对照，充分反映出1982—2010年全县人口类型发生了很大变化。

人口年龄类型标准及第三次至第六次普查指标对照表

表1—04—10

指　标	计量单位	人口年龄类型标准			人口普查的具体数据			
		年轻型	成年型	老年型	第三次	第四次	第五次	第六次
少年儿童系数(0-14岁人口占总人口比重)	%	40.00以上	30.00-40.00	30.00以下	41.76	33.45	28.91	19.93
老年人口系数(65岁及以上人口占总人口比重)	%	4.00以下	4.00-7.00	7.00以上	4.05	4.26	5.98	8.50
老少比(65岁及以上人口占0-14岁人口比重)	%	15.00以下	15.00-30.00	30.00以上	9.69	12.75	20.67	42.63
年龄中位数	岁	20.00以下	20.00-30.00	30.0以上	18.5	21.6	27.7	34.9

第三次人口普查除“老年人口系数”指标属成年型外，其余3项指标皆属年轻型；第四次人口普查，除“老少比”属年轻型外，其余指标皆在成年型标准范围之内；第五次人口普查，全县人口基本属于成

年型，因有“少年儿童系数”这项指标已进入老年型的指标范围；第六次人口普查，全县人口年龄类型发生了巨大变化，衡量人口年龄类型的4项指标全部都属于老年型，全县整体已进入老龄社会。

（二）人口再生产类型

人口再生产分为增加型、稳定型和减少型，具体划分标准与第三次至第六次人口普查相应数据对照，第三次人口普查属“增加型”。第四次普查基本属“增加型”（“15岁至19岁人口占总人口的比重”属稳定型）。第五次普查属“稳定型”。第六次普查基本上属于“稳定型”（“0至14岁人口占总人口的比重”属减少型）。

人口再生产类型划分标准及第三次至第六次人口普查数据表

表1—04—11

指　标	划分标准			全县4次人口普查相应数据			
	增加型	稳定型	减少型	第三次	第四次	第五次	第六次
0-14岁人口占总人口比重(%)	10.00	26.50	20.00	41.76	33.45	28.91	19.93
15-49岁人口占总人口比重(%)	50.00	50.50	50.00	46.95	53.03	53.46	56.54
50岁及以上人口占总人口比重(%)	10.00	23.00	30.00	11.29	13.52	17.63	23.53

（三）劳动年龄人口※比重

第五次和第六次人口普查，因是以“常住”口径进行登记，导致全县劳动年龄人口的绝对数量小于第四次人口普查数据。但从第三次人口普查起至第六次人口普查期间，劳动年龄人口占总人口的比重除第五次普查出现小的波动外，整体上是不断提升的。相应的是非劳动年龄人口占总人口的比重呈下降趋势。1982年第三次人口普查时，16岁以下未成年人和劳动年龄段之外的老年人，分别占总人口的41.23%和9.73%。2010年第六次人口普查时，16岁以下未成年人和劳动年龄段之外老年人，他们占总人口的比重分别变为21.73%和15.55%。非劳动力年龄的未成年人和老年人占总人口的比重中，未成年人的比重大幅下降，而老年人口的比重，反而还是持续上升。

劳动年龄人口数量和比重表

表1—04—12

次　序	劳动年龄人口合计		男性劳动年龄人口		女性劳动年龄人口	
	数量（人）	占总人口比重（%）	数量（人）	占劳动年龄人口比重（%）	数量（人）	占劳动年龄人口比重（%）
第三次人口普查	126103	49.06	67338	53.40	58765	46.60
第四次人口普查	156189	58.56	84547	54.13	71642	45.87
第五次人口普查	152419	58.16	84410	55.38	68009	44.62
第六次人口普查	156123	62.72	84788	54.31	71335	45.69

※“劳动年龄人口”，又称“劳动适龄人口”。它是根据人口性别，按不同年龄段划分的。我国现行规定，男性16-59岁，女性16-54岁为劳动年龄人口。

（四）年龄构成指数

人口年龄构成指数，分为国际通用和国内规定两个不同的标准和计算口径。无论是用国际标准或是用国内标准衡量，全县第三次人口普查至第六次人口普查，年龄构成指数中，总抚养比及少儿抚养比均呈下降态势，唯老年抚养比是上升的，从另一角度反映出全县人口老龄化的进程正在加快。

年龄构成指数表（国际标准）

表1—04—13

次序	人口数（人）				占总人口的比重（%）				年龄构成指数		
	合计	0—14岁	15—64岁	65岁及以上	合计	0—14岁	15—64岁	65岁及以上	总抚养比	少儿抚养比	老年抚养比
第三次人口普查	257024	107344	139282	10398	100.00	41.76	54.19	4.05	84.53	77. 07	7.46
第四次人口普查	266694	89213	166110	11371	100.00	33.45	62.29	4.26	60.55	53.71	6.84
第五次人口普查	262039	75763	170615	15661	100.00	28.91	65.11	5.98	53.58	44.40	9.18
第六次人口普查	248926	49614	178162	21150	100.00	19.93	71.57	8.50	39.72	27.85	11.87

年龄构成指数表（国内标准）

表1—04—14

次序	人口数（人）				占总人口的比重（%）				年龄构成指数		
	合计	0—14岁	15—59岁	60岁及以上	合计	0—14岁	15— 59岁	60岁及以上	总抚养比	少儿抚养比	老年抚养比
第三次人口普查	257024	107344	134404	15276	100.00	41.77	52.29	5.94	91.23	79.87	11.36
第四次人口普查	266694	89213	160049	17432	100. 00	33. 45	60.01	6.54	66.63	55.74	10. 89
第五次人口普查	262039	75763	162168	24108	100.00	28.91	61.89	9. 20	61.58	46.72	14.87
第六次人口普查	248926	49614	167627	31685	100. 00	19.93	67. 34	12.73	48.50	29.60	18. 90

三、民族构成

（一）总人口的民族构成

1982年第三次人口普查，全县少数民族人口为18642人，1990年第四次普查达20723人，2000年第五次普查增为22063人，2010年第六次普查又减为20191人。4次人口普查，全县少数民族人口分别占总人口的7.25%、7.77%、8.42%和8.11%。相应的是4次人口普查汉族人口分别占总人口的比重为92.75%、92.23%、91.58%和91.89%，其绝对数分别为238382人、245962人、239976人和228735人。总的情况是，全县少数民族占总人口的比重基本上呈上升态势。鉴于计划生育政策对少数民族有一定程度的放宽，是形成上述局面的主要原因。另是汉族和少数民族通婚所生育子女，为了享受在升学、招工、征兵

等方面对少数民族的优惠政策，在填报族别时，多填报为少数民族。

（二）少数民族的族别构成

全县少数民族人口虽还不到总人口的10%，但族别又多达20多个。族别之间人口相差比较悬殊。第六次人口普查的情况是：苗族11126人为最多，其次是布依族5428人，第三是彝族1920人。3个主要少数民族人口占全县少数民族总数的比重，分别为55.1%、26.88%和9.51%，合计占全县少数民族的91.49%。除土家族、仡佬族和侗族人口分别占少数民族总人口的2.93%、1.21%和1.13%外，其余少数民族人口占少数民族总人口的比重均在1%以下。至于少数民族的族别和族别人口在各次人口普查中增减变化的不一致，主要是由人口流动的因素造成。

第三次至第六次人口普查少数民族人口比重及增减情况表

表1—04—15

族别	第三次人口普查		第四次人口普查		第五次人口普查		第六人口普查		第六次比第三次人口普查增减百分比（%）
	人口（人）	占少数民族总人口比重（%）	人口（人）	占少数民族总人口比重（%）	人口（人）	占少数民族总人口比重（%）	人口（人）	占少数民族总人口比重（%）	
合计	18642	100. 00	20732	100. 00	22063	100. 00	20191	100. 00	+8.31
蒙古族	5	0. 03	15	0. 07	64	0. 29	67	0. 33	+1240. 00
回族	140	0. 75	96	0. 46	83	0. 38	92	0. 46	-34. 29
苗族	9863	52.91	11209	54. 07	12268	55. 60	11126	55.10	+12. 81
彝族	1887	10.12	1955	9. 43	1993	9. 03	1920	9.51	+1.75
壮族	51	0.27	44	0.21	51	0. 23	51	0. 25	—
布依族	6046	32.43	6538	31.54	6397	28.99	5428	26.88	-10. 22
朝鲜族	—	—	7	0. 03	6	0. 03	—	—	—
满族	93	0. 50	123	0. 59	55	0. 25	31	0.15	-66. 67
侗族	233	1. 25	237	1. 14	311	1.41	228	1. 13	+2. 24
瑶族	1	—	5	0. 02	7	0. 03	11	0. 05	+1000.00
白族	39	0.21	33	0.16	145	0. 66	134	0. 66	+243. 59
土家族	4	0.02	181	0. 87	364	1. 65	591	2.93	+146. 75
傣族	—	—	5	0. 02	7	0. 03	5	0. 03	—
黎族	4	0. 02	8	0. 04	31	0. 14	38	0.19	+850. 00
畲族	3	0. 02	1	—	2	—	6	0. 03	+100. 00
水族	107	0.57	72	0. 35	65	0. 29	101	0. 50	-5.61
仡佬族	33	0.18	70	0.34	125	0. 57	245	1.21	+642. 42
锡伯族	7	0. 04	10	0. 05	1	—	—	—	—
京族	20	0. 11	18	0. 09	14	0. 06	3	0. 02	-85. 00
藏族	—	—	—	—	10	—	4	—	—
维吾尔族	—	—	—	—	3	—	1	—	—

续表

族别	第三次人口普查		第四次人口普查		第五次人口普查		第六人口普查		第六次比第三次人口普查增减百分比（%）
	人口（人）	占少数民族总人口比重（%）	人口（人）	占少数民族总人口比重（%）	人口（人）	占少数民族总人口比重（%）	人口（人）	占少数民族总人口比重（%）	
哈尼族	—	—	—	—	2	—	5	—	—
土族	—	—	—	—	2	—	10	—	—
仫佬族	—	—	—	—	10	—	14	—	—
羌族	—	—	—	—	8	—		—	—
毛南族	—	—	—	—	1	—	14	—	—
哈萨克族	—	—	—	—	—	—	1	—	—
傈僳族	—	—	—	—	—	—	1	—	—
佤族	—	—	—	—	—	—	3	—	—
纳西族	—	—	—	—	—	—	1	—	—
布朗族	—	—	—	—	—	—	1	—	—
其他民族	106	0. 57	105	0.51	38	0. 35	59	0.57	+7. 55

（三）少数民族的地域分布

2010年第六次人口普查，少数民族在全县4镇6乡中均有分布，其人口数量占总人口的比重在10%以上的有大石、六屯和谷堡3个乡，分别为25.95%、12.77%和10.05%。久长镇和六广镇比重较低，分别占5.91%和5.97%。其余乡（镇）的比重相差不大，处于8%左右。

第六次人口普查少数民族在各乡（镇）分布及占总人口比重表

表1—04—16

乡镇名称	总人口（人）	少数民族人口（人）	少数民族人口占总人口比重（%）
全县合计	248926	20191	8.11
龙场镇	83215	5427	6.52
扎佐镇	40719	3152	7.74
久长镇	25276	1493	5.91
六广镇	19540	1167	5.97
谷堡乡	17172	1725	10.05
六屯乡	10099	1290	12.77
小箐乡	15698	1216	7.75
洒坪乡	10932	938	8.58
大石乡	8339	2164	25.95
六桶乡	17936	1619	9.03

境内人数较多的苗族、布依族、彝族有聚居的特点。第六次人口普查，全县217个行政村中，有13个行政村少数民族人口占总人口的比重超过30%。他们分别是龙场镇的高仓村（93.83%），扎佐镇的新民村（70.29%）和三里村（31.34%），久长镇的下堡村（34.41%），六屯乡的大木村（60.05%）、小木村（50.95%）、独山村（45.76%）和西冲村（43.81%），小箐乡的新场村（35.73%），洒坪乡的高寨村（31.18%），大石布依族乡的大寨村（85.45%）、大屯村（81.56%）和竹坪村（59.85%）。

四、文化构成

从1978年起，全县人口中文盲、半文盲逐渐减少，受不同层次教育者不断增加，受较高层次教育的越来越多。

（一）文盲和半文盲

1982年第三次人口普查，全县有文盲、半文盲57872人，1990年第四次普查有49127人，2000年第五次普查降为27325人，2010年第六次普查仍有12658人。总体情况是，全县文盲、半文盲的绝对数量日益减少。其特点：一是城镇文盲、半文盲占总人口的比重低于乡村。第四次人口普查，城镇和乡村文盲、半文盲的比重分别是12.79%和20.01%。至第六次普查，城镇和乡村文盲、半文盲的比重为2.42%和4.93%。二是女性中文盲、半文盲的比重一直高于男性。1990年第四次普查，女性文盲、半文盲占女性总人口的25.51%，男性则为11.89%，2010年第六次普查，女性和男性文盲、半文盲的比重分别为7.43%和2.9%。三是经济较发达中心地区的文盲率低于经济欠发达的边远地区。龙场、扎佐和久长3镇第五次人口普查，文盲、半文盲占15岁以上总人口的10.93%，其余7乡（镇）占19.25%。第六次普查，龙场、扎佐、久长3镇文盲、半文盲占6岁及以上总人数的3.87%，其余7乡（镇）占8.02%。

文盲、半文盲在地域分布上是不均衡的。第六次人口普查，全县6岁及以上的229264人中，文盲和半文盲12658人，占5.52%。各乡（镇）的情况差异较大：扎佐镇3%，久长镇3.95%，龙场镇4.27%，谷堡乡4.71%，大石布依族乡6.37%，六广镇6.68%，六屯乡7.53%，六桶乡9.07%，洒坪乡10.21%，小箐乡11.77%。个别行政村直至2010年第六次人口普查，文盲、半文盲的比重仍然很高。男性文盲、半文盲率在15%以上的有龙场镇的花桥村（16.38%），小箐乡的青中村（26.05%）；女性文盲、半文盲率在30%以上的有龙场镇的花桥村（32.82%）、洒坪乡的蜈蚣桥村（30.22%）、小箐乡的紫江村（33.16%）和青中村（42.55%）。

（二）具有小学文化程度人数

第三次至第五次人口普查，全县具有小学文化程度人数分别为94752人、116376人和119168人，分别占总人口的36.87%、43.64%和45.48%，无论是绝对人数或是占总人口的比重都是增长较快。而第六次人口普查时，具有小学文化程度的人数降为92052人，比重也降至36.98%，其原因是计划生育工作深入持久开展，有效遏制人口过快增长，导致学龄儿童减少。

（三）具有初中文化程度人数

具有初中文化程度人数一直稳健增长。1982年第三次普查为39327人，第四次普查增至48762人，第五次和第六次普查，继续上升至72185人和98340人。4次普查，全县具有初中文化程度人数占总人口数的比重，分别为15.3%、18.28%、27.55%和39.51%。充分反映出普及九年义务教育的成果。

（四）具有高中文化程度人数

1982年普查为9984人（含中等专业教育人数，下同），1990年为12389人， 2000年增至14293人，

2010年再增至16928人，分别占总人口的比重为3.88%、4.65%、5.45%和6.8%。

（五）具有大学文化程度人数

全县具有大学文化程度人数增长最快。1982年仅有1233人（含大学专科，下同），占总人口比重为0.48%。1990年普查升至1869人，占总人口的0.7%。2000年普查为2998人（本科733人，专科2265人）。2010年普查迅速增至9243人（本科2875人，专科6368人），占总人数的比重分别提升至1.14%和3.71%。

（六）具有研究生学历人数

2000年第五次人口普查，全县有7人具有研究生学历，2010年普查增至43人。研究生学历人数虽只占总人口的0.003%和0.02%，但反映了受最高层次教育的人从无到有，且不断增加。

全县人口文化构成变化较大，其特点：一是人口受教育的“面”不断拓宽，文盲、半文盲占总人口的比重由1982年的22.52%降至2010年的5.09%；二是人口受教育程度不断上升，具有初中及初中以上文化程度的人口，1982年为50544人，占总人口的19.67%，到2010年达124554人，占总人口的50.04%，其中，受过高等教育（含大学专科、大学本科和研究生）的人口，1982年仅1233人，至2010年已增至9286人，分别占总人口的0.48%和3.73%；三是城镇人口受不同层次教育人口的比重高于乡村人口，1990年第四次人口普查，受不同层次教育人口中，城镇人口占城镇6岁及6岁以上总人口的77.85%，而同一口径乡村人口只占65.54%。2010年第六次人口普查，城镇和乡村受不同层次教育的人口，分别占城镇和乡村6岁及6岁以上总人口的90.22%和85.69%；四是男性人口的文化程度高于女性，2010年第六次人口普查，全县6岁及6岁以上229264人中，男性118383人，女性110881人，具有不同层次文化程度的男性和女性分别为114665人和101961人，分别占6岁及6岁以上男性和女性总人口的96.85%和91.96%。从不同层次的文化程度看，情况更为突出。2010年第六次人口普查，具有小学文化程度的92052人中，男性占50.06%，女性占49.94%；具有初中文化程度的98340人中，男性和女性分别占54.88%和45.12%；具有高中文化程度（含中专）16928人中，男、女分别占55.32%、44.68%；具有大学文化程度（含大专）的9243人中，男、女分别占56.41%、43.59%；具有研究生学历的43人中，男性占51.16%，女性占48.84%。

具有高中（含中专）及以上文化程度的人口中，全县男性占55.7%，高出女性11.4个百分点。龙场、扎佐、久长和六广镇，其比重都在60%以下，龙场镇最低，占52.81%，男女比重较为接近。其余6乡都在60%以上，最高的六桶乡占62.77%，高出女性25.54个百分点。

各乡（镇）人口的文化构成差距较大，凸显了发展的不平衡。全县第六次人口普查6岁及6岁以上229264人中，剔出文盲、半文盲12658人后，具有不同层次文化程度的为216606人，占6岁及6岁以上总人口的比重，全县平均为94.48%。扎佐镇最高为97%，小箐乡最低为88.23%。具有小学和初中文化程度人口占6岁及6岁以上总人口的比重最大，除龙场镇为77.75%外，其余乡（镇）均在80%以上，最高的谷堡乡占90.43%。具有高中文化程度（含中专）人口占6岁及6岁以上总人口的比重，全县平均7.38%。龙场镇和扎佐镇高于全县平均数，分别占10.41%和12.29%。久长镇占4.25%，六广镇占3.63%，谷堡乡占3.36%，六屯乡占4.19%，小箐乡占2.43%，洒坪乡占2.86%，大石布依族乡占3.96%，六桶乡占4.74%。具有高等教育文化程度（含大学专科、大学本科和研究生）的人口占6岁及6岁以上总人口的比重，全县平均为4.05%。各乡（镇）的情况分别是：龙场镇占7.58%，扎佐镇占3.59%，六广镇占2.55%，六屯乡占2.14%，久长镇占2.01%，六桶乡占1.96%，洒坪乡占1.66%，谷堡乡占1.5%，大石布依族乡占1.47%，小

箐乡占0.92%。2010年普查，全县拥有大学本科学历的2875人中，有80.73%的人集中在龙场和扎佐两镇，他们分别占67.9%和12.83%，具有研究生学历的43人中，龙场镇24人，扎佐镇12人，久长镇3人，洒坪和六桶两乡各2人。

第六次人口普查各乡（镇）人口的文化结构表

表1—04—17

乡镇名称	6岁及6岁以上人口	其中						
		文盲和半文盲	小学	初中	高中	大学专科	大学本科	研究生
全县合计	229264	12658	92052	98340	16928	6368	2875	43
龙场镇	77063	3289	25212	34702	8019	3865	1952	24
扎佐镇	37826	1134	12339	18349	4647	976	369	12
久长镇	23097	913	9947	10792	981	369	92	3
六广镇	17940	1198	8616	7017	651	326	132	
谷堡乡	15641	737	7464	6680	525	195	40	
六屯乡	9243	696	4452	3510	387	131	67	
小箐乡	14286	1682	6897	5229	347	109	22	
洒坪乡	10076	1029	5309	3283	288	115	50	2
大石乡	7625	486	3919	2806	302	74	38	
六桶乡	16467	1494	7897	5972	781	208	113	2

五、职业构成

1978年，被称为“资本主义尾巴割得最干净”的修文县，只存在全民和集体两种所有制成分，纯粹是“清一色”的公有经济。劳动者就业全部都在全民和集体所有制的单位中。是年全县社会劳动者86988人，其中：职工18282人，占21.02%；农村集体劳动者68706人，占78.98%。全民所有制职工15531人中，从事农林牧渔业的849人，占5.47%；从事工业2138人，占13.77%；从事交通运输、邮电业151人，占0.97%；从事建筑业和资源勘探8465人，占54.5%；从事批发零售商品与餐饮业1000人，占6.44%；从事金融、保险业83人，占0.53%；从事房地产和公用事业29人，占0.19%；从事卫生、体育、文教和社会服务业1951人，占12.56%；从事机关、团体工作865人，占5.57%。城镇集体所有制职工2751人中，从事工业1473人，占53.54%；从事建筑业417人，占15.16%；从事交通运输、邮电业279人，占10.14%；从事批发零售商品与餐饮业456人，占16.58%；从事文教、卫生事业126人，占4.58%；农村集体劳动者68706人中，从事农林牧渔业67671人，从事工业1035人，分别占98.49%和1.51%。

1979年，城镇居民中出现了个体劳动者，他们多属原下放农村的返城居民、返城知识青年、干居民※

※干居民系指住在城镇，虽有劳动能力，但又无职业的社会群体。

和少数退休职工，主要是从事饮食、修理、理发、房屋修缮、板车运输和经营小百货。在当时历史背景下，上述行为被称为“闯红灯”，是很担风险的，往往成为工商行政管理部门的查处对象。随着中共十一届三中全会精神的深入贯彻，1980年一些城镇个体经营者纷纷申请注册登记，工商行政管理部门受理了他们的要求，为319户个体工商户颁发了营业执照，于是，全县纯粹公有制经济的格局被打破 。1982年中共十二大召开后，国家进一步明确对个体、私营经济鼓励发展的方针，城乡个体工商户逐年发展的同时，又出现了由数人合伙的私营企业。至1985年，全县城乡个体工商户达2233户，私营企业198户。当年全县社会劳动者96628人中，从事农林牧渔、水利业者达80424人，占83.23%；从事工业者4151人，占4.29%；从事地质普查和勘探业466人，占0.48%；从事建筑业761人，占0.79%；从事交通运输、邮电业861人，占0.89%；从事商业、饮食、物资供销2850人，占2.95%；从事房地产管理和公用事业13人，占0.01%；从事卫生、体育和社会福利560人，占0.58%；从事教育、文化、广播事业3649人，占3.78%；从事科学研究、综合服务事业96人，占0.10%；在国家机关、政党机关和社会团体中从业的200人，占0.21%；从事其他职业的2597人，占2.69%。

1985年年末社会劳动者在国民经济各部门中的供职情况表

表1—04—18　　　　单位：人

所有制性质分类 / 国民经济部门	合　计	全民所有制单位职工	城镇集体所有制单位职工	城镇个体劳动者	农村集体和个体劳动者
合　计	96628	8213	1834	1003	85578
一、农林牧渔、水利业	80424	729	—		79695
二、工业	4151	1129	610	52	2360
三、地质普查和勘探业	466	466	—		
四、建筑业	761		420		341
五、交通运输、邮电业	861	191	80	7	583
六、商业、饮食、物资供销业	2850	987	463	873	527
七、房地产管理和公用事业	13	13			
八、卫生、体育和社会福利事业	560	323	160		77
九、教育、文化、艺术和广播事业	3649	2854			795
十、科学研究、综合服务事业	96	19	76		1
十一、国家机关、政党机关和社会团体	200	191			9
十二、其他	2597	1311	25	71	1190

20世纪80年代初，全县农村普遍实行家庭联产承包责任制，农民有了生产经营自主权，劳动效率大为提高，出现越来越多的富余劳动力。一些具有开拓精神的年轻人，开始在当地或附近的乡镇企业中上班，或在县内全民所有制和集体所有制的企、事业单位中当合同工或临时工，既找到就业门路，又增加了收入。1984年国务院出台允许农民自理口粮进城务工、经商的文件，对农村大量富余劳动力转移起到很大的

助推作用。在中央精神导向下，县劳动局开始有组织的劳务输出，但被称为“农民工”的劳动力进城务工并未形成规模。1992年，全县农民工不足千人，其中由劳动部门组织输出的只有179人。是年，邓小平视察南方重要谈话发表，从理论高度深刻回答了困扰和束缚人们思想的许多重大认识问题，强调坚持“三个有利于”（是否有利于发展社会主义社会的生产力，是否有利于增强社会主义国家的综合国力，是否有利于提高人民的生活水平）和“发展才是硬道理”，大胆地进行改革，引导不同所有制成分的企业蓬勃发展，使社会用工需求骤增，全县农民工队伍扩大，很快形成一股潮流。1995年，农民进城务工达8126人，占农村全部从业人员的6.47%。2000年增至16168人，2005年增至23468人，2010年再增至32425人，分别占这3年农村全部从业人员的11.1%、15.04%和19.4%。来自农村中富余劳动力的农民工竟成为社会财富的直接创造者。

农民工是农村中大批富余劳动力转移的一个层面。随着产业结构的调整，农民商品生产意识的增强，除外出农民工外，农村劳动力向非农产业转移的情况也是突出的。1978年，98%以上的农民从事传统的农林牧渔业生产，到1985年，农村中从事农林牧渔业生产的劳力下降为93.13%，1990年又降至90.52%。到2000年全县农村从业人员145706人中，从事农林牧渔业的只有113427人，占77.84%；非农产业占22.16%，其中工业占3.62%，建筑业占2.47%，交通、仓储及邮政通信业占1.33%，批发贸易及餐饮业占1.6%，其他从业者占13.14%。至2010年，农村劳动力从事传统农林牧渔业者，还不到全部劳动力的60%，1/3以上的劳动力已转移至非农产业，从而有力地推动了全县第二、第三产业的发展。具体数据为：当年167148个农村从业人员中，从事农林牧渔业99199人，占59.35%；从事工业9058人，占5.42%；从事建筑业6688人，占4.00%；从事交通运输、仓储和邮政业4144人，占2.48%；从事批发零售、住宿、餐饮业8983人，占5.37%；其他从业人员（含外出农民工32425人）39076人，占23.38%。数据表明，当年的农村劳动力中，从事传统农林牧渔业生产的仅占59.35%；而从传统农业中转移出来的劳动力即占40.65%；其中，在本地从事非农产业的占21.25%，外出农民工占19.4%。

随着改革向纵深推进，外资企业在县境落户，多种形式非公有制企业的发展，使职工队伍日益壮大，并促进了所有制结构的深刻变化。1978年，职工队伍只有全民所有制和城镇集体所有制两种成分，分别占职工总数的84.95%和15.05%。2010年全县职工队伍中，全民所有制占56.67%，城镇集体所有制占4.07%，其他经济类型（外资和非公企业）占39.26%。全民所有制职工8065人中，企业单位职工1486人，占18.43%；事业单位职工4774人，占59.19%；机关单位职工1805人，占22.38%。按国民经济行业划分：从事农林牧渔业120人，占1.49%；从事制造业485人，占6.01%；从事电力、燃气及水的生产和供应业276人，占3.42%；从事交通运输、仓储及邮政业91人，占1.13%；从事信息传输、计算机服务和软件业51人，占0.63%；从事批发和零售商品业305人，占3.78%；从事住宿和餐饮业55人，占0.68%；从事房地产业11人，占0.14%；从事租赁和商务服务业3人，占0.04%；从事科学研究、技术服务业和地质勘察业28人，占0.35%；从事水利、环境和公共设施管理业144人，占1.78%；从事教育2954人，占36.63%；从事卫生、社会保障和社会服务业787人，占9.76%；从事文化、体育和娱乐业234人，占2.90%；从事公共管理和社会组织工作2521人，占31.26%。城镇集体所有制职工579人中，企业单位职工553人，占95.52%；事业单位职工13人，占2.24%；机关单位职工13人，占2.24%。按行业分：从事建筑业257人，占44.39%；从事批发零售商品业69人，占11.92%；从事金融业202人，占34.89%；从事房地产业25人，占4.32%；从事租赁和商务服务业13人，占2.24%；从事卫生、社会保障和社会服务业13人，占2.24%。其他经济类型5587人全是企业职工。其中从事采矿业84人，占1.50%；制造业4915人，占87.97%；批发和零售商品业269人，占4.82%；从事住宿和餐饮业36人，占0.64%；从事文化、体育和娱乐业283人，占5.06%。

2010年年末，全县个体工商户已发展至5258户，从业5600人，其中除少数手工业者外，绝大多数都是从事第三产业领域的商业、饮食业、服务业和修理业。从经营模式看，个人经营4471户，家庭经营787户，分别占个体工商户总数的85.03%和14.97%。

从全县人口就业比重看，1978年为36.1%，1990年上升至47.28%，2010年再上升至61.57%。不可否认，在劳动适龄人口中失业现象的客观存在。1996年县劳动部门开始办理失业登记，有1236人领到《失业证》，2000年办证失业人口为1372人，2010年第六次人口普查登记，有2870人为失业人口。导致失业的情况，主要是国有企业下岗职工，大中专毕业生尚未找到工作，农民承包土地被征用，个人在国有企、事业单位中主动退职后又未找到新的就业门路，还有一部分人本来就无就业意愿而在家料理家务。失业人口多集中在城镇，龙场和扎佐两镇即占全县失业人口的79.44%。

专记：元庆村民外出务工潮

坐落在六广镇境域的元庆村，原来是一个交通闭塞、世代农耕、干旱缺水、生产和生活条件都较差的边远贫困村。农村实行家庭联产承包责任制后，一举解决了群众期盼解决的吃饭问题，但大量的富余劳动力无用武之地，用钱紧缺仍然是一道没有破解的难题。

家居元庆四组的李松，1982年初中毕业后，不安现状，翌年即前往贵阳打工谋生，几年打拼学到技术和积攒资金后于1986年回村带领10多个青年先后在贵阳、安顺和云南昆明等地承揽民宅修建小工程，拉开了元庆村较大规模村民外出打工的序幕。外出打工虽然艰辛，但经济收入普遍比在家务农高出两倍以上。由此对村民产生了巨大的吸引力。三组的张国、二组的燕志伦、四组的李祥靖、李祥益等人也纷纷与村里乡亲相约结伴到城里当民工，很快就形成了一股外出务工潮。至2010年10月31日，全国第六次人口普查时，元庆村外流人口达801人（男437人，女364人），占全村户籍总人口1356人（男721人，女635人）的59.07%，远高于全县平均的30.05%和六广镇的39.18%，为全县217个行政村之冠。其中，流入省外354人，流入镇外省内447人，分别占44.19%和55.81%。流入省外者又以浙江余姚居多，共329人，占外流总人口801人的41.07%，有12个女青年和1个男青年还与当地人结婚成家。

元庆村民外流有两大明显的变化。一是初期外流人员纯粹是富余劳动力本人，他们单枪匹马，往往是年初空手出门，年末抱“财”归家，继后逐步过渡为带上未成年子女或老年人，最后发展为一部分人举家外出，长期生活在外，成了只在家乡“挂”个户口的“名义村民”。至2010年10月31日，全村举家外出者达186户，占总农户354户的52.54%，其中已有65户在外购买或修建了自己的住房。二是前期外出人员全是打工，随后部分转为经商，还有部分人通过多年打拼，实现资金原始积累后，自己办起了企业，当上了老板。如李松和赵友华分别成了可承接千万元和百万元以上工程的建筑商，徐永华兴办起电瓶厂，唐忠义开办了砂厂。至2010年，全村外出的有8人已成为拥有一定资产的老板。外出人员中有小汽车13台，其中还不乏“宝马”“沃尔沃”等名车。

由于离乡外出去处多为经济较发达地区，这对促进外出人员思想观念的转变和劳动技能的提高起到很大的作用，有一部分人外出一段时间后又返乡创业。他们紧盯市场广开经营门路，大力发展商品生

产。村主任郭其书和村民左勇在家乡投资建千亩以上的猕猴桃果园；村民郭国等3户利用家乡条件，分别饲养山羊100多只；李呈贵投资建起规模养鸡场；唐忠友种植近20亩太子参。一批产业的兴起带动了家乡产业结构的调整和农业的综合开发。2010年，全村在不放松粮食生产的同时，出栏大牲畜181头，肥猪940头，山羊198只，家禽1.88万只。肉类总产达74吨、人均产肉55.06公斤，禽蛋6.1吨，种植蔬菜630亩，并开始了盆栽观赏植物的生产。

农民外出打工（经商）促进了村内劳动力从业结构的巨大变化。至2010年，全村750个劳动力中，从事农业的395个，占52.67%；从事工业的102个，占13.6%；从事建筑业的13个，占1.73%；从事交通运输、邮电业的18个，占2.4%；从事商业的28个，占3.73%；从事饮食业的32个，占4.27%；从事其他劳动的162个，占21.6%。与1978年全村343个劳动力中，有341个从事农业，占99.42%；从事非农的劳动力只有2个，占0.58%的情况相比，从事农业劳动力比重下降46.75个百分点，劳动力的就业空间越来越大。

鉴于外出打工和经商人员比重大，全村产业结构调整效果比较显著，导致农民经济增收。2010年元庆村农民人均纯收入为5200元，高出六广镇平均4762元的9.2%，略高出全县平均数5152元的0.93%。与31年前的1978年人均纯收入120元(全县平均 141元)相比，年均递增12.5%，比同一时期全县这一指标年均递增11.9%相比，高出0.6个百分点。就整体看，元庆村群众的温饱问题已经完全解决，生活质量明显提高。近10%的农户利用现在四通八达的公路交通网购置了汽车、拖拉机或摩托车。2010年人均住房面积34.04平方米，75%的人家居住的是舒适的砖混结构房。成年人除个别老年之外都用上了手机，大多数农户都拥有一般的家用电器。全部村民都参加了新型农村合作医疗，60岁以上老年人都办理了养老保险，适龄儿童全部上了学。对于缺乏经济收入的困难户，政府都将他们纳入“低保”对象。2010年全村有4.8%的农户和3.17%的人口由民政部门按季度共发放补助2.23万元，人月均43.26元。

一部分长期在外经商或打工的人员不忘家乡，关心家乡。村里新修学校，修筑道路，建设人畜引水工程，每年春节期间开展文体活动等，他们纷纷解囊相助。对于有困难的农户，特别是老年人，还经常在经济上给予资助。共产党员李松，除承包村小学修建工程，为确保质量、主动让利导致亏损之外，还直接赞助村里公益事业和帮助困难户、慰问老年人达10多万元。2008年汶川大地震，县教育局组织实施的爱心工程以及贵阳建筑医院新建工程等，他都慷慨捐资。

元庆村出现的民工潮和人口外流，是改革开放涌现出来的新生事物，主流应当肯定，但也存在不容忽视的问题：一是学校无法维系。多年建在村里的元庆小学原有8个教师，开设6个班，有学生220人左右，后因外出务工和经商者陆续将子女带往就业地点上学，导致生源减少。至2009年仅剩学生64名，无法正常开班，迫使学校停办，校舍闲置。除34名学生被家长带往外地寄读外，剩下的30名只得前往离村3公里至7公里远的德政小学和邻县息烽的何家洞小学就读。路程较远的学生往往是“上学天不亮、回家月亮上”，对学习有很大的影响。二是空巢家庭问题凸现。2010年，元庆村有60岁及以上老年人的家庭75户，占总户数的21.17%，其中单身老人9户，1个老人与未成年亲属户2户，只有一对老年夫妇的26户，有一对老年夫妇与未成年亲属户2户。由于大量青壮年外流，形成52%的老年人家庭是空巢家庭。在尚缺乏完善的社会保障和服务的情况下，这些空巢家庭的老年人有许多方面感到不便，生活更显孤单枯燥，缺乏亲情感，无不发出感叹：“膝下儿孙进城去，留下两老守家园，宽房大屋少欢笑，要想团聚等过年”，“一日三餐饭，闲时菜园转，坐看电视磨时光，夜里只有星星伴”。三是撂荒耕地严重。外出打工、经商者留下是举家外流后的责任地，其中土质较好、管理方便的多是转让给亲友或出租给他人耕种，而土质较差和管理不便，约占总耕地面积10%的上百亩耕地是撂荒的，有地无产，严重浪费。

第四节　家庭　姓氏

一、家庭

在常规统计和各次人口普查工作中，“户数”分为集体户和家庭户两部分。集体户以企、事业单位、学校等为户名，其成员往往是单独的个体而不是完整的家庭。家庭户一直都是总户数最主要的构成，与人口总量变化趋势相一致，全县家庭户数随之不断增长。1990年第四次人口普查，全县家庭户为58947户，2000年第五次人口普查增至72030户，2010年第六次人口普查继续增长至80633户。

（一）家庭户人口规模

第四次人口普查，全县五人户最多，占家庭户的21.93%，其次是四人户，占20.59%，占13.87%的六人户位居第三。第五次人口普查，比重位列前三的是：三人户占25.95%，四人户占24.7%，五人户占16.01%。第六次人口普查，三人户继续位列第一位，占25.29%，二人户的比重猛增至24.06%，处第二位，四人户比重下降至18.31%，但仍居第三位。这种变化明显表现家庭户人口规模逐渐变小的态势。

第四次至第六次人口普查家庭户人口规模表

表1—04—19　　计量单位：户

指　标	第四次人口普查（1990年）		第五次人口普查（2000年）		第六次人口普查（2010年）	
	户数	所占比重（%）	户数	所占比重（%）	户数	所占比重（%）
家庭户总户数	58947	100.00	72030	100.00	80663	100.00
一人户	2647	4.49	6048	8.40	14456	17.92
二人户	5346	9.07	11303	15.69	19404	24.06
三人户	10606	17.99	18690	25.95	20397	25.29
四人户	12136	20.59	17796	24.70	14772	18.31
五人户	12924	21.93	11536	16.01	7029	8.71
六人户	8178	13.87	4456	6.19	2808	3.48
七人户	4234	7.18	1489	2.07	1071	1.33
八人户	1847	3.13	476	0.66	428	0.53
九人户	640	1.09	151	0.21	177	0.22
十人户及以上	389	0.66	85	0.12	121	0.15

2010年第六次人口普查，全县家庭户户均人口为2.97人，处于中心地区，经济发展较好的龙场、扎佐和久长3镇，户均人口分别为3.05人，3.22人和3.13人。其余7个乡（镇），户均人口均在3人以下。大石乡最低，户均只有2.61人。10个社区居委会中，户均2－3人的有8个，3—4人的有2个。217个行政村中，户均2人以下的1个（城南村户均1.5人），占0.46%；2—3人的127个，占58.23%；3—4人的86个，占39.63%；4人以上的3个（久长镇芦山村4.27人，龙场镇大地村4.12人，龙场镇建新村4.09人），占1.38%。

（二）家庭户类型

与家庭户人口规模逐渐变小趋势直接相关的是，1982年第三次人口普查时，全县家庭户是以三代户为主，到2010年第六次人口普查时已演化为二代户为主的户型。一代户的比重也在提升，而三代及三代以上户型的比重明显趋于下降。2010年人口普查时，全县80663户家庭户中：一代户28486户，占35.31%，二代户40446户，占50.14%，三代户11422户，占14.16%，四代户309户，占0.39%，没有五代及以上的家庭户。全县一代和二代户占家庭总户数的85.45%，三代和四代户占14.55%，但乡（镇）间差别较大。一代和二代户型洒坪乡所占比重最高，相应的是三代和四代户型的比重最低。相反，扎佐镇三代和四代户型所占比重最高，相应的是一代和二代户型所占比重又最低。

第六次人口普查各乡（镇）家庭户数及类型表

表1—04—20　　　　　　计量单位：户

指标		全县合计	龙场镇	扎佐镇	久长镇	六广镇	谷堡乡	六屯乡	小箐乡	洒坪乡	大石乡	六桶乡
家庭户	户　数	80663	26497	11253	8017	6786	5683	3477	5312	4123	3157	6358
	所占比重(%)	100.00	100.00	100.00	100.00	100.00	100.00	100.00	100.00	100.00	100.00	100.00
一代户	户　数	28486	8363	3312	2702	2843	2105	1354	1959	1837	1408	2603
	所占比重(%)	35.31	31.56	29.43	33.70	41.90	37.04	38.94	36.88	44.55	44.60	40.94
二代户	户　数	40446	14308	5706	3925	3231	2764	1546	2608	1953	1483	2922
	所占比重(%)	50.14	54.00	50.71	48.96	47.61	48.64	44.46	49.10	47.37	46.97	45.96
三代户	户　数	11422	3742	2156	1357	689	792	563	728	326	261	808
	所占比重(%)	14.16	14.12	19.16	16.93	10.15	13.94	16.19	13.70	7.91	8.27	12.71
四代户	户　数	309	84	79	33	23	22	14	17	7	5	25
	所占比重(%)	0.39	0.32	0.70	0.41	0.34	0.39	0.40	0.32	0.17	0.16	0.39

二、姓氏

（一）主要姓氏

1978年，全县人口有姓氏216姓，其中单姓213姓，复姓3姓。2010年，随着人口增加，姓氏增为284姓，其中单姓281姓，复姓3姓，即：

王、李、张、刘、杨、陈、范、朱、马、贾、罗、谌、雷、冯、邓、尹、廖、颜、严、姜、许、宋、吴、谢、赵、姚、蔡、邹、夏、高、黄、安、周、彭、袁、孟、熊、任、陶、徐、丁、胡、林、康、贺、曹、郑、蒋、金、潘、毛、孙、余、向、谭、韩、汪、晏、唐、何、杜、程、郭、田、常、苏、路、沈、顾、秦、孔、薛、梅、钱、汤、梁、魏、母、聂、曾、冉、岳、钟、龚、欧、石、韦、鲁、穆、舒、管、柳、方、万、戴、祝、董、黎、伍、毕、殷、白、温、詹、党、游、查、甘、车、陆、喻、章、傅、史、吕、鲍、卢、郎、骆、兰、易、齐、邵、樊、霍、明、段、牟、商、冷、敖、崔、江、吉、归、申、施、邱、葛、郝、应、倪、刁、凌、先、艾、翁、蒙、晋、左、班、覃、包、燕、皮、项、缪、童、尤、邬、闵、丘、单、辜、洪、巫、卓、饶、蹇、牛、裴、邢、蒲、司、焦、辛、文、耿、庹、于、肖、叶、涂、屈、萧、季、虞、花、祁、武、俞、屠、闫、但、蔺、赖、鄢、卞、闻、苟、关、鲜、沙、敬、贡、阳、阎、简、阮、侯、国、全、费、莫、纪、龙、戚、奚、窦、靳、师、匡、暨、乔、柯、华、禹、付、帅、阙、谷、古、翟、宁、容、成、柴、瞿、宁、主、蓝、卿、薄、斯、宗、阙、卯、俎、祖、印、冰、池、裘、盛、年、官、桂、仇、操、呙、荀、赢、尚、腾、卜、冒、胥、娄、盘、海、寇、庞、荣、代、矿、灰、桑、粟、银、佘、勾和欧阳、令狐、端木等姓。

（二）主要少数民族姓氏

2010年，县境少数民族人数较多的苗族、布依族和彝族有姓氏34姓。其中，苗族共11126人，姓氏有王、刘、唐、陈、邓、杨、徐、李、张、潘、马、熊、古、罗、皮、韦、祝和侯等18姓；布依族5428人，姓氏有王、李、金、罗、陈、班、葛、郭、花、潘、姚、黄、韦、蒙、江、佘和龙等17姓；彝族1920人，姓氏有杨、张、王、陈、龙、罗、马、李、车、熊和刘等11姓。

第五节　人口控制

一、组织机构

（一）县级机构

1981年1月，恢复修文县人民政府建制，原县革委计划生育办公室相应更名为县政府计划生育办公室。1984年11月，县政府计划生育办公室改为计划生育委员会。1989年7月，为使计划生育工作做到齐抓共管，成立了以分管副县长林志云为组长，县直有关职能部门负责人为成员的修文县人民政府计划生育领导小组。1992年，经县编委批复，计划生育委员会下设财务统计股、业务股和综合办公室。1995年9月在县级机构改革中，撤销县计划生育委员会，设立修文县计划生育局，下设办公室、政策法规科和宣传统计科，行政编制为10人。同月，县委，县政府调整充实了人口与计划生育领导小组，由县委书记罗筑云任组长。2004年8月，根据新时期人口和计划生育工作的需要，县计划生育局又更名为县人口和计划生育局，10人的行政编制不变，增加了制定人口发展规划，加强人口和计划生育工作的综合协调；对人口规模增长趋势，人口素质、结构、迁移等人口和计划生育重大问题进行研究；推动全县人口和计划生育工作的综合治理，促进人口与经济社会协调和可持续发展；协同有关部门实施出生缺陷干预工程；组

织协调有关部门开展出生人口性别比治理工作等职能。局本部下设办公室（含人事、监督、财务和宣传教育），科学技术科，规划统计科（含信息化工程）和政策法规科（含 计划生育“三结合”和信访工作）。此次机构调整后，一直处于稳定状态，直至2010年。人员编制也无变化。

1984年4月，县政府批准成立修文县计划生育宣传技术指导站，系计划生育委员会下独立的事业单位。为适应全县计划生育深入展开的需要，2002年县政府又决定该指导站与隶属于县卫生局的妇幼保健站进行资源整合，以“计妇合一”的方式组建修文县计划生育妇幼保健服务中心。属县人口和计划生育局下的副局级事业单位，内设办公室、保健科、临床综合科、医技科和药具科。保留县计划生育宣传技术指导站和县妇幼保健站两块牌子，实行一套人马，核定35人事业编制。但随着业务的拓展，事业人员编制又分别增加至45人和52人。

1994年9月，为加强对县境内流动人口的管理，县政府同意成立县人口稽查队，隶属于县计划生育委员会领导，人员由内部调剂使用。1997年5月，县编委下文，给人口稽查队5人事业编制。2004年8月，更名为修文县人口和计划生育流动人口管理办公室，核定事业人员编制3人。

（二）区、乡（镇）机构

1979年10月，各区、社配备1名计划生育专职人员，但无专门机构，人员由各区、社机关内部调剂。1992年“撤、并、建”，全县将原6区（镇），31乡（镇）撤并为4镇6乡，各乡（镇）设计划生育股，行政编制共30人。1996年12月，乡（镇）政府工作机构编制调整，计划生育股更名为计划生育办公室，其行政编制扩至40人。2002年6月，乡（镇）党政机关机构改革，保留计划生育办公室，但未对人员定编，所需人员由党政机关总编制中内部调剂。

1990年2月，县人民政府同意成立区、乡（镇）计划生育服务站，由县统一调配专业人员。1992年“撤、并、建”后，10个乡（镇）计划生育服务站核定事业编制60人。2004年9月，扩编为115人。

（三）村（居）计生组织

1980年7月，全县农村每个大队和生产队都设1名计划生育队长。1984年政、社分设后，各村及村民组的计划生育干部仍然保留。1988年改为在各行政村分别设立2名计划生育信息员，由村党支部书记和村委会主任兼任。1993年3月起，每个行政村和居民委员会设置1名专职计划生育员，取代原由村党支部书记和村委会主任兼任计划生育信息员。1999年起，村（居）计划生育员更名为计生专干，每个村（居）设置1名育龄妇女小组长。

二、主要措施

曾一度被称为“天下第一难”的计划生育工作，在县委、县政府领导下，通过不断探索、不断总结、逐步走上健康发展、顺利推进的轨道。

20世纪70年代末和80年代初期，基于群众中旧的生育观念根深蒂固，宣传教育工作不深不透，工作阻力极大。为了完成上级下达控制人口过快增长的任多，只好从县直机关抽人调车，各级干部齐上阵，轰轰烈烈搞突击。这种做法在当时确实也起到一定的作用，取得一些效果，但队伍的临时性，工作的季节性，更主要的是未得到群众的理解与支持，“超生游击队”闻风而动、四处躲藏，给工作造成很大的被动，浪费大量人力、物力和财力。群众评论“抓时雷声大，过后雨点小”，治标不治本。国家机关、企事业单位职工和城镇居民，因有严厉的处罚措施，对计划生育也往往是被动接受。鉴于这样的局面，县委、县政府

1986年提出：“在计划生育工作上，一要改变过去的突击性为经常性；二要稳定计生队伍；三要改管理型为服务型”。这是全县计划生育工作机制改变的转折点。关于计划生育工作中主要的政策规定，前《修文县志》297-298页已作记述，不再重复。《中华人民共和国人口与计划生育法》、国家《流动人口计划生育工作条例》和《贵州省人口与计划生育条例》先后颁布后，对原来县里制订的一些地方性法规进行清理，凡与上述“法”和“条例”不一致的，均停止执行。下列主要措施，推动了全县的计划生育工作深入开展。

（一）开展人口与计划生育工作的综合改革

2002年，根据上级统一部署，全县开展了人口与计划生育工作的综合改革。在管理体制方面：城镇变户籍地管理为主为现居住地管理为主，建立“属地管理、单位负责、条块结合、居民自治、社区服务”的新体制；农村变县、乡（镇）工作为主为“村为主”，变主要依靠计生专干工作为实现计划生育村民自治，形成“县指导、乡（镇）负责、组配合、户落实”的工作格局。一是将人口和计生管理与县直有关部门工作职责有机结合，并以签订目标责任书的形式分别予以明确，进行考核，加大管理的力量，扭转过去由计生部门“单打一”，逐步形成在各级党委和政府领导下，由计生部门牵头，20多个职能部门相互配合，齐抓共管的新体制。二是创制和发放《修文县计划生育通用卡》，当事人在办理或审验工商营业执照，暂住证、驾驶执照、营运证等证件和申请项目立项、申请贷款等手续时都必须出示此卡，达到共同把关、综合治理之目的。三是在流动人口管理问题上，坚持流入地管理为主和“谁用工谁负责、谁受益谁管理，谁的地盘谁清理”的原则，加强对流动人口计划生育管理和优质服务相结合。四是全面推行人口与计划生育村民自治。通过公开招聘村级计生专干、选配好村级计生班子，充分发挥村级计划生育协会的网络和工作优势、首创村级“计生审核专用章”的使用等措施，初步形成群众广泛参与，村民自我教育、自我管理、自我服务、自我监督的计划生育管理机制。

在工作机制方面：2002年开展的人口与计划生育工作综合改革中，又对管理工作、技术服务、考核评估等方面的机制进行改革，更加适应推动工作的需要。同时还不断建立和完善以建立符合市场经济体制的利益导向机制和社会保障制度，人口与计划生育经费投入，改革计划生育干部人事制度，完善人口与计划生育工作调控体系为主要内容的计划生育工作的保障机制。综合改革的核心是体制和机制创新。至2005年，在已建起“依法管理、村民自治、优质服务、政策推动、综合治理”5个新机制的基础上，又加上“领导决策、队伍建设和投入保障”3个机制。全县人口与计划生育综合改革工作于2007年顺利通过省级验收。

（二）加大对群众宣传教育的工作力度

一是加大宣传教育面。2004年，在全县初中以上学校开展“国策及性健康知识和新型生育文化”进校园活动，2006年又开展“国策及性健康知识”进校园活动。县委党校将人口理论、生育政策、法律知识列为教学内容。把流动人口也作为重要的宣传教育对象；二是充分发挥各级计生协会、共青团、妇联和青年志愿者的积极作用，利用县、乡（镇）、村（居）三级人口学校覆盖面宽、定期上课的有利条件开展宣传教育；三是形式多样化，让群众喜闻乐见。除常规的宣传车、宣传栏、黑板报、标语牌、挂图、宣传读物外，在《修文报》（后为《当代修文》）、修文电视台开辟“计划生育专栏”，以计划生育为中心内容的文艺演出、演讲、知识竞赛等，并利用场天搞咨询服务等形式很受群众欢迎。2009年起，县人口计划生育局创办内部交流刊物《修文人口与计生》，每月一期、免费发至村民组，反映工作动态、宣传政

策法规及生殖健康等内容，还利用手机已经普及的优势，开通了一个短信宣传平台，直接服务到人。这些创新的宣传教育形式，也取得了较好的效果。

由于宣传教育工作的深入开展，使计划生育这项基本国策和生育方面主要的政策规定，基本上做到了家喻户晓，工作阻力减小，干群关系也有明显改善。主动实行计划生育的家庭越来越多。过细的工作，人性化的服务，涉及计划生育的信访大幅下降。1996年发生信访356件，2004年陡然上升至1569件。因计生主管部门内部建立了一整套严格的制度，做到热情接待，认真处理、件件有回复。因而化解了一些矛盾，消除了一些误解，解决了一些实际问题，进一步密切了与群众的关系，致使信访件数又呈下降趋势，2010年仅有165件。

（三）将计划生育工作纳入目标管理

1984年起，县将地区下达的年末总人口、自然增长率、“四种手术”完成数量、控制多胎率等指标分解后，由县与各区签订“承包责任书”，年末总结、根据完成情况兑现奖罚。区再与乡签订“承包责任书”。1987年起，全县实行目标责任制，计划生育工作由县政府与计划生育委员会签订，年终考核后，由县政府与计划生育委员会兑现奖励或处罚。1992年“撤、并、建”后，又改为县政府与各乡（镇）人民政府签订“目标责任书”。1996年修文划入贵阳市后，不但每年都将计划生育作为目标管理的重要内容，县政府与各乡（镇）人民政府签订责任书，而且将计划生育工作作为考核干部政绩的重要内容，坚持“一票否决”制度，对没有完成计划生育指标任务的乡（镇）党政一把手要负总责，给予诫勉谈话和亮“黄牌”警告，责令限期整改，促使乡（镇）主要领导干部增强搞好计划生育工作的责任感。

2003年起，实行“双线”目标管理体制。党政线由市政府与县政府签订后，再由县政府与各乡（镇）政府签订。主要内容是政策、经费、人员等保障措施。计生线由县计生局与市计生局签订后，再由县计生局与各乡（镇）计生办签订。主要内容是人口与计划生育各项指标任务。这一模式直至2010年未变。

（四）注重计划生育队伍建设

为适应工作需要，特别是计划生育工作重心下移后，除县计划生育妇幼保健服务中心加强技术人员配备外，重点是加强对乡（镇）计生办和计生服务站的人员配备。

2010年，县计划生育妇幼保健服务中心共50人，其中专业技术人员41人，占82.0%，拥有中级技术职称的17人。50人中文化程度构成情况是：大学本科15人、占30%，大学专科29人、占58.0%，中专5人、占10%，高中1人、占2%。乡（镇）计生办和乡（镇）计生服务站共103人：大学本科11人、占10.68%，大学专科66人、占64.08%，中专23人、占22.33%，高中3人、占2.91%。乡（镇）计生服务站63人中，有主治医师6人，主管护师2人，护师7人，执业医师10人，助理医师9人，医士8人，护士10人，助产士1人，妇儿保卫生员1人，技术员9人。其中具有中级技术职称的15人，占23.81%，达到了计划生育节育手术基本不出乡（镇）的要求。此外，2010年，人口计划生育局机关配备人员12人（其中流动人口管理办公室3人），村民委员会和居民委员会有计生专干241人，育龄妇女小组长（计生中心户户长）1614人。

为提高计划生育专职人员的学历和业务水平，从2004年起，选派部分人员（包括村级计生专干）先后到贵州大学、贵阳医学院进行学历培训或进修学习；邀请有关专家到县举办培训班、培训县内各级计生干部1800余人次；积极开展岗位技术练兵活动，2007年以来在市举办的练兵大比武活动中，均取得好名次；还对乡（镇）干部和计生办人员进行开展计生工作基本能力培训；各乡（镇）组织力量对村（居）干部，育龄妇女小组长进行计生法规和应知应会知识培训，共达2100余人次。

尽力为基层计生机构和人员开展工作创造条件。除按国家《农村计划生育技术服务机构基础设施建设标准》为乡（镇）计生服务站合理配置了技术服务、宣传教育、优生监测、避孕药具、生殖保健、母婴保健、信息传输等设备外，还新建10个乡（镇）计生服务站业务用房，平均达750平方米以上。2009年，县、乡（镇）两级投入96万元，按省《计划生育技术机构统一视觉形象规范手册》标准及“亮化、绿化、美化、文化”要求，装修和改造乡（镇）计生服务站，完善功能布局，既体现人口计生人文特色，又符合医疗标准，做到科学管理、服务方便、特色突出和满足个性化的要求。还先后为乡（镇）计生机构配备了业务用车，为提高诊疗水平和管理层次，还为他们配备B超机、计算机、打印机等现代化设备。2005年，改扩建计划生育妇保健服务中心，面积达1998平方米，技术装备基本达到应有尽有，还先后建成面积不少于40平方米的村（居）计划生育室227个。

县委、县政府加强计划生育队伍建设的一系列举措、对调动全县计划生育职工的积极性发挥了很大激励作用。除长期坚守岗位、默默奉献之外，突出的表现：一是自1983年以来，涌现出52个先进集体（国家级16个、省级13个、地市级23个），1981年以来有32人（国家级11人、省级8人、地市级13人）被评为先进个人，分别受到表彰。二是在工作中有创新。如使用《修文县计生干部、村（居）级计生员考核纪实手册》、《修文县计生专用卡》，村级“计生审核专用章”；实行计划生育合同公证，推行计划生育联户管理，志愿者参与推进“婚育新风进万家”活动等，都是在实践中总结出来新的工作方法，得到上级主管部门的肯定，有的（如计划生育合同公证）还在全省推广。三是2007年2月县人口和计划生育局部署在全局干部职工中开展“修文要发展，计生干部怎么干”大讨论，此类活动在县直机关中是少见的。

（五）依法管理和人文关怀相结合

提倡一对夫妇只生一个孩子和生两个孩子全是女孩，采取绝育措施不再生育，是计划生育管理的重要内容。至2010年，全县农村有独生子女户4733户，双女结扎户952户。在营造宣传舆论环境中，在政治上使他们得到荣誉；认真落实“奖、扶、医、帮、优、保”6方面的利益导向政策、使他们在经济上得到实惠。因而由过去主要依靠“处罚多生”为主推动工作，逐步转向“奖励少生”为主，运用利益导向作用推动工作的轨道。早在1979年《修文县计划生育试行办法》就规定独生子女可以凭证享受一些优惠、优先政策，并为独生子女家庭一次性发给奖励费200元。1980年县委、县政府又决定为独生子女每月发保健费4元。1998年，根据《贵州省计划生育条例》将独生子女户家庭的奖励标准调为100—500元，将保健费标准调为5元。但因财政困难，奖励费和保健费一直没有很好兑现，后来甚至中断。2003年县委、县政府为维护政策的严肃性，取信于民，在各乡（镇）认真清理的基础上，由县财政一次性投入资金3 7.11万元，足额补发了所拖欠的奖励费和保健费。这一措施取得了很好的效果。当年全县有925户办理了《独生子女证》、主动放弃二胎生育的家庭有58户。2004年有555户办理了《独生子女证》、有52户主动放弃了二胎生育指标。1998年起，对领取了《独生子女证》，符合生育第二胎条件而不生育的，另发一次性奖励费500元以上。修文对独生子女和二女结扎夫妇启动养老保险较早，1991年开始后一直是在不断地完善之中。2004年计划生育养老保险的领取标准是：男年满60周岁，女年满55周岁，独女户家庭夫

妇每人每月领取60元；独子户家庭夫妇每人每月领取50元；双女结扎后家庭夫妇每人每月也是领取50元，直至亡故。2002—2004年，共为农村2033户独生子女户，613户双女结扎户夫妇办理了养老保险并发放了《养老金领取证》。之后，这项制度为计划生育家庭奖励扶助制度所取代，除原来养老保险的领取标准未变外，还增加了独生子女、双女结扎户家庭未满18周岁子女意外死亡的；子女未满18周岁，其父或母死亡的；子女未满18周岁，因病、因意外伤害致残的，视其伤残程度，分别一次性发给扶助金2000—5000元。独生子女和双女结扎户参加农村新型合作医疗，每户每年补助10元。对农村中因计划生育手术并发症而丧失劳力的，也列入了扶助对象。2005年“少生快富”奖励制度，2006年“关爱女孩奖”都在计划生育工作中得到认真的落实。至2010年，全县共兑现“少生快富”奖励59户、19.6万元，“关爱女孩奖”1940人，1114万元。这些奖励措施既为计划生育家庭减轻了经济负担，并极大地帮助他们解除了后顾之忧，推动了工作。此外，从2001年起，对具有农村户籍，长期居住在农村的独生子女户和双女结扎户的考生，参加全国高考、录取时给予加10分的照顾。至2010年，共为89名考生办理了加分的相关手续。

（六）加强对流动人口计划生育的管理

修文流出、流入的人口数量都比较大，对他们计划生育管理过去一直都是一个薄弱环节。1 994年成立人口稽查队（后更名流动人口管理办公室），但由于流动人口分布面广，而力量又有限，也不能完全适应工作的需要。1999年，县人口与计划生育领导小组行文，要求乡（镇）人民政府负责对进入辖区经商、务工人员进行清理登记、验证，对流出人口的办证等方面也作了明确要求，建立流动人口信息平台。按时上报流动人口数据。这一制度后转为“全国省际流动人口统计制度”。2005年，在所有乡（镇）及部分村（居）委会正式启用“流动人口管理平台”信息系统。

鉴于县城所在地的龙场镇辖区内流动人口，特别是流入经商、打工人员多，煤窑、矿山和乡镇企业又往往是流入打工人员集中的地方，为了摸清底数，2002年3月份组织上百人的队伍集中进行清理登记和验证；2006年5月，由县委分管计划生育工作的副书记兼纪委书记付涛亲自率领计生、公安、工商、国土、乡镇企业等单位和乡（镇）100余人，14台车，分5组对龙场镇范围及部分流动人口较集中的乡（镇）和特殊地段进行全面清理、整顿。发放宣传资料2000余份，共清理登记流入人口2189人。同时进行妇检54人、上环29例、引产8例、人流5例、结扎24例，年度内生育补报2人。2007年6月，县召开流动人口计划生育集中清理服务活动专题会后，各乡（镇）分别在人口计生局的配合下开展了清理和服务上门活动，至7月初结束。之后，每年5月开始开展流动人口宣传清理100天活动已成制度。再加上经常化的过细工作，确保了流动人口管理和服务无死角。2009年，县出台《关于建立流出人口计划生育管理服务联络站的实施意见》。各乡（镇）在流出人口较为集中的地点建立流出人口计划生育管理服务信息联络站。选聘自觉遵守计生政策、热心计生工作、并有一定威望的对象为信息联络员，与他们定报酬、定职责、定任务、经过培训后上岗。2010年，县招聘25名流动人员协管员，乡（镇）也招聘10余名协管员，负责对流动人口、房屋出租人进行相关法律法规和政策的宣传，采集、登记辖区内流动人口及房屋出租情况，督促房屋出租人认真履行人口、计生登记报告制度。使对流动人口的管理，逐步形成网络。通过上述工作，全县流动人口的婚育状况处于全面的掌握之中，为有针对性的计划生育管理和服务奠定了较为坚实的基础。至2010年7月31日，全县常住人口231435人，流出74545人，其中育龄妇女25023人，已婚育龄妇女16604人；流入12337人，其中育龄妇女3572人，已婚育龄妇女3033人。流出人口生小孩615人，其中政策内生育464人，政策外生育151人，符合政策生育率为75.45%。流入人口生小孩144人，符合政策生育率为100%。流出人口已婚育龄妇女办理“婚育证明”的占98.3%，流入已婚育龄妇女持“婚育证明”的占96.2%。

（七）实施出生缺陷干预工程

为提高出生人口素质，实现“少生优生”，从2003年起，在县计划生育指导站内设“出生缺陷监测和干预中心”。指导基层开展此项工作及人员培训，宣传出生缺陷的干预，遗传优生咨询，普及生殖健康教育及孕期保健。乡（镇）计划生育技术服务站内设乡（镇）级“出生缺陷干预监测站”，经常开展出生缺陷及遗传优生的咨询活动，开展群体流行病学调查及相应的检查，掌握辖区内出生缺陷的发生情况和动态变化，及时向县反馈信息。村（居）计生服务室为具体的监测点，负责宣传、咨询、走访和信息收集工作。出生缺陷干预工程的主要工作是：一是对持证待怀已婚育龄妇女发放“叶酸”“福施福”，预防新生儿“神经管畸形”。二是进行技术干预，主要是进行风疹、巨细胞、单纯疱疹、弓形体四种病毒的检测、筛查。三是对产前≥12周婴儿进行B超监测。2010年计划内怀孕妇女参加优生培训率为96.97%，优生监测档案建档率达100%，免费发放“叶酸”2695人，TORCH筛查24人，ABO溶血筛查2500人，新生儿疾病筛查1301人，有效地降低了出生缺陷发生率。此外，为了实现“少生优生”，从1989年起，根据《婚姻法》和《结婚登记管理条例>的规定，结婚当事人在结婚登记前开展婚前保健检查工作，严禁患有不宜生育的遗传性疾病的人和禁止直系血亲和三代以内旁系血亲的人结婚，严把婚前检查关。2004年，新的《中华人民共和国婚姻登记条例》实施，不再强求婚检，致全县婚前检查率大幅下降。2009年实施“计生通用卡”制度后，婚前保健检查率有所回升。2010年全，县结婚登记3102对，免费婚检1286对，婚检率为41.46%。

三、工作成效

通过30余年的不懈努力，县委、县政府在领导全县人口和计划生育工作中，认识在不断地深化，措施在不断地完善，方法在不断地改进和创新。特别是把“计划生育是我国的一项基本国策”作为贯穿始终的指导思想；把宣传群众、依靠群众作为开展工作的基本遵循；把计划生育队伍建设作为组织保障；把计划生育列入各级目标考核内容作为重要的推进举措；把政策法规的要求与人性化服务紧密结合，因而使工作由被动变为主动，并逐步转入经常化、规范化、法治化和科学化的轨道，基本达到了控制人口过快增长的目标，工作成效是显著的。

1.妇女总和生育率下降。20世纪70年代末期，全县妇女总和生育率约为5%。1982年第三次人口普查，1990年第四次人口普查，2000年第五次人口普查和2010年第六次人口普查，该项指标分别为3.4%、2.15%、1.29%和1.28%。

2.初婚年龄推迟。1980年，全县初婚年龄平均为23.44岁（男24.77岁，女22.05岁），1990年初婚年龄平均为22.14岁（男22.94岁，女21.3岁），2000年初婚年龄平均24.2岁（男25.65岁、女22.8岁），2010年初婚年龄平均25.61岁（男27.28岁，女23.89岁）。除1990年初婚年龄有反弹之外，总的变化趋势是，人们的婚育观念正逐渐发生变化，适当晚婚已蔚然成风。

3.节育率提高。20世纪70年代后期，全县育龄妇女节育率只有50%左右。1990年这一指标升至89.1%，2000年和2010年分别为90.74%和89.36%。随着宣传工作的深入开展，除育龄妇女外、育龄男性、自觉采用药物或器具避孕，达到节育目的的人也越来越多。

4.计划生育率大幅提升。20世纪70年代中后期，全县计划生育率仅为4%左右。80年代后期平均为73.7%，1990年、2000年和201 0年此项指标分别达到82.2%，88.06%和84.62%。

5.多胎率下降。开展计划生育后，全县多胎率由20世纪80年代初的47.2%降至80年代末期的17.5%。1990年多胎率继续降至11.4%。2000年和2010年持续再降至5.11%和1.94%。多胎出生人口：1980年为1895人，1990年为492人，2000年和2010年分别为163人和56人。

6.人口过快增长基本得到控制。20世纪70年代，人口出生率为35.28‰，自然增长率为25.09‰；80年代出生率和自增率分别为16.7‰和10.9‰；90年代出生率和自增率分别为17.11‰和11.22‰。进入21世纪后，2000—2010年这11年，全县人口出生率为10.13‰，自增率为4.98‰。总的变化趋势是人口出生率和自增率是明显下降的。由于计划生育工作持续深入地开展，1978至2010年全县累计少生26万余人。

专记：计划生育真抓实干　全县少生26万

1978年前，全县人口以迅猛之势增长，在生育问题上长期处于失控的无政府状态。1949年新中国成立至1977年的29年中，除3年困难时期有两年（1960年和1961年）人口自然增长率呈现负增长之外，自然增长率在10.01‰—20.00‰的有5年，在20.01‰—30.00‰的有9年，在30.01‰—40.00‰的有11年，在40.01‰以上的有两年（1965年47.48‰，1967年45.07‰）。形成这样局面的根本原因是人口的出生率远远高于人口的死亡率。1949—1977年，人口死亡率在10.00‰以下的有9年，在10.01‰—20.00‰有19年，在20.01‰以上的有1年（1961年27.21‰）。29年人口死亡率平均为11.62‰，而人口出生率在10.01‰—20.00‰的有1年（1962年13.82‰），在20.01‰—30.00‰的有4年，在30.01‰—40.00‰的有7年，在40.01‰—50.00‰的有10年，在50.01‰—60.00‰的有6年，在60.01‰以上的有1年（1965年61.25‰）。29年人口出生率平均为40.27‰，高出人口死亡率28.65个千分点，这正是29年全县人口平均的自然增长率28.65‰。

进入改革开放时期，由于县的各级党政领导人口意识普遍增强，坚持物质文明、精神文明和计划生育工作一起抓，终于赢得了经济建设大发展，精神文明建设创佳绩，人口自然增长率持续下降的可喜局面。1978至2010年的33年中，人口出生率平均为14.70‰，其中在10.00‰以下有6年（2003年最低、为7.51‰），在10.01‰—20.00‰的有21年，在20.01‰以上的有6年（1998年为最高、达27.78‰）；人口死亡率平均为5.54‰，其中在10.00‰以下的32年（1990年3.86‰为最低），10.01‰以上的1年（2005年13.18‰）；人口自然增长率平均为9.16‰，其中，10.00‰以下的18年（2004年2.67‰为最低），10.01‰以上的15年（1998年19.28‰为最高）。显而以见，人口自然增长涉及的3项指标均低于改革开放前的29年。人口过快增长势头得到有效遏制后，经济建设成果的人均水平相对提高，这是全县城乡居民收入大幅增长，生活质量明显改善，人均预期寿命不断提高最直接的原因。

如果县委、县政府不是坚持不懈地抓计划生育工作，使计划生育这一基本国策落在实处，那全县的人口形势就严峻得多。就是不按1949至1977年实际的人口自然增长率28.65‰，而是按开展计划生育后的1975至1977年年均人口自然增长率27.02‰推算，以1977年总人口236454人为基数，2010年全县总人口应为569968人，比当年实际总人口305917人多出264051人，这就是1978至2010年全县少生的人口。如果情况真是这样，2010年全县经济建设成果的人均占有水平，均在现有实际水平的基础上降低46.33%。人均GDP要由15097元改写为8103元，人均粮食产量要由341公斤改写为183公斤，人均地方财政收入要由914元改写为491元，城镇居民人均可支配收入要由15756元，改写为8456元，农民人均纯收入要由5152元改写为2765元……那将是“种粮难糊口，用钱哪里有？小康目标太渺茫，贫困伴随大家走”那样严酷的局面。

改革开放33年，全县由于计划生育工作深入持久地开展，少生26.4万人。这既是工作成效最集中的体现，更重要的是，这30余年的实践，使各级党政领导机关、各级干部及广大人民群众，不但普遍增强了人口意识，而且还不断地增强了“人均”观念，这为以后人口有计划地增长奠定了一个较好的基础。

政治建设篇

1978年12月中共十一届三中全会召开后，县委在坚持以经济建设为中心的同时，致力于民主政治建设。1981年恢复人民代表大会制度并建立人大常委会，撤销“县革命委员会”，恢复县人民政府，1983年建立政治协商会议修文县委员会，1984年取消“政社合一”的人民公社体制，人民公社不再作为一级政权机构组织，改置乡（镇）行使政府权力，生产大队建立村民委员会实行村民自治。1997年起，启动“平安修文”建设工程。通过实施“六有”工程使人民群众学有所教，劳有所得，病有所医，老有所养，住有所居，居有所安。跨入21世纪，县委号召全县人民开展生态文明城市创建活动，以此改善和提升人民生活质量。深入抓好中共建设，通过开展“三讲”（讲学习、讲政治、讲正气）教育、“三个代表”（中国共产党始终代表中国先进生产力的发展要求、代表中国先进文化的前进方向、代表中国最广大人民的根本利益）重要思想学习教育和保持共产党员先进性教育活动，着力提高党员的整体素质和基层党组织的战斗力，使党组织的战斗堡垒作用和党员的先锋作用得到充分发挥。县委重视国防建设，形成党委议军、人民拥军的良好氛围。驻军部队把人民群众当作亲人，在执行军事任务的同时，积极参与地方经济建设。2005和2010年，修文两次荣获贵州省“双拥”（拥军爱民、拥政爱民）模范县称号。

人民代表大会制度的恢复，扩大完善了政治民主。1981—2010年，县人民代表大会及其常委会作出“开展普法教育”“加强土地管理”“建立工业园区”“依法治县”和“保护环境”等决议、决定共388项，有力地加快法治进程，促进了经济发展和生态保护。

县人民政府贯彻实施县委“建设经济强县”“科教兴县”“工业强县”等一系列发展战略，确立“以工业化带富农民，以城镇化带动农村，以产业化提升农业”的战略思想，聚力发展工业主体经济和外向型经济，实施“三点两线一园区”、十里工业走廊、“扎佐物流园”建设规划，使县域经济到2010年基本实现从传统农业向新型工业的转型。

建立县政协为各界人士搭建起参政议政平台，使政协委员通过视察调研、提出提案的方式向县委、县政府建言献策。1983—2010年，政协委员共提出调研报告114份和提案1604件，报告和提案内容涉及经济、民生、生态、平安、法治等。

实行民主选举、民主管理、民主决策、民主监督，由民主选举的217个村民委员会和12个居民委员会成为村民当家作主的代表。

在县委的领导下，历届县人大、县政府、县政协和各人民团体、各级党政组织及广大党员干部，围绕县委提出的不同时期的奋斗目标，进行产业结构调整，着力招商引资，狠抓城镇改造和举办“阳明文化节”等大规模的建设实践，使修文的经济社会发生翻天覆地的变化。至2010年，体现全县经济实力的国内生产总值达到46亿元，创下历史新高。

一系列的民主政治建设和惠民举措，凝聚了全县党员干部与全县人民一道同心同德搞建设的正能量，一个稳定、民主、和谐的修文显现出蓬勃生机。在县委的领导下，历届县人大、县政府、县政协和各人民团体、各级党政组织及广大党员干部，围绕县委提出各个时段的奋斗目标，进行产业结构调整，着力招商引资，狠抓城镇改造和举办“阳明文化节”等大规模的建设实践，使修文的经济社会发生翻天覆地的变化。至2010年，体现全县经济实力的国内生产总值达到46亿元，创下历史新高。

第一章　政治体制改革

1978年12月中共十一届三中全会后，县委把政治体制改革和扩大社会主义民主摆在全县工作的重要位置。在改革进程中着力拨乱反正，不断完善中共领导方式和决策机制，健全社会主义民主制度，深化行政管理体制改革，加强对权力的制约和监督，实施依法治县方略，从而推动全县经济发展和社会进步。

第一节　民主政治建设

一、人民代表大会制度恢复完善

1981年1月，按照1979年7月1日第五届全国人民代表大会第二次会议通过的《中华人民共和国地方各级人民代表大会和地方各级人民委员会组织法》规定，召开修文县第七届人民代表大会第一次会议，恢复“文化大革命”开始后中断15年时间的人民代表大会制度。在七届一次人民代表大会上，选举产生修文县人民代表大会常务委员会。

2006年6月21日，县人大常委会听取县政府工作汇报

从1981年恢复人民代表大会制度起，每年县、乡两级人民代表大会均要举行1次全体代表会议，并按期换届。县、乡人民代表由选区选民直接选举产生，以表达选民意志，使人民民主权利得到增强。每次普选，均组建选举工作领导机构。县成立

选举委员会，下设办公室承担选举事务。各乡（镇）设立相应机构，保证选举工作顺利进行。县、乡（镇）两级选举委员会主任由同级党委或人大主要领导担任，并设副主任和委员若干人。县人民代表大会每届选举前由县人大常委会党组向县委呈送换届选举工作报告，陈述选举工作要旨、指导思想、组织机构和时间安排、代表名额分配、工作方法步骤等，由县委批转下发文件执行。接着组成工作组到选定的选区试点，总结出经验后再全面铺开。同时进行选举工作骨干培训和宣传发动。选举采用无记名投票，对居住分散和老弱病残的选民采取流动票箱投票、计票，最后由选举委员会确认并宣布选举结果，发放代表当选证书。选举结束后的两个月内，召开县人民代表大会。对代表的考察和选举，注重革命化、年轻化、知识化和参与民主管理的素质。从1981年恢复人民代表大会制度开始选举代表，全县享有选举权和被选举权的公民参选率均在85%以上。

县、乡（镇）两级人大代表来自各自辖区内的各行各业，具有广泛的代表性。每年1次的县、乡（镇）人代会议期间，代表们依据工作实际和群众意愿提出议案审议各项报告。从2002年开始，县人大常委会每年在县人代会期间，组织代表按工业经济、农村工作、社会事业和民主法治4个专题进行审议，县政府对代表审议意见的初步办理方案向主席团会议汇报。

1981年设置县人大常委会后，在县人代会闭会期间，由县人大常委会依法行使人代会的权力。常委会每2个月举行1次例会，听取和审议“一府两院”（县政府和法院、检察院）工作报告，讨论决定县内重大事项。此外，还根据需要召开临时会议，邀请有关部门负责人列席。

二、政治协商制度建立

1983年3月，为贯彻执行中国共产党同各民主党派和无党派人士“长期共存，互相监督”“肝胆相照，荣辱与共”的方针，建立中国人民政治协商会议修文县委员会，县内中国共产党和无党派民主人士等19个界别75人为首届委员会委员，对县委、县人民政府的大政方针和人民生活等重大问题进行政治协商，通过建议和批评发挥民主监督作用。至2010年，政协修文县委员会共历7届，先后有社会各界的941人作为政协委员参与政治协商、民主监督，建言献策。

在中共修文县委领导下，县政协每年举行1次全体委员会议，并按期换届。在全县大政方针以及政治、经济、文化和社会生活中的重大问题决策之前、决策执行过程中均履行政治协商。政协委员通过开展视察调研、提出提案等方式参政议政。1983—2010年，县政协组织委员视察与调研活动137次，以学习组、调研组和委员个人名义写出调研报告114份；收到委员提案1604件，归并立案1512件，提出提案的委员2865人次，使政协组织与政协委员的职能得以发挥。

三、村民自治制度实施

1984年实现政社分设，将全县生产大队革命委员会改建为村民委员会，设主任；生产队改建为村民小组，设组长。村民委员会和村民小组为农村群众性的自治单位，是村民进行自我教育、自我管理、自我服务和自我监督的基层群众性自治组织。至2010年，全县共置217个村民委员会1414个村民小组。

（一）贯彻实施《中华人民共和国村民委员会组织法》

1984年，全县普遍建立村民委员会，村民委员会在基层公共事务和公益事业中施行“四自”方针，使人民群众直接行使民主权利。从1984至1988年，村级调解组织调解山林、水利、婚姻、赡养、财产、经济等各类纠纷1.38万件，调解成功率达91.8%；防止非正常死亡76人。村民委员会发动村民制定乡规民约，组织群众联防，建设精神文明，使社会治安明显好转，群众对村委会感到满意。

1986年，全县贯彻中共中央、国务院《关于加强农村基层政权建设的通知》精神，对村民委员会进行整顿，先整顿思想，再整顿组织，然后建立健全人民调解、治安保卫、公共卫生、社会福利等工作机构和制度。村民委员会按照县委宣传部、县文明委员会和民政部门的安排部署，普遍完善村规民约，开展创建文明村和评选“五好家庭”活动。

1990年贯彻实施《中华人民共和国村民委员会组织法》，全县217个行政村通过选举建立新的村民委员会。《中华人民共和国村民委员会组织法》的实施使村委会建设步入法治化、制度化，有力地推动了各项工作的开展。新的村委会建立后，全县展开宣传民政部《关于在全国农村开展村民自治示范活动的通知》。1995年，全县启动村民自治示范活动。

2002年开展村民自治示范县创建活动，县委、县政府下文成立基层组织建设工作领导小组和村民自治工作领导小组，全县10乡（镇）亦建立相应组织。先后出台基层民主政治建设、村务政务公开、村民自治、村民委员会换届选举等专项工作文件。在创建活动中采取“一车一网两报三会”（宣传车，远程教育网，县报、墙报，村民大会、村民代表会、场天宣传会）为主的宣传方式，强化村民的民主自治意识和提高农村基层干部的民主自治能力。2002至2005年的4年间，在村民自治工作中，全县共组装宣传车110台次，建远程教育播放点217个，制作发放光碟3.1万张，出墙报、黑板报1500期，县内媒体专门宣传和刊播相关信息、资料245条次，召开村民大会、村民代表会议1400次，组织场天宣传95次，散发宣传资料6.5万份。与此同时，通过市、县、乡三级短期培训、党校学习、远程教育、以会代训等形式培训村干部5000人次。2005年，首轮村民自治示范县活动通过贵阳市民政部门达标验收。

2008年6月久长镇上寨村无公害蔬菜种植协会成立

通过贯彻实施《中华人民共和国村民委员会组织法》、开展村民自治和村务公开活动。至2010年，全县农村由村民委员会牵头建起养鸡协会、养猪协会、猕猴桃协会、蔬菜营销协会、花卉协会等46个，拥有农民会员7446户1.8万人。扎佐镇萝卜营销协会在闯市场中主动出击，取得进入贵阳市五里冲蔬菜批发市场的绿色通行证，为种植萝卜的农民打开了致富途径。村民自治破解了“三农”（农业、农村、农民）瓶颈，达到“群众得实惠”的目标，全县农民人均纯收入从2002年的2476元上升到2010年的5152元。

（二）民主选举

从1984年起，村民委员会换届均实行民主选举。1990年依据《中华人民共和国村民委员会组织法》的规定选优选强村干部。2005年初的第六届村（居）换届选举，按照县委、县政府《村（居）民委员会换届选举工作方案》，以村务公开为切入点，任期财务审计为重点，严格程序为首要，全县217个村依法选举产生村民委员会217个，选举主任215名，副主任29名，委员738名，村民委员会选举完成率为100%，村民委员会主任选举完成率为99%。选民16.9万人，参加投票选举14.02万人，参选率达83.2%，一次选举成功率为82.9%。新一届村民委员会成员中有中共党员404名，占39%；初中以上文化程度823人，占84%。2007年11月至次年3月进行的第七届村换届选举，试行选举方式改革，将洒坪乡的蜈蚣桥村、硐口村和六广镇的沙坡村以及六屯乡的全心村作为“海选”（村委会组成人员提名与选举一次进行，不事先推荐提名的选举方式）试点，4个村均实现一次成功选举出村委会班子。村民对自己能直接行使民主权利十分满意。蜈蚣桥村选民刘朝军投完票后高声地说：“这样的选举使村民享受到真正的民主权利，我们满意得很。”

通过民主选举产生的村领导班子成员，基本上能代表村民的意愿，绝大多数是农村中处事正派的能人。为提高村委的政治思想素质和办事能力，在完成选举后，县、乡（镇）两级政府都对新的村委成员进行培训。通过培训和工作实践，村干部多数成为农村经济发展的带头人。小箐乡崇恩村是一个没有经济支柱产业的贫穷村，村民“养猪为过年，养牛为犁田，养鸡为换盐巴钱”，2002年，村“两委”（村党支部委员会、村民委员会）一班人带领村民走科技兴村之路，因地制宜养殖肉牛、肉鸡、肉鸽，两年时间，全村617户家家成为养殖户，从此告别贫穷落后的日子。洒坪乡的孟树明等3名村干，2003年7月各出资5000元，在村里建起无公害肉牛养殖示范，一年时间，带动农户310户，仅肉牛养殖1项每户就增收9000元。

2007年11月30日，洒坪乡蜈蚣桥村“海选”现场

专记：龙王村村民投票罢免村干部

2001年9月4日，扎佐镇龙王村村民通过投票，罢免了村委会主任的职务。

龙王村村民杨怀亮，高中文化，人年轻，有冲劲，1999年被选为村委会主任。上任当天就向群众承诺要兴修水利、安装电话，在村里干一番事业。随着时间推移，两年多却没见承诺兑现。他放着村务不管，自己外出打工挣钱。村民们不仅听其言，而且观其行，说他是“说话的巨人，行动的矮子”，认为他不为民办事，不配当村委会主任，遂向扎佐镇党委和镇人大主席团如实反映。镇党委和镇人大主席团经过深入了解，证实村民反映情况属实，镇人大主席团决定指导村民以投票方式，表决这位村官的去留。

投票前，采取民主评议的方式在村民代表会上对杨怀亮的工作进行评议。评议中，村民代表反映最突出的问题是杨怀亮只说不干，只顾自己打工挣钱，把村里的事搁在一边，还将村委会公章交给家人，村民办事需要签字盖章由家人代办。作风不民主，村里的事个人专断独行。为此，村民代表会形成决议，由村民投票罢免杨怀亮村委会主任的职务。

9月4日，有法定选举权的村民集中投票。全村310户1075人，其中有选举权的739人，发出罢免票688张，收回680张。投票结果，590票同意罢免杨怀亮的村委会主任职务。

附：

“我们满意得很”——直击蜈蚣桥村“海选”

贾长远　陈新国

11月30日，是洒坪乡蜈蚣桥村乡亲们值得记住的日子。在第七届村民委员会换届选举中，他们通过“海选”一次投票产生了新的村民委员会，选出了他们满意的带头人。

古驿道上春潮涌

蜈蚣桥村坐落在洒坪乡偏僻的小山沟里，是一个具有民族特色和文化底蕴的地方。尽管已是冬季，暖暖的阳光依然洒在蜈蚣桥村的每个角落，从人们的脸上、从村民们新修的房屋上，无不流淌着春天般的温暖。明代贵州著名的女政治家奢香夫人开辟驿道时，率众在这里修建了蜈蚣桥，因而积淀了集中民力和智慧办大事的实践。传承古人遗风，今天的蜈蚣桥村村民们沐浴中共惠农政策和新农村建设的春风，在村党支部和村委会的带领下，发展蜜李种植、豆腐加工和酿酒业，年均纯收入已超过2500元。这里民风淳朴，700多口人中以苗族为主的少数民族就达30%以上。在第七届村委会换届选举中，蜈蚣桥村被作为全县4个“海选”试点村之一。这一天，所有在家的村民，在上午就赶来参加这一前所未有、盛况空前的庄严典礼。

苗族老人笑开颜

“海选”会场彩旗飘扬，装饰一新的石墙上贴满了贺信和公告。第六号公告写着11月30日是选举投票的日子，新的村委会班子将在这里产生。主席台铺上红地毯，后方幕布上悬挂着醒目的换届选举主题会标。选民们分5个组整整齐齐坐在指定区域，激动和兴奋洋溢在脸上。他们心里装着一把秤，要用来称出竞选人在心里的分量。66岁的苗族老人吴珍秀坐在同伴中间，她穿着一套盛装而引人注目。当村党支部书记岳玉芳宣布全体起立，奏中华人民共和国国歌时，老人神情严肃，站起来一动不动，凝神聆听……耳聪目明的老人乐呵呵地说，她家今天来开会的是祖孙3代7个人，她一大早吃了饭就催促起儿孙们快来开会。看到这么多人，她回忆起自己年轻时参加生产队大会时的情景。平时都是在电视机里听到国歌声，今天她是第一次和这么多人一起听国歌，她的脸上全是幸福的神情。老人直爽地说，报名选主任和委员的人她都认得，自己不会写字，她可以念，让代写人填选票，满意谁就投谁的一票。

选出满意当家人

村委会换届选举是人民群众当家做主、充分表达意愿、参与民主政治生活的大事。

选民们经过认真思考，在选票上写上自己满意的当家人姓名，投上了神圣的一票。选民刘朝军投完票后大声爽朗地谈体会。他说这样的选举他太满意了，国家提倡计划生育，降低人口数量，提高人口素质，群众的生活越过越好，还要免除农民子女的书杂费，免除农业税，让群众得到很多实惠。这样的选举我们满意得很。选好当家人，他有这份责任。付国珍老人今年已经94岁了，她是年龄最大的选民。她家住的地方离会场不远，由于走路不方便，是儿子背她来的，上午11点钟就赶到会场了。在投票的时候，她由工作人员搀扶着，一步一步笑呵呵地走近票箱。

当天下午，选民们一次投票选举产生了村委会班子成员。在热烈的掌声中，村委会主任赵连祥向大家深深地一鞠躬，衷心感谢父老乡亲对他的信任和支持，表示要在村党支部带领下，团结好村委会一班人，加快蜈蚣桥村基础设施建设，搞好产业结构调整，强化村务公开，推进民主管理，实现生产和生活条件明显改善，促进群众致富增收。要认认真真贯彻落实好党在农村的各项方针政策，全心全意为村民搞好服务。

时已傍晚，村民们都舍不得离开。文艺工作者们给乡亲们送上了一台精彩的文艺节目。生动的歌舞、小品充满激情，一曲曲颂歌回荡在小山村的夜空……

（本文录自2007年12月3日《当代修文》）

（三）民主管理

自1998年起，县委、县政府开始探索村民自治民主管理，使村民自我管理、自我服务、自我教育、自我监督的职能得到发挥，村民委员会逐步走上依法履行职责的轨道。至2004年，全县217个村都建立健全《村民自治章程》《村民会议制度》《村民代表会议制度》《村务公开制度》《村规民约》《民主管理和民主决策制度》等相关的村民自治制度。扎佐镇在全镇推行村级议事“两个三分之二”民主决策制度，明确规定凡涉及村内财产转移、合同签订、大额资金使用等事项，必须经村民委员会全体成员、村民小组长、村民代表、全体党员参加的会议决定，如果应参会人员不足2/3，或对所决定事项同意者不足到会人员的2/3，所作的决定视为无效。谷堡乡在全乡推行“事前公示制度”，规定凡涉及村民利益的事项如救灾救济款物发放、扶贫项目落实、茅草房改造分户指标等，事前必须向村民公示，接受村民监督。在制定制度的同时，村委会积极引导村民参与村的事务管理，坚持“村民的事村民管，众人的事大家干”。实行民主管理，办事公开，极大地增强了群众参政的积极性，也使民主监督成为实实在在的事，不再是只写在纸上和挂在嘴上的“空头支票”。2004年，全县在茅草房改造工程中，因为强化民主管理，严格执行《事前公示制度》和《村民代表会议制度》，杜绝了不正之风，没有发生群众不满意的上访，圆满完成此项民心工程，受到贵阳市委、市政府表彰。在推行和实施民主管理过程中，注重发挥村党支部和村治保、调解、青年、妇女等组织的作用，特别强调和明确村党支部在村工作中的领导地位，使村民自治工作始终在村党支部领导下进行。同时，通过村治保、调解、青年、妇女等组织，建立起与群众联系的桥梁，妥善调解民间纠纷，维护社会治安，推动计划生育和殡葬改革等工作的开展。2003年，洒坪乡、六屯乡推行“群防群治一体化治安网络工程”，村民参与社会治安管理，不讲报酬组成巡防队，坚持夜间巡逻，遏制了农村中多发的偷牛盗马案件发生。这种村民参与社会治安管理的做法，被省、市公安部门作为经验推广。至2010年，村民“四自”的自治方式仍在不断完善。

2005年4月16日，谷堡乡平寨村村民代表开会讨论村务

（四）民主决策

全县村委会2002年建起重大事项须经村民大会或村民代表会表决后才予施行的制度。村民代表按5至15户推选1人参与村的重要事项决策。至2010年，全县共有村民代表6251人。2002年，谷堡乡平寨村“两委”经过调研，计划在村里新建集贸市场活跃乡场商贸，增加集体收入，但又担心资金缺口大，实施起来困难多，不敢轻举妄动。村委会把这个打算进行公示，征求村民意见，又通过村民代表深入到群众

中搜集反映，然后召开村民代表会议表决通过村委会的动议，形成决策。开工后，全村家家出力户户上工，原预算要支付30万元的工程，结果只花19万元竣工。贵州省委常委、贵阳市委书记王晓东在平寨调研农业和农村工作时，称赞村里的干部群众是“新时期的愚公”。在实施“改茅”工程中，扎佐镇喻家街村有位村干部在村委会研究分下户去的“改茅”指标时，为自己的女儿家争得一个指标，公示后群众有意见，反映到村民代表那里，在村民代表评议会上，代表们当面锣对面鼓地指出，村里还有比他女儿家更迫切需要“改茅”的农户，这位村干部也意识到自己的做法带有私心，当场就作检讨，还上升到以权谋私的高度来认识，群众也就原谅了他，而真正需要“改茅”的另一户农家得到了这个指标。

（五）民主监督

2002年，县委、县政府出台《乡（镇）政务、村务公开规范化建设实施方案》，制订《民主评议制度》《民主管理、民主监督制度》、《财务报销制度》和与之相关的党风廉政建设、监督检查、考核奖惩等制度，做到有机构有人管理，有章程有规矩有要求办事，以村务公开为重要内容的民主监督收到了良好的效果。全县217个村的村务公开面达100%；岗位职责、工作目标等固定公开事项公开达100%；计划生育、涉农事项收费等热点焦点问题公开达100%；村务公开和村级财务公开达100%。村务公开方式以固定公开栏为主，会议公开、公告公开、明白手册（卡）公开等为辅。2004年，又将远程教育网络作为载体。村务公开的主要内容是政策法规、工作目标、村干职责、办事程序、财务管理、工程建设以及村民关注的热点、难点。3年间，县、乡、村三级共投入资金30万元，制作村务公开栏530个，重点公开群众关注的村内财务、计划生育和农村税费减免。在村务公开的基础上推行村级财务委托核算制度，村里成立民主理财小组，乡（镇）建立村级财务核算代管中心。实行村务公开，使民主监督落到实处。全县农业税减免97.4万元，种粮直补78.2万元，涉及25万群众,未出现一例上访事件。2010年，首钢贵阳新特材料循环经济工业基地落户扎佐，扎佐镇政府和三里、小堡两村村委会将项目涉及的征地、农户搬迁、主通道建设、河道改造等项目全部公诸于众，合理解决好被征地、征房农民的利益问题，拆除626户1560栋8.7万平方米住房仅用26天时间，620余万元征地款仅用4天就发放完毕。拆迁工作实现零上访。

四、城镇社区建设

2003年，按照民政部《关于在全国推进城市社区建设的意见》，县成立社区建设指导委员会，分两个阶段改革街道居民组织，推动社区建设。第一阶段是10月在县城所在地建立社区，将龙场镇原有的7个居民委员会整合，建立龙岗、宾阳、虎山、栖凤4个社区。11月进入第二阶段，将扎佐镇原有的2个居民委员会撤销，组建景阳、襄阳2个社区，在久长镇组建长久社区。11月28日，经贵阳市民政局批准，新组建的7个社区挂牌成立。继后，又增建3个社区，至2010年，全县4个镇和小箐乡所在地的居民委员会经过整合建为10个社区，即龙场镇的龙岗、宾阳、虎山、栖凤社区，扎佐镇的景阳、襄阳、万江社区，久长镇的长久社区，六广镇的松江

2010年，虎山社区居委会招募“三创一办”义务监督员现场

社区，小箐乡的小箐社区。社区居民委员会的成员由本社区居民民主选举产生，负责社区日常事务管理。社区居民委员会的在乡（镇）党政领导下组织街道居民实行自我管理、自我教育、自我服务、自我监督。龙场镇和扎佐镇属的社区居民委员会分别由本社区居民选举7名委员组成，其余社区居委会各为5名委员组成。

2004年，县委办公室、县政府办公室印发《关于进一步加强社区建设的意见》，要求全县社区按照《修文县示范社区标准》开展创建活动。创建活动结合贵阳市开展的“民主法治示范社区”创建活动进行。2005年，又结合贵阳市“十大和谐社区”评选活动深入开展示范社区的创建活动。

通过创建活动，社区“四自”的自治职能不断增强。龙场镇龙岗社区地处县城东北角城郊接合部，置有生猪交易集市，环境长期脏、乱，差。创建活动开始，社区提出“全民参与‘卫生与秩序’整治”的口号，筹集资金8000元将猪市改建成200米的文化长廊。社区对吸毒人员采取“一帮一，一助一”的方式开展帮教，2005年，成功帮助8名吸毒者戒除毒瘾。吸毒人员钟荣健因复吸被劳动教养3年，妻子含恨出走。钟劳教回来后生活无着，社区不仅给他安排街道保洁工作，还帮他介绍对象，使他回头是岸，表示要好好劳动，做个遵纪守法的公民。社区发动群众筹资建起图书室，组建合唱队、腰鼓队、健身队。居民休息时间，或到图书室看书，或参加歌咏、健身活动。扎佐镇景阳和襄阳社区的“低保”人员自动成立夜间巡逻队、街道清扫队和“殡改”宣传队，主动走上街头服务。

2004年，龙岗社区被贵阳市命名为“民主法治示范社区”。2006年，虎山社区获得贵阳市“十大和谐社区”殊荣。2008年，全县社区开展“创建充分就业社区”活动，解决零就业家庭和就业困难者的就业问题，有634人通过政府开发的公益性工作岗位实现就业。2010年，为配合全县开展的“三创一办”（创建国家卫生城市、国家环境保护模范城市、全国文明城市和协办2011年第九届全国少数民族传统体育运动会）工作，社区招募义务监督员1000多人报名参加，这些义务监督员佩戴红袖章活跃在城镇街道上开展“三创一办”监督和宣传工作。

第二节　行政管理体制改革

一、恢复县人民政府

1981年1月，召开县第七届人民代表大会第一次会议，选举产生县人民政府县长、副县长，复建修文县人民政府取代1967年“文化大革命”中建立的县革命委员会，行使政府行政职能。复建县政府后，政府职能得到充分发挥，经济建设和社会发展成果显著。1981—2010年的30年间，全县面貌发生了翻天覆地的变化，复建县政府前的1980年，全县国内生产总值仅4318万元，30年后的2010年上升为46亿元，比1980年增长107倍。

二、建立（镇）人民政府

1978年，延续人民公社体制，公社作为一级“政社合一”的行政机关。1979年，农村实施经济体制改革，针对原有的人民公社极不适应经济发展的问题，县委于1984年出台《关于县、乡（镇）两级人代会换届选举及政社分设建乡工作和选配领导班子的意见》，指导全县公社按《中华人民共和国宪法》规定建立乡（镇）人民政府32个，正式履行政府管理职能。乡（镇）政府发挥服务经济社会建设的作用，大力组织人民群众发展生产，致当年粮食产量刷新历史纪录达到5.9万吨。

三、政企分开

1984年5月7日，县委、县政府出台《关于企业经济体制改革的决定》，明确国营企业在保证完成国家计划任务后可以自主经营，并明确企业可以改革用人制度，不拘一格选拔人才，改政府任命企业领导人为职工代表大会选举。简政放权和松绑让利后，国营企业有了经营自主权。红旗煤厂仅用1年时间扭亏为盈，还清了历年所欠外债17.8万元。

三角山水泥厂

1988年后，随着市场竞争日趋激烈，县内国营企业因无拳头产品缺乏竞争力，负债累累，举步维艰。修文酒厂至1990年，已拖欠县工商银行贷款800余万元和利息200多万元。县酱菜厂靠信贷维持生产，陷入“找点吃点”的困境。针对这一状况，县委、县政府于1992年6月下发《关于加快改革开放和发展步伐的意见》，按照“宏观管住，微观放开”的原则，实行政企分开。政府主要做好对企业的规划、协调、监督、服务，企业则以转换经营机制为重点，落实“五权”（人事劳动权、资金分配权、产品定价权、投资决策权、进出口经营权），积极推行“五自主”（生产经营自主、产品定价自主、内部分配自主、劳动用工自主、技术改造自主）、“四放开”（经营放开、价格放开、用工放开、分配放开），打破“一大三铁”（大锅饭，铁饭碗、铁工资、铁交椅），把企业推向市场。与此同时，抓好股份制试点，对长期亏损、扭亏无望的国营企业关停并转，进行资产重组。1994年11月，修文酒厂因欠国家税款241.2万元无力交纳，县人民法院依法宣布破产。1997年，将已无力发给在职职工工资和退休人员退休费的红旗煤矿转让给个体业主经营。1998年，将县酱菜厂所有资产以95万元整体出售给贵州联宇公司，以有偿转让方式将负债1041.64万元的三角山水泥厂折价1750万元转让给华兴实业公司，转为民营。

第三节　机构改革

1983年12月，遵照中央机构改革精神，县成立机构改革领导小组，进行二级机改，解决机构设置存在的部门过多、职能交叉、权责脱节等突出问题，整合职能，更好地服务经济建设。机改方案明确规定单位的领导职数、年龄和文化结构，减少副职，实现干部革命化，年轻化、知识化、专业化。1984年4月结束时，二级机构由原来的61个减为53个，其中县委部门7个，政府部门28个，按照党章、宪法和有关规定设置的11个，改变性质7个。改革后的机构在原有基础上减少13.1%。

继后，县委、县政府又多次对机构进行调整，压缩事业编制。1992年为精减行政和事业单位职工，以巩固机构改革的成果，县委、县政府出台《关于分流行政机关事业单位人员的决定》，规定除学校、医院和按规定不能经商办企业的单位外，凡属县财政拨款的党政机关、事业单位和群众团体实行60%留任和40%离岗的人员分流。由于对分流人员的安置去向不落实，职工抱着“铁饭碗”不愿离岗，仅有政策允许的少量职工办理提前退休和停薪留职，个别职工与原单位脱钩去领办县属企业或乡镇企业。出于社会稳定的需要，致原计划将40%的职工停发工资分流出单位的决定终未执行。

1995年，按照政企职责分开、职能转变、理顺关系、精兵简政和提高效率的原则，县内再次进行机改，将县委工作机构由原来的12个减为8个，政府工作机构由原来的28个减为26个，事业单位3个，局改为公司1个，其他单位（县供销社）1个，按宪法和有关规定设置的机构7个，群团组织6个。将全县二级机构由1984年的53个减为46个，减少15.2%。然机构改革成果未能巩固。后又因县域经济社会发展加速，行业细分的管理需要，又新建机构或将已合并机构再予拆分，致机构又逐年增多，到2000年，二级机构从1995年的46个复增为66个。

2001年，按照政企、政事分开和“精简、统一、效能”的方针与定职能、定内设机构、定人员编制和领导职数的“三定”原则，又一次进行党政机构改革。此次改革要求机构和人员编制两不增，不再为机关增加新的自定事业编制。县政府采取召开机构改革动员会议，提前印发《机构改革“三定”方案》供单位学习了解“三定”要求，及时在《修文报》和修文电视台刊播工作信息等方式加大宣传力度，营造良好的机改氛围。同时，严格按照省、市编制办公室“三定”原则，认真对单位的“三定”方案进行初审和复审。经报贵阳市政府批准，县内二级机构核定为51个，比原有的66个减少20%。此次机改使机构设置趋向合理，编制人员相对固定，工作职责也较前明确，但职能交叉、机构重叠的问题仍未完全解决。

2010年，县委、县政府针对全县经济社会发展的实际需要和政府的功能特点，采取问卷调查和召开座谈会的方式征求对机改的意见，然后提出《修文县政府机构改革方案》，报经贵阳市委、市政府审查批准，遂于6月启动政府机改，12月结束。此次机改的重点是对县政府的二级机构整合组建，将原卫生局和原食品药品监督管理局整合组成卫生和食品药品监督管理局，将原旅游事业局和原文体广播电视局整合组成旅游文体广播电视局（挂新闻出版局和版权局牌子），将发展和改革局、科学技术局（知识产权局）、物价局、乡镇企业局（煤炭管理局）、粮食局整合组成发展改革经贸局（挂科学技术局、知识产权局牌子），将原移民工作办公室业务和水利局水利水电工程移民业务合并组成水利水电工程移民局，为政府直属事业单位。在整合组建的同时，裁撤卫生局、食品药品监督管理局、旅游事业局、文体广播电视局、发展和改革局、科学技术局（知识产权局）、物价局、乡镇企业局（煤炭管理局）、粮食局、农业办公室（扶贫开发办公室、农业综合开发办公室）、招商局和移民工作办公室等12个机构。裁撤后扶贫开发业务划归农业局，农业综合开发业务划归财政局，招商局业务划归政府办公室。此外，原人事劳动和社会保障局更名为人力资源和社会保障局，原建设局更名为住房和城乡建设局，原交通局更名为交通运输局。同时，调整原为政府直属事业单位的安全生产监督管理局为政府工作部门，原由政府办管理的信访局调给县委办公室管理。

经过机构改革，县政府置工作部门27个，比原机构减少25.1%，其中行政单位23个，即政府办公室、发展改革经贸局、教育局、民族事务局、公安局、监察局（与纪委合署）、民政局、司法局、财政局、人力资源和社会保障局、国土资源局、环境保护局、住房和城乡建设局 、交通运输局、农业局、水利局、旅游文体广播电视局、卫生和食品药品监管局、人口计生局、审计局、林业绿化局、统计局、安全监管局；政府直属事业单位3个，即档案局（档案馆）、地方志办公室（与县委党史研究室合署）、水利水电移民局。其他机构1个即供销合作社联合社。

第四节　司法制度改革

一、检察体制改革

（一）工作机制改革

1978年10月，复建在“文化大革命”中被砸烂的县人民检察院，随即迎来中共十一届三中全会召开，改革开放的重大举措为检察工作注入了生命力，使检察工作机制不断创新，检察机关的工作进一步规范。1982年，建立免予起诉、不予起诉、免予刑事处分和无罪释放4类案件复查制度，分别对4类案件涉及的28人进行复查，未发现有不合法律规定的问题。1986年后健全职务犯罪侦查一体化工作机制，规范介入侦查的范围、方式和程序，首批聘用16名检察通讯员，并相继建立扎佐林场检察室等8个检察室为县人民检察院的派出机构。1988年，制定《自侦案件内部监督程序（试行）》，改变自侦案件侦、捕、诉不分的“一竿子到底”的做法。同时，尝试介入民事案件审判程序。检察长杨中华出庭县人民法院审理六屯乡农民唐子培诉六屯乡政府企业办侵犯其茶场承包权的民事案件，首开检察机关介入法院民事案件审理的先河。1992年，制定“捕后补充侦察意见书”制度和“专人审查、集体讨论、检察长或检察委员会决定”的办案制度。2000年，改变以往逐级审批案件的行政化管理手段，由主办、主诉检察官负责案件的侦查、批捕、起诉并承担相应责任，增强干警责任意识和办案质量意识。2003年，为推进公诉改革步伐，实行主诉检察官办案责任制。2008至2010年，深化检察职能，将预防职务犯罪工作重心前移，与工商局、国土局、国税局、地税局、移动公司修文营业部、中铁七局扎南高速第一合同段项目部、首钢贵阳钢厂等部门建立职务犯罪协调机制，开展行业预防和专业预防。一系列检察工作机制的改革，促进执法方式不断创新，执法行为得以规范，司法公信力进一步提高，群众称赞“修文县人民检察院是公平正义的”，县人民检察院也被评为全省“基层检察院规范化建设先进院”。

（二）监督机制改革

1998年，开展检务公开，全面实行当事人权利、义务告知制度。完善律师会见犯罪嫌疑人，以及在侦查、审查逮捕、审查起诉过程中听取当事人及其委托人意见的制度。1999年起，实行“一岗双责”，检察长与副检察长、副检察长与科室长层层签订《党风廉政建设责任书》，与量化考核相挂钩，并推行《诫勉谈话制》《干警八小时以外管理制》。内部监督实行预警提示制度、纪检部门个案跟踪回访制度；完善检察委员会的改革，进一步改进检委会议事制度。自觉接受人大及其常委会监督，遇有重大事项以及重要工作，主动向党委和人大汇报，不定期邀请人大代表视察、评议检察工作。2003年，加强检察机关的立案监督，检察院与县工商局、国税局、地税局、质监局、药监局、烟草专卖局等20家行政执法机关建立刑事犯罪立案监督联席会议制度、监督联络员制度、信息通报制度和行政执法机关移送案件制度。

2005年建立人民监督员制度，加强检察机关直接受理侦查案件的监督，对检察机关拟作撤销案件、不起诉案件和被逮捕的犯罪嫌疑人不服逮捕决定的职务犯罪案件，由人民监督员进行独立评议，.提出监督意见。2006年5月12日，启动人民监督员工作程序，对一犯罪嫌疑人不服逮捕决定案实行监督。人民监督员通过调阅卷宗、听取案件承办人对案件情况的介绍及作出批捕决定的理由和法律依据后进行评议，作出维持批捕决定的监督意见。2007年—2010年，以维护司法公正、树立法律权威、保障诉讼参与人诉讼权利为出发点，完善诉讼监督范围，增加诉讼监督手段，突出监督重点。其间，2008年向公安机关发出要求提供法庭审判所需证据意见书72份，发出纠正违法通知书10份，纠正该捕而漏捕的8人。2009年专门召开有党代表、人大代表、政协委员、律师和人民监督员参加的刑事审判法律监督专项检查工作座谈会。2010年，在监所检察中突出重点监督，对涉及减刑、管制、假释、剥夺政治权利、暂予监外执行的146人进行全面清理。

（三）干警管理制度改革

1993年前，县人民检察院主要是采取干警退休后由子女顶替、招收以工代干人员、安置复员退伍军人、从外单位调入等方式补充检察干警。1993年，为保证干警素质，补员方式改为考试录用和干部交流，经考试录用人员5名，干部交流1名。1994年，实行招考进人，通过全省统一招考，录用人员7名。2003年起，执行公务员“凡进必考”的规定，先后通过公开招考方式新进人员11名。1998年6月首次实行检察官评定制度。2001年，根据新修改的《中华人民共和国检察官法》设立司法考试制度，对检察官的任命必须通过司法考试。同年，试行中层领导干部竞争上岗制，中层干部全员竞争上岗，至2010年，有14名年纪轻、学历高、富有进取精神的干警走上院属科室领导干部岗位。

二、审判制度改革

（一）庭审公开

1989年起，县人民法院执行《中华人民共和国行政诉讼法》《中华人民共和国民事诉讼法》和《中华人民共和国刑事诉讼法》规定，凡审理刑事、民事和经济纠纷、行政案件，除涉及国家秘密、商业秘密、有伤风化、未成年人犯罪、个人隐私和离婚当事人申请不公开审理的案件外，其余均实行公开审判。凡公开审判的案件，开庭3日前贴出公告，先期公布案由、当事人姓名或名称、开庭时间和地点。但在审理案件过程中，仍有不严格执行法定程序，应该传唤到庭的关键证人不传唤到庭质证，甚至个别案件“先定后审”的现象存在。是年依法应公开审判的案件中，公开开庭审理的刑事案件达95%，民事案件为98%，行政案件100%，经济案件100%。针对少数审判人员对庭审公开作用认识不足的问题，法院于1990年提出以公开审判为重心，实现办案质量、办案效率和社会效果“三统一”，要求在公开审判活动中，着力在调查、质证、辩论上下功夫，并开展庭审观摩评查和评选优秀审判员、书记员活动，不断提高庭审质量和执法水平。

1993年，贯彻落实第十六次全国法院工作会议精神，实施“四公开”（公开调查，公开质证，公开辩论，公开宣判），将整个审判活动置于人民群众监督之下。

1995年，在民事诉讼中推行以“强化庭审功能，实现司法公正”为目标的“一步到庭”“一步到位”的审判方式，强调当事人的举证责任（即“谁主张谁举证”），审理案件直接进入争议的焦点和重点，将审判活动置于群众的参与和监督之下进行，使法律的公正成为看得见、摸得着的事，实现当事人满意和群众满意的社会效果。是年审理何正荣诉何正林房屋纠纷案，该案原告和被告系同胞兄弟，案件的审理不仅关系房产的处理，还关系到一个家庭的和睦。县人民法院受理此案后，在庭审中先公开调查，初步了解原、被告产生纠纷原因，继而引导双方公开质证、辩论，查明该争执房屋系由原、被告共同修建的事实，系双方共有财产，依法作出双方都认可的判决。庭审前，弟弟何正荣一直认为房子是自己修的，哥哥何正林参加修建只是兄弟间帮忙，不该享有房产权，在公开质证时才知道何正林承担了修房时向生产队赊用砖瓦的债务，享有房屋产权是合法的。于是，为房子吵了十几年架的两兄弟重归于好。以庭审公开为核心的公开审判方式至2010年仍在不断完善。

（二）“诉辩式”审判方式

1997年，改“纠问式”审判为“诉辩式”审判。此前，审判人员接受案件后，要携卷调查收集证据，向有关领导汇报，共同分析案情查漏补缺，认为案情基本清楚后先组织当事人调解，久调不成才正式开庭，开庭前还要整理纠问当事人具体问题的提纲，审理时按序纠问。这种“纠问式”审判方式存在对审判工作行政化管理，审判人员无独立性，审而不判，判而不审，职责与权利错位，对裁判错误落实不到承担责任的人，错案追究形同虚设的弊端。由于无正当程序规范的有效约束，审判实践中滥权现象严重，案件审理无法保证公正与效率。实行“诉辩式”审判后，强调案件事实及当事人双方的主张由诉讼双方当庭举证、质证，法官则根据双方证据的证明程序居中裁判，当庭认证，公开宣布裁判理由和结果。实践中，“诉辩式”审判方式得到当事人认可。2002年起，在民事审判中还推行庭前证据交换制度和诉讼风险告知制度，在刑事审判中推行“普通程序简化审”的审判方式。至2010年，“诉辩式”审理方式仍继续采用。

（三）“立审分离”和“审执分离”

1998年，县人民法院开始实行立案与审案分开的“立审分离”制，改变此前民事法庭案件自立自审的做法。是年7月，撤销原有的告申庭，成立立案庭，实行统一立案，排期开庭，统一指派书记员，统一送达诉讼材料。“立审分离”使立案工作规范化，制度化，杜绝了法官自行办案现象发生。是年，法院收案明显增加，达到1178件，比1997年的502件增长1.34倍。

1987年，为解决案件判决后执行难的问题，法院成立执行庭负责执行各审判庭移送的执行案件。但因无严格的审执分离规定，审判庭也办理执行案件。2000年10月，根据最高人民法院“审执分离”的规定，县人民法院成立执行工作局，局下设执行庭，专门负责执行案件的执行工作，使审判和执行分开，各司其职。实行“审执分离”后，解决“执行难”问题成效明显，2010年受理执行案件390件，执结357件，执结率为91.54%。

2008年3月，县人民法院第一法庭在洒坪乡巡回审判点公开审理案件现场

（四）巡回法庭

2001年，县人民法院在谷堡乡成立谷堡巡回法庭，由民一庭的审判员每月定期两次巡回审理民商事案件，以解决离法庭驻地较远的群众打官司难、诉讼成本高的问题。2003年，又分别在六桶乡和久长镇

建立巡回法庭，2005年，在洒坪乡建立巡回法庭。3个巡回法庭均由人民法庭法官定期巡回审理区域内民商事案件。巡回法庭在乡（镇）政府内设办公室，门口挂有“修文县人民法院巡回法庭”衔牌，室内置法台、法椅、法桌等设施，正面墙悬挂国徽。

巡回法庭审理案件适用简易程序，办案周期短，做到就地办案，当庭宣判，当庭送达法律文书。2004年10月，六广法庭用便捷方式，4天审结92件小额借款纠纷案，为诉讼群众节约了诉讼时间。在定点巡回办案基础上，法院又创新“汽车巡回”办案方式，为六广法庭和扎佐法庭购置办案车、速录机等设备，办案车在乡间巡回，车到那里就把案办到那里。这种办案方式被群众称为“我们的汽车法庭”。

（五）监督机制改革

1989年，县人民法院建立告诉申诉审判庭（简称告申庭），负责处理告诉申诉和案件复查工作。1999年撤销告申庭建立审监庭。审监庭的建立，强化了监督职能，有效地解决了群众告状难、申诉难的问题。2000—2005年，审监庭受理申诉复查的民事案件29件，有9件进入再审程序，对其中程序违法的2件和程序、实体均违法的2件均作改判。

1993年，县人民法院出台《错案追究制度》。制度规定对因办“人情案”“关系案”，甚至徇私枉法、营私舞弊和工作失职等造成错案的，根据情节轻重给予警告、记过、降级、撤职等纪律处分，三年内不得晋升职务、职级。构成犯罪的，依法追究刑事责任。《错案追究制度》使法院的内部监督机制日趋完善，至2010年，未有属制度规定内的处罚记录。

1998年11月，在原有的信访工作基础上，县人民法院建立院长接待日制度，规定每周二下午为院长接待日。院长接待日制度的建立，使领导能更直接了解群众反映的问题责成有关庭室及时解决，有效地保护群众的合法利益。

2005年，在各庭室明确一人为信访联络员，建立起信访网络，把信访工作构建成网络化管理。同年，制订《人民陪审员管理办法》，通过公开招聘，择优选任6人为法院人民陪审员。是年，人民陪审员参加审理刑事、民事、行政案件54件，使案件的审判得到有效的社会监督。

从2008年起，推行诉讼当事人监督制，法院制作“审判纪律监督卡”发给当事人，通过当事人的直接监督促进司法公正。2010年，发放审判纪律监督卡3000张。

（六）干警任用制度改革

1984年前，县人民法院干警均通过选调方式进入，1985年开始面向社会招录5人。以后，则采取招录与选调并行的方式进人。2003年起，按照公务员“凡进必考”的原则，始实行公开招考，至2010年，通过省、市、县的公务员统一考试，共招录干警9名。

1981年前，县人民法院院长由县人委或县革委任命，恢复县人民代表大会后，则由人代会选举产生。副院长、审判委员会委员、庭长、副庭长和审判员由院长提请县人大常委会任免，助理审判员、执行员、书记员及其他干部则由院长任免。

1979年起，按《中华人民共和国法官法》规定，法官实行等级制，有3名法官获得四级高级法官证书，37名法官获得一至四级法官证书。

2005年10月起，实行审判长、独任审判员选任制。审判长和独任审判员的任职资格须经过考试、考核等程序，不合格者不再享有对案件的审判权。至2010年，仍实行此选任制。

三、律师制度改革

1980年10月建立县司法局，按照1980年8月实施的《中华人民共和国律师暂行条例》规定，司法局设法律顾问处，开展律师事务。1991年，法律顾问处改为律师事务所，后又更名为“黔文律师事务所”。从1996年5月《中华人民共和国律师法》颁布开始，律师必须具备法定条件并参加国家举行的律师资格考试通过后，方可从事其律师工作。至2010年，全县具备律师资格的专职律师共10人。

1984年，随着县域经济发展，法律服务需求增加，县法律顾问处改“等案上门”为“主动服务”。是年，开展法律顾问服务业务，接受县粮食局驴坊粮库扩建工程、县农机厂、县农具厂等单位聘请，派出律师担任法律顾问。全年，为聘请单位代理诉讼2件，非诉讼调解、仲裁5件，草拟并审查经济合同13件，提供法律咨询21件，收回各种欠款1.2万元。1990年，法律顾问通过诉讼途径为418库光华物资供销公司挽回经济损失10万元，为马家桥联合铁厂调处多年未决的联营纠纷，使铁厂恢复正常生产。1992年，律师事务所派出3名律师，协助县酒厂、县红旗煤厂、县科委、城关粮店等单位，到河北、河南、江苏、福建、湛江和南宁等地清理“三角债”15万元。1984年—2010年共接受104个单位聘请担任法律顾问。此外，律师通过接待群众来访进行法治宣传，解答法律咨询，提供法律帮助，代写法律事务文书等开展法律服务。1981年—2010年，共解答法律咨询9376人次，代写法律事务文书1184份次。

从1998年起，开展法律援助服务，为经济困难或特殊案件的当事人提供减、免费的法律帮助；2001年成立修文县法律援助中心；2002年在县妇联成立法律援助妇女工作站。1998—2010年，共办理法律援助案件74件。

2003年4月，受县人民法院指定，法律援助中心指派律师曹宽义对未成年人刘军盗窃案进行法律援助，县人民法院采纳律师关于被告具有法定和酌定从轻处罚的辩护意见，使被告得以从轻处罚。6月，谷堡乡陈永波之子陈军在谷堡中学上体育课与同学嬉戏受伤，经医院抢救无效死亡。法律援助中心接到法律援助申请后派员调查，查明陈军死亡系教师疏于管理和同学的侵权行为所致。通过出庭参加诉讼，使受援人依法获得学校和侵权人家长的赔偿。

2003年，龙场镇法律服务所被司法部、全国残疾人联合会授予“残疾人维权示范岗”称号；2004年，六广镇法律服务所被省司法厅、省残联授予“残疾人维权示范岗”称号。

专记：法律援助残疾人朱开平

2004年7月22日，残疾人朱开平向法律援助中心申请法律援助打官司。法律援助中心根据《法律援助条例》规定，依法受理其诉遵义县南白镇第一汽车队陈开法交通事故人身伤害赔偿一案的法律援助代理。

该案起因是2007年5月朱开平聘用的驾驶员驾车与贵C23280号大货车发生撞车事故，经济损失达29万元。经交警部门勘察后裁决朱开平的驾驶员负事故主要责任，承担60%的经济损失17.4万元，对方负事故的次要责任，承担经济损失40%计11.6万元。但对方支付1.9万元后就拒不给付余款。于是，援助律师按40%的次要责任起诉对方，要求支付余款9.7万元。法院立案后，援助律师再次向当事人了解情况，发现被告方行车证上的车主只是挂靠单位，非真正的购车人，事故车辆的所有权人还涉及遵义县电杆厂4对夫妻共8人，使案情变得复杂起来。援助律师立即利用法院送达诉讼文书的有限时间，四处搜集证据，终于在法院开庭前找到被告的车辆买卖合同、合伙合同、挂靠合同等有利于诉讼的证据，依法追加8人为被告人。由于代理律师事前证据搜集充分，法院审理后作出支持朱开平诉讼请求的判决。在案件审理过程中，委托的鉴定机构未能及时对申请人的二级伤残护理费用作出鉴定，造成申请人伤残后护理费请求证据不足，未得法院支持。代理律师又寻找相关法律依据，提出参照工伤条例残后护理费计算方式计算的代理意见，得到法院采纳，使朱开平的合法权益得到维护。

第五节　干部人事制度改革

一、干部选拔

从1982年起，按照革命化、年轻化、知识化、专业化的“四化”标准和干部工作科学化、民主化、制度化的要求选用干部。1984年起进行机构改革，提拔了一批中青年干部，使局级干部的年龄比原班子降低5.4岁，具有大专以上文化程度的达到57.1%；乡（镇）级干部的年龄比前降低8岁，文化程度也相应提高。1995年，按照中共中央《党政领导干部选拔任用工作暂行条例》启动干部制度改革，但步伐较缓。1999年推行干部公开选拔制，选拔团县委、监察局、乡企局、建设局、计划与经济贸易局5个单位副职5人。2000年，县委制定《股级干部选拔任用工作暂行办法》，将股级干部管理权限下放给乡（镇），简化对股级干部的任免程序，实现乡（镇）党委管人与管事的有机结合。同年，实行“干部任前公示制”，对拟任干部张榜公示，公示时间为7天或15天，同时公布举报电话，群众对拟任干部的意见可通过书面、电话等方式反映，从而加大群众对选拔干部的监督力度。2002年，中共中央正式公布《党政领导干部选拔任用工作条例》要求选拔任用干部不仅坚持“任人唯贤”和“四化”方针，更要突出德才兼备、群众公认、注重实绩。2004年，在县人民检察院、法院、建设局、文广局、农业局、林业局、工商局、农业办公室和久长镇等单位推行中层干部竞争上岗，58名干部通过竞争走上领导岗位。2005年1月21日，首次推行县委全委会对下一级党委、政府领导班子正职拟任人选和推荐人选表决制，由县委常委会主持，对5名乡（镇）党委书记、6名乡（镇）长共11人进行表决，结果全票通过。2007年，加大贯彻《党政领导干部选拔任用工作条例》力度，提出“领导干部熟悉《条例》，组织人事干部精通《条例》，广大群众了解《条例》”的要求，使干部选拔任用形成民主推荐测评、任前公示、任中监督、离任审计等制度得以实施，使民主推荐测评的方式得以实行，使群众对干部选拔任用的知情权、参与权、选择权和监督权得到保障，使配套的干部监督联席会议制度、经济责任审计制度以及打招呼、函询、诫勉谈话制度落到实处，使对领导干部行使财权和事权的监督得到强化。2008年，在二级班子调

2010年公推竞岗大会现场

整中引入“差额”机制，对所缺正、副科级领导职位按20%或30%的比例提出考察对象，严格实行差额考察，总计提名考察对象110名。同时，实行县委常委会议差额票决拟提拔人选，进一步扩大党内民主，拓宽选人用人的视野，全面推行任前公示、任期试用制度。2010年深化干部人事制度改革，县委成立公开选拔领导干部工作领导小组，下设办公室，专司公开选拔干部的工作。结合政府部门机构改革，采取公推竞岗和公推直选的方式，产生5个部门的党政一把手和龙场镇党委书记；对县委党校、县政务服务中心、县红十字会等部门所缺的副科级领导职位均采取公开选拔的方式进行配备，公选4名副科级领导干部。公选干部经过报名、笔试、面试、体检、组织考察、讨论决定等程序，每个程序进展情况均予公示，待群众无异议后才进行下一程序，通过严格把关，提高了选人用人的公信度。至2010年，共公示干部147人次，对75名干部实行1年试用期。

专记一：首次公开选拔副科（局）级领导干部

1999年6月，县委决定对团县委副书记、县监察局副局长、县卫生局副局长、县乡镇企业局副局长、县计划与经经济贸易局副局长、县建设局副局长6个领导职位进行公开选拔。选拔工作由县委组织部具体实施。组织部发出《关于面向全县公开选拔副科级领导干部的通知》，并制定《公开选拔副科级领导干部简章》，开始公开选拔副科级领导干部。

7月8日至21日，有109人报名应选。经审核符合条件的有75人，其中男性69名，女性6名；少数民族11名；研究生1名，大学本科22名，大专30名，中专11名，高中11名。7月25日，鉴于报考县卫生局副局长职位的人数达不到《通知》规定的开考人数，按应急措施第一条的规定，于7月25日发出公告终止选拔县卫生局副局长职位。8月8日，应选人员在修文中学笔试。之后，公选办公室根据笔试成绩按5：1比例分别划定各选拔职务的分数线，有26名参考人员上线进入面试（县监察局副局长职务第五名并列）。9月18日举行面试。面试采取自我介绍、宣读施政方案、现场抽题回答的方式应试。随后，按3：1比例确定16人进入组织考察（县监察局副局长职务两人并列）。9月底，考察完毕，5名年轻干部通过公开选拔走上领导岗位。王朝惠任监察局副局长、左军任团县委副书记、胡林任计经局副局长、谭永红任乡企局副局长、彭顺进任建设局副局长。

首次公开选拔干部在群众中引起强烈反响，普遍反映：“县委采取这样的方法选出来的领导干部，体现公开、公平、公正的要求，我们信得过。”

专记二：提拔干部首次实行任前公示

2000年8月，县委贯彻中共中央《领导干部选拔任用工作暂行条例》，由组织部对拟提拔任职的11名干部进行任前公示。此次公示的11名对象，有的由副局级干部提拔为局级干部，有的由股级干部提拔为副局级干部。之前，县委常委会通过集体研究决定拟提拔干部名单，然后交由组织部门将拟提拔干部的有关情况，采取张榜公示的方式进行公示。公示榜张贴于县委、县政府办公楼和公示对象所在单位、拟任职单位。公示期为15天。在公示榜上要求干部群众采取口头、书面或电话向组织部反映公示对象的品德、作风、工作、廉政等方面存在的问题，并要求反映情况者使用真实姓名，说明身份、单位和联系地址，反映问题的时间、地点、经过、证人、证据等，不准借公示之机捏造事实诬陷、诽谤他人。

张榜公示的同时，组织部还通过县内媒体《修文报》对领导干部任前公示制的目的意义进行宣传，说明任前公示制是深化干部制度改革的重大举措，是防止用人的不正之风和腐败现象的有效方法。目的是广泛听取干部群众对拟提拔干部存在问题的反映，经调查核实后，再决定拟提拔干部是否正式任命。

首次对提拔拟任新职的干部进行公示，引起群众的极大关注。公示期间，组织部收到对公示对象存在问题的电话反映2个、书面举报1个。对收到的反映，组织部即行安排专人调查核实，其结果是2个电话反映的问题存在，但事实被扩大，不影响干部任职，1个书面举报的问题属实。公示期满后，组织部将公示情况和问题调查核实情况及任用意见向县委常委会作如实报告，县委常委会于9月中旬作出正式任用公示人选的决定时，取消了书面举报问题属实的拟任人选的拟任职务。

二、干部录用

1997年开始试行按岗位需求、编制和录用计划，经上级主管部门批准，面向社会公开招收国家公务员和机关工作者的干部录用制度，但一直在摸索。2004年起，全面实行国家公务员“凡进必考”（即进入公务员队伍都必须通过考试）制度，面向社会公开招考公务员和事业单位人员。实行“凡进必考”制度，要求用人单位招录新成员必须通过笔试、面试、审核合格才能进入，从源头上保证录用人员素质。通过笔试、面试、审核三道关口，使公开、公平、公正选人用人的原则落到实处。是年，通过贵州省人事厅招考和县内自行招考方式，招录36名公务员进入县司法、县直部门和乡（镇）机关工作。此次招录的国家公务员孟捷，原是修文报社事业身份人员，被录用为公务员后，工作积极，作风正派，得到群众认可，两年后被选拔为副科级干部。2008年，试行从优秀村干部中招录乡（镇）公务员制度，县组织人事部门在村（居）支部书记和村（居）委会主任中考录乡（镇）公务员2名。至2010年，“凡进必考”仍是县内国家公务员准入的主渠道。

2004年招考事业单位职工面试现场一角

附：

修文县2004年县、乡机关统一公开招考国家公务员和机关工作者公告

为加强我县机关干部队伍建设，优化公务员队伍结构，增强机关活力，报经省委组织部、省人事厅和市委组织部、市人事厅批准同意，决定在我县县、乡机关公开招考主任科员以下非领导职务国家公务员和机关工作者。为确保这次招考工作的顺利完成，根据《贵州省2004年省、市、县、乡四级机关统一公开招考国家公务员和机关工作者简章》有关规定，现将有关招考事项公告如下：

一、招考人数

本次公招县司法局职位4个，人数4人，扎佐镇政府职位1个，人数1人，久长镇政府职位1个，人数1人，龙场镇政府职位1个，人数1人，谷堡乡政府职位1个，人数1人，小箐乡政府职位1个，人数1人，六广镇政府职位1个，人数1人，洒坪乡政府职位2个，人数2人，大石乡政府职位2个，人数2人，六屯乡政府职位2个，人数2人，六桶乡政府职位2个，人数2人（具体报考职位及资格条件在报名点公示）。

二、报考对象及报考条件

（一）报考对象

1. 贵阳市户口大专以上应届和往届毕业生（不含委培生）；

2. 普通高校本科以上应届毕业生（不含委培生）；

3. 定向到市、区（县、市）的应届毕业生，只能在所定向的市、区（县、市）报考。定向到具体单位的应届毕业生不能报考；

4. 全县各级机关、各类企事业单位职工；

5.2003年西部计划志愿者。

（二）报考条件

1. 拥护中国共产中共领导，热爱社会主义；

2. 遵纪守法，品行端正，具有为人民服务的精神；

3. 具有国家承认的大专以上学历；

4. 五官端正，身体健康，身体条件符合公务员体检标准；

5. 年龄为35周岁以下（1969年1月1日以后出生）；

6. 具备拟报考职位所需的其他资格条件。

三、报名及资格审查

具体报名工作由县招考工作办公室负责，服名时间为2004年5月26日—5月30日，09：00—17：00。报名地点在修文县人事劳动和社会保障局。

考生报名持毕业证、有效身份证或户口簿原件及复印件1份（应届毕业生持就业推荐表原件和复印件1份），在职人员持单位同意报考证明（中、小学教师持县教育局报考的证明），西部计划志愿者同时持贵州省大学生志愿服务西部计划项目管理办公室证明。省外的普通高校应届毕业生可由本人报名，也可由其他人员代为报名。考生报名时交近期同底免冠1寸照片3张。

每位考生只能报考1个职位。

经资格审查合格者，发给准考证。准考证发放时间为2004年7月8日—7月10日，在报名点发放，考生凭本人有效身份证和发票领取准考证。考生必须同时持有效身份证和准考证参加考试，无有效身份证或准考证者不得参加考试。

招考职位人数与报考人数的比例达到1：3方能开考。达不到此比例的，适当调整招考计划。如调整后，仍然达不到此比例的，则取消该职位招考计划。

四、笔试、面试、体检、考核、录用审批按省、市有关规定执行。

咨询电话：2322078

联系人：杨德静　杨云贵

监督电话：2323573

联系人：蔡延武

修文县公开招考国家公务员和机关工作者办公室

二〇〇四年五月二十一日

三、大中专毕业生分配

1978至1988年，沿袭大中专毕业生统一分配的规定。从1989年起，毕业生分配供大于求，县已无力安排大中专毕业生就业，以致出现毕业生“毕业即失业”的问题。1997年后，实行毕业生“双向选择，自主择业”，县不再统一分配毕业生。1998年，县成立人才交流服务中心，接受毕业后暂未落实工作单位和非公有制单位委托的大中专毕业生档案保管。至2010年，人才交流服务中心存管大中专毕业生档案600余份。其间，先后为百余名或落实工作单位或考上研究生的毕业生提供了原学校完整档案，使他们顺利进入工作单位或继续深造的学校。2010年9月起，开展未就业高校毕业生登记工作，对毕业后未就业或就业后又失业的毕业生登记在册，登记的毕业生享受免费求职指导、免费职业技能培训和鉴定、免费职业介绍、小额担保贷款、创业及经营场所租金补贴、失业保险金申领、申请就业困难认定和安置就业帮扶政策，对符合条件的由县劳动保障部门落实帮扶措施。

四、事业单位职称改革

（一）专业技术职称套改

1980年，县成立科技干部技术职称评定委员会，下设工程技术、农业技术、医疗卫生3个评定小组，开展专业技术职称套改工作。至1982年，将1966年年底前毕业从事技术工作的大学毕业生7人套改为助理工程师、4人套改为助理农艺师、1人套改为助理农经师、1人套改为助理畜牧师；将1966年年底前毕业从事技术工作的中专生32人分别套改评定为助理工程师2人、助理农艺师7人、助理畜牧兽医师3人和技术员20人。此外，将从事技术工作转为行政工作的大学毕业的3人套改为助理工程师1人和助理农艺师2人；中专毕业的12人套改为助理工程师1人和技术员11人。对不具备规定学历于1966年底前工资在技术13级以上的5人套改为助理工程师2人、助理农艺师2人和助理畜牧师1人；工资在技术16至14级的5人均套改为技术员。

（二）职称评定

1986年，成立县职称改革领导小组，由科学技术委员会负责技术职称评定工作。次年，组建农业、工程、卫生、财会、中学和小学6个专业初级职务评审委员会，并相应成立32个专业初级职务评议小组，由点到面，对187个企事业单位所属的1600名专业技术人员进行专业技术资格评议。年底，推荐评定高级职务11名（其中3人不占指标）、中级技术职务96名，报相应级别职务评审委员会评审。1988年，共评审任命各级专业技术职务1634人，占科技人员总数的94%。其中，高级职务29人，中级职务353人，助理级职务781人，技术员级职务471人。1989年，对农业、工程、财会等系列的16名科技人员进行评审任命，其中任命高级职务1人，中级2人，初级13人。同时对21个企事业单位499人颁发专业技术职务资格证书，其中高级职务9人，中级89人，初级401人。至1991年，有在岗评定职称科技人员2306人，其中高级职务18人，中级职务356人，初级职务1932人。1992年职称评定工作改由县人事局负责，纳入人事正常运行轨道。

五、事业单位试行聘用制

2004年年初，根据贵州省政府《关于事业单位人事制度改革的实施意见》和省政府办公厅《关于在事业单位试行人员聘用制度的通知》，全县事业单位开始人事制度改革，实行聘用制。聘用对象是政府财政全额和差额预算（核定收支和定额或定项补助）管理的事业单位中与之建立人事关系的专业技术人员、管理人员和工勤人员。10月，在文化和教育系统试点，由事业单位主管部门制定《事业单位人事制度改革工作实施方案》并组织实施。《方案》包括工作原则、改革范围及对象、工作步骤和工作程序、组织领导机构、纪律要求及设置岗位、竞争上岗、签订聘用合同等内容。在实施过程中，首先召开人事制度改革工作培训学习会议，提高认识，然后根据各单位的性质、任务和事业发展的需要，科学合理地设置岗位，明确每个岗位的职责、权利、任职条件等，具体制定岗位设置方案，最后竞聘上岗。聘用人员先从本单位现有人员中选聘，按照“公开、公正、公平”的原则，由应聘人员根据各自的特点选择适合自己的岗位，写出应聘申请，并签订合同。至年底，试点单位文体广电局率先完成人事制度改革试点工作，全局参加人事制度改革的事业单位15家共有职工74名，因任领导职务不参加签合同的21人，落聘8人，缓聘5名，签订合同聘用40名。继后，事业单位实行招聘制工作逐年全面展开。但事业单位的岗位设置管理多年积压问题较多，工作推进缓慢。县人事部门本着“尊重历史，着眼未来，从易到难，稳步推进”的方针，采取措施解决存在问题。2009年4月启动事业单位岗位设置管理工作，建立实名登记制度。按机构名称、编制数、实有人数、批准文号、事业单位法人证书号、社保登记码、组织机构代码、规格（级别）、内设机构、举办单位（主管部门）、经费形式、开办资金、宗旨和业务范围、住址、单位联系人、联系电话和实有人员姓名、身份证号、性别、出生日期、学历、民族、参加工作时间、进入本单位时间、出入编情况、岗位（职务、职称）等逐一登记，建立事业单位机构编制实名制信息管理基础数据库。至2010年，全县242个事业单位中已有87个完成岗位设置工作，并按贵阳市人事部门审核批准的最高职务档次、不同等级结构比例和各级各类岗位职数，实行公开、平等、竞争、择优的原则，开展竞聘上岗、聘用合同签订鉴证、兑现聘用人员相应待遇工作，对落聘人员作妥善安置。至此，以岗位管理为核心的竞争上岗、优胜劣汰、岗变薪变等用人机制逐步形成，全县共向社会公开招聘事业单位工作人员74名。

第二章　中共地方组织

第一节　党员代表大会

县的党员代表大会按党章规定，每5年举行一次，1978年前，全县举行过3次党员代表大会。1982—2010年，又举行过7次党员代表大会。有时，根据需要也召开党员代表会议，主要是选举出席省、市党员代表大会的代表。1988年6月6日，召开党员代表会议会议，选举出席中共贵州省第六次代表大会代表，119名党员代到会表，会议选举黄生忠和田应宜为省第六次党代会代表。1993年9月24日，召开党员代表会议，选举产生出席中共贵州省第七次代表大会代表。1999年6月10日召开党员代表会议，议选举产生陈石、毛铭彝等18名代表（含市里下选3名代表）出席中共贵阳市第七次代表大会。2006年11月3日召开党员代表会议，到会代表111名。会议选举产生袁周、韩力争、赵军、魏明禄、石洪、王成林等20名代表出席中共贵阳市第八次代表大会。

第四次党员代表大会　1982年8月26—30日，在县城召开，应到代表288名，实到286名，代表全县4799名党员。县委书记刘清德代表第三届县委作《加强中共建设，提高中共战斗力，努力把社会主义物质文明和精神文明搞上去》的工作报告。县委纪委书记王正华代表县委纪委作《进一步加强中共纪律工作，为争取党风决定性好转而斗争》的纪委工作报告。大会总结了第三届县委期间的工作，讨论了新的历史时期全县物质文明建设、精神文明建设和进一步加强中共建设的意见，号召全县各级党组织和全体共产党员团结全县人民，在政治上与党中央保持一致，坚定地贯彻中共十一届三中全会以来制定的路线、方针和政策，全力推进社会主义物质文明建设和精神文明建设，为实现全县财政经济状况根本好转、社会风气根本好转和党风根本好转而努力奋斗。大会对两个报告作出相应决议。大会选举22名委员和3名候补委员组成第四届修文县委员会，选举7名委员组成中共修文县委纪律检查委员会。四届一次全委会选举书记1名，副书记3名和常务委员6名组成县委常务委员会。继后，因人事变动进行届中调整，至第五次党代会前，县委常委会组成人员为9名。

第五次党员代表大会　1987年6月27—30日在县城召开。应到会代表280名，实到256名，代表全县5583名党员。县委书记黄生忠代表县委作《深入改革，团结战斗，大力推进修文县社会主义物质文明和精神文明建设》的工作报告，县纪委书记王正华代表县纪委作《修文县纪律检查工作报告》。大会总结了四届县委的工作，提出坚持以经济建设为中心的总任务，把改革放在首位，深入进行经济体制改革，大力发展商品生产，认真贯彻中共中央关于科技和教育体制改革的两个决定，推进社会主义物质文明建设和加强社会主义精神文明建设，全面开创本县社会主义现代化建设新局面。大会号召全县各级党组织带领全体共产党员团结各族人民，以经济建设为中心，坚持四项基本原则，坚持改革、开放、搞活的方针，埋头苦干，为实现经济持续稳定增长和精神文明建设取得新成绩，以及党风和社会风气进一步好转而奋斗。大会对县委工作报告和县纪委工作报告作出相应的决议。大会选举23名委员和4名候补委员组成第五届中共修文县委员会。选举11名委员组成中共修文县纪律检查委员会。五届一次全委会选举书记1名、副书记2名和常务委员8名组成县委常务委员会。后因人事变动，至第六次党代会前，常委会组成人员仅为9名。

1987年6月27日中国共产党修文县第五次代表大会召开

第六次党员代表大会 1990年9月18—20日在县城召开，应到会代表186名，实到177名，代表5748名党员。县委书记黄生忠代表县委作《振奋精神，团结战斗，促进我县政治、经济、社会稳定协调发展》的工作报告。县纪委书记陈海龙代表县纪委作《修文县纪律检查工作报告》。大会总结了第五届县委的工作，肯定各级党组织带领全体党员和全县各族人民认真贯彻党在社会主义初级阶段“一个中心，两个基本点”的路线，以经济建设为中心，坚持四项基本原则，坚持改革开放，使国民经济得以持续发展，党风进一步好转，社会日趋稳定，人民生活不断改善的成绩。同时号召全县各级党组织带领全体党员和各族人民坚定不移地贯彻中共十三届四中全会、五中全会、六中全会精神，以稳定总揽全局，以经济建设为中心，切实加强中共建设，进一步搞好改革开放，为实现全县政治进一步稳定，经济进一步发展而努力奋斗。大会对县委工作报告和县纪委工作报告作出相应的决议。大会选举23名委员和4名候补委员组成第六届修文县委员会。选举13名委员组成中共修文县纪律检查委员会。六届一次全委会选举书记1名、副书记3名、常务委员6名组成县委常务委员会。继后，虽人事几经变动，至第七次党代会前，常委会组成人员仍保持10名。

第七次党员代表大会 1993年4月1—3日在县城召开，应到会代表187名，实到187名，代表全县5878名党员。县委书记朱生亮代表县委作《团结奋斗，开拓进取，加速经济发展，促进社会进步》的工作报告。县纪委书记王克勤代表县纪委作《修文县纪律检查委员会工作报告》。大会总结了第六届县委的工作，一致认为，六届县委期间，县委领导全县党员和各族人民继续贯彻执行中共基本路线，不断深化改革，稳定和完善农村家庭联产承包责任制，工业转换企业经营体制，商业实行所有权和经营权分离，建成一批中外合资和外商投资企业，乡镇企业有了新的发展，交通通信有了新的突破，使修文面貌有所改观。大会号召全县各级党组织带领全体共产党员和全县各族人民紧密团结在以江泽民同志为核心的党中央周围，高举建设有中国特色社会主义的伟大旗帜，沿着中共十四大指引的航向，围绕建立社会主义市场经济体制，加大改革力度，为加速经济发展促进社会进步而奋斗。大会对县委工作报告和县纪委工作报告作出相应的决议。大会选举27名委员和4名候补委员组成第七届修文县委员会。13名委员组成修文县纪律检查委员会。七届一次全委会选举书记1名，副书记2名，常务委员6名组成县委常务委员会。继后，人事虽经变动，至第八次党代会前，常委会组成人员仍保持9名。

第八次党员代表大会 1998年4月8—10日在县城召开，应到会代表184名，实到169名，代表6868名党员。县委书记黄乃铸代表县委作《高举邓小平理论伟大旗帜，全面推进兴修富民的跨世纪宏伟工程》的工作报告。县纪委书记胡晓刚代表县纪委作《中共修文县纪律检查委员会工作报告》。大会总结了第七届县委5年的工作，一致认为，5年间，县委带领全县党员和各族人民贯彻执行中共十四大和十五大的重要决策，认真落实邓小平视察南方谈话精神，牢牢把握“抓住机遇，深化改革，扩大开放，促进发展，保持稳定”的基本方针，正确处理改革、发展和稳定的关系，全面推进物质文明建设和精神文明建设，使全县的社会生产力、整体综合实力和人民生活水平有大幅度的提高。大会号召全县各级党组织带领全体共产党员和各族人民高举邓小平理论的伟大旗帜，紧密地团结在以江泽民同志为核心的党中央周围，继续贯彻中共十五大精神，同心同德，共谋以展，为全面推进兴修富民的跨世纪宏伟工程而努力奋斗。大会对县委工作报告和县纪委工作报告作出相应决议。大会选举27名委员和5名候补委员组成第八届修文县委员会。选举13名委员组成修文县纪律检查委员会。八届一次全委会选举书记1名、副书记3名和常务委员4名组成县委常务委员会。继后，人事几经变动，至第九次党代会前，常委会组成人员为7名。

1998年4月中国共产党修文县第八次代表大会召开

第九次党员代表大会 2003年3月6—8日在县城召开，应到会代表201名，实到198名，代表7284名党员。县委书记魏明禄代表县委作《抢抓机遇谋发展，集中精力建强县，为建设繁荣文明的新修文而努力奋斗》的工作报告。县纪委书记岳建初代表县纪委作《中共修文县纪律检查委员会工作报告》。大会总结了第八届委员会5年的工作，出席大会全体代表一致认为，过去的五年，是奋进的五年，辉煌的五年。五年间，县委带领全县广大党员和各族人民开拓进取，奋力拼搏，使改革开放和各项建设取得巨大成绩，经济实力显著增强，特色产业初具规模，工业强县势头强劲，旅游产业蓬勃兴起，城乡建设强力推进，人民生活明显改善，文明程度进一步提高，民主法治逐步健全，中共建设不断加强。大会提出九届县委的总体思路：突出一个主题（建设经济强县），强化两个基础（夯实基层组织建设和基础设施建设），建设三个文明（物质文明、精神文明、政治文明），实现四大战略（科技兴县、环境立县、农业稳县、工业强县），着力五个突破（特色支柱产业突破、招商引资突破、非公有制经济突破、城乡一体化突破、经济实力突破）。大会号召全县各级党组织带领广大党员团结各族人民，高举邓小平理论伟大旗帜，按照“三个代表”重要思想要求，深入贯彻中共十六大精神，同心同德，奋发图强，为实现全面建设小康社会的目标而努力奋斗。大会对县委工作报告和县纪委工作报告作出相应决议。大

2003年3月中国共产党修文县第九次代表大会召开

会议选举26名委员和5名候补委员组成第九届修文县委员会。选举13名委员组成修文县纪律检查委员会。九届一次全会选举书记1名，副书记4名，常务委员5名组成常务委员会。继后，人事几经变动，到第十次代表大会前，常委会组成人员为11名。

第十次党员代表大会 2006年9月25—27日在县城召开，应到会代表222名，实到218名，代表7700名党员。县委书记魏明禄代表县委作《振奋精神，扎实工作，努力推进全县经济社会全面协调发展》的工作报告，县纪委书记阮晓燕代表县纪委作《中共修文县纪律检查委员会工作报告》。大会总结了第九届委员会的工作，一致认为，九届委员会期间，全县党员和全县人民在县委领导下，高举邓小平理论伟大旗帜，全面贯彻“三个代表”重要思想，团结奋斗，顽强拼搏，促进国民经济快速、健康发展，人民生活水平明显改善，社会主义法治建设和精神文明建设成效显著，中共建设不断加强，为全县全面建设小康社会打下坚实的基础。大会号召，全县党员和各族人民继续高举邓小平理论伟大旗帜，认真实践“三个代表”重要思想，全面贯彻落实科学发展观，与时俱进，开拓进取，狠抓落实，集全县之智，举全县之力，抢抓机遇，加快发展，为推进修文经济社会全面协调发展而努力奋斗。大会对县委工作报告和县纪律工作报告作出相应决议。大会选举39名委员、7名候补委员组成中共修文县第十届委员会，选举21名委员组成修文县纪律检查委员会。十届一次全委会选举书记1名、副书记2名和常务委员9名组成常务委员会。继后，人事几经变动，至2010年12月，常委会组成人员为10人。

2006年9月，选举的中国共产党修文县第十届委员会常务委员

第二节 中共修文县委

1978年沿袭1971年恢复的县委建置，领导全县人民步入改革开放和社会主义现代化建设的新时期。从1982—2010年，县委通过选举共历7届。随着行政区划调整，县委于1996年从原隶属的安顺地委划出归属贵阳市委领导，至2010年，隶属关系未变。

自1978年中共十一届三中全会起，县委励精图治，带领全县人民走改革发展之路，从探索家庭联产承包到实施工业强县战略，历经30余年风风雨雨，使修文发生天翻地覆的变化，各项建设突飞猛进，人民生活显著提高。县委不断加强中共建设，通过开展“‘三讲’教育”“三个代表学习教育”和“保持共产党员先进性教育”等一系列活动，增强党员以群众利益为根本的信念，发挥先锋模范作用。在改革开放和现代化建设实践中，县委执政能力不断提高，成为全县人民奔小康的坚强领导集体。

一、会议

（一）县委全会

县委全委（扩大）会议 1981年8月3—6日在县城召开。会议传达学习中共十一届六中全会精神和省委四届七次全委扩大会议精神，学习《建国以来中共若干历史问题的决议》。

县委四届一次会议 1982年9月30日在县城召开。会议按照《选举办法》，选举产生常委、书记、副书记和纪律检查委员会委员、书记、副书记。

县委四届二次全委（扩大）会议 1982年12月25—29日在县城召开。会议审议通过《关于实现修文县经济建设奋斗目标的方案》，讨论如何开创修文县社会主义建设新局面。

县委（扩大）会议 1983年9月12—16日在县城召开。会议传达贯彻贵州省第五次党代表大会和省委工作会议精神，研究部署修文县农村工作。

县委四届三次全委（扩大）会议 1983年11月26—30日在县城召开。会议传达贯彻中共市二届二中全会和省委扩大会及工作会议精神。

县委全委（扩大）会议 1985年9月11—14日在县城召开。会议传达学习中央整党决定精神和省委、地委关于第二期第二批整党工作的安排。

县委全委（扩大）会议 1985年12月24—27日在县城召开。会议审议通过《中共修文县委关于制定修文县国民经济和社会发展第七个五年计划的建议》（讨论稿）和1987年实现全县党风根本好转的规划。

县委四届七次全委会议 1987年6月23日在县城召开。会议讨论县委在第五次党代会上的工作报告及有关事项。

县委五届一次全委会议 1987年6月29日在县城召开。会议选举产生常委、书记、副书记。

县委五届二次全委会议 1988年2月24—25日在县城召开。会议听取并通过县委《深入贯彻十三大精神，深化改革，稳定经济，为修文县的繁荣昌盛而奋斗》和县政府《统一思想，审时度势，努力完成1988年的经济工作任务》两个报告。

县委五届三次全委（扩大）会议 1988年3月4日在县城召开。会议审议讨论县委书记黄生忠作的报告。

县委五届四次全委（扩大）会议 1988年5月30日在县城召开。会议审定修文县出席中共贵州省第六次代表大会代表候选人名单，决定召开修文县党代会的时间和选举办法，安排部署全县农村的春耕生产。

县委五届五次全委（扩大）会议 1989年3月20日在县城召开，会议审议通过《全面落实十三届三中全会精神、加快改革开放步伐，保证各项任务的胜利完成》的工作报告。

县委五届六次全委（扩大）会议 1989年6月26—27日在县城召开。会议学习十三届四中全会公报、邓小平在接见首都戒严部队军以上干部时的讲话等文件。

县委五届七次全委（扩大）会议 1990年8月1日在县城召开。会议研究召开中共修文县第六次代表大会的有关事项，安排部署下半年的各项工作。

县委六届一次全会 1990年9月20日在县城召开。会议差额选举产生中共修文县第六届委员会常委，等额选举产生县委书记、副书记。

县委六届二次全委（扩大）会议 1991年1月28—29日在县城召开。会议传达贯彻省委五届六次全委扩大会议精神，研究部署县的有关工作。

县委六届全委（扩大）会议 1993年3月23日在县城召开。会议研究召开县七次党代会的相关事宜，讨论修改七次党代会工作报告。

县委七届一次全委会议 1993年4月3日在县城召开。会议选举产生县委常委、书记、副书记。

县委全委（扩大）会议 1994年11月11—12日在县城召开。会议传达贯彻中共十四届四中全会、省委七届三次全委会议和地委扩大会议精神，研究制订加强修文县基层党组织建设的措施，安排部署1994年后50天和1995年各项工作。县委书记罗筑云在会上作题为《认真学习，深入贯彻，全面落实中共十四届四中全会精神，把中共建设提高到一个新的水平》的报告。

县委七届四次会议 1996年3月6—7日在县城召开。会议审议通过《中共修文县委关于制定修文县国民经济和社会发展“九五”计划的建议》（以下简称《建议》）和县委副书记、县长陈开域对《建议》的说明，以及《中共修文县委1996年工作要点》等文件。

县委七届五次会议 1996年12月25—26日在县城召开。会议讨论并通过《中共修文县委关于“九五”期间加强社会主义精神文明建设的实施意见》。

县委七届六次会议 1997年11月13—14日在县城召开。县委书记黄乃铸代表县委常委会作《全面贯彻落实中共十五大精神，全力推进我县改革开放和两个文明建设》的工作报告。

县委七届七次会议 1998年4月3日在县城召开。会议对七届县委任期5年来的工作进行总结并讨论七届县委工作报告。

县委八届一次会议 1998年4月10日在县城召开。大会选举产生八届县委常委、书记、副书记。会议通过中国共产党修文县纪律检查委员会第一次全体会议选举结果报告。

县委八届三次会议 1998年9月10日在县城召开。会上，县委副书记、县长魏明禄传达省第八次党代会精神传达提纲，县委书记黄乃铸就学习贯彻落实省第八次党代会精神和市委六届三次全会精神作大会报告。

1998年4月，中国共产党修文县委员会八届一次全会召开

县委八届四次会议 1998年12月12日在县城召开。会议审议通过《关于进一步加强农业和农村工作的意见》，县委书记黄乃铸作大会报告。

县委八届五次会议 2000年7月27日在县城召开。会议审议通过《县委、县政府关于加强人口与计划生育工作，严格控制人口过快增长的决定》和《县委、县政府关于改善投资环境，扩大招商引资的决定》，增补赵黔、胡昭明为县委委员。县委书记黄乃铸作大会报告。

县委八届六次会议 2000年12月26日在县城召开。会议审议通过《修文县国民经济和社会发展第十个五年计划纲要》，通过关于递补辛勇智、廖莉文为县委委员的决定草案。

县委八届七次全体（扩大）会议 2002年3月1日在县城召开。会议选举魏明禄、胡晓刚、罗永芬、罗品香、王建坤5名党员为出席贵阳市党代会代表。

县委八届八次全体（扩大）会议 2002年12月12日在县城召开。会议提出按照中共十六大总体部署和市委的总体要求，修文县实现小康目标“三步走”的发展战略目标。县委书记黄乃铸作题为《认真贯彻十六大精神，向全面建设小康社会的目标奋勇前进》的工作报告。

县委八届九次全体会议 2003年3月1日在县城召开。会议通过关于召开中国共产党修文县第九次代表大会的决议。讨论中国共产党修文县第八届委员会工作报告（讨论稿）和中共修文县纪律检查委员会工作报告（讨论稿），同意提交县九次党代会审议。

县委九届一次全体会议 2003年3月8日在县城召开。会议选举产生中共修文县第九届委员会常委、书记、副书记。会议通过中共修文县纪律检查委员会第一次全体会议选举结果报告。

县委九届二次全体（扩大）会议 2003年8月7日在县城召开。县委书记魏明禄代表县委常委会向大会作题为《认清形势 强化责任 狠抓落实 确保全年目标任务的完成》的工作报告，县委副书记、县长石洪总结上半年全县经济社会发展情况，对下半年工作作安排。

县委九届三次全体（扩大）会议 2004年1月16—17日在县城召开。县委书记魏明禄代表县委常委会向大会作工作报告，县委副书记、县长石洪总结2003年经济社会发展情况，并对2004年工作进行安排。

县委九届四次全体（扩大）会议 2004年9月3日在县城召开。会议总结十年来修文县实施西部大开发战略的工作，对贯彻落实《中共贵阳市委、贵阳市人民政府关于进一步推进西部大开发战略的实施意见》进行部署，安排部署2004年后4个月的工作，县委书记魏明禄作工作报告。

县委九届五次全体（扩大）会议 2005年1月21日在县城召开。会议听取和讨论《中共修文县委2005年工作要点》，县委书记魏明禄作工作报告，县委副书记、县长石洪总结2004年经济社会发展情况，并安排2005年工作。

县委九届六次全体（扩大）会议 2005年8月10日在县城召开。县委书记魏明禄代表县委常委会作工作报告，县委常委、常务副县长成华强作会议总结。

县委九届七次全体（扩大）会议 2006年1月16日在县城召开。县委书记魏明禄作工作报告，县委副书记、县长石洪通报《修文县国民经济和社会发展第十一个五年规划》编制情况，并安排2006年工作。

县委十届一次全委会 2006年9月27日在县城召开。会议选举产生新一届县委常委会，魏明禄当选第十届县委书记，石洪、王成林当选县委副书记。会议审议通过《中共修文县第十届纪律检查委员会第一次纪委全会选举结果报告》。

县委十届三次全体会议 2006年12月31日在县城召开。会议选举魏明禄等6人作为县出席中共十七大代表候选人初步人选，石洪等9人作为修文县出席中共贵州省第十次代表大会代表候选人初步人选。

县委十届四次全体（扩大）会议 2007年3月6日在县城召开。会议对《中共修文县委2007年工作要点》进行讨论，县委书记魏明禄向大会作《统一思想 真抓实干 推进经济社会又快又好发展》的工作报告，县委副书记、县长石洪就贯彻落实好会议精神和做好2007年的经济工作作部署。

县委十届五次全体（扩大）会议 2008年1月11日在县城召开。会议对2007年全县经济社会发展工作作总结，安排部署2008年经济社会发展工作。县委书记魏明禄向大会作《深化认识 统一思想 推动修文经济社会又好又快发展》的工作报告，县委副书记、县长石洪对贯彻落实好会议精神和做好2008年的经济工作进行部署。

县委十届七次全体（扩大）会议 2009年1月19日在县城召开。县委书记石洪向大会报告工作，县委副书记、县长蒋志伦总结2008年经济社会发展工作，并对2009年全县工作进行安排部署。

县委十届八次全体（扩大）会议 2010年1月30日在县城召开。会议对2009年全县工作作总结，并安排部署2010年全县经济社会发展工作。县委书记石洪向大会作题为《强化执行力 提升竞争力 纵深推进生态经济强县建设》的报告。

2010年1月30日，召开中共修文县委十届八次全体（扩大）会议

（二）县委常委会议

在县委全委会闭会期间，县委常委会行使县委全委会职权，执行党中央及省委、市委的指示和县委全委会的决议，传达贯彻中央、省委、市委的重要文件、重要会议精神，研究决定全县经济社会发展、中共建设等方面的重大问题，研究决定有关干部的推荐、提名、任免、奖惩，对县级领导干部的任免向市委提出意见和建议。研究决定有关单位的重要请示等事项。研究讨论召开全县党员代表大会、党员代表会议事项。研究审定县委年度工作要点、县委重要文件以及县委领导代表县委所作的重要工作报告、讲话，研究决定县人大、县政府、县政协、县人民法院、县人民检察院党组请示的问题。

县委常委会议题原则上由县委常委提出。县委工作部门及议事机构、县政府工作部门、县人大、县政协以及县人武部、县人民法院、县人民检察院及各人民团体等拟提请县委常委会研究的议题，根据县委常委会议规定，由各单位提出书面请示，报县委办公室按程序处理。县委常委会按季度定期（各季度季末县委常委会）听取县政府经济运行及重大项目建设和下步工作情况汇报，乡镇、社区经济社会发展及重点工作和下步工作情况汇报，材料以县政府党组名义报送。

需要提交县委常委会研究讨论的重大问题或重要事项，会前可先由县委书记与有关常委进行酝酿，也可由县委书记委托有关常委进行酝酿。

常委会议原则上每月召开2次，每周星期二为各单位报送议题时间，每次召开常委会议之前未报送议题的，将列入下一次常委会议讨论议题。遇到重要情况可随时召开，必要时可以召开县委常委（扩大）会议。县委常委会议召开的时间、地点、议题一般应在会议召开2天前通知到县委常委和固定列席人员，会后县委常委会议决定的事项及时编发会议纪要。一般每届县委召开常委会50~90次不等。1986年召开常委会23次，1996年召开15次，2010年召开17次。

（三）书记办公会议

书记办公会议由县委书记根据工作情况召集并主持，县委办公室负责。由书记、副书记、纪委书记参加，其他列席人员由书记根据会议内容确定。书记办公会由书记或书记委托副书记主持，可根据工作需要召开。书记办公会不能代替常委会作决定。会议议事范围：研究酝酿干部任免、奖惩事宜和需要提交常委会会议讨论决定的问题等；对常委会会议决定事项的组织实施进行协调；商议日常工作及其他重要事项。书记办公会议是否记录、编印会议纪要，由主持会议的负责人确定。

二、县委工作机构

1978年，县委工作机构共5个，继后，根据工作需要时增时减。1979年增为7个，1981年为11个，1982年为12个，1983年建1撤1，保持12个，1984年增为14个，1986年减为13个，1987年增为14个，1990年增为15个，1992年增为16个，1993年增为17个，1995年减为16个，1996年减为15个，1998年增为16个，2000年增为17个，2001年增为18个，2003年增为19个，2005年建1撤1，保持19个，至2010年，19个机构仍存。

县委办公室 1978年沿袭1976年复建的县委办公室，其主要职责是向全县传达县委的工作部署，联络、协调县属各工作机构执行县委的工作指示和要求，管理县委机关内部事务。至2010年，办公室辖管保密局、机要局，内设秘书科、信息科、政策研究室、督查室、行政科5个职能科室。

组织部 1978年沿袭1976年复建的县委组织部，负责全县党组织的建设和干部管理工作。2010年，组织部辖管远程教育中心，内设办公室、干部科、组织科、干监科、人才科、公务员管理科、信息科7个职能科室。

宣传部 1978年沿袭1976年复建的县委宣传部，负责中共路线、方针、政策的宣传和理论教育工作。至2010年，宣传部辖管文明办、新闻信息中心，内设办公室、理论科、宣传文艺科3个职能科室。

县委党校 1978年沿袭1976年3月恢复的县委党校，负责县内干部的培训和提高学历工作。2010年，党校设有办公室、教育科、行政科3个职能科室。

信访组（信访科、信访办公室、信访局） 1978年7月，建立信访组，负责对人民群众来信来访的接待处理。1980年10月改称信访科。1987年1月改称信访办公室，为县委、县政府信访工作联合机构。2007年改称信访局，属政府机构。2010年6月，明确信访局为县委工作部门。

纪律检查委员会 1979年8月，恢复“文化大革命”时期中断的县委党纪监察机构，建立县委纪律检查委员会，负责维护中共章程和协助县委加强党风建设和反腐败工作。1983年2月，县委纪委升格为中共修文县纪律检查委员会。

农村政策研究室（政策研究室） 1979年2月，建立县委农村政策研究室，职责是围绕中共中心工作开展调查研究，为县委工作决策提供参考建议。1983年3月撤销。1995年复建。1997年更名为县委政策研究室，隶县委办公室。2001年，改为县委办公室职能科室。2010年，政策研究室仍存。

档案馆（档案局） 1979年1月，恢复县档案馆建制，负责统一管理全县文书档案。1981年，建立档案局，局馆合署办公。1984年，机构改革后改为县委办事机构。1986年1月，划属县政府机构。

统一战线工作部 1981年6月建立，负责贯彻执行中共统一战线方针和政策工作。2010年统战部仍存。

党史资料征集研究办公室（党史研究室） 1981年8月，建立县委党史资料征集研究办公室，负责党史资料征集、研究和编写工作。1985年5月，与政府地方志办公室合署办公。2002年12月，改称党史研究室，仍与地方志办公室合署办公。内设综合科和业务科2个职能科室。至2010年，党研室仍存。

保密办公室（保密局） 1981年6月，建立保密办公室，负责贯彻执行党和国家保密工作的方针和政策，指导全县机关和企事业单位的保密工作，会同相关部门查处失密、泄密事件。1990年3月，保密办与政府保密局合署办公。1995年2月，撤销保密办建制，保密业务由县委办公室统管，1996年4月，恢复保密办，但仍归县委办管理。2010年，保密局仍隶县委办公室。

政法委员会　1982年6月建立，负责政法工作方针政策的贯彻执行。2010年，政法委员会辖维稳办、综治办、禁毒办、国安办，内设执法监督科、政工科、综合办公室3个职能科室。

社会治安综合治理办公室　1982年10月，成立社会治安综合治理领导小组办公室，简称综治办，为常设机构，其职责是指导、协调维护社会稳定工作，掌握、分析社会治安形势和综合治理工作进展情况；督促检查落实综合治理各项措施，研究有关方针、政策并提出建议；总结交流综合治理经验，组织综合治理宣传、理论研究工作。至2010年，综治办仍存。

农村工作部　1983年12月，复建县委农村工作部，负责党在农村工作方面的路线、方针和政策的贯彻执行。1984年10月，农工部与县政府农村工作委员会合署办公。1985年3月，党政分开，农工部又单独运作。1995年5月，农工部撤销。

老干部工作局（离退休干部工作局）　1984年1月，建立老干部工作局，负责离职退养干部的学习和生活管理。1995年10月，改称离退休干部工作局，其工作范围扩至副县级以上离退休干部。2010年，离退局仍存。

机构编制委员会办公室　1984年1月建立，负责管理全县行政、事业机构和人员编制。初与人事局合署办公，1995年10月，从人事局析出单列。内设有2001年4月成立的事业登记管理局。2010年，编委办仍存。

机要室（局）　1987年5月，建立县委机要室，负责收发传真电报和管理机要文件。1990年2月，改为机要局。1995年2月，与县委保密办公室和政府保密局合署办公；9月，撤销机要局编制，其业务由县委办公室统管。1996年4月，复建机要局，业务仍归县委办管理。2010年，机要局机构及业务仍隶县委办公室。

关心下一代协会（关心下一代工作委员会）　1990年，建立关心下一代协会于老干部管理局，其职责是依靠和发挥“五老”（老党员、老专家、老教师、老战士、老模范）优势，加强对未成年人的思想道德建设。1996年，改为关心下一代工作委员会隶离退局。2010年，关工委仍存。

台湾工作办公室　1992年4月建立，与县政府台湾事务办公室合署办公，负责对台工作，促进祖国统一大业。1996年2月，撤销台工办。

修文报社（新闻信息中心）　1993年12月建立，时称修文报社，隶县委宣传部，负责采编、出版、发行《修文报》。2005年6月更名新闻信息中心，为宣传部下属事业单位，负责《当代修文》的采编、出版、发行工作。2010年，新闻信息中心仍存。

国家安全工作领导小组办公室　1996年6月建立，隶县委政法委，负责县内国家安全和社会政治稳定工作。2010年国安办仍存。

禁毒办公室　1997年5月建立，与县综治办合署办公，实行两块牌子一套人员，负责县的禁毒工作。2010年，禁毒办仍存。

督查室　1998年6月，建立县委督查室，专司县委目标工作的督促、检查和考核事宜，隶属县委办公室。2001年10月，改为县委办公室职能科室。2010年督查室仍存。

维稳办公室　1999年，建立维护稳定工作领导小组办公室，隶县委政法委，负责指导和协调全县维护社会稳定工作。主要职责是研究分析全县维稳工作形势和社会矛盾情况，提出对策建议，协调处理群体性事件。初时无正式编制，办公室主任由政法委副书记兼任。2001年4月，定为正科级机构。2010

年，维稳办仍存。

国防教育办公室　2000年5月建立，隶县委宣传部，负责组织开展全县国防教育活动。2005年，国防教育办公室撤销。

精神文明建设指导委员会办公室　2003年建立，隶县委宣传部，主要职责是规划和实施全县精神文明创建工作。2010年文明办仍存。

远程教育管理中心　2005年建立，全称为数字信息与远程教育管理中心，隶组织部。职责是组织实施全县远程教育工作。2010年，远教中心仍存。

三、县委直属党委

直属机关党委　1984年6月复建，负责县直机关党建工作。2010年，直属机关党委仍存。

公安局党委　1982年11月，建立临时党委。1989年1月，正式成立公安局党委，负责公安部门党务工作。2010年，公安局党委仍存。

教育局党委　1998年8月建立，负责教育系统党务工作。2010年，教育局党委仍存。

党校党委　1998年11月建立，负责党校党务工作。2010年，党校党委仍存。

经委党委　1985年9月建立，负责经委系统党务工作。1995年9月，因机构变更，经委党委撤销。

计经贸局党委（发展与改革局党委）　1995年9月调整机构，将原计划委员会、经济委员会、工业办公室、商业局、轻工局和物资局整合组建计划与经济贸易局，相应建立计经贸局党委。2001年机构改革，计经贸局更名发展与改革局，党委亦相应更名发展与改革局党委。2010年6月，改革政府机构，不再设发展与改革局，发展与改革局党委工作相应停止。

农业银行党委　1999年5月建立，负责农业银行党务工作。2010年，农业银行党委仍存。

农业局党委　2009年4月建立，负责农业局党务工作。2010年，农业局党委仍存。

发展改革经贸局党委　2010年6月，县政府机构改革，将原发展与改革局、科学技术局（知识产权局）、物价局、乡镇企业局（煤炭管理局）、粮食局整合组建成为发展改革经贸局，相应建立发展改革经贸局党委，负责发展改革经贸局的党务工作。

旅游文体广播电视局党委　2010年6月，县政府机构改革，组建旅游文体广播电视局，相应建立旅游文体广播电视局党委，负责旅游文体广播电视局的党务工作。

四、县委派出机构

党组　1979年12月，为发挥党组织在机关工作中的领导核心作用，县委作出决定，恢复和建立县属机关党组，随即在公安局、法院、检察院设置党组。1981年，设置县政府党组、县人大常委会党组和工业交通系统党组。1983年，设置县政协党组和农业银行党组。1988年，设置烟草局党组和工商银行党组。1994年，设置国家税务局党组。1995年，设置建设银行党组和人民银行党组。1997年，设置工商业联合会党组。1998年，设置地方税务局党组和文化广播电视局党组，撤销工商银行党组和建设银行党组。1999年，设置交通局党组，撤销农业银行党组。2000年，设置工商局党组。至2010年，全县有党组28个。

医药产业园区党工委　2010年4月，设置医药产业园区中共工作委员会，负责园区中共建设与经济社会发展工作。园区党工委设书记1名，副书记5名（4名兼职），委员7名。

五、决策与活动

(一)发展先进生产力

解放思想大讨论 1979年9月，召开全县三级干部会议贯彻贵州省委《关于放宽农业政策的指示》精神，县委在会上提出“解放思想，走出禁区”，并出台《全县试行包产到组联产计酬的意见》发到全县1028个生产队，要求将《意见》与解放思想联系起来讨论。广大干部群众通过讨论，思想异常活跃，农村联产承包责任制得到迅速推行。至1981年，农村全面实行联产承包，生产力得以解放，当年虽遭旱灾、虫灾、雹灾的袭扰，农业总产值仍达到3260万元，比1978年的2111万元增长54.43%。

1992年，邓小平视察南方重要谈话发表后，县委即召开全委扩大会议，传达学习中发〔1992〕2号文件（邓小平视察南方谈话），联系实际又一次开展解放思想大讨论。通过学习讨论，清除了“左”的障碍和对改革开放的若干疑虑，明确“三个有利于”（是否有利于发展社会主义社会的生产力，是否有利于增强社会主义国家的综合国力，是否有利于提高人民的生活水平）作为判断经济发展是社会主义还是资本主义的标准，从而坚定培育市场经济体系的决心，使经济发展的步伐迈得更大更快。以交通通信为龙头，开工建设连接修文、黔西两县的六广河大桥，开通久长、扎佐、城关等地的程控电话，增置谷堡乡农贸市场，引进台商建成年产千吨魔芋精粉的贵州蒟蒻食品有限公司……一系列发展的举措把全县的改革开放和社会主义现代化建设推向新阶段。

1995年，县委从全县经济基础薄弱的实际出发，作出“招商引资，发展经济”的战略决策。为使干部群众统一思想，县委部署在全县开展解放思想大讨论。通过解放思想大讨论，全县干部群众深化对改革的认识，明确在改革开放过程中必然要经历的阵痛，把思想高度统一到县委的工作要求上来。曾引起全县争议的县酒厂破产案，就是全县干部群众通过解放思想大讨论，认识到酒厂破产是市场经济的必然结果，是经济改革中资产重组的需要，因而从最初的不理解到后来普遍赞同政府对酒厂宣布破产的决定，使县人民法院顺利按法律程序审结该案，没有出现因企业破产引发的群体事件。

1998年贵（阳）毕（节）公路开工建设，为抓住这次发展机遇，县委责成修文报社组织召开领导干部座谈会，以《贵毕路开工——修文面临的机遇和挑战》为主题展开讨论。6月26日，县委书记黄乃铸、县政协主席王清义和县乡领导干部42人和县内3位年轻企业家参加座谈。座谈一致认为，要抢抓机遇，攻坚克难，使修文面貌大改观。会后，《修文报》以整版篇幅刊登座谈会综述。

2000年，国家实施西部大开发战略，县委抓住机遇，提出实现修文经济跨越式发展的战略构想。4月，县委部署在全县开展“西部大开发，修文怎么办”的思想大讨论，并提出“解放思想，更新观念，乘势争先，强县升位”的目标，将修文的经济发展排位从贵阳市的挂末移至中等靠前位置，把修文建设成一个经济繁荣、社会进步、人民幸福、山川秀丽的家园。全县干部群众广泛参与，《修文报》设置《西部大开发，修文怎么干》专栏，供大家建言献策。广大党员干部和群众从投资环境、资金筹措、吸引人才诸方面提出了很多很好的意见，都表示要抓住契机，集中精力把经济建设搞上去。

2007年，县委在贯彻贵阳市第八次党代会精神，思考修文大发展的背景下，向全县领导干部特别是副县级以上领导干部发起“修文要发展，我该怎么干”的思想大讨论活动。1月18日和19日，县委召开县级班子联席会议，扩大到乡（镇）和县直部门领导参加，围绕“修文要发展，班子怎么办”“修文要发展，我该怎么干”展开讨论。会后，将副县级以上领导干部的发言集成《思路决定出路》一书出版。

思想大讨论激发了全县人民建设修文的热情，促进了生产力的发展，为修文各项建设事业迅速驶入

快车道打下坚实基础。2008年，经贵州省建强县领导小组考核各项指标后，将修文县纳入全省第三批建设经济强县行列。至2010年，全县地方生产总值创下历史新高，比1978年净增45.6亿元。

产业结构优化 1988年，为加速全县国民经济发展，县委开始探索产业结构调整，先在农业产业结构上寻找突破口。7月，批准乌栗乡下硐、红星等村寨300户农民跨村组织“下硐联户合作农场”，以种植猕猴桃为主发展经果林，引导传统农业走商品经济的道路。嗣后，又引进金秋梨、艳红桃等优良品种入境在宜种的地方种植，使产业结构调整跨进规模生产时期。1998年4月，县第八次党代会明确1998年至2002的工作目标，提出农业产业结构调整要“狠抓特色经济，促进农业产业化”，在5年任务中提出“优化产业结构，创造良好的发展氛围和空间”，使产业结构调整从农业向工业、乡镇企业及商贸服务业等多个经济领域扩展。八次党代会还作出“以旅游为主导，发展壮大第三产业”的产业结构调整战略决策。2000年，县委在实施“西部大开发” 战略中，再次对产业结构调整作出“工业强县”的决策。从1998年第八次党代会到2010年的12年间，产业结构逐步形成三种态式：一是第一产业稳中有升，到2010年，一产增加值为7.91亿元，与提出优化产业结构前的1987年的6327万元相比，增加7.28亿元，年平均增长6064万元；二是第二产业逐步提升，至2010年，二产增加值为17.11亿元，与1987年的3204万元相比，增加16.79亿元，年平均增长1.4亿元；三是第三产业增长迅速，至2010年，第三产业实现增加值51.16亿元，与1987年的3234万元相比，增加50.84亿元，年平均增长4.24亿元。各种产业之间比较，一产比重下降，三产比重上升，二产比重逐渐提高。产业结构渐趋合理，国内生产总值自1988年起，每年按15%的速度递增。

2007年1月18日，“修文要发展，我该怎么干”讨论会现场

专记：种植金秋梨　富了折溪村

谷堡乡折溪村距县城5公里，距贵（阳）毕（节）公路修文入口处8公里，区位优越，交通方便。1998年前，村民从事的多是传统农业，能赚点钱的只有烤烟种植一项，1998年国家限制烤烟种植面积后，村民收入减少到人均不足800元。是年，县委提出“狠抓特色经济，促进农业产业化”的产业结构调整方针，村“两委”（村党支部和村民委员会）结合村的实际调整产业结构，发动群众种植以金秋梨为主的经果林。1999年全村有200户栽种梨树1500亩。到2005年，全村436户家家种梨，规模达到4000亩。是年，全村人均收入达3757元，为1998年的5倍，其中仅金秋梨的人均收入就达1199元。1998年村里开始调整产业结构就种金秋梨的孟炳华，经过10年努力成为种梨大户，2008年，他家

外国友人到全国旅游示范点—谷堡折溪村观赏梨花

种梨收入就有6万元。村民蒋德军家种10亩梨树，卖梨收入达5万元。

乡里利用成片的梨园紧挨梨花湖（原名古隆水库）的地理优势，在县、乡政府的支持下，于2004年尝试举办“梨花节”，打造山水风光与田园风光为一体的乡村旅游。是年3月25日，春意盎然，梨花盛开，贵阳市举办的“百姓生活游首游式”与“梨花节开幕式”同时在梨花湖畔举行。漫山遍野白如堆雪的梨花，梨花湖水波不兴的一泓碧水，加上远近田坝里金黄的油菜花，如诗如画的田园美景，迷醉了前来参加开幕式的万余游客，使“梨花节”一炮打响。继后，村里年年举办“梨花节”，村民利用“梨花节”又办起“农家乐”，集赏花、娱乐、餐饮为一体。当年带头种梨的孟炳华，2005年投资12万元，新建300多平方米楼房专门经营“农家乐”。村民余兴明深有体会地说：“原来只晓得种梨卖能赚钱，现在才懂得只要会打算，梨树花也会赚钱。”2010年，折溪村农民人均纯收入逾5300元，超过全县农民人均纯收入100多元。

非公经济发展 1980年，县委作出“允许多种经济形式并存”的决策，促进乡镇企业和个体工商业迅速发展，当年即有319户申请办理个体工商户证照，乡镇企业出现农工商联营发展的强劲势头，马家桥乡被全省作为“两马经验”（修文马家桥、遵义马家湾）推广。1986年，县委又就发展非公有制经济作出“区、乡、村、联营、个体五个轮子一起转”的决策，使非公经济发展步伐加快，至1990年，全县从事个体经营的工商户达2155户，有乡镇企业4537个，总产值为9258万元。1998年，县委贯彻中共十五大明确的非公有制经济是社会主义经济的组成部分的精神，在4月召开的县第八次党代会上提出“加快乡镇企业、个体、私营经济发展”。2004年，县政府奖励累计纳税达1400多万元的贵州科开医药股份有限公司“奥迪”轿车一辆，并授予该公司“重点纳税企业先进单位”称号。至2010年，个体、私营、股份等非公有制经济已扩展到国民经济的各个行业，实现增加值26.56亿元，使非公经济在全县国民生产总值中的比重达到57.5%，成为县域经济增长的中坚力量。

2004年，县政府奖励给科开医药公司的“奥迪”轿车

“科技兴县”战略 1980年起，县委把科学技术作为发展先进生产力的重要手段，对科技研究、推广、应用和科技队伍建设作出一系列决策，以推进科技事业的发展。是年1月，召开科技人员座谈会，听取意见并号召科技工作者发挥才干，为全县经济和社会建设贡献力量。3月，在三级干部会议上提出“科技兴农”的口号。10月，批准成立修文县科学技术协会、科技干部技术职称评定委员会两个与科技发展和队伍建设密切相关的组织，使科研和科技推广应用逐年呈现良性发展态势。1987年在农村推广生料养猪新技术，有2100户农家饲养生猪1.5万头，出栏3800头，获利114.4万元。1988年，县委提出“尊重科学、尊重人才”的兴县方略，不断壮大科技队伍。1990年，全县有35名科技工作者获得高级技术职称。1996年，县委七届四次全会作出决议，把“科教兴县”和“开放带动”作为经济社会发展的两大战略，1998年增加“可持续发展”为“三大战略”。2000年，县委抓住国家实施西部大开发战略的契机，对发展科学技术推广运用科技再次作出决策，明确提出“2000年创建省级科技先进县”，号召全县“大力普及科

学知识，加大科技推广和投入力度”。由于县委确立“科技兴县”“科技创先”的指导思想和战略决策，促进了全县科技事业发展，使科技成果普及和转换利用率明显提高，2002年科技进步对县域经济增长的贡献率达到36.7%。2003年，县第九次党代会又再一次将“科教兴县”明确为全县经济社会五年发展的“四大战略”（科教兴县、环境立县、农业稳县，工业强县）之一。2006年12月30日，县委召开全县科技大会，再次发出“实施科教兴县战略，推动县域经济发展”的号召，要求运用各种宣传媒体大力普及现代科学知识，加大对科技的财政支持和金融扶持力度。县委有关科技发展的决策在实际工作中产生良好效应，2010年，县政府申报科技项目52项，申请专利20件获授权19件。

“建设经济强县”和决策“工业强县”　2000年，在国家实施“西部大开发”战略大背景下，县委针对县域经济总量小，在贵阳市十区、县（市）中经济发展排名滞后的实际，分析加快发展的有利因素，一是紧靠省会城市，二是交通便利，三是通过1999年“修文精神”和“修文形象”创建，全县人民迸发出加快发展的激情和干劲，于是作出修文“实现跨越式发展”“建设经济强县”的重大战略决策。围绕“建设经济强县”的总决策，根据不同阶段的具体情况，县委又作出过若干具体决策，加速经济发展。这些决策中具有代表性的是2000年提出的“发展一产，主攻二产，突破三产”，2001年提出的“一产稳县，二产强县，三产活县”，2002年提出的“工业强县”。县委不同时期的经济发展理念，高屋建瓴，统揽全县的经济运行，保障县域经济的持续稳定增长。县政府根据县委“发展一产，主攻二产，突破三产”的决策，制订“三点两线一园区”〔“三点”即龙场镇、扎佐镇、久长镇；“两线”即贵（阳）遵（义）公路和贵（阳）毕（节）公路；“一园区”即扎佐医药园区〕经济发展规划和旅游发展规划。由于加快建设步伐，扎佐医药园区和贵遵公路、贵毕公路沿线产业带当年即见雏形，六广河旅游开始接待游客。县政府围绕“一产稳县，二产强县，三产活县”的指导思想，加大产业结构调整力度，致一产稳中有升，实现增加值3.64亿元；二产迅速攀升，实现增加值4.34亿元；三产发展提速，实现增加值2.97亿元，分别比2000年增长4.1%、22.7%、11.9%。县政府以“工业强县”为发展经济的突破口，推动传统产业和新兴产业齐头并进，使传统产业中的优势产业水泥生产规模达到100万吨，15家新兴医药企业落户扎佐医药园区，形成全县经济新的增长点。2007年，全县地方生产总值达29.7亿元，人均1.03万元，财政总收入3.25亿元，城镇居民可支配收入人均1.16万元，农民人均纯收入3535元。经贵州省建设经济强县领导小组考核，达到建设经济强县的指标，从2008年9月起纳入全省第三轮“建设经济强县”行列。跻身经济强县，揭开了修文历史的新篇章，全县人民无不为之震撼，一致认为“是县委解放思想，带领广大干部群众开拓进取的结果”，纷纷表示要继续在县委的领导下，以时不待我的精神，不断推动全县的经济建设、政治建设、文化建设和社会建设永续发展。2009年，县委再次作出“强力推进工业强县”的决策，在十届七次全会上重申“没有工业化就没有经济强县的可能”，并在全省实施“工业化战略”的背景下，确立“以工业化带富农民，以城镇化带动农村，以产业化提升农业”的经济发展目标。在其指导思想下，从2006年到2010年“十一

2009年8月20日首钢贵阳特殊钢有限责任公司“新特材料循环经济工业基地”开工

五”计划的5年间，县政府通过重新编制工业园区规划、城镇建设规划和产业布局规划，采取土地适度向规模集中、农民逐步向城镇集中、产业重点向园区集中的措施，重点发展现代医药食品工业、建材业和装备制造业，促进全县加速走上从传统农业步入新型工业的转型之路。5年间，工业招商引资在全县招商引资中的比例占到95%，共引进投资超过10亿元的工业项目5个。2010年，年产200万吨特种水泥、年产10万吨氢氧化铝、年产5万吨的石油压裂支撑剂、年产2000吨白酒等项目建成并投产。还有2009年引进的首钢贵阳特殊钢新特材料循环经济建设项目，计划总投资138亿元，占地5760亩，2010年9月完成测绘、征地和进场主通道建设并启动安置房建设工程；诺亚精密铸造有限公司投资4.5亿元年产20万套精密铸件项目开工建设；贵州轮胎公司总投资71亿元年产1280万条高性能子午线轮胎异地技改项目、贵州百灵制药、台湾统一食品等一大批优强企业相继落户县内。至2010年，全县生产总值实现46.19亿元，与2000年的9.31亿元比较，10年间增长3.9倍。

（二）社会主义先进文化建设

中共十一届三中全会后，县委在各个发展阶段制订加强精神文明建设、发展先进文化的措施。1982年在全县开展以“讲文明，讲礼貌，讲卫生，讲秩序，讲道德；心灵美，思想美，行为美，语言美”为内容的“五讲四美”文明礼貌月活动。之后，又成立社会主义精神文明建设办公室、文学艺术界联合会、农村文化站、乡镇精神文明活动中心、文工团、军乐团等精神文明建设和文化文艺组织，出台《关于加强精神文明建设的决定》，采取送文化下乡、城乡结合互动等形式，促进全县精神文明建设和文化建设。

群众文化活动和繁荣文艺 1978年，县委宣传部就开展群众文化活动丰富群众文化生活于12月向全县发文，要求各机关和乡镇组织群众性的文艺活动，让群众在欢乐、祥和的气氛中欢度“两节”（元旦节、春节）。是为1976年结束“文化大革命”后，首次以县委宣传部行文传达县委关于开展群众文化活动和繁荣文艺作出的决定。之后，每逢节庆，或以县委宣传部，或以县委办公室和县政府办公室名义向全县提出开展群众文化文艺活动的要求。1980年，中共中央作出加强精神文明建设重大决策后，县委把开展群众文化文艺活动融入精神文明建设之中。1982年，县第四次党代会号召全县“努力把社会主义物质文明和精神文明搞上去”，把开展群众文化文艺活动写进县委的《工作报告》。1987年第五次党代会上，县委在《工作报告》中又一次提出“大力推进社会主义物质文明和精神文明建设”。在县委作出一系列关于加强精神文明建设的决定后，健康文明的群众文化文艺活动在县内蓬勃展开。先是传统的玩花灯形式得以恢复，继后，文化部门又搜集整理创作花灯小调小戏，供群众开展活动采用。1983年，组织县内首次花灯研讨会，对花灯在新时期的发展推广等问题展开讨论。1986年，全县花灯发展到135棚。群众喜爱的龙灯亦得到发展，城关镇群众自发组织的龙灯会就有4个，其中还有1个女子龙灯会。逢年过节，龙灯会的会员舞起彩龙，敲锣打鼓燃放鞭炮在城镇表演，气氛十分活跃。1988年，县委宣传部根据县委推动精神文明建设的要求，牵头在县内

2007年多彩贵州舞蹈大赛修文分会场比赛现场

成立文学、美术、书法、摄影和音乐舞蹈戏剧等5个文学艺术群众团体。1990年，县委批准成立县文学艺术界联合会。1993年复刊《修文报》。1997年，将原县文学协会创办的文学刊物《潮水》更名《栖霞文艺》，由县财政拨款定期出刊。1998年，按中宣部送文化、送卫生、送科技“三下乡”要求，县宣传、文化、文艺部门在开展“送文化下乡”活动的同时，还在县城举办文艺演出和比赛，组织农村群众进城参加文化文艺活动，通过城乡互动，促进全县的文化和文艺走上繁荣的道路。1999年，县委在《工作要点》中提出“在农村全面实施‘一二三四五’（一块黑板、二条标语、三份党报、四次活动、五户十星级文明户）工作计划”“掀起群众文艺活动新高潮”的要求。2000至2001年，结合“三讲”教育和“三个代表”重要思想学习教育活动的开展，县委再一次作出在全县“大力发展社区文化、村镇文化、企业文化、校园文化”和“广泛开展群众性文体活动”的要求。1998—2010年，县宣传文化部门及其他相关部门贯彻落实县委要求，组织“送文化”下乡活动达230次，全县举办的各种演出活动上千场次，举办艺术作品展览25场次，出版《修文县志》（李祖炎主编 公开发行）、《阳明胜境》（县政协主编 公开发行）、《修文史话》（朱五义著 内资）、《王阳明在龙场》（夏之奎主编 内资）、《阳明先生的故事》（陈新国著 内资）、《千古龙冈漫有名》（杨德俊编 内资）、《潮泉集》（朱五义著 内资）、《野山》（陈新国著 公开发行）、《郝承德画集》（郝承德著 内资）、《古驿行吟》（陈新国著 公开发行）、《王学之魂》（文化节组委会与贵阳王阳明研究会合编 公开发行）、《龙场墨韵—修文书画集》（陈新国主编 内资）、《栖霞文荟1998—2005》（陈新国主编 内资）、《王学之旅》（修文县人民政府与贵阳王阳明研究会合编 公开发行）等文化、文艺著作20余种。其他还有广场演出、群众自发举行的乡村和社区文艺活动数以千计。从1998年始办春节群众游演活动是县内群众文化活动和文艺繁荣的集中体现，数千群众有组织地以各种文艺形式在街头进行数小时的游行表演，欢歌狂舞，把节日欢乐、祥和的气氛推向高潮 。

2006年春节游演

专记：大红春联迎新春

为山村群众义务写春联，是文学艺术界书法家们每年春节将临的一项重要活动。进入农历腊月二十，县里书法协会的会员们就忙起来。由县文联筹资金购来文房四宝，几十位书法家按乡（镇）赶场的日子，分别下到乡场上，由乡（镇）政府预先找好场地，生上大火，再到学校借来课桌，书法家们就开始为群众书写春联。说是写，其实是送，啥子都是不要钱的。书法家们根据群众要求的内容，当场挥毫泼墨。赶场的群众见书法家在义务写春联，兴高采烈地把一张张桌子围得水泄不通，这个要写大门对那个要写小门对，这边喊那边叫，乡场显得热闹非凡。不光从县里来的书法家为群众写，本地乡村的书法爱好者也不甘寂寞，大家轮番上阵，一个场天要为群众写4000多副门对。等到大年初一，到村子里走一遭，家家户户门上都贴得有红朗朗的春联，一派喜气洋洋的气氛衬托出今日山村红红火火的生活。

县文联从1990年成立至2010年，一直坚持为群众义务写春联。20年间，有千余人次书法爱好者为群众书写春联20万副。写春联已成为县里每年必不可少的一项群众文化活动。开初，大多是由县文联组织书法家下乡去写，2007年以后，逐渐变成村委会专门请书法家进村去写。这一变化折射出人民群众生活水平的提高，对文化需求愈发强烈。2007—2010年，县文联先后应扎佐镇、久长镇、六屯乡、大石乡等乡镇的40多个村邀请到村里去为群众写春联。继后，县里把写春联作为一项群众文化活动固定下来，每年拨出经费由县文联负责组织。县里的一些单位也与县文联合作出经费出车辆，由文联写好后专程送到村民家中。

文明创建活动和公民道德建设 1982年3月，县委作出决定，在全县开展“文明礼貌月”活动。1983年，又一次部署在全县开展以“五讲四美”“三热爱（热爱祖国、热爱社会主义、热爱中国共产党）”和“三优一学（优美环境、优良秩序、优质服务，学习雷锋）”的文明礼貌月活动，使县城的“脏、乱、差”得以治理，文明礼貌得到市民认同。1987年，在全县开展文明单位和文明村寨评选活动，次年4月，县内有7家单位3个村寨被命名为“文明单位”和“文明村寨”，有2个村寨被命名为“科学普及村寨”和“荒山绿化村寨”。此项活动一直延续，其间，又增加了评选“十星级农户”“文明家庭”内容。1995年，县委制订《关于“九·五”期间加强社会主义精神文明建设的实施意见》，推动先进文化建设进一步发展。

1997年，县委、县政府表彰文明单位

1996年国庆节，县委宣传部开始有计划地在全县开展爱国主义教育活动，组织县直机关、学校、企事业单位干部、学生、工人、政法干警、武警官兵2000人在修文中学操场举行升国旗仪，旨在激发人们的爱国热情。之后，升国旗仪式成为每年元旦、国庆必不可少的重要活动。县精神文明建设委员会先后命名烈士陵园，阳明洞囚禁张学良将军处，体育馆升旗台，革命烈士梁方膏、魏怀远牺牲地德政元庆箐口丫口、六屯乡大木寨红军标语处为爱国主义教育基地。每年清明节，学校师生、机关干部、驻军部队战士前往烈士陵园扫墓凭吊，缅怀先烈。县的相关工作部门贯彻县委《实施意见》，先后举办“党史知识竞赛”“毋忘国耻，振兴中华”“光辉五十年”“走向新世纪”“保护环境，美化修文”等全县性的读书、讲演比赛和征文活动，抒发全县人民爱党爱国爱家乡的情怀。此外，还定期举办中共基本路线教育和邓小平理论学习讲座，18岁成人宣誓仪式等活动，使爱国主义教育落实在干部群众爱岗敬业上，成为修文经济社会发展的助推器。2002年，党中央公布《公民道德建设实施纲要》，县委对加强公民道德建设亦作出相应要求。县委宣传部、县文明委编制《公民文明手册》《公民文明行为图册》在全县发送，在农村组织订立《文明公约》，邀请专家学者到县作专题讲座，县内媒体开展《做合格公民》征文活动，推进公民道德建设。2003年，贯彻省市开展创建文明县的要求，提出在全县开展《创建文明县，做文明市民》活动。继后，又结合不同阶段的要求，践行“卫生与秩序整治”“整脏治乱”，以“三下乡”（文化下乡、科技下乡、卫生下乡）、“四进社区”（科教进社区、文体进社区、法律进社区、卫生进社区）活动为切入点，提升城乡群众的文明素质。2006年，开展“树立社会主义荣辱观”活动。县委中心学习组率先进行学习，继而行文要求各级领导深刻认识树立社会主义荣辱观的必要性、重要性和紧迫性，开展形式多样的学习活动，激发全县干部群众学习和践行中共中央总书记胡锦涛提出的“八荣八耻”荣辱观（即：以热爱祖国为荣，以危害祖国为耻；以服务人民为荣，以背离人民为耻；以崇尚科学为荣，以愚昧无知为耻；以辛勤劳动为荣，以好逸恶劳为耻；以团结互助为荣，以损人利己为耻；以诚实守信为荣，以见利忘义为耻；以遵纪守法为荣，以违法乱纪为耻；以艰苦奋斗为荣，以骄奢淫逸为耻）。县委宣传部举办“树立社会主义荣辱观”讲座和召开座谈会，《当代修文》举办征文活动，县文联组织创作儿歌童谣并在《栖霞》辟专栏刊登，团县委、教育局联合在学校举办朗诵会。通过各种形式的宣传学习，社会主义荣辱观深入人心。2008年初全县遭受严重凝冻灾害，社会主义荣辱观激励全县人民夺取抗灾斗争的全面胜利。2009年和2010年，县委以举办“两节一会”（中国·贵阳避暑季、阳明文化节、贵阳市旅游发展大会）和“三创一办”（创建国家卫生城市、国家环境保护模范城市、全国文明城市和协办2011年第九届全国少数民族传统体育运动会）为契机，开展“四个模范”（学习宣传模范、树立文明形象模范、保护环境模范、履职尽责模范）活动，促进全县人民文明素质得以更大提升。

2009年，修文县第八个公民道德宣传月活动现场

修文精神和修文形象 1999年5月，县委决定对修文形象和修文精神作出定位，将其内容以简洁、明了、铿锵、易记的语言进行归纳，以凝聚全县党员和干部群众的智慧和力量，推进经济发展和社会进步。指定县委副书记王真霖、县委办公室副主任汪浩、县委宣传部副部长刘元珍、修文报主编陈新国、县人大常委会办公室主任宋阳、县政协办公室主任宋文龙、地税局局长熊永忠、国土资源局局长雷华熙等8人组成临时工作机构，负责搜集广大群众对修文精神和修文形象定位和内容的意见。从5月下旬至6月上旬，临时机构共搜集整理30条来自社会各界的意见和建议报送县委。县委于6月下旬作出《关于明确修文精神和修文形象内容的决定》，明确修文精神为“团结务实，乘势争先”，修文形象为“言行一致，开明开放”。县委的《决定》作出后，宣传文化部门在县内外展开宣传，要求全县党员和干部身体力行，努力实践。修文精神和修文形象的定位增强了全县人民兴修富民的责任感、光荣感和使命感，成为鼓舞、激励全县人民热爱修文，建设修文的精神动力，也成为引进外商落户修文兴办企业的感召力。

《修文之歌》传唱 1998年3月，县第八次党代会发出“调动全县党员、干部和广大人民群众的积极性、创造性，进一步解放思想，抢抓机遇，振奋精神，奋发图强，全面推进兴修富民的宏伟工程，以崭新的面貌跨入21世纪”的号召。八届县委贯彻党代会精神，于1999年年初责成宣传、文化部门以凝集民心、调动人民群众的积极性和创造性为兴修富民而努力奋斗为目的，创作一首反映修文历史与现状、展示未来发展前景、讴歌全县人民顽强拼搏、勇往直前、争创一流风貌的县歌。是年3月，县委宣传部和县文明委在《修文报》上刊登征集县歌歌词的通知，至4月，征集到县歌歌词32首，谱曲8首。县委宣传部和县文明委于4月14日成立县歌创作小组。4月下旬，创作小组在广泛征集的基础上，以陈新国创作的《修文人民奔向明天》歌词为基础，进行修改和再创作，县委书记黄乃铸、县长魏明禄亲自修改并审定歌词后，由王真霖执笔，钟毓毅、王扬惠参与谱曲，集体创作完成《修文人民奔向明天》的县歌初稿在《修文报》上发表，县委宣传部行文将其作为全县“五月的风”歌咏比赛必唱歌曲，以便更广泛地征求意见修改定稿。在歌咏大赛上，来自乡镇、机关、群众团体的34支参赛队1000余人演唱了这首歌，在群众中激起强烈反响。之后，主创人员又深入基层采风征求意见，县委领导召集文艺界人士对歌词和曲子进行反复修改，正式定名为《修文之歌》。继后，又约请省、市词曲作家审听、修改定稿，并由贵阳市歌舞剧院乐团、合唱团作伴奏合唱录音。

1999年7月14日，县人大十二届常委会第十二次会议作出《关于在全县广泛传唱〈修文之歌〉的决定》。7月18日，在《修文人民奔向明天》的群众文艺调演晚会上，县文工团合唱队演唱了《修文之歌》，那气势磅礴，催人奋进的歌声，引起全场观众的共鸣，赢得热烈的掌声。之后，县委再次作出决定，将《修文之歌》印制在职工上岗证的背面，同时制作成镜框挂于各单位办公室。《修文之歌》唱响在全县城镇乡村，鼓舞全县人民为建设修文美好的明天而奋斗。

附：

孙儿教我唱《修文之歌》

徐克伦

我十岁的孙儿，是实验小学五年级的学生。在一个周末的下午，她做完作业后对我说："爷爷，我教你唱《修文之歌》。"当时我尚未反应过来，有点丈二金刚摸不着头脑，后经她用粉笔将原文抄写在地板上，我才明白，原来小孙儿是要教我唱那首鼓舞和激励修文人民用自己的智慧和勤劳的双手去创造美好明天的《修文之歌》。

其实，我知道这支歌，也唱过这支歌，大概是由于年龄的关系吧，总觉得唱不好，正是这样，隔一段时间不唱便忘了。可我从心底里喜欢这首歌。一来为了鼓励孙儿主动担任教我唱歌"老师"的积极性，二来因为好久没有唱这支歌了，经孙儿提醒，我倒也想放开这久闭的"歌喉"，于是孙儿唱一句我跟着唱一句。她那稚嫩的、银铃般的歌声十分动听，唱出了21世纪修文人民海阔天高任驰骋的决心、信心和气魄。使我骤然感到，祖国更有希望，我们修文的明天更有希望。这以后，我每天都要唱唱这支歌，有时还要唱上几遍，连平时不爱听我这"老鸭子"声音的老伴，也常受到我感染，随声附和地唱起来。

我觉得《修文之歌》是一首百唱不厌，百听不烦的歌。这不仅仅因为它具有豪迈、坚定有力的进行曲旋律，而且，作为老年人，特别是作为修文的老年人，我深感创造修文未来的辉煌，不仅是修文青年一代的事，我们也应在有生之年，努力学习，和全县人民一道，高举伟大旗帜，为修文的田野山川耕耘，老有所学，老有所为，以实际行动树立修文形象，和全县人民一道奔向美好的明天。

（录自2000年1月10日《修文报》）

（三）民生关注

致力解决"三农"问题　1979年9月起，县委结合修文是农业县，农村人口占全县人口80%以上的实际情况，致力解决"三农"（农业、农村、农民）问题，实施土地承包责任制，发展生产力，使农村群众生活逐年向好；1988年，针对农村经济发展步伐迟缓，县委作出一系列决策，领导和引导农民群众进行产业结构调整，加速农村经济发展。但因为经济总量小，基础薄弱，农村仍然存在"农民苦、农村穷、农业危险"的"三农"问题。2000年后，县委把解决"三农"问题放在全县工作的首位，作出一系列解

决问题的决策。2001年，在《工作要点》中提出“稳定农业基础”“千方百计增加农民收入”。是年，为农村群众6840人解决饮水困难，为300户实行计划生育的贫困户改造危房或修建新房，为808户农民修起沼气池。在全县开展的“三个代表”重要思想学教活动中，县委号召全县机关党员、干部，为农民群众办实事办好事474件，使6.2万村民从这些实事和好事中得到实惠。2003年1月，党中央召开农村工作会议就解决好“三农”问题作出重要部署后，县委把解决好修文“三农”问题列入重大议事日程，在2003年的《工作要点》中提出“扎实抓好农村工作，确保农业增效，农民增收”，在向全县人民承诺办的10件实事中，致力解决“三农”问题的就有5件，内容涉及水利建设、治理水土流失、农民群众饮水、坡改梯、退耕还林、乡村公路建设、茅草房改造、改厕、改圈、修建沼气池、建设村寨广播电视网络等。2004年，县委在《工作要点》中再次强调要“认真解决农业、农村和农民问题”，并在工作实际中强化服务“三农”的意识，把“增加农民收入”列为“三农”工作的重中之重，采取突出结构调整主线，加大投入力度，引导农民进行规模化生产、专业化加工、品牌化开发、产业化经营措施，壮大农村特色优势产业，发展区域特色经济，从而提高农业综合经济效益。在实施过程中，以深化体制改革为基础，责成县政府及其相关部门完成粮食流通、农村水价和水利产权制度、农村信用社、农村税费、林业管理体制等多项改革。2003—2010年，通过实施农业产业结构调整、减免农业税费、为群众办实事、种粮直补、茅草房改造、清理兑现农民工工资等措施，在农村开展“双带”致富（党员干部带头致富和带领群众致富）、“双千”帮扶（一千名干部帮扶一千个村）等一系列活动，使农村的经济得以发展，农业的基础地位得以巩固，农民的生产生活条件得以改善。2010年全县农林牧渔总产值达13.14亿元，农民人均纯收入为5152元，分别比1978年的2111万元和141元增长61.2倍和35.5倍。

2007年2月1日，大石乡竹坪村老鸹河村民组集体搬迁至政府帮建的新村，县农办、民宗局等单位为搬迁村民送去柴米油盐，祝贺他们乔迁新居

城镇困难群体关注扶持 改革开放后，由于市场经济冲击和工商企业改制，使国营和集体企业一批职工下岗待业。城镇一些群众因收入微薄、因残因病或意外事故发生，造成生活困难。下岗职工和低收入群众形成城镇的困难群体。县委从1998年起，把解决城镇困难群体生活问题提上重要议事日程，并采取一系列措施，对其进行妥善的安排、安置和救济。1998年2月，县委在县、乡、村三级干部会议上明确提出要“采取多种措施妥善解决下岗职工的安置、分流问题”；1999年1月召开全县工作会议再次要求各级部门要“关心群众生活”，要“紧紧围绕与群众生活息息相关的突出问题，为群众办好事办实事”；2000年，在县委《工作要点》中特别提出“要着力解决特殊困难群众的生活生产问题，加大扶贫解困力度”；2002年，在全县工作会议上更具体地提出解决城镇困难群体生活的措施，要求相关部门“进一步加大社会保障体系建设，扩大城乡低保面，力争6000人纳入低保”。县政府落实县委一系列关于解决城镇困难群体生活生产的指示和要求，实施再就业工程和低保工程，2010年,城镇新增就业1858人，纳入低保3456人。县直各部门、各单位按照县委要求，开展捐赠、送温暖等活动，使城镇生活困难群体得到社会的关爱，使最低的生活保障得以落实。

提高人民生活水平 1998年，县第八次党代会向全县人民承诺以“富民富县为目标”，到2002年“全县人民生活水平基本达到小康”。2001年党中央提出“三个代表”（中国共产党始终代表中国先进生产力的发展要求、代表中国先进文化的前进方向、代表中国最广大人民的根本利益）重要思想后，县委把发展经济和提高人民生活水平作为执政的重中之重。在制定“十五”计划的发展目标任务时，把国内生产总值确定为年均增长15%，把城镇居民人均可支配收入确定为年均增长14%，把农民人均纯收入确定为年均增长6%。从推进经济结构战略性调整、实施可持续性发展战略、加大基础设施建设力度、着力科技创新、扩大招商引资、大力发展教育等诸多方面确保经济社会发展目标的实现，以达到提高人民生活水平的目的。从1998年至2002年的5年间，随着县域经济不断增长，全县人民的生活水平亦随之提高。此间，县里完成退耕还林2.5万亩，治理水土流失156平方公里，建设小康村43个。农民人均纯收入增加到2028元，年均增长4.7%，城镇居民可支配收入达到5900元，年均增长6.57%。2003年，县第九次党代会把“实现小康”作为发展目标。到2010年，农民人均收入已达到5152元，城镇居民可支配收入达到1.58万元。通过实施小城镇建设、安居工程、农村茅草房改造、农村电网改造、电视“村村通”、移动电话“村村通”、修建村组公路、“三下乡”等系统工程来实现全县人民物质文化生活的改善。农村茅草房改造工程从2001年实施到2004年全面完成，使1.16万户居住在低矮潮湿茅草房的农户搬进砖混结构、明亮宽敞的新居，他们喜上心头，在新房门上张贴“居新屋着新装饮美酒老少同乐，小大事成大业瞻前程锦上添花”“三个代表送春风，改茅工程暖万户”“富民政策暖万家，落实改茅我受益”的大红对联表达喜悦之情。

（四）扶贫开发

1978年，全县农村没有完全解决温饱问题的贫困人口约占农村总人口数的40%。贫困人口大多出现在鳏、寡、孤、独、病和家底薄缺劳力的农户，频发的自然灾害也是导致贫困和返贫的原因。是时，县委和县革委（县政府）视贫困人口为弱势群体，明确生产队每年从决算分配中提取的“公益金”给予照顾，还通过无偿发放粮食、衣物、棉被和救济金予以救助；实行家庭联产承包责任制后，又通过农户每年向集体上交的提成中落实对特困户的生活安排。但杯水车薪，每年从民政部门发放包括实物折款在内的救济金也不过40万元左右。这种被人们称为“输血式”的扶贫方法也仅能维持极贫人口的生存，对于数以万计的贫困人口来说，简直无补于事。

1982年，根据国家年农民人均纯收入175元的贫困线（即绝对贫困线或温饱线）标准划分，全县尚有农村绝对贫困人口7.42万人，占农业总人口的36%。面临艰巨的扶贫任务，县委确立“扶贫先扶志”的指导思想，一改以往纯粹使用发放救济金扶贫的办法，教育群众劳动致富；采取以点带面的方法，总结点的经验推广到面上去。中寨公社地处边远，多山缺水，土地贫瘠，耕作粗放，粮食低产。全公社农业人口中，贫困面较大。县委和公社党委以中寨为点，组织工作组蹲点帮扶，一方面指导精耕细作，提高粮食产量，并帮助发展养鸡、养猪等家庭副业；一方面组织富余劳力到乡镇企业中去打工。经过两年努力，有过半的贫困人口初步摆脱贫困，越过年人均175元的绝对贫困线，其中还有18户修起新房，改善了居住条件。县委总结中寨经验，行文全县号召区、社（镇）学习推广。

1984年，县委遵照贵州省委和安顺地委“让贫困户尽快脱贫和尽快致富”的指示，改以往单一的救济扶贫为发展生产扶贫，从救济款和救灾款中抽出部分资金扶持有劳力和技术但缺乏资金投入的贫困户发展生产。一是选准对象，对有科学知识、有劳动技能、有劳动能力的贫困户优先扶持；二是选准项目，对投资小、见效快、效益好、周期短、能“吹糠见米”的项目先支持；三是采取有偿与无偿结合的方法安排资金，对有偿还能力者以无息有偿的方式签订合同，二至三年还本，到期收回留在所在区、社（镇）作为扶贫资金滚动使用。采用以上方法，当年签订贫困户勤劳致富扶贫合同220份，扶持对象270户，需要的项目资金48.03万元，由民政部门借助13.5万元（其中2.34万元为无偿扶持），借贷18.99万元，自筹15.54万元。至1985年，全县共扶持依靠劳动致富的贫困户1791户，扶持资金29.5万元，除民政部门的借助外，尚有县科委、税务局和烟草公司无偿投入6.0万元帮助贫困户发展种植、养殖和小型企业，其中种植烤烟的贫困户当年人均增收109.5元。发展生产使贫困户很快脱贫，全县贫困人口从1982年的7.42万人降为3.84万人，贫困发生率为18.33%。

1985年农业遭到严重旱灾，导致粮食和经济作物大面积的减产和减收，使原经过帮扶基本摆脱贫困的一部分农户返贫，贫困人口猛增为6.7万人，贫困发生率反弹至31.67%。针对因灾增贫的严峻形势，县委、县政府责成民政部门按照“三保一优先”（保重灾区的“五保”户、孤儿和残疾人，保缺乏生产自救能力、借贷无门的极贫户、保来年春耕大忙季节缺粮、缺款影响耕种的困难户，在同等条件下对烈属、军属和复员退伍军人中的残疾人优先）的原则发放救济款（含救济粮折款）44万元帮助贫困户、重灾户安排生活，恢复生产。

1986年，县委、县政府进一步明确扶贫的指导思想，将工作重点放在增加贫困户自身的“造血”功能上，在解决温饱的同时着力抓劳动致富。一举投入5.9万元购买洋芋种11万公斤和玉米良种1万公斤无偿发放给边远地区和受灾区的3911户贫困户栽种，收获洋芋63.2万公斤和玉米81.7万公斤，户均增收410公斤和344.7公斤，不仅解决了缺粮问题，还有余粮出售。此外，县政府如实向安顺行署报告灾情，行署批准减免农业税（公粮）221.3万公斤，折款71.72万元，使全县4.13万户农户获减免，其中贫困户减免全覆盖。与此同时，行署又下拨自然灾害救济款50万元和寒衣救济款2万元，还发放无息贷款5万元支持贫困户购买种子、肥料进行秋耕秋种。双管齐下，立竿见影，当年贫困人口又回降至3.73万人，贫困发生率为17.5%，1987年又降为3.51万人，贫困发生率为16.25%。

1988年，县委、县政府总结前阶段的扶贫工作，认为1984年改变单靠救济扶贫的方法是正确的，应认准方向，坚持走保生存与求发展相结合和治标与治本相结合之路，实行开发式扶贫，进一步增强“救济有限，生产无穷”的理念，开始建立农村救灾扶贫互助储金会，依靠农民自身的力量互帮互借，扶贫救灾，治穷奔富。至1990年，以行政村为单位建成储金会73个，入会9977户4.69万人，拥有周转资金23.48万元，其中农户集资14.4万元，单位赞助0.98万元，民政部门资助8.1万元。继后，储金会发展为149个，入会2.01万户9.4万人，集资71.5万元，其中民政部门资助30.5万元。后又增为159个，入会2.15万户10.11万人，储金总额78.81万元，其中会员入股30.57万元，社会捐赠2.2万元，民政部门扶持46.04万元。储金会的资金用在本村内无息借贷，多是春借秋还，帮助贫困户安排生活和发展生产。县民政局在建立扶贫互助储金会中除资助大量资金外，又牵头创办起修文县扶退残双扶公司和扶退残磷肥厂，安排了17名复员退伍军人和残疾人就业，还将厂里生产的磷肥支持厂地农民发展生产，

贵阳市南明区向修文县茅改工程捐款

帮助脱贫。因扶贫事迹突出受到安顺地区行署肯定，并出席地区扶贫表彰大会。

1990年，县委、县政府专就扶贫工作召开全县三级干部会议，传达贯彻贵州省委、省政府《关于进一步搞好扶贫开发工作的决定》，要求认真落实扶贫致富规划。会后，全县5个区辖的19个乡（镇）79个行政村在国家以工代赈项目资金的扶持下，组织贫困户启动5年内建成5万亩坡土改梯土、梯田的大型项目，使农业生产条件得以较大的改善。同时，加大农村经济体制改革力度，贫困户的劳动力，有的在责任地里精耕细作，有的从事养殖业，有的经营商业，有的上工矿企业打工。通过各自努力，到1993年全县农村贫困人口减至2.41万人，贫困发生率降至10.12%。

1994年，县委、县政府遵照国务院颁布的《国家八七扶贫攻坚计划》，集中人力、物力和财力，用7年左右时间基本解决全县农村贫困人口的温饱问题。在具体措施上，与33个县直工作部门签订《帮村扶贫目标责任书》，对口最贫困的33个行政村，派员驻村帮扶，具体组织所在村扶贫开发项目的实施，要求帮村不脱贫，部门不脱钩。扶贫资金从以工代赈项目的实施和扶贫贷款进行安排。措施有力，效果明显，全县贫困人口减为1.81万人，贫困发生率降至7.5%。

1997年，县委、县政府将扶贫工作列入当年为群众办的15件实事之一，组织10个工作队，派出88名队员分赴10个乡（镇），并明确28名副县级以上干部各包1个贫困村，又明确205名副局级和局级干部各包1户贫困户。要求全体扶贫干部真抓实干2年，队员一年一轮换，换人不换点。并投入扶贫资金419.2万元资助贫困村发展生产。经过两年扎实工作，按照1998年农民人均纯收入635元的标准线划定农村绝对贫困人口，仅有1.7万人，贫困发生率为6.64%。

1999年，贵州省委、省政府决定从是年起安排一定数量的资金给修文扶贫，当年即拨付73万元，2000年又拨付81万元，加上县财政安排的支援不发达地区资金都作为扶贫经费专项支出，用于扶贫攻坚，发展生产。资金到位，使用恰当，又予生效，全县贫困人口降至1.49万人，贫困发生率为5.68%。

2001年，县委、县政府贯彻落实国务院新颁的《中国农村扶贫开发纲要（2001—2010）》，提出新的要求：集中人力、财力和物力扶贫攻坚，尽快解决少数贫困人口的温饱问题，加强贫困乡村的基础设施建设，改变贫困地区经济、社会、文化的落后状况，为达到小康水平创造条件。从此，全县的扶贫开发进入了工作力度大、资金投入多、成效最显著的新阶段。县委、县政府以扶贫开发统揽全局，调整以县长亲自挂帅担任组长的扶贫开发领导小组，充实扶贫开发的办事机构，乡（镇）明确1名副乡（镇）长专抓扶贫开发，县直部门结合各自的职责将扶贫工作列为本部门的重要任务尽力做好，并从县直机关和乡（镇）抽出194名精壮的干部加上贵阳市委安排从市直部门和南明区、白云区、小河区抽调的干部分3批下到10乡（镇）105个贫困村实施“135”帮扶工程（组织1000人的帮扶工作队，进驻一市三县的300个经济发展滞后村，每年帮助自己所在村办成5件实事），按照“一年一轮换，换人不换点，帮扶村不达小康不脱钩”的要求进行帮扶。并根据2000年人均生产总值、人均地方财政收入和农民人均纯收入3项指标综合分析排队，确定大石、小箐、洒坪和六屯4个乡为扶贫开发重点乡，其中大石为一

2004年3月17日，贵州省委常委、贵阳市委书记王晓东在洒坪乡为改茅户修建新房奠基

类贫困乡，小箐和洒坪为二类贫困乡，六屯为三类贫困乡；确定105个行政村为扶贫开发重点村，其中一类贫困村42个，二类贫困村60个，三类贫困村3个。扶贫对象确定后，要求工作到村，帮扶到户，建档立卡，监测到位，精准扶贫。在具体操作上，以全面建设小康统揽扶贫开发，坚持“四个根本”（把加强组织领导作为根本保证，把改善民生作为根本目的，把发展产业作为根本抓手，把发挥群众主体作用作为根本动力），改变“一副药方治百病”的简单做法，建立“一村一策、一户一法”的帮扶机制，层层签订责任书，明确联系项目村的部门负责人为村实施扶贫开发的第一责任人，村“两委”（党支部委员会、村民委员会）的主要负责人为直接责任人，县对乡一月一查，乡对村一周一查，年终纳入目标考核，兑现奖惩。在资金的投入上，从2001年起，每年都有国家财政扶贫资金、国家以工代赈扶贫资金和信贷扶贫资金用于扶贫开发，10年累计全县扶贫开发总投入达9690万元，主要用于4个重点扶贫开发乡和乡（镇）下的105个重点扶贫开发村的开发项目，其中种植业占8.85%，养殖业占16.76%，林业占3.72%，基本农田建设占14.59%，水利建设占6.44%，道路建设占44.8%，村综合服务室建设占0.86%，技术培训和技术推广占1.61%，其他占2.37%。大量的扶贫资金投入扶贫开发项目，使处于贫困地区的农民尤其是贫困户获得更大的实惠，非贫困地区也从中获得一定的好处。一是农村经济发展步伐加快。经过农田水利建设，农村人均基本农田近0.5亩，新修灌溉渠道59.2公里，防渗维修渠道273.8公里，建小水窖1.12万口，解决了17.1万人和1.4万头大牲畜的饮水问题。全县一产增加值从2000年的1.63亿元增至2010年的3.48亿元，增长1.14倍，年均递增7.9%。农业总产值由2000年的1.93亿元增至2010年的5.55亿元，增长1.88倍，年均增长11.14%。农业人口人均产粮从2000年的351公斤增为2010年的393公斤，增长12.03%。农民人均纯收入由2000年的1808元增为2010年的5152元，增长1.85倍。4个扶贫开发重点乡2010的人均产粮和人均纯收入均比2000年有大幅度增长。人均粮食产量2000年大石乡222公斤，小箐乡248公斤，洒坪乡287公斤，六屯乡381公斤，2010年大石乡增为343.5公斤，小箐乡为314.5公斤，洒坪乡为381公斤，六屯乡为527公斤。农民人均纯收入2000年大石乡1360元，小箐乡1413元，洒坪乡1527元，六屯乡1541元；2010年大石乡为3308元，小箐乡为4167元，洒坪乡为4176元，六屯乡为4323元。二是社会事业进一步发展。全县农村人口自然增长率由2000年的10‰以上降至10‰以下，实现了教育“两基”（基本普及九年义务教育、基本扫除青壮年文盲）达标，乡（镇）卫生医疗机构得到改造和重建，缺医少药和看病难、看病贵的状况得到缓解，新型农村合作医疗“参合率”达到97.13%，实行农村最低生活保障使贫困人口达到“应保尽保”，组织10.9万人次的农民参加技术培训，科学种田技能显著提高，外出农民工实现单凭气力干活向靠技术吃饭的转变。三是农民生活极大改善。全县整合资金3.2亿元改造农村茅草房和危房，让1.2万农户住上砖混结构的新房，实现了住有所居；所有行政村实现通路、通电、通邮、通电话；村寨串户路基本建成，绝大多数村民组和自然村寨都能通汽车；广播电视实现村村通，家家户户都能接收广播电视节目。按照2007年以绝对贫困线的标准划分，全县贫困人口降至1.02万人，贫困发生率为4%，到2010年，贫困人口降到7068人，贫困发生率降至2.67%，比1982年的7.42万人和36%减少6.71万人和降低33.3个百分点。但从2008年起，衡量贫困人口的标准改为“两线合一”，即绝对贫困线加低收入贫困线。按此划分，2010年的贫困标准线为人均1274元，全县的贫困人口为2.07万人，贫困发生率为7.78%。

（五）小康建设

1982年12月，县委根据中共十二大提出“到20世纪末使全国人民物质文化生活达到小康水平”的发展战略，编制并经过四届全委二次会议审议通过《关于实现修文县经济建设奋斗目标的方案》，提出“到2000年实现全县工农业总产值在1980年的基础上翻两番，人民群众的经济收入成倍增长，物质文化生活较大幅度改善”的奋斗目标，是为全县小康建设的起步。为使目标在预定期内实现，决定采取“两段（1981—1990年为第一段，1991—2000年为第二段）四步（1981—1985年为第一步，1986—1990年为第二步，1991年—1995年为第三步，1996—2000年为第四步）”分期实施。

至1990年，全县工农业总产值达到32978万元（1990不变价，下同），人均1242元，年均递增12.26%，比1980年的10358万元增长2.18倍，超计划实现了第一阶段翻一番的目标。其中工业总产值占工农业总产值的72.67%，主要原因是乡镇企业异军突起，1.7万多名职工分布在4500多家企业从事采矿、冶炼、建材等生产，以超常规的速度不断创造劳动价值，致乡镇企业中的工业产值占全县工业总产值的72.12%；但农业总产值仅占工农业业总产值的27.33%，主要原因是1990年遭受严重旱灾，粮食产量跌入低谷，总产仅40569吨，人均152.8公斤。除粮食外，烤烟、肉类等主要农产品均比上年减产10%以上。尽管如此，主要指标的工农业总产值实际在1980年的基础上翻了1.59番，超计划实现了预期目标，小康建设第一阶段的两步目标如期实现，在迈向小康的征程中跨出了坚实的第一步。

第一阶段（1981—1990）奋斗目标实现情况表

表2—02—01

指　标	计量单位	1980年基数	1990年目标		1990年实绩		实绩为目标的百分比（%）
			绝对数	年均递增（%）	绝对数	年均递增（%）	
一、总　　人　　口	人	245397	270053	0.96	265579	0.77	98.34
二、人口自然增长率	‰	14.87	10.00	—	8.15	—	—
三、工农业总产值	万元	10358	22220	7.82	32978	12.26	148.42
其中：工业总产值	万元	5701	12469	8.14	23966	15.43	192.20
农业总产值	万元	4657	9751	7.67	9012	6.85	92.42
四、人均工农业总产值	元	422	823	6.91	1242	11.39	150.91
五、粮 食 总 产 量	吨	49200	73390	4.08	40569	−1.96	55.28
六、人　均　产　粮	公斤	200.5	271.8	3.12	152.8	−2.71	56.22

注：表中工农业总产值、工业总产值、农业总产值和人均工农业总产值一律使用“1990不变价”。

从1991年起，分段实施进入第二阶段。经过10年两步运作，以大力发展乡镇企业为支撑，以加强农业基础地位为抓手，到2000年，全县小康建设又呈现可喜的局面：一是工农业总产值上升为118624万元，人均4097元，年均递增12.68%，比1980年的实绩翻了3.56番，大大地越过《规划》，“到2000年实现全县工农业总产值在1980年的基础上翻两番”的目标。二是粮食生产从1993年起“八连增”，产量增至88904吨，人均307公斤，分别比1980年的49200吨和201公斤增长80.7%和52.7%。三是人们赖以生存和改善生活的农副产品普遍增多，与1980年比较，油菜籽由1613吨发展至9039吨，增长4.6倍；烤烟由431吨发展至2814吨，增长5.53倍；肉类总产由2421吨发展至17040吨，增长6.04倍；禽蛋由218吨发展至1039吨，增长3.77倍；水产品由20吨发展至303吨，增长14.15倍；蔬菜由6800吨增至57480吨，增长7.45倍；茶叶由14吨增至49吨，增长2.5倍；干鲜果由24吨增至84吨，增长2.5倍。四是财政收入大幅度上升，与1980年相比，全县财政总收入8003.09万元，人均276.43元，分别增长41.51倍和35.04倍，其中地方财政收入4853.75万元，增长24.78倍。五是群众收入成倍增加，职工人年均工资7911元，农民人年均纯收入1808元，分别比1980年的767.1元和178元增加9.58倍和9.16倍；城镇居民人均可支配收入2000年达5110元，比开始城镇居民经济调查的1996年3480元增加46.84%。六是群众生活水平有较大提高，全县农村贫困人口从1982年的7.42万人降为1.49万人，贫困发生率从36%降为5.68%，大多数贫困人口温饱问题得到解决；城乡居民消费性支出不断增长，城镇居民从1996年人均支出2730元增为3517元，农民从1981年人均支出161.43元增为984.33元；居民耐用消费品升级换代，城镇居民家庭100%拥有彩色电视机和电炊具，90%有洗衣机，50%有电冰箱，3%有移动电话。农民家庭80%有电视机，29%有洗衣机，9%有电话机，9%有自行车，3%有汽车，98%有大型家具；居民居住条件有很大改善，城镇居民人均住房19.9平方米，农民人均住房17.4平方米，其中砖混结构过半；用于精神文化生活的支出也有增加，城镇居民的支出从1996年的人均244.4元增为319元，农民的支出从1981年的3.35元增为70元；衡量居民富裕程度的恩格尔系数（即食品支出占整个消费性支出的比重），城镇居民从1996年的51.58%降为51.15%，农民从1981年的69.81%降为59.04%。均告别绝对贫困、实现温饱水平的历史性跨越。

第二阶段（1991—2000）奋斗目标实现情况表

表2—02—02

指　标	计量单位	1990年基数	2000年目标		2000年实绩		实绩为目标的百分比（%）
			绝对数	年均递增（%）	绝对数	年均递增（%）	
总人口	人	270053	289563	0.68	289516	0.87	99.98
人口自然增长率	‰	8.15	7.00	—	5.45	—	—
工农业总产值	万元	22220	52742	8.92	118624	13.67	224.91
工业总产值	万元	12469	30120	9.22	99328	17.34	329.77
农业总产值	万元	9751	22622	8.78	19296	7.90	85.30
人均工农业总产值	元	823	1821	3.93	4097	12.68	224.99
粮食总产量	吨	73390	99110	3.05	88904	8.15	89.70
人均产粮	公斤	271.8	242.3	2.34	307.1	7.23	89.72

注：表中工农业总产值、工业总产值、农业总产值和人均工农业总产值一律为“1990不变价”

为在全县营造想小康、盼小康、干小康、奔小康的氛围，使群众学有榜样，赶有目标，县委按照建成小康村的8条标准进行衡量审定，于1994年命名城关镇的城南村、城北村、白莲村，扎佐镇的兴红村，久长镇的清江村，六桶乡的盐井村为首批小康村。1996年又经贵阳市委、市政府和县委、县政府审定，全县有17个行政村为小康村。1997年编制《修文县小康建设规划》，按照贵州省农村居民小康综合评价标准逐一进行量化打分，全县217个行政村，有47个村得分在60.1分以上，占21.66%；80个村得分在40.1—60分，占36.87%；90个村得分在40分以下，占41.47%。按此情况，规划要求分年建成小康村：1998年建成30个，包括已命名的17个共47个，占21.66%；1999年建成70个，占32.26%；2000年建成100个，占46.08%。随着《规划》的出台，建立以县委书记黄乃铸为顾问、县长魏明禄任组长的修文县小康建设领导小组，提出“脱贫致富奔小康”的工作思路，将小康建设与扶贫开发结合起来，狠抓落实。经过努力，成效显著，农村贫困人口逐步减少，贫困发生率持续下降，贫困“短板”逐渐补齐，从而推动小康建设向前迈进。

2002年，县委以中共十六大确立的全面建设小康社会的目标进行对照，认为全县20年的小康建设虽然迈出了坚实的步伐，取得较大的成绩，特别是聚力扶贫开发让大多数贫困人口告别绝对贫困，使困扰若干年的温饱问题得以解决，群众颂声载道：“是社会主义制度的优越性，是县委带领全县人民奋斗的结果，是修文建设发展史上的一个新的里程碑”。但是，以“国民生产总值到2020年力争比2000年翻两番”和“经济更加发展、民主更加健全、科技更加进步、文化更加繁荣、社会更加和谐、人民生活更加殷实”的标准衡量，全县的小康建设是低水平的、不全面的、发展很不平衡，距离党中央的要求还有很大差距。于是，县委决定抓住实施西部大开发的契机，调整战略布局，采取切实措施，坚持以经济建设为中心，大开山门招商引资，走科技含量高、经济效益好、资源消耗低、环境污染少的发展工业经济之路；农业实行土地承包经营权流转的方式发展规模经营；组织农村富余劳动力向非农产业和城镇转移，使城镇人口的比重不断提高；精心打造旅游开发带动服务业的发展，不断提高第三产业在国内生产总值中的比重；加强法治建设，健全社会就业和文化教育、医疗卫生、社会保障体系，以保证群众享受到多样的物质文化需求和安居乐业的社会秩序；继续推进扶贫开发，巩固扶贫成果，尽快使尚未脱贫的人口解决温饱问题。

经过10年的攻坚奋战，又使全县的小康建设上了一个新的台阶。到2010年，国民生产总值达到257646万元（1990不变价，下同），人均8899元，年均递增17.46%，比2000年的实绩翻了2.25番，提前实现中共十六大提出“到2020年翻两番”的目标；粮食产量104336吨，人均341公斤，分别比2000年的实绩增长17.36%和25.46%；财政总收入达54387万元，人均1778元，比2000年分别增长5.8倍和5.42倍。其中地方财政收入为27960万元，比2000年增长4.76倍，人均914元，增长4.44倍；城镇居民人均可支配收入15756元，农民人均纯收入5152元，比2000年分别增长2.08倍和1.85倍；农村绝对贫困人口从2000年的1.49万人降为7068人，贫困发生率从5.68%降为2.67%；居民消费性支出城镇人均10926元，农村人均3229元，分别比2000年的3517元和984元增长2.11倍和2.28倍，其中用于食品支出的比重不断下降，用于衣着、居住、出行和游玩的比重持续上升，用于精神文化生活方面的支出明显增加；城镇化率为29.25%，在2000年21.09%的基础上提升8.16个百分点。此外，民主法治建设、社会就业、社会保障、精神文明建设、生态建设都有重大进展。经贵州省建强县领导小组考核，于2008年纳入全省第三轮建设经济强县行列。据统计部门每年对农村居民小康的综合评价：2010年得分83.21分，在1997年53.44分的基础上增长了29.77分，并有农民人均纯收入、衣着消费支出、已通公路行政村比重、用电户比重、已通电话行政村比重、享受社会五保人口比重和万人刑事案件立案件数等7项指标是满分，即达到了全面建设小康的要求，但尚有多半指标离“小康值”还有距离，其中基尼系数差7.4个百分点，恩格尔系数差0.1个百分点，人日均蛋白质摄入量差12克，钢木结构住房比重差6个百分点，百户电视机拥有量差2台，服务消费支出比重差3.3个百分点，人口平均预期寿命差1岁，劳动力平均受教育程度差1.2年，安全卫生用水差16个百分点，小康户占总农户的比重尚差一半。针对小康差距，县委决定采取更有针对性的措施，更加扎实的工作作风，进一步将小康建设驶入快车道，实现中共十六大确立的2020年全面建设小康社会的宏伟目标。

2000—2010年农村居民小康综合评价得分表

表2—02—03

指　标	评价标准		权数	各年最终评价分数　（分）										
	温饱值	小康值		2000年	2001年	2002年	2003年	2004年	2005年	2006年	2007年	2008年	2009年	2010年
1. 人均纯收入	1500元	2500元	30	19.07	20.62	22.55	24.60	28.26	30.00	30.00	30.00	30.00	30.00	30.00
2. 基尼系数	20.0%	35.0%	5	3.00	3.00	3.00	2.00	1.67	1.67	1.67	1.67	2.00	2.33	2.53
3. 恩格尔系数	60.0%	50.0%	6	0.60	1.80	2.40	4.80	4.80	4.92	4.98	5.10	5.22	5.34	5.94
4. 蛋白质摄入	47克/日·人	75克/日·人	9	7.07	3.54	2.89	1.93	2.57	2.57	2.57	2.89	3.54	4.82	5.14
5. 衣着消费支出	27元/人	70元/人	3	2.02	0.20	2.86	2.72	2.86	3.35	3.56	3.56	1.42	1.53	3.00
6. 钢木结构住房比重	43.0%	80.0%	7	1.89	2.84	3.59	3.78	3.97	4.16	4.92	5.30	5.68	5.86	5.86
7. 电视机普及率	1台/百户	70台/百户	6	3.91	4.61	4.61	4.43	4.61	4.78	4.87	4.87	5.22	5.83	5.83
8. 服务消费支出比重	2.0%	10.0%	6	3.75	3.75	3.15	3.15	3.53	3.53	3.53	3.53	3.53	3.53	3.53
9. 人口平均预期寿命	68岁	70岁	4	2.00	4.00	4.00	2.00	2.00	2.00	2.00	2.00	2.00	2.00	2.00
10. 劳动力平均受教育程度	6年	8年	5	2.00	2.50	2.50	2.00	2.00	2.00	2.00	2.00	2.00	2.00	2.00
11. 已通公路行政村比重	50.0%	86.0%	3	3.00	3.00	3.00	3.00	3.00	3.00	3.00	3.00	3.00	3.00	3.00
12. 安全卫生水普及率	50.0%	90.0%	3	0.75	0.90	0.90	0.90	0.98	0.98	0.98	0.98	1.35	1.38	1.38
13. 用电户比重	50.0%	95.0%	3	3.00	3.00	3.00	3.00	3.00	3.00	3.00	3.00	3.00	3.00	3.00
14. 已通电话行政村比重	50.0%	70.0%	2	0.00	0.30	1.70	1.70	1.90	2.00	2.00	2.00	2.00	2.00	2.00
15. 享受社会五保人口比重	50.0%	90.0%	4	3.00	4.00	4.00	4.00	4.00	4.00	4.00	4.00	4.00	4.00	4.00
16. 万人刑事案件立案件数	5件	20件	4	4.00	2.93	3.20	4.00	4.00	4.00	4.00	4.00	4.00	4.00	4.00
17. 小康户所占比重	—	70.0%		—	—	—	—	—	—	—	—	—	—	—
计划外生育（是1/否2）	—	—		—	—	—	—	—	—	—	—	—	—	—
合　　计	—	—	100.00	59.06	60.99	67.35	68.01	73.15	75.96	77.08	77.90	77.96	80.62	83.21

注：2010年前“人均纯收入”的温饱值为600元，“权数”即每项评价指标量化后的满分数

六、党员干部队伍建设

（一）“三讲”教育活动

2000年，县委贯彻落实中央〔1998〕17号文件和省委〔1998〕5号文件精神，决定从2月28日起，在县委、人大、政府、政协、纪委、法院、检察院、公安局的领导班子和领导干部45人中开展以讲学习、讲政治、讲正气为主要内容的党性党风教育活动（简称“三讲”教育活动）。活动至5月10日结束。后又于7月12日增补县委组织部、宣传部班子成员共7人作为“三讲”教育活动对象，至9月17日结束。“三讲”教育活动，按“思想发动，学习提高；自我剖析，听取意见；交流思想，开展批评；认真整改，巩固成果”4个阶段进行。阶段性活动结束后，又于10月份进行10天“回头看”。整个活动前后历时89天。

“三讲”教育活动开展前，县委于2月17日成立以县委书记黄乃铸为组长的“三讲”教育领导小组，领导小组下设办公室，从县委组织部等单位抽调21名同志集中办公。为做好活动准备，县委组织“三讲”教育对象“未讲先学”，两次集中学习中央和省、市关于“三讲”教育的有关文件和中央规定《讲学习讲政治讲正气教育读本》中的必读篇目，并结合工作实际进行“未讲先改”。2月24日，省委派出陈德安为组长的巡视组一行6人进驻修文。“三讲”教育活动在巡视组的指导下随即正式展开。

2月28日，进入“思想发动、学习提高”阶段。参加活动的8个单位在28日、29日分别召开“三讲”教育动员会。动员会后，教育对象集中到贵铝一矿矿区进行为期8天的封闭学习。学习期间，发出《征求意见表》373份，收回356份，回收率达95．44%。征求到意见和建议2003条，经巡视组整理为1167条。巡视组建议将广大干部群众反映比较集中、强烈且具备条件整改的问题进行早改、快改。3月11日，经县委常委会议研究，就涉及县委、县政府的7个整改事项明确整改期限、责任单位、责任人和整改措施，要求修文报社、县电视台及时对整改情况进行宣传报道和督促。与此同时，人大、政协、纪委、法院、检察院、公安局班子也根据自身实际边学边改。县委、县政府针对群众反映的县城老城区街道照明设施毁损严重问题，决定恢复老城区道路照明及维护管理，投入10万元新安装路灯170盏；针对群众反映供水不及时，时有停水断水问题，随即加大投入完成城南水厂建设，与老水厂合并扩量供水。针对农村群众反映化肥市场价格混乱问题，责成供销部门及时调进尿素3100吨、磷肥1800吨、复合肥250吨、磷铵206吨，对化肥市场实行总量控制，使化肥价格得以稳定。至3月8日，“三讲”教育第一阶段结束。

3月9日—4月14日，转入“自我剖析，听取意见”阶段。9日，召开第二阶段动员会。县委要求参与“三讲”的单位班子成员及领导干部严格按照中央文件精神，搞好自我剖析，做到解剖自己不怕严，听取意见不怕刺，亮出问题不怕丑，触及思想不怕痛。要在自己查、群众提、上级点、互相帮的基础上，认真剖析，撰写个人剖析材料。

剖析材料形成后，县委组织县人大、县政府、县政协、县纪委、县人民法院、县人民检察院、县公安局领导班子和县级领导干部（包括副县级以上离退休同志），乡镇和县直科局单位正职领导干部共227人参加对县四大班子和县级领导干部的民主评议。评议结果：最高的真实率和深刻率达95%，最低的真实率和深刻率分别为84%和77%。

4月15日，活动进入第三阶段——交流思想、开展批评。这一阶段至4月24日结束。参加“三讲”教育活动的各班子第一责任人与班子成员谈心交心，听取别人对自己的批评，同时，帮助班子成员正确对待批评，准确掌握本单位干部、群众的思想动态，统一认识，统一思想。期间，“三讲”教育单位还召开民主生活会进行民主评议，开展批评和自我批评。民主评议中，共发放对各班子成员征求意见材料180份，发放率和收回率为100%，满意率为100%。在此期间，贵阳市“三讲”办主任黄光聪、“三讲”教育活动指导组组长董效田和市纪委副书记周庭祥到县指导工作。

4月25日，活动进入“认真整改、巩固成果”的第四阶段。参加活动的领导干部将“三讲”教育与当前工作紧密结合，既做到敢于亮“丑”，不怕揭短，又做到“两不误，双促进”。在征求到的1167条意见和建议基础上，协助省委“三讲”巡视组召开老干部、党外人士、文卫代表、私营企业主、村党支部书记征求意见座谈会5次，又征求到意见和建议51条，梳理为44条，群众来信来访提出意见和建议30条。意见和建议涉及民主集中制、机关作风、廉洁自律、干部人事工作、中共建设等多方面。各“三讲”教育单位针对存在的问题进行查摆，边整边改，以整改真改取信于民。共制订整改措施173条，建立完善各项规章制度141项，确定整改内容179项。

2000年10月18—27日，进行“三讲”教育“回头看”。“回头看”的目的是巩固和扩大“三讲”教育成果，进一步落实整改措施。“回头看”分为学习提高、回顾自查、认真改进3个阶段。

10月18日进入学习提高阶段，由第一批参加“三讲”教育活动的单位班子集中一天时间进行学习，进一步提高对“三讲”教育重要性的认识，提高对搞好“回头看”的认识，并研究制订“三讲”教育“回头看”的意见。

10月19—22日为回顾自查阶段。采取班子自己找、群众帮助找、依靠指导组重点找等方法认真回顾检查，广泛征求意见。征求意见结果，干部群众对各“三讲”单位整改措施落实情况的满意率和基本满意率均在97%以上。共收集到意见36条，建议38条，经梳理为意见26条，建议27条，其中对县委班子的意见4条，建议3条，对县政府班子的意见4条，建议4条。市委指导组组长朱启樯带队深入到龙场镇白莲村了解情况，与农户座谈，又收集到意见15条，建议12条，经梳理为意见8条，建议8条。经市指导组督促，进入实施程序。

“回头看”认真改进阶段于10月23日开始，至26日结束。这一阶段主要是狠抓落实。经指导组回顾督查，县参加“三讲”教育的8个班子76项短期整改和55项中期整改的内容全部完成，占整个整改内容的73.2%，48项长期整改内容全部分解落实到责任人。“三讲”教育活动至此结束 。

专记：雷厉风行整改　老街有了路灯

2000年2月17日，县委成立“三讲”教育活动领导小组后，提出“未讲先学”“未讲先改”的要求，从各个渠道收集群众意见。修文报社将县城老城区市民反映《新街好漂亮，老街灯不亮》希望恢复照明意愿的读者来信，作为群众意见汇报到“三讲”办公室。此前，由于老城区照明设施损坏严重，致使夜晚黑漆一片，给市民的生活和工作带来诸多不便，并成为社会治安隐患。县委、县政府对恢复老街路灯给予高度重视，把“让老街路灯亮起来”作为“边整边改”的重要内容。

2月22日，县委副书记、县长魏明禄和副县长周毅、赵永祥率县财政、供电、城管等部门负责人到羊叉街一带挨家挨户走访群众，倾听市民意见。群众反映说：“自从路灯不亮后，夜间出门十分不便，黑猫猫的，叫人心里害怕。”环卫工人说：“没有路灯，夜间扫地吃尽苦头。”根据市民的意见和愿望，县政府于3月11日召开县长办公会议，研究并制订整改方案，决定由政府投资8万元，责成供电部门尽快着手实施。3月14日，供电局即组织施工。施工期间，政府又增拨资金2万元。施工人员加班加点，用3天时间更换路灯170盏。老街路灯亮了，群众心里也亮堂了。他们对前去采访的《修文报》记者说："县委、县政府给群众办了一件好事、实事，我们从心里感谢县委、县政府为老百姓想得周到。"市民赋诗咏赞：小街窄巷，夜黑人稀，电杆纵列不见灯。居民心里盼，亮丽老城区。"三讲"教育整改，雷厉风行，政府斥资慰民心。千灯夜放时，万众颂党恩。

（二）"三个代表"重要思想学习教育活动

2001年2月23日，县委遵照党中央和省、市委关于在农村开展"三个代表"（中国共产党始终代表中国先进生产力的发展要求、代表中国先进文化的前进方向、代表中国最广大人民的根本利益）重要思想学习教育活动的部署，成立以县委书记黄乃铸为组长的农村"三个代表"重要思想学习教育领导小组，抽调18名干部到县"学教"办公室办公。组建55个驻乡（镇）、部门督查组，224个驻村（居）指导组和4个宣讲组，分别对"学教"活动督促、检查、指导把关。贵阳市委派出由夏祥林带领的市督查组，从活动开始即驻县履行督查职责。自2001年2月26日召开动员大会始，至2002年6月20日召开总结大会止，"学教"活动历时480天，全县10个乡（镇）、90个县部门、229个村（居）共4682名干部分3批开展活动。

每批活动分3个阶段进行：

第一阶段，学习培训。三批"学教"活动举办培训班9期，培训乡镇、部门、村干部3070人次，各单位召开动员会、培训会、座谈会4000次。学习内容主要是《农村干部学习"三个代表"重要思想文件汇编》、江泽民"七一"讲话、中共十五届六中全会精神。基层干部将集中学习、专题讨论和自学相结合，撰写读书笔记和心得体会，使"三个代表"重要思想入脑入心。

全县农村"三个代表"重要思想学习教育培训班开课

第二阶段，对照检查。乡（镇）、县部门、村（居）班子和基层干部采取"自己找、出去听、集体查、领导帮"的方式，广泛征求意见，查找存在的突出问题，形成书面对照检查材料。3批活动共征集意见5.59万条，建议4.03万条。其中，乡镇征求到意见1.86万条，建议6876条；县部门征求到意见5203条，建议7206条；村（居）征求到意见3.21万条，建议2.62万条。班子成员之间采取交心谈心和召开民主生活会等方式，开展批评与自我批评。

第三阶段，整改提高。班子及基层干部针对存在的突出问题，制订整改方案，坚持边学边改、边查边改、边整边改，带着整改方案深入基层，听取群众意见，班子共制订整改措施4570条，建立健全制度2740个，均向群众公布，接受监督。

县、乡、村3批"学教"活动，共落实整改措施4150条，占落实总数的90.8%，群众满意率平均达93.3%。对未落实的措施建立限期整改责任制。新建和完善制度413个，将为民办实事纳入制度管理。

"学教"活动使干部思想和工作作风明显转变。基层干部提高了思想觉悟，增强了群众观点和服务意识，群众反映说：过去要办点事，是门难进、脸难看、事难办，现在去办事，领导干部笑脸相迎看坐端

水，能办的马上就办了，不能办的也有个答复。活动中，按省委“万名干部下基层，进村入户办实事”要求，全县先后7次组织271名县、乡党员领导干部下到基层听民声，察民情，解民忧，共建立联系点256个，走访群众12万人次，办实事4227件。洒坪乡乡政府驻地地处干山，一直流传着“洒坪干山坡，吃水靠马驮”的顺口溜，缺水是困扰群众生产生活的“老大难”。“学教”活动中，市、县水利部门筹集资金68万元，建成1座日供水量120吨的水厂，解决了1800多人的饮水困难。村民喝上白花花的自来水后感慨地说：“以前干部下村是催粮催款、结扎引产，今天干部下村是真心实意帮我们排忧解难。”扎佐镇组建农业科技服务队、医疗服务队、志愿者服务队等便民服务队，帮助农民抓农作物育苗移栽，为群众送医送药和义务修理电器。村民们说：“服务队没有架子，是我们身边的活雷锋。”2001年7月初，六桶乡遭受风暴、冰雹袭击，直接经济损失上千万元。一方有难，八方支援，全县党员、干部伸出援助之手，向灾区捐款8.2万元。县农业局组织3个工作组帮助灾区群众生产自救。供电局顾不上自身直接经济损失惨重，单位捐款2.2万元，职工捐资2050元，局党支部甚至将上级党委奖励的1000元也捐了出来，送到六桶灾区。

“学教”活动使农村经济发展步伐加快，存在的突出问题得到解决。县乡村加快建设农村小康社会的步伐，确立“企业带、市场保、先示范、后推广”的农村经济结构调整思路，共拟定涉及农业农村发展项目3160个。全县共落实农村基础设施建设和经济社会发展项目资金4331万元，各种捐款8.3万元，捐款折物35万元，新建水利工程64处，解决2.3万人和9014头（匹）牲畜的饮水问题，新修、改造公路105.7公里，架设桥梁3座，改造茅草房和为贫困户建房3708户，建起2个农村劳动力转移培训基地，转移农村富余劳力1428人，举办科技培训48次，培训人员3900人次，办结群众来信来访196起，为农村解决热点难点问题356个。龙场镇程官村村民余忠本家居住地离村较远，几十年未用上电，村两委成员捐资购买电杆12根，协调技术人员义务帮助他家接装供电照明线路，送去了光明。余忠本一家逢人便说：“要不是‘三个代表’，我家不知哪个时候才能用上电哩。”2002年1月28日全省村级“三个代表”重要思想学习教育工作电视电话会上，县委书记黄乃铸作题为《切实加强领导，认真落实责任制》的经验交流发言。

“学教”活动调动了基层干部和群众的积极性。活动期间，全县举办社会宣传854期，印发宣传资料8万份，深入宣传“三个代表”重要思想，在农村基层干部和群众中引起极大反响．基层干部破除“等、靠、要”思想，增强发展意识。谷堡乡平寨村村支书文明祥，通过学习教育后，对“来自农民，服务农民”的定位有了深层次的认识，放下经营多年的矿山，带领群众赶修进村公路和发展大蒜种植。他说：“自己富不算富，大家富才是真正的富。”村里群众在村“两委”带领下，脱贫致富奔小康的热情高涨，义务投工投劳1.1万余个，修路、改水、架桥、挖渠，改善农村基础设施。洒坪乡中明村在“学教”活动建起了新街和集贸市场，一扫群众过去赶场“晴天一身灰，雨天一身泥”的状况。在外打工的100余名中明村人得知家乡面貌发生巨变，激动万分，陆续回村投身家乡建设。春节时，农民在家门口贴上大红对联“三个代表如春风化雨群众

县委书记黄乃铸（中）在洒坪乡村级学教活动上作讲话

得实惠；富民政策似金光大道山村展新姿”，以此表达对开展“学教”活动给农村带来变化的激动心情。

“学教”活动使农村基层组织建设和党员队伍建设得到加强。活动期间，县委结合乡、村换届考察干部，对两级领导班子进行调整充实，有269名年轻干部走上县部门、乡（镇）及村的领导岗位。全县调整软、瘫村班子19个，思想整顿18个，撤换选配村干部56人，发展党员224名，新增入党积极分子783名和优秀村级后备干部1005名，使农村党员和干部的综合素质、治村管村水平得到提高，村级领导班子的凝聚力和战斗力明显增强。“学教”活动前，大石布依族乡联丰村村支书杨付平搞汽车运输，村委会主任秦正林帮人看煤厂，整天忙于自己致富，群众有意见。随着“学教”活动深入开展，两人思想认识得到提高，决心齐心协力带领群众搞产业结构调整，共谋发展大计。在两位“当家人”的努力下，村的经济发展了，群众给了他们97%的“满意”评价。

专记：黄乃铸身体力行“三个代表”

2001年2月26日上午，刚开完县里“三个代表”重要思想学教活动动员大会的县委书记黄乃铸就搭乘客车前去谷堡乡水口村。前些年，水口村经济发展较为缓慢，至今还有六七十户人家住在茅草房里。县里把水口村茅草房改造列入议事日程，最让黄乃铸放心不下的是村里群众对改造茅草房的积极性如何？是否有能力承担需要自己筹集的大部分建房资金？

黄乃铸一到水口村，就走进贫困户杨康华、马银军、陶永康家中，详细了解他们的生产生活情况。并就筹集建房资金的事为他们出主意，想办法。村民们纷纷表示只要政府支持，他们年内就可以把新房建起来。黄乃铸对闻讯赶到的谷堡乡党委政府领导说，帮助贫困户建新房要切实维护农民利益，在保证质量的前提下尽量降低成本，以最低价格建造出最好的房子。

当晚，在村民陈顺义家中，围着火炉，十多户农民群众与黄乃铸就如何寻找致富门路摆起了“龙门阵”。他对村民们说：要瞄准市场，充分利用自身优势调整产业结构，要学会利用先进科学技术增产增收。当得知村里已搞起种植大蒜基地和早熟糯玉米基地，但在栽培技术上还有一些困难时，他立即给县农业局领导打电话，要局领导协调技术员帮助解决种植技术问题。村民们和县委书记越摆心越近，越谈越来劲，晚上12点过了仍不愿离去。大家说：“黄书记为我们修房造屋发展生产出主意想办法，处处从老百姓的利益着想，我们心里感到很高兴。”

（三）保持共产党员先进性教育活动

2005年1月19日，县委按照中央和省、市委关于开展实践以“三个代表”重要思想为主要内容的保持共产党员先进性教育活动（简称先进性教育活动）的部署，成立以县委书记魏明禄为组长的先进性教育活动领导小组，领导小组下设办公室，抽调13人具体办公。1月22日，召开动员大会，先进性教育活动随即分3批在全县展开。第一批参加单位有县直属党政机关，县委、县人大、县政府、县政协机关，法院、检察院和人民团体，县直属事业单位及部门管理的事业单位的党组织。第二批是乡（镇）机关，包括街道社区和社会团体、社会中介组织、乡（镇）机关及其直属单位、县派驻乡（镇）的基层单位，国有企业和非公有制企业的党组织、中等职业学校、县直中小学校；第三批是农村和部分党政机关，以及承担先进性教育活动的组织和指导工作的县有关机关、部门。

每批先进性教育活动均分3个阶段进行。

第一阶段，学习培训。学习内容主要以《保持共产党员先进性教育读本》为基本教材，重点学习《党章》、中共中央总书记胡锦涛视察贵州时的重要讲话和关于社会主义荣辱观的重要论述等一系列指示精神。第二阶段，分析评议。采取发放征求意见表、个别谈话、召开座谈会、开展谈心活动等方式，广泛征求意见。第三阶段，整改提高。针对查找出的突出问题，自我剖析，认真制订整改方案和整改措施，建立整改工作责任制，做到明确负责人，明确整改事项，明确整改措施，明确整改时限，明确近期、中期、长期整改目标的“五个明确”。

至2006年6月30日召开总结大会止，3批先进性教育活动历时545天。活动期间，先后组建15个驻乡（镇）、部门督导组，217个驻村指导组和1个宣讲团，对活动进行指导、督查、宣讲。贵阳市委派出的督导组和巡视组一直驻县履行指导督查职责。全县467个党组织和8225名党员参加活动。

在先进性教育活动的学习阶段，采取集中学习、专题辅导、组织讨论、实地参观，以及个人自学等形式组织学习，同时，充分利用现代远程教育网络，为党员干部架起“空中课堂”。全县建立11个流动党员登记管理站，在同济堂药业等非公企业中成立9个临时党支部，对710名流动党员和部分年老体衰、文化水平低的党员，采取“寄”学、“送”学、“帮”学的形式，确保参学率和覆盖率。全县集中学时累计达48万个小时，平均每个党员集中学习时间达48小时，自学时间42小时。累计撰写心得体会9230篇。

2006年“先教”活动期间，六广镇合兴村党支部带领群众修建3公里长的进村公路

活动的第二阶段“分析评议”期间，全县共设立682个意见箱，召开2436场次座谈会，发放征求意见表3.24万份，走访群众3.83万人次，开展谈心活动2.89万人次。共征求到意见和建议2.14万条，其中涉及党组织的有1.01万条。对党员撰写的党性分析材料，严格审阅，实行“三不过关”，即：存在问题找得不准不过关，思想根源剖析不深不过关，努力方向不明确不过关，有206名党员的党性分析材料被责令重写。在参加活动的8225名党员中，有6810人撰写了党性分析材料，其他因病和没有写作能力而不能撰写的有1415人。全县共召开民主生活会、组织生活会和党员民主评议会6842次，党员参会率达96%以上。各级党员领导干部参加联系支部的评议活动3644次。

进入整改提高阶段，采取边学边改、边议边改、边整边改的方式，真正让整改实效取信于民。至2006年6月底，全县列入整改的5011个问题中，整改落实4734个，277个暂时不能整改的问题也向群众说明原因，积极创造条件争取及早解决。

先进性教育活动期间，县委在修文电视台、《当代修文》上开辟“做时代先锋·让群众满意”“努力实践‘三个代表’·保持共产党员先进性”“永葆先进性·建设新农村”等专栏，通过媒体向群众反馈活动的进展情况。同时，采取组建宣讲团、编简报、发资料、写标语、出板报，以及编写花灯调、山歌，举办展览、演讲比赛等群众喜闻乐见的方式，营造浓厚的舆论氛围。3批先进性教育活动，全县共建宣传栏405个，书写标语8263条，巡回宣讲526场次，发放资料23万份，编发简报、快讯342期。省、市先进性教育活动办公室转发县的简报、快讯90期，中央、省、市新闻媒体播发县的先进性教育活动新闻257

条，县电视台播放新闻918条和宣传标语1628条（次），《当代修文》刊登新闻420条、宣传标语264条（次）。2006年6月14日，新华社、《人民日报》、中央电视台、中央人民广播电台等6家媒体聚焦修文，对修文建立党内生活机制，增强党性意识；建立党员管理机制，强化组织纪律；建立党员学习机制，提升综合素质；建立党员教育机制，增强服务能力；建立民主参与机制，确保有效监督；建立“吐故纳新”机制，纯洁党员队伍；建立考核评价机制，激发党员热情的“八大长效机制”的成功经验进行集中报道。

每批活动结束，均进行群众满意度测评。广大群众对先进性教育活动总体评价的满意率和基本满意率达99.76%。

在先进性教育活动中，还以推进中共先进性建设为目标，召开理论研讨会、座谈会等方式开展理论研讨工作。活动期间，全县党员干部共撰写理论研讨文章200篇，从中遴选25篇编辑成《足迹——修文县保持中共先进性理论成果选编》一书出版。各个党组织加强制度建设，探索党员教育管理的长效机制，全县新建制度253个，健全完善制度1484个。

先进性教育活动使党员的思想认识明显提高，先锋模范作用充分发挥。洒坪乡轿子山村残疾党员李树荣自学种植柑橘技术后，自编技术资料20多份送给周围农户，义务帮助6户贫困户实施柑橘品种改良。六广镇广山村4名党员主动出资，为因老房子年久失修坍塌后无房居住的王文书家修建住房。各党组织还实行无职党员设岗定责制和党员承诺制，激发党员工作热情。扎佐镇石竹村党支部为申天平、彭朝学等9个无职党员分别设立了远程教育岗、勤劳致富岗等9个岗位。据统计，全县2216名无职党员设岗定责后，共为群众办实事2316件。

先进性教育活动使基层组织建设不断加强，党组织的凝聚力、战斗力、向心力得到增强。县农业局第二党支部选择龙场镇程官村作为支部活动实践基地，在程关村发展200亩旱毛豆种植，明确每个党员具体负责8户的技术指导。六广镇新中、滨江、合兴、六广村党支部切实抓好人饮解困工程实施，共解决486户1709人、818头大牲畜的饮水困难。谷堡乡折溪村党支部带领村民们发展金果林种植、经营“农家乐”，开辟致富新路。在3批活动中，全县整顿软弱涣散党支部49个，调整不胜任现职的支部书记14人，下派3名机关干部担任村党支部书记，对7名村党支部书记进行诫勉谈话，对400名村级干部和后备干部进行中专学历培训。组织160个村1500余名党员干部到革命实践教育基地、生态经济示范基地参观学习。此外，县委还举办2期乡镇主要领导、6期村党支部书记培训班。活动中，有2000人向党组织递交入党申请书，有658名申请人被确定为入党积极分子，全县发展新党员368名。

县委办公室党支部保持共产党员先进性分析评议阶段工作部署会议

先进性教育活动使党员干部工作作风不断转变，广大党员干部积极为群众办实事、解难事。县委常委坚持做到“四个带头”（带头学习，带头深入基层，带头解决疑难问题，带头加班处理工作），积极帮助基层解决工作难题。县史志办公室免费为久长镇清水村编写村志，并为该村70岁以上的51名老人照相。扎佐镇开展“合医135”活动（即村支部书记和村委会主任帮助1户、镇职工帮助3户、镇班子成员帮助5户贫困户参加农村合作医疗），捐款1.7万元帮助500户1700个贫困人口参加新型农村合作医疗。全县11个“三农”服务团深入乡村角落和田间地头开展种植养殖、劳动技能、卫生防疫、法律法规宣传632场次，发放资料12万份，现场解答群众疑问1.1万人次，培训人员1.6万人次。3批活动全县共落实帮扶资金1289万元，帮助6000户困难群众解决实际困难；投资6万元帮助20个困难企业解决实际问题；帮助2179人实现再就业；落实资金17.7万元，解决6598名家庭困难的学生入学；落实低保金234.98万元，使1万名困难群众享受低保、医保待遇；为群众办实事9879件。

附:

贵州修文县巩固先进性教育活动成果

在先进性教育活动中，贵州省贵阳市修文县针对各级党组织存在的问题，认真总结先进性教育活动的经验，按照“新建一批、整改一批、完善一批”的工作思路，从党员教育、学习、管理等方面，积极探索建立先进性教育长效机制。

针对部分农村无职党员任务不明、评议无据和农民党员不愿管事、不能办事的现状，修文县建立了党内生活机制，全县各级党组织普遍建立健全了中共组织生活会、民主生活会、党课等制度，使党员的党性意识得到加强。同时建立党员管理机制，全县217个农村党支部都实行了党员承诺制和无职党员设岗定责制。修文县还利用远程教育网络，实行周二播放日制度，组织各乡镇村书记、村委会主任、致富能手等就农村实用技术、党在农村的方针政策等方面进行培训，建立起党员学习机制。仅今年上半年，就组织培训26期，培训农村党员干部5.6万人次。修文县还建立党员服务机制，共有800余名机关党员参与了社区“共驻共建”活动，目前已开展200多次服务活动，办实事132件。

为保障党员的民主权利，修文县建立民主参与机制。扎佐镇推行两个“三分之二”工作制，即重大事项必须经三分之二的村民代表、三分之二村“两委”成员表决后方可生效实施；六广镇推行重大事项“五步议事法”，即提议、征求民意、上级审议、票决、组织实施。在评议党员干部过程中，修文县做到坚持统一组织和分类考核相结合、定性考核与定量考核相结合、共性工作目标考核与特色性突破性工作目标考核相结合、考核结果与干部使用相结合等“四个结合”，公平公正地评价每名党员干部。

在第三批先进性教育活动中，修文县各级党组织共培养入党积极分子500余名，发展新党员81名。全县共整顿软弱涣散的农村党支部19个，调整不胜任现职的村党支部书记5名，对7名村党支部书记进行了诫勉谈话，对1名党员给予开除党籍处分。

（原载2006年6月18日《人民日报》）

七、党务

（一）组织建设

党员发展 1978年后，结合全县工作重点，注重在知识分子、生产第一线骨干、妇女、少数民族中吸收新党员。各级中共组织按照县委对发展新党员提出的“坚持标准、严格程序、保证质量”要求，成熟一个发展一个。1979年，全县党员数从1978年4431名增至4593名。之后，党员人数逐年增加，党员队伍不断发展壮大，但各地发展不平衡，一些村党支部几年没有发展新党员，全县知识分子党员比例低于全省平均水平。1985年，县委提出“发展新党员步子要放大一些”“突出发展重点，培养卫生、教育行业和农村中的优秀青年”的要求，各级党组织贯彻执行县委指示，当年发展党员255名，其中知识分子85名，在农村发展初中文化程度以上新党员166名，党员队伍文化程度结构得到较大改善。1990年8月，贯彻《中国共产党发展党员工作细则（试行）》，使全县党员发展步入规范化建设的轨道。1995年，加强农村基层发展党员的工作，把发展党员与培养后备干部结合起来，重点在35岁以下和高中文化以上的优秀农村知识青年、妇女、少数民族和经济建设的能人中发展新党员，以解决农村党员队伍年龄偏大、文化偏低、村级班子后继乏人的问题。自1995年—1997的3年间，共发展农村党员543人，其中35岁以下、初中以上文化程度的279名、少数民族74名、科技带头人137名。同时还培训入党积极分子1291人，作为骨干培养的808人。通过党员发展为农村干部队伍增添了新鲜血液，为中共基层组织增强了生机和活力。从2000年起，党员发展工作始终围绕“三个代表”重要思想开展，在“巾帼建功”“远程教育”“双带致富”“双千工程”“改茅工程”“扶贫攻艰”等不同阶段全县的中心工作中发现、培养优秀人才，将符合条件的吸纳到中共组织中来。2008年1月，全县遭受雪凝灾害，各级党组织发展的入党积极分子在抗灾斗争中表现突出，有20多人被批准“火线入党”。至2010年年底，全县共有党员8967名，其中女性党员1764名，农村党员5570名。

2008年2月10日修文供电局党支部新党员在抗凝冻第一线举行入党宣誓

1978—2010年党员基本情况统计表

表2—02—04

年份	党员总数	其中				文化程度			年龄结构				
		新党员	少数民族党员	妇女党员	农村党员	大专以上	中专高中	初中	25岁以下	26至35岁	36至45岁	46至55岁	56岁以上
1978	4431		363	621	3290	21	89	597	168	1071	2675		517
1979	4593		384	640	3561	32	109	657	149	1103	2803		538
1980	4744	139	390	661	3622	35	151	779	170	1135	1373	2066	
1981	4799	112	398	643	3666	34	152	781	179	1091	1339	2190	
1982	4860	146	390	645	3631	41	189	839	149	1064	1352	2295	
1983	4909	135	371	680	3792	48	208	883	121	1053	1261	1548	926
1984	5012	216	396	703	3830	61	310	1006	113	1114	1267	1577	1001
1985	5337	350	428	764	3902	95	446	1172	145	1050	1374	1571	1197
1986	5583	339	444	804	3939	120	590	1284	217	1040	1465	1631	1230
1987	5701	243	430	830	3948	131	635	1374	246	1084	1467	1641	1263
1988	5770	200	432	841	3913	156	687	1398	188	1111	1525	1631	1315
1989	5448	164	437	832	3864	182	730	1453	218	995	1548	1478	1500
1990	5818	153	447	835	3896	228	826	1468	200	1029	1539	1523	1527

续表

年份	党员总数	其中				文化程度			年龄结构				
		新党员	少数民族党员	妇女党员	农村党员	大专以上	中专高中	初中	25岁以下	26至35岁	36至45岁	46至55岁	56岁以上
1991	5970	268	455	864	3980	242	893	1577	175	1091	1509	1460	1654
1992	6085	207	449	910	3828	264	958	1611	110	864	1555	1498	2058
1993	6187	240	462	943	3853	299	1017	1659	142	902	1553	1498	2094
1994	6304	190	465	977	3848	313	1096	1707	153	857	1593	1472	2229
1995	6752	505	506	1033	4182	367	1261	1951	226	1059	1677	1560	2230
1996	6758	366	521	1093	4156	392	1292	2014	248	1079	1541	1629	2261
1997	6868	309	520	1123	4242	450	1403	2042	221	1115	1552	1630	2350
1998	6819	228	540	1138	4188	495	1416	2034	208	1107	1519	1603	2382
1999	6875	168	550	1163	4214	571	1458	2063	222	1102	1531	1605	2415
2000	6993	208	574	1189	4312	646	1473	2178	211	1087	1558	1668	2439
2001	7111	118	581	1239	4355	720	1571	2200	242	1232	1715	1700	2222
2002	7248	137	594	1343	4422	795	1588	2245	286	1418	1783	1721	2040
2003	7364	116	596	1385	4490	833	1594	2250	305	1550	1776	1784	1849
2004	7486	122	632	1452	4566	876	1600	2258	389	1555	1782	1791	1969
2005	7700	214	636	1495	4621	985	1662	2250	413	1568	1788	1795	2146
2006	8068	368	636	1608	4814	1047	1722	2251	422	1712	1904	1822	2218
2007	8245	177	674	1568	4922	1096	1808	2253	470	1730	1935	1941	2219
2008	8452	207	677	1625	5100	1122	1865	2258	523	1857	1926	1960	2186
2009	8759	304	681	1691	5381	1303	1895	2253	581	1922	2007	2054	2195
2010	8967	208	704	1764	5570	1412	2008	2255	685	1972	2013	2095	2200

党员教育　1980年，贯彻中组部、中宣部《关于加强党员教育健全中共组织生活的意见》，分批对3369名党员（其中农村党员2903人）进行“端正党风，增强组织观念”的培训。1982年，结合中共十二大精神的学习贯彻，要求全县党员与党中央保持政治思想上的高度一致，为实现“四个现代化”而奋斗。1983年，组织党员学习新《党章》，采取集中培训和分期轮训的方式，对党员进行20天集中教育，并在党员中开展“争做合格党员、合格干部、创先争优”活动。1985年，根据《中共中央关于整党决定》，在党员中开展党性、党风、党纪教育，要求党员从思想上清除以权谋私、利己主义、个人主义。同时，分期分批对农村党员进行培训，鼓励党员带头劳动致富。1988年，在全县开展“争做合格党员”活动，要求农村党员破除小富即安的思想，树立改革创新、面向市场、面向商品经济的新思维。1989年，县委组织党员集中7天培训，旨在进行思想政治教育，要求党员与党中央保持一致。1990—1992年间，通过开

2005年3月，县委举办农村党支部书记培训班

办县乡业余党校等方式，把对党员的长期教育与短期培训相结合，主要进行增强党组织的战斗堡垒作用和发挥党员先锋模范作用教育。1993年，县委提出“抓党建促经济”，在全县建起5个党员示范点，15个电化教育点。电化教育点当年播放教育专题片10场次，接受教育的党员达2300人。1995年，对党员进行理想信念和共同致富教育，组织2450名有帮带能力的党员与4512户贫困户制订帮带脱贫计划。1998年开展“五学”（学中共基本理论、市场经济知识和法律、法规、业务知识）活动。是年，各乡镇业余党校共培训党员干部606人。2000年，结合“三讲”教育，在全县党员中开展“讲政治、讲学习、讲正气”教育培训。2001年和2002年，全县进行“三个代表”重要思想学习教育活动，两年间，先后7次组织1万名党员、干部下基层，为群众办实事。党员、干部在“学教”活动中接受党性、党风教育，转变工作作风，受到人民群众好评。2003—2004年，结合“双千工程”“双带致富工程”“远程教育工程”的开展，对党员继续进行“三个代表”重要思想学习教育，两年共培训党员1.2万人次，其中农村党员3600人次。2005—2006年在全县开展“保持共产党员先进性”教育活动，通过党员先进性教育，增强党员的事业心和责任感，提高党员的理论水平和解决问题的能力，使基层组织增强凝聚力和战斗力。2006年，结合保持共产党员先进性教育，在党员中开展“树立社会主义荣辱观”活动。

一系列的思想教育措施，使党员的党性意识得到加强，在2008年1月全县遭受50年不遇的凝冻灾害期间，党员的先锋模范作用充分体现。县委书记魏明禄和县委副书记、县长石洪在保电抢修工地上与工人一起抬电杆；乡（镇）的党员干部穿上自制防滑草鞋，跋涉几十里山路，把救灾物资送到住得分散掉远的困难群众家中；村的党员给群众送水、送蜡烛，把自家砂厂的发电机拿出来发电为村民打米、照明，将自己搞客运的汽车用来免费接送保电工地的工人；县机关1500名党员干部不顾自己家中同样停水断电,每天奋战在抗灾第一线。党员的带头作用激发了全县人民抗灾激情，同心同德，万众一心，夺取了“抗凝冻保民生”斗争的全面胜利。

2008年，修文县党员干部抗击凝冻灾害

干部教育培训 1978后，县委坚持“党管干部”的方针，始终把干部教育培训作为提高干部队伍素质、推动改革发展的基础性工程，坚持围绕大局培训干部，通过举办读书班、培训班等方式，立足实践提高干部理论水平和工作能力。1994年起，在党委、党组、总支建立中心学习组制度，定期对领导干部开展培训。1998年，建立干部月末知识讲座制度，对股级以上干部进行理论培训。自1978年至2010年，开展各类培训活动400多期次，培训干部逾万人次。2010年，选派县委党校骨干教师到乡（镇）宣讲十七届五中全会精神13场，共培训党员、干部及入党积极分子1400人。除县里开展教育培训活动外，对后备

干部和重点培养干部还采取外派学习和挂职锻炼方式拓宽教育培训内容，促进干部知识结构和能力素质随着发展要求而提升。从1978—2010年，先后选派300多名干部到贵州工业大学、省委党校、安顺地委党校、贵阳市委党校学习。先后有100多名干部被选派到江西华西村、北京房山区、贵阳南明区和省直、市直机关挂职锻炼。这些选派外出学习和挂职锻炼的干部理论水平和工作能力提升较快，多数成长为群众信任的优秀领导干部。县人民法院原审判员刘文新1997年被选派到省委党校法律专业学习，不久因审判工作能力凸显，被提拔为行政庭庭长。继后，又先后被选拔到乡镇、县委、市委领导岗位上。

1990年4月，欢送下基层干部挂职锻炼大会

干部监督　2000年建立领导干部任期经济责任审计制度，开始对离任领导干部任职期间的经济情况进行审计。至2005年对10名领导干部任期经济责任审计，10人均有违反财经纪律的行为，对其中2人给予警告处分、1人严重警告处分、1人行政记过、免职1人、调整工作1人。2002年制订《加强科（局）级党政领导干部监督工作的意见》，同时制订《领导干部八小时以外行为规范》，强化对领导干部的监督。此外，还实施领导干部任免表决无记名投票方式，实行领导干部任前公示制。对任前公示设有专门举报电话，专人负责受理群众举报。从2000年实施任前公示制至2010年，共受理9个举报电话和13封举报信。经组织部门核实，其中2个举报电话、3封举报信所举报的内容属实，2个举报电话内容不影响干部任职，3封举报信内容影响任职，取消3名被举报对象的拟任职务决定。

干部任用　自1982年中共十二大提出实现干部队伍革命化、年轻化、知识化、专业化的要求后，县委按照“四化”条件提拔任用了一批中青年干部，使全县干部队伍特别是各级领导班子出现年龄降低、文化程度提升和干部新老交替的局面。2002年，按照中共中央《党政领导干部选拔任用工作条例》要求推行干部公开选拔，在坚持“四化”方针的同时，更注重德才兼备、群众公认、实绩突出。经过考察，使一批干部走上县直部门和乡（镇）领导岗位。2007年，加大贯彻《党政领导干部选拔任用工作条例》力度，实行任用干部民主推荐测评、任前公示、任中监督、离任审计等制度，使群众对干部选拔任用的知情权、参与权、选择权和监督权得以保障。2008年，深化干部人事制度改革，县委采取公推竞岗和公推直选的方式选任干部，公选干部经过报名、笔试、面试、体检、组织考察和讨论决定等程序进行筛选择优任用，做到公开、公平、公正，使任用干部的公信度得以提高。

2005年4月19日，县委举行干部作风建设报告会，采取以会代训方式培训干部

1978—2010年干部基本情况统计表

表2—02—05

项目 / 人数 / 年份	干部总数	其中			文化程度			年龄结构				
		党员	少数民族	妇女	大专以上	中专高中	初中以下	25岁以下	26至35岁	36至45岁	46至55岁	56岁以上
1978	2046	720	117	713	193	719	1494	193	882	757	506	68
1979	2442	769	131	706	186	826	1430	144	872	747	586	93
1980	2586	778	149	764	202	1010	1374	220	869	770	641	86
1981	2694	750	154	791	217	1161	1316	344	855	745	665	85
1982	2812	794	161	832	226	1321	1265	499	789	767	672	85
1983	2716	683	151	397	231	1339	1146	455	868	728	574	91
1984	2606	630	65	778	156	977	1473	212	867	1094	390	43
1985	2568	716	148	785	298	1395	875	552	728	695	507	86
1986	2683	870	163	849	341	1510	832	624	730	693	526	110
1987	2862	720	218	921	359	1610	893	784	770	696	502	110
1988	3165	939	188	748	344	1910	911	613	971	857	626	79
1989	3157	926	168	833	359	1810	988	333	1154	1206	426	38
1990	3217	916	223	1037	485	1977	755	498	1148	835	584	152
1991	3303	1119	275	1151	578	2018	707	555	1265	778	518	187
1992	3440	1221	214	1020	633	2171	636	597	1289	857	550	147
1993	3385	1280	233	1002	696	2184	505	625	1244	878	516	122
1994	3492	1338	235	1043	766	2261	495	666	1298	889	549	90
1995	3643	1385	267	1109	887	2313	443	723	1361	896	569	94
1996	4379	1594	329	1283	1092	2875	412	2193		1359	709	118
1997	4510	1643	355	1328	1129	2980	401	2240		1378	766	126
1998	4669	1695	386	1376	1138	3121	390	2291		1402	825	131
1999	4698	1709	396	1427	1253	3136	309	2304		1413	853	128
2000	4926	1733	383	1720	1422	3234	270	2580		1391	826	129
2001	5102	1801	389	1772	1506	3343	253	675	1930	1484	882	131
2002	5269	1902	437	1849	1623	3401	245	632	1987	1549	969	132
2003	5470	2029	486	2007	1817	3427	226	628	1976	1651	1088	127
2004	5657	2104	492	2081	2107	3341	209	568	2151	1697	1094	147
2005	5858	2173	534	2173	2591	3084	183	507	2305	1734	1176	136
2006	6084	2238	539	2298	3238	2679	167	493	2427	1788	1239	137
2007	6238	2297	569	2476	3810	2269	159	462	2437	1921	1275	143

续表

项目 人数 年份	干部总数	其中			文化程度			年龄结构				
		党员	少数民族	妇女	大专以上	中专高中	初中以下	25岁以下	26至35岁	36至45岁	46至55岁	56岁以上
2008	6491	2375	587	2574	4561	1787	143	418	2554	2038	1342	139
2009	6674	2411	607	2662	5132	1417	125	357	2653	2142	1386	136
2010	6842	2544	612	2765	5715	1015	112	303	2782	2222	1401	134

注：1.2000年，26~35岁干部人数含25岁以下干部，2001年后单独计算；2.企业单位职工含派遣制、合同制用工；3.统计范围：乡镇、县属机关事业单位、垂管系统单位、驻县国有企业单位等，军事机关未纳入统计

远程教育 2003年6月，根据贵阳市委关于首批试点农村党员干部远程教育工作的部署，经县委常委研究决定成立县委农村党员干部现代远程教育领导小组，由县委书记魏明禄担任组长，县委副书记、组织部长朱桂云担任副组长，下设远程教育办公室管理日常事务。随即正式启动远程教育工作，主要职责是建立远程教育网络培训农村党员干部，向党员干部和群众宣传国家的方针政策、法律法规，组织村民学习农业实用技术走科科学致富之路。

2004年为进一步健全工作机构，形成上下联运的常态机制，成立修文县数字信息与远程教育管中心，负责对全县远程教育工作进一步统一管理、指导。机构健全后随即进行站点建设，首批建站199个，覆盖全县91.7%的行政村，未建站点的村也建起播放点。199个站点中有55.8%的站点建在当地学校由教师兼管；18.1%的站建在村里的公共场所和23.1%的站点建在村民住宅内，配有专职管理人员。各站点以周二为播放日开展“双千（在贵阳市范围内选派1000名年纪轻、文化高、能力强的机关干部任队员，进驻全市的1000个行政村）工程”，着力推进远程教育。广大农村党员干部和群众在播放点上接受农业科技教育后，把“双千工程”称为“民心工程”“致富工程”，还编山歌赞扬：“远程教育人人夸，要学技术就找它，鼠标轻轻点一下，就把专家请到家。”谷堡乡折溪村村民李峰外出打工返乡种植金秋梨，由于受技术制约收效甚微，见村里建起远程教育终端接收站就迷上远程教育，从网上学得金秋梨栽培、管护和销售等知识，便扩大种梨面积种出果大、色亮、味好且成果率高的梨子，一年就增收7000多元。在李峰的带动下，全村村民种梨积极性一下迸发出来，种植规模达万亩。依托“万亩梨园”春赏梨花，秋摘梨果的契机，折溪村迎来络绎不绝的游人，村民们又利用远程教育学到的厨艺办起“农家乐”餐饮，增添了一条致富门路，使一年的农民人均收入从原来的1000元增加到3857元，其中年收入在5万元以上的农户就有30家。小箐乡大坝村村民刘正秀与其他村民一道创办起无公害生猪养殖基地。由于缺乏养殖技术，使母猪生下的仔猪成活率不高。于是，她利用远程教育资源，从网上学习养殖技术并应用于实践中。仔猪进入市场交易后，养猪基地不但收回投资，还净赚1.6万元。在养殖基地带动下，全村养殖户发展到120户，养殖规模由原来的46头扩大到1500头，村民每户每年纯收入达2万多元。村民们尝到甜头后，称远程教育这条信息传导为“高速公路”。

经过3年运转，远程教育为深化基层党员群众教育奠定了良好基础。但由于兼职管理人员较多，且未明确固定工作经费，致远程教育操作管理素质、课件服务质量等不能及时满足党员群众的需求。到2007年，全县能够正常组织群众集中收视和教学的站点仅占23%，有设备因管理不善和更新不及时导致25%

的站点运转不正常。

2009年，为切实保障工作开展，县委落实每个远教管理员每月750元的劳务补助，并建立“两个定期服务”（定期走访服务、定期教学辅导服务）制度，要求所有站点操作管理人员每个星期用一天时间深入村寨，访困难，问需求，为群众送去种植、养殖技术和法律法规、健康知识、计划生育政策，并征求播放内容，又用一天针对群众对播放的意见进行教学辅导，从而有效地推动了远教服务职业化进程。

2010年，为深入贯彻落实中共中央关于在基层党组织和党员中开展创先争优活动的指示精神，县委根据贵州省委部署参加“百千万（在全省范围内创建100个远程教育学用转化示范村，评选1000名远程教育成绩突出站点管理员，培育1万名远程教育党员创业带富能手）工程”活动为切入点，以示范带动，提升远程教育的整体水平。

在“百千万工程”中，全县共刻录反映江苏省华西村发展经验的光盘260张和种种养殖技术光盘500张并发放到各远教站点，采用“看、听、观（临场）、送”的“四学”模式灵活组织、多措并举开展教学培训，以此帮助农民群众转变观念，提高致富技能。全县开展宣讲80场，组织收看全国远程教育卫生专用频道《纪念建党90周年》专栏300场3500人次，收看中央举办的纪念建党90周年重大活动的实况及录像230场2500人次。编辑整理“农村新风尚，宝典进万家”课件，并刻录2500余张光碟下发到农村（社区），积极推进学用转化，促进农村党员干部和农民群众提高素质，使全县涌现出一批种植养殖党员创业带富示范能手。久长镇清江村发展莲藕种植500亩，莲花白种植1500亩，全村1年人均纯收入达6000元，成为全镇的小康示范村。

2010年，全县远程教育工作现场推进会

随着全县远程教育的深入发展，到2010年底，全县共建远程教育接收站点215个（村站点205个，社区站点10个），其中92.7%的站点建在村（居）综合办公楼，基本上取消了原来建在学校和私人住宅的站点。51个村（居）站点开通了宽带，培训管理员14期3200人次。整个项目共投入财政资金950万元。

附：

农村党员干部现代远程教育情况调查

曾庆红在贵州考察时指出：“开展农村党员干部现代远程教育，是巩固农村‘三个代表’重要思想学习教育活动成果、把建立‘让干部经常受教育，使农民长期得实惠’的长效机制真正落到实处的一项重要举措，一定要把这项工作切实抓紧抓好。”

根据晓东书记的要求，2月上旬，我与组织部长等到我县7个乡（镇）的71个村，就农村党员干部现代远程教育工作开展情况进行实地调查，所到村占全县行政村总数的30%。下到村里，我们查看远教设备的管理和使用情况，与近800名村组干部、群众及“双千队员”进行座谈，了解情况，共商对策。

我县自2003年以来，并建立村远程教育站点206个，分播点1400多个。工作启动后，县、乡（镇）、

村加强组织领导，加大资金投入，完善硬件设备，建立培训制度，配备管理人员，在“双千队员”的帮助下，采取周二播放日、群众点播、“红领巾”传播等灵活多样的方式，把远程教育逐步拓展开来。通过远程教育，一是党和国家的各项方针政策、法律法规在农民群众中得到及时、有效的宣传贯彻；二是农村党员干部群众积极学习农业适用技术，直接用于生产，对农村经济发展、农民增收起到有力的推动作用；三是进一步丰富农村党员和群众的精神生活，提高了科学文化素质。村民们普遍反映：是远程教育使我们学到了技术，获得了信息，增加了收入。

从点上调研和面上掌握的情况来看，目前远程教育工作出现了一些新的情况和问题：

一是主观上出现松劲情绪。远程教育工作需要的是长期坚持才能生效，不能立竿见影，有的教育内容需要与实际操作结合起来才见分晓，但有的乡（镇）干部心浮气躁，没有见着教育效果就松劲懈怠，抓远程教育就为应付检查，工作流于形式。

二是设备运转不正常。部分硬件由于管理不善或者使用不当，导致损坏搁置；有的因承担不起昂贵的维修费，使设备故障排除不了，不能正常运转。据统计，全县设备运行正常的站点仅有146个，占71%；基本正常的8个，占4%；运行不正常的52个，占25%。

三是组织集中收看难。农村劳动力释放后，青壮年外出务工较多，留下来的老弱妇幼，观看远程教育积极性不高，特别是遇到农忙时节，村民们白天忙于干活，夜间要休息，没有观看时间。全县能正常组织教学的站点仅有48个，占23%；基本正常运转的122个，占59%；简直组织不起来陷于瘫痪的36个，占18%。

四是课件内容针对性不强。一些播放点有什么就播什么，有多少就播多少，播放的内容与群众的需求不对路，调动不起群众的参学积极性。

五是缺少专职的操作管理人员。一方面，学校兼职教师既要授课，又要照应远程教育，往往顾此失彼，两项工作均受影响；另一方面，没有建在学校的站点的专职操作管理人员素质偏低，不能熟练地使用和维护设备，使播放难以正常运转。全县有专职操作管理人员的站点为148个，占72%，操作管理能力急需提高。

六是经费保障困难。不少的站点缺乏工作经费，需支付的是水电费、设备维修费和操作管理人员的报酬等，均未列入专项开支，致使管理人员难以稳定。

针对上述问题，结合调研中搜集的意见，提出如下建议：

一要进一步提高认识。要把远程教育作为提高农村党员、干部和群众素质的重要平台来建设，作为推动农村经济发展的“助推器”长期坚持下去。

二要注重远教的针对性。村支两委和“双千队员”要相互配合，村支两委要订出技能培训计划，县远教办和“双千队员”要负责刻录课件，课件要提供群众真正想看、想知道、想学习的知识和技能；要根据每户群众经营的不同产业进行分班培训，分类教学，避免“陪坐”现象；要充分结合当地自然条件、生产习惯等选择和制作适合当地实际的乡土课件，使群众能将学到的知识用于实际生产之中，解决实际问题。

三要掌握培训的灵活性。根据农村群众生产忙闲和生活习惯，灵活调整培训时间。农闲时节增加一定的培训次数和培训内容，农忙季节可适当减少培训量。要根据村民居住分散的特点，多点组织播放，方式灵活，确保效果，不走过场。

四要加强对专职操作管理队伍的建设。一方面要加强对专职管理人员的培训，不断“充电”，熟练地掌握操作技术；另一方面要加强对兼职的村级管理人员的培训，相对稳定技术队伍。

五要整合资源，扩大覆盖面。农村远程教育服务的对象主要是党员干部，但不能仅限于此。应将远程教育扩大到全体村民，使群众都能学习党和国家政策，掌握致富本领，了解市场信息，促进增收致富。要完善硬件设备，将远程教育与计划生育、殡葬改革等工作结合起来，实行资源共享。

六要解决必要的专项经费，确保正常运转。县、乡财政要挤出资金给困难村解决设备维修、课件制作、管理人员报酬等问题。有条件的村要通过创收弥补远程教经费的不足，确保农村远教事业健康发展，为新农村建设和构建和谐社会发挥应有的作用。

（作者：魏明禄）

（二）宣传和理论学习

1.宣传

形势政策宣传 县委的宣传工作紧密结合党和国家的路线、方针、政策、法律和当前的中心工作进行，以推进马克思主义大众化，提升群众的政治素养，营造浓郁的工作氛围，凝聚民心，鼓舞全县人民为建设修文而奋斗。

1978年，结合党中央开展的“实践是检验真理的唯一标准”大讨论，在县内重点开展搞好经济建设的重要性和紧迫性宣传。1979年，随着农村联产承包责任制的推行，着力宣传农村体制改革，鼓励农村群众走改革致富、劳动致富之路。1979—1986年，以宣传社会主义初级阶段理论为主，采取办讲座、办培训等方式宣传学习“对外开放、对内搞活”的经济政策。1987年至1990年间，宣传学习党中央提出的“一个中心两个基本点”（以经济建设为中心，坚持四项基本原则，坚持改革开放的基本路线）。其间，大张旗鼓开展“五讲四美三热爱”（讲文明、讲礼貌、讲卫生、讲秩序、讲道德；心灵美、语言美、行为美、环境美；热爱祖国、热爱社会主义、热爱中国共产党）的宣传，以组织歌咏比赛、举办征文和书画展等形式，广泛宣传共产党好、社会主义好。1989年，重点宣传10年改革成果，引导干部群众学会用辩证唯物主义的观点正确看待改革的成就和问题。继后，重点结合历届全国党代会的召开，将中共十三大至十七大的大会报告以及历次全会精神作为学习宣传的重点，在党员干部中开展轮训，组建宣讲团，在全县城乡开展集中宣讲教育。1992年，邓小平视察南方重要谈话发表，以宣传学习为重点，进一步推进社会主义市场经济理论的学习，引导干部群众一心一意抓建设，聚精会神谋发展。1993年，以宣传中共十四大为重心，举办副科级以上干部学习“中国特色社会主义理论”轮训班和中共十四大建设社会主义经济体系为内容的骨干培训班。1995年，党中央颁布《爱国主义教育实施纲要》，在县城和乡镇均举办爱国主义报告会，受训达6万人次。1997年中共十五大召开后，以突出中共十五大提出建设社会主义强国三步走战略学习宣传为重心，在1998年至2000年间，组织开展“三讲三争”（讲学习、讲政治、讲正气，争当学习模范、廉洁奉公模范、开拓进取模范）活动。2001年，“三个代表”重要思想学习教育活动在全县开展，邀请省委讲师团莅县举办3场报告会，宣讲“三个代表”重要思想，5000余人受训。2002至2004年，围绕中共十六大提出的“全面建设小康社会”指导思想，先后组织讨论会、专家讲座10多场次，宣传全面建设小康社会的纲领和贯彻落实科学发展观。2005—2008年，结合县委的中心工作，分别开展保持共产党员先进性教育活动、树立社会主义荣辱观、发扬抗灾精神宣传。2007年，围绕中共十七

2005年农业普查宣传现场

大精神，宣传进一步贯彻落实科学发展观和坚持中国特色社会主义经济建设、政治建设、文化建设和社会建设的基本纲领。2008年抗凝冻期间，宣传工作紧密配合，通过县内媒体《当代修文》和修文电视台重点宣传、组织小分队深入村组宣传、利用场天在集市宣传等多种方式，凝聚全县人民的战胜灾害的信心。2009年和2010年，宣传工作以“两节一会”（2009“中国贵阳避暑季”、第四届国际阳明文化节、贵阳市第三届旅游发展大会）、“三创一办”（创建国家卫生城市、国家环境保护模范城市、全国文明城市和协办2011年第九届全国少数民族传统体育运动会）活动为载体，开展“办好文化节，争做文明人”“‘三创一办’我参与我受益”等系列宣传，以增强全县干部群众建设生态文明县的信心。

对外宣传 1978年后对外宣传工作列上议事日程，但力度不大，宣传方式单一，致外界对修文了解甚少。1996年，修文划属贵阳市管辖，外宣工作得到有力推动。1997年，县委、县政府举办“板栗节”，以办节的形式向外界推介修文。继后，外宣力度不断加大，方式增多，依托省市媒体和国家级媒体开展对外宣传成为主要形式，并制作宣传光碟、宣传画册、出版图书等，营造对外宣传氛围。其中制作宣传片《修文之旅》《修文风光》《修文—美在农业》《拓展广阔的天地—修文纪事》和航拍电视片《王学圣地》等10余种，出版宣传画册、图书《黔中宝地—修文》《王学圣地》《阳明胜境》《王阳明在龙场》《阳明先生的故事》等20余种。1999年，提出“打好阳明文化牌”，以县内独有的阳明文化为载体，筹办阳明文化节，通过办节活动更强有力地对外宣传修文。是年10月，“中国贵阳’99阳明文化节”举办，对外宣传取得明显效果。之后，又于2002年、2005年、2009年相继举办了第二届、第三届、第四届“阳明文化节”。

2009年9月3日县委宣传部举办对外宣传工作暨业务培训会

通过办节宣传、媒体宣传、制作各种宣传品宣传等多种外宣方式，修文形象日趋成熟，对外影响不断提高，“王学圣地，秀美修文”印象深入人心，为招商引资发展经济打下了基础。

2.理论学习

干部理论学习的主要方式一是集中学习，按事前制订的学习制度在规定时间内组织干部统一学习；二是在党委、党组、总支建立中心学习组进行专题讨论；三是举办月末知识讲座，集中全县副科级或股级以上干部听大课；四是规定学习篇目，由干部自行利用业余时间学习。多种学习方式使规定学习与自觉学习有机结合，形成浓厚的学习氛围。从1978年起，先后组织学习《邓小平文选》《陈云文稿选编》《马克思主义哲学学习纲要》《建设有中国特色社会主义》《社会主义初级阶段理论》《中共基本路线学习纲要》《关于社会主义若干问题的学习纲要》《中共中央关于经济体制改革的决定》《社会主义商品理论》

《市场经济理论》《中共党史学习纲要》《“三个代表”重要思想学习纲要》《公民道德读本》《人民利益高于一切》等政治理论书籍，并在不同阶段结合当时的形势任务和中心工作组织学习中央领导的讲话、中共会议文件精神等。检查理论学习的方式是组织学习考试、检查读书笔记、规定撰写调研文章。1988年，532名干部参加商品经济理论学习考试，及格率为99%。1997年，组织4000名干部参加市场经济理论学习考试，及格率为100%。2001年、2004年和2008年先后组织全县干部参加党性党风知识和理论考试。全县干部通过理论学习和工作实践，理论水平得以提高，县委先后编辑出版《足迹》《扬帆》《思路决定出路》等调研论文书籍收录县内干部论文107篇。

（三）统一战线工作

1981年成立统一战线工作部，专司全县统一战线工作，通过执行中共统一战线方针政策，团结一切可以团结的力量，调动一切积极因素，投入到经济社会发展事业中。此前，先后于1979年、1980年为1957年错划“右派”，在历次政治运动中被错误处理过的小商、小贩、小手工业者和少数民族干部中的统战对象，按中央的部署落实统战政策，改正对错误的处理，并给予经济补偿。

政协委员推荐　1983年成立修文县委领导下的统一战线组织——政协修文县委员会，至2010年共历7届。历次换届，其委员人选按统筹兼顾、全面安排的方针，德才兼备的原则和体现大团结大统一的精神，先后为政协推荐委员候选人1800人，审查明确委员1041人。

联系非公经济人士　1991年，在非公有制代表人士中开展“爱国、敬业、贡献”和“致富思源，富而思进”教育活动。之后，采取组织非公经济人士出国考察、召开座谈会、在非公企业中建立中共组织、引导非公企业参与国企改制、帮助非公企业解决实际困难等多种形式，团结县内广大非公经济人士发挥其企业优势，为县的经济发展贡献力量。至2010年，与50多家非公企业建立起联系制度，联系企业人员120人，联系1440人次。

贯彻对台方针政策　1983年成立对台工作领导小组办公室，1992年改设台湾工作办公室，与县政府台湾事务办公室合署办公。此前，于1982年开展台属台胞普查登记，时全县共有去台人员167人，台属台胞453人。2002年再次普查登记，有去台人员150人，台属570人，台胞1人。每年春节和中秋节，县委均召开“三胞两属”（台湾同胞、香港同胞、海外侨胞，台属、侨属）和各界人士座谈会，宣传中共对台方针和政策，加强对台宣传。1991至2010年接待回乡探亲台胞380人，走访慰问台属660人次。1998年和2000年，有台胞罗明忠和罗龙云回乡探亲病故，按相关政策为其处理后事，两名死者在台子女和大陆亲属均表示满意和感激。1999年和2002年，先后帮助台属任金品和余黔湘办理过境继承遗产手续，受到当事人称赞。1996年帮助台胞杨世发办理回乡定居手续，杨世发定居县内后已娶妻生子。至2010年，已为县内台属60人办理台属证。

（四）政法工作

社会稳定维护　2001年，县置维护社会稳定办公室于政法委内，开展维护社会稳定和防范打击邪教组织违法犯罪的工作。至2010年，先后打击处理邪教人员40人，教育转化人员33人；妥善处置扎佐把七村殡改事件、小箐乡紫江村计生事件等10余起群体性事件；排查化解矛盾纠纷100余起；协调各有关部门解决了南风井地质灾害、阳明老酒厂企业改制等一批重大历史遗留问题；建成乡镇综治、维稳调处中心和226个村和社区维稳信息员队伍；建立起维稳工作领导责任制、责任追究制、矛盾纠纷排查调处责任制等20余项工作制度，为维护稳定工作提供了制度保障。

2006年10月20日，贵阳市扎实推进无毒县工作会议在修文召开

在维稳工作中，县委政法委加强基层基础建设，每年及时调整充实县、乡两级维稳机构，健全以县委办、政府办、维稳办、信访办（局）、110报警台为信息枢纽，10个乡（镇）综治办、司法所、派出所为主体，226个村（社区）为辐射的维稳信息网络。2004年起，针对邪教组织向农村渗透蔓延的斗争趋势，县委政法委坚持打防结合，齐抓共管，充分利用全县综治、维稳网络，加强社会面排查和对重点人员管控，开展流动人口信息登记、楼群院落管护和夜间巡逻。在重大政治活动敏感期及节假日，均组织县公安局、县维稳办等相关部门，针对全县重点地段、重点区域、流动人口集中地等进行专项排查，及时化解不稳定因素，确保全县社会稳定。2010年，按照“预防为主、抓早、抓小、抓苗头”的原则，将发现的不稳定因素制成《近期不稳定因素分解表》，明确责任单位、责任领导、配合单位、责任人和办结时限，并先后召开14次专题维稳工作会议进行部署，把矛盾纠纷化解在基层，消除在萌芽状态。

社会治安综合治理　1982年10月，县成立社会治安综合治理领导小组，下设办公室，指导全县开展社会治安综合治理工作。1983年，县委精心部署和指导“严打”战役，坚持依法办事，尽最大努力从重从快，稳、准、狠地打击严重危害社会的各类犯罪分子，在“严打”第一阶段战役中就依法逮捕罪犯388人，判决210名，其中判处死刑立即执行的23名，死缓3名，无期徒刑6名，有期徒刑119名。在综合治理中，大力普及法律常识、增强人民群众法治观念，除在县直机关单位组织专题学习外，还在城乡广泛开辟法治宣传专栏，印发各种宣传资料，并运用广播电视报刊等多种形式进行普法教育，提升群众的法治意识。1997年起，综合治理工作结合“平安修文”建设工程开展，构建全县齐抓共管的治安防范网络。至2010年，全县已实现“110”“119”“122”报警台“三台合一”和治安“网格化”管理，获省综治委授予的“平安工程红旗县”称号。

（五）党史征研

1983年建立党史资料征集研究办公室，即开展县内民主革命时期党史资料的征编工作。至1995年，共查档1012卷，摘卡3185张，摘录报刊212份，发函调信65封，征集照片104张，走访老干部、知情者203人次，召开座谈会22场次。先后编写成《红军长征在修文》《修文县革命烈士传》《中国共产党修文县历史大事记》等书，考证明确修文解放日，撰写《风雨征程—修文党史纪略》在《修文报》连载。《红军长征在修文》共分四个部分：第一部分载综述、日志、修文籍红军战士及红军流散人员概况、采访录；第二部分为红军文献，摘录刘伯承、肖华、任弼时、关向应等回顾长征的文章和日记；

1991年，县委举办党史知识竞赛

第三部分收录19份旧政权关于红军长征过境的有关资料和文稿；第四部分附录，收录6篇红军入黔相关记事。《修文县革命烈士传》收录烈士梁方膏、商胜祥、黄兴志、罗孝昌、刘子义、徐华、陈必祥、黄少清、罗章龙、张小林等黑白照片10幅，获军功奖证书黑白照片3幅，刘子义烈士家书影印件1幅；载烈士传记13篇，烈士简介13篇，烈士英名录120人。

1996—2000年，征集、核实、编写《中共修文县组织史资料》。采用“划块分期、纵横结合”的编纂体例，以党、政、军、统、群5个系统分编，每编按3个时期立章，设置“中国共产党修文县组织史资料”“修文县政权系统组织史资料”“修文县地方军事系统组织史资料”“修文县统一战线系统组织史资料”“修文县群众团体系统组织史资料”5篇15章62节；于2001年内资出版，16开本，33印张，720千字，首次印制1000册。2002—2010年，收集300余万字资料，完成《中国共产党修县历史·第一卷》编撰，2010年10月定稿付印。全书设5篇14章38节和大事记，23万字，记述1935至1978年中国共产党在修文组织领导全县各族人民开展政治、经济、军事、科学、文化、教育等建设的历程。

在史料征编过程中，充分运用党史资料开展革命传统教育，先后举办党史知识竞赛、“勿忘国耻”演讲比赛等活动。与此同时，为省市编写党史书刊提供20余万字资料。其间，于2008年编撰成《风雨阳光路——纪念修文改革开放三十周年》。全书收录文章经济建设类14篇、政治建设类5篇、文化建设类10篇、社会建设类9篇，1978—2007年数据资料24份，彩插16页，彩照77幅，从社会、政治、文化、经济等方面展示修文改革开放30年间取得的丰硕成果。

（六）党校教育

1982年2月，开办农村干部培训班，招收学员42名，1年后毕业，全部分配至乡镇工作。1983年，县内按相关政策，吸纳40名干部职工子女顶替其父母工作，党校专门举办为期3个月的培训班，以提高其政治素质和工作能力。全年举办3期党员培训班，参加党员为县直机关、区、乡、镇党员，培训内容主要是学习中共十二大通过的新党章，提高党员对新时期中共任务和党员条件的认识。1984年，党中央明确各级党校要担负起正规化培训干部的任务后，党校的干部培训工作即从短期轮训为主转向正规化培训，1985—2010年，招收中专班6届，毕业学员200人；招收大专班4届，毕业学员340人；招收电大生311名，毕业301名。同时，短期培训干部800人次。

县委党校迎“七一”暨校庆大会

（七）信访

信访工作由县委、县政府设立的联合机构信访局（原称信访办公室）负责，其业务是接待人民群众来信来访，了解民情动态。1978—1988年，主要以处理要求落实政策的信访为主。此间，对750人按政策规定给予重新安排工作、作退职退休安置、补发工资、经济退赔或补偿、安置就业等处理。继后，随着工业企业改制、流通体制调整、事业单位改革逐步推进，以及县城拆迁改造、工业园区建设力度加大，利益大范围调整，社会矛盾集中反映，信访量呈上升趋势，最多年份群众来信来访逾500件2000人次。经过广泛宣传、领导亲自处理老大难问题、落实信访工作责任制，信访形势得到有效控制。2010年，群

众来访235起724人次，其中集体访31起357人次；群众来信148件次。

县委、县政府设有领导接待日制度，每周由1位县委常委或副县级领导到信访局接待来访群众，随机处理群众反映的问题。1999年起建立信访联席会议制度，由县委政法委主持召开有公、检、法、信访、民政等部门领导参加的联席会议，分析全县信访形势，研究重点信访问题。对重点问题由县信访局发出交办函，跟踪督查，限期处理。及时化解矛盾，减少越级上访和集体上访。2006年设置县长热线电话，2009年4月，又通过网络、邮政信件、电话、短信平台4个载体，开通“百姓——书记县长交流台”，畅通信访网络。2010年，县委、县政府领导接待来访群众25起169人次。

信访局设有信访接待室，每天安排专人接待来访群众，并严格执行首问负责制，做到有访必接，有接必办，有办必果。2008年，大石乡高山村与大寨村发生饮水纠纷，大寨村将高山村进村道路阻断。高山村村民到信访局上访，要求解决两村饮水矛盾。信访局调查获知，2007年两村建饮水工程时，系共用高山村水源点，因地质结构复杂，蓄水池底部处理不好，蓄水困难，不能满足两村饮用，发生为争水高山村毁坏大寨村引水管，大寨村因而堵塞高山村村路的群体事件。县政府随即责成水利局妥善解决，后经工程人员重新设计处理蓄水池渗漏保证正常用水，两村群众矛盾得以化解。

（八）编制管理

1981年7月，成立县编制委员会，办公室设在县人事局，负责掌握控制全县行政、事业机构和人员编制。1988年1月，原劳动工资局管理的党、政、群机关和事业单位的工资基金移交县编委办公室。1995年，县编委办从人事局分离出来单列。编委办于1996年9月独立开展业务。2002年机构改革时，编委办列入县委机构序列，是县机构编制委员会的常设办事机构，既是县委的工作机构，又是县人民政府的工作机构。2001年1月建立修文县事业单位登记管理局，2004年8月，设置修文县机构编制委员会督查室。

机构编制管理　控编补员，编制管理执行“一支笔”审批制度。1990年10月，开展党群机关控编“消肿”工作，全县党政群机关编制、人员膨胀的状况得到控制。2004年4月，印发《修文县机构编制委员会工作规则》和编制委员会、组织部、人事劳动和社会保障局共同制订的《关于严格机构编制和人事调配管理的意见》。

事业单位登记管理　2001年，根据国务院第252号《事业单位登记管理暂行条例》及省、市有关文件精神，县编委办拟定具体执行意见并以修府办通〔2001〕3号文下发有关单位，启动登记工作，凡有健全的会计制度，实行独立核算，能够独立承担民事责任的事业单位都要进行登记。要求事业单位向登记管理机关和审批机关分别报送上一年度执行《事业单位登记管理暂行条例》的情况报告。

印章管理　1995年机构改革后，县编委办统一管理县直各部门、县属事业单位印章的制发和废止印章的收缴工作，加强对机构改革后机关、事业单位的印章刻制工作和撤销、合并、更名单位原使用的印章的收缴和销毁工作。2006年3月以来，对全县90多家单位的130多枚印章进行了重新制作。编委办每年都将作废的印章统一移交给县档案局保管。

机构改革管理　党政群团事业机构分别在1995、2002、2004、2005、2010年进行重大改革。1995年机构改革，党委机构设置7个，政府机关26个。1997年，相继恢复战备办、粮食局、环保局、物价局。1998年、1999年，地税局、工商局上划为省垂直管理，隶属县政府行政机构实有28个，县政府直属事业局级机构7个。2002年，全县机构改革，中共党委机构设置8个，其中县委工作部门7个，归口管理机构1个，县政府工作部门设置24个，受政府委托行使部分行政管理职能的直属事业单位3个。经过机构改革后，县级党、政、群机关及乡（镇）机关行政编制总数由809名（不含公、检、法、司专项编制）精简为670名，减少139名。2004年，进行政府机构改革，政府工作部门整合为24个。2005年8月被列为贵州省乡（镇）机构改革试点县之一。是年进行乡（镇）机构改革，进一步把乡（镇）政府职能转到社会管理和公共服务上来，合理界定乡（镇）机构的职能及任务，理顺县、乡、村机构和组织之间的责权关系。综合设置乡（镇）党政办事机构：按照《贵州省乡镇分类标准和方法》测算，修文县一类乡镇5个：龙场镇、扎佐镇、久长镇、六广镇、谷堡乡；二类乡镇5个：六屯乡、洒坪乡、大石乡、小箐乡、六桶乡。一类乡（镇）设置的5个综合办事机构是：党政办公室、社会事务办公室、经济发展办公室、人口与计划生育办公室、社会治安综合治理办公室。二类乡（镇）设置的4个综合办事机构是：党政办公室、社会事务办公室（与社会治安综合治理办公室合署办公）、经济发展办公室、人口与计划生育办公室。乡（镇）人大、纪委、政法委、人民武装部等不专设办事机构，其具体事务由党政办公室和其他办公室承担，工、青、妇等组织按有关章程设置。2010年政府机构改革，县政府工作部门机构改为22个。

（九）老干部管理

1984年设置老干部管理局，负责管理离职退养干部的学习和生活。1995年1月改称离退休干部工作局，其工作范围扩至副县级以上离退休干部。从建立老干局起，认真落实老干部各项政治待遇和生活待遇。每年“七一”“八一”、国庆、重阳、元旦、春节等重大节日召开老干部茶话会、座谈会；定期通报情况，介绍全县政治、经济形势；坚持阅文制度，对享受县处级待遇的离退休干部，可阅读发至县级的有关文件；在重大决策出台前，主动征求老干部的意见；每年春节前夕，县委、县政府均邀请享受县处级政治生活待遇的离退休干部参加各界人士新春团拜会，欢度节日；县财政每年拨出资金为老干部征订报纸杂志；1988年对离休干部年满70周岁的享受护理费待遇，1997年实施离休干部医疗统筹精神，将企业离休干部纳入医疗保险，保证离休干部病有所医。2000年起，县委组织部和修文报社为老干部赠阅《修文报》，老干部人手一份。凡国家、省、市有关老干部工资待遇、生活补贴方面的文件，县委、县政府都贯彻落实。2008年，建立离休干部特困帮扶机制，帮助离休老干部解决生活中的特殊困难。县委、县政府创造条件组织离退休老干参加文体活动和外出参观考察、视察全县改革发展成果。2009年组织参加贵阳避暑季暨第四届国际阳明文化节开幕式、参观贵阳市环城高速公路、到扎佐工业区进行考察并参观贵阳野生动物园等活动。2010年，组织部分老干部到烈士陵园参加县开展的“清明文明祭祀、预防森林火险”和“绿丝带”志愿服务活动。老干部发挥余热，组成“五老”（老党员、老干部、老军人、老模范、老教师）网吧监督队、劝导队，对网吧进行巡查、检查，规劝违规上网的未成年人，教育、举报违规接纳未成年人上网的网吧业主，净化未成年人成长环境。

2006年1月，县委召开《修文县志》（1978—2010）编纂推进会，退休干部发挥余热投身县志编纂

（十）政策研究

县委政策研究室为县委办公室内设科室，主要职责是围绕中共基本路线、重大决策和上级党委以及

县委的工作部署，对全县经济、政治、文化、党建及社会发展等方面的重要政策问题以及带有全局性、方向性的“热点”、难点问题进行调查研究，提出意见建议，供县委决策参考。根据县委指示，组织协同有关部门起草或修改有关重要文件、报告和文稿。承担有关改革试验、试点工作任务，总结经验做法，为工作整体推进提供学习借鉴。配合完成上级业务部门开展的调研课题等。

1983年县委批转县委研究室、农办《关于武家寨七个生产队联合建设文明村寨的调查报告》，在全县因地制宜推广。1993年，形成《修文县非公有制经济发展现状、问题及对策》供县委、县政府决策参考。至2010年，县委政策研究室先后牵头完成了第一轮农村改革试点、参与全县各个“五年规划”等工作和任务，共起草各类重要文件、调研报告230余份，其中撰写《安泰模式打造贵州药谷》等较为有影响力的报告达20余篇。

（十一）督查检查

县委督查室负责督促检查上级党委的重要决策和重要工作部署的贯彻落实情况；对县委出台的全县性重要文件和县党代会、县委全会等全县性会议议定事项进行分解立项和督促检查；对县委、县政府为民办“十件实事”进行专项督促检查；承担县委和县委领导开展督促检查的组织协调及服务工作；牵头制订全县各乡镇、县直各部门年度绩效目标、调整、考核等工作，重点抓好全县各乡镇、县直部门年度保证目标和党群部门主要工作目标的日常管理和检查考核，及时下发“督办通知”“督办督查通报”“督办督查专报”督查文件，发布年度综合目标绩效考核情况通报等。

督促检查主要采取实地督查、书面督查、电话督查、督查调研等多元化方式进行，不断强化督促检查力度，每年平均发布“督办督查通报”“督办督查专报”等文件30余期，切实为县委、县政府为民办“十件实事”、重大项目和重要工作的推进提供强有力的支持和保障。

（十二）保密工作

1981年，县委建立保密委员会并置办公室，负责贯彻执行党和国家保密工作的方针和政策，指导全县企事业单位的保密工作，配合相关部门查处失密、泄密事件。1992年保密办与政府保密局合署办公，两个机构既是县委的常设办事机构，又是县政府主管保守国家秘密的职能部门，归口县委办公室管理。自保密机构设立后，每年均对县城打字复印店进行保密检查及人员保密知识培训。县委、县政府及相关职能部门出台一系列重要文件，保密办（局）开展各种宣传活动做好全县保密工作。1998年，县委办公室、县人大办公室下发《关于对〈保密法〉贯彻落实情况进行检查的通知》并开展执法检查。2003年，县委出台《关于进一步加强全县保密工作的意见》。2010年，新修订的《中华人民共和国保密法》颁布后，保密局在《当代修文》上分10期全文刊登宣传，并组织干部职工学习，在修文电视台滚动播出宣传保密知识。利用场天在新客车站发放新《中华人民共和国保密法》《关于国家秘密载体保密管理的规定》《信息安全等级保护管理办法（试行）》和《手机使用保密管理规定（试行）》等相关保密法规宣传资料。

县部门开展国家安全、保密、档案法宣传活动

（十三）关心下一代工作

1990年设置关心下一代协会隶属于老干部管理局，1996年改称关心下一代工作委员会，依靠和发挥“五老”（老党员、老专家，老教师，老战士、老模范）优势，加强对未成年人的思想道德建设。关工委在10个乡（镇）和县直部门、村（居）以及学校、企事业单位相继成立关工委或关工小组。至2010年全县仍有关工组织48个，组成人员200余人，“五老”参加关心下一代工作活动的有60余人。

关工委通过青少年思想道德教育、法治宣传教育、科技文化教育、普及科学家教知识和为青少年办实事、做好事等活动开展关心下一代工作。从成立关协组织起，为加强未成年人思想道德建设，全县各级关心下一代组织配合有关部门，对青少年进行以理想信念为核心的爱国主义、集体主义、社会主义、革命传统和艰苦奋斗教育。每年均组织“五老”报告员深入基层，结合纪念重大节日，通过报告会、讲座等形式，引导青少年树立正确的世界观、人生观、价值观，受教育的青少年每年达到3万人次。在“二五”普法到“五五”普法期间以全县普法工作为契机，组织关爱工作团、法治报告团和“五老”等，深入学校、社区和企事业单位，宣传《中华人民共和国未成年人保护法》《中华人民共和国预防青少年犯罪法》以及《中华人民共和国义务教育法》《中华人民共和国道路交通安全法》等法律法规，通过举办法治辅导报告、法律知识讲座、上法治课等，引导广大青少年从小学法、懂法、守法、用法，提高辨别是非能力，自觉抵御不良倾向，依法维护自身的合法权益。对失足青少年和“问题青少年”，组织“五老”进行结队帮教。2004年起，组织50名“五老”义务网吧监督员，配合有关职能部门抓净化学校和社会环境工作，对全县网吧、游戏厅进行检查监督。1998年开始，以县科协和县科技局为主，组织科技工作者到学校开展科技讲座，引导青少年热爱科学崇尚科学。2004—2008年，县疾控中心与修文报社合作，在少年儿童中开展地氟病防治知识征文活动，330名少年儿童通过学习写稿宣传地氟病防治知识。2010年，在野生动物园和县实验一小、二小开展首批省科普教育基地和贵阳市青少年科技教育特色学校创建达标工作，组织科普大篷车将流动科技馆送到六屯中学，通过模型、实物等现代科技展示手段，为500余名学生进行科普知识教育。2005年起，教育、妇联等部门创建家长学校普及科学家教方法，帮助广大家长树立为国教子思想。县关工委发动和组织县内单位为青少年办实事、做好事，2006—2010年，修文报社、县文联、教育局等单位先后在中小学生和团员青年中开展“文明礼仪童谣征集”“读书心得征文”“爱祖国爱家乡朗诵比赛”“少儿书画展”等主题活动，激发青少年爱祖国爱家乡立志成才的激情。重视关爱全县1000多名“留守儿童”的思想和学习、生活，在全县范围内举行各种活动，关心弱势群体中的青少年和儿童。2010年“六一”节，县妇儿工委和县妇联将价值7000元的运动、游戏器材送到县实验二小和小箐乡幼儿园，县委组织部为龙场镇马口小学、六屯小学、六桶小学的20名留守贫困儿童送去慰问金8000元。县工商联联络贵州华飞化学工业有限公司、贵州东方希望饲料有限公司等企业和贵阳市工商联南安商会和绍兴商会，为县实验小学捐助资金1.35万元，为六屯乡西冲村大路边小学捐赠电脑和运动器材等。

第三节　中共修文县纪律检查委员会

1979年8月设置县委纪律检查委员会，负责中共纪律检查工作。1983年12月，遵照中央纪律检查委员会《关于健全中共纪律检查系统，加强纪检队伍建设的暂行规定》，将县委纪律检查委员会升格为中共修文县纪律检查委员会，在县委和上级纪委的双重领导下，开展维护党纪党规，加强党风建设，检查中共路线、方针、政策和决议执行情况等工作。自1984年起，县纪委实行常委制，从县的党员代表大会选举常委会组成人员分工担任书记、副书记和常务委员。县纪委内设办公室、纪律检查科和案件审理科，1986年增置经济检查科。1988年12月改科为室，并撤销经济检查科，增设信访室。1993年6月，县纪委与县监察局合署办公，置办公室、纪检监察室、案件审理室、信访室、党风廉政建设室和监察综合室。2002年3月增设宣传教育室、干部管理室。2009年12月增设纠正行业不正之风办公室，同时更名党风廉政建设室为党风廉政室，至2010年，县纪委内设机构的8室格局未变。

一、党风廉政建设

党风廉政建设与党纪宣传和反腐倡廉宣传教育工作相结合，互为依存，相互促进，通过宣传教育，促使党风向好。

主题教育活动　1982年，作出《认真贯彻执行〈关于党内政治生活的若干准则〉的决定》，并提出“学《准则》见行动，从我做起，从现在做起，从每一件事做起”的要求，在全县上下掀起学习宣传《准则》的高潮。1989年，在党员、干部中开展维护安定团结局面，反对资产阶级自由化教育。1999年，以“三讲”教育为契机，开展党性党风党纪教育宣传。2000年，开展党风廉政“宣教年”活动，举办“党纪政纪法规百题竞赛”“清风杯”大合唱比赛、“廉政杯”书画影展、“颂祖国颂家乡”卡拉OK大赛，印发成克杰、胡长清贪污腐败案件资料对党员进行警示教育、组织2000余人次观看影片《生死抉择》。2003年至2005年，开展宣传贯彻《建立健全教育制度监督并重的惩治和预防腐败体系实施纲要》《中国共产党纪律处分条例》活动。其间，在2003年开展的“七个一”（举办一次党风廉政征文活动，制作一件廉政警示宣传品，举办一次领导干部廉洁从政教育讲座，开展一次警示教育活动，举办一次党性、党风和法规知识竞赛，出版一本党员干部撰写的廉政论文集，举办一次廉政书画展）宣传教育活动中，举办贵阳市勤政廉政模范人物先进事迹评选及修文巡回报告会，县委副书记、纪委书记岳建初参加全市巡回宣讲。2006年起，举办廉政文化进机关、进社区、进家庭、进学校、进企业和进农村的“六进”活动。围绕党性党风党纪教育，先后组织开展“《党章》再学习再教育”“学习‘三个代表’重

2003年，县举办“清风颂”文艺晚会

要思想”“学《党章》、保先进、促发展”等主题教育活动；结合厉行节约制止奢侈浪费专题教育，开展“廉洁奉公、勤政为民”主题活动。2009年，把反腐倡廉宣传教育融入到职能部门的工作中，明确纪委、组织部、宣传部、文明办、文广局等22家单位为“大宣教”联席会议成员单位，调动各职能部门的资源优势，形成大宣教合力。2010年，贯彻落实中央纪委《关于加强廉政文化建设的意见》，开展示范教育、警示教育、岗位廉政教育活动，引导党员干部讲党性、重品行、作表率。

1980—2010年，全县共组织35项党风廉政建设主题教育活动。在开展主题教育活动中，召开各种廉政教育会议246场次，播放廉政电教片200部，编印下发反腐倡廉教育资料1.7万册，开展党纪条规知识竞赛、先进典型事迹巡回演讲12次。

廉政制度建设 1980—2010年，县委、县政府、县纪委先后制订出台120项反腐倡廉制度规定，各乡镇和县直各部门结合实际，突出重点部位和关键环节，制订规章制度460多项。1982年针对招工、招生、农转非、工转干和调动工作中搞不正之风问题，制订《关于共产党员干部职工当前应遵守的几项纪律的决定》，处理了16名违纪干部。1989年，实施干部考廉制度，规定由县纪委搜集基层党组织和副科级以上党员干部党风廉政建设的情况，记入廉政档案，作为评先评优、提拔使用的重要依据。1991年推行公开办事程序、公开办事结果、主动接受群众监督的“两公开一监督”制度。1998年实行领导干部家庭财产申报制度，要求全县党政机关、企事业单位科级领导干部每年底必须申报个人家庭收入情况。2001年起，把党风廉政建设纳入各级党组织工作目标考核，县、乡（镇）、村和机关单位层层签订“党风廉政建设责任书”，把权力关在制度的“笼子”里，明确责任人，量化管理。2006年，大石乡党委与县纪委签订“党风廉政建设责任书”后，加强制度建设，以制度建设促党风廉政建设，制订“领导班子议事制度”“效能建设有关规定”“政府接待就餐制度”等规章制度，通过制度管人管事，仅政府接待一项，依靠《接待就餐制度》管住大吃大喝，当年就比上年减少就餐支出5万元。2008年制订《建立健全惩治和预防腐败体系2008—2012年工作规划》，要求坚持工作报告制度，将执行责任制和推进惩防腐败体系建设情况定期向上级党委、纪委报告。2010年，建立健全反腐败协调机制和相关工作联席会议制度，做到部门之间经常通报情况、交换意见，密切配合、优势互补。

2007年，县直属机关党委组织干部到大洞口监狱开展“现身说法”警示教育活动

二、案件查处

1979年恢复纪律检查工作至1992年，共查处违纪党员460人次，其中开除党籍87人，留党察看102人，撤销党内外职务72人，警告和严重警告196人，降级3人，开除留党察看5人，开除公职5人。1993年，纪律检查委员会与县政府监察局合署办公，至2010年，共查处违纪党员、干部955人次，分别给予纪律处分。1986年，县农业局干部王宗良、农业银行久长营业所工作人员张顺德、水塘邮电所工作人员赵英明贪污公款，经纪委查实后移交司法机关处理，4月26日，县委纪律检查委员会与县打击经济领域犯罪领导小组在县电影院召开县直机关职工大会，由检察机关在大会上对3人实施公捕。2000年3月—2001

年1月，县民族宗教事务局副局长韦金成利用职务之便，虚构拆除扎佐电影院和修建扎佐天主教教堂建筑工程的事实，与贵州省建筑公司建安二处等5家单位的经办人签订拆除和修建合同，并以支付前期工程款为借口，骗取现金25.5万元。2002年2月，韦又化名王伟，冒充贵阳市金阳新区协调办负责人，骗取湖南省对外建筑公司武汉分公司巨额工程款。经县纪委和监察局查明案情后，决定开除韦金成的党籍和公职，并移交司法机关依法处理。2002年12月，韦金成被县人民法院认定为犯诈骗罪判处有期徒刑10年，并处罚金5万元。

全县纪检监察机关在查案执纪的同时，加强信访举报工作，及时处理各种矛盾和问题。31年间，共接受办理业务范围内的信访举报1685件次，信访件按期办结率100%。

1993—2010县纪检监察案件查处情况表

表2—02—06

项目／年份	结案	党纪处分（处理）						行政处分（处理）						
		免予处分	警告	严重警告	撤销党内职务	留党察看	开除党籍	免予处分	警告	记过	记大过	降级	撤职	开除
1993	43	4	1	5	1	3	8	5	5	6	3	0	2	1
1994	48	5	3	4	0	2	2	6	12	9	4	0	1	3
1995	69	7	9	8	0	1	3	12	14	9	4	1	3	6
1996	65	1	3	15	1	4	10	11	8	6	4	23	4	6
1997	50	1	2	5	0	7	3	3	11	16	7	4	2	1
1998	42	0	6	5	0	3	10	0	11	6	5	1	5	4
1999	58	6	4	8	2	6	17	0	8	9	4	1	1	9
2000	52	2	11	9	1	3	5	3	16	2	2	2	2	5
2001	51	2	3	11	1	5	7	7	6	5	2	2	0	7
2002	56	0	10	13	1	2	3	2	19	1	1	2	4	1
2003	72	5	11	12	0	3	6	8	20	6	2	4	4	0
2004	80	7	24	19	2	2	8	10	7	3	0	4	2	1
2005	81	10	36	13	0	7	11	4	5	1	0	0	0	3
2006	36	2	9	5	1	3	4	4	9	2	0	0	0	1
2007	41	19	23	12	0	2	5	4	15	5	6	1	0	3
2008	37	0	12	7	0	1	5	0	12	4	5	1	0	3
2009	49	0	7	7	0	3	12	0	15	6	4	3	2	7
2010	25	0	2	1	1	1	7	0	5	5	4	0	2	1
合计	955	71	176	159	12	58	126	79	198	101	57	49	31	68

三、纠风治乱

1980—1985年，针对党员干部在招工、招生、农村户口转为城镇户口、建房分房中以权谋私、违反计划生育政策、参与赌博、强迫命令、打架斗殴、乱砍滥伐林木、严重官僚主义等不正之风，先后组织17个次调查组进行调查，共审理查处各类案件307件，给予378名党员党纪处分，其中：开除党籍73人，留党察看96人，撤销党内外职务49人，警告、严重警告160人；对18名党政干部参与经商办企业的行为给予纠正。1996年和1997年，对全县事业单位预算外资金进行检查，查出有问题单位督促交存专户。1998年，全县所有行政事业单位实行资金“收支两条线”管理，县纪委加强监察，预算外资金专户储存率和统一票据使用率均达100%。1999年，下发《关于严禁用公款吃喝玩乐的通知》等文件，要求党员、干部廉洁奉公。2003年，出台“禁酒令”，规定机关人员不得在上班时间饮酒；制订关于禁止党员干部大操大办“生日宴”、子女“升学宴”“搬家宴”的规定，倡导文明节俭新风。2007年起，加强对各项支农惠农政策落实情况的监督检查，严肃查处贪污、私分、截留、挤占、挪用涉农资金的行为。2009年，推进领导干部廉洁自律工作，会同有关部门加强对重点时段、重点部门、重点岗位的监督检查。查处3名干部违规收受现金问题；纠正医药购销和医疗服务中的不正之风，建立医务人员医德考评制度，推行药品和医疗器械集中采购办法，规范集中采购工作。是年，集中招标采购378个品种的药品，共362.74万元，招标采购金额占总金额的94.68%。2010年，开展“整治发展软环境，建设服务型机关”专项工作，对上班期间不认真履行职责的7名干部进行问责。

第四节　乡（镇）党委与中共基层组织

一、乡镇党委

1978—1981年，县委辖城关区、扎佐区、六广区、小箐区和久长公社（区级公社）4区1公社党委，区级以下公社（镇）党委27个。1981年，久长公社建制改为区的建制，相应改久长公社党委为久长区党委；增设程官公社、金桥公社、久长公社、清水公社和扎佐镇建制，相应设公社和镇党委。全县有区级以下党委32个。1984年4月，根据中共中央、国务院《关于实行政社分开建立乡政府的通知》，全县公社均改为乡建制，公社党委相应改称乡党委，同时，将城关区辖的城关镇建制升格为区级建制，城关镇党委相应升格为区级党委。至此，县委共辖5个区党委和1个区级镇党委及31个乡党委。1991年11月撤区并乡建镇，撤5区1镇党委及乡党委，建龙场镇、扎佐镇、久长镇、六广镇、谷堡乡、洒坪乡、小箐乡、六屯乡、大石乡、六桶乡10个乡（镇）党委。

二、党总支与党支部

1978年，全县有党总支3个，1999年有11个，2008年有15个，至2010年有党总支20个。1978年，全县有中共基层支部308个。2000年，全县党支部有442个。2004年，基层组织机构发展工作拓展到非公有经济组织，在非公有经济组织建立中共基层支部5个。至2010年经过调整，全县共有党支部429个。

第三章　人民代表大会

县内人民代表大会制度始于1954年，1966年，因“文化大革命”停止活动，至1981年才得恢复。1981年至2010年为县人民代表大会第七届至十四届任期。七至十届每届任期为3年，十一届起任期改为5年。其间，为使县级换届时间与省、市同步，第十三届任期从2003年3月起至2006年11月，未满5年。第十四届任期从2006年11月起恢复为5年。

第一节　县人民代表大会

一、县人民代表选举

县人民代表选举按《中华人民共和国全国人民代表大会和地方各级人民代表大会选举法》和《选举法实施细则》规定进行，第一步建立县选举委员会，指导全县开展选举工作；第二步由县乡（镇）举行选举培训，同时进行营造氛围的宣传动员；第三步选民登记；第四步提出代表候选人；第五步确定代表候选人；第六步以选区为单位选举产生出席县人民代表大会代表。

1981年，第七届县人民代表大会共登记选民11.85万人，选举产生第七届人大代表238名。

1984年，第八届县人民代表大会共登记选民12.95万人，选举产生第八届人大代表236名。

1987年，第九届县人民代表大会共登记选民14.11万人，全县划为87个选区提出代表候选人410名，确定正式候选人237名，选举产生第九届人大代表164名。

1990年，第十届县人民代表大会共登记选民14.92万人，全县划为96个选区提出代表候选人653名，确定正式候选人287名，选举产生第十届人大代表186名。

1993年，第十一届县人民代表大会共登记选民15.54万人，全县划为93个选区提出代表候选人676名，确定正式候选人285名，选举产生第十一届人大代表189名。

1998年，第十二届县人民代表大会共登记选民16.54万人，全县划为90个选区提出代表候选人702名，确定正式候选人272名，选举产生第十二届人大代表182名。

2003年，第十三届县人民代表大会共登记选民18.53万人，由各选区提出代表候选人551名，确定正式候选人276名，选举产生第十三届人大代表186名。

2006年，第十四届县人民代表大会登记选民18.72万人，由各选区提出代表候选人541名，确定正式候选人271名，选举产生第十四届人大代表185名。

县人大代表选举主要由乡（镇）人民代表大会执行。县人大七届一次会议产生常务委员会后，历届常委会高度重视指导乡镇人大选举工作，1987年，县、乡两级人大换届，常委会党组向县委呈报《关于1987年县、乡两级人大换届选举工作的报告》，报告对选举的组织机构、时间安排、代表名额分配以及方法步骤作了明确具体的规定。县委以县发〔1987〕1号文件批转该报告并要求各地贯彻执行。此后每届选举，常委会均以同样的方式指导乡镇换届选举工作。此外，常委会通过监督的方式指导乡（镇）选举。1990年3月10日，六屯乡在换届选举中因该乡第15选区下选的乡领导落选，即否定了当日的选举，于次日重新组织投票选举实现“领导意图”。常委会收到群众反映后，经调查反映情况属实，即作出《关于纠正六屯乡第十五选区违法选举乡代表的决议》，确认该选区10月10日选举有效，11日选举违法，无效。

二、历届人民代表大会

1981年第七届至2010年第十四届共历8届县人民代表大会，共召开会议39次。每次会议除特殊原因外，多数都听取和审议了县政府工作报告、县人大常委会工作报告、县人民法院工作报告、县人民检察院工作报告、县国民经济和社会发展计划报告、县财政预算和预算执行情况报告等六个报告并对各个报告经讨论后作出相应的批准决议。会议还听取和通过提案审查委员会关于提案审查的报告。

七届一次会议 1981年1月11—16日在县城召开，应出席代表238人，实到210人。会议除听取和审议“六个报告”外，还总结中共十一届三中全会后全县各项工作取得的成绩和经验，强调必须进一步把全县工作重点转移到经济建设上来，要求1981年人口自然增长率降至10‰以下。会议选举第七届县人大常委会组成人员主任1人，副主任5人，委员12人，并选举县人民政府县长1人，副县长4人，选举县人民法院院长和县人民检察院检察长。

七届二次会议 1982年9月2—5日在县城召开，应出席代表227人，实到172人。会议听取和审议“六个报告”。在肯定全县政治安定、经济工作成绩显著的同时，强调政府要加强经济工作的领导，号召全县人民振奋精神，同心同德，为搞好“两个文明”（物质文明和精神文明）建设而努力。会议增选人大常委会副主任1人，并调整选举县人民检察院检察长。

七届三次会议 1983年3月18—21日在县城召开，应出席代表225人，实到168人。出席县政协一届一次全委会的政协委员48人列席会议。会议听取和审议“六个报告”，提出1983年工农业总产值产值达到5983万元，比上年增长5.8%的奋斗目标。会议选举9人为贵州省第六届人民代表大会代表。

七届四次会议 1984年2月28—3月1日在县城召开，应出席代表225人，实到代表172人。出席县政协一届二次全委会的政协委员63人列席会议。会议听取和审议“六个报告”。重点讨论机构改革，调整领导班子问题。强调各行各业各部门要抓经济建设，特别要在农村中发展重点户和专业户，鼓励农民在商品生产中大胆探索和实践，为农业的进一步发展作出新贡献。会议批准1名老同志辞去人大常委会主任职务，4名老同志辞去副主任职务，同时补选人大常委会主任1人和副主任3人。

八届一次会议 1984年3月6—10日在县城召开，应出席代表236人，实到221人。会议听取和审议“六个报告”，在听取和讨论国民经济和社会发展的“七五”计划《草案》中，会议提出“六五”计划的

1985年工农业产值比上年增长14.85%的奋斗目标。会议选举第八届人大常委会组成人员主任1人，副主任5人，委员17人。并选举县人民政府县长1人，副县长3人，选举法院院长和检察院检察长。

八届二次会议 1985年9月16—18日在县城召开，应出席代表230人，实到198人。会议听取和审议“六个报告”，认为中共十一届三中全会后全县经济形势是好的，号召各行各业在改革大潮中做出新贡献。

八届三次会议 1986年3月26—30日在县城召开，应出席代表225人，实到196人，出席县政协一届三次全委会的政协委员55人列席会议。会议听取和审议“六个报告”，还听取县人民政府关于“七五”规划（草案）报告，提出到1990年全县工农业总产值达1.1亿元，粮食6.5万吨，财政收入2100万元，人口自然增长率控制在9‰以下。会议还讨论和审议县人民政府《关于加强土地管理的暂行规定》和《普及法律常识的实施意见》，并作出相应决议。

八届四次会议 1987年4月2—4日在县城召开，应出席代表178人，列席125人。会议听取和审议“六个报告”，提出1987年集中力量抓好两件大事：一是政治上坚持四项基本原则，反对资产阶级自由化；二是经济上坚持改革、开放、搞活，开展增收节支，努力实现财政收支平衡。会议还作出关于加强法治教育维护安定团结的决议。

九届一次会议 1987年8月25—29日在县城召开，到会代表162人。出席县政协二届一次全委会的政协委员101人列席会议。会议听取和审议“六个报告”，会议号召全县深化改革，重点增强农业后劲和搞活企业，努力提高经济效益，为完成1987年的国民经济和社会发展计划而奋斗。会议选举第九届县人大常委会组成人员主任1人，副主任4人，委员12人。并选举县人民政府县长1人，副县长4人，选举法院院长和检察院检察长，选举9人为贵州省第七届人民代表大会代表。

九届二次会议 1988年4月7—9日在县城召开，到会代表135人。出席县政协二届二次全委会的政协委员105人列席会议。会议听取和审议“六个报告”，强调经济工作要突出改革主题，促进农村商品经济发展，搞活企业内部经营管理，努力增加财政收入，确保1988年国民经济和社会发展计划实现。

九届三次会议 1989年3月28—31日在县城召开，到会代表150人，出席县政协二届三次全委会的政协委员104人列席会议。会议听取和审议“六个报告”，强调贯彻好中央治理经济环境，整顿经济秩序，全面深化改革的方针，采取经济的、行政的、法律的、纪律的、思想政治工作的手段五管齐下，进行宏观调控，以免出现经济生活混乱。会议补选第九届人大常务委员会委员2人。

十届一次会议 1990年4月24—28日在县城召开，到会代表181人。出席县政协三届一次全委会的政协委员105人列席会议。会议听取和审议“六个报告”，强调保持国民经济长期、持续、协调、稳定发展，圆满完成治理整顿的基本任务。会议选举第十届人大常委会组成人员主任1人，副主任4人，委员12人。选举县人民政府县长1人，副县长4人，选举法院院长和检察院检察长。

十届二次会议 1991年3月26—29日在县城召开，到会代表186名。出席县政协三届二次全委会的政协委员110人列席会议。会议听取和审议“六个报告”，与会代表就1990年全县财政收入1415.9万元比上一年1615.46万元减少12.35%展开讨论指出：县政府要依靠全县广大干部和群众，克服困难，扎实工作，为完成经济工作和社会发展任务，为实现“八五”计划努力奋斗。

十届三次会议 1992年3月26—29日在县城召开，到会代表181名。出席县政协三届三次全委会的政协委员102人列席会议。会议听取和审议“六个报告”，认真讨论、审查全县《国民经济社会发展十年规划和“八五”计划（草案）》，还讨论了《修文县实施义务教育法规划（草案）》，并作出授权县人大常委会对该规划审查批准的决定。会议补选罗筑云为县人民政府县长。

十届四次会议　1992年11月12日在县城召开，到会代表178人，列席代表24人，会议选举县出席省第八届人民代表大会代表8名。

十一届一次会议　1993年4月7—10日在县城召开，到会代表189名。出席县政协四届一次全委会的政协委员118人列席会议。会议听取和审议“六个报告”，强调县政府在今后的工作中千方百计抓好农业和农村工作；要优化产业结构，增进经济效益；要保持工业生产稳步增长；大力发展第三产业；抓好财政金融工作；大力发展科技教育事业。会议选举县人大常委会主任1人、副主任4人，县人民政府县长1人、副县长4人，选举法院院长和检察院检察长。

十一届二次会议　1994年3月22—25日在县城召开，到会代表189名。出席县政协四届二次全委会的政协委员121人列席会议。会议听取和审议“六个报告”，充分肯定1993年县政府在县委的领导下，带领全县人民努力奋斗，取得的粮食总产量、烟叶收购量、财政收入、农业总产值、工业生产计划、粮食定购入库、乡镇企业计划和计划生育工作8项考核指标获安顺地区总分第一名的成果。会议补选涂新善为县人民政府县长。

十一届三次会议　1995年3月22—24日在县城召开，到会代表188名。出席县政协四届三次全委会的政协委员134人列席会议。会议听取和审议“六个报告”，对县政府在1994年狠抓计划生育工作，使修文再一次荣获全国计划生育工作先进县称号给予高度评价。

十一届四次会议　1996年1月18—19日在县城召开，到会代表186名。此次会议是因修文县由安顺地区划出归贵阳市管辖，需增选贵阳市九届人大代表和因县政府县长工作变动出缺，需补选县长而特别召开的。会议选举出席贵阳市九届人大代表11名，补选陈开域为县人民政府县长。

1996年1月18日，县十一届人民代表大会第四次会议召开

十一届五次会议　1996年3月19—21日在县城召开，到会代表186名。出席县政协四届四次全委会的政协委员127人列席会议。会议听取和审议“六个报告”。1996年是第九个五年计划实施的开局年，会议重点讨论和审议国民经济发展“九五”计划。

十一届六次会议　1997年3月19—21日在县城召开，到会代表185名。出席县政协四届五次全委会的政协委员137人列席会议。会议听取和审议“六个报告”，对1996年政府工作给予肯定，认为是达到了在“九五”计划第一年“开好头，起好步”要求的。同时也对财政报告体现的财政赤字累计为1598.3万元表示担忧。

十一届七次会议　1997年10月28—29日在县城召开，到会代表162名。会议主要议程是选举出席贵阳市第十届人民代表大会代表，选举产生修文县出席贵阳市第十届人民代表大会代表20名。

十二届一次会议　1998年3月24—28日在县城召开，到会代表182名。出席县政协五届一次全委会的政协委员127人列席会议。会议听取和审议“六个报告”，对政府工作报告指出“五年来县的经济持续稳定发展，各项社会事业取得新进步，社会保持稳定局面，‘八五’计划圆满完成，‘九五’计划有了良好的开局”表示赞同，并对过去5年县政府的工作给予肯定。会议依法选举人大常委会主任、副主任、委员，选举县人民政府县长、副县长，选举法院院长和检察院检察长。

十二届二次会议 1999年3月30—4月2日在县城召开，到会代表184名。出席县政协五届二次全委会的政协委员128人列席会议。会议听取和审议“六个报告”，重点讨论1999年的经济预期目标和1999年县政府计划办理的16件实事，希望县政府认真抓好16件实事中的“九三”工程项目，确保1999年完成体育馆、文广大楼、人民广场等工程建设，迎接首届阳明文化节的举办。会议补选县人大常务委员会委员3名。

十二届三次会议 2000年2月23—25日在县城召开，到会代表182名。出席县政协四届五次全委会的政协委员122人列席会议。会议听取和审议“六个报告”，对1999年成功举办阳明文化节使修文知名度和影响力得以提升给予充分肯定。强调县政府要下大力做好2000年教育“两基”达标工作，以优异成绩迎接新世纪的到来。会议补选县人大常委会委员1人。

十二届四次会议 2001年2月21—23日在县城召开，到会代表179名。出席县政协五届四次全委会的政协委员148人列席会议。会议听取和审议“六个报告”和重点讨论和审议全县国民经济和社会发展“十五”规划，认为这是一个积极进取，催人奋进的规划，是全县人民奋斗的行动纲领，相信县政府在县委的领导下，一定能把修文的事情办好，带领全县人民将计划变成现实。会议补选李玉轩为十二届县人大常务委员会主任和郑炳州为县人民法院院长。

十二届五次会议 2002年3月5—7日在县城召开，到会代表178名。出席县政协五届五次全委会的政协委员146人列席会议。会议听取和审议“六个报告”，对报告提出的重点抓好以农业战略性调整为主线、以医药园区建设为突破口、以旅游开发为龙头、以公路建设为重点提出建议和意见。会议对2001年全县财政收支结束了多年赤字的历史感到满意。会议作出接受蔺新喜辞去县人民检察院检察长职务的决定，补选毛鸿为县人民检察院检察长。补选县人大常委会委员1人。

十二届六次会议 2002年11月4—5日在县城召开，到会代表178名。会议选举出席贵阳市第十一届人民代表大会代表16名。

十三届一次会议 2003年3月19—22日在县城召开，到会代表185名。出席县政协六届一次全委会的政协委员153人列席会议。会议听取和审议“六个报告”，对县政府总结过去的5年“是全县综合实力全面提升的5年，是改革开放取得突破性进展的5年，是人民生活水平不断提高的5年”表示认可，并赞同“抢抓机遇谋发展，集中精力建强县”的工作思路。会议依法选举人大常委会主任、副主任、委员，县人民政府县长、副县长，选举法院院长和检察院检察长。

在县十三届人民代表大会一次会议上，代表投票选举新一届人大常委会和政府领导班子

十三届二次会议 2004年2月11—13日在县城召开，到会代表185名。出席县政协六届二次全委会的政协委员152人列席会议。会议听取和审议“六个报告”，认为十三届人民政府在起任期首年即2003年保持了县域经济的持续、健康发展，使全县各项事业取得了新的成绩，特别是计生工作获贵阳市目标考

核一等奖，县城治理获贵阳市“黄果树杯”环境整治与综合治理城市组一等奖的成绩给予肯定。会议对政府提出实施“农业稳县，工业强县，三产稳县”的战略思路表示赞同。

十三届三次会议　2005年3月8—10日在县城召开，到会代表170名。出席县政协六届三次全委会的政协委员150人列席会议。会议听取和审议“六个报告”，就政府工作报告提出的2005年全县经济发展总体要求和奋斗目标提出建议和意见。

十三届四次会议　2006年3月1—3日举行。到会代表174名。出席县政协六届四次全委会的政协委员158人列席会议。会议听取和审议“六个报告”，重点讨论“十一五”规划纲要。会议强调，要突出坚持用工业化总揽全局，坚持建设社会主义新农村，坚持大胆创新，完善“十一五”规划《纲要》，使之成为修文县经济社会“十一五”期间的发展蓝图和全县人民的行动纲领。

十四届一次会议　2006年11月21—23日在县城召开。到会代表186名。出席县政协七届一次全委会的政协委员154人列席会议。按规定，十四届一次会议应在2008年换届时召开，遵照贵州省委全省各级统一换届时间的指示，故提前2年召开，与省、市换届同步。会议听取和审议“六个报告”肯定十三届政府的工作，认为政府工作报告重点突出、振奋人心，反映民意、贯穿民生。赞同报告提出的未来5年工作任务和目标。会议选举第十四届人民代表大会常务委员会委员、主任、副主任；选举人民政府县长、副县长，选举法院院长和检察院检察长。

2006年11月21日，县第十四届人民代表大会第一次会议召开

十四届二次会议　2007年3月21—23日在县城召开。到会代表186名。出席县政协七届二次全委会的政协委员170人列席会议。会议听取和审议“六个报告”，通过讨论，就教育、医疗卫生、环卫、金融以及城市建设、工业企业做大做强；文化旅游业及服务业发展；保障改善民生和社会事业发展；加强政府自身建设等方面提出意见和建议。

十四届三次会议　2008年3月12—14日日举行，到会代表185名。出席县政协七届三次全委会的政协委员174人列席会议。会议听取和审议“六个报告”，认为县委、县政府带领全县人民战胜了年初遭遇50年不遇的凝冻灾害，工作值得肯定。赞成政府工作报告提出的全县工作重心迅速由“抗凝冻、保民生”转移到“抓重建、保民生”，立足抗灾夺丰收，迅速恢复各行各业正常的生产和经营秩序的工作安排。会议号召全县人民紧密团结在以胡锦涛同志为总书记的党中央周围，高举中国特色社会主义伟大旗帜，以邓小平理论和“三个代表”重要思想为指导，以科学发展观为统领，进一步解放思想，弘扬“知行合一，协力争先”的贵阳精神，以奋发有为的精神状态，求真务实的工作作风，攻坚克难，狠抓落实，为建设生态文明城市、构建和谐修文作出新的更大的贡献。

十四届四次会议　2009年3月11—13日在县城召开。到会代表178名。出席县政协七届四次全委会的政协委员172人列席会议。会议听取和审议“六个报告”，强调要统一思想，围绕强县升位的建设目标，调动各方面的积极因素，突出抢抓机遇，加快发展的主题，贯彻落实科学发展观，积极应对挑战，争上项目，关注民生，扩大内需，大力推进生态文明建设，加快城乡一体化进程，保持经济持续健康发展。

会议补选蒋志伦为县人民政府县长，并增选县人大常委会委员1名。

十四届五次会议 2010年3月17—19日在县城召开，到会代表177名。出席县政协七届五次全委会的政协委员176人列席会议。会议听取和审议“六个报告”，对政府工作报告提出“全力振兴工业经济，强化经济发展支撑”的战略思想反响强烈，提出建设性的意见。会议强调，2010年要以纵深推进生态文明城市建设为总揽，围绕建设生态经济强县的目标，主抓“四大集群”（循环经济产业集群，物流产业集群，旅游文化产业集群，特色产业集群），确保全县经济可持续发展，全面完成“十一五”规划各项目标任务，切实加强民主法治建设和精神文明建设，为实施“十二五”规划奠定良好基础。

2010年3月17日，召开县第十四届人民代表大会第五次会议

第二节 县人民代表大会常务委员会

县人民代表大会常务委员会为县人民代表大会的常设机构。常委会组成人员为主任、副主任和委员，由代表大会选举产生。主任由代表大会等额选举，副主任差额选举。1981年恢复人民代表大会制度至2010年，县人大常委会共历8届，即第七届至第十四届。县人大常委会设主任，副主任职务。

一、县人大常委会议

人大常委会会议由人大常委会主任召集并主持。会议内容一是听取和审议政府、法院、检察院及政府工作部门工作报告，二是对重大问题作出决定或决议，三是制定具有行政法规性质的“规定”“意见”、“办法”，四是决定“一府两院”（县人民政府，县人民法院、县人民检察院）办事机构人事任免。至2010年12月，七至十四届人大常委会共召开214次会议。

每次常委会议都是根据当时工作的重点提出议题作出决议，以指导工作开展。

第七届人大常委共召开会议25次，其中有8次听取有关部门工作报告，内容涉及财政预决算、人口普查、林业“三定”（稳定山林权、划定自留山、确定林业生产责任制）、打击经济犯罪、打击刑事犯罪、环境保护、教育改革、城镇建设和市场管理等方面。对各部门的职责任务，经常委会议讨论并提出意见，在工作过程中督促完成，并进行有效监督。1984年第七届二十四次会议和二十五次会议听取城乡建设环境保护局关于城镇建设规划的汇报后，常委会对规划方案提出修改意见，并对工作进展迟缓提出批评，责令迅速规划，付诸实施。

第八届人大常委会召开常委会议17次，通过会议审议县政府审计、工商、税务、水利、治安、地方志、农业生产等工作报告并作出决定或决议，以保证全县工作的开展。1986年第八届八次会议听取县政府关于县志编修工作的汇报后，作出《关于加强县志工作的领导，完成编修工作的决议》,《决议》有力地推动了全县地方志工作，1999年《修文县志》公开出版发行后，先后以装帧印刷质量获国家新闻出版署优秀图书奖；贵阳市第四次社会科学优秀科研成果评比一等奖；贵州省第五次哲学社会科学优秀科研成果评比三等奖，县地方志办公室被评为全国修志先进单位，受到中国地方志指导小组嘉奖。

第九届人大常委会召开常委会议18次，会议内容涉及法治建设、审议政府相关工作报告、讨论征兵工作、学习党中央和全国人大1989年作出的有关制止北京春夏之交政治风波相关文件等。在审议政府职能部门关于科技兴农、农用物资和良种供应、农田水利基本建设安排意见、植树造林工作安排、土地清理和详查情况等报告后，通过作出决议的方式明确要求各部门牢固树立为农业服务的思想，大力支援农业，严肃查处吃农、坑农的不正之风，保护农民合法权益。1989年，城镇居民对粮食品种搭配不当意见很大，第九届十一次会议上听取县政府关于当前粮食供应情况的报告后强调指出，粮食供应涉及千家万户，关系人心稳定和社会安宁，要求政府认真解决。会后，政府一方面采取措施调整品种搭配，一方面向群众做解说工作，从而取得群众谅解，密切政府与群众关系。

第十届人大常委会召开会议22次，对全县工作产生重要影响的有1990年7月16—19日召开的第十届二次会议。会议听取和审议农业、烟草、教育等部门的工作报告，指出农业工作在推广农村适用技术上边远地区步子缓慢，引进的良种部分质量较差，良种良法推广不够普及，赊销“两杂”良种20多万元未收回等问题，建议一是把好种子关，严格执行国家有关种子法规；二是对拖欠的种子款，请区、乡（镇）协助追收；三是改革农业服务体系，加强目标管理，完善技术承包合同，树立为大农业服务的思想。烟草公司应加强对干部职工的思想政治教育、职业道德教育和业务素质培训，搞好廉政建设。要把好烟叶收购关，打击烟贩子和内外勾结吃农坑农的蛀虫，努力为发展全县烤烟生产，为完成税收任务作出贡献。教育工作要加强对教师事业心和责任心的教育，提高教学质量。要稳定教师队伍，制定学校收费标准，清理和查处乱收费现象。1992年9月15—18日召开第十届十七次会议，听取和审议县计委、公安局、综治办等单位的工作报告，提出有关建议、意见。会议指出，对受灾严重地区的群众生活安排应引起重视。在经济工作中，县属工业企业效益不好，县酒厂面临破产；国营商业企业、供销企业部分出现亏损等。提出县政府及有关职能部门要结合实际采取切实措施，努力完成各项计划。县公安局和综治办要发扬成绩，配合“二五”普法，依靠群众力量，狠抓大案要案的侦破，狠狠打击各类刑事犯罪，抓好社会治安综合治理。要抓好队伍建设，提高干警的政治、业务素质，为经济建设保驾护航。

第十一届人大常委会召开会议38次。1993年6月11—12日，十一届一次会议听取和审议教育、农业、水电3部门的工作情况汇报，分别作出审议意见。会议对教育工的成绩给予充分肯定，同时指出应重视的问题：一是继续深入宣传、贯彻《中华人民共和国义务教育法》和《中国教育改革和发展纲要》，落实全县“九年义务教育规划”，完成《纲要》中提出的20世纪90年代教育工作的主要任务；二是继续努力提高教育质量，抓好自身队伍建设，以适应教育形势发展的需要；三是进一步建立、完善、巩固教育目标管理责任制，促进教育事业发展和教学质量提高；四是狠抓学额巩固工作，尽力减少中小学生流失；五是规范收费范围和收费标准，合理收取各种费用；六是全社会都要关心、支持教育事业的发展，为科教兴县作出更大贡献。会议听取农业春耕生产情况的汇报后，要求加强农业生产田间管理，做好农业适用技术推广，管好、用好粮专资金。听取水利建设情况的汇报后，建议县政府及职能 部门强化对水

利设施的管护工作和山塘水库的蓄水保水，管好用好有关资金。对岩鹰山水库主干渠防渗施工质量差的问题，要查明原因，严肃处理。1993年11月25—27日，第十一届四次会议听取和审议县计委、监察、矿管及检察院有关工作情况报告，分别作出审议意见，要求县政府严格执行县十一届人大一次会议批准的各项计划，千方百计完成各项计划指标；要充分发挥各职能部门的作用，加强宏观调控，认真解决计划执行中的具体问题，确保全县1993年国民经济和社会发展稳定、协调、健康发展。要求监察机关进一步加强对行政执法活动的监察，促进行政机关依法行政，纠正执法中的违法违纪行为；要从监察工作角度抓好有影响案件的查处；要努力提高办案质量；进一步提高监察干部素质，充分发挥监察机关的职能作用。针对矿管工作中存在的管理不力状况，要求对全县矿产品经营企业进一步清理整顿，对无证非法开采的坚决取缔，严禁乱挖乱采，违法开采。对检察机关打击经济犯罪的工作指出，要“敢”字当头，排除困难，集中力量尽快办结一些群众反映大、有影响的经济犯罪案件。打击经济犯罪要实事求是，不应受指标限制。要加强与有关部门配合、协作，处理好既独立办案又接受监督的关系。同时要发挥检察机关的法律监督作用，加强侦查监督和审判监督，切实发挥司法机关的整体效应。1994年7月5—7日第十一届九次会议听取和审议县劳动、物价、乡镇企业等部门的工作报告，作出审议意见。会议对劳动及其劳动行政执法工作指出，县政府及其劳动部门要把宣传、实施《中华人民共和国劳动法》和安全生产法律法规同“二五”普法工作结合起来，增强宣传力度，严格执行法律。必须把“安全第一，预防为主”的方针落实到企业生产过程中去，尽量减少和避免伤亡事故发生。积极做好社会福利和社会保障工作，为建立新型的社会保障体系做出贡献。对于物价工作，县政府及物价部门要对市场物价加强监测，执行好有关法律和政策，对物价管理做到管而不乱，活而有序。对乡镇企业工作，会议要求县政府各职能部门对企业要搞好服务，兑现发展企业的各项优惠政策。利用资源优势，招商引资，综合发展，提高经济效益。

第十二届人大常委会召开会议42次。1998年7月22—24日，第十二届三次会议听取和审议县综治办、交通局、建设局等部门的工作报告。对于社会治安综合治理工作，指出当前社会生活中诱发、滋生违法犯罪的消极因素仍大量存在，社会治安形势严峻，政法部门要继续开展“严打”斗争和专项治理，进一步落实“六包”责任制，实施“平安工程”，为全县的经济发展和社会进步保驾护航，为创造稳定的治安环境作出贡献。对于交通工作，会议要求必须确保崇恩到小箐公路改造工程年内完成，对贵阳市政府要求全县村村通公路的部署尽快落实。对于建设部门汇报的住房改革，会议要求县政府及主管部门要提高对城镇住房制度改革的认识，稳步推进住房商品化、社会化，促进住宅业成为新的经济增长点，不断满足城镇居民日益增长的住房需求。1999年9月27—28日第十二届十五次会议听取和审议县公安、计经、财政、卫生、档案、建设、国土等部门的工作报告。对于公安工作，会议指出，要充分发挥公安机关的职能作用，加大侦破重大刑事案件的工作力度，严厉打击各类刑事犯罪，确保社会稳定。同时要加强公安队伍的建设，提高干警的政治、业务素质，正确行使人民赋予的权力。坚持从严治警，内强素质，外树形象。对财政工作，会议指出：一是抓好专项检查，强化日常监督；二是强化税收征管，确保财税及时足额入库；三是加强预算外资金的管理；四是开展增收节支，把财政赤字降到最低限度。对于卫生工作，会议要求，卫生部门要大力宣传卫生法律、法规，依法管理全县卫生事业；要抓好医疗卫生系统改革，认真解决全县“少、边、穷”地区看病难、吃药难的问题；要重视卫生技术人员的培训，加大在财力、物力、人力上对卫生工作的投入。对于国土局报告的矿管工作，会议要求，矿管部门要认真学习、宣传《中华人民共和国矿产资源法》，切实采取措施，努力将资源优势转变为经济优势；同时要抓好矿业与环保并重的工作，保护生态平衡；要加强对采矿企业的控批工作，认真整顿矿业秩序；加强矿管队伍管理，努力建设一支廉洁、高效的矿管队伍。2000年10月17—18日，第十二届二十二次会议听取和审议城管、司法、公安、地税、国税等部门的工作报告。对于城管工作，会议肯定自“99阳明文化节”以来，市容市貌、环境卫生管理等方面的成绩，同时指出：城管工作和创卫工作是一项社会性、长期性、群众性很强的工作，要深入持久地进行，常抓不懈。一是要加大投入，努力改善县城环卫硬件设施；二是加强宣传教育，增强城镇居民的环卫意识；三是抓好城管队伍建设，以适应新形势工作的需要；四是加强楼群院落、卫生死角的管理，保护绿化环境，解决公厕布局。对于司法局报告的“三五”普法工作，会议要求县政府要高度重视，加强领导，同时要通过宣传教育提高全社会的法治意识，领导干部、执法人员要带头学法、懂法，严格执法，依法行政；对“三五”普法、依法治县工作经费要尽力保证。对于财税工作，会议指出，目前财税形势十分严峻，财力枯竭，税源萎缩，收入进度迟缓，支出控而不下，离完成全年任务差距很大。会议要求县政府加强对财税工作的领导，千方百计完成全年的税收任务。要抓好后续财源建设，加强税收征管，防止税源流失。要严格执行有关法律、法规，坚决打击偷、漏税行为。2002年6月19日，第十二届三十六次会议听取和审议工商、宗教、供电、统计、文体广电部门的工作报告，提出建议意见。对于工商工作，会议指出，要进一步加强工商法律法规的宣传，继续抓好打击制售假冒劣房商品的工作，整顿和规范市场秩序，清理整顿网吧市场，充分发挥工商管理部门的职能作用。对民族宗教工作，会议针对全县少数民族地区建设滞后、生活水平低、文教卫生事业落后等问题指出，县政府及职能部门要加大民族工作力度，加强民族法律、法规、政策的宣传，努力提高少数民族干部素质，建好项目库，积极争取上级支持，加快少数民族地区水、电、通信设施建设，努力改善少数民族地区的生产生活条件。对于文体广电工作，会议要求职能部门要进一步理顺工作关系，建立规章制度，加大执法力度，建立电视信息网络，提高电视收视质量。要配合有关部门清理整顿文化市场，取缔非法网吧。要逐步解决电视“村村通”的遗留问题，为丰富人民文化生活，提高人民生活质量作出应有贡献。

第十三届人大常委会召开会议22次。2003年7月24—25日，第十三届四次会议听取和审议农业、建设、民政、人劳社保和质监等部门的工作报告，并相应作出“审议意见”。对于城建工作，会议要求进一步贯彻实施《中华人民共和国城市规划法》等法律法规，做到规划先行，保证规划的严格实施；对执行不严及违规问题，进行一次全面检查。对于民政工作，会议提出一要建立行政执法队伍，规范行政执法，提高办事效率，做到依法行政；二要制定具有长效机制的殡葬管理制度，要尽快选址建公墓，规范管理，积极稳妥推进工作。对于社保工作，会议提出要进一步加大社会保险金的征收力度，并要积极解决粮食系统历年欠费问题。对质监工作，会议提出要以保护人民的生命健康安全为主题，查处大案要案，真正保护人民的合法权益；要对全县烟草计量器进行专项检查，保护烟农合法权益。会议还要求县政府及主管部门对会议提出的意见要在第六次常委会议上作整改工作报告。2004年3月24日，第十三届十次会议听取和审议民宗局、教育局、司法局、农业局的工作报告，会议在肯定各报告部门所取得工作成绩的同时也指出存在问题，在民族宗教工作上，中共宗教理论、宗教政策、宗教法规的宣传力度不够，少数部门的党员、干部对宗教政策工作的重要性认识不足；一些地方宗教活动混乱，乱建寺庙、滥塑佛像、借教敛财现象时有发生，打着宗教旗号进行邪教活动等封建迷信活动情况依然存在；对不合法

进行宗教活动的场所没有彻底清理，数目不清，情况不明；宗教干部的数量、素质不适应形势需要等等。会议要求政府针对存在的问题，采取措施加以解决。在教育“两基”复查和“普实”验收工作上，会议建议教育主管部门要坚定信心，克服厌战思想，加强信息沟通，抓好技术指导，同时抓好软件资料基础工作及实验桌、实验室设备等硬件设施建设；要重点抓好初中阶段辍学问题，确保辍学率不突破3%的验收标准；要加大师资培训力度和教育教学改革力度，提高教师素质，提高教学质量；县政府要采取有效措施，加大资金投入，确保“两基”复查和“普实”验收工作顺利开展。对“四五”普法工作，会议建议：县政府及司法部门要加强领导，健全、充实普法领导小组和“普法办”工作人员，切实抓好普法工作；要修改、完善“四五”普法长远规划、年度计划，保证“四五”普法工作扎实有序，依法治县、依法行政工作顺利进行；要采取多种形式，分层次、对象进行普法考试，并注重效果；县政府要完善目标管理，建立健全督查机制，并保障经费投入，使“四五”普法工作顺利开展。对农业局作的《中药材种植基地建设工作情况报告》，因反映情况不全面、数据不翔实未获通过，会议作出“审议意见”要求其整改落实。2005年6月16—17日，第十三届十九次会议听取和审议县司法局、农业局、计生局、环保局、水利局的工作报告，提出建议意见。对计划生育工作，会议指出存在对流动人员和农村早婚、早育等没有切实有效的管理办法，有失控漏管现象，计划外生育时有发生；基层计生协会工作与全面工作结合不够，少数计生协会形同虚设；计生协会“带头、宣传、服务、监督、交流”职能发挥还有待加强等等。会议建议县政府及计生主管部门进一步宣传计生法律、法规，依法管理计生工作，建立健全各项规章制度。同时要总结计生协会的经验教训，帮助解决实际问题，使计生协会工作顺利开展，以推动全县计生工作健康发展。对环保工作，会议指出，全县生态环境保护工作形势严峻，生态环境总体恶化趋势尚未得到有效遏制。危害群众身心健康和正常生活的饮用水污染、烟尘污染、居民区噪声污染和开山采石、取土、挖矿等导致的生态环境破坏严重等，群众反映强烈。会议希望县政府及环保部门充分认识环境保护工作的重要性，彻底改变先污染后治理，先破坏后恢复的状况，尽快实现环境质量好转，实现人与自然和谐相处，确保全面建设小康社会目标的顺利实现。

第十四届人大常委共召开会议30次。2008年6月26日，第十四届十二次会议听取和审议县人大常委会执法检查第一组《关于对<中华人民共和国税收征收管理法>执法检查情况的报告》，会议原则同意执法检查组的报告。会议认为，县政府及其税务执法部门认真贯彻执行《税收征收管理法》。指导思想明确，目标任务明晰，做了大量工作，取得了一定成绩。但在执法方面还存在一些问题，与全面贯彻实施《税收征收管理法》还有一定差距，需进一步加强。会议对县政府及其税务执法部门提出要求：一是加大宣传力度，从广度和深度上加大对《中华人民共和国税收征收管理法》及配套法规的宣传，努力营造学法、用法、守法的良好社会氛围，全面提高公民税收法律意识，使纳税人能自觉、主动申报纳税，尽力减少偷税、逃税等违法行为的发生。二是提高执法人员的综合素质，加强内部管理监督机制，使广大税收征管人员树立公正执法、严格执法、文明执法的观念。采取灵活多样的方式征管，实现依法征收、应收尽收。要进一步强化责任意识，以依法征管，增加税收收入，促进经济发展为己任，加大税收征管力度。三是加强综合治税，切实转变工作作风，加大政府对税收征管的领导和协调力度，强化扣缴义务人的法定职责，进一步明确有关部门的协税责任，支持税务机关依法执行职务，提高税收征管工作效率和质量。健全税收执法责任制，促进征管水平的提高。努力提高服务意识，在促进企业发展上下功夫。四是建立有效机制，完善目标责任，确保年度任务完成。2009年10月29日，第十四届二十三次会议听取和审议县人大常委会执法检查第三组《关于对（中华人民共和国就业促进法>执法检查情况的报告》。会议原则同意执法检查组的报告。会议认为，县政府及其人事劳动和社会保障执法部门认真贯彻执行《中华人民共和国就业促进法》，做了大量工作，取得一定成绩，但在执法方面还存在一些问题，与全面贯彻实施《中华人民共和国就业促进法》还有一定差距，需进一步加强。会议提出5条审议意见并要求县政府在3个月内将研究处理的情况书面报告人大常委会，同时向本级人大代表通报并向社会公布。一是深入开展《中华人民共和国就业促进法》的宣传教育活动。充分运用媒体等多种宣传教育方式，对《中华人民共和国就业促进法》进行深入的宣传教育，提高知晓率；政府及其有关部门对法律规定的政策措施、工作职责等要进一步的明确，有关部门要认真履行各自的职责，协助县人民政府开展促进就业工作。二是县政府要把扩大就业作为修文县经济和社会发展的重要目标，纳入国民经济和社会发展规划。制定促进就业的中长期规划和年度工作计划，并认真组织实施。三是依法搞好职业教育和培训工作。规范和加强职业技能培训，要加强职业技能培训机构与企业的密切联系，坚持抓好培训实用人才和熟练劳动者教育培训，实行产教结合，为经济建设服务，以达到促进就业的目的。四是县政府要鼓励社会各方面依法开展就业服务活动，逐步完善覆盖城乡就业服务体系。要建立失业预警制度，对大规模的失业实施预防、调节和控制，要加强指导和监督并做好劳动力资源和就业、失业状况的调查统计工作。五是建立健全促进就业目标责任制。政府要建立促进就业的目标管理体系，强化对相关部门和下级政府进行目标考核和监督。

二、县人大工作机构

第七届县人大常委会机关内部工作机构仅设有办公室。第八届设有办公室、政治法律工作委员会、财政经济工作委员会、文卫科教工作委员会、民族工作委员会、代表联系工作委员会。第九届设办公室、法治工作委员会、财政经济工作委员会、教科文卫工作委员会、民族工作委员会、代表资格审查委员会。第十届改为“一室四委”，即办公室、法治工作委员会、财政经济工作委员会、教科文卫工作委员会、代表工作委员会。“一室四委”的机关机构设置一直延至2010年第十四届任期未变。

办公室　1981年1月设置，为人大常委会机关枢纽部门，负责办理常委会交办的日常工作。至2012年，办公室仍存。

政治法律工作委员会（法治工作委员会）　1984年11月设置，1987年9月改称法治工作委员会。负责联系法院、检察院、公安局和司法局有关工作，负责检查法律法规的贯彻执行情况，督促有关部门办理人民群众的申诉案件。至2010年，法治工作委员会仍存。

财政经济工作委员　1984年11月设置，负责联系财政经济部门的有关工作，监督财政经济部门贯彻执行财政经济方面的法律法规。至2010年，财政经济工作委员仍存。

教科文卫工作委员会　1984年11月设置教科文卫工作委员会，负责教育、科技、文化、卫生等部门的工作，监督教科文卫部门贯彻执行有关方面的法律法规。至2010年，教科文卫工作委员会仍存。

代表联系工作委员会（代表资格审查委员会、代表工作委员会）　1984年11月设置代表联系工作委员会，1987年9月改称代表资格审查委员会，1990年4月改称代表工作委员会。负责联系人民代表，为人民代表依法履行代表职责做好服务工作，至2010年，代表工作委员会仍存。

民族工作委员会　1984年11月设置，负责民族区域自治法和有关法规的贯彻执行。1990年4月，民工委撤销。

三、县人大常委会派出机构

人大联络组 1986年1月起，在区（含区级城关镇）设人大联络组为常委会的派出机构，接受区（镇）党委和常委会的双重领导，在本行政区域开展属人大职责范围内的工作。1990年11月撤销。

人大工作委员会 1990年11月，将设在5区1镇的人大联络组改建为人大工作委员会，工委会仍为常委会的派出机构。1992年年初，全县“撤区并乡建镇”工作完成，新建的10个乡镇相继召开人民代表大会，建立本级人大主席团，人大工作委员会即行撤销。

第三节 “三权”行使

县人大及其常委会按《中华人民共和国宪法》赋予的权力对“一府两院”工作实施监督，对县内重大事项作出相关决定、决议，在县人民代表大会闭会期间，县人大常委会可决定《中华人民共和国地方各级人民代表大会和地方各级人民政府组织法》规定的县内相关人事任免。通过履行监督权、决定权、任免权，扩大完善政治民主。

一、监督权

1990年，县十届人大常委会第四次会议通过《对“一府两院”实施监督暂行办法》并作出决议，明确监督的目的、范围和内容，规定监督的方式和程序。1992年，贵州省人大常委会颁布《监督条例》后，则按《条例》开展监督工作，通过审议工作报告、开展执法检查、视察和调查、进行工作评议和述职评议、加强信访工作等，不断拓展监督渠道，增强监督实效。

（一）听取和审议工作报告

1981年至2010年，县第七届至第十四届人民代表大会共召开会议36次，听取和审议“一府两院”工作报告194个。县人大常委会共召开会议214次，听取和审议各项报告526个。1991年，县人大十届二次会议审议政府工作报告后，提出政府对农业的投入偏少、对少数民族地区扶贫开发措施不具体、乡镇企业管理混乱、资源浪费和社会治安差群众无安全感等问题。2003年县十三届人大常委会第四次会议听取和审议县建设局的工作报告后，提出审议意见要求建设部门做到规划先行，保证规划的严格实施。对人大审议报告中提出的问题，涉及部门均认真整改着力解决。2003年，县十三届人大常委会第四次会议审议县政府民政工作报告后，提出“要制定具有长效机制的殡葬管理制度规范管理，积极稳妥推进全县殡改工作”的审议意见。县政府及政府民政工作部门认真对待，经过半年多时间调查研究、征

2003年3月县十三届人大一次会议分组审议报告

求意见，于2004年年初作出《关于进一步加强殡葬改革工作的实施意见》，要求全县在殡葬上做到“确保火化率达100%，对殡葬改革以来的违规入棺土葬行为做到力度不减，政策不变，逐步清理”。县殡改领导小组一年间组织各种宣传活动116次，出动宣传车102台次，发放殡改宣传资料10万份，制作固定标语350条，做到资料入户，精神到人。是年11月28日，县政法部门还在久长镇召开公处大会，对3名暴力阻碍殡葬执法的人员进行公开处理。2009年10月，县人大常委会专门听取县政府《2008年以来网吧管理工作情况报告》，审议后提出2条意见：一是县人民政府及有关部门要从保障青少年的健康成长这个高度来充分认识加强网吧管理工作的重要性，认真研究网吧管理的特点和规律，探索如何更好地建立网吧管理的长效机制，严格按照《互联网上网服务营业场所管理条例》的规定，抓好监督管理。有关部门要加大监督管理工作力度，对上网人员进行实名制登记，严格控制超时经营，严禁未成年人入内等，做到规范管理，常抓不懈。二是对无证经营场所，要发现一处打击一处，从严从重处罚，坚决取缔，确保网吧监管的实效性。县政府文化职能部门按常委会的审议意见，加强网吧监控管理，在3个月时间内，派出稽查执法大队共检查网吧48次，零点后行动10次，对1家违规经营的作停业整顿处理。还组织由离退休老同志等社会力量组成的义务监督员队伍，到网吧开展违规接纳未成年人的专项监督。

（二）执法检查

1988年，贯彻省人大常委会《关于全省开展执法检查的决定》，县人大常委会首次开展执法检查。之后，执法检查成为惯例，每年开展一次，亦有按上级人大要求或结合县内工作实际开展的不定期执法检查。1992年在对“一府两院”的执法检查中，发现有的执法人员执法违法，办关系案、人情案的问题，提出检查意见后得到纠正。2005年开展《中华人民共和国水土保持法》《森林法》执法情况检查时发现执法部门对滥伐、盗伐林木及非法营销木材打击不力、部门之间协调配合不好、管护经费缺乏等问题；开展《中华人民共和国传染病防治法》执法工作检查中发现经费缺乏、设施落后、专业技术人员不足、制度不健全等问题。对人大执法检查中提出的建议和意见，相关执法部门均按要求进行整改。2005年8月，县交通局针对县人大在《中华人民共和国道路交通安全法》执法检查中提出的“对县城营运三轮‘摩的’整治不力、农用车辆严重超载”等问题进行专项整治，组织执法人员100人次，出动执法车50次，10天时间共查处违章车辆110辆、暂扣营运证120个、罚款4万元、追缴规费10万元，维护了全县的交通秩序。2007年10月，县人大常委会派出执法检查组，对贯彻实施《中华人民共和国环境保护法》情况进行检查。检查中发现紧靠县城南面的三角山水泥厂和生产铝矾土的四达矿产有限公司生产中排放大量粉尘和废气，三角山水泥厂购进的除尘设备没有安装，四达公司立窑除尘项目尚在进行课题研究。县城东北面的鼎鑫公司和华航冶炼公司，虽安有除尘设备，但为节省开支，生产时不启动除尘器，听任烟尘弥漫，直接影响周边居民生活和城区环境。人大常委会将检查情况通报县政府，要求限期整改。在县人大常委会的直接干预下，县政府采取强有力的措施，于2008年6月果断关停污染严重

2010年，县人大常委会到计生局进行《中华人民共和国人口与计划生育法》执法检查

的华航冶炼公司，责成县环保部门对县内“冒烟企业”实施24小时监控，并对有可能造成环境污染的企业明确3条意见：一是必须24小时开通环保设备，杜绝污染；二是实行转产，寻找新产业；三是达不到上述2个条件坚决关停。

2008年至2010年3年间，县人大大常委会先后组织执法检查组对《中华人民共和国动物防疫法》《中华人民共和国税收征收管理法》《中华人民共和国劳动合同法》《中华人民共和国水土保持法》《中华人民共和国土地管理法》《中华人民共和国就业促进法》《中华人民共和国城市房地产管理法》等国家法规及人民群众关心的县内网吧管理问题进行执法情况检查，形成检查报告经常委会审议后，提出审议意见，县政府就常委会的审议意见作出相应整改报告。

（三）评议

从1994年起，县人常委会对“一府两院”及其职能部门工作进行评议。评议分为工作评议和对任命干部述职评议。1994年对县人民法院147件上年审结案件进行评议。通过阅卷、调查走访当事人和召开各界人士座谈会等多种方式，在了解全面情况的基础上与召开会议的形式面对面展开评议，指出法院办案中存在案件超时、法律文书质量不高、公开审判制度贯彻不够、执行难等问题。县人民法院在人大评议后，针对评议中人大代表的意见和建议，作出“完善错案追究责任制，提高审判质量；开展执行月活动，努力解决执行难问题；开展法律文书制作比赛活动，提高法律文书制作水平；加大巡回审判工作力度，方便群众诉讼；鼓励干警报考市中院法律大专和本科班，提升专业学历；将院长接待日制度由每周半天改为1天，广泛听取群众对审判工作的意见”6条整改措施，通过整改提高办案质量。是年11月7日，对棕泰联合铸钢厂诉贵阳华晓建材轧钢厂购销合同纠纷案，法院采取先予执行方式，执行标的23万元，依法保护了申请人的合法权益。1995年3月，对8名任命干部进行公开述职评议，此后，这种述职评议每年进行一次，从1995年至2010年共对27名任命干部公开评议。

专记：一次务实的干部公开述职评议

1999年6月，县人大常委会决定对监察局局长刘光祥、农业办公室主任辛勇智和计划生育局局长陈绍文3名部门领导进行述职评议。这次述职评议，坚持不评功摆好、不唱赞歌，重点找存在的不足和问题、挑缺点找“毛病”的原则，先由县人大常委会组织评议组，下到评议对象单位召开座谈会，听取意见，进行民主测评，并查阅有关资料，征求意见，实事求是地对被评议对象作出“货真价实”的评议意见。经过3个月的运作后，县人大常委会于9月13至14日在县城召开第十四次会议对3名评议对象面对面地展开评议。这次常委会除通常应出席和列席人员到会外，还有述职评议工作组成员和常委会任命的县政府各办、局负责人参加会议。

评议会议上，参会的人大代表针对被评议对象的述职报告，提出尖锐而中肯的意见。对监察局局长刘光祥进行评议时直面指出，监察局长监察业务不熟，知识面窄、深入乡（镇）少、亲自办案少；对农办主任辛勇智评议时指出工作满足现状，没有完成职能要求和任务，工作方法简单，民主作风差的问题；对计生局长陈绍文评议时针对计生法规宣传力度不够、执行不严，基层网络工作抓得不扎实，计生系统财务管理混乱等问题，提出了更严格的要求。

人大代表不讲情面，却又客观公正，一分为二看问题，谈问题，不仅使被评议对象心跳，也使列席参加会议的其他部门领导同志感到脸红。被评议对象刘光祥在评议后发言说：“原以为自己年轻，工作有闯劲，不存在啥子问题，听了评议，才发觉自己的工作离党和人民的要求还有很大差距。真是‘不评不知道，一评吓一跳’，这次评议给自己敲了一记警钟。”参加会议的县财政局局长王天镜说：“这次评议评的是别人，但我一边听一边也在心里找自己工作中的差距。在领导岗位上，真的要时时处处以人民的利益为重，你干得称不称职，人民心里有杆秤。”

（四）信访

自县人大常委会建立的1981年开始即将群众来信来访列为议事日程，至2010年，县人大常委会接待群众来访共4944人次，年均170人次；处理来信2720件，年均94件。1989年，河南信阳县公民张文和3次到县人大上访，反映他到谷堡乡杨家相亲，此前曾汇款600元及物品给杨家，后相亲不成，杨家不但不退还钱物，反诬张文和进行诈骗，致使张被公安机关收容审查。经县人大法治工作委员会调查后，将实际情况反馈给相关部门，后经法院立案审理，确认杨构成诬陷罪，对其作有罪判决，从而保护了公民的合法权益。1994年，小箐乡发生护林人员履行看护集体森林职责时，开枪打伤盗伐林木者事件，但公安、检察机关却以伤害罪将护林人员逮捕。其家属将此事反映到县人大，人大常委会依法监督，要求公安、检察机关复查该案，经复查确认系定性不当，遂作撤案处理，释放护林人员。2000年，洒坪乡北庄村12户农民上访反映自种玉米在当地无销路，雇车运至修文出售时被工商部门查收。人大财政经济工作委员会调查了解情况后，认为国家不能保证收购时，应允许农民将自产的粮食进入市场，并将这一观点与工商部门进行沟通，取得统一认识后，工商部门将查收的玉米发还12户农民。

二、决定权

1981—2010年，县人民代表大会及其常委会共作出决议201项和决定187项。1982年因拓宽修文至六广公路未及时修复县城至阳早路段而影响通车，七届人大常委会对此作出限期修复的决定，遂由县政府现场办公，督办完成工程。1986年八届人大三次会议对《修文县1986—1990年普及法律常识实施意见》（即“一五普法”）作出5条决议：一是从1986年起，用5年左右时间，有计划、有步骤地在全县公民中进行一次普及法律常识的教育，并逐步做到制度化、经常化；二是普及法律常识的重点对象是各级干部和青少年；三是普及法律常识的内容以宪法为主，结合学习其他法律法规，各部门学习本部门有关的法规，各地区根据存在问题学习有关法律知识；四是各地区、各部门要认真搞好普法试点，以点带面，全面开展；五是县、乡政府和各部门要加强领导，层层包干，分级负责，认真培训好骨干和解决普法教育工作中的具体问题，要制定实施计划，采取有力措施，保证普法实施规划的实现。县人大常委会作出决议后，县即成立法治宣传教育工作领导小组，结合实际采取多种形式开展普法宣传教育。至1990年，全县“一五”普法期间农村应普法对象16.15万人，有13.88万人参加普法学习；城镇应普法对象2万人，有1.8万人参加普法学习。八届人大常委第四次会议针对县内土地管理极度混乱问题，作出《严格依法加强土地管理的决定》，有效地制止了土地使用中的违法现象。1989年小坝、谷堡两乡换届选举乡长，有两名候选人未获半数票而大会主席团即宣布当选上报。县人大获悉情况后，即作出两乡选举无效的决定，责令重新选举。2001年7月25日，县十二届人大常委会第二十九次会议听取和审议县政府关于建立贵阳修文扎佐高科技医药工业园区议案报告后，随即组织部分县人大代表对该医药园区进行实地视察，作出《建立贵阳修文扎佐高科技医药工业园区的决定》。至2010年，扎佐医药园区已发展为全省重点工业产业园区。2003年9月18日，县十三届人大常委会第五次会议听取和审议县人民政府关于建立修文扎佐物流

中心议案的报告，认为建立修文县扎佐物流中心是关系全县经济建设和社会进步跨越式发展的大事，也是综合开发、充分利用修文县境公路、铁路交通大动脉优势的新举措，对一、二、三产业的发展具有极大的拉动作用。会议作出《建立修文扎佐物流中心的决定》。至2010年，扎佐物流园区建设已具规模，成为拉动全县经济发展的杠杆。2005年12月15日，县十三届人大常委会第二十二次会议听取和审议县人民政府关于《修文县十里工业走廊总体规划》的议案报告，作出《关于批准修文县十里工业走廊总体规划的决定》。决定指出，《总体规划》是事关全县“十一五”期间工业发展的大事，是依托交通、区位、资源优势，着力引进县外资金和技术，实现工业产业协调配套、升级，进而建立一个高技术、生态化、结构合理的产业基地，促进工业经济持续、快速增长的重要举措。实施《总体规划》必须牢固树立并认真贯彻全面、协调和可持续发展的科学发展观。认真贯彻贵阳市委、市政府建设生态经济市的决定，按照走新型工业化道路建设资源节约型、环境友好型社会和构建社会主义和谐社会的总体要求，正确处理资源、环境与发展的关系，认真做好有关工作，该规划所涉及的区域均在修文河上游，环境保护至关重要，必须严格执行国家有关环境、资源的法律法规和政策，确保资源的合理利用和可持续发展。县人大的这一决定，奠定了县人民政府实施“工业强县”战略的基础，至2010年，修文经济发展即步入从传统农业向新型工业转型之路。

此外，县人大常委会1986年作出的《关于加强修志工作的领导，坚决完成编修任务的决议》，有力地推动了县志编修进程和首轮《修文县志》顺利出版。1991年作出的《关于实施“长江中下游防护林工程”的决议》，使全县生态建设逐年向好，2010年，全县森林覆盖率已达40.3%；1998年作出的《关于深入开展依法治县工作的决议》，加快了法治建设步伐，至2010年，全县已形成以基层依法治理为基础，以行业依法治理为支柱，以地方依法治理为主体的依法治理网络；1999年作出《关于县人民政府必须认真抓好修文县城河道治理的决定》后，县政府筹集资金600万元对修文河县城段河道进行改造，至2010年，修文河从小桥河到阳明洞一段河道已是水流清澈，两岸绿树成荫。每至夜晚，镶嵌在河堤上的彩灯晶莹闪烁，倒影于微波荡漾的绿水中，朦胧夜色里宛若银河星影。1999年作出《关于在全县传唱<修文之歌>的决定》，使《修文之歌》响澈城乡，燃起全县人民热爱家乡、建设家乡的激情。2004年通过的《关于对“一府两院”工作报告意见落实情况的再审议制度》，规定“一府两院”提请常委会审议的报告，一律采用书面形式，并于常委会开会前5日送达，报告必须经“一府两院”主要领导或分管领导审定；一次审议未通过的，须将审议意见落实情况再次向常委会报告，常委会根据落实情况进行再审议表决；二次末通过的，必须继续整改落实，在下次常委会再次审议表决；如整改3次都不能通过者，常委会将依法行使提出质询，并责成有关负责人写出书面检查、通报批评、免职或撤职等职权。“再审议制度”的执行，提高了对“一府两院”的监督实效，至2010年，未出现3次整改不能通过审议的情况。

三、任免权

县人大常委会遵照《中华人民共和国地方各级人民代表大会和地方各级人民政府组织法》规定，在县人民代表大会闭会期间，可决定副县长的个别任免；在县政府县长、法院院长、检察院检察长因故不能担任职务时，决定代理的人选；决定任免县人民政府的其他组成人员。决定任免法院副院长、庭长、副庭长、审判委员会委员、审判员；决定任免检察院副检察长、检察委员会委员、检察员。自1986年1月29日县八届人大常委会第八次会议到2010年县十四届人大常委会第一次会议期间，县人大常委会共任免国家机关工作人员897人，同意辞去职务31人，决定推选代理职务12人，撤销职务1人。

县人大常委会为更好地贯彻执行人事任免的法律法规，行使好任免权，先后于1992年9月制定《人事任免暂行办法》，1998年4月制定《对任命干部任前法律知识培训和考试办法》，2003年5月制定《关于推行干部任前供职报告制度》以及《被任命干部就职宣誓制度》，强化被任命人员的法治观念，明确法定职责、权利、义务，增强公仆意识和责任感。这些制度的建立和完善，促进人事任免工作日趋规范化、法治化、制度化。

第四节　代表履责

一、议案和建议

县十四届人大二次会议代表询问会上，代表王正荣发言

从1981年1月召开第七届人民代表大会第一次议至2010年3月召开第十四届第五次会议，经历次大会议案审查委员会明确的代表议案共22件，建议共2946件。1983年，代表议案《关于禁止红旗煤矿和贵阳煤矿伸向县城区域地下采煤案》，事关县城人民生命财产安全，县政府采取措施停止两煤矿在该区域的采掘活动。1987年，代表议案《关于岩鹰山水库库区农民致富措施案》，县政府经调研后，不仅为库区农民解决口粮和化肥补贴，还拨款修复小箐乡两个村的4条沟渠和照明用电。1992年，代表议案《关于加强农业科技服务网络》案，因涉及农村经济发展，县政府根据“撤并建”后的实际情况，随即组建起乡镇农技服务站、水利站、畜牧兽医站，并在村一级建立农科组织，配备农科服务员，普及农科技术知识。1996年，代表建议“设立六桶人民法庭”，县人民法院收到建议后，考虑到六桶乡尚不具备设立法庭的条件，即采取建立巡回法庭加大巡回办案力度等措施，解决当地群众诉讼难的问题。1999年、2000年代表提出解决“农村学校危房”“农村用电难”“少数村组看电视难”等建议，县政府均通过当时正运作的教育“两基”达标、农村电网改造、电视“村村通”予以解决。2005年，代表提出“改造老城区”建议，县政府采纳后，筹资570万元，改造阳明西路和民主路。2008年，代表建议“治理县城周边烟尘污染”，县政府高度重视，于是年6月责令污染严重的华航冶炼公司停产整顿。

二、调查和视察

1981—2010年，县人大常委会组织代表围绕涉及国计民生的大小事务组织视察活动共57次，参与视察的代表除县人民代表外，还有驻县的省、市人大代表，视察内容有法律法规执行情况、国民经济运行情况和财政预算执行情况以及生产、救灾、社会治安、群众生活、工作纪律等，每次视察各有不同的主题。

1986年3月，在对桃源乡、清水乡、宝寨乡、崇恩乡视察时，发现偷盗问题严重，群众没有安全感，遂向县政府提出建议，责成县公安局着力解决偷盗严重等治安问题。县公安局于4月1日起在全县开展以反盗窃为中心的30天战役，摧毁盗窃团伙1个8人，行政拘留37人，收审25人，提请批准逮捕5人，劳教少管6人。2008年9月，对县城“整脏治乱”工作进行视察，针对视察中发现的问题，向县“整脏治乱”办公室提出推行“整脏治乱”问责制的建议得到采纳，于10月出台《推行“整脏治乱”工作问责暂行办法》，促进“整脏治乱”工作跃上新台阶，从是年第三季度在贵阳市排位最后一名跃升到第四季度的第二名。

2010年，县人大代表到龙场镇视察

县人大还组织代表开展调查活动，通过调查的方式对“一府两院”工作进行监督。1986年，对广田乡补选乡长违背《中华人民共和国地方各级人民代表大会和地方各级人民政府组织法》规定开展调查，及时予以纠正，责令重新选举。1981年至2010年，县人大常委会共组织代表开展调查活动51次。

专记：我当代表为人民

人民代表在不同的岗位上，不断实践“人民选我当代表，我当代表为人民”的承诺。

吴绍昌履职尽责不畏权

1982年，县委作出决定，凡是年满58周岁在县人大、县政协领导岗位上的干部退居二线，凡年满48周岁在县委、县政府领导岗位上的干部调整到县人大、县政协工作，未经过法律程序就宣布县级班子调整方案，并要求即时到位。当时担任县人大常委会主任的吴绍昌认为县委这种做法违背了法律规定，只有召开人民代表大会按程序选举产生新的县级国家机关领导成员才能有效。有人劝说吴绍昌：“老吴，这事县委都定了，你何必认真。”他反复思考后对劝他的同志说：“国家正在建设法治社会，我作为人民代表和县人大常委会的主任，应该带头履行好人大的监督职能维护法律尊严。我不能改变县委的决定，但有向上级反映情况的权利。”于是，他顶着压力，向省人大常委会如实汇报了这桩违背法规的事，得到省人大常委会的支持。几天后，县召开人民代表大会，经过选举产生新一届人大、政府班子领导成员。按规定退下来的同志，经大会批准辞去原职，新到任的同志合法进入县人大常委会和县政府工作。在大是大非面前，吴绍昌坚持原则，不仅维护了选举法和地方组织法的尊严，也使县委领导受到一次具体的法治教育。

谭荣先三次“上书”建大桥

1989年年初，作为人民代表同时担任县人大常委会主任的谭荣先，带着全县人民的嘱托，来到黔西县，与黔西县人大常委会的同志们协商造福两地人民的大事——联名向省人民代表大会提出议案：建议省人民政府将修建六广河大桥纳入全省公路建设项目。

六广河是两县界河，河深水急，两岸悬崖峭壁，阻断两地交通。千百年来，人们就希望能在六广河上建起一座桥，但是，从奢香开九驿起，五六百年过去了，人们依然是望河兴叹。谭荣先与黔西县的省人大代表们达成共识：为了两县人民的利益，要向省里“上书”。

1990年，修文、黔西两县的省人大代表在省人代会上首次“上书”，提交了《关于兴建六广河大桥的议案》。但省交通厅没有把建设六广河大桥列入1990年的计划。1991年，两县代表再次“上书”，在省人代会上又提交议案，引起省里的重视派员调研，但交通厅仍未立项。1992年全省人代会上，谭荣先再次联络两县代表三次“上书”。

1992年5月11日，贵州省交通厅下达《关于六广河大桥项目建设书的批复》——桥名贵州六广河大桥，桥长248米，引道6公里，单跨150米，桥面宽10米，设计荷载汽—20，挂—100，投资668万元。六广河大桥建设终于开工上马。

文明祥不负重托解民忧

文明祥是谷堡乡平寨村党支部书记，县十二、十三、十四届人大代表。1994年，为解决村里儿童上学难问题，文明祥不仅积极到县教育、建设等部门奔走呼吁，还带领群众调土地、挖基础，拿出积蓄5万元垫资买建筑材料，在教育部门支持下，建起一幢500平方米的教学楼，使孩子们终于告别了每天步行10余里路程上学的历史。2000年，又针对群众反映强烈的用电难、电价高的问题，文明祥在县第十二届人大第三次会议上提出调整农村电网改造思路，加大农村电网改造力度，切实改变农村照明难、用电难的建议，得到供电局采纳，通过农村电网改造很快把光明送到边远村组群众的家中，使村民们从此不再有用电难的慨叹。

刘正秀发展养殖为民忙

刘正秀是小箐乡大坝村的村民，县第十四届人民代表大会代表。2006年她提出建设大坝村生猪养殖基地的建议，为大坝村群众找到一条致富之路。“贵州省无公害生猪养殖基地”在大坝村挂牌建立后，群众的养猪积极性却不高。刘正秀心想，既然牵起这个头，就要做出样子来，带动大家共同发展。她通过“借猪还猪”方式，养了10头二元杂交母猪，当年收入近万元。村里的群众眼见为实，流露出羡慕的眼光。刘正秀乘机邀请大家上门参观，积极传授她的“致富经”。一时间，她家成了学习养猪技术的课堂。对村里想发展生猪养殖却缺少资金的群众，她积极主动为他们跑贷款，找资金。村民黄银秀的丈夫2004年去世后家庭生活困难，一年做来不够半年吃。刘正秀想方设法帮她贷款养3头母猪。黄银秀靠养母猪过上好日子，2010年建起120平方米的新楼房。小坝村的生猪养殖在刘正秀的带动下，规模越做越大，到2010年，全村有70%以上的村民养殖生猪，常年存栏生猪1500多头，户均年收入达2万元。

第五节　乡（镇）人民代表大会主席团

1987年乡（镇）换届选举时，按1986年12月六届全国人大常委会第十八次会议修改的《中华人民共和国地方各级人民代表大会和地方各级人民政府组织法》规定，由人民代表大会选举产生乡（镇）人大主席团。是时的乡（镇）隶属于区。1992年2月“撤区并乡建镇”后，新建的城关、扎佐、久长、六广、谷堡、大石、六屯、小箐、洒坪、六桶10个乡（镇）分别召开人民代表大会，选举产生乡（镇）人大主

席团和乡（镇）人民代表大会主席、副主席。在乡（镇）人民代表大会闭会期间，乡（镇）人大主席团按《贵州省乡镇人民代表大会主席团工作条例》履行检查、督促宪法、法律、法规及本级人民代表大会和上级人民代表大会及其常务委员会的决议、决定在本行政区域内的遵守和执行情况；听取和审议本级人民政府的经济、教育、科学、文化、卫生、民政、民族、社会治安等工作情况的报告，监督本级人民政府的工作；根据本级人民政府的建议，决定对本行政区域内的国民经济和社会发展计划、财政预算的部分变更；检查、督促本级人民政府及有关单位办理本级人民代表提出的建议、批评、意见等职权。至2010年，10乡（镇）人大主席团仍存。

第四章　人民政府

第一节　组织机构

1978年，沿袭“文化大革命”时期建立的县革命委员会履行政府政务。1981年1月，恢复县人民政府建制，隶属安顺地区行署。1996年，修文县由安顺地区析出，隶属贵阳市人民政府。

县人民政府由县长、副县长组成领导班子，主要议事形式为政府全体（扩大）会议和县长办公会议。

一、县政府工作机构

1978年沿袭“文化大革命”结束后的县革委会工作机构32个。1981年恢复县人民政府建工作机构45个。继后，政府工作机构随机构改革、工作性质和业务范围变更以及国家政策调整等诸多因素时有变化，至2010年12月，有政府工作机构23个；有直属事业单位3个；有其他机构1个；有政府办事机构10个；有县政府与上一级主管部门双重领导机构19个。

县政府办公室　1978年沿原建置县革委办公室，1981年1月复称县政府办公室，为政府枢纽机关，负责政府工作事务的联络、协调、服务和政府机关的内部事务以及公文处理等工作。至2010年12月，县政府办公室仍存。

公安局　1978年沿原建置公安局，担负预防和打击犯罪，维护社会治安，保护国家财产和人民生命财产安全职责。至2010年12月，公安局仍存。

财政局　1978年沿原建置财政局，负责管理全县财政收支工作。至2010年12月，财政局仍存。

教育局　1978年沿原建置教育局，负责管理全县教育事业。至2010年12月，教育局仍存。

交通局（交通运输局）　1978年沿原置交通局，负责全县交通建设和运输管理。2010年6月，改称交通运输局。至2010年12月，交通运输局仍存。

人事局（人事劳动局、人事劳动和社会保障局、人力资源和社会保障局）　1978年沿原置人事局，1984年1月，将劳动管理业务并入，改称人事劳动局，10月，劳动业务从人事劳动局析出，复称人事局，1995年9月，再度合并劳动业务，重置人事劳动局。2001年10月，吸纳社会保障业务，更名人事劳动和社会保障局。2010年6月，改称为人力资源和社会保障局。至2010年12月，人社局仍存。

劳动工资局　1978年沿原置劳动工资局，负责管理就业安置、安全检查和职工工资晋级工作。1984年1月，与人事局合并称人事劳动局，10月，劳动工资业务从劳动人事局析出，复置劳动工资局，1995

年9月，劳动工资局裁撤，其业务归并人事劳动局。

计划委员会（计划与经济贸易局、发展和改革局、发展改革经贸局） 1978年沿原置计划委员会，负责拟定并组织实施全县国民经济和社会发展中长期规划和年度计划，衔接、平衡各主要行业的行业规划，统筹协调经济社会发展，研究分析经济形势，提出全县国民经济发展和优化重大经济结构的目标和政策建议。1995年9月，将经济委员会、工业办公室、商业局、轻工局、物资局业务并入计划委员会，改称计划与经济贸易局。2001年改称发展改革局。2010年6月，将科学技术局（知识产权局）、物价局、乡镇企业局（煤炭管理局）、粮食局裁撤，其业务并入发展改革局，改称发展改革经贸局。至2010年12月，发展改革经贸局仍存。

工业局（经济委员会） 1978年沿原置工业局，负责管理全县工业生产。1984年改称经济委员会。1995年9月，撤销经委，其业务由计划与经济贸易局管理。

轻工业局 1978年沿原置轻工业局，负责管理全县手工业产生产，1995年9月撤销轻工业局，其业务由计划与经济贸易局管理。

商业局 1978年沿原置商业局，负责管理全县商品流通业务。1995年撤销商业局，业务由计划与经济贸易局管理。

物资管理局（物资供应公司） 1978年沿原置物资管理局，负责管理国家计划内物资。1984年5月改称物资供应公司。1985年复称物资管理局。1995年9月撤销物管局，其业务由计划与经济贸易局管理。

粮食局 1978年沿原置粮食局，负责管理全县粮油购销、加工、调运、仓储工作。2010年6月撤销粮食局，其业务归并发展改革经贸局。

社队企业管理局（乡村工业公司、乡镇企业管理局） 1978年沿原置社队企业管理局，负责管理全县社队企业生产。1984年2月改称乡村工业公司，1985年1月更名乡镇企业管理局，1996年3月加挂煤炭工业局牌子。2010年6月撤销乡镇企业局，业务由发展改革经贸局管理。

科学技术局（科学技术委员会） 1978年1月沿原置科学技术局，负责全县科学研究和科技推广工作，12月改称科学技术委员会。1995年9月复称科学技术局，并加挂知识产权局牌子。2010年6月，科技局机构不再单列，其业务归并发展改革经贸局，在发展改革经贸局加挂科学技术局和知识产权局牌子。

广播事业局（广播电视局） 1978年原置广播事业局，1984年2月增加电视业务，改称广播电视局。1995年9月，广播电视局业务并入文化局，组建文化广播电视局，广播电视局撤销。

民政局 1978年沿原置民政局，负责管理全县民政事务。至2010年12月，民政局仍存。

农业局（农牧局） 1978年沿原置农业局，负责全县农业种植技术指导工作。1984年2月与畜牧局合并，改称农牧局，11月，畜禽养殖业务析出，复称农业局。1995年9月，畜牧工作再次归并农业局，但农业局名称未变。2010年6月，接纳扶贫开发工作，加挂扶贫开发办公室牌子。至2010年，农业局仍存。

移民办公室（水利水电工程移民局） 1978年沿原置移民办公室，负责兴建水利水电工程移民安置工作。1995年9月，移民办业务归并农业综合开发办公室，机构不再单列，在农发办加挂移民办牌子。2001年11月，农发办撤销，重置移民办公室，2010年6月，撤销移民办，将水利局大中型水利工程移民安置工作的管理和监督职责与原移民办业务归并，设置水利水电工程移民局。至2010年12月，移民局仍存。

林业局（林业绿化局） 1978年沿原置林业局，负责管理全县植树造林工作。2001年11月改称林业绿化局。至2010年12月，林业绿化局仍存。

气象站（气象局） 1978年沿原置气象站，负责全县气象事业发展规划、计划的制定和气象观测、气象预报。1981年7月改称气象局，1984年4月复称气象站，1988年5月又恢复气象局名称。至2010年12月，气象局仍存。

水利电力局（水利局） 1978年沿原置水利电力局，负责全县农田水利管理、小水电工程建设和人畜饮水。2001年10月改称水利局。至2010年12月，水利局仍存。

农业机械管理局（农业机械管理服务站、农业机械管理事业局） 1978年沿原置农业机械管理局，负责管理全县农业机械为农业生产服务工作。1984年5月更名农业机械管理服务站。1987年4月复称农业机械管理局。1995年9月，改称农业机械管理事业局。2001年11月撤销农机局，其业务交由农业局管理。

计划生育领导小组办公室（计划生育委员会、计划生育局、人口和计划生育局） 1978年沿原置计划生育领导小组办公室，负责全县计划生育工作。1980年1月改称计划生育委员会。1995年改为计划生育局，2001年改称人口和计划生育局，负责全县人口控制和计划生育管理。至2010年12月，人口和计划生育局仍存。

卫生局（卫生和食品药品监督管理局） 1978年原置卫生局，负责管理全县医疗卫生工作。2010年6月接收食品药品监督局业务，改称卫生和食品药品监督管理局。至2010年12月，卫生和食品药品监督局仍存。

供销合作联社 1978年沿原建供销合作联社，为县政府管理的全县供销合作社的联合组织，其业务范围是管理农村商品购销。至2010年12月，供销合作联社仍存。

邮电局（邮政局） 1978年沿原置邮电局，经营管理全县邮政电信业务。1998年9月，析出电信业务后专营邮政业务，改称为邮政局。至2010年12月，邮政局仍存。

供电所（供电局） 1978年沿原置供电所。1992年6月改为供电局，由贵阳供电局实行行业代管。1998年，通过资产有偿转让成为贵州电网公司子公司，由贵阳供电局直接管理，负责全县供电，至2010年12月，供电局仍存。

工商行政管理局 1978年沿原置工商行政管理局，负责全县市场管理工作。至2010年12月，工商行政管理局仍存。

税务局 1978年沿原置税务局，管理全县税征业务。1994年9月，撤销税务局，其业务交由国家税务局和地方税务局负责。

知识青年上山下乡办公室 1978年沿原置知识青年上山下乡办公室，负责上山下乡知识青年安置工作。1982年1月，知青办撤销。

人防战备办公室（人防交通战备科、人防交通战备办公室） 1978年沿原置人防战备办公室，1988年8月改称人防交通战备科，1990年9月改称人防交通战备办公室。1995年9月，撤销人防交通战备办，其业务由建设局负责。1998年1月，人防交通战备工作从建设局析出，重置人防交通战备办公室。2001年6月，撤销人防交通战备办，其业务由政府办公室负责。

人民银行 1978年沿原置人民银行，负责管理全县金融事业。至2010年12月，人民银行仍存。

体育运动委员会（体育局） 1978年6月，复建“文化大革命”时期被撤销的体育运动委员会，负责

管理全县体育运动事宜。1995年9月，改称体育局。2001年10月，体育运动管理工作并入文化广播电视局，体育局撤销。

招生办公室 1978年7月建立招生办公室，负责大中专学校的招生工作。至2010年12月，招生办仍存。

城市建设局（城乡建设环境保护局、住房和城乡建设局） 1978年9月建立城市建设局，加挂基本建设工程局牌子，负责规划县内城镇建设和施工管理。1984年2月，将环保局与城市建设局合并，改称城乡建设环境保护局，1995年9月，划出环保工作归国土局管理，同时接纳住房制度改革和人防战备工作后称为建设局。1998年1月划出人防战备业务，机构名称未变。2010年6月，改称住房和城乡建设局。至2010年12月，住建局仍存。

标准计量所（标准计量局、技术监督局、质量技术监督局） 1978年12月建立标准计量所，负责对全县标准化计量和产品质量的监督管理。1986年9月更名标准计量局。1992年6月改称技术监督局。1995年9月技监局并入工商行政管理局，在工商局加挂技术监督局牌子。1999年6月，技监局从工商行政管理局析出单列更名质量技术监督局，负责全县质量、计量、标准化、组织机构代码、特种设备、认证认可、食品安全监察等工作，并行使行政执法职能。至2010年12月，质监局仍存。

建设银行 1978年沿原置建设银行，负责办理县内基本建设拨款和对拨款行使财政监督。2005年9月其业务划属金阳支行后，建设银行撤销。

畜牧局 1979年1月建立，接管农业局划出的全县畜牧兽医和畜禽养殖工作。1984年2月，畜牧局与农业局合并为农牧局，11月，农业和畜牧业务分开，复建畜牧局。1995年9月，畜牧业务归并农业局，畜牧局撤销。

档案馆（档案局） 1979年1月恢复“文化大革命”时期撤销的档案馆建置，负责全县档案管理工作。1981年10月建立档案局，与档案馆合署办公。1986年1月，档案局（馆）由县委工作机构调整为政府机构。至2010年12月，档案局（馆）仍存。

统计局 1979年7月复建“文化大革命”时期撤销的统计局，负责全县国民经济和社会发展的统计业务。至2010年12月，统计局仍存。

农业银行 1979年12月复建1965年撤销的农业银行，负责管理农村金融工作。至2010年12月，农业银行仍存。

民族事务委员会（民族宗教事务局、民族事务局） 1979年12月，复建“文化大革命”时期撤销的民族事务委员会，负责掌握全县少数民族情况和民族地区的经济文化建设。1995年9月增加宗教工作，改称民族宗教事务局。2010年6月改称民族事务局，加挂宗教事务局牌子。至2010年12月，民族事务局仍存。

司法局 1980年10月建立，专司司法行政工作。至2010年12月，司法局仍存。

农业区划办公室 1980年10月建立，负责搜集农业资料和农业调查研究工作，撰写综合区划报告供农业开发利用。1995年9月，撤销区划办，其业务交由农业综合开发办公室办理。

文化局（文化广播电视局、文体广播电视局、旅游文体广播电视局） 1981年7月建立文化局，负责管理全县文化事业。1995年9月，文化局与广播电视局合并，称文化广播电视局，统管文化广播电视业务。2001年10月，体育局并入文化广播电视局，称文体广播电视局，负责文化、体育、广播电视业务。2010年6月，旅游局并入，组建旅游文体广播电视局，负责管理全县旅游、文化、体育、广播电视工作，

并加挂新闻出版局和版权局牌子，由旅游文体广播电视局管理新闻出版和版权保护工作。至2010年12月，旅游文体广播电视局仍存。

建设银行扎佐专业支行 1981年4月，改建设银行修文支行扎佐办事处为扎佐专业支行，直隶安顺地区中心支行。1984年6月，复为扎佐办事处，扎佐专业支行撤销。

建设银行猫冲专业支行 1981年4月，改建设银行修文支行猫冲办事处为猫冲专业支行，直隶安顺地区中心支行。1984年6月，，复为猫冲办事处，猫冲专业支行撤销

农业广播学校 1981年5月建立，负责培养农业技术干部和农村技术人员。至2010年12月，农业广播学校仍存。

环境保护局（城乡建设环境保护局） 1981年7月建立环境保护局，负责全县生态环境保护和环境建设、环境监测等工作。1984年2月与城乡建设局合并，改称城乡建设环境保护局。1995年9月，环保业务划归国土局。1999年12月，又将环保业务从国土局划出，恢复环境保护局建制。至2010年12月，环保局仍存。

对外经济协作办公室 1983年1月建立，负责对外经济技术协作，促进县域经济发展。1995年9月，外经业务由计划与经济贸易局办理，外经办撤销。

老龄委员会办公室 1987年11月建立，负责宣传贯彻执行老龄工作的方针政策，为老年人做好服务工作。1996年3月，撤销老龄办，其业务交由县委离退休干部工作局管理，2001年10月复建老龄办，与民政局合署办公。至2010年12月，老龄办仍存。

烟草专卖局（烟草专卖公司） 1983年建立烟草专卖局和烟草专卖公司，实行“两块牌子，一套班子”，负责烤烟生产、购销和卷烟购销的管理。至2010年12月，烟草专卖局（烟草专卖公司）仍存。

工商银行 1984年1月建立，与人民银行合署办公，负责办理工商信贷和储蓄业务。2006年划属白云区工商银行管辖，改置白云工商银行修文办事处，工商银行撤销。

审计局 1984年2月建立，专职审计监督行政和企事业单位的财政收支。至2010年12月，审计局仍存。

物价局 1984年4月建立，负责商品调价和物价检查工作。1995年8月，物价局与工商管理局合署办公，对外仍挂物价局牌子。1999年6月，物价局从工商局析出单列。2010年6月物价业由并发展改革经贸局管理，物价局撤销。

农村信用合作社联合社 1984年9月建立，属农业银行管辖，负责管理乡（镇）信用社。1997年1月，信用联社与农行脱钩，独立建制。至2010年12月，信用联社仍存。

农村工作委员会（农村经济委员会、农业办公室） 1984年10月建立农村工作委员会，与县委农工部合署办公，负责管理农村经济改革和农业发展工作。1986年4月更名为农村经济委员会。1995年9月改称农业办公室，增加扶贫开发工作。1997年1月，烤烟生产办公室与农业办公室合署办公。2010年6月，农业办公室撤销，烟办单列，其余工作交由农业局管理，农业局加挂扶贫开发办公室牌子。

手工业生产合作社联合社 1984年复建在“文化大革命”时期撤销的手工业生产合作社联合社，与轻工业局合署办公。1986年7月将业务交由轻工业局统一管理，手联社撤销。

地方志办公室 1985年5月建立，负责地方志书和地方年鉴的编修及指导工作，与县委党史研究室合署办公。至2010年12月，方志办仍存。

人民保险公司（财产保险公司） 1985年10月建立人民保险公司，开展各项保险。1996年10月改称财产保险公司，专司财产保险业务。1999年6月，复称人民保险公司。2004年4月，又改称财产保险公司。至2010年12月，财产保险公司仍存。

土地管理局（国土资源管理局） 1986年，建立土地管理局，负责全县土地管理和土地法规宣传贯彻执行工作。1995年9月，纳入矿管局和环境保护局业务，改称国土资源管理局。1999年12月，又将环保业务划出归环保局，其机构名称未变。至2010年12月，国土资源管理局仍存。

监察局 1987年12月建立，负责监督职工遵纪守法情况和受理违纪案件工作。1993年6月，监察局与县纪委合署办公。至2010年12月，监察局仍存。

经济体制改革办公室（经济体制改革委员会） 1988年8月，建立经济体制改革办公室，负责设计改革方案、落实改革措施和督促检查事宜。1991年改称经济体制改革委员会。1995年9月，体改委工作交由政府办负责，在政府办内置体改办公室，体改委建制截止。

教育督导检查办公室（教育督导室） 1989年9月，建立教育督导检查办公室，负责对全县教育工作的督察办理。1994年9月，改称教育督导室。至2010年12月，教育督导室仍存。

矿产资源管理办公室（矿产资源管理局） 1990年2月，建立矿产资源管理办公室，负责管理全县矿产资源的开发利用。1992年8月，改称矿产资源管理局。1995年9月，矿管局业务并入国土局，机构不单列，在国土局加挂矿产资源管理局牌子。

保密局 1990年3月，建立保密局，负责贯彻执行党和国家有关保密工作的方针和政策，指导机关和企事业单位的保密工作，会同有关部门查处泄密、失密事件。1995年2月，保密局与县委保密办公室、县委机要局合署办公；9月，保密工作归属县委办公室管理，撤销保密局独立建制。1996年4月，保密局和保密办合署建置办公。至2010年，保密局仍存。

盐务管理局 1991年1月建立，行使盐务管理的行政职能，与盐业公司合署办公。至2010年12月，盐务局仍存。

酒类专卖局 1991年1月建立，负责管理酒类生产和销售。1995年9月，酒类专卖局撤销。

社会治安综合治理办公室 1991年6月建立，负责指导、协调全县社会治安综合治理工作。至2010年12月，综治办仍存。

禁毒办公室 1991年建立，负责禁止贩毒、吸毒工作，与社会治安综合治理办公室合署办公，1999年从综治办析出，改置于公安局内。2005年1月改置于县委政法委。至2010年12月，禁毒办仍存。

烤烟生产办公室 1991年12月建立，负责烤烟生产中的协调、服务工作。1997年1月，烟办与农业办公室合署办公。2010年6月撤销农办后，烟办单列。至2010年12月，烟办仍存。

农业综合开发办公室 1992年4月建立，负责指导和管理全县农业开发工作。1995年9月，农发办接纳移民工作和农业区划业务，但机构名称未变。2001年11月，撤销农发办，其管理的农业开发业务归并农业办公室，移民业务由重置的移民办公室管理。

台湾事务办公室 1992年4月建立，与县委台湾工作办公室实行“两块牌子，一套班子”合署办公，承担有关对台事务，促进祖国统一大业。1996年2月，撤销台湾事务办公室，其工作职能并入统战部。

工业办公室 1992年5月建立，与对外经济协作办公室合署办公，负责宣传县域工业资源和开发情况，提供咨询服务，办理项目审批。1995年9月撤销工业办，其业务由计划与经济贸易局办理。

住房制度改革办公室 1992年6月建立，负责对公有住房出售、评估，审批职工集资建房手续和管理住房资金。1995年9月，将房改办列为建设局内设机构。

税务局（国家税务局） 1978年沿原建税务局，1994年9月将税务局分置为国家税务局和地方税务局，分置后的国税局仍在原税务局办公地点办公室，专门负责中央税的征管工作。至2010年12月，国税局仍存。

地方税务局 1994年9月建立，负责地方税征管工作。至2010年12月，地税局仍存。

项目办公室 1995年12月建立，负责贯彻执行有关经济工作的方针政策，管理全县经济建设项目。1997年撤销项目办，其职能归并计划与经济贸易局。

旅游公司（旅游局） 1984年8月建立旅游公司，专司旅游开发管理工作。1987年4月撤销旅游公司。1996年2月建立旅游局。2010年6月，旅游业务并入旅游文体广电局，旅游局撤销。

农业发展银行 1997年2月建立，负责国家政策控制的农业金融业务。至2010年12月，农发行仍存。

人寿保险公司修文营业部 1997年3月建立，专门经营人寿保险业务。至2010年12月，人寿保险营业部仍存。

城市管理委员会 1997年3月建立，负责综合管理城镇市容、环境卫生、园林绿化和市政设施等工作。2001年10月，撤销城管委，其业务归并建设局。

社会保险事业局 1997年12月建立，负责管理全县职工社会保险业务。2001年10月，撤销社保局，其业务归并人事劳动和社会保障局。

电信局 1998年9月，将电信业务由原邮电局析出，单列电信局，专司全县电信业务。至2010年12月，电信局仍存。

移动通信公司 1998年9月建立，专司移动通信业务。至2010年12月，移动公司仍存。

督查室 1998年6月建立，负责检查督促并反馈全县乡（镇）和县直部门工作任务完成情况及工作目标考核。2001年10月，改为县委工作部门，由县委办公室管理。

依法治县办公室 1998年12月建立，统筹协调政府在依法治县工作中的相关事务和法治宣传工作，置于司法局。至2010年12月，依治办仍存。

商业银行 2000年5月建立，负责管理城镇储蓄和信贷业务。至2010年12月，商行仍存。

扶贫开发办公室 2001年11月建立，负责全县农村扶贫开发工作，机构未单列，在农业办公室加挂扶贫开发办公室牌子。2010年6月，农业办公室撤销，扶贫开发业务归并农业局，在农业局加挂扶贫开发办公室牌子。至2010年12月，扶贫开发办公室仍存。

医药局（食品药品监督管理局） 1981年1月建立医药局，负责监督药品药械工作。1984年将业务移交给经济委员会，撤销医药局。2001年新建食品药品监督管理局，负责的食品、药品及医疗器械经营的监督管理。2010年6月，撤销食品药品监督管理局，其业务改由卫生和食品药品监督管理局负责。

安全生产监督管理局 2004年9月建立，负责有证煤矿、非煤矿山、冶金、建材、危险化学品、烟花爆竹、民爆等行业安全生产，指导、协调和监督其他行业安全生产工作。原为政府直属事业单位，2010年调整为政府行政机构。至2010年12月，安监局仍存。

医药园区管理委员会 2010年4月建立，负责医药园区建设和管理工作。至2010年12月，医药园区管委会仍存。

卫生和食品药品监督管理局　2010年6月，将卫生局和食品药品监督管理局，组建成卫生和食品药品监督管理局，统一管理原卫生局和食品药品监督管理局业务。至2010年12月，卫生和食品药品监督管理局仍存。

工业园区建设开发办公室　2010年11月建立，负责园区的总体发展规划、产业布局、基础设施及重大项目建设和招商引资等工作。至2010年12月，工业园区建设办公室仍存。

二、区乡（镇）行政组织

1978年，县革命委员会下置城关，扎佐、六广、小箐4个区革命委员会和久长1个直属公社革命委员会。1980年5月，各区革委会改称区公所。1981年1月复建县人民政府后，将久长公社改置为区，公社革委会改称区公所。1984年5月，城关镇人民政府升格为区级人民政府，至1991年11月，全县仍置5个区公所和1个区级镇政府。1992年2月，撤销区一级行政建置。

1981年沿袭“文化大革命”时期建制，区革命委员会下辖公社（镇）革命委员会，即城关区革委会辖东方红（王官）、程关、马家桥、石安、阳早、新场（场坝）、谷堡、乌栗等8个公社革委会和城关镇1个镇革委会；扎佐区革委会辖扎佐、三元、清让、桃源、六屯等5个公社革委会；小箐区革委会辖小箐、马场（小坝）、崇恩、洒坪、中寨等5个公社革委会，六广区革委会辖六广、广田、德政、大石、红岩（回水）、六桶、花椒、凉井、宝寨等9个公社革委会。久长公社革委会直属县。1981年1月，将原久长公社改为久长、金桥、清水等3个公社，并将城关区公所管辖的石安公社划给久长区公所管辖，析出东方红公社的小山、高仓和马家桥公社的青龙、大地以及三元公社的清水塘等6个大队组建水塘公社，从扎佐公社析出和平、新庄、大园、中营、桥头5个生产大队和2个街道居民段组建成扎佐镇。将所有公社革委会改为公社管理委员会，至此，全县共置5个区公所、30个公社管理委员会和2个镇人民政府。1984年4月实行政社分设，将公社改为乡，建立乡人民政府；5月，城关镇升格为区级镇，直隶县管辖；6月，改桃源、大石2个乡为布依族乡，至此，全县置5个区公所和1个区级镇人民政府，30个乡人民政府（含2个布依族乡人民政府）和1个乡级镇人民政府。1985年9月，将久长、六广2个乡人民政府改置为镇人民政府，至此，全县置有5个区公所和1个区级镇人民政府、28个乡人民政府（含2个布依族乡人民政府）和3个乡级镇人民政府。1992年2月，为适应改革开放和经济发展，实行乡（镇）人民政府“小政府，大服务”的行政建制，撤区、并乡、建镇，撤销5个区公所，将1个县直管的区级镇人民政府和28个乡人民政府、3个乡级镇人民政府整合改置为县直辖4个镇人民政府和6个乡人民政府。

城关（龙场）镇人民政府　1992年2月撤销城关区公所，将原城关镇、王官乡、程关乡、马家桥乡、阳早乡合并建立新的城关镇人民政府，镇政府驻地县城民主路。1999年8月，恢复“龙场”镇名，称龙场镇人民政府。至2010年12月，龙场镇人民政府下辖36个村民委员会和6个社区居民委员会。

扎佐镇人民政府　1992年2月撤销扎佐区公所，将原扎佐镇、扎佐乡、三元乡、清让乡合并建立新的扎佐镇人民政府，镇政府驻地扎佐街。至2010年12月，扎佐镇人民政府下辖25个村民委员会和3个社区居民委员会。

久长镇人民政府　1992年2月撤销久长区公所，将原久长镇、清水乡、金桥乡、石安乡合并建立新的久长镇人民政府，镇政府驻地久长街。至2010年12月，久长镇人民政府下辖24个村民委员会和1个社区居民委员会。

六广镇人民政府　1992年2月撤销六广区公所，将原广田乡和德政乡的平营、前锋、团山、元箐、金山、岩脚等6全村并入六广镇，建立新的六广镇人民政府，镇政府驻地六广街。至2010年12月，六广镇人民政府下辖22个村民委员会和1个社区居民委员会。

谷堡乡人民政府　1992年2月，将原谷堡乡、场坝乡、乌栗乡合并建立新的谷堡乡人民政府，乡政府驻地谷堡。至2010年12月，谷堡乡人民政府下辖19个村民委员会。

六屯乡人民政府　1992年2月，将原六屯乡、桃源乡合并，建立新的六屯乡人民政府，乡政府驻地格都堡。至2010年12月，六屯乡人民政府下辖13个村民委员会。

小箐乡人民政府　1992年2月撤销小箐区公所，将原小箐乡、小坝乡、崇恩乡合并，建立新的小箐乡人民政府，乡政府驻地小箐街。至2010年12月，小箐乡人民政府下辖17个村民委员会和1个社区居民委员会。

洒坪乡人民政府　1992年2月，将原洒坪乡、中寨乡合并，建立新的洒坪乡人民政府，乡政府驻地小坝。至2010年12月，洒坪乡人民政府下辖18个村民委员会。

大石布依族乡人民政府　1992年2月，将原大石布依族乡和回水乡的回水、天桥、沙坝、红岩4个村以及德政乡的联江、联合2个村合并，建立新的大石布依族乡人民政府，乡政府驻地大石。至2010年12月，大石布依族乡人民政府下辖15个村民委员会。

六桶乡人民政府　1992年2月，将原六桶乡、花椰乡、凉井乡、宝寨乡和回水乡的石板村、平山村合并，建立新的六桶乡人民政府，乡政府驻地六桶坝。至2010年12月，六桶乡人民政府下辖28个村民委员会。

1984年政社分设，将生产大队革命委员会改建成村民委员会，村委会设主任，生产队改建为村民小组，村民小组设组长。2003年推进社区建设，改居民段为社区，街道居民委员会相应改为社区居民委员会。至2010年，全县共置217个村民委员会，1414个村民小组；置12个社区居委会。村民委员会和居民委员会为群众性自治单位，是村民进行自我教育、自我管理、自我监督和自我服务的基层群众性自治组织。

第二节　县政府会议

一、县政府全体（扩大）会议

1981年1月复建县政府，即建立县政府组成单位人员会议，1999年改称县政府全体（扩大）会议。会议议题主要有：贯彻县委战略决策和工作思路，研究落实措施；总结工作，部署任务；研究出台以县政府名义发布的重要工作计划和文件。出席人员为县长、副县长和政府成员以及各乡（镇）乡（镇）长。根据需要，有时也邀请县人大、县政协负责人以及党群部门负责人参加。1984年4月17日政府组成单位人员会议研究县内企业改革工作，会后，报经县委常委会研究同意,出台县委、县政府《关于企业改革的决定》。1998年11月4日会议，研究国有企业改制工作，决定对红旗煤矿、三角山水泥厂、酱菜厂等

国有企业实行“有偿转让”；针对烤烟限产，研究提出“一调六补”（通过调整结构，以发展经济作物、养殖业、乡（镇）企业、非公经济、组织外出务工和推广农业适用技术予以弥补）的农业增产增收措施。2002年，政府全体（扩大）会议提出“工业强县”、2007年提出“建设生态文明县”、2009年提出“以工业化带富农民，以城镇化带动农村，以产业化提升农业”等发展经济的举措。一系列通过政府全体（扩大）会议提出的具体措施，经过努力攻坚，使县域经济社会发展获得显著的成效。

二、县长办公会议

2009年9月18日，县政府第二次全体组成人员会议

县长办公会议由县长或县长委托副县长召集，对涉及国民经济和社会发展计划、财政预算、城市建设规划、宏观调控和改革开放的政策措施、社会管理事务、大型项目建设等重大问题，均通过会议进行决定、协调和部署。参加人员主要以事项涉及的乡（镇）、部门领导为主，有时也邀请县人大、县政协领导和其他部门领导参加。县长办公会议作为例会规定每月召开一次，遇有重大问题需要及时解决则临时召集，有时因县长外出则延期召开。1981年至2010年，共召开县长办公会议361次。县内人民群众关注的事项，多由县长办公会议提出解决措施。2000年，群众反映县城老城区无路灯照明，影响夜间出行。县政府于3月11日召开县长办公会议，作出由县财政出资8万元修复老城区路灯的决定。11月，县长办公会议研究安泰入驻扎佐医药园区事项，会议作出的决定，在实践中成为修文招商引资的“安泰模式”。2008年2月24日，县长办公会议研究凝冻灾害后重建工作，对全年经济工作提出“目标不减，任务不变”的要求，是年，全县国民生产总值达到3.5亿元，实现增长15%的目标。2010年5月13日，县长办公会议研究环保工作，提出“强制淘汰落后产能”的要求，会后，13家产能、工艺、设备、产品落后企业被强制淘汰。

第三节　施政纪要

县人民政府1981年复建后，不断探索发展经济和社会各项事业的职能转变，通过履行经济调节、市场监管、社会管理和公共服务的职能行使政务，促进县域经济和社会发展，经济总体水平逐年上升。至2010年，国内生产总值达到46亿元，人均1.51万元。人民物质生活走出低水平徘徊的历史。2010年，农民人均纯收入达到5152元，城镇居民可支配收入达到1.58万元。人口素质有明显提高，人均预期寿命达到70岁，成人识字率达到90%；人民精神文化生活日趋丰富，城镇居民消费性支出达到1.09万元，农村居民达到3229元。人民生活环境和城乡自然条件逐年改善，森林覆盖率超过全国平均水平，达到40.3%。

一、政务公开

1981年复建县政府后，大力推进政务公开，打造“阳光政府”。1988年，推行“三公开一监督”制度，对群众关心的招工、职工调动等热点实行公开办理、公开政策、公开结果，接受群众监督。1999年起，在工程建设项目招投标、大中专毕业生就业、退伍军人安置、预算外资金管理、土地出让等方面，建立公开办理运行机制，推行行政执法责任制、行政执法公示制、服务承诺制，增强政府的工作透明度。2003年下发《关于进一步深入实行政务、厂务、村务公开的意见》，2004年再次下发《关于做好“三公开”工作的意见》，进一步强调推行政务公开，督促县乡两级机关各部门主动对接企业和群众需求，扩大政务公开范围，制定公开办事目录、公示收费项目及标准等。

县政府政务公开内容共9项，即政策法规重要规定；政府确定当地经济建设和社会发展的重要事项；政府的职责权限、办事依据、办事程序、办事时限、办事结果等事项；政府年度工作目标及执行情况、政府财政预算及执行情况、政府领导人任免事项；政府兴办的社会公益事业建设情况，政府为民办实事项目执行情况；对重大问题实行向社会公开咨询制度；直接影响公民、法人或其他组织权益的行政执法事项；法律、法规和规章规定必须公开的政务事项；其他需要公开的事项。政务公开的形式主要有设橱窗（公开栏）、向社会公布公开电话、设立政务大厅、设置电子触摸屏、召开新闻发布会等多种形式。

2004年，县政府在政府办公楼设置电子触摸屏，将须公开的政府工作内容、各种办事程序制作成政务指南，通过触摸屏即可轻松获得相关信息；改建政务公开栏，随时更换公开内容。2005年，实行新闻发言人制度，凡县内有影响的事项，均向媒体和公众公布。至2010年，县政府及其职能部门通过《当代修文》和修文电视台先后向社会公开森林防火、防汛责任单位及责任人、享受低保人员名单、“整脏治乱”和“创卫”责任人及其电话、出租车财政补贴发放名单、“县委书记大接访”活动县领导接待日程及电话、百姓—书记县长交流平台交流方式、一村一名大学生选聘、从村干部中选录乡（镇）公务员、申请经济适用住房名单等200余件。

2009年至2010年，完善政府门户网站，网站设置“政务公开”专栏，下设“领导信息公开”和“政府信息公开”子专栏，将需要公开的事项通过网络向社会公开。

乡（镇）政府和县政府工作部门及县内其他部门按政务公开内容以设立公开栏、媒体发布等形式实现政务公开。县民政局在单位门口设公开栏，定期公布低保对象增减名单，县人民法院、物价局、供电局利用《当代修文》刊登“开庭公告”“粮油副食品每周价格报告”“停电作业公告”。县医院对所有收费项目的依据、价格全部上墙，使看病群众明白付费。扎佐镇和平村的村民给《当代修文》“读者来信”专栏来稿称：“过去到镇里办事两眼一抹黑，现在有了公开栏，办的事该找谁上面都写得清清楚楚，真是方便了群众。”六屯乡退休多年的老干部聂洪武写诗称赞：“实行‘三公开’，赢得民心来。”

二、作风教育和效能建设

自1981年复建县政府起，坚持不懈地抓好政府机关的思想、作风和制度建设，增强依法行政意识，转变工作职能，创建廉洁高效的服务型政府。1982年3月召开首次政府廉政工作会议。之后，每年均召开相同内容会议，总结布置政府廉政工作，警示政府工作人员廉洁从政。1988年，对机关工作人员德、能、勤、绩实行百分考核。1993年，县政府出台《县人民政府工作规则》和《县人民政府工作人员守则》，完善服务承诺制、首问责任制、一次性告知制、限时服务制等。明确提出加强自身建设，提高决策

2006年4月，全县直机关作风整顿会议现场

水平和管理能力，塑造“开拓、务实、廉洁、高效”的政府形象。2001年和2007年两次在政府机关中开展作风教育整顿活动。2007年还结合全县开展的“修文要发展，我该怎么干”大讨论，要求政府工作部门采取上门走访、召开座谈会、发放意见征求表、设立征求意见箱等，多渠道征求意见，查找工作中存在的问题进行整改。2009年和2010年结合推进大项目落户工作，开展“整治发展软环境，建设服务型机关”和“服务发展、服务企业、服务基层”的“三服务”活动，增强职工的服务意识。2010年年初，“整治发展软环境，建设服务型机关”领导小组办公室在部分企业中征求意见测评政府服务工作，发出测评表64张，收回64张，表示满意的51票，基本满意的13票，不满意的0票。由于“三服务” 活动的开展，不仅增强了职工服务意识，而且提升了政府的服务形象。

三、经济调节

1979年后，县政府贯彻执行中共十一届三中全会路线，全面推行改革、开放、搞活的方针，将工作重点转移到经济建设上来，对社会总需求和总供给进行总量调控，促进经济结构调整和优化，保持经济持续快速健康发展。在不同的时期分别提出经济发展的奋斗目标，1984年确定“本世纪末实现全县国民生产总值比1980年翻两番”，2001年提出“建设经济强县”，2010年提出“加速发展、加快转型”和明确“工业强县”的发展战略等。围绕这些目标，县政府根据不同阶段的经济发展要求，作出一系列经济调节的决策措施，推动全县经济发展。

（一）经济运行机制改革

1979年9月，作出《全县实行包产到组联产计酬的意见》，迈出农村经济改革的第一步。1981年，全面推行土地联产承包责任制。实行土地承包责任制凸现出强劲的生命力。1982年，全县农业总产值达到4312.2万元，比公社化时期的1979年翻了1番。1998年，在1981年农村实行土地承包的基础上，进一步深化土地承包责任制，将农村土地承包期再延长50年，将非耕地资源开发的承包使用期再延长60年，巩固完善土地承包责任制，促进农村经济继续稳定发展。2010年全县农林牧渔业总产值达到13.14亿元,比1980年的2449万元增加53倍。

1984年作出《关于企业改革的决定》，明确县内企业在保证完成国家计划任务的前提下，可以根据自身条件选择经营方式和用人制度。到1990年，再度作出对企业“松绑放权”的决定，允许企业自主经营，在企业内部实行承包责任制或目标责任制，把经营权力和经济利益结合起来，促使企业向市场经济转轨。1997年11月，针对县内国有企业因在计划经济时期负债累累，无力参与市场竞争的实际情况，作出对国有企业改制的决策，先后采取“有偿转让”等方式，对红旗煤矿、三角山水泥厂、棕刚玉厂、郭家林水泥厂、酱菜厂等国有企业进行改制，这一决策使一些濒于倒闭的企业在改变经营机制后重又焕发生机。此间，还依照国家相关政策，对流通体制、金融体制、财政体制改革作出决策，使县的经济发展逐年向好。2010年全县实现工业总产值56.09亿元，是1978年2614万元的21倍。

（二）非公经济发展

1998年4月县第八次党代会把“加快乡（镇）企业和个体、私营经济发展”写进全县工作的指导思想。从是年起，县政府加大发展非公有制经济的力度，作出简化办证程序、减税、免税等有利于发展的决定，促进非公经济迅速发展。至2010年，全县持有证照的个体经营户发展到3775户，私营企业182个，非公经济实现增加值26.56亿元，在全县GDP比重中占57.5%，成为全县经济的重要组成部分。

（三）“工业强县”经济发展战略

1999年起，县政府实施“三点两线一园区”经济发展规划，即在龙场镇、扎佐镇、久长镇和沿贵（阳）毕（节）、贵（阳）遵（义）两条过境高等级公路建设新的经济产业带，在扎佐建设医药工业园区，大力发展外向型经济，引进外资和技术，扩大对外贸易。2001年，县委提出“二产强县”后，县政府又于2005年实施“建设十里工业走廊”规划，开发国有闲置土地、厂房、荒山及贫瘠土地，引进高科技、生态化、结构合理、高速增长的产业，打造继扎佐医药园区后工业壮大发展的后续基地。2009年，县政府再次作出建设“龙场—扎佐—久长工业循环经济示范园区”规划，提升工业质量和效益。至2010年，全县已拥有规模以上工业企业45家。县政府经过10年的努力，逐步使修文走向从传统农业到现代工业的转型。“三点两线一园区”“十里工业走廊”“工业循环经济示范园区”成为“工业强县”经济发展战略中壮大县域经济的重要支撑点。

2007年5月26日，华飞公司5万吨氢氧化铝项目开工奠基

专记一：迅速崛起的修文医药产业园

1996年，县委、县政府择址在省城北大门扎佐筹建医药产业园区，最初是利用原航空工业部属011系统的304医院搬迁后闲置的房屋引进绿太阳制药厂，获得成功后，坚定了政府筹建医药产业园区的设想。选择扎佐筹办医药产业园区，主要是充分利用扎佐林场的自然资源，给入驻的制药企业提供良好的生态环境。1998年，县政府加大招商引资力度，相继制定出台招商引资优惠政策和激励措施，对外来投资者实行全程服务，鼓励投资商注重科技含量，发展新兴产业，开发化学原料药、生物化学药、新型药物制剂等。外来投资者也看重这块“宝地”，充分利用丰富的生物资源发展特色经济。

医药产业园区规划总面积4.3平方公里，分布在扎佐林场境内的贵（阳）遵（义）高等级公路和210国道沿线，由A、B、C3个功能区组成：A区主要布局制药工业，B区为综合功能区，C区为综合服务区。2000年起，县政府对外加大招商引资力度，对内加大投资软环境治理，提出“招商、安商、稳商”要求，实施“一站式”服务，以吸引投资者。2003年，园区初具规模，国家农业部将其命名为“全国乡（镇）企业科技园区”。2006年7月经国家发改委和省政府审核，列为省级开发区，并更名为“贵州修文医药产业园”。至2010年已有19家药业入驻。

专记二：安泰药业顺利入驻医药园区

2000年8月，贵州安泰药业意欲入驻修文兴建的扎佐医药园区。进场规划需占用扎佐林场林地108亩，每亩价格为4.75万元，仅此一项，企业就要投入500多万元。如果一下子付清征地款，就没有更多的资金建厂房、购设备。因资金运作存在困难，企业想放弃入驻打算。

县政府获知安泰的想法后，立即召开县长办公会通报这一情况。与会者一致认为，能不能留住安泰，是对政府招商引资能力的考验，政府应发挥服务职能，千方百计为企业排忧解难，帮助安泰解决资本运作的“瓶颈”。会议决定由副县长成华祥代表县政府与扎佐林场协商，希望林场降低征地价格。9月初，县政府与扎佐林场就安泰药业入驻的林地征地价格召开第一次协调会。但因林场的主管部门是省林业厅，其价格是由林业厅按国家相关政策确定的，林场无权改变，致协调会没有达到预期效果。是时，扎佐林场也因经济转型正在谋求发展，也有留住安泰药业的意愿。在接着召开的第二次协调会上，林场领导班子提出一个设想：安泰药业的征地款可部分缓交，但缓交部分要由修文县政府担保到期偿付。成华祥即将林场的设想向县长魏明禄汇报。魏明禄认为这个设想有利于修文招商引资工作开展，有利于安泰药业入驻医药园区，也有利于林场的发展，但县政府用什么资金担保？担保的主体是否合法？若安泰缓交的征地款到期不能偿还，政府又该怎么办？带着这些问题，两位政府领导多次召集县财政、税务、政府法治办领导会议进行调查研究。11月，在县长办公会议再次研究安泰入驻园区事项时，魏明禄、成华祥提出通过调研深化林场领导班子设想后的新建议：即安泰药业可先给付扎佐林场部分土地转让金，剩余大部分由县政府负责偿还林场，将安泰药业建成投产后为县级财政提供税金的50%，作为政府偿还部分的资金来源。此建议经县长办公会议研究形成决定并向县委常委会作了汇报。12月，县政府与扎佐林场、安泰药业再次召开协调会统一认识，最后明确由安泰药业按每亩7480元的数额，先付给扎佐林场部分征地款。这一协调结果被制作成具有法律效力的协议书，使安泰药业顺利获得入驻园区的“入场券”。协议书规定：安泰药业投产见效后，县政府每年从其为地方财政提供的财政税收中拿出50%偿付给扎佐林场，直到补足土地款为止。

扎佐医药园区的安泰药业

县政府这个举措引起很大反响，一批医药企业纷纷前来联系入驻园区。因为这个“企业低门槛入驻，地款用税收补齐”运作起于安泰药业被誉为修文招商引资的“安泰模式”，先后有17家企业仿照“安泰模式”入驻扎佐医药园区，截至2010年，入驻园区的医药企业达19家，实现总产值20.65亿元，同比增长25%。医药园区的迅速崛起，在贵州招商引资和医药产业发展史上写下了浓墨重彩的一笔。

（四）农业产业结构调整

1988年，县政府开始探索农业产业结构调整，先在乌栗、下洞两地发动农民利用荒山瘦地种植猕猴桃，力图在贫困山区引导农民从传统农业向经济农业转移。1998年，针对国家限制烤烟种植面积削减烤烟计划的实际，县政府提出“广开门路，增产增收” 的农村经济工作要求和“一调六补”（调整结构，发展经济作物、养殖业、乡镇企业、非公经济，组织外出打工和推广农业适用技术来弥补）措施，使农业产业结构调整在全县全面展开。到2000年底，仅猕猴桃种植一项就从1997年的1.2万亩发展到3万亩。1999年，县政府再次对农业产业结构调整提出“一乡一业，一村一品”的构想，全县农业产业结构调整形成强有力的发展态势，经济作物种植面积达到12万亩，经果林种植仅猕猴桃一项就使农民人均收入年增加200元，土鸡年出栏100万只以上，生猪年出栏在21万头以上，肉牛年出栏1400头以上。2010年，县农林牧渔业总产值达到13.14亿元，比1978年的2110万元增长50倍。

龙场镇中哨村的延晚番茄

专记：猕猴桃产业“蛋糕”做大了

1998年，县政府把猕猴桃种植确定为全县农业农村经济的“五大产业”之一，把发展猕猴桃产业作为全县农业产业结构调整的突破口，同时注册了“六广河”牌商标，开始实施品牌战略，并探索产业化经营方式。农业开发部门从提高品质、提高效益着眼，狠抓猕猴桃生产基地建设，在优质品牌上做文章，扩大宣传，搞好营销。这期间，中央电视台、贵州电视台、《贵州日报》《贵阳日报》《羊城晚报》等新闻媒体先后报道过修文的猕猴桃产业。贵州空港服务公司将“六广河”牌猕猴桃作为指定销售产品。1999年，县果品公司携“六广河”牌猕猴桃先后参与厦门、广州、西安、大连、北京等地举办的全国名、特、优、新农产品展销订货会或经贸洽谈会，修文猕猴桃由此被推向全国，在广州、深圳、南宁、北京、上海、吉林、长春、哈尔滨等省外城市设立销售联系点，初步建起销售网络。同时，还通过互联网把县内猕猴桃的有关信息发向全国，在网上下载猕猴桃的生产管理、市场营销、产品开发等信息指导全县猕猴桃产业发展。宣传和营销活动的扩大带来了良好效应，1999年和2000年，全县猕猴桃销售出现供不应求的良好势头，2000年9月，猕猴桃刚上市，各地客商云集修文，仅几天时间，基地生产的800万公斤猕猴桃鲜果就销售一空，实现产值2800万元。

猕猴桃产业的发展，促进了经济、社会、生态效益的协调发展。至2002年，全县种植猕猴桃的果农达5000余户2万余人，年收入在10万元以上的11户，5万元—10万元的27户，1万元—5万元的123户，一部分果农已从传统大农业中分工出来，成为从事猕猴桃生产的专业户，更多的果农因种植猕猴桃走上致富之路，有的修了新房子，有的购置了汽车、农用车，过去因为经济条件不好娶不上媳妇的人家如今已娶妻生子，广大农村呈现一派生机勃勃的景象。

一业兴，百业旺。猕猴桃产业的大发展，推动了全县的运输业、冷藏保鲜业、服务业的共同发展，同时，因为发展猕猴桃种植，给昔日的荒山草坡披上了绿装，水土流失也得到了控制。春来满山绿遍，秋来果实累累，正是猕猴桃产业发展的真实写照。

（五）非公企业结构调整

1996年起，针对县境非公有制企业发展迟缓、难以参加市场竞争的实际，县政府作出在“九五”期间加大非公企业二次创业力度调整产业结构的决策。非公企业二次创业以调整产业结构、优化生产力布局为主，从三个方面进行，一是以发展高新技术产业为重点，推进区域生产力布局相对集中。经过几年努力，逐步形成以龙场、扎佐、久长3镇连接构成的经济工业带，一批投资规模较大、科技含量较高的企业纷纷入驻，主要有以仙灵药业（后改称“同济堂”）为代表的医药工业，以福鹏麦芽糊精厂为代表的食品加工工业，以林海新材料公司为代表的新材料工业，以兰地公司为代表的养殖业等，基本形成以龙场、扎佐、久长3镇为点，沿贵（阳）遵（义）、贵（阳）毕（节）两条高等级公路为线和扎佐医药园区为园区的“三点两线一园区”为载体的非公企业工业生产布局，以扎佐医药工业园区为代表的新兴高科技术逐步形成支柱产业，并对全县经济发挥辐射带动作用。二是以培育规模企业为龙头，加快产业结构调整。在二次创业中以市场为导向，以资源为纽带，对存量资产进行战略性重组。利用20世纪60年代创建于80年代外迁的原航空工业部属庆文厂、万江厂、四一八库闲置厂区引进的仙灵药业、兰地公司、龙翔集团就是这一指导思想的产物。其次是培育林海新材料公司等一批潜力较大的高新技术企业。通过调整产业结构，培育龙头企业，使一批骨干企业的规模效应和聚集效应不断增大，至2010年，县内已有资产超千万的企业12家，年销售收入超千万元的企业20家。三是优化行业结构，促进新兴支柱产业快速成长。此前，非公企业在县域经济中虽占较大比例，但多数是利用本地资源发展起来的资源型产业，后劲不足。1998年县政府提出“改造传统产业、壮大支柱产业、发展新兴产业”的调整措施，1999年对县内17家水泥厂中达不到国家建材产业政策标准的13家限期关闭，进行技术改造。2000年，有8家水泥厂完成技改投入生产，生产能力由技改前年产不足40吨提高到100吨。同时，加速存量资产的战略性重组，对88家煤炭企业实行“关井压产”，保留38家，并按照年产3万吨能力进行技术改造，使生产要素向优势化企业聚集。

龙翔集团车间生产

2000年，全县完成对非公企业的二次创业，形成以采掘、建材、医药、食品加工、冶金、化工、耐火材料为主体的7大支柱工业产业，特别是以医药为代表的高新技术产业已成为重要支柱产业。2010年，全县非公企业完成营业收入64.02亿元，上缴税金2.65亿元。

（六）第三产业提升

从1998年起，针对县的区位、能源、交通、自然资源和人文资源优势，把发展和壮大第三产业作为扩张县域经济的目标，以旅游业为重点，提升第三产业。至2010年，“以旅游为龙头，发展第三产业”的构想从蓝图变成现实。县内旅游业以阳明文化为中心，以高尔夫度假中心—阳明洞—六广河为主线，形成东有桃源河魔幻漂流，西有六广河、回水石林，南有高尔夫度假中心、高原森林野生动物园，北有珍珠岛、苏格兰牧场，中有阳明洞、三潮水的旅游框架。

2008年全县依托旅游资源优势，大力发展旅游业，完成阳明主题公园、森林野生动物园等景点续建配套工程，野生动物园被评为国家AAAA级景区。精心组织宣传“爽爽贵阳，秀美修文”，成功举办桃园河魔幻漂流峡谷冲浪大赛。全年共接待游客66.5万人次，实现旅游总收入1.37亿元。2010年，组织参加中国国内旅游交易会和中国重庆城际国际旅游交易会，成功举办“2010生态贵阳会议企业家高尔夫邀请赛”。全年共接待游客388.6万人次，实现旅游总收入2亿元。是年，成立县旅游文化投资有限公司，为加快旅游开发和市场化运作提供保障。完成《修文县阳明主题公园建设性详细规划》《六广河旅游区总体规划》《贵阳市森林野生动物园二期建设概念规划》等的编制。启动苏格兰牧场民族生态旅游公园、六广河二期——阳明古渡建设。县政府努力培育文化产业，以阳明文化为载体，阳明书院、王阳明影视城等规划也在2010年启动。

野生动物园的大象表演

2008年，以扎佐镇为中心的物流业雏形显现，扎佐火车站仓储面积达2000平方米，修文兴达公司在扎佐火车站建成6000平方米仓库和1500平方米露天货场，贵阳盐业公司在扎佐建成盐业配送中心。2010年，集仓储、运输、配送、转运、贸易等为主的扎佐物流园区已具规模，园区铁路专用线、农资农肥转运交易中心等项目开始建设。是年，县政府加强市场体系建设，完成3个乡（镇）农贸市场升级改造。组织落实家电、汽车下乡及以旧换新政策，消费市场呈现购销两旺态势，完成全社会消费品零售总额10.13亿元。

1998年，以县城改造为契机，房地产业迅速发展，至2002年，总投资达4.4亿元，建筑面积达40.78万平方米。2008年起，房地产业发展提速，至2010年，县城“新都口岸”“明河花园”“利尔上河城”等商品房开发完成，“文城逸都”“腾晖家园”等项目开工建设，城市容量增大，城区面积拓展到5平方公里。完成县城主干道白改黑、管线入地、交通标志标识更新等工程，主城区污水管网收集系统基本完成。

至2010年，全县第三产业实现增加值21.17亿元，对GDP的贡献率达28%。

四、市场监管

县人民政府依法对市场主体及其行为进行监督和管理，以维护公平竞争的市场秩序。

（一）市场监管行政执法体系建立

1998年，县人大常委会作出依法治县的决议后，县政府对行政执法作出相应决策，建立“依法治县办公室”，加大对行政执法的监督管理和宣传。1999年，按国家体制改革相关要求，将质量技术监督业务从工商行政管理局划出，成立质量技术监督局。2001年，建食品药品监督局，从体制上完善市场监管的行政执法体系。至2010年,全县已形成工商行政管理、质量技术监督、药品食品监督、税收征管为主，企业管理部门、金融部门协同配合的市场监管体系。

（二）市场监管的行业自律与群众参与体系建立

1990年起，县内通过县政协、统战、司法部门、税务机关、工商联、个体协会、私营企业协会、消费者协会等组织的联络、宣传，在市场主体中构建起行业自律与约束机制。至2000年的10年间，县举办

2010年全县开展食品卫生检查

的税法宣传、产品质量宣传、消费者权益保护宣传等有关市场建设的宣传活动达百余次之多，组织市场主体学法守法的学习、培训、宣传活动亦在百次以上。同时，涉及市场监管的职能部门向社会公布服务电话和举报电话，动员群众参与市场监管。2001年起，以“3·15”消费者权益日、“税法宣传月”为主，加大行业自律与群众参与市场监管体系建设力度。是年“3·15”期间，以“绿色消费”为主题，县政府组织工商、消协、个协、私协、物价、国税、地税、技术监督、卫生、电信、邮政、移动、烟草、宣传、妇联、人行、工行、农行共18家单位和13家企业开展大型宣传活动，活动现场设立伪劣商品展示台、法律法规宣传服务台、企业产品展示台和受理投诉台，宣传的同时接受群众投诉。活动期间，接受群众咨询1400人次，受理现场投诉15起，发放宣传资料3.5万份，受众逾6万多人。2007年4月，县国税局和地税局联合举办“税法宣传月”税法知识竞赛，县内制药、房开、电力、商业的36家企业参加。至2010年，行业、群众参与的市场监管体系成为县政府实施市场监管的主要方式之一。

（三）市场监管的舆论引导监督体系建立

从1998年起，利用县内媒体电视台和《修文报》（《当代修文》）开辟专栏，加强舆论引导和舆论监督，新闻媒体在每年的税法宣传月、“3·15”活动期间都出增刊、专版和制作专题宣传相关法律法规，报道遵纪守法的市场主体，每年年终或年初都要刊播对县的经济作出贡献的纳税大户名单。2002年4月10日，《修文报》第四版整版刊登《税收知识有奖竞答100题》，供读者通过答题学习税法；县质监局2001年至2010连续10年与县内媒体合作，刊播有关质量技术标准和监管工作法律法规。2010年，《当代修文》和修文电视台刊播市场执法主体税务、工商、质监、物价的相关新闻信息达217条。

（四）打击制假售假、商业欺诈违法行为

工商、质监、税务、物价等部门不间断地开展打击违法经营、假冒伪劣、偷税漏税行为。2005年1月春节前夕，工商局开展对食品市场的打假宣传，共查扣涉嫌假冒“贵州茅台”酒49瓶，茅台内供酒8瓶，收缴假冒“双桥”味精22包，脑白金、含钙麦片29盒，无生产日期的干吃奶粉19包。2007年，县政府按照《贵阳市食品生产加工业整顿工作方案》，组织质监、工商、卫生、药监4个部门对县内11家米粉生产企业检查考核，结果有6家不合格，对其作出限期停业整顿的决定。2008年，轰动全国的“三鹿奶粉事件”发生后，县工商局对全县723户经营食品的超市、百货店进行检查，查获含三聚氰胺的三鹿奶粉180公斤，作集中销毁处理。在对药品、食品销售行业专项清理活动中，取缔非法行

县食品药品监督工作人员在农贸市场检查食品

医4户、吊销工商执照1户。县物价局加强价格监管，全年共查处违法案件38件，经济制裁金额达23.3万元，退还消费者21.6万元，收缴财政1.7万元。2010年，在县城开展“百城万店无假货示范街”创建活动，倡导诚信经商，营造文明健康和谐有序的消费环境，保护消费者正当权益，深受市民称赞。

五、社会管理

县人民政府通过实施社会管理职能维护社会秩序和社会稳定，加强社会治安综合治理，保障人民群众生命财产安全，建立健全处理突发事件的应急机制，应对公共危机，保护和治理生态环境，造福于民。

（一）社会秩序和社会稳定维护

从1981年复建县政府起，采取政策性措施以维护社会秩序和社会稳定。一是规范社会组织和社会事务，凡民间社会组织均需按国家统一规定办理登记注册，在国家政策允许的范围内进行活动。1990年，将社团管理纳入民政工作范围，是年对全县社会团体调查摸底，造册登记。查实全县共有学术类社团8个、行业类社团11个、专业类社团79个。2001年，开展民办非企业单位组织登记工作。至2010年，有登记社团组织29个，民办非企业单位10个。政府职能部门民政局代行政府对社会事务的管理，开展社会福利、社会救济、优抚安置、婚姻丧葬等社会事务工作。二是设立政府信访办公室（后改为信访局），接待人民群众来信来访，了解民情动态。1989年起，建立政府领导接待日制度，每周由一位政府县长到信访办公室接待来访群众，随机处理群众反映问题。三是调节收入分配，保证群众享有衣食住行。2001年起，在城镇实施居民最低生活保障制度，2008年为4472名城镇困难人口发放低保金734万元。同时，还通过民政救济帮助因天灾人祸造成生活困难的群众，仅2008年，政府发放的各类救济款项就达366.7万元，发放温暖煤7700吨，帮助7589户困难家庭渡过暂时困难。从2009年起，实施“六有工程”（学有所教、劳有所得、病有所医、老有所养、住有所居、居有所安）民生行动计划。至2010年全县小学适龄儿童入学率达99.63%，初中阶段入学率106.90%，高中阶段入学率44.51%。城乡统筹就业完成6554人，农村富余劳动力转移4696人；零就业家庭动态为零；城镇登记失业率在4%以内；失业保险扩面1126人，征缴失业保险费155.58万元。养老保险扩面2407人,完成率达215.60%。新型农村社会养老保险参保10.5万人，城镇老年居民养老保险参保185人。新型农村合作医疗共有23.9万人入保，参保率为97.13%，医疗保险扩面1658人，工伤保险扩面5398人，城镇居民医疗保险扩面1472人，辖区内所有居住满3个月的0—6岁儿童建立预防接种证和预防接种卡，对适龄儿童进行常规疫苗接种7万余人次，完成县人民医院二期工程地勘及三通一平。建成经济适用房133套（9898平方米）、廉租住房833套（4.15万平方米），累计发放租赁补贴资金144.86万元，完成8199户农村危房改造、103户以工代赈易地扶贫搬迁项目，进一步改善了低收入家庭住房状况。严厉打击“两抢一盗”和黄赌毒，加强校园周边环境综合治理，完善群防群治体系，提高街面见警率，群众安全感和满意度达90%以上。一系列民生计划落到实处，使群众能安居乐业，县境社会秩序日趋稳定。

扎佐中学校园

（二）社会治安综合治理

1991年6月，建社会治安综合治理办公室，负责指导、协调全县社会治安综合治理工作。由政府组织、动员群众广泛参与整顿社会治安，在城镇建立巡防队，在城镇社区建立治安保卫小组，在农村村寨建立巡逻组，配合公安部门建起“打防结合，以防为主”的社会治安防范体系。政府制定社会治安综合治理考核制和一票否决制，对机关、乡（镇）综合治理工作进行考核，考核不合格者，按规定处罚。1999年，荣获省级“平安工程”红旗县称号。2003年，六屯乡在村寨建起村民自治的治安防范网络后，被农村群众深恶痛绝的偷牛盗马等治安案件近乎绝迹，县政府给予表彰并总结其经验在全县推广。2005年起开展“平安修文”创建活动，至2010年仍在进行中。是年，破获“两抢一盗”案件552起，创建无毒乡（镇）8个、无毒村214个、无毒社区10个，群众安全感满意度达90%以上。

（三）安全生产

1988年，县政府设立安全生产委员会，由1名副县长担任主任，县乡企局、计经局等相关职能部门为成员单位，不定期召开会议，安排、布置安全生产工作。职能部门专门配有负责安全生产管理的领导，各乡（镇）亦明确有政府领导抓安全生产工作，定期或不定期进行安全生产检查。县政府制定有安全生产的考核措施和目标考核办法，每年年终按目标考核办法对负有安全生产责任的单位和单位领导、单位责任人分别进行考核。2002年4月25日，六广镇中坪村豪猪湾无证煤矿矿主付汉祥利欲熏心，在其煤矿不具备开采条件而被强制炸封后，仍招募民工盗采，致使发生透水事故，6名民工死亡，县政府就此承担责任，有21名责任人员受到责任追究，其中4名煤矿合伙人被移交司法机关追究刑事责任；常务副县长、分管副县长受到行政记过处分；县长被责令向市政府作书面检查；8名科级干部受到行政撤职、行政降级、行政警告处分。县政府从事故中吸取教训，明令炸封所有无证开采煤矿的矿井，并于2003年建安全生产监督管理局，落实安全生产责任制，对安全生产的防范、检查予以强化。2003至2005年的3年间，县内媒体报道政府及职能部门有关安全生产的会议、检查、处理百余次，县政府封闭、炸毁达不到安全生产条件的煤窑50座，从源头上堵住生产安全隐患。2006年至2010年5年间，县内无重特大事故发生。2010年亿元生产总值生产安全事故死亡率为0.51，实现事故起数和死亡人数“双降”目标。

（四）公共危机突发事件应对

县政府建有应对突发事件应急机制，不断提高应对公共危机的能力。1996年7月1日至5日，县境遭受百年不遇的特大暴雨侵袭，降雨量最大地区达315.3毫米，最小地区235.9毫米，暴雨造成洪涝灾害，给人民生命财产带来巨大损失。灾害发生过程中，县政府及时组织抗洪抢险救灾，出动由公安干警、武警消防官兵、民兵组成抢险队，由医院、卫生所、防疫站组成的防疫医疗队奔赴发生险情和灾情的地区，抢救人民生命财产。全县人民群众也紧急动员起来投入抢险救灾，把灾害造成的损失减到最小。在特大暴雨发生期间，由于政府应对及时，抢险措施有力，全县仅有4人死亡，1人失踪。2002年4月25日，六广镇中坪村豪猪湾煤矿发生透水事

2008年，凝冻灾害造成县城部分居民点断水，消防大队送水保障饮用

故。县政府接报后，立即组织16个相关部门抢险人员170人，携带抽水泵等物资赶赴现场抢险救人，使3名遇险被困矿工获救。是年7月4日，县城发生不法分子煽动阳明村村民冲击县政府、县人民法院的群体性事件，县政府在县委和贵阳市委的领导下，采取积极措施平息事件，维护安定团结的局面。2003年，“非典”突发，政府启动公共危机应急预案，一周内拨款54.5万元，组织卫生、医疗、防疫、公安、交通、宣传等部门“一手抓宣传，一手抓防治”，一方面深入群众宣传“非典”可防可治不可怕和“非典”防治知识，安定人心，一方面采取设卡阻源，广泛喷洒防治药水，在医院设立隔离病室等措施预防“非典”入侵。由于宣传有力，防治措施得当，在近半年的“非典”防治工作中，县内未发生一例“非典”和疑似病例。2008年初，县内发生50年不遇的冰雪灾害，全县受灾人口达24.5万人，其中受灾较重人口8.5万人，直接经济损失3.4亿元。县政府在县委的坚强领导下，组织全县人民“抗凝冻，保民生”，在20天的灾害发生过程中，全县每天有1500多名县、乡干部战斗在抗灾救灾第一线，组织群众抢修供电供水设施、发放款物、慰问群众、落实救灾措施。到灾害结束，没有出现一户受冻、一人挨饿。同年2月5日晚，扎佐镇兴红村发现饮用水源受到不明污染物污染，县环保局即要求村民立即停止取水。接着对被污染水源进行取样监测发现锰超标20倍，氨氮超标2.1倍，化学需氧量超标0.05倍，认定水源已经受到污染。水污染造成当地2000多人和6000头（只）畜禽饮水困难。县政府于2月6日上午召开应急处置工作会议启动应急预案。由政府每天派消防车、洒水车在该片区定点、定时供水，解决当地的人畜饮水问题。后经查明水源污染原因系贵州省有色地质勘查局五队在银厂坡详勘时用钻孔机打穿矿层遇到岩溶，导致钻机循环水及所带的沉砂、岩粉进入地下岩溶系统，造成饮用水源异常。由于县政府处置及时，未有人畜禽饮水中毒现象发生。

六、公共服务

县政府努力为公众生活和公众参与社会经济、政治、文化活动提供保障和创造条件，履行政府的服务职能。

（一）教育“两基”达标

从20世纪90年代中期开始，县政府加大教育投入，通过教育提供高水平的人才和高素质的劳动力。1996年，按省政府要求，开始实施教育“两基”（基本普及九年义务教育和基本扫除青少年文盲）达标工作，1997年纳入财政预算内的教育经费拨款为1262.1万元，1998年为1968万元，1999年为2066万元，3年间的财政拨款平均增长率为22.83%，这个比例高于财政年平均增长率6.8个百分点。2000年11月，经省人民政府验收为基本达标，2004年复查完全达标。至2010年，全县有中学23所、职业中学2所，小学112所、特殊教育学校1所，幼儿园10所。在校初中学生1.54万人，职业中学在校生2360人，小学生2.88万人。全县适龄儿童入学率为99.47%，初中适龄少年入学率为104%。

2007年，教师节座谈会

（二）文化、广播电视和体育事业

县政府坚持立足本县实际，走特色文化与时代精神结合的社会事业发展路子。从1998年起，以“团

结务实，乘势争先”的修文精神和“言行一致，开明开放”的修文形象为主题，广泛开展群众性的精神文明创建活动。至2010年，创建省级、市级、县级文明单位共140个，文明村寨和十星级文明农户90个。1999年抓硬件设施，投资900万元建成修文体育馆、投资300万元建成文广大楼等文化体育活动的标志性建筑。2000年完成10个乡（镇）精神文明活动中心建设。文化体育设施的改善，更丰富了群众文化体育活动的内容。1993年恢复《修文报》，1997年创办《栖霞》文艺杂志，1999年出版《修文县志》，1999、2002、2005和2009年分别举办4届“阳明文化节”并刊行一批文化图书，奠定了建设文化县的基础。至2010年，建成9个乡（镇）文化站，217个村农家书屋，广播人口覆盖率为100%，电视人口覆盖率在90%以上。

2006年大石布依族乡小学举办文艺演出欢度节日

专记：异彩纷呈文化节

1999年、2002年、2005年和2009年，在县内先后举办4届中国·贵阳（修文）国际阳明文化节。

第一届阳明文化节于1999年10月14日在新落成的体育馆举行开幕式，来自国内外嘉宾2000余人出席。体育馆2000多个座位座无虚席，满街人如潮涌，彩旗飘扬，喜气盈盈，比过春节还要热闹。王思齐、庹文升、孙国强等省市领导和担任过省领导职务的老同志苏钢、龙志毅、张玉环、苗春亭、陈行庚、徐挹江、李冀锋等莅临开幕式，来自美国哈佛大学的教授杜维明、香港孔教学院博士汤恩佳、中国人民大学教授张立文等在开幕式上发表了热情洋溢的讲话。文化节期间，举办了大型文艺《圣地·热土》的演出和《王阳明在贵州》《良知千古光》等图片、美术、书法展览，举行了“阳明遗迹寻访游”和品尝“阳明宴”等活动，一批有关阳明文化的书籍举行了首发式。13个医药、旅游项目签约。本届阳明文化节历时3天，其间，阳明学术研讨会在省城贵阳举行。

2002年10月18日，第二届阳明文化节开幕，省人大常委会副主任李万禄、徐敬原，老同志陈远武，贵阳市委副书记、市长孙国强，市委副书记辛维光等20余名领导及韩国阳明学会会长金吉洛等国内外专家学者60余人、各地来宾共2000余人出席开幕式。本届文化节历时2天，其间举行了阳明学术研讨会、阳明遗迹寻访游、阳明祭祀、开幕式文艺演出、六广河篝火晚会、龙冈秋韵书画展、花卉盆景根雕奇石展、小吃品尝、福利彩票发行和招商项目签约等活动。文化节期间，有11个招商项目签约。文化节组委会向来宾赠送了县内作者撰写的有关阳明文化研究的著作。

2005年，举办第三届国际阳明文化节

2005年9月14日，第三届阳明文化节开幕。王晓东、司徒桂美、蒙启良、李金顺等省市领导，叶辛、杜维明、汤恩佳等知名人士、来自13个国家和地区的百余名专家学者和各地来宾、群众万余人出席。本届文化节比前两届规模大、规格高，主办单位除中共贵阳市委、贵阳市人民政府外，还增加了贵州省文化厅和中国国际儒学联合会，承办单位为县委、县政府。这届文化节增加了一项颇具特色的内容——举办《良知与和谐社会》论坛，国际知名儒学大师杜维明、成中英、高柏园、杨国荣等对王阳明良知思想在建设和谐社会中产生的作用进行阐述。文化节期间，还开展阳明杯国际名人高尔夫球赛、名特优产品展销会、阳明碑苑落成剪彩、利尔之夜文艺晚会、叶辛春晖小学落成典礼、经济建设成果及发展规划展、龙冈秋韵书画展等系列活动。

2009年5月5日，第四届阳明文化节与2009中国贵阳避暑季活动同时举行。由省政府和国家旅游局主办，贵阳市委、市政府和省旅游局承办。国家旅游局副局长王志发出席晚会现场并致开幕辞，省委副书记王富玉宣布2009“中国·贵阳避暑季暨第四届国际阳明文化节”开幕。国家风景园林协会会长、城市规划协会会长、建设部原副部长赵宝江，中国气象学会秘书长王春乙，《今日中国》总编辑宫喜祥，民建中央组织部副部长李维平，国际儒学联合会副会长、美国哈佛大学燕京学院院长、教授杜维明，国际儒学联合会副会长、夏威夷大学教授成中英，国际儒学联合会副会长、香港孔教学院院长汤恩佳，应邀出席开幕式。省委常委、贵阳市委书记李军，省委常委、副省长黄康生，省人大常委会副主任傅传耀，省政协副主席伍鸿麟，贵阳市委副书记、市长袁周，市人大常委会主任李跃南，市政协主席陈石等省市领导出席开幕式。应邀出席开幕式的还有遵义市、六盘水市、安顺市、黔南州、黔东南州、黔西南州、毕节地区、铜仁地区的领导以及贵阳市委、市人大、市政府、市政协部分班子成员和贵阳警备区领导。

来自德国、美国、加拿大、澳大利亚、马来西亚、新加坡、韩国、日本、中国台湾以及全国各地的200多名王学研究专家学者参加了这次文化盛会。5月5日晚上，在阳明文化主题公园举行盛大的开幕式和文艺演出、燃放烟花、放响礼炮。那一刻，修文顿时成了歌与舞一体，烟花绽放与礼炮齐鸣的欢乐海洋。

5月6日，来自海内外的200多名与会专家学者在阳明文化主题公园参加以“知行合一与贵阳精神、阳明学与21世纪、阳明学与实心实学、阳明学与其他哲学的对话”等为主题的高端论坛。高端论坛由王晓昕教授主持。国际儒学联合会副会长、美国哈佛大学燕京学院院长杜维明，国际儒学联合会副会长、美国夏威夷大学成中英，国际儒学联合会副会长、澳大利亚大学教授李瑞智，中国哲学史学会会长、北京大学儒学研究中心主任陈来，加拿大卡城大学教授史罗一、台湾淡江大学副校长高伯园等在论坛上就王阳明“知行合一”“致良知”的哲学命题发表论见。

四届阳明文化节的成功举办，使修文知名度和影响力大大提高，中央电视台等国内众多新闻媒体报道其盛况，一些知名学者撰文称赞修文为传承优秀传统文化和阳明文化所作的努力，有人说：“办这样的文化盛会，把一个山区小县推介到海内外，一定会给今后的发展带来潜在影响。”

（三）控制人口增长速度，提高人口素质

县政府从20世纪70年代末期就致力于控制县内人口增长速度，以计划生育委员会为主体，动员全县人民参与，长期坚持不懈抓计划生育，1992年、1994年两度荣获全国计划生育先进县殊荣，从2004年开始连续7年获贵阳市目标考核一等奖，并荣获省级“计划生育优质服务县”称号。2010年，据公安年报统计，全县人口总数为30.59万人，按计生年报统计，人口出生率为12.5‰，人口自然增长率为6.7‰，人口

计划生育率为91.7%。

从1986年起，政府采取优先发展教育，鼓励社会力量投资教育，改善办学条件等措施，促进人口素质的提高。2002年，全县人口每万人中，具有大学受教育程度的为115人，与1985年比较，增加45人，具有高中受教育程度的为547人，比1985年增加121人，具有初中受教育程度的为2746人，比1985年增加915人，具有小学受教育程度的为4366人，比1985年增加187人。到2010年，全县非文盲率为97. 68%，城镇非文盲率达到99. 71%，实现基本扫除文盲。

（四）城乡卫生医疗体系

从1991年开始，县政府大力发展农村卫生事业，不断改善农村医疗条件，有效提高农村医疗卫生水平。1999年，荣获“省级卫生县城”称号。到2000年，农村医疗卫生保健已达到合格县标准。据2002年统计，孕产妇死亡率为110/10万人以内，婴儿死亡率为32.9‰，农村卫生室覆盖率达89.86%。县政府发动群众持续开展爱国卫生运动，使城乡卫生面貌明显改观。至2010年，全县有各级各类卫生医疗机构29个，医院病床583张，卫生人员776人，全县人口死亡率为5.8‰。

（五）社会保障

2001年设社会保障局，开展社会保险业务。至2010年，社会养老保险参保人数为1.04万人，全年征收养老保险费4910万元，失业保险参保人数为4351人，全年征收失业保险费174万元。城镇居民最低生活保障人数为3456人，发放低保金518万元，实现应保尽保。农村低保制度逐步建立，2010年，已为9453人发放低保金1029万元。

（六）扩大社会就业

1995年后，随着体制改革不断深入，就业矛盾日趋突出，政府采取提升“三产”等经济调节措施拓展就业空间，据第五次人口普查的资料显示，全县15岁以上从业人口比重为78%。但因就业问题面临来自城镇和农村的双重压力，又有新生劳动力和失业下岗人员的双重困扰，加之就业需求与经济发展的矛盾短期内难以平衡，社会就业问题仍是县政府致力解决的重点。2008年，开展“创建充分就业社区”活动，政府开发公益性工作岗位1000个，安置634名就业困难人员上岗。小箐社区居民陈开贵因年龄偏大，又没有文化，加上体弱有病，是典型的就业困难人员。由于求职无门，家中两个孩子还在中学读书，致使家庭生活十分困难。通过政府开发的公益性岗位，使其得到一份保洁员的工作，解决了就业难问题，他逢人便说：“还是人民政府好呀，现在我家的生活有着落了。”2010年，城镇新增就业人数为1858人。城镇登记失业人数1935人，失业率为2.9%。

2006年3月4日，县政府在县城体育馆广场组织企业用工招聘会

（七）公共设施建设

1998年，第十二届政府在《政府工作报告》中提出“以道路建设为契机，加快基础设施建设和小城

镇建设”。1999年起按“依靠地价增值，投资受益，市场运作”的模式经营城市，在县城实施“九三工程”，投资近亿元完成旧城民主路改造，新建阳明大道、玩易路、翠屏路中段、朝阳路东段、长征路中段等10条市政大道，建成县城东片区道路网络，建成龙冈广场、县城体育馆、文广大楼、社区服务中心、曲尺新桥、阳明新桥、阳明牌坊等一批建筑。完成自来水并网工程，使县城日供水量由原来的300吨增至6000吨，解决了县城居民的生活用水。扎佐镇、久长镇、六广镇、六桶乡的小城镇建设有长足发展。至2005年全县城市化水平由1997年的6%提升到18%。县乡公路全部硬化、油化，实现村村通公路。2008年，城镇建设力度进一步加快，完成县城河滨广场、河道治理、农贸市场等建设项目。至2010年，全面完成县城新客车站、综合管网改造、主要街道“白改黑”、污水处理厂、阳明大道立面整治等一批市政项目建设；新增城市绿地6277.62平方米，县城空气质量达到国家二级标准。全县城镇化率达36.5%。

专记一：交通网络连城乡

20世纪90年代初期，老百姓就流传一句民谣：要致富，先修路。1996—2000年的“九五”期间，这句民谣成为县委、县政府发展修文经济的战略举措。1997年，县政府提出以交通建设为龙头的经济发展思路，使公路建设步伐加快。在实施交通建设的过程中，大胆探索，抢抓机遇，打破长期以来由上级交通部门和财政补贴搞交通的格局，全方位开拓筹集建设资金，实现改造、新建项目双扩张。

1998—2000年的5年间，省、市、县、乡共投入资金1亿余元，完成了以管养、新建、改造、提级为主的公路交通建设。共改造公路59条，全长210公里，修建大小桥梁4座，全长178米。其中，冒沙井至乌栗的等外级公路提升为4级路面；完成六广河大桥及引道工程；县城至小箐公路改造为3级泥结碎石路面，0—3公里段为一级水泥路面，东门桥完成改建拓宽；六桶乡花椰至息烽县九庄公路被列为保畅工程，并提升为4级泥结石路面。全县实现村村通公路，客车通车率达到98%。由县列管的公路共12条，管护里程161.8公里，其中重要公路2条，一般公路5条，乡公路5条，村公路217条。加上已经通车的贵遵、贵毕两条高等级公路和210国道，全县公路通车旅程555.5公里，交通大网络基本建成。

1992年12月26日，靶（靶坳）修（文）公路二期改建工程竣工通车典礼

公路交通网络的完善，缩短地区之间的时空距离，增强社会流通功能，促进运输事业的发展。至2010年，全县已形成以私营经济为主体，国家、集体、个人一起上的客货运格局，载客汽车发展到197辆，载客量达3806客位；载货汽车1920辆，载重量为4549吨；开通营运线路26条；经营汽车维修业务的个体户发展到230户。公路交通的发展，为一大批农村、城镇剩余劳动力拓宽了就业门路，为农村农产品及时外运提供了便利，给全县经济发展奠定了基础。

专记二：小城镇建设与县城东片区开发

1991年3月，县城过境公路油箩街至长征桥段改造水泥路面工程开工，由此，全县小城镇建设与县城基础设施建设拉开帷幕。1996年后，小城镇建设与县城基础设施建设进入提速阶段，这期间，县城建成长700余米，宽21米的迎春路，建成翠屏路中段、朝阳路西段、长征路中段、玩易路等10条城区主次道路，新建占地14亩的综合农贸市场。扎佐、六桶、久长等乡（镇）小城镇建设的步伐同时加快，扎佐镇至1999年底，累计投资2500万元，新建街道3条，总长3.5公里，集镇面积由原来的1平方公里扩展到4平方公里。六桶乡建成的新集镇受到省市建设部门好评，《贵阳日报》还作过专门报道。其他乡（镇）集镇主干道亦先后建成。

扎佐镇景阳广场

1998年，随着改革开放不断深入，人民物资生活不断提高，加大城镇基础设施建设，特别是对县城的改造被列为县政府的重大议事日程。根据中共修文县委八届四次会议精神，县政府多次召开会议研究县城基础设施建设12个重点项目。12月19日,县委常委扩大会议对县政府提出的建设项目进行审定，这批项目被称为“城镇基础设施建设‘九三’工程”，即：一桥（拓宽东门桥）、一馆（兴建县体育馆）、一场（兴建龙冈广场）、一楼（兴建文化广播电视大楼）、一线（修筑贵毕公路修文联络线即阳明大道）、一中心（建设社区服务中心）、一小区（兴建安居工程河滨花园小区）、一校（建立一所九年一贯制学校）、一河（治理修文河部分河段）、三路（修筑县城道路网络建设中的翠屏东路、河滨大道中段和健身路）。“九三”工程从县委常委扩大会议后开始启动。12个建设项目按照县委提出的“精心策划、精雕细琢、精打细算、精兵强将”的“四个精”要求先后上马，对每一个工程项目都设立第一责任人、总监督员和纪检监督员，并实行向社会公开承诺制度。1998年12月28日，县体育馆举行奠基仪式，标志着“九三”工程进入实施阶段。至1999年10月，“九三”工程中的项目基本完成，体育馆于10月6日开馆，10月14日，中国贵阳99阳明文化节在馆内举行了开幕式。文广大楼、社区服务中心大楼也相继建成投入使用，东门桥拓宽工程、龙冈广场、河滨花园安居工程、修文河部分河段治理、三条道路的修建都在1999年全面竣工。阳明大道、九年一贯制学校建设也在2003年完工。

从1998—2005年，政府在城市基础设施建设和“九三”工程中总投入近亿元，使县城面积从过去的1.8平方公里扩展到3.5平方公里，极大地改变了县城面貌。投资900余万元的体育馆，已成为体育爱好者开展活动和人民群众健身的地方，还先后在此举办过全省青少年跆拳道比赛、中国女篮联赛等赛事。投资200余万元、面积1.4万平方米的龙冈广场是群众休闲的好去处。建筑面积3600平方米的文广大楼，集文化、新闻、教育、科技等单位于楼内，大大改善了这些单位的办公条件。《贵阳日报》《贵州日报》、贵州电视台、贵阳电视台先后报道过有关“九三”工程的新闻，贵阳有线电视台还派员到修文拍摄了城镇基础设施建设的系列专题片，分四个内容连续播出。2000年，《贵阳日报》载文称“修文有了让参观者惊叹不已的全省县城第一个体育馆，第一个绿地广场……”

2005年10月，投资3000多万元、占地2万平方米的客车站和商住小区新都口岸同时开工建设。新都口岸位于新春村与城区交接处，总建筑面积9万平方米，以新建客车站为中心，商圈、住宅沿河滨路、虎山路、龙山路展开，将客运口岸与商圈、住宅完美结合，从而形成多层次口岸经济带动式发展的商住区。2007年3月，新客车站竣工启用，可供停放大型客车150台的大停车场，宽敞明亮的候车大厅，5000

至1万人的日旅客流量，让乘车的人们不禁感叹："修文城发展得好快唷!"新都口岸商住区在2009年全部建成，其建筑风格浓缩了现代北欧风格和本地建筑风格的精华，奢华中不失庄重，颇受购房者青睐，预售时就基本无剩房。

2009年，县政府再出大手笔，在东片区高视河与小桥河交汇处，紧接腾晖酒店，启动"文城逸都"楼盘建设项目。项目总投资9亿元，占地面积160亩，规划建筑面积30万平方米，其中有2000户规模的住宅区，10万平方米的商业区，2公里长的"千灯水岸"不夜城，是县内首个集商业、住宅、休闲、文化娱乐为一体的大型社区。2010年8月，文城逸都开工，工地彩旗飘扬，塔吊高竖，机器轰鸣，呈现出一派热火朝天的景象。

（八）信息服务

20世纪80年代末期县政府开始探索对公众提供信息服务，1996年，以县城程控电话扩容为契机，致力信息化建设，至2010年，已建成CDMA无线基站131个，实现全县通信无盲区。全县移动电话用户14万户，联通用户2.2万户。固定电话用户达3.6万户。邮政开通24条邮路，邮路总长1049公里，邮政局、所均实现电子业务运行，邮政业务收入达750万元。随着计算机的普及，县内开通宽带、E视通、联通上网业务。2010年县政府已实现局域网、资源网、数据库建设，完成政府门户网站更新改造，使全县的信息产业得到空前发展。通过互联网发布政府信息、公共信息、市场信息、产业信息和企业信息，有力地推动了全县经济社会的发展，帮助了不少农民走上致富的道路。

七、"为民办实事"工程

从1998年起，每年年初县政府均要明确一批实事工程，向全县人民作出并完成承诺，称为"为民办实事"。实事工程项目由政府筹集资金，限定时间完成，并推行项目工作目标化、目标任务责任化，按计划实施推进。实事项目确定后，在县内媒体上和政府网站公布，并制成喷绘张贴于政府大院宣传栏，一方面公示于众，一方面提醒政府各工作部门限期完成。在实事办理过程中，县政府督查室定期对实事承办单位进行检查，对办理迟缓的部门进行通报批评。县内媒体发挥监督职能，对实事项目随时报道。自1998年至2010年，被政府列入为民办的实事项目共139件。除年初明确办实事项目外，政府随时把群众急需解决的事作为实事办理，群众获益颇多。1999年，政府针对县城自来水供水紧张，给居民生活带来不便的实际，决定修建城南水厂，并将这一决定列为当年为民办实事的一个项目。立项后，政府筹集资金，按期建成实现供水，使县城自来水供水量在原有基础上增加19倍，解决了居民经常缺水的问题，为人民群众办了一件实实在在的好事，受到群众称赞。按照国务院农村电网"两改一同价"（农电体制改革、农网改造和实现城乡同网同价）的要求，县政府全面部署实施农村电网改造工程。是年7月14日，在六屯乡都堡村举行农网35千伏工程启动暨六屯变电站开工典礼，揭开全县农村电网改造改建工程序幕。至2000年年底全县农网改造完成，总投资3700万元。农网改造给农村群众带来了实惠，农民用上放心电、便宜电，推动农村经济快速发展。为改善农村住房条件，2001年3月，贵阳市启动全市"改造农村茅草房工程"（简称改茅），县成立改茅工作领导小组，随即揭开改茅工程序幕。改茅工程分批进行，至2004年12月全面完成，整个改茅工程总投资1.4亿元，共改造茅草房1.16万户。

附：

1998—2010年为民办实事项目

1998年16件：

1. 解决23个村1.07万人的脱贫问题，实现贫困人口基本脱贫

2. 完成250户特困农户1125人的异地搬迁或就地改造

3. “创卫”达到省级卫生县城标准

4. “平安工程”达到省级标准

5. “长防林”一期工程通过部级验收

6. 开工建设修文“王阳明纪念馆”

7. 完成岩鹰山水库灌溉二期配套工程和高潮、浪潮水库灌渠配套工程

8. 新种植猕猴桃1万亩、板栗2000亩

9. 完成10个村人畜饮水工程

10. 完成修文到扎佐公路的油路铺设、改造工程；扩宽改造东门桥；建成扎佐、久长、六桶3个客（货）运站；实现村村通公路

11. 完成玩易路水泥道路建设，启动洒坪、大石集贸市场建设工程

12. 完成谷堡、小箐、洒坪、六广、大石、六桶6个乡（镇）光缆铺设工程，实现乡乡通程控电话

13. 完成县图书馆建设。新建3个乡级精神文明中心和30个村级文化广播室

14. 新增校舍5000平方米，撤除中小学危房8000平方米

15. 改建县保健站和2个乡级医院

16. 开工建设殡仪馆

1999年16件：

1. 开工建设贵（阳）毕（节）公路修文出口至县城阳明大道

2. 建成县龙岗广场

3. 建成县体育馆

4. 建成文化广播电视综合大楼（含图书馆、广播电台、电视台、报社、文联）

5. 建成社区服务中心

6. 建成县殡仪馆

7. 建成迎春花园等安居工程8000平方米

8. 完成城南水厂工程并供水

9. 建成县城翠屏东路、河滨大道中段、健身路、长征路延伸段等4条道路

10. 启动修文河部分河段治理工程

11. 新建和改造校舍1万平方米，基本消除中小学危房，在县城开工建设1所九年一贯制学校

12. 建成六广至高枧公路

13. 建成六广、小箐、大石、洒坪4个乡（镇）精神文明活动中心和谷堡、洒坪、大石3个卫生院，新建六屯、久长2个乡（镇）计生站，改造六桶、大石、六广3个乡（镇）计生站

14. 改造中低产田土1.55万亩，治理水土流失面积36平方公里．完成农村人畜饮水工程30处，解决1.5万人和5000头大牲畜饮水困难

15. 完成东门桥拓宽改建。

16. 建成80个村级科技文化广播室，实现村村通广播；建成70个村的电视转插台或有线电视网；扩大各乡（镇）光缆电视信号及电话网的覆盖面，实现修文电视台、广播电台节目通过光缆向乡（镇）的直接传送

2000年10件：

1. 建成贵毕公路修文出口至县城阳明大道

2. 实现教育“两基”达标

3. 实现创建省级科技先进县目标

4. 建成县人民医院综合大楼（4000平方米）

5. 完成龙场镇格佬寨水库除险加固工程

6. 完成农村人畜饮水工程9处，解决3000人饮水困难

7. 完成农村300户特困户、计生特困户改造危房或建新房1.5万平方米；利用财政小额扶贫资金帮助800户贫困农户、计生特困户发展经济

8. 实现村村通广播电视，新建谷堡乡精神文明活动中心

9. 建成大石乡至息烽石洞乡何家洞6．5公里道路；硬化小箐乡至六桶乡公路部分路段

10. 完成城镇电网和农村电网改造工程

2001年7件：

1. 配合贵阳市公路管理局完成修文—久长—马家桥—扎佐道路油化工程，完成冒沙井—小箐、冒沙井—水口、大石—回水—六桶、扎佐—六屯部分路段47公里道路油、硬化工程

2. 完成修文河团渔湾河道弃弯取直工程

3. 开工建设县城翠屏东路

4. 帮助300户农村贫困户（计生户）改造危房或建新房

5. 继续完善仡佬寨水库配套工程建设

6. 开工建设县城公墓

7. 实施农村人畜饮水工程，解决6840人饮水困难；建成580座沼气池

2002年10件：

1. 贫因户建新房和以工代赈建房400户，茅草房改造1200户。农村“两改一气”建设3300套

2. 完成岩鹰山水库渠系配套改造二期工程，解决2万农村人口饮水困难。完成岩鹰山、新坪、大煤厂3座病险水库除险加固工程

3. 退耕还林1.5万亩，治理水土流失90平方公里

4. 改造硬化小箐经广田至六广大桥公路、六广至高枧公路、扎佐至六屯公路、小箐经中寨至六级电站公路，全长共56．5公里。新建乡村公路30公里

5. 开工建设修文县阳明小学；修建和完善小箐乡和大石乡中学教学大楼、师生宿舍以及大石乡民族小学综合楼

6. 完成县城民主路县政府至羊叉街段道路改造

7. 建成阳明大道入口处“王学圣地”牌坊

8. 建成农村劳动力技术培训中心

9. 建设2万平方米经济适用住房，竣工验收1万平方米。

10. 完善3个乡（镇）文明中心内部设施，完成50个自然村寨广播电视工程

2003年10件：

1. 完成岩鹰山水库配套工程，治理水土流失面积20平方公里，解决2万农村人口饮水困难，完成坡改梯3000亩，退耕还林1.6万亩

2. 完成农村贫困户建房和茅草房改造2000户；“两改一气”（改厕、改灶，建沼气池）300套

3. 硬化油化改造县际公路、旅游路、经济路65.5公里

4. 建设修文河曲尺桥至小桥河段河道治理工程

5. 启动扎佐日供水2万吨水厂建设，年内完成日供水3000吨的一期工程

6. 建成4处铁路道口“平改立”工程

7. 新建经济适用住房、商品房2万平方米，完成1万平方米

8. 新建校舍9000平方米，建成修中第二教学楼，启动扎佐中学综合楼建设

9. 建成县文化馆；完成50个自然村寨广播电视工程

10. 新建7个社区居委会的办公用房

2004年10件：

1. 完成“两基”复查和“普实”验收工作

2. 实施农村现代远程教育工程，完成30个农村党员活动室、199个村级卫星接收站、18个中学多媒体教室建设；完成50个自然村寨通广播电视工程

3. 启动县级行政中心、六广镇行政中心和新集镇建设

4. 开工建设县城新客车站和久长客车站

5. 实施140公里县乡公路油化、硬化和45个贫困村320公里等级公路改造；完成3个铁路道口“平改立”工程

6. 完成4741户茅草房改造，基本消除农村人居茅草房；新建沼气池3000口，改圈3000个，改厕3000个，改厨3000个；完成坡改梯工程3000亩；实施久长镇兴隆村国家级土地整理项目

7. 启动高潮、浪潮水库除险加固和二官坝水库新建工程，完成古隆、王官、新坪等7座水库渠系配套45公里；完成人畜饮水工程26处，解决1.6万农村人畜饮水困难

8. 完成中韩造林示范项目1.25万亩；“二环”林带建设县级实施1720亩

9. 开工建设县医院综合大楼、青少年活动中心；完成县疾控中心实验大楼、扎佐镇卫生院综合楼建设

10、完成县计划生育服务保健中心办公大楼和9个乡（镇）计划生育服务站办公楼建设

2005年10件：

1. 启动金龙水库建设及配套工程，新建小水池1200口，实施农村人畜饮水工程28处，解决1万人饮水困难

2. 实施11所农村中小学危房改造

3. 完成184个行政村“模改数”，新建120个自然村通广播电视工程

4. 新增45个行政村通电话

5. 规划建设15个生态村；实施改圈、改厕、改灶及沼气池配套建设3000套，改造串户路20公里

6. 完成县城合一路至阳明洞步行街及牌坊建设；完成人民路、翠屏路、迎春路、朝阳路部分人行道彩板铺设工程

7. 完成河道治理一期工程两旁的绿化、美化工程；启动曲尺桥至长征桥河道治理工程

8. 建设30个村党员活动室、16个贫困村宣传文化室

9. 对贫困农民儿童计划免疫实行全免费，对传染肺结核患者实行全程免费治疗

10. 完成3个司法所和3个派出所建设

2006年10件：

1. 兴建大石、六广、小箐、乌栗、久长、清让、六屯7所农村中学学生宿舍用房1.33万平方米；按政策对农村学校义务教育阶段学生实行“两免一补”（免书本费、免杂费；对农村寄宿制学校家庭困难学生实行生活补助）

2. 推进新型农村合作医疗制度，覆盖全县农村农民

3. 新增就业岗位1365个；完成农村富余劳动力非农技能培训3000人，农村富余劳动力有序转移2600人

4. 实施农村人畜饮水工程5处，新建农村小水池1600口，解决农村饮水安全6500人；完成“四改一气”（改厕、改灶、改圈、改路和修建沼气池）4870套

5. 完成11个贫困村整村推进扶贫工作；实施农发土地治理项目1个、标准化农田治理项目2个

6. 完成扎佐、久长、六广、小箐4个乡（镇）客车站新建、改造；改造三里至桃源河景区公路6.5公里；完成80公里串户路硬化

7. 完成286个自然村5600户通电视和157个自然村通广播工程；建好10个村级综合室（党员活动室、宣传文化室、卫生室、计生室）

8. 建成县中心敬老院

9. 完成阳明主题公园的建设性详规，并启动建设；开工建设县城河滨路（迎春花园至拟建新客车站段）和污水处理厂；完成修文河曲尺桥至翠薇路段河道治理；新增城区绿地3000平方米

10. 建成六桶、大石、六屯3个乡计生妇幼保健站；完成2个乡（镇）基层司法所办公用房建设

2007年10件：

1. 免除农村人口和城镇低保人群子女义务教育阶段的学杂费和书本费；完成修文三中及实验幼儿园的建设及搬迁工作；实施扎佐二小标准化建设工程

2. 建成县老干活动中心；新建垃圾中转站2个；创建绿色社区1个

3. 完成县行政拘留所和六广派出所、龙场镇和久长镇司法所建设

4. 完成县、乡、村公路改造194公里；村寨串户路改造80公里；建成六桶客车站

5. 实施基本农田建设项目3个；实施11个一类重点贫困村整村推进工作

6. 解决农村饮水安全2.4万人；新建小水池2000口；完成“四改一气”建设5000套；建成无公害蔬菜基地27个

7. 新增就业岗位1600个；完成农村富余劳动力转移培训4000人，有序转移3200人；完成新一轮农技

培训3.5万人次，绿证培训1200人，颁证1000人

8. 完成新农村“万村千乡市场工程”农家店建设50个；建成村级综合楼41个

9. 完成285个自然村通电视和137个自然村通广播工程

10. 新型农村合作医疗制度农业人口参合率达90%以上，完成8个乡（镇）卫生院改扩建工程

2008年10件：

1. 完成县职业教育培训基地实训楼建设；完成洒坪乡九年一贯制标准化学校建设

2. 实施电视“户户通”2000户和村通广播90套

3. 推进新型农村合作医疗制度，2008年农业人口参合率达90%以上；启动城镇居民医疗保险工作和启动企业职工医疗保险工作

4. 新增就业岗位1600个，实施农村富余劳动力培训4700人，转移就业4200人

5. 解决农村饮水安全3.5万人；完成农村危房改造229户；完成“四改—气”农村生态能源建设2500套；完成村寨串户路硬化80公里；完成新农村“万村千乡市场工程”农家店建设15个；新建奶牛养殖小区3个

6. 启动12个一类重点贫困村的整村推进工作；实施农发土地治理项目1个

7. 完成村级综合楼建设40个

8. 启动建设海马大桥和麦架至修文公路，实施“500公里县乡公路改造与建设工程”；启动建设县乡公路4条80公里；启动实施“村级硬化公路建设”工程，建设村级公路100公里；启动谷堡、洒坪客车站和久长货运站建设

9. 启动建设阳明主题公园；完成阳明洞至翠微桥段河道治理；完成河滨休闲广场、北门桥改造、中山路改造（羊叉街至北门桥）、小街改造、玩易窝修复工程

10. 建设经济适用住房1万平方米；廉租房30套1200平方米；完成县城农贸市场升级改造；完成县城污水处理厂及配套截污干管一期工程建设

2009年10件：

1. 完成计生局、龙场镇计生站办公楼建设；完成龙场镇、扎佐镇卫生院建设；完成44个村级综合楼建设

2. 扎实推进“两基”迎“国检”工作，确保顺利通过验收；完成六桶、久长、洒坪中学标准化学校建设

3. 积极推进新型农村养老保险工作，参保扩面1.75万人；新增就业岗位1400个；实施农村富余劳动力转移培训1960人，转移就业1575人

4. 完成村级公路建设130公里；完成村寨串户路硬化建设130公里；启动大石、六屯客车站建设；建成久长货运站

5. 实施农村危房改造1482户；完成廉租住房120套6000平方米

6、实施12个贫困村整村推进工作

7、完成农村沼气池能源建设2341套；实施乡村清洁工程3个；实施2个5000头标准化奶牛养殖小区建设

8. 开工建设岩鹰山水厂，解决4.8万人饮水安全

9. 建设农家店15个，农村超市2个，乡村绿色回收站5个，农村集贸市场2个，农资配送中心3个

10. 继续实施农村广播电视户户通工程，新增电视入户4000户；建成自然村通广播站90个；建成农家书屋76个

2010年10件：

1. 完成修文中学“申示”（申报省级示范性普通高中）、修文三中扩建、修文四中规划及教学楼建设工作；建成和完善农家书屋100个；范完成3400户“户户通”电视和90个村通广播工作

2. 提高全县农村居民最低生活保障标准，每人每年不低于1300元。认真做好全国新型农村养老保险试点县工作，确保新型农保扩面8000人，养老保险扩面1000人，城镇居民医保扩面1000人

3. 全面完成8199户农村危房改造；开工建设廉租房2万平方米，经济适用房建设133套9848平方米；继续对低收入群体实行财政直补政策

4. 启动县人民医院标准化建设；完成6500个农村无害化改厕；实行乡（镇）卫生院和村卫生室全部配备使用基准药物，实现统一配送和零差率销售；启动建立城镇、农村人口健康档案信息系统。

5. 完成“雨露计划”农村劳动力转移培训1650人，转产1343人，绿证培训1600人。充分就业社区完成率40%；完成城乡统筹就业5880人，继续保持“零就业家庭”动态为零

6. 新建2个5000头大型标准化奶牛养殖基地；在洒坪、谷堡等乡（镇）实施草地生态畜牧种草养羊项目，年内投放种羊2.3万只，覆盖农户1146户；完成村寨串户路150公里；实施农业综合开发土地治理项目1个；完成农贸市场升级改造和标准化建设项目6个；新建农家店20个，新建超市3个，改造建设配送中心3个，建设农民专业合作社5个

7. 完成岩鹰山石坝库区、许家田坝水库除险加固工程，启动金龙水库建设；治理水土流失30平方公里

8. 开工建设白（云）修（文）公路、海马大桥工程；完成世行贷款项目小河沟至水口、六桶至柏茂、马家桥至驴坊共86公里道路建设；完成扎佐三元至白云落刀井11公里通乡油路建设

9. 完成6.6万平方米城区道路“白改黑”工程。完成河滨路延伸段997米和北环线1400米城市道路建设

10. 完成扎佐珍珠河河道改造，新增和改造公共绿化面积2.5万平方米；完成营造林6320亩（其中市级植被恢复项目6000亩，石漠化治理200亩，植树造林120亩），退耕还林补植补造1.16万亩，增加森林覆盖率1个百分点；完成5个规模养殖企业大中型沼气池建设，新建乡村绿色回收站5个。

第五章　人民政协

1983年3月，中国人民政治协商会议修文县委员会成立，由共产党、人民团体、民主人士和各界代表组成。按照《中国人民政治协商会议章程》，遵循“长期共存，互相监督”“肝胆相照，荣辱与共”的方针，对县内的政治生活、经济建设、文化教育和人民生活等重点问题进行政治协商，民主监督，巩固和扩大爱国统一战线，推进全县的社会主义物质文明、精神文明和政治文明建设。

第一节　组织机构

一、政协委员会

1983至2010年，县政协共历7届，每届委员会由不同界别委员组成。28年间，共有19个界别的942名委员参与政治协商，为县的经济社会发展建言献策。

政协委员会历届组成界别和人数统计表

表2—05—01

届别 界别	第一届 1983.3—1987.8	第二届 1987.8—1990.4	第三届 1990.4—1993.4	第四届 1993.4—1998.3	第五届 1998.3—2003.3	第六届 2003.3—006.11	第七届 2006.11—2010
	人数	人数	人数	人数	人数	人数	人数
中国共产党	6	7	7	8	13	12	13
无党派人士	8	7	8	5	5	7	8
共青团	2	3	4	4	4	4	4
妇联	3	4	5	7	9	10	11
工会	3	4	5	5	6	7	8
工商联	3	6	7	10	10	12	14
科技界	10	8	7	9	9	12	13

续表

届别 / 界别	第一届 1983.3—1987.8	第二届 1987.8—1990.4	第三届 1990.4—1993.4	第四届 1993.4—1998.3	第五届 1998.3—2003.3	第六届 2003.3—2006.11	第七届 2006.11—2010
	人数	人数	人数	人数	人数	人数	人数
文化艺术界	5	6	5	8	8	7	9
社会科学界	3	2	2	4	4	3	5
农业界	3	3	8	10	10	11	14
教育界	6	9	7	10	10	12	12
体育界	1	2	2	2	2	2	2
医药卫生界	3	7	7	8	8	8	10
少数民族	3	5	7	7	7	9	10
宗教界	1	2	2	2	2	2	3
经济界	—	—	—	—	10	13	15
青年联合会	—	—	—	—	4	4	4
特邀人士	9	23	26	29	33	26	31
港澳台属	3	5	6	—	—	—	—
其他	3	2	—	—	—	—	—
合计	75	105	115	141	159	161	186

二、常务委员会

政协委员会通过全体委员会议选举产生主席、副主席、秘书长和常务委员为常务委员会组成人员。常务委员会在委员会闭会期间履行政协工作职能。常务委员会主席、副主席、秘书长、常务委员数历届设置是：第一届常务委员会主席1名，副主席4名，秘书长1名（兼任），常务委员14名；第二届主席1名，副主席6名，秘书长1名，常务委员13名；第三届主席1名，副主席4名，秘书长1名，常务委员15名；第四届主席1名，副主席6名，秘书长1名，常务委员13名；第五届主席1名，副主席4名，秘书长1名，常务委员15名；第六届主席1名，副主席5名，秘书长1名，常务委员25名；第七届主席1名，副主席6名，秘书长1名，常务委员23名。

三、政协机关工作机构

县政协机关工作机构，各届设置不尽相同，1983年3月县政协建立，工作机构设置为“一办三委五组”。1987年8月至1990年4月，县政协第二届期间，工作机构调整为“一办四委四组”。1990年4月至1993年3月第三届期间工作机构又调整为“一办六委”。1998年3月第五届常委会组成后，又调为“三委两室”。2003年3月至2006年11月六届期间，在“三委两室”的基础上，增设智力支边办公室机构。2006年11月至2010年12月县政协七届期间，机关工作机构为“两室三委”：即政协办公室，智力支边办公室；提案法治社会联谊委员会，经济科技委员会，教卫文体文史学习委员会。

政协办公室　1983年3月建立，为政协机关枢纽部门，负责文书处理和行政事务管理工作。至2010年12月，政协办公室仍存。

学习委员会　1983年3月建立，负责组织政协委员学习中共路线、方针和政策，增强委员和参政意识和监督能力。1998年3月撤销，其职责并入教卫文体文史学习委员会。

文史资料委员会　1983年3月建立，负责征集、整理、研究和出版文史资料。1998年3月撤销，其工作并入教卫文体文史学习委员会。

社会联谊委员会　1990年5月建立，负责联系对外交往工作。1998年3月撤销，其工作并入提案法治社会联谊委员会。

经济建设工作组　1983年3月建立，负责联系经济开发和科学技术推广等有关事宜。1990年4月撤销。其工作并入经济科技委员会。

文化教育工作组（科教文卫工作组）　1983年3月建立，文化教育工作组负责联系文化教育工作方面的事宜。1987年8月，增加科技、医药、卫生的联系工作改称科教文卫工作组。1990年4月撤销科教文卫工作组，业务交教卫文体委员会。

医药卫生工作组　1983年3月建立，负责联系医药卫生工作事宜。1987年8月撤销医药卫生工作组，业务并入科教文卫工作组。

群众工作组　1983年3月建立，负责政协与人民群众的联络工作。1990年4月撤销。

祖国统一工作组　1983年3月建立，负责联系祖国统一大业有关事宜。1990年4月撤销。

工作组联系委员会　1987年8月建立，负责联系各区、乡（镇）政协联络组政协委员，指导在当地的参政议政工作。1990年4月裁撤。

提案工作委员会（提案法治委员会、提案法治社会联谊委员会）　1983年3月建立提案工作委员会，负责委员提案的搜集、归并、分发、督办和回复等工作。1990年5月增加法治工作内容改称提案法治委员会。1998年3月又增加社会联谊工作内容，即改称提案法治社会联谊委员会。至2010年12月，提案法治社会联谊委员会仍存。

经济科技委员会　1990年5月建立，负责联系经济开发和科学技术推广等有关事宜。至2010年12月，经济科技委员会仍存。

教卫文体委员会（教卫文体文史学习委员会）　1990年5月，建立教卫文体委员会，负责联系教育、卫生、文化和体育方面的工作。1998年3月，撤销文史资料委员会和学习委员会，将其职责并入教卫文体委员会，改称教卫文体文史学习委员会。至2010年12月，教卫文体文史学习委员会仍存。

智力支边办公室　1984年7月建立，系县人民政府设在县政协的办事机构，负责组织政协委员及科技人员赴边远地区传授文化科学知识，帮助开发农村经济，引导农民脱贫致富。至2010年12月，智力支边办公室仍存。

四、政协区、乡（镇）联络组

1983年建立县政协后，即在城关区、扎佐区、久长区、六广区和小箐区设置政协联络组。城关区所属的城关镇升格为区级建置后，亦在镇内相应设置联络组。联络组属县政协的派出机构，受县政协的指导和属地党委领导，负责联系本区域政协委员及各界人士发挥其参政议政职能。1992年2月，撤区并乡建镇后，原城关区、扎佐区、久长区、六广区和小箐区政协联络组改为城关镇、扎佐镇、久长镇、六广镇和小箐乡政协联络组。1993年4月，政协第四届第一次会议后，又在六屯、谷堡、洒坪、大石、六桶5乡建立政协联络组。各乡（镇）联络组负责联系本乡（镇）各界人士参政议政，协助地方政府搞好各项工作。1998年3月，政协乡镇联络组撤销。

第二节 会 议

一、政协委员会全体会议

县政协委员会全体会议一年举行一次。1983年3月—2010年12月县政协共历7届委员会，召开全体会议27次。每次会议除特殊情况外，都听取政协常务委员会工作报告和提案办理情况报告，并作出相应决议。应会委员还列席同时召开的县人民代表大会的会议，听取和讨论县人民政府工作报告等。

一届一次会议 1983年3月17—22日召开。应到委员55人，实到48人。会议听取《县政协筹备情况的报告》，听取和审议《提案审查情况报告》并作出相应决议。全体委员列席县第七届人民代表大会第三次会议，听取和讨论政府工作报告。会议期间，与会委员学习《中国人民政治协商会议章程》，讨论《政府工作报告》，表示要认真学习，投身四个现代化建设，为修文经济社会发展建言献策。会议选举主席1名，副主席4名，秘书长1名（由一名副主席兼任）和选举14名常务委员组成第一届常务委员会，通过一届一次会议决议。至此，中国人民政治协商会议修文县委员会正式宣告成立。

1983年3月县政协一届一次会议到会委员合影

一届二次会议 1984年2月27—3月2日在县城召开，应到委员75人，实到68人。会议听取和审议政协一届常务委员会工作报告和提案办理情况报告，并作出相应决议。全体委员列席县第七届人民代表大会第四次会议，听取和讨论会议所作的政府工作报告。会议组织委员学习新时期人民政协的性质、地位和作用，提高对政协工作的重要性和必要性的认识。全体委员表示要积极参政议政，努力把人民政协工作搞好。会议认为进行社会主义现代化建设离不开教育发展和科学进步，因而离不开知识分子。县政协要经常关心爱护知识分子，了解知识分子的情况，推动知识分子政策落实工作，进一步调动知识分子建设社会主义的积极性。因人事变动，政协领导班子缺额，会议补选主席1人，副主席4人，秘书长1人（由1名副主席兼任）。

一届三次会议 1986年3月25—30日在县城召开，应到委员75人，实到55人，本次会议按例应在1985年召开，但为了与县人民代表大会同步举行，故1985年未召开全体会议。会议听取和审议《政协常委会工作报告》等相关报告。并作出相应决议。全体委员列席县人大八届三次会议听取和讨论政府工作报告。会议对县的各项改革措施和建设工作提出了建议。会议号召全体政协委员要坚定不移地协助党和政府把改革搞好，发挥政协人才荟萃的优势，为四化建设献计出力。

二届一次会议 1987年8月24—29日在县城召开，应到委员105人，实到101人。会议听取和审议《政协一届常务委员会工作报告》《提案办理情况报告》，并作出相应决议。全体委员列席县人大九届一次会议，听取和讨论政府工作报告。会议选举产生主席1名、副主席6名、秘书长1名和常务委员13名组成政协二届常务委员会。会议强调要旗帜鲜明地坚持四项基本原则，反对资产阶级自由化。要求全体委员做维护安定团结政治局面的模范。

二届二次会议 1988年4月6—9日在县城召开，应到委员107人，实到105人。会议听取并审议《政协常务委员会工作报告》和《提案办理情况报告》，并作出相应决议。全体委员列席县人大九届二次会议，听取和讨论政府工作报告。会议要求政协委员高举爱国主义和社会主义旗帜，以中共十三大精神为指针，进一步发挥人民政协政治协商、民主监督的职能作用，努力建设“两个文明”，发展和巩固爱国统一战线，为县的经济振兴和各项建设事业贡献聪明才智。

1987年8月召开县政协二届一次会议

二届三次会议 1989年3月27—30日在县城召开，应到委员107人，实到104人。会议总结并讨论政协二届二次会议以来的工作和审议《政协常务委员会工作报告》《提案办理情况报告》，并作出相应决议。全体委员列席县人大九届三次会议，听取和讨论政府工作报告。会议认为，县政协在治理经济环境，整顿经济秩序，推进深化改革，维护安定团结的政治局面，发展全县经济，壮大爱国统一战线，组织委员学习，开展视察考察，征集、整理文史资料方面都作了大量工作，取得一定成绩。会议首次表彰政协先进单位城关镇联络组和先进委员15名，先进工作者3名。

三届一次会议 1990年4月23—27日在县城召开，应到委员115人，实到105人，应邀列席13人。三届一次会议是在全国人民深入贯彻中共十三届四中全会、五中全会和六中全会精神的新形势下召开的。会议听取并审议《政协常务委员会工作报告》和《提案办理情况报告》，并作出相应决议。全体委员列席县人大十届一次会议，听取并讨论政府工作报告。会议对政协全体委员在1989年北京春夏之交政治风波中经受严峻考验，保持自身稳定，并协助党委、政府做好维护安定团结的工作给予充分肯定。会议选举主席1名、副主席4名、秘书长1名和常务委员15名组成政协三届常务委员会。会议还表彰政协先进单位1个，先进委员18人，先进工作者3人。

三届二次会议 1991年3月25—29日在县城召开，应到会委员115人，实到110人。贵州省政协副主席宋树功莅会并讲话。会议听取并审议《政协常务委员会工作报告》和《提案办理情况报告》，并作出相应决议。全体委员列席县人大十届二次会议，听取并讨论政府工作报告。委员们分组讨论，希望县政府克服困难，扎实工作，带领全县人民为实现“八五”计划努力奋斗。会议对1990年评出的两个先进集体和20名先进政协委员进行表彰。

三届三次会议 1992年3月25—29日在县城召开，应到委员120人，实到102名。会议听取并审议《政协常委会工作报告》和《提案办理情况报告》，并作出相应决议。全体委员列席县人大十届三次会议，听取并讨论政府工作报告。会议要求政协委员和各界人士以中共十三届七中、八中全会精神为指针，认真学习邓小平建设有中国特色社会主义的一系列重要论述和中共中央政治局对我国改革和发展中若干重大问题的正确决策，坚定不移地贯彻执行中共“一个中心，两个基本点”的基本路线以及中共中央《关于坚持和完善中国共产党领导的多党合作和政治协商制度的意见》，解放思想，大胆探索，履行职能，参政议政，为完成县委、县政府提出的经济和社会发展任务而努力。

1992年，政协主席曾文学在县政协三届二次全会上作工作报告

四届一次会议 1993年4月6—9日召开，应到委员121人，实到118人。中共修文县委书记朱生亮在开幕会上作题为《承上启下，继往开来，献计献策，振兴修文》的讲话。会议听取并审议《政协常委会工作报告》和《提案办理情况报告》，并作出相应决议。全体委员列席县人大十一届一次会议，听取和讨论政府工作报告。会议选举主席1名、副主席6名、秘书长1名和常务委员13名组成政协四届常务委员会。会议号召全体政协委员为振兴修文发挥聪明才智，献计献策。

四届二次会议 1994年3月21—23日在县城召开。应到委员128人，实到121人。会议听取并审议《政协常委会工作报告》和《提案办理情况报告》，并作出相应决议。全体委员列席县人大十一届二次会议，听取和讨论政府工作报告。委员们在分组讨论中一致表示，随着各项改革措施的相继出台，政协应坚定不移地团结全县各族人民，支持政府推行深化改革的措施，并正视改革带来的新矛盾、新问题，切实参政议政，促进全县工作。

四届三次会议 1995年3月21—24日在县城召开，应到委员139人，实到134人。会议听取并审议《政协常委会工作报告》和《提案办理情况报告》，并作出相应决议。全体委员列席县人大十一届三次会议，听取和讨论政府工作报告。会议还听取薛占成等4名委员就发展非公有制经济、农业生产和环境保护以及做好政协乡（镇）联络组工作的发言。

四届四次会议 1996年3月18—21日在县城召开。应到会委员139人，实到127人。会议听取并审议《政协常委会工作报告》和《提案办理情况报告》，并作出相应决议。全体委员列席县人大十一届四次会议，听取和讨论政府工作报告。会议还听取张胜祥等6名委员就发展蔬菜生产，加速国有工业企业机制转换，大力发展非公有制经济，调整农业结构建立畜牧业生产基地，因地制宜带领农民扶贫致富奔小康和深化教育体制改革加强教学管理等方面的问题作的专题发言。

四届五次会议 1997年3月18—21日在县城召开。应到会委员141人，实到137人。会议听取《政协常委会工作报告》和《提案办理情况报告》，并作出相应决议。全体委员列席县人大十一届五次会议，听取和讨论政府工作报告。会议安排大会发言，部分政协委员分别就抓好扶贫开发与计划生育工作、办好农村医疗卫生事业、加强对青少年思想道德教育、加强农村精神文明建设和县的农业现状及其发展对策、加快发展非公有制经济等方面工作作专题发言。中共修文县委书记黄乃铸在到会讲话，要求县政协

坚持以邓小平建设有中国特色社会主义理论为指导，坚持中共基本路线和基本方针，紧紧围绕县委、县政府的中心工作，采取多种形式，开展多种活动，为修文“两个文明”建设作出新贡献，在参大政、议大事、办实事、求实效上取得新的成绩，在履行职能上有新的提高。

五届一次会议 1998年3月23—26日召开，应到委员131人，实到127人。会议听取并审议《政协常委会工作报告》和《提案办理情况报告》，并作出相应决议。全体委员列席县人大十二届一次会议，听取和讨论政府工作报告。会议选举产生主席1名、副主席4名、秘书长1名和常务委员15名组成政协五届常务委员会。与会委员一致认为政府工作报告总结“五年间县的经济持续稳定发展，各项社会事业取得新进步，社会保持稳定局面，‘八五’计划圆满完成，‘九五’计划有了良好的开局”是符合实际的。表示要在新一届政协的领导下发挥才智参政议政，为修文繁荣昌盛作出贡献。

五届二次会议 1999年3月29—31日在县城召开。应列席委员141人，实到128人。会议听取并审议《政协常务委员会工作报告》和《提案办理情况报告》，并作出相应决议。全体委员列席县人大十二届二次会议，听取和讨论政府工作报告。因为人事变动，会议补选1人为秘书长（兼任），增补6人为五届委员会常务委员。县委书记黄乃铸在大会开幕式上作题为《同心同德，抢抓机遇，努力开拓，为实现修文县跨世纪的发展而奋斗》的讲话。

五届三次会议 2000年2月22—24日在县城召开。应到委员141人，实到122人。会议听取并审议《政协常务委员会工作报告》和《提案办理情况报告》，并作出相应决议。全体委员列席县人民代表大会十二届三次会议，听取和讨论政府工作报告。会议要求政协委员加强理论学习，坚定正确的政治方向，紧跟形势，发挥政协优势为兴修富民作出新贡献。

五届四次会议 2001年2月20—22日在县城召开，应到委员159人，实到148人。会议听取并审议《政协常务委员会工作报告》和《提案办理情况报告》，并作出相应决议。全体委员列席县人民代表大会十二届四次会议，听取和讨论政府工作报告。彭文冲、张传武、薛占成、杨正明、左晓云、陈新国、张仕伦等10名委员在大会发言中就全县的经济和社会发展等方面的问题提出建议和意见。

五届五次会议 2002年3月4—6日在县城召开。应到委员159人，实到148人。会议听取并审议《政协常务委员会工作报告》和《提案办理情况报告》，并作出相应决议。全体委员列席县人民代表大会十二届五次会议，听取和讨论政府工作报告。会议要求全体政协委员要珍惜荣誉，以饱满的热情履行职责，不断提高参政议政水平，用自己扎实的工作赢得群众的爱戴和社会的好评。

六届一次会议 2003年3月18—21日在县城召开，应到委员161人，实到153人。会议听取并审议《政协常务委员会工作报告》和《提案办理情况报告》，并作出相应决议。全体委员列席县人民代表大会十三届一次会议，听取和讨论政府工作报告。会议选举主席1名，副主席5名，秘书长1名和常务委员会25名组成政协六届常务委员会。县委书记魏明禄到会讲话，对新一届政协工作提出3点意见：一是进一步提高认识，增强政协工作的责任感；二是围绕中心认真履行人民政协职能；三是加强自身建设，提高履行政协职能的水平。

六届二次会议 2004年2月10—12日在县城召开。应到委员161人，实到152人。会议听取并审议《政协常务委员会工作报告》和《提案办理情况报告》，并作出相应决议。全体委员列席县人民代表大会十三届二次会议，听取和讨论政府工作报告。会议号召全体政协委员认真学习贯彻落实中共十六大及十六届三中全会精神，提高参政议政水平；坚持以“三个代表”重要思想为指导，切实履行职能，深入调查研究，为修文实现全面建设小康社会目标献计出力。

六届三次会议 2005年3月7—9日在县城召开。应到委员161人，实到150人。会议听取并审议《政协常务委员会工作报告》和《提案办理情况报告》，并作出相应决议。全体委员列席县人民代表大会十三届三次会议，听取和讨论政府工作报告。会议号召全体政协委员牢牢把握团结和民主两大主题，为修文经济社会发展贡献力量。

六届四次会议 2006年2月28—3月2日在县城召开。应到委员162人，实到158人。会议听取并审议《政协常务委员会工作报告》和《提案办理情况报告》，并作出相应决议。全体委员列席县人民代表大会十三届四次会议，听取和讨论政府工作报告。会议号召全体政协委员与全县各界人民委实施全县“十一五”规划献策献力，为全县的经济社会更好更快发展书写出新的篇章。

七届一次会议 2006年11月20—22日召开，应到委员165人，实到154人。按规定七届一次会议应在2008年换届时召开，为遵照中共贵州省委指示，全省届期统一为五年一届，故提前2年召开本次会议。会议听取并审议《政协常务委员会工作报告》和《提案办理情况报告》，并作出相应决议。全体委员列席县人民代表大会十四届一次会议，听取和讨论政府工作报告。会议选举主席1名，副主席5名，秘书长1名和常务委员会22名组成政协七届常务委员会。会议号召全体政协委员抓住经济社会发展中的热点、难点问题，深入开展视察、考察、调研活动，重视社情民意，拓展参政议政渠道，不断加强自身建设，为推进修文经济社会发展努力奋斗。

在县政协七届一次会议上，委员们听取政协工作报告

七届二次会议 2007年3月20—22日在县城召开，应到委员186人，实到170人。会议听取并审议《政协常务委员会工作报告》和《提案办理情况报告》，并作出相应决议。全体委员列席县人民代表大会十四届二次会议，听取和讨论政府工作报告。会议要求全体政协委员深入学习贯彻《中共中央关于加强人民政协工作的意见》，进一步提高政治理论水平和履职能力，围绕中心，服务大局，为促进全县经济社会发展建言献策。

七届三次会议 2008年3月11—13日在县城召开，应到委员186人，实到174人。会议听取并审议《政协常务委员会工作报告》和《提案办理情况报告》，并作出相应决议。全体委员列席县人民代表大会十四届三次会议，听取和讨论政府工作报告。会议对县委、县政府在年初带领全县人民投入“抗凝冻，保民生”的攻坚战并取得全面胜利给予高度评价。会议号召全体政协委员创新思维，拓宽履职渠道，关注民生，反映民意，为建设生态文明城市、构建和谐修文作出努力。

七届四次会议 2009年3月10—12日在县城召开，应到委员186人，实到172人。会议听取并审议《政协常务委员会工作报告》和《提案办理情况报告》，并作出相应决议。全体委员列席县人民代表大会十四届四次会议，听取和讨论政府工作报告。会议补选七届委员会秘书长1名。会议要求全体政协委员以“关注民生，推动发展，促进的谐”为履职主线，多思发展之计，多谋富民之策、多办利民之事，为强县

升位建设文明生态经济、构建和谐社会作出更大贡献。

七届五次会议 2010年3月16—18日在县城召开，应到委员186人，实到176人。会议听取并审议《政协常务委员会工作报告》和《提案办理情况报告》，并作出相应决议。全体委员列席县人民代表大会十四届五次会议，听取和讨论政府工作报告。会议要求全体政协委员“参政议政建真言，不随声附和，反映社情民意吐真情，不回避矛盾”，积极投身建设生态经济强县事业。

2010年3月16日召开县政协七届五次会议

二、政协常委会议

县政协常务委员会议一般每季度举行1次，特殊情况可提前或推迟举行。常务委员会议组成人员为：县政协主席、副主席、秘书长和常务委员。根据会议议题需要，县政协各工作组、联络组、委室负责人列席会议。常务委员会议主要职权是：决定召开全体会议有关事项，审议提交全体委员会议的文件，主持县政协全体委员会议；执行县政协全体会议的决议，组织委员开展调研、视察等重要活动；审议通过向县委、县政府提出的建议及建议案，对有关职能部门的工作进行评议；提出常务委员会组成人员增加或变更建议名单，由县政协全体委员会议决定；决定县政协机关工作机构的设置和变动，并任免其领导成员；协商决定下届县政协委员会的参加单位、委员名额和委员人选及界别设置；协商决定县政协本届委员会增加或者变更参加单位、委员名额和人选；讨论决定县政协其他重大事项。

1983年3月—1987年8月第一届县政协共召开常委会议17次。1983年4月1—2日，召开一届一次常委会，研究明确组织机构的设置和人员分工，决定建立学习委员会，提案工作委员会、文史资料研究委员会、经济建设工作组、文化教育工作组、医药卫生工作组、群众工作组、祖国统一工作组，设立县政协办公室和文史资料研究委员会办公室等事项。

1987年8月—1990年4月，第二届县政协共召开常委会议12次。1987年9月11—12日，县政协召开二届一次常委会，学习全国政协《章程》，讨论第二届县政协的机构设置，决定成立县政协文史资料研究委员会、提案工作委员会、学习委员会、工作组联系委员会，县政协办公室和区（镇）联络组。

1990年4月—1993年4月，第三届县政协召开常委会议14次。1990年5月15—16日，第三届县政协召开第一次常委会议。学习《中共中央关于密切同人民群众联系的决定》，协商讨论《县政协常委会工作规则》、《三届委员会组织通则》及《秘书长、副秘书长工作规则》。

1993年4月—1998年3月，第四届县政协召开会议21次。1993年5月26—27日，召开第四届县政协第一次常委会议，学习全国政协主席李瑞环在全国政协八届一次全会和八届一次常委会上的两次讲话，讨论常委的分工及政协议事及工作规则，研究1993年县政协的工作要点，并进行人事任免。

1998年3月—2003年3月，第五届县政协召开常委会议19次。1998年6月2日，召开县政协五届一次常委议，通过五届政协工作机构调整为“三委两室”，即：经济科技委员会、教卫文体文史学习委员会，提案法治社会联谊委员会、政协办公室、智力支边办公室。并协商决定相关人事任免。

2003年3月—2006年11月，第六届县政协召开常委会议10次。2003年4月24日，召开县政协六届一次常委会议，传达学习中共修文县委关于转发中共贵州省委《关于认真开展学习郑培民同志活动的意见》的通知和省政协主席王思齐在省政协九届一次常委会上的讲话。通过县政协2003年工作要点和县政协常委会工作规则。

2006年11月—2010年12月，第七届县政协召开常委会议16次。2010年8月17日，召开县政协七届十六次会议，学习国务院《关于引导民间投资健康发展的若干意见》，听取县政府副县长刘瑜通报全县2010年1至7月经济运行和政府机构改革情况。

2006年6月26日，召开县政协六届五次常委会

第三节　参政议政

一、委员学习知政

政协委员的学习根据不同时期不同阶段的要求，由政协常委会提出安排意见，委员按界别组成学习组，定期或不定期进行。

一届政协针对机构新、人员新的特点，组织学习政协《章程》，使委员了解政协工作的性质、地位和作用。针对县委安排的理论学习计划组织学习《邓小平文选》《中共中央关于经济体制改革的决定》、中共十二届四中、五中全会文件等。二届政协在1989年北京春夏之交政治风波期间，组织政协委员学习《人民日报》社论及有关文件，学习邓小平在接见首都戒严部队军以上干部时的讲话，通过学习，全县政协委员坚守工作岗位，为巩固安定团结的政治局面作出贡献。三届政协将委员学习与把思想统一到建设有中国特色社会主义的目标上来、统一到坚持和完善我国基本政治制度上来、统一到发展社会主义民主和维护安定团结上来、统一到服从和服务于经济建设多作贡献上来的“四个统一”相结合，极大地发挥委员参政议政作用。四届政协在组织学习的基础上以听讲座、听辅导报告等多种形式，推动委员学习。1996年，邀请省社会主义学院教授王守君莅县作社会主义市场经济专题讲座，讲座后即组织委员参加县委开展的“解放思想大讨论”。委员们以认真负责的态度针对修文实际，提出意见和建议。五届政协结合“讲学习、讲政治、讲正气”的“三讲”教育活动和“三个代表”重要思想学习教育活动的开展，组织委员学习《中共中央关于在全党深入学习邓小平理论的通知》《中共中央关于农业和农村工作若干重大问题的决定》《公民道德建设实施纲要》等重要文件。围绕中共修文县委提出的“乘势争先，强县升位”（指县委带领全县人民经过努力建成强县跻入贵州省强县行列）奋斗目标，举办“西部大开发，修文怎么干”和“西部大开发，政协怎么干”两次研讨会，近百名委员和各界人士写出有情况、有分析、有论证、有针对性的调研报告及论文30篇。六届政协在学习中，突出抓政协领导班子中心学习组、政协委员学习组、政协机关干部职工学习主题活动，学习形式多样内容丰富，先后有委员25人次在《贵州政协

报》《贵阳日报》《当代修文》等报刊上发表学习心得体会和调查研究文章。七届政协在学习中强调结合县的经济社会发展，关注民生，并向委员提出“学以增智、学以养德、学以善政、学以修身”的学习要求。

二、视察调研问情

1983—2010年，县政协组织委员视察与调研活动共137次，以学习组、调研组和委员个人名义写出调研报告114份。参与视察与调研的委员本着参政议政促进修文发展的宗旨深入群众了解情况，实事求是向县委、县政府提出改进工作的建议和意见。

1983年6月，政协委员对全县4个区9个乡遭受水灾和雹灾后的救灾和春耕生产情况进行视察，向政府提出尽快修复水利灌溉设施，以稳定群众情绪，安定人心，树立生产救灾信心的建议，得到县政府采纳，县政府对救灾工作作出4项决定：一是千方百计恢复和发展生产，号召和动员非灾区人力、物资支援灾区；二是县民政部门立即下拨救济粮、款解决灾区群众的住房、吃饭困难；三是各区、乡镇注意防洪抢险，加强水利管理，明确责任制；四是总结经验教训，向群众宣传退耕还林，严禁乱砍滥伐和毁林毁草开荒。1987年组织委员赴德政乡就全县遭受冰雹灾后粮食减产情况进行点上调查，提出3条解决群众生活困难的措施。县政府采纳后积极落实，组织发放救济款82万元，救济粮167万公斤，救济因灾贫困群众9893户4.86万人，使群众生活得到保障。1990年11月，对六桶乡两个村民组群众生活及生产自救情况开展调查，写出《对六桶乡风联村沙塘井、樱桃井两个村民组群众生活及生产自救情况的调查报告》，向县委、县政府提出对受灾严重的农户发放生活贷款和救济粮的建议。县委、县政府高度重视，从全县角度考虑，抽调机关干部126人组成农村工作队，深入受灾地区查灾核产，安排救济粮200万公斤，救济款80万元，对灾区救济对象进行救济，从而解决了灾民的基本生活困难。1996年9月10—13日，政协13名委员组成调研组，历时4天，对城关镇、六桶乡等非公企业进行调查，了解基本情况后，针对全县非公企业发展中存在的问题，向县委、县人民政府提出成立县非公企业协调领导小组，研究和分析企业运行情况，及时协调解决企业发展中碰到的实际困难和具体问题；出台吸引投资者的优惠政策；利用县的优越地理条件和丰富的自然资源，积极调整产业结构，以建材和磷化工产品为龙头，形成地方的支柱产业；政府及其有关部门要主动帮助和支持企业多渠道筹集资金，组织企业走股份合作的道路；提高企业经营者的管理水平；广泛推广乌栗红星农场规模化栽种的做法，带动农户种植，掀起千家万户齐办绿色企业的高潮；在政策允许的范围内，千方百计减轻企业负担；放水养鱼，给企业创造一个良好的生存发展环境等7条建议。委员的建议得到县委、县政府的高度重视，作出加大非公企业二次创业力度调整产业结构的发展方针，使全县的非公企业在短短几年间获得突飞猛进的发展，营造出以龙场镇、扎佐镇、久长镇，贵遵、贵毕公路沿线和扎佐医药园区为载体的“三点两线一园区”非公企业工业生产的格局。2003年6至7月，政协组成专题调研组对县的殡葬改革进行调研，走访村（组）15个，召开座

2010年9月27日县政协开展主席视察活动

谈会28次，参加座谈的干部群众850人次。通过调研对殡葬改革提出8条建议：一是实行火化的范围不以乡镇划界，要与火葬场的距离和交通条件划定；二是实行火化的对象要以死者本人而定；三是鼓励划定范围以外的群众实行火化；四是民政部门要增强服务意识，运尸体车辆不能以盈利为目的；五是火化后骨灰一律不准再用棺木装殓再行土葬，严禁占耕地垒坟；六是有条件的乡镇和群众居住集中的村寨要选择适宜的非耕地规划修建公墓；七是组建以职能部门牵头的专业监察队伍；八是制定殡改办法要注意与相关法律法规一致，严格依法行政，并便于操作。这份调研报告以县政协建议案呈报后，受到县委、县政府高度重视，责成县民政局对建议案认真研究。县民政局参照政协委员的建议，在全县划定公益性墓地225个，实现每个行政村都有农村公益性墓地；对久长殡仪馆加强管理监督，特别是在收费项目上建立健全各项制度；帮助龙场镇城南殡仪服务站建成投入使用，满足县城群众丧事活动需要。县政府结合人大代表和政协委员的建议，出台《关于进一步加强殡葬改革工作的实施意见》，全县殡葬改革工作由此走上制度化轨道。2008年5月，政协收到群众和政协委员反映龙场镇新生村华航冶炼厂生产中偷排黑烟造成污染，严重影响当地村民生活。政协随即开展以环保和生态建设为主题的主席视察活动，通过实地查看和走访群众后，向陪同视察的环保部门领导提出两条建议，一是督促企业运行除尘设备。二是环保部门加强监控，严防企业为省钱偷排烟尘。是时，华航冶炼厂烟尘污染已引起县委、县政府和县人大常委会的高度重视，四大班子下决心治理。6月19日，县委召开常委会作出对华航公司污染处理意见，一是必须24小时内用上环保设备，杜绝污染。二是实行转产，寻找新产业。三是达不到以上两个条件，坚决关停。然后，华航冶炼厂24小时运行环保设施，做到废烟达标排放，使新生村一带恢复了天蓝地绿水清的生态环境。2010年4月16日，开展主席视察活动，针对鸿鑫水泥厂、绿太阳药业、阳明国兰文化公司等企业存在的修筑公路办理土地手续困难的问题，视察组与陪同视察的县政府有关部门领导现场协商，献计献策，帮助企业解决影响加快发展的难题，为企业营造良好的交通条件和生产环境，使落户企业更加安心，一致表示要更好地与地方政府共谋发展，共求双赢。8月17日，政协常委视察贵阳钢铁厂入驻的基地项目开工建设情况和扎佐镇大河村新农村建设情况，无不为修文发生的变化欢欣鼓舞，纷纷表示要维护好安定团结发展的局面，促进全县繁荣昌盛。

三、提案建言献策

从政协建立开始，政协委员多通过提案这个渠道对政府工作建言献策，行使政治协商、民主监督、参政议政职能。

政协委员提案多从经济发展、文化生活、党风廉政建设、社会稳定、精神文明建设、关注未成年人成长、民族宗教、市容村貌等人民群众关心问题，向县委、县政府提出建议和意见。县委、县政府及相关职能部门对政协委员提案积极采取措施办理。

1983至1986年一届政协期间，委员提出的《建议拨款修建烈士墓案》《要求筹建修文地面卫星接收站案》《要求加速修好修（文）一六（广）公路案》《建议适当增加发展林业生产资金案》等提案，均受到政府重视。1984年，拨款30万元将原烈士墓地改建为烈士陵园；1986年拨款建成卫星接收站；针对修六公路建设重置工程指挥部，加速工程进度，很快实现通车；就林业建设资金偏少的问题，及时调整预算，1985年增拨3万元资金。1987—1989年二届政协期间，委员提出《关于清理六广后街污水案》、《建议在扎佐再增一座输电线路案》，相关部门采取积极措施予以办理。1988年，对六广街道污水处理采取镇

政府出一点、部门拿一点、群众筹一点的“三个一点”的办法筹资2万元修理沿街水沟，解决污水横流问题；1989年由修文供电局协调争取省供电局支持，增设变压设备，解决了扎佐镇供电不足的问题。1990—1992年三届政协期间，委员提出《关于维修二中教学楼案》，县政府采纳后，从城镇建设基金中拨款10万元，责成县教育局筹资6万元，计16万元，对二中教学楼进行维修。委员吕国治、王敏圣、何克光针对县内教师队伍人才流失情况，提出《稳定教师队伍，控制非政策性调动案》，县委、县政府研究后作出4项决定：一是任何单位不允许从教师中调人，组织、人事部门必须严格把关；二是师范院校毕业的大专中生必须实行对口分配，不得改作他用，以充实学校师资；三是对个别确因工作需要提拔调动的教师，要征得教育部门的同意，才能办理有关手续。四是教育部门和各类学校要加强思想政治工作，教育广大教师热爱教育事业，安心教学岗位，为四化建设培养人才作出贡献。决定出台后，教师队伍得以稳定。1993—1997年四届政协期间，委员提出《在县城修建综合市场案》，县政府采纳其建议，于1995年拨款22万元建成县城农贸市场。委员伍玉秀提出《修建戒毒所案》得到县委、县政府高度重视，投资32万元，将离县城3公里的原王官公社2100平方米的办公楼改建为戒毒所，建病房12间500平方米，干警住房6间70平方米，配档案室、医务室，可容戒毒人员百余人。委员吴昌贵、丁曼、李玉珍提出《尽快规范我县领导干部公费安装住宅电话案》涉及党风廉政的大事，县委书记黄乃铸亲自办理此案，后由县委办公室下发〔1997〕5号文件对领导干部用公费安装住宅电话作出明确规定，刹住了公费安装住宅电话的不正之风。委员张寿彭提的《开辟新水源，尽快解决县城的生产和生活用水案》事关民生，县政府在财力十分紧张的情况下，向银行贷款78万元对羊落井水厂进行改造，从而缓解了县城用水紧张状况。1998—2002年五届政协期间，委员提的《关于整治县城市容市貌案》、《建议将“城关镇”名恢复为“龙场镇”名案》均得到及时办理。县政府于1999年3月以修府通〔1999〕3号文件发出《关于综合整治县城市场的通知》，又于同年8月以修府办〔1999〕27号文出台《关于集中治理城市交通秩序突出问题的实施方案》。工商部门为解决人民路摆摊设点占用街道问题，把赶场地迁往迎春路，消除了人车混杂容易造成交通事故的隐患。1999年，县政府收到18名委员联名提的《建议将“城关镇”名恢复为“龙场镇”名案》后，结合城关镇党委、政府内容相同的报告召开专题研讨会、座谈会，形成共识后将这一请求上报贵州省和贵阳市人民政府，省政府于1999年9月24日作出批复，9月27日，城关镇名正式恢复为龙场镇名。2003—2006年六届政协期间，委员提案《限制在县城燃放烟花爆竹的建议案》得到县政府重视，于2003年11月

1999年，县政府采纳政协委员《关于改造东门桥至三潮水路面的建议》案，投资300万元对东门桥进行拓宽、硬化

2010年9月27日，县政协主席会议到林业局视察林业绿化工作

发布《关于修文县禁止燃放烟花爆竹的管理规定》，划定禁放区域，明确禁放时间，具体规定烟花爆竹的生产、运输和经营事项，使县城恢复了宁静、卫生的生活环境，市民无不称好。县教育局、县物价局收到委员陈信梅提的《关于进城农民工子女入学收费问题案》后，认真分析研究，按照省市有关文件精神，制定《实施意见》和《实施细则》，把流动人口子女教育纳入普及九年义务教育管理，解决了进城农民工子女的入学问题。2006至2010年七届政协期间，委员陈廷贵提出《关于建立我县国家投资项目审批快捷机制的建议》得到县政府及有关部门重视，通过成立扩大内需增加投资工作领导小组办公室、制定《项目会审制度》和《项目追溯制度》、在项目管理中实行问责制等措施，保障了投资项目实施。委员蔡新春等提出《建议加强夜间巡逻，确保百姓出行安全》提案，得到公安局采纳，先后采取在社区新建或扩建巡逻队、调整巡逻重点地段、民警带领巡防队员开展24小时巡逻等措施，使社会治安明显改善。委员陈新国提案《应重视阳明文化的研究的建议案》得到县委宣传部重视，先后于2007年4月和2008年6月两次约请贵阳王阳明研究会的专家学者莅县商讨拟定王阳明思想研究课题，后于2009年出版《王学之旅》一书。委员徐涛提案《关于保护修文环境，促进维修行业健康发展》得到交通部门采纳，对环境脏、乱、差的维修企业坚决停业整顿，2009年就责令停业整顿13户。

县政协委员参加崇恩小学教学楼竣工暨开学典礼

自1983—2010年，县政协共收到委员提案1604件，归并立案1512件，提出提案的委员2865人次。

政协提案办理情况统计表

表2—05—02

类别 届次	提案数	立案数	提案人数	已回复	回复率%
一届一次	46	43	55	22	51.56
一届二次	27	23	73	22	95.65
一届三次	36	36	68	35	97.22
二届一次	59	59	81	59	100
二届二次	56	56	60	55	98.4
二届三次	84	84	132	84	100
三届一次	89	87	67	87	100
三届二次	82	81	89	71	86.56
三届三次	65	65	78	71	87.69
四届一次	74	72	107	72	100
四届二次	80	74	98	74	100
四届三次	79	79	93	79	100
四届四次	61	61	101	61	100

续表

类别 届次	提案数	立案数	提案人数	已回复	回复率%
四届五次	59	59	100	59	100
五届一次	64	63	89	63	100
五届二次	45	45	145	45	1000
五届三次	44	37	148	37	100
五届四次	30	24	67	24	100
五届五次	44	37	65	37	100
六届一次	40	32	89	32	100
六届二次	180	72	168	72	100
六届三次	80	71	224	71	100
七届一次	75	68	203	68	100
七届二次	48	43	104	43	100
七届三次	37	34	115	34	100
七届四次	48	47	131	47	100
七届五次	62	60	124		
合　计	1604	1512	2865		

专记：扎佐天主堂回归教会得民心

1985年，政协委员吴庆兰提交《要求归还扎佐天主教大经堂》提案，立案转由县委统战部和县民宗局办理，鉴于历史原因复杂，经历一至四届政协仍未办结，成为一件长达14年的疑难积案。其间，县委统战部和县民宗局多次深入调查，也无处理结果。

扎佐天主教大经堂建于清咸丰十一年（1861），属天主教会产业。1950年扎佐解放，大经堂一直作为区政府的办公用房。中共十一届三中全会后，正常的宗教活动恢复，当地天主教会即要求大经常回归教会。

1999年，五届政协提案法治社会联谊委员会决定将这一具有代表性，且影响较大的老案作为一件重点提案抓落实。是年5月24日，提案法治社会联谊委员会组织专委成员、县政协各委室主任，邀请县委统战部、县民宗局领导和提案人到扎佐进行现场办案，经过实地察看，召开座谈会，走访群众，与当地党委、政府沟通争取支持和理解，把归还大经堂统一到执行中共宗教政策这一认识上来。提案法治社会联谊委员会即将调查情况向县委、县政府汇报。县政府随即召开县长办公会议，研究处理《要求归还扎佐天主教大经堂》提案的意见，作出分期分批归还大经堂的决定。决定上报县委常委会议通过后，县政府又成立专门的领导小组负责协调处理，至此，历时14年的《要求归还扎佐天主教大经堂》提案得以办理。提案人吴庆兰收到回复通知时兴奋地说：政府这样关心天主教徒，我们要与政府同心同德把扎佐建设得更加美好。

第四节　文史资料征集

1983—2010年，县政协先后征集文史资料700余篇，600余万字，使用363篇（首）98万余字，编辑出版《修文文史资料选辑》6辑和贵州旅游文史丛书《阳明胜境》。6辑文史资料的第一辑、第三辑和第五辑系征集参加过解放修文和解放初期参加建设的老同志撰写的文章63篇，展现了修文解放、剿匪斗争、土地改革、教育改造起义的国民党军官、镇压反革命、抗美援朝等不同方面的珍贵史实。第二辑冠名《修文风光》，着重介绍县境的文物古迹和秀丽的人文自然景观。第四辑冠名《桥》，是在1998年六广河大桥竣工后编辑出版的。修建六广河大桥是修文和黔西两县人民企盼已久的大事，大桥建成后，两县群众欢欣鼓舞，作诗撰联表达喜悦心情。政协收录101首诗139幅楹联集成文史资料出版，不仅反映民心民意，更为后世留下珍贵史料。2001年2月出版的第6辑文史资料，是在2000年国家实施西部大开发战略后，全县政协委员和各界人士响应县委号召，为修文实施西部大开发战略建言献计的文章辑录，冠名《“西部大开发”政协委员建言集》，全书收录28名县政协委员通过调查研究从不同领域所撰写的调研文章。县政协集体名义撰写的《为了青山绿水》、委员虞顺华撰写的《对我县生态环境建设和资源保护的思考》、江少陵撰写的《对我县生态环境建设的几点建议》，为县委、县政府2008年作出建设生态文明县的决策提供参考。

县政协编辑出版的文史资料

第六章　群众团体

第一节　工　会

一、组织建设

1978年中共十一届三中全会后，县总工会按期进行领导班子换届选举和整顿基层工会组织，建设职工之家，充分发挥机构的职能作用。1979年，整顿和加强工会组织，建基层工会64个，会员2875人，占职工总数的71.9%。1984年4月，对基层工会进行整顿和验收，合格工会63个，领导成员312人。1994年，开始在非公有制企业组织职工入会。11月，成立第一家乡镇企业工会—修文久长棕刚玉厂工会和第一家中外合资企业工会—贵州四达矿产有限公司工会。1996年贯彻县委《关于我县非国有企业建立工会组织的意见》，提出“哪里有职工，哪里就建会”的要求，全年整建基层工会12个，组建非国有企业工会1个。2001年10月，县委明确乡（镇）副书记、副乡（镇）长兼任工会主席，促进工会建设，新建企业工会210个，会员4793人。2005年，开始组织农民工入会。到2010年，县总工会下属基层工会达310个，会员3.7万人。

2009年9月19日，召开县工会第十次代表大会

县总工会第五届至第十届会员代表大会一览表

表2—06—01

大会次别	召开时间	出席人数	选举委员数	选举常委数
五	1983.8.27—29	135	8	4
六	1988.9.28—29	127	19	7
七	1993.12.20	141	21	6
八	1999.5.26	86	17	7
九	2004.9.21—22	116	27	9
十	2009.10.18	121	23	9

二、主要活动

（一）参与经济建设

开展劳动竞赛 1987年，县里开展“五个一”（做一件好事，参加一项改革，提一条合理化建议，练好一门基本功，人均增产一百元）竞赛活动，全县73个工会1276名职工参加，至年底，增产资金144.5万元，实现人均增产100元的目标。1993—1996年，开展“艰苦创业，立足本职，勤奋工作，增效益，作贡献”劳动竞赛，全县评选出先进基层工会32个，先进班组12个，先进劳动者126名。1997年，改劳动竞赛为建功立业竞赛。2004年7月，贵州龙翔能源（集团）有限公司工会开展“向55周年国庆献礼立功竞赛活动”，使各项生产经营指标实现历史同期新突破。2006年，贯彻贵阳市总工会《关于团结动员全市广大职工为实现“十一五”规划建功立业的意见》，围绕“学练技术，提高素质，争做贡献，发展经济”这条主线，团结动员全县职工依托岗位投身建功立业竞赛。扎佐渝鑫水泥制造有限公司水泥粉磨车间员工虞平富认真观察，思考各个环节系统工作，努力专研，改进磨台增灶，既减轻机械运输损耗，又增加了3至5吨生料粉磨日产量，被公司评为优秀员工。2007年11月，组织贵州龙翔公司、县烟草公司、县农业局等7个单位250名女职工开展钳工、车工、磨工、产品营销、农用技术等技能竞赛，县总工会获市总工会、市文明办、市科技局、市劳动社会保障局联合颁发的女职工专项技能竞赛组织奖。2008年，深入开展“建功立业大竞赛”“百万职工大练兵”活动，共组织10乡（镇）工会和17个行业工会1300余名职工参加。2010年，动员276个单位参加“安康杯”劳动竞赛，促进了全县的安全生产。

2010年，税务代收工会费经费和工会筹备金的咨询、办理

开展技术革新活动 1979—1981年，县酱油厂青年朱家福认真学习外地经验，反复实验，试制出酿造微生物3042曲酶，达国家规定的二级酱油。1990年，贯彻全总开展“发明创造”的决定，在职工中开展技术革新、技术协作、扩大生产、争创高效的活动。2002—2003年，全县122个工会3240名职工参加技术革新活动，共创利175.2万元，其中技术攻关创利124.5万元，节能降耗25.7万元。2007年，在全县职工中进行技术培训和开展技术比武、技术攻关、技术改造、合理化建议等多形式的经济技术革新活动，有80个企业1.2万名职工参加，提出合理化建议182条，创经济效益40万元，开展技术攻关，技术开发项目4项，创价值220万元。2008年，85个企业开展“我为节能减排做贡献”和“六小”（小核算、小发明、小创造、小改革、小节约、小经验）型的经济技术革新活动，有力地促进全县的节约能源和减排污染工作。

（二）维护职工权益

1981年开始推行职工代表大会制度，维护职工的合法权益。1997年建立集体合同制度。1999年实行厂（院、校）务公开，加强企业（院、校）民主管理。

成立职工代表大会 1981年，全县建立19个企业职工代表大会，维护职工的合法权益。1983年，县邮电局建立职代会后，发动职工提合理化建议，有12项被采用后，完成国家下达的18项经济技术指标，其中有6项超额完成。1990—1997年，开展职代会提案审议活动，其间共审议提案302件，实施114件。2006年，规范完善改制企业职代会2个。至2010年，全县共建立非公企业职代会82个。

推行厂（院、校）务公开 1999年6月，贯彻县委、县政府《关于实行厂务公开的实施意见》。12月，全县实行厂（院、校）务公开的单位达34个。县教育工会采取“先试点，后公开”的措施，制定《修文县校务公开实施意见》，从2001年起，全县中、小学普遍实施公开教学计划、校园建设、职称评定、资格认定、财务收支。王官小学校务公开于2004年受到贵州省教育厅表彰。至2010年，全县实行厂（院、校）务公开的单位达160个，其中国有企业10个，集体企业12个，非公企业40个，事业单位98个。

援助困难职工 1978—1996年，多以火灾、涝灾、疾病和企业停产造成职工家庭生生活困难者作为援助对象，由职工福利费、财政拨款和社会捐资给予临时性生活救助，补助金额为30至80元。1991年，红旗煤厂、酱菜厂、磷肥厂等企业因水灾停产，带来部分职工生活困难，县总工会向受灾严重的21户职工发放补助1000元。1997年，实施“送温暖”工程，在临时救助的基础上，于“春节”均对困难职工进行救助。慰问困难职工450户，发放慰问金及食品折款5.5万元。2003年，“困难职工援助中心” 建立，县总工会通过援助中心联合有关部门制定扶贫帮困相关措施，建立起有效的帮扶机制。2010年，县总工会与人事劳动社会保障局合作，开办下岗职工再就业培训班和组织就业招聘会，帮助700人实现再就业，实施“送温暖”工程，筹措慰问金10.7万元，慰问困难职工家庭335户；开展“金秋助学”活动，向61户困难职工、农民工困难家庭考入高中、中专、大学的子女发放助学金6.55万元。

（三）劳模管理

2000年，县委、县政府贯彻市劳动模范大会精神，印发《关于开展我县建国以来劳动模范、先进人物调查登记工作的紧急通知》，县总工会按照县委指示，安排专人负责，开展深入细致的调查登记工作，分门别类造册登记，报贵阳市总工会劳模办公室审定。此后，每年都把劳模调查登记作为常规工作，明确专人管理。到2010年，全县共有劳动模范57名，其中国家级1名，省部级25名，市级31名；享受生活补贴38名。省“五一”劳动奖章5名，享受生活补贴3名。立军功者6名，其中一等功3名，二等功3名，享受生活补贴5名。

专记：全国劳动模范宋均成

宋均成，男，汉族，1947年2月出生于洒坪乡和平村，中专文化，曾担任修文县红旗煤矿井下作业班班长。全国劳动模范。1990年退休。

1970年，宋均成被招为县红旗煤矿工人，先后转战过修文、六广两个矿区，干过井下采煤、抽水和井外开卷扬机、充电工作。1971年因煤场轨道倒塌受伤离开采煤第一线。他在生产中刻苦好学，善于摸索，致技术水平不断提高。1976年被调到充电房工作，遇到矿灯封口胶短缺，直接影响到井下生产。他经过反复试验，成功地用石腊、沥青熬制成代用材料解决生产所需。1986年企业实行承包制后，主动申请重返采煤第一线，却又遇到一场暴雨造成三号井主风巷被淤泥封住而停产。他带领8名工人泡在稀泥烂窖里苦战8昼夜，提前7天完成了清淤排水，使生产得以恢复。红旗煤矿虽建矿较早，但采煤工艺落后，加上井下工人多是农村招来的农民工，要带好这个班把产量拿上去，宋均成感到除耐心的思想工作和按章管理外，关键是自己带好头。他说：“我是班长，要工人干，自己就必须带头干。”他不仅这样说，也是这样作。职工反映：宋班长无论是原来搞其他工作还是现在当班长，从来都没有误过一个班。他下井采煤，总是上班在人前，下班在人后，班班干满点，年年出满勤。1987年出勤353天，1988年出勤385天，按矿规定井下出勤一个月不低于23天的要求，他2年干了3年的工作。他经常对职工讲："社会主义是干出来的，不是混出来的，没有国家的利益就没有企业的效益，也没有个人的福利。"在宋均成的带领下，全班原煤产量和原材料降低率均居全矿之首。1988年10月生产原煤1950吨，比同井其他两个班多产500吨。1989年1—5月月均产煤458吨，月月突破矿规定的月产200吨指标，比同井其他两个班平均月产量高出54.2%。

宋均成终年采煤在井下，就是这样默默地把光和热奉献给城乡人民。1989年9月，他被评为全国劳动模范，县委、县政府召开大会，欢送他赴北京参加国庆观礼。当他与其他劳模信步走上天安门时，满脸露出从未有过的喜悦，内心发出感叹："因为有了共产党，我们煤矿工人才会有幸福的今天。"

第二节　共青团

一、组织建设

1978年健全共青团修文县委。1984年随着乡级政权恢复，全县除原有6个区团委外，新建32个乡（镇）团委，共324个团支部，有团员6386名。2002年机构改革，明确团县委行政编制4名，设书记1名，副书记1名。1992年撤区并乡建镇，10乡（镇）建立团委。2008年，团县委下属基层团委37个，团总支5个，团支部277个，团员9781名。2010年组织情况未变。

1980年4月，共青团扎佐公社第四届团代会全体代表留影

第十一次至十六次县团代会一览表

表2—06—02

大会次别	召开时间	出席人数	选举委员人数	选举常委数
十一	1980.4.28-5.3	340	33	11
十二	1987.8.7-8	115	17	7
十三	1992.4.10-11	135	19	9
十四	1997.5.21	137	19	6
十五	2004.9.22-23	112	21	7

二、主要活动

建设思想道德防线　1979年起，团县委先后开展"争做一个合格共青团员"、"立志争优"、"学雷

团县委举办增强共青团员意识教育活动竞赛

锋，学赖宁，比先进，树新风、做新人”、“重走红军长征路”、“争创青年文明号”等活动，引导青少年坚定跟党走的信念。1990年，在“学雷锋，学赖宁、比先进、树新风、做新人”活动中，全县191所中小学及县区40个单位团组织，组成200个服务小组，3200名青少年走上街头开展便民利民活动，为7000人次群众提供服务。阳早小学刘明均、王怀禄、王怀喜、宋桂林、罗青海等5位同学勇灭山火，共青团安顺地委授予“赖宁式好少年”称号。1993年，在“修文青年重走红军长征路”活动中，38名团员青年从县城出发，沿着当年红军长征经过的三元、扎佐、清让、桃源等地，历时4天徒步行程125公里，学习红军不怕远征难的英雄气概和无坚不摧的革命精神。1996年，按照团中央提出的“少年雏鹰行动”计划，在广大青少年中开展“手拉手”活动，6名少先队员获市“三级雏鹰”奖章，1名获贵阳市“十佳少先队员”称号，1名老师获贵阳市“十佳少先队优秀辅导员”荣誉。2000年，开展“走向新世纪”读书征文活动，两万名团员青年参加各种形式的学习会、报告会和专题讨论会，写心得体会8000余篇，320人参加征文，1人获全国特等奖，1人获一等奖，1人获二等奖。2003年在少年儿童中开展争当“修文文明小使者”活动，县实验小学少先队组成“小小交警队”走上街头，号召市民文明行路，引导“摩的”和汽车司机自觉遵守交通规则，帮助环卫工人打扫街道卫生、清洗街道护栏和广告牌。实小、二小少先队员“文明小使者”向经营户发放倡议书，宣传文明经营、文明交易。2006年至2010年，与当代修文编辑部、县文联、教育局等单位合作，先后在中小学生和团员青年中开展“文明礼仪童谣征集”“读书心得征文”“爱祖国爱家乡朗诵比赛”“少儿书画展”等主题活动，焕发青少年爱祖国、爱家乡立志成才的激情。其间，在2008年凝冻灾害后，团县委组成有1500多名团员青年参加的34支青年突击队，参与灾后重建宣讲、基础设施修复、帮助农民恢复生产、义诊等工作。震惊全国的“5·12”汶川特大地震后，在团员中开展“交纳一次特殊团费、帮助一位灾区群众”活动，收到特殊团费1.66万元如数汇至灾区。2010年，团县委与宣传部、文明办、教育局等单位合作，共同举办以首届校园风采展示大赛，全县有300名学生获得市级表彰。

组织青年志愿者服务社会　1996年，团县委发出《关于开展为困难群众排忧解难“一助一”志愿者服务行动的通知》，全县3000余名青年志愿者踊跃参加捐赠活动，共捐资5万元，捐物折款10万元。继后，志愿者行动成为共青团的一项重要工作，主要参与社区服务、扶贫开发、环境保护、抢险救灾、大型活动等5大类31项服务。2004年，组织200名青年志愿者服务“双千”工程，进村入户为村民义诊、检修电器和提供农业科技服务。在扎佐镇独山村，志愿者将“远程教育”“医疗保健知

2010年，修文中学共青团团员做交通引导员

识”等内容编成布依山歌教村民传唱。2006年，开展“弘扬雷锋精神，参与志愿服务”活动，全县千名青年志愿者深入社区、村寨开展家电维修、绿色环保、法律援助等。2008年，开展青年志愿服务进社区等活动，不断扩大青年志愿者工作影响力。至2010年，全县有青年志愿者5692名，注册登记2764名，“一助一”结对619对。

自2005年起，先后有百余名大学生西部计划志愿者和“三支一扶”（支农、支教、支医和扶贫）志愿者到县从事志愿服务工作，2010年尚有大学生志愿者46名。团县委通过推行志愿者安全健康管理通信卡，安全健康管理制度，信息报送管理制度的“一卡两制”，采取定期联系、定期活动、召开座谈会、建QQ群、微博等多种形式，积极做好大学生志愿者在修文的管理服务工作。

争创“青年文明号” 从1994年起，团县委组织团员青年开展争创“青年文明号”活动，引导青年诚实劳动，爱岗敬业，建功成才。1999年，县信用联社团员青年参加团市委等部门举办的全市金融系统青工比武大赛，取得手指点钞二等奖。至2010年，全县共创市级“青年文明号”13个，县级“青年文明号”29个和“青年文明岗”9个。

培训团干 1980—1981年，对全县农村团支部进行轮训，学习中共中央和省委关于农村工作的指示。1989年，团县委举办“弘扬五四精神，鲜明反对动乱”专题研讨会。2000年，开展“走向新世纪”读书征文活动，320名青年学生撰写“走向新世纪”文章。2006年8月，团县委举办团干培训班，各乡（镇）团委、县直有关团支部、县直学校及各乡（镇）中心学校团支部、少先队大队辅导员及16个新农村示范点团支部负责人共70人参加培训。2010年，80余名县、乡专、兼职团干参加培训，培训内容以新型团委的运行机制设计、工作内容及运行中所遇到的困难和问题为切入点，团省委书记陈昌旭到会指导。通过培训，坚定了专兼职团干的工作信心。

119青年志愿者行动启动仪式

创建青年联合会 1997年9月，县委建立修文县青年联合会，10月，县青年联合会第一届第一次全体会议在县城召开，出席委员71名，会议选举14人组成第一届常务委员会。从1997年至2008年，青联会领办农业项目20个，创办县级以上示范基地10个，培养农村青年星火带头人100余名，培训青年6000余人次。配合团县委全面实施青年人才工程，推进争创“青年文明号”“青年岗位能手”活动，累计创建市级“青年文明号”13家，县级“青年文明号”29家，培养县级以上“岗位能手”50余名，并协同人事劳动部门通过开展职能技术培训，组织青年外出务工等形式，帮助5000余名青年实现再就业。2010年，青联会委员100余人分赴10乡（镇）开展“乡村行”暨绿丝带活动，给10名留守儿童送去一批文具和2000元慰问金，并结成帮扶对子。

评比表彰先进 1987年，三角山水泥厂团委组织委员胡学惠受到团省委和省经委联合举办的“小发明、小改造”活动的表彰。1990年，阳早小学刘明均、王怀禄、王怀喜、宋桂林、罗青海被团省委授予“优秀少先队员”称号，团地委授予5名同学“赖宁式好少年”称号。1995年6月，县委、县政府授予洒坪中学初一学生魏先志“舍己救人好少年”光荣称号。团县委追认魏先志为共青团员，并在全县团员青

年中开展向魏先志学习的活动。1996年经县委批准，授予马道静、李继彬、叶礼贵、杨胜佳、曹成俊、刘玉华、李修平、周尚明、陈书品等9人为首届“修文县优秀青年”。2003年，六桶乡保山村青年李根书获团中央2002年度“全国农村青年创业致富带头人标兵”称号。2009年，县大学生志愿服务西部计划管理办公室获“全国大学生志愿服务西部计划优秀项目办”称号。

专记：好少年魏先志被追认为共青团员

魏先志系洒坪中学一年级学生，班上的体育委员，学校的优秀学生。父亲魏祥贵任洒坪乡副乡长，母亲是一名普通农村妇女。1995年6月，因救落水同学周登美光荣献身被追认为共青团员。

魏先志生在农村，长在农村，从小就养成忠诚老实、艰苦朴素的良好品德。在家里他体贴父母，勤做家务；在学校，他尊敬老师，团结同学。1994年9月考入洒坪中学。学习期间，他给学校留下了极好的印象。学校开展义务建校活动，他不顾天气寒冷，全身心投入劳动，在其带动下，他所在的第四组率先完成任务。学校举办运动会，他多次获奖，为班级争得了荣誉。他乐于助人，临近期末考试，同学胡景富生病不能到校上课，每天放学后他坚持给胡补习功课，使胡顺利通过考试。有一次在操场捡到一块价值100多元的手表，立即交到学校总务处，让手表很快物归原主，其拾金不昧的事迹在学校被广为传颂。由于魏先志各方面表现突出，第一学期就被学校评为优秀学生。1995年6月，魏先志、周登美等一批同学相约到青山村龙洞湾水库游泳。先到的脱衣下水，其中有不会游泳的周登美不慎跌入10米深的水中。后到的魏先志见状，当即和衣纵身跳入水中救人。由于被溺水者紧紧抓住，两人抱成一团在水中挣扎。另一同学刘刚见状也跟着跳了下去，路过的村民孟天生见后随即跳入水中施救，均被溺水者牢牢扭住动弹不得。紧急关头，青山村26岁的周光友闻声赶到，果断跳入水中，奋力把周登美拉出水面，刘刚和孟天生脱身后，协同把周登美救上岸。然因救人精疲力竭的魏先志沉入水底，光荣献身，时年仅15岁。

魏先志为抢救同学而英勇献身的事迹，在全县群众中引起强烈反响。为弘扬其舍己救人的优秀品质，1995年6月26日，县教育局向全县各级各类学校发出《关于向舍己救人的好少年魏先志同学学习的决定》。27日，中共修文县委、县人民政府亦作出《关于表彰见义勇为的魏先志等人的决定》和《关于授予魏先志舍己救人好少年称号的决定》，号召在全县范围内开展向魏先志学习的活动。共青团修文县委追认魏先志为共青团员，并发出通知，在全县广大团员青少年中，广泛开展“向舍己救人好少年魏先志”学习的活动。

第三节　妇女联合会

一、组织建设

从1978年起加强妇女组织建设，于1989年7月召开县第五次妇女代表大会，选举产生县第五届执行委员会，团结动员全县妇女努力工作，开拓进取，在建设中国特色社会主义事业中作贡献。2002年机构改革，明确县妇联行政编制4名，其中设主席1名，副主席1名。到2004年，全县10乡（镇）均建有妇女联合会，12个居民段建有妇女代表会，32个县直机关有妇委会或妇女小组。2010年，县妇女联合会和下辖33个机关妇委会、10个乡（镇）妇联以及217个村妇代会仍存。

第五次至第八次县妇女代表大会一览表

表2—06—03

大会次别	召开时间	出席人数	选举执行委员数	选举常务委员数
五	1989.7.18—20	160	31	11
六	1999.6.17—18	160	23	13
七	2004.9.20—21	117	21	9
八	2009.10.20—21	120	25	13

二、主要活动

组织妇女参与改革实践 1980年，各级妇女会组织农村妇女投身农村经济体制改革，参与实行家庭联产承包责任制。至1985年，县内以妇女为主的科技户58户，专业户2808户，联合体213户，第三产业240户。1988年，沙溪村妇女戴秀英承包开发县城西门坡荒山200亩，创办全县第一个“三八果园实验场”，获省“三八红旗手”称号。1998年，六广镇女青年李忠琼到县城创业，先是租房经营发廊，经过几年努力，创办起“六广姑娘浴都”，成为县内的女企业家。2002年，龙场镇妇女蔡新春创办嘉新酒业有限公司，生产其研发的“星丹”保健酒和获国家专利的治疗骨折苗药，被誉为“女性创业之星”。2003年，小箐乡小坝村妇女刘正秀被选为村的科技副主任，带领村民创办无公害生猪养殖基地，全村3年时间养猪户由14户发展到120户，喂养二元杂交猪由46头增加到1500多头，刘正秀被全国妇联评为“全国双学双比活动优秀女能手” 。2005年，在改革实践中成长起来的妇女创建起自己的组织“修文县女企业家协会”，至2010年，女企协有会员30余人。

2010年2月8日，全县人民团体“三创一办”绿丝带温暖行动进社区活动暨迎春座谈会

开展“双学双比”和“巾帼建功”活动 从1989年起，县妇联在全县农村妇女中开展学文化、学技术，比成绩、比贡献的“双学双比”活动。1992年，在城镇和国家机关女职工中开展“巾帼建功”活动，县妇联引导、鼓励广大女职工立足岗位建功立业。金融系统开展“学身边人——胡江”活动，转变工作态度，优质为顾客服务；粮食系统开展“学习英模曹明芬、骆邦珍”，搞好粮油供应。1993年，深入开展“双学双比”竞赛活动，到1998年，有529名妇女获绿色证书，505名获得女农民技术员资格。2002年，龙场镇沙溪村妇女戴秀英获全国和省“双学双比”种植能手。2008年，全县各级妇联组织配合乡（镇）农业服务中心举办农技培训班31期，参训妇女500余人。各“双学双比”成员单位举办绿证培训班18期，320人参训，其中妇女265人。选派谷堡乡折溪村妇代会主任周训秀参加省妇联“科技二传手”培训，选派扎佐小堡村妇女参加贵州省首届乡村女大厨比赛，获三等奖。县妇联在庆“三八”活动中评选

和表彰在各行各业中涌现出的“巾帼建功”先进工作者6名。2010年，县妇联以实施素质工程为重点，深化“双学双比”活动，先后在龙场、扎佐举办两期农村妇女农技与非农技能培训班，培训妇女200余人；配合县乡（镇）农业技术服务中心举办培训班508期2.5万人，其中妇女1.7万人，建“巾帼示范村”4个，送科技图书妇女杂志200余册。

开展“三八绿色工程”活动 1990年，县妇联制定“为十年绿化修文作贡献”的规划，在全县妇女中开展植树造林、绿化修文的“三八”绿色工程活动。至2000年，全县各级妇女组织投工10.32万个，创建妇女林32个，造林面积达1.86万亩。六广镇四寨村妇女杨成秀获贵州省1991至1992年度“林业生态建设女标兵”称号。

开展“五好文明家庭”创建活动 1981年，在全县开展“五好（爱国守法，热心公益好；学习进取，爱岗敬业好；男女平等，尊老爱幼好；移风易俗，少生优育好；勤俭持家，保护环境好）文明家庭”创建活动。至2010年的30年间，县妇联结合各个时期精神文明建设要求，不断修订“五好”家庭创建标准，与相关部门配合先后开展评选“五星级农户”“科技示范户”“学习型家庭”“好婆婆、好媳妇、好女婿、好女儿”活动和“文明进万家”“创建平安家庭”等活动，把文明家庭与扶贫济困、移风易俗、绿色环保、文明村镇、文明城市、文明行业、文明机关、“三创一办”、平安修文创建等活动结合在一起，深入开展“五好文明家庭”创建活动。先后表彰“五好家庭”“学习型家庭”“平安家庭”“环保家庭”“五星级农户”“科技示范户”共4000多户。

维护妇女儿童合法权益 从1979年开始，县妇联明确1人负责来信来访工作。1980—1985年，共收到来信464件，来访5562人。1981—1985年，妇联配合有关部门解救妇女儿童20余名。1989年，开展法律宣传培训，办班58期，培训各级妇女干部591人。1992年5月，县委批转县妇联《关于学习宣传贯彻执行妇女权益保障法安排意见》，全县张贴标语206条，出黑板报32期。2006年3月，县妇联、司法局、团县委等几家单位联手上街开展妇女维权宣传活动，宣传新修改的《中华人民共和国妇女权益保障法》，新《中华人民共和国婚姻法》、《计划生育条例》、《妇女婚前检查常见问题解答》等。2008年，贵阳市妇联、贵阳市综治办、县司法局和县妇联在县城中心街道悬挂大幅标语，制作妇女维权宣传栏，向群众发放《妇女发展纲要》、《儿童发展纲要》、《中华人民共和国妇女权益保障法》等宣传资料3700余份。2010年，县妇联共接待群众来信来访36件40人次，其中：婚姻家庭类26件30人次；人身权益类4件5人次，调处率为100%；陪审各类案件16起；利用妇女维权周活动宣传《致全省留守儿童父母的一封信》《送法到乡镇社会法律法规资料选编》，接受群众咨询，让更多的妇女学会运用法律武器维护自身的合法权益；关爱并慰问留守儿童20名，发放慰问金8000元；为实验二小、小箐乡幼儿园送去价值7000元的学习用品和运动器械。

开展评选先进活动 1979年，在全县开展争当“三八红旗集体”活动，从各条战线评出“三八红旗手”278名和“三八红旗集体”22个。1982—1986年，全县共评出“三八红旗手”722人次，“三八红旗集体”10个，“五好家庭”816户，“五讲四美”先进集体10个。1996年全县评选“三八红旗手”33名，“三八红旗集体”16个，“五好文明家庭”98户，“双学双比”女能手和“巾帼建功标兵”36名。2002年，开展评选“好婆婆”“好媳妇”“好女婿”“好女儿”活动，评选出“五好文明家庭”32户，“好女婿”20名，“好女儿”19名。2008年3月，县妇联对获得2007年度的10个先进基层妇女组织、20名“双学双比”先进工作者、6名“巾帼建功”先进个人、6名“两纲”（《妇女发展纲要》《儿童发展纲要》）

先进个人、5户“五好文明家庭”、5户“学习型家庭”、3户“节能环保”家庭和5名“抗凝冻、保民生、抗灾救灾”先进个人进行表彰。2009年，全年共表彰20户“五好文明家庭”。

专记：孝星叶茂仙赡养孤寡老人纪实

叶茂仙家住龙场镇新寨村。早在1967年，她见本村白岩寨孤寡老人刘玉珍腿脚不灵便，生活无着落，就和丈夫郑远明商量，把刘老太接到家中养老，担负起赡养老人的义务。

时光的年轮转至1985年，71岁的刘玉珍腿部出现骨肉萎缩，下肢麻木，行动十分不便。1996年起竟全身瘫痪，不能下地行走，生活起居全靠别人照顾护理。叶茂仙夫妇经常求医购药为老人诊治，省吃俭用为老人烧水做饭。白天，为老人打开住室通风透气，搀扶老人到户外晒太阳，活动筋骨；夜晚，又扶助老人进屋休息就寝。老人大小便失禁后，叶茂仙一周要为她擦洗一次身子，每天要清洗老人的尿布和裤子，经常换洗床单被褥。冬天，冰水透彻入骨，叶茂仙冒着严寒，冷水清洗尿裤，致双手开出道道裂口。有人关心叶茂仙说：“刘老太和你非亲非故，何必自讨苦吃。”叶茂仙斩钉截铁地回答：“我有心接她来挨我住，就有责任把她照顾好。”

为照料卧床不起的刘老太，叶茂仙夫妇未出过远门，每天必须留一人在家驱寒送暖。1998年初冬，郑远明生病住院，叶茂仙一边在医院护理丈夫，一边又要回家照顾老人，往返奔波。一天，她摸黑冒雨从医院赶回家里，见老人跌在床下，顾不上换掉全身雨水湿透的衣裤，赶紧将老人抱在床上换去尿裤，端来热水洗净老人全身，然后又做出热气腾腾的饭菜，一口一口地喂进老人嘴里。看着老人憔悴的面容，叶茂仙摸着她冰冷的双手，悔恨自己来晚一步，让老人受苦了。老人见叶茂仙身上湿透的衣服，想着她丢下住院的丈夫，来照顾我这个半截入土的人，就老泪纵横地说：“茂仙啊，我又不是你们的亲娘养母，你们全家对我这样好，是我拖累你们，我只有下辈子才能报答你们。你给我买包耗子药，让我吃下死去算了。”叶茂仙安慰老人道：“我们有缘走到一起，我说过您就是我的亲娘，我们要好好为您养老送终。”说到此，婆媳俩抱头痛哭起来。

叶茂仙夫妇照料老人的事迹感动着下一代，远在广东打工的长子、三儿常打电话回家问候刘老太的病情，寄回好吃的食品让老人尝鲜，虽已另住的大儿媳，也常来为老人端屎倒尿，喂水喂饭，孙辈们上街赶场也忘不了为老人买点好吃的带回来。逢年过节或老人生日，全家为老人做新衣服，祝愿老人健康长寿。叶茂仙家庭原本就不富裕，加上长期要照顾一个患病老人，负担就愈显沉重。已到成婚年龄的两个儿子都没有成家，两个儿子把敬老养老的美德作为择偶的第一标准，说不孝敬老人的女孩我们坚决不娶。

2001年刘玉珍离世，叶茂仙夫妇按照农村习俗礼葬了老人。目睹叶茂仙一家任劳任怨照顾病瘫老人34年，感动得一位邻居老大爷发出感慨：“我活了80多岁，见如此孝敬不是生母的，要算叶茂仙这家人。”2002年，叶茂仙被评为“贵阳市新世纪孝星”，受到市精神文明指导委员会的表彰和奖励；2005年又获得“全国孝亲敬老之星奖”的荣誉。

第四节　科学技术协会

一、组织建设

1980年建立县科学技术协会，至2010年先后召开代表大会3次，3次代表大会均选出科协正、副主席。2002年机构改革，明确科学技术协会事业编制4名，设主席1名，副主席1名，列入参照试行国家公务员制度范围。到2010年，县科协下置县级学会3个，乡（镇）科普协会10个，各类农村专业技术协会18个，科普志愿者517名。

第一次至第三次县科学技术代表大会一览表

表2—06—04

大会次别	召开时间	出席人数	常委数	委员数	选举主席、副主席
一	1980.9	100人	9人	21人	主席1名、副主席2名
二	2004.9	150人	19人	45人	主席、副主席各1名
三	2009.10	160人	19人	46人	主席、副主席各1名

二、主要活动

开展科普宣传　县内科普宣传主要以举办科技讲座、编印科技宣传资料、放映科技影片和场天设点宣传为主。1981年，设立农业科学技术咨询服务站，通过场天设点宣传方式，开展以农、林、牧、副、渔为内容的科技知识宣传。1981—1982年，服务站共为8.4万人提供咨询服务，被群众誉称“街道农业大学”，获省科协表彰。1996年起，每年举办培训班，组织县、乡（镇）两级科普骨干参加培训，推广农业实用技术。自2001年国务院将每年5月第三周定为全国“科技活动周”和2003年中国科协将每年6月29日定为“全国科普活动日”后，县科协每逢“科技活动周”和“科普活动日”均举办科技宣传普及活动。2004年，联合县宣传、教育、卫生等17个单位开展以“科学普及——你我共参与”为主题的系列活动，通过多媒体、模型、实物展出方式宣传现代农业、环境保护、生命科学等科技知识。在《当代修文》辟科普宣传专页（栏），在县城设立固定宣传展板，在乡（镇）建图书资料室，在村建远程教育系统等多种形式，形成全县科普宣传网络。

1997年，县委、县政府表彰科技兴农人才

2005年，配合有关部门开展送科技到农家20余次，为农民刻录科普光碟300余套，举办“科普讲

座”70余次，办科技培训班25期，参训者3751人，放科普电影10场，观众达6000余人。2008年“科技活动周”，邀请省科普专家到县作“科技教育与人才培养”等科普报告。2010年科普活动日，开展“百万公众网络学习工程——网络操作技术培训”活动和“节约能源资源，保护生态环境，保障安全健康”为主题的科普宣传活动，让节能减排、科学保护生态环境的理念和做法普及到人民群众中。

开展农村科普工作　1980—1990年，在农村重点开展科技扶贫活动，通过科技传帮带使贫困群众尽快脱贫。1985年县科协专家咨询组在桃源乡、六广镇引导农民种植柑橘2000亩21万株，有500多户农村家庭依靠种植柑橘走上致富路。1991—2010年，农村科普工作以“科技兴农”为主线，与县农业、科技部门配合开展科技培训和送科技下乡、科技进社区活动。1999年起，在农村组建农村专业技术协会。2003—2005年，共发放各类科普宣传画600张，科普宣传资料3万份，农村实用技术手册6000册，放映科教片70场，培训农村科技骨干和农技协会会员2500名。通过广泛的科普活动，使一批农民掌握了2至3门农业先进实用技术。2003年，选派3名青年农民参加贵阳市农村科普与实用技术竞赛获三等奖。2004年，洒坪乡中明村农民运用所学技术种植大蒜508亩，每亩纯收入1000元，是种植油菜收入的3倍。2008年县科协与县农业部门配合，农村实用技术培训6.5万人；举办“绿证”培训班70个，培训1700人；非农技能培训80期，培训2600人。2010年，组织15名农村科技致富带头人参加市农村信息技术培训；组织农村专业技术协会会员参加全国农民科学素质网络竞赛活动。至此，全县注册的农村专业技术协会达33个，年产值超百万元的有11个，8000余户农村家庭6万余人成为专业技术协会会员，这种“协会+基地+农户”或“协会+公司+基地+农户”的组织模式成为农民致富的推动力。

开展青少年科普教育　1999年起，在中小学开展学科奥林匹克竞赛、小发明、小制作、小论文、小实验活动，激发青少年爱科学、学科学的热情。2003年，组织学生参加全国青少年计算机奥林匹克分区联赛，修文二中初二年级学生李彦喜获贵阳市初中组三等奖。2008年“全国科普日”活动期间，邀请科普专家贵阳学院钱贵晴教授莅县作“科技教育与人才培养”报告，组织修文一中、二中、三中学生400人聆听报告。2010年，县科协会同教育局举办以“建生态文明市，做三创主人翁”为主题的第二十九届贵阳市青少年科技活动月活动，以学校为单位组织学生开展“读科普书，听科普报告，做科学小实验和小制作，写科学小论文”的科技活动。

第五节　工商业联合会

一、组织建设

1978年，因“文化大革命”影响一时尚未清除，致工商联合会组织停止活动又长达8年。直到1988年8月召开第四次会员代表大会，工商联才予挂牌恢复。2002年机构改革，明确工商联事业编制3名，设主席1名，副主席1名，列入参照试行国家公务员制度范围。从1988到2010年，工商联召开会员代表大会6次。

第四次至第九次县工商联会员代表大会一览表

表2—06—05

大会次别	召开时间	出席人数	选举执行委员数	选举常委数
四	1988.8.11-13	158	27	9
五	1992.7.8-9	100	23	11
六	1997.5.20	100	34	17
七	2001.11.29	120	66	33
八	2006.7.27	106	30	21

二、主要活动

实施光彩事业　1999年，县光彩事业推动委员会成立，启动实施光彩事业工程，广大非公经济人士积极投入，以项目为中心，开发资源，兴办企业，培训人才，安排就业，发展贸易，捐赠财物。到2005年，工商联会员参与光彩事业项目26个，涵盖冶炼、建材、采掘、制药、食品加工、养殖、耐火材料、新材料制造、房地产开发、物流等项目。投资金额4.4亿元，安排4469人就业，培训5569余人，捐赠资金60.8万元。2008年，40多家非公企业捐赠价值200万元的药品和现金380万元。嘉兴酒业有限公司捐赠价值17万元的骨伤药酒，并带领医疗小分队亲自送往四川地震灾区。2010年，发动全县非公经济人士为抗旱救灾捐款30余万元，协调香港基督教青年联合会会员刘松基为小箐乡杉林村考进清华大学的顾光超提供学士、硕士、博士8年连读的学费，每年5000元，共4万元。

1992年7月，召开县工商业联合会第五届会员代表大会

2004年县工商联会员光彩事业实施项目一览表

表2—06—06

项目名称	企业名称	法人	投资总额（万元）	脱贫人数	培训	就业	捐赠（万元）
中成药制化、化妆品	贵州绿太阳制药有限公司	沈子明	2088	73	80	90	23.6
机制红砖	修文小营砖厂	袁达明	707	65	153	172	5.9
中成药制造	贵州同济堂制药	王晓春	11376	850	1150	1100	436.8
房开、建材、装潢材料	贵州利尔房地产开发有限公司	李修平	7500	31	235	316	48.8
原煤采掘	修文三利煤厂	刘金华	250	20		48	3
蒟蒻粉	贵州日光蒟蒻食品医药化工有限公司	王乾麟	992.4		30	30	33.42
普通硅酸盐水泥	修文县三角山水泥厂	荣启华	2944	101	300	210	7.3
酱油、萝卜干	贵州联宇食品有限公司	梁光华	1100	30	100	48.	0.4

续表

项目名称	企业名称	法人	投资总额（万元）	脱贫人数	培训	就业	捐赠（万元）
生铁	修文铁合金厂	贺胜安	900	65	120	138	13
石油压裂支撑剂	贵州林海新材料有限公司	石世泽	2353	73	520	225	1
普通硅酸盐水泥	修文德荣水泥厂	王荣仿	800	67	98	115	4.2
铸造生铁	修文平泰冶炼有限公司	赵敬忠	470	8	145	160	2.1
机制红砖	修文县高坝砖厂	杨　忠	308	45	190	60	2
普通硅酸盐水泥	修文南方水泥厂	王少林	800	6	250	191	6.8
铸造生铁	修文荣达冶炼厂	黄光荣	300	65	305	140	4.1
机制红砖	修文普陀砖厂	杨富贵	100	48	200	145	2
普通硅酸盐水泥	贵阳久长建材有限责任公司	范永联	2000	73	520	280	
建材、房开	贵阳吉泓房地产开发有限公司	陈华明	420		43	99	18
普通硅酸盐水泥	渝鑫水泥制造有限公司	陈代海	1200	75	420	108	1.2
机制红砖	毛冲坝砖厂	岳玉江	100	25	150	142	6.4
铸造生铁	福贵铁厂	李俊奕	110	15	138	51	3
铸造生铁	双辉铁厂	刘瑞泉	4000		193	193	
耐火瓷球	天成陶瓷有限公司	杨国琼	300	20	50	50	
鸡蛋鸡粪加工	贵州兰地实业有限公司	罗　进	1300	30	49	49	8
普通硅酸盐水泥	六广水泥厂	冯绍康	1480	76	180	219	9.9
普通硅酸盐水泥	阳明耐火厂	曹昕惠	115	40	50	90	7

服务非公企业　自1997—2005年，县工商联组织非公有制企业参加全国区域性大型活动4次，参展产品主要有保龄酒、土鸡蛋、萝卜干、猕猴桃、苦丁茶、高麦芽糖浆、魔芋粉制品等具有地方特色产品。2003年，贯彻贵阳市委、市政府《贵阳市专业技术带头人和中青年科技骨干选择、管理实施办法》，在民营企业中开展评选工作，罗进、陈志明被市委、市政府命名为市级2004—2008年度中青年技术骨干，同时被县委、县政府表彰为2004—2008年度修文县专业技术带头人。李忠琼、温新明、冯修胜被县委、县政府表彰为2004—2008年度修文县中青年技术骨干。2004年，工商联组织非公经济人士参加省工商联举办的“民营企业迎接入世新挑战”学术讲座、WTO知识、依法治国、税法知识讲座，参加贵阳市各界人士“实施大开放，建设大贵阳”动员会和中国·西部（贵阳）民营经济论坛系列活

2010年4月6日广东贵州商会向修文捐赠抗旱救灾款10万元

动。推荐贵州兰地实业有限公司总经理周杰等5人参加贵阳市工商管理硕士（MBA）研究生班学习。

2007年，工商联组织7家企业参与“2007中国·贵阳首届新型城市产学研暨民营科技成果展示交易会”洽谈，会员陈志明研究的专利产品——电子制冷芯片、汽车刹车冷却水故障显示报警器、发动机自动保护器、电子节油器等专利产品吸引众多商家，美国博化集团投资控股有限公司代表卢元均当场表示愿投资4000万元人民币联合开发。2008年，工商联协助人事劳动局举行招聘活动，54家民营企业参与招聘，共提供55个工种1306个工作岗位，经过洽谈，现场达成意向性协议218人。2010年，帮助县内5家非公企业解决工会费缴纳问题，避免了一场官司。

参政议政　自1983—2005年，属工商联界的政协委员向政协修文县委提交提案115件，情况反映9件，撰写《修文县非公有制经济发展现状、措施及方向》等调研报告16篇。到2010年，推荐工商联会员和非公经济代表人士担任市政协委员5人，县政协委员124人，市人大代表3人，县人大代表8人。

专记：自主创业的工商联女会员蔡星春

蔡星春系龙场镇新生村人，1962年生。上初中不久因家庭经济困难辍学后在家帮助父母种地。1979年起外出贵阳、遵义打工，后又摆摊做小生意和修理钟表。是修文县工商联合会会员。

1985年，丈夫参加南疆保卫战后，带着受伤的左臂复员进厂当工人，但伤病复发，厂方无力支付医药费。为治愈丈夫的伤痛，蔡星春毅然投入对骨伤苗药的采摘和研制。她不辞辛劳，经常步行二三十里乡村小道，攀悬崖峭壁，下深涧沟壑采集药草，全然不顾跌跤摔倒，手足划破出血。把药草采回家里，将其晒干、碾细、煎熬成剂让丈夫服用，并细致观察疗效。经反复试验，于1990年年初步研制成民间苗药配方。丈夫服用后，曾多次求医都未治愈的左臂逐渐恢复知觉，进而能伸展收缩、弯曲自如，最后居然像健康人一样，随手能提起重物，可以参加繁重的体力劳动。听到蔡星春治伤成功实践，上门求索者络绎不绝。她乐施好善，对无力买药者免费赠给伤药。接着，她萌发长远打算，在炮制伤药的基础上又研制成功食疗保健酒，既能医治伤病，又能增进人体健康。一时间食疗保健酒又名声大振，蔡星春也四处扬名。

1992年，她和辞去工作的丈夫在县城创办起汽车修理厂，一边积存修理收入，一边生产食疗保健酒，命名“星丹保健酒”。2000年5月向贵州省卫生厅申报生产“星丹”酒，经卫生厅考察后，于2001年批准生产销售，使“星丹”酒正式投放市场。

2002年，蔡星春重新装修汽修厂，融资500万元兴建2800平方米的厂房和办公大楼，创办嘉新酒业有限公司，专门生产“星丹”酒。“星丹”酒上市深受群众青睐，2003年7月，获国家知识产权局发明创造专利证书，并在香港国际专利技术博览会上获得世界科学技术发展成就奖。

蔡星春从创新实践中不断总结，将若干成功的实践升华到理论上并写出有价值的文章投稿报刊，2002年论文《新经济时代女性创业者观念创新》获全国二等奖。她关爱团体，带头参加工商联开展的各项文体活动，主演的方言小品“妈妈，我要读书”获2002年8月贵阳市工商联举办的“思源思进”文艺表演一等奖。她慷慨解囊，奉献爱心，多次捐赠钱物扶弱助残。2005年9月捐款1000元资助大石乡三名贫困女孩就读修文中学，并负责承担其中一人高中三年的学杂费，后又到县特殊学校向残疾学生捐款2000元。2001年被评为优秀个体工商户。先后担任县女企业家商会会长，省女企业家商会副会长等职。经省工商联推荐，2002年在北京出席“首届杰出女性创业成就国际展示会暨女性创业经济论坛”。

第六节　残疾人联合会

一、组织建设

1990年10月，建立县残疾人联合会。12月，县残疾人联合会第一次代表大会在县城召开。大会通过《发展残疾人事业，促进两个文明建设》的工作报告，会议选举产生第一届主席团委员会。1994年12月，召开第二次残疾人代表大会。1997年，县残联升格为正科级事业单位。2002年机构改革，明确县残联事业编制5名，设理事长1名，副理事长1名，列入参照试行国家公务员制度范围。至2010年，机构未变。

县第一次至第三次残疾人代表大会一览表

表2—06—07

大会次别	召开时间	出席人数	备　注
一	1990.12	63人	主席团成员17人，选举主席1名，副主席3人。
二	1994.12	38人	主席团成员21人，选举主席1名，副主席2人。
三	2007.12	93人（其中：列席42人）	大会选举主席团委员29名，选举主席1名，副主席4名，执行理事会理事长1名，副理事长1名，理事3名。

二、主要活动

教育培训残疾人　1992年9月，在城关镇（今龙场镇）新春村玩易窝兴建特殊教育学校1所，校舍建筑面积388平方米，时收教聋哑儿童16名。2001年9月扩大学校规模，校舍面积增至1183平方米。具备开班11个，寄宿学生150人的特教设施。2002年，校长苏桂秀被评为全国特殊教育先进个人，获“江民特教园丁奖”。自2002年到2005年，在实施“扶残助学春雨行动”项目中，14名残疾人学生受到资助，受助金额1.75万元。2010年，完成城镇和农村残疾人职业培训400人次，新增残疾人就业60人。

2007年12月，召开修文县残疾人联合会第三次代表大会

2003年，六广镇举办精神病防治康复工作培训会

残疾人康复　1998年6月，县残联首次开展“光明行动”，为27人摘除白内障33例，安装晶体33例，脱盲率达100%。9月，举办聋哑儿童语言康复和智残儿童系统化家庭训练家长培训班。聘请市残联罗仕勋部长讲课，主要内容有《聋儿致病因素早期表现预防知识》《聋儿家庭培训知识》等，有

137人参加听课。到2005年通过“光明行动”，使320余名白内障患者重见光明，65名低视力残疾者提高了视力；通过开展聋儿康复训练，使65名聋哑儿童增强听讲功能；通过矫治，为36名肢残人装配假肢；为300名盲人配置铝合金反光膜标准手杖。通过开展精神病防治康复，使98名重型精神病患者得到综合治疗。谷堡乡折溪村精神病人孟启忠，患精神病多年，常被家人关锁控制，1999年经治疗康复后，能进城打工做事，成为一名自食其力的劳动者。2010年，完成白内障手术170例，送治精神病人45例，治愈出院36例。

扶残助残 1991年起，每年5月第三个星期日定为“全国助残日”。1996年5月开展第六个“全国助残日”活动，全县张贴标语180条（幅），走访慰问残疾人170人次，发放慰问金及物资（折款）3700元；为特殊教育学校捐款1200元。1998年，实施《残疾人扶贫攻坚计划》，开展残疾人康复扶贫工作，争取到中央康复扶贫指标460万元，兴办谷堡猕猴桃、板栗基地和龙场镇水塘村园林绿化果木基地，新寨村康尔绿色产品基地等8个项目。投入资金430万元，集中安置一批残疾人就业和带动残疾人脱贫；帮助600户农村贫困残疾人改造了危房和茅草房。搬进新房的残疾人书写“迁新居不忘中共大恩大德，住新房牢记中共富民政策”等门联与感谢中共好政策。开展残疾人技术培训，与有关部门配合进行种植、养殖、家电维修、缝纫、理发、盲人按摩等技术培训，受训残疾人达1355人次。谷堡乡哨上村盲人青年杜相发接受培训后于1999年在县地开办第一家“相发盲人按摩店”从事盲人保健按摩。对“三无”（无劳动能力、无经济收入来源、无亲人照顾）的残疾人，列入城乡最低生活保障对象，由地方财政供养。到2005年，全县8775名残疾人享受城乡最低生活保障。2010年，完成扶贫4500人次，危房改造50户，资助贫困残疾人就读60人。

维护残疾人合法权益 1991年，县残联配合有关单位对《中华人民共和国残疾人保障法》进行宣传，召开座谈会、报告会8场次；印发宣传资料2万份，参与部门46个。1994年，开展“一元钱”捐赠活动，40家单位共捐款3019元。2000年，县政府出台《关于分散按比例安排残疾人就业意见》后，2005年县内诺亚矿业公司聘用46名残疾人集体从业，每人月工资300至400元。到2005年，实现残疾人就业1376人次。从国务院颁布《法律援助条例》起到2005年，残联配合有关部门开展残疾人培训134人次，无偿提供法律援助25件（次），为残疾人当事人赢利经济赔偿10万余元。2004年县第一司法所，第三司法所被省司法厅、省残联命名为省第一批“残疾人维权示范岗”。2010年，共核发各类残疾证3200余份。

开展残疾人文体活动 一是文艺活动。群众性残疾人文艺活动以残疾儿童比较集中的县特殊教育学校最活跃。每年“六一”儿童节和“全国助残日”活动期间，都要组织文艺演出。县特殊教育学校自1992年成立后，创作各类形式的文艺节目120余个，演出70余场次。1996年贵阳市举办残疾人工艺美术作品展，残联每届均组织县内残疾人创作作品参展。至2008年4届残疾人工艺美术作品展期间，残联选送各类残疾人作品144件参展，有20件作品获奖。2001年，在贵阳市庆祝建党80周年残疾人文艺汇演中，县特校选送的舞蹈《阿童木》获三等奖。龙场镇肢残人朱俊水获个人演唱三等奖。二是体育活动。从1998年起，残联均组团参加贵阳市残疾人运动会和选拔运动员参加省的残疾人运动会。1998年，由38名残疾人运动员组成代表团参加市第七届残疾人运动会，5名运动员获个人项目奖，其中六广镇滨江村肢残人候俊庭获男子100米蝶泳第一名，县获得运动会组委会授予的组织奖。1999年，贵州省第二届残疾人运动会上，选派1名乒乓球女运动员和1名45公斤级女子举重运动员加入贵阳市代表团参赛，肢残人女运动员许嘉获乒乓球女子单打冠军，女运动员赵晓丽获45公斤级女子举重冠军。两名残疾人运动员分别受到市、县人民政府残工委表彰和奖励。2002年，县组团参加贵阳市第八届残疾人运动会，获得金牌1枚，银牌4枚，5个第三名和1个第四名，并获得道德风尚奖和组织奖。2010年，组团参加贵阳市第九届残疾人运动会，获得金牌2枚，银牌1枚，铜牌4枚。

第七节　文学艺术界联合会

一、组织建设

1990年9月，县文学艺术界联合会第一次代表大会在县城召开，出席代表85人，会议选举27人组成县第一届文学艺术界联合会。1997年，县文联召开第二次代表大会，出席代表86人。2002年机构改革，明确县文联事业编制3名，设主席1名，副主席1名，列入参照试行国家公务员制度范围。2009年，召开第三次代表大会，出席代表88人，选举35人组成并更名为文联委员会，同时将已成立的文学协会（后改称作家协会）、书法协会、美术协会、摄影协会纳入文联委管理。继后，又将成立的音（乐）舞（蹈）（戏）剧协会纳进文联。至2010年，县文联机构未变。

1990年9月，召开县文学艺术界第一次代表会议

二、主要活动

文学创作　县文学协会于1988年9月成立，有会员43人，选举15人组成常务委员会，7人组成理事会。1997年，第二届理事会成员增为10人。至2010年，会员发展到104人，其中省级会员3人，市级会员16人。文学协会组织喜爱文学者开展创作活动，于1988年12月创办文学刊物《潮水》，至1991年12月出版3期后停办。1997年复刊，更名《栖霞文艺》(季刊)，以发表文学作品为主，辅以其他艺术门类作品，至2010年，共出版35期。

2009年县文联举办纪念改革开放30周年诗词（美文）诵朗会

1990年9月，县文联聘请《山花》主编文志祥、《花溪》编辑叶笛和《安顺文艺》主编周清明莅县作报告，举办阳明笔会，听讲者达140余人，创作作品60余件。1998年4月，县文联与贵阳市文联合作，组织两地作家50余人到大石乡和六广镇采风，历时2天，与当地群众同吃同住，创作62篇（首）作品在《贵州日报》《花溪》杂志上发表。

2002年4月，县文联组织县内文学爱好者50人在谷堡乡举办文学讲座和笔会，聘请《山花》副主编冉正万、《花溪》副主编戴冰讲课。收到作品150件，《栖霞文艺》和《修文报》副刊先后刊载其中60件。1998至2005年共有96人发表作品217件，其中有14件被省、市级期刊选用。2006年，县文联与省文联艺术中心联合，举办“贵州修文阳明诗会”，80名省内诗人和20名县内文学爱好者参加，诗会发布“良知与责任——中国修文诗歌宣言”。2007年，与省作协合作，组织省内作家80人，县内作家30人在县城开展历时两天的“百名作家写修文”采风活动。至2010年，有7名会员出版个人作品集。陈新国短篇小说集《野山》2000年获贵阳市人民政府第五届金筑文艺奖，肖江虹的中篇小说《百鸟朝凤》2009年在《当代》发表，先后被《小说选刊》和《中华文摘》选载。

美术创作　县美术协会于1988年8月成立，会员33人。第一届理事会由12人组成。1997年第二届理事会减为10人。自1988—2005年，会员创作作品达500余件，其中有100余件被遴选为市、省和国家级的展品，有20余件入选省级以上编辑出版的美术册。2004年国庆，县美协组织书画作品80件在贵阳市阳明祠举办“修文县美术书法作品展”，省市书画界知名书画家30余人参加开幕式并观看展出作品。展出6天时间接待观展市民700余人，《贵州日报》《贵阳日报》、贵阳电视台等新闻媒体报道展况。2004年和2007年，理事郝承德分别出版《郝承德书画集》2册。

书法活动　县书法协会于1998年8月成立，会员43人。第一届理事会由18人组成，其中9人为常务理事。1997年由15人组成第二届理事会。至2005年，会员发展到86人。协会于扎佐镇、久长镇、六广镇分别成立书法协会分会。1990—2010年，文联和分会独立举办书法展览30余次，展出作品800余件。会员朱俊首的作品多次入选国家级书展并获奖。郝承德、晏才俊、杨美玉、李暄等会员的50余件作品入选省、市展品。少年书法作者孙瑜、孙崖的作品参加全国性书展并获奖。每年春节将临，书协会员都下至农村为村民义务写春联，初在场天设摊书写，只收取纸张费。从1992年起，每年由财政出资一两千元作为笔墨纸张和乘车费用，由文联组织会员开展此项活动，至2010年，为全县10乡（镇）书写春联达2万余副。

摄影活动　摄影协会于1998年成立，有会员30人，至2010年，会员发展到55人。其中省级会员2人，市级会员5人。1997年，影协配合县委宣传部和贵州摄影家协会举办“六广河风光摄影大赛”活动。2008年，文联组织影协会员深入“抗凝冻，保民生”第一线创作，在抗灾斗争结束后举办“抗凝冻，保民生”主题美术摄影作品展。1988—2010年影协会员创作作品300余件参加县文联举办的展出活动。周尚明、余岚等会员有作品在《贵州日报》《中国摄影报》发表并被收入省、市级出版的摄影作品集。

2009年9月4日，县摄影家协会换届选举

音乐舞蹈戏剧演出　县音乐、舞蹈、戏剧协会（简称音协）于1990年9月成立，会员102人。第一届理事会由19人组成。1997年第二届理事会由15人组成。至2010年，会员人数发展到210人。其中，省级会员9人，市级会员22人。1988—2010年共创作歌曲140首，创作各类剧作50余件，参加各类演出活动400余场次。1992年，刁福林创作的小戏《卖烤烟》获省文艺调演三等奖。1999年，集体创作的《修文之歌》，由县人大常委会作出决定要求全县传唱。2003年，陈新国创作的《王学圣地》电视片脚本由贵阳电

视台搬上荧屏。2006年，舞蹈《红苞谷》在贵阳市第四届群众文艺调演中获一等奖，并被推荐参加2007年全国“群星奖”大赛。会员张禧年创作歌曲80余首，贾文创作歌曲50余首。2002年，贾文创作的《木叶新歌》获团中央举办的歌曲征文奖，2004年获贵阳市第六届金筑文艺奖。

第八节　红十字会修文分会

一、组织建设

1991年12月组建县红十字会，县人民政府以修府通〔1991〕33号文明确县红十字会组成人员。2004年，县政府调整充实县红十字会组织机构，以修委干任〔2004〕04号文明确县卫生局局长胡晓明任常务副会长，卫生局干部王旅黔任秘书长。2004年，县中医院率先成立基层红十字会，由熊文欣任会长，李文峰任副会长，郭松任秘书长，会员33人。2005年，全县10个乡（镇）卫生院相继组建红十字会，乡（镇）卫生院红十字建会率达100%，红十字志愿者34人。2006年，县机构编制委员会以县机编〔2006〕07号文明确县红十字会行政编制1人，事业编制2人，由县财政全额预算管理，人员待遇参照国家公务员制度执行。2006—2007年，修文中学、扎佐中学、六广中学、百信医院、扎佐林场医院等单位成立红十字会。2008—2009年，龙场镇龙岗社区、宾阳社区、栖枫社区、虎山社区组建红十字会服务站。2010年，修文二中、修文三中成立红十字会。到2010年，红十字会修文分会仍存。

二、主要活动

2005年9月，县卫生局和红十字会、贵州省血液中心、贵航高级技工学校联合在技校举办“人间有冷暖，献血见真情”为主题义务献血，要求参加献血300人以上，实际采血352份（人），超贵阳市红十字会下达260人的35.38%。2006年1月至2月，县红十字会在卫生下乡帮扶中开展“博爱送万家”活动，对吸毒人群进行HIV监测，在全县乡村进行广泛的禁毒宣传。4月，红十字会开展“爱心关心暖人心”活动，对贫困、残疾弱势人群进行救助，救助涉及全县8个乡（镇）15个村24户104人。2007年全县献血325人，比计划数超25人。2009年，县红十字会利用“5·8”“9·12”“12·4”等宣传日，联络10乡（镇）红十字会组织开展各类宣传活动50余次，发放宣传资料4万份，积极开展《中华人民共和国红十字会法》《红十字标志使用办法》《中华人民共和国献血法》及《贵阳市捐献遗体和角膜办法》等法律法规宣传。9月组织县属各事业单位干部职工无偿献血，共有261人参与，采血量达7.6万毫升。2010年，县红十字会自筹资金1万元对县100户贫困户进行慰问，开展群众性救护知识培训1400人次，组织无偿献血2次，采集血液7.8万毫升。

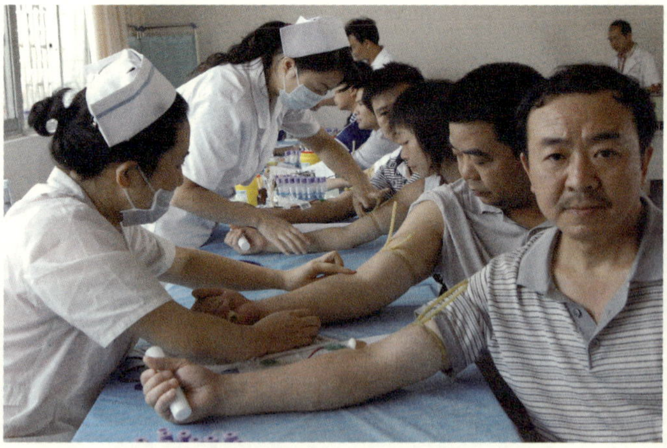

2009年，县红十字会组织干部职工无偿献血

第七章　法　治

第一节　社会治安综合治理

1982年10月，县委成立社会治安综合治理领导小组，下设办公室，提出“社会治安社会治，综合治理综合抓”的工作思路。通过综合治理，使违法犯罪活动得以遏制，使社会治安得以好转。1991年，社会治安综合治理领导小组更名为社会治安综合治理委员会。

一、“普法”教育

1986年启动“一五”（1986—990）普法教育。至1990年，全县近86%有接受教育能力的公民参加普法学习。1992年5月21日，县十届人大七次会议审议批准县的“二五”（1991—1995）普法规划。“二五”普法教育期间，确定小箐乡、城关镇城北村、修文中学、三角山水泥厂为普法试点单位。至1995年，“二五”普法结束，全县有20万人接受法律常识教育。1996年进行“三五”（1996—2000）普法教育，结合精神文明建设和严打斗争、社会治安综合治理等专项工作展开，效果明显，群众法律意识不断增强。2001年，将“依法治县”宣传教育结合“四五”（2001—2005）普法教育一起规划，先后开展依法行政、公正司法、依法治乡（镇）、依法治村、依法治校、依法治企示范点的创建工程。确定县水利局、县人民法院、龙场镇、龙场镇白莲村、城关二小、六广水泥厂为示范点创建单位，然后全县铺开。通过“四五”普法教育，全县普法和依法治理工作实现由提高全民法律意识向提高全民法律素质转变，由注重依靠行政手段管理向注重运用法律手段管理转变的“两个转变”，公民的法律素质和全社会法治化管理水平得到提高。2006年“五五”（2006—2010）普法教育期间，围绕“十一五”规划的实施和法治建设的实际，把法治教育与道德教育有机结合，以“学法律、讲权利、讲义务、讲责任”为主题，广泛开展“法律六进”（进机关、进乡村、进社区、进学校、进企业、进单位）活动，推进社会治安综合治理。

2008年，县直部门开展普法宣传

普法教育除利用广播电视宣传，举办法治讲座，发放宣传资料，举办开展法律咨询，举办法律知识竞赛，召开公捕公判公处大会等形式广泛宣传外，还针对不同普法对象采取不同的普法方式进行。一是领导干部带头学法用法治度化；二是举办各种法律骨干培训班；三是设置法治宣传栏；四是“送法下乡”；五是在青少年学生中普法经常化；六是各部门结合自身实际开展与其相关的专业法宣传。从1996年“三五”普法至2010年“五五”普法的15年间，全县共举办领导干部法治讲座21次，举办各种法律骨干培训班36期，在村（居）委会设置法治宣传栏229个，“送法下乡”370次，发放宣传资料110万份，展出图片200余张，张贴标语400幅，组装宣传车巡回宣传430台次，举办法治文艺演出18次，为学校上法治课50次，开展警示教育26次。通过普法宣传，使全县80%以上的公民受到法治教育，人民群众的法治观念和法律意识明显增强，推动了依法治县进程，进一步促进了社会治安综合治理。

2005年6月，县人民政府与省市民政部门联合在六广镇开展《行政区域界线管理条例》宣传活动

二、开展“严打”和专项治理

从1983年“严打”斗争开始后，政法部门始终坚持“从重从快”严厉打击严重刑事犯罪和经济犯罪的方针，适时组织各种形式的专项斗争和专项治理，打击犯罪分子的嚣张气焰，发挥震慑犯罪的威力和教育群众的作用。

1983年8月，遵照党中央《关于严厉打击刑事犯罪活动的决定》，公安机关开展“三年为期，三个战役”的“严打”斗争。“严打”对象主要是杀人、放火、爆炸、投毒、贩毒、强奸、抢劫、重大盗窃、拐卖人口、强迫引诱容留妇女卖淫等犯罪分子、流氓团伙和为非作歹、横行霸道、欺压群众、危害一方的新“东霸天”“西霸天”以及牢头狱霸等。8月17日深夜，“严打”拉开帷幕。9月18日，在县体育场召开宣判大会，旁听群众万余人。从1980年起，在县城称霸3年多的流氓团伙主犯田景黔、陈俊被判处死刑。宣判会后田景黔等7名被处极刑的严重刑事罪犯被押赴刑场执行枪决。11月14日，再次在体育场召开宣判大会，杨荣飞、蒋晓波等12名罪犯被处以死刑。至1986年10月，三年“严打”斗争结束。在“严打”斗争中，共收审违法犯罪人员740人，提请批准逮捕485人，判刑339人，其中死刑27人，摧毁犯罪团伙54个202人。

2007年，县开展“严打‘两抢一盗’专项斗争”期间召开的公判大会

1996年，执行党中央再次作出的在全国开展“严打”集中统一行动的决定。“严打”中，全县侦破刑事案84件，摧毁犯罪团伙9个30人，抓获作案、批捕在逃人员33人，先后有11名犯罪分子慑于法律的威严，到公安机关投案自首。

在开展专项斗争和专项治理行动中，针对什么犯罪突出就打击什么犯罪。1984年组织“打流窜”

统一行动，收审一批流窜犯罪分子。1985年建立整顿铁路治安领导小组，组织民兵护路队昼夜巡逻，打击在铁路沿线行凶抢劫的车匪路霸。1987—1990年，针对拐卖人口案件突出的实际，县打拐办、公安局、妇联等部门密切配合，解救出160名妇女和11名儿童，惩处“人贩子”64名。1993年先后开展“追逃犯，打流窜”、“打击卖淫嫖娼”、“打击车匪路霸”等专项斗争，使刑事发案下降，社会治安好转。1996年开展“追逃打流”“禁毒”“打拐”“扫黄打非”等专项行动，抓获一批犯罪人员。2002年开展“打黑除恶”斗争中，重点打击称霸一方的洒坪乡阳桥黑恶势力，维护了企业正常的生产秩序。2005年起，以打击“两抢一盗”（抢劫、抢夺，盗窃）侵财性案件为重点，严惩违法犯罪分子，有效震慑犯罪。公安部门开展打击犯罪的集中统一行动16次，出动警力4550人次，车辆1400台次。检察机关受理提请批准逮捕刑事案件163件288人。审判机关刑事收案170件304人，结案154件252人。2005—2010年，公安机关侦破刑事案件3636起，打击一批危害社会危害人民生命财产安全的犯罪人员，使社会治安明显向好，人民群众对县内社会治安的满意率达90%以上。其间，公安机关于2005年侦破以严郁华为首的黑恶势力破坏龙场镇杨寨村村委会选举案，团伙头目严郁华被判处有期徒刑20年，其余12名骨干成员分别被判处20年至2年不等的有期徒刑。此案2007年经省高院二审宣判后，引起媒体关注，2009年12月13日，中央电视台《焦点访谈》播出的《黑帮染指农村基层选举》节目，深入报道该案。

2008年8月10日，严厉打击刑事犯罪公捕大会

专记：乡村黑社会的覆灭

2004年12月，龙场镇杨寨村准备选举村民委员会主任，家住白云区的乡村黑社会头目严郁华企图让其手下罗善发的亲戚杨昌达当上村主任，以便掌控村里的铝矿开采权。选举之前，严就指使手下在村民中采取贿选手段拉选票，一个选民发给50元或100元买下投杨昌达的一票，一下发出2.3万元。但23日选举结果，杨昌达的票数低于另一候选人。未等唱票结束，严郁华就指使罗善发、文仁祥等10余名黑社会成员冲进会场砸桌子、摔板凳捣乱，迫使选举改期进行。2005年2月22日，杨寨村再次投票选举村主任，为防止黑恶势力捣乱，县委、县政府指示县公安局为此次换届选举保驾护航。

严郁华一伙为达到让杨昌达当选的目的，于选举当天清早由文仁祥等纠集白云区艳山红镇和大山洞镇的黑社会成员近百人，8时在白云大酒店门口上车，安排人买了几十根木棒，每人发1双白手套，携带几十把管制刀具及仿“六四式”手枪、火药枪气势汹汹地冲进杨寨。这帮人赶到杨寨会场时，为张扬不达目的誓不罢休的声势，竟警告上次收了钱没有投杨昌达票的村民，并频频点燃“地滚龙”土炮仗扔向会场，震得会场四周鸡飞狗叫，小孩被吓得大哭不止。紧接着，又捡起石块、砖头，砸向会场门窗，气焰十分嚣张。

严郁华等“示威”后，即离开会场想回到村外停车的上坝煤厂。孰料，接到报警赶来的百余公安干警已在这里张网以待，警车呼啸而至，将这帮人团团围住，当场抓获寻衅滋事的黑社会成员89人，收缴管制刀具31把，木棒50根，仿“六四式”手枪两支及子弹6发，双管、单管火药枪3支及轿车、面包车

18辆。

继后，贵阳市公安局成立了以局长邹碧声为组长，副局长肖家璇、刘维亚为副组长，市公安局刑侦支队和修文县公安局等单位组成“2·22”专案组对以严郁华为首的黑恶势力立案侦查。此案被公安部列为督办案件。经过专案组缜密侦查,彻底查清了以严郁华为首的黑社会性质犯罪组织的罪行,并成功将严郁华等13名组织成员抓获归案，缴获自制手枪8支、火药枪2支、各类刀具30把、木棒50根等凶器。2006年4月17日，贵阳市中级人民法院作出一审判决，严郁华等向贵州省高级人民法院提起上诉。2007年2月17日，贵州省高级人民法院对以严郁华为首的黑社会性质犯罪组织作出终审判决，维持贵阳市中级人民法院对严郁华、文仁祥、杨光华、王加义、罗善发、钱军、张卓全、柯勇等8人的一审判决。主犯严郁华因犯组织、领导黑社会性质组织罪，非法买卖枪支、弹药、爆炸物罪，聚众扰乱社会秩序罪和赌博罪，被判处有期徒刑20年，剥夺政治权利3年，并处罚金人民币1万元。以参加黑社会性质组织罪，非法买卖枪支、持有枪支、弹药、爆炸物罪，聚众扰乱社会秩序罪分别判处文仁祥、杨光华、王加义、罗善发、钱军、张卓全、柯勇7人有期徒刑20年至5年。另以参加黑社会性质组织罪，聚众扰乱社会秩序罪，非法买卖枪支、非法持有枪支罪分别判处蔡定生、刘力贵、李长顺、杨昌达、王正峰5人有期徒刑4年至2年。

2007年，贵州省高级法院二审严郁华

严郁华黑社会性质犯罪组织受到法律严惩后，在社会各界引起广泛关注和强烈反响，特别是曾受到该黑社会性质犯罪组织欺压、残害的龙场镇杨寨村和白云区麦架镇下堰村广大群众无不拍手称快。

附：

中央电视台《焦点访谈》：黑帮染指农村基层选举

前不久，全国打黑办公布了打黑除恶专项斗争三年来的成果。在破获、公诉及审结的各类案件中，有一个特点值得关注，那就是黑社会性质组织对农村基层民主选举的把持、破坏，从而达到对农村基层政权的渗透。

2005年2月22日，是贵州修文县龙场镇杨寨村村委会换届选举的日子。这一天，10多辆面包车载着100多名手持刀棍的人突然闯进村寨，给一个名叫杨昌达的候选人造声势。接到报警后，修文县公安局的民警迅速赶到了现场。在对犯罪嫌疑人进行审查后，警方认定，这是一起有组织的黑社会性质犯罪案件，团伙头目名叫严郁华，他们操纵杨寨村选举的目的是要掌控该村的铝矿。早在2002年，严郁华就插手基层民主选举。当时，在白云区的下堰村进行换届选举时，严郁华等人通过威胁和利诱村民，使一个叫卢德华的村民成功当选。卢德华一上任，便将没有任何资质的严郁华任命为工程队队长，凭着这个身份，严郁华等人包揽了多项工程。短短两年时间，就赚得80多万元。之后，严郁华又分别在白云区的麦架村、高山村和程官村上演了这一幕，把这些村的选举搅得乌烟瘴气。贵州省高级人民法院对这个黑社会性质犯罪团伙进行了终审判决。团伙头目严郁华被判处有期徒刑20年，其余12名骨干成员分别被判处

20年至2年不等的有期徒刑。

据全国打黑办发布的信息，当前我国黑恶势力犯罪还处于活跃期，对基层政权建设的危害仍然突出。当前和今后一段时期，打击黑恶势力的任务依然长期、艰巨和复杂。

（来源：2009.12.13央视网）

三、预防犯罪

县委治安综合委员会抓综合治理工作，注重发挥公安、检察、法院、司法、民政、工会、青年团、妇联、文化等综治委成员单位的职能作用，预防犯罪。检察机关根据办案中发现的问题，有针对性地向有关单位提出检察建议。1986年，在办理航空工业部属庆文机械厂一盗窃案中，针对厂基建仓库5年时间被同一人盗窃50多次，且携带赃物从值班室门口通过无人察觉的严重情况，发出检察建议，庆文厂按检察建议内部整改，加强防范，避免类似案件的再发生。审判机关利用召开公开宣判大会，对判处缓、管、免人员进行回访帮教等形式，落实“打防结合，预防为主”的方针。1999年，县人民法院在小箐乡对杀害郭田村村委会主任的罪犯胡荣坤公开宣判，执行死刑，扩大办案社会效果。2000年起，加强刑释解教人员的安置帮教工作，至2010年已形成全县上下衔接、左右配合的安置帮教网络，公、检、法、司等部门组织帮教团到劳改单位对修文籍服刑人员进行帮教，帮教率达94.4%。同时，对监外执行罪犯强化管理措施，杜绝脱管、漏管现象，有效地预防监外执行罪犯重新犯罪。

2005年5月24日，县人民法院到羊艾农场帮教修文籍服刑人员

四、平安修文工程

1997年，县综治委制定《关于“平安工程”创建活动的意见》，下达各乡（镇）创建“平安小区”“平安单位”、“平安村寨”的任务数，启动“平安工程”试点。1998年创建活动铺开，创建“平安工程”工作步入制度化、规范化轨道，获省综治委授予“平安工程红旗县”称号。至2010年，全县社会治安防控体系基本建成，10个乡（镇）均达平安乡（镇）创建标准。

五、治安防控网络

2008年起，以县委办、政府办、维稳办、信访局、公安局110报警台为综治维稳信息枢纽，10个乡（镇）政法委（综治办）、派出所、司法所为主体，全县村和社区为辐射，构建综治维稳信息网络，明确综治维稳信息员240人，确保信息畅通，及时消化各种矛盾纠纷。并在全县各级各部门建立应急分队，组织党员干部参与治安维稳防控。2009年已实现“110”“119”“122”报警台“三台合一”，接处警率达100%。

2009—2010年，坚持“打防结合，预防为主”的方针，构建起全县齐抓共管的治安防范网络。按照治安防范网格化的要求，科学设立和划分巡逻责任区（段），强化对城区街面的控制能力，在主要交通要道和区域边界设置卡口、卡点13个，在县城中心龙岗广场设报警室，对群众的报警求助及时处置。乡

（镇）综治部门在行政村成立以村组干部、退伍军人和民兵为骨干的治安联防队，构建以守村护寨为基础的农村治安防控网络。按照“谁经营、谁负责”的行业管理责任制建起行业治安防控网络，县公安、工商、文化、交通、城建、劳动等部门坚持定期对网吧、文化娱乐业和汽车租赁业等特种行业以及旅游风景区开展安全检查、涉爆涉枪安全隐患检查。2010年，开展“平安乡镇”“平安社区”“平安村寨”“安全文明校园”创建活动，激励人民群众“建一方文明，保一方平安”，全县60%村组实现零发案、低发案和80%的村组实现零上访、低上访的目标。

2008年5月，民兵在县城巡逻

第二节　公 安

一、机构设置

1978年，县公安局设置秘书股、政保股、经保股、预审股、消防科、看守所和扎佐、六广、久长、城关4个派出所。后随工作业务变动或增或减或合或拆或更名，至2010年12月，设执法勤务机构8个，即指挥中心（加挂办公室牌子）、安全与经济文化保卫大队、刑事侦查大队、交通警察大队（加挂公路巡逻民警大队牌子）、治安管理大队、禁毒大队、公共信息网络安全监察大队、巡逻（特警）大队；设综合管理机构4个，即政工室、纪检监察室（加挂警务督察大队牌子）、法治室、警务保障室；设派出机构11个，即龙场镇派出所、扎佐镇景阳派出所、扎佐镇三元派出所、久长镇派出所、六广镇派出所、六屯乡派出所、谷堡乡派出所、小箐乡派出所、大石乡派出所、洒坪乡派出所、六桶乡派出所。

二、队伍建设

（一）学习教育

1978年起，县公安局开展多种形式的学习教育活动，学习理论，宣传典型。1979年，以学习公安部《关于重新印发<人民公安机关开展先进工作者活动试行办法>的通知》为契机，开展“学先进争先进”活动。1987年，组织学习邓小平《坚持四项基本原则，反对资产阶级自由化》和《建设有中国特色社会主义》等文章，加深理解社会主义与发展商品经济、与民主建设、与改革开放的关系。1994

2007年，县公安局警察训练基地开班

年组织干警学习《人民警察法》，开展刑侦业务、政保基础工作等培训。1995年，组织学习《中华人民共和国国家赔偿法》。1996年起，掀起“学济南交警，做优秀警察”热潮，涌现出一批先进典型。2000年，在“三讲”教育活动中，组织学习上级规定的理论读本。2001年开展“三个代表”重要思想学习实践活动。2003年在全局开展“三项教育”（全心全意为人民服务的宗旨教育、实事求是的思想路线教育、严格公正文明执法的法治教育）活动。2006年起，开展社会主义法治理念教育和社会主义荣辱观教育活动。2008—2010年，开展“深入解放思想，推进科学发展”为主题的教育活动。通过学习教育，全县民警确立“立警为公，执法为民”的指导思想，努力“打造一流队伍，培育一流作风，创建一流业绩”，为全县的“改革、发展、稳定”营造良好的政治环境和治安环境。

（二）制度建设

1980起，将公安干警审批农转非户口和车辆证照发放权力集中警务岗位，实行“两公开一监督”（公开办事程序、公开办事结果，加强群众监督）制度。1992年，按照公安部《关于坚决制止公安干警刑讯逼供的决定》，制定《审查讯问工作规程》，防止违法违规行为。是年12月，全县首批33名警察被授予警督警衔，69名警察被授予警司、警员警衔。1994年，制定《修文县人民警察正规化管理暂行办法》。1995年，试行“民警警诫制度”和“错案责任追究制度”，增强民警严格执法观念。1996年，推行“警诫待岗制度”和“禁酒令”。2003年，组织学习“五条禁令”（严禁违反枪支管理使用规定，违者予以纪律处分，造成严重后果的，予以辞退或者开除；严禁携带枪支饮酒，违者予以辞退，造成严重后果的，予以开除；严禁酒后驾驶机动车，违者予以辞退，造成严重后果的，予以开除；严禁在工作时间饮酒，违者予以纪律处分，造成严重后果的，予以辞退或者开除；严禁参与赌博，违者予以辞退，情节严重的，予以开除）。2004年8月26日凌晨，猪贩万兴胡、吕大洪等5人从毕节往贵阳运猪途中，车行至修文县城,遭遇酒后上街寻衅滋事的居民宋广纠缠，车辆无法通行。经龙场派出所民警协调未果，转由交警处理,而交警部门接警后未及时出警，致使当事双方矛盾激化，宋广抢占运猪车辆的驾驶室不让车开走，因时间过久造成生猪死亡4头伤病17头的事件。事件经媒体报道后，引起县公安局重视，除赔偿猪贩损失5000元外，还对民警在办案过程中出现的过失进行深刻反省。事后，公安局举一反三，以“8·26案件”为教训，迅速在全县公安系统开展一场自查自省自纠活动。2006—2010年，先后制定出台《公安局三不准、四严禁规定》《民警执法责任制度》《民警执法过错责任追究办法》等20项制度。2010年，交警大队在整治贵（阳）毕（节）路扎佐收费站车辆拥堵和驾驶员偷逃过路费的为期5个月行动中，接受收费站按每月9000元给予的协勤人员生活补贴费用。县公安局获悉后，责令交警大队退还违规收取的4.5万元。

2008年1月，全县警力整治启动仪式

（三）创新争优

1978年，全县公安机关以学雷锋、学硬骨头六连为主要内容，全面开展争当先进工作者活动。1979年，贯彻公安部《关于重新印发<人民公安机关开展先进工作者活动试行办法>的通知》，全县公安系统开展立功创模活动。此后，创新争优、立功创模成为公安局至2010年常年开展的重要活动。其间，1995年开展“争当刑警、治安警、交警、户籍警标兵”活动。1998年，基层派出所民警罗林被公安部授予全国优秀人民警察称号。全局即以学习罗林为主线，开展争创“让人民满意公安队伍”活动，邀请罗林介绍“立足基层，建功立业”的先进事迹。2004年，在开展“远学任长霞，近学蒋庆”活动中，巡防队员刘熙于9月26日勇斗歹徒英勇牺牲，贵州省人民政府追认刘熙为革命烈士。从1998—2010年，县公安局先后被授予全市“优秀公安局”“严打先进单位”等称号，叶礼贵、杨志黔、杨军、晏正伦等97名公安民警立功受奖，涌现出罗林、王晓刚、戴宗林等一批全国、全省和市级先进民警。

三、刑事侦查

1980年，公安局建立刑事侦查队，专司刑事案件侦破工作，当年侦破案件55起，破案率达88.6%。1983年起，先后开展“打现行、破大案、挖团伙、追逃犯”，打击“车匪路霸”“打黑除恶”“利剑行动”“严打‘两抢一盗’”等一系列专项斗争，破获一批有重大影响的案件，依法逮捕一批刑事犯罪分子，摧毁一批流氓犯罪团伙。

1983—1986年“严打”期间，提请批准逮捕作案人员485名，判刑339人（其中死刑27名），摧毁犯罪团伙54个。此后，针对刑事犯罪发案趋向复杂化，作案人员手段残忍、流动性大的特点，继续保持“严打”态势，增加刑侦干警和器材设备，加大侦破力度，及时侦破大案要案。1987年发生刑事案件122起，破获88起，破案率为72.1%。其中重大案件32起，破获30起，破案率为90.9%。之后，随着县域经济不断发展，社会转型期的矛盾日趋突出，发案率增高，而破案率相对降低。1988年发案140起，比上年上升12.8%，破98起，破案率只70%。其中重大案件62起，破43起，破案率为71%。1989年刑事案件高达723起，仅破300起，破案率为41.9%。1990年，针对县内盗窃案发案率高，群众缺少安全感的实际，先后组织3次反盗窃专项斗争和2次破案会战，立刑事案件642件，破获338件，破案率从上年的41.9%提高到52.64%。1991年加大破案力度，破案率上升到72.62%。对刑案侦破的稳、准、狠，有效地遏制了县内刑案高发的趋势，其中嚣张一时的抢劫庙宇案，在修文、开阳、息烽、金沙4个县公安部门的严密协作下，仅两个星期就将列为安顺地区的要案予以侦破。1992年刑事案件下降到396起，侦破311起，破案率为78.53%。1993年，刑案又下降到278起，侦破228起，破案率为82.01%。

1998年，推进刑事侦查改革和派出所改革，实现侦审合一。3月，按照省公安厅《关于改革和加强刑事侦查工作的决定》，撤销四科（预审）组建刑侦大队，下设刑侦中队，划分侦查破案责任区，建立健全激励机制和办案责任制。是年，立刑事案381起，破229起，破案率为74.11%。2000年起，刑事案件再度呈高发现象，立案727起，发案率与1999年比较，上升90.81%。2001年，立刑事案1212起，破647起，抓获犯罪人员450名，抓获网上在逃人员46名，收缴财物折款24万余元。

2002年，刑侦工作以“打黑除恶”为主线，开展重点整治，对长期干扰、破坏洒坪乡阳桥煤厂的地方恶势力进行严厉打击，抓获以黄以军为首的7名犯罪分子，收缴火药枪5支。与此同时，加强情报信息工作，共收集犯罪信息资料2310份，为侦查破案提供有力线索。开展网上追逃，抓获网上在逃人员190名。及时破获久长镇焚尸案，龙场镇系列强奸、抢劫案。2004年，开展“命案必破”专项行动。全县发生的7起杀人案，破获6起。10月23日，龙场镇翠屏西路183号住户家中发现两男一女3具尸体。办案民警多次现场勘查和尸检勘验，调查走访，查明死者吴道群因其夫在外强制戒毒，遂与刑满释放人员张梦林姘居。在得知丈夫即将戒毒期满返家，便提出与张梦林分手断绝关系。张梦林对此怀恨在心，将吴道群及其儿子梁浩杀死后，把吴的尸体拖至床边用石灰掩埋，将梁浩的尸体焚烧后分尸，并将部分尸块丢进厕所内。之后，张梦林畏罪服毒自杀身亡。轰动全县的三尸案终于告破。

2005—2010年，刑侦工作以创建“平安修文”为载体，实施“居有所安”工程，深入开展严打“‘两抢一盗’、保卫百姓平安”行动，加大对“命案”和“恶性案件”等影响大的案件以及群众反映强烈的“多发性”案件的侦破打击力度。此间，刑事案件累计立案4105起，破案3636起，群众安全感和满意度达90%以上。2003年12月28日，扎佐镇康乐浴室一顾客在洗浴接受保健按摩时被他人持刀杀伤，送医院抢救途中死亡，嫌疑人外逃。案发后公安局成立专案组开展侦破工作。近1年半的时间，专案组民警行程数千公里，遍查嫌疑人的社会关系和家庭情况，疏理甄别大量的信息和线索。但嫌疑人好似人间蒸发，音讯全无。2005年5月26日，专案组获得嫌疑人用化名“陈勇”在广西南丹大厂镇一带打工的信息。随即组成抓捕组赶赴南丹大厂镇，于27日成功将嫌疑人抓获。此间，又相继破获影响恶劣的“6·06”洒坪凶杀案、“9·12”岩洞腐尸案、六桶“2·06”命案和残杀4岁幼女案。2010年1月13日，小箐乡境内发生1起抢劫摩托车杀害车主的恶性案件，刑侦干警经过7个月侦查，于7月12日将凶手抓获归案。

2010年8月18日洒坪乡东庄村四组村民胡大胜为洒坪乡派出所送来锦旗，感谢派出所为其追回被盗物资

专记一：系列劫庙要案侦破记

1991年，扎佐镇四明洞庙宇遭到歹徒抢劫，时任县公安局长的苏善立即指派干警前往侦破。正在调查中又传来周边开阳、息烽、金沙等地也不断发生抢劫庙宇、强奸、杀人等恶性案件，特别是金沙县的庙宇抢劫案十分残忍，除抢劫财物外，还将一个庙宇中的两名尼姑强奸后杀害并抛尸河里。对此，群众反映强烈，公安机关压力很大。1992年5月，安顺地区破案会战开始，将修文县的庙宇抢劫案件列入重点侦破案件，指定刑侦队队长吴超群任专案组长，王新华等为组员，局长苏善担任总指挥专攻此案。

5月30日由修文县公安局牵头召开修文、开阳、息烽、金沙县刑侦队破案联席会。会上，各县通报了发案情况，经过梳理，得出几个县发生庙宇抢劫案的特点是：作案目标相同，都以庙宇为抢劫对象；作案手段相同，撬门入室先打掉光源，捆绑受害人；3至5人持火管枪、菜刀、卡子刀等凶器；见什么抢什么，见女的先调戏、搜身、强奸，将室内的锅碗瓢盆、油盐米菜、菩萨盖头的红布、尼姑和尚穿的衣服等洗劫一空；团伙成员之间相互结合交叉作案，他们白天踩点，在附近藏匿到夜深人静时，突然袭击庙宇，作案后，又窜到外地销赃挥霍。

经过分析，联席会议决定将4县抢劫庙宇案件并案侦查。开阳县刑侦队提供了1个重要线索，他们在修文县久长镇追回了1个犯罪嫌疑人销赃的手表。经过深入调查、分析、排查摸清了作案嫌疑人，但无证据。会议决定，各县把抢庙宇案件再作清理，抓紧侦查，发现情况及时汇报，修文县公安局运用从传讯嫌疑人切入，然后顺藤摸瓜，以此为突破口的策略，由局长亲自召集刑侦队和久长镇派出所干警研究方案，久长镇派出所干警夜以继日地进行调查取证。在群众的协助下，仅用3天时间就查到作案嫌疑人是白窑村的史大明，当即采取果断措施对其传讯审查。

作案嫌疑人慑于法律的威严，交代了参与抢劫庙宇的犯罪事实。他交代的5起案件中与刑侦队勘察的现场情况吻合。通过审讯，还掌握了其他犯罪成员，苏善当机立断下令拘禁。并及时将情况向息烽、开阳、金沙通报。当得知参与强奸、杀害两名尼姑的凶手已潜回金沙的信息，立即电告金沙抓人。1992年6月5日杀人凶手终于在金沙落网。金沙县公安局局长陈兴瑜和刑侦队指导员罗文华专程赶到修文了解破案进展情况提审人犯。提审后，陈兴瑜感慨地说："困扰我们1年多的系列抢庙案件终于在修文告破了，这就是兄弟县并肩战斗的结果。否则，这些案件不知要拖到啥时候。"

经过两个星期奋战，摧毁一个抢劫、强奸、杀人的犯罪团伙，11名成员中抓获7人，1人投案，1人在安顺劫庙时摔死，还有2人在逃。他们共作案24起，涉及7个县、市，强奸3人，杀死2人，捆绑受害人30余人，在已破的24起案件中，有23起是抢劫庙宇案件。

专记二：8小时侦破一起绑架强奸抢劫案

1999年8月3日晚11时，罗刚、罗锡健、吴英明、朱彪4人纠合在一起，在贵阳市黔灵湖边抢劫1辆桑塔纳轿车，强行对车上1名叫高争丰的男子和1名女青年搜身，劫得现金250余元和手机2部后，由罗刚将车开往修文方向。

当晚12时，车开至白云区麦架乡六道拐处，罗刚将女青年拖下车进行强奸。次日凌晨3时，车行至久长电影院门口公路处，罗刚、吴英明下车冒充派出所干警，对一辆东风车的驾驶员强行搜身，劫得现金6300元。凌晨4时，车行至久长羊马田一打砂厂处，罗锡健等将高争丰押下车，罗刚在车上再次强奸女青年。凌晨5时许，罗刚将车开到修文小河沟大麻窝公路边停下，威逼高争丰通知妻子带20万元前来赎人。高用手机与妻子通话联系后，高妻于中午11时将15万元交到罗刚一伙人手里。巨款到手，4人驾车逃离，将高争丰3人扔在原地。

高争丰等3人当天中午向县公安局报案。

公安局接报案后，立即投入大量警力侦破。一面组织各派出所民警上路堵截，一面到小河沟煤矿附近实地调查。调查中找到被罗刚丢弃的轿车，并获悉4人已租车逃往遵义方向。

8月4日8时，公安局刑侦干警在遵义警方协助下，将正在遵义一酒店寻欢作乐的罗刚等4人抓获，缴获现金13.6万余元和用劫款购买的金戒指、金项链、衣物及手机4部。此时，距受害人报案刚好8小时。

四、户籍管理

1979年，农村以生产大队户口底卡和生产队口粮分配名单为基础，重新登记户主、户数、人口、男女等内容和数据。城镇户口由公安派出所登记。1981年清理整顿全县户口，更换户口底卡，按生产队、路段、厂矿家属区为单位装订成5948册。1985年增办暂住户口登记，规定外地人在县城居住1月以上，须办暂住户口证。是年，外地流入县境人口4735人，办暂住户口2037人。1988年，对流动人口实行"谁用人谁管理"的原则，全年办理暂住户口608人。1989年实行居民身份证，户口管理逐渐规范化、制度化。至1990年，颁发身份证16.7万个。是年，配合全国人口普查，查明全县人口为26.7万人，其中，男性13.9万人，女性12.8万人。全县有家庭户5.9万户，集体户319户。

1991年成立户政科，办理临时身份证258人，农村户口转城镇居民（简称"农转非"）95户228

人。颁发身份证2211人。1992年“建并撤”后，各乡镇派出所接管农村户口管理。至2010年，户政业务均按政策规定办理。其间，1992年以收费方式突击办理“农转非”户口，1个户口收费4500元，1个月后停办，有405人通过“买户口”的方式，从农村户口转为城镇居民户口。

五、治安管理

（一）禁毒

自1980年起，县内吸毒贩毒者骤然增多，公安机关加强查处，一经发现，立即给以打击。1987年至1989年，破贩毒案8起，种植罂粟案20起，铲除罂粟苗5300株。1990年，县公安局与民政和卫生部门联合，在县城川会馆办戒毒班两期，56名吸毒人员参加。1995年，针对贩毒严重，吸毒人员有增无减的实际，开展6次禁毒专项行动，开展“6·26”国际禁毒日宣传咨询活动，抓获种、吸、贩毒人员68人，捣毁贩毒窝点5个。1998年，将设于行政拘留所内的戒毒所迁至龙场镇建新村原王官乡政府住址，收进戒吸毒人员271人次，报劳动教养21人。1999年组建禁毒科，开展“90天扫毒大行动”，运用出禁毒墙报、办禁毒讲座、举行禁毒签名活动、发放宣传资料等在群众中广泛进行禁毒宣传教育。

2000年起，严格执行“吸毒一律强戒、复吸一律劳教、贩毒一律刑事处罚”的方针，加强“四禁”（禁贩、禁制、禁种、禁吸）工作，坚持“打零包、破大案、堵源截流”的工作思路，开展各种禁毒专项行动。2002年开展“春夏扫毒风暴”行动，2003年强化“无毒社区”创建和巩固工作，全县创建“无毒社区”10个。2004年开展“利剑行动”“飓风扫毒行动”，撤销禁毒科，成立禁毒工作大队。

2006年10月，启动3年创建“无毒县”工作，按照“抓宣传，造声势；抓禁吸，重帮教；抓打击，见实效；抓创建，强巩固”的要求，强力推进禁毒工作。公安局坚持“四禁并举，预防为主，严格执法，综合治理”的方针，以“打团伙，破大案，摧网络，追毒资，断毒源”为目标，开展“雷霆行动”，严厉打击毒品犯罪，大石布依族乡启用“五支队伍”参与禁毒宣教，确保巩固“无毒乡”称号。至2009年，在3年创无毒县期间，破获毒品案177起，抓获犯罪嫌疑人194人，缴获海洛因1198.22克。

县公安局在城镇街头宣传毒品的危害

2010年，实施“禁毒预防、禁吸戒毒、禁毒严打、堵源截流、禁毒严管”五大战役，成效显著，龙场、扎佐、久长3镇实现“无贩毒、无制毒、无复吸、无新增吸毒人员、无非法种植毒品原植物”的“五无”乡镇。

（二）禁赌

1978年后，随着经济发展和人民生活提高，加之管理工作未跟上，致社会不良现象乘虚而入，尤其是赌博竟成公害。1980年9月，扎佐镇派出所一夜查获3场赌博，抓获赌徒43人，收缴赌具6副。随后几年，由于禁赌措施不力，赌风愈演愈烈，以打麻将为主的“方城战”泛滥。1985年，公安局加大禁赌力度，投入大量警力，抓赌345起，查获赌场78个，仅县城就抓获参赌者207人。视参赌者情节轻重，分别给予罚款，行政拘留等处罚，赌风有所收敛。1986年县八届人大三次会议上，人大代表强烈呼吁狠刹赌博风，维护社会治安秩序。公安局狠抓禁赌工作，处理赌博人员168人，其中治安处罚163人，劳教5人，使赌博风得以控制。

1987—1988年，公安机关组织5次打击赌博专项行动，抓获赌徒225人，收缴赌资3万余元。1994年8月，在城关镇开展大规模刹赌风行动，处罚赌徒54人。1996年查处赌博案104起。后来，由于禁赌时紧时松，赌博之风屡禁不止，甚至出现蔓延趋势。

2004年12月8日，县公安局与贵阳市公安局刑侦支队打黑大队联手，出动200余名警力，30余台警车，端掉距扎佐镇20公里处山坡上的一大赌场，抓获违法人员120余人，现场收缴赌资30余万元，查扣涉案车辆40余台。

2005年后，人民生活水平提高较快，“小赌怡情”成为时尚，打麻将、玩扑克博一点小彩头不再认为是赌博，被称作“精武馆”的麻将馆可以公开营业，餐馆、茶楼无处不见麻将桌，甚至大街上也有人打麻将玩扑克小赌。至2010年，公安局打击赌博也只针对聚赌和赌资大的赌博行为，对500元以下的小额博彩不再制止。

（三）特种行业管理

从1978年起，属公安机关管理的特种行业经营户逐年增多，1985年全县有特种行业经营户122家。为加强管理，公安局与工商部门配合，制定特种行业的审查、登记、办证、定期换证、不定期检查等制度，确定特业户的经营范围，凭证经营，有报必查，违者必纠。1987年，查处一录像放映室播放淫秽录像牟利行为，取缔无证经营旅社1家。1989年实行居民身份证后，规定投宿者必须持身份证。

1991年，对特种行业清理整顿，查明县内旅社、出租私房、废品收购点、录像室、娱乐室、茶社、舞厅、夜市营业性舞厅、个体书摊等特业经营户124家。继后，坚持定期和不定期检查相结合加强管理。1993年，对特业检查中查出有经营户贩卖淫秽录像带和书刊，有经营户容留妇女卖淫，均按法律法规惩处。1999年，对全县娱乐场所清理检查158家次，对废品收购点清理检查20家次，对印刷、复印经营户清理检查38家次，与文化部门配合开展“扫黄打非”行动10次。清理检查中查出33家特业经营户有违规经营行为，均作停业整顿处理。2003年，县政府投资5万元专款改造县城公共消防水栓，重点在特种行业较多的龙场、扎佐、久长、六广4镇开展“禁赌、禁娼”专项行动，抓获处理一批违法犯罪人员。

2005年起，特种行业经营户日渐增多，公安局加大管理力度，除日常管理外，并对各类行业从业人员进行遵纪守法的宣传教育。是年，培训从业人员250人次，发放宣传资料2万份，开展专项检查10次，检查行业、场所340家次，下发《限期整改通知书》100余家次，停业整顿11家，取缔无证收购点2家。

2006年，按“平安修文”建设的要求，建立健全行业场所治安防控网络和以堵塞犯罪空隙为目标的监管机制，对特种行业实行“谁经营、谁负责”的行业管理责任制。与工商、文化、交通、城建、劳动等相关部门配合，坚持定期对网吧、文化娱乐业、汽车租赁业、旅社业等开展安全大检查和涉爆涉枪安全隐患大检查，有效遏制各类违法犯罪活动。每逢“五一”和“十一”旅游黄金周前，县政府安委会均要组织公安、交通、旅游部门对旅游景点、公共场所进行检查，堵塞安全漏洞，消除安全隐患。黄金周期间，相关部门均要派出人力维护交通秩序、景点秩序和公共秩序。至2010年，黄金周期间均无一例安全事故发生。

（四）危险物品管理

爆炸物品管理 按照县公安局规定爆炸物品须由使用人申请并经批准后才可使用，但在管理过程中也常有事故发生。1979年1月，六屯公社二洞小水电站工地保管员谢发举分发雷管时吸烟，烟火掉入雷管盒引起爆炸，当场炸死2人，炸伤4人。9月，三元公社水塘五队吴云华烘烤受潮雷管引起爆炸，炸死3

人，炸伤6人，毁坏房屋27间。

1983年“严打”斗争中，公安局加强对爆炸物品监督检查，收缴一批违规爆炸物品。1984年，根据《中华人民共和国爆炸物品管理条例》规定，公安局健全对爆炸物品的生产、储存、销售、运输和使用管理制度，规定销售炸药必须经公安局批准，使用炸药必须有乡政府以上单位证明，并对爆破人员进行培训，经考试合格者发给爆破证。1985年，公安局配合工商部门制订对境内鞭炮制造、储运管理制度。但管理仍有疏漏，发生犯罪分子用炸药爆炸杀人案。1990年6月18日晚，宝寨乡张福华、方正祥利用炸药爆炸故意杀人，致1人重伤，房屋炸毁。后张福华被判处死刑，方正祥被判死缓。

1992—1995年，公安局加强管理，共收缴违规炸药1562.5公斤，雷管2181枚，导火绳3447米。1996年，清理全县爆炸作业点378处，取缔非法储存炸药点31处，收缴炸药690公斤，雷管1867枚，导火绳1403米。

2003年起，由乡镇公安派出所负责民爆物品销售、运输、贮存、使用、清退库5个环节的管理，与销售、使用单位签订责任书，严格购买审批程序，将责任落实到人。是年，县政府作出县城除春节期间外平时禁放烟花爆竹的决定，违禁者由公安机关处罚。2005年5月29日，龙场镇程关村矿山工地炸药48公斤被盗，破案后抓获嫌疑人贺真贵，追回被盗炸药。2010年8月6日，一爆破公司10枚非电毫秒雷管被盗。接警后，公安局立即启动《民用爆破器材安全事故应急预案》，抽调近百名警力经7小时搜索堵截，悉数追回被盗雷管。2010年11月10日，龙场派出所民警夜间巡防时，在学宫巷听到震耳的鞭炮声即追踪寻迹，在学宫巷27号住户4楼屋顶上将燃放鞭炮的居民杨昌查获，在教育其遵守民爆物品管理规定的同时，处予500元罚款。

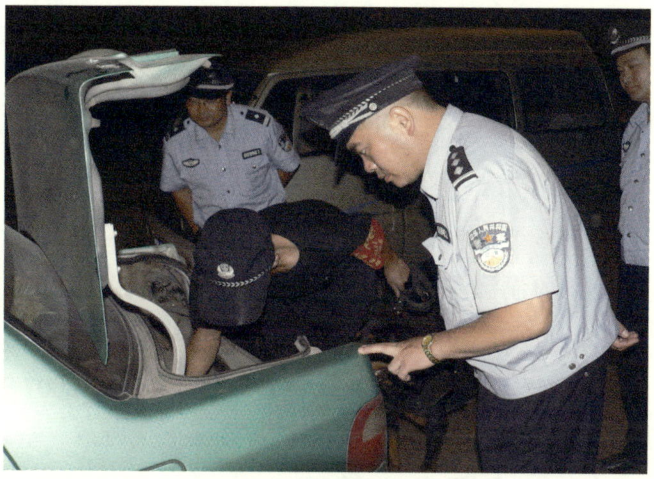

2010年8月，县公安局设卡检查过往车辆是否携带危险物品和毒品

枪支管理 从1980年起，公安机关每两年进行一次枪支清查，对非法治造、私藏枪支者，一经查实，按有关条例惩治。1982年贯彻执行《枪支管理办法》，对枪支进行全面清理、登记、收缴和换证工作。同年4月，德政公社前锋生产队金玉学制造长短猎枪34支，并私藏各种子弹，案件侦破起诉后，金被判处有期徒刑15年。9月，省政府发布《关于收缴私藏枪支弹药、爆炸物品和其他凶器的通知》，全县开始清理、收缴农村的猎枪、火药枪。此后，该项工作不断延续。1991年至2005年，公安机关共收缴火药枪、气枪、猎枪、仿真枪、自制手枪等1500余支，子弹60余发，管制刀具246把。

2006—2010年，完善金融部门、内保涉枪和各公务用枪单位的枪支管理制度，并实行择期抽查与全面检查结合,共检查单位枪库15次。

（五）治安案件查处

1979年，县公安局依照《中华人民共和国治安管理处罚条例 》的规定，对行政拘留人员由看守所拨出监室执行拘留。1980年，专设行政拘留所执行拘留。1980—1986年，通过查处治安案件实施行政拘留2817人。1987—1992年，全县发生治安案件2952起，查处2534起，行政拘留2241人，劳动教养10人，少管23人。1993—1998年，发生治安案件3553起，查处3363起，行政拘留1399人，劳动教养67人，少管6人。1999—2005年，发生治安案件4388起，查处3237起，行政拘留1208人，劳动教养85人，少管7人，其他处理54人。2006—2010年，发生治安案件4101起，查处3613起，行政拘留1346人。

（六）基层治安保卫

1978年起，在各公社生产队复建基层治保组织，由县公安局三科和区、镇派出所对治保人员进行业务培训，并适时对治保组织整顿、充实，以发挥基层治保组织在协助公安机关管理社会治安、侦破案件、防火防盗和调解民间纠纷的作用。1981年，公安局在城镇、厂矿组织联防巡逻组，参加者多是基层治保人员。1992年撤区并乡建镇后，对治保组织进行调整充实，增设治安联防队。扎佐镇马鞍村自1996年建立治安联防队至2000年整整4年的时间里，没有发生过一起刑事案件。至2010年，全县共有治保会217个，治安联防队217个，队员868人。

六、监所管理

1978年起，看守所贯彻落实监所管理规定，及时发现并整改安全隐患，确保监所安全。1979年死刑犯方道忠在水龙头上将手铐砸开，企图逃跑，被看守人员及时发现，给其加戴脚镣戒具，保证死刑顺利执行。1985年，在押人犯杨孝仁、黄煜等在监内墙壁挖洞企图越狱，经发现及时采取措施，制止了事件发展。

1990年，在检察机关配合下，开展文明看守、文明管理活动。1992年，看守所被县委、县政府授予“文明单位”称号。

1996年相继发生2起收审人员集体脱逃事件，共逃跑收审人员22名。事件发生后，吸取教训，调整班子，加强警力，推行安全目标化管理，制定岗位责任制，将确保安全的责任分解落实到每个民警身上。1997年，看守所获省公安厅“三级达标所”称号。次年，再度评为“二级达标所”。

2005年，投资273万元对看守所改扩建，2007年竣工。是年，公安部下发《看守所民警执勤行为规范》，开始以此为基础，逐层推进勤务模式改革。至2010年，已全面落实民警直接管理制度。

七、交通安全管理

1987年1月公安局置交通管理科，8月，县交通监理工作归属公安管理，公安局改置交通警察队于川黔公路过境的扎佐镇，县城设城关分队。1994年，交警队改置交警大队，下设交通管理科和一、二中队。2001年，贵（阳）毕（节）公路开通，增设三中队负责修文段的交通安全管理。

（一） 交通法治宣传

2009年，县交警检查酒后驾车

公安交警部门建立后，通过交通法治宣传，使群众安全意识增强，交通环境改善、交通事故压降。交警部门每年组织集中宣传2次以上，不定期组织车驾人员学习。1991年，举办驾驶员轮训班108期，先后有900名驾驶员参加学习；举办摩托车驾驶员培训班2期，100人参加培训。1992年11月29日，一辆由王官小学校长彭江涛兼营的个体客车在修（文）六（广）公路柿花树处翻入85米深的悬崖底，造成23人丧生的惨剧。事后，集中全县驾驶员进行“安全第一”教育，并于12月4日在事故地点召开700人的现场会，立“血字碑”警示后人。1997年，大力宣传《中华人民共和国道路交通安全法》，制作交通事故展板于街头，让群众通过观看展板增强交通安全意识，并与城关镇王官村开展共建交通安全村活动，竖立标志牌，教育村民管好牲畜，不要随意横穿马路。2001年，“王官交通安全村”通过省交警总队检查验收。2003—2005年的3年间，组织车驾人员安全学习1142人次。2006—2010年，围绕畅通工程建设，先后开展“文明从足下起步”、“不闯红灯文明交通行动”交通安全宣传“进农村、进社区、进企业、进学校、进家庭”的“五进”活动，交警大队在全县各中小学上交通安全课198次，有6万名学生和群众接受交通法规和交通安全常识教育。

（二）交通环境整治

进入20世纪80年代，交警部门每年均组织交通环境整治行动，不断改善全县交通秩序，优化治安环境。1988年，全年查车9313台，查处无证驾驶者36人，惩处肇事致死人命的驾驶员5名。1990年，检验车辆867台，审验驾驶员1460人，查车3.68万辆，查出违章车辆2500辆。1991年，对该报废的车辆实行强制报废。是年，为配合全县“严打”集中统一行动，设卡查车3500台次，查出两起制造贩运假茅台酒案，1起团伙诈骗案，抓获犯罪嫌疑人12人。1994年，对全县交通秩序进行整顿，在主要交通道口安置交通标志。2002年11月29日，贵（阳）毕（节）公路63公里+150米处发生货车与客车相撞事故，当即死亡17人，损失141万余元。继后，采取弯道处竖立标志牌，路面铺减速胶带，严格执勤监控等措施，防止类似事故再发生。2003—2005年，查处交通违章3.37万起。2006—2010年，重点开展农村道路交通安全、危险化学品运输交通安全、幼儿园接送学生车辆交通安全集中整治。其间，2009年和2010年先后开展“道路交通安全集中整治专项行动”、交通安全“三项行动（执法行动、治理行动、宣传教育行动）”、无牌无证车辆专项整治行动、道路交通安全百日专项整治行动等，从严查处各类交通违法行为。2010年，针对贵（阳）毕（节）公路扎佐收费站堵车及驾驶员偷逃过路费等问题，与收费站联合进行为期5个月整治。通过开展各项交通安全整治活动，安全事故呈逐年下降趋势，2009年，县内共发生交通事故1912起，较2008年下降10%，死亡19人，低于控制指标22人，受伤16人，较上年下降9%，实现“一降两保”（降事故，保畅通、保安全）目标。

2009年，交警取缔非法加水点

八、消防管理

（一）机构与设施

1983年，县公安局消防股改称消防科，隶属安顺地区消防支队，享受现役军人待遇。设科长1人，参谋1人，民警7人。有消防指挥车和消防车各1辆。1986年1月，组建消防中队。1997年7月，撤销消防科。2005年消防中队升格为消防大队，配置执勤车辆4台，其中25米举高喷射消防车1辆，水罐消防车1辆，斯太尔水罐泡沫车1辆，抢险救援车1辆，个人防护装备555件，特种防护装备348件，抢险救援装备44件，灭火器材288件。

（二）消防宣传

从1986年建消防中队起，针对各时期消防工作的重点和火灾特点，利用中小学安全教育日、119消防日、安全生产月等时机，强化防火检查和防火宣传，采取消防宣传进机关、进企业、进社区、进学校、进家庭、进农村等形式，动员和组织社会各方面力量，开展自查、互查、抽查、集中宣传、分散宣传等多种活动，并组织青年志愿者参与消防宣传，提高全社会消防安全意识，增强消防知识，提高社会防御火灾的能力，推动全县消防工作的开展。至2010年，共举办426期消防培训班、610次知识讲座，发放20万份宣传资料。

2009年，消防志愿者在六桶乡街头向群众散发宣传资料

（三）火灾隐患整治

1998年起，结合辖区实际，先后组织开展烟花爆竹、化工、人员密集等场所火灾隐患专项整治，发动全社会力量参与和投入到防火安全检查行动中，发现和消除一大批火灾隐患。2000年，消防大队与全县50个重点消防单位签订“防火安全责任书”。2008年，采取“四结合”方式推进农村消防工作。一是结合小水池修建与烟水配套工程，变生产性水池为消防水池；二是结合机耕道建设，变机耕道为消防通道；三是结合危房改造工作，变危改工作为安全隐患消除工作；四是结合包村干部下村指导和调查生产情况的工作实际，变农村工作员为消防安全检查员和宣传员。2009年，结合新《中华人民共和国消防法》的实施，强化消防安全宣传工作，严格落实消防安全责任制度，建立健全消防档案，积极开展各项消防安全专项检查，全年共检查各类场所和单位990次，督促整改各类火灾隐患408处，下发《责令限期改正通知书》125份和《复查意见书》121份。2010年，与工商、安监部门配合，开展烟花爆竹安全生产专项检查，严厉打击烟花爆竹无证非法经营、非法储存、销售非法产品等行为。同时将消防产品治理普查作为火灾隐患普查的一项重要内容落实，在日常的隐患普查整治工作中开展消防产品普查整治活动，采取“三个一遍”（对辖区内所有的消防安全重点单位和设有自动消防设施的单位所使用的消防产品检查一遍；对辖区内所有的消防产品维修、销售企业检查一遍；对整治期间所有申报验收的建筑工程所使用的消防产品检查一遍）的方式，查处假冒伪劣消防产品200件，全面治理和净化消防产品市场。

（四）消防业务训练

1986年起，不断加强从简易的器材装备操作到统一开展基本消防技能训练，从简单的练习到按灭火作战计划开展实地演练，使消防训练的内容、手段和方法不断充实、改进，消防官兵扑救重特大恶性火灾的实战能力得到提高。2000年后，着眼树立“练为战”的思想，扎实开展攀登挂钩梯、攀登9米拉梯救人、着隔热服破拆与疏散物资、佩戴氧气呼吸器登楼排烟、越障操作手抬泵灭火、100米消防障碍等训练，使作战整体效能进一步提高。

2007年，县消防大队组织开展消防演练

2009年11月19日，消防大队在县实验幼儿园开展消防应急演练。演习中，消防官兵对孩子们讲解和演示在火场逃生自救和自护自救方法以及教师要如何有序组织幼儿进行疏散、求救等。2010年1月7日，消防大队开展紧急拉动演练。当晚8时，警铃拉响，官兵急速着装蹬车到消防车开出库门，仅用51秒时间。当指挥员下达演练科目——修文腾晖酒店五楼KTV着火，有两名工作人员被困急需救援的命令后，两名战士组成火情侦查小组侦查火情；一队战士沿楼梯铺设水带，一只水枪直攻火点灭火；救人小组采取徒手救人和单杠梯救人两种方法营救被困人员。整个救援演练过程完成仅用11分钟。

（五）灭火救灾

消防组织建立后，总是把保障人民生命财产安全作为第一要务。1986年12月6日，久长镇川黔公路上一辆装有2.5吨液氯的汽车被撞引起燃烧，烈火与随时可能爆炸的氯气瓶威胁着久长街上2300多居民的生命财产安全。县消防中队和驻县的航空工业部属418库消防队受命赶赴现场，与烈火和泄漏的毒气搏斗1个多小时，将烈火扑灭，避免了氯气瓶爆炸的危险。事后，消防中队受到省公安厅表彰。

2006年7月12日，县境内302国道上一辆大客车与一辆满载47桶黄磷的大货车相撞造成黄磷起火，引发两车燃烧。消防大队接警后迅速赶赴现场扑救，连续战斗8小时将大火扑灭，避免人员伤亡和财产损失。县人民政府为消防大队记集体三等功1次。

2008年2月7日扎佐镇长坡村一户村民住宅发生火灾。消防大队迅速出动2辆消防车赶赴现场。面对火光冲天，浓烟滚滚，大火正向四周蔓延的现场。消防战士按照指挥员部署，迅速展开灭火战斗。仅10分钟即扑灭大火。

2010年10月14日，龙场镇民主路一民房发生火灾。消防大队接警后立即出动4台消防车和22名消防官兵赶赴现场，当即发现火场走廊上摆着一个液化气罐正处于大火烘烤，随时可能爆炸。3名消防战士不顾生命危险立即冲进火场搬走液化气罐。1个小时后大火被扑灭。

九、维护社会政治稳定

1987年9月，在六广区境内的山间田野发现“空飘”反动宣传品，县公安局组织力量收缴传单20种287张，收音机1台，以及食物、药品、衣服等。在收缴的同时向群众进行正面宣传，揭露敌人阴谋。1988年，办理出境手续14人，接待回乡探亲台胞36人次。1989年，北京春夏之交政治风波，县公安局加强信息情报工作，及时掌握敌、社情动态，并对重点人员进行审查，使社会秩序继续稳定。

1994年，根据新形势的需要，制定“处置治安事件预案”，落实应急措施，妥善处理了六桶乡顺江村与金沙县部分村民因婚姻纠纷引发的群众斗殴事件，省扎佐林校女学生自杀诱发学生准备游行请愿事件，城关新生铁厂与新生村村民因地界纠纷发生的挖路事件，并查处和取缔不法宗教组织“呼喊派”及其活动。1995年，对非法传教的“门徒会”成员进行处罚，劳教3人，行政拘留5人，治安处罚8人，收缴非法传教资料300余份。

2002年7月4日，龙场镇阳明村的几名以身试法者以政府征地修路、拆迁安置不合理为由，煽动村民扣押、殴打镇的领导干部，并将扣押者作为人质游街，又聚众闯入县政府，砸摔办公室门窗和办公设备，继而冲进县人民法院砸毁办案车和毁损大量的办公用品及文书档案。事发后，县公安局使用录像辨认印证，认定这是一起有预谋、有策划的群体性事件，导致政府直接财产损失370万元，影响县政府、县人民法院正常办公长达半个多月。针对事件中触犯《中华人民共和国刑法》而涉嫌犯罪的客观事实和涉事者，公安局展开侦查工作，收集事件参与者的人证、物证、摄录像等涉嫌犯罪的证据，于2003年7月先后将4名犯罪嫌疑人杜启文、石世菊、贺从华、石永禄抓获归案，12月25日，法院以聚众冲击国家机关罪和非法拘禁罪判处杜启文有期徒刑7年，以犯聚众冲击国家机关罪判处石世菊有期徒刑4年，以犯聚众冲击国家机关罪和非法拘禁，判处贺从华有期徒刑4年，以犯非法拘禁罪判处石永禄有期徒刑2年。

2004—2005年，公安机关查处邪教违法案7件，处理12人。配合县委、县政府维稳部门处置扎佐镇和平村、六广镇滨江村村民集体上访、县城“摩的”堵路、兴红厂退休职工上访等各类群体事件16起，有效维护全县社会政治稳定。

2006年，公安局提出以情报信息为龙头，大力加强隐蔽战线上的斗争，全力侦破邪教“法轮功”等各类邪教案件，坚决防止发生危害国家安全和政治稳定的重大政治事件、重大暴力恐怖事件。2007年，发放《反邪教形势教育提纲》由乡（镇）和单位组织学习，提高干部群众对反邪教斗争的认识。2008年至2010年，重点开展“公安局长大接访”活动，拓宽公安工作与人民群众的交流渠道，化解社会矛盾，解决突出问题。在北京奥运会、中共十七大、新中国建立60周年等重大活动期间，县内无一人进京上访；在重大项目征地拆迁中，出现“零上访”的安定局面。

第三节　检　察

1978年10月复置县人民检察院，12月正式挂牌办公。重建后的检察院依法独立行使检察权，开展刑事检察、经济检查、法纪检察等业务，为全县的改革开放、经济建设和社会进步保驾护航。

一、刑事检察

（一）审查批捕

1979年，县检察院根据《中华人民共和国逮捕拘留条例》开展审查批捕业务，共受理公安机关提请批准逮捕案件19件23人。1980年1月1日，《中华人民共和国刑法》《中华人民共和国刑事诉讼法》正式实施，检察院运用法律武器，依靠群众，密切配合公安机关、人民法院，以整顿社会治安为中心，坚持以事实为依据，以法律为准绳，重点打击杀人、抢劫、强奸、放火和其他严重破坏社会秩序的现行刑事犯罪，公安移送的批捕案件86件111人，除退回补充侦查的2件2人外，共批捕76件99人，不捕8件10人。从1982年起，坚持重大案件提前介入，了解案情，把工作做在审查批捕之前。是年5月，驻扎佐的航空工业部属兴红机械厂工人杨洪武因谈婚不成，对女方怀恨而产生杀人恶念，遂盗窃厂里冲锋枪和半自动步枪各1支，子弹24发，窜至扎佐公社把七生产大队，开枪打死女方父母和妹妹，影响十分恶劣。检察机关受理该案后及时批捕，发案仅17天即经贵州省高级人民法院终审判处杨洪武死刑，群众拍手称快。

1983年，贯彻执行全国人大常委会颁布的《关于严惩严重危害社会治安的犯罪分子的决定》，拉开

“从重从快”严厉打击严重刑事犯罪斗争的序幕。检察院坚持“严打”方针，以审查批捕、审查起诉作为工作重点，与公安、法院密切配合，对严重刑事犯罪依法快捕快诉。当年批捕人犯184人。至1990年，检察机关介入公安机关开展的“压大案、反盗窃、打流窜、抓逃犯”和查禁社会丑恶现象、打击破坏通信电力设备、拐卖人口等专项斗争，坚持突出“严打”的重点和依法“从重从快，一网打尽”的方针，严格执行依法办案和“稳、准、狠”的原则，对报捕案件，凡基本犯罪事实清楚，基本证据确实并必须逮捕的坚决批捕；对未构成犯罪或情节轻微，或可捕可不捕的不予逮捕，对事实不清，证据不足的，退回补充侦查或由报捕部门自行撤回。

1991—1999年，实施“个人阅卷，集体讨论，检察长或检察委员会决定”的办案程序，确保办案质量。期间，受理袁义华故意杀人案时，检察院提前介入，深入现场调查取证，两天内办结批捕手续，半个月即移送安顺分院起诉。1995年，配合参与围歼车匪路霸、打拐、禁娼、禁毒等专项斗争。1999年，配合公安机关开展90天扫毒大行动和“追逃”专项斗争，批捕一批毒品犯罪分子。

从2000年起，贯彻“稳定压倒一切”的方针，强化对有组织犯罪，带黑社会性质的团伙和流氓恶势力犯罪的打击力度，积极投入“严打整治”斗争，维护社会稳定。

2004—2010年，继续贯彻对严重刑事犯罪从重从快打击的方针，重拳出击危害国家安全犯罪、严重暴力犯罪、黑恶势力犯罪、毒品犯罪以及“两抢一盗”等多发性侵财犯罪。2005年，召开公捕大会3次，对盗采国家矿产资源、贩卖毒品等重大刑事犯罪案件的犯罪嫌疑人公开逮捕，有力地震慑犯罪，对维护全县社会政治稳定发挥了积极作用。2005年，在查处严郁华团伙破坏龙场镇杨寨村选举的“2·22”涉黑案件中，检察院派员提前介入，深入案发第一现场了解和掌握案情，及时批捕31人。1979至2010年，共批准公安机关和检察院侦查部门提请逮捕案犯6417人。

2007年召开公捕大会

（二）审查起诉

1979年3月，县检察院开始受理审查起诉案件。1980年1月，《刑法》《刑事诉讼法》《人民检察院组织法》正式实施。检察机关依法全面开展审查起诉工作。1981年3月，久长镇杨柳村村民廖义方因责任田纠葛与王世周发生矛盾，廖便邀集族宗20多人围攻殴打王世周及其家人，致王世周死亡，在当地造成恶劣影响。检察机关依法对廖义方、廖义章、廖笃礼、廖义忠、杨忠珍、廖祥也等人提起公诉。1983年“严打”，对强奸多名妇女，抢夺检察干警枪支的方道忠、周光贵2人提起公诉后，方道忠被法院判处死刑，剥夺政治权利终身。1985年，检察机关加大打击拐卖人口犯罪力度。王满珍以介绍对象为名，将多名妇女拐卖到江西等地，给受害人及其亲属造成严重身心伤害和经济损失。检察院提起公诉后，王满珍被法院判处有期徒刑15年。

1992—2002年，检察机关重点打击杀人、抢劫等严重犯罪，维护社会稳定。1992年，钟良云、张绍明、李德荣、伍万林、李玉林等多次结伙在公共汽车、旅社等场所持刀抢劫，依法起诉后被法院分别判处死刑和有期徒刑。1997年，被告人汤顺林、汤国友伙同他人以搭乘“摩的”为由，将县城一摩托车驾驶员骗至崇恩花桥，抢走摩托车1辆，现金13元。检察机关依法起诉后，法院以抢劫罪判处两被告各有期徒刑9年。2002年，朱友俊、朱国忠、赵启富等互相纠集，曾7次窜到六广镇永兴煤厂，大肆破坏煤矿设备、道路、水源等，并殴打该厂工人，造成损失1.5万余元，公安机关办案过程中，朱友俊等人又围攻派出所，殴打民警。检察机关提起公诉后，朱友俊等被依法判处有期徒刑、管制等刑罚。

2005年起，为保证公诉案件质量，防止冤假错案发生，坚持惩治犯罪与保障人权相统一，做好“两个告知”（告知被害人有权参加刑事审判活动，并有附带民事诉讼的权利；告知被告人有权聘请律师为其辩护的权利），坚持把公诉工作与全县工作大局有机结合。是年，对非法盗采国家矿产资源犯罪案9件11人依法提起公诉，法院对6件8人作有罪判决。2006年，办理唐厚毅等人强迫、容留妇女卖淫一案时，考虑到该案社会影响十分恶劣，向法院提出从重量刑建议，使被告人最低被判处有期徒刑3年，最高被判处15年。在办理唐文祥交通肇事案时，鉴于被告人在案发后及时报警并对死者家属进行赔偿，对唐文权作出不起诉决定。2009—2010年，起诉工作以打击农村黑恶势力犯罪和“两抢一盗”为重点，通过提起公诉依法严厉打击以李绍华、李绍雄为首的六广镇农村恶势力犯罪团伙，黄明金、徐泽贵为首的龙场镇水塘村农村恶势力犯罪团伙以及王乔国、黄利国为首的久长镇农村恶势力犯罪团伙。

二、职务犯罪侦查与预防

（一）反贪污贿赂

1980年，检察院开始查办经济犯罪案件。1981年设立经济检察科，查办新场信用社杨光清在任业务员期间，采取收入不入账手段，贪污信用社资金1.17万元的案件。起诉后，法院判处其有期徒刑15年。

1982年，贯彻执行中共中央、国务院《关于打击经济领域中严重犯罪活动的决定》和全国人大常委会《关于严惩严重破坏经济的罪犯的决定》，将打击经济领域的犯罪作为长期的重要任务。是年办理贪污案2件2人。

自1987年起，先后成立驻农业银行、县供销社、税务局、扎佐林场、乡镇企业局、工商银行检察室。各检察室协助检察机关办理经济犯罪案件，宣传法治。1996年6月，根据省检院指示予以撤销。

1982—1990年，受理各类经济案件线索266件，立案侦查131件，向法院提起公诉44件46人，为国家、集体挽回经济损失160万元。

1991—1993年，以打击贪污贿赂犯罪为重点，查办经济犯罪案件，开展反腐败斗争。3年共受理各类经济犯罪线索105件，立案侦查75件，为国家、集体挽回经济损失70余万元。

1994年，经济检察科改建为反贪污贿赂工作局，即开展“百日反贪”活动，办结经济犯罪案19件，挽回经济损失38万元。活动结束后被安顺地区检察院评为“百日反贪先进集体”。

1995年起，重点查处“三机关一部门”（党政机关、行政执法机关、司法机关，经济管理部门）

县人民检察院检察官到人劳系统开展预防职务犯罪工作

的经济犯罪案件。1996年5月，县城建指挥部出纳员张亚东携公款17万元潜逃。案件侦破后移送起诉，张被法院判处无期徒刑。1997年，通过三角山水泥厂的财务往来，一举查办县政府副县长赵吉超和原县委常委、纪委书记、贵遵公路修文指挥部指挥长陈海龙等涉及9名国家干部贪污、受贿和挪用公款的窝案串案，后经法院审理分别判处8人有期徒刑和缓刑，1人免予刑事处分，其中，赵吉超贪污、受贿2.56万元和涉案赃款9.05万元领刑3年，陈海龙贪污2.55万元和与他人共同贪污未遂5.32万元，共同挪用公款10.15万元领刑6年。1998年，检察院又查办地税局会计股股长、扎佐分局副局长、省公路五公司质检科长等贪污贿赂案件和卫生局副局长、县爱卫会副主任及会计合伙贪污扶贫款案件。1999年，查办城关烟叶站站长、副站长、会计、保管员等6人贪污挪用28万元公款的窝案串案等。这些案件的查办，受到群众一致好评。至2010年，共立案侦查70件79人，其中大要案件占80%，挽回经济损失420余万元。与此同时，积极开展预防职务犯罪工作，贯彻落实“打防结合，标本兼治”的方针，把预防工作贯穿到查办案件的各个环节。

2001—2005年，除正常查办县境发生的经济犯罪案件外，受上级检察机关指定，先后查办原贵州省交通厅办公室主任代小忠，贵州日报社基建办主任严贵全，贵州省王武监狱副政委代永富等一批贪污贿赂犯罪大案要案。其间，于2003年成立预防职务犯罪工作领导小组，狠抓职务犯罪的预防和查办。检察院介入县计经局、文广局、交通局等单位的工程项目招投标，把预防职务犯罪工作推向前沿。2005年，启动人民监督员制度，选任5名市、县人大代表、政协委员作监督员，对检察机关办理的贪污贿赂、渎职侵权职务犯罪案件中犯罪嫌疑人不服逮捕决定的、拟撤销案件的和拟作不起诉的3类案件进行监督。

2006—2010年，坚持“标本兼治、综合治理、惩防并举、注重预防”的工作方针，在查办职务犯罪的同时，采取送法上门、法治巡展，培训网络联络员，举办座谈研讨活动、进行个案预防、行业预防和专项预防等措施，促进预防工作专业化、法治化、社会化。从2006年起，对全县百万元以上的工程项目进行同步预防，个案预防，预防率达100%。2009年，针对首贵特殊钢异地搬迁工程等大项目开工建设，会同有关部门成立廉政监督组6个，积极开展专项预防工作。至2010年，县人民检察院职务犯罪预防已形成“在参与中监督、在监督中服务、在服务中预防”的模式，使职务犯罪预防落到实处。

（二）反渎职侵权

1979年设置法纪检察科，开始查办法纪案件。翌年查办三元公社武装部长苏方国捆绑吊打群众，致死人命的严重违法乱纪案。起诉后，法院判处有期徒刑缓刑。在查办法纪案件中，检察院采取召开普法教育会、安全教育会、现场会等方式，向群众进行法治宣传，将办案与法治教育有机结合，扩大办案效果。从1980年到1990年，先后查处扎佐罗汉湾煤矿瓦斯爆炸案，贵阳煤矿透水案等到重大责任事故案，六屯乡党委书记非法拘禁案等有较大影响的案件。收到良好的社会效果。

1991—1996年，将法纪检察工作作为保护人权，反击国内外敌对势力攻击诬蔑中国政府不重视人权的重要任务，重点打击渎职侵权影响极坏，后果严重，给国家集体造成重大经济损失的犯罪，对事出有因，后果不严重，情节轻微的案件，则多采取教育、疏导、调解息诉的办法处理。同时帮助有关单位建制堵漏，预防和减少犯罪。1993年，检察机关两次参加县政府组织的安全大检查，清理整顿矿山、小煤窑，落实安全生产措施。此间，每年立案查处法纪案件都在10至15件之间，案件呈下降趋势。

1997年，新修改的《中华人民共和国刑事诉讼法》《中华人民共和国刑法》实施后，检察机关法纪检察管辖范围缩小，主要查办国家机关工作人员利用职务之便侵犯公民人身权利、民主权利案件和经济领域中的玩忽职守案件。法纪检察科也于2002年改称渎职侵权检察科。这期间先后查办县公安局刑侦大队大队长和一副大队长及一中队长的徇私舞弊案，贵州省王武监狱原副政委代永福和警员苏明徇私舞弊为服刑犯人减刑案，为促进司法公正起到积极作用。2005年，进一步加强预防职务犯罪工作，与省送变电公司索丰营项目处，贵航集团技工学校等单位建立预防职务犯罪联系制度。全年发出预防职务犯罪《检察建议书》5份。2006年，立案查办渎职侵权案件2件2人。

2007年4月，撤销渎职侵权检察科，成立反渎职侵权局。至2010年，检察院强化预防职务犯罪工作，每年开展一次“群众参与、反腐倡廉、服务和谐”等主题的举报宣传周活动。同时，建立职务犯罪协调机制，先后到工商局、国土局、国税局、地税局、移动公司修文营业部、中铁七局扎南高速第一合同段项目部、首贵特殊钢异地搬迁工程建设指挥部等单位开展行业预防、专业预防，举行预防职务犯罪专题座谈、法治讲座等多种形式活动39次，促进党员干部廉洁从政，减少贪污贿赂渎职侵权案件的发生。

2007年4月16日，县检察院反渎职侵权局成立

三、监所检察

县检察院复建后于1979年开展监所检察工作。1985年设立驻监所检察室，明确专人负责监检工作。1993年设置监所检察科进行经常性的监所检察。

（一）安全检查

1979年起制定“一月一检查，节日大检查”制度，发现问题及时与看守所、武警中队联系处理。1982年国庆节前夕检查发现1、2号监室内有砖头、木棒和玻璃碎片，3号监室人犯李元明身上系有红布条，监室墙上有洞，即收缴发现的危险物品，用水泥补塞墙洞，消除隐患。1987年9月，出现人犯故意口吞刀片致病，企图逃避处罚问题。检察院写出《狱情动态》报告，配合监所采取措施制止。在历年的安全检查中，对于发现的问题都提出纠正意见，做到防患于未然。1990年，与监所密切配合，打击牢头狱霸，深化文明管理。是年关押人犯510人，监室爆满，且重刑犯多。检察院针对管理上的薄弱环节，建议监所建立罪犯出所鉴定制度、牢头狱霸登记制度和狱情登记制度。2000年开展监所检察检务宣传，将监所检察的职责、职权、任务、管辖范围，犯罪嫌疑人和被告人的权利、义务，刑事诉讼办案周期等制成宣传栏，在监区公开，并设立投诉箱，增加执法透明度，维护监管的正常秩序。2005至2006年，改建监所，人犯转移外县关押，检察院克服异地工作的困难，加强与外地监所的联系，及时全面掌握在押人犯在各个诉讼环节情况和生活情况、身体状况，及时督促办案单位和办案人员按照诉讼程序和诉讼时限完成办案工作，有效预防超期羁押的发生，维护在押人犯的合法权益。

（二）违法行为纠正

1980年，针对监所出现以拘代侦、以拘代惩问题，检察机关及时督促公安、法院清理积案，予以纠正。

1990年后案件增多，监所超期羁押现象突出，检察院及时提出尽快结案纠正超期羁押违法的建议。

1994—1995年，发出纠正超期羁押建议48人次，对4名保外就医条件消失的罪犯建议收监投劳，杜绝凭白条关押和无证关押人犯的现象。1999年，纠正超期羁押42人次，清理不符合留所服刑条件的5人，查办1件看守干警涉嫌虐待被监管人员案件。2004年，纠正3件以取保候审时间折抵刑期的案件。2005至2010年，着重配合有关部门对被管制、缓刑、假释、暂予监外执行等人员进行监督，预防社区矫正对象再犯罪，着力维护社区矫正对象的合法权益。

（三）开展“共建文明”活动

1985年起，检察院与监所执勤部队开展监所文明管理、文明看守，文明执勤的共建文明监所活动，加强对人犯的法治教育，为被监管人员上法治课4次，与人犯谈话86人次。1990至1992年，与公安、法院配合打击牢头狱霸，促使人犯遵守监规，认罪服法。1990年和1994年，协助看守所与油脂厂粮食局等单位联系，请求优惠粮油价格，以使人犯吃饱吃好。2003年“非典”流行时，对监所进行消毒，为被监管人员作体检。此间，看守所于1986年和1992年两度被县委、县政府授予“文明单位”称号。2007年起，公安机关推进勤务模式改革，全面落实民警直接管理制度，检察院与公安机关配合，深入开展创建文明看守所活动。是年7月20日，贵阳市人民检察院贯彻落实《最高人民检察院关于加强和改进监所检察工作的决定》座谈会在修文召开，推动了监所检察工作更加有效开展。2010年，进一步规范监所检察制度，检察院与公安机关、法院加强联系，严格执行换押制度，杜绝超期羁押违法现象，全年无超期羁押情况发生。

2010年2月10日，县检察院检察官到看守所进行清监检查

四、法律监督

（一）立案监督

1997年，新修改的《中华人民共和国刑事诉讼法》《中华人民共和国刑法》颁布，《中华人民共和国刑事诉讼法》，检察机关按刑诉法规定，通过审查批捕、审查起诉、信访、举报多种方式开展立案监督。1998年，通过信访渠道，对应当立案而不立案的2件2人，向公安机关提出建议立案侦查。2001年，根据群众信访线索，对久长镇下堡村一村民伤害案深入调查后，向公安机关发出《要求说明不立案理由通知书》，督促立案侦查，后经法院审理，以故意伤害罪判决。

2008年10月13日，县检察院举行人民监督员颁证仪式

2003年，开展“食品安全专项立案行动”，检察院与工商、税务、质监、药监、卫生等20多家行政机关建立行政执法与刑事执行工作衔接机制，建立“修文县立案监督联席会议”制度。此做法被作为经验推介后，最高检察院检察长贾春旺批示：“贵州省修文县人民检察院立案监督工作做法值得重视，看来不少基层检察院在强化法律监督上进行了不少探索，也创造了不少好的经验。”是年，办理立案监

督案11件12人。

2004年，检察院继续通过行政执法与刑事执行相衔接的工作机制开展立案监督工作，向公安机关提出补充侦查建议书50次，办理立案监督案件17件。

2005年起，检察院把监督的重点放在社会危害大、群众反映强烈的案件上，并加大对常规案件的审查力度，认真分析被害人提出的控告材料，从中发现线索，广辟案源，至2010年，受理立案监督案件98件，共向公安机关发出要求说明不立案理由通知书92件，向行政执法部门发出移送案件建议函79件。对行政执法部门根据检察院建议移送公安机关立案侦查的案件，检察院即派员介入侦查。

（二）侦查监督

1980年，《中华人民共和国刑法》、《中华人民共和国刑事诉讼法》、《中华人民共和国人民检察院组织法》正式实施，检察院依法对侦查活动进行监督。自1980—1996年，通过提前介入、审查批捕、审查起诉等方式，不捕219人，增捕90人，增诉33人，免诉23人，督促公安机关抓获批准逮捕在逃罪犯12人，介入公安机关重特大案件侦查活动200次，向公安机关提出纠正违法通知115次。期间,对1982年公安机关移送起诉的唐定荣抢劫一案，经认真审查，听取群众意见，查明肖远彬是被漏掉的同案犯，决定将其逮捕，提起公诉。

1997年新的《中华人民共和国刑法》、《中华人民共和国刑事诉讼法》实施后，检察机关在侦查监督工作上的力度进一步加大。从1997年到2004年的8年间，共增捕12人，追诉13人，督促公安机关抓获批准逮捕在逃罪犯2人、共增诉漏罪15次。提前介入公安机关侦查活动106次，向公安机关提出补充侦查建议书300份。

县人民检察院侦查指挥中心

从2005年起，检察院从5个方面加强对侦查活动的监督。一是对执行回执的监督。对每个案件的批捕回执进行逐个登记，回执未到位的及时沟通，督促原案件承办人在法定时间内将批捕回执送达检察院；二是介入和审查逮捕中注重审查在逃、另案处理等是否属实，防止放纵犯罪现象发生；三是对公安机关和自侦部门的办案期限严格监督，有效防止超期羁押；四是开展对刑讯逼供监督专项行动，杜绝和防止刑讯逼供现象发生；五是对证据不足或者情节轻微的案件依法不捕不诉，对遗罪漏罪依法追究。自2005年至2010年，共向公安机关发出《提供法庭审判所需证据材料意见书》97份，对于不捕案件及时向公安机关发出《补充侦查建议书》33份，《检察建议》7份。不捕87件98人，不诉22件25人，追诉70件。

（三）审判监督

刑事审判监督　1981年起，检察机关通过出庭支持公诉，对人民法院刑事审判活动进行监督，对判决裁定错误或量刑畸轻畸重的案件提出抗诉，对于审判中一般违法行为提出口头或书面意见纠正。是年，提出抗诉案1件，纠正违反审判程序1次。

1987年，对5名被告判刑偏低和1人不应判无罪的，向法院提出抗诉，使有罪的人受到法律处罚，无罪或犯罪情节轻微的人不受法律追究。

1997年后，按照修改后的《中华人民共和国刑事诉讼法》规定，进一步加强对刑事审判的监督。至1998年，对法院量刑畸轻的案件3件3人提出抗诉，二审法院均作改判。

1999年后提出的抗诉案件，绝大部分获得市人检察院支持抗诉和二审法院改判。2000年，县人民法院审理县烟草公司龙场镇烟叶站站长、副站长等5人贪污案，对5名被告均判处缓刑。检察院审查后认为量刑畸轻提起抗诉，经市中级恰民法院终审改判其中3名被告为6年、5年、4年的有期徒刑。2004年，对久长镇一农民非法行医致死人命一案，县人民法院仅判被告有期徒刑1年，处以罚金2000元。经提出抗诉后，市中级人民法院改判被告有期徒刑10年，并处罚金5000元。至2010年检察机关共提出抗诉案件25件29人，多为法院改判。2010年，检察院办了1件足以引起深刻反省的错案，其中的经验教训值得记取。2007年6月—2008年11月间，扎佐镇三元村农民滕彩荣在高尔夫度假中心球场捡拾1249个高尔夫球，被检察院批捕并以盗窃罪提起公诉，2009年3月，县人民法院对滕彩荣盗窃高尔夫球案作出一审判决，判处滕有期徒刑3年缓刑4年。一审判决结果出来后，人民检察院以适用缓刑不当、量刑畸轻为由向贵阳市中级人民法院提请抗诉。而腾彩荣也不服此判决，也向贵阳市中级人民法院提起上诉。2009年8月，贵阳市中院裁定县人民法院的判决认定事实不清证据不足发回重审。12月，县人民法院重审后作出判决：高尔夫球系抛弃物，滕彩荣的捡球行为不构成犯罪。重审后，检察院再次以“遗失球的所有权归高尔夫所有，（滕彩荣的捡球行为）是秘密窃取高尔夫的财产”“高尔夫度假中心是封闭式运动场所，四周有围墙，腾彩荣翻墙秘密潜入高尔夫球场内‘捡球’，是秘密窃取高尔夫度假中心财产”为由提请抗诉。2010年3月，市中级人民法院作出终审判决，认为“会员打出而未找回的球，在其放弃寻找并已退出球场后，此类球应为该会员的抛弃物，腾彩荣所捡拾的球为会员所放弃，故其所捡拾的高尔夫球不属高尔夫度假中心所有”“在度假中心范围内的财产都归其所有，这一理由于法无据”驳回抗诉，维持原判。终审判决结果证明，人民检察院两次提请抗诉的是一起错案。继后，检察院根据国家赔偿法向滕彩荣作了赔偿。该案在法学界、报刊和网络上引起广泛关注，中央电视台《新闻调查》2010年6月5日以《三元村的高尔夫之痛》，《今日说法》2010年10月19日以《赚小钱丢了自由 沉重的代价为哪般》报道该案时对错案成因作了深刻分析。

2009年7月29日，公诉人在县人民法院清水塘专案庭审现场

民事行政审判监督　1988年，省人民检察院、省高级人民法院发出《关于人民检察院对民事审判活动实行法律监督的通知》后，县人民检察院与县人民法院配合，选择唐子培诉六屯乡企业办茶场承包合同纠纷案开展民事审判监督。1990年10月和1991年4月，《中华人民共和国行政诉讼法》《中华人民共和国民事诉讼法》先后颁布施行，检察院按规定于1991年5月设置民事行政检察科，逐步开展民事、行政审判监督工作。

1992年起，通过控告申诉渠道受理民事、行政申诉案件，其中大多数案件认定事实、适用法律及审判程序是正确的，判决裁定并无不当。对这类申诉，认真做好申诉人的息诉服判工作，以维护审判机关形象和司法权威。对于判决、裁定确有错误的案件，一部分建议法院再审改判，一部分按程序提请抗诉。2004年经民行科审查，提请上级检察院抗诉的何金艳等5名工人诉奇峰工贸公司劳动争议案，经法院开庭再审，采纳了检察机关的抗诉意见，撤销原判，判令工贸公司在规定期限内为何金艳等5名工人交纳劳动关系存续期间的养老保险金和失业保险金。同时支付经济补偿金及赔偿金共3.6万余元，帮5名工人讨回了合法权益。至2005年，受理申诉案件205件，提请抗诉案19件，其中部分案件获得法院再审改判，保护了当事人的合法权益。

专记：检察机关帮助5名工人讨回合法权益

2002年5月8日，贵州省奇峰工贸有限公司通知何金艳等5人解除劳动关系。何等向县劳动争议仲裁委员会申请仲裁，要求工贸公司补交工作期间的社会养老金和失业保险金，支付解除劳动关系后的经济补偿及未按规定支付的经济补偿金和赔偿金。在仲裁过程中，工贸公司单方收回解除劳动关系的决定。仲裁委于7月11日作出支持工人仲裁请求的裁决，但未写明工贸公司应支付的具体金额。5名工人以没有具体金额，无法要求对方履行为由诉至县人民法院。工贸公司也以已经收回解除决定，劳动保险与其无关为由提出反诉。

人民法院一审认定5名工人的诉讼请求成立，判决工贸公司支付5人经济补偿金、赔偿金和补缴5人工作期间的劳动保险费用。工贸公司不服判决上诉，二审法院以一审对工贸公司的反诉未并案审理为由发回重审。2003年2月，县人民法院重审此案，认定工贸公司解除劳动合同的决定违反法定程序，不具法律效力，5名工人应于判决生效后立即回公司上班。5人以该判决未对劳动保险的诉请进行审理，判令工人回公司上班无法律依据为由上诉。贵阳市中级人民法院于同年6月17日判决驳回上诉，维持原判。2004年3月，何金艳等5人向贵阳市人民检察院申诉。市人民检察院将案件移交县人民检察院审查。县人民检察院审查发现，生效判决在适用法律上存在两个问题：一是判令工人回公司上班超越审判权限；二是生效判决未对工人主张公司补缴其工作期间社会养老保险金和失业保险金等费用的诉请依法审理判决，显属错误，县检察院据此提请上级检察院抗诉。

2005年4月，省人民检察院向省高院抗诉。法院开庭再审该案，采纳了检察机关的抗诉意见。于同年12月判决撤销原判，判令工贸公司在规定期限内为5名工人交纳劳动关系存续期间的养老保险金，同时支付经济补偿金及未按规定给予经济补偿的赔偿金3.6万余元。结案后，何金艳等5名工人来到县人民检察院，手捧判决书，兴奋地对办案人员说：“我们的案子改判了，该得的钱有着落了，谢谢你们。”

五、控告申诉检察

县人民检察院重建后设信访接待室，并建立检察长接待制度。1986年，改信访接待室为控告申诉科。信访内容除检察院重建之初以要求平反历次政治运动和“文化大革命”时期的冤假错案为主外，多为揭发控告国家工作人员贪污受贿、违法乱纪和不服公安、法院等有关部门处理判决的申诉等。检察院通过控申信访工作获得贪污贿赂、渎职侵权等犯罪案件的案源，也为开展立案监督、侦查监督、审判监督提供线索。

1988年成立举报中心，接受群众对党和国家机关工作人员职务犯罪及侵犯公民民主权利且属于检察机关管辖的案件线索举报，接待处理来信来访162件次，除转有关单位处理和疏导调解外，又为各业务科室提供法纪、经济、刑事等案件线索20件。

1996年起，开展创建文明接待室活动，加强控告申诉举报初查力度，对举报人的举报及时初查，做到件件有着落、事事有交代，并设立举报奖励基金，对举报有功者进行奖励。并规范接待工作，建立健全检察长接待制度、文明接待制度、受理群众来信来访制度等一系列规章制度，依法妥善处理群体性事件和集体上访，使矛盾及时化解。1999年首届阳明文化节开幕前夕，有两名群众到举报中心反映情况，声称如果反映问题得不到解决，就要在文化节期间上街喊冤。检察院对举报人说服疏导，避免了不良影响的发生。至2010年，共受理群众来信来访394件，年均43.8件，被贵阳市委、市政府授予“文明信访接待室”称号。

2005年成立处理涉检上访案件领导小组，制定处理涉检上访预案，并充分发挥控告申诉检察工作密切联系群众的作用，不断完善首办责任制和检察长接访、业务部门负责人巡访制度。精心组织举报宣传工作，上街开展法律咨询、受理群众举报。2009年“两节一会”期间，检察院出动警力130余人次参与处理水塘村群体上访突发事件,参与金久水泥厂、首贵特殊钢异地搬迁工程等维稳、安保工作，协助政府化解社会矛盾，使“两节一会”顺利举行。至2010年，共受理各种来信来访237件，年均39.5件，出动宣传车60次，发放宣传资料2.1万份。

专记：韩杼滨莅临县人民检察院调研

2000年4月15日上午，最高人民检察院检察长韩杼滨莅临县人民检察院，出席“三讲”教育动员大会。县人民检察院全体干警、贵阳市各区、县（市）检察院部分干警共200多人参加会议。

韩杼滨在动员会上发表讲话，要求基层检察院在开展“三讲”教育活动中，要紧密结合基层检察工作特点和自身实际，坚持高标准、严要求，切实解决领导班子和领导干部在党性党风方面存在的突出问题，达到坚定信念、增强党性、统一思想、强化宗旨的目的。要严格落实领导责任制，确保“三讲”教育活动健康开展；要把“三讲”教育的成果用制度形式固定下来，融入中共思想建设，组织建设、作风建设的制度体系中去。

2000年，最高人民检察院检察长韩杼滨（前排左起六位）到县调研

在听取县人民检察院的工作汇报后，韩杼滨对检察院寄予殷切期望，要求全体干警团结务实，努力工作，把县人民检察院建成全国第一流的县级检察院。当得知县人民检察院办公条件存在实际困难，韩杼滨立即指示省高检院拨款10万元，帮助县人民检察院维修办公楼，改善干警工作条件。韩杼滨还走访干警家庭，到龙场镇军民村看望村民。

第四节 审 判

一、刑事审判

1978年中共十一届三中全会后，县人民法院充分发挥刑事审判惩治犯罪、维护社会稳定的职能，开展刑事审判工作。1979—1980年，判处各类刑事犯罪案件63件83人，1981—1982年，判处196件339人。此间，严重危害社会秩序的案件呈上升趋势，团伙犯罪突出，青少年犯罪比例大，农村偷盗耕牛案件数量增多，社会治安令人忧虑，人民群众缺乏安全感。从1983年开展严厉打击严重刑事犯罪的斗争起，法院坚持“严打”方针不动摇，与检察、公安机关通力协作，积极参与“打黑除恶”“严打两抢一盗”等专项整治行动，每年都有针对性地召开公处大会，一批刑事犯罪分子受到严厉打击。

1983年“严打”期间，严惩一批严重破坏社会治安的犯罪分子，27名严重刑事罪犯被处决。法院在“严打”斗争中，结合全县治安状况，重点打击严重危害社会治安的杀人、抢劫、强奸、拐卖人口、流氓、重大盗窃和团伙犯罪“七类”犯罪以及惯犯、累犯。至1986年，召开大型公判会32次，旁听群众达14万人次。

1987年，刑事审判工作除继续打击“七类”刑事犯罪外，还突出打击严重经济犯罪，并适时开展专项斗争和集中打击行动。遵照省高级人民法院《关于严厉打击盗伐、滥伐林木犯罪活动的通知》精神审理盗伐森林案件时，在扎佐林场召开公审公判会，省电视台作录像报道。以后，相继开展压大案、打流窜、反盗窃、打拐卖、扫“六害”（卖淫嫖娼、制作贩卖传播淫秽物品、拐卖妇女儿童、私种吸食贩运毒品、聚众赌博和利用封建迷信骗财害人）等专项行动，从而维护社会秩序稳定。1989年4月，将脱逃流窜作案的强奸犯胡平安和伤害公安人员的罪犯李世祥押赴作案地处决，收到较好的社会效果。

1990年5月，中央政法委员会再次部署“严打”斗争。三个阶段的“严打”期间，县人民法院除突出打击车匪路霸、牢头狱霸、团伙犯罪外，还把非法种植罂粟、容留妇女卖淫、伪造货币等新类刑犯罪作为打击的重点。针对少年犯罪案件呈上升趋势的实际，于1991年开设少年法庭。对少年犯罪案件的审理立足教育挽救、寓教于审、惩教结合。

1993—1997年，继续贯彻“严打”方针，从重从快惩处严重刑事罪犯。5年共召开大型宣判会33次，并通过新闻媒体进行“严打”宣传，扩大“严打”效果。在打击经济犯罪斗争中，坚持“一要坚决，二要慎重，务必搞准”的原则，排除干扰，秉公办案。审结各类刑事案件691件，判处案犯974人。1993年集中宣判胡荣跃、钱兴荣等拐卖妇女、绑架儿童等案件，对胡、钱二犯分别从重判处10年以上有期徒刑。1995年审结影响较大的公安干部卢开成受贿案。

1998年，充分运用修改后的《中华人民共和国刑法》和《中华人民共和国刑事诉讼法》，严厉打击严重危害社会治安和严重破坏经济秩序的犯罪活动。依法判处小箐乡党委副书记邓天勇破坏县“煤炭五统一”政策，暴力抗拒检查，开车闯关致矿管检查人员重伤造成重大影响的故意伤害案、贵遵公路修文段指挥长陈海龙等贪污、挪用公款案和县卫生局吴削易等贪污案。1999年，依法判处县公安局李云志等贪污、徇私枉法案。

2001年，将杀人、伤害、抢劫、绑架等严重暴力犯罪，重大盗窃，拐卖妇女儿童和贩毒等带地域特点的多发性犯罪作为打击重点，开展集中打击专项斗争。，罪犯张勇、周永华酒后使用暴力和威胁手段，轮奸两名女性，并抢劫被害人现金，情节恶劣，法院判处张犯有期徒刑20年，剥夺政治权利5年；判处周犯有期徒刑15年，剥夺政治权利5年。县邮政局职工蔡健贪污储户存款和金融凭证，被判处有期徒刑16年。2003年，判处在扎佐片区多次抢劫、强奸、入室盗窃，且手段恶劣影响极坏的罪犯张福鑫、王思权有期徒刑各20年，并到当地公开宣判，震慑犯罪分子。

2006年，把维护社会稳定置于刑事审判工作的首位，打击涉黑涉恶、抢劫、受贿等严重危害人民群众生命财产安全和破坏社会经济可持续发展的各类刑事犯罪，重点打击“两抢一盗”侵财犯罪。2007年，判处杀伤缉毒民警的犯罪嫌疑人李劲松有期徒刑9年，并公开宣判，有力打击犯罪。2010年，在“严打两抢一盗，保卫百姓平安”行动中，到案发地公开宣判犯罪嫌疑人，昭示审判机关坚决打击“两抢一盗”[抢劫、抢夺、盗窃（包括入室盗窃和盗窃机动车）]犯罪的决心。

2010年8月18日县人民法院、县人民检察院在洒坪乡召开公捕公判大会

二、民事审判

1978年后，县人民法院审理民事案件多以调解为主。至1986年结案1579件，调解966件，占所结案的60%以上。1987年《中华人民共和国民法通则》施行后，逐步向“坚持着重调解，调判结合”转变。1991《中华人民共和国民事诉讼法》颁布后，则按“根据自愿和合法的原则进行调解，调解不成的，应当及时判决”的规定裁处案件。县人民法院探索调解创新，通过法庭辩论，在查清事实、明确是非责任后进行调解，改庭前就地调解为庭上调解，并组织观摩庭审方式，推进公开审判。至1995年审结民事案2072件，调解结案827件，判决结案781件。1996年，推行民事案件审理中“谁主张、谁举证”的司法理念，并深化以直接开庭、当庭宣判为内容的民事审判方式改革，当年受理民事案件451件，结案429件，结案率达96%，直接开庭宣判率达60%。1999年，以开展“审判质量年”为契机，提出审理民事案件“应当一月结案”，要求当庭宣判率必须达到80%以上。同时，将调解书、裁定书签核权限下放，改由审判长或独任审判员签发，以提高办案效率。至2001年3年，审结民事案件3270件，其中当庭宣判2776件，宣判率达85%。2002年完善法庭巡回办案制度，建设巡回法庭，解决法庭辖区大、群众打官司难的问题，至2010年，县人民法院下属的第一法庭（六广法庭）和第二法庭（扎佐法庭）人民法庭每年审结的案件80%以上是在巡回法庭审结，巡回法庭被群众称为“我们的汽车法庭”。

从2002年起，为适应因经济转轨、社会转型引发民事案件增多的实际，加大民事审判方式改革力度，进一步发挥审判调节职能。2003年，民事案件审理实行简繁分流，县人民法院决定由人民法庭受理的案件全部适用简易程序审理，以提高案件审结率，缩短办案周期。第一人民法庭2002年结案256件，适用简易程序审结185件，结案周期34天，2003年结案273件，均为适用简易程序审结，结案周期21天，2004年结案的382件，平均结案周期18天。2004年10月，第一法庭仅用4天时间就审结92件小额借款纠纷案，受到贵阳市中级人民法院表彰。2005年，县人民法院修订《案件流程管理规定》，对庭审前后的调解时限作出明确规定，防止出现案件久调不结现象，调解结案的593件民事案件，全部在规定时限内结案。2007年实施新的诉讼费收费办法，县人民法院坚持以“和谐司法”理念指导民事案件审理，坚持“调判结合”原则，不断创新司法举措，努力满足群众司法需求。2008年5月，采取电话开庭方式，成功审结一起当事人一方为四川地震灾区群众的案件。2009年，以巡回接待、调查、针对性宣传为依托，按照“先易后难、各个突破、调主判辅”的原则有序地处理涉及群体批案的案件审理方式，先后审理46件拖欠民工工资案、30件劳动争议案，调解成功率达78.18%，有效消除可能引发的社会矛盾。与此同时，办理诉讼费缓、免95案，缓免诉讼费12.7万元。2010年，在完善巡回审判机制基础上，创新民事案件审理中的调解方式，推广温情调解、分步调解、联动调解、现场自认调解及亲情互动调解等方法，民事案件调解结案和经过调解自愿撤诉案件占案件结案数的60.43%，化解了一大批矛盾。

专记：实行巡回审判 方便群众诉讼

1985年，县人民法院在管辖范围有9个乡的六广法庭推行巡回审判，把辖区分为六广、广田、大石、六桶4个片区，在广田、大石、六桶设巡回办案点，每月定时巡回到点办案，方便群众诉讼。1987年，审理大石乡78岁的布依族老人姚树珍赡养纠纷案时，法庭在当事人家里组织调解，通过对其儿子、儿媳进行法治教育和道德教育，妥善解决了老人的生活问题。旁听群众深有感触地说：“不孝老人，国法不容。这样的官司打到家门口来，脸面都丢尽了。”

1999年1月，县人民法院撤并法庭，将六广和小箐人民法庭合并成立第一人民法庭，扎佐和久长人民法庭合并成立第二人民法庭，城关和城关镇人民法庭合并成立第三人民法庭。2001年，又将第三人民法庭与民庭合并为民一庭，民二庭。法庭撤并后，辖区扩大了，虽然方便了法院的管理，但却给边远山区群众带来打官司难的问题，为打官司，有的要走上几十里路，一场官司来来回回跑两三趟，耗时耗钱耗力。为解有决边远地区群众诉讼难的问题，法院在巡回审判设置上下功夫，在法庭驻地外的乡设置巡回审判点。从2003年开始，先后在谷堡、六桶，久长、洒坪建起专供巡回审判用的标准、规范的巡回审判法庭，实现了在乡镇审理案件时，当事人、旁听群众同样可以在庄严的法庭内行使权利，履行义务，监督审判。同时，采取“末页提前制作 ”的方法，到巡回地后就地立案，就地审理，结案后立即利用手提电脑打印法律文书其他事项，实现当庭送达。使办案周期大大缩短，减少了当事人的诉讼开支。在案件处理方式上，法庭在巡回办案中坚持“能调则调，少判多调，当判则判，调判结合”的处理方式和“彻底化解纠纷，促进社会和谐”的办案指导思想。2003年1月，二法庭在久长巡回审理清江村4户村民拖欠供电局电费案中，巡回法官充分发挥调解职能，化解一触即发的矛盾，依法保护当事人双方的权益，维护供电市场的正常程序。第一、第二法庭和民一庭的调解结案率每年都在70%以上。为便捷、高效地巡回审判，法院从审判程序着手，实

2007年5月六广人民法庭巡回接待点开展综治宣传活动

行案件简繁分流。对双方争议不大、法律关系清晰、审判人员能即时调解做出处理意见的简单案件，全部适用简易程序，就地审理。2004年10月，通过巡回审判方式，二法庭1个月内成功办结100件小额借款纠纷案，一法庭适用简易程序调处92件小额借款纠纷案仅用4天时间。

三、经济审判

1982年10月县人民法院设经济审判庭，将经济案件从民事案件中剥离出来，由经济庭专审。2001年1月撤销经济庭，经济案件复归民庭审理。

全县经济案主要有法人之间的经济纠纷、法人与其他经济组织之间的货款纠纷、农村土地承包合同纠纷、企业内部承包或租赁和产品质量纠纷、金融机构借款纠纷等。1985年，审理修文农具厂诉贵阳市云岩农机修造厂购销合同贷款纠纷案，为农具厂追回货款1.2万元及一批实物配件。1988年，审理六屯乡关山茶场纠纷案时，检察机关派员出庭监督，法院通过判决制裁被告六屯乡企业办的违法行为，维护了原告唐子培的合法权益。《贵州日报》和贵州电视台均作报道。审理城关镇供销社诉久长纸袋厂货款纠纷案时，经过对濒临破产的纸袋厂清产核资，清理债权债务，最终调解结案，为供销社挽回20万元的经济损失。事后供销社向法院赠送“为政清廉，秉公执法”锦旗。秋粮入库期间，受理3起农村承包合同纠纷案，制裁不交纳公余粮的当事人，保障秋粮入库。

1989年，法院配合银行、信用社开展“依法治贷”活动，发挥审判使职能，保障国家信贷资金及时回库。

1993年，法院确立经济审判为经济体制改革和经济建设提供法律保障和服务的审判原则，成立法律服务中心，受理请求法律服务的经济纠纷，结案22件，标的达43万元。1994年审理一件涉农承包纠纷案中，发现因纠纷导致一个村寨变压器得不到使用，村民无电抽水致几百亩稻田干裂，上百户人家人畜断水。即与供电部门联系先予供电，解决人畜饮水及田土浇灌，并对群众说服疏导，妥善处理纠纷。是年，县人民法院审理县酒厂破产还债案，化解企业债务百余万元，并协助县政府安置分流下岗职工。至2000年，法院审结各类经济案件达1016件。

四、行政审判

1986年12月始建行政审判庭。1987年受理赵绍英不服县土地管理局对其违法占地处罚案，法院判决维持土管局处理的合理部分，撤销处理不当部分，赵仍不服又予上诉，后经安顺中级人民法院判决，维持原判。

1990年《中华人民共和国行政诉讼法》正式施行后，坚持“以事实为根据，以法律为准绳”原则，保护公民、法人和其他组织的合法权益，维护和监督行政机关依法行使行政职权。至1992年，受理行政案27件，全部审结。

1993年，除受理正常行政诉讼案件办理外，有针对性地受理非诉行政执行案件。此间，协助土管部门对全县土地使用情况进行集中清理，执结一批非诉土地案件。行政诉讼案共审结31件，其中判决维持行政机关决定的14件，占45.2%；撤销和变更行政机关决定的7件，占22.6%；撤诉处理的10件，占32.2%。1993年，久长镇沟边煤厂与小箐煤厂为开采边界发生纠纷，经县矿产资源管理局、乡镇企业局等调解，明确各自开采方向和范围，约定两厂之间留出30至40米的保安煤柱。后两厂又生纠纷。为防止事态扩大，县乡镇企业局于1994年向两厂下达行政指令，责令双方退出保安煤柱，在各自采区内开采。原告沟边煤厂以乡企局绘制的煤井走向图与实际不符，被告的行政指令支持了小箐煤厂的违约行为，侵犯了原告的合法权益为由提起行政诉讼。审理中，应原告申请，法院委托贵阳煤矿对原告和第三人的煤厂井下巷道走向作测绘，测绘结果认定原告在掘进中越界开采事实存在，遂判决维持被告县矿产资源管理局的行政指令。经二审判决维持原判。

1998—2005年，行政审判趋向成熟，县人民法院在行政审判中既重视保护行政相对人的合法权益，又注意维护行政机关的执法权威。审理3起诉煤炭工业局、矿管局行政处罚案，审判人员通过对当事人进行法治教育，使原告认识到自己的行为违反行政法规，因而主动撤诉，自愿接受处罚，并当庭兑现罚款，使3案一天内顺利审结，维护了县的“煤炭五统一”政策实施。

2006—2010年，县人民法院主动策应行政审判理念的变化，将诉讼调解机制引入审判工作实践之中，行政诉讼案件和解撤诉率提高。此间共受理行政诉讼案件261件，撤诉率达60%。针对土地行政类案件增多趋势，除加大审判力度外，开展依法行政的法律宣传，培训相关行政执法人员，化解行政纠纷，营造良好法治氛围。至2010年共受理土地行政类案件66件，结案率为100%。

五、执行工作

1978年，案件执行实行“审执合一”，由审判庭负责，对确需强制执行的案件，法院统一组织实施。1983年7月，归登荣与陈素荣离婚判决生效后，法院对其财产进行分割时，归对陈家抬家什的人大打出手。法院即组织强制执行，对归实施拘留措施，后以归登荣构成拒不执行法院判决、裁定罪判处有期徒刑3年。1986年，针对执行难问题，法院集中力量统一行动，先后在六广、扎佐和久长等地组织执行行动。执行中，请乡村干部配合宣传法治，促使当事人自觉执行。对个别无视法律，对抗执行的人，则依法采取拘留、罚款等措施强制执行，收到执行一案、教育一片的效果。

1987年成立执行庭后，80%以上的民事案和经济案的执行仍由各审判庭负责，执行庭受理确需强制执行的案件，既做到“审执分离”，又搞好“审执配合”。

1992年，以落实最高法院开展“执行年”活动为契机，县人民法院组织执行大会战，在县交通、土管、税务、水电、工行、农行等单位设立8个执行室，以加强执行工作。全年收执行案464件，执结403件，执行率达86.9%。

1995年，贯彻最高法院全国执行工作会议精神，实行“审执分离”。案件执行统由执行庭办理，共执行352件，执行率达96%。

1999年，最高法院再次部署“执行年”活动，县人民法院开展春、秋季执行大会战，实行一案双责制（庭长与承办人共同负责）、排期执行制、定期结案制，申请人举证和被执行人申报财产制度等，使执行难问题有所缓解。全年受理执行案801件，执结735件，执结率91.76%，。

2000年，县人民法院成立执行局，实行统一管理、统一协调和自上而下的监督制约机制，使执行工作趋向制度化。

2001年起，县人民法院探索发布执行敦促公告、冻结划拨、亲人代结、分期偿还和发放债权凭证等案件执行方式，运用司法强制措施，加大对“有钱不还”、“恶意躲债”等不良现象的打击力度，建立审判环节和执行环节的互动联系，提高案件执行效率。2002年，县机电化轻公司申请执行调解书生效已近3年被告未履行还款义务的购销合同欠款案。法院催促被执行人无果，遂采取强制措施将其拘留，拘留次日，被执行人将全部案款缴清。在案件执行中，县人民法院加强对执行干警司法服务理念教育，加强矛

盾易于激化案件的疏导工作，妥善处理案件执行与维护社会稳定的关系，提倡人性化执行。2004年，县建筑公司申请执行贵州星源净宇燃气公司欠款案，执行标的17万元。执行人员考虑到被执行人系外来企业，对县的经济发展有积极作用，不宜采取强制执行措施，且尚未正式经营，要一次给付全部标的确有困难。执行人员即动员被执行人采用分期给付的方式兑现。后被执行人在3个月内分3次将所涉标的兑现完毕。2008年，执行一起人身损害赔偿案时，办案法官在采取强制措施的同时，通过与被执行人反复谈心疏导，消除其抗拒情绪，成功处理这起多年积案，申请人向法院赠送“公正执行，和谐确保”锦旗。自1996年实行“审执分离”至2010年，县人民法院共收执行案件5569件，执结5012件，执行率为90%。仍有一批积案未能执结，执行难仍是县人民法院司法审判工作需要突破的瓶颈问题。

县人民法院副院长苏晨霞（左三）率干警到当事人家中兑现案款

六、信访与立案

1982年，县人民法院设信访接待室，负责处理群众来信来访及其所反映的告诉申请事项。至1989年接待室撤销，共处理来信2955件，接待来访4150人次，调处简易纠纷240起。

1989年，成立告诉申诉审判庭，把信访接待纳入审判工作。至1991年，处理来信1009件，接待来访2895人次。

1992年实行案件立审分离，除扎佐、久长、小箐法庭受理的案件和刑事公诉案件外，其余案件均由告申庭审查立案，而后分送相关法庭处理。至1997年处理来信1428件，接待来访2100人次，做到事事有交代，件件有着落。

1998年，撤销告申庭，成立立案庭负责信访接待和立案工作，认真落实法律援助和司法救助，积极开展诉前保全和调解，实现诉调对接；施行特快专递送达，提高送达效果和成功率。并推行“大立案，精审判，严监督，强执行”，突出“大立案”审判工作机制，告诉到法院的案件符合立案条件的当日立案。2005年，实行案件管理网络化，所有案件通过电脑立案纳入流程管理，从源头上杜绝虚假结案和指标数据差错。是年，立案庭被贵阳市中院荣记集体三等功。2006年起，县人民法院所属2个法庭实现网上远程立案。2007起执行国务院《诉讼费用交纳办法》，至2010年，对弱势诉讼当事人“减、缓、免”诉讼费40余万元。

2005年5月12日县人民法院院长郑炳州到洒坪乡接待来访群众

自1998年，实行院长接待日制度起，每周二由院领导班子成员轮流处理来信来访，掌握信访信息，处理急难案件，方便群众诉讼。信访工作由立案庭负责，对来信来访逐一登记，认真审查，分类处理。2001年改由书记官室负责，2002年复转立案庭负责。2005年加大信访工作力度，在各庭室明确一名信访联络员，建立起信访网络，实现网络化管理，并纳入目标考核。2006年起，坚持一手抓涉诉信访工作，一手抓审判质量，提高司法公信力。运用教育、协调、救济等方式，化解来访群众心结，解决信访矛盾。2008年，制定《信访责任追究制》《矛盾纠纷排查化解工作实施细则》，进一步拓展涉诉信访排查渠道，完善联（带）案下访机制，积极预防和消除社会不稳定因素。至2010年，共接待群众来来访5200余人次，处理来信3100余件。

七、审判监督

1998年，设立审判监督庭，主要审理当事人申请再审案件、县人民法院决定再审案件、上级法院发回重审案件和检察机关抗诉案件。县人民法院根据审判工作需要，制定《岗位目标管理责任制》《目标管理考核办法》《案件流程管理规则》和《案件质量评查办法》，加强对审判活动的管理和监督。2008年，进一步加强上诉案件质量评析，查找不足，切实提高案件质量。全年，上诉案件76件，二审改判率为2.52%，发回重审率为1.05%。2009至2010年，推行阳光审判，共发放《审判纪律监督卡》7000余份，主动接受当事人对案件审理的监督。

第五节　司法行政

1981年3月建立县司法局，内设法律顾问处、公证处、法治宣传股、人民调解股筹机构，开展律师、公证、法治宣传和人民调解等工作。至2010年，内设机构为办公室、依法治理办公室、政工科、基层工作科、法律援助工作管理科（法律援助中心）、公证处、律师事务所。全县10乡镇均设置司法所。

一、法治宣传

（一）“一五”普法（1986-1990）

“一五”普法重点对象是工人、农民、知识分子、干部、学生、军人、其他劳动者和城镇居民中一切有接受教育能力的公民。普法内容侧重于《中华人民共和国宪法》《中华人民共和国婚姻法》《中华人民共和国刑法》《中华人民共和国经济合同法》和《中华人民共和国治安管理处罚条例》等法律常识学习和普及。强调各级领导干部要多学一点，学深一点。采取抓试点推全县、举办普法培训班、创办农民业余法治学校、组建普法小分队、举行学法知识抢答赛等形式，开展和推进普法工作。5年共举办培训班46期，培训普法骨干5689人。全县13.88万人参加普法学习，占应普法对象的85.96%。

（二）“二五”普法（1991-1995）

重点对象是领导干部、执法人员（包括司法人员和行政执法人员）、青少年特别是中学的在校生。普法的主要内容是“以宪法为核心”，“以专业法为重点”。普法的基本目标是紧紧围绕党和国家的中心工作，组织深入学习《中华人民共和国宪法》，同时有计划、有步骤、分层次地组织学习上级规定的相关专

业法律知识，促进各项工作依法办事。“二五”普法期间，全县在继续抓好城乡群众性普法工作的同时，采取聘请专家、学者举办法治讲座的形式，重点对县、乡领导班子成员和行政执法人员进行《中华人民共和国公司法》《中华人民共和国反不正当竞争法》《中华人民共和国产品质量法》等法律法规以及经济法基础知识、社会主义法治建设理论等内容的培训学习。同时实施法律常识进课堂工程，加强对青少年的法治教育。其间，开展普法宣传80多场次，受教育者达40多万人次，有4800人次参加全省法律知识考试。

（三）“三五”普法（1996—2000）

重点对象为工人、农民、知识分子、干部、企业经营管理人员、学生、军人和个体劳动者以及其他一切有接受教育能力的公民。基本目标是通过在全体公民中继续深入进行以宪法、基本法律和社会主义市场经济法律知识为主要内容的宣传教育，进一步增强公民的法律意识和法治观念，提高各级干部依法办事和管理的能力和水平。其间，1997年，举办各类普法骨干培训班培训骨干9000多人次，举办法律知识竞赛4次，上法治课32次，组织对“一书六法二条例”（即《社会主义法治建设基本知识》，《中华人民共和国宪法》《中华人民共和国国家赔偿法》《中华人民共和国行政诉讼法》《中华人民共和国行政处罚法》《中华人民共和国刑法》《中华人民共和国刑事诉讼法》《国家公务员暂行条例》《行政复议条例》）的学习和学法考试。1998年，全县建立干部“学法日”制度，重点学习《邓小平论民主与法治建设》《依法治国论》等。全县干部职工参加贵阳市学法统一考试，召开“青少年禁毒教育大会”，组队参加贵阳市禁毒知识竞赛等。1999年办法治宣传栏750期，发放宣传资料10万份，培训骨干2000人次，举办《中华人民共和国国家安全法》法治讲座等。2000年，成立县“三八”妇女维权领导小组，开展“三八”维权周活动等。5年间，全县有22万人次参加普法学习。累计开展普法宣传100场次，受教育50万人次。

（四）“四五”普法（2001—2005）

重点对象为领导干部、司法和行政执法人员、青少年以及企业经营管理人员。普法的主要内容是宣传与整顿规范市场经济秩序相关的法律法规，宣传与加入世界贸易组织相关的法律知识，宣传与维护社会稳定相关的法律法规，宣传社会发展迫切要求普及的各项法律法规。基本目标是通过“四五”普法规划的实施，努力实现由提高全民法律意识向提高全民法律素质的转变，实现由注重依靠行政手段管理向注重运用法律手段管理的转变，全方位推进各项事业的依法治理，为依法治国、建设社会主义法治国家奠定坚实的基础。其间，开展“六个一”示范点创建工程（一个依法行政单位、一个公正司法单位、一个依法治镇单位、一个依法治村单位、一个依法治校单位、一个依法治企单位），确定水利局、法院、龙场镇、龙场镇白莲村、城关二小、六广水泥厂为示范点创建单位。全县公务员1171人参加贵阳市组织的法律知识考试，参考率、及格率均达100%。2003年将“非典”防治宣传列入“四五”普法内容，使“非典”防治宣传教育深入人心。2004年，邀请中国宪法学研究会副会长张光博讲授宪法修正案知识。

（五）“五五”普法（2006—2010）

“五五”普法从2006年开始至2010年结束，重点对象为领导干部、公务员、青少年、企业经营管理人员和农民。其间，于2006年8月启动法律“六进”活动（进机关、进乡村、进社区、进学校、进企业、进单位）；2009年5月17日，在扎佐镇举办“法律六进”系列宣传活动，以《贵州省法律援助条例》《法律援助知识问答》《中华人民共和国禁毒法》《中华人民共和国未成年人保护法》《妇女权益保障法律知识》《外来务工人员合法权益法律知识》《“送法到乡镇社区”法律法规资料选编》等法律法规知识书籍为主要内容，开展宣传咨询服务。现场搭建舞台演出文艺节目，由劳教人员现身说法，用自己的亲身经历讲述毒品的危害。活动当天，展出宣传展板10块，发放宣传资料5000份，接受群众咨询120人次。2010年4月启动“法治修文”建设活动。

“五五”普法的5年，全县共举办领导干部法治讲座4次，举办各种法律骨干培训班16期，全县229个村（居）委会均设法治宣传栏，开展“送法下乡”法治宣传46次，发放宣传资料12万份，张贴标语300幅，组装宣传车巡回宣传20架次，举办法治文艺演出14次，为学校上法治课40次，开展警示教育20次。各专业法实施部门结合实际采取多种形式开展法治宣传教育。全县受教育公民达80%以上，人民群众的法治观念和法律意识明显增强，依法办事的能力更加提高。

2006年9月18日在“法律六进”活动中，县人武部在县城街道设点宣传《国防教育法》

二、依法治县

1998年，县委作出《关于深入开展依法治县的决定》，县人大常委会作出《关于深入开展依法治县工作的决议》，县政府作出《关于依法治县的实施方案》，县建立依法治县工作领导小组，设办公室于司法局。此后，每年与10乡（镇）和县直部门负责人签订依法治县目标责任书，乡（镇）和县直部门结合实际往下逐层签订相应的责任书，形成依法治县有人管有人抓有人干的工作格局。

依法治县结合历次普法教育开展。其间，县人大常委会从1998年起，实行任命干部任前法律考试制度；县政府按行政法治“六化”（执法权限法治化、规范性文件合法化、行政管理程序化、行政执法标准化、执法检查经常化、监督机制完善化）建设要求，实施依法办事“五公开”（办事程序公开、办事时限公开、办事标准和质量公开、办事结果公开、责任追究公开）和责任追究“四不放过”（对违法违纪行为不调查清楚不放过，不严肃处理不放过，不制定整改措施不放过，不给群众答复不放过）。1999年，县水电局把严格执法，抓队伍建设和创建文明单位结合起来，行政执法中无错案，被评为“省级文明单位”。2000年，县政府对1992至2000年的1243个文件进行清理，废止7个文件，对全县行政执法部门的执法主体、执法资格、执法责任、执法程序、交叉执法和委托执法等内容进行界定。在学校开展依法治校。大石乡将8名不送子女入学的家长告上法庭，依法维护适龄儿童接受教育的权利。修文中学通过抓学校管理制度、抓教师素质教育、抓学生法治教育，实现无违法犯罪、无吸毒、无重大治安案件发生的“三无”学校。检察机关每年7月开展“举报宣传周”活动，加大预防和惩治职务犯罪举报宣传。县人民法院推出“当日立案，排期开庭，一月审结，公证裁判”的便民利民审判工作机制，被省高院评为“人民满意的好法院”。“三五”普法期间，县交通局开展公路“三乱”（乱收费、乱罚款、乱摊派）治理，对县境公路进行定期不定期检查。对六屯

2009年5月21日，久长小学开设禁毒法治教育课

乡、六桶乡擅自在公路上设卡，向过往煤车、运矿车收取管理费的行为给予纠正。2002年4月25日，六广镇发生小煤窑透水造成9人死亡的事故，从县到乡相关部门责任人15人受到行政处罚，非法组织开采的付汉祥等4人被依法追究刑事责任。继后，针对全县矿山乱挖滥采问题，县政府对185个煤矿进行检查，炸封煤窑37个，责令停产9个。是年，煽动龙场镇阳明村不明真相群众打砸县政府、县人民法院的“7·4”群体事件为首者杜启文等4人受到法律制裁。县的行业部门运用法律手段开展依法治税、依法治路、依法治校等。2005年，针对县城脏、乱、差现象开展“整脏治乱”活动，整治覆盖率达90%。在全县农村开展依法治村活动，建立健全调解委员会和治保小组，推行“四民主”（民主管理、民主选举、民主决策、民主监督）、“两公开”（村务公开，财务公开），实行村民自治。谷堡乡获贵阳市“依法治理示范点”称号，谷堡乡平寨村被司法部、民政部授予“全国民主法治示范村”称号。

2010年，启动“平安修文”和“法治修文”建设工程，依法治县取得阶段性成果。

三、法律服务与援助

1987年，按照司法部《关于乡镇法律服务所的暂行规定》,建立六广区法律服务所，为全县首家农村法律服务机构。后又相继建立久长区法律服务所、乡镇企业法律服务所等基层专业性法律服务机构，通过担任法律顾问、代理诉讼、参与非诉讼调解、参与仲裁活动、解答法律咨询和代写法律事务文书为农村群众和乡镇企业提供法律服务。乡镇企业法律服务所成立仅1年就代理诉讼24案，为5家企业追回欠款11万元，挽回经济损失17万元。

1997年，在乡镇设司法助理员履行司法行政和提供法律服务职责，撤销法律服务所。1999年，全县基层民主与法治建设步伐加快，群众对法律服务的需求增大，县司法局在全县设立3个片区法律服务所，与同时成立的乡（镇）司法所实行“两块牌子，一套人马”的管理体制，六广镇法律服务所服务范围为六桶乡、大石乡、洒坪乡、六广镇。扎佐镇法律服务所服务范围为久长镇、六屯乡、扎佐镇。龙场镇法律服务所服务范围为小箐乡、谷堡乡、龙场镇。继后，又在县城成立修文县法律服务所。法律服务所提供服务热情、周到，办案质量高，信誉好，受到群众好评。2001年，龙场镇法律服务所为该镇13个村担任法律顾问，为村委会和村民提供法律服务，解决相关法律事务，使“有事找我的法律顾问去”成为村民的口头禅。扎佐镇法律服务所每年开展向服务企业及村寨送法律服务上门活动，通过开展法律咨询、上法治课，促进企业和村民运用法律手段维护自身合法权益，被称誉为“企业、政府和村民的连心桥”。2000年开通“148”法律服务电话，以“把法律交给群众，送服务走进万家”为服务宗旨，给群众和社会组织提供便捷、高效的免费法律咨询和其他法律服务。2002年，龙场镇法律服务所获省司法厅“优秀法律服务所”称号，2005年，六广镇司法所（法律服务所）被司法部授予“全国先进司法所”称号。至2010年共处理来电咨询、求助1490人次。全县基层法律服务所共代写法律事务文书2552份，代理案件1757件，担任法律顾问130家，主持调解纠纷79件，协办公证（见证）1053件，解答法律咨询1.3万人次，开展法治宣传617次。

2001年建立县法律援助中心，在乡镇建立法律援助工作站，按照《贵州省法律援助试行办法》开展法律援助工作，为贫、弱、残及特殊案件当事人提供法律帮助，保护当事人的合法权益。法律援助案件由县法律援助中心统一受理、统一审查、统一指派律师、统一督办、统一建档，实行制度化管理。援助中心制作“法律援助便民卡”，发到全县各村组干部、人民调解员及村民手中，加大对法律援助工作的宣传力度，推动该项工作开展。2001年建立法律援助中心时，仅受理6件案件，之后，逐年增加，最多的2006年达到250件。至2010年，共办理法律援助案件863件。

办理法律援助案件,不收取当事人任何费用,办案经费由县政府按《贵州省法律援助经费管理暂行办法》规定补助，纳入县财政预算。此外，从2006年起，每年从国家分配的中（国）加（拿大）项目法律援助专项经费中获得补助5—6万元，保障法律援助工作的开展。

县法律援助中心建立后，主要对未成年人、残疾人、老年人和贫困人员提供法律援助，通过法律援助保障社会弱势群体的权益得以实现，体现法律面前人人平等。2006年，为六屯乡44户村民诉贵州丰裕种业公司经济纠纷案提供法律援助，法院采纳法律援助工作者的代理意见并当庭宣判贵州丰裕种业公司不履行合同约定，造成44户农户经济损失，依法对44户农户进行赔偿。2007年洒坪乡司法所法律援助工作人员调解的洒坪乡上坝村420余户村民与该村栗木山煤厂因煤炭开采造成自然灾害而发生纠纷案，不仅维护了当事人的正当权利，还避免了群体性事件发生。全县共办理法律援助案件863件。龙场镇法律服务所被司法部、全国残联授予“残疾人维权示范岗”称号，六广镇法律服务所被贵州省司法厅、贵州省残联授予“残疾人维权示范岗”称号。

四、人民调解

1978年后，逐步恢复“文化大革命”中瘫痪的人民调解工作。1982年，贯彻司法部《关于加强人民调解工作，进行社会治安综合治理的意见》，在全县村（居）组织建立人民调解委员会225个，调处民间纠纷634件，防止非正常死亡2人。1986年，结合“一五”普法实施，加强调解员队伍建设与制度建设，对全县228个人民调解委员会的人民调解员2500人进行培训。1990年，配合民政部门在全县15个居民委员会成立调解委员会，在15个100人以上的厂矿（场）建立调解组织，并组织全县“人民调解知识竞赛”活动，提高调解人员业务水平。2002年，成立县司法调解指挥中心，各乡镇亦成立相应组织，建立起县、乡、村三级调解网络，形成人民调解和行政调解相结合的“大调解”格局。同时，加强调解员队伍建设，调整各级调解委员会，选聘一批年纪轻、有文化、有一定法律素质的干部充实到调解员队伍，使人民调解工作逐步建立起“党委领导，政府牵头，村为基础，所为依托，部门联动”的模式，坚持“以情感化，依法调解，规范操作，灵活高效”的工作原则，使调解工作成为维护社会治安的“第一道防线”，成功调处一大批疑难、复杂、久调不决的纠纷。2002年，六广镇广义村村民与修筑高（枧）六（广）公路的施工方发生纠纷，施工方拖欠村民工钱不给，村民则将施工方修路设备搬走，将路堵死不让车辆通行，并欲集体上访。六广镇司法调解中心获知后立即介入调解，通过调查取证，做双方当事人思想工作，宣传国家有关法律法规，化解双方矛盾，最终，施工方向村民支付了工钱，村民归还了施工方设备，纠纷得以平息。至2010年，全县有各级人民调解组织委员会229个，人民调解员1349名，共调解各类民间纠纷5243件，调解率100%，调解成功率97.3%。

五、公证

1981年3月，按照司法部《关于公证处的设置和管理体制的通知》规定，建立县公证处，隶属于县司法局。公证处成立之初，没有专职公证员，由县法律顾问处律师兼职办理公证业务，直到1987年才配备专职公证员，全面开展公证业务，并建立公证联络员制度，在县直机关、工商银行、区（镇）财政所及驻县中央厂矿聘请县首批公证联络员11名。

公证处成立后，即针对广大群众和干部对公证机关性质和公证工作等不了解的实际情况，加强公证工作宣传，编写印发《公证工作问答》等宣传资料，向群众宣传公证机关的性质、任务和业务范围。1996年1月《贵州省公证条例》颁布实施，1月28日，县公证处利用场天设点宣传。2005年3月1日，《中华人民共和国公证法》颁布实施，公证处加强对公证法的宣传。之后，每年在县司法行政机关开展法治宣传时，县公证处均派人参加，宣传公证知识，使公证工作逐渐深入人心，公证业务逐步开展，业务范围逐步扩大。

《中华人民共和国公证法》实施后，公证处以经济合同公证为重点，推行公证接待“首问负责制”，开辟“农村小型水利工程改制合同书”公证、“国有土地使用权转让合同”公证，参与政府采购投标现场公证等新证源，并推行就地办证方式，确保公证事项的真实性、合法性、可行性和公证的诚信度，还做好公证后的回访、检查和监督工作，及时处理违约行为和纠纷。2006年5月，一杜姓当事人理继承权公证时，因其弟远在浙江打工不能到场，杜即喊一个人冒充其弟前来办证。公证人员在审查材料时发现问题，即深入杜所在的龙场镇宾阳社区调查核对，结果证实杜确实存在欺骗行为。在对杜进行批评教育后，要求其重新提供材料才给予办理公证，避免了一起错证的发生。至2010年，公证处根据《中华人民共和国公证暂行条例》及《中华人民共和国公证法》的规定，共办理证明合同（契约）、委托书、遗嘱；证明财产继承、转让、赠予；证明亲属关系；证明身份、学历、经历；证明出生、婚姻状况、生存、失踪、死亡；证明文件上的签名、印章属实；证明文件的副本、节本、译本、影印本、与原本相符；对于追偿债款、物品的文书，认为无疑义的，在文书上证明有强制执行的效力；保全证据；保管文件；代理与公证事项有关的文书；根据当事人的需要办理其他公证事项；涉外公证等13项各类公证46680件。

六、安置帮教

1999年，县委成立刑释解教人员安置帮教工作协调小组，下设办公室于司法局，加强对刑释解教人员的指导和管理，按照“帮教社会化”方式开展工作。

2004起，坚持“教育、感化、挽救”原则，做好刑释解教人员的衔接管控，登记建档，落实帮教。做到不脱管、不漏管、底数清、情况明、不失控，并量化帮教工作考核目标，要求全县帮教对象改好率达90%以上，重新犯罪率不超过5%。至2010年，全县共建立安置帮教领导小组10个，有安置帮教工作人员468人，结成帮教对子733对。结合刑释解教人员大多为农村人口的实际情况，安置以帮其落实责任田地为主，解决基本生活问题。2004年至2010年，全县刑释解教人员安置率达85%，帮教率达97%，重新犯罪率控制在3%以下，最大限度地预防和减少重新犯罪。

2009年，帮教对象参加社保部门举办的厨师培训

专记：帮教服刑人员

1991年4月29日，由县政协、关协、团县委和政法委、公安局、检察院、法院、司法局等部门以及服刑人员家属代表共22人组成的帮教团，到沙子哨劳改农场看望修文籍服刑人员，开展帮教活动。当

天，阳光明媚，修文籍服刑人员121人和其他服刑人员共260多人聚集在广场上参加帮教大会，他们的脸上也像阳光一样变得灿烂起来，特别是修文籍的服刑人员看到了家乡的亲人，感受到被高墙阻隔的亲情，心里有说不出的高兴。帮教会上，县里来的领导对服刑人员作帮教讲话，服刑人员家属代表进行发言，语重心长，使服刑人员感动不已，他们纷纷上台表示决心，要努力改造自己，重新做人。会上，县青年歌手苏琼还为服刑人员演唱歌曲“故乡情”，帮教团把带来的120多件礼品和法律书籍赠送给服刑人员。帮教会后，帮教团和部分服刑人员进行面对面的交谈，更使服刑人员感受到家乡亲情的温暖，要积极改造，洗心革面，争取早日与家人团聚，成了那一刻他们说得最多的话。1999年1月17日，由公、检、法、司、工商、团县委、妇联、关工委等单位组成帮教团赴金华劳改农场对修文籍服刑人员进行帮教，带去了慰问品，并向服刑人介绍家乡的发展变化，使170余名服刑人员深受教育，表示要认真改造，做一个有益于社会的人。2004年，县司法局和贵阳市司法局组成帮教团到瓮安监狱对修文籍服刑人员进行帮教，与2002年煽动群众闹事的“7·4”事件主犯杜启文进行帮教谈话。杜启文对自己所犯罪行追悔不已，并表示要努力改造，争取早日与家人团聚。

第八章 军 事

第一节 军事组织

一、机构

（一）人民武装部

县人民武装部 1978年，中国人民解放军修文县人民武装部沿袭原部队建制，隶属安顺军分区。1986年5月，县人民武装部改为地方建制，隶属中共修文县委员会，军务仍由安顺军分区领导，称“修文县人民武装部”，级别为副县级。人武部机关设置办公室和政治工作科、军事训练科。1996年6月，人武部回归军队建制，复名“中国人民解放军修文县人民武装部”，正团级建制，隶属贵阳军分区，受贵阳军分区和中共修文县委、县政府双重领导。人武部机关设置军事科、政工科、后勤科。2003年12月随贵阳军分区组建为贵阳警备区，人武部亦改隶贵阳警备区。至2010年，人武部建制及隶属关系未变。

2007年2月，修文县被省人民政府、省军区授予贵州省双拥模范县称号后，县委书记魏明禄（左二）、县长石洪（右二）、县人武部部长周明（右一）、县人武部政委柴忠元（左一）在县委大院合影纪念

1986年起，县人武部坚持以人为本，注重加强思想政治建设，发挥“一线指挥部”作用，着力提高人武部、民兵预备役战斗力，推进军事斗争各项准备；做好后勤与装备工作，增强综合保障能力；做好民兵工作“三落实”（组织落实、政治落实、军事落实），加强全县民兵预备役建设。1990年后，县委、县政府和县人武部合力共抓全民国防教育，积极开展拥军优属、拥政爱民活动。2007年和2010年，修文县相继被授予省级“双拥模范县”称号。

区（社）乡（镇）人民武装部 1978年沿袭原建制，在区和县直属久长公社设区（社）人民武装部，1981年，久长公社改建为区，原公社武装部随之改建为区武装部。1984年，城关镇升格为区级建制设镇人民武装部后，全县共设6个区（镇）人民武装部。1992年撤区并乡建镇，随即在乡（镇）设人民武装部。乡（镇）人武部属地方建制，武装干部由地方派遣，受本级党委、政府和上级军事机关双重领导。至2010年，全县10个乡（镇）人武部仍存。

（二）人民武装委员会

1979年6月恢复“文化大革命”时期停止活动的修文县人民武装委员会，1989年7月更名为中共修文县人民武装委员会。武委会在县委的领导下，协调各方力量，贯彻落实民兵工作的方针政策和完成各个时期的民兵工作任务，共同抓好民兵建设。至2010年，中共修文县人民武装委员会仍存。

（三）国防动员委员会

1996年4月，成立修文县国防动员委员会，县委书记任第一主任，县长任主任，常务副县长、人武部部长、人武部政委为副主任。1996至2010年，县国防动员委员会先后召开16次会议，并形成会议纪要。县国防动员委员会在县委、县政府领导下，负责协调国防动员工作中经济与军事、军队与政府、人力与协力关系等工作。

2003年5月，县国防动员委员会召开会议

二、驻军

贵州省警卫部队一支队四中队（贵州武警总队一支队四中队） 1978年，贵州省警卫部队一支队四中队驻贵州省广播厅扎佐发射台担任警卫工作。1982年8月，改称贵州武警总队一支队四中队，至2010年仍驻扎佐发射台。

陆军第十四军四十一师步兵第123团和炮兵团 1978年，县境马家桥驻有中国人民解放军陆军第十四军四十一师步兵第一二三团（代号0279）和炮兵团（代号0280）执行防务。1979年2月，奉调云南边境参加南疆保卫战，8月，一二三团和炮兵团均随四十一师驻防云南通海和建水。

贵州省军区独立师炮兵团 1979年7月，中国人民解放军贵州省军区组建独立师，师属炮兵团（代号35634）驻防马家桥进行军事教育训练。1981年7月调防。

贵州省军区独立团 1981年8月，新组建的贵州省军区独立团（代号35635）驻防马家桥。1983年2月，独立团整编为贵州省军区独立营（代号35636），调防贵阳市乌当区野鸭塘。

修文县人民武装警察中队 1982年12月，武警部队修文县中队驻修文县城，受安顺地区武警支队领导。1996年1月，修文县划归贵阳市管辖后,改隶贵阳市武警支队。2005年，贵阳市支队与原武警一支队合并为贵阳市支队后，县武警中队改隶贵州省总队贵阳市支队。

昆明军区后勤部（成都军区后勤部昆明办事处）农场 1983年12月，中国人民解放军昆明军区后勤部在马家桥以原部队营地建立农场，驻干部战士100余人，经营种植业和养殖业，兼营石油、采矿等企业。1985年6月，撤销昆明军区建制归成都军区，农场隶属成都军区后勤部昆明办事处，至2010年，农场仍存。

贵州省军区后勤生产基地 1983年，贵州省军区35636部队从马家桥驻地调防乌当区后，将营区组建为后勤生产基地，由留守人员经营。至2010年，后勤生产基地仍存。

修文县武警消防中队（消防大队） 1986年2月组建武警消防中队驻防修文县城，隶属安顺地区消防支队，1996年1月改隶贵阳市消防支队。1997年改建为大队。2010年消防大队仍驻修文。

贵阳陆军预备役工兵团团部　1999年新组建的中国人民解放军贵阳陆军预备役工兵团团部驻防马家桥,隶属贵州省军区和贵阳市委、市政府，实行军地双重领导。平时进行战备训练，参加地方经济建设，维护社会稳定，战时履行作战工程保障任务。至2010年，工兵团团部仍驻马家桥。

第二节　党管武装体制

一、第一书记制度

从1986年县人民武装部改为地方建制起，就实行县委书记担任县人武部党委第一书记制度。1986年至2010年，先后有王向规、黄生忠、朱生亮、罗筑云、黄乃铸、魏明禄、石洪担任人武部党委第一书记。

二、武装部主要领导参加地方党委制度

1986年起，每届中共修文县委员会均有1名县人武部政委或部长参加，乡（镇）人武部部长均为同级党委成员，各级武装干部配合所在地党政组织开展人民武装工作，为党管好武装，当好参谋。

三、地方党委议军制度

1986年起，将议军列入县委常委工作日程，实行党委议军制度化，常委会每年议军1至2次，主要议决武装工作中的重大问题。基层党委每半年召开1次议军会议，解决武装工作中的实际问题。

第三节　兵员征集

一、征兵机构

每年征兵期间，县成立征兵工作领导小组，由县人武部和宣传、公安、民政、卫生、工会、共青团、妇联等部门抽调工作人员组成征兵办公室，下设秘书、宣传、政审、体检等工作组，负责具体的征集工作。征兵工作结束，领导小组及办公室即行撤销。

二、征集实施

县征集兵员工作多在每年冬季进行，少数年份亦在春季征召。每年征集兵员开始，均采取“四定”（定片区、定任务、定时间、定对象）“三包”（包思想发动、包兵员质量、包优抚政策落实兑现）责任制，以保证兵员质量，使入伍新兵政治、文化和身体素质全部合格。征集工作分为三步：第一步，宣传动员，号召适龄青年报名登记，由乡（镇）武装干部和部队接兵人员进行目测初步审定，登记造册；第二步，体检、政审，由县统一组织进行体格检查和政治审查，合格者报县征兵领导小组审批，批准后即填发《入伍通知书》；第三步，交接起运，给应征青年佩戴大红花，敲锣打鼓，鸣放鞭炮，送县报到，由

征兵小组逐人点名交给接兵部队，起运入伍。1987年开始征兵改革，逐步完善征兵制度，使征兵工作步入法治化、制度化和规范化，征兵效率得到提高，兵员质量得到保证。县内每年征兵都要根据实际情况提出具体措施，严把兵员质量关。2000年的冬季征兵，针对时间紧、任务重、要求高的特点，将应征青年的政治素质放在首位，严格政审标准，坚持谁政审、谁签订、谁负责的原则，采取由下而上，上下结合的方式，县、乡、村三级初审与交叉联审、复审、会审结合，实行层层负责制。政审责任单位做到与每一名应征青年见一次面，摸清其政治立场、思想品德、社会交往、有无违法违纪等情况。对应征青年实行尿样检查，清除吸毒人员。为确保兵员质量，在征兵工作中建立有纪检组织和监督机制，坚持全程公开、集体定兵。2004年的冬季征兵，严格按照《关于征集公民服现役政治条件的规定》严把政审关，对187名预定兵员进行尿液特检采集，及时派专人专车送交贵阳市戒毒检测中心检测。2006年起，征兵增加心理检测，包括计算机测验、智力纸笔测验和结构式心理访谈3个方面。计算机测验采取一对一人机对话形式检测，复检者独立操作计算机，完成数字运算测验、数字搜索测验、语词推理测验和中国士兵人格测验，主要检测受检者的数字运算能力、辨别能力和反应速度，语言理解和语词类别推理能力的精神分裂样人格特征等心理障碍。若计算机检测不合格的应征青年还作智力纸笔测验，进一步检测明确智力障碍的程度，排除因计算机使用不熟练而造成的“假”不合格，最终作智力“合格”或“不合格”的结论。对计算机测验、纸笔测试不合格的应征公民，由心理访谈人员做进一步的心理访谈，通过访谈，评估其是否已患精神障碍或将来患精神障碍的危险程度，排除因不理解答题要领而造成的“假”不合格者。通过上述措施，做到每名新兵在政治上绝对可靠，在身体上、心理上符合标准，确保证兵员质量。至2010年，修文县实现连续26年27次无责任退兵。

三、征兵宣传

每年征兵工作开始，即展开广泛深入的宣传工作，号召适龄青年报名，由乡（镇）武装干部和接兵人员进行初步审定，登记造册。广大青年争先恐后应征，“一人参军，全家光荣”的政治气氛很浓。历年报名应征青年均占适龄青年的85%以上。按照上级分配的人数年年都满额完成征集任务。1986年，全县父母送子报名参军者达420人次，兄姐送弟报名者164人次，兄弟争相报名者63人次。

2000年后，出现适龄青年、预征对象外出打工多，高考入学多，报名参军人员少的实际情况，完成征兵任务难度增大。征兵宣传工作也针对性地提出“既注重面上的轰轰烈烈，又突出宣传重点和地方特色”的要求，将征兵宣传工作贯穿于全民国防教育之中，让受教育适龄青年、预征对象了解政策法规和征兵程序。将应征条件、体检标准、政审标准等及时在县的媒体《修文报》（《当代修文》）、修文电视台刊播，让广大群众掌握政策、熟悉标准。各乡（镇）征兵办结合本地实际，采取有效措施，利用宣传车、电视、展板、标语、板报等形式，大力宣传，大造声势。2004年，人武部认真贯彻落实《省政府、省军区关于做好平时征兵准备工作的意见》，牢固树立向平时要质量的意识，深入乡

2005年10月，冬季征兵期间，县征兵工作领导小组组织开展征兵宣传

（镇）调查摸底，做好兵役登记，把征兵宣传放在平时的工作中，并提前做好初检初审和病史调查，对当年确定的553名预征对象，做到来源清、去向明、联得上，有针对性地作宣传教育工作。是年，冬季征兵工作开始后，县征兵工作领导小组利用10月31日县城赶场天，在县城中心地带设立征兵工作宣传点，布置展板，拉起横幅，开展征兵宣传活动。当天，宣传工作同时在其他乡（镇）展开，全县共散发宣传提纲9640份，张贴、悬挂标语1000条（幅），接受群众咨询718人次。同时，还出动13辆宣传车，开进村寨乡村巡回播放宣传提纲，营造良好的舆论氛围。县长石洪在电视台向全县人民发表电视讲话，动员适龄青年踊跃报名参军；县电视台每晚在黄金时段滚动播放征兵公益广告，扩大征兵宣传力度。各乡（镇）专武干部不分白天黑夜到田间地头、到应征青年家中宣传动员。通过多渠道深入宣传，鼓舞适龄青年报名应征和家长送子当兵的热情，营造适龄青年踊跃参军、家长支持子女应征的良好社会氛围。2006年，接受自1993年以后第二次在县征招驻藏兵员任务，县委、县政府高度重视，责成宣传部门充分利用县内电视和《当代修文》报，对征兵工作的新规定和进藏入伍青年的待遇进行广泛的宣传，鼓励入伍青年到祖国最坚苦的地方去磨炼意志。由于宣传工作到位，圆满完成110名驻藏兵的征集任务。2010年10月31日，县人武部部长童代平、政委李利亚、县政府副县长王雄飞等领导走上街头，参加冬季征兵宣传咨询活动，给群众发放宣传资料接受群众咨询，一天就发放宣传资料5000份。

四、征集对象

历年的征集对象，因各个时期的不同情况有所侧重。1978—1980年，在农村主要征集家庭劳动力比较充裕的贫农、下中农子弟；在城镇征集部分厂矿企业、事业单位满2年工龄的青年职工。1981—1985年，在城镇征集高中应届毕业生和具有初中以上文化程度的青年。在农村征集具有小学以上文化程度的青年。1986—2010年，在城镇征集高中毕业的青年，机关、企事业单位具有高中以上文化程度的青年职工；在农村征集具有初中以上文化程度的青年。

征集兵员的年龄、体格、政治条件，历年均按《兵役法》和国家统一标准，由各级层层把关，严格审查。其中的政治条件要求，1980年前，偏重于家庭出身和社会关系，凡出身于剥削阶级家庭和有复杂社会关系的青年，一般不得入伍；1980年后，改为着重审查应征公民的现实表现，注重严把“五关”（报名关、政审关、文化关、体检关、定兵关）。2006年，全县参加应征青年506人，经体检、政审合格218人，合格率达43%。之后再经择优录取，兵员质量实现“三满意”（群众满意、接兵部队满意、征兵领导小组满意）。2010年冬季征兵中提出“坚持标准、全面衡量、好中选优”的要求，经过两个月努力，于12月13日把合格兵员送到部队，圆满完成征集任务。

2006年11月22日《当代修文》记者拍摄送子当兵情景

五、紧急动员

1979年对越自卫还击作战期间，在县进行紧急征兵。通过紧急动员，提高了广大群众和适龄青年对参军参战保卫祖国是每个公民的神圣职责和光荣义务的认识，有力地激发了大家关心国家安危，为保卫祖国而献身的激情，使广大适龄青年和退伍军人踊跃报名参军，涌现出适龄青年争相参军参战，退伍军人要求重返前线杀敌立功，干部和党员带头送子当兵，父母带子报名参军的动人情景。8天时间，经过政审和体格检查，批准230人应征，参加昆明军区第五补训团，其中还有42名复员老战士和1名女兵。

1978—2010年征集兵员数额

表2—08—01　　　　单位：名

年份	兵员数	女兵	备注	年度	兵员数	女兵	备注
1978	204	—	—	1995	105	—	—
1979	384	1	—	1996	110	1	—
1980	131	—	—	1997	115	1	—
1981	152	—	—	1998	96	—	—
1982	120	—	—	1999	137	—	—
1983	111	—	—	2000	133	1	—
1984	100	—	—	2001	132	—	—
1985	40	—	—	2002	126	—	—
1986	112	—	—	2003	129	—	—
1987	105	2	—	2004	131	1	—
1988	—	—	未征	2005	130	4	—
1989	96	—	—	2006	110	—	—
1990	190	—	春冬各1次	2007	112	—	—
1991	110	—	—	2008	116	—	—
1992	104	—	—	2009	113	1	—
1993	100	—	—	2010	113	—	—
1994	110	—	—				

第四节　预备役

一、军人登记

1981年恢复预备役军人登记。士兵预备役分为第一类预备役和第二类预备役。第一类预备役士兵包括建立民兵组织单位中的基干民兵和未建立民兵组织单位中经过预备役登记的28岁以下退出现役的士兵、专业技术人员。第二类预备役士兵包括建立民兵组织单位中的普通民兵和未建立民兵组织单位中经过预备役登记的29至35岁的退出现役的士兵。是年，全县登记一类预备役为3753人（复退军人619人），二类预备役1.5万人（复退军人662人）。编为基干连38个，下辖124个排，378个班。至2010年，服士兵一类预备役1.2万人，二类预备役4.8万人。

二、军事训练

按照规定，未服过现役的第一类预备役士兵，在18至20岁阶段应参加30至40天的军事训练。预备役军人的军事训练一般在民兵组织中进行。县人民武装部每年均通过民兵训练形式组织预备役军人军事训练2至4次。

三、工兵团组

1999年8月2日，中国人民解放军贵阳陆军预备役工兵团在县成立，标志着修文国防后备力量的建设发展又迈出新的一步。在当天的成立大会上，中共贵州省委常委、省军区政委喻忠桂向工兵团授予军旗，省军区政治部主任雷玉德宣布23名营以上军官的任职命令。贵阳陆军预备役工兵团是以现役军人为骨干，以预备役军官、士兵为基础组建的，全团部署在修文、开阳、息烽、花溪、小河、云岩、白云、清镇8个县（区、市）和开阳磷矿、贵州久联集团、詹阳动力重工有限责任公司和贵阳市肺科医院等企事业单位，团部驻马家桥。预备役工兵团建成后，除加强部队自身建设外，积极参加县的社会主义物质文明和精神文明建设。1999至2010年，工兵团官兵参加护林、防火、防洪等值勤700多人次，参与扑灭山火、抢险救灾40多起。

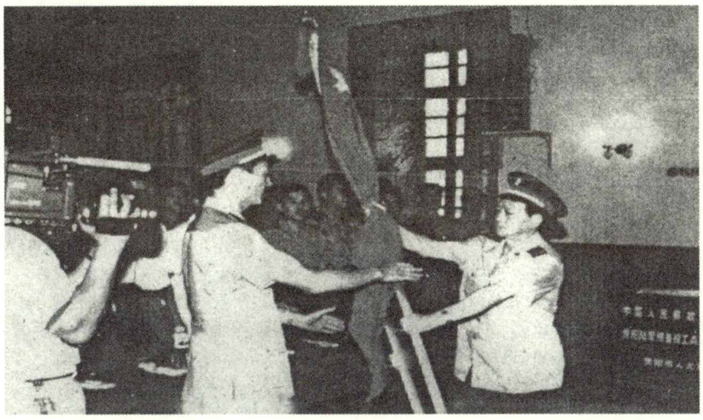

贵州省委常委、省军区政委喻忠桂（右）向工兵团授予军旗

第五节　民　兵

一、民兵组建

调整民兵组织　1981年，按中共中央、国务院《民兵工作条例》进行民兵整组，缩小组建范围，压缩民兵年龄，简化组织层次，严格民兵条件，将全县民兵调整为255个连，计有民兵1.89万名（其中基干民兵3800名，普通民兵1.51万名），占全县总人口的7.7%。从1985年起，按照中央“减少数量，提高质量，抓好重点，打好基础”的要求，全县又编为353个连，有民兵1.95万名，其中基干民兵3800名，普通民兵1.57万名，占全县总人口的6.3%。1999年开始，在民兵编组上改过去跨队、跨车间编组为以生产单位编组，使之利于开展活动。2006年，再改民兵编组为以村为单位，每村建成1个连，

2007年6月，县民兵应急分队成立

全县共建8个团，24个营，217个连，有民兵6.23万人（其中基干民兵1300人，普通民兵6.1万名），占全县总人口的20%。

建立应急分队 1996年，县人武部在龙场镇试点组建民兵应急分队，参加民兵30名。2003年，全县10乡（镇）均建立民兵应急分队，每队有民兵20名，2004年扩大到30名，以后逐年扩充。民兵应急分队是应付突发事件、维护社会稳定的中坚力量，经过几年建设已步入正规化轨道，基本实现武器装备现代化、通信工具现代化，成为一支素质优良、动员快速、战斗力强的队伍。2007年，为便于民兵应急分队快速调遣，随时执行应急任务，提高工作效率，于6月28日将原来分散在全县10乡（镇）的民兵应急分队集中组建为修文民兵应急分队。至2010年，县民兵应急分队仍存。

二、民兵武器装备与管理

1978年，除保留厂矿和县直部门的武器库外，公社武器均集中到区保管。1980年起民兵武器陆续重新装备，全部淘汰旧式武器。1984年，撤销区武器库，除保留大型厂矿武器存放点和电站执勤枪支外，武器均集中到县武器库保管。1990年后，随着国力的增强，民兵武器装备已实现国产制式化。自1990年10月起，民兵武器统由县人武部集中保管。2000年，对民兵武器装备仓库改建，增设全方位监控系统及“三维报警系统”（库房报警、值班室报警、首长报警）。同时，对库室保管员进行严格政治审查和经常性的思想考查，对出入库人员坚持审查、登记制度，定期对武器弹约进行擦拭保养，保证武器装备处于良好的战技术状态。自武器集中管理后，县人武部把安全管理工作作为头等大事来抓，至2010年已连续20年无安全事故。

三、民兵训练

1978年，沿袭就地、分散、小型、业余训练的民兵训练方式。1981年，根据总参谋部指示，改革基干民兵训练方式，民兵军事训练以民兵干部和基干民兵为重点，对普通民兵军事训练不作要求。每年只对未经训练的基干民兵进行一般基础训练。将就地、分散、小型、业余训练改为以区或公社和县或系统为单位集中训练。1984年，派民兵通讯班参加安顺军分区民兵比武大赛，荣获团体赛第三名。1986年3月5—25日，首次集中各区、乡（镇）、厂矿的140名六零炮兵到县人武部集中驻训。

农村民兵参训期间耽误的时间实行误工补贴。国家机关和企事业单位参训的民兵，其工资和其他物质待遇照常发给。

1990年起，民兵训练按《民兵军事训练大纲》和上级军事机关规定进行。2004年，将民兵军事训练列入乡（镇）年终工作目标考核内容，是年，通过正确的指导和扎实训练，25名个人和8个单位取得优异成绩，受到通报表彰。2006年，贯彻《贵阳警备区军事训练工作指示》的同时，深入开展“履行使命，献身国防”的主题教育，围绕反恐维稳和抢险救灾组织民兵军事训练3期，组织10个乡（镇）的民兵应急分队进行队列会操训练。为提高民兵和民兵应急分队的机动作战能力，县人武部还

2005年7月，乡（镇）专武干部军事训练

创新训练方式，组织小箐乡民兵应急分队进行行程150公里的野营拉练训练。1990—2010年，全县计有5.41万名民兵接受训练。

四、民兵任务

（一）参军参战

1979年南疆保卫战期间，全县民兵以临战姿态投入对越自卫还击行动，有的积极参与支前工作，有的踊跃报名参军参战，有的复退军人申请重返前线，经审查后批准384名民兵应征入伍，批准42名老战士重返前线，编入昆明军区第5补训团训练。入伍战士英勇杀敌，涌现出许多可歌可泣的英雄事迹。小箐公社民兵商胜强，1982年1月应征入伍，1984年任中国人民解放军35211部队41分队炮排排长，随部队开赴云南边陲投入自卫还击战。4月29日，攻打146号高地和34号高地战斗中，不顾个人安危，冒着越军密集炮火，架炮连续摧毁敌人4个火力点，后英勇牺牲，实践了生前“洒尽满腔青春血，报答祖国养育恩”的誓言。

（二）维护社会治安与抢险救灾

1978年，县人武部将组织民兵维护社会治安和参与抢险救灾作为民兵建设的重要工作来抓。1980年1月，公安部紧急通缉令缉拿的犯罪分子胡三娃，潜逃到马家桥石坟坝余安贵家。马家桥公社人武部长罗友华、民兵副连长刘成方和排长朱德祥，带领武装民兵配合县公安局将其擒获。安顺军分区分别给罗友华、刘成方和朱德祥各记二等功一次，公社民兵连受到贵州省人民政府通令嘉奖。1983年，在严厉打击刑事犯罪分子过程中，县人武部组织全县民兵配合县公安部门突击行动，依法逮捕一批犯罪分子，摧毁一批犯罪团伙。从1989年8月开始，县人武部调集46名民兵组成护路民兵连，于公路、铁路交叉处设立岗哨，在犯罪分子经常出没的地方设暗哨，24小时沿线昼夜巡逻维护治安秩序，确保国民经济大动脉安全畅通。1990年，处理大小事故12起，捡拾各种被盗物资价值10多万元，查出携带易燃易爆危险品上车的旅客150人次，避免一起由小孩乱扳信号机可能导致的翻车事故发生。民兵连中40名民兵受到省、地、县表彰。2001—2003年，扎佐、龙场、久长、谷堡、小箐等乡（镇）民兵20多次参与扑灭森林火灾，为国家挽回上百万元的损失。2005年夏，全县遭受旱灾，县人武部组织民兵2300多人参与抗旱保苗。2008年全县遭受冰凝灾害，500民兵战斗在“抗凝冻保民生”第一线，参与供电抢修，为山区受灾群众运送生活物资，20人受到县委、县政府表彰。

2008年县民兵参加抗击凝冻灾害

（三）参加社会主义建设带头劳动致富

1978年中共十一届三中全会后，县内民兵积极开展多种经营，先后办起采矿、烧砖瓦、运输、食品加工、饲养和种植等工副业。扎佐乡小堡村民兵李淑俊1982年开始种植烤烟，在反复实践中总结出一套提高栽培技术和烘烤质量的经验在全村推广，村里24户人家1984年种烟90亩，收入4万元，户均1500

元。金桥乡石榴村民兵排长李贤忠，1984年组织23个民兵承包荒山570亩，两年艰苦劳动，使荒山披上绿装，经县林业部门实地验收，符合造林规定标准，被评为封山育林先进集体。至1990年，全县民兵专业户达960户，以民兵为主体的联户企业30个。1991年，马家桥乡年平均产值10万元以上的38个乡村企业中，有18个企业以民兵为主体兴办，其中又多是民兵担任厂长。幸福村党支部组织以民兵为主的178个剩余劳动力，从中挑选8名民兵为骨干，接过一座亏损的原社办土砖瓦窑，改建成10门和14门的两座轮窑，两年生产红砖700万块，创产值42万元，向国家缴纳税金1.5万元，为村民创造财富18.4万元。全村199户人家中，9户盖起12间砖瓦房，15户买电视机，22户买单车，44户买缝纫机，家家都有收音机，群众生活得到较大改善。1998年调整农业产业结构，乡（镇）民兵成为主力军，六桶乡民兵李根书发展林下养鸡2万只，个人致富后又将技术传授给周围群众，带动一乡农民发展养殖业，使六桶乡成为远近闻名的土鸡养殖专业乡。2002年，全县农村民兵响应县人武部号召积极投身新农村建设，在农业产业结构调整中做典型当标兵，至2010年，由民兵经营的烤烟、经果林、中药材种植基地有13个。

第六节　国防教育

1994年12月建立修文县全民国防教育领导小组。1997年3月改建为全民国防教育委员会，下设办公室。至2000年7月，全县10乡（镇）均建立国防教育领导小组。在广大干部和群众中灌输国防知识，强化国防观念，开展国防教育活动。

从1995年起，在全县中学开设国防教育课，每周1至2节，发给学生国防教育读本，把国防知识渗透到教学之中。每年新学期开学前，派军事教官到学校，集中高一年级新生开展为期7天的国防教育，进行军事训练。

每年“八一”建军节，组织县国防教育委员会成员开展军事日活动，进行实弹射击演习，县级领导班子到县境驻军看望慰问官兵，以增强各级领导干部的“国防教育”意识。2000年7月10—14日，组织全县中、小学54名品学兼优的学生，开展国防教育夏令营活动，参观遵义会议会址、遵义红军山、息烽集中营等爱国主义教育基地，激发培育学生成才报国的热情。2001年3月22—25日，在龙场、扎佐、久长3镇举办“国防教育图片展”，参观者达5000余人。2003年，开展“双拥模范县”创建活动，把增强全民国防意识放在首位，引导人民群众树立没有国防就没有安全，没有军队就没有发展的意识。县委、县政府采取“六个结合”（国防教育与普法工作相结合、与理论学习相结合、与党员干部教育相结合、与学生素质教育相结合、与市民道德教育相结合、与企业文化建设相结合）的方式，在全县

2010年，县国防教育领导小组开展军事日活动

逐步实现国防教育网络化、经常化、制度化、深入化。2004年第四个国防教育日，县国教办下发通知，要求全县各单位部门开展国防教育日宣传活动，并作具体安排。当天，县国防动员委员会成员单位在县城设立宣传点，在大街上摆放国防教育展板，张贴标语，播放录音，发放宣传单。学校、机关、驻军和乡（镇）组织学生、民兵、战士、干部职工开展万人签名活动。2010年第十个国防教育日，贵州国防军事学校修文分校举办军事技能汇报表演，使观众受到一次具体的国防教育。

第七节　人防战备

1978年，县设战备领导小组，负责战备人防工作。1979年南疆保卫战期间，在全县人民中进行战备形势教育和战况通报，并对复员退伍军人进行普查登记。根据上级布置的任务，县人武部抽调4名现役军人到补训团执行任务，临战征集384名新兵补充作战部队，批准42名复员退伍军人重返前线。1984年4月，县战备领导小组改称人防战备领导小组，设办公室办理日常工作。1996年《中华人民共和国人民防空法》颁布后，县政府和县人武部每年10月29日举行人防音响警报器鸣响演练。演练由县政府领导和人武部领导担任指挥长，当天10时，由指挥长下令，防空警报以预先警报、紧急警报和解除警报3个阶段鸣响10分钟。1997年组织民兵150人在210国道扎佐至久长段，进行运沙填坑、清理边沟、清除障碍物的公路战备演练。

2002年设人防战备办公室，结合民用建筑修建防空设施，在县城民用建筑翰林花园拟建防空地下室，面积1200平方米，可容2400人。2005年开始征缴人防工程易地建设费，当年征缴18万元。2010年11月12日，翰林花园防空地下室通过贵阳市人防办验收合格，成为县第一个通过验收的民用建筑地下防空避险设施。至2010年，全县已建成防空疏散区217个，可容8至10万人。

第八节　拥政爱民

一、参加和支援地方经济建设

1998年起，驻县部队和民兵按县人武部提出的“五抓五带”（抓机关带基层，抓干部带民兵、抓民兵带全民、抓城镇带农村、抓集中带经常）要求，积极投入到参加和支持地方经济建设的大潮中，帮助人民群众调整生产结构，脱贫致富。2001年4月，驻县贵阳陆军预备役工兵团组织集中训练舟桥营3连官兵连续作战7天，完成谷堡乡大棚蔬菜基地1公里道路的修建任务。7月，工兵团捐资3万元，出动官兵20人携工程机械，同扎佐镇大堡村群众共同构筑长550米村路，为当地群众发展经济创造良好条件，群众称为“军民连心路”；2002年和2004年，工兵团完成县投资300万元的民主路改造任务。驻县贵州省军区后勤生产基地把生产技术和管理经验介绍给当地农民，通过技术帮扶，促进驻地附近农民增收。基地每年聘用驻地农村富余劳动力500人次，拓宽村民增收渠道。还通过观念、技术、信息等方面的优势，带动并促进驻地周边的白莲、幸福、军民3个村进行产业结构调整，2004—2010年，3个村农民群众增收达400万元。

2005年7月，县人武部为谷堡乡新堰村困难群众送去生产生活物资

2003—2010年，驻县部队官兵植树造林8.5万亩，帮助贫困群众改造茅草房45户，帮助23名失学儿童重返校园，修建乡村公路和串寨路350公里，修建小水窖和水池100余口。

二、抢险救灾

2002年4月，扎佐林场、小箐乡、龙场镇相继发生森林火灾，正在集中训练的工兵团2个连队官兵160余人，快速集结，紧急出动，连续作战，扑灭森林火灾3起，使群众的生命财产免受大火吞噬。2004年8月31日晚，停放在县城体育馆西门路边的一辆面包车突然起火燃烧，车内冒起黑烟，火苗冲出车窗外。途经该处的县武警中队3名战士立即展开扑救，20多分钟后将大火扑灭，遏制了一场意外事故发生。2005年5月7日，六广河海马村河段一机动客船被大风掀翻沉没，5人遇难。工兵团于次日派出20名舟桥专业骨干，3艘冲锋舟参与沉船搜救，经过4天连续作战，将沉船打捞上岸。2006年7月12日，县境302国道1辆大客车与1辆满载47桶黄磷的大货车相撞造成黄磷起火，引发两车燃烧。县消防大队接警后迅速赶赴现场，将大火扑灭，县政府为消防大队记集体三等功一次。是年，县人武部组织民兵450人，扑灭大小森林火灾30余次，挽回经济损失100多万元。1978年至2010年，驻县部队参与抢险救灾200余次，为国家挽回经济损失1500余万元。

2005年5月7日，县人武部、贵阳陆军预备役工兵团官兵参加六广河沉船搜救

经济建设篇

1978年后，随着中共十一届三中全会精神的深入贯彻，特别是关于真理标准大讨论，长期憋在广大干部、群众中想改变经济落后面貌的愿望，终于有一个好的氛围得以展现。以改革为动力，全县整个经济工作显现出日益向好的新局面。

20世纪70年代末和80年代初，县委、县政府认真地对县情进行再认识，一致认为县境资源丰富，区位优势明显，交通较为方便，处于国家大电网覆盖之下，具有发展经济较好的基础条件，不能再捧着金碗讨饭吃，必须大干快上。为突破制约经济发展的资金、技术和人才短缺这一瓶颈，下决心采取借鸡下蛋的策略，积极开展外引内联，多次组织力量赴经济发达地区考察学习、招商引资；聘请省、市知名专家为全县的发展“把脉”献策；充分发挥本县知识分子的积极作用，为改革和建设出力。要求县直机关围绕发展提供更好的服务，政法、公安部门为发展切实保驾护航。1982年县委编制《关于实现修文经济建设奋斗目标的方案》，提出到1990年全县工农业总产值在1980年的基础上翻一番的要求。由于家庭联产承包责任制的全面推行，使全县农业生产迅速发展，乡镇企业异军突起，从而改变全县以农为主的经济格局。1984年，国营企业开始改革，厂矿公司可以根据自身条件选择经营方式和用人制度，导致工业生产发展势头良好。从1982年起，国营企业扭转连续13年亏损的窘境，开始为地方财政上交收入。到1983年，全县地方生产总值、工业总产值、农业总产值和乡镇企业总产值分别以年均递增12.39%、5%、9.88%和17.92%的速度增长，开局良好。1984年是重要的节点，地方生产总值、工业总产值、农业总产值和乡镇企业总产值分别在1983年的基础上增长33.65%，77.77%、29.86%和156.39%。这是以往未有的过增长速度。从此，全县经济建设迈入发展的快车道。面对大好形势，县委、县政府及时制订“一产稳县，二产强县，三产活县”的发展战略，加强产业结构调整，注重非公有制经济发展，开始对县境旅游资源的开发，制订资金、人才、技术“三引进”的配套政策，加大招商引资的力度，使经济工作既保持高速发展的态势，又使第一、二、三产业及各产业内部的关系逐渐趋于协调。至1990年，全县生产总值达1.97亿元、工农业总产值2.05亿元、乡镇企业总产值9258万元，在1978年的基础上分别增长4.51倍、5.39倍和18.41倍，年均递增分别为15.28%、16.71%和28.04%。其中工农业总产值提前5年，于1985年在1980年的基础上实现翻一番的奋斗目标。工农业总产值中工业产值所占比重。由1978年的34.11%上升至45.29%。随着生产的发展，地方预算内财政收入由1978年的188.9万元增至1990年的1415.9万元，年均递增15.81%。经过13年的不懈努力，使全县经济发展水平上一个新的台阶，为继续发展打下一个良好的基础。但13年的快速发展是在低水平的基础上实现的，县委、县政府领导经济建设缺乏经验，是“摸着石头过河”走过来的。因此出现重发展、轻质量，重眼前成效、轻可持续发展的倾向。在“有水快流”的指导思想下，对资源盲目开发利用，导致浪费；提出“先上车，后补票”的口号，使一些新上项目缺乏应有的监管，高能耗、高污染的企业乘势入驻；新上项目多、骨干企业少，且布局零乱，缺乏统一的规划；在发展过程中，生态意识、环保意识比较淡薄，带来一些后遗症；采取“三不要”（不要户口、不要人事档案、不要组织手续）引进人才的办法良莠不分，甚至还有“招进女婿而气走儿子”的现象发生。这些都是比较突出的问题。

从1991年起，全县经济工作步入稳步发展之路。1992年邓小平视察南方重要谈话发表后，县委召开全委扩大会议集中学习，明确以“三个有利于”（是否有利于发展社会主义社会的生产力、是否有利于增强社会主义国家的综合国力、是否有利于提高人民的生活水平）作为判断是社会主义还是资本主义的标准，从而进一步坚定狠抓经济建设的决心，提出“以交通通信为龙头，大力培育市场经济体系，整体推进修文经济建设”的指导思想。在第八次党代会上，县委又明确提出“加速经济建设，全面推进兴修富民”的工作目标。农村工作以稳定和完善家庭联产承包责任制为核心，以加大科技和资金投入为重点，以调整农业内部产业结构为抓手，引导农民大力发展商品生产。通过这些措施，使农作物种植面积逐年扩大，复种指数突破200%大关，经济作物种植面积比重上升，粮食生产量从1993年起实现八连增，蔬菜、水果、肉类、禽蛋和水产品产量增长势头强劲。至2000年，一产增加值达3.49亿元，在1990年8204万元的基础上增长3.26倍，年均递增15.57%；农业总产值达4.57亿元，在1990年1.12亿元的基础上增长3.08倍，年均递增15.10%。20世纪90年代，县委、县政府抓住原驻县企事业单位外迁闲置大量厂房的机会，进一步加强招商引资工作，招进一批科技含量高，投资规模大，经济效益好的企业入驻；原国营工业企业改制焕发出新的活力；一大批通过外引内联新上的非公有制工业企业成为工业经济重要的组成部分。20世纪90年代后期，县委、县政府提出“改造传统产业，壮大支柱产业，发展新兴产业”为发展工业经济的新思路，为提高运行质量，对落后产能采取果断措施淘汰或改造，1999年对88家煤炭开采企业关井停产55家，对17家水泥生产企业中不达标的13家停产限期进行整改。果断的措施推动全县工业生产的健康发展。随着县城改造工作的铺开，带动建筑业的发展，使全县第二产业在生产总值中所占比重由1978—1990年平均31.45%提升至1991—2000年平均36.50%。与此同时，建机构，作规划，加快旅游业发展的步伐。以扎佐镇为中心的物流业雏形初显，房地产开发方兴未艾，城乡市场日益繁荣，信息产业发展步伐加快，从而有力地带动第三产业的发展。1991—2000年，三产对地方生产总值的贡献率达23.54%，比1978—1990年提升3.27个百分点。全社会固定资产投资2000年为3.13亿元，比1990年增长47.59倍，平均递增高达47.45%。地方预算内财政收入2000年为4853.75万元，在1990年的基础上增长2.43倍，年均递增13.12%。根据中央提出到2000年工农业总产值要在1980年基础上翻两番的要求，全县在第一阶段（1981—1990年）提前5年实现翻第一番的目标后，又于2000年出现工农业总产值达11.86亿元，实际上在1980年的基础上翻3.43番。工业产值占工农业总产值的比重由1980年的55.04%和1990年的72.67%上升至2000年的83.73%，“工业强县”目标得到有力地推进。2000年，在“团结务实，乘势争先”修文精神激励下，县委、县政府乘国家实施西部大开发战略的极好机遇，提出实现全县经济跨越式发展的构想，并在职工中广泛开展“西部大开发，修文怎么办”的思想大讨论，制订“解放思想，更新观念，乘势争先，强县升位”的目标。

2001—2010年，是全县国民经济运行最好的10年，既保持发展的高速度，又使产能、质量有明显提升。2003年在县第九次党代会上，县委提出“抢抓机遇谋发展，集中精力建强县”的主题，明确全县工作整体思路为：突出一个主题（建设经济强县），强化两个基础（夯实基层组织建设和基础设施建设），建设三个文明（物质文明、精神文明、政治文明），实现四大战略（科技兴县、环境立县、农业稳县、工

业强县），着力五个突破（特色支柱产业突破、招商引资突破、非公有制经济发展突破、城乡一体化突破、经济实力突破）。2007年县政府又站在新的高度，提出“建设生态文明县”的工作目标，2010年又作出“强制淘汰落后产能”的决定，关停13家产能、工艺、设备、产品落后的企业。在抓经济工作中，县委、县政府的环保理念、生态意识明显增强。招商引资成立专门机构，建起项目库，推行“一站式”服务，并着力树立“诚信招商，文明招商”形象，把工作重点放在投资规模大、科技含量高、经济效益好的项目上，培育自己的支柱产业。项目引进更注重布局，使规划实施的“十里工业走廊”“三点两线一园区”“工业循环经济示范园区”逐渐成形，成为“布局集中、产业集聚、资源节约、配套完善”的工业基地，使工业总产值由2000年的9.93亿元猛增至2010年的56.09亿元，年均递增18.91%，又使全县以工业为主体的二产增加值在生产总值中所占比重不断上升，10年平均达38.77%。由于商品经济不断发展，使不同规模的农产品基地不断涌现，在自愿基础上组建新的经济联合体也应运而生，逐渐形成以“菜、畜、果、药”为拳头产品的特色农业。与此同时，粮食生产一直没有放松，总产稳步增长，1978—1990年年均产粮4.7万吨，1991—2000年年均产粮7.15万吨，2001—2010年年均产粮9.23万吨。这10年中，第二、第三产业的蓬勃发展，使一产农业在生产总值中的比重逐渐下降，正体现出产业结构调整的巨大成就，但农业总产值和农业增加值的增长幅度仍然很大，2010年在2000年基础上分别增长1.88倍和1.26倍，年均分别递增6.52%和8.50%。一批对外有较大影响力的旅游项目陆续建成和投入营运，推动全县第三产业跨越式发展，使其在生产总值中所占比重稳步提升，2010年占45.82%，第一次位居第一、第二产业之上，充分体现发展第三产业的巨大潜力。这10年，全社会固定资产投资208.76亿元，其中，包括招商引资在内各渠道投入基本建设和更新改造的项目资金149.24亿元，成为全县第一、二、三产业大批新增生产能力的资金支撑。非公经济已形成以采掘、建材、医药、食品加工、冶炼、化工、耐火材料为主体的7大支柱工业产业，2010年非公企业实现增加值26.56亿元，占生产总值的57.5%，成为全县国民经济发展的一个亮点。由于经济建设持续发展，并奠定一定的基础，2007年经省建设经济强县领导小组认真考核决定，从2008年起将修文纳入全省第三轮建设经济强县之列。2001—2010年全县地方财政收入达14.5亿元，年均1.45亿元，比1991—2000年年均5626万元增长1.58倍。地方财政收入占生产总值的比重2001—2010年为5.85%，在1991—2000年5.11%的基础上提升0.74个百分点，综合反映经济运行质量的提高。至2010年，全县经济建设主要指标在全省88个县（市、区、特区）中的排位总趋势是在2000年的基础上有明显提升：生产总值由第38位升至第33位，人均生产总值由第23位升至第16位，农业总产值由第46位升至第34位，规模以上工业总产值由第60位升至第10位，地方财政收入由第40位升至第35位，人均地财收入由第24位升至第20位，农民人均纯收入由第15位升至第12位，粮食总产由第59位升至第57位，人均产粮由第53位升至第44位，肉类总产量由第38位降至第45位，油菜籽产量由第20位降至第27位，烤烟产量由第35位降至第37位。修文跻身全省建设经济强县行列后，对全县整个经济工作是个极大的推进，至2010年，在27个建经济强县（区、市）中，主要指标的排位也是在2000年基础上向前提升：生产总值绝对数的排位未变，均是第25位，但人均生产总值由第19位升至第15位，规模以上工业总产值由第26位升至第25位，农业总产值由第19位升至第15位，固定资产投资由第25位升至第18位，地方财政收入由第26位升至第21位，人均地财收入由第20位升为第19位，农民人均纯收入由第14位升至第12位。

第一章　农　业

长期以来农业一直是全县国民经济中的基础产业。由于多种原因，特别是较长时间在人民公社体制下，农业劳动者的生产积极性受到严重挫伤，产业结构不合理，生产水平低下，商品率不高，发展速度缓慢。1978年全县农业总产值仅为2111万元，农业人口人均产值116元，主打产品的粮食总产5.29万吨，平均亩产134.9公斤，农业人口人均产粮291公斤。集体经济全年总收入1455万元中、出售产品收入254万元，商品率仅为17.48%。当年农民从集体经济中人均分配收入45.97元，人均口粮196公斤，分别只占全年人均纯收入141元和人均实际占有粮食216.5公斤的32.6%和90.5%，农民家庭自营收入占有相当比重。

进入改革开放时期，1981年农村中普遍实行家庭联产承包责任制，农民享有生产、经营自主权，生产积极性得到空前的调动和发挥。在县委“一产稳县、二产强县、三产活县”战略构思指引下，响亮提出步入“一靠政策、二靠投入、三靠科技”的振兴农村经济之路，全面推行农村经济体制改革，着力调整产业结构，加大对农业的投入，在改善农业生产条件上狠下功夫，以大规模、多形式对农民进行培训为抓手，大力推广农业实用技术，提高劳动者素质，逐步推进传统农业向现代农业转化，种田为糊口向商品经济转化，使农村经济出现多业并举，持续发展的新局面。2010年，全县农业总产值达13.14亿元，在1978年的基础上增长12.34倍，年均递增8.17%，农业人口人均产值4980元，牧业产值、渔业产值和农林牧渔服务业产值的比重有明显提升，产业结构趋于合理。粮食总产10.43万吨，粮食作物平均亩产293.1公斤，农业人口人均产粮395.4公斤，分别比1978年增长0.97倍、1.17倍和0.36倍。“果、菜、畜、药”逐渐形成拳头产品，源源不断地进入市场，农产品的商品率达85.16%。尽管1978年后全县第二、第三产业有蓬勃的发展，2010年农业对全县经济总量的贡献率仍达17.13%。农业的发展确保社会稳定，为全县整个国民经济健康发展奠定坚实基础。

第一节　农村经济体制改革

一、全面实行家庭联产承包责任制

1978年，全县约有1/3的生产队仍处于“吃粮靠返销、生产靠贷款、生活靠救济”的窘境，农民对集

体经济缺乏信心，希望变革是大家的心愿，特别是在边远经济不发达的地区，试图改变集体经营模式的探索时有发生。然而，在极“左”思想影响下，县、区、社三级的一些干部形成只有“集体经营才是社会主义”的片面观念，“纠偏”也就成农村工作中的一项中心任务。就是在这样的背景下，《贵州日报》头版以显目大标题发表关岭县顶云公社《定产到组姓“社”不姓“资”》的报道立即在全县农村引起剧烈震动，要求仿效其做法的呼声相当强烈。花椰公社黄银生产队和马场公社秋收后将集体耕地安排给社员种植夏收作物，并明确谁种谁收，于次年取得较集体经营时好得多的收成。他们敢为人先的成功探索，在农村引起极大反响，并成为当年全县开展关于真理标准大讨论活动中被广泛传颂的典型事例。根据外省、外县的做法，打破由生产队统一经营的格局，包产到组、联产计酬，小段包工、定额计酬等责任制迅猛铺开。1979年7月，搞责任制的生产队已达850个，占全县1028个生产队的82.68%。面对这样的形势，各级干部看到搞生产责任制确实能调动农民的生产积极性、有利生产的发展，但又担心这种搞法是否会涉及方向、道路问题，普遍感到困惑。关键时刻，中共十一届四中全会通过《关于加快农业发展若干问题的决定》，贵州省委随即出台《关于放宽农业政策的指示》。9月县委制发《全县试行包产到组、联产计酬的意见》。11月，县委又提出“在坚持生产资料公有制的前提下，各种责任制都可实行。政策要放宽一点，办法要灵活一点，形式要多一点”，并组织200余名干部帮助生产队将集体土地分别落实到农户承包经营，承包期为3年。县委的明确态度，给基层干部和农民群众壮胆，加速全面建立生产责任制的工作进程。1980年年初，除4个生产队仍按集体统一经营外，99.6%的生产队都选择实行不同形式的生产责任制。根据群众要求，为有利生产，方便管理，县委决定将生产队的规模划小到1739个。在实行生产责任的过程中，群众通过比较、一致认为包干到户这种经营方式将生产成果和劳动者的利益更直接地联系起来，不仅克服以往分配中的平均主义弊病，而且简便易行。至1981年年底全部生产队都实行包干到户责任制，后规范称为“家庭联产承包责任制”。

实行家庭联产承包责任制除将生产队耕地按人落实到户经营外，还把集体的耕牛、农具等生产资料固定到户使用，生产队所欠贷款分摊到各户承担，生产队的果园、茶园、山林、鱼塘和加工作坊等也采取承包方式由社员经营。明确所有权和经营权后，农民家庭与生产队签订“五包”合同：一包完成国家粮食征购任务和农副产品派购任务；二包照顾烈军属、因公致残者和“五保”户的必要开支；三包生产大队和生产队干部的合理报酬；四包必要的公共积累和生产费用；五包发展经济、教育、卫生等事业所需的费用。随后，县委又出台“五不变”的政策，即生产队的组织形式不变，基本生产资料集体所有制不变，生产责任制形式在相当时间内稳定不变，农民向国家、集体承担的各项任务不变，农副产品收购价格和奖励办法不变。这些举措使农民吃“定心丸”，打消怕政策变的顾虑，一心扑在发展生产上。全面实行家庭联产承包责任制的1981年，全县遭严重旱灾、雹灾和虫灾袭击，给粮食生产造成重大损失，比上年减产31.33%，但实现农业总产值3260万元、油菜籽产量3500吨、烤烟1630吨、肉类总产2476吨和禽蛋365吨，分别比上年增长33.12%、116.99%、278.19%、2.27%和67.43%，整个农业仍获得好收成。农民人均纯收入180元，在1978年141元的基础上增长27.66%，实现大灾之年不减收。

由于推行家庭联产承包责任制的时间短、群众要求迫切，干部缺乏经验，也确实出现诸如错误认为搞责任制就是单干，基层领导班子涣散、少数队无人管理，集体财产流失，无政府主义蔓延等问题。县委根据中央和省委有关指示精神，一直将农村工作重点放在稳定和完善生产责任制的工作上，纠正在前进过程中所出现的问题。一是明确生产队的职权和干部职责，规定承包农户只有对集体土地及其他财产的使用权，纠正和制止侵犯公有制的错误行为。二是推行土地承包合同，并确保合同兑现。1983年宣布，农户承包的责任地长期稳定不变的政策。1984年根据贵州省委“耕地承包期一般应在15年以上”的文件精神，县委又再次组织力量，以行政村为土地发包方与农户签订承包期为20年的合同。同时，1981年全县还开展林业“三定”（稳定山林权、划定自留山、确定林业生产责任制）工作，对25.69万亩林地的权属予以明确，为农民划自留山11.02万亩，实现“山有主、主有权、权有责、责有利”。并明确承包荒山造林至少50年不变的政策，而且有承包继承权。1998年全县开展第二轮土地承包工作（又称“土地延包”）。第一轮土地承包到期后，承包期再延长50年。这项工作做得很细。县、乡（镇）、村三级均成立领导小组，并由县、乡（镇）抽调300余人进村入户进一步明确农村土地属集体所有，村民委员会为土地的发包方。在整个工作中，着重处理好土地承包到户经营与发展壮大集体经济的关系，承包经营与发展适度规模经营的关系，大规模土地整治与农民家庭承包经营的关系和人多地少的关系。实行“增人不增地，减人不减地”的政策。对“三户一人”（“农转非”户、死亡绝户、外迁户和已办理“农转非”手续的本人）原来的承包土地和强占集体的土地一律清理收回，由村集体经营或重新发包。对第一轮土地承包后的开荒地，本着“保护生态，承认现实，集体所有，有偿使用”的原则处理。对影响生态平衡，导致水土流失的一律退耕还林、还草；对符合耕地要求的开荒地，由村与开发农户办理承包手续。历时半年，最后以“一看、二查、三听、四议、五评”的方法通过市级验收，农户也分别在《土地承包合同书》上签字盖章认可。验收后为5.2万户农户颁发由贵阳市人民政府统一印制的《土地承包经营权益书》。通过土地承包工作，落实土地承包25.59万亩，其中耕地23.71万亩，非耕地1.88万亩（含林地1.61万亩）。在开展二轮土地承包工作的同时，落实农户应承担的村提留132.03万元，乡统筹306.16万元。农业税731.96万元，并分别分解到户，填写在土地承包合同书中，对应承担的义务，农民有一本明白账；三是进行土地承包制度改革。实行土地有偿承包或租赁经营，允许土地经营权转让。开征土地占用税和土地承包使用费，鼓励农民走专业经营道路。土地承包使用费纳入村的提留、乡（镇）统筹合并计算，并严格实行“村收乡（镇）管村用”制度，主要用于发展村的集体经济开支。1994年县政府行文，对可开发的荒山、荒地等非耕地资源，边远、不易管理的瘦薄耕地，撂荒两年以上的责任地，已搞林业“三定”但没有开发或开发差的坡地，对未实行“三定”或土地权属不明确或承包手续不完善的土地等，集体可收回向社会公开拍卖其使用权。当年全县成功拍卖土地使用权43宗，面积1.27万亩，为安顺地区首创。土地承包制度的改革，一方面突破农民只是从事农业生产的历史局限，让一些农民摆脱依赖土地的传统格局，将精力放在发展第二、三产业上。1980年全县农村劳动力资源有97.45%是从事农业生产的，到1990年为90.52%，2000年为77.85%。继后变化进一步加速，至2010年农村劳动力资源中，从事农业的只有59.35%，而从事第二、三产业的比重已提升至40.65%。另一方面促进农村土地的有序流转，不但农村种田大户和林业大户能获更多的土地经营权，开展适度规模经营、发展商品生产，就连城镇居民、外省经营者也参与其中搞土地开发利用，从面盘活土地资源，实现双赢。2007年县农业主管部门对农村耕地流转情况组织一次专题调研，全县耕地流转总面积3.34万亩，占耕地总面积的4.3%。共涉及79个行政村、5318户，多发生在人多地少和公路沿线地区。由农户自发流转的占64.37%，由村出面并经登记备案的占35.63%。流转形式主要有转包、转让、互换和出租。流转耕地用于发展蔬菜生产的最为突出：1000亩以上的基地有2个，100至990亩的有4个，20至980亩的有78个。至2010年，通过农村耕地和非耕地流转，共建成水果生产基地28个，面积突破9万亩；规模养殖场55个，涌现出种养大户146户。土

地流转使家庭联产承包责任制进一步得以稳定和完善，并成为全县农民普遍采用的基本经营方式。此种经营方式使农民乐于接受的主要原因在于他们拥有生产经营自主权，积极性得到调动，有力地推动农村经济的发展，实现农业增效、农民增收。以全面实行家庭联产承包责任制的1981年为基数，至2010年，全县一产增加值和农业总产值年均递增速度分别达7.21%和7.71%，农民年人均纯收入由1981年的180元增到2010年的5152元，年均递增达11.83%。这样的发展速度在修文农业发展史上是没有先例的。铁的事实向世人宣布：全县农民原来长期渴望解决的温饱问题已经解决，正向全面建设小康社会的宏伟目标迈进。

二、建立统分结合的双层经营体制

1978年仍沿袭“一大二公”人民公社体制，农业主要生产资料基本上全部归集体所有并支配使用。农民除按政策划有少量自留地可以经营外，就连家庭副业也被视为“资本主义尾巴”严格加以限制。是时，就是单一的集体经营体制。在实行生产责任制的过程中，县委、县政府始终坚持“宜统则统、宜分则分、统分结合”的原则，不搞“一刀切”，引导农民建立以农民分散经营与集体统一经营相结合的双层经营体制。这既取代原来单一的集体经营体制，又纠正搞生产责任初期的一些人认为“搞责任制就分田单干”，“搞责任制集体经济就不存在”的误解。明确提出在实行家庭联产承包责任制的同时，发展乡（镇）、村两级集体经济，把消灭无经济实力的“空壳村”作为工作目标，并鼓励农户兴办经济联合体。当时的农民既有以户分散经营的强烈愿望，但在扩大经营规模、拓宽经营领域问题上，因为分散经营毕竟是单枪匹马，势单力薄，统一发展集体经济也是普遍要求。于是乡（镇）办、村办企业和经济联合体有较大发展。1978年全县乡（镇）办企业298个，村办企业179个，尚无经济联合体，从业者共计4391人。至1990年，乡（镇）办企业增加到2425个，村办企业因归并等原因减少到71个，联户企业989个，全部从业人员增加至1.74万人，从集体经济获得的收入成为农民年人均纯收入的一个组成部分。1990年农民人均纯收入538元中有59元，1995年农民人均纯收入1194元中有92元，2010年人均纯收入5152元中有223元是来自乡（镇）、村两级集体企业和经济联合体的收入。

在各种形式经济联合体中，农民专业合作社的发展较好。2006年《中华人民共和国农民专业合作社法》颁布，自2008年全县第一个农民专业合作社——谷堡乡“香纯蔬菜种植专业合作社”诞生后，至2010年全县在工商行政管理部门正式办理注册登记的就有71个。其中从事种植业的33个、从事养殖业的36个，另有服务型的专业合作社2个。这些专业合作社以家庭承包经营为基础，实行横向联合，有很强的专业性。在办社宗旨上，对外以获得最大经济效益为目标；对内开展技术培训，信息咨询，农资供应，提供产前、产中和产后服务，成为农民产品进市场的桥梁和纽带，推动农业产业化和规模化经营。这种组织形式完全是在农民自愿的基础上组建的，内部实行民主管理，确实为农民带来实实在在的经济利益，深受农民欢迎。

三、农村税费改革

1978年全县征收入库公粮（农业税）原粮2409.3吨，为农民向国家缴纳的农业税。除此之外、还统购和超购原粮3315.5吨。农业税，占当年粮食总产的4.55%，还未达到税率（常年粮食总产的7%）的要求，农民人均负担13.2公斤，加上统购和超购粮食占粮食总产量的10.81%。在人均产粮只有291.2公斤情况下，农民人均负担征、购粮食任务31.5公斤。当年农业税实际入库折款55.88万元。占全县财政收入的

29.58%，农民人均3.07元。除国家税收外，集体经济为应对支付大、小队干部的报酬，保证“五保户”基本生活需求，照顾军、烈属及困难户和公益事业的必要开支，在当年决算分配中提留管理费和公益金37.59万元，农民人均负担2.07元。即全年农民税、费负担人均5.14元，占1978年农民从集体经济中实际分配所得45.97元的11.18%，占当年人均纯收入141元的3.65%。

从1979年起，对涉农税收的征收政策进行多次调整。当年实行起征点计征办法：规定以生产队为单位，水稻主产地区农民人均口粮在200公斤以上，杂粮地区人均口粮在150公斤以上，稻杂兼产地区人均口粮在175公斤以上，人均从集体分配收入在50元以上的才征收农业税；人均分配收入虽在50元以上，而口粮标准又低于起征点的适当减征；人均口粮和人均分配收入都在起征点以下的一律免征农业税。这一政策的贯彻落实，1979年全县征收公粮（农业税），比上年减征501吨原粮，减征幅度为20.8%。获得免征的生产队60个，减征的生产队769个。1980年起，农业税起征点由原来的一年一定先后改为一定三年不变和一定五年不变。1986年起，农业税可由纳税农户以现金方式按统一规定的粮食价格缴纳，从而结束农业税一律以实物（粮食）缴纳的历史。1985年起，恢复征收契税，1987年起、面向占用耕地建房或从事非农用途的单位或个人开征耕地占用税。1988年起，单列税种开征农业特产税，此前农业特产税是并入农业税中征收。1993年，根据国务院的要求，农业税征收仍以缴纳粮食为主，但用现金缴纳仍占相当比重。2003年起，农业税的征收全部实行现金折交。为减轻农民税赋，1998年起，农业税征收入库总额呈减少趋势，当年实际征收823万元，比前三年（1996—1998年）年均1107.58万元减少25.69%。

实行家庭联产承包责任制后，农民除承担随土地分摊应缴纳的农业税外，还要承担村的“提留”和乡（镇）“统筹”费用。村级是公积金、公益金和管理费，主要用于发展村级集体经济，兴办公益事业，支付大、小队干部报酬，保“五保户”生活，照顾军、烈属和大、小队管理费用。乡（镇）级有农村教育事业附加、计划生育、优抚、民兵训练和修建乡村道路等民办公助项目的款项。村的提留和乡（镇）统筹费用开始一段时间标准不高，额度不大，但在一些乡（镇）和村，干部急于求发展，改变生产和生活条件，不顾群众意愿和承受能力，提高提留和统筹费用标准；个别领导干部为彰显“政绩”，甚至搞起形象工程，所需资金摊派到户；对农村义务教育、农民建房、农村土地管理、殡葬和计划生育、农民进城务工等方面乱收费、乱罚款从个别现象逐步演化为一种“风”，而且愈刮愈烈，成为筹集资金、盲目上项目的手段。乱收费、乱罚款、乱摊派的名目繁多，严重地区农民负责超过上年农民人均纯收入的10%，导致农民怨声载道，严重影响干群关系。1996年，中共中央、国务院发布《关于切实做好减轻农民负担工作的决定》，1998年，在中共中央《关于农业和农村工作若干重大问题的决定》中再次强调减轻农民负担。要求对农民合理负担部分坚持定向、限额，一定三年不变，保持相对稳定；严禁乱收费、乱罚款、乱集资和各种摊派，纠正变相增加农民负担的做法，对违反规定的要严肃处理。根据中央两份文件的要求，全县开展对农村“三乱”和摊派进行专项整治，建立以“一事一议”为主要形式的村民民主议事机制，规定农民负担的最高上限，并确立监管的长效机制，严防反弹。对于按政策规定的合理负担，经核定后以农户为单位填写并发放“农民负担监督卡”，使农户心中有“数”。通过这些工作，农民在“费”的方面负担日益加重的问题在很大程度上得到遏制。

2001年，根据党中央和国务院的统一部署，县委、县政府成立农村税费改革工作领导小组，拉开大规模对农村税费工作进行改革的序幕。次年，此工作全面铺开。主要任务就是“三取消、两调整、一改革”，即取消乡（镇）统筹费、农村义务教育集资等面向农民收取的行政事业性收费和政府性基金、集

资，取消屠宰税和取消统一规定的劳动积累工和义务工；调整农业税和调整农业特产税；改革村提留的收取和使用方法。根据土地利用现状变化较大、粮食生产水平有较大幅度提升和物价上涨等因素，重新核实农业税的计税面积和常年粮食产量及计税价格，严格规范农业税的征收管理。除烤烟外，停征农业特产税。均衡农村不同从业人员的税费负担，健全村级“一事一议”筹资、筹劳的管理制度，把农民负担监督管理机制转入常态化，合理解决村干部报酬、村级管理经费和“五保户”的供养经费。同时处理乡（镇）、村两级的不良债务。这些政策的落实，使农民的税、费负担明显减轻。2001年全县农民税、费负担763.55万元，人均30.13元。2002年农民承担税、费总额505.95万元，人均19.99元，减少幅度分别为33.74%和33.59%。

2003年贯彻中央逐步减少农业税的决定，这是农村税费改革工作的延续。当年实际征收入库466万元，2004年实际入库395万元，分别在上年基础上减征72万元和71万元。2005年执行贵州省委决定，全部取消农业税，农业税附加也一并停止征收。至此，沿袭几千年被农民认为是“皇粮国税”的农业税征收历史宣告终结。此举在农民中反响相当强烈，一致由衷地称颂共产中共惠民政策好。

农村税费改革后，农民每年的负担要求控制在上年农民人均纯收入的2%以内，最高上限不得突破5%。2002—2010年，全县农民人均负担的实际发生数都在上年农民人均纯收入的1.8%以下。

四、农产品统派统购制度改革

1978年沿袭计划经济时期的体制，为保障供给，稳定市场，支援经济建设，国家对粮食和油料实行统购统销，对生猪实行派购，对烤烟等主要经济作物和土特产品实行统一收购的政策。随着农村改革的深入和经济的发展，其政策仍带来农产品价格背离价值，阻碍生产发展的负面作用。县委、县政府根据中央及省委、省政府有关指示精神，对原来相关政策进行调整。从1979年起、对超购粮食在统购价的基础上加价50%、并奖售化肥；1983年起，又对油菜籽的收购实行收购计划内的40%按统购价，60%按超购价（在统购价基础上增加50%），其政策措施在一定程度上缓解国家收购价格偏低的矛盾，但并未从根本上解决问题。1985年，根据中共中央1号文件，即《关于进一步活跃农村经济的十项政策》，把改革农产品统、派购制度列为首项任务，当年在全县范围内取消粮食统购，实行国家合同定购和市场收购的“双轨制”。定购粮任务的30%按原统购价执行，其余70%按原超购价收购。完成合同定购任务的余粮允许自由上市。烤烟按计划收购，实行优质优价。油菜籽分等级定价、敞开收购。对于生猪、肉牛、禽、蛋、药材、生漆、蔬菜等农产品，价格一律放开、随行就市，自由交易、不许压级压价。这些改革措施，农民不单在生产经营环节上、在产品处理环节上也享有充分的自主权，发展生产的积极性进一步得到调动。农产品价格放开，促进市场繁荣。1981年，全县城乡集市成交额865.8万元，1985年增至1231万元，1991年再增至2360万元。1985—1991年年均递增11.46%，比1981—1985年年均递增9.2%高出2.26个百分点。城乡集市成交额中尤以食品类增长最为明显。1991年与1985年比较：粮油、肉食、禽蛋、水产品、蔬菜和干鲜果分别增长24.60%、83.82%，3.53倍、68.75%和35.56%。农民对城镇居民农产品销售额，1981年仅有5.76万元，1985年为362万元，1990年增至988万元，1992年再增至1117万元，1985—1992年年均递增达17.47%；国营商业部门和供销合作社对农副产品的收购，1978年只有241万元，1985年为1008万元，1990年增至1714.7万元，1998年再增至2163万元。农产品价格放开后，1985年至1998年农副产品收购总额年均递增为6.05%。这些资料都反映进入市场的农产品越来越多，不仅农民从中增加收入，城镇居民也从中受益、分享到农村改革的成果。

粮食购、销一直都是整个农产品购、销工作的核心内容。对粮食购、销的改革也在不断地深化。1996年起，逐步退出国家对粮食收购的“双轨制”。1998年根据国务院《进一步深化粮食流通体制改革的决定》的精神，对农民手中的余粮实行按保护价敞开收购的政策，农业发展银行确保收购粮食的资金，粮食部门的粮食实行顺价销售，并深化对国有粮食企业的改革。2000年粮食收购政策又由保护价收购调整为“保优限劣”。2004年，中央决定全面放开粮食购、销市场。为此，县委、县政府责成有关部门对过去在粮食购、销方面的政策、法规进行全面清理，凡不利于粮食自由流通的一律停止执行或进行必要的修改和完善，从而结束粮食购、销业务只能由国家粮食主管部门独家经营的历史，形成国家、集体和个人都可依法经营的新局面。2008年，国家又连续两次提高粮食最低收购价的标准，以保护农民种粮的积极性。

五、农村合作组织改革

供销社和信用社均是农民入股兴办的合作组织，但受“左”的影响，1978年后一度曾仍为“官办”，村中已普遍实行家庭联产承包责任制、商品生产已迅速发展的新形式很不适应。在农村经济体制改革的过程中，全县对农村供销、信用合作社进行以恢复“三性”（组织上的群众性、管理上的民主性、经营上的灵活性）为主要内容的改革。

（一）供销合作社改革

1983年供销合作社的改革全面铺开。一是把县供销社改组为基层供销社的联合社，正式恢复供销社的合作商业性质，使其成为城乡经济交流的一条主渠道。二是加强民主管理，一改过去基层供销社领导由上级任命的做法，改为由社员代表民主选举产生。1987年县联社和基层供销社都进行换届选举，有部分社员被选进基层社和县联社的领导班子直接参与管理，还有部分社员成供销社的合同工。三是清理和扩大社员股金。在三年清理社员股金基础上，按规定补发历年积欠社员应分红利2.03万元。至1985年末，全县社员股金扩至12.41万元，在1964年4.45万元水平上增长1.79倍。四是拓宽服务领域，改革经营方式，实行自主经营。一些基层供销社还先后帮助农民成立辣椒、烤烟等生产协会这样的合作经济组织，并在资金、信息、技术、运输和销售等方面提供服务，加强与农民的联系。五是在内部普遍推行经营承包责任制，使经营者的个人收入与经营成效直接挂钩。通过这些改革，供销社已初步自成体系、遍布乡村，形成有一定经营设施和手段的服务网络。至1990年，供销社系统有县企业3个（农资公司、土产公司和日杂公司），基层供销社5个，分销点32个，饮食服务和生产加工点3个，经营点108个。1991年“撤、并、建”工作后，基层供销社由原来区设置改为按乡（镇）设置变为10个。

（二）信用合作社改革

管理体制改革　1984年根据国务院批转中国农业银行《关于改革信用合作社管理体制报告的通知》精神，经县政府批准建立县农村信用社联合社，并于当年9月召开第一届社员代表大会，选举产生首届理事会和监事会。县联社对辖区内农村信用合作社行使管理职能，但农村信用合作社包括联社在内隶属县农业银行领导的关系并未改变。直至1997年根据国务院《关于农村金融体制改革的决定》才与县农业银行脱离行政隶属关系，按照中国人民银行重新发布的《农村信用合作社联合社管理规定》进行管理，恢复农村信用社的合作性质，改“官办”为“民办”，对股权设置、民主管理、服务方向和财务管理等方面予以规范，使农村信用社真正成为由农民、农村经济组织和内部职工入股，内部实行民主管理，主要为入股对象服务，依法自主经营、自负盈亏、自担风险和自我约束的合作金融组织。与农业银行脱钩后，

各基层信用社的业务由县联社负责管理，金融监管由县人民银行承担。2003年根据国务院颁发《深化农村信用社改革试点方案的通知》精神，按照“国家宏观调控、加强监管，省级政府依法管理、落实责任，信用社自我约束、自担风险”的监管体制，明确信用社的管理由省政府负责。实际上省政府只负责直接管理省联社，省联社具体管理以下的信用社机构，银监会对信用社承担金融监管职能。在认真进行清产核资工作的基础上，由县人民银行和税务部门对“一呆两难”（呆账贷款，难以收回的呆账贷款，难以变现的抵债资产）进行检查认定，制定《修文县农村信用社增资扩股和降低不良贷款实施计划》，并启动全县农村信用社统一县级法人核算工作，结束原来县、乡（镇）两级法人核算的历史。通过改革壮大信用社的资金实力，增强抗风险能力。至2010年8月，全县农村信用社各项存款余额达11.36亿元，比1977年的184万元增11.34亿元，增长567倍，年均递增21.43%；各项贷款余额10.07亿元，比1977年的72万元增10.06亿元，增长1006倍，年均递增23%。在全县经营存、贷款业务的金融机构中，存、贷规模由前10年的倒数第一位飙升至第一位。特别是在支农工作中充分发挥主力军的作用。股金余额达6111.8万元，比1977年的18.7万元增长325.8倍。随着业务的拓展，在岗职工增至187人，比1978年的68人增长1.75倍，联社内置9个部（室）下辖18个分社和基层社。

人事制度改革 1996年起，改招收固定工为招收合同工，并实行全员劳动合同制。2009年起又改为派遣制，即联社与贵阳市劳动服务公司签订合同，由市劳动服务公司根据用人单位对新进职工的素质和数量要求进行派遣，当年派遣20人，2010年派遣10人。在基层社负责人的决定上，1984年联社负责人由社员代表大会民主选举产生，对联社的中层干部采取由联社聘任的方式决定。从1999年开始，对基层信用社负责人采用聘任予以明确。为确立“能者上、平者让、庸者下”的用人机制，2006年联社先制定《员工岗位竞聘实施方案》，成立竞聘考评组织，通过竞聘人自述、评委评分，民主测评和张榜公示等程序，最后决定联社中层干部和各基层信用社的负责人，予以正式聘任。

工资制度改革 1994年打破职工原来单一的等级工资，实行等级工资和责任目标津贴相结合的新制度。等级工资是固定的，责任目标津贴和其他津贴与工作业绩挂钩，按完成任务的比例计发，2005年，县联社根据《贵州省农村信用社劳动工资分配指导意见，（试行）》的精神，制定《修文县农村信用社工资分配方案》，将工资改革又向前推进一大步；彻底打破等级工资制度，建立起以效益为核心，符合农村信用社特点的结构工资制度，职工工资由基本保障工资、绩效工资、津贴工资和奖励工资4个部分组成。其中绩效工资根据职工岗位责任大小、技能要求高低、劳动复杂程度、履行岗位职责和完成既定工作目标考核情况而定。奖励工资则是根据联社当年盈亏情况而按比例分摊至每个职工头上的份额。除基本保障工资（按当地政府规定当年最低工资标准执行）和津贴按月发放外，绩效工资按季发放，奖励工资按年发放。

六、集体林权制度改革

2007年12月铺开对全县集体林权制度的改革工作。按照中共中央、国务院《关于全面推进集体林权制度改革的意见》建立由县党、政“一把手”任组长的集体林权制度改革领导小组和由县直接领导，乡镇组织实施，村组具体操作，部门搞好服务的工作机制。层层实行责任制，严格按照整个工作各阶段任务的时间表有序进行，深入推进。

全县217个行政村，除龙场镇的城南村无集体山林，扎佐镇的新庄、和平、桥头、大园、中营和喻家街6个村的林改方案未获得2/3以上村民通过认可外，纳入本次林改的为210个村。全县集体林地面积

68.06万亩，除不纳入本次林改范围的16.51万亩外，进入林改的集体林地为51.55万亩。通过紧张、扎实的工作，至2010年完成勘界面积47.61万亩，勘界率达92.36%。其中自留山17.64万亩，责任山16.15万亩，集体统一经营林地11.77万亩，其他类型2.05万亩。在将林改前林权摸底情况（山林的经营权归谁），制定的林改方案、勘界的林权状况，发证前的林权归属情况分别进行公示（又称“三榜定案”）这一程序的基础上，村民无异议后，核发全国统一式样的林权证。至2009年，基本完成集体林权制度改革的主体改革任务——确权发证工作，为5.47万户农民核发林权证，面积46.9万亩，确权发证率为91%，对已完成的确权发证工作通过市林改办的验收。

在勘界确权的基础上，农民必须与村集体经济组织签订承包经营合同，明确双方的责权利。林地的承包期为70年。在承包期内不改变林地用途的前提下可以转让；承包期届满可依法继续承包。此次林改前，集体林地已承包到户或已流转，符合法律规定、承包或流转合同规范的，继续有效，不再重签；承包或流转合同不规范的，要予以完善，进行补签；不符合法律规定的，要依法纠正。原林业“三定”工作中，划给农民的自留山由农民长期无偿使用，不得收回或调整。

林改开始至2010年全县发生2308起林权纠纷（涉地面积9.89万亩）。在工作中坚持逐级负责，分级调处（即户与户的纠纷不出组，组与组的纠纷不出村，村与村的纠纷不出乡、镇，乡镇间的纠纷不出县）、主动协商，着重调解的原则。在调处纠纷过程中，做耐心细致的工作，使纠纷双方都能做到实事求是，注重证据，顾全大局，互谅互让，并以民间调处为主，尽量不走司法程序，使1829起纠纷（涉地8.24亩）得到妥善处理，调处成功率达79.25%，但仍有1/5的纠纷调处不成功，影响确权发证，尚需继续做工作。

健全林权登记原始档案管理，是此次林改工作中的一项重要内容，要求之高，胜过农村两轮土地承包工作。要达到林权登记内容齐全规范，数据准确无误、图、表、册一致，人、地、证相符，贵阳市指定修文为此次林改档案管理试点县。为此，县林改领导小组下设置档案收集、管理工作组，专管此项工作，使此项工作及时介入、有效跟进，狠抓落实。在实践中摸索出在收集、使用、管理档案方面突出“早”“全”“准”“便”“严”五字要求得到上级的充分肯定。经整理至2010年年底，参加林改210个行政村中，除24个行政村尚有难以调处的林权纠纷（不是指整个村，而是这些村中存在林权纠纷），导致勘界和发证无法进行，以村为单位的档案资料不完整而不能归档入馆外，其余186个行政村涉地43.78万亩的2.96万件档案资料已移交县档案馆保存，为今后加强管理奠定基础。

林改不单要完成勘界、确权、颁证这一核心任务，按照中央部署，围绕林业生产健康发展，还要进行林权流转，政策性森林保险，林权抵押贷款，促进农民林业专业合作社发展等方面的配套改革，因此整个集体林权制度改革 安排的时限较长。2010年后还有包括遗留的勘界、确权、颁证和资料归档入馆在内大量的后续工作需要跟上，但集体林权制度改革的成效已经初显。由于已初步确立农民在发展林业上的主体地位，“山还于民，还权于民，还利于民”后，过去普遍存在的“山不归我、我不爱林，利不归我、我不营林，责不罚我、我不护林”的现象得到很大程度的扭转。“看好自家的山，管好自家的林”，“把山当田耕，把树当粮种”已成为越来越多农民的自觉行动。林业产值在农业总产值中的比重，已由开始林改时2007年的0.01%增至2010年的0.57%，发展速度有所提升，继续保持全县森林面积、木材蓄积和森林覆盖率同步增长的发展势头。

第二节 生产条件

县境地貌特征、气候条件和土壤类型均适宜农业多种经营，开发潜力较大，发展农业生产的条件是比较好的。

一、农用土地

1982年，县政府组织力量对全县自然条件、自然资源和社会经济条件进行调查查清令，县农用地面积共139.07万亩，占土地总面积的86.57%。2010年，县国土资源管理局又对全县土地利用现状进行详细统计，农用地增为142.71万亩，占土地总面积的88.44%。经过28年的耕种历程，农用土地呈现“两增”（园地和林地增加）、“两减”（耕地和草地减少）的态势。

（一）耕地

1982年，全县耕地为71.99万亩，占土地总面积的44.81%。除不能栽种的田埂、土坎外，实有种植面积为52.6万亩，其中水田15.07万亩，旱地37.54万亩，分别占实种面积的28.65%和71.35%。2010年减为64.44万亩，仅占土地总面积的39.93%，个中原因主要是城乡居民修建住宅、工矿企业占用、交通建设用地和退耕还林还草所致。

（二）园地

1982年，全县园地为1744.35亩，占土地总面积的0.11%，其中果园97.8亩、茶园1646.55亩。2010年增为3.06万亩，占土地总面积的1.9%，其中茶园增幅不大，主要是大种猕猴桃、金秋梨等水果，使果园面积大大增加。

（三）林地

1982年，全县含灌木林和苗圃在内的林地为33.81万亩，占土地总面积的21.05%。由于历年绿化造林和退耕还林，使林地面积连年增加，至2010年，林地达66.78万亩，占土地总面积的41.39%，比1982年增加32.97万亩，增幅为97.53%。

（四）草地

1982年，全县包括疏林草地在内的草地共33.11万亩，占土地总面积的20.61%。随着林业用地的扩大，致草地面积逐年减少，至2010年减为8.43万亩，仅占总耕地面积的5.22%，降幅达74.54%。

二、农业劳动力

1978年，全县有农村劳动力6.87万个，占农业总人口的37.77%，他们主要是从事以种植为主的常规农业生产，每个劳动力平均负担耕地6.08亩。是时，农活基本上全凭人工操作，加之人民公社体制束缚着大家的生产积极性，多为出工不出力，故未显现出剩余劳动力。继后，随着改良农具、农机具的逐步推广和应用，特别是农村普遍实行家庭联产承包责任制后，农民的生产积极性空前高涨，劳动生产率大幅提高，剩余劳动力日益显现。对此，县委、县政府采取积极措施，引导农村剩余劳动力向非农领域转移，为社会创造价值，为农民自己增加收入。全县较为丰富的农村劳动力资源，不但能确保农业生产的需要，还为发展第二、第三产业提供劳动力保障。30多年间，农村劳动力从业领域发生历史性的变化：1978年从事林牧渔业的劳动力占农村总劳动力的93.61%，2000年降至77.85%，2010年再降至55.22%。是为进入改革开放时期后农村发生巨大而深刻变化中的一个亮点。由于耕地复种指数由1978年的166.64%提升至2010年的275.65%，农作物种植面积大增，从事农业的劳动力平均每劳负担7.28亩，在1978年的基础上增加1.2亩。通过在农村中扫除青壮年文盲，加之经常性、多形式技术培训工作的开展，使农村劳动力的综合素质普遍提高，观念有更新，从而助推着传统农业向现代农业转型，促进商品生产的发展。

三、农用动力

在传统农业期间，大量农事活动都由劳动者手工操作，运输作业一般由人挑和背扛去完成。人力无法承担的耕作作业和笨重物资的运输主要由畜力承担。在逐步实现农业机械化的进程中，使落后的人畜动力向机械动力逐步推进。

（一）畜力

1978年全县大牲畜年末存栏2.5万头（匹），其中黄牛9485头，水牛1.1万头，马、骡、驴4875匹。当时饲养纯粹为解决农用动力问题。每年集体经济分配时都要为牲畜预留一定数量的饲料粮，除老、伤、残外严禁宰杀，受到地方性法规的严格保护。然而役畜总量仍然不足，每头役牛平均负担近17亩耕地，常需到外地购进补充。农村实行家庭联产承包责任制后，农民饲养大牲畜的积极性增长，1990年存栏3.99万头（匹），2010年达4.73万头（匹）。分别在1978年基础上增长57.84%和86.8%，大牲畜存栏量的内部结构变化：一是养牛目的不再是纯粹为使役耕田、耕地，同时也是为产肉、产奶；二是马、骡、驴的饲养量明显下降。除中心地带外，耕牛仍是农业生产的主要动力，马匹仍是部分农户生产、生活不可缺少的运输力量。

（二）机械动力

1978年全县农机总动力5429千瓦，平均每亩耕地不到0.02千瓦，主要是国有和集体拥有的拖拉机、农副产品加工机械和排灌机械。土地到户经营后，农民对既省力又能极大提高工效的各种农机具舍得投入，政府对购置农机具的农户实行补贴，也是农民购置积极性高涨的重要原因。1990年全县农机总动力2.65万千瓦，2000年增至8.15万千瓦，2010年再增至17.59万千瓦。分别在1978年的基础上增长3.88倍、14.01倍和31.4倍。1978至2010年年均递增高达11.48%。2010年每亩耕地平均拥有0.67千瓦。设计小巧且效率较高的耕种机在中心地区的农村已逐渐取代由耕牛耕地作业之势，运输机械改写由劳动力肩挑背扛的历史。

四、农田水利

全县农用水利工程多是在20世纪50年代末和60年代初修建的。1978年后，针对工程修建质量不高和投入运行后逐渐老化的问题，工作重点是放在除险加固、设备更新和配套完善上。2010年全县有蓄水工程254处、蓄水能力3931.7万立方米，引水工程164处、引水流量3.09立方米/秒，电力提灌站192站，装机容量5200.5千瓦，再加上机械提水的柴油泵、汽油泵、水轮泵和部分自流灌溉面积，全县有效灌溉面积达7.41万亩，占耕地总面积的28.28%。水利设施对抗御县内频繁多发的旱灾对农业生产造成的重大威胁发挥很好的作用。县境西北部干旱缺水，旱地分布集中，在20世纪90年代国家通过以工代赈的形式支

持农民修建小水窖、小水池，缓解人畜饮水和生产用水困难，取得一定的效果。同时，为探索节约用水、科学用水新路，先后建成幸福村节水灌溉示范工程（又称贵阳市修文节水灌溉示范园）等6处，修建蓄水池，铺设管网，进行喷灌和滴灌，灌溉面积共5080亩。

五、农用物资

（一）种子种畜种禽

随着农民素质的提高，低产或者劣质农作物及畜禽品种逐渐被淘汰，基本实现良种化。主要农作物水稻、玉米、油菜的杂交种子较长时间均由农业局种子公司调进并独家经营。进入21世纪后，这种经营权彻底放开。烤烟良种一直由烟草专卖局调入并直接发放给农户。畜禽良种原来是由畜牧主管部门调入并推广，继后引进渠道有所拓宽，但均能保证供应。

（二）肥料

全县各类化肥用量由1978年的5574吨增至2010年的1.94万吨，用肥结构也趋于合理。1978年氮肥占整个化肥施用量的45.73%，除磷肥外，钾肥及复合肥用量极少。2010年化肥施用量中氮肥占34.91%，磷肥占42.51%，钾肥占7.17%，复合肥占15.41%。原来施肥偏氮问题基本得到解决。1978年前，由于化肥供应有限，畜禽饲养量不多，为解决肥料问题，只得割秧青、烧渣土肥来补充。进入改革开放时期后，养殖业大发展，大量畜禽粪便成为量大、质优的有机肥来源。因此，用于种植业的有机肥数量及占整个施肥量的比重，都有明显上升。

（三）农药

在没有更有效防范病、虫害给农业生产导致重大损失的情况下，大量使用农药也是无奈之举。劳动者环保意识、生态意识提高后，农药使用量明显下降，特别是一些禁止使用的农药也不再供应和使用。2001年，全县使用农药66吨，2010年降至36吨。

（四）塑料薄膜

作为一项农业实用技术进行推广，全县使用量呈增长趋势。前期主要用于水稻育秧和烤烟、蔬菜、玉米育苗环节，后来逐步扩展至地膜栽培和塑料大棚栽培。2000年全县使用151吨，2010年发展至171吨。

（五）燃油

1978年全县销售柴油372吨，主要是确保80台拖拉机和126台手扶拖拉机及少量柴油抽水泵用油需要，汽油用量极少。当时全县只有县石油公司在县城设置一个加油站，用户加油极不方便。之后，国家对石油产品经营逐步放开，从而打破由县石油公司独家经营的局面，石油产品供应网点也遍及全县。至2010年全县共有加油站19个，其中国有股份制加油站14个，私营加油站5个，用户都能就近购买到所需的柴油、汽油及润滑油料。

（六）电力

1978年农村用电量432万千瓦时。随着国家电网对全县城乡的全覆盖和对供电网改造完成，农村用电条件大为改善，生产、生活用电都得到保障。2010年农村用电2561万千瓦时，在1978年的基础上增长4.93倍，年均递增5.72%。

六、科普网络

1980年组建县科学技术协会后，各乡（镇）也分别成立科普协会，其重要职责是通过各种形式将农业实用技术传授给农民，将先进技术转化为现实的生产力，推动农村经济发展。2010年共有乡（镇）科普协会10个，科普志愿者517名，还有以蔬菜生产、水果种植、畜禽养殖为主由农民自愿组织起来的专业技术协会18个。2003年农村党员干部远程教育站点建设工作启动，宣传讲解农业实用技术为重要的教育内容。至2010年，共建成远程教育接收站点215个。由于覆盖面宽，定期开展活动，设备先进，农民看得懂，学得会，实际上也成为科普教育的一个重要平台。

七、农业科技队伍

县内的农业科技队伍是在不断地发展壮大的，至2010年，农业主管部门农业局和林业局共有农业科技人员2222人，占职工总数的84.41%，平均每1万农业人口有9.08名农业科技人员。科技人员中有高级技术职称的2人，占0.9%，有中级技术职称的54人，占24.32%。他们的专业配备较为齐全，能够承担全县农业发展的技术保障任务。此外，农村中还有2913人获得农民技术职称证书，其中中级职称1人，有4550人经考核合格，也是农业科技队伍中的一支重要力量，科技部门已为他们注册并颁发绿色证书。

第三节　种植业

种植业一直都是全县农业的主体。1978—2010年的33年间，其产值在农业总产值中所占比重除6年外，其余年份均在60%以上。尽管在调整农业内部产业结构过程中，牧业、渔业和农林牧渔服务业均有较大发展，但其主体地位仍然依旧。粮食生产是种植业的核心内容，进入改革开放时期，在提高粮食总产的方式上，实现了由原来主要依靠扩大种植面积转向主要依靠提高单位面积产量来增加粮食总产的过渡，将粗放经营向集约化经营方向大大地推进了一步。1978年全县粮食作物种植面积39.27万亩，总产5.3万吨，2010年全县粮食作物种植35.6万亩，比1978年减3.67万亩，而粮食总产达10.43万吨，反比1978年增加5.13万吨。原因就是2010年粮食作物平均亩产293公斤（主要品种水稻489公斤，玉米263公斤），在1978年平均亩产114公斤的基础上增长157.02%。在发展粮食生产的同时，注重油菜、烤烟为主经济作物和蔬菜生产的发展，拓宽了农民增收的渠道。特别是蔬菜，不但种植面积迅猛扩大，以农村新型合作组织为依托、大建生产基地，沟通产销渠道，打造名牌，不但成为贵阳市重要的蔬菜供货地，还远销省外，成为拳头农产品。在调整农业内部产业结构中，种植范围不断扩大，面对市场需求，种植花卉和中药材已渐成规模，在发展特色农业上迈出了可喜的一步。除对野生中药材资源进行抚育外。2010年人工规范化种植中药材面积达1.14万亩，产量（干货）2677吨也为全县拳头农产品之一。面对农业人口人均耕地偏少的实际，为适应发展需求，合理安排农作物茬口，大力提高复种指数，使农作物种植总面积有大幅增长。1978年全县农作物种植总面积46.44万亩，复种指数为166.64%，2010年增至72.22万亩，复种指数提升至275.65%，这不失修文种植业发展的又一亮点。

一、种植结构

按常规，农作物种植分粮食作物、经济作物和其他作物三大类。进入改革开放时期后，种植结构调整，是农业内部产业结构调整的一项重要内容，致全县农作物种植结构发生了较大变化。

部分年份各类农作物种植面积及所占比重

表3—01—01　　　　　　　　　　　　　　　　　　　　　　　　单位：亩

年份	农作物种植总面积	粮食作物		经济作物		其他作物	
		种植面积	占种植总面积比重(%)	种植面积	占种植总面积比重(%)	种植面积	占种植总面积比重(%)
1978	464432	392709	84.56	57380	12.35	14343	3.09
1990	472033	338746	71.76	102981	21.82	30306	6.42
2000	547245	369495	67.52	119535	21.84	58215	10.64
2010	722220	355965	49.29	109485	15.16	256770	35.55

总的变化趋势是：粮食作物种植面积在农作物种植总面积中的比重下降，以蔬菜种植为主的其他作物比重上升，而经济作物所占比重变化不大。这种变化充分反映了全县农民在吃饭问题已经解决的基础上，在安排生产时，面对市场，积极发展商品生产，以获取更大的经济效益为目标。这种观念上的转变是深刻的。

全县各农作物产量的增长，主要靠加大种植的科技含量，提高亩产，但扩大种植面积也是重要手段。1978年农作物种植总面积46.44万亩，以后逐年有所增加，至2010年已达72.22万亩，在1978年基础上增长0.56倍。这既提高了有限耕地的产出水平，也缓解了人多耕地少的矛盾。

二、主要农作物发展概况

（一）粮食作物

在改革开放初期，县委、县政府针对农民种田吃不饱的现状，决定在恢复和发展农村经济工作中，将大力发展粮食生产摆在突出的位置上来抓，加上实行以户经营的生产责任制后，农民生产积极性空前高涨，在较短的时间内就改变了粮食总产上下波动、徘徊不前的局面。1984年粮食总产5.91万吨，农业人口人均产粮281.8公斤，从整体上一举解决了农民的吃饭问题。这之后，粮食生产一直没有放松，并以前所未有的速度发展。1991年、1996年、1998年和2004年，连跨4道“门槛”，分别突破6万吨、7万吨、8万吨和9万吨。在高起点上，2008年再创辉煌，全县粮食总产越过10万吨大关。这其中，从1993年起，实现了粮食的八连增，从1992年的5.04万吨，跃升至2000年的8.89万吨。这是修文有统计资料记载以来绝无仅有的，堪称奇迹。粮食生产发展的巨大成就，主要是一靠政策、二靠科技、三靠投入，致粮食作物亩产水平的不断提高。1978年所有粮食作物平均亩产为114.1公斤，1999年上升为153.8公斤，2006年突破200公斤，最高的2009年达298.6公斤。粮食作物种植面积呈典型的单峰驼背形（两头低、中间高）。1978—1988年每年均在50万亩以下；而1989—2005年每年却在50万亩以上，其中2005年达60.84万亩；2006—2010年粮食作物种植面积又降至40万亩以下。2010年粮食作物种植35.6万亩，因自然灾害影响，平均亩产293.1公斤，总产10.43万吨，在2009年基础上，亩产和总产分别下降1.61%和1.92%。

全县粮食作物品种较多，就其种植面积和产量而言，主要是水稻、玉米、马铃薯和小麦。多年来，他们一直是粮食总产的主要构成，其产量占粮食总产量的95%以上。

水稻 全县有稻田9万余亩，农田水利设施较多，加之气候条件均适宜水稻生产。水稻因其产量高，大米又是人们生活中的主粮，一直都是最主要的粮食作物品种。常年种植面积虽然只占粮食作物种植的1/4，但产量却占粮食总产的45%左右，是粮食总产最主要的构成。水稻生产受灾害性气候和病虫害的影响大，表现在总产量和亩产水平上有较大波动。1978—2010年的33年间，总产在2万吨以下的有4年，2—3吨的有13年，3—4万吨的有10年，4万吨以上的有6年。最高为2009年的4.42万吨，最低为2002年的1.43万吨；平均亩产在200—300公斤的有14年，300—400公斤的有10年，400公斤以上的有9年。最低的2002年为152公斤，只占最高年2009年489.6公斤的31.19%。2003年起，水稻生产的稳定性明显增强，总产和亩产记录不断被刷新，成为确保全县粮食总产稳定增长的主要因素。

玉米（俗称苞谷） 是县境旱地种植最主要的粮食作物，常年种植面积保持在11万亩左右，产量占粮食总产量的30%左右。由于它既可作人的口粮，又可作为畜禽养殖的饲料和加工生产饮料酒，农民种植的积极性一直较高。但随着农民生产的粮食自给有余后，因种玉米经济效益不高又有所放松，由1978年种植11.96万亩下滑至1988年的9.71万亩。后来全县养殖业的大发展，对玉米需求猛增，价格走俏，玉米种植有了恢复性的发展。栽植面积基本上稳定在每年11万亩左右。1988年前，玉米亩产摇摆在150公斤上下，没有重大突破。2000年亩产首次超过200公斤，2004年起基本上保持了逐年提升的好势头，2009年达264.6公斤，创历史最好水平，在1978年亩产136.9公斤的基础上增长93.28%。2010年种植玉米10.85万亩，在1978年基础上少种1.11万亩的情况下，实现总产2.86万吨，比1978年增产74.43%。

马铃薯（俗称洋芋） 适应性较强，犹以冷凉气候条件最为适宜。整体看，全县马铃薯种植面积是不断扩大。1978年6.44万亩，1990年6.89万亩，2000年和2010年分别种植7.16万亩和8.56万亩。随着单位面积产量的提高，由1978年平均亩产85.9公斤（以5：1的比例折合为原粮后，下同），升至2010年平均亩产246.6公斤，促使马铃薯总产由5539吨发展至2.11万吨，一般年景占粮食总产量的15%左右。

小麦 在人民公社制度下的集体经营时期，种植面积较大。一是为了尽量增加粮食收入，以便安排群众生活。二是为了向国家交纳公粮。1978年种植6.5万亩，总产1637吨，平均亩产仅25.2公斤，水平相当低下。1981年全面实行家庭联产承包责任制后，粮食生产有突破性的发展，亩产水平不高的小麦也就很自然地成为压缩种植的对象。1982年种植面积仅2.07万亩，1985年还不足2.0万亩。以后虽有恢复性的增长，但波动很大。一般年景，它的产量仅占全县粮食总产的5%左右，2010年全县种植小麦3.14万亩，总产3977吨，平均亩产126.7公斤。粮食主产区的龙场、扎佐和久长3镇成为小麦种植的空白镇。现在农民种植小麦，主要是为了调剂生活的需要，因面食方便而做法多样的特点，为很多人所接受。

（二）经济作物

县内种植的经济作物主要有油料作物和烟叶两类。1978年少数民族尚有种植苧麻的习俗，面积492亩，随着市场的日趋繁荣现已逐步消失。花生和土烟种植面积分别由1978年的800亩和2447亩变化为2010年的3105亩和3615亩，呈温和增长态势。但从种植面积和产品的商品率衡量，油菜和烤烟一直是经济作物的主打产品。1978年油菜和烤烟种植面积共5.33万亩，占经济作物种植总面积5.74万亩的92.74%，2010年这一比重又提升到94.06%。

油菜 它以生育期较短，又有养地作用，而为农民喜爱。解决自身食油问题和为完成国家下达的油菜籽定购任务是农民种植油菜的原因。1978年，全县种植4.1万亩，总产565吨，平均亩产13.7公斤。

1985年国家取消了油菜籽定购政策，实行分等级定价，敞开收购，并允许自由上市。这在很大程度上解决了价格与价值背离的问题。农民种植积极性得到进一步的调动。气候条件和市场价格的双重影响，油菜种植面积和总产量的不稳定性表现突出，但发展仍是总趋势。1978—1990年的13年，年均种植5.58万亩，年均产油菜籽3116吨，平均亩产55.8公斤；1991—2000年，年均种植7.48万亩，年均产油菜籽5533吨，平均亩产74公斤；2001—2010年年均种植7.79万亩，年均产油菜籽7765吨，平均亩产99.7公斤。2010年油菜生产年景欠好，共种8.11万亩，比上年增加1.42万亩，产油菜籽6305吨，亩产77.8公斤，又分别比上年减少1319吨和36.3公斤。

烤烟 全县有宜烟旱地11万余亩，又有种植基础。1978年种植1.23万亩，收烤烟904吨，成为集体经济一项重要的现金收入来源。当时粮食紧缺，粮烟争地矛盾突出，是制约烤烟发展的主因。随着农民吃饭问题得以解决和烤烟收购价格的提高，全县种植面积扩大，1985年种植3.87万亩，总产4468.4吨，创历史新高。鉴于20世纪80年代中期，全县经济尚处欠发达阶段，地方财政吃紧，而烤烟特产税税率高达38%，其入库税收实际已占地方财政收入的1/3，这无疑对地方政府发展烤烟生产的积极性是一个进一步的推动，提出“要想富得快，烤烟加油菜”的口号，每年给乡、镇下达指令性的种植计划任务，把烤烟生产计划完成情况纳入目标考核，严格兑现奖惩。农民更是直截了当的说：“种粮填肚子，种烟抓票子。”这样上下很快就形成了一股狠抓烤烟生产的合力。1988年开始，登上年种植4万亩以上的新台阶。1991年发展至5.12万亩，总产5911吨，登峰造极。出现了全部乡、镇和除城郊人多地多，屈指可数的行政村外，都争相种植烤烟的“盛况”。但由于服务跟不上（主要是在收购烟叶环节上），对农民积种烟积极性有所挫伤，曾一度出现种植面积下滑。1997年恢复至4.1万亩，当年国家出于宏观调控、出台限产政策，次年起，全县烤烟种植被压缩至2万亩左右，但对烟叶质量要求进一步提高。这对农民和地方财政收入的影响都很大。县委、县政府积极应对：一是加大农村产业结构调整的力度，引导农民大力发展水果、蔬菜和中药材等附加值和商品率都很高农产品生产，以增加收入，弥补因压缩烤烟种植而造成的损失；二是趁此时机，推动烤烟种植区域化和栽培技术标准化。烤烟生产“遍地开花”的现象已不复存在。至2010年，龙场、扎佐、久长3镇和谷堡乡已不再种植，将种植任务全部安排在基础条件好、便于烤烟生产优势更好发挥的其余6个乡镇。2010年全县实种烤烟2.53万亩，产量3821吨，平均亩产151公斤，分别为2009年的164.42%、269.46%和164.13%，有恢复性的增长，并刷新了亩产记录。

附：

要用积极的态度对待烤烟生产

——对我县烤烟生产的调查与思考

（1999年12月6日）

烤烟在我县农村经济中曾占有相当大的份额，在为农民脱贫致富和地方财政增收方面起过举足轻重的作用，有人把它喻为“支柱产业”。但今天由于各地大抓烤烟，使烟叶购销处于买方市场，直接表现为价格下跌，质量要求过高，在一定程度上挫伤烟农的生产积极性。不少基层干部认为，烤烟已成为“夕阳产业”，有的甚至说出“烤烟生产可有可无”的话。

带着这个问题，我和县政府办公室、烟办、烟草公司的同志先后在5个乡（镇）25个村的100户烟农中，对烤烟生产情况进行走访调查。被调查总人口414人，劳动力256个，总耕地面积494亩（习惯亩），实际种烟422亩（折合丈量亩）。其中烟草部门供种410亩，占移栽面积的97%，自留种3%；在5月20日前移栽的128亩，占实栽面积的30%，最晚的到6月10日才移栽结束；共投入烤烟专用复合肥7.17吨，亩均17公斤；用中上等土种烟274亩，占移栽面积的65%；加强中后期田间管理，如实进行打顶抹芽的仅占15%。调查中，预计产烟叶2.85万公斤，亩均67.5公斤；预计收入达13.39万元，亩均317元，种烟户人均收入323元。

上述调查情况表明：我县今年的烤烟生产除气候影响外，还存在5个突出问题：一是移栽普遍偏晚，在5月20日后移栽的面积达70%；二是物化投入严重不足，按每亩施用高浓度专用复合肥50公斤的标准计算，亩差33公斤，施用少的仅2.5公斤；三是瘦土种烟比重大；四是栽平土烟、烟地套种其他作物较多；五是普遍放弃中后期田间管理，导致烟叶质量、单价都很低。从现金收入看，种烟农户人均达323元，应该说在种植业上，尤其在一些边远地区农村人口中不算一个小数。从粮烟比价看，种烟与同等生产水平的玉米产出相比，还是种烟强于种粮。

从我县1985年以来14年烤烟生产的统计看，每隔2—3年就出现1次产量高峰，最高的是1997年，全县收购烟叶11.83万担，总产值达2941万元，实缴农特税547万元。除因国家调减计划原因外，往后正好遇到烤烟的“低谷期”。大体上同全国全省烟叶产销形势相同。

我认为烤烟作为农村经济的一个组成部分，特别是在我县农村经济结构中，还没有找到一个代替的产业时，无论是从农民增收的角度，还是从地方财政收入的来源考察，烤烟生产至少在5年内还丢不得。烟农只要把握季节，注重投入，实行良种良法配套输入，从真正意义上实现良种化、区域化、规范化的种植，烤烟生产是有效益的。有人作一个比喻：“烤烟价格如同国库券，其他农产品价格好比股票”。这个比喻不无道理。这些年来，尽管烤烟收购上存在这样那样的问题，烤烟基础价格起码是在产前就公布的，只要生产优质烟叶，价格是相对稳定的；而其他农产品的价格要等生产出来销售时才能准确反映，若遇丰收年，价格肯定下跌，或多或少存在一定的价格风险。

怎样抓好烤烟生产呢？我认为必须做好以下几方面的工作：

第一，加强对烤烟生产的领导。烤烟是用途比较单一的商品，而产销又不能完全运用市场的手段进行调节，还带有一定的计划性。因此，基层政府还不能放弃对烤烟生产的领导。除继续坚持县、乡政府分管领导负责制，层层签订责任书等好的做法之外，主要依靠全县烤烟辅导员这支生力军，采取分片包干、责任到人，从育苗、移栽、烘烤到收购，实行一包到底，搞好产前、产中、产后服务。产前抓宣传发动，落实计划，抓物资供应到位。要把有限的资金向能产优质烟、土地面积宽、致富门路少的乡、村、户转移；统一供种、供肥。产中抓育苗统一管理，抓适时移栽，抓连片种植，抓技术培训。产后抓建立良好的收购秩序，正确执行国家等级标准，兑现奖惩政策，打击烟贩，杜绝“人情烟”“关系烟”。

第二，强化科技兴烟，主攻烟叶质量。从我县气候、土壤等自然环境和悠久的种烟历史分析，烤烟产量和质量要上新水平都是可以办到的。但在生产计划安排时，必须确定“要种烟就必须种好烟，种不好烟就不要种烟”的指导思想。在物化投入上，要坚持烟农是投入的主体，紧紧依靠黄果树集团公司对基地生产扶持的举措，努力把烤烟作为贵阳市烟厂的“第一车间”来抓，坚持走全面推行“十大技术规范措施”的科技兴烟之路。一是烤烟品种良种化，全部做到种植优良品种。我县目前在品种上，以“K326”为主，合理搭配“北长82”，必须坚持由烟草公司统一供种，坚决杜绝劣杂品种和烟农自留种。

二是连片种植区域化。为实现规范化栽培，有利于轮作和科学管理，烟地必须做到适当集中，相对连片种植，以村、组为单位统筹规划，合理布局。以30亩为起点，有条件的地方可以达数百亩。三是闭苗全苗袋苗化。全部做到营养袋（块）假植育苗，达到苗齐、苗壮。四是抓住最佳季节适时移栽。为避免七月中、下旬出现的干旱天气对烤烟的不良影响，要抓住谷雨、立夏、小满3个节气做好移栽工作。实践证明，我县烤烟最好在5月20日前移栽结束。五是单厢高垄栽烟规范化。要根据土壤肥力、品种、气候等条件，本着肥土宜稀、瘦地宜密的原则，一般每亩地种植1100—1300株。为利于通气、通风和光照均匀，移栽时应拉线定位。为使烟株根系发育，充分吸收水肥，达到增加烟叶干物质的目的，必须实行起垄上高厢栽烟。六是科学合理施肥。烤烟是喜钾作物，氮、磷、钾以1：2：3施用量为宜。每亩施纯氮8—10公斤，配合施用500—800公斤农家肥和50公斤油枯。烤烟移栽后25天内，一定要全部施完肥料。七是彻底打顶抹芽，严格控制留叶数，提高单叶质量。“K326”等良种可控制在18片以内，及时打顶抹芽，做到烤后“一棵桩”，烤后单叶重达6克以上。八是坚持成熟采收。九是做到科学烘烤。烘烤过程中，坚持使用“三表一计”和遵循“三看三定三严三灵活”的技术原则，要严格控制变黄、定色、干筋期温、湿度变化。十是抓好以预防为主的病虫害防治。危害烤烟的主要病虫害有：炭疽病、野火病、黑胫病、赤星病、青虫和蚜虫等。在防治上，一要在培育壮苗、适时移栽、合理轮作、科学施肥、中耕除草等农业措施上狠下功夫，以预防为主；二要抓好预测预报工作，强化技术指导，做到诊断准确，喷药适时，处置得当，达到减少损失、降低防治成本的目的；三要实行连片防治，提高防治效果。苗床期普防3—5次，大田移栽后10天1次，持续3次以上。

总之，烤烟生产作为我县种植业的一个重要部分，尽管收购计划调减到4.45万担，只要合理安排，按基地县的标准组织生产，狠抓科技兴烟，集中精力把质量抓好，烤烟在我县农村经济中仍然占有一席之地。

（本文作者魏明禄）

（三）其他作物

县内主要是绿肥和蔬菜两大类。1978年它们种植面积共1.38万亩，占农作物种植总面积的2.98%。

绿肥 1978年种植6606亩，因有很好的养地效果，又是优质有机肥，还一度保持了较好的发展势头，1990年达1.59万亩。这之后，在片面追求经济效益的指导思想下，种植面积逐年萎缩，至2010年已不再有人种植。

蔬菜 改革开放初期集体经济不从事蔬菜生产，只有农民在自留地少量种植，主要提供自己食用。1978年全县蔬菜面积只有7232亩，农民户均不足0.2亩。后为确保内迁军工企业职工和驻军的蔬菜供应，才划定为数不多、从事专业蔬菜生产、吃商品粮的蔬菜队，但全县蔬菜种植面积并未因此大幅度增长，1985年也不过1.12万亩。在调整农业产业结构过程中，县委、县政府引导农民利用临近贵阳的区位优势，大力发展蔬菜生产，作为农民增收的一项重大措施来抓。至1990年，种植面积升至2.63万亩。通过进一步引进蔬菜种植企业，建立生产基地，发展蔬菜生产专业合作社，培训经纪人沟通产销渠道、加强技术指导等措施，使全县蔬菜生产不断迈上新台阶。实现了跨越式的发展。2000年种植3.98万亩，2005年跨越10万亩（10.07万亩），2010年达22.77万亩，产量为27.23万吨。大批量的蔬菜销往省内外，实现了“农业增效，农民增收”的既定目标。蔬菜种植面积占全年农作物种植总面积的比重升至31.52%。

三、栽培技术

（一）水稻栽培

播种 县境水稻种植多为一年一季，在海拔1000米以下的河谷低凹地带，采用适当的农科技术亦可种植双季稻。水稻种植在传统人工耕种的基础上不断改进，主要有以下几个步骤：

耕整稻田 种稻之前，须先将稻田土壤翻犁耙平，目的是让土壤疏松平整和让稻田保水保肥，传统的做法称之为“三犁三耙”。一犁一耙为保水，使田水不易渗漏，如遇干田或土变田还需多犁多耙，直到水田不漏水为止；二犁二耙为保肥，在第一次犁耙后数天待田泥沉紧后普施一次草肥或秧青（嫩树叶）、复合肥料等作底肥，翻犁耙平，如施用秧青，在犁后数天待秧青腐烂后再耙平；三犁三耙为田泥疏松、平整，在插秧之前，最好是当天，将水田纵横各犁一遍，第二遍称“打夹泥”，如土质好的田块可不用“打夹泥”，耙平即可插秧。如耙平后12小时内不插秧，田泥在插秧前还需再犁耙一遍。所以农谚中有“愿栽三年的黄秧，不愿插隔夜的冷田”就是这个道理。对于特殊地块的水田翻犁整地，可因地制宜，视情况而定。对土质较硬的干田和容易漏水的沙泥田可适当多犁多耙，对锈水田和烂泥田可适当少犁少耙。20世纪80年代初，农村土地包干到户后，抢水打田时间有限，平整稻田多简化为“两犁两耕”，但必须达到田泥疏松平整和保水保肥的要求。90年代，旋耕机使用在一些地势比较平坦地区逐渐普及，由于旋耕机集耕耙为一体，而且效果好效率高，一般耕整两遍即可。第一遍主要是为保水，第二遍主要是为保肥。两遍之间需相隔1—2天。

播种育秧 农谚“秧好一半谷”，意为育好稻秧可多收一半谷子。历来农民种田对育秧技术都非常重视。育好秧需经过选择秧地、浸种催芽、播种和苗间管理几个环节。

选择秧地 秧地多选择向阳、平坦、土温暖、泥脚浅、土质肥沃、渗水适中、排灌方便的地块，同时还需掌握所选择地块土壤的酸碱度。土壤pH值在5~6时最适宜水稻发芽出苗及幼苗生长，种子吸水发芽快，生理机能旺盛，可抑制立枯病菌的发展，增强幼苗抗性。当土壤pH值超过7时，水稻发芽、出苗生长显著变弱，土壤pH值低于4时水稻发芽也受抑制，特别是旱地育秧，对水稻发芽、出苗生长的影响最为明显。若选择地块土壤pH值超过7时或低于4时，还需用稀硫酸或腐质酸、草木灰等来调节土壤pH值在5~6之间。秧地耕整时间一般选择在清明前进行，育水秧田块需将秧田三犁三耙，施足底肥，泼洒清粪水，起垄荡平待播；育旱秧地块需将秧地翻犁熏烧、碎土平实待播。

浸种 浸种前需要进行晒种，晒种利用太阳光谱的短波光杀死附着在种子表面的病菌，增进种子内酶活性，提高发芽率，使其出芽快而整齐。其方法是将谷种薄薄地摊平在水泥地晒场上，晒时勤翻动，使种子干燥度一致，晴好天气可晒1个太阳日，多云天气可晒2个太阳日。晒好的稻种需进行一次精选，选取饱满的种子，有利于培育壮苗。选种的方法可采用水选、风选和筛选等，1988年开始使用水稻选种机选种。浸种一般采用小苏打、萘乙酸、赛力散、西力生溶液或生石灰水浸种，浓度为1%，浸种3至4日，让种子吸饱水后播种或催芽后播种。20世纪80年代，采用强氯精浸种，浸种48小时，浸种时推行三起三落的浸种方法，即白天浸泡，晚上捞起来，连续三次。

催芽 根据不同育秧方式的要求，可将种子催成粉嘴谷（即谷芽刚露白）或芽谷。大多数育秧方式都需要在播种前对种子进行催芽（旱地育秧可不用催芽）。根据种子发芽对温度的要求，催好芽的关键是掌握高温破胸、适温催芽、降温晾芽。一般要求3天内能催好，发芽率达90%以上。水稻催芽方法主要有：

限水催芽——将吸足水分的种子放入箩筐内，盖上草保温催芽，当芽长出时，将种子摊于木板或晒席上，约2厘米厚，每天淋温水，保持种壳不吹白，限制根芽继续伸长，天晴即播。限水催芽方法简单，但需要经常浇温水，若不翻种，发芽不整齐。

牛圈肥和火土灰催芽——将吸足水分的种子放入牛粪堆中，利用牛粪发热增温催芽，此种方法要经常检查，否则会造成烧芽烂种。或是将吸足水分的种子用火土灰（煤灰）加温水与谷种拌匀，然后盖上稻草催芽。

冷热谷大堆催芽——将吸足水分的种子的3/4用35℃—40℃温水浸泡到手握谷种有温感时，取出倒入垫有稻草的漏水挞斗内，再将其余1/4的冷谷放在中间拢成堆，上盖稻草，麻袋保温。每天早晚各翻动一次，方法是将表面上的谷种换在中间，原中间的谷种换在面上。大堆催芽主要适用于量大的种田大户应用，不适宜于一般量小家庭。此法靠谷种自然增温，保温措施较简单，但如果量小种温提高得慢，发芽时间长，发芽长短不齐。

塑料棚催芽——此法是把大堆催芽和塑料大棚工艺相结合，靠地热自然加温，种子受热均匀，发芽整齐，而且适合广大农村推广使用。

地坑催芽——在地下挖2尺深土坑，底部有排水十字沟，用纱布将吸足水分的种子包好放入其内，面上覆盖保温的稻草麻袋。此法催芽易保温，且氧气充足不易烂种。

人工增温催芽——将吸足水分的种子放在蒸气催芽室或温室催芽，此法种子受热均匀，发芽快而整齐，不易烂种、烂芽。但是催芽需要设备和燃料，技术关键较难把握，仅适用于工厂化生产，暂不宜普及到农户。

传统育秧一般选在清明至谷雨期间播种。20世纪80年代随着新品种推广，根据齐穗安全期的要求和当地气候特点及水稻品种生育期长短，适当调整提前10~15天采用两段育秧和旱育浅植育秧，一般以3月下旬至4月上旬播种为主。播种量多少对秧苗素质影响极大，同时也与育秧方式也有很大关系，常规稻育水秧，播种量一般每亩120公斤左右。湿润育秧或地膜育秧，播种量一般每亩100公斤左右。杂交水稻播湿润育秧或地膜育秧，播种量每亩20至40公斤，采用旱育浅植每平方米播干谷50—70克。

水田育秧 亦称育水秧，属传统育秧方式。耕整好的秧田整块不开沟或用人走出一路脚印分块，后发展为分厢宽1.32米—1.65米，用扁担刮平田泥。播种时放浅薄水均匀抛撒催好芽的谷种。播种2天后，遇晴天灌浅水，使谷芽扎根立苗快（常因播后无晴天，灌深水护谷芽时间长，导致缺氧而烂秧），遇雨天开缺口放水，雹雨天灌满水，雹后缓缓放水，以利秧苗生长。秧苗扎根后，施腐熟人粪尿作追肥，移栽前灌深水以便拔秧。此法虽操作简单，但不能育早秧，不利培育壮秧，若遇寒潮时易烂秧，烂秧率常在10%—30%，严重时，秧苗全毁，补撒后，错过季节，常造成生长后期秋雨影响

水田育秧

不能成熟。到20世纪80年仍有部分稻田采取育水秧方式，90年代不再采用。

旱地育秧 亦称育旱秧，有的称育“铲子秧”。方法是利用地势高朗，不易积水，向阳背风的微酸性土壤地或黄泥夹砂地作秧地。播种前犁地，深度在20厘米左右，以柴草熏土，碎土开厢1米左右，沟宽25厘左右，厢高20厘米左右，长度随地势而定。播种前普施腐熟清粪水于厢面，每亩1500公斤。每亩用稻种150公斤，做到土湿、肥湿、种湿。播后用木板轻压，使种子与细土结合，上盖一层薄土或细灰1厘米厚，再用杉枝叶或薄膜覆盖保湿保温。待稻秧苗长出1厘米高时撑高覆盖物15—20厘米，以遮阴和保温。苗长8至10厘米后可揭开覆盖物进行练苗至移栽。移栽时一般是用板锄将表层薄土连同秧根一并铲起，土层厚度不伤秧根为宜，但不宜太厚。此法育秧具有操作简单、能抗寒、能提早育秧、秧苗移栽后返青快、生长迅速等优点。弱点是稻秧对土壤pH值要求比较严格，pH值超过7或低于4的土壤不宜做秧地，否则会造成稻种不发芽、生长缓慢和烂秧等现象。

旱地育秧

湿润育秧 其做法是水耕水整，排水开厢和干耕干整开厢，一般厢宽1.3米，沟宽30厘米左右，沟深13厘米左右，用浅水刮平厢面，厢面晾至不落粒后播种，常规每亩播种量100公斤左右，杂交稻每亩播种量30公斤左右，播后将谷种轻轻压一下，然后盖火土灰或细土，再盖干绿肥、松毛。在秧苗三叶期以前，灌水不淹过田面，秧苗三叶期后灌水上厢，并随苗长高加深水层，以不淹心叶为宜。其优点可培育壮秧，缺点是不利抗低温和高温，易造成烂秧。20世纪90年代后，此法为地膜覆盖育秧所代替。

地膜覆盖育秧 在湿润育秧的基础上，使用地膜覆盖育秧，其做法前期与湿润育秧方法相同，不同的是最后加盖一层地膜，并用田泥压住四周。出苗后如遇高温，打开地膜两头通风，以防高温烧苗。秧苗三叶期后，根据气温情况，揭膜炼苗。此法育秧，更能保温，出苗率高、成秧率可提高20%至30%，并提早成熟2至3天。地膜育秧的优点是能适时早播，防寒保苗，培育壮秧。

旱育水促 20世纪70年代，针对部分地区缺水或春雨迟，为保证适时早播，确保安全齐穗，采取旱整、旱播、旱育，移栽前适期淹水促苗。此技术与湿润育秧比较，秧苗根系发达，秧根多，白根率为湿润秧的2.3倍以上，根系活力强、恢复生长快，秧苗绿叶比重、含水量高，秧苗干物质含量多、充实系数大、硬朗健壮，移栽后不出现停滞生长期，在干旱条件下抗旱力强、产量损失率低，秧龄弹性大，在长秧龄移栽条件下减产幅度小于湿润秧。

场坝育秧 20世纪70年代后期，利用集体空闲厂坝作秧地，可减少育秧用田，既省工、又省时，管理较方便，其做法与湿润育秧田基本相同，唯秧床的泥土要搬运，多取老肥泥田，插秧时带土移栽。其技术是旱育、密播、小苗带土移栽，有省秧地、幼苗扎根立苗快、成秧率高的优点。但易产生水分失调，青枯死苗，秧苗素质较差，3叶期必须及时移栽。经几年的实践，不适应培育壮苗的要求，农民不再采用。

温室蒸气育秧 1988年，开始推广工厂化温室育秧和木架小温室育秧，采用人工锅炉蒸汽调节温室内的温度和湿度。此技术能按时育秧，保证秧苗免遭寒潮的侵袭，无烂秧，不误农时，又能集中成批生产，同时省种、省肥、省劳力，育秧快、成秧率高、争季节、防烂秧、提早成熟等优点。还能统一育

秧，统一供应秧苗，防止品种混杂。但由于成本高，千家万户难以统一，故难以推广，只有木架小温室育秧小范围推广。

两段式育秧 1989年，开始推广两段育秧。第一段秧为旱秧或温室育秧，第二段秧将秧苗在3叶期移栽到秧田中，经20多天培育出3至4个分蘖的壮秧苗。其优点是秧苗弹性长，秧龄最长可达60多天，对暂时缺水的水田可延长秧龄，既能保证水稻安全齐穗又不影响产量。最大的优点是能培育多蘖壮秧，提高成秧率，生长整齐一致，穗大粒多，结实率高，增产显著，一般比湿润育秧和地膜育秧增产5%以上，比水秧增产15%左右，并提早成熟。其缺点是第二段寄秧花费的劳力较多，农户采用第二段秧进行抛秧的办法，来解决其缺点，到2005年，两段育秧占总育秧面积的三分之一以上。

旱育浅植 1995年引进水稻旱育浅栽培技术，苗床选择地势平坦、背风向阳、土壤肥沃、排灌方便的旱地或地下水位在1米以下的稻田；宜用菜园地，禁用施放过煤灰的地块。播种前施足底肥，对土壤调酸和消毒处理。播种时按150—250克/平方米当年浸制好的种芽播种，播种要均匀，播后用细土盖种。适时喷水在二叶期前，秧苗不缺水卷叶，就可不喷水，三叶期后保持一定的水分，一般叶不卷筒不补水，防止徒长。旱育浅植优点抗逆能力强，特别是抗“低温阴雨”天气；秧龄弹性大，具有迟栽稳产效果，省力省地减轻劳动强度，一亩大田只需净苗床8至10平方米；育秧成本低，苗矮壮实多蘖，移栽后返青快，一般增产5%以上。

水稻抛秧栽培技术 1997年，引进推广水稻抛秧栽培技术。做法是先用肥沃园土过筛后加适量复合肥、腐熟农家肥，并进行调酸、消毒处理后作营养土。然后装入特制的塑料秧盘，每盘先放营养土达盘深的三分之二，再用摆种器每孔摆杂稻种1至2粒，面盖1厘米营养土，压实、浇透水后将秧盘放入秧厢上，最后覆盖地膜。出苗前温度控制在35℃以内，一叶龄时控制在25℃以内，二叶龄时看天气通风炼苗，并注意浇水、施肥、防治病虫害。抛秧时水田要平整，第一次抛秧70%，第二次抛秧30%，然后下田匀密补稀。此法虽能培育壮秧，有降低劳强度、提高工效和节省劳力、秧田、水肥及利于农业化服务等优点。但由于技术要求高，首次投入费用高，故很少推广。

插秧 县境每年水稻插秧最佳时间在立夏、芒种期间，最迟不得超过夏至。所以当地有“立夏小满正栽秧”和“芒种打田不坐水，夏至栽秧少一腿”的农谚。

插秧分传统插秧和科学插秧两种。传统插秧一般是梯田栽顺田弯，大田或方田栽线秧（直行）。栽插密度讲究肥田稀，瘦田密，肥田33厘米至40厘米见方，瘦田15厘米至18厘米见方。科学插秧提倡合理密植，为控制密度，一般采用拉绳插秧，行距15厘米—28厘米，上等田每窝栽5至6株，中等田每窝栽7至8株，下等田每窝栽9—10株。杂交水稻亩栽1.5万至2万窝，窝栽1至2株（带2至3个大蘖），每亩2.5万至3万株苗。早熟组合每亩按1.7万至2万窝，窝栽8—10株基本苗。

灌排水 对有灌慨条件的稻田适时调节田水深浅，一般是插秧后深水护苗，薅头道秧时放浅水，分蘖末深水，谷穗灌浆后放浅水，成熟时排干田水。种植杂交品种后，改以浅灌为主，改满灌为沟灌，中期只轻晒或露田，后期不能断水过早。从1995年推广水稻旱育浅植以后，整个灌慨过程是以浅水灌溉和湿润灌溉为主，达到协调水气矛盾，促进地上、地下部协调生长。尤其对冷、烂田的水稻增产显著。

中耕除草 水稻中耕次数2至4次不等，多为3次，第一次在插秧后30天左右，最后一次在抽穗时薅谷花秧，并拔除毛稗。方法是采用手薅，一般要求是“头道浅，肥拌匀；二道深，薅到根；三道精，田抹平；杂草除净，肥土拌匀，窝窝薅到，精益求精”。20世纪80年代，开始使用化学除草剂，主要有敌稗、五氯酚钠、二甲四氯、除草醚等化学除草剂。1988年以后，化学除草逐步取代人工中耕除草，达到除草、省工、减轻劳动强度的目的。其做法是在插秧后5至7日内与尿素或用细泥土拌匀撒施。

施肥 水稻种植施基肥一般在栽插前同稻田耕整一并进行。肥料主要分为农家肥和化肥两大类，农家肥主要有圈肥、秧青、绿肥、青粪（人、猪粪尿）、草木灰、油枯等；化肥主要有磷矿粉、过磷酸钙、钙镁磷肥、复合肥等。水稻追肥一般结合中耕除草进行，移栽25至30天后薅头道秧追分蘖肥，促进稻秧多分蘖，提高成穗率，增加有效穗。又1月后薅二道秧再追吹穗肥，促进水稻枝梗和颖花分化，增加每穗颖花数。再1月后待稻穗出齐时追增粒肥，有效延长叶片功能，提高光合强度，增加粒重，减少空秕粒，尤其群体偏小的稻田及穗型大、灌浆期长的品种，施用粒肥效果最为明显。水稻追肥一般使用化肥，氮肥品种有硫铵、硝铵、氨水、碳酸氢铵、尿素；磷肥品种有磷矿粉、过磷酸钙、钙镁磷肥。钾肥品种有氯化钾、硫酸钾；复合肥有三元素复合肥和有机复合肥；微量元素肥料有硼肥、硫酸锌，还有磷酸二氢钾。2000年以后，仍以施尿素、过磷酸钙、钙镁磷肥、复合肥为主，并开始大量推广沼肥。

防治病虫害 县境水稻主要病害主要有恶苗病、稻瘟、穗颈稻瘟等；虫害主要有二化螟、三化螟、黏虫、稻纵卷叶螟、稻飞虱、稻秆蝇和稻苞虫等。病虫害发生面积少则3万亩，多则达9万亩，占稻田面积的90%左右。防治措施一般使用药剂防治，2000年以后推广高效、低毒、低残留农药，严禁使用高毒、高残留农药，并改单一用药为混合用药，同时轮换用药。

收获 水稻收获主要有传统和机械两种方式。传统收获方式是人工割禾，挞斗脱粒，加围席顶盖遮挡以减少掉谷损失。机械收获方式是人工割禾，机械脱粒，脱粒速度一般是挞斗脱粒2至4倍。20世纪80年代，一般使用的是脚踏式打谷机。90年代，电动打谷机、汽油机动打谷机脱粒逐步普及全县农村。

（二）玉米栽培

播种 玉米种植可与其他农作物进行间种、套种、复种和轮作。其方式有玉米与小麦或马铃薯（洋芋）套作，玉米与豆类间种，玉米与油菜、烤烟轮作等。20世纪80年代，引进杂交玉米和地膜覆盖及育苗移栽技术。到2003年，全县推广旱地分带轮作，其中马铃薯与玉米分带轮作、小麦与玉米分带轮为玉米适时早播创造条件。

玉米播种时间可在土壤耕层内5厘米地温稳定通过7℃~8℃时开始，当地农民一般是在桃花开后播种。如果是与小麦或马铃薯套种，在小麦麦穗出齐或马铃薯苗出齐时播种。较晚的是与油菜轮作，要等油菜收获后才能播种。播种前翻犁一道后打沟，或挖松土壤后打窝。底肥施用沤熟的圈肥或清粪水拌灰，亩施肥量800—1000公斤。同时适当施用一点磷肥，每亩20—30公斤。密度一般为行距1米，窝距55—57厘米，每窝保证2株，每亩2300—2500株左右。玉米种植提倡合理密植，可根据品种特性和栽培特点确定密度。单作玉米，早熟品种，植株高大，生育期长，亩栽2500—2800株，中熟品种亩栽3000至3400株。套作玉米，晚熟高秆品种，亩栽2200—2600株，中秆品种，亩栽2600—3000株。80年代，改进栽种方式，种植杂交玉米，采用宽窄行种植，宽行3—3.5尺，窄行1.5—2.5尺，窝距根据密度而定，加大玉米种植密度。平展型亩栽3000—3500株，紧凑型亩栽3500—4500株。播种玉米种子可分为栽白子和栽包衣子两种，白子即只晒种和浸种，包衣种是将晒种和浸种后的玉米种拌上桐油，再裹上一层磷肥。

1978年，县农推站在城关镇新春村三组试验玉米营养土育苗移栽技术，亩产达585.15公斤。1988年，引进地膜覆盖综合高产栽培技术，试验面积120亩，平均每亩424公斤，平均比露地玉米亩增118.2公斤。特别是海拔较高地区，采用地膜栽培效果更显著。进入21世纪，扎佐镇小堡、龙王等村每年栽地膜玉米300多亩，解决前期低温的矛盾，争夺季节优势，卖早鲜玉米增收。

中耕追肥 玉米1季中耕2—3次，多为2次。第一次在播种后30天左右秧苗4叶龄时进行，中耕时匀去多于的弱苗，每窝保留2株壮苗。同时结合施肥，可施用清粪水或尿素，量不宜太多。中耕的深度要求做到苗旁浅、行中深，定苗前浅，定苗后深，同时注意对病虫害的防治。第二次中耕在播种后50至60天左右，玉米苗开始拔节时进行。同时根据秧苗长势情况追施适量氮肥，适当培土。第三次中耕视情况而定，在玉米苗开始出穗时，若土壤板结，杂草多、苗弱可再进行一次中耕，并根据情况追施适量的化肥。20世纪80年代，开始使用化学除草剂清除玉米地中杂草，同时损去中耕劳作。化学除草逐步取代人工中耕除草，有人把这种做法称为是“种懒庄稼”。

收获 玉米种植根据不同品种和不同种植时间，收获时间不同。玉米成熟期可分为乳熟、蜡熟和完熟三个时期。鲜食玉米为乳熟，全生育期为70—80天，一般在授粉后16—22天可收获上市。蜡熟期玉米一般在授粉后35—40天，外壳开始变黄，此时的玉米做饭口感最好，但不利贮藏和做种。完熟期玉米一般在授粉后40天以上，部分玉米果穗开始下垂，此时玉米达到生理完全成熟，籽粒体积最大，干重率最高。适时收获，可以获得最高的经济产量。收获的果穗经晾晒后脱粒清选入库，一般籽粒水分要低于16%才可安全贮藏。贮藏库房应干燥通风，并经常检查，防止虫蛀、鼠害和霉变。

（三）小麦栽培

栽培 小麦种植耕作制主要有小麦与玉米、小麦与水稻、小麦与烤烟等一年两熟制。在寒露至霜降期间播种，播种前整地，一般为一犁一耙或两犁一耙。播种主要采取条播或厢播两种方式，条播又分单行条播和双行条播。单行条播行距均为40—50厘米；双行条播为两密一稀宽窄行，宽行距80厘米，窄行距20厘米；厢播为箱面70—80厘米，两厢之间相隔20—30厘米。不管哪种播种方式的行距均为来年开春时以便套种玉米或烤烟。稻田种植小麦多采用单行条播，行距可缩小到30—35厘米。特殊情况的山地种植可采用窝播，一般行距40—50厘米，窝距10—15厘米。播种量一般点播4公斤/亩，条播6公斤/亩，厢播8公斤/亩。

施基肥一般在小麦播种时一并进行，主要用圈肥或土皮灰拌清粪水，每亩施肥750—1000公斤。施圈肥是将其铺在沟底或厢底，肥面播撒麦种，再盖上3—5厘米泥土。施土皮灰拌清粪水有两种做法，一是与施圈肥方法相同，二是将麦种与灰粪拌匀，将其均匀的播撒在沟底或厢底，再盖上泥土。来年开春看麦苗长势，若苗势弱可再追施一次清粪水或氮肥。

小麦种植较为粗放，一般不用中耕、不需灌溉，只需注意防止麦苗不受鸟、兽、畜及病虫害即可。小麦病虫害防治主要应防治白粉病、锈病和蚜虫。一旦发生病虫危害，就及时喷洒农药防治。

收获 一般在6月上中旬小麦基本成熟，整个麦田2/3的麦穗发黄时收割，小麦蜡熟末期是最佳收获期。但小麦不可过于成熟，以免籽粒脱落而减少收成。小麦收获方式大致与水稻收获方式相同，若是量小亦可将其割回家中晒干脱粒。

（四）薯类栽培

薯类的传统种植方式一般在地势较高的瘦地上实行一年一熟制，在中上等土地上，实行马铃薯、玉米间套作，马铃薯、红苕一年二熟制。随着耕作制度改进，主要有单套单，即马铃薯、玉米单行间作。双套单，即双行玉米套作单行马铃薯，及马铃薯、玉米、马铃薯（秋薯）三熟制。1980年实行三熟制分带间套作，即马铃薯、玉米、红苕（或蔬菜），1990年后又推广马铃薯、水稻种植方式。其栽培特点是由单作向间套作发展，由一季向二季发展。

洋芋种植一般在立春前后开始。种前将地翻松耙平，按每行50厘米的行距开沟，每亩施放农家肥2500至3000公斤做底肥。洋芋种需切成种块，方法是从顶芽为中心点纵向切破，洋芋小一切二，洋芋大再分切，每个种块不得小于30克，1种块至少要有1个以上芽眼。切好的薯块用草木灰拌种，既有种肥作用，又有防病作用。栽种时在沟内按20至25厘米窝距施化肥，化肥上面施有机肥，在有机肥上面每窝播放2个种块，尽量使芽块与化肥隔离开。随后盖土起垄，覆土需达6—10厘米以上。

苗期中耕培土2至3次，以增强土壤的通透性，为马铃薯根系发育和结薯创造良好的土壤条件。春播洋芋，一般到5月底6月初成熟。当大部分茎叶由绿转黄，继而达到枯黄，地下块茎即达到生理成熟状态，即可收获。

（五）油菜栽培

油菜在秋末霜降前后播种，冬、春生长，全县各地均可种植。传统种植方式为旱地行距50至60厘米，窝距40至45厘米，每亩施腐熟农家肥或草皮灰400至500公斤；水田在水稻收获后翻犁板田耙细打窝播种，有的不耙细打窝，直接将草皮灰拌清粪水和种子播撒在泥坯间，用锄欠细盖土。1个月后间苗，每窝留壮苗4至5株。为提高单位面积产量，在传统种植的基础上提倡精耕细作、合理密植，每亩施农家肥1000公斤左右，并增施磷肥。80年代，进一步提高规范化栽培技术，加大甘蓝型品种推广，并提倡育苗移栽。2000年，推广稻田免耕油菜栽培技术，采用移栽器破口移栽，管理时不需中耕。

油菜生育期一般为180天，每年5月中、下旬成熟。当全株80%的角果呈黄绿色后人工收割堆垛和晾晒，以便籽粒后熟，经过后熟及时晒干、脱粒、扬净。

（六）烤烟栽培

育苗　苗床选用背风向阳、地势平坦，水源方便，水质洁净，排灌方便，交通便利，没有种茄科、蔬菜等作物的稻田或旱地。传统做法是将苗床土壤翻松，用柴草熏烧地面，烧后碎平，开1米左右厢面压平，施用腐熟清粪水，播种后盖一层细土，面盖茅扇、草帘、杉枝叶之类遮光。继后引进外地经验，采取低厢薄膜覆盖育苗，省工省时效果好。20世纪80年代中期推广营养袋、块球、假植育苗技术成功，此后在全县普遍推广。烤烟育苗播种时间一般在2月份立春后进行，4月份清明后移栽。

移栽　全县除冰雹灾害多的地区外均可种植业。移栽前翻松土地，开厢起垄，一次性施足底肥，每亩施用量为农家肥2000公斤左右和专用烤烟复合肥30至50公斤。最早4月上旬即可移栽，最晚不超过5月下旬。厢窄种单行，厢宽种双行。种植密度每亩1200至1600株，瘦土多种，肥土少种。

田间管理　栽后一星期及时查苗，发现漏栽、死苗、病弱苗立即补栽预备壮苗。栽后15天左右，进行第一次中耕扒蔸培土。栽后第二个月结合烟苗长势进行第二次中耕，揭去地膜，摘除2—3片底脚叶，然后锄松垄底两侧，锄尽垄表杂草，深锄沟底，将垄培高达40厘米以上，培高茎基部。适时打顶抹杈。在中心花开放时打顶，营养过剩烟田可在盛花期打顶。正常栽培条件下，留叶20—22片，中等肥力烟田现蕾后下部叶片出现落黄,留叶18—20片，肥力较低烟田，现蕾前脱肥呈现落黄的留叶数16片左右。打顶后一段时间，在烟叶腋部易生长出腋芽，最好在腋芽3厘米左右时将其抹去，以后每隔5—7天抹一次。

收获　识别烟叶成熟的方法，传统的做法是掌握成熟叶片的五大特征，即烟叶绿色变成黄绿色，叶面茸毛脱落，叶尖下垂，烟筋变白，叶片柔软不粘手。20世纪80年代中期以后，对烟叶成熟度要求提高，增加要求烟筋主脉、侧脉变白，叶耳退绿，叶尖要干枯等采收标准。烟株各部分烟叶成熟期不一致，下部叶成熟叶龄一般为50—60天，中部叶60—70天，上部叶70—80天。每次采收叶片数量3—4片，整株烟叶分5次左右采完。

烘烤 烘烤前将采收的烟叶分为成熟、欠熟和过熟三类分别编杆。编烟要求烟叶背对背，大叶两片一撮，小叶3片一撮。一般杆长1.5米，每杆编烟叶50至60撮。上炕时成熟烟在中层，欠熟烟在下层，过熟烟在上层。烘烤一炕烟叶需要5天左右时间，其过程分为变黄、定色、干筋三个阶段。变黄期以较低的温度和较高的湿度，温度范围42℃至55℃，相对湿度范围30%至70%；变黄阶段完成后转火定色，以固定烟叶在变黄期所得到的优良品质和色泽，进一步促进优良品质的形成；干筋期进一步提高温度和降低湿度，温度范围55℃至70℃，相对湿度30%以下，把烟叶的主筋烤干。烟农将其总结为“小火捂汗吊黄，拔火敞汗蔫黄，追火收张定色，大火响壳干筋”。1984年，执行《贵州省“烤烟烘烤”地方标准》要求烘烤烤烟。1996年，贵州省开展“中美合作改进中国烟叶品质试验”后，进一步提高对变黄烟叶变黄程度的烘烤要求，普遍采用“低温慢变黄”的烘烤方法。

（七）蔬菜栽培

种植 县境地处云贵高原东部，大部分地区海拔1200—1300米之间，气候属亚热带季风性气候，无霜期269天，最长324天（大屯），一年四季均有露地蔬菜栽培。根据气候条件、地力及各种蔬菜品种习性等，耕作制度可安排为一年两熟至三熟，最多可安排为四熟，可间作、套种、单种和轮作，亦可与玉米、小麦等粮食作物间作、套种和轮作。传统蔬菜种植较为粗放。20世纪80年代，随着市场需求增大，蔬菜种植面积增加，县农业局每年都要对农民进行科学种植蔬菜进行技术培训，不断提高菜农蔬菜种植技术和品种更新。

育苗技术 为提高土地利用率，缩短蔬菜种植时间，增加单位面积的产量，绝大部分蔬菜品种栽培都需要经过育苗。苗床选用背风向阳，两年内未种植过同类蔬菜（最好选用种过豆类和葱、蒜类）的土地做苗床。肥料以选用农家肥为主，但需充分腐熟回凉后才能用，使用未腐熟的农家肥会产生大量有害气体伤害幼苗。苗床在播种前深翻土地，深度在20厘米以上，有条件可以用柴草熏床土，再碎土开厢，厢宽80至100厘米，沟宽25厘左右，厢高15至20厘米，长度根据用苗量而定。播种时先在厢面施放一层腐熟的农家肥，为避免幼苗伤根，可在农家肥面上撒上一层草木灰或细土，厚度根据蔬菜品种而定。种子播撒完后掩盖一薄层细土，有的品种可不用掩盖。浇一次透水，盖上遮光材料以遮阳光和保温。育苗时间一般1个月左右即可移栽。20世纪80年代，采用塑料薄膜拱棚育苗，营养袋块育苗和营养钵育苗。

栽培 栽培主要有露地栽培和保护地栽培两种方式。县境地处亚热带地区，全年都有可进行露地栽培的蔬菜品种，传统习惯多以这种栽培方式为主。20世纪80年代，为提早蔬菜成熟季节，解决前期气温低的矛盾，达到保温、保水、保肥，促进作物高产，逐渐推广塑料薄膜覆盖栽培，90年代又出现大棚蔬菜种植。2000年以后，市场需求扩大，为满足市场需求，大力发展反季节蔬菜种植。一方面在乌栗的大塘、六广的滨江和大石的大屯利用当地海拔底、气温高的特点发展早熟蔬菜种植；另一方面利用县境东部地区高海拔冷凉气候的特点，在龙场、扎佐、久长、小箐等乡镇发展延晚番茄种植。从2002年起，对蔬菜质量要求提高，蔬菜生产严格按照贵阳市无公害蔬菜技术规程操作，从过去重产量轻质量，忽视食品安全转变为安全、质量第一，生产中科学防治病虫害，采取预防为主，综合防治，以农业防治为主，化学防治为辅，生物防治相结合。严禁高毒、剧毒、高残留农药的应用，严格掌握农药的安全间隔期，浓度和使用次数，推广使用频振式杀虫灯，减少农药的使用。同时采取科学施肥，坚持重施腐熟农家肥，适量施用化肥，并控氮、稳磷、增钾，大力推广沼肥。

四、品种改良

（一）品种资源

1980年，对农作物品种普查，基本摸清全县农作物品种资源，至2010年又陆续引进各种农作物新品种。

水稻品种有96个，主栽品种58个，种植面积6.5万亩。其中，耐寒籼稻19个（新品种3个），粳稻8个（新品种5个），糯稻12个；耐旱性籼稻12个（新品种2个），粳稻5个（新品种2个），糯稻8个；适宜冷烂田种植的籼稻16个（新品种2个），粳稻7个（新品种3个），糯稻12个；适宜煤锈田种植的籼稻2个，粳稻4个（新品种2个），糯稻11个；陆稻4个，其中糯型、籼型各2个。1980年至2010年新增杂稻品种44个，常规籼稻2个，粳稻3个，糯稻2个，本地老品种逐步被淘汰。玉米品种21个，其中糯玉米3个、杂交玉米8个。1980年至2010年新增交杂交玉米品种42个，其中甜玉米3个、糯玉米3个。小麦品种20个，其中地方品种5个，引进新品种15个。1980年至2010年新增小麦品种8个。高粱品种2个。大麦品种5个。荞子品种2个。红苕品种3个。洋芋品种8个，其中地方品种4个、引进新品4个。1980年至2010年新增品种8个。大豆品种24个，种植面积较大的品种有大白水豆、小白水豆、早黄豆。1980年至2010年新增大豆品种8个。花生品种1个品种为珍珠豆型。油菜品种13个，其中甘蓝型品种6个、白菜型油菜4个、芥菜型油菜3个。1980年至2010年新增杂交油菜品种10个，常规种5个。烤烟品种3个。1980年至2010年新增烤烟品种5个。

（二）良种繁育

杂交水稻的配制　1978年，县派人到海南岛繁殖杂交水稻“29南1号A”和“29南1号B”，种植90亩，收种2.3吨。从海南回来后制种42亩，在乌栗大塘制种攻关田亩收种63.5公斤。1979年制南优2号631.5亩，其中大塘制种112.1亩，平均亩产22.03公斤。六广制种259.3亩，平均亩产12.45公斤。桃源制种167.1亩，平均单产19.4公斤，大屯制种93亩，平均单产16公斤。以后因杂稻制种要求技术性强，对光照和气温等自然条件要求高，制种技术力量和自然条件跟不上，造成种子生产水平低，数量、质量不保证，次年停止杂稻制种。

杂交玉米的配制　20世纪70年代，县派人到海南岛建良种繁育基地配制杂交玉米种。1978年，配制“黔单4号”和“中单2号”284.5亩，收种27.8吨；繁殖玉米“关岭花山”和“自330”共45亩，收种478公斤。1980年县派3人随同地区制种队到云南繁殖杂交玉米“莫17”“自330”和“墨白群”改种，制种360亩，其中收“修顶72”种子1572公斤，制“黔单4号”4851斤，“中单2号”16894.5公斤。1983年，在六桶制杂交玉米种共1265亩，平均单产136.75公斤，其中“中单2号”355亩，“黔单4号”65亩，“郧单1号”583亩。1984年在六桶制种1512亩，其中，“郧单1号”1062亩，“黔单4号”438亩。因制种技术要求高、成本高，制出的种子栽后植株高度不整齐，增产不显著。同时，外地进入的商品良种比自制效果好，次年停止杂交玉米的制种，多用外地商品良种。

（三）良种引进

水稻　1978年，县内原有引进良种主要有黔农5782、农育1744、西农175、川大粳、庆丰、湘东、台北8号和南优2号等。初引种杂稻的南优2号在城关镇新春大队试验种植，平均单产474公斤，比粳稻310公斤多产164公斤。1979年，全县杂稻种植9500亩，在当年的品比试验中，南优2号亩产527.5公斤，比庆丰亩产417.5公斤、庚湘445公斤、台北8号427.5公斤、农育1744亩产405公斤，南优2号亩产最高。1981

年，县种子公司引进水稻桂朝2号种2500公斤，在六广、大石、洒坪、桃源、红岩、六桶等6个低海拔公社的22个生产队、115户科技示范户的200亩土地上进行示范种植。尽管当年大旱，仍获较好收成。一般单产550公斤，最高727.5公斤，最低425公斤，比推广多年的庆丰稻种增产28%。继后陆续引进威优64、汕优63、汕优64、桂朝2号，亩产量在485公斤至682公斤之间。1985年引进威优481、威优77，亩产450公斤至650公斤，从而促进杂稻的推广。1988年推广中矮秆良种6.56万亩，占水稻面积69.3%，其中推广优质稻金麻粘0.7万亩，亩产350公斤至582.5公斤，推广优质稻银桂粘0.6万亩，亩产420公斤至510公斤，虽金麻粘、银桂粘品质优，但亩产不及同期引进的其他优质杂稻品种高。90年代水稻种植多以威优64、威优77、威优481、汕优晚三、金优207、岗优12等品种为主。2000年以后，水稻种植从单纯追求高产高转向追求优质方向发展。2004年，推广品质优良的金桂99、新香优80、岗优22、金优413、金优404、2优363等杂交水稻品种达8.467万亩。占水稻种植面积的90.4%。经验收杂交水稻优质米品种比常规良种亩增100公斤左右。在常规稻推广方面，部分农户还恢复台北八号和安粳314，利用这些品种米质优的特点，提高经济效益。

玉米 原有引进良种罗马尼亚、黔单4号、中单2号、京杂6号等。1979年，在城关镇新春大队验收72.7亩黔单4号玉米种植，平均单产363.8公斤，比本地玉米平均亩产235.6公斤，亩增56.3%。1981年，引进玉米群体改良种“墨白94”250公斤，在城关镇新春大队的11户科技示范户的100亩土地上进行示范种植。一般单产200公斤至300公斤。产量虽然不高，但有抗旱耐瘠薄、满尖不易霉烂、籽粒硬口感好、抗倒伏、成熟早等优点。继后陆续引进推73单交、陕单1号、成单1号、黔西4号、兴中、兴黔、掖单13号、息单7号、六玉1号、黔群1号，亩产在300至668公斤。1988年，推广玉米良种种植10万亩，其中杂交玉米4万亩，群体改良种6万亩。90年代玉米种植多以73单交，兴中、兴黔双交种、贵毕301、贵毕302、黔西4号、六玉301等为主。2000年推广海禾1号亩产738.7公斤，临奥1号亩产700.6公斤，农大108亩产693.1公斤，金21亩产664.5公斤，黔玉1号亩产664.3公斤，安单136亩产645.8公斤，高油115亩产563.9公斤，毕单4号亩产559.3公斤，黔单10号亩产602公斤、登海3号亩产636.9公斤、遵玉3号亩产567.5公斤、黔兴4号亩产606..7公斤、西山7号亩产468.2公斤。2005年至2010年，主推黔兴4号、安单136、遵玉3号等品质较好的杂交玉米达6.5697万亩。占玉米种植面积的63.6%。

小麦 原有引进良种矮粒多，阿波、内乡5号等。1979年引进推广百泉565、阿夫、泰山4号、新育4号、武麦3号、三月黄等品种。1985年推广百泉565、占小麦面积80%。1988年推广贵农10号，面积3.5万亩，其余为百泉565、绵阳26等。2000年以后小麦品种主要以贵农10号为主，占小麦栽种面积的80%，以后引进兴麦17、贵花1号、贵花5号、川麦和绵阳26等品种进行推广。

马铃薯 原有引进良种威宁河坝洋芋、米粒、马尔科、阿昆纳、马铃铛、金苹果、红豆沙、克新1号，亩产1500至2000公斤。1978年全县种植主要以米拉洋芋为主，直至20世纪末。2000年开始大面积推广脱毒洋芋种植，品种主要有大西洋、中薯3号、费乌瑞它、六引95—1、威芋2号、威芋3号等品种。

油菜 原有引进良种胜利油菜、黔油23、矮架早等。1979年，引进黔油8号在红岩公社沙坝示范推广50亩，最高单产151.3公斤，比本地竹丫油菜增产2倍以上。1985年引进黔油9号、云油7号、湘油2号，平均单产105公斤。1986年推广杂交油菜托尔、奥罗，平均亩产129.3公斤。但因生育期长植株较高，未能大面积推广。1988年推广黔油9号、西南1005，79-1、78-4-1和白菜型的北京油菜。20世纪90年代，先后推广油研7号、油研5号、黔油12号、贵杂2号，杂选1号。2003年稳定种植5.5万亩。占油菜种植面积的70% 。继后至2010年，又新推广德油8号、德油12号、黔油17、黔油18。常规油菜推广的品种主要有杂

61、油研1号、油研2号、贵油7号。经验收杂交油菜比常规良种亩增30公斤左右。

烤烟 原有引进良种特字400号、大黄烟、小黄烟、春雷3号、红花大金元等。1978年全县种植主要以春雷3号为主，1985年以后主推k326，1988年以后主推 Nc82和G28。2000年起，主推云烟45、云烟47、K326等品种。

（四）良种管理

1978年，县置有种子公司，隶属县农业局，负责全县农业技术推广和良种配制、引进及质量管理等工作。1991年成立种子管理站，与种子公司合署办公。2003年，县种子公司因注册资金不足撤销。种子管理工作由种子管理站负责。

20世纪70年代末80年代初，良种经营采用以公粮指标实物调换，将检验合格的良种缴在国家仓库，农民于次年在播种推广时再将稻谷换种，以粮换种。1985年，国家对良种经营实行改革，免除营业税和工商所得税，同时粮油良种经营改为议购议销，粮食部门与农业种子经营脱钩。良种生产、收购、调拨、销售由农业部门规划安排，实行自主经营，并直接参与育种繁殖，与需种单位签订购销合同。供应良种，采取现金购买或以粮换种方式；不再抵顶粮油计划定购任务。同时，省规定对农作物种子的引种、调剂、销售和推广工作一律由种子公司统一经营管理，非种子部门和个人不得经营。2004年起，实施《中华人民共和国种子管理法》规定：凡经营种子的单位和个人，必须持有工商行政管理部门发给的营业执照。必须有种子公司委托书、种子产品合格证，并到当地农业管理部门备案。要求经营种子保证质量，必须接受当地农业、工商行政部门的监督，种子检验人员和植检部门的检疫人员有权对种子进行抽查。并规定经营种子要按国家或省的种子分级标准、按质论价、优质优价，种子销售单位和个人均应执行国家规定的种子价格，不得任意加价。

从良种收购开始，检定合格标准纯度必须是96%以上，所含杂质物在0.5%以下，充分干燥，并无掺砂土者。检验方法，起初是有经验的技术人员用牙咬，带有清脆的断裂声音。对备荒种子的质量，要求充分纯洁干燥，新鲜饱满，无其他夹杂物及病菌寄附者。收购前作发芽试验，其发芽率在85%以下者不得作种使用。1987年，县建立种子检验室，配备检验员，添置水仿测定仪、发芽箱、烘干厢、天平、显微镜等设备。种子检疫按照“农作物分级标准”和“农作物种子检验规程”进行。种子检疫按国家“植物检疫条例”规定进行。检疫范围为预约繁殖种子、生产自用的种子、救灾备荒种子、市场销售种子。检验分田间检验和室内检验。田间检验，主要鉴定品种纯度，检查病虫危害，异作物，杂草混杂程度、并观察生育状况。室内检验，分入库前检验和出库检验，经检验合格签证后方可销售。

（五）培养良种基地

位于县城西南1.5公里。培养良种基地良种场，统称为“县农场”。1978年有场长1人，技术员2人，工人19人，配备有农机东方红（履带式）、27型和35型拖拉机各1台。主要研究农业生产中的良种推广、化肥施用和养殖业生产中的品种改良、饲养技术及各种先进农业科学技术的引进、试验、示范、推广等工作。良种场工人属农业工人，每月按国家事业单位管理人员和工人工资标准发给工资，年底按各专业队的收入分别进行核算，工资与工作任务挂钩实行超产奖励，减产罚扣工资的生产制度。良种场生产的种子交给国家，由种子公司和粮食部门负责经营销售或以粮换种供给农村。

1984年实行联产承包责任制，将土地、耕牛、农具等承包到专业队，专业队再承包给工人。职工每人承包田1.2亩，土2.9亩；未享受商品粮供应的子女按每人承包0.7亩土。农具、耕牛又按承包土地分配到承包到户。土地承包时有在职工人44人，其中退休职工9人，有场长1人，副场长1人，管理技术人员2名，

分土地的职工家属子女47人。土地承包后，工人达到退休年龄，由县人事部门批准，办理退休手续，财政部门按规定发给退休金，所承包土地交还单位，由单位另行安排生产。

2004年县编委批准核定县良种场管理编制3人，设场长或副场长，管理人员2人。良种场工人维持原状，不予增加和减少。2010年末，良种场有退休职工41人，在职职工11人。退休职工由县财政负担每月拨款3.7万元发工资，在职工人以承包土地创收作为基本生活资料，未办理退休的职工的养老保险由个人承担。农场管理人员有场长1人，管理人员2名。单位管理的土地有120亩，由单位承包给农户耕种，收入用于办公开支和补贴职工差额。

五、肥料利用

传统农业生产，多以施用农家肥为主。20世纪70年代末，肥料使用以农家肥为主，化肥为辅。化肥多为追肥施用，仅有磷肥和复合肥作底肥。80年代，化肥使用量逐步增加，并出现农家肥与化肥配合施用，提高肥料的有效利用，促进农作物增产。1983年钾肥肥效试验获安顺地区科技成果四等奖。90年代，推广平衡配方施肥方法。1997年推广平衡施肥增产，获省农业厅丰收一等奖。

（一）农家肥

是主要的肥料资源，常见的有人畜粪尿、圈肥、灰肥（柴灰、火土灰、草木灰、岩灰、煤灰）、堆肥、沤肥、土杂肥、绿肥、秧青、秸秆、油枯等。圈肥、堆肥、沤肥、土杂肥、绿肥、秧青、秸秆为粗肥主要用做农作物底肥，人畜粪便腐熟后称“清粪水”主要用于追肥，土皮灰拌清粪水可做旱地作物底肥，油枯可做底肥亦可做追肥。农家肥多为底肥施用，稻田底肥以撒施为主，旱地以窝施为主。稻田施放底肥多用圈肥，施用量一般为一挑田两挑肥，即亩施800至1500公斤。旱地作物每亩施底肥人畜粪尿拌火土灰500至1000公斤，结合中耕每亩追清粪水300至500公斤。20世纪80年代，实行家庭联承包责任制后，多养牲畜多积肥成为广大农民的自觉行动，绿肥逐步恢复、发展，秸秆还田得到推广。农家肥的数量大幅度增加，每亩用肥量达1000公斤以上。1998年以后，随着外出打工人员的增加，年轻人出去多，农村劳动力减少，加上使用化肥省事，农家肥施用量减少，有的甚至只用化肥，不用或少用农家肥。

传统积肥多采用割草垫圈，铲土皮灰，割秧青，集蓄人畜粪便等方法。集体化时期基本上采取积、养、种、制的方法积制农家肥，并提出多养牲畜多积肥的口号，要求把养畜、积肥、搞好环境卫生三个方面工作结合起来称为“三结合”。要求“六尽”，即野粪拾尽，稻桩捡尽，沟坎路旁杂草割尽，路上肥泥铲尽，邻田土秧青采尽，阴沟肥泥掏尽。还要求做到牛有栏、猪有圈、粪有坑、坑有盖、人有厕、禽有舍、灰有棚。制肥方法除传统的积肥方法外还有高温堆肥法。做法是在田边地角或房前屋后选择一小块不影响交通和环境而且平坦干燥的地块做堆肥场，场面底部开挖20×20厘米的十字沟至堆场外。采用稻草、玉米秆、油菜秆、杂草、秧青、落叶等原料加清粪水、牛马粪、石灰、肥泥或泥炭等做配料。堆制前用石片或长秸秆盖住十字沟面，并将原料用铡刀切成5至8厘米长。堆制时在十字沟中心立一根竹竿或木棍，以便通风透气。然后铺一层原料泼洒一层配料，堆至4—5层，边堆边压实，堆高1米左右。堆完后淋透水，外盖一层细土，再用稀泥密封。半月后从顶部淋一次透水。再半月翻堆一次，方法是将里面翻到外面，外面翻到里面，堆实浇水、稀泥密封。再过1个月腐熟后即可开封施用。20世纪80年代，使用化肥逐步普及，积肥观念逐步淡化，农作物秸秆多被放火焚烧。90年代，为保护生态环境和防止水土流失，禁止割秧青和铲草皮灰，提倡秸秆还田和种植绿肥。

底肥亦称基肥，占施肥总量的60%左右。可作为底肥的农家肥主要有圈肥、堆肥、绿肥、秧青、火土灰、青灰（柴草灰)、油枯、垃圾、石灰等。稻田基肥以撒施为主，并结合耕翻进行。旱地基肥多为窝施或条施。种肥是把腐熟有机肥用来拌种、盖种、穴施、条施，以及用作水稻的粑面肥。追肥主要在植物生长过程中施用，可作为追肥的农家肥主要有清粪水（人畜粪尿)、青灰、油枯等。追施一般选择阴天或晴天的早晨、傍晚无露水时进行。追施量根据作物的长势和土地肥力而定，长势弱适当多施，长势旺盛的少施或不施；肥地少施，瘦地多施。追肥方法主要有泼施、窝施、粪包秧和随水灌施多种方法。水稻育秧时可用清粪水泼施或灌施，移栽时可用青灰抹根或用腐熟并踩细的圈肥包秧根（俗称栽坐粪)。旱地作物追肥主要用清粪水、油枯肥进行条施或窝施。

（二）化肥

氮肥有尿素、碳酸氢铵、硝酸铵、硫酸铵、氯化铵等。磷肥有过磷酸钙、钙镁磷肥、磷矿粉等。钾肥有氯化钾、硫酸钾。复合肥有三元复合肥、有机复合肥、生物复合肥。底肥主要以复合肥和磷肥为主，可单独施用亦可与农家肥混合施用，一般用量亩施20至50公斤。施肥方式可采取窝施、沟施或撒施。钙镁磷肥还可直接用于水稻抹秧根。可用1%至3%过磷酸钙作水稻、小麦、番茄的根外追肥。磷矿粉同堆肥、圈肥堆沤发酵作基肥，还可用来种植绿肥作底肥，起到以磷增氮的作用。在土壤严重缺钾或种植高钾作物的情况下钾肥也可作为底肥施用，一般亩用量15至25公斤，多与农家肥混合施用。氮肥也可与农家肥混合作底肥，但使用不普遍。追肥一般分为根部追肥和叶面施肥，多以氮肥为主，施用量根据氮肥品种氮含量及作物需要而定，一般亩施15至20公斤。水稻追肥多采用撒施，施时注意不要使化肥留在叶面。旱地作物则多采用窝施，窝施时注意覆土，并避免与根、叶，直接接触，以免灼伤植株。钾肥作追肥，可直接施于根部，每亩10公斤。硫酸钾主要施用于烤烟、茶叶，氯化钾用于粮食、油料和蔬菜作物。复合肥作追肥，亩用量10至20公斤。叶面施肥一般采用喷洒，兑水根据施肥浓度0.5%至1%。

六、植物保护

（一）病虫害防治

1.病虫害种类

县境位于贵州省中部，自然条件有利于多种农作物生长的同时也易发生多种虫害。2000年起，开始农村产业结构调整，果蔬生产得到长足发展，虫害种类也随之增加。特别是一些外地品种引进，产生一些新虫害。

境内农作物主要病虫害一览表

表3—01—02

类别	品种	病　害	害　虫
粮食作物	水稻	真菌性病害主要有稻瘟病、纹枯病 、胡麻叶斑病 、小球菌核病、恶苗病、霜霉病、稻曲病、叶鞘腐败病等；细菌性病害主要有水稻白叶枯病、条斑病、基腐病等；病毒性病害主要有条纹叶枯病、黑条矮缩病等	水稻螟虫、稻飞虱、稻蓟马、稻苞虫、蝗虫、黏虫、稻杆潜蝇、负泥虫、稻叶蝉等
	玉米	黑穗病，大、小斑病	玉米螟、黏虫、小地老虎
	小麦	锈病、赤霉病和白粉病	主要是蚜虫
经济作物	油菜	菌核病、霜霉病、白锈病和病毒病等	蚜虫、跳甲等
	烟草	有青枯病、黑胫病、花叶病、炭疽病、立枯病、野火病和猝倒病等	有小地老虎、大地老虎、黄地老虎、烟蚜、烟蛀茎蛾等

续表

类别	品种	病　害	害　虫
经济作物	茶树	有茶饼病、茶园赤星病等	有小绿叶蝉、茶毛虫、茶牡蛎盾蚧、卷叶蛾、尺蠖、刺蛾、蓟马、叶螨等
果树	猕猴桃	有根结线虫病、花腐病	有叶蝉类、金龟子类
	梨树	有梨黑星病、梨黑斑病、梨锈病、梨轮纹斑病等	有大食心虫、梨虎和梨茎蜂等
	柑橘	有柑橘溃疡病、炭疽病、脚腐病等	有大实蝇、潜叶蛾、疣壁虱、锈壁虱、天牛、蚜虫、尖尖蚧、柑橘红蜘蛛等
	苹果	有苹果腐烂病、苹果褐斑病、苹果白粉病、苹果炭疽病等	有苹果小食心虫、介壳虫和叶螨等
	桃	有桃缩叶病、桃流胶病等	有桃蚜、桃蛀螟、红头天牛、吸果夜蛾等
	李	有黑斑病、流病胶、炭疽病	有介壳虫、小食心虫
	葡萄	有葡萄霜霉病、褐斑病、炭疽病、白粉病、黑痘病等	有葡萄透翅蛾、十星叶甲、三星叶蝉、天蛾等
	板栗	有板栗干枯病、板栗白粉底、板栗叶斑病、种实霉烂病	有古毒娥、黄刺娥、金龟子、黄枯叶蛾、栗实象鼻虫、象桃蛀、螟栗实娥、栗透翅蛾、栗瘿蜂、栗大蚜、栗花翅蚜、栗红蜘蛛
蔬菜	白菜	有白菜软腐病、白菜霜霉病、黑斑病	有小菜蛾、菜粉蝶、菜螟、菜蚜、小地老虎、红蜘蛛、小菜蛾、菜青虫、跳甲等
	瓜类	有霜霉病、白粉病、炭疽病、病毒病、枯萎病、灰霉病等	有瓜蚜、黄守瓜、白粉虱、蜗牛、蛞蝓、小地老虎、蛴螬、金针虫等
	番茄	有番茄晚疫病、番茄病毒病、青枯病、灰霉病等	有棉铃虫、蚜虫、白粉虱等
	辣椒	辣椒疫病、枯萎病、青枯病、病毒病、炭疽病、白绢病、叶斑类病、白星病等	有烟青虫、蚜虫、红蜘蛛等

稻瘟病　水稻病害中危害最大，每年县境各地均有不同程度的发生。其属真菌性病害，以菌丝或分生孢子附着在稻草或稻种子上越冬。带病稻草产生的分生孢子借风传播，侵染秧苗和本田水稻，在病株上不断产生孢子再浸染；带病种子传播后直接引起秧苗发病。每年有两个流行期，即6月下旬水稻分蘖和7月中下旬水稻孕穗期。

水稻螟虫　危害较大，以二化螟、三化螟和稻纵卷叶螟为主，全县各地都有发生。一般年发生二代，冬种面积大，绿肥种植多，越冬虫量基础大，为害重。水稻迟插，为害重，杂交水稻比常规水稻危害重。稻纵卷叶螟为迁飞性害虫，每年4至6代。每年4至5月第二代成虫由南方迁入，第三代成虫5月下旬至6月中旬迁入县境，时值水稻分蘖期，第四代成虫6月下旬至7月上旬，甚至到8月上旬，多本地虫源繁殖，一般年份三代重于四代。第五代成虫于8月中旬发生北迁，第六代成虫由北往南迁。县境稻纵卷叶螟虫害成灾偶尔发生，1994年发生最重，全县9万多亩稻田普遍受害，水稻产量比上年减22%。

稻飞虱　为县境主要害虫之一，全县各地均有发生，主要以白背飞虱为主，每年发生4至5代，一般5月中旬迁入，7月上中旬随西南气流向北迁移。8月中下旬随东北气流向南回迁。白背飞虱的主害代在第三代和第四代，为害盛期在6月中下旬。褐飞虱主害期一般在8月中旬至9月中旬。

黏虫　以危害水稻、玉米为主。5至6月间，黏蛾迁入量大，发生严重。6月份相对湿度大，有利黏虫幼虫的成活，高湿干旱不利粘黏虫生长。耕作制度上，小麦套种玉米重于单作玉米。

小地老虎 为旱地农作物主要害虫，是春播作物玉米、烟草、蔬菜等苗期的主要地下害虫，常造成缺苗断行。其年发生3至4代，以第一代幼虫为害最大，4月中下旬是危害盛期。冬季气温高年份，次年虫害发生早，危害大。

玉米螟 是危害玉米主要害虫，年发生3至4代。危害主要是因为叶片被幼虫咬食后，降低其光合效率；雄穗被蛀，常易折断，影响授粉；苞叶、花丝被蛀食，会造成缺粒和秕粒；茎秆、穗柄、穗轴被蛀食后，形成隧道，破坏植株内水分、养分的输送，使茎秆倒折率增加，籽粒产量下降。

2.预测预报

1985年县农业局在城关镇新春村建观测场点，进行病虫预测预报。1992年观测场地取消，改为冬前、冬后作物生长各个阶段进行调查。2000年以后，在各地安装频振式杀虫灯一方面杀虫，一方面测报。通过在不同海拔高度进行调查，发布病虫预测预报。

测报对象主要是水稻二化螟、三化螟、稻苞虫、玉米螟、黏虫、小地老虎、稻飞虱、稻纵卷叶螟、小麦白粉病、稻瘟病、小麦赤霉病等。

病虫预测 一般在冬前冬后作物生长各个阶段进行调查，结合历史资料，参考农作物品种布局、气象预报等情况，作出发生量、发生危害程度预测。

病虫预报 内容包括发生期、发生量、发生危害程度，提出防治时期、防治办法及建议。预报工作，每年年初分别对夏收作物和秋收作物主要病虫害作出发生趋势预报。

水稻病虫害普查

3.防治方法

耕作上采用轮作可以减轻病害发生，如玉米实行轮作，可有效地降低玉米丝黑穗病的发病率。因小地老虎、黏虫成虫易在杂草和枯叶上产卵，要经常铲尽田边地角杂除草，适时中耕；冬前翻耕土地，消灭越冬幼虫，冬春季节处理玉米秸秆，减少玉米螟幼虫。稻苞虫幼虫在游草、茭白、柳叶蓑杂草上越冬、结合兴修水利、积肥，消灭幼虫。清除烧毁稻桩、玉米桩，枯叶和麦桩，消除和减少卵量，减轻危害。开春以后，处理病毒草，减少稻瘟病病源。可选用抗（耐）病虫高产优良品种降低稻瘟病的发生。20世纪70年代引种的杂交稻南优2号抗稻瘟病，80年代引种的常规稻桂朝2号抗稻瘟病，90年后期引进的金桂99抗稻瘟病。加强水肥管理、控制，水稻生产实行沟灌、浅灌、晒田，可减轻病害的发生；合理施用氮肥、增施磷钾肥可控制稻瘟病的发生。

人工防治 主要是手工捉虫，特别是对水稻、玉米螟虫害防治效果显著，经常早晚到稻田、玉米地中巡视，一经发现即时捕杀。手工捉虫可最大限度减少农药污染，适用于部分食叶类害虫幼虫捕杀。2001年谷堡乡红星村300多亩板栗园发生严重螟栗虫灾，发动农民手工捉虫，防止虫害的蔓延。

种子处理 采用农药浸种和拌种，杀灭种子内病原物，防止病虫危害、促进种子发芽和幼苗健壮。浸种方法有清水浸种、温汤浸种、药剂浸种，拌种是将药剂、肥料和种子混合搅拌后播种。20世纪80年代，县内普遍使用强氯精为水稻种子浸种，使用桐油加石灰或钙镁磷肥为玉米拌种。90年代，广泛使用

强氯精、浸种灵和玉金刚、吡虫啉、多菌灵等农药浸种和拌种。

物理防治 是一种发展时间较长又较容易掌握的防治手段，主要采用物理措施来减轻或消灭病虫害的方法。根据昆虫具有趋光性的特点，诱集昆虫，集中杀灭。最早采用的有煤油灯诱虫，20世纪80年代又采用白炽灯、汞灯、发光二极管等诱虫。杀灭方式一般为电击、水溺、毒杀等。90年代后又推广使用频振式杀虫灯杀虫。此外，还采用糖醋诱杀，即在蔬菜地或果园中用糖醋诱杀螟蛾；草把诱卵，集中烧毁；推广隔离法，对水果进行套袋处理等。

化学防治 即使用农药防治动植物病害的方法。农药具有高效、速效、使用方便、经济效益高等优点，但使用不当可对植物产生药害，引起人畜中毒，杀伤有益微生物，导致病原物产生抗药性。农药的高残留还可造成环境污染。20世纪70年代末使用的农药品种主要有西力生、赛力散、硫酸铜、六六六、滴滴涕、稻瘟净、敌敌畏、乐果、敌百虫等。80年代增加甲胺磷、氧化乐果、杀虫双，杀螟松。90年代增加乐斯本、杀虫王、敌杀死、速灭杀丁等农药。2000年以后，严禁使用剧毒、高毒、高残留农药，以前常用的六六六、滴滴涕等20种剧毒农药停止使用，甲胺磷、氧化乐果等18种高毒、高残留农药停止使用。施药方法主要有喷雾法、喷粉法、种子处理、土壤处理、熏蒸法、烟雾法，此外，杀菌剂还用于涂抹、浸果、蘸根、树体注射、仓库及器具消毒等。

中草药防治 即采用中草药防治农作物病虫害，主要有用马桑叶防治食根叶甲，用耗子头（草乌）防治地老虎；用石灰防治稻瘟病，用烟秆、烟筋防治螟虫、地老虎；用鸡蛋菜油乳剂治烟蚜；用石灰、山烟茎秆研细放在秧根下，毒死小豆虫，用耗子头、苦参根研细加石灰泡水，滴入玉米苗心和用马桑叶、野棉花或五朵云熬水冷却，淋在受害植株上防治钻心虫。

生物防治 生物防治是利用有益生物或其他生物来抑制或消灭有害生物的一种防治方法。防治方法主要有以虫治虫、以菌治虫和养鸭治虫等。20世纪80年代曾推广养鸭治虫，采用养鸭捕食稻田中的稻飞虱、叶蝉、稻纵卷叶螟、稻苞虫。90年代使用生物农药BT乳剂防治蔬菜害虫。县境内农作物病虫害天敌资源，主要有草蛉、瓢虫、步行虫、畸螯螨、钝绥螨、蜘蛛、蛙、蟾蜍、食蚊鱼、叉尾鱼以及食虫益鸟等。

（二）草鼠鸟兽害

1.农田害草

（1）害草种类

县境农作物普遍危害严重的害草主要有眼子菜（水案板）、稻稗（毛稗）、四叶萍、牛毛毡草、鸭舌草、马唐（熟地草）、牛筋草、狗尾草、繁缕（鹅儿肠）、牛繁缕、看麦娘、香附子、马兰、艾蒿、白茅、狗牙根。坝田杂草主要有牛毛草、稻稗、水绵、鸭舌草等13种，冷烂田主要有眼子菜、长瓣慈菇、黑藻等11种。麦地杂草主要有看麦娘、棒头草、繁缕等8种。油菜地杂草主要有早熟禾、看麦娘、繁缕等7种。蔬菜地杂草主要有马唐、辣子菜、婆婆纳等17种。果园杂草主要有草艾蒿、飞蓬、马兰、双穗雀稗等23种。其他旱粮和经济作物主要杂草有马唐、牛筋草、狗牙根、白茅根等23种。

（2）除草方法

人工除草 农谚有“要得庄稼好，铲尽地边草”。人工除草一年四季均可进行，各种农作物在播种前铲除干净田边地头杂草；农作物生长过程中适时中耕除草；农作物收获后将地中及周边杂草除尽焚烧或堆沤成肥料。水田除草的方法还有就是施足农家肥，有谚语说：“田肥草稀，田瘦草密”。眼子菜（水案板）多的水田还可采用多耙1至2道田泥，将草根耙漂在水面使其难以着泥生长。

化学除草 20世纪80年代中期，县境开始出现使用禾大壮除草剂清除稻田杂草。以后化学除草剂品种逐渐增加，主要的有除草醚、草枯醚、稻田一次净、灭草王、稻草隆、扑草剂、敌草隆、草甘膦等。化学除草，稻田多于旱地。2010年，全县稻田化学除草面积已达70%。约7万亩左右，除草效果达90%左右。大多数化学除草剂具有选择性除草的特点，稻田杂草中最难治的眼子草（水案板）可选用扑草剂、敌草隆防治。对稗类草、狗尾草、看麦娘、牛筋草、马唐、猪殃殃等一年生杂草，可选用草甘膦。

2.农田鼠害

全县每年都有不同程度农田鼠害发生，危害损失在1%至10%之间。其中，1983年、1986年、1994危害较重，严重的田块损失达15%左右。

农田灭鼠较早采用磷化锌、安妥、广氟乙酰胺等。20世纪80年代，推广使用敌鼠钠盐、杀鼠迷、氯敌鼠、毒鼠磷、灭鼠优等药剂。90年代，推广使用溴敌隆、杀鼠灵、大隆等药剂。防治方法改过去一家一户防治为大面积成片防治、乡村联合防治。同时，杜绝使用对人畜有害的高剧毒鼠药四亚甲基二砜四胺（毒鼠强）。

3.鸟兽害

危害农作物的鸟兽，主要有麻雀、乌鸦、黄豆雀、野猪、刺猬、野兔、獾等。主要危害水稻、玉米、红苕、马铃薯等。20世纪80年代，县境鸟、兽害情况不很严重，麻雀、乌鸦、野猪、刺猬等有害鸟兽数量锐减几近灭绝。90年代后，县境自然环境条件逐步改善，有害鸟兽数量逐步增加，特别是麻雀之类的害鸟数量陡增，进入2000年后，几近成灾。有害鸟兽对农作物的危害逐步加大。防治方法，以器械捕捉、毒饵诱杀，在稻田中插上稻草人防鸟害等。

农作物主要鸟兽害及防治一览表

表3—01—03

<table>
<tr><th>类别</th><th>名称</th><th>危害农作物</th><th>防治方法</th></tr>
<tr><td rowspan="5">鸟类</td><td>麻雀</td><td>以谷物为食，主要危害水稻的种子和成熟稻谷</td><td rowspan="5">1. 在田间安放稻草人，或以长竿插在田间，梢端挂反光材料或能发出声响的东西，恐吓鸟类
2. 人工驱鸟，在田间不定时地放鞭炮、敲打，以随时驱赶田间害鸟
3. 可在田间作物上喷洒驱鸟剂，也可在播种子时用辛硫磷类颗粒剂施撒田间或喷洒一些气味浓的杀虫剂</td></tr>
<tr><td>黄豆雀</td><td>以谷物为食，主要危害小米、山谷（旱稻）等</td></tr>
<tr><td>乌鸦</td><td>啄食瓜果、谷物、农作物种子等</td></tr>
<tr><td>喜鹊</td><td>啄食瓜果、谷物、农作物种子等</td></tr>
<tr><td>八哥</td><td>啄食水果及蔬菜等</td></tr>
<tr><td rowspan="5">兽类</td><td>野猪</td><td>食性很杂，主要是对新播种的玉米、番薯、马铃薯等破坏较大</td><td rowspan="5">1. 用稻草人、反光材料或能发出声响的东西吓阻
2. 选用农药拌种，毒杀或驱赶害兽
3. 用捕捉器械捕捉</td></tr>
<tr><td>刺猬</td><td>啃食农作物，危害瓜果</td></tr>
<tr><td>野兔</td><td>啃食禾本科、豆科植物茎叶和番薯、蔬菜等</td></tr>
<tr><td>獾</td><td>俗称泥猪，主要拱食玉米、蕃番、马铃薯的种子和种块</td></tr>
<tr><td>鼠</td><td>俗称耗子，主要有山耗子和水耗子</td></tr>
</table>

第四节　养殖业

养殖业历来都是农业重要的组成部分。体制问题、市场需求、粮食短缺是导致改革开放前全县养殖业发展缓慢、生产水平低下最主要的制约因素。直至1979年，大牲畜年末存栏2.5万头，生猪年末存栏7.3万头、年内出栏3.1万头，各种肉类总产1680吨，禽蛋184吨，水产品4吨，实现畜牧业产值420万元，占农业总产值的比重为16.25%。20世纪80年代初，农村家庭联产承包责任制的确立，农民有了生产、经营自主权，城乡居民随着经济发展、收入增长、对畜禽产品的需求猛增，在较短时间内，农民生产的粮食自给有余，从1985年起，全县养殖业以前所未有的速度发展。当年大牲畜年末存栏3.38万头，生猪年末存栏8.32万头、年内出栏5.3万头，各种肉类总产4569吨，禽蛋441吨，水产品93吨，实现畜牧业产值1738万元，使其在农业总产值中的比重提升至33.31%。面对这样强劲的发展势头，县委、县政府通过引进骨干养殖企业，带动规模养殖；通过科学规划、资源整合、推动建设养殖小区；通过对养殖业内部产业结构调整，扩大养殖范围。在扶贫攻坚战中，通过在资金、技术上对贫困户进行扶持，把发展家庭养殖作为重大的扶贫措施来抓。这些主要措施，促进全县养殖业的健康发展。特别是在养殖结构和养殖方式上发生了深刻的变化。2004年获得“全省生猪养殖示范县”的荣誉称号。至2010年，大牲畜年末存栏4.7万头、当年出栏1.4万头，生猪年末存栏9.68万头、当年出栏1.59万头，各种肉类总产1.72万吨，产禽蛋3155吨，水产品产量658吨，产牛奶（鲜奶）9752吨，实现畜牧业产值3.41亿元，占全县农业总产值的25.95%。大宗的畜、禽、蛋、鱼、奶产品，已成为省会贵阳重要的生产基地县。2010年全县农民人均家庭经营收入4642.59元中，养殖业收入为831.5元，占17.91%，不失为农民增收的一个重要渠道。

一、家畜饲养

（一）牛

1978年，全县牛存栏2.04万头，主要是以役牛为主，属生产队集体财产。生产队安排给队内责任心强、有一定养牛经验的人家饲养。放牧分集中放牧和单独放牧两种，集中放牧称“放伙牛”，放牧人称“伙牛匠”，放牧牛群10至20头不等，报酬按中等劳动力标准记全年工分。对养牛户集体每年按1个中等劳动力全年1/5左右的标准记工分作报酬。秋后集体分配时留足一定数量的玉米作耕牛饲料，主要在寒冬和耕地时饲喂耕牛。集体的稻草和玉米秸秆按耕牛的数量比例和大小分配给养牛户作饲草。

1981年农村经济体制改革，全县农村全面实行包干到户，耕牛折价按承包土地的人口分摊固定到户，成为农民的私有财产。1983年，中寨乡东庄村村民在三岔河边马岩山下兴办畜牧场，养殖耕牛18头，开启民办养殖场先河。继后六桶乡保坪村农民发现牛肉市场看好，遂购进一些老、弱、病、残牛饲养，育肥后作肉牛出售，获利丰厚。至2000年，六桶乡先后办起宏兴、长兴和山保肉牛养殖场，年出栏肉牛300余头。2002年10月，在市、县政府的扶持下，由政府投入大部分资金，群众自筹部分资金，建起大石乡天桥村种草养牛基地，饲养能繁母牛172头。随后大石乡又建起红岩、回水养牛基地。

2003年，县引进“好1多”奶牛养殖企业入驻久长镇清水村，全场饲养奶牛600头，年产鲜奶3600吨。公司帮助清水村25户村民办起养殖规模200头的村办奶牛场，当年购进75头饲养。县内奶牛养殖从无到有，并逐步向扎佐、谷堡和六桶等乡镇发展。2004年，谷堡乡折溪村建立肉牛饲养基地，国家提供无息贷款3万元，发动蛇田农户26家，养牛105头。由于当地养牛效益不及种植猕猴桃、金秋梨等水果明显和饲养技术跟不上，最终未能成功。2005年，在县政府财政贴息扶持政策支持下，在六广镇沙坡、合兴、四寨村和六屯乡高峰村先后建起肉牛养殖场，共计投入种牛116头，其中六广镇64头，六屯乡52头。2010年，全县除个体养殖外，另建有肉牛养殖基地8个，奶牛养殖基地6个，成牛年末存栏数42385头，年末出栏12482头，年产鲜奶9752吨，牛肉产量1373吨。

县境当地牛种分为黄牛和水牛两类。其中，黄牛属黔中类型，分布全县各地，主要在西部和北部以旱地作物为主的六广、大石、六桶、洒坪和小箐等乡镇。黄牛主要作役用，用以耕犁中等硬度以下的旱地为主，亦可耕犁水田，日耕地1.5至2亩，负荷量为150—200公斤。连续耕地4小时后，脉搏有明显增高，休息15分钟后即恢复正常，出肉率36%。黄牛1.5至2岁性成熟，初配年龄为2.5岁，繁殖年龄到16岁左右，发情持续1至2天，怀孕期为275—290天，一般每胎产仔1头，母牛繁殖年限为12至13年。黄牛的特点是耐粗饲，适应性和抗病力强、性情温顺、耐热耐寒、吃苦耐劳。水牛属黔南型。主要分布于龙场、扎佐、久长、谷堡和六屯等乡镇，中心区在龙场镇的王官、程关、马家桥和扎佐的清让及久长镇清水等地。水牛体型中等，体躯粗壮，腰大且园，四肢粗壮结实，关节明显，角质黑色，较为粗壮，角尖向内，毛被多为灰黑色。为役用型牛，其饲养管理与黄牛类似，系圈养与放牧相结合，役用年限为15年，主要用以耕犁水田和中等硬度以上的旱地，日耕2至2.5亩，负荷量为200—250公斤。产区内每100亩耕地有水牛7.97头，有能繁殖母牛1.73头。母牛3岁初配，性周期19—24天，发情持续1至2天，怀孕期320—330天，母牛繁殖年限为15年。水牛特点怕高温不耐寒，高温季节喜欢到水塘和泥潭打滚，借以散热和防止昆虫叮咬，寒冬季节要注意防风保温以防冻伤冻死。

黄牛、水牛

除本地牛外，20世纪70年代，县多次组织到关岭购买耕牛，补充县内畜力。1979年5月，又从清镇农牧场引进3头爱沙尼亚种公牛，安排在县畜牧站和六广区畜牧站作耕牛品种改良，其中县站2头，六广站1头。通过爱沙尼亚种公牛培育的后代在役用性能、体形外貌、体尺体重等方面都有明显的提高和改进。1998年从关岭引进黄牛10头（公牛2头，母牛8头）、辛地红公牛2头、爱沙尼亚公牛2头。

2001年从省品改站引进西门塔尔种公牛1头，投放给六桶乡大兴村饲养培育。西门塔尔牛是世界著名大型温带肉用牛种之一，原产于瑞士和法国、德国和奥地利等地，为黄白花或红白花头及腹下部白色。肌肉发达，无过多脂肪，体型大、产肉性能好、产乳量高、役用性能也很好，是乳、肉、役兼用的大型品种。种公牛体重1100公斤，成年母牛650公斤，在半肥育状态下，母牛屠宰率达53.55%，肥育后公牛达65%，日增重800—1000克，是肉牛饲养和品种改良的理想选择之一。2003年，好1多乳业入驻久长建清水奶牛场，引进荷斯坦牛(中国黑白花牛)43头饲养。荷斯坦牛属大体型奶牛，产奶量最高，年产鲜奶8000公斤左右。继后，又先后从吉林、陕西等地引进秦川和西门塔尔、利木赞、泥里水牛、夏洛来黄牛共600头，促进县内牛的品种改良。

（二）马

1978年，全县有马4835匹，主要用于驮运、拉车和代步乘用等，大部分属生产队集体财产，也有部分属农民私养。集体部分的马，一般是承包给个人搞运输，承包费每月30—50元不等，集体按1个上等劳动力标准记工分。承包的由承包人负责饲养，未承包的按养牛标准给饲养户记报酬。1981年，全县农村包干到户后，集体饲养的马折价变卖给农户自养自用。

养马比养牛精细，一般需要有马棚（俗称马圈），不能与其他牲畜混养，马棚要经常打扫干净，要保持棚内干燥卫生，冬暖、夏凉。饲喂要有食槽（俗称马槽），饮水要有专门的水缸。马的饲料分粗、精两类，粗饲料主要有青草和稻草、玉米秸秆等，精饲料主要有玉米、大豆、小豆、豆渣和饼粕等。精饲料一般在役用下力时饲喂，其他时间少喂或不喂。20世纪80年代，随着市场经济发展，县境乡场增多，在边远的六桶、大石、六广、洒坪等地的马帮又开始形成，主要以驮运货物为主。2000年代前后，全县实现村村通公路，机动运输逐步成为主要运输工具，畜力运输退居次要位置。2010年，全县仍有马1491匹。

马

境内马属西南马中贵州马，全县各地均有，主要分布在西、北部地区，中心产区在六广、六桶、大石、小箐等乡镇，产区内每平方公里拥有马匹达16.53匹，其中能繁母马5.82匹。其主要特征为体格中等，躯体呈近高方形结构，外表清秀、体质结实，头直而方，耳小而立，颌凹宽，头颈结合良好，毛被以栗、骝色为主。特点是短小精悍、行动敏捷、役力超强、善于爬山，适于山地驮运。马驹生后1.5岁龄开始性成熟，2.5岁初配，发情周期长短不一，平均21天左右，发情持续5至7天，孕期340天左右，繁殖年限和使役年限均为12至15岁。境内无阉割公马的习惯，公母马约各占一半。成年公马体高为116厘米，体长为114厘米。成年母马体高为113厘米，体长为114厘米。境内马多为役用，长途驮运载重60至70公斤，日行35—40公里；短途驮重可达100公斤。单马驾车可载重400至500公斤。

另有马和驴杂交的后代称为骡子，公驴和母马所生称为马骡，公马和母驴所生的后代则称为驴骡。马骡像马，驴骡像驴。马骡力比马大，善驮运和拉车；驴骡善于奔跑，利于代步乘用。一般马骡可役使20年左右，驴骡可役使30年左右。

（三）猪

1978年，生猪养殖主要在广大农村，一般为农户家庭喂养，大多数农户1户1头猪，少数农户1户2头，极少数农户1户3头，也有极少数的无猪户。部分生产队集体办有养猪场，养猪10至20头不等。部分城镇居民家庭为贴补家庭生活也少量饲养生猪。在广大农村为鼓励农民养猪，提出“1人1头猪，1猪1亩地”的发展目标，同时划拨每个家庭1至2分旱地作为养猪饲料地。由于当时受粮食产量的影响，生猪养殖一直发展缓慢。是年，全县生猪年末存栏仅为6.79万头。国家对生猪养殖实行“生猪派购，购五留五，肉猪统一经营，严禁私宰生猪”的政策。1979年起，政策逐步放宽。

1985年，国家取消派购，猪肉价格放开，增加对城镇居民的肉价补贴。取消生猪派购后，收购价格有的实行指导价格、适当浮动，有的随行就市，销售价格也相应放开。农民养猪积极性提高，年末生猪存栏数达8.32万头，年内出栏5.3万头。之后起，生猪养殖主要受价格波动、需求变化和疫病影响，但总体趋势生猪存栏数不断上升。1995年，全县年末生猪存栏达10.06头，年内出栏7.63万头。

2004年，县被定为全省优质肉猪基地，全县共建生猪养殖基地8个。至2006年，生猪养殖数量创历史最高水平，年末存栏22.85万头，年内出栏28.5万头，肉类总产量3.3万吨，但价格走低，严重挫伤农民养猪积极性。2007年，生猪年末存栏减少至8.25万头，年内出栏减少至13.2万头，肉类总产量减少至1.47万吨。为确保生猪生产稳定发展，国家提出鼓励发展标准化规模养殖政策，大力发展生猪标准化规模养殖，积极推进生猪规模场和养殖小区的标准化改造，改善饲养和防疫条件，实行统一良种、统一防疫、统一操作规范，降低养殖成本，提高生产能力。同时政府实行补贴政策，对规模化养猪补助标准为：年出栏500—999头补贴20万元；年出栏1000—1999头补贴40万元；年出栏2000～2999头补贴60万元；年出栏3000头以上的为80万元。对能繁母猪补贴政策2007年为每头能繁母猪发放标准为50元，2008年提增加到100元。2009年生猪价格开始回升，2010年国家对能繁母猪的补贴停止，但对生猪标准化规模养殖场继续实施补贴。全县生猪养殖年末存栏9.27万头，年内出栏15.25万头，肉类总产量1.71万吨。

1.生猪品种

生猪品种主要分为本地品种和引进品种两大类。本地品种主要为黔中型和黔西北型猪种，毛被多黑色，少数为黑白相间和棕色（俗称“黄毛猪”）。其中典型代表品种为乌栗猪，主要产于乌栗以西的大塘、平滩和绿水一带，故名乌栗猪，全县各地均有分布。乌栗猪属肉脂兼用型，按其毛色：黑色占18%，“六白”占40%，“六白”夹大花点41%，有少量黄毛猪。乌栗猪的头中等大小，耳大向前下垂，嘴筒长而直，腹大下垂呈秽状，后驱较高且丰满，斜厩较多（占55%），四肢开张直立，骨骼结实，少数踏蹄（6.5%），毛中等长短，奶头平均为12.5个，成年公猪75至100公斤，母猪50至80公斤。乌栗猪性成熟早，初配年龄为四个月，性周期20天左右，妊娠期约114天，最高繁殖年限为20年。母猪繁殖性能为：初胎产仔数5至6头，2—3胎产仔数7至8头，4胎以上产仔数8至10头。乌栗猪均为圈养，人们习惯喂以熟食，多以青绿饲料为主，搭配少量精料，育肥多为吊架子方式，催肥期增加精料，幼龄阶段增重迅速，肥猪到80公斤左右则生长转缓。乌栗猪具有耐饲，抗病力强的特点。但由于无计划引种杂交，品种纯度降低，较引进优良猪种优势减弱，逐步被淘汰。

1978年从浙江省金华地区引进种公猪99头（其中长白猪50头，苏白猪6头，约克猪43头）；从江苏东海县引进长白猪16头（其中母猪6头，公猪10头）；又从外地引进巴克夏猪19头。全县有长白、约克、巴克夏、苏白、荣昌五个种猪品种。1979年，开始推广生猪人工授精技术，当年人工授精达288头，受孕率达89.6%，一般产仔6至8头，最高产仔19头。1985年，生产一代杂交猪，1998年生产推广杂交猪11万头，2003年增加到15.8万头。2004年，先后在久长石安、六屯西冲、小箐大兴、小箐大坝建二元杂

交母猪小区，养二元杂交母猪2592头，为全县提供优良种源。2005年，又引进优质二元杂交母猪1750头，国外良种杜洛克种公猪20头。年底，全县杂文猪达18.7万头。以后至2010年，每年都要引进一批优良猪种，提高良种优势，防止生猪品种退化，推动生猪生产发展。

2.生猪饲养

主要分为传统饲养和科学饲养两种方法。其最大的区别是熟食和生食，传统饲养又称为熟饲料养猪，讲究的是要把猪喂饱喂好；科学饲养又称新法养猪，讲究的是饲料营养的均衡搭配，降低生产成本，提高经济效益。

传统饲养　饲料分为精饲料和粗饲料。精饲料主要有玉米、马铃薯、番薯、杂豆和大麦等。用量根据猪的大小和不同的生长阶段适当调整。刚开食的乳猪和育肥期精料比例可高一些，甚至以喂精料为主，其余阶段可少一些。以1头50公斤重的架子猪为例，一般1天有0.5至1公斤玉米分两次饲喂。粗饲料分为青饲料和干饲料两种：青饲料俗称猪草，包括蔬菜、番薯藤和无毒且适口性好的野菜、树叶、水牛植物、嫩牧草、绿肥等；干饲料主要有米糠、麦麸、油枯等，也可用豆类叶、树叶、葛藤叶等晒干粉碎后称为“干糠”作喂猪的干饲料，主要在冬季缺少青饲料时替代青饲料养猪。饲喂方法一般是将精料磨为半细，青料切为1至2厘米长，按照一定的比例放在大锅（俗称猪食锅）中煮熟成稀粥状，待温度降至温热时饲喂。一般饲喂一日两次，少数有一日三次。

传统养猪的圈舍分为板圈和草圈两种。板圈一般是上为猪圈下为粪池，中以耐水耐腐蚀的木枋铺平，猪就养在铺平的木枋之上。在广大农村农民习惯将厕所和板圈合并修建，共1个粪池，以便积蓄人猪粪便作农家肥使用。草圈一般为坑状式畜圈，坑为方形，长宽3×3米左右，深1.2至1.8米，坑壁有土壁和石砌两种。圈壁多为土墙，少为石墙，极少为砖墙。圈顶多为盖草，亦有少数盖瓦。圈内铺垫稻草、玉米秸秆、秧青、杂草等。铺垫物每次铺垫10至20厘米，要经常保持圈内干燥。圈内可单独饲养生猪，也可猪、牛混养。其中的铺垫物与猪、牛粪便混合发酵后为优质农家肥，可作农作物底肥使用。板圈夏凉冬冷，冬季要注意防寒保暖。草圈夏凉冬暖，有利于牲畜过冬。

种公猪、母猪、肥猪、架子猪、仔猪分圈饲养，经常保持圈舍清洁干燥。所以有农谚总结为：“喂猪不用巧，只要圈干臊食热。”生猪的传统饲养，一般周期为一年，少数为两或两年以上。屠宰多在春节前1个月内宰杀，少数在喜庆、春耕和秋收时宰杀，平时除上市销售的外一般不予宰杀。

科学饲养　进入20世纪80年代，随着农村经济体制改革的不断深入，农产品产量提高，农民养猪观念发生变化，由过去的喂猪过年改为喂猪赚钱。养猪从过去的不计成本改为降低成本，提高经济效益，科学养猪技术得到逐渐推广。首先将传统的吊架子育肥改为直线育肥，即根据猪各个生长发育阶段所需的营养进行饲料调配，如对仔猪采取提早断奶，提早补料，促进猪的迅速增长发育，满100公斤左右屠宰，以提高肉猪出栏率和养猪经济效益。对公猪进行专门饲养、种公猪日粮喂量为2.5—3公斤配合料和2公斤青饲料。配种时还要加喂鸡蛋，实行单圈分槽饲养，每日除供给清洁水外，还采取外放运动，增强体质。对未孕母猪日喂两次，以青绿饲料为主，少喂精料。怀孕后适当增加一点糠麸，以免母猪过肥，同时喂少许食盐，日喂三次。母猪临产前喂精料，并单独隔养，减少放牧，不与合群，以免殴斗堕胎流产。产后母猪还需用黄豆或豌豆磨浆催奶。仔猪产出20日龄开食少量精料，为双月断奶逐步过渡。60日龄断奶后每天喂3—4次。1983年县科委引进配合饲料配方技术列入科研项目，交原畜牧局和粮食局合作实施试制成功后，随即交与粮食局青年综合社投产。80年代中期，逐步改进生猪饲养方式，改熟喂为配合饲料生喂，一是减少燃料，二是减少劳力，三是营养全面，为猪生长创造条件。同期，在久长镇石安村率先出现生猪养殖专业户，有的烤酒用酒糟养猪，有的采用先进技术用配合饲料养猪，每户年出栏生猪20至30头。在其带动下县内的久长镇上堡、下堡、小箐乡的大兴、大坝和六屯乡西冲等村先后发展成为养猪专业村。为降低养猪成本提高养猪的经济效益，县还先后引进生猪饲料的发酵、氨化、青贮等技术，大大提高生猪饲料利用率。

90年代，新法养猪得到广泛推广，群众将其总结为“四良四改三提高”。即推广良种，改一般品种为优良品种；推广良料，改单一饲料为配合饲料、混合饲料和全价饲料；推广良法，改熟饲为生饲，减少营养损失，饲料不必经过蒸煮，直接生喂；推广良舍，改深坑圈为向阳干平圈饲养。其目的是要提高出栏率，提高饲料利用率，提高个体产肉率。进入21世纪在原有基础上又提出“三推广”“三普及”和四提高养殖新技术：即推广林草畜、粮草畜、畜沼粮结合的生态养殖技术，推广优质畜产品标准化技术，推广小区规模养殖技术；普及畜禽人工授精杂交改良综合配套技术，普及人工种草、天然草场改良和饲料青贮、秸秆氨化技术，普及动物疫病综合防治技术；提高家畜个体生产能力，提高牧草、饲料转化率和秸秆利用率；提高动物疫病防治能力。同时，结合农村“四改一气”工程，进行改圈，保证养猪圈内清洁、干燥，减少疾病的发生。养猪专业户不仅有圈舍，圈舍外还连有活动场，配有自动饮水装置头，促进生猪生长。

（四）羊

县境养羊因农民嫌放牧麻烦，又易损坏庄稼，加上羊肉膻味不受人喜欢，故养羊不多，仅有少数农户零星养殖。1978年，全县养羊417只，1979年发展至459只。1981年，全县农村包干到户后，养猪比养羊有利可图，养羊户多弃羊养猪，至1986年全县羊存栏数下降到209只。20世纪80年代后半期，由于羊肉小吃的兴起，羊肉价格提高，市场需求增大，羊肉多由外地购进。中寨乡东庄村农民在马岩山兴办畜牧场成群饲养山羊，产量逐年增加。至1990年全县山羊存栏增至388只。进入90年代，政府引进黑山羊鼓励农民养殖，至1993年存栏数增加到780只。1995年起，结合扶贫开发项目，政府从资金上给予大力帮扶，全县养羊数量激增，至1996年全县养羊存栏数达10020只。继后养羊发展势头持续增长，1999年全县养羊存栏数达16071只，为历史最高水平。次年起逐年减少，至2010年全县养羊存栏数回落至9865只。

黑山羊养殖

1978年，县境山羊品种主要有白山羊和麻羊两种。公羊3至4月龄性成熟，初配多为6至8月龄；母羊4至5月龄性成熟，初配多为8至10月龄配种。一般成年公羊体重平均为32公斤，成年母羊平均为30公斤出肉率可达45%左右。主要分布在石安、中寨、六广、大石、凉井等偏僻山区和少数民族聚居的地方。20世纪90年代，引进贵州黑山羊养殖。黑山羊品种优于原来的白羊和麻羊两种山羊。一般成年公羊体重达35公斤，成年母羊体重达34公斤，胎产羔率为148.81%。出栏羊出肉率达46.36%。

（五）兔

1978年，县境内仅有极少数人家养殖家兔，全县总数不足1000只。1984年，发展农村多种经营，引

进长毛兔养殖，城关区马家桥乡还出现专门养殖长毛兔专业户。至1987年，全县有兔1341只。继后由于养兔专业户技术跟不上，加上兔毛价格回落，养兔专业户亏损转产。20世纪90年代中期，养兔业再次兴起，多以养殖肉兔为主，主要涉及城关、小箐、六广、大石和六桶等乡镇，养殖专业户多与餐饮业挂钩，沟通产销渠道。至2000年，全县养殖兔存栏量5000余只。2003年，引进康庄牧业养兔公司落户小箐乡崇恩村。基地占地面积100余亩，种草面积达60亩，建有标准兔舍1200平方米。养殖优质种兔600余只，当年开始产种兔。2004年，外出务工人员苏贵荣返乡创办盛鑫养兔公司，在龙场镇木厂村修建养殖场，当年引进优良种兔300只饲养。2005年，市、县政府再次倡导并扶持养兔，在石头、来鹤、宝坪三村设置肉兔养殖小区，投放种兔67组。年底，多数已产仔兔。贵阳市政府把宝坪村肉兔养殖作为市级示范点，在保坪召开肉兔养殖现场会，推动全市养兔业的发展。至2010年，康庄牧业养兔公司采取“公司+农户”模式与农户签订“三包”养殖合同（即包技术，包产品销售，包种兔供应），实行产前、产中、产后服务。在龙塘、崇恩、尖山等村发展养殖专业户，全县建成养兔小区17个，养殖种兔共1097组13164只，涉及全县10个乡镇1000余户农户。 盛鑫养兔公司采取“企业+基地+小区+农户”的模式，坚持“统一品种、统一投入、统一标准饲养、统一免疫程序、统一销售”，养殖户只管精心养兔，技术、服务、市场等均由企业承担。盛鑫公司养兔发展辐射带动包括县内龙场、大石、六桶等乡镇及白云区、清镇市、花溪区等地3000多户农户养殖兔，成为贵阳市养兔龙头企业。

商品兔养殖

县境本地家兔品种多为白兔，另有本地兔与其他品种杂交后代兔，也属本地兔，毛色有白色、黑色、黑白花和灰色等。本地兔毛短，眼球红色，喜打洞而居，多为笼养，以蔬菜、嫩草、豆叶为食。母兔受孕一月后产仔，以腹毛垫窝，一胎产仔4至6只，年产3至4窝。成年兔重1.5至2公斤。

2003年，县农业局从昆明引进齐卡巨型兔333只在崇恩花桥康庄养殖场繁育成功，同年7月原种兔开始产种兔。齐卡肉兔全身洁白，眼呈粉红色，后驱较高，四肢粗大，胴体背腰宽，后躯肌肉丰富，属巨型兔。其特点是发育早，生长快，适应性好，抗病力强等特点。成年兔体重6至8公斤，屠宰率60%以上，肉质细嫩。每胎平均产仔8—16只，肥育成活率为93%。齐卡肉兔优于其他兔种，产出率高，是集约化，规模化养殖的理想肉兔品种。

2005年，引进加利福尼亚大型种兔饲养，此兔身躯白色被毛，而鼻端、两耳、四肢下端和尾部杂以黑色。其特点是性早熟、温顺，母性好，适应性强，抗病、繁殖力强，遗传性稳定，适于营养较高的精料型饲料。身躯匀称，头大小适中，耳小直立，眼红色，嘴钝圆，胸部、肩部和后躯发育良好，肌肉丰满四肢短细，为中型肉用兔品种，肉质鲜嫩。成年兔重4至5公斤，屠宰率52%—54%。。

2010年，县境内零星饲养多以本地兔种为主。养殖场及养殖小区饲养均系齐卡巨型兔和加利福尼亚兔。

二、家禽饲养

（一）鸡

1978年，境内农村家禽饲养主要以鸡为主，一般饲养量不大，每户饲养量在10只左右。全县年出栏

18万羽，禽蛋产量171吨。1981年，全县农村包干到户后，农民思想观念发生变化，开始出现养鸡专业户，规模每户在50至100只左右。20世纪80年代中期，在城关区马家桥一带建起几个养鸡场，规模每场2000至3000只。此后至90年代下半期，全县各地养鸡场不断兴起。但由于养殖技术跟不上，大多数养殖场是养殖第一批鸡赢利，第二批保本，第三批亏损停产，究其原因主要是防疫技术差，养鸡死亡率高。

1997年，六桶乡山保村村民李根中和下坝村村毕成国在乡政府的扶持下，学习外地经验采用林下养鸡，兴办林下养鸡场取得成功，并带动一批100只以上的养殖户120多户。1999年，结合贵阳市菜篮子工程项目在扎佐镇三元村成立贵州兰地实业有限责任公司，专门从事蛋鸡养殖，是一家专业从事现代农业生产和现代农业技术推广的高科技民营企业，项目包括12万蛋鸡养殖场、家禽孵化厂、家禽饲料厂、生物有机复合肥厂、禽肉制品加工厂和200亩优质果园及木本花卉园艺场等。2007年，久长镇清水村外出务工农民回村在清水村三湾子建立起一个规模20万羽蛋鸡养殖场，当年饲养蛋鸡8万羽。2009年谨成农业有限公司落户山岔村，当年养鸡1.5万羽。2010年，全县鸡存栏110万只，禽蛋总产量达3155吨，比1978增加17.45倍。

县境本地鸡属黔中类型，公鸡毛色红颈绿尾夹黑色，单冠，冠大峰高，冠齿为5至7个。成年公鸡重2至2.5公斤。母鸡毛色多为麻黄，8月龄左右开始产蛋，产蛋率低，年产蛋80至120枚，就巢性强，就巢期为20至30天，成年母鸡体重为1.5至2公斤。本地鸡肉质细嫩，味道鲜美。全县各地均有饲养。1978年，境内鸡品种除本地鸡外还有来杭鸡、芦花鸡、乌骨鸡、陈鸡（斗鸡）、九斤黄、贵农黄、星布罗、澳洲黑、伏巴特、红育京北等品种。

1983年，县畜牧站先后在贵州农学院引进贵农黄鸡种3.3万只，并实施贵农黄育种计划。经过亲本选育、杂交筛选、横交固定和继代选育四个育种阶段，到1993年培育出理想型种鸡4万只。每只年产蛋量175枚，比本地鸡多产40至50个蛋，蛋重55克，母鸡重2.25公斤。另外还通过市场从外地引进优良肉鸡和蛋鸡品种鸡苗饲养，其品种主要有艾维茵、爱拔益加（AA鸡）、红布罗、狄高黄等。此类品种大多系鸡苗引进，一般不自行繁育。为提高养鸡经济效益，此后境内饲养鸡品种主要从良种化和土鸡化两个方向发展。2005年又从湖南引进闵中麻鸡60万只，从广西引三黄鸡、铁脚麻脚各60万只在县内饲养。2009年，引进绿壳蛋鸡在久长镇茶山村饲养。

（二）鸭

境内养鸭多分布在龙场、扎佐、久长、谷堡、六屯和小箐等乡镇有水域的田坝地区，占家禽饲养量的8.82%。1978年集体化时期，养鸭人家不多，因养鸭习惯群养，养鸭户一般养鸭10至20只，最多的可达40至50只。集体养鸭300至1000只，称为“鸭棚子”，每棚鸭由2至3人负责管理。一般多以养鸭产蛋为主，宰杀多为公鸭和老鸭。1981年，全县农村包干到户后，集体鸭棚折价拍卖给私人，部分农民承包山塘、河段大批养鸭。20世纪90年代后，因养鸭污染环境，山塘、河流养鸭逐渐减少。2010年，全县存栏数达2.4万只。

江西麻鸭

境内养鸭品种多为黔中麻鸭。公鸭紫灰、黑颈、绿头，叫声沙哑；母鸭全身为栗麻色。成年鸭体重1至2公斤，公鸭

较母鸭略重。母鸭7至8个月开始产蛋，年产蛋100至200枚，在水域广阔、饲养水平较高的条件下，年产蛋也可达180—210枚。母鸭不会孵蛋，繁殖鸭苗小批量可用母鸡代孵，大批量可用炒谷壳成批孵化。除此外，尚有部分人家饲养有北京鸭及火鸭（疣头鸭），一般批量不大，只有几只到几十只不等。

（三）鹅

境内各乡镇均有零星饲养，占家禽饲养量的4.2%，但多集中在有水域的田坝地区，1978年存栏4850只，一般为农户家庭少量饲养。食物主要是谷物、嫩杂草、蔬菜和水生植物等。鹅习性群居，宜成群放牧，让其自由采食鲜嫩杂草，早出晚归，补以精料，如玉米谷物麦糠麸之类，就可迅速成长。鹅适应性强，饲养管理容易，经济效益好。20世纪80年代中期，在龙场、扎佐、久长、谷堡、六屯和小箐等乡镇出现一些养鹅专业户，每户养鹅30至50只。1995年，在久长、龙场、六广、小箐、洒坪等乡镇的一些平地、土坡上种植三叶草、黑麦草等优质牧草养鹅试验成功，证明鹅能适应地理环境和气候的变化，高海拔山区亦可养鹅。到2010年全县存栏发展到25万只。

灰鹅

20世纪70年代末，境内养鹅品种以灰鹅为主，其中部分为狮头鹅，另有部分白鹅。本地灰鹅主要为肉用，成年公鹅体重4—5公斤，母鹅3—4公斤。母鹅一般就巢期为20—30天，每窝可孵蛋6—8枚，亦可用母鸡代孵。90年代，养鹅大多购买商品鹅苗饲养，一些外地优质鹅苗随商贩传入县境。其品种主要有平坝灰鹅、织金白鹅、荣昌白鹅等。

三、养蜂

县境蜜蜂养殖历史悠久，多为农家小规模饲养，一般以木桶、木箱、竹篓做蜂房，俗称蜂桶。饲养蜂种以中蜂为主，1978—1988年，全县养蜂在1800群左右，一般农户多则6至10群，少则1群，基本无养蜂专业户。20世纪90年代，常有外地养蜂专业户转地饲养蜜蜂路过县境，部分有在县境逗留半年以上。2010年，全县人工养蜂在2000群左右，年产蜂蜜8吨。

县境人工饲养蜜蜂品种为中华蜜蜂，简称中蜂，俗称糖蜂。全县各地均有分布，其中洒坪、六屯、六桶、大石、小箐等乡分布较多，占全县总群数55%以上。另有野生蜜蜂，疑为家养蜜蜂分群逃出在野外自然繁殖，亦可招回人工饲养。野生和人工饲养蜜蜂均称为本地蜜蜂，经历长期自然选择，适应当地复杂自然环境，各地饲养蜜蜂品种在形态特征和生物特性，生产能力上略有差异。整体上看本地蜜蜂适应性强，在早春晚秋，天气多变寒潮频繁的情况下，都能安然无恙。冬天，外界虽有积雪，气温在2℃—3℃，少量工蜂也能出巢采水。本地蜜蜂产卵育虫灵活，蜂群能根据外界蜜源及气候条件来调节产卵虫数量，若蜜源丰富，气候适宜，蜂王产卵多，工蜂育虫积极；若气候寒冷，蜂群结团而缩成

土蜂箱养蜂

小圈，节制育虫，有利于节约饲料。一年当中的补喂饲料数量较少，在一般情况下，即使蜜源条件稍差，管理粗放，蜂群也能维持活动。

县境各种野生和栽培的蜜源植物极为丰富，种类繁多，一年四季花开不断，各类蜜源花前后相继交替开放，是发展养蜂的优越条件。被广泛利用的蜜源植物中农作物有水稻、玉米、油菜、向日葵、花生和豆类、麦类、荞麦类及各种瓜菜等；绿肥作物类主要有紫云英、苕子（野豌豆）、田菁等；果树类主要有梨、桃、李、杏、柿、葡萄、板栗、枇杷、山楂等；经济植物类山茶、油桐、漆树等；林木类主要有洋槐、乌桕、女贞、泡桐、梓木、柳、马尾松、盐肤木、香薷（木浆花）和柃木等；野生花草类有三叶草、黄荆条、野坝子、益母草、杜鹃花、茅栗、金樱子、火棘、野山楂、野蔷薇类、野菊类及蓼属植物等。一年中春夏秋三季蜜蜂源较为丰富，冬季蜜源较少。县境冬季蜜源植物主要有野菊类植物可为晚秋初冬蜜源。林木类中的盐肤木、香薷和柃木等为冬季花粉蜜源。在各类蜜源中，苕子蜜堪称蜂蜜中之上品，因其结晶时宛如雪脂又称“雪脂莲蜜”，既有普通蜂蜜的解毒润燥作用，又有清凉养颜、滋润肌肤的独特功能。

县境养蜂尚未形成产业，多为农民小规模少量养殖，全县最多时可达2000群左右。养殖方法多采用传统技术，管理较为粗放。饲养蜜蜂的蜂房一般用圆木、木板、木条或竹篾做成，圆柱体，长80至100厘米，直径40至50厘米，中空似桶状，故又称为蜂桶。每只蜂桶可养1群蜜蜂，所以民间计算蜂群一般按桶计算。蜂桶为密闭不透光，用木条或竹篾做成的蜂桶外面要糊上一层稀泥或牛粪，一般安放在遮风避雨屋檐下或阳台上。在蜂桶向外一侧桶壁近底部处钻留10个左右蜂洞，蜂群大可多钻，群小可少钻，蜂洞大小要大于工蜂小于蜂王，目的是以利工蜂出入避免蜂王逃走。

传统饲养蜜蜂，只取不喂，蜜产量较低，一年仅取蜜1—2次。一次在春季油菜花后期，另一次在秋季10月。取蜜时用烟熏蜂离脾，将蜜脾割下。蜜脾用棕片包裹，或置于竹淘萝中，用手反复揉捏，将蜜挤在容器内，余渣按传统养蜂法熬蜡。由于毁脾伤子，影响蜂群发展，不能多次取蜜，每群蜂一年仅取蜜3—5公斤。饲养规模，少则1户1至数桶，蜜源较好的地区，多则可养数十桶。由于缺乏养蜂科学知识，分蜂季节常任其自然飞出，再行收捕，接入另桶饲养。

中蜂易受巢虫危害，蜂群被害后常飞逃，群众在长期饲养过程中，对防治巢虫不断总结经验。每次取蜜时将蜂巢割一半，留一半。割去的一半因榨蜜、熬蜡，潜藏于蜂巢中的巢虫幼虫被杀死。到下一次割蜜时再割去上次留下来的另一半蜂巢，将新造的脾留下。即使脾中蜜不太多，也要割去一半，群众称此为洗窝。这既有防治巢虫的作用，也可促进巢脾更新。此方法符合现代换脾杀虫，防治巢虫的科学道理。以上传统养蜂法在全县广大农户中仍在沿用。

四、水产养殖

县境自然环境适宜发展淡水鱼类生长，水资源丰富，但水产养殖起步较晚。1978年，全县渔业水产品产量仅4.9吨，产值不到1万元，占农业总产值0.05%。随着改革开放的不断深入，社会主义市场经济的形成，推动县境水产养殖业的发展。2006年，水产品产量创历史最高，达956吨，产值921万元，占农业总产值1.09%。以后逐步回落，2010

水产养殖场

年全县水产品产量658吨，产值982万元，占农业总产值0.75%。

全县总水面12.21万亩，占全县总面积的7.57%，宜养水面达38169.7亩，占水域面积的31.26%。其中，山塘水库254座，其中小Ⅰ型水库7座，小Ⅱ型水库21座，山塘226座，正常高水位面积7059.7亩；河流水面20710亩；稻田9.43万亩，可用于养鱼稻田1.04万亩。另有丰富的地下水资源，主要分布在久长镇杨柳村、六屯乡西冲村和龙场镇新春村等地，常年储量达100亿立方米，水温8℃—20℃，水质良好，适宜发展虹鳟、欧鳗、鲟类等高品质冷性鱼类养殖。

2006年，经对县境各类水质监测分析，地表水矿化度范围均在300—500毫克/升之间；碳酸盐硬度和非碳酸盐硬度均在170—250毫克/升之间；水化学类型为重碳酸类水（C），PH值7.5~8.5之间，水型为Ⅲ型。水质监测现状评价为Ⅲ类水质占15.6%，Ⅳ类水质占33.6%，Ⅴ类水质占22.6%，劣Ⅴ类水质占28.2%。地下水监测结果矿化度浓度均值467毫克/升，总硬度均值281.8毫克/升。水化学类型为重碳酸类水（C），PH值7.5~8.5之间。县境水质符合淡水鱼类养殖条件。

1981年，经调查全县共记录鱼类203种，隶属于鳗鲡目、鲤形目、鲶形目、合鳃目和鲈形目等6目20科98属。其中以鲤形目的鲤科、鳅科、平鳍鳅科鱼类以及鲶形目的鲿科鱼类居多。仅鲤科鱼类就有120多种，占鱼类总数的61%，其次为鳅科鱼类，有17种，占总种数的8.4%。在丰富的鲤科鱼类中，又以适宜生活在亚热带山区河流的鲃亚科鱼类居多，计有44种，占鲤科鱼类种数的35.5%。

全县主要经济鱼类多为捕捞鱼种，主要有鲤科中的鲤、鲫、三角鲤、乌原鲤、刺鲃、倒刺鲃、南方白甲鱼、小口白甲鱼、厚唇鱼等，鳅科鱼类中的长薄鳅、斑带条鳅、红尾条鳅、泥鳅等种类，鲶科鱼类中的越鲶和鲶等。系统养殖鱼类中有鲤、鲫、鲢、鲔、草鱼等品种，以放养鲤鱼较为普遍。稻田放养的鱼类主要有鲤、鲫、草、鳙鱼等，放养鲤鱼中有高背鲤、镜鲤、河鲤、玉鲤、红鲤等种类。

1985年，县先后从花溪、清镇等地引进鳊鱼放入六广河，继后又在扎佐镇兴红村人工试养获得成功，养殖12个月后平均个体长150克，最大个体达250克。次年，引进在扎佐三元饲养并繁殖鱼苗供应县内各地。1987年，在广东、遵义引进革胡子鲶，在池塘混养后移入水泥池中加强越冬，次年春繁殖出苗，投方池塘饲养，最大个体达2.3公斤。1990年在清镇引进30万尾三杂交鲤（荷元鲤）种苗25万尾供应扎佐的青塘水库及县内池塘和稻田放养。

县境除鱼类外，具有较高经济价值的水生动物还有两栖动物、爬行动物、甲壳动物和软体动物资源。其中主要有：两栖动物大鲵（娃娃鱼）全县蕴基蕴藏量约1500公斤，2001年在县的红旗煤厂捕获1条鱼重达12公斤。蛙类有青蛙（田鸡）、蛤蟆、石蚌和蟾蜍等。鳖类有鳖和山瑞鳖2种，生活在河流、水库和池塘中。虾、蟹类有河虾、河蟹，其中锯齿华溪蟹分布最广。螺、蚌类有中华圆田螺、胀肚圆田螺、铜锈环楼螺、梨形环棱螺和河螺等和沙蚌、三角帆蚌，其中三角帆蚌还可用于淡水育珠。为保护水生动物资源，避免过度捕捞，从2002年开始，规定每年2月1日—5月31日为禁渔期，禁止捕捞野生水生鱼类。

（一）鱼类

县境人工养殖鱼类品种先后有鲤鱼、鲫鱼、草鱼、鲢鱼、鳙鱼、桂鱼、鳊鱼、青鱼、鲶鱼、江团（角角鱼）、黄颡鱼（黄腊丁）、罗非鱼等。人工养殖鱼类品种中除六广鲶鱼外其余均为外地引进品种或人工繁殖。鲤鱼、鲫鱼、江团、黄颡本地有天然野生，养殖一般从外地移植驯化后人工繁殖或自然繁殖。草鱼本地无天然野生，20世纪80年代初在岩鹰山水库养殖场人工繁殖成功。其他品种多靠从外地购进鱼苗养殖。鱼类养殖中较普遍的主要有鲤、鲫、草、鲢、鳙、鳊、青、鳜、鲶鱼等。

1.品种

鲤鱼 虽有天然野生，但生长缓慢，人工养殖多为移植驯化后人工繁殖或自然繁殖。鲤鱼适应性强，分布广，生活在河流、湖泊、水库、池塘等多种水域，常栖息于松软的底层和水草丛深处，杂食性、生长快，种类和数量多，是塘、库、稻田的主要鱼类。据1991年调查，1龄鱼平均体重87.9克，2龄鱼204.9克，3龄鱼464.3克，4龄鱼917.0克，5龄鱼3至4公斤，多年生最大个体可达10至15公斤。

鲫鱼 虽有天然野生，但个体小，生长缓慢，多年生长野生鲫鱼个体最大少有超过250克，不宜人工养殖。20世纪80年代引进外地鲫鱼品种经人工移植驯化后人工繁殖或自然繁殖。引进鲫鱼品种多系杂交，适应性强，能在不良环境条件下生长和繁殖，对温度、水质变化、低溶氧量等均有较大的忍受力。多年生最大个体在1至1.5公斤左右。

草鱼 属中下层鱼类，一般喜栖居于河流水库中、下层和近岸多草水域。草鱼具有流水洄游的习性，境内六广河乌江电站大坝蓄水后创造流水洄游条件，可以自然繁殖。草鱼性情活泼，游泳迅速，常成群觅食，性贪食，为典型的草食性鱼类。其鱼苗阶段摄食浮游生物，幼鱼期兼食昆虫、蚯蚓、藻类和浮萍等，体长达10厘米以上时，完全摄食水生植物，其中尤以禾本科植物为主。草鱼生长迅速，1龄鱼体重可达500克左右，2龄鱼2.5公斤，3龄鱼3至5公斤，4龄鱼达性成熟后，增长就显著减慢，体重约6至7公斤，多年生最大个体可达40公斤左右。

鲢鱼 俗称白鲢，属中上层鱼，为典型的滤食性鱼类，靠腮的特殊结构滤取水中的浮游生物。有时也吃浮游植物，并喜食草鱼粪便和投放的鸡、牛粪。亦吃豆浆、豆渣粉、麸皮和米糠等，更喜吃人工微颗粒配合饲料。生长速度快、产量高，如果饵料充足，当年鱼可长到500至600克，3龄鱼体重可达3至4公斤，在天然河流中多年生最大个体可达30至40公斤。

六广鲶鱼

鲶鱼 鲶鱼同鲇鱼，并非鲢鱼，主要生活在河流水库中下层，多在沿岸地带活动，白天多隐于草丛、石块下或深水区，夜晚觅食活动频繁。属肉食性鱼类，捕食对象多为小型鱼类、虾类、蛙类和水生昆虫等。境内有六广河鲶鱼，属县域特产，形态不同于其他鲶鱼，嘴上胡须仅见上面2根，下面2根几乎完全退化，较其他鲶鱼嘴大、眼小，多为野生，亦可人工养殖，但对水质要求较高。肉质鲜美，被认为类似鱼翅、甲鱼珍品。

鳙鱼 俗称花鲢，习性与鲢鱼相同，个体比鲢鱼稍大，最大个体可达40至45公斤。

鳊鱼 俗称三角鲂、武昌鱼，本地无天然野生，多为引进鱼苗养殖。喜栖于底质为淤泥，石砾及沉水植物丰富的水域。杂食性，幼鱼主食浮游动物，软体动物和昆虫幼体，成鱼主食水草。一般当年鱼体重可达100至200克；2龄鱼体重可达300至500克，以后生长速度逐渐减慢，多年生最大个体可达3至5公斤。

青鱼 俗称倒刺鲃、青鲤，为中下层鱼类。食物以螺蛳、蚌、蚬、蛤等为主，亦捕食虾和昆虫幼

虫。在鱼苗阶段，则主要以浮游生物为食。青鱼生长迅速，个体较大，成鱼常见最大的个体重约15至20公斤。

鳜鱼 俗称桂鱼，多生活在水清的河流水库中的近底层，特别喜欢藏身于水底石块之后，或繁茂的草丛之中。为肉食性鱼类，主食小鱼虾。鳜鱼为典型的肉食性鱼类，喜食活饵料，常吞食超过自身长度的鲢鱼、草鱼、青鱼、鳊等活鱼苗。一般当年鱼体重可达100至200克；2龄鱼体重可达300至500克，以后生长速度逐渐减慢，多年生最大个体可达2至2.5公斤。

2.养殖方法

库塘养鱼 1978年，全县水库养鱼由县水利电力局统一管理，除岩鹰山水库有专人管理外，一般水库只是投放鱼苗，任其自然生长，鱼长大后统一捕捞，是年全县水产品产量5吨。1979年，省水利电力厅拨款31万元，在岩鹰山水库万兴库区南面建成鱼种场一个，次年人工繁殖家鱼成功，解决水库鱼苗种源缺少问题。

1984年6月28日，召开全县养鱼工作会议，推行水面养鱼经济承包责任制，67人承包21个水库，宜养面积3060亩，220人承包220个小山塘。是年水库养鱼收入达52万元。1985年起，政府加强对水库渔业基础的扶持力度，实行标准化养殖，在蚌壳堰水库70亩水面两年捕鱼1.75万公斤，年平均单产达125公斤；扎佐高潮水库面积6亩，1986年亩净产达到575公斤，年获利润6516元。1987年至2006年，全县水库共建成孵化点11处，鱼种培育池150亩，年生产鱼苗鱼种2520万尾，投放鱼种250万尾。水库水产品产量从年产11吨发展到252吨。继后，由于加强环境污染治理和城乡人畜饮水工程建设，许多水库被列为人畜饮用水源，有的取消原有的养鱼承包合同，或因环境污染治理养鱼受到限制，全县水库养鱼承包面积减少，产量降低。2010年，全县水库养鱼虽未减少，但全年水产品产量减少至30吨。

池塘养鱼 1984年，推广池塘养鱼高产技术和苗种培育技术。首先是马家桥部队农场将原来的操场和训练场改建为养鱼池塘54亩，继后又在蚌壳堰、万江厂、新民村等地建成养鱼池塘200亩。池塘养鱼多采用放殖大规格中成鱼饲养，并实施多品种混养，投饲施肥，防病治病，轮捕抢放等技术措施，次年收鱼5500公斤。1986年，在县城北面的庆文厂和城东罗家寨穿山堰河边建成养鱼池塘40余亩，当年投放鱼苗养殖，次年收成鱼1.6万公斤。1987年，城关镇青龙村二组，建成养鱼池塘41亩，次年收成鱼产鱼1.65万公斤。1995年，久长镇沙雁村建鱼池18亩，次年收鱼4.5万公斤，平均亩产2500公斤。1996年，久长镇石安、下堡村民在河边修筑养鱼池塘20余亩，引河水养殖网箱成鱼，每亩放养网箱成鱼1200公斤，当年养殖当年见效，每公斤增值7至8元。

池塘养鱼的品种，一般以鲤鱼、草鱼、鲫鱼为主，稍大一点的池塘还混养有鲢鱼、鳙鱼。从20世纪80年代中后期开始陆续引进养殖团头鲂、罗非鱼、荷元鲤、丰鲤、白鲫、草胡子鲶等移植驯化鱼类。基本形成"塘中养鱼鸭、塘上种瓜果、岸边养猪鸡"的模式。2002年，开始以推广以渔业为基础的鱼猪结合、鱼鸭结合、菜猪鱼结合的池塘养鱼方式迅速发展。2003年对全县以平地村为主的4200亩生态渔业项目进行调查：项目区鱼凼建设面积22.68平方公里，年产鱼495.6吨，占全县水产品产量的65.6%，仅渔业就增纯收303.198万元，共有1272户农户（5476人）参与鱼凼实施，户均增加纯收入2383.5元，人均增加收入554元，亩均增加收入722元。

稻田养鱼 全县有水田9.43万亩，其中保灌面积7.6万亩，宜养面积近3万亩。1981年，全县农村包干到户后，当年放养稻田100亩，1982年放养稻田275亩。

1983年，县畜牧局把加强对养鱼重点户的技术指导工作列为重点，共讲授养鱼技术9次，印发稻田养鱼资料500余份，全县选择10户作典型，从田块选择、鱼种放养到饲养管理都派技术人员进行辅导，收到良好效果。龙场镇新春村重点饲养户刘国武，1982年放养稻田6.8亩，放养鱼苗7000尾，次年10月收，产鱼377.5公斤，平均亩产55.5公斤，出售鲜鱼302.5公斤，收入现金1200余元。是年，对全县原4个区、9个公社、10个生产队60户稻田养鱼户进行调查，其放养稻田170.6亩，投放鱼苗8.47万尾，平均每亩放养量为496尾，总产鲜鱼4925公斤，平均亩产29公斤，最高亩产45公斤，最低亩产9.5公斤；平均亩产稻谷474公斤，最高亩产达617.5公斤，最低亩产350公斤。与不养鱼稻田相比，稻谷最高增产30%。原程官公社青龙大队，有10户稻田养鱼16.13亩，投放鱼苗1.66万尾，每亩养1000尾，共产鲜鱼555.5公斤，平均亩产34.5公斤，亩产稻谷544公斤。亩产稻谷与上年相比，增长7%—19.5%，与当年非养鱼稻田相比，增产10%以上。是年，全县放养稻田面积为2347亩，为上年的8.5倍，放养鱼苗91.3万尾，其中鲤鱼苗种80万尾，秋后收鱼1.25万公斤，平均亩产5.5斤。

1984年，全县放养稻田面积为4016亩，为上年的1.7倍，成为安顺地区稻田养鱼最大的一个县，产鲜鱼2万多公斤，比上年增加1倍。扎佐乡大堡村牛角弯组有稻田养鱼15户，放养稻田32.3亩，放养鱼苗28950尾，每亩放养896尾，总产鲜鱼823.5公斤，亩产25.5公斤，亩产稻谷450公斤，与当年非养鱼稻田相比，一般增产10%左右，最高增产19.5%。1985年全县稻田养鱼4717.9亩，投放鱼苗180.7万尾，并着重抓鱼苗孵化和一次鱼苗突击放养工作。全县重点孵化鱼苗户10户，孵化鱼苗100万尾；引进和经营鱼苗2户，引进鱼苗66万尾。1986年，计划发展稻田养鱼5000亩，实际稻田养鱼2542.8亩，比1985年减少2175.1亩，下降46.1%。引进鱼苗3.85万尾，其中鲢鱼苗1万尾，草鱼苗2.3万尾，鲤鱼苗3万尾，总产量为64841.4公斤，平均亩产25.5公斤。1987年早期干旱，少数地区因缺水打田给稻田养鱼造成困难，积极性受挫，影响发展，计引进苗105万尾，稻田养鱼1341亩，低于1983年以来各年稻田养鱼面积。

稻田养鱼除饲养鲤鱼外，还饲养草、鲢、鳙、罗非鱼、草胡子鲶等。各地又相继出现垄稻沟鱼，厢沟养鱼，田凼结合养鱼，稻茭鱼、稻藕鱼等多种形式的饲养方法。1988年至1993年，全县推广垄稻沟鱼3215亩，普遍获得稻、鱼双增收。龙场镇红旗村周孝芝进行垄作与平作养鱼对比试验，平作亩收稻485公斤，鱼35.7公斤；垄作亩收稻571公斤，鱼97.1公斤，稻谷增产17.7%，鱼增产1.72倍。2002年龙场镇、小箐乡、久长镇、扎佐镇兴起田凼结合养鱼（生态渔业），即田头挖坑养鱼，坑深一般1米至1.5米左右，坑面积占田面积的8%—10%，全县共推广4200亩。2001年，县农业局水产站验收平地村农民毕先祥家田凼结合养鱼10.4亩，平均亩产稻谷569.5公斤，鱼36.7公斤。2002年，在龙场镇新生村进行稻、茭、鱼试验面积6亩，稻谷平均亩产494公斤，鱼28.9公斤，茭瓜168.5公斤，亩产增值253.96元。

稻田养鱼

2005年，在田凼结合养鱼的基础上引种指导投放大规格草鱼种（100—150克）600公斤，云班鮰（50—100克）200公斤，鲤鱼苗1.5万尾，草鱼苗2万尾。同年由省农业厅、市农业局验收的稻田生态养

鱼，亩均产鱼112公斤，稻谷折干亩产量533.8公斤，生态带水果、蔬菜产值300元，合计亩产值1820.84元，实现稻田增粮、增鱼、增收目标。

随着农业产业结构调整，稻田养鱼产值不及种植蔬菜和瓜果，2006年起，县内不再开展稻田养鱼。

鱼苗繁殖 县境繁殖鱼苗技术以鲤鱼为主，在稻田中繁殖或库、河采卵繁殖，大批量生产时，则配备产卵池，卵化池或孵化架，淋水设备等。繁殖前，将鲤鱼亲鱼分雌雄专池进行春季强化培育。产卵池、孵化池用生石灰消毒，把棕片龙须草或废旧化纤网衣等扎成鱼巢，消毒后待用，如采用淋水孵化，还需搭好孵化架，架好淋水设备。清明前后，当水温回升到16℃以上，就开始并池繁殖。选择壮健的亲鱼，按雌雄配备1：1—2放入产卵池，同时放入鱼巢，2—3天内即自然产卵于鱼巢上。之后将附卵鱼巢放到孵化池中自然孵化或放到孵化架上淋水孵化，3—4天后鱼苗即破膜而出。1978年，县畜牧局分别派人到四川省合川、贵阳等地学习水产技术和人工繁殖鱼种培育技术。次年，省水利电力厅投资31万元，在岩鹰山水库万兴库区南面建成鱼种场一个，有孵化池、排水设备、培育池33.7亩。

鱼苗养殖场

青、草、鲢和鳙四大家鱼不能在静水池塘和水库中自行繁殖，须通过人工注射催产药物辅以孵化技术等，1980年人工繁殖草鱼成功，孵化鱼苗100万尾，解决水库鱼苗种源。但由于技术含量高，一般农户不易掌握，所以四大家鱼苗大部分靠从外地引进培育饲养。

1982年三元彭启明，张道书等利用稻田作鲤鱼产卵池，把附有受精卵的鱼巢放在箩筐中淋水孵化，等胚胎出现眼点，就用湿稻草包好出售，每年销售“鱼蛋”2500多包。全县农户生产的鲤鱼苗种除供应本县1万多亩稻田养鱼外，还销往邻县。鲤鱼繁殖季节常出现倒春寒天气，为抵御倒春寒的侵袭，1983年彭启明采用搭塑料棚，装孵化架，棚内生炉火增温的办法，收到良好的效果，提高出苗率。

1985年，全县孵化各种鱼苗261万尾，其中岩鹰山渔场孵化鱼苗35万尾，鲤鱼苗65万尾，鱼苗重点户生产鲤鱼苗160万尾；1988年，除自繁鱼苗254万尾外，还引进鱼苗200万尾；1990年77万尾，引进250万尾；1993年自繁鱼苗550万尾。

1998年首次在岩鹰山水库试用网箱试养鱼苗，11月进种，仅20天时间1.5万尾草鱼种5厘米增至8.4厘米，收获1.1万尾，成活率70%左右。

由于鱼苗繁殖技术含量高，小规模繁殖利润不很显著，2000年后，个体鱼苗繁殖户逐步退出。到2010年，仅存岩鹰山1处，鱼种培育池60亩。当年全县生产鱼苗鱼种1000万尾，投放鱼种500万尾，生产成鱼550吨。

（二）特种水产

牛蛙 1995年，有部分农户从外地引进牛蛙饲养，大多因管理不善而失败，仅龙场镇新水村孟华一户养殖成功。年初，孟华从江西购进牛蛙苗2000只饲养，养殖面积2.3亩，投喂米糠、蝇、田螺、鱼虾、蚯蚓等饲料。一年后获成蛙1500只，最大个体长到300克，有的已产卵繁殖，1997年，除出售种蛙和蝌蚪外还发展食用蛙500多只。后来因市场滞销影响，导致无法继续饲养。

鲶鱼 1987年，从广东、遵义引进革胡子鲶，在池塘混养后移入水泥池中加强越冬。1988年春繁殖出苗，投方池塘饲养，最大个体达2.3公斤。六广鲶鱼为南方大口鲶，是县内特产，有很高的经济价值。20世纪90年代中期，大石乡大屯村民收购野生六广鲶鱼半成鱼饲养，由于养殖技术跟不上和饲料成本高，养殖1年后作罢。此后六广河沿岸的渔民或餐饮业主采用暂养箱养殖捕捞或收购来的野生六广鲶鱼，待价而售。

大鲵 俗称娃娃鱼。2009年，在六屯乡大木村兴建小清大鲵养殖场开始养殖大鲵，养殖规模达2000平方米，养殖大鲵2000尾。继后又在龙场镇潮水村、水塘村和六屯乡独山村相继兴建顺兴大鲵养殖场、盛鑫龙洞娃娃鱼繁殖示范基地（后更名为碧源大鲵养殖场）和桃花源生态娃娃鱼繁殖示范基地繁殖饲养大鲵。至2010年年底，全县有养殖大鲵企业4家，养殖规模达8000平方米，共养殖大鲵1万余尾。

碧源公司大鲵鱼苗繁殖

鲟鱼 2008年，修文县布依渔庄有限责任公司在六屯乡下西冲兴建水产养殖场开始养殖鲟鱼。2010年，养殖场占地5亩，年养殖虹鳟8万尾、清鳟3万尾、中华鲟3万尾。

观赏鱼 2009年，为促进生态文明城市建设，调整农业产业结构，根据贵阳市《关于促进农业稳定发展，农民持续增收的实施意见》的总体部署，由贵阳市农业局组织，在修文县幸福村水院庄建设观赏鱼养殖示范基地，发展观赏鱼养殖。项目由水院庄水产养殖专业合作社具体实施，建成连片占地80亩的饲养池塘，投放锦鲤、锦鲫苗种70万尾，是贵州省最大的锦鲤养殖基地。另外，岩鹰山水库养殖场30亩标准养鱼池塘也承包给个人养殖观赏鱼类，饲养锦鲤和锦鲫等30多尾。之后，由于县建阳明文化园，水院庄观赏鱼养殖项目作罢，仅存岩鹰山水库标准养鱼池塘观赏鱼养殖场。

五、养殖饲料

1985年，经调查全县拥有各类农作物秸秆的总产量1.6亿公斤（以1984年粮食产量计、平均粮草比为1∶1.6），农副产品总产量为0.36亿公斤，饲料粮0.14亿公斤，以此推算全县饲料干物质总量为1.2亿公斤，其中含粗纤维300.96万公斤，粗蛋白质102.99万公斤，消化能2.62亿兆卡，合7489.63万玉米单位，理论载畜量46342头。按牛单位计，按每头牛单位日需4.428玉米单位，年需1616.11玉米单位，占全县54358头的85.25%。

（一）农副产品饲料

谷物类 玉米为能量饲料的主要产品，常年产量约2万吨，分布全县各地，每年约有60%（1.2万吨）用做牲畜的饲料，同时还需从外地调入2—3万吨，主要用于配合饲料、混合饲料。稻谷全县常年产量约3.5万吨，每年用作饲料的不足6%（0.2万吨）。豆类常年产量0.2万吨，但用作饲料的不足0.1万吨。

糠麸类 统糠由于全县稻谷产量80%是由农村加工，其副产品统糠约有1万吨，全用作饲料。米糠全县约有副产品米糠9235吨用作饲料。麦麸全县约有麦麸（以小麦麸为主）277吨可作为饲料。

块根块茎类 番薯（红苕）全县常年产量约0.3万吨，大部分用作饲料。马铃薯（洋芋）全县常年产

量约1.5万吨，主要产于龙场、扎佐、六屯、久长等乡镇，约有1万吨用作饲料。芭蕉芋主要生产于六屯、扎佐、六桶等乡镇，年产约2.1万吨。

秸秆饲料　全县粮食常年产量近10万吨，可供利用的秸秆8万吨，其中稻草4万吨，玉米秸秆4万吨，均可作为牛、马、羊饲料。同时，每年约有25万吨麦秆和菜籽秆也可利用氨化和微贮加工饲料，但由于秸秆太多，群众改不习惯，多被放火焚烧，利用率很低。

藤蔓　包括番薯藤、花生藤、瓜类藤叶等，全县年产量约有15万吨，大部分作为猪的饲料。

蔬菜脚叶　全县年产蔬菜脚叶3.5万吨，大部分为猪的饲料。

瓜类　全县年产瓜类2.5万吨，其中约1/3用作猪饲料。

绿肥　全县绿肥有紫云英，光叶紫花苕，常年种植4.5万亩，产绿肥15万吨，但由于传统习惯，大部分用作肥料，而作为饲料的约只10%—20%。

（二）工副产品饲料

油枯　主要以菜籽油枯饼为主，系高蛋白质饲料，全县油菜籽常年产量约0.7万吨，可得到菜籽枯饼0.5万吨。同时还从外地引进作配合饲料用约0.5万吨。20世纪70年代末，由于脱毒技术尚不成熟，将大部分菜籽饼直接下田作肥料。80年代初，脱毒技术及加工手段均有所提高，因而菜籽饼大部分用作饲料。

酒糟　全县年产饮用酒0.1万吨左右，产酒糟0.2万吨，折干物质0.1万吨。1984年，酒糟总产量1450吨，饲用量1410吨，饲用率99.22%，消化能674.05万兆卡，载畜量1192头。1985年起，由于粮食产量逐年增收，酿酒业不断扩大，酒糟产量迅猛增加。2000年以后，年产鲜酒0.111万吨，产酒糟0.195万吨。

此外，全县每年尚有酱油糟110吨、糖糟400吨、豆腐渣2000吨、粉渣1万吨等工副业产品均可作畜禽鱼饲料。

（三）动物性饲料

骨粉　每头肥猪屠宰可有骨4公斤，每头牛可有17.5公斤，每只羊可有2.5公斤，按全县年屠宰猪、牛、羊数计，可得生骨0.03万吨，可生产饲料骨粉0.017万吨。据样品测定，杂骨含粗蛋白质28.5%，粗脂肪5.5%，粗纤维2%，粗灰分64%。

肉骨粉　主要由屠宰后的下脚料及病死畜尸高温处理而成。每头猪平均可制0.5公斤左右，每头牛可制4.9公斤，每只羊可制0.5公斤，按全县年屠宰猪牛、羊屠宰数计，可产肉骨粉0.07万吨。据贵阳样品测定，肉骨粉含粗蛋白质56.7%，粗脂肪30.1%，粗纤维2.2%，无氮浸出物1.5%，粗灰分9.5%。

血粉　据测定，每7.5公斤鲜血可产粉1公斤，每头肥猪可产鲜血3公斤，每头牛可产7公斤，每只羊可产1公斤。全县年屠宰猪约20.7万头，牛0.05万头、羊0.05万只，可产鲜血0.46万吨，可制成血粉0.018万吨。据贵阳样品测定，猪血粉含粗蛋白质94%，粗脂肪0.4%，粗灰分5.6%，是很好的蛋白质饲料。

（四）水域野生饲料

县境河流、库塘、池沼、沟渠、稻田等水域生长有许多水生植物可做畜禽饲料。水生饲料茎叶柔软，细嫩多汁，营养价值较高，但水分含量特别高，一般在92%以上。水生饲料主要的有水白菜、水葫芦、水花生（水马桑）、浮萍（有绿萍、紫萍）、凤眼莲、鸭舌草、雨久花、水烛（香蒲草）、虾藻、穿叶眼子菜、泽泻、矮慈姑、慈姑、黑藻、水车前等。水生饲料是畜禽养殖上好饲料，但长期饲喂，易感染姜片吸虫、蛔虫等寄生虫疾病，从而影响生长发育，严重的还会导致死亡。为预防畜禽感染寄生虫病，水生饲料不宜生喂，最好是经过发酵，以杀灭虫卵后再饲喂，而且还要定期对猪进行驱虫。

（五）陆地野生饲料

陆地野生饲料主要分为喂猪和喂牛、马、羊两大类，喂猪的称为猪草，喂牛、马、羊的称为牧草。

猪草 猪食性杂，能够饲喂猪的植物种类较多，包括草本、木本和藤本植物等。

草本类主要有白蒿、米蒿、马兰、野苋菜、灰菜、苣荬菜、马齿苋、刺菜、苦菜、扫帚菜、木耳菜、鱼腥草、荠菜、饭包草（竹叶菜）、繁缕（鹅儿肠）、老鹳筋、灯笼菜、糯米藤、何首乌、锯锯藤、牵牛花、马蹄草，鼠曲草（清明菜）、蕨菜、天胡荽（星秀草）、蒲公英、薄荷（鱼香菜）、紫苏、酢浆草（酸咪咪）、三叶草、车前草、千里光、牵牛、牛膝、鬼针草、十字马唐草（熟地草）等。

木本和藤本植物主要以叶为主，嫩叶可作青饲料直接喂猪，老叶可青贮或切碎晒干以备冬季饲喂。木本植物主要有洋槐、紫穗槐、构树、马尾松、胡枝子、盐肤木、野樱桃等。

藤本植物主要葛藤、野葡萄等。木本植物中松针粉含有丰富的粗蛋白质、脂肪、微量元素和维生素等，是新型的畜禽饲料添加剂，用作畜禽饲料添加剂或直接饲喂畜禽，不仅能节省饲料，降低成本，而且对促进畜禽生长发育、增强抗病力和提高生殖功能等均有明显的促进作用。

天然牧草 全县有草山草坡可利用面积32.367万亩，占全县总面积的20.15%。其中，有连片草场61片共8.38万亩。连片草地中草山草坡71867亩，疏林草场11906亩。其中，5000亩以上有2片；3000—5000亩5片；1000—3000亩19片；165—1000亩的35片。分布全县各地，以东南部、东北部和西部较为集中。仅禾本科、豆科牧草中优质牧草就有100余种。

禾本科牧草主要有云香草、硬秆草、荩草、马塘草（熟地草）、狗尾草、白茅（毛针草）、四脉荃草、野古草、箭秆草、黄背茅、狗尾草、扭黄茅、拂子草、丝茅草、五节芒、画眉草、鼠尾草、牛筋草、笔筒草、过江草、斑茅草、黑燕麦、高羊茅、竹叶草、早熟禾、金丝草、棒头草、鹅观草、拟高粱、三毛草、茼草、扁穗雀麦、菰（茭瓜）等。

豆科类牧草主要有紫云英、野毛扁豆、地八角、野扁豆、野大豆、五叶草、野苜蓿、红三叶、白三叶、野豌豆、雀野豆、野豇豆、柔毛山黑豆、水皂角等。

莎草科牧草主要有莎草、珍珠茅、香附子、水蜈蚣、异型莎草、水莎草、碎米莎草、红鳞扁莎、萤蔺等。

菊科天然牧草主要有红果黄鹌菜、毛莲菜、鹅不食草、马兰、洋姜、鼠曲草（清明菜）、千层塔、梁子菜、一点红（羊蹄草）、旱莲草、鱼眼草、野菊、肥猪草、三叶鬼针草、牡蒿等。

此外，苋科有鸡冠花、皱果苋、繁穗苋、凹头苋、尾穗苋、空心莲子草（水花生），藜科有扫帚菜、灰灰菜等，蓼科有野荞麦、扁蓄、金荞麦等，灯芯草科有淡花地杨梅，车前科有车前草，旋花科有兔耳草，石竹科有麦蓝菜，荨麻科有糯米草等均属优质牧草。

人工种植牧草 1984年，开始种植牧草试验成功，先后引进种植紫云英、串叶松香草、籽粒苋等牧草面积100亩。1986年，新增种植牧草50亩，其中红三叶草15亩，白三叶草3亩，黑麦草27亩，串叶松香草5亩。1987年，全县有种植农户93户，播种面积为91亩，其中三叶草12亩，黑麦草44亩，串叶松香草35亩。1988年至1993年全县种植优质牧草为：粮草间作光叶紫花苕15125亩（其中留种地2350亩），苏丹草、黑麦草、串叶松香草等共70亩，改良草场800亩。1995年至1996年种植饲用绿肥26170亩，种植优质牧草、红白三叶草、黑麦草、苏丹草、甜菜等共2090亩；2010年推广优质牧草2.55万亩，大多数

连片种植，其中品种主要有红三叶、白三叶、紫云英、黑麦草、籽粒苋、串叶松香草、苏丹草、紫花苜蓿、黄竹草等。此外还引进种植粮草兼用型和粮油兼用型玉米品种植。从中科院引进“中玉10号”和“R2926”粮草兼用型玉米品种，在六桶、酒坪两乡部分养殖户试种128亩。两个品种亩产玉米472公斤和567公斤，产秸秆1400公斤，比常规玉米秸秆增加一倍以上，为青贮、氨化、微贮饲料的制作提供丰富的来源。粮油兼用型高油115杂交玉米是由中国农业大学选育而成，其特点是籽粒含油量为普通玉米一倍以上，秸秆产量可达1500公斤以上，是粮、草兼用型作物，县引进首先在洒坪乡小坝村和六桶乡林下养鸡试验种植215亩。

6.鱼饲料

县境鱼饲料资源较为丰富，分布广，主要分为水生饲料资源和陆生饲料资源两类。

水生饲料　水体中可供鱼类及较大水生动物食用的饲料资源包括浮游生物，底栖动物和水生维管束植物（水草）。(1) 浮游生物种类繁多，数量丰富，分布广泛，以池塘最为丰富，山塘水库次之，江河较少。池塘中的浮游生物大多为喜有机物质种类，有浮游植物中的绿藻、蓝藻，隐藻，有浮游动物中的砂壳虫、钟形虫、镖水蚤和剑水蚤等。浮游生物繁殖快、数量多，当地多数池塘属中营养型，少数属富营养型。山塘水库的浮游生物比池塘少，大多数山塘水库属贫营养型，少数属中营养型。(2) 底栖动物包括软体动物，水生昆虫，水生寡毛类三类。软体动物中的蚌、蚬、螺，水生昆虫中的蚊科、摇蚊科幼虫及蜉蝣目幼虫，水生寡毛类的水蚯蚓是一些鱼类的天然饵料。池塘因富含有机质，底栖动物较丰富，主要种类有螺类、蚌类、蚬、水蚯蚓及摇蚊幼虫，生长繁殖较快，常与鱼类争夺饲料及水中溶氧。底栖动物种类共有50余种（属），隶属于腹足类、甲壳类、寡毛类、蛭类和水生昆虫近25科45属。(3) 全县有水生维管束植物近100种。稻田管束植物40余种，主要分布在坝田、滥田的湿生、沼生和水生的主要杂草有稗、水莎草、泽泻、矮慈、长瓣慈姑、眼子菜、鸭舌草、金鱼藻、槐叶等18种。

陆生植物　陆生饲料是水产业的重要饲料，境内陆生饲料丰富多样，主要分为野生和栽培的青饲料、粮油饲料、农工副产品、畜禽加工副产品等。(1) 青饲料主要饲喂草鱼、团头鲂、鳊等草食性鱼类。主要有各种野菜、野草、人工牧草、蔬菜、禾本科豆科绿叶等。(2) 粮油饲料主要有玉米、大豆、麦类、谷类及薯类等。

农副产品下脚料　农工副产品有谷糠、麦麸、油枯、酒糟、糖糟、酱油糟、菜油脚、豆渣、粉渣、果渣和中药渣等。畜禽加工副产品有屠宰畜禽的下脚料及骨粉、骨肉粉、血粉等。

六、畜禽疫病防治

1978年，县、区、公社各级均建有畜牧兽医站，专门防治畜禽疾病。1979年，县畜牧局组织人员对全县畜禽疫病进行调查，发现全县畜禽各种疫病共84种，其中传染病25种，寄生虫病32种，中毒病24种，猪、牛疑难病3种。县疫情调查总结：仅上半年全县共死猪4115头，占年存栏83845头的4.9%，其中以猪瘟、猪肺疫、猪丹毒、仔猪副伤寒、仔猪白痢等五种传染病为主，占总死亡数的50.03%。牛以普通病为主，牛出血性败血症（牛出败）、气肿疽、牛传染性胃肠炎、恶性皮下水肿，均在不同地区都有发现，肝片吸虫病据镜检牛粪2096头，检出肝片吸虫422头，占总检头数的20.1%。1981年，认真贯彻落实“预防为主，治疗为辅”的疫病防治方针，每年从一年一次春防培训到一年春、秋两防培训和因病设防培训。从单一的牛、猪瘟病预防培训到牛、猪、鸡、鸭、鹅、兔、羊、狗、猫等畜禽疫病疫苗预防注射接种培训，牲畜“Ⅱ号病”“五号病”“牛出败”“马鼻疽”“炭疽病”“狂犬病”等疫苗预防注射，猪瘟、猪丹毒、猪肺疫三联苗预防注射等技术培训，每年培训均在500人次以上。1988年，县畜牧局再次组织人力对全县农村畜禽流行病进行调查，查出全县畜禽主要传染病有牛出败、气肿疽、马鼻疽、猪瘟、鸡新城疫等36种，并对其分布流行区域，发生规律及危害情况及其资料进行整理汇编。全县畜禽疫病防治实行“以防为主、防治结合”的方针，加强宣传，科学预防各种畜禽疾病发生。同时，建立健全畜禽疾病报告制度，使许多疾病得到及时扑灭，有效预防和控制各种畜禽疾病危害。

（一）畜禽常见病

猪瘟 猪瘟俗称“烂肠瘟”，是一种具有高度传染性严重威胁养猪业发展的主要传染病，具有高度传染性和致死性。一般情况猪瘟死亡率占猪死亡总数的30%—40%。1978年，扎佐区5个公社中的扎佐公社处于川黔要道，猪瘟死亡占猪死亡总数的百分比最高，占41.3%。1979年占65.8%，其余4个公社只占10%。另外在县境边远并与邻县交界的一些社队，猪瘟发病死亡率也较高，占猪死亡总数的百分比分别为1978年占29.1%、1979年占47.4%。到1980年，由于防控严格，当年猪瘟死亡占猪死亡总数的31.2%。1981年起猪瘟死亡占猪死亡总数的百分比分别为：1981—1991年占23.1%，1992—2000年占9.8%。继后至2010年，猪瘟在部分农村时有零星发生，主要源头是从外地引进的仔猪和逃避防疫的农户所致。

猪肺疫（猪巴氏秆菌病） 1978年，发生猪肺疫的大队有158个的368个生产队发病961头，死亡597头，占死总数6.75%。1979年有120个大队的216个生产队发病429头，死亡271头，占猪死亡总数的6.50%。1980—1990年10年间，全县有159个村发病死亡猪平均每年150—179头，占猪死亡总数的4.3%和3.1%。1991—2010年经过多年预防注射，使该病得到有效控制，死亡占总数的1.9%。

猪丹毒 1978年，猪丹毒有110个大队的217个生产队发病515头，死亡250头，占猪总死亡数的2.83%。1979年，有74个大队的136个生产队发病358头，死亡124头，占猪死亡总数的2.96%。1980—1990年，猪丹毒发病死亡157头，占平均每年猪总死亡数2.1%。自1990年起通过综合防治发病率和死亡率逐渐下降，至2010年，全县平均每年猪丹毒死亡占猪死亡总头数的0.8%。

仔猪副伤寒 1978年，有120个大队的220个生产队发病874头，死亡675头，占猪死亡总数的7.64%。1979年，有98个大队的140个生产队发病460头，死亡326头，死亡率77.6%。据查，1980至2010年间，全县每年死亡于仔猪副伤寒的仔猪在1000—1200头之间。

仔猪白痢 主要发生在各地养猪场和饲养母猪的地区。1978年，有101个大队的177个生产队发病2395头，死亡503头，占猪死亡总数的5.69%。1979年，有92个大队的161生产队发病1478头，死亡243头，占猪死亡总数的5.83%。1980—1990年间，全县平均每年发病1000—1300头，平均每年死亡100—150头。1991—2010年，全县每年发病500—1000头，死亡50—120头之间。

猪传染性水泡病和猪腹泻病 全县各地农村均有不同程度的发生，据调查，两病易治愈，所以死亡较少，1978—2010年，32年间平均每年死亡于这两种病的猪在100头左右。

牛气肿疽 1978年，牛气肿疽是地方性流行病，由于实行“因病设防”，积极采用疫苗预防接种，控制疫病发生，逐年加强进行地区性预防注射，至1997年未发生牛气肿疽疫病。1998年6月中旬，在城关镇花桥村和尚洞组发生牛气肿疽疫情，感染死亡牛5头，经市、县、镇业务部门及时采取有效防疫措施，控制疫情的传播与蔓延。此后至2010年未有发生。

牛出血性败血症 1979年，牛出败病有37个大队的55个生产队发病耕牛81头，死亡65头，占死亡总数的11.46%。1980年，有23个大队的40个生产队发病耕牛72头，死亡60头，占死亡总数的12.27%。

1981年，有8个公社10个大队的12个生产队发病耕牛24头，死亡9头。1983年发病59头，无死亡。此后至2010年，再没有牛出败病发生。

炭疽病 1991年发生过一次，首先在六广镇六广村松江组发生，然后蔓延至大石乡大屯村，两地共死亡牛5头、猪1头、犬1只，感染4人。继后至2010年再无炭疽疫病发生。

口蹄疫（五号病） 1998年3月30日，在久长镇驴坊村发现疑似病猪，猪蹄部、嘴唇出现水泡症状，经化验确诊为“0型”阳性。次月又先后在久长、扎佐、城关、六屯等乡镇中的40村、45个组、93户，466头猪，31头牛染上“口蹄疫”。1999年，在龙场、扎佐、六屯、小箐、六桶、谷堡七个乡（镇）相继发生本病，计738头猪，1245头牛。1998—1999年两年间发病疫点58个，计感染病猪1204头，扑杀1204头；染病牛1276头，死亡6头，扑杀深埋38头,隔离治疗73头。继后至2010年没有此疫病发生。

鸡新城疫 鸡传染病中以鸡新城疫最为普遍，发病快，死亡率高。1978年，有92个大队的207个生产队发病4805只，全部死亡，占鸡死亡数的51.50%。1979年，有57个大队的107个生产队发病1689只，也全部死亡，占鸡死亡总数的33.89%。1980—1986年调查51个村，103个村民组，平均年发病1500只，还是全部死亡。1987年起，积极加强疫苗预防，使鸡新城疫得到有效控制，以后至2010年全县平均每年发病控制在1000只左右。

鸡白痢 1978年，有45全大队的95个生产队发病1678只，全部死亡，占鸡死亡总数的17.98%。1979年，有57个大队的84个生产队发病1186只，也全部死亡，占鸡死亡总数的17.08%。1980年—2000年，各地均有发生，但主要在养鸡场流行。2000至2010年，由于农户对鸡传染病危害增强意识，购进鸡必打防疫针，鸡发病和死亡也逐年减少，实际每年全县发病不到1000只。

禽霍乱 危害仅次于鸡新城疫。1978年，有67个大队的123个生产队发病2198只，全部死亡，占鸡死亡总数的23.50%。1979年，有36个大队的70个生产队发病738只，也全部死亡，占鸡死亡总数的16.35%。1980—1990年，在全县各地农村均不同程度的发生，年均发病1000只，病死率82.3%。1991—2010年，年均发病800只左右，病死率68%。

（二）畜禽疫病检疫

市场检疫 1978年，为防止畜禽疫病传播和流行，县畜牧家禽业委员会行文规定：从4月1日起，凡进入牲畜交易市场的牲畜，一律要经兽医部门人员检疫和注射预防苗；未经检疫和预防注射的牲畜，一律不准进入市场交易。至年底，全县组织畜牧兽医技术干部、工商、税务、食品、公社兽医人员、农村防疫员，在城关、久长、扎佐、六广、小箐5个大场区，检疫进入市场大小生猪。1981年，检疫注射工作又增加牛炭疽病和鸡瘟检疫。至1988年，年均市场检疫和防疫检疫注射猪瘟4200头，牛马炭疽210头（匹）次，鸡瘟5600只。1989年，扩大检疫范围，增加六桶、洒坪、乌栗市场，全县检疫市场增至8个。至2010年，年均市场检疫和防疫注射牲畜3万头次，家禽10只次。

运输检疫 1978年，县在久长区设置有畜禽运输检疫检查站，检疫工作主要由久长畜牧兽医站负责。1982—2005年，除久长站外相继增设城关、扎佐、六桶、大石、小箐、六广等站，全县共计7个运输检疫站开展运输检疫工作。检疫分为铁路运输、公路运输、水路运输和赶运等检疫。其目的是为防止畜禽疫病跨地区传播和减少途病途亡。

市场肉类产品卫生检验 1985年，根据国务院发布《家畜家禽防疫条例》规定，县畜牧局分批派员到省、地进行肉品卫生检验技术培训，逐步在全县开展对农贸市场的肉类产品卫生检验工作。是年全县肉品检验共3538头（只），其中猪肉3447头、牛肉64头、羊肉27只。检出猪瘟肉254头；猪丹毒肉184头，猪囊虫病肉725头。1986—1996年11年检验猪肉1.23万头，检验牛肉816头，其中年均检出病猪386头，大牲畜检出病畜9头。1997—2010年，年均检验猪1.622头，合格1.621头，合格率达99.94%。

（三）主要传染病防治

猪瘟 猪瘟历为县内家畜中最严重的传染疾病。县内各级兽医站每年春、秋两季都要组织人力对畜禽进行全面预防注射。1980年，建立畜禽疫防治网，县、区、公社设兽医门诊工作站。1981年，实行防疫注射奖励，注射一头猪，国家奖励0.05元，注射一头大牲畜，国家奖励0.10元，注射畜禽实行收费70%归集体，30%归防疫员。至1988年，平均每年注射猪瘟10万头次，防疫率均在90%左右。1989年起，大部分农民对预防畜病观念逐步发生改变，由过去的被动变为主动，免疫接种猪瘟疫苗平均免疫率达91%以上，以后逐年提高，猪瘟发病率和死亡率均大幅度下降。据2003年10个乡镇217个村的普查，发病率仅在1.8%至2.5%之间。至2010年，虽然猪瘟在一些乡镇仍时有发生，但仅为局部零星发生，流行情况极为有限。

炭疽病 炭疽病俗称“飞疔”，是由炭疽杆菌引起的人畜共患的急性、热性、败血性传染病。特别是牛马等大牲畜容易感染，一年四季均可发生，夏季多发。从1978年起，每年普遍开展春秋两次给牛马等大牲畜进行炭疽预防注射，至1990年全县无炭疽病例发生。1991年6月23日，六广镇六广村松江组1户村民家中死亡两头猪，剥食后感染4人，经六广卫生院初诊为“皮炭疽”。由于村民缺乏对炭病疽病知识解，猪死后又从邻近村寨借来两头牛关在自己死猪的圈内，致牛亦感染炭疽病。6月30日1头牛死亡后丢于六广河沙坝，当夜水位上升，此牛被洪水冲到离此相距4公里的大屯村，造成大屯村死牛3头，猪1头，犬1只，感染1人，经济损失约1.5万元。县立即启动紧预案，组织人员开展扑灭工作。紧急调入牲畜炭疽病疫苗0.9万头份，人炭疽病预防疫苗1300头（份）。在疫区普遍为大牲畜注射炭疽病疫苗，其中牛403头、马53匹、猪2015头。对污染的猪圈、场地进行严密消毒。同时在通往疫区交通要道设卡对过往车辆进行消毒，对过境活畜及畜产品进行严格的检疫，有效地切断疫源的扩散。从1992年开始，每年在疫区平均注射炭疽疫苗为1.79万头（匹）次，注射密度均在95%以上。至2010年，县内再无炭疽病疫情发生。

口蹄疫（五号病） 1983年，根据中央、省、地严格控制牲畜“五号病”的病源传播途径，加强牲畜市场检疫和出境检疫的要求，县组织兽医专业人员重点对5区13公社（镇）42个大队92个小队及9个居民段和烽光厂、久长火车站家属区的2487户农户和居民户饲养的猪、牛、羊进行登记检查，历时1个月，共检查猪5507头，牛1271头，羊6只；同时对扎佐、久长、六广赶场天进行市检登记，市场检查生猪497头，牛163头，普查结果未发现口蹄疫病。次年起，每年春、秋两次普查，加强监测，至1997年年底未发现口蹄疫病。

1998年3月30日，在久长镇驴坊村发现疑似“五号病”猪，县组织“防五”指挥部，启动紧急预案。经查，病源系3个猪贩子从广西贩运仔猪270头到扎佐、久长、城关、小箐等设点销售，最先在久长驴坊发现一头疑似病猪。随后到省化验的病样结果出来确诊为“0型”阳性病，即口蹄疫（五号病），随即展开全县性扑灭疫情工作。经跟踪调查，先后在久长、扎佐、城关、六屯等乡镇发现有466头猪、31头牛染上“口蹄疫”。县立即采取措施封锁疫区，禁止病畜输出、输入，控制疫病扩散。同时，在扎佐、久长、龙场等主干公路线上设临时公路检疫卡6处，对过往动物及产品、运载工具进行检疫、消毒；使用消

毒石灰坚持疫点严格消毒，封闭全县的8个牲畜交易市场。此次疫情发生后，对病猪一律扑杀，1头不留；对病牛进行隔离监控治疗，直至痊愈；对未感染的猪、牛、羊等偶蹄牲畜进行一次普遍的“五号病”0型疫苗预防接种，疫情很快得到控制。

1999年，在龙场、扎佐、六屯、小箐、六桶、谷堡等乡镇相继又发生“五号病”疫情，计738头猪，1245头牛染病，县再次启动紧急预案，组织应对，因已有上年经验，疫情很快得到控制。

2000年以后，县农业局把牲畜“口蹄疫”病作为每年春秋两防的工作重点，要求注射率达100%，通过严格控制和预防，至2010年全县再无“口蹄疫”病畜出现。

（四）寄生虫病防治

1979年县畜牧局对全县畜禽疫病的普查中，共查出畜禽寄生虫病有32种，其中主要的有肝片吸虫病、疥癣病、消化道蠕虫病等10余种。全县各乡镇均有，危害严重的以牛、羊肝片吸虫、疥癣及各种畜禽消化道蠕虫病为主。

肝片形吸虫病 肝片形吸虫是一种寄生在哺乳动物胆管内的常见寄生虫，又称肝蛭病，是一种危害严重的蠕虫病，草食性动物中的牛、羊等反刍动物最易感染。牛、羊感染后临床表现为食欲减退，反刍异常，腹胀，很快贫血、消瘦，被毛粗乱，颌下水肿，腹泻等。1979年畜禽疫病普查后发现，六广区、城关区、扎佐区较为严重，其中黄牛感染率为38.5%，水牛感染率27.9%，羊感染率0.7%。随即开展一次大面积牛羊肝片吸虫病的驱虫工作，对28个公社，136个大队，533个生产队，4362头牛羊进行驱虫（其中黄牛1626头、水牛2733头、羊13只）。1980年起，县畜牧兽医部门一方面加强防治宣传，另一方面对属地范围内的牛、羊定期或不定期进行驱虫，使感染率大幅下降。2000年后至2010年，境内家畜肝片吸虫病仅有零星偶发。

前后盘吸虫病 前后盘吸虫病是由前后盘吸虫引起的一种寄生虫病，主要发生于牛、羊等反刍动物的胃和小肠里，严重者易导致病畜死亡。1979年，对28个公社，122个大队，320个生产队的耕牛采用前后盘病镜检，查出病牛1217头，占牛总数的5. 81%。防治措施与肝片形吸虫病相同。1980年后，耕牛感染率逐年降低。2010年，据查全县前后盘吸虫病感染为2.8%。

胰阔盘吸虫病 是由阔盘属吸虫寄生在哺乳动物的胰脏、胰管内所引起的寄生虫病，牛、羊最易感染，还可感染猪、兔、猴和人等。县内各地均有流行。据1979年调查，全县耕牛感染率24.4%，感染强度为15—239条，是耕牛体内较大的寄生虫种之一。

消化道蠕虫病 消化道蠕虫病是最常见的肠道寄生虫病，包括蛔虫病、钩虫病、蛲虫病、绦虫病、包虫病及肝吸虫病等。1979年，对全县耕牛寄生虫调查，消化道蠕虫病感染率56%，感染强度41—210条。此病是耕牛体内寄生的优势病种之一，主要分布在六广、六屯、大石等乡镇的极少数村寨，其余地区仅有零星偶发。

疥癣病 1979年普查统计，羊疥癣发病率12.4%，猪为13.6%—15%，牛为0.06%—0.07%。采用的治疗药物，主要用杀灭菊酯、杀螨灵、辛硫磷、林丹乳油、消虫净、杀螨剂及伊维霉素等。1986年，始用敌百虫防治，效果显著。至2010年，全县大部分地区不同程度得到有效控制，少数地区达到消灭羊疥癣病的目标，猪、牛疥癣病仅有部分零星偶发。

焦虫病 1978—2003年，在全县范围内，累计治疗和治愈牛焦虫病1.5万余头次，主要防治采用黄色素、雷凡诺尔、阿卡扑林、贝尾尔、苯脲咪噻等。在用药的同时采取夏、秋季节积极灭碑等措施防治，到2010年全县十个乡镇的农村只有偶尔发生。

蛔虫病 蛔虫病是畜禽常见多发病，是专性寄生虫，各畜禽之间的蛔虫互不感染，较常见的有猪、鸡、牛蛔虫病。猪蛔虫病在县内各地均有发生，1997年7月，剖检猪小肠35例，其中有蛔虫者29具，感染率高达82.86%。另外发现仔猪蛔虫也有感染，感染率一般在30%—60%，个别地区感染率可达60%以上，强度在8—23条。鸡蛔虫感染为72.1%，严重感染时，肠管或肌胃完全被虫体充满和阻塞；以1—3月龄小鸡感染率高，死亡大，危害重。牛蛔虫病水牛、黄牛均可感染蛔，其中水牛感染为29.5%，黄牛18.7%。畜禽蛔虫病的防治每年春秋各进行1次预防性驱虫。驱虫药主要有驱蛔灵、丙硫苯咪唑、甲苯咪唑、左旋咪唑、噻咪啶等。

球虫病 球虫病是一种对畜禽肠道有损害的寄生虫病之一，其中对鸡、兔影响最大，特别是放养鸡、兔，患病死亡率高，甚至可全群死亡。其他畜禽也易感染。1996年6月，小箐乡畜牧兽医站在贵阳调进946只2—3月龄雏鸡全部感染球虫而发病，死亡561只，死亡率59.3%。1999年6月小箐乡的崇恩购进雏鸡数百只，死亡39.0%。1984年，在城关（龙场镇）、扎佐、久长3镇的23个村检查6064头牛，牛球虫阳性感染率为33.4%，1991年33个村调查，牛球虫阳性感染37.4%。1982年，在城关扎佐两区调查，猪球虫阳性感染率为47.4%（37/78）。1996年六广、六桶两乡镇调查，猪球虫粪检感染率为45.7%，经鉴定为猪艾美尔球虫等四种猪球虫。磺胺类药物对本病有特效，磺胺二甲嘧啶、磺胺喹恶林、磺胺-6-甲氧嘧啶、对防治球虫均有良好的效果，二甲氧苄氨嘧啶（DVD）与磺胺二甲嘧啶（SM2）合剂也有良好的防治效果。

猪囊虫病 1989年，县畜牧局兽防站和城关区畜牧兽医站在农贸市场肉品检验4720头，检出囊虫病猪83头，感染率1.8%。2000年起，全县农村开始实行四改一气后，猪囊虫病感染率下降。

食道口线虫病 食道口线虫病是由多种线虫寄生于家畜结肠中引起的线虫病，虫体主要寄生于羊、牛、猪等家畜。1997年抽查检验，绵羊感染率33.3%，猪感染率为28.0%，牛感染率为50.0%。治疗可使用驱虫药物，均有较好效果。

（五）普通病防治

牲畜主要普通病的种类 根据全县各诊疗单位对应诊牲畜病例分类统计，县内牲畜主要普通病约30余种，其中有少数病具有较明显地方特征。马内科病主要有消化不良、胃肠炎、风气疝、胃扩张、便秘疝、痉挛病、感冒、气管炎、咽喉炎、鼻炎等。其中，消化系统疾病占48.2%，疝气病占内科病的21.1%，马痉挛病占14.5%。除此之外马病还有四肢风湿、产科、外伤、肿疡、眼病等，其中四肢风湿最多，要占50%以上，这与当地环境有关。牛内科病以瘤胃臌气、前胃弛缓、瘤胃积食、三胃阻塞、肠炎、口腔炎等消化系统病居榜首，占内科病的67%，其中4种胃疾病占内科病的55.7%。牛外科病以四肢运动器官疾病为最多，占外产科病的53.5%。其次是外伤肿疡、眼病及胎产病。80年代后，牛前胃疾病逐年明显增加，由占总病例的18.62%增加到36.8%。其原因主要是每年春耕期间，不少农民不愿割青草和用稻草喂牛，而代之以大量秕谷、玉米面、谷糠等干精饲料，造成停滞胃内而引起。猪病主要有胃肠炎、感冒、肺疫、流行性腹泻、猪瘟、丹毒、副伤寒、水肿病、蛔虫病、仔猪黄痢、仔猪白痢、胃肠炎、气喘病、链球菌感染和荨麻疹、风湿病、直肠脱出、仔猪脐带发炎、脐疝、腹股沟阴囊疝、湿疹、结膜炎、皮炎、猪乳房炎、母猪瘫痪、不孕、胎衣不下、仔猪贫血等。其中以胃肠炎、感冒、肺炎为多。

中毒病 栎树叶中毒 又称青杠树叶中毒，主要发生在耕牛身上，一般年份不易发生，在出现严重干旱的春末夏初季节，由于缺乏嫩草，放牧牛采食青杠树嫩叶和花占日粮一半以上即易引起中毒，严重的可导致死亡。1982年7月，城关区谷堡、阳早和王官3个公社6个生产队发生耕牛青杠叶中毒68头，其中谷堡公社折溪大队蛇田生产队发现30头。经治疗除1头死亡外其余治愈。1983年以后，青杠树叶中毒现象极少见，仅个别乡镇偶尔发生，采用中西结合治疗很快痊愈。发霉稻草中毒多发生在水稻产区，因牛采食发霉稻草而发生，主要是水牛，其次是黄牛。冬季为高发期，其余季节很少发病。治疗可采用碘化钾和荆防败毒散加减治疗有一定疗效。1994至2010年未此病发生。黑斑甘薯中毒主要发生在盛产红薯的六桶、六广、大石、六屯等乡镇，中毒的原因是牛、猪吃霉烂的红薯所致。中毒后发病快，死亡率高。牛中毒典型症状是呼吸困难，呼吸音如拉风箱，故俗称牛喘气病，喷气病，扯炉症等。治疗采用高锰钾（克）10%，葡萄糖500毫升，静滴和10%安那加5×10×2支肌注。预防黑斑甘薯中毒病，主要是妥善处理烂薯，不使牛、猪误食。耕牛代谢性酸中毒主要是因为过量饲喂精饲料或牛偷食过量稻谷、玉米、小麦等所致。因牛属草食性动物，过量采用精料不反胃引起消化功能障碍，且可致瘤胃内环境改变。轻者可引起胃积食、膨胀，重者在胃内产大量乳酸，而致牛产生酸中毒。猪亚硝酸盐中毒俗称“饱潲病”或“饱食瘟”，因猪食入含有过量亚硝酸盐饲料所致。青绿饲料或块根饲料富含硝酸盐，当慢火焖煮、枯萎霉变的青绿饲料或块根饲料时，硝酸盐可被硝酸盐还原菌还原为亚硝酸盐，猪食入后即易中毒。1983年，六屯公社下西冲生产队1户农民家饲养的4头架子猪突然死亡，经确诊为亚硝酸盐中毒。据查，该户农民的猪饲料煮熟后放在木桶内加盖长时间存放，使青饲料中的硝酸盐转化为亚硝酸盐，猪吃食后引起中毒。治疗可使用美蓝或甲苯胺蓝等。预防措施，青绿饲料宜新鲜生喂，发热腐烂后不要饲喂。需要烧煮时，切忌闷于锅里过夜。

（六）疑难杂病防治

猪应激综合症 应激综合症牛、马、猪及家禽均可发生，尤以猪最为常见，特别是初引进的良种幼猪最易发生，有人称是水土不适原因所致，严重者可突然死亡。20世纪80年代，六屯乡独山村曾发现5头病猪。1991年，小箐乡小箐村发现3头。治疗可用盐酸氯丙嗪、维生素C、E、D和碳酸氢钠组成抗应激添加剂，10天为1疗程，一般1—2个疗程，治愈率达90.9%。

猪尿结石病 常见于种公猪泌尿系统病，排尿困难或淋结，经用利尿通淋药治疗无效。1986年，扎佐区兽医站对所收治11例病猪的年龄、体重、季节、地理环境等因素作过调查，以6—9月雨季发病最多，主要发生在石灰岩分布地区，猪易尿结石症，甚至有因尿闭造成膀胱破裂。治疗采用手术切开，直接取出结石。

（七）兽医专业防治

专业队伍 1978年，县置有兽医防治站，隶属县畜牧局，设站长、副站长各1人，时有兽医专职人员7人。全县5区32公社（镇）置有5个畜医联合诊所和32个兽医站，计有兽医人员171人。1981年12月28日，成立县畜牧兽医协会，计有会员25人，其中国家技术干部22人，社办兽医人员3人。1984年2月机构改革，兽防站隶属农牧合并的农牧局，11月农牧分开，兽医防治站隶属畜牧局。是年，原公社兽医站更名为乡镇兽医站，全县32个乡镇，除城关镇外，其余皆建兽医站，拥有兽医专业人员129人，其中有29人兼管行政事务，负责境内牲畜疾病防治。到1991年，全县5个区，32个乡镇，共有兽医人员210人，有联合诊所5个，参加协会的有147人。

1992年撤区并乡建镇后，除县兽医防治站外其余合并建立10个乡镇畜牧兽医站，原小乡镇的兽医人员变为片区兽医防疫人员。片区防疫人员每享有国家每人每年180元的报酬，其余报酬主要靠防治病畜、市场检疫、牲畜配种和双轨防疫责任制适当收费来解决。

1995年10月，畜牧局并入农业局，兽防站随之隶属于农业局。2004年4月，县兽医防治站析建为兽疫防治检疫站和兽医卫生监督检验所，分别负责对县境内兽疫防治检疫和兽医卫生工作监督管理，确保人民群众身体健康。2010年，全县共有兽医专业技术人员增到72人。

预防 1978年，全县农村畜牧兽医站属集体事业单位，实行自主经营、自负盈亏的管理方法，推行合作医疗制度。实施家畜家禽预防注射，当年对全部生猪和半数大牲畜进行疫苗注射预防。由于国家兽医技术干部人数少，防疫力量不足，县畜牧局组织民间中兽医建立兽疫防治队伍开展防疫工作。

1981年，实行预防注射奖励办法，对民间防疫员按注射1头猪奖励0.05元，注射1头大牲畜奖励0.1元发给奖金。收费按大牲畜每头收0.3元，家禽每只收0.05元，其收入70%归集体，30%归防疫员。公社兽医人员，划片包干，进行预防。1982年，在农村普遍执行大包干责任制后，公社兽医站对兽医人员实行畜禽预防承包，开展春秋两季定期预防注射，防疫人员深入农村一家一户进行防疫。据1986年调查，畜禽发病率大大下降，就生猪发病率比1977年减少4.4个百分点。

1987年防疫资金短缺，停止秋季防疫注射。有的畜主将病死的牲畜拿到市上出售，加之市场检疫工作不力，造成当年牲畜疫病流行。六屯乡中山村一周内死亡耕牛5头、猪18头。据调查，全县家畜发病2777头，死亡2372头，死亡数占发病数的85.4%。县畜牧局组织人员突击对全县9万多头牛进行一次牛出败为主的预防注射；同时各乡镇兽医站紧急治疗病牛2100头、病猪1500余头、病马560匹，治愈率80%以上。此后吸取此次惨痛教训，县增加和保障防疫经费，加强预防工作，使全县畜禽疫病得以控制，至2010年全县再无重大疫情发生。

治疗 1978年，县内兽医治疗多采用中西结合方式给畜禽治病。中兽医讲究阴阳、五行和脏腑、经络学说，按辨证施治原则进行畜病的诊断和治疗。西兽医检验手段多样准确，治疗多采用服药、打针和输液等方式，效果快而明显。一般兽医人员，中、西兽医技术都掌握一些，就诊时根据具体情况而选择治疗方案。当时县内比较权威的兽医技术人员主要有县兽医站的彭朝相和王仲修等人，他们除坚持站内日常兽医诊治外，还承担对全县兽医技术人员的业务培训和指导。是年8月，为总结发扬老中兽医临床实践经验，县农业局举办中兽医培训班，专门请彭朝相、王仲修等老兽医讲课，传授技术并和与会人员进行经验交流。11月，县兽医站彭朝相、王仲修等同志在县畜牧站作中兽医技术交流，介绍10余种牲畜常见病和牛病针灸穴位及治疗方法。80年代，全县各乡镇兽医技术人员及民间兽医人员开展畜禽诊治，年均治疗各种畜病，大牲畜0.5万头（匹、次），猪4万头（次），禽80000羽（次）。1994年8月，县兽医站冷先贵关于治疗马劳伤血尿的经验，参加全国在荔波县召开的中兽医协会经验交流会上交流。次月又参加四川乐山中兽医经验交流会。继后至2010年，全县中兽医技术人员在实践中不断总结经验，普遍具有比较成熟的兽医技术，能治疗猪、牛、马、羊等21种疾病，治疗有效验方59个。

七、鱼病防治

1. 鱼病种类

县境易患鱼病主要有5类18种，以池塘养鱼发病较多，山塘、稻田养鱼次之，水库病害较少。细菌性鱼病有烂鳃、赤皮病、肠炎病、打印、竖鳞病、白头白咀病、白皮病。寄生虫病有锚头鳋病、中华鳋

病、鱼虱病、鲤嗜子宫线虫病、舌状绦虫病、复口吸虫病、小瓜虫病、车轮虫病、指环虫病、碘孢子虫病、鱼怪。真菌性鱼病有水霉病、鳃霉病。病毒性鱼病书血病、痘疮病。非寄生性鱼病青泥苔、浮头、跑马病以及温差过大引起的“感冒”等。

2. 防治方法

鱼病防治重在预防，以防为主。池塘养鱼，放养之前，需要进行消毒，以减少鱼病的发生。其方法可将池水全部排干，让池底暴晒或冰冻，以消灭各种病原菌、寄生虫和敌害。或是用漂白粉、生石灰等消毒药物彻底消毒。养鱼要坚持巡塘，每天早、中、晚到池塘边看看，观察池塘里的鱼有无浮头现象、鱼群活动情况、水质变化、有无疾病和敌害等。特别是每年的5—9月份，是鱼病流行的高发季节，要及时发现鱼病，及时诊断、及时治疗、对症下药。

1979年扎佐镇烂木桥山塘杨树贵试用扑草净防治塘中的青泥苔取得良好效果。1984年刘国武、陈依祥用乌柏、辣蓼、铁苋菜干成粉，拌入麦麸中喂鱼，在发病季节每周一次，多年来草鱼未发生鱼病。1995年张道书对自养的两口池发生草鱼烂鳃、赤皮病的鱼塘连续观察，发现其病因是鱼虱危害。1996年采用“治虫为主、治病为辅”的防治措施，对所有养鱼池进行防治，迅速治愈草鱼鱼病。2002年马家桥渔场发现先发生中华鳋病，随后出现草鱼烂鳃病，赤皮病几种病的发生多与锚头鳋的寄生和鱼虱病引起。县良种场周昌孟用虎杖（酸汤秆）舂细熬水，全池泼洒治疗水霉病，久长镇的娄韦华用砍碎的芭蕉茎叶泡在池中治疗锚头鳋。扎佐镇兴红村彭启明用松针、敌百虫和硫酸铜治疗猫头鳋。小箐乡的李厚明用艾叶、菖蒲、辣蓼拌饲料喂鱼防治草鱼烂鳃病、肠炎病和赤皮病都取得较好效果。

第五节　林　业

1978年农业集体化时期，由于集体林木管护不到位，年年造林不见林，加上部分地方毁林开荒和偷砍盗伐现象不断发生，致林业生产不见发展反而退化，水土流失严重，在六广、小箐等地区的一些地方还出现石漠化问题。1981年，进行森林资源调查，全县森林覆盖率15.4%。实行林业“三定”（稳定山权林权，划定自留山，确定林业生产责任制）后，山林承包到户，责任落实到人，调动农民造林育林的积极性。1982年3月成立县绿化委员会，统一组织指挥全县林业生产，各地加强植树造林、抚育幼林和封山育林工作。林业生产开始步入健康发展的轨道，森林资源和绿化面积逐年增长。

1990年6月，县政府制订《1989—2000年造林绿化规划（草案）》，作出《关于十年基本绿化修文的决定》，并与各区（镇）签订造林绿化“5年消灭荒山”的责任书，同时启动“长江中上游防护林体系建设”工程（简称“长防林工程”），以工程建设推动造林绿化。同时，制定优惠政策鼓励造林和采取拍卖非耕地使用权兴办绿色产业等一系列措施，在全县掀起新一轮植树造林高潮，1996年县境基本消灭荒山秃岭，全县森林覆盖率达24.36%。至2000年，长防林工程完成，除抚育幼林外营造林面积达54万亩。

2001年，林业绿化又进入新高潮，县委、县政府把退耕还林还草，加强西部生态环境保护和建设作为西部大开发的重要工作来抓，成立县“退耕还林（草）领导小组”，制订《退耕还林还草实施办法》，规定凡25°以上坡耕地，分年度有计划退耕植树或种草。落实“退耕还林(草)、封山绿化、以粮代赈、个体承包”政策和实行“谁退耕、谁造林、谁经营、谁受益”的政策，把退耕还林还草与扶贫开发、农业综合利用和水土保持等结合起来统筹安排。2002年和2003年，县委、县政府又先后实施贵阳市“二环”林带工程造林和中韩合作喀斯特石质山造林。至2005年“中韩合作造林”完成人工造林1.95万亩，至2010年，完成贵阳市二环林带造林营造生态公益林2.8万亩，全县森林覆盖率达40.3%。

全县林业产值从1978年的63万元，发展至2010年的752万元。年均递增8.06%，是农业内部四大产业中发展速度最慢、商品率最低的一个产业。在其它产业均有蓬勃发展的情况下，林业产值在农业总产值中所占比重还呈下降趋势，由1978年的2.98%降至2010年的0.57%；但是，通过30多年来的不懈努力，已造就的60多万亩青山，使全县生态环境得到明显改善，巨大的生态效益已经显现，这是无法用简单经济指标来衡量的。从这个意义上讲，林业生产发展的巨大成就，是全县人民共同拥有的一笔宝贵财富。

2010年，全县森林覆盖率达40.3%

一、林权制度

（一）林业“三定”

人民公社时期，除国有山林外，一般山林属生产队集体所有并由集体经营，部分属公社或大队集体所有集体经营。由于集体林权制度产权不明晰、经营主体不落实、经营机制不灵活、利益分配不合理等问题逐步显现出来，部分农民为其自身利益，乱砍滥伐集体林木，严重影响林业生产发展。随着农村联产承包责任制的实行，1981年6月县贯彻中共中央、国务院《关于保护森林发展林业若干问题的决定》精神，决定在保持集体林地所有权不变的前提下在全县农村开展林业“三定”工作。6月13日，县委组织47人的工作队，以阳早公社为试点，进行林业“三定”，于7月20日结束。9月，又在清让、六屯、桃源、金桥、小箐、花榔6个公社开展第一批林业“三定”。11月中旬，“三定”工作全面铺开，全县组建959人的“三定”工作队，分赴各公社开展工作。首先查清森林资源，调解山林纠纷，明确山林权属。经清查统计，全县有林地面积（习惯亩）15.84万亩，折合丈量亩25.69万亩（包括灌木林8.77万亩），占总面积的15.88%。填发集体山林所有证1897张。同时查明，全县有荒山荒坡20.42万亩，占总面积12.62%。通过“三定”明确权属及作用，并划出其中的11.02万亩给社员作自留山。同时，还确定集体山林管理责任制，并由公社填发集体山林管理证（或合同）2008份。在“三定”工作中，全县恢复和巩固

社队林场58个，其中社办12个，大队办44个，生产队办2个，共有林场人员187人。“三定”期间清理并处理乱砍滥伐山林和毁林开荒案件154起，没收木材47立方米，罚款4226元，收回影响水土保持的私人开荒地1.56万亩。12月底，林业“三定”工作全部结束，落实林业生产责任制，做到“山有主、主有权、权有责、责有利”，调动起群众发展林业积极性，当年全县育苗191亩，造林2.09万亩，为造林任务的139.36%。

鉴于林业“三定”中尚有部分国有山林和难以确定权属的林地未予确权，县政府又于1990年经过调查核准县属国有山林定权，发证29张，面积1.03万亩；1997年又对省属扎佐林场国有山林进行核准定权，发证11张，面积2.1万亩。至此，全县尚有16.31万亩（含灌木林地12.98万亩）未发林权证。其中省属扎佐林场未发证的有3.8万亩，因其他原因未发证的有2.2万亩，存有权属纠纷的1.6万亩。

2008年7月，贯彻落实《中共中央、国务院关于全面推进集体林权制度改革的意见》和《贵州省人民政府关于开展深化集体林权制度改革工作的意见》和《贵阳市人民政府关于全面推进集体林权制度改革工作的意见》精神，县委、县政府根据工作的需要成立县集体林权制度改革工作领导小组，并出台《关于开展深化集体林权制度改革工作的意见》《集体林权制度改革工作实施方案》和《关于强力推进破坏森林资源案件查处工作的通知》指导全县集体林权制度改革工作。到2010年，确定林权的集体林地面积45.45万亩，占纳入林改范围集体林地46.14万亩的98.5%。

（二）非耕地拍卖

林业“三定”后，县委、县政府为实施土地利用的总体规划，达到合理节约用地的目的，采取法律、行政和经济综合措施进一步开发利用土地资源。1994年8月，县人民政府发出《印发<关于拍卖荒山荒地等非耕地使用权的规定>的通知》，对“可开发的荒山、荒地，没有充分利用的水资源等非耕地的使用权和边远、不易管理而又瘦薄耕地及撂荒两年以上责任地的使用权”进行公开拍卖，对全县荒山非耕地4500亩和工矿废弃地900亩进行扩垦增殖开发。同时，还规定：对已搞林业“三定”的荒山荒坡等非耕地，“没有开发或开发差的，以及开发虽较好但土地权属尚不明确或承包体制不完善的由集体统一收回拍卖”；对未实行林业“三定”的集体荒山等非耕地的使用权，可由集体统一进行拍卖；撂荒两年以上的责任地由土地所有权拥有者收回拍卖。拍卖期限由双方协定，但至少不少于一个使用期限（15年），一般为30—60年。非耕地拍卖后，买方享有经营自主权，生产管理及收益分配、产品处置权利，开发后可转让、出租、抵押贷权（含附着物）、继承和捐赠等。8月23日，县政府在久长镇芦山小学召开非耕地现场拍卖会，当日拍卖成交21宗面积1129.5亩，每亩单价最低45元，最高145元。9月15日，又在谷堡乡举行非耕地使用权拍卖，现场拍出非耕地13宗，1114.95亩，成交金额9万余元。至年底全县共拍卖非耕地80宗，11660亩，拍卖金额28.94万元。

非耕地资源拍卖后种植的猕猴桃

1996年1月16日，六屯乡成功拍卖山王庙、黄泥坡2宗非耕地使用权。山王庙地块75亩，竞拍价每亩175元；黄泥坡地块68亩，竞拍价每亩275元。截至2004年年底，全县共计拍卖非耕地174宗，面积

18256亩，拍卖金额52.36万元，平均每亩拍卖价28.68元，最低每亩10.47元，最高1041.67元。

二、森林资源

（一）林业用地

1984年森林资源调查，全县有林业用地33.81万亩，占全县土地面积的21.05%。其中，森林11.82万亩，灌木林12.91万亩，林木覆盖率为15.4%。1999年，第二次森林资源现状调查，全县有林业用地面积61.29万亩，占土地总面积的38.0%。有林面积达35.41万亩，占林业用地面积的57.78%；疏林地2.83万亩，占4.62%；灌木林地13.81万亩，占22.53%；未成造林地2.02万亩，占3.3%；无林地7.18万亩，占11.72%；苗圃地301.5亩，占0.05%。全县森林覆盖率30. 50%，其中有林地覆盖率21.95%，灌木林覆盖率8.56%。活立木蓄积量增长到49.5万立方米，林业生产迈上新的台阶。

2001年，结合国家西部大开发的重要战略决策，县把退耕还林还草，加强生态环境保护和建设作为重要工作来抓。从2002年正式启动退耕还林（草）工程造林，凡25°以上坡耕地，分年度有计划退耕，全部植树种草。至2005年年底，全县4年退耕还林造林79100亩，其中25°以上坡耕地造林5.01万亩，荒山造林29000亩。2010年，全县各类林地68.14万亩，占全县土地总面积的44.06%。其中，有林地42.03万亩，灌木林19.62万亩，林木覆盖率达40.3%。

（二）资源分布

县境属黔中用材林和水土保持林区，据林业区划，全县主要划分为5个林业区。

1. 西北部水土保持林、经济林区

猫洞河以北地区，包括六广、洒坪、大石、六桶4个乡镇全部和小箐大部。区内属岩溶低中山地貌类型，山峦起伏交错，岩石裸露较大，西面以六广河和猫跳河与金沙、黔西、清镇三县交界。林区有林业用地面积17.04万亩，占整个区划面积的38.54%，其中：有林地1.97万亩，占林业用地的11.55%；疏林地2.27万亩，占13.33%；未成林造林地0.16万亩，占0.96%；灌木林地7.42万亩，占43.55%；无林地5.21万亩，占30.6%。活立木总蓄积为4.51万立方米。森林覆盖率15.78%，其中有林覆盖率为3.3%，灌木林地覆盖率为12.43%。用材林占绝对优势，其优势树种有杉木、马尾松、华山松、柏木、阔叶树等，总面积1.87万亩，活立木蓄积量2.49万立方米。

水土保持经济林

2. 西南部针、阔用材林区

包括谷堡乡全部、小箐乡东南部和龙场镇北部、西部及西南部，共36个村。境内地形由东向西倾斜，近猫跳河一带河谷发育明显，多为石灰岩分布。土壤多为中层黄壤、中薄层黄色石灰土，薄层酸性紫色土和硅铁、硅铅质黄壤。林区有林业用地12.73万亩，占整个区划总面积的39.6%。其中，有林地面积2.81万亩，占22%；疏林地2.05万亩，占林业用地面积的16%；灌木林地2.86万亩，占22%；无林地4.95万亩，占39%。活立木总蓄积量为5.96万立方米，森林覆盖率17.65%。用材林中天然马尾松占

93.78%，较集中连片分布在谷堡乡、场坝乡、阳早乡、崇恩乡和王官乡的木厂、茶田村一带。阔叶树多呈散生状分布于河谷地带和村寨周围。其优势树种有杉木、马尾松、华山松、柏木、阔叶树等，总面积2.8万亩。活立木蓄积量4.64万立方米。

3. 东北部松、杉用材林区

包括久长和六屯2个乡镇的33个村。区内地形由北向南倾斜，主要山脉为东西走向。有林业用地面积13.66万亩，占全区总面积43.56%。其中，有林地3.33万亩，占林业用地面积的24.39%；疏林地1.5万亩，占11.01%；灌木林地1.69万亩，占12.4%；未成林造林地1.18万亩，占8.66%；苗圃地238亩，占0.17%；无林地5.93万亩，占43.47%。活立木总蓄积8.69万立方米，森林覆盖率16.06%。用材林占绝对优势，其优势树种有杉木、马尾松、华山松、柏木、阔叶树等，总面积3.24万亩，活立木蓄积量7.82万立方米。

4. 中部农田防护林区

包括龙场镇东北部、中东部和扎佐镇北部、东部，共43个村。区内多中山、丘陵、坝子地，丘陵散布，谷地与山间较为平缓。有林业用地面积5.91万亩，占全区总面积的23.66%。其中，林地2万亩，占林业用地面积的33.85%；疏林地0.36万亩，占16.3%；灌木林地0.47万亩，占7.89%；未成林造林地0.14万亩，占2.37%；苗圃地113亩，占0.19%；无林地23278亩，占39.4%。有活立木总蓄积4.5万立方米，森林覆盖率9.87%。其优势树种有杉木、马尾松、华山松、柏木、阔叶树等，总面积1.95万亩，活立木蓄积量3.82万立方米。

5. 南部松、杉用材林区

包括扎佐镇南部及龙场镇东部、东南襄阳，共10个村，区内山峦起伏，沟谷明显，地形南高北低。有林业用地面积5.9万亩，占全区总面积的47.18%。其中有林地面积1.71万亩，占林业用地面积的28.92%；疏林地0.47万亩，占8%；灌木林地0.47亩，占8%；未成林造林地0.17万亩，占2.91%；苗圃地595亩，占1.00%；无林地3.02万亩，占51.23%。有活立木总蓄积5.01万立方米，森林覆盖率为17.36%。优势树种主要有杉木、马尾松、华山松、柏木、阔叶树等，总面积1.69万亩，活立木蓄积量5.012万立方米。

1999年全县资源调查，森林资源分布呈北少南多之势，西北部五乡（镇）有林地11.34万亩，东南部五乡（镇）有林地20.89万亩。优势树种组结构上，针叶林较多，有24.37万亩，占有林地面积的68.8%；阔叶林有3.79万亩，占有林地面积的10.7%；针阔混交林3.95万亩，占11.2%；经济林3.3万亩，占9.3%。

（三）林种结构

1. 用材林

1978年，各地区均有用材林，主要分布在县境西南部、东北部和南部地区，特别是省属扎佐林场重点营造用材林，树种主要有杉木、华山松、马尾松、黑松、檫木、梓木、滇杨、泡桐、水杉、柳杉等。全县共有林地面积14.11万亩，蓄积量21.38万立方米，其中有林地面积11.14万亩，蓄积量14.78万立方米；疏林地2.97万亩，蓄积量4.12万立方米；散生木蓄积21.38万立方米。从1984年起，开始建立用材林基地。至1987年，全县用材林共有11.55万亩，活立木蓄积量29.23万立方米，森林覆盖率15.03%。1995年，全县有用材林共20.41万亩，活立木蓄积量42.95万立方米。

1995年，全县森林资源二类调查，活立木总蓄积量为49.49万立方米，其中有林地蓄积44.21万立方米；占总蓄积量的89.34%；疏林地蓄积1.16万立方米，占2.35%，散生木蓄积0.61万立方米，占1.23%；

四旁植树蓄积3.51万立方米，占7.08%；在有林地各林种中，用材林蓄积量41.79万立方米，占有林地蓄积的94.52%；防护林蓄积量1.59万立方米，占3.6%；薪炭林蓄积量0.83万立方米，占1.88%。用材林蓄积中，马尾松最多，占58.50%；其次是华山松，占18.03%，杉木14.03%；再次分别是栎类、阔叶混、桦类、柏木、针阔混交、针叶混交、杨树、杂木、软阔类、柳杉、硬阔类、水杉、杨树组、檫木、泡桐和枫香等。

2010年，全县共有用材林29.91万亩（含疏林地），占全县林地总面积的40.96%，木材蓄积51.34万立方米，占全县木材蓄积总数的48.87%。

2. 经济林

主要经济林木有油桐、油茶、生漆、茶叶、柑橘、猕猴桃、梨子、核桃、板栗、桃子、李子、枇杷、杨梅等，绝大部分经济林木属于零星分散型，成片生产不多。1987年，乌栗乡下硐联户合作农场建立，入场农户联户合作开发非耕地5000多亩，连片种植猕猴桃、板栗等经济林木。继后，在全县推广。1994年，全县开始推行非耕地使用权拍卖，极大地促进经济林木生产发展。1999年，经济林发展至3.3万亩，主要树种有猕猴桃、板栗、梨子、苹果、杜仲、茶叶、柑橘、桃子、李子、枇杷、杨梅等。到2004年，全县已建成各类经济林总面积9.4万亩，大部分经济林木基地已开始产出。2010年，全县生产各类林产品主要有水果2.46万吨、茶叶55吨、板栗77吨、核桃31吨、油桐籽28吨和生漆10吨。

3. 薪炭林

薪炭林树种多为青杠、毛栗等杂树灌木。20世纪80年代初，县境一些交通不便的边远地区仍有燃烧薪炭的习惯。1985年，全县共有面积956亩，占全县林种面积0.5%，蓄积1263立方米，占全县蓄积总数的0.55%。随着农村农民生活水平不断提高，农村基础设施不断完善，林区管护不断加强，燃烧薪炭的农民逐步减少，在面积没有增加的情况下炭林蓄积量逐年增加。1995年森林资源二类调查统计，全县薪炭林蓄积量8310立方米，占1.88%。进入21世纪，只有极少数的农民燃烧薪炭，薪炭林的功能完全变成增加植被覆盖和防水固土作用。

4. 防护林

1987年，县被列为“长江中上游防护林体系建设第一期工程”（简称“长防林一期工程”）建设重点县。工程从1990年开始启动，当年完成造林1621亩。至1997年，全县共落实荒山承包造林625处8.56万亩，拍卖荒山43宗1.27万亩，引进外地投资11宗200万元。新营造林总面积46.63万亩，人工造林18.63万亩，低效林改造0.54万亩，封山育林27.46万亩。

二环林带防护林

2000年年底，县境被划入贵阳市第二环城森林带（简称“二环林带”）建设范围。从2002年开始，到2010年完成。全县新造林3.09万亩，编制“二环”林管护方案，落实管护人员25名管护人员，签订管护合同，完成7725亩幼林抚育。

5. 特种用途林

主要是风景林，树种以硬阔叶树为主，松、柏类次之。一般树龄较大，最大的有500多年树龄。主要

分布在龙场、扎佐、谷堡等乡镇。1999年，全县计有172亩，蓄材500多立方米。

6. 竹林

境内各地均有，分野生和人工种植两类，野生一般呈零星分布，人工种植多为成片生长，规模一般为0.5至2亩之间。品种有绵竹、苦竹、慈竹（钓鱼竹）、金竹、斑竹、黔竹、楠竹、水竹、黑竹（又名紫竹）、刺竹、箭竹、箬竹和棕竹等。2010年，全县有人工种植成片竹林110余亩，竹材蓄积20万株。

（四）树种

县境地处北亚热带季风性湿润气候区，平均海拔1240米，植被属亚热带常绿阔叶森林类型，种类繁多。常见乔木树种有33科84种，其中阔叶树30科63种，针叶树3科21种。用材树品种主要以针叶树中的松、杉为主，阔叶树常见用材主要有梓木、柏杨等。经济林木树品种主要有油桐、油茶、茶叶、梨树和板栗等。灌木林科种较多，据不完全统计有100余种。一般喀斯特（石山）地区多为常绿灌木，其余地区多为落叶灌木或混交灌木。竹类品种有2科13种，比较常见的主要是绵竹、苦竹、钓鱼竹等。

三、营林

（一）种苗生产

1. 种子

（1）采种

本地采种主要有马尾松、杉、梓木和杨槐等。1978年，由林业部门发动群众按照“适地适树”的原则，进行自采、自育、自造。因林业用地权属不明确，群众造林信心不足，采种积极性不高，当年仅收购树种6.5公斤。1981年的林业“三定”后调动群众的造林积极性，采种热情高涨。1981年全县收购树种1700公斤，1982年收购树种700公斤，1983年7950公斤，1984年为9000公斤。本地采种因成本高利润少，从1985年起，收购树种开始减少，所需优势树种大多从外地调入。

（2）引种

主要有两种方式，一种是从外地引进种子本地育苗，另一种是直接从外地引进树苗种植。1985年，县从外地引进的树种主要有柳杉、台湾杉、水杉、湿地松、雪松、黑松、葵花松、火炬松、铁肩杉、红花梓木和大叶梧桐柏等品种，继后又引进喜树、川樟等。1987年，乌栗下硐村农民组织兴办合作农场，引进板栗和猕猴桃“贵长”种植，继后又引进猕猴桃“米良”“川蜜”“秦美”等品种，经优选推广到全县种植。1993年，引进水蜜桃、艳红桃在乌栗一带种植。1999年，谷堡乡政府引进金秋梨、红花梨种苗，发动折溪村村民种植，形成千亩连片梨园。此外，20世纪90年代至21世纪初，还先后引进四川红橘、江西蜜橘、布朗李、安徽砀山梨、太湖枇杷、巨峰葡萄、福建茶、文旦柚、巨森苹果等。

2. 育苗

1978年，县内具有育苗技术和能力的单位主要有贵州省扎佐林场、县久长林场（二关坝林场）和部分社队集体林场。其中，久长林场主要以育苗为主，承担全县80%的植树造林所需树苗；扎佐林场和社队林场一般是自育自用，偶尔作一些调剂。二关坝林场属县国营林场，有宜林荒山1000余亩，辟有苗床40亩，主要培育松、杉、梓木等用材林树苗，每年要为全县提供树苗2万多株树苗，一直是县内植树造林育苗主要基地。

1981年林业“三定”后，用苗量大增，县将原有社办林场调整为合作林场，并出现一批联户林场和林业专业户、重点户、科技户，当时被称之为“两场、三户”。林业部门分别与“两场”“三户”签订育苗协议，无偿提供育苗种子、技术和化肥。每年11月验收，根据苗木生长情况，分为三等按每亩50、45、30元付酬。自然灾害造成损失，视其情况给予适当补偿。1984到1987年，“两场、三户”育苗面积累计1452.4亩，向县内提供各种苗木1985.4万株。

1999年，二关坝林场改制，贵阳市白云区顺兴园艺有限公司出资11.8万元购买，将其改建成顺心苑苗圃场，性质改为私营企业。经营项目为园艺和绿化，种苗主要有桂花、香樟、紫微、雪松、银杏、金弹子、樱花等70多个品种，苗木量达2000万余株。树苗除供应县内外还为贵阳金阳新区等地的园林、公路、城市和二环绿化提供大批树苗。

二关坝林场苗圃

（二）造林

1978年，大力提倡植树造林，但年年造林不见林，加上部分地方毁林开荒和偷砍盗伐现象不断发生，林业生产不见发展反而退化，水土流失严重，在六广、小箐等区的一些地方还出现石漠化现象。1981年随着农村经济改革，全县林业“三定”对山林权属进行明确，并建立“权、责、利”相协调的生产责任制，实现“山有主、主有权、权有责、责有利”，使社员吃“定心丸”，调动营林、护林的积极性。促进林业生产发展，当年造林2.09万亩，为造林任务的139.36%。

1982年3月4日，县成立“绿化委员会”，统一领导指挥全县林业生产，并与各区签订“林木育苗责任书”，对林业生产实行目标责任管理。继后，林业专业户、重点户、林科户（简称“三户”）和合作林场、联户林场（简称“两场”）不断涌现。1985年5月，县与黔西两县政府达成协议，共同发起以退耕还林、植树造林保护植被、防止水土流失为主要内容的治理乌江流域六广河段行动。1990年6月，县政府制订《1989—2000年造林绿化规划（草案）》，作出《关于十年基本绿化修文的决定》，并与各区（镇）签订造林绿化“5年消灭荒山”的责任状；同时启动“长江中上游防护林体系建设”工程（简称“长防林工程”），以工程建设推动造林绿化。

从1990年起，县委、县政府多次行文，继续实行荒山荒坡承包责任制，坚持“谁造谁有、合造共有，荒山造林允许继承，长期不变”的政策。实行非耕地使用权公开拍卖，调动广大干部群众的造林积极性。至1996年，全县基本消灭荒山秃岭。1999年贵州省重点生态工程区森林资源调查，全县有林地达35.41万亩，森林覆盖率达到30.5%，活立木蓄积量增长到49.5万立方米。

2002年和2003年，县又先后被列为贵阳市“二环”林带工程造林和中韩合作喀斯特石质山造林重点县。至2005年，完成“中韩合作造林”人工造林1.95万亩；至2010年，完成贵阳市二环林带造林营造生态公益林2.8万亩。

1. 国营林场造林

县境内国营林场主要是贵州省扎佐林场和县久长林场（二关坝林场），其中扎佐林场为贵州省人工造林松、杉用材林基地，久长林场以育苗为主。扎佐林场经营范围涉及修文、开阳、息烽三县和白云、乌当两区。在县境部分，跨县属龙场、扎佐、六屯三个乡（镇）。林场建立后，年年有计划地种植松、杉等

用材林木，不断引进优良树种种植。至2010年，全场累计造林12万亩，保存面积10.5万亩，活立木蓄积量达42万立方米。

2. 集体林场造林

1978年，全县社队集体林场有90个，植树21.4万亩。1981年林业“三定”，将继续保存的社队集体林场改为合作林场，实行定面积、定管理、定收益、定报酬的责任制，把造、育、管、护工作和责、权、利紧密联系起来，进行植树造林和抚育幼林。对解散林场的林地，则由公社承包给农民管护。整顿后，全县尚有合作林场40个，专业人员175人，常年组织群众造林。至2010年，全县有集体林场47个，有林地面积8.49万亩。

3. “四旁”植树

1978至1981年，“四旁”（路旁、水旁、宅旁、村旁）植树，年均植树34.1万株。1982年，县将宅旁植树列为四旁植树重点，要求机关、学校、医院、厂矿、城镇街道两侧、居民住宅周围都要植树，所植林木数量和质量较前提高。1982年到1990年，年均植树近90万株。90年代年均植树100万株以上。县委机关大院、县政府机关大院和阳明洞、三元贵阳高尔大度假中心、久长珍珠岛休闲中心等单位企业院（园）内绿树成荫，成为清新和谐的园林化环境。进入21世纪，县内各中、小学在“两基”达标工作中，也把校园绿化作为一项重要工作，纷纷植树种花、草，美化校园，成效显著。至2010年，全县“四旁”零星植树共2315万株。

4. 示范点造林

1990年县委、县政府作出“十年绿化修文”的决定后，为推动群众性造林，要求县、区、乡（镇）领导深入农村办造林示范点。由林业部门作出规划，领导带领机关干部组成承包集团，组织发动规划区内的农户按统一树种，统一规格，统一质量要求植树造林，1992年，全县共办示范点15个，造林3425亩。到1997年，仅领导承包办示范点211个，新造林5.9万亩。

5. 工程造林

（1）长江中上游防护林工程造林

简称“长防林工程”。从1990年开始，至2000年结束，共11年完成营造林面积53.59万亩(抚育除外)，占总体规划建设规模30.8万亩的173.9%，其中人工造林21.27万亩，封山育林29.70万亩，低效林地改造2.59万亩。四旁植树574.16万株，义务植树267.43万株；抚育补植10万株；公路绿化120公里，河流绿化26公里；育苗2989亩。

（2）贵阳市“二环”林带工程造林

简称“二环林带造林”。为落实亚欧森林会议和《贵阳宣言》精神，将贵阳打造成“森林之城、休闲胜地”，中共贵阳市委七届四次全会《关于制定贵阳市国民经济和社会发展第十个五年计划的建议》决定建设贵阳市第二环城森林绿带。县政府抓住被列为工程建设重点县的机遇，认真组织实施。从2002年开始，到2010年完成。全县共投资3187.62万元，营造生态公益林28337.1亩，封山育林1万亩，义务植树400亩。

（3）中韩合作喀斯特石质山造林

简称“中韩合作造林”。2001年12月26日，中国国家林业局与韩国国际协力团签署《中韩合作中国西部五省造林项目实施协议会谈纪要》，韩国国际协力团出资500万美元，无偿援助中国西部地区五省

（区）生态建设。2003年9月，修文被列为项目建设县，安排在大石、六广、小箐、洒坪4个石漠化较为严重的乡（镇）营造，总投资200万美元。其中韩方援助100万美元，中方配套100万美元。2005年完成人工造林1.95万亩，修建沼气池1000口和蓄水池300口，培训人员1万人次。

中韩合作造林

（4）退耕还林（草）造林

1996年出台《修文县土地利用总体规划》指出：全县大于25度的坡耕地8587公顷，占耕地面积的20.97%，占旱地29724公顷的28.89%。这些耕地坡度大，保水保肥能力差，水土流失重，土层薄，肥力低，有碍农业生产的发展。

2000年9月，贯彻落实国务院发布《关于进一步做好退耕还林还草试点工作的若干意见》。县委、县政府把退耕还林还草，加强西部生态环境保护和建设作为西部大开发的重要工作来抓。2001年，成立由县长魏明禄担任组长的“县退耕还林（草）领导小组”，同时制订《退耕还林还草实施办法》和《修文县退耕还林（草）实施意见》。落实“退耕还林(草)、封山绿化、以粮代赈、个体承包”政策，把退耕还林还草与扶贫开发、农业综合开发、水土保持等结合起来，统筹安排。在确定土地所有权和使用权的基础上，实行“谁退耕、谁造林（草）、谁经营、谁受益”的政策。农民承包的耕地和宜林荒山荒地，植树种草以后，承包期一律延长到50年，允许依法继承、转让，到期后可按有关法律和法规继续承包。

2002年1月5日退耕还林工程正式启动，总任务为3.5万亩，其中退耕地2万亩，荒山造林1.5万亩。采取统一部署、政府补贴、群众实施的凡25度坡耕地分年度、有计划地退耕，全部植树种草。经检查验收合格，由政府一次性补助种苗款50元/亩；退耕地每年补助粮食150公斤（原粮）/亩，现金20元（补助年限为：生态林补助8年、经济林补助5年）。由于补助政策的兑现，调动群众退耕还林的积极性，至2010年全县退耕还林造林7.61万亩，其中荒山造林29000亩，25度以上坡耕地退耕造林47100亩。为全县土地利用的调整和合理使用、保护土地资源奠定良好的基础。

1978—2010年植树退耕情况表

表3—01—04

年度	造林（亩）	零星植树（万株）	年度	造林（亩）	零星植树（万株）
1978	22172	40	1995	27840	92
1979	24509	67.2	1996	22395	63
1980	8910	42.9	1997	10455	82
1981	8475	74.2	1998	15960	83
1982	28626	166.9	1999	38355	90
1983	51613	431.4	2000	33165	89
1984	43690	140.2	2001	25335	90

续表

年度	造林（亩）	零星植树（万株）	年度	造林（亩）	零星植树（万株）
1985	59400	136.1	2002	43170	90
1986	25821	65.5	2003	18000	90
1987	19534	50.9	2004	15495	90
1988	14363	59.6	2005	18000	40
1989	14086	56.2	2006	4900	30
1990	7824	59.2	2007	3400	50
1991	31451	62	2008	1005	50
1992	22545	62	2009	5000	40
1993	37875	71	2010	2000	40
1994	29685	95			

（三）育林

1. 封山育林

1978年农业集体化时期，虽然也提封山育林，但由于乱砍滥伐，森林破坏严重。1981年，实行林业“三定”，调动农民造林育林的积极性。1982年，县、区、乡政府发动村民订立《乡规民约》、《村规民约》，在封山育林区设立警示标志，依靠群众自我约束，禁止在封育区内放牧、砍伐、铲草皮烧灰和打秧青，当年全县封山育林面积2.14万亩。继后每年都要新增一批封育林区，其中2007年和2008年封育面积最多，分别为7.6万亩和8.1万亩。2010年，全县封山育林3.6万亩，累计达79.57万亩。

1982—2010年封山育林情况表

表3—01—05　　单位：万亩

年份	封育面积	年份	封育面积	年份	封育面积
1982	2.17	1992	2.12	2002	1.34
1983	2.50	1993	3.04	2003	0.80
1984	3.60	1994	3.48	2004	7.65
1985	3.83	1995	6.83	2005	8.16
1986	3.83	1996	4.08	2006	0.50
1987	2.80	1997	2.86	2007	0.80
1988	1.18	1998	1.00	2008	0.50
1989	2.30	1999	1.25	2009	0.10
1990	2.45	2000	1.66	2010	3.60
1991	2.63	2001	2.51		

2. 幼林抚育

1981年实行林业“三定”后，各地更加重视抚育幼林，当年抚育350亩。1983年增为2080亩。1984年，“三户”林场和自留山植树，抚育幼林达5353亩。1986年抚育幼林面积达1.5万亩。继后，每年抚育幼林面积皆在幼林抚育作业面积的85%以上。因植树、抚林成效显著，1987年10月，省绿化委员会命名金桥乡石榴村为全省绿化先进单位和扎佐乡马鞍村罗甲云为全省绿化先进工作者。

1990年，县作出“十年基本绿化修文”的决定后，全县上下“乔、灌、草”并举，“封（山）、补（植）、造（林）、抚（育幼林）”结合，抚育幼林成为群众的自觉行动。特别是1992年县委、县政府出台《关于全面推进农业综合开发的安排意见》和《关于绿色产业开发的安排意见》后，各地更加精心抚育幼林。谷堡乡下硐联户合作农场、折溪村千亩连片梨园、龙场镇马口村邵文龙果木场等，每年都要对幼林进行松土、剪枝、施肥。2003年，全县抚育幼林创历史新高达5万亩。1978年至2010年，全县累计抚育幼林30.74万亩。

1979—2010年幼林抚育一览表

表3—01—06　　单位：亩

年份	面积	年份	面积	年份	面积
1979	6183	1990	1549	2001	16000
1980	1100	1991	—	2002	25000
1981	—	1992	—	2003	50000
1982	350	1993	—	2004	40500
1983	2080	1994	1555	2005	—
1984	5353	1995	40155	2006	5000
1985	2481	1996	5840	2007	8000
1986	14149	1997	10230	2008	4995
1987	12932	1998	—	2009	1000
1988	—	1999	10000	2010	22665
1989	—	2000	20250		

四、护林

（一）严禁乱砍滥伐

1981年，结合林业“三定”，严肃处理偷砍盗运案件154起，没收木材47立方米，罚款4224元。使毁林开荒者退耕还林，偷砍林木者受到处罚。1985年，木材市场放开，允许林农和集体木材自由上市，实行议购议销，随行就市，木材采伐一度失控。程官乡程官村农民1人6天就砍伐集体林木72株。计12立方米。次年冬，六屯乡村民300多人进入贵州省扎佐林场六屯分场林区哄砍林木600多立方米，折价27万元。对此，县委、县政府作出决定，一方面广泛宣传《中华人民共和国森林法》，一方面集中力量迅速开展打击破坏森林资源的犯罪活动，依法逮捕9名犯罪分子，刑事拘留17人，罚款2270元，有力制止乱砍滥伐现象。

1987年2月，为维护林业生产秩序和切实保护林业资源，县林业局建立林业公安派出所，配备公安干警4人。省扎佐林场亦充实林区派出所力量，使林业的治安保卫工作得以加强。为发挥群众护林的积极工作，实行专门机关与广大群众联防群治相结合。1989年12月13日，县人民政府与扎佐林场召开护林联防会议，将国有林护林工作承包给林区周边的区、乡（镇），并签订承包合同，明确责权利。再由区、乡（镇）将任务逐级承包到毗邻林区的村、组。凡有承包任务的乡、村、组建立护林队伍，将任务落实到人，护林任务重的乡，还配备一名专职护林人员从事护林工作。实行联防护林后，林区山林火灾、偷砍盗伐林木案件减少，森林资源得到有力保护。

1994年，市场对木材需求增加，一些木材经营加工企业和个人为寻求自身利益，不顾国家限额采伐森林的规定，无证经营或擅自进入林区进行黑市交易，导致林木过量采伐。为保护森林资源，1995年3月县政府发出《关于加强木材经营加工管理的联合通知》，决定从3月1日起，全县实行木材经营加工许可证制度。凡从事木材经营、加工的单位和个人，需办理经林业主管部门（林业局）审核同意发给《木材经营加工许可证》和经工商行政管理机关审发的《营业执照》，严格持证、照经营。除国营木材经营单位可在林区收购木材外，其余只准在林木市场交易，严禁收购无证采伐的木材。凡农民房前屋后的木材，需持有村委会或乡（镇）林业站证明方可交易，其余上市木材，必须持有砍伐证、运输证，外县进入县境市场的木材还需持有检疫证。

1998年，为进一步落实“一本账”计划，合理开发利用森林资源，县林业局作出《关于抚育间伐、更新采伐实行专人负责制的决定》，要求各乡（镇）要严格采伐审批制度，明确专人负责，认真进行规划设计。认真执行《森林采伐更新管理办法》，采伐的林木当年必须更新造林。批准砍伐后，乡（镇）林业站人员现场监督，严格执行砍伐证规定不能超过的数量；批少砍多、批小砍大，异地、异种砍伐视为乱砍滥伐，追究有关人员责任。对规划不当，追究负责设计人员的责任。《决定》执行，对保护森林资源起到积极作用。

2000年12月，根据国家林业局森林、公安局省林业厅、公安厅“在天然林保护区内开展严厉打击破坏森林资源违法犯罪活动专项斗争（代号‘天保行动’）”精神，县林业局、公安局对开展“天保行动”作出部署。行动从15日零时开始在全县范围内展开，经过调查摸底、集中打击、整章建制三个阶段，至次年2月10日结束。共出动警力300余人次，车辆60台次，共查处各类案件32起，林业行政罚款18137元，收缴木材96立方米，挽回经济损失10万元。同时还查处破坏野生动物案件3起，收缴蛇60公斤（其中毒蛇40条）和花面狸1只。收缴作案工具斧头6把、木锯4把、柴油锯木机4台。清理整顿木材市场及加工场点和宾馆酒家83家，收缴木成品、半成品120余件。整个“天保行动”对震慑犯罪，教育群众，维护林区治安，保护森林资源起到推动作用。

乱砍盗伐

2005年，为加大对林地的保护力度，对县内26家矿山、104家采石（采砂）场、2家取土硅厂进行排查，对其中违法占用林地的，发出停止违法行为的通知书，限期改正，并到林业主管部门接受违调查处理。对26家毁林开荒的业主依法进行处理，有效地保护林地。

2006年，由于煤炭价格大幅上涨，煤矿所需木材大增，不法人员铤而走险趁机倒卖木材，致林木乱砍滥伐现象又死灰复燃。针对此种情况，县开展森林资源专项整治行动，严厉打击乱砍滥伐林木、乱征滥占林地等违法犯罪行为。2009年，县破获1起乱砍滥伐，倒卖木材团伙大案。六广广田李氏四兄弟网络部分社会上的一些闲散人员共20人，盗伐贩卖木材，牟取暴利。在六广镇、小箐乡、扎佐镇及贵阳市白云区等地盗伐国有林场、集体林场和个人所有的林木，或滥伐集体所有和个人所有的林木，并非法收购农民非法砍伐的木料牟取暴利，使得其所到之处林木大量被盗伐，生态植被受到严重破坏。对犯罪团伙打击，有力地震慑乱砍滥伐现象。2010年，县内乱砍滥伐现象基本得到遏制。

（二）森林防火

县境山林火灾每年均有，特别是冬暖春旱的年份最易发生，尤以春节过后半月和清明前后10天是山林火灾的高发时期，全县年均5起左右。引起山林火灾原因主要是人为因素造成，20世纪70年代末，在一些偏远落后地区仍有个别放火烧山现象；农民铲土皮烧灰积肥，防火不慎易引发山林火灾；当地有春节、清明上坟的习惯，上坟人员燃烧纸、烛和燃放鞭炮不慎导致火灾；闲杂人员在林区玩火、抽烟若遇天干草枯也易导致山火；更有甚者少数个别道德缺失者，以图好玩人为故意放火。火灾原因中因上坟人员而引起的火灾要占所有山林火灾的2/5以上。1981年，落实林业“三定”政策后，调动起广大群众护林防火的积极性和主动性，各地采取发布护林防火公告，制定护林防火公约，订立村规民约等实行联防群治，山林火灾急剧减少，1984年，获安顺地区林业局颁布的护林防火二等奖。

1987年，县成立护林防火指挥部，林业局成立森林防火指挥部办公室（简称“森防办”）与公安派所合署办公，各区、乡（镇）亦成立相应组织，国营和集体林场还雇有专人负责山林管护工作，全县共有4000多人分别守护各林场，基本做到山山有人管，林林有人护，一旦发生火警，及时组织扑救，使山林火灾基本得到控制。1988年，贯彻国务院发布的《森林防火条例》及省人民政府发布的《森林防火条例实施办法》。县林业局采取宣传车巡回宣传，散发宣传资料，张贴公告等形式，加强对群众进行护林护火法律知识及技能的教育。1989年3月，县政府转发《关于加强野外用火管理防止山林火灾的通知》，并规定：不准在林区烧灰积肥；在林区上坟不准烧纸钱，点烛和燃放鞭炮；不准在林区野炊；不准携带火种进入林区。一旦发生森林火灾，必须彻底清查原因，严肃进行处理，森林火灾得到明显遏制。

县林业局组织森林防火

1990年春，由于长期干旱，草木枯干，山林火灾发生次数达34起，创历史最高纪录。火场面积达30多公顷，受害森林面积28.63公顷，经济损失60多万元。县森林防火指挥部统筹协调，在全县建立县、乡（镇）、村三级森林防火组织，形成网络系统，把防火宣传教育，排查火灾隐患，火险报警，组织扑救作为常规性的工作来抓。1994年3月县人民政府再次发出《关于加强野外用火管理严防山林火灾的紧急通知》，对野外用火再次进行规范。

2000年3月又在县林业局成立有30名队员的森林防火专职扑火队，发生火警，即赶赴现场，扑救灭火。在冬春火警易发季节，县森防办实行专人24小时值班，加强县域内的火警监控。一旦发生火灾，迅速组织扑救，控制火势蔓延，降低损失。

2003年春旱，草木枯燥，极易引起火灾，全县发生森林火灾次数仅次于1990年，达19次。其中重大火灾13次，由于扑救及时，全部经济仅为4000元，将损失降到最低点。2005年，森林火灾发生又呈上升趋势，全年火灾次数达13次。究其因多以人为因素为主，经查实后，行政处罚2人，治安拘留10人，刑事处罚2人。其中比较典型的1起是六屯乡全兴村村民吴道华放火烧毁大木村杨家大田背后山林，经群众举报，县林业派出所派员勘察，过火面积30亩，烧毁后砍伐面积2亩，吴被依法刑事处罚。此后全县进一步加大森林防火宣传的力度，并结合典型案例，加强法治教育等。次年起，森林火灾发生得到有效控制，2008年发生次数最少，全县仅有3次。

2009年年底，县境暖冬干旱，到2010年春季，天干风大，极易引起森林火灾，全县发生森林火灾次数高达12次。由于事前县及各乡镇均制定有森林防火预案，做好充分防火准备，一旦火警发生，及时扑救。12场火灾过火面积仅为14.4公顷，直接经济损失4.51万元。

（三）森林病虫害防治

境内影响林木生长病虫害有237种。其中，病害70种，主要病种有杉树黄化、炭疽、落叶病和松树棕锈、赤枯病和立木腐朽病等；虫病167种，危害较大的有象鼻虫、天牛、金花虫、螟、毒蛾、蚧和蚜虫等。森林病虫害防治工作，贯彻“预防为主，防重于治，积极消灭”的方针，由林业主管部门积极开展森林植物检疫，病虫害普查等工作防患于未然。一旦发生，及时组织技术力量，采取“土洋结合”的办法，进行灭治。1991年，县林业局专门设立森林病虫害防治站，具体负责苗木检疫和病虫害防治等工作，使森林病虫害防治步入专业化、经常化的轨道。

1.苗木检疫

1992年5月至10月，县林业局组成12人普查组，对全县范围的森林资源检疫对象普查。普查确定具有代表性普查片区15个，调查小区12个，调查树种15个。普查对象除按国家规定的20种检疫对象病虫外，还根据省府办公厅〔1986〕119号文件确定的马尾松疱锈病、泡桐丛枝病、毛竹枯梢病、板栗疫病、青杨天牛、光肩星天牛、日本松干蚧、坡面材小蠹、暗枝材小蠹九种危害较大的病虫作调查，对一般性森林昆虫作采集。普查发现，县境有马尾松疱锈病、青杨天牛、光肩星天牛3种检疫病虫；有云斑天牛、星天牛、松褐天牛、二星叶甲、楸螟、杉炭疽、松赤枯病7种危害较大的虫害和病害。

1996年9月，对各乡（镇）苗木进行产地检疫调查。共调查地块23处，面积74亩，检疫苗木209.6万株（其中马尾松133.6万株，柏木50万株，柳杉4.8万株，杉15万株，华山松6万株），检疫发现，因洪涝害感病苗木3万株。1997年4月，由县林业局森林病虫害防治站牵头，组织各乡（镇）林业站专兼职检疫员共12人分乡（镇）全面铺开野外调查，历时9个月，共踏查10个乡（镇），75个村，2.44万亩林地。完成国家林业局发布的35种森林植物检疫对象调查，发现锈色粒肩天牛、双条杉天牛、菊花叶枯线虫病、板栗疫病、柑橘溃疡病、松疱锈病等6种森林植物检疫对象在县境分布，并查清其危害情况及发展规律。

2005年对林业有害生物进行踏查监测，全县共踏查24.6万亩，踏查监测覆盖率为93.9%。还对400亩林木种苗地进行林木种苗产地检疫，占应实施检疫面积的92.5%，保证种苗产出质量。7月在全县范围内进行为期1个月的森林植物检疫执法行动，出动人员126人次，车辆40余车次，发放宣传资料300余册，开展检疫执法20次，检查松、杉、杂木等圆木、板材187万立方米。2006年起，开始对苗圃产地检疫，检疫苗木品种主要有柳杉、滇柏、刺槐、女贞、香樟、桂花、小叶女贞、红叶石楠等。至2010年，累计检疫苗圃8790亩次。

2、病虫害调查

1978年6月，省、地、县联合组成森林昆虫调查组，在城关小营林场、久长驴坊林场、六广中心林场和阳早天然松林等4个点进行森林昆虫调查。共采集昆虫标本31件167种，其中较多的有金龟子22种，金花虫类16种，蝽类15种，瓢虫类13种，象鼻虫类11种，天牛类6种，鳞翅目幼虫5种。同时查出主要森林病虫害有马尾松肿瘤病、马尾松赤枯病、杉木黄化病、杉木落叶病、杉木炭疽病等。

1980年8月，县林业局抽调23名林业干部组成森林病虫害调查组，在全县范围内开展森林病虫害普查。调查森林面积7924亩，有1895亩发生病虫害，并详查病害树种26个，发现病虫害70种和虫害170个，采集病虫害标本182个。1982年组织10名林业技术人员进行复查，调查森林面积4400亩，采集标本74个，发掘主要树种27株，发现病虫害45种。

2000年，抽调23名林业干部经过培训后在全县范围内开展全面经济林病虫害普查工作。共普查经济林面积6.33万亩，发现有经济林病虫害有21种，其中危害较大的病害有板栗白粉病、栗芽枯病、梨黑星病、黑斑病、桃褐叶穿孔病、流胶病、缩叶病、花椒锈病等8种；主要虫害有栗瘿蜂、柑橘瘤鼻虱、柑橘天牛、尖尖蚜、白蜡蚧、潜叶蛾、花椒肉蝶等7种。采集制作标本31个，其中干标本17个，浸泡标本14个；又分为病害标本14个，虫害标本17个。

2001年10月，按照贵阳市林业局的统一部署，在全县范围内开展松材线虫害普查工作。经调查，全县受害面积0.7万亩，枯死木1.71万株，濒死木1.08万株。较为严重区域有谷堡乡折溪、下硐、六屯乡全兴、龙场镇白莲和六广镇合兴等村。除及时采取救治措施外，还作出加强林区管理，严禁带病木材流通，林管员分片定点做好监控等决定，防止病源的传播蔓延。

2005年，县森林病虫害防治检疫站对全县17.2万亩松森全面实施松材线虫病的监测预防工作，全年共镜检样品781个，未发现松材线虫病。至2010年，全县累计监测调查森林资源2300万亩次，预测预报发生林业有害生物7.14万亩次，测报准确率达93.9%。经检测调查，县境尚未发现检疫性林业有害生物。

3、病虫害灭治

1978年，发现小营林场200亩华山松遭象鼻虫害，即用6%可湿性六六六溶液喷杀；中心林场100多亩马尾松遭松纵坑切梢小蠹虫，施撒6%六六六粉于根部；驴坊林场有双条杉天牛和苹果枝天牛，用90%敌百虫溶液喷射树干，使3个林场虫害得到制止。

1991年，县林业局设立森林病虫害防治站，以各区、乡（镇）林业站为病虫害监测报警点，在林地相对连片地点聘请兼职检疫员，建立森林病虫害检疫防治网络，对防治工作进行经常化、规范化管理。经调查发现县内森林病虫害主要有松毛虫、银杏大蚕蛾、松褐天牛、金龟子、栗实象和松赤枯病，危害树种主要是马尾松次生林。防治措施一般采取伐出衰弱木、清理林区卫生、对伐倒木及时进行加工处理等防止蔓延；对虫害采取喷施农药速灭杀丁、摘茧、捉虫、间伐或间移等措施。1996年，城关镇木厂片区暴发马尾松毛虫害，采用“林丹”烟剂熏蒸，使林区有虫害株率从96%下降到15%。2001年，在六屯、六广、大石、洒坪等乡镇的部分林区发生银杏大蚕蛾虫害，面积达2000亩。采取人工防治与生物防治、化学防治并举，发动群众折茧1500公斤，用50%马拉松乳剂、5%杀螟松乳剂、90%敌百虫晶体加水防治，防治效果80%以上。2002年，发生病虫害面积7330亩，其中云南松毛虫害30亩，银杏大蚕蛾害2300亩，松褐天牛害5000亩，发动群众摘茧4767公斤集中烧毁，喷洒百僵菌1000公斤，防治率达75%；为防止松材线虫病传入县境，应用天牛引诱剂监测防治天牛，采用M99—131诱剂（液态）折叠式撞板型诱捕器开展引诱天牛试验工作，降低虫口密度，收到很好的预防效果。2003年，在六广、洒坪、谷堡等乡（镇）发生虫害面积共1.42万亩，其中松褐天牛5000亩，云南松毛虫害30亩，银杏大蚕蛾害300亩，尺蠖害300亩，蛴螬害9190亩。当年采用人工摘茧和喷洒百僵菌、辛硫磷进行防治。

森林虫害防治

2005年，在龙场、谷堡、六桶、久长、扎佐等地发生松褐及银杏大蚕蛾等森林虫，成灾面积600亩，主要采用释放“肿脚蜂”6.4万只防治松褐天牛和施放白僵菌5100公斤防治银杏大蚕蛾。至2010年，全县森林病虫害累计防治7.01万亩次，占林业有害生物发生面积的98.3%。其中无公害防治面积6.98万亩次，占累计防治亩次的99.6%。通过防治，全县未暴发林业有害生物灾害。

五、林产品

（一）林木产品

原木　为县内主要林产品，用途广泛，主要用于城乡房屋修建、矿山坑采及电力传输等。建房用圆木主要有房梁、立柱、楼枕、檩子、椽子和架材等，大料多以杉木为主，椽子多为杂木。矿山坑采主要用作坑道支撑坑木，木材以松木为主，因其内含油质耐腐蚀为一般木材所不及。电力传输主要用做木质电杆，一般以杉木为主。20世纪90年代，城乡建房砖混结构逐步取代其他结构，木材使用逐渐减少，电线杆亦被水泥电杆和铁塔式电杆所代替，仅有矿采坑木还继续使用。

原木

木枋　俗称“枋子”，多为20厘米以上圆木解成，厚度一般在3厘米以上，最厚可达8至10厘米，特殊用途的木枋可达15至20厘米厚。木枋材质主要有杉、松、梓木、柏杨等。可用于制作为家具、门窗、农具等，也广泛用于建筑、运输等领域。

木板　俗称“板子”，多为15厘米以上圆木解成。厚度一般为2.4厘米（俗称八分板），最薄的有0.8至1厘米厚。板长规格一般2米长，也有按特殊要求大于或小于2米长的木板。材质和用途大致与木枋相同。

制材 主要有较为标准的木枋和椽皮。标准木枋一般为松、杉木制成，规格一般为200×12×5厘米。一般木材商店均有销售。主要用于建筑和制作家具等。椽皮一般为松木制成，规格为200×12×2.5厘米，主要用于房屋盖瓦之用。建造瓦房时，将椽皮按“4寸椽皮5寸沟”规格固定在檩、梁斜面上。20世纪70至80年代在木材市场有大量椽皮销售，90年代后椽皮逐步消失无人使用。

柴薪 砍伐的灌木或采伐圆留下的枝杈多用作柴火，是缺煤地区民间主要燃料，其余地区也将其作为辅助燃料。民间砖、瓦和泥陶烧结均需将其作为引火材料或燃料。

木器制品 农具主要有犁、耙、风簸、挞斗、秧盆、粪桶等，家具主要有如床、柜、屉、桌、橙、椅等。木制农具可定制或在农资商店购买，家具可定制或家具商店购买。

原竹 主要有绵竹、苦竹、金竹、慈竹、桂竹、楠竹、水竹、刺竹等种类。分2厘米以上和以下两种，2厘米以上竹子可辟竹篾编制农具、家具等；2厘米以下称为竹条条，可编竹篱笆、竹楼笆或为垂直蔓生蔬菜的攀爬物等。原竹一般在各个集镇场天竹木自由市场有售，也有专门的竹木商店销售。

竹制品 县内主要有竹席、箩筐、背篼、撮箕、提篮、簸箕、竹筛等竹制农具和家具。

（二）林副产品

茶叶 全县各地均有，多产于龙场、扎佐、六屯、久长和谷堡等乡镇。其中，六屯茶具有色红、味浓、清香特点，为境内茶叶之特产。采茶多在清明摘第一道，夏初摘第二道。传统制茶时用大火炒软、手工揉搓，文火焙干。1978年全县办起大、小茶园22个。六屯公社和久长公社茶园，采用机械化制茶，提高产品质量。1979年，茶园地达900多亩，收购16.3吨。实行土地联产承包责任制后，各地茶园实行承包，分散茶树转入家庭联产承包，农民在责任地中不断扩大种植。2010年，全县茶叶种植1200亩，产茶55吨。

水果 全县各地均有出产，品种有梨、桃、李、杏、柿、樱桃、花红、石榴、枇杷、山楂、枣、拐枣、柑橘、猕猴桃和葡萄等。特产早些年有王官梨、扎佐大红袍花红、六广河边柑橘，近些年有乌栗红星猕猴桃、古隆金秋梨和六广白花桃。2010年，全县各类水果种植面积达22.77万亩，水果产量2.46万吨。

生漆 全县各地均有出产，多产于西北部河谷地带。1981年林业“三定”后，程官乡高仓村建立漆树基地，全村自留山植漆树2000多亩，20多万株。洒坪乡猫洞河两岸村民，亦大量种植漆树。到2010年，全县生漆产量10吨。

五倍子 县内大部分地区出产，农业合作化时期，毁林开荒，产量大幅度下降，后结合整社、宣传“三忌一留”，即忌在林地铲草积肥，忌采倍叶喂猪和垫圈，忌砍断倍树或扳折倍枝采摘，并在采摘时每株留1至2个五倍子，让其自然爆裂，使倍蚜虫来年繁殖。至2010年年产量50吨。

桐籽 主产区在西北部河谷地带，原多为自然生长繁育。1978年，“小秋收”农民采集桐籽，全县收购桐籽3000多吨。1981年实行家庭联产承包后，部分村民认为田边地角的油桐树影响粮食生产，纷纷砍树，致桐籽产量下降，1982年全县仅收购桐籽40公斤。1994年，为发展少数民族聚居地区经济，大石乡党委、乡政府因地制宜，发动村民种桐籽1000亩。2010年，全县收购桐籽28吨。

干果 盛产于县境西北部乡镇，主要是核桃和板栗。板栗多为林间自然生长繁育，核桃多植于农家房前屋后。家庭联产承包后，政府组织群众开发非耕地，调整农村产业结构，发动群众连片种植，到2010年，全县板栗种植8000亩，核桃2000亩，核桃产量31吨，板栗产量77吨。

第六节 农田水利

农业集体化时期，水利设施建设坚持以“小型为主，配套为主，社队自办为主，加强管理，狠抓实效。”的方针，冬春季节全县大搞农田水利建设。当时兴修的大批水利设施，由于设计标准偏低，工程质量差，配套不全，老化失修，水库病险，以致留下很多后遗症。1980年，水利方针改为“搞好续建配套，加强经营管理，狠抓工程实效；抓紧基础工作，提高科学水平，为今后发展做好准备”。随着中央和地方财政体制改革，实行“划分收支、分级包干”体制，水利投入开始逐步减少，基建投资、防汛维修费大部分、农田水利事业费全部由县财政安排，水利建设受到很大的影响。1984年，为巩固农田水利设施的效益，政府通过以工代赈重点支持农村水利建设。1986年，水电局增设水土保持办公室，县财政增加水利投入，水利资金基本恢复到1980年财政包干时的水平。同时在区乡建立水利管理站、工程专管机构和群众管水组织三个层次的基层服务体系，并按标准解决基层水利和水保管理服务机构人员编制。

1988年，贯彻《中华人民共和国水法》，规范水资源开发、利用、防治水害，促进水利事业的改革与发展，水利事业走上依法治水的轨道。1989年，贯彻国务院《关于大力开展农田水利基本建设的决定》精神，进一步加强水利建设，县把农田水利基本建设作为一项长期任务列入计划，把水利建设作为重要工作来抓。“八五”期间，提出“加强经营管理，提高经济效益为主”的治水方针，水利投入逐年增加，建设明显加快，并提出走“水利为社会，社会办水利”的思路，采取多元化、多层次、多渠道筹集水利建设资金，保障水利建设事业发展。

1996年，县由安顺地区划属贵阳市管辖，水利事业发展迎来机遇，水利建设再兴高潮，工程标准提高，资金投入加大，水利建设又上一个新台阶。1999年，县结合全国西部大开发机遇，做出全县水利建设的长远规划，制定新的水利发展战略部署。在2000年制定的“十五计划”中将水资源可持续利用提高到保障经济社会发展的战略高度，执行中央提出的“全面规划，统筹兼顾，标本兼治，综合治理。坚持兴利除害结合，开源节流并重，防洪抗旱并举，下大力气解决洪涝灾害、水资源不足和水污染问题”新的治水方针。

2000年实施“百村人畜饮水工程”，2001至2004年实施国家二期“渴望工程”和国家农村饮水解困工程。资金采取政府投入为主、农户自愿投入、其他社会投入为补充的多元化投入机制，实行“一事一议”开展农村基础设施建设。至2005年，全县农村人畜饮水困难问题基本解决。2006年，水利建设把坚持节约资源和保护环境作为工作重点，着重加强水、大气、土壤等污染防治，改善城乡人居环境，兴修水利突出防治水患。至2010年，县把农田水利作为农村基础设施建设的重点任务，严格

岩鹰山水库

水资源管理，注重科学治水、依法治水，突出加强薄弱环节建设，大力发展民生水利，不断深化水利改革，加快建设节水型社会，促进水利可持续发展。

一、水利建设

（一）蓄水工程

县内绝大部分水利设施为20世纪50—70年代修建，规模较大的主要有岩鹰山、蚌壳堰、高潮、浪潮、烂沟、和阁老寨等水库。80年代，全县水利工作主要以加强经营管理、发挥工程效益为目的。但是，由于之前修建的大批水利设施设计标准偏低，大多是土法上马，设施不配套，年久失修，水库病险，以致留下很多后遗症。1985年香巴房水库建成后，水利工程建设重点转移到工程管理和除险加固及配套建设上来。至1990年，全县共建蓄水工程247处，蓄水量3750万立方米，有效灌溉农田面积3.96万亩。其中，小Ⅰ型以上水库7座，总库容2891万立方米；小Ⅱ型水库20座，总库容653万立方米；山塘220口，总库容206万立方米。

1996年，县划归贵阳市管辖后，水利项目任务和规模逐渐加大，特别是1998年后，对水库除险加固、渠系配套等工程项目逐渐增多，资金投入越来越大。2001年进一步加大水利建设投入，新建小山塘、小水池、小水窖“三小”水利工程226个，使全县蓄水量增加12.25万立方米。2003年，政府通过国家开发银行贷款，解决农村基础设施建设问题，先后新建小箐龙塘、龙场金沟、中哨坝、扎佐新民4座山塘和箐沟小Ⅱ型水库。到2010年，全县共建各类水利工程619处。其中，蓄水工程254处，蓄水3931.7万立方米，保证灌溉面积6.07万亩，有效灌溉面积5.45万亩；引水工程164处，引水流量2.55立方米/秒，灌溉面积2.1万亩；电力提灌站192站，总装机204台，容量5200.5千瓦，总灌溉面积3.1万亩。

小Ⅰ型蓄水工程概况表

表3—01—07

工程名称	所在地（村）	集雨面积（平方公里）		总库容（万立方米）	兴利库容（万立方米）	设计灌面（万亩）	有效灌面（万亩）	保证灌面（万亩）	坝型	正常高水面（亩）
岩鹰山	小箐乡新场、万兴、凤凰村	石坝	4.3	930	440	2	1.57	1.27	砌石拱坝	873
	小箐乡新场、大林村	土坝	10.2	825	800				均质土坝	1038
蚌壳堰	久长镇金桥、驴坊、中心村	15		500	338	1.3.	0.85	0.71	均质土坝	780
高　潮	扎佐镇丁官、龙王村	6.5		112	90	0.4	0.35	0.22	均质土坝	225
浪　潮	扎佐镇石竹、三元、大山村	8.5		245	138	0.27	0.23	0.14	均质土坝	480
烂　沟	谷堡乡谷堡村	4.5		135	111	0.6	0.55	0.43	均质土坝	194
阁老寨	龙场镇水塘、高仓村	14.7		114	60	0.51	0.30	0.25	均质土坝	214
香巴房	六屯乡独山村	156.6		138	138	原用于发电，2003年改作旅游			砌石重力坝	348

小Ⅱ型蓄水工程概况表

表3—01—08

工程名称	所在地（村）	集雨面积（平方公里）	库容（万立方米）	兴利库容（万立方米）	设计灌面（亩）	有效灌面（亩）	坝　　型	正常水面（亩）
营盘山	龙场平地	1.75	84	63	600	500	均质土坝	161
黑　山	龙场小营	0.5	24	20	400	400	均质土坝	100
古　隆	谷堡折溪	2.1	58	34.5	782	600	均质土坝	144
许家田坝	谷堡上花	0. 563	28	22	610	610	均质土坝	54
把　七	扎佐把七	0. 75	30	22	600	550	均质土坝	87
清　塘	扎佐马鞍山	0.51	27.8	17	700	600	均质土坝	102
西　苗	扎佐双月	1.2	16.4	10.8	692	692	均质土坝	49.5
黄土冲	扎佐双月	0.5	10	6.8	403	403	均质土坝	30
后　洞	扎佐长坡	4.8	24.7	16.4	1100	700	重力砌石	58
石　桥	六屯高峰	2.55	40.5	29.34	500	500	均质土坝	105
林　场	六屯高峰	1.33	14.4	7.66	300	300	均质土坝	42.7
流白水	六屯安全	1.2	34	22.5	500	500	均质土坝	83
盐井冲	久长芦山	1.2	46.6	40.5	1300	700	均质土坝	126
孟　冲	久长栋青	2.25	72	59	1300	1200	均质土坝	171
田家寨	久长金桥	2.38	42	31	500	500	均质土坝	97.5
烂木桥	久长栋青	2	22	16.2	300	计入孟冲	均质土坝	84
小　河	小箐大林	1.2	17.3	12.85	1200	400	均质土坝	50
新　坪	六广新坪	0.51	20	14.5	500	500	均质土坝	51
大煤厂	大石回水	0.58	26	20.7	590	590	均质土坝	59.4
煤幺寨	六桶金星	0.65	13.8	10.65	525	525	均质土坝	37.5

（二）引水工程

全县绝大部分引水工程为20世纪50至70年代修建，其中规模最大的是岩鹰山水库渠系配套工程与水库建设同期进行。1978年，县专门成立岩鹰山水库配套工程指挥部，进行渠系配套工程建设后期工作。1985年年底，配套工程所有项目全部完成。共建有支渠12条长89.96公里，电力提灌站10站，电灌渠5条长28公里。但由于工程修建时，质量标准低（渠道大部分为石灰泥浆砌筑），加之干渠支渠不少地段处于岩溶发育和山体易滑坡地段，常有渠段垮塌和拉裂现象，影响水库效益的正常发挥。

从1985年开始，引水工程建设重点以防渗维修配套为主，同时动工修建大石岩湾排坡引灌工程。工程位于县城西北面大石乡岩湾村，水源位于邻县息烽县石硐乡大洪村边境，最枯流量0.08立方米/秒，集雨面积3.5平方公里。水源地处边界，地势较低，在大洪村排坡便流入溶洞汇入乌江。经相邻两村、两乡相互协调，同意大石乡岩湾村引用石硐乡大洪村排坡水源灌溉岩湾村耕地。工程由县水电局设计，在大洪村排坡修建拦水堰一座，配套渠道4.8公里，将水引到岩湾村的湾子、麻窝等组，灌溉耕地720亩。工

程分两期进行：一期工程于2003年年底动工，修建拦水堰1座，灌溉渠道2公里，2004年4月竣工；二期工程建渠道2.8公里，2005年建设完成投入使用。

2010年，全县共有引水工程165处，引水流量计3.09立方米/秒,有效灌面21770亩,保证灌面19640亩,其中灌溉面积100—500亩的小Ⅱ型引水工程10处，引水流量1.59立方米/秒，主灌渠25条75公里，有效灌面8510亩，保证灌面7840亩，引水灌面500亩以下的工程154处，引水流量1.5立方米/秒，主灌渠250条350公里，有效灌面14290亩，保证灌面12800亩。

小Ⅱ型引水工程概况表

表3—01—09

工程名称	所在地	所在河流	引水流量（立方米/秒）	设计灌面（亩）	渠长（公里）
长　堰	龙场镇幸福村	修文河	0.12	700	6
千功堰	龙场镇白莲村	修文河	0.12	600	4
水塘大堰	龙场镇水塘村	穿山堰河	0.05	500	4
瓦罐窑头堰	龙场镇新寨村	小桥河	0.1	850	5.3
瓦罐窑二堰	龙场镇新寨村	小桥河	0.1	600	2.2
洋霍堰	扎佐镇中营村	鱼梁河	0.2	1000	3
西冲堰	六屯乡西冲村	桃源河	0.3	1300	4.8
擦耳岩堰	六屯乡星中村	龙井河	0.1	850	4.4
天生桥工程	谷堡乡哨上村至洒坪乡新乐村	花桥河	0.32	1700	18.3
二道响水堰	大石乡大屯村	六广河右岸龙洞泉水	0.2	600	3.5
大石岩湾排坡	大石乡岩湾村	六广河水系地下水	0.08	720	4.8

岩鹰山水库渠系配套工程概况表

表3—01—10

渠　道		起止点	全长（公里）	渠道断面（高×宽米）	设计灌面（亩）
主干渠		从石坝2号隧洞至六广镇龙窝村水淹塘	19.16	±2×2	20000
引水支渠	小箐支渠	小箐大兴村尹家寨四号隧洞出口至郭田村	6.25	0.7×0.7	600
	马场支渠	小箐大兴村尹家寨至小坝村敖家丫口	11.3	1×0.8	2000
	洒坪支渠	大兴村一号渡槽上口至洒坪乡蛇场小坪上	12.7	1×1	3000
	宝山支渠	小箐大兴村石坎组至宝山村龙山	6.6	0.7×0.7	1000
	龙塘支渠	杨泗河下田坝接“八一”支渠至龙塘芦稿冲	9.2	1×1	1800
	大石支渠	从广田水淹塘主干渠至大石	8	1×1	1000
	红缨支渠	从广田水淹塘主干渠至兴中坪上水库	6.9	0.8×0.7	1000
	茶山支渠	从红缨支渠冒儿田分渠至洒坪蛇场坪上	9.6	0.8×0.7	1000
	中寨支渠	从红缨支渠关庄分渠至洒坪高寨村老鸦洞	10.1	0.8×0.9	1500
	后山支渠	从大石支渠广田岩湾处分渠至后山	3.5	0.8×0.9	1000
提灌支渠	崇恩支渠	从土坝右侧提水引至小箐尖山村黄泥田	7.35	0.9×0.6	1000
	八一支渠	从土坝前摇儿石提水至龙场镇放马坪	10.6	0.7×0.7	1200

（三）提水工程

全县提水灌溉主要集中在城关、扎佐和久长3个区，1981年全县有汽、柴油泵共260台，其中汽油泵170台，柴油泵90台；电力提灌站共有218座，装机221台，总装机容量6932千瓦，灌溉面积3.3万亩。继后，因部分提灌站管理不善导致报废，至1990年，尚存193座，装机206台，总装机容量5885千瓦，灌溉面积2.1万亩。其中，装机容量100千瓦以上的小Ⅰ型电灌站10座20台；装机容量20—100千瓦的小Ⅱ型电灌站22座25台；装机容量20千瓦以下的电灌站161座161台。1990年至2010年，全县先后又新建电力电灌站9座，其中小Ⅰ型电灌站1座、小Ⅱ型电灌站3座、小Ⅱ型以下电灌站5座，总装机287.5千瓦；此间农村用电普及，两厢电动水泵取代汽柴油泵。2010年，全县共有电力提灌站193座，装机202台，总装机容量6030.55千瓦，灌溉面积3.099万亩。其中，小Ⅰ型电灌站10座15台；小Ⅱ型电灌站23座25台；装机容量10千瓦以下的电灌站160座162台。另有小Ⅱ型以下电力提灌站160座，装机162台，总容量24.61万千瓦，灌溉面积1.46万亩。

2010年全县小Ⅰ型电力提灌站一览

表3—01—11

站　名	站　址	装　机（千瓦/台）	扬程（米）	设计灌面（亩）	有效灌面（亩）	设计流量（立方米/秒）	渠　长（公里）
蚌壳堰站	久长镇金桥村	600/4	33.5	10000	750	0.8	29.8
龙塘站	小箐乡龙塘村	100/1	95	300	300	0.048	2
鱼久（二级）站	扎佐镇葛马村	155/1	36	2800	2300	0.25	3.8
鱼久（三级）站	久长镇清江村	200/2	29.8	2200	1700	0.15	3.7
崇恩站	小箐乡新场村	100/1	32.2	1500	1500	0.16	8.6
洋坝田站	谷堡乡尖山村	120/1	60	200	180	0.02	1.3
兴隆站	六广镇龙窝村	100/1	92.3	300	250	0.03	1.6
后洞站	扎佐镇长坡村	175/2	45、54	1100	1050	0.1、0.3	9
轿子山站	洒坪乡轿子山村	100/1	175	300	200	0.03	未配
老虎洞站	谷堡乡平滩村	135/1	150	1200	580	0.05	2
合　计	10站	1785/15	—	19600	8810	—	53.75

2010年全县部分小Ⅱ型电力提灌站一览表

表3—01—12

所在乡镇	站　名	站　址	装　机（千瓦/台）	扬程（米）	设计灌面（亩）	有效灌面（亩）	设计流量（立方米/秒）	渠　长（公里/条）
龙场镇	城北站	县城北修文河	40/1	28	300	200	0.016	1.6/1
	岩脚河站	新水村岩脚河	28/1	28	300	250	0.05	1.5/1
	建新站	建新村祖师店	40/1	47	320	250	0.03	2/2
	龙滩站	建新村龙滩	30/1	47	300	260	0.03	1.7/1
	路家河站	新生村路家河	20/1	15	300	250	0.008	1/1
	艾家湾站	白莲村艾家湾	40/1	42	350	300	0.03	1/1

续表

所在乡镇	站　名	站　址	装　机（千瓦/台）	扬程（米）	设计灌面（亩）	有效灌面（亩）	设计流量（立方米/秒）	渠长（公里/条）
龙场镇	军民站	军民村	40/1	55	300	250	0.03	1.5/1
	龙井站	普陀村龙井	40/1	30	400	400	0.05	5/3
	水牛坡站	大地村水牛坡	38.5/2	28	400	400	0.06	4.5/3
	马关站	马关村马关	40/1	35	700	600	0.06	4/3
	高榜站	马关村高榜	37/1	50	300	300	0.027	1.5/1
扎佐镇	大桥边站	三里村大桥边	37.5/2	38	450	430	0.028	1.44/2
	丁官站	丁官村	40/1	32	600	400	0.032	5.5/3
	杨家寨站	葛马村杨家寨	40/1	35	500	300	0.05	3.8/2
	花鱼坑站	泗溪村	55/1	69	400	350	0.03	2.5/2
久长镇	上堡站	上堡村	40/1	47.6	400	300	0.047	1.5/2
	烽光清坑站	杨柳村	55/1	46	800	600	0.05	3/1
	清坑站	杨柳村	40/1	40	700	650	0.075	3.7/3
	洗马塘站	清水村洗马塘	30/1	19	500	500	0.06	4/2
	栋青站	久长镇	55/1	80	600	500	0.05	1.5/1
	茶山站	茶山村	55/1	57	400	300	0.04	1.3/2
六屯乡	石桥站	六屯乡	40/1	51	300	300	0.02	2.7/1

（四）农村人畜饮水工程

县境属黔中中低山地带，自然排洪效果较好，故当地有“不怕淹，只怕干”的农谚，所以人们不太重视防洪排涝工作。加上国家财力有限，防洪排涝工程一般是由群众自办，国家补助少量经费，效果不很显著。1996年7月，县境遭受百年不遇的洪涝灾害，直接经济损失达2300多万元。从1997年起，国家每年投入大量经费修建防洪排涝工程，到2010年，完成清江排洪等7处较大型工程，防洪排涝灌溉面积达3584亩。

清江排洪工程照片

清江排洪工程　久长镇清江村地形独特，全村大部分水田集中在两山之间，面积1500多亩，中部有一小溪，积雨面积6.5公里，一般流量0.02立方米/秒，溪水流过田坝至三坝入消水坑经地下汇入葛马河。凡因连续降雨80毫米以上，消水坑泄洪不及，小溪两岸的清江坝子千亩稻田就要被洪水淹没8—9天才能消退。集体化时期，清江大队群众动工兴建清江排洪

隧洞，长680米，横断面1.5×2米。国家补助经费10余万元，投入劳动力2000个，隧洞进出口进尺300米，工程由于资金不足干干停停至1982年全面停工成为半拉子工程。1991年7月8日、9日两天降雨155.8毫米，7个村民组受灾，淹没面积1070亩，淹没10天的洪水才退完，清江坝子种植的水稻不同程度受灾，造成粮食大幅度减产，绝收面积240亩，少收粮食40万公斤，直接经济损失30余万元。1996年7月初，清江村又遇特大暴雨，最长淹没49天，1000余亩水稻绝收。1997年，国家投资120.6万元，兴建排洪工程，工程1997年2月动工，11月完工建成排洪隧洞680米，成型断面1.5×1.95米，排洪渠2100米，最大断面2.2×1.5米，防洪排涝面积1070亩。

阳明河段治理工程 工程位于龙场镇阳明村境内，距县城3公里。工程主要目的是保护国家文物单位阳明洞和阳明山庄及河道两岸百余亩稻田免受洪水侵害。工程由贵阳市水利水电勘测设计研究院设计，贵州省水利水电勘测设计院承包公司施工，总投资52万元。从2001年1月5日动工，修建河堤2道96.5米，河岸护坡346.5米，片石小路380米，过河跳墩2处，拦河堰2道长58米。2001年5月23日竣工。

阳明河流取直改道工程

小坝排洪渠工程 工程位于小箐乡小坝村，距县城24.6公里，距小箐乡政府7公里，为县小坝流域水土流失综合治理工程之一。渠道全长1000米，断面2×1.5米，侧墙顶宽0.5米，底宽0.8米，高1.5米。工程投资20万元，于1998年11月开工，1999年4月竣工，防洪排涝面积300亩。

谷堡水口防洪排涝工程 工程位于谷堡乡水口村，距县城19公里，由县水利局设计，贵州省江河水利水电建设有限公司承建。工程于2001年10月15日开工，2001年12月10竣工，总投资28.9万元。完成工程项目有水口公路桥至拦河坝段河堤护砌154米，拦河坝1座10米，拦河坝上游河道疏浚与垮塌部位补砌长1160米。工程效益防洪排涝面积900亩。

修文河团鱼湾改道工程 修文河团鱼湾改道工程地处县城东北边缘，穿山堰河汇入修文河河口处。改道工程主要目的是将原河道截弯取直，使河水从长征桥下游直接进入主河道，改道河段长90米，宽30米。工程由县水利局设计，贵州省江河水利水电建设工程有限责任公司承建。工程2001年12月18日动工，2002年2月5日竣工，投资32.8万元。

木厂排洪渠工程 工程位于龙场镇木厂、干坝两村境内，距县城7.5公里。由县水利局设计，县建筑公司承建。于2002年10月4日动工，2002年12月30日竣工。建成排洪渠3.15公里，最大断面2.2×1.3米，工程总投资40万元，工程效益防洪排涝面积234亩。

（五）节水灌溉工程

县境节水灌溉工程从20世纪90年代初开始起步，1992年在六桶乡下坝村建小水窖138个，容积2898立方米，蓄水池20个，容积2038立方米，并配置部分管网，浇灌旱地1270亩，但由于当时种植结构单一，工程效益不明显。1996年，县划归贵阳市管辖，旱地节水灌溉工程建设围绕农村产业结构调整进程，修建一批技术含量相对较高的节水灌溉工程。至2010年，全县共建有小水窖4942个，蓄水容积达12.36万立方米，灌溉经果林、蔬菜地和常规种植旱地达面积1.9万亩。

驴坊节水灌溉工程 工程设计在久长镇驴坊村5组（龙灯坡）引水，引水流量0.011立方米/秒，用直径110塑管2740米引至2组贵遵公路左侧一山头，修建200立方米蓄水调节池1座，在灌区内建容积为35立方米小水窖60个，经调节池，用管网相互联通，接蓄水灌溉，并配置移动式喷灌机具10套，节水灌面1020亩。工程于2000年3月8日动工，2000年6月底全面完成投入使用。

谷堡乡水口节水灌溉工程 工程位于谷堡乡水口村，灌区属烂沟水库控制旱坡地灌区。工程设计在烂沟水库南北干渠水口村境内，干渠下建有容积300立方米蓄水池5个，利用自然落差在灌区旱坡地中配置输水管网11公里，设置喷水点280个。工程于2001年6月4日动工，2001年9月20日完成，灌溉面积为450亩。

马关节水灌溉工程 工程位于龙场镇马关村，设计灌溉面积1100亩。其中，果园1000亩，蔬菜地100亩。蔬菜灌区设计取马关河水，经高榜电灌站提到灌区制高点进入调节池，再由调节池通过管网，利用自压方式喷水灌溉；果园区主要通过修建集水池集水，局部水池以泵站提水辅助灌溉，共计修建90立方米水池14个，50立方米水池4个，30立方米水池11个，10立方米水池13个，配套管网1.73万米，设置喷水点80个。工程2002年3月28日动工，2002年6月10日建成投入使用。

大屯节水灌溉工程 工程位于大石乡大屯村，六广河右岸。设计在二道水灌渠下建蓄水池5个，容积550立方米，铺设管网18.6千米，以自压的方式进行喷灌。工程设计建喷灌站400个，灌溉蔬菜地400亩，经果林500亩。工程2002年8月动工，12月底建成投入使用。

平寨梭坡节水灌溉工程 工程位于谷堡乡平寨村梭坡，是全县无公害蔬菜种植基地之一。设计在村内莫家湾取水，用管道引至陈家湾，修400立方米蓄水调节池1座。在灌区内布置小水池（窖）151个，每个25立方米。用管网将其与调节池连接，整个工程共铺设管网2767米，设置闸阀控制进行灌溉。工程于2002年7月动工，2003年3月25日完成投入使用，灌溉蔬菜地250亩，经果林200亩。

幸福村节水灌溉示范工程 工程位于龙场镇幸福村境内，为贵州省节水灌溉应用示范与研究基地，属集科研试验、节水技术示范与技术培训为一体的高标准、高起点的节水灌溉示范工程。工程包括渠道防渗2.8公里；新建提水泵站一站，装机3台96千瓦，流量320立方米/小时，扬程50-81米；安装100千伏安变压器一台；铺设管道D200—D250型铸铁管1750米；建调节池3座，蓄水容积300立方米；建小水池20口；田间输水塑料管道26.36公里；大棚7个，其中塑料大棚5个，规格为6×80米，日光温室大棚2个，规格为7×80米；建灌溉自动化管理系统，新增节水灌面1660亩，其中喷灌300亩、滴灌110亩、低压管灌420亩；渠道防渗630米，旱地浇灌200亩。工程于2002年1月动工，至2004年底建成投入使用。

擦耳岩排洪灌溉工程 工程位于六屯乡星中村，距县城40公里，距乡政府2公里。由贵阳市水利水电勘测设计研究院设计，贵州省水利机械化实业总公司承建。2003年8月30日动工，2004年5月竣工。建成星中排洪渠5公里（含拦水堰坝、涵洞、人行桥等渠系建筑物），长田灌溉渠5.5公里（含拦水堰坝、涵洞、人行桥等渠系建筑物），工程总投资75.3万元。工程效益排涝面积460亩，灌溉面积520亩。

二、水土保持

（一）水土流失

农业集体化时期，片面强调粮食产量，大量毁坏森林植被，盲目垦荒，以至陡坡越开越贫，越贫越垦，水土流失严重，堰、河、塘淤积，生态系统恶性循环。1980年，全县森林覆盖率仅占总土地面积的9.3%。1982年调查，全县的流失面积达24.6万亩，占全县总面积的15%。1983年，县政府通报全县水土

流失情况，耕地面积只占土地总面积的51.86%，其中坡度在25度以上旱地占18.2%。土壤侵蚀类型以水力侵蚀和重力侵蚀为主，由土壤侵蚀引起的石漠化现象日趋严重，平均每年以1600亩的速度增加。全县水库、山塘因泥沙淤积而减少蓄水量140万立方米，减少灌溉面积3500亩，其中报废山塘54座，减少蓄水量29.32万立方米，减少灌溉面积1357亩。

20世纪80年代，采取退耕还林，坡改梯等措施治理水土流失虽取得一些成绩，但由于乡镇企业发展，大量建厂、挖煤、采矿等破坏森林植被，使边坡稳定性降低，引起滑坡、塌方、泥石流等严重地质灾害，水土流失治理依然严峻。2000年，全县水土流失面积318.13平方公里，占全县总面积1075.4平方公里的29.57%，其中轻度流失面积为262.06平方公里，占全县总面积的24.36%，中度流失面积为53.90平方公里，占全县总面积的5.01%，强度流失面积2.17平方公里，占全县总面积的0.2%。全县总土壤流失量达95.6万吨，年平均侵蚀数为每平方公里3005吨。

（二）水土流失治理

集体化时期也提倡治理水土流失，但均无实质性措施。1982年，县成立水土保持委员会，进行水土保持治理。1983年，县政府下发《水土保持工作的意见》，提出采取生物措施与工程措施，以植树造林为主的方法治山治水，保持水土。在制止毁林毁草开荒，乱砍滥伐，放火烧山，乱采矿山的同时，必须有水土保持措施，对违反规定，造成水土流失的，按《水土保持条例》、《中华人民共和国森林法》、《中华人民共和国环境保护法》追究责任；有领导、有计划，分期分批进行陡坡退耕，还林、还牧、还草，严禁任意开荒、扩大耕地面积，对35度以上的坡耕地一律停止耕种，25度至35度的坡耕地采取修造梯土，实行林粮、林果间作，对25度以下的坡耕地，逐步建成基本农田；大力植树造林，种草、封山育林，对灌木林、稀疏林进行补植，加强幼林抚育管理，明确水库、山塘、渠道、公路、村寨、铁路的绿化责任。8月，县水土保持委员会做出《小箐乡大桥沟小流域治理规划》，规划治理面积13.4平方公里，经安顺地区水土保持委员会和地区财政局批准实施。治理内容为：植树造林，涵养水源，对原有410亩用材林和178亩稀疏林实行封山育林，对已有2716亩乔木和灌材，实行轮流封山，作为薪炭林，逐步更新，满足农户烧柴需要；陡坡耕地退耕还林2559亩，修造梯田梯土1200亩，防止水土流失；发展多种经营，建苗圃30亩，发展以桃、李、杏为主的果园225亩等。至1985年年底，完成除部分退耕还林外其余治理项目全部完成，至1990年退耕还林任务全部完成。

1991年6月，实施《中华人民共和国水土保持法》及配套法规，为防治水土流失提供法律依据。1996年修文划归贵阳市后，水土保持工作力度进一步加大，县将水土保持办公室更名为水土保持监督站，负责全县水土保持日常工作，行使水土保持法律法规赋予的行政执法职权，对全县水土保持工作实施监督管理。是年县政府组织农业、林业和水利等部门在小箐、洒坪建立山、水、林、田、路小流域综合治理，规划治理面积4平方公里，涉及小箐乡、洒坪乡的3个村14个村民组771户3443人。1997年6月，县政府根据具体情况划大石和六桶两

山水林田路气综合治理

乡为水土保持“重点治理区”，面积159平方公里；划龙场、扎佐、久长和六广4镇为“重点监督区”，面积514平方公里；六屯、小箐、洒坪和谷堡4乡为“重点预防保护区”，面积398平方公里。主要采取生物措施与工程措施并举的办法，增大投入，采取积极有效措施治理水土流失。

1996年开始，采取以小流域为单位进行“山、水、林、田、路、气综合治理”，至2005年，共治理面积44.91平方公里，坡改梯及坡面整治0.24万亩，营造水土保持林2.43万亩。其中，1996年在小箐、洒坪乡交界部分治理面积4平方公里，1998年在小箐小坝治理3.88平方公里，2000年穿山堰河流域8平方公里，2001年马关河流域14.57平方公里，2002年六广松江小流域13.4平方公里，2005年修文河流域1.06平方公里。

同时县政府还制定治理开发“四荒”（荒山、荒沟、荒丘、荒滩）资源各项优惠政策，鼓励和支持对“四荒”资源进行治理，抓好农业综合开发，水土保持农民增收两不误。全县治理开发“四荒”5.44万亩，仅谷堡乡红星果园场种植猕猴桃、金秋梨等经果林达7000多亩，成为科技成果的示范基地和科技兴农的典型。至2005年，全县实施坡改梯工程6.626万亩。使坡土变梯土，减少水土流失，让过去的“三跑”土变成“三保”土，改善农业生产条件，提高土地生产能力。实行退耕还林（草）造林，凡25°以上坡耕地，分年度有计划退耕，全部植树或种草。到2010年年底，全县累计退耕还林造林7.91万亩，其中25°以上坡耕地造林5.01万亩，荒山造林2.9万亩。累计开发非耕地12万多亩，其中开发荒山荒坡11万多亩，共建经济林4万多亩，用材林7万多亩，培植中草药1万多亩。农业综合开发增加治理范围的植被覆盖率，减少水土流失，改善生态环境。

三、农田基本建设

农田基本建设主要是通过改良土壤提高单位面积产量，其措施主要有兴修水利改土造田，为保持水土避免流失大力开展坡土改梯土，为增加土壤肥力和结构采用生化手段改良土壤等。目的就是要充分挖掘和发挥土地资源的最大潜力，使农民增产增收。

（一） 改土造田

改土造田俗称“土变田”，目的是使耕地更加保水保肥，增加单位面积产量和产值。土变田在集体化时期均为人力施工，造价比较高，1亩土变田需要数十乃至数百个人工，但人多力量大，当时曾大量开展改土造田。1982年土地承包到户后，由于土变田改造成本高而逐渐减少。90年代随着农村产业结构调整，土地资源科学合理利用，种植经济果树和蔬菜，产值比种水稻要高得多，部分甚至高出数倍。有的农民将原有的水田改种经济价值较高的农作物，大幅度增加农民收入。水田优于旱地的价值就不十分明显，土变田的价值和意义也就不大。进入21世纪，可以采用挖掘机、装载机等机械化改土造田，减少人工，降低成本，但也仅限于挖筑鱼塘和改土造藕田方面，很少用于稻田改造。

专记：愚公式的大屯人

大屯村位于大石布依族乡西部。村境地形北、东、南三面环山，西邻六广河。过去唯有一条小路从手爬岩出入至大石。村内山多、石多、泥土少，曾被人们称为“石头上的村寨”。原本就是人多地少的大屯，1978年六广河下游乌江电站建成关闸蓄水，沿河边仅有的50多亩水田和部分旱地被淹没。

为解决村民的吃饭问题，当时的大队干部带领群众开始大规模改土造田运动。老支书陈国均说：“只要山上还有石头泥巴，我们身上还有两只手，又可以从头干嘛。”话虽好说，但实际情况是村内最大的特

点就是石头多泥土少，“田坎好砌，泥土难聚”成为摆在大家面前的一道难题。大队党支部召开群众大会，大家讨论解决问题的办法。最后决定发扬愚公移山的精神，先用石头砌田坎，再从远处搬运泥土来造田。大屯人造田采用的工具是“钢钎+铁锤+背篼”。大队干部带头，发动群众采取人背马驮的运输方法从远处搬运泥土来造田。为衡量工作量大小，他们采取按量计酬，搬运来的泥土用大秤称过计数，故称之为“称土造田”。这样艰辛的搬运过程是一般地方没有的事情，至今大屯人还依稀记得田中泥巴的斤两。大屯人“称土造田”的故事便由此传开，但六广河对面邻县寨子里的人却笑话他们说：“照你们这样搞法好费力哦，是我们宁愿饿肚皮吞苞谷饭咯。”大屯人说：“气力哪会有乱用的，今天辛苦，今后终有回报。”从70年代末到80年代初，在荒乱的石头上大屯人硬生生地造出300多亩水田和500多亩耕地，群众的吃饭问题基本解决，真让六广河对面的人们羡慕。

（二）坡土改梯土

集体化时期，大搞基本农田建设，开垦荒地，大量森林植被遭受破坏，造成严重的水土流失。1978年贯彻全国农田基本建设会议精神，全县开展山水林田路综合治理，一个冬春出工共6000多万个，搬运土石562万立方米，坡改梯328处，面积达1.87万亩。1981年，全县土地承包到户，林权尚未落实，大量森林被砍伐，毁林开荒现象死灰复燃。

1982年调查，全县森林覆盖率为9.3%，水土流失地24.6万亩，占总面积的15%；土地肥力下降，裸岩不断扩大，大于25度的坡地增加。为此县政府做出加强水土保持工作的决定，制定三年完成综合治理规划，组织群众修拦山沟、封山育林、垒砌梯土。1983年县成立水土保持委员会，领导和组织治理水土流失，要求大于25度的陡坡耕地一律退耕还林还草，在15至25度缓坡耕地进行坡土改梯土。至1988年全县坡改梯2500亩，水土流失的治理初见成效。1990年，进一步加大治理的力度，县由农办牵头，组织全县坡改梯工作。全县坡改梯4.9万亩，占全县旱地面积的27.95%。1991年国家对贫困地区开展“以工代赈”，县成立坡改梯建设指挥部，下设办公室，抽调精干的技术人员组成工作班子，专门负责全县坡改梯工作。严格按照统一规划、统一选点、统一测设、统一培训和统一实施的办法进行。选择10—25度的坡土地段，进行实地测设，绘制施工图纸，同时搞好同步工程和配套工程设施。根据小流域的特点，山、水、林、田、路综合治理，生物措施与工程措施相结合、综合治理与开发同步进行。有水源条件的地方，治理中一步到位、坡土改为梯田。对水土流失的坡耕地，砌筑土埂（水泥砂浆石墙），平整土地，改良土壤。配套修建机耕道、拦山沟、蓄水池、小水窖，变“三跑土”为“三保土”，对四面环山的槽子地，修建排洪沟，防止水打沙壅耕地。1992—2003年，全县集中大面积实施坡改梯工程，面积累计达8.75万亩。通过坡改梯工程，将坡耕地改造成为保土、保水、保肥的梯土，同时配合山、水、林、田、路的综合治理，有效地控制水土流失，提高土地生产能力，增加农作物单位面积产量，促进全县农业的可持续发展。

全县坡改梯实施至2005年国家各级财政累计投入资金1662.43万元，农民投工855.89万个，按每个工日10元计，折款8558.2万元。计划实施面积88762.1亩，测设图斑622个，实际完成92300.4亩，其中净增耕地面积20086.6亩。施工中，累计完成土石方478.6万立方米，砌筑土埂36328条1437.19千米；修筑机耕道及乡村公路113条123.57千米；修建排洪沟、拦山沟286条91.404千米；配套建设引水渠23条4.07千米；小水窖（水池）2724个25209立方米；结合坡改梯建设水保林7200亩，种植地埂树计62.38万株，有效治理水土流失面积62.3平方千米。全县坡改梯项目实施区共72112户、96990人受益，户均增加基本农田1.28亩，人均增加0.95亩；年人均增加粮食40.9公斤，增收46.50元。

（三）改良中低产田

县内耕地土壤类型多样，多数为黄泥田、黄沙土、黑砂土和砾质土，其中部分土地耕作性、适用性较差，跑水、跑肥、跑土属所谓的“三跑”土地。对土壤瘠薄，肥力条件差的耕地，进行改土培肥，通过增厚土层、增施有机肥等方式改良土壤，提高耕地生产力。对酸性较强的煤山地和锈水田施用生石灰调整酸性土壤的pH值。施用量根据土壤的pH值而定。

对“天晴一把刀，下雨一包糟”的胶泥重黏土土则掺和大量的垃圾灰、煤灰等沙性物质，使土壤结构疏松透气。掺混作业可与土壤耕作的耕耙或旋耕结合起来进行。对地势较高的瘠薄砂质土壤，采用客土法改良，挖掘塘、沟、岩洞等肥泥改良。但改良工程量大，一般宜就地取材，因地制宜，亦可逐年进行。也可在进行土地平整、道路与排灌系统建设时，有计划地搬运土壤进行客土改良。对山间糟谷、盆土低洼处和河沟边低洼积水地方或煤山泉水露地等的冷水田、烂泥田、锈水田，针对其化学性状及农业性状采用开沟排水、沉水的方法进行改良。并在冷烂锈水田中，采用半旱式栽培技术，有效地提高中低产田的产量和产值。施腐熟性圈肥、秧青，施锌、钙、镁、磷等有机肥及施石灰等方法以提高土壤肥力和降低毒性。

四、水利管理

（一）工程管理

1. 管理制度

1978年，由水电局管理股负责全县工程管理，下置高潮浪潮水库管理所、鱼久电力提灌工程管理站和岩鹰山水库管理所管理具体水利工程，其余一般工程按属地管理的原则进行管理，最小的由生产队或组管理，跨区域的由上一级管理。1981年5月，管理股改为灌溉管理股，专门负责全县灌溉管理工作。随着农村经济体制改革的不断深入，全县水利工作重心从水利建设转到水利建设与工程管理并重上来。

1982年，贯彻省水利厅《关于推行水利管理责任制的初步意见》，明确水利设施管理权属，制订管理措施，实行管理责任制，全县90%以上的水利工程都制订有工程管护制度。1983年，县政府颁布《关于划定水利工程保护范围的规定》，重新划定水利工程的保护范围，打桩定界，竖立标志，颁发土地管理证，并规定不准在水库、山塘内蓄水位以下耕种；凡小Ⅱ型以上水库土坝下游外延30米至50米，两端半径20米至30米和水库山塘保护区，25度以上坡耕地禁止耕种，已种者必须退耕还林、还草；石砌干渠、支渠两侧1—2米和干渠两侧外坡脚2—3米渠道保护区亦不得耕种。1985年，蚌壳堰水库纳入国营灌区由县水利电力局直接管理，同时香巴房电站也划属县水利电力局管理。

2003年8月，县政府又发文规定：根据工程规模、受益范围按照分级管理原则进行管理。小Ⅰ型水利工程由县水利局主管，设立水利工程管理所（站）；小Ⅱ型及其重点部位蓄水1万立方米以上的小Ⅲ型水利工程由乡（镇）政府管理；小Ⅲ型以下水利工程由受益单位或个人进行管理。各类水利工程设施受县水利局行业监督管理和技术指导。根据国家对水利工程实施保护的要求，继续执行1983年《关于划定水利工程保护范围的规定》，并进一步强调所有水库、山塘正常蓄水位以下和工程保护范围内严禁耕种。任何单位和个人不得将这些土地作为责任地承包耕种或划做自留地、饲料地。已经占有的，必须退耕还库还塘或停耕还林还草。蓄水100万立方米以上的岩鹰山、蚌壳堰、高潮、浪潮、烂沟、阁老寨、香巴房等

小Ⅰ型水库，大坝背水面坡脚外延30至50米，两端扇形半径20—30米作为水库的保护范围。蓄水10万立方米以上100万立方米以下的王官、营盘山、黑山、古隆、许家田坝、把七、清塘、西苗、黄土冲、后洞、石桥、林场、流白水、盐井冲、孟冲、田家寨、烂木桥、小河、新坪、大煤厂、煤幺寨等小Ⅱ型水库，大坝背水面坡脚外延15—30米，两端扇形半径10—20米作为水库的保护范围。蓄水10万立方米一下的山塘，土坝背水面坡外延5—10米，两端扇形半径5—10米作为水库的保护范围。蓄、引、提水利工程干、支渠两侧的保护范围应根据渠道大小和所在地形及地质确定。一般石砌干支渠道两侧1—2米，土渠外坡脚2—3米以内作为渠道保护范围。

2. 运行调度

1979年11月，岩鹰山水库土坝放水管断裂，漏水达58.5升/秒。险情发生后，水库管理所向县水利电力局紧急汇报，同时采取向石坝库区输水措施，降低水位，由于措施果断，险情得到控制。

1981年3月1日，水利部颁发《水库工程管理通则》后，要求小型水库参照《通则》编制科学运行调度方案。根据要求，县水利电力局安排各工程分别制订年度用水计划和防洪调度预案，进行科学的运行调度。岩鹰山水库在未实行计划用水前年亩均耗水1000—1200立方米，实行计划用水后，年亩均耗水464立方米。

从1982年开始，全县落实水利工程管护责任制，小Ⅱ型以上水库均订立申报用水计划，按计划供水、用水，轮班灌溉等用水制度，改善过去混乱的用水局面。同时要求各工程制订年度用水计划和防洪调度预案并严格执行，汛前在确保大坝安全的前提下，做好蓄水、保水和灌溉工作，汛期各工程要服从县防汛抗旱指挥部的统一调度，结合工程实际和气象预报，指挥水库管理人员蓄水或放水。

2000年4月，王官水库大坝引水涵洞出现浑水，工程管理人员向水利局汇报后，水利局请专家现场分析鉴定，发现险情重大并有垮塌可能，决定放空库水处理险情，未造成危险事故。

2006年10月，六屯乡石桥水库大坝右端迎水面发生地陷，洞径3米，深1.5米。县水利局接六屯乡水利站报告后局领导和技术员立即赶赴现场，采取开闸放水并注意观测等措施，控制险情，随后对其进行灌浆防渗处理。

3. 维修养护

农业集体化时期，蓄水、引水工程的维修、岁修，一般由工程所在公社、大队组织社员在冬春季节进行，工程量大的由县水电利局组织维修。1978年，县水利局争取安顺地区财政专项资金，对岩鹰山水库土坝进行培厚加固处理。1979年夏，发现施工导流管右管闸阀水胶损坏，漏水9升/秒。采取从坝顶钻孔灌浆，将两根直径为300毫米的导流管封堵，并用厚为0.8米的混凝土将出口两个闸阀浇筑堵死。11月，发现土坝放水管断裂，漏水58.5升/秒，放水失控，水库管理所采取向石坝库区输水的措施，降低水位。随后，县水利电力局做出设计，报省水利电力厅和地区水利电力局批准，将放水管灌浆封堵后，在大坝右岸山体开凿一座长90米，宽1.7米，高1.9米，过水流量3立方米/秒(灌溉用水量0.5立方米/秒) 的椭圆形混凝土构件衬砌拱隧洞，在隧洞进口安装直径600毫米双向转动闸门，并由省水利机械化施工处对土坝进行帷幕灌浆处理。同时对2号隧洞进口侧漏水点进行灌浆处理。

1981年农村实行家庭联产承包责任制后，一般水利工程的维修养护由工程所在区、公社和大队组织受益农户集资投劳在冬春季节进行。工程量大、投劳多、受益区农户难以筹集大量资金修复的水毁工程，由县在小型水利经费中适当补助。提水工程的检修、养护，由管理单位负责。若雷击、凝冻损坏的高压输电线路、机械设备，受益区农户无力修复的，由县在小型水利经费或抗旱经费中酌情补助。1981至1986年，水利部水电九局、省水利机械化施工处三次对蚌壳堰水库大坝、溢洪道基础进行帷幕灌浆，总进尺2700米。处理后，渗漏量由59.5升/秒减小到10升/秒。1983年，六屯乡流白水水库，因泄洪冲垮大坝左岸基础及溢洪道，县水利电力局补助物资，乡政府组织群众修复。1986年，由县水电局补助物资，群众投工投劳分别对营盘山、古隆、孟冲、煤幺寨等四座水库的涵管及闸门进行维修改造。对阁老寨水库、蚌壳堰水库、把七水库、清塘水库、西冲引水渠、擦耳岩引水渠、岩鹰山水库干渠、红英支渠、龙塘支渠、天生桥引水渠道等工程进行维修、防渗处理共2.3公里。1987年，又对杨家寨电灌站、西苗水库、孟冲水库、西冲引水工程、桃子沟引水工程等蓄、引、提工程渠道进行防渗维修，共计10.7公里。1988年冬至1989年春，完成蓄、引、提工程渠道防渗43公里，检修电力提灌站44站。

从1989年冬开始，一般水利工程的维修养护从防渗补漏、除塞清淤为主转变为以预防为主，首先是对一些病险水库进行除险加固，提高工程质量标准。对石桥水库和黄土冲水库进行除险加固处理，对蓄、引、提工程渠道进行防渗维修共42公里，整修山塘32口，检修电力提灌站48站。至1995年，对全县大部分小Ⅱ型以上水库进行除险加固处理和对全县小Ⅱ型以下的山塘水库全部进行完整治处理。同期，对全县的提水、引水工程进行常规养护维修，保证其全部正常运行。1996年7月，县大部分地区发生百年不遇的暴雨洪灾，全县的水利工程仅有蚌壳堰水库溢洪道尾端遭到冲坏，其余山塘水库均无大碍，经受住一次百年不遇特大洪灾考验。1996年下半年至1997年，全县的水利工程维修主要针对大洪灾造成的损坏。

1998年，首先从高潮水库开始对全县小Ⅱ型以上水库进行渠系配套处理，至2005年全部完成。2006年，第二次对小Ⅱ型以上水库进行除险加固处理，2007年完成石桥水库大坝灌浆防渗及修复处理，2008年完成高潮、黑山、烂木桥水库除险加固。至2010年，全县小Ⅱ型以上水库二次加固处理全部完成。

加固后的蚌壳堰水库大坝

（二）水费征收

1978年，全县用水仅有高潮水库和岩鹰山水库计收水费。其标准是高潮水库自流灌溉每亩每年1.2元，电力提灌每亩每年0.8元，由水库调节灌溉0.6元/亩。岩鹰山水库石坝库区6号隧洞前0.7元/亩，加粮食0.5公斤；6号隧洞后0.6元/亩，加粮食0.5公斤；提灌0.4元/亩，加粮食0.25公斤 。1979年调整为：6号隧洞前1.0元/亩，加粮食0.5公斤；6号隧洞后和洒坪支渠0.8元/亩，加粮食0.5公斤；提水灌溉按0.4

元/亩，加粮食0.25公斤不变；土变田的三年内按自流灌溉的50%收费；土坝库区底孔放水调节灌溉0.2元/亩，加大米0.25公斤。1984年又调整为：自流灌溉2.5元/亩；电力提灌和土坝、石坝下游改善面积1.2元/亩；旱地浇灌0.8元/亩。特殊灾害造成减产或绝收的，报经县政府批准后酌情减免。

其他蓄水、引水工程，根据当地实际情况，制定相应的收费标准。电力提灌工程，一般以抽水所耗电量计算，每千瓦时电除电费外，加收0.02元—0.05元作为水费。1985年2月14日，县政府根据省政府〔1983〕111号文件，重新制定水费征收标准：自流灌溉按2.5元/亩；提水灌溉，扬程在50米以下的按1.3元/亩，扬程在50米以上的按0.8元/亩；放库水调节灌溉的1.2元/亩，全县水利工程均按上述标准执行，当年共收水费1.26万元。

1989年，农用水费实行以粮计收，由灌区农户将水费粮随定购粮入库。县政府以修府〔1989〕14号转发省政府〔1989〕7号文件规定："农用水费实行以物计价，以粮计收。"农用水费计收粮食标准是自流灌溉每年每亩计收大米不低于6.5公斤；提水灌溉的，扬程小于50米的，计收大米不低于3.3公斤，扬程大于50米的，不低于2.3公斤。计收办法由工程管理单位根据当年灌溉用水情况，通知用水户（单位）应缴数额，秋后随定购粮一次交当地粮管部门。结算方法为粮食部门收取水费粮，除工程管理单位留出部分维护工程所需外，由粮食、水利部门参照当地当时的粮食议购价确定价格，报经县政府批准后进行结算，一次付给水管所或区水利管理站。结算后的粮食由粮食部门作议价经营。除农用水费以粮计收外，其余各类用水的计收标准和使用办法，仍按黔府〔1983〕111号和黔府〔1986〕85号文件执行。按照新标准执行后，当年即收取水费粮13.95万公斤，折合人民币19.86万元。1998年，随粮计收水费，改为水管单位自行收取。

2003年，全县水利工程农用供水执行新的收费标准。新标准是根据财政部、水利部和贵州省政府关于农用水收费规定，经市物价局、水利局和县政府审批通过。对小Ⅰ型蓄水工程农业自流灌溉供水综合成本水价为48元/亩/年；提水灌溉工程水价为48元/亩/年（机电提灌的燃料和电费另计）。按三年逐步调整到位的原则，2003年调24元/亩/年；为供水成本的50%；2004年调整到36元/亩/年；为供水成本的75%；2005年起调整到供水综合成本水价。对小Ⅱ型蓄水工程农业自流灌溉供水综合成本水价为44元/亩/年；引水灌溉水价为35元/亩/年；提水灌溉工程水价为48元/亩/年（机电提灌的燃料和电费另计）。按三年逐步调整到位的原则，2003年自流灌溉水价调整22元/亩/年；引水灌溉水价为18元/亩/年；提水灌溉工程水价为19元/亩/年，为供水成本的50%；2004年自流灌溉水价调整33元/亩/年，引水灌溉水价为26元/亩/年，提水灌溉工程水价为29元/亩/年，为供水成本的75%；2005年起调整供水综合成本水价。对小（Ⅲ）型及其以下农业灌溉水利工程，参照小Ⅱ型蓄、引、提水利工程综合成本水价执行。

（三）多种经营

县境气候温和湿润，水域辽阔，适宜各种水生动植物繁衍生长。民间素有利用堰、塘、田、池养鱼和在江河打鱼捞虾，利用河水、溪流碾米、磨面、榨油生产洋芋粉。20世纪70年代末80年代初，岩鹰山水库管理所在管理所周围、新村、2号隧洞管理房、土坝管理房周围已征拨的土地上种植玉米、水稻、洋芋、油菜、蔬菜，每年可收玉米1000公斤，水稻750公斤，蔬菜5000公斤。1979年，部分土地退还生产队，从管理人员中抽出部分人员养猪，年收入1500—2000元，并为养鱼和农作物生产提供饲料和肥料。省水利电力厅投资31万元，在岩鹰山水库万兴库区南面兴建一个鱼种场，建有孵化池、培育池33.7亩,管理房600平方米。每年培育草鱼、鲢鱼、鲤鱼鱼苗1500多万尾，产值近40万元。

1982年，贯彻水利电力部制定的水利从为农业生产服务，发展到为整个社会服务的方针和省人民政府《贵州省渔业生产管理条例》及省水利电力厅《关于在水电上普遍推行经济承包责任制和积极持续两户的通知》精神，放开搞活开展多种经营，利用县内水利资源和管理人员的技术特长，因地制宜开展水库、山塘、稻田养鱼，饲养家禽、家畜，种植农作物，开展农副产品加工，安装检修提水机械等，大力提倡“以水养水”“以电养电”的发展思路。

1984年6月28日，经县政府批准，召开全县渔业工作会，传达贯彻省人民政府和省水利电力厅有关发展淡水养鱼的精神。之后普遍推行承包水面养鱼的经济承包责任制。全县27个小Ⅱ型以上水库中，有21个被67人承包；220个小山塘全部被人承包；还有12人承包三段河流（4500米）养鱼，当年全县渔业收入5.2万元。同时，蚌壳堰水库管理所与金桥乡农户合资联办1个酒厂，农户每年包干交管理所2000元。管理所人员在已划定的工程保护范围内种植粮食、蔬菜，在库内养鱼。渔久电力提灌站安装3台打米机，为周边群众服务，年收入近3万元。1984年成立检修小组，为农村检修提水机械，年收入3000多元。还与葛马村联办小煤窑，年收入2000元左右。1998年，蚌壳堰水库管理所在发展渔业的同时，还发展山鸡养殖，年均产值达5万多元。2000年，又开展鸡鱼和生猪养殖，年均产值近6万元。之后至2010年，全县的蓄水工程，除部分未蓄水的水库和饮水水源外，大多数都已承包开展多种经营。

岩鹰山水库渔场

第七节　农业机械

1978年，全县农机总动力达5429千瓦，范围涉及农灌、农耕、栽插、植保、收获、农副产品加工和运输等方面。除简单的人力机械外绝大部分农机产权属公社、生产大队或生产队集体所有。全县农业机械由各公社经营，各公社办有拖拉机站管理拖拉机营运和维修。5个区农机管理站负责辖区农机安全生产管理工作。

1981年，全县普遍实行联产承包责任制，农业经营形式由集体统一经营转变为包干到农户分散经营，大马力拖拉机和大型耕整地机械等农机无用武之地，大部分被闲置下来，农副产品加工和运输等机械承包给个体经营。1983年1月，贯彻中共中央《当前农村经济政策的若干问题（草案）》文件精神，允许农民个人或联户购置农副产品加工机具、拖拉机和汽车从事生产和运输。原集体农机除电灌设施外大部分折价或拍卖转归私人经营。

1996年，县划属贵阳市，每年从市级财政拨付专项资金对农民购置耕作机械实行补贴，标准为25%，以后逐年提高。1998年5月，全县第一个“市级”农机化示范区暨第一支农机合作服务队在龙场镇幸福村成立，继后全县又相继建立起14个农机合作服务队，拥有各类耕作机械、排灌机械和加工机械等。实行有偿服务，取得良好的社会效益和经济效益。

进入21世纪，农业机械化步入快速发展时期。从2001年开始，由政府部门出资，受益村民投劳，大力修建机耕道。2004年，颁布实施《中华人民共和国农业机械化促进法》，不仅为农机化提供法律保障，而且中央财政、省级财政还分别安排专项资金，对农民和农业生产经营组织购买国家支持推广的先进适用的农业机械给予补贴。到2010年，全县建设机耕道2401公里，建有农机合作服务队18个，累计发放农机补贴619.8万元，农机总动力达17.59万千瓦，机灌面积7.86万亩，农机化水平达到30%以上，有力推进农业机械化进程。

进入21世纪农村普遍使用小型耕整机耕地

一、农用机械

（一）排灌机械

县内传统排灌工具有龙骨车（水车）、竹龙（大竹打通吸水用）、龙秆、戽水篼、戽水桶、枧槽、筒车等。1978年，较普遍使用汽柴油泵和电力提灌机械，传统排灌工具逐步退出历史舞台。是年，全县农机总动力5429千瓦，机灌面积2.38万亩。1990年，总动力达2.65万千瓦，机灌面积2.64万亩。2000年，总动力发展到8.15万千瓦，机灌面积3.89万亩。2005年，总动力升至11.53万千瓦，机灌面积4.89万亩。2010年，全县机灌总动力1.29万千瓦，机灌面积9万亩。

1. 汽、柴油机灌溉

柴油机抽水机 1978年，全县有柴油抽水机65台238千瓦，1990年，有340台1315千瓦，2000年有451台1947千瓦。2005年有580台2156千瓦。2010年，有102台336千瓦。全县推广的柴油泵机型及马力主要有175-5，190-10，195-15-12，2105-20，F160-3，R180-6等类型。

汽油机抽水机 1978年，全县有汽油泵108台238千瓦，1990有205台513千瓦，2000年有122台295千瓦，2005有104台262千瓦。2010年，有95台260千瓦。全县推广的汽油泵机型主要有F176-3，IE50-3，Q581-3.5，162-3，AK10型-10，R175-5，F175-5，IE40-3等类型。

2. 电力排灌

1978年，全县电力提灌站主要集中在城关、扎佐和久长3个区。全县共有电动抽水机280台415千瓦。20世纪80年代，因部分提灌站管理不善导致报废，至1990年，尚存193站，装机206台，总装机容量5885千瓦，灌溉面积2.1万亩。90年代，全县先后又新建电力电灌站9个，其中小Ⅰ型电灌站1站、小Ⅱ型电灌站3站、小Ⅱ型以下电灌站5站。总装机287.5千瓦。至2010年，全县共有电力提灌站193站，装机202台，总装机容量6030.55千瓦，灌溉面积3.1万亩。

3. 农用水泵

1978年，县内使用农用水泵主要是由县农机厂生产的3kg水泵，是年全县共有345台，1990年增加到435台。20世纪90年代初，县农机厂破产改制后，3千克水泵停止生产，县从外地引进农用水泵物美价廉，随着农村经济的发展，农用水泵品种逐年增多，主要有离心泵、水轮泵、水轮机、潜水泵等各种类型的小型农用水泵。2000年，全县农用水泵增加到1173台。到2010年，全县共有农用水泵2028台。

4. 喷灌机械

1978年，县农机局从遵义购进1套喷灌机械在县农场试验成功，但由于成本费用高，效果不甚明显，未推广普及。进入21世纪，农业节水喷灌技术随着农村产业结构调整，蔬菜、水果种植的需要又重新提上议事日程。2000年至2004年，县先后在久长镇驴坊、谷堡乡水口、平寨、龙场镇马关和大石乡大屯兴建节水灌溉工程，并逐步在全县推广。

2010年，全县喷灌管网长度64.19千米，喷灌点1921套（个），喷灌面积达5580亩。

（二）耕作机械

县境传统耕作工具主要有锄、钯、犁、耙等。自20世纪50年代末开始引进拖拉机耕整土地，到1978年全县已有大、中型轮式、履带式和手扶式拖拉机194台，并广泛用于农耕和运输。80至90年代，拖拉机主要从事运输，从事农耕较少。20世纪末21世纪初，国家加大对农民购买农机补贴力度，调动农民购买农机的积极性，农耕机械在农业生产中得到广泛应用，甚至有的地方出现取代传统牛耕的趋势。

1. 拖拉机

1978年全县拥有各类拖拉机194台，总功率3013千瓦。型号主要有热托—25A型、热托—25K型、D—40型履带式、东方红—54履带式、丰收35型、丰收27型、手扶式等拖拉机。主要分布县境中、东部地区的城关、扎佐、久长等区的东方红、马家桥、阳早、扎佐、三元、久长、清水等公社。有拖拉机的公社还办有拖拉机站负责管理拖拉机营运和维修。是年春耕前，县农机局从绥阳县请来两名手扶拖拉机技术员，在配有手扶拖拉机的10个公社组织手扶拖拉机耕地巡回表演，举办手扶拖拉机训练班。嗣后，阳早、东方红、久长等公社部分大队还成立机耕队，阳早公社手扶拖拉机12台下田，完成耕作1739亩；久长公社中型拖拉机4台下田，完成耕作3450亩。1979年，阳早公社农机站及东方红公社建新大队机耕队荣获贵州省农机局表彰。

1983年，随着农村经济体制改革深入，原公社和大队的拖拉机卖给个体户后绝大部分改变其用途，主要用以跑运输为主。从1985年开始，又大量新购和从外地购买二手拖拉机，一时间拖拉机几乎成县内运输主要工具。1987年，全县各类型拖拉机总数增达377辆，比1978年增加183辆。1988年起，原有一部分拖拉机因年久失修和长期超载缺乏维护保养而逐步报废，有的升级换代改购农用汽车运输，拖拉机数量逐步减少。至1990年，全县拖拉机总数减少为114辆，同期农用汽车增加至150多辆。

1996年县划属贵阳市管辖后，政府逐步加大对农民购买农机补贴，拖拉机数量开始恢复并逐步增加，1999年大、中型拖拉机发展到244台7448千瓦，手扶拖拉机发展到252台、2575千瓦。2000年大、中拖拉机发展到337台8602千瓦，手扶拖拉机增至415台4417千瓦。2005年大、中型拖拉机发展到675台、1.61万千瓦，手扶拖拉机增至687台、8492千瓦。2010年，大、中型拖拉机发展到1119台、2.91万千瓦，手扶拖拉机增至553台、7889千瓦。大、中型手拉机主要是用于农业运输，手扶拖拉机主要是用于耕地，从而促进机耕面积增加。

2. 配套机械

1978年，县内配套拖拉机使用的耕作机械主要有2铧犁、3铧犁、4铧犁、圆盘耙、钉齿耙、旋耕机等。手扶拖拉机主要配单铧犁和旋耕机。1979年，全县有大中型拖拉机配套农具271套，其中机引犁176套，机引耙28套，旋耕机67套；小型拖拉机配套机具30套，其中机引犁20套、旋耕机10套。全县机耕

面积达2万多亩。

1981年实行家庭联产承包责任制以后，拖拉机配套农具明显减少，1986年大、中型拖拉机配套农具仅2套，全县机耕面积仅42亩，拖拉机以运输为主，农机耕作处于低谷。到1990年大、中型拖拉机配套农具增到7套，其中机引犁5套，旋耕机2套：小型拖拉机配套机具30套，其中机引犁15套、旋耕机15套，全县机耕面积恢复到4572亩。1993年耕作机械增加，机耕面积达1.62万亩。

小型旋耕机

1996年，修文县由安顺地区划归贵阳市管辖，贵阳市委、市人民政府从市级财政拨付专项资金对农民购置耕作机械实行补贴，标准提高到25%；1998年购农具部分的补贴标准从25%逐年上升，到2000年购农具部分的补贴标准提高到40%，其中农民原来购有主机和单独购买的犁、铧、耙、旋耕机等同样按同一标准予以补贴。政府多渠道的购买农机补贴，提高广大农民购买耕作机械的积极性。小型耕作机械从1998年的17台发展到2000年的114台。其中，小型耕作机械（简称微耕机）型号有：中山—6型耕整机、桂花牌耕整机，丹霞—61型耕整机、凯马牌耕整机等，加上部分上海—50型、川农—15型、丰收—180型等大中型耕作机械。2000年大中型拖拉机配套农具12套，其中机引犁6套，机引耙4套，施耕机2套：小型拖拉机配套机具114套，其中机引犁30套、机引耙43套、旋耕机41套，全县机耕面积达3.21万亩。2005年，全县有大中型拖拉机配套农具12套，其中机引犁7套，机引耙4套，施耕机1套；小型拖拉机配套机具369套，其中机引犁190套、机引耙153套、旋耕机26套，全县机耕面积达4.83万亩。

2010年，全县有大中型拖拉机配套农具25套，其中机引犁7套，机引耙3套，旋耕机15套；小型拖拉机配套机具490套，其中机引犁490套、机引耙204套、旋耕机606套，全县机耕面积达12万亩。

（三）栽插机械

县内栽插机械主要是插秧机，1959年“大跃进”中开始使用县内农机厂生产的简易竹夹式插秧机，20世纪70年代中期，插秧机使用达到高潮。1978年，全县共有手动插秧机1220台，机插面积达1.8万亩。涉及21个公社，72个大队。1981年，实行家庭联产承包责任制，农户独立承包、自主经营、生产规模缩小、不利于机械操作，放弃机械插秧。此后，再未使用机械插秧。

（四）植保机械

20世纪50年代“大跃进”时期，县内开始推广使用手动圆筒式单管喷雾器，主要用于农作物病虫害防治。70年代，圆筒式喷雾器使用比较普遍。1978年，县内开始引进机动喷雾器。80年代中期后，背负式喷雾器逐步取代手动喷雾器，机动喷雾器主要在农场、茶场和林场使用。

1. 手动喷雾器

1978年，一般1个生产队配有2至3台圆筒式单管喷雾器，喷药前先打足气后再背在身后单手喷药，待气耗尽药液雾面变小时又放在地上打足气，再背起喷药，如此反复多次，耗时费力，工效不高。1981年，农村一般是3至5户农民使用1台圆筒式单管喷雾器。

手动喷雾器

1982年，遭受不同程度的病虫害，县政府购置工农—16型背负式喷雾器99台，无偿送到灾区灭虫，农资公司调进背负式喷雾器607台。背负式喷雾器克服圆筒喷雾器喷药停机打气的缺点，只需兑装好药水即可直接背在背上，一手打气，一手喷药，使用极为方便。1986年，县境遭遇历史罕见的虫灾，虫势猛，虫种多，受灾面积大，据县植保站调查，全县水稻病虫害面积为7.23万亩，占插秧面积的79.9%，苞谷病虫害面积为2.56万亩，占种植面积的20.5%，县委、县政府组织召开灭虫紧急会议，并成立县扑灭虫灾指挥部，组织各科局有关人员及农科干部36人分赴各区宣传和指导扑灭虫灾。同时县财政局拨出专款购买各种农药320吨，喷雾器374台分配到各受灾地区，经过全县人民的一致努力，战胜特大病虫害。1990年，背负式喷雾器增加到1288台，1999年市级财政补贴购背负式喷雾器150台防虫救灾，2000年有3010台，2005年有4365台。2010年，全县背负式手动喷雾器发展到1.49万台。

2. 机动喷雾器

1978年，县内购进5台担架式机动喷雾器，设计为一机带双管，射程远、工效高，特别是油菜在结夹期遇蚜虫，使用效果最好，但机体大而笨重一般要4人以上操作，田间转移不方便，维修较困难，此后未再引进。

1980年，引进东方红—18型机动喷雾器进行灭虫。此机具有一机多用、不用水、工效高、使用方便等特点。主要用于水稻、玉米、小麦、油菜等大田作物的虫害防治、也可用于林木虫害防治

1987年，县内引进背负式机动喷雾器30台。背负式机动喷雾器使用小型汽油机作动力，工作效率高，喷雾效果好，使用方便。不足的是自重大、噪音大、污染大、机温高、机手作业环境差，维修专业技术要求高，加上汽油成本高，农民使用不很普遍。1990年，全县增加到44台。1999年，市财政补贴购背负式机动喷雾器20台。到2010年，全县背负式机动喷雾器共有137台。

（五）收获机械

传统农作物收获工具主要是镰刀和挞斗（俗称贯斗），一般采用镰刀割禾，挞斗脱粒。1959年，县农机厂从安顺购进一台脚踏打谷机并仿制成功，此后县内使用的脚踏打谷机绝大部分属县农机厂生产。20世纪70年代中期又引进和生产机动打谷机生产技术。80年代，全县农村已较普遍使用脚踏打谷机和机动打谷机，使用挞斗脱粒很少见到。90年代县农机厂破产后，县内使用打谷机由外地购进，机型多以机动打谷机为主。1996年，开始对购买打谷机农民实行补贴，农民购买和使用机动打谷机的积极性大增。进入21世纪，全县农村普遍使用机动打谷机，大多数为汽油机或单相小型电动机自制改装的动力打谷机。

1. 人力打谷机

1978年，全县较平坦的田坝地区生产队，部分使用脚踏打谷机，最多的生产队可达5台左右，全县共有1000多台。1981年，打谷机随土地折价变卖给个体农户或分配给几家农户共同使用。到1984年，全县拥有1056台。继后，因县农机厂停止生产和有的打谷机时间过长、损坏严重、缺少配件、废弃较多，

1987年全县仅存622台。1988年，县推广使用安顺地区农机科研所和万江机电厂生产的737型人力打谷机。1995年以后，全县范围推广的人力打谷机主要是国营万江机厂和息烽农机厂生产的短筒，小斗式737型人力脱粒机。

1996年修文县的行政区域划归贵阳市管辖后，由市级财政对购打谷机的农民实行补贴。1996—1998年农民购买一台737型人力脱粒机可获补贴20元，1999年对农民购机补贴标准作调整，从每台补贴20元调整为补贴30元。2000年全县人力脱粒机拥有量达4010台。到2010年，全县人力脱粒机的拥有量达5980台。

人力打谷机

2. 机动脱粒机

1978年，全县已有稻麦两用弓齿式脱粒机19台，同时县农机厂将打谷机加上皮带轮及电动机，改为电动打谷机，1979年发展到43台。1981年，全县农村实行联产承包责任制后，农户因耕地少劳力少，不适宜使用脱粒机，所以人力脱粒机仍被大力推广。

1988年，安顺地区农机局下拨1台杭州产“东抗HL—2020型”履带式联合收割机在县试用，经试验虽然性能好，工作效益高，在正常情况下8小时收割面积约12—15亩，而且从收割、鼓风、除草、装袋均为自动化。但因县境地处山区，机耕道路不通，田、土块面积小，坎坷不平，加之收割机工作前要用一辆农用运输车拖送到收割地点，并要找平台搭跳板卸下车，然后再搭跳板进入田块作业。运输、选点、过沟、上坎等极为不便，工作量大，投入人力较多，加之零配件缺乏，不适宜在山区地带推广使用。

1992年，从安顺地区农机研究所引进试验使用两台安顺产三厢动力电动稻、麦脱粒机，由于机身全铁，笨重难移，加上采用三相异步电动机，受场地、电源等因素制约，故未推广。

1999年，县推广使用万江机电厂生产以小型汽油机作动力的机动脱粒机，厂价1200元/台，市农机局补贴400元，农民实付800元。但因此机使用故障较多，至2001年全县才推广出20余台。

2005年，全县普遍使用的脱粒机，大多数为汽油机或单相小型电动机作动力的自制改装的动力脱粒机。这种机动脱粒机比人力脱粒机工作效率高，改装结构简单、方便，还能起到一机多用的效果，既能脱粒，又能改用于抽水、加工等用途。2010年，全县共有各类机动脱粒机422台。

3. 谷物烘干机

农作物收获后，一般要经干燥处理后才能收藏。县内传统方法是晾晒和用烘房炕干，如遇阴雨连绵季节，干燥处理不及时，造成大量粮食发芽或霉变。1979年，在城关镇新水大队砂锅寨生产队试用庆丰型烘干机效果良好。1980年，省农机局先后拨给县庆丰型堆放式谷物烘干机60台，安装59台，分布在全县19个公社、45个大队及县良种场和城关粮管所等。其中水稻主产区的水塘、王官、马家桥、扎佐、三元等5个公社安装最多。1981年秋收时节，县境连续受阴雨46天，严重影响谷物收获及公粮入库，烘干机发挥很大作用，全县烘干机共烘干稻谷133万公斤，使公粮入库得到保障。水塘公社一台烘干机就烘干稻谷6.45万公斤，实绩曾刊载《贵州日报》。

1982年，县农机局农机研究所吸收和学习遵义等地经验，进行粮、烟两用烘干机的试验，在六屯、王官公社选点进行烤烟烘烤试验成功。能提高烤烟质量，达到黄、鲜、净的要求，受到群众欢迎。农机科研所还为城关粮管所设计安装面条烘干房，采取热空气由上往下吹，吸气机从下部吸气排除的技术措施，解决烘烤面条弯曲的问题。1983年，由于烘干机是国家无偿投资，加之责任制后，土地承包到户，无人管理，被偷、盗、损坏，各大队安装的烘干机名存实亡。

2002年，贵州省农机局在县无偿投放3台大型电动烘干机，安装在久长镇兴隆村、扎佐镇大堡村和龙场镇平地村调试使用。经省农机局、市农业局专家和技术人员现场对谷物、辣椒、萝卜等进行烘干比对，所烘产品均达到标准技术数规定的指标要求，适宜在县境推广使用。但由于近几年天气好，农户收获的农作物晒得干。加上烘干机耗电高、耗劳力多，农户不是很需要，所以未大量推广。

（六）农副产品加工机械

传统农副产品加工工具和机械制米有擂子、水碾和石碓，磨面有石磨，榨油有木榨等。20世纪60年代逐步引进打米机、磨面机、榨油机等加工机械。70年代，又引进淀粉加工、制作米粉等机械。1978年安顺地区农机局下拨给修文揉茶机、炒茶机各2台，在六屯茶场、久长二关坝茶场试验推广应用，其工效高，质量好。70年代末，农副产品加工几乎是以机动加工机械为主，每个公社和部分生产大队安装有电动打米机，电动磨面机、榨油机也基本能满足县内需要。传统农副产品加工工具除石磨和石碓在广大农村还常用外，其余很少见使用。

1981年，全县农村实行联产承包责任制后，集体的农副产品加工机械承包给个体户经营。80年代中期，政策放宽，部分农民家庭购买农副产品加工机械经营致富，发展为农副产品加工专业户。90年代，部分农副产品加工专业户生产规模扩大，由过去的家庭生产发展为作坊生产，农副产品加工机械也随之升级换代。进入21世纪，农副产品加工机械向大小两个方面发展，一方面部分农副产品加工作坊需要扩大生产，加工机械产能需要提高；另一方面是农副产品加工机械小型化，以适用于农民家庭自用。

1. 粮食加工机械

碾米机 1978年全县已较普遍使用电动碾米机碾米，当年全县已有150台。1990年发展到465台，2000年发展到643台，2005年发展到950台，2010年发展到6530台，2.2万千瓦。

磨面机 主要用于磨面和饲料加工等。1978年，全县已有各种型号磨面机160台。1990年发展到320台，2000年发展到583台，2005年发展到1062台，2010年发展到1625台。

2. 油料加工机械

传统榨油方法是用石磨或水碾将油料碾碎，再用木榨采用挤压方式将油料榨出油来，此种方式劳动强度大、出油率不高。1962年，县开始引进2台电动榨油机榨油。1978年，全县已有榨油机15台，木榨榨油已全部淘汰。1980年全县拥有各型榨油机30台，1983年发展46台。20世纪80年代，随着县内外大型食油加工厂的出现，其加工设备先进，出油质量好，农村榨油机逐渐减少，到1988年仅有13台。1989年又开始发展，次年发展到90台，2000年

人工油榨

发展到131台，2005年发展103台，2010年发展212台。

3. 饲料加工机械

包括饲料粉碎机、铡草机和饲料颗粒机等。从60年代末期县内引进第一台饲料加工机械起，到1978年全县已有饲料加工机械15台、225千瓦。1990年发展42台、770千瓦。

20世纪末，随着农村产业结构调整，养殖业的发展，小型饲料加工机械需求不断增加。2000年全县饲料加工机械发展到794台、1385千瓦。2005年发展到1130台、2906千瓦。2010年发展到5445台、1.15万千瓦。县内历年使用过的饲料加工机械机型主要有湘农—440型，湘农—329型，FS—32型，红旗270型，风雷—1型，FS—306型，90—400型等。

（七）运输机械

传统运输工具主要有扁担、扦担、箩筐、粪篮、粪桶、背篼等，因其使用方便，至今仍在使用。非机动运输机械主要有独轮车（俗称鸡公车）、手推车和马车。其中，独轮车已于20世纪80年代被淘汰手推车和拖拉机运输成为农村运输主力。90年代后，农用汽车运输成为农村运输主力。

1. 非机动运输机械

独轮车 为一种古老的运输工具，俗称鸡公车。全木制成，独轮。载重为100至150公斤，最大载重为250公斤。20世纪50—60年代鸡公车的使用较为盛行。70年代胶轮手推车出现后，独轮车逐渐减少，80年代被淘汰。

手推车 最早的手推车为全木制成，左右各一木轮，俗称木制手推车，简称为手板车。此名一直沿用。20世纪70年代，充气胶轮取代木轮，车身轻便，载重量增大。胶轮手推车一般载重量为250公斤最大载重量右达600公斤。80年代交通方便的农村使用较为普遍，用作运输各种农家货物。进入21世纪，广大农村仍普遍使用，部分农民还专门到县城从事手板车运输服务。

马车 早先的马车均属木制胶带轮车，俗称“花角轮车”。一般载重量为500—600公斤。20世纪70年代，花角轮改装成充气轮胎，称作胶轮马车。此种马车要比原来的花轮马车的载重量提高30%以上，一般载重量为700—800公斤，最高时可达1000公斤。80年代，在县城出现有在胶轮马车上装上木架或铁架，周围和顶上用布遮阴的马轿车，有的还在车前部分加装一对板车胶轮做成四轮马轿车，人坐上去比两轮的更加平稳，专门运送县城至王官方向和马家桥方向的客人，继后部分乡镇也有出现。90年代县内各乡镇短途客运汽车开通后又逐步被淘汰。至2010年，县内仍有极少数使用充气胶轮马车。

农用胶轮马车

2. 机动运输机械

拖拉机 20世纪70年代末至80年代，县内拥有的拖拉机一机多用，农忙时从事农耕，农闲时跑运输增加副业收入。1980年，全县拖拉机的年运输量达811万吨公里。80年代，拖拉机除农业运输外，多数还从事矿产品、煤、砖、瓦、水泥、石料等建筑材料运输，成为县内运输主力。1987年，县内运输各大中小型拖拉机发展到264台，8727马力。90年代初期，农用汽车大量增加，拖拉机运输逐步减少。2000年至2010年，仅有一些小型拖拉机（俗称“狗儿车”）从事短途运输和工地转运。

农用汽车 从1983年开始，允许农民购买农用汽车，到1985年全县农用汽车增至58辆，到1990年发展到150辆。20世纪90年代，农用汽车运输取代拖拉机运输，成为县内运输主力，为县境内农村主要短途运输工具。至2010年，全县农用汽车增加到1576辆，总载重达7880吨。

二、农机供应

1978年，县置有农机供应站，隶属于县农业机械局管理，经营属国家计划管理。1980年，为方便群众，利用扎佐交通便捷的区位优势，在扎佐区设置农机销售供应点，继后又在县城马落坑设置农机零配件销售点。1984年4月，县农机供应站改建为农机供应公司，属县农机局下属国营企业，财务独立核算、自负盈亏，具有独立的经营管理权。业务主要销售中小型拖拉机、推土机、机耕耙、机耕犁、插秧机、柴油机、汽油机、电动机、水泵、各型农副产品加工机械、农用运输车、各种抗旱器材及各型机具的零配件等。至1994年，县农机供应公司在激烈的市场竞争中逐步衰退下来，经营仅能维持企业职工工资发放。与此同时，民营农机经营顺势崛起，1995年县农机供应公司遭受广东汕头不法商人许仁汉诈骗后，导致公司损失金额120多万元后垮台停业，民营农机经营发展成为县内农机经营主力。至2010年，国内一些农机生产厂家委托的代理商发展成为主流，主要销售企业有贵州吉华农机有限公司、贵州合盛农机有限公司、贵阳市农业机械公司、贵州天云农机有限公司、贵州国豪农机有限公司、贵州和协农机有限公司、贵州金色硕果农机有限公司、贵州省农业机械总公司、贵阳群力物资有限公司、贵州中甲农机有限责任公司和黔南州农业机械有限责任公司等。经营农机品种主要有拖拉机、微耕机、挖掘机、装载机、榨油机、机械脱粒机、秸秆燃气灶、粪水分离器、农产品加工和畜牧、植保、排灌等机械。

三、农机技术推广

1978年，县农机局下设有农机技术推广站（简称农推站）。在全县开展农业机械引进、试验、试制、推广等工作。推广大、中、小型拖拉机、农用车、犁田机、打谷机、粉碎机、烘干机等各种农用机械应用。

1979年，县农机科研所参加省山地农机研究所联合设计庆丰型烘干机，在城关镇新水大队砂锅寨生产队试用效果良好。每炕稻谷1000公斤水分在20%以上需3小时，水分在20%以下需2小时。水分均达到国家规定的13.8%以下标准。受到省山地农机研究所奖励。

1983年春，县农机局从江苏引进工厂化育秧新技术在县农场进行工厂化育秧新课题试验取得成功，当年试验5个品种，验收亩产达400公斤。次年在县推广工厂化育秧技术，解决全县长期以来育秧时节受倒春寒影响烂种烂秧的问题。保证不违农时，为水稻获得丰收提供保障。1987年4月，省工厂化育秧现场会在王官乡召开现场会，接待参会人员学习参观。

小型旋耕机

1988年，县农机推广站购进水田耕整机10台，在城关、扎佐、久长等地示范推广，由于耕整机体积小、易搬运，不需要机耕道，不要求稻田成片，

机用油单位购油，凭农用柴油供应证到农机管理部门申报供油。供应量多少，由县农机管理服务站统一安排。

1986年，为加强农用柴油管理，制定《油料及监理规章》，要求拖拉机驾驶员必须具有驾驶证、机车年审合格证、机车保险证，才能办理油料供应证。

1987年初，贵州省人民政府颁发关于完善粮食订购合同制度的几项规定，将“粮油挂钩”柴油指标交给农机部门管理。根据这一规定，由县农机局按计划分配，石油公司按分配计划将挂钩平价柴油和供应范围转为议价销售，议价油每公斤1.1元，所得差价收入转由粮食部门补贴给售粮农民。

1991年1月，国务院发布《国务院批转农业部、水利部、机电部关于加强农机生产和使用管理工作报告的通知》。根据农业发展的实际需要，增加农用柴油、电力和维修材料、零配件供应。农用柴油继续实行计划管理，农业(农机)部门负责分配。完善粮油挂钩管理办法，保证挂钩柴油兑现，既让农民得到实惠，又能使挂钩柴油真正用到农业生产上。

1992年第三季度起，农机用油取消计划供应，完全走向市场化。

四、农机安全监理

1978年，全县农机安全监理业务由县农机局配合县交通监理站管理，联合进行路检路查和处理农机事故等。农村经济体制改革开始后，农村拥有拖拉机和农用车辆的逐渐增多，1984年，国务院发布《关于农民个体或联户购置机动车、船和拖拉机经营运输业的若干规定》。“农民个体或联户的农用拖拉机，由县、市以上农机监理部门负责检验，并办理报户、过户、发牌证手续；其驾驶人员，必须按有关规定进行考试、考核，取得合格证”。1985年3月，县农机局成立农机安全监理站，负责对全县农用车、拖拉机和驾驶员的安全监理，严格执行机务规章、操作规程、交通规则、驾驶员管理制度、培训及考试制度、年检审制度、交通安全活动制度等一系列规章制度。农用车、拖拉机与驾驶员的年度检审工作，每年进行一次检验审核，不合格者不能上道路行驶。各种车辆必须在年检前将机车进行一次修理或保养，保证机车技术状况良好、安全设施齐备。主机和拖斗（箱）喷漆一新，安全可靠，才能签证。机车驾驶员按区域集中学习有关安全生产的文件和规章制度，评比安全生产的优秀驾驶员。一年不参加年审的驾驶员，处以罚款20—30元，停止供油。两年不参加年审由监理部门吊销驾驶执照。

1986年5月，县农机监理站在“安全月”活动中，组织全体农业机械管理人员在全县五区一镇建立起安全学习联组13个，以安全联组为单位按季度召开安全员会议，组织驾驶员学习，检查车辆，纠正违章。其农机监理站到安全联组指导学习培训，参与交通部门事故处理，以当年实情考核安全联组的工作。通过路检路查及每年开展“安全月”活动，全县违章车辆越来越少，促进农机安全生产。1987年9月，贯彻执行公安部、农业部发布《关于农用拖拉机道路交通管理问题的通知》精神规定：“凡上道路行驶专门从事运输和既从事农田作业又从事运输的拖拉机及其驾驶员，由公安机关按机动车辆进行管理。有关道路行驶安全技术检验、驾驶员考核、核发全国统一的道路行驶牌证等项工作，公安机关委托农机部门负责，并有权进行监督、检查。”每年进行一次拖拉机年度检验和驾驶员年度审验。对在道路上行驶的拖拉机的检查、纠正违章、处理交通事故等，统一由公安交通管理部门负责。在道路外发生的拖拉机事故由农机监理部门处理，需给予治安管理处罚和追究刑事责任的由公安机关处理。

1992年9月，贯彻执行国务院办公厅发布《国务院办公厅关于加强对拖拉机运输交通管理的通知》精神规定：在市区、旅游风景区、主要干线公路及其他公路的交通拥挤地段，规定一定的区域、路段和时间，不准拖拉机上路；拖拉机从事运输在道路上行驶时，遇到后边车辆发出超车信号时，驾驶员必须靠右行驶，并减速让行；拖拉机从事运输，必须向中国人民保险公司投保第三者责任险。1992年10月，进一步加强乡镇农机管理服务站（农机站）管理，健全和完善农机社会化服务体系，促进农业生产发展、繁荣农村经济，农机站以为农业生产、农民生活和农村建设提供综合服务为根本宗旨，坚持“以农为主，综合经营、有偿服务、增强活力”办站方针，实行管理、服务、经营一体化的经营管理机制。充分发挥农机效能，提高经济效益和社会效益。

2004年，对拖拉机、农用汽车实行登记制度，未经登记不得上公路行驶。对登记后上道路行驶的机动车，根据车辆用途、载客载货数量、使用年限等不同情况，定期进行安全技术检验。检验合格并办有第三者责任强制保险的拖拉机及农用汽车公安机关交通管理部门发给检验合格标志。2007年，农业机械安全生产工作被列入政府工作考核内容，建立健全农业机械安全生产责任制，落实安全生产监管主体职责，强化生产经营者的主体责任。2009年贯彻执行国务院《农业机械安全监督管理条例》，农机监管坚持以人为本、预防事故、保障安全、促进发展的原则，进一步加强农机日常监管。

农机监理执法

第二章 工 业

1978年，全县全部工业总产值为2614万元，其中县级及县以下工业总产值1093万元（当年价），占当年全县工农业总产值3204万元的34.11%。从1980年开始，县政府逐步通过放权让利等措施，调整政府和企业的关系，调动企业和职工生产积极性，1983年县属工业企业总产值1786万元。1984年，工业经济体制改革全面铺开，在国有企业中实施利改税，加速工业经济发展。与此同时，乡镇企业异军突起，采取乡办、村办、乡村联办、个体办、联户办多种形式，掀起大办工业热潮。1985年10月，时任省委书记胡锦涛莅县，重点视察马家桥乡镇企业，并给予充分肯定，称“两马”（修文马家桥和遵义马家湾）是全省乡镇企业的两面旗子，其经验推荐全省。1990年，全县乡镇工业企业达1593个，是1978年社队工业企业223个的7.14倍，总收入达6206万元，是1978年309万元的20.8倍。在全县工业经济中占“半壁河山”，成为县域经济的重要支柱，与县办工业、中央和省驻县工业企业齐肩并进。20世纪90年代，中央驻县工业企业陆续搬迁出县，工业经济发展重点转向招商引资上来，并将扎佐列为经济开发区。90年代末，县属绝大多数国营工业企业相继改制为民营，成为民营非公有制经济，在县委加强引导、政府全力服务、司法保驾护航、社会积极支持下得到较好发展。进入21世纪，县委、县政府按照高起点、高标准要求规划建设扎佐医药、食品工业园区和“十里工业走廊”，引进制药、食品和新材料精工企业入驻，使工业走上以高新外向型产业为支撑的工业经济发展之路，成为“修文未来经济引擎”。2009年，县委、县政府实施省工业强省战略和构建贵阳至遵义产业带发展规划，展开以“政府主导、市场运作”的方式建设“一区三园”（贵州修文工业园区、龙场工业园、扎佐工业园和久长工业园）。到2010年园区形成“布局集中、产业集聚、资源节约、配套完善”的势态，成为以医药、食品、新材料、新型建材、特殊钢、轮胎、精密铸件、机械加工等行业为主导的新型工业循环经济区，规模以上企业实现总产值51.24亿元。

贵州扎佐医药工业园（修文医药产业园）

第一节　体制改革

1978年，县内国营工业企业均为政企合一，实行计划经济运行模式，集体工业企业受计划经济的指导。1980年，县委、县政府执行省政府《关于扩大企业自主权若干问题的具体规定》，放宽工业企业经营自主权，迈出工业体制改革第一步。但依然沿袭计划经济下的公有制经营模式。1982年，党中央提出“以计划经济为主，市场调节为辅”发展国民经济的战略决策和制定国民经济“调整、改革、整顿、提高”的方针，县政府成立国营企业整顿领导小组，关停长期亏损的县化肥厂，落实国务院《国营工厂厂长工作条例》，国营工业企业实行厂长负责制、企业经济责任制和“利改税”新税制，改革企业管理体制。1991年9月，县经济体制改革委员会以改革工业企业经营体制增强企业活力为重点，推行多种形式的经营承包，分离企业所有权与经营权改革企业经营体制，把企业推向市场。同时，县委、县政府进一步解放思想，在思想观念上放心、放胆，政策措施上放宽、放活，工作方式上放手、放开，改革工业企业投资体制，吸纳各方投资发展工业。

1993年，县政府根据中共十四届三中全会提出建立现代企业制度要求，让企业在市场竞争中优胜劣汰，批准县磷肥厂有偿转让为私营，同意县酒厂依法破产，三角山水泥厂兼并县农机厂，率先对一批国营企业产权进行改制。同时在国营企业普遍实行承包责任制，变国营企业为国有企业。1997年，贯彻贵阳市委、市政府《关于放开搞活国有小型企业实施意见》，成立县国有工业企业改制领导小组，对县属国有工业企业进行由浅入深、由表及里的产权体制改革。之后国有工业企业陆续转型，出现职工下岗、再就业与安置，国有资产流失，资产保护与置换等问题。到2001年年底，县属11个国有工业企业除县粮食局直属面粉加工厂和油脂化工厂外其余9个企业进行资产权和经营权的改制。其中，除农机厂已被三角山水泥厂兼并外，出售其余8个企业经营权和资产权，转让金额共3386万元，初定涉及改制职工1344人，一次性补偿解除劳动关系职工1024人，办理退休手续纳入社会保障的职工294人，当时未能享受参与领取补偿和另谋职业者73人。继后落实政策，其中部分人员得到补偿，实际涉及1391人。从此，县属9个改制国有工业企业即为独立的经济实体，转为非公有制工业。

一、产权体制改革

（一）股份合作

1984年，县委、县政府按照安顺地区行署提出的乡办、村办、联办、联户办、户办发展乡镇企业方针改革乡镇企业产权体制，鼓励发展股份合作企业。当即有小营村、县乡镇企业局和“418”库劳动服务公司3家股份合作，创办箐口铝矿煅烧厂；马家桥乡政府和铁二局第三材料厂合股创办马家桥铁厂，成为县内首批股份合作企业，带动乡镇集体工业和户办工业逐步向股份合作迈进，随后股份合作的范围、规模和数量逐渐扩大。1991年5月，县三角山水泥厂和贵州省冶金矿产进出口公司、美国C—E矿产公司实行股份合作，投资500万美元创建贵州四达矿产有限公司，年产6万吨特级耐火铝矾土生产线，成为县内第一家中外合资股份合作企业。1995年年底，县乡镇企业局与个体投资商王晓春、贵阳市北供电局、贵阳市经委供销公司联合入股，投资1864万元，在久长镇沙雁村创办久长黄磷厂，建成年产2500吨现代化

黄磷生产线。到1999年，股份制企业步入多种产业，全县共引进资金1935.64万元，办起冶炼、建材、化工等上档次、上规模、产值高、效益好的现代化股份合作制企业。2002年，引进集药品开发、生产、销售为一体的民营股份制企业——贵州维康药业有限公司落户扎佐医药工业园区。建成第二年，产值达4000万元，纳税300万元。同年入驻医药园区的科开医药股份有限公司，完成企业内部股份改制后，2004年销售收入净额1.5亿元，创税1240万元，获得县委、县政府奖给“奥迪”轿车一辆，并授予“重点纳税先进企业”称号。贵州仙灵药业进行内部股份制改制，更名为贵州同济堂制药股份有限公司，当年生产总值1.56亿元，纳税2200万元，荣获贵阳市委、市政府“十强纳税大户”称号。在工业产权体制改革中诞生的股份合作制企业迅速发展，成为县工业经济主要组成部分。2005年，全县22家年营业收入500万元以上规模工业企业中，有股份合作制企业9家，占规模企业的41%。2007年，股份制工业总产值达8.27亿元，2008年，增至9.5亿元，其中，营业收入达500万元以上规模股份有限公司企业受世界金融危机影响致生产下滑，总产值仅7697万元，比2007年的1.05亿元下降26%。工业增加值1841万元，比上年下降60%。2009年，规模以上股份公司企业工业增加值为1672万元，比上年下降12%，到2010年规模以上股份公司企业工业增加值开始回升，达到1840万元，比上年增加12%。

专记：马家桥联合铁厂股份合作由弱变强

1984年，马家桥乡政府实行内联外引，创办股份合作企业。当年由乡政府利用支农无息贷款38万元，铁二局第三材料厂出资40万元，两家共同向县农业银行贷款10万元，双方单位职工个体集资5.5万元，共计93.5万元，联合兴建年设计生产能力为6000吨的马家桥联合铁厂。翌年8月，铁厂建成投产，年末生产生铁100吨。由于生产设备简陋，技术力量薄弱，生产一直不正常，至1987年5月，累计亏损22万元，被迫停产。9月，县政府为改变联合铁厂处境，召集投资方协商，分析研究对策，决定扩大联合，增加投入，又引入铁五局物资公司以补偿贸易方式出资60万元，铁厂偿还银行贷款和退掉个体集资15.5万元，剩余资金用于铁厂维修和购买原料。从此铁厂成为铁五局物资公司、铁二局第三材料厂和马家桥乡政府3家共同经营的股份合作企业。12月4日，铁厂再次点火恢复生产，当月生产生铁373吨，继后生产逐年上升，到1990年，年产量均在6000吨左右，达到设计生产能力，年均创税12万元。

1993年，铁五局物资公司退出股份，自筹资金400万元另创办城关镇新生铁厂。马家桥联合铁厂又投资金300万元，扩建容积为28立方米炼铁炉1座，股份从93.5万元增长到400万元，固定资产增加，技术含量提高，使联合铁厂年生产能力提高到1.8万吨，比1990年年产量增长2倍。

（二）依法破产

1986年，县酒厂异地改造，在龙场镇干河桥建起阳明酒厂。1989年投产后，时遇酒类市场供过于求，竞争激烈，产品多为赊销，购销业务混乱，资金不能及时回笼，还造成多起“三角债”，严重影响生产，亏损严重。1990年，亏损额高达11.9万元，1992年亏损上升到240万元。到1993年年底，外债累计达200万元。

1994年3月10日，酒厂法人代表王宗俊书面向县人民法院提交破产申请，县人民法院随即将破产案报安顺地区中级人民法院，地区法院认为：修文酒厂破产案尚为全区首例，影响面广，必须慎重对待，既要依法受理，又要考虑企业职工的出路。县委、县政府根据地区法院的意见，采取由酒厂职工决定企业出路的办法。经过学习《中华人民共和国企业破产法（试行）》，权衡各方利弊，最终选择依法破产。5月14日，酒厂再次向县人民法院提交破产申请。法院根据《中华人民共和国企业破产法（试行）》和最高人民法院《关于<中华人民共和国企业破产法（试行）>若干问题的意见》，于5月20日正式受理，国营阳明酒厂正式进入破产程序。经清理确定固定资产总额83.5万元，总债务212.9万元，法院依法作出资不抵债、依法破产的判决。遂成为全省国有工业企业依法破产的第一家。

阳明酒厂破产后，贵阳龟龄寿酒集团以500万元价购买该厂。县政府用厂出售款解决174名在岗职工一次性安置补偿，解除职工劳务关系。另有38名退休职工纳入社会保险，安养终身。

（三）产权出售

1993年9月，县国土资源管理办公室和县经济体制改革委员会根据中共十四大关于国营企业从放权让利进入转换企业机制的要求，经县人民政府研究同意将长期亏损的县磷肥厂作为安顺地区国企转换机制的试点。由资产所有方（县政府）将该厂以481万元有偿转让给原三角山水泥厂厂长吴昌明领办民营企业，改为久长水泥厂转产水泥，为县内第一家国营转民营的工业企业。新产权法人吴昌明从1994年起，在5年内分期付款，结清转让资金，并承担原磷肥厂银行贷款和债权债务，接收该厂职工保留国有企业职工身份继续在厂里参加生产，支付劳动报酬，开创国企职工在民营企业上班的先例。继后，为缓解县财力困难，新产权方又承担职工养老金的25%。

1997年7月9日，贵阳市委、市政府下发《关于放开搞活国有小型企业实施意见》，要求1997年各区（县）小型企业改革改制面必须达到90%。县政府采取因企制宜、点面结合、务求实效的措施，做出“总体安排、逐步推进”的改革部署，于10月成立县国有企业改革改制工作领导小组及其办公室负责具体工作。并组织改革改制领导小组成员31人赴重庆考察学习合川市国企改革改制经验，返县后结合县国有工业企业实际采取“一厂一议，一厂一策”方法，以县三角山水泥厂作为国企产权体制改革试点，经过宣传动员、摸底调查和资产评估，遂将资产总价1935万元的三角山水泥厂公开招标整体出售。经多家私企角逐竞标，最终敲定除职工宿舍外，以1750万元出售给华兴实业公司总经理荣启华。11月，县政府从部门抽调人员组成4个工作组分别进入县国有工业企业，产权改制全面铺开。1998年2月，按照修府〔1997〕2号文批准酱菜厂整体出售方案，酱菜厂以95万元整体出售给贵州联宇食品有限公司法人代表王文。县改制小组将出售收入扣除该厂债务后剩余的59万元一次性安置职工47人和遗属4人。经过计算需安置费69万元，尚欠10万元，县政府从其他国有企业改制后的出售款中调剂补齐。领取补偿款职工不再保留国企职工身份，原企业与政府脱钩。

1998年改制出售的修文酱菜厂

至2001年12月，属县计划经济贸易局管辖的9家企业，除兼并1家、破产1家和出让经营权3家外，其余4家均按产权出售方式完成改制任务。此次改制虽然减轻政府的负担，但造成国有资产流失，产生不良的社会后果。

专记：三角山水泥厂产权出售前后

1983年，县政府成功将下马企业县化肥厂改建为水泥生产厂，厂名更为修文县三角山水泥厂。1986年10月建成年产4.36万吨普硅水泥生产线，产品普通硅酸盐“甲秀牌”425号水泥创下省优名牌，占有一定市场。曾获贵州省水泥行业“标杆企业”、安顺地区“优秀企业”称号。1987年推行承包经营责任制，实行“包死基数，确保上缴，超收多留，歉收自补”办法，使之成为县属国营龙头企业。1993年，又投入技改资金271.5万元完善第二条生产线，形成年产8万吨的水泥厂。时逢国家基础设施建设项目增加，水泥畅销，企业效益显著，使全厂职工从352人增到405人。同年兼并县农机厂，并将其与外资联营合资共建四达公司。1995年8月，三角山水泥厂从四达公司退出，所属资产交由县政府统一安排。1996年，县政府将三角山水泥厂采用工资、住房、工龄、房籍作为“风险抵押”承包给县计划经济贸易局副局长唐林经营管理。

1997年11月，在全国国企改制的大背景下，县国有工业企业改制领导小组采取“靓女先嫁”办法，决定以三角山水泥厂作为企业产权改制试点。由县委副书记王赤兵带领改制小组成员进厂，召开职工动员会和各方面座谈会，讨论分析企业存在问题及解决办法，印发调查征询意见问卷200份。调查结果，85%的职工赞成改制。县改制小组初步核出企业总资产额为1885.42万元，负债1152.57万元，账面净资产732.85万元。改制小组综合全厂职工意见，决定整体出售三角山水泥厂，正式向县国有工业企业改制领导小组提交整体出售申请。12月，县资产评估事务所对三角山水泥厂资产评估计算整体资产总额为1935万元。

1998年2月23日，县改制领导小组在县政府四楼会议室举行三角山水泥厂产权出售竞标答辩会，宣布竞标资质、竞标办法、公开资产评估结果和企业债权、债务后。当即有久长水泥厂、华兴实业公司和贵州贫困山区资源开发公司参加竞标答辩。其中，久长水泥厂提出按资产评估价值出资1850万元，采取先支付部分资金，职工补偿部分的资金由职工自愿合股暂不支付，作为改制后加入新产权企业的入股，职工作为股东在厂继续上班，按月领取工资，按季或年分别计发入股分红收益，由于此方案事先未纳入竞标程序，政府解除企业与员工的劳务关系为原则，出售资金到位是关键而没有采纳。最终经县政府批准将水泥厂除职工宿舍外的全部资产以总价1750万元整体出售给华兴实业公司法人荣启华。华兴公司首期付款700万元，承接水泥厂全部资产和债权、债务。双方协定付款时间和方式：华兴公司必须于1998年5月28日前将首期付款足额汇至县计划经济贸易局银行专户，余款待计经局和华兴公司清理三角山水泥厂债权、债务后结算，方法为“一是华兴公司首付700万元+（债务－债权）大于1750万元，则大于部分由计经局退还华兴公司；二是华兴公司首付款700万元+（债务－债权）小于1750万元，则不足部分由华兴公司补足计经局；三是余款待计经局、华兴公司双方债权、债务清理结束，并从双方签字认可之日起7日内全部汇至双方账户”。

1998年改制拍卖的三角山水泥厂

华兴公司首期付款转到县计经局账户后，县国有工业企业改制领导小组于1998年5月31日向政府提交三角山水泥厂改制后职工社会保障和安置实施意见，经县政府研究同意，分别以在册职工、离退休职工、合同制工和伤残职工的不同情况，实行工龄补偿，正式职工以工龄每年1122元计算，合同制工人按每年250元计算。全厂除36名退休职工移交社会保障外的362人，用华兴公司首期付款700万元一次性发放，实际发放662万元，另有14人因欠销售款和离岗，暂扣发补偿，未发补偿款存于华兴公司，事后为落实14人补偿，则由县财政补发。至此，原企业与职工劳动合同关系解除，三角山水泥厂正式转为民营企业。

改制后，水泥产量曾一度上升。继后华兴公司以三角山水泥厂的固定资产作为抵押担保分别向贵阳市白云、金阳和乌当3家商业银行贷款共625万元。向白云区农村信用联社艳山红分社和贵阳市农业发展银行南明支行为修文联合磨料厂（法人荣启凤）和贵州荣氏食品有限公司及贵州省高速公路开发总公司修文有限公司担保贷款共903万元。并欠修文农业银行和工商银行以及建设银行转入农业银行的呆账款共747万元，欠修文国税局和地税局税款共114万元。累计债务2389万元。

2005年10月，华兴公司将企业转租给四川省江油市中坝镇人程新发经营。2006年4月，出租经营改为合伙经营，企业变更法人，由法人程新发组建贵州省修文县三角山水泥厂普通合伙企业，以1000万元资本重新注册、登记营业期限2006年4月—2012年9月，继续生产水泥。2008年8月，企业原法人荣启华与新法人程新发正式签订合伙协议书，明确企业合伙股份，整个合伙企业出资总额为1000万元。其中，荣启华以三角山水泥厂结存固定资产折价100万元入伙，占合伙出资10%；程新发以资金入伙，含已付荣启华的押金150万元，超付原租赁租金210万、租赁期间投入的设备费共290万元和现金250万元，合计900万元入伙，占合伙出资的90%。10月，程新发与贵阳市商业银行白云支行签订还款协议，三角山水泥厂以每月提供500吨水泥，由商业银行回收销售款，以支付白云、乌当和金阳3家支行的贷款。修文各银行的贷款成为呆账。12月，华兴公司荣启华与三角山水泥厂法人程新发签订股份转让合同，华兴公司将持有的三角山水泥厂10%的股份转给程新发，由程新发于12月31日前支付给荣启华转让费100万元，全部接受三角山水泥厂资产独资经营。而原改制时华兴公司除首期支付用于发放职工安置一次性补偿款662万元外，尚欠1088万元。县国有资产办公室、县计划经济贸易局与华兴公司一直未按双方1998年5月出售协定予以结算。

至2010年，三角山水泥厂企业债务沉重，生产下滑，已到难以维持地步，一个总额1935万元的三角山水泥厂资产无形中流失殆尽。

（四）主辅分离

20世纪90年代中期，国家航空工业部属国有企业中国贵州航空工业（集团）有限公司下属物资储备中转企业418库，在市场经济发展流通渠道畅通的情况下逐步取消计划管理业务，企业与主厂贵航集团万江机电有限公司的主辅关系名存实亡。为求企业生存，418库另组建为云天航空工贸有限公司，开发摩托车凸轮轴和包装箱生产，因利润微薄，难以维持企业职工生活，累计负债1000多万元，面临倒闭。

2002年云天公司根据国家经贸委、财政部、劳动和社会保障部等八部委《关于国有大中型企业主辅分离，辅业改制分流安置富余人员中的实施办法的通知》，与驻地人民政府联系，要求主辅分离，脱离贵航，转移地方，改制分流。2003年4月3日在贵阳市贵龙饭店举行移交仪式，仪式由万江机电有限公司董事长刘承民主持，贵航集团董事长周万成，县委书记魏明禄代表交接双方出席，贵航集团副总经理楚海涛、县政府县长石洪在《关于贵阳云天航空工贸有限公司移交修文县人民政府的协议》上签字，万江公司副总经理练希平、县常务副县长成华强在移交清单册上签字，将其全部资产，债权债务，以及在岗职

工188人、退养职工49人、离休职工4人、退休职工143人移交县人民政府变更企业产权。

分离后，县人民政府为盘活云天资产，安置企业职工，经两次招商引资，兼并云天。10月，最终引入贵州龙翔铝业有限公司，双方于28日签订《关于贵州龙翔铝业有限公司兼并贵阳市云天航空工贸有限公司协议书》，云天公司原董事长、党委书记李学军主动提出继续在龙翔公司（民营企业）工作，愿与改制职工一起拼搏，担任龙翔公司副总经理。他说：“职工就业，我就业，职工安心，我就安心。”经过一番努力，先后建起5栋1.2万平方米新职工住房、办公综合大楼和集贸市场等基础设施，使云天面貌焕然一新。产品凸轮轴销售量逐年上升，由移交前年生产60万套，销售收入1500万元，到2007年生产154万套，销售收入2081万元。2008年，因在遭受凝冻灾害停电停水，仍生产93万套，销售收入1474万元，成为县工业企业中的纳税大户之一。云天分离后翻天覆地变化，职工总结三个因素，一是县委、县政府的关注与支持；二是龙翔集团有个好的领导班子；三是原企业（云天）领导与职工携起手来一起拼搏。2010年，生产凸轮轴336.62万套，产值7.84亿元。

（五）转让嫁接

1978—1982年，县水泥厂（郭家林水泥厂）逐年接纳新职工，一个年产量不足1万吨的小型厂竟有国企职工、合同制工和大集体工200多人。进入90年代，工厂设备老化，富余人员累赘，周转资金短缺，长期负债经营，企业运转艰难，导致1998年拉闸停产，职工离岗。是年9月面对步履维艰的处境，县国有工业企业改制领导小组作出县水泥厂面向社会招标租赁经营的决定，由县计划经济贸易局出面，将企业以每年租金40万元租给私营业主吴学明，召回职工恢复生产。吴学明承租后只恢复简单再生产，无力解决设备老化问题，难以兑现租赁合同，职工因领不到工资而频繁上访。

2000年8月，县计划与经济贸易局终止与吴学明的租赁协议，将水泥厂转让给广西个体经营户邹炳泉，收取转让费240万元，一次性安置职工187人，其中138名在册职工领取安置费，49名退休职工移交县社会保障部门供养。邹炳泉接手后，随即利用该厂厂址和原料基地以及技术熟练的工人等条件，再度用厂嫁接给广西鸿鑫公司，引来省外资金1000万元联合组建修文鸿鑫水泥厂，对原厂进行技术改造，同时又筹建一条年产8.8万吨的特种水泥生产线，并集中主要的人、财、物投入厂区建设，修筑围墙、堡坎，扩展厂区范围，改观厂容厂貌。经过改造的原普硅水泥生产线恢复生产，产量逐步上升，2005年生产水泥1.48万吨，2006年达1.74万吨， 2008年达2.03万吨。2009年7月，鸿鑫水泥厂年产60万吨熟料新型半干法JT窑水泥生产线开工建设。2010年JT窑生产线尚在建设中。

（六）分离重组

1981年，从事制鞋、打铁、木工、缝纫的久长综合社率先分割资产，自动解体，从业者转为个体家庭作坊或另谋他业，成为县内第一家分离重组的城镇集体工业企业。至1990年，全县7家集体工业及165个从业人员，因设备落后、资金短缺，生产发展缓慢。至2003年，又有5家企业走上资产分离、人员分流、重组经营的道路，2家厂房闲置、设备部分转卖、职工分流自谋发展。其中尼龙衫厂解体，70名职工自谋生路。县农具厂资产分离，有技术的工人办起私人作坊，生产农业机械配件和锄头、镰刀等小农具。服装厂变卖厂房，按职工工龄分配卖房款，全厂48人中有32人走上个体经营道路。县建材厂分割资产，在册职工16人，多数重组参加县建筑公司，个别自办砂石厂和水泥预制件加工厂。扎佐农具厂将建筑面积820平方米的厂房6栋32间、解放牌汽车2辆以及刨床、气锤、车床等设备变卖，分割资产，1998年将矿粉车间转让给个体户王克华，将刨床等卖给罗万模，所得转让费用作还贷和解决老职工的生活费，2003年，将厂房、车间全部卖给个体户段吉士，至此资产全部分离，职工自谋他业，扎佐农具厂不复存在。虽未解体的修文皮鞋厂，由于鞋价上涨，生产成本增加，销售市场疲软，致部分技术工人退出集体，自立门户，谋求个体发展。县印刷厂资产闲置，部分机器设备转卖，职工为谋生路分流自行创业，使一厂变四厂，职工朱桂英、查远文、陈维贵、胡桂兰等自筹资金办起迎春印刷服务部及栖枫、修文中学、南门等4家印刷厂，各厂通过工商、文化管理部门取得印刷许可证和工商经营执照，接承全县企事业单位和党政机关的表册、凭证、信笺、信封、公文纸、宣传刊物，以及中小学试卷、复习资料等印刷业务。2010年，分离重组的修中印刷厂、南门印刷厂在竞争中倒闭，迎春印刷服务部、栖枫印刷厂经营有方，效益较好，业务遍及全县各部门和各乡（镇）。

（七）兼并移植

进入90年代，由于激烈的市场竞争，县农机厂因资金不足、管理松弛、产品滞销等问题导致停产。1992年，三角山水泥厂将县农机厂兼并，接纳职工75人，安排在职职工53人在水泥厂上班。利用农机厂厂区35.87亩用地作为参与贵州四达矿产公司组建入股资本，将兼并后的县农机厂及部分职工转移到贵州四达矿产公司，被转移的农机厂从此归四达公司所有，职工保留国有企业工作籍。1994年1月，四达公司投产，成为县内首家与外资联营的股份企业。1995年8月县政府主持三角山水泥厂从四达公司退出股金，按国有资产由政府统一安排使用，职工仍留四达公司上班。1998年6月三角山水泥厂产权整体出售，被移植到四达公司的职工返厂参加改制，领取一次性安置补偿，解除国企职工身份。

县属国有工业企业经营权、资产权改革情况表

表3—02—01

企业名称	地址	建厂时间（年）	改制时间（年）	改制方式	转让金额（万元）	一次性补偿（人）	新产权方安置职工数（人）
县农机厂（新厂）	龙场镇新寨村	1984	1993	被三角山水泥厂兼并后移植	—	—	53
棕刚玉分厂	龙场镇水塘村	1987	2000	转让经营权	200	128	—
久长磷肥厂	久长镇驴坊村	1978	1993	产权转让	481	—	33
县水泥厂	龙场镇郭家林	1971	2000	产权转让	240	138	—
三角山水泥厂	龙场镇新寨村	1986	1998	一次性出售	1750	362	21
耐火材料厂	龙场镇程关村	1971	2001	转让经营权	40	78	21
综合酱菜厂	龙场镇潮水村	1958	1997	一次性出售	95	47	12
红旗煤厂	龙场镇西门坡	1963	1997	转让经营权	80	64	—
县阳明酒厂	龙场镇干河桥	1986	1995	依法破产后出售	500	174	—

二、投资体制改革

1984年，县委、县政府解放思想，改单一的全民所有和集体所有公有制经济成分向多种经济成分并存，共同发展，从而调动起各种经济成分参与投资工业生产的积极性。90年代，又鼓励企业相互参股、职工持股、外资入股，对外招商引资，建立多元化、开放性的投资体制，使县域工业经济从公有经济为主逐渐转向非公有制经济占主导地位的格局。2008年，全县非公有制工业企业增加值达9.98亿元，占整

个工业经济增加值的75.2%，多元化投资的工业企业中规模（营业收入500万元）以上非公有制企业总产值就达24.95亿元，规模以上国有企业工业增加值4.68亿元。规模以上非公有制私营企业、有限责任公司、股份制企业、外商投资企业、港澳台企业工业增加值达7.51亿元，改变工业投资结构和工业经济成分。2010年，县内工业企业，除电力工业为国有企业外，其余均改为各种形式投资的非公有制企业，非公规模以上工业企业增加值达12.71亿元，其中，股份有限公司企业1840万元，有限责任公司企业5.51亿元，个体私营工业企业2.47亿元，港澳台投资企业1842万元和外商投资企业4.37亿元。分别占规模以上工业增加值的1.45%、43.3%、19.42%、1.45%和34.38%。

（一）农村集体投资

1978年，农村社队经营的冶炼、采煤、砂石开采、饲料、砖瓦及农具制作等集体工业多为手工和半机械生产方式，生产效率较低，经济效益有限。1980年，马家桥公社贷款15万元，集体投资兴建全流程机械化生产的马家桥水泥厂，指派公社干部罗贵祥、岳光明主持建厂和组织生产，从而带动社队一批新的集体工业诞生，仅两年时间全公社就办起社队集体工业企业88家，1983年工业总产值达1030.4万元。在马家桥公社的带动下，全县农村集体工业蓬勃发展，企业达130家。

1984年社队企业改称乡镇企业，县委、县政府根据农业部《乡镇企业产权制度改革意见》，进行乡镇集体企业经营和产权体制改革。关、停队办小煤窑，采掘、砖瓦、砂厂生产小企业进行横向联合，矿产从采掘转向矿产品加工，农村集体投资企业通过拍卖和有偿转让等方式逐步转为户办、联办及股份合作的民营企业，改变乡镇企业投资体制。到1995年，全县乡镇集体工业企业从90年代初的220家减为124家。2000年，随着民营企业发展，股份合作企业扩大，大量吸纳转化集体投资资产，使农村集体企业再度减少为29家。2003年仅存12家，其中有6家挂着乡镇集体企业的牌子，向乡（镇）缴纳一定数量的利润或管理费，实际已转为民营企业，被称为“挂户”企业。2005年清理“挂户”企业时停止上缴利润和管理费，“挂户”企业正式转为民营企业，农村集体工业仅存属村组所有的砂石厂和石灰厂共6家。管理上均采用承包方式转手给个体经营，集体无资金继续投入对设备进行技改和维修，资金由承包者垫付，承包期满结算，集体无能力偿付承包者垫付资金，只得用企业抵债由承包者接收，集体企业顺理成章地就成为私人企业。至2010年，原集体企业经营得好的转变为私营企业，经营得不好的自行下马，集体企业就此消亡。

（二）城镇集体投资

1980—1986年，由城镇街道集体继续集资和部门继续资助兴办的印刷厂、服装厂、农具厂、砖瓦厂、尼龙衫厂、皮鞋厂、建材厂均为城镇集体工业企业，属县轻工业局管理。6年间，城镇集体工业投入建设资金114.7万元，其中1980年3月，轻工局主持筹集资金20万元，招收工人70人，购置针织机37台和络丝机、锁边机、缝合机、崩丝机各2台，创办尼龙衫厂；12月，扎佐皮鞋社集体和轻工业局筹资42万元，在扎佐街购置厂房，设产品销售门市部，增添气压黏合机、氯丁胶搅拌机、胶粘气泵、红外线烘柜进行生产，正式命名修文县皮鞋厂；1983年，县印刷厂继续投资增添四开印刷机2台，铜模2付，切纸机1台，使企业固定资产达到14.3万元；1984年，县劳动服务公司组织城镇待业青年30人，自筹资金1.73万元，劳动服务公司拨款2.1万元，县科委拨科研费3000元，王官乡投资5.3万元，集体向银行贷款9.5万元，共筹集资金21.03万元，购置球磨机、颚式机、山砂机、制砖机，组建修文建材厂；1986年，扎佐农具厂自筹资金17.4万元，配置汽车2辆、空气锤1台、化铁炉1座，并配置厂房32间。至此，城镇集体投资工业壮大，企业增至10家，从业332人。

80年代后期，随着乡镇企业产权制度改革深入和民营经济发展迅猛之际，城镇集体企业也分离个体经营，走上民营企业道路。扎佐砂锅厂、城关砖瓦厂、城关农具厂等人员分流，自行关、停。到1990年，城镇集体企业尚存7家，从业人员165人。90年代中期，在市场激烈竞争中生存艰难的7家企业有5家逐步走上关、停、并、转、售之路，集体资产分离，职工分流，创办个体经营企业。其中，划归县乡镇企业局管理的建材厂，于2001年7月进行资产重组，转为股份制企业，更名为贵阳修文建筑工程有限公司。至2010年，城镇集体投资工业企业只存2家，其中印刷厂资产闲置，部分转卖，除留守人员外，有的职工分流创业，有的转为社保养老。皮鞋厂职工一部分留厂生产，一部分走上个体经营之路。

（三）县财政投资

1978年，县财政投资创办的地方国营工业有县化肥厂、县水泥厂、红旗煤厂、县酒厂、县农机厂、久长磷肥厂、综合酱菜厂、耐火材料厂、城关菜油厂和城关面粉加工厂。

1978年坐落在阳明西路的县农机厂

1984年，城市经济体制改革全面铺开，县级财政陆续投资改建、新建和续建地方国营工业。当年投资686万元改建县化肥厂为三角山水泥厂，投资350万元续建县新农机厂，1986年投资600万元建新阳明酒厂，1987年投资500万元新建水塘棕刚玉厂，1990投资120万元续建久长驴坊面粉加工厂，1991年投资298万元续建马家桥油脂化工厂（菜油厂）。继后，将老酒厂、城关菜油厂、城关面粉加工厂、农机厂分别并入续建新厂。此间县级财政共投入建设资金2554万元，全县地方国营工业企业为11家。

1993年，地方国有工业企业进行经营权、资产权改革，到2001年12月，县计划经济贸易局所属的三角山水泥厂、县水泥厂、红旗煤厂、耐火材料厂、棕刚玉厂、磷肥厂、酱菜厂均经过拍卖和有偿转让等方式转为民营企业，酒厂依法破产后将资产出售款安置补偿职工。县农机局管理的县农机厂被三角山水泥厂兼并后转移到贵州四达矿产公司。到2010年，县粮食局管理的油脂厂、面粉加工厂未改制，因原料短缺和管理不善停产。

附：

未改制的国有工业企业

修文县油脂厂

1991年，经安顺地区经委同意，投资298万元，在城关区马家桥乡幸福村建占地45亩，年加工菜籽9000吨，日产菜油50吨的修文县油脂厂，同时撤除建于20世纪50年代的城关菜油厂，新产品以市场价销售至贵阳市区及周边县。1995年，由于周转资金不足，农村油菜籽生产从计划生产转为市场调节，农民

种油菜面积减少，加之个体油厂大量收购菜籽，使油厂原料短缺，加上企业内部管理措施不力，购销经营环节失控，使企业负债930万元，欠交企业职工养老保险金190万元，沉重的压力迫使企业关闭。时至2010年，企业闲置总资产1151万元，全厂82名职工靠出租厂房分领租金维持基本生活。

城关面粉加工厂

1981年，县粮食局将建于县城的下属企业打米厂和面粉厂合并为城关面粉加工厂，其产品按计划供应居民。1990年，厂址迁至久长镇驴坊国家粮食储备库区旁，以利面粉加工转运。新厂占地4亩，总投入建设资金120万元，其中县财政拨款60万元，粮食局筹资34万元，贷款20万元，驻县厂矿赞助6万元。1996年因设备陈旧，无品牌产品，原料无保障，产品无销路，生产下滑，负债96万元，欠交职工养老保险金28万元，被迫停产。2010年，企业闲置总资产188万元，退休职工15人纳入社会保障，在职职工17人靠出租厂房收取租金维持基本生活。

（四）中央、省级投资

1978年，驻县万江机电厂、兴红机械厂、烽光电机厂、华文电工厂和庆文标准件厂均为中央部级投资的工业企业，隶属国家航空工业部。红枫电厂三、四、五、六级电站和贵铝一矿、贵阳煤矿则为省级投资驻县的工业企业。1985年，航空工业部属企业实施经营体制改革，统一由联合投资组建贵航集团在生产军工产品同时开发民用产品。为增强企业竞争实力，于20世纪90年代中期相继分别迁往贵阳市小河区、白云区、乌当区。1998年，贵阳煤矿因茶田和小河沟矿井煤源枯竭，便搬迁黔西县泰莱异地改造。2001，落实贵州省“十五”西电东送计划，由省乌江开发有限责任公司在六广河上游兴建索风营电站，工程概算动态总投资31.24亿元，装机容量600兆瓦，年发电量20.11亿千瓦时。2002年7月始建，2005年8月14日第一台机组投入运行。2006年6月第二、三机组发电。至2010年，县境尚存省级投资的驻县国有企业电厂5家和贵铝一矿1家共6家。

2002年索风营电站建设开工典礼

（五）个体投资

1985年10月，贵州省委书记胡锦涛视察马家桥乡镇企业指出：“乡镇企业由政府所有，阻碍企业积极性。”在省委领导讲话的启发下，乡镇企业增添个体经济成分，个体经营户王廷贵投资，利用普陀村硅砂创办玻璃厂；个体户贾明华投资，租用驻马家桥部队迁移后闲置的营房办起硫酸铝厂；黄光荣投资创办铝合金厂、精锌厂。1989年，个体户贺胜安自筹资金3万元，并以补偿贸易方式筹资建起马关铁合金加工厂，置容积13立方米的炼铁炉一座，设计年生铁生产能力6000吨，面向市场采购原材料及燃料，带动一批个体“矿老板”“煤老板”投资办矿。

进入90年代，原县计委干部李修平下海，集资600万元创办年产8万吨的利尔水泥厂，又带动一批个体投资者办起生产红砖、生铁、砂石、包装袋、白酒和生物化肥等行业，使个体企业迅猛发展。90年代末，全县个体民营企业发展到1000家。其中证照齐全的个体民营企业煤炭开采有278家、小煤窑400个，砂石厂80家，冶铁厂10家，酿酒户150家。另有小矿点、小砖厂、小铝矿煅烧厂、预制件工场等个体企业。全县在个体户和民营企业从业人员达到1.3万人。

2000年起，县政府根据国发〔1999〕43号文件要求，进行煤矿关井压产治理，凡年产量在3万吨以下的小型煤矿全部关停，取缔和炸封无证煤窑及事故多发煤矿，至2002年累计关停294家，仅存合法煤矿48家。2004年，经整顿后年产3万吨以上达标煤矿有27家。

这一时期，国家要求对一些产能过剩和环评不达标企业进行整顿，大多数个体企业相继关、停、并、转。石灰在建筑中被水泥、磁粉取代，县城东蛤蟆坡、城南三角山石灰厂停办，仅存观音山一处小土窑6只。个体酒厂在阳明酒厂和安酒集团停止收购白酒勾兑中级酒后，销量大减，逐渐停办。冶炼厂受世界金融危机冲击，铁矿开掘量下降，产品滞销，纷纷关停。2008年，年产6万吨达标煤矿仅存16家。除关、停外，一部分走上联合经营道路，使内资个体投资小型工业企业不足100家。2010年，年产6万吨煤矿改造升级，未能改造的煤矿淘汰，铁厂关停，铝矾土煅烧企业一部分关停，一部分转产。是年，年营业收入100万元以上中、小型个体投资工业企业17家仍然生气勃勃，总产值2.4亿元。

专记：个体投资企业——高坝砖厂

1993年，乌当区东风镇个体经营户杨时文到修文谋求发展，承包久长矿产实业有限公司高坝砖厂，当年红砖产量不足80万块。杨时文面对设备陈旧、工艺落后的砖厂，经过反复论证思考，于1997年下决心用承包5年的积蓄和多方面筹资将砖厂所有权买断，转制为个体民营企业，更名为修文县高坝砖厂。为实施砖厂技术改造杨时文于1998年变卖家乡自己经营多年的养殖场，筹集资金200万元，将原厂推倒重建。2000年，又筹资100万元，进行二次技改，引进制砖流水生产线。建成后具有先进制砖流水生产线1条、焙烧窑32门、干燥室11道，并置制砖机1台、对辊机3台、顶车机1台、窑车500台、东风牌142型翻斗汽车2辆、国产挖掘机1台、推土机2台，又置办公楼1幢和员工宿舍数间，企业固定资产总额达320万元，拥有稳定职工150人，年产红砖2500万块。经过一番拼搏，企业逐步发展，2001年被评为县先进民营企业，2002年获得贵阳市“生产建设水土保持先进单位”称号。随着房地产业的发展，产品畅销于扎佐、修文、久长及贵阳市城区，销量增加使2005年纳税上升到24万元。2006年，生产红砖1290万块，纳税19万元。2007年生产红砖1500万块，纳税18万元。2008年，生产红砖2300万块，纳税24万元。直到2010年，产量保持不减，是全县个体投资企业的纳税重点户。

企业富，不忘回报社会。高坝砖厂接收兴隆、高坝、猪头山农民工达120人，每月按时计酬发放工资。同时面向社会伸出援助之手，投入当地公益事业，慷慨解囊为群众办实事，先后用企业生产的红砖支持猪头山小学、兴隆小学修建教室，给猪头山村委会、兴隆村委会和久长镇派出所建起办公楼，又为村里建成提水站，出动企业机械设备为猪头山小学、兴隆小学修建校园和道路。出资6000元支持村文化建设和扶持失学儿童返校读书，抗灾期间踊跃捐款，慷慨解囊累计捐资12万元。

（六）股份联合投资

1984年，县委、县政府根据安顺地区行署制定“五轮（乡办、村办、联办、联户办、户办）驱动”发展乡镇企业的方针，鼓励联合投资办企业。马家桥小营村党支部书记韩荣真带头“试水”，与“418”库劳动服务公司和乡镇企业局联合投资31万元，建成总容积810立方米，2窑1囱的箐口铝矿煅烧厂；接着县矿产公司、县建筑社、马家桥部队农场、县教育局劳动服务公司分别与个体投资者联合创办起股份制企业。到1990年，全县股份联合企业发展到136家，从业者2937人，创收989万元。

1992—1996年，根据省委、省政府《关于加快推行乡镇企业股份合作制的意见》，贵州省军区后勤部与贵阳耐火材料厂、中寨企业管理站与河北故城县化工厂、基建承包商石世泽与林海公司、个体投资商王晓春与贵阳市工业供销公司和贵阳市北供电局等分别联合投资创办股份制企业。

进入21世纪，股份联合规模越来越大，相继成立股份公司制企业。2002年，个体户杨凯胜与4户股东联合投资230万元，兴办三茗食品有限公司，建成年产200吨低糖猕猴桃果脯生产线。2003年，“好一多”乳业利用“公司+基地+农户”的运作方式吸收丁官村和清水村农户入股，公司实力壮大，又投入资金2000万元，在扎佐镇建成日处理鲜奶200吨的乳制品生产线。2004年，“仙灵药业”完成资产重组，成立同济堂制药股份公司，固定资产达5000万元。同年，中方马胜与外资（美国·中国陶粒支撑剂有限公司）联合投资4000万元，在扎佐镇兴红村建石油压裂支撑剂生产线。随后股份联合企业逐步向股份公司化迈进，到2005年年底，全县有股份公司制工业企业11家，总产值5.4亿元。2006年发展到13家，总产值7亿元。2008年又增加新建的华飞氢氧化铝有限公司、贵州康亚轩食品有限公司和创试冶炼有限公司，股份公司制工业增至16家，总产值7.6亿元。2009年，规模以上股份有限公司工业增加值达1672万元，2010年上升到1840万元。

（七）外商投资

1991年5月，美国C—E矿产公司与县三角山水泥厂和贵州省冶金矿产进出口公司联合投资500万美元组建贵州四达矿产公司，建成年产6万吨特级耐火铝矾土生产线，成为县内第一家中外合资股份制企业。1995年8月，三角山水泥厂和省冶金矿产进出口公司退出股份，四达矿产公司由美国C—E矿产公司独资经营。继后美国C—E矿产公司又与瑞士斯坦伯格公司联合经营，四达矿产公司成为外商联营企业。

四达矿产公司

1998年，捷克F投资公司出资1750万元购下久长黄磷厂建外资独资企业，更名为贵州富捷化工有限公司。捷克F投资公司拓宽销售渠道，产品多为出口，2000年黄磷产量突破2000吨，2001年上升到2240吨，年均纳税160万元。至2008年，全县2家外资企业总产值达8.7亿元，占全县36家规模以上的企业总产值34亿的25.4%。2009年，规模以上外商投资工业增加值为3.36亿元，2010年达4.37亿元。

专记：县内首家外商投资企业——贵州四达矿产有限公司

1991年5月，贵州省冶金矿产进出口集团公司看准修文铝土矿资源丰富及其煅烧铝矾土的优越条件，与县三角山水泥厂商议开发耐火材料铝矾土生产，经过省冶金矿产进出口集团公司联系引进美国C—E矿产公司，3家决定联合投资筹建特级耐火铝矾土生产线，产品直接销售国际市场。时逢三角山水泥厂正寻求企业发展之路，厂长吴昌明果断决定兼并与本厂一路相隔，面临生产资金不足、产品滞销、导致停产的县农业机械厂，以农机厂占有的35.87亩土地作为组建铝矾土煅烧的股金。三角山水泥厂兼并农机厂后，省冶金矿产进出口集团公司、美国C—E矿产公司和三角山水泥厂3方共同出资含三角山水泥厂土地折价在内共500万美元兴建年产6万吨特级铝矾土生产线，定名贵州四达矿产有限公司，于当年10月破土动工，1994年1月竣工投产。

公司投产后，年产棕刚玉2万吨，产品质量达到特级耐火铝矾土标准，质量名列世界前茅，产品直接打入国际市场，经济效益较高。全公司常年稳定员工170人，其中工程技术人员8人，管理人员25人，工人137人。员工中有大学专科以上学历20人，大部分员工来自县内和原农机厂工人。

1995年8月，省冶金矿产进出口集团公司和县三角山水泥厂退出股份，由美国C—E矿产公司独资经营。为拓展国际市场，解决生产原料短缺问题，美国C—E公司又与瑞士斯坦伯格公司合资经营，成为外资联营股份制企业。两家外资联合后，在县境谷堡乡上、下屯开办铝土矿储量达500万吨的矿山一个，采矿专供公司生产专用。由于矿源得以解决，产量逐年增加，2004年生产熟铝矾土2.32万吨，总产值达2788万元，出口营业收入1731万元，纳税突破100万元。2005年销售大增，纳税达360万元，其中国税283万元，地税77万元，为县境工业企业纳税大户。2007年生产熟铝矾土3万吨，纳税450万元，2008年，虽受世界金融危机影响致销售不畅使产量降为2万吨，但仍纳税318万元。至2010年产量保持3.2万吨，产值6858.5万元，纳税400万元。

（八）港台投资

1991年3月，香港德利贸易公司与县经济贸易局协议开拓修文硅铁的销售渠道，将个体户陈顺隆经营的修文硅铁厂与港商合作，组建文德矿冶有限公司，注册资金122万美元，投资比为原硅铁厂占60%，德利公司占40%。文德公司组建董事会，双方派代表共同经营管理，成为县境首家与香港的合资企业。当年产硅铁2000吨，产值600万元，产品远销日本、韩国、美国和中国香港、台湾地区。继后，文德公司采取租赁、承包等经营方式，生产基本稳定。1994年，台商王乾麟和唐起麟投资125万美元，在扎佐镇大山村建起年产1000吨魔芋精粉的日光蒟蒻食品有限公司，为驻县台商合伙企业。公司有固定员工25人，魔芋收割加工季节聘用季节工100余人。产品外销为主，是县内一家较早出口创汇企业之一。同年，台商徐吉顺投资300万元买断扎佐喻家街由厦门和湖南投资商联合经营的双星铁厂，改造建成年产1.2万吨铸铁的东海铁厂。投产后因管理不善，效益较差，于1996年停办。2001年，港商徐频投资3356万元，率先入驻扎佐医药园区，按照国家药业CMP标准进行技改建成贵州安泰药业公司，开创县境招商引资的“安泰模式”，为县内港方独资工业企业。2005年，公司在岗职工92人，其中大中专以上学历的占75%，高、中级技术职称16人。其产品消炎利胆胶囊载入《国家卫生部颁发的国家药品目录》，为国内外推广使用产品。2008年，港台投资规模以上工业企业总产值达5988万元。2009年，规模以上港台投资工业企业增加值为5902万元，2010年降为1842万元，比上年下降68.79%。

港商徐频投资在扎佐医药园区建成的安泰制药厂

三、经营体制改革

（一）联合经营

1985年10月，贵州省委书记胡锦涛视察马家桥乡镇企业，在赞扬其艰苦创业精神，在肯定乡镇企业成绩时指出："乡镇企业为政府所有的体制，容易挫伤企业积极性和阻碍横向联合，行政干预就会弱化企业市场竞争意识，管理部门与企业的矛盾冲突直接影响企业再生机会和发展后劲。"他要求"各级领导干部更新观念，实行企业重组，从分散作业的'小字号'企业向市场化、规模型、联合经营方向发展"。县委书记王向规按照省委领导指示，带领县属乡镇、工商和税务等部门负责人对马家桥乡乡镇企业进行为期1个月的考察调研，撰写出6万多字的《马家桥乡乡镇企业考察与分析调查报告》，以政府名义出台一系列乡镇企业面向市场化、规模型、联合经营发展的政策和措施。马家桥乡政府利用闲置地建厂的条件和支农无息贷款与铁二局第三材料厂联合建起马家桥铁厂；小营村利用本地山地资源优势，联合县乡镇企业局和"418"库劳动服务公司兴建箐口铝矿煅烧厂；马家桥白莲村6户村民共同出资，利用本村待开发的山地与县乡镇企业局矿业公司联合兴办白莲水泥厂；个体户贺胜安、陈顺隆寻找扩大经营之路，贷款98万元与县乡镇企业局矿业公司、县建筑公司、马家桥部队农场联合经营，建成年产6000吨的修文硅铁厂。1987年，县耐火材料厂与贵阳第三砂轮厂联合开发耐火材料，组建修文棕刚玉冶炼分厂，分别以土地或持有资金参加联合，土地以使用价值折算入股，按资产投入比例参与税后收入分配。至1990年，全县联营企业发展到136家，涉及轮窑铝矿煅烧窑、水泥厂、冶铁厂和煤炭开采等行业，均为村民联户或与其他经营企业联合经营。一批小打小闹的小铁厂、小砖厂、小煤厂、小水泥的个体企业走上联合经营道路。小营砖厂联合经营后，经济实力增强，股东在厂长袁达明的带领下，不惜重金加大技改，使产品的技术含量攀升，红砖从国标100号上升到150号，增强企业在市场竞争中的实力。此外，联合后的硅铁厂从生产型转变为生产经营型。联合后的棕刚玉分厂，产品可以不通过中转环节直接销售给贵阳第三砂轮厂，增加企事业收入，从而推动企业发展。

1986年，马家桥乡联合企业白莲水泥厂

（二）承包经营

1987年，县属国营工业企业的管理者以"包死基数，确保上缴，超收多留，歉收自补"的税利指标为基础向政府承包企业经营，使自负盈亏成为企业经营体制改革的核心，将企业的资产所有权与经营权分离开来，以调动企业生产经营的积极性。于是，企业的厂长纷纷要求承包。县水泥厂厂长李世银，棕刚玉厂厂长朱永彬，三角山水泥厂厂长吴昌明、方德明，红旗煤厂厂长应锡文，耐火材料厂厂长高忠志乘势而上。但是，承包经营后，因利益分配矛盾，职工生产积极性调动不起来，在承包期内强化生产，加速企业设备损耗，导致承包者未能完成承包税利基数，政府只得收回企业多次转承。红旗煤厂承包后，承包方应锡文未能按协议履行责任，长期拖欠职工工资，引起职工上访，县政府当即终止承包协议。县水泥厂承包后在企业富余人员多、负担重、设备老化、资金短缺的情况下，被迫停产向社会转租经营。耐火材料厂承包后，生产仍然滞后，又转包给贵阳云岩区个体户王林经营，承包期6年，机器带病运行，仅一年时间，承包方自动放弃承包。县三角山水泥厂经过两轮厂长承包退出后，又由企业主管部门县经济贸易局副局长唐林以工资、家电、住房、工龄、党籍“风险抵押”方式再次承包，形成主管部门既是发包方，又是承包方，承包者既是政府行政领导，又是企业承包经营者，企业仍然依赖政府，所谓“风险抵押承包”没有约束力，没有抵押价值，承包者无风险，职工待遇无改善，职工与承包者矛盾日益加重，企业生产难以维系，造成承包流产。暴露出承包经营治标未治本的弊病，迫使国营工业企业走上经营权转让和资产权出售的道路。

1988年，承包经营时县红旗煤厂厂区

（三）租赁经营

1998年，以税利包干形式承包经营的县水泥厂（郭家林水泥厂），因基础薄弱和缺乏资金投入难以维持生产，导致青年技术职工纷纷离岗到外地打工，企业停产。为解决在厂职工和退休职工的生活，县经济贸易局采取面向社会招标租赁经营方式，将该厂租给私营业主吴学明经营。双方达成租赁协议由出租方负责提供生产厂房和设备，召回离岗工人，并为承租方提供生活设施和办公设施，负责与主管部门联系，提供用户和客户信息资料。承租方在承租期间承担年租金按年付给，每年总额40万元，租赁期6年，承租方负责支付厂方原银行贷款利息，计发职工工资，交付职工养老金和负责生产安全。由于承租者将就陈旧机器带病运行，在强化生产中加速设备损耗，到2000年承租方不能按合同支付银行利息累计达18.19万元，生产设备到再也不能运行的地步，职工反响强烈，纷纷要求县主管部门解决。县经济贸易局为深化企业体制改革，达到治本目的，经研究终止与吴学明的租赁协议，将该厂产权以240万元转让给广西玉林私营业主邹炳泉，经就地改造后继续生产水泥，改造后的生产线从2005年至2008年产量逐步上升，年均生产水泥1.6万吨。

（四）转让经营

1997年，县政府以接收红旗煤厂工人继续上班，发放退休工人工资，缴纳职工养老金为条件，以零转让费将厂经营权转让给原承包厂长应锡文经营，改为私营企业。但应接手后仍拖欠工人工资，欠交职工养老金，职工意见大，反响强烈。2000年年初政府收回转让的经营权，派县经济贸易局干部郑光祥任临时厂长恢复国营企业身份。2001年，县工业企业改制领导小组针对红旗煤厂资源枯竭、设备报废，再采掘已严重影响到县城西门坡一带地层安全等因素予以关闭，采取异地搬迁方式选六广镇丁家寨、扎佐镇双月村作为搬迁建厂地，但因资金困难和技术力量不足，县政府召开常务专题会议决定将

2001年，改制出售的县耐火材料厂

红旗煤厂丁家寨分矿的经营权以40万元有偿转让给浙江温州投资人林昌亩，把双月村分矿经营权以40万元有偿转让给扎佐镇三元村村民赵高文。两人接手后分别投入资金600万元，在两地各建成年产6万吨的煤矿。政府将转让费一次性安置红旗煤厂在职职工64人，并将退休职工45人纳入社会保障，红旗煤厂原矿址及办公地、职工宿舍地等仍属国有资产。是年，县国有工业改制领导小组根据县国有工业企业改制“一厂一策、一厂一议”方案，针对棕刚玉冶炼厂因生产亏损21万元，欠债务741万元、欠留守人员工资10万元，共772万元，恢复生产无望，经过市场协议定价将厂矿山开采权、经营权和冶炼厂土地使用权标价200万元，转让给民营贵阳金星冶炼厂经营。金星冶炼厂接手后，投入技改资金260万元，继续冶炼棕刚玉和生产耐火砖，转属县乡镇企业局管理。同时，县工业企业改制领导小组根据修府通〔2001〕42号文《关于县属国有企业改革改制的实施意见》，结合耐火材料厂资源枯竭、厂房设备陈旧、工艺技术落后的具体情况决定该厂生产转型，将厂的土地经营使用权折价40万元转让给个体经营户虞兴安进行生产转型改造。虞接手后投入1200万元资金将原厂改造建成年产8万吨的特种水泥生产线，划归县乡镇企业局管理。

四、管理体制改革

（一）“松绑”到“解绑”

1981年，县委、县政府贯彻落实贵州省政府《关于扩大企业自主权若干问题的具体规定》，从简政放权入手，改革管理体制。政府对企业进行宏观管理，企业在完成政府下达生产指标的基础上，实行保量不保价的企业产品自销制度，企业产品可直接进入市场成为商品。县红旗煤厂根据市场供求，自定产品价格生产经营良好，当年扭亏为盈，并还清上年欠款17.5万元。县化肥厂回收次品化肥，再次精炼，以销售收入发放日班奖和交接班条件奖，凡当班人员，包括生产、维修、门卫、后勤等岗位，日班每人0.5元，使当班职工人人关心生产、努力出勤。随后继续松绑，放开化肥价格，实行“内部价”、“出厂价”、“零售价”多种价位，产品不经调拨可直接面向农民出售，农民还可用肥猪直接换取化肥，既方便农民，又使企业解决劳保食肉短缺，互相实惠，扭亏为盈。

1984年县经济委员会、乡镇企业局对企业下达的计划指标开始减少，产品由市场需求调节生产。铁矿、水泥、红砖、白酒、酱油等16个产品均取消指令性计划，以指导性计划给予调节，实行产品经销“双轨制”，企业产品直接和用户签订购销合同，企业自找买主，自寻运输途径。乡镇企业局矿产公司、供销公司、六屯乡矿产公司和扎佐农具厂等均持有自寻的火车皮运输计划。“松绑”放权给企业带来实效，推动全县工业经济发展。“松绑”放权阶段，政府只改变部分职能，未改变机构，撤掉“香火”未撤“庙”，虽然下放部分权力、让出部分利益，但在放权的同时又相伴随政府管理部门增加，机构重叠设置，机关冗员保留权力，使权力仍停留在各行政部门之间的“分权”上，企业的“婆婆”有增无减，企业松开手，仍套着绳索。1995年“松绑”转变为“解绑”，产品生产销售完全由市场调节，企业生产什么，生产多少，根据市场需求变化组织生产。在1997年出现亚洲金融风暴和2007年出现世界金融危机中由于国家宏观调控、企业自我调节度过危机。2008—2010年，工业企业在社会主义市场经济条件下，根据资源的社会配置和产品的市场需求情况，进行自我调节、自我约束、自我发展，产品产量随资源配置、市场需求而变化，产品产量稳步上升，企业充满生机和活力。

（二）以税代利

1983年，县政府按照全国统一部署，改革企业财税管理体制，把企业上交给国家的利润款改为向国家缴纳税金。将企业以利润的形式向国家提供剩余产品改为按国家规定的税种和税率缴纳税金，县水泥厂、红旗煤厂、耐火材料厂及不需补贴的县供电所作为第一批新税制改革单位。

1984年10月利改税全面铺开，开征企业产品税、营业税、增值税和所得税，原则是："包死基数，确保上缴，超收多留，歉收自补。"税后利润归企业自行安排，保证"国家得大头，企业得中头，职工得小头"，使企业从政府包揽逐步走向市场。为使企业完税后又可获利，县政府采取减税让利办法，征收比例分步推进，激发企业活力。至1989年，6年间全县工业企业向国家累计纳税7764万元，比利改税前1978—1983年的6年累计上交利润203万元增加37.25倍。2008年，全县年规模以上企业实现利税总额5亿元，其中，利润总额2.7亿元，缴纳国税、地税共计2.3亿元。到2010年，国家税和地方税均稳定，随企业营业收入增加而增加，是年国有控股企业纳税7493万元，内资私营企业纳税5959万元，外资企业纳税1.17亿元。

（三）用工制度变革

1981—1991年，劳动部门将就业人员、安置对象以合同制工、大集体工分配到企业。1992年实行政企分离，放开企业择人权和用人权，实行先培训后就业，结束企业招收学徒工传统和统一分配安置模式，打破职工的"铁饭碗"。1998年，县劳动人事局和县总工会举办就业培训班，以学习驾驶、维修、计算机操作技能为主，同时学习《中华人民共和国劳动法》《失业保险条例》，并注重强化参训者的职业道德意识、职业责任感、职业纪律要求和职业礼仪素养，共培训238人，培训后由参训人与用工企业对接，根据"双向选择"原则就业上岗。是年，贵州胜兴发展有限公司建设、经营的修文殡仪馆（火化场）根据其用工专业性，采取文化知识考试方法招聘工人和从湖南省长沙殡葬管理中专学校招聘应届毕业生共16人，派往清镇市殡仪馆学习培训，组建企业员工队伍。2003年4月，县劳动局组织81名待业人员到贵阳市花溪宏信药业学校学习，为扎佐医药园制药企业输送技术工人。2004年，贵州龙翔能源（集团）公司接收就业前培训人员30人到公司上班。2006年，县劳动局与县总工会组织105人培训计算机操作和电工、维修工，其中有60人被企业录用。2007年5月，县社会保障局与县工商局联合举办民营企业用工招聘活动，全县25家企业参加，2000人报名应聘，初步达成协议356人，后由企业考核正式录用60人。2009年，贵州金久水泥有限公司、贵州鑫益陶粒支撑剂有限公司和贵州"好1多"乳业股份有限公司等38家企业，在县体育馆广场举行为期一周的"2009年民营企业用工招聘会"，为寻求就业人员提供1134个岗位。其间报名求职398人，经企业用工选择，达成录用协议141人。企业经过对员工实行"三定"（定员编制、定部门职能、定岗位规范），以竞岗答辩择优聘用企业管理人员，实行先培训、后就业的员工录用做法，彻底改变企业劳动人事制度，推进企业管理体制改革深化。

1998年县人事劳动局就业前培训班计算机操作培训

专记：联宇食品有限公司广聘管理人员

1998年，由股东王文、曾铭辉和陈霖组建的贵州联宇食品有限公司创办起下属企业联宇食品厂、兴

红原料生产场和息烽水产养殖场，均按公司化广聘管理人员，跳出供奉式、家庭式用人框框，把企业人事用工管理摆到企业管理的核心位置上，在贵阳市范围内广纳管理人才，聘用企业管理人员9人，使企业用人达到科学化。

公司董事会经过考核，以聘书方式聘任已退休的县政协原主席林志云任公司顾问；聘已退休的县委党校原副校长、经济管理讲师罗国通任公司办公室主任，受公司董事会委托代经理主持公司全面工作，直接为董事会、股东负责；聘贵阳市电力局退休会计师李发民任公司主管会计，分管财务；聘修文邮政局退休职工葛正厚分管公司基础设施建设；聘贵阳市味纯园酱菜厂退休厂长解学成任联宇食品厂厂长；聘原酱菜厂改制企业职工郑大义返岗任生产副厂长；聘息烽761厂下海职工姜彦明任食品厂经营副厂长；聘贵阳市调味品协会会员余佳任食品厂化验室主任；聘城关镇退休干部陈明芳任兴红原料生产场场长，使一批有专长，懂业务的退休、下海、下岗人员在联宇公司得到用武之地。

公司管理机构组建后，由公司办公室制定出公司管理章程，部门职能职责、科室人员编制和生产岗位规范等各项规章制度，聘用人员各负其责，各守其职，相互配合，内抓管理，外拓市场，开发出袋装、瓶装、礼品盒特醇的香菇酱油系列产品10余种，并被认定为贵州省调味品协会和消费者协会推荐的产品。1998年，实现营业收入比1997年增长1.2倍，实现利税比1997年增长1.4倍，固定资产比1997年增加120万元，聘任的管理人员为公司发展打下坚实的基础，使公司成为县国有企业产权改制后，生产运行12年保持不断壮大的非公有制企业。

（四）一体化管理

1995年，随着县工业企业发展，开发项目增多，县委、县政府将招商引资创办企业工作纳入议事日程，使招商引资开始从民间转为政府部门的工作范畴。但投资者申办企业仍需要跨过多道门槛，需经县计划经济贸易局、环境保护局、城乡建设局、国土资源局、技术监督局、水资源办公室、工商局、税务局、公安局以及供电企业多家审批，带来程序复杂、手续繁琐、权力分割等诸多弊病，甚至有的部门门难进、脸难看、事难办。进入2000年，县委、县政府下决心改革管理体制，强调政府从行政管理转向行政服务，走上“规划、协调、监督、服务”一体化管理轨道，实行并联审批、主办负责、抄告相关、一次办结的操作程序，为企业营造良好的投资环境。2001年，县政府履行一体化服务职能，开创“一站式”办公，采取“一体化”操作，成立县招商引资办公室，印发《投资指南》，将拟定开发的项目明细化，分设旅游、食品、医药、建材、化工、物流、房地产和现代农业等行业，标明相关工作部门电话号码、水资源费征收标准、电力销售价，规范各部门收费“明白卡”，使投资者手握《指南》若指掌。项目申办由县招商引资办、计划经济贸易局代权受理。同时政府简化土地征用手续，申办企业只需先交征地费，剩余款项待企业投产后，从每年所缴纳给地方财政税额的减免部分逐年付给土地持有者；工商部门为方便企业创业，放宽出资限制；税务部门开设“绿色通道”，实施优惠政策运作。2002年6月，县供电局在转变管理职能中，建成全省县级第一家“95598”计算机网络一体化服务体系，履行“客户只需打入一个电话，其余的事由我们来做”的一站式服务，受理报装申办、电费查询、用电扩装、业务咨询、侵权投诉、意见建议、违章举报等，建起由局统一指挥的7个供电所和39个农村服务站网的一体化管理体制，实行一体化操作，方便用电企业，使客户感到满意。通过一系列方便措施引进安泰医药企业落户扎佐，成为县创建医药工业园引进多家项目入驻的“安泰模式”。到2010年，“一体化”管理、“一站式”操作的服务不仅引进19家上规模、上档次的医药生产企业，还引进“好1多”乳业、龙翔能源、华飞化工、金久水泥、贵阳钢厂、贵阳吉隆单宁化工、贵阳怡丰精细化工、贵酒公司、贵州轮胎等规模工业落户县境。

（五）公司化管理

1995年，县乡镇工业调整产业结构，促进企业横向联合，提倡组建公司制企业，建立董事会（股东会）领导下的厂长（经理）负责制，按权力、决策、执行、监督等各自的职能组建相互独立、相互制约的管理机构，形成产权明晰、责权分明、管理科学、激励和约束相结合，由董事会、监事会、经理等管理层共同组成的企业公司化管理体制。1998年，白莲水泥厂列为县内第二期小型水泥企业技改对象，企业面对两种选择：要么组建公司，走大联合，筹集资金投入技改；要么终止小合作，解散或各自转入其他联合公司。企业管理者岳玉贤经过利弊权衡，选择企业走公司化管理之路，动员企业股东继续扩大联合，筹措资金400万元，把分散的资金集中统一使用，企业员工重新调配，分为生产和技改两块，各施其权，各尽其责，相互促进，实行利益统一分酬，风险统一承担，将年产1万吨立窑技改成年产6万吨新型机立窑生产线，使企业内部资产结构发生根本变化，经济效益逐渐增长，跻身县内中型企业之列。其余未实行公司化管理的强力水泥厂、复退残水泥厂、扎佐水泥厂、环北水泥厂被迫转产和关闭。

1999年，全县按公司组建的条件和标准，批准成立公司制工业企业的有贵州四达矿产公司、修文文德冶炼公司、贵州联宇食品公司、贵州林海实业公司、贵州瑞达生物工程公司、贵州利尔建材公司、贵州奇峰工贸有限公司、贵州日光蒟篛食品有限公司和贵州富捷化工有限公司等9家，注册资金共7912万元。进入21世纪，落户县内的17家药业企业和“好1多”乳业、龙翔能源、华飞化工、金久水泥、贵酒集团等均按公司化管理体制组建，一批非公有制公司化的骨干企业诞生，使修文的工业企业呈现腾飞的态势，成为全县经济社会发展的擎天柱。

（六）领导任聘变革

1981年，实行党委（支部）领导下的厂长负责制和党委（支部）领导下的职工代表大会制，党委集体领导，职工民主管理，厂长负责行政指挥和行使企业生产经营权。县委委派蔡显明任县化肥厂党委书记主持全面工作，提拔原厂中层干部唐群担任厂长负责生产管理。1986年，按照干部革命化、年轻化、知识化、专业化标准，县经济委员会和党组任命晏政国任三角山水泥厂郭家林分厂厂长和党支部书记，吴昌明任总厂厂长，并完成全县7家县属国营企业领导班子整顿，明确由厂长主持企业全面工作。

1987年8月，县委根据中共中央办公厅、国务院办公厅《关于认真搞好国营企业领导体制改革试点工作的通知》，对县内国营企业三角山水泥厂进行领导体制改革试点，推行承包经营责任制，坚持“包死基数，确保上缴，超收多留，歉收自补”原则，由原厂长吴昌明负责承包，实行生产经营和行政管理负责制。同时，县委、县政府派局级领导干部谢恒信进厂任党委书记，协助、支持厂长吴昌明工作，并明确吴是企业法人代表，对企业全面负责。党委侧重抓贯彻执行中共路线、方针、政策和职工政治思想、精神文明建设及基层支部、党员自身的建设，党委的政治主张通过党员的先锋模范作用体现，促使全厂职工觉悟普遍提高，使遵纪守法、维护设备、爱护公物、文明礼貌风气大增，有力地支持、协助厂长吴昌明狠抓生产经营、技术革新、生产调度、员工启用、生活福利等全盘工作，创下省优“甲秀牌”425号水泥品牌，打入贵阳市区，使企业在市场站稳脚跟。在试点的带动下，推进全县国营工业企业领导体制改革，至1989年，全县地方国营工业企业普遍推行承包经营管理负责制。

1997年，加快县级工业企业改革步伐，将县属工业企业产权出售，把原国有企业改制成非公有企业。改制后，企业厂长或经理实行公开招考、竞岗答辩、择优聘用及解聘制度，使企业领导体制有新的突破，增强公平、民主、竞争、敬业意识，彻底摧毁企业领导干部的“铁交椅”。

第二节　产业结构

1978年，县内工业已有航空工业部属011系统5厂1库、省属5个梯级水电站和贵铝一矿、贵阳煤矿，县工业局创办的“五小工业”（小煤窑、小水泥、小化肥、小机械、小钢铁），县粮食局创办的粮油加工企业，农村社队创办的社队企业，除省、部开发的电力、采矿、机械和电器工业行业外，县属五小工业、社队工业初步形成以建材、原煤、小化肥生产为支柱的工业行业结构。1984年，乡镇企业中的小炼铁厂、铝矾土煅烧厂、水泥厂、水泥预制构件厂、砖厂等逐渐兴起，磷化工开始起步，增添工业行业的种类。1995年，县政府引进山西环海实业有限公司共同组建县创办的“全国光彩事业东西部合作示范项目”开发金属镁生产线，还未正式投产就下马。进入21世纪，贵州林海新材料企业诞生，联宇食品、日光食品、金格食品相继投产，15家制药企业落户扎佐医药工业园，使工业行业结构更为丰富。2008年，已建成以水力资源开发的水电站及建设的供电网；以普通硅酸盐水泥生产为主，制砖为辅的建材工业；以铁矿、铝矾土矿为原料的冶炼企业；以磷、煤为原料的化工企业；以绿色植物为原料的食品工业；以地方民族医药（贵州苗药）开发，并已获国家GMP药业认证制药企业；以铝矾土为原料生产石油压裂支撑剂的新材料工业。到2010年首都钢铁公司贵阳特殊钢厂、贵州贵酒公司、化工企业贵阳吉隆单宁、贵阳怡丰精细、华飞氢氧化铝、贵州轮胎和新材料生产企业贵州鑫益能、贵州泽希、贵州自立、贵州宇丰、修文银星等先后落户县境，使工业行业结构更为完善。

一、电力

（一）水电站

1978年，县境有县自建的香巴房、二洞河、白水、洞口河、大屯小型水电站和贵州省电力局在猫跳河上建的河口、三级、四级、五级、六级梯级电站，具有水电明珠之称。1990年，县自办的大屯电站因水源不足而停运，其余继续运行。从1998年至2004年，随着农村电网建设和改造完成，实现全县城乡电网联网，同网同价，供电充足，县办电站除香巴房电站随桃源河漂流开发转交给桃源河峡谷神州漂流公司经营发电自用外，其余陆续关停。省建的河口电站并入三级电站统管，三、四、五、六级电站运行完好。

1960年建于猫跳河干坝村石门坎的三级电站

2002年2月，按照贵州省“十五”计划，开工建设西电东送的六广河索风营电站，于2006年6月全部建成投入营运，其装机容量为3×200万千瓦，年发电量2011亿千瓦时，使全县电站装机容量升为798.5千瓦，到2008年全县发电量达到历史最高的22.4亿度。2009年起，因猫跳河流域水位下降和国家南方电网调控，当年全县发电量达仅为20.7亿度，2010年再降为13.01亿度。

专记：胡锦涛视察索风营电站建设

2005年2月10日，时值新春佳节之际，在索风营电站建设者们不顾天寒地冻，紧张地工作在建设工地上，进行着电站建设的最后冲刺。此时，中共中央总书记、国家主席胡锦涛在贵州省和贵阳市党、政领导的陪同下，冒着凛冽的寒风，莅临索风营电站建设工地，视察电站建设，慰问日夜奋战在电站建设中的全体员工。视察中胡锦涛肯定乌江开发公司对“流域滚动梯级开发”的战略思想，要求“电力开发要像索风营建设一样，必须考虑环境保护，走持续发展、滚动发展之路，继续编写乌江事业的下篇”。

2005年胡锦涛视察索风营电站建设

在胡锦涛的关怀和鼓励下，电站建设加快进度，视察后仅半年时间，建成总库容2.012亿立方米水库大坝和电站引水洞，并安装完内径为9.9米的压力钢管，以及尾水隧洞10×16.3米的城门洞，又建起长133.2米、宽24米、高57.72米的地下厂房，安装完3台单机容量为200兆瓦混流式水轮发电机组，完成土建工程挖山覆盖层234.3万立方米，开挖石方153.2万立方米，开凿隧道洞石97.28立方米，浇灌混凝土129.83万立方米，安装金属构件7791吨，帷幕灌浆15万立方米，固结灌浆13.4万立方米，完成110千伏输电线路安装。当年8月14日，电站第一台机组投入运行，16日下午3时强大的电流联网输往南方，实现当年开工，当年截流，首台机组并网发电的目标，使电站成为“工期短，投资少，绿化早，环保好，移民少”的生态型企业。随着第二台机组组装完毕，进入调试，第三台机组安装进度加快。12月23日第二台机组投入运行。2006年6月6日，第三台机组安装完毕投入营运。电站建设告竣，装机容量3×200兆瓦。电站投入运行后，生产一直正常，先后荣获全国“安康杯”竞赛优胜企业、贵阳市生态文明创建示范点和贵州省企业文化建设示范基地等称号。

（二）输变电

1978年，县境建有久长变电站和阳明变电站正常运行。两座变电站均为110千伏，有35千伏线路8条，110千伏线路5条，10千伏线路9条。1979年建广田变电站，设主变2台，35千伏进线1条，10千伏出线回路间隔6个。继后又增建和平变电站，供电线路35千伏8条、10千伏9条、110千伏5条。1999年开始进行农村电网改造，又增建小营、六屯和六桶3个变电站，共建有663个变压器台区，加上原有变电站有10千伏项目改造线路599.4公里、0.4千伏以下项目改造线路1876.8公里，电网覆盖全县217个行政村，覆盖面达99.8%。2000年年底，全县农村电网改造告竣，实现城乡电网同网同价。2004年又建扎佐220千伏变电站。2005年又在扎佐镇喻家街建110千伏变电站，使全县供电容量达8万千伏安，售电量4

亿千瓦时，比1998年的1.57亿千瓦时售电量增加1.3倍。2008年全县供电量为6.45亿千瓦时。到2009年，县境共有110千伏变电站3座，35千伏变电站7座，主变总容量301.5兆伏安，110千伏输电线路6条，总长77.1千米；35千伏输电线12条，总长163.15千米；10千伏输电线48条，总长1106.64千米，配置变压器1490台，总容量171.47兆伏安，供电面积1075.7平方公里，用电户达7.03万户，通电率为99.98%，供电量6.26亿千瓦时。2010年，供电量达8.25亿千瓦时。

2010年全县电力工业企业概况表

表3—02—02

	企业名称	地址	装机容量（千瓦）	主管单位	建设时间（年）	投产时间（年）
发电	河口电站（修文老电站）	龙场镇干坝村	1.5	红枫电厂	1942—1951	1951
	三级电站（修文电站）	龙场镇干坝村	2万		1960	1961
	四级电站（窄巷口电站）	谷堡乡平寨村	4.5万		1965	1971
	五级电站（红林电站）	谷堡乡水口村	10.2万		1965	1979
	六级电站（红岩电站）	洒坪乡轿子山	3万		1971	1974
	索风营电站	六广镇沙坡村	600万	乌江开发	2002	2005
输变电	久长变电站	久长镇沙雁村	110千伏	县供电局	1962	1963
	阳明变电站	龙场镇阳明村	110千伏		1969	1972
	广田变电站	六广镇广田村	35千伏		1980	1985
	和平变电站	扎佐镇和平村	35千伏		1989	1990
	小营变电站	龙场镇小营村	10千伏		1998	1999
	六屯变电站	六屯乡都堡村	35千伏		1999	2000
	六桶变电站	六桶乡盐井村	35千伏		2001	2003
	喻家街变电站	扎佐镇喻家街	110千伏		2005	2005

专记：农村电网改造

1999年，按照国务院农村电网“两改一同价”(农电体制改革、农网改造和实现城乡同网同价)的要求，县政府全面部署实施农村电网改造工程。是年7月14日，贵阳市北供电局与县供电局在六屯乡都堡村举行农网35千伏工程启动暨六屯变电站开工典礼，标志着全县农村电网改造改建工程进入实施阶段。六屯35千伏变电站首台变压器容量为3.15万千伏安，连同供电线路架设，总投资400万元。

农网改造工程开始实施后，县供电局走村串寨摸底调查，进行改造规划设计。之后，通过招标组织13个施工作业队，打响农网改造大会战。

农网改造至2000年年底完成，总投资3700万元。农网改造给农村群众带来实惠，农民用上放心电、便宜电，为农村经济发展注入活力，农民群众对此感慨万端。龙场镇的马关村在农网改造前，村里人家多从事农耕，农网改造后电压稳定，供电量足，不少农户利用电力在道路沿线开起粮食加工房、汽车维修点，经营红红火火。小营村做豆腐生意的村民袁昌兴家以前因为用电扯皮，电压不稳，买电磨也用不上，农网改造后，一户一表，不再因用电扯皮，电压又稳，白日夜晚都有电，磨豆腐的生意兴旺起来。村民刘兴祥家以前因为电压不稳，点电灯还没有煤油灯亮，就把电灯换成煤油灯，农网改造后，他家又把煤油灯换成电灯。广大村民用上农网改造后的方便电后，由衷地称赞：农网改造利村民，电源引到我们家，照明生产都方便，农民心里乐开花。

二、建材

（一）水泥

1978年，县境建有县郭家林水泥厂和马家桥水泥厂。1986年，县办三角山水泥厂和白莲水泥厂先后建成投产，1988年修文二中校办水泥厂建成投产。20世纪90年代，又陆续兴建起渝鑫、久长、利尔、荣利达、贵遵、潮水、北流、强力、扎佐、环北、复退残和国康等水泥厂，到1998年，全县有水泥生产企业17家，年生产能力30.5万吨。在激烈的市场竞争中，部分企业在90年代末，进入技术改造，到1999年，久长建材有限公司完成10万吨水泥生产线技改；利尔建材有限公司8万吨生产线技改完毕；南方水泥厂10万吨生产线技改告竣；三角山水泥厂第二套生产线建成。同时宏华水泥厂、贵阳市德荣水泥厂、贵州建源水泥厂、渝鑫水泥厂及国康水泥厂进行技改后，都分别达到年产6万吨生产能力。进入2000年，经济效益欠佳的强力水泥厂、扎佐水泥厂、环北水泥厂、复退残水泥厂关停，全县生产水泥为60.1万吨。经过技改后的水泥产量稳步上升，到2008年，全县有水泥生产企业14家，年生产水泥88万吨，产值1.4亿元。2009年7月1日，鸿鑫水泥厂年产60万吨熟料新型半干法JT窑水泥生产线开工建设，12月31日，年产200万吨新型干法回转窑熟料水泥贵州金久水泥厂一期工程日产4000吨生产线点火投产，使全县年生产水泥翻过百万吨大关，达118万吨，2010年达211万吨。

1996年，由原成久耐火厂改建成的贵遵水泥厂

专记：一座现代化的建材生产项目——金久水泥厂在久长诞生

2008年7月29日，贵州黔桂发电有限责任公司独资注册2.4亿元，组建贵州金久水泥有限公司落户久长镇，利用原航空工业部属烽光电工厂厂址兴建年产200万吨大型水泥生产项目。厂区距贵阳市40公里，距县城16公里，涉及金桥村和上堡村的5个村民组，征拨土地113亩和矿山710亩，搬迁企业5家、砂石场2个和农户60户。

项目规划建设两条4000T/日新型干法回转窑熟料水泥生产线及配套7.5兆瓦余热发电站，四条年产30万立方米加气混凝土新型建材生产线，预计总投资15亿元。工程分两期进行，第一期于2008年9月完成厂区“四通一平”，12月正式开工建设。建设中按照国家对水泥工业生产“控制总量、调整结构、提高质量、保护环境”的原则，综合利用粉煤灰、硫酸渣、脱硫石膏、磷渣等工业废弃物生产水泥，年计消耗废渣73.36万吨，建成一道现代化的循环经济型干法水泥生产线。项目建设中，得到县委、县政府重视和

支持，贵阳市委副书记市长袁周和市委副书记李涛、县委书记石洪、县长蒋志伦经常到建设现场办公解建设情况，察看工程进度，协调解决建设中的具体问题，使工程建设进度加快，进展顺利。

2009年12月，第一期工程完工，吸收300余人就业，当月31日点火烘炉，随即试产。项目建设实现建厂环境优美、原料来源稳定、工艺技术先进、人力资源丰富、市场前景良好的效果，使县境水泥生产水平显著提升，产业结构合理调整，产品质量得以升级。2010年1月至12月累计实现产值1.23亿元，利税2500万元。

2008年，落户于久长镇的金久水泥厂

2010年水泥生产企业概况表

表3—02—03

企业名称	地址	年产量（万吨）	投资规模（万元）	企业性质	建设时间（年）	备　注
郭家林水泥厂	龙场镇沙溪村	8.8	1240	联营	1972	2000年改制
南方水泥厂	龙场镇白莲村	10	800	个体	2000	2001年8月跨入规模以上企业
三角山水泥厂	龙场镇新寨村	8	1750	个体	1996	1998年改制
宏华水泥厂	龙场镇白莲村	8	277.5	联营	1984	—
建源水泥厂	龙场镇普陀村	8	400	联营	1988	1999年产权转让
渝鑫水泥厂	扎佐镇中营村	10	600	个体	1992	2000年技改
久长水泥厂	久长镇驴坊村	10	481	个体	1993	1994年技改
利尔水泥厂	龙场镇小营村	18	1400	联营	1994	—
荣利达水泥厂	龙场镇小营村	8	700	个体	1996	—
北流水泥厂	龙场镇潮水村	8	1000	个体	1998	2003年技改
德荣水泥厂	龙场镇潮水村	8	500	私营	1998	产权转让
奇峰水泥厂	久长镇兴隆村	30	1400	联营	1996	2005年8月改建
国康水泥厂	六广镇中心村	2	400	私营	1998	2000年改建
金久水泥厂	久长镇金桥村	200	15	联营	2008	2010年投产

（二）火土砖

1981年马家桥幸福砖厂建成制砖轮窑，开始生产机制红砖，1983年又建一座“自来风”轮窑，带动其他砖厂从手工制砖向机制砖轮窑发展。1985年全县制砖轮窑发展到17座，生产红砖4563万块。1994年，小营砖厂建26门轮窑一座，置400型制砖机，年生产能力达3000万块。1998年，高坝砖厂技改，新建18门焙烧轮窑一座，年产量提高到1500万块，2000年第二次技改，引进先进制砖流水线一条，轮窑扩为32门，生产能力达年产3000万块。与此同时，黔丰、毛冲坝、对门山和杨家湾等小型砖厂相继技改，生产能力大幅度提高。2005年，全县制砖企业达18家，形成年产红砖多条生产线，将红砖产量提升到1.95亿块，产品销至贵阳市辖各区县。2010年，部分砖厂关停，全县生产红砖1.42亿块。

2010年制砖生产企业概况表

表3—02—04

企业名称	地址	产品	年产量（万块）	投资规模	企业性质	建设时间（年）
幸福砖厂	龙场镇幸福村	红砖	1000	逐步投入	联营	1981
黔丰砖厂	龙场镇普陀村	红砖	400	5000万元	联营	1983
响水洞砖厂	龙场镇普陀村	红砖	800	5000万元	联营	1983
小营砖厂	龙场镇小营村	红砖	1400	400万元	个体	1985
杨家湾砖厂	龙场镇白莲村	红砖	未定产	小规模	私营	1988
对门山砖厂	龙场镇白莲村	红砖	1000	逐步投入	联营	1993
何家湾砖厂	龙场镇马家桥	红砖	未定产	小规模	私营	1993
毛冲坝砖厂	马家桥毛冲坝	红砖	未定产	小规模	私营	1994
高坝砖厂	久长镇高坝村	红砖	3000	600万元	私营	1997
坤泰页岩砖厂	龙场镇普陀村	页岩砖	1500	400万元	私营	2001
高原耐火材料厂	扎佐镇三元村	耐火砖	5万吨	700万元	私营	2003
茶田砖厂	龙场镇茶田村	发泡砖	—	—	联营	2004

（三）砂石

1978年，县境建筑用砂以山砂为主，产砂点主要在县城蛤蟆坡和马家桥马官丫口、小山坝倒马坎等处，年产山砂1万余立方米。1985年，城乡基础设施建设加快，砂石需求量增加，县内一批砂石厂应运而生，成为乡镇企业重要组成部分。至1990年，全县山砂销售量达15万立方米。龙场镇马关村、普陀村采砂山成为村民致富的“金银山”。进入90年代，贵（阳）遵（义）、贵（阳）毕（节）高等级公路建设铺开、乡村公路硬化、城镇道路改扩建，促使砂石生产扩展到其他乡镇，又诞生一批砂石厂，共开采石灰石393.78万立方米，其中1999年县城基础设施“九三”工程建设期间采石就达176.70万立方米。到2000年，全县有砂石厂37个，砂石开采量达887.8万立方米。从2003年起随着城乡建设需求量减少以及房开公司自办商砼混企业，砂石产量呈下降趋势。全县采砂石量仅145万立方米。到2010年，全县持有开采证的砂石厂有56个，但多数处于停产。

（四）石灰

1978年，原建的县城东蛤蟆坡、王官公社三角山、马家桥公社小营的石灰窑继续生产。1985年新建马关、小营、程官等村办石灰厂。继后因基础设施建设、房屋建筑有新型墙面涂料、水泥、瓷粉应市，全县石灰产量长时间徘徊在年产3000吨左右。从1995年起，石灰成为工业原料，需求量开始上升，到1999年全县累计生产石灰16万吨。2003年，以石灰作为电石生产原料的贵阳华宏冶炼有限公司落户于久长镇，使石灰需求量大增，年产量达到3万吨。2005年，全县生产石灰已达4万多吨。直到2010年年生产量一直稳定在3万吨左右。

（五）水泥预制件

1982年，因县境楼房建筑楼面、屋面开始使用水泥预制板，县建筑公司在县城东门蛤蟆坡建起水泥预制件厂，专门生产水泥预制空心板供楼房建筑用。随后水泥预制件从空心水泥板发展到水泥砖、水泥瓦、走廊花板和挑梁等水泥预制构件。到1985年，全县水泥预制品工场竟达100多处。进入90年代，城乡建设加快，安居工程、商品房开发进一步推动水泥预制构件生产。2001年，农村茅草房改造铺开，水泥预制件生产又呈现好的势头。至2006年年均生产预制件24万立方米。继后由于房屋建筑楼层和屋面采取整体浇灌，使空心预制板生产量逐渐减少，至2010年，仅剩龙场镇水泥预制厂5家，年产板6万立方米，扎佐镇预制厂12家，年产板8万立方米，六广镇水泥砖厂1家，年产砖30万块。

专记：崛起的马家桥乡建材业

20世纪70年代末，城关镇马家桥公社的社队企业在全县尤为突出，除公社水泥厂外，还有幸福、白莲的队办砖瓦厂和马官队办砂厂等。1981年实行家庭联产承包责任制，队办企业采用承包方式承包给社员个人或部分社员联合经营。1983年，幸福砖厂引进自来风轮窑生产红砖，年产350万块，村民收入骤然增加，激励起队办企业的积极性。1984年，全乡工业企业发展到151个，其中建材生产企业包括小水泥厂、砖厂、水泥预制厂、砂石厂就有84个，占全乡工业企业总数的55.6%，用工1675人，占全乡劳动力资源的49.36%，建材产值300.93万元，占全乡工业总产值的83.9%，一跃而为全县独占鳌头的建材之乡。

1984年，安顺地区乡镇企业工作现场会选在马家桥乡召开，地委书记陈远武对马家桥乡建材业的迅猛发展和取得的成绩加以充分肯定，并赞扬："这是农村致富的希望。"现场会议促进马家桥乡的建材业更上一层楼。在上级党委、政府的鼓励下，充分利用乡境蕴藏的马血泥、石灰石和页岩大办建材工业。1985年，全乡制砖轮窑发展到17座228门，山砂场23个，打砂机24台，石灰窑16个，兴办石粉厂、水泥预制件厂和白莲水泥厂，使全乡建材企业增为92个，占工业企业总数的53.18%，产值584万元，占工业产值的77.9%，获得省委农村工作部授予"建材之乡"荣誉称号。省委书记胡锦涛亲临马家桥，对马家桥乡镇企业发展业绩赞不绝口，并将兴办乡镇企业的"两马"（遵义马家湾、修文马家桥）精神和经验推荐全省。省委领导的鼓励和鞭策进一步推动马家桥乡建材企业的发展。当年，全乡工农业总产值达1030.4万元，人均年纯收入达1114元，为全县农民人均年纯收入305元的3.65倍，走在全县乡镇的前头。

三、采煤

1978年，全县原建的社办煤厂、队办煤厂、县社队企业局接管煤厂和国营煤厂共21家继续生产。进入80年代，随着冶炼、水泥、烤烟等生产发展，对煤炭需要量增大，拉动一批手工开采的私营小煤窑诞生。到1988年，国营贵阳煤矿搬迁黔西、红旗煤厂处于半停产状态，全县乡镇有煤厂192个，其中使用机械化生产采伐年产达2万—3万吨较大煤厂有广田松山煤厂、二关坝煤厂、六广镇煤厂、扎佐镇煤厂和洒坪乡煤厂。1994年，全县有证煤厂发展到230个，矿工2568人，年采煤59万吨，产值1763万元，原煤销往省外，煤炭产业成为乡镇企业的重要支柱。

1995年，全县拥有大小煤窑包括村民在房前屋后自挖的煤洞400多个，其中经营性无证开采煤窑就有151个，持证开采率仅为25%。小煤窑存在既破坏生态环境，浪费资源，又诱发地质灾害，时有伤亡事故发生。当年4月，县设置煤炭工业局，组建稽查队，行使煤炭行业行政管理督查权，负责煤炭生产和经营整顿，强化煤炭“五统一”（统一订货、统一运输、统一票据、统一结算、统一管理），保护煤炭资源，强化安全生产，维护经营秩序，加强税费征收。但乱挖乱采的小煤窑泛滥，屡禁不止。县煤炭工业局行使对煤炭行业管理职能，加强对煤炭生产企业的整顿，经过整顿建立起扎佐镇三里河、大石乡红岩、六广镇朱家坝3个煤炭生产示范点。全县有证煤厂208个，比1994年减少22个，生产原煤62万吨，比1994年增产23万吨。1998年，县煤炭工业局进一步加强煤炭行业管理，采取关井压产措施，依法清理关闭无证非法开采、安全无保障、规模小、事故多的煤窑104家，取缔封闭无证和不规范煤井418处（含隐蔽煤窑和房前屋后自挖煤洞），拆除作业工棚33处，没收乱挖煤窑的设施9处，处理非法采挖者15人，处以罚金8970元。经整顿后全县原煤年产量虽降至78.39万吨，但保障煤炭资源合理开采，减少环境污染和安全事故发生。

1999年，县政府根据国发〔1999〕43号文件精神，出台《关闭非法和布局不合理煤矿安排意见》，组织县煤炭工业局、国土局、经贸局、总工会、公安局和乡镇企业局联合统一执法，清理炸封关闭无证矿井28处，吊销未能达到办矿条件煤窑29家的生产许可证。2000年8月，县煤炭工业局发出《关于加强煤矿改造、做好关井压产工作准备通知》，经过整顿全县仅保留煤矿矿井48个。随后逐年检查，对不能达标的矿井责令关闭。到2004年，年产3万吨以上达标矿井降至27个，取缔无证煤窑61个，其中谷堡乡17个，六广镇5个，六桶乡6个，龙场镇12个，扎佐镇7个，大石乡2个，久长镇10个，洒坪乡2个。2008年全面关停小煤窑，年产6万吨达标煤矿仅存16家，生产原煤106.3万吨。虽然矿井减少，但生产能力提高，产量大幅上升。2009年，达标煤矿年设计产量定为9万吨，将年产6万吨煤矿16个改造升级到9万至15万吨。2010年新建15万吨和30万吨煤矿各1个，全县达标煤矿为18个，达到年产量9万吨以上继续生产的煤矿9个，生产原煤167万吨。

2009年，改造后的洒坪乡栗木山煤矿

2010年九万吨以上达标煤炭生产企业概况表

表3—02—05

企业名称	地址	年产量（万吨）	投资规模（万元）	企业性质	建设时间（年）	备　注
红星煤矿	谷堡乡红星村	15	技改300	私营	2005	2009年完成技改
天治煤矿	谷堡乡平寨村	15	486	联营	2005	按达标煤矿要求建设
栗木山煤矿	洒坪乡上坝村	15	技改1291	联营	2004	2009年完成技改
双月煤矿	扎佐镇双月村	9	技改1500	私营	2001	2009年完成技改
清水沟煤矿	六桶乡花椰村	15	2000	私营	1968	原为村集体，1988年转为私营
丁家寨煤矿	六广镇前丰村	15	726	联营	2003	2005年完成技改
黔丰煤矿	六广镇前丰村	15	技改450	私营	2005	2009年完成技改
三利煤矿	六广镇广义村	9	技改450	私营	2000	2009年完成技改
龙窝煤矿	六广镇中山村	9	技改1000	私营	2005	2009年完成技改

四、冶炼

（一）生铁

1984年，县内开始兴建小炼铁厂，到80年代末稍具规模的修文联合铁厂建成，年产量均未超过6000吨。90年代中又办起修文新生铁厂、阳明铁厂、裕黔铁厂、双星铁厂、荣达冶炼厂，使全县生铁年产量由1994年2.89万吨上升到2001年的6.65万吨。2003年，县外民营经济入驻，开办起贵阳双辉钢铁有限公司、新宇冶业有限公司和金阳冶业有限公司，使全县生铁产量达到7.4万吨。到2004年，全县落户铁厂10家，生产生铁达13万吨。2005年起因矿源逐减和环境保护需要，小铁厂生产不稳定。2008年全县生产生铁8.9万吨。2009年，全县产生铁8万吨，2010年全县产生铁18万吨。

（二）铁合金

1989年，县内建有修文硅铁厂、河口铁合金厂，开始冶炼铁合金。1991年，硅铁厂与香港德利公司合资经营，将厂名更为贵州文德矿冶有限公司，生产铁合金，产品远销中国台湾地区和菲律宾、韩国、日本。2003年，年产3.6万吨贵阳鼎鑫电冶有限公司、年产5.4万吨贵阳龙源实业有限公司、年产3.6万吨贵阳文乐冶炼有限公司和贵阳三阳冶炼有限公司等铁合金冶炼企业相继入驻县境。全县6家铁合金冶炼企业，年生产能力达10万吨。2010年由于原料缺乏和环境达标的要求，企业处于半停半生产状况，产量逐年下降。2009年4.9万吨，2010年3万吨。

（三）特殊钢

2008年8月，贵阳钢铁厂落实贵阳市“退二进三”（第二产业退出贵阳市区、第三产业进入贵阳市区）战略部署，与首都钢铁厂联手开发首钢贵阳特殊钢新材料循环经济项目，落户在扎佐镇工业园区。特殊钢项目由首钢总公司、贵州省国资委、中国信达资产管理公司分别以60%、32.19%、7.81%的投资比例进行资产重组。由首钢控股，计划投资138亿元，组建首钢贵阳特殊钢有限责任公司。特殊钢项目建设，顺应国家钢铁工业联合重组潮流，充分利用资源，盘活国有资产，实现保值增值。

2009年3月3日，项目建设进场主道动工，8月20日，生产基地动工，占地面积5764.5亩。2010年，完成基地进场道路扎（佐）六（屯）公路改扩建，厂区“三通一平”（水、电、路通，场地平），厂房建设进入实施阶段。当年完成投资38亿元，一期工程顺利竣工。基地建成后采用国际领先设备、工艺，通过对资源和能源再循环，达到年产钢、锻钢、棒材、扁钢、车轮钢、模具钢等100万吨，产值150亿元，增值税10亿元。整个项目拟定3年完成，实现技术、质量、产品、环保一流的循环经济冶炼工业。

2009年3月，首钢贵阳特殊钢厂奠基开工典礼

（四）铝矾土煅烧

1985年，全县共建起6家铝矾土煅烧企业，建有煅烧窑37座，将铝矾土烧成熟料，制成耐火材料半成品，产品远销国内外，成为县内工业创汇的大宗产品。2000年，新增铝矾土煅烧企业4个，使全县铝矾

土熟矿产量达23万吨。2005年煅烧企业发展到48家，共生产铝矾土熟矿30万吨。2010年产量上升为31万吨。

（五）棕刚玉

1988年，在铝矾土煅烧基础上兴办起生产棕刚玉冶炼厂，用一级铝矾土熟矿冶炼棕刚玉，产品大部分经省进出口贸易公司远销国外。生产棕刚玉的企业主要有年产4500吨的联合磨料厂、年产5000吨的久长棕刚玉厂、鑫火棕刚玉厂、鲁黔银星磨料有限公司和县属棕刚玉冶炼分厂和年产6万吨特级耐火铝矾土的贵州四达矿产有限公司。其中联合磨料厂的产品经对外贸易经济合作部批准，于1999年10月荣获具有进出口经营权生产企业资格，产品直销美国、韩国、日本以及中国香港地区，为贵州省产品出口创汇名列前茅的棕刚玉生产企业，2003年，产量达7900吨，产值2102万元。2010年，规模以上的棕刚玉厂只有四达矿产有限公司和银星磨料有限公司，其余企业关停，年产棕刚玉5.2万吨。

专记：金属镁厂建设始末

1994年10月，被誉为“中华锅炉王”的全国优秀青年企业家、山西省环海实业有限公司董事长兼总经理梁文海，随全国光彩事业考察团千里迢迢赶到贵州考察扶贫项目，当即受到县委、县政府领导谋发展的激情打动，深入修文考察。梁文海看到原航空工业部属烽光厂迁出后的厂区环境、地理位置和交通运输等优越条件，表示投资意向。县委、县政府采取“引进一个企业，出去一批干部”的策略，派员前往山西联系，并成立由县委副书记牛熹（贵州省委统战部社会主义学院干部挂任）为组长，县有关部门干部为成员的协调组，从已买断烽光厂产权的绿原公司手中，再次以310万元将烽光厂转让给山西环海实业有限公司，组建起贵州环海实业有限公司。公司聘用牛熹为总经理主持工作，作为修文县创办的“全国光彩事业东西部合作年示范项目”。

1995年初，公司首先论证年产10万吨道路水泥生产线项目。此时又遇国内出现金属镁生产的好势头，于是在没有经过充分论证的情况下，盲目将水泥生产线改上金属镁生产线。计划投资1120万元，其中山西环海总公司一次性投资642万元（含实物折抵和设备投入），向银行贷款405万元，向贵阳市政府借乡镇企业发展资金50万元，筹集其他款项73万元，共到位总资金1170万元，开始建设冶炼金属镁厂。在牛熹的主持下，因缺生产技术人员、土建未按招投标程序办理、建设工程未按计划实施、子项目和其他费用超支、采购业务不熟造成购进的真空机组设备纯属下马淘汰设备，以及公司总经理牛熹两头担任职务、政企不分和在修文挂职期满返原单位等因素，项目建设处于半停顿状态。

1997年年初，山西环海总公司派高级会计师到厂监督，县政府调整环海公司管理人员，聘请原011系统418库主任徐耀山出任总经理，指派县纪委干部唐德华为副总经理，并派土建工程师临场指导，调整公司人员后又投进资金100万元继续建设。8月，检验设备效果，进行小规模试产，生产金属镁5吨。11月，基本建成年产1000吨金属镁生产线。随即山西环海总公司指派张爱果等人接管该厂，而此时金属镁市场价已降至该厂生产成本临界点，导致生产长期搁浅竟达10年。时至2008年7月，才由贵州金久水泥有限公司将瘫痪多年的金属镁厂接过来，改建成年产200万吨大型的现代化水泥生产企业。

2010年冶炼企业一览表

表3—02—06

企业名称	地址	产品	年产量（万吨）	投资规模（万元）	企业性质	建设时间（年）	投产时间（年）
联合铁厂	龙场镇马家桥	生铁	6	155	联营	1984	1985
文德矿冶	龙场镇马家桥	硅铁	6	（122美元）	联营	1984	1991
华航冶炼	龙场镇新生村	生铁	3	200	私营	2002	2003
双辉钢铁	龙场镇潮水村	生铁	6	4000	私营	2003	2004
诺亚矿产	龙场镇军民村	生铁	4.68	3000	私营	2003	2004
金阳冶业	龙场镇王官村	生铁	6	2000	私营	2003	2004
新宇冶炼	龙场镇王官村	生铁	2.5	1000	私营	2003	2004
福贵冶炼	龙场镇白莲村	生铁	5	300	私营	1995	1999
新生冶炼	龙场镇新生村	生铁	1.5	300	私营	1993	1994
兴胜冶炼	龙场镇新生村	生铁	6	447	联营	1993	1994
华宏冶炼	久长镇上寨村	电石	10	1000	私营	2004	2004
三阳冶炼	久长镇新民村	镍钼合金	3.6	3000	私营	2004	2005
鲁黔磨料	龙场水塘村	棕刚玉	2	1000	私营	2005	2005
联合磨料厂	龙场镇潮水村	棕刚玉	0. 5	800	联营	1988	1990
新宇冶业	龙场镇王官村	生铁	2.5	1000	私营	2002	2002
鼎鑫电冶	龙场镇阳明村	硅锰合金	3.6	1500	私营	2004	2004
文乐冶炼	龙场镇新生村	铁合金	3	2000	私营	2003	2004
龙源实业	龙场镇新生村	生铁	3.6	1500	私营	2004	2005
鑫火实业	龙场镇水塘村	棕刚玉	2	技改260	私营	1987	2004
赣发铁合金厂	龙场镇马家桥	铁合金	0. 7	技改500	私营	2000	2000
国森冶炼厂	龙场镇	生铁	—	技改160	私营	2000	2001
宏和矿业	龙场镇	电溶锆	—	440	私营	2002	2002
修文铁合金厂	龙场镇马关村	铁合金	0.6	1000	联营	1989	1993
四达公司	龙场镇新春村	耐火材料	6	500(美元)	联营	1991	1994
阳明铁厂	龙场镇阳明村	生铁	1.2	400	联营	1993	1994
双辉钢铁厂	龙场镇潮水村	生铁	6	1200	私营	2003	2004

五、机械制造

（一）县属机械工业

20世纪80年代初，县农机厂生产农用水泵、打谷机、插秧机、托轮式球磨机、粉碎机及粉碎机平板、锰合金耐磨球铁、砂石机销往全县农村社、队集体和社队采掘企业。城关铁器社生产的小型农具、农具配件、小五金畅销县内外。扎佐农具厂生产小农具和修理车辆。80年代末，城关铁器社在市场竞争中被淘汰，企业停产，职工各寻门路生产锄头、镰刀小农具。扎佐农具厂转卖厂房，分割资产，职工另谋他业。县农机厂在农村实行联产承包以家庭为单位生产经营，使用农机概率减少，企业在周转资金不足的影响下停产，1993年被三角山水泥厂兼并。从此县属机械工业走向个体加工农机配件之路。

（二）驻县机械工业

1978年，航空工业部驻县企业有烽光厂、万江厂、兴红厂、华文厂、庆文厂和储备原材料的418库。1985年，改革开放逐步深入，从生产军工产品转向生产民用机械，产品有心脏按摩机、各类电机、电梯接插件、汽车雨刮器、测速机、高压纺织计量泵、油剂计量泵、综合式卷烟机、疲劳测试机、轧面机、包装机、摩托车凸轮、钻床配件和变压器等。其中心脏按摩机获空军科技成果二等奖和国家优质产品金龙奖；洗衣机电机获航空工业部和贵州省优质产品奖；CS27—05交流伺服测速机组获国家银质奖；纺织计量泵、油剂计量泵填补国内空白。20世纪90年代上半期，烽光、华文、庆文厂和万江大部先后迁往贵阳市小河、乌当和白云区，仅留下兴红厂、418库和万江的世星机械厂。1998年，兴红厂宣布破产下马。2003年，418库脱离贵航集团转移地方后并入民营企业贵州龙翔集团公司，主要生产“云天牌”摩托车凸轮轴组件，产品获ISO9001：2000质量管理体系认证，批量生产，成批销往南京、济南、常州、重庆、宁波、上海等摩托车生产厂家，入围国家摩托车行业最佳零部件明星阵容。2005年，全县机械工业产值6857万元，占工业总产业值的3.86%。为发展县内机械工业，县政府拟建的开发项目库，将开发年产3万吨不锈钢冷轧和年产3万吨连铸连轧热轧卷，年产200万套车用铝合金轮毂等项目开始招商，采取产业扶持措施，以推动机械工业的发展。2010年，全县机械工业产值7889.4万元，其中万江世星机械厂3105.2万元，龙翔凸轮轴4784.2万元。

航空工业部驻县企业万江厂生产车间

六、食品

（一）粮油加工

1978年，县粮食局下属的城关打米厂、面粉厂、榨油厂和扎佐、久长、六广粮管所打米、面粉加工车间均属地方国营企业，产品按计划供应城镇居民。1990年，城关打米厂和面粉厂合并迁驻久长驴坊国家粮食储备库区旁，占地4亩，投资120万元，修建“四皮一心”（4台皮磨、1台心磨）面粉生产车间，设计年产标准粉1万吨。建成后利用国家计划进行面粉加工，日产面粉300吨，产品按计划供应城镇居民。1991年，粮食局投资298万元，在城关区马家桥幸福村建年加工油菜籽9000吨，日压榨菜籽50吨，产精炼菜油20吨和油饼30吨的油脂厂。厂建成后，原城关菜油厂与新厂合并，产品除计划供应城镇居民外，其余议价销售。1994年，国家取消粮食计划供应，粮油加工企业面向市场，因原料无保障、产品滞销、购销混乱、管理失控、生产下滑、亏损严重，于1996年停产。

2004年，贵阳领先食品有限公司和修文金格食品有限公司分别投资300万元，在扎佐镇食品工业园建

起方便食品厂，生产面食方便食品。为提高产品质量，增强市场竞争，2008年两厂分别进行改造、续建，到2010年生产基本正常。

（二）风味食品

1992年，县库区经济开发公司（县移民办）投资1400万元，利用扎佐原航空工业部属304医院搬迁留下的场地，建野珍食品厂，成为县内首家以工业化生产方式加工本地山珍野果，生产精美风味食品的规模型企业。“野珍”系列产品中的“宝中宝”“玖瑰牛肉干”“山珍果”“精三蛋茹酥”“小米鲊”曾获1994年贵州食品荟萃展中最受消费者欢迎的产品。后来由于政企不分、行企合力办厂，致企业没有活力，生产难以维系，1996年被迫停产。

1993年建成的野珍食品厂厂部

2000年，联宇食品有限公司在生产风味香菇酱油的基础上，开发风味油辣椒、风味萝卜干、风味蕨菜、风味竹笋等，产品年产500吨，被誉为“绿色食品”，2002年国际阳明文化节，产品列入旅游商品，成为县内首家旅游食品定点企业，产品销往省内外。至2010年，公司经营正常。

（三）乳品饮料

1999年，众福特色食品有限公司使用扎佐芭蕉芋、马铃薯和玉米为原料，在扎佐镇和平村兴建年产5000吨液体葡萄糖、3000吨高麦芽糖浆生产线，同时开发猕猴桃粉、苦丁茶粉和苦荞粉冲剂型饮料产品。次年生产麦芽糊精560吨，液体葡萄糖800吨。2000年初，因原料短缺，生产下滑，处于半停产状态。

2003年，由杨凯胜牵头联营组建贵阳三茗食品有限公司，采用谷堡乡独特的“贵长”猕猴桃果就地建成年产200吨低糖猕猴桃果脯生产线，生产果酱、果酒、水果罐头等系列饮料。年加工猕猴桃500吨，产品打入旅游商品市场。后因生产工艺及宣传促销因素影响，果脯销路不畅，生产处于停产状态。

2004年，贵州好一多乳业有限公司利用下属久长镇清水和扎佐镇丁官奶牛养殖场为基础，在贵（阳）遵（义）与贵（阳）毕（节）高等级公路交汇处建设现代化乳品加工厂。生产乳制食品50余种，产品销往贵阳市区和周边县市。

2009年，贵州三金圣果饮品有限公司，开发出“猕露”牌系列富硒猕猴桃饮料，在2010年5月贵阳市“第四届旅游发展大会”时，由大会将该饮料作为指定饮品，受到参会嘉宾一致好评。至此产品大量推向市场，销路良好。2010年，乳产品产量8079吨，产值7727.7万元。

专记：跳跃前进的好一多乳业有限公司

2003年3月，贵州好一多乳业有限公司落户久长镇清水村，投资1400万元建成占地40亩的饲养棚5栋、饲料库1座、挤奶机台5个和可饲养奶牛600头的奶牛基地。经过1年努力，第一批荷斯坦奶牛160头于2004年3月入场。基地建设初期，公司依托“好1多”乳业协会采取“公司+基地+协会+农户”方式，由公司投资建饲养场，基地集中圈养，协会承担贷款购牛，农户种草喂牛的运行机制，使“好1多”乳业迈出可喜的第一步。

2004年7月，协会建起“四统一”（贷款、建圈、防疫、挤奶统一）和“两分户”（饲养、结算分户）合作经济组织，组建清水奶牛养殖小区。有25户村民参加协会贷款100万元，建起2000平方米圈舍，购入奶牛75头，使公司养殖规模扩展，“好1多”乳业向前跳跃一步。

“好1多”乳业有限公司

随后，为推动公司乳业发展，又在扎佐镇丁官村和息烽县青山乡建起与清水基地同等规模的奶牛饲养基地各一个。在扎佐贵（阳）毕（节），贵（阳）遵（义）高等级公路立交道口旁征地50亩，投资2000万元，建起建筑面积1.2万平方米，日处理鲜奶200吨现代化乳品生产线，品种50余种，年加工鲜奶7.2万吨，年产值达5.7亿元的大型乳业制品加工厂，使公司又向前跳跃一大步。

2005年，久长清水村基地饲养的奶牛增至600头，年产鲜奶3600吨，协会发展奶农增至120户，饲养奶牛280头，全村牧草、鲜奶出售纯收入565万元，人均4843元。2010年又在六桶乡新建奶牛场，配置挤奶机台和鲜奶储存罐，鲜奶直送公司乳品加工厂，三级跳跃使“好1多”乳业的“蛋糕”越做越大，立足省内乳业市场经久不衰。

（四）酒类酿造

1978年，国营修文酒厂在县城、六广和扎佐建有分厂，生产白酒计划供应县内居民。1979代，国家对酿酒业放宽政策，酒类专卖转向市场营销，给农村社队酿酒带来契机。1980年，个体户也加入酿酒行业，全县小酒作坊发展到200多家。其中，久长镇石安村个体酿酒专业户就有20户，酿造县内闻名的“石安酒”。继后，扎佐镇办起桥头联合酒厂，年产“景阳窑酒”120吨，“景阳大曲”400吨。六广镇粮管所酒厂，年产苞谷酒500吨，其酒甘醇浓烈、清冽香甜，有“六广小茅台”之称。马家桥桂花树酒厂生产的“黔井窖酒”在贵州省商业粮食系统“习水杯”酒类大赛中获得铜奖，县政府为此给予表彰，发给酒厂奖金2000元。到1985年，马家桥酒厂的“三游洞”瓶酒、桂花树酒厂的“黔井窖酒”、扎佐将军山酒厂的“将军山”瓶酒和小坝乡牟尼酒厂的“文绿窖酒”上升为中级酒，分别在工商部门注册商标受到法律保护。

1978年，国营修文酒厂一角

1986年，国营修文酒厂看到酒类市场兴旺，贷款600万元在城关镇干河桥征地55.3亩，建起建筑面积1.86万平方米的阳明酒厂。生产“阳明窑酒”“阳明大曲”“阳明小曲”“蜜源花粉酒”“三潮老窑”和“夜郎村酒”，成为县内多项产品获优胜奖的先进企业。进入90年代，酒类市场竞争激烈，企业产品走向赊销，带来“三角债”使企业严重亏损，欠下外债高达200万元，于1994年依法破产。其资产由贵阳龟龄酒集团收购，生产被誉称为“东方人头马、亚洲马爹利”的保健酒——“龟龄寿酒”。龟龄酒刚试产便遭到亚洲金融风暴冲击而停产，继后将场地出租给通汇铝业公司。

2009年，贵州贵酒有限公司投资14亿元，在县城郊外的城北村和潮水村、阳明村交界处征地331亩，建起年产1万吨麸曲酱香型白酒生产线。县委、县政府为支持项目建设，组建县直有关部门领导共37人组成的贵州同济堂产业园建设项目协调小组，在县协调小组协调、配合下首期工程于2010年1月5日启动，建年产麸曲酱香型白酒2000吨生产车间，12月9日竣工并顺利投料试产，年底投入生产，同时启动建设第二期年产麸曲酱香白酒4000吨的生产线。

1990—2010年主要食品生产企业概况表

表3—02—07

企业名称	地址	产品	年产量（吨）	投资规模（万元）	企业性质	建设时间（年）	备注
联宇食品厂	龙场镇潮水村	酱油、风味食品	4200（酱油） 500（风味食品）	150	私营	1998	改制企业建
联宇食品焦糖厂	龙场镇潮水村	焦糖	1500	100	私营	2001	2001
龙山乳业	扎佐镇丁官村	鲜奶	1000	500		2003	2005
领先食品厂	扎佐镇新民村	方便面	—	300	联营	2005	2007年续建
金格食品厂	扎佐镇石竹村	食品加工	—	200	联营	2006	2007年续建
好一多乳业	扎佐镇和平村	乳制品	7.2万	2000	联营	2004	2007年运行
日光蒟蒻食品厂	扎佐镇大山村	魔芋精粉	1000	125	私营	1995	2005年半停产
众福特色食品厂	扎佐镇和平村	麦芽糊精	1800	509	私营	1996	1997
三茗食品厂	谷堡乡谷堡村	果脯	200	230	联营	2002	—
扎佐蹄膀食品厂	扎佐镇三元村	蹄膀	未定量	1000	联营	2005	—
县油脂厂	龙场镇幸福村	菜油	1.8万	1151	国营	1991	1996年停产
县面粉厂	久长镇驴坊村	面粉面条	1（标准面粉）	188	国营	1990	1996年停产
野珍食品厂	扎佐镇万江小区	野珍食品	—	1400	国营	1992	1996年下马
康亚轩食品厂	扎佐镇和平村	淀粉、面制品	—	1500	私营	2008	—
绿原食品厂	久长镇金桥村	牛肉干	350	107	联营	1995	1995年出售转产

专记：昙花一现的食用菌工厂

1984年，安顺地区乡镇工业经济会议在县马家桥乡召开后，县科协主席朱明龙从母校江苏无锡轻工学院得知工厂自动化生产食用菌的信息，学院还提供食用菌工业化生产的机械设备，如果建厂，年产食用菌可达720吨。县委对此信息十分重视，由县长王向规带领朱明龙等10人亲赴无锡考察，返县后在县委常委会上提议开发食用菌工业化生产，经过讨论决定立项建厂，充实乡镇工业的产业门类。县政府决定厂址落地马家桥，由城关镇政府负责建设。

城关镇接手该项目后，镇党委、镇政府组成食用菌项目建设领导班子，直接与无锡轻工学院联系。学院提供江苏省文教局〔1984〕004号《关于金针菇生产技术鉴定书》，称该项目技术属国内首创，适用于其他食用菌生产。于是双方协议：无锡轻工学院提供食用菌生产机械设备，价值12万元，工业化生产食用菌技术转让费4万元，学院派周勇等2名设备安装师傅亲临马家桥帮助安装调试。经过项目建设领导班子和施工人员80余人花1年多时间，食用菌厂于1985年4月竣工。县政府、城关镇政府选定5月1日国际劳动节举行投产仪式，邀请省科学院领导和工程技术人员参加，县属机关、单位也派代表前往祝贺。

在投产仪式上省科学院工程师胡志仔细观察食用菌生产设备后发现："这套设备根本不可能生产食用菌。"他指出："只有微波炉能起到消毒的作用，更谈不上工业化生产。"然而县领导和城关镇项目建设班子，对胡志的话半信半疑，随即开机生产。经过反复试产，生长不出食用菌。问题暴露出来，安装调试师傅无能为力，事后又请江阴食用菌指导站的站长解难。经过多次调试，仍无回天之力，食用菌工业化生产竟成过眼云烟，就此作罢。经法院民庭调解认为:无锡轻工学院将仅有实验依据，未进行工厂化试验的技术、设备出售转让，是项目建设流产的主要责任方，应赔偿经济损失18.4万元；县政府盲目引进项目，未经认真考察，自负经济损失985万元，留下沉痛的教训：前事不忘，后事之师。

七、化工

1978年，县五小工业中化工企业有县化肥厂和磷肥厂，县化肥厂产品销售价格远低于生产成本，亏损严重，人说："不产不亏，生产就亏。"1982年累计生产碳酸氢铵2万吨，虽支援农业，但包袱沉重亏损达554.6万元，被迫停产下马。磷肥厂利用磷矿生产磷矿粉，产品不易溶解，肥效极低，销路不好，1993年又改生产水泥。1994年，福建商人投资210万元，在久长镇沙雁村建年产4万吨的钙镁磷肥生产线，又因未取得生产许可证而夭折。

1995年，贵州开磷集团走矿（磷矿）、肥（磷铵）结合之路，拓展企业经营范围，拟建年产48万吨磷铵建设项目，选址县境扎佐镇黑山坝。县委、县政府为使磷铵项目落户，采取筑巢引凤方法，于9月组建县磷铵项目选址协调小组，由县委书记罗筑云任组长，代理县长陈开域、县人大常委会主任王克勤、县政协主席林志云和副县长何松，赵吉超任副组长，相关部门领导为成员，在县财力十分困难情况下，与开磷集团合资征地109亩开发长2.17公里的 "磷铵大道"，总投资2040万元。继后，建设规模为年产磷铵200万吨和磷铵二酸60万吨，项目总投资28.2亿元。后因资金不能及时到位，管理人员违纪、磷铵大道建设日趋缓慢，加上国家宏观调控，贵州已有瓮福磷矿化工基地，避免重复建设，致使磷铵项目告吹。

1996年5月，县乡镇企业局与贵阳市供销公司、私营业主王晓春联办黄磷厂，投资1864万元，在久长镇沙雁村建年产2500吨黄磷厂，一举试产成功，带动一批磷化工企业迅速发展。接着就有富捷化工有限公司落户久长，投资1800多万元，建成修文黄磷厂。1997年，贵州黄果树企业（集团）有限公司下属分公司在马家桥创办永昌化工有限公司，租用搁置的县油脂厂，投资75万元，应用高新技术建成年设计生产50吨的粗烟醇生产线。1998年，华祥矿产有限公司投资300万元，将福建商人在久长镇沙雁村的钙镁磷肥厂生产线买断，重建年产3万吨的过磷酸钙和6万吨磷矿粉的修文磷肥厂。与此同时，在扎佐、马家桥先后又建起磷化厂，其中腾达蒸磷厂利用马家桥驻军闲置营房，投资20万元，建蒸熬车间，回收黄磷。2001年，黔鑫磷化工有限公司投资65万元，仍在马家桥部队闲置营房办起磷酸、磷酸二氢钙各3000吨的磷化工产品生产线，随后又投入20万元，新增生产线1条，使生产能力得以提高。2002年，谷堡乡村民集资30万元联办年产300吨黄磷盐酸厂，因设施简陋和工艺、技术跟不上而停办。2007年5月在龙场镇原105地质队场址开工的华飞化学工业有限公司，项目计划投资8亿元，依托县境丰富的铝矿资源、能

源及产业基础优势，建占地365亩氢氧化铝生产线。2010年4月首期工程竣工点火试产，7月26日，第二期年产10万吨建设工程接着开工。

2010年8月，贵州轮胎股份有限公司根据贵阳市政府“退二进三”战略决定，异地搬迁改造落户扎佐镇工业园，建中国最大的轮胎及配套产业基地。公司在丁官工业小区征地2300亩，投资71亿元，建设年产高性能子午线轮胎1280万条生产线，预计年新增产值106亿元，销售收入90.56亿元，可获利润14.34亿元，纳税5.73亿元。项目分三期建设，一期建设年产250万条全钢载重子午轮胎生产线，二期建设15万条全钢工程子午轮胎和15万条农用子午轮胎生产线，三期建设1000万条半钢子午轮胎生产线，整个项目计划在两年内完成。2010年年底完成建设征地，拆迁工作已完成85%。

专记：华飞化学工业有限公司落户修文

2006年3月，上海华飞投资集团有限公司考察西部资源开发渠道，拓宽公司投资经营项目，到修文考察区位、资源、交通、电力优势，决定氢氧化铝项目选址在龙场镇小营村原105地质队驻地。与县政府签订落户协议后由县政府组织相关业务部门办理立项、报批手续。2007年4月，县委书记魏明禄和县长石洪带领相关部门领导到上海浦东新区洽谈具体事宜。随后，上海浦东新区区委常委、上海市磁浮交通发展有限公司总经理臧新民、上海华飞置业集团有限公司董事长石晓飞、上海浦东新区北蔡镇党委书记吴凤飞和新区唐镇党委书记夏天惠亲赴修文，于5月26日举行氢氧化铝建设项目开工典礼挂牌贵州华飞化学工业有限公司，县委、县政府领导和华飞集团负责人共同举镐为氢氧化铝厂建设奠基。

项目占地365亩，计划投资8亿元，分3期建设氢氧化铝生产线。首期拟定投资4亿元，建成年产10万吨氢氧化铝生产线，第二期投资2亿元，第三期投资2亿元，最终形成年产20万吨氢氧化铝企业，年产值达10亿元。生产流程采用德国拜耳发生产工艺。经过铝矿破碎均化、矿浆磨制、添加石灰烧碱分离和高压脱硅工艺，最终产出氢氧化铝产品。2008年10月底，项目已完成投资3亿元的工程计划，40米高的生产烟囱，30米高的分离器，破碎厂房，一排排储槽罐，赤泥分解车间相继竣工。一个科技含量重，现代化程度高的化工厂，在县内展现雏形，2010年4月首期工程竣工，顺利点火试产，7月26日，二期年产10万吨建设项目开工。

1978—2010年化工生产企业概况表

表3—02—08

企业名称	地址	产品	年产量（吨）	投资规模（万元）	企业性质	建设时间（年）	备注
修文化肥厂	龙场镇新春村	碳酸氢铵	3000	470	国营	1972	1981年下马转产
久长磷肥厂	久长镇驴坊村	磷肥	3000	350	国营	1972	1993年出售产权
富捷化工厂	久长镇沙雁村	黄磷	3000	1750	外资	1996	—
华祥磷化厂	久长镇沙雁村	磷酸钙	3000	300	联营	1998	2005年整改
永昌化工厂	龙场镇马家桥	粗烟醇	50	125	联营	1998	1999年7月投产
黔鑫磷化工厂	龙场镇马家桥	磷酸	3000	85	股份合作	2001	2001年5月投产
		磷酸二氢钙	3000				

续表

企业名称	地址	产品	年产量（吨）	投资规模（万元）	企业性质	建设时间（年）	备　注
谷堡乡磷化厂	谷堡乡	黄磷盐酸	300	30	联户	2002	已下马
宏和矿业	龙场镇	电熔锆	—	440	—	2002	2003年6月投产
宇丰建材厂	扎佐镇兴红村	铝酸钙粉	10万	200	联营	2004	—
怡丰日化厂	扎佐镇兴红村	石油添加剂	—	3000	—	2005	—
吉隆单宁化工厂	扎佐镇	食品添加剂	—	2500	股份	2005	—
怡丰日化厂	扎佐镇兴红村	石油添加剂	—	3000	股份	2005	—
创试冶炼厂	小箐乡	五氧化二钒	—	2000	联营	2006	—
华飞氢氧化铝厂	龙场镇小营村	氢氧化铝	20万	80000	联营	2007	2010年4月投产
宏达塑胶厂	扎佐镇万江厂区	塑胶	—	200	联营	2007	—

八、医药

1978年，县卫生局在县城马落坑置有一家药厂，生产生理盐水、注射用水、葡萄糖注射液、红汞、紫药水、碘酒、止血粉、烫伤粉、感冒茶、冻疮膏、风湿丸、蛔虫丸、胃痛丸、牙痛水、癣药水、跌打药酒、止咳糖浆、风湿跌打丸和舒筋镇痛药水等。后因设备差和技术跟不上，所生产药品质量不稳定，企业自负盈亏、接连亏损，1979年年底停办下马。

1997年7月，贵州绿太阳制药有限公司投资800万元，将原扎佐珍珠井“野珍食品厂”闲置厂房和场地改造成制药厂，致力于地方民族药（贵州苗药）开发研究，生产肤痔清软膏、貂胰防裂膏和日晒防治膏3个民族药，以及磁疗祛斑按摩乳、补天胶囊、绿格尔顽癣敌、绿格尔粉刺净、葆肤康软膏、痔舒安软膏6个保健品种,是贵州省内唯一生产膏霜剂的制药企业。产品曾荣获“星火计划”实施十周年优秀项目金奖和98’中国新产品新技术博览会金奖，为中国民族医药学会推荐产品。绿太阳制药企业落户扎佐，开启县委、县政府利用万江机电厂、304医院迁出后留下的大量国有土地、房舍，抢抓国家强制药业进行GMP技术改造的机遇，作出规划开发“扎佐医药工业园区”的构想。

2000年3月，《扎佐医药工业园区规划》在贵阳市第一届药业协会成立大会上亮相，引起制药企业的关注。8月，又在全国乡镇企业经贸洽谈会期间，以沙盘模型展出“规划”，园区分为A、B、C三个功能区，规划面积4.3平方公里，由生产、生活、服务、绿化4个部分、9个地块组成。县政府采取“一站式”服务和各部门“零费率”优惠政策，开创“低门槛入驻，税收补地款”的办法，使安泰药业于2000年12月率先入园，称之为“安泰模式”。

2001年入驻县境的仙灵药业有限公司（后更名贵州同济堂制药股份有限公司）生产的仙灵骨葆系列药品：有仙灵骨葆胶囊、仙灵骨葆片、心脑康胶囊、胶体果胶铋胶囊、枣红安神胶囊、补肾益脑胶囊、润燥止痒胶囊。其中的心脑康胶囊、胶体果胶囊被列入《国家基本药物目录》。“仙灵骨葆胶囊”荣获吉隆坡世界骨伤科理事会一等奖和中国骨伤科理事会特别贡献奖。

2003年，已有安泰、源隆、奥新、光正等制药企业和科开药业公司入驻扎佐医药园区，进行国家GMP标准改造建设。2004年4月1日，由省乡镇企业局副局长蒋先宏主持，副省长肖永安代表农业部授予

扎佐医药园区全国乡镇企业科技园区称号，并颁发园区匾牌。于是园区建设形成高潮，又有吉隆丹宁、杏林堂中药、香港龟龙等企业入园筹建。

2005年，园区共13家药业GMP技改完毕，获得国家标准认证资格，其中有12家企业投产，经过国家医药GMP标准认证企业有和仁堂、维康、绿太阳、天方、德昌祥、浩成、恒和、长生、安泰、同济堂、光正、喜儿康等12家药业企业，获得贵州苗族验方研制成功、具有知识产权、被批准为国首准字药品达41个，主导产品类型包括：喷雾剂、膏霜剂、颗粒剂、水针剂、栓剂、冲剂、酊剂，产品销往全国，市场稳定。总产值达6.8亿元，占全县工业总产值的38.31%，纳税5709万元。2006年7月6日，贵州省政府将扎佐医药工业园区更名为贵州修文医药产业园，并以国家发改委第41号公告将贵州修文医药产业园列为省级开发区。

修文医药产业园内的天方药业

2008年，全县制药企业生产片剂药3.8亿片，中成药2238吨，医药产值14.69亿元，占县规模以上工业企业总产值的48.4%，实现销售收入10.06亿元，上缴税金1.12亿元。2009年，贵阳市政府、市规划委员会审核通过《贵州修文医药产业园区控制性详细规划》，将医药产业园规划面积修订为5.17平方公里。园区规划批准后，通过与太平洋集团合作，采取BT模式修建园区的“1号路”“希望路”“万喜路”。2010年，“园区1号路”竣工通车，华德斯药业投资7200万元，济生药业投资5800万元，康纳圣方药业与杏林堂药业联合投资3000万元，相继落户园区。至年底，县境建成、在建和拟建制药企业19家。其中通过GMP标准认证药品生产13家，在建企业3家，拟建企业5家。园区已扩展成为以中成药制药为主，集生物制药、化学制药与中草药种植于一体，有4000多从业人员的地方经济支柱产业。拥有根据苗族验方研制成的自主知识产权的药品，获准字号的品种有380余个。生产中成药2642吨，实现工业总产值20.65亿元。

2010年修文医药产业园生产企业及产品一览表

表3—02—09

企业名称	主　要　产　品
绿太阳药业	肤痔清、日晒防治霜、貂胰防裂膏、痛经软膏、复方辣椒碱乳膏、磁疗去斑按摩乳、补天胶囊、葆肤康软膏、痔舒安软膏、绿格尔系列顽癣敌、绿格尔系列粉刺膏剂、胶囊
安泰药业	通迪胶囊、消炎利胆胶囊、妇平胶囊、皮净气雾剂、心脑灵胶囊、伤痛一喷灵、冰扼伤痛雾剂
同济堂药业	仙灵骨葆胶囊、润燥止痒胶囊、枣仁安神胶囊、复方牙痛酊、诺氟沙星胶囊、阿咖酚茶、滇白珠糖剂、氨咖黄敏片、小儿氨酚黄那敏、盐酸左旋咪唑宝塔糖、处长方甘草口服液
光正药业	小针剂、板蓝根冲剂、板蓝根粒剂
天方药业	杜仲颗粒、补肾强身片、清脑隆压液、克感敏、雷尼替丁（片、冲、液）、富马酸亚铁干糖颗粒
维康药业	骨康胶囊、肿痛消喷雾剂、妇科调经胶囊、眼安宁、风湿定胶囊
和仁堂药业	泌淋清胶囊、康妇灵胶囊
恒和制药	枇杷止咳胶囊、精制银翘解毒胶囊、丹参舒心胶囊

续表

企业名称	主　要　产　品
德昌祥药业	妇科再造丸、止喘灵气雾剂、杜仲壮骨丸、天麻灵芝口服液（丸剂、气雾剂、口服液）
长生药业	妇炎清、布洛芬缓释胶囊、克胶囊
浩成药业	三七胶囊、老得生胶囊、阿归养血颗粒、妇科止带片、苦生片、柏枝祛温泻剂、柏枝祛湿喷雾剂
喜儿康药业	葱芽健脾凝胶、续参酒、天泉道酒剂、喜乘龙酒剂、强力镇痛磁疗贴、绿色凝胶膏剂酒剂
科福丽康制药	胶囊剂、乳膏剂、流浸膏剂、肤舒止痒剂、板蓝根颗粒、保胃胶囊、酮康唑乳膏

九、新材料

1991年，林东矿务局多种经营公司研究产出橡胶促进剂M新材料（硫化促进剂），得到省化工厅新成果研究肯定。1993年，公司利用扎佐镇林东技校旧址，投资283.5万元建成年产500吨橡胶促进剂M生产线，其产品填补西南地区的空白，市场前景乐观。后因公司管理人员走马换将，后来者无建树，企业失去商机，以亏损而告终。

2000年，贵州林海新材料制造有限公司投资2300万元扎佐镇中营村建占地3.3亩的生产场地，利用铝矾土生产新材料石油压裂支撑剂，产品经中国石油勘探开发研究院廊坊分院实验和评价，以及美国STIM—LAB实验检测，多项指标达到世界先进水平，以省内最高分入围新产品推荐行列。2004年，又有中方业主马胜与美国·中国陶粒支撑剂有限公司联合投资4000万元，在扎佐镇兴红村建成年产6000吨石油压裂支撑剂生产线。与此同时，个体经营户杨国林、杨国琴兄妹投资300万元，创办天成热陶瓷有限公司，在王官村利用铝矾土深加工生产耐磨陶，建起年产3000吨高强度耐磨瓷球生产线，产品质量达到国内同行业先进水平，填补省内该产品的空白。随后又投入80万元资金建4孔窑形长度22米的推板窑，将生产能力提升到年产4000吨。

贵州林海新材料有限公司

2008年，扎佐镇境内形成由贵州省科技厅、省经贸委授牌的新材料产业园区，已入驻贵州林海新材料公司、贵州中陶公司、贵阳天龙摩擦材料有限公司、贵州怡丰精细化工有限公司为代表的新材料生产企业，先后开发出一批具有高新技术含量、市场前景广阔、处于国内先进水平的新材料产品。

贵阳天龙摩擦材料有限公司

2009年，县政府为开发县内以铝矾土为原料的新材料工业，引导贵州鑫益能、贵州泽希、贵州自立、修文银星、贵州中陶、贵州宇丰等企业，对铝土矿焙烧熟矿实施能源就地转化，开发新材料产业，促进县域内资源优势转化为产业优势，在扎佐镇三元、龙场镇小山建立新材料基地。国家科技部创新基金管理中心公布2009年度国家创新基金第二批立项项目名单有贵州鑫益能陶粒支撑剂“86MPa高强度陶粒支撑剂”和修文天成热陶瓷“利用贫瘠铝土矿与废弃耐火材料生产高强度耐磨瓷球技术”，分别获国家创新基金75万元和60万元，并获省级资金25万元和20万元。其无偿的资助为全县历史之最。

2010年新材料生产企业概况表

表3—02—10

企业名称	地　址	产　品	年产量（吨）	投资规模（万元）	企业性质	建设时间（年）	投产时间（年）
林海新材料厂	扎佐镇中营村	石油压裂支撑剂	5000	2300	股份	1997	1999
天成热陶瓷厂	龙场镇王官村	耐磨瓷球	4000	500	私营	2003	2006
天龙摩擦材料厂	扎佐镇兴红村	刹车带	未定产量	2000	联营	2005	2005
高新盛远厂	扎佐镇喻家街	玻璃钢锚杆	未定产量	2000	私营	2005	2006
扎佐化工厂	扎佐镇和平村	硫化促进剂	500	283.5	私营	1993	1994
中·美陶粒支撑剂厂	扎佐镇兴红村	石油压裂支撑剂	6000	4000	合资	2005	2005

十、铸造

20世纪80年代初随县水利工程建设告一段落，社队铸铁厂相继停办。80年代中期，为适应社队采掘业和城镇楼房建设所需，扎佐农具厂和修文农机厂增设铸造车间铸造球磨机铁球和楼房下水管。进入90年代，随水泥生产企业发展，球磨机增多，扎佐镇三元村丁富荣兴建三元钢球厂，邓书德办起伟宏铸铁厂铸造钢球，年产3000吨。2010年，贵州诺亚精密铸造有限公司落户龙场镇马家桥，计划投资4.5亿元，占地60亩，建设年产电动机、发电机、水泵、低压电器和电动工具外壳等各类精密铸造件20万吨。项目预计年产值21.5亿元，于12月19日，开工建设，各项工作有序推进，运转正常。

专记：三线建设在修文

1978年，诞生于20世纪60年代的“三线建设”企业驻县的有航空工业部属011系统华文、庆文、烽光、万江、兴红和418共5厂1库，成为县内工业化进程的骨干企业。1985年，在生产军工产品同时开发民用产品。其中烽光电工厂系航空工业部航空微特电机制造、国家医疗器械定点生产厂，为航天、航空、电子、兵器、舰船、汽车、医疗、电器、机械提供产品。华文电工厂生产低压、高压、耐温、密封、屏蔽、小型联接插头座件，为航天、航空、航海、通信、地质、机械提供电子、电器配套设备。该厂自行设计研制的XKE系列插头座是80年代国内最新产品，获得国家和贵州省科学大会奖励。兴红机械厂系航空工业部属重点企业航空恒迷装置厂，承担设计制造航空用电机、电器冲压件，其冷冲压技术先进，置有完整的配套设备、检验仪器、电器冲压件专供军工生产企业，在军工生产任务减少时又开发生产民用汽车水箱总成、油剂计量泵、高压纺织计量泵、挤压模具和减速机械。万江机电厂系航空工业部属011基地航空电动机件、空气活门的专业辅机制造厂，军用产品有10个，航空机种配套件产品有19种，为空军、海军及011系统主机厂生产配套件和零部件，其自研产品新型力臂自动调节器获贵州省科学大会奖、部优产品奖、国家银质奖。庆文机械厂系航空工业部属航空标准件生产厂，按照国家GB标准、航空HB标准、联邦德国DIN标准专业生产国防、化工、矿山、纺织、运输、建筑等机械用标准件、专用连接件，产品具有高强度、高精密、耐高温、耐腐蚀的特点，销往全国27个省市区和出口德国、美国、东南亚各国及中国港澳地区。四一八库系国家航空工业部属企业，直接隶属万江机电厂，专为011基地在修文境内周转储备生产物资的企业，置有库房40幢，建筑面积1.8万平方米，并在扎佐火车站建有站台及库房，承担平衡汇总011基地在修文各厂原料订货计划、批量供应和储备物资的任务。

"5厂1库"建成后在修文招收一批知识青年和复员退伍军人进厂就业，并对县办地方国营企业给予技术援助，其中庆文机械厂帮助县水泥厂、县化肥厂培训电焊工安装仪器仪表，烽光电工厂帮助县化肥厂建设进行设备测试、高压管道探伤、高压焊接，使县地方工业加快建设步伐。80年代中期，军工企业转轨变型，实行军品、民品生产结合的经营体制改革，由军品计划生产向民品市场需求转轨，开发民用产品。其主要产品有：各类电机、心脏按摩机、电梯接插件、汽车雨刮器、汽车玻璃升降器、测速机、高压纺织计量泵、油剂计量泵、综合式卷烟机、疲劳测试机、轧面机、包装机、压力锅、钻床配件、彩电显像管插件、万能保险插头座以及变压器等。其中，心脏按摩机获得空军科技成果二等奖、国家优质产品金龙奖；CS27—05交流伺服测速机组获国家银质奖；纺织计量泵、油剂计量泵填补国内空白。航空工业艰苦创业，从军品生产到民用产品，曾开创出县境工业史上一派生机勃勃的局面，促进县域经济发展，推动社会进步。

航空工业部属万江厂办公楼

进入90年代，011系统在县企业调整生产结构，采取联合组建贵航集团，驻县的华文、烽光、庆文、万江四厂分别搬迁到贵阳市小河区、白云区和乌当区进行扩建和改造。兴红机械厂主要从事设计制造航空用电机电器冲压件，虽技术设备力量雄厚，但在军品生产任务大量削减的情况下，企业生产吃不饱，便全力开发生产民用产品，实行独立核算，自负盈亏。企业面临市场经济产品结构全面调整的挑战，不能迅速适应市场需求，经济效益差，走向关停最后破产，移交地方。418库因市场物资供应充足、物资流通渠道畅通，所建仓库全部闲置失去物资储备功能，并组建起云天航空工贸有限公司，开发摩托车凸轮轴和包装箱生产。但效益低、利润薄，累计负债高达1000万元，面临倒闭。

2002年，云天公司根据国家政策脱离贵航，移交地方，改制分流。县政府为盘活云天公司资产、安置云天职工，于10月引入民营贵州龙翔铝业有限公司兼并云天公司，重组建成贵州龙翔集团公司，转为民营企业，继续生产摩托车凸轮轴，2010年生产凸轮轴336.62万套，产值4784.2万元，销售收入达到2100万元。

第三节　工业产业园区建设

2009年，县委和县政府根据贵阳市委筑党发〔2009〕14号《关于振兴工业经济若干政策的意见》和筑党发〔2009〕15号文《加快全市工业园区建设的意见》，以及市委和市政府出台的振兴铝加工业、现代生物药业、煤化工业、特色食品业、物流业的战略举措，开发建设修文工业产业园区。园区位于县境扎佐、久长、龙场3个镇的三角地带，距贵阳市区35公里，210国道、贵遵高速公路、贵毕高等级公路、川黔铁路等穿境而过，区位优越、交通便利。园区按照“一区三园”（即贵州修文工业园区，含龙场工业园、扎佐工业园和久长工业园）规划布局。总规划面积50平方公里，先期实施20平方公里。建设以科学发展观为指导，以生态文明建设为统领，以“政府主导，市场运作”为原则，建成“布局集中，产业集聚，资源节约，配套完善”的工业基地。依托修文区位优势、产业基础和承载空间，利用现代科学技术，围绕快、转、高的发展要求，发展高新技术产业和现代制造业。重点发展以高品质特种钢、高性能橡胶制品、铝矾土深加工产品为主的新材料产业；以生物医药及特色食品为主的现代医药食品产业；以智能制造、轨道交通、装备制造为主的精工制造产业；以新型建材及固废综合利用为主的节能环保产业，配套发展现代物流等生产性服务业。以龙场镇、扎佐镇、久长镇为核心，县域交通网络为骨架，沿贵遵高速公路、贵毕高等级公路、龙麦、龙扎、龙久等城市干道两侧的城镇带发展，形成3条轴线产业空间结构。同白云、观山湖、高新、综保同城化发展，构建“沙文—扎佐—久长”高新技术走廊，“龙场－麦架”现代物流通道，打造贵阳北部高新技术产业和现代制造业的工业基地。

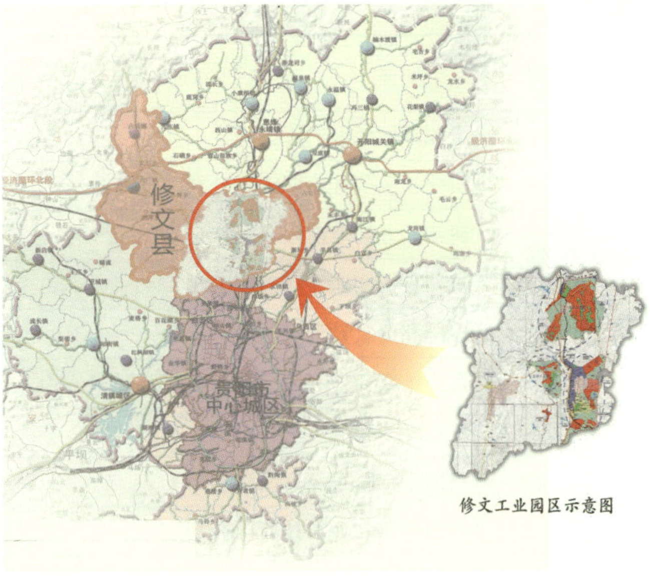

修文工业园区示意图

一、扎佐工业园

位于扎佐镇中、西南部，距贵阳市中心30公里。以现代生物制药、食品加工、特殊钢、轮胎、新材料和现代物流为主导产业。已有生产贵州苗族中成药19家企业、贵阳统一食品、贵州好一多乳业、首钢·贵阳特殊钢厂、生产各类子午轮胎的黔轮胎厂、贵阳泽希、自立、鑫能和林海等新材料企业以及贵州兴达物流、永盛和置业、东方钢材市场等现代物流业落户其间。

扎佐工业园区主要企业总投资及2010年实现产值情况表

表3—02—11

类　别	企业名称	厂　址	总投资（万元）	产值（万元）
制　药	贵州绿太阳制药有限公司	扎佐医药园区	5000	11224
	贵州安泰药业有限公司		5000	11511
	贵州德昌祥药业有限公司		5000	36712
	贵州恒和制药有限公司		3000	7433
	贵州光正制药有限责任公司		4000	8902
	贵州喜儿康药业有限公司		3000	3149

续表

类　别	企业名称	厂　址	总投资（万元）	产值（万元）
制　药	贵州浩诚药业有限公司	扎佐医药园区	3000	1437
	贵州长生药业有限责任公司		2500	4648
	贵州天方药业有限公司		5000	5000
	贵州科福丽康制药有限公司		3000	4000
	贵阳和仁堂制药有限公司		4000	11486
	贵阳维康药业有限公司		3000	42261
乳　品	贵州好一多乳业股份有限公司	扎佐镇和平村	4000	7728
食　品	贵阳康雅轩食品有限公司	扎佐镇和平村	2000	400
饲　料	贵州通邦农业科技有限公司	扎佐镇石竹村	2500	3938
	贵阳东方希望动物营养有限公司	扎佐镇大山村	3000	5905
新材料	中陶支撑剂(贵州)有限公司	扎佐镇兴红村	3000	6520
新材料	贵阳天龙摩擦材料有限公司	扎佐镇兴红村	2500	921
新材料	贵州鑫益能陶粒支撑剂有限公司	扎佐镇三元村	7000	12063
—	贵州林海陶粒制造有限公司	扎佐镇中营村	3000	2578
机械制造	贵阳万江世星机械有限公司	扎佐万江工业园区	3000	3105
磨　料	贵州宇丰熔料有限公司	扎佐镇兴红村	3000	3096
磨　料	修文县银星磨料有限公司	扎佐镇三元村	3000	7957

二、龙场工业园

位于龙场镇东北部、中部和南部，距贵阳市中心38公里。以精密铸造、机械加工、氢氧化铝、白酒生产为主导。已有贵州龙翔机械加工企业、贵州华飞氢氧化铝企业、诺亚精密铸造企业、天成热陶瓷有限公司以及贵州同济堂产业园的贵酒有限公司白酒生产线和同济堂制药企业入驻。

龙场工业园区主要企业总投资及2010年实现产值情况表

表3—02—12

类　别	企业名称	厂　址	总投资（万元）	产值（万元）
制　药	贵州同济堂制药股份有限公司	龙场镇城北村	8000	61200
酿　酒	贵州贵酒有限公司	龙场镇城北村	100000	60000
机械制造	贵州华飞化学工业有限公司	龙场镇小营村	100000	20000
化　工	贵州龙翔铝业（集团）有限公司	龙场镇小营村	4000	4784
建　材	贵阳利尔建材有限公司	龙场镇小营村	3000	3490
建　材	修文县荣利达水泥厂	龙场镇小营村	3000	2610
建　材	南方水泥厂（原马家桥水泥厂）	龙场镇白莲村	1000	2500
铸　造	诺亚精工铸造	龙场镇马家桥	计划（4.5亿元）	尚未投产

三、久长工业园

位于久长镇中东部，距贵阳市中心42公里。以新型建材生产加工、磷化工为主导。有以贵州金久水泥为主、以久长建材公司以及奇峰工贸公司、高坝红砖厂为辅的水泥建材生产企业；有富捷磷化工和永新产业转移承接基地的后备区。

久长工业园区各主要企业总投资及2010年实现产值情况表

表3—02—13

类 别	企业名称	厂 址	总投资(万元)	产值(万元)
新材料	贵阳修文华宏冶炼有限公司	久长镇上寨村二关坝	4000	21935
水泥生产	贵州奇峰工贸有限责任公司	久长镇上寨村二关坝	6000	7326
水泥生产	贵州金久水泥有限公司	久长镇金桥村	150000	18633
水泥生产	久长建材有限公司	久长镇驴坊村	2000	6000
机制砖	久长高坝砖厂	久长镇高坝村	600	1200

第四节 企业管理

一、职工管理

（一）干部竞聘

20世纪80年代初期，工业企业贯彻国务院《国营工厂厂长工作暂行条例》，实行党委领导下的厂长负责制和职工代表大会制，采取党委集体领导，厂长行使行政指挥的管理方式。1986年，国务院颁发《全民所有制企业厂长工作条例》，县政府按《条例》要求结合企业情况，以三角山水泥厂为试点，改革企业领导干部管理体制，完善水泥厂生产经营责任制。企业管理干部按“四化”（革命化、年轻化、知识化、专业化）方针和德才兼备原则选任。厂长由企业主管部门任免，副厂长由厂长提名，企业党组织推荐，报主管部门任免。企业中层干部由厂长或党委（支部）推荐，由厂长任免。1987年，全县工业企业实行厂长负责制企业22个，其中国营企业17个，城镇集体企业5个。

1993年12月国务院颁布《中华人民共和国公司法》，企业逐步申办为有限责任公司，实行产权明晰、权责分明、管理科学、激励和约束相结合的管理体制。在职工管理方面，先从干部启用加强管理，给员工做出榜样，打破长期以来干部终身制，使干部的聪明才智得到发挥，达到“火车跑得快，全靠车头带”领军作用。企业管理干部由公司董事会考核聘任厂长（经理），企业副职以及中、低层干部采取竞争上岗，竞选答辩，招聘考试，择优聘用，取消干部和工人的界限，只要是有用之“才”，不论其资历，唯一的择用标准是看其人的知识、才能，工作中是否真抓实干，干出成效。通过考核，择优，使一批确有真才实学的干部分别走上企业的领导岗位。1994年10月，县乡镇企业局与县人事劳动局联合，请县委党校教师命题、评卷，对乡镇企业管理人员进行考试，内容包括政策、法律、法规，文化基础，时事政治等，择优聘用24名乡企管理干部。同时全县实行公司化管理，聘用管理干部的企业有四达矿产公司、文德冶炼公司、环海实业公司、瑞达有限公司、龟龙公司、联宇食品公司、绿源公司、棕刚玉冶炼分厂、联合磨料厂共9家。到2005年，有全县规模以上工业企业独资公司4家，国有控股股份制公司1家，非公有制有限责任公司8家，外商投资有限公司2家，均按《中华人民共和国公司法》规范，实行企业管理干部竞聘运行机制。2010年，增加制药企业8家、新材料企业9家以及贵阳钢厂、贵酒集团、贵州轮胎等企业实行管理干部竞聘上岗。

（二）员工择优录用

1979年，企业用工沿袭统一分配办法，出现把只会“吃斋”不会“念经”的人也安置到企业，县办“五小”工业郭家林水泥厂是一个年产量不足1万吨的企业，拥有国有企业职工、合同制工、大集体工共200人，庙小僧多粥少企业人满为患，实难管理。

1994年企业实施《中华人民共和国公司法》，由于企业产权转移，劳资关系明确，企业对员工的管理置于核心位置上，凡是招用员工和在职员工续业均参加劳动技能、专业知识、法律法规培训。特殊工种、关键岗位均进行专业考试，待取得合格证后持证上岗。乡镇企业局管理的采掘企业持上岗证的矿长、安全员、瓦检员、爆破员、电工等达140多人，均实行员工录用、升降、培训、工资、奖罚、考核、淘汰制。1997年9月，县三角山水泥厂实施定员工编制、定部门职能、定岗位规范，裁减管理岗位人员、分流富余职工。聘请县委党校讲师罗国通为全厂职工讲授在市场经济条件下，企业、职工如何双向选择，如何体现企业择人权、职工择业权以及企业定编、定职、定岗的必要性和必然性。随后企业分流富余职工20多人从事附属产品开发，机关人员根据自身条件和能力从管理岗位转入生产岗位，使企业负担减轻，企业活力增强。

（三）职工代表大会

1978年，国营企业中建立的工会组织是企业联系职工群众的桥梁和纽带，主要开展组织职工集体活动、帮助职工排忧解难和反映职工群众的各种意见和要求，维护职工合法权益。1980年，县总工会将企业建立职工代表大会制度提上工作日程，经过民主选举出来的职工代表大会代表全体职工对企业实行民主管理，组织职工参与本单位的民主决策、民主管理和民主监督。进入90年代，国有企业，股份制企业、联营企业均建立健全工会组织。企业通过职工代表大会职能、职权与公司董事会、监事会相互衔接，形成激励、制约机制，履行职工代表大会对企业生产经营、产品开发、技术更新、人员启用和资金流动的建议权、监督权，既保证企业高层管理的拍板、定案决策权，又保证企业员工监督、建议权，使企业呈现又有集中、又有民主、又有统一意志，又有个人心情舒畅、生动活泼局面。至1997年，县总工会培训职工代表352人，提高职工代表参与企业民主管理水平。组织开展职代会提案审议活动、审议提案302件，实施114件，其中生产方面71件，评议领导干部91人。1998年，县三角山水泥厂、郭家林水泥厂、红旗煤厂、耐火材料厂等职工代表大会重组改制，重新登记组建、发展新会员。到2006年，规范、新组建企业职代会2个，2007年12月，规范、完善改制企业职代会4个，建立非公有企业职代会4个。2010年新建工业企业职代会22个，全县工业企业职代会发展154个。

二、厂务公开

1999年，根据贵阳市委办公厅〔1999〕19号《关于国有企业实行厂务公开、民主监督制度工作的通

知》和县政府县办发〔1999〕21号《关于实行厂务公开的实施意见》，开始在全县国有、集体企业实行厂务公开，向职工公开企业发展规划、生产经营目标、改革改制方案、物资采购、职工安置、劳保福利等关系企业、职工切身利益的重大问题，旨在扩大企业民主管理，调动职工积极性，监督领导成员廉政自律，推动企业稳定发展。6月，县委、县政府成立厂务公开领导小组。8月，领导小组召开国有、集体企业厂长（经理）、工会主席共50人参加的厂务公开工作会议，强调“厂务公开，企业的主管部门是第一责任人，从解决不愿公开，不敢公开入手切实搞好厂务公开，严禁搞形式走过场”。到年底，全县实行厂务公开的企业达34个，占计划公开41个企业的82.4%。

2002年8月，县建筑公司因管理不善、效益差、干群关系紧张，导致职工集体上访，面临破产边缘，在县厂务公开领导小组推动下，依法民主选举企业法人（经理），公开企业改革方案、发展规划、财务收支，使职工明白、满意，企业回到正常运行轨道。2004年5月，县总工会主持召开厂务公开工作会议，将林海新材料制造有限公司、县供电局等10户企业开展厂务公开检查情况进行公布，从而推动企业厂务公开制度化、规范化。同时，县乡镇企业局对整改后保留的27家煤矿安全生产问题，开展“人人事事保平安”为主题的“安全月”活动，采取“自己找、出去听、集体查、职工帮”的方式，公开查找企业安全生产存在的问题，设置意见箱，广泛收集反馈意见，梳理意见完善制度，加强整改。通过厂务管理公开活动，共查出安全隐患1761件，提出整改意见1783条，使煤矿企业牢记“安全生产并非小事”。2005年7、8月，贵阳市厂务公开领导小组成员黄德琴、曹希平先后两次莅县检查厂务管理公开工作，对六广镇三利煤矿和石笋煤矿实行瓦斯检测、防护用品、安全责任等的执行情况公开给予肯定。2007年10月18日，贵阳市厂务公开检查组组长赵永祥带领11人，到县检查厂务管理公开和厂务民主管理工作，听取县工会及13个企业情况汇报，并以问卷形式调查抓重点、促深化、抓制度，促规范、抓落实、促提高的“三抓、三促”，推进厂务管理工作开展。贵州龙翔能源（集团）有限公司以企业职代会为基本形式，开展厂务管理，把涉及职工切身利益的重大问题都交职代会讨论，将公司新建100套职工住房分配方案经职代会讨论公布,职工认为合理、透明、公平，得到市厂务公开检查组的肯定和赞许。至2010年，厂务公开制度一直坚持，增强企业民主管理意识，使企业走上规范管理道路。

三、物资管理

（一）管理体制

1980年，企业物资包括生产原料、基建三材（钢材、木材、水泥）和设备构件等的分配和管理，增加省人民委员会的物资分配权限，凡是中央驻县的国防军工企业和省、县所属的地方企业所需物资，不论是国家经济委员会的全国统一分配物资（统配物资），或是中央各部所管的统一分配物资（部管物资），仍按系统和隶属关系进行申请和分配，省人民委员会有权根据当地情况和需要的缓急，在各企业之间进行数量、品种和分配时间进行调剂。军工企业所用的特殊原材料，若地方政府要求调用必须得到中央主管部门同意。县属国营企业向县工业局，城镇集体企业向县轻工局，社队企业向社队企业局逐级申报，又经主管部门向上级物资供销部门申报，取得物资分配的调、购、拨指标后，到物资供货单位购拨。国防军工驻县企业011系统物资供应、储备的管理工作由所属企业418库承担储备和中转，按计划调入和拨出。县社队企业局设立物资供销公司，由公司按年度将物资供给计划告知发给企业，再由企业将物资需求汇总后向企业局申报，经批核后再由供销公司组织供应物资，调、购、拨程序繁锁，手续复杂。

1985年，随着乡镇企业的发展，私营、联营企业应运而生，物资供、需量骤然增加。时逢国家取消企业物资统一分配改为市场调节供求，企业所需物资直接进入市场采购。在转入市场调节初期，国家采取指导性价格调控，随着市场逐步放开，进入90年代，物资全由市场调节，实行市场价格，出现物流灵活、物源丰富、物资管理简化便捷的局面。物资供求从计划管理到市场调节后，航空工业部属企业与物资储备、中转企业418库的主辅关系减弱，致418库大量设备和库藏功能资源闲置，企业亏损，不得以组建云天公司，从物资储备供应企业转变为生产型企业。

（二）物流管理

20世纪90年代末，县内商品市场、物资市场繁荣兴旺，物资专销店、连锁店、仓储、批发店、零售店雨后春笋般发展起来，物资流通部门遍布各乡镇，构成物资流通网络，电信购物、邮政购物、网上购物普遍展开。2000年，县物资供销部门和县内企业依托川黔铁路，贵（阳）遵（义）、贵（阳）毕（节）高等级公路在扎佐火车站交汇的交通优势，设立的物资转运站，毕节地区也在此设立物资转运办事处，从而激活县内物流业发展，为企业物资供、求和管理提供有利条件。

2004年，贵州兴达物流公司在扎佐火车站建起货场面积6.5万平方米，配置两条铁路专线、10吨行吊装载机和30吨、100吨地磅贵阳北郊物资集散旱码头。使县内企业的购、销物资包括钢材、设备、水泥、红砖、铝土矿、煤炭、农产品、食品、药品均在此购进运出。到2007年，扎佐物流集散基地形成卸载、转运、发送各种机械设备，原材料、产品的物流园，企业通过物资购销网络直接购进售出，大大地减轻企业物资管理的工作量，使企业的物资管理工作重心转向企业内部生产现场物资管理环节。至2010年，扎佐物流园扩建规划修编通过评审，已完成设计总工程的37.5%，累计投资7997万元，以增强物资流通能量。同时建成农村现代物流服务网，创办农家超市208个，物流配送中心8个，覆盖全县99%行政村，使物流管理更为便捷。

（三）生产现场管理

1985年起，物资供应由市场调节，随着物流业发展，物资供应充足，生产企业供、销环节的物资管理得到简化，物资管理重点逐步转向生产现场环节。1990年，落实《贵州省工业企业现场管理规范》，企业“外抓市场”“内抓现场”，对生产现场设备、原材料、产品加大管理力度，开展降物耗、保质量、求效益为中心的物资管理工作。驻县航空工业部庆文机电厂、万江机械厂、烽光电机厂及县属国营企业三角山水泥厂、县水泥厂、酒厂、耐火材料厂都结合自身实际，相应制定生产现场物资管理办法，以达到物资流动规范，设备高效运行，产品优质低耗的效果。1991年，县乡镇企业局，经贸局举办TQC培训班，帮助建材、冶炼企业进行TQC基本知识普及教育培训，使产品质量管理原材料质量管理由“人治”转向“法治”。2000年，贵遵水泥厂、联宇食品公司、久长建材公司、华宏冶炼公司和绿太阳药业，开展“质量、品种、效益年”活动，抓住生产环节的物资管理，培养提升企业素质，使企业从速度效益型向质量效益型转变，从粗放经营向集约经营转变，加强对企业生产环节设备、原料、产品等物资的管理，通过国家ISO9000和ISO9001质量管理体系认证。2003年，全县工业企业开展走新型工业化道路活动，各家企业从生产现场物资管理入手，施行设备、原材料、半成品、再制品、成品等物资定置管理，对生产现场流动物资实行定量化管理，按规定及时转序或入库，达到物资标志清楚，账、物、卡相符的要求。使物资的生产现场管理成为整个物资管理的落脚点，成为企业物资管理工作的重心。

四、财务管理

（一）利改税

1978年，县属国营企业向县财政上交利润，县财政弥补企业亏损。至1983年，县属国营工业企业6年累计上交企业利润203万元，县财政弥补给企业亏损累计金额888万元，交补相抵，年均弥补给企业资金114万元，占6年间地方财政年均收入389.04万元的29.3%。

1983年，按照国家《国营企业利改税试行办法（草案）》，对全县国营企业实行利改税，将企业上缴给国家的利润改为企业所得向国家纳税。县耐火材料厂、农机厂、红旗煤厂、郭家林水泥厂、久长水泥厂列为第一步利改税企业试行。1984年10月，实施第二步利改税，征收企业产品税、增值税、营业税、所得税后，税后利润由企业自行安排，用于再生产、设备维修更新、产品开发和员工工资。为激发企业积极性、扩大企业税后利润，地方政府采取减税让利措施。从1984年到1989年6年中，全县工业企业向国家累计缴纳所得税7764万元，年均纳税1294万元，比利改税前6年累计上交利润203万元增加38倍。2000年，企业纳税5629万元，2007年2.72亿元。到2010年规模以上工业企业实现利税总额3.87亿元。

（二）拨改贷

随着利改税制度实施，企业基本建设资金、新产品开发资金和技术改造资金筹集，由财政拨款改为企业向银行贷款，企业承担贷款本、息偿还。1983年，县化肥厂转产生产水泥，组建三角山水泥厂，向银行贷款686万元，利改税实施后，由企业税后利润逐年偿还本息。1986年，县酒厂贷款600万元异地改造，修建阳明新酒厂。1994年，因经营管理不善申请破产，法院依法作出资不抵债依法破产的判决，县政府以500万元将阳明酒厂转让给贵阳龟龄寿酒集团。1997年，三角山水泥厂改制，整体出售给华兴实业有限公司，其贷款及债权、债务由新产权方承担。“拨改贷”降低财政风险，减少财政负担促使企业加强财务管理。2001年黔丰矿产工贸公司向县信用联社贷款13万元，将原制砖轮窑改为环保型轮窑，改造后年产红砖800万块，经济效益提高，2003年，如期如数归还贷款本、息。贷款投资回笼，得到保障。

（三）工资管理

20世纪80年代初，改革国营企业劳动分配制度，套改职工工资，按职工工龄、技术、文凭等进行评定。80年代中期，部分企业实行基本工资加超产奖励，少数企业实行定额工资或包干工资，个别企业推行奖励工资，同经济效益挂钩，上不封顶，下不保底的分配办法，改革收入分配制度，加强工资总额的宏观调控。但平均分配和分配不公拉大差距并存，“上班拿工资，干活要奖金”，能多不能少的变相“大锅饭”仍然存在,使企业工资总额大大突破。1987年，三角山水泥厂本着资产所有权与经营管理权分离的原则，推行承包经营责任制，按照“包死基数，确保上缴，超收多留，歉收自补”的十六字方针，进行国家与企业之间的分配。接着全县县属国营企业均采取包干基数，超收分成效益工资方式进行企业与职工之间分配。但在与企业承包经营者在签订承包合同时，使承包基数和浮动比例随意性增大，收入只与利润挂钩，未与效益联结，挂涨不挂落，负盈不负亏，出现企业员工工资和效益增长比例“倒挂”问题。同时大幅度拉开职工与承包者的收入分配差距，致承包人年收入高于职工收入1至5倍。在对未完成合同，扣减经营者奖金、浮动工资，连续两年不能完成合同者，虽终止合同，重新招标但承包有“风”无“险”，是人人敢于承包，勇于承包的根源带来工资管理混乱。民营企业员工工资则按国家劳动部门规定的确保最低工资标准，采取基本工资、定额工资、计件工资、岗位工资多种形式，以效益工资为核心，破除“铁交椅”“铁饭碗”、“铁工资”的劳动分配制度。1998年，随着经济体制改革深化，国有企业转为民营企业，企业职工的工资收入分配改为“效益型”，即与经济效益挂钩；部分民营企业员工的工资分配由“效益型”向着“市场型”转化，按照社会劳动力价值进行劳动收入分配。至2010年，国营企业县供电局实行职务工资、岗位工资；民营企业实行效益工资，包括岗位工资、基本工资、定额工资、计件工资和超额完成生产任务的奖励工资。

（四）财务核算

1980年开始，企业改变过去一收一支收付记账的财务管理方式，统一按照“增减记账法”进行企业财务核算，建立健全企业账簿核算制度。随着市场经济发展，企业加强财务管理，以财务核算、资金活动作为企业管理的主要内容，用财务核算去检验财务计划的制定、组织、实施、控制和调整情况，以财务核算去分析企业固定资产、流动资产、物资、产品、货币在生产经营中的使用效果，充分发挥财务核算的功能。企业销售收入总额上缴税金后，以税后利润按比例提取管理费用，在利润收入中列支，分月分季提成，年终结算。其余利润用于企业发展基金、扩大再生产、支付员工工资、设备更新、产品开发、职工教育培训，并分别设置会计科目，进行财务收支核算，制止企业财务资金混乱，以及“两本账”、“小金库”，使企业财务核算规范化、制度化。

1987年7月，县乡镇企业局为贯彻落实《乡镇企业财务制度》《乡镇企业会计制度》《乡镇企业成本开支范围的规定》，加强对企业财务核算制度的执行和培训，参加省财政厅、省乡企局、安顺地区财政局、地区乡企局共同举办为期15天的市、县财政系统会计、乡企主管会计、骨干企业会计财务核算知识和财务制度执行培训，全县乡镇企业72名财务人员参训。1991年，全县44名乡企财务人员参加会计资格考核。1994年全县乡企财务人员90人参加省乡企局“现金流量表”操作培训。1995年乡企局组织100人参加县财政局组织的“工业成本核算”培训。到90年代末，全县工业企业财务人员全部实现持证上岗，促进企业财务管理规范化。至2010年，县财政局组织全县会计人员400余人（含工业企业财会人员）在网上参加会计继续教育培训，学习财务知识和管理制度，组织会计从业资格、专业技能考试报考工作。继续执行《财务通则》《会计准则》，使财务核算制度执行落实有序、有效。

五、安全管理

（一）宣传教育

20世纪70年代末，社队企业采矿使用土法开采，挖“神仙土”“鸡窝洞”时常踏陷，安全系数极低。煤窑流传“挖煤汉子不要犟，二四八月灯不亮”的谚语，全凭经验自保，井毁人亡事故不断。县“五小”工业冶炼厂、化工厂、机械厂爆炸、中毒、灼伤、砸伤事故时有发生。从1980年起，安全生产列为企业效益考核，职工级别升降的措施，把安全生产的重点放在用电安全、消防安全、机械操作安全、有毒有害物质安全、易燃易爆物质安全、井下施工安全等环节，加强对驾驶、起重、电工、电焊、司炉、瓦斯爆破等技术岗位的管理。

1982年县政府以每年5月为“安全生产活动月”，成立 “安全月”活动领导小组。劳动局、乡镇企业局、工业局、检察院联合成立矿山安全检查组，抽调人员组建安全生产办公室，大张旗鼓开展安全生产宣传教育。1985年，成立县安全生产委员会，为县最高层次安全生产行政管理机构，广泛开展安全生产执法和宣传。进入90年代，采矿业大发展，无证矿山、煤窑遍处皆是，屡禁不止，安全生产形势严峻，

县安全委员会将“安全生产活动月”改为“安全活动周”，定于5月中旬第一周进行声势浩大的宣传，组织宣传车深入矿山、井区巡回宣讲，制作安全生产案例资料和图片，利用赶集天，散发宣传资料。1991年小箐乡人民政府针对新场、崇恩、大林村村民自挖自用煤窑，宣传《中华人民共和国矿产资源法》，使村民自动关闭，煤窑停止挖采。1997年，整顿煤炭开采，县政府召开全县煤矿安全生产教育专题会7次，与会470人次，出动26辆车次，深入矿山宣传。1999年3月，针对工矿企业乱挖采和污水乱排放，造成人畜饮水枯竭和水源污染、安全事故隐患严重，县水利局、水资源监察大队结合“3·22”世界水日和第二十届“中国水周”，以饮水安全为主题宣传“水法”，印发宣传资料5800份，宣传面达25万人次。2002年4月，六广镇人民政府针对中坪村非法盗采原煤，导致死亡9人事故，通过新闻媒体披露，扩大教育面。2003年安全月活动中，县乡镇企业局在县城迎春路、翠屏路、人民路悬挂醒目的安全生产横幅标语，制作煤窑事故典型案例宣传教育展板，设置宣传点发放安全生产宣传资料4000份。2004年，县劳动局和乡企局联合开展“人人事事保平安”为主题的安全月活动，深入展开《中华人民共和国安全生产法》的宣传，在县城赶场天设点宣讲。2005年至2008年，县总工会为企业安全生产开展安全管理的宣传教育，配合省总工会，市总工会组成的安全检查组深入六广镇大桥沟煤矿、丁家寨煤矿进行安全生产宣传；配合县安监局、供电局、龙场镇等28个单位在县城举行“安全生产，国泰民安”大型宣传活动，发安全法规资料2000份；组织县煤炭行业工会举办有20家煤矿企业参加的“煤矿安全知识竞赛”，并为六广镇龙窝煤矿、中心煤矿、黔丰煤矿、福利煤矿，谷堡乡大营煤矿，六桶乡清水沟煤矿6家获胜者颁奖；组织“安康杯”竞赛，着力增强煤矿工会劳动安全意识，与工会签订安全生产集体合同。县总工会在安全生产管理中开展的宣传教育活动，荣获贵阳市总工会“筑牢安全防范网，劲吹和谐劳动风”工作创新奖。2010年，县监察局组织首届“安康杯”小品大赛和安全生产应急知识竞赛，大力开展“安全生产月”活动，采用悬挂安全生产横幅、张贴图片和发放宣传资料等方式加大宣传力度，弘扬以人为本，关爱生命的主旋律。

（二）培训上岗

1981年，县劳动局安检科开展对企业特殊工种驾驶、起重、电工、电焊、司炉、瓦斯、爆破岗位进行技能培训，建立考试、考核持证上岗制度。到1985年共培训煤矿安全员97人次、化验员29人次和司炉、焊接、仪表技术工26人次。1992年，小箐乡抽调1名乡干部兼任乡企业安全员，组织矿山、煤窑从业人员学习矿井空气条件、矿井瓦斯、矿井水管理、矿井顶底板管理和安全用电常识。1997年，县安监局、劳动局在举办全县安全生产宣传教育活动中配用电视录像，以身边发生的典型安全事故案例，开展企业安全生产全员培训，县公安局举办矿山爆破员培训。2000年，实行安全生产“包保”责任制，对采矿企业进行全员培训，共培训矿工1642人。2004年5月，县乡镇企业局为加强煤炭生产安全管理，在煤矿基层选出59名矿工作为“群众安全监督员”集中学习培训，由市煤炭局专家授课，建立起煤矿新的安全监督机制，加强安全管理。并把矿山安全员培训内容从一般安全基础知识提高到安全掌握应用设备、设施，应对突发事件的处置能力和自我保护能力，培训矿工916人。同时贯彻执行《中华人民共和国安全生产法》，建立特种作业人员必须持证上岗备案制度，全年举办特殊工种培训25期，共培训技术工人达946人。2005年，县乡镇企业局制定《煤矿职工培训计划》，培训中，教员不仅严格按照授课预案讲解，还结合县内井下施工实际情况讲授，普及安全生产知识，举办培训班24期，考试合格工人830人，特殊岗位全部实现持证上岗。2010年,贵阳市安监局在县举办矿山安全标准化自评人员培训,有170人参加。县安监局培训中心组织矿山、矿井从业人员培训班3期，培训人员128人；水泥生产企业安全生产培训班8期，培训人员393人；危化行业安全培训5期，培训人员227人。进一步提高工业企业从业人员安全素质和安全生产技能。

（三）监督检查

1982年，县劳动局、检察院、乡镇企业局、工业局联合成立矿山安全检查组，进行安全生产监督检查群防群治，对采矿企业安全生产联合执法，防治结合，查封有事故隐患矿井20处，责成采矿企业、小煤窑设置安全监督员，购置安全检测仪器42台，矿灯87盏，杜绝井下明火照明。80年代末，矿井施工、开采安全生产监督检查、防范治理形成经常化、制度化。进入90年代，工业企业主管部门推行安全生产责任制，县乡企局制定《乡镇煤矿安全生产管理制度》，开展群防群治。各生产企业内部制定《岗位安全操作规章制度》，按制度规范操作、施工。2001年，针对已撤销、关停的矿井死灰复燃情况，县乡企局、矿山安全检查组耗费炸药60箱、雷管500枚、汽车75辆次、人员500人次和资金8万元，“反复炸，炸反复”，有力地制止安全事故反弹。2003年，7月，县乡镇企业局对已经技改，只持单证（无生产许可证）的10家煤矿，经省煤炭生产验证组复核，重新进行验收。在贵阳市乡镇企业局和安全生产技术专家指导下，督促14家煤矿装置起瓦斯监测监控系统、配置探水设施，全年进行12次安全设施大检查，下达安检指令书291份，提出整改意见1367条。2004年5月，县乡镇企业局为加强煤矿监督检查群防群治，在全县煤矿基层选出59名矿工作为“群众安全监督员”，请煤采专家讲授安全监督课，建起煤矿群众性的安全生产监督机制。2005年4月，由县乡企业、安监局、国土局联合成立处置突发事件小分队，配置越野汽车、摄影机和紧急装备器材，开展群防群治。6月，全县投入141万元建成煤矿瓦斯监测监控系统网，使用中国联通CDMA网络体系的24家煤矿实现联网运行，对瓦斯浓度变化进行监控。开展矿山、矿井安全生产评比考核工作，对安全生产无事故企业给予奖励，对有安全隐患，未及时整改企业进行处罚，使企业安全生产意识得以增强。2010年,在安全检查中，排除安全隐患100条次，责令停产整顿企业4家，挂牌监办重大安全隐患1处，由隐患单位整改后报市安监委办理销号。安全生产“金安”工程项目建设完成并投入使用，实现省、市、县三级安全监管之间的互联、互通。

（四）事故处理

20世纪80至90年代，工业生产安全事故处理主要对煤矿安全事故追究事故直接和间接责任人的责任，其中有扎佐石堰河煤矿透水事故导致10人遇难，六广茶林煤矿瓦斯爆炸6人死亡，大石联丰煤矿井下二氧化碳超标6人窒息身亡，谷堡红星煤矿瓦斯爆炸7人死亡，分别追究经营直接责任人刑事责任和乡管企业的行政领导间接责任，给予撤职或警告处分，但生产安全事故仍然频发。

进入2000年，在县政府组织下，由县计划经济贸易局、乡镇企业局、劳动局和公安局联合执法，采取对企业生产安全事故产生的原因潜在隐患不分析，查不清不放过；对事故治理处理措施不落实不放过；对事故责任直接和间接相关人员未追究应负责不放过；对企业职工未受到安全生产教育提高安全生产责任，树立安全生产意识不放过的“四不放过”原则处理事故。2002年，六广镇中坪村豪猪湾煤厂在未取得采矿许可证、安全生产许可证、煤炭生产许可证、营业执照及矿长资格证的情况下,组织工人违规采煤。其间,六广镇镇政府曾责令其停止开采,但矿主置若罔闻,仍继续开采，致煤窑突发透水事故,造成9名工人遇难，经调查认定为非法监采不具开采资质所致。事故发生后采取疏导群众、安抚死者家属、炸封矿井和追逃责任人等措施处理。同时还对影响生产和生活环境的其他安全事故有针对性地采取不同措施

进行处理，其中对六广镇龙窝煤矿和洒坪乡上村煤矿采矿导致团岩地面塌陷依法炸封煤井；对久长镇富捷日化黄磷厂安全防范措施不力导致17名工人中毒，依照劳动保护法支付伤者医疗费外，另补偿精神安抚费；对谷堡乡白泥田联营矿山、三峰铝业和惠源矿山疏干排水挖采造成地下水沉降，使人畜饮水枯竭，除支付赔偿金外，还责令为村里修建人畜饮水水池；对久长镇永兴村杨正贵的砂厂采砂损坏蚌壳堰水库沟渠，给排放水造成安全隐患责令停产。

2009年，在安全事故处理中进一步分析明确事故发生的原因，使职工受到安全生产教育，以吸取教训，其中当年5月贵州煤矿安全监察局林东监察分局对六广镇银山煤矿“4·22”机电事故作出处理：维修工邱天福违章操作导致事故，是事故直接责任人，因其在事故中死亡，未追究责任。安全员白希沙，当班负责维修现场监督，未落实现场安全监督职责，对事故发生负有重要责任，根据《安全生产违法行为行政处罚办法》第44条规定，给予罚款4000元行政处罚。矿长彭代强，是事故当班带班负责人，未认真履行带班负责人职责，对事故发生负有重要责任，根据《中华人民共和国安全生产法》第80条规定，给予罚款2万元行政处罚。对银山煤矿未落实安全生产责任制，未及时消除安全事故隐患，违反《煤矿安全规程》第732条规定，导致安全事故，根据《生产安全事故报告和调查处理条例》第37条规定，给该矿罚款12万元的行政处罚。7月，贵州煤矿安全监察局林东监察分局下达对六广镇黔丰煤矿“6·3”顶板事故处理决定：工人严同学是事故发生当班班长，负责回风巷掘进施工作业，当掘进工作面放炮之后，未认真执行“敲帮问顶”制度，在未采取安全措施情况下，私自处理炮后倾倒的临时支护，导致事故发生，是事故直接责任人，鉴于其在事故中死亡，不再追究其责任。安全员赵怀忠是跟班安全检查和现场安全监督人，未认真履行职责，现场监督不力，并未及时采取措施，消除事故隐患，对事故发生有重大责任。根据《安全生产违法行为行政处罚办法》第44条规定，给予罚款2000元行政处罚。副矿长林天波是事故发生当班负责人，在支护倾倒、顶帮存在开裂情况下，未及时督促消除事故隐患，负有重大责任，根据《安全生产违法行为行政处罚办法》第44第规定，给予罚款3000元行政处罚。矿长赵怀书是安全生产第一责任人，管理职责不到位，矿级管理人员职责分工不明，未建立安全隐患排查治理制度和现场安全监督管理制度，对事故发生负主要责任，根据《贵州省安全生产条例》第58条规定，给予罚款5000元的行政处罚。其矿违反《煤矿安全规程》第3条、4条、41条规定和《生产安全事故报告和调查处理条例》第37条规定，给该矿罚款11万元行政处罚。2010年，共发生各类安全生产事故18起，其中煤矿安全事故2起、死亡2人，冶炼安全事故1起、死亡1人，均按《安全生产违法行为行政处罚办法》给予处理。安全事故同比下降39%。

专记：豪猪湾矿难九人身亡

2002年4月25日上午10时，六广镇中坪村豪猪湾小煤窑发生透水事故，井下矿工困于井内，矿主逃离现场。村民得知透水事故，即向六广镇政府电话报警，镇政府当即组织人员于25日中午12时赶到现场。与此同时，县长魏明禄和常务副县长成华强、县委常委、纪委书记陆秀祥，副县长周毅奔赴豪猪湾，立即组建由县安委办、乡镇企业局、国土局、计经局、公安局、建设局、供电局、水利局、卫生局、民政局、物资局、交通局以及县人民法院、检察院、消防等共170人的抢险指挥部和事故处理领导小组。由县长魏明禄直接担任指挥长和领导小组长，设置抢险技术组负责抢险具体事宜，后勤组负责抢险物资调配，群众工作组负责疏导群众，安抚死者家属，追逃组负责追查外逃责任矿主。

次日晚，经过30个小时紧张的抢险排水，找准井下情况，组织人员下井，找到6具遇难矿工尸体后便炸封矿井。27日，据生还者忆述和多方解，得知井下还有矿工，即组织挖开已炸封的煤洞，再次组织人员下井，又找到3具尸体。整个抢险搜救工作历经3天，查明9名矿工罹难，3名矿工致伤。事后县委、县政府召开会议，县长魏明禄通报六广镇豪猪湾煤矿非法盗采，发生透水事故及县抢险工作，并责令各乡镇展开地毯式的安全检查，决定对不具备开采资格的煤窑进行炸封。事后，对违法盗采造成事故责任人付汉祥、付汉发、吴学林、吴学伦4人由〔2003〕筑刑终字第11号分别判刑6年的惩处，并对相关行政机关管理人员等17人给予行政处分。

第五节　企业选介

一、贵州龙翔能源（集团）有限公司

贵州龙翔能源（集团）有限公司是贵州龙翔集团公司在2003年11月兼并贵州云天航空工贸有限公司（原418库）后组建的民营企业，落户在龙场镇小营村，公司占地400亩，注册资金8948万元，总资产2.8亿元。下属子公司有云天航空工贸公司、贵州巨能电力发展有限公司、贵州金石磨料制造有限公司和贵州丰汇贸易有限公司。2004年，公司已发展为集矿业开发、化工冶炼、机械制造、国际贸易为一体的综合性民营集团企业。主要产品有凸轮轴、包装箱、电熔氧化锆、棕刚玉磨料、工业硅和煤炭。其拳头产品“云天牌”摩托车凸轮轴组件，获国家ISO9001：2000质量管理体系认证，产品批量销往南京金城、济南轻骑、重庆隆鑫、常州光阳、宁波太阳、虹桥动工、上海欧翔等摩托车生产厂家，入围到国家摩托车行业最佳零部件配套体系明星阵容。

2004年组建初，公司员工200人，次年增为357人，到2007年队伍壮大到800人，因此荣获“贵阳市再就业工作先进单位”称号。员工中大专以上学历者占30%，具有专业技术人员的百人中，有高级企业管理人员，有享受国家特殊津贴的高级工程师，有专门从事国际贸易的营销员，是一支能创业、能创新、能干事的员工队伍。2010年，《puaqt通用机凸轮轴产品技术攻关》项目获得省、市创新基金20万元重大项目支持，生产凸轮轴336万套，产值4784.2万元。

二、贵州林海新材料制造有限公司

贵州林海新材料制造有限公司位于扎佐镇中营村的川黔铁路、贵（阳）毕（节）、贵（阳）遵（义）高等级公路交汇处，占地面积50亩。1997年3月，公司投资2300万元，建成年设计能力7000吨压裂支撑剂（陶粒），专供石油、天然气开采施工使用。2000年5月竣工投产，2003年2月产品通过ISO9001：2000国家质量体系认证，各项性能指标均达到国家石油行业SY—PS108—1997标准和美国石油协会API标准。用于塔里木油田阿克1#井进行压裂施工，日产天然气从7.3万立方米上升到51万立方米，使林海陶粒知名度得以提升，并荣获贵阳市人民政府授予“科教兴市示范工程”称号。林海陶粒不仅结束我国石油压裂支撑剂依赖国外进口的历史，而且出口哈萨克斯坦、俄罗斯、加拿大。《中国石油报》以“国产优质陶粒登陆北美市场”为题作专题报道。

2004年，公司拥有专利2个、产品品牌2个、产品规格4种。年生产能力提高到8000吨，纳税260万元，跻身县内纳税大户行列。2005年生产支撑剂5857吨，产值2097万元，实现营业收入1152万元，纳税122万元。在贵州省名牌产品推荐评比活动中，林海陶粒获得贵州省人民政府颁发的“名牌产品”证书。2010年，生产陶粒8797吨，产值2578.3万元。

三、贵阳富捷化工有限公司修文黄磷厂

简称修文黄磷厂，驻久长镇沙雁村305省道北侧，靠近川黔铁路、贵（阳）遵（义）高等级公路，交通十分便利。黄磷厂始建于1996年5月，由贵阳市经委下属供销公司、修文县乡镇企业局、贵阳市北供电局和个体户王晓春共同投资建成年设计生产能力2500吨现代化黄磷生产线，次年5月点火试运成功，当年生产黄磷2000吨，达到设计生产能力。1998年，为有利于黄磷的生产经营管理，县乡企局、贵阳市经委供销公司和贵阳市北供电局退出联营，由个体投资者王晓春独资经营。因黄磷市场价格下降，资金回笼困难，生产受到影响，王晓春将厂转让给捷克投资公司经营。

黄磷厂转让后于2000年恢复正常生产，部分产品出口销售。产量达2000吨。2001年产黄磷上升到1万吨，大大突破生产能力。2004年生产量又下降为2244.94吨，销售收入2632.1万元，纳税160万元。2005年由于原料紧缺，导致生产量下降到1534吨，加上2004年积压产品使销售收入达3088万元，纳税达166万元。从2005年起至2008年，虽受原料短缺制约，但企业仍坚持生产，为来自沙雁当地农民工和久长镇复员退伍军人100余人提供就业场所。2008年，因受世界金融危机影响，产品失去销路而停产。

四、黔鑫磷化工有限责任公司

黔鑫磷化工有限责任公司是一家股份制企业，2001年利用原驻龙场镇马家桥的部队闲置营房，投资65万元建成磷化工生产线。由于设备不配套，达不到年产磷酸、磷酸二氢钙能力各为3000吨产能。2004年，年产量各1000吨，销售收入500万元，纳税20万元。在生产经营中，锻炼出一支能管理、会经营、懂生产的员工队伍，为企业增添活力。有一定积累后，公司又制定以磷化工为主的发展规划，投入资金20万元，新增1条磷化生产线。2005年，生产磷酸3000吨，销售收入增至701万元，纳税增至25万元。企业由小到大、由弱到强，逐步发展。黔鑫公司虽然步履艰难，但不忘回报社会，每年都使用部分资金购买学生学习用品、体育器材赠予当地的马家桥小学，“六一”儿童节都到马家桥小学与学生欢度节日，“八一”建军节都到马家桥驻军慰问部队官兵。2010年，因环保评审不达标而停产。

五、众福特色食品有限公司

公司于1996年3月建立，驻地扎佐镇和平村，地处210国道旁，邻近贵（阳）毕（节）、贵（阳）遵（义）高等级公路入口处。翌年2月建成试产，由贵州省轻工科研所专家现场指导、试机、调运，于4月取样首批产品麦芽糊精，经省轻工科研所检测，各项指标均达国家标准。

麦芽糊精选用优质玉米淀粉、大米为原料，采取酶法水解工艺精制而成。产品用于食品、轻工、医药行业，麦芽糊精上市后即与省内多家糖厂、食品厂、制药厂建立起稳定的供货关系，部分产品销往云南。

1999年，公司进行技术改革，扩增年产5000吨液体葡萄糖和3000吨高麦芽糖浆生产线。技改后，厂区面积扩增为1.2万平方米，生产厂房和库房达2200平方米，综合办公楼400平方米，企业总资产达1000万元。2000年，生产麦芽糊精560多吨，液体葡萄糖800余吨，销售收入260万元，纳税14.5万元，企业

获利35万元。2008年，随金融市场波动，与多家食品厂、药厂供销关系链中断，生产下滑，2010年处于半停产状态。

六、贵州联宇食品有限公司

1998年，在国营企业改制中，县政协职工王文以95万元整体购买原修文县酱菜厂改造组建贵州联宇食品有限公司，1999年年底投入130万元资金进行年产4200吨酱油生产线技改，推出“瑞其尔”牌系列酱油，获得省调味品工业协会监制证书，成为省消费者协会推荐产品，销往贵阳、黔南、黔东南等地。公司以酱油系列产品为龙头，又开发油辣椒、水豆豉、糟辣椒等风味食品。同时利用扎佐特产大白萝卜生产萝卜干，产品通过ISO9001：2000国际质量管理认证，获国际阳明文化节指定使用产品。2000年10月，“萝卜干”被选入参加武汉食品展销贸易洽谈会，受到与者青睐。公司固定资产增至620万元，占地面积20亩，建起年产1800吨低盐固态发酵工艺酱油生产线1条和800平方米包装车间配置有先进食品包装设备、设施齐全的化验室，另有闲置厂房2500平方米，可用于扩大再生产。至2010年企业成为生产运行12年保持不断壮大的非公有制企业。

七、贵州文德矿冶有限公司

1991年，个体户陈顺隆和马家桥驻军农场、县乡镇企业总公司共同经营的修文硅铁厂与香港德利贸易公司联合后组建的铁合金冶炼厂注册名称定为贵州文德矿冶有限公司，位于龙场镇马家桥。公司为县与港商合资企业，注册资金122万美元，资产比例为原厂方占60%，港商占40%。公司聘有常年在岗工程师7人、厂外咨询服务工程师7人和企业管理干部2人，员工总数187人。当年生产硅铁2000吨，销售收入600多万元，纳税70万元，出口创汇200万美元，产品远销日本、韩国、美国及中国香港、台湾地区。

1993年，马家桥部队农场、乡企公司退出联营，文德公司由个体投资户陈顺隆与港商联合继续经营。2004年，生产硅锰合金687吨，销售收入1262万元，纳税80万元。2005年，因产品销售不畅，导致产量下降，生产硅锰340吨。之后文德公司采取租赁、承包多种经营方式，基本维持生产。2007年因受到亚洲金融风暴及世界经济危机影响，产品失去市场，生产告吹，工厂闲置。

八、贵州利尔建材有限责任公司

1994年，由原县计委干部李修平停薪留职在龙场镇小营村创办利尔水泥厂，年产普通建材水泥6万吨。1997年到1999年先后两次技改，累计投入资金600万元，改建成年产8万吨水泥生产线，开创“利尔”水泥品牌。随后将利尔水泥厂申办为利尔建材有限责任公司。

2000年，公司法人李修平将公司转给股东周明贵和骆成碧经营，周明贵任经理兼法人代表。2002年，公司又投入资金800万元扩大再生产，建起年产10万吨水泥生产线，使生产能力达到年产18万吨的规模。2003年公司场地扩大到64.5亩，固定资产达3700万元。2004年7月，公司为确保产品质量，特邀中国进出口质量认证中心专家对公司30余名技术、管理人员进行产品质量体系ISO9001：2000标准培训，引进质量管理体系设施进行产品质量监测，一举通过ISO9001：2000国际质量体系认证。2005年生产水泥13万吨，销售收入2280万元，纳税99万元，跻身于县内工业企业纳税大户之列。2010年，生产水泥13.59万吨，产值3490.4万元。

九、贵州奇峰工贸有限责任公司

1989年9月，中国人民解放军成都军区后勤部征用久长镇二关坝干桥的部分林地，投资1960万元兴

建成久耐火材料厂，厂区占地面积54.2亩，建筑面积5398平方米，1991年9月建成投产。1994年，耐火材料市场疲软，水泥市场看涨，成都军区后勤部再投入资金200万元将原厂改建成水泥厂，设计能力年产水泥7万吨，厂名更改为贵遵水泥厂，于1996年11月正式投入生产，所产水泥抗震和防渗性能好，广泛运用在高等级公路和高层房屋建筑上。1998年，按照国家关于军队办企业改制的有关政策军队停止办企业，整体将贵遵水泥厂移交地方，改为省经贸委下属国有控股企业贵州奇峰工贸有限责任公司，继续生产经营。

2005年，公司拥有主机设备φ2.5×43.3米新型干洁旋窑1台、φ2.5×6.5米生料球磨机2台、φ1.5×12米烘干机1台、φ3×13米水泥磨机1台，主辅生产设备共200余台（套），固定资产原值5092.5万元，年生产能力30万吨，产品质量上成，通过国际ISO900：2000质量体系认证。公司利用工业废渣生产的环保水泥产品，荣获贵阳市科技进步二等奖，是县内水泥生产行业一流上规模工业企业。到2010年，公司划归修文工业园区久长工业园，企业总投资已达600万元，产值达7326万元。

十、南方水泥厂

南方水泥厂前身为县境内首家乡办的马家桥水泥厂，位于龙场镇马家桥艾家湾，距县城6公里、距修（文）开（阳）公里0.5公里。原厂设计能力年产普通硅酸盐水泥5000吨。厂区在原料斜坡上，山上开采原料、经粉碎、配料、磨碎、成球、煅烧、熟料磨细工序顺坡而下出成品，其优点是减少机械提升和设备转运，降低生产成本。原厂属马家桥公社社办企业，后转属马家桥乡。

1988年1月，个体户王绍林承包经营该厂，又投入资金200万元对设备进行系列改造，将生、熟料磨机改为φ183型，使生产能力提高至年产2万吨。1990年，在水泥市场疲软、销路不畅情况下，经营仍产销两旺，生产水泥1.5万吨，盈利30万元。1992年，王绍林将水泥厂产权购断，厂变成自己的私人企业后更加放开手脚，对企业进行全面规划。1994年重新筑窑，更新设备，将年生产能力扩大到4万吨，成为县内乡镇企业水泥生产规模最大、最有竞争实力的企业。

1996年，水泥厂按国家建材行业管理规范要求，又出资580万元，推倒土窑，修成新型机立窑生产线，经过3年努力，到1999年新型机立窑竣工投产，形成年产10万吨水泥生产线，所产“风林”牌水泥价廉实惠，受到用户好评。2000年将厂名更为“南方水泥厂”，生产步步上升。2004年，产出水泥4万吨，总产值678万元，纳税79万元，成为县内工业企业纳税大户之一。2010年，生产水泥5.08万吨，产值1266.4万元。

十一、丁家寨煤矿

丁家寨煤矿坐落在六广镇前丰村，有修（文）六（桶）三级公路与矿井道路相连。煤矿原属国营红旗煤厂改制后的异地改造矿井，为解决改制后退休职工生活费来源而创办。矿井交通运输、地质构造、水文条件、煤层赋存、矿藏储量和开采条件都较优越。从2001年起，经过几翻领办、转办，到2003年将矿开采权和经营权转给吉林省白山市个体经营户袁凤友，按照省、市煤炭办矿标准进行技改和设备更新，改造成年产6万吨原煤的生产企业，正式获得《煤炭生产许可证》。

煤矿遵循“以人为本、安全第一”方针，从矿长到矿工、层层落实安全生产责任制，投入资金10万元安装瓦斯监测控制系统，将安全生产管理落实到井下，成为全县煤矿工业示范矿井。2004年，生产原煤5.46万吨，达到设计生产能力。2005年，提交扩界开采申请，得到审批，展开全面的矿井技改和扩能工作，将生产能力提升到年产原煤15万吨，使煤矿产量逐年上升。2010年，成为县内关井压产后保留的11个达标煤矿之一，年产原煤21万吨，产值1.01亿元。

十二、栗木山煤矿

栗木山煤矿位于洒坪乡上坝村，距洒坪乡政府驻地2.5公里，有县乡沥青道路与矿山道相连。矿井蕴藏煤炭资源100万吨，地质构造简单，煤层倾斜角度较大，须用斜井提升的长臂式采掘法，以挖掘机械、安全设施大量投入。1999年实施煤炭企业“关井压产”，周边矿井被关停，该矿进行整改保留。经贵工勘察设计院设计，制定年产3万吨整改方案，但因经营者无力承担技改任务而暂停生产。2003年，贵州宏和矿业有限公司接管后，按省、市煤炭办矿标准制定技改方案，在方案实施过程中又将煤矿转让给个体经营户刘华财和秦钲武联合经营，前后累计投入技改资金700万元，将该矿改造成年产原煤3万吨规范型矿井。

2004年，煤矿面貌改观，矿部设办公室、生产科、安监科、经营科，职工总数100名，其中正副矿长3人、技术员4人、后勤人员23人、矿工70人。到2010年，经过技改生产能力达到年产原煤15万吨。当年产煤6万吨。

十三、贵州同济堂制药股份有限公司

贵州同济堂制药股份有限公司系原贵州仙灵药业有限公司更名创立。公司前身仙灵药业始建于1994年，1999年由贵阳花溪蔡冲迁驻龙场镇原航空工业部属庆文机械厂搬迁后留下的场地，厂区占地面积403亩，公司生产的“仙灵骨葆胶囊”荣获吉隆坡世界骨科理事会一等奖，产品获中国骨伤科理事会特别贡献奖。1999年7月投资3100万元，按国家医药GMP标准进行“仙骨葆”系列药品生产技术改革，2000年建成胶囊车间、片剂车间、颗粒剂车间以及药品库房，置有胶囊剂、片剂、颗粒剂3种剂型6条生产线。2000年后连续3年被贵州省委、省政府评为先进乡镇企业给予表彰。2003年7月，贵阳市委、市人民政府授予公司“十强纳税大户”称号。

2004年公司进行股份制改制，更名为同济堂制药股份有限公司，生产总产值1.56亿元，销售收入2亿元，纳税2200万元，利润2100万元。2005年销售收入达2.11亿元，纳税2900万元。为保证生产原材料，先后投资2000万元在修文、息烽、雷山等县建立中药材保护、种植、抚育基地2万亩，同时研究、开发惊天宇注射液、肾炎康胶囊、肝脂清胶囊、骨参原料胶囊等新品种。2007年获贵阳市最高科技创新奖，并与美国信纳克医学研究中心在北京联合发布历时两年的临床试验结果，成功通过国际权威机构认证。2008年，公司中药文化入选“第二批国家级非物质文化遗产”名录，成为国家重点保护的非物质文化遗产。2009年，公司经贵州省科学技术厅审定为高新技术企业，并颁发高新技术企业证书。至2010年企业生产步步腾飞，生产药品777吨，创产值6.12亿元。

十四、贵州绿太阳制药有限公司

贵州绿太阳药业创建于1993年，原生产基地位于贵阳市龙洞堡，1997年迁驻扎佐镇修文医药产业园A区，入驻时投资800万元兴建起县内医药产业园第一条现代化药品生产线。

公司产品由贵州苗药制作配方开发，主要有膏霜中药制剂“绿格尔”系列，拥有肤痔清软膏、貂胰防裂膏、日晒防治膏3种民族特色药以及磁疗祛斑按摩乳、补天胶囊、葆肤康软膏、痔舒安软膏、绿格尔顽癣敌和绿格尔粉刺净保健系列品种。其产品日晒防治膏送至北京赠予天安门国旗护卫队试用后，成为

国旗护卫队首选护肤品，产品畅销全国23个省、市、区，还远销至加拿大、荷兰、俄罗斯、越南等国家和中国香港地区，曾荣获“星火计划”实施十周年优秀项目金奖和’98中国新产品新技术博览会金奖，成为中国民族医药学会推荐产品，也是旅游商品中的畅销药品。公司董事长沈子民荣获贵州省2000年度“优秀乡镇企业家”称号。

2004年6月，公司技改、扩建的医药生产线取得国家药业GMP标准认证。销售收入达到2906万元，纳税257万元。2005年，增至3456万元，纳税364万元，公司总资产达到5464万元。到2010年公司有员工75人，其中高级职称10人，大专以上员工25人，拥有资产总额7039万元，年生产总值1900万元，纳税300万元。

十五、贵州维康药业有限公司

贵州维康药业有限公司兴建于1999年，系骨伤科药品开发、生产和销售为一体的专业化民营股份制企业。2002年4月迁入修文医药产业园区后根据南京医药设计院规划设计，于2004年完成国家药业GMP改造，建成一个新型现代化花园试药品生产厂，设有胶囊、颗粒、酊剂3条生产线，厂区建设占地80亩，投入建设资金3368万元。

公司生产的主导产品“骨康灵”和“肿痛消”是挖掘苗药秘方，结合现代中药药剂、药理学、临床研究而成，为贵州苗药系列药品之一。产品经北京、上海、广东、江苏、浙江等地100多家三甲医院临床验证，医疗效果显著。“骨康灵胶囊”“肿痛舒喷雾剂”获得国家保护专利，产品覆盖全国28个省区，并在50多个城市建有营销网络。2002年4月迁入医药园区边建设、边生产，当年实现销售收入2475万元，纳税160万元。2003年，销售收入到达4000万元，纳税300万元。2005年，销售上升为1.06亿元，纳税增至772万元，跨入亿元以上产值企业。2006年，公司被贵阳市政府列为全市23家重点扶持上市企业之一，被贵州省科技厅授予“贵州省高新技术企业”称号。2010年，拥有职工263人，其中大中专学历176人占70%，中高级职称14人，资产额2.4亿元，年销售收入6亿元，纳税2500万元。

十六、贵州光正制药有限公司

公司前身系国有老牌企业贵阳制药厂，改制后为解决职工再就业而组建贵州光正制药有限公司。2001年5月，公司迁驻修文医药产业园区。厂区地处扎佐林场，周边地势平坦、森林茂密，近邻贵（阳）遵（义）、贵（阳）毕（节）高等级公路、210国道和川黔铁路。公司投资4800万元，经过18个月建成，建筑占地20.5亩，建筑面积1.6万平方米，其中GMP标准厂房5280平方米，绿化面积2.56万平方米，道路及活动场所1万平方米，成为布局合理、新颖别致的花园式的药品生产企业。2003年2月，公司经国家药品监督管理局验收，取得药品GMP标准论证。全公司有员工226人，其中制药专业人员186人。员工学历比例中专占64%，大专占21%，本科占15%。聘请有GMP体系管理科技人才组成完善的药业生产和管理机构。公司置有质量保证部、生产部、工程部、物科部、销售部、财务部和人事劳动部，各部职责分明，生产经营秩序井然。

公司建有固体制剂和小容量注射剂两个大型生产车间和生产配套流水线，其中小容量注射剂是西南地区最大的一家，也是省内唯一上规模、上档次的企业，年产小容量注射剂12亿支，胶囊剂1.5亿粒，片剂10亿片，颗粒剂6000万袋。2003年创产值2592万元，营业创收719万元。2004年营业收入达1320万元。2005年上升为2174万元，纳税突破100万元，跻身于县内工业企业纳税大户行列。至2010年，公司生产经营逐年上升，拥有资产总额3.5亿元，年生产总值7000万元，实现利税490万元。

十七、扎佐重晶石粉厂

1981年5月，扎佐镇居民何贵书在扎佐镇中营村向银行贷款10万元和争取到国家支农资金16.8万元，动工建设扎佐重晶石粉厂，1982年4月建成投产。厂区占地3.6亩，建筑面积838平方米，置有4123216型磨机2台，包装机1台，运输汽车2辆。当年采矿4.9万吨，生产重晶石粉1000吨。1983年，国际钻井需要重晶石粉数量大，但厂生产能力较小，加之包装费、出港费高昂，产品只得受托于贵州省矿产品进出口公司转销国外。由于产品质量保证，吸引10个国家前来订货。国内胜利油田采用该厂产品后推荐加入中国石油部昆山供应网，成为扎佐镇首创外汇的企业。1986年，企业获利12.4万元，偿还银行贷款和国家支农资金。随后企业扩展经营范围，增添设备，增建年产1万吨磷矿粉车间，产品销往山东、福建，企业效益又有提升。1988年5月，厂长何贵书获贵州省人民政府授予“优秀乡镇企业家”荣誉。1990年，生产重晶石粉5.8万吨，其中钻井级5万吨，化工级8000吨，纳税32万元，盈利65万元，创外汇4万美元。1994年，企业注册为贵州修文兴达有限责任公司，扩大生产规模，买断六屯乡重晶石矿的开采权，从此采矿、加工于一厂，年采矿2万余吨，年产重晶石粉1.2万吨，产值达300万元。

进入2000年后，由于重晶石矿受到可开采的资源逐步减少及受亚洲金融风暴的影响，使重晶石粉生产加工下滑。2006年，因与政府签订的开采、生产合同期满，企业乘此停产，随着将企业厂房出租。

十八、联合磨料厂

1985年经营铝矾土煅烧的个体经营户荣启凤，在城关镇（今龙场镇）潮水村征地20亩，合股投资兴建冶炼棕刚玉2000千伏安冶炼炉1座，年产棕刚玉4500吨，产品得到安顺、珠海等地客户信任，销路扩大。1989年扩建万吨初级制品生产线，企业资产达到1800万元，产品年产值2500万元。

20世纪90年代初，因受国外垄断集团干扰，产品出口受到制约，企业面临下马。处于困境中的荣启凤毅然决定增资270万元，随后又追加到400万元，再上优特粒生产线，使产品由粗放生产转为深度加工，提高产品价值，增强企业的市场竞争力。1993年，新建的制粒生产线投入运行，由于使用先进的振动碾压、切割、破碎工艺，产品质量远远超过对辊和球磨的产品，并使用水洗烘干，提高棕刚玉的洁净度，在同行业中处于优先地位，产品由省进出口公司远销国外。企业走出困境，成为县乡镇工业重点企业之一。1999年10月，企业经外贸经济合作部批准，获得具有进出口经营权的生产企业资格，产品成为日本、韩国、美国C——E矿产公司的合作伙伴。2003年，生产棕刚玉7900吨，创产值2102万元，排位贵州省出口创汇增长前十名，受到省人民政府的表彰。2004年，企业法人荣启凤重病离世，管理失控，加之银行贷款累积，导致生产日趋下滑，企业陷入停产状态，2005年产值仅为918.1万元，2006年停产。

十九、天成热陶瓷有限公司

2002年，生产经营铝矾土煅烧的杨国林和杨国琴兄妹为与省外客户建立稳定的供销业务，亲赴省外考察。经过观察访问，发现建筑业使用陶瓷市场前景良好，尤其是建筑陶瓷中的耐磨陶瓷市场需求量较大，返厂后立即进行利用铝矾土生产耐磨陶瓷的论证，以铝矾土深加工生产耐磨陶瓷拓展企业产品结构。2003年，兄妹俩投资500万元在龙场镇王官村征地30亩，创办天成热陶瓷有限公司，建容积90立方米倒烟窑2座，生产耐磨陶瓷球，年生产能力3000吨。经过1年实践，产品质量已赶上省外同行业水平。到2004年，杨氏兄妹又认为倒烟窑虽然能生产出高密度的耐磨陶瓷球，但能耗高、产量低、生产周期

长，难以进入规模生产，产品质量虽然赶上同行业水平，但合格率不高，档次上不去。

2005年，兄妹两人再次出省考察，寻求先进煅烧技术，参观无数煅烧窑后，经过分析对比，选定推板窑煅烧。经过半年试烧，产品质量提高，产量上升，又投入资金80万元，建起4孔22米长的推板煅烧窑，使企业生产能力达到年产4000吨，生产成本降低的同时开发出具有高新技术含量、市场前景广阔的新材料产品，企业实现将资源优势转化为产业优势，一举成为县内拔尖的工业企业。

2009年，企业利用贫瘠铝矾土矿与废弃耐火材料生产高强度耐磨瓷器球技术，荣获科技部创新基金奖60万元，获省级科技创新基金奖20万元，至2010年，生产一直稳步前进。

第三章 交通运输

1978年，县境公路有国道、省道、县道共9条，全长178公里，贯通5个区驻地及部分公社，另有过境铁路一条，长34公里。建有汽车客运站2个，货运企业3个，火车站4个，年汽车客运量28万人次，汽车货运量29.3万吨。

20世纪80年代，随着改革开放的开展，运输市场放开，农村掀起“要致富、先修路”热潮，拉开乡村道路建设序幕。1992年，县委、县政府确立“改变投资环境，振兴修文经济”的发展思路，提出以交通、通信为龙头发展县域经济，全县乡村公路建设的力度加快。1996年划归贵阳市管辖，增加县内乡村公路建设的投入，使乡村公路建设进入高峰期。2001年，县以过境高等级公路建设为契机。启动乡村公路改造升级，将砂石路面改造为柏油路面，建设国家四级公路，增建县、乡（镇）汽车客运站，开通六广河水路航线。到2010年，全县公路有高等级公路、国道、省道、县道、乡村公路及专线公路，另有铁路和水道，交通运输网络建成，已构成贵阳市城区半小时交通经济圈，在建的白（云）修（文）公路、海马孔大桥等项目，构成新的交通经济产业带，拉动全县经济持续快速增长。

贵（阳）遵（义）高速公路与贵（阳）毕（节）高等级公路于扎佐互通

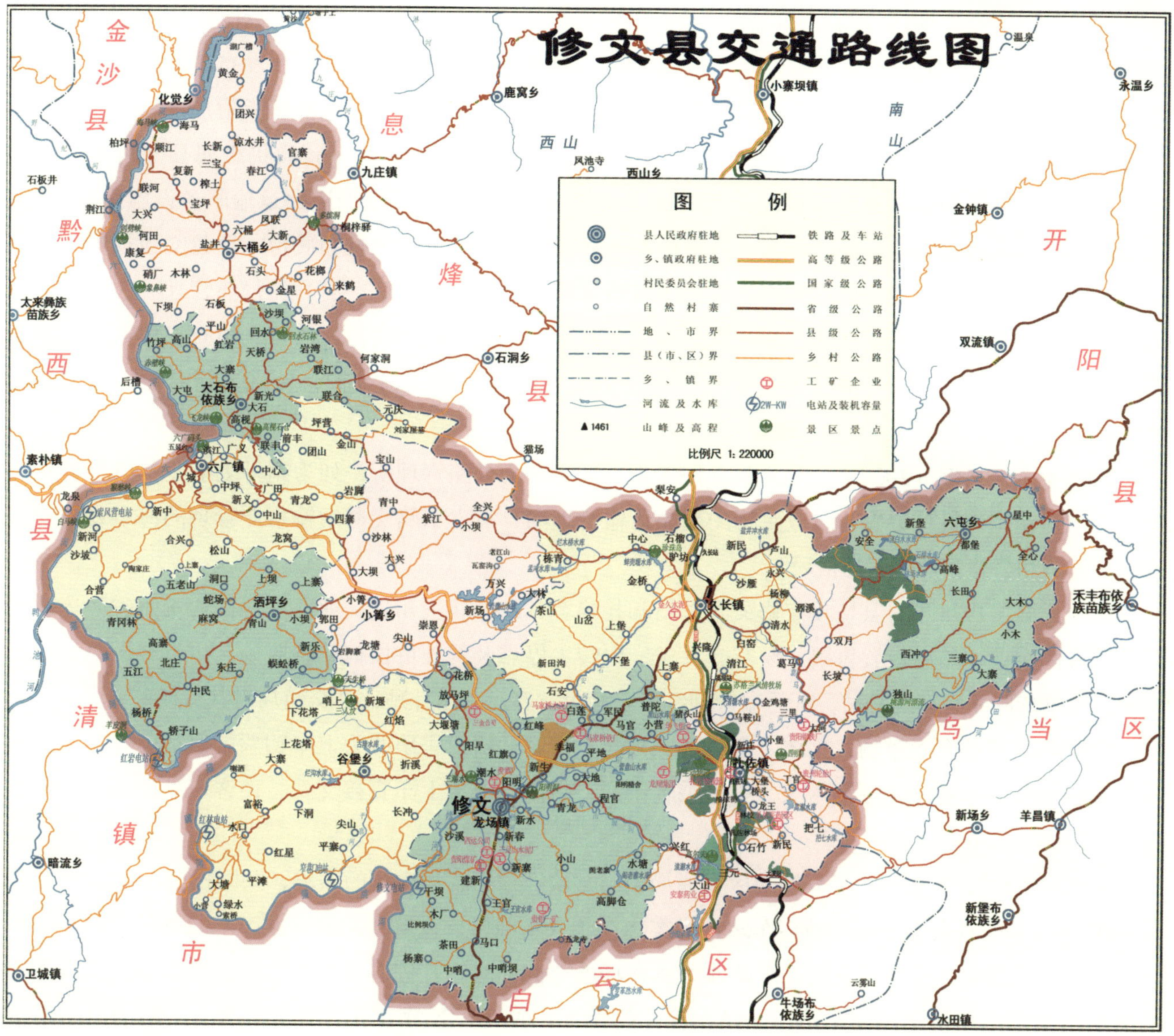

第一节　体制改革

一、机构改革

行事分置　1978年，保留县交通局建制，主管全县交通运输行政管理。1988年，经县机构编制委员会决定分离行政机构与事业机构，设置港航监督站、公路运输管理所、公路管理工区3个事业机构。

2002年6月，根据县委、县政府《关于县级党政机关“三定”工作的实施意见》，将交通运输局列为县政府行政工作部门。12月，根据省、市港航部门实施航管和航运分流精神，将县港航监督站更名为县地方海事处，为正科级事业机构，道路运输管理所、公路管理工区（所）不变。海事处纳入县财政预算管理，主要职能是贯彻执行国家《内河交通安全条例》及水路运输政策、法规；对水路运输企业审批、核查运输船舶及服务配套设施；监督水运经营活动，协调处理航运事务；汇集和发布航运技术、水文信息，维护航运安全；协调船舶和港埠、码头平衡衔接。公路运输管理所在取消客货附加费、交通发展基金征收后，由中央转移支付资金委托县财政支付，为自收自支事业机构，行政仍隶属县交通运输局管理，其职责是审批和审验道路运输经营者资格，经营项目范围；统筹规划道路运输服务设施配套建设；发放、审核道路运输营运证件、标志；监督检查运输经营行为、运输工具和质量，征收交通规费；受理道路运输违法违规和纠纷处理；实施道路运输驾驶员和运输车辆维修厂（店）的行业管理。公路管理工区为事业机构，主要职责是宣传贯彻公路路政管理法律、法规，对路政行使监督、检查；负责对公路及控制区排水、道涵、道牙、高架桥、护栏、指示牌等路政设施巡查、维护；负责公路养护的施工作业秩序。

2006年，修机编〔2006〕11号文将公路管理工区更名为公路管理所，列为副科级事业单位。至2010年，交通运输组织机构分置为行政主管的交通运输管理局，负责水路交通运输事业管理的海事处、公路运输管理所和公路管理工区的格局。

事企分离　1978年，县境设有修文客车站和扎佐客车站，属贵州省交通厅下属机构贵州省客运总站直接管理的企业，站内设置售票、候车、发送、中转、停靠及驾驶员住宿就餐服务，由省客运总站负责调配，车站依附于省客运总站，其运输管理经费差额由省客运总站补贴，县交通局对其行使监管。

1985年，开放客运市场，集体、个体客运兴起，将客运窗口售票改为上车购票，票证由省客运总站制作。1988年后，客流量逐渐增大，中途乘客不断，售票又改为上车直接交费，使客车站售票，候车业务告停。

1989年10月，省交通厅、安顺地区交通局会同县政府根据客运市场的需求，共同投资57万元在县城建5300平方米的社会停车场和新客车站，供客运汽车入场经营，设置售票厅、候车室、办公室、小卖部等服务，并将原有太极桥黄土坡客车站改为货车场。与此同时，扎佐客车站改为社会停车场，其设施由县交通运输管理站接管。客车站与上级主管部门经济上脱钩，经营管理体制由事企合一转为自主经营企业。

二、企业改革

县车队　1978年，县交通运输管理站管理的县国营汽车队，由县财政拨款6万元，置运输货车3辆。1980年，车队贷款购置货车3辆，增设汽车维修经营部，定名为“双定厂”，即定汽车统一维修点，定材料统一配给。1982年，车队进行经营体制改革，实行承包责任制，将车辆与驾驶员签订“包干合同”，车队按油料计划定额，每消耗100公斤油料收取承包费250元，除指令性运输统一安排外，由驾驶员自行从事货运。1984年，客运专营松绑，自1985—1986年，车队共置客车6辆投入客运。仍实行车辆营运承包责任制，承包者以每消耗100公斤油料，缴纳车队350元承包费。由于承包经营中车辆超载营运，维护保养差，使车况下降，加之车队管理不善，在营运市场失去竞争力，故停止营运业务，变卖汽车，只经营汽车维修。随即车队部分管理人员返回交通运输管理站，部分驾驶员调离。

到2010年，车队退休职工全部纳入社会保障，将汽车修理厂车间及其场地出租，收取租金发放在岗职工基本工资和上交养老金。企业年均纳税1万余元，账面固定资产34万余元，车队牌子保留。

联合（营）车队 1981年9月，县交通局为贯彻落实中央和省“封车节油”指示，将县国营车队汽车7辆、城关运输社汽车5辆、扎佐运输社汽车6辆和县化肥厂汽车2辆组建交通运输联合车队。实行车权、财权、人权不变，货源、调度、核算、加油统一管理，由交通运输站、县车队派员管理营运，负责调度，理货、结算、收费和油料供给。1983年，个体运输进入运输市场，因车队产权各属，货源难以统管，造成车辆各自为战，调度极为困难，竞争缺乏活力，经营效益极差，被迫解体。

1986年，集体、个体运输大量涌现，交通局为维护运输秩序和交通安全，决定统一管理交通运输市场，报经安顺行署同意，成立县联营车队。由相关参营单位、个体运输专业户代表组成车队领导班子，交通局指派局干部杭朝林任队长，县石油公司经理王立顺和交通监理站吴贵生任副队长，将参加联营的145辆汽车分为扎佐、久长片区和城关、小箐、六广片区进行管理。1988年石油供应放开，县成立个体运输协会，改由县工商行政管理局监管，参加联营的个体车辆退出，致车队实力下降，参加联营的车辆返回原单位，联营车队又予解体。

运输社 1980年，城关运输社复苏，集体经济积累逐渐增加，于1983年购置货运汽车4辆、大客车2辆和畜力双套马车8辆，并设汽车维修车间。1985年，扎佐运输社在集体资产壮大时，拥有运输汽车11辆、拖拉机2辆和畜力双套马车10辆、设汽修厂1处，房屋建筑3栋，面积788平方米，固定资产33.47万元。

随着交通运输业发展和营运市场开放，由于运输社管理不善，无力与个体运输户竞争，企业难以为继。1990年和1997年，扎佐运输社、城关运输社分别破产，各自变卖车辆、马匹、房产，将变卖款按职工参加集体企业的工龄长短分给安置费，职工自谋生路，有技能者走上个体经营道路。直至2010年，城镇集体运输社无存。

三、管理体制改革

工程建设招投标 1978—2000年，交通运输设施建设工程均由县政府和交通局联系施工单位，或由施工单位上门承接。2001年8月，根据《中华人民共和国招投标法》和《贵州省建设招投标管理条例》。县交通局开始实行建设工程招投标。首次招投标在总投资202万元的扎佐至六屯K0—K2段2公里改造工程进行。由投标单位介绍施工资质、技术设施、施工方案，建设单位拟定工程等级质量、建设工期，经过开标评审，工程由贵州省公路建设公司中标承建，贵州省交通厅咨询服务有限公司监理。

继后，全县公路建设总投资额在500万元以上（含500万元）的项目，均由贵阳市交通局和县政府共同组织实施。项目总投资额在500万元以下，由县政府委托有资质的中介评估机构评估后，按基本建设程序和招投标法规组织实施。到2002年年底全县公路改造项目10个，计138公里，全部招投标施工。

2004—2010年，贵阳市计划委员会下达到县的县际路、经济路、旅游路改造项目共17条，全长143公里，贫困村道路改造共63条，全长321公里，经县公路建设领导小组、交通运输局会同发展改革局、审计局、监察局、财政局等相关部门根据道路勘查、设计、评估资料，出台各条道路建设招标书，在《贵阳日报》《修文报》刊出进行招标，共有省内外建设施工单位31家投标，经过评审有县建筑公司及四川合江牛脑驿建筑公司等5家中标承建，确保公路建设工期和质量。

投资引进结合 2000年，贵州省交通厅投资300万元在县修建国家二级客运车站，几番选址论证均未能确定项目建设地。2004年，县政府引入贵州泰维房地产公司，签订引进资金8000万元开发修文地产协议，将建设国家二级客运车站项目与房地产开发项目结合，拟定县城新开发区在黄秧寨、马掌坡、小桥河建设以客运、商贸、住宅、绿地为一体的建设项目，定名“新都口岸”建设工程。其中，国家二级客运车站建有站前广场、停车场、办公楼、售票候车厅和站内附属建筑，于2006年12月1日投入营运。使城市建设、交通运输和住宅建设同步规划，统一建设，是交通运输建设管理体制改革中投资和引进相结合范例。

2006年建成的县城国家二级客运站

公路分级段管理 1996年1月，修文县划属贵阳市管辖，县交通局公路管理工区，业务改由贵阳市交通局公路管理处管理。在县境内高等级公路建设竣工和国道、省道改造，县际公路、县乡公路、乡村公路扩建为柏油路面后，公路养护转为护理、清洁和绿化。公路管理体制转为分级段管理：从2001年起，县际公路、县乡（镇）公路、乡（镇）村公路由贵阳市交通局公路管理处统一管理；县公路管理工区（所）具体负责管理修文至六广、冒沙井至水口寺、小箐至中寨、广田至六桶县道4条；县乡（镇）公路、乡（镇）村公路由县公路管理工区协助乡（镇）政府管理；210国道、107省道、305省道修文段由省交通厅公路管理处息烽公路管理局管理；贵（阳）遵（义）、贵（阳）毕（节）两条高等级公路由省高管处直接管理。

四、经营体制改革

货运市场化 1978年，由县国营车队和城关、扎佐两个集体运输社，包揽全县计划内物资和各乡（镇）生产、生活物资运输。

1984年，随着经济体制改革力度增大，物资流通量增加，流通渠道增多，县交通局执行国家“放宽、搞活”政策，放开货运市场，使国营车队、集体运输社、个体运输户、工矿企业车队共180辆货车投入全县货运，并按贵州省交通厅关于农用拖拉机在农闲期间参加社会运输的规定，办理短途货运拖拉机24辆，1985年货运总量达28.3万吨，货物周转量113.2万吨公里。

1990年，运输市场完全放开，全县共有货车371辆，另有拖拉机114辆参加营运，由货方自找运方，车主自找货源，双方按市场经济协商运价。由于运输车辆逐年增加，货运市场一度成为货方市场，车主相互杀价竞争货源，货运市场竞争激烈。2010年，全县货运汽车增为1920辆，货运量达510万吨，货运市场一派兴旺。

客运公司化 1978年，县内客运由贵阳市客车站经营，全县每天有10班次客车往返于贵阳至修文、六广、扎佐。1981年，商品经营放开、小商品经营户涌出，乡（镇）到县城、县城到贵阳客流量急剧上升。1982年，县交通局组织县内运输单位参加客运，投入客车5辆，按车站安排路线、时间出车。1984年，根据旅客滞留抢搭乘车状况，交通运输部门委托县内工矿企业内部使用客车参加营运，往返于企业驻地乡（镇）、县城和贵阳。1985年，为缓和客运流通难的问题，改变国营车站独家经营状况，准许个体运输户置客车营运。到1987年，个体客车共45辆，客运线路由贵阳至修文，修文至扎佐、久长、六广发展到全县22个乡（镇）。1988年，随个体客运不断发展，又开通县城至凉井、宝寨、马场、宝山、蜈蚣桥、岩鹰山、小山坝线路。1989年，为制止客车各自为战，抢班争客、快跑揽客现象，10月县政府投资

57万元在县城环城北路新建5300平方米社会停车场作客车站，分为贵阳、扎佐、六广三个方向线路停车区位，客车按入场先后顺序停放，按排列班次时间出车，车主自行收费，基本规范客运秩序。

2002年3月，贵（阳）毕（节）高等级公路开通，修文经白云到贵阳营运客车多数愿走贵（阳）毕（节）公路，为适应路线和旅客需要，6月，个体客运户组建修文黔通联营公司，置“依维柯”快巴11辆，专营修文经贵（阳）毕（节）公路线至贵阳。是年全公司共有客车30辆，分为3个车队经营全县客运，实行公司统一管理，使客运走上联合经营公司化管理道路。2005年，公司壮大，客车发展到164辆，营运线路遍及全县10乡（镇）。2006年12月，修文国家二级客车站建成，公司转入客车站营运，由车站统一车次，统一售票。并将“依维柯”快巴更换为“金龙”旅游大巴，直开贵阳市金阳客运站。至2010年，黔通联营公司置有客车156辆，开发线路36条，日发送350班次，日均旅客发送量5000人次，年客运量380万人次。城区内的交通又分别组织起永兴、客运、盛鑫、残专协会等出租车公司运营。客运公司化经营、使客运秩序井然，运输风险防护能力也得以提高。

途经贵（阳）毕（节）高等级公路修文收费站的修文快巴

第二节　路网建设

一、公路

1981年，农村经济体制改革使乡镇企业大量涌现，为打开与外界的联系，在20世纪80年代中期开始修筑乡、村、寨连接干线公路的砂石路汽车道。1992年，在县委、县政府提出“以交通通信为龙头振兴经济”的推动下，乘贵（阳）遵（义）、贵（阳）毕（节）公路建设之机，加快乡村公路建设，至1999年修建乡村公路185条，长1141公里，实现全县村村通公路。1996—2004年，在贵阳市政府支持下，改造硬化乡（镇）村公路29条，长290公里，实现县管公路升级换代。2000—2005年，工矿和旅游企业修建专线公路41条，长128公里，与乡（镇）公路相连，共同筑起县境交通网络。同时启动通往村的公路升级，至2009年的9年，全县131个贫困村74条砂石路改造为水泥路，长317公里，并增修乡村公路117条，长784公里。到2010年，全县公路共463条，通车里程1602公里，与1978年的178公里相比，净增8倍。

（一）高等级（高速）公路

贵（阳）遵（义）公路　1993年9月，第一期工程开工，该路起于贵阳，止于遵义，途经县境扎佐、久长两镇的大山、三元、和平、猪头山、高坝、兴隆、久长、驴坊、石榴等村，过境全长22.6公里。设有贵阳高尔夫度假中心进出口，扎佐、久长收费站匝道口，连通210国道和305省道以及修（文）扎（佐）

公路、麦（架桥）肖（家寨）公路。该路扎佐大山村至和平村立交桥段为一级公路，宽21米，双向6车道，长10公里，立交桥至久长镇石榴村段为二级公路，宽12米，长12.6公里。1997年11月全线贯通。

2005年3月，实施贵（阳）遵（义）高等级公路第二期工程，修筑扎（佐）南（遵义市南北镇）段为双向车道。途经县境内扎佐镇和平村和猪头山村、久长镇兴隆村、上寨村、久长村、金桥村、驴坊村、石榴村，在兴隆村段建有服务站。经扩建后贵（阳）遵（义）高速公路全程双车道宽增至21.5米。于2007年12月竣工运行，实现县内高速公路“零”的突破。

贵（阳）遵（义）高速公路扎佐段与贵毕高等级公路交汇处

贵（阳）毕（节）公路 1995年，交通不畅的毕节地区获得国家专项资金，计划沿明洪武年间修建的龙场九驿，修建到贵阳的高等级公路。1998年8月由贵州省交通厅公路局承建开工。该路由贵（阳）遵（义）高速公路扎佐站起，经修文、黔西、大方3县进入毕节市，全长178.5公里。途经修文县境扎佐镇和平村，龙场镇小营、马官、平地、幸福、新生、红烽、放马坪、花桥村，小箐乡崇恩、全兴、凤凰、大兴、小箐、大坝村，六广镇四寨、广山、中山、中坪、广城、新中村，至六广河大桥与黔西县交界，县境全长47.5公里。其中，扎佐镇和平村至龙场镇石坟坝为一级路面，长9.5公里；石坟坝至六广河大桥为二级路面，长38公里。县境段设扎佐、修文、小箐、六广4个进出收费站匝道。建有冷水沟、石坟坝、三板桥、半沟、垭口、龙洞、洞门坡等公路桥，在出县境六广河上建有公路大桥，全长564.2米，主跨240米，桥高103米，距水面306米，有“桥梁博物馆”之称。2001年10月竣工通车。按照1999年贵州省九届人大常务委员会颁发的《高等级公路规范建设条例》规定，实行全封闭和半封闭公路进行管理。

（二）国道省道路面升级

210国道 1981年，川黔公路列为国道210线，可北上四川、陕西、甘肃、宁夏、内蒙古包头，南下广西南宁。穿越县境久长镇、扎佐镇，北起于久长镇羊马田，经驴坊、久长、兴隆、高坝、猪头山、扎佐、三重堰、石板哨等村寨，全长25.5公里。2003年，经过改造，路基宽增至9米，路面宽扩至7米，最小平曲半径14米，最大坡度9%，三级柏油路面。连接修（文）扎（佐）公路、305省道和久铜（麦肖）公路。为县境东部扎佐、久长二镇交通主干线。

107省道 1986年，改造省道粑（粑坳）修（文）公路王官新场至杉树林段，扩宽路基6.5至7.5米，路面宽5.5至6.5米，柏油路面，长5.9公里。1990年，省公路管理局拨款改造白云区大坝至修文县城段，修筑三级柏油路面。途经龙场镇的城南、新春、新寨、建新、王官、马口、中哨等7个村，全程10.5公里。2001年，因贵（阳）毕（节）公路通车和白（云）修（文）公路建设启动，致粑修公路大坝至修文段养护减弱，损坏严重，车流量减少。至2010年，道路破损状况仍然存在。

305省道 2002年，贵州省交通厅和贵阳市政府拨款，将该道修（文）开（阳）公路段，由修文县城到开阳县，途经修文县城、马家桥、普陀、久长、沙雁、芒山至开阳县白马洞，过县境段长20公里，改造成路基宽7.5米的四级柏油路面。2008年，修建久长至开阳段的新公路，在久长镇210国道、贵（阳）遵（义）高速公路久长匝道处，建由白云区麦架桥至瓮安肖家寨的麦肖公路，穿过久长村至芦山村

到达开阳县境，路基宽7.5至8米，路面宽7米的三级柏油路面，全长9.48公里，使原305省道久长至开阳更加便捷。

（三）县道改造升级

1996年起，在贵阳市政府支持下，启动县管公路改造，提升公路等级，采取加宽路基，平整路面、铺足碎石、挖砌边沟、修筑堡坎、铺设道牙、浇灌路面等措施，使县际公路、县乡公路、经济路、旅游路达到四级公路标准。2001—2006年，市县财政逐年投入公路改造资金，到2007年完成27条公路的改造升级，总里程293.2公里。2008年又对乡村公路进行扩建改造，硬化路面，到2010年，全县四级公路达383条，总里程114.73公里。

2009年，改造的进村四级公路

2001—2007年境内公路升级改造一览表

表3—03—01

所属管辖类别	路名或道路起止点	里程（公里）	路面材料	路面宽（米）	开工时间（年）	竣工时间（年）
省　道	修开路（县城至芒山）	20	柏油	7.5	2002	2003
县际路	六桶盐井至海马孔	13	柏油	6.5	2003	2005
	火石丫至桐枝驿	6.5	柏油	6.5	2003	2005
	六屯至香火岩	9	柏油	6.5	2003	2004
	丫口田至何家洞	4.7	柏油	6.5	2004	2005
县　道	广六路（六广至六桶）	19.5	柏油	6.5	2001	2002
	修六路（县城至六广）	38.2	混凝土、柏油	6.5-8	2001	2002
	小中路（小箐至中寨）	13	柏油	6.5	2002	2002
	马扎路（马家桥至扎佐）	9	柏油	6.5	2002	2002
	修久路（县城至久长）	15	柏油	7.5	2002	2002
	扎六路（扎佐至六屯）	22.1	柏油	7.5	2002	2002
	冒乌路（冒沙井至乌栗）	15	柏油	6.5	2002	2002
乡（镇）路	久长至大石高枧	28.5	柏油	6.5	2004	2006
	扎佐至干龙洞	8.24	柏油	7.0	2005	2006
	久长至龙塘坝	7.5	柏油	6.5	2005	2006
乡村路	阳明洞至三元	16.1	柏油	6.5	2004	2006
	崇恩至栋青	13.1	柏油	6.5	2004	2007
专线路	六广至高枧	4	柏油	6.5	2001	2004
	六广街至六广河码头	2.6	柏油	6.5	2002	2003
	省林场至珍珠井	2.5	混泥土	7.5	2002	2002

续表

所属管辖类别	路名或道路起止点	里程（公里）	路面材料	路面宽（米）	开工时间（年）	竣工时间（年）
专线路	久长至珍珠岛	4.5	柏油	6.5	2002	2004
	三里至香粑房	6.5	柏油	6.5	2005	2006
	中寨至六级电站	5	柏油	6.5	2004	2007
经济路	扎佐街至501厂	4	柏油	6.5	2003	2003
	石猫猫林场至安全村	4	柏油	6.5	2004	2005
	猪头山至华飞铝业	1.6	混凝土	6.5	2005	2005
	贵钢农场至丁官村	1.1	混凝土	6.5	2005	2005

（四）乡村公路建设

1996年，市、县政府投资改造，修建乡村公路，到2000年共计投入资金868.5万元，实现全县217个行政村公路村村通。2001至2008年，对全县131个贫困村村级公路62条，长317公里进行改造，将砂石路面改造为混泥土路面，路面宽统一增至4.5米。至2008年年底，全县共修建乡村公路117条，计784.5公里。2009至2010年，对乡村等外级公路继续升级改造为四级路面50公里，使乡村四级公路总里程达662公里，等外级村道公路仅存122.7公里。

2001—2008年境内等外级公路改造一览表

表3—03—02

乡（镇）名	路名或起止点	里程（公里）	路面材料	竣工时间（年）	投资（万元）	过境行政村
龙场镇	新生村至放马坪	5.1	混凝土	2005	220	新生　阳明　红峰　放马坪
	新水村至兴红村	12	混凝土	2005	240	新水　小山　高仓　兴红
	潮水村至长冲村	6.2	混凝土	2005	116	潮水　长冲
	幸福村至平地村	4	砂石	2005	24	幸福　平地
	贵铝一矿至中哨	2.8	混凝土	2004	56	中哨
	三级电站至干坝	4.2	混凝土	2004	84	干坝
扎佐镇	扎佐至大堡	1.5	混凝土	2005	19.76	扎佐　大堡
	扎佐至小堡村	3	混凝土	2005	46.23	扎佐　小堡
	三元至大山	1.5	混凝土	2005	10	三元　大山
	大堡至大河	2	混凝土	2005	15	大堡　大河
	大堡至月牛坝	5.3	混凝土	2005	102	大堡　大河　小堡
	金鸡塘至新庄	2.23	混凝土	2005	106	金鸡　新庄　小堡
	茅洪至小冲	8.2	混凝土	2005	64.6	大山
	顺兴场至西苗	3.26	混凝土	2005	164	双月

续表

乡（镇）名	路名或起止点	里程（公里）	路面材料	竣工时间（年）	投资（万元）	过境行政村
扎佐镇	猪头山至金鸡塘	7.4	混凝土	2005	65.2	猪头山　马鞍　金鸡
	扎佐至新庄	2.3	混凝土	2005	6	新庄
久长镇	久长至小谷龙	6.84	混凝土	2005	148	久长　杨柳
	石安至桃子山	8.85	混凝土	2005	84	石安　桃子山
	石安至马道子	3.5	混凝土	2005	15	石安　兴田
	崔家寨至茶山	4.2	混凝土	2005	136.8	中心　茶山
	猫冲至夹角山	13.4	混凝土	2005	84	山岔　茶山
六广镇	六广至中心	0.4	混凝土	2004	8.8	六广　中心
	六广至下南江	2	混凝土	2004	19.5	六广
	猫洞至团岩	6.65	混凝土	2004	133	龙窝　中心　四寨
	十字岭至烂窑	3.28	混凝土	2004	65.6	松山　中心
	青龙至四寨	4.72	混凝土	2004	94.6	青龙　广山　四寨
	广城至五老山	6.4	混凝土	2004	128	广城　合兴　五老山
六屯乡	石猫猫林场至武家寨	6.8	混凝土	2005	136	新堡　都堡
	小木至牛背上	2.3	混凝土	2005	46	小木
	三寨至大寨	6	混凝土	2005	120	三寨　大寨
	高峰至下寨	2.57	混凝土	2005	51.4	高峰
	大木至全兴	6.6	混凝土	2005	132	大木　全兴
谷堡乡	谷堡至放马坪	12	混凝土	2005	239	谷堡　折溪　大堰　红焰　放马坪
	平寨至犁田湾	6	砂　石	2001	40	平寨
	三处至绿水	7.5	混凝土	2006	150	绿水　大塘
	谷堡至下花塔	7.9	混凝土	2008	158	谷堡　上花塔　下花塔　哨上
	谷堡至平寨	5.5	混凝土	2005	110	谷堡　尖山　平寨
	平寨至柏枝	2.25	混凝土	2001	30	平寨
	折溪至古隆	5	混凝土	2003	30	折溪
洒坪乡	小坝至上坝	7.95	混凝土	2006	159	小坝　青山　上坝
	青杠林至阳桥	3.8	混凝土	2006	76	阳桥　五江　中明
	中明至五江	7.2	混凝土	2006	144	中明　五江　青杠林
	蛇场至青杠林	7.33	混凝土	2006	146	青杠林　蛇场　硐口
	新乐至小坝	6	混凝土	2006	19	新乐　小坝
	洒坪至上寨	8.5	混凝土	2006	30	洒坪　上寨

续表

乡（镇）名	路名或起止点	里程（公里）	路面材料	竣工时间（年）	投资（万元）	过境行政村
小箐乡	新场至大林	6.03	混凝土	2005	120.6	新场　大林
	杉林至四寨	5	混凝土	2006	76.3	杉林　四寨
	杉林至大兴	5	混凝土	2005	70	杉林　大兴
	大坝至青中	6.77	混凝土	2005	135.4	大坝　青中　紫江
	崇恩至龙塘	5.72	混凝土	2006	114.4	龙塘　崇恩　尖山
	崇恩至栋青	5	柏　油	2005	15	大林　栋青
	杉林至四寨	5	混凝土	2006	76.3	杉林　四寨
大石乡	大石至大屯	6.5	混凝土	2006	130	大石　大屯
	大石至老鸹河	10.14	混凝土	2005	202.8	大石　大寨　高山　竹坪
	丫口田至联江	5.21	混凝土	2005	104.2	岩湾　联江
	新光至联江	4.72	混凝土	2005	94.4	新光　联江
	天桥至回水	6.44	混凝土	2005	128.8	天桥　回水　沙坝
	联江至元庆	5	混凝土	2005	100	联江　联合　元庆
六桶乡	盐井至官寨	10	混凝土	2005	200	大石　大屯
	宝坪至大兴	4.85	混凝土	2005	97	盐井　大林
	花椰至来鹤	6.6	混凝土	2005	132	花椰　来鹤
	六桶至大兴	5	混凝土	2006	15	盐井　大兴

（五）专线公路建设

县境专线公路有水力电站线路、航天工业部011厂矿线路、医药园区线路、林场专用线路、风景名胜旅游线路。其中水力、工矿、医药、林区专线公路29条，全长82.5公里。随开发贵阳—扎佐高尔夫—修文阳明洞—六广河峡谷—息烽温泉旅游线。建设辅助公路12条，全长59.7公里。到2010年全县专线公路共41条，总里程1460公里。

1.主要工矿企业专用公路

电站专用线　位于县西南龙场镇、谷堡乡境内，东起龙场镇新寨村小河沟接粑（粑坳）修（文）公路（S107），西至五级电站机房，途经龙场镇新寨、建新、木厂、沙溪村和谷堡乡长冲、平寨、平滩、红星、水口、大塘村。全程28公里，四级公路，水泥路面，道宽6米。主要连通红枫发电厂猫跳河上三级（修文）、四级（窄巷口）、五级（红林）3个电站。

六级(红岩) 电站用线　位于县西部洒坪乡境，东起中明村中寨接小中公路（X188），西至六级电站大坝，途经洒坪乡中明、阳桥、轿子山村，全长6.7公里，四级公路柏油路面，道宽6.5米。

贵州铝厂一矿用线　位于县境南部龙场镇境，西起王官村接省道粑修公路（S107），东至小山坝五龙寺，途经王官、小山村，全长6.7公里，四级公路，柏油路面，道宽6.5米。

郭家林水泥厂用线 位于县城西面，东北起接县城北门桥中山北路，向西南至郭家林水泥厂，途经龙场镇城北、沙溪村，全长2.5公里，等外级公路，泥沙路面，道宽6米。

航空工业部418库用线 位于县中部龙场镇小营村境，北起小营团坡接马扎公路（X156），向南至418库厂区，全长1.2公里，等外级公路，水泥路面，道宽6米。

扎佐工业园区公路 位于扎佐镇东南部龙王、石竹和新民村境内，分别由药区大道、长生路、万江路、德昌路和恒生路组成。药区大道西起210国道接扎佐襄阳南路，东至杨家井与长生路、万江路、德昌路和恒生路交汇，全长1.9公里，一级公路，双向四车道，柏油路面，道宽25米；长生路西起快活林接210国道，东至杨家井与德昌路和恒生路交汇，往西北回连药区大道，继往东为万江路。长生路、万江路实为一条路中两段，长生路长1.3公里，万江路长0.9公里，四级公路柏油路面，道宽6.5米；德昌路和恒生路为一条道路，德昌路西南起光正药厂，东北至杨家井0.3公里，过交汇处称恒生路，继往东北0.5公里至珍珠井接新民村乡村道路，二级公路柏油路面，道宽9米。

贵阳特殊钢厂大道 位于扎佐镇中部和平、新庄村境，西起扎佐铁路桥接210国道，往北绕过小长田、新庄，东于大堡村洞上接扎六公路，全长2.8公里，双向四车道，中无隔离带。二级公路柏油路面，道宽25米。

501厂用线 位于扎佐镇东部大堡、丁官村境，西起洞上接扎六公路，东至501厂接乌当区X136县道，全长3.6公里。四级公路柏油路面，道宽7米。

航空工业部533技校用线 位于县境东南龙场镇高仓、水塘村和扎佐镇大山村境，东起大山村接X195县道，往西3.1公里至校区后，转向北3公里至兴红机械厂接X195县道，全长6.1公里，等外级公路，水泥路面，道宽6.5米。

硝厂医院用线 位于县西北六桶乡盐井、木林、何田村境，东起六桶坝接X186县道，西至硝厂医院，全长4.5公里，等外级公路，泥沙路面，道宽6.5米。

2. 主要景区景点专用线

一般景区景点与主干公路之间有一段距离，为开发旅游修有专用公路。

天生桥景区用线 位于县西部谷堡乡折溪、红焰、新堰、哨上村境，东接蛇田冒乌公路（X190），北至景区附近，全长7.6公里。其中蛇田至红焰村后寨3.1公里为四级公路柏油路面，路宽6.5米，其余4.5公里为等外级泥沙路面。

六广河旅游用线 位于县西北六广镇新中、六广、滨江村境，南接贵毕高等级公路六广收费站，北至六广河边方家坝。全长5.1公里，三级公路，柏油路面，道宽7至8米。

桃源河景区用线 位于县东六屯乡独山村境，西接三里至长田X078县道，东至桃源河景区大门，全长1公里，三级公路，柏油路面，道宽7米。

苏格兰风情牧场度假中心用线 位于县东久长镇兴隆、清江村境，西接高坝210国道，东至景区大门口，全长1公里，四级公路，柏油路面，道宽6.5米。

珍珠岛度假中心用线 位于县北久长镇驴坊村境，东接王家河210国道。西至珍珠岛度假中心大门前，全长2.3公里，四级公路，柏油路面，道宽6米。

多缤洞景区用线 位于县西北六桶乡金星、石头、大新村境，西接火石丫广六路（X186）县道，东至修文、息烽两县交界处，全长6.9公里，四级公路，柏油路面，道宽6.5米。

2010年全县公路网概况表

表3—03—03

管理级别	条数	线路	境内里程（公里）	技术等级
省高速公路管理局	2	贵（阳）遵（义）公路	22.6	一级双车道宽21米
		贵（阳）毕（节）公路	47.5	一级长双车道9.5公里
				二级长单车道38公里
省　　管	3	210国道	25.5	三级柏油路面
		107省道	5.9	三级柏油路面
		305省道	20	三级柏油路面
县　　管	21	含县际路、县道、乡（镇）路、经济路	362	四级柏油路面
乡（镇）管	43	含乡村、镇村路	205.6	四级柏油路面
村　　管	353	村寨路	785	四级路面662公里
				等外级路面122公里
工矿企业管	29	含企业内部及驻地通往乡镇和干线路	82.5	水泥和柏油路面
旅游企业、景区（点）管	12	旅游景区（点）通往干线路	45.6	水泥和柏油路面
合　　计	463		1602.2	

二、铁路

1986年，川黔铁路开始电气化改造，将内燃机车改为电力机车，1991年改造完成并投入使用，列车时速由50公里/小时，提速到70公里/小时，使重庆至贵阳的时空距离缩短。1993年，随着贵（阳）遵（义）高等级公路建设和后来210国道改造升级为三级公路，县内久长和扎佐增开至贵阳客运班次，乘坐列车乘客逐渐减少。到2000年，原设在跨县境的久长、扎佐普快列车不再停靠。

2003年，县境段铁路建设重点转入维护和车站建设，铁路运输以货运为主。到2010年，久长站置停车道4条，建货运站台5个。扎佐站建成贵阳市北物流旱码头，是成都铁路局战略装（卸）车点，停车道增至6条，实现铁路与公路联运，辐射贵阳市、遵义地区、毕节地区、铜仁地区，县境铁路已成为设施配套齐全的区域型交通运输主骨架。

三、水路

（一）乌江渡库区六广河段

1979年，乌江电站大坝建成蓄水，使乌江上游六广河水面增宽，最宽处达100余米，水深20余米。1984年，贵州省移民办公室调拨油泵船2艘给六广镇组织水运。拉开六广河航运序幕。1996年3月，贵阳市交通局组织开发六广河至乌江电站大坝水路航道，投资40万元，爆破六广河石门坎河道暗礁，经一个月余，清除石块80立方米，使长30米的芭蕉沟湾通航，开辟出从六广河渡口到乌江电站大坝全长74公里的航道，其中县境段长41公里，经过大屯、联合、顺江、海马等村，建有货物装卸码头和旅游码头，置有水运汽船63艘和游船39艘，揭开全县航运事业的新篇章，常年均有旅游和货运船只运行。年运量达6000余吨，载客量1500余人次。

（二）索风营库区猫跳河段

2005年，六广河上游索风营电站大坝建成蓄水，使船舶顺江而上直通猫跳河六级电站和鸭池河，构成县境水路观光旅游航线和沿江村民货运航线，其中索风营大坝至猫跳河阳桥与清镇市交界处航道长13公里，谷堡乡水口村五级电站至洒坪乡轿子山六级电站15公里，形成县交通网络中旅游观光航线组成部分。

（三）桃源河旅游航道

2005年，贵州神州漂流有限公司开发桃源河旅游航道长9.5公里，其中一期开发4.5公里，开创惊险刺激、富有魔幻魅力的峡谷漂流航线水路。水上漂流航道由贵州神州漂流公司经营，县地方海事处管理。2010年，航道漂流达20.88万人次。

第三节　交通设施

一、车站

（一）汽车客运站

1978年，全县仅有2个汽车客运站和1个代办站，1984年起随着改革开放的开展，汽车运输市场放开，县内陆续新建6个乡（镇）客车站，到2010年，县境有客车站8个。

县客车站　1978年为省汽车客运总站下属车站。1986年因改革车站售票为上车售票，站内售票业务停止，车站设施交县运输管理站。1989年10月，贵州省交通厅、安顺地区交通局和县政府共同投资57万元，异地新建于县城环城北路，占地12亩建成5300平方米的县客车站，社会停车场设客运售票厅、候车室、车站办公室和小卖部。2005年，贵州省交通厅安排300万元建设修文县国家二级客车站，选址于县城新建的河滨路南段“新都口岸”，占地30亩。2006年12月1日投入营运。2010年，车站开设36条客运线路，客运汽车156辆，日发送350班次，旅客日均发送量5000人次。

扎佐客车站　1978年沿用，属省汽车客运总站管理。1988年因改革售票制度，站内售票和接待客车业务告停，该站由个人承包经营。2005年，扎佐镇开发建设襄阳新区，贵阳市客运站将该站迁至大园村珍珠河旁，建4000平方米车站，停车位增至30个。2010年，县政府为提升扎佐镇城镇化水平，开发建设珍珠河小区，以土地置换方式在襄阳路至210国道的支线上修建为三级客车站，用来置换大园村客车站场地。车站建设由县交通局补助资金40

2005年修建的扎佐客运站

万元，建成车场面积3500平方米，建筑面积2200平方米和停车位40个的客车站，开设14条客运线路，仍由贵阳市客运站经营管理。

久长客车站 1978年到2004年，过往久长镇的客车，均在川黔公路与修开公路交汇路口停靠。2005年，在镇农贸市场投入使用的同时，将老街场坝菜市改为客车停车点。2009年，县交通局和久长镇政府投资124.4万元，在修开公路与龙山路交汇处旁边建占地25亩的镇客车站。车站营运建筑楼2400平方米，停车位20个，开设至贵阳、修文、开阳、息烽和扎佐、小箐、石洞、栋青线路，始发客运班次176班。2010年客车日往返43辆，180班次，旅客往返量600人次。

2009年建成的久长客运站一角

六桶客车站 2006年前，开往六桶的客车均停靠在六桶街口。2007年，县运输管理所与六桶乡政府主持，在新建的盐井村集镇广田至六桶公路旁建客车站。建设资金由县运输管理所投入40万元，乡政府征用站址，建成停车场2000平方米，30个停车位。日旅客往返量500人次。

乌栗客车站 2008年前，开往谷堡乡及其辖地乌栗的客车均停靠公路旁边。2009年，县交通局与谷堡乡政府主持，利用世行贷款100万元在谷堡乡富裕村修建乌栗客车站。站址落地在冒（沙井）乌（栗）公路进入富裕村处，占地6亩，设有开往修文、贵阳线路，每天往返24班次，旅客往返量750人次。

洒坪客车站 2008年前，开往洒坪的客车均在公路旁边停靠。2009年，由县运输管理所和洒坪乡政府主持，向世行贷款100万元修建乡汽车客车站。站址位于小（箐）中（寨）公路线上的小坝，占地6.5亩，设有开往修文线路，每天往返车次9次，以及至贵阳、枫香桥、蜈蚣桥、六级等班次，日往返14班次，旅客往返量400人次。

六广客车站 1978年为代办站，1986年改为乘客上车售票，代办售票遂停。到1995年前，六广镇只设有客车停靠点在街口，1996年，县交通运输管理所租用六广镇粮管所场地改建成客车站，建有停车位30个，除开往县城、贵阳线路外，还开通黔西素朴及六广镇辖区的德政、元庆、沙坡等线路。车站建设由县交通局补助40万元，车站营运利用客车停车费和车站服务费收入支付场地租金。每天客车往返30班次，旅客往返量800人次。

小箐客车站 1984年前，小箐乡汽车客运只设代办点代售车票和客车停靠点。1985年，客运市场放开，客运汽车逐渐增加。到2000年每天除经过小箐客车25辆外，乡内定点客车有11辆25班次。为发展客车运输业，县交通局补助40万元，由小箐乡政府调剂乡供销社闲置场地改建为客车站。设开往县城、贵阳线路，每天往返28班次，旅客往返量600人次。

专记：国家二级客运修文客车站

2000年，贵州省交通厅针对修文县城扩展，人流量剧增的情况，为合理布局，配套建设，安排300万元资金为建设国家二级客运汽车站。由于县城建设规划几番调整，一直没有选定客车站建设地。

2004年，县委、县政府提出“践行科学发展、打造宜居修文”“把城市做优做强”的战略决策，决定

在县城东南开发黄秧寨、马掌坡、小桥河畔，把建设国家二级客运站和房地产开发项目合为一体，拟定为新都口岸客运、商贸、住宅小区建设项目。客运汽车站位于小区中心地段，占地2万平方米，站前建广场2500平方米，广场中建花园1200平方米，绿化率为整个车站的3.5%，广场两侧建车辆出入车道和人行道。站中建办公、候车厅3930平方米，附属建筑750平方米，配置旅客安检通道，车辆放行检验道，车辆检车处。站后建有停车场，设停车位100辆，日发送旅客量5000至1万人。站旁设置汽车配件、饮食服务、商务办公、经营商铺、保安物业等服务。车站投入营运后，每天进出车辆上百车次，带动百余家商旅服务，人来车往，一派繁荣景象，车站竟成为修文县城步入城镇化的一大亮点。

（二）汽车货运站

2008年，贵阳通源运输公司与久长镇政府利用久长镇为修（文）、开（阳）、息（烽）三县交通连接的优势修建汽车货运站。站址坐落在修开公路与镇区龙山路交汇处，建站资金为世行贷款，由镇政府征地5亩，县交通局协调，通源公司经营。站内设有货物转运仓库、站办公楼、停车场，建筑面积1800平方米。2010年，货运站由久长村委会代管，收取货车停靠费，承接210国道、305省道和麦（架桥）肖（家坳）公路以及贵（阳）遵（义）公路货运汽车停靠和转运业务。

（三）火车货运站

1978年，川黔铁路沿线货运由途经县境的久长、高坝、扎佐、大关冲4个火车站办理。1996年至2010年，各站多以货运列车停靠为主。

久长火车站 站内原铺设车道4条，筑起0.8公里连线接川黔公路，除始建的车站客、货运站台外，1986年到2000年分别建有761矿，开阳磷矿、开阳县久长农资配送中心、省公路管理局沥青转运和国家粮食储备库转运等专用货运站台。

高坝火车站 站内铺有停车道3条。1991年启用客运，供贵阳至遵义短途慢车停靠。2000年，随贵（阳）遵（义）高速公路建成和210国道改造升级，旅客多乘汽车，高坝站乘客稀少，从此客运业务停止，专供临时货运。

扎佐火车站 原建有1.11公里联络公路连接扎佐街，置有停车道4条，供普通旅客列车和货运列车停靠。2003年，成都铁路局在站内建起战略物资装卸点，到2010年建成贵阳市北物流中心，其站内铁道增至6条，建客运站台3个和货运站台4个，实现铁路与公路联运，辐射贵阳市和毕节地区、遵义地区、铜仁地区，成为设施齐全的区域型物流旱码头。

大关冲火车站 站内原建有停车道2条，分设客运、货运站台。至2010年除停靠普通旅客慢车和节假日加班列车外，主要用于货物转运。

专记：在公路和铁路交汇点构建起物流园

扎佐镇是贵阳市的北大门，扎佐火车站有川黔铁路、贵遵、贵毕两条高等级公路，321、210国道以及县道修扎公路在此相汇。南距贵阳市中心38公里，北距息烽县35公里，东距开阳县42公里，西距毕节市180公里。扎佐地处要冲，具有进滇入川，通江达海的功能，从此启运北可上遵义、重庆、成都、西安、兰州、银川、包头，南可下广东、广西，西入云南。

2001年，贵州兴达物流公司瞄准扎佐火车站独特的区位和交通优势，创建公路、铁路、仓储结合的贵阳市北部物资集散地——扎佐物流园。经过10年建设、扩展，到2010年园区日益完善，占地2966亩，拥有铁路专用线950米，进场道路1350米，货场面积5万平方米，10吨行车装载机各1台，10吨、30吨地磅各1台，商务大楼1.8万平方米，形成集公路、铁路联运、转储配送、装卸搬运、包装加工、物流信息、金融商务、生活服务等功能为一身的物流园。承接全国各地运往扎佐的煤炭、医药、农资、钢材、机电、建材、食品、粮油、矿产、机械和生活物资的集中、分流和储存。园区还建有驻县工矿企业和县内农资公司、盐业公司物资转运站，县外的毕节地区还在园内设有物资转运办事处。园区服务辐射到贵阳市、毕节地区、遵义地区和铜仁地区。营运开始后是贵阳市北郊规模最大的旱码头。

二、渡口码头

（一）渡口

1979年，乌江电站建成蓄水，使乌江上游六广河段水位上升，继而在六广河沿岸建起六广河1号渡和2号渡及大屯、野鸡河、焦家坪、周家堰和海马渡口。渡口处河面宽为200米至590米，水深达26米至53米。1984年，渡口始用机动渡船，经县政府主持渡口检查，认定六广河2号、大屯、野鸡河、焦家坪、海马和周家堰6个为安全渡口。1996年，六广河大桥建成，连通修文、黔西两岸，将六广河1号渡改建为旅游码头停靠游船，六广河2号渡停用。其余渡口保留，供修文、黔西、金沙三县邻江村民往来和运输。至2010年，未变动。

联通修文与金沙两县的海马渡口

六广河渡口一览表

表3—03—04

渡口名称	位　置	河面宽（米）	水深（米）	渡船吨位（吨）
上马渡	六广镇新河村钟家河坝与黔西县卞家寨之间	100	30	10
六广1号渡	六广镇滨江村龙王庙与黔西县五显台之间	200	26	12
六广2号渡	六广镇滨江村洪家滩与黔西县五显台之间	380	28	12
大屯渡	大石乡大屯村与黔西县花苗寨之间	400	35	10
转龙滩渡	大石乡高山村笔架山与黔西县马鬃岭之间	400	35	10
六桶河渡	六桶乡何田村吊狗岩与黔西县箐口乡之间	420	35	10
野鸡河渡	又名三岔河渡，六桶乡联合村灾江湾与金沙县小田坝之间	420	40	10
焦家坪渡	六桶乡顺江村锈水田与金沙县白果坪之间	560	53	10
海马孔渡	六桶乡海马村与金沙县戛渡凹脚之间	570	53	10
周家堰渡	六桶乡黄金村周家堰与金沙县箐口寨之间	590	53	10

（二）码头

1992年，县交通运输局主持在六广河方家坝修筑码头，为5级梯形，长20米，设泊位2个，可容20吨船只停靠装卸。1998年，贵州省公路工程总公司与县政府联合开发六广河峡谷旅游，投资1000万元在六广河滨江村洪家滩大沙包处修建长400米的阶梯式码头。码头占地4.23亩，分置5个泊位，配游轮6艘。建竹楼宾馆5444平方米和公园式停车广场5000平方米，入口由贵（阳）毕（节）高等级公路六广收费站匝道口直达，是六广河货运和旅游码头，年货运量6000吨，旅客量50万人次。2005年，索风营电站大坝蓄水，在大坝上游建索风营码头，长300米，船可顺江而上，直抵猫跳河六级电站和鸭池河。

三、桥梁

1978—2010年，全县除对县城北门桥、东门桥等桥梁进行维修和扩建外，共建有公路桥梁35座，竣工33座，有两座尚在建设中。

（一）六广河大桥

1991年，修文、黔西两县申请修建六广河公路大桥，由省交通厅纳入全省公路桥梁建设项目。1992年5月，省交通厅批准安顺、毕节两地区编制的“建桥建议书”。大桥坐落于六广镇滨江村青龙嘴，连接黔西县素朴镇五显台村的六（广）素（朴）公路。桥式为预应力桁式组合拱桥，长298米，单跨跨水面150米，桥宽10米，距水面高100米，承载量20吨，挂车100吨。由贵州省交通厅勘察设计院设计，省宏达路桥公司承建，投入建设资金668万元。于1993年3月30日破土动工，1996年10月10日竣工通车。

1996年10月竣工通车的六广河大桥

（二）六广河特大桥

位于六广河边擦耳岩。桥型从德国引进，桥面用美国万宝公司伸缩钢，采用凝缝连接成单箱连续钢构“T”型桥，全长564.2米，主跨240米，桥身高103米，桥面宽12米，距水面高306米，为亚洲同类桥梁之最。由贵州省交通厅勘察设计院设计，贵州省桥梁公司承建，投入建设资金6000万元，工程于1999年11月动工，2001年10月竣工通车。

贵（阳）毕（节）公路六广河特大桥

（三）扎佐互通式立交桥

1998年12月始建，坐落在贵（阳）毕（节）和贵（阳）遵（义）两条高等级公路交汇处，为贵（阳）毕（节）公路专用桥，跨越210国道和修（文）扎（佐）公路。其中跨修扎公路桥为1孔，宽

贵（阳）遵（义）贵（阳）毕（节）扎佐互通立交桥

27米，高6米，长36米。跨贵遵高速桥为8孔，宽29.6米，高6米，全长541米。贵遵高速进入贵毕公路收费站横跨贵毕公路桥为10孔，宽11米，高6至10米，长700米。组成贵毕、贵遵公路相汇互通式立交桥。2000年10月投入使用。

（四）大寨桥

2010年9月，修（文）六（广）公路改道，过往车辆避开东门桥蛤蟆坡农贸市场入口处，改在阳明河大寨段修建跨河大桥。桥为钢筋混凝土结构，全长65米，宽24米，车行道宽15米，两侧人行道各宽3米，桥面有护栏，主跨1孔，距水面高50米，两端引桥孔各宽5米。工程由贵州省建工集团第四建筑工程公司承建，至年底该桥仍在建中。

（五）人民桥

原名为东门桥，位于县城东门外，跨修文河。1998年，扩建，由中建四局承建，次年1月18日动工，5月18日完成主体工程并通车，投入资金84.16万元。

改扩建后净跨38.5米，宽21米，车行道宽15米，两边人行道各宽3米，载重负荷车重20吨，挂车100吨。1995年10月，鉴于改建的人民路延至东门桥，遂更名为“人民桥”。

（六）新曲尺桥

系原曲尺桥的改建，离原曲尺桥下游10米，属阳明大道建设项目，是阳明大道起点。2001年开始修建，为钢筋混凝土浇灌平式桥。桥身3孔，每孔跨度9米，横跨小桥河、高涧河交汇处，桥全长40米，宽20米，高5米，西南接河滨路与朝阳路交汇处，东北为阳明大道。2002年8月竣工通车。新桥改建后，市民休闲、散步常到桥头，游览两岸风光，百姓惯用原名仍称“曲尺桥”。

（七）阳明桥

位于阳明村，跨阳明河，紧靠阳阳洞而得名。1991年改造修（文）久（长）公路时亦将原建桥改造重建。重建后桥孔跨40米，桥宽12米，为县城通往久长、扎佐二镇的公路干道桥。2002年，修建贵（阳）毕（节）高等级公路联络线阳明大道时在原桥的东南侧2米处建起一座与之规模、式样相同的复线桥，两桥并列组成形似一桥的阳明新桥，使整个阳明桥宽度增为25米。两桥桥面相连处建起隔离带护栏，来往车辆复线行驶，各行其桥（道），畅通无阻。

（八）翠屏桥

2003年9月，修建县城翠屏东路延伸段时修建。桥由中国西南市政设计院设计，中建五局承建。混凝土轻拱形单孔平桥，净跨25米，两端引桥各长1米，桥宽21米，两侧人行道各宽3.5米。桥面两侧设护栏，护栏间安装桥面路灯，总投资225.6万元。工程于2004年7月12日竣工验收通车，为县城新、老城区跨小桥河，连接东西片区的主要桥梁。

（九）翠薇桥

系县城东片区跨过高涧河的桥梁。2006年，建于阳明大道商贸、住宅街支线的朝霞路，跨过高涧河连接新建的第三中学和县实验幼儿园，直通拟建中的县城外环路。桥长26米，宽20米，车行道宽14米，两侧人行道各宽3米，投入建设资金330万元。桥面两侧设置桥面护栏，站立桥头南面可观高涧河曲径通幽和翰林花园树木青翠风景，向东可览秀丽壮观的阳明洞景区主题公园，成为阳明商住街的一道风景线。

1978—2010年公路桥梁建设一览表

表3—03—05

桥名	过桥公路	坐落地点	结构	孔数	长(米)	宽（米）	高（米）	建设时间(年)
香粑房桥	香粑房电站公路	扎佐镇香粑房电站	石拱	1	—	—	—	1978
光渡河桥	六开公路	六屯乡白果寨	石拱	1	24.7	5.4	5.5	1978年建,2004年重建
新花桥	修六公路	龙场镇花桥村	石拱	1	7	8	5	1985年另建
王家湾桥	修六公路	龙场镇潮水村	石拱	1	14.2	5	3.8	1985
新春平桥	新春村道	龙场镇新春村	坝桥	1	—	—	—	1988
沙溪平桥	沙溪村道	龙场镇沙溪村	石拱	1	—	—	—	1989
阳明桥	修扎公路	龙场镇阳明村	钢砼	1	40	12		1991年重建
六广河大桥	修黔村道	六广镇滨江村	钢砼	1	150	10	100	1993—1996
扎佐桥	贵遵高速	扎佐镇和平村	钢砼	1	10	30	5	1993—1997
铜广井桥	贵遵高速	久长镇铜广井	钢砼	1	8	12	12	1993—1997
驴坊桥	贵遵高速	久长镇驴坊村	钢砼	1	8	12	5	1993—1997
久长桥	贵遵高速	久长镇久长村	钢砼	1	8	12	8	1993—1997
襄阳桥	扎佐联络线	扎佐镇大元村	钢砼	1	39	34	8.3	1995—1996
蒙山桥	修六公路	小箐乡东家湾	钢砼	1	7	8	5	1996年另建
扎佐桥	贵毕高速	扎佐省煤校处	钢砼	1	35.5	27	5	1998—2000
扎佐立交桥	贵毕高速	扎佐省煤校处	钢砼	8	541（含引桥）	29.6	6	1998—2000
石坟坝桥	贵毕高速	龙场镇幸福村	钢砼	1	7	21	5	1998—2000
二支线平桥	扎佐二支线	扎佐镇大园村	钢砼	1	12.8	19.5	6.5	1998
人民桥(原东门桥)	修六公路	龙场镇东门	钢砼	1	38.5	21	5	1998—1999
三板桥大桥	贵毕公路	小箐乡崇恩村	钢砼	1	100	13	75	1999—2001
白岩脚大桥	贵毕公路	小箐乡凤凰村	钢砼	10	100	13	10	1999—2001
下半沟大桥	贵毕公路	小箐乡凤凰村	钢砼	4	140	13	25	1999—2001
龙洞大桥	贵毕公路	小箐乡大坝村	钢砼	5	150	13	20	1999—2001
洞门坡大桥	贵毕公路	六广镇新中村	钢砼	7	210	12	25	1999—2001
擦耳岩大桥	贵毕公路	六广镇新中村	钢砼	8	200	12	20	1999—2001
六广河特大桥	贵毕公路	六广镇擦耳岩	钢砼	1	240	12	103	1999—2001
索风营倒张拱钢索桥	电站公路	六广镇索风营电站	钢索	1	155	12		2001—2002
新曲尺桥	阳明大道	龙场镇曲尺桥	钢砼	3	40	20	5	2001
阳明桥	阳明大道	龙场镇阳明村	钢砼	1	40	25	5	2002
一支线平桥	扎佐一支线	扎佐镇景阳苑	钢砼	1	4.4	20	4.5	2003

续表

桥名	过桥公路	坐落地点	结构	孔数	长(米)	宽(米)	高(米)	建设时间(年)
栖凤桥	翠屏东路	龙场镇小桥河	钢砼	1	25	21	4.4	2003—2004
翠屏桥	翠屏东路	龙场镇翠屏路	钢砼	1	25	21	—	2003—2004
翠薇桥	曲尺桥至三中公路	龙场镇阳明大道东	钢砼	1	26	20	—	2006
大寨桥	修六公路	龙场镇大寨	钢砼	3	65	24	50	2010
海马孔大桥	修文至金沙公路	六桶乡海马村	钢砼	1	180	11.5	—	2010

专记：六广河大桥通车　千载阻隔变通途

自有史记载，六广早就有“水西门户”之称，为黔中贵阳进入黔西、毕节要道。以六广河为界，东为六广，西是黔西。明洪武十七年（1384年），贵州宣慰使奢香承诏开辟九驿进入黔西、毕节，在六广设立第二个驿站，受到六广河阻拦，依靠船只摆渡过河开辟黔西。隆庆四年（1570）贵州总兵安大朝在六广驿艰难摆渡过河进剿水西。清光绪二年（1876年）知县贾芳筹款造船在六广河建义渡备受挫折。千百年来六广河阻隔两岸，过往行人只能靠摆渡过河。

1983年，省交通厅在六广组织修文、黔西两县领导商讨修建六广河大桥会议，拟定投资160万元建桥方案。会后进行征地、拆迁、勘探等前期准备工作，后因资金不到位，只好告吹。1988年，修文、黔西两县省人大代表、省政协委员联合提案向省政府请求修建六广河大桥，提案由省政府转交省交通厅办理。

1992年5月11日，省交通厅下达《关于修建六广河大桥建议书的批复》，拉开六广河建桥序幕。是年12月8日，省交通厅和安顺、毕节两地区及修文、黔西两县负责人联合商定，成立大桥建设领导小组，下设大桥建设工程指挥部，修文县委常委、纪委书记王克勤担任指挥长，修文、黔西两县交通局局长担任副指挥长，展开大桥建设准备工作。1993年3月30日，举行声势浩大的大桥建设开工仪式，六广河两岸彩旗飘扬、锣鼓喧天、鞭炮齐鸣、欢声雷动震撼六广河谷，数十名书法爱好者书写楹联挂满六广镇大街小巷。

1996年10月10日，六广河大桥建成通车。大桥号称六广河上第一桥，连通修文六广镇和黔西素朴镇。自此一桥飞架两岸，让千年天堑变从此通途。通车典礼上，修文、黔西两县领导和群众数千人参加剪彩仪式，两岸锣鼓喧天，鞭炮齐鸣，共同欢呼大桥的建成结束千年靠摆渡的历史。有的群众还编顺口溜表示庆贺：社会主义好，天堑变通道，物资畅交流，城乡换新貌。

1998年，修建贵（阳）毕（节）高等级公路，在六广河上建起当时为亚洲同类桥梁之最的六广河上特大桥。从此车辆川流不息，古驿道上的六广驿已敞开胸怀笑迎过往行人。

六广河大桥通车

四、匝道收费站

（一）贵遵公路扎佐收费站

位于扎佐镇和平村黄土坡连接210国道处。为贵（阳）遵（义）高速公路扎佐进出口站。建于1997年11月，年均出入汽车21万辆。

（二）贵毕公路扎佐收费站

位于扎佐镇和平村挖煤冲连接贵（阳）遵（义）公路、210国道，修（文）扎（佐）公路连接处，为贵（阳）毕（节）高等级公路扎佐进出口站。建于2001年3月，年均进出汽车260万辆。

（三）贵遵公路久长收费站

位于久长镇久长村大龙滩连接210国道、305省道、麦（架桥）肖（家坳）公路处，为贵（阳）遵（义）高速公路久长出入站。建于1997年11月，年均出入汽车29万辆。

贵（阳）遵（义）高速公路久长收费站

（四）贵毕公路修文收费站

位于龙场镇幸福村与平地村交界处，是贵（阳）毕（节）高等级公路连接305省道、县城阳明大道。建于2002年3月，年均进出汽车20万辆。2009年取消收费。

（五）贵毕公路小箐收费站

位于小箐乡小箐村连接修（文）六（广）公路处，为贵（阳）毕（节）高等级公路小箐街进出口匝道。建于2002年10月，年均进出汽车7.3万辆。2009年取消收费。

（六）贵毕公路六广收费站

位于六广镇新中村，系贵（阳）毕（节）高等级公路六广镇进出口匝道，连通修（文）六（广）公路、六（广）素（朴）公路及索风营电站专线路和六广河旅游专线路。建于2002年10月，年均进出汽车21万辆。2009年取消收费。

（七）高尔夫度假中心匝道收费站

2001年贵阳高尔夫度假中心投入营运，在贵（阳）遵（义）高速公路扎佐三元村设置进出口匝道收费站，专供进入高尔夫度假游和高尔夫球爱好者及赛事车辆进出。

五、车辆检车场

1992年，县交通警察大队第二中队在扎佐镇设置机动车年审和交通事故处理站。1997年3月贵阳市交通警察大队在扎佐喻家街210国道旁占地8亩，修建扎佐车辆检车场，以电子计算机检测汽车外形、电路、底盘、制动装置和尾气排放，并承担修文、息烽、开阳3县的汽车检测。1998年8月检车场建成投入使用，到2010年，年均检车3500辆。

六、公共停车场位

2010年，县城10条主街混凝土路面改为沥青路面，使城市交通网络和市政设施得以提升，城区街道设置便民临时公共免费停车车位846个，城区房地产开发地下层建成收费停车位254个，房开住宅小区公共绿地、院落设置收费停车位1519个，县直机关、企事业单位办公楼宿舍区院落设置停车位450个，合计车位3069个，仅占城区小车8000辆的38.36%。于是城区大街小巷小车拥挤停靠，街道便民临时停车位竟成长期固定停车位，街面小车一条龙，双条龙不断出现，人行道往往被小车停靠占用。为维护车辆停靠秩序，部分单位停车位实行收费管理。

第四节　运　输

一、客运

（一）公路客运

1978—1983年，由贵阳客车站发往县内城关、扎佐、六广客运班次每天10班，年均客运量36万人次。1984年，随着旅客增多和运输经营体制改革，客运松绑，允许县内工矿企业和个体户置客车参加营运，改变以往客运由国营车站垄断的状况。到1986年1月，仅两年时间，全县拥有客车39辆，其中驻县工矿企业10家15辆，县属工矿企业7家11辆，个体运输户3家3辆，国营客车站和国营汽车队10辆，开设经营路线至贵阳和县境22个乡（镇），每天开出76班次，运量6300余人次。

1990年，大小型客车增加到119辆，3370座。其中，国营企业10辆，集体52辆，个体57辆，每天开出班次187班次，运量1.43万人次。全年客运总量为138.7万人次。

1996年，启动客车村村通工程，发展乡村客运，到2000年实现全县村村通客车。2002年10月，贵（阳）毕（节）高等级公路开通后，原修文经白云开往贵阳的客车，一部分改由贵毕公路经扎佐到贵阳。个体运输户将车型更换成宽敞、舒适的依维柯直达贵阳，组建起营运火爆的“黔通快巴”车队，每天上午6点30分发车，每间隔20分钟一班，下午8点收班。

2006年12月，县城国家二级客运站落成，组建起黔通联运公司，将修文至贵阳线路客车更为“金龙旅游大巴”，除开通全县乡镇村和贵阳外，还开通修文至邻县开阳、息烽、黔西的客运线。至2010年，县客运站日发车350班次，日均发送旅客5000人次。全县年客运量达528万人次。

2000年，实现全县村村通客车

1978—2010年公路客运一览表

表3—03—06

年份	客运车数（辆）	客运量（万人次）	年份	客运车数（辆）	客运量（万人次）
1978	10	—	1995	121	192
1979	10	—	1996	121	197
1980	10	—	1997	125	215.4
1981	10	—	1998	122	202
1982	10	—	1999	256	206
1983	10	—	2000	174	325
1984	40	57.6	2001	278	360
1985	40	61.84	2002	289	376
1986	44	69.16	2003	295	384
1987	56	120.7	2004	272	425
1988	70	145.5	2005	276	483
1989	78	126.2	2006	278	301
1990	109	183.7	2007	256	308
1991	109	133.4	2008	234	400
1992	101	122.4	2009	200	490
1993	118	154.9	2010	197	528
1994	119	161.6			

2006—2010年县城二级客车站客运线路及发车班次一览表

表3—03—07

线　　路	车辆数（辆）	日发班数	线　　路	车辆数（辆）	日发班数
修文至贵阳金阳站	53	212	修文至猫冲	2	6
修文至扎佐站	12	60	修文至新寨	4	20
修文至久长站	4	20	修文至贵铝一矿	8	48
修文至六广站	10	40	修文至洒坪中寨	3	9
修文至六桶	6	6	修文至乌栗	6	24
修文至回水	1	2	修文至宝山	2	6
修文至联江	1	2	修文至新乐	1	4
修文至花榔	1	1	修文至德政	2	4
修文至海马孔	2	2	修文至三元	2	10
修文至大石	1	2	修文至郭田	1	4
修文至高山	1	2	修文至上坝	1	3

续表

线　　路	车辆数（辆）	日发班数	线　　路	车辆数（辆）	日发班数
修文至凉井	2	2	修文至马家桥	8	40
修文至马场	2	3	修文至杨寨	1	4
修文至小箐	1	4	修文至小河沟	4	40
修文至岩鹰山水库	3	12	修文至开阳县	2	4
修文至花塔	1	3	修文至息烽县	2	4
修文至下花塔	1	3	修文至黔西县	1	1
修文至龙塘	1	3	修文至白云杉树林	5	30

（二）铁路客运

1978年，川黔铁路有贵阳至重庆普通旅客列车1对，1987年，增开贵阳至遵义慢车1对，开设县境大关冲、扎佐和久长客运站，旅客发送量日均分别为82、140、98人。

川黔铁路久长火车站

2000年，随着川黔铁路实行电气化改造列车提速和贵（阳）遵（义）高等级公路通车，公路客运增开贵阳至重庆、贵阳至遵义线路，加上久长、扎佐增加到贵阳的客运班次，使县境多数原铁路沿线短途乘客改乘汽车，铁路乘客随之下降，贵阳至重庆普快不在县境各站停靠，只有贵阳至遵义普通慢车和贵阳至桐梓临时加班列车在扎佐、久长站停靠，日均乘客仅百人。

（三）水路客运

1984年，六广河渡口使用小拖轮供往来旅客渡河，日均100人次。1990年，上马、大屯、转龙滩、野鸡河、六桶河等5个渡口以木船摆渡旅客日均3000人次。六广河1号渡、2号渡和焦家坪、海马孔、周家院渡口以汽轮运客，日均640人次。1996年，六广河旅游航道开通，旅游公司和个体船运经营户置客轮供游览六广河七峡，客船载客20至100人，节假日期间，日均运量1000人次。2005年游客增加，39艘水运游船，日载客1500人次。2008年，六广河上游开通从索风营电站大坝顺河而上，直抵猫跳河六级电站和鸭池河，扩展水路旅游航线，客运逐年增加。2010年，全县水路客运达10.23万人次。

二、货运

（一）公路货运

1978年，有国营县车队和城关、扎佐集体运输社从事公路货运。1981年，农村马车参与货运。1984年，允许农村拖拉机从事运输。到1990年，全县有运输马车794辆，货运量2.7万吨；拖拉机114辆，吨位达239吨；大小货运汽车338辆，货运量66.1万吨。2008年，实现村村通公路，马车和拖拉机运输自然

淘汰，村民购置货运汽车647辆，使全县货车增为1320辆，年货运量410万吨，主要从事燃煤、水泥、砂石、钢材、化肥、矿产品、机制砖和建材预制品的运输。2010年，全县货运汽车增为1920辆，货运量达510万吨。

1978—2010年公路货运情况表

表3—03—08

年份	车辆数（辆）	货运量（万吨）	年份	车辆数（辆）	货运量（万吨）
1978	18	29.3	1995	499	178
1979	20	41.3	1996	438	161
1980	40	38.1	1997	644	240.3
1981	75	35	1998	720	192
1982	95	26.1	1999	872	210
1983	110	33.5	2000	988	330
1984	118	22.1	2001	1078	353
1985	163	28.3	2002	1163	401
1986	317	30.2	2003	1317	432
1987	305	75.5	2004	1109	269
1988	315	87.9	2005	1245	303
1989	317	67.4	2006	1195	359
1990	348	66.1	2007	1244	373
1991	298	57.2	2008	1320	410
1992	371	93.6	2009	1551	455
1993	363	108.8	2010	1920	510
1994	446	149.8			

（二）铁路货运

1978年，启用县境大关冲、扎佐、久长火车站，其中大关冲车站年发送货物量5万吨，扎佐、久长站各10万吨。1980年3个站发送量仅为30万吨。1991年，增加启用高坝火车站。运输货物主要是原煤、建材和矿产品。其中久长站承担国家粮食储备库粮食转运以及磷矿、沥青、农资、生活物资的转运，年转运粮食3万吨、磷矿40万吨、沥青2万吨、黄磷3万吨、农资3万吨和生活物资7000吨。扎佐站1978年至1989年货运量10万吨，1990年30万吨。2003年，扎佐站建成贵阳市北物流旱码头，修建铁轨6道，货运站台4个，日吞吐量1800吨，辐射贵阳、毕节、遵义、铜仁的物资转运业务。2010年，全县铁路货运量上升至100万吨。

（三）水路货运

1978年，县境水路货运仅有六广河部分航段，主要是沿江村民运输农副产品到集市出售，运回村民生产、生活物资。

1996年，乌江渡库区六广河航道开通，由六广渡口顺江下至乌江电站大坝，六广河营运货轮增加，村民购置载重量12吨的油泵机动船，在长达74公里河道从事货运。2005年，有货轮63艘，2010年，因水路货运物资少，货轮未增未减。

三、运输工具

（一）客运

马轿车 1990年，因经过县城的省道改为柏油路面，以及县城区段加宽为25米的混凝土路面，使1978年前被淘汰的运输马篷车复出，成为城郊短途客运工具，往返县城至三潮水、王官、马家桥的3条线路，有车8辆行驶，分段收费每人0.5元至2元。1996年，改观城市容貌和整顿交通秩序，马篷车营运被取缔。

摩托 1993年，县城环城路改造竣工，一批待业人员购置双轮摩托载客营运，1车乘坐1人，城内收费1元，城郊2至3元。继后改成三轮摩托，置有车箱、座位，1车承载3人，每人起步价2元，城郊加费。1998年，扎佐、久长集镇和县城城郊村民也置双轮摩托入城载客，接送进城村民往返。2003年，摩托客运发展到双轮摩托80余辆，三轮摩托2000辆。

2009年，三轮摩托穿行于县城大街小巷，被人们称之为“摩的”，带来交通秩序混乱，县交通局抓住开展“三创一办”（创建国家卫生城市、国家环境保护模范城市、全国文明城市和协办第九届全国少数民族传统体育运动会）活动的契机，加强城市交通管理，取缔“摩的”客运。

出租车 2000年，轿车的士进入县城客运市场，1车乘坐4人，每人3元起价，城郊加费。2008年，起步价增为4元，由经营专营公司管理，从城郊营运发展到长短途兼营，县城办理营运资质“的士”74辆。2010年，县城和扎佐镇、久长镇共有营运“的士”150辆。

县城客运出租车

客车 1978年至2006年，县境客运汽车几经变化从简易棚车演变为大巴、快巴、面包车。其中金龙大巴载客40人，依维柯快巴载客20人，昌河面包车载客8人。2010年，县城取消小型客运面包车，全县大中型客运汽车共197辆。小型客车只有8辆，经营扎佐至久长210国道专线短途客运。

客运列车 1978年有川黔铁路普快列车过境。1991年，列车动力一律改内燃机为电气化，有普快、慢车、节假日加班列车，内置软座、硬座、软卧、硬卧，车厢并设有空调，还有餐厅、洗手间。每节车厢乘客120余人，全列可载1200余人。主要供长途旅客乘坐。2010年，有电气化列车贵阳至重庆、贵阳至遵义，贵阳至桐梓旅客列车经过。

客运轮船 1996年，六广河航道启用客运机动轮船，大客轮双层载客160人，内设吧台、小吃、酒水、客房、会客室，配有空调。小客轮载客30人，船舱置有座位。另有供游客游玩的快艇，分别乘坐5至20人，船速由驾驶人员根据航线掌握，一般时速为10至30公里。2010年，航道有各类客运轮船100艘。

（二）货运

裹底背篼 约高80厘米，上圆下方，上大下小。1998年，农村、城镇作为人力搬运的工具。至2010年，城镇住房业主及装修公司均由背篼运输装修材料和装修渣土垃圾上下楼，每天待运背篼100余个，主要分布于县城和扎佐镇等集镇，农村仍有使用。

手板车 20世纪80年代，城镇有人力手板车穿行巷弄院落，用于搬运杂物。1990年，农村以农用机动车取代手板车，大量手板车转入城镇，为城镇居民临时运送物品。2010年，县城区辟有手板车运输市场停靠待运点，共有人力手板车80余辆。扎佐镇分布零星人力手板车20余辆。

马车 1980年，全县有300辆，每辆由双辕、车架、车厢组成，分为单、双、三套（马匹数）几种，载重量分别为500、700、1000公斤，日程30公里，用于县境短途运输。1990年增至800辆。2000年，整顿城镇市容市貌，马车运输市场被机动运输车代替，到2010年，城区马车运输消失，乡村仍有马车载运。

20世纪80年代的畜力马车

拖拉机 1984年，农用拖拉机卸犁，挂拖斗投入运输，分为大、中型和手扶式，分别载重4吨，2吨，1吨，每小时运行10至20公里。1990年，参与营运拖拉机114辆。2000年，农用拖拉机被农用汽车和电动三轮车取代。

电动三轮车 1984年，城镇开始使用电动三轮车从事货运。每车配有小型货箱，载重500公斤至800公斤，时速15公里。用于城镇和城乡接合部短途货运。到2010年，电动三轮车在农村主要用于农田生产运输，在城镇主要为商铺转送货物及快递邮件。

货车 1980年，县属国营企业和集体运输社有货运汽车24辆，分为大、中、小型，配置有载货车厢，用汽油或柴油发动牵引，每小时运行20至40公里。大型10轮车载重10吨至20吨，中型6轮载重5吨至10吨，小型（微型货车）4轮载重3吨至5吨。大中型用于长途货运，包括煤炭、砖石、化肥、矿产品及生活物资。小型用于城镇生活物资转运。1984年，个体运输户置车参加运输，全县货运汽车增至180辆。1990年370辆，2010年增至1920辆，货运量达510万吨。

货运列车 1978年至1990年，县境川黔铁路有货运列车，分别停靠于大关冲、扎佐、高坝、久长货运站。列车车厢挂拉数不等，每节载重60吨，时速50公里。1991年，提速达70公里。2010年，年货运量80万至100万吨。

货运油轮 1984年，六广河启用油泵船从事货运，船载重量12吨。1996年，六广至乌江河道开通，货运油轮逐年增加，2010年增至63艘，年运量1万吨。

四、车辆维修

1978年后，运输车辆连年增加。县国营汽车队维修厂和城关、扎佐两个集体运输社汽车维修点不能满足车辆维修需要，1985年城镇相继建起个体汽车维修厂（店），1990年发展到105家，分布在县城、扎佐镇和久长镇路段以及修（文）六（广）公路和305省道、107省道路段。

2000年，县交通局、工商管理局和公安交警队针对汽车维修厂不规范、占道经营、维修资质低、维修质量差等问题，对汽车维修厂（店）进行清理，取缔无证维修厂（店），全县仅存车辆维修厂（店）81家。

2004年，按照相关规定，对汽车维修厂（店）实行资质审核换证，经过长期整治，取缔不具资质维修厂（店）后，全县正式办理汽车维修营业厂（店）82家。

驻县城内的时新汽车修理厂

2010年，经交通运输管理所认可，办理汽车维修登记维修厂（店）30家。

2010年经认可的汽车维修场店概况表

表3—03—09

维修厂（店）	法人代表	经营场（店）址
贵州颖林全自动清洗美容有限公司修文分公司	刘　颖	县城阳明大道利尔上河城商业7号楼
修文县龙场镇瑞丰汽车修理厂	谢　萍	龙场镇新春村107省道旁三小路口
贵阳双林汽车修理有限责任公司	李国荣	扎佐镇和平村
修文宏达汽车二保场	徐　涛	龙场镇阳明大道
扎佐小张汽车修理厂	刘　松	扎佐镇学苑路
修文县扎佐昌远汽车修理厂	聂　强	扎佐镇大园村
修文县龙场镇南方汽车修理厂	潘应荣	龙场镇油萝街107省道旁
贵阳市修文新力达（时新）汽车修理厂	叶时新	龙场镇阳明东路232号
修文县城南汽车修理部	李廷卫	龙场镇新生村三组
贵阳宝达马迪汽车服务有限公司	陈泰安	龙场镇阳明东路232号
修文宏昌汽车修理厂	陈　军	龙场镇潮水路消防大队旁
修文县恒达汽车修理厂	黄以甦	龙场镇人民南路乡企局旁
修文县兴旺汽车修理厂	叶春龙	龙场镇阳明村
修文县恒通汽车修理有限责任公司	杨　军	龙场镇新生村
修文四达汽车修理厂	郭友波	龙场镇新春村五组
贵州盛鑫工程机械服务有限公司	焦万荣	龙场镇阳明大道
修文县桂林汽车修理厂	黄桂林	龙场镇潮水村94号
修文县绍明汽车修理厂	任连芬	久长镇川黔南路
修文县合明汽车修理店	唐合明	久长镇久长村六组
修文县新动力汽车修理厂	秦　天	龙场镇幸福村

续表

维修厂（店）	法人代表	经营场（店）址
龚太原汽车轮胎修理店	龚太原	久长镇贵遵公路匝道口旁
曾世江汽车轮胎修理店	曾世江	久长镇贵遵公路匝道口旁
四兴汽车修理厂	张四林	扎佐镇210国道
修文创阳汽车维修服务中心	兰贵军	龙场镇翠屏路学宫巷
龚太学汽车电器维修店	龚太学	久长镇久长村6组210国道旁
尹彦维汽车修理店	尹彦维	小箐乡小箐街
润贵汽车修理厂	周润贵	龙场镇油萝街107省道旁
修文九龙汽车服务中心	李仕龙	扎佐镇前进南路191号
修文红生汽车修理厂	付　洪	龙场镇新春村
修文永嘉汽车服务中心	孙安国	龙场镇人民北路154号

第五节　管　理

一、路政执法

（一）落实路政法规

1982—1983年，农村实行家庭联产承包制，出现有村民在靠公路沿线承包地开挖公路路基、堡坎、水沟，有的横穿公路开沟引水灌田，砍伐行道树增强土地光照，还有企事业单位基本建设施工侵害公路，造成安全隐患。针对这些问题，1984年初，县交通主管部门组织人员对修（文）六（广）、广（田）六（桶）、小（箐）中（寨）、扎（佐）六（屯）、冒（沙井）乌（栗）等县级公路损坏情况进行调查，公路路基被吞食7926平方米，挖横穿公路引水沟渠11条，砍伐成材行道树10棵，受损桥涵2道。3月，县政府为治理公路被损坏问题，根据国务院《关于加强公路路政管理，保障公路安全畅通的通知》和《贵州省公路路政管理暂行办法》，组织区、乡分管领导和公路工区管理人员学习路政法规，以中央和省的文件作为路政管理的法律依据，落实路政执法。对造成公路交通安全，损害公路所涉及的单位和村民作出按公路技术标准限期恢复的决定，使公路损坏状况得以制止。

1999年贵阳市政府颁布《公路路政管理规定》，2001年贵州省政府颁布《公路路政管理规定条例》，给路政执法进一步提供法律保障和具体的管理依据。县交通局为落实路政执法，相应制定出贯彻落实路政执法的法规细则，发放路政法规宣传资料。到2010年，建立起路政管理制度，包括“超限运输申请”“增设非公路标志申请”“增设管线申请”和“增设平交道申请”等，制定出“治理超限运输实施方案”“桥梁抢修应急方案”“路政档案管理制度”“路政管理统计制度”“路政管理公示制度”“路政票据制度”以及“损坏公路赔偿收费标准”等，有力地维护公路产权，推动路政执法。

（二）清除公路路障

1984年，县交通安全委员会为加强路政管理，在5月“安全月”活动中组织县交通局、公安局、司法局、工商行政管理局、城建局联合执法，对影响公路交通安全的堆积物、建筑物、摊点、店铺、广告牌等进行清除，共拆除路障点107处，面积376平方米，其中主要有县耐火材料厂建于扎佐街至扎佐火车站公路交叉路口（K0+100处）磅房侵占公路10米×2.5米；县水利局修建烂沟水库在冒（沙井）乌（栗）公路11公里处淹没公路1公里，在修（文）六（广）公路K23+500处修建横穿公路混凝土拱涵1道；108厂企业在冒（沙井）乌（栗）公路10K至11K处堆放生产、生活垃圾，侵占公路路基699平方米；城关镇居民赵凤鸣在修（文）六（广）公路K0+800处修建住房阻毁涵洞1道。县交通安全委员会根据路障情况，作出处理意见，规定公路穿越城镇路段建筑、店铺须离公路两侧边沟3米之外，严禁在公路留地范围内修建各类停放场点；禁止在公路上和留地范围内晒粮，堆放农作物、肥料；搬迁公路交通沿线公路贸易市场。经过长期坚持路障治理，县际公路、乡村公路面貌得到改观。2010年在公路沿线清除路障垃圾堆放点760处，共8785立方米，清除违规建筑22处，共168.8平方米。

清除公路路障宣传牌

（三）治理公路“三乱”

1993年，因修筑贵（阳）遵（义）公路和改造210国道，致四川、遵义至贵阳货运汽车由修文沿107省道至贵阳，使107省道修文段损毁严重，车辆经常受堵，有村民在房前屋后或承包地内开辟便道让车通行，有村民在公路损坏段铺砂、填石、设卡，让车通行收取过路费。有的管理人员将超载卸货放行变为超载交钱放行，并出现接收公路改造受益地企业“赞助”和改造道路村民投劳。一时间公路乱设卡、乱收费、乱摊派现象凸显。2009年，贵阳市交通局和县交通局狠抓治理公路“三乱”，要求路政管理人员严格执行路政管理规章制度，并对违规人员严肃处理。2010年，“三乱”得到彻底治理，乱设卡、乱收费、乱罚款得到遏制。只依法收取道路修复费，其中设立平交道口费2631元，路产赔（补）偿费3665元，占用公路埋设光缆费6930元。

二、公路养护

（一）工区养护

1985年，县境210国道和107、305省道的养护管理均由贵州省公路局息烽公路养护工区承担，在全县设立公路养护道班6个。1996年1月，县地方公路工区养护工作划归贵阳市交通局公路管理处领导，行政隶属县交通局，具体负责对县管公路的养护组织、实施，承担县道5条和专线公路4条的养护，将县道改造升级为柏油路。过县境的210国道和107、305省道由省公路局息烽公路管理工区养护。贵（阳）遵（义）、贵（阳）毕（节）两条高等级公路由省高速公路管理局养护。

至2010年，公路养护一直坚持执行贵州省交通厅提出的“全面规划、加强养护、重点发展、科学管理、保证畅通”养路方针，由公路工区承担主要养护任务，职责从“修、补”为主转为巡察、监督、保

洁和绿化为主，养护工作重心由养转管，使好路率达到98%，比1985年的65.5%上升32.5个百分点。

（二）村民养护

1978年，根据“以路养路、以农促路、农路结合、全面发展”的养路方针，将县管修（文）六（广）、扎（佐）六（屯）、冒（沙井）乌（栗）、小（箐）中（寨）、广（田）六（桶）公路和通往电站、火车站的专线公路，共119.5公里列为群养公路，设立固定群众养护班，由公路管理工区派技术人员指导，分段划给公路沿线公社、生产队。公社派村民农闲养护，养护经费由县交通局拨给公社，公社下拨给队，队实行养路评工记分，统一分配。1982年，农村实行家庭联产承包责任制后，村民不再承担公路养护，固定性村民养护班即行解散。

（三）承包养护

1985年，县道养护实行承包责任制，承包给公路沿线的32户村民。养护任务由县交通局下达年度养护计划指标，制定季度公路养护检查标准，经检查合格支付给承包人的养护费。对养护优良者给予承包费额的10%至20%奖励；若养护不达标，则扣罚10%至20%承包费。经年终检查良路率27%，差路率22.8%，养护综合值为51.3%，与1984年相比，良路率提高16.9个百分点，差路率下降25.2个百分点，养护综合值上升12.4个百分点。1988年，县成立公路管理工区，具体制定和组织实施公路养护计划，仍采取承包养护方式，直至1995年停止承包。

（四）政府养护

1996年，启动县际公路、县乡（镇）公路改造升级，到2007年，县际路、县乡（镇）路和专线路共27条升级为四级柏油路，养护工作重点转为维护、保洁和绿化。2008年完成贫困村公路改造62条，根据《贵阳市贫困村村公路建设改造工作实施办法》第九条规定，公路养护管理由公路所处地的乡（镇）人民政府负责。政府明确专人管理，在市、县交通局指导下开展维护保养工作。县、乡（镇）政府负责养护资金的管理，确保公路养护资金按期拨付，专款专用。

2009年，为进一步完善农村公路管养运行机制，增强公路沿线单位和村民对公路的管养意识，通过招标将公路行道树栽种发包给有种植技能的专业队伍，实行行道树管理权和所有权挂钩，政府与公路沿线村民签订行道树管护责任书。全年种植行道树全长327公里，清理公路边沟353.6公里，疏通涵洞30道，清运塌方790立方米，修复挡墙1380立方米，修复路基6770平方米。经贵阳市公路处检查，县管公路养护综合值为81.26%，乡管公路为80%，村管公路为78.3%，全年投入养护资金138万元。

县管公路养护施工

三、运输事务

（一）公路货运事务

1981年9月，县交通局为落实中央和省“封车节油”指示，将分散的20辆货运汽车组成联合车队，实行统一货源、统一结算、统一加油、统一调度。1984年，县交通局按照“放宽、搞活”政策，实行国营、集体、个体货运一起上。于10月又将个体货运专业户组成联营车队，分为城关片区和扎佐片区开展货运业务，油料实行统一管理，按完成货运任务量分别核定供油量，运费按公路路线三类等级收取，统一结算。

1988年，成立县个体运输专业户协会，货运进入市场化，货运事务转由县工商行政管理部门管理，负责办理货运营业登记，征收货运税费，以及对驾驶员和车主的思想、职业道德和法律法规教育。油料放开，按国家油价自购，运价由货主与车主按市场经济规律议定，具体货运事务由车主自行管理，运输协会负责协助工商行政部门行使依法营运和依法纳税等事务。

（二）公路客运事务

1984年，县交通局为缓解客运紧张状况，吸纳县内工矿企业客车参与客车营运，统一使用交通部门客车票。1985年，允许个体购置客车参与营运，收费按照交通运输部门规定的里程定价。1987年，全县有客运汽车70辆，其中个体客运汽车45辆。为使客运正常，县交通局将所有参加营运客车的车型、座位、线路、里程、收费、出发和返程时间列表公布，以使互相监督，共同遵守。为保证客运安全，严把客运市场准入关、车辆质量技术关、驾驶员从业资格关，对全县客运汽车作出4条规定：必须遵守交通运输主管部门规章和划分的营运线路挂牌营业；按批准的线路和班次准时出车，不准争客挤班、抢点；遵守客运管理规定，做到运输手续齐全，使用交通部门统一印制客车票，按里程计费；为确保旅客安全，严禁超速、超载。

1989年，客运汽车统一进入新落成的社会停车场经营，分为贵阳方向、扎佐方向、六广方向营运线路，按运管所排定班次、时间依序入场，依次出车。

2002年，对由个体运输户组成的黔通快巴车队经营沿贵（阳）毕（节）公路至贵阳路线，指定龙山路为停靠点，由车队管理人员组织指挥，按排定班次、时间发车，营运秩序井然。

2006年，组建修文黔通运输公司，对进出县城客车统一在县国家二级客运站经营，实行公司化管理。将客运汽车分成3个车队，由车站统一售票，设立老、弱、病、孕、军人优先窗口和返乡农民工服务站，履行旅客入站行李安全检查，车辆进站排队，出站放行登记执行到2010年未改变。

（三）水路航运事务

1985年1月，县交通局根据《全省水上交通安全工作会议纪要》精神，向县政府呈报《成立乌江库区六广河航运管理站的报告》，提出航管、航运分治，组建航运管理机构负责航运事务。5月，县政府批准成立修文县航运管理站。1986年4月成立县乌江库区六广航运管理站，开展清理渡口和办理民运船牌照，进行驾驶员身体健康检查。11月，贯彻贵州省政府《关于立即制止客（渡）船违章超载确保旅客安全的意见》，对渡口船及客、货船进行清理整顿，核定载重量定额，划定载重线标志，禁止船舶超重渡运。

1987年12月，县政府执行“安全第一，预防为主”方针，制定并公布内河渡口守则，维护渡口安全。1998年9月，航运管理站对办理检验合格的货船、游船、快艇营业牌照，准予营运。继后按制度规定每年对船舶进行年审。

四、交通安全

（一）公路安全

1980年，公路交通安全由贵阳市交通警察队管理，县里相应成立交通安全管理委员会，贯彻“安全第一，预防为主”的交通安全方针，进行交通安全检查，对不良带病车辆、无证车辆给予罚款和扣证、封车处理。

1982年，县交通安全管理委员会和县交通局开展公路交通安全优秀驾驶员和驾驶标兵评比，评出安全集体11家，先进个人531人。县石油公司驾驶员王家骏获安全行车80万公里以上“驾驶标兵”，县车队驾驶员唐开文获安全行车30万公里以上“优秀驾驶员”称号。1984年充实完善交通安全管理组织，在公路沿线区（镇）成立交通安全领导小组，加强交通安全管理。1987年，县公安局成立交通警察大队，城关镇、扎佐镇设立交警中队，负责组织驾驶员学习交通法规，维护交通秩序。1990年，持续开展三个月交通安全宣传活动，审核驾驶员1460人，年检车辆867辆，接受交通安全教育人数15万人次。全年车辆肇事104起，死亡7人，受伤32人，经济损失13.6万元，与1987年相比分别下降43.5%、77.4%、41.8%和48.7%。

1997年7月，县交通警察大队与龙场镇王官村共建交通安全村，竖立标志牌，给王官中、小学生讲交通安全常识课，向村民宣传交通安全知识。2001年12月，贵州省交通警察总队副政委徐崇茗到“王官安全村”检查、验收。2002年，省高速公路交警、县交警队、县交通局分别对公路沿线小箐、六桶等中学生上交通安全课，展示交通安全展板，组织驾驶员观看交通安全录像。县政府在重大交通安全事故发生点竖立“血字碑”警示后人，在17条客运线路的易发交通安全事故地段装置警示牌42块。

县交警队交通警察到学校对学生进行交通安全宣传教育

2010年，全年出动公路交通安全执法车6000车次，投入执法人员3000人次，检查各种机动车辆1556辆次，组织学习交通法规、培训12期400余人次，使驾驶人员安全意识得到进一步提高。

专记：立下血字碑　警示后来人

1992年11月29日，城关镇王官小学校长彭江涛经营的贵03-06244号大客车，雇用无客运驾驶证照的拖拉机驾驶员吴维均驾驶。该车从六桶开往县城，行至修（文）六（广）公路小箐乡柿花树村段下坡处，因操作失误，至客车翻坠，掉进85米深的悬岩坑底，当即死亡23人，伤9人，其中重伤8人，轻伤1人一起重大交通事故在此发生。

事故发生后，小箐乡政府、县交通局当即电告上级相关部门，省、地、县分管领导闻讯赶赴现场组织抢救，将伤员送往医院治疗，协调处理遇难者善后事宜，通知死者亲人认领遗体，发给死者家属3000元丧葬费。事故直接经济损失10余万元。

12月4日，县委、县政府主持在事故发生地召开交通安全教育现场会，到会700余人。认定这起特大恶性交通事故系漠视交通安全法规的事故。无客运资质的驾驶员吴维均因在事故中死亡未追究刑事责任，车主彭江涛由〔1993〕修刑初字第40号处刑期1年零6个月，缓刑2年的刑事责任。为吸取血的教训，特意在事故发生地公路旁竖立“血字碑”昭示后人。

（二）水路安全

1987年12月25日，县政府批准并公布《内河渡口守则》规定渡口的位置，必须经县人民政府批准；

渡船必须经港监部门检验，标有载客（货）定额，标明船名牌，并划载重线；渡船操作人员必须持有港监部门制发的渡工证书，严禁无证和残疾以及酒后船工驾船；遇洪水暴发，大风大浪及雾罩视线不良或其他危及安全过渡情况，必须停渡；乘客要自觉服从管理，维护渡运秩序，不得强行要求过渡或自行驾船过渡；乘客和渡工都有责任执行“安全第一、预防为主”的方针，互相监督，维护渡口安全。《守则》公布后，港监站按规定抓船舶年检，航运重点抓旅游季节和节假日水运安全，配置救生器材，配备专人加强周末水运安全监控。到2010年，县海事处、港监站每年均进行“水上运输秩序”“船舶航行秩序”“船员管理秩序”和“通航秩序”整顿。乡（镇）政府分别与船主签订《安全责任保证书》。是年检查船舶127艘次，出动执法人员138人次，出动检查执法车辆和巡逻艇46辆（艘）次，巡查里程4097公里，确保水上船只安全运行。

专记：海马孔翻船五人遇难

2005年5月7日，六桶乡部分职工和海马村部分村干部共14人，乘坐村民任其鼎驾驶的“黔南白客”27号客船，从海马孔渡口起航顺六广河直下，到息烽县黄沙渡口出水洞野炊。下午5时30分用餐完毕原线返程。当客船行至海马渡口1130米处，突遇从西北角的金沙县入侵修文的大风，强风中心位于六广河海马峡一带，乘船者将玻璃窗关上，随船继续前行。窗外狂风肆虐，河浪翻腾。6时50分距海马渡口仅40米接近靠岸时，客船便遭狂风夹着冰雹袭击，河浪掀起1米多高将船翻倒，驾驶员被风刮离驾驶台，机舵下沉，船舱进水。顿时，船内发出一片呼救声。一发千钧之际，驾驶员的儿子任金舟用脚使劲蹬玻璃窗，呼喊大家从窗口钻出逃生。除9名男子潜水逃出外，其余5人困于舱内。河对岸金沙县化觉村“黔金”19号客船的船主和海马孔部分村民听到求救声连忙赶往出事地点，见1人爬上岸，将8人救出险境，其中6人安危无恙，2人轻伤，5人未见身影。经核实，遇难者系乡计划生育站职工余正仙、蒋维波和聘用人员余春群及其12岁的儿子，以及海马村委会主任任中平。

海马孔翻船事故沉船搜救上岸

翻船事故发生后，县委书记魏明禄和县长石洪当即带领县级有关领导、部门负责人和医护人员赶至海马村，贵阳市海事局和安监局的领导同时奔赴现场。于海马渡口成立搜救指挥部，制定搜救方案，一方面组织力量展开搜救工作，一方面求助省、市和兄弟县增援力量参与搜救。省委常委、市委书记王晓东和市长袁周批示，举全力打捞沉船和搜救失踪人员。

至5月11日下午5时21分，经过4天的紧张打捞，沉船浮出水面，向岸靠拢，5位遇难者尸体均在船轮中找到，一一由家属认领。根据贵阳市气象台和修文气象局监测数据显示，“黔南白客”27号客船沉水时，风力已达10级。专家指出，就六广河情况而言，船舶抵御风力的能力最高只能达到7级，超过7级河浪翻滚，船只必定遇险。据此，贵阳市事故调查组结论：海马孔翻船系受风暴影响，属重大风灾事故。

（三）铁路安全

1989年4月，县人民武装部按照省护路办公室要求，组建县川黔铁路护路队，在川黔铁路经过的久长、扎佐成立护路队，每队配有10名队员分为两班，每天巡逻3次，负责铁路护路保路的治安管理。防止不法分子用石块乱砸旅客列车和爬车盗窃货运物资。护路队挑选政治素质良好、身体强壮和年龄在30岁左右的民兵组成，日夜巡逻在县境30.4公里的铁道线上。

1990年11月7日，1515次货运列车行至K387+100米处，有盗窃者扒车推下10捆涤纶布匹，被巡逻在铁道线上的护路队员郭光华、陈绍恒发现，窃贼见护路队员后惊慌逃遁。二人在守护赃物的同时，上报车站，车站转告货主，收回布匹，挽回损失。

1991年9月18日深夜，3193次列车行至K382丛林处，突然停车，接着从林中奔出4人跑向车头，再从车上推下11袋物品后，列车启动开走。这一情景被巡逻队员赵高学发现，他立即通知其他队员赶到事发点，将4名犯罪嫌疑人连同赃物一起抓获。经铁路公安侦察审讯，确认系列车司机与乘务员勾结犯罪分子共同作案。案件侦破后赵高学受到成都铁路局表彰。

1996年8月，在宜宾至广州397次旅客列车上，一位四川女乘客不慎从车窗掉下列车，当即已摔得头破血流，被护路巡逻队员杨家武、韩廷俊发现，立即送往医院救治。

1997年，县人民武装部民兵护路工作移交给县综合治安办公室。至2010年铁路运输安全由县政府综合治安办公室管理，组织护路队巡逻，严防破坏和盗窃。

巡逻在川黔铁道上的护路队

五、规费征收

（一）养路费

1978年，根据国务院《关于整顿公路养路费征收标准的报告》精神，养路费征收率由运费总收入的12.5%降到10%。1981年，又将养路费恢复为12.5%；企业车辆按载重吨位征收，每月每吨85元。1985年增到105元，并于10月1日将养路费率提高到15%。1986年，县成立养路费征收站，统一征管，费率执行1985年规定的15%。

2009年，将养路征收改为汽车燃油附加费，把养路费和其他收费一道按每购1公升燃油交1元的比例纳入汽车燃油费中，至2010年未变。

（二）运输管理费

1980年3月，根据安顺地区行署《关于交通运输管理费管理办法的请示报告》精神，运输管理费由地区总站管理改为县运输管理站直接管理。管理费收入按月提取管理费总额的10%上交地区交通局，作为统一印制票据和其他管理活动的费用，其余由县运输管理站自行支用。1982年，执行贵州省交通厅、财政厅《关于运输管理费几个问题的规定》，管理费率以运费收入总额向承运车辆收取，2吨以上汽车按1%至1.5%、2吨以下按1.5%计征。1985年执行贵州省《公路运输管理费征收和使用规定》，凡汽车运输每月每吨按500元征收营业管理费。

2009年至2010年，运输管理费征收中取消客、货运输附加费和交通发展基金费以及各项办证工本费。

（三）公路占用补偿费

1993—2008年分别执行黔交〔1993〕04号、黔价费〔2003〕113号、黔价费〔2006〕60号文件对公路占用、损害赔补偿收费规定。

2009年，执行贵州省物价局和财政厅关于公路路产占（利）用，损害赔（补）偿收费项目标准的通知》（黔价费〔2009〕63号），县交通运输管理局向社会公示各项收费标准。2010年收取增设公路平交道口费2.63万元，路产赔（补）偿费3655元，收取占利用公路埋设光缆费6930元，共收补偿费3.7万元。

（四）运输服务费

1978年，恢复交通运输管理服务收费，包括客运、货运附加费，运输行政管理费，水运行政管理费，养路费和交通发展基金费。2009年，改革交通运输管理体制，将客运和货运附加费、交通发展基金费、养路费、水运管理费和公路运输行政管理费纳入机动车、船燃油费之中，以每消耗1公升油料收取1元费用，由中央财政统一提取后，按比例返还给地方财政。其运输行政服务性收费有港务费、船检费、车检费。社会服务性收费由交通运输企业根据县物价局制定和县发展改革局监制的社会服务收费项目、费率、标准收取，包括旅客服务费、车站服务费、车辆服务费，其中，旅客服务费分摊在车费中，车站和车辆服务费分为按客车座位数收服务费，每辆车年均6480元，每辆年均停车费1300元，每辆年检车费180元。2010年收运输服务费110万元。

第四章　信息产业

1978—1982年，县邮电局人、财、物归贵州省邮电管理局管理，贵州省邮电管理局委托安顺地区邮电局代管。1996年，修文县划归贵阳市管辖，贵州省邮电管理局委托贵阳市电信局代管县邮电局。1998年9月县邮电局析建为邮政局和电信局。1999年8月，电信局固定通信与移动通信分营。

中共十一届三中全会后，党和国家把邮电通信建设列为经济发展的战略重点优先发展，提出“统筹规划，条块结合，分层负责，联合建设”的十六字方针和资金投入的政策措施。全县邮电部门抓住机遇，充分用好用活各项政策，加快发展。

1980—1993年，邮政网络增加，服务网点延伸到公社（乡、镇）和村（居）委会，邮件传递速度加快，除少数步班邮路外，普遍采用自行车、摩托车、委办汽车和自办邮车相结合的邮运方式。邮政业务范围逐步扩展，除常规业务外，新开办集邮、邮政快件、邮政特快、邮政广告、邮购业务、国际邮政、邮政金融、代理业务等。业务量、业务收入每年以10%至15%的速度增长。

电信大楼

1995年6月28日，国家重点建设工程福州—杭州—贵阳—成都光纤电缆工程建设修文段破土动工，县委、县政府用汽车拖着物资，敲锣打鼓到马家桥慰问施工的解放军官兵。这项工程途经县境杉树林—王官—修文—马家桥—普陀—上寨—久长—驴坊—石榴。10月16日县邮电局程控电话接入这条长途光纤电缆。

电信业从完全垄断到引入竞争，从政企合一到政企分开，从两个竞争主体到多个竞争主体，走过一条“在发展中改革，在改革中发展”的成功道路。1994年以联通公司成立为标志，使电信业打破垄断，引入竞争机制。1998年后，进一步加大改革力度，实行政企分开、邮电分设，重组电信和联通，成立移动公司。

2001年，以打破固定电信领域的垄断为重点，实施企业、资源、业务和市场重组，全县形成联通、电信、移动3家基础电信企业竞争的格局。

2008年5月24日，工业和信息化部、国家发展和改革委员会、财政部联合发布《关于深化电信体制改革的通告》，实施电信重组。以发展第三代移动通信（简称3G）合理配置现有电信网络资源，既防止垄断，又避免过度竞争和重复建设。从而使电信资源配置进一步优化，竞争架构得到完善；自主创新成果规模应用，后续技术不断发展，自主创新能力显著提升；电信行业服务能力和水平进一步提高，监管体系继续加强，广大人民群众充分分享电信行业发展改革的成果，实现电信收购联通CDMA网（包括资产和用户），联通与网通合并，铁通并入移动的营业格局。

第一节　邮　政

一、邮路

1978年，县邮电局邮件业务邮路有省内邮路和县内邮路。省内邮路是省邮政局至县邮政局之间运输邮件的路线。县内邮路是县邮电局至各邮电局（所）之间运输邮件路线。

（一）过县境省内邮路

1978—2002年，贵阳至瓮安的自办汽车邮路通过县境，途经扎佐、修文、马家桥、久长。扎佐、修文、马家桥、久长等邮政局所进口邮件由该趟邮车运输。修文、马家桥的出口邮件，由该趟邮车运到久长卸下，然后由久长连同县局的出口邮件一起发当日瓮安至久长至扎佐（扎佐局出口邮件也发该趟邮车）至贵阳的自办汽车运输。

2003—2010年，贵阳至瓮安的自办汽车邮路改为贵阳至息烽自办汽车邮路。县境扎佐、修文、马家桥、久长等邮政局所的进口出口邮件接发照旧。

（二）县内邮路

在县邮政局的县内邮路中，原有自办汽车、摩托车、自行车、步班邮路，也有委办汽车，摩托车邮路。经过20多年的改革，基本上把自办邮路全部改为委办邮路。

修文至小箐至大石至六桶邮路　1978—2002年2月，小箐、大石、六桶等邮政局、所的进出口邮件由修文至六桶委办汽车运输，邮局派押运员押运邮件。2002年3月起，小箐、大石、六桶等邮政局、所的进出口邮件，县邮政局直接委托修文至六桶客车运输，邮局未派邮件押运员。2006—2010年，修文至六桶邮路自行派车运送。

修文至六广邮路　1978—2002年2月六广邮政支局的进出口邮件由该局派员用自行车运送到广田与修文至六桶委办汽车交接。2002年3月起，县邮政局将六广邮政支局的进出口邮件委托修文至六广客车运输，邮局未派邮件押运员。

修文至谷堡至乌栗邮路　1978—1979年，谷堡、乌栗邮电所的进出口邮件由修文至谷堡至乌栗至猫冲至修文的自办汽车运输。1980—1982年，由修文至谷堡至乌栗的自办摩托车运输。1983—1985年，由贵阳至修文至谷堡至乌栗的委办汽车运输，邮局派有押运员押运邮件。1986—1997年，由修文至谷堡的自办摩托车运输到谷堡，然后由谷堡派员用自行车将邮件运送到乌栗。1998—2002年2月，由修文至乌栗委办汽车运输，邮局派有押运员押运邮件。2002年3月起，县邮政局直接委托修文至乌栗客车运输，邮局

未派邮件押运员。2010年起，自办汽车运输。

修文至猫冲邮路 1978—1979年，猫冲邮电所的进出口邮件由修文至谷堡至乌栗至猫冲至修文的自办汽车运输。1980—1985年7月，由贵阳至猫冲的委办汽车运输，邮局派有押运员押运邮件。1985年8月—1989年5月，由谷堡邮电所派员步行送到猫冲。2010年起，由乌栗投递员投递。

修文至小山坝邮路 1978—1993年，小山坝邮电所的进出口邮件由修文至小山坝自办摩托车运输。1994—1998年，由承包人王宗祥用自行车运输。1999—2003年，由县局派员用自行车运输。2010年起，由水圹段投递员用摩托车投送。

修文至中寨邮路 1978—1983年，中寨邮电所的进出口邮件由修文至六级电站的委办汽车运输，邮局派有押运员押运邮件。1984年1月至5月，由小箐邮电支局派员用摩托车运输。1984年6月至1988年6月，由承包人步行送到小箐邮电支局交接。2010年起，由小箐支局投递员投送。

扎佐至天星桥邮路 1978—1979年，天星桥邮电所的进出口邮件由扎佐邮电支局派员用摩托车运输。1980—2003年，由501厂派员用摩托车运输。2010年，由扎佐投递员用摩托车投送。

扎佐至新民邮路 1978—1981年，新民邮电所的进出口邮件由扎佐邮电支局派员用摩托车运输。1982—2003年，由万江厂派员用摩托车运输，由邮局按行程补助厂方汽油和按天数补助厂方驾驶员出差费。2010年，由扎佐支局三元的投递员用汽车投送。

扎佐至水塘邮路 1978—1982年，水圹邮电所的进出口邮件由扎佐邮电支局派员用摩托车运输。1983—2003年，由兴红模具厂派员用摩托车运输。由邮局按行程补助厂方汽油和按天数补助厂方驾驶员出差费。2010年，由扎佐支局三元段投递员用自办汽车投送。

扎佐至高峰邮路 1978—1983年，高峰邮电所的进出口邮件由五三三技校派员用自行车、摩托车运输。1984—2003年，由五三三技校用摩托车运输，由邮局按行程补助校方汽油和按天数补助校方驾驶员出差费。2010年，由扎佐支局三元段投递员自办汽车投送。

扎佐至箐门口邮路 1978—2003年，箐门口邮政所的进出口邮件由该所用自行车运送到扎佐邮政支局交接。2010年起，由扎佐支局投递员自办汽车投送。

久长至金桥邮路 1978—1991年，金桥邮电所的进出口邮件由该所用自行车运送到久长邮电支局交接。2010年，由久长支局投递员用摩托车投送。

1978—2010年修文县邮路一览表

表3—04—01

序号	邮路名称	交通工具	班期	单程（公里）	实际行程
1	扎佐—修文	贵阳—开阳（息烽）自办邮车	逐日	17	17
2	修文—马家桥—久长	贵阳—开阳自办邮车—修文自办	逐日	17	17
3	修文—小箐—大石—六桶	修文—六桶委办汽车—修文自办	逐日	54	108
4	修文—谷堡—乌栗	委办汽车—修文自办	逐日	15	30
5	修文—小箐—六广	委办汽车—修文自办	逐日	40	80
6	小箐—洒坪	自行车—修文自办	间日	5	10
合计				148	262

（三）投递路线

县邮政局所至用户之间传递邮件的投递路线除人员班期变化外，一般变化不大。到2010年县邮政局有投递路线28条1229公里。

1978—2010年修文县投递路线一览表

表3—04—02

序号	投递线路名称	交通工具	班期	单程（公里）	实际行程
1	县城一段	自行车—摩托车	逐日	20	40
2	县城三段	自行车—摩托车	逐日	20	40
3	县城五段	自行车—摩托车	逐日	20	40
4	修文—王官	自行车—摩托车	间日	48	48
5	修文—程关	自行车—摩托车	间日	51	51
6	修文—新场	自行车—摩托车	间日	44	44
7	修文—阳早	自行车—摩托车	间日	38	38
8	修文—河口—小山坝	自行车—摩托车	逐日	38	38
9	谷堡—四级电站	步　班—摩托车	间日	10	20
10	乌栗—大寨	步　班—摩托车	间日	19	19
11	乌栗—大塘	步　班—摩托车	间日	20	20
12	马家桥—平地	自行车—摩托车	间日	40	40
13	马家桥—普陀	自行车—摩托车	间日	22	44
14	久长—石安	自行车—摩托车	间日	25	50
15	久长—清水	自行车—摩托车	间日	23	46
16	扎佐—把七	自行车—摩托车	间日	40	40
17	扎佐—六屯—桃源	自行车—摩托车	间日	44	88
18	扎佐—三元	自行车—摩托车	间日	41	41
19	小箐—洒坪—中寨	步　班—摩托车	间日	29	58
20	小箐—马场—崇恩	步　班—摩托车	间日	28	56
21	六广—沙坡	步　班—摩托车	间日	29	58
22	六广—广田	步　班—摩托车	间日	23	46
23	大石—大屯—高山	步　班—摩托车	间日	23	46
24	大石—回水—德政	步　班—摩托车	间日	23	46
25	六桶—凉井—宝寨	步　班—摩托车	间日	22	44
26	六桶—花椰—木林	步　班—摩托车	间日	27	54
27	六广—索风营	步　班—摩托车	逐日	17	34
28	扎佐镇投递段	自行车—摩托车	逐日	20	40
合计				804	1229

二、业务

（一）经营范围

邮政业务分为主营业务与代办业务两大类。主营业务为函件、包件、机要文件、特快专递、汇兑、报刊发行、邮政储蓄、集邮等。代办业务为代收电话费、代办身份证、代办驾驶执照、代售火车票、代售飞机票、代办物资流动等。

（二）邮件处理

业务窗口

邮件按内件性质分为函件和包件。函件包括信函、明信片、邮简、印刷品、盲人读物、邮送广告等；包件包括包裹、直投包裹。邮件按传递时限分为普通邮件和特快专递邮件。普通邮件是按照一般时限传递处理的邮件，包括普通函件、普通包件。特快专递邮件是以最快速度传递处理的邮件，包括特快专递函件、特快专递包件。按处理手续分为平常邮件和给据邮件。平常邮件收寄时不给收据，处理时不登记，投递时不需收件人签收，不接受查询，不承担赔偿责任。给据邮件收寄时出具收据，处理时进行登记，投递时需收件人签收，并接受查询及承担赔偿责任。给据邮件按邮政局所负的赔偿责任，分为保价邮件和非保价邮件。对保价邮件，承担按保价金额赔偿责任。对非保价邮件，按规定限额承担赔偿责任。函件按寄递区域分本埠函件和外埠函件。本埠函件以地级以上城市，以及所属城区（不包括市辖县和飞地）为范围；县（含县级市）以县（市）境内（不含飞地）为范围；在上述范围内互寄的函件为本埠函件，范围超过本埠函件互寄范围的函件为外埠函件。

（三）邮政储汇

1.邮政汇兑

邮政汇兑网点　1978—2001年8月，县邮政局所属邮政支局、邮政所（除大石外）均为传统邮政汇兑网点。县邮政局及龙场、扎佐、久长、六广等邮政支局、所为电子汇兑联网网点。小箐、六桶、谷堡等邮政支局、所为电子汇兑手工网点。

邮政电子汇款业务种类　按时限分为投单通知汇款、24小时汇款、2小时汇款、实时汇款、次日入账汇款、实时入账汇款。

运用现代信息技术改造传统邮政汇兑业务　2001年7月1日，国家邮政局在全国开办电子汇兑业务，9月1日县邮政局正式开办邮政电子汇兑业务。邮政电子汇兑由国家邮政局汇兑中心、省邮政局电子汇兑中心、县（市）邮政局电子汇兑中心和汇兑网点四级机构组成。

2.储蓄

储蓄网点　1987年7月26日，县邮电局邮政储蓄网点开业。1992年12月11日，扎佐邮电支局邮政储蓄网点开业。1994年12月18日，久长邮电支局邮政储蓄网点开业。1994年4月18日，六广邮电支局邮政储蓄网点开业。2004年12月24日龙场镇邮政所邮政储蓄网点开业。截至2005年12月31日，全县有4个邮政储蓄网点。

储蓄种类 储蓄种类分为定期储蓄、活期储蓄、定活两便储蓄、邮政储蓄延伸业务等。定期储蓄包括整存整取、零存整取、存本取息、整存零取、通知存款等。整存整取以50元起存，多存不限。存期分3个月、半年、1年、2年、3年、5年6个档次。邮局发给存单，到期凭存单或密码1次支取本息。零存整取以5元起存，多存不限。存期分1年、3年、5年3个档次。零存整取定期储蓄有两种存款方式：第一种每月存1次，每次存款金额固定；第二种每月存款次数和存款金额都不固定。两者计息结果一致。邮局发给存折，到期凭存折或密码一次支取本息。存本取息以5000元起存，一次存入本金，分次支取利息。存期分1年、3年、5年3个档次。邮局发给存折，储户凭存折分期取息，到期时一次取回本金。整存零取，一次存入本金，存期分1年、3年、5年3种，邮局发给存折，以后凭存折分期支取本金，利息于到期结清时一次支付。通知存款，本金一次存入，不约定期限，可一次或分多次支取部分本金利息。起存金额500元以上，多存不限，最长存期3年，支取时可全部支取，也可以多次部分支取，且未支取部分仍按原存入日计息，取款金额在规定数额以上的需要提前通知邮局。活期储蓄随时可存，随时可取，存取次数和金额不受限制，灵活方便。活期储蓄存款1元起存，多存不限。邮局发给存折，凭存折可以随时办理存取款。定活两便储蓄储户在存款时不确定存期，随时可以支取，利率随存期长短而变动。邮局发给存单，存单金额固定为50元、100元、500元、1000元4种，并在一定范围内（如县、市内）实行通取。邮政储蓄延伸业务主要包括11185电话银行业务、代收代缴业务、邮政储蓄绿卡等。2010年，县邮政储蓄余额1.82亿元，占全县金融市场份额的6.58%。

邮政储蓄

用现代信息化的技术发展邮政储蓄业务 1987年县邮政局开办邮政储蓄业务是手工操作，储蓄户仅410户，余额为26.7万元。2002年9月邮政储蓄和邮政电子汇兑实现全国联网，国家邮政局进行邮政储蓄计算机系统应用软件的统一版本工程建设 。将邮政储蓄业务系统和中间业务系统相对隔离并有机结合，以邮政储蓄业务处理为基础，以客户为管理中心，将客户账户数据集中于省(区、市)中心，并充分考虑与全国数据大集中的衔接，建立一整套包括邮政储蓄业务处理、会计核算、资金清算、信息管理、事后监督在内的和将风险控制贯穿始终的邮政储蓄应用软件统一版本，实现邮政储蓄全国通存通取。2004年9月1日，县邮政局各储蓄网点和全国邮政储蓄统一版本计算机系统联网，特别是实现全国邮政储蓄和邮政电子汇兑联网，扩大邮政储蓄余额来源。为保证邮政储蓄资金安全，重要地方都安装监控摄像设备和布设报警系统，并与110报警系统联网，且用的是数字监控系统设备。由于设备优化，扩大 储源，储户增多。至2005年，储户3.02万户，邮政储蓄余额达9053万元。

三、邮政编码

1989年，邮电部根据《中华人民共和国邮政法》第二十五条“寄递邮件逐步实行邮政编码”规定，在全国推行邮政编码，以便于邮件分拣和传递。

邮政编码采用四级六位数编码，分别代表省、邮区、县（市），投递点四级。其中，前二位表示省，前三位表示邮区，前四位表示县（市），最后两位表示投递局（区）。

1989年县内邮政编码顺序排列一览表

表3—04—03

单位名称	邮政编码	单位名称	邮政编码
县邮电局	550200	谷堡邮电所(108厂)	550213
扎佐邮电支局	550201	小箐邮电支局	550214
天星桥邮电支局(501厂)	550202	六广邮电支局	550215
新民邮电所(万江厂)	550203	大石邮电所	550216
高峰邮电所(航空技校)	550204	六桶邮电所	550217
水塘邮电所(166厂)	550205	马家桥邮电所	550218
庆门口邮电所(418库)	550206	猫冲邮电所(水电九局)	550210
久长邮电支局	550207	中寨邮电 所(六级电站)	550211
金桥邮电所(峰光厂)	550208	乌栗邮电所(五级电站)	550212
小山坝邮电所	550209		

四、邮政资费

1978年县邮政局执行的邮政资费是邮电部1953年5月国家币制改革时颁发的邮政资费标准，平常信函每20克或其零数，本埠0.04元，外埠0.08元，挂号信每件0.2元（挂号费0.12元+平信费0.08元）。

1990年7月31日经国务院批准，邮电部从即日起进行邮政资费调整，这次调整的主要是平常函件、印刷品、挂号信、包裹资费。平常函件，每重20克或其零数，本埠由0.04元调为0.10元，外埠由0.08元调整为0.2元。挂号信由0.2元调为0.5元。

1992年6月30日经国务院批准，邮电部从即日起，调整部分邮政资费。每10克航空费由0.05元调为0.1元，邮件快件费由0.8调为1元。

1996年12月经国务院批准，邮电部从即日起，调整部分邮政资费，外埠平常函件每20克或其零数由0.2元调为0.5元，挂号函件由0.5元调为0.7元。

1999年3月1日起经国务院批准，国家邮政局从即日起，进行邮政资费调整。国内信函首重100克内，每重20克，本埠0.6元，外埠0.8元。挂号费调为2元。

2005年2月贵州省邮政局出台《邮政资费手册》对某些邮政资费进行调整。挂号费由2元调到3元。

第二节　电　信

一、电报

（一）电报种类

1978—1984年分为防空电报、天气电报、水情电报、军政电报、新闻电报、普通电报、汇款电报、公电8种；1985年起改为天气电报、水情电报、公益电报、政务电报、新闻电报、普通电报、汇款电报、公电8种。1991年后，电报退出公共通信领域。

(二) 电报服务与时限

1978—1991年，县邮电局的电报服务水平为县城的电报直投（白天随到随投）。直投范围：东至阳明洞，南至县农场，西至县政府，北至酱油厂。各邮电支局的电报直投范围以支局所在地集镇为界。不属于直投范围的电报，按邮政班期投递。其间县邮电局到邮电支局利用电话电路话传电报，县局电报房收到的来报，可以随收随传到支局投递。支局收受的去报可以随收随传到县局电报房拍发。除邮电内部话传电报外，水电九局、航空工业部166厂、355厂、3117厂、1028厂、418库、533技校、501厂，贵州省105地质队等单位发出的电报，由该单位指定通过培训的专人直接将电报话传到县邮电局电报房拍发，全国各地传来单位的电报，由县邮电局电报房直接话传给单位指定的专人。电报在收、发报局之间的时限为：加急电报4小时，普通电报6小时。1992年县邮电局收发电报设备改为微机收发电报，可译五笔字型汉字。1997年县邮电局收发电报的微机可以自动诠译电码。传输设备接入数据通信网（DDN），用“英特网”的一个通道收发电报。发报局发出去的电报，由发报局加密通过“特英网”发对方局。收报局收到的电报，通过解密后按规定投送给收报人。电报全程时限规定加急电报240分钟，普通电报360分钟。但局与局之间的实际时限一般只需要30分钟左右。

(三) 电报处理

1978—1991年，县邮电局有专职报务员3人，电报投递员1人，各邮电支局由话务员兼办电报业务，各邮电所由营业员兼办电报业务。县局使用的电报设备是两台电传打字机和1条通过插报机修文—贵阳的载波电路。各分支机构使用电话电路话传电报。其间年来报收电报量1.4万至1.9万份，年去报发电报量1.2万份至1.8万份。继后，电话逐渐普及，电报业务减少，1992—2000年每年电报量降到5000至6000份，2001—2010年每年仅300份左右。

(四) 传真

1979年县邮电局配置传真机1台办理传真业务。由于传真业务费用较高，基本上无用户，传真机主要供邮电内部使用。继后，传真业务分为公众传真和用户传真两种，随着办公设备现代化，县委、县人民政府和中央、省、市驻县大型企业陆续自购传真机利用邮电网络传递内部文件及资料，也有市民到县电信局发传真传递相关证件身份证、结婚证、独生子女证、图纸、图片、照片等。

二、长途电话

(一) 人工长途电话

人工长途电话交换机和长途电路 1978年，县邮电局设置长、市、农合用人工磁石式电话交换机2台，容量200门。有一端LW-204型三路晶体管载波电话终端机用架空明线和贵阳对开。有修文至贵阳长途电路3条和修文至贵阳至安顺长途电路3条。1984年7月，省邮电管理局配给县局一端ZD-26型12路晶体管载波电话终端机用架空明线和贵阳对开。有修文至贵阳长途电路6条和修文至贵阳至安顺长途电路6条。1986年，县邮电局长、市、农合用交换机扩容为300门，总容量达到500门。1987年7月，川黔同轴电缆建设工程途经县境的三元、扎佐、久长、驴坊、石榴，长途电话线路使用同轴电缆。1989年8月，省邮电管理局配给县邮电局两端LFFD24路载波电话终端机用同轴电缆线路和贵阳对开，配给县邮电局一端LM305A12路载波电话终端机用同轴电缆线路和息烽对开，配给县邮电局一端LM305A12路载波电话终端

机用架空明线和开阳对开。有修文至贵阳长途电路8条，修文至贵阳至安顺长途电路6条，修文至开阳长途电路2条，修文至息烽长途电路2条。

长途电话人工台交换处理 长途电话人工台实行迟缓的接续方法，即用户挂号后要挂机等候，由话务员按照规定的接续顺序通报受话局，再由受话局找到受话人后回叫发话局接通用户通话。1978至1992年7月县邮电局长途电话人工台是长途电话、市内电话、农村电话合设的200至500门磁石式电话交换机，每班由2名话务员值守，实行昼夜值班每班8小时，1名负责长途电话和农村电话的接续处理，1名负责市内电话的接续处理，在工作中互相协作配合，共同完成长途电话、市内电话、农村电话的接续处理工作。县邮电局经办的长途电话分为去话（县局用户发往各地的长途电话）和来话（各地发往县局的长途电话）。

长途电话人工台的交换处理程序 受理用户挂号先是按排列顺序向对方局通报，然后接续发、受话人通话。在开始通话和通话过程中进行监听，通话完毕计算并向用户通报通话分钟后拆线。

长途电话接续顺序 长途电话按照业务种类和计费等级排列接续顺序。同一接续顺序的电话按挂号时刻先后通报接续。长途电话顺序为：防空情报电话，特种电话，紧急调度电话，政务电话，加急普通电话、加急公务电话、加急业务电话，普通电话、公务、业务电话。若遇电报电路阻断则经长途电话电路话传电报时，分别列入天气电报、水情电报、特急电报、加急电报、普通电报顺序接续处理。国际电话在国内电路上的接续顺序为国际遇险电话，国际政务电话，国际加急业务、加急私务电话，国际业务、私务电话。人工运作的长途电话经转的长途台多，处理程序多，接续顺序多，要挂一个长途电话，要等候许多时间，有时还挂不通，故长途电话业务发展较慢。

（二）半自动和自动长途电话

1986年11月1日，县邮电局长途台至安顺地区邮电局长途台半自动电话开通，仅限于修文长途台和安顺长途台之间互相拨电话。

1989年3月28日，修文至贵阳至安顺半自动长途电话开通，省邮电管理局通知县邮电局启用08637区号，县邮电局长途台直拨贵阳市内和安顺市内的电话用户。与此同时，两城市的用户也可以直拨修文县邮电局长途台接通受话人。

1992年8月22日凌晨3时，县邮电局正式割接开通从日本引进的纵横制1000门自动电话。

1993年1月9日，邮电部批准县邮电局自动电话进入全国长途电话自动化网，区号为08637。此时，县城市内电话用户可以直拨已进入全国长途电话自动化网的用户。

（三）长途程控电话交换设备和传输设备

1993年5月24日12时，久长邮电支局开通河北保定模拟式64门数字程控电话。8月20日零时，扎佐邮电支局开通奔吉HJ-10D200门数字程控电话。9月28日零时，县邮电局开通贝尔S-1240数字程控电话1000门。1994年9月29日17时20分，六广邮电支局开通奔吉HJ-10D128门数字程控电话。1995年6月28日起，福州—杭州—贵阳—成都光纤电缆建设工程，先后途经县境内杉树林—王官—修文—马家桥—普陀—上寨—驴坊—石榴。10月16日，县邮电局长途电话电路全部使用光纤电路。同日省邮电管理局通知县邮电局分组交换网直接进入贵阳分组交换网，长途电话区号改为0851。此后，中央、省、市驻县境内的355厂、501厂、166厂、533技校、418库、贵铝一矿等单位，申请进入县邮电局电信通信网，数千个用户安装程控电话。程控电话经过历年扩容，到2004年，程控电话交换机总容量达到3.41万门；程控电话用户达到2.13万户；长途电话业务收入达到200万元，是1978年1.4万元的143倍。

（四）IP长途电话

2001年1月，县电信局开办IP长途电话业务（17900），在固定电话机上使用电话卡业务。用户可以在任何一部双音频电话机上使用该项业务，所产生的电话费通过IP电话卡记账扣出。此后推出IP电话卡（17908）业务，开放范围为市内固定电话、国内和国际长途电话。用户可利用市内任何一部双音频电话机使用，所产生的IP通话费，通过IP电话卡记账扣除，对所使用的电话不计费。

（五）可视电话会议

1997年6月24日，县邮电局开通可视电话会议义务，利用数字传输电路，两个或两个以上地点实时传递点对点或一点对多点的活动图像和声音。主会场和分会场可以互相看到图像，使电话会议进入现代化。继后又安装有投影设备。

三、市内电话

（一）市内电话设备

1978年，全县市内电话杆路，使用的是水泥电杆和木电杆。市内电话线路主要是架空铁线和部分电缆。市内电话用户261户。1986年县邮电局长、市、农合用磁石电话交换机扩容300门，总容量达到500门。

1991年7月，县人民政府与安顺地区邮电局签订《修文县程控电话建设协议书》。

1992年县委、县人民政府提出“以交通通信为龙头，全面发展修文县经济”的战略目标，在人力、物力、财力上给邮电部门大力支持。各级邮电部门积极主动的把县城程控电话建设所需的资金、物资、设计、施工、安装等工作做到位。由于各级邮电部门与地方政府配合默契，县城程控电话建设前期工作进展顺利。但程控电话交换机主机不能及时到位。1992年8月22日凌晨3点，纵横制自动电话交换机1000门开通。市内自动电话号码为五位（22000-22999）。1993年1月9日零时，邮电部批准修文县城自动电话进入全国长途电话自动化网，区号为08637。9月28日零时，县城S-1240型1000门程控电话交换机开通，县电话号码由5位升6位，即原电话号码22006升322006。至此，县城电话用户甩掉手摇电话机。1995年10月30日扩容S-1240型1000门。1996年7月13日，修文县电话号码由6位升为7位，原电话号码为322018号升为2322018号。此时，县城的主要线路设备为地埋光缆和电缆。1997年7月26日扩容S-1240型3000门。1998年9月6日扩容S-1240型5288门。1999年11月10日县城机关单位、职工宿舍、街道居民宿舍户线工程开工，12月29日竣工。该工程把三层以上楼房（含机关单位、职工宿舍、街道居民宿舍）不论安装电话或未安装电话的用户，邮电局都把安装电话用的电缆线安装到每家每户门边，方便安装，方便维修，保证质量。程控电话加上光缆电路，接续时间快，通话质量好，很受用户欢迎。2002年7月4日扩容S-1240型2952门。到2004年12月31日，县城程控电话总容量达到1.33万门，程控电话用户达到8285户，2010年增到2.62万户。

（二）IC电话卡（无人值守公用电话）

IC卡又叫集成电路卡，形状与名片相似。1997年首期在县境扎佐贵阳高尔夫度假中心开通10门IC电

话卡，2002年在县城开通512门IC电话卡，到2007年因业务萎缩及城市建设影响IC电话全部拆除。开通期间持卡人通过卡正面镶嵌的集成电路（IC）芯片与IC话机内读卡器的接触实现通话，只要不划伤芯片都可以使用。由于芯片是金属制造，故易受空气氧化，芯片若氧化就会与话机读卡器接触不良而影响卡的有效使用，如果话机显示出“错卡”字样，只需用橡皮擦把芯片表面氧化物擦净就可继续使用。

（三）有人值守公用电话

电信部门为方便未安装电话的用户和流动用户使用电话，推出有人值守公用电话。1993年前，公用电话主要安装在邮电机构的营业窗口，用户使用公话，要到邮电机构营业窗口办理。1994年城乡开通程控电话，公用电话普及到城乡报刊亭和商业门面，县城出现多家公话超市，到2004年全县城乡的公用电话达到511户。继后，由于程控电话和移动电话普及，到2010年有人值守公用电话仅存15户。

（四）200电话卡业务

1996年，县邮电部门开通200电话业务全称为密码记账式电话卡业务，凡持有200卡的用户，可在贵州省内各地公用电话、用户小交换机、住宅电话和单位的任何一部双音频电话机上，通过卡号记账的方式拨打本地电话和国内、国际长途电话。200业务卡除将呼叫产生的费用记在账卡账号上外，还具有依目的码进行限制、限值指示、密码设置、连续进行呼叫、卡号和密码转入次数的限制、修改密码、防止欺骗、查询余额、缩位拨号、修改缩位拨号、设置重拨、设置和使用缩位拨号、余额转移等功能。200电话业务资费与固定电话收费标准相同。

（五）201校园卡

2001年在扎佐省林业学校开通300门201电话，用户通过拨打201特服号，在本网指定范围内的双音频电话机上以自动密码记账方式拨打市内电话、国内长途电话、国际长途电话业务。201卡与200卡类似，用户在规定的双音频电话机上依次转入账号和密码，通过电信网络系统确认后即可打电话，且能拨号上网。201卡具有修改密码和查询余额等功能。持有201电话卡者，可拨打本地网电话、国内长途电话和国际长途电话。继后，受移动电话普及影响，该业务逐步萎缩，到2008年201业务全部退出。

（六）300卡电话

中国电话卡300业务是在智能网上向社会开放的记账式电话卡业务。县邮电局于1996年开通，用户通过任何一部双音频电话机，以密码记账方式拨打本地网电话、国内和国际长途电话。300卡电话业务比200卡电话业务功能更多，还实现全国范围内的联网，做到一卡到手，走遍全国均可拨打电话。300电话卡可以在全国县（市）级以上城市使用；每一步都有语音提示引导用户拨号；用户自设密码，并且可以随时修改密码；提供缩位拨号、修改密码、查询话费余额、连续呼叫和限制呼叫等多种功能服务。

四、农村电话

（一）人工阶段农村电话主要设备

1978年县邮电局为适应修文县工农业生产的发展，对农村电话通信设备进行更新改造，县至扎佐、久长、小箐、六广区中继线电话杆路由木杆改为水泥杆，杆路总长224杆公里；电话线路由铁线改为铜线，线路总长349对公里，除实线外，开通单路载波电话终端机，修文至扎佐开通三路载波电话终端机。时有扎佐、久长、小箐、六广、六桶5个交换点，5台磁石电话交换机，交换机总容量210门；电话用户149户，农村电话通话4.4万张。从1986年起县邮电局至区乡交换机之间陆续实现半自动拨号。

（二）农村电话人工台交换处理

县邮电局农村电话人工台的交换处理程序首先是受理用户挂号，然后按排列顺序向对方局通报，接续发、受话人通话，在始话时和通话过程中进行监听，通话完毕即计算向用户通报通话分钟并拆线。

（三）农村电话接续顺序

农村电话按照业务种类和计费等级排列接续顺序。遇同一接续顺序的电话则按挂号时刻先后接续。农村电话接续顺序分为防空电话、中央首长电话、特种电话、紧急调度电话、特级公务业务电话、中央各部委各省省长地方首长电话、加急军政电话、加急新闻电话、加急公务业务电话、军政电话、新闻电话，普通电话、公务业务电话。若遇长途电话在农村电话电路上接续时则接在同类农村电话之前。

2009年乡村入户线路检修

（四）程控电话阶段主要设备

传输设备 1997年1月5日贵阳市电信局建设部与城关镇、扎佐镇政府召开联席会议，就城关镇、扎佐镇程控电话扩容改造工程中的光缆工程挖沟补偿问题达成协议，32沟公里光缆工程由城关镇、扎佐镇组织民兵施工，邮电部门补助23万元，其余由地方政府负责。工程于当年2至5月完成。1998年3月10日，谷堡、小箐、洒坪、六广、大石、六桶等乡（镇）光缆工程进场施工，5月14日竣工。该项工程由中国人民解放军56274部队80分队施工。至此，全县10个乡（镇）全部通光缆。继后光缆又向中央、省、市驻县厂矿企事业单位和村级接入网延伸。到2003年全县光缆达到263皮长公里。为解决好“三农”通电话问题，县电信局架通多数村的光缆电缆线路，全县电缆长度为560皮长公里，光缆和电缆资产原值达到2900多万元。

程控电话设备 1993年5月24日12时，久长邮电支局开通河北保定模拟式64门数字程控电话。8月20日，扎佐邮电支局开通奔吉HJ-D200门程控电话。1994年9月29日，六广邮电支局开通奔吉HJ-D128门程控电话。1996年9月8日，久长邮电支局扩容为奔吉HJ-D128门程控电话。1997年2月3日，万江厂开通540线对光环程控电话。1998年11月26日改为S-1240型模块，同时开通6芯光纤电缆。1997年2月27日，修文至扎佐12芯光纤电缆开通。同时，扎佐邮电支局扩容S-1240型1000门程控电话。8月1日，修文至马家桥6芯光纤电缆开通。11月6日，修文至久长6芯光纤电缆开通。1998年7月1日，小箐、洒坪、六桶512门程控电话6芯光纤电缆、广田496门程控电话6芯光纤电缆、大石256门程控电话6芯光纤电缆、回水224门程控电话6芯光纤电缆和六广6芯光纤电缆同时开通。8月1日，马家桥1280门程控电话6芯光纤电缆开通。9月28日，六屯512门程控电话6芯光纤电缆开通。10月21日，761矿500线对光环程控电话6芯光纤电缆开通。11月30日，501厂500线对光环程控电话6芯光纤电缆开通。12月24日，533技校564门程控电话6芯光纤电缆开通。12月26日，高尔夫1000门程控电话6芯光纤电缆和418库336门程控电话6芯光纤电缆开通。1999年1月1日，谷堡256门程控电话6芯光纤电缆开通。1月28日，1028厂756门程控电话6芯光纤电缆开通。8月1日，乌栗256门程控电话6芯光纤电缆开通。11月28日，扎佐扩容S-1240型1000门程控电话。2000年12月6日，平滩128门程控电话6芯光纤电缆开通。2001年5月22日，马关256门程控电话6芯光纤电缆开通。26日六广扩容华为HONET型1024门程控电话。30日中寨208门程控电话6芯光纤电缆开通。6月1日，崇恩159门程控电话6芯光纤电缆开通。27日，马场128门程控电话6芯光纤电缆开通。2002年1月28日，中哨128门程控电话6芯光纤电缆开通。4月10日，县电信局借省内二干光纤电缆直埋工程途经修文至久长的机会，直埋修文至久长方向光纤电缆24芯。其中修文至马家桥12芯，马家桥用6芯，马家桥至下堡用6芯；修文至久长12芯。5月6日，扎佐扩容S-1240型1968门程控电话。16日久长扩容华为HONET型2048门。21日清让432门程控电话6芯光纤电缆开通。28日，索风营500门程控电话6芯光纤电缆开通。9月14日，上寨224门程控电话6芯光纤电缆开通。11月14日，清水224门、场坝224门程控电话各6芯光纤电缆开通。12月28日，把七128门程控电话6芯光纤电缆开通。2003年3月3日，扎佐开发区1536门程控电话6芯光纤电缆开通。5月22日，驴坊622门程控电话6芯光纤电缆开通。8月8日，中心224门程控电话6芯光纤电缆开通。2004年1月6日，修文至扎佐用架空方式新增36芯光纤电缆和修文至久长用架空方式新增12芯光纤电缆。12月8日，下堡224门程控电话6芯光纤电缆开通。到2004年底，农村有程控电话接入网点37处全部通光纤电缆，程控电话在线容量达到2.09万门，比1978年的210门增长99.5倍。程控电话用户达到1.39万户，比1978年的149户增长93.3倍。仅久长镇驴坊村就有程控电话435部，超过1978年全县农村电话用户的总数。

五、程控电话接入网

自1993年开通程控电话后，逐步把长途电话、市内电话和农村电话接入程控电话交换机，并架通全县各乡镇光缆，组建本地电话网，实现传输数字化，交换程控化。

（一）县局母局程控电话接入网

1978年，县局母局是长途、市内和农村合设的200门磁石电话交换机。1986年扩容为长、市、农合设500门磁石电话交换机。1992年8月22日开通从日本引进的二手设备纵横制C23型1000门自动电话交换机。1993年9月28日开通S-1240型1000门程控电话交换机，同时停用C23型1000门交换机。1995年10月30日扩容S-1240型1000门程控交换机。1997年7月26日扩容S-1240型3000门程控交换机。1998年9月6日扩容S-1240型5288门程控交换机。在县局（即城关片区）管理维护范围内，2004年有程控电话交换机在线容量1.66万门，其中县局母局1.29万门，河滨花园2952门，马家桥1088门，马关256门，一矿512门，谷堡256门，乌栗256门，崇恩160门，中哨128门，平滩176门，场坝288门，观音山200门。从2005到2010年，固定电话用户从1.27万户增到1.4万户，宽带用户从2420户增到3125户。手机用户2009年始办，到2010年达到1.03万户。剔除扎佐、久长、六广3个支局的收入后，县局电信收入从2005年的774万元增到2010年的1550万元。

县局程控交换机

（二）扎佐母局程控电话接入网

1978—1992年，扎佐母局使用的是1台50门磁石交换机，1992年5月22日县人民政府召开办公会议研究扎佐镇程控电话建设，达成在扎佐镇建设程控电话的共识，10月21日县邮电局与扎佐镇签订《程控电话建设协议书》。1993年8月20日零时扎佐母局开通奔吉HJ-10D200门程控电话。1997年2月27日扩容S-1240型1000门程控电话。同时开始使用修文-扎佐12芯光纤电缆。2002年5月6日，扩容S-1240型1986门程控电话。2004年8月17日，扩容华为接入网928门。在扎佐母局维护管理范围内有程控电话交换机在线容量9784门，其中母局2976门，六屯512门，清让432门，把七160门，扎佐开发区1536门，万江厂1512门，兴红厂756门，418库336门，533技校564门，高尔夫1000门。共有电话用户6623户电信业务收入196万元。从2005到2010年，固定电话用户从6856户增到7384户，宽带用户从952户增到1185户，手机用户从2009年开始到2010年达2568户。全局电信收入从283万元增到452万元。

（三）久长母局程控电话接入网

1978—1992年，久长母局使用的是1台40门磁石电话交换机，1993年5月24日开通河北保定模拟式64门程控电话。1996年9月8日扩容为HJ-10D型128门程控交换机。1997年11月16日修文至久长6芯光纤电缆开通，2002年4月10日县局借省内二干直埋工程途经久长的机会直埋修文至久长方向光纤电缆24芯，其中修文至马家桥12芯，马家桥使用6芯，其余6芯由马家桥至下堡使用；修文至久长12芯。2002年5月6日久长母局扩容华为HONET型2048门程控电话，原模拟式64门程控电话交换机停用。在久长母局维护管理范围内，2004年有程控电话在线总容量3849门，其中久长局2048门（含761矿），凤凰山204门，上寨224门，驴坊608门，清水320门，中心224门，下堡224门。共有电话用户2572户，电信收入84万元。2005年到2010年，固定电话用户从2688户增到2805户，宽带用户从185户增到276户，手机用户从2009年始办，到2010年达726户。全局电信收入从98万元增到135万元。

（四）六广母局程控电话接入网

1978—1993年，六广母局使用的是1台50门磁石电话交换机。1994年9月29日开通奔吉HJ-10D型128门程控电话交换机。1998年7月10日开始使用广田-六广6芯光纤电缆。2001年5月26日六广扩容为华为HONET型1024门程控电话。在六广母局维护管理范围内，2004年有程控电话在线容量3936门，其中母局1024门（含索风营电站），马场128门，小箐512门，洒坪512门，中寨256门，广田496门；大石272门，回水224门，六桶512门。共有电话用户2433户，电信业务收入128万元。从2005年到2010年，固定电话用户从2487户降到2043户，宽带用户从62户增到105户，手机用户2009年开始办理，到2010年达398户。全局电信收入从132万元降到116万元。

（五）其他程控电话接入网

1978—2003年，除母局程控电话接入网外，全县还有贵航集团533技校、兴红厂、万江厂、418库和贵铝一矿、小箐、六桶、马家桥、谷堡、河滨花园、中哨、马关、乌栗、平滩、场坝、崇恩、马场、洒坪、中寨、广田、大石、回水、凤凰山、驴坊、中心、上寨、清水、高尔夫、扎佐经济开发区、六屯、清让、把七、761矿、索风营电站、观音山、下堡等36处程控电话接入网。2004年2月，中哨介入网扩容，2006年7月新建龙场镇木厂接入网，2007年11月新建平营接入网和久长镇清江接入网，2008年8月新建扎佐镇三里接入网，2010年4至6月，又在部分村寨、公司、生活区增建NGN局等站点73个，至年末固定电话用户达到7264户，宽带用户达3392户。

六、电话号码资源

电话号码资源是县电信企业文化的重要组成部分，电话号码分为长途电话区号和本地网电话号码两部分。

（一）长途电话区号

长途电话区号是邮电部按照国家划定的行政区来编排的自动电话号码。1989年3月18日，修文县的长途电话区号为08637，08代表贵州省编号，63代表安顺地区编号，7代表修文县编号。1995年10月16日，修文县的长途电话区号为0851，08代表贵州省编号，51代表贵阳市编号，贵阳市管辖的一市三县五郊区均使用0851长途电话区号。

（二）五位数电话号码分配

1992年8月22日，县邮电局正式割接开通从日本引进的二手设备纵横制1000门自动电话交换机，县城电话用户使用上自动电话，自动电话号码为5位数即：22000—22999。电话号码前1位数的“2”代表修文县编号，第2位数以后的号码代表用户编号。

（三）六位数电话号码分配

1993年3月3日，县邮电局出版第二部电话号码簿时，电话号码由5位数升为6位数。5月24日12时，久长邮电支局开通河北保定模拟式64门程控电话交换机。8月20日零时扎佐邮电支局开通重庆奔吉HJ—10D200门程控电话交换机。9月28日县邮电局开通上海贝尔S—1240型1000门程控电话交换机。1994年9月29日17时20分六广邮电支局开通奔吉HJ—10D128门程控电话交换机。上述地区的程控电话开通后，全县各地区使用的六位数电话号码，前1位数代表修文县编号，第2位数代表程控电话接入网编号，第3位数以后的号码代表用户编号。当时的电话号码分配：县邮电局程控电话接入网320000—349999，扎佐邮电支局程控电话接入网350000—359999，久长邮电支局程控电话接入网360000—369999，六广邮电支局程控电话接入网550000—559999。

（四）七位数电话号码分配

1996年7月13日，县的电话号码由6位数升为7位数，与贵阳联网。县城、谷堡、扎佐、六屯、久长、小箐、洒坪等地在原号码前加“2”；六广、大石、六桶等地去掉原号码头“5”加“24”。升位后，前两位数号码代表修文县编号，第3位数号码代表程控电话接入网编号，第4位数以后的号码代表用户编号。电话号码分配：县邮电局母局程控电话接入网2322000—2329999，2330000—2332287，河滨花园程控电话接入网2370000—2372927，马家桥程控电话接入网2310000—2311087，观音山程控电话接入网2311800—2311999，一矿程控电话接入网2312000—2312511，谷堡程控电话接入网2410000—2410255，场坝程控电话接入网2411000—2411223，平滩程控电话接入网2415000—2415911，乌栗程控电话接入网2413000—2413255。扎佐邮电支局程控电话接入网2260000—2260927，2352000—2353999、2353920—2353967。扎佐高尔夫程控电话接入网2351000—2351999，扎佐经济开发区程控电话接入网2354000—2355535，扎佐533技校程控电话接入网2356000—2356499、2367512—2367575，扎佐1028程控电话接入网2356500—2356999、2366000—2366255，扎佐万江程控电话接入网2357000—2357999，六屯程控电话接入网2358000—2358511，扎佐418库程控电话接入网2359000—2359335，清让程控电话接入网2430000—2430431，把七程控电话接入网2430500—2430659，久长邮电支局（当时称谓）程控电话接入网2362000—2364047，凤凰山程控电话接入网2361000—2361200，清水程控电话接入网2434000—2434319，上寨程控电话接入网2435000—2435223，驴坊程控电话接入网2436000—2436607，中心程控电话接入网2437000—2437223，马关程控电话接入网2300000—2300255，六广邮电支局（当时称谓）程控电话接入网2452000—2453023，小箐邮电支局（当时称谓）程控电话接入网2420000—2420511，崇恩程控电话接入网2422000—2422159，马场程控电话接入网2423000—2423127，回水程控电话接入网2424000—2424223，洒坪程控电话接入网2440000—2440511，中寨程控电话接入网2443000—2443255，广田程控电话接入网2456000—2456495，索风营程控电话接入网2456500—2456999，六桶程控电话接入网2470000—2470511，大石程控电话接入网2490000—2490271，下堡程控电话接入网2416000—2416223。

（六）编辑出版电话号码簿

自开通自动电话、程控电话后，用户使用自动电话、程控电话必须有电话号码。为方便电话用户查找电话号码，县邮电局于1993年、1994年、2000年先后编辑出版《修文县电话号码簿》送给本地固定电话用户使用。还将修文县电话号码资料提供给省、市电信部门，供他们编辑出版全省全市电话号码簿，供广大电话用户使用。

七、数据通信

（一）分组交换

1997年开通分组交换业务，将用户发送的信息分割成若干定长的数据段，在每个数据段的前后加上控制信息、地址信息，形成一个分组，以存储转发的方式在网络各个节点上传输。每个节点交换机可以根据这个分组的地址信息，按预先设置的路由，将它转发到下一个节点，直至收端。组成用户信息的各个分组到达收端后，再按原顺序还原成用户信息，传送到下一个节点，传送给收端用户。分组交换可分为不同速率、不同类型的终端与终端，终端与计算机，计算机与计算机之间通信，以及数据库资源共享提供的高效优质的数据通信业务，并为各电子信息、电子数据交换、可视图文等新业务的开放提供必要的网络环境。

2009年电信网络维护

（二）电子信箱

2001年开通电子信箱业务，该业务是一种基于计算机网络，以存储、转发形式交换各种电文、信件、传真、图文及其数字化信息的处理系统。电子信箱的实现方法是在电信网设“电子信箱系统”（实际上是一个计算机系统），每个用户都有属于自己的1个电子信箱，通信的过程就是把信件传送到对方的电子信箱中，由收信用户使用特定号码从信箱中提取。如发信人需要将信件直投到非信箱用户终端，信箱系统可利用存储转发。主要功能是收发信件、处理信件、直接投递、布告栏、电子格式程序、远程用户代理、安全保密。接入电子信箱的用户终端可以是各类计算机，也可以通过电话网、互通信件等方式接入。

（三）计算机互联网

2001年开通计算机国际互联网，它是建立在计算机网络上的网络，是符合TCP/IP协议网络组成的网间网，各式各样的计算机、微机、Untet工作站、大型计算机及各类计算机局域网、广域网都可以和Inter-

net互连。用户可以通过Internet登录使用在地球另一端的资源，也可以同世界范围内成千上万计算机交换文件和传达电子邮件。中国公用互联网和邮电部门经营管理的全国性业务网，具有提供多种工具扩展用户对通信的多层次需求，包括电子信箱、交谈和多人聊天等功能。通过电话拨号、交换网、过帧中继网、专线入网。

（四）数字数据网

1998年开通，由光缆（数字微波和卫星）数字传输电路和相应的数字交叉复用节点组成的数字数据传输网，可以为用户提供各种速率的高质量数字专用电路，以满足用户组建、中高速计算机通信网和发展中的多媒体通信网的需要。数字数据网的基本业务是向用户提供多种速率的数字数据专线服务。同时为用户提供一点对多点通信、虚拟专用网和帧中继业务等。采取用户终端设备接入、用户网络与数字数据互连方式接入。

（五）帧中继宽带业务网

1998年开通，帧中继技术利用帧对数据进行封装，使之在网络中传输，并可使多个用户同时使用一条线路的数据业务。它的网络时延和数据传送速率质量高，而且在一条物理连接上能够提供众多的逻辑连接，从而大大提高线路和宽带的利用率。以异步的方式处理接续和用户的宽带分配，实现在网络中的高速传输和交换。处理多种类型的网络流量，如语音、视频图像和数据，是宽带高速通信的主要模式。主要有局域网互联、图像传送、虚拟专用网。

（六）县电信部门开办互联网接入

县电信部门1997年开办互联网接入业务，有县委、县政府、县金融系统、省林校、索风营电站等单位和个体网吧及广大市民采用各种方式使用互联网接入业务。其中宽带互联网接入业务ADSL宽带业务，自2003年3月18日县电信局推出主题为“将梦想接入现实”的“宽带极速之旅”系列活动，普及宽带业务知识，将宽带梦想接入每个用户的现实生活中，让用户感到全新的高速度上网体验，尽享互动精彩的数字娱乐生活，逐步实现“宽带中国”的远大目标。

第三节　移动通信

一、网络

县内移动通信建设始于1999年，利用无线移动通信网连接公众市话网，开通无线寻呼。1990年4月建成无线寻呼台（BP机），开通无线电话集群系统，实现全区漫游。1993年，开通手提电话（俗称“大哥大”），实现全省联网漫游。

1995年10月，县建成第一个移动无线基站，地点在修文中学龙岗山顶。1996年建成龙场镇观音山、久长镇凤凰山、扎佐镇邮电办公楼顶3个。1997年建成扎佐镇高尔夫、龙场镇移动公司楼顶2个。1998年建成龙场镇文广大楼、人民法院老楼、龙场镇供电局大楼顶3个。1999年建成小箐乡旧小箐大坡、六广镇贾家洞、六屯乡政府对面山、六桶乡盐井村山头等6个。2000年，全县共建基站196个，基本实现“村村通”，行政村、高速路，国道、省道、县道全覆盖。2001年起，逐年解决自然村和城镇居民小区“弱覆盖”问题，到2010年12月，全县共有移动无线基站2017个，其中2G基站237个，3G基站60个。同时7个TD—SCDMA室外基站和6个TD—SCDMA室内分布系统的投入使用，使县城3G网络得以完善。县城可使用3G网络实现视频通话，真正让广大市民畅享3G带来的新生活。

2010年开始试运营的移动3G修文网络

二、无线寻呼

1992年，县内发展数码寻呼机用户8000户。1993年，对无线寻呼系统进行改造，由人工到自动，开通5000台，由数码机到汉字机，实现全省漫游，用户达到9000户。1995年5月，无线寻呼升级，开通5000台，实现全国联网漫游。到1998年年底，无线寻呼用户达到1.2万户。2004年无线寻呼业务终止。

三、小灵通

2002年开办“小灵通”无线市话业务，用户在本市电信网络服务范围内可以拨打和接听市内电话、国内和国际长途电话，并实行单向收费。有移动电话功能、固定电话的资费待遇。小灵通电话号码由贵阳市电信分公司分批分配给一市三县五郊区电信部门使用。7800000至7899999、8700000至8799999、8800000至8899999和8900000至8999999号段，一市三县五郊区电信部门均在使用其中号码。到2010年小灵通业务仍存。

四、移动电话

（一）号码资源及用户

2000年，县内开通移动A网，2008年4月开通G网，经营的主要业务有：全球通、神州行、本地通、数字数据业务及其他语音信箱、短消息、信息点播、IP电话、手机银行等。

移动公司电话号码资源有139、138、137、136、135，后逐步增加151、153、159号段。联通公司“C网”建成，分配号段有131、132、133、134。具有上述号码资源，县移动公司、联通公司依靠自身的网络优势和号码资源，积极发展移动通信业务。在地、县以自建自营厅为骨干，以业务代办点、代售处、合作营业厅为依托，构建社会化营销渠道网络体系。

1996年，国内联网漫游达到全国所有省、市、县城市，开通与国外及港澳地区7家公司的GSM自动漫游。截至2000年年底，县内移动用户达到4万户，年收入7000万元。

2007年1月，修文移动公司正式启用光纤互联网数据接入。12月，位于六广镇索风营电站接入开通光纤数据接入，开始修文移动对外集团数据接入服务。至2008年5月，集团客户增至10家。6月，铁通以互联网运营资质和移动公司合作，共同管理互联网数据接入业务。

2009年5月，针对个人客户启动宽带互联网接入业务。至年底，个人客户达272户，与关联的中国移动本地手机号共享资费。当年本地净增客户2.51万户。

2010年，积极开展产品创新和业务推广，把握信息化机遇，以行业应用为切入点，充分发挥“移动性、个人性、实时性、安全性”的信息化优势，向各行业提供全方位的新业务方案及应用，带动企业信

息化市场，逐步把移动信息服务做大、做好、做实。截至12月底，互联网接入集团用户23户，个人用户617户。集团客户达到485户，比上年增长78%。公司共拥有短信厅达到60个，村级代办30家，空中营业厅105家，合作厅6家。公司拥有在网客户12.79万户，营运收入8438.71万元，其中新业务超2000万元，市场份额达89.16%；

（二）热门业务

飞信　2001年开通，系中国移动的综合通信服务，即融合语音（IVR）、GPRS、短信等多种通信方式，覆盖完全实时的语音服务、准实时的文字和小数据量通信服务和非实时的通信服务的客户通信需求，实现互联网和移动网间的无缝通信服务。除具备聊天软件的基本功能外，通过PC、手机、WAP等多种终端登录，实现PC和手机间的无缝即时互通，保证用户能够实现永不离线的状态；同时飞信所提供的好友手机短信免费发、语音群聊超低资费、手机电脑文件互传等更多强大功能，令用户在使用过程中产生更加完美的产品体验；使用飞信能够满足用户以匿名形式进行文字和语音的沟通需求，为使用者创造不受约束、不受限制、安全沟通和交流的通信平台。移动通信致力于通过飞信为用户重新诠释多彩动感的移动生活为广大用户提供更完善更人性化的服务。

无线音乐　2001年开通，无线音乐专区提供全网用户无线音乐体验，是综合彩铃下载、新歌抢听、歌迷俱乐部的专业音乐专区，有全国最新最炫的彩铃、最IN的音乐资讯、最宽广的音乐交流空间，为用户打造个性化的回铃音。

来电提醒　2001年开通，来电提醒业务是基于呼叫转移来实现的话音增值类业务。来电提醒业务针对被叫开通，用户可人工设置呼叫转移状态，如遇忙转移、无应答转移、不可及转移和无条件转移，将呼叫转移到来电提醒业务平台。呼叫被转移到来电提醒平台后，系统会向被叫用户发送主叫用户的来电信息，从而满足被叫用户实现来电提醒和避免打扰的需求。客户开通来电提醒业务后，系统将为客户默认为遇忙、不可及或关机两种状态呼转到13800851309，客户可拨打96139修改默认设置。在手机关机或不在服务区时，将来话转移到自动短信平台，在手机开机或有信号时将收到在关机或无信号期间来电号码为内容的短信通知的业务。

新业务　从2001年起还开通短信、彩信、手机上网、随e行、手机报、手机地图、手机导航、手机证券、手机钱包、手机电视、手机动漫、百宝箱、号簿管家、手机邮箱、12580综合信息服务门户和航信通等16项新业务。2010年新业务收入为2191.75万元，占营业总收入的25.97%。

（三）业务品牌

全球通　2000年9月开通，其核心理念为“我能” 源于“全球通”值得信赖的实力，代表着“全球通”与客户一起不断进取的决心，是坚韧不拔、超越自我的勇气，坚持梦想、不懈追求的动力，自信、乐观和笑看人生的胸怀。2010年全球通用户2.57万户。

神州行　2001年9月开通，享受同普通全球通客户一样的网络覆盖和通话服务，在全国所有城市都可开通，并可在这些城市间漫游。为满足大众市场的需要，以“限制型，灵活及实惠”为原则，针对不同细分客户推出不同的资费套餐。所有这些资费套餐被统称为“神州行”本地营销案。“神州行”品牌包括“神州行”标准卡（基于智能网，无月租费，标准资费0.6元/分钟，预付费，不需签约）和“神州行”本地营销案两大部分。“神州行”本地营销案包括“神州行大众卡（黔中游套餐）”“神州行本地卡”“神州行新轻松卡”“神州行大众卡”“神州行大众卡旅游套餐”“神州行彩铃IC卡”“村通农话”和“移动公话”等。随着品牌建设工程的系统化，神州行正带着“轻松由我”的主张继续更好地为大众客户群体服务。2010年全县用户有3.13万户。

动感地带 2003年8月开通，开设学生套餐、娱乐套餐、时尚办公套餐。2010年全县用户2.7万户。

黔中游 2003年8月开通，深受客户喜爱，2010年全县用户达4.72万户，占全县客户规模的36.94%。

五、移动通信企业

1994年3月，修文联合通信有限公司（简称“联通公司”）成立。1998年9月28日县邮电局遵照信息产业部（1998）96号文件和贵州省邮电管理局《贵州邮电现业分营工作实施方案》正式分置县邮政局、县电信局。县邮政局于10月1日正式挂牌成立。2000年8月，县电信局亦称“电信公司”正式挂牌成立。2002年1月，中国移动通信集团贵州有限公司（简称“移动公司”）修文分公司成立。

第五章　城乡建设

1978年，全县5个区（社）的集镇总面积共为2.8平方公里，街道总长1.25万米多为砂石路面。居民人均居住面积4.0平方米。农村建有乡村马路59条，总长283.5公里，村民住房简陋，有茅草房住户1.2万户，1.5万人饮水困难，10%的农户未用上电，通信条件极差。

1994年，县政府贯彻执行省发〔1994〕2号文《关于加快小城镇建设的决定》，率先修建县城私营经济一条街，拉开城镇建设的序幕，到1997年，县城区面积扩大到1.8平方公里。1998年，县委、县政府提出："加快以县城为中心，扎佐、久长、六广3镇为重点，其他乡（镇）各具特色"的城乡建设发展思路。以1999年县城实施基础设施建设"九三"工程为起点，掀起城乡建设热潮，奏响一曲气势恢宏的城乡建设华彩乐章。

到2010年，全县城乡面貌焕然一新，10个乡镇的集镇总面积上升为15.95平方公里，是1978年的5.7倍，居民住房人均面积达42平方米，是1978年的10倍。其中龙场镇（县城）面积达5平方公里，人口城镇化率从1998年的13.88%提升为36.5%，一座可持续发展，秀美生态县城呈现在世人面前。农村建起四级公路189条，总里程1311.34公里，实现村村通公路；危房、茅草房改造和新农村建设使村民人均住房面积达30.6平方米；建成人畜饮水"渴望工程"132处，"百村人饮"工程14处，解决人畜饮水困难，农村电网建设和改造，实现城乡电网一体化管理，电网覆盖率100%；新农村建设使电视通讯覆盖全县217个行政村，农村正向小康社会迈进。

2010年，县城一隅

第一节 县城建设

1978年，县城面积仅1平方公里，布局有主街1条，次街3条，街道总长5.5公里，居住1.8万人，房屋累计面积7.6万平方米。1986至1993年在环城路东侧建起3.7万平方米单位公房。1994年，县政府决定开发县城东片区，走“政府创造环境、社会投资建设”大规模、大动作、大投入、大合作新城开发道路，掀起县城建设热潮。率先修建“私营经济一条街”，随后开发虎山路、黄秧路。到1997年，城区面积扩大到1.8平方公里，人口增至3万人。1999年，实施城市基础设施建设“九三”工程，县政府将加快城镇建设与改善民生结合起来，把城镇规划、建设、管理与县域经济发展结合起来，把提高城市化水平与打造“王学圣地，秀美修文”品牌结合起来，提出建设宜居修文的城市建设理念，让市民休闲有去处，娱乐有场所，购物有中心，努力实现建一片、绿一片、美一片的目标，使城区面积达到2.5平方公里，常住人口达3.2万。2005年，阳明大道商贸住宅街建成，城区面积扩展到3.7平方公里，人口增为3.5万。2007年，新建街道15条，城区面积增至3.8平方公里，新建住房累计8.68万平方米，人口达4万人。2008年，城南新都口岸商贸、住宅、运输综合区建成，城区面积升为4平方公里，人口增到4.2万。2010年，“利尔上河城”、“新都口岸”第二期商贸住宅建设项目和城南廉租住房工程竣工，“文城逸都”“腾晖家园”商品住房开发，使城区面积达5平方公里，县城10条主街道6.6万平方米“白改黑”（混凝土路面改为沥青路面）和城市综合管网入地工程实施，使人口城镇化率提升为36.5%，常住人口达4.8万。2010年，随着新建商品房的出售，县城常住人口增加至5.2万人。

一、旧城改造

环城路扩改建 1990年12月，县政府在“人民城市人民建”的方针指导下，制定《改建县城过境公路段集资办法》，筹集资金200万元，对位于旧城区东侧，南起油萝街、东抵东门桥的环城路沙石路面进行混凝土路面扩、改、建。扩改工程由中建四局机械施工公司承建，1991年3月动工，1992年竣工投入运营。使道路总面积达3.54万平方米。

街道路面硬化 1981年，县财政拨款10万元，由县城建局组织对中山路、民主路和龙井巷（前半段）、学宫巷路段进行混凝土硬化。1984年，采取县财政投资和机关企事业单位集资办法，对阳明路、龙井巷（后半段）、玩易路、顺城街、栖凤路、长征路进行混凝土硬化，从而结束县城老街泥沙路历史。继后，因改造环城路重车经过中山路、民主路，使两路压损。2003至2005年，对损坏的中山路、民主路进行彻底改造，改造后街道统一扩至6米宽，修建沿街人行道，街面护堤道牙，筑起单道预制砼管地下排水道，使旧城街道路面状况得以提升。

1981—2005年旧城区部分街道混凝土硬化改造工程概况表

表3—05—01

名 称	起止点	改造年份	长度（米）	宽度（米）	面积（万平方米）
阳明东路	人民路林业局门口——阳明大道丰阳加油站	1981	180	21	0.38
阳明西路	人民路阳明宾馆门口——中山路羊叉街	1982	660	4.5	0.3
学宫路	翠屏西路龙岗广场——修中宿舍	1987	300	3.5	0.11
人民路	油萝街——东门桥	1991	1415	25	3.54
翠屏西路	县政府大院前——翠屏路龙岗广场	1997	300	14-21	0.51
文化路	实验小学——修文中学	1997	400	4	0.16
栖凤路	民主路供销社——四川会馆旧址	2000	300	4.5	0.114
中山路	翠屏西路县政府大院前——北门桥	2003	1300	6	0.78
民主路	翠屏西路县政府大院前——南门口人民路	2005	500	6	0.3

县体育场拆迁 1998年体育场面积7700平方米。1999年，县政府实施县城基础设施“九三”工程建设，异地新建体育馆，将原体育场连同周边房舍占地改建为龙岗绿地广场1.74万平方米。

2001年至2002年在广场西面和北面分别建起文化走廊式的龙岗花园商住楼、粮贸花园商住楼；广场东南侧紧靠人民路、翠屏西路，建道牙、绿篱与街道人行道相隔。2004至2006年在广场南，位于翠屏西路的企业单位，纷纷拆旧新建商住楼，糖业公司、医药公司、土产公司、农资公司等一批新楼拔地而起，使绿地广场四周环境大为改观，旧城街道踪影从此告别市民，令人无迹可寻。

校园改造 20世纪90年代末，从文化路的实验小学起，过察院坡到龙岗山修文中学地段，建有县实验小学、县实验幼儿园、修文中学、县职业高中、修文师范、县教师进修学校以及电大工作站等教学单位。构成县内教学教育基地。

1999年，实施县城基础设施建设“九三”工程，在新城区新建九年一贯制学校1所，2000年改造在建设中的修文中学改为独立高中，分离出初中部，于2002年8月迁入新建九年一贯制学校校址，校名为修文三中。2006年修文中学申办省级示范高中，拟定全校整体搬迁，随后决定就地改造，将职业高中迁至油萝街县委党校内，把留下的16亩校舍用地作为修文中学改、扩、建之用。同时县政府又将占地1652平方米的实验幼儿园，迁至县城东片区高涧河畔，实验幼儿园部分用地和龙场镇城南村第六组的2231平方米土地征划给实验小学进行校园扩建。至年底，实验小学占地面积达1.27万平方米，校舍建筑面积6700平方米，除教室、办公室、会议室、食堂、教师宿舍外，还置有自然实验室、微机室、音乐室、图书室，并建学生活动场地1400平方米，配置校园大门和周边围墙，将1997年改造硬化的实验

1999年，落成的修文中学逸夫楼

小学至修文中学的文化路、学校生活区与教学区隔离，使学校环境一改旧貌。修文中学占地面积3.46万平方米，建有教学楼3幢、综合楼1幢、学生宿舍公寓2幢、教师宿舍4幢、二层楼食堂、餐厅1幢，并置有阶梯教室、化学实验室、物理实验室、生物实验室、图书室、阅览室、微机室、画室、音乐室、会议室及50余间教室，使教学用房面积达1.93万平方米，并投资7万余元改建学校运动场，投资110万元改造校园道路，面积3.62万平方米，总长1080米。2008年继续扩建修文中学，校园占地92亩，新建教学楼2幢，于2009年70年校庆投入使用。2010年，完成贵州省省级示范性普通高中办学标准的硬件建设。

专记：环城马路旧貌换新颜

县城环城马路是粑（粑坳）修（文）公路经县城路段，南起油萝街、东至东门桥，为砂石路面，雨天泥泞，晴天尘飞。1986年前，路西侧拥有零星居民住房及县轻工业局、工商银行、工商局、土产公司、城关镇医院等参差错落的砖木结构建筑。东侧是城南村菜地，仅有县电影院突兀于菜园中。

1986年，县启动环城路东侧建设分为两个片区逐步实施。其中一片区，南起油萝街北端，北至县委大院前长征路口，南北长220米，东西宽95米，占地30亩，沿路旁建起县供电局、农业局、水利局、人事劳动局、交通局、信用联社、国土局、乡镇企业局、人民银行、建设银行等13个单位办公楼，建筑面积共1.8万平方米，投入资金363万元。二片区，南起县委大院前长征路口，北至长征桥桥头，南北长700米，东西宽80米，占地80亩，沿路旁修起县农业银行、自来水公司、保险公司、县医院、粮食局、民政局、农机局、疾控中心、县车队、县客车站等12个单位办公楼，建筑面积共1.9万平方米，总投入资金320万元。1990年12月，县委、县政府针对该路东侧的发展情况，实行财政投资一点、争取上级补助一点、沿街单位集资一点的办法筹集改造资金。具体集资方式：一是责任集资，凡住环城路两侧机关单位，按单位房屋所占路面长度，以每米600元征集；县内各种机动车辆按载重吨位每吨100元，大小客运车、小车按车内座位每座10元征集。二是义务集资，县、镇机关、事业单位，按1990年9月底预算外资金提取5%；企业单位按自有流动资金提取5%征集。三是赞助集资，包括县、镇机关职工、个体企业、个体商户、城镇居民、驻县单位、部队及各界人士捐助，数量不限。3种方式共计筹资金200万元。1991年3月扩改建动工，1992年竣工投入使用。改造后的环城路长1415米，宽25米，其中车行道宽15米，两侧人行道各宽5米，总面积3.54万平方米，混凝土路面。两侧间植行道树，沿路装置长臂照明路灯，修筑1×1.6米浆砌石地下排水道。在与翠屏路、阳明路交叉路口设高杆照明灯和交通红绿灯。

环城路东侧的改造，带动西侧居民相继拆旧新建住宅楼，楼层均在3层以上，一层为经营商铺，二层及其以上为起居室。与此同时，西侧供电实业公司、县计划经贸局、土产公司、邮电局、五金公司、百货公司、县国税局等单位相继拆旧建新，群楼耸立。仅仅3年，一条千米过境马路，住房鳞次栉比，道旁绿树成荫，道上人来车往，热闹非凡。昔日环城路，今日人民道，竟成为县城老城区与新城区的分界线，路西老城留痕，路东新时尚，见证着历史变迁。1995年10月，县政府批准县地名委员会报告，经过改造后的环城路正式命名为“人民路”。

二、新城区建设

私营经济一条街 1994年5月25日，《修文报》刊登县政协委员熊永忠“修建私营经济一条街建议”，引起城关镇党委、镇政府高度重视，镇党委书记张华政、镇长王成林立即组织相关人员到桐梓县考察城镇开发，拟出“借鉴桐梓县统一规划，统一征拨用地，统一标准建设，分期分步实施的城镇建设方案”上报，县委、县政府立即作出“启动县城城镇建设”决定，成立县城市建设综合开发指挥部，抽调人员拟定规划、制定方案和绘制图表。11月9日，指挥部发布1号公告，启动私营经济一条街建设，12月10日破土动工。

私营经济一条街南起县人大办公楼前长征路、北抵新长征桥桥头，与1992年改造的人民路平行并列。在与东西走向的翠屏路、朝阳路交汇处分别设十字交叉路口。征用土地130亩，涉及2个村民组，62户农户。建设采取“总体规划、分步实施、逐步推进、滚动发展”步骤，“以资本置换土地”方式，把除街道路用地之外的两旁土地，以挂牌方式公开出售，分路段以每平方米120—150元置换价出售，售地收入除支付被征地农户出让土地金外，其余用于街道建设。

1995年6月，街道道路雏形显现，招徕县城居民、个体经营户、机关单位职工、企事业单位踊跃购地建房。全路段共售出土地257宗，7万平方米，收取出售金980万元。街道房屋建筑基本统一，高4至6层，外墙装饰贴白色釉砖。全街除企事业单位建办公用房外，私房有400多户，每户占有2至4个经营门面，拥有个体商铺562个，形成拟建中的私营经济一条街。建设中，城建指挥部投入滚动资金5000万元，其中道路建设投资800万元，完成路面硬化、水泥砖砌人行道、供电、给排水和两旁绿化。1995年10月20日，县地名委员会将此街命名为“迎春路”，意会县城建设迎接着明媚的春光，拉开新城区建设的序幕。

翠屏东路 1998年，县人民政府以第一届“99”国际阳明文化节举办的契机，拟定完善县城道路网主骨架翠屏东路建设。该路段西起翠屏中路与迎春路交汇的十字路口，东至县体育馆与河滨路交汇处，全长500米，道路占地1.05万平方米。从1999年初路面开通起，城镇居民、企事业单位、房开商争相在道路两旁购地建房。道路东端北侧临路建造占地21亩的全省县级首家体育馆，9月举办阳明文化节时，道路、体育馆建成投入使用。

2003年9月9日，动工修建翠屏桥，同时修建翠屏东路延伸段。延伸段经翠屏桥跨过小桥河，直抵城东片区罗家寨，路段长336.2米，2004年7月投入使用。延伸段南侧建起青少年活动中心、县人民医院，北侧建起全城第二高层建筑腾晖大酒店。翠屏东路竣工与翠屏中路连接，再接翠屏西路，成为新、老城区的连线，为县城交通网路中东西走向的主骨架。

河滨大道 系县城基础设施“九三”工程建设项目，也是县城街道的主骨架之一。1999年年初破土动工，9月，“99”阳明文化节投入使用。路段东

贯穿全城东西的骨架翠屏路示意图

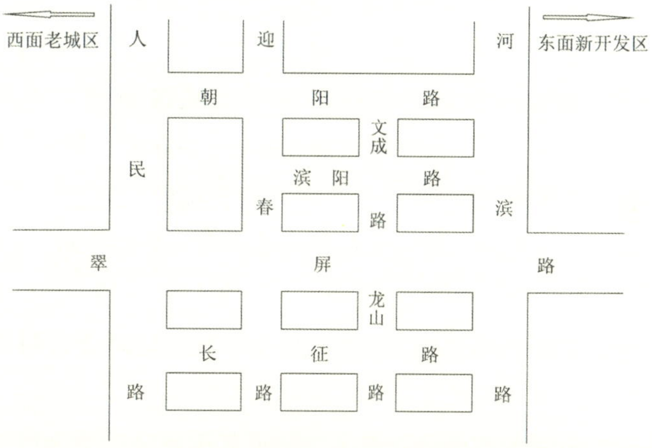

河滨大道交通骨架示意图

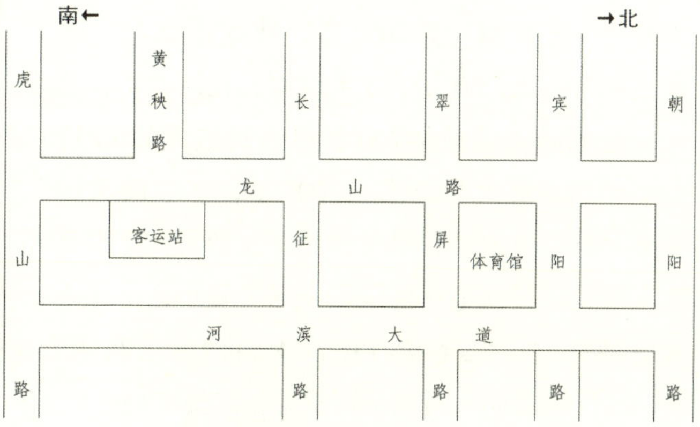

起阳明大道“曲尺桥”，南至翠屏东路为河滨大道东段，西靠县体育馆和广播电视大楼，东临小桥河畔华兴花园住宅区。在华兴花园小区至“曲尺桥”段临河面，筑有高5米河堤路基，并建人行道护栏。全路段占地面积8400平方米，车行道宽21米，两侧人行道各宽5米，路长400米。

2003年，于河滨大道东段与翠屏路交汇处向南延伸，与长征路交汇，延长段长100米为河滨大道中段。2005年3月，启动集商贸、客运、住宅为一体的新都口岸建设，河滨大道又由长征路口继续向南段延伸，直抵黄秧寨与虎山路延长段相汇，南段长250米。2006年年底全线贯通，在曲尺桥头连接2003年建设的阳明大道。成为新城区贯穿南北的主骨架。

新都口岸住宅　2000年，贵州省交通厅安排300万元资金，为修文修建国家二级客运车站。2004年初，县长石洪带队参加第十届厦门国际贸易洽谈会，与贵州泰维房地产公司拟订投资8000万元，在修文开发房地产协议。县政府针对修文的发展潜力和交通、商贸、住宅实际，结合修建国家二级客运车站项目；提出“践行科学发展，打造宜居修文”的思路；强化环境意识，把城市做美”的城市建设理念，决定在城南村小桥河畔把房地产开发和构建国家二级客运站项目合为一体，拟定客运、商贸、住宅结合的小区建设项目，鉴于是坐落在县城新城区，又是旅客、货物和交通工具出入的通道和车辆停靠地，故取名“新都口岸”。

新都口岸小区建设，由贵阳宇航建筑设计事务所设计，以客车站为中心，沿河滨大道延伸段、龙山路延伸段，虎山路延伸段和长征路辅以商、住楼建设。工程于2005年5月破土，2006年12月第一期建设工程竣工投入使用。整个口岸共占地118.62亩，其中客运站用地30.03亩，置站前广场2500平方米，场中建花园1200平方米，绿化率3.5%，广场左右分别建车辆出入道和人行道。停车场设车位100辆，旅客日发送量5000至1万人，车站办公楼、候车厅3930平方米，其中站附属建筑750平方米。小区住宅楼，首期工程建房18幢，占地63.06亩，建筑面积1.87万平方米。住宅户型分为A、B两类，A型建筑面积125.21平方米，B型建筑面积93.73平方米，取样北欧低楼层建筑风格，三面采光，幢与幢之间气流通畅。商务面积1.84万平方米，经营铺面风格统一，分别进驻医药食品、百货家电、五金建材、时装鞋帽、汽车配件、餐饮住宿等经营户和商务办公室。小区内设物业管理，承担保安、保洁、维修等服务。

2007年，城乡建设局在口岸入口临小桥河畔建起5400平方米的河滨休闲广场和1900平方米街心花园、草坪，休息亭、水冲式公厕，使人居环境，口岸情趣浓郁。从2008年起口岸已成为经商、落户、投资、休闲、消费合一的功能区、生活区。

阳明大道商贸住宅街　街道起于阳明大道南段“曲尺桥”头，止于阳明大道转盘处，全长820米。2003年8月开建，到2005年，建起占地1333平方米，建筑面积8.89万平方米的翰林花园商贸住宅小区，建成居民商住楼200多户，共占地128.25亩，建筑面积19.3万平方米。2006年，在“曲尺桥”、阳明大道三角地带，建起碧璟花园商贸住宅小区和明河花园商贸住宅小区以及安居工程小区。整个街道商铺林立、住宅楼有序。街道房屋层高4至6层，底层临街面人行道排列整齐，二楼统一挑出1.5

县城阳明大道上的商住楼

米，三楼以上退进错落多样化，建筑组团以“绿”为主色调，与阳明洞自然风景相陪衬，使人居环境、城市建设与大自然相协调。整齐的商铺、明亮的住宅，通畅的街道与住宅观景阳台、院落绿色走廊相统一，形成开门见景，推窗见绿，景观景点与阳明文化水乳交融的丰富多彩的生态建筑。

2008年2月，启动阳明大道转盘处西北侧利尔上河城小区开发。小区占地面积69.52亩，修建住宅700套，建筑面积13万平方米；商业建筑1.5万平方米，内有农贸市场、商务中心、社区医疗等设施。是年年底首期工程完成，小区雏形已见，2009年启动第二期工程，继续向北延伸建设商贸住宅街和机关办公楼，2010年县人民法院、检察院、人口和计划生育局、残疾人联合会和盐业公司先后入驻。

2010年县城新城区主要道路概况表

表3—05—02

道路名称	起　止　点	建设时间（年）	长度（米）	车行道（米）	人行道宽（米）	总面积（万平方米）
迎春路	长征路县人大大楼——阳明路长征桥	1994	1000	21	5	2.6
朝阳路	人民路春华酒家——河滨路“曲尺桥”	1997	500	21	5	1.3
翠屏东路	迎春路移动公司——县人民医院	1999—2003	836	21	5	2.17
河滨路	朝阳路“曲尺桥”——虎山路新都口岸	1999—2006	750	21	5	1.95
滨阳路	迎春路农贸市场——河滨路体育馆	1998—1999	350	10	1.5	0.35
虎山路	人民南路交通局——原科委	1997	110	12	2.5	0.16
滨河路	河滨花园——朝阳路	1998	100	7		0.07
黄秧巷	人民南路烟草经营部——黄秧寨	1998	110	12	2.5	0.16
永乐巷	朝阳路——翠屏东路	1998	600	5		0.30
龙山路	翠屏东路体育馆——长征路	1999	100	12	5	0.17
永安路（巷）	新长征桥——长征路	1999	600			
良知路	朝阳路——翠屏东路	1997	370	10	3	0.37
长征路	人民路农业银行——河滨路小桥河	1999	500	13	3	0.8
知行路	龙山路——玩易路	1999	115	红线宽10米		0.15
健身路	朝阳路邮政花园——翠屏东路体育馆	1999	300	21	5	0.78
文成路	人文巷——翠屏东路	1999	400	12	2.5	0.58
阳明商住街	“曲尺桥”——阳明大道转盘	2003	800	21	5	2.08
正心路	阳明洞——阳明新村	2003	110			
格致路	阳明大道转盘——外环路	2005	270	21	5	0.57

三、房屋建筑

单位公房　1986年，县城启动环城路东面开发，有县农业局、交通局、供电局、人事劳动局、国土资源局、乡镇企业局、国税局、工商局、粮食局等35个行政企事业单位在环城路修建单位新办公楼。1994年开辟私营经济一条街建设，县信用联社、农发办、移民办、建设银行、工商局等在该路修建单位公房。1999年，翠屏东路和河滨大道建起移动通讯公司、龙场镇派出所、物资局、社区服务中心、民政局、农业发展银行、文化广播电视大楼。2003年在阳明大道上建起残疾人联合会、县计划生育委员会、法院、检察院等单位办公楼。单位办公楼均具高层，框架式砖混结构、外形新颖美观，装饰华丽。楼内功能齐全，水、电、消防设施完善，开启县城房屋建筑新局面。

从1986—2010年，县城单位公房建筑面积达6.5万平方米，投入建设资金3000万元。

县城部分单位公房概况表

表3—05—03

公房名称	位　置	建成时间（年）	投资（万元）	结构	规模	
					楼层	面积（平方米）
县人大、政协大楼	长征路	1989	23	砖混	4	1130
烟草专卖局大楼	翠屏路	1992	140	框混	9	2964
粮贸大楼	人民北路	1994	120	框混	8	2500
电力大楼	人民南路	1996	345	框混	9	3927
国土局大楼	人民南路	1998	150	框混	5	3203
工商局大楼	迎春路	1996	93	框混	7	1600
地税局大楼	翠屏中路	1997	76	框混	6	1642
县建设银行	迎春路	1998	120	框混	6	2794
国税局大楼	人民南路	1998	150	框混	5	3203
县农业银行	人民南路	2000	473	框混	5	1068
县民政大楼	河滨路	1999	198	框混	8	2798
文广大楼	河滨路	1999	412	框混	8	3900
疾控中心	人民路	2005	75	框混	5	757
县法院大楼	阳明大道	2005	500	框混	庭院式	5000
人口计生局	阳明大道	2005	110	砖混	4	2000
交通局大楼	人民南路	1988	26	砖混	5	859
邮政大楼	人民南路	1986	32	砖混	4	1271
残联大楼	阳明大道	2005	65	砖混	4	785
移动通讯	翠屏路	2002	31.5	框混	6	1200
社会停车场大楼	人民北路	1989	57	砖混	3	5300
乡镇企业局大楼	人民南路	1990	80	框混	5	3200
水利局大楼	人民南路	1994	85	框混	5	2000
县中医院	翠屏东路	1995	100	砖混	4	4072
县医院综合门诊楼	翠屏东路	2004	960	框混	6	1077

公益建筑　为满足机关单位和企事业单位职工、城镇居民精神文化生活需要，使离退休干部老有所乐、青少年文化娱乐和残疾人康复，县政府将公益文化设施建设提上议事日程。1979年，修建起占地5

亩，建筑面积1463平方米，内设1167个座位，可供放映、演出的电影院。1984年建成老干活动室，建筑面积800平方米，内设娱乐室、棋类活动、报刊阅读室、老年书画室，并办起老年大学。1985年，建起县工会职工俱乐部，建筑面积856平方米，成为职工业余活动处所。1998年12月9日，县委、县政府根据县委八届四次全会精神和贵阳市人民政府批复《修文县城市整体规划》要求，拟定县城基础设施建设12个重点项目进行审定，将其归纳为县城基础设施“九三”工程建设项目，其中修建县体育馆是基础设施建设项目之一。建设项目经县计划经济贸易委员会批准立项，工程由县城市建设综合开发指挥部统一指挥、组织实施。工程由中建四局设计院设计，中建四局承建。体育馆位于县城新城区翠屏东路与河滨路交汇处，东临河滨路，南靠翠屏路，西抵文成路，北挨宾阳路。占地21亩。12月28日举行奠基仪式，经过9个月奋战于次年9月28日竣工，是为贵州省第一家修建的县级体育馆。馆东门头镶嵌有贵州省体育局原任局长、国家乒乓球运动健将王家声亲笔书写的“修文县体育馆”匾牌。馆东、馆西两门设阶梯上二楼进入馆内看台，四周看台设置座位2360个。南北两门从一层入馆，一层内设综合运动场、健身房、休息室、办公室、更衣室、洗手间。工程建设投入资金1199.4万元。馆外四周建起附属活动场，设置篮球场和多种多功能健身器材，场外临街建有绿化带，花台和绿篱与街道相隔。1999年10月6日正式开馆。2004年，建有占地5亩，主体建筑面积3557平方米，内设有球类、棋类、微机、图书、美术、阅览、放映、音乐、舞蹈等活动的青少年活动中心。2008年，重修老干部活动中心，建筑面积1500平方米，成为离退休干部聚会、娱乐、健身的好去处。

县城体育馆

1979—2008年县城主要公益建筑概况表

表3—05—04

名　称	位　置	建设时间（年）	建筑面积（平方米）	投资（万元）	结构	备注
电影院	人民路	1979	1463	43	框混	2003年开发翠屏小区时拆除
体育馆	翠屏、河滨路交汇处	1999	5900	1199.4	框混	
县工会俱乐部	学宫巷	1985	865	35	砖混	
县残疾康复中心	阳明大道	2005	785	65	砖混	
县文化馆	阳明洞景区	2003	1633	166.6	框混 砖混	
青少年活动中心	翠屏东路	2004	3557	311.9	框混	
阳明文化园	阳明洞景区	1998	850	475	框混	
老干活动室	长征路	1984	800	30	砖混	
老干活动中心	阳明东路	2008	1500	165	框混	

民用住宅 1978年，县城民用住宅多数是解放前留存下来的青瓦木板房和20世纪60至70年代修建的青瓦石墙房、砖木结构房，累计建筑面积7.6万平方米，人均住房4.1平方米。

1994年修建县城私营经济一条街，居民私人建钢混结构的住宅楼400多户。1999年至2002年，市民相继在新辟的翠屏东路、文成路、龙山路、滨阳路、朝阳路修建住宅楼。2003年，又在新开辟的阳明大道修建商贸住宅街，居民200多户又建起民用住宅楼，建筑面积达19.3万平方米。与此同时，城市建设部门还建起经济适用安居房、安置房、兼租房，新建静园、紫荆、河滨、虎山、思源等民用住宅小区，住宅面积6.5万平方米。房开公司开发的民用住宅商品房，建民用住宅花园小区13处，住宅建筑面积15万平方米。是年底，于县城原电影院处修建星河银座大厦，建筑为A、B、C3幢楼中的主楼，以品字型布局，以"T"字型将翠屏商业步行街3幢楼连为一体，构成翠屏小区，2004年投入使用。由贵阳市建筑设计有限公司设计、贵州星河房地产开发有限公司开发，故名"星河银座大厦"。大厦框架结构，设计地下室1层，地面16层，建筑总面积1.36万平方米，其中商务使用面积2188平方米，住宅面积1.04万平方米，地下室面积756平方米。大厦内置垂直电梯2部，一部供商务、住宅使用，一部为消防安全专用。大厦为县城首家设有电梯的民用住宅楼，被人们称之为"电梯房"。大厦东、南面建有步行街禁止车辆通行，道路全长194.6米，南北方向一条宽9.9米，东西方向一条宽8.8米，路面用彩砖、大理石块、青石板铺成线条和几何图案。街道中装置杆式园林型路灯23杆，46盏，两侧一楼商铺门前埋置地灯。道路中安置座椅和简易健身运动器材，供住户及徒步人群休闲。小区西面入口置地板大理石石刻"翠屏商业街"，北面入口竖立大理石碑刻"翠屏商业步行街"，使主体星河大厦建筑更加靓丽多彩、现代大方，成为凸显县城的重要地标建筑。至2007年，县城民用住宅累计面积91.8万平方米，人均住宅为29平方米。2010年，又升为42平方米，是1978年的10倍。

县城中心电梯楼星河银座大厦

1978—2010年县城部分年份民用住宅建设发展情况表

表3—05—05

年份	累计面积（平方米）	人口数（人）	人均居住面积（平方米）
1978	76233	18591	4.1
1983	160139.6	21071	7.6
1988	261414.6	23551	11.1
1990	306787	24543	12.5
1995	432368	27023	16
2000	575640	29520	19.5
2004	713600	29000	24.6
2005	898000	32000	28.1
2007	918088	35000	28
2010	2016000	48000	42

宾馆建筑 20世纪90年代，为适应县旅游业发展，先后修建阳明宾馆、阳明山庄。阳明宾馆位于县城人民路与阳明路交汇处，由县粮食局投入资金420万元，建成建筑面积4280平方米，高7层的框架结构房，集餐饮、客房、桑拿、会议、购物、KTV歌舞为一体的综合服务大楼。阳明山庄位于阳明洞后面河边，依山傍水，整个建筑高3层，大厅部分为框架结构，客房楼为砖混结构，两楼相依，总面积2200平方米，集食、宿、玩为一体的山庄式宾馆。

2007年，引进贵阳腾晖酒店管理有限公司投资1500万元，在县城翠屏东路翠屏桥边建占地8000平方米，建筑面积9195.3平方米，设地下室1层，地面10层，框架结构高45米的“腾晖酒店”。一层为接待大厅、二层至三层为餐饮部，四层为会议室、五至十层为客房部。内设电梯4部，安全通道5个。2008年11月3日竣工投入营运。

四、阳明文化建筑

王阳明纪念馆 1998年9月，为弘扬圣地文化、传承阳明学说，贵阳市政府投资400万元，县政府自筹75万元，在阳明洞景区东南侧修建王阳明纪念馆，当时命名为“阳明园”。该工程由中建四局机械化施工公司承建，主体建筑850平方米，砖混结构，仿古式，屋面盖青灰色琉璃瓦，翼角鳌尖，雀替均匀，形状各异的卷草，馆正大门为仿古庭院式，饰以乳钉，其余侧门为格扇式，万字花格棂木乃伊窗。广场入馆进正大门建12级石梯，馆通面宽共11间、进深7间、前后左右相通、正堂（享堂）砌大理石台，塑有高3米的王阳明青铜像，形象威武、巍然屹立。馆内左侧为贵宾接待室，右侧为阳明文化陈列室，布展陈列面积达2400平方米。馆外建有4000平方米草坪广场，塑有高5米的王阳明与龙冈书院学子陈宗鲁、汤伯元、叶子苍群雕铜像。2005年广场扩建，场地面积占7910平方米，其中青石板地铺面积6516平方米，绿地面积1394平方米，命名为“阳明主题公园”。园内的王阳明纪念馆为当今最大的阳明文化专题纪念馆。

1999年10月，阳明园落成暨开馆剪彩仪式

阳明精舍 1997年，深圳行政学院教授蒋庆出于对阳明文化的热爱和崇仰阳明先生的人格精神，自筹资金在龙场镇平地村营盘山修建由桂竹园、性天园、俟圣园、乐道园、奉元楼、退藏巷等组成的阳明精舍。建筑沿袭中国书院文化传统，选址在山林、湖水之地占地180亩，建筑面积1800平方米，沿精舍周围建起阳明果园，展现出中国文化儒雅人文气息，其布局道出闲适清雅的田园情趣。2000年夏精舍还在建设中就迎来第一位外国客人加拿大卡加利大学教授史罗一先生，2003年精舍竣工又迎来北京“一耽学堂”青年。至2010年，有来自日本、韩国、加拿大等国家和中国香港、台湾地区学者、记者以及北京、上海、浙江、广东、福建等省市的

阳明精舍全景

学者前往精舍论学，感受精舍不亦乐乎的阳明文化传播场所。

王学圣地牌坊 2002年3月5日，在贵（阳）毕（节）高等级公路通向县城的阳明大道入口处，修建“王学圣地”牌坊。该牌坊由浙江璜店古建筑设计院设计，贵州省建工集团以86万元投标承建。工程施工招贤纳才，在深圳、广州、广东、云南、山东、四川等地招聘长于古建筑施工的能工巧匠，历时205天，一座造型别致的“王学圣地”牌坊巍然耸立在县城东北面，成为城区和郊区分界的界碑。牌坊地基深为7至8米，最深处8.7米，可承受20层大楼之重，所使用的钢材、焊接材料均作抗折抗拉检测，地面石料质优，打磨精细。牌坊为门栏式，似如大院门庭三门、四柱、五顶，高17.1米，宽28米，中间正门上方镌刻着中国书法家协会主席沈鹏书写的“王学圣地”四个大字，下方雕刻腾龙、跃虎，左右两门上框雕刻吉祥图案。立柱上由省著名书法家戴明贤书写的四副对联。牌坊建成不仅引人跨进县城就追思阳明良知之说，同时也是向人们推介修文的一张名片。

坐落在阳明大道上的“王学圣地”牌坊

阳明书院 2003年在阳明园东北侧，配合阳明文化的传承，投资166.6万元修建阳明书院并设文化馆于其中。书院建筑面积1633平方米，分前后大院，两院以大厅相隔，大厅为框混结构，两院两侧建砖混结构二层楼厢房对称。整个建筑红柱、灰墙、琉璃瓦、屋檐翼角。大院前门石阶入院，跨过院门，步青石板行道上阶梯进大厅，两旁辟有绿地、置有花坛。建筑外形仿古、室内装修时尚，设有阅览、娱乐、休闲场所，是人们避开城市喧嚣，挣脱繁杂事物后进行学术研究，养性修身的好去处。

五、仿古步行桥

建于高涧河畔文城逸都商住区绿地花园地段，是通往阳明洞景区的河中观赏副桥，跨越高涧河东、西岸，搭接在两岸沙堤坝之上，是由河中岩层钻孔、栽筋、立墩的多孔、外石、内混的钢筋混凝土结构自然式仿古曲形桥，桥长8.5米，桥面宽1.8米。由安顺康达工程建设有限公司承建，于2009年4月动工，5月竣工，投入资金18.6万元。

六、供水与排水

（一）供水

1985年，对县城供水总管进行改造，形成两个闭合环组成“8”字形的供水环。因老城区供水支管锈腐，加之住户增加水压不足，致高楼层、高地势经常断水。1995年，县水利局根据县城供水需求和供水现状，经贵州省水利厅黔水农〔1995〕8号文批准立项，投资343.88万元在城南陶家龙潭建日供水量4800吨的南门水厂一座。1997年建成水厂但无供水权，致厂闲置。2000年，县政府为解决县城供水短缺难题，提出把南门水厂与东门水厂联网供水的设想，但因水厂产权各属，利益分配存在异议，致联网供水搁浅。2001年8月，县城乡建设局根据市民建议，提出水厂资产有偿转移，重组国有资产方案，将水利局权属的南门水厂产权转给县自来水公司。11月，县政府按照城建局提出的方案，作出两水厂联网供水决定。

2002年1月1日，两水厂正式并网供水。自此，城区供水能力上升到日供水9000吨。截至2010年，县城有直径100毫米以上供水管长20公里，供水范围4.2平方公里，供水2300余户，人口4万人，人均日供水量190升。

（二）排水

1990年前无正规排水系统，雨污合流由高向低排入河道。1991年到2003年，城区经过环城路改扩建和旧城街道硬化以及私营经济一条街、河滨大道、阳明大道建设，形成五大总水沟组成的城区排水系统，分别承担新老城区街道路面雨水和生活污水排放，排水方式为雨污合流，经过截污沟直接排入城区河道，造成修文河的污染。到2007年，城区五大排水总沟长1.24万米。加上系统内主要街道排水沟渠，总长度3.01万米。继后续建思源路碧景苑花园、明河花园、河滨大道新都口岸和翠屏东路落户腾晖酒店、县人民医院，排水沟共长1200米，使城区排水沟渠长达3.13万米。

2008年，修建污水处理厂于王家湾，占地24亩，建厂房面积600平方米，日处理污水量5000立方米。污水沿小桥河、高涧河、修文河、三岔河、东门河、北门河段直抵潮水村王家湾厂址。河堤铺设地下排水管道，建排污沟3万米，截污沟3920米，分别连接阳明大道商贸住宅街、河滨大道、迎春路、人民路、中山路五大排水沟。年底铺管完成90%，投入资金7680万元，2009年3月建成，6月投入使用。2010年3月通过贵州省环保监测总队验收，4月通过贵州省环保厅建设工程验收。城区生活污水经处理后达到排放标准。

2009年竣工的县城污水处理厂一角

1.老城区排水

人民路排水沟　人民路排水沟为老城区排水主干渠，1991年前干渠为明沟，1991年环城路改造时将单侧明沟改为双侧暗沟，筑浆砌石1×1.6沟渠，单面全长1400米。主干渠在老城区的主要汇入点有：南门油萝街北段和民主路南段雨污汇入主干南段洗脚塘处；民主路城关二小经城关镇卫生院汇入主干渠；城南殡仪馆水沟向东经公安局原址大门前汇入大龙井出水处，穿民主路和龙岗路南段在县烟酒公司处汇入翠屏西路南侧大沟，再向东流入环城路主干渠；中山路实验小学处向南至县百货公司，转向东经原城关粮店，龙岗广场南侧注入环城路主干渠。

羊叉街天然雨污冲沟　位于老城区中山路与阳明西路交界处。天然冲沟主要汇入有中山路实验小学校址以北，文化路、温家坡北面和阳明西路西段的雨污水，在阳明西路与中山路交界处汇合流入月亮井、杨柳井出水天然冲沟，流入北门河白马滩。

2.城东新区截污沟

1991年环城路改造后，逐步开发城东新区，排水系统按城区建设规划展开建设，在街道两侧修筑浆砌石排水沟汇合后分别流向河道处，结合城区河道治理，在河堤筑截污沟。到2005年，已修筑截污沟的河段有：小桥河翠屏桥至曲尺桥段，修文河的曲尺桥至新长征桥段，新长征桥至三岔河段。截污沟均建于河堤西侧，单面。新城区的雨污部分汇入人民路东侧排水主干渠，注入东门河，部分流入河道截污沟，注入三岔河。城东新区大道排水系统自成体系，以预制混凝土管在大道双侧铺设，有4条排水分支沟汇入预制总管，汇合后排入修文河曲尺桥处。

县城区排水沟渠概况一览表

表3—05—06

城　区	名称	单、双面	沟长（米）	沟渠类别	雨污流向
老城区	民主路排水沟	中道（单）	700	预制砼管（直径1米）	北段汇入翠屏西路大沟，南段流入人民南路干渠。
	中山路排水沟	中道（单）	1300	预制砼管（直径1米）	北段流入北门河白马滩，南段流入翠屏西路大沟。
	阳明西路排水沟	单面	660	浆砌石沟	西段流入月亮井出水天然冲沟，东段流入人民北路干渠。
	文化路排水沟	单面	400	浆砌石沟	流入中山路排水管沟。
	翠屏西路排水沟	双面	600	浆砌石沟	自西向东汇入人民路干渠。
	人民路排水沟	双面	2800	浆砌石沟	从油萝街北，由南向北流入东门河。
新城区	虎山路排水沟	双面	220	浆砌石沟	由东向西流入人民南路干渠。
	黄杨路排水沟	双面	220	浆砌石沟	由东向西流入人民南路干渠。
	长征路排水沟	双面	1000	浆砌石沟	东段流入小桥河，西段流入人民路干渠。
	迎春路排水沟	双面	1200	浆砌石沟	从南至北流入长征桥截污沟。
	朝阳路排水沟	双面	1000	浆砌石沟	自西向东流入修文河截污沟。
	翠屏东路排水沟	单面	1000	浆砌石沟	西段流入人民路干渠，东段流入小桥河截污沟。
	宾阳路排水沟	单面	350	浆砌石沟	由西向东流入小桥河截污沟。
	文成路排水沟	双面	800	浆砌石沟	汇入翠屏东路排水沟。
	永乐巷排水沟	单面	600	浆砌石沟	汇入翠屏东路排水沟。
	健康路排水沟	单面	600	浆砌石沟	汇入翠屏东路排水沟。
	河滨路排水沟	双面	800	浆砌石沟	自南向北流入曲尺桥截污沟。
	龙山路排水沟	双面	200	浆砌石沟	由南向北流入翠屏东路排水沟。
	河滨巷排水沟	单面	100	浆砌石沟	由南向北流入朝阳路排水沟。
	玩易路排水沟	单面	380	浆砌石沟	南段汇入虎山路水沟，北段汇入黄杨巷水沟。
	阳明东路排水沟	双面	360	浆砌石沟	自东向西流入修文河长征桥。
	知行路排水沟	单面	160	浆砌石沟	自南向北汇入虎山路排水沟。
	潮水路排水沟	双面	6000	浆砌石沟	分多段分别排入修文河。
	阳明大道排水沟		5600	浆砌石沟	由东向西流入修文河。
	居民小区排水沟		3000	浆砌石沟	分地势排入街道主沟。

城区街道五大排水系统一览表

表3—05—07

系统名称	所处城区	总长（米）	规格（米）	材质	单双面	系统内沟渠数	流向河段	最终流入
中山、民主路改建系统	旧城	2000	直径1	预制砼管	单	4	北门河 东门河	北门河王家湾污水处理厂
迎春路系统	新城	1200	1×1.5	浆砌石	双	6	东门河	北门河王家湾污水处理厂
河滨路系统	新城	800	1×1	浆砌石	双	4	修文河	北门河王家湾污水处理厂
人民路系统	新、旧两城区	2800	1×1.6	浆砌石	双	6	东门河	北门河王家湾污水处理厂
阳明大道系统	东片区	5620	直径1	预制砼管	双	4	修文河	北门河王家湾污水处理厂

七、河道治理

1996年7月初，连续两天暴雨使修文河河水猛涨，洪水淹没原“曲尺桥”上游高涧河两岸大片良田，小桥河上漂浮物顺河而下，挂满长征桥孔，水流不畅，河水淹至桥面，团鱼湾河段县职业高中教师宿舍内40多人困于“孤岛”。1998年，县展开对修文河的治理。

小桥河与修文河段 1999年修建河滨大道时，实施治理小桥河翠屏桥至修文河长征桥河段一期工程，在河段西岸修筑高5米混凝土河堤，全长580米。并在“曲尺桥”至长征桥段西侧建河道绿地河滨花园。2003年2月，启动河段治理二期工程，对小桥河围堰至翠屏桥两岸，翠屏桥至长征桥东岸进行治理。其中小桥河围堰至翠屏桥西岸筑混凝土河堤，高5米，长100米；小桥河围堰到翠屏桥，至曲尺桥东岸沿河用天然石料修筑河堤，总长665米，河堤上建宽20米绿化带间置垂柳。河道清淤时保留河底天然岩石群体，分段修筑混凝土拦河坝，提高河道水位。治理后的小桥河段河面净水宽20米，修文河段净水面宽达30米。2007年，开发思源路明河小区、碧璟园小区建设时，进行修文河段东岸曲尺桥至长征桥治理，采用天然石料修筑河堤，长200米，河堤上建起20米宽的绿化带。

阳明河段 距县城中心1.5公里，流经阳明洞风景名胜区内的阳明山庄、阳明大桥、阳明新村、利尔上河城商贸住宅小区。2001年1月，县水利局展开对该河段的治理。修筑河堤2道长96.5米，筑河岸护坡长346.5米，建片石小路长380米，修建过河跳墩2处，拦河堰2道长58米。治理工程5月竣工。2008年，在阳明山庄至阳明桥段建沿河堤草坪、种竹，面积1000平方米。

团鱼湾河段 2001年2月，治理长征桥下游团鱼湾段。治理后使修文河段河水从长征桥不再经过羊落井饮用水源水厂处团鱼湾，取直道流入东门河。治理工程挖土石方1.18万立方米，筑浆砌石河堤1677立方米，形成河面宽30米，长140米的人工河道。河道两岸建步行道各宽2米，绿化带宽10米，植有垂柳、竹木。投入资金28.2万元，工程于2002年2月竣工。治理后河水清澈，两岸碧绿，成为市民休闲、垂钓之处。

高洞河段 2008年，抓住举办2009年国际阳明文化节和中国·贵阳避暑季在修文举行开幕式的契机，启动高洞河段，阳明大道曲尺桥至阳明洞风景名胜主题公园的河道治理。拓宽河道、修筑河堤，绿化河岸，建起花园、草坪、凉亭，修建过河仿古桥和朝霞路翠薇桥。改扩建后河道长960米，河道宽30至40米，净水面宽20米，投入改扩建资金480万元。治理后的高洞河两岸绿草花圃树木青翠，河道曲径通幽，成为市民晨练、傍晚散步之处。

高洞河

八、市政设施

人行道 1991年，改扩建环城路，开启按城市建设要求、规划，标准化修筑街道中的人行道。继后新建的街道均建有人行道，其中主街人行道宽5米，次街人行道宽3米，均铺设人行道混凝土道板。从1997年起至2002年的5年，市政人行道由居民人均占有3.2平方米，上升为7.63平方米。至2005年，人行道总面积达29.66万平方米，居民人均占有量达到8.5平方米。

2005年迎接第三届国际阳明文化节，对城区主要街道翠屏路、迎春路、人民路、河滨路、朝阳路、文成路、宾阳路、阳明商贸住宅街进行人行道改造，换铺彩板和设置盲行道，换铺面积4万平方米，投入资金220万元。

2006年，新都口岸商贸、客运、住宅区街道铺设彩板人行道，面积2500平方米。至此，城区居民人均占有人行道面积达9平方米。2009年，趁启动城市综合管网入地工程的机会，再次更换人民路、翠屏路、阳明大道商住街、迎春路、河滨路、朝阳路、长征路、龙山路、宾阳路、文成路10条街道人行道透水道板4.5万平方米。2010年，在利尔上河城商住小区北环路段和阳明大道段铺设彩板人行道，面积2200平方米，使城区居民人均占有人行道面积增加为9.5平方米。

路灯 1978年，健康路、中山路、民主路在街道电杆上置有简易杆式路灯。从1991年开始在人民路、新建的迎春路、河滨路、翠屏东路、朝阳路等均设置街道长臂式路灯。小街小巷、旧城区均更换杆式路灯。人民路与翠屏路、人民路与阳明路、迎春路与朝阳路交汇十字路口分别安装高杆组合式照明灯。河道护栏、桥面护栏、翠屏小区步行街、体育馆绿化带、龙岗广场、阳明仿古步行道、河滨休闲广场、河滨花园均装置园林式路灯及框架组合式水晶灯。长达2.82公里的阳明大道两侧装有高10米双臂型路灯，共179组，416盏，投入路灯建设资金74.74万元。2006年，新装市政路灯270盏，线路长7000米。2009年在城镇综合管网入地之际，为方便市民增设千米路灯线，增装路灯15盏。到2010年，有城区街道路灯865盏，园林照明灯200盏，路灯均由县城乡建设局市政科按市政设施统一管理。路灯启、闭实现自动化，全城路灯亮灯率为95%。

2009年，城市建设“更换路灯”

环卫 20世纪80年代初，城区街道开始设置果皮箱，材质从

砖、铁皮发展到不锈钢、玻璃钢。每年更换、维修、添置。90年代后期，开展创建文明卫生县城活动，县体育场始建城区第一个水冲式公厕，全城大街小巷、院落、机关单位建半封闭和全封闭垃圾池。县财政、贵阳市环卫局共投资51.6万元，修建城区长征路垃圾中转站1座，日处理垃圾50吨。2007年，由县财政投资，县城乡建设局在阳明路、虎山路各增建1个垃圾中转站。到2008年，全城区除单位公厕外，共建街道水冲式公厕13个，每0.35平方公里有公厕1个。2009年，县政府拟在扎佐镇和平村菜地煤矿旧址，建垃圾填埋场工程项目，未获批准。另拟定贵州省危险废物和贵阳市医疗废物处置中心建设，其项目选点于县境小箐乡凤凰村上半沟，距县城17公里，占地287.9亩，规划使用年限23年，属省级综合性危险废物和医疗废物集中处置中心，由贵阳市城市建设投资控股有限公司建设，总投资2.19亿元。中心承接贵阳市三县一市七区的医疗机构1350家医疗废物回收处理。其中，承接修文县境内238家，县城区内16家医疗机构医疗废物处理。到年末，县城共有果皮箱（垃圾箱）220个，全封闭或半封闭垃圾池353处，垃圾中转站3座；街道水冲式公厕14个，每0.35平方公里达到1个，危险废物和医疗废物处理项目建设工程接近尾声。

绿化 1990年，城区街道无行道树，只有过境公路环城路一侧及体育场植有少量绿化树木。1992年，在扩改建后的人民路植行道香樟树450株。1999年年初开始，有规划在主要街道种植行道树，开展庭院绿化，建绿地、花园、草坪，其中新建的主干道迎春路、翠屏东路、朝阳路、河滨路和次干道虎山路、文成路、长征路种植香樟、玉兰、梧桐行道树。10月，建占地1.74万平方米的龙岗绿地广场，草坪面积9000平方米，间植多种优质风景树。同时在阳明纪念馆前建4000平方米的草坪广场；在修文河西岸曲尺桥至长征桥建800平方米的河滨花园绿地；在县体育馆南、北、东三方馆外广场沿植杨梅、玉兰、竹和灌木绿篱。县委、县政府、县人大等党政机关办公大院、庭院绿化突出，县委大院建绿地草坪800平方米，县政府大院建草坪500平方米，县人大办公楼旁建健身草坪250平方米。县气象局、老干局、供电局、实小、二小等10个单位获县庭院绿化先进单位。2001年，分别在小桥河、修文河、三岔河、团鱼湾人工河、高涧河河堤植树、种草坪、栽花等进行河道绿化，种植常绿灌木、垂柳、竹、香樟、玉兰等，绿化总面积达2.4万平方米。2002年10月绿化阳明大道，第一期全路段种植行道香樟树1400株，第二期绿化分两部分，一部分在阳明大道隔离带，从“阳明圣地”牌坊至大道转盘处，长1420米，宽9.6米，分7个板块，总面积1.36万平方米，种植松柏和小乔木；另一部分是在大道转盘处直径50米，总面积1963平方米的转盘中央带，植高9米、胸径30厘米白皮松1株，四周植常绿小乔木，转盘东西两面，分别用红叶女贞，红花继木镶植嵌出“言行一致，开明开放”八个大字，以此表现修文精神。2007年，在新都口岸河滨大道东侧，小桥河畔建面积5400平方米、绿地900平方米的休闲花园草坪。到2010年，全城绿化面积5.78万平方米，其中草坪面积1.25万平方米。

专记：全省县城第一个绿地花园——龙岗广场

1999年，县将位于人民路与翠屏西路两条城区主干道交汇处的原县体育场建成绿地广场。广场为贵州省县城中的第一个绿地广场，是城市标志性设施之一，市民把这亮丽工程视为城区交通的地标。

工程由贵州省环美绿化有限责任公司设计承建，县政府为建设单位，派副县长赵永祥任项目第一责任人，县人大副主任何先祥任总监督员，县纪委常委王邦椿任纪检监督员。工程于4月动工，8月28日竣工，总工期142天，投入建设资金220万元。广场总面积1.44万平方米，以高标准草坪为主，分7大地块，共9000平方米。每块草坪地块之间建花岗石地板人行道，道牙、绿篱沿途置有石条凳，人行道面积3000平方米。广场中部建直径20米的喷水池，池中设置高位喷水龙头10组50个，低位喷水龙头20个，彩灯20组40个。草坪中间植多种优质风景树，设有杆式园林照明灯、地射彩灯、框架组合式水晶灯。广场东、南两侧临街面以绿篱和道牙与街人行道相隔，西、北两侧建有与之相陪衬的文化走廊式龙岗花园、粮贸花园商住楼。

位于县城中心的龙岗广场

广场建成后成为市民休闲之处，夕阳老人到此摆谈说唱，儿童嬉戏玩乐、年轻人聚集转悠，外来宾客也不忘到此浏览观赏。一位来自马口村抗美援朝退伍老兵李奎，亲临广场无限欣喜，高声感慨道："昨天的体育场、大饭店算个啥？这才是我们今天的新修文！"

管网 2008年，县城街道只有地下排雨沟和供水管入地。2009年9月23日，在国家扩大内需、增加投入的政策指导下启动县城综合管网改造项目，县政府向社会发出公告，由县政府向国家开发银行贷款，投资4500万元，进行城市街道雨污分流和包括自来水供水管、供电线路管、通信线路管、广播电视线路管入地的管网改造，以改善人居环境，提升城市品位。

管网入地工程包括对阳明大道、翠薇路、人民路、迎春路、阳明东路、翠屏路、长征路、虎山路、朝阳路、河滨路、文成路、宾阳路、格致路等13条街道改造排污管沟，修建强、弱电管路，管路规模长10.84千米，换铺人行道道板4.5万平方米。对流经城区的高涧河、小桥河、大寨河进行净水、河水分流、铺设排污管线。

管网入地工程于10月7日在迎春路北路口启动，分为4个标段推进，施工采取封闭或半封闭方式运作。2010年1月27日工程竣工验收，铺设地下管网分别长：人民路1300米，迎春路800米，朝阳路500米，文成路270米，龙山路120米，河滨路700米，翠屏东路100米，格致路300米，翠微路200米，阳明大道2800米，共投入建设资金4357万元。管网建设结束，一改以往电杆林立，蛛网密布的旧貌，使城市现代化建设又向前推进一步。

第二节　小城镇建设

1978年，全县区所在地的城关、扎佐、久长、小箐、六广集镇总面积为2.8平方公里，街道均为砂石路面，总长1.25万米。1992年，县行政区划改制，撤区并乡组建为10个乡（镇），其中城关（县城）、扎佐、久长、六广为镇建制，六屯、谷堡、洒坪、小箐、大石、六桶为乡建制。1994年，根据贵州省委、省政府〔1994〕2号《关于加快小城镇建设的决定》，开始启动小城镇建设。到2004年，全县除县城之外，乡（镇）总面积上升为9.85平方公里，其中建制镇扎佐、久长、六广集镇总面积达5.5平方公里，其余6个乡集镇总面积4.35平方公里。

2009年，县委、县政府根据贵阳市委“加快发展，加快转型，推动跨越”促进城市建设的主基调，实施贵阳市工业强市和城镇化带动战略，委托华中科技大学城市规划研究院拟定《修文县城市总体规划（2010年—2020年）》，制定“一主两副、一环双轴、点线结合”的建设方略，“一主”即以龙场（县城）、扎佐为核心区，其中龙场镇为全县政治、文化、商贸、旅游服务中心城镇，扎佐为产业经济、物流中心城镇；“两副”即久长为发展建材、加工制造及康体休闲旅游镇，六广为发展能源、旅游建设镇，以及其余乡集镇各具特色的城镇建设体系。自此城镇建设按照规划，先抓城镇水、电、路、通信等基础设施，采取市场化运作模式，利用BT和BOT方法集资开发。到2010年，小城镇建设取得初步进展，为提升全县城镇水平打下基础。

一、扎佐

扎佐乃黔中腹地，集镇位于县城东部，距贵阳城区中心32公里，距县城15公里，1994年集镇面积0.75平方公里。210国道穿集镇段长2.5公里；贵（阳）遵（义）、贵（阳）毕（节）两条高等级公路在集镇交汇，过境段长3公里，以及集镇支线路，构成“四横四纵”交通网。2001年，贵（阳）毕（节）高等级公路通车，使扎佐镇至县城距离缩短为9.5公里。2003年，集镇面积扩大到3.5平方公里，为全省32个重点镇之一，2004年由国家六部委列为全国重点镇。镇区建有工业园、物流园和医药产业园，全国唯一的高原森林高尔夫度假中心和全省唯一的森林野生动物园落户扎佐。

2009年，在首钢贵阳特殊钢厂、贵州轮胎厂落户扎佐，建设麦架—沙文—扎佐高新技术走廊之际，全镇完成县属固定资产投资5.8亿元，招商引资8亿元，加快城镇基础设施建设，完善城镇服务功能。到2010年集镇面积达3.8平方公里，正向《修文县城市总体规划（2010—2020）》的“一城两区”迈进。

扎佐新貌

（一）街道

扎佐集镇有街道共14条，其中1993年前的老街7条，分别为：于襄路、景阳路、古驿路、书院街、经堂后街、砂锅巷、场口街。从1994年启动小城镇建设开发襄阳大道起到2010年新建街道7条，分别是：

襄阳大道 1995年2月，县委、县政府为推动扎佐小城镇建设，按照贵州省人民政府办公厅（黔府办函〔1994〕106号）文件精神，征用扎佐镇和平、中营、大园、喻家街、桥头等5个村的部分土地，修建贵（阳）遵（义）高等级公路扎佐联络线。采取“以地生财、以财修路、以路促发展”思路，引进房地产开发商，鼓励镇区居民和企事业单位投资，开发联络线两旁土地，修建商住一条街。

大道起于贵（阳）遵（义），贵（阳）毕（节）两条高等级公路立交桥、210国道、川黔铁路、修（文）扎（佐）公路交汇的周家坟山处，止于210国道省林校，全长2.31公里。道路沿途设4个平交路口，与镇区老街相连。大道建双向车道宽25米，双向车道中间建绿化隔离带宽1.5米，两旁人行道各宽4.5米，道路共宽35米。工程于1995年2月24日开工，1997年竣工，投入资金1800万元。大道开通后，镇机关、企事业单位和居民相继建起居民商贸住宅楼200多户，建筑面积8万平方米和安居工程住宅楼建筑面积2.72万平方米，大道高楼成排，铺面林立，人们称之为“商业大街”，是扎佐镇政治、商业、文化中心。

广场路　2003年始建，2005年建成。东起于210国道、景阳北路，西至襄阳路转盘处，为集镇横向支线，建设时列为“一支线”，全长500米，宽100米（含房舍）。该路旁建有景阳园广场，故为广场路。

育英路　2003年始建，2004年竣工，2005年街道形成，是集镇横向支线街，建设时作为“二支线”。东起于210国道砂锅巷街头，西至襄阳路转盘处，全长500米，宽100米（含房舍）。该路经过扎佐中学、中心小学和幼儿园，故名育英路。

中营路　1998年始建，1999年开通，是集镇横向支线。东起于210国道和景阳路路口，西至扎佐火车站入口，长1.2公里，宽100米（含房舍）。该路穿越中营村，故名中营路。

东兴路　是集镇扩展开辟的新路，建于2000年至2003年。西起于210国道皂角树街口处，东至干河沟，长1公里，宽150米（含房舍）。该路东段已建成集镇新街，取旭日东升，兴旺发达之义，命名为东兴路。

西门桥街　是2000年至2003年开辟的集镇新街，由小路和弄巷扩改建。东起于西门桥，向西转南至重晶石粉厂厂门，连接中营路。长600米，宽80米（含房舍）。该路起于扎佐河西门桥老地址，故称为西门桥街。

大园街　2000—2003年由大园村居民住房、弄巷拆出改造新建。东起于襄阳路猪市坝，经大园坝至襄阳路第二小学人行天桥处，长1公里，宽60米（含房舍）。路穿过大园村境内，故称大园街。

（二）房舍

单位公房　据1990年统计，集镇机关、企事业单位公房共4.4万平方米。1997年10月，扎佐镇政府在襄阳大道新建的办公大楼落成，带动镇机关、企事业单位在襄阳大道修建办公楼，相继建有社区办公楼、农业服务中心、老年活动中心、精神文明中心、城管环卫站等，建筑面积达4500平方米。

2000—2005年，扎佐中学、扎佐中心小学、扎佐第二小学、扎佐镇幼儿园、珍珠幼儿园、叮当幼儿园和景阳中学等增扩建校舍共2.1万平方米。新建贵阳市人民医院扎佐协作医院大楼2500平方米，镇医院续建住院部600平方米。2010年集镇共有公房7.3万平方米。

居民建房　1997年襄阳大道开通，两旁建起居民商住楼200多户，建筑面积达8万平方米，每户楼下设置3至4个经营铺面，成为集镇“商业大街”。1998—2005年，居民在新开辟的大园街、广场路、育英路、中营路、东兴路建住宅楼，建筑面积达6万平方米。到2010年，居民建房达15万平方米。

商品房　从2004年起到2010年，贵州清镇小城镇建设房开公司，利华房开公司等开发“珍珠铭园”、“恒鑫园”等商品房，共建商品房2.6万平方米。

安居房 从1997年12月，镇政府修建首批安居工程，2000年实施第二期安居工程，2002年修建紫竹园经济实用住房，到2010全镇共建安居、经济实用住宅2.7万平方米。

（三）广场

2002年10月，在襄阳大道旁建占地8300平方米集镇中心广场，取名为景阳园广场，场内种植花木、草坪，置有简易体育、休闲器材。2003年6月，在社区建二居广场，占地面积2000平方米。到2010年，可供市民休闲娱乐的广场达1万平方米。

珍珠河社区广场

（四）绿化

从1997年开始进行集镇绿化，以点、线、面结合展开，采取以住宅小区、楼庭院落、机关单位的公共场地绿化为点，新建的襄阳大道种植行道树和珍珠河河堤种植防护林绿化为线，景阳广场、社区广场种植花木、草坪为面全面开展。由于集镇处于开发和基础设施建设阶段，绿化未同步跟上，加之河道防护林植树成活率较低，集镇绿化率仅为20%。

（五）集贸市场

1991年，为改变集镇马路市场经营状况，扎佐供销社、扎佐粮管所分别利用单位场地建起供销社综合市场8200平方米，粮贸市场320平方米，2004年，在新开通的大园街建成大园农贸市场8405平方米。2010年，集贸市场总面积达1.7万平方米。

（六）河道治理

从1998年起开始治理被污染的扎佐河，其中，珍珠河段至一支线襄阳路转盘处于2000年竣工。2003年治理一支线至红卫桥段，于2005年完成第一期工程。治理工程由贵阳市建设局和镇政府集资250万元，在长达680米的珍珠河部分河段修筑起高5米的石料混凝土河堤，清除河道沉污，疏通河床，使河面宽增至20米，河堤沿岸敷设污水截污沟管，种植河道防护树，使河道污染初步得到控制。

（七）供水供电

供水 1997年始建日供水量5000吨水厂1座，集镇90%居民用上自来水。2005年，随集镇面积扩大，乘扎佐医药园区建设之际建大堡村高潮水厂，供水能力1.5万吨，使集镇自来水普及率达98%，日供水量3500吨。

供电 1989年，集镇用电依靠久（长）扎（佐）10千伏电压线路供给。1990年12月建扎佐和平变电站，设35千伏线路，置4000千伏安变压器。2005年，扎佐电网已建有小营220千伏变电站1座、易家街110千伏变电站1座、和平35千伏变电站1座，用电负荷占总容量的60%，实现用户一户一表。

专记：建设新扎佐　打造卫星城

扎佐镇地处贵阳市北大门，且有210国道、川黔铁路、贵（阳）遵（义）、贵（阳）毕（节）两条高等级公路穿境，四纵四横集镇交通网优势，1996年，扎佐镇党委、镇政府以一年抓整合、二年打基础、三年上台阶的城镇建设思路，采取依托资源、面向市场、规划区域、重点突破的开发建设措施，着力实施“四区、三业、一城”规划。以原万江片区为主的医药园区，以高尔夫度假中心为重点的观光旅游区、以扎佐火车站为中心的物资仓储集散区、以黑山坝待开发地段为后备的工业园区作为镇区建设重点，拉动全镇蔬菜、药材种植业，家畜养殖业，三产服务业发展，向贵阳市建设“大贵阳”“两城三星”规划迈进。

到2010年，经过13年开发建设，扎佐已有占地3.8平方公里集镇。拥有19家医药生产企业，建成全省最大医药产业园；建成“好1多”奶制品、日光蔺篘食品、领先食品等5家食品生产企业；建成占地3000亩，全省第一家高尔夫度假中心；全省第一家森林野生动物园；“森林之城、休闲胜地”贵州绿之春生态园；建成贵阳市北物流旱码头贵州兴达物流公司；黑山坝后备工业园接纳首钢贵阳特殊钢厂落户筹建。镇区已开辟青菜稳定种植面积1500亩、地萝卜300亩、白皮优质萝卜3500亩，专业蔬菜基地法定面积达1040亩；建成1500亩大河艳红桃基地；320亩葛马人工草场苗圃；饲养500头奶牛丁官养殖基地；拥有25户餐馆“快活林”饮食一条街。一个融医药、食品、商贸、储运、旅游、饮食、种植、养殖为一体的贵阳新兴卫星城雏形展现在世人面前。

年底，又在贵阳市开发麦架—沙文—扎佐高新技术走廊之际，贵州轮胎厂落户工业园区，县、镇政府完成固定资产投资5.8亿元，招商引资1.78亿元，加大城镇基础设施投入，为《修文县城市总体规划（2010—2020）》构建“一城两区”打下基础。

二、久长

久长集镇位于县城东北部，距县城15公里，有川黔铁路、210国道、贵（阳）遵（义）公路、修（文）开（阳）公路穿过。1998年，省建设厅根据久长镇三县相邻的特殊位置，交通便捷，物流畅通的区位优势，明确为全省小城镇建设试点镇。2001年，始建集镇市政道路，使集镇面积从0.45平方公里扩展至1.5平方公里。

2009年，贯彻落实贵阳市筑党发〔2009〕14号文和15号文精神，县政府根据久长矿产和旅游资源情况，将久长规划为发展建材，加工制造及康体休闲旅游镇。到2010年集镇面积达2平方公里，是1978年0.4平方公里的5倍，为县内第三大集镇。

远眺久长

（一）街道

1978年，集镇有川黔公路、修（文）开（阳）公路过境，建有以两条公路相交的“十”字公路街，

街道沿公路朝东、西、南、北四个方向伸展。1981年，川黔公路列为国道210线，改造为柏油路面后，过境段街道从1978年的300米延伸为1600米，其中：以“十”字路口为中心，川黔北路街抵达铜矿井长700米，川黔南路街至丫叉田长900米；修开公路街经过1990年、2001年两次改造硬化为柏油路面后，修开东路抵龙山脚久长中学长700米，修开西路达虎山脚粮管所长200米。

2000年7月，投资271.9万元，历时1年零4个月修建集镇首条市政道路“龙山大道”，北起210国道黄土坡县石油公司加油站，东接修开公路与久（长）清（水）公路交汇处，全长332米，宽30米，其中两侧人行道各宽5.6米。2004年10月，投资78万元，修建明珠路、北连龙山大道，西接210国道，全长246米，宽13米，其中两旁人行道各宽2.5米，成为集镇新区。新区建成使集镇街道总长达3000米，集镇面积上升到1.5平方公里。到2010年，居民逐步向街道各端延伸段和在新开辟的麦（架桥）肖（家堡）公路两旁建房，使街道长增至3630米，集镇面积达到2平方公里。

（二）房舍

1978年，集镇房屋建筑总面积1.9万平方米，以砖木、木架、石墙、茅草杂聚，砖混结构房仅有420平方米。1982年，久长供销社投资18.5万元在210国道与修（文）开（阳）公路交汇“十”字路口建办公经营楼1幢，砖混结构5层，面积1200平方米，成为久长历史上最高标准性建筑。2005年，随龙山路、明珠路建成，所建房屋皆为砖混，最高达6层，其造型和装修日趋现代。

单位公房 1978年，单位公房总面积8100平方米，多为砖木结构。20世纪80年代中建公房，面积1.01万平方米，以砖混结构为主，少数砖木。90年代建公房1040平方米，均为砖混结构。进入2000年，新建镇文化中心、财政所、司法所、客车站、卫生院、农业中心和久长中学等建筑面积达到8600平方米。到2010年，单位公房达5万平方米，是1978年的6倍。

居民建房 1978年，居民住房以木架瓦房、木架茅草房、石墙石棉瓦房和砖木瓦房修建，其中木架结构3040平方米，石墙结构120平方米，茅草房4740平方米，砖混结构420平方米。从80年代中期开始，居民沿210国道、修（文）开（阳）公路新建和拆旧改造住房，均为砖混结构，共建1.23万平方米。2005年，龙山大道和明珠路建成，居民建商住房7.9万平方米，最高楼层达6层，使居民建房总面积上升至10万平方米。到2010年集镇已彻底清除茅草、石墙房，尚存少数木架房。

（三）供排水

供水 久长集镇所在地水源贫乏，1978年，机关单位集资修建铜矿井高位水池，部分单位用上自来水。20世纪80年代初，集镇接通011系统烽光厂供水管，单位自建蓄水池备水饮用，街道设供水点，供居民排队挑水。1984年3月，国家投资12.7万元将金桥村三叉泉井水提升引至集镇，铺设水管总长5627米，使集镇居民用上自来水，结束久长街挑水饮用历史。

1999年，县政府利用国家“渴望工程”资金建久长镇水厂，由县水利局设计修建，装直径150毫米主管，改造街道支线供水。2002年，利用世界银行农村改水项目贷款216.5万元，由县自来水公司主持实施久长镇集镇饮水工程改造，水源取自金桥村地下泉水和蚌壳堰水库容水，建二级提升站，铺直径100毫米供水管道长7公里，日供水能力1000吨，彻底解决久长集镇饮水困难。

排水 1978年，久长街生活污水与雨水合流，明沟直排入下街东南侧川黔铁路涵洞水塘，流入白窖村至清水村河沟。2005年修建龙山大道、明珠路时街道两侧筑浆砌石排水暗沟，其中龙山大道排水沟单边长330米，明珠路排水沟单边长236米，两路排水雨污合流由北向东南流入川黔铁路涵洞低凹水塘，部分雨污自然消沉，部分流入白窖至清水村河道。2009年，镇政府投资1.4万元，清理改造210国道、修（文）开（阳）公路街两侧排水沟，筑浆砌石暗沟长660米，雨污合流汇入川黔铁路涵洞两侧水塘。

（四）供电照明

1978年，集镇有110千伏久长变电站1座，34千伏线路2条，110千伏线路3条，电力充沛。街道置有木质电杆并安装路灯供街道照明。1984年，集资3.5万元，将街道木质电杆改为水泥电杆，安装街道路灯共48盏。2005年，龙山大道、明珠路建成，政府投资15万元，安装街道路灯。2009年，镇政府投资3.1万元修复和增设街道路灯52盏，使集镇街道入夜后通明。

（五）集贸市场

2002年，镇政府投资110万元，在修（文）开（阳）东路建综合农贸市场，占地8.95亩，设经营门面71个，摊位64个。2005年市场初步形成文化娱乐、蔬菜饮食为主的集贸场所。

2009年，政府实施商务部“双百市场工程”项目，在龙山路旁龙山下建标准化农贸市场，占地17.59亩，硬化场地5600平方米，场内建起钢架结构经营大棚2016平方米，棚内设有8米×0.8米固定式摊位16个，分为食肉、粮油、干菜、水产、百货、活禽、果蔬、副食8个经营区。总投资170万元，可容5000人同时购物。

三、六广

六广集镇位于县城西北部，与黔西、金沙两县隔六广河相望，距县城35公里。1978年，集镇面积0.3平方公里，1990年集镇面积增为0.5平方公里。随开发贵阳—扎佐高尔夫—修文阳明洞—六广河峡谷—息烽温泉旅游风景线、索风营电站建设和落实省、市小城镇建设的精神，2000年县政府将六广集镇以园林式旅游服务区定位，列为县小城镇建设重点镇，成立六广旅游开发、小城镇建设、索风营电站建设前期工作领导小组，加大旅游基础设施建设。到2010年，集镇面积达到1.5平方公里，是1978年的5倍；居民住户达650户，是1978年的2倍；房屋建筑达9.3万平方米，是1978年的6倍，已成为县域西北边缘重镇。

山城六广

（一）街道

六广街处于六广河峡谷地带，地势由东向西倾斜，两端窄，中间宽，呈鱼肚状，给街道建设带来困难。1978年有前街、中街和后街，均为毛石泥土路面，总长1200米。1983年区政府投资3.8万元进行道

路混凝土硬化4200平方米。1988年，政府出资，单位、居民集资共3.7万元混凝土硬化街道场坝和3条支巷4500平方米。

2001年，在县开发领导小组协调下，镇政府投资18万元，改造硬化六广派出所至堰塘的街道，长350米，作为六广街对外的窗口。2004年，镇政府为加快小城镇建设步伐，将六广建设为县的重镇，改扩建松江大道，建成长300米，宽15米混凝土路面；开辟南江路，长320米，宽10米混凝土路面。新路建成后，机关单位，居民相继在此建房，形成由北面进镇公路到龙口山腰，南面至兰江田坝的房屋建筑带，初步形成新街，使六广街道总长达1720米，成为六广镇松江新区。2010年，常住户达650户、2900人。

（二）房舍

1978年，街道部分居民将木结构旧房改建为砖木结构瓦房。进入20世纪80年代，居民在集镇北面沿公路两旁建房多为砖混结构2层楼房，北面向龙口山，南面向兰江田坝发展。单位公房建设较少，只新建电影院、供销营业楼、邮政营业楼和电视差转台站。1992年，县行政区划改制，加大六广集镇建设力度，一批单位公房，居民商住楼相继在新开辟路段建成。到2010年六广镇房屋建筑达9.3万平方米。

单位建房 1978年，六广街公房只有政府办公房，学校教学用房，粮管所，供销社和电影院等共2万平方米。1980年，邮政所率先修建营业办公楼和职工宿舍，供销社建成三楼一底供销大楼，六广中学建校舍。

1992年，镇机关、企事业单位新建和扩建公房，相继建起幼儿园546平方米，六广小学教学用房2000平方米，卫生院2300平方米，敬老院850平方米，供销社经营和办公新楼1050平方米，六广中学新校舍3094平方米以及镇政府办公楼、信用社营业楼、烟叶站等一批公房，到2010年新建公房达2万多平方米。

居民建房 1978年，六广集镇居民住房多为木架和砖木结构，有少数茅草房，人均住房19平方米。进入80年代居民开始修建砖混结构房，至1990年统计有3层砖混结构房13栋，土墙茅草房尚存10户。2000年起，居民沿松江大道和南江路建房，改造老街危房和茅草房。形成老街北面公路口到龙口山腰，南面至兰江田坝的住房带，到2010年居民建房总面积7.3万平方米，人均住房30平方米。

旅游服务房 1998年，开发六广河峡谷旅游，在滨江村建起10栋2层的竹楼宾馆，共5444平方米。内设各类房间200间，可供150人住宿，其中大厅面积达400平方米，可供600人就餐 。2001年，在集镇新行政中心旁建起“松韵山庄”，建筑面积600平方米，设客房36间，可接待100人就餐，30人住宿。

（三）供水排水

1978年，集镇建有从水浸沟母猪洞至六广街引水管，将泉水引至中街蓄水池供水。1988年，取水浸沟祝家荒地地下水，引至区财政所和区公所处，分别建160立方米和40立方米蓄水池，再由3000米管道输往上，中、下街，向居民供水。

2004年，为保证供水量和水质，由贵州省水利水电勘测设计研究院设计，贵州省建工集团第三建筑工程公司施工，利用白水和水浸沟双水源建自来水厂。水厂占地2亩，修厂房500平方米，建过滤净化二级提升泵站，铺管6200米至集镇，日供水量1000吨，投入资金500万元。解决集镇及邻近村5000余人饮用水，人均日供水量80升。

集镇老街地势倾斜狭窄，新区地势较高，排水采取自然冲沟排放，雨污合流，由东向西流入黄水沟，自然沉积之后，经黄水沟流入六广河大桥东侧六广河之中。

（四）供电与照明

1979年，建成白水电站，装机2台容量150千瓦向集镇供电。1981年，扩建白水电站，装机容量增为320千瓦，年发电量30.77万千瓦时，基本满足集镇用电和街道照明。1984年，区政府组织集资3.5万元，改造街道路灯。1987年，区政府、白水电站和县移民办共同投资，将供电木质电杆更换为水泥电杆，拆换街道供电和照明线路。

2002年，改由国家电网广田35千伏变电站供电。电力充足，电压稳定，满足单位办公、居民生活、街道照明和企业生产用电。2004年，镇政府投资15万元，安装新区街道路灯，使集镇成为昼夜通明的小山城。

四、谷堡

谷堡位于县城西部谷堡村，1992年，由原乌栗、场坝、谷堡3个小乡合并组建为谷堡乡，利用国防工业华文电工厂搬迁移交给地方政府的场地及房屋建筑作为乡政府驻地，是全乡政治、经济、文化中心。乌栗是传统集市贸易的古老集镇，人口相对集中，形成一乡两个集镇。

新镇谷堡

新集镇开发　1992年组建谷堡乡时，将华文电工厂移交的厂址及房屋建筑1.7万平方米，原厂房、办公房改建为乡政府机关和乡属行政、事业单位办公用房。新集镇有冒乌公路（X190）穿过，距县城10.3公里。1998年乡政府对新集镇进行规划，居民沿冒沙公路谷堡段修建住房，形成长800米集镇街道。2003年，县、乡部门投资200万元建库容量500吨水果冷藏库和占地5亩的水果批发市场。是年，贵阳三茗食品有限公司投资200万元，建猕猴桃果脯生产线和公司大楼。与此同时，居民相继在冷库和水果批发市场旁建房，形成与冒沙公路垂直相交的十字街1条，全长300米，使集镇面积达到1平方公里。

在华文电工厂搬迁后，中断谷堡自来水供给。1997年，为解决新集镇饮用水，由贵阳市政府补助10万元建集镇供水设施，修抽水泵房1座，置15千瓦抽水泵2台，建120立方米高位水池1座，铺输水管道1300米，向集镇供水。2004年，为扩大供水面，增修调节水池1座，容量170立方米。继后修建龙井塘湾水厂，铺设供水主管4000米，日供水量为300吨，使集镇年人均生活用水达30吨，自来水普及率达90%。新集镇谷堡面积已达1平方公里，建街道2条，全长1200米，同时建起农贸水果批发市场、水果冷藏库和猕猴桃果脯生产线，成为县域内观光农业、园艺旅游、果品加工的新集镇。

老集镇续建　1978年，乌栗老集镇已有街道2条，集镇面积0.2平方公里。20世纪80年代中期富裕起来的村民在集镇冒沙公路旁新建住房，形成一条公路街全长260米。1997年，富裕村修建因山体滑坡搬迁村民安置点，建起外观统一的民居住房50户，建筑面积4500平方米。1998年，在原乌栗乡政府旧址建乌栗中学新校舍，占地3200平方米，建筑面积2200平方米，活动场地1800平方米。与此同时改扩建乡直属乌栗小学，新建教学楼1050平方米，使学校总建筑面积达5150平方米，活动场地3050平方米，其中硬化场地2000平方米。2004年，在集镇王家大院修农贸市场1个，面积8000平方米，设摊位90个。2007年，县政府落实市发展改革委员会“2006年农村卫生服务体系建设方案”，在乌栗建谷堡乡卫生院业务大楼，投入资金33万元，其中中央预算内专项资金25万元，省、市、县配套资金分别为5万元、2万元、1万元，并得到香港“佛光国伟”捐资15万元，建成占地面积300平方米，建筑面积500平方米，内外装饰现代的乡卫生院大楼。2009年，县交通局与乡政府主持，利用世界银行贷款项目贷款100万元，修建谷堡乡乌栗汽车客运站，占地6亩，设有乌栗至修文、贵阳线路，每日往返车次24次。到2010年，乌栗集镇面积为0.25平方公里。有街道3条，全长870米，农贸市场1个，客运汽车站1个，医院1所，中小学各1所。

五、六屯

六屯集镇位于县城东部都堡村，地处修文、开阳、乌当三县（区）交汇部位，距县城38公里，有扎（佐）六（屯）公路（X192）穿过，连通至开阳县香火岩。是县域内东部地区传统的物资交易地。1996年，集镇街道改造、扩建，建有集镇街道2条，全长1200米，集镇面积0.26平方公里。2010年，集镇常住居民450户，常住人口3000人，居民建房3万平方米，成为以农副产品，土特产生产加工、商贸、旅游服务综合性集镇。

六屯鸟瞰

街道改造 1996年8月，县、乡政府进行六屯集镇街道改造、扩建，将扎（佐）六（屯）公路集镇街道拓宽为12米，长900米的混凝土路面为集镇主街，另修建分支街宽8米，长400米，与主街形成“十字形”交叉街道，使全集镇街道共长1300米。沿街设置环卫设施垃圾池、果皮箱，安装沿街路灯，整个扩、改建工程于1997年9月30日正式竣工，结束六屯街砂石路面历史。2003年，扎（佐）六（屯）公路路面改造，铺筑沥青路面，并进行街道绿化。

房屋建筑 1996年，集镇街道扩、改建，居民拆除旧房36户，共2160平方米，修建砖混结构楼房，建筑面积1万平方米，投入建设资金3150万元。乡政府及乡属机关单位在集镇主街修建单位公房，建筑面积共8500平方米，投入建设资金950万元。相继修建集镇农贸市场1个，占地1780平方米，建筑面积1143平方米，设商铺22间，摊位80个，投入建设资金200万元。到2005年，居民相继续建住宅和商铺兼用房21栋，建筑面积共计1365平方米，其中经营商铺面积682平方米。2007年，县政府落实贵阳市发展改革委员会2006年农村卫生服务体系建设，投入专项资金23万元扩建乡卫生院业务用房350平方米，使乡卫生院业务用房建筑面积增为800平方米。2010年，筹建中的六屯乡客运汽车业务用房建筑面积800平方米，已进入工程建设招标程序。

供排水 1997年，乡政府投资28万元，修建集镇饮用水工程，采取电力提升方式，铺设输水总管2000米，日供水100吨，解决全集镇居民、机关、餐饮商户共600户饮用水。2010年，集镇日供水能力132吨，年生活用水4.83万吨，自来水普及率98%。1996年8月实施集镇街道扩改建，于街道两侧修筑起封闭式排水沟，雨污合流，全长1900米。后又修建污水处理厂1座，日处理污水能力80吨。

供电 1978—1995年，由扎佐和平供电站供电，供电不稳定。1996年争取到贵阳市“村村通电”资金，接通久长变电站电网，建一条10千伏线路长14公里，用电得到保障。2004年，农村电网改造增建六屯变电站，实现城乡电网同网同价，一户一表。集镇街道安装路灯，通宵照明。

六、小箐

小箐集镇位于县城西北小箐村，1978—1992年，为区政府驻地，有修（文）六（广）公路（X184）穿集镇而过，距县城19公里，是洒坪、石洞、六广毗邻地物资交易的传统小集镇。

1992年，撤小箐区，建小箐乡。乡政府机关设于小箐街，为全乡中心集镇。乡政府按照县委、县政府城乡建设发展思路，小箐集镇以农副产品加工，集市贸易为主的集镇展开建设。到2010年，集镇面积达0.35平方公里。常住户750户，常住人口0.6万人，房屋建筑面积13万平方米。

远眺小箐

街道 1978年，小箐集镇只有老街1条，长400米。1979年起，居民沿修（文）六（广）公里（X184）老街口从东至西沿线修建住房，到1992年建成长1000米公路街。从2003年起在老街南街口起至贵（阳）毕（节）公路匝道口路段修建住房，到2005年已初步形成间断街。随后沿修六公路南侧逐步开发，到2010年，集镇共建街道4条，总长2000米，街域面积1.68万平方米，街道铺面面积0.96万平方米。其中，迎宾路为集镇主街，从修（文）六（广）公路小箐段消极洞至大丫口，全长1000米，宽8米；太平路为集镇老街，从老街口北端至油脂仓库段，全长400米，宽7米；兰谷路从老街南街口至小箐小学段，全长200米；石景路东从集镇农贸市场起，西至小箐中学段，全长400米。

房屋 1978年，小箐街公房有：小箐粮食仓库1栋、粮管所办公经营房1栋，小学1所房屋2栋、初中1所石墙房1300平方米，区公所办公房1栋，供销社房屋1栋，均为小青瓦木房、砖木结构房和石墙瓦房，总面积2000平方米。居民多数为土墙茅草房，少数木板青瓦房，住户250户，人口1600人。从1985年开始兴修一批单位公房，相继建有供销社办公经营楼1栋2层，建筑面积2040平方米；区公所办公楼1

栋3层，建筑面积972平方米。以及区法庭、公安派出所、农技站、工商所、信用合作社、烟叶站、税务所等单位公房。居民拆除土墙瓦房和茅草房，相继建起一批砖混结构1至2层小平房。

1992年，乡属机关事业单位为改善办公环境，相继修建单位公房，是年小箐乡卫生院建业务用房1栋建筑面积200平方米，继后建病房1栋建筑面积477平方米；1993年小箐粮管所建粮贸大楼1栋3层，建筑面积800平方米，小箐中学扩建校舍1栋，使校舍建筑面积增为2188平方米；2001年乡政府建精神文明活动中心大楼1栋4层，建筑面积1900平方米；2002年小箐中学建教学楼1栋5层，建筑面积5436平方米；2003年乡政府财政投资建集镇农贸市场1个，面积3500平方米，设经营商铺22个，摊位80个，水冲式公厕1座面积50平方米；2005年公房建筑面积达6.55万平方米，总投资达3100万元。居民建2层以上楼房82幢，已消灭土墙茅草房，住户620户，人口2480人。2007年，县政府落实贵阳市发展改革委员会2006年农村卫生服务体系建设，扩建乡卫生院业务用房，建筑面积550平方米，使乡卫生院建筑面积达1227平方米。除机关、事业单位建公房外，居民在新开发路段修建住房，底层为经营铺面，楼层为住宅，其中2至5层楼层100余栋，建筑面积共5.5万平方米。到2010年，集镇房屋建筑面积达13万平方米。

供电　1978年，由修文至广田路线供电，电压基本正常。2000年农村电网改造，实行城乡同网同价，一户一表，户通率达100%，集镇街道改装水泥电杆和路灯，电压稳定。

供水　1979年5月，由县水利局设计在集镇南的兰花岩建提水站，装机40千瓦，修蓄水池1座，容量40立方米，从蓄水池再提升至学校坡丫口，再筑蓄水池1座，容量50立方米，经100毫米铸铁管输至街上。投入建设资金3.05万元，解决2000人饮水。

1992年，乡政府根据集镇建设之需，筹集资金16万元，在两蓬岩建装机34千瓦提水站。将龙洞水与兰花岩提水站连接，经两级提升，扬程达115米输至街上。1998年，又将学校坡蓄水池扩大为213立方米。2000年，乡政府投资12万元，在凤凰村上半沟大山脚建蓄水池1座，容量30立方米，铺设输水管6.1公里引至小箐街学校坡蓄水池，增加水量。

到2010年的31年，已累计投入供水建设资金50万元，对供水工程进行改造、扩建、铺设分支管线，共建蓄水池5座，总蓄水容量473立方米，解决小箐集镇750户，5000人饮用水。日供水能力4500吨，自来水覆盖集镇，普及率100%。

七、洒坪

洒坪集镇位于县城西北部小坝村，距县城26公里，有小（箐）中（寨）公路（X188）穿镇而过。1992年，县行政区划建制改革，设为洒坪乡乡政府驻地。2003年，《洒坪乡总体规划（编修）》拟定乡集镇为旅游业及农副产品生产加工为主的集镇，自此，洒坪集镇建设按《规划（编修）》展开。到2010年，形成以洒坪老街为中心向新镇区东面扩展、连片的集镇居住小区，东抵文笔山脚，西达杉林坡的集镇新街。使集镇面积增为0.24平方公里。街道总长1260米，街域面积1.25万平方米，常住户500户，常住人口0.3万人，居民住房3.2万平方米。

老街改造　1978年，洒坪老街房屋建筑以木板青瓦房为主，间有部分土墙瓦房和茅草房。1980年居民开始修建砖墙房，同时改造土墙茅草房。1984年，乡政府建砖混结构大楼336平方米。1990年，居民在街头新建住房，使老街扩展，长达300米，街道面积3300平方米。2002年，洒坪乡集镇依托过境小（箐）中（寨）公路（X188）改造之机，对老街进行改造、扩建，投入资金16万元，将老街改造成宽7.5

洒坪街景

米，长314米的混凝土路面，使老街与新街道相连。自此，结束洒坪街砂石路，无排水沟，雨天一街泥，晴天满街灰的历史。

新区建设 2002年，洒坪集镇建设以过境公路改造，硬化为契机，修建一条长960米，宽13.5米集镇新街。在新街两侧建人行道，筑排水沟，铺设自来水管，电信电缆，植行道树，装置路灯。修建起乡政府行政中心大楼、乡财政所、公安派出所、生态移民中心、精神文明中心、计生妇幼保健服务中心、乡卫生院、中小学教学楼、集镇农贸市场等建筑，2006年底，单位公房建筑面积达3万平方米，总投资1800万元，形成集镇建设重心向新区倾斜。在新街利用以工代赈移民异地扶贫搬迁项目修建移民住房120户，每户由政府补助建设资金1万元，使户均建筑面积达85平方米，形成长1000米的移民一条街。继后，吸引本乡和外乡居民陆续前来新区建房，其中平房130栋，建筑面积1.3万平方米，二层楼以上楼房48栋，建筑面积0.96万平方米。新区房屋建筑总面积达到6.3万平方米。

供排水 1997年在乡境青龙山洞湾水塘筑水渠，以明渠自流式引水至集镇，修建蓄水池，经简易处理，由分支管道输至用户，水卫生质量极差。2000年，县水利局投资80万元，从小箐乡鲤鱼塘取地下水，建提水站1座，以封闭管道输水至集镇，铺设输水管19.2公里，设置蓄水池2座，其中低位水池容量150立方米，高位水池200立方米。基本解决集镇饮水。继后，为彻底解决集镇用水，国家投资67万元在太阳坪（天星桥引水工程项目）建水厂1座，铺设输水管16.47公里，引水至集镇，日供水能力2100吨，年人均生活用水6吨，自来水普及率98%。2001年前，洒坪集镇街道没有排水设施。2002年老街改造，新区建设修筑街道排水沟，总长2500米，雨污合流，由县城乡建设局规划设计室设计，县建筑公司承建。排水系统以集镇地形、地势划分排水区域，采用沿街道铺设矩形沟渠，浆砌石607立方米，用混凝土预制板封盖。生活污水采用化粪池沉积消化，流入雨污沟渠分片区排放，汇合后排入镇旁天然消坑。

供电 1978年洒坪街用电由修文至广田高压输电线供电，1999年农村电网改造，木质电杆改为水泥电杆，按标准更新输电线路，实现城乡电网同网同价，一户一表，供电稳定，户通率100%。

八、大石

大石集镇位于县城西北部大石村，距县城37.6公里。有广（田）六（桶）公路（X186）经过。1990年，场坝面积3000平方米，赶集人数每场1400人，置有摊位40个，是县域内西北部传统的物资交易地。

1992年，乡政府按照县委、县政府提出的“十五”期间以科学规划为先导，要素聚集为基础，产业发展为支撑，城乡一体化为目标，提高城镇化水平，缩小城乡差距，促进城乡协调发展思路，将大石集镇建设定位为以农副产品加工，旅游服务和集市贸易为主的集镇。到2010年，集镇主干街道形成，居民住户460户，人口0.25万人。

大石一隅

街道扩建 1996年，乡政府按照《大石乡总体规划》展开集镇建设。2004年，根据大石绿色石林景区旅游景点开发，对总体规划进行修编，集镇以贸易、农副产品加工和旅游服务为主，开展以修（文）六（桶）公路（X186）街为主骨架的集镇建设，集镇范围东北面至大石村与大寨村交界处，东南面至坡脚组山下，西南面至乡砖厂与田湾组交界处，集镇面积1.2平方公里。2010年，完成主干一条街改造，南起木踏石路口，北至关牛洞旁路口，全长1300米，路宽8米，街道两侧修筑排水沟，全长2000米。其中，中街北端两侧建有宽2至3米人行道。随街道扩建，使集镇面积达到0.25平方公里。

房屋建筑 1992年，乡政府投资建大石乡小学教学楼，设置班次10个；邮电所修建砖混结构单位公房160平方米，置业务房6间。1993年，建公安派出所办公楼，占地200平方米，砖混结构房1栋2层，建筑面积400平方米；农村信用社占地456平方米，建2层办公楼，设业务用房150平方米。2000年，县卫生局投资10万元为乡卫生院建业务房200平方米。2001年，贵阳市政府拨款修建大石中学教学大楼1栋，建筑面积4275平方米，设教室14间，办公室、实验室等共10间。2002年，六广供销社大石分社建经营门面房2个。2003年建大石集镇农贸市场，占地6800平方米，建筑面积2000平方米。2006年，司法所购置民房1处，改造为2层办公楼，面积380平方米。2007年，建乡计划生育妇幼保健站2栋3层楼，建筑面积共800平方米；县政府、县卫生局落实贵阳市发展改革委员会2006年农村卫生服务体系建设，为乡卫生院扩建业务房400平方米，使乡卫生院建筑面积共计达1070平方米。同时，大石乡居民根据乡集镇建设规划修编，为适应乡旅游产业发展之需，相继在街道修建商贸、住宅房，底层门面经营，楼上或后院为住宅，使牛肉粉馆、面馆、餐饮店、小商品店布满街道。共有商住房建筑面积3万平方米。2009年，投资20万元对集镇房屋进行立面改造，到2010年全部完成改造40户，使街道房屋焕然一新。

基础设施 大石为全县唯一的布依族乡，也是全省一类重点少数民族贫困乡。随着省新一轮扶贫攻坚的实施，大石乡建设在政策、项目、资金得到省、市、县扶持。

1997年到2005年，相继4次对大石集镇生活供水设施进行改造、扩建。其中：1997年，为解决1981年建的响水洞引水供水不足，县水利局重新设计，从距离集镇5.5公里的联合村何家洞引水至大石街，投入“渴望工程”资金24万元，安装输水管5500米，筑蓄水池2个，容量178立方米。2002年，县水利局再次勘察设计，从六广镇竹营村叫化洞引水至大石，铺设输水管6643米，建蓄水池3个，容量335立方米，投入资金46万元。2004年，利用国家“解困工程”项目资金10.2万元，增建蓄水池2个，容量150立方米，铺输水管长9650米。2005年，第三批“渴望工程”投入资金5.39万元，县民政局投入2.4万元，又增建蓄水池3个，容量204立方米，铺输水管8633米。经过改造、扩建使集镇生活用水每天每人达到160升，年供水量4万吨，年人均生活用水36.5吨，自来水普及率100%。

2003年，集镇街道，铺筑沥青路面，进一步改善集镇镇容，净化环境。县、乡政府投资95万元，建乡集镇农贸市场1座，占地面积6800平方米，建筑面积2000平方米。2004年，在农村电网改造建设中，完善、更换集镇供电设施，用电线路架设规范，用上安全、放心电，实现城乡电网同网同价，用电户装表率100%。2005年，建电视差转台1座，电视普及率100%。2010年，程控电话进入百姓家达90%，移动通信信号、联通通信信号覆盖全乡。

九、六桶

六桶集镇位于县城西北六桶坝。距县城50公里，是修文、息烽、金沙、黔西四县邻近区域物资集散地。1994年集镇整体搬迁至原街面相邻的盐井村，到2010年，集镇面积扩大到2平方公里，新集镇常住800户，人口5000人。

沿边重镇六桶

街道建设 1978年，六桶集镇仅有寒婆岭至小木林300米长的一条街，街下面建一个既停车又赶场的小坝子。由于地势低洼，地形狭窄，交通堵塞，制约着当地经济发展和居民生活环境的改善。1994年乡级机关和集镇整体搬迁至盐井村，建成街道6条，分为行政商贸、文化教育、自然生态、交通报务、工业5个区块，规划建设占地2460亩，其中建设用地995.25亩，占40.46%。2005年街道建设基本完成，2010年新街住宅建筑完成85%。

基础设施 1995年起，新集镇建设中，乡政府投资260万元建5000平方米集镇农贸市场，修经营大棚，设置摊位，修建公厕等设施。修筑集镇街道排水沟，其中主街采取由临街面单位、住户、商铺以建房占街道长度按比例出资统一修建，筑浆砌石沟渠，盖水泥预制板，人行道铺设供水主管，埋设电信电缆，种植行道树。次街由贵阳市政府、乡政府共同投资27万元，修建排水沟，与主街排水沟相连，利用地势走向，雨污合制排入刘家沟凹地。到2005年排水项目全部完工。

1998年起，县供电局进行农村电网建设和改造，建六桶变电站，并改造35千伏六桶变电站供电线路，完成集镇电网建设，实现一户一表，用电线路覆盖每条街，并且在集镇主街，次街人行道单侧均安装钢管杆式路灯，共计80余盏。至2003年新集镇供电工程全部完成。

2005年，由县水利局投入资金26万元建新集镇自来水厂1座，铺设供水干线5.86千米，由乡水利站负责管理。2006年11月，为保证集镇供水面，增加供水量，县水利局启动“饮水安全”工程，利用煤幺寨地下水建提水站，筑高位水池输水至水厂，扩大供水量，工程由县水利局投入建设资金80万元，利用移民搬迁经费40万元，共投入建设资金120万元。2010年，集镇供水能力380吨/日，年人均生活用水16.2吨，自来水普及率100%。

专记：六桶集镇异地搬迁

六桶乡是1992年由原六桶、花椰、凉井、宝寨4个小乡合并组建，乡级机关设于六桶坝。由于原集镇三面环山，地势狭窄，不宜发展。乡政府重组后，按照民众意愿，决定搬迁。立即成立集镇建设委员会和搬迁实施领导小组，选址于原集镇南面相邻且地势开阔的盐井村盐井组。同时对新址进行测量和规划，确定以发展商贸、农副土特产品加工为主的综合性集镇，新集镇中部为行政办公区、商业贸易区，东西部为文化、教育区，西北部为自然生态景观区，南部为对外交通服务区，东北部为工业区，规划面积共2460亩，其中建设用地995.25亩。

1994年9月7日乡政府办公楼率先破土动工，拉开新集镇建设序幕。新集镇以过境的广（田）六（桶）公路（X186）盐井村段，南起六桶变电站，北至乡卫生院，长1500米，宽17米公路为主街，两侧各建3米宽的人行道。另以主街分支建4条次街，即主街中段分叉至东面多缤洞和息烽县九庄方向，街长670米，宽8米；主街东侧分叉至乡国土所，街长300米，宽7米；再分至六桶中学，分支为“Y”形再连接东北面次干街，长300米，宽7米；乡派出所至六桶小学，再往北接主街，长200米，宽7米。各条次街两侧建2—3米宽人行道，允许本乡及邻乡居民在人行道外购地（限宽12米内）建房。到1995年集镇道路基本形成，乡属电信、邮政、财政、农村信用社、派出所、工商所、粮站、烟草、供电等机构及250户居民相继在新街建房搬迁。是年8月30日启动新集镇农贸市场赶集。为使后人不忘惠及千秋的搬迁大举，1997年7月1日乡党委、乡政府在办公大院门前着文刻石为记。

六桶新集镇一角

2005年，再扩建120米长的移民新街，并投资27万元修建排水沟渠，投资26万元建设集镇供水，县供电局对六桶变电站35千伏线路进行改造，实现一户一表。是年底，已形成主街一条，次街5条，街道总长3090米，房屋总建筑面积18万平方米，农贸市场、供电、供排水完备，常住居民696户，流动住户35户，集镇人口2454人的新兴集镇，邻县邻乡群众纷纷入市摆摊经营，在建的海马大桥竣工后，新集镇成为金沙县化觉、柏坪和息烽县九庄途经修文到贵阳的交通枢纽地。

第三节　乡村建设

1979年到1995年，在实施“要致富，先修路”战略和以工代赈、移民异地扶贫搬迁等工作的推动下，乡村建设虽有起色但步伐较缓慢，全县多数乡村只有马车道入村，通电村组仅1364个，占总村组数的95.1%，通电户4.52万户，占总户数的90.1%。政府虽投资100余万元修建乡村人畜饮水工程90余处，但仍有1.5万人存在饮水难的问题，有1.16万农户居住茅草房。

1996年，修文县划属贵阳市管辖，乡村建设步伐加快，1998年起先后实施茅草房改造，扶贫建房，危房改造，“四气一改”，新农村建设，乡村道路改造硬化，实施国家农村饮水“渴望工程”和贵阳市“百村人饮工程”，农村电网建设和改造等，掀起乡村建设热潮。到2010年，全县农村人均住房面积达30.6平方米；实施“渴望工程”132处，“百村人饮工程”14处，人畜饮水困难得到解决；农村用电实现城乡一体化管理，同网同价，电网覆盖率100%；全县共建乡村公路189条，总里程1311.34公里，实现乡村公路村村通。

折溪村新貌

一、道路建设

（一）进村路

2004年4月16日，启动首批4条贫困村公路修建通过招标方式实施；28日，第二批贫困村公路12条开工；5月18日第三批贫困村公路12条建设启动；31日第四批贫困村公路15条动工。至2005年，共修建贫困村公路66条，全长475.8公里，投入建设资金6244.1万元，覆盖全县144个村。同时，对已通村公路砂石路进行混凝土硬化10条，扩宽道路5至5.5米，全长135.5公里。还改造通往乡村旅游景点公路12条，全长45.6公里。经过进村公路建设，使龙场、扎佐、久长、六广4镇实现村村通水泥路，六屯、谷堡、小箐、洒坪、大石、六桶6乡进村主干道硬化共计40条。

2008年，全县建有乡村公路158条，总里程1141.34公里。其中，拓宽、改造、硬化四级路面公路28条，共计214.64公里；等外路面公路117条，共计784.5公里，处于施工中道路13条，长442.2公里；2009年，新建进村公路130公里。2010年，改造、新建、续建村级公路25.9公里，是年全县通村道路长1311.34公里，实现全县217个行政村村村通，等外级道路仅存122.7公里。

2002—2010年全县扩改建四级乡村道路一览表

表3—05—08

起止点	长（公里）	起止点	长（公里）
久长镇——大石乡高枧	29.32	小箐街——小坝	6.5
久长镇——久长镇清水村	4	冒沙井——下花塔	8.6
久长镇王家河——赵家坝	12	谷堡——大塘	12.5
龙场镇——扎佐镇三元	5	谷堡乡乌栗——红星	3
扎佐镇三里——六屯乡桃源村	12	龙场镇青龙——岩脚寨	4.7
六广镇广城——沙坡	7	谷堡集镇——平寨	5.3
小箐乡崇思——久长镇栋青	13.5	谷堡乡乌栗——下花塔	10
六桶集镇——海马孔	10	六广镇中山——五老山	7
六桶乡六桶坝——黄金村	9	德政——元庆	3
六桶乡——官寨	10.8	谷堡乌栗——尖山	2.7
六桶乡花榔——长岭冈	8	合兴——十字岭	4
猫洞——新义	8	大寨——下花塔	8
松山——烂窑	3	谷堡下洞——大寨	6
久长金桥——马家桥	10	红星——平寨	3

2004—2005年贫困村进村道路建设情况表

表3—05—09

项目 乡镇	公路数（条）	里程（公里）	投资（万元）	涉及村（个）
龙场镇	7	99.3	755	17（镇外村1个）
扎佐镇	10	37.6	598.7	16
久长镇	5	95.4	651.8	10
六广镇	6	23.5	449.5	13（镇外村1个）
六屯乡	5	24.3	485.4	8
谷堡乡	8	40.5	764.7	20
小箐乡	8	44.3	637.2	17（乡外村1个）
洒坪乡	6	40.8	574.6	15
大石布依族乡	6	38.0	760.2	16（乡外村1个）
六桶乡	5	32.1	567.0	12
合　计	66	475.8	6244.1	144

专记：广山村打通村公路促进运输业发展

广山村坐落于六广集镇东面，东连四寨村，南邻中山村、西接新义、中心村，北靠青龙村。往东经小箐至修文，往南经六广抵黔西，往西经大石至六桶，往北经德政到息烽县。村居委会驻地广田街上，距六广集镇8公里。1992年，行政区划改制，划编六广镇管辖。

全村耕地人均占有量仅0.6亩，但煤炭资源丰富，产煤量大。原煤除供县境外，还销至贵阳、开阳、息烽、黔西等地。2001年，修文至六广、六桶、德政公路改造和通村公路扩建后，外地进村运煤车辆骤增。村党支部书记李学开见运煤车辆多装快跑，昼夜不停，便购置1辆汽车搞运输，年收入3万余元，在其带动下部分村民也购车搞起运输来。

2004年，村民抓住全县进村公路进行扩宽、硬化改造，改善村交通环境的契机，相继购车50辆，把煤炭、水泥制品往外运，把农资化肥和生活日用品运进来，一改单一的种植业为种植运输并举，共同发展。

2005年，运输红红火火，车辆增至93辆，平均3户村民有1辆运输车，村两委为发展集体经济，筹资15万元建起3000平方米的大牲畜交易市场，投资25万元建起3000平方米社会停车场，投资16万元建起村农贸市场，设置铺面103个，引进外地商家70余家入驻，所经销的商品全由村运输户承运，使全村经济又上一个新台阶，农民人均纯收入达2200元，超过全县平均水平。

（二）串户路

2001年初，贵阳市市长孙国强到久长镇石安村调研，目睹远近闻名的石安古寨，受到村民酿酒、养猪影响，污水横流，臭气冲天，道路稀烂，环境脏、乱、差。当即提出对石安古寨环境综合治理。3月20日县政府成立石安村村容村貌治理领导小组，展开对石安的环境治理。到年底村寨道路硬化、扩宽村组道路200米，村民串户路5公里。2003年4月，久长镇驴坊村干部容弟伦、叶兴伦为开发村苗木基地和发展蔬菜种植，组织村民筹集资金11万元，修建全村串户路。2004年，县委、县政府贯彻落实贵阳市筑党发〔2003〕28号文件，全面展开全县村寨串户路修建，其中：扎佐镇乘工矿企业建设“三通一平”修建公路之机，修筑与工矿公路相连的户通路21条，100公里；久长镇清水村为发展饲养鹅鸭、奶牛和改变村容村貌，修建串户路24条，2534米。大石乡为配合石林旅游景区开发，修进村民组路11条，长11公里，使84个村的大多数农户门前有路，随着又修串户路1.5公里。小箐乡大坝村遵照《贵阳市创建生态示范村实施意见》改善村容村貌，硬化串户路6公里。

2009年，县委、县政府为改善农村人居环境，促进城乡一体化建设，全面铺开串户路建设，共修建串户路175公里。地处山重水复的洒坪乡入组串户路硬化达85%，花繁果香的谷堡乡进寨通组没有回头路，相互串通，串户路硬化达90%。

洒坪农村串户路

2010年，继续村寨公路和串户路硬化。全县农村共建串户路140公里，使人居环境大幅度改善，呈现“走遍村寨不脏鞋、车子开进院坝来”可喜的局面。

（三）机耕道

2003年，县委、县政府贯彻《贵阳市贫困村村公路建设改造工程实施办法》，把农村农田管理的机耕道纳入农村道路建设范围，先在龙场、扎佐、久长3镇展开，市级投入资金19.5万元，县级投入1.95万元，共建机耕道13公里。2004年起机耕道建设在10乡（镇）铺开，至2010年，全县投入建设资金828.56万元，其中市级资金376.61万元，县级匹配1.95万元，村自筹450万元，共建机耕道长95.6公里。

2003—2010年全县机耕道建设情况表

表3—05—10

年度	修建机耕道里程（公里）	市、县政府补助资金（万元）
2003	13	市级19.5，县级1.95，共21.45
2004	15	市级37.5
2005	22.5	市级50.75
2006	13.7	市级36
2007	6.7	市级72.36
2008	2.7	市级17.5
2009	21	市级136.5
2010	1	市级6.5
合计	95.6	378.56

二、住宅修建

（一）移民建房

1997年，谷堡乡率先在富裕村建起因山体滑坡受灾移民搬迁安置点，修住宅50户，4000平方米，成为外观统一的新农舍。2001年，洒坪乡开创利用以工代赈、移民异地搬迁项目修建移民新居120户，每户由政府补助建房资金1万元，户均面积达85平方米，形成一条排列整齐的移民住房街。六桶乡开发盐井村新集镇修建长达166米的移民新街，还利用以工代赈移民异地搬迁资金建移民安置小区住房65户。与此同时在县境西部山区修建因灾、因贫移民搬迁住房，其中相对集中的建有小箐乡崇恩、大林移民住房46户，所有移民住房均为砖混结构小平房，每户建筑面积在80至90平方米，外墙贴瓷砖，内墙刷涂料，地板浇铸水泥清光，有的农户贴上地板砖。至2010年，全县移民搬迁建房797户，3272人受益。

（二）扶贫建房

2000年，全县10乡（镇）党委、政府贯彻落实县政府修府发〔1999〕223号文件精神，展开对农村中的特困户、受灾户、复员退伍军人、残疾人住房进行扶持修建，六广镇先行帮助32户贫困户建房81间，建筑面积3184平方米，接着各乡（镇）相继启动帮助贫困户163户，复员退伍军人47户，灾民9户，五保户305户，残疾人8户建房，每户补助建房资金1万元至3.6万元。到2010年，全县扶贫建房564户，解决2000人住房困难。

（三）茅草房改造

1998年，由贵阳市启动茅草房改造，户补助3000—4000元不等。2000年，县委、县政府提出“改造茅草房”要求，展开对全县农村茅草房的普查工作。2001年，根据市委“在三五年内消除茅草房”的指示，决定对全县农民居住的茅草房进行改造。到2004年的4年，全县消除农村茅草房1.16万户。

专记：农村茅改暖人心

2000年12月28日，贵州省委常委、贵阳市委书记王晓东和市委常委、市委秘书长许朗莅县调研农业、农村、农民工作，县长魏明禄陪同到谷堡乡水口村，见到村民居住在土墙茅草房时，王晓东深切地说：“解放50多年，我们的群众还住在茅草屋里，作为市、县干部，我们内心有愧，一定要采取措施由县财政安排点、市直部门挤一点，动员干部、职工捐一点，村民自己筹一点，争取三五年时间消除农村茅草房，改善农村贫困群众居住环境。”县委、县政府遵照王晓东的讲话，立即组织县机关500多名干部深入全县217个行政村展开调查，查清2001年居住在茅草房的尚有1.16万农户。县政府成立以县长魏明禄为组长、分管农村工作县委副书记、县政府副县长为副组长，县财政局、建设局、农办等部门负责人为成员的“修文县帮助农村贫困户改造茅草房工作领导小组”，出台《帮助农村贫困农户解决茅草房实施方案》，提出6个坚持：坚持农户自力更生，投工投劳和尽最大努力集资为主，政府补助每户4000元资金；坚持建房面积每户不低于80平方米；坚持因地制宜，适当集中，原则上以原宅基地为主，结合小城镇建设、小康村建设，建房地块由乡、村调剂解决；坚持先解决挨邻集镇和旅游景点周边的，再解决靠公路沿线的，最后解决边远地区的住户；坚持计划生育户、双女结扎户、优抚对象户、少数民族户优先；坚持除市、县直属部门帮助解决外，所余茅改，以农村特困户危房改造和以工代赈，移民搬迁项目在4年内加以解决。同时制定茅草房改造土地使用原则、建房标准、资金补助、区域规划、简化手续等办法，要求就地改造、异地搬迁、先行试点、分步实施、普遍展开、层层落实。

贵阳市委书记王晓东在水口村调研

从2001年到2004年，改造茅草房1.16万户，建成户均面积80平方米的砖混结构平房，70%采取外墙贴瓷砖装饰，建筑面积达93万平方米，投入茅改资金1.38亿元。其中：市财政投入扶助资金1368万元，市级部门帮扶资金2066.54万元，市领导帮助解决64万元，县财政投入资金436.8万元，县属部门帮扶资金311.2万元，县领导班子成员帮扶解决24.2万元，启动灾民建房资金112万元，使用以工代赈移民搬迁资金210万元，农民自筹资金9200万元。

茅改结束农村居住茅草房的历史。六桶乡盐井村民刘长志新房落成门联上所题：“三个代表落到实处谢党恩，大好政策落实茅改我受益”，洒坪乡一农户门联：“三个代表送春风，茅改工程暖万户”，表达农民感谢党和政府的心声。

（四）危房改造

2005年，首先在大石布依族乡实施，以改善农村人居环境，到2007年，共改造农村危房89户，国家投入改造资金35.6万元。2009年2月16日，县政府召开全县农村危房改造工作会议，全面展开农村危房改造，对危房改造工作进行具体安排部署，要求年内按计划完成第一批改造任务1482户。2010年继续开展农村危房排查、改造，两年共改造危房9911户。

2009—2010年全县农村危房改造概况表

表3—05—11

乡　镇	合计	省级补助改造危房（户）	市级补助改造危房（户）	危房改造中异地搬迁（户）
龙场镇	1686	237	1449	—
扎佐镇	893	—	—	—
久长镇	965	42	923	—
六广镇	1564	—	—	—
六屯乡	1023	—	2009年541 2010年482	—
谷堡乡	558	51	507	—
小箐乡	866	33	2009年370 2010年463	—
洒坪乡	445	—	390	55
大石布依族乡	919	—	2009年451 2010年408	60
六桶乡	992	2009年44 2010年365	518	65
合计	9911	—	—	180

（五）农房立面整治

2009年，开展对全县主要交通干道贵（阳）遵（义）和贵（阳）毕（节）公路、210国道、麦（架桥）肖（家寨）公路沿线可视范围内两侧农民住房立面景观整治，统一改造成外观白墙、坡形屋面、赭石色木梁结构样式，院前花池小路格调统一，呈现一派社会主义新农村景象。其中扎佐镇在贵（阳）遵（义）公路三元村、猪头山村段；久长镇在贵（阳）遵（义）公路兴隆村、久长村、驴坊村段、麦肖公路久长村段；龙场镇在贵（阳）毕（节）公路马关村、小营村、新生村段临路农房全部立面改造共320户。与此同时，龙场镇阳明村、新生村临阳明洞景区立面改造农舍40户，六桶乡海马孔生态旅游村寨立面改造农舍50户。全县农舍立面整治达410户。

立面改造后的农舍

三、人畜饮水

1980年，有取水垂直距离超100米，水平距离超1000米，人畜饮水最困难，干旱山区小箐乡率先实施兰花岩人畜饮水工程建设。20世纪90年代又对小箐饮水工程进行改造，再建小箐大坝饮水工程，解决小箐村、大坝村4000人，大牲畜1980头饮水困难。2000年开始实施贵阳市“百村人饮”工程和国家二期“渴望工程”，建起扎佐镇三元、黑山坝、新庄3个饮水工程、小箐乡崇恩饮水工程、久长镇金桥饮水工程等项目。至2004，全县凡在水平距离超过1000米，垂直距离超过100米饮水困难的村寨均建起人畜饮水工程，共实施“百村人饮”工程14处，总投入资金125.63万元，解决7922人，大牲畜4100头饮水困难；实施“渴望工程”132处，总投入资金1290.9万元，解决5.87万人和1.59万头牲畜饮水困难，至此，全县农村人畜饮水困难基本解决。2009年建成中央预算内资金水库饮水工程扎佐镇丁官村1—3组的9个工程，解决5387人饮水安全。全县建成第一批省级财政投资农村饮水安全工程14处，解决5513人饮水安全。是年11月13日，县人大、县政府对竣工的全省农村集中饮水安全规模最大的岩鹰山供水工程进行视察，察看工程质量和供水效果，对工程予以肯定。其供水范围覆盖小箐、洒坪、六广、大石4乡（镇）的48个行政村5.5万人，日供水量4500吨，总投资2636万元，使县域西部干旱地区群众喝上安全水、卫生水。

全县主要农村饮水工程概况表

表3—05—12

工程名称	工程位置	供水范围	建成时间	投资（万元）	受益	
					人口（人）	牲畜（头）
大石乡饮水工程	响水洞	大石乡政府所在地及附近村寨	1982.4	6.8	2000	740
六桶乡芭蕉沟工程	刘家沟	六桶坝及附近村寨	1986.7	25.21	2000	500
久长镇饮水工程	金桥村	久长镇区及附近村寨	1985.12—2000	228.9	3000	600
扎佐镇高潮水厂	大堡村	扎佐集镇及工业厂矿、村寨	2005.12	800	—	—
龙场镇城南水厂	毛栗园	县城区及附近农村	1997—2000	343.88	—	—
岩鹰山水厂	岩鹰山	小箐、洒坪、六广、大石48个村	2009.	2636	55000	—
小箐集镇饮水工程	兰花岩	小箐街及附近村寨	1980.3	3.05	2000	935
轿子山饮水工程	轿子山	中寨轿子山村	1982	—	700	150
清让饮水工程	付家墓龙滩	清让顺兴场村	1985.5	—	1654	650
沙堰饮水工程	沙堰田坝	沙雁、永兴村及久长变电站	1982.10	—	—	—
三元饮水工程	对门寨	三元村村寨及工矿企业	1990.10	16	1600	983

干旱山区小箐乡人畜饮水工程概况表

表3—05—13

工程名称	规模		效益		投资（万元）	建成时间（年）	地点（村）
	蓄水（立方米）	管线（千米）	人口（人）	牲畜（头）			
小箐街饮水工程	473	66	3200	1615	49.8	1999	小箐街
大坝村饮水工程	200	5.1	785	366	18	1996	大坝村
崇恩村饮水工程	230	22.5	1080	861	25.2	2002	崇恩村
全星村饮水工程	50	6.2	920	486	6	1996	全兴村
高坡饮水工程	100	2.2	142	38	2.2	1998	宝山村

续表

工程名称	规模		效益		投资（万元）	建成时间（年）	地点（村）
	蓄水（立方米）	管线（千米）	人口（人）	牲畜（头）			
大林村饮水工程	180	4.5	386	162	5.2	1999	大林村
老鸦坪饮水工程	80	3.6	260	182	1.6	1998	紫江村
干冲饮水工程	80	2.8	155	86	4.2	1997	凤凰村
龙塘饮水工程	100	3.2	366	222	12	1999	龙塘村
小坝饮水工程	100	6.6	670	480	11	2000	小坝村
中坝饮水工程	65	3.6	200	115	4.6	2003	杉林村
马场饮水工程	55	4.2	380	216	4.7	2002	紫江村
郭田饮水工程	180	6.2	670	485	6.8	2003	郭田村
半沟饮水工程	30	2.2	160	80	2.3	2003	凤凰村
宝山饮水工程	220	8.1	810	667	15	2003	宝山村
新村饮水工程	60	4.2	470	311	10	1998	新场村
万兴村饮水工程	240	12.5	713	428	17.5	2004	万兴村
王武桥饮水工程	45	5.6	315	155	7	2004	新场村

四、农村电网

（一）农网建设

1993年起，全面启动农村电网建设，至1996年，电网覆盖全县214个行政村，占98.6%，通电户5.88万户，户通率达93%。1998年，按照省计委建设首批10千伏以下农村电网的规划，新建龙场镇小营10千伏变电站，设变压器11个台区。1999年，建六屯乡都堡10千伏变电站。到2000年，第一期建设告竣，全县设变压器534个台区。2003年，新建六桶乡盐井村新集镇35千伏（低压）变电站，设变压器118个台区，共计新建10千伏电路403.53公里，0.4千伏以下电路1270.4公里，实现全县用电村村通户户通。

（二）农网改造

1999年，按照国务院《关于加快农村电力体制改革，加强农村电力管理意见的通知》和国务院办公厅转发国家计委《关于改造农村电网，改革农电管理体制，实现城乡同网同价请示的通知》精神，贵阳市北供电局与修文供电局在六屯乡都堡村举行农网35千伏工程建设暨六屯变电站建设开工典礼，启动全县农村电网改造。2002年完成第一期改造工程，建10千伏项目12个，10千伏电路219公里，0.4千伏电路206公里，0.2千伏电路1129公里，改造后新电网覆盖全县行政村的70.5%。2003年，农网改造四期工程全部完成，共建10千伏项目改造线路599.4公里，0.4千伏以下项目改造线路1876.8公里，安置变压器729个台区，新电网覆盖面达99.8%。全县5.35万农户安装电表占农户的99.96%，达到一户一表，实现全县城乡电网同网同价。按全县电力一体化管理，下设龙场、扎佐、久长、六屯、小箐、六广、六桶7个供电所，农村设置39个电费收费服务站，承担全县4镇6乡217个村联网供电。2005年，全县农村电网覆盖率达100%，装表到户100%。农村农灌、植保、养殖、加工、基础设施建设以及村民生活都用上电。生产、生活向着农业现代化迈进。

2010年全县变电站一览表

表3—05—14

时　间	变电站	位置（乡村）	规模（千伏）	线路条数或公里数	供电范围及变压器台数
1998年农网改造前建	阳明变电站	龙场镇阳明村	110	35千伏4条 110千伏2条 10千伏9条	县城区、龙场镇附近村寨工矿
	久长变电站	久长镇沙雁村	110	35千伏2条 110千伏3条	久长镇区附近村寨工矿
	和平变电站	扎佐镇和平村	35	35千伏1条	扎佐镇区附近村寨工矿
	广田变电站	六广镇广田村	35	35午伏1条	六广镇区、六桶乡
1998年农网改造后建	小营变电站	龙场镇小营村	10	10千伏83.99公里 0.4千伏27.15公里	11个台区
	六屯变电站	六屯乡都堡村	10	10千伏290.54公里 0.44伏1135.25公里	534个台区
	六桶变电站	六桶乡盐井村	35	10千伏29公里 0.44千伏108公里	118个台区
2000年	扎佐喻家街变电站	扎佐喻家街	110	—	扎佐镇新开发区
2004年	扎佐变电站	马关村	220	—	供龙场、扎佐部分片区

五、沼气能源

1997年，县政府成立农村能源环保办公室，利用人畜粪便、田间杂草、农作物茎叶等发酵产出清洁、环保可燃性沼气，供农户作燃料和照明能源。该项工作配合农村“三改一气”（改厕、改圈、改厨）进行，农户建沼气池8立方米、改厕1.2平方米，改圈12平方米，改厨用瓷砖装饰内墙。政府拨付建设补助资金每户建池800元，改厕200元，改圈300元，改厨200元。按照国家《户用沼气池标准图集》《中国沼气质量检查验收规范》《户用农村能源生态工程南方模式设计施工与使用规范》《农村家用沼气发酵工艺规程》《沼气生产工艺国家职业标准》严格实施，验收资料一池一档，归档保存，合格沼气池使用期20年。首先在龙场镇马口村试点，到1999年先后建沼气池20多口。2000年起，全面铺开，当年完成沼气能源3300套。2003年完成3038套，2005年完成3000套。连续5年全县累计投入资金3519.4万元，建成沼气能源1.37万套。根据县能源办测算，每户每年节约燃煤3吨，折款1000元，节约照明用电每天平均0.6度，沼肥利用每户年平均增收节支1200元。

2006年2月，县委、县政府在谷堡乡折溪村举行全县“四改一气”农村生态能源建设启动仪式，在改厕、改圈、改厨基础上增加村寨道路改造，把“三改一气”扩展为“四改一气”。2007年，投入资金1926.9万元，完成“四改一气”工程5000套。2009年，在全县农村进一步开展建设，完成2341套，其中，扩大内需新增133套，巩固退耕还林成果建208套，利用国债项目建2000套，同时还在“龙山”乳业有限公司、好一多乳业有限公司等5个规模养殖企业建大、中型沼气池项目，开发沼气能源。由于沼气建

设是一次性投入，并纳入乡（镇）目标考核，仍出现领取补助而无实际使用户状况，加上养牛、养猪户减少，电力充沛、液化气充足和农村劳动力外出务工无人管理等因素，到2010年，使用户逐减。

2001—2005年全县农村沼气能源建设套数一览表

表3—05—15

乡镇名称	合计(套数)	2001年	2002年	2003年	2004年	2005年
龙场镇	1830	282	500	348	300	400
扎佐镇	1145	71	300	304	250	220
久长镇	1207	37	300	300	300	270
六广镇	1263	53	250	305	305	350
大石乡	843	0	250	175	218	200
六桶乡	1651	111	400	410	350	380
六屯乡	1153	52	300	221	300	280
谷堡乡	1582	166	400	448	317	250
小箐乡	1481	160	300	311	360	350
洒坪乡	1203	88	300	215	300	300
合　计	13700	1020	3300	3038	3000	3000

专记：新农村建设进一步夯实农村基础设施

2006年2月，县委、县政府根据贵阳市委、市政府《关于加快建设社会主义新农村的决定》，制定《关于加快建设社会主义新农村的实施意见》，以农村“四改一气”（改厕、改圈、改厨、改路，开发沼气能源）为突破口，以路、气、房、庭院广场、电视通信等基础设施建设为重点，打一场新农村建设攻坚战。

县委、县政府成立新农村建设工作领导小组，选择27个村进行试点，建立起县委、县人大、县政府、县政协领导和县直部门领导与试点村的联系制度，到村指导，围绕各村基础设施建设具体情况进行资源调查，选定建设项目，集中人、财、物力量，进行基础设施配套建设。以建好一个点为示范，带动一大片的思路，推进全县新农村建设。在27个试点村中有省级示范点龙场镇中哨村和谷堡乡折溪村2个，市县共建示范点洒坪乡小坝村、小箐乡杉林村、谷堡乡平寨村、久长镇永兴村4个，县级自建示范点21个，共投入新农村建设资金5703.6万元。其中久长镇重点建设永兴“春晖家园”基础设施，建起绿地休闲广场和棚式灯光篮球场，新建村民住房20户，使永兴村面貌焕然一新；谷堡乡折溪村用于基础设施建设资金90.56万元；龙场镇中哨村投入基础设施建设资金129万元，使基础设施建设上一个新台阶。

到2010年，仅5年时间，示范点完成“四改一气”工程2867套，修建和硬化进村公路5公里，进组公路15.3公里，机耕道31.7公里，村寨串户路168.63公里，改造危房321户，建“三小”（小山塘、小水池、小水窖）工程366口，人饮工程6处。修建村级综合楼21栋，建休闲广场20个共2.67万平方米，其中篮球场9个，完成村村通电视，实现用电一户一表。新农村建设取得明显成效，进一步夯实农村基础设施。

第四节　城镇住房制度改革

1978年，县城人均居住面积仅4.1平方米。除街道居民户住房外，职工多数住在机关单位因陋就简改造宿舍。1987年，县政府提出机关单位集资修建职工住房方案，以福利性方式分配。到1990年，县城人口增为2.45万人，住房累计面积达30.68万平方米，人均面积为12.5平方米。

1992年，县委、县政府贯彻执行国发〔1991〕31号和国办发〔1991〕73号文件精神，实行住房制度改革，首先改革职工福利分房，出售单位公有住房给职工，使住房逐渐步入商品化，出现新兴的房地产业。在出售公有住房的同时各种住房相继问世，建立多渠道投资、多形式开发的城镇住房建设机制。到2008年，县城出售单位公有住房12万平方米，居民自建住房50万平方米，房地产开发公司建成商品房25万平方米，政府开发经济适用住房17万平方米，单位职工集资联合建住房10万平方米，政府建廉租房1.3万平方米，使居民住房累计面积达115万平方米，人均38.1平方米，比1990年翻3番，是1978年的9倍。人口较为集中的扎佐镇、久长镇共出售单位公房9410平方米外，建起居民自建住房、经济适用房、集资房、商品房共计23.8万平方米。2009—2010年，县城房地产进入高峰期，利尔上河城商品房二期工程和新都口岸商品房二期竣工出售，腾晖花园商住楼、文城逸都商住楼一期建成出售，政府财政投资的廉租住房1200套分配出租，使居民人均住房面积上升为42平方米。

一、公有住房改革

住房提租补贴　1992年，全县党政机关、企事业单位及中央省直单位驻县职工有3182户，6121人，加上家属人口共1.03万人，住房3290套，人均居住面积仅24.5平方米。职工月均交房租2.23元，每平方米租金合0.05元。为改革职工公有住房低租金、高福利分配的制度，县实行公有住房提租补贴。提租范围包括县境内不分隶属关系所有的公有住房。提租系数标准从是年起逐步调整，以砖混结构单元式套房为准，新房每平方米使用面积月租金0.3元，旧房0.25元；同时实行住房补贴，由职工所在单位按其月工资的2%一次性核定金额，按月发给。1995年新房提为0.55元，旧房提为0.45元；1998年新房提为0.75元，旧房提为0.65元。到2000年，每平方米租金为2元。其他各类住房租金依据住房结构、房内设施、地段环境等情况进行增减调剂。住房租金提取控制面积按国发〔1983〕139号文件规定，一般职工为50平方米，县处级及相应中级职称职工为60平方米，地师级及相应高级职称职工为75平方米，超过面积即增收租金。所提取的租金由房屋所有权单位存入银行住房信贷部设立的专户，用于公有住房维修和管理。

提取住房公积金　为鼓励职工建房或购房，建立住房公积金制度，规定凡在县内工作并具有常住户口的党政机关、群众团体、企事业单位固定职工和合同制工人，无论是住公有住房，租赁住房、还是私有住房均提取住房公积金。公积金由个人和单位共同承担，最初提取比例按职工个人上年度工资总收入的5%为基数提取，属于财政负担、企业负担的单位按职工提取的5%金额值数为准，给职工补贴相应金额，一次性核定，按月补贴。凡领取公积金补贴的职工一律取消单位自发的各项住房补助。财政全额拨款单位给职工公积金补贴列入财政预算支付；差额拨款单位由财政拨款和单位自收自支两类按比例提取；企业单位由房屋折旧费、大修理基金、管理费中列支，不足部分列入企业生产成本计支。职工退休

后不再提取公积金，已提取部分金额还给职工个人。职工和单位共提取的公积金划归县住房资金管理委员会办公室统一管理。

1994年，县直机关、企业单位开始按6%比例提取住房公积金。2005年乡（镇）机关、学校、医院等部门开始执行。提取公积金比例先后两次提高，到2006年执行10%（单位和职工各5%）。

2008年1月，成立贵阳市住房公积金管理中心修文管理部，代行县住房资金管理委员会职能，管理全县住房公积金。规定凡已连续提取公积金6年以上者，年龄男60岁、女55岁以下的可申请以公积金贷款购房或建房，贷款年限在30年内，贷款金额在40万元之内。购买第一套商品住房并已付房价20%的可贷房价金额的80%；购第二套商品住房已付房价30%的可贷款房价金额的70%。购买第一套二手房者已付房价25%的可贷房价金额的75%；购第二套二手房已付房价40%的可贷房价金额的60%。如果职工用住房存量补贴支付房屋全产权中土地收益金不足时，可用公积金支付。在职工离退休、返还银行住房贷款、一次性购买商品房、经房管部门批准自建住房、死亡以及重大病患者均可使用住房公积金。至2009年，县住房公积金管理部办理提取住房公积金开户单位199个，交缴住房公积金职工6952人。2010年全县缴纳、提取滚动积存公积金5953.96万元。

公有住房出售　1992年初，县政府贯彻执行国办发〔1991〕73号《关于全面推进城镇住房制度改革的意见》和黔府发〔1992〕3号《贵州省城镇住房制度改革实施方案》，成立县城镇住房制度改革领导小组，组建县房改办公室处理日常工作。接着，再出台修府〔1992〕14号《关于推行住房制度改革工作的意见》，对全县城镇住房制度改革作出总体部署，深入宣传、改革低租金、高福利的住房制度，使干部和群众从思想上确立"住房付钱，多住多出，住好房多拿钱"的消费观念。同时，启动公有住房勘测、量算、填表完善档案。

1993年，县政府出台优惠政策，鼓励职工购买自住房，促进职工福利性住房向商品房过渡。房改办公室参考安顺地区所辖县（市）公有住房售价，结合本县情况，以1993年4月1日为界，此前所建的公有住房为旧房，以重置价每平方米177元出售，4月2日起所建公有住房为新房，以标准价每平方米187元出售。同时对军残、离休、困难户购房和提租补贴采取优惠措施，对住房面积超标户采取增收租金措施。连续5年零6个月，全县出售1993年4月1日前所建旧房1845套，出售1993年4月2日以后集资所建新房605套，其中县城528套，久长镇23套，扎佐镇54套，全县出售包括单位职工集资在内的职工公有住房共计2450套。

1993—1995年，以改革职工公有住房低租金、高福利分配为基点，按公有住房建造价的70%房产出售给住户，住户享有70%产权，先达到国家、单位、职工三级出资，共同占有房屋产权，此阶段出售的公房称为"半产权房"，不能转让、抵押。1996—2000年，为实现住房资金良性循环，既让城镇职工每户有一套住房而安居，又使国家积累部分建设资金，将单位公有住房留存的30%产权，再次出售给职工住户，使职工拥有房屋建造价100%的所有权，由"半产权房"改为"全产权房"，职工可以依法继承，如果居住5年以上并付清房款者还可将房出售，出售增值扣除税费后，按照当时所付房款占市场价比例与原产权单位分成。2000年1月1日起停止住房实物分配，住房销售全部转向商品化和市场化，其房屋的维修费、管理费、折旧费、投资利息、房产税、保险费、利润、地租等完全纳入房产，可以按市场议价出售。职工购买的"全产权住房"、集资合作建房和经济适用房均要缴纳国家所有资产部分的土地收益金，已缴纳收益金的房屋即彻底转化为完全商品房。

至2005年的8年，出售经济适用房1061套，建筑面积共为13.36万平方米，出售金额838万元。到2008年，全县已办理缴纳土地收益金的完全产权房2160户，2010年增到1.08万户。既结束低租金、高福利的住房分配的历史，又满足职工购房的渴望。

实施住房货币化制度 2008年，县政府落实贵阳市政府〔2000〕54号文件批准清镇市、开阳县、息烽县、修文县实施住房分配货币化制度，对1998年12月31日前在全民所有制或集体所有制单位就业的在册职工包括离退休职工，在实施房改前工资构成中的住房消费含量不足部分，以职工住房存量补贴方式给予职工补偿，将存量住房资产按2000年现值评估，并结合职工工龄给予一次性补贴。其补贴对象和工龄年限由县劳动人事部门提供，最高工龄计算限定为40年，以时任职务级别计算年补贴标准，一般干部320元，副局（科）级380元，正局（科）级级410元，副县（处）级和中级职称480元，正县（处）级及高级职称550元，副地级及正高级职称600元，正地级750元，职工可用存量补贴缴纳土地收益金，不足者自补，剩余的政府财政以挂靠形式暂欠职工。与此同时，将国家和单位每年用于职工住房建设投资的各种隐性支出转化而来的资金，以住房增量方式补贴给职工，用于职工住房消费，逐步纳入职工工资之中，其补贴从1999年1月1日起在全民所有制和集体所有制单位职工中实施。鉴于县财力实际情况，县财政承担的单位职工的增量补贴从2007年1月1日起计发，发放标准为在职职工月工资总额扣除西部补贴后的20%，离退休人员按月离退休费总额扣除西部补贴后的25%计算。1999年1月至—2006年12月应补发给职工的增量补贴，政府财政暂欠。

截至2008年9月20日，第一次增量补贴发放工作结束，累计归集增量资金4667万元，其中属财政负担的行政事业单位144个，归集资金3392万元；工矿、商贸等企业12个，归集资金1275万元。兑现给职工的增量补贴资金共计2531万元，兑现人数4860人，其中属于财政负担人员4656人，兑现补贴2119万元；企业负担人员204人，兑现增量补贴412万元，自此职工住房实现货币化配置。城镇低收入人群、无房户和住房困难户由县经济适用住房建设中心和廉租住房保障中心统一规划，统一建设，统筹分配，城镇住房制度改革工作重点即转入对原出售公房的土地收益金补缴和办证阶段。2010年，兑现离休干部，国家省、市劳动模范，调离县的干部共84人的住房存量补贴，计发补贴资金98万元。同时收缴土地收益金946万元，其中行政事业单位447万元，企业单位499万元。存量补贴建账5165人，其中财政负担人员4433人，企业负担人员732人，全年回收住房贷款8万余元。

发放房屋产权证 1985年，县成立房地产管理站，隶属城乡建设局。1998年7月1日起，执行《贵阳市房地产管理办法》，全县机关部门和企事业单位公房和职工购买的房改房、集资建房、经济适用房、居民私人自建住房进行登记、核查、发证。并对驻县航空工业部属8个单位累计房屋建筑面积31.44万平方米，贵铁分局火车站房屋面积9060平方米，林东矿务局贵阳煤矿房屋面积3.5万平方米，林东煤矿技校房屋面积6439.27平方米，贵铝一分厂房屋面积6.18万平方米，扎佐林场房屋面积2.23万平方米，以及驻县部队营房，县人民武装部

房屋产权证

住房都进行产权登记、归档、发放全国统一的房屋所有权证，明确房屋的产权关系。当房地产因买卖、交换、赠予、继承、折产、划拨、转让、判决等房屋转移和房地产权利人法定名称改变，或者房屋坐落的街道门牌号发生变化以及房屋部分改造、拆除、倒塌、焚毁而改变原状，房地产抵押、典让以及房屋或土地失灭、土地使用年限届满等，一律由权利人在规定的期限内持有关证件到房屋所在地人民政府房地产登记机关申请登记，注明产权变化。从1998年12月31日起可以进入市场交易。截至2005年，登记办理全国统一房屋权属新证9781件。2008年，按修委办字〔2008〕60号通知，经县城镇住房制度改革办公室核定，由产权人缴纳住房土地收益的房屋，由政府房管机构发放县房地产交易市场准入许可证，纳入商品房范围。发放房屋产权证后，既可依照法律保护自己的房屋所有权，又可上市转让、变卖，从而获得房地产增值实惠。

截至2010年，全县共计发放房屋交易市场准入许可证1.08万件，其中房改房、集资房、经济适用房共2160件，居民自建房、商品房共8670件。

二、集资建房

成本价集资　1992年，县政府针对机关、企事业单位职工住房长期失修、陈旧破烂问题，出台《集资建房实施办法》，由单位积极组织，统一规划，统一修建，职工自愿参加。采取“先集资，后建房，定向预售”办法，由职工先交集资款，当集资数额达到建房预算资金准价的60%以上，房产管理部门即办建房手续，房屋建成后按户建筑面积计算，补足建房成本价，办理住房使用权。参加集资建房的对象首先照顾单位住房困难户和危、旧、破房户，然后逐步扩宽。政府出台集资优惠政策，免征住房建设固定资产投资调节税、一次性契税、房产税、城镇土地使用税以及能源交通基金和预算调节基金，建设单位提供的建房用地，作为政府和单位对集资建房的投资，职工个人按住房成本价出资，获得房屋70%产权，但不能转让、出售。到1997年，全县按成本价集资建房528套，建筑面积4.8万平方米，其中县城451套，面积3.9万平方米；扎佐54套，面积7800平方米；久长23套，面积1610平方米。

全额集资　1998年，住房制度改革进一步深化，单位公有住房按建造价100%出售产权之后，集资建房转入按建造价100%由居住方全额集资，政府把集资建房纳入城镇建设基建计划，出台建房用地征地政策，在一定时期内免征部分税收。集资建房对象从单位扩大到城镇社区居民，共同组建合作建房组织，面向社会筹集资金，建房分房，维护管理。房屋建成后房管部门办理房产手续，住房即获得建造价100%产权，可继承、转让和出售。到2003年底停止集资建房的6年建全额集资房813套，建筑面积6.1万平方米，投入资金1亿元。

三、私人建房

1994年，根据县办通〔1994〕10号文件精神，启动县城私营经济一条街建设，在长1000米的街道上由城镇居民、个体经营户、机关企事业单位职工私人建房400多户，建筑面积18万平方米，一条取名“迎春路”的新街率先崛起，带动城镇住房建设驶进快车道。1995年，扎佐镇开发襄阳大道，私人建房200户，建筑面积8万平方米。到2000年在县城新城区6条共长1860米的主要街道上，相继建成700户私人住房，建筑面积达40万平方米。2003年，在长800米的阳明大道商贸住宅街，私人建房200多户，建筑面积19.3万平方米。2004年，久长镇开发龙山路和明珠路，私人建房130户，建筑面积7.8万平方米。到2008年，全县城镇新开发的街道上有私人建房1700户，建筑面积达95万平方米。2010年，县城建局办理私人宅基地申请建房65件，私人住房建设项目51个，总用地面积8108.88平方米。

自建自住 从1992年起，县城以及扎佐、久长、六广3镇市民个体出资自建住房，其款式多为前、后两楼，中置天井，前楼底层为铺面，楼上为住房，后楼也是住房，故称“商住楼”。楼层按县建设局统一规划、新城区不低于4层、老城区不低于3层。县城相对集中建在小吃街（良知路）、朝阳路、龙山路、健身路（文成路）、迎春路，占私人建房总数的35%。扎佐镇相对集中在襄阳路、东兴路、育英路和大园街，久长镇在龙山路、明珠路和川黔路，六广镇在南江路和松江大道，此三镇私人建房基本都为自建自住房。

联户共建 1995—2003年，县城和扎佐镇私人建房出现多户自愿联合，共同出资征地建住宅房。出资者按自身需要及经济实力预出资金，统一规划、统一修建，户型基本统一保证房屋整体结构，公用部分造价费用共同分担，共同所有。房屋建成后按各户实际建筑面积结算，产权所有者独立申报住房产权登记。此类房屋高4至6层，集中在县城新区，多建在阳明大道和朝阳路，占私人建房总数的20%。扎佐镇集中在襄阳大道，为数较少。

住售结合 1992—2010年，在私人建房中有个体出资者利用自身原有土地使用权或征拨的土地，分楼层分户建4至5层住宅式楼房。建筑临街面采取底层设门面经营铺，二楼以上分别为住宅。房屋建成后出资者申办产权证，除留出自身居住部分外，将其余部分按市场价出售。此类房屋分散在县城的多处街道和扎佐镇襄阳路、大园街，占私人建房总数的30%。

先建后售 1998年，落实《贵阳市房地产管理办法》，县房地产管理站发放房屋产权证开始，对凡持中华人民共和国房屋所有权证和县房地产交易市场准入许可证的房屋可以出售，在县城和扎佐镇出现私人建房中的先建后售情况。一是出资者先建自住房，嗣后嫌环境不适，或经济发生困难将房转手出售；二是出资者预先投资建房，建成后转手出售，以获房产增值收益。此种先建后售的私人建房主要分布在县城新城区的阳明大道、朝阳路、翠屏路路段临街面，一般高4至5层，老城区内一般是拆掉老住宅重建高2至3层，占整个私人建房总数的15%。

四、保障性住房

经济适用房 1998年，县政府针对单位职工少，既无空置土地，又缺资金而无法组织职工集资建房问题，决定修建经济适用住房。由县住房制度改革办公室拟定建设项目报经县城乡建设局备案，然后向银行贷款筹资修建。建成后由住户付款购买。当年首批经济适用住房在县城建成，取名“虎山小区安居工程”，共4幢，72套，建筑面积6600平方米，投入资金270万元，不分机关职工和街道居民，配置给缺房户和经济困难户，以每平方米430元出售。1999年，建成6幢，48套，建筑面积2.3万平方米，投入资金895万元。2000年，经济适用房建设资金实行由住户预交启动资金，政府安排用地，建成后按房屋成本价结算补交购房款，平均房价每平方米540元。至2004年，县城共建经济适用住房项目6个，住宅楼53幢，1259套，建筑面积16.9万平方米，投入建设资金1.27亿元。与此同时，在人口多，居住集中的扎佐镇，镇政府主持从1998—2004年，由贵州明兴房开公司承建“紫竹园”，清镇小城镇建设房开公司承建“珍珠铭园”、“皂角树经济适用房”和“照前值苑”A、B栋共4期经济适用房，建筑面积共2.7万平方米。2005年，进一步改革住房制度，住房全部进入市场，经济适用房停建。2008年，县政府为解决既无经济能力购买商品房，又不具备租赁廉租房条件居民的住房问题，再次启动经济适用住房建设，在县城新开发的思源路建房185套，建筑面积1.1万平方米，以每平方米1300元出售，低于商品房价30%，使城镇灵活就业低收入人群和中低收入的企事业职工得以购置经济适用住房。安有所居的弱势群体购得住房后纷纷感谢党和政府的关怀："昨天住着破瓦房，刮风下雨难抵挡；今日搬进广厦间，寒士安居感谢党"。

1998—2008年县城经济适用住房建设概况表

表3—05—16

建设时间（年）	投资量（万元）			建设规模		
	合计	个人	贷款	幢	套	建筑面积（平方米）
1998	270		270	4	72	6600
1999	895		895	6	48	23368
2000	593	593		10	48	13988
2001	1737	1737		15	527	44060
2002	765	765		5	96	17000
2003	7074	7074		6	217	23880
2004	1350	1350		7	251	30094
2008	由政府主持修建后出售				185	11193

廉租房 2007年，为解决城镇低收入人群和社会低保户住房的困难，县政府成立廉租房管理中心，由县财政出资在思源路建成每户55至60平方米的廉租房247套，建筑面积1.25万平方米，投入资金1400万元。以使用面积每平方米1元，面向社会低收入户廉价出租。2008年，在阳明大道曲尺桥三角地段建廉租房33套，建筑面积1492平方米，解决33户低收入家庭的住房，使城镇保障性住房累计面积达18万平方米。2009年，县政府又在县城城南五大块建廉租住房311套，新春村建54套，思源路（二期）建24套，扎佐镇大园村建192套，扎佐镇三元村建72套，扎佐林校建149套。同时回收2008年所建经济适用住房38套作为廉租住房处理，使全县廉租住房建成802套。

2008年，廉租房入住启动仪式

2010年，在县城城南良种场国有农用地11.89亩，启动399套建筑面积2万平方米廉租住房建设，预计次年6月分配出租。届时城镇低收入人群和社会低保户基本实现安有所居。住进到廉租房的群众连声称赞党和政府送的温暖：城镇社会低保户，安居高档暖室中，街上没有卖炭翁，我们感谢温伯公（温家宝总理）。

五、商品房开发

开发公司 1998年，利尔建材公司由生产水泥转向房地产开发，以销水泥赚积起来的资金投入县城经济适用住房建设，先后建起静园、紫荆、河滨、迎春等住宅小区，锻炼出一支开发房地产业的队伍，于1999年挂牌贵州利尔物业房地产开发公司。2000年，县内部分建筑施工企业瞄准市民对住房的需求和房地产市场前景步入房地产开发之路。县建筑公司陈华明组建起修文华明房地产开发公司，随后更名贵阳吉泓房地产开发公司。在利尔、吉泓公司带动下，有的个体经济实体也进入房地产开发行列，纷纷申报注册经营房地产，先后组建起利华、国康、深宏等公司，甚至持有贵州省建设厅颁发的入黔施工许可证，长期在县内承包建筑施工的四川合江牛脑驿建安公司法人刘明清和四川藉个体建筑工人王明，也分别组建起贵州明兴房地产开发公司和贵州标大房地产开发公司。

2004年起外地房产地产开发企业贵州星河、贵州林云、贵州绿丰、贵州新进、贵州泰维和清镇小城镇建设房开公司，也相继打入修文房地产开发市场。2007年，有贵州腾晖房地产开发公司，2009年，又有贵州弘晋、冠荣房地产开发公司进入修文开发房地产，至此县境内的房地产开发公司先后拥有19家。

开发项目 1998年，利尔、利华、华明建筑商在县城开始修建商品房，建筑面积3916平方米，面向社会出售。到2002年年底，先后建起阳光、千禧、世纪、华兴、龙岗、翠园、玩易等商品房住宅小区，共建商品房617套，建筑面积9.26万平方米，投入开发资金4350万元。扎佐镇开发大园村商品房1.5万平方米，投入资金480万元。自此把商品房开发推向高潮。到2003年，商品房累计建筑面积达13.6万平方米，2004年在新建的阳明大道商贸住宅街，一次性开发建设翰林花园商贸住宅小区占地13.3亩，建起商品房6幢，建筑面积8.89万平方米，投入开发资金3988万元。扎佐镇开发珍珠铭园商品房1.1万平方米，投入资金600万元。2005年在县城中心区黄金地块开发翠屏小区商品房，以A、B、C三幢楼品字型布局建住宅174套，建筑面积2.7万平方米，投入开发资金1843万元，其中小区主楼星河银座大厦地面16层“电梯楼”为城区最初出现的最高建筑，建筑面积1.36万平方米。2006年开发的新都口岸商贸住宅小区，建商品楼18幢，建筑面积3.7万平方米。同年开发的碧璟苑商贸住宅小区，占地6亩，建筑面积1.51万平方米，投入开发资金440万元。2007年，启动利尔上河城商住小区开发，占地68亩，计划建商品住宅房700套，建筑面积13万平方米。2008年，小区已见雏形，并向市民开盘。同年吉泓房地产开发公司在县城建设明河花园商住房小区，建房140套，建筑面积2.6万平方米、投入建设资金2000万元。明兴房开公司在县城思源路开发商品房1幢，建筑面积3891平方米。

2009年，贵州腾晖房地产开发公司在县城翠屏东路开发建设腾晖花园小区商品房，用地面积9729平方米，规划建商住房建筑面积4.59万平方米，投资6000万元，其中2幢于2010年完成工程60%，开盘出售。

同年，弘晋房地产开发有限公司进驻修文开发“文城逸都”房开项目，后与冠荣房地产公司联合开发拓展“文城逸都”建设，该项目位于县城东片区，西紧抵小桥河、高涧河，南靠翠屏东路翠屏桥，北挨阳明洞景区，东以拟建的白（云）修（文）公路相邻，占地175亩。工程分为A、B、C三地块，总建筑面积31.37万平方米，其中商业性10万平方米，住宅性20万平方米，计划投资6亿元。项目A区紧临阳明文化园，建筑以居住为主，商铺为辅，临河面建绿化带，B区建东高西低建筑群，以居住为主，C区以公共服务性为主，打造人文景观与旅游休闲为一体的建筑。2010年，一期商住房868套初现规模，其中B1至B6、B7至B11、B12至B17已竣工，完成工程量的33%。8月，第二期工程住宅1200套动工，已向社会预售，平均售价每平方米3300元。

环境恬静的文城逸都住宅小区

部分房地产开发公司建房及销售价格概况表

表3—05—17

公司名称	商品房名称	建设时间	开发房屋面积（平方米）	开发房屋（套）	投资（万元）	售价（元/平方米）
贵州利尔房地产开发公司	千禧商住楼	2002	3000	25	100	510
	阳光商住楼	2002	3600	30	120	520
	翠园、邮政花园	2003	29000	242	1466	630
	翰林花园	2004	88900	6幢	3988	870
	上河城	2008	13000	700	建设中	1800
贵阳吉泓房开公司	华兴花园	2003	8300	74	427	700
	明河花园	2004	26000	140	2000	1850
贵州星河房开公司	翠屏小区A楼	2005	13576	174套	1843	700
贵州林云房开公司	翠屏小区B、C楼		13096			1200
贵州新进房公司	龙岗花园	2003	2400	25	190	780
贵州标大房开公司	玩易花园	2003	5500	37	206	500
修文国康房开公司	世纪园小区	2002	14000	114	780	600
贵州绿丰房开公司	粮贸花园	2003	5854	54	454	776
贵州深宏房开公司	碧璟园	2004	15080	—	440	950
贵州泰维房开公司	新都口岸	2006	37071	18幢	—	1600
贵州明兴房开公司	富都商住楼	2005	10500	—	880	1720
贵州腾晖房开公司	腾晖花园	2009	40000	第一期120套	6000	3150
贵州利华房开公司	扎佐镇大园村	2004	15000	—	480	650
清镇小城镇建设房开公司	扎佐镇珍珠铭园	2004	11000	占地3.6亩	600	760
贵州弘晋房地产开发公司	文城逸都	2010	313740	12868套	6亿元	3300

1998—2008年全县商品房开发概况表

表3—05—18

地址	开发时间（年）	投资（万元）	开发规模			开发类型	
			幢	套	面积（平方米）	纯住宅	商住结合
县城	1998-2000	984	8	425	52300	住宅	—
	2001	400	1	50	8000	—	商住
	2002	550	1	84	12288	住宅	—
	2003	500	2	103	16000	—	商住
	2004	2900	6	380	56274	—	商住
	2005	1843	3	174	26622	—	商住
	2006	—	20	—	52151	—	商住
	2007	2000	—	140	26900	—	商住
	2008	—	—	840	156000	—	商住
扎佐镇	2002	480	—	—	15000	住宅	—
	2004	600	—	—	11000	—	商住

专记：李修平与利尔房开公司

1993年，县计划委员会干部李修平下海办企业，组建贵州利尔建材有限责任公司，建起年产8万吨的水泥生产线，开创“利尔”品牌水泥，畅销全县及贵阳市区，赢得用户信赖。1998年，李修平把经营视线转向房地产开发，将建材公司转给股东周明贵、骆承碧经营，自己专营房地产开发。当即接手县政府主持下的经济适用住房安居工程建设，从中摸索经营房地产经验。1999年，挂牌贵州利尔物业房地产开发有限公司，李修平任董事长兼总经理，继续承建政府计划建造的经济适用住房。2000年，利尔公司独立开发房地产，建起商品房住宅楼，分别取名“千禧花园”“阳光花园”“翠园”和“邮政花园”，建筑面积达3.6万平方米。2004年在阳明大道商贸住宅街修建占地13.3亩、建筑面积8.89万平方米的翰林花园商住小区商贸住宅楼6幢，在小区投入使用时公司遵照建设部《城市新建住宅小区管理办法》和国务院《物业管理条例》，联合贵阳市顺和物业管理公司，以甲方利尔公司、乙方业主、丙方顺和物业组成翰林花园小区物业管理委员会，使翰林花园成为环境优美、秩序井然、邻里和睦、居家安全的住宅小区，受到住户青睐和市民信任，公司声誉扬名县内外，经济实力也随之增强。2005年，利尔公司打入贵阳市小河区房地产市场，开发紫竹苑和瑞和家园商品房共15万平方米，工程荣获“花园式住宅”之称。2007年，在县城开发上河城商贸住宅综合小区，占地460亩，修建住宅700套，建筑面积13万平方米，其中商贸经营面积1.5万平方米，内设农贸市场、商务中心、社区医疗等设施齐全的多功能商贸楼。2008年上河城商住楼开盘，面向市民销售。

经过一番拼搏，利尔物业房地开发公司连续在2000年、2003年和2004年荣获贵州省质量检验协会“质量诚信”企业奖，其中的2003年还获得贵阳市首届“十佳优美人居环境楼盘”综合大奖。李修平获1998年贵阳市第三届十佳杰出青年、2002年贵州省“五四”优秀青年、2003年首届贵州省杰出青年企业家的称号和2004年共青团中央“一级星星火炬”等殊荣。利尔公司10年的发展历程，在修文城市建设史上留下不可磨灭的篇章。

六、房地产交易

旧房转让　为适应房地产转让、交易业务需要，1998年成立中介机构修文县房地产评估事务所，进行房地产值评估。其服务对象系单位和企业大宗房地产交易转让项目，至于私人个体旧房和二手房交易定价多为交易双方根据市场价商定。嗣后评估事务所因未与行政机关脱钩即被撤销。1999年，经县政府同意，成立修文县房地产交易中心，属县房地产管理站的经济实体，承接各类房地产产值评估，担任房地产转让、交易的中介人、见证人。到2006年交易中心共评估各类旧房房产交易228套，面积2.65万平方米，办理私人个体双方房产权交易32件，面积4000平方米，交易金额138.6万元。

经济适用房销售　1998—1999年，由住房制度改革办公室修建经济适用住房，以成本价每平方米430元向市民出售。2000年采取先交付预购款，然后由开发单位将预购款作为住房建设启动资金，待房屋完工交付时按每平方米预售价和实际建设面积建造成本进行核算，通知购房者补交差额，在缴纳房屋建造价100%房款后办理购房正式手续并领取产权证。到2005年销售经济适用住房1259套，建筑面积15.9万平方米，销售金额6084万元。2008年，在县城思源路再次启动经济适用房建设，建住房185套，建筑面积1.1万平方米，以低于商品房价30%的价位，面向既无能力购买商品房，又不具备租赁廉租房条件的城镇居民出售。

商品房销售 房开公司凭持有房地产开发管理部门颁发的商品房预售许可证，按照商品房所处地段、环境、配套设施、房屋结构等向房地产管理部门提交的预售计划、预售方案、预售价位，经房地产管理站到开发现场勘察、审核，再由县城乡建设局统一发布预售公告，房开公司公布户型，每平方米售价，再经购房者选购，交付预购款，签订预购协议，待房屋竣工交接时按实际建筑面积结算，交付全额资金，领取房屋产权证。从2000—2005年，全县销售商品住宅房817套、建筑面积9.3万平方米，平均售价每平方米700元。2006年销售2660平方米，平均售价每平方米1300元。2007—2008年销售3200平方米，预售商品房登记135件、面积1.4万平方米，平均售价每平方米1800元。2009年，县房地产管理部门发放商品房预售许可证7个，商品房销售备案登记482件，建筑面积4.95万平方米，预售面积7.7万平方米，平均售价每平方米3200元。

第五节　管　理

一、规划管理

1984年，县人民政府根据省政府要求，制定出城镇建设规划管理的具体措施：城镇所进行的一切建设都必须纳入城镇建设规划，建设必须经过规划部门审批，否则不准施工。凡新建或拆除重建的房屋不得越过规划确定的红线。新建街道、居民点由规划部门先作出详细规划，经批准后方可按详规建设。旧城区房屋重建，必须保持新建房与原建筑群体之间的关系，方位一致。对违反城镇建设规划的单位和个人一律追究责任。

1990年，实施《中华人民共和国城市规划法》，规划管理转入正轨。2002年，县政府印发修府办通〔2002〕45号文件，设立城乡建设局规划管理科，负责对全县城镇体系、城镇总体规划、开发区总体规划进行编制和申报；对城镇建设编制详规和组织实施；参与县土地利用总体规划的审查和重点建设项目的选址；核发《建设项目选址意见书》《建设用地规划许可证》《建设工程规划许可证》；拟制城镇建设规划的中长期计划；对城镇建设项目的统筹安排和建立项目库；对城镇管网建设进行协调和建档；指导城镇供水、供电、燃气和垃圾、污水处理等的建设管理；会同有关部门审查城市基础设施建设的立项、设计和概算；会同文化、旅游部门对风景名胜区进行规划、保护和开发的管理。同时，设立建设局规划设计室，承担全县城乡建设勘察、规划和设计业务。设立建设局村镇建设管理股，指导集镇、村庄的规划管理，包括村镇基础设施建设、供水和燃气建设、污水处理、移民搬迁等。并在全县10乡（镇）相应设立村管所，列为乡镇财政全额预算管理的事业单位，行政上划为乡（镇）政府机构，业务上归属县城乡建设局。全县各级规划管理机构按其职责和乡镇体系进行管理。

2010年，开发“文城逸都”商品房建设。该项目位于县城东片区，商品房建筑沿高涧河、小桥河河边建造。其建筑违反城市建设规划和城市河道管理法规，背离县委、县政府2009年提出建设“生态优先，环境制胜”的生态保持和自然生态魅力之乡的规划理念。开发时将小桥河于1999年列为“九三”工程建设项目修筑的天然石料宽20米绿化河堤降低2.5米，造成建筑物地面与河床水位接近，商品房临河面只有2米，甚至出现小桥河与高涧河交汇处的建筑直接伸入河道的问题。这种置规划不顾的行径不仅损失已经建成的市民休闲之地，而且破坏城市的自然环境和河道的防洪功能，市民对此隐患反响十分忧心，多次多方面向有关部门反映未果。

二、城镇建设管理

市政工程 1978—1998年，县无市政工程建设方面的管理规章。1999年4月，实施县城基础设施建设“九三”工程，拆迁县体育场、县文化馆和县体委宿舍，建设县城第一个大规模的市政工程“龙岗绿地广场”。县委、县政府决定该项目分两期进行，第一期建1.44万平方米（体育场面积），第二期待文化馆和体委宿拆迁后建。工程建设违背决议，将广场二期工程用地改为商品房开发，使原规划的广场面积缩小1/3，就此引起市民和县政协委员反对，政协委员联名提交提案，反对将地块广场二期工程用于房地产开发，但最终未得解决，仍建成商品房出售。2004年，建设局设立市政管理站，根据《贵阳市市政设施管理办法》《贵阳市城区河道管理暂行办法》《贵阳市环境噪音防治规定》《贵阳市建设工地施工管理规定》对市政建设进行管理，包括参加市政设施建设工程竣工验收，对市政设施维修保护，按建设规划控制对市政道路的占用、改动和挖掘，保障市政设施功能完好正常运转，编制市政设施建设项目计划，市政设施维修计划，办理占用、改动、拆迁和临时接用市政设施的管理手续。

2005年2月，为迎接2005年阳明文化节，城乡建设局成立市政管理领导小组，将阳明大道上的建筑工地纳入市政管理重点，要求施工单位围墙施工，控制渣土，减少噪音，清除占道场地。同时加强城区干道、重点公共设施的定时巡查。2006年，创建文明县城，拆除不规范广告牌（架）87处，查处不文明施工建筑工地15个，下发限期整改施工工地通知书28份，拆除占用人行道面积162平方米的报刊售货亭25个，整顿规范洗车场15家，拆除违章建筑1086平方米，增设学校入口、入城街口提示牌19块，新装市政路灯270盏，线路长7000米。2008年，为迎接2009年阳明文化节，对市政环境进行彻底整改，清理排污沟泥沙淤积、更换排污沟盖板、维修河道围栏、清除河道漂浮物、安装河道和休闲广场彩灯、对阳明大道房屋立面改造，拆除违章建筑5236平方米，查处不文明施工工地5起，取缔占道经营摊点88个。安装主街道路灯850盏，阳明大道路灯346盏，园林照明灯200盏，实现启闭自动化，使全城路灯亮灯率达到95%。城区人行道面积30万平方米，居民人均占有9平方米。

城管监察 1997年3月，县政府组建城市管理委员会。其职能：接受县城乡建设局、工商行政管理局、公安局、林业绿化局、民政局、环境保护局和交通运输管理局授权委托，对城市实施监察管理。6月，城管委落实县政府批转《关于整顿县城城区市容市貌，道路交通的意见》，配合交警队、交通局规范县城客运机动车和出租车停靠点，发放交通法规宣传资料3000份，用制度管理公交秩序。8月，又与运管所联手整顿市容市貌，在县城散发关于加强机动车、三轮车、人（畜）车的管理通告1000份，对主街道日巡日查，加强对城市交通秩序的监察管理。11月，再根据《修文报》曝光的电影院、人民路与翠屏路交汇路口的饮食小吃摊位占道经营，影响市容市貌和交通问题，城管委对饮食摊采取强制性拆离。取缔沿街面饮食店的露天明火煤灶170个，全部更换为燃气灶。1999年，为迎接阳明文化节，县政府出台综合治理规定11条，县电视台开办“红绿灯下呼唤文明”电视节目5期，“曝光台”舆论监督节目6期，提高市民“改陋习、树新风”维护市容市貌意识。

2002年10月，城管委划归县城乡建设局，成立城建监察大队，在扎佐镇、久长镇、六广镇成立城管监察分队，行使城管职能。2007年，在县城配备城管监察协管员，县政府组织下岗、待业人员协助道路

交通警察执勤，组成“4050”人员执勤岗位，分成24个班组、22个路口，由71人身着协警背心，佩戴上岗证分班执守。同时县直机关单位配合，分街道设立文明守法监督岗，社区创办文明专栏30处，推出平安文明院落1128个，形成多控、联治、共管的城镇管理监察体系。

2009年，县城管局集中力量开展市容市貌专项整治，采取定人员、定路段、定岗位、定时间、定职责、定奖惩的“六定”原则进行管理。使城管工作落到实处，城市管理水平得以提升，市容市貌大大改观，获得全省城管专项行动督查综合排名第十二位，全市排名第三位的好成绩。

环境卫生 1980年，为抓县城环境卫生治理，成立环境卫生管理站，隶属县爱国卫生委员会，有环卫工人5人，1982年增至9人，1986年增至15人，随后划归城关镇政府管理。1989年，改环境卫生管理站为城镇管理监察站，下设环境卫生清洁队和城镇环卫监察队。1994年开展创建省级文明卫生县城活动，县政府组建创建省级卫生县城指挥部，进行县城环境卫生整顿，通过“人人动手、建设文明卫生新修文”和“修文是我家，净化美化靠大家”的宣传教育，创建文明卫生县城已成为全城市民的共识和行动。

2004年，设立扎佐、久长、六广3镇环境卫生管理站，由镇政府管理，负责街道的环境卫生。到2010年，县城380个垃圾池，3个垃圾中转站，1个垃圾填埋场，12个公厕，230个果皮箱，20条街道，4处休闲广场的保洁工作都有人承担。

专记：“三创一办”促进城镇建设管理

2009年12月，中共贵阳市委八届八次全会作出“力争2010年获得全国文明城市、国家卫生城市、国家环境保护模范城市和协办第九届全国少数民族传统体育运动会”决议，在全市开展“三创一办”活动。县城建局组织城管、市政、环卫投入三创活动，制发《“三创一办”宣传手册》5000册，发给机关、企事业单位、建筑工地及市民。龙场镇党委、镇政府翻印贵阳市发出的《扎实开展“三创一办”，纵深推进生态文明城市建设》倡议书，由社区居委会发至市民家中，做到“三创一办”家喻户晓。为抓好文明工地建设，城建局组织施工单位、监理部门、建筑公司、建材公司、建材预制企业40人参加创建文明工地现场活动，实行建筑工地办公区、生活区、施工区“三区分离”，硬化工地进出口道路、封闭运送建筑渣土，清洗运输车轮，控制建筑垃圾抛、洒、滴、漏，一律围墙施工，防止建筑噪音影响市民，工地现场悬挂醒目的宣传标语，一场“三创一办”的攻坚战首先在建筑工地打响。

2010年4月，县城建局整顿经营市场，改造街道环境，拆除农贸市场占道经营摊点，取缔饮食经营户明火炉灶42个，增加冲洗街道力度，更换街道垃圾箱150个，新增路灯线路5千米，一改县城旧貌，市民精神为之一爽。

8月24日，县委、县政府组织启动“三创一办”义务监督仪式，由100名学生、100名县直机关义务监督员和100名社区街道居民义务监督员组成交通值勤岗、环卫监督岗、城管监察岗，开展爱护

武警战士清扫街道归来

公共卫生、保护生态环境、执行绿色消费、减少白色污染的“绿丝带”活动，把“三创一办”推向高潮。与此同时，县政府把“三创一办”纳入城镇建设管理目标考核，制定《修文县“三创一办”工作问责规定》，并在电视台和《当代修文》宣传报道，营造从机关到社区人人关心创建，人人参与创建，争当文明市民的氛围，使城镇市政设施明显改善，市容环境明显改观，市民文明素质明显上升，一个整洁、亮丽、有序的城镇呈现在市民面前，促进城镇建设管理的新常态。

三、乡村建设管理

乡村公路 1983年10月，县政府为加强乡村公路建设管理根据国发〔1983〕105号《关于加强公路路政管理、保障公路安全畅通的通知》和黔府〔1983〕122号《贵州省公路路政管理暂行办法》，结合县境内乡村公路建设实际，抽调县、乡、村人员组成乡村公路建设工作组，采取县、乡、村多级筹资、群众出劳、路政部门和群众护养的方式进行乡村公路建设和管理。1984年，针对扎佐、久长、清让、洒坪、广田、大石、红岩等乡集镇场期，以马路作集镇贸易市场影响交通的情况，乡政府组织工商行政管理部门规范赶场区域，拆除公路旁经营占道建筑、堆积物、维修点等路障107处，面积376平方米。1985年贯彻县乡公路“全面规划，加强养护，重点发展，科学管理，保证畅通”的管理方针，将6条县通乡公路采取承包责任制方式包给公路沿线32户村民养护，3条乡通村公路由村民进行季节性养护，良路率比1984年提高16.9个百分点。1986年，设置乡村公路界桩110.5公里，完成公路边界造册登记，绘图建档，并报送县政府备案。

2001年，公路建设工程实行招投标制，第一个招标工程是扎佐至六屯K0+K2公路改造，工程质量达到设计标准。2004—2005年，由贵阳市计划委员会下达经济路、旅游路改造14条，长111公里，贫困村公路54条，长325公里的等级升级改造，均由县交通局、发展改革局、审计局、监察局、财政局等部门组成公路建设领导小组进行建设管理，按村级公路建设质量管理“五级负责制”进行建设，把公路质量技术指标的要求印成小册子300份，发给公路沿线村民以之监督。到2010年招投标制度未变。

村民住房 20世纪80年代，村民住房建设由村和村民共同管理。进入90年代，移民搬迁、新集镇建设，进行统一规划设计、统一管理修建。

2001年，县政府将茅草房改造归入全县建设综合目标进行考核和管理，按照一个原则，即坚持自力更生为主，适当补贴为辅的原则；两个优先，即优先考虑抗美援朝复退军人和少数民族村民；三个公开，即公开申报审批程序，公开补贴对象名单，公开补贴标准；四个结合，即茅改与乡村公路建设结合，与村集镇建设结合，与经济园区建设结合，与小康村建设结合。由县农办统筹协调，城乡建设局负责质量监督和技术指导，县财政、审计、监督部门负责补助资金专账管理，专款专用，建立“放心卡”和资金补助清册，乡（镇）和村组负责建设用地协调、监督，新房落成后茅草房撤除。

2006年，城镇和农村建设双轨运行，实施城乡建设一体化管理。县城乡建设局分点负责抓落实。实施前先拟定建设项目，绘制环境整治方案图，房屋立面改造效果图、施工材料表和工程预算表，使村民直观解整治改造内容和要达到的效果。经过16个新农村建设试点，城乡建设一体化管理得到市政府的肯定，在贵阳市属区、县、市推广。到2010年，县城乡建设双轨运行制正有序地向前推进。

沼气能源 2002年，成立县农村沼气能源办公室，各乡（镇）政府相应成立农业服务中心，抓沼气能源的建设和管理，按照审批、资金、施工、验收等程序入手开展工作。先由农户申请，经村委会汇总

报乡（镇）农业服务中心，由服务中心实地勘察初审，再报县沼气能源办公室审批、备案。财政补助资金实行专户管理，专款专用。乡（镇）沼气建设施工人员先经过技术培训，取得培训合格证。再按照《修文县农村沼气能源建设实施方案》《施工人员管理制度》《档案管理制度》《物资管理制度》《沼气池及配套工程验收制度》，实行行业准入、持证上岗、签订合同、接受监督等管理措施。整个工程完成，由各乡（镇）农业服务中心和县沼气能源办验收，建立一池一档资料，记录施工地点、户主、施工人员、建池容积、建设质量、验收时间、验收人员签名等，由乡（镇）农业服务中心和县沼气能源办各1份长期保存。至2010年管理制度未修改。

人畜饮水 20世纪80年代，县境农村人畜饮水建设管理侧重于对水源的保护和取水点的维修。进入90年代，解决饮水困难将建设管理提到县政府工作日程，重点解决农村群众取水在垂直距离大于100米，水平距离大于1000米的人畜饮水，以设置集中供水点为主，条件好的村寨则引水入户。1999年起实施国家农村饮水“渴望工程”，由县水资源办公室和县水利局、爱卫会联合，乡、村配合争取国家、市、县专项资金及世界银行贷款，发动村寨群众投劳，水利局负责饮水工程设计，乡村委组织实施。

2005年，县政府根据中央保障农村人畜饮水安全，从工程的水量、水质和方便程度上进一步提高建设管理标准，决定在2009年前全面解决全县农村饮水安全问题，将饮水安全工程纳入县政府实事目标进行考核和管理。2006年，对全县已开发的水源和取水工程划定保护范围，在保护范围内严禁耕种，任何单位和个人不得将取水工程范围内的土地作为责任地承包或划作自留地和饲料地，对已占用的必须退耕还林、还草。2008年，县水利局根据贵阳市水利局下达的实施农村饮水安全3500人的计划指标，饮水安全工程88处，纳入贵阳市级计划目标，组织实施，按市政府对农村饮水安全的要求进行管理。2010年，农村饮水安全由县卫生监督局履行监督职责，对饮水卫生进行专项检查，对有20户以上人家饮用水源点252口进行抽查，抽查达标率96.5%，其中有132口设有专人管理，6口建立健全卫生管理组织、制度和卫生档案。

四、房地产管理

房屋产权管理 1985年，县成立房地产管理站，隶县城乡建设局下属事业单位。房管站根据《修文县城镇和工矿区房屋所有权登记及核发证实施办法》，对县属机关、企事业单位的公有住房和驻县工矿企业房产进行普查，将普查结果载入《贵州省城镇房屋普查结果资料汇编》。1998年，县政府按照建设部建房字〔1998〕136号文件精神和贵州省、贵阳市人民政府要求，成立房屋产权验证换证领导小组，于6月19日授权给县建设局房管站办理县域内房屋权属管理登记和发证。7月1日开始对全县所有房产权进行登记、归档，发放全国统一的房屋所有权证，至2005年年底办理9781件。继后陆续办理，截至2010年年底，累计办理房屋交易市场准入证1.08万件，凡持有产权证的房屋，均可以依法进入房地产交易市场。

房屋拆迁管理 1998年前，县政府根据国务院305号《城市房屋拆迁管理办法》，对建设所涉及的房屋拆迁、补偿、居民安置进行妥善管理，使拆迁工作顺利展开。

1999年，扎佐镇开发襄阳大道、磷铵大道，由于宣传动员、补偿兑现工作不到位，以及工程管理人员违纪，造成部分拆迁户上访，经县、镇两级政府协调后得以解决。2001年，县城开发阳明大道，因拆迁户的要求未予落实，出现拆迁纠纷引起群体打砸县政府、县人民法院的“七四”事件，由公安机关立案侦查，息烽县人民法院按法律程序作出处理，判处4名被告人有期徒刑2—7年。县政府根据贵阳市人大常委会市人大字〔2001〕11号《贵阳市房屋拆迁管理办法》为依据，从城镇建设规划编制需要出发，遵照对被征用地人的房屋所拆迁的面积以及等级给予公平、合理的补偿，对其居住生活给予妥善安排的总原则，对阳明大道较为集中的拆迁，采取统一规划修建安居小区方式安置拆迁户，在阳明大道旁集中建起占地61.5亩，民用住宅80多户的阳明新村。

到2004年年底，全县涉及房屋拆迁的龙场镇（县城所在地）、扎佐镇、六广镇、久长镇共计拆迁335户，拆迁房屋建筑面积34048.16平方米。2005年，全县拆迁98户，拆迁面积7340.28平方米，其中久长镇明珠路建设拆迁1户，拆迁面积111.3平方米，龙场镇（县城区）新都口岸建设拆迁31户，面积1455.48平方米，扎佐镇扎南公路建设拆迁66户，面积5773.5平方米，各项拆迁工作到位，房屋拆迁顺利完成。

2008年8月，首钢贵阳特殊钢循环经济项目落户扎佐镇，在扎佐工业园区开发管委会和镇政府的协调管理下，由县级领导成员参加开发管委会的组织领导，建设单位为保证拆迁进展顺利，向国家开发银行贷款2.73亿元，用于项目征地、房屋拆迁和村民安置。首先征用拆迁户建房安置区用地307.315亩，保证村民拆迁后建房。在拆迁面广、涉及村民多、建筑面积大的情况下，由于政府重视、资金到位、补偿及时、措施得当，顺利拆迁村民住房612户，1560栋，拆迁面积8.71万平方米。

2009年11月，贵州同济堂产业园建设项目——贵州贵酒有限责任公司年生产10000吨白酒生产线异地技改落户龙场镇，经县委常委会研究决定成立贵州同济堂产业园建设项目协调领导小组，设立项目协调领导小组办公室，直接负责项目建设的协调管理。遵照筑府发〔2009〕99号文和101号文的规定，调高拆迁补偿，增加社保安置，拆迁补偿安置采取“两公开”原则，即安置补偿政策公开，利益信息兑现公开，以化解拆迁矛盾，顺利拆迁村民住房21户。

2010年8月，贵州轮胎股份有限公司异地搬迁改造项目落户扎佐工业园区，在工业园区开发管委会和镇政府协调管理下，按照筑府发〔2010〕6号文件规定，对拆迁房屋给予合理补偿，村民给以妥善安置，拆迁房屋292栋，建筑面积2000平方米，至年底拆迁工作完成85%。

2000年拆迁房屋补偿标准一览表

表3—05—18

房屋类别	结构形式	建筑补偿价元/平方米	最低补偿价元/平方米
主房	框 混	300	150
	砖 混	260	130
	砖 木	240	120
	石 木	220	110
	土 木	160	70
畜棚、厕所	砖 混	140	70
	石 木	100	50
	土 木	80	40
工棚	一次性补偿30元/平方米		
主房基础	砌石式、砼修筑一次性补偿40元/平方米		

注：此方案经2000年11月6日县政府2000年第九次常务会议通过

2002年房屋拆迁土地基准地价一览表

表3—05—19　　　　单位：元/平方米

区　域	用途	金额			
		一类	二类	三类	四类
龙场镇	畜业	785	470	270	160
	住宅	280	250	200	155
	工业	240	210	180	150
久长镇	畜业	560	410	170	
	住宅	260	200	150	
	工业	220	180	140	
六广镇	住宅	270	220	170	
扎佐镇	住宅	280	230	180	

注：此地价于2002年5月30日以修建呈〔2002〕3号文上报贵阳市审批得以批准

五、建筑业管理

行业执法监察　1991年起，为打造一流县城，县政府组建工程指挥部对财政投资建设项目进行管理，直接对建设项目的规划用地、工程立项、施工合同、造价定额、预算决算履行监察。城乡建设管理部门只是对工程建筑的质量严格把关，其中对扎佐镇卫生院办公楼和病房建设工程中存在的安全隐患作出责令限期拆除的处理；对县体育馆柱基钢筋不符合设计测试质量作出拆柱更换，重新施工的决定；对县文广大楼基础圈梁断裂、墙体裂缝，实施行业执法监察职能，拒绝签字验收。

2001年《中华人民共和国建筑法》颁布，打开修文建筑市场，县城乡建设局明确建筑管理科的执法监察职责，制定《建设用地规划许可证审批程序》《建设工程规划许可证审批程序》《建设工程报建登记备案程序》《建设工程竣工验收申请备案程序》，对建筑行业和建设工程进行全面执法监察。2005年8月，对全县房地产建筑市场进行全面检查。9月，针对检查中发现的问题，组织房地产开发公司开展诚信经营、维护建筑市场秩序，推动修文房地产业，开展建筑市场健康发展的“光彩事业”和“信誉宣言”活动，并对违章违规的建筑工程实行执法监察，查处省建九公司承建的扎佐中学教师宿舍楼、贵阳林云安装公司承建的翠屏小区B栋商住楼和贵州标大房开公司开发的玩易花园住宅楼存在安全隐患、未按工程建设强制性条文标准规定的施工和工程偷工减料等违法违规，并作出限期整改的处理。

2009年11月18日，县委、县纪委配合行业执法监察针对工程建设中仍在用地、质量、造价、安全方面存在的问题，召开工程建设领域突出问题专项治理会议，对专项治理工作进行部署，将其纳入各乡（镇）各部门的目标管理。

2010年6月30日，县城乡建设局根据《建设工程规划许可证审批程序》规定，对扎佐镇襄阳大道7家建筑未办理《规划许可证》和未提供施工图资料，作为违章建筑处理，建筑面积1.4万平方米，责令停止施工。

取消政府代理代建　1991年，县城环城路改造，由县政府分管城乡建设的副县长任工程指挥长，代表政府对改造工程实施管理，开启政府对县财政投资，政府集资建设项目的代理代建先河。随后扎佐镇襄阳大道、磷铵大道建设，县城基础设施“九·三”工程建设，均由政府领导任项目第一责任人，全权代表政府行使建设项目的管理。

2001年国家《中华人民共和国建筑法》、《中华人民共和国招标投标法》颁布后实行建筑行业管理，将建设工程项目管理纳入城乡建设局工作范畴。对建设工程立项、规划用地、工程报建、建筑安全、工程招标、造价定额、预算决算、工程验收和工程质量进行全面管理。县政府成立国有资产办公室和国有资产投资经营有限公司，使财政投资项目以国有资产形式由国有资产投资经营公司作为法人投资，对投入资金的使用进行监督。其工程项目的建设各项管理则由县城乡建设局建管科具体实施。2002年，取消由政府领导组成的工程指挥部代理代建，所建的“王学圣地”牌坊、阳明大道绿化工程、翠屏东路延伸段工程、青少年活动中心等建设项目，均由国有资产投资经营有限公司作为投资法人，由城乡建设局建管科负责管理，严格禁止无证设计、无证施工、无建设手续的“三无”工程，有力地遏制政府官员在代理代建中干预工程项目和在土地转让的权钱交易。

工程招投标　2001年1月，《中华人民共和国招标投标法》颁布，贵州省建设厅相应出台《建设招投标管理条例》、《房屋建筑和市政施工招投标办法》。县城乡建设局明确建筑管理科专职人员管理工程招投标，并把《招投标法》纳入“四五普法”活动，印刷宣传资料6000份在城镇发放，开展咨询服务。2003年，县内建筑工程招投标进入贵阳市工程交易中心，实行公开招标，到2004年，进入贵阳市工程交易中心招标项目有扎佐中学学生宿舍楼、修文中学第三教学楼、县人民法院审判大楼、县计经局综合楼、县计生妇幼保健大楼、县残疾人综合服务中心等16个项目，总建造价4557.92万元。其中有14个项目依法委托招投标代理机构组织招标事宜，依法委托比例达87.5%，突破当年建筑工程委托招投标比例需达30%的要求。2005年，建筑工程在招投标限额之内的有移动通信大楼、县职业中学教学楼等24个建设项目，总建造价4131.35万元，均进入贵阳市工程交易中心公开招标，依法委托比例达100%。从实行《中华人民共和国招标投标标法》到2006年依法按照招投标限额进行的招投标项目累计为62个，项目总建造价1.18亿元，招投标率为100%。2007—2008年，由贵阳市政府在县内主持的建设工程项目均由市政府委托招投标机构进行招标代理。

2009年8月，县纪委组织召开全县建设工程招投标管理工作会议。发展改革局和城乡建设局提出4条管理措施：一是建设项目立项审批备案开始即严格审查项目申报资料和投资金额，进入招投标者必须具备勘察、设计、施工、监理等据实资料；二是完成项目申报前期工作后，确定招标代理机构、监理单位、对招标文书、资格、资质预审和对开标、评标、工程的进度、质量、款项等应全程跟踪；三是对财政投资和财政担保投资项目，要严格选择代理机构，审查代理资格，严禁行政干预和“暗箱”操作，实行“阳光招标”；四是建设工程投资在限额以上工程均应按招标程序进入贵阳市建筑市场交易中心，发布招标公告，抽取评标专家意见进行评标。

2010年，县城建局共办理报建登记备案项目47个，总投资金额3.3亿元，总建筑面积24.65万平方米，按照建设项目投资金额进入贵阳市工程交易中心公开招标项目22个，建筑面积15.04万平方米，招投标率为100%。

建筑市场管理　1984年，县政府批准成立县建筑管理站，隶属县城乡建设局，负责全县建筑监督，审核施工队伍的技术力量、固定资产、流动资金、机械设备、建筑施工场地条件、资质级别、建筑材料

等，对建筑工程的质量和安全进行管理。1985年，建筑管理站对县内各乡（镇）10个建筑施工队伍和外来20个建筑施工队的资质技术力量进行审定，具有合格施工资质的施工队县内7个，外来2个。对此，作出建筑施工队整改处理意见。

2002年8月，县建设局拟制《修文县整顿和规范房地产市场秩序工作的实施方案》，将房开企业列入建筑业规范管理之中。对利华、新进、吉泓、利尔、明兴、国康等房开公司开发6万平方米的商品房和4万平方米的经济适用住房进行检查，发现施工中存在安全隐患和偷工减料，商品房销售面积和实际建筑面积有“短斤少两”等问题并进行查处，对使用的建筑材料进行检测，对房屋的分项工程和隐蔽工程进行抽查，对竣工的项目进行综合评价。经过两年整顿，从2004年起，全县所有的房地产建设工程质量和建筑施工均实现“零上访、零投诉、零安全事故”，市民满意指数上升。

2009年，建筑管理站对建筑市场、建设项目展开的管理和服务，共办理报建登记备案手续项目34个，总投资9219.34万元，总建筑面积4.25万平方米；办理工程施工许可证手续15个，总合同造价3843.72万元，总建筑面积5.82万平方米。对续建项目20个和新开项目31个进行全过程跟踪监管，排查建筑工地22个，排查各类工程隐患53条次，下达整改通知书22份，使建筑市场正常秩序得以维护。

清理工程款项 2005年，县政府为维护农民工合法权益，成立清理建筑工程拖欠工程款和农民工工资领导小组办公室，清理拖欠工程款862.83万元，使工程建设付款比例达到44.3%，清理拖欠农民工工资190.44万元，使支付农民工工资比例达到96.6%。其中清理政府财政性投资拖欠工程款591.63万元，清欠农民工工资100.64万元，涉及农民工600人；清理房开公司房地产开发项目拖欠工程款70万元；清理其他建设工程项目拖欠工程款201.2万元，清欠农民工工资89.8万元。

2009年，县政府着力排查建设工程拖欠农民工工资，全年共追欠农民工工资125.9万元，分别是建工集团五公司拖欠扎佐奶牛场建设工程农民工工资80万元，建工集团六公司拖欠县职业高中综合大楼工程农民工工资8万元，修文建筑材料公司拖欠水堰庄房屋立面整治工程农民工工资11万元，省建联合公司拖欠久长明珠路建设工程农民工工资17.4万元，贵州广颢城乡建设有限公司拖欠新都口岸建设工程农民工工资3万元，中国有色金属第十一冶建工程公司拖欠华飞氧化铝建设工程农民工工资6.5万元。

2010年，全年共追回拖欠农民工工资及工程材料款233.5万元，其中，建工集团三公司166.5万元，修文建筑建材公司4万元，七冶建筑公司0.5万元，省建三公司4.5万元，广西五鸿建筑公司19万元，扎佐镇新庄新农村建设款7万元，广西河池市都安县第三建筑公司15万元，贵州林云建安公司12万元，贵酒项目建设5万元。

六、物业管理

2003年，县城诞生以“服务”为主的进宏物业管理公司，服务住宅小区环境卫生、庭院绿化、安全防护、水电维修等。2004年，一大批融商铺、商务办公、会议、打字楼、宾馆、酒店、娱乐、住宅为一体的新型建筑应市，物业“从服务”型向“服务、管理、经营”型转变，按照国务院颁布的《物业管理条例》履行管理职责，形成多层次、全方位、规范化的物业管理格局。

进宏物业 2003年，由张元宝、方德祥、叶林、张远祥等组建，名称为修文进宏物业管理公司，标志着物业管理新兴行业在修文诞生。公司承接虎山安居小区、翠园、邮政花园、粮贸花园、龙岗花园和河滨花园等住宅楼的物业管理。主要开展住宅楼环卫保洁、值班传达、水电维修、代收水电费等服务性业务。物业服务兴起初期，业主对物业服务性管理认识不足，服务性消费理念尚未形成，致物业服务收费与服务项目支付难以平衡，公司资金运行不能达到良性循环，亏损较大、无利可获。2006年，公司停业，管理业务转交小区业主委员会。

永恩物业 2005年，县城翠屏商住小区建成，房开公司联系贵阳市永恩物业在修文成立永恩物业管理公司，招聘县城待业人员承担翠屏小区A、B、C三幢商住楼的物业管理。服务对象有商铺、宾馆、餐饮、商务、娱乐和居民住户，涉及经营户48户，住宅户160户，对象复杂，服务面广。其中A楼星河银座大厦楼高17层、地面16层、地下室1层，地面1至3层为经营、宾馆、商务、娱乐，4至16层的民居兼营餐饮、理疗、培训、美发等服务，造成往来人员频繁，电梯使用频率高，费用大，经营与生活废弃物多，给公共设施、环境卫生、值班传达、安全防护的管理增加难度。到2010年，公司运作处于艰难的维持状态。

顺和物业 2005年，县城翰林花园小区占地13.3亩，建筑面积8.89万平方米商住楼投入使用，小区开发商利尔房开公司联合贵阳顺和物业管理公司进驻翰林，组建顺和物业修文分公司注册挂牌，资质等级为三级。2006年4月，公司与业主签订物业服务协议，由甲方利尔房开公司、乙方业主、丙方顺和物业公司共同签订翰林花园物业管理公约，制定签发业主手册，明确三方之间相互关系、责任和权益。物业公司以“服务”为核心，把业务向经营和管理展开，从日常环卫保洁、防护安保、庭院绿化、水电维修的服务，扩展到为业主代理、代办和家政等有偿服务，使物业管理从单纯的服务向经营服务转变，以诚、以勤、求善、求美作为公司的发展目标。到2010年，公司管理日益完善，把小区营造出环境优美、秩序井然、邻里和睦、居家温馨的氛围。

翰林花园小区物业管理手册

新兴物业 2007年8月15日，贵阳新兴物业在县城成立“修文县新兴物业管理有限公司”，有员工12人，承担县城新都口岸住宅面积1.87万平方米，商务面积1.84万平方米，入住2000人的物业管理工作。为搞好对象众多的物业管理，着力提高服务质量参与贵阳市物业协会组织的活动，接收物业管理新信息，不断增强物业管理能力和服务意识。针对部分业主对物业管理认识不到位、物业消费理念欠缺等问题，主动上门咨询服务，发放管理温馨提示、住户防范防护资料和贺年慰问卡等，还举行茶话会征求管理意见，寒冬凝冻时帮助老弱住户提水，协助城管部门开展“整脏治乱”，从而得到业主的信任。

七、景区管理

1987年起，县城乡建设局根据建设部关于风景名胜实行分级管理的规定，承担起县域内风景名胜区的管理工作。

2002年，县建设局作为全县风景区行政主管部门，决定由建设局规划管理科和建筑管理科具体负责全县风景区的规划、开发、建设和保护。根据国务院国发（1985）26号《风景名胜区管理暂行条例》和建设部《风景名胜区管理暂行条例实施办法》规定，配合、协助县文化局对文物古迹进行管理、配合县旅游局对旅游观光资源进行管理，参与和指导全县风景区建设、开发和利用，配合县文化、环保、林业部门对风景区的文物古迹、古建筑遗址、奇特溶洞、古树名木、古堡、石刻碑文、革命遗址、历史人文景点进行普查、评价和鉴定，采取定期维护、挂牌保护措施。在规划管理范围内开发、利用和扩建风景

区时，保持风景区原貌特征和自然环境，防止风景区开发中的人工化、城市化倾向。其中，阳明洞景区修建阳明书院、阳明文化馆、阳明步行道、阳明牌坊等新建筑时，都远离阳明洞景点达100米之外。新的建筑工艺外形仿古与阳明文化相陪衬、统一。既丰富阳明文化内容，又防止风景区建设城市化。对三潮水古寺的维修、保护，则针对修（文）六（广）公路车辆往返频繁，管理难度大的问题，修筑起与古庙配套的仿古围墙。玩易窝、三人坟、蜈蚣桥、古竹索桥等古迹，除竖立文物保护牌外还采取与当地村委会、村民配合看护管理，严禁在景点保护范围开垦种地、放牛牧马、采石挖砂。开发高枧、回水石林，六广河七峡、桃源河漂流等风景区，加强河道、石林、峡谷、溶洞的地质原生态环境和植被的保护，严禁开发单位任意改造。在开发高尔夫度假中心、珍珠岛避暑中心、苏格兰风情牧场、野生动物园、岩鹰湖景区，重点加强景区地型、水体、植被的保护，制止随意改变水体源头和流向，严禁砍伐景区四周树木。旅游配套建设中的建筑物、停车场、娱乐场、餐饮设施在建设局建管科指导、监督下逐步实施，定期对景区环境进行测试和综合评价。

2007年，建设局根据黔建景通〔2007〕156号《贵州省建设厅关于2007年风景名胜区和城市公园“整脏治乱”专项行动实施方案》，召开风景区整脏治乱工作会议，成立风景区整脏治乱专项行动领导小组，提出风景区整脏治乱要求并作具体安排，严禁在风景区内摆设饮食摊点和乱搭乱建，严禁暴露垃圾，景区内一律使用水冲式公厕，污水集中处理等，以一个文明的旅游环境迎接2009年阳明文化节。

八、人口城镇化管理

1986年县城总体规划时，人口仅2万人，随着城区建设发展和农村联产承包责任制实施，农村部分剩余劳动力从承包土地中释放出来寓居城里，使城镇流动人口增加。县政府随之改革城镇户籍管理制度，实行城镇暂住户口登记，吸纳流入县内城镇人口4735人，办理暂住户口2037人。是时，包括中央省市驻县工矿企业职工及家属2万人在内，全县城镇人口有所增加，人口城镇化率为24.52%，比全国人口城镇化率17.9%的比重高6.62%。1988年，随着经济发展、物流畅通，大量农村人口进入城镇谋生。1991年，县政府推出收取城镇建设费方式办理“农转非”户口政策，吸引农村人口买城镇居民户口长期在城镇定居，办理“农转非”户口228人，1992年增办101人，1993年又增办474人。1994年，取消城镇人口粮油供应，粮油放开由市场供应，农村户口与城镇户口差别缩小，城镇户籍管理政策再度放宽，使县内人口外流，出现人户分离、有户无人状况，加之中央，省市驻县企业搬出县境，使城镇人口减少，到1998年，县城区总人口为3.2万人，扎佐集镇人口2.5万人，久长镇集镇人口1.8万人，六广镇集镇人口1.2万人，全县集镇非农业人口共3.6万人，人口城镇化率仅为13.88%，低于全国人口城镇化水平。

1999年，县委、县政府按照县第八次党代会提出的“加快以县城为中心，扎佐、久长、六广三镇为重点的城市建设”新思路，加强城乡一体化建设，以人口城镇化管理为抓手，推动城镇建设，为达到2020年人口规划目标，县城6万人、扎佐镇5.5万人、久长镇5万人、六广镇2万人，采取农村人口从分散村寨向中心村集中，村寨向乡集镇集中、乡集镇向城镇集中逐步转移推进的战略。政府着重抓城镇市政基础设施、文化教育设施、交通运输、住房开发、供水供电的建设，鼓励农村人口进城经商、务工、居住。在户籍管理上以人为本，实行人口属地管理，外来人员入县只需持有《身份证》、《流动人口婚育证》、《结婚证》、《节（绝）育手术证》便可在城镇社区登记、居住，其经商、务工、子女入学等与城镇常住户同等相待，以推动人口城镇化进程。到2010年，县城城镇区内人口发展到6万人，其中常住人口5.2万人，流动人口8000人，人口城镇化率为18%，与全国人口城镇化率44.9%仍有较大差距。

目　　录

文化建设篇

社会建设篇

人　　物

附　　录

第六章 商 业

1978年中共十一届三中全会后，全县商品流通在“改革、开放、搞活”方针的指引下，一是进行体制改革，发展个体商业；二是调整购销政策，取消分配式、多层次、统购包销的三级批发方式；三是对国营商业和供销社商业实行“商品分工，城乡开通”的新体制，开展以城乡贸易为中心的商品流通，实行以承包经营为主的多种形式经济责任制。从1992年起，经过3年营运，到1995年全县商业彻底步入从国营商业垄断经营到经营放开、激活组织、培育市场的轨道，实现国营商业所有权和经营权的分离，全县社会商品零售总额增到1.21亿元，首次跨过亿元关。

2004年9月，入驻县城中心的合力超市

1996年，贯彻大市场、大贸易、大流通和坚持综合与专业结合、批发与零售结合的方针，进一步完善多种所有制并存的市场流通体制，使全县商品流通领域出现历史上未有过的生机与活力。至2010年，全县社会商品零售总额达10.13亿元，比1978年的2472万元增长40倍，32年的年均增长率为12.3%。

第一节 体制改革

一、经营机构改革

（一）建立国营商贸公司

1978年，全县国营商业有百货、石油、食品、五金、糖酒、蔬菜、药材、饮食服务等8家公司，经营店柜76个，职工320人。1981年1月恢复盐业公司，分置医药公司（西药）与中药材公司，划归县医药局归口管理。糕点、酱菜加工分别从糖酒、蔬菜公司划出建立综合食品厂，由商业局直接管理。并建立针纺、日用百货、文化用品、五金、交电、糖酒、食盐、糕点、中西药等10个批发部（属三级站）,承担全县生活日用品的采购和调拨分配。

2001年11月，根据县政府〔2001〕28号文件精神，将早已资不抵债的百货、糖酒、蔬菜、五金、食品和经营煤炭的燃化等6家公司进行资源整合，组建县商贸公司进行物业管理。至2010年，商贸公司经营商铺和屠宰场出租收入达37.1万元。

（二）粮食商业政企分置

1978年，县粮食局为行企合一机构，有职工273人，其中局机关32人，粮油加工业49人，各区粮管所及仓库192人。1994年改为政企合一的粮油总公司。1999年将粮油总公司撤销重新组建，置粮食局为行政管理机构，内设办公室、粮管科、会统科，行政编制12人，负责管理全县粮油收购、销售、调运、储存、加工、建仓和财务等方面的业务。设立事业机构军粮供应站，编制5人，管理和发放军用粮油。企业机构设1库2个公司，即驴坊粮食储备库和粮食购储责任公司、粮油工贸有限责任公司。驴坊粮食储备库有职工18人，承担国家各级储备粮油和县公司商品粮、救灾、救济、军用粮的保管工作，有固定资产232万元，流动资产2011.2万元。粮食购销有限责任公司下辖龙场、扎佐、久长、小箐、六广5个分公司，员工187人，主要承担国家和地方专项粮油储备、调拨、轮换和定购粮、保护价粮食的收购、批发以及政府安排的大宗粮油调剂等，有固定资产710万元，流动资产2009万元。粮油工贸有限责任公司下辖龙场、扎佐、六广工贸公司和面粉加工厂、饲料工业公司、筑潮米业公司、油脂化工厂、阳明宾馆共8家核算企业，有职工252人，固定资产2088万元，流动资产13万元，从事商业性的粮油购销、加工及国家政策允许范围内的其他商业或服务等经营性业务。从1999年12月起实现粮食商业的政企分开和人、财、物彻底分离，企业成为独立自主、自负盈亏、自主经营、自我发展的经济实体。

1999年，置于阳明综合市场的军粮供应站

（三）供销商业复建理事会

1978年，全县供销系统有企业管理和经营单位68个，职工328人。1983年3月，根据省政府专员、州长、市长会议精神，县供销合作社属5个区的基层社先后召开社员代表大会，选举理事会、监事会和出席县第四届社员代表大会代表，7月召开有104名代表参加的县供销社社员代表大会，通过《供销社章程》，审议经营计划，民主选举理事会和监事会，选举班耕书任理事会主任委员，副县长曾文学为监事会主任委员。同时将县供销社改组为联合社，恢复供销社的“三性”（组织上的群众性、管理上的民主性、经营上的灵活性）职能。8月，各基层供销社清查社员股金的名册、账本、凭证，并组织老社员代表、老理事和老干部认真核实后重新造册，换发新社员证，补发红利3.03万元。至2010年入股社员达5000多人，社员股金扩大到180余万元。社员们高兴地说：“我们自己办的供销社又回来。”

（四）物资商业实行公司制

1978年沿袭原建制，县物资局为政企合一机构。1984年4月改为物资供应公司，划属县经济委员会管理，承担县团级内的重点工程所需的钢材、机电、水泥等一类物资的供应。1995年9月根据县政府机构改革方案，物资公司改为物资总公司，并入县计划与经济贸易局管理。2008年1月，公司挂牌贵阳市鑫筑民爆经营有限公司修文分公司，实行两块牌子、一套人马的运作方式，公司下设办公室和综合科、民爆物品管理科以及龙场爆破站，有职工60人，承担火工材料的专业营运。至2010年，物资总公司和民爆经营分公司的建制未变。

（五）医药销售机构

1978年，中药材和西药均由药材公司独家经营，承担全县医疗机构的药品供应，设有中、西药批发部（三级站）各1个，零售部1个，业务人员12人，归属商业局管理。1979年西药业务划出单独组建医药公司，仍为商业局领导。公司从县城健康路（今翠屏西路）迁到中山路办公，主要经营药品（器）批发业务。1981年药材、医药两公司从商业局析出，划归新成立的医药局管理。后将医药管理局并入县经济委员会。随着县经委改置，医药机构管理又归属计划与经济贸易局，再后又由县发展改革局领属，至2010年，医药机构体制未变。

2010年，仍存的县药材公司门市部

（六）服务业改制

国营服务业 1978年，县国营饮食服务公司经营有餐饮、旅社、浴室、照相等业务，职工20余名，盈亏全由国家负担，1981年实行国家所有、集体经营、自负盈亏的管理和经营方式，到1990年，企业退休人员增为21人，养老负担沉重，公司陷入困境，只得拆除马路围墙修起13个简易门面，安排13个职工承包经营,暂时缓解养老金无来源的问题。1999年趁县城改造之机，县政府将饮食服务公司转型，职工达到退休条件的按规定办理退休手续，由县社会保障局按月发给养老金；在岗职工分别由盐业公司、自来水公司和物资总公司各安排1名，其余17名转到城管委安置。至此，饮食服务公司消亡。

合营服务业 1978年，城关、扎佐、小箐、六广区和久长公社驻地均有公私合营服务业，从事饮食、旅社、理发及修理等业务。1993年，随着市场经济体制的建立和市场的激烈竞争，合营服务业因设备陈旧、资金困难等原因，全部转型为个体经营，原有房屋和场地陆续有偿转让，所获资金归还贷款和支付股金、股息，所余部分按从业人员工龄长短进行补偿，职工最高的得到3000元，最低的100元，公私合营体制即行消逝而退出历史舞台。

（七）发展个体商业

1978年，城乡商业全被国营商业和供销社垄断，全县仅有个体工商2户和代销店4家。1983年12月建立县个体劳动者协会，城关、扎佐、久长、小箐、六广成立分会，加入个体协会会员2216人，从而推动城乡个体经济发展。

1984年贯彻落实县政府《国营商业、企业改制方案》，废止对个体工商户长期执行的“利用、限制、改造”政策，解下束缚私营商业的“七不准”（不准扩大经营范围、不准增加经营网点、不准增加从业人员、不准自行定价、不准跨地区流动购销、不准在集市贸易采购原材料、不准批发）。县工商局也解放思想，放宽政策、疏通渠道，促进交流，鼓励支持个体经济发展。1985年，全县个体工商达1483户，从业人员2375人，营业收入1132万元。

1993年，贯彻执行贵州省政府《关于加快个体私营经济发展的通知》，除金融等10种行业外，其余商品允许个体工商户生产和经营。到2010年，全县个体工商户增为4508户，从业人员7232人，营业收入达4.56亿元，成为县域商业的主体。

二、用工制度改革

（一）企业职工择优录用

1987年前一直沿袭计划经济体制的用人制度，招收的职工经过1年试用期即转正为正式工。1988年7月，按照国发〔1984〕67号《关于进一步扩大国营企业自主权的暂行规定》，县烟草公司根据工作需要，通过考试择优录用40名职工充实到一线岗位。1992年，贯彻执行省政府黔政办发36号文件要求，一是企业职工实行“三制”（干部选举制、职工合同制、技术人员聘用制）、“三岗”（经考核合格者实行在岗，不合格者实行试岗，试岗期间不合格者待岗）的管理办法。二是清退临时工，县食品、百货、烟草、糖酒等公司共清退16名，按每工作一年补偿1个月的工资标准进行补偿。三是鼓励部分职工自主分流，凡自主分流者根据其工作年限，按每年1个月的基本工资一次性计发安置费，2001年8月，县烟草公司7名职工主动申请自主分流，与公司解除劳动合同关系，补偿人民币24万元。

（二）粮食企业减员增效

2003年7月，为把粮食企业建成“自主经营、自负盈亏、自我约束和自求发展”的市场竞争主体，对属于政策性经营的粮食购销公司实行减员增效改革：第一步进行清产核资，对粮食购销公司、驴坊仓库、5个报账分公司和21个购销点的资产进行产权界定，并办理产权证。经核资粮食购销公司和驴坊仓库总资产为6488万元，其中固定资产942万元，流动资产5546万元，负债6542万元，资不抵债54万元；第二步由社会保障等相关部门对职工进行登记，按每个参改职工资金1万元的标准，由省财政划拨5000元、市财政4000元和县财政1000元作为粮改资金。粮食购销公司定编41人，驴坊粮食储备库定编18人；第三步实行竞聘上岗择优录取，对竞聘前的196名职工全部解除劳动合同关系，然后采取自愿报名、文化考试、面试竞职演讲、民主评议和组织考察打分的办法定人，有68名职工重新与公司（仓库）签订劳动合同，3名残废军人由县粮食局安排适当工作，对35名符合内部退养条件者，经本人申请，每人每月按最低工资标准290元计发生活费，由企业按规定向社保机构缴纳基本养老保险和其他社会保险，到法定退休年龄办理退休手续，享受基本养老保险待遇。90名另谋职业，自主分流，企业给予一次性补偿。改制当年，粮食购销公司从市场上收购粮食2895吨，比上年增加1604吨；粮食销售1284吨，多销481吨。2010年收购粮食（含省外购进）3716吨，销售粮食4041吨。上级下达粮食系统亏损计划20万元，盈亏相抵仅亏损18万元，实现减员增效的目的。

三、经营方式改革

（一）商品多渠道流通

1978年，国营商业掌控商品的分配和营销大权。1979年实行放开搞活，一是改单一流通为多渠道流通，各公司既可在贵阳二级站进货，又可到省外采购；个体工商户可在贵阳市西路批发市场以及江浙、沿海一带进货。二是改商品批发、零售各自独立经营为批零兼营，主动上门批发，给顾主提供方便。三是改隔着柜台售货为开架售货，顾客可以上柜自由挑选商品，若购置大型家用电器，还用车送货上门，

并负责安装和调试。四是开展灵活多样的促销手段，商家经常开展凡购物金额达到一定数额即给予打折、优惠或奖励等的促销活动。至2010年，商品购销多渠道的经营方式一直坚持。

（二）粮食收购订购价改保护价

1978年沿袭原定的粮食统购政策。1985年贯彻中共中央、国务院《关于进一步活跃农村经济的十项政策》，取消粮食统购，对稻谷、玉米、小麦实行合同定购，价格以三成按原统购价，七成实行超购价，其他粮食品种允许自由上市议购，当年粮食部门向农民签订定购合同3.89万份。为确保完成粮食合同定购任务，县政府对区、乡政府实行奖励办法，一旦完成或超额完成任务的，则按定购总价款的4%—6%奖励。1990年为解除对合同定购的误解，执行国务院决定的指令性计划，改粮食合同定购为国家定购。至2002年全县按合同定购收购粮食总计9.89万吨，年均5496吨。从2003年起取消粮食定购，粮食部门按保护价敞开收购农民余粮，至2010年，保护价收购余粮的办法未变。

（三）粮食销售步入随行就市

1978年沿袭原定的统销政策，城镇居民购粮凭《供应证》定量供应或凭粮票购买，享受平价供应。1980年成立粮食议价公司，开展议购议销活动，除挂牌在市场上收购粮食外，还从省外调入议价粮平抑粮食市场，满足消费者的需求。1991年起个体粮商增长较快，仅县城就有22家个体户经营粮食，加上农民自产的粮食也进入市场销售，与粮食部门销售议价粮竞争。1995年“议价粮油”被“随行就市”取代，粮食议价公司也随之消逝。2010年全县个体粮油收购、加工、销售店有21户，人们可在市场内自由选购粮油食品。

（四）国营商业改制

1978至1986年，商品购销均是由公司经营。1987年按照所有权和经营权分开和责权利相结合的原则，推行承包经营责任制。国营商业有上缴利税递增包干、基数包干、定额包干、超收定比分成包干或还贷，对亏损企业有定额减亏包干和节亏全留，到1990年承包期满企业可顺延承包2年。由于市场疲软，1993年除盐业公司略有盈利外，其余企业均出现亏损，故改由职工个人承租柜台经营。

2001年11月起全部改制为个体经营，公司不再进行管理。

（五）供销商业“四自一包”

1987年，城关、扎佐有4户供销企业63名职工承包工业品经营。1993年全县供销社8户企业120个柜组实行自主经营、自负盈亏、自我约束、自主分配和包上缴国家利税及企业利润的“四自一包”经营制，以商品折抵铺底资金共400万元，每年按一定比例扣回，到2004年铺底资金全部收回，所剩商品变成承包人的资金积累，续租门店、柜台经营，至2010年未变。

（六）医药商业经营承包

1987年推行中药材经营承包制，先由公司管理向计划与经济贸易局承包，再由职工分柜组或个人向公司承包。1996年停办医药批发业务，公司将余货分给职工销售。1999年还清银行贷款本息共15万元，再由6名职工各出资1万元作资本，租赁公司门面及货柜合资合劳经营。2010年销售收入40万元，纳税1.6万元。

（七）物资公司承包经营责任制

1982年将业务人员分为建材机电和金属化工两个组承包销售。1983年改为盈亏包干责任制，分股室考核，按比例分成计奖。1984年又实行承包经营，公司先向县经委承包，再由各股室向公司承包。1987至1990年为上交利润包干，超收全归企业的承包经营责任制。从1991年起，计划分配物资逐渐取消，最后只留下火工产品（炸药、雷管、导火绳）实行专营。到2010年，承包经营制完全消失。

（八）农村网上经销

新网工程 1978至2004年农村各商品销售点均由自己上门进货。2005年12月至2010年，随着开展“万村千乡”（全国在1万个村各建1个符合标准的农家店，在1000个乡各建1个农业生产资料超级市场）市场工程建设，供销部门在全县建起称为“新网工程”的货物配送中心和回收废旧物资站，先后在县城、扎佐火车站、久长、小箐和六广等地建立7个配送中心，对新建立的农家店实行信息购物和货物配送；并在县城、扎佐、六屯 、久长、小箐、六广、六桶和扎佐林场建立16个再生资源绿色回收站，年均回收废旧金属、书报等物资2000吨，直送工厂加工利用。

2010年仍存的县城人民南路供销社农家店化肥直销点

农业产业化经营 2009年3月，为提高农产品生产组织化程度，全县供销部门参与或创办农民养牛、养猪、养兔、香纯蔬菜种植等专业合作社19个，入社农户1218户，实现销售收入785万元，帮助农民增收80多万元。县供销社（团体会员）与天合养殖专业合作社丁文胜、鑫盛养兔农民专业合作社苏贵荣、香纯蔬菜种植专业合作社王吉健作为首批会员加入贵州省农民合作经济组织联合会，成为农业社会化服务的骨干力量。

（九）物业租赁

1991年，县供销社改造扎佐供销社采购站，投入资金450万元，次年建成建筑面积9000平方米的农贸综合市场，有商业门面（柜）177个和摊位300个出租。1995年投入营运，年交易额1.02亿元，创税利218万元。继后又采取集资、合资等方式筹资500万元，扩建小箐、洒坪、中寨、六广等4家农贸综合市场1.5万平方米，有摊位750个，门面（柜）300个。此外，还引进资金750万元，开发县城世纪园（县土产公司商住楼）、扎佐景阳家园等，全部出租给供销社职工和个体工商户经营。2010年，全县供销系统自有产权农贸市场3个，托管市场1个，建筑面积2.4万平方米，门面477个，摊位1100个，销售收入2.5亿元，收取租金256万元。属于供销系统的职工大部分进入市场内租赁门面经营。

第二节 市 场

1978年，县境仍沿袭历史上惯有的群众赶乡场售货购物习俗，全县有17个乡场，集市门店由国营和

集体企业经营。1979年起，县委、县政府解放思想，打开山门，抓市场建设促商品流通。1992年中共十四大明确提出把建立社会主义市场经济体制作为改革和发展的目标，使集镇孕育出农贸综合市场，开启商品展销。2000至2005年，超级市场、农家店开始萌发并迅速扩展。至2010年，全县共有集市18个，农贸综合市场15个，超级市场11家，农家店158个，街道商铺4118户，接纳入境商品展销9次，形成一个促使商品顺畅流通的市场体系。

一、集市

1978年，全县有区和公社所在地集市17个，上市商品主要是农副产品土烟、干辣椒、鸡鸭和生活用品煤油、盐巴、日用百货等。1985年县工商部门征得城南村在修文饭店门口（今翠屏东路）的土地12亩扩建集市。1995年六桶乡在坪上建起新集市，县城迎春路亦建成私营经济一条街，城关集市即从体育场迁入，扎佐、久长、小箐、六广等乡（镇）相继拓宽集市面积。2007年农业局投资5万元，将原清让乡群众自发兴建的葛马牛马集市拓宽为1000余平方米，招徕开阳双流和息烽石硐等邻地的客商，初期每场上市牛马约200头（匹），成交额55至60万元。2008年，县城新辟东面蛤蟆坡集市8000平方米，并将南面虎山路延至新客车站4000平方米作为集市。7月，久长镇石安村自筹资金3000元在石安寨门口建公厕、平场地、修建围栏，建起800平方米的牛马集市。至2010年，全县共有集市18个，其中牛马集市2个，百货集市16个，集市的振兴有力地促进商品流通和农村经济发展。

1978年和2010年全县集市基本情况一览表

表3—06—01

集市	场期（星期）	1978年				2010年				备注
		面　积（平方米）	摊位（个）	赶集人数（人）	场均成交　额（万元）	面　积（平方米）	摊位（个）	赶集人数（人）	场均成交　额（万元）	
龙场	日	6000	335	25000	1.1	21000	900	48000	139.00	即县城集市
乌栗	四	1000	30	500	0.3	2600	50	3000	8.42	
猫冲	五	300	20	300	0.2	1500	30	300	6.95	
扎佐	日	4000	240	20000	1	26400	700	41000	124.76	
六屯	三	1500	15	300	0.3	4500	150	2400	39.96	
桃源	五	1000	30	500	0.2	2000	50	1000	13.32	
久长	日	2000	60	15000	0.8	14500	240	20000	45.17	
小箐	六	1500	80	12000	0.7	15000	230	15000	39.81	
洒坪	二	1000	20	800	0.3	8000	80	3000	18.39	
马场	一	500	15	300	0.2	1800	40	800	9.19	
中寨	四	1000	20	500	0.2	5100	60	1300	13.76	
六广	日	2500	160	10000	0.8	15600	440	20000	62.01	
广田	三	1000	30	1400	0.2	4000	90	3000	22.74	
大石	五	1000	25	1300	0.3	4500	60	3000	13.78	
德政	二	500	15	300	0.1	1200	20	800	4.59	

续表

集市	场期(星期)	1978年				2010年				备注
		面积(平方米)	摊位(个)	赶集人数(人)	场均成交额(万元)	面积(平方米)	摊位(个)	赶集人数(人)	场均成交额(万元)	
六桶	四	1200	120	10000	0.6	19400	360	14000	55.89	—
红岩	六	1000	30	500	0.1	—	—	—	—	1992年停
葛马	六	—	—	—	—	1000	20头(牛马)	300	61.25	1985年建
石安	二	—	—	—	—	800	20头(牛马)	100	7.66	2008年建
合　计		27000	1245	98700	7.4	159900	3500	177000	686.65	—

附：县政协关于六桶集市贸易调查报告

沿边集市——六桶
——关于六桶集市贸易的调查报告

政协修文县委员会

六桶位于修文县西北面，距县城50公里，周边与黔西、金沙、息烽3县为邻，分别距九庄、化觉17公里、20公里。六桶坝自古即为县西北角的商品集散地，每逢子、午（鼠、马）赶场天，四面八方的人便拥挤在狭窄的街道上进行交易。解放前，市场面积仅800平方米，入市交易的有粮食、土烟、鸡鸭、仔猪等农副产品，工业品有日用百货、盐巴、布匹等。解放后的1966年9月，广（田）六（桶）公路通车，接着贵阳客车直达六桶，给边远山区人民的出行带来方便，沿边的九庄、化觉群众也从六桶乘车出行，赶六桶场的人猛增，从商者也拥在公路两旁摆摊。1978年中共十一届三中全会后，农村实行家庭联产承包责任制，市场更趋活跃，县工商管理部门将市场往六桶小学旁拓展达1200平方米，有摊位120个，场均入市1万余人次，交易额0.6万元。1992年12月六桶乡党委、乡政府迁往盐井村坪上，乡党委书记余长武、乡长宋庆豪主持规划新建集贸市场，于1993年12月启动，1995年8月竣工开业，将集市划分为百货、粮食、蔬菜、鸡鸭、农贸综合、牛马牲畜等市，街道两旁店铺鳞次栉比，烟酒食品、日用百货、彩电冰箱、时装面料、鞋帽雨具、装饰材料、摩托车等商品一应俱全。新集市开业招揽大批来自九庄、六广、化觉的客商，他们在划定区域内摆摊，推销自己运来的商品，使市场更加繁荣兴旺。至2010年，集市面积扩展为1.94万平方米，摊位增至360个，赶集者场均1.4万人，场均交易额达55.89万元，分别比1981年增长15.16倍、2倍、0.4倍、79.3倍。

六桶新集贸市场的建成,给六桶乡带来新的发展机遇：

——从传统的种植业向养殖业转变。自古以来，六桶村民一向过着“一把锄头一张犁，春种秋收冬天闲”的农耕日子。六桶新集市开市以后，出现“山上鸡鸭叫，圈中猪牛壮”的喜人景象。山保村青年李根书自费外出学习养鸡技术回村，1998年自筹资金2万元,建鸡舍120平方米,养鸡1000羽，经滚动发

展，2005年存栏3万羽，出栏8万羽，年产值130万元，获利40万元，并带动村民参与饲养，集六桶“土鸡”放养、圈养为一体，养殖业遍布全乡28个行政村，其中兴农、富民等养鸡场年产土鸡5万余羽，至2010年，全乡有大、中型养殖场20多处，养鸡鸭50羽以上的达600余户，每逢周四赶六桶，有土鸡6000至7000羽入市，贵阳客商驾着商车前往收购，一车连一车地将活鸡、活鸭运进省城蛋禽市场，丰富市民的菜篮子。根据市场需要，六桶的养殖户在养殖鸡鸭的基础上又向肉鸽养殖发展。2008年11月，牛角土外出打工青年张峰从省外引进种鸽1818对，带动村民饲养肉鸽，使六桶乡的养殖业增加一项新的产业。此外，肉牛、肥猪、驮马等牲畜每场竟有300余头上市交易。2010年全乡出栏鸡鸭20万羽，大牲畜3160头，肥猪28962头。

20世纪80年代，六桶老街集市一角

——引导农民向经果蔬菜拓展。种植商品烤烟本是六桶乡的支柱产业，也是全乡经济收入的主要源，1994年种植1.01万亩，生产烟叶1100吨，产值5500万元，最高的1997年达1.35万亩，产量1613吨，产值8065万元。从1998年起，为提高烟叶质量减少种植面积，使烤烟栽种逐年递减，最少的2001年仅4000亩，产量430吨，产值5400万元。面对严峻形势，六桶乡政府不得不从传统种植烤烟向“换品种、反季节”上转移，带领农民走发展经果蔬菜致富之路。从1999年起，依托特色旅游产品“六广河”牌猕猴桃，大力发展猕猴桃种植，2000年种植面积即达1300亩,别具特色的宝坪“百亩桃林”已展现春来黄花遍山、夏日苍翠满园、秋天果实累累的自然景观，形成一道靓丽的风景线；抓住国家实施退耕还林契机，在联合、顺江、海马等村建成100亩柑橘生产基地，并种植金秋梨、樱桃、麻竹等；建成3000亩的辣椒基地，17个村从事反季节蔬菜生产，种植早熟玉米、大蒜等。2010年蔬菜产量达9853吨，水果产量223吨，全乡实现农业产值1.1亿元，农民人均纯收入4716元。

——拉动小城镇的建设。1993年5月，六桶乡党委、乡政府为搞好新集贸市场建设，遵照土地管理法规研究土地费转让标准，制定实施办法，召开领导成员联席会议作出决定：为鼓励街道居民、村民、职工和机关单位以及外来户参与新集市的开发，机关单位购地按4800元/亩，其他住户按3600元/亩的价格优惠，村民、居民及个体工商户限购临街门面长12米，户占地面积不得超过120平方米。公告张贴后，村民、工商户、职工积极筹集资金，有的找亲朋好友借钱，有的向信用社贷款，购者排成长龙办理登记手续。经过紧张有序的施工，建成长1500米、宽17米的主街一条；宽10米至14米的次街4条，全长2500米，并完善地下排污、自来水、闭路电视等设施，从15万元的启动金拉动社会资金5600万元，建起楼房700多幢，建筑面积达17万平方米，至2010年已有住户700余户，3000余人。从此，盐井村坪上成为六桶乡政治、经济、文化的中心。

六桶乡新集市农贸市场

自从六桶新集市投入使用后，息烽县九庄镇每天就有5班农村公共汽车开行六桶。据六桶乡集镇管理办公室曹廷科同志介绍：凡是城市有卖的物品，在六桶新集市上都能买得到；不论什么土特产品，在别处卖不出手的在这里都能推销。个体商彭维贤把六广镇国康水泥厂生产的水泥运到六桶销售，生意十分火爆，大有供不应求之势，他情不自禁地说："没有六桶集市的大发展，我哪有今天的好生意。"

市场作导向，六桶换新颜，装点此江山，明天更灿烂。用地600亩饲养5000头奶牛的"好1多"养殖场已落户六桶并于2008年启动兴建，横跨乌江上游六广河连接修文、金沙两县的海马大桥已于2010年6月开工建设，具有峡谷风光特色的海马孔旅游正在开发……这些项目的实施必定带来更加广阔的商机。到时，金沙的原煤、陈醋、回沙酒将源源不断地取道六桶运销外地，黔中及省内外的工业产品也将源源不断地路经六桶运往黔西北。可以预言，不久的将来，六桶既是车船南来北往的交通枢纽，更是一个重要的商品集散地。它带给六桶人民的是富裕，是和谐，是幸福。

二、街道商铺

1978年，全县共有商铺65户分布在县内集镇街道上，也驻有国营公司和供销合作、公私合营和代销商店，全部从业者400余人。经营百货、针纺、五金、烟酒、食品、医药、餐饮、粮食、食油和化肥、农药、农具等农业生产资料，年营业额2446.5万元。1981年在中央对外开放、对内搞活的方针指引下，实行国营、集体、个体一起上，允许各种经济成分进入商业流通领域，鼓励、支持私营经济发展，一改过去商业领域沉寂的局面。1983年3月贯彻执行国务院《关于发展城乡零售业、服务业的决定》，一批城镇待业青年投向商海，仅城关公私合营商店就招收125名职工参与经商，城镇居民也利用自家临街房舍改成铺面办起商店，致商业网点普遍增加，到1989年全县商铺发展到2059户，从业2760人。

进入20世纪90年代，继县城建成私营经济一条街后，六桶、六屯、大石、洒坪等乡镇驻地均扩建商业街道。原在农村代销的人家也迁往街上经营，住在县城老街的经营户也迁入新街发展，经常挑担赶"转转场"的行商也在集镇买地建商铺。到2010年，全县商铺已发展到4118户，从业者增为7628人，经营商品除百货、日杂外，出现家用电器、时装、鞋帽、烟酒、金银饰品等专营店，年营业额达3.24亿元。

专记：繁荣的私营经济一条街

1994年5月，城关镇（今龙场镇）党委、政府采纳县政协委员对在县城修建私营经济一条街的建议，决定由镇党委书记张华政和镇长王成林带领班子成员和城南、城北两村支部、村委以及县政协等部门领导一行12人赴桐梓县考察城镇开发建设，借鉴桐梓统一规划、统一征拨用地、统一标准和分期实施城镇建设的经验，建设商业大街。县委、县政府听汇报后当即作出启动县城城镇建设的决定，并以县办通〔1994〕10号文成立县城市建设综合开发指挥部及其办公室，由县委常委、县纪委书记胡晓刚任指挥长，城关镇垫资20万元作启动资金，并对原县城建设规划进行修改，绘成图纸，报经安顺行署批准。11月9日，指挥部发布第一号公告：私营经济一条街南起县人大门口，北抵新长征桥，在离农贸市场和春华酒家门口100米处各辟十字路口1个，街道总长1000米，宽21米。占地130亩，涉及被征地农户62户、拆迁户2户和机关单位建筑物4处，需迁坟4座。开发运作采取总体规划、分步实施、逐步推进、滚动发展和以资本置换的方式，将大街两旁土地挂牌出售，每平方米单价120元至150元，所获资金除付给农户土地出让金外，其余全部用于街道和公共设施建设。12月10日，在春华酒家门前破土动工，次年6月，大街雏形展现。一时间城镇居民到指挥部争相购地建造商住楼，指挥部共计售出土地257宗，7万平方米，收取资金980万元，除7家企事业单位外，其余均是个体工商户、城镇居民、单位职工。与此同时，启动农贸市场建设，建筑面积2万平方米，置铺面和摊位302个。1997年4月，大街命名“迎春路”，正式投入使用。迎春路与人民路并列，横贯翠屏街，又入驻一批商店。全街布满商店562个，有餐饮、旅馆、烟酒糖、时装布艺、鞋帽、办公用具、家用电器、电器维修、汽车租赁、摩托车行、饰品、美容化妆、美发发廊、音像影碟出租、药品销售、医疗诊所、洗染、陶瓷装饰、灯具、手机公话超市、五金交电、管道、粮油销售、饲料兽药、农业生产资料等门店，店内商品林林总总，应有尽有。开店的多来自县内，也入驻一批四川、湖南、浙江等地的商户。个体户王正义原在老城民主路开饭馆，后迁新大街建起四层大楼一幢，挂牌“黔龙酒家”经营餐饮，十多年经久不衰。饲料兽药个体户彭中武原在老城南门摆摊，1996年8月出资6万元购建门面1个，专营重庆正大饲料和兽药，销至邻地沙文、黔西等地，月销售饲料25至30吨，他采取灵活经营方式，扶持千余户村民养鸡、喂鸭，助推农村养殖业的发展。迎春路的赶场天，贵阳、白云、息烽等地流动商贩云集大街，全街日均销售额50万元至60万元，每年向国家缴纳税费800万元至1000余万元。

1997年，建成的县城私营经济一条街

三、农贸综合市场

1978—1988年，县城每天的蔬菜均是菜农挑担沿街叫卖，或占道经营，肉市则设在狭窄的龙岗路上，市民上市买菜拥挤不堪。1989年，县城开始在新建的翠屏东路设置农贸综合市场，后又按照规划要求，改建于迎春路西侧的阳明农贸综合市场，总面积2万平方米，置摊位302个，一举改变历史上的马路市场为全县第一个小商品集散地，使经营者有一席之地，又给居民购买农副产品和日用生活用品带来极大方便。在此带动下，扎佐供销社利用原土产收购站场地相继扩建起1万平方米的综合市场。久长、小箐、六广、六桶等乡（镇）也将市场拓宽。至2010年，全县共建有农贸综合市场15个，置摊位1200余个。市场从早到晚，天天开市，既方便附近农民直接入市销售新鲜的农副产品，又方便市民购买所需的鲜菜、鲜肉、鲜蛋、活鸡、活鸭以及加工制作过的熟食品。据阳明农贸综合市场营销统计，日均在市场摆摊和挑担入市售货者250余家，购置副食品市民5000人次，仅鲜猪肉日销量达3000公斤，各种商品日销售总金额达60余万元。

四、农家店

1978年，县境各区和人民公社的农业生产资料、盐巴、布匹、百货等生活日用品，均由区供销社和32个公社（镇）分销店承担。1980年起，市场逐渐开放，个体工商户快速发展，供销社（店）业务量逐渐缩小，只得将商店承包给职工经营。2005年12月，贯彻执行商务部〔2005〕258号文件精神，县供销部门启动农村新网工程，在全县选点建设“万村千乡”农家店。每个店的房舍由国家助资5000元，建筑面积80平方米以上，门面装修和货柜安装按照建设图纸统一施工。至2010年，全县共投入资金253万元，其中省、市供销社补助74万元，调动社会闲散资金179万元，建成农家店196个，总面积为1.91万平方米，覆盖90.3%的自然村寨，服务对象近20万人之多。店房建起后，即挑选有一定文化、头脑精明、家居适中的村民，经市供销社业务培训，考试合格发给证书正式担任店长。由县农资公司统一配送货物，统一标识商品，统一规定价格，统一计划管理。店里经营的化肥、农药、烟酒、食品和日用百货，具有价格实惠、采购方便、质量保证等好处，年均销售收入4000万元。村民们满意地说：告别多年的供销社又回来，想买生产资料和生活用品都能买到，太方便！

五、超级市场

2000年9月，下岗职工虞野于县城建起首家由顾客自我选购商品的“笑容超市”，开县境兴办超级市场的先河。2004年9月，颇具规模的合力超市又在人民北路和翠屏西路交汇处兴起。继后，接踵而至的又有山羊、华联、大昌隆等超市入驻。超市一改以往商品与顾客被隔开，由营业员取商品给顾客又由顾客付款给营业员的售货方式，让顾客进店在货柜上自选商品，拿到收银处付款，钱货点清后顾客即可提货出店。市场商品除日用百货外，还有鲜肉、蛋禽、蔬菜等。到2010年，全县有烟酒、食品、日用百货、家用电器等超级市场10家，其中的家电超市还可在顾客选定商品付齐货款后，由超市派车将物品送到顾客家中并安装试用运转正常才予结。全县在超市从业者267人，当年销售额近1亿元，向税务机关缴纳税金700万元。

专记一：笑容超市兴衰记

笑容超市为下岗职工虞野以月租4500元租得位于县城迎春路的天地人公司大楼底层180平方米营业用房，自筹备资金30万元装修和备货建起的全县第一家超级超市。2000年9月开业，自任经理，出售卫生纸品、洗涤用品、文具、烟酒、糖食和饮料等日用生活用品。由于经营方式灵活，为顾客提供很多方便，经营1年销售额达250万元，生意非常火爆。

2002年10月，因天地人公司大楼转让给县信用联社，笑容超市迁到体育馆南面继续经营。由于场地小、商品少，又不在街对面，光顾的顾客不多，使生意从红火转为清淡。2003年初又以年租金28.2万元租得位于翠屏路与人民路交汇处的城北村综合大楼，装修后于7月开业，由于没有调整好自己的经营策略和疏于管理，进货没有适销对路，加上房租高额、流动资金短缺，致亏损不断增加，只得低价处理余货，在付清所有费用后还亏损14万元，虞野迫于生计远走他乡另寻门路。

专记二：讲诚信的修文合力超市

2010年的县城文成逸都合力超市

2004年6月，开阳县人张昌勇看准修文市场，决定在县城兴办合力超市分店，租用位于人民路与翠屏西路交汇处的城北村街面房一楼一底，共500平方米面积作营业厅，招收员工40名，9月开业，经营食品、百货、家用电器、时装、鞋帽等商品万余种。超市以讲诚信为理念，处处为顾客着想，严格执行“不是正规厂家生产的商品不进店，破损、过期商品不上柜台”的店规，上柜商品必有完整的商标，并向顾客承诺：凡从店中购到假冒伪劣、过期变质的商品，由商店赔偿5至10倍的补偿金，让

顾客进合力买到的是放心商品。同时还把超市办成爱心商店，更加赢得顾客的好评和赞誉。经与县民政局商定，凭民政局发给的低保证到商店购买生活日用品，可享受低保金内9至9.5折的优惠价格。从开业至2010年底，有500余名低保人员到店购买商品获得优惠差价3000余元。城北村低保户刘国才欲购年货过春节，特地到合力超市购买菜油、面条和日用杂货得到优惠，感动地说："合力超市说到做到，是我们信得过的商店。"

合力超市为贵州大型超市之一，在全省各地设分店连锁经营，县境除县城置分店外，尚有扎佐分店，顾客持"购物卡"在各店均可自由选择需要的物品付现款或刷"购物卡"。据统计，合力超市开业之后，日均入店顾客500人次，日均销售金额1.6万元，每月向国家缴纳税费5000余元。群众感受是：高兴而来，满意而去。

2000—2010年全县超级市场一览表

表3—06—02

名　称	所在地址	商场面积（平方米）	员工数（人）	开业时间	经营商品	日均顾客（人）	日均销售额（元）	备　注
修文笑容超市	县城迎春路翠屏路交汇处	180	10	2000年9月	糖食 文具 家用小电器	300	8000	2004年3月停业
修文大昌隆超市（阳光便利店）	县城朝阳路中段	150	5	2001年5月	烟酒食品日用百货	100	2000	
修文万家隆超市	县城人民南路皂角树	300	10	2004年5月	食品日用百货家用小电器	200	5000	
修文合力超市	县城人民北路与翠屏西路交汇处	500	40	2004年9月	食品日用百货家用小电器	500	16000	
扎佐合力超市	腾飞路东段	400	12	2004年10月	食品日用百货家用小电器	100	5000	
修文国银家电	县城阳明大道西段	600	8	2006年9月	彩电冰箱洗衣机电磁炉	300	2000	
扎佐华联购物广场	县城新东路中段	800	15	2007年9月	食品日用百货家用小电器	15	3500	
修文山羊家电建材五金城	县城新都口岸进口右边	800	6	2007年12月	冰箱彩电五金建材	5	2000	
修文华联购物中心	县城迎春路与长征路交汇处	1600	26	2008年9月	烟酒食品日用百货	500	8000	
修文惠客便利店	县城阳明大道西段	200	5	2008年9月	食品烟酒日用百货	100	1500	
修文福乐多超市	县城上河城	4000	130	2010年6月	食品和生活用品	1000	50000	

六、商品展销

1999年10月，县城街道拓宽，县境果农借首届阳明文化节的举办，在健身路、翠屏路摆摊设点展销金秋梨、猕猴桃等水果，开修文展销商品之先河。同时，贵阳市市西路商品展销公司也看中修文县城的商机，租用新体育馆南广场撑起活动大棚，设立货柜和摊位，连续10天展销日用百货、五金交电、鞋帽、时装、图书、化妆用品及粮食、饮料等。此后，每年春、秋两季都出现商品展销会，除省内商户外，先后有上海、武汉、江西景德镇、广西北流、湖南醴陵、内蒙古等地的商家在迎春路、健身路和原汽车客运站举办商品展销，每次设有摊位250个至300余个，销售额达500余万元，使一向为普通群众经营的草根市场一跃而为外地商家参与的大市场，商圈的扩大是历史上没有过的。2008年3月，上海帅增贸易有限公司于健身路举办让利于民的商品展销活动，在长达200米的大棚内设置摊位300余个，仅10天销售额即达800万元。由于帅增公司让利给受凝冻袭扰的灾民，工商部门免收工商管理费，商家主动捐款2万元救济遭受凝冻灾害的灾区和灾民，以感谢政府的支持。

县城商品展销市场

第三节　行业经营

一、农产品购销

（一）粮食购销

粮食收购　1978年，沿袭第二个“一定五年”的粮食统购政策。1985年粮食市场开始放开，除稻谷、玉米、小麦实行定购外，其他粮食品种自由上市议购，遇市场价格低于原统购价时，粮食部门仍按原统购价敞开收购。1987年实行定购粮食“三挂钩”（粮肥、粮油、预购定金挂钩）。1990年全县完成统（定）购3750吨，议价收购390吨，从省外购进190吨。1993年国家对定购粮食实行价外加价，在原标准每50公斤大米5.2元，小麦、玉米4.2元的基础上，加价补贴每50公斤大米13元（稻谷9元），小麦和玉米每50公斤各补贴8元。1997年10月，为减轻农民负担，按照贵州省粮食厅和农业厅联合规定收购粮食时不得代各单位和各部门收扣提留、统筹费、农业特产税、屠宰税及烟挂粮、烟挂钱。2001年因退耕还林、定购粮调减为2910吨。定购品种只为中晚籼稻、不分定购价和保护价，中等收购价每公斤1.1元，对交售陈粮者每超过1年，每公斤降0.10元。2003年取消粮食定购，由粮食购销公司在市场上收购，2007年收购粮食仅70吨。

2009年9月，利用粮油购销有限公司扎佐分公司大坡粮站储备粮库成立县穗丰粮油储备有限公司，承担县级粮油储备。11月，完成县级储备库储备稻谷1000吨。2010年增至1816吨。稻谷入库后按照《县级储备粮油管理办法》进行管理，以备应急供应。

粮食销售　1978年，城镇居民供应标准按系统分等级定量供应。1980年成立粮食议价公司，至1984年共议价销售1.07万吨。1990年因伏旱粮食减产，议价市场价格上扬，仅销售议价粮236吨。1992年根据外地做法，凡要求农转非户籍的每人可以缴纳城镇增容费4500元，凭公安部门发给的蓝色户口簿办理

474人城镇居民粮油供应证。

1993年5月，根据国办〔1993〕25号文件精神，对在粮改中产生的军粮差价、费用和补贴由各级财政承担。差价每公斤大米补贴1元，面粉补贴1元，大豆补贴1.6元，由粮食部门收取军用粮票，按标准补给购粮单位的差价。6月，粮食取消凭票证购买，城镇居民很少到粮店买粮。是时，全县有个体粮店21个，销售品种有惠水大米、安顺旧洲大米及从国外进口的泰国米等。面条有六广面条、绥阳面条、阳关面条等。据城关镇（今龙场镇）冬季1个场天的调查，上市粮食总量3万公斤。

2002年，实行退耕还林，采取“以粮代赈”办法对退耕还林户每亩年补助150公斤稻谷或玉米，补助期为经济林5年，生态林8年，还草2年。全县退耕还林（草）2万亩，销售粮食3000吨，2003年达4500吨，购粮资金由省粮食局和省财政厅负担，由县农发行支付90万元给购销公司。2004年起补助粮可以领取粮食，也可以领取现金。2010年销售粮食4041吨。

（二）油菜籽收购和菜油销售

油菜籽收购 1978年沿袭定购制度，对油菜籽完不成任务的生产队仍采取“斗硬”办法，责令农民在市场上买菜籽交任务，或按大米与菜籽的折算比例，以大米顶油菜籽任务。

1990年收购价分别按70%作定购价和30%作议购价。1992年收购油菜籽不分计划内计划外，实行综合计价敞开收购。1993年取消计划定购，次年油菜籽产量减产，为防止县际之间哄抬菜籽收购价格，安顺地区规定每100公斤按65—70元价格收购。1994年对市场实行监管，在国家粮食部门未完成收购计划前，不准他人或企业在市场上收购。同时县政府于7月决定油菜籽价格从每100公斤210元调高到240元。1995年因夏季受灾，为确保新建的油脂厂生产需要，收购价格又比邻近的息烽、开阳、金沙等县每公斤高于0.2至0.4元，促使外县油菜籽大量流入县内，但因收购菜籽时水分掌握不严导致发霉，翻晒后数量短少，出油率下降，损失达45万多元。1998年又规定在粮食部门未完成菜籽的收购任务之前，其他单位或个人不准在市场上抢购，违者一律作没收处理，是年共没收45户在市场上收购的油菜籽1.96万公斤。2000年起，省、市不再出台菜籽收购指导价，收购计划逐步缩小，购销随行就市。2006—2007年县粮食购销公司一粒菜籽都未收到。2008年，上级业务部门下达1500吨油菜籽收购任务全部完成。2009年收购按菜油统计，当年收购100吨，2010年完成150吨。

菜油销售 1978年，菜油销售沿袭原定量供应标准，城镇居民每人每月0.4公斤，1980年提高到0.5公斤，1990年油菜籽丰收，从8月起实行“平价销售，定点供应，保留定量，价格不变，多购不限”的原则，对城镇居民当年4月以前的存油量，每公斤在当时价2.18元基础上下降0.2元给予优惠。为扩大销售，粮食部门组织职工到缺油区推销。1992年向河南、浙江等省销售油菜籽300余吨。1993年菜油销售价又调到每公斤4.3元，国家价格与市场价格持平参与市场竞争，当年销售菜油1469吨。继后，随着油脂市场放开，食用油从单一的菜油增加瓶装花生油、小磨芝麻油等，从个体油

2010年县城人民南路个体粮食销售店

店扩大到综合超市。2007—2010年，除军粮供应站仍按国家价格供应驻县部队菜油外，其余居民和行业均到市场上自购。

（三）烤烟收购

1978年，烤烟由各供销社收购，县土产公司对外调拨。1984年1月县置烟草专卖局，城关、扎佐、久长、小箐、六广5个区置烟叶站，28个乡设烟叶收购点。1998年4月贯彻执行国家烟草专卖局规定，实行“市场引导，计划种植，主攻质量，合理布局”的烟草生产指导方针，烟草种植计划大大削减，县委、县政府作出“调整布局、稳定面积、主攻质量和提高单产”的决策，把烤烟种植安排在六屯、六桶以及杉林等老烟区，面积稳定在2万亩，从资金、化肥及科技方面进行扶持。13年间亩产最低的1999年74.5公斤，最高的2001年119.4公斤。2010年收购烤烟3821吨，比1997年的最高年产量5911吨减少2090吨。

1978—2010年主要农产品收购情况一览表

表3—06—03　　　　单位：吨

年份	粮食	油菜籽	烤烟	年份	粮食	油菜籽	烤烟
1978	5370	400	904	1995	5391	10139	2955
1979	5850	610	1243	1996	6355	5974	4982
1980	5990	1590	431	1997	5529	1699	5911
1981	3310	3430	1603	1998	5000	3724	3194
1982	8480	6470	3021	1999	3373	6515	2884
1983	8210	3080	1525	2000	6371	2352	2814
1984	4620	2630	3695	2001	5277	3447	1667
1985	3200	60	4468	2002	5743	1501	1614
1986	4710	1210	2839	2003	2860	1145	2138
1987	4970	2980	2605	2004	5047	4157	1977
1988	4830	4340	4814	2005	37822	1541	2329
1989	5220	3260	4823	2006	70	—	2105
1990	6720	3280	3213	2007	70	—	2058
1991	10999	6266	3932	2008	34377	1500	2284
1992	4505	2598	4305	2009	1000	313	1418
1993	5006	2631	4823	2010	816	469	3821
1994	5979	2032	2778				

注：1. 2005年和2008年粮食收购数含省外调入

2. 2009年和2010年油菜籽收购为菜油折算

1978—2010年粮食、菜油销售统计表

表3—06—04　　　　单位：吨

年度	粮食	菜油	年度	粮食	菜油
1978	11977	173	1995	9155	109.6
1979	12085	176	1996	6475	134.5
1980	11252	196	1997	8133	635
1981	12198	340	1998	6265	101
1982	17420	638	1999	5416	10
1983	11146	721	2000	2377	698
1984	16908	878	2001	5427	355
1985	12577	332	2002	2929	14
1986	11808	483	2003	4982	23
1987	11514	412	2004	6795	229
1988	12903	401	2005	6656	—
1989	12475	268	2006	50	—
1990	12891	369	2007	50	—
1991	14548	192	2008	167	—
1992	12033	644	2009	141	—
1993	9166	1469	2010	4041	—
1994	9672	329			

二、农业生产资料销售

1978年，化肥、农药（械）、中小农具等农业生产资料由供销社经营，化肥按计划供应，竹木农具按国家下达的计划加工成风车、挞斗、龙骨车等供应。从1980年起改革流通体制，实行市场调节，多渠道经营农业生产资料。

（一）化肥

1978年由农资公司经营，化肥品种有尿素、碳铵、硝铵、磷肥、钾肥等。1981年销售化肥1024吨。1984年生产厂家增多，销售出现多渠道经营，价格有平价、计划外议价和市场价。1987年为稳定价格，县实行综合计价销售。1990年销售1.2万吨。20世纪90年代在扎佐建立转运站后，由扎佐直运销售点。2005年又加强农村网点建设，首先在六屯建立农资专卖店，全县较集中的村寨建农家店销售。2010年销售量达2.3万吨，主要品种有尿素、

2010年仍存的贵阳农资扎佐储备配送中心

复合肥、普钙和钾肥等，销售金额2700万元。

（二）农药

1978年由农资公司专营，主要品种有666、滴滴涕、赛力散，农药械有单管和双管手摇压缩喷粉器。农药销售1985年为164吨。20世纪90年代末，停止使用有机磷农药和剧毒性农药。2000年起农民种植蔬菜改用菌治病和养鸭治病等新技术，致销量下降，到2005年出售农药2.5吨。

（三）农用塑料薄膜

1978年由农资公司和基层供销社经营，生产厂家少，流通渠道单一，年均销售20吨。进入20世纪80年代起生产厂家可以自销，经营渠道增多，1990年全县销售达256吨。1991年后推广农业实用技术，需求量增大，个体经营户增多，致农资公司销量锐减，最高的1997年销售46吨。2007年减为6吨，收入9万元。2008年农资公司停止经营，农资个体经营户直向贵阳经销商店进货销售。2010年全县销售量40吨，销售收入600万元。

（四）良种

1978年种子销售由种子公司承担，主要品种有杂交水稻和杂交玉米。2000年7月全国人大常委会第十六次会议审议通过《中华人民共和国种子法》开始执行，放开经营权，允许个体经营。2003年种子公司改为植物保护站，负责对种子经营权的审批和监督。到2005年全县种子经营有50余户。玉米品种有“鲁三3号”“毕单13号”“贵单8号”，水稻品种有“杰优8号”“吉优9号”“香草单优2017号”等。至2010年种子经营增为75户，销售玉米种10万公斤，每公斤均价35元；水稻种3万公斤，每公斤均价50元。

2010年，县城迎春路个体农资销售店

（五）中小农具

1978年，由供销社销售的木制农具有风车、挞斗，铁制农具有锄头、镰刀、铧口等。1979年起转为多渠道经营，供销部门销售量逐年下降，1990年由1985年前7年年均9.1万件降至3.7万件。进入20世纪90年代，国家不再下达木材计划，供销社也不再加工木制农具，个体手工业者则制作打谷机、铁制犁头供应农民，全县年销售打谷机近400部，每部售价200至250元；铁犁头近80部，每部售价160至180元。至2010年，农具仍由个体户经营，除小型农具继续使用外，木制风车接近消失，铁制犁头逐渐被小型耕作机械取代。

（六）农机具

1978年由县农业机械公司组织销售，主要品种有大、中、小型拖拉机，机耕犁、耙，柴油机，汽油机及农用运输车等，销售总额达106.5万元。1981年起农

2004年起实行财政补贴的县城小型耕作机销售点

民经济收入增加，农机具销售量逐步上升，到1990年全县销售拖拉机255台，运输机械203部，加工机械666台。2004年11月贵阳市政府贯彻执行《中华人民共和国农业机械化促进法》，对购买农机具实行38%的价款补贴，个体农机具经营户延伸到乡（镇）。2010年全县有农机经营户32家，从业人员73人，销售农机具1014台，销售金额达728万元，农户获补助款277万元。

三、日用商品销售

（一）百货

1978年由县百货公司经营，各区供销社及公社分销店设专柜经销，商品实行计划调拨。1979年起县百货公司扩大经营范围，放开工业品自销和个体经营，百货花色品种逐渐增多，特别是江浙、两广等地百货日用品涌入县内市场，逐步形成专业化经销。到1990年全县建立兼营百货综合市场10个，零售兼营百货网点260个，同时取消指令性计划商品，实行按市场需求多渠道进货，按市场规律灵活制定批发和零售价格，至1990年，年均销售额为762万元。1991年起百货商品敞开供应，展开市场竞争，百货公司因受传统组织形式、经营思想等因素影响，经济效益连年下滑。1994年10月县城建立私营经济一条街，经营日用百货的个体门面约占60%，经营户多由贵阳市西路批发市场进货，或与生产厂家订货，或从省外采购进货供应。2005年建成兼营百货的自选超市10个。2010年全县有百货店铺200余家，从业人员320人，销售收入达3000万元。

县城迎春路日用小百货个体经营店

（二）针纺织品

1978年，沿袭棉布计划销售，凭票购买，由县百货公司和供销社负责经营。1983年1月，随着纯化纤中长织物和涤棉品混纺布品进入市场，逐步取代纯棉制品。5月，针棉织品免收布票。1986年，根据县政府办16号文件精神，县百货公司对全县1.48万户贫困户7.41万人每人赊销纯棉布10米共74.1万米。至1990年，全县年均棉布销售74.2万米、呢绒2万米，床单9115条，化纤布及涤棉混纺布16.2万米。由于化纤布滑爽挺括，仿制逼真，免烫易干，色泽牢固，逐渐成为全县纺织品市场的主要品种，到20世纪90年代中期已占家庭用布的50%，到90年代末期上升到80%。2000年起，针纺织品经营以私营和个体商业为主，厂家自销也形成网络，直接向经营商家销售，零售商多从贵阳进货，品种繁多，应有尽有。至2010年，县境有针纺织品店35家，时装店110家，从业者400人，年销售收入9900万元。

（三）五金交电

1978年，五交化行业沿袭条条管理，由五金公司经营，供销社设专柜销售，商品按计划分配调拨。1979年起五金市场放开，个体专营商店逐渐涌现。2010年全县有经营户150家（含超市电器经营部），年销商品30万件，销售收入2.2亿元。

家用电器　1978年由县国营五金公司经营，区供销社设专柜销售，调入商品由省、市公司计划供应。1979年计划外商品允许三级批发企业和零售企业出省采购或向二级站择优选购，调入14英寸黑白电视机，当年销售107台。1980年开始销售收录机，1982年洗衣机进入市场，1987年电冰箱问市。至1990年，年均销收录机109台，电视机（含彩电）388台，洗衣机220台，电冰箱78台。1991年起货源充足，由国营转为个体经营，敞开供应。又增加音像类的DVD、VCD、投影机及家用石英炉、空调器、饮水机、洗浴器、抽油烟机、微波炉、消毒碗柜、电饭煲等品种，商品逐渐普及。2008年6月，为刺激家电下乡消费，对彩电、冰箱、空调和洗衣机由地方财政按每件总额的13%补贴，县财政年均补贴200万元，让人民群众得到实惠。到2010年，年均销售家用电器15万件，销售收入1.5亿元。

县城国银家电销售店

交通工具 1978年，县五金公司及区供销社专柜经营有自行车、手推车、三轮车及其配件，“永久”“飞鸽”“凤凰”牌自行车实行凭票供应。从1985年起逐步取消票证，打开店门敞开销售，至1990年年均销售自行车870辆。1991年起摩托车、摩的进入市场，并逐步发展为个体经营，有的还直接为生产厂代销。2005年5月，个体户廖伦义在阳明大道开起“嘉陵摩托车”销售店，主要销售两轮摩托车和三轮农用车。继后，“大运”“本田”等销售店也陆续进驻。2010年，仅县城就有“雅马哈”“比齐亚”“豪爵”“天马”“铃木”等车辆销售店10户，年均销售900辆，销售收入700万元。

装饰材料 1978年，装饰材料中的五金、门扣、合页、风钩以及涂料等由五金公司和区供销社专柜经营。1990年县城民主路开起第一家个体装饰材料店，但只销售简易的外墙和内墙瓷砖。继后，随着城区开发和危房改造，先后增加陶瓷、木地板、家居装饰配套设施专卖店。2000年起又陆续增加安全门、卫浴门和楼宇对讲门等门业。2010年仅县城就有家居装饰材料店85户，从业人员300人，年销售收入1.5亿元。

（四）副食品

食盐 1978年，由糖酒公司批发，供销社和公私合营商店零售，均按计划调入供应，零售为散装加碘盐。1981年复为盐业公司专营，实行塑料袋包装加碘食盐零售，每袋500克售价0.2元，盐业公司对食盐销售店颁发许可证，供应一般比较平稳。1988年市场物价上涨出现暂时抢购食盐现象，曾进行过限量供应。1989年又敞开供应。1990年全县食盐供应网点981户。之前至是年的13年，年均销售食盐1430吨。1991年起县内计划内和计划外用盐，一律由盐业公司统一组织购进和批发销售。海味盐、调味盐等品种也投放市场。销售方式逐步实行配送制，由盐业公司派车运到网点保证市场供应。2010年全县销售食盐1468吨，销售收入368万元，上缴税费27万元。

糖食 1978年，糖食由国营糖酒公司和供销社经营。至1985年，全县共销售食糖2040吨，年均销售255吨。食糖除安排劳动保护、糕点生产及产妇、婴儿外，余下部分每人按0.25公斤分配供应到人。县糕点厂因缺乏原料，只能生产芝麻圆饼、糖条和夹沙饼等。1984年白糖市场放开，传统的沙琪玛、鸡蛋糕、桃片糕等进入市场，每逢中秋佳节还有“五仁”“水晶”“椒盐”“火腿”月饼供应。1997年县城农贸综合市场及迎春路私营经济一条街落成，外地客商落户制作糕点销售，他们采取前门开店、后屋作坊的模式营运，花色品种有西式和中式之分，味道有广味、江浙味、川味及黔味等。还能应顾客的需要制作生日蛋糕或为老年人祝寿的寿桃等。2010年仅县城就有糕点营销店12家，从业人员40人，销售收入150万元。

酒 1978年，由糖酒公司和供销社经营，年销售酒450吨，其中散白酒系本地生产，瓶酒来自贵阳、安顺、遵义等地。1979年起市场放开，全县酒类出现多家生产、多渠道经营的状况，国营主渠道销售逐年下降。消费从一般白酒转向高中档白酒，散白酒逐渐被瓶装酒代替。1980年销售480吨。1985年全县有销售酒店95户，酒类批发11户，1990年散白酒仅销售20吨。进入20世纪90年代，随着群众生活水平的提高，消费转向以高中档窖酒为主，其品种有阳明大曲、安酒、湄窖等。2000年起，全县习酒、董酒、茅台、五粮液、金沙回沙酒销量上升，散白酒多在农村销售。至2010年，酒类销售点有612个，从业人员1989人。年销酒732吨，销售收入1.46亿元。

县烟草公司卷烟配送

卷烟 1978年，卷烟系糖业烟酒公司批发经营，由贵阳、遵义烟厂供货，并分甲、乙、丙、丁4个等级，丁级烟有兰雁、大三元、向阳花、模范，主要消费在农村，城镇以乙级、丙级为主，品种是芦笙、乌江、朝阳桥、花溪、云雾山、黄果树等，1980年全县销售卷烟5376箱。1985年改由烟草公司批发经营。甲级过滤嘴卷烟销量不断上升，黄果树、遵义、云雾山等市场供应趋紧，连续6年销售卷烟11.4万箱，年均1.9万箱。继后，县内销售的卷烟品种陆续增至数十种，中华和贵州磨砂黄果树、精装遵义仍很走俏，云南卷烟红梅、阿斯玛、红河、红塔山也相继进入市场，深受消费者青睐。2005年县烟草公司成立配送中心，对全县1192个网点卷烟批发实行送货上门，销烟9855箱。2010年卷烟销售达到巅峰1.21亿箱，销售收入1.75亿元。缴纳税费3502万元。

食肉 1978年食肉由食品公司经营。1979年在完成“购五留五”派购任务后，剩余的肥猪允许上市出售或宰杀销售。居民和机关干部职工凭票供应。1980年猪肉市场开放，允许个体屠宰上市敞开供应，价格随行就市。从1985年4月起生猪购销放开，猪肉取消定量供应，零售价格调高后出现价差，政府对城镇居民进行食肉补贴，每人每月补助0.8元，年底一次性领取。1990年上市猪肉仅5134吨。1992年猪肉供应由食品公司经营转向个体屠商经营为主。1996至2001年城镇居民每人每月补助又提高到1.5元。2002年食肉补贴取消，生猪采购、屠宰全由个体工商户承担，县城还出现牛肉专卖户。2005年全县食肉供应量1.2万吨，年人均消费量39公斤。2010年增至1.72万吨，比2005年增加0.52万吨。

禽蛋 1978年禽蛋实行派购，由供销社代购，收购鲜蛋每公斤奖售粮食0.5公斤。1983年改为计划收购，原奖售粮食改为奖励粮票，每公斤鲜蛋另奖售标准化肥1公斤。国营食品部门完成鲜蛋收购计划后可展开议购议销。1984年收购鲜蛋136吨全部上调。1985年鲜蛋经营放开，购销实行多渠道经营。久长区清水乡还出现“清水蛋帮”，贩运鸡鸭蛋到贵阳出售。一些科技示范户禽蛋养殖场开始萌发并迅速扩展，禽蛋销售量逐年上升。1990年全县禽蛋上市产量达303吨，1995年增至606吨。至2010年，全县有1000只以上蛋鸡养殖场18个，上市鲜蛋达3155吨，销售收入4.73亿元。

牛奶　2002年前，县内牛奶供应全由境外调入。2003年2月贵阳“好1多”奶牛场落户久长镇清水村，养奶牛600头，2005年产鲜奶3600吨，销售收入288万元。此后六屯乡石猫猫、谷堡乡红焰村、六桶乡石头村先后办起奶牛场，产奶由“好1多”奶牛场加工，批发给商场或个体户销售。至2010年，全县有奶牛场7个，养奶牛7000头，年产鲜奶9752吨。农民自养奶牛售奶3000吨，除在县内市场销售外，还大量供应闯入省城贵阳，销售收入792万元。

辣椒　1978年由供销社收购，至1980年的3年全县收购干辣椒23.7吨，年均7.9吨。1981至1990年中有6年收购总量达49.2吨，年均8.2吨。1997年起调整农业产业结构，县政府把发展辣椒产业作为一项内容，到2000年种植面积达6233亩，集中在龙场、扎佐、久长3个镇和谷堡、六屯2个乡种植，当年收干辣椒1558吨，收入2340万元。2010年，全县各乡（镇）普遍种植辣椒，面积达1.25万亩，上市产量2717吨，销售收入7475万元。

（五）果蔬

蔬菜　1978年，蔬菜销售由国营蔬菜公司和蔬菜合作商店经营。1980年起发展多种经营，到1990年，蔬菜种植面积达2.2万亩，总产量2.7万吨。1993年，王官乡马口村农民自发向邻近的白云区摆茅村引进晚番茄，扎佐镇大堡村引进白萝卜种植成功并迅速向周边发展。又先后引种黄瓜、大葱、蒜薹等品种。1996年蔬菜种植扩大到全县10乡（镇）。到2010年复种面积达22.77万亩，品种有76个，上市产量达27.21万吨，平均吨价1630元，销售收入4.43亿元。除本县供应外，主要销往广州、珠海、深圳和重庆等地。其中：晚番茄种植面积9694亩，销售总量4.24万吨，销售收入7755万元；白萝卜种植面积4.53万亩，上市总量6.08万吨，销售收入5549万元。

水果　1978年县境主要有梨子、酥李、桃子等品种，产量较少。1988年马怀麟将猕猴桃引进乌栗乡下硐村种植成功，开创全县发展水果种植新局面，到1990年全县果木栽种达6867亩，挂果面积2660亩，上市量647.3吨，销售收入6.47万元。1992年在下硐联户合作农场的带动下全县大量种植猕猴桃，同时引进金秋梨、艳红桃、葡萄、酥李、枇杷、柑橘、杨梅等品种，种植面积迅速扩大，栽培技术逐渐提高。至2010年，全县果树种植面积7.5万亩，挂果面积6.27万亩，上市产量2.46万吨，销售收入1.77亿元。其中猕猴桃创下名品牌，在省内外都占有市场。

县城水果销售店

四、药材药品

（一）中药材收购

1978年由供销社收购后调贵阳市药材公司，主要有续断、杜仲、黄柏等20多个品种，年收购量约100余担。1981年起市场放开，改由药材公司负责购销，国家收购价格低于市场价格，收购量逐年减少，有些个体工商户出面在市场上收购中药材运到贵阳出售。1987年供销社停止对中药材收购。1997年起，县招商引资引进医药制造业，厂家需要大量的中药材原料，农业部门抓住契机，在小箐、六屯、大石等地规模种植半夏、淫洋霍、板蓝根5000多亩，直接销给厂家，2010年产量175吨全部售出。

（二）药品销售

1978年由县药材公司经营，年销售收入32万元。1990年医药经营放开，个体药品经营户增加，有些药厂以出厂价直接送货到医疗单位，致药材公司销售金额降至16万元。2010年，仅县城就有药品零售店15户，年销售收入达4500万元。

五、燃油（气）销售

1978年，燃油系国家计划物资，由石油公司经营，每年的销售指标均由计划部门下达。1981年县石油公司从商业局划给县计划委员会管理，后又随机构撤并，依次划属县经委、计划与经济贸易局和发展改革贸易局。1999年6月，又上划归中国石油公司贵州省公司管理，置中国石油化工有限公司修文县支公司，2010年县境置加油站19个承担燃油经销业务。

汽油　1978年，汽油按计划调入供应，型号以70号油为主，年销售量3000吨。1980年起运输市场放开，公、私车辆增多，于1982年实行统购统配，先后使用购油折、油票定量供应。由于需求量与计划供应的差距太大，县石油公司直接去广东茂名购得月均3至5个车皮汽油补充，型号有70号、80号、85号，到1991年每年销售量4000—5000吨，从而缓解供需矛盾。1992年三级市场放开，取消凭证供应，允许其他企业和私人开办加油站参加产品销售，型号减少70号增加90号，年销售5000—8000吨。1999年6月，石油公司加入石油集团，投资205万元购进马家桥部队和扎佐武装部加油站改建成城南加油站，新建扎佐立交桥和广田加油站，实现程控化加油和24小时加油制。2010年，全县有国有股份制加油站14个，私营加油站5个，主要销售90号、93号、97号汽油，全年销售汽油3.32万吨，销售收入2.63亿元。

县石油公司加油站

柴油　1978年柴油销售372吨，大都使用于农机具抽水灌田，由县计委统一分配到区，再按农机具分配供应。1982年年初改由农业部门分配。1985年至1990年乡镇企业发展，柴油汽车大增，6年销量达8400吨，年均1400吨。1992年取消凭证供应，至2010年的19年总销量为1.61万吨，年均销售847吨。

煤油　1978年前，煤油大部分用于农村照明，到1979年，煤油灯多被电灯所取代，但煤油炉具逐渐增加，至1990年的11年销量达3900.6吨，年均销售354.6吨，1991年起因农村用电普及，炉具亦被淘汰，煤油销量随之下降。2002至2010年，以煤油作燃油基本消逝，仅有洗涤、溶剂少量使用。

燃化气　1984年11月，县石油公司在县城皂角树建起首家燃化气供应店，销售液化炉、燃化气和抽油烟机。1999年贵州星原净宇燃化气开发有限公司投资480万元，于南门粑（粑坳）修（文）公路侧征地10亩建燃化气供应站，将外地运来的气源在站内分装入钢瓶，再分运到全县各乡（镇）站供应用户。至2010年，全县已建燃化气供应站18个，覆盖县境各乡（镇），用户从1998年的450户上升到3万户。年销液化气913吨，收入730万元。

六、文化用品销售

（一）图书

1978年，县境图书统一由新华书店修文店和扎佐分店经销，主要发行国家出版的教学课本、文艺书籍和科普读物。1989年，个体书店“知行书屋”在县城开业，首开私营书店之先河。至2010年，全县除国有新华书店外，私营书店已发展为7家，从业者15人，年均销售收入1500万元。

（二）文具

1978年，文具由县百货公司和供销社经营，货源主要靠省公司按照计划分配、调拨，经营范围大多是传统的笔、墨、纸和文体用具中的常规乐器、球类等几十个品种。1980年起文具市场逐步放开，允许个体户参与经营，品种逐步增加，到1990年全县国营、集体、个体文具增到150个，从业者268人，货源靠省、市文化用品公司进货近80%，近20%属自行采购。进入20世纪90年代，文具市场形成以私营和个体经营为主，货源由经营者按市场需求自行采购，除高档的钢琴、手风琴、管乐器、电子计算机等无经营外，其他商品多有商家经销，2010年全县仅专营文具网店就有26个，从业者66人，年营业收入901.78万元。

（三）音像制品

1978年只有县广播站使用交流和直流收音机。1985年收录机、电视机及歌带进入市场，1990年5月待业青年袁琴开办的第一家租、售磁带店于县城开业，接着个体影碟经销店相继涌现，商品逐渐增多。至2010年，全县有“天地人”“晓军”“碟友”“美美”“中华”等音像销售店11家，从业员工15人，年销售收入70万元。

七、信息工具销售

（一）固定电话

1978年，固定电话和电话器材系邮电局经营，市内和农村用户共410户。20世纪80年代后期电信市场放开，允许个体户参加销售。1993年9月县城程控电话开通，经几次扩容，逐步扩大到城镇和农村住户，固定电话市场迅速扩大，销量大增，到2000年除原用户更新电话机外，新用户购机安装就达2.17万部，2001年至2010年再新增0.76万部，累计共达2.93万部，在1978年基础上增加71.5倍。久长镇清水村村民廖庆礼说：“我家两个儿子在浙江打工，过去要与儿子通电话得走几公里上街才办得到，现在自家安上程控电话，一拨就通，互报平安，真是太方便。”

（二）手机

1992年11月，县邮电局始推出TK-348无线电话机（人称“大哥大”），每部售价高达1万元以上。接着国外进口产品摩托罗拉、诺基亚、索尼爱立信、三星等手机进入修文市场，国产的首信、波导等品种也相继问市，以三星手机销量最多，价格最高的摩托罗拉每部达2万余元，国产的波导牌手机最低也是1000多元。1999年起新增国产的康佳、华为、金立、联想、天语等诸多品牌。2002年5月再增加各种型号的小灵通，并开展小灵通信用保底赠机和各种形式的预存话费送机等营销活动，扩大市场销售。由于手机市场发展速度惊人，销售价格也相应下降，每部名牌手机最高1万余元，多数品种一般在5000元以下，普通的仅几百元，最低的老年人用机99元。2010年，全县电信、移动、联通3家公司直销或代销手机商店有131家，年销售手机5000部，营业收入250万元。

（三）寻呼机

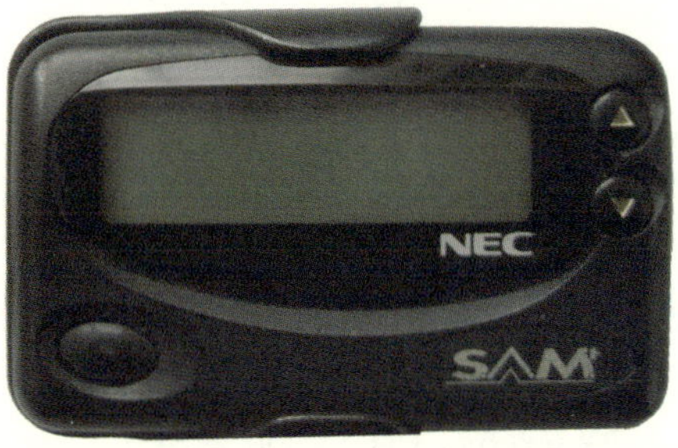

20世纪90年代销售的寻呼机

1992年县邮电局开通无线寻呼系统，即有销售寻呼机（BP机）的商店24家，当年出售寻呼机3000部，每部售价最少近500元，最高3000元。到1996年累计售机3000部。继后由于移动通信普及，从2004年起寻呼机退出历史舞台。

（四）电脑

县境使用电脑始于1993年，用户直接到贵阳购买。2008年1月，宏洋电脑公司在县城人民南路落户，销售的电脑有台式和手提式（笔记本电脑）两种，其品牌有联想、戴尔、方正等。至2010年，县城有宏洋、苏宁、新世纪等电脑销售店5家，年销售电脑400台，销售总收入160万元。

八、家具销售

2010年县城家居办公用品个体经营店

1992年前县境内无家具销售店，机关、居民所需家具须到贵阳家具店购买，或自备材料制作。1993年首家小胡家具店于县城开业，出售文件柜、写字台、床、座椅及沙发等。继后，由于人民生活水平的提高和住房时尚化，吸引商家涌入县城经营家具。到2005年，仅县城家具店就发展到21家，各家年销售收入15万元至40万元不等。随着家具用量饱和，导致有的家具店逐渐改业经营其他，至2010年，县城家具销售店仅剩10家，年均销售总收入仅200万元。

九、废品物资回收

1978年，在沿袭供销社回收社会零星的废旧物资的同时，县物资局启动经营废旧金属回收业务，回收废旧金属、橡胶、书报、塑料、针织品和玻璃等。1982年县内更新报废汽车统一由物资局收购后再集中上交金属回收公司。1983年物资局增办报废机电产品回收业务，凭企业主管部门核批的报废清单到企业核对付给残值费再拉回上调。与此同时，准许个体户过街串乡收购废旧物资。到1990年供销部门回收各类废旧物资200余吨；物资局回收废旧金属2000余吨和废旧汽车131辆；个体户收购废旧钢铁、书报、纸壳、铜、铝等900余吨。1991年后汽车敞开供应，报废汽车转由交警部门负责处理。由于供销、物资部门坐班收购，回收量逐年下降，1993年物资局停止收购报废机电产品，1995年只停止收购废旧有色金属，供销部门也同时停止废旧物资回收业务。2010年，县境废旧物资收购全由个体户经营，自找销路调出。

十、对外贸易

（一）出口

1978年，县境外贸出口处于起步阶段，出口产品仅有煅烧的铝矾土特级矿，通过贵州省进出口贸易公司对外销售，销量较小。

1983年，利用县内资源加工半成品或成品销售。是年，油漆级重晶石粉由省矿产品进出口公司销往英国、西德、日本、新加坡、苏联、捷克。由于产品质量上乘，吸引10余个国家进口公司到厂订货。1987年仅铝矾土熟矿外销创汇近50万美元。

进入20世纪90年代，新增棕刚玉外销美国、韩国、日本和中国香港地区。硅铁由合资经营的香港德利公司直销美国、韩国、日本及中国香港、台湾地区，1991年出口创汇近200万美元。黄磷产品部分外销，成品药远销加拿大、荷兰、俄罗斯、越南和中国香港。

1999年10月，县联合磨料厂获国家外贸经济合作部批准，取得进出口经营权，产品由第三方转销改为企业直销。2000年起再增石油压裂支撑陶粒产品出口哈萨克斯坦、俄罗斯、加拿大等国家。云天牌摩托车凸轮轴组件也随主车配套出口。由于受企业内部资金等因素和国际市场环境影响，出口种类有所减少，出口量时增时降。2010年具有进出口经营权的企业7家，其中有出口实绩的企业仅3家，按贵阳市商务局对外公布数据，全县出口创汇2483万美元，其中兴达物流公司通过湛江港出口重晶石粉5万吨，创外汇50万美元。

（二）进口

改革开放33年间，全县有的企事业单位除因生产（业务）需要，偶尔进口少量的机械或医疗设备外，还有个人通过网购、代购间接方式进口部分手机、照相机、电脑、家电用品、泰国米、烟酒、奶制品、香水、化妆品、保健品等。

第四节　服务行业

一、餐饮

1978年全县经营餐饮业10家，从业职工159人，其中国营1家27人，公私合营9家132人，分布在县城及各区公所驻地。1980年起市场放开，个体餐饮店逐渐涌现，公私合营餐饮业转为个体经营，全县饮食网点达到68家，从业173人，菜饭、小吃品种繁多，各具特色。其中扎佐林场门口的川黔公路上就有餐馆22家，时称“快活林”，以蹄膀火锅最有名气，往贵阳、遵义的司乘人员多在此进餐，生意十分红火。到1990年全县餐饮业达220家，从业者357人，年营业收入339万元。1993年起餐饮以私营和个体经营为主，网店遍布城乡，总数增到330家，从业935人。县城餐饮酒楼（店）主要承办宴席，各旅游风景点谷堡乡折溪村，扎佐镇独山村、大河村，大石乡大屯村也办起农家饮食店，用自种的蔬菜，自己腌制的腊肉、香肠，自酿的米酒接待游客。落地扎佐的贵阳高尔夫度假中心还能根据国外游客的需求制作西式餐饮。到2010年，全县仍有餐饮业220家，从业者高达1300余人，年营业收入1.2亿元。

二、旅社

1978年，县城仅有国营饮食服务公司、公私合营的旅马店及各区供销社开办的旅社共12家，从业者25人，有床位300张，年营业收入5万余元。从20世纪80年代起，县粮食、邮电等部门利用多余的房屋办起招待所，设普通房间接待旅客。90年代后，阳明宾馆、阳明山庄、高尔夫度假中心、久长珍珠岛休闲避暑处、索风营营地，腾晖酒店相继建立旅馆，配有电话、电视、空调、卫生间及各种不同档次的标准间或套间，其中的珍珠岛为三星级。六广河大峡谷、桃源河漂流都设有床位供游客食宿，腾晖酒店还置有集住宿、餐饮、洗浴、娱乐等服务项目。至2010年，全县有宾馆、旅社35家，床位3000张，从业人员500人，年营业收入5000万元。

三、洗浴

（一）沐浴

1978年，国营饮食服务公司设有洗澡堂，分大池和淋浴，用人工在马落坑抽井水烧热使用。1985年县城个体杏林春浴室开业，设有大池、盆池、淋浴等。继后机关招待所也增设卫生间和洗澡间供客人和职工沐浴。1993年，国营修文饭店澡堂随着体制变革停业。随后有六广姑娘浴都、阳明大道的月光海岸（后改称湘水湾湾）和腾晖水会等一批上档次的洗浴室出大户，设有大池、小池，浸泡、冲浪，桑拿浴和蒸气浴等，有的还增设修脚、推拿、按摩项目为顾客服务。2010年，全县经营洗浴业的有30家，从业员工321人，年收入3000万元。

（二）足疗

2001年县城栖凤路开办首家足疗室，置床位12张，员工7人，用药水泡足修脚，每次收费10元。接着顺心足疗、大众足疗相继开业，采用药物足疗和中式、泰式足疗，治疗香港脚、灰指甲病，还可修剔老茧、角质等。至2010年，仅县城就有全国连锁顺心足肢堂、丽雅苑足疗中心和聚缤缘足疗城等15户，从业者45人，年营业收入50万元。

（三）美发

1978年共有45人从事理发业，分布于县城和区公所驻地。20世纪80年代末至90年代，一部分农村剩余劳动力外出打工学艺，掌握技术后回乡创业开设发廊，外地江浙和沿海打工者也涌入县内租房营业，为女士做发型、焗油、倒膜、染发、烫发等。到2010年，全县有美发店105家，从业者250人，年营业收入3000万元。

四、修配雕刻

1978年，补鞋、补锅、配钥匙、雕章和修理单车、钟表等均属县城综合社经营，从业者21人。1980年起，随着家用电器进入家庭，修理业务就扩展到录音机、影碟机、电饭煲、微波炉、电磁炉、洗衣机、冰箱、彩色电视机、计算器、手机和电脑等，单车修理也从打气、补胎扩展到摩托车及各种大小汽车的维修和保养。至2010年，全县从事家电和汽车修理、钥匙配制、印章雕刻等行业修理者有310家，从业1500人，年营业收入3000万元。

2010年，县城个体雕刻修配店

五、家政

1978年至2000年，县境仅有个别家庭请用保姆在家同吃同住。2001年起随着经济迅速发展，社会分工越来越细，群众生活水平不断提高，家政服务逐渐成为兴新行业。2009年

3月贵阳煤矿工人家属李红参加贵州省妇联在贵阳举办的家政服务培训班结业，邀约3个农村姐妹，首创红姐家政，以诚信服务取信于民，每月有上百户的顾主签订合同，服务项目有在病床边照护病人、在家当保姆、带小孩、上门打扫清洁卫生等，2010年，县城又增添顺心保洁服务有限公司，从业者25人，月均服务150—200户，员工月工资一般是1200—1500元。

六、中介拍卖

1994年8月，久长镇政府应炉山村民要求，主持拍卖本村荒山，成交21宗。1996年7月，六屯乡、谷堡乡仿效运作，贵阳市委副书记罗大林亲自带市属相关部门领导临场观摩，认为做法值得推广。继后凡转让小山塘、小矿山和县城改造出售的地块一律实行公平、公正、公开挂牌拍卖，但拍卖中有政府行为。2009年7月贵阳宏运拍卖公司入驻县城，成立同春和信息服务部，至2010年共成交二手房14套，成交额250万元。

七、殡仪服务

2005年，县城城南村在原四川会馆馆址修建殡仪服务中心，占地5亩，投入150万元建有灵堂、吊唁厅、接待室、家属休息室和宾客就餐厅，还提供为死者沐浴、更衣、整容以及哀乐悼念、灵车送葬等服务，解决丧家占用街道操办丧事的问题。至2010年，6年共接待殡仪活动210起，年均35起，营业总收入147万元，年均24.5万元。

建在县城内的城南殡仪服务中心

八、物流

1999年，贵州兴达有限公司利用扎佐独特的交通和区位优势，将公路、铁路货物运输和仓储有机结合，在扎佐火车站货场侧面置兴达物流公司，修建铁路专用线，置货场配备行吊、装载机、地磅等，承担修文、开阳的矿石、煤炭、药品、建材等物资装运和黔北、黔西北矿产品和农产品的转运。2010年5月，贵阳宏运物流公司又在修文成立子公司，承接贵阳东站嘉润路、市西路百佳商场、头桥海马冲及三桥批发市场等收货点及修文普陀客户托运的货物中转，一般以件为单位计收运费和服务费，每件5元，大型货物按吨位计价或占用空间计价。2010年底，兴达物流公司货物吞吐量达214.2万吨，营业收入2800.5万元，上缴国家税金678万元。宏运物流公司月均转运货物15万件，扣除汽车运费及货物装卸费，月均收取服务费5万元。

专记：前进中的兴达物流公司

贵州兴达有限公司始建于1994年12月，选址在扎佐镇中营村，主营重晶石开采洗选后由都拉营火车站运出境外。1999年3月，公司利用坐落在省城贵阳北面，距贵阳市区仅35公里的里程和210国道、贵（阳）遵（义）和贵（阳）毕（节）高等级公路和川黔铁路的交汇处扎佐，加上县供销社、国防工业四一八库（后为云天工贸公司）、贵阳煤矿及毕节地区（在扎佐）建的仓储不能满足物流发展的需要，决定增设储运贸易子公司，与四一八库在扎佐火车站的货物集散场合用发运矿产品，年货物吞吐量25万吨。2003年迎着建设“大贵阳”的契机，公司投资1868万元购进原云天工贸公司扎佐铁路专用线，扩宽货物集散场，陆续添置装卸机械及设备，提高公路、铁路的转运能力，年货物吞吐量增到80万吨。2007年又根据贵阳市大物流规划和铁道部《关于建设铁路战略装车点工作意见》，被列入全国20个战略装车点中唯一参与建设的民营企业。公司筹资4150.3万元将原物资集散场和铁路专用线改建为战略装车点，承载起整列货车的装卸，年货物吞吐量增到100万吨。到2010年，递增为200万吨，跻身于贵阳市大型民营物流企业行列。公司拥有铁路专用线2条1353米，硬化货场13万平方米，装载机7台，卸货机2台，挖掘机3台，100吨电子衡2台，10吨行吊1台和办公楼1569平方米，职工增为80人，发货量和货物吞吐量在2007年的基础上增加77%，年收入增加1.5倍，缴纳国家税金增加71.2%。拟建的农资农肥转运交易中心、粮食转运交易中心和商务调度中心业已动工，第三条铁路专用线正在规划中，建成投产后的年货物周转量将达500万吨，可安排就业300余人，直接服务于黔北、黔西北和黔东等地区，将西南地区与沿海港口通过铁路、公路、长江水域连成一体，从而促进黔中及全省的资源优化配置、产业结构调整以及物流业向专业化、规模化、现代化发展。

2010年位于扎佐火车站旁的兴达物流仓储物资部

2007—2010年物流业主要指标统计表

表3—06—05

年份	发货量（万吨）	货物吞吐量（万吨）	收入（万元）	税金（万元）
2007	60.5	121.0	1120.0	396.0
2008	61.5	123.0	1140.0	438.0
2009	75.7	151.4	2377.3	591.1
2010	107.1	214.2	2800.5	678.1

九、其他服务

（一）广告制作

县内广告制作始于1992年5月，第一家是县电影公司停薪留职职工郝 浩在人民南路开业，为商家制作商品广告、标牌、彩旗和会标等。1994年11月县城私营经济一条街落成，相继涌现傲蕾一兰、世纪汇美、工艺美术等广告公司，增加商店匾额、广告灯箱等制作业务。1999年，县广播电视台开始传媒广告，分为公益性和商业性：公益性有通告、通知，如寻人启事、部门停水或封锁道路等；商业性广告主要是为商家介绍商品、宣传商品和为消费者提供承诺等，根据播出时数、次数收取费用，播放时间均安排在地方自办节目中插播，年均播放115条，收取费用10余万元。2010年，全县广告制作公司发展到20家，从业者50人，营业总收入90万元。

（二）文书打印

1993年待业青年曾成双在修文饭店门面开设首家办公用品打印部，承接各种文书打印。1994年又有新源、田园等打印部挂牌经营，先后增加发送电子邮件和传真业务，并按期纳税。2001年田园打印部店主田志英由于打印文书注重质量，诚信经营被评为县级文明个体工商户，2005年荣任县政协第七届委员会委员。2010年，全县有打印店15家，从业者50人，营业收入120万元。

（三）摄影

1978年，仅有县国营饮食服务公司内设照相部，从业人员7名，使用座机拍摄黑白照片。另有扎佐一个体从事照相业务。1981年起饮食服务公司从业人员多因年老相继退休，到1990年仅剩2人，其中1人承包，1人停薪留职，致国营照相部消失。1991年起县城先后有晓青、阳明、卓映等个体彩色扩印店在县城开业，从黑白、彩色胶卷照相逐步过渡到数码相机及录像和婚纱摄影，并对新郎新娘和演员化妆。2010年，全县有照相馆15家，从业人员35人，营业收入达120万元。

2010年，县城人民南路晓青照相馆

（四）鲜花配送

2000年，县境第一家文碧鲜花店在县城民主路开业，经营家居装饰、个人饰品，后又购进鲜花配送，为客户制作开业花篮、会议插花、装饰婚礼花车、生日用花、胸花、捧花，白喜事花篮、灵堂用花以及开展回收花篮等。继后又有浪漫花海、时尚鲜花店开业。2010年，县城有鲜花配送店3家，从业者12人，营业收入30万元，缴纳税费1.2万元。

2010年，县城文碧鲜花配送店

（五）缝纫

1978年，有集体缝纫社两家，缝纫机78台，职工66人，主要为县百货公司加工服装。1982年服装市场放开，从江苏、浙江、四川等地入驻个体缝纫户，制作款式新颖，收费低廉，很受顾客青睐。1988年原缝纫社解体卖掉固定资产，按职工工龄和级别分配，工人改在家中或小街小巷给顾客改衣服、上拉链等。2010年全县共有个体缝纫店15个，从业者25人，营业总收入50万元，纳税4万元。

（六）洗涤

1978年，市民穿的毛料衣服多是送到贵阳洗染店洗烫。1982年县城首家余昌敏洗染店在栖凤路开业，从事衣物洗涤，一改以往使用烙铁烫熨为电熨斗熨烫。1994年起县城小敏、乘洁等洗烫店相继挂牌营业，县外一些设备先进、技术上乘、服务态度好的洗烫店也入住县境，洗涤分为水洗和干洗，还提供衣裤改制和卷边、上拉链，皮衣清洗、上色、打油等服务。2010年，全县有各种洗涤店15家，从业者40人，营业总收入120万元。

第五节 管　　理

一、计划管理

1978年，商品进货渠道单一，国营商业经营的商品绝大部分由二级站统一调拨；供销社经营的商品则按经济区划进行调拨和余缺调剂。粮食实行统一计划，分级管理。1979—1984年改革计划管理体制，计划管理商品逐步由指令性改为指导性，以致计划管理的商品逐渐减少。同时放开市场，实行多渠道经营，市场开始放开。1985年起扩大企业自主权，各种行业有权根据市场变化制定自己的经营计划。1987年全面推行承包经营责任制，县商业行政部门只对商业流通企业下达指导性的商品流通计划和财务计划。1990年为保证粮食任务的完成，将合同定购改为国家定购，属指令性计划。1994年国有商业流通企业推行国有民营，取消凭票供应，全面按市场规律由职工自主经营、自负盈亏、照章纳税。到2010年一直延续市场调节，群众自由选购，商业计划已失去计划经济时期的作用。

二、财务管理

1978年，商品流通企业实行经济独立核算制，盈亏纳入县级财政，盈利上交，亏损拨补。1983年起实施国营商业企业利改税后，对企业税后留利、减亏分成、奖励和福利基金的使用企业可在规定的范围内自行支配；企业对固定资产折旧基金、大修理基金、企业发展基金有权合并使用；企业对占用的流动资金有权按规定使用；企业有权按计划和经营范围组织商品进销；企业在留利中开支必要的业务造成亏损由财政补贴，但经营管理不好造成的亏损一律由企业自负。粮食商业实行粮食财务双包干，结余分成。1994年国有商业推行国有民营，按照自筹资金、自主经营、自负盈亏和企业性质不变、隶属关系不变、职工身份不变、服务宗旨不变的原则，实行职工个人或全员风险抵押租赁公司的柜台经营。2001年11月起百货、糖酒、蔬菜、五交化、食品、燃料6家公司重组为商贸公司进行核算，原公司收入只有物业租赁租金。至2010年除盐业、烟草、石油等少量专营公司仍按国有企业核算外，其余商品流通企业核算制度一概消失。

三、价格管理

1978年，沿袭原统一定价销售制度，企业无制价权。1980—1983年开放食肉、鲜蛋、蔬菜市场，放开三类农副产品价格，日用工业品实行国家定价、指导价、浮动价、协商价、自由价等多种价格。1984年扩大企业制价权，放宽价格管理权限，饮食行业按照核定的毛利率自定产品价格，部分小食品价格下放给生产和经营企业自主确定，食品工业和饮食业用议价原料生产的制成品允许高进高出、低价低出。1990至1994年市场放开，商品价格和服务价格实行明码标价。1998至2010年按照国家《中华人民共和国物价法》规定，对少数紧俏商品除实行政府指导价或政府定价外，其余全部实行市场调节价，由买卖双方议价成交。

四、票证管理

1978年，沿袭原实行的凭票证供应制度，每人每年发给布票1丈5尺7寸，棉花票3市斤，布票、棉花票分别由县商业局、供销社专人保管，粮票、油票由粮食部门专人负责，其余限量供应的商品票证则由经办单位负责管理。1982年粮油票实行统一计划、统一收发、统一保管、统一建账、专室或专柜保管。石油公司对汽油先后实行凭票、凭折供应。1984年商品放开，品种增多，取消布票、棉花票，除燃油和彩色电视机等少数高档商品继续凭票限量供应外，其他商品均敞开供应。1992年取消汽油票(折)，1993年6月粮食、食油取消凭票证购买。至此，全县市场全面敞开，购物票证即成为历史。

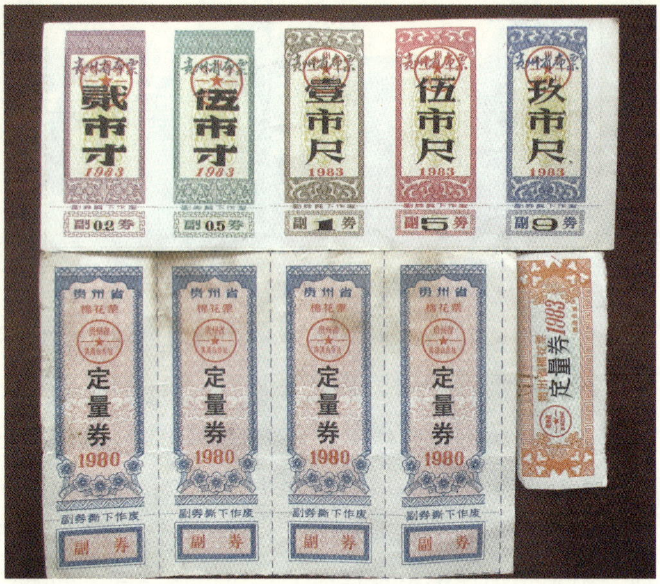

上为1983年使用的布票；下为1980年和1983年使用的棉花票

五、商品管理

1978年，沿袭原计划经济的经营体制，商品供应品种、数量有限。1979年2月恢复酒类专卖，加强对白酒的经营管理。1981年置烟草专卖局管理烟草专卖业务。食盐、石油及火工产品的雷管、炸药、导火索仍实行专营，在保障市场商品供应的同时，商业部门还配合工商、公安、税务、物价、质监等部门对流通环节进行专项治理，于1994年1月在210国道久长段查扣贵州省供销汽车场无证运卷烟两车。1995年9月取消酒类专卖，放开经营。1998年8月捣毁扎佐镇三元村假烟制造窝点，收缴YG14大型卷烟设备1套、小型卷烟机1台、切丝机2台、烘干机1台、咀棒15件、盘纸12件、烟叶2吨、成品假卷烟11件、小汽车2台、移动电话1部，3名犯罪嫌疑人被追究刑事责任。2000年5月又捣毁久长镇境原烽光厂内假烟厂1个，缴获PG14型卷烟机2台、3000型包装机1台、柴油发电机1台、真空泵2台、筛选机1台、成品假烟46件。至2010年共查处制假、贩假卷烟案件10起，罚没收入28万元，使市场秩序得以维护。

县烟草专卖局正门

第七章　旅　游

1984年1月，贵州省科学院山地资源研究所洞穴考察组莅县考察花榔乡“躲兵洞”和大石乡的回水石林、高枧石仓。测定“躲兵洞”为当今全国实测长洞之冠，对石林的“奇石、幽洞”、“曲径、绿境”秀色景观开发旅游给予充分论证和高度评价，引起县委、县政府重视，提出“旅游搭台、经济唱戏”的战略方式，组建起旅游开发指挥部和旅游公司，并将明代留存的省级重点文物胜迹纳入旅游开发项目，揭开发展旅游业的篇章。后因资金匮乏和交通制约，使开发一度搁浅。

1996年，县由安顺地区划属贵阳市管辖，县委、县政府抓住开发旅游业契机，成立县旅游事业局、组建旅游产业发展委员会，面对贫困财政，拓展思路、引资开发，借鸡生蛋，使旅游业重整旗鼓驶入快车道。至2007年，先后引进旅游企业7家，分别开发贵阳高尔夫度假中心康乐游、六广河峡谷观光游、苏格兰牧场康乐游、珍珠岛避暑中心休闲游、贵州绿色石林景观生态游、贵阳森林野生动物园科普游和桃源河魔幻漂流奇景游等项目。同时，将贵州省政府批准命名的修文阳明洞风景名胜区以“王学圣地、秀美修文”作为旅游形象定位进行打造，推动民族风情游、农业观光游、乡村生活体验游和红色旅游开发。

2009年，全县各类旅游企业发展到20家，构筑起以“爽爽的贵阳”为依托、“王学圣地文化”为中心、高（速）等级公路和六广河航道为纽带，形成五大旅游片区，即阳明洞风景名胜区、六广河峡谷风景区、猫跳河喀斯特地貌水电坝型博览区、岩鹰山湖风景区、扎佐林场康乐休闲区为骨架的文化游、观光游、休闲游、风情游等相互交融旅游网，展示出森林之都、避暑之城、人间仙境、天然氧吧、圣地文化、秀美修文的多彩风貌。成功举办“2009中国·贵阳避暑季”开幕式和第四届国际阳明文化节，极大地提升修文旅游城市的形象和知名度，全年接待游客322.71万人次。2010年，接待游客388.6万人次，旅游点收入19.95亿元。修文已成为“爽爽贵阳”的后花园，是旅游者心向往的地方。

县境旅游景点分布图

第一节 旅游开发

县境旅游资源丰富，以国家《旅游资源分类调查与分析》分类，计有主类8个、亚类31个、基本类155个。1995年，贵州省政府批准“修文阳明洞风景名胜区”为省级风景名胜区。

县境旅游资源构成表

表3—07—01

主 类	亚 类	基本类型	旅游资源单体概况
A类地文景观	AA类综合自然旅游地	AAA山岳型旅游地	龙冈山 翠屏山 观音山 岩鹰山 凤凰山
	AB类	ABA断层景观	逆掩断层
		ABB褶曲景观	拖拖褶皱
	AC地质地貌过程形迹	ACB独峰	姊妹峰
		ACD石（土）林	回水石林 高枧石林
		ACE奇石、象形山石	象鼻石 双月岩 老人石 猴祖石 石老龟 史目之任 阳明妙笔 坐石弄溪
		ACF岩壁、岩缝	剑壁岩
		ACG峡谷段落	七峡 六广河大峡 桃源河峡谷 猫跳河峡谷 箱型峡谷 两蓬岩
		ACL岩石洞、岩穴	阳明洞 贾家洞 玩易窝 观音洞 四明洞 多滨洞
	AE类	AFA岛区	珍珠岛
B类水域风光	BA河段	BAA观光游憩河段	猫跳河 六广河 桃源河 海马三叉河
	BB天然湖池沼	BBA游憩湖区	金湖 逍遥湖
		BBC潭池	犀牛潭
	BC瀑布	BCA悬瀑	金银瀑 银滩瀑布 三道响水瀑布
	BD泉	BDA冷泉	情人泉 高洞寒泉 扎佐珍珠泉
C类生物景观	CA树林	CAA林地	扎佐林场
		CAB丛树	龙冈山古树群
		CAC独树	文成柏 大屯黄连木 洒溪朴树 胡子田光叶榉古树 六屯大木银杏树 龙场皂角树 黄嵛树
D类天象、气象景观	DB天气与气候	CBB避暑气候地	扎佐高尔夫度假中心 珍珠岛避暑中心 久长谷凉都避暑 苏格兰风情高山牧场 扎佐冷水沟林场（各旅游景区均有分布）
E类遗址遗迹	EB经济、文化活动	EBD废弃生产地	白岩厂古矿遗址 六桶河银汞矿遗址
		EBE交通遗址	古驿道 六广驿旧址 滨江六广驿古渡遗址

续表

主　类	亚　类	基本类型	旅游资源单体概况
E类遗址遗迹	EB经济、文化活动	EBD废弃生产地	白岩厂古矿遗址　六桶河银汞矿遗址
		EBE交通遗址	古驿道　六广驿旧址　滨江六广驿古渡遗址
F类建筑与设施	FA综合人文旅游地	FAC、宗教、祭祀活动场所	三湖水知非寺　谷堡水口寺　雨花寺　佛光寺　刺目寺　古佛洞寺　金凤寺
		FAD园林游憩区	猕猴桃基地　金秋梨果园　珍珠岛兰花公园　扎佐艳红桃基
		FAF建设工程、生产基地	三、四、五、六级电站　索风营电站（猫跳河、六广河梯级电
		FAH动植物展示地	贵阳森林野生动物园
		FAI军事观光地	高仓古堡　石安古院落
	FB单体活动场馆	FBB祭拜场所	王文成公祠
		FBD体育健身场馆	贵阳高尔夫球场　县体育馆
	FD居住地与社区	FDA传统、乡土建筑	石安古寨　独山布依山寨
		FDC特色社区	大屯布依村寨　滨江苗寨　苏格兰牧场
		FDD名人故居与历史纪念建筑	何陋轩居　君子亭　宾阳堂　阳明纪念馆　阳明精舍　张学良陈列馆
		FDE书院	龙岗书院
	FE归葬地	FEB墓（群）	三人坟　海马孔古墓　赵德全墓
	FF交通建筑	FFG桥梁	贵毕公路大桥　古竹索桥　蜈蚣桥　秀水桥　古渡飞虹（六广大桥）
	FG水利工程	FGA水库观光游憩区	蚌壳堰水库　岩鹰山水库　银燕水库　云盘山水库　索风湖
G类旅游商品	GA地方旅游商品	GAA菜品饮食	骗鸡豆腐　扎佐蹄膀　扎佐豆花鸡　六广鲶鱼　扎佐萝卜干　俄罗斯汤
		GAB产品与制品	扎佐魔芋精粉　蜈蚣桥豆腐干　灵芝鲜鸡蛋　猕猴桃饮料　金秋梨　郭田酥李　日晒防治膏（药品）　葆肤康软膏（药品）　布依风情雕刻　海马造纸　苗族服饰
H类人文活动	HA人事记录	HAA人物	王阳明　张学良　蒋介石
	HC民间习俗	HCA地方风谷与民间礼仪	哭嫁　丧歌　下堡苗家跳花坡　大屯布依“六月六”歌会　谷堡搂查节
		HCB民间节庆	“六月六”“四月八”春节　元宵　端午　中秋
	HD现代节庆	HDA旅游节	阳明文化节　风情斗牛节　漂流节　梨花节

1998年，贵阳市政府划定修文为贵阳市卫星城开发旅游服务业。县政府随即委托贵州省城乡规划院对阳明风景名胜区作《修文阳明风景名胜区总体规划》，构成以王学圣地文化为主体，与爽爽的贵阳、秀美的修文风光相结合的旅游线。

2006年，贵阳市建设局委托贵州省城乡规划院对阳明风景名胜区现状进行调查，提交《修文阳明风景名胜区调查报告》。根据全县旅游资源情况再次调整，细化资源开发，将景区建设分为3区：一是云泉碧水景区，从六广河大桥至与息烽县分界处，包括飞龙峡、赤壁峡、象鼻峡、剑劈峡、海马峡等5峡30景，其范围东起周家田垭，西至郭家里，南起大坪上，北至大坝田，面积48.6平方公里，其中属修文县境28.3平方公里，属黔西县境13.3平方公里，属金沙县境7.0平方公里。景区以乘船游览为主，在大屯布依山寨设立码头，建服务设施，开发民族风情和田园生活休闲游，并在适当地段选刻王阳明诗作《六广晓发》于岩壁之上，展现阳明文化供游客欣赏。二是石林荟萃景区，以高枧石林和回水石林景观为主，东起石牛山，西至大石板，南起周家田垭，北至江家大山，面积10.4平方公里，景点11个，在回水村、高枧村设立旅游服务部，为游客提供就餐和茶水，建游览步道、休息点，保持农业用地，突出“绿色石林”特征。三是三镜映月景区，将珍珠岛避暑中心景区扩展，使面积增至10.2平方公里，东起王家河，西至火石头，南抵龙孔，北至畜牧场，以湖泊景观为主，发展水产养殖和野生动物养殖，使休闲避暑功能充分发挥。

2009年12月，县政府和贵阳市旅游局委托北京大衍至用旅游规划设计院制定《贵州省修文县旅游产业发展总体规划》，其范围涉及全县10乡镇1075.7平方公里，东及东北与开阳县连接，东南与乌当区毗邻，南与白云区相连，西南以猫跳河与清镇为界，西北与黔西县、金沙县隔六广河对峙。旅游产业定位为贵阳支撑性旅游地、“爽爽贵阳”品牌旅游地和贵州品牌旅游地，国内养心观光地和特色养生度假旅游地。旅游品牌定位为爽爽贵阳，不老修文；阳明水城，养心修文；奇峡山水，秀美修文；世外山乡，休闲修文。旅游产品定位为养心体验旅游产品，养心度假旅游产品，乡村旅游产品，康体休闲旅游产品，生态旅游产品，修文科普旅游产品。经过打造的修文是凉爽的修文，是心学的圣地，是智慧的源泉。至2010年，全县旅游容圣地文化游、休闲康乐游、生态观光游、民族风情游为一体，使爽爽的贵阳、秀美的修文笑迎天下宾客。

第二节　景区景点

1984年，县境旅游资源揭开开发的序幕，1995年批准为省级风景名胜，统称“阳明风景名胜区”。至2010年，逐步形成以阳明文化为龙头，中沿贵（阳）毕（节）公路抵修文县城，以阳明洞为中心，感受阳明文化，使游者体验历史人文饱经沧桑的阳明遗迹名胜区；东部沿贵阳、遵义、毕节经贵（阳）遵（义）高等级公路、贵（阳）毕（节）高等级公路抵扎佐镇，以扎佐林场为轴心，游览高尔夫度假中心、野生动物园、景阳森林公园和桃源河峡谷漂流，享受康乐的休闲娱乐区；北部沿贵（阳）遵（义）高等级公路和210国道抵久长镇，以珍珠湖（蚌壳堰水库）为轴心，游览珍珠岛、苏格兰风情牧场、岩鹰山湖，享受休闲观光的避暑度假区；西北部沿贵（阳）毕（节）高等级公路到六广，以六广河峡谷为轴心，浏览七峡风景、索风湖风光、贵州绿色石林和体验大屯布依山寨风情、观赏六桶多缤洞岩溶艺术风景名胜区；西南部沿专线公路，以猫跳河为轴心，欣赏全国著名的水电坝型博览，观赏流金溢彩的水电明珠，分享绿色花果园艺的科普观光区。这五大片区构成修文旅游大框架。

一、人文景观

（一）阳明遗迹

从1995年起，县旅游产业发展委员会和旅游局利用阳明文化旅游资源，将明正德年间兵部武选清吏

司主事王阳明谪官龙场，任驿丞时悟道讲学，留下的玩易窝、阳明小洞天和明、清建筑的何陋轩、君子亭、龙岗书院、宾阳堂、摩崖石刻等国家重点文物作为阳明文化展现。经过10年开发建设，到2005年阳明洞风景名胜区成为修文旅游业主体，被誉称为“王学圣地”，先后在阳明洞景区建起阳明先生及子弟群体塑像、王阳明纪念馆（阳明园）、王学圣地仿古牌坊、阳明景区仿古步行道、阳明精舍、阳明碑苑、阳明书院、阳明主题公园等，形成一组规模宏大的建筑群，诸多建筑造型各异，工艺精巧，与阳明洞景区明、清建筑浑然一体。吸引日本、韩国、加拿大及国内150多名学者慕名前往论学。阳明主题公园占地11.87亩，青石板地铺面积9.77亩、绿地面积2.1亩、园前还建仿古阳明牌坊，投放建设资金1.1亿元。整个园区以阳明洞景点为依托，向四面辐射。景区内栖霞山古树密布，古建筑、古文化遗址缀在其间。东侧一片田畴，阡陌纵横，阳明河水潺潺缓流。南侧面临商贸楼群林立的阳明大道和曲折通幽的高洞河水，渊然黛，泓然静，气象万千，既有秀丽多姿的风光，又具灿烂的历史文化，融自然风光与人文景观为一体，形成一个独特的阳明文化圣地，为全国最大的阳明文化园区，它泱泱乎修文圣地文化秀美之景。从1999到2009年举行4届国际阳明文化节，有来自日本、韩国、美国、加拿大、巴西、新加坡、马来西亚、印度尼西亚、澳大利亚、俄罗斯等15个国家和中国香港地区的学者参加节日庆典，每届节日都有国内外和省内外的嘉宾2000余人莅临。美国哈佛大学教授杜维明、香港孔教学院博士汤恩佳、国际儒学家成中英、高柏园、杨国荣，日本九州大学名誉教授冈田武彦、日本京都论坛事务局局长矢崎胜彦、台湾中国文化大学教授曾春海、中国人民大学教授张立文、中国作家协会副主席叶辛等专家学者,均在节日期间进行“良知与和谐社会”“良知与道德”“天人合一与生态文明”、知行合一与贵阳精神”“阳明学说与中国文化”的研讨。4届阳明文化节均有中央电视台、天津《今晚报》、香港《大公报》载文评述。《贵州日报》、贵州电视台、贵州广播电台、《贵阳日报》、贵阳电视台等新闻媒体报道节日盛况，介绍“王学圣地”，招来八方游客，使圣地的知名度和影响力得以扩展。2009年8月2日，贵阳市举行“2009十大影响力风景名胜区”和“2009十大魅力旅游景区”评选活动颁奖典礼暨景区图片展，阳明旅游景区以“王学圣地文化”的丰富内涵荣获“2009十大魅力旅游景区”称号。

2009年，世界著名儒学文化名人汤恩佳在第四届阳明文化节接受采访

（二）古驿文化

1985年，县旅游开发工程指挥部将明洪武十七年（1384）贵州宣慰使奢香开辟龙场驿道经过的木阁箐山、蜈蚣山雨花寺和成化五年（1469）贵州宣慰使安观在龙场驿道上修建的秀水桥、蜈蚣桥，开辟的六广驿站、六广古渡，以及正德四年（1509）由京都准备去赴任的吏目主仆3人在龙场驿道旁死后留下的“三人坟”纳入县旅游资源开发之列。其中有古驿道上被称为“十桥之冠”的蜈蚣桥，虽经数百年风雨剥蚀但仍安如磐石，以及留下还依稀可辨的《建十桥记》《重修十桥记》《蜈蚣桥彝文碑文》；明正德四年（1509）在龙场悟道讲学的龙场驿驿丞王阳明率弟子为死于驿道旁的吏目主仆3人筑冢掩埋后撰写的《瘗旅文》，并由清道光十九年（1839）县人刻碑，后又由贵州省文史研究馆馆员陈福桐书写的碑文竖于坟侧，都是龙场古驿道上留下的珍贵历史文化。

至2010年，古驿道上的蜈蚣桥及建桥碑文、雨花寺遗址、“三人坟”及《瘗旅文》、马鞍山垭口和谷堡蜈蚣山坡古驿道遗迹、六广滨江六广驿渡口及龙王庙遗迹，都是研究和考察明代古驿道、水道、桥梁、人文风情的历史资料，成为历史文化旅游者回味、追溯古人业绩的好去处。

古驿道上的蜈蚣桥

（三）宗教寺庙

1996年起，县旅游资源开发公司和民族宗教事务局明确宗教祭祀活动场所贾家洞佛洞山寺、三潮水知非寺、四明洞佛光寺和观音山金凤寺纳入宗教祭祀文化游之地，供游客憩息观赏。

贾家洞佛洞山寺 坐落在六广河猴愁峡右岸贾家洞内，是一座两厅相通开有天窗的天然溶洞，洞口西向，下邻六广河，距河面高200多米，对岸与黔西县隔河相望。洞庭湖中建一寺庙名为佛洞山寺，始建于明朝末年，清代和民国年间进行过重修和补修。2003年于东面后山选新址建新庙宇， 2009年六广河旅游公司在贵阳市开展“避暑季”期间在此举办系列旅游活动，更为佛洞山寺增辉添彩。游人可从后山或河边进入洞中于洞口眺望六广河峡谷两岸风光，亦可观瞻贵（阳）毕（节）公路横跨在六广河之上特大桥的巍然雄姿。在洞下悬崖有“悬挂泉水”流出注入六广河。至2010年，佛洞山寺仍然香火不断，游人不绝。

佛洞山寺

四明洞佛光寺 地处扎佐镇东2公里的翠屏山山麓有一天然石洞称为四明洞，洞中宽敞，洞高10多米，宽20多米，洞周茂林修竹，苍翠葱茏，幽雅清奇。原洞内建一佛教寺庙，20世纪60年代废弃，1984年恢复活动，香客和游人逐渐增多，1996年县政府明确四明洞为佛教活动场所，次年更名为佛光寺。2003年冬在洞内石壁上增塑五百罗汉像，2008年又增塑白色3面观音圣像，施工中还发现距今1万年至4万年的新石器时代古人类遗址。四明洞为扎佐地区的一游览胜地，每逢佛教盛会，香客游人爆满，热闹非凡。

三潮水知非寺 位于县城西北郊1.5公里的观音山南麓。三潮水属间歇泉，寻常每日潮水3盈3缩，故名。明崇祯年间贵州总兵王国桢建有凉亭、水池，泉水自岩隙中流经石雕龙嘴喷涌而出，泻于扇形池内。池中伏一大石如龟，每当潮水，淹没龟

知非寺

背，水始退去。池上方为一翼角攒尖顶四角凉亭，名潇洒亭，又名观潮亭。同时建1寺庙称潮水寺，清顺治年间更名知非寺。1985年列入省级文物保护单位，1995年纳入贵州省政府批准为阳明风景名胜旅游资源之一。1999年贵阳弘福寺投资100万元，新修大雄宝殿，改造配殿，增设十八罗汉菩萨塑像，修僧侣房、筑游览山道和寺庙仿古围墙。2010年，观音山上林木葱郁，山下古刹森森，潮水寺庙已复旧观，游人观赏游览，观者众多，每逢观音盛会更是香客游人如织。

观音山金凤寺　距县城北1.5公里的观音山，山势挺拔高耸，山上林木葱绿，近观挺拔雄峻，远观端秀峥嵘。登临峰顶俯眺，县城尽收眼帘，四顾群山皆小。东南麓有一寺庙，红墙黄瓦，梵舍俨然。寺庙为20世纪80年代新建，原名观音寺，90年代又多次增建，2000年又大兴土木，2008年竣工更名为金凤寺，为县境内规模较大，香客最多的1座寺庙，每逢观音盛会公安机关均要派人到金凤寺维持秩序。

（四）科普观光

岩鹰山水库　位于小箐乡境内。1998年由贵州省城乡规划设计院编制的《修文阳明洞风景名胜区总体规划》，将岩鹰山水库纳入旅游资源开发范畴，以休闲观光和科普文化游产品定位。水库绕过70座高山峻岭，跨过20道深谷沟壑，大坝造型似一道长虹横跨在岩鹰湖上，精心设计之作由水电部列入重要科技资料收存，是自然环境和现代化水利开发相统一的典范，也是具有较高科普教育价值的旅游资源，迎来全国22个省区水利石拱坝建设代表和外国友人考察以及贵阳地区游人参观。2010年，岩鹰山湖已成为“爽爽的贵阳，避暑的天堂”县内五大旅游片区之一，是水利观光科普文化的游憩区。

岩鹰山湖

喀斯特岩溶　1984年，经贵州省科学院山地资源研究所考察，认定六桶乡境内的“多缤洞”是一座具有发育完整的巨型石灰岩溶洞。大石乡境内“回水石林”“高枧石林”是两亿多年前海洋波浪作用形成的碳酸岩，具有极高的旅游价值和科普价值。1985年县拟定为旅游开发区，随着县旅游业的发展，又将县境内的猫跳河、六广河、桃源河、二洞河、天生桥、兰花谷等悬岩褶皱，逆掩断层、拖拉褶曲的喀斯特岩溶地质，地貌列为科普旅游资源进行开发。2001年3月，贵州省教委，贵阳一中等6所中学选定修文县境内猫跳河流域典型的喀斯特河谷为贵阳市中学生科普教育基地，迎来数以计千的学生、学者、游客参观考察。2003年《贵阳市修文县旅游发展总体规划》将猫跳河峡谷列为科普生态旅游区。

生态水电站　1999年5月，《修文阳明风景名胜区总体规划》评审，认为猫跳河流域开发建设的生态梯级电站具有中国水电坝型博物馆之称的人文景观，生态环境独特的坝型作为科普教育资源纳入规划。2003年10月，《贵阳市修文县旅游发展总体规划》将猫跳河流域水电站坝型博物馆列为科普生态旅游区。至2010年，因县财力短缺，开发进度缓慢。

森林野生动物园　2007年，位于扎佐冷水沟林场的贵阳森林野生动物园已成为集野生动物异地迁移养殖、动物保护、动物繁育、森林植被保护、生态环境建设，以及环境、植被、动物协调生存科普教育基地和观光休闲、科普文化相结合的旅游处。2008年4月，举办“2008年青少年生态体验，爱动物科普教育日活动”，吸引贵阳市区中、小学生游览，感受动物的兽性、野性和灵性，以及与大自然协调生存自然规律，接受科普教育。

（五）特色食品

从1996年起，随着旅游业的开发，饮食业在旅游景区迅速发展，出现“快活林”饮食一条街、桃源食府、赖家食府、黔龙酒家、龙场驿食府等。1999年8月1日，成立“阳明宴研究学会”，研制阳明宴菜肴。10月，举办首届阳明文化节，来自四方宾客在县城餐馆品尝“阳明宴”，感受阳明饮食文化，受到来宾的赞赏。2002年10月和2005年10月举办第二届、第三届阳明文化节，有地方风味特色菜骟鸡豆腐、西山蕨菜、幽竹劲节、五盏春光、瓦蒸腊肉、六广鲶鱼、扎佐蹄膀、香椿煎鸡蛋、风豆豉蒸腊肉、酸菜小豆汤、古隆鸡、老鸭汤、酸汤鱼及风味特色小吃野味烧烤、臭豆腐、豆腐圆子、春券、黄粑、二块粑等，深受嘉宾青睐。其中骟鸡豆腐用骟鸡肉与豆腐浑然为一体烹制，白里润红、清香四溢、汤清不腻，是敬请贵客和老人的佳肴。六广鲶鱼用六广河、猫跳河特产淡水鱼制作，其鱼肉质细嫩、富含营养、味美鲜香、色泽洁白，是县内特有菜肴，成为省、市电视节目中推荐的不用任何调料的野味鱼。扎佐蹄膀皮泽红润、糯脆鲜美、肥而不腻，享有“肉食之王，十里飘香”美誉，远销省内外，2005年被指定为第三届国际阳明文化节贵宾专用礼品之一，继后被列为贵阳市非物质文化遗产。

扎佐蹄膀

（六）历史人文

1984年，县旅游公司和县文物管理所协同配合进行县旅游景点前期开发，把民国政府军事委员会委员长蒋介石三次游览阳明洞古迹和蒋介石题书刻于阳明洞摩崖上的“知行合一”墨迹，以及爱国名将张学良被蒋介石囚禁在阳明洞的历史遗迹作为参观和考察历史人文旅游资源进行开发利用，使游人重温那段难忘的历史。

1996年，由县政府组织县旅游局和县文化广播电视局配合，将民国27年（1938）至30年（1941）张学良被囚禁在阳明洞文成祠东厢时的旧址复制还原历史原貌。囚室里竖张学良和赵一荻的硅胶像，置有梳洗台和留存的实物竹木结构“将军桌”，展现将军研读阳明学说时赵四小姐陪伴的场景，作为爱国主义教育瞻仰处。2005年，在阳明洞栖霞山下占地2亩，修建阳明西苑四合院仿古建筑，面积500平方米，设前门古戏楼、后正殿、两侧厢房作为张学良将军经历陈列馆，馆内陈列着含囚禁期、军事生涯、晚年生活三个方面内容的文献，包括文史资料、图照、书信。2010年，张学良囚禁旧址和陈列馆被列为中国国防大学和贵州省爱国主义教育基地，参观游览者达3.5万人次。

阳明洞文成祠复制还原的张学良和赵一荻硅胶像

（七）知青故居

2005年9月，全国作家协会副主席叶辛（叶承喜）响应共青团贵州省委发起“在世界上只有一种最亲切的声音，那便是母亲的呼唤”的“春晖行动”，携同在上海有识之士徐林宝、朱胜杰、王铭槐等，重返20世纪60年代他们插队落户的久长公社永兴大队（今久长镇永兴村），回忆当年用汗水浇洒的这片土地和留下的丰富生活经历。叶辛在曾经破旧的永兴小学里，见到他的学生袁兴开已走上讲堂上课的情景，昔日师生情谊顿时涌上心头，遂回上海邀约8家企业慷慨解囊捐资35万元修建永兴“春晖小学”。春晖小学陈列有叶辛足迹图照、叶辛题书“修文立志”书券墨迹。校园旁建有600平方米的绿地草坪、棚架灯光篮球场，塑有知青群体塑像，崖石数处书题“反哺故土，回报社会”“岁月蹉跎志犹存”“饮水思源”等石刻，村民在改造后的农舍中仍保留着叶辛居住过的土地庙破旧居室，供人们参观，感悟知青上山下乡生活经历。

2006年，久长镇政府和县旅游局利用永兴知青文化，开展乡村旅游，创办“春晖家园”“山谷凉都避暑”“知青文化游”。村民袁廷春、姚应荣、黎生贵、全兵等结合村老地名“砂锅寨”，办起有“砂锅宴”和香猪、瑶山鸡等特色菜的乡村游接待站。久长镇、永兴村共同举办以知青文化为题材的“乡情、亲情、友情”“爱久长、情久长”等文学、艺术、笔会等活动。仅1年就接待游客4万人，旅游收入400万元。2009年4月8日，共青团贵州省委“中国知青纪念林”植树活动在永兴村举行，来自全省各地200多名老知青在永兴回味知青经历之后参加植树活动，种下知青纪念树。5月2日，久长镇利用“春晖家园游”暨贵州省青少年夏令营基地授牌仪式在永兴村举行，将知青文化春晖行动与青少年夏令营活动相结合，推动旅游业发展。9月9日，共青团中央青农部副部长郭祥玉在永兴调研“春晖行动”，参观春晖家园，春晖小学、春晖广场和叶辛旧居，对久长镇开展的知青文化游给予充分肯定。2010年，贵州电视台《天下旅游》栏目、中国扶贫杂志社的记者分别下到久长永兴参观、采访、拍摄“春晖家园”，报道春晖行动开发知青文化旅游。全年接待游客3万人次，旅游收入280万元，从此永兴已成为贵阳市避暑地和学生夏令营基地，是回味知识青年上山下乡，插队落户经历的知青文化旅游地。

春晖广场叶辛题书“岁月蹉跎志犹存”的雕塑

二、康乐旅游

贵阳高尔夫度假中心 位于扎佐镇贵（阳）遵（义）高等级公路旁三元村，距贵阳市区35公里。1996年，县政府引进香港英皇有限公司和广东揭阳金华实业有限公司联合投资开发康乐旅游，占地3015亩。其中，森林面积1500亩，人工湖水容量245万立方米。

中心利用天然森林资源和水域资源，建起18洞72杆国际高尔夫球场2个、会员大酒店2000平方米和九龙戏珠喷泉、挥杆少女雕像、700米长文化长廊、松涛山庄、会员别墅等建筑物，有击球练习场2万平方米，另有网球场、壁球室、台球室、游泳池、夜总会、舞厅、卡拉OK歌厅及棋类等设施，在一片湖水、草坪、花丛中依山靠湖建起浪潮湖泊亭、果岭球道、钓鱼台。整个中心垂柳依依、清风徐徐，水波粼粼，体现生态环境和现代文明的有机结合，为全国最凉爽的绿色高尔夫度假之地。1998年5月，经省旅游局批准成立县内第一家旅行社“贵阳高尔夫旅行社”，多次举办全国性高尔夫球公开赛，有来自全国选手、高尔夫球爱好者到此展示球艺，搭起修文与外界文化交流的桥梁。2006年举办“信天翁杯高尔夫球邀请赛”“开磷杯”多彩贵州“两赛一会”“联通杯”西部业余高尔夫球巡回赛，“中国移动全球通VIP高尔夫俱乐部业余差点排位赛”等，获世界经济人周刊社颁发“最具影响力和最具潜力的十大GOLF球场”荣誉证书。

贵阳高尔夫度假中心球道

2009年5月9日，在2009中国·贵阳避暑季系列活动中举办贵阳移动全球通VIP高尔夫俱乐部“移动杯”高尔夫联谊赛。中心以开展高尔夫球各种赛事推动高尔夫度假旅游发展。2010年接待游客7.37万人次，旅游收入4421.88万元。

专记：挥杆绿茵以球会友

贵阳高尔夫度假中心，是冬无严寒、夏无酷暑的旅游度假胜地，拥有难易兼容、娱乐和挑战并存的贵州高原唯一、全国最佳的18洞72杆标准森林湖泊高尔夫球场。1号洞前一片碧绿湖水、沙坑环绕；2号洞临陡然下陷果岭松林；3号洞前一望无垠、一览无余绿坪如茵；4号洞前山峰耸峙、层林翠叠……小小银球使人在高原森林里纵横驰骋、展示毅力、智慧、技巧比拼，在绿茵挥杆中感悟和谐、幸福人生。特有的真山真水魅力、凉爽宜人气候、浓厚高尔夫文化、一流服务设施，迎来高尔夫赛事连连，商务会议、企业经营论坛时时举办，国内外各界人士、高尔夫爱好者数度往返，“挥杆绿茵，以球会友”。

2000年，“贵阳杯”全国高尔夫业余公开赛，2001年，全国高尔夫精英赛、2002年“泛鹰杯”贵州省高尔夫球公开赛、2004年西南高尔夫业余巡回赛、世界旅游小姐皇后年度大赛中国赛区总决赛配对赛，2005年“阳明杯”国际名人赛等赛事在此举办，迎来国内外高尔夫名流和爱好者。2006年“将军杯年庆邀请赛”迎来20位中国将军与贵州各界精英进行配对赛。田纪云、张思卿、曾荫权、邵逸夫、冯巩等各界人士先后到此参观考察、挥杆击球、交朋会友。全国人大常委会原副委员长程思远、国家体委原副主任荣高棠到此感受挥杆快乐，欣然分别提笔书下“挥杆贵高、以球会友”、“挥杆绿茵、怡情健体”，彰显高尔夫充满友爱的社交理念，让所有的高尔夫会员、爱好者以及国家政协原副主席罗豪才、博鳌亚洲论坛秘书长龙永图等各界人士感受高尔夫文化神韵，赞叹修文人民开明开放、真诚友爱、锐意进取的精神风貌。随着高尔夫活动和赛事开展，贵州省组建起高尔夫球队、青少年高尔夫球队，贵州省、贵阳市分别成立高尔夫球协会，搭起以高尔夫

2005年西部业余高尔夫球赛贵州队夺冠

球会友、广泛人际交流的平台，贵阳高尔夫挥杆连宾朋、银球传和谐这张修文人民持有的名片传遍国内外。

珍珠岛避暑中心 2000年，贵阳市人民防空战备办公室投资，将地处贵（阳）遵（义）高等级公路和210国道旁的久长镇金桥村畔壳堰湖畔，占地120亩（其中水域面积3平方公里）库区建成“平战结合人口疏散基地”，取名“珍珠岛避暑中心”。中心既是战备疏散场所，又是避暑旅游区。中心设置避暑别墅9栋，内设标准间80间、床位220个，为三星级旅游餐饮店，另置啤酒广场、网球场、羽毛球场、游泳池、多功能厅、棋牌室、台球室、健身房、钓鱼船台、游船等，成为生活、休闲、避暑、康乐、公务为一体的旅游服务中心。总投入开发建设资金达4000万元。

珍珠岛避暑中心

2003年5月1日正式开放，当年就接待游客1.5万人，营业收入92.3万元。2008年，游客5.5万人次，收入553万元。2010年，游客达到9万人次，收入增到2699万元。

岩鹰山湖游憩区 1998年，岩鹰山水库管理所将水面宽阔、湖映群山、峡跨长虹锁蛟龙的人造景观向游人开放。整个湖区由小六广湖、万兴堡湖、岩鹰山湖毗连而成。小六广湖，烟波浩渺、形如菱角，有王五岗巍然耸立，与大林坡、茶山相依。湖的南面一道土坝长堤连接两座郁郁葱葱的小松山，截断大雁河，把一湾绿水积留在小六广群山之中。湖心并列大、小两岛，相距百余米，大岛重岩叠翠，绿树成荫；小岛地势低平，浅滩甚多，白鹤、斑鸠、鹭鸶在此静守觅食，追逐戏水。万兴湖湖水清澈，湖岸青山倒影，仿佛是水中之山在流动，有令人心醉，柔和、沉静的爱恋。坐落在湖西南岸边有“石锣山”和“石鼓山”。石锣山正面岩壁上还有摩崖石刻：石锣对石鼓，金银二万五，谁人识得破，买通万兴堡，但无从考证其作者和篆刻年代。1971年修水库时，在石锣山和石鼓山炸取石材，水库建成后，万兴堡片片旱地变为良田，人们终于识破谜底：在中国共产中共领导下，众志成城治山治水，使万兴堡变出良田二万五。岩鹰山湖沉睡在岩鹰山、白虎山、青龙山和凤凰山之间的狭长深谷中。用1道人工弓形大石坝闭锁峡谷湖水，相映成趣，展现自然环境与人造景观巧妙的结合。

岩鹰山湖游憩区一角

湖区刚开放，游客临湖游览、垂钓、聚会，引来贵阳、白云和县内游客和垂钓者300多人。库区10多户村民就地办起饮食服务接待站，县运输部门增开县城至库区客运班车，库区管理所增设库区游船。2003年管理所向贵阳市财政申请房屋改造资金30万元，修起库区游客住宿、饮食、娱乐、休闲场所。是年县政府主持编制《贵阳市修文县旅游发展总体规划》，将库区列为休闲度假旅游区。2004年，县交通局投资300万元，硬化库区16公里围库道路。2006年，岩鹰山湖已沿久（长）高（枧）公路连接珍珠岛水库，县旅游局将岩鹰山湖规划为岩鹰山旅游区并开辟库区湖泊景观游之道，迎来新疆、黑龙江等省市的90多个参观团以及阿尔巴尼亚客人游览。2010年，岩鹰山湖列为“爽爽的贵阳，避暑的天堂”修文五大旅游片区之一，是理想的水库风景康乐游和水利科普观光游憩区。

桃源河魔幻漂流 2001年7月，扎佐镇民营企业家翁先明与县政府签订开发位于六屯乡境内距贵遵高等级公路扎佐站10公里的桃源河峡谷旅游资源合同，成立贵阳市修文神舟漂流有限公司，投资200万元开发，建成集湖、泉、河、瀑、山、涧、峡和古生物化石为一体的桃源河峡谷漂流旅游。2002年，开始营运，但景区窄，规模小，后续资金有限，拓展受到制约。10月，贵阳市旅游局引进重庆民营企业家张元亮到景区考察。以180万元资金向翁先明买断桃源河峡谷的经营权，挂牌“贵州神州漂流有限公司”，并投入1500万元对桃源河景区进行整体开发。2003年，神州漂流公司委托西南师范大学旅游规划研究院编制《贵阳市修文桃源河生态旅游区发展规划》，对景区进行资源开发评估、客源市场分析、游玩项目打造和游览规划定位。

2005年，公司在宽30米、落差40米的桃源河“三道响水”大瀑布右侧开凿出长达5公里的魔幻漂流滑道和观光车道，添置500多艘橡皮船和4台游览观光车以及游客接待中心，日最大接待游客量达1000人。首创全国最惊险刺激和富有魔幻魅力的峡谷漂流。游客在急流波涛中乘一叶皮筏弄水，经“三道响水”三级瀑布，进入天然隧洞，再经过岩石筑就的人工明渠，跨越架空滑道而下，顺河欣赏两岸曲折多变、怪石交错、奇峰峭壁与飞泉凸现的喀斯特奇景和魔幻漂流项目外，神州漂流公司还开发香粑房水库、珍珠滩瀑布、苗王头、麒麟岩、神龟戏水和相亲岩等景点供游客游览。

2007年6月，由县政府和贵阳市旅游局、市体育局联合主办，神舟漂流公司承办的“2007迎奥运贵阳（修文）首届漂流节暨桃源河魔幻漂流大赛”，有200名漂流爱好者赶至峡谷参与漂流竞技，吸引数以计千的游客前来观赏。

2009年3月，桃源河景区抓住举办中国·贵阳避暑季、贵阳市第三届旅游产业发展大会 和中国·贵阳（修文）第四届国际阳明文化节的契机，迎来重庆市68家旅行社在桃源河景区采点，绘制出桃源河旅游线路。6月27日，贵阳（修文）第二届漂流节暨2009桃源河魔幻漂流大赛在桃源河景区举行，将全国首创的桃源河峡谷魔幻漂流推向省内外。2010年，峡谷漂流游客增至20.88万人次，景区营业收入达5221.05万元。

桃源河魔幻漂流

六广河码头乐园 1996年2月，县旅游局利用全长74公里的六广河峡谷开发康乐观光游，购置旅游船1艘用于旅游接待服务，因受资金和交通制约导致搁浅。1998年，承建贵（阳）毕（节）高等级公路建设的贵州省公路公司对风景旖旎的六广河七峡情有独钟，决定投资开发六广河峡谷旅游，便与县政府旅游开发指挥部签订开发合同，成立六广河旅游公司。公司在六广河边滨江村占地4.23亩，于河面宽38米，水深25米处修建长400米的旅游码头，使用楠竹修建起5444平方米的竹楼宾馆，并建起公园式停车场和花园草坪的阳明广场，整个码头气派富有河谷特色。码头水面宽阔，机动游船乘坐游客在河面穿行，既可休闲，又可观景。游客可饱览“遥看烟波锁二桥”的秀丽景色。

2003年修建六广河上游索风营电站，下游乌江电站开闸放水，水位下降，竹楼码头旅游经营受到影响。2008年，电站建成，水位回升，但因中断经营期间码头管理不善，宾馆失修，游客减少。2009年8月，六广河旅游公司抓住贵阳市开展“避暑季”系列旅游活动契机，举办“六广河杯”大力士大赛，迎来全国百余大力士参加角逐，吸引数以计千游客观看，同时游览七峡，实现游客数量历史性的突破。随后公司委托北京达沃斯巅峰旅游规划设计院重新规划景区，对竹楼码头进行全新改造，并开发温泉，增设避暑休闲酒店，观光栈道和峡谷探险。

六广河旅游码头

2010年12月，公司在六广河码头广场举行“阳明古渡”项目建设奠基仪式，投资2亿元对码头升级改造，增添景观，以达到设施齐全、结构优化的旅游乐园。

专记：沧桑古渡变乐园

六广河自古即为水西门户，以河为界，东为修文县六广镇，西为黔西县素朴镇。从明洪武十七年（1384）贵州宣慰使奢香承诏开辟九驿时起，六广河渡口即有木船摆渡两岸过往行人。过渡人们为求过河平安，在河边修起一座龙王庙，常年烧香化帛，以求神灵保佑。

1979年，六广河下游乌江电站大坝建成，河道水深20米，水面宽处达100米。1996年，贵阳市交通局拨款40万元爆破石门坎暗礁，使巴蕉湾河段常年通航，形成从六广河渡口到乌江电站大坝长达74公里的水上航线。1998年，县政府看好六广河峡谷前景，开发旅游商机，与省公路工程总公司联合组建六广河峡谷旅游开发有限公司，投资1000万元，建设公园式码头。2001年10月，码头竣工，命名为阳明码头，使奔流咆哮的古渡变成高峡平湖。呈现“汇三峡之险，集漓江之秀于一体，从乌龙滚滚劈山谷呼啸，到此而风平浪静”的态势，敞开胸怀笑迎四方游客。

六广河阳明码头位于六广镇滨江村方家田坝，由贵（阳）毕（节）高等级公路六广收费站匝口，经长3公里、宽11米的柏油路直达。码头入口处建有高13米四柱三门三楼的石牌坊，中间行车道宽7.8米，两侧人行道各宽2米。进入牌坊大门，河岸边塑有布衣素服、腰束布带、高髻于顶、颜下长髯、左手托书、右肩挎伞的王阳明石雕像，给游客吟诵“遍行奇胜才经此，江上无劳羡九华”诗句赞赏六广河美景。临河岸建有长100米，高1.2米的石栏栏间嵌有60块长1米的青石板，石板两面雕刻有花鸟鱼虫、飞禽走兽、松竹梅兰各种图案。码头处建有占地7.5亩的阳明广场，草坪场上植有桂花、芭蕉、翠竹和各种名花。码头右侧建有占地6亩，建有10栋面积5444平方米的翠竹二层楼群宾馆。整个建筑以楠竹作柱、作枋、作瓦、作墙，室内陈设、设施全为竹桌、竹椅、竹凳、竹篱、竹刻。馆内置有现代化健身器材，辅以保健按摩、中药足疗、芬兰桑拿、水床躺浴、冲浪干蒸，游客可享受现代休闲旅游康乐服务。馆外配有竹楼休闲亭、水上游泳池、烧烤场、儿童乐园、射击场、沙滩排球、儿童足球以及300辆车位的停车场，游客可尽享悠山、绿水之清闲。除广场、宾馆设施外，还建有5个泊位，配有游轮6艘。其中，阳明1号、2号、3号游轮为全空调，每艘载客160人，轮内配设吧台，小吃、酒水、有棋牌室和客房供游客休闲。阳明4号游轮载客60人，提供小吃、酒水服务。阳明5号双层游轮，一层可休闲娱乐、二层供商务会议，配置空调，可载100人。另有小型游轮1艘，载客30人。还有可载25人，9人、5人快艇各1艘，1次供820名游客乘坐尽情观赏沿河峡谷7峡42景。

2005年，索风营电站建成蓄水，从电站大坝乘船逆水而上，直抵猫跳河六级电站以及鸭池河，使水路旅游航线扩展，游览者逐年增加。2008年，游客为5万人次，旅游收入741.72万元。2010年，增为10万人次，旅游收入2046万元。

三、生态旅游

贵州绿色石林 坐落在大石布依族乡境内，由回水石林和高枧石林两部分组成。1997年，县旅游局投资15万元开发高枧石林。1998年7月建成100米景区公路、景点步行道、景区公厕及100平方米的停车场，后因资金短缺搁置。2001年，《贵州日报》刊登韩进撰文描述回水石林："环拥诸峰如犬牙锋锐直指苍穹，谷中巨石零落横放，如牛、如大象、如鲸鱼，其形不可胜数，或石之上，或石之后、或石中间，便有人家茅屋瓦房坐落，竹树掩映其间，如巨大盆景……"高枧石林分布集中，有"石仓"之称。石林奇形怪壮具有石林难见石、林木树葱葱之奇，地缝纵交横、曲径又通门之幽，天坑洞庭深、八卦处处生之险，石笋似千军，万马将前立之状，天成石兽园、拟态万象存之趣。游客孔令华吟诗赞美"夫妻吻"巨石："我赞叹你俩有这般勇敢，让情魂弥漫月下清寂山间。凝目黑夜精灵，我向有情人呼喊：与其夜夜做化蝶的幻梦，不如学石人相拥长吻千年。""夫妻吻"是情人相约留影、海誓山盟、定情相守的好地方。有《恋石》以"相望想闻又相拥，磐石妆成撼莎翁，世代同根生不息，欢歌载舞六月里"的诗句赞美高枧石林。2005年3月，贵州泽源公司与回水村签订回水石林开发协议，投入开发资金126万元。后因资金不足放弃开发。2007年6月，贵州金州公司与回水、天桥、沙坝3个村签订回水石林开发协议，投入资金700万元，建成回水石林景区围墙、接待大厅、停车场、景区大门、牌坊以及6.5公里的游览步道。由于金州公司资金跟不上，且开发范围和规划未按专家考察定名，又未与县政府签订开发合同而停工。

高枧石林景观"夫妻吻"巨石

2009年5月21日，县政府为推动石林景区开发，在大石乡回水村举行"踏青避暑，石林有约"采风活动，来自省、市、县艺术界100多名美术、书法、摄影、音乐艺术家一睹贵州绿色石林神奇魅力，观看乡村酒吧茶艺表演和民歌对唱，在感受"端午粽香、情满石林"时，展示浓浓墨香乐趣。整个采风活动分为"生态之旅""文化之旅""智慧之旅""青春之旅"4个部分，以游绿色石林、观生命奇迹、品农家风味、悟百态人生为主题打造乡村

"六月六"布依歌会

游。7月27日（农历六月初六），县旅游局和大石乡政府在石林举办“千年之恋”布衣歌会，以舞动布依风采、唱响绿色石林为主题，开展“山水画廊，魅力大石”书画摄影展和“寻梦回水潮，牵手六月六”布依歌王歌后争霸赛，邀请县内扎佐新月和六屯独山，开阳县禾丰、乌当区偏坡和新堡，金沙县化觉等地布依歌手参赛，赛前6对金婚夫妇和6对新婚夫妇一道漫游石林，并在“夫妻吻”景点留影共祝夫妻感情天长地久。

2010年年初，金州公司重整旗鼓按景区总体规划进行开发，找到实力伙伴组建“贵州黔中绿色石林开发有限公司”，与县政府签订开发协议。县政府为确保景区建设达到高标准、高品位和高档次的要求，提出按国家4A级旅游景区标准予以开发，将景区打造成以休闲娱乐、观光度假和布衣风情为一体的生态旅游区。12月，开发项目进入编制及协议谈判，预计投入资金2亿元。

绿色石林景点概况及主要景点一览表

表3—07—02

石林名称	概　　况	景　　点
回水石林	位于大石乡回水村境内，原属天然水塘，水干缩之后露出石峰，四周田园千亩，一派田园风光，农舍坐落其间	回水塘——田园风光景色
		将军峰——原名“观音峰”
		双洞天——高柱构成井腔
		穿洞三仙——穿洞下尊三石峰
		绿荫石林——石林处于绿荫中
高枧石林	高枧石林位于大石乡高枧村境内，占地300亩，石林分布集中，有石仑之称。犹如存放奇石之库，石形各异，无石不奇，各石似景。	阳明布道——原名“鸟兽聚会”
		无言石门——原名“凯旋门”
		拥抱千年——又名“夫妻吻”
		鸳鸯石——形如鸳鸯鸟
		美发仙子——原名“母亲石”
		横空出世——一条石斜指南天

六广河七峡景观　位于六广镇和六桶乡境内。1995年，贵州省政府批准六广河七峡纳入修文阳明风景名胜区。1996年，县旅游局开始对六广河峡谷旅游进行开发，后因受交通和资金制约而中断。1998年，修筑贵（阳）毕（节）高等级公路跨六广河猴愁峡时设高等级公路匝道线与六广河相连。承建贵毕公路建设的贵州省公路工程建设总公司考察六广河峡谷后，决定开发六广河七峡景观旅游资源，成立“六广河旅游公司”，在六广河古渡建旅游码头，置游艇，建宾馆，开凿七峡游航道。

白马峡之大鹏展翅景观

2002年贵阳市开发旅游业，构筑起贵阳市区—扎佐高尔夫度假中心—修文阳明洞景区—六广河峡谷景区—息烽温泉旅游风景线，其中的六广河峡谷长74公里航道上，一览白马峡、猴愁峡、飞龙峡、赤壁峡、象鼻峡、剑劈峡和海马峡及其42景，同时感受到滨江花苗村寨和大屯布依村寨的民族风情，使七峡景观更加多彩多姿。

六广河七峡景观一览表

表3—07—03

序号	名　称	位置与范围	规　　模	景点名称	景点概况
1	白马峡	白马峡至桔子寨长3公里	峡高差250—300米，宽10-20米。	白马滩	乌江水库静水起点，水从乱石中似脱缰白马奔驰
				苍鹰搏击	老鹰岩巨大断壁形同雄鹰展翅，大有搏击长空之势
				雏鹰回首	老鹰岩处小群山形如一群雄鹰、仰望雏鹰展翅之姿
				一线天	河两岸山岸并立，从河谷底仰望，只见蓝天一线
2	猴愁峡	橘子寨至六广河大桥长4公里，包括古度飞虹、危岩高耸、猿猴愁攀总景观	峡高差300—350米	贾家洞	洞内存寺庙，有碑刻、悬岩上可俯望峡谷风光，高洞流泉
				高洞寒泉	泉水每日流水2514吨，从贾家洞流出沿悬岩而下、悬挂泉水
				观音坐莲	擦耳岩上天然一图案、形同观音坐于莲花之上
				坐石弄溪	高耸断岩，形同老翁头像观看溪流河水景观
				猿猴嶂谷	河西岸河谷壁立、树木葱翠、有猿猴常嬉戏于此
				双月岩	裸露山岩层向下弯曲形成两道弧形犹如两轮弯月
				金扁担	河南岸悬岩有如扁担状岩石，传说为神仙所用
				悬棺葬	悬崖壁上有悬棺，具传说是神仙所遗
3	飞龙峡	滨江村至大屯村长3公里	峡顶峰与水面高差250米，宽10—20米	白水飞龙	距河水60米处一洞、白水流出、量大，其景似一条白龙。
				明阳妙笔	河岸岩柱顶生小树，似观音手中净瓶，有阳明诗文“陆广晓发”、“过天生桥”记述
				金龙闹瀑	白水电站下游瀑布经过褶皱岩石，形成了无数金龙游动。
				镇龙峰	白水瀑布对岸，数峰凸起，犹如屏障
4	赤壁峡	大屯村至老凹河长5公里	包括峡河岩石三迭景、夜郎组类、呈肉红色赤壁。	苗女彩裙	悬岩接近水面处，褶皱岩石，红黑相间，似如苗女彩裙
				滨江苗寨	苗女彩裙开阔处有一面悬岩，一面临水的苗家风情小寨
				布依桃源	大屯村三面环山，一面临水，农家幽美，布依山寨，似如世外桃源
				五老八仙	大屯后山峰、上游看五峰如五老，下游看如八仙。
				珠帘叠翠	高60米瀑布景、山顺陡岸洒入河中，如一幅美丽的壁挂
				银丝细雨	河西岸瀑布从数十米高呈丝状、细雨飘下、水珠万点
				拖拉褶曲	典型的受压力变成的岩层地质景观，具观赏性、科普性
				赤壁白鹭	岩壁呈红色、裂纹交错如画，似火炼常有白鹭停留于此

续表

序号	名　称	位置与范围	规　　模	景点名称	景点概况
5	象鼻峡	老凹河至班家寨长4公里	主景：峡中有如象鼻岩石伸下	象鼻石	象鼻峡处一岩石伸入河中，形如象鼻吸水
				逆掩断层	岩石受地质压力作用形成地质景观，具有科普价值
				峡谷挑源	河峡谷裂缝可乘小船进出，环境幽深，似如桃源
				观音洞	河岩一溶洞可乘小船入内，深数十米，有乳石似如观音
				黑龙洞瀑	百米高崖上，黑龙洞流水喷泻而下，形成瀑布
6	剑劈峡	班家寨至石盖路长7公里	水面宽变化大，窄处10米，宽处500米	翠屏春峦	河岸边一排山峰林立，植被茂盛，如同屏障、幽峦
				悬崖天梯	梯子崖悬岩上有梯阶小路，沿绝壁攀缘到岩顶，直上云霄
				剑劈石	河岸岩层褶曲断裂，形如斧砍剑劈之势
				卧狮啸天	三岔河口交汇处一山锋似如雄狮昂首，向天长啸
				玉柱双瀑	在支流野记河岸，断层崖，两岸各有一飞瀑流下
				彩崖悬链	一凹型绝壁上一缕白水倾流直下，如同彩链悬空
				白滩怪石	河东大白滩寨下，岸上怪石林立，神奇的姿态各异
7	海马峡	剑劈岩至峰子岩，县境内长9公里	县境段峡谷长9公里	碧水涌泉	瀑布水从60米高悬崖处洞中涌出，形成飞瀑
				白鹭惊水	在宽阔的河面上常有白鹭飞过，高旋俯冲姿态万千
				蛤蟆岩	河西岸箐口寨山形如蛤蟆状，俯视江面，其形逼真
				藏书岩	河东岸岩石千层万叠，龙如万卷书，叠放存于山中
				青龙岩	藏书岩下游岸边40米高处一洞地下水涌出，飘下如青龙
				姊妹峰	两座山峰伫立湖中，犹如翘首比肩依偎的姊妹

景阳森林公园　2001年5月，贵州省林业厅将扎佐林场的台墩坝、三元、冷水沟和珍珠井4个分场组成省级森林公园。其中三元分场取名为“景阳公园”，它既是贵阳市环城防护绿化带重要组成部分，又是市民休闲度假、避暑吸氧、康体健身的好去处，作为省级森林公园向市民开放。公园占地1.7万亩，其中森林面积1.5万亩，整个园区森林覆盖率达90.43%，满园苍松翠柏，一片林海。偶尔几点空处，也被青草铺成绿地。空地四周低矮的灌木丛除常见的映山红和火棘外，尚有药用植物113种，观赏植物95种，可食用野菜类植物65种。公园内的浪潮湖，集水245万立方米，湖面被青翠茂盛的森林植被环绕。公园周围，连绵起伏的“馒头山”轮廓浑圆层次丰富，蜿蜒的山峦构成公园风景的主骨架。冬末春初，万木复苏，野花偏处，多姿浪漫，生机盎然；盛夏林木葱茏，随风起舞，暑气消散，清凉舒适；金秋天高云淡，枫叶红火棘果熟，尽显“万绿丛中一点红”；隆冬时节大雪压青松，松枝挂冰条，似乎来到别有情趣的银色世界。公园常有游人到此荡涤城市尘灰，开心色喜，清神醒脑。2010年，景阳森林公园已成为贵阳市郊大型的野营理想之地，是游客结伴而来休闲度假、避暑吸氧、康体健身的旅游地。

苏格兰风情牧场

苏格兰风情牧场 2007年，县政府利用地势海拔1330米，年平均气温13.6℃的久长镇清江、兴隆两村的森林草场和水域湿地开发生态旅游。通过招商引资由海南投资商冷静组建贵州黔秀农业开发有限公司，创办苏格兰风情牧场度假旅游村。规划用地3000亩，按照生态旅游景点开发建设，内设苏格兰风情度假酒店、老年疗养院、康乐活动中心、高尔夫球练习场、马术俱乐部、户外拓展训练基地、特色养殖场、滑草场。至2008年累计投放资金2397万元，建成牧场圈舍400平方米，种植香麦草、三叶草300亩、滑草30亩、优质果园70亩、楠竹54亩、柳树200株、香樟树400株、杨梅树15株，建起科普蔬菜大棚6亩及旅游配套设施，牧场雏形已见，集生态农业观光、旅游度假、休闲娱乐、疗养居住为一体，启动高尔夫球练习，马术、草场戏牛羊，草上飞、石阵螟想、垂钓、烧烤、草地露营，登山等活动。牧场显现出英国苏格兰地区小镇克罗夫特海得牧场风格，融入大量英伦文化元素，处处具有浓郁的异域风情。牧场山清水秀，草丛葱绿，景色十分优美，是“爽爽的贵阳，避暑在久长”的生态旅游之地。县旅游局规划将苏格兰风情牧场和农业生态园纳入贵阳—扎佐高尔夫度假中心—久长苏格兰牧场—久长珠珠岛旅游线路。

2009年9月28日，苏格兰风情牧场一期工程竣工并试运营。同时接待北京、海南、重庆及省内游客5000人次，营业收入15万元。

2010年，黔秀农业开发公司又投资3.6亿元启动第二期工程，计划建成能容300至500人的四星级准五星级宾馆，能容200人居住的青年公寓，沿湖建别墅60幢，增设游艇，开水上娱乐项目。拟建苏格兰风情小镇一条街，设置小镇酒吧、娱乐室、音乐茶室，以填补贵州异域风情旅游空白，拓展生态旅游内涵。是年，由县旅游文体广电局、久长镇政府主办，苏格兰牧场承办的“浓情九月，情系你我”和牧场举办中秋文艺晚会，吸引省、市部门领导，贵阳旅行团和市民自驾游，顿时牧场人欢车鸣，游人川流不息，日最大接待游客4000人。全年接待旅客12万人次，营业收入达3552万元。

贵阳森林野生动物园 2001年，趁修文开发旅游资源之际，云南民营企业家张彦军亲临省级森林公园扎佐林场考察，发现地处贵（阳）遵（义）、贵（阳）毕（节）两条高等级公路旁的冷水沟林区地貌独特、其间有缓坡、山坳、宽谷、山峰、石林、溶洞等自然景观，而且森林茂密，空气清新，是野生动物栖息繁衍的理想家园，于是决定投资于此开发森林野生动物园，供游客游览享受人与自然，动物与自然和人与动物和谐相处的乐趣。后经贵阳市政府和国家林业局批复立项为旅游资源开发项目。项目规划占地5000亩，投资2.6亿元。2006年5月1日，野生动物园正式向游客开放，园内放养大熊猫、金丝猴、斑马、长颈鹿等200多种5000多头（只）。内设有珍稀动物园、动物表演场、科普教育馆、儿童动物园、大型动物散放区，以及游乐场、宾馆餐

森林野生动物园

厅、停车场，是全国唯一的为公众提供旅游观光的高原森林野生动物园，是集生态、观光、科普为一体的综合性生态园。游客进入园内观赏以野生动物和森林景观为主线，从中解野生动物的野性、兽性和灵性，迁地繁殖和保护，同时观赏世界上珍稀动物和观看动物表演，还可走进科普教育馆满足求知欲望。

动物园开放即与周边的高尔夫度假中心、桃源河峡谷魔幻漂流中心、珠珠岛避暑中心和阳明洞王学圣地共同构成黄金旅游区，使“林城贵阳”“秀美修文”游人络绎不断。2008年，园区新建华南虎园和国宝熊猫馆，与成都熊猫繁殖研究基地合作，引入熊猫“乐水”“珠珠”移居；与上海动物园合作，引进具有贵州血统的华南虎“珍珍”“妮妮”“敏敏”和“浩浩”入住，日最大接待量突破4万人次。

2009年1月13日，野生动物园获国家旅游局〔2009〕4号文批准为国家AAAA级旅游景区，也是县内第一个国家级AAAA旅游区。5月5日，由贵阳市委、市政府主办，市旅游局、县旅游局承办的“贵阳市第三届旅游产业发展大会”在野生动物园举行，国家旅游局副局长王志友，国家风景园林协会、国家城市规划协会会长赵宝江、贵州省旅游局副局长李三旗、省建设厅副厅长姬保山以及贵阳市各区（县、市）领导，使森林野生动物园的美誉度和知名度得到较大提升。2010年，接待游客83.7万人次，实现旅游收入1.8亿元，创下县内旅游景区营业收入之最。

生态电站博览馆　2003年10月，县政府委托贵州省旅游经济研究所、贵州师范大学地理研究所和贵州省建筑设计院共同编制《贵阳市修文县旅游发展总体规划》，将贵州省水利电力厅于20世纪70年代，在修文县境内猫跳河段建成个性独特、雄伟壮观的河口（修文老电站）及三级（修文电站）、四级（窄巷口电话）、五级（红林电站）、六级（红岩电站）等梯级电站，列为全县7个旅游片区之一的猫跳河峡谷坝型博物馆科普生态旅游区。电站建设从荣获“贵州第一”“世界第一”的称号起，便成为游客游览、参观和接受科普教育之地。它既是中国水电坝型的“橱窗”，又是流金溢彩的艺术长廊，构成修文河流域的水电明珠链。随着县旅游业的开发和电站专线公路硬化，游客漫步在幽深的历史小巷，似觉跨进一座偌大的电站博物馆，听着解说员的介绍，体味到岁月流逝和世事变化，感悟到建设者的智慧、游览电站生态秀丽风光，实在是价值所在。

2005年，六广河段修建索风营电站大坝关闸蓄水，形成索风营湖。其设计独特的地下电站被称为“生态电站”，是水力资源持续、滚动式开发的典范。电站还未对外开放，便有游客到此览胜。至2010年，索风营电站还是旅游资源开发的处女地。

六级电站库区水域风光

专记：未开发的生态旅游处女地——索风营湖

2002年，在县境与黔西县交界的六广河上游，六广河七峡首峡——白马峡上端兴建索风营电站。2005年，电站大坝建成，蓄水总库容量2.01亿立方米，坝高121.8米、坝顶长167米、河床坝段设有5孔、宽13米的敞开式溢流口，最大下泄流量1.6万立方米/秒，引水发电地下厂房的隧洞分为3洞3机单元供水，隧洞钢管内径分别为9.9米和7.6米。发电厂房宽24米、高57.7米、长133米，由3台单机容量200兆瓦混流式水轮发电机组构成。索风营电站的建成除为来访者参观巍然屹立的大坝和独特的生态形电站外，还为游客乘船游览美不胜收的峡谷风光和烟波浩淼的索风湖景观，以及号称世界第一的倒张拱钢索桥和亚洲之最的六广河特大桥。

索风湖大坝上游的深山峡谷中，奔驰的鸭池河和猫跳河河水被高耸的大坝锁住，呈现出山清水秀的大湖水域，连接着修文、黔西、清镇三县。湖面周围青山连绵，湖水波平如镜，湖中野鸭戏水，渔翁荡舟布网，游船破水而行，游客到此陶醉于幽静迷人的美景中，流连忘返。

从大坝逆流而上，进入二屯峡。峡谷左岸岩呈红色，故名“红岩脚”，右岸山形似一艘帆船，故称“船山”。二屯峡内有斧劈刀砍的二屯岩，往前进行到黔西境有滴水岩，常年一股清泉泻入河中。岩左下有一渔洞，渔民常年搭棚在此捕捞。渔洞上方又有两个小岩，形状半圆，外形好似罗汉。经过5公里的二屯峡段，便到三岔河口，右为鸭池河，左为猫跳河，河水汇合泻入乌江。

沿猫跳河顺河逆上进入猴儿峡。猴儿峡河面狭窄，沿河两岸挂满丛丛藤蔓，满壁翠绿。右岸山上有一巨石，酷似顽皮猴儿眺望对岸，欲想跃跳过河。过猴儿峡进入黑塘峡，岩壁上有一瀑布飞流直下，泻入潭中。右岸有岩形同一巨大的半边蚌壳竖立于岸。经蚌壳岩逆水而上到猫跳岩，岩石犹如一只巨虎准备起跳过河。猴儿峡左岸有笋子岩，高峻挺拔，直指苍穹。从石笋岩一侧看去宛若观音静瓶，故称“静瓶峰”。瓶颈古树茂密，虬枝蔓绕，瓶顶绝壁高30多米，游人欲攀，但望洋兴叹。

过静瓶峰，进入一线天。此处河道和山谷既窄又长，河水穿流于悬崖峭壁之间，游船到此擦岩而过。悬岩上方树木葱郁，常有猕猴结伴来到人工投食点进餐。河的左岸有一尖峰，峰顶又分成两峰，伊如一对依偎的恋人。河的右岸又有相连的双峰，似马鞍又似驼峰。在一线天中段右岸崖壁上有一洞，称为“羊皮洞”，洞口形成竖立的四边形，高约80米，瀑水如珠帘倒挂，泻于崖下深潭，飞散出轻盈缥缈的水雾。羊皮洞内宽敞，进洞道路奇岖险峻，游人惊叹：“仰视天际远，俯视若海滨”。瀑布下方百米处溪涧有平整的天然大石块，供游客在此开怀畅饮，抚琴弈棋。

从石桌上游200米，有宽达25米的瀑布喷出。再往上游200米处，又有水面宽20米瀑水飞流直下数丈。再往上游只见3座尖山，如同三位将军屹立在岸、守卫着猫跳河六级电站。电站大坝旁的大山形似大花轿，名为“轿子山”，旁立8个小山头，恰似八人抬轿，游客到此可“乘轿”上岸，参观雄伟的六级电站中孔射流式双拱壮观的大坝。亦可乘舟返游，再览胜景。

索风湖猫跳河一线天

农业生态旅游园　20世纪80年代初，谷堡乡红星村创建园艺场，折溪村和平滩村也相继建场种植猕猴桃、金秋梨、板栗、柑橘、艳红桃走上果园经济的致富道路。到2003年，种艳红桃3000亩，猕猴桃6000亩，金秋梨1500亩，美国布郎李5000亩，小叶苦丁茶1000亩。大塘村建有50亩的花卉大棚，场坝村建有15亩的盆景培植场，形成“协会+基地+农户”的生态园艺绿色产业。

2004年4月，县政府以折溪村万亩梨园为载体，在梨花湖畔举办首届梨花节，吸引上万市民进园赏花，品尝农家餐饮。7月，折溪村被国家旅游局评为全国农业旅游示范点，也是贵阳市首家出炉的全国农业旅游示范点。

2009年3月22日，“贵阳·修文第五届梨花节”在折溪村梨花湖举行开幕式，吸引贵阳市“汽车之家”俱乐部组织百辆轿车临湖参加活动，顿时游客爆满，湖畔热闹非凡，整个生态园接待收入达2174.3万元。扎佐镇大河村、久长镇上寨村、六广镇滨江村、大石乡回水村、六桶乡海马村也利用本村的生态、河流、交通等优势，栽种艳红桃、葡萄、晚熟酥李、柑橘、樱桃、荷花等经果林园，修建停车场及果园行道，办起农家乐，开展田园观光、生态旅游、农家娱乐、科普教育为一体的农业生态游，接待春赏花、夏摘果、河边垂钓、烧烤、观景的游客。

农业生态旅游示范点—折溪

2010年，仅谷堡乡折溪、扎佐镇大河、久长镇上寨、六广镇滨江、大石乡回水、六桶乡海马等6个村就有农家乐旅游示范户39家，接待游客53.5万人次，旅游总收入达4905万元。

专记：从猕猴桃到花果乐园的谷堡乡

1988年，乌栗乡（今谷堡乡）下硐村村民联户创办红星合作农场，利用非耕地种植猕猴桃。1998年，县委、县政府将猕猴桃种植定为全县农村经济的“五大产业”之一，作为调整农业产业结构的突破口，产量达1000多万公斤，远销广州、深圳、北京、上海、长春、吉林、重庆等地。1999年，猕猴桃鲜果注册“六广河”商标，作为旅游商品进行开发。2000年，贵州省农业厅授予“六广河”猕猴桃“贵州省优质农产品”称号，到2004年猕猴桃种植发展到6万亩。中央电视台、贵州电视台、《贵州日报》《贵阳日报》《羊城晚报》等新闻媒体相继报道修文的猕猴桃。从而使谷堡红星农场名扬省内外。为保证农村经济持续发展，谷堡乡把果木种植从山上移到山下，从非耕地扩展到耕地，建园建场，种植柑橘、桃、李和梨，形成“协会+基地+农户”的模式发展生态园艺绿色产业，打造全省著名的花果之乡，被列为贵阳市第一个国家农业旅游示范点。全乡种植板栗1400亩、猕猴桃6300亩、金秋梨3000亩、桃3000亩、美国布郎李5000亩和65亩花卉培植场，园区出现月月有花香、季季有果品的花果乡，每年梨花盛开和金秋品果上市，不断吸引四方客人赏花摘果，人人乐在其中。

春来，梨花盛开，踏青赏花者来到谷堡乡折溪村，村里的梨花湖碧波荡漾，周围一片“雪山”，恰似皑皑白雪的连绵山峦围绕着不着边际的海洋，正如唐代诗人岑参在《白雪歌送武判官司归》所描绘的景象：“忽如一夜春风来，千树万树梨花开。”

夏末秋初，梨园硕果挂满枝头，沉甸甸地压得树枝低下头来，艳丽的红桃，金色的秋梨，脆甜的酥李诱惑游人信手采摘，让大家在果园里尽情享受丰收的喜悦。

多缤洞岩溶艺术 1984年3月，县委、县政府重视县人大七届四次会议通过《关于开发回水石林和花榔躲兵洞旅游区》的提案，随即组建县旅游开发指挥部，进行旅游资源开发。据贵州省科学院山地资源研究所考察组实测考察躲兵洞洞长20.5公里，洞内岩溶雄壮多姿、五彩缤纷，巍然屹立，遂将民国年间当地绅民命名的“躲兵洞”改称为“多缤洞”。

多缤洞位于六桶乡大兴村与息烽县交界的凤凰山，是一座石灰岩溶洞，有13个洞口、66个洞厅，一般洞空高5至20米，最高的“潘家天窗”空高110米、洞宽30米，最大洞厅面积1100平方米。洞内有石林、石台、石门、石柱、穿洞和溶井等奇特景观。其中仙境台犹如一座富丽堂皇的仙人舞台，棚顶倒挂石笋、石幔，恰似舞台悬挂的幕布银屏；莲花洞里荷花盛开，洞顶晶莹水珠下滴，好似一幅春雨荷花塘图；石琴厅有形似手风琴叠层石块的巨石，轻击石块即发出悦耳之声；彩虹桥好似“天桥”飞虹，洞顶白玉般钟乳石水珠下散，就像“小桥流水人家”田园风韵；南天门景观的“擎天柱”石笋，宛若定海神针……。众多的喀斯特岩壁、洞穴、石林，规模宏大，气势磅礴，是地质考察、科普、生态、观光旅游佳地。1985年，县政府正式拟定多缤洞为旅游开发区，获省政府拨款兴修大石至多缤洞公路。后因县财力不济，续建资金短缺，开发告吹。1987年8月3日《人民日报》报道称多缤洞为“天下奇观”，是世界一流的喀斯特洞穴艺术宝库，是举世无双的地下岩溶艺术博物馆。从《人民日报》报道起到2010年，每年都有游客驾临观光“天下奇观”的岩溶艺术宝库。鉴于交通因素制约，多缤洞有待开发。

四、民族风情游

大屯布依风情园 2002年，随着六广河峡谷旅游开发，不断有游客到坐落在六广河下游东岸“赤壁峡”的大屯村游山玩水，感受布依山寨的民族风情。

2003年7月，在村主任李昌勇带动下开办乡村游农家乐接待站4个。大石乡干部汪忠炳与他人合资建起“布依不老寨”避暑山庄，购置游船，建起码头和露天游泳池接待游客。2008年12月，贵阳电视台《天下旅游》栏目组深入大屯村现场采访和录制节目，分两期在贵阳电视台播放，宣传大屯布依山寨，推动大屯民族风情游发展。

2009年，根据贵阳市委、市政府统一部署，以开展2009中国·贵阳避暑季系列活动为中心，以弘扬阳明文化为主题，由县旅游局牵头，于7月27日（六月初六）将大屯村寨中的“石生树”“树抱石”古树奇观，无名古墓，“手扒岩”等迷人景观和布依风情结合组织“六月六”布依歌会，吸引周边布依歌手和游客，使大屯乡村民族风情游收入大增。2010年，因六广河河水下降，水位较低，导致旅游受到影响，大屯游客减少，全村接待仅2.5万人次，旅游收入229万元。

独山布依山寨 2005年，桃源河峡谷景区启动魔幻漂流后，地处景区香粑房水库湖口山丘之上的六屯乡独山布依山寨，常有游客在此歇脚、观赏，不时向村民询问食宿。村民们看好接待游客开设乡村接待站的前景，便利用寨后一条通往景区的石阶道路和寨内布依村民居住的具有民族特色的小青瓦四合院，办起乡村游和民族风情游。并引进贵阳牂牁旅游工艺品厂在独山落户开发民族工艺，以布依风情为素材生产皮雕、竹雕、蛋壳画。同时办起农家乐接待站。游客漫步在林荫道上、游古寨，赏桃花，观茶

花，品尝布依农家茶饭菜，感受布依农家风情，观览民族风情立体画廊。2007年进行新农村建设，又硬化进寨路、串户路和休闲广场，并修复通往桃源河景区500米长的石阶游览步行道，对名扬村内外的布依族“葛氏祠堂”，使全村环境大为改观，农家乐接待站增为8个。

布依族六月六歌会

2008年举办首届“六月六”布依文化歌会，吸引数以千计到桃源河漂流游客和市民观看演出。全年接待游客3.5万人次，旅游收入360万元，2009年接待3万人次，收入365.65万元。2010年，接待2.2万人次，收入206万元。

下堡苗族跳花场 1995年9月，日本日中艺术文化交流协会理事岩田十士及其同道的日本友人，不远万里驾临久长镇下堡村苗寨，纵情观赏苗族芦笙舞、斗角舞和板凳舞。他们为质朴、粗犷和具有浓郁民族特色的苗族歌舞而倾倒，提出把苗族歌舞推介到日本广大观众中去的要求。1996年6月，岩田十士又千里迢迢赶到下堡，与同道的7名日本朋友考察苗族风情，欣赏苗族歌舞，正式邀请以王军、王敏兄妹为核心的下堡苗族歌舞队一行10人，于是年10月18日乘日海轮“燕京号”东渡日本，在神户、名古屋、岐阜和东京等地演出歌舞14场，受到日本人民热情欢迎。至2009年，下堡苗寨花场一直以奏芦笙、敲小鼓、跳苗舞、喜迎中外宾客。其中“苗族斗角舞”和“下堡苗族舞”分别被列为贵州省和贵阳市非物质文化遗产，“斗角舞”还参加2009“多彩贵州”舞蹈大赛，使下堡苗舞传遍全省，但亲临下堡观赏的游客不多。下堡民族风情旅游资源，有待开发。

久长苗族花坡跳场

高脚仓苗族古堡 1985年，县政府将建于清康熙三年（1664）坐落在龙场镇营盘山山坳里的高仑苗寨古堡被列为县级文物保护单位。高仓古堡原是苗族村民为避兵乱、匪祸和保护家园修筑的石城堡，堡墙周长138米，高2.6米，厚1.8米，建造结构和布局巧妙，有西、北两大石门，自西向东开排水沟，堡内还有锅台炉灶，兵祸临头时寨民集中饮食。北门建有通道，供避兵、匪之用，易守难攻，具有“一夫当关，万夫莫开”之势。还备有独特的粮仓，木质结构，粮仓四周有走廊，仓脚由石柱支撑离地，石柱高2米，具有通风、防潮、防鼠、防火等功能。寨民因此称之为“高脚仑”，寨名也因此故称为“高仓”村。

2010年，古堡尚存，苗家青年常在古堡旁的古树下欢歌笑语，芦笙、唢呐、笛子、月琴和姐妹箫伴随轻歌曼舞传承着千百年的苗族人风情。高仓寨旁建有蓄水114万立方米的阁老寨水库，水库左临的鱼洞泉清澈见底，林木蔽荫、雀鸟呼鸣，古堡、水库相辉映，构成一幅美丽的自然景观，列入县招商引资项目，是有待开发民族风情游的一片宝地。

石安古院落 1996年，县文物管理部门和县旅游局将坐落在久长镇石安村的古院落列为县的古建筑加以保护，该古院始建于明代万历年间。相传江西吉安庐陵杨氏家族被追杀逃亡至石安寨，建起12座结构、布局、形状一致的四合院和祠堂，同时在石安河上架桥和石龙山下修塔。古院建筑砖木结构、外墙为青砖、墙体灰缝细致、四棱上线。内墙壁木板扣缝，为典型的“金包银”建筑。每个院落有正房3间、两侧厢房两间对称。院内屋基、院坝、围墙均为统一尺寸，由平滑石块砌铺，方正整齐。古寨四周建石砌围墙，寨门分设在建筑群左右两侧，远望竟似一族大户之家。院落之间修筑宽2米石块道路，弯曲回转，形成巷道，把院落连接起来，可相互通往。行人经过巷道，会发出咚、咚、咚的脚步声。巷口处设垛口，可观看山寨外四周，院外却难见院内。整个寨子犹如迷宫，使人步入感到阴森，不敢往前再走。杨氏搬进新居后，其子考中进士，进入翰林院，其家重新安定下来，一家人官位和金钱已安磐如石，便把寨子取名为“石安寨”。

至2010年，古院历经数百载，仍留存着标准的中式“金包银”建筑，成为人们游览处所。桥、塔虽毁，遗迹尚在。经过改造后的村寨水泥路与古院青石板路同在，新建农舍与古老四合院共存，今古相衬，谱写着岁月的流逝和时代的变迁。石安古寨所保留的居住房舍、防御体系和建筑工艺是研究明代文化、民族风情、建筑风格的重要资源，有待发掘。

五、红色旅游

20世纪80—90年代，县地方党史、志书和文史刊物已将中国工农红军二万五千里长征两次经过修文，红迹遍及全县8个乡镇，109个村寨，行程250公里的歼敌、惩恶、济贫和播下的革命火种记入史册。县政府将红军长征留在六屯乡大木寨的红军标语列为县级文物重点保护单位，使红军长征在修文的遗迹成为人们见证长征历史和接受革命教育之处，开始吸引人们游览和老红军回顾长征历史的处所。

1983年，原红军六军团卫生连连长、中国人民解放军总后勤部副政委李真重返长征时曾战斗过的扎佐镇，即兴书写下毛泽东诗词《七律·长征》，存于县委办公室作为纪念。1984年，原红六军团16师师长、中央顾问委员会委员、中国人民解放军海军副司令员周球保（周仁杰）重游长征时奋战过的扎佐镇，留下回忆录《奔袭贵阳北部重镇——扎佐》。1985年，修文籍老红军、河南省安阳市政协主席段文华返故乡，重温红二、六军团长征经过修文的史实，给县政协提供珍贵的历史资料。1994年，原红军六军团团长萧克，重返曾战斗和留宿过的扎佐，在县领导陪同下到军团指挥部旧址“景阳书院”和军团政治部住所旧址“云霖堂”药铺回忆长征史，并到他曾经住过的老住宅处探询故人。

进入2000年，游览红军在修文的遗迹，红色旅游起步。2005年，县政府在谷堡乡举办第二届梨花节，将红军长征为冲出国民党军的围追堵截，横渡谷堡乡绿水村猫跳河时借渡的古竹索桥进行维修，着力打造县内红色旅游，作为革命传统教育红色旅游景点招来数百人游览。2009年，贵阳市警备区政治委员孙峰一行莅临修文，在县委和县人民武装部领导陪同下参观六屯乡大木寨红军标语，对这经典历史文物的保护和教育后人给予肯定和称赞，使县开发红色旅游坚定信心。到2010年《县旅游志》将红军长征在修文的遗迹纳入旅游资源，列为县旅游业开发的组成部分，为开发红色旅游提供详实的资料。

（一）中央红军遗迹

1935年4月2日至4日，中央红军一军团一师三团、三军团、五军团和军委纵队长征进入县境，经过六桶官寨和久长、清水、清让、六屯、桃源、扎佐等地行程77公里。红五军团在六屯的长田、大木书写许多宣传标语，其中大木寨李忠良住房墙壁上的“红军是干人的军队”、“取消一切高利贷”、“只有苏维埃才能救中国”，红军走后村民用柴火堆积才保护下来。红军曾宿营久长和桃源，其中红一团和军委纵队

大木村保留的红军标语“红军是干人的军队”

在桃源时，朱德司令夜宿净慈寺，给乌江北岸九军团发报“我今天在扎佐东南地区”，并在寺庙墙上书写“月华山”三字。离开修文时经底窝寨逼近贵阳，留下红军长征“兵临贵阳逼昆明，调虎离山弃金沙，我军乘胜追赶路程”的赞歌。

（二）红二、六军团遗迹

1936年1月31日，红军二、六军团在贺龙、任弼时、萧克和王震的率领下进入修文县境，红迹遍及久长、扎佐、龙场、谷堡、洒坪、小箐、六广等地，行程173公里。其中，六军团进入扎佐把七、丁官、牛角湾、龙王寨，攻克扎佐镇，驻扎“景阳书院”和“云霖堂”。二军团经程关、盛官、罗家寨进入县城，驻扎“学宫”。2月2日离开县城，经谷堡绿水索桥过猫跳河进入清镇。留下红军攻克贵阳北部重镇扎佐，进占修文县城，抢渡猫跳河索桥，转向黔西北建立根据地，进滇入川北上等可歌可泣的遗迹。

索桥古渡

第三节　旅游设施

一、景点公路

1999年，县政府紧紧抓住贵州省建设旅游大省和贵（阳）遵（义）、贵（阳）毕（节）两条高等级公路穿越县境的契机，大力建设乡村公路和旅游景点公路，经过5年奋战，到2005年有景区专线公路12条，2010年，增至16条，均与县内干线公路连通。

2010年通往景区（点）专线公路一览表

表3—07—04

景区名称	起、止点	长度（公里）	道宽（米）	路面材料	主要游览景点
阳明洞名胜区	阳明大道至阳明主题公园	0.8	15	柏　油	瞻仰阳明小洞天、龙冈书院、宾阳堂、君子亭、何陋轩、文成祠等
玩易窝古迹	油萝街至玩易窝	0.5	6	混凝土	瞻仰王阳明初到龙场悟道的穴居处
六广河七峡景区	1.修六公路终点至六广河风景区	3	6	柏　油	参观六广河竹楼码头，乘船观赏七峡风光
	2.贵毕公路兴中至码头	1.6	6.5	柏　油	游览六广河七峡
	3.兴中隧道至猴愁峡	7.6	6.5	柏　油	参观赏索风湖和电站大坝
回水石林	大石至回水	4	5	混凝土	观赏石林全景

续表

景区名称	起、止点	长度（公里）	道宽（米）	路面材料	主要游览景点
高枧石林	六广公路高枧至石林	0.5	5	混凝土	观赏“石仑”奇形怪石
多缤洞景区	六广公路火口垭至多缤洞	6.5	5.5	柏　油	参观赏全国长洞之冠全貌
三人坟古迹	冒乌公路蛇田至新堰哨上	3	5	砂　石	参观明代三人坟、蜈蚣桥、古驿道
岩鹰山湖	修六公路苗坝至岩鹰山水库	10	6	混凝土	畅游岩鹰山湖和参观峡跨长虹的水库大坝
高尔夫度假中心	兴红厂至浪潮水库	1	5.5	混凝土	观赏高尔夫度假中心全景
阳明精舍	马关至营盘山	13	5.5	混凝土	参观桂竹园、性天园、俟圣园、乐道园、奉元楼等
大屯布依风情园	广六公路木踏石至大屯村	6.5	5	混凝土	观看古寨、古树及民族风情
桃源河漂流	扎六公路桃子湾至香把房库区	2	5.5	混凝土	观赏桃源河峡谷风光、船支漂流、桃源花
珍珠岛避暑中心	210国道金桥村至珍珠岛	2	5.5	混凝土	参观青山绿水环抱的旅游避暑别墅
苏格兰风情牧场	210国道兴隆村至牧场	2	5.5	混凝土	参观苏格兰风情草场，特色养殖和欣赏异域风情

二、宾馆酒店

1994年起，随着旅游资源的开发，县境宾馆酒楼得到较快发展。2010年，全县有大小宾馆酒店69家。因修文距贵阳市中心仅38公里，又有贵（阳）遵（义）、贵（阳）毕（节）高等级公路开通，莅县的游客多数不留宿，或返程或选择到贵阳住宿，在一定程度上制约着县内宾馆住宿业的发展，全县置有20人以上住宿客房的仅有8家，其中规模较大、档次较高的3星级宾馆1家。

（一）阳明宾馆

1994年兴建，是县城最先建成的宾馆，坐落在县城人民北路与阳明路交汇处。宾馆主体高7层，建筑面积4280平方米，内设餐饮、客房、桑拿、会议、KTV歌舞、购物等服务项目。餐饮部菜肴有川、黔、粤等风味，一次可容150人就餐。客房部有标准客房50间，内设电视、电话、暖气、洗浴。设有大、小会议室。1996年，阳明风景旅游综合开发服务中心在宾馆开设餐饮、客房作为县旅游宣传服务的窗口。后因经营不善出现亏损，即采取承包方式增加服务项目，但几经周折仍无法经营导致停业。

（二）望阳山庄

1996年，县政府为配合旅游业开发，提升对外接待水平，由县财政投资702万元，在阳明洞景区旁的阳明河畔建起2501平方米的宾馆，取名“望阳山庄”。山庄内设餐饮部，含大小餐厅各1个，包房餐室10间，客房部含标准间12间，3人间4间，4人间3间，豪华套间3间，以及娱乐部有卡拉OK厅1间，娱乐包房5间。山庄于2000年和2003年两次承包经营，承包方分别更名为“阳明山庄”“圣泉山庄”。2004年，山庄亏损严重，终止承包，一直停业，继后由县政府将此改为县林业局办公楼。

（三）六广河码头竹楼宾馆

1998年在六广河旅游码头建成竹楼宾馆，置有迎宾厅、客房、商务中心、会议室、歌舞表演场、餐厅、包房，桌、椅、凳、壁画装饰皆以楠竹编制而成。共有竹楼10栋，宾馆大厅400平方米，能同时接待宾客300

人就餐。客房可容150人住宿。独特、别具一格的宾馆可为游客提供芬兰风情桑拿、干蒸、水床躺浴、冲浪服务。

（四）高尔夫会员大酒店

2000年建成的高尔夫会员大酒店坐落在高尔夫度假中心，酒店集饮食、住宿、娱乐、购物为一体。内设豪华客房、标准客房共120套，大、中、小各类会议室、商务活动室、高档餐饮部、桑拿浴室、美发厅、咖啡厅、购物中心、KTV歌舞厅。酒店环境秀美，既可挥杆绿茵怡情健体，又可休闲度假交际娱乐。

高尔夫会员大酒店

（五）黔龙酒家

系县城老字号个体私营饮食企业。酒家继承修文传统红、白两案菜肴，推出具有地方特色的清蒸蹄膀、盐菜肉、八宝饭、脆皮鱼等，为节假日宴席、婚宴最受青睐的餐饮。1999年首届阳明文化节，节日组委会要求酒家接待宾客餐饮要凸显修文饮食文化特色，由老经理王再明组织红、白两案厨师研究“阳明宴”菜谱，利用本地材料，按照传统烹调工艺，做出可口宴席，宾客赞不绝口。2002年和2005年阳明文化节，酒家分别承担宾客接待达600人次。

（六）珍珠岛饭店

2003年，在珍珠岛避暑中心内按三星级饭店标准建设，内设置餐厅、包房、大小会议室、配备多媒体投影仪，为各类会议和培训接待业务服务。2004年经贵阳市旅游局组织评定为三星级饭店。饭店餐厅特别推出适合避暑休闲所需的家常饭菜和农家特色菜。店区环境幽静，设计别具风格，步入啤酒广场既可畅饮各类啤酒，又可尽情享受珍珠岛美丽的湖光山色。2010年，“中心”达到避暑型酒店的标准，列为贵阳市第一批避暑型酒店。

（七）龙场驿食府

2004年建在阳明洞景区内的阳明洞东后侧。分前后两个对称小院组成的仿古建筑，内有山石、草坪、花圃、水池，外设停车场。食府有大小餐厅20间，另设台球室和棋牌活动室，一次可容200人就餐，可供阳明洞游客品味修文特色饮食。2005年阳明文化节，接待游客500人次。是游览阳明洞后休息、就餐的方便处。2010年为开展县文化馆业务和保护阳明洞景区环境，食府停业。

（八）腾晖酒店

位于县城翠屏东路翠屏桥头。2007年，按三星级酒店标准建设，店内服务部设有停车场，有客房标准间、单人间、豪华标准间、观景间、豪华套房共118间，还有腾晖水会桑拿洗浴中心、多功能宴会厅、商务中心、大堂吧、小客厅、大小会议室，置有电视、录像、投影、活动舞台、会议背景等多媒体服务。一次可容600人就餐。酒店设施齐全，豪华典雅，宜餐宜住。

三、休闲山庄

1999年，阳明山庄依托阳明洞风景名胜，率先在阳明河畔阳明大道旁建成，开展旅游、休假、餐饮、住宿、娱乐服务。继后县旅游局根据山庄建设规模、功能，将其划归为旅游宾馆。2000年在三潮水景点依托观音山自然风光、间歇泉景观和潮水寺祭祀优越条件，建起潮水山庄，使短期游客、节假日市民出游光顾于此。继后，又随着县境旅游景点开发，在各景区（点）分别办起松涛山庄、唐人山庄、松韵山庄、桃源山庄、一合山庄和熙苑山庄。有的山庄位于城镇近郊，有的坐落山间峡谷，构成一幅幅各式各样的画券，为忙碌一周工作的人们提供轻松愉悦的处所，为喜欢河岸垂钓、爬山踏青、品味绿色果蔬的游客提供度假休闲的场所。2010年，全县休闲山庄仍存8个。

四、乡村游接待站

20世纪90年代初，随着农业产业结构的调整，激发农民发展第三产业的积极性。他们转变观念，开发乡村服务业、兴办起乡村旅游接待。2004年，谷堡“花果之乡·休闲乐园”被列为全国农业旅游示范点，开展以“美在农家、吃在农家、学在农家、乐在农家”为主题的农业生态观光游。接着县旅游局组织有条件开发乡村游的乡村外出参观、考察、学习，并举办农家旅游服务技能培训，制定乡村游规划，修建村寨道路，进行村寨环境整治和风情风貌建设。使“农家乐”接待站、“乡村游景点”、“农家旅社”犹如雨后春笋迸发出来，接待站先后推出大屯布依“六月六”歌会、下堡苗族歌舞、谷堡梨花节、大河村采果、回水塘避暑、上寨新农村风貌、独山布依风情和永兴知青文化等乡村游活动。

2008年，全县开办起折溪、滨江、大河、大屯、独山、上寨、大堡、回水等8个乡村旅游接待点，70个农家乐接待站，31家农家旅舍，接待乡村游客45万人次，收入4500万元。2010年，全县乡村旅游接待点增为9个，收入5820万元。

专记：火爆的大河村农家乐接待站

2000年，扎佐镇党委和镇政府落实县委、县政府大力调整农业产业结构的战略措施，在坐落在镇东南依山傍水的大河村组织村民发展产值高的经果林，种植艳红桃、葡萄和糖梨13.6万亩，果熟季节果园地头飘香，果农腰包鼓胀。

2005年，桃源河峡谷漂流开始营运，带来大河村新的发展生机，使前往漂流的游客路过大河村都要留步歇脚。2006年的一天，一位游客带领全家进到村党支部书记徐若家果园里采摘艳红桃，向徐若打听道：“你家有饭吃没有？”徐若答：“有”。随即与家人做一桌农家饭菜请游客进餐，客人赞美饭菜可口。徐若因此得到启发，便产生办“农家乐”的念头。于是，“缘缘农家乐”欣然应市。半年时间，徐若接待游客4000人，创收6万元。2007年，光临徐家果园摘果、就餐的游人络绎不绝，徐若便投入资金美化庭院环境，拓展经营规模，办起“住农家屋、吃农家饭、品农家菜、观农家景、享农家乐”的一条龙服务，旅舍每天每人包吃包住收费60元，8个房间入住率在95%以上，周末，节假日还需提前预约。在徐若的带动下，全村相继办起经县旅游部门注册备案、挂牌经营的农家乐接待站10个，成为县内外知名的乡村旅游点。镇党委书记刘元珍深入村里要求农家乐接待站服务人员改善服务态度，提升服务质量，更新经营理念，按照新农村建设的要求办好农家乐。在县旅游局和镇党委的组织下，大河村的农家乐接待站越发兴旺，成为县旅游业的重要增长

大河农家乐

点，为大河农民开辟出一条有效的增收途径，使村里300名村民靠山吃山，就地创业，年创收达40万元之巨。2009年，全村农家乐接待收入上升为513.58万元。2010年达1594万元。村民周春菊直言："旺季的农家乐，每天都有7至8桌外地游客到我家吃饭，光是这项每天就可以收入500—600元。"到村民吴学明果园里采摘葡萄的游客不断，每斤葡萄售价2.5元，年收入3万至4万元。一位来自重庆游客刘伦明高兴的说："我们来这里既避暑、游玩，又享受采农家果、干农家活、吃农家饭、交农家友的喜悦"。一位息烽游客何德利深有感受地说："我是朋友介绍来的，这里山清水秀，乡风纯朴，进入园区既能品尝鲜果，又可享受村游之乐，使我感到物有所值"。

第四节　旅游服务

一、旅游企业

旅游公司　1984年8月，县成立旅游公司，为局级国营企业。县财政划拨经费，购置大客车2辆，设置经营门市部，负责办理县内旅游景区前期开发事宜。后因资金短缺，开发工作搁浅，于1987年4月撤销公司。1996年8月，经县政府批准，县旅游局制发修旅字〔1996〕1号文件成立阳明风景旅游综合开发服务中心，旅游局副局长何小萍兼任中心经理，租用办公地点，以阳明酒家为经营基地，招用员工23人，启动餐饮、客房作为旅游宣传服务窗口。1999年县工商行政管理局根据工商管理规定吊销"中心"营业执照，公司停止经营。到2006年，先后引进香港英皇和广东揭阳金华联营开发贵阳高尔夫度假中心，创办集康乐、健体、娱乐、避暑、度假为一体的综合性旅游公司；贵州省公路工程公司创办六广河峡谷旅游开发有限公司经营六广河码头及峡谷旅游；贵阳野生旅游开发有限公司开发贵州扎佐森林野生动物园；贵州神州漂流有限公司开发桃源河生态旅游区；贵阳黔秀农业开发有限公司开发苏格兰风情牧场生态旅游；修文县珍珠岛饮食娱乐有限责任公司经营珍珠岛避暑休闲旅游。2007年又引进贵州阳明国兰文化发展有限公司，2009年，启动开发建设的阳明兰花生态旅游区，各公司为独立的企业管理运行机构，均在贵阳市区设立旅游办事处。2010年各公司共接待游客149.16万人次，旅游收入3.68亿元。

2010年主要旅游公司（景区）运营情况一览表

表3—07—05

旅游景区、旅游公司名称	接待游客人（万人次）	服务收入（万元）
阳明洞景区（县文广旅游局）	6.16	492.976
六广河峡谷旅游开发公司	10.24	2046.52
贵阳野生旅游开发公司	83.68	18410.19
贵阳高尔夫度假中心	7.37	4421.88
贵州神州漂流有限公司	20.88	5221.05
珍珠岛饮食如乐有限公司	8.99	2699.34
贵阳黔秀农业开发有限公司（苏格兰风情牧场）	11.84	3551.7

旅行社 1998年5月起，自贵阳高尔夫旅行社成立后，中国旅行社、美嘉旅行社、海外旅行社、原野旅行社先后在县城设立办事处，经营到云南大理、丽江，广西桂林、北海，四川成都、九寨沟，西安、华山、华清池，华东五市以及贵州省内黄果树、天星桥、龙宫，荔波，剑河等多条线路旅游业务，组织城乡居民外出旅游。2009年，贵州百事通旅行社有限公司在县城设立营业网点。

2010年2月，贵州多彩旅行社有限责任公司在县城文广大楼设立修文分社，开展国内旅游、出境旅游和咨询服务。以逛上海、瞻古都、游山水、赏名园、玩绍兴、登黄山为主要景区，开展北海、南京双飞五日团体游，厦门、鼓浪屿双飞五日团体游和省内黄果树、天星桥、龙宫一日游，花溪、天河潭、青岩古镇一日游，遵义会议会址、息烽集中营一日游，天龙山、天龙屯堡、红枫湖一日游等。到年底，全县有1家旅行社和13家旅行社营业点开展接待旅游团体，组织市民外出旅游代售机票以及会议接待服务。

二、旅游线路

1996年6月，经贵阳市旅游组织评审，将修文旅游评为“1个旅游区”和2条旅游线，即阳明风景文化旅游区和贵阳—阳明洞—三潮水—三人坟—天生桥峡谷—贵阳、贵阳—六广河峡谷—息烽温泉—贵阳旅游线。

2005年又形成4条旅游线路：

——贵阳（遵义、毕节）至修文阳明洞、玩易窝、三潮水、梨花湖、三人坟、古驿道、天生桥、蜈蚣桥线。沿线游览阳明文化、奢香文化、绿色园艺。

——贵阳（遵义、毕节）至修文猫跳河三、四、五、六级电站以及索风营电站、绿色石林、六广七峡、乌江水坝线。沿线观览水电坝型博览馆、岩溶石林、典型喀斯特地质遗址。

——贵阳（遵义、毕节）至扎佐高尔夫度假中心、野生动物园、景阳森林公园、桃源河生态漂流线。沿线享受康体、娱乐、观光、避暑游。

——贵阳（遵义、毕节）至久长珍珠岛避暑中心、唐人山庄、知青文化村、苏格兰风情牧场线。沿线参与生态观光、避暑、康乐、休闲、农家乐等活动。

2007年5月，建成对外开放的6个旅游景区，根据景区特点和交通情况，县旅游局推出一日游，二日游和三日游的旅游线路。

一日游：

A线贵阳（遵义、毕节）至扎佐高尔夫度假中心、野生动物园。

B线贵阳（遵义、毕节）至六广七峡、绿色石林。

C线贵阳（遵义、毕节）至六屯桃源河峡谷魔幻漂流。

D线贵阳（遵义、毕节）至修文阳明洞、玩易窝、三潮水。

E线贵阳（遵义、毕节）至野生动物园、苏格兰牧场。

二日游：

A线贵阳（遵义、毕节）至扎佐高尔夫、野生动物园、桃源河漂流。

B线贵阳（遵义、毕节）至六广七峡、绿色石林、高尔夫度假中心、野生动物园。

C线贵阳（遵义、毕节）至阳明洞、野生动物园、桃源河峡谷魔幻漂流、苏格兰牧场。

D线贵阳（遵义、毕节）至阳明洞、野生动物园、珍珠岛避暑中心。

三日游：

A线贵阳（遵义、毕节）至六广七峡、绿色石林、阳明洞、高尔夫度假中心、野生动物园、桃源河魔幻漂流、苏格兰牧场。

B线贵阳（遵义、毕节）至六广七峡、绿色石林、阳明洞、高尔夫度假中心、野生动物园、珍珠岛避暑中心、苏格兰牧场。

C线、贵阳（遵义、毕节）至阳明洞、猫跳河、高尔夫度假中心、野生动物园、桃源河魔幻漂流、苏格兰牧场

三、旅游推介

1996年起，县委、县政府分别组织县政协、县委宣传部、旅游局、文化局、文联、地方志办公室、修文报社和邮政局编纂各类书刊和制作音像推介修文旅游。随后又与旅游企业和景区共同举办各类旅游活动进行宣传推介，吸引游客。到2010年已采取书刊文本、音像制品、旅游节庆、旅游赛事和承办旅游产业会等多种形式，提升修文旅游的知名度和影响力，成为开发利用旅游资源开展旅游服务，发展旅游产业的重要举措。

书刊 1996到2010年，分别制作《阳明风景名胜区》《优越的区位·迷人的资源》《修文旅游》《城乡和谐游·欢乐在修文》《爽爽贵阳·生态修文》等旅游景区景点折页共13.5万册。编辑《贵州旅游时尚》“王学圣地，秀美修文”专刊，印刷《王学圣地·秀美修文》宣传册300册，制作《爽爽贵阳·生态修文》旅游景区宣传台历4000册，编辑《六广河诗词楹联集锦》《贵州旅游文史系列众书》修文券《阳明胜境》《阳明先生故事集》《王阳明在龙场》《修文名胜风光诗文选》《阳明学术研讨会论文提要汇编》书刊，以及《秀美修文·心向往的地方》邮资明信片文化册。与此同时，县委书记魏明禄主编《王学圣地》展示修文名胜、历史人文、阳明文化、山水诗情和民情风物；贵阳市委宣传部组织市、县共同编纂《王学之旅》推介阳明文化、古驿站道、山水洞瀑和民族风情，由贵州民族出版社出版。其书刊文本、宣传折页和明信文化册除在各景区景点散发给游客，赠送给嘉宾外，又发至贵阳市各旅行社及遵义、毕节和重庆等地，并在“2010年中国国际旅游交易会”和“2010年中国重庆城际旅游国际交易会”向省内外发放推介。

音像制品 1997年，除由贵州电视台国际部在修文拍摄的“贵州旅游风光”专题片，在省电视台播放外，还参加在大连举办的全国旅游博览会展播。县电视台与贵州省电视台合拍的“修文之旅”专题风光片，先后在全国16个大中城市滚动播放。1999年，制作“修文风光”光碟500张在“中国贵阳99阳明文化节”作为礼品赠送给嘉宾。2009年，制作歌颂修文自然风光及旅游景区的歌曲专辑《修文风》和创作的《秀美的修文·神奇的地方》音像制品，在“2009中国贵阳避暑季暨中国国际阳明文化节”赠予嘉宾。

宣传展览 1997年，县委、县政府与贵州摄影家协会联合举办“贵州修文阳明风光摄影赛”拍摄修文旅游景观，其优秀作品80余幅在省影协会展出，又与贵州华联集团有限公司在贵阳市中华路等处连续展出一周。当年县旅游局参加香港旅游促销会和中国昆明国际旅游交易会，发放宣传资料2000份。1999年，县旅游局投入资金10万元，制作旅游风光大型宣传广告牌和景区（点）示意图版16块，展示修文风光。2004年，分别在“贵阳·修文2004梨花节”“贵阳市第八届中国国际风筝节”以及在重庆市举办的“森林之城——贵阳联盟贵州黄金旅游线清凉夏季游”，展出修文旅游展板和喷绘广告。

2007年3月和2009年4月，县内旅游企业组织旅游促销团，分别参加贵阳市旅游局组织的“2007年首届（贵阳）避暑季——乡村体验游启动仪式”“贵州人游贵阳”宣传展销活动，共发放宣传资料4万册。

四、节庆赛事

阳明文化节　1999年10月，由贵阳市委、市政府、贵州省文化厅和国际儒学联合会主办，县委、县政府承办的首届“中国贵阳99阳明文化节”在县城举办，历时3天。节日期间举行由300名文艺工作者演出的大型文艺节目“圣地·热土”。大型展览“王阳明在贵州”“王阳明谪黔遗址”以及书画展，举办“阳明遗迹景点游”，迎来中外嘉宾2000人。2002年10月第二届阳明文化节举办阳明学术研讨会、阳明遗迹寻访游、阳明祭祀、圣地迎宾演出，龙岗秋韵书画展。除迎来中外游客外，还在此举办世界旅游小姐年度皇后大赛中国赛区总决赛，24名佳丽莅临阳明洞传播旅游文化。2005年9月，第三届阳明文化节举办《良知与和谐社会》高端论坛，有10多个国家和地区学者180余人参加，迎来扮演中国革命领导人著名影星王琪、王伍福、郭连文、刘劲和卢奇到场献光，使游客达到5.6万人次。2009年5月，第四届阳明文化节在阳明主题公园举行开幕式，将本届阳明文化节中国·贵阳避暑季活动结合举办，是阳明文化与旅游有机结合在修文旅游的创举。花儿乐队和美丽音符女子乐团前来助兴，迎来游客数以万计。

2005年，第三届阳明文化节开幕现场

梨花节　2004年4月，县政府主持在谷堡乡折溪村的梨花湖畔举办首届梨花节，吸引数以千计的游客到万亩梨园赏花拍照，使梨花湖名扬县内外，打造出谷堡乡金秋梨品牌，推进折溪村乡村旅游的发展。随后在2005年4月、2006年4月、2008年4月、2009年3月，分别举办二、三、四、五届梨花节。在举办第五届梨花节时，节日前组委会组织召开有新华社、中央人民广播电台、贵州人民广播电台、贵州电视台、贵州日报、贵州都市报、贵阳人民广播电台、贵阳电视台、《贵阳日报》《贵阳晚报》《文汇报》、金阳时讯、金黔在线网、当代修文和修文电视台等15家媒体参加新闻发布会，使梨花湖游客达4万人次，极大地推介修文的旅游。

桃源河漂流节　2007年6月，由县政府、贵阳市旅游局、贵阳市体育局联合主办，贵阳修文神州漂流有限公司承办首届桃源河漂流节，有200名漂流爱好者参加漂流竞技，举办“徒步溯溪竞走”，把旅游与体育结合起来，吸引大量游客到桃源河景区。2008年7月，“2008中国·贵阳避暑季之修文桃源河魔幻漂流及峡谷冲浪大赛”和“多彩贵州歌唱大赛修文赛区决赛”在桃源河景区举行，成为人无我有的“中国魔幻漂流”“桃源河峡谷冲浪”的品牌，增添漂流节的内容，有来自贵阳、遵义、重庆的200名漂流爱好者和26名多彩贵州歌唱大赛选手参加活动，吸引游客数以千计观看。2009年6月，举办“贵阳（修文）第二届漂流节暨2009桃源河魔幻漂流大赛”。节日期间还举办漂流爱好者参加的“铁人三项”漂流赛，游客参加“家庭冲浪擒鸭”趣味赛，迎来游客5000人。

六广河杯摄影赛 2008年8月，贵州省摄影家协会、贵阳市旅游产业发展委员会和县委、县政府和六广河旅游公司主办的贵州省“六广河杯”摄影大赛在六广河景区举办，摄影爱好者登上游船手举相机，用镜头捕捉六广河峡谷美景，展示六广河风光，吸引大批摄影爱好者和游客参加，为六广河景区的旅游宣传、推介起到积极的作用。

旅游产业发展大会 2009年5月，贵阳市委、市政府主办、市旅游局、县政府承办的“贵阳市第三届旅游产业发展大会”在贵阳森林野生动物园举行。大会贯彻落实贵州省委、省政府关于加快旅游产业发展的重要举措，不仅把修文旅游推介出去，为建成以阳明文化旅游为核心集文化、康体、休闲、生态游为一体的旅游产业起到积极推动作用，使修文旅游上一个新的台阶。

六广河杯大力士赛 2009年8月，由贵阳市旅游局、县政府主办，县旅游局、六广河旅游公司承办的“六广河杯大力士赛”在六广河景区举办，有来自全国各地100名选手参加“大力士拖车”“手掷啤酒瓶”“翻运大轮胎”的角逐，游客参加老公背老婆、拔河、极限等趣味性比赛，聚集来自全国各地游客数千人。活动持续14天，拉动人气，增加旅游收入，为六广河旅游推介起到轰动效应。

“六广河杯”大力士比赛

五、旅游商品

食品 1992年，县移民办下属库区经济开发公司，利用山地野果创办野珍食品工业生产厂，生产野珍食品系列产品玫瑰牛肉干、山珍果、小米酢、精三蛋茗酥等，获1994年贵州食品荟萃产品最受欢迎品奖，推向旅游食品市场。2000年，联宇食品有限公司生产油辣椒、风味萝卜干、风味蕨菜、风味竹笋纳入“绿色食品”系列，是国际阳明文化节指定的旅游商品，颇受游客青睐，企业获准为贵阳旅游食品定点生产企业。2002年，贵阳三茗食品厂利用县内丰富独特的猕猴桃果，生产低糖猕猴桃果脯，打入旅游市场。落户在扎佐食品工业园的“扎佐蹄膀”批量生产，誉为“十里飘香，肉食之王”，被指定为2005年国际阳明文化节专用礼品，并列为贵阳市非物质文化遗产。

2009年，随着县旅游业的发展，县内养殖企业看到旅游市场销售旅游商品的商机，将养殖的禽、兔及蛋加工包装进入旅游商品市场。其中，贵州兰地实业有限公司生产加工的灵芝低胆固醇鲜蛋、卤香鸡肉，修文盛鑫兔业有限公司生产加工的“兔大哥”有机系列产品，包装精美、携带方便，成为旅游者购买馈赠亲朋好友的礼物。2010年，贵阳三金圣果有限公司生产的“猕露”牌系列富硒猕猴桃饮料，由贵阳市第三届旅游发展大会指定为大会饮品，推向旅游市场。

水果 1981年，小箐乡郭田村寻找致富路子，利用本地特色酥李果大核小、色泽艳丽、入口酥脆、风味甜香、饱满圆润的特点和具有去解郁毒、活血生津引饮、祛痰利尿、润肠通气之功能，属“肝病宜食之果”，有“黔中第一李”之称的郭田酥李，规划种植1.2万株，面积300亩。每年5月底开始上市，六七月份酥李大量入市供游客购买。1998年，乡政府组办郭田酥李节，有贵阳、白云、修文水果经营商300多人云集郭田，洽谈酥李购销，产品打入贵阳市水果批发市场。2005年全乡种植酥李4000多亩，年产100万公斤，产值达300万元。郭田酥李竟成为小箐乡特色产品支柱进入旅游市场。

1984年，桃源乡村民宋聚熙、宋致焕等在树林砍伐一空、坡陡土软的山坡上，引资建起柑橘基地，种温州蜜橘350亩，5.3万株。20世纪90年代初蜜橘年产5万公斤。2005年柑橘基地依托桃源河峡谷风景区旅游的开发，推出游客进园观景采橘活动，使蜜橘成为旅游商品售量大增，是年销售收入10万元。

1991年，谷堡乡红星村村民在村党支部书记黄国祥带领下，创办“谷堡红星农场”，带动全乡种板栗1400亩、猕猴桃6300亩、金秋梨2000亩、桃子3000亩和美国布郎李5000亩。1999年，猕猴桃鲜果注册“六广河”牌商标，作为旅游商品进行开发。2000年，省农业厅授予“六广河”猕猴桃“贵州省优质农产品”称号，销往广州、深圳、北京、上海、长春、吉林、重庆等地。2004年，谷堡乡“金秋梨”吸引四方游客游园观赏、实地购梨成为游客馈赠亲友的必带礼品，全乡果品销售收入140万元。

1999年，扎佐镇大河村种艳红桃1500亩。成熟艳红桃肉质细腻，香脆可口。每至夏末秋初，前来扎佐高尔夫度假者、野生动物园参观者和到桃源河源漂流者均进果园采摘购买。

药品　2000年开发建设的贵州修文医药产业园拥有17家制药企业，其中维康药业“骨康灵”，天方药业“杜仲颗粒”，同济堂药业“仙骨灵葆”等均属贵州野生动植物资源研制的康体保健苗药产品，具有“千年苗医，万年苗药”之誉，成为旅游者选购向亲友送健康的礼品。

贵州绿太阳药业生产的“日晒防治膏”、“磁疗祛斑按摩乳”、“葆肤康软膏”等远销加拿大、捷克、荷兰、俄罗斯、东南亚及中国香港、澳门地区。其中“日晒防治膏”是指定的旅游专用医药产品，“磁疗祛斑按摩乳”和“葆肤康软膏”是中国民族医药协会推荐的旅游用品，可预防夏季强烈阳光紫外线热辐射灼伤，是夏季旅游，游泳、户外活动、防暑最佳护肤品，成为主要旅游景区（点）设专柜销售的商品。

工艺品　2004年9月，利用龙场镇红板桥美人峰下传说是伏羲老祖化身的巨石“石老人”命名的贵州修文石老人旅游工艺品经营部，位于县城迎春路，专门经营县境内旅游工艺品：雕刻、刺绣、贴烙、卡通玩具、纺织、腊画、竹器。

2007年3月，建在六屯乡独山村的修文牂舸旅游工艺品厂，通过招商从贵阳市小河区迁入独山，依托桃源河峡谷风景和独山布依风情开发山水花鸟，布依风情激光皮雕，竹雕、蛋壳画、沙画等旅游商品。2009年，黔府发〔2009〕30号文和筑府发〔2009〕72号文将龙场镇平地、六桶乡黄金村的苗族服装制作工艺列为省、市非物质文化遗产，参加省、市旅游商品设计比赛，增添县内旅游商品开发的种类。

纺织工艺品销售

花卉盆景　1999年起，久长镇建旅游休闲、苗木花卉科技型公司顺兴莞园艺场，植木本花卉50多种，培植盆景1万多盆。谷堡乡场坝村张显明建占地12亩盆景培育场，植盆景万盆，大塘村张峰建20个占地75亩的花卉大棚。

2002年，国际阳明文化节举办花卉盆景展，游客参观络绎不绝。同时参加贵阳市花卉盆景展和贵阳白云区风筝节花卉盆景展活动，推出修文花卉盆景佳品，获得金、银、铜奖，自此花卉盆景走上旅游商品市场。时至2010年，每逢星期六、星期日都有外地游客光临县城花卉市场，挑选修文独特的“火辣”“黄秧”“水杉”等盆景。

第五节　旅游管理

一、管理机构

1996年成立县旅游局，负责对全县旅游规划和旅游资源开发的协调服务工作，并根据县政府的安排编制出《修文县旅游经济发展“九五”计划》。随着高尔夫度假中心的球场和宾馆以及六广河旅游公司的码头宾馆建成营运，旅游局的工作开始由协调服务转入旅游行业管理。2002年，县政府以修府办通〔2002〕37号文明确旅游局为全县旅游业管理机构和具体的职责职能，旅游局根据其管理职责职能对旅游景区和旅游企业行使行政管理，开展对景区的等级评定、申报，协助景区建设提升景区档次，履行旅游市场监管，负责旅游安全、旅游经营秩序和旅游投诉等方面的管理。

2007年，为适应全县旅游业发展需要，加强对旅游服务质量的管理，县政府以修编制〔2007〕17号文成立“旅游质量监督管理所”，行使旅游行政执法，净化旅游环境，使旅游的服务质量得以提高。

二、市场管理

2007年，县旅游局和旅游质量监督管理所在全县各旅游景区和宾馆酒店设置旅游投诉电话，接受游客的监督，制定《旅游质量监督检查制度》尤其是对旅游黄金周的检查监督执法加强管理力度；制定《旅游投诉管理处置制度》由专人进行投诉调查、核实和取证，帮助游客处理解决投诉的问题，使游客乐意接受；制定《旅行社管理制度》加强旅行社经营准入验证的管理，并配合贵阳市旅游局开展打击黑旅行社、黑导游、黑旅游交通车辆的非法经营，杜绝骗客、宰客、拉客等情况的发生。

2009年9月，县政府成立以县旅游局为主的县整顿和规范旅游市场秩序专项行动领导小组，由文化广播局、工商行政管理局、物价局、城乡建设局、卫生局、公安局和县委宣传部配合，集中力量开展对旅游企业、景区整顿和规范旅游市场秩序的专项行动，使旅游企业遵守市场秩序，根据自己经营类型和范围分别制定企业内部管理制度，以达到自我调节、自我约束、自我管理、自我发展。到2010年年底，全县受理旅游投诉累计40起，经过协调解决，处理率和游客满意率为100%，既维护游客的合法权利，又保障旅游企业的合法利益，树立起良好的修文旅游形象。

三、经营管理

从1996年开始开发建设旅游景区，至2008年，组建起旅游经营公司6个，后因景区宣传推介不力，公司各自为战，旅游未形成互动，旅游人数较少，未达预期效应。2008年，为打破旅游滞后的局面，县旅游局经过调查研究，找到解决问题的突破口，引导企业转变经营观念，采取多种形式的经营方式，使旅游形成一条线，连成一片，互动发展。

（一）发放旅游代金券

2008年，县旅游局配合森林野生动物园以回馈方式，推出面值80元代替100元的旅游代金券30万张，使野生动物园游客爆满，日最大接待游客量达4万人次。2009年，动物园抓住举办“2009年中国·贵阳避暑季”、“中国·贵阳（修文）第四届国际阳明文化节”和“中国·贵阳第三届旅游发展大会”的机会，又发放面值70元代金券20万张。六广河旅游公司发放面值80元代替110元旅游代金券50万张，游客只需补30元既可游览六广河峡谷风景，又可就餐吃六广鲢鱼，观看民族风情表演，参加篝火晚会。与此同时，贵阳市政府为推动全市旅游业发展，印制面值30元旅游代金券，县旅游局获4000张，发放给动物园和桃源河景区。通过代金券发放两景区游客数量大增。2010年，六广河旅游公司又推出面值70元一日游消费券和当年高考学生全免费游优待券，收到极大的旅游宣传效应。

（二）实行折价销售

2006—2008年，森林野生动物园游览门票由物价部门核定为100元。2009年，根据市、县旅游局文件精神，实行折价销售，以6折定门票价格为60元。同时贵阳市政府推出旅游打折优惠卡，将野生动物园、桃源河魔幻漂流列入打折卡之列，其中动物园凭卡5折优惠，桃源河漂流凭卡8折优惠。门票打折销售使动物园游客成倍增加，当年门票收入达2000万元，实现企业扭亏为盈。桃源河魔幻漂流迎来游客20万人次，营业收入突破5000万元。随着珍珠岛避暑中心推出住宿打5折优惠，并免费提供各种球类活动和健身活动的场所设施，把游客留住，接待达7.5万人次，企业收入大增。2010年，野生动物园将门票打8折优惠，直接调为80元，使景区游客持续增长，全年接待游客达80万人次。

（三）采取错峰通票

2009年，县政府为迎接2009年中国·贵阳避暑季、中国·贵阳（修文）第四届国际阳明文化节和中国·贵阳第三届旅游发展大会的举办，采取措施加强对旅游的经营管理，由旅游局牵头，组织旅游企业成立“旅游行业互动组”相互配合，促使旅游资源整合和互动。其中桃源河景区为缓解高峰期压力采取错峰通票方式把节假日和周末游客分散，实行周末和节假日期间全价经营，周一至周五原价225元降为125元的低价位漂流、冲浪和乘坐观光车的通票，不仅减轻景区高峰期的压力，使游客数量稳步上升，又把外地到桃源河漂流的游客先分流到其他景区游览然后进行漂流，从而收到旅游互动的效果。

四、安全管理

县旅游局根据旅游行业管理的规定，分别对景区、星级宾馆酒店进行安全管理，包括旅游交通运输、旅游设施、消防、食品卫生等方面，分别与景区旅游企业、宾馆服务单位签订旅游安全目标责任书，明确责任人；与消防、交通、海监、城管、安监和卫生等部门联合开展“全国安全月宣传活动”，出动执法车巡查，并采取积极有效的措施：一是开展综合治理，加强对旅游景区和宾馆酒楼的用电、消防、游乐设备、食品卫生和废弃物的管理，设立安全监控网，配备救生器材，厨房食品生、熟分离，设置安全通道及标志，防火禁烟标志，悬挂安全防范宣传标语，加强节假日高峰期值班护卫；二是加强安全防范，对旅游企业的游乐场，旅游水上航道和漂流船等设施的操作，向维护人员进行安全意识教育，提高熟练操作设备和应对突发事故的处理能力，树立安全责任感；三是建立长效机制，成立县旅游安全工作领导小组，明确安全管理的责任人，制定《修文县旅游系统突发事件应急预案》和旅游安全检查措施，包括行业检查、联合检查时间上采取定期、不定期、临时等形式。至2010年年底，旅游景区和宾馆酒店实现杜绝安全隐患的目标，未发生旅游安全责任事故，县旅游局获得安全生产目标考核先进单位称号，有力地保障游客和企业生命财产的安全。

第八章　金　融

1978年，全县有金融业务机构43个，年末存款余额1044万元，贷款余额1680万元。从1980年起对金融业进行一系列的改革，至2010年，仍存人行、银监办及工商银行、农业银行、农业发展银行、邮政储蓄银行、商业银行、农村信用合作社联合社；有经营金融业务机构26个，年末银行存款余额27.73亿元和贷款余额19.31亿元，在1978年的基础上分别翻7.6番和6.5番。

保险业于1981年恢复，1996年改制， 2010年保费收入从1986年的27万元增至3730万元，理赔支出由1986年的10万元增至668万元，分别翻7.3番和6.1番。

第一节　体制改革

改革开放33年间的金融业改革，将人行剥离出来成为独立国家银行，银监办专司金融监管职能，各专业银行改制为国有商业银行，合作金融逐步健全并迅速扩大，形成以中央银行为领导，国家银行为主体，与其他金融机构并存的金融体系。

一、机构改革

（一）管理机构独立

人民银行县支行　1978年，县人民银行沿袭原有建制，领属13个基层机构，负责掌管货币发行，调节货币流通，管理信贷资金和金融市场，经营信贷和储蓄，代理财政金库等业务，隶属人行安顺地区分行。办公地址在县城健康路（今翠屏西路）。1980年1月，将支行农村金融干部及其农金业务和5个区驻地业务机构移交给中国农业银行县支行经营，农村信用社亦随之转隶县农行管理。

1990年建成的人民银行县支行办公楼

1984年1月执行中国人民银行“县级不设人民

银行”的决定，支行及下属9个基层机构全部划属中国工商银行县支行，采取一个机构、两块牌子、资金分开、两套账目过渡的办法，分别核算人、工两行业务。至此，人民银行终止对外经营城镇工商信贷和储蓄业务。

1986年9月1日县人行独立，专门行使以金融管理为职责的中央银行职能，加强信贷资金集中管理和综合平衡。原在县工行专办人行业务的杨晓莉等5人跟随业务转入。1990年8月，人行迁人民南路18号新建办公楼办公。1996年1月随县划归贵阳市管辖，改隶人行贵阳市分行。次年1月起代管农村信用合作联社。3月成立农村合作金融监督管理科，专司农合行业管理与监督。1998年前获得县级和省级“文明单位”殊荣后，1999—2010年继续坚持群创群建业绩突出，成绩斐然，连续荣获中国人民银行“文明单位”荣誉。12年间，该行先后获得中国人民银行先进集体、先进基层党组织、“五四”红旗团支部和全国金融“五一劳动奖章”、全国模范职工小家及贵州省2人先锋号各1次，涌现出县级以上先进个人41人次，其中王华获2001年中国人民银行“优秀团干部”称号，蒋丽萍分别获得2001年、2003年、2005年人民银行贵阳中心支行、成都分行和总行“青年岗位能手”称号。至2010年行内置3股1室，职工23人，配正、副行长和纪检组长各1人。

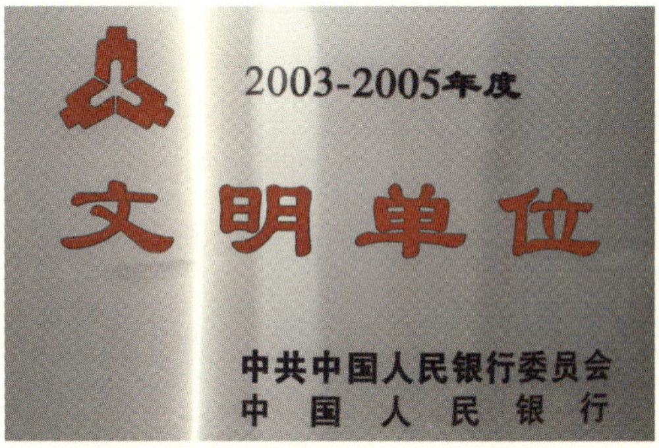

人民银行县支行获得的文明单位奖牌

银监办事处 2003年中国金融监管体制进行改革，实行银行、保险、证卷分业经营、分业监管。银行业由国务院成立中国银行业监督管理委员会（简称“中国银监会”），省、县相应设置监管局、监管办事处。12月23日，县银行的业主要监督管理职能从人民银行析出，在人行五楼成立中国银行业监督管理委员会贵州省监管局修文办事处（简称“银监办”），直属贵州监管局，原负责监管工作的4人同时划转，负责监管辖区内银行业金融机构市场准入、高管任职、风险评级等，并本着中国银监会管法人、管风险、管内控，提高透明度的监管宗旨，寓监管于服务之中。至2010年银监办仍存，人员未变，配主任1人。

（二）政策性银行分置

1997年2月，县农业银行原代理的农村政策性金融业务并20名业务人员析出，成立中国农业发展银行修文县支行，隶属中国农业发展银行贵州省分行，专司国家规定的农村政策性金融业务，并代理财政性支农资金拨付。支行建立后，在县城河滨路自建办公楼独立办公。至2010年，行内置有会计股和信贷股分别办理业务，共有职工13人，配正副行长各1人。

位于县城河滨路的农业发展银行县支行办公楼

（三）专业银行改制

1980年起，县建设银行、农业银行及后置的建行扎佐专业支行和猫冲专业支行均称为专业银行，共有对外服务机构22个。1984年执行国务院关于专业银行改制为商业银行的决定，专业银行即向商业银行转轨，以总行为独立核算单位，以效益性、安全性和流动性为经营原则，实行自主经营，自担风险，自负盈亏，自我约束，并以其全部法人财产独立承担民事责任。2004年起再由国有独资的商业银行改制为国家控股商业银行，2010年县工商银行、农业银行及农行下属的扎佐营业所仍存，共有职工58人。

建行县支行 1978年沿袭支行建制，办公地点在县城人民南路。下属猫冲办事处，共有职工8人。负责基本建设拨款监督。1980年改革，由单一财政监督职能转为财政监督和银行服务双重职能。同时增设扎佐办事处。次年为加强基本建设资金管理，将扎佐办事处升格为专业支行，隶属建行安顺地区中心支行，猫冲办事处升格为专业支行由县支行代管。1984年7月，扎佐专业支行复为办事处，猫冲专业支行撤销，业务并入县支行。8月，人员由县管转为系统管理，向商业银行转轨。1988年始办现金收付和储蓄业务，陆续增设服务机构。1990年在人民南路从原址迁入新建办公楼办公，始设营业厅对外服务。1992年受县政府委托独家办理住房改革金融业务，至1995年内设5个职能机构，下属4个基层处（所），有职工53人。

1996年1月随县划归贵阳市管辖，县支行改隶建行贵阳市分行，3月26日行名由原中国人民建设银行修文县支行改为中国建设银行修文县支行。1999年7月机构改革划归省分行营业部。2000年7月划属金阳支行，2003年4月改隶省分行。并由人民南路迁迎春路和翠屏路交汇处新址办公。

2004年建行率先实行股份制改革，改称中国建设银行股份有限公司修文县支行，机构收缩，人员实行竞聘上岗，扎佐办事处异地搬迁并入乌当支行改为五〇一办事处。2005年9月县支行撤销并入金阳支行，储蓄存款和住房公积金业务分别移交县农村信用联社和贵阳市商业银行县支行接办，在职正式职工1人和储蓄员4人随业务调到县农村信用合作联社，其余人员划转金阳支行。退（离）休（含内退）人员统一划归省分行管理。至2010年未变动。

农行县支行 1979年12月，根据国务院《关于恢复中国农业银行的通知》精神，将原县人行农金业务和经办人员及下辖5个区营业所划入恢复农业银行，支行内设6个股（室），职工63人，作为经营农村金融及储蓄业务的专业银行，领导农村信用社，隶属农业银行安顺地区中心支行。办公地点置于县城人民南路。1984年起逐步向商业银行转制，人员收归系统管理。1994年代办农村政策性金融业务。1996年1月改隶农业银行贵阳市分行，机构收缩，人员精减，2009年1月实行股份制改革，挂牌为中国农业银行股份有限公司修文县支行，职工竞聘上岗。至2010年，仅存县支行及扎佐营业所，支行内置2部，年末职工45人，配有行长1人、副行长2人。

县城人民南路农业银行股份有限公司县支行办公楼

工行县支行 1984年1月，根据国务院《关于建立中国工商银行的决定》，接收原县人行建制，内设6股1室，下辖11个基层处（所），职工86人由系统管理，办理工商信贷和储蓄业务，代办县人行委托现金管理、工资基金管理和管理流动资金业务，隶属工商银行安顺地区中心支行。办公地址在县城健康路（今翠屏西路）。1986年9月县人行委托业务终止。1996年1月改隶工商银行贵阳市分行，8月进行机构改革，收缩机构，将18个正副科级（原称“股级”）干部精减为7人。2002年6月再次改革，人员由56人减为35人，实行全员竞聘。2005年实行股份制改革，10月改称中国工商银行股份有限公司修文县支行。由于机构向城市收缩，业务量下降。2007年1月，保留原机构和行名，内部降格为白云支行下属机构。

2010年仅有机构1个，职工13人，配负责人1名主持全行工作。

（四）邮政储蓄银行建立

1987年下半年，县邮电局根据主管局部署在营业厅增设储蓄柜办理储蓄业务，执行金融法规，接受县人行管理。继后，县城、扎佐、久长分别增设储蓄点，加上局本部共4个营业机构。同时办理小额质押贷款业务。2008年随全国邮政储蓄银行建立，由国家邮政总局全资控股，6月6日省邮政局下文通知改置为中国邮政储蓄银行有限责任公司修文县人民南路支行，由邮政储蓄局领导分别担任行长和副行长，隶属邮政储蓄贵阳市分行，地址设于县城人民南路。至2010年，全行有服务机构4个，职工17人，其中行领导2人。

（五）合作金融变革

农村信用合作联社　1978年沿袭28个社（镇）农村信用合作社建制，职工共68人，经营农民储蓄和部分农业存款、贷款业务，隶属县人民银行。1980年1月改隶县农业银行。1984年9月从农行析出农村信贷业务，建立县农村信用合作社联合社，办公地点在人民南路农行县支行内，民主选举产生理事会和监事会，由县农行副行长、行长分别担任理、监事会主任。1987年在5个区和边远的六桶乡置中心社，领导各管辖片区的基层社。1988年监事会主任改由县政府分管副县长担任，人行副行长、农行行长任监事会副主任。1992年1月，按县改建的10乡（镇）各置基层社，并随业务扩大增加网点。

2002年4月县联社迁迎春路揭牌仪式

1997年1月，县信用联社与县农行脱离隶属关系，划归县人民银行代管，成为由农民入股、社员民主管理、主要为入股社员服务的合作金融组织，依法自主经营，自负盈亏，自担风险，自我约束。2002年办公地点迁迎春路。2004年改隶省联社贵阳办事处。2005年对联社中层干部和基层社领导由任命改为聘任，法人统一，以县联社为股份制核算单位，结束基层社独立核算的历史。

2009年5月25日，贵州省联社党委下达黔农信党干任2号通知，组建中共修文县农村信用合作联社委员会和纪律检查委员会。2010年，联社内置9个部（室），下辖18个分社和基层社，在岗职工187人，配主任1人，副主任2人，主任助理1人。

商行县支行　2001年9月，贵阳市商业银行延伸到修文建立支行，办公地址在县城迎春路，为集资兴办的股份制商业银行，在国家金融方针政策指导下实行民主管理，灵活经营，自负盈亏，自担风险。2010年，内设4个部（室），在岗职工35人，配正副行长各1人。

（六）保险改制

国有财产、人寿保险机构分设　1980年11月，执行国务院《关于恢复国内保险决定》，县设保险特别代办处，业务由人民银行代理。1985年6月建立中国人民保险公司修文县支公司，接办人行代办业务，隶属人保安顺地区分公司，办公地址在县城人民北路。1992年和1993年分置扎佐办事处和六广办事处。

1996年全国保险业自成系统，人保支公司和六广办事处撤销，按原有业务分置中保人寿保险公司修文营业部和中保财产保险公司修文县支公司，分别改隶各自的贵阳分公司，成为互不从属的国有股份制保险企业，不敷人员从社会招聘营销员办理业务。至2010年，人寿支公司内置3个部，下辖2个办事处，正式职工7人，配正副经理各1人；财保支公司内有2个部，职工9人，配正副经理各1人。

县城人民北路人民保险公司县支公司办公楼

股份制营销保险机构入驻 2004年12月，平安人寿保险公司率先入驻，建立营销服务部后，又有安帮财产、新华人寿、泰康人寿保险公司先后建立，办理营销业务。至2010年，除平安营销服务部注销外，其余3家仍存。

2004—2010年入驻县内保险机构一览表

表3—08—01

机构名称	起建时间	办公地址	业务项目	隶属上级公司
平安人寿保险修文营销服务部	2004.12	县城迎春路建行五楼	人寿保险	平安保险贵阳分公司
安邦财产保险修文营销服务部	2007.11	县城阳明大道11号	财产保险	安邦财产保险贵州分公司
新华人寿保险修文营销服务部	2008.05	县城翠屏小区A栋三楼	人寿保险	新华人寿保险公司
泰康人寿保险修文服务部	2008.10	县城文成路邮政花园二楼	人寿保险	泰康保险贵州分公司

注：平安人寿保险修文营业部2007年10月注销

二、用工制度改革

正式工改合同制 1980年前，银行用工一律实行统招统配，招进的人员试用期满即转为正式工，人事管理权归县。1980年起，县农行，工行、建行及保险公司管理权先后收归系统。1994年员工改称“行员”，实行行员等级工资制度改革，行员工资分为11级46档，人、工、农、建4行按员工级别、工龄、从事业务岗位进行套改。

1996年执行县政府《关于企业全面实行劳动合同制实施细则》，将正式工改为合同制，由支行与职工签订劳动合同，明确双方的权利和义务，依法确认劳动关系，从此打破“铁饭碗”，结束“进行定终身”的历史。1999年，工、农、建3行再次对人事制度和报酬分配制度改革，建立与行政级别脱钩，与岗位职责、工作绩效、服务年限等相联系的行员级别体系，使员工报酬与劳动增加值紧密挂钩，经营者收益逐步与所创利润挂钩，实行按月考核计发工资，延续至2010年一直执行。

银行招用储蓄员 1987年，为适应金融业务发展需求，工行、农行、建行陆续招收储蓄员（又称“代储员”或“代办员”）办理储蓄业务，工资收入低于正式员工，如有招工指标，即通过考试录用为正式工。从1991年起国有商业银行储蓄员经济收入与正式工接近，统一缴纳养老保险，以解决后顾之忧。1996年起储蓄员均作为合同制职工。2005年县建行撤销，接办业务的县联社按照移交方要求对划转的4

名储蓄员办理转为正式工手续。2008年，储蓄人员由自行接收改为派送制，即由接收银行与联系的贵阳市劳动服务公司协商并签订合同，劳动服务公司按合同派送劳务人员，试用两年经业务考试合格即转为合同制用工。2010年仍存的工行、农行、商行、联社和邮政储蓄银行共有派送职工76人，占5行职工总数288人的26.39%。

贵阳市劳动服务公司派送到县联社的员工正在办理业务

保险招用营销员 1996年，改制后的人寿保险公司和财产保险公司，始招收营销员拓展保险业务，凡取得保险代理资格证和保监会颁发的展业证并愿从事保险业务者，自愿与保险机构签订代理保险合同，缴纳保证金500元，即可成为营销员从事保险业务。个人经济收入则按照自己代办保费收入和规定比例计提，人员可以随进随出，保险机构仅作为外勤人员统计，不记入职工之列。2010年末，人寿支公司和财保支公司共有营销员42人。

三、信贷资金管理体制改革

差额包干 1980年改革信贷计划管理体制，将原多年推行的指标管理改为“统一计划，分级管理，存贷挂钩，差额控制”。贵州省统一实行存贷款差额控制，逐级下达差额指标，安顺地区中心支行对县支行下达年末差额指标。至年末，县人行出现存款增长、贷款下降的问题，存差额为143.8万元。1981年恢复县农行，将差额控制改为差额包干。7月，人、农行之间各种资金管理实行“归口清算，加强考核，存欠资金，互计利息”。至年末实现存差75.2万元。到1983年，从差额控制到差额包干，扩大基层行的经营自主权，消除指标管理、死扣贷款计划，使经济发展受到瓶颈制约的弊端。

实贷实存 1984年，信贷资金管理改为“统一计划，划分资金，自主经营，互相融通”办法。工、农两行信贷资金统一纳入国家综合信贷计划，财政性存款划归人行使用，吸收的企业存款和农村存款、储蓄存款按比例缴存存款准备金，资金往来实行上存下贷、实贷实存方式进行管理，各行自办系统联行往来和跨系统资金清算。此改革虽然改变计划指标原由各系统逐级下达的办法，但又出现通过转存款、汇兑在途等方式虚贷虚存变更年末基数的情况。即年终县工行内部轧差检查发现贷款规模有结余，在未进行贷前调查就于当晚贷款100万元给乡镇企业局矿业开发公司，转给公司经理王忠兰之子刘智发展第三产业，造成38.19万元的损失。

20世纪80年代老信合员魏元明（右一）在农家现场办理存贷业务

1985年11月21日至次年2月25日再次改革信贷计划，将建行原执行的收支轧差后的差额纳入国家综合信贷计划，改为收支两方全额纳入信贷计划，与工、农两行一并执行“统一计划，分级管理，差额控制，实借实存，存差上缴”办法管理。自1986年2月26日起自筹资金营业，出现县农行营运资金不足，向县建行拆借资金150万元解决，借款期限1个月。1987年，为进一步完善信贷计划管理体制，改为“合理供给，确定期限，有借有还，周转使用”办法，以货币供给制约资金需求，使专业银行成为相对独立、具有自筹信贷资金能力的经济实体，其贷款规模所需资金自行筹措，多存多贷，少存少贷，县人行不再包揽资金供应。县农村信用社执行省人、农两分行通知，新增存款按比例缴纳存款准备金。到2010年，存款准备金制度仍延续执行。

专记：刘智贷款一百万　银行损失近一半

1984年12月31日下午近6时，县工行内部轧账检查发现贷款规模有结余，为扩大年终贷款基数，使次年贷款规模宽松，主持工作的副行长毕长惠与退居二线的原行长陈德富商定，安排信贷股长通知事前要求贷款的乡镇企业局矿业开发公司到行办理贷款手续，并在审查贷款收据时，连贷款单位名称和印鉴不符都未察觉便签字同意贷款，导致乡镇企业局以下辖矿业开发公司名义贷款330万元，其中230万元通过联行在途资金占用（已于次年1月28日收回），余下100万元留公司，次年1月15日公司将款转汇贵阳给乡企局副局长王忠兰之子刘智经营。

4月，工行安顺地区中心支行获得知情人反映上述情况后，立即与中共安顺地区金融纪检组、中共修文县纪委组成工作组进驻县工行查账、追款，并立案侦查，于6月收回31万元，尚欠69万元，行长沙宗兴以法人代表身份向贵阳市中级人民法院提出民事诉状，诉请判令乡镇企业局返还贷款。1987年6月27日中级人民法院以刑字第106号判决书判决：乡镇企业局收取刘智虚报利润7.75万元如数退出归还贷款；检察机关随案移送法院处理的赃款及赃物折款发还20.34万元归还贷款；个体商户张天光（在逃）欠刘智借款和货款11.84万元，个体商户宋顺文（在逃）诈骗刘智货款9万元，本案被告刘智、林忠开、刘应祥三人下欠赃款14.61万元，已判决在案，由司法机关依法继续追缴上缴国库；以上3项共计63.54万元，下欠银行贷款5.46万元由乡镇企业局负责赔偿，如数归还贷款。至此，该贷款实际收回两项案款13.21万元，另案款15.02万元，赃物处理收回还贷2.57万元，加上存款户余额扣收抵贷款100万元和原收回31万元，累计收回61.81万元，尚差款35.44万元和赃物处理损失2.75万元无法收回，实际损失38.19万元，报经主管行批准于1989年12月核销。

1987年6月，贵阳市中级人民法院以106号判决书判决：刘智犯贪污罪判处有期徒刑10年，犯诈骗罪判处有期徒刑15年，犯玩忽职守罪判处有期徒刑3年，总和刑期28年，决定执行20年，剥夺政治权利5年；林忠开犯贪污罪判处有期徒刑15年，剥夺政治权利3年；刘应祥犯贪污罪判处有期徒刑5年；王忠兰犯玩忽职守罪判有期徒刑5年；毕长惠犯玩忽职守罪判处有期徒刑1年，缓刑1年。

银行发放贷款历来坚持贷前调查、贷时审查、贷后检查“三查”制度，但县工行在“实贷实存”信贷管理体制改革中，漠视制度规定，仅凭个人意志放贷，导致案件形成，给银行造成无可挽回的经济损失，使涉案者依法负刑。教训严重，以戒后人。

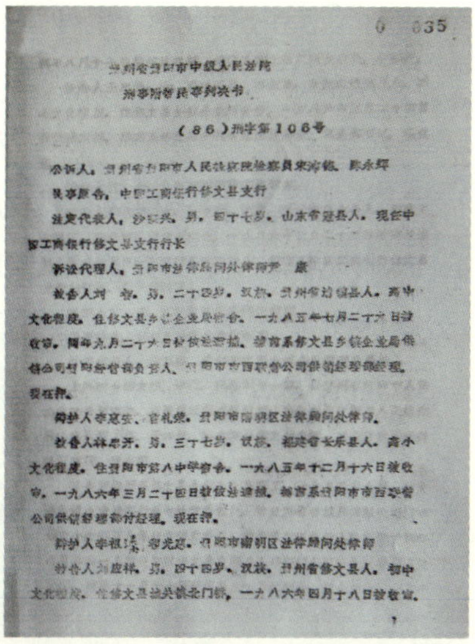
(86)刑字第106号

刘智案判决书

限额管理　1988年，按照中国人民银行《深化信贷资金管理体制改革的意见》，金融宏观调控仍以控制信贷规模为主，除部分贷款限额仍由专业银行管理外，人民银行对短期贷款管理由收支两条线改为限额控制和限额管理，审批贷款实行专业银行最高限额、贷款投向、清仓挖潜三挂钩，限额不得突破。农村信用社信贷收支不纳入国家综合信贷计划，作为一个单独层次监控。1989年，为抑制通货膨胀，人行不再下达专业银行存款计划，年度贷款最高限额作为指令性指标，由人行和专业银行“双线控制”，人行实行“全年亮底，按季监控，按月考核，适时调节”，专业银行实行“控制总量，调整结构，保证重点，压缩一般，适时调节”。至年末全县短期贷款仅比上年增加64万元，增长0.75%。此项改革，虽能拓展融资渠道，促进金融竞争，但业务交叉不能互通信息，出现多头开户和多头贷款以及存款派生，仅1990年5月县人行检查发现18户企业多头开户，5户企业多头贷款。1992年人民银行对专业业银行备付金缴存比例提高到5-7%进行控制，防止储备过少出现支付困难。1995年又实行贷款卡管理，专业银行凭人民银行签发的贷款卡发放贷款，杜绝多头贷款发生。此贷款卡管理一直执行到1997年为止。

间接调控　1998年3月，执行国务院《改革金融机构存款准备金制度》，将各金融机构代理财政性存款中的机关团体存款、财政预算外存款划归金融机构一般性存款，计缴存款准备金；金融机构将人行法定存款准备金账户和备付金账户合并为存款准备金账户，按金融企业法人实行按旬考核；降低中央银行对金融机构存、贷款利率。5月，人行恢复公开市场业务，正式参与商业银行国债回购；取消对国有商业银行贷款规模控制，在推行资产负债比例管理和风险管理的同时，实行“计划指导，自求平衡，比例管理，间接调控”的信贷管理体制，综合运用利率、公开市场业务、存款准备金、再贷款、再贴现等货币政策工具，间接调控货币供应量，使其实现货币供给目标。至2010年制度未变。

县工商银行设置的对公业务柜台

四、基本建设拨款改贷款

1978年，国家预算内基本建设沿袭拨款制度，县内拨款监督由建行履行，1979年8月，按照国务院批转国家计委、建委、财政部《关于基本建设投资试行贷款办法报告》的精神，对基本建设管理体制进行改革，将建设资金由拨款改为贷款，实行有偿使用，贷款业务由建行经办。1980年，建行安顺地区中心支行和县支行先在县境猫跳河五级电站配套建设工程试点，1982年按照国家计委、中国人民建设银行《关于进一步实行基本建设拨款改贷款通知》精神，再推广到独立核算并具有还款能力的企业。1984年拨改贷全面实施，1985年再对拨改贷范围作调整，调整后行政事业单位不再实行拨改贷，对已贷款项目按程序报经批准后豁免。

1980年拨款改贷款建成的猫跳河五级电站

1988年，国务院批准国家预算内基本建设投资实行基金制管理，基本建设基金分经营性和非经营性两类，经营性项目仍实行拨改贷，非经营性项目则实行基金拨款。至1990年的11年，县建行累计发放基本建设贷款2987.36万元，其中，中央预算

贷款2855.82万元，地方预算贷款131.54万元。收回2750.34万元，其中，中央预算贷款2738.84万元，地方预算贷款12万元。1999年后，随着银行改制和计划体制改革，基本建设拨改贷制度取消，改由市场调节，至2010年，固定资产贷款降为单位和个人贷款中一个小项。

第二节　银　行

1978至2010年，随着金融体制改革逐步深入，金融业务和经营品种逐渐增多，业务管理和服务亦渐加强，存款余额增长220.6倍，贷款余额增长113.9倍。

一、人民币发行

继1978年前发行第一、第二、第三套人民币后，中国人民银行又于1987年4月—1988年9月分次发行9种券面新版人民币，即第四套人民币，其中50元券和100元券为1987年4月27日和1988年5月10日首发。1999年10月1日—2004年7月30日陆续发行第五套人民币，面额有1元、5元、10元、20元、50元、100元和5角、1角纸币及1角、2角、1元金属硬币。2005年8月31日起再次奉命发行“2005年版”第五套人民币，面额有5元、10元、50元、100元纸币和1角金属硬币。每套人民币发行均与继续流通人民币同值流通。

为纪念重大历史事件，宣传爱国主义和社会主义精神文明，展示改革开放的伟大成就，县人行自1979年起陆续发行全国统一制发的流通纪念币和不流通纪念币，流通纪念币与现行人民币等值流通，但多数品种发行量少，多为民间收藏。

1978至2010年，全县累计发行人民币677.21亿元，收回634.18亿元，年均发行和回收分别为20.52亿元和19.22亿元，有力地推进县域经济的快速发展。

二、银行存款

1978年，全县存款余额1044万元，吸收和组织机关、团体、企事业单位存款主要靠行政措施。1984年，专业银行开始向商业银行转制，各行提出“存款立行，存款兴行”的工作方针，充分利用利率杠杆作用进行市场竞争，其间一度出现存款中的“水分”。由于国家及时对金融秩序整顿，使银行间的不正当竞争在1996年得到遏制。2010年，全县存款实现27.73亿元，33年间年均增长19.06%。

财政存款　1978年为县人行业务，年末余额34万元，在全县银行存款中占3.26%。1984年改为各国家商业银行代理，1990年余额实现459万元，1991年后存款余额有增有降极不稳定，到2000年降至147万元。2001年贵阳市商业银行在县建立机构，财政存款基本纳入该行办理，由于财政资金宽松，存款余额猛增，2010年实现1.65亿元，占当年全县银行存款总额5.94%，在各项存款中居第四位。

企业存款　1978年，工商企业存款主要由县人行经营，年末余额501万元，在银行存款中占47.99%，居各项存款之首。1984年县工商银行接办。1985年增加单位定期存款等品种，存款额上升，到1990年达2045万元。1991年起中小企业不断增加，国有商业银行重点抓存款大户，帮助企业催收贷款，同时以优质服务接待客户，到2000年达到1.7亿元。2001年后国防工业011系统驻县企业和医院迁往贵阳，幸有贵阳市股份制商业银行进驻修文，以灵活的经营方式办理金融业务，致存款大幅增长，至2010年全县达到4.77亿元，占当年全县银行存款总额的17.21%，在各项存款中居第二位。

农业存款 1978年为县人行经办，年末余额45万元，仅占全县银行存款的4.31%。1980年县农行接办，继县人行之后开办有奖储蓄，筹集资金保障存款客户支取。至1990年余额达到812万元。1992年有农村信用社存款列入银行存款，存款业务逐步向农村种植、养殖等领域扩展，2000年实现1176万元。从2001年起，国家为彻底改变农村落后状况，财政大量向农村投入资金，县农行和农村信用社也加大扶持和服务，到2010年余额增至3.63亿元，占当年全县银行存款总额13.09%，在各项存款中居第三位。

储蓄存款 为金融企业共办业务，1978年余额为155万元，在全县银行存款中占14.85%，排位在企业存款之后。1987年和1988年邮电局和建设银行开办储蓄，加上工行、农行陆续举办的各种有奖、摸奖、实物销售储蓄，促使全县储蓄存款连年增长，到1990年达到4090万元。1992年又增农村信用社存款，加上各行为增加更多的市场份额，分别增设储蓄网点，创新储蓄品种，拓展储蓄领域，开展通存通兑，任务到柜到人，虽存款额有所上升，但一度出现存款发钱发物的变相提高利率和公款私存、公款转储蓄等不正当的竞争。到1996年，刹住银行间不正当的储蓄手段，各金融部门认真贯彻执行调整后的储蓄利率，加强宣传力度，改进服务争取客户，在国防工业011系统驻县企业及其医院迁出和银行机构收缩的情况下，全县储蓄存款仍以前所未有速度增长，到2010年达到15.71亿元，在当年全县银行存款中占比升到56.65%，33年间年平均增长24.15%，从1986年起连续25年一直排列在银行各项存款的第一位。

县农村信用合作联社营业厅

专记：县联社存款跃居金融部门之首

1996年，农村信用社仍为国家银行的助手，办理农民储蓄和部分农村金融业务。存款余额仅3809万元，在各金融企业存款总余额中占11.08%，居工、农、建3行之后，排位第四。1997年，县联社执行国务院《关于农村金融体制改革的决定》，脱离农行的隶属关系，成为独立自主、自求发展、自我约束、自主经营、自负盈亏的集体所有制合作金融组织。紧紧围绕“外抓发展拓空间、内抓管理增效益”的经营理念和“存款立社、存款兴社”的指导方针开展工作，1月接办县农行撤销的小箐营业所各项存款120余万元，7月增办财政性存款和单位存款，又将个人储蓄存款从农村拓展到城镇，加上着力改善服务，提高服务质量，至年末余额实现6911万元，比1996年增长81.44%，在各金融企业存款总余额中占12.56%，超过建设银行位居第三。

2001年，在普遍推行计算机操作，提高办事效率的同时，对中层干部实行竞聘上岗，增强员工责任感；开展送电影下乡活动，在全县10乡（镇）和住户集中村寨放电影50场大力宣传储蓄利国利民等好处。2003年12月再次开展建社以来规模最大、内容最丰富宣传活动，组装宣传彩车在全县巡回宣传，在《修文报》办专刊，在省内新闻传媒报道宣传文章，使储蓄见红利家喻户晓。至年末，存款余额达到1.53

亿元，比2000增长1.2倍，在各金融企业存款余额中占19.41%，超过农行和股份制商业银行跃居第二。

2004年5月，全县聘请419名驻村联络员，帮助信用社组织存款和提供贷款发放信息。同时，抓住国有商业银行改制网点向城镇收缩的契机，接办县建行扎佐办事处各项存款1992.43万元和农行六广营业所各项存款643万元。2005年又接办县建行各项存款1.11万户，余额5357.7万元，并大力发展新客户，巩固老客户，至年末存款余额增至3.33亿元，又比2003年增长1.2倍，在各金融企业存款总额中占比增到28.3%，跃居各银行之首。到2010年，存款余额为12.59亿元，自1997年起年平均增长28.45%，在全县银行存款总余额中占45.41%，位居第一。令人瞩目的存款余额充分说明是农村金融体制改革促使全县信合员努力开拓创新的结果。

扎佐信用社吴光惠（左）走街串巷义务为商户兑换零钞

1978—2010年全县金融机构财政、企业、农业存款余额统计表

表3—08—02　　单位：万元

年份	财政存款	企业存款	农业存款	年份	财政存款	企业存款	农业存款
1978	74	501	45	1995	85	8661	544
1979	63	373	47	1996	1	9984	844
1980	150	500	77	1997	364	9472	289
1981	162	583	71	1998	879	11046	168
1982	241	843	116	1999	57	13653	1118
1983	132	964	4	2000	147	16954	1176
1984	590	1342	53	2001	123	20583	1788
1985	147	1629	106	2002	405	23655	3366
1986	39	1366	266	2003	86	20558	4557
1987	165	1793	357	2004	1539	31831	9306
1988	381	2325	762	2005	1269	24265	12581
1989	341	1896	662	2006	4384	37136	14545
1990	459	2045	751	2007	2197	50660	15938
1991	426	2170	839	2008	5520	74341	19378
1992	299	3554	1718	2009	11619	44514	27099
1993	188	3854	1288	2010	16459	47729	36296
1994	658	5666	644				

全县银行存款余额增长图

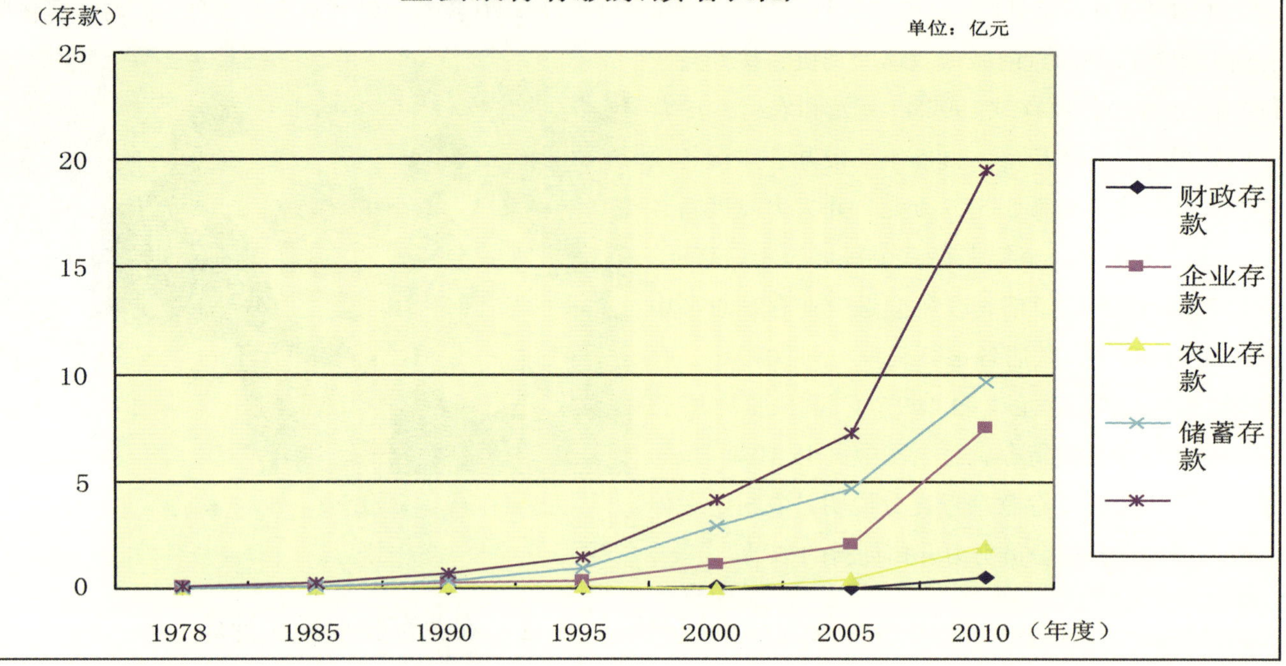

三、银行贷款

1978年，贷款仅限于工商企业流动资金，年末余额1680万元。1984年起贷款领域扩大到乡镇企业、建筑业、私营企业、个体工商户以及群众建房和生活住宅、消费等范围。2002年贷款称谓改变，即一年以内流动资金贷款改称短期贷款，超过一年以上的称中长期贷款。2010年指标变更，短期和中长期贷款由按行业区分改为个人、单位、普通并购、银团和贸易融资5项，贷款余额达19.31亿元，自1978年起年均增长15.98%，其中，短期贷款7.04亿元，在贷款总额中占36.46%；中长期贷款12.27亿元，占63.54%。

（一）短期贷款

工业企业贷款 1978年为系人行经营，年末余额520万元，在全县贷款余额中占29.58%。1984年1月改由县工行经营，1985年坚持“区别对待，择优扶持”和“保重点，压一般”的原则，优先支持市场适销对路产品，特别是优质、名牌产品的生产。县三角山水泥厂“甲秀”牌水泥，郭家林水泥厂425“黔阳”牌普通硅酸盐水泥得到贷款扶持，产品一时供不应求。

1986年，县工、农、建3行按照“少贷多清，清贷结合，力求平衡”的原则，组织力量协助企业清理“三角债”。9月，县工行召开企业洽谈会，债权、债务双方见面，银行从中撮合，双方达成谅解，历经两个多月，共清理出人欠货款804万元，欠人货款508万元，清理中发放流动资金贷款225万元，归还欠人货款80%，收回人欠货款637万元，解开“三角债”链。1988年，再协助企业挖掘内部资金潜力，县工行派信贷员与万江和五0一两厂人员分赴贵阳、云南、广西、江西等省、市协助清理收回货款201万元，通过函件或催款单间接收回货款近300万元，帮助开户企业挖掘出资金潜力1502万元，收回3户地方企业风险贷款34.2万元。1991年进行二次清理“三角债”，从9月到10月，由县工行开户的12家工商企业参加，累计循环清欠金额376.6万元，其中收回省外货款338.7万元，清付欠人货款244笔，金额138.7万元，使一时严重困扰企业的“三角债”得到摆脱。

1996年，执行中国人民银行、国家经贸委、财政部、中国工商银行《关于帮助困难企业解决拖欠工资问题的通知》，县工商银行破例向兴红机械厂发放2笔基本生活费贷款70.7万元，列入国务院特定贷款。1999年工行、建行处置不良贷款，到2004年累计处置工业企业不良贷款本息1377.42万元，其中剥离724.32万元给各自省分行清收公司负责清收，核销653.1万元。加之驻县011系统企业迁出，贷款余额随厂划转，地方国有工业企业改制，贷款相应减少，至2009年，全县工业企业短期贷款余额为9104万元，与1978年相比增加16.5倍。

商业企业贷款 1978年为县人行经营，年末余额752万元，在全县贷款余额中占42.77%。1984年改由县工行经办，根据统购、派购、计划收购、定购、选购等不同的购销形式，分别采取保证供应、按计划供应、按合同协议掌握贷款等方式，对企业核定贷款限额，按年、季下达贷款指标掌握发放。县百货公司获70万元进货贷款，商品进入市场即售完，本息按期全部归还。1986年承担两棉赊销贷款，期限5年，由县百货公司对1.48万户贫困户7.41万人赊销纯棉布74.1万米，金额133.38万元，连续5年由省财政贴息49.72万元，其本金因农民无力归还最后作剥离处理。

1988年上半年经济过热初露苗头，县内出现“抢购风”，县工行增加贷款50万元给五金公司补充库存物资保证市场需求。1990年上半年再发放贷款45万元，解决2户商业企业清欠付款。1992年国营粮食商业企业贷款改由县农行经营，连续5年积极组织资金保证农副产品收购，增加地方库存储备，解决连续几年收购“打白条”的问题。继后，国有商业企业经营机制改变，实行柜组承包、租赁承包，收回贷款难度大，1995年县工行信贷资产质量检查，查出国有商业企业贷款余额614万元，其中呆滞384万元，呆账153万元，累计占87.46%。

1997年，县农行农村政策性金融业务移交县农发行办理，县工行对物资供销企业贷款采取边收边贷办法支持，两年购进和卖出近200辆农用山地车和解放牌142载重汽车。又针对烟草市场不景气、化肥价格不稳定的情况，采取贷款与库存、组织存款、信用回笼三挂钩进行控制。2000年5月工行对五金、烟酒、百货、蔬菜4家商业企业不良贷款734.59万元剥离并划转给省分行华融公司负责清收。至2005年的15年，银行对国有商业企业累计发放贷款13.14亿元，其中，烟草5.78亿元，粮食6.06亿元，供销及农资1.3亿元，促进全县市场稳定。到指标变更前的2009年全县商业贷款余额为6235万元，比1978年增加7.3倍。

农业贷款 1978年由县人行经营，仅有农业生产设备、农业生产费用及社员个人贷款，年末余额290万元。1980年县农行接办，1986年清理1978年以前农业贷款积欠，豁免34.4万元。此后，由于农村实行家庭联产承包，贷款转向农业科技和农业现代化领域，1988年起谷堡和乌栗两乡得信用社贷款扶持3000户农民科学种植猕猴桃和经果林3万亩，成立全县乃至安顺地区首个联户农场——修文县下硐联户合作农场，至1990年，全县贷款余额增到1283万元，其中乡镇企业贷款余额419万元，占32.66%。

1991年起，农业贷款转向农村企业和农技推广，扶持农村多种经济发展。1997年起六桶信用社连续6年贷款150万元，扶持六桶乡山保村300户农民科学养鸡，仅李根书兴农养殖场年均放养土鸡超过1万只，年均收入10万元，获“贵阳市共青绿色示范基地”称号，2000年扎佐镇信用社扶持丁官村111户农民种植金秋梨1013亩，投产后年均产梨80万公斤。同时清理出120户不良贷款本息5680万元，划剥给省分行长城公司负责清收。

2001年，贷款扩展到农村基础设施建设和地方经济领域。县联社先后贷款38万元支持小箐乡小坝村和六桶乡共82户农家在规划的新街修建新居。2002年再开展诚信贷款活动，久长镇石安村村民诚实守信，被评为全县首个“信用村”，全村90%的农户得到贷款支持发展科学养猪，成为贵阳市远近闻名的养猪村。2003年久长信用社贷款支持清水村23户农民喂养奶牛116头，月产牛奶3.5万公斤，月收入4万元。

2005年县联社开展评级授信活动，对6万户农民评定信用等级，解决农民贷款担保难的问题，获得省联社于2008年授予的业务创新奖。2009年3月，县农行系统始办农户小额贷款，列入全国153家试点行，次年全面铺开，马官村农民还款守信，获取全县独家、全省第二家信用村的荣誉。县联社还同时增办互保乐贷款，发放1670万元支持农户购进奶牛1000头，到年末，农业贷款余额增到2.66亿元，在全县贷款余额中占17.98%，居短期贷款中各项贷款之首，与1978年相比增加90.6倍。

农村信合贷款支持全县万头奶牛发展一角

专记：信用小额贷款让农民致富

信用社的小额贷款具有金额小、时间短、利率低等特点。1996年全县信用贷款余额实现1875万元，比1978年的49万元增加1826万元。1997年把支农小额贷款作为各项贷款工作之首，除按传统方式发放外，先后推出“资信卡贷款”“联保贷款”“创建信用村、组贷款”“农户小额信用贷款”“互保乐贷款”等类种。2005年对全县6万农户评级授信，被评为优秀级可借贷款1—3万元，较好级可借贷款0.5—2万元，一般级可借0.3—1.5万元，不超过前述授信额度不用担保抵押，凭信用在辖区内信用社贷款；贷款超过信用等级额度，采取“互保乐”贷款，由村民自愿参加互保会成员共同承担风险，信用社根据互保会开设互保风险金专用账户余额，按1:10比例匹配信贷资金支持，并在贷款环节上给予方便，以解决农户需借较大金额贷款担保抵押难问题。仅2009至2010年累计发放5.48亿元，有2.5万多种植户、1万多养殖户、5000多经商户得到贷款扶持，先后走上脱贫致富之路。龙场镇中哨村农户靠小额贷款扶持种植延晚番茄远近闻名，带动邻近村民种植延晚番茄发家致富。扎佐镇大河村有115户共贷款80万元，种植经果林2500亩；帮助8户农民发展乡村旅游，办起农家乐餐饮业。久长镇清水村农户获贷款99万元发展奶牛养殖，奶牛从116头增到250头。是年6月，龙场镇、谷堡乡、小箐乡饲养奶牛农户借小额贷款700万元购买优质奶牛600头。六桶乡政府驻地异地搬迁到盐井村，信用社积极发放贷款支持农户在乡政府驻地兴建住房和门面经商，使新建集镇变成近1万平方米，居住着数百户居民的新兴集镇，促进地方经济繁荣，推动农民致富。到2010年全社小额贷款余额达到3.21亿元，比1996年翻4.2番。

小箐信用社职工深入农户发放贷款

附：

县信用联社扶持农户发酿酒养猪财

段　纲

走进修文县久长镇石安村，映入眼帘的是进村水泥路通向各家各户，很多农户家肥猪满圈，苞谷酿出的酒味芳香扑鼻，一栋栋砖混结构的楼房拔地而起，家家户户用上自来水，很多农户都用上手机或电话，屋里的装饰和家用电器与城里人没多大差别。村民们笑呵呵地说，这些巨大的变化主要与农村信用社的大力扶持分不开。

石安村酿酒、养猪也有多年历史，但过去经营养猪只有少部分村民，且是靠小打小整作为副业去做，发展缓慢。2001年，久长信用社为重点扶持一批农户先富起来，以此带动更多农户致富。决定选择石安村部分有酿酒、养猪经验的农户走专业化之路发展酿酒、养猪致富。杨祥华、高应忠等村民是信用社首批贷款扶持的酿酒、养猪户，户均贷款1万多元办起酿酒作坊、购进10余头小猪试养，通过科学养猪，精心照料，当年就获得明显的经济效益。村民们看着眼红，一户户跟着养猪，部分办起酿酒作坊，对申请要求借贷款发展的农户，信用社及时给予贷款支持。2002年，石安村有农户260多户，其中就有近百户在信用社贷款的支持下办起养猪场，户均养猪10头左右，一下子就比上年增加几十户养猪户。村民们积极按还款期限归还贷款和按期付息。由于村民守信用，2002年修文县信用联社在全县农村首批开展评定“信用村”中，被评为全县第一个“信用村”。被评为“信用村”后，信用社立即按照“信用村贷款手续适当简便，利率优惠”的规定为村民办理贷款。借贷款在5000元以下的取消担保抵押手续，凭信用方式借款，5000元以上的采取担保抵押或联保方式办理，且“信用村”贷款利率低于非“信用村”的0.2个百分点左右。贷款手续的简便和利率的优惠，调动石安村村民发展养猪、酿酒致富的积极性，走养猪致富的农户逐年增加，规模逐年扩大。截至2005年，全村270户人家户均养猪10头左右，其中有70户左右养猪在30头左右，有10户养猪在60头左右，最多的一户养猪上100头。猪的品种以优质二元杂交猪为主，猪的分类有种猪、仔猪、架子猪、肥猪，村民养的主要销往贵阳等地，酿的酒主要销往本县和周边县。全村农户养猪年收入500万元左右，人均年收入4000多元，15户酿酒户户均年收入1万元以上。酿酒、养猪全是宝，良性循环实在好。苞谷酿酒后酒糟供喂猪，猪粪肥耕地或卖给农户种果树或种庄稼用，种地收入的苞谷又成为酿酒原料。逐步富裕起来的农户开始改变居住环境，从2003年起，全村农户开始大兴土木，逐步改变居住环境。如今，全村80%以上的人家已居住在宽敞、明亮的砖混结构楼房里，很多人家购有农用汽车。过去脏、乱、差，猪粪乱堆乱放臭气熏天的现象得到改变。村干部们满有信心地表示：我们要带头继续遵守信用，同时要继续监督村民们遵守信用，长期保住“信用村”这块光荣牌子，把石安村建设成为生态良好、村风文明更加宜业宜居的社会主义新农村。

（原载《贵州日报》2005年10月24日第五版）

私营企业及个体企业贷款　1982年起，贯彻执行国营、集体、个体一齐上的方针，县人行及各专业银行陆续开办私营及个体贷款，但数额极少。1985年私营企业生产正常，产品适销对路，经济效益较好，用房屋、机器设备作抵押均可贷款；个体贷款用贷款行定期存款单抵押，并开立定期零存整取专项储蓄存款户，每月存入固定金额，贷款到期将其支取归还贷款，1991年贷款余额达101万元，在当年全县短期贷款余额中占0.9%。1997年个体经济贷款实行定期存款单抵押为主，财产抵押为辅，工行发放贷款151笔，金额446万元，有收有贷年末余额303万元。2001年县股份制商业银行建立即经营该项贷款。2006年，县邮政储蓄始发放小额质押贷款金额612.03万元，收回327.5万元，到指标变更前的2009年，全县私营和个体贷款余额为1.26亿元，在全县贷款总额中占8.54%。

建筑安装企业贷款 1985年由县建行经营，解决建筑安装企业短时间资金不足的问题，1986年末余额15万元。1992年起随着住房制度改革，集资建房逐渐增多，建筑安装企业流动资金需要量增大，贷款余额增至121万元。1997年起商品房和基础设施建设速度加快，建筑安装企业流动资金贷款快速上升，到2006年本贷款余额增到3250万元。由于贷款及时回收，至2008年，余数仅162万元，在当年全县贷款总额中仅占0.15%。2009年无余额。

消费贷款 1993年起配合住房制度改革，县建行始办个人住房贷款，支持城镇职工集资建房。1998年县工行正式开办个人住房贷款业务，建行增办汽车贷款由贵阳市分行统一办理。1999年2月中国人民银行下达《关于个人消费贷款的通知》，住房贷款作为消费贷款，各中资商业银行在继续办理原有住房贷款业务的同时，陆续推行小额存单抵押贷款、住房抵押贷款等业务，工行累计发放个人住房贷款217万元，解决邮电等6个单位87户住房建设。继后，各商业银行先后增办助学贷款、个人住房按揭贷款、住房装修贷款等项目，2001至2002年工行累计发放553户，金额1830万元，收回572万元。2008年全县消费贷款余额为1235万元，2010年除个人中长期消费贷款1.94亿元外，个人短期消费贷款增为1.24亿元，两项合计3.18亿元，占当年全县贷款余额的16.47%。

（二）中长期贷款

基本建设贷款 1980年配合基本建设管理体制改革，县建行始办基本建设拨款改贷款，先在县境猫跳河五级电站配套建设工程试点然后全面推行，至1983年的4年贷款共2600万元，连续6年全部收回本息。1985年国家对信贷计划进行改革，基本建设项目资金改由银行吸纳信贷资金发放贷款。1990年县建行利用发行金融债券资金发放特种贷款30万元。

1994年起，各国有商业银行集中资金确保重点项目，由省、市主管行在下达基本建设贷款规模内发放。1999年开工建设过县境的贵（阳）毕（节）高等级公路，就由建行省分行营业部发放贷款7.5亿元，促进公路建成，县建行只承担县境土地征拨款拨付业务。继后，县内上马程控电话扩容设施建设、移动通信公司基站和网站建设、农村电网改造等，均属建行集中资金发放项目。2001年县商行贷款1000万元建成2.8公里的县城阳明大道。2004年又贷款4200万元支持修文中学扩建。至2010年贷款项目变更，固定资产贷款列为单位普通贷款中的一个小项，年末余额5.32亿元，在全县贷款总余额中占27.56%。

建行贷款建成的贵（阳）毕（节）高等级公路扎佐至修文段一角

技术改造贷款 1981年系县人行经办，至1983年累计发放284.4万元，支持中央企业军品转民品生产和县尼龙衫厂、建材厂等6个技术改造项目。由于当时受行政指令影响和银行贷前审查不严，造成21万

元呆账贷款。1984年贷款业务由工行接办，贷款称谓由中短期设备贷款改为技术改造贷款，连续两年分别向县酒厂发放集体工业设备贷款220万元，专用基金贷款180万元进行扩建，生产“阳明大曲”、“阳明酒”等品种一度热销省内外。

1985年，按照“区别对待，择优扶持”和“保重点，压一般”的原则，从1986年起连续4年贷款1740万元支持万江机电厂研制、开发、生产“桑塔纳”轿车零部件，逐渐进入批量生产，被国家纳入“七五”计划国产化重要项目，并列为国内重点生产厂。1991年坚持“三保三压”（保计划内压计划外，保重点压一般，保生产性压非生产性）方针，再次贷款5000万元支持万江厂完成四期技术改造，生产轿车手摇玻璃升降器、电动刮水器、电动玻璃升降器，其质量、性能及生产能力、技术水平均进入全国同行业前三位，曾多次被评为部优产品，该产品市场占有率分别占上海大众、一汽大众、一汽红旗和神龙富康轿车同类产品市场的48%—73%。同年12月又贷款200万元支持邮电局安装1000门“长市合一”程控交换电话，从此告别40多年全县电话“摇把子”。2002年起县建行先后发放2396万元支持五O一厂、绿太阳药业、奇峰水泥厂完成技术改造贷款。由于011系统驻县企业迁往贵阳，贷款余额随厂划转，使余额由1996年7165万元降到2009年的300万元，仅占全县贷款总余额的0.2%。

1978—2010年短期、中长期贷款年末余额统计表

表3—08—03　　　　单位：万元

年份	短期贷款								中长期贷款			
	小计	工业	商业	农业	建筑企业	乡镇企业	私营及个体	其他	小计	基本建设	技术改造	其他
1978	1680	520	752	212	—	—	—	196	—	—	—	—
1979	1759	635	746	230	—	—	—	148	—	—	—	—
1980	2219	590	628	822	—	39	—	140	932	932	—	—
1981	2324	795	754	744	—	31	—	—	1496	706	—	790
1982	2367	540	891	847	—	40	—	49	2095	1301	—	794
1983	2284	475	742	944	—	46	—	77	1605	1601	—	4
1984	2929	967	666	802	—	419	—	75	1663	1436	—	227
1985	3675	1250	1712	421	15	200	—	77	1078	749	21	308
1986	6304	3221	2396	384	15	249	—	39	582	582	—	—
1987	7851	4092	2597	621	11	290	—	240	500	211	2	287
1988	7652	4262	2509	293	32	337	—	219	980	127	853	—
1989	8123	4336	2681	300	46	269	—	491	1433	115	1318	—
1990	9078	4914	2871	494	84	420	—	295	2031	120	1631	280
1991	9538	4617	3485	560	84	691	101	—	1710	160	1460	90
1992	12714	5551	3687	1767	121	1190	109	289	2303	—	2213	90
1993	13786	6661	3414	1746	151	1534	64	216	2289	80	2009	200
1994	16010	7094	4354	1498	191	1872	12	989	4429	—	3210	1219

续表

年份	短期贷款								中长期贷款			
	小计	工业	商业	农业	建筑企业	乡镇企业	私营及个体	其他	小计	基本建设	技术改造	其他
1995	21203	8529	6456	1971	120	2680	68	1379	5816	89	5045	682
1996	21710	7148	6680	2610	70	3398	68	1736	8954	—	7165	1789
1997	25693	7142	9366	1611	290	3800	350	3134	9940	85	6780	3075
1998	33711	10929	9110	3814	285	5627	704	3242	4362	81	4060	221
1999	34272	8052	9893	5110	285	5520	713	4699	11778	859	3218	7701
2000	34943	8605	8150	6332	410	2566	420	8460	12336	691	1719	9926
2001	34672	8077	5468	10083	271	1661	125	8987	16120	423	3198	12499
2002	31715	5446	5775	10447	231	3293	328	6195	20687	545	5963	14179
2003	28564	2192	6101	8510	222	2195	673	8671	18072	181	2488	15403
2004	37651	1142	3548	18781	1000	390	1388	11402	20213	4650	2396	13167
2005	36616	1529	8445	14535	890	420	1987	8810	32908	5104	2483	25321
2006	63950	1321	18039	11304	3250	2574	1297	26165	45710	7534	—	38176
2007	50475	899	22527	10788	750	2086	341	13084	80718	7000	—	73718
2008	51063	896	6916	23947	162	2310	116	16716	60282	4600	—	55682
2009	65916	9104	6235	26557	—	8098	12605	3317	81765	9300	300	72165
2010	70379	—	—	—	—	—	—	—	122676	—	—	—

注：①1985年和1992年县建设银行和信用联社信贷资金纳入信贷计划，故本表对信用贷款不予单列。②表列分项数来源于县人行及各行年度决算报表。③2010年指标调整，短期贷款分项数为：个人贷款及透支4.37亿元（其中个人消费贷款1.24亿元），单位普通贷款及透支2.59亿元均为经营贷款，银团贷款700万元。中长期贷款分项数为：个人贷款4.71亿元（其中个人消费贷款1.9417亿元），单位普通贷款6.51亿元（其中经营贷款1.19亿元，固定资产贷款5.32亿元），银团贷款1.05亿元，票据融资50万元均为贴现

全县银行贷款余款增长图

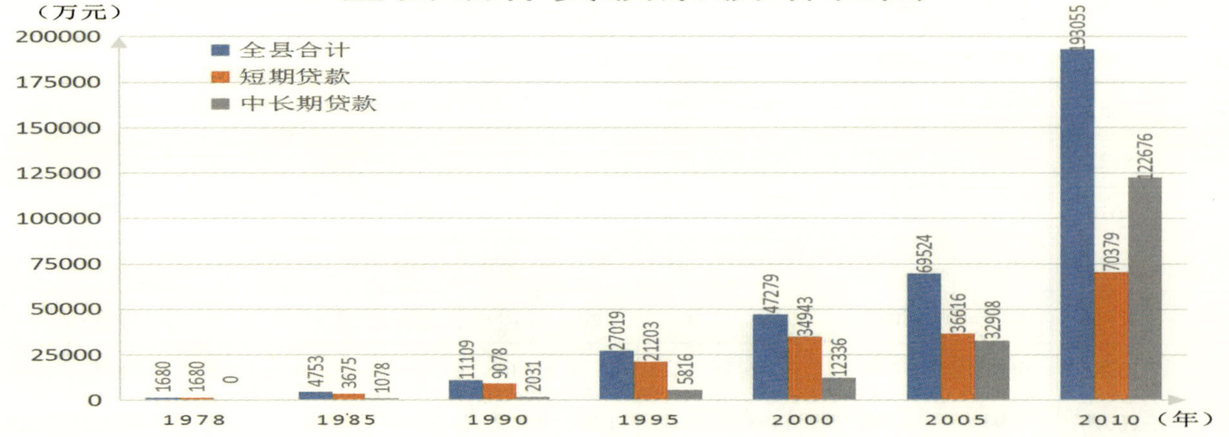

四、中间业务

1983年前，仅有代理财政存款、代发行国债和委托贷款等项目，获取的手续费列为其他收入。1984年专业银行向商业银行转制，均从存贷款业务以外渠道开发新的收入源，1985年增加代理发行国家债券、财政债券、金融债券、国家重点建设债券等10个项目。进入20世纪90年代，中间业务扩大到代办保险、代理收费（款）、代发工资及国债买卖、单位或个人汇款、跨行存取等范围共数十个品种，收入逐年增加并逐步规范统一。到2008年仅代发工资就达82.54亿元，按月平均为6.88亿元，全县银行中间业务总收入实现290万元。至2010年增到524.06万元，增幅为80.71%。其中收入最多的县农行达262万元，占该行当年总收入的49.99%。

五、金融管理

（一）人民币管理

1978年人民币基本保持稳定。1980年起随着市场开放对现金需求量增大，先后采取提高结算起点、现金管理范围放宽等方式进行管理。1988年为遏制突然出现的物价上涨， 实行一个单位只能在一家银行开立现金结算户。1995年7月又实行大额现金支付登记备案制度，除对工资和农副产品采购支付现金外，其余在开户银行一次支付现金达3万元，或一个月内累计对同一开户单位支付现金达10万元的进行登记备案。2000年2月国务院颁发《人民币管理条例》后，县人行即按照条例进行管理，至2010年未变。

（二）人事管理

专业技术职称评聘　1982年，按照国务院《经济专业干部职称暂行规定》，人行系统由省分行成立评审委员会开展评审工作，县人行徐光惠被评为经济师，另有10人被评为初级职称。1983年10月执行中共中央办公厅、国务院办公厅《关于整顿职称评定工作的通知》，评定工作暂停。1987年贯彻执行中央关于职称改革工作的指示，人、工、农、建4行和保险公司按系统进行职称评定，有12人获中级职称，其余专业人员评定为初级职称，取得职称资格者由主管行按照人事分管权限实行聘任。继后，评聘工作步入正常化、规范化，该晋升者照实晋升，该评未评者进行评聘。1994年起专业技术职称须经全国统一考试获取，再由管理机构聘任。2010年，全县金融保险在职人员中共有中级职称21人，初级职称120人。

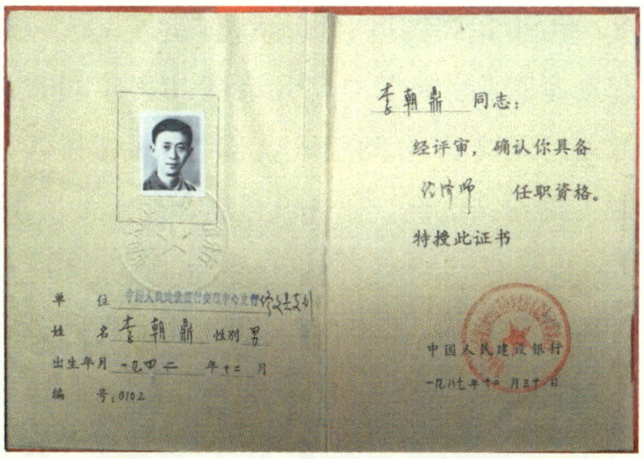

1987年颁发的专业技术职称任职资格证书

职工竞聘上岗　1986年，县工行率先聘任支行行政领导干部。进入20世纪90年代，各行聘任逐渐由支行正、副行长扩大到中层干部以及员工。2002年起，县工、农、建行及县联社先后推行全员竞聘上岗，领导干部职位公开竞争、任前公示、受聘人员与支行签订目标责任合同，如不履行职责违规违纪者，轻者扣发奖金、津（补）贴等经济处罚或下岗，重者则辞退或开除，执行到2010年未变。

专记：县联社实行竞聘上岗　存款大幅增长

2005年前，历经51度春秋，农村信用社员工一直是统一调配，由主管银行或县联社下文执行。2006年破例以县联社统一法人，联社改革用工制度，员工从统一调配改为岗位竞聘，建立起“能者上，平者让，庸者下”的科学选人用人制度，3月颁发《员工岗位竞聘实施方案》，成立竞聘考评委员会，按照公开、公正、公平原则择优选用业务人员，凡辖区内在岗员工连续两年综合考核为称职以上和竞聘前无不良贷款者均具备竞聘资格，对竞聘中层干部还要求学历为高中以上和从事金融工作4年以上或相关经济工作8年（其中有2年金融工作）以上，年龄在45周岁以下，有经营管理和创新能力者均可参加员工和中层领导干部竞聘。经过资格审查，凡符合条件者可对照公示职位、职责和条件，每人书面申请两个竞聘岗位，并写出10分钟就职稿阐述岗位认识、个人优势和任职的工作思路、办法、措施、经营指标，再经过业务考试、民主测评、公开述职及答辩，考评出优秀、称职、基本称职、不称职进行公布，优秀和称职人员竞聘入围后进行任前公示、谈话，中层干部还须上报审批择优聘任。由于中层领导职数有限，作为该竞聘职位拟聘人员和下一轮竞聘职位推荐人员则入人才库管理。对不参加岗位竞聘的员工可选择退休、退养、退职、调离；对落聘和竞聘前有不良贷款的人员一律作为待岗处理，只发基本保障工资，期满经考核合格可参加竞聘上岗，否则限期3个月调离。

农村信合员工竞聘上岗前业务知识考试

11月9日竞聘工作结束，全社员工146人，除联社领导5人外，余下141人全部参加岗位竞聘，有1名工作员竞聘到中层领导岗位，1名中层副职竞聘为正职，1名中层正职领导干部降格为一般工作员，2名员工落聘待岗。

由于竞聘制度动真格落到实处，大大地调动员工的工作积极性和增强责任感，使存款快速增长，从起动竞聘头年的3.33亿元增至2010年的12.59亿元，在各银行中的名次从第二位跃居第一位；贷款余额从3.24亿元增到10.38亿元，连续9年保持各行之首。广大员工无不赞许用工制度改革的举措，深有体会地说：端着铁饭碗，业务没进展，改革治慵懒，经营大改观。

高级管理人员管理　1998年实施高级管理人员管理制度，对县内商业银行、政策性银行、保险公司的行长（经理）、副行长（副经理），农村信用联社理事长、监事长、主任、副主任，邮政储汇局长、分管副局长一律定为金融机构高级管理人员，经人行资格审查后即可任职。当年全县复查任职高级管理人员13人，按照《商业银行授权、授信管理暂行办法》规定实施逐级授权、授信制度，规定各级领导（行长）职权范围。2003年政策性银行副行长改为上报备案，不列入高级管理人员。至2010年，全县银行高级管理人员共有15人，其中县人行3人，农行3人，农发行2人，信用联社3人，商行2人，邮政储蓄2人。

（三）金融服务管理

票据交换　1988年6月，各银行之间的跨行汇划款项均为相互转汇。为解决跨行资金及时畅通，从是年7月县人行始办票据交换业务，县工、农、建3行票据统一由县人行每天派员送贵阳参与票据交换，返回后再转给各行。1989年12月为减少每天往返麻烦，由县人行设票据交换所，各支行设票据交换员，每天定时在票据交换所进行交换，从而加速银行的资金周转，此办法一直执行到2010年未变。

计算机运作 1988年7月前，银行业务均是手工操作，全用算盘计算办理业务。8月，人行省分行安排修文县支行为全省首批装配微机的20个行之一，运用计算机处理账务，接着工、农、建3行也先后开通计算机运作，从此结束手工操作的历史。1995年4月，县人行计算机运用于国库、发行、统计、劳动工资、金融管理等专业。1996年县工行所属服务网点也全部使用计算机办理对外业务，接着农、建两行及其他金融保险服务网点陆续推行，促使操作速度加快，办事效率提高。至2010年全县金融机构共置计算机187台，达到坐岗职工人手一机。

通存通兑 1990年前，各银行储蓄存款只能在开户行（处）存取。1991年，县工行率先发行牡丹储蓄卡后，农业银行金穗卡、建设银行龙卡相继发行。继后来又增加长城卡、信用卡、复合卡、磁条卡、绿卡等诸多品种。1996年起银行储蓄卡已先后在辖区内通存通兑，后又扩大到全省乃至全国以及跨行支取。2002年3月起，各行普遍发行银联卡，客户既可在全国范围内通存通兑，又可跨行支取，还可到商场刷卡购物结算。到2010年，全县金融机构发行银行卡总量已达13.6万张，从而推动全国个人信用体系，大大方便客户，提高整个金融系统信息处理效率。

实行柜员制 1995年前，银行对外业务均沿用双人坐柜、交叉复核制度。1996年县工行率先在各服务网点安装计算机系统，推行柜员制，接着其他金融机构也相继推行。至2010年，县工行已实现综合柜员制，县农行及扎佐营业所各设综合柜员1个，即1人坐岗办理本行开办全部对外业务，从而减少客户办理多项业务要跑多柜的麻烦。

电子汇划 1996年前，银行汇划业务系通过信汇和联行划拨方式进行结算。1997年1月，县人行电子联行“天地对接”开通并投入使用，实现网络传输方式下的“地上三分，天上三秒”。3月中央银行会计核算系统电子计算机启动运行，4月开始运行电子联行同城资金清算系统，实现磁介质方式下的“天上三秒，地下三小时”。6月，人民银行市、县发行事务处理系统电子运行启动，实现以国家统一标识代码和用计算机开立、管理账户，考核银行结算资金，客户资金划拨通过电子汇划方式办理，汇款输入计算机对方即可收到。1998年建行系统率先推出个人电子汇款业务，2001年6月正式命名为“速汇通”，接着工行系统“汇款直通车”和农行系统“通汇宝”业务相继推出，个人可办理100万元以内现金、活期储蓄存款账户、储蓄卡汇款实现24小时到账。2005年县人行开通大额支付系统，凡在银行开立结算户、汇款金额在5万元以上汇划业务。2006年又开通小额支付系统，办理5万元以下收款业务。2007年再次开通支票影像系统，凡在银行开立结算户单位或个人使用银行支票，均在全国范围有效。电子汇划业务普遍运用，突破时间和地域限制，为客户提供安全、快捷和个性化服务，加速资金周转，提高资金使用效益，从而助推经济的发展。

推行电子银行 1994年前，金融业务只能在开户行（处）柜台办理。1995年县工行利用网络技术向客户提供网上银行个人客户服务，利用通信和计算机技术提供9.56万个客户电话服务。之后，县建行的95533、县农行的95599个人客户电话服务相继开展，通过网站（点）和电话向个人客户提供金融信息服务和金融产品销售，并允许客户通过网站或电话进行查询、转账、缴费、结算、支付、

县工商银行营业厅电子银行

证券、基金等金融交易。1996年县工行又在营业厅一角增置ATAM自动取款机，每天24小时提供客户自助服务，在另一角增置电子银行，为客户办理业务提供票据服务。到2010年，全县金融机构已置有自助银行1个，电子银行2个，装置自动取款机16台，自助终端1台，仅县工行个人电子银行客户就有1.68万户，连续两年位居贵阳市工行系统同业第一名。此外，各网点还在等候区域设置调号机和沙发供客户使用，解决排长队办理业务的问题。

（四）金融风险管理

市场准入 1984年，建立中央银行与专业银行二元银行体制及多种所有制金融机构体系。10月起银行机构实行市场准入制度，县人行对解放后建立并存在的20个金融机构登记上报，其中工行12个，农行6个，建行2个，12月分级颁发《经营金融业务许可证》。对31个农村信用社由主管行登记上报，经农行安顺中心支行审查后，由同级人民银行批准发证。1985年3月县人保支公司列入发证范围（至省保险业监管委员会成立终止）。之后，延续执行批准机构发证，撤销机构收回，保留机构定期换发新证。至2010年，全县准予经营金融机构共23个，其中工行1个，农行2个，农发行1个，县联社14个，商行1个，邮政支行4个。

执行“约法三章” 从1984年起，专业银行向商业银行转轨，银行机构快速增加，业务扩大迅速，违反金融秩序情况时有发生。1993年7月，贯彻执行全国金融工作会议提出整顿金融秩序“约法三章”：一是立即停止和认真清理一切违章拆借，已违章拆出资金的要限期收回；二是任何金融机构不得变相提高存贷款利率，不准用提高利率办法搞“储蓄大战”，不得向贷款对象收取回扣；三是立即与银行自己兴办各种经济实体脱钩。为此，县人行召开县内各金融机构负责人会议，签订同业公平竞争协议，县农行开办多种经营公司与支行脱钩，其他支行准备开办经济实体一律停止。1997年为整顿金融秩序防范金融风险年，人行与工、农、建、农发行、县联社、人寿保险和财产保险公司签订《金融系统执法、风险防范化解目标责任书》，把防范和化解金融风险作为全年工作重点。1998至2010年，银行经营逐步转入正轨，按规经营。

2005年8月7日，省联社副主任宋锐（右一）、副理事长陈齐奎（左二）到扎佐丁官村了解贷款支农情况

处置不良资产 1995年5月《中华人民共和国商业银行法》出台前，国家商业银行处于转轨过程中，控制贷款质量方面缺乏有效的内部控制，从而产生一定规模的不良资产。为消除逐渐孕育着的金融风险，县工、农、建行按照上级部署，对不良资产进行清理上报。1999年4月和9月建、农、工3行分别按系统成立中国信达，长城、华融资产管理公司，负责接收、管理和通过出售、置换、资产重组、债转股、资产证券化等方式处置下属行剥离的不良资产，县工行剥离并划转县轻工系统3户贷款本金186.12万元，贷款利息193万元。2000年5月再次剥离并划转商业系统4个公司贷款本金371.45万元，贷款利息363.14万元；县农行剥离并划转不良资产120户，本金4460万元，表内利息155万元，表外利息1065万元。2003年县建行核销不良资产贷款3户，金额62.4万元（含息烽县支行撤销划入的贷款21.5万元），工

行核销兴红机械厂贷款590.7万元，所欠利息同时处理。2004年6月建行再剥离划转贷款本息345.2万元（含息烽县支行贷款10万元）。至此，工、农、建3行累计核销和剥离并划转贷款本息7792.01万元，占3家银行1998年末贷款总额的28.12%，让国家商业银行卸下包袱，轻松上阵。

贷款卡管理 1995年前，银行业务交叉，带来企业多头开户和多头贷款问题。1996年4月县人行执行总行决定，始对辖区内银行发放贷款实行“贷款卡”管理。凡申请贷款的企业和个人，须持贷款申请书、企业代码证、营业执照、税务登记证、验资报告、法人及担保人身份证、上年和最新财务报告，先到县人行办理“贷款卡”，银行凭“贷款卡”发放贷款，以便全面掌握企业贷款情况，优化资金配置，提高贷款效益和监控率。1999年7月至2010年累计颁发贷款卡284个，从而制止银行之间因不正当竞争导致企业多头贷款的弊端。

贷款卡

授权、授信 1997年，贯彻执行中国人民银行《商业银行授权授信管理暂行办法》，凡批准成立具有独立法人地位的中资商业银行实行一级法人体制，建立法人授权管理制度，在法定经营范围内对有关业务职能部门及其分支机构和关键业务岗位进行授权，被授权人在授予的权限范围内开展业务活动；同时根据国家货币政策和各地区金融风险及客户信用状况，对各地区及客户在最高授信额度内进行授信。商业银行总行对有关业务职能部门和管辖分行直接授权、授信后，管辖分行及其以下再逐级实行转授权和转授信至支行，签订授权、授信书，期限一年。到2010年县内各银行一直沿袭由各自主管行转授权、转授信，年终进行考核，从而强化国有商业银行统一管理与内部控制，增强防范和控制风险能力，保护社会公众和银行自身的合法权益。

2007年10月26日，县信用联社聘请20名行外人士为行风监督员

城乡反假货币网络 2007年，根据贵阳市中心支行《关于在三年内逐步落实农村反假货币网络建设》的要求，县人行深入县辖各乡（镇）和村组建起农村反假货币网络，至2008年完成龙场镇、扎佐镇、久长镇、六广镇、谷堡乡、六屯乡各村的组建工作。2009年继续开展小箐乡、洒坪乡、大石乡、六桶乡77个村反假货币网络建设，全县10乡（镇）农村信用社建立反假货币宣传站，217个村委会和12个居民委员会建立反假货币宣传点，每个点聘请1至2名义务宣传员并签订协议书，由人行集中培训，颁发义务宣传员聘书，运用贵州省反假货币联络员管理信息系统建立健全个人档案，陆续配置伪钞鉴别仪、放大镜等机具。至此，全县实现乡（镇）有组织、村寨有人管、宣传经常化目标，成为贵阳市辖三县一市村级反假网络全覆盖的县。

（五）金融监管

1986年9月县人行独立，专门行使中央银行赋予的职能，对银行机构进行监管，先后于1993年7月对市场准入、经营范围、经营行为的监管。1995年6月以银行风险为核心监管。1998年4月对3家金融机构上年四季度至当年一季度高息揽存、公款私存、高息揽储内部规章监管，查出公款私存16户132笔33.7

万元，变相提高利率382笔余额422.5万元，作成本列支付手续费1.8万元，多付利息0.3万元，当即对违规银行机构处以3万元罚款；对公款私存和公款转储蓄，按公款存款额每天万分之五罚息。2004年起银行机构监管由银监办执行，至2010年未发现严重违规行为。

（六）金融稽核

1988年起施行金融稽核，由中央银行对商业银行采取全面稽核和专项稽核方式进行。1995年县人行开展存款准备金缴存专项稽核，核出工行截至6月的8个月利用县辖往来发生在途资金14笔，金额8850万元，导致漏缴存款准备金1066万元。开展银行资金来源和资金运用专项稽核，核出6月底挂账挤占信贷资金90万元，低质量资产1417万元，占贷款总额26.4%。1996年开展储蓄业务专项稽核，核查出邮政储蓄1至5月对半年以上定期存款按5‰支付酬劳费4.5万元；储户透支2笔，金额3.3万元。2002年开展现金、账户管理专项稽核，查出股份制商业银行出借账户套取现金90笔，金额764.1万元；化整为零套取现金165万元，违规开户套取现金52.8万元，公款私存202.2万元，受全省金融系统通报批评和经济处罚。2004—2010年未核出严重违规问题。

2009年6月，县人行行长杨晓莉（中）、副行长王洪（右一）、纪检组长宋文（左）在县联社河滨路分社指导工作

（七）反破坏和伪造人民币

1979年，贵阳、都匀、凯里等地发现绢布绘制假钞，经人行省分行调查多数由修文、息烽等地流入。1980年9月县人行与公安局、工商局联合召开座谈会，侦破流入修文境内伪造人民币案。1983年11月24日，又与农行、公安局联合印发《关于坚决打击变造、破坏人民币的紧急通知》，要求一经发现，认真组织侦破。1991年11月28日，人行再与公安局联合破获久长镇驴坊村三组特大假钞案，当场缴获伪造人民币成品、半成品共13张，历史货币2400张及作案工具等，依法判处3名罪犯有期徒刑。1994年5月，破获小箐乡境内贩卖伪造人民币案，抓获罪犯3人，缴获伪造人民币50元券75张，面值3750元。1999年6月，贯彻执行国务院反假工作联席会议决定，全县金融机构从上至下开展“99反假币宣传周”活动，唤起全社会共同反假。此后，每年“3·15”消费者权益日都举行反假币宣传，防止假人民币流通。2007—2009年，在贵阳市辖三县一市率先完成农村反假货币网络建设，分别在10乡（镇）农村信用社置宣传站，217个行政村和12个居民委员会设置宣传点，每个站（点）聘请宣传员1至2人，陆续配备伪钞监测仪和放大镜等机具，成为贵阳市辖三县一市独家村级反假网络全覆盖的县。至2010年止的4年累计收缴假币4221张，金额

2005年10月县联社利用场天开展反假币宣传

32.23万元。

专记：驴坊假钞制作案破获记

县境驴坊假钞案系广西壮族自治区东南县武占乡弄辉村农民崔德寿、久长镇驴坊村三组村民黄大权在贵阳做股票生意亏本后的协商共谋：以崔德寿的制假技术，黄大权出资购买制假纸张、药水等材料，分别在黄大权、李大成家用黄、李2人提供的人民币作底版伪造人民币，先后将伪造币拿到贵阳、修文等地购物被识破。10月6日李大成又吩咐其弟李忠拿1张100元面伪造币到农行久长营业所兑换被发现。事发后，久长派出所当即组织警员侦察获取线索，10日立案侦破，在摸清作案人员基本情况和获取重要脏证后，29日抓获涉案者4人，随即对人身和住所搜查，计缴获伪造人民币100元票面5张，50元票面2张，半成品5元票单面各1张，2角票单面2张，1角票单面2张，历史货币2400张，大洋3块，伪造人民币人物图印章3枚，伪造用工具1套8件，纸胶水3瓶，伪造用纸3件，证书3份，药水4瓶，国库券5元，美术本4本。在确凿的证据面前，涉案者认罪不悔，经县人民法院1992年2月25日开庭审判，判决崔德寿、黄大权、李大成犯伪造国家货币罪，依法分别判处有期徒刑7年、5年、3年，从而维护国家金融秩序，保护国家货币正常流通。

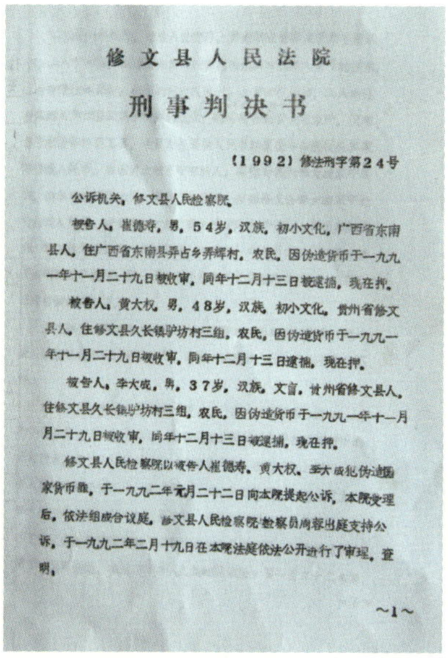

修文县人民法院

刑事判决书

（1992）修法刑字第24号

公诉机关，修文县人民检察院。

被告人，崔德寿，男，54岁，汉族，初小文化，广西省东南县人，住广西省东南县弄占乡弄辉村，农民。因伪造货币于一九九一年十一月二十九日被收审，同年十二月十三日被逮捕，现在押。

被告人，黄大权，男，48岁，汉族，初小文化，贵州省修文县人，住修文县久长镇驴坊村三组，农民，因伪造货币于一九九一年十一月二十九日被收审，同年十二月十三日逮捕，现在押。

被告人，李大成，男，37岁，汉族，文盲，贵州省修文县人，住修文县久长镇驴坊村三组，农民，因伪造货币于一九九一年十一月月二十九日被收审，同年十二月十三日被逮捕，现在押。

修文县人民检察院以被告人崔德寿、黄大权、李大成犯伪造国家货币罪，于一九九二年元月二十二日向本院提起公诉，本院受理后，依法组成合议庭，修文县人民检察院检察员肖蓉出庭支持公诉，于一九九二年二月十九日在本院法庭依法公开进行了审理，查明，

~1~

县人民法院判决书

第三节　证　券

1981—2010年，为筹措资金支持国家经济建设和地方经济发展，先后发行各种债券、基金和不同形式的有奖定期储蓄，累计筹集资金2.7亿元。

一、政府债券

国库券　1981年起，为适当集中各方财力，促进国民经济稳步发展，县工行、农行、建行根据国务院统一部署，每年对国营企业、集体企业、事业单位、机关、团体、部队、农村富裕社队和个人发行国库券。发行期为每年1至6月，个人购买延至9月，起息日期为购买年7月1日，债券不记名，不挂失，不准上市转让。1982年起属单位购买只开收据不发券。1985年起单位和个人购买千元以上均开收据，可记名，可挂失。对个人购买1985年以后发行的国库券，在兑付之前已持券2年以上，如因特殊急需用款，可将其转让给银行办理“贴现”（贴现国债券），贴现期从贴现月计算至到期月。至1990年，县工、农、建3行累计代理发行452.8万元，超任务6.44%。其中单位购买79.67万元，占15.51%；个人购买434.13万元，占84.49%。1989起发行特种国债，国库券不再对单位发行。1991年起推销方式改为集团承购包销，由各国家商业银行总行承购，基层网点联网销售，任务不再下达到县，县内银行不再统计，当年全县完

成个人购买61万元。1998年国库券停止发行。

1981—1991年全县国库券发行任务及实际完成情况统计

表3—08—04　　　　单位：万元

年份	任务			实际完成				
	合计	其中		合计	占任务%	其中		
		集体	个人			中央企业	县内集体	县内个人
1981	1.50	1.50	—	2.47	164.67	—	2.47	—
1982	37.00	3.20	33.80	39.21	105.97	—	3.75	35.46
1983	37.00	2.10	34.90	31.21	84.35	0.85	2.30	28.06
1984	27.00	3.10	23.90	33.24	123.11	3.50	1.55	28.19
1985	46.00	4.05	41.95	48.10	104.57	3.50	4.05	40.55
1986	46.00	3.00	43.00	46.04	100.09	—	5.67	40.37
1987	46.00	4.70	41.30	52.08	113.22	—	10.24	41.84
1988	60.00	7.00	53.00	69.72	116.20	—	12.50	57.22
1989	60.00	7.00	53.00	65.49	109.15	—	14.05	51.44
1990	64.90	14.90	50.00	65.24	100.52	—	15.24	50.00
1991	—	—	—	61.00	—	—	—	61.00
合计	425.40	50.55	374.85	513.8	106.44	7.85	71.82	434.13

凭证式国债　1994年起，为筹集资金用于经济建设，县工行、农行、建行每年分期面向社会公众发行。债券为记名国债，购买时填写“中华人民共和国记账式国债收据”，可挂失，可提前兑付和办理质押贷款及出具存款证明书，但不得更名，不可上市转让，自购买之日起计息，到期一次还本付息，不计复利，逾期不再加计利息。2004年9月起，县建行已实行贵州省分行联网发售和兑付，工、农两行也相继推行。1997—2005年，仅县工行累计代理发行22期，金额3250.46万元。

记账式国债　2002年6月开始发行，县工、农、建3行经办，由投资人持有效身份证券在承办银行办理持有国债份额登记，领取购买国债收据或对账单证明其所有权，根据财政部通过招标方式确定的利率按年付息，计息日期从登记日起算。发行结束，国债可上市流通，通过银行网点进行买卖交易。到2010年仍继续执行。

二、财政部债券

国家重点建设债券　1987年，为筹措国家重点建设资金，县内专业银行代理发行29.4万元。发行对象为企业、事业单位及个人。债券期限3年，单位购买开给购买债券收据，可记名，可挂失，年利率6%；个人购买发给统一印制债券，年利率10.5%。计息日期自购买之日起算，到期一次还本付息，不计复利，逾期不另计息。

财政债券　1988年，为筹措国家建设资金，弥补财政赤字，面向金融机构发售，县内金融单位共购债券49.3万元，由县人行代收，债券期限分为2年、5年，均计单利，从购买年7月15日起息，到期一次还本付息，债券可记名，可挂失，可在银行和其他金融机构之间作抵押进行资金拆借，可向人民银行申请4个月以内的短期抵押贷款。

保值公债 1989年全国物价涨势过猛，为吸引投资者和保护群众经济利益，县工行、农行、建行代理发行。债券面额分为20元、50元、100元3种，期限3年，利率与储蓄存款利率和保值贴补率挂钩。始终高于3年期定期储蓄存款利率1个百分点加保值贴补率。从10月4日起开始发行，累计完成76.49万元，超任务0.4万元。

特种国债 1989年，为筹措财政资金，县工行、农行、建行代理财政部面向各种企业及主管部门、事业单位、社会团体及个人发行。发行期为9月30日前，国债期限5年，年利率15%，从交款之日起计息，到期一次还本付息，不计复利。债券收款单据可记名，可挂失，可向银行申请抵押贷款。至1990年累计发行37.44万元，其中1989年17.73万元，1990年19.71万元。

三、银行债券

金融债券 1985年至1990年，为筹措资金用于企业效益好、产品系社会急需的特别贷款，县工行、农行、建行面向社会公众发行，其中，县工行除1988年未发行外，其余5年均发行1年期债券，年利率9%；县农行除1985年和1988年未发行外，其余4年发行1年期债券，年利率为9%和13.34%；县建行仅1987年发行2年期债券，年利率10%，发行收入用于发放特种贷款，到期一次还本付息，不能提前兑付，不能流通和转让，至1990年累计发行230.11万元，其中工行115.61万元，农行100万元，建行14.5万元。

累进利息金融债券 1987—1990年，为吸收社会闲散资金用于经济建设，县工行、农行、建行面向社会公众发行。债券期限5年，利率与期限挂钩，进息采取累进制，即第一年为年利率9厘，第二年1分，第三年1分1厘，第四年1分2厘，第五年1分3厘，利息按对年对月对日计算，不足年部分不计息，超过5年部分不另计息。至1990年累计发行98.33万元，其中工行1987—1988年发行51.13万元，农行1988年发行29.2万元，建行1988—1990年发行18万元。

贴水金融债券 1988年，县工行和建行发行，为固定期限浮动利率，固定期限为3年零3个月，利率不在券面上标明，通过发行价格确定，即价格为：100元券收款75元，500元券收款375元，1000元券收款750元，面额与发行价格之差即为利息。全年累计发行32.15万元，其中工行28万元，建行4.15万元。

四、有奖储蓄凭证证券

1981—1989年，为筹集资金支持地方经济建设，县人行、工行、农行、建行、联社、邮政储蓄先后开办9种有奖（销售）储蓄，发售有奖定期储蓄凭证证券32.17万张，筹措资金794.08万元。

1988年农村信用社发售的定期有奖存款单

定期有奖有息存款单 1981至1982年，县人行共发售4组，存期1年，每张存款单面额10元，各组设一至末奖4项，通过摇奖确定中奖号码，每个奖金1元至400元。1987至1988年，县农行及其下辖的城关、扎佐、小箐、六广营业所发售4组，存期仍为1年，存款单面额为10元和30元两种，每组奖项分3种等级，每等奖项2个、3个、4个，中奖号码摇奖确定，奖金最高1000元和2000元，最低1元至200元。县联社下辖城关、扎佐、久长、小箐、六广、六桶、王官7个信用社发售7期8组，存期1年，每张面额10元，各组分别设奖项3个和4个两种等次，奖品有现金和实物。以上16组存款单到期时，每张付利息有0.1元、0.2元、0.3元、1元等。累计发售存款单14.62万张，筹集资金166.2万元，其中人行3.12万张，筹资31.2万元；农行3.5万张，55万元；联社8万张，80万元。

定期有奖存款单 1982年8月，县农行发售1组后，又于1987至1988年再与城关、扎佐、久长、六广、六桶营业所（处）发售5组，县工行发售5组，邮政储蓄发售2组（含地区局主办1组）。存期均为1年，到期一次还本。每张存款单面额有5元、10元、20元、30元共4种，每组设奖分两种等级，每等奖项3个和4个，奖品除邮政储蓄1987年发售1组为现金30至1000元外，其余均为实物，分别有18寸彩色电视机、落地式电风扇、台灯、自行车、气压热水瓶、收录机等。全县累计发售存款单12.39万张，筹集资金257.84万元，其中，工行发售5万张，筹资120万元；农行发售5万张，筹资120万元；邮政储蓄发售2.39万张，筹资17.84万元。

定期定额贴现有奖存款单 1987年3月至5月，县农行发售1组，存款单5000张，存期1年，每张面额100元，购买时贴现5元，实收95元，实际筹集资金47.5万元。存款单不记名、不挂失、不提前支取，售完开奖，奖项设4个等级，奖品1至4等依次为价值2000元20寸进口彩色电视机、价值500元双卡收录机、现金50元、6元。到期按面额还本。

住宅有奖定期存款单 1987年6月，建行安顺地区中心支行举办，在县发行，县建行发售存款单1247张，每张面额30元，筹集资金3.74万元。存款单不记名，不挂失，不能提前支取，存满2年一次还本。奖品分5个等级，7月2日在安顺摇奖确定中奖号码，龙场镇徐永发购买75380号中2等奖，获安顺市内住房一套，因本人不要住房则领取该房折款1.3万元。

积零存整有奖有息定期存款单 1988年6月，农行县支行与下辖的城关储蓄所合办1组，发售存款单3000张，每张月存30元，全年360元，累计筹集资金108万元。售完开奖，奖项设4个等级，除末奖为现金10元外，其余奖品分别为电冰箱、自行车、电子琴。每张存足1年还本并付利息1.87元。

实物销售定期存款单（实物销售储蓄） 1988年11月至1989年4月由县工行经办，存款凭证为普通定期存款单，储户存入规定数额资金，银行卖给所需物资。历时6个月，累计卖出贵州赤天化尿素10吨，24K金首饰982.17克，18吋华日牌电视机17台，风华牌电冰箱20台，宝石戒指40枚，筹集资金52万元。

定期有奖销售存款单（有奖销售化肥储蓄） 1988年11月起，全省农业银行系统开办，县农行参与，存款凭证为普通定期存款单，起存金额100元，多存不限，存期1年，不提前支取，每存100元奖励平价尿素票10市斤，储户凭票在当地指定销售点购买。1989年停办。

摸奖定期存款单 1989年3月，县工行举办两期，全部以奖代息。第一期存款单1000张，每张面额10元，存期1年，奖品有茅台酒、董酒、平坝窖酒、热水瓶、枕巾、毛巾、牙膏、铅笔、文具盒、手巾。第二期存款单面额20元，存期2年，设奖7个，奖金分别为500元、200元、50元、5元、3元、2元、1元，由储户伸手到袋内摸奖号，以号兑奖，开办不久即停办，实际吸储仅9万元。同月，县农行开办，存期为1年，存款单每张10元，全部以奖代息，奖号可重复摸，奖品为实物，可以部分变换。当众兑现开奖，累计发售存款单1.23万张，收储资金12.3万元。

“月月乐”定期定额活期有奖有息存款单 1989年6月，由农行修文、息烽两支行合办，共发售存款单3万张，每张面额30元，筹集资金90万元。存款单存期虽定1年，但储户可随时支取，又具有活期性质，每月由两家银行开奖一次，每次均设奖项4个等级，奖品各期不同。

五、证券投资基金

1999年起，为满足基金市场发展需要，帮助有理财需求但没有充裕时间、有意参与证券投资但缺乏证券知识、风险承受能力较低需回避股票等高风险投资品种、拥有一定闲置资金并希望保持资金较高流动性的个人理财者，县工行、农行、建行开办代销证券投资基金业务，凭投资人有效身份证件及证件卡办理开放式基金认购、申购、赎回。代销品种有博时、长城、银华、华夏、银丰、华安等，至2010年累计销售证券投资基金2.18亿元，其中工行代销461支，金额1.6亿元；农行代销153支，金额5800万元。

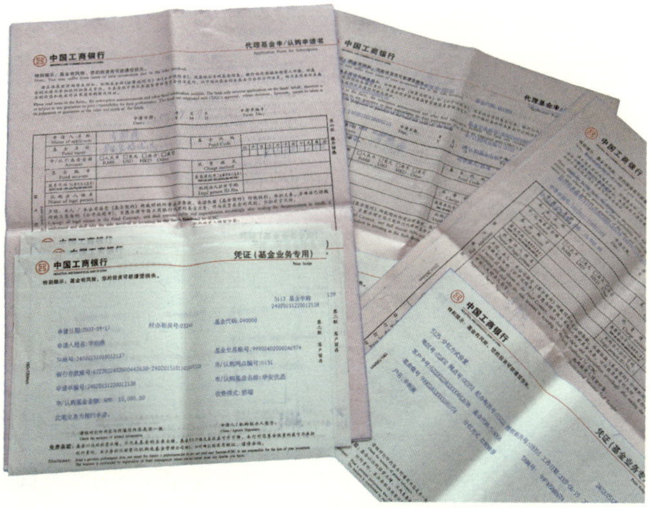

2007年县工商银行发售的证券投资基金凭证

六、企业债券

三角山水泥厂债券 1992年11月17日，县人行依照国务院《企业债券管理暂行条例》规定，批准发行40万元，发行对象为本企业职工，债券期限2年，年利率9%，自文到1月内发行，筹集资金用于企业生产线“填平补缺”项目资金不足，到期一次还本付息。债券不得上市流通，不能转让或作抵押贷款。

万江机电厂债券 1992年12月27日，报经人行安顺地区分行批准，发行100万元。1993年4月17日，再次批准发行100万元，两笔债券期限均为1年，年利率8.5%，限于本企业职工认购，于文到1月内发行，筹措资金用于企业流动资金不足，到期一次还本付息。债券不准上市流通，不能转让、不能作为抵押贷款。

第四节 保 险

1980年11月，县内恢复保险业，冠名人保修文特约代办处，业务由县人行代理。1985年成立县人民保险支公司专营保险业务。1996年分置财产保险和人寿保险。至2010年，保险品种发展为120余个，当年保费收入3730万元和理赔支出668万元，其中财保分别占38.77%和80.99%，人保占61.23%和19.01%。

一、财产保险

1980年，县内仅有企业财产保险、家庭财产保险和机动车辆第三责任险3种。至1985年，保费收入仅74万元，理赔支出43万元，占保费收入的58.11%。从1987年起陆续增加货物运输险、农业险和人寿险。1991年县政府统一办理全县烤烟保险，当年因灾损失赔付26万元，为该项保费收入15万元的1.7倍。1992年全县烤烟继续投保，赔付率仍占该项收入的124%。1993年下半年增办农房长效还本保险，全县2.27万户农民投保。1994年4月大石乡大寨村11户农家遭受严重火灾，每户获赔800元。六屯乡遭受冰雹和暴风雨袭击，房屋严重受损，对135户受灾农户赔付1.35万元，帮助灾民渡过难关。至1995年全县保费收入实现336万元（含人寿保险），为1986年的12.4倍。

1996年体制改革，财产保险分设，一边抓收入，一边抓赔付，大力拓展保险领域，增加保险品种，致保险业务快速发展。2007年起再增办国家扶持“三农”（农业增收、农村发展、农民增收）养殖奶牛保险、能繁母猪保险，保险费由各级财政匹配资金补助80%，养殖户只承担20%，支持养殖业尽快发展，使保费收入跨过千万元。至2010年除停办少数品种外，仍存有企业财产险、机动车辆险、家庭财产险、货物运输险、金牛险、船舶险等60余个险种，当年保费收入1446万元，为1996年325万元的3.4倍；理赔支出541万元，为1996年182万元的2倍，充分发挥保险防灾的重要作用。

专记：财政投保扶持生猪奶牛发展

2007年，为使生猪、奶牛快速发展，保障人民生活需求，由国家财政投入资金，财保支公司9月25日起开办能繁母猪养殖保险，凡饲养场所在当地非蓄洪、行洪区饲养1年以上和存栏30头以上，猪龄8个月至4周岁，无伤残和疾病，有县级畜牧防疫部门审定免疫程序接种，且能识别身份统一标志母猪的均可办理。每头保险费60元，由国家财政补贴48元，养殖户承担12元，保险金额1000元。如在保险期内因暴雨、冰雹、泥石流等自然灾害或火灾、爆炸、口蹄疫等意外事故造成母猪直接死亡，养殖户只承担40元查勘费，财保支公司按照保险合同约定负责赔偿。截至2010年，4年全县累计入保2.44万头，保费收入146.56万元；死亡赔付1561头，赔付156.1万元，占该项收入106.51%。

2008年12月18日开办奶牛养殖保险，每头保险费240元，国家财政补贴192元，养殖户承担48元，保险金额4000元。至2010年止除2009年因财政未拨补助款而未办理外，全县累计入保892头，保险费收入21.41万元，死亡赔付2010年有70头，赔付金额28万元，占该项收入130.78%。

财政投保扶持养殖的奶牛

二、人寿保险

1995年前，为人民保险支公司开办险种。1996年体制改革，人寿保险分业经营，但业务仍由财保支公司代理。1997年将人保业务析出，组建人寿保险机构，经办人员随业务划转，另招聘一批营销员办理保险，不断扩展保险领域，增加诸多保险品种，认真办理赔付，使业务快速发展，到2002年，保费收入达257万元，在全县保险收入中占36.77%，理赔支出85万元，占收入的33.07%。2005年收入超过千万

元。到2010年除停办少数险种外，仍存有团体人身险、子女教育险及国寿、康宁、祥和、祥运等67个主险种和附加险，使保费收入记录刷新，全年达到2284万元，在全县保费收入中占61.23%，跃居首位；而理赔支出仅127万元，占当年该公司保费收入5.56%。

1980—2010年保费收入和理赔支出统计

表3—08—05　　单位：万元

年份	保费收入				理赔支出			
	合计	人民保险公司	财产保险公司	人寿保险公司	合计	人民保险公司	财产保险公司	人寿保险公司
1980—1985	74	—	—	—	43	—	—	—
1986	27	27	—	—	10	10	—	—
1987	52	52	—	—	21	21	—	—
1988	80	80	—	—	50	50	—	—
1989	97	97	—	—	51	51	—	—
1990	112	112	—	—	56	56	—	—
1991	143	143	—	—	120	120	—	—
1992	196	196	—	—	123	123	—	—
1993	209	209	—	—	104	104	—	—
1994	298	298	—	—	134	134	—	—
1995	336	336	—	—	179	179	—	—
1996	325	—	325	—	182	—	182	—
1997	406	—	406	—	176	—	176	—
1998	432	—	432	—	265	—	265	—
1999	377	—	377	—	215	—	215	—
2000	413	—	413	—	217	—	217	—
2001	309	—	309	—	150	—	150	—
2002	699	—	442	257	297	—	212	85
2003	684	—	532	152	319	—	294	25
2004	1254	—	804	450	454	—	383	71
2005	2151	—	852	1299	698	—	587	111
2006	2410	—	1044	1366	772	—	682	90
2007	2156	—	1170	986	887	—	574	313
2008	3166	—	1197	1969	973	—	727	246
2009	3268	—	1519	1749	755	—	584	171
2010	3730	—	1446	2284	668	—	541	127

第九章　招商引资

1981年，县政府成功引进重晶石粉生产技术和砖瓦窑电抽风工艺。1983年，成立县对外经济协作办公室，负责地方产品协出和所需物资协入。1984年制定“三引进”（资金引进、技术引进、人才引进）配套政策，开展横向联合引资。1993年采取内引外联举措推动招商引资，在携带部分地方产品外出招商推介的基础上，县委、县政府于1998年补充修订招商引资优惠政策和措施。1999年确立“团结务实，乘势争先”为修文精神和“言行一致，开明开放”为修文形象，打开山门，降低门槛，外出招商。2000年成立县招商引资机构，创造性地推行“一站式”服务，营造出良好的投资环境，构成亲商、安商、富商的良好氛围，使一批又一批商家和企业先后落户县境。

第一节　项目库设置

1984年，对外经济协作办公室始编《修文县资源情况简介》，至1992年项目资料均根据企业需要临时编写，规格极不统一。1993年8月，“中国黄果树山水风光游暨中国国际名酒节”在省城贵阳举办，县政府责成县经济委员会和乡镇企业局编写部分《项目简介》，作为参加招商引资资料。1995年12月建立县项目办公室，1996年于乡镇企业局置项目库，协助项目办公室编制项目建议书10个，其中建材类3个，化工类3个，冶炼类2个，食品类2个。1997年库内资料增至43个，包括能源类4个，建材类10个，化工类10个，冶金类6个，医药类2个，机械类3个，轻纺类6个，旅游类2个。

1998年，贵州省政府和贵阳市政府拨给专款购置微机、复印机等设备，开始对外发布项目信息，进一步为招商引资提供资料。2004年5月县正式建立项目库。2006年6月成立招商引资局，项目资料逐渐增加，内容不断完善，至2010年项目库资料增至135个，其中工业类29个，农业类27个，旅游类42个，房地产类2个，食品类11个，医药类5个，基础设施类13个，电力类1个，物流商贸、节能减排等项目5个。项目库发挥信息功能，较好地为招商引资服务，使投资商充分解县情和打算开发的资源，增强落户修文的决心和信心。贵阳森林野生动物园落地县境，就是商家首先从项目资料中解到县境扎佐有丰富森林资源、良好的气候条件、便捷的交通和位于省城贵阳北大门的区位优势以及宽松的投资环境，然后经

过现场查勘敲定将动物园园建在扎佐林场，赓续于2004年10月起建，历时1年工期，于2005年10月建成，2006年6月开园，至2010年累计接待游客216.89万人次，旅游综合收入4.66亿元。入驻龙场镇潮水村的双辉钢铁有限公司从项目库资料中掌握到县内铁矿藏量和交通条件后下决心建厂，于2003年6月破土动工，次年投产，仅2005年就产出生铁2.76万吨，实现产值5942万元，销售收入5236万元，纳税250万元，排位在县域纳税大户前10名。

专记：双辉钢铁有限公司落地潮水村

2002年，福建籍人刘文华，从项目资料中得知修文县紧靠省城贵阳，交通便捷，电力有保障，水资源和铁矿资源丰富，招商引资政策优惠等条件后，决定选址距县城3公里，贵（阳）毕（节）高等级公路入口仅6公里的龙场镇潮水村，征地75亩，累计投资4000万元兴建1座炼铁厂，取名“双辉钢铁有限公司，刘文华自任经理。公司建成128立方米冶炼高炉一座，18立方米环式烧结机一台，年设计生铁生产能力6万吨，2004年8月投产，年销售收入从2005年的5236万元增到2010年的1.8亿元，纳税从250万元增到6599万元，连续保持年营业收入500万元以上的工业企业和全县纳税大户排位前十名。先后吸收当地农村剩余劳动力就业360人。

公司投产后，充分利用自身的技术人才，坚持以环保排放达标和提高生产效率的底线，达到“生产要上去，环境不污染”的目的，对不适应生产的设备进行改造，投资550万元专项治理环保设施，配备高炉冶炼高效废气净化系统，使处理后的废气排放达到国家规定的标准；用闭路循环冷却水处理系统对高炉冶炼废水进行净化处理，循环使用，不让废水排出厂区；安装高炉水冲渣系统，使处理后的冶炼废渣变废为宝，供作水泥生产的原料。2005年5月，双辉公司成为县域首家正式通过国家环保验收合格的冶炼企业。至2010年，有职工276人，当年实现产值2.1亿元，销售收入1.8亿元，缴纳国家税金660万元。

第二节　软环境建设

1994年始编《投资指南》进行宣传。1995年组织服务单位到入驻企业现场办公。2005年置便民服务中心，服务单位抽人集中办公。至2010年《投资指南》历经几次改版，宣传范围已覆盖到一产、二产、三产。入驻企业仅在一道门内即可办完开工前所需办理的事宜。

一、编印《投资指商南》

1994年由县委宣传部主笔、乡镇企业等部门配合，编写出县内首期招商引资的《投资指南》，简要介绍修文环境资源、经济发展、投资导向、优惠政策及服务措施，使外来投资者从中对县的区位优势、资源状况有所解。1999年改编为折叠式开本，内容较前翔实。2001年又由县招商引资办公室主持编制《投资指南》，设计精美，用大量图片展示修文，投资导向栏目精选37个项目列表逐个反映；专辟审批程序栏目，载明投资项目审批由招商办、计经局、乡镇企业局全权受理代办，限期办理完毕；并刊载有县政府招商引资优惠政策。

2004年版为《修文投资项目》，内容分旅游、食品医药、铝工业、建筑材料、物流服务、房地产开发、农业开发、资产转让、通信录、电水价10个部分，分别对25个招商项目进行介绍，其中扎佐医药食品工业园、久长铝工业园等。扎佐物流中心还载有规划平面彩图，使投资者既读文，又看图，印象深刻。

1999年出版的《投资指南》

2007年，由招商引资局编印，新增外来投资企业《办事指南》，内容分为修文概况、自然风光、投资优势、投资导向、政策法规、投资项目、投资程序、社会服务等。8个栏目，对70个投资项目用表予以介绍，并载入扎佐物流园、扎佐医药工业园2007至2025年总体规划图。还告知投资者办事程序和应出示的资料以及相关部门的联系电话，为投资企业提供很多方便。

二、“一站式”服务

1994年前办理项目申报，涉及立项、审批等手续时，基本是各守门户、各自为阵，坐机关、卡脖子、推诿扯皮的事时有发生。1995年，县政府多次召开部门协调会，要求部门增强服务意识，下到企业现场办公，为其排忧解难，首例解决引进的黄磷厂各项手续的办理，使企业顺利落户于久长镇沙雁村。

2000年，扎佐医药产业园区招商启动，县政府成立园区协调领导小组，组织国土、工商、环保、公安、规划等部门下到园区服务，办理项目申报、立项、审批等事宜。要求部门提高办事效率和服务质量，简化审批程序，缩短办事周期，兑现服务承诺，规范收费行为。凡上级明令取销的收费项目坚决不收，周边区县停收的项目一律停收，有征收幅度的项目一律按最低标准优惠收取。并主动出面协调入驻企业与扎佐林场以及周边的关系，将收费“明白卡”制度和倡导多年的“人人都有招商形象，处处都是招商环境”的口号落到实处，创造性地推出引进、申报、落地、建设、生产“一站式”全方位服务，形成“一站式接待，一条龙办理，一揽子解决问题”的模式，使办事效率显著提高，确保商家引得进、留得住、能发展，一致感到“满意在修文”。2003年引进的龙翔能源集团有限公司深有感触地说：“我们企业在短期内能迅速发展，是得益于县委和县政府优质高效的服务。”

三、设立便民服务中心

2005年，县政府结合《中华人民共和国行政许可法》的实施，在招商引资办公室设立便民服务中心，从发改、公安、国土、环保、工商、建设等部门抽调政治素质好、业务水平高、办事能力强的中层干部进驻，设立办事窗口，以窗口服务形式受理、履行各部门相关行政许可等职能和提供行政服务。各部门服务事项为：发展和改革局办理建设项目核批、备案及转报上级局的行政许可事项；公安局办理户籍变动、身份证、出国（境）、边境通行、制印等行政许可事项；国土资源局办理社会法人、个人土地使用行政许可事项；环境保护局办理建设项目环境保护评价、环保行政审批事项；工商行政管理局办理申请人申请投资生产、经营项目工商行政审批事项；建设局办理各类建设项目规划、用地选址、工程施工

行政许可事项。服务工作实行“一道门进，一道门出，一个窗口对外，一个漏斗对内”办法，操作人员除用10%的精力办理行政许可服务事项外，其余90%精力用在项目追踪、协调、落实、服务上，让“亲情修文”形象留在客商的脑海里，使之树立“投资就在修文”的信心。

第三节　招商引资活动

1978—1981年，县委、县政府实施引进人才、技术、资金的举措。1984年始派对外经济协作办公室人员参加全国性的商品交易会、洽谈会以及宣传推介，先后采取政府部门协调、中介搭桥、产品布展推介、入境考察洽谈、外出布展引商、文化搭台招商等方式开展招商引资活动。1998—2010年共引进180个企业入驻，其中第一产业21个，第二产业126个，第三产业33个，累计到位资金54.8亿元。

一、政府部门协调引资

1984年，县委书记王向规率县科协主席朱明龙一行赴江苏省无锡市考察，引进食用菌工业化生产线。因该项目尚处实验阶段，设备仅属试制，技术也未成熟，加之缺乏生产食用菌经验，造成32万元的直接经济损失。继后，遇上国内经济过热，通货膨胀加剧，县政府总结经验教训，抱以审慎态度，放缓招商引资步伐。1992年通货膨胀得以遏制，县政府加大招商引资力度，得知台商王乾麟意欲在贵州投资的信息，县乡镇企业局与扎佐企业管理站跟踪，诚信相邀与之达成共识，引进资金125万美元，在扎佐镇大山村建成年设计能力1000吨魔芋精粉生产线，从而开创招商引资新局面，至年末全县引进项目21个，其中年产值50万元以上的8个。1993年铁二局第三材料厂在原有基础上投资300万元，扩建马家桥联合铁厂，建成容量28立方米炼铁炉一座，使年设计生产能力提高到1.8万吨。同时引进铁五局物资公司投资400万元，建成年设计能力1.2万吨生铁的新生铁厂。此外，马家桥乡柯达铁厂和扎佐镇双星铁厂也是县政府进行协调引进资金建起来的。继后5年，县委、县政府还对招商引资有突出贡献单位和个人，在经济上给予重奖，获奖额1500元至5万元，以肯定能人的作用，继续招商引资。

2000年9月正式成立县招商引资领导小组，从工商、计划经济、国土、乡镇企业、环保、财政、人事等部门抽调干部到领导小组办公室办公，进一步将招商引资纳入政府工作日程。2004年，根据国家制定对社会经济发展加强宏观调控的决定，县委、县政府明确经济工作的思路首先突出招商引资，必须在引进大项目上下功夫，从而培育工业支柱产业和拉长产业链。在引进华飞铝氧化项目中，县主要领导分头多次与投资者洽谈，邀请公司决策层莅县考察，甚至参加业主董事会，使其下决心把项目落地修文。但因招商心切，考察粗疏，导致腾源铝业行骗案件的发生。2006年6月起，责成招商引资局专司招商引资工作，至2010年认真履行政府决策，参与发展县域经济，负责对引进国内外资金、技术、人才及投资项目的考察和洽谈，并协同有关部门促进招商引资，使其工作步入健康轨道。

专记：腾源铝业的覆灭

腾源公司系山西省太原市人王飞龙和柳林县人张钰（女），于2002年9月用1万港元注册资金在香港注册成立腾源集团投资有限公司（简称“香港腾源公司”）。年底，王飞龙等乘修文招商引资开发县域矿藏资源，发展地方经济之机，意欲在县辖的久长镇投资生产氧化铝，并与美国丰泽财务管理与投资有限公司共同聚资2980万美元，成立修文腾源铝业有限公司，其中商定香港腾源公司出资1937万美元，丰泽公司出资1043万美元，由王飞龙出任董事长，张钰任总经理，霍安安任副总经理，办事处设于贵阳。

2003年1月10日，县政府由于招商心切，在未严格考察情况下，由副县长成华强带招商办、乡镇企业局及久长镇等部门的主要负责人共7人，在遵义由县招商办出面与腾源公司代表张钰、霍安安签订《投资兴建氧化铝项目协议书》。29日，贵阳市发展计划委员会以筑计农字34号文明确建设规模为年产氧化铝80万吨，资金自筹，项目实施年限为2003年的批复。5月15日贵阳市工商行政管理局受理登记，并通知5天内办理手续和领取执照。于是腾源公司以零注册方式取得企业法人执照，29日又拿到贵阳市政府《台港澳侨投资企业批准证书》。《证书》明确“企业类型为外资，经营范围为生产、销售本企业产品，经营年限为50年”。

《协议书》签订后，县政府先后召开研讨会评估项目，并对相关问题专题研究，腾源公司也先后通过国外投资者和香港腾源铝业投资财团到县考察。在没有投入相应资金，又未按程序办理公司运作氧化铝项目需要的投资许可证、基本建设计划书审批、土地征用、环保评估等相关手续的情况下，公司竟对市、县明确表示不许收取建筑安装保证金的意见置之不理，采取对外发包工程方式借款和收取报名费、认定金、保证金、合同履约金、质保金、联营费、图纸费等共40户1248.8万元。11月3日，氧化铝项目在久长镇久长村金鸡山脚举行开工庆典，破土动工兴建，占地共34亩。19日，贵州省政府土地清理督查组临县检查提出，氧化铝建设属违法用地，责令立即停工，立案审查。于是，王飞龙、张钰离开贵阳，公司日常工作由霍安安负责，霍仍然采取收取资费方式向4个单位索取资金124万元。12月，被索取资费者报案，公安机关立案侦查。

2004年3月，贵阳市工商行政管理局以资金不到位为由依法吊销营业执照。4月，贵阳市公安局侦查发现公司收取上述资金后并没有用于项目审批等事宜，而是移作与项目无关的支付，先后购买各种类型汽车14辆，价值400万元；王飞龙和张钰以个人名义在深圳购买两套房产，价值75万元。遂由公安机关派警赴深圳将王飞龙、张钰抓获。在公安机关调查期间，霍安安故意隐瞒公司财务资料，并将其转移到海南省海口市交给他人保管。2005年4月，公安机关将资料追回，霍安安也于当月被抓获归案。

经贵阳市中级人民法院审理认为，腾源公司以非法占有为目的，在签订合同过程中骗取对方当事人

行骗未建成腾源铝业有限公司

保证金、报名费等资金共13家523万余元，其行为已构成合同诈骗罪，被告人王飞龙、张钰、霍安安作为公司主管人和直接责任人，应当承担相应刑事责任。王、张对全部涉案金额负责，分别判处有期徒刑15年，各处以罚金1万元；霍安安应对其签订合同手段骗取保证金124万元负责，并故意隐匿公司会计资料，其行为构成隐匿会计凭证、账簿罪，数罪并罚，判处有期徒刑11年，并处以罚金。2005年10月11日，新华网贵州频道以《"空壳公司"设局狂骗》为题，对法院审判情况专题报道。

案件终结后，司法机关办案人员指出：该案中被骗子们"请君入瓮"的被害单位之多，被骗金额之大，令人匪夷所思。随着市场竞争加剧，一些公司使用诈骗伎俩频频出招。而地方政府发展经济的招商心切，对前来投资者不仅不认真审查，反而违背规定为其大开绿灯。殊不知不少骗子就是抓住这种心理，投其所好，利用政府的"信誉"大行其道。需要提醒的是：地方政府在招商引资中千万要保持清醒头脑，谨防自觉不自觉地成为犯罪分子的"帮凶"。

二、中介搭桥引资

1984年，为解决企业资金的缺口问题，马家桥联合铁厂得到四川省綦江县赶水镇个体户蒋再宜提供信息，由白莲村村民华端钰上门联系，引进铁二局第三材料厂资金40万元与之联办。后又通过县政府协调，引进铁五局物资公司资金60万元与铁二局第三材料厂、马家桥乡政府三方联营，更名为联合铁厂，年产6000吨生铁，达到设计生产能力。1985年小营村通过乡镇企业局引进四一八库服务公司资金15.5万元，与乡镇企业局矿业公司投资15.5万元建成箐口铝矿加工厂，次年实现利润26万元，创外汇8万元。继后，城乡之间、地区之间、不同所有制之间横向联合陆续展开，项目和资金数额逐年增多，至1990年，全县累计引进资金2000万元，使乡镇企业固定资产从1985年的688万元增至4634万元，增长5.7倍。1993年后，招商引资工作逐步展开，中介搭桥引资相应减少。2006年欲投资修文房地产开发的上海老总石晓飞得知县政协干部王文介绍县内铝资源丰富的信息后，改变原有打算，利用龙场镇小营村原一〇五地质队遗留闲置场地，投资8亿元建成年产20万吨铝氧化项目，至2010年投产，实现产值2560万元，销售收入1750万元。

2010年华飞铝氧化项目投产

三、产品布展推介

（一）贵阳布展推介

1993年8月8—15日，中国黄果树山水风光游暨中国国际名酒节在贵阳举行，县政府编成部分项目简介，责成乡镇企业局和县酒厂等部门组团并带部分产品参加布展和招商引资。由于首次组团参与大型活动，地方资源不凸显，参展产品一般化，致招商未见成效。

1998年5月28—31日，贵阳龙洞堡国际机场通航，贵州省政府举办贵州招商旅游暨贵阳机场通航庆典，开展经贸洽谈。县政府抓住机遇，组团随带部分特色产品参展推介，让参加庆典商家大开眼界，从而提高修文知名度。此后，县委、县政府增强招商引资观念，从坐等投资者上门转为走向全省乃至全国招商。

2000年，责成县乡镇企业局在详查县境闲置资产基础上，重新整理编写招商项目资料，随带部分工农业名优产品参加8月18日在贵阳举办的全国乡镇企业东西合作商贸洽谈会，以此推介吸引众多客商，当即与投资商签约27项，意向投资8.4亿元，其中协议23项，签约金额含国外资金6640万元在内共5.5亿元。

2001年，贵阳（香港）投资贸易洽谈会专设修文展区，县政府组成12人的代表团前往，共接待客商70多家，签订旅游投资项目2个，意向投资2730万美元；经销代理1项，意向金额3500万元；销售协议1项，年销售额1000万元。2005—2010年，一年一次的中国贵阳医药博览会召开，县政府均组团参加，虽无签约项目，但对扶持县境医药业做大做强起到积极作用。

（二）长沙、西安布展推介

2006年9月，招商引资局副局长朱启军带领先食品有限公司人员及产品，赴湖南省长沙市参加中部国际贸易博览会。2007年4月，县政府常务副县长魏燕飞率招商引资局、乡镇企业局及恒和制药有限公司人员及产品，参加在陕西省西安市举办的国际贸易洽谈会。两次参会主要是布展推介产品，提高产品知名度，将产品推向全国。

四、对外招商推介

（一）省内招商

1985年，外协办派员参加贵阳召开的全国经济技术洽谈会、国际经济技术合作和贸易洽谈会，广泛宣传县内资源及发展经济的有利条件。1997年，招商引资逐步由横向联合转向内引外联。1998年5月，县政府组团参加贵州省经贸洽谈会，回县后采取“一事一议、一厂一策”的方式进行招商，对不同投资商和不同投资项目制定不同的招商政策。

2000年9月，县招商引资办公室着手规划医药产业园和物流园等经济园区，并在医药产业园建立协调领导小组，由县委常委、常务副县长成华强担任组长，从14个相关部门选派干部进驻园区实行“一站式”服务，为企业办理立项、审批等手续。至2002年8月，累计引进县外资金形成固定资产投资3.9亿元，涉及建设项目116个，分别占全县工业、交通运输业、旅游业等产业固定资产投资5万元以上项目总投资和项目总数的70.42%和39.59%。此后，入驻企业陆续增加，截至2010年，仅医药产业园落户企业即达18家，园区内德昌祥、绿太阳、科开、维康、天方、光正等药业均是从省城贵阳迁入的。维康药业有限公司原住乌当区新添寨，县政府从市政府获知属于迁出单位信息后，便责成招商引资局上门推介，邀请企业领导亲赴扎佐医药产业园实地考察，因选定扎佐林场去万江厂路边地块，但该地中间被农民耕地相隔，县即出面协调，由公司按每亩7480元价格征得后面山地换取农民熟耕地，总计补偿农民2.2万元，使征用的地连成一片，遂于2002

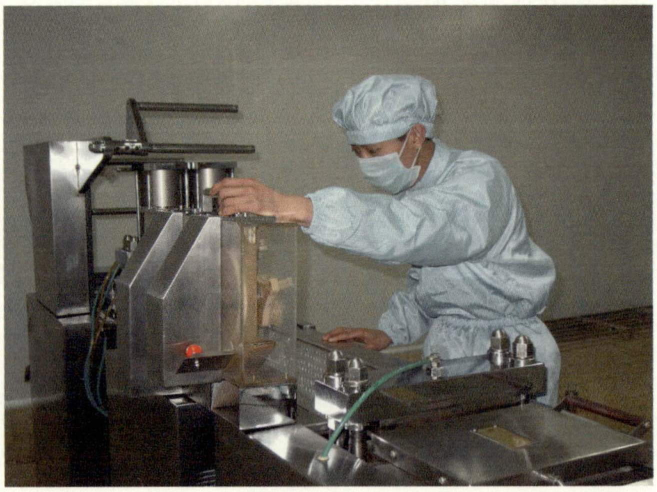

天方药业制药车间

年4月动工进行GMP异地技术改造，边建设边生产，当年实现销售收入2475万元，纳税160万元。2010年实现 产值4.2亿元，年销售收入3.6亿元，缴纳国家税收2557万元后盈利3081万元，成为县内纳税大户。

（二）省外招商

县组团出省招商 1997年前，招商引资基本是在县境周边打转，有投资者上门才予洽谈。1998至2002年，县政府先后10次组织招商引资团参加全国和省、市大型经济贸易洽谈活动，签约30余个。后又于2004年先后组团赴山东、新疆、四川、福建、广东、浙江、上海等省（自治区、市）考察学习，进行招商推介，引进新投资项目17个，合同引资3.48亿，当年全部开工建设。

2005年，着力打造“诚信修文、诚信招商、文明招商”的形象，以亲情、友情感动外来客商。2006年立足县境地域优势和产业现状，以华飞铝氧化项目为重点，保留16家煤炭企业为基础，原破产航空工业一六六厂园区引进企业为依托，重点发展制药、物流、新材料、机械制造、铝产品精加工和深加工和房地产、旅游业，通过精选项目以小分队招商形式，瞄准上海、福建、浙江、重庆、长三角、珠三角等地区招商，在全县第一、二、三产业上形成一批发展势头好、产业带动强、具有强大市场竞争力的特色支柱产业。至2010年，先后组团赴福建、西安等地参加招商引资推介洽谈会，累计签订新投资项目73个，续建项目68个，实际到位资金19.74亿元，多数项目按预定期限建成投产。

2010年9月9日，县政府在福州招商推介会

随市团出省招商 2005年5月，抓住贵阳市政府组织大型团队赴福州招商推介的机遇，副县长成华强率招商引资办和乡镇企业局负责人参加，与贵州天龙摩擦材料有限公司签订协议，投资2000万元建设工业用摩擦材料生产线。2006年4月、5月和9月，县政府又组织相关部门负责人参加招商团随贵阳市招商团赴杭州、昆明、广州进行展招商推介，与福建、浙江、上海、广州等省（市）客商签订投资协议6个，合同金额17.5亿元。2007年3月和6月再组团随市招商团赴上海、苏州、成都招商推介，与投资方签订意向协议1项，意向投资9.2亿元；签订投资协议1项，投资金额3000万元。

随省团外出招商 2006年6月，县政府县长助理张华政率招商引资局、乡镇企业局负责人参加贵州省赴哈尔滨经贸代表团招商推介，与吉林省投资商袁凤友签订投资3500万元开发六广镇丁家寨煤矿、大桥沟煤矿、永兴煤矿项目协议。2010年，3个煤矿年销售收入超过1亿元，纳税602万元后盈利1070万元，全部跻身规模以上工业企业。

（三）香港招商

2005年11月，贵阳市政府组织大型招商团赴香港招商推介，副县长成华强率招商引资办等部门负责人参加，与泛亚细安香港有限公司签订意向性协议，投资1000万元人民币在扎佐镇大山村建设魔芋粉精加工项目，2008年生产魔芋粉120吨，产值2277万元，营业收入287万元，缴税1万元，盈利4万元。后因效益不佳停产。

（四）国外招商

2007年5月，县长石洪率相关企业负责人参加贵阳市政府代表团赴新加坡和马来西亚招商推介，与新加坡客商签订投资4500万元人民币在扎佐镇兴红村原一六六厂内兴建宇丰净水剂生产项目，在久长镇黄磷厂投资500万元人民币贸易流通项目。2010年宇丰公司产值达到3095万元，实现营业收入1233万元，纳税187万元，列入规模以上工业企业。

五、文化搭台招商

1999年10月14—15日，举办首届阳明文化节，节名为“贵阳99阳明文化节”，在县城搭建900平方米摊棚展销地方产品，举办投资贸易洽谈会，接待客商63个，散发宣传资料数千份，与投资方签约14项，金额3.28亿元，其中协议6项，投资金额9914万元。

2002年10月18—19日，举办第二届阳明文化节，节名为“2002中国贵阳（修文）阳明文化节”。举办前期由副县长成华强带领有关部门负责人，赴省内制药企业宣传招商优惠政策及优越投资环境，欢迎商家节日聚会参加投资洽谈，至月底共落实签约项目11个，投资金额2.93亿元，随即全部办完土地征用手续，其中7个项目当年开工。

2005年9月13—17日，举办第三届阳明文化节，节名为“中国·贵阳（修文）第三届国际阳明文化节”。按照乡（镇）报送洽谈项目举行签约仪式，到会客商100余人，签约项目66个，投资金额27.7亿元，其中意向投资50个，金额22.18亿元。与河南省客商签约投资4000万元，选址扎佐镇大关冲建成银星磨料有限公司。2009年四届阳明文化节的成功举办，扩大招商引资，拉动修文城市基础设施、文化基础设施、旅游基础设施建设，城乡面貌得到改善和提升，人的精神和素质得到提振，助推县域经济发展和生态文明城市建设。至2010年，公司在岗职工98人，当年实现产值7956万元，年销售收入7495万元，纳税160万元后盈利35万元。

第四届阳明文化节招商引资签约仪式

六、引进考察洽谈

1997年，县政府诚邀拟寻求更大发展空间的贵州绿太阳药业有限公司总经理沈子明到县考察，看到扎佐镇珍珠井原野珍食品厂闲置厂房、场地，离210国道仅1公里，交通条件和园林绿化非常优越，当即决定将公司生产基地从贵阳龙洞堡迁入，用4个月时间投资800万元建成县境内首条现代化药品生产线，致力于贵州苗药开发与研究。

请进考察的同济堂制药

1999年春，再邀贵州仙灵（2004年更名为“同济堂”）药业股份有限公司董事长王晓春至县考察，对与县城相邻的原贵州航空标准件厂搬迁后留下的闲置场地颇感兴趣，当即一锤敲定，以310万元转让费买下，7月起投资3100万元将花溪蔡冲生产场地迁入，按GMP标准进行异地技术改造，2000年建成胶囊剂、片剂、颗粒剂3种剂型六条生产线，成为县内又一家规模以上工业企业，2010年销售收入达4.39亿元，纳税5200万元，为园区3家销售收入超亿元的企业之一。

专记：绿太阳公司首家入驻修文医药产业园区

绿太阳公司创建于1993年，原生产基地置于贵阳龙洞堡，致力于贵州苗药开发，初期产品尚无知名度。为使产品占有一定市场，董事长沈子明亲自外出跑销售，携“日晒防治膏”至北京武警总队，将产品赠予天安门国旗护卫队试用，护卫队员感觉良好，特致函感谢并索购。此后，“日晒防治膏”成为国旗护卫队的首选护肤品，北京大小报纸争相报道，给该产品打免费广告。为寻求更大发展空间，1997年沈子明应邀到县内考察，看中扎佐林场境内原野珍食品厂闲置厂房和场地，于7月将生产设备从龙洞堡迁入，投资800万元兴建现代化药品生产线，厂区占地48亩，厂房和辅助设施建筑面积1.3万平方米，绿化面积1.18万平方米，绿化覆盖率达37.37%，10月竣工投产，成为修文医药产业园区较早入驻的企业，省内唯一生产膏霜中药制剂生产商。所开发绿格尔系列产品拥有肤痔清软膏、貂胰防裂膏和日晒防治膏3个民族药及磁疗祛斑按摩乳、补天胶囊、葆肤康软膏、痔舒安软膏、绿格尔顽癣敌、绿格尔粉刺净6个保健系列品种。产品畅销于全国23个省、市、地区，部分产品远销至加拿大、荷兰、俄罗斯、越南等国家和中国香港地区。拳头产品肤痔清软膏系苗药验方应用现代技术精制乳化的纯中药制剂，经贵阳医学院和四十四医院、北京中日友好医院、中国中医研究院等多家医院对数百名患者临床验证，皮肤病显效率为73.33%，痔疮显效率86.66%，妇女带下病显效率76%，曾荣获国家“星火计划”实施10周年优秀项目金奖、1998中国新产品新技术博览会金奖，为中国民族医药学会推荐产品。公司还生产有集磁疗祛斑按摩乳集美容面膜、中药祛斑乳液、磁疗按摩、养颜护肤、内服外擦为一体的美容保健品，被誉为“微型家庭美容院”。新开辟葆肤康软膏等4个品种主要销售在海外市场。2001年肤痔清软膏入选国家重点产品暨特色药品，被贵州、新疆、大庆油田等省、区和企业列为公费医疗报销用药，当年营业收入达到1300万元。

进驻修文医药产业园区的绿太阳制药公司

2002年，公司投资1800万元扩展场地，就地进行技术改造，新建3条生产线。2004年6月取得国家GMP标准认证资格。到2010年，公司员工增至182人，年产值和营业收入均达到1.1亿元，缴纳国家税金1170万元后获利773万元，成为年销售收入上亿元的大户。

第四节　人才　技术　资金引进

1981年开始引进人才、技术和资金，1984年县委、县政府制定《“三引进”互惠条件》和《奖励暂行规定》，对投资者在土地和税收方面给予优惠，对引进者实行一次性奖励。1996年，县委、县政府加大招商引资力度，于2000年和2008年两次调整招商政策，在产业扶持基础上，对符合国家产业政策且固定资产投资达1000万元以上项目，符合土地利用总体规划的按缴纳土地出让金的30%、50%、100%额度奖励企业用于扩大再生产；非公有制企业在一个会计年度内对财政贡献额达100万以上，分别给予3万元以上定额扶持和增量扶持，从而促进招商引资和入驻企业快速发展。

一、人才引进

1980年前，企业职工均是就地录用，技术人才十分匮缺。1981年起，随着企业数量增加和生产技术含量逐渐增大，有的企业采取送出去委托培训或代为培训方式提高技术工人水平；有的企业采取聘进工程技术人员帮助解决生产中的技术问题。1987年投产的马家桥铁厂，由于设备陈旧和技术落后被迫停产，后与铁五局联办，由铁五局选派技术精、懂管理的人才担任厂长，负责对全厂生产和技术的管理。12月4日点火，当月产出生铁373吨，合格率达86.5%。1988年修文硅铁厂（后改名文德矿冶有限公司”）聘请7名编外工程技术人员，每周上班两天，其余时间如遇技术难题则到厂处理。落户小营村箐口铝矿加工厂与军工企业四一八库联营，改由四一八库懂技术会管理的潘吉成任厂长，将整体装窑计费改为进窑生矿计费，每窑多装生铝矿30吨，使能耗和成本降低，每窑增加产值2000元。

1991年，有的企业聘用国营企业和科研部门工程技术人员在本企业兼职，或聘请已退休的工程技术人员参加管理。原帮助联合磨料厂建厂工程师李乐勇系贵阳市国营企业职工，在原工作单位办理退职手续后，全身心投入厂内管理生产和技术长达16年，企业一直蓬勃发展。文德矿冶有限公司与香港德利贸易公司合资，先后聘请在岗工程师7人，厂外咨询服务工程师7人，管理干部2人，加强对生产和技术的管理，是年生产硅铁近2000吨，产值600万元，纳税70万元，出口创汇近200万美元，使企业扭亏为盈，产品远销日本、韩国、美国及中国香港、台湾等地区。河口铁合金厂聘请贵阳科研部门退休工程师进厂管理，生产一直保持正常。

1993年起，县委、县政府着重抓好外引内联，重视发展“能人经济”，使之起到“领头雁”的作用。县政府在财政不太宽裕情况下安排40.75万元资金，奖励1992至1995年引资落地生产单位和有功人员。作出较大贡献的“十佳”厂长（经理）和年纳税百万元以上企业的厂长（经理），以肯定能人在发展经济中的作用。至1995年年末，全县民营集体企业中，除兼职指导的工程技术人员外，还引进专职工程技术人员39人。

1996年起，企业生产从粗放型向集约型转变，大部分建材企业引进沿海企业的先进生产工艺，安装自动化生产设备，采用微机配料跟踪反馈系统，所需技术人才和管理人员多是进入人才市场择优录取。先是利尔水泥厂率先吸纳大专院校毕业生20人进厂操作，其他企业纷纷仿效，使企业人员文化素质和专业素质显著提升。

2000年起，引进企业逐渐增多，企业把人才智力开发、高科技产品开发作为立厂之本，在社会上广招专业人才。2008年全县40家年营业收入500万元以上规模工业企业职工7264人中，拥有研究生57人，占0.76%；大学和大专文化2205人，高中和中专1915人，分别占30.36%和26.36%；高中及中专以上学历职工共4177人，占职工总数57.48%，其中高级技术职称67人，中级技术职称248人，初级技术职称364人，高级技术工18人，高级工和中级工310人，合计1064人，占职工总数14.65%。2010年企业专业技术人员达到974人，占企业职工总数7662人的12.71%。

二、技术引进

1980年前，县内企业数量少，且多是产品粗加工，产品单一，技术含量低。1981年，马家桥幸福砖厂在湖南引进电抽风工艺建起制砖轮窑，一改以往采用立窑烧砖的传统技法。1983年又投资17.5万元引进四川广汉“自来风”（自然通风）轮窑工艺获得成功。继后，新上马的砖厂均采用幸福砖厂引进的技术兴建，使陈旧的“马蹄窑”砖厂和电抽风工艺逐渐淘汰。1985年，城关镇沙溪村唐昌明自费外出考察，引进贵阳电视机厂技术，聘请3名工程技术人员对12名员工进行3个月培训，办起星光电器接插件厂，使用熟练工35人，为贵阳电视机厂生产24万套电视机匹配器和连接线，质量合格率达99%。贵州文德矿冶有限公司投资40万元引进75号硅铁生产技术，扩大年设计生产硅铁能力达3000吨。河口铁合金厂、久长棕刚玉厂、联合磨料厂等高能耗企业引进冶炼炉电极助烧工艺，使企业生产技术上升一个档次。

1991年，技术引进以建材工业、能源工业、原材料、农业企业为重点，通过技术改造调整产业结构。1992年，联合磨料厂引进国内较为先进机械振动碾压、切割、破碎工艺，总投资400万元新建一条制粒生产线，使产品质量攀升，企业摆脱困境，在同行业中具有较强的竞争力。

1996年起，技术引进又由结构调整转向提高经济效益，引进沿海地区先进技术和设备，扩大企业生产能力。1997年利尔建材有限公司，引用湖北宜昌实用技术研究所高级工程师汪诗谊研制的环保型纸质地膜技术，就地建厂生产纸塑复合编织袋。1998年年初电价上浮，硅铁厂和河口铁合金厂采取承包经营，引进江西省赣发公司经营者承包两厂，主要生产硅锰合金，年实际产量达到1.2万吨设计生产能力。乌当区东风镇杨时文买断承包多年的高坝砖厂，自筹资金200万元进行技术改造，将原厂立窑推倒重建18门焙烧轮窑一座和五道干燥室一栋，配窑车500台用窑烟余热烘干砖坯，使红砖年产量从80万块提高到1500万块。2000年又筹资100万元进行二次技改，引进先进红砖流水生产线一条，提高坯砖抗压耐折强度，并将焙烧轮窑扩大到32门，改建烘干室为11道，年设计生产能力提高到3000万块，红砖质量达到国标150号以上。

进入21世纪，加大振兴工业经济力度，加快工业小区建设。以体制创新和科技创新推动产业结构优化升级和可持续发展。11年共引进16家规模大、实力强、前景好的药品企业进行技术改造，其中有14家先后取得国家GMP和GSP认证资格，投入正常生产。维康药业有限公司2004年完成异地技术改造，年产值和年销售收入稳步增长，2005年跻身于县内亿元以上产值和营业收入的工业企业。兰地实业有限责任公司入驻扎佐镇新民村，始终坚持以科技进步为企业生存和发展之本，在扩大生产规模的同时，以科技为导向，发展产品多元化、管理科技化，采取“基地+农户”方式，带动农户发展高油玉米种植和林下养鸡增加农民收入，并进行大型养殖场废弃物无害化资源化利用、灵芝在降低畜禽产品胆固醇中运用、亚高原地区提高蛋鸡孵化率研究、新型禽肉制品开发等项目的研究，建立起蛋鸡高效养殖技术综合体系和适应高原特点养殖模式，总体达到国内领先水平，居西南地区同行业之首，被国家科技部评选为国家星火项目基地，贵阳市政府命名为科技示范基地，董事长罗进被评为全国星火科技先进个人。2008年公司拥有职工50人，实现营业收入1630万元，缴纳国家税金30万元后仍获利120万元。2009年至2010年，市场价格逐渐攀高，养殖成本增加，公司压缩规模、经济效益有所下降。

专记：注重人才和技术的维康药业

贵州维康药业有限公司于1999年在贵阳高新技术开发区建立，为集骨伤科药品开发、生产、销售为一体的民营股份制企业。2002年4月，通过招商推介迁入扎佐医药产业园区，征地80亩，按照国家《药品生产质量管理规范》标准，委托南京医药设计院设计进行GMP异地技术改造，2004年建成生产车间5680平方米，加上办公大楼和空压房、冷冻站、配电房等配套建筑共1万平方米，厂区绿化9861平方米，道路及广场面积有7000平方米，总投资3368万元，成为医药产业园一个新型现代化花园式药品生产厂。是年6月顺利通过国家GMP标准认证。

技术改造后，公司继续坚持以“内抓产品质量，外抓企业形象”和“维护人类健康”为宗旨，以保证患者用药安全有效为根本，不断提高产品的知名度和信誉度。生产经营过程，一是注重知识人才开发。公司总职工160人，配有大学、大专毕业生101人，加上高中毕业生54人共155人，占总职工人数96.88%，至2008年已有34人获得中、初级职称资格，成为企业技术骨干。二是设立课题组，聘请贵阳医学院专家和公司骨干组成，由药学院院长王永林和公司经理况明伦负责，对骨康胶囊、肿痛舒喷雾剂、妇科调经胶囊等产品进行专题研究，解决产品制作工艺和产品质量稳定性问题，并按照《中成药西药产品注册管理办法》规定，由医学院专家协助制定产品质量标准。三是开展新药研制与开发，挖掘苗药秘方，结合现代中药药剂学、药理学精心研制和临床试验，至2005年已申报产品“缓释透皮剂”为国家级二类新药。产品骨康胶囊和肿痛舒喷雾剂为贵州苗药系列之一，经北京、上海、广东、江苏、浙江等省（市、区）100多所三甲医院临床验证，有效率高达98%，由地方产品升格为国家标准，获得国家保护专利，销往全国28个省、区、市，原国家骨伤协会主席、骨科专家尚天裕教授称赞公司产品解决若干年骨伤患者疼痛难题。以2010年与2005年相比，职工从112人增到236人；年产值从1.08亿元增到4.2亿元，增加2.9倍；营业收入从1.06亿元增到3.6亿元，增加2.4倍；缴纳国家税金由772万元增到2557万元，增加2.3倍，为全县年营业收入超亿元大户。

三、资金引进

1981年开始，由政府部门和企业自由运作。1984年县政府正式制定“三引进”配套政策，采取合营、独资经营等方式引资。至1990年，经外协办牵线并审批项目10个，总投资1730.5万元，其中引进境外资金占89%，使具有一定规模和科技含量的硅铁厂、棕刚玉厂、铁合金厂和一批矿产品深加工企业得以建成，加上乡镇企业共办起各类联合企业15家。香港德利贸易公司投资50万美元联办文德矿冶有限公司，为县内首家有产品出口权的企业。

1991年起，世界经济财团对中国口岸实行经济封锁，冲击出口产品外销，而硅铁厂与香港德利公司仍冒风险合资经营，由港方投资120万元港币负责销售，并对冶炼炉进行技术改造，使年设计生产能力由3000吨提高到6000吨，产品远销中国台湾地区和菲律宾、韩国、日本等国，从而摆脱世界经济财团经济封锁。1992年，联合磨料厂成功引进技改资金270万元和年生产能力1万吨的棕刚玉砂、段砂制粒生产线。1993年引进铁五局资金447万元改建新生铁厂为兴胜冶炼厂，由铁五局派出从事冶炼工作多年具有丰富冶炼经验的成善清任厂长，仅7个月就试运成功投入生产，投产后坚持以“优质、高产、低耗”冶炼方针进行管理，使产出生铁、球墨铁、炼钢铁符合国家标准，销往贵阳、四川、湖南、杭州等地，1996年在小高炉冶炼评比中获贵阳市质量第一和贵州省质量第二的名次，县委、县政府表彰并奖励成善清1万元。继后，绿原公司投资107万元在久长原烽光厂区兴建年产牛肉干350吨的食肉加工厂，福鹏公司投资600万元兴建麦芽糊精厂。至1997年的5年，全县新上投资额10万元以上项目投资3.24亿元，其中引进境外资金2.56亿元，占79%。

1998年，确立“以资源换技术、以产权换资金、以市场换项目、以存量换增量”的办法进行招商引资。次年举办阳明文化节，用“文化搭台、经济唱戏”的举措引进仙灵药业有限责任公司投资3100万元入驻龙场镇原庆文厂区，又引进绿太阳制药有限责任公司投资1700万元入驻医药产业园，还有兰地实业有限公司、永昌化工公司、久长黄磷改装厂、高尔夫度假中心颐湖苑别墅建设等入驻项目陆续开工建设。2001年县政府制定医药产业园规划方案，开展前期基础建设。次年又规划11个工业小区，以医药生产、野生动物园、铝矾土深加工为重点进行引资，又有安泰、光正、科开、维康、天方、和仁堂、恒和、长生共8家医药生产（销售）企业入驻医药产业园，累计投资2.39亿元进行异地技术改造，万方生态资源开发有限公司修文万亩苗圃等引进项目也开始启动，至2002年8月的4年零4个月，全县工业、交通运输、旅游等产业固定资产投资额在5万元以上项目总投资5.5亿元，其中引进境外资金3.9亿元，占总投资的70.42%。

1996年，引进港资在扎佐三元修建的贵阳高尔夫度假中心

2004年，实施“农业稳县、工业强县、三产活县”战略，把发展作为第一要务，领导带头跑招商引资，争取项目，争取资金，以“诚信”赢得客商信任，使“好一多”乳业有限公司投资1400万元建成投产，扎佐物流仓储运输中心，贵阳森林野生动物园以及浩诚、中际、德昌祥等药业相继开工。2005年又着力树立“诚信”修文、文明招商形象，优化招商环境，营造“亲商、富商”良好氛围，增强招商吸引力。2006年拟订《外来投资企业与周边群众矛盾纠纷调处制度》《外来投资企业与周边环境保障制度》，保护投资者合法权益。2008年借贵（阳）遵（义）、贵（阳）毕（节）高等级公路、麦架至修文快速干道、金沙至修文公路沿线区域划作优化开发区之机，以高新技术带动现代药业、能源产业、铝及铝加工等高新技术产业发展。至2010年的7年全县累计引进新项目120个，实际到位境外资金42.42亿元。

2007年在扎佐冷水沟建成的贵阳森林野生动物园

专记：环海公司金属镁项目建设始末

环海公司金属镁项目系1994年10月山西省环海实业有限公司董事长兼总经理梁文海应邀莅县考察，查阅招商引资资料并实地察看地处川黔公路和川黔铁路沿线绿原公司（即原烽光厂闲置厂区）后，即敲定以310万元投资买断组建贵州环海实业有限公司。为培养人才和探索机构改革新路，县委、县政府采取“引进一个企业，出去一批干部”的办法，从县委、县计委、公安局、乡镇企业局抽调干部建立工作协调领导小组，由省委组织部抽调到县挂职锻炼的县委副书记牛熹任组长带领驻厂工作。环海实业公司经中

共安顺地委特许批准。聘任牛熹为总经理。

1995年年初，论证建设悬窑年产10万吨道路水泥项目，前期准备资金到位，即进行地质勘探、水电修补、暂住人口登记，成立护厂队等工作。8月，由于金属镁价格暴涨，环海总公司决定一次性投资642万元，并向银行贷款405万元，加上摊入固定资产成本的其他款73万元，共计1120万元，改为金属镁项目。到1996年11月，基本建成年设计能力1000吨金属镁生产线，耗资土建工程115.43万元，安装工程60.75万元，购置设备405.95万元，原厂房、车辆、利息、技术转让、地勘等319.52万元，累计形成固定资产901.65万元，余下资金除支付原材料195万元，无形资产、递延资产、待摊费用35.1万元后，只剩11.7万元，还不够21.6万元的预付账款，形成入不敷出的尴尬局面。眼看生产已无资金保证，加上牛熹挂职期满回省，导致厂建处于停工状态。

1997年，县政府针对金属镁生产线没有专业技术人员，造成工程未按计划进行，且超计划投资；土建未按招投标程序办理；配置财会人员又无专业技能；采购的真空机组设备纯属淘汰旧货；原银行计划贷款300万元流动资金不能到位等实际情况，迅速调整人员，聘请航空工业部属418库原主任徐耀山为总经理，指派财政局干部唐德华为副总经理，高级工程师刘润祥为土建项目工程技术指导把守质量关，又聘请一名有多年实践经验的会计师接管和清理财务账目和设备问题并追究供货方责任；山西总公司同时指派1名高级会计师负责监管，增加含贵阳市政府支持发展资金50万元在内共投资100万元新建一座竖窑。是年8月，用竖窑发生煤气，启动两台还原炉进行小规模试产，产出5吨镁，样品送山西环海总公司检测，质量达到国标GB/3499—1995一级精镁标准。后又因再无资金投入而停产。11月，山西环海总公司指派张爱果等人接管公司，但又遇金属镁市场价格下降到生产成本临界线，再生产下去已无利可图，只得停产关闭。时隔10年后的2008年，将公司有偿转让给贵州金久水泥厂。

第五节　经济园区建设

2000年县委、县政府决定依托扎佐林场拥有的7万亩森林资源和良好的生态环境，于川黔铁路、川黔公路、贵（阳）遵（义）和贵（阳）毕（节）高等级公路途经的扎佐开始规划建设经济园区，2001年招徕客商入驻，2010年于扎佐镇境建成有18家企业入驻的医药产业园区，又开建物流园区，实现年产值达20亿元。

一、医药产业园

2000年，利用扎佐林场、万江机电厂、三〇四医院闲置大量国有土地和房舍，抓住国家强制制药企业GMP改造和贵阳市两城区医药生产企业异地改造的机遇，规划建设医药产业园。

是年3月，园区规划首次在白云区召开的贵阳市第一届药业协会成立大会亮相，8月规划沙盘在全国乡镇企业经贸洽谈会展示，以独特区位、便捷交通和绿色环境等优势吸引药业界商家。贵阳市委、市政府领导带领直属相关部门到园区现场办公，贷款300万元建设基础设施。县成立协调领导小组，实行“一站式”服务，为企业代办立项、环保、建设等审批手续，对园区实行统一规划、统一建设、统一配套、统一管理、统一服务，使园区里的广场、花园、喷泉、雕塑、绿化等景观具有一定艺术含量和文化品位。历经海南召开的贵阳市第二届药业协会、渤海经济园和长三角开展招商推介，拓展园区，贵州同济堂制药股份有限公司入驻县城北门外原航空工业部属庆文机械厂搬迁后留下的场地。至2003年招徕医药企业15家入驻，总投资5.5亿元，建成面积2.4平方公里，完成道路扩建改造、电信宽带光缆铺设、供电供水网路、排污管网设施、中心广场及停车场、标志性建筑等建设，于2003年4月获农业部授予“全国乡镇企业科技园区”称号，成为省内规模较大的省级医药产业园区之一。2006年7月经国家发改委和贵州省政府审核，列为省级开发区，更名为贵州修文医药产业园。2008年10月28日被农业部评为第三批全国农产品加工业示范基地。园区以制药、食品加工为主导产业。贵阳市政府要求在“十二五”期间按照二类工业园区进行建设。至2010年入驻企业增达18家，除杏林堂、科福、华德斯、华芝宝、济昇5家药业在建外，尚有天方药业有限公司因特殊原因停产，其余企业生产经营正常，药品以消化系统、泌尿系统、心血管系统、妇科用药、解毒、广谱抗菌中成药制造为主，累计拥有注册商标433个。省、市名牌产品有同济堂药业“柔壹”仙灵骨葆，德昌祥药业妇科再造丸，绿太阳药业“绿格尔”系列，恒和药业枇杷止咳胶囊、维康药业骨康胶囊，安泰药业妇平胶囊等。其中同济堂药业主导产品仙灵骨葆胶囊填补中成药治疗骨质疏松的空白，荣获世界骨伤科联合会科技进步一等奖、中国骨伤科协会特别贡献奖、贵州省优秀产品一等奖。整个园区是年完成产值20亿元，占全县规模以上工业企业产值的39.77%，其中，德昌祥、维康、同济堂3家药业年营业收入超亿元，实现9.8亿元，缴纳税金8300万元，分别在全部规模以上工业企业中占23.19%和21.47%。

二、扎佐物流园

扎佐系省城贵阳北部大门，南距贵阳市中心35公里，往东42公里与开阳相接，西至毕节170公里，北往息烽35公里，向西北延伸360公里和向北延伸350公里即可到达四川合江和泸州以及重庆，又是川黔公路和川黔铁路必经之道，历为重要商品集散地，素有“旱码头”之称。1978年前县供销社、航空工业部属四一八库、贵阳煤矿先后在扎佐建仓储货，年转运进出物资达5万吨，20世纪80年代增到10万吨。90年代贵（阳）遵（义）和贵（阳）毕（节）高等级公路开通，毕节地区也在扎佐设办事处转运进出物资。

2001年，县政府决定引进物流企业入驻，将扎佐打造成辐射黔北、黔西北，承接重庆、四川、云南等省、市集散物资的黔中现代物流基地，带动商业、运输、仓储、加工配送、信息服务等现代服务业快速发展。贵州兴达物流公司看中其独特的优势，将公路、铁路货运与仓储有机结合，发展贵阳市北郊物资集散业务。2004年投资3000万元，修建扎佐火车站货场侧面A、B两区的两条铁路专用线，全长450米，拥有货场5万平方米，配有10吨行吊和装载机各1台，100吨和30吨地磅各1台，连续3年完成卸载、转送、发送矿产品、机电、建材等物资80万吨。

2006年，贵阳市政府将扎佐物流园列为全市物流建设项目之一，成都铁路局批准川黔线扎佐站建一条长950米、能满足整列货车停靠的专用线。

引资建成的扎佐物流园铁路专线

2008年贵阳市政府再次将该园规划为今后15年重点建设的物流园之一，规划面积3795亩，分商流、物流商务、流通加工、公路、仓储、生活配套服务、公路铁路联运共7个区（港）。到2010年园区总体规划通过省、市专家初步评审，核心战略装车点已建成铁路专用线1355米，货场硬化13万平方米，仓库2000平方米，总投资8050万元。农资农肥、粮食两个转运交易中心和商务调度中心即将开工建设，兴达物流公司和贵阳东方钢材市场已落户园区，是年发货量达到107万吨，货物吞吐量增到214万吨，缓解贵阳物流的压力。

第六节　招商效益

一、促使全县综合经济实力增强

1978至2008年，县委、县政府利用自身区位、交通、资源优势，引入诸多企业落户，在稳定发展第一产业的同时，推动第二、第三产业快速发展。至2010年，全县生产总值达到46.18亿元，与1980年比较增长106倍，其中，第一、第二、第三产业分别增长39.7倍、114.6倍、143.2倍。年人均国内生产总值从177元增到1.51万元，增长84.3倍。

二、助推农村产业结构调整

1981年起，率先在乡镇企业中资金、技术和人才，然后扩大到项目引进，从乡办工业延伸到种植业和养殖业，使农村产业结构得到合理调整。到2010年，全县农林牧渔业总产值实现13.14亿元，比1980年的2449万元增加52.7倍，其中种植业产值9.52亿元，增加48.1倍；林业产值752万元，增加11.7倍；牧业产值3.41亿元，增加75.1倍；渔业产值982万元，增加490倍。从1980年与2010年各业在农业总产值中占比看，种植业由72.46%降到9.22%，林业由0.57%增为2.41%，牧业由25.95%降为18.29%，渔业由0.75%降为0.08%，服务业从无到有占到0.27%。

产业结构调整后的猕猴桃产业

三、加快非公经济发展

1988年起，招商引资引进一批批资金雄厚、技术先进的企业落户县境，从而改变全县经济结构，加快非公有制经济和各种混合经济的发展，使非公经济在全县经济总额中的比重不断上升。2000年全县非公经济增加值实现4.78亿元，2010年增到26.65亿元，占GDP比重为57.5%，10年年均增速为18.7%。其中，各产业非公经济增加值和在本产业增加值中的比重分别为：第一产业4.96亿元，占62.7%；第二产业12.22亿元，占71.4%；第三产业9.38亿元，占44.3%，非公经济的发展明显快于国有经济。

专记：引入龙翔公司　盘活云天资产

云天公司的前身为国营四一八库，1965年迁驻龙场镇小营村，系中国贵州航空工业集团〇一一基地下属的物资储备中转库，1980年前曾发挥物资储备中转的重要作用。继后，由于市场经济发展，公司职能逐步减弱，遂并入贵航集团万江机电有限公司作为辅助企业。公司想尽办法生产民用沙发、铁皮文件柜等，但没多久产品销售不畅，仅包装箱和摩托车凸轮轴项目成气候。然市场竞争激烈，利润微薄，难以养活云天职工，到2002年负债达1000余万元，并长期拖欠职工工资和社会保险费等，陷入濒临倒闭地步。

龙翔生产车间一角

2003年，贵航集团和万江公司将云天公司分离出来，于4月3日整体移交给县政府，18日兼并给引入的贵州长久铝业有限公司，但因前期运行资金不到位和产业政策制约，致兼并搁浅。6月13日县政府解除长久公司的经营权和资产所有权。10月28日将云天公司兼并给引入的贵州龙翔铝业公司，利用云天公司现有场地、设备和职工以“诚信、民主、求实、创新”的治厂理念，以2003年获得质量管理体系认证的“云天牌”摩托车凸轮轴作为拳头产品，对云天职工全部接纳安置，并吸收精干的职工进入管理层，在确保原凸轮轴、纸箱、贸易项目继续正常运转的同时，一边改善职工居住条件和工作条件，一边开发生产项目，兼并宏和矿业有限公司，又投资1800万元兴建年设计能力2000吨氧化铁生产线。2005年再引入山东北金集团有限公司先后投资2000余万元对摩托车凸轮轴项目进行技改扩建，新建厂房6000平方米，新增用于新产品开发无靠模凸轮轴磨床等设备，使凸轮轴实际设计能力增加到250万套，厂房容量规模可达到500万套，预留足够发展空间。2006年起连续3年投资3亿元，分别在大方建设年产9万吨和纳雍、修文各建年产30万吨规模的煤矿。2007年，凸轮轴年生产量从2003年的60万套增到154万套，增加156.67%。继后，由于在建煤矿未予投产，致2010年营业收入只实现2500万元，缴纳国家税金130万元后出现亏损610万元，待原煤进入销售后将扭亏为盈。

四、壮大第三产业

1997年起，依托境内独特的旅游资源，紧扣“王学圣地，秀美修文”的区域定位，大力发展旅游业，并以“阳明文化节”、“梨花节”、“漂流节”、“高尔夫赛事”、“和谐城乡游”、“避暑季”等活动进行招商引资，开发、配套建设投资约6亿元，初步建成各类旅游企业20余家。至2010年累计接待游客388.6万人次，旅游总收入19.95亿元。旅游带动交通运输、餐饮服务、商品流通、邮电通

谷堡梨花节

信等第三产业快速发展，房地产及社会服务等新兴产业也逐步壮大。第三产业实现增加值21.16亿元，在全县生产总值中所占比重由1997年的20.67%上升到45.82%，对GPS贡献率达到38%。

五、促进财政金融稳健增长

由于招商引资引进人才、技术、资金和项目，从而开辟财源，加快县域经济发展，使地方财力不断增强，财政收入连续翻番。2010年，全县财政总收入达5.44亿元，上缴中央、省、市财政收入后，地方财政收入为2.8亿元，在1978年基础上翻7.4番。经济发展加快银行筹措资金速度，2010年全县银行存款余额由1978年的1044万元增到27.73亿元，增长264.6倍，有力地保证和促进县域经济正常运转和各项事业发展。

六、扩大劳动就业

从1988年起，引进企业入驻，所需劳动用工多为就地招聘，从而拓宽就业门路，加大城镇失业人员就业和农村剩余劳动力转移到厂就地从业，连续11年引进企业陆续建成投产。兰地实业有限责任公司带动4500余户农民发展高油玉米种植，户均年增收1008元，100余户农民发展林下养鸡，户均年增收6000元。到2010年，全县规模以上工业企业共45个，职工年平均9343人，其中有43个系招商引进企业，从业人员多由周边地区招聘。

第十章　经济管理

1978年12月，中共十一届三中全会作出“把党和国家工作的着重点转移到经济建设上来”的决策，让国营、集体、个体经济共同发展。县委，县政府在保留原有计划、财政、税务、工商、物资综合机构的同时。又陆续增加物价、统计、劳动工资、质量技术监督等办事机构，加强对经济工作的管理，促使国民经济从计划管理转向计划指导和市场调节。由于市场化程度不断提高，促进农业经济结构调整日趋合理，工业经济发展步伐加快，第三产业成为新的经济增长点。2010年，全县国内生产总值实现46.18亿元，与1978年相比翻7番，年均增长16.4%。其中，第一产业达7.91亿元，所占比重由38.52%降至17.13%；第二产业17.11亿元，由41.62%降为37.06%；第三产业21.16亿元，由19.86%增至45.81%。财政总收入达到5.44亿元，比1978年的188.9万元翻8.5番。经济发展，带来人民生活水平的提高，城镇居民人均可支配收入和农村居民人均纯收入分别为1.58万元和5152元，比1996年的3480元和1978年的141元增长3.5倍和35.5倍，越来越多的人家正在由温饱型奔向小康型。

第一节　计划管理

1978年沿袭计划委员会建制，计划管理偏重于经济指标。1979年起改革体制，从指标管理转向宏观调控。至2010年，累计编制并完成5个五年计划、2个长期计划以及各年的年度计划，从而推进县域经济快速发展，全县三次产业顺序由二、一、三转为三、二、一，产业结构不断改善。

一、体制改革

1979—1984年重点转变计划工作指导思想和改进计划管理方法。在放开农村集市贸易和小商品价格基础上，积极发展集体、个体商业。1984年，对生产计划指标中的农业部分和工业品除供电量、木材等少量重要产品外全部变指令性为指导性；物资分配缩小统配范围，发挥市场调节作用；商业取消农副产品统购，对粮食等主要商品实行合同定购，放开生猪购销，开展以城市、集镇为中心的商品批发；基本建设实行拨款改贷款，资金专户存储，简化审批手续；文教卫生除中 小学入学率和人口自然增长率、计划生育率等少数指令性指标分解到部门外，其余计划全部实行指导性和市场调节。

1985—1991年，重点抓长时间实行的指令性计划为主的管理体制改革。按照国务院“大的方面管住管好，小的方面放开搞活”的要求，通过减少指令性计划，扩大指导性计划和市场调节，使政府对经济管理由直接控制逐步转向间接控制；以编制年度计划为主转向编制中长期计划和行业规划为主，提高计划管理的科学性；拓宽计划管理内涵，把计划管理工作转到抓大事、抓经济协调服务和综合平衡上来，集中精力抓好全县资源开发和经济建设中成效显著的项目，注重横向联合，外引内联，促进县域经济发展。

1992—2010年，在重点建立计划管理体系的同时完善宏观调控体系，加快社会主义市场经济的发展。1993年起强化计划指导性和市场调节的方向性，重点研究全县经济发展的大问题，使计划更加符合县情，更加贴近市场，突出总需求与总供给平衡的分析预测。2001年起重点突出战略性、综合性、超前性及指导性。按照市场经济要求，对计划期内需要解决的问题开展专题调研分析。2010年，全县已建立起计划调节与经济规模调节、经济政策调节与法律手段调节相结合的调节体系。

二、年度计划

每年年初编制的年度计划，经县人民代表大会批准下达执行，执行中如遇自然灾害等特殊情况于下半年进行计划调整。33年间出现的拐点年度有1982年农村普遍实行家庭联产承包制、1992年撤区并乡建镇、2002年开展农村税费改革。

1982年农村体制改革后，对农业发展迅猛和工业稳步增长预测不足，致使完成实绩与计划指标出入很大。全县工农业总产值实现6715.2万元，超计划11.92%。其中工业总产值为2403万元，超14.43%；农业总产值为4312.2万元，超10.57%。还有烤烟产量3021.2吨，超54.93%；油菜籽产量6517.2吨，超43.55%；地方财政预算收入635万元，超55.63%。

1992年，对10乡（镇）重组后重视乡镇企业，放松农业种植管理，导致部分计划指标不能完成。全年农作物播种面积较上年减少1万亩，生产总值实现2.1亿元。为计划的91.1%。其中，第一产业增加值8480万元，为计划的80.76%；第二产业增加值7469万元，为计划的95.76%；第三产业增加值5004万元，超计划6.47%。国民收入总额1.66亿元，比上年减少6.59%。工农业总产值2.17亿元，为计划的89.29%。其中农业总产值1.17亿元，为计划的81.01%；工业总产值9951万元，超计划18.99%。农业主要产品中，粮食总产量5.04万吨，油菜籽产量4355吨，生猪年末存栏8.15万头，均未完成计划任务。烤烟产量4305吨和大牲畜年末存栏4.26万头，超计划2.5%和1.46%。财政收入1849.38万元，完成97.33%。

2002年，计划制定较为贴近县情，全县农村经济发展缓慢，年营业收入500万元以上规模工业企业比重偏小，资源优势尚未转变为经济优势，实际完成不够理想。全年生产总值实现12.18亿元，占计划的99.19%，其中第一产业增加值3.81亿元，超计划0.53%；第二产业3.9亿元，占计划的73.72%；第三产业4.47亿元，超计划39.69%；县及县以下工业总产量12.87亿元，超计划4.63%，其中规模以上工业产值2.86亿元，超5.9%；社会固定资产投资完成6.07亿元，占计划的97.41%；县级财政预算收入7086万元，超13.29%；农民人均纯收入2028元，超计划24元；城镇居民人均可支配收入5899元，超计划41元。

三、五年计划

1978—1980年为“五五”计划期间。自1981—2010年的30年间，除未编制“六五”计划外，共编制“七五”“八五”“九五”“十五”“十一五”共5个五年计划（2005年起改称“五年规划”），每个五年计划均经过县人民代表大会审议批准下达执行。各个五年计划执行结果是：“七五” 计划指标与完成实绩出入较大，其中生产总值仅完成70.45%。“八五”计划至“十一五”规划编制较贴近实际，全县生产总值均超

额完成各计划指标，其中第一产业发展较为稳定，3个五年计划都超额完成，1个五年计划完成99.92%，年均增长速度从“十五”规划的6.89%增到“十一五”规划的9.64%；第二产业发展较慢，“八五”计划超额完成，其余3个五年计划都未完成，最低的“九五”计划仅完成55.73%，年均增长速度则从“十五”计划的26.76%降到“十一五”规划的21.88%；第三产业起步晚、发展快，除“八五”计划完成90.19%外，其余3个五年计划都超额完成，最高的“九五”计划超1.9倍。年均增长速度从“十五”的15.27%增到“十一五”的15.76%。其余主要指标除县级预算收入和粮食总产量完成较好外，大牲畜和生猪年末存栏仅完成60.63%和32.26%。

“五五”至“十一五”计划主要指标完成情况统计表

表3—10—01

指标		计划期	计量单位	“五五”计划末期（1980年）	“六五”计划末期（1985年）	“七五”计划末期（1990年）	“八五”计划末期（1995年）	“九五”计划末期（2000年）	“十五”计划末期（2005年）	“十一五”计划末期（2010年）
全县生产总值		计划数	万元	—	—	28000	39000	75712	190100	450000
		实际完成	万元	4318	10222	19725	45895	93104	200071	461839
		完成占计划	%	—	—	70.45	117.68	122.97	105.25	102.63
其中	一产增加值	计划数	万元	—	—	—	14000	35000	45100	79170
		实际完成	万元	1945	4111	8204	19491	34973	49162	79100
		完成占计划	%	—	—	—	139.23	99.92	109.01	99.92
	二产增加值	计划数	万元	—	—	—	16000	41734	82800	202800
		实际完成	万元	1481	4044	7689	18227	23255	76609	171130
		完成占计划	%	—	—	—	113.92	55.72	92.53	84.38
	三产增加值	计划数	万元	—	—	—	9000	11926	62200	168030
		实际完成	万元	892	2067	3832	8177	34876	74300	211609
		完成占计划	%	—	—	—	90.86	292.44	119.45	125.94
工农业总产值		计划数	万元	4100	—	14017	33500	115300	310400	—
		实际完成	万元	4146	8849	20477	52596	145153	268780	—
		完成占计划	%	101.12	—	146.09	157.00	125.89	86.59	—
其中	工业总产值	计划数	万元	1600	—	6800	21500	74076	237400	—
		实际完成	万元	1697	3469	9274	23843	99297	177451	560900
		完成占计划	%	106.06	—	136.38	110.90	134.05	74.75	—
	农业总产值	计划数	万元	2500	—	7217	12000	41224	73000	—
		实际完成	万元	2449	5380	11203	28753	45669	76264	131404
		完成占计划	%	97.96	—	155.23	239.61	110.78	104.47	—
地方财政收入		计划数	万元	—	—	1400	2100	3268	8552	30600
		实际完成	万元	188	963	1416	2203	4854	12828	27960
		完成占计划	%	—	—	101.14	104.90	148.52	150.00	91.37

续表

指标 \ 计划期		计量单位	"五五"计划末期(1980年)	"六五"计划末期(1985年)	"七五"计划末期(1990年)	"八五"计划末期(1995年)	"九五"计划末期(2000年)	"十五"计划末期(2005年)	"十一五"计划末期(2010年)
粮食总产量	计划数	吨	55000	—	57500	60000	82200	93300	100000
	实际完成	吨	49200	39002	40569	67600	88904	97677	104336
	完成占计划	%	89.45	—	70.55	112.67	108.16	104.69	104.33
油菜籽产量	计划数	吨	750	—	4500	5500	5600	7500	7100
	实际完成	吨	1613	1386	4992	4164	9039	8855	6305
	完成占计划	%	215.07	—	110.93	75.71	161.41	118.07	88.80
烤烟产量	计划数	吨	550	—	5000	4200	5000	2820	2250
	实际完成	吨	431	4468	3213	2955	2814	2329	3821
	完成占计划	%	78.36	—	64.26	70.36	56.28	82.59	169.82
大牲畜年末存栏	计划数	头	30000	—	40000	46000	54000	—	78000
	实际完成	头	25832	33751	39958	48835	57469	72807	47288
	完成占计划	%	86.11	—	99.90	106.16	106.42	—	60.63
生猪年末存栏	计划数	头	78000	—	90000	110000	160000	—	300000
	实际完成	头	74706	83235	80204	100638	157128	218551	96765
	完成占计划	%	95.78	—	89.12	91.49	98.21	—	32.26

注：20世纪80年代，原国民经济计划改为国民经济和社会发展计划，计划指标体系调整和完善，加上县未编制"六五"计划，故表内少数指标无计划数和完成数及占计划的比例

四、长期计划

（一）1976—1985年国民经济和社会发展规划

系1978年前根据"工业学大庆""农业学大寨"和粮食上《纲要》的战略要求制定，主要指标为粮食总产量11.5万吨，油菜籽4200吨，烤烟2000吨，生猪存栏30万头，人口控制在25.24万人以内，工业总产值达到1000万元。由于对实行改革开放战略决策带来的县域经济发展取得巨大成就难于预测，致使完成实绩与计划指标增减幅度较大。到1985年除人口25.16万人控制在规划指标内和"五小"工业产值2057万元超105.7%以及烤烟产量4468吨超113.4%外，粮食总产量和油菜籽产量因天旱减产，只完成3.9万吨和1386吨；大牲畜和生猪年末存栏3.38万头和8.32万头，仅占规划指标的28.75%和29.37%。

（二）1991—2000年十年规划

1990年12月，根据中共中央《关于制定国民经济和社会发展十年规划及"八五"计划的建议》，县编制《国民经济和社会发展第八个五年计划及2000年远景目标规划纲要》，经1991年3月县十届人大二次会议审议通过执行。主要指标为国内生产总值6.6亿元，工农业总产值6.7亿元（其中工业4.94亿元，农业1.76亿元），财政收入8000万元，粮食总产量8.5万吨，油菜籽产量8000吨、烤烟产量5800吨、大牲畜和

生猪年末存栏16万头和18万头。到2000年实际完成国内生产总值9.31亿元，超41.06%；工农业总产值14.52亿元，增加1.2倍；粮食总产量8.89万吨，超4.59%；油菜籽产量9039吨，超12.99%；烤烟因国家控制种植面积，仅完成2814吨，占48.52%；县财政收入和生猪年末存栏均未完成规划指标。

第二节　财政管理

1978年沿袭原财政局建制，全年财政预算收入188.9万元。1979至2010年财政稳步推进一系列改革，财源不断扩大，财政收入连续增长。33年累计收入32.72亿元，年平均收入1.02亿元。其中，2010年收入5.44亿元，为改革开放之初1978年的87.9倍，从而保障县域经济正常运行和各项事业持续发展。

一、体制改革

（一）财政体制

1. 县级财政体制

分级包干制　1979年前实行“定收定支，收支挂钩，总额分成”制，1980年改为“划分收支，分级包干”（分灶吃饭）制。将收入和支出划分为中央和地方两级，给地方财政确定一个收入和支出包干基数实行包干，收大于支的多余部分上解中央，支大于收的给予定额补给。是时，修文属于支大于收的县，预算收入全部留用，收不抵支部分由安顺行署补助。改革从“一灶”吃饭改为“分灶”吃饭，从“条条”分配改为“块块”分配，使地方财政权力扩大，地方财政的责任也随之增强。

1985年，贵州省对地（市）实行“划分税种，核定收支，分级包干”制。由于第二步利改税形成的税制尚不完善，不能完全按税种划分收入，故安顺地区对县增加“总额分成”。即电税县分成30%，烟叶和酒类产品税比上年增收部分留存60%，其余税和收入全部上解中央。于是，全县收支相抵为收大于支，成为上解县，其上解比例1986年和1987年分别为6.5%、6%，1988年调为10.41%，至1993年累计上解1524.32万元。

分税制　1994年1月起，按照中央政府和地方政府的事权划分规定，将国家全部税种划为中央税、地方税、中央和地方共享税，以此界定中央财政和地方财政收入范围。建立中央、地方两级税收征管体系和分级预算制度，合理调节地区间的财力分配。改革后，贵州省上划中央和中央返还的税收各级财政按比例分成，中央留给地方25%的增值税中省为10%、县为15%；国有土地有偿出让收入、土地增值税、土地使用税、资源税，省、地各50%，在地区50%中县分成20%。1996年划归贵阳市管辖后改为市分成20%、县30%，2001年再改为市10%、县40%；烤烟税除5%上缴中央外其余全留给县，其他各项收入原属各级的一律不变。至2010年分税制继续执行。

2. 基层财政体制

1982年前，试行屠宰税由公社征收，县税务局、财政局、公社按20:40:40比例分成。1982年始建区级财政管理体制，次年起财政局按区级事业单位支出指标和支援社队农业拨款由财政所统管。1985年实行“核定收支，定额或比例上解，超收分成，减收减支，超支不补，结余留用”的管理体制。1992年撤区并乡建镇，乡镇财政所改按“核定基数，分级负担，按实际收入总额分成”进行管理。由于全县10乡（镇）财政所初建，财政局仍实行统一管理，以规范财政预算运作行为。

1994年改为“确保收入计划和支出基数，定额补助和上解，超收按比例分成，歉收扣减可用财力”管理体制。

2003年改按“划分收支范围，确定上解基数，保障正常运行，实行以奖代补、自求平衡”的管理办法。2004年进行补充，将收入按收入基数或收入完成数减去支出基数作为上解基数，对超收乡（镇）兑现奖励政策。2006年11月又调整和完善县、乡两级预算收支范围和财政管理权限，使县乡事权与财权相统一。

2010年改为“划分收支范围，核定收支基数，保障基本支出，明确转移支付，超收实行分成，歉收扣减财力”管理。将收入按税种划分，以上一年乡（镇）财政收入剔除城市维护建设税、建筑安装营业税、教育附加和养征罚没收入为基数，年增幅20%为当年任务数；支出以当年12月乡（镇）负担为基数一年一定。超收分成比例为：小箐乡80%，谷堡、六屯、洒坪、大石、六桶乡50%，龙场、扎佐、久长、六广镇40%；实现当年收支平衡奖励5万元。管理结束，有8个乡（镇）完成任务，2个乡达到收支平衡，按管理办法计算兑现。

（二）政府委派会计

2000年，由县财政局派出会计人员到县人民法院、民政局、交通局试点。2001年6月组建教育局会计结算中心，办公地点在县农业银行三楼，总揽教育系统全部会计业务。其中修文中学等13个独立核算会计单位为一级核算制，取消单位会计，只设一名报账员办理本单位经费收支向会计结算中心报账。基层辅导站管理的学校实行二级会计核算制，学校财务仍由辅导站管理，统一对会计结算中心报账。2002年委派范围扩大到检察院、计划生育局、文体广电局、县政协、县委宣传部、县农办。

2003年8月组建县会计管理中心，地址在县商业银行四楼，对全额拨款的县直行政事业单位实行财政资金集中管理，统一开户，分户核算，10月1日正式挂牌办公，计有74个单位纳入管理范围，驻县城的单位职工工资全部由商业银行代发，其他会计业务全由中心统一办理。2005年纳入管理的单位增为90个，覆盖面100%。同时，乡（镇）会计管理中心相应建立，负责办理本乡（镇）财政拨款单位会计业务，对财政资金进行管理和监督。

2005年12月13日，县编制委员会批准会计管理中心加挂县级财政国库支付中心牌子。实行两块牌子一套人马，履行国库集中支付职能，办理相关国库资金收付结算和凭证审核。

2010年9月，实施国库集中支付改革，撤销会计管理中心，保留县级财政国库支付中心，原会计管理中心经理的会计业务还回拨款单位经办。

2010年，县会计集中支付中心一角

（三）农村税费改革

2001年1月启动税费改革，县成立领导小组和办公室经办。计税面积增减以第二轮土地承包为依据；常年产量以1998年前5年种植的农作物平均产量，按规定比例折算稻谷产量后合理确定。全县按照自然条件、耕地优劣和基础设施配套，划分龙场镇、扎佐镇为一类地区；久长镇、谷堡乡、六屯乡、六桶乡为二类地区；六广镇、小箐乡、洒坪乡为三类地区；大石乡为四类地区，并以乡（镇）为单位抽好、中、差3个村、分别测算出3个等级的常年产量。

2002年4月，税改全面展开，以报刊、电台、文艺演出等方式进行宣传。县有关部门对1999年（基数年）农业税和“三提五统”（提取公积金、公益金、村管理费，统一民兵训练费、民政优抚费、乡村道路修建费、教育费附加、计划生育费）征收进行核实公布。5月以村、组为单位召开动员大会，9月各乡（镇）张榜公布县预批方案，经农民签字认可。全县签字率达100%。10月县下达《农业税征收管理暂行办法》，成立农业税征收管理局和乡（镇）分局。分别在龙场镇幸福村、扎佐镇马鞍村、谷堡乡平寨村、六广镇新义村、小箐乡青中村、大石乡天桥村、六桶乡海马村召开农业税及附加征收现场会，农户到会率和完成任务户均达100%。至年末同时免征对农民征收的农业特产税，全县217个行政村，1415个村民组，25.03万农民，负担额由改革前的1999年实收1269.5万元降到763.55万元，减负率达39.85%；人均负担由50.72元降到30.09元，减负率为40.67%，其中最高的六屯乡减负率高达48.28%，最低的六桶乡为28.2%。2003年起，遵照中共中央、国务院逐步减免农业税的指示，逐年减少农业税征收。2005年执行省政府决定全部免征农业税，结束历代沿袭下来农民缴纳“皇粮”的历史。

2002年6月，农村税费改革宣传

专记：农业税彻底退出历史舞台

农业税，亦称“公粮”，为古老税种，历来以户为单位缴纳，农民心目中已形成“皇粮国税，不可抗拒”和“种地交皇粮天经地义”的观念。

2001年开启农村税费改革，农业税逐年减免，是年实征入库466万元，2004年减到395万元，2005年全部免征。至此，沿袭2600多年的“皇粮国税”彻底退出历史舞台，全县地方财政每年减少农业税479.52万元和农业税附加95.91万元，正附税合计575.43万元。为弥补免征的农业税收入，县委、县政府决定大力发展工商税财源。到2010年，全县地方财政预算收入增为2.8亿元，比免征农业税前的2004年1.04亿元翻1.2番。

农业税免征后，广大农民喜形一色，结合农业产业结构调整，在耕地上猛下功夫。久长镇清水村大种玉米、黑麦、燕麦供给驻村“好1多”奶牛场奶牛饲料，形成家家种牧草、户户养奶牛的局面，2005年全村经济收入333万元，为1977年的4倍。杨柳村村民把责任地出租给珍艳有限公司，劳动力给公司打工，农家肥由公司收购，2006年7月—2008年7月，全村总收入达332万元，户均收入4980元。龙场镇王官至中哨千亩农田改种晚番茄远近闻名，年户均收入上万元。广大农民赞不绝口地说：“农民种田不纳税，倒转还领补助费，子女上学不交费，看病还要减免医药费，只有今天的农民才有这样的福分。”清水村88岁的老共产党员王方俊说："我活这么多年，无论是听说的还是亲自经历的，都没有哪个朝代的农民种田不交粮，只有中国共产党敢为天下先。"

（四）政府集中采购

2001年前，预算管理单位购物实行社会集团购买力标控制，由单位自行购买。2002年，按照《贵阳市政府采购管理暂行办法》，国家机关、预算管理的事业单位和社会团体使用财政资金购物、租赁、委托或雇用等方式获取货物、工程和服务的行为改为政府集中采购。2004年8月财政局设政府集中采购中心。2005年统一办理行政事业单位413辆公车续保。2002—2010年累计采购470次，支付采购金额1.21亿元，比预算采购金额减少1997.4万元，节约率为16.51%。

（五）乡财县管乡用

2004年11月，贵州省财政厅决定在修文县进行"乡财县管乡用"财政管理方式试点改革，以谷堡乡和小箐乡为试点单位。2005年1月，试点启动，财政局预算科设乡财政总预算会计，乡财政所设财政结算会计、综合业务管理、出纳，将原乡党政机关、事业单位和财政所共13个银行账户改为4个，8名职工上划财政局管理， 12个临时人员经费停止支付；乡财政811万元债务就地消化。6月启用电算化管理，实行网上申请、网上审批、网上监督。至年末，谷堡乡财政收入完成414.01万元，比上年增长42.24%；小箐乡完成200.4万元，比上年增长54.15%。两个乡财政支出及其他考核指标均达计划要求，财政局按照试点改革财政激励约束机制，从试点乡新增财力中安排30%的资金，以奖励方式分别补助谷堡乡21.73万元，补助小箐乡19.9万元。

2006年1月，"乡财县管乡用"扩大到六屯、洒坪、大石、六桶4个乡。2010年再次将乡财政总预算会计业务退回乡财政，按照"三统一"（统一账套设置、统一银行账户、统一核算软件）进行规范管理。

二、财政收入

（一）中央财政收入

1996年起，增值税须上缴中央75%，排污费、土地有偿使用收入、探矿权采矿权使用费及价款收入、矿产资源补偿收入按比例上解。至2010年，全县累计上解中央财政11.4亿元，占同期财政总收入的37.18%，年均上解7601.53万元。

（二）省级财政收入

1996年起，增值税上缴省财政10%，资源税、城镇土地使用税、土地有偿使用收入、排污费、探矿权采矿权使用费及价款收入、矿产资源补偿费、煤炭资源收入均按比例上解。至2010年，全县累计上解2.58亿元，在同期财政总收入中占8.4%，年均上解1716.59万元。

全县纳税大户科开药业

（三）市级财政收入

1997年起，资源税、城镇土地使用税、土地增值税、土地有偿使用收入、排污费、探矿权采矿权使用费及价款收入、煤炭资源收入纳入市级财政分成， 2010年止，全县累计上解3339.57万元，在同期财政

总收入中占1.09%，年均上解238.54万元。

（四）县级财政收入

1978年起，县在积极发展经济增加财源的同时，按照上级统一部署进行税制改革，恢复和新增20个税种、3个基金及附加，停征2个税种，至1995年全县累计财政预算收入2.07亿元，年均收入1150.11万元。

1996年起，县在巩固好原有财源的同时，努力培植新兴财源，建立后续财源，开展“三长”（分管财政工作副县长、财政局长、税务局长）理财，使财政收入剧增， 到2010年增至2.8亿元，比1995年的2203.1万元增加11.7倍，比1978年的188.9万元增加147倍。1996至2010年全县累计收入16.35亿元，在同期财政总收入中占58.53%，年均收入1.1亿元。自1978年至2010年年均增速16.9%。

专记：三长理财促征收

翻开全县财政收支记录，1978年预算收入只有188.9万元。历经19年的改革和发展，到1997年增至3147.56万元，收支轧抵滚存财政赤字7764万元。1998年县政府实行“三长”理财，促进收入增长：与各乡（镇）政府签订目标责任书，把财政预算收入纳入乡（镇）目标考核，与年终奖金挂钩，实行县长、财政局长、税务局长三长一票否决；实行财政、税务局长和乡（镇）长负责制，乡（镇）长负责发展经济扩大财源，税务局长负责征收入库；规范乡（镇）财政管理体制，实行划分收支范围，核定收支基数。对一类乡（镇）执行定比递增，定额上解，专项补助，超支予奖。二类乡（镇）执行定比递增补助，超收全留。三类乡执行自求平衡，超收留用；推行1+3管理，三长实行征管责任制，定期召开会议分析研究，分片组织，集中征收，让乡（镇）集中精力谋地方经济发展；龙场、扎佐、久长3镇侧重发展工业和蔬菜生产，其余1镇6乡主要发展经济作物种植及养殖。乡镇拟报财源建设发展项目，获批后县采取资金匹配、贷款贴息或拨给适当资金组织实施，推进项目建设；调整不适宜的代征业务。启动之年即招商引进项目17个，到位资金2.5亿元，90%的乡(镇)实现超收，使全县财政、税收连续大幅上升，财政收入成本从1998至2001年的20%降到2003年的8%。2005年县财政预算收入突破亿元大关，2010年全县财政预算收入由1997年的3147.56万元增到2.8亿元，增加7.9倍，收支轧抵由滚存赤字转变为滚存结余1895.7万元，初步扭转县财政收支不平衡的局面。

（五）补助收入

1978—1996年财政收入来源有专项补助、调整任务增减补助、上年结余补助、其他补助。1997年增加税收返还补助，2003年起再增一般性转移支付补助、民族地区转移支付补助、调整工资转移支付补助、农村税费转移支付补助、取消农业特产税降低农业税转移支付补助等项目，1978—2010年全县累计上级补助收入为25.47亿元，年均获取补助7716.78万元，其中2010年补助4.17亿元，相当于县财政自身收入的1.49倍。

1996—2010年各级财政收入及所占比重统计一览表

表3—10—02

年份	全县总收入（万元）	占比（%）	中央财政		省级财政		市级财政		县财政	
			收入（万元）	占比（%）	收入（万元）	占比（%）	收入（万元）	占比（%）	收入（万元）	占比（%）
1996	4006.30	100.00	1293.90	32.30	171.20	4.27	—	—	2541.20	63.43
1997	5660.73	100.00	1828.48	32.30	604.55	10.68	80.14	1.42	3147.56	55.60
1998	6566.28	100.00	2103.85	32.04	630.23	9.60	91.04	1.39	3741.16	56.97
1999	7174.73	100.00	2128.78	29.67	668.98	9.33	107.78	1.50	4269.19	59.50
2000	8003.09	100.00	2361.13	29.50	690.76	8.63	97.45	1.22	4853.75	60.65
2001	9202.95	100.00	2815.39	30.59	709.89	7.72	42.67	0.46	5635.00	61.23
2002	11746.00	100.00	4054.00	34.51	565.00	4.81	41.00	0.35	7086.00	60.33
2003	13214.00	100.00	3565.00	26.98	993.00	7.52	64.00	0.48	8592.00	65.02
2004	17122.51	100.00	5434.80	31.75	1178.68	6.88	110.03	0.64	10399.00	60.73
2005	21382.49	100.00	7036.98	32.91	1378.89	6.45	138.62	0.65	12828.00	59.99
2006	28580.47	100.00	11575.80	40.50	2212.46	7.74	239.21	0.84	14553.00	50.92
2007	32453.53	100.00	13940.36	42.95	2513.75	7.75	208.05	0.64	15791.37	48.66
2008	43062.37	100.00	18340.29	42.59	4883.51	11.34	747.43	1.74	19091.14	44.33
2009	44065.37	100.00	16651.34	37.79	3757.58	8.53	628.45	1.43	23028.00	52.25
2010	54386.79	100.00	20892.77	38.42	4790.24	8.80	743.70	1.37	27960.08	51.41

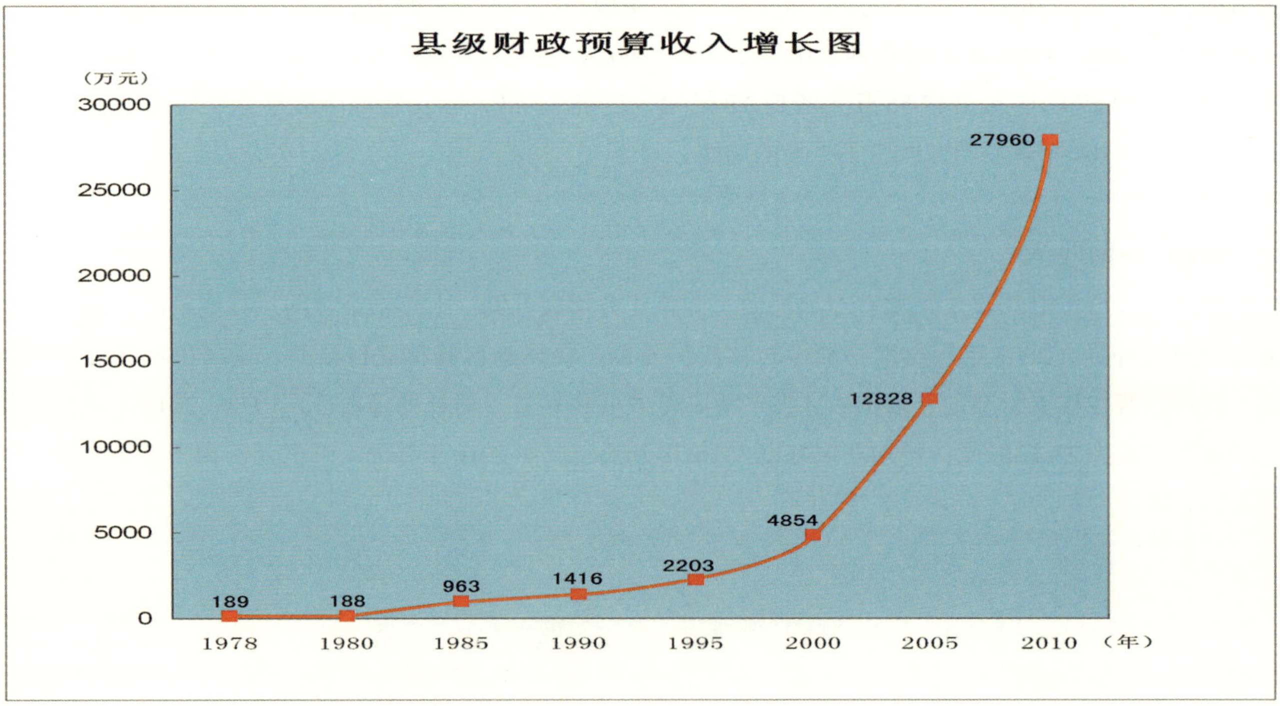

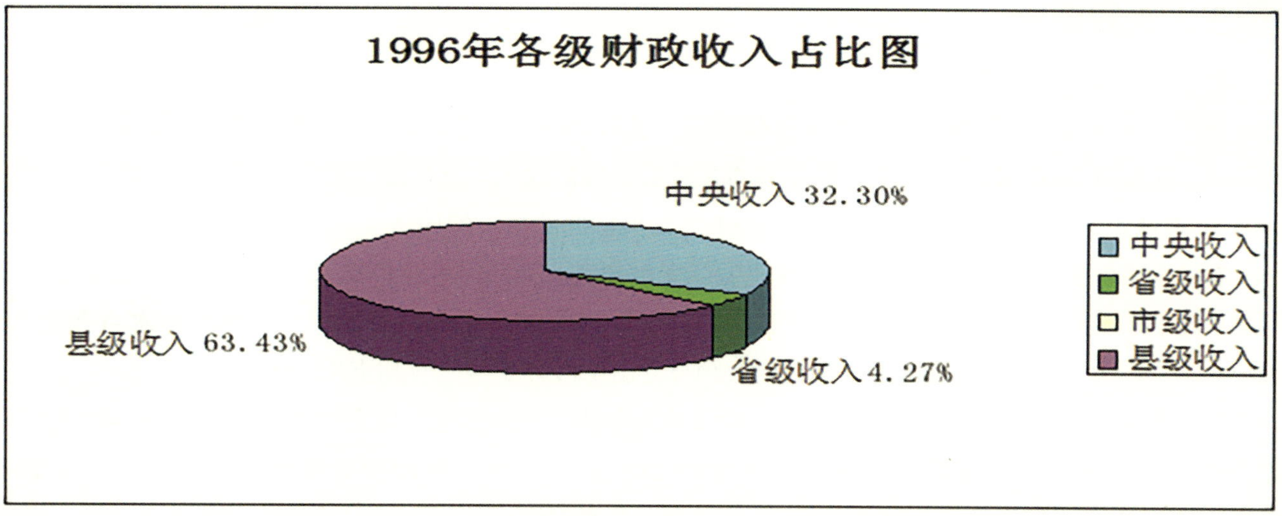
1996年各级财政收入占比图
中央收入 32.30%
县级收入 63.43%
省级收入 4.27%
中央收入
省级收入
市级收入
县级收入

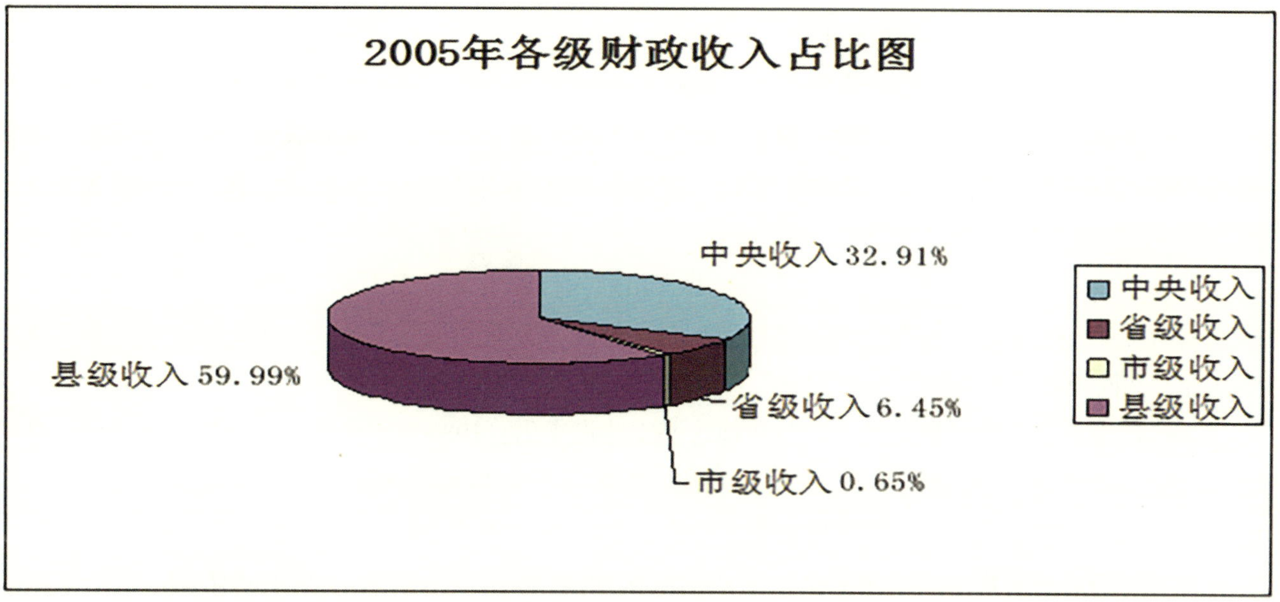
2005年各级财政收入占比图
中央收入 32.91%
县级收入 59.99%
省级收入 6.45%
市级收入 0.65%
中央收入
省级收入
市级收入
县级收入

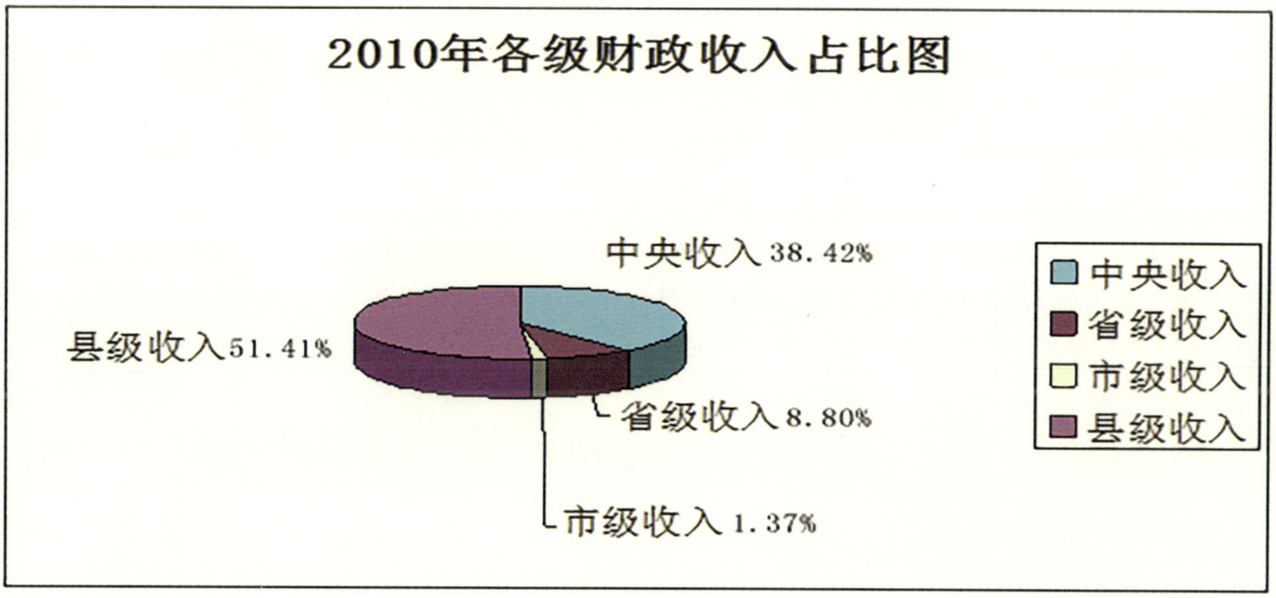
2010年各级财政收入占比图
中央收入 38.42%
县级收入 51.41%
省级收入 8.80%
市级收入 1.37%
中央收入
省级收入
市级收入
县级收入

三、财政支出

（一）县级财政预算支出

1978年全县支出492.28万元，1979年起坚持“量力而行，从紧安排”的原则，在保证正常经费支出的同时，加大对农业、教育、卫生、科学技术、社会保障的投入，支出连年增加。至2010年的33年累计支出42.49亿元，年均支出1.33亿元，其中2010年支出8.98亿元，在1978年的基础上年均增长17.66%。

农林水事务支出 1978年列有支援农业生产支出和农业类部门事业费支出。1995年单列农业综合开发支出项目。2007年增设环境保护项目和扶贫项目，同年财政支出项目调整，统称农林水事务支出。1978—2010年累计支出6.59亿元，在同期财政预算支出中占15.51%，年均支出1996.62万元。

教科文卫支出 含教育、科学技术、文化体育与传媒、医疗卫生、计划生育、党校教学、档案管理及干部培训事业费。1978至2010年累计支出15.28亿元，占同期财政预算支出的35.97%，年均支出4631.23万元，其中教育总支出10.13亿元，占同期财政预算支出的23.84%，为县内各项支出之首，医疗卫生支出3.36亿元，在同期预算总支出中占7.92%。

一般公共服务支出 原称行政管理支出。1978至1985年含公检法司经费支出。2007年调整财政支出类别，原列入其他部门的统计、财政、税务、审计、人事劳动、商贸、工商和农业类的国土资源、气象等部门均划入行政类，统称一般公共服务支出。1978至2010年累计支出7.86亿元，在同期财政预算支出中占18.5%，年均支出2382.21万元。

公共安全支出 1978—1985年公检法司经费支出列入行政管理费支出类，1986年单列为支出项目，2007年起增加武警、国防（民兵）及办案经费项目，统称“公共安全支出”，至2010年的25年累计支出2.66亿元，在同期财政预算支出中占1.42%，年均支出237.08万元。

城乡社区事务及住房保障支出 1978年前为基本建设支出。1986年增加城市维护费支出项目，县城和小城镇建设资金多以城市维护费支出项目列支。2007年改称城乡社区事务及住房保障支出。1978至2010年累计支出1.22亿元，占同期财政预算支出的2.87%，年均支出368.85万元。

社会保障与就业支出 1978至1990年，仅有抚恤和社会救济福利支出。1991年增加社会保险基金，为国营企业职工缴纳养老保险基金和失业保险基金。1997年再增军队离（退）休干部移交地方安置经费。1998年推行城镇和农村居民最低生活保障制度。至2010年的33年累计支出2.98亿元，在同期财政预算支出中占7.01%，年均支出902.23万元。

工交商和其他部门支出 为上述各支出项目以外的部门事业费支出，1978—2010年累计支出1.68亿元，占同期财政预算支出的3.96%，年均支出510.27万元。

其他支出 包括支援不发达地区资金、政策性补助、城镇青年就业补助及专项支出中的排污费、教育费附加、其他杂项支出。2003年起增加村民委员会经费项目支付村干部工资。1978—2010年累计支出4.22亿元，在同期财政预算支出中占9.93%，年均支出1277.9万元。

（二）上解支出

1978—2010年，仅有总额上解支出和专项上解支出两项，累计上解支出6367.9万元，年均上解199万元。

1978—2010年县财政预算支出所占比重统计表

表3—10—03　　　　　　　　　　　　　　　　　　　　　　　　　　单位：%

年份	农林水事务	教科文卫	一般公共服务	公共安全	社会保障和就业	工交商和其他部门	城乡社会事务及住房保障	其他支出
1978	33.10	29.49	14.84	—	2.91	10.83	3.04	5.79
1979	33.48	33.09	15.71	—	5.48	9.63	0.19	2.42
1980	27.27	38.11	17.62	—	6.42	5.35	—	5.23
1981	28.08	39.52	16.89	—	6.59	2.74	—	6.18
1982	18.59	39.17	20.64	—	5.08	10.59	—	5.93
1983	24.36	37.32	17.33	—	5.31	7.53	1.06	7.18
1984	13.22	38.61	17.09	—	6.14	12.21	9.79	2.94
1985	11.17	45.58	22.17	—	9.40	4.70	1.29	5.69
1986	10.84	44.64	20.67	3.03	8.03	6.73	2.18	3.88
1987	11.06	38.85	23.17	3.19	7.12	4.78	3.36	8.47
1988	10.46	38.29	19.70	4.19	5.75	8.07	4.06	9.48
1989	12.00	34.80	16.99	4.16	8.10	4.62	6.44	12.89
1990	11.90	38.46	19.37	5.36	8.29	5.24	6.55	4.83
1991	12.21	36.68	16.36	4.64	4.63	3.33	3.70	18.45
1992	13.31	33.96	17.22	3.97	3.62	7.56	5.37	14.99
1993	16.80	34.88	18.77	4.49	1.99	7.85	1.18	14.04
1994	12.29	33.99	16.84	3.96	3.04	9.93	2.88	17.07
1995	12.64	34.65	18.02	6.05	2.89	6.88	1.15	17.72
1996	15.42	35.87	21.99	6.28	6.61	4.80	0.88	8.15
1997	18.23	30.37	20.02	7.28	3.87	4.18	1.24	14.81
1998	19.91	39.22	19.44	5.81	4.12	3.64	1.44	6.42
1999	12.32	41.34	22.35	8.44	1.08	3.40	2.92	8.15
2000	12.45	50.05	16.73	6.51	3.19	5.28	2.19	3.60
2001	11.27	45.48	17.93	6.63	4.82	6.30	2.75	4.82
2002	9.06	40.39	17.50	5.97	5.06	6.38	5.06	10.58
2003	9.76	42.66	17.05	5.40	2.10	5.66	1.49	15.88
2004	9.41	41.36	17.63	5.25	3.21	4.13	2.85	16.16
2005	11.74	40.05	20.11	6.22	3.68	3.29	1.88	13.03
2006	8.99	39.67	19.58	8.18	1.83	3.03	4.07	14.65
2007	14.26	36.70	20.92	7.18	6.68	2.10	3.05	9.11
2008	16.98	35.52	18.91	6.15	8.47	2.92	3.65	7.40
2009	17.07	30.93	18.51	6.70	11.15	3.93	2.06	9.65
2010	20.97	32.26	16.69	5.96	9.31	3.86	2.97	7.98

四、财务管理

（一）预算资金管理

经费定额包干　1978至1979年，行政事业单位公用经费实行总指标控制，1980年改为定额包干，至1985年，县委、县政府、人大、政协、纪委及区、乡（镇）机关每人每年282元，公检法部门320元，其他部门225元。1989年分别提高为320元、440元、320元。1990年再提为440元、520元、400元。以后包干指标随市场物价变化和财政收入情况而变。2008至2010年人年均定额公用经费：县委、县政府、人大、政协及政法部门500元，镇400元，乡700元，其他部门400元。

农业投资改有偿使用　1978—1980年，县财政扶持农村社队的资金为无偿投入。1981年改部分投资为支农周转金实行有偿投资，由受援方与财政签订借款合同，财政收取不超过银行同类贷款项目利率的资金占用费。

1992年9月，财政局置财政信用资金管理所，将支农周转金作为财政信用资金发放。1990至1993年，全县共投放资金494.23万元，其中含省级财政项目383万元，县级财政项目110.22万元。1994年8月止，累计收回349.5万元，占发放数的70.72%。

2002年，将支农周转金列入统筹范围，由财政部门专项储存，统一管理。2000—2010年累计发放4538.1万元，收回2762.05万元，核销93.98万元。

实行信用担保　1999年，财政局设国有资产投资经营公司，始办委托银行贷款扶持县域中小企业发展。2002年起扶持方式逐步由委托贷款转为信用担保。1999—2008年共支持企业35家，金额7553.41万元，并为16家企业（单位）办理信用担保1.64亿元，解决企业资金不足的困难。扶持的企业除阳明山庄（圣泉山庄）外，其余均投产见效。2009年至2010年，发放5笔3.18亿元给农业银行县支行，解决白（云）修（文）公路建设和贵阳特殊钢厂前期资金供应。

2003年3月获县国投公司担保贷款130万元经营的贵州联宇食品有限公司

国有资产产权登记　1990年县财政始对国有企业国有资产进行清理。次年认定全县国营企业国有资产存量1499.2万元，其中工业企业867.6万元，交通企业30.3万元，商业企业363.4万元，农林水企业21.4万元，文教卫生企业74.2万元，城市公用86.5万元，其他55.8万元。

2002年，登记国有企业国有资产产权，全县产权占有国有企业19户，资产总额1.12亿元，其中国有资产1312万元，负债总额9866万元。

从2003年起，每年上半年对上年行政事业单位国有资产产权年检登记，到2010年全县行政事业单位全部资产总额共8.88亿元，比2007年5.69亿元增加56.22%。主要实物资产有行政事业单位累计占地1154亩（县级300亩，乡（镇）级855亩），房屋建筑物44万平方米（县级18万平方米，乡镇级26万平方米），交通运输设备598辆（县级455辆，乡镇级143辆），大多数单位虽占有使用，但没有按规定办理房屋产权证和土地使用证。

2010年全县地方国有资产产权登记情况统计表

表3—10—04

项目		登记户数	全部资产			年末固定资产原值			主要财产情况				
			资产总额	负债总额	国有资产净值	合计	房屋、构筑物	交通运输设备	土地占用面积	房屋构筑面积			公用车辆
										合计	办公用房	用于经营房屋	
计量单位		户	万元	万元	万元	万元	万元	万元	万平方米	万平方米	万平方米	万平方米	辆
合计		140	88846	34881	53965	34781	14619	6593	77	44	19	1	598
按部门分	教育	30	15072	4832	10240	9339	5109	225	64	24	7	—	18
	卫生	14	9384	2911	6473	4609	2826	274	2	4	1	1	19
	广播电影电视	11	2997	2117	880	527	93	129	—	—	—	—	13
	行政管理	62	21235	10276	10959	8264	2977	2943	7	11	7	—	243
	公检法	5	8319	1645	6674	4496	703	1748	1	1	1	—	201
	抚恤和社会福利	1	2903	567	2336	241	86	96	—	—	—	—	10
	工交建	2	5383	4346	1037	232	28	136	—	—	—	—	12
	农林水	4	22057	7483	14574	6358	2425	868	3	4	3	—	70
	其他	11	1496	704	792	715	291	174	—	—	—	—	12
按单位性质分	行政	67	29554	11921	17633	12759	3780	4691	8	12	8	—	444
	事业	61	57590	22218	35372	21229	10637	1728	69	32	11	——	141
	社团	1	206	38	168	78	11	—	—	—	—	—	1
	其他	11	1496	704	792	715	291	174	—	—	—	—	12

注：科研、商粮贸、金融部门未登记

（二）预算外资金管理

1987年5月经县政府批准，行政事业单位预算外资金实行“专户储存，计划管理，财政审批，银行监督”；企业及主管部门预算外资金实行“计划管理，政策引导”。

1991年，县财政局与人民银行县支行商定，自11月1日起财政专户储存的预算外资金由不计利率改为计付利息。从1993年5月起，在乡（镇）所在地银行机构开设预算外资金财政代管专户储存，纳入单位财务统一管理，统一制定收费发票，预算内和预算外资金合并编入预算支出计划。1994年3月，全县13个系统41个行政事业性收费项目及罚没收入纳入预算内管理，收入缴国库，开支列财政支出。1998至2010年仍实行收支两条线管理不变。

2000—2010年全县预算外资金收支统计一览表

表3—10—05　　　　单位：万元

年份	收入	支出	年份	收入	支出	年份	收入	支出
2000	2052	2854	2004	2572	2250	2008	1274	1124
2001	1745	1668	2005	1639	1516	2009	951	863
2002	1523	1151	2006	3031	2833	2010	1120	1016
2003	2105	2283	2007	1220	1318			

(三)会计事务管理

职称确认和聘任　1978—1986年未评定技术职称。1987至1989年，财政局对会计专业人员评审确认技术职称，实行聘任制度。1990—1993年评审确认改由部门组织考试获取。1994年实行全国统一考试获取职称资格。至2010年全县经考试取得中级职务资格22人，取得初级职务资格52人，加上原评定确认职称部分全县共有会计专业技术人员140人，其中中级32人，初级108人。

会计认证　1990年3月始办，对经申报、考试、考核符合条件的发给《会计证》，持有《会计证》者可从事会计工作。1999年对持证会计人员进行培训，每人每年参加学习不得少于48小时。至2010年全县持《会计证》人员781人。

(四)财政监督

1981年财政局置监察股，对行政事业和工建交企业进行监督检查，至1982年查出违纪金额26.51万元，检查中入库4.61万元。其余继续追缴入库。

1985年起，贯彻执行国务院决定，每年开展税收、财务、物价大检查，9月至12月检查当年违纪金额71.19万元，应补缴税金和利润21.9万元，检查中入库6.9万元。

1989年起全国物价上涨，收费混乱，县政府遵照中共“治理整顿，深化改革”的方针，责成财政监察部门连续4年共查出违纪资金265.46万元，其中应补缴税金和上交财政资金231.51万元当即补缴入库。

1990年，根据国务院通知和贵州省政府电话会议精神，饬令200个行政企事业单位和17户个体工商户中首先自查，然后重点检查，共查出违纪资金131.91万元，应入库91.88万元，没收2.5万元，检查中入库63.95万元，完成没收和应入库资金的67.76%。

1991年，有209家应查户进行自查，查出22家偷税漏税、乱发补贴，共违纪支付46.53万元，应入库29.52万元。接着由监察部门重点检查税务、财务、物价91家，查出违纪资金40万元，收缴入库39.81万元。1995年市场物价开始下滑，检查的重点转向清理“小金库”，在普遍自查的基础上重点检查12个单位，查出4个单位收款2.05万元未入账，分别给予限时纳入财务预算处理。

1996年和1997年重点清理检查预算外资金，查出应缴未缴财政预算外资金16万元，应缴未缴财政专户资金191万元，责令立即入库和缴存。六广土管所仅2名职工，1997年超标准发放资金实物1650元和岗位津贴1650元，超标报销旅差费818元，白条收费达3857元，共计违纪金额7975元，六广镇政府下发整改通知，限期归还违规支付资金，并处以单位500元和负责人50元罚款。

1998年，税收、财务、物价检查工作停止。2000年10月，财政局置监察室，专门行使财政监察职

责，每年开展一次财政内部财务检查，对两个行政事业单位开展会计信息质量检查，要求整改达40余次。至2007年查处违纪资金51.55万元；清理全县领导干部拖欠、借用公款157万元，检查中收回124万元。小箐、谷堡、大石3个财政所职工贪污、挪用公款案调查结案，有4名职工共贪污28.65万元，挪用公款5.8万元，被移交司法机关判处有期徒刑，另有5人受纪律处分，处予经济罚款。至2010年监察工作连续进行，未发现重大违纪问题。

财政监督工作人员履行监督职责

第三节 税务管理

1978年沿袭税务局原有建制，工商税由税务局征收，农业税由财政计征。1983年和1994年分别进行国营企业利改税和分税制改革，将原来单一的工商税制逐步改为多种税、多次征收的复合税制。2005年取消农业税，2010年工商税收从1978年的182万元增到4.43亿元，在1978年基础上年均增长率为18.74%。

一、体制改革

（一）机构改革

1978年，县置税务局，下设税收股统管税收征收、管理和检查，基层由5个区税务所负责本区域的征收管理。1990年1月征管、征收分置机构，局置直属稽查队，专司税务稽查职能。1994—2010年推行分税制，原税务局和基层税务所分成国税局、地税局两个机构分别征收中央税和地方税。

国税系统 分置初期，局置征管股、征收股和直属稽查队，基层按区置5个税务所。1996年年初，局征收分局与城关税务所合并组建为直属征收管理分局，负责县以上企事业单位及城关片区的征收管理。1997年10月裁撤扎佐、久长两个税务所，置扎佐征收管理分局；撤小箐、六广两个税务所，置六广征收管理分局。分别承担原税务所辖区的征管业务。1999年县局及分局设置办税服务厅，将税务员上门征税改为纳税人到服务厅自缴。2003年6月再撤六广征收管理分局，业务移交扎佐征收管理分局接办。2005至2010年复置六广税务分局，与扎佐税务分局同时升格为副科级单位。

税务办公设施

地税系统 分置初期，局置征管股、征收股和直属稽查队，基层按乡（镇）置税务所共10个。

1996年初将税务稽查队改为税务稽查分局；撤城关、谷堡两所及局征收股，置直属征收分局；撤扎佐、六屯两所，置扎佐税务所；撤小箐、洒坪两所，置小箐税务所；撤六广、大石、六桶3所，置六广税务所，并建后各自负责本区域地方税的征收管理。2001年又根据省编制委员会办公室关于乡（镇）地税机构原则上按经济区域设置的要求，撤扎佐、久长税务所，置扎佐征收管理分局；撤小箐、六广税务所，置六广征收管理分局。县局及分局置办税服务厅办理纳税业务。2003年7月至2010年，扎佐、六广分局复为税务所。

（二）税制改革

国营企业利改税 1983年5月启动，分两步进行，第一步主要对盈利的国营企业征收企业所得税，把企业原来向国家上交的利润大部分改为以所得税形式上交。全县地方国营企业24户，除4户因亏损或定额上交利润外，其余20户均实行利改税。其中百货、石油等8户划为大中型企业，缴纳所得税后的利润征收调节税。耐火材料厂、农机厂等12户划为小型企业，税后利润留归企业。

第二步于1984年10月与工商税制改革同步进行，主要是将企业原来上交国家财政收入分别按11个税种纳税，使国家参与企业分配方式由税利并存过渡到完全以税代利。除国家规定的军工、邮电、粮食、农牧等企业暂时不实行外，全县25户地方国营企业，除蔬菜、食品两公司因亏损暂不划定类型，其余23户中百货公司批发部等3户为大中型企业，征收国营企业所得税，税后利润征收调节税。耐火材料厂、农机厂等20户为小型企业，按照超额累进税率征收国营企业所得税，税后利润原则上留归企业。执行到2010年，税务依率征税，企业照章纳税。

分税制 1994年起实施，其主要内容：一是全面改革流转税制，实行以增值税为主体，消费税、营业税并存，内外统一的流转税制；二是改革所得税制，将原来对国营企业、集体企业、私营企业分别征收的所得税合并为统一的企业所得税；三是改革个人所得税制，将原来对外国人征收的个人所得税、对中国人征收的个人收入调节税、个体工商户所得税合并为统一的个人所得税；四是对资源税、特别目的税、财产税、行为税作大幅调整，扩大资源税征收范围，开征土地增值税，取消奖金税、建筑税等税种。同时，根据中央政府和地方政府的事权划分，将全部税种按中央、地方划分开来分别征收，执行到2010年未作变动。

专记：税制改革促进税收翻番

历史上修文一直处于欠发达地区，经济发展滞后，税源竭蹶，1978年工商税收只有182.34万元。1979年起的16年历经国营企业利改税改革，工商税增至2621万元，净增2438.66万元。1994年分税制改革，县政府采取有效措施：加强交通和水、电、路为主的基础设施建设，促进物流畅通；利用自身区位、地理、资源优势招商引资，从1998年起连续13年共引进项目216个，到位资金54.85亿元，已有45个入驻企业年缴纳税金2.59亿元，分别占规模以上工业企业纳税总额的97.78%和全县工商税收总额的93.82%；采取"一厂一议，一厂一策"办法对县属国有企业分别进行异地改造、有偿转让、引资改造，抑或破产处理，使其焕发活力；实行"三长"理财征管责任制，分片组织，集中征收，使税收及时入库；大力发展非公有制经济，允许非公资本进入垄断行业、公用事业和公共基础设施领域。全县非公经济实现增加值26.56亿元，占GDP的比重达57.5%。1999年，国、地税务局和基层分局置办税服务厅，纳税由上门征收改为纳税人主动申报，明白纳税。2004年全县税收翻亿元关，2010年实现4.43亿元，比1994年增加14倍，比1978年增加227.8倍，上解中央、省、市财政后，县留1.96亿元，县财政由1997年

滚存赤字7764万元转变为2010年滚存结余1895.7万元，彻底摆脱财政拮据的窘境。

二、农业四税

（一）农业税

1. 征收

农业税历来由财政负责征收，实行依率计征，征收以实物为主，税率比较低；农业税附加随农业税征收，多用于财政预算未予安排的农村公益事业。1979年农业税征收改革，恢复起征点征收，起征点为水稻区农户平均收入200公斤，杂粮区150公斤，稻杂兼产区175公斤，分配收入50元以上的生产队实行征收，起征点以下的不予征收，分配收入在标准线以上但人均口粮在标准线以下适当减征。1980年起征点征收又由一年一定改为一定三年不变。1983年对达到起征点的队又实行一定五年征收。1986年取消粮食统购，农业税征收逐步由征粮改为用现金折抵。1993年根据国务院决定征收恢复以粮食为主，2003年起农业税征收全部实行现金折交，并逐年减少征收额。2005年起全部免征农业税，农业税附加也随同停交，从而结束缴交农业税的历史。从1978至2004年，全县累计征收入库6031.81万元，年平均增收223.4万元。2005—2006年农民补交尾欠26万元。

2. 减免

灾歉减免　每年对农作物自然灾害导致歉收，根据灾情轻重实行轻灾少减，重灾多减，特灾全免。

社会减免　每年对无劳动力家庭生活困难、因受意外伤害等原因交税有困难、少数民族聚居的生活困难地区、不发达贫困山区，通过减免扶持发展生产。

起征点减免　1979年，以生产队为单位计算，起征点上征收，点下免征。是年全县1089个生产队，全免60个，部分减免769个，减免队占总队数76.12%，累计减免税额117万元。

鼓励发展生产减免　凡垦种新荒地和熟荒地，自有收入之年起免征1—3年；非耕地种植农林特产免征3年；新开辟桑园、茶园、苗圃及农户自留地、饲料地等零星种植农作物全部免征。

基建占用耕地调剂减免　凡属批准征用耕地进行基本建设的，实行调剂减免解决。

退耕还林减免　凡属国家规定25度以上坡耕地退耕还林还草的，自退耕之年起减征。

增加农民收入减免　2002年起国家为减轻农民负担，增加农民收入，逐年减免农业税，2005年全部免征，将这部分收入让利于农民。

农业税实行依法减免和先减后征，通过减免平衡农民负担，减免指标逐级下达，一直落实到纳税户。1978—2002年中有22年累计减免折稻谷1909.9万公斤。

（二）农业特产税

1978年前纳入农业税征收。1988年单列税种开征。1994年原工商税中产品税征收的烤烟、毛茶、精制茶、晒烟、原竹、原木、生漆等农业特产划入农业特产税征收。2002年面向农民征收的农业特产税除烤烟外全部废止。之后，征收对象仅有县烟草公司和落户非贫困乡的企业。2006年烟叶税从财政局转由地方税务局征收。至2010年农业特产税仍存。

（三）耕地占用税

1987年开征，凡占用耕地建房或者从事非农业建设的单位和个人均应缴纳。2008年该税从财政局转地方税务局征收。至2010年税种仍存。

（四）契税

1985年恢复征收，税率为买契3%—5%，赠予契6%，典契3%，2008年该税从财政转由地方税务局征收。至2010年契税仍存。

1978—2002年农业税征粮统计

表3—10—06

年份	依率计征（万公斤）	减免（万公斤）	减免后应征税额（万公斤）	地方附加		正附税合计（万公斤）	实际完成			农业人均负担（公斤）
				征收比例（%）	征收额（万公斤）		合计（万公斤）	正税（万公斤）	附加（万公斤）	
1978	376.00	85.0	291.0	8.00	24.0	315.0	314.50	291.00	23.50	16.6
1979	377.00	147.0	230.0	8.00	19.0	249.0	248.50	229.50	19.00	12.6
1980	374.00	147.0	229.0	8.00	18.0	247.0	246.50	228.50	18.00	12.4
1981	376.00	225.0	216.0	8.00	17.0	233.0	232.50	215.50	17.00	11.5
1982	376.00	117.0	258.0	8.00	20.0	278.0	278.50	258.00	20.50	13.5
1983	376.00	4.0	367.0	8.00	29.0	396.0	395.50	366.50	29.00	19.1
1984	376.00	29.0	364.0	8.00	29.0	393.0	395.50	364.00	29.00	18.7
1985	376.00	205.0	183.0	8.00	15.0	198.0	197.50	183.00	14.50	9.4
1986	406.25	105.0	301.0	8.00	24.0	325.0	325.40	301.30	24.10	15.2
1987	406.25	101.0	305.0	8.00	24.0	329.0	329.20	304.80	24.10	15.3
1988	406.25	69.0	337.0	8.00	29.0	366.0	366.20	337.20	29.00	16.3
1989	376.00	43.0	333.0	8.00	27.0	360.0	359.30	332.76	26.60	15.9
1990	376.00	130.0	246.0	8.00	20.0	266.0	365.80	346.10	19.70	11.5
1991	263.18	90.9	172.3	8.00	13.8	186.1	186.06	172.27	13.79	8.0
1992	263.18	17.2	262.1	8.00	21.0	283.1	281.10	281.10	—	11.1
1993	263.20	16.2	247.0	8.00	19.8	266.8	266.76	247.00	19.76	11.1
1994	263.20	10.5	252.7	8.00	20.2	272.9	272.92	252.70	20.22	11.3
1995	263.20	47.6	215.6	8.00	17.3	232.9	232.85	251.60	17.25	9.4
1996	263.20	53.7	243.1	8.00	19.5	263.1	263.10	263.10	—	10.6
1997	263.20	24.1	238.8	8.00	24.3	263.1	263.10	263.10	—	10.7
1998	263.12	24.4	241.5	8.00	24.6	266.1	266.09	241.45	24.64	10.8
1999	263.20	16.4	246.8	8.00	19.3	266.1	266.07	246.81	19.26	10.6
2000	263.20	37.6	225.6	8.00	24.7	250.3	250.28	225.64	24.64	9.9
2001	263.20	92.6	170.6	10.52	18.0	188.6	188.59	170.63	17.96	7.4
2002	376.55	166.7	209.9	20.00	42.0	251.9	251.88	209.90	41.98	10.0

注：1. 常年产量：1978至1979年4185万公斤，1980至1990年4144万公斤，1991—2001年2901万公斤，2002年5379万公斤；2. 因农业税征收年报表缺失，1992、1996、1997年数系财政局测算，实际完成数为粮食部门征收数

1978—2010年农业“四税”收入统计

表3—10—07　　　　　　　　　　　　　　　　　　　　　　单位：万元

年份	合计	农业税	农业特产税	耕地占用税	契税	年份	合计	农业税	农业特产税	耕地占用税	契税
1978	55.88	55.88	—	—	—	1995	680.00	308.00	352.50	14.40	5.10
1979	53.00	53.00	—	—	—	1996	1013.40	462.60	531.10	13.70	6.00
1980	52.80	52.80	—	—	—	1997	1195.10	414.90	723.80	7.10	49.30
1981	49.76	49.76	—	—	—	1998	1116.00	497.00	540.00	37.00	42.00
1982	51.92	51.92	—	—	—	1999	823.00	422.00	321.00	50.00	30.00
1983	84.72	84.72	—	—	—	2000	896.00	374.00	387.00	75.00	60.00
1984	84.09	84.09	—	—	—	2001	611.00	259.00	89.00	173.00	90.00
1985	58.89	58.89	—	—	—	2002	855.00	538.00	253.00	36.00	28.00
1986	85.20	84.36	—	—	0.84	2003	848.00	466.00	296.00	32.00	54.00
1987	105.34	104.34	—	—	1.00	2004	753.00	395.00	250.00	57.00	51.00
1988	119.85	115.47	0.55	—	3.83	2005	530.00	23.00	453.00	9.00	45.00
1989	159.17	155.19	1.11	—	2.87	2006	619.00	3.00	425.00	—	191.00
1990	119.99	113.70	3.84	—	2.45	2007	1312.00	—	488.00	660.00	164.00
1991	123.28	113.79	6.86	—	2.63	2008	1345.00	—	631.00	543.00	171.00
1992	187.05	171.40	11.70	—	3.95	2009	2732.38	—	627.30	1114.45	990.63
1993	230.99	212.00	11.68	—	7.31	2010	2431.51	—	526.16	1461.99	443.36
1994	614.50	334.00	251.20	14.00	15.30	—	—	—	—	—	—

三、工商类税

（一）税种

1978年至1982年沿用原税种4个，1983年起先后开征（复征）税种23个，加上沿用税种共27个，停征税种13个，至2010年仍保留税种14个。

1. 流转税类

工商税　1978年沿用，以行业为项目，按产品执行不同税率。1984年10月分解为产品税、增值税、营业税，同时停征工商税。

产品税　1984年10月开征，系原工商税中工业和农、林、牧、水产品采购部分的延续。适用税率3%至55%共38个。1989年部分产品改征增值税，1994年课税项目全部改征增值税，产品税即时

地税局工作人员到企业检查纳税情况

终止。

增值税　1988年1月开征，以生产经营中增值额为课税依据，先在中央国营工业企业中试行，1989年起逐步扩大征收范围，增值率为12%至18%。1994年征收范围改为商品生产、批发、零售和进口，增值率从0至17%，2010年征收1.86亿元，在国税和地方税收总额中占42%，为全县税收的主体。

营业税　1984年10月开征，以行业设置税目，分经营业务设置税率，课税对象主要是第三产业营业收入，税率1.5%至10%。1994年1月执行税率提高到3%至20%。2010年营业税征收7542万元，在全县国税和地方税收总额中占17%，是工商税收中仅次于增值税的主要税种。

资源税　1992年1月开征，仅对煤炭资源实行定额税。1994年起征收范围逐步扩大到原油、天然气、固体（液体）盐和其他非金属矿原矿、黑色和有色金属矿原矿等。2010年资源税仍存。

消费税　1994年开始征收，属中央税种，县内应税产品有白酒、鞭炮，税率分别为25%、15%。2010年消费税仍存。

2. 企业所得税类

工商所得税　1978年沿用，以集体企业和个体经营盈利所得征收的税种，实行两套累进办法和五种不同税率。1985年4月按照经济性质分解为国营、集体、私营3种企业所得税，工商所得税即时废止。

国营企业所得税　1983年1月开征，系原国营企业上交利润改征的税种，大中型企业比例税率55%，小型企业及县以上供销社分八级征收，税率7%至55%。1994年9月分税制改革并入企业所得税。

集体企业所得税　1985年1月开征，课税对象为集体企业利润所得和主管部门向企业提取的管理费结余，实行新的8级超额累进税率，税率10%至55%。1994年9月并入企业所得税。

私营企业所得税　1988年开征，课税对象是资产属私人所有并雇工8人以上的私营企业从事各项经营的利润所得，税率比例统一为35%。因查账阻力大和专管人员业务水平有限，仅1989年至1990年征收37万元，1991年后无该税收入。1994年9月并入企业所得税。

企业所得税　1994年9月由原国营企业所得税、集体企业所得税、私营企业所得税合并组成。1995年1月开征，实行33%的比例税率。为不增加利润较低的企业税收负担，另置18%和27%两档低税率。2008年税率实行25%。2010年企业所得税仍存。

3. 个人所得税类

城乡个体工商业户所得税　1986年1月开征，以从事工商、服务、交通运输、建筑安装及其他行业和经工商部门批准的个体工商业户为纳税人，税率为7%至60%分10级征收。1994年税制改革并入个人所得税。

个人收入调节税　1989年正式开征，以国境内取得收入的中国公民为纳税人，根据收入来源分别采取超倍累计税率和比例税率征收。1994年并入个人所得税。

个人所得税　1994年由城乡个体工商业户所得税和个人收入调节税合并组成，税率按所得类别分为9档，最高45%，最低5%。2008年10月9日起储蓄存款利息所得税免征。2010年个人所得税仍存。

4. 财产与行为税类

房产税　1987年1月开征，先在城关、扎佐两镇实施，后扩大到公、私房产，按房产原值征收的以原值一次减除30%后余值计征1.2%，按租金征收的以租金收入金额计征12%。2010年房产税仍存。

城镇土地使用税　1990年开征，计征时间起于1988年10月，以土地管理部门核准的土地使用证书确定的使用面积为计税依据，先从建制镇开始，再扩大征收范围。初期每平方米0.2元至2元，1996年分为

6级税额0.4元至3元。2010年城镇土地使用税仍存。

土地增值税 2002年开征，凡转让国有土地使用权、地上建筑物及附着物并取得收入的单位和个人均按四级超额累进税率计征，税率最高60%，最低30%。2010年土地增值税仍存。

车船使用税 原名称“车船使用牌照税”，1978年停征，1986年10月复征，以拥有并使用的单位和个人为纳税人，年征收税额为：乘人汽车10座以下120元，每增10座增加40元；载重汽车每吨36元；摩托车20元至40元。非机动车中兽力车12元至32元，人力车18元。2010年车船使用税仍存。

印花税 1988年12月复征，以国境内书立和领受性质的凭证、财产转移书据、权利和许可证书、营业账簿和经财政部门确定征税的其他凭证单位和个人为纳税人，实行比例税率0.05‰至0.5‰和按件贴花（5元）办法征收。至2010年印花税仍存。

建筑税 1983年10月开征，凡使用国家预算外资金、地方机动财力、企事业自有资金、银行贷款及其他自有资金进行基本建设和更新改造项目中的建筑部分按10%税率纳税。1991年12月改征固定资产投资方向调节税，建筑税即时终止。

固定资产投资方向调节税 1992年1月开征，系建筑税的延续，课税对象为固定资产投资项目实际完成投资额。税率分3种：农、林、水利、能源、交通运输、邮电等9类44项执行0%税率；轻工、商业、供销、物资、金融等4类6项执行5%税率；建材、轻工、城市建设等4项执行30%税率。1999年7月1日起立项或完成的投资额减半征收。2000年1月起对新发生的投资额暂停征收，2002—2010年全县无固定资产投资方向调节税收入。

奖金税 1984年开征，课税对象为国营、集体企事业单位发放各种形式奖金及超过规定标准发放各种带奖金性质的工资津（补）贴，税率30%至300%。1994年停征。

屠宰税 1978年沿用税种，对经营屠宰业的国营、合作企业征收猪、牛、羊定额税为3元、2元、0.4元。1985年扩大到收购环节。2002年5月取消屠宰环节和收购环节征收，2003年至2010年全县无屠宰税收入。

牲畜交易税 1978年沿用税种，以牲畜交易额为计税依据，税率5%。1994年停征。

城市维护建设税 1985年1月开征，凡缴纳产品税、增值税、营业税的纳税人以其纳税额计税征收，县城和集镇税率5%，农村1%。至2010年该城市维护建设税仍存。

车辆购置税 原为车辆购置附加费，2001年改为车辆购置税，由交通部门代征。2005年1月改由国家税务局征收，凡购置汽车、摩托车、挂车、农用运输车均实行从价定率计征，税率10%。2010年仍存。

教育费附加 1986年6月开征，凡缴纳产品税、增值税、营业税的纳税人以其税额计算征收，附加率3%。至2010年教育费附加仍存。

专记：为国聚财的纳税大户科开公司

科开公司建于1995年，前身为贵阳医学科技开发药品经营部，从创建开始，一直秉承“敬业、求实”的经营理念，坚持以人为本，以质量为生命，从严管理的高标准发展企业。2002年为加速企业发展，从省城贵阳迁入扎佐，在医药园区征地50亩，投资1000多万元，按照国家《药品经营质量管理规范》进行GSP改造，新建大型药品储备库1908平方米，办公及医疗服务综合楼1806平方米。2003年，首批通过国家药品监督管理局在贵州的论证、验收，取得认证资格，经贵州省政府批准为贵州科技开发医药股份有限公司，经营范围有中成药、化学制剂、抗生素、生化药品、诊断药品、生物制品、二类精神药品等3000多种，是省内药品批发企业大型经营商和制药企业药品总代理。2004年实现销售收入净额1.5亿元，缴纳国家税金1240万元后实现利润610万元，成为推动贵州医药事业发展的主力军，为地方经济腾飞作出重大贡献。11月，县委、县政府授予“重点纳税企业先进单位”称号，奖励“奥迪”轿车1辆。2005年销售收入增到1.81亿元，纳税1794万元后利润达1986万元，纳税额比上年增长44.68%，名列全县纳税大户榜首。之后，公司紧紧抓住西部大开发和地方政府发展地方特色经济的机遇，不断拓展业务和经营渠道，促进“规模、结构、质量、效益”协调发展，以优质服务把经营理念覆盖到全省，连续5年累计为国家提供税收共计7137万元，在全县同期工商税收总额中占4.39%。

工商各税演变示意图

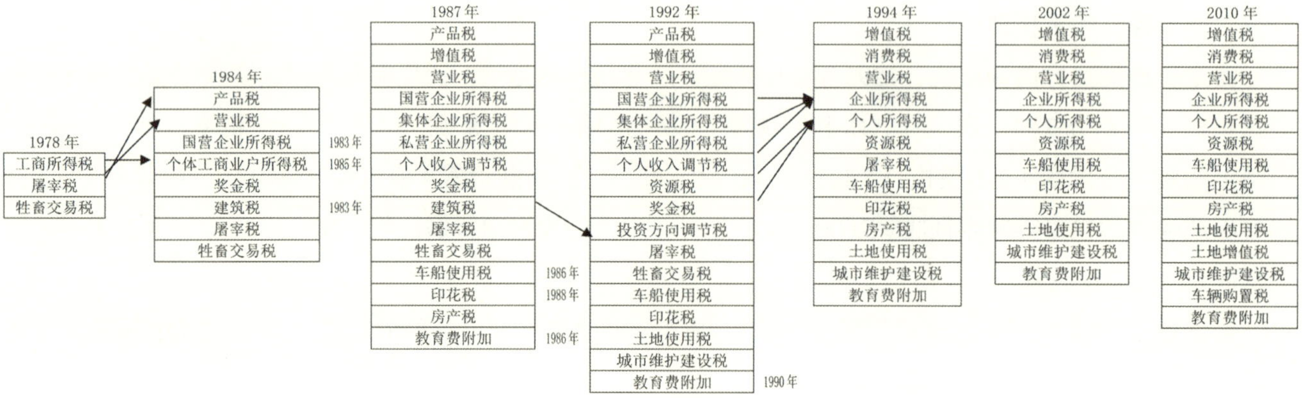

（二）专项基金

能源交通重点建设基金 1983年1月开征，凡国营企事业单位、机关、团体、部队和地方政府预算外资金及上述单位所属城镇集体企业所得税后利润均属征集范围。征收率10%，9月提高到15%。1995年停征。

国家预算调节资金 1989年1月开征，凡地方财政和行政事业预算外资金，国营企业及其主管部门提取各项专用基金，其他未纳入预算管理资金，县属集体和国营企业、事业单位及各企业主管部门所属集体企业和预算外企业缴纳所得税后的利润，均按10%征收。1996年1月停征。

价格调节基金 2006年8月开征，按营业收入的1‰征收。2010年仍存。

1978—1994年工商税分税种收入统计一览表

表3—10—08　　　　单位：万元

税种 \ 年份		1978	1979	1980	1981	1982	1983	1984	1985	1986	1987	1988	1989	1990	1991	1992	1993	1994
合计		182	200	170	297	580	703	891	1315	1131	1297	1680	1799	1582	1807	2086	2362	2621
流转税类	工商税	163	182	150	273	556	645	823	—	—	—	—	—	—	—	—	—	—
	产品税	—	—	—	—	—	—	—	1060	812	957	1207	1140	794	1056	1174	1254	
	增值税	—	—	—	—	—	—	—	—	—	—	68	155	185	241	308	414	1460
	消费税	—	—	—	—	—	—	—	—	—	—	—	—	—	—	—	—	8
	营业税	—	—	—	—	—	—	—	130	184	203	259	275	326	311	313	444	301
	资源税	—	—	—	—	—	—	—	—	—	—	—	—	—	—	14	23	343
企业所得税类	工商所得税	13	10	12	14	13	16	15	—	—	—	—	—	—	—	—	—	—
	国营企业所得税	—	—	—	—	—	30	35	42	51	49	44	49	29	46	121	73	255
	集体企业所得税	—	—	—	—	—	—	—	21	17	14	20	36	28	22	7	18	24
	私营企业所得税	—	—	—	—	—	—	—	—	—	—	—	7	30	—	—	—	—
个人所得税类	城乡个体工商业户所得税	—	—	—	—	—	—	—	—	1	—	4	6	7	10	9	11	—
	个人收入调节税	—	—	—	—	—	—	—	—	—	—	—	5	20	18	14	18	—
	个人所得税	—	—	—	—	—	—	—	—	—	—	—	—	—	—	—	—	35
财产及行为税类	房产税	—	—	—	—	—	—	—	—	—	4	4	4	6	7	9	9	11
	土地使用税	—	—	—	—	—	—	—	—	—	—	—	—	17		26	14	16
	车船使用税	—	—	—	—	—	—	—	—	1	5	5	7	8	5	4	5	5
	印花税	—	—	—	—	—	—	—	—	—	—	4	8	2	—	—	4	2
	投资方向调节税	—	—	—	—	—	—	—	—	—	—	—	—	—	—	22	15	27
	建筑税	—	—	—	—	—	4	8	34	23	20	19	32	63	47	—	—	—
	奖金税	—	—	—	—	—	—	—	6	4	2	1	3	2	—	—	—	—
	屠宰税	6	8	8	9	9	6	9	6	4	3	3	3	2	2	2	1	5
	牲畜交易税				1	2	2	1	2	4	4	3	3	3	3	1	1	
	城市维护建设税	—	—	—	—	—	—	—	14	17	18	23	30	22	22	43	48	109
	教育费附加	—	—	—	—	—	—	—	—	2	7	7	7	10	17	19	10	20
	其他	—	—	—	—	—	—	—	—	11	11	9	29	28	—	—	—	—

注：1. 1983至1985年国营企业所得税收入，前志列入企业收入，本志纳入税收收入。2. 其他栏为基金和滞纳金、罚款收入

1995—2010年国、地税务局分税种收入一览表

表3—10—09　　　　单位：万元

税种 \ 年份		1995	1996	1997	1998	1999	2000	2001	2002	2003	2004	2005	2006	2007	2008	2009	2010
全县合计		2900	3510	4016	4963	5471	5629	6732	8409	9253	12618	17078	22990	27219	33891	34707	44340
国家税务局	合计	1899	2017	2345	2852	2800	3116	3717	4695	5004	7105	9357	12851	15855	19828	16976	21945
	增值税	1719	1957	2204	2759	2674	2960	3497	4478	4795	6746	8769	12255	14700	18811	13722	18621
	消费税	6	10	11	5	4	4	6	3	1	—	—	1	1	1	1185	1002
	营业税	20	—	—	88	70	74	53	28	5	—	—	—	—	—	—	—
	企业所得税	—	—	40	—	39	6	29	65	90	232	449	412	949	889	2016	2304
	个人所得税	40	—	—	—	—	72	12	121	113	127	139	183	205	127	53	18
	其他税	114	50	90	—	13	—	120	—	—	—	—	—	—	—	—	—
地方税务局	合计	1001	1493	1671	2111	2671	2513	3015	3714	4249	5513	7721	10139	11364	14063	17761	22395
	营业税	394	529	838	1063	1132	1272	1625	1813	1854	2242	3020	3682	3741	4544	5380	7542
	资源税	419	458	348	414	472	450	373	543	445	556	664	1009	1153	1112	1227	1638
	企业所得税	76	177	62	104	121	64	229	338	708	932	1503	1339	1455	1455	2115	2163
	个人所得税	16	49	46	98	247	225	320	366	584	1001	1423	2021	2405	3216	3656	5063
	房产税	14	41	75	65	97	84	75	136	139	146	210	237	348	243	361	295
	土地使用税	17	37	41	41	51	33	45	68	76	84	117	122	251	621	530	577
	车船使用税	9	11	16	13	13	15	16	20	19	22	23	34	68	113	54	114
	印花税	4	2	5	7	10	10	16	31	19	13	24	45	79	106	156	210
	投资方向调节税	18	44	30	93	240	75	3	—	—	—	—	—	—	—	—	—
	屠宰税	1	9	9	18	32	29	17	14	—	—	—	—	—	—	—	—
	土地增值税	—	—	—	—	—	—	—	11	2	5	11	95	141	464	247	524
	城市维护建设税	28	93	158	137	185	174	196	230	250	300	439	687	739	938	797	1143
	教育费附加	5	43	43	58	71	82	100	144	153	212	284	443	496	620	506	695
	其他	—	—	—	—	—	—	—	—	—	—	3	425	488	631	2732	2431

注：2006至2010年，地方税务局征收的烟叶税、耕地占用税、契税，改列本节“农业四税收入内”

1995-2010年国地税收入增长图

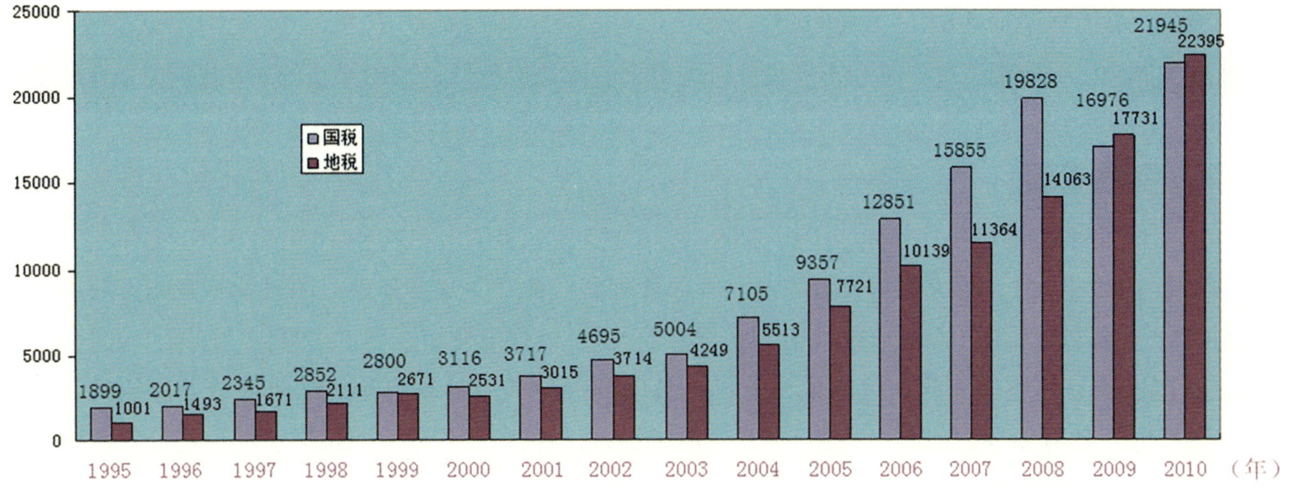

（三）税收减免

1978年，税收减免沿袭原有6种类型。

补贴型减免 1978年起对安置待业青年、知识青年达到规定比例企业定期减免营业税、所得税。2001年12月扶持下岗人员再就业，对招收下岗人员达到规定比例，并签订3年以上劳动合同的服务性企业定期减免营业税、所得税、城市维护建设税，对下岗人员从事个体经营实行定期减免。2002至2005年共减免264户，减税额达40.3万元；对退役士兵就业优惠3户，减免税款3400元。

残疾人就业率较高获减免营业税的诺亚矿业有限公司

税基型减免 系指通过提高免征额或起征点，以及扩大税前列支项目范围等，以缩小纳税免税人的税基达到减免的目的。

恢复型减免 企业因客观原因造成经营亏损，在税收上予以减免照顾，帮助其恢复生产。如系主观原因造成亏损减免则从严。

导向型减免 1985年2月，为鼓励发展直接为农业生产服务的生产项目，对生产销售磷肥的久长磷肥厂减免产品税。1987年2月为抑制使用黏土烧砖，对页岩、砂石、石灰石为原料制砖企业减免产品税。

推广型减免 1989年6月，经贵州省税务局批准给予国营三八五厂已通过省级鉴定的SYJ-1型电动手持牙钻，定期减免增值税30%；1993年12月对万江机电厂列为省级新产品的桑塔纳轿车玻璃升降器，定期减免增值税80%。

救济型减免 2003—2005年，地方税务局减免从事生产经营的残疾人31户，税金9900元。2005年对诺亚矿业有限公司安置“四残”人员（盲人、聋哑人、肢残人、智残人）办理退税29万元。

2005年8月，国家税务总局再次以国税发〔2005〕129号文件明确，减免税按类型分为两类，即：

报批类减免 应有税务机关审批减免税项目，2010年的8年共减免389户营业税、个人所得税、城市维护建设税、教育费附加共67.13万元。

备案类减免 为取消审批手续和不需税务机关审批的减免税项目，2010年止的9年共减免企业所得税3户，减免金额236.96万元。

四、税收管理

（一）干部垂直管理

1978至1983年9月，税务机构人员编制、干部管理和经费开支归县管理，10月执行贵州省政府黔府〔1983〕121号通知改为垂直管理。1984年2月，按照全国统一规定在编人员正式着装。1994年9月分税制实施，县国家税务局隶属安顺地区国家税务局，县地方税务局由县政府和安顺地区地方税务局双重领导，以同级人民政府领导为主。1996年1月至2010年县划归贵阳市管辖，国税局、地税局分别隶属贵阳市国家税务局和贵阳市地方税务局。

（二）征收管理

税收登记 1982年始办税务登记和申报，向纳税人核发税务登记证。1993年实施《中华人民共和国税收征收管理法》，1994年9月实行“统一代码，分别登记，分别管理”。1997年2月起对纳税人或扣缴义务人采取不申报手段或不缴纳税款者按偷税论处。2001年纳税方式由传统的税务专管人员上门征税转变为纳税人自行申报纳税，在办税服务厅集中征收。2010年全县税务登记5763户，其中国家税务局2521户，地方税务局3242户。

发票管理 1978至1980年国营企业和供销企业使用的发票由主管部门管理，其余经营发票一律由税务机关统一印制和管理，管理办法由县制定。1989年4月安顺地区税务局统一发票格式、统一编号、统一印制，县税务局负责辖区内的发票统管和核售。1994年9月县国税局置发票管理所，地方税务局指定征管股（科），下属税务所指定专人分别负责发票领购、保管和发售。普通发票的印刷由贵阳市国、地税务局发票管理所统一办理，有固定生产经营场所、财务和发票管理制度健全、发票使用量大或统一发票式样不能满足业务需要的企业，应报经税务机关审批，并签订发票管理使用责任书，方可由指定的印刷厂凭发票管理部门签订的发票印刷通知单印制。

税收信息化 1990年，县税务系统仅有1台386微型计算机，用于计划、会计、统计核算制表，税收征管全是手工操作。1998年县国家税务局对征收管理机构配置新型计算机7台，纳入中国税收征收管理（CTAIS）系统。地方税务局连续4年配置计算机17台，基本实现与贵阳市地税局和各税务所联网销售发票、单机填开税票、交通运输发票征收税款。2001年市、县国税系统采用512KDDN网络连接与全国联网。2002年国家税务总局在贵阳市进行税收征管信息系统试点，县国税局被列为试点单位之一，龙场、扎佐、六广征收管理分局与银行网点申报成功上线运行，委托商业银行县支行和县信用联社代收税款。2003年征管数据向贵阳市国税局集中，规范税收征管流程。同年，县地税局启动贵州省地税信息管理系统建设，实现在一个统一广域网络支持下的立体税收征管和行政事务处理系统。6月完成信用社代征税款和会计核算数据集中。2005年县国税局综合征管软件上线运行，征管数据向省局集中，在岗干部64人已达人手一机。县地税系统在岗53人，已配计算机52台，基本实现执法人员一人一机。至2010年全县税收

征管信息系统运转正常。

专记：地方税务局获全国先进集体殊荣

2002至2004年，县地方税务局以组织收入为中心，以“建一流班子，带一流队伍，创一流业绩，造一流环境”为目标，在“依法治税，从严治队，科学管理”的工作实践中，狠抓“六个加强建设”促征管。

——加强征管制度建设。先后建立83项制度，分月按季考核，与工作业绩挂钩兑现奖惩，连续3年完成地方税征收1.35亿元，超任务8.76%，年均增长22.44%，被评为县综合目标管理先进单位。

——加强行风建设。2002年县局被列入县第二届“阳明文化节”12家窗口执法形象行风社会评议单位，在县机关中率先实行指纹考勤，职工着装配证上岗，使用文明敬语，严禁文明忌语，从接好每个电话、接待好每个纳税人做起，实行首问负责制，与年度公务员考核挂钩。至12月考核总分98.67分名列第二。

——加强信息化建设。2003年2月贵阳市地税系统信息化建设全面铺开，县局4月完成基础资料收集、鉴定、录入，5月实现同市局核算数据大集中和上下级机关税收执法行为全过程监控，被贵州省地税局定格为信息化建设典范。7月省局以现场观摩会形式向全省推广。2004年4月，贵阳市政府授予2002至2003年度信息化建设先进单位。

——加强征管基础建设。2004年1月，县局被贵阳市地税局确定为全市征管基础建设试点单位，2月获得中国质量认证中心ISO 9001：2000征管质量现场认证，增加硬件和软件培训及资金投入，实现一人一机和落实一人多岗，一岗多责，岗责交叉，协作配合，互相监督，做到“满负荷工作”状态下热情、周到、细致服务。10月与云岩区地税局顺利通过市局现场验收，并召开观摩会在全市推广。

——加强党风廉政建设。县局始终把监管与预防职务犯罪同步进行，对人事、财务、大宗物品采购改事后监管为事前、事时监管，实行“阳光稽查”，公开监督电话，聘任特邀和兼职监督员，让税收全过程置于纳税人监督之中，未出现税务人员违规违法问题。2003至2004年度获市局考核一等奖，中共贵阳市委授予2002至2004年度先进基层党组织称号。

——加强征管文明建设。以“三优一满意”（优质服务、优良作风、优美环境、让人民满意）为主题，开展多种形式的活动。2003年，直属征收分局大厅获市级“青年文明号”、直属征收分局获“全市财源建设青年突击队”和贵阳市2000—2003年度“文明窗口”称号。2004年10月经过明查暗访，市文明办授予县局机关和扎佐、六广税务所“创建文明城市”流动红旗，市委和市政府授予县局2002至2004年“文明单位”奖牌。2005年先后获得全省和全国税务系统先进集体称号。

2005年7月，修文地税局获国家级表彰

（三）税收监管

税法宣传 1978—1980年，税法宣传缺乏力度。1981年起为推进税制改革，税务部门利用宣传栏、有线电视等方式进行税收宣传。1991—1995年，在县司法局配合下，全面开展以宪法为核心、以专业法为重点的法治宣传教育第二个五年计划（“二·五”普法），税务局大张旗鼓地开展宣传，当年全县受教育公民达20万人次，被国家税务总局评为全国税法宣传教育先进单位。1996年，国、地两税务局先后举行税法颇具规模的宣传游行、拔河、卡拉OK赛、税法知识竞赛、有奖征文等多种形式拓宽宣传面。2000年4月，国税局又在扎佐一小举办税法知识讲座，全场500余名学生在“全国少年朋友都来做小小宣传员”横幅上签名加入税法宣传队伍。2003年4月，国、地税务局与共青团县委联合，在全县共青团员中开展“税法宣传志愿者注册活动”，第一天就有纳税人主动向国税局补缴税款1.03万元和滞纳金723元。至2010年，税务宣传方式注重实效，使宣传既融洽税企关系，又能支持企业发展。

1996年国、地税务机关在县城开展税法宣传

税收检查 1978年，沿袭税务专管员对纳税户进行季度、半年、一年的周期性检查。1983年查出漏税面达75%，补税24万元。1985年起开展一年一次的税收大检查，查补税额52万元。1990年成立专职稽查队，采取自查、互查、抽查、重点检查、专项检查等方式对违章案件、大案要案，配合司法机关进行查处。1993至2010年，除对纳税义务人进行检查外，还将扣缴义务人代扣代缴、代收代缴税款及有关经营情况纳入检查范围，经县税务局局长批准，检查员可以查询纳税人和扣款义务人的银行账户。经地、市税务局局长批准，检查员可以查询案件涉嫌人员的储蓄存款。如发现纳税人有逃避纳税义务的行为，可按照《中华人民共和国税收征收管理法》规定，采取税收保全或强制执行。

专记：一场遏止住的肉市风波

1999年11月18日，县城发生以罢市行为公开抗税的肉市风波。这次风波起源于地税局和工商管理局执法人员18日清晨检查，发现县城食品公司定点的屠宰场杀多报少偷税证据后，通知屠商到地税局开会，向其宣传有关税收政策，按规定每宰杀一头猪（按50公斤鲜肉计算），应缴纳国税20元和地税23.84元的税款，考虑到屠商实际情况，仅收地税15元，少征8.84元。并对6户严重偷税屠商各作补交每头15元税款，各罚款200元予以处罚，屠商即以税重为借口不杀猪上市。在少数人煽动下，几十名屠商用水浇熄杀猪用的灶火，换新锁将屠宰场大门锁上进行罢市抗法。工商局副局长胡利斌闻讯最先赶到，责成聚众罢市屠商迅速恢复市场供应，并组织推选代表到工商所办公室反映意见。地税局局长熊永忠到场明确指出：任何偷税漏税行为都是要被严厉打击的，不得扰乱市场秩序，必须立即恢复市场，维护市民生活稳定。龙场镇工商所所长罗继忠也找行业分会人士谈话疏导。但罢市屠商不仅不恢复市场，还提出“要继续闹下去，不闹政府不会重视”的话继续抗拒。据调查，这次事件实为几名带头闹事屠商向每个屠商收取20元钱作为“活动经费”，派人四处窜村和堵截城外猪肉进入县城，并收取押金，必须不在县城卖肉才退给押金，并阻止县城四面的村寨也不得运肥猪入城宰杀。面对严峻形势，县委、县政府连夜召开紧急会议，责成工商所和食品公司迅速组织猪源保证猪肉正常供应，并由相关部门召集屠商开会学法守法守纪，照章纳税。

19日早晨，工商部门组织人员深入村寨，动员养殖户供应生猪，农户在工商干部护送下将活猪运到

县城屠宰，又被20余名闹事屠商把住屠宰场大门不让活猪进场，并站在杀凳上威胁宰杀工人，阻拦宰杀工作开展。龙场派出所和110指挥中心立即派干警赶到现场控制事态发展。上午10时，各部门再次召集屠商开会表明政府态度，重申有关政策。中午，公安干警和有关部门负责人共同将鲜肉护送进入农贸市场，几十名屠商又围住不准猪肉摆上案桌销售，也不让市民买肉，护送的公安干警严阵执法，并规劝开导，晓之有理，一个个才悄悄离去，肉市开始经营。下午3时，县政法委书记殷建忠亲临现场召集会议，要求食品公司发挥主渠道作用，在工商、地税等部门协同下，继续组织活猪确保市场供应。

20日，肉市风波平息，猪肉市场恢复正常营业，副县长周毅指出，这是一起由少数人操纵，以偷税漏税抗税为主要目的，煽动多数不明真相屠商参与的不法行为，是得不到广大人民群众支持的，必须旗帜鲜明地反对和打击。市民也对有些屠商欺行霸市，偶尔还玩点“手脚”深恶痛绝。对这次罢市事件发生，市民们纷纷表示，宁可不吃肉也不能助长这股歪风。一部分参与闹市的屠商也有所悟地说：“我们受蒙骗和被利用，今后一定守法经营，再也不干这种蠢事。”

依法治税 1987年，县人民检察院设立驻税务局检察室。1993年，县公安局和人民法院分别在税务局设立公安执勤室和法院执行室，行使打击偷税、抗税和其他违反税法行为的职责。至1996年，受理税务案件67起，立案查处15起，其中，偷漏税案15起，查补偷漏税款62万元。1997年国、地税务局分别成立领导小组，每季安排一次专题法律知识讲座，开展税务执法权限法定化、税务规范性文件合法化、征收管理程序化、税务处罚标准化、执法检查经常化、监督机制完善化的行政法制“六化”建设，确保税收征管活动“法治、公平、文明、效率”。8月，对全局税务执法开展重点检查，其中，税务稽查分局共检查纳税户203户，立案21件，结案17件，全部符合稽查程序。11月，根据修改后的《中华人民共和国刑事诉讼法》规定，检察机关不再直接受理涉税犯罪案，税务检察室、公安执勤室、法院执行室相应撤销。之后，涉税案件由公安机关查处，至2010年未变。

第四节　审计管理

1984年建立县审计局，依照法律法规独立行使审计监督，至2010年的27年，通过专项审计、财务收支审计、定期审计、审计调查等方式，累计完成审计项目723个，审计出违规违纪资金3240.58万元，应上缴财政资金211.69万元，管理不规范资金1.07亿元。

一、业务审计

（一）行政事业财务收支审计

1984年始办，先后审出农业机械局1982年举办拖拉机驾驶员培训班挤占培训经费1374元和农业局以权谋私贪污支农周转金案件。1987年置行政事业审计股，专司财政拨款的行政机关、事业单位、社会团体财务收支专项审计。1993年审出城乡建设局前两年漏提漏缴预算调节基金和国家能源交通重点建设基金3.27万元。1998年审计发现10个林业站1990年至1997年长江防护林工程款，只有扎佐、小箐两站账目清晰，其余8个站均无完整账目可查，有的连流水账都未见到，对谷堡站站长兼出纳期间挪用工程款1.25万元予以追回。

县审计局办公大楼

2009—2010年，按照“揭露问题，规范管理，促进改革，制约权力，提高效益”的工作要求，坚持审深、审透、审细、审严的原则，审出县级财政2009年总预算未按规定列报支出，致使总预算一般预算支出中地方安排数超过人民代表大会批准的调整数323万元。

（二）企业、基建财务审计

1987年，审计局置工商企业审计股，专司国有企业、国营资产占控股和主导地位企业、商贸公司资产、负债、损益的审计监督，对国家和县属建设项目概算执行、决算情况监督，受上级审计机关授权审计国际组织和外国政府贷款、援助、赠款和财务收支。1990年审出县烟草公司连续2年3个月违规发放工资、补贴、奖金7.02万元。1999年发现谷堡乡财政所全额集资职工宿舍20套，总面积由设计1640平方米增至2385.48平方米，总投资由54.4万元增到117.82万元，每平方米造价由合同价320元增到468.75元，擅自扩大建筑面积和投资，造成挤占使用财政预算资金12.75万元，财政所负责人擅自挪用村提留和乡统筹资金22.64万元用于宿舍修建。2000年开展煤炭“五统一”收费专项审计，查出全县煤炭工业连续两年收费中由于制度不健全、不完善，存在不同程度的违规返还维简费、降低维简费返还比例、收取扶持费等问题，违规违纪金额共199.44万元。

2009—2010年，重点抓好群众普遍关注的“热点”“难点”审计，完成农田基本建设资金、新农村建设项目资金、村寨道路建设资金、农村危房改造专项资金审计，审减工程款524.3万元和管理不规范资金28万元，使工程投资领域的经济秩序得以维护。

（三）财政金融审计

1987年始办，先后与安顺地区纪委配合，对工商银行县支行1979—1986年费用开支审计，审出财务管理上弄虚作假、伪造会计凭证转移资金、虚列支出等违纪资金17.2万元。与财政局联合审计城关区财政所1985—1987年上半年财政收支，发现乱发奖金及补贴等违规问题。

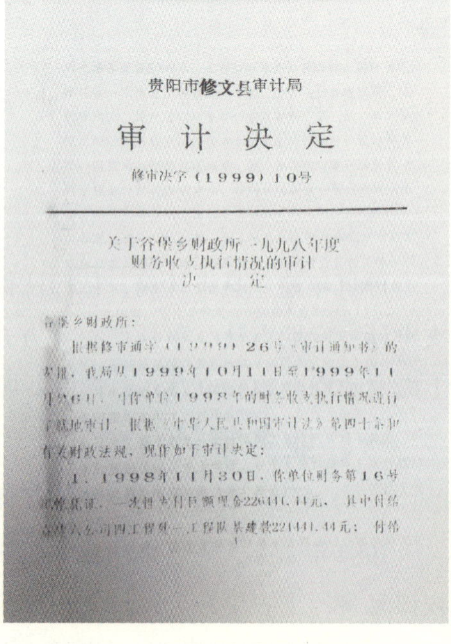

贵阳市修文县审计局

审　计　决　定

修审决字（1999）10号

关于谷堡乡财政所一九九八年度
财务收支执行情况的审计
决　　定

1999年，对谷堡乡财政所的审计决定

1995年实施《贵州省财政收支审计试行办法》。1996年县审计局置财政金融审计科，行使同级预算执行情况、地方税收征管、同级国库办理、同级预算资金收纳拨付和财政预算执行、财政决算、乡（镇）财政决算审计，受上级审计机关授权审计在县的国家金融、保险机构的资产、负债、损益情况和专项审计，发现县级财政资金紧迫，调度困难，为保吃饭和正常工作运转，存在不同程度的项目资金拨付不及时或转移用途问题，加之少数欠缴税款又未及时

组织征收缓解财政资金压力，至2003年，一直出现财政收支不平衡，财政连年赤字，到2004年起至2010年才有所缓解。

（四）经济责任审计

1998年始办，对各级领导干部离任审计。2002年审计局增置经济责任审计科，受组织、人事部门和纪检监察机关委托，对党政部门正职领导干部任期届满或任期内办理调任、转任、轮岗、免职、辞职、退休等事前审计，对改制、改组、兼并、出售、拍卖、破产的国有企业重组进行经济责任审计。至2010年止累计完成党政领导干部审计27项，对国有企业领导人员任期审计2项。其中2006年8月对大石乡乡长李祥任职期间经济责任就地审计，发现李祥没有认真履行职责，监管严重失职，导致乡财政财务管理混乱，以致出现截留挪用、贪污等违纪行为。

专记：大石乡违纪窝案告破

大石布依族乡为县内少数民族聚居最多、经济发展滞后的贫困乡，一年财政预计收入不足百万元，自2002年县审计局对乡财政管理和会计核算审计后，2006年又对2003年起的3年零7个月财政财务审计，受县委组织部委托对乡长李祥任职期间经济责任履行情况审计，审出乡财政财务管理失控，总预算、农业四税、会计核算中心财务核算基本处于无会计账簿核算状况；内部控制失效，财政所长严同军一人负责多项会计、出纳，与刘城溢未办理相关单据移交手续，本人用于公务和个人借款共计48万元；部分记账凭证与所附原始凭证不符，记账凭证差错较多；编造不真实、不完整的虚假财务会计报表；大量财政性资金被乡政府工作人员借出，部分资金被个人长期占用，乡政府和财政所有14人借用财政性资金150.12万元；部分会计凭证中发现有违规或不合规行为；多年的农业四税账、部分固定资产和收支原始凭证未进行会计核算；会计档案管理不合规。

审计结束，审计局对相关责任人存在的违纪及失职问题，按程序分别移送相关部门处理。县纪委和监察局分别对副乡长金志明、财政所长严同军、林业站副站长张祥文三人给予开除党籍、开除工作籍处分。李祥任乡长和乡党委书记期间，未认真履行职责，监管严重失职，导致出现财政财务管理混乱，涉及弄虚作假截留挪用财政资金，个人挪用财政资金、违规收取并挪用养兔农户保证金，对严同军、金志明、张祥文贪污受贿的犯罪行为失察等违纪行为，对涉案资金共143.69万元负有领导责任和直接责任，但本人能积极配合调查和深刻认识，决定给予党内严重警告和行政降级处分。乡党政及其机关其他领导至工作人共涉案20人，除移送司法机关的3人外，其余17人分别受到行政警告、党内严重警告、撤职、行政记过和免予行政处分。

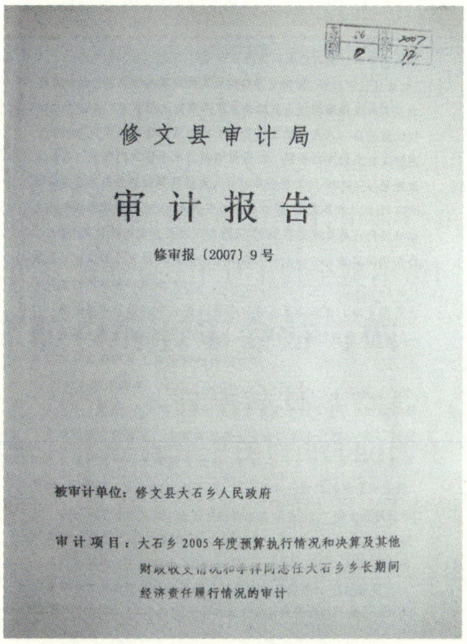
修文县审计局

审计报告

修审报（2007）9号

被审计单位：修文县大石乡人民政府

审计项目：大石乡2005年度预算执行情况和决算及其他财政收支情况和李祥同志任大石乡乡长期间经济责任履行情况的审计

2006年，对大石乡财政所审计报告

2007年3月，县审计局在修审报〔2007〕9号《审计报告》中提出审计评价意见：一是3年多来大石乡财政财务工作存在管理失控、内部控制失效、财务核算基本处于无会计账簿进行核算；二是由于多年财政财务管理混乱，财政财务核算不真实和不完整，而少数国家工作人员对国家财经法律法规学习不够、执行不力等原因造成大量数额的国家财政性资金被个人长期占用；三是多年来由于主管部门对财政财务的监督管理不够深入，极少数人员严重的工作失误，是形成大石乡多年来财政财务出现严重问题的原因；四是针对大石乡政府财政总预算会计、农业“四税”财务会计、乡政府单位财务会计存在会计核算和财务管理混乱问题李祥应承担直接责任，对乡属部门财务核算和管理存在的问题李祥应负管理责任。

2008年8月5日，贵阳市中级人民法院筑刑二终字第162号《刑事判决书》认定，2003至2006年严同军在任乡财政所所长前后，利用职务便利，以虚开发票、虚列支出方式贪污公款9.29万元，依法判处有期徒刑6年。

县人民法院〔2008〕修刑初字第24号《刑事判决书》认定，金志明任副乡长、张祥文任林业站副站长期间，利用职务上的便利，非法收受他人回扣、采取收款不入账、保留虚列支出的行为已构成受贿罪、贪污罪。案发后，金志明、张祥文已全部退清涉案款4.87万元和4.71万元，均被依法判处有期徒刑2年。

二、审计协作与回访

县审计局成立，先后与县经委及财政、税务、、农行县支行等部门联合审计，审出烟草公司1984年违规挤占费用13.46万元，占费用总支出的47.9%，成本计差0.24万元，两项合计13.7万元，人为地减少10万元利润，掩盖企业的真实盈亏。同年审出农业局以局领导、会计、出纳为主的6人，采取虚报冒领、以领代支、做假账、转移资金等手段贪污农业投资4.47万元，占当年财政拨给用款的62%。1986年耐火材料厂账务混乱、乱挤乱摊成本2万元，重复记账4.33万元，违规多发职工工资7.35万元。1992年粮食企业超亏挂账395.7万元，比原账面挂账多26.47万元。在审计协作的同时，对反映较大的被审计单位进行回访，使审计报告得到落实，缓和审计与被审计单位的关系。2010年，审计协作与回访业务未终止。

三、后续审计与复审

（一）后续审计

1990年始办，至2010年先后对1993—2001年世界银行贷款支持农村卫生人力开发项目、1996—2003年卫生疾病预防项目计划免疫子项目、2000—2004年第九个卫生发展项目妇幼子项目、1999—2004年第四期中国农村供水与环境卫生项目资金进行续审，未发现违反国家法规和贷款协议的问题。

（二）复审

1984—2010年间，仅1986年6月对县物资局1985年度财务和钢材、水泥、汽车等品种审计，审出有问题资金23.72万元，其中应上交财政13.42万元，但物资局有异议。1986年8月经安顺地区审计局复审，维持县审计结论，审计局结合单位实际情况酌情考虑从宽处理，让物资局基本执行审计决定，向税务部门缴纳奖金税1万元，纠正账务方面存在的问题。

四、社会审计和内部审计

（一）社会审计

1989年12月，县成立审计事务所，归属审计局，负责管理、指导、监督、检查和接管政府、法院、检察院、主管部门、乡镇企业委托的审计事项；承担部分国营企业厂长任期经济责任审计；帮助企事业单位建账建制，提供财会咨询；办理工商企业注册资金验证和年检；银行贷款抵押物查证；国有企业会计报表年鉴。因注册资本不足30万元和注册审计师或注册会计师少于5人，于1998年6月撤消，原经办社会审计业务终止。

（二）内部审计

1985年始建内部审计制度，至1998年，全县有8个单位设立内部审计机构，配审计人员14人。2004年县烟草公司按照省烟草办和烟草专卖局指示精神，对2000—2004年8月烟草专卖罚没收入和2001年至2003年公司（局）财务收支进行内部审计，六屯、小坝、大石、六桶站一组作为重点审计点，审减卷烟经营部装修款3260元。至2010年，内部审计继续运转。

第五节　统计管理

一、体制改革

1978年沿袭原计划委员会兼理统计业务，1980年1月将统计业务析出专置统计局，区、乡由秘书经办统计业务。1988年各区（镇）始建统计工作站，分别由分管区（镇）领导和秘书兼任正副站长，半年报、年报由下属统计人员集中办公综合上报。1992年新组建的乡（镇）置统计站。2001年建立县统计执法大队统一着装执法。至2010年查处违反统计法单位7家。

二、统计调查

（一）农产量抽样调查

1980年8月以县为单位抽选7个调查点试行水稻产量抽样调查后，1983年起每年都以县为单位进行夏、秋两季农产量抽样调查，验证农业全面统计数据，报省统计局、计委、农业厅、粮食厅共同研究确定。

1990年，调查以乡（镇）为总体，将小麦、水稻、玉米、薯类、杂粮列为统计调查项目，采用两个阶段等距抽样；第一阶段在乡里抽定村民组，抽出的调查单位一般5年不变，以便连续观察：第二阶段在已抽出的村民组中抽选农户或地块。当年全县抽样调查点167个，调查农户1670户。1993至2010年调查方式改为按人平均推算粮食产量，中途视其情况对调查点作适当轮换。

（二）农村住户经济调查

1981年7月采取抽样调查方法从全县215个大队中抽出潮水队、沙雁三队、中山六队为全县上、中、下3种类型调查点，每个点抽选有代表性的10户农家进行典型调查。次年起调查点先后增加扎佐镇中营大队、马家桥公社白莲一队、小箐公社大坝大队、崇恩公社大丫口队、六桶公社落邦队5个点，加上原有3个共计8个80户列入贵州省的调查点。调查项目包括家庭基本情况、家庭生产、出售商品、家庭经济收支、粮食及现金收支平衡、食物消费量、购买商品等。调查资料实行手工汇总上报安顺地区农村调查队。

1996年，以乡（镇）为单位，在保留省调查点的基础上，10乡（镇）抽选25个调查点，每个点调查10户，全县调查点达33个330户。继后，结合各个时期的实际情况对调查点进行调整。至2010年全县列为省的调查点有龙场镇潮水村和新寨村、六广镇中山村、洒坪乡小坝村、小箐乡大坝村、谷堡乡新堰村、久长镇白窑村和扎佐镇双月村，调查户80户。乡(镇) 调查点调整为21个，加上省调查点共29个290户，各调查户基本能如实填报数据为政府决策提供依据。

（三）单项调查

1978年沿袭原统计调查制度，至1985年先后进行工业企业用电设备拥有量、水稻生产及收获、县和县以上统计人员编制及事业费开支等项调查。1986年7月，县委、县政府组织11个单位参加的联合调查组对马家桥乡的自然资源、农业劳动力、乡镇企业历史沿革及现状、乡镇企业生产、经营、管理、税收、劳动力等情况全面调查，成稿《马家桥乡镇企业观察与分析》上报贵州省政府和安顺地区行署。1987—1998年因统计力量不足，单项调查暂停。

1999年，启动扎佐镇第一居委会和第二居委会、六广镇合营村、小箐乡新村村、大石乡新光村的人口变动情况抽样调查，发现人口出生率比原摸底调查数高出10.32个千分点。2003—2010年，先后开展城镇低保户问卷调查、从事医药制造和医疗仪器设备及器械制造工业企业调查、人口变动情况抽样调查、群众安全感调查、城镇劳动力就业状况抽样调查、公共安全感调查、城市住户普查，城镇居民大样本调查、贵阳市民幸福感指数调查等，为县委、县政府以及中央和省、市制定政策提供依据服务。

统计局工作人员在农村培训住户调查员

（四）城市住户调查

1996年，采取等距抽样办法在全县城镇居民住户中抽取30户作为调查户，调查主要内容为家庭可支配收入、消费支出等，调查数据处理由贵阳市城市住户调查队专职统计人员负责。2004—2008年，住户调查资料的编码、录入、审核、上报等工作改由县统计局专职统计人员负责，贵阳市城市住户调查队于季度、年度对主要统计指标进行评估、定案。至2010年仍保持30个调查户。

三、国情国力普查

（一）人口普查

继1953年和1964年第一次和第二次全国人口普查后，从1978—2010年进行第三次、第四次、第五次和第六次全国性人口普查。

第三次 1981年5月—1982年12月进行，普查登记标准时间为1982年7月1日零时。此次普查项目多，规模大，首次使用电子计算机进行数据处理。为便于与国际对比，除满足国内需要项目外，有的项目还按照联合国统一要求制定。在认真做好宣传、户口整顿、工作规划等前期准备工作后，于1982年4月在阳早公社的潮水、阳早、红旗3个大队和庆文机械厂、城关镇第五居民委员会试点。5月正式开展普查，至普查时点，全县总人口从第一次普查11.1万人和第二次普查13.18万人增到25.7万人，分别增长131.61%和94.96%。

第四次 1989年9月至1990年12月进行，普查登记标准时间为1990年7月1日零时。先后经过前期准备、户口整顿、培训普查干部、登记和复查、手工汇总、编码、资料分析等环节，圆满完成各阶段工作任务。普查标准时点全县总人口为26.67万人，比第三次普查增长3.76%。

第五次　1999年2月开始，2002年4月结束，普查登记标准时间为2000年11月1日零时。此次普查是在社会主义市场经济条件下的首次人口普查，普查规模大，项目多，涉及面广，工作队伍庞大，使用的先进技术为国内外前所未有。选调普查指导员250人，长表普查员234人，短表普查员930人，加上县、乡两级普查办公室人员共1500余人，在完成普查区域划分、普查区域地图绘制、户口整顿、宣传动员后，先对“居无定所”人口提前登记，然后全面铺开。2001年4月，在《修文报》以公报一号公布普查时点全县手工汇总人口共26.2万人，比第四次普查减少1.76%。同时公布人口分布、家庭户人口、年龄结构、性别构成、民族构成、受教育程度。接着以公报二号公布机器录入汇总的民族构成、人口在业、在业人口的行业构成、人口婚姻构成状况，育龄妇女生育状况、人口住房状况等。

验收第五次人口普查表

第六次　2009年11月县政府制发《人口普查实施方案》，2010年1月全县开展普查宣传，引导普查对象配合登记。9月分两期对401名普查指导员和1025名普查员培训后，即以村配指导员和小区配普查员开展普查工作。10月进行普查摸底登记，12月8日县完成普查表非专项编码转入专项编码，至2010年11月1日零时普查登记标准时间。全县常住人口24.9万人，比第五次普查减少4.99%。其中65岁及以上人口2.04万人，在总人口中的比重为8.2%；居住在城镇人口7.31万人，居住在乡村人口17.59万人。城镇人口比重比第五次普查上升8.26个百分点。

普查员入户登记

第三至第六次人口普查主要指标数据统计一览表

表3—10—10

项目		单位	第三次普查		第四次普查		第五次普查		第六次普查	
			数量	与第二次比%	数量	与第三次比%	数量	与第四次比%	数量	与第五次比%
一、总户数		户	49074	+70.62	59311	+20.86	73074	+30.20	75618	-3.48
二、总人口		人	257024	+94.96	266694	+3.76	262039	-1.74	248926	-4.99
三、按性别	男	人	132565	+98.32	138784	+4.69	138196	-0.42	129621	-6.20
	女	人	124459	+91.50	127904	+2.77	123843	-3.18	119334	-3.64
四、性别比		%	106.51	+3.66	108.51	+2.00	111.59	+3.08	108.62	-2.97
五、按民族	汉族	人	238382	+88.26	245956	+3.18	239976	-2.43	226628	-5.56
	少数民族	人	18694	+112.67	20732	+10.90	22025	+6.24	22327	+1.37
	民族不详	人	106	—	105	-0.94	38	-63.81	—	—

续表

项目		单位	第三次普查		第四次普查		第五次普查		第六次普查	
			数量	与第二次比%	数量	与第三次比%	数量	与第四次比%	数量	与第五次比%
六、按文化程度	大学	人	1233	+519.60	1869	+51.58	3005	+60.78	11212	+273.11
	高中	人	9984	+1560.61	12389	+24.99	14293	+15.37	17754	+24.21
	初中	人	39327	+931.63	48762	+23.99	72185	+48.04	95243	+31.94
	小学	人	94752	+201.19	116376	+22.82	119168	+2.40	91816	−22.95
	不识字或识字很少	人	57876	—	43227	−25.45	28807	−33.23	11387	−60.47

（二）农业普查

第一次 1995—1997年开展，普查主要内容包括：农业生产经营单位数量、规模、结构；农业用地在各生产经营单位的分布和使用情况；农业生产性固定资产数量、结构、性能；农业劳动力数量、素质、从事的行业和流动情况；乡镇企业和建制镇基本概况。普查时点为1996年12月31日零时，时期指标为1996年1月1日—12月31日。普查分为前期准备、普查登记、数据处理、总结表彰4个阶段。普查指标共38项678个。

1995年6月县建立普查办公室，次年7月派3员到息烽县永靖镇参加市级农业普查试点，8月县进行试点，10月全县铺开，划分为217个普查区，1414个普查小区，每个普查区配1名普查指导员，每个普查小区配1名普查员进行现场登记。1997年2—4月县普查办手工汇总。普查结果，全县农村住户为5.29万户，农村人口23.05万人，其中，男性12.17万人，女性10.88万人。从业人员14.04万人。在校学生4.72万人。农村住户农业用耕地26.81万亩，其中水田9.6万亩。农作物种植面积5.61万亩。

第二次 2005年启动，2008年结束，由贵阳市政府统一组织实施。普查内容包括：从事第一产业活动单位和农户生产经营；乡（镇）、村委会及社区环境；农业土地利用；农业和农村固定资产投资；农村劳动力就业及流动；农民生活质量。普查标准时点为2006年12月31日。时期资料为2006年度。县、乡（镇）成立普查办公室负责本区域普查工作，逐级签订责任状，依法进行普查。

2008年5月，贵阳市农业普查办公室和市统计局将普查主要数据分6期予以公报，普查全部资料以《贵阳市第二次农业普查资料汇编》统一印发。普查结果，全县4镇6乡217个行政村，登记住户5.53万户（集体200户，家庭5.51万户）。家庭户中常住5.49万户，本村户5.3万户。常住人口17.54万人，其中男性9.19万人、女性8.35万人。全家外出1.61万户4.48万人。耕地面积46.85万亩，其中水田13.14万亩。常住户中有4.8万户从事农业生产，其余为非农业生产或兼营，有农业技术人员2507人，

老农认真学习第二次农业普查资料

拥有各种类型拖拉机517台，配套农具136台，联合收割机8台，年末存栏生猪7.9万头，牛3.23万头，羊1572只，农村人均居住面积23.5平方米。

（三）工业普查

继第一次全国性工业普查后，1978至2010年先后开展两次工业普查。

第二次　1985年2月开始，普查范围为全部工业企业（含乡镇工业）。普查内容包括企业基本情况；生产、销售与库存；新产品和产品质量；工业置备；主要工业产品生产能力；原材料、燃料、动力消费与库存；能源；主要技术经济指标；专业化与协作；劳动工资；财务成本价格；矿山资源开发和利用等。普查时间：产品产量、产值、销售量、销售额、工资总额、利润、税金等指标填报1985年全年数，其中的重要指标填报1985年、1984年和1980年的全年数；工业设备拥有量、主要产品生产能力、产品成品库存量、原材料和燃料库存量、固定资产等指标填报1985年12月31日数。历时1年完成全部普查任务。

第三次　1995年9月开始，普查内容包括工业企业资产状况、所有制结构、主要产品结构、行业结构、财务状况等。普查时限为1995年。1996年7月普查全部结束。普查结果，全县拥有工业企业1830个，从业人员1.33万人，总产值按1990年不变价计算为2.24亿元，年末资产3.12亿元。

第三次全县工业企业基本情况统计表

表3—10—11

项　目	企业数（个）	从业人数（人）	总产值（万元）	年末资产原值（万元）
合　计	1830	13317	22405	31249
一、乡及乡以上	143	6427	13421	27621
1. 国有企业	18	1118	1583	7204
2. 集体企业	93	3229	6595	9439
3. 股份和“三资”企业	4	451	2110	5015
4. 联营和其他经济类型企业	28	1629	3133	5963
在乡及乡以上企业中：乡办企业	94	4059	8318	14016
二、村及村以下企业	1687	6890	8982	3628

注：表内所列的系1995年的数据

（四）基本单位普查

第一次　1996年1月开始，普查对象包括所有的法人单位及法人单位所属的产业单位，各类企业、事业、机关、社团法人和其他法人，以及法人所属的农业、工业、建筑业、交通运输业、批发零售贸易业、餐饮业、服务业、行政事业单位和社会团体等产业活动单位。普查内容主要有单位基本信息、主要属性、基本经济活动和其他信息。普查登记标准时间为1996年12月31日零时。历经一年半时间，园满完成准备阶段、调查及数据处理阶段、资料开发阶段的全部任务。

第二次　2001年12月启动，普查登记标准时间为2001年12月31日，普查对象和普查主要内容与第一次普查相同。历经1年半完成普查任务。普查结果，全县共有1560个基本单位，其中法人单位657个。在基本单位总数中，农林牧渔业42个，工业125个，建筑业3个，交通运输、仓储及邮电通信业29个，批发零售贸易和餐饮业51个，金融保险业24个，房地产业2个，社会服务业6个，卫生、体育和社会福利业53个，教育、文化艺术及广播电影电视业170个，科学研究和综合技术服务业2人，国家机关、政党机关和社会团体338个，其他行业4个。从业人员总计3.83万个，其中，男性2.5万人，女性1.33万人。

（五）第三产业普查

1993年9月开始，普查年度为1991年和1992年。普查范围除农业、工业、建筑业外，隶属关系在县境内所有行业单位。普查内容包括第三产业机构和人员、生产经营活动、实物资产3部分。至1994年全部结束。

第三产业普查全县分行业单位数及从业人员数统计表

表3—10—12

行　业	单位（个）	从业人数（人）	行　业	单位（个）	从业人数（人）
全县合计	3993	14626	社会服务业	439	815
农林牧渔服务业	46	203	卫生、体育、社会福利业	54	692
水利管理业	15	54	教育、文化及广播电视业	217	3361
交通运输、邮电通信业	476	1483	综合技术服务业	4	30
批发零售贸易、餐饮业	2266	4714	国家机关、政党机关、社会团体	403	2799
金融保险业	37	403	其他行业	35	70
房地产管理业	1	2			

注：表内所列系1992年的数据

（六）经济普查

第一次　2004年5月开始，普查对象是从事第二产业、第三产业的全部法人单位、产业活动单位和个体经营户。普查范围有采矿业、制造业、电力、燃气、水生产与供应业、建筑业、交通运输、仓储与邮政业、信息传输、计算机服务与软件业、批发与零售业、食宿与餐饮业、金融业、房地产业、租赁与商业服务业、科学研究、技术服务与地质勘查业、水利、环境与公共设施管理业、居民服务与其他服务业、教育、卫生、社会保障与社会福利业、文化、体育与娱乐业以及公共管理与社会组织、国际组织等19个行业门类，90个行业大类。普查标准时点为2004年12月31日，时期资料为2004年。

普查实行“全国统一领导、部门分工协作、地方分级负责、各方共同参与”原则。县组建普查办公室，分别抽调指导员33人，普查员165人，历经1年多完成登记填表、数据审核汇总工作，县统计局分3次向社会发布普查公报：2004年年末全县共有第二、第三产业法人单位669个（企业236个，机关事业190个，社会团体5个，其他238个），产业活动单位856个（二产279个，三产577个），个体经济户6917户（二产3132户，三产3785户），全县就业人员2.95万人（二产1.29万人，三产1.66万人）。就业人员中，单位就业人员1.89万人，占64.15%；个体经营人员1.06万人，占35.85%。企业实收资本有二、三产业347个企业法人单位，实收资本28.06亿元（国家投入19.83亿元，集体投入1.65亿元，个人投入6.31亿元，港澳台和外商投入资本0.27亿元）。

第二次　2009年5月开始，普查标准时点为2008年12月31日，时间资料为2008年度，普查对象是县域内从事第二、第三产业全部法人单位、产业活动单位和个体经营户，普查主要内容包括单位基本属性、从业人员、财务状况、生产经营情况、生产能力、能源消耗及科技活动情况等。普查结果，全县有法人单位694个（企业275个，机关事业166个，社会团体和其他法人单位253个），产业活动单位289个（二产21个，三产251个），有证照个体经营户3775户（二产205户，三产3570户）。全县工业企业法人单位192个，从业人员1.09万人，有证照个体工业经营户256户，从业人员982人。

2008年，第二次经济普查培训

第六节　物价管理

1980年4月，县始设物价局，按照中央改革部署对价格体系进行改革。至2010年，县内市场经济体制已经形成，实行政府定价、政府指导价和市场调节价并存的管理，物价局根据各个时期发展变化，实行宏观调控，对违价行为依法查处，使市场价格稳定发展。

一、价格改革

（一）酝酿、准备、探索阶段

1979年，引入市场价格机制，重点调整价格结构，实行调放结合，以调为主。在1978年提高大豆等23种农副产品收购价格基础上，再次提高粮食、油料、生猪等18种主要农副产品收购价格和肉类、蔬菜等8种主要副食品销售价格，全面调整纺织品价格，提高部分重要原材料、燃料价格。1982—1984年先后放开549种商品价格和小食品价格。

（二）向市场价格过渡阶段

1985年价格改革全面展开，重点放开物价管理权限，转换价格形成机制，实行以放为主，调放结合。1987年按照国务院《价格管理条例》，实行国家定价、国家指导价、市场调节价并存的价格管理模式，赋予企业一定的定价权。1988年改变五交化商品作价办法，由倒扣作价改为顺加作价。1989—1991年发生通货膨胀，物价以治理整顿为主，建立和完善价格宏观调控体系，控制物价总水平。对关系国计民生的重要商品实行最高限价，对人民生活关系密切的商品和服务实行提价申报制度，规范市场价格秩序。

（三）改革全面深化阶段

1992年，目标是建立以市场调节价格为主，有政府宏观调整的社会主义市场经济价格体系。对自主定价的70户颁发《贵州省企业定价证》和《贵州省物价员合格证》，保障企业的价格自主权。1993年在实现粮食购销同价的同时，取消城镇居民平价定量供应粮食办法，对国家用于粮食生产的化肥、柴油由平价供应实物改以货币方式在收购价格之外将平议差价以加价形式付给农民，旨在调动农民种粮积极性。1994年全县推行商品和服务明码标价，增加市场交易透明度。1998年5月，对国家《中华人民共和国价格法》规定的大多数商品和服务性价格实行市场调节价，对与国民经济发展和人民生活关系重大的资源稀缺的少数商品、自然垄断经营的商品和重要公用事业、公益性服务价格实行政府指导价或政府定价，实现从集中的计划价格体制向市场形成价格转换。2003—2010年，除对省政府界定的重要储备物资、国家专营物资等18类商品和服务价格实行政府指导价或政府定价外，其余商品和服务价格均实行市场调节。

物价局在县城设点开展《价格法》宣传

二、商品价格管理

（一）农业生产资料价格

国家重点管理的有化肥、种子、农用塑料薄膜3类。

化肥价格 1984年前销售价格由供销部门统一定价。1985年起实行“双轨制”，计划内化肥执行全省统一零售价，计划外价格批货批价，由县供销社制定统一零售价报物价局备案。1988年改由县农资部门专营。1989年3月调整化肥销售计划内尿素每吨由521元提到549元，硝酸铵每吨392元；计划外实行最高零售价，尿素和硝酸铵每吨限价1130元和920元。由于价差大，投机商囤积计划内产品，到计划内无货时拿出来按计划外销售，坑害农民。为制止私商投机行为，1990年将计划外尿素全县统一综合销售价格管理，执行全县一价。到1992年计划内统配尿素每吨销价742元。

1994年5月，取消计划内、计划外出厂价格，实行中准价格，由省（或地）、县农资公司和基层供销社3级经营，各个环节经营费率为：省（或地）、县农资公司各4%，基层供销社6%，销售实行顺差作价。11月将省、地、县3级批发改为省级批发，县农资公司及基层供销社批发零售结合，尿素经营费率10%并实行送货制，全县尿素零售价统一为每吨1440元。1995年尿素货源偏紧，价格暴涨，5月县核定综合零售价每吨2550元，11月又降为2225元。

1996年为控制化肥价格持续上涨，实行定期审价制度，县的综合价每半年调整1次，3月至7月尿素每吨2625元，1997年再降到2200元。硝酸铵每吨1875元。1999年3月，全省放开化肥零售价格，授权给县物价局必要时可制定最高限价管理。2002年全部实行市场调节，由经营者自主定价销售，物价部门以市场监测进行管理，必要时可启动临时作价（限价）干预，至2010年12月，赤天化尿素市场零售价每吨2100元，西洋复合肥每吨2900元。

种子价格 1978—1987年杂交水稻和玉米良种价格极不统一。1988年起实行预约供种，销售价格由国家和政府按照“保本微利”原则定价，预定内和预定外供种保存合理差价。每公斤杂交水稻预约内3.6元，预约外4元；杂交玉米预约内1.6元，预约外1.8元。1996年实行分品种、分等级定价。1998年改为综合销售价格全县一价，每公斤杂交水稻12.5元，杂交玉米7.5元。2002年又恢复优质优价，分品种定价。2004年取消种子价格审批，销售价格由经营者自主定价，至2010年未变。

农用塑料薄膜价格 1978—1988年由县供销社制定全县统一零售价。1989年改按农业生产年度一年一定，计划内和计划外统一实行综合销售价，全县一价。2001—2010年放开由经营者自主定价，实行市场调节。

（二）农产品价格

粮油价格 1978年执行原粮油统购统销低价收购政策，购销价格倒挂，购进价高于销售价。1979年起收购价格陆续提高，至1985年基本理顺农村粮食购销价格，以标准等级为例，籼稻谷定购价每公斤0.322元，粳稻谷每公斤0.338元。1987年起经过5次调整粮油品种价格，至1992年实现粮食购销同价，大米、面粉、玉米3种粮食标准等级统销价格，平均每公斤由0.458元调为0.674元。提高后给予城镇居民粮价补贴，补贴对象为机关和企事业职工每人每月5元，中、小学民办教师3元。

1993年国家放开粮食价格和经营，保留粮食定购数量，全县粮食定购任务按原“一定五年”基数不变，按照市场价格水平确定价格。同时放开食油购销价格和经营，取消食油收购计划和城镇居民粮油平价定量供应，保留居民粮食平价定量供应关系。1994年市场粮油价格上涨，国有粮食企业实行大米每公斤1.4元，菜油每公斤6元挂牌销售平抑物价，城镇居民凭购粮证月供应大米15公斤，菜油1公斤。之后，经过两次调整政策性粮食销售价格，到1998年11月，政策性粮食销售价格每公斤大米2.3元，稻谷1.58元，玉米1.36元。

县物价局检测员调查市场农户产品价格

2004年5月，国务院颁布《粮食流通管理条例》，粮食经营放开，粮油价格主要由市场供求形成，物价局对市场进行监测管理。2008年市场粮油价格波动，物价局于1月31日召开新闻发布会，对籼米、菜油、猪肉等居民生活必需品实施临时价格干预，控制严重凝冻灾害造成的物价上涨。至12月1日解除价格干预。继后，受市场价格波动影响，到2010年12月大米市场销售均价每公斤4.6元，粳米每公斤5元，晚粳米每公斤4.8元，面条每公斤4.6元，散装菜油每公斤14元。

烤烟收购价格 1978—1990年为15级标准收购，在收购价外对上、中等烟实行价外补贴。1990年7月，烟叶生产扶持费为每50公斤上等烟补助30元，中等烟补助25元，以调动烟农种优质烟的积极性。1991年全县试行烤烟40等级制收购标准试点。1993年烟叶生产扶持费并入收购价格，1996—1998年对烟叶生产实行奖励，到1999年烟叶生产补贴仍并入烟叶收购价格内。2001年为发展优质烟，调高大部分上等烟和部分中等烟收购价，调低部分下等烟收购价进行调控。2005—2010年贵州省执行二价区烤烟收购价格，全县按二价区价格进行收购。

（三）轻工业品价格

食盐价格 食盐零售价历来为省物价局和商业厅共同管理，实行国家定价和政府定价相结合。1980年每公斤0.3元，1985年调为0.34元。1988年9月全国物价波动，对城乡居民实行定量凭证供应，每人每月0.6公斤，零售价每公斤0.36元。次年恢复城乡食盐差价和实行包装销售，集镇辖区外的区、乡供应点散盐零售价每公斤0.4元。1994年5月20日取消城乡差价，实行全县一价，精细盐每公斤0.9元，包装食盐随之提高，碘盐加碘不加价。2001年2月，小包装食盐改用复合膜包装，县城零售价0.5公斤袋装1元，1公斤袋装2元，县以下0.9元和1.8元。2002年12月取消1公斤包装，全县统一供应0.5公斤包装。2003年起再次执行全县一价销售，每袋0.5公斤1元。2006年分0.5公斤和0.25公斤包装两种，零售价1.3元和0.8元。2010年12月全省统一零售价，0.65公斤和0.3公斤袋装零售价分别为2元和1元。

1994年起实行食盐包装零售

药品价格 1978—1988年药品价格较为稳定，变动较小。1989—1990年3次调整部分药品销售价格，制定190种规格药品出厂价和批发价的销售价格。1991年3—7月整顿中药材价格，对150种中药材实行经营差率控制，进销差率最高不超过14%，批零差率为25%至35%；对20种中药材收购实行指导价格，10种销售价格调升调降。

1996年9月针对药品价格上涨过快问题，改药品价格由倒扣作价为顺加作价，由中央和省两级管理，国家计委管112种，省物价局管176种，首批放开50种药品由医疗单位自主定价。1997年药品价格秩序混乱，零售价格不断上涨，调查整改医疗机构13个，药品批发和药品零售商店12个，个体诊所71个，督促其认真执行中央管理价格目录中18类85个药品批发价、零售价。1998年7月县物价局和卫生局制发《关于加强药品价格管理的通知》，要求药品经营企业和医疗机构药品销售价格按照实际进价加规定差率确定。县医药公司药品批发可以实行批量作价，给购货方5%以内折扣。同时实行药品价格公示制度，物价局对药品价格进行监测。

2000年7月，改革药品价格管理办法，实行政府定价和市场调节价，国家只管药品零售价，不再制定出厂价和批发价，列入基本医疗保险药品目录的药品实行政府定价，其余药品实行市场调节价，取消流通差率控制，由经营者自主定价。至12月，列入国家计委定价药品和制剂、计生药具共464种。2003年，实行省、地、县3级医疗机构联合招标采购，由省物价局核定中标后临时零售价格。到2010年5月18日为控制药品价格，减轻患者负担，乡（镇）及社区医院实行药品零差价销售。

（四）重工业产品价格

电力价格 1978年沿用原价，照明用电每千瓦时收费0.2元。1984年动力用电每每千瓦时收0.085元，次年1月每千瓦时加收0.0011元，农业灌溉用电按扬程分每千瓦时0.06元、0.04元、0.03元3种。1988至1989年两次调整水库管理所及小水电电价格后，到1999年启动农村电网改造和农电管理体制改革，电力销售价格由县物价局和水电局共同管理，实行国家定价和政府定价，以国有电站供电价格为主，其他小水电站比照执行。电网改造期间，农村居民用电到户电价实行最高限价，每千瓦时居民生活用电0.74元，非居民照明用电0.88元，营业性照明用电0.9元，农业生产用电0.4元，农业排灌用电0.2元，非工业和普通工业用电0.56元。

2000年启动县城电网改造，取消用电量总表管理，全县分3个电价区统一执行省物价局批准的综合过渡电价。2003年起城乡居民生活用电实行同网同价。同价水平每千瓦时0.403元，其余仍执行过渡电价。2004年9月城乡用电，抄表到户的调为0.45元，未抄表到户的按台变同价每千瓦0.45元，最终到户最高不

超过0.5元，同时停止执行综合过渡电价按省目录电价执行。至2010年12月，城镇居民照明用电每千瓦时0.4556元。

成品油价格 按照“中央统一领导，地方各级分级管理”原则，成品油销售价格实行国家定价和政府指导价。1988年3月，对计划内高价成品油实行最高限价管理，70号汽油每公升1.51元，0号柴油每公升1.39元，灯用煤油每公升1.45元，各地不得超过限额。1990年为减少农民经济压力，于11月将计划内煤油销售价格由城乡一价改为城乡差价，全县分为3个价区，每公斤销售价格分别为0.8元、0.64元、0.74元。

1991年3月物价管理权下放，计划外议价成品油销售价格改由县石油公司会同物价局共同制定，灯用煤油批零差率为煤油10%，汽油、柴油、润滑油11%。12月对平价油以外的汽油、柴油实行综合销售价，根据市场价格走势适时进行调整。

1992年4月又对计划内平价、计划外高价、议价3种价格的煤油改为综合销售价，一价区每公斤1.54元，二价区1.64元，三价区1.74元。1993年4月除军队和农用成品油按平价供应外，其他用户计划分配的成品油一律改为按高价销售，70号汽油每公斤2.15元，灯用煤油和0号柴油每公斤2元。

物价人员检查加油站成品油销售价格

1994年5月，改革成品油价格管理，对汽油、柴油、煤油等统一实行国家定价和政府定价，恢复由中央和省两级制定，县内执行省的销售价格，70号汽油每升零售价2.3元，0号柴油每升2.25元，煤油每公斤为：县城2.78元，乡镇2.9元。

1997年后成品油价格坚持以市场为导向，建立国内与国际石油价格接轨办法，随国际市场油价变化定期调整国内市场成品油销售价，一般每月调整一次，至2010年12月22日零时起93号汽油每升零售价6.97元。

液化气价格 1978—2002年销售价格由经营者自主定价。2003年起纳入物价部门管理，由贵州省物价局制定作价原则，授权市、县政府管理。2004年9月又改为政府指导价，标准瓶装净重14.5公斤零售价68元，钢瓶检验费计入生产成本，送气劳务费按自愿有偿原则,每瓶1元至2元。同时配套建立成本监测制度，掌握市场供求状况和价格动态，在进货成本大幅度变化时相应调整销售价格，到2010年年末，由于国际市场油价影响，14.5公斤零售价每瓶高至125元。

（五）供水价格

1978—1987年，县城居民生活用水每吨0.16元，1988年调整供水价格，县城不分用水类别每吨0.2元。1991年8月改按用水类别实行差别水价。按管径大小收取增容费和停水损失费，个人100—500元，单位300—2000元，县城公用设施建设和敬老院、托儿所、幼儿园、中小学校的用水酌情缓、减、免。

2009年9月8日，受市局委托县物价局召开县城供水价格和污水处理费标准调整听证会

1993年起，增加行政事业用水、经营服务用

水、特殊用水类别。2002年3月和2009年8月县物价局两次召开城区供水价格决策听证会，论证县城供水价格调整方案。乡镇居民供水价格本着“补偿成本，合理收益，节约用水、公平负担”的原则制定。执行到2010年未变。

1978—2010年县城供水价格统计一览表

表3—10—13　　单位：元/吨

用水类别＼年份	1978年	1988年	1991年	1993年	1995年	1997年	2002年	2009年
居民生活用水	0.16	0.20	0.25	0.35	0.60	1.00	1.20	2.10
工业用水	—	0.20	0.30	0.60	0.80	1.20	1.40	2.50
行政事业用水	—	0.20	1.00	0.80	1.20	1.50	—	2.40
经营服务用水	—	0.20	1.00	0.80	1.40	2.00	—	3.70
特种用水	—	0.20	1.00	0.80	1.40	5.00	—	5.20
市政用水	—	—	—	—	—	—	—	1.50

三、服务性价格管理

（一）公路运输价格

1978年沿袭政府定价，按线路分3个等级作价，到1986年旅客运输基本运价一、二等公路人/公里0.027元、三等公路人/公里0.033元；货运基本运价：吨/公里0.18元、0.2元、0.23元。1989年8月，运输乱涨价、滥收费严重，实行最高限价管理控制，旅客运输8座及以上人/公里0.045元至0.06元，7座以下不分路等，车/公里0.6元。

县物价局检查春节客运票价

1992年10月，执行贵州省物价局、交通厅《汽车运价规划实施细则》，客运票价由基本运价、交通发展基金、油料差价组成，一至三等公路基本运价人/公里0.038元、二等0.043元、三等0.048元，交通发展基金每人公里0.015元，油料差价人/公里0.01元。

1993年，随着路面质量提高，运价项目由单一客车改为普通客车、中级客车、高级客车、小型客车、普通卧铺客车、高级卧铺客车及小轿车出租、包车等类，1997年6月运价由按线路等级定价改为按车辆类型定价，实行中准价管理，乡与乡、县与乡及夜班客车票价可在20%以内上浮，微型小客车以中型客车票价为基础可上浮30%，客运包车实行市场调节价。货运价格上浮按中转价10%至40%。

2002年12月，再次改革汽车运价旅客运输价格，以国家指导价为主，按优质优价原则实行差别运价。同时放开货物运价，实行市场调节，由承托双方协商确定，执行到2010年县城至金阳（高速公路）客运价格每人15元，至白云（老水泥路）每人8元，至扎佐、至久长每人4元。

（二）邮电资费价格

邮政资费　由国家统一管理，实行国家定价和政府定价。1978—1989年按邮件性质、寄达地区、邮件重量、邮局办理手续、邮件运输方式、邮局所负补偿责任等条件综合确定价格，国内平信每重20克0.08元，明信片每张0.04元，其他项目资费均低，导致行业亏损。1990年和1992年两次调高资费。1996年12月邮政资费进行结构性调整，清理各种乱收费、乱加价，取消邮政附加费。国内平信每20克由本埠0.1元、外埠0.2元调整为不分本、外埠一律0.5元，其他项目资费也大幅提高。

1998年优化邮政资费结构，平信、印刷品计费方式由递重等额累进计费改为分区（本埠、外埠），分首重（100克以内）、续重（100克以上至限重）分别计费，明信片和挂号信不分本外埠，每件0.6元、2元。同时，降低5000元以上高额国内汇款汇费，每笔超过50元的一律按50元计收。执行到2010年除国内汇款逐步转入邮政储蓄汇兑外，其他收费未变。

电信资费 1996年前，县内电话资费分长途、市内、农村3类，长途电话按空间距离划分12个等级，执行每分钟收费0.1元至1.2元不同资费标准。1995年县城2000门程控数字电话投入使用、安装及改制实行优惠。1996年资费改为市内、本地网、长途3类。

1997年1月改革电信价格，实行城乡同价。用户基本月租费为甲种7.6元，乙种12元；市内电话通话费提高为每3分钟0.168元；停止农话资费标准。本地网营业区执行市内电话资费标准；长途电话计费等级由12级简化为4级；公用电话收费分本地网营业区内、区间和国内长途，资费标准为0.3元、0.7元和1元。

1999年3月，电信资费实行“三降一理顺”（降低因特网拨号上网资费、降低固定电话初装费和移动电话入网费，降低国内出租电话和国际及港澳台电话资费，理顺本地网营业区内电话资费），取消本地网营业区内、区间加收的邮电建设附加费。

2001年，再次进行结构性调整，计费单元由1分钟改为6秒钟，国内长途电话计费等级再由4级降为1级；基本月租费分为县城住宅电话每月每部12元，农村10元，办公电话25元。同时取消邮电建设附加费，放开导呼机服务费和IP电话业务资费，由经营者自主定价，扩大固定电话本地网营业区范围，实行城乡通话费同价，至2010年未变。

四、行政事业性收费

（一）医疗服务收费

1978—1990年主要执行贵州省卫生厅1964年制定的省、地、县三级收费标准。1991年7月省卫生、物价、财政部门联合调整收费标准595个，新增收费标准696个，常用挂号费每人次县级医院0.2元，区级0.15元；急诊0.3元、0.25元；住院每床日2元、1元。但出现的药品经营和医疗单位擅自提高药品和服务价格的问题，导致患者看病贵、看病难。

1999年6月，再次规范和调整收费标准，对不同等级医疗机构部分服务价格实行分等定价。挂号费不分医院等级、初诊复诊，普通门诊和急诊每人次0.5元和1元；住院费县级医院按每间床位分5元、4元，乡镇医院2.5元。手术费由按病种收费改按手术易难程度，分为特大、大、中、一般、小5类，每类再分一、二、三等，实行分类定价。另增

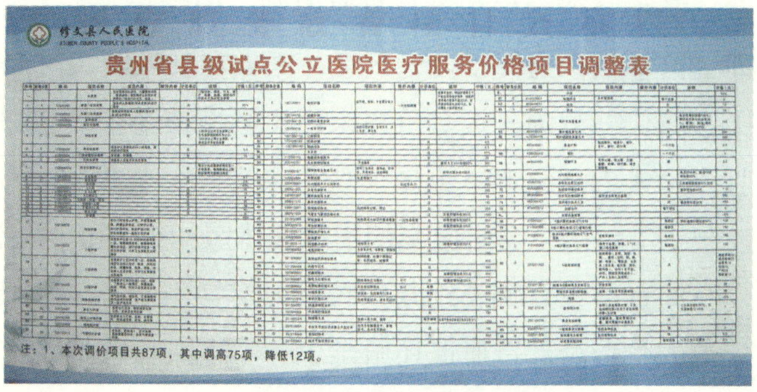

县人民医院收费公示牌

诊察费，降低大型检查收费标准，进一步界定医疗收费项目。

2003年6月，按照国家宏观调控和市场调节相结合的原则，取消政府定价，实行政府指导价和市场调节价，县、乡（镇）非营利性医疗机构分别在《贵州省医疗服务价格》《贵阳市乡镇和社区医疗服务价格》范围内确定本医院执行标准；营利性医疗机构实行市场调节价，由医疗机构根据实际服务、成本、市场供求情况自主制定收费标准。执行到2010年除少量调整外未作大的变动。

（二）中小学收费

1978至1988年，全县中小学、幼儿园执行贵州省人委〔1964〕教张字第48号文件规定标准。1989年7月小学、初中实行义务教育，只收杂费、免收学费。11月，开展全县中小学收费项目清理整顿，学校自行收取的补习、留级、转学、考务、管理、辅导、复习资料、试卷、公物押金、卫生、班费等费饬令制止。

1990年春季开学执行新收费标准，学杂费县城4元至8元，农村3元至7元。1994年春季开学全县中小学统一杂费收费标准。执行到1997年，镇所在地和镇以下学校执行相同收费标准，高中不分县城和农村每学期杂费30元、学费40元。1999年秋合并初小、高小收费项目，统称小学杂费。

2004年秋，物价、教育、财政在全县义务教育阶段推行“一费制”收费办法，包括杂费、课本费、作业本费、信息技术教育费统一为“一费制”，其他收费改为服务性收费。修文中学定为普通中学，执行高中学费收费标准，秋季开学学费每学期每人高一600元，高二和高三380元。

2006年秋，县内部分乡镇义务教育阶段公办学校免收书费、杂费，取消服务性收费。2008年全县实施，到2010年未变。

专记：一封举报信　牵动局长心

2005年4月25日，县物价局局长聂天义收到小箐乡崇恩村18位村民联名反映崇恩小学乱收费举报信后，立即与县纪委、监察局、纠风办、教育局商定，组成联合调查组于26日下午深入学校调查处理。根据举报，调查组走访学生、家长和村民，查看学校财务，对照国家有关学校收费政策法规，认定2003年11月至2005年1月，崇恩小学接受香港友人3次捐资人民币2.42万元，2004年9月和11月两次支付贫困学生书杂费7682.5元，属正常开支，余款1.65万元未挪作他用；学校收取学生每人书本费55元、杂费25元、教育资料费一至二年级4元和三至六年级5元、蒸饭费2.5元、驱虫费1.5元，三至六年级信息技术教育费10元，是按照“一费制”规定，经县物价局核准收费项目和标准，收费时出具正规收费票据，属正常收费；学校将应收消毒费2.5元改收驱虫费1.5元，是合理收费项目；学校收取学生蒸饭费为服务性收费，必须坚持学生和家长自愿原则，但学校收取138名未在校蒸饭的学生每人2.5元，共345元，责令立即退给学生；为便于食堂蒸饭，派人在县城购买统一规格的饭盒111个，每个5元，照价卖给学生自愿购买，属代办行为，饭盒价格未超出县城市场平均价格；学校当年有六年级毕业生41人，由学校财务统一收取每人21元，除5人属欠费生未交外，共收36人756元，属学校自定项目标准收费，收取的费用由学校统一支付每个学生应交的毕业集体照相2元和个人照相5元后，尚余14元应退给学生。

调查结束，调查组与学校领导交换意见，对收费出现的问题进行批评，学校领导虚心接受，有两项应退的收费全部造册退还给学生。学生家长感到“实行阳光收费我们放心”，也表示今后应当积极支持学校的正常收费，化解学校与学生、家长之间的矛盾，消除学校在群众中的不良影响。

（三）行政事业单位收费

1978年收费项目较少，沿用政府计划部门原定标准，未纳入物价管理范围。1979年起收费项目逐渐增多，标准不统一，出现乱收费问题。1987年起执行国家《价格管理条例》，收费纳入物价部门管理和监督，步入清理整顿，核发收费许可证管理，至1989年共清理、整顿、规范46个部门收费，发放《贵州省收费许可证》100本。

1991年2月，奉国务院指示开展治理“三乱”（乱收费、乱罚款、乱摊派），经过自查自纠、重点检查、审查处理、整章建制4个阶段，清理审查省、地、县制定收费项目136个，收费标准592个，取消纠正乱收费项目15个，办理收费许可证159本。

1993年6月开展收费年审及收费许可证验证，全县年审部门28个，验证150本，年审收费金额350万元，取消4个收费项目和8个收费标准，降低4个收费项目和6个收费标准，暂停收取房屋登记费、勘察丈量费、过户手续费和工本费。自11月1日起，收费单位必须持物价部门重新办理的新证和财政部门统一印制的收费票据收费，收费标准公开，收入金额上缴财政，纳入财政预算管理。

1995年1月，按照《贵州省行政事业性收费管理条例》及实施细则，收费实行统一领导，分级管理，由中央和省两级审批，财政和物价部门审核立项，确定收费标准，收费年审一年一次，违反规定乱收费者由物价和财政部门查处，至2005年全县共取消不合理收费项目82个，降低收费标准1个，保留收费项目81个。2005年起全面推行收费公示制度，所有收费部门在收费窗口的醒目位置公开收费项目、收费标准、收费范围、收费依据、计费单位及价格举报电话，让社会监督。至2010年，全县费单位共176个，核发收费许可证290本。

五、物价监督检查

1981年恢复物价监督检查工作，1984年成立物价检查所，与工商、税务、质量技术监督等职能部门配合，监督检查物价1988至2010年累计检查2926次（个），立案查处违法案件437件，实行经济制裁379.82万元，其中，退还消费者71.42万元，没收290.8万元，罚款15.6万元。

（一）市场物价检查

1978—1985年市场物价稳定，仅进行常规性的价格检查。1988年下半年起物价涨速较快，乱涨价现象突出，物价局印发商品标价笺25万张，发放给经营公司和商店，实行商品明码标价。糖业烟酒公司以每公斤2.5元零售价批发白糖3160公斤，获非法收入7374元作为没收并罚款200元处理。1994年，国家计委颁发《关于商品和服务实行明码标价的规定》及实施细则，县物价局利用赶场天开展宣传和咨询，发放明码标价笺4万张，使商品标价笺挂柜率从1990年的80%增到90%以上。

物价员在县城发放“创建百城万店无假货示范一条街”倡议书

2000年建立健全价格监督举报制度，在全县各乡（镇）和县城街上醒目位置分别悬挂价格监督举报牌，公开“2326936”价格监督举报电话，2001

年在县城步行街示范明码标价。2003年在全县建立农村价格网络，10乡（镇）设立价格义务教育监督站，201个村设价格义务监督员。同时开展“价费阳光工程”“诚实规范标价，禁止价格欺诈”“百城万店无假货”活动，重点对与人民生活密切相关行业进行检查。2009年农村市场价格趋于稳定。2010年受市场价格整体波动，物价涨幅较大，检查重点转向涉农、涉企和教育收费，全年市场价格检查10次，立案查处违价案件2件，没收违法所得7.47万元。

（二）物价大检查

1985年起贯彻执行国家物价局《关于在税收财务大检查中同时开展物价大检查的通知》，每年下半年进行一次税收、财务、物价大检查，物价方面重点检查商品销售价格违法。1988年重点转向违反物价政策和规定，钻“双轨制”价格空子乱涨价、乱加价、乱集资、乱收费、抬价抢购紧缺物资等，纠正县百货公司和农资日杂公司不合理的计价方式，处理违价案件2件，没收违法所得7544元，罚款230元，全部上缴财政。

1990年起，商品价格逐步放开，检查重点由流通领域转向行政事业性收费，治理“乱收费、乱罚款、乱摊派”，全县165个单位全面自查，重点检查63个单位，查出各种违纪金额49万元，当年入库31万元，占应入库数的87.8%。1994年商品价格基本放开，实行市场调节，重点治理乱收费和农业生产资料价格检查，查出一般违价行为112件，价格违法案件6件，涉价金额6.2万元，纠正70个单位无证收费、乱收费行为。贵阳煤矿在扎佐地区长期超价格标准收取电费2万元被立案查处。1995年重点检查131个单位和685户个体工商户，查出各种违纪金额150.5万元，当年入库135万元。1996年重点对前几年未检查到的违价案件进行清查，查出违价金额3.7万元全部没收入库。1997年税收、财务、物价大检查停止，但常规性的物价检查列入商品和服务价格检查继续进行。

（三）商品及服务价格检查

1980年起开展，1988—1989年检查车辆、食盐、药品、粮食、烟叶共5次，没收非法所得34.67万元，罚款2354元，奖励举报人140元。1990年重点检查与人民群众密切相关的生活必需品和服务价格。1991—1998年查出医药公司提高中成药批发价所得1.23万元，作上缴财政6746元处理。自来水公司提高水价获非法所得1605元全部没收，并罚款1605元。

1999—2005年，针对群众反映的热点问题，先后检查全县药品、水电、民爆物品销售和食盐、自来水价格12次，发现提价收费突出。中医院推迟执行政府定价多收药品价款、供电局自立项目收取222户用电许可证款和297户缴费手册工本费，物资公司在销售炸药、雷管、导火绳收取劳务费及发票工本费，盐业支局在批发环节向70户食盐零售经营户收取300元、500元保证金等。7年累计查出违规多收价款27.71万元，除盐业支局违法收取经营户保证金2.9万元全部退还经营户外，其余全部没收缴入国库，对较严重的经营户给予经济罚款5.24万元。2008至2010年药品及服务价格检查，未发现大的违价问题。

物价人员检查超市商品价格

（四）行政性收费检查

1978—1987年收费项目少，由经济主管部门管理。1988年纳入物价部门统一管理，进行清理、整顿、发证，连续5年为255个补办和申办单位颁发《贵州省收费许可证》。1990年遵照中共中央、国务院《关于坚决制止乱收费、乱罚款和各种摊派的决定》，清理整顿“乱收费、乱罚款、乱摊派”，连续两年对收费单位进行自查自报、重点检查、审核处理、整章建制专项治理，发现自立名目自立收费项目、提高收费标准和重复收费7273元，当年收缴财政2195元，退还用户1125元。1993年又按照国务院指示把治理乱收费作为反腐败斗争的主要内容，至1994年年审验证，重新核发收费许可证154本，取消收费项目24个，降低收费标准4个，暂停收费项目4个。

1995年起，对人民群众关注的中小学、医疗、行政事业、公路运输及涉农收费进行专项治理，至2005年累计查出价格违法金额198.08万元，没收37.91万元，退还消费者65.58万元，对严重违法者罚款4.22万元。其中中小学乱收费较为严重，采取提高标准收费、擅自立项收费、扩大范围收费、集资收费等手段累计乱收费75.28万元，占违法金额总数的37.98%，当即有50%的学校退还给学生和学生家长。继后，全面推行收费持证公示制度，学校认真落实“一费制”收费政策，行政事业性收费已转入正轨。到2010年，全县176个收费单位中除个别学校出现变相乱收费外，其余收费单位都能正确执行国家价格法律法规，依法收费，明白收费。

第七节　工商行政管理

1978年，沿袭原工商行政管理局的建制行使对全县工商业管理职责。1979年起在坚持以公有制为主体的前提下，放宽政策发展多种经济。2010年各类企业由43户增为847户，个体工商业者从2户代销商店增为6457户。

县工商局办公楼

一、经济合同管理

（一）合同鉴证

1978年仅对县内经济合同鉴证。1982年7月实施国家《经济合同法》，经济合同鉴证工作全面展开。1984年12月—1985年，依法鉴证经济合同1万份，总金额1154万元。1986年在180个企业内置专职或兼职合同管理员管理经济合同，到1990年共依法鉴证经济合同215份，总金额2370万元。已履行198份，占鉴证数的92.09%。1994年根据修改后的《中华人民共和国经济合同法》在万江机电厂举办企业合同管理员培训班，核发和换发经济合同授权委托书84份，发放示范文本200本。

1999年3月实施全国人大通过的《中华人民共和国经济合同法》，对经济合同鉴证不强制执行，而县仍继续办理。2001—2008年，全县共鉴证经济合同482份，鉴证金额3.4亿元，核发经济合同授权委托书46份，散发各类文本120套。2010年1月实施《贵州省合同监督条例》，将合同鉴证改为合同条款格式备案，有3家旅行社和15家门面租赁户提交合同格式条款备案。

（二）经济合同仲裁

1984年11月成立县经济合同仲裁委员会，当年调解经济合同纠纷2件。1986—1990年仲裁合同纠纷1件，案值金额12万元；调解34件，涉及金额385.5万元，无复议和申诉。1991年按照《中华人民共和国民事诉讼法》规定订立合同应有仲裁条件，凡未订立仲裁条件的合同仲裁部门不予受理。1995年9月实施国家《仲裁法》，县不再设仲裁委员会，原仲裁业务终止。

（三）财产抵押登记

1999年开办。2001—2002年累计办理抵押登记57份，主债权金额1.56亿元，抵押金额1.8亿元。2010年又办理登记60件，主债权金额1.27亿元，抵押金额3.84亿元。

（四）“重合同，守信用”活动

1987年开展，在全县企业中每年评选1次。评选条件为内部管理制度完善；有分管领导、专（兼）职管理人员和合同管理机构；经常学习有关法律、法规并有记录；依法纳税；合同履行率必须达100%；在同行业中经济效益较好。评选由企业自愿申请，县工商局初审，地区工商局核批，县政府公布和颁发“重合同守信用单位”铜质牌匾和荣誉证书，之后符合条件者保持命名，不符合者取消资格并收回牌匾和证书。至1989年，全县有16户企业获得“重合同守信用单位”称号。2001年有2户获省级、4户获市级、10户获县级“重合同守信用单位”称号。2002年分国家、省、市三级授牌。2010年有4户企业获省级“重合同守信用单位”称号；25户企业获市级“守合同重信用单位”称号。

2010年县工商局局长胡利斌（左）为企业授牌

二、工商业登记管理

（一）登记注册发照

1978年县内仅有国营企业15户，集体企业28户，经营代销商贩2户。1980年进行工业企业普查登记，发照102户，职工2328人，注册资金931.7万元。1981年新增个体工商业319户。1985年对党政机关和党政干部经商办企业清查处理，全县共14户31人，投资77.1万元，将10户转为非党政机关经营，由企业部门归口管理，4户作注销或吊销营业执照处理。至1990年全县有工商企业213户，注册资金1.55亿元，从业1.66万人；个体工商业2943户，从业3645人。

1993年，对边远地区个体工商户“先发展，后规范”，边远贫困地区“只发照，不收费”或“只登记，不发照”。1995年对农村中申办种植、养殖等企业上门办照免收登记费。1996年对机动运输车辆先作交易验证，然后办营业执照。1997年对下岗人员就业只凭企业证明书和身份证即可办证，免收登记费。

2003年起开设注册绿色通道，促进就业和再就业，对计划生育户、下岗职工、应届大中专毕业生、残疾人、复员退伍军人、返乡农民工自主创业提供快速、便捷准入通道。连续8年为454名下岗职工，28名残疾人，9名复退军人，101名应届高中毕业生优先办理设立、变更、注册登记和验照，为148名返乡农民工自主创业办理个体工商户营业执照，共减免注册登记费、工本费、管理费20万元。到2010年全县工商业登记注册增至7304户，其中有限责任公司363户，内资分公司124户，企业法人45户，内资非法人企业和非公私营企业216户，个人独资企业及分支机构99户，个体工商业6457户。

（二）年度检验

1981年试行企业年度检查制度，次年起每年年终进行1次。1990年对私营企业实行定期年审，个体工商户验照贴花，审查其资金、经营状况、经营行为是否与登记项目相一致，4年换发1次营业执照。1994年执行国务院决定，每年1至4月对公司进行年度检验。1995年年检438户，验照贴花个体工商业2460户，对长期停产的18户企业扶持恢复生产，限期整改11户，对名存实亡的28户注销营业执照，对未验照贴花的120户个体工商作变更登记61户，补办登记23户，注销登记36户。2000年起，年检、验照贴花与专项治理结合进行，未参加年检的企业和验照贴花的个体工商户，依照法规进行处罚。2002年立案查处涉嫌有抽逃、虚假出资行为的公司3户，其中1户被罚款1800元处理，另两户责令更正；对擅自变更登记的企业3户和个体工商16户罚款3.2万元；注销登记企业5户，参与炸封无证小水泥、小煤矿64户。2003年清理出无照经营者410户，对其中303户罚款42万元。2004—2010年，年检和验照工作达到规范，未发现违反程序和规定的行为。

注册科干部正为来办事者办理年检业务

2002—2010年企业年检和工商户验照统计表

表3—10—14　　　　单位：户

年份	合计	年检	验照	年份	合计	年检	验照
2002	1134	224	910	2007	3326	458	2868
2003	1555	294	1261	2008	2539	402	2137
2004	1946	350	1596	2009	2590	464	2126
2005	2602	426	2176	2010	4053	487	3566
2006	2970	447	2523				

三、商标管理

（一）注册登记

1979年10月国家恢复商标注册，凡必须使用注册商标的商品，须报县工商局初审，省工商局复审，国家工商行政管理局统一复审合格后办理注册手续。注册期限为10年，期满不再补办注册即自行注销，至1990年全县累计核准注册商标26个。继后每年利用“3·15”活动，组织人员上街进行商标、广告宣传和咨询，提高群众对商标的认识。对商标注册单位进行登记备案。2002年，又对全县注册商标进行摸底调查，有15家企业注册商标18个。

2010年实行“一县一牌，一所一标”目标，推荐的贵州好一多乳业股份有限公司“好1多”商标，被省工商局认定为贵州省的著名商标。1979—2010年，全县累计注册商标87个。

（二）保持注册商标专用权

自1979年始办注册商标起，工商局对注册商标专用权进行保护，查处并销毁3户企业违法冒用他人商标25万份和县酒厂违规印制“贵州名酒”标志后，1987年起每年利用“3·15”活动宣传《中华人民共和国商标法》，不断提高群众对注册商标的认识。

1990年8月执行国家工商总局规定，商标印刷必须由取得县工商局“指定印刷商标单位”资格的印刷企业或个体工商户承担。1999年5月又对注册的文字商标与知名商标名称中的字号产生混淆的，一律不予受理，并要求申请人说明理由。

2001年按照“标本兼治，重在治本”的原则，配合市场巡查、企业回访、登记审查，对注册商标进行监管。2004年各工商所对注册商标建立台账管理，在保护注册商标专用权行动中执法人员检查经营者235户，商品交易市场5个。2008年开展保护奥林匹克标志、清理“老干爹”注册商标和打击“傍名牌”不正当竞争专项整治。1997—2010年累计立案查处63件违法印制商标、假冒他人注册商标等商标违法行为，没收侵权商品201公斤和仿冒“玉蝶”电线49圈，仿冒“金立牌手机、苏泊尔电磁炉及电饭煲”等侵权商品237件，罚款金额共计21.6万元。

四、广告管理

（一）户外广告登记

1995年2月，《中华人民共和国广告法》实施，县工商部门在组织宣传的同时，对户外广告审查登记，对广告经营单位进行全面检查。1997年起广告经营单位由县初审，报贵阳市工商管理局复审合格者准许经营。2002年广告执法工作权限下移，县工商局对辖区内店堂牌匾进行审查登记，全县登记发布户外广告商10户，店堂牌匾广告商7户。2003—2010年强化和规范广告行政执法，办理广告登记704件，其中户外广告118件，店堂牌匾广告586件，受理并查处广告案件53件。

（二）广告市场整顿

1994年至1995年，县工商局开展户外广告清理，清除各种未经审批，擅自张贴广告828张。对未经审查的广告加盖“未经审查，谨防受骗”印章，查处并清除虚假广告207份。1997年开展11项专项检查，查处违法广告5起。2001—2010年，严格广告经营单位登记管理，加强和规范广告行政执法，累计立案查处虚假、误导、未登记、不良文化广告102件，罚款8.74万元，清除违法广告30块，没收制假药品及印刷品广告资料3000份，撕毁野广告1500张。

五、市场管理

（一）“3·15”宣传

自1987年全国开展“3·15”国际消费者权益日纪念活动起，每年3月15日前后的赶场天，县工商部门都自办或联合各有关部门共同举办宣传活动，增强消费者防假识假意识和能力，促进全社会关心和支

持消费者权益保护工作。活动较突出的1994年3月12—16日，工商局、消费者协会、物价局、质量技术监督局、修文报社和电视台，利用县城、扎佐、久长、小箐、六广赶场天开展“3·15”宣传咨询活动，展出并销毁价值12万元的假冒伪劣商品。

2004年“3·15”国际消费者权益日，工商局与消费者协会、文体广电局、移动公司联合主办，邀请县委宣传部、县人大、县政协和物价局、质量技术监督局、新闻、电视等14个单位260人参加，开展以“诚信·维权”为主题的宣传活动，特邀一支民族风情演出队在台后的工商局门口表演《七月火把节》、《芦笙舞》等10余个精彩节目，开展有奖消费知识问答，发出纪念品500份。参会的10名县领导身披绶带和宣传员一起向消费者散发《中华人民共和国消费者权益保护法》、《中华人民共和国行政许可法》、《中华人民共和国商标法》等宣传资料3800份及消费者维权卡2500张，共接待咨询3600人次，现场受理并解决投诉3起。

2009年，工商部门在赶场天设点宣传识别伪劣商品

2009年和2010年3月的13—15日，为加大“消费与服务”年主题宣传活动的力度，会同40家政府职能部门和企业开展赶场天宣传，出动流动宣传车，执法人员手机24小时开机值守“3·15”热线，活动期间开展市场检查31次，公开销毁价值9万元的假冒伪劣商品，省、市、县电视台对活动全程报道，增大宣传效果。

专记：一次深入人心的“3·15”宣传活动

1994年3月12—16日，为纪念“3·15”国际消费者权益保护日，县工商局与消费者协会、物价局、质量技术监督局、修文报社及电视台联合，利用赶场天开展《中华人民共和国消费者权益保护法》大型宣传活动。活动于12日开始在县城举行，会场设在县工商局办公楼门前，四周悬挂大幅宣传布标，场内置政策法规宣传台、咨询服务台、现场投诉台和假冒伪劣商品曝光台，场外置市场检查组，由60余名宣传队员表演节目，播放《中华人民共和国消费者权益保护法》，摆出假香烟58条，假董酒、假湄窖、假鸭溪等瓶装酒3000瓶，冒牌永久101型自行车1辆及劣质香皂、加盐味精、假棉絮等，共计价值12万元。先后到场听众达7000人次，散发消费知识和识别15种假冒商品宣传资料3421份，接待咨询2158人次。市场检查组抽查200个摊点，查处无照经营者10户，短斤少两者3户，超范围经营者2户，共罚款300元。其中1户使用8两当1斤的“短命秤”坑害消费者被罚款100元，消费者当即拍手称快。宣传结束，曝光的假冒伪劣商品全部销毁，

2009年，城郊分局工作人员在县城开展“3·15”宣传

群众个个拥护，都说“是侵害消费者的经营商应受到的惩罚”。15日晚，县广播电台和电视台分别播放宣传活动实况，让全县人民都知道《中华人民共和国消费者权益保护法》是保护消费者权益的法律。宣传活动的震慑力很大，不仅使广大群众知道消费者有保护自己消费的权利，而且让经营商户明白销售假冒伪劣商品坑害消费者是违法的，有的商户当即表示：今后一定要坚守职业道德，诚信经营买卖。

在基层各工商所和消费者协会分会也与县工商局同步组建宣传组，利用当地赶场天开展宣传，全县共贴挂大幅标语155幅，散发宣传资料5000份。时值小箐乡召开人民代表大会，会议上播放《中华人民共和国消费者权益保护法》录音磁带，并列入会议讨论内容。很多代表都说：“以前我们还不知道消费者有这样大的权益，回村后我们要向群众宣传，买到假货的人就有地方告状。”

（二）市场检查

1980年，县内恢复农村集贸市场，允许农民入市经营小百货、饮食、蔬菜等，工商人员常年进行检查监督。1983年组织巡回检查组出动执法人员728人次对各个集市进行检查，查出无证商贩236人，当即对其补办登记注册领取《营业执照》经营。1993年，开展定期或不定期大检查和节假日检查，共检查22次2245户，查出无证经营127户，短斤少两343户，假冒伪劣商品18件，折价4万元，作没收销毁处理。

1995年采用专项治理与市场大检查相结合的办法开展为期74天的夏季饮料市场整治，与卫生、防疫等部门共组织235人检查生产厂、批发部、个体工商128户，查出有重大问题的11户，罚款2580元，销毁变质饮料876瓶。

1996年成立“打假”领导小组，先后对化肥、农药、农膜、种子、药品回扣进行专项检查，取缔非法经营种子的个体户3户，立案查处1户，没收假种子35公斤。

1998年推行市场管理巡查制度，11月工商局成立粮食市场监管巡查队，工商所置巡查组，加强粮食市场监管。次年2月，六广巡查组在粮食市场严打中查获不法商贩贩运玉米2.4万公斤。

1999年7月工商与公安、文化等部门配合，对县城邪教“法轮功”出版物进行检查清理，收缴邪教“法轮功”书籍和手抄本453册，录音和录像带176盒，图牌和徽章41件。

2000—2001年，先后开展娱乐及电子游戏专项治理和“百日打假”行动，出动执法人员378人次，检查经营户1792户次，自愿关闭和取缔电子游戏场所10个，端掉制假饮料窝点4个，查获饮料生产设备1套、粮食4.5吨、没收物品涉及案值180万元，对违法者罚款11.3万元，查获和查扣假冒伪劣商品进行销毁处理，成品假饮料173箱，包装箱150个，价值2万余元；查扣涉嫌不合格钢材10吨，假冒草坪专用复合肥5吨，假乙草胺甲除草剂180瓶，涉嫌金额28万元。没收假冒“相宝山”牌高级卫生纸234包，假洗发液50公斤，假冒豪华鸡精8包，假冒双桥味精289包，假平坝窖酒10瓶，假冒万能胶30瓶，“三无”（无生产日期、无厂址、无生产厂名）香皂216块，过期饮料142瓶，过期食品158袋，过期月饼70公斤，劣质水果75公斤，土炮竹25团。

国家工商总局直销局副局长沈根申（中）和省市局领导莅县检查食品安全

2003—2004年，先后开展旅游景点安全、餐饮、美容美发、文化市场、传销、农资等检查26

次，出动检查人员1504人次，检查经营户4550户次，取缔兴红厂区传销窝点和传销据点14个，取缔无照经营户40户，遣散非法传销人员130人，没收传销有关资料200本及现金3万元，累计各项经济罚款46.09万元，为农民挽回经济损失3000元，当地农民赠送给工商局“消费者之保护神”锦旗1面。

2008年结合全国产生的“三鹿奶粉”事件，对全县723户食品经营户进行快速检测5000户次，集贸市场90个次，定点屠宰场50个次，取缔2户，查处制售假冒伪劣食品案41件，没收假冒伪劣食品6004公斤，罚没金额1712万元。

2009至2010年开展“无传销县”“扫黄打非”、销售地沟油及滥用食品添加剂等专项整治，与从事糕点、米面、油菜籽加工经营户签订《不滥添加非食用物质承诺书》140份，确立29家“食品安全示范店”，取缔黑网吧5户，没收电脑、显示器、键盘和鼠标38套，使市场秩序得以维护。

六、协会管理

（一）个体劳动者私营企业协会

1983年12月成立县个体劳动者联合会，选举产生常务委员16人，选出主任1人，副主任2人，秘书长1人，任期2年。1985年12月换届，并在城关镇及5个区设立分会，分会下设20个小组。全县会员共有2216人。

1986年12月将原个体劳动者联合会改称个体劳动者协会，委员会改称理事会，主任、副主任改称会长、副会长，废止原联合会章程，统一执行全国个体劳动者协会章程。1991年和1999年增加六桶分会和食肉行业分会，小组增到43个，会员2338人。

1991年5月3日，县私营企业协会成立，并在7个工商所辖区设分会。

2004年4月，同时召开个体劳动者协会第六届第二次理事会和私营企业协会第三届第二次理事会，决定将个体劳动者协会和私营企业协会合并为县个体劳动者私营企业协会，简称“个私协会”，选举产生理事会和会长、副会长、秘书长，下设5个分会，分会以下设小组。2010年，有分会4个，个体会员4304人，私营企业会员386个。协会实行自我教育、自我管理、自我服务，围绕协会章程开展活动。

文明诚信活动 1990年前，以小组为单位组织会员学习工商法律法规，开展遵纪守法教育和各种形式的“文明诚信促和谐”活动，把“爱国敬业、守法经营、诚信服务、奉献社会”落到实处。

1994年开展“消费者信得过企业、信得过摊位、信得过商店”活动。有3家荣获安顺地区“消费者信得过企业”、8家获县“消费者信得过企业”、41户获“文明个体工商户”、10人获县“十佳乡镇企业厂长（经理）”称号。

1996年开展“优质优惠”活动，全县420户个体工商业销售优质产品，优惠让利2.1万元。1997年开展“文明个体工商户”活动，1998年扎佐汽车修配厂陈志明发明汽车刹车专用控制品，试用电气控制刹车，专利成果价值500万元，获国家专利局实用新型专利证书和澳大利亚新世纪博览会金奖，并获得美国爱迪生发明中心、香港科学院荣誉发明评选委员会和中国发明城集团公司的国际金奖。个人分别荣获贵阳市、贵州省“十佳杰出青年”称号。2006—2010年，有210户次获“文明个体工商户”和28户私营企业被誉为“光彩之星”企业。有28户家电、建材、医药、百货、烟酒、超市和店铺，自己出资制作25幅布标悬挂，向消费者让利3.6万元，受到社会广泛称赞。

送温暖献爱心活动 继1990年久长镇个体工商户李光明5年为办学、办医院、助贫和亚运会等捐资8万元，受到国家个体劳动者协会和工商总局表彰后，1994年起个体工商户和私营企业通过协会组织、或自发捐助资助灾区失学儿童、学校、孤寡老人等，尽自己微薄之力，至2010年累计捐款21.3万元。其中

2008年5月四川省发生汶川大地震就捐出6.47万元，占30.38%。

（二）消费者协会

1989年12月成立，设会长1人，副会长2人，正、副秘书长各1人。各工商所辖区设7个分会，按行业或系统设9个监督站，对市场的商品和服务进行社会监督。为提高各分会和监督站人员政策水平和执法、用法能力，开办培训班2期14次，培训人员2210人次。至1994年受理投诉案件284件，涉及电器、钟表、服装、家具、建材、香烟、修理等，协商解决282件，为消费者挽回经济损失13.7万元。龙场镇白莲村岳玉贤用6万元在河南省太康县农机经营部购造纸机1台，4月安装完试机不到3小时烘缸机就开裂10厘米，协会现场调查属实，发函联系，获换新机1台。

1995年10月，县城待业青年刘建新用3.5万元在息烽县农机供应店购买1辆农用运输车，次年1月发现驾驶室与车厢结合部前后位置的左右侧断裂不能使用，协会派人依法与卖方力争，由卖方换上价值3000元的大梁，恢复正常使用。

1996年8月，龙场镇阳明村伍西华在贵阳市源声摩托车经营部购买洪都牌摩托车1辆，10月16日深夜停在家中无端起火烧毁，协会立即请公安、消防等单位到现场察看，再请专业人员检测，查准属于质量问题，经省消费者协会与卖方协商，赔偿伍西华2000元。从2004年至2010年，协会受理调解投诉案件270件，为消费者挽回经济损失29.11万元，上报贵阳市消费者协会典型案件7件，其中2件曾在《贵州日报》披露。

专记：不法商用“黑心秤”坑害农民遭处罚

2009年8月，该案系广东省商贩王林华自带磅秤和包装纸箱到龙场镇马口村收购西红柿，议定每公斤购价3元，收购第一天和第二天王在自带的秤上搞假，短斤少两遭农民质疑，第三天卖西红柿的农民聚集在收购点与王论理讨公平。为防止事态扩大，村“12315”农村维权联络站联络员即电话投诉请求援助处理，工商局城郊工商所执法人员立即赴村进行调查，发现王称西红柿使用的磅秤吊砣底部“增生”出一块吸附很隐匿的磁铁，若将磁铁取下每箱重量称出21.5公斤，加上磁铁称则为19.5公斤，一箱足足相差2公斤，与部分农民在家称过后再拿到该磅秤称的西红柿重量差数相符合，即每箱少付给农民6元，连续3天共收购286箱，总计少付1716元。执法人员现场公开揭露事实真相后，王无话可辩。

调查结束，执法人员根据《中华人民共和国消费者权益保护法》第四十九条规定和收购支付现金无详细记录，很难计算对个人赔偿的实际，就地组织购售双方当事人经过4个小时调解，最终达成一致意见：王向所有农户当面赔礼道歉，并按当天收购的60箱西红柿价值3870元，用现金1次赔偿给农户。

2009年8月城郊工商所现场查处使用黑心秤坑害农民

通过该案的曝光和处理，活生生的事实让群众感到国家《中华人民共和国消费者权益保护法》虽已执行多年，但少数经营者仍不顾国家法律的尊严，采用“黑心秤”短斤少两的手段进行欺诈获利，从而受到加倍补偿是“木匠戴枷，自作自受”。

第八节　质量技术监督管理

1979年，始置县标准计量管理所，1986年升格为计量局，1999年更名为质量技术监督局，依法行使标准化、计量、质量及特种设备安全监管职能。至2010年，全面完成市制计量器具单位改制，推行法定计量单位；统一组织机构代码标识；实行工业产品生产许可制度，推进县域经济稳定、健康发展。

一、标准化管理改革

（一）推行法定计量单位

1978至1983年使用市制计量单位。1984年改为统一实行法定计量单位。改革后，长度计量单位由市尺、公尺兼用统一为米（公尺），以下为分米、厘米、毫米，以十进位。公路里程以千米计。耕地面积因全县未经过丈量，仍沿用习惯亩，而征拨使用的土地则以丈量亩计算。境域面积以平方公里计。体积计量仍使用立方米不变。容量统一为升，升以下为分升、厘升，以十进位。液体零售用的量提由市斤改为公斤或毫升。质量和重量的计量统一为千克（公斤），千克以下类推为百克、十克、克，以十进位。1000公斤为1吨，农村家庭一般使用杆秤，集贸市场台秤、杆秤兼用，中药计量用戥子。矿产品和企业大型产品用地衡，以吨为单位，吨以下为公斤。石油加油站用加油机，以升计量。至2010年，全县16个加油站有加油机55台，加油枪98把，企业有地秤（地衡）80台。经批准制造杆秤的个体户仅有扎佐镇大园村的刘燕祥一户，产品均以公斤制秤。

（二）统一组织机构代码

1993年，县执行统一代码标识制度，凡批准成立的国家机关、事业单位、企业、社会团体、外省（市）驻县机构和其他依法成立的组织，一律办理代码登记，颁发代码证，代码证自发证之日起4年内有效，期限届满前30天办理换证手续，在有效期内由县质量技术监督局进行年检验证。2001年起实行统一网上赋码，县质量技术监督局自行制证。至2010年，全县组织机构代码仍存1560个。

二、计量管理

（一）计量器具

1979年，标准计量管理所始对县内衡器进行检测和管理。1986年8月根据国务院改革计量单位的要求，在供销合作系统推行市制计量单位改制，1987年投放市场合格公斤秤500把，到1990年基本普及法定计量单位。1992年6月开始对万江机电厂配3名计量检查员，委托对厂内贸易结算计量器具监督检查。

1998年，县城阳明综合市场设置的公平秤

1998年，为加强社会对计量器具监督，先后在人口较为集中和贸易往来多的龙场、扎佐两镇农贸

市场增设社会公用计量标准秤各1台。2002年，新增建筑材料检测项目，当年检定计量器具746件（次），覆盖率达95%。帮助8户企业完善计量检测体系及定量包装商品企业通过确认、评价的咨询服务。

2003年起对38台30吨以上的地衡每年检验1次，次年起对14个加油站使用的68支加油机实行每半年检定1次，经调试合格发给检定合格证。2008年9月至2010年，龙场镇和扎佐镇的政府所在地所有商店和主要集贸市场固定摊点禁止使用杆秤，免费检定龙场镇超市及农贸市场用计量器具654台（件、次），10乡（镇）14家医院用计量器具实行强制检测，经维修合格率达100%，检定加油机枪245把、电子汽车衡92台（次）全部合格。

（二）特种设备检测

1999年8月质量技术监督局接办劳动安全部门特种设备安全监督管理职能，增置特种设备安全监督科，行使对县内锅炉、压力容器、电梯、起重机械、客运索道、大型游乐设施及设计、生产、安装、维修、改造、使用的安全监管。2001年上半年对40台锅炉、11台压力容器和13套儿童游乐设施进行检查，达不到规范标准的作限期整改或停止使用，土锅炉一律取缔。

2002年进行普查登记，县内拥有锅炉67台，压力容器67台，压力管道3030米，其他特种置备29台，换发使用证57个，对锅炉实行定期检查。2004年建立特种设备安全档案，实行安全责任管理，对有安全隐患的37户下发《安全监察指令书》限期整改，有严重隐患的5户停业整顿，取缔自制锅炉（土锅炉）2台。2009—2010年，重点对17户耗能企业的能源计量器（水表、电表、电子汽车衡）进行监控，检定周期合法有效，计量数据准确。累计检查使用特种设备单位140户次，特种设备381台次，压力管道2127米。对5户未按时完成整改的作立案调查处理。

（三）集贸市场治理

1988年全面推行法定计量单位后，县计量部门采取定期或不定期对市场计量器具检查检测。1993年，检查发现县城市场定量包装食品重量不足，水果摊贩短斤少两问题严重，计量器具90%不合格。关岭县花江人在县城开的3家狗肉馆每公斤短少0.4公斤，人称“狗八两”；上市烟花爆竹无燃放说明和厂址厂名，火炮500响的实有420响或460响，1000响的实有870响至890响，并存在燃放不安全问题。计量部门对不符合标签通用标准的食品限期整改，停止销售，对短斤少两包装的食品责令降价销售，将1500多公斤问题食品全部没收销毁。2001年校检生产企业和经营摊点天平28台、地衡20台、案秤150台，对不合格的进行处理。2008年县质量技术监督局与食品生产企业签订《食品安全承诺书》《食品生产企业质量安全目标管理责任书》，开展食品生产非法添加非食用物质和滥用食品添加剂及桶装饮用水专项整治，加大对食品生产企业日常监管，从源头重点打击和防范危害人民群众生命健康安全的制假行为。到2010年，县内11户生产企业未发生过制假行为。

计量管理所人员检查集贸市场计量器具

三、标准化管理

（一）产品标准登记备案

1978至1987年，县内地方工业生产的白酒、酱油、水泥、皮鞋等产品是按照国家规定的产品标准进行生产的。1988年12月，颁布《中华人民共和国标准化法》，企业生产的产品标准执行国家标准、行业标准、地方标准、企业标准4种，县质量技术监督局对国家标准、行业标准、地方标准实行标准登记。企业标准由企业先报文字材料，质量技术监督局组织专家审查后登记备案。质量标准有效期为3年。质量技术监督局登记的有农业产品标准、旅游产品标准等，以县为标准化示范区，谷堡乡折溪村为标准化示范点，2002年至2010年企业报送备案的《贵州省企业产品执行标准登记证书》累计有188本，其中国家标准117本、企业标准71本。

（二）消灭无标准生产县

2000年，贵州省将修文县列为消灭无标准生产县之一，县政府制发《消灭无标准生产工作实施方案》。举办3期企业厂长（经理）和企业管理人员标准化培训班，78个企业105人参训，经考试合格。11月通过省级验收，认定全县114个工业企业的140个生产产品进入标准化，使产品的标准覆盖率由23.57%提高到100%。共备案登记标准140个，其中执行国家标准79个，行业标准12个，企业标准49个。抽查产品89批次，合格率为75.28%，达到消灭无标准生产县的标准，由省质量技术监督局颁发验收合格证书。

2002年，县质量技术监督局对消灭无标准生产的93家企业71个产品以及201个标准（执行国家标准86个，企业标准91个，行业标准16个，企业标准备案8个）进行复查，产品标准覆盖率达到98%，使企业经营的标准意识得到增强。

四、质量管理

（一）工业产品核发生产许可证

2002年起，县始对境内工业企业产品实行市场准入和开业审查制度，对准入产品核发国家生产许可证，建立企业质量档案。至2008年获准生产并建立质量档案的有久长建材、利尔建材和德荣、南方、鸿鑫、奇峰工贸，建源、三角山、宏华、金星、荣利、渝鑫水泥制造，宇丰燃料和国康水泥厂生产的普通硅酸盐水泥，金旺达和华祥矿产的磷肥，富捷化工的工业黄磷，华宏冶炼公司的碳化钙，天龙摩擦材料公司的摩擦材料，东方希望动物营养公司的饲料等获得县质量技术监督局颁发的生产许可证。扎佐神力面粉厂的小麦粉、联宇食品公司的酱油、“好1多”乳业的饮料和液体乳、新泉的瓶（桶）装饮用水、康雅轩公司的食糖、领先食品公司的罐头、龙场镇山野人家饼屋的糕点、扎佐镇调味品厂的酱油获贵阳市食品生产许可证。阳明实业有限公司的白酒产品虽获生产许可证，但没有产品投放市场。

城郊工商所对食品进行检测

2009至2010年，贵州“好1多”乳业的蛋白饮料、贵阳新泉公司的瓶（桶）装饮用水、贵州三金圣果公司的饮料、贵州金久水泥有限公司的水泥获国家质监总局生产许可证书。扎佐镇调味品厂的酱油、久长镇隆华食品厂的糕点、扎佐惠子郎食品厂的果冻、龙场镇春燕糕点厂的月饼获省质监局生产许可证。

（二）质量监督检查

1986年标准计量局开展产品质量监督检查，至1990年县五金公司销售“日芝”牌劣质电冰箱、水电安装队经营存在问题电器产品和县内生产的胶粘皮鞋被查处，1993年检查涉农产品，参观谷堡乡境内销售假化肥，县科技市场和马关、阳早、扎佐等地经销无证种子，马家桥有不符合国家标准的农用塑料膜均被处理。县科技市场销售的杂交玉米“辽原一号”发芽率仅为21.5%。1994年抽查水泥生产企业，全县9个水泥厂的产品全部合格的仅一家，其中的扎佐水泥厂、复退残水泥厂和成志水泥厂为无证生产，被责令补办生产许可证和经济罚款。

1999年，对县城21家个体汽车零件经营户检查，有13家存在质量问题，其中9家作罚款和没收处理。2002年抽查经营户1088户次，建材产品合格率达83.33%；食品合格率达90%；农产品合格率60%；其他商品合格率为83.33%，给县质监局抽检不合格7家企业下发整改通知，对当年复查合格3家恢复经营。2004年按照国家标准建立78家企业产品质量档案。

2006年起，将食品作为重点抽检商品，对食品生产企业模底登记，签订《食品质量安全打假责任书》和《食品质量安全承诺书》，建立台账和档案，聘请食品质量协管员和信息员进行管理，质量技术监督局不定期巡查、回访。2008年不合格“竹园”牌桶装水和国内“三鹿奶粉”事件发生，质量执法人员对县内11个送水站和1个饮用水生产企业逐一检查，抽样不合格2家供水站被立案查处。派出5名监管人员进驻贵州“好1多”乳业股份有限公司进行全过程质量监管，检查销售企业原奶215批次，成品1010批次，合格率100%。

“三鹿奶粉事件”发生后县质监进驻“好1多”乳业监管

2010年开展“质量提升年”活动，检查53家预应力混凝土空心板生产企业51个产品，合格率仅占41.18%。针对发现的问题，质量技术监督局帮助企业规范质量标准，提高产品质量，完成产品检验191个批次，合格率上升到77.49%。

专记：质监局进驻“好1多”确保乳制品质量安全

2008年发生“三鹿奶粉事件”后，全国开展乳制品专项整治活动，县质量技术监督局遵照国家质检总局统一部署，于9月17日派出5人进驻贵州“好1多”乳业股份有限公司进行乳制品质量监管。入驻当天召开监管工作部署会，传达对驻厂监管工作的要求和进厂后的工作安排。18日再次开会明确监管工作的职责。21日对全体员工进行食品质量安全知识和职业道德培训。在增强质量安全意识的基础上，从原料进厂验收、生产过程控制、成品出厂检验等环节实行24小时全程监控，还帮助企业建立原材料和半成品进厂检验制度、生产过程质量责任制度、出厂产品检验制度，不能自检的三聚氰胺，均与有条件的检测机构建立固定委托检验关系，要求企业在获得QS证（含生产许可证）后，每批原料奶检验合格才能投入生产；成品奶经企业自检和法定机构检验合格方能出厂销售，做到监管措施到位，服务工作到位。对公司存在的生产设备消毒记录不全、非生产工人随意进出生产车间、生产工人进车间未洗手和消毒等不规范问题，责令企业限期整改，确保产品合格和安全。至次年2月，累计检验原料奶690批（次）共3553吨，乳制品产成品液态奶3515批（次）共3354吨，合格率均达100%，确保乳制品质量安全。当广大市民目睹质监部门认真履职，确保乳制品质量安全后深为感动，普遍反映："我们能够喝到放心奶，首先应当感谢的是质监局和职工。"

（三）打假治劣

1978—1988年，伪劣商品由工商部门查处。1989年4月27日，县成立打击经销伪劣商品办公室于质量技术监督局。至1990年，先后查获假茅台酒50件，标值10.8万元。1993年对全县调味品市场进行整顿，对糕点糖果生产企业监督检查，销毁伪劣酱油3000公斤。

1999年起，加大对生产、销售假冒伪劣商品的打击力度，先后开展"查市场，保两节（元旦和春节）""查农资，保春耕""查建材，保建设"和百日打假活动，检查重点系商品质量。至2002年共检查生产企业和销售商4326户，查出521户生产或销售劣质商品，标值216.6万元，立案调查202件，受理群众投诉43件，处理508户，经济罚款7.6万元，捣毁生产或销售劣质商品窝点30个，查封和取缔27户，销毁标值4万元的假冒伪劣商品。

工商执法人员销毁假冒伪劣商品

2004年，先后捣毁久长镇金源铁合金厂和龙场镇王家湾铸件厂生产、销售国家禁止的地条钢窝点，没收地条钢11.9吨，罚款1.9万元。

2006年起，以食品质量作为打假制劣的重点，3年查处生产加工伪劣食品商11户，捣毁制售黑窝点2个，查处伪劣食品案值5000元。

2008年4月7日，工商部门开展食品安全专项检查，发现4户个体经营者从贵阳市购进不合格泡椒鸡爪在县城销售。经过专项检查人员快速检测和贵阳市疾病预防控制中心检测为不合格产品，当即查处并销毁。

执法人员监督销毁劣质泡椒鸡爪

2009—2010年，先后开展桶装饮用水、农业生产资料、建筑及装饰材料、家电下乡产品、絮用纤维制品、机动车辆、起重机械及食品质量专项整治，办理行政案件47件，涉案货值23万元，没收和罚款10.39万元，为企业和消费者挽回经济损失

14万元，使消费者的合法权益得以维护。

专记：惩处违法经营商品　教育广大工商户

2008年4月7日，工商部门开展食品安全专项检查，发现4户个体经营者在贵阳市威西门市场购进不合格泡椒鸡爪在县城销售，共计数量181.5公斤，每公斤进价17元。运回后分别在龙场镇阳明综合市场6个摊点以每公斤18元或19元价格销售，至检查发现时已售出12.2公斤，获违法所得227元。经过专项检查人员快速检测和贵阳市疾病预防控制中心检测结果，此泡椒鸡爪甲醛含量每公斤达20mg，为不合格产品，产品货值金额共计3337元。

14日，工商行政管理局完成调查取证后，向当事人下发《行政处罚告知书》，当事人未在法定期限内提出陈述、申辩。18日根据《中华人民共和国产品质量法》第三十九条、第五十条规定当事人在从事食品经营中，未按照规定认真检查所销售的食品质量是否合格，未严格履行当事人与工商行政管理局签订的《食品安全责任书》所要求食品质量自查制度，所销售过期食品给人民群众身体健康造成一定危害，应依法惩处。分别下达第46号、第47号、第48号、第49号《行政处罚决定书》，责令停止销售，没收违法销售不合格泡椒鸡爪169.3公斤和违法销售所得227元，对当事人处以罚款4773元。

一次惩戒4户食品经营者销售不合格泡椒鸡爪的违法行为现场教育一批工商户，大家纷纷表示：要以诚信经营，以道德立身，决不去做丧失天理良心的买卖。

第九节　土地管理

1978年，土地沿袭国家和集体所有，使用土地实行无偿划拨和有偿使用的制度。1987年《中华人民共和国土地管理法》颁布实施，土地管理局代表政府对土地使用实行统一征拨、有偿出让，对违法占地者依法清查处理。1992年改革土地管理制度，开始挂牌拍卖土地，实行土地使用限期制。

2001年，为满足城镇建设用地，县政府对土地实行收购储备，土地使用通过招标拍卖、挂牌出让方式确定。到2010年的23年，全县办理土地统征265宗，征拨面积1.4万亩，其中耕地0.95万亩，占67.48%。

一、土地使用制度

（一）计划管理制

1978年，土地管理沿袭原先的政府分级管理制，即土地使用未纳入国民经济计划范畴，也未办理土地使用证。1987年非农业建设用地开始纳入国民经济和社会发展计划，实行指令性计划管理，连续4年全县共批准非农业建设用地560亩，占安顺地区下达用地计划指标2160亩的25.93%。

1988年3月，贯彻执行贵州省《土地管理实施办法》，改过去分散、多头管理为在政府领导下实行行政、经济、法律的集中统一管理。县政府审批用地权限仅限耕地3亩以下，或1个建设项目征用耕地或其他土地10亩以下。同时始办城镇宅基地审批和国有土地使用申报。1989年又增办乡村宅基地审批，次年

填发城镇国有土地使用证。到1990年全县完成申报3948宗，占应申报宗地4427宗的89.18%。

进入20世纪90年代，实行城镇住房制度改革，导致土地开发热且逐渐升温。为严格控制建设用地管理，县土地管理局遵循“一保吃饭，二保建设”的方针，采取用地与节地相结合，按照“三个坚持”（坚持计划管理，坚持宏观调控，坚持“一支笔批地”）的原则，切实做到立项前参与、实施中核定、手续齐审批，把建设用地纳入法制化管理。至1997年，5年全县共审核报批国家、集体和个人建设用地1018宗，面积699.11亩，其中国家用地81宗426.73亩，集体用地27宗162.97亩，个人用地910宗109.41亩，均未突破地区（市）下达的计划指标，使建设用地管理宏观调控初见成效。

1998年，建设用地改为预报、预审管理，每年先预报下年用地计划，保障建设用地所需。1999年1月实行新修订的《中华人民共和国土地管理法》，按照“十分珍惜和合理利用土地，切实保护耕地”的基本国策，实行占用耕地与开发复垦挂钩。6月，县国土局和县农办作为甲方，与县城市建设指挥部（乙方）签订《耕地开垦协议》，由乙方按照县政府当年造地计划实施开垦造地521.97亩，使供给引导和制约需求统筹兼顾，实现耕地利用占补平衡。

2007年，为解决县内土地使用多，于本县开发、整理增加耕地弥补不足的问题，耕地占补平衡扩展到异地开展，由使用土地单位申请和投资，经县国土资源局报省、市主管部门批准，再由县的经办单位在异地（仅限本省内）购买新增耕地指标予以弥补。至2010年，4年累计投资8900万元，先后在开阳县、印江县、玉屏县、石阡县购买增加耕地指标6720.14亩，县内自行开发2408.48亩，实现耕地总量动态平衡。

（二）有偿使用制

1978年，土地市场尚不完善，仅对铁路建设以外的其他建设用地占用耕地实行有偿使用，由征用方按照被征地前三年常年产量计算补偿费补偿给耕地被占用单位，补偿标准由政府制定。

1982年5月，县政府根据国务院颁发《国家建设征用土地条例》规定，征用土地应当由用地单位支付补偿费（包括土地、青苗、附着物补偿费和安置补助费）和1984年根据贵州省政府以黔府〔1984〕46号文件规定补偿标准，结合县内的统计年报数，以及农业技术推广典型试点产量和不同地区复种产量分析，拟定征用土地的补偿费实行包干补偿，并以被征地的年产值和补偿倍数计算，耕地每亩平均年产值最高为上等蔬菜地1000至1380元，最低为下等旱地232至348元，土地补偿费为蔬菜地、稻田上、中、下3个等级分别按六、五、四倍补偿；旱地、园地上、中、下3个等级分别按五、四、三倍补偿；青苗补偿按年产值1倍补偿；安置补助费蔬菜地按8至10倍补助，稻田按7至9倍补助，旱地、园地按6至8倍补助。到1988年县档案局办公楼和1994年县城建私营经济一条街建设，均征用城南和城北村蔬菜地和稻田，以该耕地被征用前3年平均亩产值1000元为基数计算，补偿青苗费为1倍，土地补偿费为6倍，安置补助费为10倍，3项补偿费共计17倍，合人民币1.7万元，双方表示接受。

1996年1月，修文县划属贵阳市管辖，7月贵阳市土地管理局与市物价局、市粮食局、市蔬菜工作办公室联合下发筑土字〔1996〕41号文件，调整五区一镇（云岩区、南明区、花溪区、乌当区、白云区和小河镇）征地年产值计算标准，明确自8月1日起修文县、开阳县、息烽县依照此计算标准下调30%执行。2002年6月26日和2009年12月31日，贵阳市人民政府又先后下发筑府通〔2002〕52号和筑府发（2009）100号文件调整征地年产值计算标准，由一个县一个标准改为按征地区片价补偿标准，致补偿费逐步提高。同时，为解决县城及乡（镇）建设资金，自1991—2010年县内小城镇建设用地，也采取市场调节价出让，就2007至2010年政府收购储备土地通过挂牌出让，每亩平均出让价达到14万元以上，相当于政府制定价的3倍多。

1996—2009年征地年产值计算标准统计表

表3—10—15　　　　单位：元/亩

开始执行时间	文件字号	菜地			稻田			旱地		
		上等	中等	下等	上等	中等	下等	上等	中等	下等
1996.8.1	筑土字（1996）41号	—	—	—	793.45	630.35	467.25	531.65	405.65	279.65
2002.7.1	筑府通（2002）52号	2710.00	2038.00	1533.00	1067.00	843.00	657.00	714.00	565.00	369.00

2010年征地年产值补偿标准及征地养老补助标准统计表

表3—10—16

区域范围	统一年产值标准（元/亩）	征地类型	合计（倍）	土地补偿（倍）	安置补偿（倍）	综合补偿标准（元/亩）	社保资金标准（元/亩）
龙场镇 扎佐镇	1500	耕　地	24	10	14	36000	12000
	1500	建设用地	7	4	3	10500	4800
	1500	林　地	10	7	3	15000	4800
	1500	牧草地	8	5	3	12000	4800
	1500	其他农用地	8	5	3	12000	4800
	1500	未利用地	4	4	0	6000	4800
	1500	园　地	10	7	3	15000	4800
久长镇 六广镇 谷堡乡	1500	耕　地	22	10	12	33000	10000
	1500	建设用地	7	4	3	10500	4000
	1500	林　地	10	7	3	15000	4000
	1500	牧草地	8	5	3	12000	4000
	1500	其他农用地	8	5	3	12000	4000
	1500	未利用地	4	4	0	6000	4000
	1500	园　地	10	7	3	15000	4000
六屯乡 小箐乡 洒坪乡 大石乡 六桶乡	1500	耕　地	20	10	10	30000	8000
	1500	建设用地	7	4	3	10500	3200
	1500	林　地	10	7	3	15000	3200
	1500	牧草地	8	5	3	12000	3200
	1500	其他农用地	8	5	3	12000	3200
	1500	未利用地	4	4	0	6000	3200
	1500	园　地	10	7	3	15000	3200

注：土地补偿、安置补偿按统一年产值标准计算

（三）土地使用限期制

1990年5月，贯彻执行《中华人民共和国城镇国有土地使用权出让暂行条例》，始对土地使用实行限期制，按其土地使用权出让和转让用途确定使用年限为：商业服务用地（包括商贸、旅游、餐饮、娱乐等业）40年，社会事业用地（包括工矿企业、教育、科技、文化、卫生、体育等业）50年，住宅用地70年。到2010年，土地使用限期的制度未变。

二、土地市场

从1978年起，县境开辟土地市场，其中有政府经营的一级市场和城市建设指挥部经营的二级市场。

（一）土地一级市场

土地统征　1978年，实施土地统征制度，经用地单位向土地管理部门申请批准，由规划部门选址测绘，再由征用方和被征用方签署《征地协议书》，按照统征价格出让，付清补偿款项，土地买卖手续即成交完结。至1983年，全县补办土地统征手续3宗，面积102.09亩，其中耕地8.14亩，荒山93.95亩；承办征地报批手续11宗，面积7136.86亩，其中耕地1261.96亩，荒山5874.9亩。

1986年10月设置县土地管理局，为县政府办事机构，专司土地管理，承办土地统征、出让、划拨等事宜，将城镇和农村居民宅基地纳入土地市场管理范围。到1991年全县累计统征出让土地70宗，面积374.46亩，其中耕地237.58亩，占63.45%。

1992年8月，县政府遵照贵州省土地管理局转发国家土地管理局《关于进一步加快土地使用制度改革的通知》要求，提出“对新区开发要推广统一规划、统一征用、统一开发、统一出让、统一管理”，“土地部门要代表政府高度垄断土地一级市场，二、三级以下市场由政府宏观调控，充分搞活”。自1994年起，县土地管理局陆续将县城和扎佐镇、久长镇、六屯乡、六桶乡的小城镇建设用地先征为国有，然后再出让或划拨。到2000年，累计统征出让土地142宗，面积6853.08亩，其中耕地4886.59亩，占71.31%。

2001年8月，按照贵阳市人民政府制发筑府发〔2001〕38号文件精神，允许“实行土地收购储备，建立政府收购—储备—出让土地的运作方式和土地供应制度”。从2006年起始办土地收购储备，即由政府先将待开发地进行统征，然后通过挂牌出让或划拨方式出让。到2010年，累计全县统征土地53宗，面积6769.89亩，其中耕地4321.36亩，占63.83%。除统征和划拨出让部分土地外，其余均按照政府规定价格计算补偿费。至2010年，全县挂牌出让土地30宗，面积1529.2亩，收入2.21亿元，亩均出让价14.43万元，从而促进县域经济快速发展。

非耕地拍卖　1994年，根据中共贵州省委2月农村工作会议“要把开展非耕地资源作为振兴农村经济的新增长点”的要求和“可以有组织地拍卖非耕地使用权”的精神，县土地管理局借鉴遵义地区拍卖非耕地使用权的经验，于8月启动在久长镇芦山村和9月在谷堡乡政府召开两次拍卖非耕地使用权现场会，引导村的集体土地进入市场，从而促使全县乃至安顺地区非耕地拍卖工作的开展。到年底全县共拍卖非耕地使用权80宗，面积1.17万亩，拍卖总金额28.84万元，每亩平均卖价24.82元。到2004年，全县拍卖非耕地增到174宗，面积1.83万亩，拍卖金额52.36万元，每亩均价26.68元，亩卖价最高1041.67元，最低10.47元。拍卖现场颁证兑现，做到土地权属明确，地块界定清楚，协议图件齐全，既维护法律的尊严，又保护土地使用者的合法权益。与此同时，全县还拍卖公房23宗，用地面积1.5亩，拍卖金额48.8万元。

专记：芦山村非耕地拍卖成功举办

1994年8月23日，县土地管理局按照贵州省农村工作会议精神，在久长镇芦山村成功举办首场非耕地使用权拍卖现场会。拍卖现场会在芦山小学举行，参加单位有县土地管理局、县林业局，县农业开发办公室、县区划办公室。现场会由久长镇非耕地使用权拍卖领导小组组长石光亮主持，县司法局公证处杨忠兴、李登义、姚学文对拍卖活动现场监督公证。现场会还邀请安顺地区和县级领导班子有关领导莅会指导，各乡（镇）分管土地管理的领导也到会观察。拍卖活动开始前，先由公证人员对卖方芦山村村委会和竞买方梅锦玉、刘志等10人的身份进行验证，然后由县土地管理局局长雷华熙宣读《县拍卖非耕地使用权规定》和交代非耕地拍卖的有关事项，接着宣布拍卖荒山的名称、坐落地点、面积、使用期限。竞买鸣锣开始，每宗地都经过激烈竞争，最后一锤定音确定买主。拍卖非耕地21宗，面积1129.5亩。每亩卖价最低45元，最高145元。当即由公证员进行公正，现场颁发使用证书。为修文县和安顺地区非耕地的管理和使用历史揭开新的篇章。

现场拍卖活动自始至终依照法律程序进行。通过拍卖，使人民群众的土地法律观念得到提高，成交者一致认为现场拍卖公开、公正、合理；参加竞买但未竞拍到的竞买人也感到现场拍卖竞争公平，心服口服。

（二）二级市场

县城东片区土地拍卖 1988年，县政府规划拓展县城扩建东片区，11月获省政府黔府通228号文件批准，征用城关镇城南村第五组和第七组菜地12.7亩。先将原健康路（今翠屏西路）延伸段建成农贸综合市场，街道两侧商贸用地由城市建设综合开发指挥部以一宗门面为出让单位协议出让土地使用权，每平方米置换价120至150元。

1993年，县政府根据贵州省土地管理局〔1992〕黔土办字14号文件“积极创造条件培育地产市场，促进经济发展和政府垄断一级市场，开放二、三级市场”精神，将拟开发的迎春路私营经济一条街两侧的商贸用地纳入土地二级市场出让土地使用权。1994年12月在未获批准的情况下先与城南、城北两村签订《征地协议》，征拨用地113.12亩，由城建指挥部以一宗门面为出让单位协议出让。1995年4月发布通告面向社会公开拍卖，迎春路中段起始价每平方米150元，经过公开竞价，东侧最高出售价达到每平方米290元，西侧中段则涨到400至450元，到4月15日公开拍卖8宗。19日又协议出让3宗，每平方米400元。南北两段因地块位置次于中段，价格差异较大。1997年3月至5月出让16宗，每平方米协议价为90至483元。1998年1月县国土局才作为出让方（甲方），县城建指挥部作为受让方（乙方），签订《城镇国有土地使用出让转让合同》，将坐落于城南、城北村的地块88.38亩出让给乙方开发，乙方按合同规定向甲方一次交付土地使用权出让金1064.99万元，使用期限50年（1995年3月15日至2045年3月15日），出让金由乙方全部付清。

1998年，随着县体育馆的兴建，县城由原中医院往东扩大到河边，称为东片区建设，2000年贵州省政府以黔府函205号文批准征地77.82亩，各路段商贸用地均由城建指挥部采取协议出让和公开拍卖方式出让土地使用权。其中各路段每平方米出让价为：良知路110至380元，文成路120至800元，龙山路330至500元，河滨路中段最高价720元，优惠10%后为648元，最低480元，翠屏东路及其余地段价位最低，多以每平方米120至150元出让。至2010年，东片区全部建成投入使用。

阳明大道土地拍卖 1999年，县委、县政府议决兴建贵（阳）毕（节）公路修文出口至县城曲尺桥

的阳明大道。2001年3月按照县政府规划，阳明大道自曲尺桥至进阳明洞分路的两侧为商贸用地，推出一期国有土地向社会公开出让。经过1个月准备，在农业银行县支行五楼会议室召开拍卖会进行拍卖。2002年3月，对2001年出让给利尔公司阳明大道北侧土地，经国土局3次催交出让地价款无果，遂报县政府同意收回重新拍卖，将底价提高到每平方米650元分段拍卖。先推出电信局用房第一宗地块，以每平方米930元成交，第二宗地居曲尺桥道路交叉口段，以每平方米1460元出让，成为当时土地出让启动的最高价。到2002年6月，阳明大道两侧国有土地使用权共出让108宗，面积63.73亩，其中公开拍卖方式出让95宗，面积26.17亩，金额1457.76万元，亩均价55.7万元；协议出让13宗，面积37.56亩，金额864.53万元，亩均价23.02万元，为财政增收2322.29万元。

拍卖阳明大道北侧土地过程中，由于阳明村有的村民提出拆迁安置补偿价低和要求在规划红线内修建住房，引发出政府与村民之间的矛盾，导致突发2002年为首者煽动村民打砸县政府和县人民法院的“七四”事件，4名犯罪分子分别获有期徒刑2至7年。

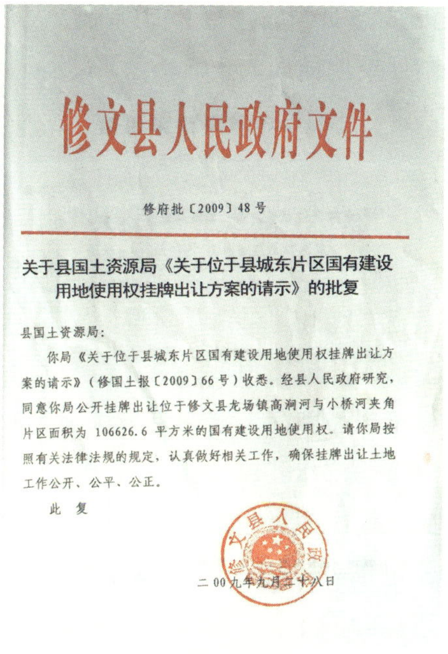

修文县人民政府文件

修府批〔2009〕48号

关于县国土资源局《关于位于县城东片区国有建设用地使用权挂牌出让方案的请示》的批复

县国土资源局：

你局《关于位于县城东片区国有建设用地使用权挂牌出让方案的请示》（修国土报〔2009〕66号）收悉。经县人民政府研究，同意你局公开挂牌出让位于修文县龙场镇高涧河与小桥河夹角片区面积为106626.6平方米的国有建设用地使用权。请你局按照有关法律法规的规定，认真做好相关工作，确保挂牌出让土地工作公开、公平、公正。

此复

二00九年九月二十八日

东片区出让批复

专记：征地拆迁中发生在阳明村的“七四”事件

阳明大道系拓展县城的重点工程，建设这条贯通龙场镇阳明村与贵（阳）毕（节）高等级公路相连接的大道，是2000年4月29日贵州省政府以黔府〔2000〕296号函批准的项目，征拨土地544.007亩，涉及龙场镇阳明、新生、幸福、城北4个村，县政府对村民拆迁安置补偿等问题曾作出规定，但有的村民认为“补偿价太低”，其中阳明村有的村民要求“在规划红线内修建房屋”。因未达目的，拒不拆迁，多次围攻工程指挥部迫使停工。

2002年3月，县建设局下达行政裁定书，要求村民们履行拆迁义务。因村民拒绝拆迁，县建设局又于7月2日向县人民法院申请，法院审查认定“拆迁合法”，作出准予强制执行的裁定。

4日下午，龙场镇镇长金松和综治办主任舒涛，与县人民法院干警去到阳明村送达行政裁定书。开始张贴公告时，即遭到村民围攻，情急之中，有一名干警鸣枪示警，不慎误伤3个村民。村民石永禄、贺从华将来不及离开现场的金松和舒涛抓住，并进行殴打、谩骂。为首的杜启文便对村民们称：“拆迁是由县政府作出的，要找就找县长。”并扬言“打倒娃儿大人就会出来”。

在杜启文的鼓动之下，石永禄、贺从华等人将金松和舒涛双手反扭，押着上街并分别押往县政府，要求县长出面解决。一行众人到县政府，未见着县长，即对县政府大楼办公室进行打砸抢，将20多间办公室门窗砸碎和办公设备砸毁，经济损失10余万元还不解恨，又冲向法院，一边用石头砸毁办公楼，一边进办公楼砸抢，导致法院办公设备被毁，3辆办公用车被砸，法院卷宗、档案及文件资料损毁或丢失，使机关工作一度瘫痪，接着又将金松和舒涛押回村里作人质。

事件发生前，杜启文曾多次裹挟村民“要顶住”，并鼓动大家“把石头搬到房子上”，只要政府敢来强迁，就用石头和狼牙棒（钉子钉在木头上的木棒）对付他们。杜启文等如此置法纪于不顾，主要是要挟政府提高拆迁补偿费，达到自己的利益诉求。

“七四”事件发生后，公安机关当即立案侦查，对为首者实行拘捕。经息烽县人民法院审理，于是年12月25日当庭宣布一审判决：认定杜启文、贺从华的行为构成聚众冲击国家机关罪和非法拘禁罪，分别判处有期徒刑7年和4年；认定石仕菊参与打砸政府行为构成聚众冲击国家机关罪，判处有期徒刑4年；认定石永禄参与押送执法人员行为构成非法拘禁罪，判处有期徒刑2年。

扎佐联络线主营线土地出让 1995年，贵（阳）遵（义）高速公路扎佐联络主线（今“襄阳大道”）开建，由县贵遵公路工程建设指挥部先将坐落于扎佐镇和平、中营、大园、桥头、喻家街等村境内需新建公路两旁地块，以150至220元/平方米价协议出让或转让，到1998年11月26日才由县国土局作为出让方，与受让方贵遵高速公路开发总公司修文有限公司签订《城乡国有土地使用权出让转让合同书》，共出让土地使用权面积371.28亩，出让金额1856.4万元，亩均出让价5万元，高于向农民征用土地价。出让金按县政府安排用于主营线区域内市政设施建设。

扎佐联络线主营线

（三）基准地价

1998年，为配合土地市场运作，县土地管理局委托贵阳市土地估价事务所承担和县土管局参与组成课题组在龙场镇试点。根据县城规划和土地定级规程，采取收益还原法和成本逼近法测算和推算出商业、工业和住宅地价价位，从而建立龙场镇城区基准地价体系，分为三类四级，于11月完成龙场镇土地分等定级、基准地价工作。

2000年，着手小城镇开发试点——久长镇地价评估工作。县政府成立土地基准地价评估领导小组，国土局拟定《久长镇土地基准地价测算工作方案》，经贵阳天辰房地产评估事务有限公司论证、测算，确定基准地价分别为三类三级，在久长镇土地开发中实施。同时，严格按照国家土地管理局《城市土地估价规程》，对县城阳明大道曲尺桥段两侧用地地价进行测算，认定其土地价格为每平方米466元。

继后，因财政经费紧张，其他乡镇建立基准地价工作尚未开展，仅参照执行，到2010年未变动。

龙场镇、久长镇城区基准地价一览表

表3—10—17　　单位：元/平方米

镇别	类别	用途	I级	II级	III级	IV级
龙场镇	一	商业用地	785	470	270	160
	二	住宅用地	280	250	200	155
	三	工业用宅	240	210	180	150
久长镇	一	商业用地	560	410	170	—
	二	住宅用地	260	200	150	—
	三	工业用宅	220	180	140	—

三、土地执法监察

（一）建立执法监察网络

1986年县土地管理局未建执法监察机构，清理乱占耕地由县成立领导小组承担。1992年5月构建村级土地监察网，全县217个行政村各聘请1名监察员，加上居民委员会聘请的监察员，全县共有土地监察员224名，经培训后按照岗位目标职责实行违法监督。11月，经安顺地区中级人民法院安中法政字（1992）27号文件批准，建立县人民法院驻土地管理局执行室。

1996年下半年，由贵州省国土厅统一向国家土地管理局申报领取并组织发放土地《监察证》，按省国土厅黔国土法监（1996）1号文件规定，颁发《监察证》给各级政府主要领导和主管国土工作的领导，各级国土部门领导和各处（科）负责人，土地监察专职干部以及乡（镇）街道办事处国土管理所负责人。

2002年8月，县国土资源管理局组建执法监察大队，单列编制8人，属参照试行国家公务员制度范围，专门行使执法工作，至2010年，执法监察大队仍存。

（二）坚持全民国土观念教育

1987年，《中华人民共和国土地管理法》颁布实施，县土地管理局组装宣传车，在全县5区1镇以及区辖的28个乡（镇）、厂矿、部队进行宣传，将《土地管理法》印制成册发到区、乡、村及各部门，并利用有线广播播放土地法问题解释及典型案例，经检查验收有80%以上干部群众知道土地管理有法规。

1991年“二五”普法教育第一年，国务院第八十三次常务会议作出决定，每年6月25日为全国“土地日”。县土地管理部门借庆祝第一个土地日之机，组织16人，出动宣传车3辆，在全县掀起以宣传土地国情、国策、国法为中心的全民国土观念教育宣传月活动。通过土地管理法律法规及典型案例的宣传教育，增强广大干部群众“五个观念”，即人多地少，耕地资源不足的国情观念，依法管好用好土地的守法观念，土地公有制和有偿使用观念，土地管理在国民经济建设中的地位观念，违法占地要受法律制裁的法制观念，让85%以上的干部群众再次受到土地管理法规教育。

1993至1997年的全国“土地日”县政府均举行大的宣传活动，运用传媒、司法、专题新闻、书画展等方式进行宣传，出动宣传车24台次，发放宣传资料51万份，宣传期间分管土地管理的副县长发表电视讲话，强调加强土地管理的重要性和必要性，特别是《土地管理法》颁布10周年的1997年纪念日，召开县四大班子主要领导参加的座谈会。通过学习国务院总理李鹏《保护耕地就是保护我们的生命线》的电视讲话，并把讲话精神落实到业务工作中去。

2000年，抓住“十分珍惜，合理利用土地和切实保护耕地”的基本国策，按照中央召开的人口、资源、环境工作座谈会提出的国土资源的保护和管理“必须严而又严”，坚持“在保护中开发，在开发中保护”，实现“资源开发和节约并举，把节约放在首位，努力提高资源利用效率”的总方针开展宣传，把各种思想统一到法律法规上来，转变全社会用地、管地观念，形成珍惜土地、保护耕地的良

1991年起国土部门每年开展一次“6·25”大型宣传活动

好氛围。

2001至2010年，利用每年“4·22”地球日、“6·25”全国土地日和“12·4”法制日，采取赶场天设立宣传咨询点、悬挂横幅、书写张贴标语、电视广播、流动宣传等方式，宣传有关土地管理的法律法规，让“节约集约用地，坚守耕地红线”的主题贯彻到县、乡（镇）、村，不断增强社会对保护国土资源可持续发展的意识，合理使用土地，积极保护耕地。

（三）依法查处违法占地

20世纪80年代，随着农民生活提高，乱占耕地建房和租赁、买卖土地时有发生。1986年县政府遵照中共中央、国务院《关于加强土地管理、制止乱占耕地的通知》和中发〔1986〕7号文件精神，成立土地清查领导小组，对1982年5月起的非农业建设用地进行全面清查。至1987年年末共清出各项非农业建设用地4302宗，面积3457.05亩（含耕地1884.35亩），其中未经批准的违法占地4203宗，面积2056.82亩，分别占97.7%和59.5%。违法占地的手段有买卖、租赁、非法转让、越权审批及其他违法行为占地。县土管局按照修府〔1986〕50号《关于在清理非农业用地中处理违法占地的意见》，分别进行补办手续、罚款、收回土地、处理违法占地，理清应收各种款项33.06万元，扣除免交3.11万元后实际收回12.35万元，占应收29.94万元的41.24%，基本制止住乱占耕地和越权审批土地问题再发生。

1990年，奉贵州省政府和安顺行署指示，县土管局配合县清房领导小组依法清理干部职工“三违”（违法、违纪、违建）修建私房。通过实地勘丈，调查取证，清出“三违”建私房47户，其中批少占多33户，超占土地面积0.36亩，除6户补办手续和2户不准再建房外，余下的39户均受到相应处罚，拆房270.83平方米，退地1.35亩，罚款7.27万元，至次年6月全部兑现。

进入20世纪90年代，农村一度掀起“建房热”，部分农户违法占地建房。1991年县土管局清查占地，对乡镇企业用地按照“过去从宽，现在从严；主动申报从宽，隐瞒假报从严；积极兑现从宽，顶着不办从严”的原则，以区为主，重点实地勘丈乡镇企业发达的城关、扎佐两区，视其违法程度进行处理。对农村非法占地建房，在普遍教育的基础上集中力量突击查处，全县共清出个人违法占地307宗，其中马家桥乡92宗，占29.97%。对213宗分别不同情况予以处理，拆除违法建筑6宗，占地面积0.59亩；罚款49宗2938元，退地5宗516.24平方米，补办用地手续153宗，扼制违法占地建房的不法行为。

1992年，按照县委、县政府〔1991〕24号文件指示，开展“农转非”人口的退地工作，仅小箐和洒坪两乡184户318人农转非，清退土地564.94亩，其中责任地367.1亩，自留地37.64亩，责任山68.3亩，自留山60.5亩，荒山26.8亩，宅基地4.6亩。

1993年，继续强化行政执法，对六屯乡三寨村13户村民侵占公地建房，占地0.14亩，乡政府向法院申请强制拆除。经过审理，县人民法院执行庭和法院驻县土管局执行室于8月4日亲临现场强行拆除，既维护法律尊严，又保护土地社会主义公有制度。

1997年，遵照中发〔1997〕11号文件精神，开展全县非农业建设用地大清查，清查时限为1991至1997年4月。清查的主要项目：一是用地手续是否合理，是否有违法批地和超占面积；二是建设项目是否符合规划和环境保护；三是土地利用是否合理，有无闲置浪费现象；四是有否非法转让土地使用权、违法出租土地及土地抵押等。6月3日，县政府成立清查领导小组，10日至7月15日开展登记清查，以交通沿线经济发达的城关、扎佐、久长3个镇及几个大型建设项目为重点。清查结果，全县5年零4个月共发生非农业建设用地4913宗，面积2981.25亩，其中占用耕地2179.2亩，占建设用地总面积的73.1%。非农业用地中批准用地3630宗，占地841.2亩，其中耕地406.6亩；未经批准用地1283宗。占地2140.05亩，其中耕地1770.6亩。在未经批准用地中，国家建设用地25宗，占地1421.25亩，其中耕地1357.95亩；集体建设用地168宗，占地577.2亩，其中耕地324亩；个人建设用地1090宗，占地141.6亩，其中耕地88.65亩。清理的特殊项目有高尔夫度假中心1家，占地1372.84亩，其中耕地429亩；高速公路项目1个，占地2238.83亩，其中耕地1830.32亩。

10月20日至12月20日，按照黔国土监检〔1997〕2号、黔土通〔1997〕7号和9号文件精神，县委、县政府提出对过去的违法用地立足教育为主的原则进行查处，对国家建设用地督促其补交有关税费后完善用地手续；集体建设用地在作出适当处罚后补交有关税费和补办用地手续，对无证开采和乱挖乱采的煤窑坚决予以关闭或强行进行整改；个人建房用地视其违纪程度，先从轻处罚再补办用地手续，对个别面积大和影响大的采取拆除和没收等重罚；对清查中发现中央11号文件下发后发生的19宗农民个人建房，全部拆除和停建恢复耕地。至12月全县共处理违法用地1304宗，其中上报省处理7宗，县处理191宗，乡（镇）处理1106宗。1998年非农业建设用地大清查扫尾时又发生土地违法8宗，面积11.55亩，其中占用耕地6.45亩，全部立案查处，罚款3.6万元，达到依法行政，促进社会安定和经济发展的目的。

2000年，根据贵阳市政府筑土地〔2000〕4号文件要求，在全县开展对农村宅基地的专项清理，从954户清查对象中查出违法用地121户，面积16.84亩，其中耕地9.8亩。经过分类处理，勒令13户拆除建筑，恢复耕地1.88亩；2户处以罚款350元。同时加派力量巡回检查，拆除非法占地建筑，恢复耕地15宗2.95亩，罚款1.12万元。

2003年，根据中央提出的国土资源保护和管理“必须严而又严”的总要求，县国土局成立巡查领导小组，拟定巡查制度，实行动态巡查和行政执法结合。2004年成立治理土地市场秩序领导小组，重点进行基本农业保护、征用农民集体土地补偿费管理使用和经营性国有土地招拍挂的专项检查，至2005年共立案查处违法用地45宗，巡查处罚21宗，收回土地159.24亩，罚款262.34万元，使违法用地者受到应得的经济处罚。

执法人员依法拆除违法占地建房

2007年，在坚持县、乡、村、组4级网络国土资源动态巡查的同时，开展“土地执法百日行动”，清查出“以租代征”土地违法案件2宗，其中创诚冶炼有限公司租用小箐乡尖山林集体土地47.22亩建冶炼厂，由贵州省国土厅直接查处；贵州修文净园文化有限公司占用潮水村集体荒山80亩建公墓，县国土局按每平方米25元处以133.34万元罚款，并责令依法补办用地手续。加上从2009年起通过土地卫星图片执法检查数据，至2010年全县共查处土地违法案件36宗，拆除恢复耕地1.35亩，处以罚款457.19万元，追缴地价款36万元，对有相关违法责任的10人向纪检监察部门提出处分建议，从而维护土地法律法规的尊严。

第十节　物资管理

一、体制改革

1978至1979年，沿袭原计划物资管理体制，计划物资实行统一供应，由生产企业和物资部门两级库存，直接供应到施工工地和生产企业，水利基建用的水泥由施工单位持县水利局分配介绍信到物资局购买。

1980年起，逐步开放物资流通，实行计划分配与市场调节相结合的“双轨制”，计划分配物资品种由256个减少到20个，分配范围缩小到重点生产建设单位、技术改造项目和直接关系到人民生活需要的部分。对供大于求的二类机电产品逐步实行敞开供应，可以合同订购或自由采购，不再纳入计划分配，生产企业在完成国家分配计划和供货合同后，超产分成产品、自行组织原材料生产的产品、试制的新产品、物资部门不收购的超计划产品，均由自行浮动价转向市场调节价。至1986年县内初步形成生产资料计划分配与市场调节相结合的流通体制。1990至2010年除主要民爆物品炸药、雷管、导火索实行专营外，其他物资一律实行市场调节，敞开供应。

二、物资调配

1978年沿袭计划分配制度，每年所需统配物资由物资局编制计划申请调配，水泥、煤炭、木材、生铁、废钢材、硫酸和火工产品中的炸药、雷管、导火索在国家统一计划下，实行地区平衡、差额调拨、品种调剂、保证上缴的管理模式。1982年起水泥、沥青、钢材、汽车等实行计划调配和市场调节“双轨制”的进货办法。1990至2010年，除炸药、雷管、导火绳3种火工产品外，其余物资均取消计划统配，放开自行采购。

三、物资供应

1979年前，国家一、二、三类物资由物资局按计划供应。1980年，执行国家物资总局供应办法，试行通用钢材票供应管理，供应票由国家物资总局金属材料公司统一印发，在全国通用。票种分为铜票、铅票、锌票、铝材票和小型材票、薄钢板票、焊接管票以及调度、调剂用的一般钢材票等，各种供应票又分为不同数量票额。县物资局按分配的计划指标，向安顺地区金属材料公司领取各种金属材料票，到省金属材料公司提货供应用户，其他统配物资不采用供应票，只按国家下达计划提货供应。

1982年停止凭票供应。1984年计划内和计划外两种物资在市场上流通，两种价格在市场同行。民用爆炸物资由国家统配改为统销。1987年对计划内金属材料供应价格由定额收费改为按定额率收费，县物资局销售的电工材料等综合费率为5.7%，汽车为10%。民用爆炸品改为国家专营物资，除国家物资部门外，其他任何单位不得经营，县物资局为全县民用爆破物品的供应、保管、管理的部门。

1991至2010年，原统配物资除民用爆炸物品外，其余物资大多已形成买方市场，供大于求，供应价格实行指导价，随行就市上下浮动销售。

第十一节　劳动工资管理

1978年沿袭劳动工资局原建制，1984年劳动局和人事局合并称人事劳动局，内置劳动工资管理机构行使劳动工资管理职能。至2010年全面完成第三次、第四次、第五次工资制度改革和历次工资调整，推行公务员工资、绩效工资、企业工资制度。国有在岗职工年人均工资收入从1978年的660元增到2010年的3.49万元，增长51.9倍。

一、工资制度改革

自1952年第一次和1956年第二次工资改革后，县内于1978—2010年先后进行过第三次、第四次、第五次工资制度改革。

（一）第三次改革

1985年7月实施，改革的主要内容：一是工资管理体制实行政企分开，分级管理；二是政府机关人员、专业技术人员改由基础工资、职务工资、工龄工资、奖励工资组成的结构工资；三是事业单位人员、专业技术人员工资由行业制定，可实行结构工资制，亦可实行其他工资制；四是政府机关和事业单位的工人可实行岗位（技术）工资为主的结构工资制，亦可实行其他工资制；五是企业职工工资同企业经济效益挂钩、同职工个人贡献大小挂钩的多种形式的管理办法。

是时，县由四类工资区改为五类工资区，基础工资每人每月39元；职务工资按担任职务和任职年限确定，随职务变动而变更；工龄工资每工作1年每月0.5元，最高计到40年；奖励工资为每年终发经费节约奖。当年行政机关和事业单位有2837人理顺工资，月增资5.37万元，人均月增18.93元；37个企业1202人理顺工资，月增资1.23万元，人均月增10.23元。

此次改革旨在理顺工资关系，解决原工资制度中存在的劳酬脱节、吃大锅饭、职级不符、难以体现按劳分配原则；工资管理制度上权力过于集中，政企不分；工资能上不能下，能增不能减的终身待遇；工资标准过多过繁，同一行业多种工资标准等弊端。

（二）第四次改革

1994年8月，按照国务院1993年79号文件对国家机关工资制度进行改革。改革主要内容：国家机关工作人员（不含工勤人员）工资主要由基础工资、级别工资、职务工资、工龄工资组成，共分高、中、初三个档次15个级别，高低之比约为8:1，即1200元至155元。事业单位工资分专业技术人员和行政管理人员两类，各种津贴占30%。

此次改革，全县行政事业单位有5500名职工按新工资标准套改增资，每人平均月增资135元。在国家机关和事业单位中建立起正常升级增资制度，每年年终进行考核，称职者增发一个月基础工资作为年终奖，连续两年考核称职者晋升一档职务工资。退休人员每人月增加20元。同时，对新参加国家机关和事业单位的工作人员试用期工资待遇调整为初中毕业生170元，高中和中专毕业生180元，大学专科毕业生195元，大学本科毕业生205元。

（三）第五次改革

根据黔府发〔2006〕45号文件精神于2006年7月1日起实施。

公务员工资制度改革 一是机关单位除工勤人员以外的工作人员实行职级工资制，基本工资由职务工资和级别工资组成，职务工资按现任职务套改，级别和级别工资档次按现任职务、任职年限和套改年限确定；二是机关技术工人实行岗位技术等级工资制，基本工资由岗位工资和技术等级（职务）工资组成，技术等级工资按考评（聘任）的技术等级套改，岗位工资档次按现任技术等级、年限和套改年限确定。机关普通工人的岗位工资档次按套改年限确定。改革后，全县66个机关单位1337人月增资45.82万元，人均增资342.68元。继后，实行正常晋升工资，晋升职务执行新任职务工资和相应级别工资；按年度考核结果累计5年称职及以上晋升一个级别，两年称职及以上晋升一个工资档次；对新录用人员工资待遇，初中学历至博士学位的研究生学历为570元至845元。

事业人员收入分配制度改革 一是实行岗位绩效工资制，工资由岗位工资、薪级工资、绩效工资、津贴补贴组成，其中岗位工资和薪级工资为基本工资，岗位工资按当时聘用专业技术岗位套改，薪级工资按套改年限、任职年限、所聘岗位结合工作表现套改，绩效工资以工作实绩和贡献进行分配并合理拉开差距，取消年终一次性奖金，津贴补贴分为艰苦边远地区津贴和特殊岗位津贴补贴。二是工资实行分类管理，基本工资执行国家统一的政策和标准，绩效工资按单位分类管理。改革后，75个事业部门3907人月增资106.61万元，人均增资272.88元。之后，则实行正常调整工资，年度考核结果为合格及以上增一级薪级工资，岗位变动执行新聘岗位的工资标准，基本工资和津贴补贴根据经济发展、财政状况适时调整。新录用人员工资待遇仍按初中学历570元，初中以上按各类毕业生分别确定。

改革的同时，对2006年7月1日后离休人员离休费，按本人离休前职务工资和级别工资（或岗位工资和薪级工资）之和全额计发。退休人员退休后的退休费和事业部门人员、机关技术工人、普通工人退职后的退职生活费，按本人退休（退职）前基本工资一定比例计发。2006年6月30日前已办理离退休手续或达到离退年龄未办理离退休手续的人员，按照级别标准增加离退休费。全县机关单位和事业部门离退休1599人，月增离退休费13.45万元，人均增加280.48元。

此外，根据贵州省艰苦边远地区津贴制度，将县列入一类区，全县机关事业单位在职人员月提高艰苦边远地区津贴13.45万元，人均增加25.65元；离退休人员月提高3.11万元，人均增加19.47元。

（四）企业自行确定内部工资分配

1978至1984年，企业职工的工资管理、调整、改革均按国家统一规定执行，企业无自主权。1985年根据贵州省劳动局《关于企业内部工资改革实施办法》，各类企业职工工资实行工资总额包干，增人不增资，减人不减资，或实行企业工资同经济效益挂钩的浮动工资，国家不再统一安排企业职工工资调整和升级增资，企业内部工资分配仍实行按劳分配原则，工资及津（补）贴都由企业自主确定。当年全县各类全民、集体企业53户，首批实行挂钩的仅有物资总公司和三角山水泥厂两户，当年经济效益显著，给职工兑现效益工资。继后，工效挂钩企业逐年增加，1992年达到15户，占县属企业27%，职工1093人，占县属企业职工数49.25%，综合计算为39.2%，超过安顺地区劳动局和县劳动局原定要求和目标。1994年，挂钩企业40户，其中国有企业34户，占全县国有企业85%，职工1791人，占86%；集体企业9户，占全县集体企业55%，职工183人，占51%，均按照挂钩规定给职工增资，减亏的企业职工晋升级别增加工资。凡按挂钩规定指标兑现上浮给职工增加的工资，由企业主管部门审定，送人事劳动局备案，人事

劳动局对企业职工实行宏观调控的政策管理。

2005年起，为解决企业退休人员工资偏低的问题，国家规定连续给企业退休人员增加生活费，到2010年已执行6年，逐步缩小工资分配差距。

二、工资调整

1978年12月起遵照国家劳动总局《关于给工作成绩特别突出的职工升级的通知》，对行政事业单位工作成绩突出的2%职工晋升一级工资，企业优秀学徒工提前转正定级，1977年调资中缓调人员表现好的补调补增工资。

1979年11月，遵照国务院批转《全国物价工资会议纪要》给部分职工调整工资，全县1589名劳动态度好、技术高、贡献大的职工升级，增资面41.2%。县为四类工资区，每级增资1元至4元。

1981年10月，遵照国务院《关于调整部分职工工资的通知》，中、小学教职工、部分卫生人员和体育工作者先补足级差，达到相应级别再升级调资，凡属调资范围者人人调升工资。

1982年，遵照国务院《关于调整国家机关、科学、文教、卫生等部门部分工资人员工资问题的规定》给机关事业单位、科教、卫生部门71,7%的职工988人升级，人均月增资6,59元。其中升两级的114人，占调资人数的11.5%。

1983年10月，遵照国务院《关于企业调整工资和改革工资制度问题的报告的通知》，对全民企业71%的职工1543人调升工资。其中9人升两级。调整后人均月增6.38元。同时对1977年调资不超过7元的补齐级差。

1986年7月，遵照国务院《关于国家机关和事业单位工作人员工资制度改革的通知》和贵州省劳动局《关于企业内部工资改革实施方案》进行工资套改（“理顺工资”），全县机关事业单位2837人增资，人月均增18.93元；37个全民企业87.1%的职工升级增资，人月均增10.23元。其中升两级894人，升3级224人，升4级6人。同时将县四类工资区类别改为五类工资区。

1987年1月，根据国务院《关于提高中小学教师工资标准待遇的通知》，给全县中小学、幼儿园、特殊教育学校教师在原工资标准的基础上提高10%，升级范围人月均增7.3元。

1988年10月，根据人事部、卫生部、财政部《关于提高护士人员工资标准的实施办法》和《关于适当解决部分老干部、老专家工资问题的实施办法》，将护士人员现行工资标准提高10%。对1957年后未升过级、现仍在职工作的原四级以上老专家和行政十级以上老干部，按现行职务工资标准晋升一级工资。其中老专家现行工资达到或超过现行工资标准一级的每月增加工资50元。1985年工资改革前离退休的可在离退休时工资级别基础上增一级工资。

1989年10月起，根据国务院批转人事部、国家计委、财政部《关于1989年调整国家机关、事业单位工作人员工资实施方案》，对9月30日在册职工调整工资，离退休人员增加离退休金。全县行政事业单位3319人升级，调资面占97.8%，其中2853人升二级。调资后人月均增13.85元，离退休人月均增13.11元；全民企业单位38个，参加调资1599人，调资面97.38%，调整后人月均增9.32元，离退休人员人均月增13.77元。

1995年10月，首次给机关、事业单位中连续两年考核称职的职工晋升职务工资，离退休人员增加生活费，全县4838名职工月增加工资10.73万元，其中行政与事业职工3710人晋升工资，增资面87.1%，月增7.58万元，每人月均增20.44元；离休75人，人月均增22元；退休905人，人月均增20元；公安干警

136人，人月均增78.7元；人民武装干部12人，每人月均增87元。

1997年7月，根据黔人发〔1997〕91号、107号文件给4096名行政机关单位和事业部门职工调整工资标准，月增发8.68万元，人月均增21.2元。同时，将基础工资由90元增到110元。10月，再给1189名离退休人员月增加生活费4.8万元，人月均增40.39元。

1998年，根据黔人发〔1998〕2号文件，给行政事业人员晋升1档职务工资，调资面达85.8%，全县3837名职工月增加8.5万元，人月均增22.2元，从1997年10月起计发。

2001年1月，根据国办发〔2001〕14号和黔府办发〔2001〕41号文件精神，给行政机关单位和事业部门6106人调整级别工资和基础工资以及艰苦边远地区津贴，给1370名离退休人员调增生活费及艰苦边远地区津贴。10月又给810名干部职工调升职务工资标准，给两年考核称职职工晋升1级职务工资，给872名符合条件的干部办理浮动工资转固定工资的手续，给357名干部办理因职务变动和职称升级的晋升工资手续。

继后，不再统一调资，每年都对两年考核称职职工晋升1档工资，连续5年考核合格增加1级工资。执行到2010年未变。

三、津贴　补贴

粮价补贴（亦称“老粮贴”）　1978年沿用，1979年后调整工资冲减，是年11月1日起新参加工作的人员不再享受粮价补贴。

副食品价格补贴　1979年10月国务院决定对职工每人每月补贴5元，1985年工资改革，行政事业单位将该补贴计入工资，企业单位仍计入成本。

班主任津贴　1979年国务院批准从11月起在公办学校试行，中学每班学生35人以下，班主任每月5元，36人以上6元，51人以上7元；小学每月分别为4元、5元、6元；1989年调整为中学8元、10元、12元，小学为6元、8元、10元。无论中学或小学，每班学生20人以下酌减2元至4元。

教龄、护龄津贴　1985年国务院决定对从事教师、护理工作人员，工龄满5年以上每人每月补贴3元，满10年以上5元，满15年以上7元，满20年以上10元。

书刊费　1984年贵州省政府决定对行政事业单位在册正式职工，每人每月发5元，知识分子和中、高级职称人员每人每月10元至30元。1988年扩大到行政事业中的干部、工人，工龄满5年以上每人每月5元，满20年以上10元。

洗理费　1985年8月，对没有浴室和理发室的行政事业单位职工每人每月4元，后又提高到10元。

交通费　1989年按财政部、劳动部规定，在职职工每人每月7元，后增为12元，再增到30元（退休人员减少5元）。

菜篮子补贴　1996年5月起每人每月30元。

岗位津贴（西部补贴）　2004年起在公务员和事业单位行政管理人员中按级别，事业单位人员和机关事业单位技术工人按技术职称和等级低于行政人员1档次，离休人员按离休时的职务（职称），办事员至正处级每人每月100元至300元。2005年，在上年标准基础上提高100元。

除以上项目外，还执行艰苦边远地区津贴、通信补贴、政法岗位津贴、司法助理岗位津贴、纪检监督办案人员补贴、医疗卫生防疫津贴、工商税收津贴、特教津贴、计划生育岗位津贴、环境保护监测津贴、城市环卫工人岗位津贴、知识分子生活补贴和档案管理人员保健津贴。

四、浮动工资

浮动工资转固定工资 1983年，县属全省65个边远县之一，根据省政府规定，从7月1日起，凡在区、乡农、林、牧、渔、农田水利和农业机械等事业部门从事农林科技专业技术人员，在原工资基础上浮动一级作为岗位津贴，满8年后转为本人固定工资。至2010年，全县各乡（镇）符合条件的2765名职工均转浮动工资为固定工资。

企业与效益挂钩浮动升级 1984年，为搞活企业，对县内企业的奖金、工资总额，实行与经济效益挂钩的浮动工资和浮动升级，即企业把职工的一部分工资（约20%）与奖金捆在一起，随企业经济效益好坏和职工劳动成果大小上下浮动，即在职工现行工资等级的基础上，按照企业经济效益和职工的技术业务水平、劳动态度、贡献大小，用企业的一部分自有资金给职工晋升工资等级，升级面控制在20%以下。1994年全县36个企业实行与工资挂钩，其中有30个企业按挂钩规定提取上述工资14.7万元给职工增资，工资增长幅度为20.27%。1997年国有集体企业挂钩45户，其中有27户获得上述工资23.33万元。2户未完成挂钩指标，下浮工资7600元。继后，县辖地方国有企业陆续改制，至2010年仅有物资总公司执行企业与效益挂钩浮动升级。

五、奖励工资

1978年5月执行国务院通知，恢复企业奖金制度，年终发放奖金；企业按完成各项经济指标补发，未实行企业核算管理的事业单位，按固定职工每人10元提取评定发放。1984年国家对奖励工资制度进行改革，机关、事业单位年终增发增收节约奖，奖金额不超过在职职工1个月的标准工资，有业务收入的单位不超过一个半月标准；企业实行利改税后，奖励基金从税后留利中提取，与企业经济效益挂钩浮动。

1985年，增收节约奖人均80元，称谓改为“奖励工资”，发放标准作适当调整。

1990年遵照省、地指示，给行政事业单位符合条件的朱明扬、杨德书、薛占成、卢永康、刘易发、周孝昌、陈福英、邓彩林、朱德志和在教学战线上作出贡献的李新民、周兴国各晋升1级奖励工资。

1992年起，行政事业单位奖励工资由原半年或年终累计发放，改为每人每月17元随工资发给。至1993年止的5年，除1991年外，县批准国营企业3%的奖励指标126个（格），给符合条件的252名职工升级增资1173.6元，人均增资4.66元。

1994年启动国家机关、事业单位工资改革，奖励工资形成发放正常制度。2001年起凡年度考核称职的，增发一个月基本工资作为当年奖励工资，无须评定；离、退休人员按基本离退休费50%计发。2006年7月至2010年全年，行政机关实行年终一次性奖金，年度考核为称职（合格）及以上发放当年12月的基本工资作为年终奖金。

文化建设篇

1978年中共十一届三中全会后，县委、县政府着眼于大文化建设，坚持教育优先的发展战略，把社会主义精神文明建设提上重要议事日程，全面推进科教文体等各项社会事业的发展。着力打造文化品牌，建设文化强县，实现科教兴县，文化惠民，使文化产业呈现多元化发展的格局。加强教育基础设施建设，壮大并提升师资队伍，推进教育教学改革。使九年义务教育、普通高中教育、职业教育等教育教学质量稳步上升。电视、网络等新型文化传媒迅速发展，文化市场日趋繁荣兴旺。地方特色文化传承和保护力度加大，阳明洞提升为国家级文物保护单位。把科技作为第一生产力，加强科技队伍建设，开展科技交流，推进科技创新，普及科技知识，保护知识产权。群众以思想道德建设为主要内容的公民素质显著提高，城乡体育事业进一步发展，全民健身工程向前推进，体育竞技屡创佳绩。方志编纂、图书出版发行经销和档案工作规范运行。

修文文化建设的创新发展，使全县精神文明建设得到全面推进，县境文化软实力显著增强，极大丰富与满足了人们的精神需求，为全县的改革开放和现代化建设提供了精神动力和智力支撑。

第一章　教　育

1978年中共十一届三中全会后，全县教育秩序逐渐步入正轨。20世纪80年代，县委、县政府坚持以“三个面向”（教育要面向现代化、面向世界、面向未来）为指导，认真贯彻落实《中共中央关于教育体制改革的决定》和《中华人民共和国义务教育法》，在实施教育体制改革的同时，逐步推进教育普及，1986年实现基本普及初等教育的目标。90年代，深入贯彻实施《中国教育改革和发展纲要》和《中华人民共和国教育法》，教育改革稳步推进，教育普及步伐加快。1993年高标准扫盲验收合格，随即启动“两基”（基本普及九年义务教育，基本扫除青壮年文盲）工作。进入21世纪，坚持教育优先发展战略，全面深化教育改革，使全县教育事业跃上新台阶。2000年“两基”验收基本合格，2004年“两基”复查和普及中、小学实验教学验收合格，2009年“两基”通过国家检查验收。至2010年，全县基础教育改革纵深推进，教育结构趋于合理，师资建设成效明显，素质教育全面实施，育人环境更加优化，教育事业呈现科学发展的良好态势。

第一节 教育体制改革

一、办学体制改革

（一）分级办学

1978年沿袭原有体制，分别由县、区、公社和生产大队办学。20世纪80年代初、中期，办学主体虽未改变，但调整了办学权限：完全中学主要由县办，初级中学主要由区和公社（乡、镇）办，生产大队（村）只办小学。《中华人民共和国义务教育法》颁布后，明确了县、乡（镇）两级政府的办学责任。80年代后期，大多数村办小学逐步划归乡（镇）办。1992年3月，县委、县政府下发《关于基础教育实行分级办学分级管理的实施意见》，全面实行县、乡（镇）两级政府办学。“分级办学”虽调动了地方办学的积极性，但在实施普及九年义务教育上暴露出诸多问题，特别是教育经费的投入，乡（镇）财力薄弱，感到压力很大。2003年，县委、县政府出台《关于贯彻〈国务院关于基础教育改革与发展的决定〉的意见》，明确学校由县主办，教育普及、经费投入、教师编制和学校布局调整等均由县政府承担，组织适龄学生入学、控制辍学、维护学校治安和划拨教育用地等则由乡（镇）政府负责，村民自治组织协助乡（镇）大力实施义务教育。至2010年，由县主办学校的办学体制未变。

（二）多元办学

1978—1984年，继续执行地方政府办学和群众办学“两条腿走路”，县、区（公社）在积极发展公办学校的同时，采取国家补助、地方集资和群众投工献料的方式，在地处边远、就学困难的生产大队和公社分别建立民办小学或民办公助的戴帽初中。直至1985年，县内仍有民办小学79所，戴帽初中9所。继后，由于农村经济发展，交通条件改善，民办小学和戴帽初中陆续撤并，或过渡为公办。1986年，退休教师李永福和个体户王仕英等在县城租赁房舍开办初中补习班和幼儿园，为县内继农村集体办学后出现的新的办学模式。20世纪90年代初期，县政府贯彻落实国家关于教育体制改革的政策，鼓励企、事业单位和其他社会力量在政府统一管理下，举办各类学校。1993年，经县政府批准，由退休教师史作经和董登荣分别筹办的私立学校破茧而出，在县城和扎佐办起华驿中学和景阳中学，打破了单一由政府办学的格局，呈现公立学校和私立学校并存的局面。1997—2001年将此办学方式称为“社会力量办学”，2002年又改称为“民办教育”。全县民办教育以学前教育和普通中学教育居多。从20世纪90年代中期至2005年，先后办有春蕾、南方、寓教、叮当等幼儿园和华驿、景阳、龙岗、兴林、紫邮、英才、良知等中学。民办教育补充了县域基础教育资源的不足，在推进教育普及和发展的过程中发挥了积极作用。但有的学校因办学条件差，师资流动性

2009年全县基础教育均衡发展工作会

大，导致生源不稳定，最后只得停办或向外转移。2006年，县政府出台《修文县民办学校管理办法（试行）》，贯彻“积极鼓励，大力支持，正确引导，依法管理”的方针，使民办教育得以健康发展，民办学校趋于稳定。至2010年，经县政府同意并报贵阳市教育局审批备案的民办学校共11所。

2010年民办学校概况一览表

表4-01-01

学校名称	校　址	办学类别	获证时间（年）	学生数（人）	教职工数（人）
春蕾幼儿园	龙场镇新春村	学前教育	1998	147	16
叮当幼儿园	扎佐镇腾飞路	学前教育	1998	314	35
南方幼儿园	县城民主路	学前教育	2002	356	33
工会学前班	县城学宫巷	学前教育	2002	146	4
寓教幼儿园	县城温家巷	学前教育	2003	80	4
六桶小花幼儿园	六桶乡盐井村	学前教育	审批中	120	10
修文文武学校	久长镇兴隆村	学前、小学教育	2003	432	20
久长春晖文武学校	久长镇永兴村	学前、小学、初中教育	审批中	64	11
景阳中学	扎佐镇和平村	小学、初中、高中教育	1993	908	49
华驿中学	龙场镇王官村	初中、高中教育	1993	610	36
小海龟艺术培训学校	县城翠屏东路	非学历培训	2010	动态	7

专记：崛起的民办学校——景阳中学

20世纪90年代，民间办学在县境兴起。1993年，退休教师董登荣在扎佐创办私立景阳中学，校址坐落在扎佐街金家园子，与扎佐一小仅一墙之隔。学校创办之初，董登荣将私房改成教室两间，面积80平方米，任课教师除董本人外，还聘请1人。当年6月，学校经修文县政府批准，为县内获批较早的民办学校之一。秋季开学，报名就读初中一年级的学生130余人。由于校舍容量受限，只得择优录取40人，随后在有些家长的迫切要求下增录8人。1994年，添建教室两间，学生增至98人，除来自扎佐当地外，尚有周边的六屯、久长和百里之遥的六桶等地，分初一、初二两个年级，教师8人多由外地引进。当年秋季临近开学，县委书记罗筑云亲赴学校视察，面对董登荣说：“你作为一个共产党员，退休后并没有忘记党的教育事业，还为培养新一代贡献余热，精神可嘉，我代表县委、县政府感谢你!”罗筑云还鼓励他一定要加强管理，引入竞争机制，与公办学校一道发展，办出特色，办出成效。县委书记一席话，让董登荣吃了定心丸，他深信民办学校将会迎来广阔的前景。董登荣退休前担任扎佐一小校长，退休后创办的景阳中学与扎佐一小挨邻，在同样的环境中，他却有着不同的身份和岗位，但对教育事业的执着追求是共同的。他积多年管理学校的经验，建立管理制度，聘用优质师资，添置教学设备，想尽一切办法创设一个良好的育人环境。

1995年7月，经县政府同意，扎佐镇政府决定将原扎佐乡政府所在地的10亩土地转让给景阳中学，扩大学校规模。1996年，学校采取自筹和贷款的方式，耗资96万元在新址建起4层教学楼1栋，建筑面积1500平方米，置教室18间和办公室6间，学校迁入新址上课。与此同时，经安顺地区教育局批准，学校

景阳中学全景

开始招收高一年级新生，办成一所完全中学，生源除来自县内，还有县周边的白云、乌当和开阳等地。当年，首届初中生毕业，32人参加中考，总分500分以上的12人，占参考人数的37.5%，办学初见成效。1997年，又增办小学，成为从小学、初中到高中“一条龙”的大型私立学校，在校学生400余人，教职工30余名。继后，学校又筹资新建办公楼、学生宿舍、食堂和运动场，办学条件得到更大改善，并实行全封闭式管理。1997年和1998年，全县中考总分第一名均出自该校。1999年，学校首届高中毕业生32人参加高考，81.3%的考生上大专以上分数线，其中上本科线的考生就有16名。消息不翼而飞，轰动县内外。更为可喜的是，扎佐当地的大堡村、龙王村等地的农村子弟跨进了大学校园，填补了这些地方历来没有大学生的空白，从而调动了当地农民送孩子上学的积极性。2001年，在校学生增至800余名，校舍又不敷使用。于是，学校又与邻近村民协商，就近置地20亩，进一步扩大办学规模。2002年，学校高三年级99名学生参加高考，96人达到大专以上分数线，上线率达96.97%。2003年，142人参加高考，131人达到大专以上分数线，其中一类本科大学上线18人。显著的办学成绩令人震撼，学校的知名度不断上升。2005年，在校学生突破千人大关，拥有1043人，生源来自全省10多个区、县，70余名教师中，中、高级职称近50%，校舍总面积达1.1万平方米，累计投资达1100多万元。是年高考，总分600分以上的考生6名，全县文科总成绩前10名中该校占8名，理科总成绩前10名中该校占7名，学校又迈上了一个新的台阶。至2010年，学校已有17年的校龄，累计向各级大中专学校输送学生2000余名。

17年间，学校从初创建设到发展完善，已有教学楼2栋，综合大楼1栋，学生公寓1栋，标准教室40间，并有计算机网络系统、多媒体教学系统和双向闭路系统等现代化教学设施，物理、化学、生物等实验室齐全，藏书达到3万余册，成为县内规模最大的全日制寄宿制民办学校。学校先后获得全国先进民办学校、贵阳市文明单位和贵阳市先进学校等荣誉称号。17年间，学校在充满艰辛的办学历程中崛起，以“认认真真读书、堂堂正正做人”为校训，以“立足基础、注重特色、全面发展、服务社会”为宗旨，严格管理、严谨治学，以德为首、以人为本，从学生身心、人格、能力等方面进行全面塑造，注重学生综合素质提高，取得卓越的办学成绩。

二、管理体制改革

（一）分级管理

1978—1985年，教育工作系县级统一管理。1985年12月召开全县教育工作会议，贯彻实施《中共中央关于教育体制改革的决定》，县委、县政府制定《关于推进我县教育体制改革的意见》，在加强宏观管理的同时“简政放权”，按照“地方负责，分级管理”的原则，对县、区、乡（镇）、村的管理职责作出明确规定，形成分级管理的体制。1992年3月，县政府出台《关于基础教育实行分级办学分级管理的实施意见》，进一步明确县、区、乡（镇）、村的管理范围，使“分级管理”继续深化。继后，随着“撤区并乡建镇”调整区划和教育改革的不断推进，全县教育工作改由县、乡（镇）两级管理。“分级管理”明确了地方各级管理教育的职责，对全面推动教育发展起到积极作用，但“分级管理”在一定程度上削弱了县一级政府的统筹协调作用。2003年，县委、县政府制发《关于完善我县教育管理体制的意见》，实行“分级管理、以县为主”的管理体制，加大了县政府的统筹力度。县政府在积极承担普及九年义务教育和巩固“普九”成果的同时，协调发展其他各项教育事业，使全县教育事业步入科学、健康的发展轨道。至2010年，“以县为主”的管理体制继续实行。

2005年，县委常委会专题研究教育工作

（二）校长负责制

1978年，取消“文化大革命”时期由工人宣传队或贫下中农宣传队领导的“学校革命委员会”，建立在学校党支部领导下的校长负责制。1984年，县教育局制发《关于加强学校管理工作的意见》，提出学校实行校长负责制，进一步明确校长的职责和任期，要求逐步落实。1996年，县政府制定《修文县中学校长负责制试行方案》，要求乡（镇）政府加强对实施校长负责制的领导，并以扎佐中学为试点率先实行。此后，在不断积累经验的基础上，校长负责制在中、小学全面推开，校长的管理水平不断提高，校长作为学校法人代表的地位亦逐步落实。至2000年，所有学校均实行校长负责制。2003年起，贯彻落实县委、县政府《关于贯彻〈国务院关于基础教育改革与发展的决定〉的意见》，使校长对学校管理的责任更加明确，具体实行学校年度目标管理。为使校长能够实现年度目标，县、乡（镇）政府和教育主管部门给予更多的办学自主权，促进其对人、财、物、事的科学管理。与此同时，进一步加强对校长的培训力度，建立定期交流机制，着力提高校长的管理能力和办学效益。2005—2008年，全县校长中有130余人次参加上岗培训，并选派10名校长到贵阳市区学校挂职锻炼。同时，每年定期对学校年度目标任务完成情况进行考核。2010年，在岗校长参加县级培训145人次，接受市级培训22人次，参加省级培训并派往大连、深圳等地挂职锻炼的有5人。通过培训和挂职锻炼，使校长的履职能力逐步增强，当年签订目标责任书的29个学校经考核均基本完成年度目标任务。

三、投资体制改革

1978年沿袭原有规定，教育经费由县、区、公社、生产大队根据办学主体共同承担，公办教师工资和学校办公经费等由县财政全额划拨。20世纪80年代初期，实行“划分收支，分级包干”的新财政体制，全县教育经费根据安顺地区下达到县的收支指标，由县财政具体安排。1983年，县财政根据年度教育事业计划和规定的各项经费指标预算定额，下拨经费到县直学校和各区。1985年，县财政以支出指标的形式直接划拨经费到县直学校和各区包干使用。同时，为解决教育投入渠道单一和教育经费不足的问题，决定拓宽办学经费来源，成立以县委书记为主任的集资办学委员会筹集社会资金，年内筹资达8.6万元。1986年，根据国家税政规定开征教育费附加。至1990年，全县共征收33万元。1991年，县政府制定《关于多渠道筹措办学经费暂行办法》，提倡“人民教育人民办，人民学校人民建，办学基金人民筹”，要求除按规定征收教育费附加外，倡导社会力量及个人自愿捐资助学。同时，县政府成立多部门组成的教

育基金委员会征收教育基金，并界定其使用范围。1994年，县政府下达给乡（镇）教育费附加征收确保完成数为80万元。当年，全县教育经费总支出913.73万元，为1990年的2.14倍。1985—1995年，筹集社会资金178万元投入教育基本建设。随着《贵州省基础教育实行分级办学分级管理的暂行规定》出台，教育投入执行“两个增长”（财政拨款的增长高于财政经常性收入的增长，在校学生人数平均的教育费用逐步增长）原则，教育经费支出按照事权和财权相统一的原则在县级财政预算中单独列项。

1996年，县委、县政府制订《关于贯彻〈中国教育改革和发展纲要〉的实施意见》，继续执行多渠道筹措教育经费政策，进一步改善办学条件，强调切实保证教育经费拨款逐步做到“三个增长”（财政拨款的平均增长速度高于财政收入的平均增长速度，预算内生均教育事业费逐年增长，预算内生均公用经费逐年增长），逐步形成以财政拨款为主渠道，征收教育基金和筹集社会资金等为辅助的多元投入格局。当年，征收教育费附加96.9万元，社会捐资58.4万元。1997—1999年，征收教育费附加763.66万元，城市维护建设税按5%划拨23.98万元，教育基金49.48万元，上级补助专项经费976.75万元，全部用于教育，经省、市审计部门审计认定，预算内教育经费投入达到“三个增长”标准。同期，全县教育经费总支出（含预算内外）中县财政预算内拨款占63.18%。2001—2003年，县财政预算内教育经费投入经审计认定仍实现“三个增长”，财政教育拨款占教育总支出的比例达90.67%。期间，上级补助教育专项经费2423.26万元，2002年实行农村税费改革后，中央转移支付资金按50%投入教育，每年445万元。随着“普九”的深入实施，县政府逐步建立和完善教育经费投入保障机制，教育支出总额中仍以财政拨款为主，确保上级专项资金和县级配套资金落实到位，继续将中央转移支付资金的50%投入教育。2004年4月起，按照《贵州省人民政府关于修订〈贵州省教育经费筹措管理办法〉的决定》征收城市教育费附加和地方教育费附加。2006年，教育各项收支全部纳入预算管理。2006—2008年，教育经费投入3.21亿元。2010年，全县教育经费总支出已达2.03亿元。

XIU WEN BAO

风雨人生路 农行诚相助 修文农行

2000年9月18日 星期一

修文供电 人民电业为人民

“两基”达标获得入场券

我县“两基”教育经费通过省级审计

头条新闻竞赛

修文农村信用合作联社 提供赞助

手拉手的合作 心贴心的服务

2000年，《修文报》关于教育经费审计的报道

专记：“两免一补”惠及城乡义务教育学生

20世纪70年代末期，中、小学生入学的费用主要有学杂费和书本费，住校学生还需缴纳生活费。1986年颁布实施《中华人民共和国义务教育法》，依照规定免收义务教育学生的学费，但并未免除杂费。1992年颁发《义务教育法实施细则》，仍规定实施义务教育的学校可收取杂费。杂费主要用来弥补学校公用经费不足，以减轻地方财政压力。由于入学仍需缴纳杂费、书本费和生活费，有的家长无力承担，导致城乡部分家庭贫困的学生辍学，以致中、小学辍学率居高不下，90年代初有的学校辍学率竟达10%以上。90年代中期，县启动实施普及九年义务教育，为切实降低辍学率，学校收费时大多采取“缓、减、免”的方式留住学生，或动员校内外职工捐资帮助家庭经济困难学生完成学业。由于采取多种措施控制学生流失，2000年小学和初中辍学率分别降至0.4%和2.73%。2003年《国务院关于进一步加强农村教育工作的决定》颁布，要求财政确保农村中、小学校公用经费，给靠收取学生杂费维持运转的学校减轻了

经费压力，同时在《决定》中还明确，对农村义务教育阶段家庭经济困难的学生实行“两免一补”（免书费、免杂费，补助寄宿生生活费），努力做到不让学生因家庭经济困难而失学。

2004年，贵州省教育厅在省内100个一类扶贫开发重点乡启动“两免一补”，县内的大石布依族乡名列其中，该乡当年即有接受义务教育的学生2378人次领到免费教科书，1564人次免除杂费，总金额15万元。次年，除大石乡外，县内其他乡（镇）的部分义务教育学生也享受“两免”政策并获寄宿生生活补助费，受益学生3.09万人次，金额126.73万元。2006年，城镇低保家庭接受义务教育的子女亦享受“两免一补”，全县春秋两季领到免费教科书的学生增至3.53万人次、金额137.76万元，免杂费8万人次、金额379万元，有7382人次的寄宿生享受每人次100元的生活补助费、金额73.82万元。到2007年，凡县内公办学校农村义务教育学生均享受“两免一补”，共有15.42万人次受益，总金额763.02万元。次年对民办学校接受义务教育的农民工子女亦实行“两免”，共免费3.22万元。2009年，提高寄宿生生活补助费额度，小学生每人每年500元，初中生每人每年750元，当年即下拨补助费249.28万元。2010年，在免费教科书扉页上加盖“本书由国家免费提供”印章。从2004年开始实施义务教育学生“两免一补”政策至2010年，全县共有75.55万人次受益，总金额达4770万元。“两免一补”政策的实施，解决了城乡贫困家庭的燃眉之急，保障了适龄儿童少年接受义务教育的权利，使“普九”成果得以巩固，广大学生家长从依法送子女入学接受义务教育中发出对党和政府的感言：种地不上税，读书不交费，党的政策好，人民得实惠。

2010年，民办学校学生领取补助费

四、学制改革

1978—2010年，县内幼儿园学制皆为3年。1984年，部分小学附设1年的幼儿学前班，继后全县推广。至2010年，幼儿学前班学习时间仍为1年。

1978年，小学和中学沿袭“文化大革命”时期的“五三二”学制，即小学5年，初中3年，高中2年。1983年秋，修文一中（今修文中学）高中恢复3年制，次年所有高中学制均为3年。1984年秋，县直小学及各区中心小学恢复6年制，次年所有小学学制亦为6年。到1989年秋季，原实行“五三二”学制的学生全部毕业，“六三三”学制全面恢复。至2010年，“六三三”学制继续实施。

五、课程改革

（一）幼儿园课程

1978年，幼儿园开设的课程有语言、计算、常识和活动（音乐、体育、美术）等。20世纪80年代起，改幼儿教学为幼儿教育，教育内容增设生活卫生习惯和思想品德，划分小班、中班和大班各科的具体教育内容与要求，强调通过上课、游戏、观察、娱乐和日常生活等形式完成教育任务。2001年起，执行教育部《幼儿园教育指导纲要（试行）》，将课程划分为健康、社会、科学、语言、艺术共5个领域，不再细分小班、中班和大班的不同目标，根据5个领域提出总括性目标，各领域内容相互渗透、有机联

系，注重综合性、趣味性、活动性，寓教育于生活、游戏之中，从不同角度促进幼儿情感、态度、能力、知识和技能等方面的发展。至2010年，继续实施《幼儿园教育指导纲要（试行）》。

（二）小学课程

1978年，恢复“文化大革命”前的分科课程模式及开设的主要课程，执行教育部《全日制十年制中小学教学计划（草案）》，三年级起增设英语。1981年秋，实验小学和各区中心小学试行贵州省教育厅《小学教学计划》，其他小学执行教育部《全日制小学教学计划》，课程设置除语文（讲读、作文、写字）、数学、英语、体育、音乐和美术外，以思想品德取代政治课，三年级以上设自然取代自然常识课，四年级设地理课，五年级设历史课，四年级以上增设劳动课，并将科技、文艺、体育和班队活动纳入课程计划。1984年起，推行六年制，执行贵州省教育厅新颁《全日制六年制农村小学教学计划（草案）》，取消英语课，开设常识课（三至五年级设自然常识，五年级设地理常识，六年级设农业知识和历史常识），劳动课从四年级起开设，在原有活动的基础上新增集体教育活动，其他课程与五年制相同。1994年秋，执行国家教委《九年义务教育全日制小学、初级中学课程计划（试行）》，教学计划改称课程计划，改革课程结构和各学科课时比例，增加课程的灵活性和多样性，将全部课程分为学科类和活动类，并留出一定空间设置地方安排课程。学科类开设思想品德、语文、数学、自然、体育、音乐、美术等7科，三年级起增设劳动，四年级起增设社会，具备条件的学校开设外语；活动类主要有晨会（夕会）、班队活动、科技文体活动、社会实践活动和学校传统活动。地方安排课程由学校根据实际和需要自定。1995年，执行国家教委《实行新工时制对全日制小学、初级中学课程（教学）计划进行调整的意见》，原有课程设置总体不变，适当调整各类课程的课时，减少周活动的总量。随着教育部2001年推行基础教育课程改革，县教育局根据《贵州省教育厅推进基础教育课程改革的实施意见》和按年度分期分批实施的原则，于2004年启动义务教育课程改革实验，实施教育部《义务教育课程设置实验方案》，以综合课程为主，除开设语文、数学、体育、艺术（或选音乐、美术）和地方与学校课程外，一、二年级开设品德与生活，三年级起开设品德与社会以及科学、英语、信息技术和综合实践活动。2008年，执行《贵阳市基础教育课程改革义务教育课程实施方案》，从三年级起开设外语和科学，艺术定为音乐、美术，体育改为体育与健康，综合实践活动包含信息技术（四年级以上）、劳动（三年级以上）和研究性学习，地方课程从四年级起每周1节，学校课程为文体活动、班会。2010年，《贵阳市基础教育课程改革义务教育课程实施方案》继续实施。

（三）中学课程

1978—1980年，全县中学统一执行《贵州省全日制五年制中学教学计划》，将农业基础知识课改为生物课，初中三年级增设生理卫生。1981年秋，执行贵州省教育厅《全日制五年制中学教学计划》，初中一至三年级均开设政治、语文、数学、英语和体育、音乐、美术、劳动技术，初一、初二增设历史、地理、生物，初二、初三增设物理，初三还增设化学和生理卫生。高中开设政治、语文、数学、英语、物理、化学、历史、地理、体育和劳动技术，从高二起划分文科班和理科班，文科班开设历史和地理，理科班开设物理、化学和生物。1984年，执行教育部《全日制六年制重点中学教学计划（草案）》，课程无变化，高中阶段从高二起仍实行文、理分科，在历史、地理、物理、化学和生物5科中，文科侧重于历史和地理，理科侧重于物理、化学和生物。1993年秋，将高中课程从中学课程体系中分出，初中执行国家教委《九年义务教育全日制小学、初级中学课程计划（试行）》，全部课程分为学科类和活动类，亦留出一定空间设置地方安排课程。学科类开设思想政治、语文、数学、外语、历史、地理、物理、化学、生物、体育、音乐、美术、劳动技术共13科，部分中学开设短期的职业指导课。活动类主要有晨会（夕会）、班团活动、体育活动、科技文体活动、社会实践活动和学校传统活动。地方安排课程由学校根据实际和需要自定。高中阶段则过渡性实施国家教委《现行普通高中教学计划的调整意见》，课程结构由学科课程和活动两部分组成，学科课程分必修课和选修课两种，活动包括课外活动和社会实践活动。必修课为政治、语文、数学、外语、物理、化学、生物、历史、地理和体育，选修课有高一、高二开设的单科性选修和高三开设的分科性选修；课外活动包括体育锻炼、知识讲座、科技活动、各类兴趣小组活动、校班会、时事教育等，社会实践活动每学年安排两周，采取分散或集中的形式进行。1995年，执行国家教委《实行新工时制对全日制小学、初级中学课程（教学）计划进行调整的意见》和《实行新工时制对高中教学计划进行调整的意见》，原有课程设置总体不变，适当调整各类课程的课时，减少周活动总量，初中增设健康教育，高中开设艺术学科。2000年，执行教育部《全日制普通高级中学课程计划（试验修订稿）》，将课程分为必修课和选修课，必修课为思想政治、语文、数学、外语、物理、化学、生物、历史、地理、信息技术、体育和保健、艺术以及综合实践活动，选修课有数学、物理、化学、生物、历史、地理和信息技术。选修课是在必修课的基础上，为拓宽和增强学生有关学科的知识和能力而开设的。2004年，全县启动义务教育课程改革实验，实施教育部《义务教育课程设置实验方案》。将初中一、二、三年级改称为七、八、九年级，设置分科与综合相结合的课程，开设思想品德、语文、数学、外语、历史与社会（或选历史、地理）、科学（或选生物、物理、化学）、体育与健康、艺术（或选音乐、美术）、信息技术和综合实践活动，并根据需要设置地方与学校课程。2008年，执行《贵阳市基础教育课程改革义务教育课程实施方案》，将历史与社会定为历史、地理（初一、初二），科学定为生物（初一、初二）、物理（初二、初三）、化学（初三），艺术定为音乐、美术，综合实践活动包含信息技术、劳动技术和研究性学习，地方课程各年级每周1节，学校课程为文体活动、班会，其他未变动。2010年，全县启动基础教育高中课程改革实验，课程设置依照教育部《普通高中课程方案（实验）》执行，分为必修和选修两部分，通过学分描述学生的课程修习状况。课程由学习领域、科目、模块3个层次构成，学习领域设语言与文学、数学、人文与社会、科学、技术、艺术、体育与健康和综合实践活动8个，每个领域由课程价值相近的若干科目组成，8个领域共包括语文、外语（英、日、俄等）、数学、思想政治、历史、地理、物理、化学、生物、艺术（或音乐、美术）、体育与健康、技术（信息技术、通用技术）等12-13个科目，综合实践活动含研究性学习、社区服务和社会实践，每一科目由若干模块组成，每个模块有明确的教育目标。

六、学校布局调整

从1979年起，县革命委员会根据全县学校布局紊乱状况整顿和规范办学行为，遏制不顾条件遍地办学的现象。至1980年，共撤并中学（完全中学、初中、戴帽初中）55所和小学106所。为巩固整顿成果，实现普及初等教育目标，又制订“压缩高中、调整初中、充实和加强小学”的方案，进一步调整学校布局。至1985年，将完全中学压缩为3所，初中调整为16所（含戴帽初中9所），小学减为105所，加上村级民办小学79所，共184所。1986年普及初等教育验收，其后继续撤并一部分学生人数少、办学条件差的学校，改部分小学为教学点。经过10年努力，至1995年，全县有完全中学1所，初中19所（含戴帽初中5所），小学167所（含教学点15个），新建职业高中和特殊教育学校各1所，公办幼儿园从原有的

1所增至5所。20世纪90年代中期启动实施普及九年义务教育，县政府出台《调整小学学校布局方案》，旨在压缩小学数量，提高办学质量。同时，鼓励民间办学，形成公办和民办学校并存的局面。2000年，小学由156所调整为121所。次年，在《调整小学学校布局方案》的基础上出台《中小学布局调整方案》，扩大义务教育学校的办学规模，继续撤并因学龄人口结构变化导致生源不足的学校，调整高中阶段教育结构，增加学前教育资源，将扎佐中学恢复为完全中学，六桶中学增设高中。2002年，将修文中学初中部剥离出来只办普通高中，新置修文三中为初级中学。至2005年，全县有普通高中1所，职业高中1所，完全中学2所，初中增至20所（7所为戴帽初中），小学调整为完小71所和教学点45个，特殊教育学校1所，幼儿园增至7所。继后，一面继续调整学校布局，另一面整合闲置校舍资源，加强乡村农民文化技术学校建设，开展实用技术培训，巩固扫盲成果。同时，着力发挥乡（镇）中心小学和初级中学的办学效益，将办学条件成熟的小学和初中并为九年一贯制学校，加强寄宿制学校建设，为学校撤并后上学较远的学生入学提供方便。至2010年，全县公办学校中，有普通高中和职业高中各1所，完全中学2所，初中10所（不含戴帽初中3所），九年一贯制学校2所，特殊教育学校1所，小学50所、教学点14个，幼儿园7所。民办学校中，有完全中学1所，小学、初中和高中并设的学校1所，学前、小学和初中并设的学校1所，学前和小学并设的学校1所，学前教育学校6所，艺术培训学校1所。

2002年，学校布局调整后新设修文三中，县委、县人大、县政府领导为学校授牌

第二节　教育结构

一、学前教育

（一）幼儿园

1978年，县内公办幼儿园仅存实验小学附设幼儿园，入园幼儿200余人。1980年，扎佐小学附设幼儿园重新开办，共两个班50余人。1981年，成立县托幼工作领导小组，设办公室于县妇联，管理各区及县属部门开办的幼儿园，并以民办公助的方式发展学前教育，当年久长和小箐各办幼儿园1所。此后幼儿园发展较快，至1983年增至11所，入园幼儿22班960人。其中除实验小学附设幼儿园为公办外，其余皆为民办公助幼儿园，有扎佐、六广、县商业系统和驻县厂矿各办园1所，城关、久长和小箐各办园2所。1984年，实验小学附设幼儿园析出独办，更名实验幼儿园，入园幼儿300余名。20世纪80年代中期，因办学条件尚不具备，部分民办公助幼儿园时办时停。1988年，明确学前教育统属县教育部门管理。1990年，全县入园幼儿763人，适龄幼儿入园率9.27%。1992年，县内尚有民办公助幼儿园5所，17班443人。次年，扎佐、久长、小箐和六广幼儿园由民办公助转为公办，公办幼儿园增至5所，共计24班805

人，适龄幼儿入园率达34.98%。至1997年，又增加六屯和马家桥两所公办幼儿园，全县入园幼儿为24班771人。继后，为缓解幼儿教育资源供求矛盾，县政府倡办私立幼儿园。1998年，私立春蕾幼儿园和叮当幼儿园分别在县城和扎佐建立。次年，全县4至6周岁幼儿入园率达41.34%。接着，县城又办起工会幼教班和寓教、南方等私立幼儿园。2000年，全县公办、私立幼儿园达12所，共40班1446人。2001年9月起，施行教育部《幼儿园教育指导纲要（试行）》，确立幼儿教育在基础教育中的重要地位，促进幼儿园快速发展。2002年，叮当幼儿园投资420万元重建新园，建筑面积3400平方米，时为县内规模最大、办学条件最好的私立幼儿园。2003年，扎佐幼儿园改扩建完成，办学条件和规模全面提升，学生容量增加到400余人。当年，全县学前三年入园率达到56.58%。2005年，县内公办、民办幼儿园已达14所，但幼儿教育资源仍显不足，以致出现一批未获办学许可且条件简陋的民办幼儿园。为进一步规范办园行为，县政府一面扩大公办幼儿园规模，另一面对民办幼儿园进行整顿。2005—2007年，各幼儿园积极挖掘潜力、增加就读幼儿，同时取缔部分不具备办学条件的民办幼儿园。2008年，实验幼儿园迁址阳明大道新建，共投入资金700万元，占地面积10亩，并完善办学设施，办学规模扩大至400余人。当年，全县幼儿园人数达到2292人，将学前三年入园率提高到60.05%。2010年，县内公办幼儿园仍为实验幼儿园和扎佐、久长、小箐、六广、六屯和马家桥幼儿园7所，获办学许可的民办幼儿园6所，入园幼儿共73班2825人，学前三年入园率上升到65.37%。

2008年，选址新建的实验幼儿园

（二）学前班

1983年，依照贵州省和安顺地区教育主管部门规定，在条件较好的小学附设1年的学前教育教学班，招收6周岁幼儿入学，以缓解幼儿入园难的问题。到1985年，县内学前班学生共计373人。20世纪80年代后期至90年代初，学前班在县内各小学逐渐铺开，入学人数大幅度增加，到1991年已有29班1102人，1994年竟达64班2481人。1996年，规范学前班管理，实行登记制度，各小学在保证小学阶段适龄儿童入学的前提下，积极创造条件举办学前班，当年有学前班98个3336人。次年，扩大到111班3536人。2001年，全县适龄儿童学前一年入园（班）率为34.82%。此后，虽学龄人口结构变化而致学前班生源有所减少，但学前一年入园（班）率上升较快。2005年有79班2497人，入园（班）率突破80%；2008年为58班1577人，入园（班）率升至85.18%。到2010年，全县学前班44班1257人，学前一年入园（班）率已达98.37%。

1991—2010年学前教育统计表

表4—01—02

类别 年份	幼儿园						学前班	
	公办			私立			班级数(班)	学生数(人)
	学校数(所)	班级数(班)	学生数(人)	学校数(所)	班级数(班)	学生数(人)		
1991	1	8	361	无私立幼儿园			29	1102
1992	1	8	378				36	1368

续表

类别 年份	幼儿园						学前班	
	公办			私立			班级数(班)	学生数(人)
	学校数(所)	班级数(班)	学生数(人)	学校数(所)	班级数(班)	学生数(人)		
1993	5	24	805	无私立幼儿园			41	1642
1994	5	25	833				64	2481
1995	6	23	724				91	3309
1996	6	26	791				98	3336
1997	7	24	771				111	3536
1998	7	26	681	2	6	141	106	3392
1999	6	26	842	2	12	339	95	2874
2000	7	27	961	5	13	485	83	2103
2001	7	28	893	6	20	906	87	2523
2002	7	26	873	8	18	951	92	2682
2003	7	26	873	8	18	951	96	2763
2004	7	25	975	7	16	683	91	2602
2005	7	28	1103	7	30	1113	79	2497
2006	7	31	1220	6	40	1336	78	2234
2007	7	30	1217	5	27	846	64	1725
2008	7	35	1439	5	28	853	58	1577
2009	7	35	1950	5	24	870	46	1422
2010	7	39	1662	6	34	1163	44	1257

二、义务教育

（一）小学

1978年，县内有公办小学101所和民办小学104所，学生1071班3.9万人，厂（场）办小学8所，学生96班4009人。1980年，县革委出台《关于普及全县小学五年制教育的意见》，按照普及初等教育的目标，对小学进行充实和加强。1984年，公办和民办小学为185所，1088班，学生3.97万人，厂（场）办小学13所，109班，学生4410人。次年，县政府制发《关于普及初等教育的安排意见》，确定以乡（镇）为单位分步推进、分类实施，将全县32个乡（镇）分为4类并确定每类的“四率”（入学率、普及率、巩固率、毕业率）指标。1986年，县内有公办和民办小学181所，1182班，学生42154人，全县入学率达94.75%、普及率达92.39%、巩固率达96.76%、毕业率达93.98%，普及初等教育经贵州省教育厅验收合格。继后，县政府要求各小学采取措施巩固普及成果，稳定“四率”指标。到1988年，入学率达95.1%、普及率达95.1%、巩固率达95.8%、毕业率达95.0%。20世纪90年代，厂（场）学校随厂外迁，学生总数有所减少。1990年，全县小学（含厂办）174所，1267班，学生3.96万人，至1994年仅为158所1162班3.37万人。1995年，全县小学适龄儿童入学率为96%。次年，县政府实施《修文县普及九年义务教育规划》，“普九”工作全面展开，各乡（镇）更加注重适龄儿童的入学和巩固。1997年，全县小学入学率上升为97.58%，辍学率为1.52%。2000年，全县有公办小学（含教学点和特殊教育学校）135所，在校生3.64万人，7至12周岁适龄儿童入学率达99.55%，辍学率仅有0.4%，顺利通过贵州省政府基本普及九年义务教育验收。继后，县政府采取措施巩固“普九”成果，稳定入学率，降低辍学率。2004年，全县有小学122所（含教学点50个和特殊教育学校、民办小学各1所），在校生2.85万人，入学率99.21%、辍学率0.41%，“普九”工作通过省政府复查。2008年，全县有小学86所（含教学点22个和特殊教育学校、民办小学各1所），651班2.24万人，入学率99.11%，辍学率0.19%。次年，“普九”通过国家督导检查。2010年，全县有公办完全小学52所和教学点14个，在校学生1.83万人，入学率99.63%。

2009年，贵阳市对修文县的“两基”督导检查

2010年公办小学概况一览表

表4—01—03

属地	学校名称	类　别	班级数（班）	学生数（人）	建校时间（年）	学校地址
县直	实验小学	完全小学	30	1939	1902	县城文化路
	第二实验小学	完全小学	23	1411	1963	县城民主路
龙场镇（14）	中心小学	完全小学	10	380	1964	新春村
	新水小学	完全小学	6	202	1964	新水村
	马家桥小学	完全小学	12	441	1941	白莲村
	阳明小学	完全小学	7	255	1950	县城阳明大道
	阳早小学	完全小学	5	116	1939	阳早村
	小营小学	完全小学	6	189	1952	小营村
	程关小学	完全小学	6	191	1958	程关村
	中哨小学	完全小学	6	98	1953	中哨村
	王官小学	九年一贯制学校	12	569	1938	建新村
	普陀小学	教学点	3	70	1941	普陀村
	大地小学	教学点	6	166	1952	大地村
	马关小学	教学点	5	117	1951	马关村
	八一小学	教学点	5	116	1964	放马坪村
	红旗小学	教学点	6	130	1964	红旗村

续表

属地	学校名称	类 别	班级数（班）	学生数（人）	建校时间（年）	学校地址
扎佐镇（7）	中心小学	完全小学	19	1188	1906	扎佐街古驿路
	扎佐二小	完全小学	21	1153	1972	大园村
	高潮小学	完全小学	4	103	1934	丁官村
	兴红小学	完全小学	6	43	1969	兴红村
	三元小学	完全小学	6	141	1952	三元村
	清让小学	完全小学	6	213	1950	双月村
	葛马小学	教学点	4	71	1954	葛马村
谷堡乡（5）	中心小学	完全小学	9	255	1939	谷堡村
	乌栗小学	完全小学	12	428	1915	富裕村
	大塘小学	完全小学	6	166	1950	大塘村
	场坝小学	完全小学	6	109	1951	新堰村
	平寨小学	教学点	6	105	1950	平寨村
六屯乡（5）	中心小学	完全小学	9	363	1947	都堡村
	桃源小学	完全小学	3	123	1932	三寨村
	大路边小学	完全小学	6	98	1932	西冲村
	星中小学	完全小学	3	37	1960	星中村
	六安小学	教学点	3	38	1957	安全村
久长镇（7）	中心小学	完全小学	17	906	1906	久长街川黔南路
	清水小学	完全小学	6	178	1921	清水村
	石安小学	完全小学	6	264	1935	石安村
	兴隆小学	完全小学	6	219	1937	兴隆村
	金桥小学	完全小学	8	312	1956	金桥村
	芦山小学	教学点	3	83	1963	芦山村
	栋青小学	教学点	5	131	1950	栋青村
小箐乡（4）	中心小学	完全小学	12	424	1906	小箐街兰谷路
	崇恩小学	完全小学	7	175	1952	崇恩村
	新村小学	完全小学	6	147	1960	新场村
	小坝小学	完全小学	6	233	1972	小箐乡小坝村
洒坪乡（4）	中心小学	完全小学	12	501	1943	洒坪乡小坝村
	中寨小学	完全小学	6	242	1926	中明村
	红星小学	教学点	2	28	1947	蛇场村
	五老山小学	教学点	2	18	1962	五老山村

续表

属地	学校名称	类　别	班级数（班）	学生数（人）	建校时间（年）	学校地址
大石乡（5）	中心小学	九年一贯制学校	8	309	1945	大石村
	连丰小学	完全小学	6	115	1950	连丰村
	新庄小学	完全小学	6	76	1955	新庄村
	高山小学	完全小学	6	86	1963	高山村
	回水小学	完全小学	6	95	1912	回水村
六广镇（6）	中心小学	完全小学	12	476	1906	六广街前街
	沙坡小学	完全小学	6	145	1953	沙坡村
	广田小学	完全小学	6	205	1948	广山村
	中松小学	完全小学	3	35	1971	中山村
	四寨小学	完全小学	6	110	1952	四寨村
	德政小学	完全小学	6	189	1943	坪营村
六桶乡（7）	中心小学	完全小学	16	755	1942	六桶街迅文路
	花榔小学	完全小学	6	162	1952	花榔村
	凉井小学	完全小学	6	138	1954	凉井村
	宝寨小学	完全小学	6	104	1954	复兴村
	顺江小学	完全小学	6	73	1963	顺江村
	关寨小学	教学点	1	16	1962	关寨村
	凤联小学	教学点	1	11	1954	凤联村

（二）初中

1978年，县内有公办和厂（场）办初中167班，学生7726人，66所小学设有戴帽初中。1981年，办有初中的公办学校44所，其中有戴帽初中的小学37所，初中学生总数为9064人。后经过调整，将部分戴帽初中从小学分出单独设立。1983年，除修文一中（今修文中学）、修文二中和扎佐中学为完全中学外，分出军民小学戴帽初中设马家桥中学为初级职业中学，尚有王官、清让、久长、小箐、六广和六桶为初中，保留乌栗、六屯、中寨、洒坪和大石为戴帽初中，其余戴帽初中一律停止招生。1985年，公办初中有148班，学生7962人。后又将乌栗、洒坪、大石等初中单列。1988年，又在谷堡、桃源和程关设戴帽初中，公办初中学生升至8267

修文县第二中学

人。1990年，全县公办学校中除3所完全中学有初中部外，尚有普通初中13所，戴帽初中6所，共150班，学生7181人；厂（场）办初中8所37班1159人。20世纪90年代，厂（场）办中学陆续迁出，民办教育兴起，初中阶段入学率逐年提高，至1993年达73.57%。1995年，全县公办中学20所，其中有1所完全中学、14所普通初中、5所戴帽初中，初中有186班，学生7959人。次年，普及九年义务教育全面启动，提高初中入学率为当务之急，各乡（镇）加大动员入学力度，学生数量增多。1997年，有198班，学生8567人，小学毕业生已按要求全部升入初中，初中入学率接近80%，辍学率为4.75%。此后，抓入学、堵辍学成为"普九"的工作重心，各乡（镇）将动员入学任务责任分解到人，入学率得以迅速提升，辍学率有所降低。2000年，全县公办学校有初中15所，另有教学点（戴帽初中）4个，在校学生1.52万人，初中阶段入学率上升到98.47%，辍学率降为2.73%，通过贵州省政府"普九"验收，认定"基本合格"。继后，在巩固"普九"成果的同时，调整学校布局，进一步扩大乡（镇）初中办学规模，压缩教学点。2002年，修文中学初中部析出，新设修文三中。2004年，初中在校生1.72万人，初中阶段入学率为104.77%，辍学率2.66%，通过贵阳市政府复核后，即申请贵州省政府"普九"复查，获得"合格"等次。从2005年起，"控辍保学"成为常规工作，虽民办中学逐渐减少，但对初中教育影响不大，全县初中阶段入学率仍然稳定。2008年，初中255班，在校生1.29万人，初中阶段入学率104.94%，辍学率2.43%。次年，"普九"通过国家督导检查。2010年，全县公办学校除2所完全中学保留初中部外，尚有普通初中12所，戴帽初中3所，民办学校的2所完中有初中部；初中在校生1.39万人，初中阶段入学率106.9%。

2010年公办初级中学概况一览表

表4—01—04

学校名称	类　别	班级数(班)	学生数（人）	独立建制时间（年）	学校地址
扎佐中学	完全中学初中部	44	2314	1957	扎佐街学苑路
六桶中学	完全中学初中部	18	936	1984	六桶街黄金路
修文二中	普通初中	34	2063	1971	县城中山路
修文三中	普通初中	24	1479	2002	县城阳明大道
谷堡中学	普通初中	7	294	1992	谷堡乡谷堡村
乌栗中学	普通初中	9	474	1987	谷堡乡富裕村
六屯中学	普通初中	6	339	1990	六屯乡都堡村
久长中学	普通初中	21	1345	1971	久长街修开东路
小箐中学	普通初中	18	936	1971	小箐街兰谷路
洒坪中学	普通初中	10	493	1987	洒坪乡小坝村
六广中学	普通初中	11	619	1971	六广街毓秀路
马家桥中学	普通初中(农业中学)	9	460	1983	龙场镇白莲村
大石中学	普通初中(九年一贯制学校)	12	665	1987	大石乡大石村
王官中学	普通初中(九年一贯制学校)	11	550	1983	龙场镇建新村
广田小学初中部	戴帽初中	2	62		六广镇广山村
沙坡小学初中部	戴帽初中	1	62		六广镇沙坡村
中寨小学初中部	戴帽初中	5	216		洒坪乡中明村

（三）特殊教育

1978—1990年，县内未设特殊教育学校，盲、聋哑、弱智残疾（简称“三残”）儿童少年中，仅有少部分智力残疾者在普通小学随班就读，由于师资、设备等专业教学资源奇缺，接受的是与健康学生相同的教育。1991年，经县人民政府批准，县教育局在县直属的新春小学试办聋哑班。次年，为统筹规划全县义务教育工作，县政府决定单独设立全日制寄宿性质的特殊教育学校，纳入义务教育范畴。学校初建时，仅有砖混平房5间，设听力残疾（聋哑）班和智力残疾（弱智）班，共招生12名，盲童则送到贵阳的专业学校就读，当年全县“三残”儿童少年入学率不足20%。继后再加大力度，除办好特殊教育学校外，在有条件的乡（镇）小学开设随班就读点，招收更多的残疾儿童少年到校学习。1997年，全县开设随班就读点71个，入学87人，加上在特殊教育学校就读的24人，共计111人，全县7至15周岁“三残”儿童少年入学率56.34%。2000年，在特殊教育学校及县内普通小学随班就读、加上在县外就读者共计174人，入学率达91.1%，超过贵州省规定的“普九”验收指标30余个百分点。并随着特殊教育学校新教学楼的落成，学校增至5班，学生99人。次年，特殊教育学校又增修综合楼和学生宿舍，校舍建筑面积达1600平方米，在校学生突破百人。“普九”验收后，特殊教育步入规范化发展轨道，特殊教育学校对学生的服务功能逐步增强，发展成一所教育功能完备的全日制寄宿学校。2004年，全县7至15周岁“三残”儿童少年入学率为91.42%，其中特殊教育学校在校学生增至127人。继后，特殊教育稳步发展，全县义务教育阶段适龄“三残”儿童少年入学率稳定，至2008年为89.6%。2010年，入学率仍达到90.79%，特殊教育学校在校学生125人。

修文县特殊教育学校教学楼

专记：城乡义务教育普及全面实现

1986年，修文普及初等教育后，继续向普及九年义务教育的目标迈进。1992年，拟定《修文县1993至1998年义务教育规划》，并于1994年经县人大审议后批准实施。县委、县政府将“普九”工作纳入重要议事日程，积极稳妥地予以推进。1996年10月，重新修订《修文县普及九年义务教育规划》，提出“整体要求、分类指导、分步实施、分乡（镇）推进”的原则，县成立领导小组，县长担任组长，形成主要领导亲自抓、分管领导具体抓的格局。1998年，依照“分级办学、分级管理”的体制，县政府明确各乡（镇）和县直单位部门的工作职责，分别签订目标责任书，提出“抓住重点、主攻难点、全面推进、夯实基础”的工作思路，把“加快危房改造、改善办学条件”作为重点，把“提高初中入学率、降低初中辍学率、提高17周岁完成率”作为难点。与此同时，建立县级班子领导干部联系学校工作制度，切实加强对教育工作的领导和指导，协调解决存在问题。各级各部门在工作中做到感情到位、认识到位、领导到位、投入到位和工作到位。通过努力，当年即新建和维修校舍1.55万平方米，消除危房6914平方米，初中入学率从上年的73.57%上升至82.37%，初中辍学率从上年的4.75%降至2.94%，17周岁完成率从上年的59.98%上升至71.29%。特别是在控制辍学方面，实行“双线五级”目标管理，即“县政府-乡（镇）政府-村（居）委会-村民小组-村民”为一条线，“教育局-教辅站-学校-班主任-科任教师”为一条线，

层层落实责任，各乡（镇）、学校组织本单位干部职工进村入户，向广大群众大力宣传《中华人民共和国义务教育法》和《中华人民共和国未成年人保护法》，使这些法规深入人心，控辍效果良好。1998年6月，大石乡政府经过反复动员，对仍不送子女入学的8位家长，依法向六广法庭提起诉讼，状告这些家长侵犯子女受教育权，法庭受理后对案件进行了公开审理，叛令被告停止侵权，立即送子女入学接受义务教育。此类案件在县法院的审判史上尚属首次，开启以执法的形式保障适龄儿童入学的先河，在社会上引起巨大反响，《法制日报》《中国妇女报》《贵州日报》和《贵州都市报》等均进行了报道。1999年3月，县委、县人大、县政府和县政协听取“普九”情况汇报，对前期开展的各项工作给予充分肯定；5月县政府对“普九”进行自查，各项指标基本达到省定标准；8月县委、县政府组织召开专题会议，要求乡（镇）和部门认真履行职责，理清工作思路，全力以赴打好“普九”攻坚战；12月县委、县政府再次听取汇报，重点对下一阶段工作进行安排部署。2000年“普九”工作进入倒计时，县委、县政府将实现“普九”列为当年要办的10件实事之一，于3月召开攻坚会，县委书记黄乃铸作《统一思想，提高认识，狠抓落实，全面实现“两基”达标》的讲话，县政府与各乡（镇）和县直部门签订目标责任书，全县上下努力营造出良好的齐抓共管的“普九”氛围。从启动“普九”到2000年8月，投入资金3280万元，新建和改扩建中、小学105所。“普九”的主要指标完成情况为：小学入学率99.55%，初中阶段入学率98.47%，三类残疾儿童入学率91.10%；小学辍学率0.40%，初中辍学率2.73%；15周岁完成率96.38%，17周岁完成率82.25%。9月，贵州省政府教育经费审计组来县审计1997—1999年教育经费投入，认定为基本合格；10月，贵阳市政府对县“普九”进行复评后，同意县政府向省政府申请评估验收；11月，省政府评估验收团到县，通过对普及程度、师资水平、教育经费、办学条件和教育质量等指标的核查，基本达到验收标准，认定修文县“普九”基本合格。2001年2月，国家教育部公布全国第七批基本普及九年义务教育的111个县（市、区）和县级行政区划单位，修文县名列其中。“普九”验收后，县政府要求“机构不撤、人员不减、干劲不松”，全力抓好整改工作，制定三年提高规划，采取措施巩固“普九”成果。2004年经过省政府复查，认定修文县普及九年义务教育为合格，“普九”又迈上新台阶。此后，县政府贯彻落实“地方负责、分级管理、以县为主”的新体制，针对“普九”薄弱环节加以强化，从整体上提高基础教育水平。2009年，修文县顺利通过国家的督导检查，“普九”任务全面完成。实现“普九”在修文县教育事业发展史上树起一座丰碑，书写出前所未有的教育发展新篇章。

2008年，全县“两基”迎“国检”工作推进会

三、普通高中教育

1978年，全县有公办和厂（场）办高中教学班41个，在校生1686人。1980年，将修文中学更名修文一中，全县有公办完全中学6所。1981年，高中有32班，学生1438人，其中厂（场）学校14班476人。继后压缩完全中学，六广中学、乌栗中学和清让中学停止高中招生。1983年，仅有修文一中、修文二中

（原城关中学更名）和扎佐中学为完全中学，共计15班，学生799人，厂（场）学校11班516人。1988年，修文一中恢复修文中学校名。

20世纪80年代中期至90年代初，县内公办完全中学皆为3所。1990年，全县高中有16班，学生633人，其中厂（场）学校3班129人。1993年和1994年，先后裁撤扎佐中学和修文二中高中部，完全中学仅存修文中学，全县高中办学规模缩小。90年代中期起，部分厂（场）中学迁出县境，民办中学兴起。1996年，修文中学有高中9班，在校生385人，私立景阳中学1班11人。到1998年，公、私立学校高中17班597人，2000年增至20班886人。紧接"普九"验收，发展普通高中教育提上县委、县政府的议事日程。2001年，扎佐中学恢复高中招生，六桶中学办学规模扩至高中。次年，修文中学初中部析出独办，学校成为独立的普通高级中学。2004年，县内有公办普通高中1所、完全中学2所，民办完全中学5所，高中在校学生达3831人。同年，县政府决定启动修文中学申办省级示范性普通高中，进一步扩大学校办学规模。次年，全县高中增加到95班，在校生4542人。此后，部分民办中学停办或迁出，在校学生人数有所减少。2008年，全县高中有87班，在校生4204人。至2010年，县内公办学校中有修文中学为普通高中、扎佐中学和六桶中学为完全中学，民办学校中有华驿中学和景阳中学为完全中学，高中共有88班，在校生4447人，其中民办学校18班839人。

修文中学校园一角

专记：修文中学教育质量迈上新台阶

从20世纪80年代起，修文中学一向是全县普通高中教育的领头羊，历年的高考成绩一直是全县高中教育效果的试金石，其间风雨兼程，广受城乡群众的企盼和关注。80年代中后期至90年代初期，由于学校办学条件较差，师生纷纷外流，生源越来越少，严峻的形势使人忧心忡忡。1995年高考最初划线时，学校只有4人达到本科最低控制分数线，而被媒体《修文报》以"今年高考惨兮兮"为题撰文曝光，最后调整划线后，全县地方考生也仅有9人被本科院校录取（含艺术院校2人，保送1人）。燃眉之急，县委、县政府领导深入学校现场办公，深找原因，针对学校存在的问题采取措施：一面调整充实学校领导班子，一面在外地招聘教师，广纳贤能，解决师资匮缺问题，并下定决心改善学校办学条件。县委书记罗筑云提出："集中全县财力、物力和最优秀的师资办好修文中学。"次年，学校103名应届生参加高考，有14人上本科线。后随时间推移，学校班子逐渐健全，师资力量不断壮大，办学条件日趋改善，各项工作渐入佳境，教学质量显著提升。1998年，全校155名学生参加高考，重点大学上线16人，一般本科大学上线68人，专科以上录取率是全省平均水平的两倍，在贵阳市所辖的"一市三县"和三郊区普通高中、完中名列第一。2001年，学校高考文、理科总平均分分别高出全省总平均分32分和48分，在贵阳市辖"一市三县"完全中学中综合排名第一，本科录取101人（其中重点院校19人），录取率高出全省平均水平23个百分点,专科录取39人。2002年，学校专科以上上线率达92.7%，再次在市辖"一市三县"和三郊区完全中学中名列第一。同年，学校的初中学段剥离，修文中学成为全县唯一的普通高中，从而迎来新

的发展机遇，办学效益再上新台阶。2003—2006年，连续4年荣获贵阳市一般普通高中教学质量“入出口”成绩评估一等奖。2007和2008两年，又分别获得二等奖和三等奖。2009年，学校二本以上上线人数达到308人，创历史新高，再获市一般普通高中“入出口”成绩评估一等奖。当年，修文中学举行建校70周年庆典，县委、县人大、县政府和县政协四大班子主要领导亲临庆贺，县委书记石洪对学校取得的成绩高度肯定，并题词“风雨七十年，阳光育人路”。2010年，学校814名学生参加高考，一本上线70人，二本上线239人，高考教学质量“入出口”评估总分在全市排名第二，再获二等奖。与此同时，学校申报省级示范性普通高中相关准备工作圆满就绪，通过市级评估获得“优秀”等次，12月中旬已进行了省级评估，正待公布验收结果。修文中学曾荣获“贵阳市五好学校”“贵阳市体育先进集体”“贵阳市文明单位”和“贵阳市先进党组织”等称号。面对荣誉，全校教职员工表示不骄不躁、稳扎稳打，努力把学校办好、办优，为地方经济社会发展多作贡献，为国家输送更多的建设人才。

2009年，县委书记石洪为修文中学建校70周年题词

四、中等职业教育

1979年，安顺地区卫生局在县医院举办护士班，招收县内和清镇县学员40名。同年，县卫生局租用贵州省地矿局驻县105地质大队职工宿舍开办卫生技术培训班，先后培训170余人。20世纪80年代初、中期，县政府针对全县教育结构单一状况，进行结构调整，发展职业教育。1983年，马家桥军民小学析出戴帽初中班建成马家桥农业中学，学校结合农村实际开展职业技术教育，先后举办医士、农学、畜牧等职业班，毕业学生百余名，学校还培训食用菌栽培、家电维修等学员。1986年，经安顺地区教育局批准，在修文二中挂牌组建县职业高级中学，招收工业会计专业学生36名。次年，县职业高级中学借用县教师进修学校校舍，招收商业会计专业学生38名。1988年，县职高从修文二中迁入教师进修学校，招医士专业学生60名和林业专业学生46名。此后两年，又分别招农学专业学生37名、工交专业学生68名和文秘专业学生56名。1990年，在马家桥农业中学开办职业高中班，招畜牧专业学生45名。次年，六广中学亦办职业高中班，招果蔬专业学生30余名，后合并于县职业高中。1991—1994年，县职高共招收中师、财会、烟草等专业学生276名。1994年，马家桥中学停止职业高中招生，改为普通初中。12月，县政府决定将电大修文工作站、教师进修学校和县职业高中合并，成立修文县职业教育培训中心，为县直属职业教育学校，时有在校生412

修文县职业教育培训中心学生实习操作

人。1994—1999年，培训中心先后招收会计电算、市场营销、工业与民用建筑和旅游等专业学生162名。2000—2004年，培训中心发挥一校多能作用，除正常开展职业教育外，还与高校联合办学，开展成人专科、本科层次学历教育，共有1011人次在校学习。2005年起，培训中心与贵州省贸易经济学校、建筑工业学校和贵州航空工业技师学院等联合办学，并于2006年迁至县城油萝街。至2008年，培训中心与联办单位招收中专层次学历教育学生1767名，开展农村富余劳动力技能培训和引导培训近4600人次。2009年，培训中心建成教学楼、实训楼和学生宿舍、食堂等，办学条件大为改善，办学规模不断扩大。2010年，培训中心在册学生1015人，开设加工制造类、信息技术类和医药卫生类等7个专业。

专记：铸造技术人才的贵州航空工业技师学院

贵州航空工业技师学院原为贵航高级技工学校，前身系国家航空航天工业部属011基地技工学校。学校于1977年10月始建于县内扎佐区三元公社大山村，其办学宗旨是为国家航空企业培养高技能人才。从创办至20世纪90年代初，学校招收县内的中学毕业生数百名，学成后分配在相关厂矿和企业就业。90年代中期，学校实行转制办学，在原国家重点技工学校贵航高级技工学校基础上发展升级为一所培养中、高级技能人才的技工院校，每年均有县内学生自愿选择在该校就读。学校占地面积260亩，建筑面积5万平方米，教学楼、实验楼、师生宿舍和运动场一应俱全，图书馆藏书3万多册，备有远程卫星网络系统，开通了校园网，向着现代化教育技术的目标迈进。学校有机械制造工程、机械装配与维修工程、电气工程3个系，有供教师教学和学生实习的各种实验、实训设备500余台（套），可满足2000名学生的实习教学；开设的专业（工种）有机床切削加工、数控加工、机械设备装配与自动控制、工量具制造与维修、模具制造、机械装配、焊接加工、热表处理技术、工具钳工、装配钳工、机械设备维修、汽车钣金与涂装、汽车维修、计算机应用与维修、电机电器装配与维修、电子仪器仪表装配技术、电子技术应用、现代物流、酒店服务等近20个，有教职员工300余名。2000年，学校先后组建贵阳小河分校、安顺黎阳分校，形成跨地区、跨部门的集团办学模式。2005年学校招生近1500名，并开始与县职业教育培训中心联合办学，县职教中心定期将本校学生送入该校委托培养，两校优势互补、协同发展，共享教育资源。2007年改称贵州航空工业技师学院后，每年招生一直稳定1200人左右。2008年，招有技师4个专业，高级技工9个专业，中级技工3个专业，学生1430人。学校已发展成一所集预备技师、技师、中级技工、高级技工培养以及初级技工技术培训和技能鉴定为一体的多层次、多专业、多学制的技工院校。2010年，在册学生达4000余名，学校累计已为航空工业和省内外其他单位培养和输送近2万名中、高级技术工人和管理人才，不少已成为企事业单位的生产骨干，为贵州航空工业和地方经济社会建设作出突出贡献。由于成绩显著，学校荣膺国务院授予“国家技能人才培养突出贡献奖”。

贵州航空工业技师学院扎佐校区

五、成人教育

（一）自学考试

1984年，修文、开阳和息烽3县联合设立成人自学考试考点。1987年，修文单独设立考点。报名参加自学考试的学员不受年龄、职业、学历限制，根据自身实际选择报考专业和科目，学习不脱产、不交费，采用专门教材自修，到时统一考试，考试合格者国家承认学历，学历层次有本科、专科和中专，证书类别有学历证、单科合格证和专业合格证3种，学制可分段完成，也可连续完成，具有“单科独进、成绩累计、零存整取、分段完成”特点。1988—2006年，修文考点考生报考专业总数330个次，报考科目3.74万科次，合格科目1.6万科次；获本科学历56人，专科627人，中专1人。2006年，由于报考人数未达设考点要求，修文考点撤销。

（二）广播电视教学

1979年，修文筹建广播电视大学，招收第一期理工班学员10人，借县师范学校教室上课，主要依靠广播、电视等媒体进行教学，学员备有专门教材，学校聘辅导员面授。1982年和1984年，先后招收文科班和党政干部专科班学员20余人。1985年，授课地点改在县委党校。1987年，于县师范学校正式建立贵州广播电视大学修文工作站，先后开设汉语言文学、中文、英语、财会、党政和文秘等专业。至1990年，共毕业学员111人。1994年12月，电大工作站合并在新建立的县职业教育培训中心。1995—2008年，学员报名踊跃，电大共招收汉语言文学本科生416人，行政管理、农经等专业专科生422人。2009年春、秋两季均招生，采取开放教育和网络教育模式。从学校合并至2010年，共毕业本科生78人，专科生143人，专科升本科16人。

（三）教师进修

1987年，修文县师范学校第十一届学生毕业，学校停办，随即利用校舍设备，聘用教师，成立县教师进修学校，招收县内在职教师中未达中等师范学历者21名，学制2年。1989年，第一届学员毕业，招收第二届学员17名。1991年，第二届学员毕业，学校停止招生。1994年，学校合并到新建立的县职业教育培训中心。

（四）中师函授

1985年，设立中等师范函授广播学校修文工作站于县师范学校，招收学员287名。学员为县内未达中等师范学历的在职教师、代课教师和其他社会青年，学制3年。学员平时利用专门教材自修，寒、暑假期间学校聘请教师集中面授辅导。1987年，招收第二届学员221人。次年，招收第三届学员160人。1990年，学校业务移交教育局教育股管理，并在扎佐、久长、小箐、六广和六桶等地设立授课点，聘当地教师面授辅导。1998年，停止招生。学校从成立至停办，共招收学员8届914人，登记注册635人，毕业421人。

（五）农业广播教学

1981年，始设中央农业广播学校贵州省修文县分校。1984年，正式设立修文县农业广播学校，隶属县委工作机构。1988年，学校纳入成人中等专业教育系列，为县政府工作机构。1996年，始招大专学员。县农业广播学校的学员为在职机关职工和农村青年，以广播电视为媒体进行教学，兼及录音、录像资料，以自学为主，辅以集中面授，学制3年，开设专业主要为农业、林业和畜牧业。从建校至2010

年，共招收农学、畜牧兽医、淡水养殖、林学、财务会计和现代乡村综合管理等专业的中专19期44班次，学员1413名，毕业787人；招收农业技术综合运用、畜牧兽医、农学、林学和财务会计等专业的大专6期11班次，学员312人，毕业181人。

（六）党校培训

1978年，县委党校仍存。至1982年，党校主要是对县内领导干部进行短期培训。1983年，举办公社干部培训班，有学员51人，是为党校首次开展1年以上的培训。1984年，党校建在县城油篓街，始有固定办学场所。1985年，贵州省委批准党校试办两年制中专班，招收行政管理班学员42人，学校被纳入中等专业学校管理范围。接着又独立承办电大党政管理专科班。1993年，学校设立函授站开始招收学员。1995年，始办函授本科班。1996年，明确学校为副县级规格的事业单位。1998年，县委决定兼办县行政学校，将培训学习与学历教育结合起来。从1985—2010年，招收两年制脱产中专班5届，毕业学员153人；电大脱产专科班4届，毕业学员52人；与省委党校联办函授中专班1届、专科班10届和本科班9届，分别毕业中专、大专和本科学员23人、816人（另有38人在读）和420人（另有45人在读）；办中央党校函授本科班2届，在读学员134人；办贵阳市农村党员干部远程教育中专班1届，招收学员417人，在读377人；与县农广校共同承办村级干部和村级后备干部中专班，毕业学员548人。

（七）扫盲学习

1978年，县教育局教育股配专人主管业余教育，开展扫除文盲工作。1982年，县委、县政府落实全省农民业余教育工作会议精神，成立工农教育委员会，加强领导，调整和发展农民教育。经过普查，全县有文盲、半文盲4.68万人，占青壮年总数的43%。全县开办业余夜校29所，学员1472人，其中出现小箐杉林和六屯武家寨等夜校典型。同年，安顺地区农民业余教育汇报会和省农民业余教育现场会在修文召开，杉林夜校的办学经验得到与会者认可，受到省、地领导赞许。次年进行文化普查，以生产大队为单位建立《文化户口册》：全县青壮年文盲1.9万人，占青壮年总数的20.47%；32个公社（镇）中有12个达到脱盲标准，11个接近标准，9个离标准差距较大。1984年，县政府召开农民教育工作汇报会，建立扫盲岗位责任制，明确业余教育专职干部职责，继续开展扫盲工作，全县青壮年文盲数下降至1.37万人，占青壮年总数的14.5%，次年又降至12.6%。1986年，经省教育厅验收，全县青壮年文盲率仅为8.22%，达到基本无盲县的标准。此后，在继续扫盲、巩固成果的基础上，将农民教育工作重点转移到提高文化科技素质上来，扫盲学习转化为农村实用技术学习和培训，各区相继开办农民文化技术学校，向农民传授农业科学技术。

1991年，乡（镇）有农技校，村有扫盲班，形成全县农民教育网络。1993年，县政府印发《关于高标准扫除青壮年文盲工作的安排意见》，采取“一堵、二扫、三提高”的方法开展扫盲。全县10乡（镇）普建农民文化技术学校，学员642人；建村级校、班、点177个，学员6521人。同年，非文盲率已达98.2%，高标准扫盲通过贵州省政府验收，成为安顺地区第四个、贵州省第十九个实现高标准扫盲的县。次年，全县农民文化技术学校达183所，3.5万人次学员参加各种形式的学习培训。1996

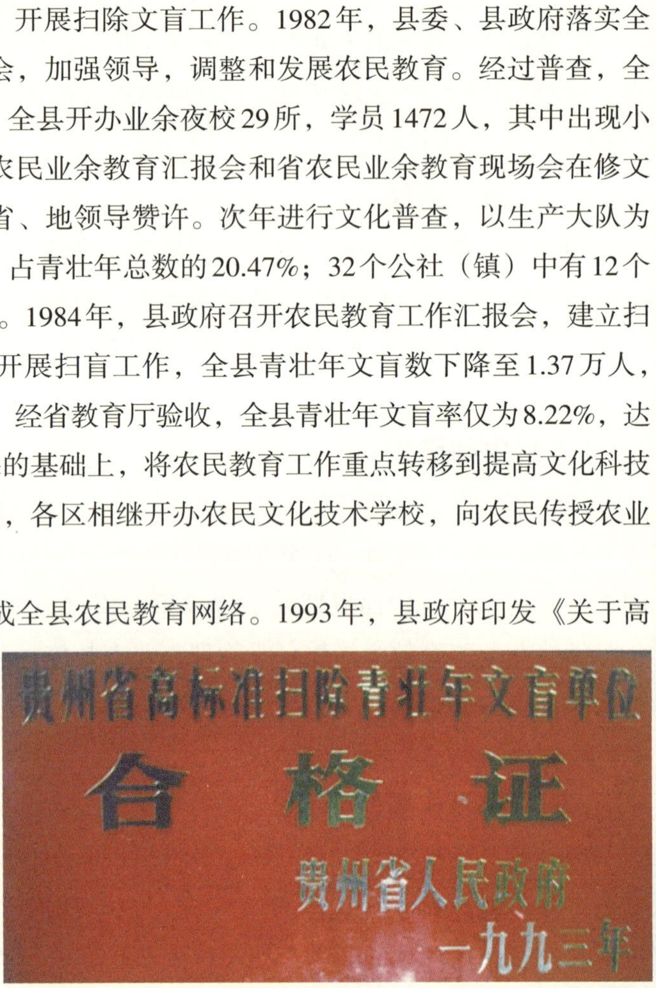

1993年，贵州省政府颁发的高标准扫盲合格证

年，县“两基”工作全面展开，将扫盲推向高潮，在工作中做到组织落实、教师落实、学员落实、制度落实、教室落实和经费落实。各乡（镇）抓脱盲巩固的同时，大力扫除新文盲，六桶乡扫盲成绩突出，迎来贵阳市扫盲工作现场会的召开。1997—1999年，全县脱盲5285人，其中脱盲后巩固5104人，巩固率达96.58%；完成农村科技知识培训35.8万人次。六桶乡花椰小学获国家教育部颁发的中华扫盲奖，小箐小学教师包富仙获全国妇联、教育部授予的第五届巾帼扫盲奖。2000年，全县已建乡（镇）、村农民文化技术学校（点）209所，凡1949年10月1日后出生的年满15周岁以上人口，其非文盲率达到97.79%，所有村（居）均达到贵州省基本扫除青壮年文盲验收指标，通过省政府验收。此后，农民文化技术学校将脱盲巩固、农技培训与道德法制建设相结合，在学文化、学技术的基础上增加公民道德、法律法规学习和培训，进一步提高学员的综合素质。2003年，培训结业5569人，其中妇女2488人。次年，扫盲工作通过省政府复查。2005年起，扫盲工作重点转为“以堵为主、堵扫结合，送教上门、科技下乡”。各地充分利用农村远程教育资源组织学习和培训，同时加强农村富余劳动力的转移培训，学员经过培训由县劳动部门输送外出务工。2005—2008年，年均培训6811人次，脱盲巩固率96.94%。2009年，建有乡（镇）、村农民文化技术学校202所，专兼职教师375名，全县227个行政村（居）均达到非文盲标准，通过国家检查。至2010年，农民文化技术学校仍继续发挥作用。

2008年，县教育局、科技局联合开展农业实用技术培训

专记：办学成效明显的杉林夜校

1981年贵州省农民业余教育工作会议召开后，县委、县政府即对全县扫盲工作安排部署，决定建立或恢复各地农民夜校，继续开展扫除青壮年文盲工作。3月小箐公社杉林生产队闻风而动，办起以扫除文盲为主的农民夜校，参加夜校学习的青壮年共45人，其中男19人，女26人，学员当中36人为文盲或半文盲。经过1年学习，脱盲34人。1982年，夜校在扫盲的基础上办起业余小学班和初中班，参加学习的学员增加到60人。夜校不但通过扫盲提高学员文化，而且结合农业生产需要，传授农业技术知识。学员们将学到的烤烟栽培知识和烟叶烘烤技术用于实践中，使全队的烤烟产值从原来的3600元上升到3.15万元；学到薄膜育秧和科学施肥、灌溉后，水稻亩产从原来的250公斤上升到575公斤；学到选用良种知识和条播密植免耕法后，油菜亩产从原来的82.5公斤上升到150公斤，现金收入从原来的9540元上升到2.9万元；学到玉米杂交法后，亩产从原来的100公斤上升到192.5公斤。由于夜校紧密结合农业生产组织农民学文化、学技术，推动了生产发展，改变了生产队的落后面貌。1982年，全队45户人家，90%以上有存款、有余粮，其中现金收入在1000元至2000元的有35户，2000元以上的有7户，6户出席全县劳动致富会议；全队购有手表25只，自行车2辆，缝纫机4部，录音机和收音机16台。

杉林夜校办学成效明显，一是区、社党委和大队党支部重视。夜校从开办起，小箐区委多次指派领导干部深入检查、指导和帮助，公社党委领导和大队党支部书记亲自发动群众，动员和组织学员学习，并经常到夜校听课，帮助解决办学中遇到的困难和问题，学校的夜间照明、办公用具得以解决，从而使学员安心，教员热心，群众放心。二是紧密结合实际，既学文化，又学技术，推动生产。夜校为适应发展生产需要，在组织青壮年学文化的同时传授农业科学技术知识，并把所学知识用到发展生产和增加农民收入中去，以收立竿见影之效。学员们尝到了学文化、学技术的甜头，迸发出学习热情，越学劲头越足，夜校越办越巩固。三是教员认真负责，积极工作。夜校教员由民办教师周继山和代课教师尹宜邦担任，他们白天在学校教书，晚上到夜校上课，积极主动协助发动和组织青壮年学员入学；他们专心备课，认真教课，根据生产需要，结合实际自编教材，没有现成材料，就在报纸杂志上查找摘录；他们为了推广新技术，先在自己的责任地上作试验，成功以后才推广，被群众称为“科学种田带头人”。此外，县、区、社业余教育专职干部的积极协助、主动配合也是夜校办学成效明显的重要原因。

1982年，小箐乡杉林开办农民文化技术学校业余初中班

杉林夜校的成功经验得到各级党委的充分肯定。1982年3月，县委批转《关于杉林业余夜校开展情况的报告》，号召全县各地认真学习其经验；继后，中共安顺地委下达《通知》，要求各县扎实学习和推广；7月，中共贵州省委办公厅下发《情况通报》指出：修文县杉林夜校的实践证明，办夜校是提高农民科学文化水平的一条有效途径，也是建设社会主义文明农村的一种重要形式。

第三节　教师队伍

一、教师结构

1978年，全县中、小学仍任用原在岗教师。继后，一批“文化大革命”中被错误处理的教师重返工作岗位。时全县教师仍分为公办、民办和代课3类。1979年，全县有公办教师887人、民办教师807人、代课教师483人。此后，按照贵州省和安顺地区的规定，将师范院校毕业生全部充实到教师队伍，并对民办教师进行整顿，合格者逐步转为公办教师。至1982年，共有师范院校毕业生300余人加入教师队伍，有29名民办教师转为公办教师，教学岗位缺额仍由代课教师补充。1984年，县委出台《关于落实知识分子政策的规定》，广开才路，招聘引进教师解决缺额问题，至1985年，招聘34人，调入40人。1986年，有47名民办教师转为公办教师，全县公办教师增加到1211人，民办教师经过整顿后减为454人，代课教师有750人。1986年起，控制民办教师数量，停止补充民办教师，至1988年，又有15名民办教师转为公办教师。1989年，从湖南聘用代课英语教师11名。1990年，全县有公办教师1372人，民办教师373人，代课教师704人。此后，公办教师逐年补充，民办教师转为公办教师的力度加大，部分代课教师转为聘用教师。至2000年“普九”验收时，补充小学教师699人和初中教师199人，先后6次将251名民办教师转为公办教师，3次将70名代课教师转为聘用教师。与此同时，县政府常务会议决定，对不能转为公办的

85名民办教师，按照相关规定发给一次性生活补助费，不再继续任用。至此，学校已无民办教师。继后，县政府出台《关于完善教育管理体制的意见》，教师实行聘任制，缺额面向社会招聘。2004年起，公办学校已无代课教师。从“普九”验收至2009年，全县共补充小学教师332人，初中教师149人，招聘引进高中教师73人。2010年，全县公办学校有教职工2422人，其中专任教师2256人，专任教师中幼儿园教师97人，小学教师1228人，特殊学校教师29人，普通中学教师847人，职业初、高中学校教师55人。

2007年，全县“师德专项教育年活动”动员大会

二、文化素质

1978年统计，772名中、小学公办教师中，大专以上文化程度79人，占10.23%；中专和高中345人，占44.69%；初师和初中309人，占40.03%；小学及其以下39人，占5.05%。20世纪80年代，国家大量分配大中专毕业生进入教师队伍，并鼓励教师在职学习、脱产进修等，以提高教师队伍整体文化素质。1990年，1518名中、小学公办教师中，大专以上文化程度235人，占15.48%；中专和高中1101人（其中高中92人），占72.53%；初中182人，占11.99%。90年代，由于实施“普九”工作，对小学和初中教师学历提出严格要求，必须分别达到中师（中专）和大专以上。为使教师学历达标，除新增教师学历必须合格外，还组织学历不合格的在职教师通过“三沟通”（高师函授、卫星电视教育、自学考试）培训学习以提高学历。

1994年，参加培训学习的初中教师达140名，其中中文专业61人，政治48人，数学13人，物理和英语各9人。次年，小学教师学历合格率为75%，中学为48%。随着补充合格学历教师不断增多和“三沟通”学员毕业，至2000年，小学专任教师1419人，中师（中专）以上学历1263人，占89.01%；初中专任教师602人，大专以上学历534人，占88.70%；小学教师大专以上文化程度占5.14%；初中教师本科以上文化程度占9.14%；补充的小学教师699人和初中教师199人，学历全部达标。后继续将教师学历达标列为重中之重。至2004年，小学专任教师1615人，学历合格1533人，占94.92%；初中专任教师697人，学历合格653人，占93.69%；小学教师大专以上文化程度占35.36%；初中教师本科以上文化程度占38.90%；2000—2004年补充的小学教师305人和初中教师122人，学历全部达标。

2008年，全县教师技能大赛现场

2005年，全县2678名教师中，大专以上文化程度1808人（其中本科353人），占67.51%；中专和高中856人（其中高中104人），占31.96%；初中14人，占0.52%；小学专任教师大专以上学历占51.07%；初中专任教师本科学历占25.96%。此后，

又将学历达标列为聘用教师的前提条件之一，并在教师学历达标的基础上，注重学历提升。至2008年，全县680名初中专任教师中，本科以上学历361人，占53.09%；1417名小学专任教师中，大专以上学历1055人，占74.45%；105名幼儿园专任教师中，大专以上学历75人，占71.43%。

2010年，全县公、民办中、小学（园）专任教师2412人，其中研究生学历1人，本科906人，大专1214人，中师（中专、高中）281人，高中以下10人；高中专任教师中本科以上学历占96.14%，初中专任教师中大专以上学历占98.39%，小学（含幼儿园、特校）专任教师中大专以上学历占80.58%。

三、政治待遇

（一）提高教师政治素质

1978年，全县教育系统有中共党员60余人，修文中学、扎佐中学、六广中学建有党支部，教育局机关与实验小学、县师范学校等建立联合党支部。20世纪80年代中期，县委贯彻落实党的知识分子政策，消除知识分子入党难问题，许多教师积极踊跃加入党组织，全县教育系统党的基层组织和党员队伍不断发展壮大。1984年，教育局成立党总支，县直属学校及各区教育办公室或区中学、区中心小学设立党支部，共有基层党组织11个。1986年，教育系统有党员288人；1990年为321人，占教职工总数的13.1%。1992年随着撤区、并乡、建镇，各乡（镇）教育辅导站及乡（镇）中学、中心小学均先后建立党支部。1995年，教育系统基层党组织增为41个，党员497人，占教职工总数的22.2%。1998年8月，撤销教育局党总支，成立教育局党委，局机关设支部。至2005年，教育系统有党支部43个，党员人数增至701人，占教职工总数的26.2%。继后，大力推进党的基层组织建设，在大型片区学校及民办学校亦设立党支部。2009年，修文中学建立党总支，学校有党员80人，为全县党员人数最多的学校。2010年，全县教育系统党支部数量增至65个，公、民办中、小学（园）教职工中有党员741人，其中女党员282人，党员人数占教职工总数的27.6%。

2008年，学校党的基层组织建设推进会

（二）表彰教师工作业绩

1979年，县委拨乱反正，为“文化大革命”中的124件教师冤、假、错案平反。1980年，贵州省政府表彰全省教育战线先进工作者，扎佐公社红旗小学赵真武和修文中学虞赓禹榜上有名。1984年起，贵州省政府每年给30年以上教龄的教师颁发荣誉证书。1985年，全国人大常委会决定每年9月10日为教师节，为迎接第一个教师节，县委、县政府成立庆祝活动筹备领导小组，对活动作周密安排，并号召各单位、各部门为教师办好事、办实事，县四大班子领导和35个单位、部门对教师进行慰问，120名教师分别受到省、地、县表彰。次年，又有140名教师受到各级政府表彰。此后，各级政府和教育

2008年，全县首届“师德之星”表彰会

主管部门均定期对教师进行表彰奖励。1989年，修文中学校长卢永康和后勤工人朱明扬被评为全国优秀教师和优秀教育工作者。1993年，共有8人次获地区级以上表彰。次年，17人次获地区级以上表彰，其中修文中学虞庚禹获特级教师称号，另有91人次获县级表彰。1995年，获全国表彰1人，省级表彰1人，地区级表彰7人，县级表彰80人。至2010年，获省政府颁发30年教龄荣誉证书的教师800余人，获国家级表彰的有李新民、陈福英、苏桂秀、吴道明、杨柏明、包富仙和屈冠翡等近20人，获省部级表彰的50余人次，获地（市）级和县级表彰的分别达200余人次和1000余人次。

专记：扎根乡村小学三十五年的苗族女教师杨柏明

杨柏明，女，1945年出生在石安乡下堡一个苗族家庭里。1960年起年仅15岁的杨柏明开始从事教育工作，先后在马家桥小学和石安小学当教师，1963年转到西冲小学工作。20世纪60年代的西冲，是一个贫穷落后的布依族村寨，仅有一条简易公路通往五六公里以外的桃源。当时，西冲小学处于初创阶段，办学条件十分困难，教室是群众腾出来的一间粮仓，桌凳是用木板搭在砖头上。在西冲小学，杨柏明每月只领取国家补助的4元生活费。学校开学时，仅有19个学生到校报名，为此，杨柏明白天上课，晚上手持火把，挨家挨户动员学生入学。由于她的不懈努力，第二年学生增加到40多人。虽然过的是烧柴煮饭、油灯照明的生活，但杨柏明铁了心肠，一心扎根西冲。辛勤的工作，换来了社员们的信任，将她留下当民办教师，并作为女劳动力记评工分。后来，她不但在情感上和当地社员水乳交融，真正置身这个布依族村寨，而且还深深地爱上这个地方。她在一则日记中写道："西冲有我难忘的许许多多乡亲，我爱这里土地肥沃，山清水秀，人民勤劳。"婚后，远在40公里之外的丈夫就近联系了一所学校，她前往执教。但到达新校后，她心里却始终惦记着西冲的一草一木，牵挂着那里活泼可爱的少数民族孩子。短暂的一年后，她同丈夫商量，毅然返回西冲。就这样，她艰难地度过一年又一年，学生换了一茬又一茬。西冲的群众看到学校有了"永久牌"教师，纷纷把孩子送到学校，就连原来在外地就读的学生也悄然返回。学生增加了，原有的校舍容纳不下，一个现实困难又摆在杨柏明的面前。在她多方奔走呼吁下，学校得以批准进行改扩建，她又走村串寨动员群众投工献料，并亲自带领学生参加建校劳动。1973年，新校舍终于落成，西冲小学面貌焕然一新，并结束长达10年的复式教学历史，代之1个拥有200多名学生的完全小学。由于地处边远，车辆运输十分不便，每个学期开学，杨柏明总是与其他教师一道，从15公里远的扎佐将书本背到学校。她关心爱护学生，经常利用课余时间给基础较差的学生指导和补习功课，有时遇到恶劣天气学生不能返家，就留下与自己食宿。她生第二个孩子时，仅仅8天就返回学校。1984年，杨柏明光荣地加入中国共产党，1987年，组织上将杨柏明转为正式教师。由于对教育事业无限忠诚，她浇灌出丰硕的成果，1988年西冲的适龄儿童入学率为100%，普及率为90%，巩固率为97.6%，毕业率为93.5%，升学率达80%以上，西冲小学历年毕业生有17人考入大中专院校。但是，她并不因为身份变化并取得骄人成绩而产生丝毫懈怠心理，反而更加严格要求自己，时时处处作出表率，无怨无悔教书育人，多次被评为修文县及安顺地区"三八"红旗手、优秀共产党员和优秀教师，并当选为乡党代表、人大代表，县第九届、十届人大代表。1989年，杨柏明被评为贵州省优秀教师；1990年，又荣获全国民族团结进步先进个人称号。1995年，杨柏明从西冲小学光荣退休，回到家乡安享晚年。至此，这个平凡而普通的乡村苗族女教师，为人民教育事业倾注和热整整35年。

（三）遴选教师参与理政

从20世纪80年代至2010年，广大教师立足本职工作，并积极参政议政，一批有突出贡献者当选为县人大代表或提名推荐为县政协委员，有的还直接从教育工作岗位上被委以重任，担任县四大班子领导。从县第九届至第十四届人民代表大会，共有40余人次的教师当选为县人民代表；政协修文县第一至七届委员会，共有40余人次的教师被提名推荐为县政协委员。修文中学校长卢永康先后担任县委常委、宣传部长、县委副书记和贵阳市委宣传部副部长，实验小学校长刘朝文先后当选县政协副主席和县人大常委会副主任，修文中学教师袁慎伦当选县人民政府副县长，刘国平、虞庚禹、陈信梅、杨正明分别当选县政协副主席，实验小学教师邓惠仙当选县人大常委会副主任。

四、培训学习

1978—1982年，针对教师业务素质参差不齐的问题，县教育局先后组织英语、物理、化学、数学、音乐、体育等学科的培训，参训者300余人次。1983年，利用暑假，分别组织中、小学教师集中到县城和各区开展为期15天和10天的培训辅导，准备教师教材教法过关考试，1000余人次参训。次年，为进一步提高考试合格率，再次利用假期开展大规模培训工作。经培训后统一考试，小学语文科合格率从4.32%上升到46.73%、数学科从2.89%上升到50.82%，初中各科总体合格率从25.16%上升到70.68%，全县689名中、小学教师达到文化、业务双合格标准，取得《教师教材教法过关考试合格证》。此后，每年均进行不同形式的培训，直至1987年所有教师考试合格。至1990年，县教师进修学校举办教师业务培训班3期，培训小学教师60余人次。20世纪90年代初、中期，主要针对教师学历达标进行学习与培训，中、小学教师近千人次参加，200余人取得合格学历。1995年，成立小学教师继续教育工作领导小组，正式启动小学教师继续教育工作，其中以培训作为主要内容。在进行培训时，县直属学校以校为单位，其他以乡（镇）为单位，进行“三字一话一画”（钢笔字、粉笔字、毛笔字，普通话，简笔画）培训。1998年，又组织小学教师集中开展“三新”（新教学计划、新教材、新大纲）培训。次年，中学教师继续教育工作启动，亦将组织教师学习培训作为主要内容。2000年，小学教师继续教育第一阶段工作告竣，经贵州省教师继续教育工作领导小组验收合格。接着开展中、小学教师继续教育（2001—2005）工程，加强教师业务知识、法律法规和信息技术等培训工作，全县2000余名中、小学教师参加。其中，结合普及中、小学实验教学，开展实验教师业务培训，参训500余人次，100余名教师经培训合格取得上岗证。2005年，在组织教师培训和自学的基础上，1000余名教师参加信息技术考试，合格率90%以上。同年，经省级验收，中、小学教师继续教育工程获贵阳市二等奖。至此，全县2000余名教师除新参加工作者外，绝大多数分别获得继续教育合格证、普法教育合格证、普通话等级证和信息技术等级证。2006年起，结合基础教育课程改革，组织教师参加贵州省“十一五”（2006—2010）中、小学教师继续教育工程，开展以“一德三新”（师德教育，新理念、新课程、新技术）为主要内容的全员培训，全县2500名中、小学教师参加。2010年，“十一五”中、小学教师继续工程通过省级验收，由于成效显著，修文县被评为省级先进单位。

专记：中小学教师“十一五”继续教育工程纪实

2006年5月，《贵州省“十一五”（2006—2010）中小学教师继续教育工程实施意见》出台，强调新一轮中、小学教师继续教育工程以提高教师特别是农村教师队伍素质为重点，以“一德三新”（师德教育，新理念、新课程、新技术）为主要内容，借助现代远程教育培训为平台，全面提升中、小学教师实施素质教育的能力和水平。为保证新一轮教师继续教育工程顺利实施，县教育局成立以局长为组长、分管副局长任副组长、相关科室负责人为成员的教师继续教育工程领导小组，制定实施方案，形成县、乡（镇）、校3级管理格局，并按照《贵州省中小学教师继续教育（2006—2010）考试考核标准及办法》的要求进行考试及考核。

此次中、小学教师继续教育工程，全县有88所中、小学的2490名教师参加培训，参训率100%，培训分为全员培训和专项培训。全员培训方面，一是师德教育培训，以《新时期师德修养》为教材，结合师德建设中的薄弱环节以及社会焦点和热点进行校本培训，每位教师集中培训达50学时以上，统一考试参考率100%，合格率99.85%；二是新理念、新课程培训，以《校本研修面对面》和《新课程推进中的问题与反思》为教材，以“决战课堂、新教材在练兵”为抓手进行学科教学业务培训，每位教师培训达120学时以上，统一考试参考率100%，合格率99.96%；三是新技术培训，以《教育技术培训教程》为教材，主要培训教师教育技术应用能力与学科教学整合能力，每位教师培训达70学时以上，统一考试参考率100%，合格率99.86%。专项培训方面，一是组织24名骨干教师参加省内外培训，分别认定市级、县级骨干教师37名和78名，培训完成率100%；二是坚持“不培训、不上岗”的原则，培训新教师97名，达120学时以上，培训完成率100%，组织县级班主任培训290人次，乡（镇）、校组织班主任进行全员培训，培训完成率100%；三是通过在职自修、脱产学习等方式，使小学（园）教师专科以上学历达1058人，占总数的75.12%，初、高中教师本科以上学历631人，占总数的68.06%，均超过全省的平均水平。此外，还组织80名校（园）长、116名教导主任或教研组长、80名实验教师、78名心理健康辅导教师和20名图书管理员进行专项培训。整个培训过程，校、乡（镇）和县每个阶段均定期进行自查，边查边改，确保培训质量。与此同时，建立经费保障机制，县教育局、各学校和教师个人合理分担培训经费，全县共计投入培训经费1163万余元，其中教育局投入243.82万元，学校投入356.94万元，教师个人投入562.25万元。

2010年工程结束，按照《贵州省教育厅关于对全省“十一五”（2006—2010）中小学教师继续教育工程进行评估验收的通知》要求，各校、各乡（镇）分别对本校、本乡（镇）开展继续教育的情况进行自查并申请县教育局验收，然后以县为单位进行自查并向贵阳市教育局申请评估验收，最后由市教育局申请省教育厅验收。年底，省教育厅验收组一行莅县，从组织管理、全员培训及专项培训3个方面，采取听取汇报、查阅资料、随堂听课、填写问卷、座谈走访、随机抽测等方式进行全面评估验收，认定为合格。在全省总结表彰时，修文县获省级先进单位，3人获省级先进管理人员。紧接着县政府召开表彰会，17所学校获先进单位、36人获先进管理人员、29人获县级先进教师的称号。

2010年，全县教师继续教育“十一五”总结表彰暨“十二五”启动会

五、职称评聘

1987年，县内开始评定教师职称，推行中、小学（园）教师专业技术职务任命制。教师专业技术职

务分中学教师和小学教师（含幼儿园教师）两个系列，高级、中级和初级3个级别。县政府成立职称改革工作领导小组，负责组织和领导初级教师职称评定和中、高级教师职称推荐上报工作，初级职称由县评定，中、高级职称报安顺地区评定。6—10月，在修文中学和实验小学试点。10—12月，又在13所区级以上中、小学（园）扩大试点范围。次年，全县铺开，并于6月结束职称评定工作。全县评定高级职称教师21人、中级275人、初级824人。评定为高、中级职称的教师，县政府颁发任命证书，安顺地区职称评审部门颁发专业技术职务资格证书；评定为初级职称的教师，县教育局颁发任命证书，县职称评审部门颁发专业技术职务资格证书。教师评定职称后，与所在学校签订协议（职责）书，由学校聘任，聘期3年。至1990年，全县在职教师评定高级职称17人，中级239人，初级975人。1993年，教师职称评定转入经常化，实行评聘结合，且限定各校高、中级专业技术职务岗位设置数量。至1997年，已评聘专业技术职务教师的情况为：高级6人、中级173人、初级994人。2001年，教师专业技术职务实行结构比例管理，各级职务按比例确定，实行评聘分开、竞争上岗。

2003年，根据教师履行职责情况，对专业技术职务资格证书进行审核，此后每3年审核1次，未经审核的证书无效。至2004年，共审核资格证1681人次。2005年，全县教师的职称构成情况为：高级职称36人、中级471人、初级2117人，教师聘期仍为3年，期满后重新考核聘用。至2010年，全县累计评定高级职称100人，中级职称1204人。2010年，全县各级各类学校专任教师专业技术职务构成情况为：幼儿教育专任教师中，中级职称18人，初级职称71人，未评职称65人；小学专任教师中，中级职称302人，初级职称919人，未评职称38人；特殊教育专任教师中，中级职称10人，初级职称19人；职业初、高中专任教师中，中级职称18人，初级职称35人，未评职称2人；普通中学专任教师中，高级职称44人，中级职称234人，初级职称583人，未评职称54人。

六、年度考核

1991年，已评聘专业技术职务资格的教师首轮聘任结束，县教育局、县人事局等部门结合教师任职条件和职责范围，一面复查，一面对其聘期内工作目标完成情况进行考核。同时，对专业技术人员进行年度考核，以定量和定性相结合的方式从“德、能、勤、绩”4方面进行考核，分为优秀、称职、基本称职和不称职4个等次，并将考核结果与个人的职称晋升、奖惩相结合。全县1186名公办教师参加复查考核，优秀等次258人，称职872人，基本称职53人，不称职3人；230名民办教师参加复查考核，优秀等次47人，称职151人，基本称职32人。此后，每年均对评聘专业技术职务资格的教师进行年度考核。1996年，全县参加考核的教师1769人，获优秀等次177人，占总数的10%。1998年起，专业技术人员年度考核纳入事业单位工作人员年度考核统一安排，考核时先由教师进行自我评鉴，然后学校根据教师履行职责情况进行量化测评并提出考核等次，最后上报县教育局考核委员会确定考核等次。当年，全县参加考核的2062人，优秀等次244人，称职1656人，不称职7人，未定等次（主要为新参加工作者）155人。2001年起，教师年度考核按照《贵州省事业单位工作人员考核暂行办法》要求，考核内容仍分“德、能、勤、绩”4个方面，重点考核工作实绩，考核结果分为优秀、合格、基本合格和不合格4个等次，并将结果与个人职称评定、工资晋升和年终奖金挂钩，从此作为续聘的重要参考条件。次年，全县2666名教师参加考核，优秀312人，合格2100人，基本合格3人，不合格2人，未定等次249人。2010年，教师年度考核仍在实施，全县2469人参加考核，优秀492人，合格1962，基本合格1人，不合格1

人，未定等次13人。

七、资格认定

1997年，根据国家教委《教师资格认定的过渡办法》和贵州省教委《关于做好在职教师资格认定过渡工作的实施意见》，县内启动教师资格认定过渡工作，认定对象和范围是1993年12月31日前已在岗的各级各类学校和其他教育机构中从事教育教学工作的教师（统称在职教师）、承担教育教学任务的其他专业技术人员和教育职员（统称其他人员），以及1986年底以前任教至省教委1996年8月8日发文之日并经省教委1992年整顿认可、发给《任用证》或《试用证》的民办教师。认定首先由教师自愿申请，然后由教师资格认定领导小组对其思想品德、学历、身体等条件和普通话水平进行审核，并组织参加教育教学能力测评且合格后，方认定相应资格。当年认定教师资格1957人，其中县教师资格认定工作领导小组认定幼儿园教师资格55人、小学教师资格1391人、初级中学教师资格401人，报送贵阳市教师资格认定工作领导小组认定高级中学教师资格84人、中等职业学校教师资格26人。经县、市两级认定教师资格者，均颁发相应的《教师资格证书》。至此，过渡工作结束。在教师资格认定过渡工作中，还对1993年12月31日前办理退休手续的教师进行资格认定，在此时段之后办理退休手续者，与在职教师一并认定。2003年1月，成立修文县实施教师资格制度工作领导小组，按照贵州省教育厅印发的《贵州省面向在职教师推行教师资格制度实施细则（试行）》规定，面向在职教师认定其资格。次年，又按照《贵州省面向社会推行教师资格制度实施细则（试行）》规定，开始面向社会认定教师资格。2003—2005年，全县认定在职教师资格1515人，其中认定幼儿园教师资格103人、小学教师资格922人、初级中学教师资格329人，报贵阳市教师资格认定领导小组认定高级中学教师资格109人、中等职业学校教师资格40人、中等职业学校实习指导教师资格12人；面向社会认定教师资格28人，其中认定幼儿园教师资格5人、小学教师资格13人、初级中学教师资格6人，报贵阳市教师资格认定领导小组认定高级中学教师资格4人。2006—2010年，共认定教师资格362人，其中面向社会认定教师资格143人。

八、工资福利

（一）工资

1978年，县内公办教师工资沿袭职务等级工资制发放。1979—1981年，两次为40%的教师提高工资。1980年，加发班主任津贴和食品补助，并对工作量之外的兼代课给予报酬。同时，增加民办教师补助费，平均每人每年50元。1983年，对1979年年底前参加工作的教师调升一级工资。次年，加发知识分子补贴、报刊补贴、边远地区工作补助。

1985年起，实行以职务工资为主的结构工资制，根据不同任职，按照基础工资、职务工资、工龄津贴、奖励工资4项总额发放，人均月增资20元，并还按从事本职工作的年限计算加发教龄津贴。1987年10月起，教师按当时的各级工资标准提高10%，人均月增资7.3元。民办教师则按国家年补助额（中学440元、小学400元）增加10%。1990年，教师普调一级工资，人均月增资12元，每人另增标准工资的10%。

1993年起，实行中小学教师专业技术职务等级工资制，工资水平大幅提高，人均月增资含交通费、洗理费和书刊费在内共计130余元，其中职务等级工资标准增加10%，继续执行教龄津贴、班主任津贴和特殊教育津贴，超课时酬金并入津贴中的课时津贴。同时，建立奖励制度和正常增资制度，凡年度考核合格者发给奖金（相当于12月份职务工资与教龄津贴之和），凡连续两年年度考核合格者每两年晋升一个工资档次，职称晋升者工资亦相应增加。1996年8月起，享受菜篮子补贴，每人每月30元。1997年，提高工资标准，高级、中级和初级职称教师职务工资均在1993年基础上增加14元，同时每人每月增加基础工资20元，并按比例增加活津贴。1999年，再次提高工资标准，高级和中级职称教师职务工资在1997年基础上分别增加112元和93元，小学一级和中学二级增加81元、小学二级和中学三级增加72元。2001年，第三次提高工资标准，高级、中级和初级职称教师职务工资分别平均增加130元、78元和70元。同时，实施艰苦边远地区津贴，县内执行一类地区标准，高级、中级和初级专业技术职务教师分别津贴60元、47元和40元。2003年，第四次提高工资标准，高级、中级和初级职称教师职务工资分别平均增加203.5元、103.5元和76元。

2009年起，实行以岗位绩效为核心的绩效工资制，以岗定薪，岗变薪变。岗位绩效工资由岗位工资、薪级工资、绩效工资和津贴补贴组成。岗位工资每个岗位设置不同等级，每个等级对应1个工资标准，个人按所聘岗位和等级执行；薪级工资每个薪级对应1个工资标准，不同岗位规定不同的起点薪级，个人按照套改年限、任职年限和所聘岗位结合工作表现，套改相应薪级；津贴补贴分艰苦边远地区和特殊岗位两种，前者每月人均70元、按不同岗位享受不同数额，后者为特殊岗位人员享有。绩效工资制首先在义务教育学校教师中实行，绩效工资总量按教职工2008年12月份的基本工资额度（含提高的10%部分）和规范后的津补贴确定为平均每人2.4万元（含年终奖金1078元），分基础性绩效工资和奖励性绩效工资两部分，前者占总额的70%并按月发放给教师，后者占总额的30%并由教育局考核各学校年度目标任务完成情况后分等次划拨给学校，学校再通过考核教师履行工作职责情况分等次发放。2010年，非义务教育学校教师也实行绩效工资制。

（二）福利

1978—2010年，公办教师享受的福利主要有医疗、住房和假期等方面。

医疗　1978—2004年，县内公办教师享受公费医疗，其生病治疗产生的相关费用按规定予以报销。2005年6月正式启动实施机关事业单位职工医疗保险制度，开始缴纳基本医疗保险费，次月起教师享受医疗保险待遇。教师的基本医疗保险费，由教育局和教师按月缴纳，教育局以上年度职工月平均工资总额为基数按7.5%的比例缴费，教师本人以上年度月平均工资总额为基数按2%的比例缴费。大额医疗补助费，由教育局和教师个人每年各缴纳48元。教师的基本医疗保险费按月划入其个人账户即社会保障卡内，购买药品时到定点药店刷卡，入院治疗则按规定报销。至2010年，教师仍然享受医疗保险待遇。

住房　20世纪90年代初实施住房制度改革，县政府鼓励教师购买公有住房和集资建房。1993年，县城学校将教师宿舍（公有房）出售给居住的教师。1994年，县政府建立住房公积金制度，县财政按应承担比例为县直属学校教职工缴存公积金。次年春，县政府在县城内选址新建教师安居小区，建成两栋宿舍共48套住房，建筑面积3480平方米，以成本价出售给住房困难的教师。与此同时，采取多种形式为城乡教师解决住房困难，其中主要方式

1995年建成的教师安居小区

是形成政府、单位和个人共同投资建房的新体制，即在校园内划定土地、学校力所能及给予补助，政府与教师共同投资或教师全额投资建设住房。至2003年停止集资建房时，修文中学、实验小学、六桶中学、中寨小学等10余所学校集资建设教师住房近1.7万平方米。2005年，县政府办公会议决定按《住房公积金管理条例》规定，对乡（镇）学校教师开始实行住房公积金制度，由县财政按3%的比例为教师缴存住房公积金，其后许多教师利用住房公积金贷款在县城购买商品房。2008年，县政府落实住房货币化政策，对1998年12月31日前在册的教职工按职务（职称）确定数额、以年度为单位给予住房存量补贴补偿，并从1999年1月起按月工资数额相应比例计发教职工住房增量补贴。至2010年，继续执行教职工住房公积金制度和增量补贴。

休假　1978—2010年，县内教师除按国家规定享有寒、暑假和其他法定节假日外，还享有一部分特殊假期。教师按法定结婚年龄（女20周岁，男22周岁）结婚的，可享受3天婚假，符合晚婚年龄（女23周岁，男25周岁）的，假期还可增加10天；教师与配偶或父母相距较远，不能在公休假日团聚的，视情况给予探亲假；教师直系亲属死亡，给予3—5天丧假，返家路程较远的还可适当延长。此外，对于女职工的产假，县教育局均按照国家和省、地（市）的相关规定执行。

第四节　教学活动

一、教学内容

（一）德育

1978年，中共十一届三中全会召开后，学校德育一改以往“以阶级斗争为纲”的教育，要求教师引导学生“好好学习，天天向上”，把青少年培养成为“四有”（有理想、有道德、有文化、有纪律）新人。20世纪80年代，贯彻《中学生守则》和《小学生守则》，加强爱国主义教育、理想信念教育和道德品质教育，开展“五讲四美三热爱”（讲文明、讲礼貌、讲卫生、讲秩序、讲道德，心灵美、语言美、行为美、环境美，热爱祖国、热爱社会主义、热爱中国共产党）活动。教育局组织开展“文明礼貌月”评比、小学生诗歌朗诵和中学生演讲等活动，实验小学、城关小学、扎佐二小和久长小学等建立升降国旗制度，修文中学把德育工作纳入对班主任工作考评范围。90年代深化学校德育工作，在继续进行《小学生守则》和《中学生守则》教育的同时，贯彻落实《中共中央关于改革和加强中小学德育工作的通知》和《中共中央关于进一步加强和改进中小学德育工作的意见》，学校建立以校长为首的德育

2010年，在扎佐中学召开全县未成年人思想道德建设工作现场会

工作管理体制，将德育工作落到实处，认真落实《小学德育纲要》和《中学德育大纲》要求，以《中学生日常行为规范（试行）》和《小学生日常行为规范（试行）》教育为重点，以“五爱”（爱祖国、爱人民、爱劳动、爱科学、爱社会主义）为基本内容，培养学生成为爱国的和具有社会公德、文明行为习惯、遵纪守法的好公民。期间，县委、县政府将烈士陵园和阳明洞张学良囚禁处列为县首批爱国主义教育基地，县教育局建立德育工作考核评估制度，先在实验小学和修文中学进行德育工作评估试点，然后全县铺开，全面完成乡（镇）以上中、小学的评估工作；德育的内容和形式更加多样化，教育局先后开展“爱国主义教育”系列活动、“爱祖国·爱家乡”知识竞赛、学生夏令营、迎接香港回归、重走长征路和法制纪律教育等活动近20次；学校德育工作成效明显，学生受地（市）级表彰者近200人，县级表彰500余人；学生道德素质呈现出从思想向行动的转化，先后涌现出洒坪中学学生抢救落水同学献身、阳早小学学生勇灭山火、六桶中学学生为亚运会捐资、扎佐中学学生见义勇为和久长中学学生拾金不昧等典型。进入21世纪，创新学校德育工作，管理体制更加完善，学校确立以学生为本的理念，将德育工作充分融入学生的学习和生活之中。中学设立德育处，小学充实少先队管理队伍；全县乡（镇）中、小学以上学校聘请政法部门干警担任法制副校长，定期给学生上法制课。学校严格执行《中小学德育工作规程》，以新颁布实施的《中小学生守则》和《小学生日常行为规范（修订）》、《中学生日常行为规范（修订）》为教育重点，贯彻执行《中共中央国务院关于进一步加强和改进未成年人思想道德建设的若干意见》、《公民道德建设实施纲要》，加大德育工作力度。2003年，实验小学、六广小学少先队获省级表彰。2004年，召开全县德育工作会，把弘扬和培养民族精神作为新形势下学校德育工作的首要任务。2005至2008年，落实并实施《修文县中小学德育工作考核评比实施方案》，每年对中、小学德育工作进行考核评比，县内学校有52班次获市级文明班级，353人次获市级“三好”（思想品德好、学习好、身体好）学生，366人次获市级优秀学生干部，县内通报表彰411人次优秀德育骨干教师。至2010年，学校德育的针对性、实效性和主动性更加突出，符合时代特征的专项教育活动内容更加丰富，爱国主义、民族精神、法制纪律、实践创新、网络文明、诚实守信、生命安全、远离毒品和反对邪教等教育全面纳入对学校德育工作的考核内容，使学生思想道德建设步入规范化管理的轨道。

（二）智育

1978年，恢复各区中心小学，县教育局确定修文中学和六广中学为县属重点中学，并要求具备条件的高中试行文、理分科，中、小学可根据学生成绩编班，小学试办重点班，中学办好重点班。同时，学校成立领导小组，加强对毕业班工作的指导，实行统一考试，强抓教学质量。1980年，贯彻落实教育部修订颁发的《全日制小学暂行工作条例》和《全日制中学暂行工作条例》，进一步整顿教学秩序，坚持实行以教学为主的原则。学校强调重点科目学习，小学阶段特别注重语文和算术两科课程，语文注重识字、写字和作文教学，算术注重计算、推理和解答能力培养；中学则重视数学、物理和化学等科目，并加强基础知识教学和基本技能训练，当时在师生中流行一句话：学好数理化、走遍天下都不怕。与此同时，妥善安排中学生参加社会实践活动，为其毕业就业和继续升学奠定必要的文化和实践基础。1984年，县教育局先后出台《关于教育改革的几项具体决定》和《学校工作管理意见》，明确要求学校加强教学工作，增强质量意识。此后几年，各学科统考成绩稳步上升。1986年小学毕业班升学考试，语文和数学两科及格率分别为20.6%和16.2%，1989年分别提高到37.15%和34.63%。中学方面，1985年高考和中考，大专以上录取73人，中专（中师）和中技录取245人，1990年则分别录取92人和330人。但由于受

应试“指挥棒”的影响，学生只重视统考科目学习，学校追求升学率成为风气，初中补习班遍地开花，高中生复读层出不穷，种种现象反映出教学面临的新问题。20世纪90年代中期，教育部倡导推行素质教育，鼓励中、小学进行教学改革尝试。各校采取措施，从开齐课程、开足课时切入，减轻学生过重的课业负担，改进教师的教学方式和授业手段，采取多种途径掌握知识，引导学生全面发展，提高整体素质。经过几年努力，成效比较明显，教学质量得以提升。1994年小学六年级统考，语文科及格率和平均分分别为76.6%和61.53分、数学科分别为48.27%和55.15分，1998年语文科分别提升8.05个百分点和7.56分、数学科分别提升13.89个百分点和5.37分；2000年与1997年相比，初中毕业生统考的6科中，平均分亦呈现上升趋势，其中上升10分以下、10至20分和20分以上的各为两科；1999年高考录取大专以上人数在1995年的基础上增加100人，中考录取中专（中师）人数则在1995年的基础上增加523人。进入21世纪，素质教育全面推行，不再以学生考试成绩作为对学校办学水平和教师教学质量评价的唯一标准，促进学生全面发展的意识渗透到学校管理的各个侧面和教师教学的各个环节。2004年小学和初中全科合格率分别为80.54%和36.7%，2008年分别提高至87.63%和77.54%。2008年，全县教育工作会议召开后，确立了全面提升教育质量的目标，县政府确定每年拨款100万元作为教育质量奖励资金。2010年，全县中、小学课程改革全面推进，各校以此为契机，稳步提升教学质量。

2008年，全县教育工作会

专记一：社会关怀让贫困学子王霄圆了大学梦

王霄出生在小箐乡新场村一个贫困的苗族家庭里，刚满周岁母亲因患癌症离开人世。“穷人的孩子早当家”，年仅10岁的王霄即开始承担家务劳动，砍柴割草、洗衣煮饭、喂猪放牛样样都干。上小学时，王霄学习十分勤奋和刻苦，考试成绩始终名列前茅。每天放学回家做完家务，都自觉完成老师布置的作业。在她幼小的心灵里，也向往着像别的孩子一样长大后能上中学甚至大学。1999年，王霄实现梦想的第一步，如愿上了初中。学校离家有8公里之遥，往往是天亮即出发，日落才归家，但她却利用这遥远的路途作为温习功课的宝贵时光，边赶路边看书。初中的学习任务十分繁重，回家后常常学到半夜鸡叫，需家人多次催促才上床休息。继母心疼她，劝她住在学校，但她却担心增加家庭负担而迟迟不肯，后经多次劝说才勉强住校，可宿舍人多嘈杂，影响学习，不久她又恢复走读。期间，没钱买参考资料，便借别人的书来抄，抄了一本又一本；

2007年，县领导参与资助贫困学生活动

没钱买作业本，便将老师用剩的粉笔头，在地上一次又一次做练习题。勤奋和努力终于有了回报，2002年王霄以优异成绩考上高中，需到更加遥远的县城就读，这一来更增加了家庭的困难，父母既要赡养年近七旬的祖母，又要抚育在初中上学的弟妹，王霄产生了放弃继续上学的念头。为了避免这个优秀的学生辍学，她的母校和小箐乡政府在捐资帮助的同时，成功地申请到1万元的“桦渊助学金”，为她的家庭解决后顾之忧，使面临困境的王霄重新点燃希望。进入高中后，王霄学习更为勤奋和刻苦，入校的第一学期即被评为“三好”学生，第二年参加修文、开阳、息烽3县高中数学竞赛荣获第二名。2005年高考，她以619分的优异成绩被四川大学录取。考上大学后，父母因上学费用拮据一筹莫展，家庭又一次陷进困境。贫困学子上不了大学引起社会的极大关注，县委书记魏明禄得知后，当即捐资1500元助其入学，在县委主要领导的义举带动下，县移动公司干部职工捐资1000元，小箐乡机关支部20余名党员捐款750元，县妇联和团县委捐资500元，为王霄筹集学费。社会的关怀，终于圆了王霄的大学梦，这个苗族女孩成为新场村有史以来的第一个大学生。开学后，王霄满怀希望，带着亲人的嘱咐和家乡父老的期望，走向人生新旅途，跨进全国重点大学四川大学的土木工程系，去实现她更大的人生梦想。

专记二：勤奋学子周政旭的成才路

1984年，周政旭出生在一个普普通通的知识分子家庭，父亲当中学教师，母亲是医护人员。由于家庭的熏陶，年幼的周政旭便在父母引导下开始识字，随着识字的逐渐增多而爱上读书。到上小学时，家中存放的各种书籍都被他“底朝天”翻了一遍，而且每到亲友家作客，最吸引他的就是人家的书柜，遇到喜欢的书总是爱不释手，借回家中仔细阅读。除喜欢读书外，他还喜欢与同龄小朋友一道游玩，经常邀约邻家孩子一同上山下河疯玩一通，时不时也犯一些诸如踩坏庄稼、摔伤胳膊之类的错误，但开明的父母并未一味指责，而是既严肃批评又鼓励其多接触大自然，激发多种兴趣，形成良好习惯，努力培养其探知自然和勇于面对困难的个性。

上小学期间，周政旭是班上年龄最小的几个孩子之一，但他的学习劲头不小，遇到不懂的问题，一定要“打破砂锅问到底”，直到弄个明白才罢休。小学6年，他的成绩一直名列前茅，多次荣获学校表彰。1996年，周政旭考入修文二中，时值学校招收首届实验班，他如愿就读该班。学校极其重视实验班的教学和管理，集中最好条件扶持，安排最优秀教师任教，晚自习统一安排教师辅导，并有教师在寝室值班，学生学习上遇到的问题随时都能给予解决。实验班的任课教师十分敬业，每人都满怀成功的希望，尽心尽力地引导和培养每个学生。实验班的同学也很努力，整个班级学风良好，教室里的电灯一直是最晚熄灭，晚自习后回到寝室，同室的同学还就当天的学习内容讨论一番，往往争得面红耳赤。在这样的学习氛围里，周政旭受益匪浅，他深知一分耕耘就有一分收获，只有经过不断努力，才能攀上理想高峰。良好的学习环境更加铸就周正旭踏实、勤奋和刻苦的学习性格，除教室里和寝室内，学校的草坪上、树荫下、花池边都成为他学习的场所，每天都在静静地看书和思考。紧张学习之余，周政旭也喜好体育锻炼、郊游等，寻找机会放松自己。初中三年，他的学习成绩总是名列前茅，曾多次获数学、英语、物理等学科的竞赛奖励。1999年，周政旭获全县中考第一名，被省级名校贵阳一中录取。进校后，周政旭又跨入一个新的学习环境，学校聚集了若干来自全省各地的学习尖子，竞争十分激烈，学习压力很大，但他很快就适应下来，不仅学习刻苦，而且活学活用、思维缜密。一次，数学老师课堂上解题，认为所讲授的方法是最简单的，周政旭下课后告诉老师，自己也有一种简单的解题方法，经老师验证后确实如此。老师对他勤于思考的行为给予肯定，并鼓励他再接再厉，往上攀登。在老师的谆谆教导下，周政旭一直迈着坚实的脚步，向着自己追求的目标奋进。高一期间参加全国中学生英语能力竞赛获三等奖；参加“希望杯”全国数学邀请赛获银牌。高二期间参加“希望杯”全国数学邀请赛获银牌；参加贵州省第六届青少年生物与环境科学实践活动获一等奖；参加全国中学生化学竞赛获贵州赛区三等奖。高三期间参加全国数学联赛获贵州赛区二等奖；参加全国中学生物理竞赛复赛获一等奖，并作为4名成员之一，代表贵州赴海南参加全国决赛，获贵州省第一名、全国三等奖；参加全国中学生化学竞赛复赛获一等奖，又作为5名成员之一，代表贵州省赴山东参加全国决赛，获贵州省第一名、全国二等奖。在海南参加全国物理竞赛时，周政旭偶遇清华大学和北京大学两校招收保送生的老师，两校都当即答应将其保送入学。过了两个月，在山东举行的全国化学竞赛现场又再次相遇，招生老师十分惊讶，同一个学生在物理、化学两个学科的竞赛中，都代表全省参加全国决赛，而且还取得骄人的成绩，真是罕见。清华大学的老师拍着周政旭的肩膀打起了包票：“小伙子不错，来我们清华吧，挑个你喜欢的专业。”而此时北京大学的预录通知书，则已经快递到母校贵阳一中，如果他想去，只需把回执填妥寄回即可。周政旭年少时，阅读过一本清华大学建筑系开山祖师梁思成的书，书中闪烁的建筑光辉和呈现的学者风范深深地吸引着他。最终，他选择了清华大学建筑系，立志将建筑作为毕生的追求，并于2002年3月顺利拿到清华大学建筑系的录取通知书，此时距高考尚有4个月。其后的时间里，有人劝他说，你反正都已经被名校录取了，就轻轻松松地玩一下，他斩钉截铁地说：“我不但要参加高考，而且一定要考好，以事实证明是凭自己能力进入清华的！”于是，全身心地投入到迎考准备中。7月，高考成绩揭晓，他以699分排列全省第五名，其中数学科以146分居全省之冠。虽然取得不凡的成绩，但他却非常平静，在和同学外出游玩几天后，又开始思索大学的学习和生活。

2002年9月，周政旭跨进清华大学的校门，这里有最丰富的学习资源，最优秀的教师和出类拔萃的同学，他认定要将这一切作为进一步学习和成长的动力，而且交出一份几乎完美的答卷：大一总成绩列全班前五名，获学校二等奖学金；大二总成绩列全班第一、全年级第一，获国家一等奖学金；大三总成绩列全班第三、全年级第三，获学校一等奖学金；大四又列全班第一，获学校一等奖学金。2006年1月参加“80筑家”金地大学生建筑设计大赛获优秀奖，9月又获年度五合国际奖学金，该项奖学金面向全国建筑与规划学院的本科生设立，从数十所建筑院校挑选5位学生颁奖；10月又参加中国建筑学会全国大学生建筑设计竞赛，获三等奖。在大四期间，他获推荐报考研究生资格，并在快速设计考试中取得第一名，最终以推研总成绩全年级第一被城市规划专业免试录取为直博研究生，师从我国城市规划与建筑界泰斗、两院院士吴良镛先生。此后他进入清华大学特有的直接攻读博士研究生阶段，并参与多项重大研究课题，在学术领域里继续努力奋斗，开始他新的人生旅程。

（三）体育

1978年，军体课复称体育课，教师按照《体育教学大纲》的要求组织教学。1979年，执行《中小学体育暂行办法》，县内各校大力开展体育、劳动“两课”和眼保健操、课间操“两操”，以及体育、文艺“两活动”。1982年，贯彻教育部修订的《国家体育锻炼标准》，在县直属学校开展体育达标活动。次年，各学校在上好体育课的同时组织体育活动，鼓励学生积极进行体育锻炼，促进体育达标，对达标学生发给《体育合格证》；凡不积极参加体育锻炼，体育成绩不合格者，不能评为“三好”学生。1985年，为继续推进体育达标，教育局设专人管理学校体育工作。1987年，修文中学率先将体育考试合格作为学生毕业的条件之一，随后大部分中学纷纷推行。1990年起，实施国务院批准颁布的《学校体育工作条例》，学校保证学生每天1小时的体育锻炼时间，执行新的《国家体育锻炼标准》，除小学一、二年级外，统一使用《国家体育锻炼标准学生成绩册》，将其作为对学生身体素质追踪的依据。1995年，首次将体育科列为中考科目，全县参加考试的学生2351人，3个项目（50米跑、掷3公斤铅球、立定跳远）考试均及格者1095人，及格率46.58%。次年，教育局组织全县中学生田径比赛，17所学校34支代表队204名男女运动员参加。1997年，组织县直学校学生参加“贵阳市环城赛跑修文赛区”比赛，并举办中学生篮球赛。次年，县教育局、体育事业局联合制发《修文县推行〈国家体育锻炼标准施行办法〉工作意见》，提出3年工作目标为实施面88%以上和达标率76%以上。在开展“达标”工作的同时，教育局分别组织篮球、乒乓球和田径等比赛，并获贵阳市政府授予“体育工作先进单位”称号。2000年，全县实施《国家体育锻炼标准》的学校超过90%，学生达标率80%以上，全面完成3年工作目标。2002年和2003年均举办中、小学生田径比赛，千余人次的男女运动员参赛。2003年，以体育项目跆拳道为特色的文武学校在久长创办，该校学生多次在省、市比赛中取得优异成绩。2004年，全县推广第二套全国中、小学生（幼儿）广播体操。2005年，全县实施教育部颁布的《学生体质健康标准（试行方案）》，各中、小学按照标准测定学生成绩并汇总，年底通过互联网直接上报教育部。同年，举办中、小学生广播体操（录像）比赛。2006年起，学校体育工作实行规范化管理，教育局与各学校签订目标责任书，保证学生每天1小时以上的体育锻炼时间，开足体育课程并上好每一堂课，学生每天做课间操，学校每学期开展综合性体育活动1次，每年将学生体质健康测试结果上报教育部。至2010年，仍然按照学生体质健康标准测定学生成绩上报。

2010年，全县中小学生田径运动会开幕式

专记：凸显体育特色的修文文武学校

修文文武学校是一所属于民间办学性质的寄宿制小学，创办于2003年，坐落在久长镇兴隆村，校舍及场地系租赁。学校的办学宗旨是以文化为主，以武术为特色，文武双修。学校除对学生进行普通小学教育外，侧重指导学生学习和训练跆拳道以强身健体，培养学生战胜困难、顽强拼搏的精神。2004年7月，学校刚创办1年即作为修文县的代表队参加贵阳市青少年跆拳道锦标赛，夺得1枚金牌、2枚银牌和3枚铜牌。次年再次代表修文组队参赛，又夺4枚金牌、6枚银牌和1枚铜牌，并获团体第一。2006年，学校被贵阳市体育中学列为跆拳道项目训练基地。5月，学校被评为贵阳市体育工作先进集体。6月，学校组队代表修文县参加贵阳市第十届运动会，获得3枚金牌、5枚银牌和6枚铜牌，并获团体总分第四名及赛会唯一的“体育道德风尚奖”。2007年1月，学生李祥和母光勇在贵州省青少年跆拳道冠军赛中获得金牌，实现在省级比赛中夺取金牌的目标。7月，在有各区、县（市）23个代表队456名运动员参加的贵阳市青少年跆拳道锦标赛上，该校学生摘取5枚金牌、6枚银牌和6枚铜牌，参加比赛的李利苹、张亮等还

获体育道德风尚奖。在2008年贵阳市举办的“全民健身与奥运同行”青少年跆拳道锦标赛中，学校组织50余名学生参赛，为“一市三县”中人数最多、阵容整齐的参赛单位，比赛结果夺取9金、8银、5铜及10个第五名的成绩，学校获县（市）代表队团体第二名和道馆学校团体第二名。其中年仅10岁的戚贵南、刘祥品分别将竞技女子丙级32公斤级和男子丙级53公斤级金牌收入囊中。学校取得的不凡战绩，受到贵阳市和县教育、体育部门的赞许，贵阳市选拔北京奥运会圣火火炬传递手，学校校长周建理有幸当选。2008年8月，学校再次组队参加贵州省举办的跆拳道锦标赛，荣获4金、3银和3铜的好成绩。同年12月贵阳市体育中学网点学校评估，该校被评为一等网点学校。2009年3月，学校首次跨出省外参加第七届香港国际武术节比赛，分获4金、2银和2铜。7月，又参加贵阳市青少年跆拳道锦标赛，获13金、8银和6铜，还获两个级别团体总分第二，一个级别团体总分第三。8月，参加贵州省青少年跆拳道锦标赛，夺取3金、2银和2铜，并获团体总分第一。2009年12月，北京体育大学武术学院院长莅校考察，将学校确定为北京体育大学武术训练基地和实习基地。同年，学校被再次评估为贵阳市体育中学一等网点学校。2010年，学校又分别组队参加贵州省青少年跆拳道锦标赛和贵阳市第十一届运动会，省级比赛获3金、2银、4铜及团体总分第一，市级比赛获5金、12银和6铜。学校从创办到2010年，已在各类比赛中获金、银、铜牌150余枚，获团体奖近10次。修文文武学校白手起家，在基础薄弱、条件困难的情况下起步，经过7年的艰苦跋涉，不断发展壮大，取得令人瞩目的成绩，为学校的特色发展探索出一条新的途径。

文武学校师生武术表演

（四）卫生

1978—1984年，县内各校根据教育部、卫生部《中小学卫生工作暂行规定（草案）》，抓好卫生检查和学生的防疫、体检等工作，初三年级开设生理卫生课程。1985年，县教育局设专人管理学校卫生工作，使学生的卫生保健和学校的卫生环境管理步入正轨。此后，教育局在大型学校建立卫生室，并拨专款为部分学校新建或改扩建厕所；卫生部门在县城学校设立学生健康检查点，并加强中、小学生的防疫工作；学校环境卫生管理日益加强，定期开展大扫除及卫生检查评比活动。1990年，执行国家教育委员会、卫生部颁布的《学校卫生工作条例》，根据《条例》要求监测学生健康状况，对学生进行健康教育，培养学生良好的卫生习惯，改善学校卫生环境和教学卫生条件，加强对传染病、学生常见病的预防和治疗。县教育、卫生部门联合对县直和区级小学进行防疫检查，学校建立学生健康卡片，将预防学生近视纳入卫生工作管理。1995年，始设健康教育课程，全县统一配发课本。次年，县教育部门配合卫生部门在全县中、小学生中开展集体服驱虫药、强化补碘，并对6周岁以下的儿童进行体检，建立健康卡片。1997年，加强对学生集体用餐卫生的监督与管理，并对参加体育中考的学生进行体检。次年，实施国家教育委员会《学校健康教育评价方案》，加强健康教育宣传，严格执行贵州省教育厅《〈学校卫生工作条例〉检查评估细则》，开展对学校卫生工作评估，督促学校认真贯彻《中华人民共和国食品卫生法》和

《中华人民共和国传染病防治法》。县教育局和卫生局联合制发《关于加强托园所及学校预防急性肠道传染病的通知》，要求学校加强食品卫生和饮水卫生管理，防止肠道传染病流行和食物中毒事件的发生；在学校倡导禁烟活动，校园内设禁烟标志，并集中开展灭“四害”（蚊子、苍蝇、老鼠、蟑螂）。1999年，县教育局制发《关于做好学校卫生工作的意见》，要求学校全面落实健康教育课时计划，保证开课率达100%，使学生健康知识知晓率和行为形成率分别达85%和75%。次年，中、小学配备卫生器材，中学建立卫生室，各校组织学生体检，完成学生健康监测任务。2003年“非典”流行，县教育局及各校建立领导小组，积极配合卫生部门开展预防“非典”，学校建立疫情零报告制度，坚持每天测查学生体温，加强宣传教育，整治校园环境，消除卫生死角，定期对教室、办公室、宿舍、食堂、餐厅杀菌消毒。由于预防措施严密，全县学校均未发生“非典”感染病例。2004年，在贵阳市食品卫生监督量化分级管理首批评级中，民办华驿中学和南方幼儿园获一类B级单位。2005年起，县教育局制定多项学校卫生管理的规章制度，定期督促检查和评价。学校开展健康教育，适时举办知识竞赛和演讲活动，着力培养学生良好的卫生行为习惯，并将性教育、预防艾滋病等纳入健康教育范畴；协同卫生部门每年开展防疫、体检和食堂食品安全检查；幼儿园和小学新招学生，在报到注册时须查验预防接种证，并将查验情况如实登记造册。至2010年，学校健康教育开课率为100%，中、小学生健康知识知晓率和健康行为形成率均在90%以上，各级各类学校未发生重大卫生事件。

2009年，全县中小学生卫生知识演讲比赛

（五）美育

1980年，全县学校恢复音乐和美术课程，使用统编教材，教师按照教学大纲教学，让学生学习和掌握音乐、美术的基础知识，培养学生的欣赏、感受和观察能力，从而形成正确的审美观点和情趣。1986年，开展全县性的“班班有歌声”活动。次年，教育局为乡（镇）以上小学补充音乐和美术教育器材，并在大型中学举办学生书画竞赛。继后，在小学和中学分别组建腰鼓队、舞蹈队、合唱团和书法、美术兴趣小组，并在“五四”“六一”“十一”“一二·九”这些节日和纪念日开展丰富多彩的文艺活动。20世纪80年代后期至90年代初期，音乐、美术专任教师匮缺，加上应试教育影响，学校音乐和美术课程普遍被当成副科，未受到应有的重视。1993—1997年，县教育局通过引进充实、委托培养方式，先后给中、小学配备专职音乐教师和美术教师，师资不足问题得以缓解。同时又通过实施“普九”、加大“减负”力度、推行素质教育等举措，严格要求学校按照课程计划开设音乐课和美术课。学校亦结合实际，组织开展形式多样的艺术活动。1997年，全县21所学校1000余名学生在县城举行“颂祖国，迎港归，唱家乡”歌咏比赛。1999年，组织开展音乐、书画和演讲文艺系列活动和庆祝新中国成立50周年、迎接澳门回归系列活动。同年，实验小学四年级学生张程《我的学校》获全国小星星杯第七届东方少儿美术大赛金奖，县内19名儿童参加全国首届少儿书法临帖大赛，10人获铜奖、9人获优秀奖。2000年，全县中、小学音乐和美术专任教师基本满足需求，县教育局统一为学校添置音乐和美术器材，以迎接“普九”验收。当

年，实验小学创编的舞蹈《莲蓬娃娃》获贵阳市文艺汇演优秀创作奖和表演二等奖，学校选送学生作品参加全国青少年书画大赛，书法作品获一等奖，美术作品获金奖。2002年，教育部《学校艺术教育工作规程》颁布实施，学校将艺术教育列为实施美育的重要途径、内容和推进素质教育的有机组成部分。为认真贯彻落实《规程》，县教育局2004年举办首届师生书画展，2005年建成县青少年活动中心，以此为平台组建校外艺术教育培训、辅导机构，把艺术教育推到一个新阶段。2006—2010年，艺术活动多姿多彩，成果丰硕。县教育局先后开展全县性艺术活动8次，其中2006年10月的首届中、小学艺术节，乡（镇）中、小学以上的37所学校1500名师生参加，举办14场风格迥异、精彩纷呈的声乐、器乐、舞蹈表演和文艺晚会以及书法、绘画展览，对学校开展艺术教育的成果进行检阅和展示，县城10万人次观看，省、市媒体均报道活动盛况。至2010年，全县有8校次获省、市文艺活动表彰，23个艺术作品获全国及省、市比赛奖励。

2007年，“多彩贵州舞蹈大赛”教育系统海选赛

专记：多功能的青少年活动中心

修文县青少年活动中心系县境内首家公办的青少年校外教育机构，位于县城翠屏东路,2004年启动建设，次年5月竣工，2006年3月启用。中心占地面积7.2亩，建筑面积4800平方米，总投资526.5万元，有计算机、钢琴、体育器械和图书等各类教学设备价值百万元。中心具备多种功能，设有音乐、舞蹈、美术、计算机、科技活动等教室32间，开展声乐、器乐、舞蹈、书法、绘画、棋类、跆拳道、英语、作文、计算机等10余类课外辅导活动；有专业教师9人，外聘教师21人。中心坚持公益性原则，以“发挥特长，张扬个性”为宗旨，服务青少年，服务社会；以活动为载体，积极推进素质教育，探索校外教育新机制，努力构建青少年校外成长乐园；开展活动突出兴趣，彰显天赋，形成特色，注重青少年全面发展和学有专长，让其在活动中受到锻炼。周一至周五的课外时间、双休日及寒暑假，免费开放图书室、计算机室、科技室、器乐室、舞蹈室、绘画室、体育室，并开展写作、英语等辅导活动，安排专、兼职教师免费辅导。中心设有阳光舞蹈团、器乐部、书画部、体育部、文学部和外语部，各部独立开展特色活动。为保证各类活动正常开展，中心制定外聘教师管理制度、班级管理制度、安全管理制度、户外活动制度、器材管理制度和教师业务考核办法、学生基本行为规范，充分利用自身资源，为青少年提供服务。从2006年启用至2010年，中心除举办学生艺术月活动和首届钢琴音乐会外，还配合县相关部门参与组织策划多场文艺演出，开展舞蹈、合唱、体育、书画、科技、演讲和经典诵读、小记者采访等各类活动56次，数以万计的学生参与。中心的阳光舞蹈团与北京舞蹈学院联合开展中国舞等级培训

修文县青少年活动中心

已有上千人次受训，该团2008年编排的民族舞《林城的花儿笑了》、现代舞《春天来了》、民族舞《好热的天》在“多彩贵州舞蹈大赛”修文赛区海选赛中，分别获得一、二、三等奖。2009年编排的舞蹈《阳光下的花朵》在北京参加“魅力校园暨校园春节晚会”展演获表演金奖。2010年编排的舞蹈《布依竹鼓操》《谷场欢歌》参加贵阳市第九届少数民族运动会表演获金奖和银奖。文学部辅导的一批文学少年在国家级及省、市、县各级报纸杂志发表文章36篇，各级作文竞赛获奖15人次。体育部训练的学员参加贵阳市跆拳道比赛，10人次获前三名。中心于2008年荣获“全国校园文化先进单位”称号。

（六）劳动

1978—1980年，中、小学继续贯彻执行“教育与生产劳动相结合”的方针，组织学生在校办农场劳动或到学校临近的生产队参加劳动。小学三年级以上开有劳动课，中学开设劳动技术课。20世纪80年代初，学生以学为主，劳动课主要是培养劳动观念和劳动习惯，劳动时间减少，劳动强度减轻，并且将劳动与勤工俭学相结合。小学每周有1至2节劳动课，对于低年级只安排力所能及的自我服务性劳动；中学的劳动技术课，初中每学年两周、每天4课时，高中每学年4周、每天6课时。中学劳动技术课的内容包括工农业生产、服务性劳动及公益劳动，以劳动实践为主，适当安排一定时间讲授生产、劳动技术原理，培养学生基本生产技术知识和劳动技能。中、小学将“爱劳动”作为对学生思想品德的基本要求列为评选“三好”学生的条件之一。1987年，国家教委先后印发《全日制普通中学劳动技术课教学大纲（试行稿）》和《全日制小学劳动课教学大纲（试行稿）》，次年又印发《义务教育全日制小学、初级中学教学计划（试行草案）》，学校严格按照《大纲》和《计划》设置课程和确定教学内容，上课采取现场参观、示范引导和动手操作对学生进行教育。同时，组织学生开展植树造林和积肥、制作营养袋支援农业生产等活动。1990年，全县师生植树5.6万株，制作营养袋333万个，积肥54万公斤。90年代中期，启动实施“普九”，根据新修订的《大纲》，部分学校配备或自制简单的教学器材进行辅助教学。1998年，遵照教育部颁布的《关于加强普通中学劳动技术教育管理的若干意见》，县教育局对各中学落实课程课时、安排师资、征订教材和成绩考核方面，加大督促指导力度，实施规范化管理。2003年，县委、县政府贯彻落实贵阳市委、市政府要求，在农村学校创办小基地，全县建成以种植和养殖为主的小基地65个。学校以此为契机，将基地作为学生劳动教育和劳动技能实习实验场所。2004年，全县启动义务教育课程改革实验，将劳动技术课和劳动课归并在新增设的综合实践活动课程中，作为学生社会实践的重要组成部分。学校大胆实验，积极创新，使综合实践活动收效较好，其中以县实验小学最为突出，该校2009年获全国先进实验学校荣誉。2010年，县域高中启动课程改革，劳动技术课分设于综合实践活动中的社区服务、社会实践以及技术课程中的通用技术中；学生每学年参加1周社会实践、高中3年内参加不少于10个工作日的社区服务，通用技术为考试科目，设现代农业技术、家政与生活技术等选修内容。

实验小学奖牌

专记：劳动教育实践基地建设

1978年，修文中学、六广中学等校的农场仍存。建有农场的学校定期组织学生在农场参加生产劳动，作为学生劳动教育和社会实践的组成部分。20世纪80年代，文化知识学习愈加突出，劳动教育形式变化，除要求学生参加学校扫除、帮助家庭做一些力所能及的劳动外，仅在一些特定的时间开展植树造林、帮助“五保”老人等公益性劳动，学校多未组织学生开展劳动实践活动。80年代后期至90年代，有的学校虽办有种植和养殖场，但仅将其作为勤工俭学的一种形式，学生并未参与实践，使劳动及劳动技术课程的书本学习与实践脱节。进入21世纪，由于素质教育全面实施，对学生劳动教育又予重视。2003年，针对学校没有学生劳动实践基地以及部分学生离家较远、中午就餐比较困难的问题，贵阳市委、市政府提出在中、小学实施小伙房、小基地和小厕所“三小”工程。县委、县政府按照市委、市政府的部署，将“三小”工程建设列为政治任务加以落实。截至2005年5月，全县共建设种植和养殖小基地65个，种植基地面积485亩，主要栽种白菜、洋芋、南瓜和四季豆等时令蔬菜；养殖基地内养有猪、鸡、兔、肉鸽等畜禽。基地除满足学生劳动实践教育需要和就地取材解决4000名学生中餐菜肴问题外，还将其创收资金弥补学校办学经费。红岩小学建猪圈4间、养二元杂交猪2头，种草1.5亩，24只种兔产小兔40余只。三元小学建养鸡场140平方米、首批出栏肉鸡500余只；建食用菌培育场100平方米，制作香菇菌包1000个。石竹小学投入资金6万元，建养兔场56平方米，笼舍840个。谷堡小学将学校9亩荒山种植600株金秋梨。大塘小学征地24亩建4个标准钢架大棚种花卉。金桥小学种生姜2亩，年收千余斤，建猪圈140平方米，养猪30头。红旗小学种葡萄1000株和金秋梨300株。特殊教育学校种草2.5亩，养种兔276只。建立劳动教育实践基地的学校，针对学生实际，定期组织参加适量的生产劳动，培养学生正确的劳动观念和热爱劳动、热爱劳动人民的感情，并掌握简单的劳动技能。但是，由于学校劳动教育实践基地土地多属租赁性质，租赁期满后未能续租，加上师生教学和学习负担过重，种养管理经验不足，以致多数学校的“小基地”难以为继，进而不复存在。至2010年，仅有属国有土地的原学校农场存在。

2005年，县长石洪向“三小”工程建设示范点授牌

二、教学研究

1978年，县教育局沿袭原有建置设教研室主管教学业务，开展教学研究。教研室分设中教组和小教组。在区一级设语文、数学教研员，对辖区内小学的教学进行指导，并组织开展本地区的教研活动。从而在全县形成县、区、校为一体的教研网络。1979—1983年，教研的主要任务是恢复和建立学校正常教学秩序，指导学校按照新课程计划和教学大纲开设课程、规范教学，组织教师学习业务知识，迎接教材教法过关考试。1984年建立教研工作责任制，加强对各区教研员和各校教导主任的业务指导。20世纪80年代后期，教研组织大力指导学校进行教学改革尝试，努力提高教学质量，于1989年组织开展“改革课堂教学结构、提高课堂教学效益”为主题的教研活动，历时两月，全县千名教师参加，教研活动围绕小

学语文、数学和中学语文、数学、物理、化学等统考科目进行。继后，先后出台《中小学教师常规管理意见》《中小学教师常规管理要求》和《中小学教学工作管理考评细则》。90年代初、中期，加强学习交流，除邀请相关专家莅县开展培训讲座外，还组织开展观摩和研讨活动，集中开展好课评选。1991—1995年，共组织培训、讲座、观摩和研讨活动8次，开展好课评选4次，县区教研员及学校教导主任、教研组长和骨干教师500人次参加。1995年，正式启动教育科研工程，在各级各类学校大力倡导“科研兴校”，将教研工作深化到新阶段。次年，邀请贵阳市教科所专家开展教育科研方法培训，县、乡（镇）教研员和中、小学教导主任、骨干教师百人参训。此后出台《修文县中小学、幼儿园教育科研管理办法》，并遴选科研论文参加全国评选活动，其中1篇获优秀奖。1997年，县教育局成立教育科研领导小组，编制科研计划，确定课题立项和子课题立项，并建立科研经费保障机制。当年，六桶中学教师明长勇撰写的论文《中学语文教学中的审丑教育》获贵州省一等奖，扎佐中学江洪滨发明的教具“三等分圆弧曲线规”获国际金奖。1998年，贵阳市教科所莅县视导，对扎佐中学科研课题“从素质教育的角度对教师教学进行综合监控评估”和“对农村中学生进行素质分层次的教育”给予高度评价。2000—2004年，举办各种教研活动50次，参加教师3000人次；邀请省、市专家进行专题讲座20场次，参加教师千余人次。扎佐中学选定的市级教育科研课题“农村家庭教育现状调查分析及教育对策”，获贵阳市市级教育科研评比一等奖，6人次获科研成果奖8项。在此期间，教育局建立课题研究领导小组，承担国家级教育科研项目，申报重点课题“整体构建学校德育体系的深化研究与推广实验”二级子课题，根据新课程师资培训策略的有效模式研究与实验，选定子课题“如何有效地对教师进行学科培训、改进传统的教学行为”，课题均顺利结题，取得一定的研究成果。2004年，教研室确定“学生自主、合作、探究学习方式的试验”为研究课题，并选定5个实验班级为研究对象，为新课程实施创造条件，获得阶段性的成果。1995—2005年，有3篇论文获教育部奖励，45篇获省级奖励，60篇获市级奖励，303篇在国家及省、市级刊物上公开发表。2006—2008年，开展各种教研活动60次，教育科研指导18次，专题调研11次；参加贵阳市第四届优质课评比，有4人获一等奖、9人获二等奖、29人获三等奖、21人获优秀奖；1人获全国英语精品课大赛二等奖。扎佐中学承担的国家级课题“农村学校积极心理健康教育活动课形成性评价体系与应用研究”，有25人次获科研成果奖35项，并获中期科研课题成果一等奖。与此同时，县教育局出台《关于促进我县“校本教研”的建设意见》，鼓励学校大力开展校本教研活动。至2010年，在各级对教学论文、教学案例、教学设计的评比中，获省、市一等奖220项次，二等奖300项次，三等奖550项次。修文中学完成省级课题研究项目2个、市级项目1个、校级项目13个；贵阳市教科所对县承担的“课堂教学有效性研究”课题已进行验收结题；实验小学承担的教育部重点课题“综合实践活动研究与实验”子课题“小学综合实践活动课程校本开发”通过贵阳市教科所评审。

2006年，扎佐中学教育科研课题交流展示会

三、学科竞赛

20世纪80年代，为达到“以赛促学、以赛促教”的目的，县内学校大多选拔学生参加国家及省、地

（市）组织的各种学科竞赛活动。1986—1990年，选拔参加竞赛者以中学生居多，竞赛科目为数学、物理和化学，先后有20人次获各级竞赛奖励。

90年代，各类竞赛名目繁多，中、小学生均为选拔对象，竞赛科目文、理皆有，学生以参赛获奖为荣，校际之间亦互相攀比获奖人次。1992年，组织学生参加各类竞赛活动9次，获全国一等奖1人次、二等奖2人次、三等奖12人次、优秀奖21人次，获省级一、二等奖和优秀奖分别为4人次、15人次和15人次，获地区级一、二等奖和优秀奖分别为3人次、9人次和9人次。1993—1999年，选拔学生参加各类竞赛23次，先后有162人次获各级等次奖励，修文中学获团体奖励2次。由于竞赛获奖受到热捧，为提高竞赛成绩，部分学校举办各类培训班，选拔少量成绩拔尖学生作为重点培养对象，部分教师利用课余时间举办辅导班，招收学生进行专科辅导，部分家长更是希望子女出人头地，将孩子送进省城接受名师指导。

从2001—2005年，全县有280人次获各类竞赛奖励。由于学科竞赛盛行，使学生不堪重负，引起社会舆论广泛关注。2005—2006年，县教育局顺应社会呼吁，采取措施严格控制参加各类竞赛的次数和人数，切实减轻学生过重的课业负担；各级各类学校落实“减负”要求，使学科竞赛热降温。2007年，参加各类竞赛的初、高中学生获省级一、二、三等奖154人次，获市级一、二、三等奖75人次。2008—2010年，参加各类学科竞赛的主要是高中学生，180人次参加10科次竞赛，获奖51人次。

四、减轻课业负担

从20世纪80年代中期起，在社会关注和家长期盼下，追求升学率和上重点学校风靡一时，“唯考分论”成为学生的学习指向，考分高低成为教学成败的衡量标准。在考试指挥棒的挥舞下，学校为提高应试水平，将学生分成重点班和快慢班，采取题海战术训练学生；学生为追求高分，夜以继日啃读书本、完成练习。过重的课业负担致学生身心健康受到损害。

90年代，县教育局采取措施，在课程设置、学生作息、考试次数、作业数量以及开展课外活动方面进行规范，摒弃“唯考分论”，推行素质教育，以减轻学生过重的课业负担。但传统的应试教育观念根深蒂固，学校在具体实施中面临巨大压力，学生家长不理解、不支持，以致“减负”成效不显。1998年，贵阳市教委调查，42.3%的初中学生睡眠不足8小时，72%的在校时间达8小时以上，74%的学生作业时间2小时以上。为强力推进“减负”，自1999年起，全县取消小学升初中的升学考试。

进入21世纪，县教育局加大“减负”力度，将“减负”纳入学校日常管理。2002年，严格要求各中、小学按照课程计划开设课程和安排课时，不准延长上课时间和挤占学生课外时间。次年，禁止假期安排和组织学生补课，少量“补差辅导”须经学生自愿且不得收取费用。2004年改革考试制度，对部分学科实行监测考试，初中历史、政治和高二政治实行开卷考试，普通中学除高三年级外，监测考试和学期考试的科目最多不超过7科。次年，除对课程设置加强监测外，还将课时安排、作业数量及考试次数也囊括在内。

2006年起，遵照贵州省教育厅《关于减轻中小学生过重课业负担保障学生身心健康的意见》，县教育局将“减负”作为行风建设的重要内容，对中、小学的“减负”提出具体要求：不以升学率作为衡量学校办学水平的唯一标准，不以考试成绩和升学率高低作为评价、奖励教师的唯一标准；不准学校增减课时和科目，不准随意增加考试次数，不准选用用书目录范围外的学生教学用书；教师不得以学科成绩判定学生好差，不公布学生考试成绩，不以考试成绩排定学生名次；小学一、二年级不留书面家庭作业，其他年级完成书面家庭作业的时间不超过1小时，初中一、二年级不超过1.5小时，高中不超过2小时；

取消统一的早自习，倡导学生早锻炼，学校上午上课时间不得早于8点，小学生每天在校时间含自习、活动在内不超过6小时，初中生不超过7小时，高中生不超过8小时，保证学生每天至少有1小时的体育活动时间。此外，要求各校丰富学生的课余生活，组织形式多样的课外活动，促进学生身心健康和全面发展；义务教育阶段学校不以考试方式选拔新生，公办小学及初中招生实行就近免试入学，学校不组织新生进行考试分班。与此同时，教育局还建立“减负”督促机制，将其纳入对教师的业务考核和对学校的年度目标考核。至2010年，学校层面的“减负”仍在深入推进，然学生家长和社会对此仍存片面认识，观念难以更新，“减负”任重道远，尚需继续努力。

五、推广普通话

1978年至20世纪80年代初期，小学语文课加强汉语拼音教学，任课教师大多采用普通话上课。80年代中后期，贯彻落实“大力推行、积极普及、逐步提高”的方针，各级教育行政部门加强教师语言文字教学基本功训练，学校要求教师使用普通话教学。

1994年，国家语委、国家教委和广电部发出《关于开展普通话水平测试工作的决定》，并修订《普通话水平测试等级标准》，把普通话水平划分为一、二、三级，每个级别又划分甲、乙两等。当年，县教育局成立普通话水平测试领导小组，在教师中进行测试工作。1997年，举办小学教师第一届普通话比赛，实验小学和六广镇教育辅导站分别获得第一名和第二名。1999年，教育局制定贯彻落实《中华人民共和国国家通用语言文字法》的《实施意见》，成立语言文字工作领导小组，拟定实施目标，确定5年内基本完成全县中、小学教师的普通话培训及测试工作，并持证上岗，规定普通话作为校园语言。与此同时，将语言文字工作列入对各站、校的考核和评估内容，将教师普通话达标列入评职、评优和晋级条件之一。当年即举办第一期培训班，凡1953年1月1日后出生的教师均参训，并对279人测试，获普通话二级水平的人数占测试总数的57.35%，其中二级甲等9人，二级乙等151人。继后又举办小学教师第二届普通话比赛，县直及乡（镇）的18所学校参赛，春蕾幼儿园和龙场镇教育辅导站分别获得一等奖和二等奖，实验小学、扎佐一小和六广镇教育辅导站获三等奖。

2000年，举办第二期培训班，组织561人测试，获二级水平的人数占测试总数的67.59%。次年，县教育局转发贵州省教育厅《关于在全省各级各类学校教师中实行坚持普通话水平等级证书上岗制度的通知》，并举办第三期培训班，对1228人进行测试，合格1145人，合格率94.78%。2002年举办第四期培训班，补训1953年1月1日后出生的此前测试未合格者，后对319人进行测试，合格307人，合格率96.24%。同年举办中、小学教师第三届普通话比赛，30所学校组队参加，修文中学和实验幼儿园获一等奖，另有4所学校获二等奖，6所学校获三等奖，9所学校分别获得优秀奖或组织奖。2003年，举办第五期培训班，对105人进行测试，其中二级以上42人，三级甲等63人。至此，中、小学教师普通话培训和测试工作告竣，在职教师全部获得普通话水平等级证书，全员持证上岗。其后，新聘用的教师，必须按要求提供普通话水平等级证书。

2008年，第五届中小学教师普通话比赛

2004—2005年，教育部门配合相关单位，举办

4期公务员普通话培训班，先后培训1080人次，测试1044人次，合格958人次，合格率为91.76%。2005年，举办中、小学教师第四届普通话比赛，30所学校组队参加，10所学校分别获得一、二、三等奖，6所学校分别获得优秀奖或组织奖。至2010年，普通话已成为教师、学生工作、学习的交流语言，普通话在校园内外广大师生中达到普及。

第五节　教育设施

一、校舍建设

20世纪70年代后期，学校遍及社队，规模较小，校舍陈旧，多为砖木和石木结构。1981年，全县校舍总面积为7.63万平方米。80年代对学校布局调整，加紧校舍建设，改善办学条件，取消小学复式班，达到“班班有教室”的要求。1981—1985年，县政府投资250多万元新建校舍3万平方米。1986年安排建设项目40个，使校舍总面积增至10.18万平方米。1988—1989年，实施建设项目25个，建筑面积1.37万平方米。1990年，校舍总面积达12.19万平方米，基本满足教学需要。90年代，启动普及九年义务教育，校舍建设投入资金较多，建设规模颇巨、覆盖面广，所建校舍多为砖混结构。1990—1995年，全县新建和改扩建学校61所，建教学楼57幢3.93万平方米，新增校舍面积4836.44平方米。1995年，全县学校占地总面积560亩，校舍总面积达15.64万平方米。其中教学用房13.97万平方米，占89.2%；办公用房3284平方米，占2.1%；师生住房1.13万平方米，占7.3%；附属用房2190平方米，占1.4%。1996—2000年，投入资金5400万元，新建和改扩建学校105所，建筑面积9.22万平方米。2000年，全县校舍总面积达20万平方米，小学生均2.82平方米，初中生均3.34平方米。2001—2004年，投入资金4390万元，新建教学楼、综合楼、学生宿舍和教师宿舍计13校次5.1万平方米，扩建教学辅助用房2.68万平方米。2004年，学校占地总面积1583亩，生均19平方米，校舍总面积24.1万平方米，生均4.2平方米。其中小学、初中校舍总面积14.92万平方米，生均面积分别为3.72平方米和4.19平方米。同年，启动农村寄宿制学校建设工程，为8所农村初中建设学生宿舍和食堂。2005—2008年，继续建设寄宿制学校，并启动实施薄弱学校建设工程和标准化学校建设工程，总投资1812万元，为9所中、小学建设教学楼和学生宿舍2.33万平方

20世纪80年代初小箐中学校舍

2005年建成的小箐中学校舍

米。2008年，校舍总面积增至28万平方米，其中小学和初中校舍增至22.36万平方米，生均面积分别达到5平方米和8.7平方米。2010年，完成洒坪中学、六桶中学和久长中学标准化学校建设工程，全县学校占地总面积1175.5亩，校舍总面积28.4万平方米。其中普通教室10.8万平方米，占38.03%；专用教室3.2万平方米，占11.27%；学生宿舍和食堂5.4万余平方米，占19.01%；教师宿舍2.5万平方米，占8.8%；其他房舍6.5万平方米，占22.89%。

专记：农村寄宿制学校建设

2004年12月，贵州省教育厅召开农村寄宿制学校建设工程启动会，正式启动农村寄宿制学校建设工程，旨在改善乡（镇）学校学生基本的学习和生活条件，缩小城乡教育资源配置差距，巩固“两基”成果。其后，按照省、市要求，成立县实施“工程”领导小组，由县长任组长，分管教育工作的副县长任副组长，教育、发改、财政、建设、国土、审计等部门负责人以及扎佐、久长、六屯、谷堡、小箐、洒坪、六广和大石8乡（镇）负责人为成员。领导小组将建设任务分解到相关部门和乡（镇），各负其责，确保“工程”顺利实施。按照省、市安排，修文县确定为农村寄宿制建设工程项目的学校共8所，均为乡（镇）初级中学。“工程”除建设学生宿舍、食堂、浴室外，还配置学生生活设施及教室课桌凳。根据贵州省教育厅、省发改委、省财政厅《关于2004至2007年全省“农村寄宿制学校建设工程”项目规划的批复》及省、市安排部署，“工程”首先于2005年在洒坪中学启动，2006年5月告竣。随即在清让中学、久长中学、六屯中学、乌栗中学、小箐中学、六广中学和大石中学破土兴建，次年8月全部建成并通过省级验收，9月投入使用。8个“工程”项目共建学生宿舍、食堂1.58万平方米，可入住学生2650人，投资1097.54万元，其中中央专项资金700万元，县自筹资金397.54万元。农村寄宿制学校建设工程的实施，使农村中学的办学条件进一步改善，离校较远学生就学难的问题得以缓解，其举措深得民心，广大人民群众发出肺腑之言：“孩子上学真周到，吃饭睡觉在学校，家长安心搞生产，还是党的政策好。”由于实施“工程”工作扎实，成效显著，修文县获得贵州省“农村寄宿制学校建设工程特优县”的荣誉，是为全省唯一获此殊荣的单位。

2007年建成的大石中学学生宿舍和食堂

二、校园建设

20世纪70年代后期，县内学校多是校园敞露、泥土操场、简易厕所，一些社队的民办学校更是杂草丛生，乱石遍地。80年代初、中期进行学校布局调整，实施普及初等教育，但着重解决的是校舍及学生课桌凳，校园建设无力顾及，致办学基础仍显薄弱。

1987年，县政府提出努力改善办学条件，在乡（镇）级以上学校逐步做到“一无五有”（校校无危房，班班有教室、学生人人有课桌凳、教师有办公室、学校有简易活动场地、校校有厕所）。次年，出台《关于巩固和发展我县普及初等教育和农民教育工作的意见》，要求在条件较好的区和乡（镇）落实办学

配套设施，逐步达到“一无六有”，即在原“一无五有”的基础上增加“学校有围墙”。但因经费不济，落实颇为困难。

20世纪90年代久长中学校园

90年代初期，部分学校在争取资金投入的同时，自筹经费并组织师生义务劳动，改造和美化校园。中期，执行国家教委《中小学校园环境管理暂行规定》，将校园建设列入工作计划并采取措施组织落实，要求合理布局校园内的教学区、体育活动区、生活区和生产劳动区，避免相互干扰，校园要绿化、美化。继后在实施普及九年义务教育中，根据《贵州省实施九年义务教育第一阶段必备办学条件（试行）》的要求，在政府增加对校园建设投入的同时，学校不等不靠，就地取材，自力更生，掀起校园建设热潮。1996—2000年，硬化活动场地3.55万平方米，砌围墙6810米。仅1999年和2000年，就完成65所学校的校园配套设施。2000年，全县121所小学有99所校园设施达标，达标率81.82%，15所中学有10所达标，达标率66.67%。随后，县政府提出巩固和发展已有成果，落实工作目标责任制，继续加强校园建设，加大资金投入力度，使学校朝着规范化、标准化的方向迈进。县教育局制定《校园环境建设检查评估要点》，将校园环境建设与管理纳入对中、小学的目标考核，规定各校投入校园建设的资金比例。2001—2004年，完成18所学校校园附属设施。其中的2002年，就完成14所学校的校园配套设施，建厕所770平方米，硬化活动场地3.32万平方米，砌围墙3100米，砌保坎6320立方米，绿化校园6000平方米。2004年，小学校园设施达标率上升至94.37%，中学达100%。此后，县教育局又制定《中小学校园文化建设方案》，对校园实行规范化管理，增强文化氛围。2005—2008年，投入校园建设资金508万元，修建校门、围墙、保坎，并硬化活动场地5万平方米，绿化1万平方米。2010年，全县中、小学均有校门、围墙，校园内分区布局和硬化、绿化基本合理，学生运动场总面积达17.5万平方米，占学校总面积的23%左右；学校对校园绿化、美化和净化实行常规管理，并加强校园文化建设，使每所学校都成为当地文化建设不断向前发展的标志。

2008年建成的久长中学校园

三、危房消除

20世纪70年代后期，学校土木、石木结构的房舍由于年久失修，有的竟成危房，存在安全隐患。据1981年资料显示，全县学校危房面积达2.79万平方米，占校舍总面积的36.57%。80年代初，启动普及初等教育，要求达到“校校无危房”的目标，大力改造小学特别是农村小学校舍，采取乡镇企业资助一点、村级组织拿出一点、群众自愿解囊一点、献工献料帮助一点的办法筹集资金，消除危房。经过努力，1986年危房面积下降到1.79万平方米，危房率降至17.61%。次年，贯彻落实贵州省委、省政府提出的“三年内完成中、小学现有危房改造和维修任务”的指示，采取中央和省拿一点、地县拿一点、群众集资一点的分级负责原则筹资解决危房问题。1988—1990年，新建、维修校舍和改造危房2.41万平方米。1990年，危房面积仅剩6670平方米，危房率占5.47%。90年代，随着时间推移，原先不属危房的又形成新增危房。1990—1995年，虽然消除危房1.57万平方米，但1995年年底尚有危房2.01万平方米，占校舍总面积的12.82%，其中极危房有9115平方米，村级学校危房1.05万平方米。鉴于此，推进“普九”时，将消除危房列为重点任务之一。1996—2000年，共投入资金3481.28万元新建校舍，消除危房2.38万平方米。2000年，全县仅有危房943平方米，危房率为0.61%。2001—2004年，消除原有和新增危房3892平方米。2004年，全县中、小学已基本无危房。此后，将消除新增危房实行常规化管理，纳入年度建设任务。至2010年，全县中、小学危房率仍为零。

专记：新时期兴起的希望学校

1991年，县政府出台《多渠道筹措办学经费暂行办法》，鼓励社会集资办学，单位和个人捐资助学。并规定集资捐资者，可以采用树碑、颁发荣誉证书和挂匾等形式予以褒奖。1993年，县政府再次明确，对捐资办学者予以表彰。次年，扎佐镇即有4位个体户捐资3.5万元建设清让中学教学楼，县政府为其颁发荣誉证书。从1995年起，县内各地在当地政府不投入或投入较少的情况下，一面利用贵阳市实行部门对口帮扶政策寻求帮助，一面广泛动员社会力量捐资助学和引进外资办学，将这种通过开展社会公益活动而建设的学校称为“希望学校”。1995年，香港九龙狮子会在扎佐镇大山村捐资建设大山日光希望小学，这是县境第一所希望学校。次年，汕头澄海服装厂厂长蔡启昌和贵阳市客运管理处又分别捐资在城关镇马口村、大石乡新光村建成马口希望小学和新光希望小学。至1997年，建成学校11所，在希望学校入学的学生共计3160名。从1995—2006年，共建成学校32所，所建校舍总面积2.94万平方米，总投资1427.15万元，其中引进或募捐资金达735.8万元，占总投入的51.56%。2007—2010年，未建设并命名新的希望学校。希望学校建成后，极大地改善了县内学校特别是农村学校的办学条件，方便学生就近入学，为全县的教育普及发挥了积极作用。

2004年建成的久长镇“好1多”希望小学

1995—2006年希望学校建设一览表

表4—01—05

年度	学校原名	学校所在地区	学校建成后新命名	建设规模（平方米）	投资额（万元）		捐资人
					总额	其中：捐资额	
1995	大山小学	扎佐镇	大山日光希望小学	550	23	23	香港九龙狮子会
1996	马口小学	龙场镇	马口希望小学	476	14.5	9	汕头澄海服装厂厂长蔡启昌
1996	新光小学	大石乡	新光希望小学	418	16.5	16.5	贵阳市客运管理处
1997	城关小学教学楼	县城	未新命名	1400	45	30	贵阳市电信局

续表

年　度	学校原名	学校所在地区	学校建成后新命名	建设规模（平方米）	投资额（万元）		捐　资　人
					总额	其中：捐资额	
1997	崇恩小学	小箐乡	崇恩希望小学	854	26.7	26.7	筑居香港政协委员孙佛富等
1997	大河小学	扎佐镇	未新命名	220	6	6	贵阳妇幼保健院
1997	紫江小学	小箐乡	紫江筑邮希望小学	570	19.2	19.2	贵阳市邮政局
1997	硐口小学	洒坪乡	未新命名	200	7	7	澳大利亚籍教师
1997	六桶小学	六桶乡	迅文希望小学	2174	76.1	20	贵阳卷烟厂
1997	长田小学	六屯乡	未新命名	395	10	8	贵阳市民宗局
1997	联合小学	大石乡	未新命名	400	15	15	贵阳南明区遵义路办事处
1998	修文中学综合楼	县城	修文中学逸夫楼	2900	137	50	香港邵逸夫
1999	沙溪小学	龙场镇	福慧贤恭小学	240	6.5	4.3	香港福慧基金会
1999	中哨小学	龙场镇	中哨希望小学	410	16	13.5	香港张济根
1999	中松小学	六广镇	中松中日友好小学	790	27	21	日本水月会
1999	元庆小学	六广镇	未新命名	424	15	7	澳大利亚籍教师
2000	扎佐中学综合楼	扎佐镇	未新命名	2300	95	50	新加坡佛教居士林
2000	新村小学	小箐乡	未新命名	900	40	35	日本驻华使馆香港福慧基金会
2002	凤联小学	六桶乡	江侯立德小学	524	22.6	22.6	香港谊安集团
2002	小箐中学	小箐乡	许潘玉仪希望中学	3310	166	40	香港许亮华夫妇
2002	芦山小学	久长镇	未新命名	680	40	20	张家港骏马集团
2002	栋青小学	久长镇	侨心小学	870	47	20	广东佛山市侨联
2002	特殊学校综合楼	县城	未新命名	600	40	20	美籍华侨邹作雄
2004	金桥小学	久长镇	“好1多”希望小学	1500	81	12	久长“好1多”乳业公司
2005	大木小学	六屯乡	金叶希望小学	541	45	30	贵阳市烟草专卖局
2005	红峰小学	龙场镇	未新命名	640	50	20	天津大学
2005	石安小学	久长镇	真维斯希望小学	1480	95	20	香港真维斯集团
2005	永兴小学	久长镇	叶辛春晖小学	581	55	35	上海知青叶辛及上海中华企业等
2005	关寨小学	六桶乡	玛葵苗圃希望小学	522	33.05	20	香港苗圃行动民间助学团体
2006	大兴小学	六桶乡	文俭希望小学	400	45	30	香港何文俭
2006	新春小学	龙场镇	新春明德小学	1020	52	45	台湾台塑集团王永庆
2006	王官小学	龙场镇	王官明德小学	1100	60	40	台湾台塑集团王永庆

四、仪器和图书

1978—1983年，县内学校的教学仪器和图书多为自购，其中完全中学备有部分物理和化学实验仪器。20世纪80年代中期，县教育局指定专人管理教学仪器配置，随即为久长中学、实验小学和城关小学配置部分常用教学仪器。1987—1989年，在区级以上中学添置实验仪器，区级以上小学配齐教学仪器，并为大型学校补充成套图书。至1990年，全县3所完全中学和2所初级中学配齐物理、化学实验仪器，1所初级中学配备演示实验仪器，7所区级以上小学和28所乡级小学配置教学仪器。90年代中期，实施“普九”，贯彻落实《贵州省实施九年义务教育第一阶段必备办学条件（试行）》，县政府按照标准为中、小学配备教学仪器和补充图书。1996—2000年，投入教学仪器和图书的专项资金达370万元。2000年，小学教学仪器达标学校有102所、达标率84.3%，初中达标13所、达标率86.67%；全县中、小学图书总数为27.72万册，小学达标学校107所、达标率88.43%、生均图书4册，初中达标学校7所、达标率46.67%、生均图书8册。2001—2004年，为普及中、小学实验教学，县政府又投入资金，将小学分成3个类别、初中分成两个类别，为70所小学和16所中学配置仪器和图书，并发动师生自制教具6381件，新购和面向社会征集图书17.32万册。2004年，中、小学实验仪器和图书达标率均为100%。小学自然实验仪器品种配备率和数量配备率分别为94.69%和91.17%。中学物理实验仪器品种配备率为94.08%，数量配备率为96.55%；化学实验仪器品种配备率为95.52%，数量配备率为97.4%；生物实验仪器品种配备率为95.28%，数量配备率为95.23%。图书总数54.6万册，其中小学生均图书7册，初中13册。2005—2008年，投入284万元，按照《中华人民共和国教育行业标准》(JY/T标准)，为中、小学配置教学仪器和图书。2008年，教学仪器分类达标率小学为96.47%，初中为100%；图书总量增至71.6万册，小学和初中生均图书分别为14册和31册。至2010年，全县中、小学教学仪器分类达标学校66所，图书74万册。

修文二中物理实验室

实验小学学生借阅图书

专记：实验教学普及全县中小学

20世纪70年代末至80年代初，县内仅完全中学备有少量实验仪器，由于没有实验室，只能做简单的演示实验。80年代中期，为进一步提高教学质量，实验教学在各中学备受重视。1986年，修文中学率先将1幢教学楼改建为实验楼，并开设学生实验课程。次年，教育局召开全县实验室工作会议，提出中学要达到“校校有实验室”的要求，并开始在区级以上中学配置实验仪器。至1990年，全县3所完全中学和2所初级中学建有实验室并开设学生实验课程，其余中学因校舍有限未建实验室只能做演示实验。90年代中、后期，具备条件的中学均设置实验室。2000年“普九”验收时，全县尚未普及实验教学，按照《贵州省教委关于贯彻〈“九五”期间全国中小学实验室工作的意见〉的实施意见》要求，必须在“普九”复查中通过省级检查验收实现普及实验教学。为实现“普实”目标，县政府成立以县长为组长的领导小组，大力推进“普实”工作。2001—2004年，共投入资金1075.5万元，其中新建和改扩建实验用房1.06万平方米，建设实验室96间，配置设备96套，并逐步完善实验教学必备条件。为使“普实”校校达标，教育局发动师生自制教具6381件，组织实验教师培训千余人次，237名教师通过考试考核合格而取得上岗资格。各学校严格按照教学大纲和教材要求开设实验课程，将学生实验技能作为素质教育的重要组成部分，培养学生动手操作能力，获得感性认识。为使每个学生都能熟练完成实验，学校全天候开放实验室，由任课教师或实验教师指导学生开展课外实验活动，保证每个实验训练5次以上。与此同时，学校加强实验室规范化管理，完善档案资料，建立实验教师职责、实验室规则、仪器设备管理等相关制度，并落实实验教师待遇。2004年，全县初中物理、化学和生物科教师演示实验开出率分别为98.22%、99.37%和100%，学生分组实验3科开出率分别为99.83%、99.23%和98.76%；小学自然科教师演示实验和学生分组实验开出率分别达到97.78%和95.47%。同年9月，贵州省政府对县“普实”工作检查验收，认定为“合格”，经专家评定，修文中学、修文三中、大石中学和实验小学、六广小学获得“实验教学达标示范学校”称号。2005—2010年，继续推进“普实”工作，教育局将实验教学纳入学校年度目标管理，每年进行考核。各中、小学将实验教学常态化，通过实验课增强学生学习兴趣，鼓励学生积极探索，着力培养其观察问题、分析问题和解决问题的能力，每年教师演示实验和学生分组实验的开出率均分别达到95%和90%以上。

修文二中学生化学实验

五、电教设备

20世纪70年代末，多数学校置有广播，主要用于集会、通报情况和做课间操，大型学校备有照相机、幻灯机用于教学。80年代，由于英语、音乐、美术科目的教学需要，有的学校自购录音机、幻灯机，条件较好的配有投影仪、放像机、电视机等。是时，县教育局虽安排专人管理电教工作，但由于经费不济，学校的电教设备仍未统一配置。90年代中、后期，影碟机已在中、小学教学中普遍使用，有的学校和教师自行购置计算机、打印机，用于处理文档资料。进入21世纪，实施以教育信息化带动教育现代化战略，坚持政府引导、学校为主、讲究实效、重点突破、整体推进的方针，加大教育信息化力度，学校的电教设备突飞猛进。2001年，县城

修文中学信息技术教育课堂

学校率先建立计算机教室。次年，全县教育工作会议召开，就全面启动计算机教育工程进行部署，后经县政府批准，六广中学、小箐中学和六广小学、扎佐一小等10余所学校以贷款方式购置计算机300余台，设置计算机教室，对学生进行信息技术教育，使农村学校学生也有了动手操作计算机的机会。2003年，贵阳市实施农村党员干部现代远程教育工程，县教育局以此为契机，积极参与教育信息化建设，大力推进信息技术教育普及。次年，全县11所乡（镇）中学、2所县直中学、2所县直小学建多媒体教室17间，视频会议室10间，远程教育地面卫星接收站111个；56所小学开设信息技术教育课，开课学生1.38万人，占应开课学生1.83万人的75.37%，所有中学均开设信息技术教育课、开课率100%，计算机生机比小学、初中和高中分别为49比1、28比1和8比1；开始实施“校校通”工程，2所学校建起校园网；学校备有电子图书光碟、录音录像带等1460件。2004年5月，县教育局成立现代教育技术管理中心，负责管理中、小学信息技术教育，并启动教育局局域网建设。当年，完成乌栗中学、六桶小学多媒体教室建设，修文中学和实验小学等5所县城学校通过ADSL接入互联网。年底，乡（镇）以上中、小学基本实现“校校通”。2005—2008年，教育信息化建设与应用同步推进，学校开始将信息资源与教育教学融合，通过共享网络教育资源，丰富了教学形式，开阔了学生视野，提高了师生教与学的能力。2008年，全县中、小学配有计算机1500台，设置计算机教室20间，多媒体教室72间，20余所乡（镇）中、小学接入互联网，5所学校建起校园网，存有电子图书光碟、录音录像带等1.15万件。2009年，投入130万元，继续推进中、小学信息化建设。2010年，全县有81所学校接入互联网，27所学校开通并使用教育信息化平台和建立门户网站，并实现“家校通”，37所学校建起校园网、出口总宽带70M，10所学校建立校园监控系统，高中学校48个班级实现“班班通”；信息技术与教育教学和学校管理融合程度显著加深，中、小学共有计算机1800台，计算机教室23间，多媒体教室80间，数字资源3000GB，有专、兼职信息技术教师60人，中、小学信息技术开课率达100%，计算机生机比小学、初中和高中分别为47比1、22比1和15比1。

第六节　教育管理

一、机构设置

（一）县级机构

1978年，由县革命委员会教育局总揽全县教育工作，县直中、小学和各区中学由教育局直管。1981年1月，县革委教育局更名县教育局，为县政府所属工作机构，履职全县教育行政管理，统筹规划和协调发展全县教育事业。2010年县教育局仍存，其内设办公室、教育科、人事科、计划财务基建科和纪检监察室，尚设有事业机构教育教学研究管理中心、招生考试管理中心（加挂学生资助管理中心牌子）、现代教育技术管理中心、青少年活动中心和会计核算中心。

（二）区（乡、镇）级机构

1978年，县革命委员会教育局在区一级设置学区，协助管理本区所属中、小学。1983年，将区设置的学区改为区教育办公室，管理职能不变。1992年撤区并乡建镇，撤销区教育办公室，新建乡（镇）教育辅导站，协助县教育局履行本乡（镇）教育管理职责。20世纪90年代中、后期实施“普九”，将原属教辅站管理的部分乡（镇）中学析出归县教育局直接管理。2005年撤乡（镇）教育辅导站，建立乡（镇）中心校，负责管理本乡（镇）内的小学和幼儿园，将乡（镇）中学全部归属教育局管理。乡（镇）中心校除设校长外，另设教研员、教育专干和财务人员。至2010年，管理体制未变。

（三）学校机构

1978年，县内大、中型学校设置管理教育教学的教导处以及管理后勤的总务处。小型学校只设教导处管理教学业务，指派教师兼管后勤工作，有的学校则由校长全权管理。20世纪90年代，县直和乡（镇）中、小学均设教导处和总务处。2003年起，中学内设教导处、总务处、德育处和办公室。2008年起，片区以上的小学内设1至2个机构，规模小的中学内设3个机构，规模较大的中学仍设4个机构，修文中学和扎佐中学还设有教科处。至2010年，机构设置未变。

二、教育督导

1989年9月，教育局设督导检查办公室，负责对全县教育工作的督促检查，并遵照省教委安排成立检查组，对全县教育经费和公、民办教师待遇情况，以及中、小学校舍危房改造和维修工作，中、小学学生流失的制止情况进行督查。次年，改督导检查办公室为局督导室，指定2人负责日常工作。1991年，制定《修文县普通中小学教育评估方案》，以实验小学和修文中学为德育评估试点，并指导各区教育办公室对所辖中心小学进行评估。次年，配合安顺地区教育局，按照《贵州省完全中学学校工作评估方案》，对修文中学进行督导评估，评估结果为优良；接着又对各中、小学升降国旗制度执行情况进行检查。1993年，县直中、小学和乡（镇）中学、中心小学完成德育评估，督评工作获安顺地区第三名。次年，撤销教育局督导室，成立县人民政府教育督导室并明确为二级局，确定编制并任命督导室主任、副主任和督导室办公室主任，聘任首批督学12名。1994—1996年，督导室先后3次对乡（镇）政府的教育工作进行检查评估，同时集中开展对实验小学、城关小学和新春小学的督导评估，以及对实验幼儿园和六广幼儿园的分类复查评估，并配合安顺地区行署教育督导室对县职业教育培训中心开展办学水平督导评估。1997—2000年，加强对乡（镇）政府和各中、小学“两基”的督促和指导，要求对照验收标准逐项达标。2000—2002年，进一步充实督导队伍，先后任命专职督学5名。2003—2004年，对10乡（镇）“两基”巩固情况进行检查，并于2004年底根据《修文县乡（镇）教育工作考核评估办法》对乡（镇）政府教育目标完成情况进行考核，将考核结果提供县政府兑现奖惩。2005—2010年，教育督导工作在巩固“两基”成果、提高“两基”水平的基础上，根据《贵阳市中小学办学水平评估试行意见》和相关评估办法以及实施素质教育的评估要求，先后对25所学校进行评估，督促学校改善办学条件、提高办学水平和教育质量，大力推进素质教育。同时，配合县教育局对各中、小学实行年度目标管理，制定考核方案，确定考核内容和标准，并定期检查指

2008年，县政府与乡镇和部门签订教育工作目标责任书

导，年终将定性考核结果反馈教育局，作为兑现年度奖惩的依据。

三、经费管理

1978—1982年，教育经费由县财政局划拨，县教育局具体管理。1983年，教育局制定《关于我县教育经费管理的意见》，对县直学校及各区的预算指标，由教育局根据当年的教育事业计划和规定的各项经费指标定额安排下拨给校、区，校、区本着勤俭办学方针妥善安排，使用时需按要求编制分季度用款计划，报教育局审核批准，并按月将财务报表上交。1985年，县政府将教育经费以支出指标的形式直接划拨、包干使用，县城学校由教育局管理，区属范围内学校由区财政所管理，学校实行报账制。1992年撤区并乡建镇，由乡（镇）财政所管理属地教育经费。1995年，执行县委、县政府制定的《关于贯彻〈中国教育改革和发展纲要〉的实施意见》，改革教育经费管理体制,实行预算单列并由县财政局直接管理，教育局汇总各校预算后报审，并履行经费使用监督的职责。此后，在加强对预算内资金管理的同时，财政局于1998年制定《关于预算外资金管理的暂行办法》，教育局亦先后制定《关于我县教育经费管理的意见（试行）》《财会工作管理制度》和《学校财务财产管理办法》。2001年9月，县政府建立教育系统会计结算中心，管理学校的财务会计工作，实行统一核算、集中管理，学校仍实行报账制。中心建立后，教师工资、教育税费、中央转移支付资金和上级专款等由其统一管理，并按照教育局用款计划划拨资金。中心还负责编报各项经费预算、决算及各类财务报告，提供政府决策所需的财务会计信息，并制定《财产物资管理制度》《票据领发登记制度》《内部签字制度》《物资采购验收分发制度》和《主管会计职责》《资金管理会计职责》《出纳员职责》。2004年，教育系统会计结算中心归并县会计管理中心，按照“预算管理体制不变，资金的管理权、使用权、审批权不变，经济责任主体法律责任不变”的原则，实行“集中管理，统一开户，分户核算”；中心设置专柜核算教育经费，县直中、小学和乡（镇）中心校实行二级核算；中心制定《财务监督职责》《报账办法（试行）》《备用金管理制度》《会计单位报账工作规则（试行）》《票据管理规定》和《固定资产管理规定》。2006年，教育各项收支全部纳入预算管理。2008年，县审计、财政、纪检等部门开展农村义务教育保障经费专项审计。2010年，成立教育局会计核算中心，教育经费由教育局集中管理，各中、小学报账时票据由教育局审核报销。

2002年，财政部教科文司检查县教育投入情况

1978—2010年县级财政教育投入统计表

表4—01—06

年份	县级财政投入经费（万元）	占县级财政支出比重（%）	年 份	县级财政投入经费（万元）	占县级财政支出比重（%）
1978	95.04	16.36	1995	984.00	23.17
1979	114.54	20.75	1996	1268.60	31.44
1980	130.61	25.22	1997	1652.60	21.42

续表

年份	县级财政投入经费（万元）	占县级财政支出比重（%）	年份	县级财政投入经费（万元）	占县级财政支出比重（%）
1981	156.98	25.17	1998	2153.90	21.83
1982	197.10	19.61	1999	2791.60	21.59
1983	219.57	17.86	2000	4474.30	25.69
1984	299.51	20.41	2001	4498.80	28.27
1985	327.23	27.70	2002	5049.90	33.02
1986	336.09	27.49	2003	5029.50	27.42
1987	315.05	26.27	2004	5472.10	23.71
1988	396.02	26.09	2005	6512.10	22.54
1989	397.43	22.34	2006	7083	20.66
1990	426.86	24.63	2007	11128	20.60
1991	508.40	26.71	2008	13867	25.23
1992	590.10	28.16	2009	15678	21.57
1993	657.90	27.43	2010	20335	22.64
1994	913.73	26.98			

四、人事管理

（一）教职工编制

1978—1983年，学校教职工编制以基本保证正常教学秩序为原则，按需调配。1984至1993年，实行“以校为单位按班级核定教职工数量”的编制标准，高中每班教职工3.6人（教师2.6人、职工1人），独立初中每班3.25人（教师2.25人、职工1人），戴帽初中每班2.5人（全部为教师），县城小学每班2人（教师1.7人、职工0.3人），区级小学每班1.7人（教师1.5人、职工0.2人），乡级小学每班1.5人（教师1.3人、职工0.2人），乡以下小学每班1.32人（全部为教师），实验幼儿园每班2.5人（教师2人、职工0.5人）。1994—2002年，仍实行“以校为单位按班级核定教职工数量”的编制标准，但班级学生有定额，高中每班学生45至50人、教职工4.1人（教师3.1人、职工1人），初中每班45至50人、教职工3.7人（教师2.8人、职工0.9人），县城小学每班40至45人、教职工2.4人（教师2.1人、职工0.3人），乡（镇）中心完小每班40至45人、教职工2.2人（教师1.9人、职工0.3人），农村一般小学每班30至45人、教职工1.7人（教师1.4人、职工0.3人），教学点每班10至30人、教师1人。2003年起，执行“根据高中、初中、小学等不同教育层次和城市、县镇、农村等不同地域，按照教职工与在校学生的一定比例核定教职工编制”的规定，全县公办学校教职工编制总数2832人。其中3所高中127人，21所初中1011人，35所片区以上小学（含所属村小及教学点）1578人，4所幼儿园72人，特殊教育学校24人，职业教育培训中心20人。2008年对编制进行调整，核定教职工编制总数为2487人。其中，3所高中289人，22所初中728人，31所片区以上小学（含所属村小及教学点）1310人，4所幼儿园102人，特殊教育学校33人，职业教育培训中心25人。在控制总量的前提下，根据各校学生人数确定教职工数量，总量实行动态管理，3年调整一次。至2010年，仍在期限以内，未作调整。

（二）学校领导任免

1978—1983年，学校校长按干部管理权限由县委组织部任免。1984年，实行分级负责制，乡（镇）以上各级各类学校校长任免由县教育局局长提名，组织部审批下文，其余公办学校由区公所、乡（镇）政府和区教育办公室商定，村级民办学校由乡（镇）政府决定；校内其他领导由校长提名任免，县教育局审批。1986年，乡（镇）及以上学校领导班子由县教育局任免，村级学校由区教育办公室和当地党政领导商定报县教育局任免。1990年起，区教育办公室（乡、镇教育辅导站）领导及其所属中、小学领导的任免权归于区（乡、镇）。1999年，县委、县政府出台《关于进一步加强全县教师队伍建设和管理的意见》，对学校领导班子的管理进行规范，明确修文中学和职业教育培训中心的正副职、修文二中正职由县委组织部任免；乡（镇）教育辅导站站长，修文中学、职业教育培训中心的中层，修文二中副职和县直其他各校（园）的校（园）长，由县教育局党委确定，人事劳动局任免；学校的其他负责人，涉及乡（镇）的须征得乡（镇）党委、政府同意，由县教育局党委任免。2003年，县委、县政府《关于完善全县教育管理体制的意见》进一步明确，修文中学、职业教育培训中心正职由县教育局提名，县委组织部、县教育局共同考察，按干部管理权限任用或聘用；修文中学、职业教育培训中心副职，乡（镇）教育辅导站及乡（镇）中心小学（园）以上的正副职，由县教育局决定任免，报县人事劳动局备案；乡（镇）中、小学（园）以上的中层及乡（镇）以下小学校长，由学校（园）或教育辅导站确定，县教育局任免。2004—2010年，逐步改革学校领导的选拔任用制度，建立校长公开选聘、竞争上岗机制；高级中学和完全中学领导由县教育局提名、考察或参与考察，按干部管理权限任用或聘用，其他中、小学（园）领导由教育局选聘；推行中、小学（园）校（园）长聘任制，明确其任职资格，实行任期制。

2007年，全县第六期小学校长任职资格培训

（三）教师调配

20世纪70年代末至80年代初，在县委统一领导下，中、小学公办教师调动须经教育局同意，在本县范围内由教育局办理；小学教师跨县、跨地区调动由教育局直接联系办理，中学教师跨县、跨地区调动由教育局提出意见报安顺地区教育局审查办理。80年代中期至90年代后期，全县公办教师的调动均由教育局研究决定，具有大专以上学历的教师如因特殊情况要求调出县的，须报地区教育局同意，新分配任教的大、中专毕业生在5年内不考虑调动。1999年，县委、县政府《关于进一步加强全县教师队伍建设和管理的意见》规定，在乡（镇）辖区内调动教师，先由乡（镇）教育辅导站提出建议并征得乡（镇）党委、政府同意后，再由教育局与县编办研究核准调入学校编制后教育局审批行文，送县人事劳动局备案；跨乡（镇）调动（含调入县直中、小学）教师，由教育局党委征求有关乡（镇）党委、政府意见后提议，送县人事劳动局与县编办研究核准调入学校编制后提交县政府党组研究审批，再由县人事劳动局

行文。满编超编学校不再调进教师，教师改行由县委常委会议研究决定。2004年起，进行人事制度改革，严格实行编制管理，全面实行教职工聘用制，教师职务聘任与岗位聘任统一，建立“能进能出、能上能下”的教师聘用新机制。此后，缺编学校聘用教师或者教师交流，须报经教育局党委研究同意并行文，学校缺额教师可面向社会招聘。2005—2008年，面向社会招聘教师48名，推荐60人次乡（镇）教师交流到县城学校锻炼，选派100人次优秀教师到农村薄弱学校支援教学。至2010年，教师聘任和交流的制度未变。

五、教学管理

1978年，县教育局出台《关于进一步办好我县重点中、小学的意见》，强调学校领导要深入教学一线，研究掌握教学规律，精通业务，抓典型，树样板。1984年，印发《修文县学校工作管理意见（试行草案）》，明确校长领导学校教学工作，教导主任组织管理教学工作。1988年，先后出台《修文县中小学教师常规管理意见》《修文县中小学教师常规管理要求》和《修文县中小学教学工作管理考评细则》，强调加强教学常规管理的同时，结合考评细则对学校教学管理进行检查与指导。通过强化管理，取得明显成效，县中考成绩在安顺地区连年名列前茅。20世纪90年代中期，对教学进行规范管理，强调促进学生全面发展，在加强传统重点科目教学的同时，重视引导学生对音乐、体育和美术之类非传统重点科目的学习，中、高考时录取的体育和艺术类学生逐年增加。90年代后期至21世纪初，以实施素质教育为重点，进一步明确教学管理方向，全县城乡学校围绕素质教育进行教学改革尝试，特别是县城学校发挥了示范带头作用，修文中学高考取得新突破，修文二中中考成绩大幅提升，实验小学县内统考连年夺魁。2004年，实施基础教育课程改革，强调在教学目标上知识与技能，过程与方法，情感、态度与价值观的三维并重；在教学方法上注重学生的参与、探究与合作，指导学生开展综合实践活动；在评价方式上不以考试成绩作为唯一手段，而是采取多元评价方式激励学生，促进学生个性化发展。在探索课改的道路上，开展教育科研为学校教学特色，全县中、小学共承担国家及省、市科研课题8个，上千人次教师参与，其中扎佐中学尤为突出，两次获贵阳市一等奖，31人次获科研成果奖43项。2008年，县政府出台《教育工作考核激励办法》，县财政每年拨付100万元对学校教育质量进行考核激励。为贯彻落实《办法》，加强质量管理，2009年教育局制定《义务教育阶段教学常规管理基本要求》《义务教育阶段教学常规管理考核细则》和《教学质量责任追究制度》，将教学质量与学校年度目标考核挂钩，通过考核兑现奖惩。2010年，教学质量考核制度仍在施行。

2008年，县教育局与学校签订工作目标责任书

六、学籍管理

20世纪70年代末至80年代初，将学生学籍纳入教育管理范畴，要求学校对在校学生造册登记，完善转学手续，控制学生流失，减少留级数量，放宽毕业要求。1984年，县教育局制定《学校工作管理意见（试行草案）》，明确学校教导主任管理学生学籍，教务员具体负责。次年，为迎接普及初等教育验收，

完成全县小学学生学籍档案健全工作，并在验收的基础上继续推进。1989年进一步完善学籍管理措施，实行“一生一号一卡”制度，即每个学生设置一个学籍号，建立一张学籍卡，并认真整理归档。次年，高中实行毕业会考制度，高中学校一律执行《贵州省普通高中毕业会考学籍管理暂行办法》。1992年，安顺地区教育局下发《关于加强小学学籍管理的试行意见》，县教育局根据《意见》要求制定《小学学籍管理办法》，规范小学生学籍号编号方式，同时要求加强初中生学籍管理，明确规定初中生学籍号编写办法，同样实行“一生一号一卡”制度。同时，中、小学实行学生学籍收费管理，小学一年级和初中一年级新入学须缴纳学生学籍管理费，但只执行2年即取消收费。1996年，为推进普及九年义务教育，禁止学校开除义务教育阶段学生，继后又取消义务教育学生的升留级制度。次年，县教育局出台《中小学生学籍管理暂行办法》，使学籍管理更加严格和规范。此后，在“普九”工作中，教育局组织专人对各校学籍管理情况进行专项检查，重点对学生人数、流动情况等进行核实，以及对学籍档案规范化建设进行督促。2001年，教育局将原《暂行办法》进行修订，新出台《修文县中小学生学籍管理暂行规定》，次年又转发《贵阳市普通高中学籍管理规定》。至2010年，两个《规定》仍在继续执行。学生学籍管理实行分级负责制，高中学校学生学籍由县教育局审核后报贵阳市教育局审批管理，初中和县直小学由学校审核后报县教育局审批管理，其余小学由乡（镇）中心校审核后报县教育局审批备案，由审核单位管理。

七、招生工作

（一）幼儿园（学前班）招生

1978—1980年，全县公办幼儿园仅有县实验小学幼儿园，每年招生不足百人。幼儿园招生除进行体格检查外，不进行任何形式的考试或测查，学生入学年龄为4至6周岁。1981年，县成立托幼工作领导小组，办园数量增多，招生规模扩大。1983年，全县幼儿园增至11所，招生300人，有的小学还附设1年的学前教育教学班并招收6周岁儿童入学。1985年，全县学前班招生373人。幼儿园在定额招生的同时，实行平时缺额补招。20世纪90年代，学前班增多，幼儿园有所减少，两者招生差距明显。1993年，幼儿园招生247人，学前班招生竟达1642人。1996年，执行贵州省教委规定，规范小学附设学前班管理，实行办班登记制度，条件基本具备者颁发《学前班办学许可证》。当年全县6所幼儿园招生260人，98个学前班招生3336人。次年，学前班达110个，招生3536人。90年代，公办幼儿园严重不足，招生数量少，学前教育发展不协调。为缓解幼儿入园难的问题，县政府鼓励民间兴办幼儿园，让更多幼儿入园接受教育。1998年，全县办有2所民办幼儿园，招生141人，约占当年全县招生数的1/3。继后，公办幼儿园每年招生基本稳定在300人左右，民办幼儿园发展迅速，招生逐年增多。2001年起，幼儿入园年龄降至3至5周岁，学前班降至5周岁。2004年，14所公、民办幼儿园在园幼儿达1658人，学前班招生2602人。2008年，12所幼儿园在园幼儿2292人，学前班招生1577人。2010年，全县幼儿园招生673人，在园幼儿2825人，学前班招生1257人。

（二）小学招生

1978年，小学基本按照就近入学的原则招生。小学招生无须考试，学生入学年龄为7周岁。1980年9月，县政府《关于普及全县小学五年教育的意见》出台，本着普及的原则，要求学校将适龄儿童全部招收，对少量未入学者，实行动员入学。次年，招生1.04万人（未含厂场子校）。1985年，为使小学入学率达95%左右，全县计划招生1万人，原则上凡属适龄儿童只要不因残疾丧失学习能力者均须招收。次年，

普及初等教育验收合格，小学适龄儿童入学率达94.75%。其后招生正常推进，入学率基本稳定。1990年招生7866人。1993年秋，实行义务教育入学通知制度，按照乡（镇）调查登记本地区应入学就读一年级的适龄儿童，由地方政府填发《入学通知书》送达入学对象的家长或监护人，督促其按时送子女或被监护人入学，申请缓读的学生须经县教育局同意，实行隔年招生的学校由县政府审批。当年全县招生8216人。1996年，重新划定各小学的服务片区，实行区域招生，凡属本校服务片区内的适龄儿童，学校均应招收入学。次年，县直小学、扎佐一小、扎佐二小和久长小学开始招6周岁半儿童入学。2001年，全县小学生入学年龄降为6周岁，当年招生5070人。此后，政府管理力度逐渐加大，家长法律意识不断提高，小学招生进展顺利，全县适龄儿童均按时入校接受义务教育，特殊情况者经批准暂缓入学。2010年，全县小学招生2566人，实现适龄儿童入学全覆盖。

（三）中学招生

1978年，中学招生仍实行统一考试制度。初中招生考试由县教育局组织，各学区具体实施，招生学校根据教育局下达的计划数划线录取；高中招生考试由安顺地区教育局组织，县教育局具体实施，招生学校根据县教育局下达的计划数划线录取。1980年，全县初中和高中分别下达招生计划3200人和450人。继后，对中学进行压缩与调整，要求各校不得任意扩大或缩减招生计划数，以致招生数量有所减少。1983年，初、高中招生计划数分别为2400人、400人。次年，初、高中分别招生2550人、350人。1985年，高中招生数占初三毕业生数的16.54%。20世纪80年代中、后期，初中招生基本稳定，但高中招生面临新的问题，许多录取进入高中的学生因担心高中毕业考不上大学而不愿就读高中，选择滞留初中补习准备考入中专、中师和中技，修完学科毕业后即可就业，致使初中补习班爆满而高中招生不足。1989年，高中仅招生225人。90年代初、中期，再次压缩高中学校，全县地方学校仅剩修文中学办有高中。1993年，高中招生数降至163人，其中还包括厂场子校的32人。1996年，全县初中招生3630人。是年，修文中学计划招高中学生135名，但开学仅有50名学生报到注册，为解燃眉之急，学校只得降低录取分数线招录学生，尽管标准降低，也只增加32名。后学校又将报名时间再次推至10月份，并对家庭贫困学生减免学杂费，方完成招生任务。次年，首次实现小学毕业生100%升入初中的目标，但高中招生仍处低潮，只招到168人。90年代后期，中专招生实行双向选择，取消统一分配，使毕业生就业政策发生变化，加之高中办学规模扩大，高中招生数量有所回升，但总体数量仍然不多。1999年，取消初中招生考试，小学毕业生凭《毕业证书》到就近学校就读初中，初中学校必须将服务片区内的小学毕业生全部招入。2000年，全县2987名初中毕业生中报考高中者达1800人，尽管已在招生计划的基础上扩招450人，但最终录取仍不足千人。进入21世纪，初中招生实行规范化管理，小学毕业生均升入初中。2002年，高中招生首次突破千位达1086人，2005年又增至1808人，初中毕业生就读高中比例已达64.8%。此后，中学招生进入稳定时期。2010年，初中和高中分别招生4581人和1718人。

（四）大中专招生

1978年县成立招生办公室，在县招生委员会的领导下负责组织实施大中专招生考试。招生实行“自愿报名，统一考试”的原则，分别在省、地招生工作管理部门的组织和具体指导下运作。由于刚恢复招生考试制度，为照顾因“文化大革命”而被耽误学习的青年，考生无年龄限制。后随着招考不断推进，对考生年龄加以限制，初中学历报考中专（中师、技校）者不得超过18周岁，高中学历招考中专（中师、技校）者不得超过22周岁，所有报考大学（大专）者不得超过25周岁。1980年，高中学历报考大学和中专（中师、中技）不得兼报并分别划线录取，县师范招收民办教师单独划定录取分数线。次年，中师只招初中学历和民办教师，中专未予限制。1983年，省外户籍迁入者高考受限，高考实行“一条龙”录取，考生可同时兼报大学和中专，考分达到何档学校最低控制线则录取在该档学校。次年，县外户籍迁入者中考受限。20世纪80年代中期，中专、中师招生实行预选考试，预选上线者方能正式参加升学考试，中专、中师不得互为兼报，考试在同一时间分别进行，分别录取，中专录取名额由地区控制，中师、技校名额分配到县；大学始招自费生和委培生，打破此前单一的计划招生体制，形成以招收国家计划生为主、自费生和委培生为辅的招生新模式和录取上的“双轨制”，后又招收定向生。1989年，县内录取自费生2人。次年，执行贵州省教委规定，普通高中实行毕业会考制度，学生须经会考合格后方能参加高考。20世纪90年代初，技工学校改为学校自行招生。1991年，农牧中专实行单独招生，指标到县。继后，中师、中专招生时初中应届和往届毕业生各占50%。1993年，中专学校亦招收定向生，继后又招收委培生。次年，经省教委批准，修文中学为安顺地区具有保送大学本科学生资格的学校。1996年，修文中学保送1名学生就读贵州师范大学。90年代后期，中专学校亦实行自行招生，大学扩大招生规模，且不再按招生计划和调节计划（即双轨）分别划线录取，而只能按总计划划定一条线（即单轨）录取，将原来的两种计划两种收费并为一种，录取的学生需缴纳部分培养费。另外，国家不再包揽大中专毕业生分配，实行个人在就业政策指导下自主择业。此后，就读中专者渐少，报考大学者渐多。2001年，全县录取大学本科以上121人，就读中专（中师）287人。后大中专招生取消年龄和婚否限制。2005年，实行“阳光招生”，高考招生有关信息向社会公开，次年高考招生实行网上录取。2007年，全县录取大专以上751人，就读中专（中职）506人。2010年，录取大学重点院校79人，一般本科443人，专科（高职）369人。

1978—2000年大、中专及技工学校录取学生概况表

表4—01—07

年度	大专及以上(人)	中专(人)		技校(人)
		总数	其中:中师人数	
1978	62	139	50	93
1979	57	170	90	103
1980	56	140	90	77
1981	39	156	90	107
1982	53	134	90	101
1983	101	140	85	103
1984	75	155	81	124
1985	73	137	59	108
1986	74	186	59	121
1987	71	194	59	141
1988	74	201	50	126
1989	49	159	51	107

续表

年度	大专及以上(人)	中专(人)		技校(人)
		总数	其中:中师人数	
1990	92	174	51	156
1991	44	154	51	学校自行招生
1992	85	128	54	
1993	73	136	55	
1994	66	122	62	
1995	54	135	91	
1996	99	284	83	
1997	110	448	147	
1998	128	470	136	
1999	154	658	150	
2000	121	615	97	

2001—2010年普通高考报考及录取概况表

表4—01—08

年度	报考人数(人)	录取人数(人)				录取比例(%)
		总数	其中			
			重点本科院校	一般本科院校	专科(高职)院校	
2001	251	203	22	99	82	80.88
2002	282	214	17	126	71	75.89
2003	449	342	25	178	139	76.17
2004	807	575	48	279	248	71.25
2005	1356	642	38	326	278	47.35
2006	1456	583	39	253	291	40.04
2007	1469	751	73	315	363	51.12
2008	1690	716	66	345	305	42.37
2009	1738	927	87	417	423	53.34
2010	1310	891	79	443	369	68.02

第二章　科学技术

从1978年改革开放起，县委、县政府在发展经济进程中始终抓住“经济建设必须依靠科技进步，科学技术必须面向经济建设”这条主线。1980年，提出“科技兴农”“尊重科学、尊重人才”的口号，旨在壮大科技队伍，推动科技发展。1995年，第一个民营科技企业—修文县瑞达生物研究所成立，至2010年，全县有民营科技企业13家，民办科技合作组织3个。1996年，县委七届四次会议作出在全县实施“科技兴县”战略决策，后又增添教育内容，上升为“科教兴县”。通过广泛深入持久的科技普及、咨询与示范，加上强有力的政策导向，全县形成科技兴工、科技兴农、科技兴事业的热潮。2000年，县委、县政府又提出“创建省级科技先进县”的目标，在全县大力普及科学知识，加大科技推广和投入的力度。2001年，涉及龙场、扎佐、久长3镇范围内共28个行政村的农业科技示范园区建成。2006年在全县科技大会上，县委、县政府再次发出“实施科教兴县战略，推动县域经济发展”的号召，要求运用各种宣传媒体大力普及现代科学知识，加大对科技的财政支持和金融扶持，同时，在全县实施科技示范村建设，为农村搭建起更加广阔的科技创新平台。县委、县政府一系列科技发展战略和具体措施给修文带来深刻变化，使农村经济发展的果、蔬、药种植和奶牛、肉牛、生猪、土鸡养殖的科技内涵得到不断提升。2001—2002年度、2003—2004年度，修文县连续两次被表彰为全国“科技进步先进县”。

1985年7月，贵州省人民政府授给修文县科委“科技战线先进集体”奖旗

第一节　科技队伍

一、队伍构成

本土培养　1978年，县内有各类种专业技术人员374名，其中，工程技术人员104人，农业技术人员80人，卫生技术人员155人，大专以上文化程度的中学教员35人。继后，随着“科教兴县”战略的实

施，充分利用县的党校、行政学校、农业广播学校、职业高中、农业培训中心和职业培训中心等教育场所及其设施培养乡土人才。至2010年，共培养本科生154名，专科生2666名，中专生4289名，短期培训2.82万人次。使科技队伍不断壮大，全县有初级职称以上的科技人员3258人，其中获得高级职称的57人，中级职称596人。此外，通过建立农村科技协会和科技志愿者队伍、在行政村和县属骨干企业中配备科技干部等方式，扩大科技队伍，使科技服务体系和科普网络体系日趋完善。至2010年，全县建起农技协会40个，吸收有一技之长的土专家会员4382人，有科普志愿者517人。

人才引进 1985年，县政府建起“专家咨询组”，聘任贵州农学院等8个单位的11位专家为成员。2000年4月，成立县科技经济专家顾问组，聘请23名专家为县的科技经济顾问。2004年5月，成立县农业科技专家院，聘请16位专家为农业科技专家院专家。专家们深入村寨田间了解民情，帮助农民就“蔬、果、花、畜”等科技难题进行攻关，推进科技知识和农村实用技术的普及。

2000年起，实施“项目引才”“事业引才”工程，至2010年，全县共引进人才1229人。贵州林海新材料制造有限公司于2002年引进高级工程师关昌烈等专家后，一举攻破高科技产品高强度石油压裂支撑剂技术难关，生产的86Mpa高强度压裂支撑剂填补了国内技术空白。2006年实施“专家库”建设，形成一支具有实力的专家队伍。至2010年，专家库有县外专家25名，本土青年科技骨干55人。

专记：“土专家”马平忠带领村民栽花致富

1996年，谷堡乡大塘村村民马平忠到贵阳一家花卉栽培园打工，学到大棚栽培技术后于1999年回到大塘，联合几户村民种植大棚蔬菜，当年即获效益。看到马平忠种蔬菜赚钱，村民上门讨教栽培技术，但联合户要马平忠留一手，不要把技术全部教给别人，给自己制造竞争对手。马平忠说：“大家掌握技术，全村都能致富，有什么不好？”对前来求教的村民，他耐心传技，从不保守，白天忙不过来，就晚上到农户家中指教。经过两三年时间，村里群众大都掌握了栽培技术，早熟蔬菜的种植规模逐渐扩大，发展早熟蔬菜成了大塘村群众增收的主渠道。

正当全村人要大干快上的时候，专家却告诉他们：经检测，大塘村土壤背景值达不到标准，不适宜发展绿色农副产品。专家的话像晴天霹雳，让马平忠吃不香睡不着。为找新的发展路子，他在家里查资料，又到外地去考察，几经周折，决定改成大棚花卉。但搞花卉投入多、困难大，他不想让村民跟着担风险，决定自己先干起来，探索出一条稳妥的发财路，再带领大家一同发展。马平忠的想法感动了打工回乡的青年谢大江，谢拿出自己打工的积蓄说：“要闯咱俩一起闯，要倒霉咱俩一起倒霉，大不了再出去打几年工。”2002年底，两人投资修建简易大棚，引进栽培剑兰等花卉品种，5个月后，运往贵阳销售，批发价1元钱1支，还供不应求。一年下来，两人投入1万多元，收入3万多元。旗开得胜，马平忠信心大增，2004年，便与谢大江投入11万元建起占地4.5亩的14个大棚，引进非洲菊、康乃馨、玫瑰等品种进行科学种植。马平忠种植的玫瑰花花蕾强壮、花瓣肥大、花色艳丽、花香浓郁、花期长，颇受花商青睐，当年就收入10余万元。他把种植技术、经验传授给乡亲们，在其带动下，大塘村的村民们或养花或种菜，依靠科技走上了致富之路。

二、科技人员待遇

1978年后，县委、县政府落实科技人员相关政策，重奖科技人员，激励科技工作者振兴县城经济的积极性。1980年成立县科技干部技术职称评定委员会，将125名符合条件的科技人员套改为助理工程师以上的技术职称。1982年，县政府专门召开职称资格证书颁证大会，对批准晋升职称的156人颁发技术职称资格证书。与此同时，组织部门还选拔53名科技人员到相关部门担任领导职务。1984年，将25名用非所学、专业不对口的科技人员调到能发挥其专长的单位；给在区、乡（镇）基层工作的科技人员向上浮动1级工资。1987年，县政府出台《关于鼓励科技人员向农村流动和兼职从事有偿技术服务的暂行规定》，1988年县委、县政府制发《关于放宽放活科研机构和科技人员政策，鼓励科技人员积极投入经济建设的意见》，允许科技人员停薪留职、兼职、辞职和从事有偿技术服务、技术入股、技术培训和技术咨询，并对科技人员通过科技服务、承包科研项目等获得的收益分配作出宽松规定。是年，县科委1名畜牧师率先停薪留职，到马家桥承包成都军区后勤部昆明办事处修文畜牧饲养场。随后，县农业局38名科技人员下乡承包种植良种小麦、油菜和病虫防治，既让生产单位获得收益，又让科技人员增加收入，取得双赢的结果。1991年，给予388名科技人员年度考核“优秀”荣誉。自1978至2010年，全县科技人员中有360人次受到县以上党委和政府的表彰，分别获得“优秀科技工作者”、“科技工作先进个人”称号，其中66人次获得省、市的表彰奖励。县设立科技成果奖，对科技人员的研究成果给予奖励，重大成果组织向市、省、国家申报。到2010年，全县累计有110项科研成果分别获得国家、省、市、县奖励。电影公司放映员陈志明下岗后刻苦钻研，发明解放牌142型汽车刹车专用控制器，荣获“新世界、新产品、新技术世界博览会”金奖和第二届“爱迪生世界发明博览会”金奖，县委随即组织《修文报》报道，报社主编陈新国撰写报告文学《山区小镇科研迷》大力宣传科研精神。与此同时，县科技局向省、市申报先进事迹，嗣后陈志明被评为“贵阳市十大杰出青年”、“贵州省十大杰出青年”和“贵阳市国有企业下岗职工再创业明星”，荣获贵州省五一劳动奖章。

1996年县委、县政府领导与科技兴农人才奖获得者合影

第二节　科技进步

一、机构建置

1998年，成立以县委书记为组长，县人大、县政府、县政协领导和有关经济、科技综合部门领导参加的“科技兴县”领导小组，县政府配备科技副县长，乡（镇）配科技副乡（镇）长，由农业和科技部门派出科技人员蹲点联系全县各村，形成从上到下的科技组织网络。1999年创建省级科技进步先进县，增设创建科技进步先进县活动领导小组，下设科技进步考核办公室。2001年，开展创建全国科技进步先进县活动，仍由创先活动领导小组负责全县创建工作的组织领导、指导、检查和考核工作。至2010年，

创建工作继续进行。

二、科普宣传

1981年6月，成立农业科技咨询服务站，采取定点和巡回相结合的方式，深入全县5个区16个公社30个生产大队开展为时9天的科技普及宣传，受众万余人次。是年，县作为全省先进集体出席在云南昆明召开的全国农村科普经验交流会。1991年，开展科普宣传进村入户活动，放映科技电影183场，办科技墙报648期，接受9.2万人次种植、养殖技术咨询。宣传结合实际，大力推广杂交水稻、杂交玉米、水稻地膜育秧、两段育秧、玉米地膜覆盖和玉米袋块栽培等农业技术。1996年3月18日全省第一个科技日，组织开展科技宣传咨询活动，印发资料13种5000份，接受咨询1万人次。1997年3月，在县城开展“科技一条街”活动，340名科技工作者参加，接受2万人次群众咨询，发放各类农技资料1.8万份。2000年3月，举行“青少年科普电视周”活动，在学校播放科技光碟40场次，组织开展“新世纪的挑战”主题讨论会，县电视台组织科技专题节目滚动播出。2003年11月，贵州省农业科技下乡活动确定修文县为贵州省的分会场，省、市100名农技专家组成农业科技下乡团，分5个小分队，赴龙场、扎佐、洒坪、小箐和谷堡5乡（镇）的12个宣传咨询点，开展科技宣传咨询，向群众赠送科技图书及光盘资料，在县农业培训中心举办“修文县农业发展专家论坛”。科技下乡活动重点在龙场镇举办“科技大集”，贵州省副省长禄智明、省农业厅厅长陶性潜、贵阳市副市长罗筑云出席开集仪式，省、市农业专家15人和科技人员100人，在集市上开展专家现场咨询，向群众赠送有关农业科技书籍3万册；省农科院组织园艺专家和贵州大学农学院园艺系果树专业的大学生到久长镇兴隆村开展科技宣传。是年，还在全县开展主题为“依靠科技，战胜非典”的科技宣传周活动。2004年5月，开展主题为“科技以人为本、全面建设小康”的科技活动周，省、市、县51个单位712名科技工作者参与，通过办黑板报、开展讲座、利用远程教育网络讲授农业科技课等多种形式开展科技宣传。2010年，先后举行“防灾减灾”科普宣传活动6次，向群众发放宣传资料4.5万份。

2005年，科技宣传周现场一角

三、专家库建设

2006年实施专家库建设，建起县外专家库和本地专家库。县外专家库采取“以专家带项目、以项目找专家”方式，结合县内经济发展，在医药、新材料、农业和环保等科技领域遴选专家入库。县外专家库的专家以高新科技注入县内经济建设，使产品科技含量显著提升。贵州科学院、贵州大学、贵州农业科学院和天津大学等院校25名县外专家入选县外专家库。本地专家库遴选县内中青年科技骨干55人入库。县外专家介入县内经济建设，促进了科技成果转化，增强了企业自主创新能力。留日博士张高与扎佐医药园区中际、安泰等企业合作，建立研究平台，使企业产品的科技水平得以提高；建筑学和力学专家钟蜀晖、李泉珍、黄质宏与高新盛远公司合作，在高新技术产业玻璃纤维增强塑料杆材的开发与应用上获得成功；材料学博士莫莉萍引进贵阳天龙摩擦材料有限公司和贵阳吉隆单宁化工有限公司等4家企业入驻县内。专家们发挥专长帮助修文发展经济的同时，还在群众中普及科学知识。畜牧专家顾怀均在久长镇清水村奶牛养殖基地先后举办奶农培训班4次，培训奶农200人。

四、科技“创先”

省级科技先进县创建　1999年5月，县成立创建科技进步先进县活动领导小组，召开“创先”专题会议3次，县财政投入科技三项费25万元。2000年，县委、县政府将创建省级科技先进县列为十件实事之一，成立“科技经济专家顾问组”，聘请李桂莲等20位专家为科技经济顾问。6月9日，召开全县科技工作大会，县长魏明禄与各乡（镇）和县直各部门签订“修文县创建省级科技工作先进县目标责任书”。是年投入科技三项费34万元。2001年11月贵州省人民政府授牌，命名修文县为“贵州省科技进步先进县”。

贵州省人民政府授予县“贵州省科技先进县”奖牌

国家级科技先进县创建　2002年4月，县委、县政府下发《关于开展争创全国科技进步先进县考核工作的安排意见》文件，启动创建工作，明确目标，制定措施，落实任务。投入科技三项费99.2万元，占当年县财政预算支出的1.32%。2003年4月，县政府召开全县科技进步考核工作会，与各乡（镇）及县直有关单位签订“创建国家科技进步考核先进县工作目标责任书”。投入科技三项费125万元，比2002年增加25.8万元。创建工作两年间，召开科技工作会议13次，专题研究扎佐医药科技工业园区、农业科技综合示范园区的建设和农业科技创新和科学技术发展十五计划纲要等重大科技问题。2004年1月，国家科技部授予修文县2001—2002年度“全国科技进步先进县”称号。2003—2004年度再度获得“全国科技进步先进县称号”。

科技部授给修文县“2003—2004年度全国科技进步先进县”奖牌

五、高新技术引进

2000年，县政府制定“三点两线一园区”的经济发展思路，沿贵（阳）遵（义）、贵（阳）毕（节）两条高等级公路线，在龙场、扎佐和久长3镇引进高新技术产业。当年12月，扎佐医药园区规划成型，先后有16家医药企业入驻。2005年，县政府充分利用破产企业的存量资产，依托贵阳市科技风险投资有限公司开展科技风险招商，建立贵阳新材料基地修文板块（即贵阳科技风险投资产业园区）,引进高新技术产业企业贵阳天龙摩擦材料有限公司、贵阳吉隆单宁化工有限公司、贵阳怡丰精细化工有限公司和中国陶粒（贵州）有限公司。贵阳天龙摩擦材料有限公司主要从事“编织型石棉树脂刹车带”生产，年产刹车带100吨出口欧洲和中国香港地区市场，年总产值1500万元。贵阳吉隆单宁化工有限公司主要从事以五倍子为原料的精细化工产品生产，年产高纯度单宁酸100吨，工业级单宁酸300吨，年总产值1400万元。贵阳怡丰精细化工有限公司主要从事年产3000吨石油抗震剂生产，出口非洲市场。中国陶粒（贵州）有限公司为外商独资企业，主要生产和出口高强度石油压裂支撑剂产品，规划在3年内达到6万吨的生产规模，产值达到1.5亿元。

一批以高新技术产业研发、生产为主的企业落地修文，开创了高新技术引领科技发展的局面。自

2000年起，先后有仙灵骨葆、86Mpa高强度石油压裂支撑剂、高强度超细陶粒、肤痔清软膏、纺织型石棉树脂刹车带、高铝瓷球、凸轮轴、白水泥、棕钢玉等项目被列入省、市星火计划项目。2002年，兰地实业公司“20万蛋鸡规模养殖技术综合开发”和“果树良种示范基地”两个项目被列入国家级星火计划项目，实现县内国家级星火项目零的突破。2003年，扎佐医药工业园区被农业部命名为“全国乡（镇）企业科技园区”，医药业成为县的重点支柱产业。2009年，贵州同济堂药业、贵州安泰药业获授省级高新示范企业，《超高强度超高密度陶粒支撑剂制造研究》和《污泥页岩轻集材料的工业化应用技术开发》项目获县级科学应用技术研发经费资助10万元。高强度石油压裂支撑剂、仙灵骨葆胶囊、杜仲降压片、高密度耐磨瓷球等高新技术产品荣获省、市科学成果奖。高新技术的引进，促使传统产业的升级换代和结构调整，对产业结构优化升级发挥了积极作用。至2010年，全县高新企业增加值占规模以上企业增加值的比例平均达到67.1%，最高的2005年达87.71%，最低的2008年为43.64%。

2002年引进的国家级星火项目兰地实业公司“20万蛋鸡规模养殖技术综合开发”

六、修文医药产业园

2000年8月，县政府抓住制药企业按GMP标准改造的契机，推出扎佐医药工业园区整体规划，并在招商引资中采取“国有土地有偿转让，简化土地征用过程”办法，探索出一条“安泰模式”园区建设路子。12月16日，贵州安泰药业投资5000万元，兴建GMP标准生产线破土动工。2001年，光正药业、绿太阳制药、和仁堂制药和科开药业等8家医药企业按“安泰模式”运作相继入驻园区。是年，实施园区项目立项、科技项目申报、配套经费投入“三优先”措施，为园区企业申报新技术开发项目3项，新产品开发4项。同时，引入贵阳市科技风险投资公司投资2000万元，县投入科技三项费30万元，支持多菲利特、三T胶囊、肤痔清等新产品和电子磁疗按摩新技术的开发。

2002年，县申报贵阳市科技项目6项，园区项目即占3项。县科技项目6项，园区占5项。贵阳市财政局和市乡镇企业局分3批下拨药业专项扶持资金650万元，县财政匹配资金162.5万元，用于入驻园区企业的GMP改造。当年，医药园区创工业总产值1.5亿元，销售收入1.1亿元，实现税收600万元。2003年4月，一座新兴的医药科技园区屹立在县境东部扎佐，被农业部命名为“全国乡（镇）企业科技园区”。到2004年，扎佐医药工业园区共引进15家药业入驻，其中10家完成GMP改造，总投入达5.5亿元，创工业总产值4.8亿元，销售收入3500万元。2005年，仅贵州同济堂药业一家年产值就达4.6亿元，年销售收入3.34亿元，利税2557万元。2006年经国家发改委和贵州省政府审核，将园区更名为“修文医药产业园”，并列为贵州省

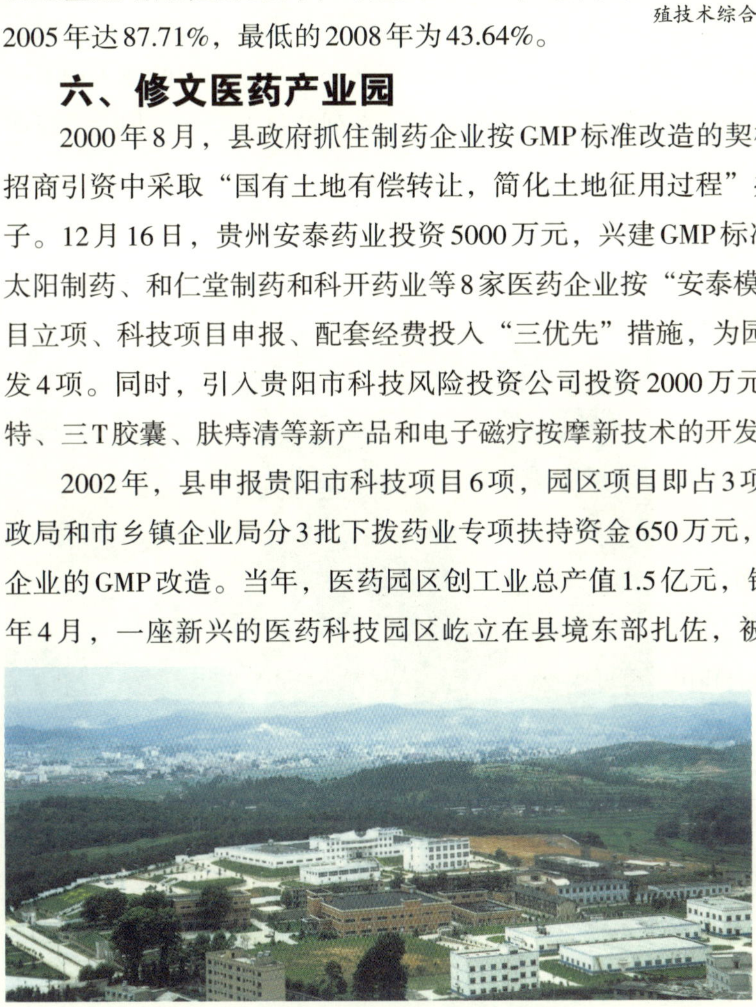

落地扎佐的修文医药产业园区

的省级开发区。至2010年，园区入驻企业18家，其中，销售企业1家，园区实现销售产值逾14亿元，上缴税金逾1.5亿元。制药业成为县的支柱产业。

第三节　科技服务

一、科技合作

1978年起，县政府组织科技成果参加各种博览会、交易会，组织企业开展高科技攻关活动，与高等院校和科研院所联合，建立基地，长期协作。先后与贵州大学、贵州农科院、天津大学等多家院校研究所签订技术合作协议，以其为人才培训基地、科研攻关基地和新产品开发基地。通过联合攻关、共建实验室和科技成果转化等方式，建设产学研联合体。2004年成立修文县农业科技专家院，省科技厅副厅长、高级农艺师高贵龙等16位专家成为首批专家院成员。贵州华德斯生物制药有限公司建立科研所，与贵阳医学院和四川大学联合研发生物菌系列产品。2009年，县科技局与贵州大学合作申报《修文县“六广河”牌猕猴桃产业化关键技术开发与应用》项目，得到贵州省科技厅农业科技重点攻关项目立项资金25万元扶持。2010年，贵阳华芝宝生物科技有限公司牵头建立以医药园区药企为战略联盟的技术创新平台，与省内外高校及科研院所建立产学研合作基地研发新药系列产品。一系列的科技合作，加大了新产品开发力度，为县域经济发展提供了强有力的科技支撑。

二、科技咨询示范

（一）科技咨询

从2000年起，县内每年开展科普宣传周和科技活动周科普活动，组织科技专家走上街头、走进田间，就种植和养殖技术、动物植物防病防疫等技术问题解答咨询。2010年5月全国第十届科技活动周期间，县科技、农林、卫生和环保行业专家和省市专家100多人，在县城现场开展技术咨询服务，发放科普资料万余份。专业技术人员还深入到扎佐、大石、六屯和洒坪等乡（镇）集市、农户家中和田间地头，接受农村群众的技术咨询。2009年，针对扎佐镇金鸡村蔬菜种植面积逐年增加，但产量和质量都上不去的问题，县科协和科技局专门组织蔬菜专家进村为群众讲解蔬菜种植技术；针对谷堡乡折溪村金秋梨种植户多，种植面积大的特点，专门邀请专家为种植户编写《梨树病虫害防治技术》，果农按专家编写的技术规范操作，果树病虫害得以防治。

2003年，省农科院专家莅县开展科技咨询活动

（二）科技示范

创办科技示范园　2001年，创办农业科技示范园区。园区落地在龙场、扎佐和久长3镇境内，覆盖

28个行政村9352户3.4万人，入园耕地面积3.75万亩。核心区地处龙场镇小营、马官、平地、大地、幸福、军民、新水和白莲8个行政村。至2010年，园区实施的项目有龙场镇放马坪村“生态园林基地”，大地村“无公害生产基地”，马口、中哨、茶田、王官和建新村“延晚番茄基地”，马官村盘龙山“猕猴桃生产基地”，平地村“养牛基地”，白莲村“山鸡养殖场”和小营村“科技园区渠系配套”及“科技园区节水灌溉”示范基地，还有龙场镇和扎佐镇科技园区生态林建设工程，龙场镇“科技园区农机具配套”和“优质苗木苗圃基地”。

2001年农业科技示范园规划咨询会

培养科技示范户 1988年开始培养农村科技示范户，至1999年，全县217个行政村平均每村有科技示范户2户。谷堡乡科技示范户陈明忠带头示范种植杂交水稻和杂交玉米，个人组织科技培训100多人次，使全村100%栽种杂稻并实现宽窄行插秧，80%栽种杂交玉米，荣获县科技兴农人才奖。

2002年，县政府制定《关于创建科技示范乡（镇）、示范村、示范户的实施意见》，实施“请一个专家，找一个龙头，争一个项目，建一个基地，富一方农民”工程。至2010年，龙场镇落实《实施意见》到位，成效显著，率先跻身科技示范乡（镇），全县还建成22个示范村，20个示范点，220户示范户。

创建科普示范基地 从2005年起创建科普示范基地，至2010年，全县创建基地4个：一是龙场镇高科技节水灌溉示范园科普基地，面积200亩，使用固定中喷、固定微喷、半固定微喷、半固定中喷、露地滴灌、大棚滴灌、软管拖灌、多功能灌溉、移动喷灌和果树滴灌，是一个集科研、节水教育宣传、作物品比试验研究、新品种引进试验和节水技术推广为一体的综合性科普示范基地，由水利部、教育部和全国节水教育办公室联合命名为“全国节水教育基地”。二是六屯乡贵阳佳惠药业基地，由贵阳佳惠药业在六屯乡新埔村建成，以种植板蓝根、瓜蒌、玄参等中药材为主，面积逾千亩，辐射带动周边都堡村、星中村和长田村发展中药材种植2000余亩。三是洒坪乡小坝村无公害蔬菜科普基地，主要种植大葱和大蒜，面积380亩，年产量逾25万公斤，年收入60余万元。四是六广镇早熟蔬菜科普基地，面积300亩，主要种植早玉米、早茄子、早辣椒、早毛豆和早番茄蔬菜。

三、科技培训

农业技术培训 1982年，县农业局科技人员在县、区、乡“三干会”上对与会干部进行农业技术培训。随后，通过召开农业新技术推广应用会议，多层次、多门类、多形式培训农民，每年有3万多人次接受适用技术培训，培养致富骨干达万人。1996年，请省农科院、农学院专家给农业技术干部和蔬菜种植大户上课，传授早熟蔬菜种植新技术。全年参加科技培训1.47万人次。继后，每年开展“三下乡”活动组织科技下乡，仅1997年就举办农技培训556场次，受训群众5.38万人。从2000年起，每年在村选拔1名30岁以下具有初中以上文化程度的青年参加农业知识培训。至2010年，共培训300人。六桶乡青年李根书通过培训掌握养鸡技术致富后，又把技术传授给村里群众，帮助大家共同致富，获团中央和农业部颁发的“全国农村青年创业致富带头人”荣誉证。龙场镇城南村村民苏贵荣参加培训后，利用学到的技术办起“盛鑫养殖场”，成为一名青年企业家。

非农技能培训 2002年起，开办非农技能培训班，指导农民进城就业。至2010年共培训3.1万人次。

先后向贵阳老干妈春梅酿造有限公司等企业输出务工人员6700人，实现技术培训与岗位就业的有机结合。2007年起，结合县内乡村旅游的发展，组织以“农家乐”乡村旅游相关知识为特色的培训科目，每年在各乡（镇）有乡村旅游条件的村就地举办非农技能培训，至2010年，先后在扎佐镇大河村、久长镇上寨村、六屯乡独山村、谷堡乡折溪村等地举办20场次，有600人接受培训。谷堡乡折溪村80%的村民家办有“农家乐”，通过培训后，掌握了服务过程中的基本礼仪，服务工作走上规范化轨道，每年吸引游客达3万余人。

2006年8月，县科技局组织县内专家到六屯乡小木村开展农业科技培训

科技技能培训 2008年起，实施以转移就业为核心，扶持和帮助贫困人口增加就业发展机会和提高劳动收入的“雨露计划”，县科技、农业、人事劳动、职业培训中心等部门通力合作，开办初级电（焊）工技术、种养殖技术、计算机知识、农业产业化方向等多项培训活动。2010年，实施科技扶贫工程，先后在龙场镇小山村和中哨坝村，扎佐镇大山村和双月村，小箐乡尖山村，洒坪乡中明村，六广镇合兴村，六桶乡来鹤村、大石乡高山村，谷堡乡平滩村举办科技技能培训班10期，培训农民1072人。举办外出务工人员法律知识培训2期，培训农民300人。至2010年，通过实施“雨露计划”和科技扶贫工程，共培训4000人。参加培训的农民学到一技之长后，纷纷从传统农业向现代农业、农业产业服务和向二、三产业转移，有的通过劳务输出到县外就业。

四、返乡农民工创业就业服务

从2008年起，县科技局设置返乡农民工创业就业服务窗口，采集农民工培训和择业需求，通过举办技能培训班和向企业推荐方式解决返乡农民工创业就业问题。2009年举办农民工返乡实用技术培训6期，培训返乡农民工165人，开展咨询宣传活动4次，接受农民工200人次咨询。对带项目、带技术返乡创业的农民工，为其开通绿色通道，并提供科技项目资金扶持。龙场镇马口村返乡农民工宋萍实施《优质二杂母猪标准化养殖示范》项目，获得3.75万元的创业资金。2010年，罗家铭等10户返乡农民工的种植养殖项目被列为返乡农民工创业示范项目，分别获得一次性资助资金3000元。

第四节　科技成果

1978年，建起科研成果登记、评审、推荐、上报和奖励制度。1981年9月，成立科研成果评审委员会，出台《修文县科学技术奖励试行办法》，科研成果登记、评审、推荐、上报和奖励制度趋于完善。1978—2010年，共获得国家级奖1项、省级奖23项，市级奖31项，县评定科技成果奖59项。

1978—2010年获地（市）以上科技成果奖一览表

表4—02—01

序号	成果名称	时间	级别	获奖人
1	岩鹰山砌石拱坝设计施工	1978年	国家级	李家平
2	普通立窑试烧矾土水泥	1978年	省级	县水泥厂
3	天生桥高扬程倒虹管设计施工	1978年	省级	陈治国
4	四病调查	1978年	省级	县医院
5	《修文地理》	1978年	省级	叶锡鳌
6	《学算术用算术》	1978年	省级	胡启贤
7	修文县畜牧区划	1978年	地（市）级	县畜牧局
8	中医药对精神病临床分型治疗初探	1981年	地（市）级	聂承先
9	水泥自动配料机和风送入库机	1981年	地（市）级	县水泥厂
10	椭圆形素磷拱顶制件隧洞衬砌	1981年	地（市）级	唐　彦
11	砷剂高温雾化疗法	1981年	地（市）级	张士学
12	修文县林业区划	1981年	地（市）级	县林业局
13	修文县主要农作物品种资源调查	1982年	省级	县科委、县种子公司
14	修文县主要农作物品种资源调查	1982年	地（市）级	县科委、县种子公司
15	水稻玉米病虫测报工作	1982年	地（市）级	县植保站
16	水浸盐析法取油	1983年	地（市）级	小箐粮管所
17	猪的人工授精改良工作	1983年	—	—
18	无害无臭厕所设计	1984年	省级	霍明书
19	修文县20年雹灾初步分析	1984年	地（市）级	杨朝栋、卢振常
20	水稻工厂化带土育秧	1985年	—	—
21	硅酸盐砖新矿源的发现与利用	1985年	地（市）级	县经委、102地质队
22	修文县能源综合区划	1987年	省级	县农机站
23	修文县万亩烤烟良种“NC82”推广	1988年	地（市）级	毛高富、王志远等5人
24	修文县烤烟优质适产攻关	1988年	地（市）级	毛高富、王志远等5人
25	修文县蜜源花粉酒系列产品	1988年	地（市）级	蒋天华　王忠俊
26	松针粉的开发利用	1989年	地（市）级	杨大文等3人
27	修文县采用综合配套技术高山杂稻获丰	1992年	省	谭玺等6人
28	农业旱地多熟丰产综合开发研究	1994年	地（市）级	谭玺等6人
29	轿车雨刮器的研制	1995年	地（市）级	万江机械厂
30	旱地分带轮作多熟制	1995年	地（市）级	县科委
31	修文、开阳两县稻田养鱼技术	1997年	省级	林德荣

续表

序号	成果名称	时间	级别	获奖人
32	高强度石油压裂支撑剂	2001年	地（市）级	贵州林海新材料制造有限公司
33	“FA-旱地龙”试验示范	2001年	省级	许定莉
34	加味承气汤治疗急性胰腺炎43例体会	2001年	中医疗科技	肖庆贵
35	甘露醇慢滴治疗脑梗死的疗效观察及护理	2001年	中医医学	张　宜
36	旱地节水灌溉技术成果推广	2002年	省级	县水利局
37	多囊卵巢综合征的超声诊断	2002年	中华医学	余本英
38	优质牧草工程	2003年	地（市）级	熊绍林
39	小鹅瘟病分离研究	2003年	地（市）级	县农业局
40	优质“三元”杂交瘦肉型猪及配套饲养技术推广	2004年	省级	游忠琼
41	国家二类新药多非利特合成工艺的技术创新	2005年	地（市）级	天方药业
42	贵州苗家紫金莲野生变种研究	2005年	地（市）级	安泰药业
43	修文县实施夏季反季节蔬菜示范及推产	2005年	地（市）级	县农业局
44	柔壹牌仙灵骨葆胶囊	2007年	省级	贵州同济堂药业
45	妇科再造胶囊	2007年	省级	贵阳德昌祥药业
46	杜仲降压片	2007年	省级	贵阳德昌祥药业
47		2007年	省级	贵州同济堂药业
48	高密度耐磨瓷球加工工艺及生产项目	2008年	地（市）级	修文天成公司
19	仙灵骨葆胶囊开发项目	2008年	地（市）级	贵州同济堂制药有限公司
50	新药妇科再造丸的深度研发	2008年	地（市）级	贵阳德昌祥药业
51	仙灵骨葆胶囊技术成果转化	2010年	地（市）级	贵州同济堂制药有限公司

第五节　知识产权

一、知识产权保护

2001年2月，县成立专利管理工作小组，同时建立县知识产权保护服务中心，启动专利管理和知识产权保护。7月，县委组织部、县科技局和县人事劳动局联合举办修文县领导干部知识产权保护培训会，县直有关部门领导及大中型企业分管科技负责人62人参加，接受《知识产权保护制度的基础知识》《中华人民共和国专利法》和《专利权属案例分析》等内容的培训。继后，由县知识产权保护服务中心引导，县内企业贵州林海新材料制造有限公司、贵州同剂堂药业股份有限公司、贵州福鹏实业有限公司、贵州联宇食品有限公司和贵州绿太阳制药有限公司先后建立起以专利为主的知识产权管理和保护制度。2004年9

月12日，县科学技术局联合贵阳市知识产权局对县城合力超市、好德隆超市、万家隆超市开展专利商品检查。抽检14个专利产品，经检索全部符合专利产品要求，未发现侵权行为。

2006年8月，“贵阳市创建全国知识产权示范城市”业务知识培训班在开班，县科技局派员参加培训。

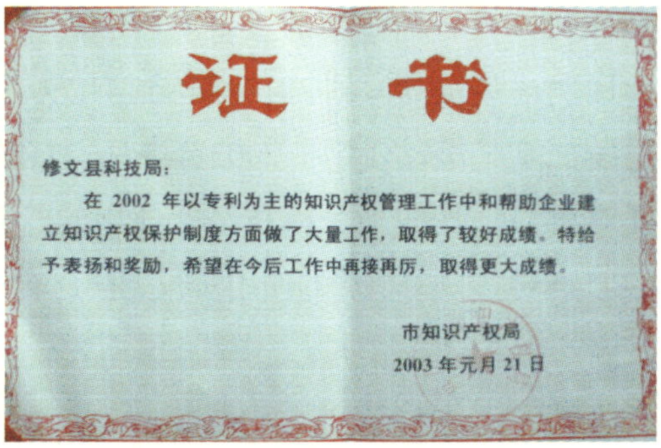
证书

修文县科技局：

在2002年以专利为主的知识产权管理工作中和帮助企业建立知识产权保护制度方面做了大量工作，取得了较好成绩。特给予表扬和奖励，希望在今后工作中再接再厉，取得更大成绩。

市知识产权局

2003年元月21日

2002年县科技局荣获贵阳市知识产权局表彰

2008年5月，县科技、工商、新闻出版、公安部门联合开展“雷雨”知识产权专项执法行动，对县城的商场、超市、药店经营的食品、电器、学习用品、药品进行抽样检查，共抽查924件，发现94件涉嫌假冒、冒充专利或专利号标注不规范的商品，按相关法律法规给予查处。6月24日，县知识产权局挂牌成立，与县科技局合署办公，两块牌子，一套班子。至此，县的专利工作体系进一步完善。

2010年机构改革，县知识产权局归属发展改革经贸局，其行政管理职责亦相应改由发改局负责。同时，明确贵州鑫益能有限公司和贵州华芝宝药业有限公司为“知识产权试点企业”，扎佐中学为市级知识产权学校。在“科技活动周”和“4·26”世界知识产权宣传日期间，采取摆摊设点和散发资料方式，开展《新专利法》和《新专利法实施细则》宣传，邀请国家知识产权局专家莅县举办知识产权专题培训讲座，并组织科技、工商、文化、公安部门参与专利执法检查。

二、专利申报

1988年，县内始有专利申报，驻县的304医院樊如彪申请旅客列车专用活动皮壳集除器专利。2004年1月，开始实施专利申请资助及专利项目扶持，先后对温新明、贺丛友和徐湘的专利申请给以资助。2005年设立专利发展基金，鼓励发明创造，使发明创造者积极申报专利，对贵州安泰药业有限公司申报的《止痛胶囊及其制备工艺》、《心脑宁胶囊及其制备工艺》、《治疗妇科炎症药及其制备工艺》和《治疗烧烫伤的气雾剂及其制备工艺》分别给予专利补助800元。

2006年，县政府制定《修文县知识产权专项资金使用管理办法》，对个人申请发明、实用新型、外观设计专利的申请费和发明、实用新型专利的授权费用给予资助。资助额度为发明、实用新型专利每件资助申请费分别为800元、500元，授权费用为800元、500元；外观设计专利每件资助申请费300元。

至2010年，有126项专利申请获授权。

第六节　科技经费

一、科技三项费

1978年，县财政投入的科技三项费（支持科技进步与创新设立的新产品试制费、中间试验费和主要科学研究补助费）为无偿使用，1983年，改为有偿、部分有偿和无偿相结合使用，但投入量较少，多用于开展科技培训活动的支出。“九五”“十五”计划期间，科技三项费投入增长较快，在财政预算支出中的比例逐年提高。到2010年达到412万元，累计1291万元。其间，2000年，县政府专门拨款20万元作科技发展基金滚动使用。2003年5月，县政府出台《修文县科技三项费使用管理办法（暂行）》，进一步加强对科技项目实施、科技经费使用的管理，按照“突出重点、注重实效、科学评估（评审）、择优支持”的原则对科技三项费的使用实行无偿、有偿和贷款贴息相结合的方式，将有偿使用回收的资金，用于补充科技发展基金。

1978—2010年县科技三项费投入情况统计表

表4—02—02　　　　单位：万元

年　度	科技三项费	年　度	科技三项费
1978	1.55	1995	0.5
1979	1.5	1996	0
1980	1.5	1997	0
1981	1.17	1998	1.0
1982	2.92	1999	25.0
1983	2.03	2000	34
1984	2.56	2001	64
1985	4.2	2002	99.2
1986	7.2	2003	125
1987	2.25	2004	133
1988	2.0	2005	140
1989	2.0	2006	155
1990	2.0	2007	220
1991	3.9	2008	247
1992	2.0	2009	265
1993	1.6	2010	412
1994	1.2		
总　　计			1964.28

二、企业科技经费

1978—1998年，县内企业在生产实践中也有专门的科技经费投入，但数量少，一般只用于科技培训。1999年起，以供电、建材、冶炼等为主的骨干企业和药业、工贸等规模以上企业，在技术改造、新产品研发上开始投入大量科技经费，为企业发展提供强有力的保证。

1999—2010年县内骨干企业和规模以上企业科技经费投入统计表

表4—02—03　　　　单位：万元

年　度	投　入	年　度	投　入
1999	113.03	2005	2573.3
2000	410.422	2006	7648.9
2001	1466.6	2007	7221
2002	739.49	2008	12410
2003	1236.58	2009	10684
2004	1279.6	2010	9328.2

三、省市科技资助费

1978—2010年，通过申报实施各类科技计划项目，获得地（市）以上各类科技资助经费1.15亿元，其中无偿资金6400万元。贵州安泰药业《贵州苗药紫金莲规范种植研究》、县科技局《扎佐镇大河村乡村旅游引导示范》、《“蜈蚣桥”豆腐标准化生产体系建设及产业链延伸》、贵州华德斯生物制药有限公司《替考拉宁生物菌工艺研究》、贵州同济堂药业《淫羊藿灾后重建种植技术》、贵州吉隆单宁化工公司《新增生产工艺用水处理系统》、修文天成公司《节能环保型推扳窑余窑灾后重建项目》、贵阳福鹏实业有限公司《麦芽糊精研究》、贵州林海新材料制造有限公司《石油压裂支撑剂中试》、贵州绿太阳制药有限公司《肤痔清规模生产》、贵州省兰地实业有限公司《20万蛋鸡规模养殖技术综合开发》和《果树良种示范基地》项目均是在市、省以至国家科技经费支持下获得成功的科技项目。2010年，县内有19个项目获得国家、省、市立项，共获得上级资金411万元的无偿支持。

第三章　文化艺术

1980年，中共中央作出加强精神文明建设决策后，县内文化文艺活动围绕精神文明建设和建设文化强县的目标，立足县情，传承优势，创新发展。

修文是王阳明成道讲学之地，县委、县政府抓住这个人无我有的特色，着力打造“阳明文化”品牌。从1999年起至2010年，先后举办过4届阳明文化节，使“王学圣地”的美称享誉国内外。县内的花灯、龙灯历史悠久，为群众喜闻乐见，逢年过节，花灯会、龙灯会的会员们敲锣打鼓燃放鞭炮在城乡表演，营造欢乐祥和的节庆氛围。1994年和1996年，举办两届民族民间文艺调演，推动传统文化文艺的传承与发展。1995年，芦笙歌舞队编排苗族芦笙舞《庆丰收》，代表贵州省参加北京市举办的第九届“龙潭杯”全国优秀民间花会大赛获二等奖。1996年，久长镇下堡村芦笙歌舞队与北京风雷京剧团由文化部批准联合组成“中国艺术团”走出国门东赴日本访问演出长达35天，在异国展现修文传统民间文化的风采。

在弘扬传统特色文化的同时，以发展文化产业为主线，建立县、乡（镇）、村三级文化网络和各类专业文化文艺协会，加快发展文学、书法、美术、音乐、戏剧、舞蹈等各类专业文化事业，全县涌现出在省、市有一定知名度的文学、艺术工作者及其作品，以及一批有建树的书画名人，并多次在省、市和全国大赛中获奖。

第一节　文化体制改革

一、文化市场

1978年，县内文化市场为国营或集体企事业单位垄断，电影放映由县电影管理站独家经营，图书销售由县新华书店独揽，音像制品销售仅有五金公司一家，文化经营活动单一，文化市场没有生机，群众文化生活枯燥。1979年，县委在全县三级干部会议上提出“解放思想，走出禁区”号召后，全县文化单位开展“解放思想大讨论”，在全国经济体制改革的大环境下逐渐放开文化市场，允许个体业主参与市场竞争。

个体放映　1980年，经县电影管理站同意，在城关、扎佐、久长、德政等地，由联户或个人办起8个个体电影队。电影队实行自负盈亏，打破区域界限，自辟放映点，影片由电影管理站提供。个体电影队

以走村串寨放映的方式活跃在农村，使农民群众特别是边远山区群众的文化生活得以丰富。1983年，在扎佐街上有外地人开办个体录像放映室。到1984年，全县办理营业执照从事录像放映个体经营的有20家。继后，因电视、网络普及，看电影、录像观众锐减，个体放映无利可图，逐渐退出文化市场。

私营书店 1980年，县内市场有小贩设摊销售图书，但多属无照经营。1982年，团县委在县城租门面开办“三味书屋”代销图书，属集体性质。1987年，“三味书屋”转让给退职教师夏之行更名“知行书屋”改为个体经营。继后，县内相继有5家私营书店经营图书销售。私营书店销售方式灵活，视读者需求进货，销售中可与购书者讨价还价，且一人兼几职减少劳务成本，在市场竞争中取得一席之地，至2010年，5家私营书店仍活跃在文化市场上，年图书销售额近50万元。

台球活动室 1980年，县文化、工商部门批准个体户经营台球娱乐业，至1988年，全县办理台球活动室营业执照的个体户达100多家。继后，光顾者不多，活动室逐渐减少，至2010年尚存4家。

音像制品销售出租 1983年，始有销售出租音像制品的个体商户，至2010年，执照经营的有两户。

歌舞厅 1984年，批准14家个体业主经营歌舞厅，至2010年，持有营业执照的歌舞厅有10家。

电子游戏室 1988年，县城两家游戏室获得经营许可开业，多为少年儿童喜好，随后发展加快，最多的2000年全县办证经营的游戏室逾20家，至2010年尚存6家。

个体印刷厂 1992年，县印刷厂解体转为个体民营经济，职工筹资办个体印刷厂，至2010年，印刷行业持证经营的有3家。

打字复印店 1995年，一温州人在县城办证经营打字复印，至2010年，全县个体打字复印店发展为9家。

网吧 2001年，8家个体业主获批经营网吧，至2010年，全县持有营业执照的网吧有13家。

二、事业改企业

1978年，全县电影放映由县电影管理站经营，站属县的事业单位，实行“条块管理”，行政上隶属县文化局，人员进出和干部任免由局行使，影片发行放映则由安顺地区电影发行放映公司负责。1981年，电影管理站改为电影发行放映公司，由原来的县属事业单位改制为企业，实行经理负责制，自负盈亏。1983年，县设广播电视局管理电视业务，后机构改革，广播电视局并入县文体广电局，由文体广电局下设的局属事业单位专司电视网络管理工作。1988年，根据国家经济委员会和国家经济体制改革委员会经企〔1987〕519号文件精神，将原为地方事业单位的县新华书店改制为由省新华书店管理的企业，县政府不再管理新华书店的人事和经营，由上级新华书店行文任命书店经理，实现企业自主。2008年，电视网络实行分制管理，将县城电视网络管理从县文体广电局析出，交由贵州省广播电视信息网络股份有限公司直接管理，省公司在修文设立分公司负责具体业务，电视网络管理人员由原来的事业性质身份改制为企业性质身份，公司实行自收自支。

三、承包经营

1980年，在全国经济体制改革的大环境下，县内有经营性质的文化单位开始探索经营体制改革。

县印刷厂 1980年，县印刷厂将原执行的计时工资制改为计件工资制，取消“大锅饭”，鼓励职工主动联系印件，增扩业务范围，使生产收入由此前的不足10万元提高到12.27万元。继而又于1984年推行经济承包责任制，由厂长以签订合同的方式将经营和管理的权利、责任、利润层层承包给车间、班组或职工个人。承包者懂技术，会管理，生产有起色，当年产值达16.38万元。

电影发行放映公司 1981年县电影管理站改为电影发行放映公司后，采用“片租承包，超租留成”的方式提高职工积极性，当年放映电影661场次，企业收入比上一年增加6541元。此后，公司又以预交全年片租的方式与下属放映单位签订承包经营合同，1982年和1983年放映场次和发行收入指标均列安顺地区榜首。

县新华书店 1985年，县新华书店在扎佐分店试行承包经营，扎佐分店承包后，图书销售发行额由1985年以前的8万元增加到10万元。1988年，县店实行承包经营，向作为财产所有权代表的发包单位安顺新华书店承包，并由县司法局公证处对承包合同作法律公证。承包经营后，书店改善服务态度，提高服务质量，仅用两个月时间就完成全年承包任务的53.6%，实现利润3.1万元。

四、聘用制

2004年，根据贵州省人民政府《关于事业单位人事制度改革的实施意见》和省政府办公厅《关于在事业单位试行人员聘用制度的通知》精神，县文体广播电视局试行人事制度改革，推行人员聘用制度。10月，文体广电局出台《事业单位人事制度改革工作实施方案》，详细制定包括改革在内的原则和目的、范围和对象、步骤和程序、组织机构和纪律要求及设置岗位、竞争上岗、签订聘用合同等内容。参与改革的有局属广播电视中心、文化馆、图书馆、文物管理所、体育事业中心、乡（镇）文化服务中心共15家事业单位。文体广电局成立以局长为组长,副局长、纪检组长为副组长，各事业单位负责人为成员的人事制度改革工作领导小组，下设办公室负责开展工作。改革分3步进行，先是提高认识。组织召开全局干部职工和乡（镇）文化服务中心负责人参加的人事制度改革工作培训学习会，继而按各单位的性质、任务和事业发展需要设置岗位,明确每个岗位的职责、权利、任职条件等，接着按照“公开、公平、公正”的原则实施竞聘。在竞聘上岗中,先由本单位应聘人员根据各自特点选择适合岗位提出应聘申请，然后组织考察，签订合同。参加人事制度改革的15家事业单位共有职工74人，除担任领导职务不参加签订合同的21人外，其余53人参与竞聘。竞聘结果，有40人签订聘用合同，5人缓聘，8人落聘。

第二节　传统文化

一、阳明文化

（一）研究与宣传

研究组织 1995年6月16日，修文县王学研究会（阳明学研究会）在阳明洞召开成立大会，通过组织章程，选举产生第一届理事会。王学研究会为群众性民间学术团体，以研究王阳明在修文期间的活动及影响为重点，兼及其哲学思想 、教育思想、书法诗文等。研究会组织学术研讨活动，与国内外阳明学研究机构及学者交流研究成果。研究会办有《良知》会刊。2010年研究会尚存。

活动与成果 1987年，王阳明研究活动拉开帷幕，先是由贵州师大、贵州大学等院校尝试举办王学

研讨会，县内王学研究爱好者或应邀或受委派参加。1995年成立县王学研究会后，研究活动逐步在县内展开。随着研究活动的开展，县人朱五义、陈新国、杨德俊、李祖炎、夏之奎、雷华熙等也相继在报刊发表研究文章。至2010年，县内组织的王阳明研究活动已涉及世界15个国家和国内12个省以及中国香港、台湾地区。县人的研究成果也从最初的在报刊发表小文章到著书立说。

县人组织或参加王学研讨会的重大研究活动一览表

表4—03—01

时　间	活动名称或内容	主要活动地点	备　注
1987.12	王阳明学术研讨会	贵州师大	派员参加
1989.4	王阳明国际学术讨论会	浙江余姚	派员参与
1993.8	祭奠阳明先生	阳明洞	派员协助组织并参与
1994.8	贵阳阳明祠修复暨王阳明像揭幕仪式和王阳明在贵阳学术座谈会	贵阳阳明祠	派员参加
1994.9	中、日、韩学者祭奠阳明先生和阳明心学暨良知工程论证会	阳明洞	派员协助组织并参加
1995.5	王阳明学术座谈会	贵州师大	派员参加
1995.11	王阳明学术研讨会	贵州大学	派员参加
1996.7	中国贵州王阳明国际学术讨论会	贵州大学	派员参加
1997.11	王阳明铜像揭幕仪式	阳明洞	县阳明学会组织
1999.10	第一届阳明文化节　王阳明纪念馆开馆仪式　王阳明学术讨论会	阳明洞	县阳明学会组织学术讨论会在贵阳举行
2002.10	第二届阳明文化节　国际学术研讨会	阳明洞	县阳明学会组织
2004.3	王学圣地·世外桃源论坛	阳明洞	县阳明学会组织
2005.10	第三届阳明文化节　良知与和谐社会高端论坛　国际学术研讨会	阳明洞、文化馆	县阳明学会组织
2009.5	第四届阳明文化节　纪念王阳明“知行合一”500周年高端论坛、国际学术研讨会	阳明洞、文化馆	县阳明学会组织
2009.5	龙永图易中天修文“论道”	阳明洞	县阳明学会协助贵州电视台组织

县内研究王学主要成果一览表

表4—03—02

时　间	名　称	类　别	编著者	备　注
1996.3	《良知》第一期	论　文	县王学研究会　编	—
1996.7	驰名中外的王学圣地—修文阳明洞	宣传册	县文管所　编	—
1997.10	王阳明在黔诗文注释	注　释	朱五义　著	内资出版
1999.8	《修文县志·王阳明在龙场》	方　志	县志编辑部　编纂	公开出版
1999.10	阳明先生	连环画	朱五义撰文、丁国才绘图	内资出版
1999.10	阳明先生的故事	文　学	陈新国　著	内资出版
2000.8	阳明洞诗文注释	注　释	朱五义　著	内资出版
2002.10	阳明胜境	文　集	县政协　编	公开出版

续表

时 间	名 称	类 别	编著人	备 注
2002.10	王阳明居夷诗今译与赏析	译 注	陈新国 著	内资出版
2002.10	千古龙岗漫有名	文 集	杨德俊 主编	内资出版
2002.10	王阳明在龙场	资 料	夏之奎 主编	内资出版
2005.11	王学圣地	图文集	魏明禄 主编	公开出版
2009.5	王学之旅	论文集	白陈新 主编	公开出版
2010.10	阳明先生法书集	书 法	县委宣传部 贵阳市文联 编	公开出版

主要宣传活动 1994年起，县委、县政府充分利用各级传媒、对外交流和自办活动加大对阳明文化的宣传力度。

1.媒体宣传 1996—2010年，县委、县政府借助各级媒体优势扩大阳明文化宣传。其间，先后协助中央电视台“中华文明之光”、“天涯共此时”和“走遍中国”栏目组拍摄《王阳明与明代心学》《中国古代思想家——王阳明》《王阳明与贵阳》3个专题片有关修文部分场景。与贵州电视台、贵阳电视台合作，拍摄制作《龙场古道寻阳明》《龙冈山上一轮月》《王学圣地》《阳明洞怀古》等专题片和《一个城市的文化记忆》节目。与《贵州日报》《贵阳日报》合作，推出阳明文化专版等。

1996年，中央电视台“中华文明之光”摄制组莅县拍摄《王阳明与明代心学》电视片部分场景，“天涯共此时”剧组莅县拍摄《中国古代思想家—王阳明》专题片，贵阳市旅游局与贵州电视台合作制作《贵阳风光》专题片摄制组到县拍摄阳明洞等名胜风光，县委、县政府派出县委宣传部、县文体广电局工作人员为剧组提供资料协助在阳明洞等阳明遗迹找景。1997年，《人民中国》记者莅县拍摄阳明洞等名胜风光图片，县委宣传部部长卢永康充任向导陪同记者跋山涉水采访拍照，后《人民中国》(日文版)在1998年第一期以5页篇幅刊登介绍修文阳明文化的彩色图片共12幅。1999年，县举办阳明文化节，组委会与贵州电视台合作莅县制作《龙场古道寻阳明》专题片播出。2002年举办第二届阳明文化节，为扩大宣传，县委、县政府邀请贵阳电视台拍摄专题片《龙岗山上一轮月》播出。2003年，贵阳市委宣传部与中央电视台合作制作的外宣电视系列片《走遍中国—贵阳·阳明文化》专辑，在修文拍摄期间，县政府予以协助。贵阳电视台与县政府合作制作大型航拍电视片《王学圣地》，县委、县政府派出宣传部部长严贵钧、副部长贾长远和县文联主席陈新国配合开展摄制工作，《王学圣地》在贵阳电视台播出后观众反响强烈，后贵阳电视台连续制作两期专访节目约请观众谈观后感。继后，县政府

县文联主席陈新国向记者介绍阳明文化遗迹

又派出县旅游局和县文联工作人员协助贵州电视台拍摄重点介绍“阳明宴”的“修文美食之旅”专题片。2005年举办第三届阳明文化节，县委、县政府与《贵州日报》《贵阳日报》等多家媒体合作，推出宣传阳明文化的专版和专题文章。2009年，与贵州电视台《论道》栏目合作，在《论道》开播两周年之际，以阳明洞为背景，制作《一个城市的文化记忆》节目，博鳌亚洲论坛秘书长龙永图与著名文化学者、厦门大学教授易中天就文化与经济社会发展的联系进行高端对话。

2.借助外力宣传 1994年9月，中、日、韩三国民间组织的“阳明心学暨良知工程论证会”在贵阳召开，县政府邀请与会代表莅县参观阳明遗迹。这是修文首次借助外力宣传阳明文化。百余名中外专家学者通过实地参观，更加深了对王阳明“良知”思想的了解，表示要在哲学领域和其他领域加强对王阳明思想的研究和宣传。1997年6月，日本岐阜县援助未就学儿童访问团莅县访问，县政府接待时特意组织访问团参观阳明洞。此后，有外地来县交流工作、参观访问的团体，县内接待单位均在允许的情况下组织到阳明洞等阳明遗迹参观，使阳明文化的宣传渠道得以拓宽。

3.拓展宣传方式 1994—2010年，修文自办宣传阳明文化活动频繁，除举办阳明文化节外，还以书画影展、诗歌朗诵、征文、祭奠王阳明等多种方式开展活动。1996年11月在阳明洞王文成公祠举行王阳明铜像揭幕仪式，阳明学研究大师、日本九州大学名誉教授冈田武彦和日本企业家矢崎又次郎、矢崎胜彦等专程从日本莅临参加，县政府邀请省市媒体报道扩大宣传。1999—2009年举办4届阳明文化节期间，县政府均组织县内艺术家以阳明文化为主题开展创作，先后举办《良知千古光》《龙场墨韵》等美术、书法、摄影展。2003年，县内艺术家在县文联举办的元宵晚会上朗诵王阳明龙场诗歌、现场书写王阳明诗作和写意绘画。《修文报》（《当代修文》）设有《了解王阳明了解阳明文化》专栏，连续宣传阳明文化。2009年，县委宣传部、贵阳人民广播电台、县文联、县文体广电局和修文移动公司联合举办的诗词（美文）朗诵会上，王阳明诗文成为参与朗诵者的首选。至2010年，县委宣传部、县文联、县教育局、县文体广电局、团县委、修文报社等部门或单独或联合举办以宣传普及阳明文化为主要内容的诗歌朗诵、征文和文艺演出活动40余次。

2005年，专家学者在王文成公祠祭奠王阳明

（二）阳明文化设施

王明阳纪念馆 1998年9月兴建，次年10月竣工的王阳明纪念馆，当时命名为“阳明园”。纪念馆位于阳明洞大门前东侧，坐东向西。纪念馆前为4000平方米的草坪广场，阳明洞与纪念馆之间塑有高5米的王阳明“龙冈论道”暨龙冈书院学子陈宗鲁、汤伯元、叶子苍的群雕铜像。朝门为古阙形式，4柱3门，门柱顶部分别镶有青龙、白虎、朱雀、玄武石雕。大门至纪念馆之间为青石板铺就院坝，每块石条之间留有10厘米间距植草。

纪念馆为砖混结构四合院形式仿古建筑，屋面是青灰色琉璃瓦。飨堂大门为板门，饰以木乳钉，其余为格扇门，万字花格棂木窗。纪念馆通面宽11间，进深7间，前面正中3间为飨堂，屋顶为歇山式。整个建筑850平方米，前后左右相连通，便于参观。

飨堂正中黑色大理石台上，塑有3米高的王阳明站式青铜像，左侧为贵宾接待室，备有放映设备，播放有关王阳明资料片供游人观看。右侧进门为陈列室，门侧有电脑触摸屏，储存包括王阳明生平简介、谪黔行迹、石刻碑记等资料。

陈列展厅布展面积2400平方米，分为王阳明生平、王阳明在贵州、王学长流远播3个部分。王阳明生平主要介绍其哲学思想、军事思想和书法艺术。陈列图片26张，图表5张，文字介绍20幅，王阳明书法墨迹复印件拓片7幅，实物5件。王阳明在贵州部分主要介绍谪黔纪事，分为忤奸遭贬、龙场悟道、知行合一、山民情谊、授业育才、黔中弟子、黔中遗迹、师生道义8个小节。陈列有图片44幅，文字介绍26幅，王阳明书法墨迹复印件《何陋轩记》《象祠记》《镇远旅邸书札》及其他碑刻拓片6幅，模型1组。王学的长流远播分为5节，介绍王阳明的“心学”思想，王学分支学派，后世影响，王学研究和成果展。陈列有明、清、民国及当代出版的《王阳明全集》，中国大陆及香港特区、台湾地区，日本、欧美等国出版的阳明学研究专著100多册，图片24张，文字介绍8幅，图表3幅，贵州清代所雕刻的《阳明先生集要三编》木刻板数块。2009年第四届阳明文化节举办前，对展厅陈列有所改动，增加了实物陈列，但陈列路径基本未变。

西园　1995年，在阳明先生谪居龙场时种菜的西园征地6亩，2005年筹资50万元建成西园。园内建有200平方米的四合院1座，从扎佐街上原四川会馆易地迁至园内修复保护的清代建筑戏楼1座。

阳明碑苑　1995年，县文物管理所和阳明学研究会集资在阳明洞侧面修建王阳明龙场诗文碑苑，刻诗碑30余块。2005年重修阳明碑苑，占地12.5亩，建筑面积1025平方米，碑廊长90米，系仿古建筑，刻王阳明所著诗文和书法手迹35篇（首）。2005年9月14日，在西园举行阳明碑苑落成仪式，知名王学专家、学者杜维明、汤恩佳、成中英、张立文、高柏园、梁燕成、葛荣晋出席并剪彩。

阳明精舍　坐落在龙场镇平地村营盘山水库旁，距县城6公里，为深圳行政学院教授蒋庆自筹资金于1997年启动修建，2002年落成。精舍占地180余亩，其中建筑占地30亩，余为果园。精舍建有桂竹园、性天园、俟圣园、乐道园、奉元楼、退藏庵等仿古建筑。朝门门楣上“阳明精舍”匾额为国际阳明学研究大师、日本九州大学名誉教授冈田武彦题书。门侧竖有“客座私祝”石碑。

从大门首先进入桂竹园，园内建有3栋房舍，分别取名为松风馆、水云轩、仰山房，门前种有桂树和竹子，建一小池名两仪池。从桂竹园草坪中的石板小道前行，便到奉元楼，楼檐下挂有“奉元复性”匾额；楼下为复夏堂，堂内正中供奉孔子行教画像，两旁供奉孟子、荀子、王阳明、董仲舒、朱熹、陆九渊等16个先贤的牌位，左面墙正中供奉王阳明坐像，两旁供奉著名先儒罗洪先、邹守益、钱德洪、罗汝芳、刘宗周、魏源、梁漱溟、康有为、熊十力、牟宗三、钱穆、唐君毅等25人牌位。楼上是繙经阁，四周书架上摆放中国传统文化书籍，主要是国内外出版的各种版本阳明学研究专著和刊物。

奉元楼后是性天园，园内建有存心斋、何言居、诚明居。园内草坪中按天圆地方建一圆一方两个祭台，作祭祖祭天地之用。楼西南面是乐道园和俟圣园。乐道园内建有勉仁堂、静一居、思贤居、明德居。与乐道园一墙之隔是俟圣园，园内建有明夷堂，左间为“正志居”，右间为精舍主人居室，左侧“无闷居”是精舍主人读书作著之所。在乐道园和俟圣园后松林中，另建有一独立的房屋退藏庵，分为归寂居和养倪居。

精舍各建筑门柱和檐下均挂有匾额和对联，匾额共12块，对联共20副，除“阳明精舍”“兀坐培根”为冈田武彦撰书外，其余为蒋庆自撰，书法家冯楠、王萼华、戴明贤、郝承德等所书。

精舍建成后，先后有日本、韩国、加拿大等国家和中国香港、台湾地区以及北京、上海、福建等省、市的学者前来论学。

王阳明铜像 1996年，由日本将来世代国际财团理事长矢崎胜彦出资铸赠，系中央美术学院副教授田世信创作，成都蜀海青铜工艺研究所铸造。像高2米，重700公斤，造价25万元，安放于阳明洞王文成公祠。

王学圣地牌坊 2002年，在阳明大道与贵（阳）毕（节）高等级公路连接处修建“王学圣地”牌坊。牌坊高17.1米、宽28米，仿古建筑。牌坊上的“王学圣地”名匾为中国书法家协会主席沈鹏题写。牌坊四柱两面刻有4幅楹联，由县人朱五义、陈新国、雷华熙、熊永忠撰联，省著名书法家包俊宜等书写。4幅楹联分别为：

修明政治，日出迎宾，携手同走阳明大道；
文著春秋，礼遇待客，齐心共树圣贤新风。

—朱五义　撰

学仰儒宗，道悟龙场，知行合一传中外；
时超先进，文兴故驿，天地更新耀古今。

—陈新国　撰

阐理修文，道学宗邹鲁，一代师儒光日月；
探幽访胜，洞天号阳明，千秋圣地谒龙冈。

—雷华熙　撰

王学经天地，问海外域中，点古衡今谁继统；
圣地启人文，看黔山越水，兴邦尚德共承先。

—熊永忠　撰

龙场古驿景观 2009年在阳明洞“后山”建成驿道、驿站，占地58亩，驿站建筑面积848平方米，题名“龙场古驿”。在“古驿”景观旁张学良被囚禁阳明洞时钓鱼的小河边建有张学良钓鱼台。

阳明主题公园广场 2005年开建，2009年建成，场地8.69万平方米，可容纳2万人。

其他项目 2009年实施阳明大道转盘至曲尺桥、阳明村泥竹寨、幸福村水堰庄共355户居民房屋立面改造工程，统一规划通电、通信、数字电视等设施，房屋墙面呈古风古韵景观，与阳明主题公园相呼应。2010年，县政府努力培育文化产业，以阳明文化为载体，先后制定阳明书院、王阳明影视城等规划，引进贵阳旅文集团投资王阳明电视剧的拍摄及影视城建设。

（三）举办阳明文化节

1999—2009年，于县内先后举办4届阳明文化节。第一届阳明文化节于1999年10月14—16日举行，主要活动有开幕式、大型文艺演出、阳明学术研讨会、《王阳明在贵州》和《良知千古光》图片美术书法展、阳明遗迹寻访游、品尝“阳明宴”、有关阳明文化的新书首发式、招商引资项目签约等。第二届阳明文化节于2002年10月18—19日举行，主要活动有阳明学术研讨会、阳明遗迹寻访游、阳明祭祀、开幕式文艺演出、六广河篝火晚会、龙冈秋韵书画展、花卉盆景根雕奇石展、小吃品尝、福利彩票发行和招商项目签约等。韩国阳明学会会长金吉洛等国内外专家学者60余人参加阳明学术研讨会等活动。第三届阳明文化节于2005年9月14—16日举行，主要活动有开幕式文艺演出、《良知与和谐社会》论坛、阳明杯国际名人高尔夫球赛、名特优产品展销会、阳明碑苑落成剪彩、利尔之夜文艺晚会、叶辛春晖小学落成典礼、经济建设成果及发展规划展、龙冈秋韵书画展等。来自13个国家和地区的百余名专家学者参加《良知与和谐社会》论坛，国际知名儒学大师杜维明、成中英、高柏园、杨国荣等对王阳明良知思想在建设和谐社会中产生的作用进行阐述。第四届阳明文化节于2009年5月5日与“2009年中国·贵阳避暑季”活动同时举行，历时3天。来自德国、美国、加拿大、澳大利亚，马来西亚、新加坡、韩国、日本、中国台湾以及全国各地的200多名王学研究专家学者参加以“知行合一与贵阳精神、阳明学与21世纪、阳明学与实心实学、阳明学与其他哲学的对话”等为主题的高端论坛。杜维明、成中英、李瑞智、陈来、史罗一、高伯园等国际知名儒学大师在论坛上就王阳明“知行合一”、“致良知”的哲学内涵发表论见。举办4届阳明文化节期间，计有中外专家学者500余人次莅临修文并参加学术研讨和论坛活动，有力地推动了阳明文化的传承、研究和普及。

专记：王学高端论坛在修文

2009年5月，在县文化馆举行纪念王阳明“知行合一”500周年高端论坛。百余名来自中国、日本、韩国、美国、瑞典、俄罗斯、乌克兰、马来西亚、印度尼西亚等海内外著名的“王学”专家、学者参加论坛活动。论坛以“知行合一”为主题。海内外著名学者杜维明、成中英、汤恩佳、方俊吉、高柏园、崔在穆、史罗一、小川晴久、陈来、钱明、解光宇等围绕王阳明的“心学”历程，对儒学的发展与传播，以及对当今社会发展的影响等各个层面作主旨发言。有的学者指出，龙场悟道是中国学术思想发展史上具有重要意义的里程碑。王阳明远眺孟子，直承象山，针对程朱理学的弊病，开辟了另一条与朱子不同的成德之学，拓宽了主体自立的精神价值世界，展示了道德自律与人格挺立的实践精神及具体路径。他的各种人生努力与致思方向都代表了儒家重新调整内在发展道路的一种尝试，也是佛家力求改变衰弊颓废社会风气的一种努力。他的影响后来远及日本、朝鲜及世界各国。阳明学作为一种国际性的学问，已经超越了国界而引起各国学者的广泛重视。有的学者指出，在经历了充满苦难、战争和冲突的20世纪，越来越多的人认识到，只有良知超越国家、宗教和民族的狭隘和偏见，“宽以居之，恕以行之”，多给别人一点关爱和尊重，才能构建和谐社会；“君子之爱若人也，推及于其屋之乌”，反思西方“己所欲、施于人”的价值观，在东方智慧中寻找答案，才会有世界的和平与安宁。王阳明学说以“致良知”为核心，侧重于人的道德修养，通过“事上磨炼”的工夫，存善去恶，使天赋良知复明，从而使个人身心和谐，进而促进人与自然的和谐，处理好人与人的关系，求得社会的和谐。

200多名王学研究爱好者和贵州大学、贵州师范大学、贵阳学院等院校的学生参加论坛活动。大家通过论坛活动，更加领悟到阳明学说对提高人的道德水平，保持生态平衡，构建和谐社会，都有重要的现实意义。

二、民间文艺

文艺调演 1994年和1996年在县城分别举办两届民族民间文艺调演，挖掘民族民间文艺精华，推动农村文化事业健康发展。第一届于1994年12月30日举行，第二届于1996年12月18日举行。两届文艺调演参演节目均为乡（镇）农民自编自演的原汤原汁作品，有苗族花歌、花灯新唱、金钱棍、苗族男女对歌、芦笙舞蹈、吹木叶、布依民歌、唢呐演奏等。

苗族芦笙歌舞队出境演出 1993年，以久长镇下堡村苗族歌舞为基本元素，兼及其他地方苗族歌舞形式，组建成一支展现苗族文化的苗族芦笙歌舞队。歌舞队成立后，于1995年代表贵州省参加北京市第九届“龙潭杯”全国优秀民间花会大赛，表演的苗族芦笙舞《庆丰收》获大赛二等奖。

1996年10月，苗族芦笙歌舞队应日本艺术文化交流协会邀请，经文化部批准，与北京风雷京剧团联合组成“中国艺术团”前往日本访问演出。歌舞队在日本巡回演出14场，1.5万多人次观看了歌舞，表演的芦笙舞、花棍舞、板凳舞、斗牛舞和苗族歌谣，受到日本观众欢迎，在异国他乡展现修文苗家儿女的风采。

吹奏芦笙迎客人

2000年，在中国凯里国际芦笙赛会上，芦笙歌舞队荣获第一名。后因歌舞队队员多外出打工，歌舞队于2001年后自行解散。

花灯会重建 花灯在修文已有500多年历史，以六广镇最为普及，村村寨寨都有玩灯的人，被誉为“花灯之乡”。1978年玩灯活动逐步恢复，县文化馆及时引导群众组织花灯会，又搜集整理创作花灯小调、小戏，供活动时采用。1983年，文化馆召开花灯研讨会，对花灯在新时期的发展推广展开讨论。至1986年，全县花灯会发展到135个。继后，因农村青年大多外出打工，多数花灯会相继解散。文化馆结合花灯发展中的新情况，引导花灯会整合，使灯会更具传承发展花灯表演的能量。1998年六广花灯协会建立，拥有300余名会员和500多人的演出队伍，年龄最大的70多岁，最小的仅7岁。2004年，协会收集整理民间流传的花灯曲调100多首，以文字的形式汇编成册。2006年，协会派出一支花灯队参加全省首届花灯大赛，荣获优秀花灯剧和花灯小戏两个奖项，花灯表演艺人汪忠发和刘昌祥荣获花灯大王称号。至2010年，全县有花灯会22个，主要集中在六广镇。

龙灯展演 1978年后，群众喜爱的龙灯复苏，1980年，城关镇（今龙场镇）群众自发组织4个龙灯会，其中一个女子龙灯会。1999年，龙灯会整合为2个，有城北村和小街2支舞龙队，一条为黄龙，一条为青龙。逢年过节，龙灯会的会员舞起彩龙，敲锣打鼓燃放鞭炮在城镇表演，男舞黄龙，女舞青龙，黄龙上下翻飞，青龙穿插游走，令人眼花缭乱，节日气氛很浓。龙场龙灯不仅在县境表演，还应邀到遵义、开阳、息烽等周边20多个城镇游演。贵阳市每年举行春节游演，县文化广电局均组织龙灯参加，龙场龙灯成为贵阳市民喜爱的表演艺术之一。

玩龙灯

三套文艺集成 1985年起，县文化局组织专人收集整理县境民间故事、民间谚语、民间歌谣，统称“三套文艺集成”。至2000年共收集民间故事106个25万字；民间谚语按时政、事理、修养、社交、生活、自然、生产和歇后语、隐语、俚语分类共15.4万字；民间歌谣以传统山歌、新编山歌、布依族歌谣、传统花灯、建房歌谣、婚姻歌谣和儿童歌谣分类共37.5万字，编辑成《修文县三套文艺集成》，按民间故事、民间谚语、民间歌谣成册，于2008年出版。

三、文化遗产保护

（一）非物质文化遗产

2006年始，启动非物质文化遗产（以下简称“非遗”）调查、申报和保护工作。县文体广电局成立调查、申报小组，对全县非物质文化遗产进行调查和申报。调查组多次深入实地走访挖掘，对所有非遗的的起源、历史、传承及其发展进行梳理，总结归纳，陆续申报。至2010年，纳入贵州省非物质文化遗产名录3处，纳入贵阳市非物质文化遗产名录3处，纳入县非物质文化遗产名录5处。

1.省级非遗

下堡苗族舞蹈　久长镇下堡村苗族舞蹈斗牛舞具有史诗性和叙事性特点。舞蹈形式是：一老者面对东方，边吹芦笙边跳舞，4个青壮年男子围着老者，手持牛角埋头单跪默语，男子两旁分别有两组女子，头盖黑布坐在小板凳上，双手放于膝盖拍打。其间，一男子拿鼓棒击鼓与苗家祖先通灵，一女子神色凝重，唱歌乞求祖先保佑。舞蹈过程中，通过与牛对峙、翻滚、叠罗汉等动作表现苗家人民勤劳的品质和坚韧不拔的精神。

黄金花苗服饰工艺　六桶乡黄金村花苗服饰具有丰富的工艺色彩。其生产工序有6道。一是制麻纺纱，将火麻制作成麻皮，再将麻皮纺成纱；二是织布，将纺好的纱用织布机织成布；三是蜡染，在织成的布上用黄蜡绘制图案，制成单色蜡染或彩色蜡染；四是编织花带，在绣床上将麻和上色的羊毛编织成花带；五是绣图，用各色彩线在土布上绣出具有本民族特色的几何形图案。最后将蜡染、编织的彩带、绣片缝制成一套完整的花苗服装。

黄金村青苗手工机织麻布

平地青苗服饰制作工艺　龙场镇平地村青苗服饰制作工艺主要是挑花刺绣。制作以加工过的土布为底，按照布纹的走向，先用色线挑出轮廓，再按图案隔一针或几针插针。挑花的手法有正面挑花反面看，反面挑花正面看。挑花时，要细数针纱，针针压纱，讲究其图案简洁明快，对称和谐。图案的设计寓意深长，方格代表田园，方格中的红线代表鱼类，花纹代表田螺，弯条代表树木等。

六桶海马孔造纸技术

2.市级非遗

海马孔造纸技术　六桶乡海马孔村造纸技术历史悠久。清乾隆年间任姓祖先任天思由播州迁至海

马孔居住，并建有造纸作坊。造纸的原料系六广河边盛产的构皮，其生产工序多达数十道。任姓造纸色彩洁白，光洁透明，称为“白纸”，因有平滑绵软不易损坏的特点，亦叫“皮纸”。皮纸在生产、生活中用途广泛，学生写作业、家庭包裹食物、银行捆扎钞票、工厂擦洗机器都能使用。白纸在市场上销量很大。造纸技术是任姓的传家宝，代代相传至今。

大屯布依古乐　大石乡大屯布依古乐主要是当地布依人民在长期的生产和生活中通过与汉文化、苗文化不断融合，不断发展起来的一种民间音乐形式。以单人用月琴、二胡和笛子等乐器演奏为主，乐器多为自制。演奏场合多在当地的婚礼、丧礼上。曲调有筒筒调、唢呐调等。代表性的曲目有《娘娘赶场》《孟姜女哭长城》《八月桂花香》等。

扎佐蹄膀　扎佐蹄膀起源于明代中叶，因食味可口成为佳肴而传承至今。蹄膀主料用猪前腿根部1个约750克，清油、甜酒酿或蜂蜜，配料有料酒、糖、盐和八角、草果、山柰、砂仁，白扣、生姜等香料。制作时将蹄膀烧刮干净，涂上甜酒酿（或蜂蜜），入清油锅，将皮炸成金黄色起锅，置于容器中并加少许水和盐及佐料上笼蒸到蹄膀酥烂即成。

3.县级非遗

独山布依风情　六屯乡独山村布依风情包括布依山歌和布依婚俗。婚俗的主要程序分为提亲、安媒、送期、结婚。先是男女青年选中对象后，经男青年父母认可，即请被称作“行媒”的媒人到女方家提亲，提亲成功后，女方家另请一称为“坐媒”的人为媒人，然后举行“安媒”仪式明确最终的媒人，由“行媒”带两只公鸡到女方家，一只送给“坐媒”，另一只由女方家用于宴请“坐媒”吃“烧香酒”。往下由男方请命理先生择期书写期程，经“行媒”送交“坐媒”并与男女双方商定结婚时间，最后举行婚礼结婚告成。

小山制陶工艺　龙场镇小山制陶起源于20世纪50年代，经历数十年生产，至今仍保存较好的手工拉坯、笼窑烧制过程，是中国传统制陶工艺的缩影。其工艺流程主要是取土—晒干—粉碎—制成陶泥—拉坯—修坯—风干—上釉—入窑—烧制。

唢呐吹奏技艺　六桶乡木林村杨家唢呐吹奏技艺留传至今已有百余年历史，其曲调有《花谱》《草谱》《道谱》《筒筒谱》《川牌谱》《笛之调》《云南调》《将军调》《四门调》《贺调》《丧调》等，每调又有若干曲，今保存的曲调有百余首。

铧口铸造工艺　六桶乡花椒村铸造铧口工艺系传统技艺，为李氏宗族世代相传，李氏家族从祖辈至今在当地均有“李铧匠” 称号。

六广花灯　六广花灯出自六广，起于明洪武年间，距今已流传500多年。当地群众不但把它作为自娱自乐的艺术，还认为它能驱邪避凶。每逢修房造屋，办红白喜事，都要敲锣打鼓跳花灯以讨吉利。花灯是当地群众喜闻乐见的艺术形式。每年正月，灯会从初一出灯，一直要玩到正月十七才收灯。玩花灯已成为六广民间重要的文艺活动。

（二）文物保护单位

1982年贵州省公布第一批文物保护单位，县境的蜈蚣桥、阳明洞、索桥列在其中，1985年，三人坟、三潮水又列入省第二批公布的文物保护单位。2006年，国务院核定并公布第六批全国重点文物保护单位，阳明洞由“省保”升格为“国保”，至此，县内有全国重点文物保护单位1处2个点，省级文物保护单位5处5个点，县级文物保护单位3处3个点。

1.全国重点文物保护单位

阳明洞　位于县城东1.5公里龙冈山腰，为明正德年间王阳明谪居龙场驿时的山洞。1958年即被列为省级文物保护单位，1982年，省人民政府重新公布为省级文物保护单位，并划定保护区范围7万平方米。1996年，贵阳市政府和县政府共投资42万元对阳明洞部分建筑物、碑刻、展品等。1998年，投资400万元在阳明洞大门前东侧修建阳明园（即“王阳明纪念馆”）。2005年，建西园、碑林、牌坊。2006年5月25日国务院公布阳明洞为“全国重点文物保护单位”。同年，县被评为“全国文物工作先进县”。至2010年，又先后在阳明洞保护区范围内建成龙场驿站、阳明文化主题公园等。

2006年6月6日，县委、县政府在阳明洞举行全国重点文物保护单位揭幕仪式

玩易窝　是县城南郊吴家湾与毛栗园之间的一座小孤山里的一个洞穴。小孤山距县城约1公里。王阳明初至龙场就在洞口搭了1件草棚栖身，并成天静坐洞中研读《周易》，反复推求，终于悟出了“心即理”之道。王阳明就此命洞名为“玩易窝”，并撰《玩易窝记》叙其悟道之事，还吟《初至龙场无所止结草庵居之》的抒情怀。1982年县政府公布玩易窝为县级重点文物保护单位，1996年升格为贵阳市级文物保护单位，旋又升为贵州省级文物保护单位，2006年随国务院公布阳明洞为全国重点文物保护单位时玩易窝也成为全国重点文物保护单位。

2.省级文物保护单位

蜈蚣桥　位于距县城15公里的洒坪乡猫洞河上，是明代龙场驿至六广驿的要津。桥为明成化五年（1469）贵州宣慰使安观所建。毁后又于万历十九年（1591）由贵州宣慰使安国亨重建，历时3年竣工，更名“龙源桥”，世人仍称“蜈蚣桥”。蜈蚣桥为龙场九驿古驿道上十桥之冠。桥系3孔石拱平桥，每孔跨度8米，连同桥墩和引桥共长40米，宽11米，高9米。其工艺采用“T”形块石建造。建桥至今，经过近400余年的河水侵蚀和数百次的山洪冲击，桥身仍安然无恙。桥面两旁装有石栏杆，栏杆由24根方体石抱柱和22块长方形石栏板装成，每根抱柱雕有形态各异、栩栩如生的石狮子，每块栏板正面皆刻有云龙和卷草图案。桥头抱柱附有抱鼓，造型美观。1982年贵州省人民政府公布为省级文物保护单位。

索桥　位于距县城20公里的乌栗，凌空横跨在修文与清镇两县之间的猫跳河上。河宽20米，水色深蓝，夹岸峭壁，桥似一条长龙腾空于两山之间。索桥的桥系绵竹捻索而成，索粗8厘米，拴在两岸悬岩凿成的“牛鼻孔”中。桥索离水面十余米，上套短竹筒，筒上吊一形象“牛枷担”的曲木架。索渡的人自缚于曲木架上，仰向天空，双手握索，缓缓移握前进。索渡悬空，望之心惊胆战。有精于索渡者，则以双手紧握竹筒，将身稍微一纵，即溜至彼岸。遇不善于索渡者或渡实物，则将其装入筐内

索桥古渡

吊于竹筒下，由对岸的人用绳牵渡。据明崇祯三年（1630）兵部尚书兼五省总督朱燮元《督黔善后事宜疏》中“在小索桥设哨”的记载，证明该桥远在明代即有。清道光十年（1830），里人修渡口竖功德碑谓：此桥历为修文、清镇两县人往来之捷径。同治二年（1863），何得胜义军经此索渡克清镇威慑贵阳。民国25年（1936）中国工农红军二、六军团由此渡口搭便桥过河挥师黔（西）大（定）毕（节），建立根据地。是时，国民党中央军围追堵截红军，用飞机在此掷炸弹数枚，但人、桥均无损。1982年贵州省人民政府公布为省级重点文物保护单位。

三人坟　位于县城西北12公里的蜈蚣坡山腰间古驿道西侧，坟茔三座并列，坟头均约高1.6米，直径4米。明正德四年（1509）秋月三日，有自京都赴任之吏目携一子一仆过龙场，投宿土苗家。翌日，三人相继死于蜈蚣坡，时任龙场驿丞的王阳明前往掩埋，并撰《瘗旅文》致祭。清乾隆八年（1743）秋，东鲁孙谔会同知县王肯谷至坟前凭吊，眼见坟地荒烟蔓草，三座坟茔均难辨认，孙即捐金垒土封墓，并赋诗撰文勒石于坟前。清道光十九年（1839）县人将《瘗旅文》勒碑竖于坟侧古驿道旁，后称此处为大碑丫口，以供后人追忆凭吊。《瘗旅文》碑毁于“文化大革命”时期，后恢复，碑文《瘗旅文》由贵州文化老人陈福桐书写。1985年贵州省人民政府公布为省级重点文物保护单位。

三潮水　位于县城西北1.5公里观音山南麓，属间歇泉，因泉水每日三盈三缩，故名“三潮水”。明崇祯年间即建有凉亭、水池，泉水自岩隙中流经石雕龙嘴喷涌而出，泻于池内。池中原有一形如龟状大石，潮水每淹至龟背即退去。三潮水西侧有明崇祯年间所建潮水寺，后由清顺治年间隐居于此自号“知非居士”的副都御史兼贵州巡抚钱邦芑改名“知非寺”。1985年，贵州省人民政府公布为省级文物保护单位。

3.县级文物保护单位

红军标语　民国24年（1935），红军长征经过修文时，红五军团一部宿营腊脖乡（今六屯桃源）大木寨，红军在寨内书写的标语“红军是干人的军队”至今保存完好。1982年，县政府公布为县级重点文物保护单位。

六广驿　位于距县城36公里的六广镇广城村，地处大山之顶，雄踞六广渡口。明洪武年间奢香所开龙场九驿中之六广驿站即设于此。崇祯二年（1629），贵州上六卫副总兵王国祯为防水西军叛乱，责成参将方国安、刘镇藩修筑石城。石城北门外一里许的夹夹关，形势险要，有“一夫当关，万夫莫及”之势。崇祯三年（1630）置敷勇卫，为卫属濯灵守御千户所驻地。城内建有驿站、千户所署、营盘、仓库、市街和庙宇。清康熙废卫建县置信顺里，即为里治，改称六广城。是时，贵州省绿营兵黔西营分防修文县六广汛外委署驻城中。咸丰九年至同治五年（1859—1866），连年兵燹，城内建筑物多为灰烬，遂将市街移至山腰龙口山前。民国年间，城墙皆毁，仅存城门。今为村寨，但历代建筑物的基础还依稀可辨，太平寺僧墓群尚存。1982年4月，县政府公布为县级重点文物保护单位。

六广驿旧址

高仓古堡　位于龙场镇程官云盘山顶，距县城7.5公里。清康熙三年（1664）聚居在县东南面高山间的苗民在山上修建木架粮仓一座，外围石垣，形似堡垒，命名“高脚仓”。后人又称“高仓古堡”。每遇兵祸匪患，全族聚居其间躲避。高仓古堡场地呈不规则四边形，所筑石垣，东面长25.6米，南面长43.8米，西面长17.9米，北面长50.6米。厚1.8米，高2.6米。总面积约1200平方米。垣内挖有21米长的排水沟，垒有炉灶。今堡已毁，惟石垣残存。1985年县政府公布为县级重点文物保护单位。

（三）文物普查

2003年启动编修第二轮《修文县志》后，县地方志办公室派员对县内文物开展过调查，2007年7月，根据全国第三次文物普查工作的部署，县文体广电局相应开展文物调查，至2010年，文物和方志工作者新发现文物有摩崖、碑碣、古寺庙、古墓、古驿道、古井、古树、遗迹、遗物等55处（件），其中重点有19处，均只作普查登记，未申报文物保护。

1.摩崖

多缤洞摩崖 位于六桶乡多缤洞洞口石壁和石门柱，为民国13年（1924））的碑文和楹联，碑文残缺，存80余字，对联为“觅得桃源这座落，能安梓里我补天”，落款“王道陈书”。

鹿子冲摩崖 位于久长镇永兴村刘世选墓侧石壁，高2米，宽1.4米，顶部横刻“逮嬗无穷”4个大字，其余竖刻279字。落款为“乾隆二十四年岁在己卯五月十五谷旦立”。

高王洞摩崖 位于大石乡岩湾村麻窝组高王洞石壁，以红色颜料书“高王洞”3字，另书有“抗战，建国，孙中山先生，大家同心，一心炸掉日本”等文字。为当地人王子华在抗日战争时期书写。

2.碑碣

濯灵所标志碑 位于六广镇广城村杨贤祥家门口，为残碑。碑高1.2米，宽0.62米，碑顶部为弧形，中间为太阳，两边为云彩纹。系康熙十二年（1673）立。

回龙寺石工碑记 位于六屯乡桃源三寨回龙寺，碑高67厘米，宽103厘米，书刻“乾隆二年（1737）丁已岁仲春月吉日立”字样。

宋母凤氏墓划地界碑记 位于久长镇清水村宋家林，为宋母诰受考夫人凤老太君冢墓碑，高1.25米，宽0.65米，刻有“合族集议，今将地名塘家湾山土荒幅，刊明界址……大清道光十四年岁次甲午花月中浣丁未吉日建立”字样。

陈济堂井碑记 位于久长芦山村七组，碑高0.65米，宽0.45米。碑顶部书“洁白”二字，碑中部书刻“龙王神”3字，碑左面书刻“众议以上井吃，中井洗菜，下井洗衣服、鞋，不准人上井洗菜，有人洗者，罚银一两入众”。碑右面书刻“见人洗不说，罚银五分入众。道光十七年冬月众立”。

手爬岩“岩书” 位于大石乡大屯村后山岩上，离大屯村约1公里。岩壁上有呈红色“图章”样图案，内有文字，字迹依稀可辨。

元庆村烈士纪念碑 位于六广镇元庆村箐口坡，系1997年11月20日六广镇人民政府和元庆村委会为1950年3月5日在该地抗击土匪牺牲的烈士梁方膏、魏怀远竖立的纪念碑。

岩鹰山水库一号隧道工程碑 位于小箐乡新场村二组偏坡寨岩鹰山水库一号隧道出口处上方。碑高2.2米，宽1.14米，厚0.27米，碑顶为半圆形，高0.5米，碑下部为长方形，高1.7米。碑顶刻有北京天安门城楼图案浮雕，两下角刻有两株松树，下部刻卷草纹，碑文内容系工程建设介绍。有“1972年9月30日立”字样。

血字碑 位于修（文）六（广）公路17公里300米处。系修文县人民政府1993年4月勒石竖立的一

口警示碑，书刻“牢记‘11·29’特大恶性交通事故血的教训,活着的人们可千万要警惕啊!”字样，世人称“血字碑”。1992年11月29日，个体车主彭江涛雇请仅持大货车驾驶证的吴维均驾驶“贵州03／03244号”大客车从六桶返回修文，行至修（文）六（广）公路大兴村小米沟处，客车坠入85米深的谷底，造成23人死亡、9人受伤和车辆粉碎性报废的特大恶性交通事故。

3.古井

陈济堂井 位于久长芦山村七组，井分为三，深均为1米。上井长3米，宽1.1米，中井长1.45米，宽1.2米，下井今已填没。井周围为圆形，用石板铺地石条砌边。此井水质好，供附近80户人家约400人饮用，还可灌溉附近20余亩稻田。从井旁碑记“道光十七年冬月众立”可知此井清代即已存在。

四方井 位于久长镇清水村清水寨北面白虎山下的田坝中间，由四口井组成，据《清水村志》记载清代即有此井。2002年改井为大水池，使用电力抽水供清水寨人畜饮用。

4.遗迹

悬棺葬 位于谷堡乡索桥下游1公里处叫猫儿夹朝的悬崖绝壁上，为古代悬棺葬，今能看见两处，棺一部分置入崖壁洞中，一部分有木桩斜撑悬于洞外绝壁上。

石塔 位于久长镇石安寨少将坡顶，为明代建筑，今已圮，仅存塔基。塔基高3米，分三层，第一层为四边形，边长6.8米，周长27.2米；第二层基础为八边形，边长2.73米，周长21.84米；第三层基础为八边形，边长2.67米，周长21.36米。

长官司 位于扎佐镇石堰河附近，系明洪武五年（1372）设扎佐长官司驻地，今地名仍称长官司。

古堡 位于扎佐镇把七村将军山，为明清时屯兵之地。东西长310米，南北宽45米，周长430米。

营盘 谷堡乡境内有2座明清时屯兵营盘，一名大营上，位于大塘村青山组背后山坡上，东西长90米，南北宽30米，周长240米，面积2700平方米。营盘围墙已圮，今可见其基础。营盘内原存有房屋，上世纪60年代仍有人居住，今无存，营盘已垦为耕地。其一名小营上，位于大营上左前绿水村小营组背后圆形土山上，东西长120米，南北长70米，面积8400平方米，周长400米，营盘围墙已圮，土地多种植果树。

祠堂 位于六屯乡独山村的葛家祠堂，面阔3间11.5米，进深7米，明间宽4米，两次间各宽3.75米，前檐为走廊，宽1.8米，柱础下部为六边形，中部为八边形，上部为鼓形。柱础直径0.43米，高0.35米，柱周长1.2米，檐柱高4米，檐高3.7米，廊柱中上部有圆形浮雕图案，次间廊为靠背椅式栏杆，雕有图案。

附：

修文“古人类遗址”探秘

新华网贵州频道1月5日电 修文—神秘的“天书”,“九十九堆”的乱石，2.4米长的石棺，上百处人类居住的断墙残垣，留下了一个个难解之谜——

神秘的土地

在修文县六桶乡，至今遗留着近百处残墙断壁，几十堆不明含义的石块建筑物，几千米用石块垒砌的小路和重叠几层的石板墓……日前，记者与文物工作者一道，踏上了这块神秘的土地。

六桶乡榨土、山保村距修文县城53公里，位于修文、金沙、息烽三县交界处，北面可通遵义、四川，向南可通贵阳，向西可通毕节、云南。与记者同行的修文县文管所所长赵星介绍：在清代甚至更早的年代，这里是一条非常重要的民间交通要道，无论是商业流通，还是人口流动，都比官道上的六广更繁荣。赵星推测，这里也许就是清代甚至更早时期的川盐入黔通道。从目前发现的地上、地下遗迹分析，这里兴盛之时，人口众多。奇怪的是，乾隆《贵州通志》、道光《贵阳府志》、民国《修文县志》均未见记载。

“天书”模糊难辨

在榨土村青山寨，有一座高100米的大山，当地人称为黄鹰岩。在半山腰处，有一段宽约1米的平台，平台上方约3米高处分布着若干似字、似画、似符号的图案，当地人称为看不懂的“天书”。记者一行爬上山腰，仰望那些怪异的图案，这些图案历经风雨剥蚀，少数形状依稀可见，多数模糊不清。在南面第8个图案旁，有后人用墨书写着“国太平之祝方□□去”字样，其中有两字已不能辨认。赵星说，这些“天书”图案从风化程度看，为同时代所绘，但由于没有纪年难以判断其书写年代，其书写人、颜料、意义尚待考证。

古老的“村落”

就在黄鹰岩以南2公里处，保存着一处古人类活动遗址，有房基、通道、墓葬等遗存，方圆达5平方公里。

我们在榨土村郭家寨、金竹坡、狮子山一带的山上看到，林间残存着大量人工砌筑的石墙基脚，无固定朝向，随形附势，依山而建。赵星推测这可能是先人居住的遗址。从断墙的遗存推测，房屋多为正面3间、进深1间，每户还有一院坝。建筑材料均为块石，无任何黏合材料，无钎锤加工痕迹，墙体厚约80厘米。在周围的几个山头之间，有宽约1.5米石头铺就的通道相互连接，四通八达。从整个布局看，房屋、道路的修建似乎有一个总体规划。

令人费解的“九十九堆”

在郭家寨东北方向500米处的两山之间，有一块2万多平方米的平地，地里伫立着无数大小不等、形状不一的石堆，高1.8米至2.5米，当地人称之为“九十九堆”，并一直成为这一带的地名。当地80多岁的王炳华老人说，他小时候就知道这个地方叫“九十九堆”，祖辈们都这样称。记者走近“九十九堆”，看见一堆堆乱石像坟包一样，顿时毛骨悚然，试着数了一下石堆的数量，却怎么也数不清。当地有一个传说，称这其中“最后一堆”有金银财宝，但谁也弄不清哪是“最后一堆’。于是，“九十九堆”招来了不少寻宝人。当地村民雷光祥说，十多年前，他和许多放牛娃曾在乱石堆里寻宝，只找到半块手镯。以前最高的石堆有三四米高，都被掘宝人掀倒了。

“巨人”部落？

在榨土村、山保村、大苗寨等地约5平方公里的地方，分布着大量石棺葬。石棺的6个面均为整块石板扣成，无雕刻纹饰、文字符号，也无随葬品，当地人称之为“苗坟”。当地村民吴文刚说，近几十年来当地多次出土石棺材，分布在“九十九堆”周边5公里范围内。他说：“幼年前，我曾两次看到从土里挖出石棺材，1999年，本村叶家在‘九十九堆’旁一块地里犁土时，从一石壕里犁出一具人骨，腿骨、头盖骨都很大，捡起小腿骨往自己的小腿上一比，竟高出膝盖有20多厘米。”村民吴元友也向记者介绍道，

4年前他家挖屋基时，曾发现重叠着三具石棺，有2.3米至2.4米长，且棺内人体骨骸很长。村民们也称，1958年“大跃进”搞深耕时，也曾挖出多副巨型石棺。只因这些石棺材质较好，都被抬去砌土坎、修路了。

据调查，当地现在没有如此高大的“巨人”，也没有用石棺葬人的习俗。

数年来，赵星在“九十九堆”一带的耕土层中发现一些印纹陶瓷片，上有同心圆圈纹、圆形斜格纹，同心圆点纹等，初步分析为罐、碗之类的生活用具残片。但因为资金匮乏，一直没有条件进一步测定残片的年代。根据当地所有遗迹综合分析，赵星认为，此处是一个居住时间较长，居住年代较早的人口稠密聚居区。具体早在什么年代，还需进一步考证。

贵州省修文县发现一处古人类遗址

2009年新华网贵阳5月7日电（李劲峰、娄辰）贵州省修文县近日发现一处古人类遗址。考古专家认定该遗址距今已有1万至4万年历史，处于旧石器时代晚期。

此次考古发现缘起于修文县境内的四明洞佛光寺的一次施工建设。佛光寺为移动寺内一尊佛像，在施工中意外发现一个碗口大小的洞穴，施工人员在洞内抓住了一条直径约6厘米的大蛇。随着施工的推进，蛇洞内竟别有洞天：一个藏有许多动物化石、石制工具的大洞出现在人们眼前。

贵州省博物馆考古专家迅速赶到现场，根据洞内石器初步认定为一处1万至4万年前的旧石器时代晚期古人类活动遗址。古遗址的发掘价值有待专家进一步考察确定。

据贵州省博物馆研究馆员蔡回阳介绍，贵州是发现古人类遗址较多地区之一，在此次新发现遗址附近，就曾发现过同时期的化石和石器。

第三节　群众文化

一、文化网络

（一）县级文化艺术单位

行政管理单位　1981年，县置文化局，为全县文化事业行政管理单位。后名称几经变更，2010年称旅游文体广播电视局。

文化馆　1978年，县文化馆设文艺辅导、文学创作、美术、摄影等组室。2003年在阳明洞景区新建文化馆，分置演艺大厅、多功能厅、展厅、创作室、美术室、音乐室、舞蹈室。至2010年，文化馆举办各类艺术培训班80余期，培训学员2000余人。组织文化下乡各类演出活动400余场次，观众达50万人次。

图书馆　1978年建县图书馆，设有书库、借书、阅览、收藏、采编等组室，至1985年藏有图书3.1万册，持证读者600余人。1999年文广大楼建成，图书馆迁至新址办公，设有借书、成人阅览、儿童阅览、采编等室。至2010年，图书藏量逾6万册，报刊100多种。年内，共计接待成人读者7158人次，儿童3895人次，图书流通9486册次。

电影公司 1978年，县电影事业管理机构为电影院管理站，1981年改电影院管理站为县电影发行放映公司，有职工9人，实行经理负责制，下设财务、放管、发行、修理组，管理全县电影发行放映业务。1984年，按贵州省电影发行放映公司《关于文化系统国营放映单位的隶属关系与管理的通知》，将县城、扎佐、久长、六广4个公办影院和农村公办电影队归属县电影公司直接管理。电影公司建立岗位责任制，实行经济承包，建立“奖优罚劣，奖勤罚懒”制度，调动放映人员工作积极性。公司积极组织影片，采取到机关单位、学校宣传，组织包场、学生专场等办法提高影片发行放映率。1986年，全县6家影院、22个放映队和厂矿、企业14个放映队共放映8446场次，观众达445万人次，电影公司被评为安顺地区年度先进单位。1992年起，随着电视普及、录像点和卡拉OK厅等娱乐场所不断增加，全县电影放映走向低谷，放映队从1986年的36个减至17个。继后，电影公司虽采取在电影院设置包间、开展保值电影有奖活动等措施，但电影观众有减无增。至2000年，县电影院已难以为继，出租给修文联宇食品公司改为购物超市。2002年，电影院交由开发商作地产开发。

2001年起，电影公司贯彻国家实施的2131工程计划（即21世纪每村每月放1场电影），组织参加贵州省举办的农村放映节，开展送电影下乡活动，至2010年，10年共放映1.2万多场次。

新华书店 1978年，县新华书店主要负责境内图书发行经销，属事业单位。固定资产仅12万元。1987年底，书店经理改由省新华书店任命，实现企业自主。次年，书店率先在全省新华书店系统试行招标承包，年内实现图书销售额416万元，比1978年的28万元增长15倍。1998年，在县城迎春路和扎佐襄阳路分别修建1268平方米和611平方米的图书发行综合楼，书店的固定资产达到195.5万元，比1978年的12万元增长16倍。2008年又在阳明大道修建图书发行综合楼，当年竣工，总投资292万元，建筑面积3033平方米。

文艺协会 1988年，建立县文学、书法、美术、摄影4个文学艺术专业协会。后又于1999年建立音（乐）舞（蹈）剧（戏剧）协会，2004年建立阳明诗词学会，并改文学协会为作家协会。几个专业文艺协会团结、组织县内文艺工作者和爱好者开展文艺活动，推动县的文艺事业发展。

文艺界联合会 1990年，成立县文学艺术界联合会，至2010年，文学艺术界联合会下辖作协、书协、美协、摄协、音舞剧协和阳明诗词学会5个团体会员组织。县文联与其他文化单位密切合作，组织开展各种文化文艺活动，使县的群众文化显露出勃勃生机。

（二）乡村文化单位

文化站（室） 1982年起，按照贵州省文化厅县有文化馆、乡有文化站、村有文化室的要求，全县启动乡（镇）和村文化站、室建设。当年在扎佐、久长、六广、王官、水塘、石安、阳早、六屯、马家桥、桃源、清让、中寨、大石等13个社（镇）建起文化站，60%的村建起文化室。1984年，为巩固乡（镇）文化站，县文化局以招聘方式为马家桥、久长、扎佐等站增加专职工作人员，使乡（镇）文化站得以稳步发展。1992年“撤并建”后，将乡（镇）文化站和原有的广播电视站合并，改建为文化广播电视站。2003年3月改称为文化服务中心。2004年村建精神文明活动中心后，将村文化室功能并入精神文明活动中心。

精神文明活动中心 1994年在谷堡乡建起全县第一个乡（镇）精神文明活动中心，之后，10乡（镇）精神文明活动中心相继建成，活动中心内设广播室、棋牌室、图书室、全民健身室，配备有音响、电脑、复印机、速印机、录像机、摄影机，成为群众文化活动的重要阵地。

（三）群众文艺团体

进入20世纪90年代，县委宣传部和文化部门根据不同时期县内文化艺术工作的需要组织群众文艺团体，与专业协会配合，推动全县文艺事业发展。

文工团 1997年12月成立修文县业余文工团，设声乐组、舞蹈组和后勤组，有团员百余人。1998年7月，业余文工团改建为修文县文工团，团员减少到46人，分声乐、舞蹈、军乐组。文工团主要参与送戏下乡演出和县的节庆演出，活动经费以企业赞助为主。2000年因经费难以为继，文工团改散。

甲秀军乐团 1999年，县文化馆与三角山水泥厂组建修文甲秀军乐团，团员多为在校学生。军乐团建立后，主要参加县内节庆联欢和庆典演出活动。至2003年因团员参加工作或就读外地高校，难以聚拢，军乐团改散。

中老年合唱团 2002年，县文化馆组建中老年合唱团，团员60余人。主要参加县的歌咏比赛、节庆联欢演出活动。2010年尚存。

二、文艺活动

（一）文艺演出

文艺演出是县内群众文化活动的重头戏。各类演出繁多，每年逾500场次。演出活动主要有4类。一是由县委宣传部牵头，文化艺术部门承办的文艺调演、节庆晚会、比赛等。1988年举办的全县文艺调演，1999年举办的"五月的风"歌咏比赛和"修文人民奔向明天"群众文艺调演，每年春节县委、县政府举办的联欢晚会，2010年举办的千人广场舞大赛均属此类。二是由乡（镇）和单位部门举办的宣传庆典演出。大石布依族乡每年举办的"六月六"歌会，2002年县文联举办的庆元宵文艺晚会，2005年县纪委举办的"清风颂"文艺晚会，2010年县文体广电局举办的"庆中秋—我们的节日"文艺晚会，县政协每年举办的各界群众春节联欢晚会等即为这一类型的演出活动。三是"三下乡"（送科技、文化、卫生下乡）演出。自1988年开展"三下乡"活动起，"送戏下乡"成为活跃农村群众文化生活的重要形式，此类演出规模虽小，但节目多是精挑细选，很受农村群众欢迎。2008年，参加过全国"群星奖"大赛的优秀舞蹈《红苞谷》就作为"送戏下乡"的节目，到乡间为群众演出。四是群众自发演出。此类活动十分普遍，无须组织，随时随地都可表演。搬家造屋、红白喜事跳花灯、吹唢喇和21世纪兴起的广场舞、社区纳凉晚会都属这类演出形式。

2010年社区纳凉晚会

专记一：川戏表演乐村民

走进六屯乡三寨村，老远就会听到锣鼓声和笑声在山谷间回荡。进到农家小院，只见人头攒动，原来是村里的群众正在院子里搞文艺活动—唱川戏。几个演员在院子的空地上聚精会神地表演《空城计》段子，观众全是村里的老老少少，大家看得津津有味。演员地道的唱腔和生动的表演，赢得观众阵阵喝彩。小院里充溢着祥和欢乐的氛围。

六屯乡三寨村川剧队由60多位农民组成，年龄最大的78岁，最小的17岁。他们能完整的演出《夜归》《惊梦》和《陈姑赶潘》等50多个川剧段子。每逢节日或是村里的庆典活动，川剧队员们就会拉开场子，为村民们带来欢乐和笑声。这个川剧队的表演没有特别的场地要求，无论是在田间地头，还是村寨院落，一旦需要，他们就能来上一段。每到逢年过节，是队员们特别忙的时候，他们从大年初二开始，一直要唱到十五。这段日子是村里的群众和川剧队员们最尽兴、最开心的时刻。这支川剧队与村里群众的文化生活息息相关，村里人家有红白喜事，都会请他们去表演。村民们只要一听见川剧锣鼓的响声，就会聚集到办事的人家来。这支业余川剧队不仅给三寨村带来了蓬勃的生机与活力，他们还被乌当区、开阳县、独山县及周边村寨邀请“巡回”演出。

专记二：“红苞谷”亮相“舞蹈世界”

2006年11月，应中央电视台文艺部“舞蹈世界”栏目邀请，修文县20多名妇女排演的大型原生态歌舞节目“红苞谷”赴京参加“大地之舞—民族民间舞蹈”节目拍摄。

《红苞谷》取材于县辖龙场镇平地村，由贵州省女企业家商会副会长、修文县女企业家商会会长蔡星春出资5万元打造。因为要参加当年举办的贵阳市第四届群众文艺调演，蔡星春邀约部分机关干部、社区群众和城镇个体工商户一起到苗族群众聚居的平地村采风。演员们和村里的苗族同胞拉家常，说农事，一起扳苞谷用背篼背回家，然后与苗族老乡一家老小在院子里磨新苞谷做饭会餐。演员们虽然有过在农村生活的经历，但离乡多年后再参加这样热闹生动的丰收劳作，创作灵感油然而生。大家围绕取材和选题展开热烈讨论，你一言我一语地谈论自己的想法，纷纷给即将编排的舞蹈取名，最后确定用人们耳熟能详而又通俗易懂的“红苞谷”来命名。她们从省城请来专业舞蹈老师指点，经过几个月精心创作和排练，大型原生态歌舞节目“红苞谷”逐渐成形。演员们利用业余时间集中排练，反复打磨这个舞蹈节目的内涵，反复推敲每一个动作细节，直到满意为止，没有一个人哼累喊痛，热情十分高涨。“红苞谷”出炉后，在2006年9月8日举行的“贵阳市第四届群众文艺调演”中获得舞蹈组一等奖和创作奖。继后一举成名，引起媒体关注。在贵阳市舞蹈新作品展演上受到北京舞蹈专家好评，并推荐参加2007年3月举行的全国“群星奖”大赛。11月25晚贵州省举行舞蹈创作比赛，“红苞谷”参赛获得展演奖。随后，她们收到中央电视台文艺部信函，被邀请参加“舞蹈世界”栏目“大地之舞——民族民间舞蹈”拍摄。演员们充满激情，经过认真准备，于11月29日登机从贵阳起飞赶赴北京，11月30日起参加为期4天的拍摄活动。这次演出，“红苞谷”在原来的基础上加以提升，展现妇女们辛勤劳动在社会主义新农村建设中获得丰收后的喜悦、欢快和幸福情景，集乐、舞、游戏情节等元素为一体，节奏明快热烈，令人赏心悦目。

《红苞谷》剧照

“红苞谷”走上中央电视台，面向全国播映，社会反响良好，为修文争了光，为修文人长了志气，修文城乡家喻户晓，在随后的各种文艺演出中都受到观众好评。2009年4月1日，“红苞谷”又登上贵州省第六届“贵辣杯”中老年舞蹈大赛舞台，表演赢得观众阵阵掌声，并获得一等奖励。

（二）书画摄影展览

1990年建立县文联后，每年举办书法、美术、摄影作品展。2004年国庆节，组织书画作品80件，在贵阳市阳明祠举办“修文县美术书法作品展”，贵州省和贵阳市书画界知名书画家包俊宜、王小竹等30余人参加开幕式并观看展出作品。展出6天时间接待观展市民700余人。《贵州日报》《贵阳日报》、贵阳电视台等新闻媒体均报道展况。2008年，县文联组织摄协、美协、书协会员深入“抗凝冻、保民生”第一线创作，在抗灾斗争结束后举办“抗凝冻保民生”主题美术书法摄影作品展，作品极具艺术感染力，受到观展者好评。至2010年共举办展览30次。

（三）征文　朗诵　演讲比赛

1978年后，县宣传、文化艺术部门联合党史、地方志、政法、教育、计生等单位通过开展征文、朗诵、演讲比赛等多种方式活跃群众文化生活，从中发现、培养文化艺术人才。2009年初，县委宣传部与贵阳人民广播电台、县文联、文体广电局、移动公司联办的“移动杯”纪念改革开放30周年诗词（美文）朗诵比赛，50余名参赛者以“颂改革春风·扬时代旋律”为主题，用文学朗诵形式激发人们对美的追求和向往。通过两轮角逐，11名选手获奖。至2010年，共举办征文比赛20期次、朗诵比赛11期次和演讲比赛45期次。

“颂改革春风·扬时代旋律”诗词（美文）朗诵比赛现场

（四）文学创作

中共十一届三中全会后，文艺复兴，县人和寓居县境者以及在县内工作的一些同志对修文这片热土情有独钟，信笔写修文的事，写修文的人，出现县内文学创作活动日渐兴盛的局面。初时，文学创作以个人自发为主，县委宣传部、县文化馆加以引导。县文化馆组织作者参加安顺地区和省的文学创作座谈会、讲习会，帮助作者提高创作水平。期间，卢永康、陈新国的小说、散文在省市级文学刊物发表。1990年文联建立后，以组织举办采风、文学讲座、笔会等多种形式，提高作者创作热情和作品质量。相继有朱五义、李祖炎、黄竹、李嘉宁、唐育文、李嘉颖、贾长远、赵昊鹏、肖江虹、余漫、宋东雁、李小龙、何小平等一批作者创作的小说、散文、诗歌、戏剧等作品见诸报刊。至2010年，县作家协会会员由1988年的43人扩大到60人，有中国作协会员1人，省作协会员3人，市作协会员16人。卢永康、陈新国、黄竹、朱五义、李小龙等有文集由出版社公开出版。陈新国的短篇小说集《野山》，2000年获贵阳市政府第五届金筑文艺奖。2009年，肖江虹的中篇小说《百鸟朝凤》在全国大型刊物《当代》发表，被《小说选刊》和《新华文摘》等全国知名刊物选载。

文学作品选录

小　说

荒土的悲剧

陈新国

"许长发吊死了!"

这天早晨，我正伏在桌上赶写一份给公社党委的汇报材料，房东王大伯推门进来，把这个不幸的消息告诉了我。

我的头轰的一声，只觉得无数金星在眼前迸跳。在闪烁的金星中，我仿佛看见一个身材高大、满脸络腮胡的中年农民，含着悲苦的微笑向我走来……

这是发生在一九七六年春天的事。

一个月前，公社党委派我到石桥生产队蹲点。石桥是闻名全县的穷队，去年大秋分配，基本口粮每人只有六十八斤，一个劳动日的收入仅五分七厘。正是春耕大忙季节，这里却在闹粮荒，集体生产濒于瘫痪。

叫我这个刚由知青提拔上来的公社干部去收拾这副烂摊子，真感到束手无策。真巧，报上登了一篇《狠抓路线这个纲，人换思想地换装》的经验报道，我读了后，心里总算有了谱儿。

一来到石桥生产队，我就根据那篇报道介绍的经验，依样画葫芦，先向全队宣布：如果谁还不出工，就不供应回销粮，这一手倒也灵验，第二天，全队的劳动力都参加改土变田了。接着，便是大造政治气氛—在墙壁上、田坎上、山坡上到处刷标语。

一天下午，我正在一匹光秃秃的山坡上写"学习大寨"的标语时，突然看见从坡背后升起一股淡蓝色的火烟，心里一惊，莫非有人没出工，在坡背后烧灰?我几步攀到坡顶，向下—望，果不出所料，只见坡脚有一个人，正端着一撮箕草皮，步子蹒跚地向一堆冒着浓烟的灰堆走去。灰堆周围是一片刚翻过的荒土。

开荒，这还了得?我急忙走下山坡，朝那儿奔去。开荒的人正弯腰拨弄着火堆，没有看见我。我站在一块大青石上，双手叉腰，厉声责问："谁在这里开荒?"那人吃惊地撑起身来，扭头看我，显得惊慌失措，使劲地搓着两只手上的泥巴，结结巴巴地说道："哦，黄，黄同志，这土原是我家的自留地，队上收去后嫌瘦了，不愿种，我见荒着可惜，想刨出来，种，种点土荞……"我打量着他：这人身材高大，穿一件破烂衣服，肩头露出黑红的皮肉，头上戴一顶发白的蓝布帽子，边沿有一圈油黑的汗渍，帽遮阳下那张泛黄的脸上，长满了络腮胡，一双无神的眼睛流露出惊惶的目光。

我认出他来了。他叫许长发，是石桥村有名的大力士，我还是小娃娃时，就听说过不少关于他的传闻：他用机公车推一石煤炭，走七八里路可以不歇气；他能够用牙咬着—桶水，绕村子走一圈；更惊人的是，有一次他挞谷子，谷子太多，箩筐装不下，他竟把挞斗举到背上，连谷子带挞斗背回晒坝。

大概是儿时曾对他产生过敬佩的感情吧，我没有批评他。我走过去拍了拍他的手臂，很亲热地说：

“长发叔，回去出工吧，开私荒是走资本主义道路，要批判的。以后不要再来搞了。”

他厚厚的嘴唇嗫嚅了一下，想说什么，却没有说出来，只是长长地叹了一口气，默默地收拾起工具，走了。

我望着他有些伛偻的背影，不禁想道：这个巨人怎么衰老得这样快？

这天晚上，我来到生产队长何二叔的家里，向他了解长发叔的情况。

坐下后，何二叔把烟锅往鞋帮上磕了磕，慢吞吞地说：“长发这几年遭整得恼火喽，大前年死妈，去年死老子，婆娘又拖个月后寒的病，屋头有点家底都抖空了。生产队这几年的情况你是晓得的，哪家不是越搞越穷?像长发这种老实人，不会去外头搞弄钱，日子过得就更苦了。去年分配时，工作队又卡超支户还钱，他家那点基本口粮还不够抵账，屋头真是锅儿挂起当钟打，娃娃崽崽要吃没吃，要穿没穿，造孽得很呵!”何二叔说话时，脸色十他阴沉。

“照这样，更要好好参加集体生产才行，锅里有了，碗里才会有嘛。”我说。

“他天天都在队上做活路，从没偷过懒。”

“今天我就亲眼看见他开私荒，你晓得不!”

“他给我讲过。”

“是你同意的?”

“嗯”

“二叔，你昨个不坚持原则?要是叫上边晓得了，你我都脱不了爪爪。”

何二叔见我发了脾气，不开腔了，闷着脑壳吧嗒吧嗒地咂叶子烟。 ‘

稍停，我又对何二叔说：“这样吧，二叔，明天你去跟他讲，叫他把那块荒土交给生产队，由生产队给他记几天工。”

“记几天工？你说得轻巧，要讲你去讲，我说不来这话。”何二叔吐了一口烟，撑起身出门走了。

我愣在那里，又气又急。

何二叔这人就是这样，对上级的指示总爱打折扣；你要是批评他，他就闷着不开腔，说多了，扯起脚就走。真拿他没办法。第二天，我只好亲自去找长发叔。刚走到晒坝边，就见他过来了。他提着一把挖田用的两齿锄，走路的样子显得十分疲乏。我迎上去和他打个招呼后，便把昨晚上想好的意见告诉他。我原以为他会冒火的，谁想到他并不感到惊讶，也没表示反对，沉默片刻，他点了点头，算是同意了。我高兴地抓住他的胳膊，说：“长发叔，这才像个贫下中农嘛，我早就知道你会坚持走社会主义道路的。你家有困难，我们慢慢想办法解决。”

我这番热情话，并没有感动他，他只是苦笑一下，然后和三三两两走过来的社员—起出工去了。

这件事过去半个月。谁会想到，意料不到的情况竟会在昨天发生呢?

昨天早上，我陪着下队来检查生产的公社副书记老汤到田边地角去转悠了一圈。汤副书记虽说是个老农村干部，这几年不知咋搞的，嘴巴上也爱挂着“阶级斗争”呀，“资本主义”呀、“唯生产力论”呀、“反击右倾翻案风”呀这些政治名词。当他看到我写在田坎上、山坡上那些标语时，着实夸奖了我一番，说我“年轻有为”“有政治头脑”，我听着这些赞扬的词儿，心里感到乐滋滋的。

我和汤副书记一边走，一边胡扯乱谈着。忽然，汤副书记指着前边说道：“喂，小黄，那不是许长发吗?他一个人在那里干什么?是不是开私荒?”

我抬头一看，心里咯噔一跳，凉了半截。

前边正是长发叔开的那块荒土，只见长发叔弯着腰在捡土里的石块，“唉，这人真是，怎么偏偏在今天……”我气极了，隔老远就朝他大喝：“长发叔，你咋个又来整啦!”他听见我的声音，连头都没抬，绕到坡那边不见了。我跑过去一看，这块荒土已经变了样子，土块砸得细细的，里面一根杂草也没有，平平整整的厢垅里，一片青嫩的土荞苗苗倔强地拱出地面。

汤副书记也走拢来。我知道这种事情是瞒不过他的，只好照直把事情的原委向他作了汇报，末了，我说：“汤书记，你看，这件事该怎么办呢?”

汤副书记嘿嘿一笑，轻松地说：“你呀，硬是豆渣捏的脑壳，这种资本主义尾巴，一刀就砍了嘛!今天下午派几个人把土荞苗苗挖了，再开会批判批判，一来断了他走资本主义的路，二来教育教育群众。”

我望了望土里那一片鲜嫩的青苗，有些不情愿地说：“他已经种上了，就让他收这一季吧，反正这土也是荒着的。”

汤副书记脸色严肃起来了，他说：“小黄，这就是资本主义，搞阶级斗争，可不能手软呵!”

听汤副书记这一讲，我也觉得应该这么办了，和资本主义斗争，当然不能手软，何况我正在争取入党哩。再说，长发叔这人也太自私，不打击他一下，怎么把人心扭在集体上呢?想到这里，我打定了主意。

送走汤副书记后，我找了几个知识青年，向他们交代了任务，便向长发叔的“资本主义荒土”进发了。

消息跑得真快，不一会，队里就传开了。只有长发叔自己不知道，我早就把他打发到大队猪场出圈肥去了。社员们三三两两站在屋檐脚，冲着我们议论：

“自留地收了，场也不准赶，刨点荒土又是资本主义，总要给人留条路啊!”

“许长发太老实，要是我，就把婆娘娃娃拖到公社去，张着嘴巴要吃，看他们咋个办。”

一到长发叔的荒土里，我指挥几个知青三下五除二，不到一刻钟，就把一块平平整整的土挖得乱七八糟。我舒了一口气，正要掏手巾擦汗，只见何二叔急急忙忙跑来。他喘着气问我：“你真的挖了?你呀，唉!你咋个不想一下，长发晓得会出哪样事!”

说完，气冲冲地走了。

何二叔的话，使我有些担忧起来。

吃过晚饭，我到长发叔家去。好些人站在他家门口，七嘴八舌地在说什么，一看见我，阴一个阳一个地溜了。

长发叔蹲在一块石头上，正捧着大土碗吃饭，见我过来，他态度漠然地指着一条小板凳，说：“黄同志，你坐。”

待我坐下去后，他又朝我苦笑一下，说道：“我吃这个饭，实在请不起你。”

我眼朝他的大土碗里望去，心里不禁一颤：那哪里是饭?清汤寡水，黄糊糊的，几片菜叶漂浮在里面。想不到这个巨人吃的竟是这种饭食!我为自己下队二十多天，没注意到群众的困难，感到万分内疚。

“长发叔，你那块荒土上的荞子……”

“挖了算罗，怨不得你。”长发叔打断我的话，抬起头苦笑一下。稍停，又说：“都怪我没出息；害了

你们……唉!我也晓得上头不准开荒，不准刨自留地，我实在是没办法呀，屋头连耗子偷的粮食都没得，娃娃崽崽饿得淌清口水，你叫我咋个办!……”他沉重地叹息着，把头埋了下去。

忽然，从屋里钻出两个光屁股的娃娃—二毛和三毛，各人端着个土巴碗，望着长发叔怯生生地叫着：

“饿，爸爸，我饿!”

“爸爸，我还要!”

长发叔望了望眼里噙着泪水的娃娃，扭头对我说：“连这样的饭，娃娃们都吃不饱。”

二毛和三毛又叫起来。

长发叔的手颤抖着，把剩下的半钵稀饭分给了他们。

“二毛!三毛!把饭给爸爸，他做了一天活路，还没吃东西哩!”一个瘦弱的女人—长发叔的妻子，站在房门口吼道。

二毛和三毛望着妈妈冒火的样子，急忙把碗又端到长发叔面前，懂事地说：“爸爸吃，吃了做活路。”

长发叔的脸异常痛苦的抽搐着，他突然从石凳上跳下来，用筷子朝二毛劈头一下。二毛被吓得“哇哇”地哭起来，

手里的碗啪地摔碎了，糠菜稀饭洒了一地。我忽然发现有两颗晶莹的泪珠在长发叔的眼眶里滚动。他突地蹲在上，捧着头呜咽起来。

我的心猛地一紧，好像掉进冷水里，浑身都冒起鸡皮疙瘩。我走过去安慰他：“长发叔，不要难过了。二天不要去开荒，有困难就依靠集体。”

我和长发叔正说话，只见何二叔领着公社的小通讯员朝我们走来，说：“到处都找不到你，这是汤副书记给你的通知。”

我打开纸条，上面写着：

小黄同志：

关于许发长开荒一事，发生在普遍学习大寨经验的时候，我们认为性质是极其严重的，对这种资本主义自发势力，必须给予坚决打击。经公社党委研究，决定许长发进公社学习班检查交代。见条后，请立即通知本人，自带口粮，被子，于明天上午来公社报到。

汤世昌　即日

仿佛被人抽了一皮鞭，我的每一根神经都颤动起来：要长发叔进学习班，这一家人怎么活?再说，他又从哪里去“自带口粮”!我不由倒抽了一口冷气，心里想，该怎样把这件事告诉长发叔呢?

何二叔看出了我的神情，不安地问道：“小黄，出了哪样事?”我迟疑了一下，把“通知”递给他。

何二叔看完“通知”，发出一声沉重的叹息。

“二叔，究竟出了哪样事?”长发叔的妻子似乎预感到了什么，也从旁问道。

“通知长发进学习班交代。”

“进学习班?咋个得了嘛!”长发叔的妻子被这个晴天霹雳震惊了，她捂住脸，转身跑进屋去。“唔唔，唔唔!”草房里传出她的抽泣声。

长发叔撑起身来，直瞪瞪地望着我，嘴唇颤抖着：“黄，黄同志，这是，真的?”

我的心咚咚直跳。他那呆滞的目光，那愁苦的面容，使我觉得自己做错了什么事。我不敢看他，低下头喃喃地说：“长发叔，是公社党委研究决定的。”

长发叔的嘴唇急剧地抽搐着，半天才吐出一句话：“这简直是不要人活啦！”

那绝望的声音，使我的心都要裂了。不知道为什么，我忽然想到荷包里的皮夹，急忙掏出来，从里面取出一张十斤的粮票，默默地塞到他手里，然后转身走了。

我万万没有想到，长发叔竟会在这天晚上上吊自杀了。

当我赶到长发叔家时，屋子里已挤满了村里的社员群众。长发叔的尸体停在院子里，他高大的身躯上盖着一件蓑衣，一双异常长大的脚裸露在外面。他的妻子扑在尸体上，一边号啕，一边诉说着：“晤……，长发呀，你就这样去了，丢下我们孤儿寡母依靠谁?你一生一世没做过亏心事，咋个落得这个下场?唔……，长发呀!你死得好惨，连话都不留一句，唔唔……”。周围的人抹着眼泪，叹息着。

二毛和三毛站在妈妈的背后，扯着妈妈的衣襟，连声呼唤：

“妈妈，我要爸爸，要爸爸!”

“爸爸起来!爸爸起来!”

我的心一阵绞痛，眼泪夺眶而出，挤出了人群……

啊，眼前是哪里？这不是长发叔开的那块荒土吗？一霎时，二十多天来的往事，都一起涌到我的心头；我仿佛看见长发叔正弯着腰在捡土里的石块，他猛地扭头对我苦笑着说：“连这样的饭，娃娃们都没有饱的吃。”我仿佛看见汤副书记站在土边边，严厉地说：“这就是资本主义!”

我无力地蹲在地上，抓起一把泥土使劲捏着、捏着……

（原载《边疆文学》1980年第2期）

山　那　边

卢永康

乡下来人讲，幺嫂撇下男人，跟一个四川裁缝跑了。她男人不报案，也懒得去找，说：“脚生在各人的肚皮上，跑了算了。”

我曾在那个边远的山村当知青。到生产队的第一天，刚腾出杂物的小石墙房里外挤满了人。大家看稀奇。脏兮兮的娃儿们，眼睛滴溜溜转，好亮。女人们走来走去，摸摸这样，看看那样，叽叽喳喳。一个瘪嘴老奶的眼泪包都包不住：“造孽哟，独巴丁一个娃儿，为哪样遭下放?”顿时把我的革命豪情浇灭了一半。还是男人们稳重，叼着叶子烟杆站在圈外边，吧嗒吧嗒，很少开腔。

“等我看一回，等我看一回!”

她扒开众人，咋咋呼呼挤进来，话音未落，已冲到我的鼻子底下。我赫退了一步。她愣了一会，随后咯咯笑：“搞半天，知青是个人不是?我还说是哪样东西!”

她的牙齿好白，整齐，乡下少见。

这就是幺嫂，河对门的人，年纪比我小，头个月嫁来的时候，差点从手扒岩摔下去。她男人是生产队会计，文化高，会用算盘打加减法，会算工分，半个寨子喊他幺哥。幺哥做活路勤快，打婆娘也勤快。乡下人多用赶场计算日子。幺哥说在明处：“婆娘些嘛，一场打顿把两顿就够了，打多了不管用。”他爱在男人们面前炫耀：“我家婆娘肉多，打起舒服!”

幺嫂对别人凶，却任随男人打。打过的第二天，照样嘻嘻哈哈。她肉多。

那天下大雨，队长没得喊做活路，一寨子石磨响。她独自撑一把红油纸伞进了我的小石屋。根本没有征求主人同意的打算，她把箱子、柜子、抽屉一个个打开，看一下又砰地关上。嘴里不停：“天，你有五双鞋，比我还多!”“妈也，这个是哪样东西?像个芭蕉扇，碰到细线就响，怪眉日眼的。”“可惜，这样好的衣柜装书。这样多书，你的脑壳装得完?”“喂哟，还有姑娘的照片呢，是你家屋头的?”直到她兴味索然地离开，我除了喊两声幺嫂外，没来得及说一句话。

我长得矮小，瘦，开始做活路只配和女人们一起。薅二道苞谷最苦，腰杆几乎要折断，天热，苞谷叶在脸上手臂上割开一道道血路路，汗水一浸，痛得难熬。随便到哪块地，幺嫂总占我旁边的一沟。薅着薅着，眼看我被拉下，她的锄头便伸过来，帮我一大截。婆娘们都笑我，她不笑。

那件事，我看得清清楚楚。在大麻窝薅苞谷，刘老二家婆娘像往常一样，把嫩娃娃捆在树上。娃儿抱着树干睡着了。幺嫂轻手轻脚走过去，看了好一阵，突然伸手在娃儿屁股上掐了一下，大概很重，娃儿惊咋咋嚎。幺嫂躲了。等刘老二家婆娘跟头扑趴地赶来，幺嫂才闪过来责怪：“你不会找一棵蚂蚁少的树?”我没有揭发。我感激幺嫂对我的关照，也同情她不会生崽。会计三天两头骂：老母猪都下得好几窝了。

在晒坝上分黄豆。我可怜家中只有一口破铁锅的车麻哥，把称给我的一份倒进他家口袋。幺嫂把我拉到烘房背后，咬牙切齿地骂：“少充好人，车麻哥懒得很，只会烧死老蛇吃，穷死活该。”

我终于盼到了和男人们背牛粪的那一天。把牛从圈里赶出去，用钉耙挖，草粪臭得新鲜，臭得好闻。粪水从背篼底往下滴，湿透了屁股，淌到脚杆弯，灌满了解放鞋，走起来滑溜溜的。我一咬牙，一次背起一百五十六斤半。幺嫂不知从哪里钻出来，把我的背篼抬下靠在坎子上，拿一个用苞谷壳编的背搭子给我套上，大声武气警告那些出粪的、掌磅秤的：“大男蛮汉的，不要欺人家知青噢。”刘老二斜眉吊眼地说：“儿喽，知青又不是你家老公。”幺嫂抓一把牛粪甩过去：“你小龟儿把我谅死了不是?我还不愿找这种老公，难得养活!”我想笑，又想哭。

我爱好文艺。公社开大会，我请了中学一位教师搭档，讲了一段相声，讲计划生育的，方言。幺嫂坐在最前排，笑得拜天拜地，嘴里直哼哼：“妈也，我的妈也。”会后，公社书记慧眼识珠，要我搞一个宣传队，长贫下中农的志气。幺嫂天天缠我，死活要参加，说她在河对门就喜欢看花灯。没办法，我编了个不伦不类的山歌齐唱，她参加，唱得很卖力。吃完晚饭，男人蜷在柴火灶旁咂叶子烟，她就跑到小学校来唱。回到家，早吹灯睡饱了觉的会计爬起来，揪起头发打她一顿，然后骑上她的肚皮，弄得她像被杀的猪一样嚎。第二天，她还来，还唱。

那天，县里来的宣传部长要看边远山区农民的演出。公社书记高度重视，说要化起妆演。没有颜料，我拿什么化妆?万万没想到，幺嫂救了急。她用红纸剪两个圆，蘸了水，往两边脸蛋一贴，过会儿把纸撕开：“嗨，这不是红了么?”

我傻乎乎看着幺嫂脸上的两团红印，马上想起了木偶戏《半夜鸡叫》里周扒皮的老婆，觉得胸口好闷。可是幺嫂高兴，公社书记也高兴，演员们都觉得是个好办法，我只得让大家剪红纸，蘸了水甚至口水往脸上贴。幺嫂很得意，窜前跳后教别人。

我的知青生活就要结束了，我要回城了。临走那天晚上，寨子里男女老少又塞满了我的小石屋。一群姑娘媳妇每人送我一双鞋垫，幺嫂不在她们当中。有人说，会计又在打她。

第二天，好大的雪，漫天遍野白茫茫。幺嫂大清早来拍我的门，她对着门缝说：“你们这些人转来转去都是城里的。往后，带起你家爱人下乡来玩。啊?”我头一次听她说“爱人”这种文绉绉的词。等我穿好衣服打开门，只看到一串深深的脚窝。

我一直没有带妻儿去看幺嫂。

现在，她快40岁了，却跟着四川裁缝跑了，到哪儿找去?

（选自《山那边》贵州人民出版社1999年出版）

家　　谱

肖江虹

一

母亲把日历翻过去，回过头对我说，下个礼拜就是七月半了，该给老人们写包了。

在母亲眼里，没有比七月半更重要的节日了。七月半到来的前半个月，母亲就开始变得小心翼翼，见到窗棂上停只蝴蝶，就说那一定是回家过月半的先人的化身，总之是这个时段出现在房前屋后的生灵都是幸福的，它们在家里健在的老人们的荫庇下，可以无忧无虑的逍遥好一阵子。

我们无双镇一到七月半就这样子，除了供奉饭食，打扫庭院这些仪式外，最重要的就是给逝去的先人们写包了。写包又叫封包，程序十分复杂。把买来的纸钱用专门的工具打制成有钱孔的冥币，再用白纸把分放均匀的纸钱用统一的方式包裹起来，最后用毛笔在白纸上书写好收包先人的辈分、姓名、纸包书写以及火化的时间。纸包书写格式要求是极其严格的，比如收包者是父亲，就要写成“故显考某某老大人收用”，母亲则写成“故显妣某氏老孺人收用”。除了格式要严格遵循，字迹还要端正，错别字是一定不能出现的，小时候我问过母亲为什么写错字不行呢，母亲就摸着我的头说：写错了先人们就收不到了，那该多可惜啊!

格式虽然严格，但对封包的数量却没有统一标准。这要根据死者和封包人的关系亲疏来决定封包的多少。每年封包的时候，父亲和母亲故去的直系亲人是最多的，每个人的摞在一起，都到我脖子处了。关系疏远一些的，比如父亲的舅舅、舅妈一类的就少了许多，五六个就成。我上了高中后，写包的任务就落到了我的头上，用父亲的话说，送你读书，还不是图个家里有个写写画画的。

我把桌子搬到院子里，太阳很好，安安静静的朗照着，树叶儿也泛着油亮亮的光，几只蜻蜓在院子上空追逐盘旋，一切祥和得像母亲的脸。

我铺开白纸开始封包。母亲颤巍巍的从屋子里出来，端出来一碗面粉熬成的糨糊放在桌子上，就拉条凳子坐在旁边静静地看着我封包。我从五岁开始和父亲一起封包，这些年来，把封包这门活计练得又快又好。母亲看着我，眼神里全是赞赏和自豪，她把封好的包拿在手里，轻轻的摩挲，然后把它们码得整整齐齐。

晌午，包终于封完了。母亲早就把毛笔和墨汁准备好了，最后母亲从里屋取出来一个红布包裹，包裹平平整整的，像我们无双镇用来盖房的薄石片。坐下来，母亲剥笋子样的一层层揭开一方猩红，包裹就真相大白了。那是我们老许家的家谱。家谱是线装的，纸张是我们无双镇自己漂出来的黄表纸。无双镇有十多个纸坊，造纸方式虽然原始，工序却复杂，这里好多上了年纪的老人都是造纸的好手。无双镇造出来的纸像这个地头上姑娘们的脸皮，薄得连阳光都包不住的。薄是薄些，但韧劲很好，时间再久也

不会变脆的。这样的纸张用来做家谱纸是最好的了。

母亲把家谱递给我的样子神圣般严肃，双手托举，腰弓一样的弯曲着。我伸出一只手，母亲使劲摇头，脸也涨得红了，我转过身子，双手高过胸，母亲才把那方淡黄递过来。我看见母亲眼角竟然湿润了，像是完成了某种神圣的交接。

我双手托着线装书，一股柔软的冰凉在指缝中游走，我似乎闻到了一种遥远的气息，淡淡的，散发着陈旧的墨香，还有一些涩滞的，让人呼吸不畅的尘土味儿。我小的时候，看见父亲写包的时候用家谱，就问父亲家谱是什么东西？父亲就停下手里的笔，眉头紧锁，很想给我一个圆满的解释，最后还是无奈地说长大你就知道了。

无双镇的纸质地再好，终究敌不过岁月的侵蚀。家谱还是泛黄了，面容呈现出可怜的憔悴，要不是封面上“许氏家谱”几个柳体字还筋强骨健的话，就真没有精气神了。我掀开它，动作轻柔而缓慢，怕把它弄疼了。扉页上的楹联是颜体字，上联是：不求金玉重重贵。下联是：唯愿子孙个个贤。第一页记述的是一个叫许闻达的。我刚念出这个名字，母亲在一旁迫不及待地插了话：“是你爷爷的爷爷的爷爷，做过康熙皇帝平藩的将军，是个很大的官呢！”母亲说这话的时候脸上有阳光一样的颜色。

看得出，这是我们老许家的大人物，有关他的记述占了整整一页。官名处还用红笔画了圈，字体也大了好几号。

夜晚。我伏在桌案上端端正正的书写着。母亲依旧坐在我旁边，父亲在墙角的躺椅上吧嗒吧嗒地吸着旱烟，他的眼睛微闭着，烟雾浸漫在一脸的沟壑里，像大雾弥漫时的无双镇。

“许正文？”我把头扭过去问。

父亲喷出一口烟雾，缓缓睁开眼，说就给个月月红吧。父亲说完又把眼睛合上了。我知道，这个时候看上去安详的父亲其实和安详无关。父亲小时候上过私塾，是我们无双镇为数不多的文化人，无双镇谁家有个写写画画的都会来请父亲，请的时候态度也极其的谦恭。长年累月的谦恭也让父亲的心气越来越高，眼长期半闭着，神情也变得和无双镇的石板路一样冰凉。话也越来越少，最后每句话都拐弯抹角的暗藏机锋，让老实巴交的乡人头疼不已。

我说月月红是多少个呢？母亲说一年有几个月？我说十二个月啊！母亲说那就写十二个嘛。

我依旧写得很慢，很认真，虽然手开始有些犯软，还是咬牙坚持着。倒不是我有多虔诚，而是稍稍潦草一点，母亲的手指就会如期而至，在我的脑门狠狠一戳。抖了抖酸麻的手，我懒懒地翻开了家谱新的一页。

我有些惊讶了。

家谱上每一个成员的籍贯、经历、出生和死亡年月日时，死亡原因，安葬地都有详细记录。唯独这一页除外。

页面上只有一个叫“许东生”的名字，名字后面是一片辽阔的淡黄。像无双镇秋天西地的那片草场，几个土丘，再向西延伸，就是一望无际的秋意。

“许东生？”我对母亲说。我当时距离母亲很近，清楚地看到了母亲听到这个名字时的反应。她先是一怔，安详的眼神里像是扔进了一块巨石，砸起一人多高的水柱。母亲那一刻是慌乱的，甚至有点魂不守舍了。喘气也变得粗壮起来，气息拂过我的脖颈，像刀刃从肤发上掠过。这一次，母亲没有照例转过头询问躺椅上的父亲，而是粗暴的伸过手来把这一页淡黄揭过了去。

我回头看了看躺椅上的父亲，除了嘴角有一些淡淡歪斜的痕迹，他依然纹丝不动。

“下一个。”父亲的声音像雪夜从门缝里挤进来的寒风。

二

冥包封写完毕了，它们被母亲规规矩矩的堆放在堂屋的大桌上，和水果、猪头一起变成了供奉品，香烟缭绕中，这些冥包被赋予了一种神秘而特殊的含义。母亲依然平静地穿梭在各个屋子之间，父亲仍旧躺在院子里晒太阳。一切平静如水。

我却被那方神秘的淡黄困扰住了。

许东生是谁？为什么在那页纸面上只有一个突兀的名字？在详细的家谱中，这个名字显得是那样的神秘和另类。那厚厚的一摞冥包中，居然没有一个是属于他的。父亲和母亲为什么在遭遇这个名字的时候会那样的惶恐和不知所措？

这些疑问让我格外的亢奋。

我搬了个凳子坐在父亲旁边。

“许东生是谁?”我的口气很舒缓。

父亲睁开眼，侧过头看着我，不说话。

“许东生是谁?”我在音调里掺杂了一些不屈不挠的味道。他的样子有些奇怪，我在他的面前成条蛆虫了，因为他的眼神里尽是厌恶。好半天，他的眼睛又合上了，像一块幕布，戏还没有开始，那面黑色就拉上了。

父亲那天再没睁开过眼，他的沉默没有让我有丝毫放弃的意思，弄清楚这个人物来龙去脉的念头反而愈加强烈。

半夜，蚊虫们在房间异常的活跃，我的大脑和它们一齐在黑暗里欢歌。“许东生”几个字在我的额头上跳来跳去，然后从我的眼眶里钻进大脑，先是在大脑的左边形成一个人影，影子高大干瘦，像一根失去水分的竹竿；紧接着影子愈发清晰，我努力的想看清楚横在面前的那张脸，可脸部的五官却一塌糊涂，我竭力的往前凑，凑近了也没有用，那张面孔还是模糊得像暗夜里的无双镇，你可以感觉到它的存在，甚至可以准确地说出哪儿是山，哪儿是水，哪儿是房屋，哪儿是土丘，可你就是看不明白。

这一夜，这个影像一直折磨着我，他时而高时而矮，时而远时而近，时而清晰时而模糊。直到公鸡在鸡窝里把带有粪味的打鸣声扔满了整个无双镇，我仍然没有摆脱这个影像的困扰。

我从床上爬起来，母亲已经把院子扫完了一大半。我过去接过扫帚，装得很是孝顺的样子说妈您歇着我来扫。母亲的眼睛鼓得大大的，以为我又要给她讨钱赶集，慌忙把口袋捂得紧紧的说要钱是没有的。我笑笑说妈您别大惊小怪的，我就想知道许东生到底是谁？母亲没有接我的话，而是一把抢过扫帚，呼啦呼啦的又开始扫地，她的脸色也不好，和堆在墙角的茄子叶一样的颜色。

“把牛赶上坡去。”母亲扔给我一句尖厉干燥的话。

我和我们家老牛一前一后地在无双镇后山的山脊上缓缓的移动着。我家的老耕牛都快九岁了，无双镇像它这样高龄的耕牛已经不多了。可能是上了年纪的原因，老牛走得特别慢，目光也格外的悠闲，隔一阵子还会抬起头来欢欢的吼两嗓子。老牛是我一手带大的，我不知道它的来历，只知道是父亲在集市上花钱买回来的，到我们家的时候个头还小，怯怯地站在院子里，眼神里充满了不安，小蹄子不住的刨着地。父亲说刚断奶的犊子都这样，慢慢把娘忘掉就好了。

老牛悠闲的在野地里吃草，我坐在石头上看天。无双镇的天遇上朗照就显得特别的高，山啊树啊看起来离天就远了，远得呼吸都畅快起来。神奇的还是远处那些云朵，打着滚似的变来幻去，刚才还是一整牛，眨巴个眼就变成僵硬的石块了。我的眼睛就在云端上奔跑，希望看见一些自己神往的东西。果然，西边一株高大的杉树顶着一个人，干瘦的，两条胳膊长长地垂着，脑袋半歪着，薄薄的像风中的剪纸。我想那一定就是我们老许家家谱里头的那个人了，他该是个瘦子，五官也不好看，走起路来还没有精神劲儿。

许东生！一会儿在我脑子里，一会儿又爬到了云端上，就这样上蹿下跳的没完没了。

我想我应该去问问爷爷的。我们老许家以前人丁兴旺，到爷爷这里就开始悬乎起来，三代单传让爷爷在一惊一乍中抖抖索索战战兢兢的过了大半辈子。在爷爷眼里，我肩负着重振老许家的神圣使命，所以我从小就被爷爷当宝贝蛋子惯着。再老眼昏花，一见到我他就两眼放光。关键的是，这么多年来，他对我几乎就是有求必应。

爷爷和奶奶住镇西头，那里住的大多是老年人。我们无双镇就这样，孩子娶了媳妇就成横生出去的枝干了，得分家，分家出来的儿子们就往东建房造屋，形成了无双镇东边儿子西边爹的独特格局。

西头全是长长的胡同，胡同一个接一个，循环往复的缠绕着。我顺着胡同一直走，胡同沟子里尽是新鲜青苔的味儿，我特别喜欢这个味道，有些幽远，又有些厚实，像用鼻孔去阅读一本厚厚的古书，苍凉中透着清雅。

果然，推开门爷爷的眼睛就亮了。两只手还在空中兴奋的乱摇，像见到了阔别多年的故友。连他屁股下的藤椅也发出嘎吱嘎吱的快乐的响声。一进门我就迫不及待地蹲在他的藤椅边问。

许东生是谁？

爷爷的眼睛在那一瞬间就黯淡下去了，像一汪到了尽头的烛火。然后他把干枯的身子紧紧地贴住藤椅，眼睛定定地望着挂满灰尘的屋梁。

好久，那汪烛火又开始慢慢升腾起来，爷爷侧了一下身子，我就听见了他骨头枯朽崩塌的声响。

“他是我的父亲，长得嘛……高大，特别高大，是我们这一带有名的袍哥，手下有好几十名兄弟，都是些狠人呢。”

“都干些啥事呢？”我问。

“杀富济贫，就是抢富人的钱物来帮助穷人。”

“真的？”

爷爷点点头，花白的脑袋像夯土墙时的大锤，沉重得足以敲碎灶上的那口大铁锅。

“那家谱里为什么不写呢？”

“袍哥是啥？土匪！有啥好写的。”

回家的路依旧要穿越那些胡同，青苔的味儿还在，无影无踪的弥漫在细窄的胡同里。伸手在空中捞一把，在鼻子边把手一松，竟然有些闷人。胡同实在太长了，最后我被闷得连脚步都变得踉跄起来。

三

我不信。

我们无双镇的花灯调子里，杀富济贫的都是当英雄来歌颂的。四处宣扬还来不及呢！哪有连家谱都语焉不详的道理。再说，你看父亲和母亲，我一提到许东生这个名字，两张脸都快成煤块了。

我连续几夜照例看见那个人影，还是干瘦干瘦的，没有一点高大威猛的痕迹。我想这样的体形哪能做袍哥呢？一阵风怕就没影儿了呢！

吃完晚饭，我对母亲说，我想把我们老许家家谱写完整。

正在灯下纳鞋底的母亲惊讶地抬起头，半截棉线还叼在嘴里。她把棉线从嘴里抽出来，说写家谱？就你？再说家谱也是完整的啊，没有地头空着啊！我说许东生那个地头空着呢！母亲说你也不知道这个祖宗的事情，你咋写呢?总不能胡乱写吧。我说我知道，爷爷告诉我的。母亲一笑，把凳子挪到我旁边，饶有兴致地问我爷爷是怎么给你说的呢?

我把身子端了端，表情也整理得严肃些说：许东生，生于某年某月某日，卒于某年某月某日，无双镇人氏，是本地有名的袍哥，手下好汉云集，常行劫富济贫之义事，为时人所敬仰……

我还没说完，母亲就笑了，笑得五官都挤成了一堆。她摇摇手说这是爷爷给你说的，我点点头，母亲笑得更欢了，最后连腰都直不起来了。

我不信。我冷冰冰的说。

母亲不笑了，她捋直身子，说一个死人和你有什么关系呢？你干嘛这样刨根问底哟?

我说是我祖宗呢！祖宗的事情我该知道吧！

妈，你就给我说到底是怎样的，好不好？我哀求。

母亲往父亲屋子里看了看，嘴唇动了动，还是摇了摇头。最后母亲把嘴凑到我耳朵边说去问问你大伯公吧！

大伯公是爷爷的堂兄，身体比爷爷好，头发也不见白，都八十的人了还能担担水在镇西头的胡同里四平八稳的行走。大伯公脾气不如身体，火爆得像六月正午的日头。

寻着大伯公的时候，他正在镇西头的大杨树下对和他下棋的赵家老头挥以老拳。远远地就听见他喝骂的声音和赵家老头哀号的声音。赵家老头往东逃遁的时候和我擦肩而过。

“你个狗日的许老鬼，赢得起输不起的老东西。”赵家老头边跑边骂。

我过去拉住宜将剩勇追穷寇的大伯公。劝他说下棋就下棋，干嘛打架呢?

是他被我打，小崽子你搞清楚了。大伯公吼。

我慌忙点头。

帮他捡起一地的棋子儿，我把他扶到石凳上坐下。

关于许东生的事，母亲让我来问大伯公是对的。在我的印象里，大伯公是我这辈子见过的最没有撒谎天赋的人，他的话就像射出去的响箭，呼啦有声。我们无双镇讲究礼节，去谁家遇到吃饭，主人总要问“吃过了吗?”，客人不管吃没吃过都会客套地说吃过了吃过了，有些还会拍拍干瘪的鼓气肚子说你看刚吃过还胀着呢！只有大伯公，遇到这种情况主人问吃过了吗？他就答还没吃呢！主人说那吃点吧！大伯公就往饭桌上瞅瞅说妈的菜太孬了老子不吃。这个世界如果连大伯公的话都不可靠，那就真没可靠的了。

我拍了拍他身上的尘土，看来两个老头在地上肉搏过。问，许东生是谁啊?

大伯公抬起头，说你问他干啥啊？我说随便问问。

“是你爷爷的爹，就是我的叔公，我父亲是你爷爷的大哥。”果然是一串响箭。

我心头一喜：“他是不是高个子?”

“去，妈的，矮得像坨牛粪。”

“粗壮吗?”

“瘦得像根豇豆。”

“他是不是当过袍哥?”

大伯公笑了，露出两排猩红的牙床，牙床上点缀着几颗稀疏的黄牙。

“袍哥？就他哪样？在村子里耍耍狠还差不多。”

我吞了一口唾沫，继续问。

“他是咋死的呢?”

大伯公不笑了，也不应我的话，转而狠狠地骂：“和老子下棋敢耍赖，看老子明天不扒了你的皮。”

“许东生是咋死的呢?”我嗓门大大的问。

“姓赵的，最好别让老子看见你，那样你就等着睡棺材吧!”大伯公站起来用手指着远方继续骂。

我沮丧的埋下头。大伯公走了，他的步伐还是很稳健，夕阳把他的影子拉得长长的，变形成了一截冬日的老枯树。

四

日历又被母亲揭去了好几页。看得出母亲揭日历时的急迫心情，她恨不得一把抓掉中间的日子，一步踏入七月半。随着日子的临近，父亲和母亲也越来越虔诚，连平素架子大上了天的父亲也变得面色温和，整天把个脸整得笑模笑样的，好像祖宗们真的已经大驾光临了一般。

一大早，父亲就把扫帚绑在竹竿上拂扫屋梁上的尘埃，这个事情每年这个时候都是要做的，大约是想给回家的祖宗们一个相对舒适的环境，让他们吃得好住得好一些。我还在床上，屋子里弥漫着一股浓浓的灰尘味儿，我爬起来，父亲狠狠地瞪着我，像是我睡懒觉让他在祖宗们面前丢了脸似的。

我蹲在院子边刷牙，天空依然高远，风懒洋洋的摇着院子里几棵枣树。我心里空闹闹的，那个名字依然在我脑海里盘旋。我想也许此刻，他就立在某一个角落里，探头探脑地打量着这里的一切。转念一想又觉得不太可能，因为在我们老许家那本家谱里，他是最不受人待见的了，这样的境遇下，他八九怕是不会来的了。

有人猛拍了一下我的肩膀，连牙刷都给拍掉了。回过头，我看见了刘光荣。

刘光荣是我小时候的玩伴，因为家穷，小学毕业就回家跟父亲下地了。十一岁那年，他父亲在追小偷的时候被小偷捅死在镇西街的石板路上。我还记得那天天气很好，一大摊血在阳光下红得分外的耀眼。我仰起头，刘光荣的脑袋特别大，把一个天都遮住了。我说你干嘛呢光荣。他说找你啊！我说找我干嘛。他说我们家包还没写呢，这不来请你了吗。我站起来说没问题。

出门的时候，父亲说话了。

“你上哪儿去?”父亲声音低沉。

“去帮光荣他们家写包!”我答。

“不许去!”父亲的脸色陡然变了。

“为什么?”我问。

“我说不许去就是不许去!”父亲把手里的扫帚狠狠的掼在地上吼。

父亲的火也把我的火点起来了，从他拒绝让我知道家谱上那片空白的真相开始我就有火了。作为老许家的人，我觉得我有权利知道这个真相，可是所有的人对这件事都遮遮掩掩。一团火在我的心里开始旺旺的燃烧起来。

“我就要去，看你能把我怎么样？”我撂下狠话拉起刘光荣拔腿就走。

路上刘光荣说你老爸怎么会发这样大的火啊。我说鬼才知道呢！大约是我抢了他的饭碗吧。

光荣家的包没有我家的多，一小堆可怜巴巴的堆在墙角。家谱薄薄的一小本，油腻腻的不说，字迹也歪歪扭扭的。

屋子里光线不好，我叫光荣拉开了灯。

光荣妈给我倒来一碗水，老人好像老了不少，一蓬头发乱糟糟的像个鸟窝，手也格外的黑，把水放在我面前的时候，我看见她黑乎乎的指头正浸泡在水碗里。我写得很潦草，这样速度就快了许多。刘光荣坐在我旁边啧啧的羡慕，说这有文化就是好，要不是家穷，我说不定也能上高中、上大学的，那样写个包就用不着求人了。

我笑了笑，很快，我的笑容就凝固了。凝固住笑容的是刘氏家谱上的一行字。

刘新松，光绪三年生于无双镇，幼时蛮横好斗，成人后更是为祸乡里，与同乡许东生合称“无双二霸”，而立年伙同许东生在村西老树林奸淫过路女子，被愤怒乡邻双双乱棍击毙，尸首被野狗分食。谨为记。

“这个许东生不会是你们老许家人吧？”刘光荣指着家谱上的那个名字问。

“不是，肯定不是！”

我握笔的手一抖，白纸上慢慢绽开了一朵黑梅，在一方雪白间妖艳地盛开。

（原载《山花》2009年第12期）

江　湖

赵昊鹏

二更梆子响起之时，城内已是黯黑一片。

城外凤徙坡上，瑟瑟秋风已然透着一股寒意。远望昏黄月色笼罩下的临安城，艮琅思忖：义兄想必已调处妥当，立马就要出城了。

数日前，艮琅与义兄茯薪趁月黑风高之便，着实做了一票，把和记当铺掌柜富三的银库搬了个底儿朝天。待得天明发现失窃之时，平日高坐柜上冷眼观人泪流的富三顿时哭了个大雨倾盆，连滚带爬直奔知府衙门，差点就没把府衙外的羊皮鼓擂穿。大堂之上，富三一面痛陈所失之物，又如捣蒜泥般磕头恳请知府大人尽早破案，直把大堂上铺的西夏花砖砸出一道缝来。

这是艮琅在临安城做的第二票“营生”。第一票是九九重阳艮琅初到临安的夜里—那日一进临安，艮琅就到府城河边的漱玉坊走了一遭。虽则坊中薰香绣被春暖红绡，老鸨唤出的当家姐儿黛卿更是抚琴拈箫美目送盼，别具一番风情，艮琅却丝毫未起淫邪之念，艮琅记得师父所言：“盗亦道也，悟道之人贵心无旁骛。”熟了夜里要行的道儿，漱玉坊自无久留必要。

那夜营生做得倒也十分顺手，半支香的功夫，艮琅就把老鸨儿房中金钗珠子元宝细软尽收囊中。收拾停顿，艮琅燕子抄水飞出栏外脚尖尚未点地，但见一黑影掠上，雷霆闪电间艮琅已被点中檀中要穴，

连人带物被人掳于腰间飞奔而去。

睁眼之际，艮琅环顾四下，已然到了似是临安中上人家客厅堂上，一中年汉子正作解穴之举。

“兄若为囊中物之故，弟愿悉数奉上!”艮琅转身欲走。

“贤弟留步，吾候弟已多时也。”顷刻，肥羊花雕上桌，艮琅与那汉子喝了开来。

酒酣时刻，大汉自腰间掏出铭牌，艮琅方知其乃临安府衙捕头，江湖人称“铁手飞擒”的名捕茯薪，大惊之下作俯首就擒状。

“贤弟且莫惊恐，兄非有此意也。目下金人南侵已成必然之势，当今朝廷朽腐不堪，兄早生解甲养老之想。日间于弄玉坊观弟，眉宇自有侠义之相，兄欲与弟成就大事，以期共享荣华。”茯薪豪言既出，自是合了艮琅心意。

“敢问兄台何以识得弟之行径?”初出山门，第一票营生即告覆舟，艮琅愧感有辱师门，犹自心有不甘。

茯薪呵呵大笑，道：“漱玉坊黛卿姐儿风流无限，坊间嚣传‘房中秘术堪使仙翁思凡’，弟少年翩翩雅游坊中且作壁上观，若非盗者，或乎道哉?”

是夜，艮琅与茯薪义结八拜金兰之交。

翌日，艮琅茯薪夜入和记当铺银库，漫屋金银古玩，直让艮琅和茯薪搬了两个来回。临去，依义兄茯薪移人眼目误指金人所为之意，艮琅于壁上题留“燕山盗圣”之名。

“只此一票，待风平浪静，吾与贤弟开一饭庄，且过富贵快活日子。”茯薪对艮琅道：“明日子时，弟可携元宝少许登城西凤徙坡，兄带役使作抓捕状，弟可呼‘燕山盗圣去也!’自后山山洞假奔金人营寨而去，兄自会于洞口备马接应。而后兄可报盗案乃金人所为，弟可即时复归临安，吾与弟亦安享富贵也!”

如是，天一放黑艮琅就上了凤徙坡。趁着早，艮琅又把义兄告知的山洞走了一遍，艮琅犹加佩服义兄的侠肝义胆和细微周致。

山崖上数点昏鸦惊起，直冲云天而去。艮琅知道，义兄带着人马上来了。

“临安府的差役们听着，爷乃‘燕山盗圣’是也，受吾主金兀术差使，取富三些许银两以充军用，爷爷去也!”感觉来人已摸至跟前，艮琅把手中拎着的元宝袋子往周遭猛一撒，立时叮叮当当滚了满山遍野。差役慌抢之际，艮琅飞身而退。

茯薪果然如约等在洞口，“义兄……”—艮琅话音未落，一柄小刀已插入他的胸口。

倒下的那一刻，艮琅想起了离开山门时师父告诫他的话：“江湖险恶，恶于人心之难测，故盗者宜独行天下。”

“江湖……”临闭眼时，艮琅嘴里嘟囔着这两个字。

靖康十年春上，茯薪风光告老。

是年腊月初九，临安城铺陈极尽奢华的义字饭庄开张，掌柜的就是艮琅的义兄茯薪。

（选自《金山》2008年第十期）

散　　文

梦见祖母

李嘉宁

近来几次在梦中见到已故去十多年的祖母。昨晚，梦到已在外工作的我回家去看她，我要买些可口的菜与她在一起吃顿饭，她听后很高兴，拉着我的手说就要我和她一起吃。似乎有许多话要对我说，似乎要享受祖孙一同进餐的天伦之乐。醒来之后，我的眼角竟噙着泪花。

躺在床上，过去那有关祖母的一幕幕便浮现在眼前。小时候听祖母讲，她和祖父在青年时代便从大方来到修文一个叫“清水”的村寨教书。虽然人地生疏、举目无亲，但当地农民却对前来从事启蒙教育的“文化人”十分敬重。他们尊称祖父为“老师”，尊称祖母为“师母”。祖父教书，祖母便挑起了生活的重担，在那民不聊生的年代，以辛勤的劳作维持着一家人的生计。解放后，在身边只有父亲一个儿女的情况下，祖父和祖母仍义无反顾地支持父亲外出工作，去“奔自己的前程”。由于积劳成疾，祖父在父亲成家前就于“三年困难时期”的饥荒年代作古，遗骨至今还留在清水的土地上。

长期的生活重压，使得祖母的脊梁成了弓形，但她又义不容辞地肩起了拉扯孙辈一代的任务。待我们初谙人事后，她又给我们讲做人的道理，讲她在贵阳达德学校就读时如何与王若飞一同接受黄齐生先生的教诲，讲木兰从军的故事……记得讲到“落霞与孤鹜齐飞，秋水共长天一色”的妙处有由来时，她竟可讲得眉飞色舞。祖母就这样在我们幼小的心灵中播下了道义与文化的种子。

祖母的暮年，正值“文化大革命”结束后不久。当时，父亲因被极“左”分子诬为“与‘四人帮’有牵连的人”而正处于“被审查”阶段。祖母便是在家庭承受着经济和精神双重压力的境况下撒手归西的。祖母生前没有留下任何遗产，却给后代留下了可贵的品质—我认为这是比任何价值千万金的遗产都值得珍藏的财富。

工作之后常常想起祖母：祖母生前一些基本的物质需求都未能得到满足，要是她还健在该有多好，我一定倾己所有让她得到应该得到的。但，这已是不可能的了。每每想到这些，我就觉得是对祖母深深地欠下了一笔心债，感到愧疚不已。

无以为报，谨以些许文字表达自己的怀念与赎意。殷殷此情，不知祖母的在天之灵能得知否？

（原载《安顺日报》1993年7月8日）

烂漫樱桃花

李嘉颖

一夜春风，樱桃花竞相开放。我只能看见异乡的樱桃花了，而梦萦魂牵的，却是家乡庭院中莹白烂漫的樱桃花。

几年前，告别老屋，迁入新居，哥哥的同学送来一株拇指粗细的樱桃枝，我和妹妹欣喜若狂，挽上

衣袖就挖开了树坑，忙活了整整一个下午。常言说："樱桃好吃树难栽"，也许是诚心感动了上帝，樱桃树竟成活得很好，日渐粗壮。花树下，合家团聚，品茗谈笑，其乐融融。花谢吐叶，一片嫩绿，沐浴春风，倍增精神。结果了，红彤彤缀满枝头，上学前，翘嘴含上一颗，清甜满口。就是在寒冬，几杆虬枝刺向长空，无畏无惧，也让我驻足凝望，久久思索。我们几兄妹读书、工作，相继离开了家乡，终日陪伴父母的，就是这棵樱桃树了。

当初，我高考连年受挫，饱受煎熬的父母百般安抚。第二次失败的消息袭来，我藏进被筒。当我睡眼惺忪走出房间时，妈妈正披衣倚在樱桃树下，一夜之间已是两鬓染霜。现在，妈已退休，爸却舍不得放下那杆命运坎坷的笔。妈的手摔折了，家中没有告诉我，当我偶然得知消息冲进家门时，二老劈头就问："回来干啥？"爸告诉同事："此生所得，三个孩子一部书（《修文县志》）。"爸的生日，我因为工作没能回家，匆匆去邮局发了一封电报："三十年哺儿女呕心沥血鬓发早白；花甲岁纂志书食草伏枥壮志未已。"后来爸爸冷冷地说："花那些冤枉钱。"可哥哥悄悄告诉我，看完电报，爸已是热泪盈盈了。

中学时代，门前的小院是同学聚会的场所，樱桃树总是慷慨地伸出繁枝茂叶为我们遮风蔽日，倾听书生意气般的"人生宣言"。现在，我不常回家，朋友们也已各散一方，偶尔遇见，都用疲惫的眼光打量对方，双手紧紧相握，不约而同地说："好久不见。"前日学着给友人写了一首诗，开句是："江湖颠沛七八年，疏离不辨故人颜。"可欢言同聚日，把酒论英雄，我的朋友们一定会大有作为的。

樱桃花开了，故乡的樱桃花一定更加烂漫。

（原载《修文报》1994年3月25日，作者"穷达"系李嘉颖笔名）

箐口杜鹃红

李元明

阳春三月，正值"吹面不寒杨柳风"时节，我和德政乡党委副书记刘永友踏着羊肠小道向元庆村走去。路过箐口时，映入眼帘的是满山竞相绽放的杜鹃花，天然地把箐口坡围成一道屏障。

顺着弯弯曲曲的石板路爬到大丫口。放眼望去，莽苍苍，郁葱葱，火红的杜鹃花海十分壮观。人们常说"箐口三月杜鹃红似火"。红是杜鹃花的本色，红是箐口坡的灵魂，红是箐口人的骄傲。它是道德、理想、情操的象征。身置箐口花海，我的思绪回到40年前这里发生的一件可歌可泣的往事中。

故事的主人翁是时任六广区长的梁方膏和区武装委员会主任的魏怀远。1950年3月5日，梁方膏和魏怀远按照县委安排，由留任的原国民党德政乡乡长李永芳带路，从德政乡公所前去铁厂坝召开征粮动员大会。他们万万没有料到，这个李永芳已于头一天串通息烽刘法政匪部在箐口伺机伏击。

他们离开德政乡公所在地烂泥山，爬上大丫口时，忽然听到左面山上有人大喊："牛吃麦子喽！牛吃麦子喽！"两位干部不知是土匪发出的暗语，仍顺着山路走下去。

临近箐口坡脚三岔路口，李永芳借故小解，钻进了煤硐口，埋伏在附近树林中的土匪朝二人疯狂开枪射击，紧接着周围山上的也响起了枪声。二人知道中了埋伏，随即拔枪还击，边打边向铁厂坝方向撤退。终因寡不敌众，身上多处受伤。他俩打完最后一粒子弹时，终因伤势过重倒在了箐口坡下。

李永芳一伙逃走后，铁厂坝的几个农民想到两位南下干部千里迢迢来到此地，为了穷苦人民的翻身事业而遇害牺牲，便在原处守灵一夜，第二天将自家的木楼板撬起来做成棺材，将两位烈士的遗体入棺安葬在箐口山坳。

但土匪仍不死心，返回来丧心病狂地扒开两位烈士的遗体，用手榴弹炸得粉碎。土匪离开后，几位农民冒着风险，又将烈士尸骨捡来入土。烈士长眠在火红的杜鹃花林带，伴随着年年岁岁花开花落。梁方膏和魏怀远两位烈士为人民的解放事业而英勇献身，他们无私无畏的精神一直激励着后人。如今，当地群众能够回忆得起这件感天动地的史事。

伫立箐口，深深地感受到先烈们用鲜血和生命换来了我们今天的幸福。我们采了一束最红最红的杜鹃花，轻轻放在烈士墓碑前，虔诚地告慰烈士：六广人民在党的领导下，继承你们的革命精神，踏着你们的足迹勇往直前，开拓进取，建设美丽六广，使贫瘠的山区发生了翻天覆地的变化。两位烈士定会含笑九泉。

六广年年春光美，箐口岁岁杜鹃红。叩拜烈士安息！

（原载1997年修文县文联出版《栖霞》第三期）

永远的楷模

卢永康

抗洪抢险的紧张战斗过去了，我站立在岩鹰山水库大石坝上。迎着猛烈的山风，看着碧绿的水面，环视生机盎然的田野，眼前仿佛又出现了当年千军万马修水库的场面。听，这是钢钎二锤号子声和阵阵松涛构成的雄壮交响曲；看，他带着民兵抬着石块走过来了！高大的身躯、鲜亮的红五星、浸透汗水的军装，溅满污泥的解放鞋，是他，是他，是我们尊敬的张政委，是曾经担任中共修文县委书记的张锡林同志！

岩鹰山水库润泽九乡，惠及众多百姓，这座巍峨丰碑铭记着：张锡林是个好书记，张锡林是个好公仆，张锡林是为官者永远的楷模！

沉重的1971年，身为武装部政委的张锡林在这特殊的历史时期就任县委书记。他对借空头政治翻云覆雨的伎俩深恶痛绝，嗤之以鼻，他首先把关注的目光投向贫困的百姓。小箐、六广一带属于干山地区，土地贫瘠，老百姓勉强以苞谷饭度日，当地流传着“要想吃大米，除非生大病”的民谣。这使张锡林心酸，心痛，心如刀绞，他想起了自己从小在河南林县老家讨饭的日子，但这毕竟是在共产党坐了几十年江山之后啊！家乡人民修红旗渠的精神激励着他，他决心带领修文人民重新安排河山！

于是，他亲率科技人员跋山涉水，反复论证，以军人的果敢与县委一班人迅速拟定了修岩鹰山水库的方案；于是，他力排众议，亲自请来省水电厅已“靠边站”的高级工程师任施工指挥；于是，他亲任指挥长，在荒山野地里的工棚内、在面盆接雨的嘀嗒声中，开始组织这场改天换地的大会战！

施工民兵队伍集结那天，是他，腾出了自己蜗居的工棚，在食堂的灶头上过了一夜；为了提前完成“三通”工程，是他，头一个走上工地，和民兵一块抢修道路。

石坝清基时，寒流侵袭，人们犹豫了。又是他，第一个跳入冰冷刺骨的水坑。

修水库的11个月内，他没有回过一次家，大年三十都在工地上苦干。

当有人以“唯生产力论”攻击他，罗织种种罪名要斗争他的时候，他冷静地回答：“等水库修完再打倒我也不迟嘛。”

正因为有这样的好带头人，岩鹰山水库以惊人的速度和可靠的质量建成，震惊了全省，改变了半个县滴水贵如油的面貌，哗哗的流水灌溉着田地，滋润着人民群众的心。有一天，灌区一位70多岁的老太婆在山路上巧遇张锡林，她嘴唇哆嗦着说："您……您是共产党的好人啦！"然后通的一声长跪在地，久久不起……

张锡林严格要求自己，生活上非常俭朴。他一年四季都穿布军装、解放鞋，差不多顿顿吃素面条，碗里几乎没有油星。在公务活动中，他从来不陪客人喝一次酒，吃一顿饭。他在修文当了6年的县委书记，居然没有报销过一分钱的差旅费。

张锡林对待人民群众比亲人还亲，老百姓也非常爱戴他。

一个老干部的母亲生病想吃猪心肺，他自掏腰包买了亲自送上门；一个农技人员的妻子生病，他用自己的钱买油买肉送到病床前；一个农民进城被扒窃，他留农民吃了饭，买好车票送农民上车。

80年代初期，张锡林从领导岗位上退了下来。有一次，小箐乡一个农民抓了几只鸡，风尘仆仆赶到县城，千方百计找到"修水库的张政委"家，反复说这鸡是修了水库后打的粮食喂大的，非要送给张政委不可。张锡林和老伴百般推辞，最后，这位农民提着鸡，大哭着，三步两回头地离去。

1988年，中国人民解放军总政治部授予张锡林解放勋章，以表彰他全心全意为人民服务的精神。第二年11月，他不幸因病去世。自发前来参加追悼会的干部群众不计其数。不少农民背着大米从几十里外赶来送他，纷纷要求把他的骨灰盒埋到岩鹰山水库，说要为他修亭子、立碑、栽常青树。颂扬悼念他的挽联和花圈在大操场上绵延了很长，很长。

张锡林是一座大山，使我感到了崇高。

张锡林是一泓清泉，时时涤荡着我的心灵。

张锡林是一口警钟，天天告诫我不能懈怠。

张锡林是一面明镜，常常提醒我怎样全心全意为人民服务。

在张锡林的面前，我羞愧，我着急，我振奋，我也感到自豪。自豪的是，我们伟大的党培养出了张锡林这样的好干部，而我，你，我们，都是这支队伍里的一员！

（选自《山那边》贵州人民出版社1999年出版。本文在1996年贵阳市"公仆杯"普通话演讲赛上获创作二等奖，作者获演讲一等奖）

生亮，你不该走

李祖炎

生亮走了……

"朱生亮书记不行了！"县委办公室主任李红雨同志语调沉重地告诉我你走了的噩耗。我简直不相信自己的耳朵，不肯承认这个现实。然而，你确在尚未完成法国学习考察任务的时候就病倒回国，遽然离开了人世。

当我在子婿的搀扶下，疾步踏入景云山殡仪馆太平间时，你已安详地躺在洁白的床单上了。顿时，我鼻子发酸，泪流满面，心中充溢着不可名状的悲恸。

往事历历在目……

我与你认识是在1981年安顺地委召开的办公室主任会议上，你给我的印象是：神情端庄，衣冠整洁，语言流利，为人随和。

九年后你调任修文县委副书记，后任书记，你把县委办公室安排的宿舍让给离休的老同志居住，自己一家三代却挤在仅56平方米的窄屋里。从此，我们成了朝夕相处的邻居。春节那天，你提着烟酒到相邻的职工家拜年，拱手感谢大家为修文的两个文明建设作出贡献，这可把住在你楼上的书画家郝承德老师惊呆了，连声说：“哪有县委书记来给我们拜年的？搞颠倒了，搞颠倒了！”

进办公室的第一天，你到史志办来向我要《修文县志》。我告诉你，县志尚未成书，只有稿本，你说稿本也行，连同《农业志》《交通志》《邮电志》《城建志》，你抱走一大摞。保密局的董扬同志对我讲，他住在你办公室的对面，每当夜阑更深，县委周围的灯光一盏盏相继灭去，只剩你的窗户灯火通明，临窗望去，你还在翻县志，看材料，作记录。

通过读志，你了解到修文有的地方还是“马路不平，电话不灵，电灯不明”，就在县委常委会上提出建设修文的思路：以交通通信为龙头，尽快改善投资环境，筑巢引凤；加快重点乡（镇）建设，搞活大流通，培育市场体系；积极开发旅游业，带动发展第三产业。常委分头调查论证，把这个思路称叫“三部曲”去运作。“三部曲”像一曲经济建设的交响乐，互为渗透，互相促进，形成了修文经济和社会全面发展态势，为今天修文的发展奠下坚实的基础。

“要得富，先修路，要发达，先把桥来架。”你把这个口号喊得修文的干部和群众心里热乎乎的，大家跑安顺，上省城，找交通部门，求有关领导，终于使修建县城“长安街”的数百万元资金到位。开工那天，风和日丽，人欢马叫，你与县长刘毓文同志带领我们，在环城路上挥锄挖土，持锹铲泥，稀泥甩得满脸满身。有的人看见说：“这才是真抓实干的书记和县长。”仅10个月，包括巴修、修久进城路段改造在内，东起阳明洞，西至王官乡，路宽10米（城内路宽25米），长近6公里横贯县城的“长安街”硬化通车，改变了“晴天一身灰，下雨满街泥”的交通面貌。街道两旁高楼林立，商店遍布，歌厅舞榭，彩灯辉煌，一派繁荣景象，令人耳目一新。面对新的市街，你归功于修文人民，将“长安街”命名为“人民大道”。

你不止一次地在大会上讲：“要吸引外资引进项目，改变修文面貌，缺少现代的通信工具怎行？”于是，你亲自到省、地邮电管理部门求援，决心安装程控电话，结束民国年间就使用的手摇电话的历史。资金、设备、技术到了，8个月就有自动交换机投入使用。程控电话开通那天，《安顺日报》以《修文有了“顺风耳”》为题报道了这一特大喜讯，大街上鞭炮声不断，人们弹冠相庆，不少人连声称赞：“说朱生亮是在讲实话，办实事，见实效，我算服了。”

又是一个春和景明的日子。六广河两岸响起了惊天动地的炮声，修文、黔西数以万计的群众云集六广河岸参加修建六广河大桥开工盛会，大家把你当成呼风唤雨的“神仙”，有的说“是你‘上蹿下跳’才有了这炮声”，有的说“是你‘兴云布雨’才有了这样的欢腾”。就在这令人难忘的喜庆日子，你激情涌动，挥毫书写一副楹联：六广依绿水，伴松韵，跨彩虹，西行进滇入川；七峡藏奇境，听辕声，涌碧涛，东去通江达海。对联字里行间，反映出你盼望大桥早日建成造福修文、黔西人民的夙愿。难怪黔西素朴镇农民王观印老人要在《好官录》上工工整整地写上“朱生亮”三个字，实实在在地记录上你为修文、黔西两县人民办的这桩功德无量的大事。

1993年11月，你奉调安顺行署。临行时，县委门前排着好多闻讯而至的人群和车辆，异口同声说要

送你到新上任的地方。一双双滚烫的手伸向你，一双双含泪的眼睛看着你。你哭了，你谢绝了大家的好意，你说你对修文有深厚的感情，无论去到哪里，都不会忘记在这块土地上生活的3年零7个月。汽车缓缓驶出县委大院，你两眼含泪频频挥手，留下的只是依依难舍的惜别之情。

光阴荏苒，又是十年，你到黔中安顺，又转乌蒙毕节。无论去到哪里，你都在践行“当官一任，造福一方”的承诺。日前，《贵州日报》头条显著位置报道了你在毕节地区不举办大型会展，不邀请歌星舞星和笑星，而是以“务实的作风、走出去的战略和抢抓机遇的意识”，引进了一批国内外优秀大企业入驻毕节：中国第一矿—山东兖矿集团开进大方和黔西进行高度机械化采煤；山西晋城煤业集团步入织金大规模生产煤基合成油；香港港冠国际有限公司走进威宁加工马铃薯淀粉；美国汉氏公司和CDM公司入驻金沙和纳雍高科技处理污水，填埋垃圾……人们把这种招商引资方法看作“特殊模式”，称为“毕节现象”。读过这则报道，感到改变毕节贫困面貌在出成绩、出经验，我不禁拍案叫道：生亮，好样的！

然而，天不从人意，就在你雄心勃勃大展身手的时候，病魔竟无情地把你活活地抢走了。这些年，由于伏案劳作，与你见面的机会极少。我恨自己没有去毕节与你畅叙别后的一切，恨自己没能赶到医院与你再见一面。

生亮，你不该走，不该走得那么早！

昨天，听说你要回毕节，我赶到贵（阳）毕（节）高等级公路遥望灵车，眼睛又一次湿润了。回到居室，草成七绝一首，愿你一路好走。

一夜寒风折劲松，挥泪顿首唤朱公；
纵然千古留遗恨，满目青山荡晚钟。

（原载《修文报》2003年6月2日）

感受六广大峡谷

余　漫

走进六广大峡谷后，我完全感到自己卑微和渺小了。

大自然就这般鬼使神差，凿劈了一些令人难以置信的境地，亿万斯年已过，人类在其面前仍不寒而栗。谁能说在这茫茫苍苍崇山峻岭中蠕动的就是万物之灵长？在六广大峡谷里，你什么也不是。不信，你振臂而呼，或仰天长啸，除了双耳还回响刚才单薄无助的声音，没有谁接纳你的呼唤。孤独刹那间涌上心头，恐惧甚至绝望占领了思想。面对群山沟壑荒山野岭，卑微和渺小突然而来，并扰乱你的神经。你或认为自己在贴近自然。蜗居斗室，你曾经拟过郊游、远足、登山、观海等等不一而足。但你现在已闯进六广大峡谷，站在特大桥上，举目四方，你又感到离自然之遥如河外星月。那些山起伏连绵着从你眼帘消失了，你没有去想象山外是什么，或者压根儿不曾敢去想山外的世界。你身不由己，面前的悬崖陡壁使你害怕得腿软了，眼底一落千丈之距使你眩晕。你开始自叹勿如，很多豪言壮语信誓旦旦的颂词后面，你如蚁般的身形此时淡若秋草。顶多你还算一个饮食人间烟火的可怜家伙，又还能做些什么！

苍茫和渺远在一些人的眼里是无边荒凉，而六广大峡谷呈现的不仅于此，荒凉无边中透着酽酽的悲壮。

时值荒冬，恰阳光送暖，枯山野岭便显得芜杂、浑浊。其时没有雾，也无风吹过，暗暗黄黄的植被

被伏在褐色泛黄的地表，顿生了荒凉。绿色仅有一丝，是被夹在谷底的一湾流水，抑或太深，像深秋的落叶上那股叶脉呈在枯黄叶面。峰峰岭岭沟沟坎坎显得小家碧玉，六广大峡谷在群山起伏里走向从容，走向苍茫与渺远，走入了悲壮。

曾经去过一段六广河谷，井底之蛙般地让六广河两岸的俊秀感动得思绪连连。因了那水、谷、瀑青青娟秀奇巧百态而将内心尘封的渴美逶迤而出。现在站在六广河特大桥上览俯，六广河如溪流穿行山涧，显得小气多了，根本没有临高望去的浩阔，气壮和雄浑。稳住情绪朝下游方向望去，峰峦相接进入云霭，不知山藏进云里还是已消失，看不见瓦屋人家，不知自己身居何地，心系何方。这时，人就难免为自己的存在而悲哀了。可以遣走或忽视甚至遗忘周边的事事人人，却因了这境地带来的感触让人欲说不清欲罢不能。无可奈何中是失落，失落中是人在自然面前的软弱和格格不入。

几百年前的王阳明公曾垂钓河边，赋诗赞曰："百鸟去边回驿路，青岩缺处见人家。行遍奇胜才经此，江上无劳羡九华。"他没有亲临登高观望六广大峡谷，一个人徘徊河边，只见到白鸟驿路，青岩人家，便顿生行遍此地无须羡慕九华之逍遥的喟叹。现在让我看来，先生若能在这季节，亲自攀顶远眺，还会生胜境之奇的感慨么?！先生的遭遇和眼底景物带来的感触，是有诸多叹息留予六广峡谷的。先生乃同样一凡人，要超越这苍莽和凄荒不见得高明到哪里去。他身处劣境困难疑虑险恶重重，要美化自己若神仙般漂游，只有在崖底沙洲，河湾水岸。怕是在这高处，四下的苍凉让他想不着神仙的身影吧！况且，他的的确确不能站在我现在的位置，目睹六广大峡谷而带给人的内心的卑微和渺小了。

穿越时空，岁月转移，六广峡谷仍不曾更改山岭赋予她的存在，顶多吸纳人类临水或蜗居的生命。人在峡谷野岭里生存，就必须有一股勇气——至少有一股忍受因山隔绝而出的寂寞的勇气。一顶茅草，半围篱笆，在山的腹地峡谷缝边安顿了大自然中这支生灵。或许他们没有注意过自身置于山中峡谷，也就没有去联想山外的山外了。日起月落陪伴的是山，望眼欲穿的是山，连梦里也还是山。要不是那淙淙流水打破沉睡的死寂，或许世上本已消失了声音。山牵山连，没有想过山始于斯止于斯。太熟悉了山的影子，也就不用（也不去想）爬至山顶看山看岭了。如此这般，当然不知自己置身于苍茫而生出的卑微和渺小了。

据说没有六广河特大桥和公路桥以前，连接两岸的只是一座铁索桥，桥面由木板铺成，人行走在上面左右晃动，令人胆战心寒。在现代人把这类生命过载的物体视着寻游怪异的饰品时，我越加想亲近它的原始模样。只可惜，后来拆掉了。生息繁衍在这块土地上的人们不忍再见到那些疼心回首的往事，拆除了，远远将之从视野里除去，从记忆深处消退，重先承接生命而延续。

由此上溯，明代女杰奢香，为归顺朝廷安抚黎民，劈水西之道以求交通往来朝令顺畅，在六广大峡谷里置了第二驿站。他一路风尘，来不及看一眼河湾沙洲、青岩人家的美景，更没有想到去登高览胜，错过了六广大峡谷的凄荒苍凉带给人内心的震撼，留予后人功过评说而去了。之后，史书上只隐约见着一些词句，说她当年开凿驿道是如何的艰辛。当时往来东西靠船涉渡，没有铁索吊桥，水势不像现在乌江关闸蓄水的平缓，湍急凶猛。后来出现的铁索吊桥，我有幸从一朋友的照片上见过，至于始建何时如何形状，没能亲见已成憾事。

再是后来散见一些描写记载六广的文章，多是些着眼于六广河里的山水之意，或传说断章。即使以后有了六广公路桥，也少见有关六广大峡谷的全貌带给人的真切感受。因为公路桥之于特大桥而言，实在是不能相提并论，人在两座桥上所得的心灵动感，当然迥然不同。一如这篇文章，我也只能蜗居在寝

室将那份感触写出来。那缕情愫久居不去，怕是积淀心里寝食难安，不如将此说之而后快，还可与去过六广大峡谷的人交流切身体验。胡说也罢，谁让自己钟情这方土地呢?!

从六广大峡谷回来之后，我仍感到自己在大自然面前的卑微和渺小，甚至我们人类。只是猛然回想到站过的那座特大桥时，便叩问自己：“是不是多余!”。

（原载《山花》2003年增刊第2期）

露天电影

黄　竹

20世纪60年代出生的人，对露天电影有一种难以割舍的情结。

站着或坐在麦秆上，爬上不高的树杈骑在枝梗上，我们都看过电影。电影对生活在文化围剿和文化荒漠年代的人是精神上难得的享受。那时，看一场电影是很不容易的。要逢什么节日，或有什么重大的政治活动，才能看上一场电影。逢电影队来家乡的晒谷场上放映时，大家都很高兴。吃过饭，早早地搬条板凳或小椅子，为的是占一个看得比较清楚的位置。去晚了，眼前人头攒动，只能站在自己搬去的板凳上，才能够穿透黑压压的一大群人看电影。那时在心底有个愿望：有一天，一个人在家里放自己喜欢的电影，美美地享受一回，足足地过一把瘾。

那时放映的电影不多，中国片就《英雄儿女》《地道战》《奇袭》，国外的影片还多些，如阿尔巴亚的《勇敢的人们》《临死不屈》《地下游击队》，后来，罗马尼亚的电影又超过了阿尔巴尼亚，如《巴布什卡历险记》《多瑙河之波》，再后来是朝鲜电影《卖花姑娘》《看不见的战线》《摘苹果的时候》和《金姬和银姬的命运》。粉碎“四人帮”的第二年，南斯拉夫的电影《桥》《瓦尔特保卫萨拉热窝》又让我们饱了眼福。放电影也反映了那个时代的政治背景，与哪个国家交好，那个国家的电影自然就放得多些。

随着年龄的增长，已经不满足于电影工作队送电影下乡或一些文化使者的慰问放映了。我们便去寻找露天电影。那时，我家乡的附近驻扎着两个团的解放军，一个步兵团、一个炮兵团。炮团常放电影，大约一个月有几次，于是我们便走十几公里路去看露天电影。解放军整整齐齐地坐在中央，我们只能靠边和靠后站着看，解放军待人还热情，对附近的人去看电影一般持欢迎态度。

大凡看露天电影，当然没有进电影院那样舒服和安逸啦。风大了吹皱银幕，银幕上的人讲话都是时断时续的，还有天公有时不作美，刚放映一会儿，便淅淅沥沥地下起雨来。于是，只好停放，待雨停后再放，至于天气的酷热和寒冷就顾不得那么多了。只要有电影看就行，何况还是免费的。70年代中期，我们搬进了县城居住。不大的县城只有一座不大的电影院，简陋破旧，座位是那种一长排的连椅。

看露天电影的年代，进电影院较少，因为一是要花钱，二是票难买。买票的场面回忆起来仍然惊心动魄。买票凭蛮力，你争我抢，为了能买到电影票，有些人不惜动用“轻功”，从拥挤的人群头上踩过，一只手抓着屋顶，一只手伸到了那个圆圆的小洞里，人说这叫“倒挂金钩”。走后门，拉关系，也能购得一两张座位居中的电影票，但只能偶尔为之。一是别人不可能次次买你的账，二是你自己也不好意思。所以，请人看电影是很体面的事。还有，一部好电影或有影响的大片，你会发现居中正坐的都是当地有头有脸的人物。看电影，也是地位的尊贵和实力的显示。

童年时代，看的电影特别记得牢，一方面是一部片子反复看了十几遍，多的甚至几十遍，还有是年少记性好的原因。有时，大家用电影里的台词开玩笑，什么“高，实在是高”、“我胡汉三又回来啦”！反正，许多台词和人物对话可以信手拈来，随时运用到生活中。进入80年代，电视进入家庭，露天电影从生活中逐渐淡出，取而代之的是装修典雅、有软席高靠背座位的影院，随时都可以看的电影。的确，比露天电影高档了许多。在空调的作用下，冬暖夏凉，还可以边吃东西边看电影，一副惬意的样子，甚至还有24小时的通宵电影让人饱尝电影“大餐”。

然而，不论条件如何好，不论音响如何美，不管是欧风美雨的大片，还是中国电影明星的作秀，反而没有了那种兴致，体会不到那份露天电影的情趣。总觉得还不如看露天电影的舒服。渐渐地，竟远离了时尚影院，甚至几年不进一次。在繁忙的重压下，有时，竟奇怪地冒出想看一场露天电影的奇想，可哪里去寻找呢?

（选自《流金岁月》贵州人民出版社2004年出版）

祝福六广

宋东雁

六广是我的家乡，生于斯，长于斯，对其认识应该是很深刻的，但或许是少不更事，对她的认识甚是模糊，谈不上有什么深刻的印记，对别人的赞美也只能淡淡的附和一声：“还行吧!”

孩提时喜欢与小伙伴们到六广河边拾圆宝石，大包小包的往家里带，那时最大的乐趣也不过如此。时间久了，裤包往往都被磨破，为此没少被父母打骂，但还是乐此不疲，因为那时实在没有比这个更好玩的。进入小学后，这项活动就渐渐地少了。一是因为有很多小孩子落河而死，父母为此千叮嘱万叮嘱，我们想想也后怕；二还是怕父母的“大刑”伺候，也就不敢再造次了。

稍稍记事的我们，既无电影，更无电视，甚是无聊；坐在屋檐下吹牛成了大人们打发时光的最大兴趣，我总闲不住，更怕冷清，哪里热闹就往哪里凑，挤进大人堆里，老老实实的蹲在地上听。可我总是没有开口的份，大人们谈来谈去，不外乎就是昨天哪个把哪个喝翻了……谈起河对门的姑娘，顿时心花怒放，腔调也变甜润了许多，因为娶到河对门的姑娘就是一件无比荣耀的事。也有泼冷水的：“有哪样稀奇嘛，只要不残不废，找个河对门的姑娘简直就是小菜一碟，本来河对门的姑娘就向往我们六广，喜欢我们六广的娃儿”。喜形于色，自信满满。

在我的印象中，六广并没有什么特别之处，也还只是“苞谷饭当顿”的生活标准，怎么就成了河对门姑娘的憧憬之地呢？我当时就想，可能是因为六广面条好吃，六广白酒醇香，六广花灯好看吧！于是，我带着这种唯我独知的幼稚走出了六广，到外地去求学了。

说到六广，我总是遮遮掩掩，就怕别人知道我来自贫穷落后的六广。

几年时光辗转而逝，我又回到了这片土地，在六广中学任教。天空还是一如既往的蔚蓝，人还是一如从前一样的热情厚道。也许是被一种虚荣心驱使，我也找来了王阳明先生的《六广晓发》等诗开始专研阅读；对此也只是一知半解，只是其中的“遍行奇胜才经此，江上无劳羡九华”让我为之一震，先生对六广的风景是高看一筹的，我却置身于此不识君，不能不说是一种审美观的缺失。

那会儿，我等不得下课，就把学生们带到六广河，要求大家以《六广河》为题写一篇作文。我也在心里认真琢磨，希望找到一点触动心弦的东西。山无言，水无声，“平淡”两字几乎就此蹦到了嗓子眼。

多年以后，陪同新闻媒体界的朋友到六广河采访，两位老记虽见多识广，却依然对六广赞不绝口：“六广河是‘长在深闺人未识’的大家闺秀，纯朴自然，不施粉黛，将来发展旅游业定是一枝独秀”，我也认同他们的看法。正如一位友人说过：要跳出六广看六广，才能读出她的独有韵味。也许正是走出了六广许多年，经历了许多事，浮躁的心平静了，才能有所思，有所得。

六广河依旧碧波荡漾，执着地奔向大海，誓有不达目的不罢休之势。六广因六广河而改变，以往宁静的小镇多了几分热闹，大多是冲着六广温泉而来，六广面条、薛家凉粉成了游客馈赠物品，总不忘往回带上一些。历史在向前发展，淳朴的六广人也没有故步自封，停止不前，经过时势的洗礼，思想也在蝶变，闲谈的话题也发生了根本性变化，既要加速发展，更要守住底线，把美好的山水留给子孙后代，绿色、生态、开放、共享等词汇不时脱口而出，并付诸行动，敢与不义之举抗争。记得曾有一个外来企业落户六广，但建设与协议相悖，带有污染，当地人积极主动站了出来，以坚决的态度抵制，最终让污染企业落荒而逃。企业老板临走，狠狠地骂了一句:不开窍的六广人，让你守着这个鬼地方穷一辈子。

常言道：一方水土养一方人。六广人还固守淳朴、厚道，认真而不较真，平凡而不平淡。六广正以开放的胸怀迎接新的发展机遇，黔贵公司携几十亿资金入住，拟打造温泉风情小镇、温泉酒店、养老社区等绿色项目。支持项目建设，就是支持地方发展，我们六广人都会有这种家乡情结、发展理念，积极支持，让未来的六广更具魅力。

凝眸云天，祝福我的家乡未来更加美好。

（选自《栖霞文荟》修文县文联2005年出版）

镜　鉴

朱五义

镜，可以正衣冠。

但凡爱美的人，常常照镜。或穿着打扮，或搽脂抹粉，做到浓妆淡抹总相宜，不失为一件美事。

在现实生活中，人们境况不同，心态各异，对镜的需求也不一样。一般来说，年轻人比老年人，女人比男人，美人比丑人尤爱照镜，而年轻美貌的女郎对镜情有独钟，随身携带，不时照照。反之，则不大照镜，这是人之常情、亦无可厚非。

为官的较之老百姓尤需照镜。百姓个人的美丑只涉及自我，顶多波及周边之人。而为官的美丑则关系一方，官越大，涉及的面就越大。然而，为官的比老百姓不爱照镜，这并非他的身上没有肮脏的东西，而是他常拿镜子照别人，不容百姓用镜去照他的缘故。或因怕照镜，便粉面涂金，乔装打扮，貌似正人君子，其实面目可憎。有如《镜花缘》中多九公游两面国所见的那样。

也有不怕照镜的。一是满脸横肉的泼皮无赖，仗势凌人：“我就这副嘴脸，你敢怎样?”二是不修边幅的人，玩世不恭，照与不照亦无所谓。三是心地光明磊落的人，莫说用一般镜子去照，即使用哈哈镜、照妖镜去照，他都无所畏惧、依然故我。所谓真金不怕火炼、身正不怕影子歪嘛！

镜，鉴也。以古为镜、可以鉴今。以前事为资考，即所谓“前事不忘，后事之师”，不要只图近利，火烧眉毛只顾眼前，少于从长计议。以成事为法戒，以之作前车之鉴，不要只向“钱”看，有奶便是娘，因而丧失人格、国格。古时，一座阿房宫，反映了“秦爱纷奢”，不爱他的百姓而招致速亡。齐楚燕赵魏韩六国相继而亡，“弊在赂秦”，而不是“以赂秦之地，封天下之谋臣，以事秦之心，礼天下之奇才”。这都是以为鉴戒的典范。

“清如水，明如镜”，这是百姓对清廉官吏赞誉之词。若政治不修，便贪多廉少。真能大言不惭如此称诩的能有几人？人称包文正为“青天”是他为官清正严明，铁面无私，至今家喻户晓、铭记百姓心间。有的人拿镜不照自己，只照他人，看不见自己的后颈窝，专指别人的背脊骨。对于属下的批评、动辄报之以“小脚鞋”，乃至作“异己”排除。唐太宗却不这样，魏征劝他居安思危，戒奢以俭，深得太宗器重，把他作为镜子，故有贞观之治。人贵在顺境的赞歌声中而能自律自持。古时邹忌欲与徐公比美、问妻、妾和客人，都说他比徐公美，他并不沾沾自喜，而是面对徐公内审外察，认定自己不及徐公美，得出“吾妻之美我者，私我也；妾之美我者，畏我也；客之美我者、欲有求于我也”的结论，并以此劝齐王广泛听取国人意见，修明政治，收到“战胜于朝廷”的良效。

批评与自我批评是面镜子，是优良作风。可如今被淡忘而不大用了。百姓心中有杆秤，可称出谁轻谁重。人民心里是面照妖镜，是妖是圣必显明。世上多少聪明入，聪明反被聪明误。水可载舟亦复舟、尽管他“机关算尽太聪明”，到头来“反误了卿卿性命”。被弄得猪八戒照镜子—里外不是人。

爱美之心人皆有之。爱美不仅听其言，还要观其行，不仅修其表，还要养其心。这不仅是个人私事，而且是维系国家民族的大事、切不可等闲视之。我们都来照镜，“日参省乎己”，让每个人的心灵美丽起来，你美了、我美了，他也美了，我们的国家民族还有不美的吗?

（选自《栖霞文荟》修文县文联2005年出版）

山村夏夜

贯长远

太阳转到坡背后的时候，月亮浮到了小村上面。蛙声从远远的池塘里传来。月色在片片禾叶上流淌，滑落。晚风里浮游着稻禾的缕缕清香。玉米灌浆了，籽粒开始丰满。蛐蛐穿越所有的瓜地。

正是晚饭时候，山村广播里送出音乐。在树下歇足了，院中已摆上土漆方桌，碗筷和瓜豆端上桌来。就着月光，龙门阵与敲碗的声音响成一片，一道嚼进肚里。

忘却玉米叶在肌肤上勒下的道道伤痛，和手心里的老茧。瓜豆和辣椒水是最好的安慰；鲜豆花裹一团苞谷饭，放进嘴里满口香，汗水已不再苦涩。

饭后各有分工，厨房里的往往是婆媳，她们抹净桌椅，继续操持家务；白天上坡下力的男人们在院中拣一干净之处，或仰躺或席地而坐，闲嗑一些话题，扯一些家常事。

父亲说他饭后的这一斗烟还香，于是叼着烟嘴儿端水喂牛。圈里那头壮牛懒懒的站立起来，把头乖乖地伸向父亲。墙根下忠实的大黑狗摇头摆尾走到牛栏前睡下了。

夏夜的山村是祥和的，依山而立的每处农舍，却都有热闹的场面。所有的心事，被装进了苦丁茶里。山村广播开始说休息，在通往山腰水井的小道上，扁担与绳索在交织一段美好的渴望；山泉被舀进木桶，撞击一串串长长的脆响；挑水的男人唱起粗野的山歌从山腰上走下来，不知疲倦。

小村入睡的时候，梦就做到了太阳升起。

无数个梦之后，我离开了小村，到了另外一个地方。

回头看看几架山梁环抱的小村，父辈们已然衰老。山间小道已变得平坦而宽阔，不时有飞快地马达声遛过；山歌已走远。而每一个壮实的家庭，都在不断分解，又进行着新的组合。

择一个夏日回小村看看。坐在空空的土漆方桌边，喝父亲为我烧制的苦丁茶，想聆听父亲对我的教诲。

院里的月光下，我与父亲隔着桌子，没有多余的话。

（原载《贵阳日报》2009年10月12日）

六广印象

李小龙

六广人

六广人站着是山，躺着是脉。

是山，就有山一样的旷达，于是六广人喝起酒来，不折不扣，不醉不休。是脉，就有脉一样的胸怀，于是六广人对外地人总是热情、亲切，让人处处感到温暖。六广的男孩豪放得如脱缰的野马；女孩却漂亮得似出水芙蓉。

六广人走进去是山沟沟，走出来是山沟沟，走了几千年的山沟沟，终于走出了山沟沟。六广人的祖先们化成肥沃的泥土，养育着子孙，他们的子孙又化成肥沃的泥土，养育着子孙，一代养育一代。

六广人应了句古话：靠山吃山、靠水吃水。在六广人的面前有一条大河，他们与他们的祖先都以此河为生命河，因为她的名字本身就叫—

六广河

六广河曾像一把无情的利剑，将大山辟开，分出了龙岗山与象鼻山，成了隔在修文与黔西之间的屏障。如今，它却成了系住贵阳与毕节的纽带，唱出了绿水围着青山转的动人歌谣。

六广河不仅仅是一条河，它更是一个景区的浓缩。它具有漓江之秀，剑门之险，华山之奇，青城之幽。人们将六广河称着“小三峡”，我看一点也不过分。如果我们将她比作美女，那无疑是闭月羞花的了。

旅游码头的建成，索风营电站的投资兴建，给六广河插了丰满的双翼，将让她飞出大山，名扬天下。那时六广人的一些特色产品也将扬名了。不信，你去尝一尝—

六广酒

六广酒与其他酒并没有太多的不同，是乎只是多了一份浓烈，容易让喝酒的人“醉倒在家门口”，“不知何处是他乡”。

六广酒是用本地苞谷与水浸沟的水精制而成的一种散白干。闻起来香，喉咙发痒，想喝，不喝不止痒；喝起来就醉，眼睛发昏，想吐，却又不醉不罢休。于是大凡好酒者到六广旅游都是慕名而去，尽兴而归。

在六广喝酒，你还可尝到六广的名小吃—

六广臭豆腐

臭豆腐以臭著名。闻起来越臭的，吃起来越香。

六广臭豆腐是“色、臭、味”俱全的，让人吃起来回味无穷。我刚到六广时并不吃臭豆腐，那里是不了解六广臭豆腐，还没尝到它的“臭”头。有一次同事拉着我去吃，我试着尝了一点点，谁知这一尝便让我与之结了缘，后来常常去吃。现在离开六广了，回想起来，总是直吞口水。

六广臭豆腐的制作过程，如同老中医看病，讲究“望、闻、问、切”。只是顺序略有不同，它是“切、问、望、闻”。闻起来臭了就可以烙来吃了，所以是“闻”在最后。

离开六广，就不容易吃上六广臭豆腐了。还想抽时间去六广看看，喝点小酒，品尝小吃。回来时还要带上那里的另一特产—

六广面条

到过六广的人都知道六广有一条面条街。远远地就能听到隆隆的机器声，那是在打面粉，在制面条。一逢场天，法庭、派出所的外面直到下街全是卖面条的。车水马龙，一派繁华景象。

六广面条讲“三纯”。即色纯、味纯、汤纯。色纯是说看起来是灰白色，顺眼，没有黑的；味纯即吃起来可口；汤纯是指煮面条后的汤不粘。只是目前尚未形成规模，亦没有占据市场。相信将来，六广面条会走俏贵阳的，在此预祝其走好。

（选自《深谷乡音》作家出版社2009年出版）

清风送爽

何小萍

一

飞机，徐徐降落在龙洞堡机场。

“乘客，您好！欢迎您来到中国避暑之都——贵阳”。空姐的话语清晰明亮，我的心充满阳光。

“绿绿的贵阳，爽爽的贵阳—和和的贵阳，爽爽的贵阳，徜徉在你的怀里，我回到了童年的时光—”孙楠的歌声亲切悠扬，好一阵清风送爽。

贵阳，一座森林环抱之城，一座生态文化之城，一座与巴黎、维也纳、圣彼得堡等城市齐名的“全球十佳避暑旅游名城”。

三年前，为品尝一道道避暑大餐，我怀揣着这座城市发出的一张张名片，寻着避暑季的轨迹，便如候鸟般在彼地和此地间来来去去。

每一次都以为是我最后的旅程，可每一次我又都情不自禁,情不自禁地投入这座城市的怀里。

我已经被她感动，为她冲动，为她深情向往……因而，“猫夏” 贵阳，已成为我生活的一段美好时光；来贵阳“猫夏”，已成为我朋友圈里的时尚。

二

在明净淡雅的花溪，我知道了山的玲珑奇巧，苍翠欲滴；我明白了水的灵动飘逸，神奇旋旎；我感悟了总理、元帅赋诗对弈的闲情雅趣，还有巴金、萧姗结为连理的缕缕情愫；解读了身为青岩人的清朝大员周渔璜编辑《康熙字典》，因思念故土作诗托画《西崦春耕图》的故事。……花溪浪漫的一夏，让我真的在“花溪河里捧起了欢乐的月亮”，看到了“花仡佬河”里蹦出的一个个“水姑娘”。

在清凉秘境的开阳，乘一叶扁舟，在南江大峡谷激情竞漂，再打开“中国最美的乡村—十里画

廊”—欣赏。……开阳自在的一夏，让我对这黔地高原上最纯美的秘境生出了无限的遐想……

在秀美神奇的修文，“六广河白鹭衔着七彩梦幻飞翔，动物园珍禽合着四季欢歌竞唱；桃源河感悟自然的神奇，高尔夫迸发超越的梦想。……阳明洞孕育了深厚的文化，龙场驿书写跨越的辉煌。……”的歌声四处回荡。五百年的儒雅圣地，千古大师的良知光芒，已成为我心向往的地方……修文轻松的一夏，让我爽透心房。

三

为进达王安石“求思之深”的境界，为求正刘伯温“五百年后看，云贵胜江南”的预言，也为抹去世人“天无三日晴，地无三里平，人无三分银”的印象，每次盛宴之余，我都忍不住会悄悄歇步，想独自看看贵阳城的周遭风貌，细细品品她四围的独有味道。

从外到内，我自由的走走听听看看；从内到外，我自在的看看听听走走。“贵阳印象”已然是渐行渐近，清晰可辨……

城内。到处是灵山秀水，绿茵绵绵，流水涓涓，充盈着诗的低吟，流动着舞的丰姿。天空有悠悠的鸽哨，还有各式各样的风筝在飘。

城内有整洁的林荫大道，有舒适的绿色广场，也有一个个经典时尚的招牌广告和一座座个性雕塑。空气中还飘着异国的咖啡豆香。

黔灵古刹充满神秘的暮鼓晨钟，甲秀楼茶苑浸透着儒雅的箫声筝曲。多彩的霓虹透射着城市的富足和繁荣。

我看到红男绿女在旋转，听到南明河在欢畅，Shopping mall内的摩登男女们更显气派和风光。

城外。一条条宽阔的大道，把这座城市延伸到无数个角落，使她变得更大；一座座伟岸的大桥把这座城市贯穿到江河湖泊的另一方，使她走得更远；一个个宏深的隧道，把这座城市带到了大山的终端，使她显得更幽；一条条航线把这座城市推到众多的国家登台亮相，使她的名气更响。

斑驳的光影铺撒在金阳大道上，透着满满的温暖、和蔼和荫凉，游弋着幸福的时光。金阳新区的夜晚似银河千条，繁星浩渺。

《多彩贵州》《大地之舞》把贵阳的美淋漓尽致的展现挥洒。

在这里，城市不再仅仅是一个概念，正如市民们所言：她除了要有“知行合一 协力争先”的城市精神，还要有如“避暑之都”的品牌形象。2010提出的“三创一办”目标，一定会使贵阳更加丰韵多彩，魅力飞扬。

为了离她更近，与她更亲，贵阳城动起来了，贵阳人情动贵阳。城市在白天有了更多的人与她同行，夜里有了更多的人与她呼吸。她更充满活力，生命也变得更加旺盛年轻。

美景留人，景随人行；真情动人，情随心寄。

贵阳的美景真情随着游人八方流动，四面吟咏。情系四海，景动五洲。大地起舞，江河欢歌。我相信，2010的避暑庆典会把贵阳城装扮得更炫更酷更爽。

四

飞机，徐徐降落在龙洞堡机场。

我走进贵阳，好一阵清风送爽。

（原载《贵州日报》2010年5月5日，原标题为《贵阳印象》）

遇见岩鹰山

肖伦文

谈及岩鹰山，县人大多是熟悉的，不是因山之隆望，而是因水之灵秀，一般说岩鹰山，定是指岩鹰山水库。也有人称之岩鹰湖，倒也多了几分雅致。

出县城往西北不足十公里，小箐地界，丛山之中，高峡平湖，三潭叠翠，那便是岩鹰山水库了。相传，阳明谪居龙场期间，一日晓发六广，途径四面坡古道，闻说有地名小六广，即亲往探之，路过凤凰山下，见一石山孤傲自立，高耸入云，形如神鹰待发，便与当地苗民攀谈，拟取山名，因当地土话称鹰为“岩鹰”，故起名岩鹰山，阳明仙风道骨，飘然而去。岩鹰山水库也叫作“七一”水库，一者是七一年所建，二者“七一”是党的生日，时移事易，后来习惯性地叫作岩鹰山水库了，及至现在又有了岩鹰山村。库区所及，尚有老蒋山、凤凰山、青龙山、白虎山、王五冈、小六广、大林山、茶山等，终究是没有岩鹰山的雄壮豪迈，逐渐少被提起，岩鹰山便独享其尊，声名在外了。

山为水之魂，水为山之灵。岩鹰山山水依依，魅影绰绰，得几分杭州西子湖的婉约隽秀，也胜似北京十三陵的粗犷大气，蔚为大观！

岩鹰山畔，凤凰山下，即是石坝库区，坝体紧扣青龙、白虎两山，如涧卧祥龙，似水映穹庐。万兴林海孕育滋滋细流，涓涓潺潺，源源汇聚；报国古寺遗存佛心善缘，念念不忘，声声回响；半山深处飘香袅袅炊烟，曲径通幽，鸡鸣犬吠。晴日金光熠熠，碧水清波，鸟欢鱼跃；雨天烟波浩渺，微风徐来，神清气爽。动如鹰凤双飞，龙腾虎跃；静若皎皎玉兔，柔柔处子。

茶山水头，小六广旁，是为土坝库区，坝体横亘大堰河故道，如水关长城，似中流砥柱。茶山龙孔源出汪汪清泉，日添夜漫，绵绵不绝；库区传神状如心字异变，契合阳明，此心光明；美丽乡村回望烟花村落，疏疏离离，水墨神韵。白昼阳光初照，潭映花影，一湖斑斓；是夜月华流银，雾起薄霜，梦回华清。风来落英缤纷，满湖飞花；人去一袭清香，花随人动！

万兴堡肩挑两库，娇小玲珑，沟通里外，暗送清泓，得土坝之滋养，受石坝之仰望，偏安一隅，不干不涸，休养生息。库虽娇小，却有肩挑日月、手转乾坤之气势，缺之不得。岩鹰三潭，虽是人工开凿，然则自成一体，风景如画，浑然天成。

岩鹰山故事，始终烙印张锡林圣名，凡此乡民，均颂称张政委。时任修文县委书记、县革委主任、县人武部政委的他，心怀“改变修文河山”之壮志，效法其老家林县红旗渠之精神，力排众议，克服万难，启动水库建设。政委率干部民工万余，吃住于工地，卧榻于工棚，举能于乡野，筚路蓝缕，战天斗地，砌石为坝，垒土为墙，仅十一月余，水库即告建成。千山流清泉，高峡出平湖；泽被十余乡，万物得甘露。一举改变了六广小箐“滴水如油”的现状，也终结了“六广小箐苞谷当顿，要想吃米除非生病”的历史。万民宏望，欢呼雀跃。政委下乡，路遇老妇，竟行大礼，长跪不起。1989年，政委与世长辞，此间乡民，莫不悲恸，扶老携幼，提米带物，前往跪拜。遥想当年，高山深壑，缺资少物，车马不通，加之政治敏感，上纲上线，的确千困万难！政委及广大人民之丰功伟业，早已定格于修文山水，定格于圣地历史，定格于万众民心，并留下了“自力更生，艰苦奋斗”之宝贵精神。

十六年前，刚工作之际，同校学长工作在此，访友之余，初次见得岩鹰山水库真容。干山坡长大之人，对水总是感觉亲切向往，水库之清澈、之秀美、之雄壮，很是令人激动、赞叹、感怀。后因工作关

系去得多了，但每一次总要去到石坝、土坝看看，沾沾灵气，闻闻花香，也很是惬意！总之，与岩鹰山的缘分着实不浅！

奇山秀水是自然之眷顾，历史人文是精神之遗存。岩鹰山婀娜多姿，本不该如此寂寞。明明一块璞玉，偏偏虚却万山。相信，古老的岩鹰山将见证美丽乡村的美丽新世界，“岩鹰花海”终将花香四溢、四季芬芳，一个个最乡愁、最世界的湖边小寨将镶嵌在国家湿地公园的桃红柳绿当中，令人趋之若鹜，忘情流连。

文末，作岩鹰春色小诗两首，平仄不顾，韵律不周，算是对岩鹰山美好的希冀。

其一

村落款款一水碧，
半是初阳半烟雨；
东风最解百花意，
不待花催早来急。

其二

昨夜天寒送归雪，
今朝日暖动花期；
岩鹰湖畔春潮起，
正是人间三四月。

山迢水漫，风轻云淡，我们一直奔跑在追求幸福的大道上……

（原载《贵阳日报》副刊版）

诗　　词

游阳明洞有感

朱生亮

一

自古苦寒吐清香，不独仲尼与文王；
谪人龙冈栖迟悟，始信正道是沧桑。

二

洞古山深水含烟，谪囚两臣似有缘；
潮涨潮落风云事，记取王张百十年。

三

轩名何陋古柏森，鬼哭云翻玩易经；
君子腹空戏节现，熬尽霜雪见阳春。

四

夕照青山几度秋，初晴晓岚独自游；

龙蛰豹隐历炼地，谁说龙冈气已收。

（选自《修文名胜风光诗文选》）

九七感赋

宋　鼎

南海百年恨失珠，舜尧十亿痛无呼；

满清腐败横遭辱，帝国强梁最庄殊。

改革兴邦增实力，收回割地是吾图；

落花无奈英夷叹，赤县腾欢正气舒。

（原载《修文报》1997年6月15日）

喜香港回归

谭荣先

一

历史沧桑愁百年，国耻民辱记心间；

香港回归洗国耻，十亿神州庆团圆。

二

又是紫荆飘香时，华夏连心庆回归；

百年祈盼今实现，花好月圆热泪盈。

（原载《修文报》1997年6月15日）

卜算子·惜别《修文报》

李祖炎

报苑群芳艳，修文一枝俏。纵论沧桑七百年①，共渡风雨桥。　　千古良知光，任重征程遥。放眼龙场换新颜，猎猎军中纛②。

①七百年：指修文元代开始有行政建置至今的历史跨度，《修文报》复刊后，作者曾与报社主编陈新国合撰介绍修文历史的《往事悠悠》连载报上。

②纛：音dào，意为大旗。

（原载《修文报》2003年12月29日）

为修文县志而作

陈福桐

一

自珍心事北南冬，一睨人才海内空；

苦劝天公重抖擞，龙冈先得惠熏风。

二

婴儿堕地报平安，放纵呱呱满室欢；
想到编书如孕子，刊成问世始心宽。

（选自《龙山吟—梧山诗词联集》贵州省文史研究馆编）

寄修文黔西合作年会

王向规

闻言西上兴欲狂，只言力微未能尝；
翘首乌蒙心往疾，常忆昆仲赋华章。
杜鹃映映添春意，农台巍巍壮民康；
纵途横楼济长短，齐习比翼任翱翔。

（选自《行吟集》贵州人民出版社出版）

送别向规同志赴安顺上任

丁治学

春早枝头绿，又闻百鸟啼；
调令昨日下，送君赴安西。
来修十五月，相外多受益；
依依惜别意，前程共努力。

（选自《行吟集》贵州人民出版社出版）

咏修文组诗

熊永忠

三潮水

当年兴旺何处寻，断垣碎瓦掩残林；
知非何必归山野，觉悟还须赖本心。
淙泉尚知间歇涌，宦案焉能长寄身；
我来诚焚香三炷，谁为逝翁证因果。

玩易窝

依稀童时几度来，绿树青山映亭台；
偶请师长谈往事，曾为碑碣慕前才。
此番难寻旧时貌，古迹多引今人哀；
忽听杜鹃啼易语，拭目春风花又开。

过三人坟

荆棘满山狐兔藏，残碑荒冢古道凉；

杯土深埋白骨怨，三瘗遍传翰墨香。
瘴疠有天终王化，知行无境细评量；
偶经凭吊难招魂，抚石空滴泪几行。

六广河

玉带碧波山滴翠，舟轻林密猿身娇；
竹隐茅舍炊烟渺，日照深谷紫雾飘。
迁客晓发张吟帜，虹桥临空启风骚；
兴废涨落千年事，江山逢时更妖娆。

阳明洞怀古

山深洞暗暂栖迟，凤毛蛮乡呈艳姿；
谪臣三载苦居夷，觉悟通宵乐吟诗。
启民龙岗开教化，传道东山究行知；
五百年后翻旧卷，且将阳明比退之。

（选自《栖霞文荟》2005年修文县文联出版）

狗吠声穿过涂满松香味的山村

周　荣

狗吠声穿过涂满松香味的山村
在我的骨头里歌吟
而我是一株不会唱歌的
一种植物
月儿在天空，高旷的天空
又在呼唤我清瘦的名字
唉！这可恶的月又在抚摸我的胡须
我激动却在他的许诺里老去
我已沉落于岁月的深底
常常蹲在潮湿的泥坑里
吐出一大堆狼藉的梦
漂浮在月光之河
月儿啊，你曾骑着我的岁月狂奔不息
不要月亮，不要他的清辉
我只要冷冷的风
和一双眼睛
放在狗嘴巴里储存

（选自《栖霞文荟》2005年修文县文联出版）

乡音景致

文清武

黄昏
村外的田野
尽现一派派生机
春意盎然

斜径上
背着箩筐的老者
擦破了血红血红的夕阳
扯得一片彩霞
披在身上

归巢的候鸟
扑入树林
叽叽喳喳的鸟语
逗引着墙角光屁股的孩童
烧好饭的媳妇
倚门而立
等待晚归的汉子

圆月初上
邻家女孩
对着月亮梳妆
远处的山顶
牛背上吹笛的牧童
肩担月亮
口吹天音

灯下
晚归的我
仍旧伏案疾书
写着工作
写着希望

（原载《修文报》2007年3月19日）

词三首

张丽梅

减字木兰花

柳烟缥缈，宿雨横枝愁遍绕。帘幕轻凉，墙外梨花携梦扬。流年暗度，词冷诗凄何处诉？缺月风寒，永夜离歌清泪弹。

阮郎归

踟蹰春半彩蝶追，曲桥岸柳垂。罗帏风入泪抛谁？无言掌上杯。 山未断，水难回，流年残月推。轻敲浮键又熹微，参商各自悲。

菩萨蛮

卷帘钩月花枝瘦，心飞目断青山后。清影半窗寒，离人犹自怜。柔情和泪凑，蜜意如垂柳。欲醉恐难眠，风敲心上弦。

（原载《中国诗赋》2010年10月第3期）

君莫问

祝　琼

君莫问，女何方
山深处，野花一朵

莫叹息，出身悲
春到时，醉透一方

莫怜惜，今朝瘦
谁相依。心事暗存

自飘零，自凋谢
随风起，欲盼朝夕

（原载《修文报》2010年11月）

楹　　联

贺六广河大桥开工二十联

朱生亮　联

六广依绿水伴松韵跨彩虹西行进滇入川

七峡藏奇景听猿声涌碧涛东去通江达海

王克勤　联

古道劈新线促国脉畅通经济繁荣

高桥酬夙愿赖各方携手领导关心

谭荣先　联

改革开放求发展奔小康先筑宽广致富路雄关漫道驿站古

建功立绩为人民谋大业须构宏伟关键桥天险通途面貌新

李玉轩　联

千秋伟业为民立绩

万代奇功修路建桥

王清义　联

修黔毗邻自古洪流为巨阻

路桥宏达指日险隘变通途

甄燕驰　联

蜈蚣桥卧古道百姓颂奢香

六广河腾巨龙万民歌尧舜

涂新善　联

六广架金桥素朴新田无天堑两县发财财道富

川黔添捷径黔西修文有通途一方致富富路宽

廖昌瑜　联

单拱跨过一百五十米神仙未必做得到

投资要花六百几十万菩萨难有此心肠

姚明槐　联

六广大桥兴建指望四通八达

修文小康起飞抛却一穷二白

杨美玉　联

小舟横渡过激流险滩心惊胆战如闯鬼门关

长桥直跨越峡谷深涧神泰情闲似逛游乐园

雷华熙　联

贵边隅之生灵筹大计重开九驿从此川滇黔桂连一线喜今日秋高气爽挥锄破土万民腾跃

毕百年之宿愿绘宏图再造山河自来汉藏苗彝是一家待明朝春和日丽把盏庆功千乘竞驰

邓文涛　联

水可成河土可成坷此河已免水阻赖上倡下和竭献民力平坎坷

木乔为桥马乔为骄其桥并非木造乃钢筋铁骨巧夺天工应矜骄

宋　鼎　联

磐石累累千寻悬崖两岸雄傲截断水西古道

坦途迤迤万里公路一桥飞渡接通云贵高原

朱五义　联

一声春雷石破天惊贯长虹利及河上河下

万众颂歌山呼岭笑庆新功福荫水东水西

谭　玺　联

水翻浪浪击石石阻道道难行行已千年

峡上桥桥连路路通车车奔驰驰向四化

宋文龙　联

一道彩虹飞天堑连通四海

两岸新桥跨关隘接连五洲

朱　屏　联

六广长桥接通平坦公路形成滇东黔西国道线

乌江大峡拦住汹涌河水造就播南筑北电力站

朱　杰　联

如奢香夫人站在桥上俯视滔滔河水奔流峡谷灌田发电必引吭高歌今非昔比

若阳明先生坐于车中仰望绵绵公路回旋岭际运货载人定挥毫急书人定胜天

刁福林　联

雄鸡高唱迎宾曲聚四方志士迎八方贵客促彩虹早现

芦笙频奏祝酒歌赖两县携手喜三地同筹铸玉龙腾飞

陈新国　联

几代梦幻只盼长虹卧波连通天堑路迎八方来客

数载辛劳定要绝岭坦途修成富民桥谱四化新歌

（选自《桥·修文县文史资料第四辑》修文县政协出版）

《修文县志》首发式赠联一联

陈福桐

政通民和喜看修文古史今朝妙手裁成一县志

天造地设难得龙场人文自然巧工联缀两景观

（选自《龙山吟—梧山诗词联集》贵州省文史研究馆编）

题修文名胜风光三联

王向规

修文革命公墓

碧血浇琼花已结丰收硕果

丹心建华厦方兴改革狂飙

阳明洞

一水抱城西遗有将军垂钓处

双树荫庭东尚有哲人讲学堂

六广河

汇三峡峻险漓江秀丽为一体成乌龙滚滚劈山穿谷呼啸而来，到此风平浪静

自禹贡梁州春秋牂牁至九驿历青史茫茫桑田沧海因革启进，于今文盛骚兴

（选自《行吟集》贵州人民出版社出版）

小　　品

“无”中生“有”

胡光胤

地　点：久长镇驴坊村办公室外院子里

人　物：胡二爷，男，40余岁，村主任

李老幺，男，30余岁，村民

蔡大娘，女，50余岁，村民

（布景：“中共久长镇驴坊村支部委员会，久长镇驴坊村村民委员会”牌子，一桌一椅）

（村主任胡坐着写字）

李：（急促而上）二爷，二爷，拐喽，没得喽，没得喽，到处都没得喽。

胡：你慌个啥子，我不是还在喽嘛！

李：龙洞沟、大堰塘、凉水井、田坎脚，到处都没得水喽，到处都干喽。

胡：水源干了，昨天我看到水窖中还有些水的嘛。

李：哎呀，我的二爷，水窖也干咯，现在啊，水窖是白天装太阳、晚上装月亮了。二爷，你说哪个办嘛！

胡：哪个办，凉拌。你着那样急？你以为就是你一个人晓得着急啊？半个月前，政府不是就带起我们修池子、窖管子，想法子、发种子、送票子？哪个不着急？

李：着急有啥用？这个水天上不落地下不生，光靠政府，政府还能挑水给我们吃啊？

胡：你娃儿晓得干着急没用哈。前两天你说的那个洞，搞到点水出来没得？

李：你说的哪个洞？

胡：山脚的那个。

李：山脚的好几个洞，人家水利站的陈站长都下去看过，特别是前天，哪个都不敢下去，还是陈站长拿几根牵牛的绳子捆起腰杆下去的，结果呢，也是细细娃儿拜义父—干爹（的）。

胡：干了就干了嘛，我还不信真要干死人！

李：二爷，你是不是要丢下我们不管喽？

胡：我哪个会丢下大家不管呢？

李：二爷，你不要麻我喽！

胡：我麻你哪样？

李：不要以为我不晓得，你肯定想另做打算！

胡：作甚么打算？

李：你是不是要搬家？

胡：搬家？

李：你不想搬家，咋个会约起支书商量，还说什么要先出二万五的材料款。你不是想搬到水源好的地方去才怪。咦，二爷，没看出来哈，你老人家给群众苦了一辈子我晓得，大家都记得到你，但在危难关头你却要逃跑啊？

胡：你说哪样？

李：哪样？你太过分了，要跑自己跑，还要以权谋私，我听到你亲口讲的，你还说加上政府给的二万二，买材料勉强够了！你不要公款私用哈。

胡：我懒得给你说！

李：懒得给我说？你不说我就不晓得啊，你硬是二两米做十个人的饭，只有你才做得出！平时口口声声说带领大家致富，关键时候就各人自谋出路！你自己的二万五我们管不着，政府拿的那二万二，你不要想独吞！

胡：那你要想啷个做？

李：啷个做，隔山打鸟、见者有份，拿出来、平分！

胡：平分！你笑死人！一分都不可能！

李：你才笑死人，想吃独食，我到政府告你！（气愤而下）

胡：你告、你告……

（村主任胡二爷追李出门，看看院子，开始扫地）

（蔡大娘挎着一篮子鸡蛋路过）

胡：蔡大娘，你要走哪里去？是不是你家缸子头又没得水喽，今天几个党员都没得闲给你家挑水……

蔡：不着急、不着急，我要去蚌壳堰水库！

胡：是哪个亲戚生娃娃喽，你提起鸡蛋要去吃满月酒？

蔡：不是得，我是给那些修沟的娃儿些送鸡蛋的！

胡：大娘，你一个人，好不容易凑得几个鸡蛋，你自家留起慢慢吃嘛！

蔡：我是不容易，哪个又容易得很？天干几个月，你天天带起那些党员打起轮子给我送水，你们家水缸都干峡，我屋头哪天断个水？你们几十亩几十亩的苗圃干起，哪息不是先把我那几小块菜地淋了再去给基地浇水？说是要去蚌壳堰水库窖水，你不喊大家斗钱，各人先拔二万五买材料……这些容易啊？再说，要不是你们上次发绿壳蛋鸡鸡苗给我养，我又哪里得这鸡蛋嘛！

胡：大娘，哪个叫我们是干部、是党员呢？

蔡：我晓得你们是党员、是干部，我更晓得你们不是神仙，天不见亮就去挖沟窖水，大晌午喽，都还没得回家吃饭！

胡：大娘，我们党员干部只是带个头，大事还是要靠大家，我原本喊40个人，结果一上就是100多！只是还有人不理解啊！还说要去政府告我。

蔡：你说李老幺那个鬼崽崽不是嘛？他刚才在二组讲，我都说他良心遭狗吃了。你不要管他。

村长啊，这样大的活路、这样多人，不吃东西啷个要得？

胡：我安排了馒头的！

蔡：几个馒头抵不到事，这是煮熟的鸡蛋，快拿去分给大家吃！趁热和。

李：（边跑边喊）二爷，有喽、有喽……

胡：那样有了？

李：（上气不接下气）有水喽、有水喽！

胡：哪点来的水。

李：从蚌壳堰水库窖过来的水通咯！

胡：窖通了？

李：通喽！

蔡：通喽。你不是去告状去喽嘛？

李：（不好意思地）我，我，是我以小人之心想二爷你老人家了哈（打自己嘴巴），二爷才不会和我计较呢！啊？

蔡：你不是说人家看到天干就想搬家？

李：不是搬家是为大家！

蔡：还说村长要吞二万五的材料款？

李：哎吆，蔡大娘，我都知道错怪二爷咯，那是给大家引水的材料款！

蔡：那喊人帮忙呢？

李：那是发动大家投工投劳！

蔡：你晓得是投工投劳哈。人家张老五到洞头找水受伤了，都去挖沟了，你好手好脚的还不快去？还在这些说三道四的？还要告人家。

李：告哪样告，我替大家谢谢他！

蔡：不要在这里花口花嘴的喽，（把篮子一抵）快去分给大家吃了！

李：好，我马上去，马上去。（提篮子下）

（选自2009年“多彩贵州”相声小品大赛修文赛区创作奖作品）

纪实文学

保卫河口电站

夏之奎

1950年3月27、28日两天，国民党残余势力勾结的土匪1500多人围攻修文县城，两次进攻均未得逞。29日，匪首李胜华、吴必瑞竟勾结清镇、贵筑土匪300余人攻打河口电站。其余匪众仍留原地，妄图引诱我驻城部队增援河口电站，以便乘虚而入，攻占县城。

河口电站位于修文河和猫跳河交汇处的东面，地势险要，北面修文河谷深流急，西面猫跳河谷深100余米，两岸石壁更如刀削，南面山谷谷深50至100余米，山势陡峭，唯有东面地势较为平缓，是土匪可

以进攻之处。年初县境出现匪患后，河口电站在军代表姚希顺的组织领导下，已做好了防匪的周密部署，在电站的东南面用石蹬子修建了1座碉堡，沿电站东面一线修筑防御工势，工势前200米范围内的杂草树木全被砍光。省军区军械处又拨给一批枪支，其中有1挺机枪，8支步枪。

29日清晨有消息来报，在电站东面的干坝、木厂一带发现有众多的土匪活动，种种迹象表明，土匪是来攻打河口电站的。姚希顺立即下令做好战斗准备。10点钟，土匪开始进攻了，先是听到“啪！啪！”两声枪响，接着众多土匪从电站东面的几座山头冲了过来，匪徒们端着步枪，火枪，还有人举着长把钩刀和梭镖，黑压压的一大片。但多数匪徒怕死不敢往前冲，吆喝一阵就躲了起来，只有少数胆大的匪徒边躲边冲，冲到前沿阵地的只不过几十个人。这边的守军严阵以待，姚希顺亲自掌握机枪，沉着冷静，等敌人靠近不到100米时他才扣动扳机，一梭子打了出去，其他的同志也跟着射击，一时间机枪声、步枪声响成一片，跑在前边的几个匪徒应声倒下，其他的匪徒吓得掉头就往回跑。就这样土匪的第一次进攻被轻易地打退了。

下午3点过钟，土匪又开始了第二次进攻，他们组织了有50多人的敢死队往前冲，其余的匪徒在后边摇旗呐喊，有的“嘟-，嘟-”地吹着牛角助威。这次敌人的进攻没有像前一次那样轻易地被打退，前边的匪徒被打倒两个后其余的匪徒迅速散开，隐蔽在石头后面和土坎下面，还不时地往这边射击，一时间战斗形成了胶着状态，这边有的战士还受了伤，情况十分紧急，稍有不慎，土匪有可能攻进电站，后果不堪设想。战斗一直持续到太阳快落山时，只听对面山顶上的牛角“喔-嘟喔”的响了几声后，土匪才停止进攻撤退了回去。

土匪虽然停止进攻，但仍然将电站围得水泄不通，从修文河电站大坝左岸至猫跳河右岸的石门坎一带都有土匪在活动。土匪不撤，单靠电站的10多条枪和几十个工人，难以抵抗土匪的多次进攻，黄昏时，姚希顺找来几个工人，给他们布置了任务，要他们把电站被围的消息带到修文去，请求县委派兵增援。天刚黑，这几个工人从电站北面的修文河涉水过河，从山林中绕道经中半坡，过沙溪，再从西门坡进入修文城，把电站被围的消息报告了县委。

县委书记夏树屏得知土匪进攻电站的情况后，立即和县长史可鉴赶到军大五分校校部，与校领导姜思毅，匡赋等人召开紧急会议。大家分析了当前的形势，县城和河口电站两处被围，相比之下河口的形势更为紧急。如果县城派大部队驰援河口，势必会造成城内兵力空虚，围城土匪会乘虚攻入县城；如果不派兵增援，河口有可能失守。会议最后决定：一方面派张参谋率领两个班的兵力驰援河口，坚守电站阵地，另一方面火速将情况报告省军区请求增援。

张参谋率领增援河口的两个班战士先到弹药库领取弹药，有的扛一箱子弹，有的扛一箱手榴弹，有的用四五条子弹袋装满子弹交叉挂在肩上，反正是能拿多少就拿多少。增援部队由电站工人作向导摸黑出西门，经过沙溪涉水过河，又经中半坡，穿过一片没有道路的青冈林，抵达修文河河口右岸。工人向导叫大家停下，随即向对岸扔了一块石头后，双手在嘴前做成一个喇叭筒状，对着对岸发出“咕嘟咕、咕嘟咕”两声信号，对岸也同样发出同样的信号回应。工人向导对张参谋小声地说：“首长，可以过河了。”张参谋挥手下令：“走！”大家一起蹚过河，再爬过一处悬崖，终于赶到了电站的前沿阵地。张参谋立即找到姚希顺研究作战方案。天逐渐亮了，匪徒们发现电站的阵地上又多了许多穿黄军装的人，大约不少于100人，原来是军代表姚希顺在天亮前叫战士们把自多余的军装都拿出来换给工人们穿上，以此壮大军威。匪徒们不知底细，认为是夜间增援的解放军大部队到了，再加上昨天的两次进攻都没有占到便宜，所以不敢轻举妄动，只是远远的放冷枪。

另一方面派往省军区请求增援的人让县委和军校的领导们研究了许久，在出南门到贵阳方向40公里的路程中有30多公里范围内是土匪的活动区，派谁去比较适合，能派去的人要么说话口音不适合，要么不熟悉情况，要么容易被敌人识破，要么……待到快天亮时才决定由文工队年纪最小的湛芝（15岁）和李佩琼（14岁）两个女演员去比较适合。命令立即传达到文工队，文工队的同志们把两个小同志化装成乡下姑娘，把告急信缝在袜子里，并找来两个小竹笆斗篷和两个夹背，还找来一个可靠的马车夫。天刚亮他们就出发了，马车夫对两个小同志说：“在路上遇到生人，你们不要讲话，让我来对付。”三人坐上马车出南门朝贵阳方向一路紧赶。走到三角山时遇到了一伙土匪，匪徒们把马车拦了来，有几个匪徒看到车上坐着两个姑娘，嬉皮笑脸地说：“哟，两个姑娘还长得蛮漂亮的嘛。”两个小同志只是低着头，做着害羞的样子。马车夫说：“这是城里头陈二老爷（陈镜秋）家花溪的两个亲戚，现在兵荒马乱的，陈大爷叫我把他们两个送回家去。”匪徒们一听说是城头陈参议长家的亲戚，都不敢哆嗦。领头的一个说：“好了，你们慢走。”下午3点钟他们来到了省军区驻地，向军区首长汇报了修文县城和河口电站被围的情况。

军区政委苏振华接到情报后，立即派出两个连的兵力，连夜火速赶赴河口增援，土匪闻风溃逃，在河口电站的守军也乘机杀出，打垮了土匪的包围，取得了保卫河口电站的胜利。这次战斗共计打死匪徒7人，打伤10多人，受到中央燃料工业部嘉奖，奖给“护厂模范”锦旗。

（原载《贵阳党史》2006年第4期）

猫跳河畔凶杀案

唐育文

三级电站坐落在修文县王官乡境内的猫跳河畔。依山傍水建立起来的办公室和家属宿舍，一层层环绕在江边一个大的山头上。山头上解放前修造的一个碉堡，依然完整地保留下来，孤零零地站在山尖顶上。山头的上部是家属宿舍，靠山脚临江处是办公室，宿舍与办公室之间的山腰里是职工食堂，家属宿舍是一排一排的平房，几排平房之间的空地是职工家属们茶余饭后聊天、下棋、打扑克的“乐园”。

一个黑影

1985年劳动节这天，食堂照例增加几个小炒。下午下班后，职工们有的在食堂，有的在家里，尽兴畅饮，酒精刺激得满脸通红。收拾完碗筷已是华灯初上时分，不上夜班的职工乘着酒兴端个小凳泡杯浓茶陆续到“乐园”寻找各自的乐趣。

电站的电灯“近水楼台先得月”显得格外明亮，将办公室家属区照耀得如同白昼，有光明就不可避免地有阴暗，此时聊天的人们海阔天空地正吹到精彩处，下棋的正全神贯注地看着棋盘。谁也没有注意到在一个阴暗角落里有一个“黑影”正探头探脑地窥视着“乐园”里的人们，看到人群并未减少，“黑影”又无声地缩回到阴暗保护区里。夜深了，人们三三两两地各自往家里走，最后的两个象棋迷也打着哈欠走了。“黑影”乘机溜到第八栋家属宿舍，靠近一家房门，从口袋里拿出什么东西，在房门上只几下便麻利地把房主人离家时锁在门上的“铁将军”卸了下来，一闪身“黑影”钻入更阴暗地方，和整个阴暗处融为一体。

她怎么一去就不来

职工食堂离家属区约有40—50米，这天是杨秀琴与王学珍当班。下午把饭煮好后杨秀琴在食堂里称了半斤豆芽，看看表才五点三十五分，离开饭时间还有二十多分钟，“还有点时间，我把豆芽拿回家去，马上就回来”。杨秀琴给王学珍说：“快点来呕，马上要开饭。”正准备炒菜的王学珍下意识地看了一眼手腕上的表。“很快就来”，杨边走边答。“怎么一去就不回来”，打了菜又忙打饭的王学珍，满头大汗嘴里在埋怨着杨秀琴，职工们吃完饭离开饭堂，王学珍一个人在收拾着饮具，边干边想：“都快七点钟了，她怎么还不来呢？可能她家里来客，走不开，我一个人干完算了，哪家没有点事情呢。他们关系一直处得很好，做完最后一件工作，王学珍也加入到“乐园”的行列里，直到睡觉也没有再去想杨秀琴一事。第二天其他职工都按时到了，只差杨秀琴一个人没有来，早餐后仍然不见来上班，王学珍似乎预感到什么，急忙给电站领导说：杨秀琴昨天下午五点钟回家，以后一直没有见到她。站领导也觉得蹊跷，顺便叫个人去找一下，十多分钟后寻找的人上气不接下气的结结巴巴地说：“杨……杨……杨秀琴被人杀死在屋里了。”什么！在场的人都不约而同地朝杨秀琴家奔去“注意保护现场，马上打电话向公安局报案”。站领导指挥职工们分头忙起来。

公安局值班民警接到三级电站的电话报案，记录本上报案时间一栏里写上。1985年5月3日八时四十分。十时十五分刑侦队赶到现场，现场上杨秀琴头南足北仰卧于卧室的地板上，头部被窗帘和三件衣服遮盖得严严实实，揭去衣服窗帘，呈现一幅不忍目睹的惨状。整个头部布满了大大小小的伤口十三处，血肉模糊，面目全非，室内的大立柜、蚊帐、电视机柜等处有明显的喷射状血迹，经法医鉴定杨是被利器损伤颅骨，脑颅骨骨折致死。“是一起凶杀案”出现场的同志们得出了共同的结论。

是谁杀死她

出现场的同志们返回县局。向地区公安处和省公安厅汇报了案情。请求技术支援，公安局副政委卓英才同志从县局一科、二科抽调干警，立即赶到三级电站，5月3日下午二时三十分省厅派工程师罗登贵率刑技人员赶到现场，立即和县公安局的同志对现场进行仔细认真的勘察。到5月5日上午从中心现场到半径50米的区域内，取到罪犯的两个鞋印，作案时使用的一只带血的白沙手套，一把有血迹的小斧头和一把带搭扣的小挂锁。

电站领导介绍情况，死者杨秀琴，四十八岁，食堂炊事员，平时工作积极，作风正派，死前未发现反常现象，也没有外边的人来找她。丈夫廖正祥身体不好在红枫湖疗养，杨秀琴的左邻宴志恒今年到乌江电站去了，家里没有人，右邻刘全贵1984年10月调红枫电站工作，全家搬走此房空着。

廖正祥被通知回来清理家中物资，发现放在柜里的现金185元，一个活期存折，一串钥匙不见了，“这把斧子和小挂锁是你家的吗”？侦察员把小斧子和带搭扣的小挂锁递给廖辨认。“不是我家的，我家没有这两样东西”。不是，那么这两件东西是哪家的？扩大现场范围，发现宴志恒家伙房的门上搭扣被撬走后留下有新印。将拾到的搭扣拿来比对，证实是从这个门上撬走的，室内壁柜被撬坏，翻得乱七八糟。宴家伙房内、窗台上、阳沟塑料纸上留下清晰的鞋印，与杨秀琴被杀现场所留鞋印相同，宴志恒接到电话通知，赶回三级电站，清理了物资后说：这里没有什么值钱的东西，只是放在壁柜内的一把小斧头不见了，侦察员将小爷头和小锁给宴辨认，宴确认自己常用的，将带血的手套和斧子送省厅进行技术鉴定，认定手套和斧头上的血与杨秀琴的血型同一，根据现场勘察确定，案件性质为盗窃杀人，且系一人所为。

“5·3”凶杀案侦破组以修文县公安局为主，从红枫电站保卫科、三级电站抽调干部共13人组成，卓英才任组长，是谁杀死杨秀琴？作案者是什么样的人？侦破组根据勘察现场的数据资料，首先为案犯画像：凶手男性，身高一米六0至一米六六，对电站家属区及杨秀琴上下班的情况较熟，贪婪、心毒手狠、摸排对象范围划在电站内部职工、子女、邻近的地质勘探队，附近的农民村寨，这些单位村寨中有过盗窃、偷摸、赌博行为和无正当职业，长期游荡的人。着重查清5月2日下午五点半以后到3日天亮前的活动情况，侦破组分成5个小组深入到群众中开展广泛细致的调查。

通过一段时间工作初步确定的15个嫌疑对象，排除了8名，剩下的7个送省厅技术鉴定否定6名，只剩下一个名叫魏荣的对象，魏荣符合画像特征，是不是他作的案？进一步查清杨秀琴被杀时间，他在干什么？调查的材料证明魏在5月2日下午六时左右曾到过第八栋宿舍，但还有个姚X与他同行，5月2日晚的活动情况一直有人证实，没有单独活动过，魏荣没有作案时间。最后一个对象不得不最后否定。至此案件的侦破陷入一片迷茫，十多个日日夜夜的辛劳，同志们两眼布满血丝，凶手还未找到，上下班总是提心吊胆，家住偏僻的职工往“安全”地带搬家，往日聊天的“乐园”里查无一人，天黑不敢出门，全家闭门守户，一派恐怖气氛笼罩着三级电站的家家户户。

是他的指纹

组长卓英才看到这种状况，召集全体人员开会，首先坚定大家的破案决心，我们一定要把凶手抓到，让杨秀琴的冤魂得以安息，使群众的情绪得以稳定，然后大家献计献策讨论侦破新方案。“电站有没有人外出”会议上不知谁提出一个新问题，电站的同志说：“有职工子弟朱吉忠1983年因盗窃被判刑，刑满后一直在外做生意，没有回来过，案发前后也没有发现他回来”，“我们食堂今年4月曾被人偷过一次，因被偷的东西不多，没有向公安局报案，案也没有破”，电站同志补充说，经过热烈讨论统一了两个侦破方案，一是将4月食堂被盗案和“5·3”凶杀案并案侦破；二是对长期流窜在外，又符合画像条件的朱吉忠的活动情况调查清楚。同志们又鼓足了劲，兵分两路齐头并进，侦破食堂被盗窃的同志在现场上取到了作案留下的指纹脚印。与“5·3”凶杀案现场留下的脚印比对，认定是同一个人的脚印，初步判断盗食堂、盗窦家和盗窃杨秀琴被杨撞见而杀人的罪犯均系一人，将取得的指纹与原定嫌疑对象—比对，又—排除，朱吉忠下落不明，没有找到，朱的情况不清，指纹脚印是不是他的，也无法比对，在并案侦破中刚有点进展又陷入了僵局，大家都在冥思苦索，食堂里留下的指纹究竟是谁的呢？“嘿！朱吉忠不是被判过刑吗”，刑侦队队长吴超群若有所悟地说：“判刑前在我们看守所关过，看守所一定会有他的指纹”，立即派人到看守所，结论两枚指纹同一，是他的指纹，可以确定朱吉忠是“5·3”凶杀案的重大嫌疑对象。

黑影亮相

“5·3”凶杀案有了决定性的突破，当务之急是要抓住不知下落的朱吉忠，“就是逃到天涯海角也要将他捉拿归案”，侦破组全体同志都下定了决定，侦破组变成4个追捕组，明确了任务范围，第一组在电站及附近农村守候，张网以待；第二组负责修文、息烽及乌江电站；第三组负责乌当区、白云区；第四组负责清镇县、贵阳市、鸭池河、南盘江。凡是朱吉忠可能落脚，途径的地方都布下了天罗地网，同志们不顾十多天夜以继日工作的疲劳，不放过一个可能的机会，连续9天的追捕守候，追捕组的同志没有吃过一顿舒心饭，没有睡过一夜安稳觉。1985年5月25日第四组张佩山和陈德之在贵阳市西路派出所的协助下，终于将朱吉忠抓获。

朱吉忠被依法刑事拘留。审讯室，侦察员与朱吉忠的较量正在激烈地进行着“朱吉忠老实交代，你从5月1日到3日都到过那些地方”，“这几天我在贵阳，一直贵阳做生意，哦，到过息烽”，朱吉忠眨着一双狡黠的眼睛回答，“到过三级电站吗？回过家没有”，侦察员单刀直入地直击薄弱点，“没有，没有到过”，慌乱中朱断然否认，声音却在颤抖，“没有到过，怎么会留下你的脚印”，侦察员的声音不高，但这种毋庸置疑的语气却给朱形成一股强大的压力，只见他手足无措，额上渗出了大颗大颗的汗水，“你看这是不是你留下的”，侦察员看准时机，出示了现场取得的脚印照片和白沙手套，朱吉忠下意识地看了一眼，汗如雨下，脸色灰白“我交代，我交代”，他的精神防线被这颗“重型炮弹”彻底垮了。

5月1日夜闪晃在三级电站家属区的“黑影”正是朱吉忠，1983年犯盗窃罪被判刑，刑满释放后在外做生意，生意蚀本，准备回家又身无分文，怕父母面前无法交代，于重操“旧业”。5月1日潜回电站，在山头的旧碉堡内等到天黑，人们都回家睡觉时撬开窦志恒家门锁，准备大捞一把，谁知窦家值钱的东西都搬走了，除一把小斧子外一无所获。他颓丧地倒在窦家床上，一觉睡到5月2日下午，贼心不死，还是要捞一把，他知道隔壁杨秀琴的丈夫在红枫疗养，此时杨秀琴正在上班，贪婪的欲望使他无法等到天黑再动手，潜入杨秀琴家正在翻箱倒柜地寻找钱财时，杨秀琴拿着豆芽突然回到家中，无法躲避，又是认识的人，于是举起手中的斧子对准杨的头一下又一下的砍去，直到完全断气。朱吉忠找到了自己需要的东西，在杨秀琴家等到天黑，又借阴暗的掩护神不知鬼不觉的离开三级电站，连夜赶到贵阳，在这期间从贵阳逃到息烽、湄潭、贞丰等地。

“我以为没有人看见，你们无法找到我，谁知……”朱吉忠耷拉着脑袋无可奈何地说，盗窃杀人犯朱吉忠终于被押上了审判台。职工们交口赞誉“公安局的人真了不起，这种无头案都破了”。三级电站做了一面大红旗送到公安局，旗子上“人民公安为民除害”的八个大字闪放着耀眼的光芒。

（选自《修文县公安志》稿）

（五）艺术创作

书法 1978年后，县内书法爱好者日渐增多，涌现一批较有建树的书法名家，其中有中国书协会员1人，省书协会员10人。朱俊首的作品多次入选国家级书展并获奖。郝承德、晏才俊、杨美玉、李暄等人的50余件作品参加过省、市展出。少年书法作者孙瑜、孙崖的作品参加过全国教育系统学生书法展并获奖。县文联每年举行书法美术摄影作品展，1988—2010年，共展出书法作品800余件。

美术 1978年后，县内有郝承德、沈兴华、杨劲松、吴道学等被省美术家协会吸收为会员，成为县内美术界的佼佼者。1988—2010年，县内美术作者创作有600多件作品参加各种展出活动，有100余件作品入选市、省和国家级的展出，郝承德、沈新华、杨劲松、吴道学、刘柏元等作者的20余件作品被收入省级以上编辑出版的美术图册。郝承德先后出版个人作品集《郝承德画集》《郝承德画选》2本。县文联出版《龙场墨韵—修文美术、书法作品集》。

摄影 1978年后，随着生活水平提高，县内摄影爱好者日益增多。1988年8月摄影协会成立，县内作者的摄影作品开始登上省级报刊和国家级报刊，有余岚、周尚明和杨翠等人50余件作品先后在《贵阳日报》《贵州日报》《文史天地》《中国摄影报》等报刊上发表。1997年，县委宣传部和贵州摄影家协会举办"六广河风光摄影大赛"，以此推动县内摄影创作水平的提高。此外，还通过参加"美术书法摄影作品展"活动来推动摄影创作的普及。1978—2010年，有250余件摄影作品参加县内和省市展出，参展作者50余人次。

篆刻 1978年后，县内喜爱业余篆刻的人逐渐增多，先是修文中学丁满、扎佐中学汪炯堂和扎佐二小谭德明等篆刻的印章日积月累共有60多方，于1989年春节参与蛇年新春书画篆刻展览，深受群众喜爱，获得良好的社会反响和认同。进入20世纪90年代，国画家郝承德除坚持绘画创作外也做成"云山之外"等篆刻作品。更喜人的是一批篆刻新秀脱颖而出。龙场镇纪委书记冯祥篆刻的"知行合一"、县书法协会主席孙新民篆刻的"学到老"、金桥小学教师吴乾辉篆刻的"翰墨千秋"、扎佐青年李文颖篆刻的"超然"、修文三中教师郑永篆刻的"不负所学"和张仕山篆刻的"千里共婵娟"等作品均富有一定的艺术品位，深受人们青睐，有的还在省市的书法篆刻展中入展获奖，成绩斐然。

音乐 县内歌曲创作以张禧年和贾文的成果较丰，张禧年创作歌曲80余首，贾文创作歌曲50余首，其中贾文2002年创作的《木叶新歌》在第四届全国乡村青年歌手大赛时演唱获优秀奖，2004年获贵阳市第六届金筑文艺三等奖。1999年集体创作的《修文之歌》，由县人大常委会作出决定在全县传唱。

书法作品

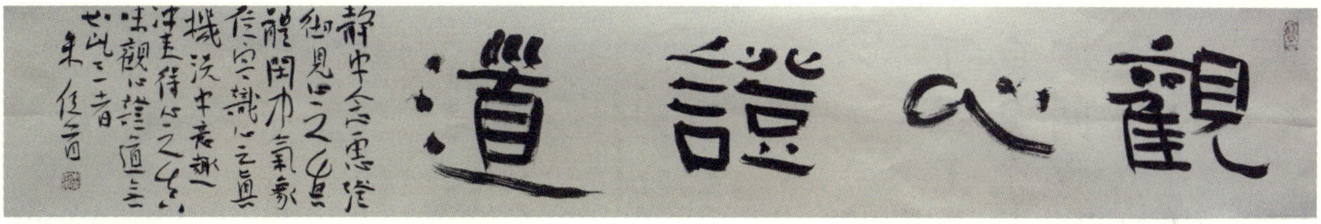

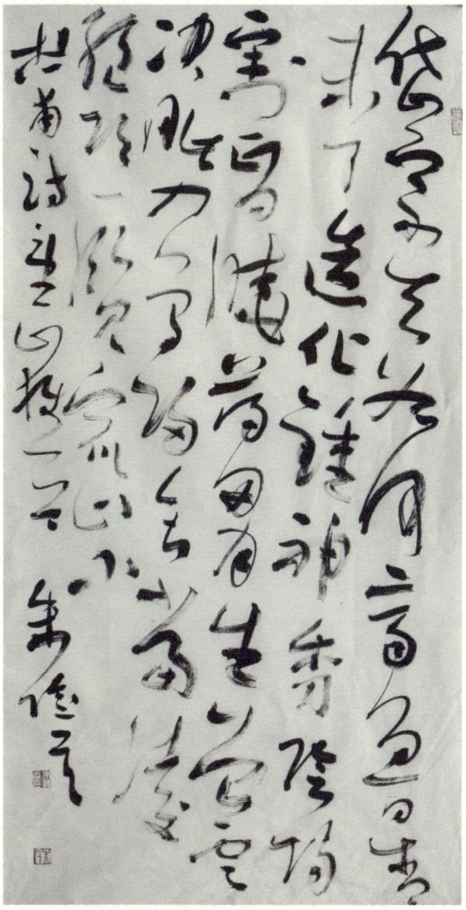

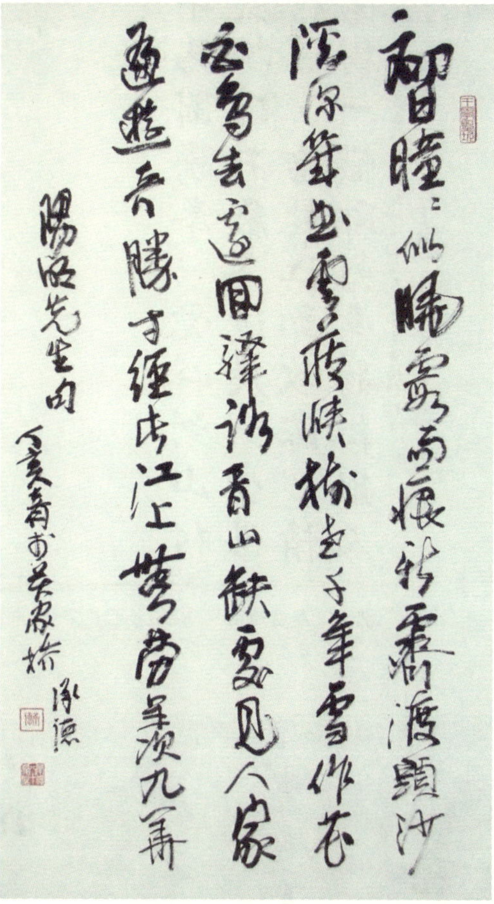

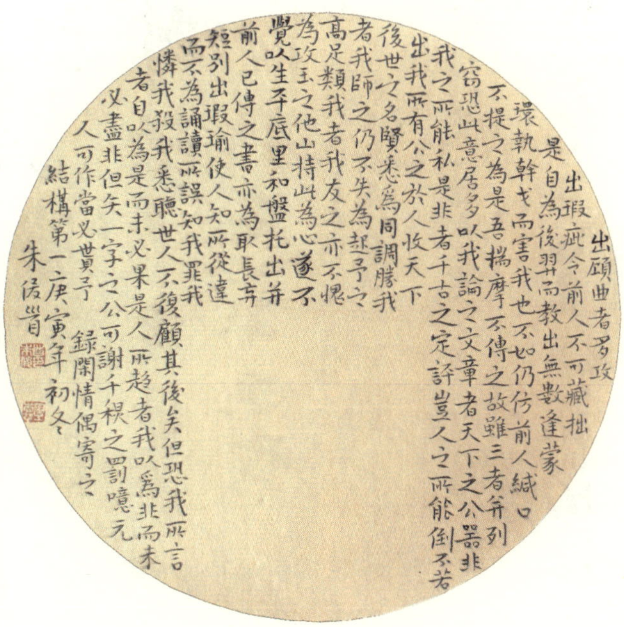

隶书·朱俊首书

草书·朱俊首书

行书·郝承德书

楷书·朱俊首书

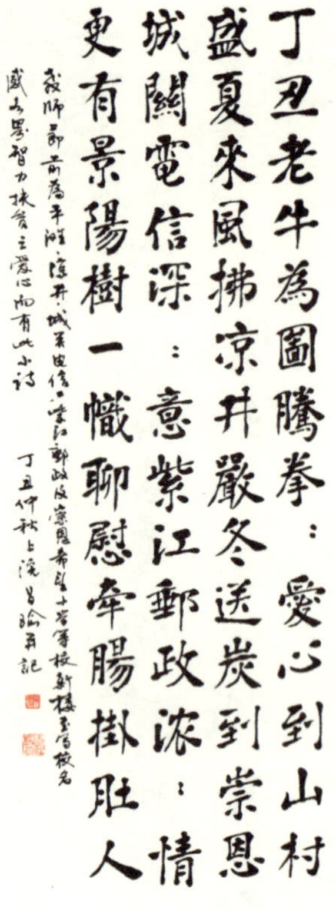

楷书·廖昌瑜书

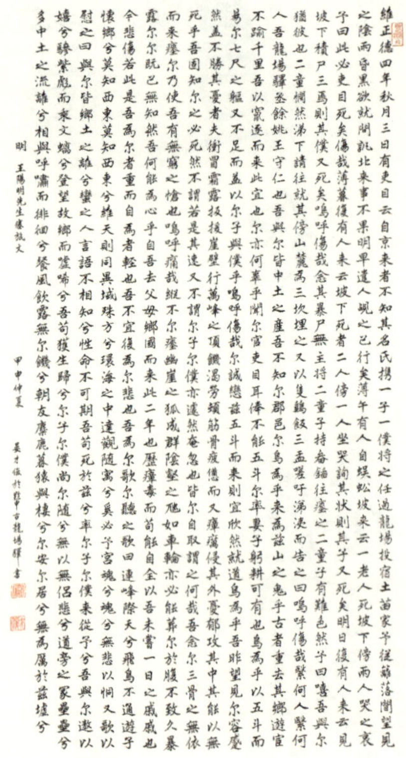

楷书·晏才俊书

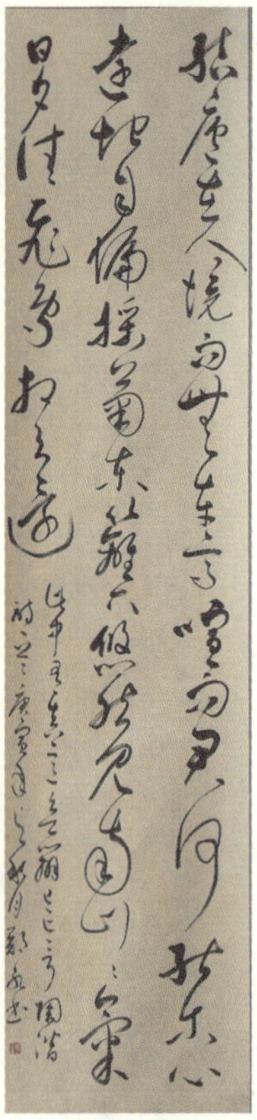

草书·郑永书

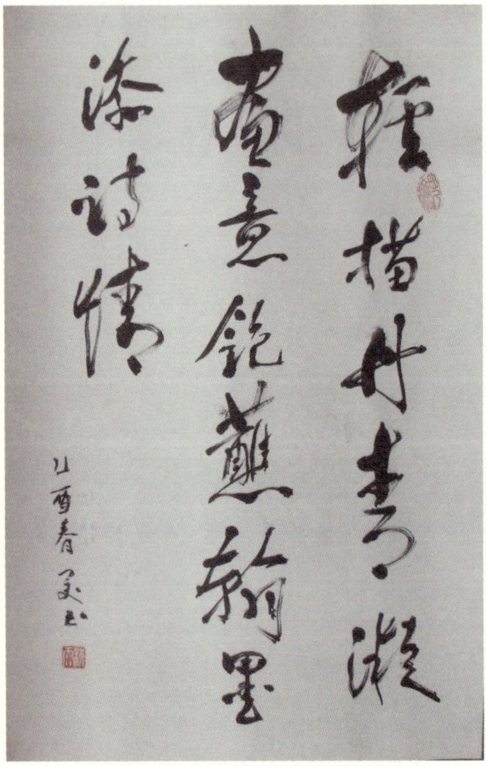

行书·杨美玉书

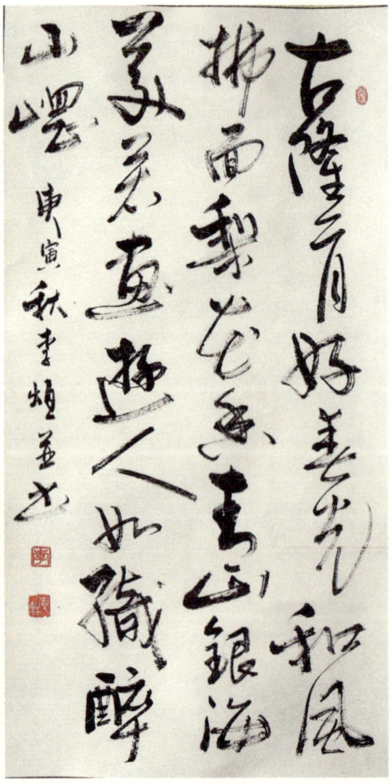

行书·李暄书

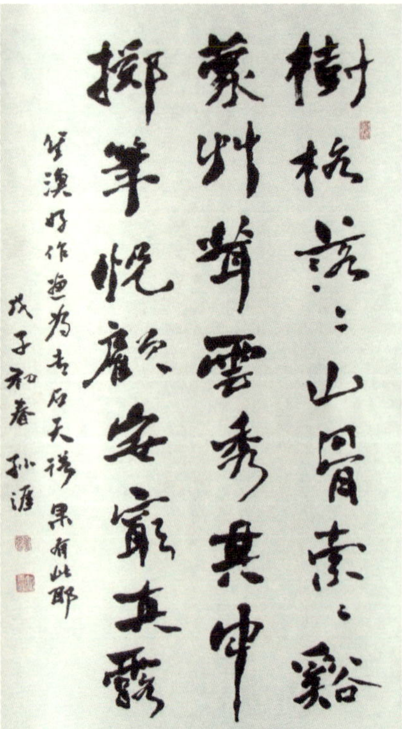

楷书·孙涯书

美术作品

油画《王阳明先生》 吴道学作

国画《幽谷深居》 郝承德作

国画《布依人家》 郝承德作

国画《蕉荫下》沈兴华作

国画《老树新花》 郝承德作

工笔画《万里祥和图》沈兴华作

国画《春山烟雨》杨劲松作

工笔扇面《荷韵》沈兴华作

油画《党旗下的笑靥》郑秀娟作

漆画《蒙古族妇女》刘柏元作

摄影作品

跨越——六广河特大桥　余岚　摄

晨曲——苏格兰牧场　朱文捷　摄

仙境——六屯乡新中村　岳金平　摄

农家希望——洒坪猕猴桃基地 周尚明 摄

湖光山色——大石乡回水湖 周尚明 摄

桃源河沐浴三道响 徐涛 摄

穿越——桃源河 杨翠 摄

篆刻作品

承德翰墨　郝承德刊

修文人　丁　满刊

翰墨千秋　吴乾辉刊

何陋之有　吴乾辉刊

千里共婵娟　张仕山刊

知行合一　冯　祥刊

学到老　孙新民刊

厚德载物　孙新民刊

不负所学　郑　永刊

砚公　冯　祥刊

超然　李文颖刊

云山之外　郝承德刊

音乐作品

修文之歌

1=F4/4　　　　集体 词曲

坚定自豪地 ♩=108

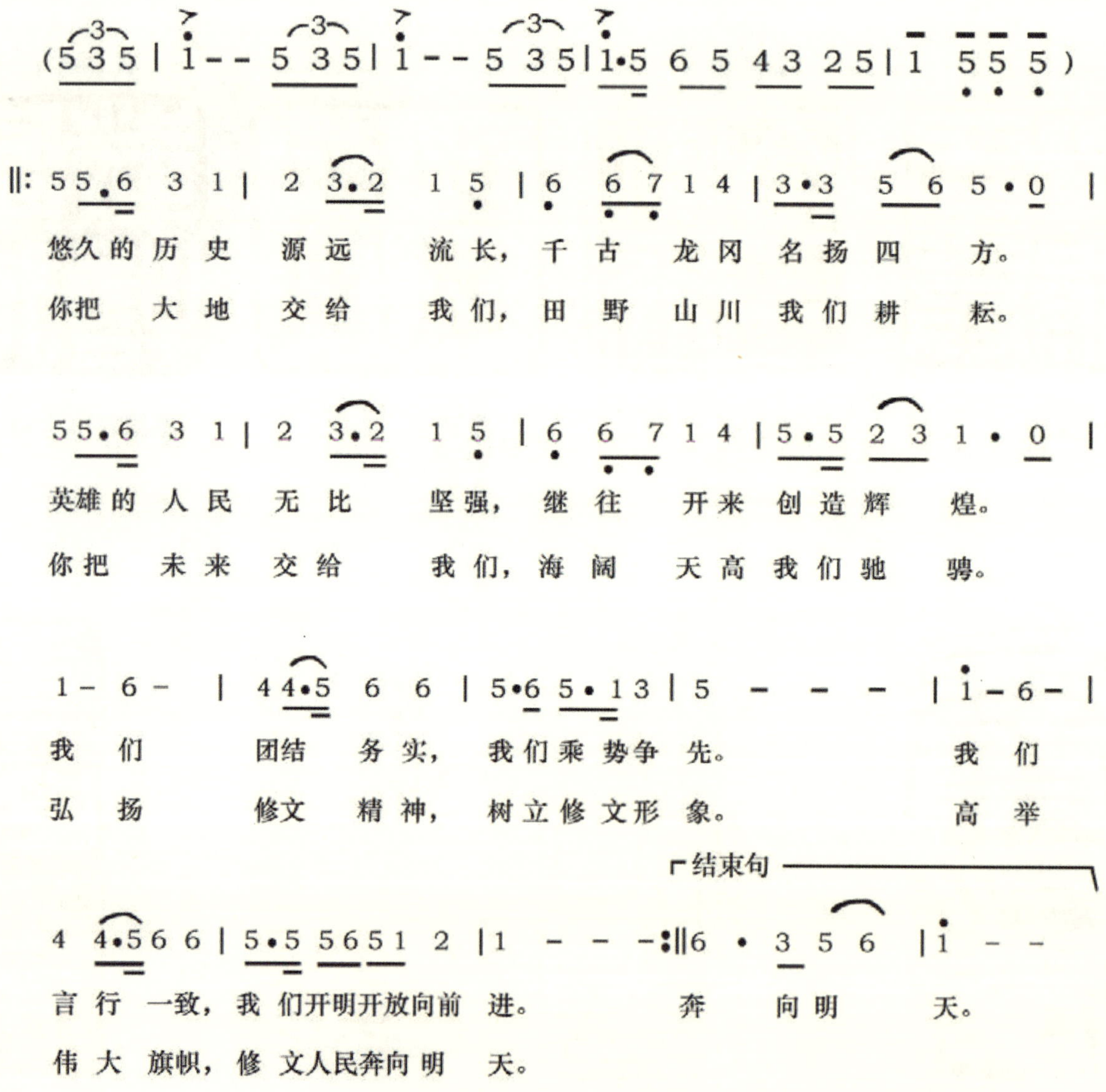

我爱中国梦

（独唱）

1 =C $\frac{2}{4}$

张禧年 词曲

民歌风　稍慢

党啊，您就是我的母亲

（合　唱）

1=♭E $\frac{4}{4}$

张禧年 词曲

深情地　稍慢

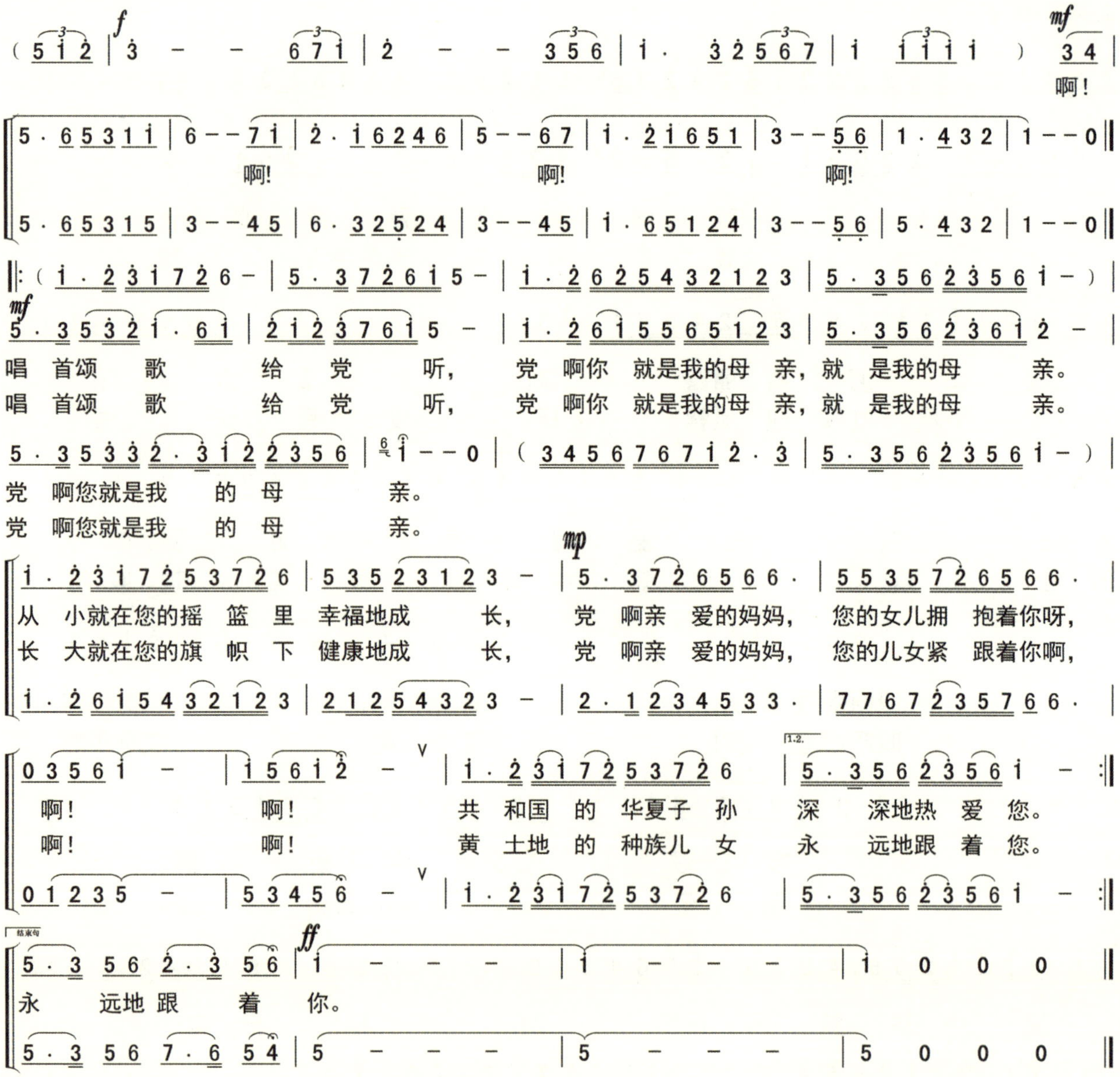

木叶新歌

（独唱）

贾文　词曲

1 =F $\frac{4}{4}$

♩=100　民歌风

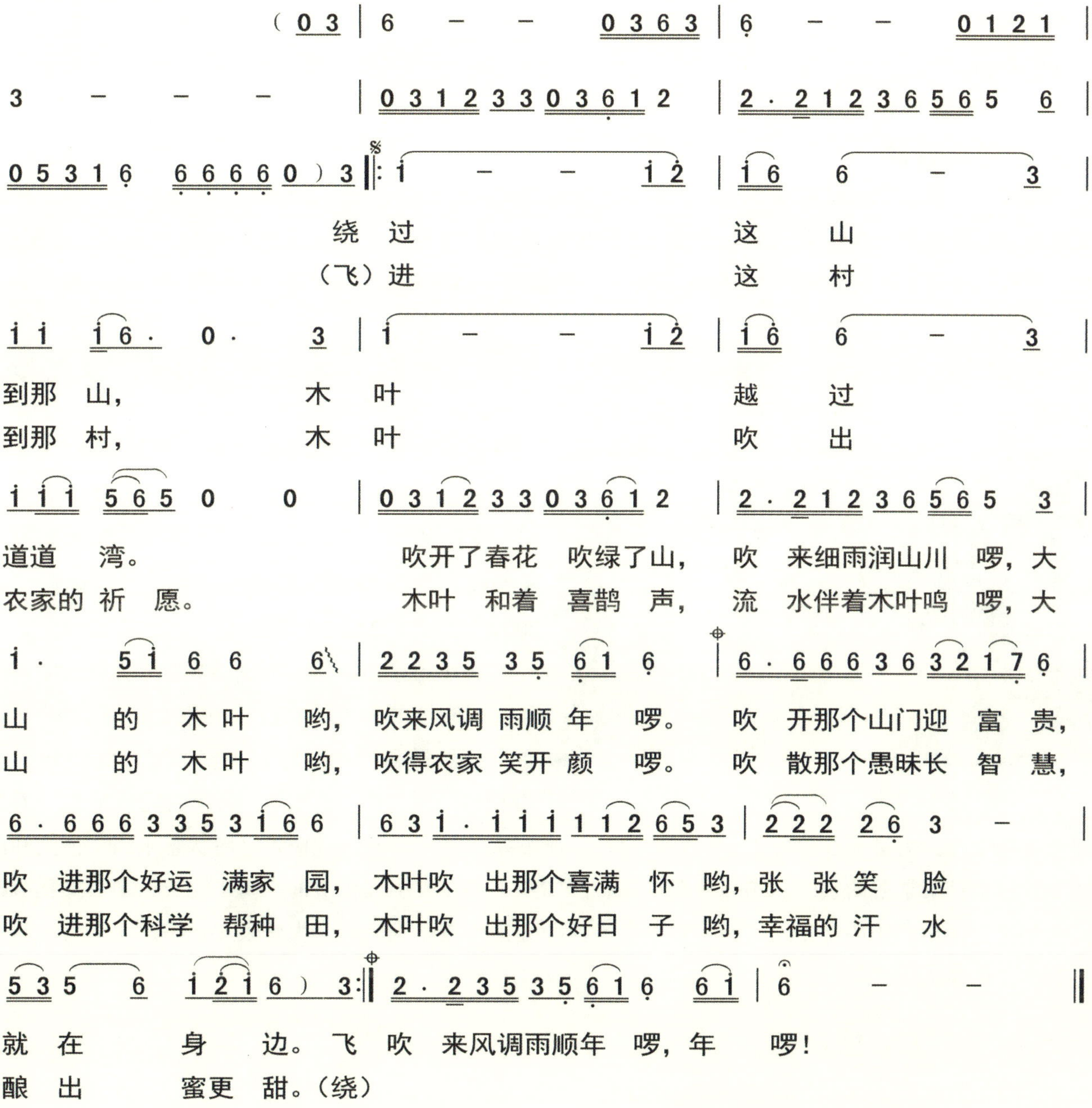

《阳光下的花朵》剧照

舞蹈戏剧 1978年至2010年，县内创作编排舞蹈100多个，各类剧作80余个，获奖20余个。1990年，陈新国创作的小品《家事》获安顺地区文艺调演二等奖，1992年，刁福林创作的小戏《卖烤烟》获省文艺调演三等奖。2003年，陈新国创作《王学圣地》电视片脚本由贵阳电视台搬上荧屏。2007年，县女企业家协会创作舞蹈《红苞谷》获贵阳市第七届金筑文艺奖，并参加全国“群星奖”大赛。2009年，胡光胤、李小龙等创作、表演的小品《周末》获贵阳市文艺调演二等奖，2010年，由县青少年活动中心和音舞剧协会创作少儿苗族舞蹈《阳光下的花朵》参加“魅力校园第四届全国校园文艺会演暨第九届校园春节联欢晚会”获金奖。

三、文化设施

1978年起，县内文化设施逐年增加，1995年后进入高潮时段。1997—2000年，全县10乡（镇）相继建成文化活动综合楼—精神文明活动中心。1999年建成文广大楼。大楼建筑面积3600平方米，集文化、新闻、教育、科技等单位于楼内。2000—2008年，全县217个村文化活动设施——村精神文明活动中心全部建成。期间，还相继建成青少年活动中心，县城文化广场、扎佐文化广场。新建的文化馆于2003年投入使用。文化馆占地面积6亩，总建筑面积为1643平方米，投资241万元。建筑风格为院落式仿古建筑。设置有演艺大厅、多功能厅、展厅、创作室、美术室、音乐室、舞蹈室等。

久长镇上寨村农家书屋

2004年起，全县掀起建设“农家书屋”（即村级图书室）的高潮。是年底，有8个村建成农家书屋。文化部门向扎佐镇和大石乡农家书屋赠送图书千余册，并举办农村图书室业务人员培训班。至2009年，全县217个行政村全部建起农家书屋，共有图书10万余册，基本能满足群众学文化、学科学和娱乐阅读的需求。在行政村建农家书屋的同时，亦在自然村和村民组建起农家书屋，2010年，在100个自然村建农家书屋，当年内完成配送、安装和图书上架工作。为进一步搞好农家书屋建设，县还举办“书香农家”、“快乐书屋智慧乐园”征文和演讲比赛，营造读书学习的氛围。2009年阳明文化园二期工程在阳明文化节前夕基本完成，阳明文化节开幕式大型文艺演出在阳明文化园广场举行。由于各种文化设施建成完善，为繁荣文化搭建起平台，从而促进县内文化事业的发展。

第四节　文化惠民

一、电影下乡

2001年起，实施“2131工程”（即21世纪每村每月放1场电影）。县电影公司在国家资金支持下，坚持送电影到农村，解决边远地区群众看电影难的问题。当年送电影下乡放映440场次，有的村达2场次。公司还与县信用联社等单位合作，筹措放映经费，组织科教片、革命传统教育影片下乡放映。2001—2010年，共送电影下乡放映1.2万场次，年均1100场次。

2009年，县文化部门在大石乡开展送电影下乡活动

二、送戏下乡

从1988年开展“三下乡”活动起，文化部门将送戏下乡纳入议事日程，但多是以完成上级文化部门和县委下达的任务为主。2001年，在“三个代表”重要思想学教活动中，县委提出在全县“大力发展社区文化、村镇文化、企业文化、校园文化”和“广泛开展群众性文体活动”的要求后，全县掀起送戏下乡高潮，不仅文化部门把送戏下乡作为工作重心，县的单位部门也积极参与。至2010年，宣传文化部门及其他相关部门举办的各种演出活动上千场次，一些上档次的演出不仅到乡（镇），还到了村组。2006年，谷堡乡折溪村举办梨花节，县的宣传文化部门和乡政府邀请贵州省武警部队文工团到活动现场演出，让村里的群众不出家门就能欣赏到在城里要一两百块钱买票才能看到的精彩表演。贵州省的著名表演艺术家卜小贵在县组织的送戏下乡活动中先后到谷堡乡、大石乡、六屯乡、扎佐镇的村组为群众演出，村民们能亲眼看到喜欢的艺术家就在身边的舞台上表演都笑得合不拢嘴。

2009年，在洒坪乡开展“三下乡”活动

三、送书下乡

在“三下乡”活动中，送书下乡是宣传文化部门的主要活动之一，逐年均有开展。2004年村组兴建农家书屋后，全县送书下乡文化惠民形成高潮，各单位、各部门不仅自身组织图书，还联系省市上级单位送书下乡。至2010年，全县共组织以科普图书为主的各类图书6万余册送到村、组，丰富农村群众的文化生活。

四、春联下乡

县文联组织的义务写春联活动从1990年起年年开展。至2010年，书法家和书法爱好者到乡（镇）村组为群众写春联达20余万幅，年均逾万幅。从开始的义务书写，到后来的直接赠送，使送春联下乡成为倍受群众欢迎的文化惠民活动。

2003年，县文联在洒坪乡送春联

五、数字信息服务

2004年，县成立数字信息与远程教育管理中心。至2010年，全县10个乡（镇）共建成11个视频终端接收系统，10个多媒体教室，206个村级卫星接收站，217个远程教育教学站，并在1400个村民组建立播放分点或流动播放点。其设备由10乡（镇）的文化中心负责管理和维修。农村远程教育成为群众致富路上的“排头兵”，小箐乡郭田村地处偏远河谷，气候条件优越，李子等经济作物种植面积大。以前因种植技术落后，产品外销价格跟不上市场变化，群众致富步伐迈不快，远教站点联网后，村民们通过网络学习果树种植新技术，了解市场行情，不仅使酥李种植水平上了一个新台阶，价格也一路飙升，2010年全村酥李年销售收入突破300万元。村民们说“不出门也能了解市场行情，远教网络又给村里修了一条进山的‘新公路’”。

第五节　文化市场

1978年后，随着县域经济的发展，文化市场日趋活跃。歌舞厅、游戏室、个体书店、录像放映室、网吧等新生文化业态相继出现，在30多年的发展中此生彼落，逐步形成县内文化市场的三类载体：一是包括歌舞厅、游戏厅、台球室等的娱乐市场；二是包括图书经营、印刷行业等的书刊和印刷市场；三是包括音像制品、录像放映、网吧等的音像市场。

一、文化行业

（一）娱乐业

歌舞厅　1984年，县总工会在职工俱乐部设歌舞厅，继后，全县先后办起14家歌舞厅。歌舞厅经营一般分设大厅消费和包房消费，顾客可以自行选择。至2010年，注册登记的歌舞厅有风暴、紫罗兰、帝豪、阳光、夜君美、老地方、浪翻天、友情、腾飞和金色文都10家。

电子游戏室　1988年，电子游戏业开始在县城出现，有两家游戏室开业，随后发展较快，扎佐、久长、六广集镇也有经营户，到2000年全县有证经营的逾20家，尚有无证经营者。游戏室多开在校园周边，光顾游戏室的多是青少年。由于玩游戏对青少年的学习产生较大影响，家长反应强烈，县内多次整顿取缔无证经营和校园周边经营，对无证经营者发现一家处理一家。至2010年，经注册登记的游戏机室有朝阳、卫东、才明、罗兴祥、罗斌和柴志富6家。

台球娱乐室 1980年，县内出现台球娱乐业，散见于城乡街头巷尾，多为露天经营。1988年，办证营业的台球活动室有100多家。但因不少打球者将台球作为赌博工具，致业主时被处罚，加之歌厅兴起，业主难以赚钱只得改行，至2010年，仅存4家台球娱乐室。

（二）音像业

音像制品租售 1983年，收录机普及，随后，影碟机也成为家庭必备电器，磁带盘和影碟销售出租业务随之兴起。经营者销售出租的音像制品基本是盗版或非正规渠道出版，故多属无照经营，文化管理部门虽不间断地取缔无证经营，但屡禁不止，大街上仍见流动摊贩销售歌碟影碟。至2010年，全县注册办证销售出租音像制品的仅有碟缘、田兴婷2家。

录像放映室 1983年，扎佐街上有外地人租用邓姓街面房放录像，前来观看者每人收费2角，为县内首家录像放映室，播放的录像带多为香港武功片，观众踊跃，深夜一两点钟才散场。至1984年，全县办理营业性放映证照的录像放映室有57家，1990年减至16家。1992年后，电视普及，录像放映室无利可图，纷纷退出市场。

网吧 2001年，县内有8家网吧办证经营，2003年按照国务院《互联网上网服务营业场所管理条例》和《贵阳市上网服务营业场所管理办法》中上网服务营业场所“县（市）不小于80平方米，上网计算机应不少于40台”的规定，将“网吧”经营户压缩到3家。因经营网吧利润空间大，从2004年起，县内网吧又逐年增多，至2010年，全县注册登记网吧有星际、宏洋、天乐、金豪、星愿、志伟、快浪、天和、苏宇、明朗、星宇、俭儿和世际13家，其中拥有100台以上计算机的网吧4家，其余均在50台以上100台以下。

（三）书刊印刷业

个体书店 1982年市场开放，县内即有个体书店“三味书屋”开业，至2010年，办理注册登记的个体书店有知行、行知、田园、华中和鹏鹏5家。

印刷 1978年，县内仅有修文县印刷厂1家从事印刷业务的集体企业。1992年改体，资产分离重组转为个体民营经济，部分职工自筹资金办起个体印刷厂。1995年，修文中学开办学校印刷厂。至2010年，全县办理注册登记的印刷厂有金汇印刷有限公司、县文光印刷厂、迎春印刷部3家。

打字复印 1995年，县城出现第一家由温州人经营的打字复印店。至2010年，全县注册经营的打字复印店有宏业、田园、迅捷、大通、唯达、星科一体、刘太银、星雨和永琴9家。

二、文化稽查

从1980年起，县委、县政府及其文化管理部门在繁荣文化市场的同时，针对文化市场出现的混乱现象不断加大管理力度，先后制定出台《修文县文化经营活动规则》《非经营舞厅的管理规定》《关于制止利用台球进行赌博的规定》《关于整顿我县录像放映，查禁淫秽音像制品的紧急通知》《关于营业性录像放映管理规定》《修文县网吧等互联网上网服务营业场所专项整治工作方案》和《关于整顿我县中小学校及周边治安秩序的实施方案》等10多个文件，并采取专项整治、安装监控软件技防、建立依法管理长效机制等措施，促进文化市场健康发展。1991年成立文化稽查队，文化稽查成为常态工作。通过稽查，发现问题，作出查处决定。1993年11月，对文化经营活动较为集中的城关，扎佐、久长、六广、小箐及工矿区进行检查，取缔无证经营者9户，对27户证照不全的责令关停补办证照，收缴非法音像带56盒，查收明令禁书13册和淫秽内容书刊24册。1998年，对文化市场进行48次检查，取缔7户无证经营户，收缴非法音像制品172盒和非法书刊652册。2005年，出动检查13次，取缔无证经营6户，收缴非法出版物5096张（册），其中淫秽光盘132张，迷信书刊362册，有害卡通画册172本，并对全县8户网吧进行1800多次巡查。2010年，在日常检查和突击检查中，共收缴非法音像制品1211张，非法图书215册，取缔黑网吧6家。在对文化市场存在的违法违规行为进行查处的同时，文化稽查队采取举办文化经营户法律法规培训班、制定文化娱乐场所管理办法等措施，增强经营者的守法经营意识，从源头上净化文化市场。

查禁淫秽音像制品 1985年，有县内营业性录像放映点57个，有的放映单位不服从管理，放映趣味低下的节目，甚至放映淫秽录像，严重毒害人民群众特别是青少年身心健康，诱发犯罪，妨碍治安。针对录像放映存在的问题，县委、县政府当年5月作出决定，全县所有营业性录像放映单位从24日起一律停业整顿，将所存有录像带送交县广播电视局审查，凡有淫秽内容的录像带，必须主动交出，隐瞒不交者，一经查出从严处理。并由县纪委、县委宣传部、县广播电视局、县公安局和县工商局联合将此决定形成《关于整顿我县录像放映，查禁淫秽音像制品的紧急通知》文件下发。《通知》规定：所有持有录像制品的企事业单位（包括非营业性的）都要自行清理，并将清理结果于5月31日前报县广播电视局登记注册、分类处理，如发现有淫秽制品隐瞒不报，将追究单位领导责任。专项整治工作持续到1986年3月告一段落，期间，查出全县录像放映点此前播放的190部录像节目中，有151部未经过省文化厅审片，按照规定查封录像放映点8个，停业整顿11个，收缴有淫秽内容录像制品60盘（盒）。

规范录像放映 1991年，根据中共中央办公厅、国务院办公厅《关于压缩整顿音像单位的通知》文件精神，对全县营业性录像放映点开展专项整顿。整顿期间，一律停止放映，并封存原有录像带。由县政府组成检查组对全县12家营业性录像放映点及厂矿有线电视进行检查，收缴录像带28盒，取缔录像放映点2家，责令停业2家。

非法出版物收缴 2004年，根据贵州省“扫黄”办《关于开展校园周边非法出版物专项治理的通知》精神，县开展校园周边非法出版物专项整治行动，1周内检查出版物市场20家次，收缴封建迷信读物370册，有害卡通画册40册，取缔无证经营2户。

整治网吧专项 2004年4月，根据贵州省文化厅《关于加强春节、寒假期间互联网上网服务营业场所管理工作的通知》要求，县委、县政府决定由县文体广播电视局、工商局、电信局、教育局、邮政局、法制办、文明办和团县委联合成立“修文县网吧等互联网上网服务营业场所专项整治工作协调小组”，制发《修文县网吧等互联网上网服务营业场所专项整治工作方案》，开展全县网吧专项整治统一行动，规范“网吧”经营行为。整治行动中，采取开展“专项整治统一行动周”活动、组织网吧经营户学习《互联网上网服务营业场所管理条例》，督促网吧业主建立网吧场内巡查制度和上网登记制度等措施，营造大张旗鼓地整治行动声势。4月，在县城龙岗广场举行“专项整治统一行动周”活动启动仪式，千余名中、小学学生在写有“告别网吧”的横幅上签名，表达约束自己到网吧上网的决心。在专项整治行动中，共出动执法人员246人次，出动执法车辆40台次，对城乡结合部、学校周边进行拉网式排查，检查经营户160户次。依法取缔无照经营户1户，停业整顿4户，对1户有违规行为的给予1000元罚款处罚。继后，采取安装网吧管理软件，通过技术措施防控网吧违规经营，在网吧设置“未成人禁止入内”标志，成立“社区绿色上网劝导队”，组织以学校德育教师为主的“纠风队”和聘请50名“五老”义务监督员，规劝违规上

网的未成年人，教育、举报违规接纳未成年人上网的网吧业主等措施，使网吧经营活动趋向规范。

三、扫黄打非

1993年，成立有文化、公安部门参加的县扫黄打非工作领导小组，开展以扫除淫秽色情、封建迷信等危害人们身心健康和污染社会文化环境的文化垃圾，打击非法出版物活动。领导小组每年召开专门会议，制订“扫黄打非”活动方案，组织联合执法行动，对收缴的非法音像制品及非法书刊进行集中销毁。1999年，组织“扫黄打非”集中行动5次，取缔无证经营者5户，停业整顿13户，收缴非法出版物（邪教《法轮功》书刊）364册，VCD光盘480张，取缔1户在学校内经营的电子游戏室。2005年，组织文化、公安、工商、城管、消防、环保、教育、电信等部门开展扫黄打非集中行动，取缔无证经营8户，收缴非法书刊1610册，收缴非法音像制品3246张（盒）。2010年，在扫黄打非行动中，重点开展校园周边环境整治，将中小学周边200米内的歌舞娱乐厅和电子游戏室全部清除，为中、小学生学习创造良好环境，并在中小学生中开展“争做文明网络少年”主题班会活动，让青少年树立正确、文明的网络意识。

第四章　传媒　出版

第一节　广　播

网络建设　1979年，全县架设的广播线路共219千米，使用高音喇叭传输广播信号，乡通率为100%。1983年，建起调频广播台。至1990年，建成县广播站1座，区广播站4座，乡（镇）广播站16座，有59个村通广播，占27.1%。1993年起，建设村级广播室，因受资金制约，进展缓慢。1999年，实施“村村通”广播电视工程，9月18日，建成村级广播室61个（150瓦扩音机），全县实现村村通广播。县被评为贵阳市“村村通”先进单位。

自办节目　1978年县建有广播站，广播站以转播中央和省电台节目为主，1986年增加无线调频转播后，开办自办节目。自办节目呼号为“修文广播电台”，设置有《修文新闻》《广播站联播》《赶场天》《民族团结》《对农村广播》《每周一歌》《天气预报》《经济信息》和《观众点播》栏目，节目采用盘带播出方式。1993年开始采用MD播出，2005年起采用音频播出后，信号质量日益提高。采编的新闻节目在各类评选活动中均有获奖。《关山林茶场为何被哄抢》获贵州省好新闻一等奖，《听到母鸡叫，先到鸡窝里去摸蛋》先后荣获全省优秀广播节目二等奖和全国优秀广播新闻三等奖。

第二节　电　视

网络建设　1978年，县内收看电视节目系通过差转台发射信号，因信号不稳定，收看质量较差。1986年，县城建成卫星地面接收站。1989年起，全县乡（镇）建起小型卫星地面接收站，同时在县城安装有线电视，继后有线电视逐步扩大到乡（镇）。1997年，全县有卫星地面接收站34座，实现电视信号全覆盖，有线电视用户达1.14万户。有线电视系统能容纳59个电视频道，传输28套电视节目。2003年改造县城电视网络，建成带宽为860MHZ双向回传的HFC网，传送的节目从7套增加至44套，节目传输质量大大提高，同时开展“E视通”业务，使县城有线电视用户从1992年的1200户发展到5500户。1999年，实施广播电视“村村通”工程，至2008年，全县“村村通”工程告竣，电视网络覆盖全县。

自办节目 1992年开播《修文新闻》，每周一期，时长10分钟。主要报道县内重大时政活动。1996年成立修文电视台，自办节目增多。新闻类节目有《修文新闻》《今日聚焦》和《喜进新农村》等，专题类有《阳光时代》和《市场指导》等，栏目类有《黄金剧场》《经典看台》《经典回放》《原声影院》和《科技大篷车》等。1996年至2010年，制作电视新闻3000余期，播出新闻2.5万余条。向省、市电视台提供外宣稿件万余条，多有获奖。《关山林茶场为何被哄抢》《爱心谱写敬老歌》《家乡变化我是记录人我是见证者》获贵州好新闻奖；《修文县400多农民获“绿卡”》和《梨子熟了农民笑了》获贵阳市好新闻奖；《修文县先进性教育活动开展有声有色》获贵阳市先进性教育活动优秀新闻作品奖；《家乡变化我是记录人我是见证者》获贵阳市播音作品奖。

第三节　报　刊

修文报（当代修文） 1993年，复刊1958年创办1959年停办的县委机关报《修文报》，四开四版，半月报。是年12月4日复刊后的《修文报》出版第一期。1995年改为旬报，1998年改为周报，四开八版，1999年改为对开四版周报，2001年增设月末版，亦为对开四版。2004年，《修文报》更名《当代修文》，四开八版，一、五版为新闻版，二、三版为经济版，六、七版为社会版，四、八版为政文、副刊版。修文报（当代修文）的办报宗旨是：坚持党的新闻方针，唱响主旋律，弘扬真善美，鞭挞假丑恶，反映县内经济社会发展，凝聚民心，为修文改革发展聚力聚智。修文报（当代修文）不断刊载有影响的作品。《当一天“破烂王”》《“我们满意得很”—直击蜈蚣桥村“海选”》获省好新闻奖，《家长不送子女入学，政府依法提起诉讼》《扎佐萝卜干怎样香起来》获贵阳市好新闻奖，《村官去留，村民作主》获全国法制协会好新闻奖。修文报（当代修文）每期发行量3000份。1993年复刊至2010年，共出版694期。

县内编辑出版的报刊

栖霞文艺 《栖霞文艺》是县文联机关刊物，原名《潮水》，1988年由县文学协会创办，1990年县文联成立由县文联主办，至1991年出版第三期后停办，1997年复刊，更名《栖霞文艺》，季刊，以发表文学作品为主，辅以其他艺术门类作品。《栖霞文艺》办刊宗旨是：积极宣传党在新时期的文艺路线、方针和政策，反映修文文艺界的活动情况，展示县内文艺工作者的创作成果和精神风貌，传递各地文艺界的创作动向，积极发挥桥梁和纽带作用，大力促进修文文学艺术的繁荣发展。设有“龙冈杂谈”“修文旅游文化”“青年作者作品小辑”“修文履痕”“尖尖角”“综合艺术”等栏目。至2010年，共出版35期。

第四节　网　站

2000年后，逐渐有县的单位通过互联网设立网站，开展宣传活动，但发展缓慢。2009年，县人民政府门户网站“贵阳·修文”建成，带动网站建设快速发展，至2010年，全县有县直部门和工商企业等的网站60多个。主要有县人民政府门户网站和中共修文县委网、修文党务公开网、修文组工网、修文青年网、修文司法行政网、修文计生网、修文国土资源网、修文住建网、修文教育网、修文中学网、修文招商引资网、修文移民网、修文人才网、修文公安为民网、修文科技网10乡（镇）网站等。

县政府门户网站“贵阳·修文”（www.xiuwen.gov.cn）设有经济发展、地域文化、修文旅游、政务公开、在线交流等栏目，着重介绍全县经济建设和对外开放取得的成就，展示修文“三个文明”建设成果和扩大开放新形象；设立政务新闻、最新信息、政府公报、政府规章、工作职责等栏目发布各类政务信息；设立在线办事和便民查询等栏目，将政府“窗口”部门提供服务的事项按行业进行分类整合，直接列出，方便用户查询和公众办事；开通书记县长交流台、县长信箱等栏目，建立公众直接向政府反映问题的网上渠道。门户网站从2008年开通至2010年的3年间，访问量达50万人次，年均13万人次。

县政府门户网站

第五节　图　书

一、著述出版

1978—2010年，县内或个人或单位经贵州省新闻出版局批准内资出版和出版社出版各类书籍86种，分文艺类、史志类、政文类、资料类。文艺类有《山那边》《野山》《郝承德画集》和《修文县三套文艺集成》等38本；史志类有新编《修文县志》《修文年鉴》《修文县组织史》《红军长征在修文》《修文革命烈士传》和民国《修文县志》点校本等33本；政文类有《王学圣地》《思路决定出路》《风雨阳光路》和《足迹》等13本；资料类有《修文县地名录》。公开或内资出版的书籍中不乏精品。新编《修文县志》出版当年即入选全国新编地方志成果展，获国家新闻出版署优秀图书奖；2000年获贵阳市第四次社会科学优秀科研成果一等奖；2001年获贵州省第五次哲学社会科学优秀科研成果三等奖。陈新国著短篇小说集《野山》2000年获贵阳市人民政府第四届金筑文艺奖。夏之奎主编《王阳明在龙场》2003年获贵阳市第五届哲学社会科学优秀科研成果奖。郝承德《郝承德画集》2005年获县文明委文艺作品特别奖。魏明禄主编《王学圣地》2008年获贵阳市第七次哲学社会科学优秀科研成果奖。

县内编辑出版的部分图书

1978—2010年出版图书一览表

表4—04—01

类别		名称	编著人	出版时间和单位	备注
文艺	回忆录	修文文史资料选辑第一辑	政协文史委员会　编	1984年政协	内资
	散文　特写	修文风光(修文文史资料选辑第二辑)	政协文史委员会　编	1985年政协	内资
	诗歌　散文	修文名胜风光诗文选	朱五义　主编	1986年地方志办公室	内资
	回忆录	修文文史资料选辑第三辑	政协文史委员会　编	1989年政协	内资
	注释	王阳明在黔诗文注释	朱五义　注释	1997年贵州人民出版社	公开
	小说　散文	山那边	卢永康　著	1998年贵州人民出版社	公开
	诗词　楹联	桥(修文文史资料选辑第四辑)	政协文史委员会　编	1999年政协	内资
	小说	野山	陈新国　著	1999年内蒙古远方出版社	公开
	回忆录	解放初期修文县的民主革命（修文文史资料选辑第五辑）	政协文史委员会　编	1989年政协	内资
	连环画	阳明先生	丁国才　绘图 朱五义　撰文	1999年第一届文化节组委会	内资
	民间故事	阳明先生的故事	陈新国 著	1999年第一届文化节组委会	内资
	散文	潮泉集	朱五义　著	2000年	内资
	小说　散文	小镇故事	黄　竹　著	2000年贵州人民出版社	公开
	散文	古驿行吟	陈新国　著	2001年新世纪文化书社	公开
	散文	千古龙冈漫有名	杨德俊　编	2002年第二届文化节组委会	内资
	注释评论	王阳明居夷诗今译与赏析	陈新国　著	2002年第二届文化节组委会	内资
	民间故事	神秘的六广河—六广河民间传说故事集	陈新国　著	2002年第二届文化节组委会	内资
	故事传说史料	修文史话	朱五义　著	2002年第二届文化节组委会	内资
	散文　杂文	流金岁月	黄　竹　著	2002年贵州人民出版社	公开

续表

类别		名称	编著人	出版时间和单位	备注
文艺	小说	撒二名传奇	董登荣　著	2004年贵州人民出版社	公开
	小说　散文 诗词	栖霞文荟	陈新国　主编	2005年文联	内资
	书法　绘画	龙场墨韵—修文书画集	陈新国　主编	2005年文联	内资
	绘画	郝承德画集	郝承德　著	2006年文联	内资
	诗歌	河山颂歌	谭荣先　著	2006年文联	内资
	诗歌	燃情岁月	苏善　著	2007年文联	内资
	散文诗词	大山里的灵秀—六广河诗文选集	陈新国　主编	2007年六广镇政府	内资
	回忆录	铁血忠魂	张元恩　著	2008年文联	内资
	特写摄影	抗凝—2008修文“抗凝冻保民生”纪实	白陈新　名誉主编 陈新国　执行主编	2008年新闻信息中心	内资
	特写摄影	冰雪作证—2008“抗凝冻保供电”纪实	陈新国　主编	2008年供电局	内资
	民间文艺	修文县三套文艺集成	杨德俊　主编	2008年文体广播电视局	内资
	绘画	郝承德画选	郝承德　著	2009年文联	内资
	散文随笔	人生絮语	黄　竹　著	2009年香港文汇出版社	公开
	散文随笔	玩在那个年代	卢永康　著	2010年 贵州人民出版社	公开
	书法	王阳明法书集	县委宣传部 贵阳市文联　编	2010年贵州人民出版社	公开
	散文随笔	深谷乡音	李小龙　著	2010年作家出版社	公开
政文类	特写专稿	修志文汇	李祖炎　主编	1990年地方志办公室	内资
	特写专稿	修文改革开放20年	夏之奎　主编	1998年地方志办公室	内资
	文论	“西部大开发政协委员建言集(修文文史资料选辑第六辑)	县政协文史委员会　编	2000年政协	内资
	特写专稿	阳明胜境	赵永忠　主编	2002年贵州人民出版社	公开
	特写专稿	王阳明在龙场	夏之奎　主编	2002年地方志办公室	内资
	特写专稿	修文县志编修纪实	夏之奎　主编	2002年地方志办公室	内资
	论文	扬帆—党建与党风廉政建设文集	岳建初　主编	2005年纪委	内资
	论文	王学之魂	王晓昕　主编	2005年贵州民族出版社	公开
	特写专稿	王学圣地	魏明禄　主编	2005年贵州民族出版社	公开
	论文	足迹—修文县保持党的先进性理论成果选编	严贵均　主编	2006年委组织部	内资
	文论	思路决定出路	县史志办公室　编	2007年地方志办公室	内资
	特写专稿	风雨阳光路	夏之奎　主编	2008年地方志办公室　统计局	内资
	论文	王学之旅	王晓昕　主编	2009年贵州民族出版社	公开

续表

类别		名称	编著人	出版时间和单位	备注
史志类	志鉴	修文县志	李祖炎　主编	1999年方志出版社	公开
		修文年鉴(2010)	胡光胤　主编	2010年地方志办公室	内资
		民国《修文县志》点校本	罗再麟　点校	2009年地方志办公室	内资
	乡(镇)志	修文县六广镇志	李祖炎　主编	2007年六广镇人民政府	内资
		修文县小箐乡志	国远明　主编	2007年小箐乡人民政府	内资
		修文县扎佐镇志	王正礼　主编	2007年扎佐镇人民政府	内资
	村志	修文县清水村志	夏之奎　主编	2007年清水村村民委员会	内资
	部门志	修文县人民代表大会志	葛恒希　主编	1986年人大常委会	内资
		修文县工商行政管理志	余文治　主编	1987年工商局	内资
		修文县卫生志	熊兴明　主编	1987年卫生局	内资
		修文县税务志	陈君生　主编	1987年税务局	内资
		修文县邮电志	徐　湘　主编	1987年邮电局	内资
		修文县水利电力志	陈文祥　主编	1987年水电局	内资
		修文县物资管理志	朱　杰　主编	1988年物资局	内资
		修文县轻工业志	邹　钊　主编	1988年轻工局	内资
		修文县农业机械志	李　锐　主编	1989年农机局	内资
		修文县工会志	朱五义　主编	1991年总工会	内资
		修文县财政志	葛恒希　主编 邓鉴录　主编	1994年财政局	内资
		修文县粮食志	蔡文广　主编	1995年粮食局	内资
		修文县交通志	朱　屏　主编	2006年交通局	内资
		修文县税务志(1978—2005)	陈君生　主编	2007年地税局　国税局	内资
		修文县乡(镇)企业志	林明礼　主编	2007年县乡镇企业局	内资
		修文县人民代表大会志(1986—2005)	王作伦　主编	2008年人大	内资
		修文县教育志	李明祥　主编	2008年教育局	内资
		修文县水利志	邓朝文　主编	2008年水利局	内资
		修文县工会志(1978—2007)	胡昭明　主编	2008年总工会	内资
		修文县民政志	陈新国　主编	2009年民政局	内资
		修文县军事志	陈新国　主编	2009年人武部	内资
		修文县农村信用合作志	刘　毅　主编	2010年11月成稿付印 信用联社	内资

续表

类别		名称	编著人	出版时间和单位	备注
史志类	党史	红军长征在修文	党史研究室　编	1986年党史研究室	内资
		党史资料汇编	党史研究室　编	1989年党史研究室	内资
		修文革命烈士传	党史研究室 县民政局　编	1989年党史研究室 民政局	内资
		中国共产党贵州省修文县组织史资料 贵州省修文县政军统群系统组织史资料	李祖炎　主编	2000年组织部 党史研究室 档案局	内资
		中国共产党修文县历史第一卷（1935—1978）	夏之奎　主编	2010年11月定稿付印 贵州人民出版社	公开
资料	名录	修文县地名录	刘柏林　主编	1989年地名办公室	内资

专记一：魏明禄主编《王学圣地》发行

2005年4月，担任《修文县志》顾问的贵州文化老人陈福桐向县委书记魏明禄建议，在编纂县志的同时编辑一本反映修文人文资源、自然风光和经济社会发展的书，以展示修文昨天和今天的发展变化。魏明禄即于5月召集《修文县志》主编李祖炎、《当代修文》主编陈新国、县长助理雷华熙和县委宣传部、县史志办公室的同志共襄其事。为弘扬历史文化和宣传今日修文，书名定为《王学圣地》。由魏明禄主编，相关同志负责征稿、撰稿、搜集照片。

经过半年努力，共征得稿件82篇、图片210幅，再三筛选，选定14位作者的51篇文章共26.3万字入书，并随文配制图片108幅。全书分为历史人文、阳明文化、山水诗情、民情风俗、利为民谋5个部分。

《王学圣地》一书采用图随文走的编排形式，开本和设计与国际接轨。中共贵州省委常委、贵阳市委书记王晓东题写书名，陈福桐和全国作家协会副主席叶辛为书作序。由贵州民族出版社出版。

2005年11月17日，适逢修文解放56周年纪念日，《王学圣地》公开发行，即被出版单位以装帧印刷质量上乘选送参加广州南国书香节书展。《王学圣地》面世后读者评价甚高。贵州历史学家史继忠在《贵州日报》著文称该书“是历史的画卷，时代的赞歌”。浙江省衢州市地方志办公室主任韩章训点评该书具有3点长处：一是说古道今，深入浅出；二是述议结合，彰往昭来；三是图文并茂，雅俗共赏。修文读者则反映该书体现“三个第一”，即县委书记领衔亲自编书在修文县是第一位，将文化与当今建设有机结合著文成书在修文县是第一部，出版图文并茂适应读图时代要求的书在修文县是第一本。

专记二：陈新国五本著作出版

中共十一届三中全会后，文艺复兴，县内涌现一批文艺创作者，他们坚持业余创作，用文学艺术形式讴歌改革开放，歌颂真善美，鞭挞假丑恶，为县的文艺繁荣作出贡献。县文联主席陈新国是这批文艺创作骨干之一。

1978年，陈新国即开始文学创作，先后在《安顺文艺》《边疆文学》《北京文学》《山花》《青年文学》《花溪》《贵州日报》副刊等报刊上发表60余万字的小说、报告文学、散文，其作品《乡场人物速写》《荒土的悲剧》《野山》《虎胆女儿英雄魂》等在读者中有一定的影响，有读者和评论家在《文艺报》

《贵州工人报》《安顺日报》上撰文评价其作品是“流动的乡村生活画卷”，“具有乡土文化的魅力”。

1998年，由贵阳市作家协会结集，内蒙古远方出版社出版了陈新国的短篇小说集《野山》，收录陈新国从1979年至1997年创作的15篇短篇小说共14万字。该书出版后，于2000年获得贵阳市人民政府“金筑文艺奖”。1999年，陈新国出于对本土文化的热爱，在修文首届阳明文化节前创作5万余字的中篇故事《阳明先生的故事》，成稿后，由贵州省新闻出版局批准内部发行。该书在首届阳明文化节期间作为县人民政府的礼品之一赠送来宾，受到欢迎。2001年，陈新国的本土文化散文作品集《古驿行吟》出版；2002年阳明文化研究和普及读物《王阳明居夷诗今译与尝析》和《神秘的六广河》出版。《王阳明居夷诗今译与尝析》共12万字，该书对王阳明在黔诗作作出注释和白话翻译，并拟出了每首诗的赏读要点。贵州“文化老人”陈福桐为该书作序。

二、发行经销

1978年，境内图书发行经销主要由县新华书店负责，1980年后，文化市场放开，允许个体业主参与图书销售市场竞争。1978年县新华书店图书销售额仅28万元，1988年实行招标承包后，图书销售额逐年上升，2010年达到579万元，最高的2006年为628万元，是1978年的16倍。1982年，县内首家个体书店“三味书屋”开业，至2010年，注册登记个体书店有知行、行知、田园、华中和鹏鹏5家。此外，集市上也常有流动书摊经营图书。个体图书经销的规模不大，且多为兼营，较大的知行书屋店堂180平方米，经营图书逾千种，年销售额在10万元至15万元间。

第五章　体　育

第一节　体育设施

一、运动场所

1993年成立县全民健身运动委员会后，县内体育设施逐年增加，先后建成县体育馆、大石少数民族体育运动场等较大的公共运动场所。至2010年，全县有水泥篮球场33个，足球场1个，排球场6个，训练房2间，游泳池2个，乒乓球室和棋室405个，门球场2个，游乐场6处，健身房（室）5个，街道、社区健身点66个。

县体育场　1978年后的10年，群众体育活动的动场所多在民国时期修建的县体育场内，1999年县城改造将体育场改建为龙岗广场，供市民休闲娱乐。

县体育馆　县体育馆正东面紧靠县城河滨路，占地21亩，设置座位2360个，总投资1199万元。1999年9月竣工投入使用。馆内设有篮球、羽毛球、乒乓球、棋类、歌舞等活动项目。体育馆四周安装有健身器材。是集体育运动、大型集会、文娱活动为一体的多功能场馆。

大石少数民族运动体育场　2006年由县投资6万元，在大石布依族乡政府驻地建成少数民族运动体育场，占地0.6亩。2007年，又投资5万元，安装户外运动设施和修建器材库并配备器材。

专记：全省首家建起的县市级修文体育馆

1998年，县政府根据县委八届四次全会精神和贵阳市人民政府以筑府通〔1998〕54号文件批复的《修文县城市整体规划》要求，提出“统一规划，合理布局，因地制宜，综合开发，配套建设”的方案，拟定县城基础设施建设重点项目12个。是年12月19日，县委常委扩大会议对12个项目进行审定，将这批项目统称为城镇基础设施建设“九三工程”，这批工程均为改变古驿龙场旧貌的标志性建筑，其中之一为修建修文体育馆。

体育馆工程经县计划与经济贸易局批准立项，于1998年12月28日举行奠基仪式，县委、县政府主要领导亲自主持，省体委副主任蔡国祥莅县参加。工程由县城建指挥部组织实施。按照县委提出“精心策划，精雕细琢，精打细算，精兵强将”的要求，选定中国建筑第四工程局设计并承建。它是一个综合性多功能的四层建筑，主体建筑采用大跨度钢架结构，立面造型、平面组合都达到省内先进水平。其配

1999年建成的县体育馆

套设施还有办公室、休息室、更衣室、体育器材室、健身房、卫生间等。馆内既可举办体育赛事，又可举行文艺演出，还可召开大型集会。全馆占地面积21亩，建筑面积5700平方米，总投资1199.4万元。施工单位克服重重困难，日夜兼程，周密安排，于1999年9月28日竣工，整个建设周期9个月，其速度之快，深受群众称赞，创下修文建筑史上的奇迹。10月6日正式开馆，14日，馆内即举办落成后的第一场盛大活动—修文首届阳明文化节开幕式。

体育馆建成后，省市多家媒体争相报道，县内广大人民群众更是因为有了属于自己锻炼身体和休闲娱乐的好去处而高兴不已，纷纷奔走相告。《贵阳日报》载文称“修文有了让参观者惊叹不已的全省县城第一个体育馆”。

修文体育馆坐落于县城东片区的小桥河畔，东临河滨路，南靠翠屏路，西抵文成路，北接宾阳路，其馆名由省体育界知名人士、省体育运动委员会原主任王家声题写。馆东西两门设阶梯上二楼入馆内看台，二楼外沿四周建有走廊相通连。沿阶而上，即可从东南西北4个入口进入馆内，馆内正中为近千平方米的综合运动场地，东侧主席台设座位60个，其余四周有阶梯形固定座位2300个。馆内视野开阔，回声较低，观众观看比赛或演出感到舒畅。

体育馆外建有附属活动场，四周绿茵环绕，空气清新。场地东面建有旗台，凡重大节日均集市民于此，举行升国旗仪式。2000年，县向省、市体育部门争取到价值10万元的多功能健身器材安装于馆外四周，以方便群众活动。每日清晨，朝阳初升，轻风拂面，早起的人们聚此锻炼，或练球，或打拳，或舞剑，或做操，有朝气蓬勃的青年，有鹤发童颜的老人，有天真烂漫的儿童，个个精神抖擞；入夜，华灯初上，人来人往，广场上轻歌曼舞，台阶上三五成群，或站，或坐，或漫步，谈学习，话工作，摆家常，人人笑逐颜开，一片欢乐祥和的景象。折射出修文人民意气风发，昂扬向上的精神面貌。

二、运动器材

1993年后，随着全民健身运动深入发展，运动器材不断增加和更新。2000年，在全民健身路径上增加高低双杠、双杠、高低单杠、天梯、腹肌架、太空荡步器、鞍马训练器、梅花桩、爬杆与滑杠、手攀云梯、仰卧起坐、三人扭腰盘、浪板、漫步器、呼啦桥、云梯、迪斯科跳跃架、双人秋千、三人休闲椅、儿童标准独臂篮架等，使健身内容更加丰富，健身市民不断增加，健身效果比较明显。2003年，县政府给全县学校统一添置一批运动器

六屯乡安装的体育健身器材

材，新增跑步机、磁控健身车、椭圆机、推举架、多功能推胸训练器、哑铃练习凳、可调式哑铃凳、可调式腹肌练习板、夹胸器、小腿训练器，坐推训练器、高低位训练器、卧式屈腿训练器、腿部屈伸训练器、双层组合哑铃架、杠铃架、杠铃多功能深蹲练习器、哑铃、臂部屈伸练习凳、腓肠肌训练器、腰腹训练器、下拉训练器、史密斯机等，基本能满足教学、训练、健身的需要。

第二节　体育队伍

一、运动员　裁判员

县内体育运动主要以群众体育为主，专业竞技体育发展缓慢，至2010年，达到国家规定等级的运动员仅有篮球二级2人，体操三级1人。达到国家规定等级的裁判员10人，其中篮球二级7人，田径二级1人、排球二级1人、体操三级1人。

二、体育团体

1978年后，县内相继成立县体育协会、老年人体育协会、信鸽协会、武术协会等体育团体，乡（镇）和一批机关单位及企业也建立相应的组织，至2010年，有各类体育协会34个，会员1400多人，坚持正常活动的有县体育协会、老年人体育协会、谷堡乡体育协会、六广镇体育协会等。2007年，久长镇上寨村成立上寨村体育协会，是县内首个村级基层体育协会。各类体育协会遵照党和政府的体育规章，团结体育工作者和爱好者，广泛发动群众参加体育锻炼，推动体育事业发展。

乌栗乡农民体育协会　1988年乌栗乡成立农民体育协会，为县内首家农村群众体育团体。成立当年即组织举办乡农民篮球运动会。之后，每年组织一次篮球比赛，各村和乡机关组队参加。1990年“撤并建”撤销乌栗乡建制，乡农民体育协会自然消失。

谷堡乡体育协会　谷堡乡体育协会成立于1991年，建立之初主要是组织乡的篮球比赛，后于2001年至2003年，在县体育局和乡政府的支持下，连续3年组织3次“索桥农民运动会”，为谷堡乡体育运动的发展奠定了基础。

六广镇体育协会　六广镇体育协会成立于1997年，成立当年6月举办象棋比赛，县内机关、乡（镇）和邻县黔西县的钟山、素朴两乡共11支队伍参赛。体育协会经常组织篮球队参加县内和毗邻的黔西县素朴乡、息烽县九庄镇的比赛。

老年人体育协会　1984年，成立县老年人体育协会，初时有50余人，到1987年增至1300多人。下设中老年健身辅导站、腰鼓队、太极拳队、柔力球队、木兰拳队、秧歌队、羽毛球队、门球队、舞蹈队、钓鱼协会等多个分支机构。1988年和1989年，老年人体育协会连续两年被评为安顺地区老年人体育工作先进集体。1995年，会员多达1400多人。至2010年，老年人体育协会有13个分会，1支门球队，1个合唱团，1支秧歌队，2支腰鼓队，1支铜鼓队，2支舞蹈队，2支武术队，1支柔力球队，会员1000多人。

中老年健身辅导站　1993年8月成立中老年健身辅导站，主要是为晨练的群众作舞蹈和武术方面的指导。至2010年，辅导站舞蹈队有队员70多人。

武术协会 武术协会始建于1988年，成立后即举办3期青少年武术培训班，2004年后，武术协会陆续分设太极协会、木兰协会和健身气功指导站。太极协会成立于2004年，至2010年有会员200余人。健身气功指导站成立于2006年，有会员90余人。木兰协会成立于2007年，有会员30余人。

武协多次组队参加省市武术比赛。在2002年3月4日举行的贵阳市迎“三八”百万妇女健身活动木兰拳比赛中，武协中老年健身队获集体表演第一名，集体全能第二名。2006年，在贵阳市第十届运动会武术比赛中，代表修文参赛的岳丽萍获太极拳第二名（银奖），刘本荣获第三名（铜奖）。2007年10月组队参加上海国际木兰拳邀请赛获一等奖。2008年3月参加香港国际武术邀请赛获三等奖。

信鸽协会 1984年成立信鸽协会，有会员70余人。信鸽协会参加过1990、1994、1995和1999年4次省市竞赛。

第三节 体育项目

一、球类

篮球 篮球是县内体育普及发展最广泛的项目，乡（镇）、机关、工厂和中、小学校均组建有篮球队，有的村寨也有篮球队。至2010年，全县有近百支篮球队、近千名运动员活跃在篮球场上。篮球赛事频繁，全县性和跨行业跨地域的比赛每年2至3次以上。1995年在县城举办“交通杯”职工篮球赛，男子组有30个单位组队参加，女子组有9个单位组队参加，比赛155场次，观众达50万人次。2004年全国女篮联赛贵阳赛区有4场赛事在县体育馆举行，促使县内“篮球热”升温，使篮球项目不仅在城镇，在乡村也得到普及发展，久长镇上寨村还筹资修建达到比赛标准的篮球场，2008年，贵阳市百村农民篮球赛在上寨村篮球场开赛。继后，“职工篮球赛”和“百村农民篮球赛”成为县内篮球项目的主要赛事。

篮球运动在城乡成为农村青少年休闲运动的重要项目

乒乓球 1978年后，县内乒乓球运动稳步发展，各乡（镇）文化中心都置有乒乓球室，机关、工厂、企事业单位和村（居）都设有乒乓球室或乒乓球台。中、小学乒乓球运动较为盛行。1998年至2002年间，教育部门连续举办5届中小学生乒乓球比赛。2008年，在全县“乘奥运之风，展乡村新貌”活动中举办全县乒乓球赛，机关、学校、乡（镇）和企业的40名运动员参加角逐。

台球 台球运动在县内颇受青少年青睐。20世纪80年代，全县随处可见台球桌，1988年，台球活动室达100多家。后因有的活动室将台球作为赌具，使此项运动在县内未能健康发展，至2010年，仅存4家台球活动室。

羽毛球　羽毛球在县内是群众喜爱的健身运动项目，晨练时运动场地上随处可见打羽毛球的人。县内从2000年起至2010年相继举办过5次羽毛球比赛，先后有300多人次群众运动员参与。

门球　门球作为健身运动项目主要在老年人群中开展，且多为退休干部职工。县内在2000年和2008年举办过两次老年门球比赛。

二、田径

田径运动在县内较为广泛。参加田径运动的有六七十岁的老人，也有七八岁的儿童，主要人群是中小学校的青少年。从2001年到2010年，县体育部门与教育部门共举办5次全县中小学生田径赛，参赛运动员最多的一次达600多人。至2010年，全县建有各年龄组田径队12个。

三、体操

县内的体操运动以广播体操为主，多是锻炼身体，基本没有竞技内容。1997年全国推行第八套广播体操，县内举行过3次广播体操比赛。至2010年，体操项目在县内仍发展缓慢，仅中小学有教学内容，县内未举行过竞技体操赛事。

四、棋类

1982年，县老干部管理局设有棋室，开展棋类活动。1998年起，县体育部门每年春节期间都举行全县象棋、围棋比赛活动。

五、武术

1985年起，县体委开办武术培训班，招收学员训练。1986年，从训练班中选出5人代表安顺地区出席贵州省第六届运动会。1999年县体育馆建成后，先后有跆拳道、散打项目在馆内举办训练班挂牌招收学员。2000年，私人办学的修文文武学校成立，至2010年，共招收学员2000余人，文武学校多次参加省、市比赛和表演，共夺得省级金牌2枚、市级金牌16枚，省、市级银、铜牌33枚。文武学校现为县的武术后备人才训练基地。

第四节　体育赛事

一、市级以上赛事

2000年起，修文开始尝试承办省、市级比赛。是年2月，由贵州省体委主办、县体育局承办的贵州省“利尔杯”少年跆拳道公开赛在县城体育馆举行，来自全省10个专州市及省内9个武术学校的70余名运动员参加为期4天的比赛。此后，先后承办过贵州省“迎接新世纪”青少年羽毛球比赛、贵阳市老年人羽毛球赛、全省“仙灵杯”散打选拔赛、“仙灵杯”木兰拳选拔赛、“贵阳杯”全国业余高尔夫球公开赛、贵阳市“贵州力力”杯老年人羽毛球赛、贵阳市少数民族运动会大象拔河项目比赛、贵州省青少年跆拳道锦标赛、全国女篮联赛贵阳赛区黑龙江—吉林、浙江—北京、四川—重庆、火车头—黑龙江4场比赛等20

余场省市级赛事。各种赛事的举办，打开修文山门，迎来省内外嘉宾，连起互相之间的情谊，使修文知名度得以提高。运动员们为修文的热情接待发出感言：秀美的修文，好客的修文，还想今后再相会。

二、县级比赛

县内体育赛事较频繁，全县性的比赛每年在2次以上，其中篮球比赛为多。

篮球比赛 县体育部门每年均举办篮球比赛，推动篮球运动不断发展，活跃群众业余文化生活。20世纪80年代末，县内以县体育部门牵头，由部门组织内部篮球赛事，教育部门组织的“园丁杯”篮球赛和乌栗乡农民体育协会组织的乡村篮球赛规模较大，“园丁杯”篮球赛共举办3届，每届有40支男女球队参加。进入20世纪90年代后，县体育部门直接组织全县性的比赛活动，1995年举办“交通杯”职工篮球赛，全县工矿企业、机关单位共组织39支男、女球队参加，比赛155场次，观众达50万人次，每场比赛都有三四千观众涌到体育场观赛，为各自喜欢的球队呐喊助威，吆喝声、欢呼声震耳欲聋。继后，县的乡（镇）、机关也组织跨县、跨乡、跨部门的赛事，1997年，六广镇举办“八一”篮邀请球赛，来自贵阳、黔西和县内的11支代表队200余名运动员参赛。1998年县直机关举办“邮电杯”篮球赛，26支球队参加。1999年10乡（镇）联合举办“兴农杯”篮球联赛，每个乡（镇）各组织一支男、女球队参加，扎佐镇获男子组冠军，龙场镇获女子组冠军。2000年后，随着县体育馆的建成，以及篮球场地的增多和完善，篮球赛事更加兴盛，全县性的比赛有2000年举办的“贵遵杯”篮球赛，组队参加的单位涉及县的机关、企业、学校、乡（镇）、武警和消防，23支男队，8支女队于每周五、六在体育馆进行5场比赛，赛期历时半年，比赛151场次。2003年举办的“质量杯”篮球赛，来自机关、乡（镇）和企业的26支球队参加。2007年，贵阳市举办首届“百村农民篮球赛”，县内也相应组织同名赛事，且每年举行，由乡（镇）和村组队参加。该项赛事至2010年已开展4次，其间，2008年贵阳市百村农民篮球赛选在久长镇上寨村篮球场开赛，2009年起县体育部门又组织全县“职工篮球赛”，两项赛事有力地推动全县篮球运动的普及。

广播体操比赛 1999年在修文中学举行首届广播体操比赛，来自县直机关单位及学校的11支代表队参加，老年健身站代表队夺冠。后于2000年和2001年相继举办两届广播体操比赛。

羽毛球比赛 2000年在县体育馆举行冠名“修文县首届羽毛球比赛”的赛事，80多名选手参加。此后，又在2002年、2007年、2008和2010年举办羽毛球比赛，但均未以连续届次冠名，2002年冠名“地质环境杯羽毛球赛”，50名选手参赛，2007年举办两次羽毛球赛，分别冠名“阳明杯”羽毛球邀请赛和“国土资源杯”羽毛球邀请赛，除县内选手外，还邀请市直机关选手参加。2010年举办“修文县羽毛球赛”，县内选手60余人参加。

2007年，举办“国土资源杯”羽毛球邀请赛

乒乓球比赛 全县性的乒乓球比赛仅在2002年和2008年举办过两次，均只设单项比赛，未设团体赛，参赛选手基本是中小学生。

老年门球比赛 2000年和2008年举办过两次老年门球赛。2000年由县政协和供电局在县城联合举办“供电杯”老年门球赛，参赛者有省人大、省老年大学、省供电局、市政协、市北供电局、市南供电局、南明区政协、县政协联谊队共8支老年门球队，县政协联谊队获第一名。2008年县老龄委组织庆祝第21届老年节门球赛，县政府队获一等奖，县邮电队获二等奖，县委队获三等奖。

桃源河漂流大赛 2007年，县政府与贵阳市旅游局和体育局联合在桃源河景区举办“迎奥运贵阳（修文）首届漂流节及桃源河魔幻漂流大赛”。当天，桃源河两岸游人如织，200名男女青年身穿救生衣乘着漂流船在湍急的河水中勇往直前。有10支啦啦队在岸边助威，“加油！加油！”的呐喊声响彻山谷。200名参赛者经过1个多小时的紧张角逐，有12名选手分获一、二、三等奖。继后，桃源河景区又于2009年举办第二届桃源河魔幻漂流大赛。

贵阳（修文）首届漂流节暨桃源河魔幻漂流大赛

第五节　参赛获奖

1978至2010年，修文县籍运动员共获得国际单项比赛金牌（冠军、第一名、一等奖）1枚，国家级金牌（冠军、第一名、一等奖）3枚，省级金牌（冠军、第一名、一等奖）10枚，获市级金牌（冠军、第一名、一等奖）51枚。

国际单项比赛金牌（冠军、第一名、一等奖） 1995年，修文籍运动员罗文代表国家队参加A级拳击赛，战胜俄罗斯、印度、韩国和中国台北4名对手，获得冠军。

国家级金牌（冠军、第一名、一等奖） 1994年，修文籍运动员罗文在全国拳击锦标赛上获64公斤级金牌，1996年在全国拳击冠军赛上获60公斤级冠军，1997年在全国第八届运动会上获60公斤级拳击冠军。

省级金牌（冠军、第一名、一等奖） 1992年8月，罗文在贵州省第八届运动会上获青少年男子52公斤级拳击金牌，刘文华获青少年男子52公斤级举重金牌，谌宏丽获青少年女子皮划艇金牌。1999年10月，许嘉、赵小丽在贵州省第二届残疾人运动会上，分别获得乒乓球女子单打冠军和女子44公斤级卧举冠军。2007年，文武学校组队代表修文参加贵州省武术比赛，获得金牌2枚。2008年，修文民间武术爱好者组队参加香港国际武术节，获太极拳集体项目冠军。在上海举行的国际木兰拳邀请赛中，修文代表队荣获2个集体项目一等奖。

市级金牌（冠军、第一名、一等奖） 1987年周继获安顺地区田径比赛男子3000米赛跑第一名、鲍崇德获安顺地区田径比赛女子3000米赛跑第一名。1988年肖显尧获安顺地区钓鱼比赛单尾重量第一名。1997年，罗文获贵阳市第八届60公斤级拳击金牌。修文代表团获贵阳市第五届少数民族传统体育运动会射弩项目金牌，表演奖项目一等奖1个。1998年，肢残人候俊庭获贵阳市第七届残疾人运动会男子100米蝶泳第一名。2002年修文代表团获贵阳市第九届运动会暨第六届民运会田径项目金牌1枚和表演奖项目一等奖2个。获贵阳市第八届残疾人运动会金牌1枚。2003年，修文代表队获贵阳市妇女长跑比赛第一名。2006年，修文代表团在贵阳市第十届运动会上获9枚金牌。2007年在贵阳市青少年田径锦标赛上，修文代表团获区（市）县团体总分第一名。2008年，在贵阳市青少年跆拳道锦标赛中获8枚金牌。在贵阳市青少年游泳比赛中获2枚金牌。2010年，组团参加贵阳市第九届残疾人运动会，获金牌2枚。在贵阳市第十一届运动会上，修文代表团获16枚金牌。此外，修文文武学校多次组队参加贵阳市的各类武术项目比赛，2002年至2010年共获得金牌16枚。

第六节　全民健身活动

1978年起，县内积极开展群众性体育活动，随后参加体育锻炼群众逐年增加。1993年，县建立全民健身运动委员会，在机关、街道和农村建立领导小组，形成组织网络，并抽调专业人员组建服务队伍。每年4至6月举办全民健身宣传周活动，充分发挥组织作用。1999年县体育馆建成，县政府购置价值10万元的全民健身体育器材安装在体育馆四周供群众健身使用。2003年，在扎佐镇社区广场安装价值5万元健身器材。2006年至2007年，先后投资11万元在大石乡建成400平方米少数民族体育运动场，配有器材库、户外民族运动设施。至2010年，全县各乡（镇）均有全民健身工程点，覆盖面达100%。共安装健身器材1400多台（套）。

县四大班子领导参加2009年元旦全民健身环城赛跑活动

随着群众健身意识的提高，晨练、晚练的人数不断增加。从1998年起，县体育部门在全县建起60多个晨（晚）练点。至2010年，每天有近3万人次参加跑步、舞蹈、剑术、球类等健身娱乐活动。

在全民健身工程中，县内常年开展的有元旦环城健身跑等体育活动。

元旦环城健身跑　从1996年起每年均开展元旦环城赛跑健身活动，有来自机关、学校、农村、公检法等各界群众组织的队伍上千人参加，参加人数最多时逾3000人。至2010年，先后组织14次元旦环城健身跑，参与者达2.8万人次。

中小学生越野跑　2007年，县体育和教育部门开始组织中小学生越野跑。分初中组（1992年1月1日后出生）男子10公里、女子5公里和小学组（1995年1月1日以后出生）5公里比赛，取前6名为优胜者，给予奖励。从2007年起，每年举行一次。2010年，有20所学校400多名选手参加男子10公里、女子5公里角逐。

“新春乐”体育活动　从1998年起，县体育部门每年春节期间都举行“新春乐”体育活动，在县城和乡（镇）驻地及各村寨开展拔河、短跑、象棋、围棋比赛。2002年正月初一，扎佐镇泗溪村举行新春乐扳手劲、拗扁担、踢毽子等活动，200多名群众参加。2003年正月初二，久长镇兴隆村举办拔河比赛，全村男女老少分组轮番上阵，呐喊声、欢呼声此起彼伏，欢乐气氛弥漫山村。在县城和乡（镇）驻地，每年春节期间都举行新春乐趣味体育活动及围棋、象棋比赛，2010春节期间，由县委宣传部、文体广电局等单位组织的新春乐活动在县城体育馆举行，来自全县各地的2000多群众参与趣味体育活动，40多名象棋、围棋爱好者参加象棋、围棋比赛。

节庆体育活动 每年“三八”妇女节、“五一”劳动节、“五四”青年节，县内都举行群众体育活动。1996年五一节，由县委宣传部、县总工会、文化广播电视局和体育局组织开展全县职工拔河比赛，21个单位组队参加。2001年“三八”妇女节，县委办公室和县妇联联合举办县直机关妇女运动会，开展拔河、跳绳、踢毽等比赛。2007年“三八”节，由县妇联牵头组织举办乡（镇）和县直机关妇女趣味体育运动会，48个单位300多名女职工参加乒乓球、接力、跳绳、绑腿踢球、踢毽子比赛。2010年，久长镇、六屯乡等乡（镇）在五四青年节举办篮球、乒乓球、象棋比赛等体育活动。

索桥农民运动会 2001年8月，谷堡乡政府在索桥组织举办首届“索桥农民运动会”，主要比赛项目为篮球，相邻村寨和县机关、企业共组织12支代表队参加。运动会连续3天，6000多人观看比赛。后于2002年、2003年接连举办，不断把群众喜爱的篮球运动推向高潮。

迎奥运全民健身活动 2008年4月30日是北京奥运会倒计时100天，全县举行迎奥运倒计时100天全民健身活动，各地、各单位开展拔河、跑步等体育健身运动庆祝奥运倒计时100天，并在县城体育馆举行迎奥运全民健身活动启动仪式，1000多名机关干部、社区居民和学校师生千余人参加。

第六章　精神文明建设

1982年，县委在第四次党员代表大会上作出“把社会主义物质文明和精神文明搞上去”的工作部署，社会主义精神文明建设由此被纳入与经济建设同等重要的工作内容。随着改革开放逐步深入，精神文明建设日益得到重视，县委、县政府在不同时期结合阶段工作重点，相继开展抓教育、搞创建、树典型、扬新风等各种文明创建活动，并在特色上着力，在改革中推进，在创新中发展，营造了良好的社会环境，逐步建立起社会诚信体系，涌现出被评为全国敬老模范村的龙场镇城北村，被司法部、中国残疾人联合会授予“残疾人维权示范岗”的六广镇法律服务所和龙场镇法律服务所，被评为全国孝亲敬老之星的六广镇沙坡村村民殷华利等一批先进集体和先进个人。

第一节　组织与活动场所建设

一、精神文明建设领导小组和建设委员会

1978—1987年，全县精神文明建设工作由县委宣传部兼管。1987年，县委设立社会主义精神文明建设工作领导小组于宣传部，精神文明建设工作由领导小组与宣传部共同负责。1990年，改精神文明建设工作领导小组为精神文明建设委员会（以下简称“文明委”），并置办公室于宣传部。

二、精神文明建设指导委员会

1997年，改精神文明建设委员会为精神文明建设指导委员会，仍在宣传部设办公室（简称文明办），文明办与宣传部共同负责具体工作，但文明办未纳入机构编制，未配备专职干部。2003年3月，县委贯彻党中央公布的《公民道德建设实施纲要》和省、市创建文明县的要求，将县精神文明建设指导委员会办公室即文明办列为编制内机构，隶县委宣传部，主要职责是规划和实施全县精神文明创建工作。

三、乡（镇）精神文明活动中心

1994年，县委、县政府在文明乡（镇）和文明村寨创建工作中，开始在乡（镇）筹建精神文明活动中心。活动中心即是乡（镇）党委、政府设立的精神文明建设指导机构，也是文化活动集中处，是集办

公和娱乐为一体的现代文明活动场所。是年，谷堡乡精神文明活动中心建成，为全县乡（镇）建成的第一家精神文明既文化活动场所。但因乡（镇）精神文明活动中心的建设涉及征用土地和资金投入等实际问题，进展较为迟缓，直至2006年，全县乡（镇）精神文明活动中心才建成。活动中心内设多功能活动厅、小会议室、广播室、棋牌室、图书室、全民健身室，并配备音响、电脑、复印机、速印机、录像机、摄影机等设备，还配置有图书、乐器、羽毛球、拔河等健身器材和象棋、围棋、弹子棋等娱乐用品。

久长镇文化中心

四、村级精神文明活动中心

1994年，抓住全县开展文明村寨创建活动的契机，开始筹建村一级精神文明活动中心。开初，将村党员活动室与精神文明活动中心一道筹建，2000年后，随着省市对村基础设施要求加大和投入增加，便将村委办公室、村党员活动室、计划生育办公室、精神文明活动中心统筹建设，一楼（室）多用。1996年城关镇城北村村委会办公楼即村精神文明活动中心建成，至2010年，全县已建成村级精神文明活动中心118个，在建9个。已建成的118个村精神文明活动中心总投资1308.74万元，其中省、市投资273.26万元、县投资433.84万元、乡（镇）投资142.88万元、村自筹458.76万元。

村级精神文明活动中心建设一览表

表4—06—01

乡（镇）	名称	修建年份	投资（万元）				
			省、地	县	乡	村	合计
大石乡	联丰村活动室	2004	—	4	—	—	4
	高枧村活动室	2004	—	5	—	—	5
	大屯村活动室	2005	—	8.5	—	—	8.5
	天桥村综合楼	2004	—	8	—	—	8
	回水村活动室	2004	—	6	—	—	6
	红岩村活动室	2006	—	9	—	—	9
谷堡乡	平寨村综合楼	2003	4	—	—	16	20
	富裕村综合楼	2003	4	—	—	16	20
	折溪村综合楼	2005	—	8.6	1	—	9.6
	上花村综合楼	2005	—	8.6	1	—	9.6
	红星村综合楼	2006	—	9.5	0.5	—	10
	谷堡村综合楼	2007	—	10.6	6	—	16.6
	下硐村综合楼	2007	—	10.6	0.5	—	11.1

续表

乡（镇）	名称	修建年份	投资（万元）				
			省、地	县	乡	村	合计
谷堡乡	新堰村综合楼	2007	—	10.6	0.5	—	11.1
	哨上村综合楼	2007	—	10.6	0.5	—	11.1
	大塘村综合楼	2004	3	3	2.4	—	8.4
六广镇	滨江村活动室	2003	—	—	—	6.61	6.61
	广山村活动室	2004	3	1	—	9.04	13.04
	新义村活动室	2004	3	1	—	2.8	6.8
	新中村活动室	2004	3	1	—	10.87	14.87
	广义村活动室	2004	3	1	—	2.65	6.65
	沙坡村活动室	2004	3	1	—	7.49	11.49
	广城村活动室	2005	—	6	2	1.8	9.8
	团山村活动室	2005	—	6	2	1.34	9.34
	四寨村活动室	2006	—	6	2	3.97	11.97
	松山村活动室	2006	—	6	2	2.1	10.1
	新河村活动室	2005	—	6	2	2	10
	岩脚村活动室	2007	10.6	1	—	0.22	11.82
	青龙村活动室	2007	10.6	1	—	—	11.6
	合兴村活动室	2007	10.6	1	—	—	11.6
	元庆村活动室	2007	10.6	1	—	0.25	11.85
六桶乡	盐井村活动室	2005	4	—	—	—	4
	何田村活动室	1997	—	0.9	—	—	0.9
	春江村活动室	1997	—	0.9	—	—	0.9
	凤联村活动室	2005	4	—	—	—	4
	黄金村活动室	2004	4	—	—	—	4
	团兴村活动室	1997	—	0.9	—	—	0.9
	凉井村活动室	1997	—	0.9	—	—	0.9
	长新村活动室	1997	—	0.9	—	—	0.9
	山保村活动室	1997	—	0.9	—	—	0.9
	来鹤村活动室	2005	4	—	—	—	4
	河银村活动室	1997	—	0.9	—	—	0.9
	石头村活动室	2006	4	4.6	—	—	8.6
	金星村活动室	1997	—	0.9	—	—	0.9

续表

乡（镇）	名称	修建年份	投资（万元）				
			省、地	县	乡	村	合计
六桶乡	顺江村活动室	2004	4	—	—	—	4
	海马村活动室	2006	4	5.6	1	—	10.6
	联合村活动室	1997	—	0.9	—	—	0.9
	大新村活动室	1997	—	0.9	—	—	0.9
	复兴村活动室	1997	—	0.9	—	—	0.9
	宝坪村活动室	1997	—	0.9	—	—	0.9
	榨土村活动室	1997	—	0.9	—	—	0.9
六屯乡	都堡村活动室	2005	—	—	7	—	7
	高峰村活动室	2005	—	8.6	—	—	8.6
	安全村活动室	2006	—	8.6	—	—	8.6
	新埔村活动室	2007	3.44	5.16	3	—	11.6
	星中村活动室	2007	3.44	5.16	4.49	—	13.09
	全心村活动室	2006	—	8.6	—	—	8.6
	长田村活动室	2007	3.44	5.16	5.9	—	14.5
	独山村活动室	2005	—	8.6	—	—	8.6
	西冲村活动室	2005	—	8.6	1	—	9.6
	大寨村活动室	2004	—	8.6	—	—	8.6
	三寨村活动室	2004	—	—	4	—	4
	大木村活动室	2007	3.44	5.16	0.1	—	8.7
	小木村活动室	2007	3.44	5.16	5.19	—	13.79
久长镇	久长村精神文明活动中心	2002	—	—	—	70	70
	上寨村精神文明活动中心	2004	—	4	—	6	10
	驴坊村精神文明活动中心	2004	—	4	—	7.9	11.9
	石安村党员活动室	2003	3.2	—	—	3.6	6.8
	白窑村精神文明活动中心	2002	6	—	—	1.48	7.48
	清水村党员活动室	2004	—	—	—	1.34	23
	中心村精神文明活动中心	2004	—	4	—	0.5	4.5
扎佐镇	大河村精神文明活动中心	2004	—	3	2	—	5
	新民村精神文明活动中心	2004	—	3	2	—	5
	泗溪村精神文明活动中心	2005	6.3	2	1	—	9.3
	猪头村精神文明活动中心	2005	6.3	2	2.4	—	10.7

续表

乡（镇）	名称	修建年份	投资（万元）				
			省、地	县	乡	村	合计
扎佐镇	三元村精神文明活动中心	2005	6.3	2	1	—	9.3
	葛马村精神文明活动中心	2006	6.6	2.9	3.5	—	13
	金鸡村精神文明活动中心	2006	6.6	2.9	1.5	—	11
	中营村精神文明活动中心	2007	5.16	5.64	25.4	—	36.2
洒坪乡	中明村党员活动室	2003	—	4	2	0.5	6.5
	北庄村综合楼	2007	—	8	3	1	12
	五老山村综合楼	2007	—	8	3	1	12
	五江村综合楼	2006	—	6	2	1	9
	轿子山村综合楼	2005	—	2	1	1	4
	小坝村党员活动室	2005	—	4	2	2	8
	青山村党员活动室	2006	—	5	2	2	9
	蛇场村党员活动室	2005	—	4	2	2	8
	蜈蚣桥村党员活动室	2003	—	2	2	1	5
	麻窝村综合楼	2006	—	5	3	1.8	9.8
小箐乡	小箐村党员活动室	2004	—	7	3	2	12
	大坝村党员活动室	2004	—	7	3	1	11
	小坝村党员活动室	2004	—	7	3	1	11
	大兴村党员活动室	2005	—	8	4	2	14
	杉林村党员活动室	2005	—	7	3	1	11
	凤凰村党员活动室	2005	—	4	3	1	8
	新场村党员活动室	2006	—	7	3	2	12
	大林村党员活动室	2007	—	7	3	2	12
	尖山村党员活动室	2007	—	7	3	2	12
龙场镇	平地村综合楼	2007	5.2	3.5	—	—	8.7
	白莲村综合楼	2007	5.2	3.5	—	5.3	14
	红峰村综合楼	2007	5.2	3.5	—	3.3	12
	红旗村综合楼	2007	5.2	3.5	—	4.3	13
	程关村综合楼	2007	5.2	3.5	—	3.3	12
	阳明村综合楼	2007	5.2	3.5	—	6.3	15
	沙溪村综合楼	2007	5.2	3.5	—	2.3	11
	军民村综合楼	2007	5.2	3.5	—	5.3	14

续表

乡（镇）	名称	修建年份	投资（万元）				
			省、地	县	乡	村	合计
龙场镇	新生村综合楼	2007	5.2	3.5	—	16.3	25
	花桥村综合楼	2007	5.2	3.5	—	0.3	9
	新水村综合楼	2007	7.2	3.5	—	23.3	32
	小山村文化室	2003	5.5	—	—	—	5.5
	中哨村文化室	2003	3.5	—	—	—	3.5
	建新村党员活动室	2004	4	—	—	14	18
	潮水村党员活动室	2005	8.7	—	—	9.3	18
	杨寨村党员活动室	2004	6.8	—	—	3.2	10
	马口村党员活动室	2005	10	—	—	4	14
	放马坪村党员活动室	2005	4	—	—	1	5
	马关村党员活动室	2005	9	—	—	5	14
	木厂村党员活动室	1994	2.5	—	—	—	2.5
	城北村综合楼	1996	—	—	—	149	149
合　　计			273.26	433.84	142.88	458.76	1308.74

五、群众创建组织与活动场所

县委、县政府重视群众性精神文明创建活动，支持群众在文明委的指导下自发建立文明创建组织，并为其提供活动场所。至2010年，全县精神文明创建的群众性组织百余个，以文艺、运动健身和科普为主。经常开展活动的群众组织有六广镇体育协会和花灯协会、谷堡乡体育协会、县老年人体育协会、龙场镇城北村龙灯会、扎佐镇健身队、六屯乡三寨村川戏表演队、县女企业家协会和县农村科技协会等。这些群众组织在文明委和相关行业部门的指导下，组织广大群众开展体育健身、文艺演出、科普学习和读书活动，活跃群众的业余生活。1999年到2010年，先后修建县城体育馆广场、龙岗广场、河滨广场，扎佐镇文化广场，大石民族运动体育场和县图书馆、文化馆、农家书屋等活动场地，为群众晨练、跳广场舞、举办夏日纳凉晚会、科技文化学习和排练表演文艺节目创造条件。

县城龙岗广场

第二节　宣传教育

从20世纪80年代初期开始，县委把社会主义精神文明宣传教育摆上重要议事日程，组织全县群众开展社会公德、职业道德、家庭美德教育和遵纪守法教育，使干部群众的思想道德素质逐步提高。

一、道德教育

文明礼貌教育　1982年3月，在全县开展“五讲”（讲文明、讲礼貌、讲卫生、讲道德、讲秩序）、“四美”（心灵美、语言美、行为美、环境美）、“三热爱”（热爱祖国、热爱人民、热爱社会主义）为内容的“文明礼貌月”活动，通过开展活动抓好以社会公德、职业道德、家庭美德为重点的思想道德教育，着重解决文明言行、环境卫生、服务质量、交通秩序等方面存在的突出问题，使广大干部群众的思想道德水平和文明程度得到提高。1983年3月开展“三优一学（优美环境、优良秩序、优质服务，学习雷锋）”为内容的文明礼貌月活动。继后，文明礼貌月活动逐年开展，使县城的“脏、乱、差”得以治理，文明礼貌得到市民认同。

爱国爱乡教育　1987年，在县第五次党员代表大会上，县委又一次作出“加强社会主义精神文明建设”的部署，号召全县人民“为实现经济持续稳定增长和精神文明建设取得新成绩，以及党风和社会风气进一步好转而奋斗”。县委宣传部开始有计划地在全县开展爱国爱乡教育活动，激发全县人民建设家乡的热情。县委党史办公室充分运用党史资料开展革命传统教育，先后举办党史知识竞赛、“勿忘国耻”演讲比赛等活动。还编辑出版《红军长征在修文》《修文县革命烈士传》《中国共产党修文县历史大事记》等书籍。1996年国庆节，县委宣传部首次组织在修文中学操场举行升国旗仪式。之后，升国旗仪式成为县内每年元旦、国庆必不可少的重要活动。2003年，县文明委命名烈士陵园，阳明洞囚禁张学良将军处，体育馆升旗台，革命烈士梁方膏、魏怀远牺牲地六广镇元庆、六屯乡大木寨红军标语处为爱国主义教育基地。宣传部、团县委、教育局、文联、文体广播电视局、修文报社等相关工作部门先后举办“光辉五十年”“走向新世纪”“保护环境，美化修文”等全县性的读书、讲演比赛和征文活动，激发全县人民爱党爱国爱家乡的情怀。此外，还举办重走长征路、18岁成人宣誓仪式、清明节祭奠先烈等活动。通过一系列爱国爱乡教育活动，使广大干部群众爱岗敬业、为修文经济社会发展作贡献的意识不断增强。

2003年，县文明委命名的爱国主义教育基地—阳明洞张学良将军囚禁处

公民道德建设　2001年，中共中央《公民道德建设实施纲要》颁布后，县内通过广播、电视、报刊、座谈会、图片展览等途径大力宣传，将每年的9月20日至26日定为公民道德宣传周，广泛开展社会公德、职业道德、家庭美德教育，提高干部群众的思想道德素质。2002年1月1日，县委举行元旦升旗仪

式，县城社会各界群众代表千余人在五星红旗下庄严宣誓，要宣传好贯彻好《公民道德建设实施纲要》，做“爱国守法、明礼诚信、团结友善、勤俭自强、敬业奉献”的合格公民。继后，县委宣传部发放《修文县文明市民读本》《市民守则》和《市民行为规范》组织市民学习。宣传教育有针对性地对城镇市民开展城市意识教育，对农村群众开展“改变村容村貌，树立文明新风”教育。县教育局、团县委还在学校开展“小手拉大手，文明路上一起走”活动，以学生促家长、以学校带家庭，共建精神文明。2003年6月28日，县四大班子领导与近千市民一起在“改陋习，树新风”誓师大会上发出“向陋习宣战”的誓言，在全县开展集中整治随地吐痰、随地便溺、乱倒垃圾、乱扔废弃物、违反交规横穿马路、乱停乱放、违章占道经营的陋习，县文明办、爱卫办向全县人民发出“改陋习，树新风”倡议书，号召全县市民努力建设文明、卫生、美丽的新修文。从2003年开始，公民道德宣传教育成为常态，每年均结合不同时段的要求，先后在全县开展卫生与秩序整治行动、争创文明城市共建美好家园活动和整脏治乱宣传教育活动，倡导文明礼貌、助人为乐、爱护公物、保护环境、遵纪守法的社会公德，倡导爱岗敬业、诚实守信、办事公道、服务群众、奉献社会的职业道德，倡导尊老爱幼、男女平等、夫妻和睦、勤俭持家、邻里团结的家庭美德。县内新闻媒体在公民道德宣传教育工作中，先后开设“加强公民道德建设，树立良好社会风尚”“创建文明城市，打造秀美修文”和“行动起来整脏治乱”等专栏，配合一系列公民道德宣传教育活动的开展。2008—2010年，全县深入开展公民道德建设工程——“满意在修文”主题活动。文明委号召全县市民学习道德模范、践行公民道德、助人为乐、见义勇为、诚实守信、敬业奉献、孝老爱亲，遵守公德、恪守职业道德、弘扬家庭美德、注重个人品德，知荣辱、讲正气、树新风、促和谐，从我做起，从小事做起，为提升修文县的形象贡献自己的一分力量。

社会主义荣辱观教育 2006年，在全县开展树立社会主义荣辱观教育活动。各乡（镇）和县直机关单位组织党员干部召开座谈会、讨论会，让党员、干部成为“八荣”的倡导者和实践者。乡（镇）通过以会代训的方式，把村组干部、农村党员培训为宣传骨干，再通过党员、干部的辐射，让“八荣八耻”（以热爱祖国为荣、以危害祖国为耻，以服务人民为荣、以背离人民为耻，以崇尚科学为荣、以愚昧无知为耻，以辛勤劳动为荣、以好逸恶劳为耻，以团结互助为荣、以损人利己为耻，以诚实守信为荣、以见利忘义为耻，以遵纪守法为荣、以违法乱纪为耻，以艰苦奋斗为荣、以骄奢淫逸为耻）为主要内容的社会主义荣辱观家喻户晓，深入人心。从3月20日到4月15日，全县发放“八荣八耻”宣传资料1.2万份，刷写标语400余条，进村入户开展宣传活动120场次。4月27日，县文明委行文建立由县委副书记朱桂云为主任的“文明礼仪，和谐修文”万首童谣（民谣）征集活动组委会，并在全县开展童谣（民谣）征集活动。至6月30日，共征集到1100多名作者创作的童谣（民谣）7200首，《栖霞》杂志和《当代修文》陆续选择刊登。6月16日，县委邀请市委讲师团莅县举办社会主义荣辱观知识讲座，全县副科级以上干部300余人听讲。6月19日，县委宣传部、党史办、团县委联合举办“走长征路，树荣辱观”活动，百余青年报名参加。全县通过开展广场演出、电视讲话、知识宣传、征文竞赛等活动，使市民受教育率达80%以上，社会主义荣辱观深入人心。

二、法治教育

1986—2010年，修文县历经“一五”普法到“五五”普法教育的全过程，“一五”普法（1986—1990）的5年全县有13.88万人接受《中华人民共和国宪法》《中华人民共和国婚姻法》《中华人民共和国刑法》《中华人民共和国经济合同法》和《中华人民共和国治安管理处罚条例》等法律常识学习和普及。

"二五"普法（1991—1995）期间，县内共开展普法宣传80多场次，受教育者达40多万人次。"三五"普法（1996—2000）的5年间，全县有22万人次参加普法学习。2001年到2010年10年的"四五"普法（2001—2005）和"五五"普法（2006—2010）期间，主要开展"六个一"示范点创建工程（一个依法行政单位、一个公正司法单位、一个依法治镇单位、一个依法治村单位、一个依法治校单位、一个依法治企单位）和法律"六进"活动（进机关、进乡村、进社区、进学校、进企业、进单位）。2009年5月17日，在扎佐镇举办"法律六进"系列宣传活动，以《贵州省法律援助条例》《法律援助知识问答》《中华人民共和国禁毒法》《中华人民共和国未成年人保护法》《妇女权益保障法律知识》《外来务工人员合法权益法律知识》《"送法到乡（镇）社区"法律法规资料选编》等法律法规知识为主要内容，开展宣传咨询服务，现场有数千群众接受普法教育。25年的普法宣传教育，全县受教育公民达80%以上，人民群众的法治观念和法律意识明显增强，依法办事的能力更加提高，遵纪守法，做合格公民成为全县群众的共识。

2007年，县交警大队到修文二中开展法制教育进课堂活动

三、禁毒教育

2004年，县禁毒委员会出台《关于贯彻落实〈国家禁毒委员会2004—2008年禁毒工作规划〉的实施意见》，禁毒宣传教育随即在全县展开。县禁毒委员会围绕"抵制毒品，参与禁毒"的主题，在全县范围内开展轰轰烈烈的禁毒宣传教育活动。除常规的宣传教育外，每年"6·26"国际禁毒日期间，全县中小学校均要开展"六个一"（学校每学期出一期禁毒知识宣传专栏黑板报，组织一次禁毒知识讲座或专题班会、队会，读一本禁毒方面的书籍，写一篇禁毒教育心得体会，看一场禁毒专题片，举办一次禁毒知识竞赛或"珍爱生命、远离毒品"图片展览）活动，强化中、小学生毒品预防教育。县禁毒办公室、公安局、司法局、宣传部在禁毒宣传活动中，采取发放禁毒宣传资料、编辑禁毒宣传栏和禁毒黑板报、制作禁毒资料图片、悬挂张贴禁毒宣传标语、在城乡集镇公共活动场所设置固定禁毒宣传栏和放映禁毒专题片等方式扩大禁毒宣传面。检察、审判机关选择有影响的毒品犯罪案件召开公捕公判大会，打击毒品犯罪，教育警醒群众"拒绝毒品，珍爱生命"。2005年"6·26"禁毒宣传日，禁毒办在县城体育馆滚动放映禁毒宣传片《毒品—致命的诱惑》和《黑白记忆》，吸引3000多群众观看接受禁毒教育。

2006年，县长石洪参与禁毒宣传活动

2006年，县委、县政府提出"一年打基础，两年上台阶，三年争创无毒县"的工作目标。县禁毒办、宣传部除开展常规宣传外，还聘请专业医护工作者到学校举办毒品与艾滋病预防专题知识讲座，在社区（村）开展"不让毒品进我家"活动。创建无毒县期间，宣传教育工作方式更加创新，先后举办禁毒游演、《中华人民共和国禁毒法》知识有奖竞赛等活动，2008年，编印《禁毒知识手册》20万

册，做到职工人手一册，人民群众一户一册。

强大的禁毒宣传教育，使群众充分认识到毒品的危害，“珍爱生命，拒绝毒品”成为大家的自觉行为，至2010年，龙场、扎佐、久长3镇实现无贩毒、无制毒、无复吸、无新增吸毒人员、无非法种植毒品原植物的“五无”镇,还创建无毒社区10个、无毒村204个、无毒单位250个，全县学校均为无毒学校。

第三节　创建活动

一、文明城市创建

2006年，全县开展“争创文明城市，共建美好家园”和“卫生与秩序整治”活动，县委设立文明城市创建办公室，通过大会动员，媒体宣传，拉开修文文明城市创建的序幕。2月初，县政府出台《修文县禁止燃放烟花爆竹管理规定》，对县城燃放烟花爆竹划定燃放区域规定燃放时间，并由县委宣传部牵头，组织公安、工商、城管、供销、电视台等单位，悬挂宣传标语、组装宣传车进行下到城乡宣传。3月14日，县委召开常委会议，专门研究创建工作，要求各单位、各乡（镇）指定专人负责文明城市创建和“卫生与秩序”整治。会后，龙场镇就组织600余名乡（镇）干部群众清理垃圾100余吨；扎佐镇对公路沿线的6个村进行整治，清运垃圾400余吨；久长镇整治公路沿线的7个村，清运垃圾200余吨。县直机关单位则参加县城整治。创建办提出“优美环境、优良秩序、优质服务”的创建口号，并将县城街道路段划分到各单位，实行责任制，对创建不力的单位亮“黄牌”。责任部门落实“门前三包”，机关干部深入临街单位、门市，宣传“门前三包”内容和要求。创建行动中，印发倡议书万余份，《城市市容和环境卫生管理办法》宣传资料1.2万份，悬挂创建宣传标语300余条，县的媒体集中报道创建活动新闻200余条。全民动员的创建行动，使全县环境卫生和秩序大大改观，街道上干净、整洁，车辆乱停乱放堵塞交通的现象没有了，行人过马路自觉走斑马线，小贩不再占道经营。农村村寨村容村貌更是令人刮目相看，村道上再也看不到猪屎牛粪，家家庭院整洁清新。是年，修文的“卫生与秩序整治”工作获得贵阳市全市检查排名第三的好成绩。继后，文明城市创建工作持续开展，2010年，结合贵阳市提出“三创一办”（创建国家卫生城市、国家环境保护模范城市、全国文明城市和协办2011年第九届全国少数民族传统体育运动会）工作要求，县委于2月10日在县城召开“三创一办”志愿服务活动启动大会，提出要以纵深推进生态文明城市建设为总揽，以落实贵阳市委、市政府提出的“三创一办”为抓手，细化目标，强力推进，提高修文的城市规划、建设、管理水平，转变经济发展方式，促进产业生态化、

2010年，县委县政府与县属部门签订创建文明城市目标责任书

生态产业化，创造一个更加宜居、宜业、宜游的良好环境，提高城市文明程度，改善城市形象，提升城市品位的创建要求。会后，干部、群众、学生等万余人组成的志愿服务队，手系“绿丝带”，在县城打扫大街小巷，拉开了全县以“三创一办”为抓手，纵深推进文明城市创建和生态经济强县建设的序幕。至年底，文明城市创建仍结合“三创一办”持续开展。

二、文明单位（行业）创建

行风评议 1995年，县内启动开展文明单位（行业）创建活动，是时，主要是推荐文明单位参与省、市评选，1999年起，以开展行风评议为契机，掀起文明单位（行业）创建热潮。县委宣传部与县纠风办配合，制定完善文明单位、文明行业管理制度，要求服务单位（行业）自查自纠，采取措施自己管，组织群众监督员队伍大家管、主管部门经常明察暗访长效管，在全县开展行风评议活动。3月，明确公安局、供电局、信用联社、教育局等4家单位为首批行风评议单位，12月末检查验收。期间，纠风办组织人大代表、政协委员、群众代表和媒体记者组成评议小组，随时开展对评议单位的明察暗访和监督工作。10月，评议小组组织“行风评议问卷调查”活动，发动社会对全县各大行业文明服务情况进行评价，让群众说话，促进行风建设，推动全县精神文明创建工作。参与行风评议的单位制定制度，聘请群众代表、机关干部为行风监督员，通过齐抓共管，行风得到群众认可。之后，行风评议工作每年有计划开展，成为文明单位创建的重要标志。

创建活动 2000年起，文明单位（行业）创建活动进入制度化管理，县文明办先后制订了精神文明创建的规章制度和评选标准，使文明单位创建有章可循，活动开展得有声有色。县人民法院把审判改革融入到文明单位创建中，2001—2005年，先后在谷堡乡、六桶乡、久长镇和洒坪乡成立巡回法庭，解决离法庭驻地较远的群众打官司难、诉讼成本高的问题。适用简易程序审理的案件，法官把审判法庭搬到汽车上，搬到当事人的家门口，让边远山区的群众就地就近完成诉讼，这些做法，被老百姓亲切地赞誉为“我们的汽车法庭”“我们的院坝法庭”。修文供电局把行风建设和文明单位创建与自身业务结合起来，在单位内部开展“人民电力为人民”“以客户为中心”活动，2009年3月，按上级规定实行“限电”。“限电”对用电企业意味着停产、减产，会给生产经营带来损失。局领导和员工并没有用简单的“拉闸”处理问题，而是“急客户之所急，想客户之所想”，他们走访客户调研，想方设法调整应急方案，把最困难的事留给自己做，把最大的方便让给企业。在“限电”期间，14家水泥厂和8家冶炼厂仍然有序生产，产量达到正常生产时的90%以上，其中被列在停产名单上的双辉铁厂和金阳铁厂也保障正常生产。在文明单位创建中，很多单位（行业）还把创建活动与县政府的“三公开”（政务、厂务、村务公开）工作要求相结合，县民政局在单位门口设公开栏，定期公布低保对象增减名单，物价局利用县的媒体《当代修文》刊登“粮油副食品每周价格报告”，县医院对所有收费项目的依据、价格全部上墙，使看病群众明白付费。文明单位创建成为关注民生，权为民用，利为民谋的特殊载体。

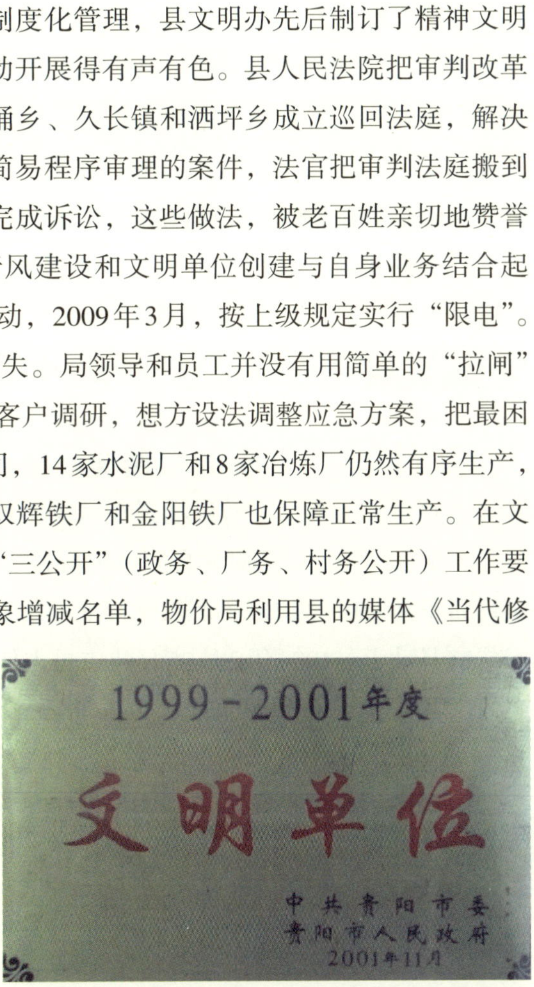

贵阳市委市政府授予县属部分单位的文明单位牌匾

到2010年，先后有县水利电力局、人民银行、纪委、农办、县委办、国税局、贵遵路扎佐征费站等13个（次）单位被评选为省级文明单位。有县政协办、国税局、供电局、地税局、质监局、县妇联、检察院、宣传部、文体广电局、气象局、财政局、政府办、人大办、综治办、高尔夫度假中心、六桶中学、大石乡财政所、小箐乡供电所、扎佐镇景阳派出所、龙场镇、久长供电所、六屯乡计生办、贵毕路修文征费站、修文移动通信公司、修文电信公司、贵毕路六广征费站、人事劳动和社会保障局、档案局、县委机要局、修文中学、私立景阳中学、扎佐中学、扎佐计生站、六广镇卫生院、法院等101个（次）单位被评选为市级文明单位。有59个单位被评选为县级文明单位。

三、文明村镇创建

1995年开始文明村镇创建工作，创建结合县内开展的中心工作进行，先后通过新农村建设、茅草房改造、卫生与秩序整治和整脏治乱等工作推进创建工作深入开展，提升农村文明程度。是年，城关镇城北村村委综合大楼竣工，即被命名为精神文明活动中心，成为不仅是修文县更是安顺地区首家农村群众开展精神文明活动的场所。

在文明村镇创建中，发展农村经济，改善村容村貌，提升农村群众幸福生活指数成为创建工作的重头戏，各村镇以此为重点抓创建。2002年，谷堡乡平寨村投入19万元在村里新建集贸市场，活跃乡场商贸，增加集体收入。2003年，小箐乡崇恩村村“两委”带领村民走科技兴村之路，因地制宜养殖肉牛、肉鸡、肉鸽，两年时间，全村617户家家成为养殖户，告别贫穷落后的日子。2007年，龙场镇争取县交通局筑路资金，硬化新春村至大寨5公里公路，解决了沿路2000多村民的出行困难。2010年，首钢贵阳新特材料循环经济工业基地落户扎佐镇三里、小堡两村，两村村委合理解决好被征地、征房农民的利益问题，拆迁工作中无一户群众上访。

农村经济发展倒逼文明村镇创建工作蓬勃发展，1995年到2010年，全县先后有扎佐镇、龙场镇、谷堡乡、小箐乡、谷堡乡平寨村、谷堡乡折溪村、龙场镇马口村、龙场镇新水村、久长镇白窑村、久长镇上寨村、洒坪乡中明村、六广镇沙坡村、六广镇中坪村、六广镇六广村、六桶乡榨土村、六屯乡西冲村、六屯乡独山村等17个村镇获得贵阳市文明村镇称号。有扎佐镇、龙场镇、谷堡乡和龙场镇城北村、沙溪村、新水村，久长镇白窑村、永兴村，洒坪乡中明村、上寨村，六广镇沙坡村、广城村、中坪村，大石乡大屯村，六屯乡西冲村、独山村，六桶乡榨土村、复兴村，谷堡乡谷堡村、折溪村，小箐乡杉林村、凤凰村等22个村镇获得县级文明村镇称号。2006年，龙场镇城北村被评选为全国孝亲敬老模范村。

专记：城北村成为文明创建的排头兵

1992年，县委、县政府选择在城关镇城北村建县内第一家村级精神文明活动中心，省、地财政支持资金3万元，其余款项由村自筹。中心位于环城路北段西侧，占地1亩，建筑5层楼房，总投资20万元，建筑面积为1300平方米，底层是商业门面，二层以上为报刊阅览室、广播室、歌舞厅兼会议室和办公室等。11月动工，1994年2月25日建成投入使用。1996年，村委会又自筹149万元重建综合大楼，次年7月25日完工。新综合楼建筑面积为2330平方米。1997年7月25日，村精神文明活动中心搬至新建的综合大楼。

1995年12月，村里成立一支40多人的男子龙灯队。成立后即在春节期间为群众表演，深受欢迎，1997年，龙灯队参加县里举行的庆祝香港回归活动。1999年8月，为迎接县第一届阳明文化节的举办,村里又成立一支87人的花环队，被活动组委会定名为“迎宾礼仪队”。2001年1月村里又组建女子龙灯队。男女两支龙灯队每年参加县里的春节游演活动，增加了春节欢乐祥和的节日气氛。龙灯队曾3次应邀到省城贵阳，1次到息烽县参加春节游演活动，2004年，还到金阳参加贵阳市举办的全市花灯、龙灯表演。

城北村在精神文明创建活动中，积极倡导科学、文明、健康、和谐的生活方式，大力弘扬尊老爱幼、男女平等、夫妻和睦、勤俭持家、邻里团结等优良传统美德。村委会和全村群众长期对村里无劳动能力、无生活来源、无法定赡养人的“三无”老人给予关心照顾，体现孝亲敬老美德，受到社会称赞。1992—1994年，省委、省政府授予“文明单位”称号。1997年，县委、县政府授予“文明村寨”称号。2006年，在中央文明办等6家单位举办的孝亲敬老先进评选活动中，被授予全国“孝亲敬老模范村”称号。

四、文明社区创建

2004年，全县街道居委会整合为社区后，县委办公室、县政府办公室印发《关于进一步加强社区建设的意见》,全县社区随即开展文明社区创建工作。文明社区创建结合贵阳市开展“民主法治示范社区”创建活动、“三优精品社区”创建活动和“十大和谐社区”评选活动进行。

创建活动中，全县社区以居民安居乐业为目标，以扩大社会服务为纽带、以完善基础设施为重点，把创建优美环境、打造优良秩序、提供优质服务作为载体，从治理“脏、乱、差”入手，通过基础设施配套建设和不断完善服务功能，把文明社区创建重点放在提高社区居民的文明素质上。2007年，龙场镇龙岗社区在“卫生与秩序整治”行动中筹集资金8000元将原来是个烂泥窖的猪市坝改建成文化长廊，还组织起合唱队、腰鼓队、健身队。2010年，县城开展“三创一办”活动，1000多名社区居民成为义务监督员，他们佩戴红袖章活跃在城镇街道上开展监督和宣传工作，受到贵阳市委宣传部领导的称赞，《贵阳日报》的记者还专门写报道，赞扬他们是“城市的一道亮丽风景线”。至2010年，全县12个社区先后建成公益性服务设施广场6个、医疗服务点8个、宣传文化室10个、图书室12个、老年学校（业余党校）12个，龙场镇和扎佐镇的社区还建起公益性健身场所，配置健身器材100余套（件）。全县社区绿化面积达3万平方米，城市亮丽工程覆盖率100%。社区已创建成生态环境优美、文体活动丰富、道德风尚良好、群众放心满意的文明社区。先后有龙场镇的龙岗、虎山和扎佐镇的万江社区被评选为贵阳市的“三优精品社区”，龙场镇的宾阳、栖凤，久长镇的长久，六广镇的淞江社区获得贵阳市“民主法治示范社区”称号，龙场镇的虎山社区被评选为贵阳市的“十大和谐社区”。

专记：龙岗社区文明创建展新颜

龙岗社区地处县城东北角城郊接合部，面积96万平方米，居住着2710户6970人，其中外来人口303户816人。这里曾经是县城赶集的猪市，集脏、乱，差、穷为一体。自2003年11月整合成立社区以后，社区党支部、居委会一班人励精图治，带领群众克难攻坚，营造出一个文明和谐的生活环境。

针对环境卫生差的问题，社区党支部、居委会集思广益，明确班子成员和党员职责，实行包片、包段责任制，充分发挥群众的积极性，开展“卫生与秩序”整治活动。社区自筹资金8000元建成200米文化长廊，既美化环境，又起到宣传教育的作用。关爱吸毒人员是社区工作的一项重要内容，社区采取“一帮一，一助一”的方式开展帮教活动，帮助吸毒者重新树立积极的生活态度，2005年，社区成功帮助8名吸毒人员戒除毒瘾。吸毒人员钟荣健因复吸被劳动教养3年，老婆含恨离去。钟荣健劳教回来，生活无着，社区党支部、居委会的同志多次上门开展“一帮一，一助一”活动，安排他当了保洁员。钟荣健在老党员李贵良的帮助下，戒除了毒瘾，并重新组建了家庭。社区为118名吸毒人员建立档案，实行“一人一档”，明确专人对社区内25名吸毒人员帮教，定时组织尿检，从源头上遏制新增吸毒人员。做好低保工作，事关困难群众的切身利益，社区高度重视，明确责任心强的党员负责，认真落实国家政策，共为245户困难群众办理低保手续。社区内的月亮井年久失修，严重影响群众的正常生活,社区积极争取社会支持，发动群众，对月亮井进行改造，工程竣工那天，群众齐聚月亮井鸣炮致谢。2005年8月，群众胡学文家里突发急事，社区“两委”一方面向有关部门争取补助，一方面带头捐款，共筹集200斤大米和1000元现金，帮助胡学文家解难。90高龄的孤寡老人汤显玉谈起多年来的生活，满脸喜悦，说“社区领导和群众经常来家问寒问暖，不是亲人胜是亲人”。社区群众的手里握有《龙岗社区便民服务卡》，服务内容在卡上写得一清二楚，群众有什么急难事，只要一个电话，就有专人上门排忧解难。党员干部带头做出榜样，群众积极效仿，邻里间和睦相处，互帮互助，同享社会发展成果。为拓宽群众活动场地，社区还建起图书室，并筹资万余元，建起社区合唱队、腰鼓队、健身队。群众或到图书室看书，或参加合唱队、健身队活动，置身于欢声笑语的娱乐圈里，越发感到社区的温暖。

五、文明家庭创建

20世纪80年代起，县内就开展有“五好家庭”评选活动。20年间，县委宣传部、县文明办、县妇联根据不同时期工作重点和县委的工作要求，不断深化“五好家庭”“文明家庭”创建活动，将活动由城市延伸到农村，使众多家庭的文明程度不断提升。

创建活动中，先后开展过“五好家庭”“十星级文明户”“书香人家”“美在农家”等文明家庭评选活动，通过各种评选活动，促进千家万户和睦团结，涌现出一大批尊老爱老、乐于助人、崇尚科学的先进文明家庭和个人。六广镇沙坡村村民殷华利一家赡养无血缘关系的老人，龙场镇白岩寨叶茂仙把非亲非故的刘老太太接到家中当作自己母亲供养孝敬，家居县城的胡林家庭参加中央电视台“神州大舞台”家庭秀表演，在县内传为佳话。2006年，县文明委给予1236个家庭“十星级文明户”荣誉称号，六广镇沙坡村的殷华利还被评为全国孝亲敬老之星。

专记：胡林家庭登上“神州大舞台”

2003年3月9日，胡林夫妇和女儿在庆“三八”修文县首届家庭才艺展示中获一等奖。经县妇联推荐，胡林家庭又于当年12月16日参加了全国妇联、中央电视台联合举办的“神州大舞台”家庭秀表演，获得“优胜奖”奖牌和证书。

“神州大舞台”是全国“欢乐之家”电视竞选栏目，是由中央电视台文艺部与全国妇联、中国家庭文化研究会联合主办的综艺性栏目，从家庭的视角反映全国各地的地域特色、人文环境、经济社会发展面貌。在第一次家庭秀表演中，胡林一家在修文阳明洞采集阳明古迹照片，约请县内人士撰写宣传解说词，在中央电视台大屏幕上宣传推介家乡修文和阳明文化。

2003年12月胡林家庭登上央视“神州大舞台”

有了前次的经验积累，胡林家庭又参加全国妇联、中央电视台联合举办的神州大舞台2005魅力家庭大赛，获得“演播纪念”牌。此次，胡林家庭按照日程安排作了充分准备，先后经历了试音、录音、录像等准备环节。他的家庭编为4号家庭，会场播放家庭服饰展示音乐，一家3口上场进行服装展示。主持人朗诵“偃武修文境如仙，世外桃源山外山，侗汉一家有盛会，欢乐祥和三月三”的歌句。

在第一板块“服装展示”中，主持人介绍说，修文因明代大思想家、教育家王阳明先生被贬至此悟道讲学而闻名于世，素有“王学圣地”之称。这里山川秀丽，气候宜人，被誉为“天然氧吧”“世外桃源”。

胡林家庭是侗汉结合的家庭，他们“服装展示”的主题是侗族传统节日“欢乐祥和三月三”。女儿胡睿是一名初中二年级的学生，曾参加过全国的少儿歌手比赛，取得优异成绩。妻子潘红梅系侗族，是一名初中教师。丈夫胡林是家中唯一的汉族，是一名国家公务员，从事经济管理工作，爱好体育和书法。

在第二板块“共创佳绩”中，胡林一家表演歌曲《美丽的侗乡》，胡林展示了书法“留有山河秀，侗家情意浓”。他们一家通过才艺展示，创意表现，将开心、默契、健康的家庭展现在观众面前，展示家庭兼赋才艺与制造快乐的能力来鼓励快乐生活、勇于创新，使广大观众感受“魅力家庭”的感染力。他们一家对家庭的热爱、对艺术的追求和对生活的积极态度，在精彩的节目中展示了精彩的生活，赢得观众赞誉，获得阵阵掌声。

六、争创“青年文明号”

从1994年起，团县委组织团员青年开展争创“青年文明号”活动，引导青年诚实劳动，爱岗敬业，建功成才。1999年，县信用联社团员青年参加团市委等部门举办的全市金融系统青工比武大赛，取得手指点钞二等奖。至2010年，全县共创市级“青年文明号”13个，县级“青年文明号”29个和“青年文明岗”9个。

七、城乡联动创建

送文化下乡　2001年，县委提出“广泛开展群众性文体活动”的要求，全县掀起“送文化下乡”活动高潮，通过城乡互动，开展精神文明创建，活跃农村文化生活。至2010年，送戏下乡千场次、送书下乡6万余册，送科技下乡开展科普宣传百余场次，送电影下乡1.2万场次，送春联下乡20余万幅。

2007年，贵阳市送文化下乡活动启动仪式在修文举行

结对共创　2006年，全县开展新农村建设，县文明委提出“文明进村镇、共建新农村”。结合新农村建设，以县内开展的结对帮扶为基础，实施城乡联动结对共建工程，推进文明创建。全县机关单位（行业）分别与217个村结对共建文明村寨。在共建过程中，机关单位为结对共建的村举办科普、理论、阳明文化讲座60多场次，向农村送电影400多场次，送文艺演出30多场次，兴建新农村建设宣传栏百余块，先后有40多家单位（行业）向共建村捐款7万余元帮助改善村容村貌。县文联还根据建设社会主义新农村培育文明乡风要求，组织作协会员编写弘扬农村新风，宣传“八荣八耻”社会主义荣辱观和“创业、道德、法纪、和谐、家庭、卫生、新风”等

内容融为一体的快板、顺口溜等通俗易懂的文艺作品在《当代修文》和《栖霞》发表，供群众传阅。2008—2010年，结对共建工程又结合县里开展的“四在农家”持续进行，以美化村容村貌构建和谐新农村为重点，把创建活动推向新台阶。

附：《中小学生文明礼仪快板》

快扳甲说：

清晨离家上学校，出门问候父母好，
上街要走人行道，靠右慢行不乱跑，
横过马路左右看，绿灯通行红灯停，
盲人叔叔行不便，一脚踩到香蕉皮，
我们赶快来帮忙，主动上前搭把手，
避免危险除后患，捡起扔进垃圾筒，
叔叔夸我真懂事，大家开心我欢喜。

快扳乙说：

过马路走斑马线，不要逞能跨护栏，
走天桥，下通道，保持距离是关键，
向人问路先称呼，文明用语不可少，
有人问路要帮忙，热情应答讲礼貌，
知道告诉正确路，不知也要道声歉，
排队候车讲次序，不争不抢不挤闹，
先下后上多礼让，遇到碰撞把歉道，
车上不能扔垃圾，不能随手窗外抛，
坐车不吵不打闹，保持安静有礼貌，
遇到老人把座让，相互体谅多协调，
谢谢再见对不起，文明用语要记牢。

快扳甲说：

衣装整洁到学校，互相问好不能少，
遇见老师行个礼，见到同学问声早，
要想显出精气神，站要如松坐如钟，
颈要伸直腰要挺，两肩打开手摆正，
女生姿态要稳当，动作不宜太张扬，
穿裙入座要并膝，两手不能放腿间，
坐着不宜倚和靠，站立不要把腿抖，
好的仪态从小养，严格要求是关键。

甲、乙同说：

上课时间快要到，提前备好工具书，

精力集中认真听，举手提问尊师长，
进入老师办公室，喊声报告等回复，
如果没有应答声，不能偷听不乱闯。

甲、己同说：

同学们，听仔细，在家也要讲礼仪，
在校是个好学生，在家当个好儿女，
认真学习写作业，适当做些家务活。

快板甲说：

客人来访要接待，主动上前问个好，
请入客房请上坐，双手递杯热茶水，
父母到来我撤退，大人谈事不打扰，
不去偷听不插嘴，说声再见就告退。

快板乙说：

接待外宾要礼貌，事先准备事项多，
献花时候要微笑，右手拿着左手托，
菊花纸花黄色花，都是忌讳不要犯，
惹来变脸与麻烦，及时提醒多注意，
了解花语与禁忌，以免费力又尴尬。

快板甲说：

就餐礼仪讲究多，大人先坐我后坐，
左侧入座左侧出，互不妨碍都方便，
大人动筷再动筷，筷子不能乱指点，
不挑不拣不乱翻，乱敲乱插是忌讳，
站起夹菜不礼貌，转到面前再来吃。

快板乙说：

想替别人把菜夹，使用公筷受欢迎，
给人敬酒要适量，不要灌酒出洋相，
礼字当头度为先，热情过头惹人嫌，
安静就餐多和谐，我们大家都做到。

甲、乙同说：

礼貌礼节用处广，律己敬人是关键，
中华复兴礼当先，发扬光大靠大家，
弘扬传统讲美德，倡导文明树新风，
共建修文文明县，文明礼仪代代传。
文明礼仪代代传！

（原载《当代修文》2006年4月10日）

八、军民共建

1998年起，驻县部队与驻地乡（镇）、村寨结成帮扶对子，以密切军政军民关系，参与地方经济建设，帮助人民群众脱贫致富为目标，开展文明创建活动，至2010年，先后建成“军民共建”单位36个。

2001年，驻县贵阳陆军预备役工兵团与谷堡乡、扎佐镇、龙场镇结成“军民共建”单位，4月，该团为谷堡乡大棚蔬菜基地修建富民道路1公里，7月，出资3万元和工程机械，出动官兵20人，同扎佐镇大堡村群众共同构筑长550米村路，为当地群众尽快脱离贫困创造良好条件，群众称村路为“军民连心路”。驻县贵州省军区后勤生产基地与龙场镇白莲、幸福、军民3个村结成共建单位后，注重与驻地农村建设协调发展，基地每主推一个蔬菜品种或发展一项产业，均把生产技术和管理经验介绍给村里的农民，通过技术帮扶，促进3个村农民增收。基地每年在共建村聘用富余劳动力500人次，为村民增收拓宽渠道。还通过观念、技术、信息等方面的优势，带动并促进3个村的村民调整产业结构。谷堡乡上花村是县内的贫困村，全年人均收入不到800元，交通条件差，自然条件恶劣，8公里进村公路多年失修，制约该村经济发展。2002年，县人民武装部与上花村结成“双带”扶贫“军民共建”点后，人武部结合上花村实际情况，帮助村支两委拟订中长期发展规划，赠送种植养殖农业技术书籍45种500余册，协调县农业部门给村民举办农业知识培训班5期、培训技术骨干60余人，还采取组织村干部和村民代表外出参观学习等方式扶贫扶智。通过3年努力，于2005年为上花村完成进村公路硬化工程，建起村综合办公楼，帮助33户贫困村民改造茅草房。3年间，人武部共为上花村贫困群众送去化肥25吨、水泥30吨、农用工具30件、树苗3万余株、课桌100套、教材200套、棉被180床，资助13名失（辍）学儿童重返校园。2005年，人武部与久长镇清水村结成共建帮扶对子，确定将清水村建设成为“军民共建社会主义新农村”示范点。至2010年，共筹资20余万元，援助清水村整修村组公路、村容整治，为23户村民改造危房和旧房。

2005年，县人武部与久长镇清水村结成共建帮扶对子，为该村硬化道路

第四节　文明新风建设

一、革除殡葬陋习

1978年，“文化大革命”时期一度放任的殡葬陋习继续蔓延，城乡有的群众办丧事大张声势地搞封建迷信和铺张浪费，有的竟大搭灵棚做法事；有的看风水、选时辰择期下葬、有的大摆酒席，借机敛财；有的大张旗鼓进行土葬。1997年，县委、县政府遵照国务院《殡葬管理条例》在196个村划定集中安葬

区，在217个村建立红白喜事理事会。1999年2月23日，县编制委员会行文批准成立殡葬管理所，10月12日，建在久长镇的殡仪馆投入使用。2003年，全县贯彻贵阳市委、市政府《关于殡葬改革工作实施情况的意见》，深入开展殡改法律法规宣传，组织大型宣传活动5次，出动宣传车辆12台次，发放宣传资料7万余份，接受群众咨询1000余人次。通过大规模的宣传和强化殡葬执法，全年火化率达52.3%。2004年，县委、县政府出台《关于进一步加强殡葬改革工作的实施意见》，全县结合精神文明创建，通过出动宣传车，发放殡改宣传资料，制作固定标语，做到资料入户，精神到人。强大的宣传教育，使群众对革除殡葬陋习的认识大大提高，加上采取果断措施，不允许在县内生产和经营棺木，引导群众将骨灰放入形似棺木的骨灰盒安葬死者，坚决制止办丧事搞封建迷信活动，县城内办丧事不得燃放鞭炮，不得随地抛撒纸钱。农村红白事理事会同时履行职能，制止丧家在丧事中搞迷信活动。民政部门加快公墓建设，完善殡葬改革基础设施。全县公益性墓地增至225个，每个行政村都有农村公益性墓地，还引进贵州静园文化公司投资经营性公墓，在龙场镇建成城南殡仪服务站，满足了县城群众丧事活动需求。强大的殡改宣传和各种殡改措施的落实，人们真正认识到殡葬改革的意义，办丧事的人家从强制火葬到自觉要求火葬，2005年，全县死亡1619人，火化率为100%。至2010年，文明办丧事蔚成风气，土葬陋习彻底革除。

县民政局开展殡葬管理法律宣传

二、婚育新风进万家

1998年，按照中央宣传部、国家计生委统一部署，全县深入开展婚育新风进万家活动。县委、县政府成立婚育新风进万家活动领导小组，由宣传部牵头，县文明办、计生局、教育局、民政局等部门为成员单位，明确责任人和联络员，形成每年定期召开情况通报会议的综合决策机制。各乡（镇）党委、政府和县直机关、企业把婚育新风进万家活动纳入精神文明建设的主要内容，以宣传倡导破陋习，以文化建设促共识，使科学文明进步的婚育观念走进百姓家，成为群众的普遍共识。活动中，全县各地广为张贴、散发《致育龄夫妇的公开信》、婚育新风进万家、关爱女孩和法律法规宣传资料，县计生部门在每年“5·29”中国计生协会成立纪念日，给新婚夫妻发宣传袋，内装婚姻知识、生殖健康和避孕节育知识资料，使新婚夫妇获取生理卫生知识；“7·11”世界人口日纪念活动期间举行“关心母亲健康，关爱女孩成长”活动；春节期间利用外出打工人员返乡与家人团圆的机会，向打工者的家庭发放宣传资料；“三八”妇女节期间，利用村精神文明活动中心和人口教育学校开展计划生育知识宣传培训；三、四月均进行计生优质服务下乡活动，县和乡（镇）妇幼保健站的医护人员带上检查器械下到村组，为育龄妇女免费“三查”（查环、查孕、查病），把真情送到育龄妇女家中。2001年5月27日，县政府在县

2009年，龙场镇开展婚育新风进万家知识竞赛活动

城举行纪念中国计生协会成立21周年大型宣传活动，省、市领导司徒桂美、王惠业和宗大尧等莅临参加，县计生协会和龙场镇计生协会组织近万人的宣传游演队伍，沿街演出两个多小时，省、市、县计生部门还在街头设立宣传咨询台，向群众宣传介绍生殖保健知识，当天免费向群众发放价值3.5万元的避孕药具和2.5万份宣传资料，还为300多名妇女义诊。继后，为推进婚育新风进万家活动，建立县、乡、村婚育新风进万家活动三级网络，组织起一支200多人的志愿者队伍，广泛开展计生政策法规和婚育知识宣传培训。2003年6月22日，县城再次举行《倡导婚育新风，参与志愿服务，做计生表率》的婚育新风志愿者推进会。贵阳市委、市政府领导，共青团贵州省委领导，省、市计生委领导和县四大班子领导与数千群众一起参加宣传游演。社区建立后，县里又在社区为流动人口开辟婚育新风流动课堂，帮助流动人口解决子女入托、就学、劳动就业等生产、生活、生育问题，为流动人口送科技、送服务、送温暖，实行动态化的宣传和服务，提高流动人口自我教育、自我管理、自我服务的意识和能力。2004年，开展关爱女孩、综合治理出生人口性别工作，建立起“政府为主、部门参与、社会捐助”的计划生育利益导向体系，把建设和完善计划生育利益导向机制作为一项惠民政策、民心工程来抓，全县单独女孩家庭均享受到优惠政策。2010年，2000余户单独女孩家庭被纳入养老保险、1000多户获得奖励扶助，真正使生育女孩的家庭在社会上有地位、经济上有实惠、生活上有保障，切实改善女孩的生存和发展环境，确保计划生育利益导向机制可持续发展。

从2001年开展婚育新风进万家活动到2010年，全县计生宣传品进村入户率达98%，群众对政策、法规、新型生育观念和避孕节育科普知识知晓率达97%。县的计划生育工作从2004年起连续7年获贵阳市目标考核一等奖，并荣获贵州省“计划生育优质服务县”称号。2005年获得由中宣部、中央文明办、国家人口计生委等中央10部委联合授予的2001—2005年“全国婚育新风进万家活动先进县”的荣誉。

三、“百城万店无假货”活动

2000年起，全县开展“百城万店无假货”活动，以提高商贸企业职工道德水准、打击制售假冒伪劣商品行为和保护消费者合法权益为宗旨，引导商贸企业员工和个体工商户严格遵守“诚信、公平、情义、服务”的商业道德准则，倡导“为人民服务、对社会负责”的良好道德风尚。从2001年到2010年，县举办税法宣传、产品质量宣传、消费者权益保护宣传等有关市场建设的宣传活动达百余次。还利用县内媒体电视台和《当代修文》开辟专栏，加强舆论引导和舆论监督，县质监局连续10年与县内媒体合作，刊播有关质量技术标准和监管工作法律法规。工商、质监、税务、物价等部门不间断地开展打击违法经营、假冒伪劣、偷税漏税行为。2001年5月，县政府组织质监、工商等部门开展“联合打假百日行动”，仅县卫生系统就出动卫生执法人员468人次，对食品、医疗卫生市场进行整顿。6月8日，县物价局、纠风办、卫生局联合发出《在全县开展药品医疗服务价格检查的通知》，经过1个月的检查，使药品医疗卫生市场得以规范。2008年，轰动全国的“三鹿奶粉事件”发生后，县工商局对全县723户经营食品的超市、百货店进行检查，查获含

2009年，县工商局开展“3·15”商品质量检查

三聚氰胺的三鹿奶粉180公斤，当即销毁处理。2010年11月，县政府决定将翠屏路商业步行街作为“百城万店无假货示范街”，在县城开展“百城万店无假货示范街”创建活动。力图通过示范作用，倡导诚信经商，营造文明健康和谐有序的消费环境。15日，县委宣传部、文明办、工商局等单位与30多家商户代表在步行街举行“诚信宣誓”，由此拉开示范街商户“共铸诚信联盟行动”的序幕。示范街商户还与相关职能部门签订“百城万店无假货示范街”活动承诺书，立下经营活动中讲诚信，不销售假冒伪劣商品，做文明商营户的誓约。活动期间，合力超市等示范店还推出“零风险购物”“无障碍退货”等便民措施，并在店内建立抵制假冒伪劣产品进入的关卡，严把商品采购关和销售关，杜绝未经安全认证的产品进店。随后，工商、质监等部门开展为期两个月的服装、家电、药品“查假打假”专项整治行动。至2010年年底，“百城万店无假货”活动仍在开展中。

四、乐于助人

支援长江流域人民抗洪救灾捐赠 1998年8月，长江流域江西、湖南、江苏等省遭受洪涝灾害，县委、县政府发出《关于开展扶贫济困支援灾区活动的通知》，号召全县开展支援灾区社会捐赠活动，并在民政局成立接收捐赠办公室，要求以捐钱为主，适用于救灾的食品、药品、化肥、水泥、钢材、木材等物资亦可捐赠。县委、县政府于8月20日在县城迎春路举行向灾区人民献爱心的捐款仪式，300多名机关干部、政法干警排成长队走向捐款箱，向灾区人民献上自己的一份爱心，当天收到捐款6万余元。至10月13日，全县共向灾区捐款22.52万元，衣物1763件。刚刚改制的三山水泥厂50多名只能领到有限生活费的职工也慷慨解囊，向灾区人民捐款1万元。

支援汶川地震灾区捐献 2008年5月12日汶川地震发生后，县委、县政府即于14日向全县人民发出《向汶川地震灾区伸援手献爱心倡议书》，号召全县人民为灾区同胞捐款捐物，奉献爱心，县红十字会和县民政局也向全县人民发出倡议书，县委组织部向全县党员发出《发挥党组织和广大党员作用支持汶川地震灾区抗震救灾工作的通知》，一个向汶川地震灾区捐款捐物献爱心活动在全县展开。14日，首次捐款活动在县城体育馆举行，捐款人群中有捧着存钱罐的小朋友，有拄着拐杖白发苍苍的老年人，有坐着轮椅的残疾人……数以万计群众怀着对灾区人民无比深厚的感情献上爱心。捐款捐物活动一直持续到6月份，活动中涌现出很多感人的事。栖凤社区68岁的李健华老人，独自一人居住，生活还要靠国家发的低保金，但听到向灾区捐款的倡议后，立即到红十字会捐款10元，并深情地说“我没有更大的能力，只能拿出这么一点，算是为灾区人民尽一点心意。”六广镇敬老院的10位“五保”老人每人凑了5块钱去捐赠，他们对工作人员说“钱太少，我们不好意思拿出手，但灾区人民受难，我们总得尽力帮他们一把”。龙场镇潮水村党支部81岁的老党员王登云在村里组织的捐款活动中已向灾区人民捐款100元，后得知县委发出广大党员通过交纳特殊党费支援灾区的号召，他叫家人带他到组织部，将平常省吃俭用节约下来的1200元钱交到工作人员手中。全县共产党员响应县委组织部交纳特殊党费支援灾区人民的号召，15天共交纳特殊党费50多万元。

2008年，修文二中组织学生向汶川地震灾区捐款

抗凝冻灾害救助 2008年1月，县境遭受50年不遇的冰雪灾害，1200根电杆被冰雪压断，20多万人用不上电。为了保电，供电局的职工早上6点钟起来，晚上12点还未归家。冰冻的山路，零下五六度的严寒，山路全被封冻，给施工带来极大困难，但他们没有被困难吓倒，一处处地换电杆，一处处地接电线，用冻僵的双手，用战胜困难的意志，连接起城乡的光明。大雪凝中，贵（阳）遵（义）、贵（阳）毕（节）高等级公路全被告冰雪封锁，2万多司乘旅客被滞留在公路上。县交警、交通部门紧急行动，先给滞留人员送去饼干、方便面、矿泉水和棉被、药品等物资，接着撒盐除冰，警车开道引路，把滞留在公路上的乘客送回家过年。冰冻使贵阳电煤告急，县政府并没有因为自己受灾严重而坐视不理，而是组织6600吨电煤送到省城贵阳。扎佐镇三元村的村主任在村民缺电打米的时候，将自家砂厂使用的发电机发电为村民打米照明。乡干部们穿上防滑草鞋，跋涉几十里山路，把救灾物资送到住得分散边远的困难群众家中，县机关1500名干部每天奋战在抗灾一线，而他们的家中，同样停水断电。700名农民兄弟参与保电抢修，有人问“一天能挣多少钱?”他们回答“抗灾救灾，给不给钱我们都要干!”据《当代修文》报道，县民政部门抗凝冻期间先后收到捐款和物资折款达百万元。

抗旱救灾献爱心 2009年10月到2010年3月，县境连续干旱少雨，全县农作物受灾13.97万亩，10万多群众和3000多头大牲畜饮水困难，生产生活受到严重影响。县委、县政府号召开展“抗旱救灾，爱如春雨”活动。县农业局组织一支抗旱突击队，到各乡（镇）寻找水源，为群众义务送水。六桶乡山宝村方圆几公里内河流干断，水井枯竭，村属烂泥沟组一户留守家庭里的76岁老人任洪柱带着两个孙女在家，受灾期间，老人每天到4公里外的马落坑背水解决祖孙3人的生活用水，背一次水要用六七个小时。为了节省用水，两个孙女3天才洗一次脸。抗旱突击队到山宝村后，几名队员把水送到老人家里，老人流着眼泪激动得连声说“感谢党，感谢政府”。大石乡政府成立的党员送水队一天要跑四五个村子，来来回回一两百里路，连吃饭的时间都用来赶路，饿了就以饼干充饥。谷堡乡新堰村的付业贵、吴学俊等9名党员为村里找到水源后，又每人捐出500元购买引水设备，把水引到村里，解决了全村87户400余人的用水困难。3月25日，县委、县政府举行“抗旱救灾，爱如春雨”捐赠活动，当天收到捐款近45万元，其中，县内24家非公企业捐款27万元，各界群众捐款18万元。乡（镇）当天也在各自驻地举行捐赠活动，共收到捐款逾10万元。继后，还有企业和群众到民政部门捐款，中石油贵州公司一次捐赠就达10万元。

志愿者服务社会 1996年，团县委发出《关于开展为困难群众排忧解难“一助一”志愿者服务行动的通知》，全县3000余名青年志愿者踊跃参加捐赠活动，共捐资5万元，捐物折款10万元。继后，志愿者行动成为共青团的一项重要工作，主要参与社区服务、扶贫开发、环境保护、抢险救灾、大型活动等5大类31项服务。2002年起，志愿服务活动从青年、团员扩大到机关干部职工，进而成为全县人民助人为乐的一项群众活动。2003年，县政府在全县招募计划生育工作志愿者，先后有600多人报名参与婚育新风宣传和计划生育工作志愿服务活动。六屯乡从2003年起就创建有由各村村民自发组织的村组巡逻队，在夜间值班巡逻，保护村寨平安，这

社区居民参与志愿者服务

种村民相互自愿服务保平安的做法，还被省综治部门作为经验推广。2004年，组织200名青年志愿者服务“双千”工程，进村入户为村民义诊、检修电器和提供农业科技服务。志愿者在扎佐镇独山村将“远程教育”“医疗保健知识”等内容编成布依山歌教村民传唱。2006年，开展“弘扬雷锋精神，参与志愿服务”活动，全县千名青年志愿者深入社区、村寨参与维修家电、绿色环保、法律援助。2008年，在“三创一办”活动中，扎佐镇的低保对象200余人主动向镇政府请缨，组成志愿服务队，参与打扫大街和卫生监督；龙场镇千余社区居民参与“三创一办”志愿服务。至2010年，全县有青年志愿者5692名，注册登记2764名，“一助一”结对619对。

五、孝亲敬老

孝亲敬老是境内传统美德。自20世纪80年代起，全县“五保”制度趋于完备，农村先后建成7所敬老院，将部分“五保”老人集中供养。1995年，县人民政府下发修府〔1995〕19号文件《修文县农村五保户供养工作实施办法》，采取集中供养和分散供养的办法保障五保老人的衣食住行。2000年后，对“五保”老人不断提高供养标准，至2010年提升到每人每年逾2000元。2006年，龙场镇城北村被中央文明委表彰为“敬老模范村”。在家庭中，敬重长辈、孝敬老人蔚然成风。六广镇沙坡村的殷华利不但伺奉年迈的继奶奶，还把邻村没有家人照料的弱智老人杨世华留住家中奉养，被中央文明委表彰为“孝亲敬老之星”；小箐乡计生站的罗文秀十几年如一日悉心照料夫家鳏寡孤独的叔叔，大石乡大寨村老寨组村民金志斌自己也是60多岁的老人，伺奉家中老母亲却丝毫不懈怠，他们的事迹在当地被群众模仿学习，被县里推荐参加“全国孝亲敬老之星”评选。

2008年建成的县中心敬老院

专记：孝亲敬老谱新篇

殷华利爱心唱响敬老歌

殷华利自幼丧父，母亲远走他乡，与哥哥随继奶奶生活。兄弟俩先后娶妻成家后，为了侍奉已经年迈的继奶奶，两个家庭同锅舀食，直到2006年才分家。分家后，两家争着伺奉继奶奶，哥哥殷华忠才把奶奶接过来住得没两天，殷华利家又要把奶奶接过去。继奶奶日子过得好，不愁吃不愁穿，两个孙子虽不是亲生的，却争着奉养她。老人家人逢喜事精神爽，80岁的人，精神矍铄，身板硬朗，还能下地薅苞谷。

六广镇的合营村有个叫杨世华的人，60多岁，是个弱智，没有成家，整天就在附近几个村子里晃来荡去，遇到谁家有粗重活路，就喊他干干，然后给顿饭吃，晚上就让他歇在牛圈楼上。2005年5月，杨世华到沙坡村，东家晃一天西家晃一天，但这哪是长久之计呢，谁家没有个烦心的时候，有时连自己都顾不过来，谁又来管这个倒风不颠的老人。殷华利和哥哥商量后，把杨世华接到了自己的家让老人住了下来。要侍奉一个头脑有些不正常的人，这里面的困难有多大呀，老人无缘无故会大吵大闹，还会摔东西，衣服穿了好久，没有人招呼他从来就不洗，三天两头他还会跑出去，一去就是好几天。但殷华利却不管怎样都将就着杨世华，十天半月就哄着他换衣服、洗澡。为了照顾好杨世华，殷华利与合营村的村主任商量，又征得镇上领导同意，把杨世华的户口迁到了自己家来。2006年4月的一天晚上，杨世华突然病了，发高烧。殷华利走了四五里山路赶到新河村把村医路喜富接到家来，给杨老人打针输液，折腾了一晚上，杨世华的病才松活下来。有一天下午，杨世华不知在哪里喝多了酒，跌跌撞撞的回来，一不小心栽到了沼气池里，殷华利一家人把杨老人拉上来后，顾不得一身的臭，马上烧水给他洗澡换衣裳，害怕老人会受凉，殷华利还专门叫妻子用红糖熬姜汤给老人喝。2006年，殷华利被评选为全国孝亲敬老之星。

罗文秀真情伺奉夫家叔叔

小箐乡计生站的罗文秀是个有苗家女子，工作踏实认真，多次获得县、乡“计生优秀工作者”称号，生活中的罗文秀，心地善良，十几年如一日悉心照料夫家鳏寡孤独的叔叔，在小箐街上有口皆碑。2006年，县里推荐她参加由中央文明委等单位举办的“全国孝亲敬礼老之星”评选。1994年，24岁的罗文秀嫁到小箐街上的姚志国家。夫家的幺叔姚志华，60多岁了，没有结过婚。年轻时靠帮别人干农活和打临工维持生计。随着岁月的流逝，年事已高的姚志华无力再帮别人干农活了，生活十分艰难。看到幺叔的生活窘状，罗文秀毅然决定将幺叔接进家门，照料幺叔的衣食住行。十多年来，她悉心照料幺叔的生活起居。幺叔有个头痛脑热什么的，她就像女儿一样精心伺候幺叔吃药打针。姚志华逢人便夸，“罗文秀真是一个好媳妇，没想到还会享受到儿孙的福呢”。

这十多年来的生活经历中，让姚志华感动的事太多。当初，姚志华新到罗文秀家时，罗文秀家只有新修的两间房子，仅能让夫妻俩容身，姚志华怕自己住在这个家里会影响两个年轻人的生活，就悄悄离开了。罗文秀急得四处打听、寻找，找到后她苦求道：“幺叔，你不要想这么多，没房子，我们先到外面找地方住，你就住我们的房子吧。”一次，罗文秀去看望幺叔，发现幺叔躺在床上，面容有些异样。可是，幺叔一直坚持说自己没啥问题，休息一会就行了。身为医师的罗文秀一看就知道幺叔说了假话。其实，幺叔是怕给她带来太多的经济负担才这样说的。给幺叔做完检查后，罗文秀迅速将幺叔送到县医院治疗。罗文秀一家并不宽裕，每年她不仅要负责公婆、小姑小叔和自己一家的生活开支、医疗费用，同时要拿出900多元钱来负责幺叔的生活费用，还要承担幺叔的医疗费。一提起这些，姚志华老人就感动不已，说：“我的生活全靠罗文秀一家，平时头痛脑热、衣食住行都是她们负责，她就像我的亲生女儿一样!”在十多年的岁月里，罗文秀对待幺叔就像对待自己的父亲一样，十几年如一日，在平淡的岁月中写就了孝亲敬老的真情。

金志斌孝敬父母传佳话

大石乡大寨村老寨组村民金志斌孝敬老人的事，在当地是家喻户晓。金志斌家有兄妹三人，其妻家是姐弟两人。对父母的赡养按理说是三兄妹的责任，对岳母的赡养也是妻子两姐弟的事。但是金志斌却把自己的父母及岳母一并赡养。他不仅尽到赡养义务，而且尽心尽力孝敬两家的老人。2000年初，金志斌将岳母接到自己的家里赡养，家里就有了三个老人，但三个老人性格、生活差异大，经常发生矛盾。金志斌就单独给岳母安排了一间房，每天都要去给岳母担水、和煤。对两家老人，他都一视同仁，哪怕是购买衣物，几位老人的衣物件数、质量都一样，从不分彼此。2004年6月份的一天，他父亲忽患重病卧床不起，大小便都不能自理。他不嫌脏、不嫌臭，精心照料父亲的饮食起居。父亲大小便失禁，常常会把裤子弄脏，每一次金志斌都不声不响地给父亲清洗。他就这样照顾父亲，直到父亲去世。2005年

初，他的岳母也去世了，家里只剩下母亲一位老人，金志斌夫妻更是无微不至地照料。每次吃饭的时候，夫妻俩总是先给老人盛好饭，其他人才端碗吃饭。他的母亲已经80多岁，手脚不灵活。他们夫妻俩早晨起来总是要给老人梳头、洗脸后才出门做活。母亲有个头疼脑热，哪怕再晚，他都要去请医生。一天晚上，母亲高烧不退，他半夜跑到离家四五里路远的乡卫生院去请医生来给母亲看病，还一直守护在母亲床前，直到母亲有所好转才肯去休息。金志斌自己也是60多岁的人，这样尽孝，难怪当地群众教育孩子孝敬老人时，都会拿他做榜样。金志斌经常在自己的弟妹及小辈的面前说：尊老敬老是我们的美德，既然父母生育了我们，我们就要尽心尽力的赡养老人。赡养老人不是做面子上的事情，不是做给别人看，而是要做到心里孝敬，要落实在行动上。

第七章　志鉴　档案

第一节　志书编纂

1985年5月，成立县地方志编纂委员会，下设办公室和编辑部，分别负责行政管理和编纂工作，并指导乡（镇）、村和县直部门的志书编纂。至2010年，全县出版各级志书28部。

一、县志编纂

1985年启动首轮县志编修，全县投入编修工作人员220人。至1990年，成稿部门志、专志60部，资料长篇12册，共576.4万字，为县志进入总纂打下基础。1993年，县志初稿形成，下发征求意见。先后召开审稿会10余次，征求到修改意见近千条。至1998年，经三易其稿后定稿送审。1999年，由贵州省地方志办公室审定批准，交付方志出版社出版发行。

新编首轮《修文县志》全书190万字，上限始于元至元二十年（1283）有行政建置起，下限断至1998年，记述跨度共716年。

二轮《修文县志》于2003年11月开始规划编纂，2004年启动。全志的编纂分为事前筹备、培训编辑、搜集资料、编写志稿、审查验收和付厂印刷等6步进行。至2010年，二轮《修文县志》已完成150万字分纂稿，进入总纂阶段，计划2018年成书出版。《修文县志》续志上限起于1978年，下限断至2010年，记述跨度33年。

1999年编辑出版的《修文县志》

经过两轮县志的编纂，培养锻炼出一支修志队伍，其中的李祖炎、夏之奎、陈新国、胡光胤等成为这支队伍的骨干。李祖炎和夏之奎分别担任两轮县志的主编和副主编，胡光胤担任二轮县志副主编。首轮志书编纂告竣，李祖炎被评为贵州省地方志系统先进工作者，受到贵州省人民政府表彰。他所撰方志论文和志书评论文章50多篇20余万字在《中国地方志》、《广西地方志》以及贵州《史志林》和《人文贵阳》发表，其中《重大运动如何入志》《续志应当记述好政治文明建设》和《二轮修志应当做好改革这篇文章》被《中国地方志》摘登和采用。《优化体式，提高品位——试论二轮志书体式改革》获贵阳市第八次哲学社会科学优秀成果三等奖，受到贵阳市人民政府嘉奖。二轮修志启动后，李祖炎被聘为贵州省方志协会（学会）顾问，先后应邀到贵阳市、花溪区、息烽县、安龙县、六盘水市钟山区和六枝特区等地讲课，并参与《铜仁市志》《盘县志》《六盘水市志》《六盘水三线建设志》《铜仁地区通志》和《遵义市志》等志稿的审改。

二、乡（镇）志编纂

全县乡（镇）志编纂工作于2003年与二轮《修文县志》编纂同步启动。至2010年，已出版《六广镇志》《小箐乡志》《扎佐镇志》。

《六广镇志》上限起自元至元二十年（1283），下限止于2005年12月。采用篇章节体，共18篇74章267节，97万字。置六广镇政区图1幅，彩色照片99幅。2007年6月出版，首次印刷1200册。

《小箐乡志》上限起自元至元二十年（1283），下限止于2005年12月。篇章节体，16篇53章197节，77万字。置小箐乡政区图1幅，黑白照片5幅，彩色照片30幅。2007年7月第1次印刷1000册。

《扎佐镇志》上限起自元至元十九年（1282），下限止于2005年12月。篇章节体，共12篇47章66节，90万字，置扎佐镇政区图1幅，扎佐医药食品工业园区示意图1幅，红军长征经过扎佐路线图1幅，黑白照片1幅，彩色照片92幅，书画、印刻作品17幅。2007年9月第1次印刷1000册。

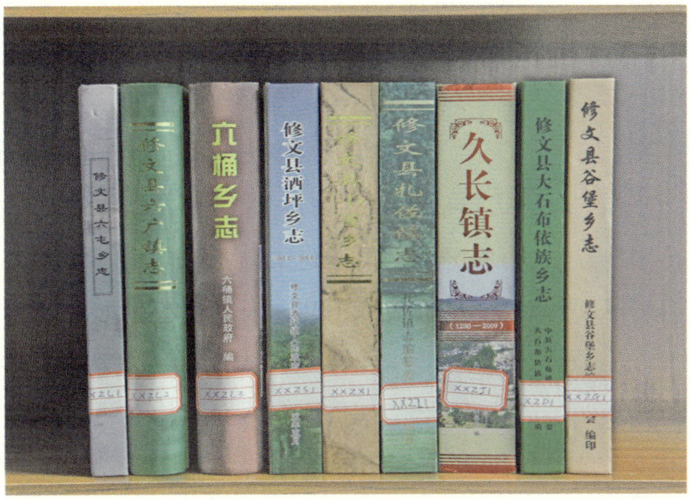

已编辑出版的部分乡镇志

2010年已进入总纂的尚有《龙场镇志》《久长镇志》《谷堡乡志》《大石乡志》，计划2015年前成书出版。

在抓乡（镇）志编纂的同时，还出版1部村志—《清水村志》。《清水村志》为贵阳市首家出版的村级志书。章节体，19章90节。上限起自元至元二十年（1283），下限断至2005年12月（限外要事延至2007年8月）。置清水村地图1幅，黑白照片2幅，彩色照片37幅，36万字。由中共清水村支部、清水村村民委员会编纂，村民集资出版。

三、部门志编纂

1985年启动县志编纂工作时，同步展开部门志的编纂，先后成书出版《修文县人民代表大会志》《修文县工商行政管理志》《修文县卫生志》《修文县税务志》《修文县邮电志》《修文县水利电力志》《修文县物资管理志》《修文县轻工业志》《修文县农业机械志》《修文县工会志》《修文县财政志》《修文县粮食志》《修文县交通志》《修文县乡（镇）企业志》《修文县教育志》《修文县水利志》《修文县民政志》《修文县军事志》《修文县信用合作志》等19部部门志，以及《修文县税务志（1978—2005）》《修文县人民代表大会志（1986—2005）》《修文县工会志（1978—2007）》3部续志。至2010年，尚有《修文县移民志》《修文县物价志》《修文县公安志》《修文县审判志》《修文县检察志》《修文县司法志》等10余部部门志稿进入总纂。

四、民国《修文县志》点校

2009年，民国《修文县志》点校本由县地方志办公室刊行。民国《修文县志》成书于民国37年（1948），虽为残本，但仍留存自然、政治、文化、军事等内容，是了解和研究修文500年历史概貌、山川地理、民物风情、名胜古迹、人物建树、社会风云的历史借鉴。县委、县政府把点校该部志书作为抢救地方文化资源的重要工作，于2008年成立以县委书记、县长领衔的“民国《修文县志》整理点校领导小组”，由县地方志办公室启动点校工作，约请贵州方志界知名专家罗再麟点校，陈福桐、史继忠、侯绍庄审读。点校本对原书错字、漏字、衍文和模糊不清者作改、补、删、正，对段落按现行行文规范和志书的内容实际改造，合理分段。点校本于2009年4月经省新闻出版局批准出版刊行。

民国《修文县志》点校本

专记：修文县地方志办公室被评为全国方志先进集体

2005年，人事部和中国地方志指导小组在全国地方志系统开展评选表彰先进活动，决定评选出一批全国地方志系统先进集体、先进工作者。

修文县地方志办公室于1999年编纂出版第一轮《修文县志》。志书以装帧印刷质量获国家新闻出版署优秀图书奖、贵阳市第四次哲学社会科学优秀科研成果评比一等奖和贵州省第五次哲学社会科学优秀科研成果评比三等奖。第一轮修志完成后，县志办于2003年转入第二轮志书的编修。

根据中央精神及自身取得的成绩，修文县地方志办公室决定参与评选全国先进，如实组织材料逐级上报。经过贵阳市地方志办公室、贵州省地方志办公室和中国地方志指导小组层层筛选，最终被中国地方志指导小组评定为先进集体。2006年4月1日，全国地方志系统表彰先进大会在北京人民大会堂举行，修文县地方志办公室主任夏之奎代表办公室赴京出席会议。

第二节 年鉴编写

《修文年鉴》是由县人民政府批准，县地方志办公室主办的年度性地方大型资料工具年刊，2010年创刊。县政府当年落实出版经费，地方志办公室成立《修文年鉴》编辑部，通过召集会议和行文部署任务，组织业务培训。全县各乡（镇）、各部门按编写纲目要求搜集资料，以信息条目形式提供文字材料和彩页图照。首部《修文年鉴》资料收录时限为2009年1月1日—12月31日。采用分类编辑法，以事业为主分类。全书设大事记、特载、概况、政治、军事、法制、综合管理、财税、金融、农业、工业、乡

(镇)企业、贸易、交通、信息产业、城建城管、教育、科技、文化新闻、卫生体育、社会生活、乡(镇)概况、法规选编、统计资料、附录共25个类目,按类目、分目、子目、条目4个层次编排,总容量45万字,采用图随文走图文并茂体式记述上一年度全县各行各业改革开放、生产建设的新成就和新经验,全面、生动地反映修文的经济和社会发展现状,对内为各级领导科学决策提供借鉴,对外作为修文名片,发挥窗口和桥梁作用。

第三节　档　案

一、档案管理

1979年1月,恢复县档案馆,整理“文化大革命”时期被造反派毁损的档案归档工作。1981年10月成立县档案局,档案管理步上正轨。1989年,投资31.6万元修建占地1.65亩的综合性档案馆,1991年投入使用。馆内设有库房4间,办公用房15间,并增加档案装具和消防设备,配置照相机、录影机、吸尘器、电视机、录像机、去湿机、消毒柜、电脑、复印机等设备。2003年,编制著录卡片、资料目录、归档文件目录、全引目录、全宗介绍、档案馆指南等10种检索工具及部分参考资料,同时安装档案管理电脑软件。

县档案馆恢复后,相继接收各单位的档案进馆。1981年始,按统一领导、统一任务、统一时间、统一方法和统一质量的“五个统一”,开展档案鉴定、整理、销毁、抢救等工作。成立档案鉴定小组,对档案逐卷、逐件、逐份鉴定,对无保存价值的予以销毁。至1986年,通过鉴定、清理,销毁重(废)份文件、资料、组卷2861卷共500余公斤。至1993年,抢救整理馆藏民清档案1039卷,重新组存民国档案1237卷,于1993年11月全部对外开放。1990年,全县开展档案管理标准化、规范化建设和创优争先活动,至2004年,有89个单位档案室达标,其中达一级标准16个,二级28个,三级42个,先进企业3个。有7个乡(镇)和1个社区达三级标准,4个税务所达二级标准。在创优争先活动中,有72个单位被评为档案管理先进单位,77人被评为先进工作者。继后,档案管理规范化建设不间断地开展,逐年均有单位档案室、库达标。2010年,在开展档案规范化建设中,档案局、馆对全县档案人员进行专门培训198人(次),指导46个村(社区)完成档案规范化建设。

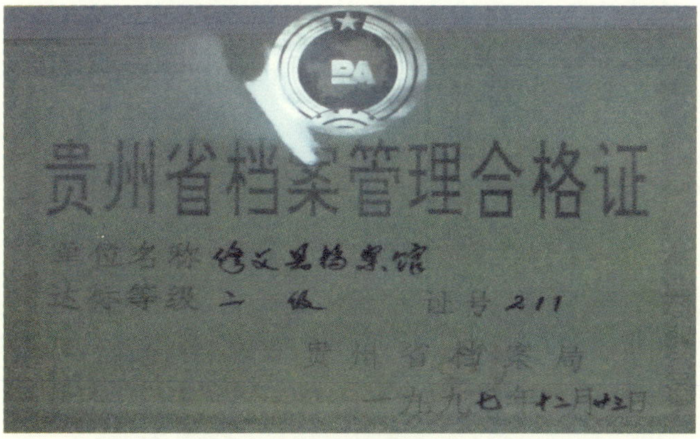

1997年,省档案局认定县档案馆为档案管理合格单位

至2010年,县档案馆馆藏永久、长期档案30万卷(件),资料逾4000册。全县有单位档案室、库120个。

二、档案利用

1978至1983年落实政策期间，县内外进馆查阅档案逾千人次。有227名在反右派、“反右倾”“四清”和“文化大革命”运动中被处分的干部，通过调阅档案甄别事实，得以平反。1981到1990年，县委党史办公室通过查阅卷宗和有关文献，编印出《红军长征在修文》《修文县革命烈士传》《中国共产党修文县历史大事记》和《中共修文县组织史资料》《修文县政军统群系统组织史资料》等书籍。1985年开始编纂地方志和2003年启动第二轮地方志编修，提供档案资料3万多卷次供编纂人员查阅、核实史实。至2010年，县档案馆共接待查档利用2.8万人次，提供档案6.17万卷次，复印档案2.25万份。

社会建设篇

县属多民族杂居县，民族数最多时达33个，居民以汉族为主，占91%以上，人口较多的少数民族主要有苗族、布依族和彝族。33年间，在改革开放总方针的指引下，全县各族人民在县委和县政府率领下，团结一致，开拓奋进，进一步营造出社会和谐稳定、人民幸福安康的大好局面。

全县社会事务主要由县民政部门负责管理，随着改革开放不断深入，管理水平不断得到新的提高。优抚安置、烈士褒扬、救济救灾、帮困助残充分体现党和政府关怀，使群众深感社会大家庭的温暖；婚姻登记进一步规范，实现了由婚姻登记管理到婚姻登记服务的转变；殡葬改革，移风易俗，推动绿色殡葬，促进 了人与自然和谐相处；基层政权建设实行村（居）民自治，由广大农民群众直接行使民主权利，依法自我管理、自我教育、自我服务，使基层民主建设逐步完善和不断提高。

20世纪80年代，社会保障属于“单位保障制”，内容包括职工退休、公费医疗和福利住房等，主要是城镇居民中的机关和企事业单位人员享有。90年代做过一些改革尝试，但未取得实质性的突破。2003年起加快改革开放步伐，坚持以人为本、注重改善民生，在社会保障制度建设方面迈出新的步伐。先后建立城镇居民基本医疗保险制度、新型农村合作医疗制度、农村最低生活保障制度，进一步完善城镇职工基本养老保险制度。相关制度的建立和落实，让广大城乡居民得到实惠，有了获得感和幸福感。至2010年，全县社会保障体系基本建立，并逐步趋于完善，基本实现社会保障制度全覆盖。

改革开放30多年，人民生活水平得到显著提高，逐步从温饱型迈向小康型，越来越多人家正步入小康。1978年，全县农村居民人均纯收入仅为141元，恩格尔系数68.37%；职工年人均工资收入仅为580.5元。到2010年，农村居民年人均纯收入达5152元，恩格尔系数为50.1%；城镇居民年人均可支配收入达1.58万元，恩格尔系数为36.6%。人们衣、食、住、行等物质条件大为改善，人口素质和文明程度大大提高，多项指标上已经达到或接近小康标准。

第一章　民族　宗教

1978年，县境共居住着19个民族，其中汉族人口居多，超过千人的少数民族有苗族、布依族和彝族，全县民族数量最多时增加到33个。县委和县政府历来重视民族工作，县政府建有民族事务委员会，先后开展落实干部政策、建立民族乡、恢复民族传统节日、培养少数民族干部等工作。从1996年起，民族工作重点转到扶贫开发上来，发展少数民族地区交通、兴修水利、调整农业产业结构、改善居住条件、兴办教育、加强文化建设、完善医疗卫生条件等，使少数民族地区经济、文化建设大为改观。

境内民俗属西南黔中风俗区，以汉族风俗为主，少数民族风俗除苗族、布依族和彝族尚有部分留存外，其余大部分已消失或汉化。改革开放30多年，各族人民齐心协力，共同为建设和发展家乡经济献策献力，相互间通婚已无民族界线，族别仅在个人信息中有所保留，大部分少数民族的生产、生活基本与汉族相同。随着改革开放不断深入，社会文明不断提高，传统美德得到弘扬和发展，当代新风普遍成为人们的行为准则，优良风尚始终是社会主流。

第一节　民　族

1978年，县境居民以汉族为主，另有苗族、布依族、彝族、侗族、回族、水族、满族、壮族、白族、仡佬族、京族、锡伯族、蒙古族、土家族、黎族、畲族、瑶族和其他民族等18个少数民族。1982年第三次人口普查，汉族人口238382人，少数民族人口18642人。少数民族中人口超过千人的有苗族、布依族和彝族。1990年第四次人口普查增加朝鲜族和傣族，苗族人数超过万人增至11209人。2000年第五次人口普查增加藏族、维吾尔族、哈尼族、土族、仫佬族、羌族和毛南族。2010年第六人口普查，总人口达248926人，其中汉族人口228735人，少数民族人口20191人。少数民族又增加哈萨克族、傈僳族、佤族、纳西族和布朗族，除汉族和未识别民族外少数民族有31个。少数民族中人口超过万人的有苗族，超过千人的仍为布依族和彝族。

全县第三至第六次人口普查各民族人口数一览表

表5—01—01

民族		第三次 1982年	第四次 1990年	第五次 2000年	第六次 2010年
汉族		238382	245962	239976	228735
少数民族		18642	20732	22063	20191
其中	苗族	9863	11209	12268	11126
	布依族	6046	6538	6397	5428
	彝族	1887	1955	1993	1920
	侗族	233	237	311	228
	回族	140	96	83	92
	水族	107	72	65	101
	满族	93	123	55	31
	壮族	51	44	51	51
	白族	39	33	145	134
	仡佬族	33	70	125	245
	京族	20	18	14	3
	锡伯族	7	10	1	0
	蒙古族	5	15	64	67
	土家族	4	181	364	591
	黎族	4	8	31	38
	畲族	3	1	2	6
	瑶族	1	5	7	11
	朝鲜族	—	7	6	0
	傣族	—	5	7	5
	藏族	—	—	10	4
	维吾尔族	—	—	3	1
	哈尼族	—	—	2	5
	土族	—	—	2	10
	仫佬	—	—	10	14
	羌族	—	—	8	0
	毛南族	—	—	1	14
	哈萨克族	—	—	—	1
	傈僳族	—	—	—	1
	佤族	—	—	—	3
	纳西族	—	—	—	1
	布朗族	—	—	—	1
	未识别民族	106	105	38	59

一、少数民族

1978年全县有18个少数民族，2010年增加到29个（含1个未定民族），少数民族族种增加多系就业和婚姻迁入。超过千人的有苗族、布依族和彝族，其中苗族人口还超过万人。

（一）苗族

苗族是县内少数民族中人口最多的民族，1982年人口总数为9863人，1983年总数超过1万人，到2010年增至11126人。全县各乡镇均有分布，人口超过千人以上的乡（镇）有龙场镇、谷堡乡、大石乡、久长镇、六桶乡、小箐乡、洒坪乡和六广镇，其中以龙场镇居多，达3468人。苗族非本地土著，大多为清康熙年间应征随军迁入，部分为周边地区自然播迁，故支系较多。主要有青苗、六寨苗、素苗、白苗、大花苗和小花苗6种，语言均为西部苗语方言，今多以说汉语为主。

青苗　因其服饰颜色多以青色为主，故称“青苗”。自称由江西吉安府随军迁入，今主要居住在龙场镇高仓村、程官两村和六广镇龙窝村。妇女服饰以青色为主，间以白色；善于刺绣，衣服、肩褡、围腰均有绣花；下装为裙子全是青色，腰带以红、白色丝线绣花；头饰较为讲究，要包头巾，插8至10根银簪，银簪上有各种银花；流行戴银手镯，此装扮称为上方。上堡、龙窝服饰称为下方，衣服式样相同，但围腰不绣花，用单色布做成，妇女头上梳髻，用一块牛骨作簪穿过，包青色头帕。青苗精通药草，善用草药治病。

龙场镇平地村青苗服饰

六寨苗　为四川苗兵随军迁入，今主要分布在龙场镇新水村、新春村和沙溪村。其服饰较之简单，头上包青色折叠头帕，上穿无领短衣，有的绣花边，有的不绣，下着麻织蜡染裙子，裙边花纹为水波浪。

素苗　相传“吴王剿水西”从广西征苗兵入县境，今主要分布在小箐乡旧小箐和洒坪乡蜈蚣桥、老蛇坝一带。以穿着素静而称著，妇女较为讲究头饰的装扮，梳头时将头发上卷后进行盘髻，包丝质头巾，上身着不绣花短衣，下身穿麻织长裙，裙边花纹为水波浪。腰系长带，白布蜡染，折叠缝制，拴系时要一层压一层地拴在腰间，称“花老蛇”。素苗服饰最大的特点是讲究腰带和头饰盘髻。

节庆苗族服饰

白苗　为广西苗兵随军迁入，今主要分散在谷堡乡白泥田、乌栗索桥和久长镇上寨等地。妇女穿戴以白色为主，故称“白苗”。服装以白麻布作底，绣五彩花纹，上穿短衣，下着蜡染白褶裙，头包折叠巾，上盖一块绣花方巾，首饰有细小的菱角、五谷子以及小银器等。

大花苗　由黔西北经黔西自然搬迁而入县境，

今主要分散在大石乡高山、竹坪、老鸹沟一带。服饰特点红色元素较其他支系多而称著，妇女服装绣有各种花纹，着装上穿内衣，外披背褡，下穿麻织蜡染白褶裙，花纹为“波浪形”，小腿束的白色绑带，头上插牛角或木梳一块，用羊毛纺线盘在头上越多越好，成为一种独特的头饰。

小花苗　又称红线苗，主要以马家桥为中心分布在龙场镇白莲、军民、普陀和久长镇的上、下堡等村寨 。据下堡村苗族老人王永贵介绍：他们是江西吉安起祖，于明末清初先到云南，后迁毕节，住一段时间后又迁来老鸹堡（今下堡），到2010年已繁衍12代，今族人口已有500余人。其妇女头饰用红色毛线扎结，服饰以红色和黄色为主，麻布蜡染，白色衬底。服饰图案以城池、山川、河流、房舍等为主题；装饰花纹有九曲江荷花、鱼花、火镰花等10余种。妇女善于挑花刺绣，服饰蕴含着丰富的历史文化，被喻为苗族同胞“穿在身上的历史书”。

（二）布依族

县境人口较多的少数民族之一， 1982年，第三次全国人口普查有6046人。2010年第六次全国人口普查为5428人，居全县33个民族人口排名第三位。主要聚居在大石布依族乡的大石、大寨、大屯、高山、竹坪和六屯乡的独山、西冲、大木、小木等村，另有部分居住在六桶乡花榔村的石头寨、六腊寨和扎佐镇大河村的鱼井坝、新民村的磨盘新寨等地。人口最多的大石乡有1700多人，其次是六屯乡有近1400人，再次是扎佐镇有1160多人，其余乡（镇）均在千人以下。境内布依族非本地土著，据考证为清康熙年间平定吴三桂后迁入。语言属汉藏语系壮侗语族布傣语支第二土语区，今布依语基本失传，多以汉话为主。

布依族习惯聚族而居，房屋多为木架瓦房。其建筑风格，六屯、扎佐一带受古代黔中水东文化影响，木架、板壁、小青瓦屋面较为普遍；独山、西冲一带至今仍保留其原有风格；大石、六桶一带受古代黔西北水西文化影响，木架、土墙间有，屋面多以盖草为主，至今普遍改为砖混结构，与当地汉族住房建筑无异。

服装多为蓝、青、黑、白等色布料，男子多包头巾，上穿对襟衣服，下着直筒裤。妇女头盖头巾，上身穿蓝色右扣式父母装短衣，胸前系青色吊挂式围腰，下穿青色或黑色布裤。妇女喜欢蜡染、刺绣，在头巾、领口、袖口、腰带、围腰边及裤口等处均有精美刺绣或蜡染，图案明快大方，不像苗族刺绣那么复杂。讲卫生、善整洁是布依族的生活特点。在布依村寨内，无论是公共环境还是家庭内外，给人的感觉是干净清新，个人身着朴实素净，雅而不俗。

（三）彝族

系县境人口较多的少数民族之一， 1982年，第三次全国人口普查有1887人。2010年第六次全国人口普查增为1920人，居全县33个民族人口排名第四位。先祖乃黔西北夷族，以六广河为界，史称“水西”，俗称“倮倮”，宋、元时部分东迁六河以东地区。明末水西反叛朝廷战败，水东的势力退回水西，仅少部分留在水东，即今县境中西部地区，新中国建立后定名为彝族。今主要分散在龙场、谷堡、小箐、洒坪、六广、大石和六桶乡（镇）。其中龙场镇最多有350人，其次为小箐乡213人，再次为洒坪乡160人，其余乡镇均在百人以下。

彝族语言属汉藏语系藏缅语族彝语支，今县境彝族已无人会讲彝语而通用黔中县境方言。彝族虽有较为成熟的文字，但今除研究彝文专家外，一般人均不认识。尚存大石乡大屯的安氏古墓彝文对联和蜈蚣桥彝文碑记对研究古代历史和揭开历史之谜起到重要作用。

彝族人口居住较为分散，多与汉族杂居相处，住房与汉族相同。服饰颜色以黑色为主，间以红、黄、蓝、绿等色。原本男子上穿黑色父母装窄袖斜襟上衣，下穿黑色四块瓦长筒裤，头包黑色丝帕，肩披羊毛披毡；妇女通常上穿黑色父母装窄袖斜襟上衣，下装多为百褶裙，由几种不同颜色的布料连接，并贴有花边。衣裤下摆、袖口和领口等处均刺有各种花纹和几何图案，中老年妇女头上挽髻，包青丝帕。由于长期与汉族杂居相处，今已完全与汉族同化，除族别外其余无异。

彝族服饰

二、民族工作

1978年，民族事务工作由县革委民族卫生办公室兼管，主要负责落实民族政策、纠正冤假错案、加强民族团结等，并对比较困难的少数民族家庭进行临时解困。1979年12月，复建县民族事务委员会，民族工作步入正轨。随着改革开放不断深入，民族事务工作和资金投入力度随之加大，注重对少数民族贫困家庭的帮扶，缩小贫富差距，促进少数民族地区经济发展。1995年9月县机构改革，民族事务委员会工作增加对宗教事务管理，特别是1996年县划属贵阳市管辖后，工作力度和经费投入进一步加大，资源得到整合，进一步推动了民族地区的经济和文化建设。2000年实施西部大开发战略，给民族工作带来新的发展机遇。到2010年，少数民族地区的经济和文化、教育、卫生等事业形成良性发展新格局。

（一）落实干部政策

1978年中共十一届三中全会后，县委作出“解放思想，打开禁区，加快落实干部政策”的决定，派出干部认真调查研究，掌握实情，对在“四清”和“文化大革命”运动中受到不公正待遇的28名少数民族基层干部进行平反，发给经济损失补偿金共3400元。优秀布依族干部扎佐区区长罗树臣，“文化大革命”期间被“造反派”诬为“走资本主义道路的当权派”遭受批判斗争。夺权时，他拒绝交出扎佐区公所公章，又被残酷批斗，并撤销其区长职务后送农村监督劳动，1975年含冤离世。1979年10月由组织落实政策，并为受其株连的儿媳张成仙恢复工作，对罗树臣遗孀莫永珍按相关规定予以抚恤。干部政策的落实在少数民族干部中引起强烈反响，群众称颂“党的民族政策回来了！”

（二）建立民族乡

1983年3月，民族事务委员会承办县第七届人民代表大会第四次会议的代表提出建立民族乡的提案，深入到少数民族居住较为集中的桃源、大石两个公社召集少数民族群众代表座谈，宣传党的民族政策，广泛征求各方面意见。并根据群众要求，向县人大、县政府上报建立少数民族乡的报告。1984年3月17日，县人大常务委员会召开会议，依照《中华人民共和国宪法》第一章第四条有关规定和中共贵州省委（1984）3号文件讨论决定：以1982年人口普查数为依据和公社规模为基础，建立大石、桃源两个民族乡，并呈报安顺行政专员公署转报贵州省人民政府。省政府以〔1984〕黔府发104号文批复同意撤销修文县大石、桃源两个公社，分别建立大石布依族乡和桃源布依族乡。在县民委的帮助下，两个公社的党委和公社管理委员会根据《中华人民共和国地方各级人民代表大会和地方各级人民政府组织法》《中华人民共和国全人民代表大会和地方各级人民代表大会选举法》规定，选举乡人民代表，召开乡人民代表大会，选出乡人民政府的领导成员，并分别于5月13日和20日召开民族乡成立大会。首任桃源布依族乡乡长班启华（布依族）和大石布依族乡乡长陈国邦（布依族）分别在会上汇报民族乡的基本情况，以及建乡以后的工作任务。

1992年撤区并乡，根据“小政府，大服务”的原则撤销原桃源布依族乡，将其所辖的独山、西冲、大寨、三寨、大木和小木6个村与原六屯乡合并建立新六屯乡；原大石布依族乡所辖9个村与原回水乡的回水、天桥、沙坝、红岩4个村和德政乡的联江、联合2个村合并建新大石布依族乡，新建乡共辖15个村、77个村民组，面积50平方公里，人口12314人，其中少数民族人口3560人，占总人口28.91%，乡人民政府设在大石板。

大石布依族乡人民政府

（三）恢复民族传统节日

县内原少数民族传统节日主要有农历正月十三苗族“跳年厂”、四月初八“芦笙节”和布依族六“六月六歌会”，六月二十四彝族“火把节”等民族节日，在“文化大革命”期间被当作“四旧”全部废除。改革开放后，为尊重少数民族风俗习惯，落实党的民族政策，1981年5月，县委以县发〔1981〕19号文件明确恢复苗族“跳年厂”“四月八芦笙节”和布依族“六月六”歌会以及彝族“火把节”等。在石安公社下堡花坡、桃源公社独山和大石公社的大石均恢复民族传统节日活动，还与周边区、市、县联谊交流。每当举办民族节日时，周边清镇县卫城，白云区牛场、沙文，乌当区新场，息烽县九庄，金沙县化觉和黔西县素朴等地的少数民族都前往参加节日活动。县委、县政府和县民委领导亲临现场祝贺，与民同乐。久长镇下堡村苗族芦笙歌舞经改编提升后，受到省内外民族艺术界专家和领导关注，1996年作为中国文化使者应邀到日本访问演出。布依族的“六月六”歌会则是结合旅游业发展，年年在六屯乡的独山，大石布依族乡大石、回水石林、高枧石仓、大屯布依族古寨轮流举办，其内容不仅有传统布依族歌舞，还有斗鸟、体育竞技等。大石布依族乡还把民族节日活动开展与宣传党的民族政策、检查落实民族政策执行情况和表彰好人好事结合起来，从而增进了民族团结。

（四）培养民族干部

1978年，全县中共党员4431名中有少数民族党员363名；行政和事业单位4135名干部中有少数民族干部203人。少数民族党员、干部在生产和工作中起到模范带头作用，成为党和少数民族群众之间的纽带，促进了各民族的团结。1981年，全县农村普遍实行家庭联产承包责任制后，少数民族党员干部带头贯彻党的方针政策，实行科学种田，带领群众勤劳致富，有力地推动少数民族地区经济体制改革。为适应改革开放需要，县委、县政府大胆放手选拔使用少数民族干部，通过重点培养，凡符合条件的则吸收发展为中国共产党党员。对少数民族干部的培养，一是选择政治素质好、有培养前途的干部，采取重点培养办法，并给予一定引导，使其在实际工作中逐步锻炼成长；二是提高学历，选拔少数民族干部保送到县委党校干部培训班或少数民族补习班学习提高。1984年二级机构改革，县四大班子24名成员中就有少数民族干部6名，占总数的1/4。2010年，全县党员8967名中有少数民族党员825名，占9.2%；行政和事业单位4958名干部中有少数民族干部441名，占9.6%。其中，有3名担任乡（镇）党委书记，2名担任乡长，有4名担任县部门主要领导职务。县级班子成员中有少数民族领导干部2名。

部分年份少数民族党员和干部一览表

表5—01—02

年份	中共党员			干部		
	全县合计（名）	其中少数民族党员		全县合计（名）	其中少数民族干部	
		人数（名）	占党员总数比重（%）		人数（名）	占干部总数比重（%）
1978	4431	363	8.20	4135	203	4.90
1980	4744	390	8.20	2299	111	5.10
1985	5337	428	8.00	2541	152	6.00
1990	5818	447	7.60	3150	204	6.50
1995	6752	506	14.30	4129	289	7.00
2000	6963	574	8.20	5408	401	7.50
2005	7965	653	8.40	5032	483	9.60%
2010	8967	825	9.20	4958	441	9.60

三、少数民族地区经济发展

1978年，县内少数民族大多分散居住在农村，主要聚居地在大石、回水一带和石安下堡、程官高脚仓以及桃源独山、腊鲊坝、大木和小木。由于历史和环境等原因使经济发展较其他地区滞后。农村普遍实行家庭联产承包责任制后，党和政府更加重视少数民族地区的经济发展。首先加强民族地区交通和水利建设，引导少数民族村民脱贫致富。2000年后，结合实施国家西部大开发战略调整少数民族地区农业产业结构，引导农民种养结合走农业市场化道路，改善农村居住环境。同时充分挖掘民族民间文化，开发旅游资源，促使少数民族地区经济发展。至2010年，大石乡的大屯、回水，六屯乡的独山、西冲等地农村面貌焕然一新，新农村建设取得显著成效。

（一）发展交通

大屯布依族村进村公路

1978年，县内少数民族地区交通运输多靠人背马驮。特别是大石布依族乡的大屯从无公路，进村出村必经山道手爬岩，因道路崎岖坎坷制约着经济发展和群众生活的改善。1981年实行家庭联产承包责任制后，大屯村流传着“要得福，先修路”的口号。先是自发组织修筑进村公路，从而引起社会的关注，县委、县政府把改善少数民族地区交通提上议事日程，作为重要工作来抓。至1995年，共投入民族经费520万元兴修大石至大屯、县城至高脚仓、马家桥经石安至久长、小箐经洒坪至轿子山、扎佐经独山至桃源、大石至苦竹坪、六桶至凉井至宝寨的公路计25条，全长

209公里。1996年县划属贵阳市管辖，市政府加大拓展边远山区交通道路的扶持力度，至2010年共拨付资金近4亿元，先后对少数民族聚居贫困村道路进行改造，实现全县村村通公路，形成村连村、寨连寨四通八达的道路网络。乡村公路的修建，加速了农村机械化进程，促进了少数民族地区经济快速发展。

（二）兴修水电工程

大石人畜引水工程 大石布依族乡环境独特，山多地少、水源缺乏，人畜饮水较为困难。为解决群众用水问题，1981年由县民委补助民族经费2万元，加上县水电局拨付专用款共计6.8万元，并由水电局设计和指导安装，从距大石公社所在地4公里的响水洞引水，安装直径150毫米水泥预制管道4200米，工程于1982年4月竣工，解决了大石附近几个村2000人和800头大牲畜饮水问题。继后又安装高山至大寨、小坝至龙山、小坝至石丫口等引水工程7处。此外，还修建小箐乡的宝山、老鸦坪，龙场镇的姚家寨，六广镇的陶家庄、金山，六桶乡的凉井、宝寨等人畜饮水池15个，总蓄水1.5万立方米，解决了含汉族村民在内的3万多群众和1万多头大牲畜饮水问题。

除险加固阁老寨水库 龙场镇高仓村系苗族聚居村，位于村境的阁老寨水库，因年久失修，库容量下降。2001年被列入贵阳市市级除险加固工程，投资306万元，项目以招投标形式决定由贵州省水利水电设计院工程承包公司承建，对大坝及两岸进行灌浆处理，扩建溢洪道，改善放水涵洞，并对1万米的干渠进行防渗处理。

兴建大屯电站 1978年，由县民委和水电局投资4.2万元，在大石布依族乡大屯村村口利用二道水引水工程修建大屯电站，距白水电站3公里，次年8月建成投入运行。设计装机容量55千瓦，保证出力32千瓦，年平均发电量2.8万千瓦时，主要供应大屯村民照明和动力用电。1986年，因电机损坏和水力不足停止运行，此后村民用电纳入国家电网供应。

修建香巴房水库 位于扎佐区桃源公社独山大队（今六屯乡独山村）境内，原设计为小水电站，1978年12月动工修建，1986年2月建成投产。工程总投资500万元，大坝为浆砌石溢流坝，坝高17.3米，顶长106米，库容138万立方米，总装机容量320千瓦，主要供桃源乡及扎佐乡部分村寨照明和动力用电，并可灌溉农田1500亩。2000年农村电网改造，电站停止运营，2003年转为旅游开发项目，改作神州漂流公司水量调节水库，同时改造成为旅游风景区。

香巴房水库

建立提灌站 1981至1990年共补助民族经费5万元，先后在久长镇上堡村、六广镇龙窝村和扎佐区独山等村建立电力提灌站9个，总装机440千瓦，有效灌溉面积达3000多亩。

架设输电线路 1998年开始，结合农村电网改造，至2005年先后在谷堡乡场坝村至水落岩，大石布依族乡所在地至高山、竹坪，六桶乡花榔村至金星等村寨架设输电线路17条，全长120公里，补助民族经费17万元，使地处边远村寨的各民族人民都用上国家电网民用电。

（三）调整农业产业结构

1996年县划属贵阳市管辖后，县民族宗教局为帮助少数民族群众早日脱贫致富，采取内引外联先后引进资金在大屯、河湾、苦竹坪种植柑橘400亩；贵阳市蔬菜公司投资3万元在桃源村建成蔬菜基地120亩，在龙场镇高仓村建起漆树基地50亩，在小箐乡郭田村建立酥李基地150亩，在谷堡乡下洞、平滩、红星、折溪、新堰等村种植猕猴桃420亩。贵阳黔灵山公园在谷堡乡大寨村计生户中种植火棘3.5万株，并负责技术指导和回收火棘苗。贵阳市蔬菜公司在乌栗建立早熟蔬菜生产基地，市政府在水口村投资13万元建设占地2亩的次早熟蔬菜批发市场，辐射大塘、绿水、平滩、水口、富裕、红星等6个村的蔬菜销售。贵阳兰地公司在三元村新寨兴办养鸡场，年产鸡蛋530万公斤和活鸡40万羽，带动周边农户大量种植高质优良玉米和提供饲料生产的机会，户均年增收1000元以上。仙灵药业公司在红星、折溪、新场、红焰等村猕猴桃园套种中药材淫洋藿2500多亩，达到果药双丰收，实现农业增产，农户增收。

民族农业产业结构调整

2003年，县政府和贵阳市民族宗教局先后投入民族经费283万元，在洒坪乡中明村养殖肉牛460头和二元杂交猪1000头，种草养殖“川白”鹅400只，受益农户户年均增收达2600元以上。

（四）改善居住条件

1998年，县农委和县民委共出资65万元，在六桶乡禾田村屯上（原硝厂医院）修建砖木结构住房1400平方米，共计8幢平房（2户1幢），另有配套设施猪圈、牛圈、厕所及院坝等，年底建成投入使用，解决了16户异地搬迁少数民族农户的居住问题。

2000年，市民族宗教局集中少数民族建房经费269万元，帮助县境少数民族地区改造740户居住的茅草房，其中大石布依族乡665户（含杂居汉族）、谷堡乡大塘村25户、散居少数民族农户50户，建筑面积6.15万平方米，户均82.2平方米。2008年，县政府又投入经费365.06万元，改造厕所626间，改造牛圈和猪圈626间，改造炉灶238座，修建沼气池2369口，使边远山区的2000多户各族农民受益。

少数民族新居

四、少数民族地区文教卫生事业

（一）兴办教育

1. 教育设施建设

1978年，少数民族聚居地区学校有大石、大屯、大寨、高山、回水、红岩、高峰、下堡、桃源、独山、西冲等小学，其中大石和桃源两校附设初中班，又称“戴帽中学”。1982年，经县政府批准大石小学改为大石布依族小学，县民委3次拨款11.8万元修建校舍，增建教室20间和教师宿舍24间。1987年，大石布依族小学初中部析出建大石民族中学。至1990年，全县少数民族居住地开办的小学有49所，并对少数民族贫困生发给助学金和寒衣补助费，对少数民族子女入学放宽年龄招生和减免学杂费，为少数民族子女提供更多的学习机会。同时还在大石、六桶、桃源等乡开办7所初级中学；在六屯、谷堡、程官等小学办有戴帽初中5个班，使少数民族子女小学毕业后能就地就近升入初中学习，推进了少数民族地区九年义务教育的普及。

1997—2001年，贵阳市政府和县政府先后投资200万元为大石民族中学选择新校址，建设新校园，添置新设备。2002—2003年，县政府又拨款按“两基”标准配套完善学校各项教学设备。至2010年，市、县先后投入民族经费62.8万元，帮助大石布依族乡石板小学和扎佐镇石竹小学修建教学楼1148平方米；帮助大石民族中学、大石民族小学、红岩小学、大路边小学、水塘小学进行校园建设，平整学校场地，修建校门和围墙。在帮村扶贫中，有27家单位和个人资助155.4万元，帮助少数民族地区的24所学校新修和维修校舍，购置教具和桌椅，兴建图书室、实验室，修建操场、厕所，美化学校环境，使教育设施日臻完善。

专记：颇具规模的大石布依族乡九年制义务教育学校

1978年大石小学附设初中班，称戴帽学校，有教职员工30人。小学部有6个班，学生326人，其中少数民族学生122人。初中部8个班，学生481人，其中少数民族学生246人。1984年，小学部发展到10个班，学生422人，初中部12班学生618人，教职员工增加到61人；1987年中小学分开，在原址建大石民族中学，时有中学教师31人，开设12个班，学生611人。学校大部分教室为初中部使用，小学部仅有5间教室，教学采用二部制。1991年，县为小学在王家丫口征地6.1亩修建新学校，其中校舍建筑占地3.2亩，并修建学生活动场地800平方米和绿化场地826平方米。建有教学楼和综合楼各1幢，其中普通教室13间960平方米，办公室3间171平方米，实验室151平方米，微机室20平方米，少先队活动室70平方米，教学仪器和体育器材保管室各1间共69平方米，图书阅览室151平方米。置有远程教育设备1套，电脑23台，课桌凳430套。1993年3月，大石小学迁新校舍上课，原校舍划归中学使用。1997年，县民宗局拨款3万元给中学修建200平方米的食堂，解决600多名师生的进餐问题。1999年，县政府拨款72万元

大石布依族乡九年制义务教育学校

在王家丫口征拨土地23亩给中学修建砖混结构4层教学楼1幢，建筑面积1860平方米。2001年，县民宗局又拨款13万元，将生活区砖木结构的旧教室改造成钢混平顶房，并平整新校操场。9月，贵阳市政府市长孙国强到大石调研，拨款110万元用于大石中学校园建设和教师宿舍改造，将原旧教学楼改造成学生宿舍。2003年，县政府拨款又建教师宿舍1幢16套，建筑面积1280平方米。贵阳市政府赠送学校电脑24台，建立远程教育站。县民宗局拨款在校园内建有864平方米的少数民族体育训练基地。2007年开办寄宿制，置床100套，桌椅50套。并对寄宿的少数民族贫困生204人每人每年补助生活费100元，使其能完成初中学业。2008年3月，将大石中学大石小学合并，成立九年一贯制大石民族学校。2010年，校区占地52亩，建有教学楼2幢、综合楼1幢、学生宿舍2幢、食堂1幢，教学用房建筑面积1.93万平方米；有普通教室50间，课桌凳2400套，电脑86台，教学、实验，体育器材按一类中学配备，图书室藏书3.12万册。小学部有教师22人，开设8个班，学生309人。中学部有教师33人，开设12个班，在校学生665人。

2. 创办民族职业班

1983年7月，县政府以〔1983〕修字35号文批转县民委和教育局报告，在县一中和二中各开办1个民族班，招收少数民族子弟100人，学生免交全部费用住校学习。开办之前，专项拨款制作床、桌、椅100套供给学生使用。学制3年，达到高中水平。在校学习期间，可以参加招工、招干和升学考试，按国家规定标准录取。鉴于少数民族子弟多来自边远山区，基础知识较差，第一年以补习为主，第二年起学习高中课程。1986年7月学生全部毕业，其中有34人先后考入安顺卫生学校、安顺师范学校和黔南、黔西南民族干部管理学校学习，期满毕业由国家统一分配工作。

（二）文化建设

1. 安装广播电视设备

1984—1990年，县政府先后投资5万元在大石、桃源、石安等少数民族比较聚居的地方建成有线广播站，架通至各村的线路，安装喇叭，按时转播中央台和贵州台的节目。随着电视普及，1991年又在各地建立电视差转台，使边远山区少数民族群众能收看电视节目。1999年起，又开通闭路电视。到2008年，实现“村村通”广播和电视，丰富了边远山区各民族的文化生活。

2. 研究民族文化

发掘文化遗产 2001年5月，县民族宗教局根据民国《修文县志》记载，并结合在当地布依族群众中调查，于大石乡大屯村发现彝族安氏古墓遗址。遗址占地约两亩，由于多年无墓主祭扫，“文化大革命”时已夷为平地，今已辟为水田。当地村民及世人不知墓主，只相传称之为“安家墓”“宣慰坟”“倮倮坟”和“火烧灰”等。据调查考证：坟墓为大块石灰石砌成，横向长方形，面宽5米，进深4米，高2米。墓正面为石材4柱3门，中2柱上刻有彝文对联，经贵州省民族学院文化系副主任、讲师陈仕军根据彝文墓碑翻译，意为：“贵山贵水安位，荣施荣令绘凿”。此次发现引起省内外史学界

安氏古墓复原图

学者关注，县民宗局邀请省彝族学会领导和专家再次对其进行详细考察论证，基本认定该墓葬为明朝贵州宣慰使安贵荣墓。

传承布依文化 2005年县民族宗教局组织15位布依族退休老同志走村串寨，收集、发掘、整理县境布依族历史、语言、节庆、婚礼、葬礼、祭祀、酒歌、花歌等文字资料50万言，为编写《贵阳布依文化》一书提供资料，还将布依婚俗“祝袍咪”（歌伴舞）撰文发表，引起少数民族文艺爱好者关注，并提出修改意见，由县民族、文化部门组织独山、大屯民族文艺表演队进行排练，作为接待游客的主要节目。

创新芦笙舞 县境苗族历来喜好歌舞，内容丰富多彩，表演活泼粗犷。1981年恢复民族传统节日后，每逢节日和喜庆均以歌舞欢度。其形式主要有唱山歌、吹芦笙、跳蹲鸡步舞、斗牛舞和打鼓舞等，多在院落或场地表演。久长镇老歌手王永贵（苗族）在下堡村带领苗族青年组织芦笙歌舞队参加省城贵阳的“四月八”活动，由于精心排练，不断创新，并得到专业人士指导，其歌舞不仅具有浓郁民族风味，而且还有较高的艺术价值。新编的苗族歌舞将男鼓手伴奏改为女青年打鼓，上场与吹芦笙的男演员共同表演，阵容整齐，技艺精湛。吹奏曲谱主要有如泣如诉的叙事曲、凄婉含蓄的悲哀曲和阳刚铿锵的欢乐曲等。改编歌舞中最为有名的是下堡苗族歌舞“恭冗冗”（庆丰收），受省内民族艺术界专家和领导关注，1995年春节推荐代表贵州省少数民族参加北京“龙潭杯”表演，获得观众好评。1996年又作为中国文化使者，应邀到日本访问演出，在日本往返月余，巡回演出14场，观众1.5万人次。

下堡苗族牛角舞

3. 保存民族工艺

县境苗族同胞素有种麻织布的习惯，自种苎麻、火麻，绩麻捻线，机织麻布，然后用五色线在布上数纱刺绣各自喜欢的图案。传统的苗族少女从六七岁开始就学习纺纱、织布、刺绣、印染等手工技术。用织出来的花布做腰带、筒裙、上衣、头巾、花帽、花带、胸挂、挂包、被子和壁挂等，成品一般多为家庭自用，有的用于交换或赠送。每逢民俗节日或庆典盛会，姑娘们都要穿戴自己亲手织绣的服装，以示自己心灵手巧。从20世纪80年代起，随着经济社会发展，少数民族文化受时代影响，日趋汉化。手工艺术仅有苗族蜡染、刺绣或被作为非物质文化保留下来。2009年8月，县民宗局和县文化部门配合开办苗族服饰工艺传习所，选拔30名当地苗族女青年进行培训，主要设置有纺织、刺绣、服饰展示及苗族语言等课程。教学由当地有专长技艺者负责传授。通过培训，学员每人都制作一套盛装，每逢举办带有民族性质的庆祝活动，他们都要穿着自制服饰展示自己的才艺。

苗族纺织 县境苗族织布原料多以苎麻为主，苎麻茎皮纤维细长，韧性较好，质地洁白，富有光泽，是纺织麻布的较好材料。一般人家可根据家庭需要种植适当面积的苎麻，每年夏秋各采收1次。新采苎麻含胶质较重较为粗硬，需用石灰水浸泡去掉胶质，搓洗漂清，再经数天日晒夜露使其变软变白才能使用。经处理后的苎麻即可用捻子手工捻成细纱，一般苗族妇女均善绩麻捻纱。制好的麻纱可根据需要染成各种不同的颜色，再上织机手工织成布。新织麻布较粗硬，须用石灰水或碱水浸泡，放在锅中用火煮练，取出用衣槌捣练和漂洗使其柔软。成布幅宽60至70厘米，长200至300厘米不等。麻布具有透气性好，传热散热快，吸水强易散湿的特点，麻布织品夏天穿着凉爽。麻布还不易受霉菌腐蚀和虫蛀，且轻盈，同容积的苎麻布与棉布相比要轻20%。不足之处在于工艺原始，质感不及现代机织布细腻光亮，而且工艺复杂成本高，随着少数民族生活水平提高多被淘汰。至2010年，县内六桶乡黄金村有少数苗族村民尚存机织麻布工艺，仅就其自身具有民族文化价值作为非物质文化遗产被保留下来。

苗族纺织

苗族刺绣 苗族妇女擅长刺绣，她们用各种颜色纱线在头巾、腰带、衣襟、袖沿中绣上精美的花纹图案，具有较强的民族特色。刺绣技法主要有平绣、挑花、堆绣、锁绣、贴布绣、打籽绣、破线绣、钉线绣、皱绣、辫绣、缠绣、马尾绣等。在工艺上可分正绣反看或反绣正看。一般是按照服装的各个部位对花纹、色彩的要求，先绣成布片，然后再拼接。苗族服装分便装和盛装两种，便装制作简朴，供平时生活或劳动时穿用；盛装制作工艺精细、复杂，要花2至3年才能制成1套，一般来说苗族女子一生之中只有一套盛装，平时不穿，要在新婚大喜或走亲访友、参加喜庆节日才着装。1981年，县民族事务委员会挑选3种服饰送国家民族文化宫参加全国少数民族服饰展受到好评。后又送法国巴黎、日本东京展出，得到国际友人的称赞。20世纪90年代，平地村苗族妇女主任唐明琴还带领苗族女青年学习刺绣，由于制作精细，受到县文化部门关注。2010年5月，平地村在县文体广电局的帮助下成立龙场镇平地村刺绣传习所，由有经验的苗族老人指导，传授苗族刺绣技艺。

苗族刺绣

布依族刺绣 在布依族聚居人口较为集中的六屯独山、西冲、大木和大石大屯等地较为盛行。技法主要有平绣、绉绣、缠绣、挑绣、编绣、骑绣、剪贴绣等。图案有人物、花草、飞鸟、虫蝶、动物等，图案多用几种颜色绣出，花纹栩栩如生，有写实、写意，也有各种几何图案。一般用作服饰、背带、围腰、账檐、被面、枕套、头帕、荷包、鞋面、手帕等。布依族刺绣对研究布依族信仰、生产方式、民风习俗等都具有重要价值。

蜡染 境内布依族、苗族妇女擅长蜡染。其工序先将布料经过浆洗、熨烫平整，再用蜡刀在不需染色的部分封涂上蜡液，待蜡凝固定形后放入染缸中浸泡染色，色染好后用清水冲洗，再用热水去蜡、漂清、晾干即成。蜡染用蜡早先普遍采用蜂蜡，今多采用石蜡、蜂蜡、木蜡等混合蜡。色料采用植物染料，多为蓝色。一般用自种的蓝靛加上适量的野生盐肤木（肤炎树）叶和马桑苔一起捣碎，熬制成蓝色的染色溶液。盛装染色溶液的缸称为染缸。染制出

布依蜡染

的图形主要有树木花草、鸟兽鱼虫等。蜡染还可采取多次上蜡，多次染色，染制出两种以上的颜色。还可根据蜡液自然龟裂现象，染制出“冰纹”图案。蜡染图案丰富，色调素雅，风格独特，用于制作服装服饰和各种生活实用品，显得朴实大方、清新悦目，富有民族特色。其产品主要有服装、床单、被面、包袱布、包头巾、背包、提包、背带和丧事用的葬单等。

4. 参加民族体育竞赛

1997年11月2至4日，县民委和县体育局组队参加贵阳市举办的少数民族传统体育运动会，有射弩、陀螺、押加、高脚竞速4个项目参赛。其中，射弩个人获立姿、跪姿、全能第三名，混合团体获第六名，押加获个人60公斤级第一名，53公斤级和68公斤级各第三名，80公斤级第四名，76公斤级第五名，团体获第三名。下堡苗族芦笙队编排《打排牛》参赛表演，获三等奖。

（三）改善医疗卫生条件

从1980年开始，县财政每年逐步拨款给居住有少数民族的大石、桃源、新场、金桥、中寨等公社新建和修缮卫生所，并添置必要药品和设备。1982年起连续3年，先后定点定向从大石、桃源、三元、花榔、场坝、中寨、石安等公社招收少数民族子弟送往安顺卫生学校民族医士班学习，学制3年，学习期间的伙食、衣服、被盖以及常用生活用具全部由国家负担。学习期满经考试合格，发给中专文凭，分配回当地公社卫生所工作。1984年，县民委拨付民族经费扩建大石、桃源民族乡的两个卫生院，设置病床，增配医生和增加医疗设备。1992年，随县撤区并乡工作的开展，将原大石和回水两乡卫生所合并建立大石布依族乡卫生院，院址设在大石街上，全院占地1亩，有业务用房320平方米。1994年，县民族事务委员会出资5万元又为大石卫生院扩建业务房150平方米。2000年，县卫生局拨款10万元，为大石乡卫生院扩建业务用房200平方米，使大石乡卫生院占地增至1.35亩，建筑面积达670平方米。2006年，县启动新型农村合作医疗，村民每人每年筹资10元医疗经费，国家每年每人补助45元，对经济困难的少数民族所需费用由民族宗教事务局缴纳，此后国家补助逐年增加。

2007年3月，县政府落实贵阳市发展改革委员会制发《农村卫生服务体系建设方案》，对全县10个乡镇卫生院中8个卫生院进行改扩建时，拟定大石乡卫生院扩建规模400平方米，投入建设资金26万元，其中中央预算内专项资金20万元，省配套4万元，县配套2万元。建设工程由县乡（镇）卫生院改扩建工作领导小组统一安排，进行工程招投标，中标价为19.81万元。年底主体工程完工，2008年投入使用。

大石卫生院

2010年，大石乡卫生院占地面积达2.4亩，业务用房建筑面积1070平方米。置有内科、外科、妇科、手术室、化验室、放射室、药房、防保、财务和院办公室等科室。有医务人员14人，病床位7张。

第二节 宗 教

县内宗教主要有佛教、道教和天主教。1978年，由于受“文化大革命”影响，宗教仍被视为迷信活动、精神鸦片。1981年6月，县委统战部落实宗教政策，恢复、开放宗教活动场所；推动爱国宗教界人士队伍建设；支持宗教界积极开展对外友好交往，防范境外利用宗教进行渗透；建立健全宗教工作机构，加强宗教工作干部队伍建设，提高在改革开放条件下处理宗教事务的能力。1982年3月，贯彻落实中共中央《关于社会主义时期宗教问题的基本观点和基本政策》，提倡“信仰宗教自由，有序管理”。1986年，县政府设立宗教科，专门负责全县宗教管理工作。

1991年，贯彻中共中央、国务院《关于进一步做好宗教工作若干问题的通知》，全面落实宗教信仰自由政策，境内各家宗教都出现了较快的恢复性增长，但有的地方出现宗教发展过热，乱建、滥建庙宇等活动场所，有的还利用宗教从事非法活动。1995年8月，根据国务院《宗教活动场所管理条例》，县委统战部、县公安局、县宗教科联合开展治理“两乱”（乱建寺庙、乱塑神像），取缔非法宗教活动，捣毁窝点16处，对42个骨干分子进行批评教育，净化社会环境。经清理、整顿并报经安顺行署宗教局批准，县内宗教活动场所属正规、合法的有佛教派寺庙知非寺、佛光寺、佛洞山寺和天主教堂圣母堂。为进一步加强宗教管理，结合机构改革，县人民政府将县宗教科与民族事务委员会合并组建民族宗教事务局。继后，县的宗教工作步入规范化、制度化、法治化，政府依法管理宗教事务，宗教工作干部队伍和爱国宗教界人士队伍得到加强。

2003年，贯彻落实中共中央、国务院《关于加强宗教工作的决定》，县政府出台《关于进一步加强宗教工作的意见》，积极引导宗教活动与社会主义现代化建设相适应，经常对宗教界人士进行政策法规教育，要求做到“维护法律尊严，维护人民利益，维护民族团结，维护祖国统一”。从2005年3月起，贯彻落实国务院发布的《宗教事务条例》，切实依法管理宗教事务，在全县范围内建立起县、乡、村三级责任制，加强对宗教的管理。各家宗教活动场所按照遵守法纪好、民主管理好、正常活动好、服务社会好、环境美化好的“五好”标准开展活动。为维护正常的活动秩序，每年常规佛教法事活动和天主教圣诞节，县公安、综治、卫生等部门加强安全保卫、饮食卫生、防火、防盗、防毒等工作，确保宗教活动顺利开展，至2010年，宗教场所从未发生过安全事故和社会治安案件。

一、佛教

1978年，县内佛教仍被视为封建迷信，偶有信奉者，其活动只能秘密进行。1982年，贯彻落实中共中央恢复宗教信仰自由政策，信奉者活动由秘密转为公开。1985年11月，知非寺被公布为省级重点文物保护单位，对原有建筑进行部分修缮，接纳香客进寺内烧香还愿。继后，在六广贾家洞和扎佐四明洞也恢复香客进庙。20世纪90年代，境内出现信教热，最崇敬的神是观世音菩萨，每年农历二、六、九月的十九日，是烧香拜佛最热闹的日子。信众不仅祈求菩萨保佑自己无灾无难，而且还祈求赐予富贵。有的企业老板也加入信众行业，并慷慨捐资修建寺庙。1996年开始，进一步加强对佛教管理，得到贵阳市佛教界的支持，使佛教事业步入规范化、合法化。2005年3月起，依法管理宗教事务。对寺庙、主持进行注册登记，经过资格审核属正规、合法者发给证书。同时还协助各寺庙订立寺庙办公、殿堂管理、财务管理、客堂管理、年检和来人报告等规章制度。

（一）佛教寺庙

县境历史上曾先后建有各类大小寺庙137座。至1978年，寺庙建筑除三潮水知非寺部分建筑和扎佐把七的观音阁有所保留外，其余寺庙仅存遗址。20世纪80年代恢复党的宗教政策，寺庙建设亦随之恢复。至1995年，全县有寺庙49座，一些不法者趁机而入利用宗教从事违法活动。8月，经县宗教管理部门清理、整顿，报经安顺地区行署宗教局批准，合法的佛教活动场所只保留知非寺、佛光寺、佛洞山寺。1996年起，境内佛教事务管理规范，设施完善。2005年按照国家《宗教事务条例》重新对寺庙进行登记。至2010年，全县在寺庙建设、人员配置和宗教事务等方面合法、正规的佛教寺庙增加了金凤寺，连同原有的3座寺庙，全县共有寺庙4座。

1. 知非寺

三潮水知非寺

位于县城西北面2.5公里处观音山南麓三潮水，为境内古老寺庙，原名潮水寺，后更名为知非寺。寺庙原为四合院落，庙前有4柱3门3楼石牌坊。庙门横额书有“知非禅林”4个大字；横梁下面中间刻有“太极图”，两边刻“帝道遐昌”，“凰图巩固”8字；门柱上刻有对联“举足宜寻中正路，入门俱是过来人”，“履山径之斜歆知非决不蹈前辙，参水源于活泼动念释然悟化机”。牌坊上刻有龙、凤、鸟、兽等浮雕图案，刻工精巧细致，是县境唯一遗存的石牌坊，惜早已倾倒掩埋于泥土之中。“文化大革命”时期，知非寺遭到严重破坏，房舍被移作他用。1982年落实宗教政策，知非寺及三潮水被列为县级重点文物保护单位，交给县文化局管理，由县财政划拨资金逐年进行维修。1985年11月，知非寺又被列为省级重点文物保护单位。1997年秋再次拨款维修，在原正殿处修大雄宝殿，西厢修韦驮菩萨殿和客室、僧寮，原址前新修山门，周围修围墙圈围知非寺和三潮水景区建筑。2000年，又由四川成都开发商出资扩建，至2004年竣工。增修观音殿和财神殿，在大雄殿后增修藏经楼、罗汉堂、观音塔、药王殿，并塑露天神农、卧佛神像，使寺院扩建成三重殿式规模。全寺占地面积30亩，建筑面积5000平方米。

2. 佛光寺

位于扎佐镇大堡村翠屏山旁四明洞中，距县城16公里，为新建寺庙。1996年明确该寺为佛教活动场所后，当地信众即募集资金修葺寺庙。洞口垒石为台，填平洞厅为堂，堂中按照地形高低分别修建大佛殿供奉释迦牟尼佛；修建观音殿供奉观音大士；观音殿旁还供关圣帝君和阎王菩萨。2005年，将后洞门打开，新修山门和配殿，面对扎（佐）六（屯）公路辟有水泥道路直达山门。另在洞顶山上修建具有标志性的“三面观音”佛像一座。全寺占地面积从过去的1.5亩扩大到15亩，建筑面积3000多平方米。

3. 佛洞山寺

位于六广镇新中村范家坡贾家洞中，距县城35公里，为一古老寺庙改建。原寺庙修筑在悬崖峭壁上的贾家洞中，“文化大革命”被废弃。20世纪80年代复有香客，后逐渐增多。1990年，信众集资复修大佛殿于洞中，供奉释迦牟尼佛像。殿旁修僧寮、客厅和斋堂。前洞厅垒砌为二级平台，下平台维修左右二厢，右厢为禅堂，左厢为僧寮。上平台建上下两殿，上殿垒土为龛，供有观音大士、十二园觉、下殿供三教圣人和韦驮诸神，岩壁上还供有石佛。下殿为木架吊脚楼，楼上供诸神牌位10多座。后洞厅新修玉佛殿，内供七彩观音和地藏王菩萨神像。洞口有将军殿，供监雹神李三将军像。2003年，得贵阳市佛教界资助，重选新址于范家坡东麓新修寺院，命名“佛洞山寺”。新寺院为上下两重式，占地1.3亩，建筑面积604平方米。

贾家洞佛洞山寺

4. 金凤寺

位于观音山南麓小地名鸡爬坎处，距县城北门1公里，为新建寺庙。原鸡爬坎有一石笋略似人形，有人称其为观音菩萨神像，于是烧香许愿，相传非常灵念，致香客逐渐增多。20世纪80年代末，信众积资为神像修造房舍遮蔽风雨，称其为观音庙。1996年，信众又募集资金修建砖木结构的观音殿，内供观音大士神像。继后又再募集资金在观音殿后兴修砖混结构的大佛殿和山门，供奉大佛和韦驮菩萨。两侧修僧寮，形成1座二重殿式庙宇。2000年，再度募集资金在观音殿右侧和殿下继修砖混结构的会客厅、药王殿、万佛殿、罗汉堂和天王殿等。2008年竣工，寺庙更名为“金凤寺”，全寺占地20余亩，建筑总面积达3500平方米。

观音山金凤寺

（二）祭祀活动

20世纪80年代初，刚恢复信仰宗教自由，尚无专门主持佛教祭祀活动的人，多由信众自己烧香拜佛求菩萨，许愿菩萨保佑达到自己祈求，将会报答菩萨，有给菩萨挂红、捐资修庙、烧香化纸等，统称这种做法为“烧香换水”。一旦许愿者祈求目的达到，就要履行之前给菩萨许下的诺言，俗称“还愿”。80年代后半期，由于烧香换水、还愿信众增多，开始出现一些专门从事主持祭祀活动的人，起初这些人并非出家、专职，仅为临时主持。90年代初，从外地入境一些和尚逐步替代了原来的临时主持人，专门从事寺庙的宗教事务活动。至2010年，境内各寺庙有和尚1~5人不等。世人称寺庙住持为方丈，称一般和尚（不分男女）为师傅，称有资历的和尚为法师。佛教祭祀活动分为日常祭祀、节日法事和个人佛事。

寺庙每天都要烧香礼佛、诵读经文、打扫佛堂，每日一小祭，农历每月初一、十五要大祭。民间也有少数虔诚信众将一尊菩萨（多为观世音菩萨）请到家中供奉，每日上香礼拜，每逢初一、十五要上香、燃烛、烧纸钱和更换供品，以求神灵庇佑全家富贵平安。大多数信众每逢初一、十五相约聚集到寺庙烧香礼佛，祈福求安。

佛教节日法事是每年定期隆重举行的祭祀活动，主要有农历正月初一弥勒佛诞辰日、二月初八释迦佛出家纪念日、二月十五释迦佛涅槃日、二月十九观音诞辰日、二月二十一普贤诞辰日、三月十六准提

诞辰日、四月初四文殊诞辰日、四月初八释迦牟尼佛诞辰日、六月初三韦驮诞辰日、六月十九观音成道日、七月十三大势至诞辰日、七月十五盂兰盆会日、七月三十地藏诞辰日、九月十九观音出家纪念日、九月三十药师佛诞辰日、十月初五禅宗初祖达摩祖师诞辰日、冬月十七阿弥陀佛诞辰日、腊月初八释迦佛成道纪念日等。由于佛教节日太多，根据贵阳市佛教协会规定，每年节日7个，即二月十九观音诞辰日、四月初八释迦牟尼佛诞辰日、六月十九观音成道日、七月三十地藏诞辰日、九月十九观音出家纪念日、冬月十七阿弥陀佛诞辰日、腊月初八释迦佛成道纪念日。实际上参加人数最多、最热闹的是每年农历二、六、九月的十九与观音菩萨有关的几个节日，其中尤以九月十九观音出家纪念日最为隆重。

除以上常规祭祀活动外，有的寺庙僧人还应一些信众个人要求，为其已故亲人超度亡灵或求学、求子、求财、求寿、求福等举行求佛之事，称之为个人佛事。1998年农历四月十六至十八，知非寺举办的“放生大会”，整个过程包括诵经、打表升疏、施焰火、施斋饭、礼佛许愿等。最后将信众买来的鱼、龟和鸟类放归河流、山林，称可为参加放生的信众获得无量福德。继后每年，各地大小寺庙均要定期或选择日子举行放生活动。

附：修文佛教源流简介

宋、元时期佛教已零星传入黔中地区，今县境东部当时称之为功州，之后历史上曾有贵州佛教协会功州分会。明永乐年间贵州建省，开始建立流官制度，实行土流并治。因受中原文化影响，四川、湖南一带部分僧人陆续进入黔中宣扬佛法，弘教开宗。明万历年间，社会相对稳定，在人口较为集的一些地区兴建了一批寺庙，然规模较小，有的还利用山洞作庙宇。崇祯年间，朝廷于今县境地驻扎重兵平定水西叛乱，水西战败投降后献出六广河以东地区。总兵王国祯下令广修寺庙，大兴佛教，以求一方平安。明末清初，有著名僧人语嵩大师和钱邦芑等于三潮水知非寺开堂说法，致宗风大振。清康熙二十六年(1687)修文建县后，佛教禅宗大兴，在县境广修寺院、悉数70余座，后增至137座，拥有僧尼230人，教徒274人。境内禅宗派系多以临济宗为主，曹洞宗次之。据考证，临济宗派僧人所建寺庙主要有乌栗、谷堡一带的水口寺、报国寺，洒坪蜈蚣桥的雨花寺，六屯三寨的回龙寺等；曹洞宗派僧人所建寺院主要有扎佐镇把七村永寿寺、六广镇广城村太平寺。著名僧人属临济宗的有雨花寺求悟陆公禅师，水口寺清泓、普智，桃源回龙寺慧峨、性通、海平、永庆、昌悦及知非寺大错、语嵩、剖石、云峰祖高，扎佐佛光寺香裕等；属曹洞宗的有六广太平寺海池、仙翁等。民国时期，人们开始崇尚科学，佛教日趋衰败，寺庙香火不及以往。解放后，佛教被视为封建迷信，大部分寺庙无人料理，庙产充公或为集体财产，有的庙宇改建为学校。僧尼部分还俗，未还俗的也都参加土地改革和集体生产。20世纪80年代落实党的宗教政策，允许信仰宗教自由，要求有序管理致佛教再次恢复发展。至2010年，全县建有佛教寺庙49座，其中规范、合法的有龙场镇知非寺、扎佐镇佛光寺、六广镇佛洞山寺和龙场镇金凤寺4座寺庙。4座寺庙与贵阳黔灵山弘福寺有密切往来，在基础设施建设上曾得到弘福寺大力资助。弘福寺资深方丈、法师曾多次亲临寺庙讲经说法，弘扬佛教精神。

二、道教

1978年，境内道教被视为封建迷信，称从事道教活动者为道士先生，全县有道士30余人，他们活动不公开，只在一些偏远地区帮人家治丧时给死者招魂、开路做道场。1982年，落实宗教信仰自由政策，道士的活动逐步从隐蔽转为公开。1995年组建民族宗教事务局后，依法管理宗教事务。由于道教无固定活动场所，无固定神像，道士基本是农村村民兼职，故道教未列入治理范围。2000年，部分从道者开始在县城和乡（镇）所在地开设门面，销售丧葬物品。继后，有的发展为集销售丧葬物品、为死者招魂、开路做道场等一条龙服务。2004年根据贵阳市民族宗教事务管理局筑民宗字〔2004〕49号文件精神，县民宗局组织力量对从教者调查统计，各乡镇均有分布，共有从教的道士71人，一直未纳入规范化管理。

（一）活动场所

境内道教神祇的庙宇称宫、殿、观、阁和庙。“宫”类有学宫、文昌宫、忠烈宫、川主宫和万寿宫，“观”类有玉皇观；“阁”类有玉皇阁、观音阁，“殿”类有三官殿、祖师殿；“庙”类有关帝庙、城隍庙、龙王庙、东岳庙、马王庙、牛王庙、财神庙、真武庙、鲁班庙、宾王庙、黑神庙、宝王庙、灵官庙等。全县有道教各类大小庙宇50多座。道教神祇虽多，但实际经常供祀的神祇仅20多座，其他小神祇都附设于大神祇的宫观之内。1978年，道教庙宇仅存县城学宫两厢砖木结构危房，其余全为废墟，仅存遗址。20世纪80年代恢复信仰宗教自由后，道士先生的祭祀活动均在自己家里和事主家中。至2010年，原县城学宫两厢砖木结构危房也都被拆除改建校舍。

（二）祭祀活动

县境道教多为正一道派，奉张天师为道首，尊元始天尊为最高尊神，以《正一经》为主要经典。祭祀活动以符箓斋醮、降神驱鬼为主，分为节日祭祀和民间日常祭祀两类。

1. 节日祭祀

祭祀道教诸神，每年正月初一玉清元始天尊诞辰日、正月初九玉皇诞辰日、正月十五张天师诞辰日和上元天官诞辰日、正月十九长春邱真人诞辰日、二月十五上清灵宝天尊诞辰日、四月十四吕祖吕洞宾诞辰日、夏至太清道德天尊诞辰日、七月十五中元地官诞辰日、十月十五下元水官诞辰日、腊月二十二王重阳祖师诞辰日及二、六、九月十九慈航会。慈航是观世音菩萨道号，慈航真人是道教人士对观音菩萨的称呼，慈航意为“救度众生，使其安乐”，民间信众非常崇拜观世音菩萨，故每年的慈航会最为隆重，参会信众最多。

2. 民间日常祭祀

正一派道家允许道士有家室，可以不住宫观，与民间信众接触机会多，常受信众请托做禳灾祈福法事。信众家中有的供观音菩萨、财神、药王及其他行业神位，有的设“天地君亲师位”或“天地国亲师位”等神位。若遇干旱灾害，信众集资请道士竖立“当年得道行雨龙王水司真宰”神位，祈求降雨，称打雨水醮；腊月二十三灶王菩萨生日，信众要扫除家中灰尘，有的请道士竖立“九天东厨司命灶王府君玉池灰合夫人神位”做道场，祈求灶王菩萨保佑家人平安富贵。此外，有的还请道士打醮做会祈神保佑消灾免难、发财发富、延年益寿等；有的根据个人愿望许愿还愿，庆坛神，请道士烧化纸钱，呈词拜表；有家人去世的，要请道士做道场，为死者招魂开路。特别是农村为死者招魂开路做道场较为普遍。

三、天主教

清咸丰年间由法国传教士传入县境扎佐，“文化大革命”中受到冲击，称其为“国际间谍分支机构”，神甫黄霞飞被污为“间谍”，遭游街示众和批判斗争，并被判刑入狱。1981年6月，县委统战部派干部上门走访，看望宗教人士，落实党的宗教信仰自由政策，为黄霞飞平反，赔偿其经济损失。1984年4月，成立县天主教教务管理小组，由扎佐教民杨良平具体负责筹划复教。其间，杨良平代表宗教界当选为县政协委员。1986年教会恢复活动，负责人为鲁宗芬。

（一）活动场所

天主教在扎佐活动场所原有大经堂和小经堂两处，大经堂又称天主堂，供普通教民礼拜之用，小经堂又称圣母堂，专供女性教民作礼拜。大经堂曾长期被占为扎佐区公所办公用房和扎佐电影院，小经堂在“文化大革命”中也被没收充公。20世纪80年代落实党的宗教政策后，县财政于1985年划拨5万元专款修复扎佐小经堂，次年竣工仍称圣母堂，交由天主教会使用。1992年，撤扎佐区新建扎佐镇，镇政府仍在原大经堂处办公。2000年，扎佐镇政府迁驻扎佐襄阳大道后，于10月县政府以修府专议〔2000〕26号文明确物归原主，将大经堂退还给扎佐天主教会使用。

（二）教会活动

1978年，扎佐天主教会教民因受“文化大革命”影响均未开展教会活动。1986年小经堂修复竣工后，交由扎佐天主教会管理，由鲁宗芬负责主持教务活动，组织教民每周举行礼拜。1999年，成立县天主教爱国委员会，简称“爱国会”，选举产生委员5名，其中主任委员1名，秘书长1名，委员3名。时有教民400人，活动每天早晚课读《圣经》，唱赞美诗和祷告。每年4月15日的“复活节”、9月8日“圣母圣诞节”、9月18日“圣母蒙世升天节”和12月25日“圣诞节”都要齐集教民唱诵圣歌和经文，进行瞻礼活动。2008年，“爱国会”举行第二届委员会换届选举，推荐常委、委员、代表出席省、市天主教爱国会会议。天主教会还热衷于爱国活动和慈善事业，在全国喜迎香港、澳门回归及新中国建立60周年大庆时，组织教民开展爱国文娱体育活动，歌颂中国共产党和祖国建设事业。2008年凝冻灾害和四川汶川地震期间，教民们还积极参与捐款救助活动。

扎佐圣母堂（小经堂）

县境另有部分信奉耶稣基督的教民，自称属基督教，1979年恢复活动，主要以家庭聚会的形式开展。2004年发展到3个聚会点：一是扎佐红兴厂，负责人申礼贵，有信徒18人；二是六屯乡三寨村，负责人朱青琴，有信徒28人；三是谷堡乡绿水村，负责人张仕芳，有信徒60人。因没有固定活动场所，均未纳入规范化管理。

第二章　社会事务

1978至1987年，社会事务由县民政局和乡（镇）民政所承担，主要是负责助残帮困、优怃安置、烈士褒扬、救济救灾、婚姻登记和基层政权建设，其宗旨是“上为中央分忧，下为百姓解难”。

1988年，根据全国人民代表大会《中华人民共和国村民委员会组织法（试行）》，选举产生农村基层法定的自治组织村委会。1990年，遵照全国人民代表大会《中华人民共和国城市居民委员会组织法》，对全县城镇居民委员会进行调整、充实。2003年根据城镇发展需要，将城镇居委会整合后建立城镇居民社区，成为城镇居民基层自治组织。同时县政府将乡(镇)民政所改为社会事务办公室。自此，县民政局、乡镇社会事务办公室、村（居）委会共同开展救灾、救济、救助、扶贫、优怃、抚恤、遣送、安置、助残、捐赠募捐、婚姻计生和殡葬改革，以及社会团体、地域管理等社会事务工作。

一站式服务办证大厅

第一节　社会福利

一、社会供养

（一）供养孤老

1.城镇孤老

1996年，城镇推出居家养老服务，加大老年公寓、老年活动中心和社区服务中心建设，实现“老有所养，住有所居”的民生计划。街道孤老由乡（镇）民政所发给供养费，由街道居民委员会代管，负责对孤老日常照顾。1997年，根据国务院〔1997〕29号文和黔府发〔1997〕66号文精神，启动全县城镇居民最低生活保障，将城镇孤老列入城市居民最低生活保障对象，使孤老供养向标准化、规范化、制度化转变。从1999年10月起，每月人均120元。2000年，供养标准在1999年基础上提高30%。2005年再次提高，使供养随社会经济发展逐步改善。2006年，对孤老供养扩展为年满60岁并无经济来源老人的供养，对年满70岁的老人提高高龄补贴，基本实现老有所依。

2009年，按照县老龄事业发展“十一五”规划和县委办、县政府办印发的《居家养老服务试点工作方案》要求，以村（社区）“居家养老”和村（社区）老龄工作为重点开展老有所依工作。在5月18日全县老龄工作会议上，县委、县政府对全县老龄工作全面布置。县老龄办和龙场镇、小箐乡、谷堡乡、六屯乡负责老龄工作的领导参加省举办的“居家养老”培训班，并前往江苏省学习“居家养老”工作经验。6月组织全县10乡（镇）老龄办负责人进行“居家养老”工作专题培训，并组织龙场镇虎山、龙岗、宾阳、栖凤社区相关人员到清镇市青龙办事处新民社区和贵阳市云岩区阳光托老所参观学习。全县9个乡（镇），5个社区，7个行政村分别启动“居家养老”服务工作。乡（镇）组织医务人员上门为90岁以上老年人免费体检，对全县90至99岁的老龄人和年满100岁以上的老龄人每人每月分别发放高龄补助费100元和200元，对全县生活不能自理特困老人12人，每人每月发给护理补助费200元。全年发放高龄补助30多万元。

县中心敬老院

2. 农村孤老

1978年，在农村对无劳动能力、无生活来源和无法定扶养义务人的孤老人员由生产大队和生产队实行“五保”供养政策，即保吃、保穿、保住、保医、保葬。1981年11月，经普查登记，全县共有五保户451户517人。随着农村经济体制改革，根据农村孤老不同情况采取不同供养方式：一是分给供养田地，由生产队集体代耕，收成归生产队，再由生产队对孤老保吃、穿、医、住、葬；二是由公社或大队在社队企业收益中提成，按月、按季发给五保户钱、粮；三是由村民代耕孤老供养地，每年定量付给五保户口粮300至250公斤；四是由孤老亲友代耕其供养地，收益归孤老；五是不分给供养地，由社队统一发放救济粮款、衣物照顾；六是有条件的乡（镇）集体办农村敬老院、将所辖范围的孤老在自愿原则下收住入院，由乡（镇）负责供养。

洒坪乡敬老院

1983年，再次对农村五保户普查登记，并调整供养标准：每人全年供给口粮150—250公斤，最多为400公斤；零用现金20至50元，最多为80元；燃煤1000—1500斤，最多3000公斤。其供养方式：一是由孤老所在生产队或大队供养；二是乡（镇）敬老院由国家包干供养，社办敬老院由孤老所在队负责孤老口粮，社负责补助孤老零用钱；三是分给孤老供养田土、可由其亲属代耕，代耕者对孤老保养到底，并可继承孤老的房产和可续耕承包期内的供养土地；四是对有劳动能力的孤老的供养田，允许自种自吃，免交农业税；五是国家以救济方式定量发给每人每年180元救济款和寒衣、棉被等物。1989年，全县农村集体供养五保户476人，发给供养金4774元，人均100.3元；国家供养189人，供养金额（包括临时救济）共计1.32万元，人均69.8元。

1990年，全县60岁以上老年人达2.66万人，占人口总数的10%，老有所养问题十分突出。针对养老问题，县政府将其列入议事日程着力解决，扩大对孤老供养的投入，增建农村敬老院。在县民政局组织下，对孤老人群较为集中的乡（镇）采取“国家补助点、集体投入点、群众自筹点、社会捐点”的办法建起城关镇、扎佐镇、久长镇、六广镇、大石乡、六桶乡和县中心敬老院共7所，收养在院孤老33人。对散居孤老364人发放养老金25万元。

（二）孤儿供养

1978年，县在县城川会馆置有孤儿院收容孤儿，临时解决孤儿供养问题。1992年，根据贵州省民政厅《关于办理收养登记有关问题的通知》，对孤儿供养进行改革，使孤儿进入家庭感受家庭温暖和接受家庭教育。从此，孤儿由国家、集体供养转向社会家庭分散收养。按照收养政策规定，凡在省内查找不到生身父母的孤儿和福利机构抚养的孤儿，不管是国内公民或外国人收养孤儿作为养子，均需到县（市、区）民政部门办理收养登记。同时县民政局派专人参加安顺地区民政局举办的孤儿收养登记培训，学习《中华人民共和国孤儿收养法》。对孤儿收养实行正规化、法治化管理。至2005年，全县家庭收养孤儿39人。2006—2008年办理孤儿收养登记21人。

二、社会助残

（一）助残机构

1990年10月11日，县政府批转县民政局《组建修文县残疾人联合会报告》，批准成立县残疾人联合会，设立县常设机构执行理事会。县残联根据《中国残疾人联合会章程》，以“弘扬人道主义、发展残疾人事业、保障残疾人平等，充分参与社会生活，投身祖国建设，共享社会物质文明成果”为宗旨，履行代表残疾人的共同利益，维护残疾人的合法权益，团结教育残疾人，为残疾人服务，承担政府委托管理和发展残疾人事业任务的职能。

1996年，机构改革，县残联与县民政局合署办公。1997年11月，县政府根据《中共中央关于党政机构改革方案及实施意见的通知》和中编办《关于地方机构改革实施中若干问题的意见》，将县残联设为独立局级机构，并恢复残联执行理事会，把助残、残疾人事业列为政府工作职责。

（二）残疾儿童教育

1992年，县政府将对残疾儿童的教育纳入社会助残工作，投入建设资金500万元创办特殊教育学校1所。校舍为1182.93平方米，置有必需教学设施。配置教师13名接收“三残”（聋哑、智残、盲

县特殊学校教学楼

残）儿童入学，开设语文、数学、美工、体育、劳技、常识和职业教育等课程。1997年，首届毕业学生13人，其中1人从事矿产经营管理，4人开办发廊，5人从事养殖，3人开店经营，全部走上自食其力之路。到2005年，入学残疾儿童累计2250人，通过长达5年学习、教育，经县保健站测查，绝大部分“三残”智商比入学前大有提高，毕业后就业率达100%。

特殊学校助残教育得到社会肯定，校长苏桂秀被评为全国特殊教育先进个人，荣获全国残疾人联合会与北京江民新科技有限公司联合授予“江民特教园丁奖”。为使助残教育坚持不懈，在县教育局特殊教育调查和预测小组组织下，逐年对5至15岁的“三残”儿童调查、摸底、登记造册，将其列入助残教育对象。

（三）残疾康复

1990年，县残联开始组织实施残疾人“三项康复”工作，主要抓残疾人听力和语言训练，矫治小儿麻痹症，治疗白内障，使三残人在身体、精神和谋职方面得到改善。

县民政局向特殊学校捐赠学习、生活用品

2005年，国家和地方财政投资65万元，建起785平方米残疾人康复中心大楼，再后又投入600万元配置肢残人装配假肢、聋哑听力语言测试仪和残疾娇型器，开展对残疾人康复治疗和训练。城镇社区亦办起残疾人康复训练室，其中阳明大道残疾人康复训练室，置有价值15万元的康复训练器具18种，免费向残疾人开放。

到2010年，全县有6000名残疾人受益，其中“光明行动”使400名白内障患者重见光明，130名低视力患者提高了视力，60名聋哑儿童提高了听、讲能力，20名小儿麻痹患者进行矫治手术，提高了行动能力，40名肢残人装上假肢；30名躯残人装配娇型器，得到肢残椅车45辆。

（四）助残活动

1. 宣传

1991年5月，县人大常委会组织司法、民政、残联、工会、团委和妇联领导专门学习《中华人民共和国残疾人保障法》，并开展宣传，在第一个“全国助残日”就有全县各乡（镇）和县直30个部门参加的助残宣传，共设置宣传点7个，悬挂张贴宣传标语512条，发宣传资料2万份。县民政局和县残联出动宣传车播放录音广播，深入到集镇、乡村、工矿巡回宣传，听众达到7万人次。县广播电台全文播放《中华人民共和国残疾人保障法》连续2天共6次。

从1991年《中华人民共和国残疾人保障法》颁布到2010年，全县利用全国法定助残日活动，累计散发助残宣传资料20万份，社区居委会办墙报、黑板报宣传专栏500期，悬挂助残宣传条幅标语100幅，报刊、电视刊播助残活动的信息文章200条（篇），使关心残疾人的活动深入人心，成为社会的新风尚。

2. 捐献

1991年，根据《中华人民共和国残疾人保障法》规定每年五月第三个星期日为全国助残日。5月17

日全县开展第一个“助残日”活动，共有47个部门参加，为残疾人捐款3.4万元，慰问残疾人170人次，为残疾人办实事60件。1994年9月14日，县政府批转县残联理事会《关于开展为残疾人事业捐赠“一元钱”活动报告的通知》，全县掀起为残疾人排忧解难的助残热潮，活动当天，县直机关25个部门为残疾人踊跃捐赠，为残疾人办实事70件。

2005年6月7日，县民政局奉办“慈善一日捐”活动捐赠仪式，现场就收到52家单位900名干部职工捐赠4.2万元。从第一个“助残日”活动起到2005年底全县收到各类助残捐赠款11万元。2006年3月，修文嘉兴酒业董事长蔡心春等3名企业家向残疾人特殊学校捐现金3300元，支持残疾人事业。2007年5月助残日活动，县民政局、贵阳市残联、县残联和六桶乡政府筹资捐赠1万元为残疾人张兴得修建新房。随后对残疾人资助纳入社会保障，列为城乡居民最低生活保障之中，使助残捐赠转为向残疾人送温暖活动，以捐物、慰问方式为主展开。

3. 维权

1991年5月，县人大常委会将《中华人民共和国残疾人保障法》纳入县“二五”善法，对群众进行普法教育。县民政局组织开展的“平等共享、保障残疾人合法权益活动”在全县铺开。进入2000年，城镇社区居委会、社区残疾人协会和农村村委会开展为残疾人提供法律援助，维护残疾人合法权益的维权活动。其中设于龙场镇宾阳社区的县司法局第一司法所，无偿为残疾人提供法律援助的案件20件，提供法律咨询120人次，为残疾当事人获经济赔偿10万元，获得贵州省司法所和贵州省残联命名的“全省残疾人维权示范岗”称号、获司法部中国残联命名“全国残疾人维权示范岗”的荣誉。设于六广镇松江社区的第三司法所获得贵州省司法所和贵州省残联命名的“全省残疾人维权示范岗”称号。同时，县政府为维护残疾人合法权益，出台《关于分散比例安排残疾人就业的意见》，将残疾人就业工作纳入政府工作日程和法治化轨道体现残疾人就业权。2007年，贵阳市人大常委会视察团莅临修文视察残疾人权益保障工作开展情况，进一步推动了残疾人维权工作的开展。

4. 培训

2003年县，残联举办助残工作者120人参加的助残知识培训，继后开展帮助残疾人学习掌握技能，包括钩针编织、电子装配、保健按摩、书画摄影、养殖栽培，培训城镇残疾人职业技术、农村残疾人实用技术，以提高就业水平和谋生能力。到2010年，城镇残疾人就业培训120人，农村残疾人实用技术培训250人，全县各类残疾人培训含特殊学校学生共3000人次。与此同时，县政府和残联培训、指导和扶助残疾人参加省、市残疾人运动会、文艺汇演、书画美术和工艺制作比赛，并取得优异成绩，提高了残疾人自强其力的能力。县残联还推荐参加省、市特奥会运动员30人，被选中1名残疾运动员参加贵州省残奥会运动集训。经培训，残疾人参加的各项赛事曾荣获贵州省、贵阳市举办的残运会、工艺美术赛、文艺汇演、书法摄影和技能比赛多项奖励，共22人次。

残疾人职业技能培训

三、特殊病医治

1983年5月，县政府改革麻风病的防治，将麻风病医院（硝厂医院）隔离治疗改为社会防治，由防治医务人员送药上门进行家庭为主的治疗。1984年8月，成立县皮肤病防治所，抽调硝厂医院医生和护士日常办公，开展麻风病的调查、治疗、管理和科研。

截至2008年，硝厂医院共医治病人868人，治愈出院631人，还未治愈病人67人，医院尚留患者24人，散居患者43人，没有增加新病人。在院病人吃、穿、住、用、医全由县民政解决。病人的药品充足，日常生活用品齐具、粮油食品保障供给，自来水、电视、电话安装就位。医治经费纳入县财政预算，超出部分由市民政局补助。2009年，县卫生部门和县疾病预防控制中心按照《全国麻风病防治规划（2006—2010）中期评估方案》，对全县（2007—2009年）三年麻风病防治项目评估，5月完成评估报告。同时开展对麻风病治愈者的监测，在1月30日“麻风病防治日”组织人员到麻风病医院对病人和医务人员进行慰问，使患者和医生从组织的亲切关怀感受到无限的温暖，病人从内心深处发出感言：是党和政府的关爱，才使我们活命几十年。

麻风病防治硝厂医院

四、福利彩票推销

1990年3月，县政府根据贵州省社会福利有奖募捐委员会《关于认真做好社会福利有奖募捐基金使用和管理的通知》和有关章程，成立由副县长王正华任组长的县有奖募捐推销领导小组，具体领导社会福利有奖募捐卷的发行和销售，计销售即开型有奖募捐卷10万张，筹集社会福利资金2.6万元。1992年销售奖券筹资34万元，1993年销售40万元。

从1995年起，将社会福利有奖募捐卷销售改为发行社会福利彩票。1996年，发行彩票400万元，吸引县内及周边县（区）群众抽奖，两天时间全部售完。1999年11月，由县民政局主持发行450万元的社会福利彩票，持续5天，销售410万元。2001年，销售福利彩票90万元。2002年，参加贵州省“星光五一”福利彩票大联销活动，集中在县城推销5天，销售彩票51万元。继后，因受到“西安体彩宝马事件”影响，即停止即开型彩票的发行。

2005年起，将社会福利彩票销售改为电脑发行，全县设有福利彩票销售点10处，不间断地进行社会福利彩票销售募捐。销售彩票筹集的款项按5%的比例纳入县地方福利基金。县所获部分用于全县扶孤助残和敬老院、特殊学校以及残疾人康复中心的活动经费，弥补地方财政助残扶孤经费的不足，赢得社会各界群众的认可和参与，上为政府分忧，下为群众解愁。2010年，全县设福利彩票销售点13个，销售彩票78万元。

专记：两天销售彩票四百万元

1996年，贵州省社会福利募捐办、贵阳市民政局和县政府联合在县城推出400万元福利彩票有奖募捐活动。彩票销售之前，《修文报》、修文电视台、白云电视台、贵州电视台播放彩票销售消息。全县百辆客运汽车挂着彩票销售标语往来贵阳城区、白云区以及全县乡（镇）深入宣传，并制作布标60幅、纸标200幅、印发宣传单6万份，大小彩旗200面和红色飘带巨型氢气球2个布满县城大街小巷。标语中最吸引人的是“爱心使你乘中巴车而来，幸运让你开长安车而归”。为加强销售的组织工作，成立以县长陈开域为组长的彩票销售领导小组，负责具体的销售组织工作。并聘请省民政厅副厅长龙英玉、市民政局长王辅衡为顾问，组织县直机关职工100人担任销售员，组成颇具声势的“大兵团”销售阵容。

2月10日，在县城新开发尚未竣工长达850米的私营经济一条街（迎春路）搭台、设摊销售彩票。在领奖台奖品公示牌上标示：设400万元福利彩票有奖募捐特等奖2名，每名奖单排座长安微型货车1辆；一等奖40名，每名奖松下29寸画王牌彩电1台；二等奖40名，每名奖松下录像机1台；三等奖60名，每名奖长虹21寸彩电1台；四等奖80名，每名奖小天鹅全自动洗衣机1台；五等奖200名，每名奖51型永久牌自行车1辆；六等奖3000名，每名奖三色纯毛毛毯1床；七等奖6000名，每名奖被套1件；八等奖13.2万名，每名奖现金2元。销售现场彩旗飘舞，人群攒动，很快拉开了400万元福利彩票有奖募捐活动的序幕。

上午9时，数以计万的人流涌入一排排销售摊，购票、刮奖、兑奖者络绎不绝。全城大街小巷成群结队的人多在谈彩票、议奖品。毗邻市、区、县群众驾车纷至沓来，加入到有奖募捐行列里。不时，阵阵传出销售现场播音员的重奖快播和重奖者领奖的鞭炮声。大街上又是工作人员驾着挂红花的长安微型车，车上载着笑容满面的获奖者缓慢穿行。人声鼎沸，气氛热烈，销售现场不断推向一浪又一浪的摸彩高潮。11日下午，400万元福利彩票全部售完，创下了全省县级单位承办福利彩票销售的最高记录。

第二节　社会救济

一、救济改革

（一）救济储金会

20世纪70年代，在一些机关单位工会支持下建立起互助储金会，组织工会会员自愿集资，以储金借贷的方式开展互救互济活动，共同克服自然灾害及其他困难。80年代，部分农村群众也仿效建立起带有救灾、救急性质的互助储金会。1988年，根据省民政厅指示，在农村广泛建立起救灾、扶贫性质的互助储金会，开展“有灾救灾，无灾扶贫，帮助灾民治穷奔富”互帮互助。农村互助储金会由村民自愿参加，以村、寨为单位，投入钱或粮作为基金。年底在城关区就建立起农村互助储金会7个，参加农户1014户、6151人，入会资金20209元。1990年，全县发展到73个，入会村民9977户，46862人，拥有储金23.5万元，其中村民自筹14.4万元，县级单位赞助9847元，县民政局资助8.1万元，自筹粮食32.9万公斤。储金会由参股村民选举管理成员，实行民主管理，进行救灾备荒、扶危济困、应急解难、服务生产、促进安定和互助自救。当年储金会发放借款12.6万元，借粮24万公斤，使万户村民受益。

1991年9月，县政府根据贵州省政府办公厅转发省民政厅《关于发展我省农村救灾扶贫互助储金会的报告》精神，批转县民政局、县粮食局《关于下拨一九九一年农村救灾扶贫互助储金会粮食的报告》，对当年新建的40个储金会一次拨给玉米22.5万公斤支持储金会发展。1995年，储金会发展到149个，入会农户2万户，筹集资金71.5万元（含粮食折款20万元），其中民政部门资助30.5万元和粮食50.85万公斤。1996年，发生洪涝灾害，储金会借出储备金40万元，帮助4984户村民渡过难关。

1997年整顿储金会，全县保留159个，入会2.15万户，持有储金总额78.87万元。2000年，按照国家金融政策规定和建立农村最低生活保障、农村医疗保障制度，农村储金会不再发展。原建储金会功能逐步消失，自行解体。

（二）社会化捐助

1990年，全县大旱，秋粮收成大减，县政府收到省、地两级下拨的捐赠款16万元和粮油、食品、化肥、衣物、水泥等物资，均及时分发到灾民手中。9月，收到北京市捐赠的衣物3.6万件，县政府将其分送给1395个村寨的1.7万户受灾群众。1994年，发起全国抗洪救灾，县委、县政府倡议向灾区伸出援助之手，县机关、城镇居民为灾区捐赠衣物3.4万件。1998年8月，长江流域抗洪救灾，全县人民向灾区捐款22.52万元和衣物1763件。

2002年，县政府出台《关于救灾救济社会捐助经常化意见》，规定每年春节假满上班的第一周和十月中旬的第一周为“扶贫济困送温暖捐赠活动周”活动，由县民政局和乡（镇）社会事务办设立捐赠接收点，将所收的捐赠物品由民政部门统一转赠。继后将接收点改为“社会捐助接收工作站”，开展日常性的捐赠工作。并由县文明办、县总工会、团县委、县妇联、县工商联和县民政局联合印发《关于开展经常性社会捐助活动倡议书》，举行社会捐助活动仪式，县委书记黄乃铸、县人大常委会主任李玉轩、县长魏明禄和县政协主席王清义在启动仪式上带头捐款，然后职工、市民踊跃捐赠，当场收到捐赠款5297元。2008年四川汶川地震，县城街道居民为灾区捐款5.66万元。2010年，县境175个村受旱，农作物绝收2.84万亩，灾害直接经济损失2.23亿元。县委、县政府、县人大、县政协和乡（镇）、县直机关在县体育馆启动“搞旱救灾，爱如春雨”捐赠活动，现场收到捐款41万元，活动结束时共收54.3万元，全部汇往灾区赈济灾民。

社会化捐助

专记：政协委员解囊赈灾记

2008年，四川汶川遭受“5·12”地震特大灾害，县政协闻讯后积极投入抗震救灾社会化捐助。在政协正副主席的带动下，委员们纷纷伸出援助的手。贵州“好1多”乳业有限公司董事长柳云松慷慨解囊，一举捐款20万元和价值15万元的物资，贵州绿太阳制药业董事长沈子民捐献价值30万元的药品。利尔建材有限公司董事长周明贵捐款5万元，嘉兴酒业有限公司董事长彩新春捐款5000元。县政协机关中共党员积极响应号召交纳支援灾区的特殊党费8800元。捐赠结束，178名政协委员共向灾区捐款45.06万元和价值5.7万元的药品。

同年，县境遭受五十年不遇的凝冻灾害，为赈济灾民，县政协发挥联系各界人士的优势，开展“抗凝冻、抓重建、保民生”的捐赠活动。在政协七届三次会议的3天时间，全体到会委员捐款7.14万元和价值5.58万元的药品，于会议闭幕之前及时将捐款和药品转交县民政局支援灾区灾后重建。会议闭幕后，政协又组织30名委员到六屯乡开展“抓重建，保民生，送温暖”活动，进行文艺义演、医疗义诊、法规宣传、慰问灾民。活动开始当天就给300名群众义诊，并向六屯乡政府和学校捐赠灾民急需药品10件和灾民维修住房资金5万元，资助受灾学生助学金4000元和图书437册。继后，政协领导又带领政协委员和机关工作人员分别深入全县10乡（镇）查灾情、看灾民、抓重建，资助特困灾民抗灾资金5900元，灾后重建水池、道路资金1万元，拯救灾后民族文化资源资金1.3万元。同时县政协联系省、市政协，得到抗灾援助资金20万元和帮助灾区儿童助学资金2万元，展现出政协联系各界人士在抗灾斗争中“一方有难，八方支援”的正能量，深受群众赞扬，普遍反映：“政协知民情、助民力、解民忧，大灾之前保民生，真是县委、县政府的好帮手”。

（三）造血扶贫

1983年，县民政局根据第七次全国民政工作会议关于“规划扶贫是帮助贫困户改变贫困面貌的正确途径，各级民政部门应会同有关单位做好这项工作”的要求。针对以往有的贫困户把受助的救济金用来挥霍浪费，把救灾种子当成口粮食用等问题，反思扶贫得失，采取措施，对扶贫工作进行规划。1984年，县政府又根据第八次全国民政工作会的扶贫扶优精神，既帮助贫困户脱贫，又帮助劳动致富，采取帮技术、增收入，提高抗拒灾害袭击能力的造血扶贫措施，对有志气、懂知识、有能力、会打算的优抚对象优先扶持。明确指导思想的同时，坚持以国家扶助为辅，自力更生为主的方针，准确选择扶贫对象，以投资少、见效快、吹糠见米的项目给有作为的贫困户先运作起来，以点带面推开。贫困户朱明国和谢正言选择深山老林办牧场，3年创造财富18.4万元，向国家纳税1.5万元。1986年，县民政局“扶持发展生产，增加造血功能，解决长期温饱，引导劳动致富”原则，抓花钱少、扶贫面宽、见效快、收益高的种植业予以援助。使因受灾给予扶持的1576户，脱贫了751户，致富195户，收入过万元的18户。1988年，县委、县政府提出“救济有限，生产无穷”的方针，走“造血型”救助扶贫道路，引导受灾贫困户自力更生，发展生产，增强自身抗灾脱贫致富能力。1991年，实施国家“九五”扶贫攻坚计划，县政府主持全面开展“双扶”（扶贫扶优）工作，把社会救济从输血变为造血。1997年，全县贫困村开展县级干部包村，科局干部包户的造血扶助工作，形成举全县之力打扶贫攻坚战的态势，全年投入扶贫资金419万元，使35个贫困村1.9万贫困人口脱贫。至2010年，干部轮流到村到户扶贫一直持续。

二、自然灾害救助

20世纪80年代，各类自然灾害频发，涉及面广，又相对集中在县境西北贫困地区，救助工作量大，困难重重。其救济措施主要是民政部门发放救济粮和救济款。1980年，全县13个公社遭暴雨和冰雹，受害农作物3.83万亩。1982年4月16个公社遭冰雹伴雷暴雨，使30个生产队农作物颗粒无收，7月又遭虫灾，受灾农田达10.3万亩。1983年，25个公社遭冰雹、暴雨，损毁农作物3141亩、房屋3688间、伤牲畜410头。1985年春旱、伏旱，全县干旱面积达17万亩，冰雹灾害农田受灾20.6万亩。1988年，六广和小箐两个区虫灾，受灾面积2.4万亩，受灾农户上万户5.2万人。1989年，洪涝和虫灾，受灾农田24.8万亩，冲毁房屋185间。县委、县政府面对这一连串的自然灾害，分别部署了抗灾救灾工作，采取的主要措施有：一是组织灾区干部、群众千方百计展开生产自救，动员非灾区人力和物力支援，解决恢复生产的种子和种苗。二是民政部门立即下拨救济粮和救济款，首先任务是解决灾民的吃、住困难。三是各区、乡加强灾后检查，排除潜在的隐患，防止次生灾害发生。四是加强防灾抗灾宣传，动员群众退耕还林，保护生态环境，总结经验教训。

20世纪90年代，县境发生1990年旱灾、1991年洪涝，1992年、1994年和1995年三年冰雹灾害，1996年洪涝灾害，由于政府和群众总结了80年代自然灾害的教训，防灾的科学技术提高，增修提灌站和排洪渠道，设有六桶、六屯、小箐和久长4个防雹站，以及准确及时的天气预报，采取了防范措施，使受灾程度大减，无重大损失，救济工作量也逐渐减轻。

进入21世纪，自然灾害防治、救助工作列入各级政府的工作职责，增强防灾、救灾力度改救济为救助，其中2001年六桶乡遭雹灾，县委书记黄乃铸、县长魏明禄和六桶乡党委、政府率农业、烟草、民政、财政等部门组成抗灾救灾工作组深入到农户现场办公，发放信用小额贷款，组织化肥、种子、燃油、农药等物资帮助灾民恢复生产。2003年六屯和桃源河遭暴雨，副县长魏燕飞率政府机关干部赶往灾区调查灾情，安抚灾民，县委副书记县长石洪组织相关部门负责人到六屯组织群众生产自救。2007年7月，全县三次普降暴雨，县水利局组织技术人员赶赴抗灾第一线抢修水利设施，保障抗灾救灾顺利进行。2008年，县域全境遭受五十年不遇的凝冻灾害，从1月12日至2月14日持续长达1个月时间。县委、县政府遵照贵阳市委“抗凝冻、保民生”紧急会议精神，提出“凝冻在持续，灾情在加重，措施要得力”的部署要求，出台“抗凝冻、保民生”12条具体措施，要求全县人民发扬雪凝无情人有情的精神，开展灾情就是命令，民生就是政治的抗冻战役，每天有1500名县、乡干部在抗冻第一线，为群众办抗灾救助实事3216件，解决生产生活难题1862个，发放救灾款432万元，使群众度过严寒的凝冻难关。

自然灾害救济

1980—2010年自然灾害及救济一览表

表5—02—01

受灾年份	主要灾害	受灾农田面积范围（亩、村、乡）	直接经济损失（万元）	损坏房屋（间、户）	伤亡人数（人）		救灾款（万元）	救济粮（万公斤）	救助灾民	
					死	伤			户数	人数
1980	冰雹、暴雨	38277	—	725	7	5	18.65	—	—	—
1981	干旱	32203	—	—	—	—	32.7	—	—	—
1982	冰雹	10.3万亩	—	268	—	3	10	—	—	—
1983	暴雨、冰雹	3141	20	3688	1	23	36.4	—	—	—
1984	凝冻	11832	54	—	4	9	28.4	—	—	—

续表

受灾年份	主要灾害	受灾农田面积范围（亩、村、乡）	直接经济损失（万元）	损坏房屋（间、户）	伤亡人数（人）		救灾款（万元）	救济粮（万公斤）	救助灾民	
					死	伤			户数	人数
1985	冰雹	206375	50	—	—	—	45.5	—	—	—
1986	洪涝、虫害	249605	—	—	—	—	93.45	270	7718	30000
1987	冰雹	7550	—	207	—	—	82	167	9893	48594
1988	干旱、虫灾	24086	—	—	—	—	—	484	10324	52414
1989	洪涝、虫灾	248000	—	185	—	—	—	—	10620	52331
1990	干旱	9个乡	—	—	—	—	80	200	11787	57154
1991	洪涝	—	—	356	7	4	60.8	166	1300	95645
1992	冰雹、洪涝	—	—	—	—	—	—	65.2	14560	65987
1994	冰雹	169942	3121.5	5299	3	6	—	74	2616	11272
1995	雹雨	244个村	6280	3896	8	11	46	42.5	9300	42000
1996	暴雨、洪涝	217个村	4200	—	5	—	144	95	7045	30000
1997	暴雨	2800亩	—	—	—	—	—	—	—	1.5万人
1999	暴雨	3036亩	301万元	227	—	—	—	—	—	—
2000	暴雨	20869亩	—	320	失踪2人 死亡1人		—	—	—	—
2001	干旱	232000	5316	57	—	—	58	—	1670	12000
2002	洪水、冰雹	116000	3899	196	—	—	206	—	—	13600
2003	暴雨、洪水	102000	1145	99	—	—	106	27	—	12000
2004	暴雨	81000	146.58	50	—	—	129	50	—	47000
2005	雹雨、洪涝	41000	1679	228	—	—	178	22	—	8000
2006	暴雨	—	—	—	—	—	69.5	—	3566	10594
2007	暴雨	—	1582	58	—	—	72.4	—	—	3620
2008	凝冻	—	1亿元	328（户）	—	—	432	—	—	
2009	干旱	—	—	—	—	—	122.57	7.0	—	8000
2010	干旱	21.97万亩	5441	—	—	—	165.5	400吨	4000	—

三、农村特困救济

1982年，农村实行家庭联产承包责任制，政府将丧失劳动能力、生活贫困人员列为社会救济的重点，建立起农村特困群众救助制度，主要由社、队（乡、村）进行特困群众的生活帮救，民政部门辅以生活补助，解决特困户的生活困难。

农村贫困救济

2003年10月，县民政局贯彻贵阳市民政局《建立和完善农村特困群众社会救助制度实施方案》，组织工作组协助乡（镇）对农村需要救助的特困对象摸底排查并造册登记，对救助对象进行分类，核定救助标准。经过排查、审核，全县因残、因病和因灾的特困对象1084户1494人。接着由民政局统一签发《贵州省农村特困户救助证》，按季度将救助款拨发到乡（镇）社会事务所，发给特困户。当年预算发放金额33.5万元，分别由省、市、县三级按4:2:4比例承担，实际发放37.2万元，救助特困人口1510人。

2005年4月，县政府召开全县乡（镇）长和民政干部会议，界定农村特困救助对象，根据农村不断变化的情况对全县特困对象摸底调查，做到确实特困者不能遗漏，以促进社会的稳定和谐。经过再次排查，全县特困对象为3027户，5087人。根据黔府办〔2005〕29号文件规定，特困人员每人每季救助75元，于当年1月起计发，救助费由省财政拨付，全年救助金共116.5万元。此外，对持有《贵州省农村特困群众救助证》的特困户家庭成员给予医疗救助，对住院治疗费满500元以上（含500元）的给予25%的救助费补贴，个人全年累计享受医疗救助金额原则上控制在3000元之内。自此，农村特困群众的救济即纳入社会低保统筹管理。

四、城镇贫困救济

（一）老弱病残对象救济

1980年，对城镇老弱病残贫困对象除每年给予衣物补助外，还定期定量发放救济费每月每人5.5元至7元。1984年，定期定量补助标准调为10至15元，经过调查核定全县城镇贫困户122户293人，其中享受定期定量救济90户103人，按月发给10至15元生活救助费，全年发救助费1.3万元。1990年，享受城镇贫困补助和定期定量救济共计154人，其中享受定期定量救助55人，救济标准每人每月30元。1998年改革城镇贫困救济工作，实施城镇居民最低生活保障制度，将城镇居民生活困难纳入城镇居民最低生活保障范围。临时发生特殊困难者，可向社区居委会提出申请，由乡（镇）社会事务所给予临时困难补助。

发放城镇居民最低生活保障金

（二）退职职工救济

1982年，县政府根据国务院“关于进一步做好60年代初被精减退职老职工生活困难救济工作”精神，对虽已按退职时工资的40%给予救助，但仍然生活困难的情况给予医疗费救助，全年按24元计发死亡丧葬补助费，按生前4个月救助费的总额计算给予补助。1982年，享受原工资40%救济的有13人，随后逐年审批办理，1983年批准16人，1984年批准32人，1985年批准67人，当年年底享受40%救济的老职工共118人持有《退职职工救济证》。1992年根据贵州省民政厅〔1992〕36号文，退职老职工定期救济证统一更换为《六十年代初精简退职老职工定期救济证》，1995年为退职老职工发放一次性救济金每人225元。

对未能按标准办理享受原工资40%救济的其他退职老职工生活困难的给予社会救助，使其生活水平不低于一般居民。生活困难者从1989年开始每年补助90元，1991年提高为100元，随后逐年提高，到2005年增至272元，全县补救对象共298人。随后逐步纳入城镇低保对象，按低保标准给以救助。

五、流浪乞讨救助

1985年恢复1973年撤销的收容遣送社会流浪乞讨人员的收容遣送站，由县民政局和公安局管理，负责收容人员在收容期间的生活救助和遣送回原籍等事宜。1985—1986年收容29人，其中县内直接收容入站17人，外地收容转入12人，县里转交到相关的收容、福利机构17人，遣送回原籍12人。1987年至1989年收容70人，送回原籍43人，转交相关机构27人。1990—1997年收容遣送72人都分别给予临时救助。

2003年，县收容遣送工作依照国务院《流浪乞讨人员救助管理办法》，改革收容遣送，坚持流浪乞讨人员自愿接受救助，政府无偿救助的原则，帮助县内流出返乡的乞讨人员解决生产、生活困难。对外地流入县内的乞讨人员动员返乡，给予返乡路费和返程期间生活补助费。其具体的管理措施为：一是将救助经费纳入县财政预算，以保障工作经费；二是采取开放式管理，对流浪中的残疾人、孤寡老人和未成年人救助须通知其家属认领或由专人送护回乡；三是外地因灾流入县内的乞讨人员，给予返程车费和生活补助，实行自动返乡；四是精神病患和痴呆流浪人员转交精神病医院和社会福利院。从此，对流浪乞讨人员的救助不再称作收容遣送救助。

2005年，县政府将农村特困人员救助对象纳入社会最低生活保障，对每户人均收入未达到60元的给予补差，全县平均补差29.7元，同时政府将救助扶贫工作列入为群众办实事，特困人员基本生活得到解决，使县内流浪乞讨人员大幅度下降。外地流入县内的乞讨人员也相应减少，其个别乞讨者以升学、丧葬、返乡和治病方式在城镇乞讨，分别经县民政局和镇社会事务所劝返。从2005—2010年，确因灾乞讨救助75人，对县内和邻近县的给予车费和路途生活费补助自行返乡，对外省和较远的县、市采取一级救助方式，负责转交至贵阳市民政机构的车辆交通费和路途生活费，对生病的乞讨人员就医住院，由民政支付医疗救助费，累计发放救助费6.5万元。

第三节　优　抚

一、烈士褒扬

（一）烈士陵园扩建

1984年，县城北门外的烈士陵园多年失修，县七届人大二十一次会议作出《扩建烈士陵园的决议》，8月1日，扩建开工。陵园占地16.7亩，依山布局。内筑7级平台。第一级为园门，用青石嵌“革命公墓”弧形横额；第二级为群众悼念广场；第三级竖“革命烈士永垂不朽”纪念碑；第四级为革命烈士墓群，包括红军烈士墓1座共5室，解放初期因剿匪牺牲的烈士墓31座，革命干部墓16座；第五级为松柏、花草园地；第六级为纪念馆；第七级为殡仪馆，内有400平方米的骨灰存放处。陵园中央竖起高19.5米红棉磨石修建的纪念碑，碑上刻有中国工农红军六军团团长萧克题书：“革命烈士永垂不朽”，碑下方刻有中共修文县委和县人民政府撰著的纪念碑文。1985年8月，县人民政府主持将散葬在县境的烈士迁入陵园。1998年，县委将烈士陵园命名为爱国主义教育基地。

2005年县政府拨款29万元，再次修建陵园，平整园区场地5116平方米，人工凿平地基60立方米，素土夯实地基2280平方米，辅青石板2100平方米，植木塔柏、黑松等优质树15种共1000余株营造出一片良好的氛围。步入园林式的烈士陵园，映入眼帘的是颇具特色的林木葱茂、环境幽静、布局端庄的祭祀场所，瞬时即呼唤起对烈士的肃然致敬。

（二）祭奠活动

1984年扩建“烈士陵园”告竣，1985年迁入散葬烈士遗骨后，每年祭扫活动如期进行。1987年4月5日清明节，县委、县政府在烈士陵园举行盛大的悼念活动，县直机关职工、学校师生、公安干警和驻县部队官兵1200人前往烈士墓前祭扫，缅怀革命先烈的丰功伟绩。

1998年，县委将烈士陵园命名为县的“爱国主义教育基地”，每年清明节、“八一”建军节、“十一”国庆节，县城中、小学生和幼儿园小朋友轮流到陵园祭扫烈士墓，接受革命传统教育。2005年4月5日，县人民武装部、县文明办、县民政局、团县委、县教育局组织千名团员、青年、武警、消防战士、少先队员瞻仰烈士墓，在烈士纪念碑前举行共青团入团、少年加入少年先锋队宣誓活动。请离退休老同志给青少年讲述革命故事，接受革命传统教育，鼓励大家学习革命先烈精神、继承烈士遗志认真学习、努力工作，为建设富强、民主、文明的祖国贡献力量。2009年4月3日，县精神文明办公室组织县直机关和县城中、小学学生代表为烈士扫墓，县四大班子主要领导和离退休老同志代表前往烈士陵园举行清明祭扫活动，深情缅怀为人民利益英勇献身的革命烈士。

祭扫烈士墓活动

（三）烈士追认

2004年4月，贵州省政府授予在1995年6月执行抓捕罪犯过程中牺牲的六桶乡社会治安综合治理办干部余春跃和罗永杰革命烈士称号。2007年2月，贵州省政府将2004年9月在县城巡逻执勤时被罪犯杀害牺牲的公安巡防队员刘熙追认为革命烈士。3月28日，县政府将烈士刘熙的骨灰安葬在县烈士陵园。随着县政府为在社会主义建设新时期，维护社会治安与罪犯作斗争中献身的烈士家属颁发《革命烈士证明书》。2008年，县民政局编纂的《修文县民政志》，将新时期牺牲的烈士记入全县革命烈士名录，成为人们永远敬仰的英雄，永垂不朽。

二、军烈优抚

（一）抚恤

1980年6月，县政府遵照国务院《革命烈士褒扬条例》，将烈士抚恤金标准在原有基础上均增加300元，由县民政局对牺牲、病故的军人实行一次性抚恤计发给牺牲、病故军人的父母、配偶或子女。1985年，县民政局根据民政部、财政部《关于调整革命烈士一次性抚恤金标准的通知》，一次性计发抚恤金以牺牲时月工资标准的40个月计发。1986年3月27日根据民政部、财政部《关于调整军人、机关工作人员、参战民兵、民工、因公牺牲、病故一次性抚恤标准的通知》、再次调整抚恤金标准，从当年7月1日起分别按新标准计发：军队干部、志愿兵、机关工作人员因公牺牲一次性抚恤按其牺牲时的月工资20个月计发；军队干部、志愿兵、机关工作人员病故一次性抚恤金按其病故时的10个月工资计发；义务兵、参战民兵、民工和工资低于所在部队23级正排职干部牺牲的，按20个月工资计发，病故按军队23级正排职干部的10个月工资计发；被军委或大军区授予英雄模范称号的军人，因公牺牲或病故增长一次性抚恤金的1/3；立二等功以上军人，因公牺牲或病故，增长一次性抚恤金的1/4。离休、退休军人，机关工作人员因公牺牲或病故，一次性抚恤标准也按此规定执行。除一次性抚恤外，其家属还享受定期定量抚恤，以每人每月计发：烈属22元，病故军人家属16元。从1990年至1998年，农村烈属和因公牺牲军人家属每人每月68元，病故军人家属63元。1999年农村烈属和因公牺牲军人家属每人每月95元；城镇烈属和因公牺牲军人家属每人每月105元。2002年农村烈属和因公牺牲军人家属每人每月160元，城镇烈属和因公牺牲军人家属每人每月185元。2003年农村烈属195元，因公牺牲军人家属190元；城镇烈属255元，因公牺牲军人家属250元。其中2001年县人民武装部在职军人尹研斌病故享受一次性抚恤1.2万元外，其在三穗县农村的父母享受定期定量抚恤每月250元，使他们精神得到安慰，生活得到保障。

2004年8月1日，根据《军人抚恤优待条例》，确定军人死亡一次性抚恤金：烈士按其工资的80个月计发，因公牺牲按其工资的40个月计发，病故按其工资的20个月计发。并对获得中央军委授予荣誉称号的增发35%，获军队军区级单位授予荣誉称号的增长30%，立一等功的增发25%，立二等功的增发15%；立三等功的增发5%。2005年，全县享受一次性抚恤的军人共21名。截至2010年，有29名已故军人享受一次性抚恤。

（二）优抚

1984年，按照民政部、财政部对残疾军人优抚进行调整的意见，在原标准的基础上分别提高35元至75元。1994年，根据民政部、财政部《关于提高部分优抚对象抚恤补助标准的通知》精神，对在乡伤残军人优抚标准在原基础上分别提高160元至1400元，在职伤残军人分别提高50元至300元。

优抚证

2004年10月，遵照国务院、中央军委《军人抚恤优待条例》，对残疾军人的优抚标准进行调整、提高，优抚不再分在乡、在职，实行统一标准，全县计发残疾军人优抚（保健金）21万元。2005年，全县86名残疾军人，计发优抚金35万元。2008年，残疾军人增至89人，计发51.67万元。2010年全县伤残军人85人，发优抚金59万元。

2009年，县政府不断深化、完善优抚机制，针对县境优抚对象年龄普遍

偏大、体弱多病的实际，将包括在乡的老复员军人等优抚对象在内全部纳入新型农村合作医疗保险，采取大病统筹资金与大病救助相结合的办法，解决重点优抚对象看病难的问题。并出台《修文县优抚对象保障实施办法》，完善优抚保障机制。为确保优抚对象生活水平与社会经济发展同步提高，对在乡老复员军人优抚金每人每月增加65元，人年定补增为5040元，全年共发定补金97.71万元，并发慰问金372万元。2010年人年定补上升为6080元，全县复员退队军人276人，计发优抚金146万元，并发慰问金463万元。

（三）优待

1984年5月，县政府根据《中华人民共和国兵役法》制定现役军人家属优待标准：城关区、扎佐区为一类区，每户年均150至200元；久长区为二类区，每户年均120至150元；小箐、六广区为三类区，每户年均80至100元。有条件的乡和企业单位为鼓励青年参军和军人在部队立功，还自筹资金增发优待金。马家桥乡发给现役军人家属的优待金占全乡人均劳动收入488元的19.4%。驻县国防工业部属五三三技工学校还从工会费、职工福利费中提取部分资金，增发军人家属优待费。1999年7月29日建军节前夕，贵州省委副书记、省长钱运录在贵阳市委副书记、市长孙国强陪同下莅临修文，慰问看望老红军战士邓绍明和革命伤残军人黄远华。向他们致以节日的问慰，并赠送慰问金。

2008年，全县有城镇现役军人27人，计发军人家属优待金1.16万元；农村现役军人186人，计发优待金3535元。有复员军人299人，其中解放前复员军人月发给优待金330元，解放后复员军人月发给优待金325元；带病退伍军人34人，每季度发给优待金387元，共发复退军人优待金125万元。有牺牲军人家属29户，病故军人家属5户，牺牲军人家属优待金每户每季度发给优待金1500元，病故军人家属每户每季度发给1275元，共计发牺牲、病故军人家属优待金15.18万元。全县所有的军人优待共计发优待金142万元。2009年，按照上年度城镇居民可支配收入，农村村民人均纯收入标准兑现义务兵家属优待金，共发放优待金97.7万元。2010年，全县义务兵现役军人家属74户发放153.8万元。

三、故亡职工抚恤

（一）一次性抚恤

1978年5月起，故亡职工的抚恤由民政转为县劳动局管理，以死者1年的工资或退休金总额给予抚恤，并给予丧葬补助火葬300元，棺材葬400元。至1990年优抚标准未变。继后，随着社会经济发展抚恤标准逐年调整、提高。2007年，县政府执行贵州省人事厅、财政厅黔人通〔2007〕117号文新规定，调整一次性抚恤对象和标准。其抚恤对象包括县直机关事业单位职工、社会灵活就业人员、企业交纳社会保障金人员（含贵阳市直管的工商、税务、质监、邮政、电信、供电和金融部门的故亡职工）。其标准为：党政机关、事业单位的职工病故后，按其生前基本工资或退休费的20个月计发，同时给予离休人员2000元、一般职工1600元的丧葬补助。抚恤费金额由县人事劳动社会保障局核算、审批，由县财政局一次性拨发。企业职工和社会灵活就业人员参加社会保障者病故后，根据黔劳厅文件规定，一次性抚恤费由社会保障部门发给，标准为1.64万元，包括抚恤费1.4万元和丧葬补助费2400元。当年，社会保障部门办理故亡人员优抚33名，共计发一次性抚恤金38.71万元。2008年办理25人，计发42.36万元。2009年，故亡职工25人（含离休人员2人），计发4.08万元。办理社会灵活就业人员参保病故者家属生活补助7户，计发2.6万元。2010年，故亡职工51人（含离休人员3人），计发一次性抚恤金2.88万元。办理社会灵活就业人员参保病故家属生活补助9户，计发3.35万元。

（二）定期定量补助

1978年初，执行对故亡职工没有劳动力的家属定期定量补助，其标准为：家居农村者每人每月6至10元，家居城镇者10至15元，由县民政部门管理。当年5月定期定量补助统一上调为30至40元，由县劳动部门管理。至1990年标准未变。2007年起，县政府根据贵州省人事厅、财政厅黔人通〔2007〕117号文和贵州省劳动社会保障厅黔劳社〔2008〕13号文的规定，对故亡职工和社会灵活就业人员及企业交纳社会保障金人员其家属无经济来源、生活困难者给予定期定量补助。其中党政机关事业单位故亡职工的家属无经济来源者，按职工生前供养家庭成员按月计算享受定期定量生活补助，一般职工家属补助310元，离休人员家属补助410元。补助金由县财政逐月发给。企业职工和社会灵活就业人员参加社会保障者病故，其家属无经济来源者享受补助，其中企业已退休病故职工的家属每月补助310元，企业在岗职工和社会灵活就业人员病故，以参保者个人累计交纳的社会保障金计算，由社会保障部门补发给家属。截至2008年，社会保障部门计发企业职工和社会灵活就业人员参加社会保障病故者家属生活补助金68.8万元。2009年至2010年，故亡职工的家属定期定量补助以一次性抚恤金发放。其中，2009年办理故亡职工家属一次性抚恤金补助25人，计发103.06万元；2010年办理27人，计发120.55万元。

第四节　安　置

一、复员退伍军人安置

1980年，县革委按照“从哪里来，回哪里去”的原则安置复员退伍军人。农村入伍的军人退伍后，一般都回乡从事农业生产，其中部分有专业技术者，可在企业单位招用工人时优先录用。带病返乡军人和二、三等伤残军人及城镇居民入伍军人可安置到企业或事业单位工作。城镇中在单位就职入伍军人，退伍后可返回原单位复职。

1987年，为鼓励军人安心服役，对“从哪里来，回哪里去”安置原则进行调整，提出把军人个人专长、服役期的表现与退伍安置挂钩，使在职军人积极参加部队“军地两用人才”的锻炼，努力学习技术。是年，安置退伍军人17人，其中，农村入伍军人6人。到1990年，复退军人中的军地两用人才成为农村经济建设的带头人，他们返乡后带领农村群众走致富道路。退伍军地两用人才朱德全于安全用在部队学到的管理知识和技能，以军人的魄力和作风，担任马家桥水泥厂正、副厂长，仅用半年时间使该厂扭亏为盈。退伍军地两用人才杨富贵，贷款自办砖厂做出成绩，光荣地出席贵州省军区民兵致富“双先”代表大会和县“双扶”先进代表大会。

1993年，随着企业的经营机制、人事制度、产权体制改革，出现城镇退伍军人安置难的问题。1999年，贯彻贵州省人民政府黔府发〔1999〕49号文件精神，提出试行安置任务有偿转移的办法，鼓励退伍军人自谋职业，当地政府对自谋职业者给予帮助。2001年，按照省人民政府下发《关于做好退役士兵接收安排工作的通知》要求，采取政府安排工作与退伍军人自谋职业相结合，执行“按系统分配安置和包干安置”的政策，由省、地、县三级负责，以县安置为主。2002年，执行省人民政府《退役士兵安置任务有偿转移和自谋职业试行办法》，县政府实行指令性安置与经济补助自谋职业相结合，共接收退伍义务兵、复员转业士官135人，其中农村回乡104人，按政策安排工作31人。其中指令性安置13人，自谋职业18人，发给自谋职业一次性补助金47万元。

2003年，县政府根据《中华人民共和国兵役法》、贵阳市人民政府《城镇退役士兵安置任务有偿转移和自谋职业实施意见》制发《城镇退役士兵安置任务有偿转移和自谋职业实施意见》，规定自谋职业者一次性经济补偿金发放标准：城镇退役士兵按上年城镇居民人均可支配收入的3倍、退役士官按5倍进行一次性补助。其中一期士官一次性补助基数增发20%，二期士官增发30%，西藏服役的增发10%。凡荣立一等功的增发30%，二等功增发20%，三等功增发10%。凭退伍军人《自谋职业证书》领取一次性补助金，凡领取一次性补助的退伍军人，政府不再安排工作。自谋职业者按国家税务总局《关于退役士兵自谋职业享受有关税收优惠政策的通知》规定享受相关税收优惠。至2005年，安置城镇退伍军人113人，其中计发63名自谋职业一次性补助金144万元。2006年，安置96人，城镇退伍21人，城镇士兵安置9人，自谋职业12人。2007年，安置124人，城镇士兵安置22人。2008年，安置156人，计发自谋职业一次性补助金73万元。2009年，接收退役士兵126人，其中城镇退役士兵34人（含转业士官）中有5人根据个人意愿安置就业，29人自谋职业，自谋职业率为85%，发放待安置期间生活补助费2.08万元。2010年，接收退役士兵123人，其中城镇退役士兵24人（含转业士官），有4人是根据个人意愿安置就业，20人自谋职业，自谋职业率为85%，发放待安置期间生活补助费1.92万元。

二、工程建设拆迁安置

（一）电站移民安置后扶工作

1979年，继续开展对猫跳河梯级水电站修文库区移民进行搬迁安置的后扶工作，主要是帮助移民改善生产、生活条件。至2008年，共投入后扶资金212.9万元，其中县财政投入11万元，县农业局投入180万元，相关部门资助21.9万元，帮助移民兴修水利，兴建提灌站，建设饮水小水窖，安装输电线路，改善居住环境，开发非耕地，购置树苗，化肥。

2009—2010年，县水利水电建设移民局逐年筹集移民资金共126.5万元，开展移民安置后扶工作。其中，帮助安置在六广镇滨江村移民进行住房改造，开发建设滨江码头；帮助谷堡乡红星村移民发展生产，开发建设果木经济园，派技术人员指导改良品种，给村民购买优质树苗和化肥，支持库区创办乡镇企业2个，家庭副业26户等脱贫改造项目。

大中型水库移民搬迁新址

（二）公路建设拆迁安置

1998—2001年修建贵（阳）毕（节）高等级公路，对县境段沿线村民住房拆迁、耕地占用进行直接补偿、帮助村民重建住房。其中涉及拆迁较多的小箐乡崇恩、凤凰、大兴、小箐、大坝等村共58户村民的住房，采取直接补偿方式，共发补偿金97.6万元，由村民就地另建住房安置。

2002年，县城开发建设贵（阳）毕（节）公路修文联络线——阳明大道，县政府执行贵阳市人大常委会人大字〔2001〕年11号文《贵阳市房屋拆迁管理办法》，从城镇建设需要出发，按照联络线被征地的拆迁房屋等级、面积给予合理补偿。对较为集中的阳明村拆迁，从妥善安排居民生活出发，采取统一规划修建村民安置小区，建起占地61.5亩，建80余户民用住宅的阳明新村。

2003年，扎佐镇扎南公路建设，拆迁村民住房66户，拆迁面积5773.5平方米。2004年，修建久（长）大（石）公路，拆迁小箐乡全兴村6户村民住房，均采取直接补偿方式，按住房面积每平方米补偿200元，由村民另建新居。

（三）索风营电站建设拆迁安置

2004—2006年建设的索风营电站是国家西电东送重点项目，电站库区建设涉及县境拆迁安置的有六广镇、洒坪乡辖的6个村，142户629人。库区集水后淹没土地767.45亩，淹没住房5015.06平方米。县水利水电建设移民局按照国家移民政策，实行有土安置和经济补助结合，分别采取就地后靠安置、投亲靠友安置、分散与集中安置多种方式，对黔西县境迁入修文的移民全部采取农业安置，以有土安置为主，生活直补为辅的办法，帮助解决住房。采取大集中，小分散方式安置在生产条件好、地理环境优越的龙场镇9个村，并在集中安置点进行了水、电、路等基础设施配套建设。

继后，县委、县政府根据国务院《关于完善大中型水库移民后期扶持政策意见》、财政部《关于大中型水库移民后期扶持基金征收使用暂行管理办法》和国家发改委、水利部办公厅《大中型水库移民后扶持政策有关配套文件的通知》，组织各级党委、政府及移民局、水利局、财政局、发改局、扶贫办、农业办对索风营电站建设移民齐抓共管，使移民安置从转移性向开发性改变，从“输血”向“造血”转变，达到移民搬迁得出，迁出后稳得住，从解决温饱走上致富。对安置在六广镇新中村、松江村、沙坡村的移民修建住房给予补助；为安置在六广镇六广村和龙场镇幸福村、新生村的移民修建水池、解决人畜饮水、安装输电线路、修筑农用机耕道和串户路；为六桶乡顺江村11户移民的房屋开裂，补助每户修缮费3000元；此外，还为移民培训农业实用技术2500人次，缝纫、家政服务技术300余人次，组织移民劳务输出83人。

（四）贵阳特殊钢厂建设拆迁安置

2008年，贵阳钢铁厂决定迁至扎佐，随后又与首都钢铁厂联手组建首钢特殊钢贵阳钢铁公司。县委、县政府为迎接首钢·贵阳特殊钢新材料循环经济项目在县落户，开拓扎佐工业园建设，抽调政府、人大、政协领导组建首钢贵阳特殊钢新材料循环经济项目建设指挥部，开展项目征地、拆迁和安置工作。项目规划区征地4940.63亩，河道征地267.78亩，扎（佐）六（屯）公路扩建征地81.13亩，村民搬迁安置征地307.32亩，进场道路征地161.48亩，涉及搬迁村民612户，住房1560栋，拆

三里村移民安置点扎佐珍珠河社区

迁房屋面积8.71万平方米，拆迁安置采取直接一次性补偿方式。对完全没有土地的村民允许自由择业或进厂打工或开店经商，向城镇居民转移。2010年，工程建设方案开始实施，征地、拆迁，安置工作全面展开。年底完成进场道路扎（佐）六（屯）公路改扩建，完成厂区“三通一平”（水通、路通、电通、场地平）一期工程竣工。

（五）同济堂产业园建设拆迁安置

2009年11月，贵州同济堂产业园贵酒项目落户龙场镇，项目建设涉及城北、潮水、阳明3村农户545户。县委、县政府成立该项目建设协调领导小组，负责项目建设拆迁安置工作。2010年1月，协调小组与贵酒公司按照“有利于化解矛盾、有利于统一政策标准、有利于项目建设推进、有利于失地农民利益保障”原则，制订出《贵州同济堂产业园贵酒项目征地拆迁安置补偿方案》。方案按照筑府发（〔2009〕99号和〔2009〕101号文规定，调高土地补偿标准，并给被拆迁户增加社会保障安置。成为贵阳市首家按新政策执行拆迁安置补偿的项目。该项目在87天有效时间里使红线内房屋21户全部拆迁，支付房屋拆迁费和村民建房过渡费158.99万元，为首批拆迁户90人办理社会养老保险。

（六）贵州轮胎股份有限公司异地改造拆迁安置

2010年8月，贵州轮胎股份公司异地改造落户扎佐工业园区，在丁官村征地2300亩，建年产高性能子午线轮胎1280万条生产线。改造项目涉及农户500户，拆迁房屋292栋，拆除房屋面积2000平方米。并涉及拆迁天主教圣地坡墓地迁坟400余座。拆迁安置按照筑府发〔2010〕6号文规定，新征地补偿安置政策，给予被征地和房屋拆迁补偿。同时，在扎佐镇新庄村征用荒山19亩给天主教圣地坡墓地置换搬迁。年底，完成征地，拆迁进展达85%。

三、地质灾害搬迁安置

20世纪80年代至90年代，政府对地质灾害救助给予一定补助，由灾民就地搬迁，村委会协调搬迁建房用地。2000年，县政府对地质灾害搬迁分灾害不同程度，采取不同措施，其中对死亡3人以下，经济损失100万元以下的小等级地质灾害，采取就地补助安置；对死亡3—10人，经济损失在100万元—500万元的中等级地质灾害，采取以有土安置、搬迁安置和直接补助相结合。

2005年，县政府依照《贵阳市自然因素造成重要地质灾害隐患治理搬迁方案》的规定，对地质灾害的补助出资比例以市级承担40%，县级和受益人共同承担60%进行组织、匹配。对中级地质灾害需要搬迁安置的受灾户，市财政每户补助4000元，不足部分由县政府出资，并协调受益人共同解决。搬迁安置所需要的建房宅基地由村委会、乡政府协调解决。户数较多集中的搬迁由乡政府择地统一安置。按照标准，对受中等级地质灾害较集中的谷堡乡山地滑坡受灾村民50户，由乡政府统一规划，在富裕村修建统一的移民住房，每户面积80平方米。对六桶乡联合村的中心组、麻窝组、白石组、丰收组、水沟组因山地滑坡受灾村民120户，统一安置在盐

地质灾害移民安置

井村新集镇的移民一条街。对小等级地质灾害，以村为安置地，就地另择地修建住房，政府给予建房补助。2007年，对六广镇广义村龙洞滑坡，受灾村民23户，市财政补助9.2万元，县民政局、交通局、发展改革局共筹资补助50万元，帮助灾民就地另建住房。2008年，对小箐乡2户、大石乡2户、六桶乡3户、龙场镇2户和六广镇1户遭受分散地质灾害的受灾村民，根据各户受灾程度给予补助2000元至5000元，就地安置。

第五节　村（居）委会建设

一、组织建设

（一）村民委员会

1978年，全县农村普遍建有“政社合一”的基层组织，公社下置生产大队，大队下置生产小队。生产大队建革命委员会，主要负责人为主任，管理大队日常事务和民事等；生产小队设小队长一职，主要负责管理农业生产及村民事务。

1984年，全县农村实行政社分离，建立起由上级推荐村民选举村主任、副主任和委员组成的群众性村民委员会。1988年7月，县政府根据《中华人民共和国村民委员会组织法（试行）》，在小箐乡郭田村进行村民民主选举试点，把干部选举权完全交给村民，由村民自主选举村委领导，组建农村自治组织基层政权。试点工作结束，于1989年3月由县民政局组织在全县铺开第一届村委会的法定选举。选举前组织村民代表学习和培训，广泛向村民宣传《中华人民共和国村民委员会组织法》，讲解村委会的性质和任务，进行年满18周岁的法定选民登记。由乡（镇）党委和选举筹委会提出村委主任、副主任和委员建议名单交选民酝酿讨论，集中反馈意见后，于正式选举前5天公布候选人。选举原则上实行村主任等额选举，副主任和委员差额选举，凡得到参选选民数或选民代表数过半的，以票多者当选。任期3年，届满换届。

1992年和1995年分别进行第二届和第三届选举。1998年，第四届选举正值《中华人民共和国村民委员会组织法》正式颁布。为搞好本届选举，县政府成立由分管民政工作的副县长任组长，县政府办、民政、农办、司法、财政、公安、妇联和民族宗教等部门为成员的换届选举工作领导小组，乡镇也相应组建指导小组。县民政局翻印3000册《《中华人民共和国村民委员会组织法》，发至全县1056个村民组组织村民学习。由于宣传、组织工作到位，县乡齐抓共管，村民选举意识增强，踊跃临场

六广村换届选举

投票，彻底改变前三届提着票箱走家串户和到田间地头投票的现象，使选举正规化、法治化，保质按时完成换届任务，选出新一届村委会主任211人和副主任817人。

2001年第五届选举，村委会主任、副主任和委员的年龄、文化结构发生变化，所选成员有高中文化程度的39人，有30岁以下年轻人19人，31岁至40岁73人。候选人的提名亦有变化，不再由乡（镇）党委或选举领导小组（筹委）提名候选人，而是由村民直接提名，并实行差额选举，使一批具有政治、文化素质、年富力强、热心为村民办事者，充实到村委会中去。

2004年10月，第六届选举，县委、县政府成立由县委副书记和分管民政工作的政府副县长分别担任指导小组组长指导选举工作。县、乡两级财政投入选举经费30万元进行选举宣传、登记和培训，使全县217个行政村的换届选举一次成功率达82.9%，换届选举完成率为100%。

扎佐镇村民换届选举工作全面展开

2007年，第七届换届产生的村委会，加强建章立制，完善班子建设，认真履行工作职责，使村务步入正轨。2008年，在127个村的两委（村党支委、村民委）推行“两推一选”（村党支委、村民委推荐村民投票选举），有34个党支委和村委会实行“一肩挑”，282名两委委员交叉任职，使村委会的班子结构得以优化。成为村民自我教育、自我管理和自我服务的基层群众自治组织。

2009年，按照贵阳市委实施“双百工程”（百名基层干部上机关，百名机关干部下基层）的要求，从村干部中公开选拔副科级领导干部，有符合条件的22名村干部报考，经审查、笔试、面试、体检、考察，本着“敢抓敢管理、敢作敢为、敢闯敢试”的条件，全县从村干部中选拔5名乡（镇）副科级领导干部，同时选派4名乡（镇）干部到村挂职。8月，县委常委、组织部部长陈雄标到六桶乡调研农村基层组织建设，实地查看复兴、春江两个村的两委建设情况，从点到面对六桶乡基层组织建设给予肯定。10月19日，按照省委组织部、省人事厅组织农村优秀青年提升学历的要求，全县启动2009“一村一大”（一个村一名大学生）学历提升，在全县217个行政村中挑选60名农村优秀青年，参加贵州广播电视大学农村行政管理大专班学习，为加强村委会建设培养一批留得住、用得上、懂科学、有技能、会管理的基层管理人才。

（二）社区居委会

1978年，在县城及扎佐街道按照《城市居民委员会组织条例》要求，全县共建有7个街道居民委员会。居委会由3至5人组成，设主任一职负责主要日常工作，下设若干居民组，设组长承担街道事务管理。

1990年初，县政府按照《中华人民共和国城市居民委员会组织法》要求，针对城镇居民委员会规模小、管理范围窄、工作职责不明确而影响社会经济发展需要的问题，对居委会进行调整、充实，分别在居民人口集中的城镇和街道设置居民委员会，居委会的选举与村民委员会选举同步进行。其中城关镇（县城）6个，扎佐镇2个；久长镇1个，六广镇1个，小箐乡1个，马家桥街道1个。全县城镇街道居委会共设12个，选出居委会主任12人，副主任及委员50人。至2002年，街道居委会建制未变。

2003年，随着城镇经济发展，大量农村人口涌进城镇，其中有的转成居民，进城经商、务工的人口不断增加，县城（龙场镇）人口从原来的2.8万人增至3.5万人。城区面积从原有的1.8平方公里拓宽为3.7平方公里。扎佐、久长、六广3镇分别列为全国、全省和县的卫星城、试点镇和重点镇，据此情况县政府根据国家大力推进城镇社区建设和国家基层政权建设的战略部署，进行新形势下的城镇管理体制改革。11月，在社区建设指导委员会和县民政局的组织下，进行社区居民委员会的选举。经贵阳市民政局审批将县城（龙场镇）街道委员会整合成为龙岗、宾阳、虎山、栖凤社区，扎佐镇街道建成襄阳、景阳社区，久长镇建长久社区，六广镇建松江社区，小箐乡建小箐社区，全县共建9个社区。

2005年，根据城镇发展需要拟增置3个社区，其中龙场镇增置阳明社区和马家桥社区，扎佐镇增置万江社区，后来，阳明社区和马家桥社区未建，只增置万江社区。增置的社区与原建的社区同时选举社区居委会。每个社区设5至7名委员组成社区居委会。社区班子成员有来自街道先进工作者和热爱社区工作的积极分子、下岗待业人员、机关退休干部。龙场镇虎山社区选举精力旺盛的原三角山水泥厂下岗职工赵金祥（中共党员）、热心为居民办事的原街道居委会成员李玉仙（中共党员）、和城关镇党委原书记何兴友组成社区居委会班子，增加了领导班子中共党员的成分，使社区党务工作开展打开新的局面。龙岗社区，选出破产企业县酒厂职工、街道待业人员朱福云、薛占琼、郑贵兰、马正凤、陈燕、高伦海等热心为群众办实事的青壮年，使居委会班子呈现年轻化，增添了居委会的新鲜血液，保持了贵阳市政府授予的“民主法治示范社区”“三优精品社区”的殊荣。

2009年，县、乡（镇）政府选派4名乡（镇）机关干部到村（社区）挂职，创建“三优精品社区”，利用既有创建成果，推进“学习型社区”建设，确保“学习型社区”达标30%的要求。龙场镇和扎佐镇申报的2个“三优精品社区”和1个“民主法治示范社区”，按标准得到验收。与此同时，为探索农村社区建设，创建农村社区管理体制和运行机制，按“生产发展、生活宽裕、乡风文明、村容整洁、管理民主”要求，县民政局拟在村民较集中居住的龙场镇中哨村建起农村社区，从中取得经验，以利面的推广。

二、政务公开

2003年，全县217个村委会和9个社区居委会逐步建立健全村（居）委会各项规章制度，其中包括《村务公开制度》和《社区政务公开制度》规定的民主管理，把村（居）重大事务决定权、日常事务参与权、干部评议的知情权交给村（居）民，增加行政管理透明度，极大地调动群众参政的积极性，使村（居）委会成为名副其实的自我管理组织。村（居）委会采取公示专栏和明白手册（卡）方式公开村（居）委会的事务，使群众放心。谷堡乡谷堡村公示专栏设有“事前公示”、“重大事项公示”、“群众点击”“有问必答”等栏目。平寨村“两委”拟在村里建设集贸市场，活跃乡场商贸，增加村民收入，鉴于资金难以筹措，不敢轻易决策，便将方案公诸于众，广泛征求村民意见。方案得到村民赞同，纷纷表态出资出力，使原先预算需30万元建设的集贸市场，在村民支持下仅花去19万元便建成了。

2004年，洒坪乡和六屯乡实施社会治安“群防群治一体化”，建设治安网络，拟成立有村民参加的联防队和巡防队加强治安管理。乡党委和乡政府将此思路向村民公示，征求意见和建议，走群防群治维护治安秩序之道路。公示得到村民赞成，联防队、巡防队当即建立，治安秩序得以维护。这一做法被省、市公安部门作为典型经验在全省推广。10月，扎佐镇喻家街村一位村干部为女儿争茅草房改造资助款，村委会张榜公示，征求群众意见，群众认为村里比她困难的人更需要“茅改”资金，这种锣面对鼓面的公开、评议，促使干部放弃指标。按此作法全县1.16万户“茅改”资金分配全部圆满完成。

社区居委会将社会低保发放、殡葬情况、救灾救助捐赠、计划生育、环境卫生、黄赌毒查处、临时困难补助、安置优恤、劳务推荐、财务支出和党支部建设等一一公示，使居民在选人、议事、管理、监督等方面成为社区真正的主人，人人关心社区、个个热爱社区。同时规范社区干部行为，消除群众对社区工作的误解，使干群关系得以改善，“三自”（自我管理，自我教育、自我约束）的自觉性不断提高。

2005年，在村务公开的基础上，实行村级财务委托核算制度。村里成立村民民主理财小组，乡（镇）建立村级财务核算代管中心，使村级财务更加公开透明，更便于广泛监督。城镇社区居委会把远程教育网络作为政务公开的载体，将社区的工作目标、职责职能、办事程序、财务管理、工程建设和热点、难点等30个项目在宽带网络上公开。从实行村务公开到2005年的3年中，县、乡、村三级共投入资金30万元，建政务工作公示专栏530个。全县217个村和挂牌的10个社区（含1个农村社区）的岗位职责、工作目标、办事程序等固定公开事项，公示率为100%；农村茅草房改造、种粮直补、计划生育、涉农收费公示率和村（居）事务、财务公示率亦达100%。

2006年，村（居）委会根据中办发〔2004〕17号文件精神，落实开好两会（村民大会、村民代表大会）、做好三项工作（村务公开、民主评议、督促检查）、落实四项权利（选举权、管理权、知情权、监督权）、推广五项制度（村级议事两个“三分之二”制度、村级财务乡代管制度、村级财经委员会制度、村支两委坐班制度、民主评议制度）的要求，开展村（居）政务公开管理活动，活动推出“咨询日”和“解答日”，加强对群众意见的收集和解决，使村（居）务公开经常化、正规化，深受村（居）民的拥护。

虎山社区居委会布置政务公开

2009年，县委、县政府针对农村不断发展变化的新形势，印发《修文县2009年村务公开管理安排意见》，制发年度村务公开目录，使村务公开民主管理目标和任务进一步制度化和规范化，使村务公开的范围和内容更加完善。4月，召开全县基层组织工作培训会，将民主管理村务作为对村委会干部培训的主要内容，使基层干部不仅知道村务公开的目的意义，而且掌握具体的实施办法。与此同时，两次组织力量对全县村务公开进行专题检查，及时发现并解决存在的问题和不足，对排查出的“难点村”14个，按贵阳市村务公开指导小组的《通知》要求，县委连续下文，就“难点村”的治理问题建起领导干部联系制度，并印发《村务公开和民主管理“难点村”治理实施方案》。9月15日，贵阳市纪委综合室主任刘佐带队莅县检查基层党风廉政建设，深入六屯乡独山村和扎佐镇大河村，采取调查问卷、开座谈会、实地察看方式，检查农村基层“党务、事务、财务”公开情况，营造农村基层组织风清气正环境。10月，县委、县政府又拟订《“难点村”治理工作验收标准》，以督促指导为抓手，采取多种措施强化村务公开制度。经过一年努力，14个“难点村”已有7个村达到验收标准。

三、自治工作

（一）村民自治

1984年政社分设，将农村生产大队革命委员会改建为村民委员会，生产队改建为村民小组，建立起

六广镇村民自治培训

村民自我服务、自我教育和自我管理的基层群众性自治组织。2002年3月，县委、县政府成立基层组织建设领导小组和村民自治工作领导小组，在全县10个乡（镇）建立村民自治领导小组。在乡（镇）自治领导小组领导下开展治保、禁毒、调解、青年、妇女、计生、殡葬等自治工作，实行村民自我教育、自我管理。2003年，把文明村寨建设、党务工作、科技兴村、创建和谐社会、发展生产等纳入自治工作范围，旨在实现村民的自我服务。久长镇清水村开展文明村寨建设，村委会狠抓树立清水新形象工作，以改变村民的精神面貌为抓手营造"平安清水"，加强村、组的治安防治，做到村民小纠纷不出组、大纠纷不出村，排解矛盾靠自身，使全村治安秩序井然，村民安居乐业。为实现村民自我管理和自我服务，村"两委"发动村民每户出资35元，投工23个，将村人畜饮水站迁至四方井，保障全村人畜饮水安全。同时在村中修建垃圾池8个，进行村寨环境治理。村里老共产党员谌贻康去世、村"两委"组织全村男女老少参加遗体告别，火化葬于村公墓，改变殡葬习俗。小箐乡崇恩村村民长期过着"养牛为犁田，养猪为过年，养鸡为换盐巴钱"的农耕生活。在村"两委"的带领下，选择科技兴村道路，因地制宜发展肉牛、肉鸡、肉鸽养殖，全村617户村民家家都成养殖专业户，2005年摘掉贫困帽，实现村民自我服务。六广镇的六广村"两委"在开展村民自治活动中重视妇女和老年人工作。村妇女组织不仅服务于保护妇女儿童权益，还增添构建和谐家庭、敬孝老人的内容。妇女更新观念，提高自身素质，开展"双学双比"（学文化、学技术，比成绩、比贡献）活动。妇女们在外为孤老做实事，在家孝敬父老，使全村老人老有所居、老有所依。大石乡沙坝村青年文清友在周边"麻将"群影响下，东游西逛，参赌成癖。村委会领导抓住他的弱点，有的放矢地进行耐心说服教育。文清友觉悟后决心戒掉赌癖，远离赌场走正道，向信用社小额贷款，购进制砖机一台办起小型砖厂。适逢村民"茅改"和危房改造，大大方便村民购砖建房，又使自己就地售砖、找到致富门路。2009年，县委、县政府推出"平安村（社区）"创建活动，并纳入乡（镇）、村（社区）综合考核目标责任，采取"一票否决"的奖惩制度，深化村（社区）自治工作。村（社区）在开展村（社区）自治、维护社会和谐、稳定工作中，查办团伙违法案件3件，查办农村"三改一气"工程中职务犯罪5件5人。建立起党委、政府引导，政协参与村（社区）居民自我教育、自我管理的长效自治体系。

（二）社区自治

1990年1月，贯彻实施《中华人民共和国城市居民委员会组织法》同时，把居民自治管理纳入居委会重要工作议事日程。2003年，居委会改建为社区，社区自治工作范围不断扩大。2004年2月，县委办、县政府办印发《关于进一步加强社区建设的意见》，要求按照《示范社区标准》建设和谐社区。社区居委会一改以往单纯负责街道环境卫生、调解民事纠纷、维护院落治安、计划生育的工作职能，把社区党建、构建和谐社区、关心青少年成长、劳务培训就业、建设无毒社区、抚优助残、社会募捐、居民生活保障都纳入社区自治工作范围。到2008年，党务工作成为社区自治重要工作。社区党支部根据城镇经济发展需要，在个体经营户中发展党员，接收外来经商、务工的党员参加社区组织生活，吸收入党积极分子参加社区党员大会，接受党的知识教育。龙场镇龙岗社区发展党员15人，虎山社区发展党员11人；栖凤社区发展15人，宾阳社区发展13人。在关心下一代工作中，各社区制定出培养、关怀少年的规划，鼓励少年学文化、学知识；开展讲文明、讲科学、讲道德、讲和谐的“四讲”教育，营造出少年无辍学、无犯罪、无吸毒、无不孝顺、无进网吧的良好氛围。社区居委会依靠老干部、老战士、老教师、老社工、老专家的协助，在社区设立学校岗、法制教育岗、禁毒教育岗、文化娱乐监督岗。龙场镇龙岗社区根据入驻社区境内实验小学、修文二中和修文中学的情况，与学校联手加强对学生的管理。节假日免费让学生上网社区远程教育，配合学校开展“6·26”禁毒宣传，上学放学时维护通往学校门前路段车辆的交通秩序。虎山社区针对社区境内网吧密布的情况，明确专人佩戴贵阳市统一颁发的网吧巡查证，制止学生到网吧。聘请老教育工作者和离退休干部给社区内的学生补课，把讲道德、树新风、爱祖国、遵纪守法搬上故事会，寓教于乐，使学生受到革命传统教育，关心下一代活动呈现出“朝阳、夕阳共同拓起一个太阳”，“老少共建”和谐文明社区的新气象。

2005年，社区居委会积极培训待业人员，推荐待业者就业。虎山社区推荐就业人员76人；栖凤社区安排贫困人员零就业家庭公益性岗位就业67人，龙岗社区利用远程教育网络培训新东方厨师、家政服务和电焊工技术，向社会推荐保安、家政服务和厨师岗位就业人员50人，因培训、推荐成绩突出，获得贵阳市“零就业家庭援助”先进社区称号。宾阳社区安排公益性岗位就业人员39人，使零就业家庭12户有业可就。

2006年，为进一步达到社区居民“三自”（自我管理、自我教育、自我服务）的要求，社区居委会分别办起市民学校、禁毒学校、科普学校、老年学校、计生人口学校。成立残疾人协会、科普协会、老年协会、老年体协、信鸽协会、花鸟协会、计划生育协会、关心下一代协会组织。栖凤社区科普协会、科普学校成绩显著，荣获贵阳市“百万公众网络学习工程”示范社区称号。龙岗社区老年太极拳队获2006年贵阳市老年太极拳比赛第二名成绩。宾阳社区的老年鼓乐队、龙灯队和腰鼓队每当节假日都要上街风光，成为县城一道亮丽的风景线。同时社区居委会把调解民事纠纷作为社区安定团结的重要工作来抓，龙岗社区和栖凤社区位居县城老城区，在旧城改造、房屋拆迁、居民拆旧翻新住房中矛盾突显，居委会主动上门调解，减少法律起诉，避免冲突，化解矛盾30起。针对社区居民就业、子女上学、计划生育、社保医疗、困难补助等事务，居委会都详尽调查处理。仅此工作，虎山社区给群众出示的证明、证件达2000份，尽了为政府排抚和为群众解难之责。

2008年“5·12”汶川地震抗震救灾，社区居委会全体工作人员上街设点、走家串户为灾区募捐，一星期内虎山社区居民捐款3000元，党员交特殊党费（为“5·12”救灾）2800元，退休干部鲍崇德、离休干部张怀成交特殊党费各为1000元；龙岗社区居民捐款8000元，交特殊党费800元；栖凤社区居民捐款2.4万元，交特殊党费2000元；宾阳社区居民捐款1.5万元，交特殊党费2000元。

2010年，贯彻落实中央《关于进一步净化社会文化环境促进未成年人健康成长的若干意见》和全省净化社会文化环境集中统一行动电视电话会议精神，实施“社区育人工程”，开展“做一个有道德、有知识的人”主题活动，县政协委员田志英在龙岗社区龙岗花园文化走廊创办“亲近知识，享受阅读”的田园书屋。书屋面积130平方米，推出阅览园地、借阅之窗，置有自然地理、科普知识、生活百科、亲子园地、儿童文学、艺术鉴赏和绘图漫画等青少年阅读书籍2万册，成为西南最大西西弗书店的合作书店。每日进店购、阅图书者达200多人，节假期间，书屋坐无虚设，中、小学生居多。学生家长也常进店咨询可供儿童阅读图书，经营者热情介绍，提供服务，为丰富青少年文化生活提供一块净土，为开展社区自治工作起到积极的推动作用。

第六节　婚姻管理

一、婚姻法宣传

1980年9月，县政府为贯彻执行第五届全国人民代表大会第三次会议通过的《中华人民共和国婚姻法》，全面展开婚姻法宣传，提倡晚婚和计划生育，开展保护妇女和儿童合法权益活动。1988年，县政府贯彻贵州省政府认真贯彻婚姻法、禁止早婚早育工作会议精神，组织县民政局、县妇联、县计生办和司法局在全县开展禁止早婚早育宣传活动。1989年6月，针对不登记同居、婚姻登记率下降问题，县直有关部门和乡（镇）配合进行全面广泛的《中华人民共和国婚姻法》宣传教育活动，对违法婚姻进行清理，宣布无效婚姻154对，依法处理362对，补办婚姻登记手续1776对，从而增强广大群众的婚姻法制观念。11月，在申请办理结婚登记的青年中宣传贯彻安顺行政公署民政局、卫生局和妇女联合会《关于在城关镇范围内开展婚前保健检查的规定》，并成立县婚前保健领导小组，负责宣传贯彻婚前体检。

1990年，纪念中华人民共和国第一部婚姻法颁布40周年，第二部婚姻法颁布10周年，全县结合计划生育工作，大规模宣传《中华人民共和国婚姻法》。县民政局、计生办和城乡居（村）委会通过墙报、电影、电视进行宣传，组织宣传队员121人，出动宣传车10台次深入村寨、发放宣传资料2100份，使全县80%的成年人受到《婚姻法》的教育，增强了群众新的婚姻家庭观念，一定程度控制了非法同居。

2000—2008年，把《中华人民共和国婚姻法》宣传与计划生育、创建和睦家庭结合起来，在全县开展“婚育新风进万家”活动，投入宣传资金300万元。经过宣传、教育和学习，使新的婚姻观念、优生优育观念、晚婚晚育、婚前体检、孝敬老人和创建和睦家庭走进千家万户。全县相继评出“五星级农户”“五好家庭”共2400户。

二、婚姻登记

1980年11月，按照民政部发布新的《婚姻登记办法》，明确区公所或街道办事处、农村人民公社管理委员会为婚姻登记机关。1984年恢复乡的建制后，乡（镇）民政所为婚姻登记机关。为贯彻贵州省《婚姻登记办法的实施细则》，对婚姻登记人员进行培训和考试。随后实行逐年培训持证上岗。1991年，全县培训31名婚姻登记人员，对考试合格的30人颁发婚姻登记员资格证书。

1992年8月，县民政局印发民政部《婚姻登记管理人员规则》至各乡（镇）民政所，同时全县统一使用民政部制作的《结婚证》、《离婚证》、《夫妻关系证明书》、《解除夫妻关系证明书》等婚姻关系证件，使婚姻登记工作规范化、法治化。1996年，全县建立婚姻登记网档案。2001年在全县普遍推行婚前体检，对婚前患有影响婚姻家庭疾病的不予办理或推迟办理婚姻登记。2002年，实行《计划生育通用卡》，育龄青年需要登记者持卡方可办理结婚登记手续。

2005年，全县婚姻登记1904件，民政办理协议离婚171件。2007年，办理婚姻登记224件和协议离婚217件。2008年办理婚姻登记2655件和协议离婚237件，在不包括法院判决的离婚案件在内，全县结婚与离婚比率中，离婚比率逐年增加，以1985年离婚82对与结婚比率1.5%相比，增至16%。其中，县、科局级干部离婚比例大，除社会、经济和家庭观念变化外，不良婚姻观影响突出，缺乏化解矛盾调解机制，单亲子女增多。2009年5月，县民政局按照《中华人民共和国婚姻法》和《婚姻登记条例》进一步规范婚姻登记工作，提高婚姻登记服务质量和登记人员业务素质，举办2009年婚姻登记工作培训班。8月，派婚姻登记专职人员到贵阳市民政局参加专业培训，增加家庭婚姻矛盾调节内容，全年办理婚姻登记2023对，办理离婚登记263对。2010年，全县办理婚姻登记2500对，其中县民政局办理982对。全县办理离婚登记470对。

婚姻法宣传和婚姻登记现场

第七节　收容救助

1978年，县置有收容站，专门负责对外来流入灾民、流浪乞讨人员的救助、教育、安置和遣返工作。1979年执行贵州省民政厅、公安厅《关于收容遣送工作中几个问题的通知》，撤销县收容站，对暂不能返乡的流浪人员转送安顺地区收容所。1985年恢复设立收容遣送站，隶属县民政局，配备专职管理人员，具体负责收容工作。负责收容遣送社会流浪乞讨人员的，由县民政局和公安局管理，负责收容人员在收容期间的生活救助和遣送回原籍等事宜。1985年至1986年收容29人，其中县内直接收容入站17人，外地收容转入12人，县转交到相关的收容、福利机构17人，遣送回原籍12人。1987年至1989年收容70人，送回原籍43人，转交相关机构27人。1990—1997年收容遣送72人都分别给予临时救助。

进入2000年，流浪乞讨者以所谓的“返乡”“求学”“就医”“葬母”进行乞讨，给收容救助工作增加困难。2003年，县收容遣送工作依照国务院《流浪乞讨人员救助管理办法》，改革收容遣送，坚持“流浪乞讨人员自愿接受救助，政府无偿救助”的原则，帮助县内流出返乡的乞讨人员解决生产、生活困难。对外地流入县内的乞讨人员动员返乡，给予返乡路费和返程期间生活补助费。其具体的管理措施为：一是将救助经费纳入县财政预算，以保障工作经费；二是采取开放式管理，对流浪中的残疾人、孤寡老人和未成年人救助须通知其家属认领或由专人护送回乡；三是外地因灾流入县内的乞讨人员，给予返程车费和生活补助，实行自动返乡；四是精神病患和痴呆流浪人员转交精神病医院和社会福利院。县财政把收容、送返流浪乞讨人员的救助经费纳入财政预算，救助主要对象是：家居农村流入城镇的乞讨人员，城镇中流浪街头的乞讨人员，露宿街头生活无着的乞讨人员。对流入城镇的残疾人、孤寡老人和未成年人实行无偿救助，联系家属认领或护送返家；对因灾、因病生活困难流入城镇的乞讨人员实行返乡车费、生活费补助、动员返乡；对流浪的痴呆人员、病情危重人员、精神病人员，发扬人道主义精神，护送安置到社会福利院或精神病医院；对无法查明姓名和家庭住址的流浪人员，民政部门负责协调安置，杜绝遗弃和相互推诿，并将当年收容救助的流浪人员情况和人数年终上报贵阳市民政局备案。

2004年，随着社会经济发展，农村、城镇启动基本生活保障和新型农村合作医疗，致流浪乞讨人员减少。2005年，县政府将农村特困人员救助对象纳入社会最低生活保障，对每户人均收入未达到60元的给予补差，全县平均补差29.7元，同时政府将救助扶贫工作列入为群众办实事，特困人员基本生活得到解决，使县内流浪乞讨人员大幅度下降。外地流入县内的乞讨人员也相应减少，其个别乞讨者以升学、丧葬、返乡和治病方式在城镇乞讨，分别经县民政局和镇社会事务所劝返。2005—2010年，确因灾乞讨救助75人，对县内和邻近县的给予车费和路途生活费补助自行返乡，对外省和较远的县、市采取一级救助方式，负责转交至贵阳市民政机构的车辆交通费和路途生活费，对生病的乞讨人员就医住院，由民政支付医疗救助费，累计发放救助费6.5万元。

第八节　社会团体与民办非企业管理

一、社会团体管理

20世纪80年代，县内社会团体逐年增加，诞生各类民间社团组织，1988年国务院明确社团组织由民政部门统一管理。1990年，县民政局按照国务院办公厅转发民政部《关于清理社会团体的请示报告》和贵州省民政厅对清理社会团体的工作部署，开始对县内社会团体的复核、清查、登记，对非法成立和存在严重问题的社会团体给予取缔或不予登记，计核实全县有社会团体98个，其中学术类团体8个，行业类团体11个，专业类团体79个。

1991年10月，县政府针对社会团体存在的混乱状况，组建由副县长王正华任组长的社会团体整顿领导小组，召开社会团体清理整顿工作会议，制定出对社会团体撤、并、留的具体整顿措施开展清理整顿工作。经过清理整顿，对符合社会团体申办条例的16个社团正式办理登记手续。1999年，民政局贯彻落实国务院《社会团体登记管理条例》和贵州省委办公厅、省政府办公厅《关于加强民间组织管理的意见》，对社会团体分支机构，包括县计划生育协会、消费者协会和个体劳动者协会分别设立在全县10个乡（镇）的24个分支机构进行登记注册，使全县社会团体管理工作步入规范化、法治化。2005年全县有社会团体29个。2009年发展到41个，其中农村科技类种植、养殖协会27个，行业协会7个，民间协会4个，公益和谐类协会3个。2010年经审核仅存39个。

2010年社会团体一览表

表5—02—02

名　称	机构代码	主管单位	名　称	机构代码	主管单位
修文县计划生育协会		计生局	修文县摄影家协会	58067100—2	县文联
修文县个体私营企业协会	7366360—1	工商局	久长镇永兴村果树协会	58413375—4	县科协
龙场弘驿果蔬种植协会	750171036	县科协	农民合作经济组织联合会	58725966—X	县供销合作社
新农夫绿色产业协会	750172776	县科协	农业生产资料流通协会	58725961—9	县供销合作社
修文县煤炭行业协会	76137736—3	县煤炭管理局	六屯乡安全村果树产业协会	59418650—X	县科协
驴坊反季节蔬菜协会	761397321	县科协	修文县食品流通行业协会	59418101—2	县工商局
扎佐无公害萝卜种植协会	785472410—0	县科协	修文县幸福小箐公益协会	59638098—X	小箐乡政府
扎佐大河村艳红桃种植协会	785472437	县科协	修文县旅游行业协会	—	县工商联合会
六广滨江村蔬菜种植协会	79529226—1	县科协	谷堡乡平滩村猕猴桃种植协会	59938562—0	谷堡乡政府
流管沙坡肉牛养殖协会	780187354	县科协	久长镇永兴村香猪养殖协会	59937729—2	久长镇政府
龙场镇延晚番茄种植协会	78548436—6	县科协	修文县书法家协会	06990901—X	县文联
新埔顺祥肉牛生猪改良协会	79525132—0	县科协	六广岩脚村果蔬种植协会	07200201—3	县科协
六广镇广城村果蔬协会	79529454X	县科协	贵州省修文县商会	—	县工商联合会
龙场镇马口村蔬菜协会	67540437x	县科协	修文县见义勇为工作协会	08565622—7	县综合治理委员会
修文县猕猴桃协会	68843571—4	县农办	修文县特种设备行业协会	09032005—8	县质监局
六屯都堡村蔬菜种植协会	692705406	县科协	六屯布依文化发展协会	31429214—9	旅游广电局
修文县斗牛协会	565011698	旅游广电局	龙场镇安全生产协会	31422983—6	安全生产监督局
修文县信鸽协会	565046460	旅游广电局	修文县志愿服务联合会	32215596—1	团县委
龙场镇水塘村养殖协会	58067131—X		谷堡乡上硐村猕猴桃种植协会	34702836—01	县科协
和谐修文促进会	569248430	县委统战部			

二、民办非企业管理

2001年4月，县政府贯彻落实国务院1998年10月颁布的《民办非企业登记管理条例》，加强对民办非企业登记管理工作，成立民办非企业管理领导小组，由县民政局民政科负责民办非企业登记管理的日常工作。6月，县民政局下发《关于民办非企业登记工作的通知》，开展对民办非企业登记广泛宣传和复查登记，到年底已为教育类民办非单位春蕾幼儿园、寓教幼儿园、南方幼儿园、叮当幼儿园、县工会学前班、景阳中学、英才中学和华驿中学等8个民办学校进行复核登记。2003年，对农村经济协会组织龙场弘驿果蔬种植协会、贵阳市修文县新农夫绿色产业协会进行登记，到2005年种植、养殖类民办非企业协会已发展到7个。

社会团体管理机构

2007年9月，县民政局依照国务院《民办非企业登记管理条例》制发〔2007〕1号《（民办非）登记驳回通知》：“认定1995年组建的股份制县属医疗事业单位县中医院国家所有资产部分还未界定清楚，没有进行国有资产验证，医院的法人代表没有进行选举，与现有法人代表不符”，驳回中医院登记民办非企业的申请，履行对民办非企业登记管理职责，县中医院民办非企业登记一直搁置。至2010年，全县登记民办非企业18个，其中教育类7个，医疗类5个，科技类3个，文化服务类3个。

2010年民办非企业一览表

表5—02—03

名　称	机构代码	主管单位	名　称	机构代码	主管单位
贵阳是修文县叮当幼儿园	430378185	县教育局	修文协和医院	58068374-0	县卫食药监督局
修文县春蕾幼儿园	78979853-0	县教育局	修文百信医院	79881575-0	县卫食药监督局
县工会学前班	07203091-1	县教育局	新春骨伤科中药民营科研	56503238-4	县科技局
修文县景阳中学	429970165	县教育局	修文汤斯德生物研究中心	761364909	县科技局
修文县华驿中学	42997079-8	县教育局	修文康庄桑果食品研究所	68843317-x	县科技局
修文县寓教幼儿园	785482969	县教育局	修文林业科技服务中心	69750706-	县科技局
修文县南方幼儿园	77531021-5	县教育局	修文县半边天老年公寓	—	县民政局
修文县中医中药临床研究会	56924247-7	县科协	修文县民政社区服务中心	—	县民政局
修文民生医院	57713004-5	县卫食药监局	修文阳明文化研发中心	56501715-x	旅游文体广电局

第九节　地域管理

一、县界勘定

1983年12月，修文、开阳两县组成联合调查组，对县境与开阳县临边界处的相互的插花地进行实地踏勘，签订《修文、开阳两县境界调查修正协议书》，确定修文县的沙坝、大林坡、沙溪、田坝、干燕等处插入开阳县境之地属于开阳县，开阳县的高程（胡子田与田坝之间处）、百花山、大田坝、猫洞等插入修文县境之地属于修文县。至此，县界边域为北纬26°45′—27°12′，东经106°21′—106°5′，全县地域面积为1071.7平方公里。

1991年1月20日，县政府要求解决扎佐区三元乡与贵阳市乌当区新场乡边界纠纷，以修府报〔1991〕1号文向安顺地区行署提交《关于请求解决我县扎佐区与乌当区新场乡边界权属纠纷的紧急报告》。因争议地涉及贵阳市和安顺地区，未能及时解决。7月，县国土资源管理局和贵阳市白云区国土资源管理局就修文与白云交界地土地资源调查情况召开座谈会，明确双方相连的界线。会议商定由双方各自绘制地界调查图和标注相互接壤边界。因各自绘制的地界存在分歧，争议一直搁置未了。

1997年1月，县政府为加强地域边界管理，根据贵州省政府黔府发〔1996〕65号文件精神，成立由副县长何先祥任组长的县勘界工作领导小组，领导小组下设办公室，由县民政局、土地管理局抽派6人负责勘界事务。6月6日，修文、清镇两县勘界工作领导小组召开勘界办公会，根据国务院〔1996〕32号文和黔府发〔1996〕65号文有关勘界工作的要求，以行政区域管辖现状为基础，本着尊重历史、注重现实、协调争议、利于管理、稳定边界、利于开发、发展经济，关全大局、互谅互让、友好协商方式制定联合勘定清镇、修文两县（市）行政区域界线实施方案。8月22日，修文与贵阳市乌当区、白云区勘界工作领导小组签订勘界边界交汇点协议，绘制边界附图，重新核定界点，建立界桩，制定联合勘定实施方案，上报贵阳市勘界工作领导小组。9月10日，贵阳市勘界工作领导小组以筑勘发〔1996〕37号文下发《关于同意〈联合勘定白云区、修文县行政区域界线实施方案〉批复》。

1998年12月3日，白云区、修文县召开核界工作会议，对双方的飞地、插入地按国家法规、政策在不影响群众生活前提下不改变原有的权属关系，明确管辖范围，管理方法，使原争议、分歧得到协调，对县域与乌当相邻边界争议界线再次核勘，协议解决了争议。

2000年，省政府分别以黔府函〔2000〕608号、黔府函〔2000〕610号、黔府函〔2000〕796号、黔府函〔2000〕798号和黔府函〔2000〕806号文批复同意修文与清镇、黔西、金沙、开阳、息烽、白云、乌当等7个区、县（市）签署的地界贯通协议书，核定县境法定界线，拟定地域界边文书，汇总边界资料，绘制地界图，竖立边界界桩，确定边界走向及交点，标绘土地权属。县域西南面与清镇、黔西，南面与清镇、白云，东面与开阳、乌当，西北面与金沙、黔西，北面与息烽、开阳的5条边界定向界点分别为：011325022524界点位于县龙场镇杨寨村与白云区麦架乡摆茅村、清镇市麦格乡谷当坪村交界处；242325022524界点位于县六广镇合营村与黔西县素朴镇马路河村、清镇市暗流乡矿山村交界处；24232424524界点位于县六桶乡联合村与黔西县泰来乡荆江村、金沙县化觉乡下坝村交界处；242425232524界点位于六桶乡黄金村与金沙县化觉乡下坝村、息烽县九庄镇柏茂村交界处；011225222524界点位于县六屯乡小木村与开阳禾丰乡王车村、乌当区新场乡杨梅村交界处。县界勘定由贵州省地质矿产勘查开发局测绘院提供《技术设计书》《界桩点成果表》《界桩图照》《界桩登记表》《界桩位置和边界线走向说明》等技术资料。同时与边界各县（市）区共同制定管理措施，严禁在界桩两侧各5米地段建房和修建永久性建筑，严禁移动界桩，加强界桩护理，及时填写清楚界桩文字，每隔5年双方联合检查边界1次。

县民政局维护县界碑

2010年5月，根据筑发〔2010〕45号《关于开展第二轮行政区域边界联合检查工作的通知》，分别与县域周边7个县（市）区联合开展边界检查，联合检查工作于12月完成。按照核定界线全县土地面积为1075.7平方公里。

二、地名地标

1981年4月，县政府根据贵州省政府“全省地名普查会议”要求，成立由副县长刘正明任组长的县地名普查领导小组，下置办公室铺开普查工作，对全县已有的3000余个地名逐个核查、登记，制作地名卡片，绘制地名图。遵照国务院《关于地名更名暂行规定的通知》，对部分重名、不尊重习俗名和不规范、不健康者进行调整和更改。村级地名更名经县政府审查批准，公社（乡）更名报请省政府批准。

1985年组建县地名普查办公室启动县地名录的编辑，1988年8月出版《修文县地名录》，其中县名1个，乡（镇）名32个，街道名15个，街道办事处名1个，自然村寨名1527个，名胜古迹名15个，河道名31个，桥梁名12个，水库名26个，山峰名184个，洞穴名19个，地片名68个，企事业单位驻地名54个，消失地名51个。普查工作结束后，县地名普查办公室即行撤销。

1992年5月，组建县地名委员会，下设常设机构地名管理办公室于民政局。7月，县人民政府批转地名委员会《关于在全县开展地名管理工作的报告》，将城关（龙场）、扎佐、久长、六广4镇作为地名标志设置试点，竖街、路、巷标志牌。并召开全县地名工作会议，布置地名普查工作和地名标志设置，使地名管理规范化。1995年，县地名委员会根据国发〔1986〕11号文和黔府发〔1992〕61号文规定，对县城道路网的各条道路命名和更改，经广泛征求各界人士及相关部门意见，反复磋商后上报县人民政府。县政府于1995年9月以修府批〔1995〕33号文批准。并分别设置街道名标志。

县城街道命名更名一览表（1995年9月22日）

表5—02—04

路　名	起止点	命名更名	原　名
中山路	翠屏路（健康路）县货公司路口至北门桥	保留名	中山路
龙岗路	翠屏路小街口北至中山路，南至民主路。	保留名	龙岗路
王家巷	中山路至西门坡	保留名	王家巷
阳明西路	阳明路西段羊叉街至环城路（人民北路）	原名划分	阳明路
阳明东路	阳明路东段环城路口至丰阳加油站	更名	修扎公路
人民南路	人民路南段洗脚塘至翠屏路（健康路）路口	命名	环城路
人民北路	人民路北段翠屏路（健康路）口至东门桥	命名	
翠屏西路	翠屏路西段中山路县政府处路口至环城路	命名	健康路
翠屏东路	翠屏路东段环城路口至迎春坝	命名	系新建
长征路	人民南路乡企局路口至马掌坡	命名	新改造路
玩易路	长征路县人大处至县农业局	命名	新开通
黄秧路	人民南路县供电局处至黄秧寨	命名	新改造，原无名
迎春路	长征路人大处至阳明东路长征桥	命名	拟建时称为私营经济一条街
学宫巷	翠屏西路粮店处至修文中学食堂	命名	改造路，原无名
温家巷	中山路原城关区路口至温家坡	命名	改造路，原无名
文化路	中山路实验小学处至修文中学	命名	改造路，原无名
秀水路	中山路北门桥处至郭家林水泥厂	命名	厂矿路，原无名
栖风路	民主路供销社处至川会馆	更名	龙井巷
响鼓山路	洗脚塘至关家湾	命名	新建路，原无名
民主路	翠屏路供销社处至南门口洗脚塘	更名	玩易路

续表

路　名	起止点	命名更名	原　名
朝阳路	人民北路春华酒家至曲尺桥	命名	新建路
虎山路	拟建中的人民南路县信用联社处至县科委	命名	新建路
沙溪路	民主路南门项家湾至五大块	命名	原无名
潮水路	北门桥至三潮水	命名	原修六公路

1997年3月，县政府发布《加强地名管理和保护地名标志的通告》，到1998年，全县在国道、省道、县道共设置地名牌标志175块，其中行政村名92块，自然村寨名27块，公路交叉道口指示牌32块，乡（镇）名24块。

1999年9月29日，县政府以修府报〔1999〕31号文件，命名新开发的县城东片区街道，其中曲尺桥至小桥河为河滨路，朝阳路至翠屏东路为良知路，翠屏东路至长征路为龙山路，河滨路至迎春路为宾阳路，迎春路至修文河边路为人文巷，长征桥至长征路为永安巷，人文巷至翠屏东路为文成路，虎山路至玩易窝为知行路，原体育场改造的绿地广场为龙岗广场。

2002年9月28日，县政府以修府报〔2002〕37号文件，对新开发的以阳明大道为中心路段分别命名为：阳明大道，南起曲尺桥，北接贵（阳）毕（节）高等级公路，全长2800米，宽34米；格致路，东起规划的外环城路，西与阳明大道交叉继续向西延伸，全长800米，宽15米；诚意路，东接规划的外环城路，西至阳明东路，全长500米，宽15米。正心路，东起阳明洞风景区，西与阳明大道交叉后继续延伸至阳明新村，全长800米，宽10米。

2004—2005年，对县境内的扎佐镇、久长镇、六广镇及小箐乡集镇街道命名和更名。其中，扎佐镇于2005年8月16日由县政府批复同意扎佐镇人民政府对新街命名和老街更名共14个，包括襄阳路、于襄路、景阳路、古驿路、广场路、中营路、育英路、东兴路、书院街、经堂后街、沙国巷、西门桥街、大园街、场口街。废除原四清路、革命路、红卫路、前进路的街名；久长镇新开发建设市政道路新街道分别命名为龙山路、明珠路，并将原川黔公路街与修（文）开（阳）公路街相交路口处的北段命名为川黔北路，南段命名为川黔南路，原修（文）开（阳）公路街与川黔公路街交叉路口处的东段命名为修开东路，西段命名为修开西路；六广镇索风营电站大坝建成道路修通和镇集镇街道改扩建后，老集镇保留上街、中街、下街名称，新建道路命名为松江路、南江路；小箐乡集镇修（文）六（广）公路街道消极洞至大丫口命名为迎宾路，老街口北至油脂仓库为太平路，老街口南至小箐小学段为兰谷路，农贸市场至小箐中学段为石景路。

县城街道名牌

至2010年，龙场、扎佐、久长、六广4镇及小箐、六桶、大石、洒坪、六屯、谷堡6个乡集镇街道、道路均设置街道名牌和道路标示牌。

第十节　殡葬管理

一、殡葬改革

1980年初，县政府为贯彻执行内务部《关于殡葬改革的意见》，加强殡葬管理，责成县民政局调查全县丧葬情况，调查结果为：旧的丧葬观念根深蒂固，大办丧事，土葬遍行。4月，县委、县政府将丧葬改革纳入议事日程，制定改革5项措施：一是加强宣传教育，利用各种形势宣传殡葬改革的重大意义，向群众讲解遗体火化是既科学又卫生又节约的丧葬；二是要求各级干部、共产党员在丧葬改革中以身作则，带头从俭治丧，做到自己的亲人死后实行火葬；三是国家机关职工（含离休、退休人员）死后，如家属执意土葬，要耐心做思想工作，说服火化，如不听劝告造成家庭经济困难的，国家不予补助；四是农村群众实行火葬要积极支持，给予适当帮助和提供交通工具，对优抚对象和救济对象火化开支费用，由县民政局给予补助；五是端公、道士、阴阳先生搞封建迷信应予取缔，对于诈骗财物造成严重后果的应依法处理。5项措施推行后，促进机关职工、城镇居民从简办丧，葬法采取火化。但火化率较低，有的遗体火化后又用棺木重葬。1990年，全县遗体火化仅有17具。

1996年，县境划属贵阳市管辖后，丧葬列为火化区。4月，县政府为贯彻落实《贵阳市殡葬管理办法》，推动殡葬改革，召开专门会议，出台《九五期间殡葬改革规划意见》，要求逐年提高火化率。1999年2月，为加强殡葬管理，由县机构编制委员会行文建置县殡葬管理所，为县民政局下属事业单位，定编3人，配所长或副所长1名。其职责是：负责贯彻执行党和国家关于殡葬改革的方针、政策和法律法规，负责全县殡葬管理，督促检查各乡（镇）和部门的殡葬管理工作任务完成情况，制止丧葬中的封建迷信活动和违背殡葬管理规定的行为。

2001年3月，县委、县政府行文《调整充实县殡葬改革工作领导小组》，组建由县委副书记王成林任组长、县政府副县长周毅任副组长的县殡葬改革工作领导小组，进一步加强对殡葬改革的领导。2003年，县政府印发〔2003〕05号文，对丧葬提出“十不准”，并在乡（镇）成立殡葬改革工作领导小组，把殡葬改革纳入各级政府工作目标责任，签订目标责任书予以考核。2004年，县委、县政府出台《关于进一步加强殡葬改革工作的实施意见》，全面推行遗体火化，要求全县殡葬确保火化率达100%。11月28日，县政法机关在久长镇召开公处大会，公开处理以暴力阻碍殡葬改革工作的“栋青事件”3名涉暴人员。搬掉障碍后，有力地推动殡葬改革，当年全县死亡1302人全部实行火化，遗体火化率达100%。截至2010年累计全县遗体火化2.1万具。

二、殡仪馆建设

1996年，修文、开阳、息烽3县纳入贵阳市遗体火化区后，带来贵阳市殡仪馆出现火化预约和排队现象。1998年，县政府为落实《贵阳市殡葬管理办法》，方便丧家治丧，特向贵阳市政府申报建设含遗体火化场在内的修文殡仪馆。市政府根据修文、开阳、息烽3县相邻，距离贵阳市区较远的实际，报经贵州省政府批准，由贵阳市计划委员会立项，在修、开、息3县相邻的久长镇域修建群众治理丧事的殡仪馆，同时满足靠近修文的贵阳市乌当区、白云区部分群众丧葬需要，整个覆盖区域面积为1500平方公里，总人

口100万。

殡仪馆选址在修（文）开（阳）公路旁的凤凰山下，距久长镇中心1公里，距县城15公里。工程建设于1998年12月动工，由县城乡建设局规划设计室参照江西省火化设备研究所的有关资料，结合县的实际审批签发殡仪馆征地、建设许可证。由县建筑公司承建，整个工程占地8亩，投入资金200万元。修建综合楼245.22平方米，火化操作车间384.22平方米，并置营业厅、传达室、办公室、丧家休息室、冷冻室、化妆室、停尸间、卫生间、骨灰存放室、吊唁厅以及停车场。置有YQ——欧式火化机2台，并建空置机位1处，年火化遗体可达5000具。殡仪馆由贵州省胜兴发展有限公司投资建设和经营，经营活动涉及的殡葬政策、法规由县殡葬管理所管理、指导，经营服务收费和服务质量由县工商局、物价局监督。1999年10月5日，殡仪馆投入营运。2003年，开阳县、息烽县自建殡仪馆，两县遗体火化业务终止。到2010年，殡仪馆已接承遗体火化2.1万具，馆务运转正常。

三、公墓

1991年，县政府将公墓建设列入议事日程，责成县民政局在县城东北面观音山建设占地100亩的示范性公墓，在县城北烈士陵园后山建遗体骨灰存放楼堂1幢2层300平方米。1994年年底骨灰存放堂仅存遗体骨灰13具。1996年，从群众入土为安习俗着眼，县政府作出“九五”期末建成县级经营性公墓1个，在扎佐、久长、六广3镇分别修建公益性公墓各1个的决定。

2000年修文殡仪馆火化遗体121具，火化后使用骨灰盒安葬58具，占火化数的48%，存放骨灰3具，其余仍为棺葬。2001年4月13日，贵阳市殡葬管理所在修文召开清镇、乌当、白云、息烽、开阳、修文殡葬管理所长会议。会议根据1997年民政部召开的第三次全国殡葬工作会议精神，进一步明确殡葬工作的指导思想，强调注重葬礼和葬法改革并重，遗体处理和骨灰处理并重，殡葬合理消费和满足不同层次需要并重，推行遗体火化后采取树葬、壁葬、草坪葬、花坛葬、盆景葬、公墓小墓艺术葬处理骨灰和骨灰存放。鼓励修建不超过1平方米的小墓位公墓和艺术园林式公墓。7月，贵阳市民政局、市物价局、市国土局、市林业局、市工商局联合以筑民发〔2001〕75号文规范骨灰安葬中的土地、物价、工商的法律规定，使遗体骨灰安葬改革工作得到有序推进。县殡仪馆拟定在修（文）扎（佐）、贵（阳）遵（义）公路交汇的扎佐冷水沟林场内建容纳1000个墓位的公墓，在县城新开发的阳明大道建殡葬礼仪服务中心，后因征地未落实和县城市建设总体规划未定而搁浅。

2004年，全县全面实行遗体火化，火化率达到100%，但火化后棺木入土、大修墓地仍然未断绝，甚至为逝后准备葬地而修建空墓穴呈上升趋势。据民政部门调查，死者采取棺葬占地每年达6000平方米，耗费棺木4320立方米。为减少土葬占地保护土地资源，县殡葬管理领导小组办公室制发修殡改〔2004〕1号《关于进一步加强公路主干线两侧散葬坟墓治理整顿的通知》，禁止在风景名胜区、文物保护区、水资源保护区以及贵（阳）遵（义）、贵（阳）毕（节）高等级公路和通往各乡（镇）公路主干线两侧可视范围内乱埋乱葬。与此同时县政府引入贵州修文净园文化有限公司，在县城西北潮水村朱家大坡修建天龙山经营性公墓，开展骨灰丧葬业务。

天龙山公墓距县城1.5公里，是以陵园为主的园林式公墓，定名“天龙山陵园”，由净园公司投资1.2亿元，规划陵园总面积30万平方米，其中陵园墓地面积12万平方米，陵位2万个，包括树葬、花坛葬、壁葬和艺术小墓穴葬，绿化面积13万平方米，道路面积4万平方米，广场面积1万平方米，含停车位400个，服务性建筑面积2000平方米。

2005年，进一步采取从源头上加以治理遗体乱葬措施，推进殡葬改革，全县217个行政村规划公益性墓地225个。县民政局与乡（镇）政府配合相继在有条件的村建设村级公益性公墓。至2010年，已建成清水、永兴、下硐、三里、新庄、小箐、崇恩等较为规范的村级公益性公墓，竖立起村级公益性公墓碑，小坟头修建较为规范。天龙山公墓已有贵阳市城区和白云区、乌当区、息烽县、开阳县以及本县逝者1500位骨灰入葬。

天龙山公墓墓群

第三章　社会保障

1978年，社会保障基本上属单位企业保障制，就业、劳动保护等业务分属人事局和劳动局管理。1995年并为人事劳动局，统管全县劳动力资源的开发利用和劳动就业工作；研究制定机关、事业、企业单位工作人员社会保险的改革方案和政策，并组织实施；综合管理全县行政、事业单位社会保险工作，实施城镇职工养老、失业、医疗、工伤、生育等保险；协调管理机关、事业单位工作人员离休、退休和退职工作；管理机关、事业单位和企业职工福利工作。1997年12月，人事劳动局下设社会保险事业管理局，负责全县社会保险各项事务。民政局先后启动城乡居民最低保障制度，从此社会保险有了统一管理的部门，社会保障也开始由单位保障向社会保障转变。2003年，随着改革不断深入和机构职能的变化，人事劳动局又改成“人事劳动和社会保障局”。2006年，中共十六届六中全会明确提出建立覆盖全民的社会保障体系，全县基本养老保险、基本医疗保险、失业保险、工伤保险、生育保险和最低生活保障等社会保障事业改革相继启动。到2010年，全县社会保障体系基本建立，并逐步趋于完善，群众生活有救助，劳动有保护，疾病有医保，老来有保障的优越性逐步实现。

社会保障服务大厅

第一节　保障体制改革

1984年，始对企业用工制度和保障制度进行改革，到2010年实行固定工改为合同制，劳动力随市场流动，实施社会保障。

一、用工制度改革

（一）统包统配制改劳动合同制

1981年前，全民和集体所有制企业沿用“统包统配”用工制度，招收职工均为固定工，并限制在城镇劳动力中统筹安置。1984年改用劳动合同制，但仅在国营企业新招工人中实行，采取用人单位与劳动者订立劳动合同，明确双方责、权、利。劳动合同一经订立即具有法律约束力，双方必须遵守。

1995年9月，遵照县政府出台《企业全面实行劳动合同制实施细则》规定：凡落户在县域各种经济组织，都必须与拟用人员在平等自愿、协商一致的基础上签订劳动合同书，依法确定劳动关系。到1996年10月，劳动合同的签订和鉴证结束，累计签订劳动合同3233份。这一制度的实施，消除了在同一企业中固定工与合同工之间的差异。继后，凡进企业必签劳动合同的规定至2010年一直推行。

（二）企业职工协商调动

1983年前，全民、集体、机关和事业单位的正式工人，如因工作需要或家庭生活困难、父母老年体弱多病身边无人照顾、夫妻长期分居等需要调动工作，经组织批准后由劳动部门办理调动手续。1984年至2010年，又改由调进调出单位自行协商办理，向劳动部门备案。至于机关事业单位的工勤人员余缺调配则改为劳动转移，不再称为调配。

2008年返乡农民工现场招聘会

二、建立社会保障体系

1978年起，保障制度逐步从运行机制、模式类型、项目构成、待遇水平、管理社会化等方面进行深层次改革，建立包括社会保险、社会救济、社会福利的社会保障制度。

基本养老保险制度　1978年，沿袭城镇职工退休养老制度。1986年10月始建城镇职工养老保险，先在国有企业劳动合同制工人中实施，再扩大到固定职工，由职工所在单位和职工缴纳养老基金统一管理。2000年6月起养老金统一实施社会化发放，覆盖范围又逐步扩大到城镇个体工商户及其雇工、自由职业者、灵活就业人员、城镇和农村居民，达到法定退休年龄并办理退休手续，即可领取基本养老金。到2010年除1892人领取离退休保障金外，有4968人享受养老保险待遇。

国有企业职工失业保险制度　1986年7月，劳动局下属的劳动服务公司承担保险基金的筹集和管理，用于待业人员临时生活救济和医疗补助。1995年《中华人民共和国劳动法》颁布实施，待业改称失业。2000年7月起，参保范围扩大到当地驻军机关事业单位职工，2010年，全县有126人领失业保险。

医疗费用社会统筹 2005年7月，县始建城镇职工基本医疗保险制度，将机关、事业、社团及其他组织人员公费医疗改为医疗保险，同时开展大额医疗补助和新型农村合作医疗。2008年至2010年统筹范围扩至企业、城镇居民和灵活就业人员，使有职业和无职业人员都能得到医疗保障。

办理社会保险征缴业务

企业职工工伤保险制度 2005年7月启动，至2010年县内各类企业及个体工商户均纳入保险范围，按行业风险实行差别费率和浮动费率。

生育保险制度 2008年9月，机关事业单位和企业统一参加职工生育保险，城镇居民纳入基本医疗保险，农村居民除纳入新型农村合作医疗外，财政还设立专项经费对农村孕产妇住院分娩给予补助。

城乡居民最低生活保障制度 1998年5月在龙场镇试点，1999年10月全县铺开，惠及居民1.51万人，至2010年继续实施。

第二节 劳动保障

1978年沿袭城镇就业安置和工伤保险制度，1984年实行就业培训，1986年始建劳动保护机构，并建立劳动保险制度和劳动保护制度，至2010年制度继续实施，使劳动者的合法权益受到保护。

一、劳动就业

1978，沿袭统招统配制度。1984年改用劳动合同制，其范围从城镇扩大到农村。2010年，企业用工全为市场配置。

（一）城镇失业人员安置

1.待业失业人员就业

1978年前统由政府安置。1979年成立劳动服务公司，实行离（退）休后子女顶替政策，连续16年对离（退）休、退职或死亡的职工，可由一个子女顶替，全县使用顶替办法安置832人就业。1993年起，安置实行劳动部门介绍就业、自愿组织起来就业、自谋职业方式就业“三结合”，在劳动局置职业介绍所，对外出务工人员进行登记，实行《务工许可证》管理。1996年起大中专毕业生不包分配，实行用人单位和就业人员双向选择。2003年，将农村富余劳动力转移列入劳动部门统一管理，统称城乡统

为就业失业人员办理的失业登记证

筹就业。2008年提出消除“零就业”家庭，要求“产生一户，消除一户，稳定一户”，帮助解决65户零就业家庭。从1984年至2010年，全县累计安置待业、失业人员4.98万人。

1984—2010年待业、失业人员安置情况表

表5—03—01 单位：人

年份	安置	年份	安置	年份	安置	年份	安置	年份	安置
1984	1150	1990	1106	1996	1367	2002	1120	2008	1289
1985	1165	1991	1316	1997	1389	2003	3484	2009	1702
1986	607	1992	1197	1998	765	2004	7142	2010	1858
1987	1120	1993	1225	1999	1378	2005	4800	合计	49818
1988	1130	1994	1287	2000	1404	2006	6147		
1989	904	1995	1026	2001	1410	2007	1330		

注：1979—1994年退（离）休顶替832人未列入表内数。

2.上山下乡知青安置

1978年，全县尚有未安置的上山下乡知识青年1732人，至1981年，除死亡8人外，其余1724人全部安置，其中求学毕业分配408人，进工厂982人，参军67人，回城安置141人，转点后安置13人，其他安置113人。

3.下岗职工再就业

1994年2月，县酒厂破产，下岗151人，其中38人作为交养老保险金到退休年龄办理退休，其余为自谋职业。1997年12月起，对国营企业 执行“抓大放小”“一厂一议、一厂一策”方针，实行改制或有偿转让，对每年的下岗职工，劳动部门将其列为“民心工程”优先安置。

2003年，按照《贵州省下岗失业人员再就业管理暂行办法》，对有劳动能力和就业愿望的，报经市级劳动保障部门审批，颁发省印制的《再就业优惠证》。持《再就业优惠证》，可享受5项扶持政策：一是从事个体经营（国家限制行业除外），3年内免征营业税、城市维护建设税、教育费附加、所得税，免收管理类、登记类、证照类行政事业收费；二是建立贷款担保基金，为下岗自谋职业、自主创业提供小额贷款担保；三是简化开业手续，提供“一条龙”服务；四是统筹解决自谋职业，自主创业经营场地；五是以非全日制、临时性、弹性工作等灵活形式就业，保障其合法权益。至2008年，全县累计发证2301人。2009年起停发。

吸纳下岗失业人员企业（国家限制行业除外），属服务型的可享受3项优惠政策：一是当年新招收人员达到职工总数30%以上，并签订3年以上劳动合同，3年内根据招用人数按年度减征一定比例的企业所得税；二是新办企业达到第一项优惠政策，3年内免征企业营业税、城市维护建设税、教育费附加、企业所得税，当年新招用人员不足30%，根据招用人数，按年度减征一定比例企业所得税；三是新招用国有企业下岗失业人员并与其签订3年以上期限劳动合同，从再就业资金中按招用人数提供为限3年社会保障补贴（个人应缴养老保险费和失业保险费仍由本人负担）。属国有大中型企业通过主辅业改制分流安置本企业富余人员举办经济实体，利用原企业主要流动资产、闲置资产或关闭破产企业有效资产，独立核算、产权清晰并逐步实现产权主体多元化，吸纳原企业富余人员到30%以上，与安置职工变更或签订新劳动合同，3年内免征企业所得税。截至2010年，连续12年累计安置再就业职工3271人。

专记一：龙翔兼并云天 职工全部安置

贵阳云天航空工贸有限公司（原418库），原为国家航空工业部属的企业，驻地龙场镇小营村，1978年前曾在物资储备中转工作中作过巨大贡献，1979年起随着实行改革开放和发展市场经济，公司自身功能逐步衰退。曾采取军品民品共同生产，后又并入万江机电厂作为辅助企业，但仍不能拓展，经营难以养活全部职工，到2002年负债超过千万元，每个职工才六七百元工资不能按月发放，超过法定退休年龄人员因欠缴养老金不能及时办理退休手续。2003年4月，根据国经贸企改〔2002〕859号文件精神，将公司与主厂整体分离，移交给县政府改制。11月政府引进龙翔公司将云天兼并，由国有转型为民营。对此，职工纷纷议论说："不改我们等死，早改我们早死。"

龙翔公司接管后，将云天公司职工384人全部安置，其中4名离休人员由县管理，在岗188人留公司继续就业，退养49人由龙翔公司续交养老金至退休，退休143人参加社会养老保险，安置率为100%，被贵阳市政府授予"再就业工作先进单位"的称号。为避免职工后顾之忧，在维持正常生产、按月足额发放职工工资的同时，连续3年修建5栋1.2万平方米职工住房，6层办公大楼，并置卫生所、单身职工宿舍、商店、浴室、农贸市场、绿化广场、龙翔大道等，从根本上改善职工生活与工作环境，使厂区面貌焕然一新，从而调动职工生产积极性，企业经济效益逐年攀升。至2010年，每人每月收入一千一百元都能按月发放，获贵阳市政府表彰，职工们高兴地说："企业改制是改革发展需要，也是我们云天职工生存之路。"

龙翔集团生产车间

专记二：小额贷款扶持再就业

2003年，为解决下岗职工自谋职业资金不足困难，县政府在财政局国资办设置小额担保贷款中心，对下岗失业人员自谋职业、自主创业提供小额担保贷款资金扶持。对持《再就业优惠证》，个人或合伙经营实体自筹资金不足（自筹资金不得低于贷款本金30%），经人事劳动和社会保障局就业办公室认定，可办理额度在3000至2万元贷款。合伙经营和组织就业，可根据人数适当放宽，但最高不超过10万元。贷款期限分为6个月至18个月5个档次，最长期限一般不超过24个月。如因特殊情况申请延期一次，最长不超过12个月。扶持就业，人均贷款2.27万元。享受扶持贷款后，贷款人正在领取的基本生活费和失业保险金自取得贷款第三个月起停发，已领取城镇居民最低生活保障金自第三个月起重新核实确定。到2010年累计为299人再就业担保贷款677.5万元。受扶持的下岗职工高兴地说："我们虽无工作，得到贷款支持有业可就，一定好好经营感谢政府。"

（二）就业培训与服务

1.就业培训

在岗职工和农村劳动力职业培训 从1981年起，县劳动部门对“文化大革命”时期及后来招收的青年工人进行文化、技术补课的同时，并与职工教育管理部门配合，采取开班授课、实地指导、辅导自修等形式对工人进行技术培训、转岗培训、晋级培训、创业培训、高级技术培训和岗位培训，以促进劳动技能的提高。开展培训项目有职业道德、基础知识、专业知识、劳动技能等。2001年，增办农村劳动力培训，与职工培训统称为城乡统筹培训，2004年6月，根据中共贵阳市委、市政府《关于实施农村劳动力转移就业工程意见》，县人事劳动和社会保障局会同教育局、农业办、农业局、职业技能培训中心在小箐中学举行农村劳动力培训班，由福建省石狮市鹏程技工学校对参训的167名学员采取“送教上门”就地培训与异地培训相结合方式进行，就地指导培训和技能培训7天，后转到厂方实习。学员经过培训考评鉴定合格发给初级职业资格证书或上岗证，由培训单位组织到相应岗位就业。至2010年累计培训5.42万人。

就业培训

1984—2010年就业培训人员开展情况表

表5—03—02 单位：人

年份	培训人数	年份	培训人数	年份	培训人数	年份	培训人数	年份	培训人数
1984	202	1990	714	1996	2400	2002	2313	2008	5650
1985	310	1991	813	1997	2431	2003	1793	2009	6229
1986	146	1992	792	1998	245	2004	4770	2010	3638
1987	655	1993	774	1999	820	2005	902	合计	54220
1988	713	1994	1617	2000	950	2006	4831		
1989	656	1995	1534	2001	2308	2007	6014		

下岗工人再就业培训 1994年起，国营企业和集体企业改制后出现下岗职工再就业问题。1998年5月，县人事劳动局遵照中共中央、国务院号召全党动手，全社会共同努力，做好下岗职工基本生活保障和再就业工作精神，拟订培训计划、教学课程，备齐培训资料和学员登记册，报经贵阳市培训中心审核合格即行开班，培训结束由贵阳市培训中心对合格者发给结业证，市鉴定中心发给职业资格证书。至2010年，累计培训下岗职工3644人，其中安置就业2493人。

2.就业服务

职业介绍 1993年5月县建立职业介绍所，在对大中专毕业生、失业人员、下岗职工、在职流动人员选择职业深入了解和合理选择职业基础上进行职业介绍，服务项目一是求职登记，对用人单位进行用工调查；二是为用人单位提供劳动力资源信息；三是为城镇求职人员和进城务工农村劳动力提供用工信息，进行就业指导咨询和介绍工作单位；四是为城镇家庭介绍服务人员；五是为从事教育和就业培训单位提供需求信息，推荐需要人员；六是对劳动力供求双方相互自愿选择达成协议后，指导其按照国家有关规定签订劳动合同；七是向有关决策部门提供劳动力资源信息，为制定就业规划和政策提供依据。1996年至2010年，除资料缺失的3年外累计全县求职登记2.39万人，职业介绍成功8292人。

民营企业招聘周活动

部分年度职业介绍情况表

表5—03—03　　单位：人

年份	登记数	获职者	年份	登记数	获职者	年份	登记数	获职者
1996	1044	116	2002	590	290	2007	3635	2302
1999	1320	680	2004	1912	243	2008	3237	4008
2000	600	240	2005	714	157	2009	3774	
2001	520	256	2006	2801		2010	3704	

核发失业证　1996年，10乡（镇）劳动就业服务站始对持有城镇户口，年满16周岁以上，有劳动能力且有就业愿望或有就业经历，需在县内就业的其他失业人员，凭本人身份证、户口簿、照片、社区居委会或村委会出具未就业证明、与原企业解除（终止）劳动关系协议人员，填写《贵阳市失业登记表》、《辖区人员求职登记表》，领取《贵州省失业人员失业证》。1996—2010年，累计全县获发《失业证》1.86万人。

为方便失业者异地就业，从1988年起至2003年累计办发《外来人员就业许可证》535份、《外出人员就业登记卡》938个。2004年停办两证业务。

企业职工档案托管　1997年，启动企业流动职工人事档案托管有偿服务。凡在县登记的失业职工、从事个体经营并与原企业解除劳动关系职工、在工商行政管理部门登记注册集体企业、乡镇企业、“三资”企业、民营企业工作的原国有企业职工，市劳动行政部门授权委托管理的企业流动职工人事档案均可办理，每份月托管费6元。到2010年托管档案共3096份。

（三）失业保险

1993年5月，县劳动服务公司贯彻国务院《国有企业职工待业保险规定》及依法宣布破产企业职工、破产企业整改期间被精减职工、按国家规定被撤销和解散企业职工、停产整顿企业被精减职工、终止或解除劳动合同职工、企业辞退和除名及开除职工、依法律法规或经省政府批准享受待业保险其他职工均属待业保险范围。由企业按全部职工（机关单位按劳动合同制工人）工资总额1%缴纳保险金，救济标准为每人每月50元，医疗补助每人每月4元。1998年7月1日，失业保险改由企业、职工共同负担，企业

2%，职工1%，由企业代收代缴。2000年7月扩大到军队机关事业单位职工。2002年9月起，所在单位和本人缴费满1年，非因本人意愿中断就业，已办理失业登记并有求职要求3项具备，可按月领取所在县最低工资标准70%失业保险金、每月10元医疗补助金。领取期限按累计缴费时间计算，缴费满1年不满2年为3个月，满2年不满3年为6个月，满3年不满4年为9个月，满4年不满5年为12个月，满5年不满6年为14个月，满6年为15个月，以后每增1年增1个月，最长不超过24个月。2004年10月，失业保险金标准从203元升到224元并延续执行。2000—2010年，累计征收失业保险费852.88万元，累计支出78.58万元。

2000—2010年失业保险参保及缴费统计表

表5—03—04　　单位：人、万元

年份	参保人数	缴费	年份	参保人数	缴费	年份	参保人数	缴费
2000	1648	9.14	2004	5894	102.61	2008	7726	130.00
2001	3536	33.82	2005	5988	45.65	2009	3248	144.00
2002	3795	22.21	2006	6385	76.30	2010	4351	174.00
2003	5713	34.71	2007	7222	80.44			

二、劳动保护

1986年成立劳动仲裁委员会，1992年成立劳动鉴定委员会，2001年组建劳动监察大队，至2010年办结诉讼案件53件，为民工追回被拖欠、被克扣工资618.25万元，使劳动者的合法权益得到保护。

（一）劳动仲裁

劳动合同鉴证　1990年5月，县劳动局印发《关于劳动合同鉴证问题通知》，要求用工单位及其职工签订劳动合同，送劳动行政机关仲裁机构办理鉴证。7月又与工商行政管理局联合转发两家省主管局《关于对私营企业、个体工商劳动合同进行鉴定通知》，推出三项要求：一是所有私营企业、个体工商户用工必须签订书面劳动合同，送劳动局仲裁股予以鉴定，凭鉴定劳动合同核发营业执照；二是不得使用在校生和童工；三是企业必须建立必要的规章制度，提供劳动安全、卫生设施，实行八小时工作制，保证职工安全健康。8月组建人事劳动争议仲裁股，承担劳动合同鉴定。至2010年，累计办理劳动合同鉴证5.6万份。

县设置的劳动人事争议仲裁庭

建立劳动争议调解组织　1991年10月，县劳动局与经济委员会、总工会联合通知，要求各企业依法建立、完善经职工代表大会讨论通过的厂纪厂规，凡没有建立调解委员会的企业必须建立。同时组织人员亲赴企业督促，至年末，全县共充实、完善和建立劳动争议基层组织30个，建立16个企业厂纪厂规。

1993年10月，再次要求各类企业必须执行《劳动争议处理条例》，凡从业人员达到10人以上，必须成立有职工代表、企业代表、企业工会代表组成的劳动争议调解委员会。到1996年11月，全县80%企业建起劳动争议调解委员会。之后，由于企业对调解工作掉以轻心。至2010年，仅有各乡镇设立劳动争议调解机构履行调解职能。

受理劳动争议仲裁案件 1986年11月，县成立劳动争议仲裁委员会，下设办公室于劳动局，行使劳动争议仲裁职能。1990年8月劳动局专设劳动争议仲裁股（后改“科”）。2002年8月增加人事仲裁职能。2008年，乡（镇）建立劳动争议调解委员会。1990年至2010年，全县累计受理并立案处理解除劳动合同、退款、伤残补偿、工伤认定、超时加班等劳动争议案件768件，通过调解、裁决、撤诉等形式全部结案。

专记：劳动争议仲裁为农民工解困

2000年10月，黔西县雨朵镇一村一组农民尤国志，与小山耐火厂签订劳动合同在厂务工。2002年12月6日与几名工友在井下作业，约14时矿井顶棚塌方受伤，先后送贵阳医学院附属医院、贵航黔江骨伤科医院、黔西县中医院住院治疗，诊断为左股骨干段骨折，作内固定术后，左大腿外侧出现血液假性动脉瘤，2003年3月31日作截肢手术， 11月28日劳动鉴定委员会鉴定受损伤为四级伤残。因工伤补偿支付问题与小山耐火厂发生争议，双方于2004年1月6日向劳动争议仲裁委员会申请仲裁。仲裁委员会于1月13日立案并组成仲裁庭审理，经两次调解无效，劳动争议仲裁委员会于3月25日以修劳仲裁字2号裁决书裁决：被诉人支付申诉人住院期间伙食补助费1350元，护理费1836元，工伤津贴9600元，一次性伤残补助金1.44万元；被诉人按月发给申诉人伤残抚恤金600元，直到申诉人死亡；被诉人2003年3月18日支付给申诉人1.62万元为在黔西县中医院住院治疗医疗费，另还应支付申诉人医疗费557元；仲裁费520元由被诉人承担500元，申诉人承担20元。4月16日，尤国志从劳动仲裁科领到由小山耐火厂付给上述补助费后深为感动地说：“劳动争议仲裁真正为我们农民工解了困。”

（二）劳动监察

劳动用工年审 1997年起，县劳动局仲裁监察科始对用人单位用工情况年审，其内容包括职工工伤、职工医疗、社会保障、工作时间、安全健康保障设施、女职工健康保护、是否使用在校生和童工以及工资支付等。2001—2010年，累计年审用人单位1436户次，对31户下达《劳动监察询问通知书》和《劳动监察限期整改指令书》，不合格的26户中有22户饬令整改，有4户被罚款3.5万元。

劳动检查 1996年3月，县劳动局仲裁监察科始对用人单位劳动用工情况进行检查。1998年至2000年，先后开展用人单位工资支付和民工流动情况检查、外来用工大检查、劳动合同专项执法检查，通知用人单位补签劳动合同1482份，补办就业证卡310个，补缴调节金9138元、失业金7.6万元和养老保险金38.8万元。

2001年，将劳动监察职能划出成立劳动监察大队，监督劳动法律、法规、规章的执行，先后对用人单位社会保险费征缴、《禁止使用童工规定》实施情况和美容美发、保健按摩、中式烹调、汽车修理行业进行检查，对非劳动用工进行专项整治。2004年起，对存在问题单位采取书面通知方式告知，至2010年，累计下达询问通知书177份，限期整改指令书97份，行政处罚告知书14份，行政处理事先告知书5

份，补签劳动合同5405份，补缴养老金1182.32万元，补缴失业保险金83.35万元，补缴社会保障金119万元，补办用工备案435户次，查出并辞退童工1人。

受理投诉案件 1996年起，县劳动局仲裁监察科始办群众来信来访，对群众反映和投诉问题立案处理。2001年，劳动监察职能改由劳动监察大队行使，对劳动法律、法规、规章执行情况就地监督，纠正和查处违法行为。至2010年，累计受理投诉案件535件，涉及6428人，全部结案处理。投诉案件绝大部分为拖欠、克扣民工工资投诉。

追讨民工工资 1997年起，民工工资作为监察重要内容，通过年审、检查、专项清查、投诉等方式，对用人单位、建筑施工单位、矿山、煤矿开展检查或专项检查。至2004年，累计为民工追讨被拖欠、被克扣工资247.58万元，涉及民工4344人。2005年，县成立清理拖欠民工工资办公室，与劳动监察大队合署办公，专事接待群众来访和清理拖欠民工工资。至2010年，为1961名民工追讨工资618.25万元，加上2004年前追讨工资共计865.83万元。

专记：两局联袂为民工讨回血汗钱

2003年4月，业主方金星水泥厂没有进行施工许可证报批报审，就与工程承包人邓国扬签订工程承包合同进行施工，因工程款拨付等原因导致承包方拖欠民工工资10.6万元，拖至阴历腊月未于兑付。人事劳动和社会保障局接到投诉后，立即责成劳动监察大队会同建设局组成调查组，历时10多天，4次进厂了解。在摸清情况的基础上，两次在建设局清理拖欠民工工资办公室召开有业主方代表和承包人参加的协调处理专门会议。按照民工工资支付由“谁用工，谁负责”的原则和任何用人单位不得以工程款或分包款未审计、未结算等理由拖欠农民工工资的要求，商定由业主方出资6.6万元和承包方出资4万元，支付民工工资，使投诉得到圆满解决。工资到手后来自四川、重庆及县内民工周远金、金代元、夏明玖等10余人深情表示：感谢政府为民工做主讨回干活血汗钱，使我们能高高兴兴地回家过年了。

（三）工伤保险

1986年起，对22个企业职工建立健康档案。1992年4月，县置劳动鉴定委员会，负责对辖区内职工伤、残、病、职业病、丧失劳动能力的确认、鉴定和审批。2005年7月启动企业职工工伤保险制度，对各类企业及有雇工的个体工商户，依照国务院《工伤保险条例》和贵阳市《工伤保险实施办法》参加保险，以本单位全部职工工资总额为缴费基数，按行业风险程度分别按0.6%、1.2%、2.4%3个档次为职工和雇主缴纳工伤保险费，并根据企业工伤保险费使用和工伤发生率等情况定期调整缴费率。凡因工作原因受到事故伤害、暴力等意外伤害、患职业病、发生事故下落不明、上下班途中受到机动车事故伤害都认定为工伤，凡工作时突发疾病死亡或在48小时内抢救无效死亡、抢险救灾受到伤害、在军队服役负伤致残的旧伤复发亦视为工伤，均享受工伤医疗和医疗期间生活待遇、残疾待遇、死亡丧葬及抚恤待遇。2005—2010年累计全县收缴工伤保险费888.04万元，由县社会保险收付管理中心统一管理，上报市级统筹支付，6年累计支出1350.21万元。

第三节 医疗保障

1978年，沿袭城镇职工公费医疗制度。2005年，推行城镇职工医疗保险和新型农村合作医疗。2008年，启动职工生育保险，保障覆盖面扩大，城镇居民分娩和农村孕妇生育也纳入基本医疗保险和新型农村合作医疗给予报销。至2010年，城镇职工、居民和农村居民均可享受医疗保险待遇。

一、公费医疗

1978年沿用公费医疗制度，仅限城镇职工，财政拨款单位由卫生局财会人员凭发票掌握支付，企业职工则由企业承担。1985年1月，改由新成立的公医办负责报销，财政拨款单位患病职工凭就诊发票附处方笺报销。1998年，财政局设立社保科接办全县公费医疗经费审核报销。到2005年7月，原享受公费医疗的在岗和退休人员转入城镇职工基本医疗保险，离休干部仍执行公费医疗，至2010年的6年累计支出601.99万元，年平均支出100.33万元，比2004年少支付20.34万元，使公费医疗经费得到合理使用。

二、基本医疗保险

（一）城镇职工、居民基本医疗保险

2005年7月启动，先在事业单位、机关团体、民办非企业单位、退休人员及城镇个体经济组织业主及从业人员中执行。患者在门诊就医、定点药店购药，使用社会保障卡在社会保险收付管理中心拨到个人账户的款支付，住院费由社会保险收付管理中心于统筹基金账户支付，超过基本医疗保险最高限额部分用大额医疗补助经费统筹支付。

2008年，保险范围扩大到灵活就业人员和城镇居民。新参保的灵活就业人员实行6个月“待遇等待期”，从期满次月起享受医疗保险待遇，并开始计算“待遇享受期”。待遇享受期在12个月内按正常支付标准30%、超过12个月至24个月按60%和超过24个月按100%享受。未按时缴费者，从次月起停止享受医疗保险待遇；中断不满6个月可续保补足欠费，自补清欠费次日起享受保险待遇。中断时间连续计算，超过6个月保险关系自行终止，以后可重新参保。参保城镇居民只享受住院或门诊大病医疗保险待遇，除个人负担部分其余由统筹基金支付。缴费年限与保险待遇挂钩，连续缴费年限每增加12个月，统筹基金支付标准增1%，增加到80%为止。首年统筹基金最高支付限额4万元，连续缴费年限每增12个月，最高限额增0.15万元，增到6万元。

社会医疗保险业务办理

2007—2010年，全县支付城镇职工、居民医疗保险费7308.58万元，其中基本医疗支付1925.14万元，大额医疗支付284.84万元，重症协议支付436.36万元，个人账户支付2593.38万元，药店购药支付2068.36万元，让有职业和无职业人员均享受到医疗保障。

（二）新型农村合作医疗

2005年7月至2010年，参保村民到定点医疗机构就诊按比例报销，连续5年6个月累计全县报销

8921.53万元，占发生医疗费的45.35%，其中门诊报销3883.12万元，住院报销5038.41万元，使村民真正享受到参加合作医疗的实惠。广大农民赞不绝口地说：我们种地不交税，学生入学不交费，合作医疗好，农民得实惠。

2005—2010年新农合门诊及住院报销标准表

表5—03—05

年度	在各级医疗机构门诊报销比例					在各级医疗机构住院报销比例			
	省、市%	县%	乡%	村%	最高补偿（元）	省、市%	县%	乡%	最高补偿（元）
2005			30	40	100		30	40	1600
2006		20	30	40	200		30	40	2500
2007		20	30	40	200		30	40	2500
2008	30	40	50	60	300	40	50	60	4000
2009	30	40	50	60	300	40	50	60	5000
2010	30	40	50	60	300	40	50	60	5000

2006—2010年新农合大病统筹报销标准

表5—03—06

年度	个人承担医疗费用（元）	大病报销（%）	大病报销封顶线（元）
2006—2007	6000—10000	30	2006年 15000 2007年 20000
	10001—20000	40	
	20001以上	50	
2008—2010	5000—15000	40	2008—2010年60000
	15001—30000	50	
	30001—50000	60	
	50001以上	70	

2005—2010年新农合医疗费减免情况表

表5—03—07

年度	合计		门诊			住院			在住院数中：二次减免	
	发生医疗费（万元）	减免（万元）	就诊报销（人次）	发生医疗费（万元）	减免（万元）	就诊报销（人次）	发生医疗费（万元）	减免（万元）	就诊报销（人次）	减免（万元）
2005		4.92	5915		4.92					
2006	934.09	270.01	258358	419.85	128.92	6203	514.24	141.09	82	18.42
2007	2153.60	740.60	446512	933.10	292.60	10066	1220.50	448.00	323	176.40
2008	4044.75	1926.89	740422	2180.06	865.15	9957	1864.19	1061.74	444	332.46
2009	5736.03	2770.60	1009442	2688.59	1341.46	11279	3047.44	1429.14	659	538.30
2010	6805.37	3208.51	853757	2731.30	1250.07	12642	4074.07	1958.44	910	652.15

注：2005年门诊栏中含住院发生数

专记：新农合让吴义琴死中得活

龙场镇干坝村五组村民吴义琴，30多岁即感到心区隐痛，因家居农村，经济条件较差，孩子年幼，认为有点病不吃药忍一忍会好的，根本没把心区的痛放在心上，年复一年的就这样拖着过日子。2009年4月20日，病情突然暴发晕厥倒地，顿时面色苍白，手脚冰凉，当即送往贵阳医学院附属医院抢救，诊断为风湿性心脏病二尖瓣关闭不全，必须施行手术治疗，治疗费需10万余元，如果不施手术就有生命危险。时仅46岁的吴义琴得知后，因家中无力支付这笔巨款，坚持要开药出院。正当病人病入膏肓，无钱手术的危急时刻，家人咨询得知大病可享受新型农村合作医疗6.5万元的信息后，决心卖掉家里唯一能从事运输挣钱维持全家生计的面包车及其他能换钱的物品，并向亲朋好友借贷凑足治疗费，随即住院手术。经护理月余康复出院，全家人喜出望外，无不感激医护人员的精心理疗。出院结账累计支付9.1万元，其中龙场镇社会保障所按规定给报销6.47万元，自负费用2.63万元，家人得到救助后感激涕零地说：大头部分合医给我家支付了，剩下的欠账压力不大，要不多久就可以还清。吴义琴逢人便讲：我的病也好了，又不给家里添累赘，好得有新型农村合作医疗才使我从死亡线上拖救过来，是党的合作医疗政策救治了我，让我终生难忘。

（三）生育保险

1.城乡居民生育保险

2000年起，为保障城乡孕产妇正常分娩，降低孕产妇死亡率，2001年结合降低孕产妇死亡率和消除新生儿破伤风基础项目，2004年实施的农村卫生人力开发项目，2008年推行的农村孕产妇住院分娩补助项目，对农村贫困家庭孕产妇住院分娩的住院费、生活费、危重抢救费实行经济救助，至2010年的10年累计有1.43万人获得救助365.14万元，让危重孕产妇顺利转为安全分娩。

2.职工生育保险

2008年9月启动列为贵阳市统筹保险项目的职工生育保险，先在国家机关、人民团体、企业、事业单位实施，11月扩大到民营企业。由女职工所在单位按照上一年度月平均工资总额为基数，以0.7%比例为职工缴纳保险费，职工个人不缴费。保险范围包括符合国家和省计划生育政策及基本医疗保险药品目录的生育医疗费、产前检查医疗费、接生费、手续费、住院费、药费、计划生育手续费，费用支出由县社会保险收付管理中心登记上报，贵阳市社会保障部门统一在生育保险基金内报销。至2010年，全县3年累计征收保险费122.58万元，2010年全县参保人数达7408人。

第四节　最低生活保障

1998年，开始在龙场镇试行最低生活保障，随后逐步在全县推开。至2010年，累计发放低保金额8272.03万元，其中发的城镇居民4684.32万元，占56.63%；农村居民3587.71万元，占43.37%。

一、城镇居民低保

民政局工作人员对龙岗社区城镇低保对象入户抽查

1998年6月，由民政局启动城镇居民低保。先在龙场镇试点，确定因智力、身残和其他原因，家庭基本无收入来源，须靠政府救济和亲邻相帮的28户39人纳入低保，保障标准90元，不足部分人月均补差32.8元。1999年10月，根据县政府《实施城乡居民最低生活保障制度暂行办法》和民政局《实施细则》，保障标准提高到月人均120元，即对家庭人均收入低于标准线之差数实行保障。确定城镇无劳动能力、无生活来源又无法定赡养、抚养、扶养义务人，或虽有法定赡养、抚养、扶养义务人而该义务人又无赡养、抚养、扶养能力；领取失业救济金或失业救济金期满仍未重新就业人员、在职或下岗人员、离退休人员及其他家庭月人均收入仍低于当地城市居民最低生活标准均为保障对象。当年人月均保障42.6元。2000年保障金标准提高30%，同时扩大保障面，要求做到“应保尽保”。是年，月人均保障标准为39.52元。2004年对三无人员（无生活来源、无劳动能力、无法定赡养人或抚养人）、70岁以上老年人、残疾人、一人户和二人户家庭、有子女上学家庭、长期患重（大）疾病病人等家庭给予政策优惠，保障金标准提高10元，提高后人月均补差达到65.7元。继后，保障金随生活水平提高而增加，从2005年135元增到2010年210元。13年全县累计支出4684.32万元。

二、农村居民低保

1999年10月启动农村居民低保，保障标准为月人均40元。按照《贵阳市农村低保实施意见》，在农村定居、农村居民户口与城市居民户口混合家庭，符合本市当年城市居民最低生活保障条件的城市户口家庭成员，享受城市低保待遇；符合农村最低生活保障条件农村居民户口家庭成员，享受农村低保待遇；夫妻一方为本市农村居民户口，其配偶及女子为非本市居民户口，在现居住地定居一年以上，其家庭人均收入低于户口所在地农村低保标准人员属于保障范围，由民政局和乡（镇）社会事务办公室严格审批，做到政策公开、补助标准公开，接受群众监督，确保离任老干部、孤老、残疾人等特殊困难群体能享受到最低保障。2005年6月，按照贵阳市政府统一部署，将农村特困户救助对象纳入农村低保范围，保障标准为每户人均月收入达不到60元的予以补差。是年平均补差29.7元。同时，县对符合计划生育政策生育女孩的贫困户、丧失劳动力残疾人、70岁以上老年人提高补助标准5元。是年发放优惠金16.5万元。2008年保障标准再提高到70元。

民政局工作员对六桶乡城镇低保对象入户抽查

至2010年的13年累计支出3587.71万元。

1998—2010年全县城乡居民最低生活保障金发放情况表

表5—03—05

年份	合计(万元)	城镇			农村		
		户	人	金额(万元)	户	人	金额(万元)
1998	1.54	28	39	1.54	—	—	—
1999	50.70	114	212	26.92	816	1143	23.78
2000	53.33	296	604	28.64	—	1194	24.69
2001	66.20	383	787	40.30	931	1321	25.90
2002	270.70	1763	4659	236.70	1091	1410	34.00
2003	268.98	1895	4758	235.48	1084	1494	33.50
2004	353.90	2444	4953	326.00	—	1510	27.90
2005	566.60	2485	5017	428.20	3027	5087	138.40
2006	775.43	2496	5079	537.11	4020	6778	238.32
2007	1086.73	2528	5170	675.01	5731	12696	411.72
2008	1757.62	2279	4533	809.62	6020	13233	948.00
2009	1588.20	2320	4638	718.20	5937	13249	870.00
2010	1432.10	1904	3839	620.60	5154	11298	811.50

注：表内数据由民政局提供

第五节　养老保障

1978年，沿袭职工退休养老制度，1986年起陆续建立和完善社会保障体系，保障范围从城镇扩大到农村。到2010年全县3.34万老年人均享受到养老保险和医疗保险待遇，使老有所养、老有所医、老有所学、老有所乐成为现实。

一、离退休保障

（一）离休保障

1980年11月实施离休养老保障，凡1949年9月30日前参加工作并达到法定退休年龄者，均可享受离休待遇。到1990年，全县117名老干部已办理离休107人。行政事业单位离休费由县财政发放，地方国有企业因单位不景气逐步改为财政拨款支付，后落实政策回新华书店的离休干部童日久进入县社会养老保险。2003年3月24日和2005年10月20日，驻县国防工业企业四一八库和兴红机械厂离休干部移交县管，离休费由省社会保险收付管理中心发放，到2010年年末，由县财政支付离休费的老干部仍有37人，年发放离休费210.18万元；由县社会保险管理中心支付的1人，年支出2.75万元、国防工业9人和其他企事业7人的离休费，省社会保险收付管理中心和所在单位均按月足额支付。

（二）退休保障

1978年，遵照国务院104号文件精神，行政机关和事业单位退休人员退休费以本人退休时标准工资和工龄计发，即参加工作时间为抗日战争时期按90%，解放战争时期80%；新中国建立后工龄满20年75%，满15年不满20年70%，满10年不满15年60%，无论干部、工人，凡因公（工）伤残或患二、三期矽肺病退休80%，生活需要扶助的计发90%。获全国劳动英雄、劳动模范、战斗英雄称号或革命建设有特殊贡献，退休时仍保持荣誉的提高5%—15%。确认完全丧失劳动能力又不具备退休条件准予退职，生活费按40%计发。

1984年，贵州省对省外来黔工作20年以上直至退休的知识分子退休费提高10%。1985年对1952年底前和1953年1月1日后参加工作分别提高10%和5%。1988年又对1952年前参加工作工龄满30年按95%，不满30年按90%；1953年1月1日后参加工作满30年按90%，不满30年85%。

1994年，根据黔人退字〔1994〕5号文件规定，凡1952年底以前参加工作工龄30年以上的按100%，满20年以上95%；1953年1月1日以后参加工作工龄满30年95%。获省政府颁发30年教龄荣誉证书并在教师岗位退休的按100%。1998年筑人字5号文又规定，从事专业技术或科学管理工作满30年，在乡镇以下从事科技管理工作满25年，具有中级以上技术职务科技人员，退休费可按100%。省人通4号文又明确，自1979年6月16日以来生育一个子女并领取独生子女证的退休金加发5%。期间，还对异地安家的增发一次性安家费，70周岁以上增发高龄津贴，死亡后发给丧葬费、抚恤费和遗属生活困难补助费等，

2010年年末，全县累计行政事业单位办理退休手续1870人，年计发退休金5891.87万元。退职5人，未参保人员退休金由所在单位负责，参保企业人员由社会保险收付管理中心统一发放。

退休养老业务办理

二、养老保险

（一）企业职工和城镇居民

1986年10月，县劳动局置社会保险事业管理股管理城镇职工居民的养老保险。规定从1984年年底起招收合同制工人，自报到之日起按本人标准工资3%和所在单位按合同制工人工资总额15%缴纳养老保险金。1988年扩大到国营企业固定职工，在有条件的单位开始办理。

经过1992年和1994年两次改革，保险费又从国家、企业承担改为国家、企业 、个人共同负担，个人缴费由企业代为收缴；基本养老金由社会性和缴费性两部分组成，社会性养老金以职工离退休时本省上一年职工月平均工资为基数，按企业职工缴费年限分段计发，即满15年及其以上按25%，满10年不满15年按20%，不满10年的每满1年一次性发给本人指数化月平均缴费工资3个月生活补助费；缴费性养老金

以职工本人指数化月平均缴费工资为基数，缴费10年的每满1年计发1%。同时，制定城镇集体企业职工、临时工、“三资”企业中方职工、私营企业职工社会养老保险统筹试行办法，进行一体化社会养老保险。

1995年9月办理养老保险金补缴，其标准按每人每月计算，1993年年底前的25元（单位20元，个人5元），1994年1月以后行政单位55元（单位46元，个人9元），企业单位48元（单位40元，个人8元），并颁发养老保险手册，实行社会统筹与个人账户相结合。1997年3月1日起，从企业缴费中划入个人账户比例由8%降为7%。

1998年1月起，国有企业和国有改制企业均列入保险范围。9月，由贵州省统一统筹支付项目。2000年6月，县社会保险事业管理局委托农业银行县支行为离退休人员设立账户，发放储蓄卡（折），采取通存通兑方式代发离退休费。

2002年5月，将保险范围扩大到个体工商户和灵活就业人员，实行社会统筹和个人账户相结合，城乡个体工商户及其从业人员、自由职业和自谋职业及其他非工薪收入者，按全省上一年在岗职工月平均工资的60%至300%作为缴费基数，城镇个体工商户和自由职业人员按缴费基数20%，城镇个体工商户为其从业人员按12%，个体工商户的从业人员本人按8%比例缴纳，其中11%记入个人账户，其余部分作为统筹基金。

以上参保人员凡属1998年9月30日及以前参加工作（参保），实际缴费年限与视同缴费年限累计满10年以上的；1998年10月1日及以后参加工作（参保），实际缴费满15年及以上的，凡符合法定退休年龄可以办理退休，并享受养老保险待遇和国家规定死亡丧葬补助费。

2010年1月贵阳市在全国未推行之前，率先启动城镇居民养老保险，境内60岁以上老人参保并缴保险费，次月起享受养老保险待遇，至年末，全县累计参保1.04万人，征收养老保险费4910万元，已有1838人办理退休享受养老保险待遇。

1986—2010年城镇养老保险缴费统计表

表5—03—05

年份	参保数（人）	养老缴费（万元）	年份	参保数（人）	养老缴费（万元）	年份	参保数（人）	养老缴费（万元）
1986—1987	737	10.25	1995	2931	169.16	2003	2271	462.25
1988		8.78	1996	5351	732.72	2004	2457	1125.60
1989	987	11.70	1997	5418	800.81	2005	3383	793.00
1990	1060	15.06	1998	3849	817.01	2006	4018	993.71
1991	1509	27.54	1999	4180	769.53	2007	5705	2183.30
1992	1557	37.59	2000	1640	350.89	2008	7341	2508.38
1993	1768	39.17	2001	1809	329.92	2009	8402	2851.78
1994	1803	58.85	2002	2118	211.76	2010	10397	4910.42

（二）农村居民

2008年7月启动新型农村社会养老保险，凡县内农业户口，年满18周岁以上（在校学生除外），且未参加被征地农民社会养老保险或城镇企业职工基本养老保险人员均可参保。缴费方式可按月、按季、按年。缴纳标准为本县上年农民纯收入，确定月缴23.57元。18周岁以上至60周岁以下缴费年限在15年以上，领取养老金标准随缴费年限增长而增加，每多缴1年增发1%养老金；45周岁以上至60周岁以下缴费不足15年可一次性补足，次月起计发养老金，也可顺延缴至15年的次月起计发养老金。60周岁以上按参保时本县农民年纯收入，一次性缴15年保险费4242.6元，次月起每月领取养老金94.4元，往后随经济增长和农村居民最低生活保障标准变动适时调整。在乡复员退伍军人参保15年及以上，以军队服役年限作为增发养老金的依据，每满1年增发1%基础养老金。年满60周岁领取养老金独生子女户、双女计生户夫妻每人每月增发100元养老金。如参保者在缴费期间死亡，个人账户本息全部退还；如在领取养老金期间死亡，从次月起停发养老金，同时一次性支付500元丧葬补助金，并将个人账户本息余额退还给法定继承人。到2010年，全县参保2145人，征收保险费519.1万元，已有1206人享受养老保险待遇。

新型农村养老保险宣传

三、老年人事业

（一）老有所养

1985年前，沿袭城镇职工退休养老制度，离退休职工通过领取离退休费来体现。1986年执行贵州省《国营企业职工退休金统筹办法》，县始建养老保险制度，以县为单位按照“以支定收，略有结余”原则，从企业工资总数中提取退休金交县统一管理，企业之间实行“余额上交，差额拨付”办法进行调剂。1988年推行国营企业职工退休金社会统筹制度，较好地克服企业间退休金负担畸重畸轻矛盾，1998年又启动城乡居民最低生活保障制度，农村以无生活来源老人为保障重点。继后，社会养老统筹范围逐渐扩大到城乡居民。2005年起在提高老年人最低生活保障同时，对百岁老人每人每月发给100元高龄保健补贴，列入县财政预算。至2010年除县属行政事业单位离职休养人员仍在本单位领取离休金外，其余均实行社会统筹，已享受养老保障老年人2.86万人，占当年全县老年人的85.66%。

（二）老有所医

2005年6月前沿袭公费医疗制度，离退休老年人患病治疗费用实行公费报销，其余老年人患病无力治疗则实行社会救助，部分单位实行定期或不定期对老年人进行体检，发现病态及时治疗。7月，按照中发〔1998〕44号《关于建立城镇职工基本医疗保险制度决定》和贵阳市贯彻执行《实施意见》，启动城镇职工基本医院保险制度，对重病实行大额医疗费用报销，减轻老年人经济负担。同时启动新型农村合作医疗，老年人患病治疗费用按比例报销。继后完善对老年人就诊免收普通挂号费，为“五保”（老、弱、孤、寡、残）老人、低保老人、复员退伍军人医疗补助和农村医疗救助，开展对老年人就医、住院、取药等优惠服务，对90岁以上老人每年一次免费体验。2008年，将医疗保险范围再扩大到城镇居民和灵活就业人员，至2010年医疗社会统筹制度全部建立，使老年人患病治疗得到保障，从而提高预期寿命。

（三）老有所乐

1990年县成立老年体育协会（简称“老体协”）后，建成3个老年门球场，组建中老年健身辅导站、老年羽毛球队、老年门球队、钓鱼协会及中老年文体组织，举办安顺地区东五县门球赛、县内4次钓鱼比赛、5届综合运动会和老年节室内体育比赛。1991年起，为进一步保障老年人老有所乐，延年益寿，县主要从5个方面开展工作。

建立老年文体组织 1992年10乡（镇）成立老体协分会，全县老体协会员从1990年949人增至1400多人。1997年12月和2002年5月，分别组建有老年人参加的业余文工团和老年合唱团。至2010年全县仍存县老体协及下属13个分会、1支门球队、1个合唱团、1支秧歌队、2支腰鼓队、1支铜鼓队、2支舞蹈队、2支武术队、1支柔力球队、1支威风锣鼓队，有成员1000余人。

建立老年活动场馆 1994—2010年，中央、省、市、县、乡财政累计投资849.98万元，村自筹458.76万元，建成乡（镇）精神文明活动中心和118个村党员活动室供老年人活动。1998年县城建设全省首家县级体育馆后，河滨花园、龙岗花园、瀚林花园、河滨休闲广场、扎佐镇紫竹园广场、万江厂老年活动中心陆续建成，10乡（镇）驻地和龙场镇普陀村建成健身场并安装健身器材，供老年人休闲和健身锻炼。

开展老年文体活动 1996年复归贵阳市管辖，至2010年县老体协先后承办或协办老年体育比赛活动3次，组队参加市、县举办老年体育运动比赛10次，有58项分别获奖。1998年10月，由县举办10乡（镇）及机关、厂矿离退休老年人“夕阳红”卡拉OK声乐大赛，每年“九九”重阳老年节均在体育馆举办室外趣味性综合运动会，开展项目有夹弹子、摸“福”字，投飞镖、赶猪、钓瓶（鱼）、丢圈、弄铅球、踢毽子等，成功者均给予肥皂、牙膏等物资鼓励。

老年人象棋比赛

组织中老年人早晚锻炼 县体育馆和龙岗花园等场馆建成，为老年人锻炼场所，每天锻炼者约五百人，长年不断，晨练项目有太极拳、中老年保健操、健身操等20余种。晚练项目分室内羽毛球、乒乓球，室外有广场舞及其他舞蹈。乡（镇）六广有花灯，扎佐有腰鼓，马家桥有金钱棍等。2006年起县体育馆免收室外锻炼所用电费，更方便老年人锻炼。

享受老年人优待 凡60周岁以上老年人可至县老龄委办理《老年优待证》，2004—2010年，除在省、市老龄委办理部分外，县累计办证5447个。其中，甲证（60—69周岁）2597个，乙证（70周岁以上）2850个。持本人《老年优待证》在县内老干部活动中心、活动站（室）、公园、体育馆、文化馆、图书室可实行半价或免费优待，游阳明洞景区和贵阳森林野生动物园对60—69岁老年人门票减半，70岁以上全免。

（四）老有所学

1990年秋，县成立老年人大学，校址设在老干局，校长由县委书记兼任，县委副书记和老体协副主席为副校长，开办初期分设政治、卫生、花卉、摄影、绘画、太极拳共7个班。继后，陆续增办健身操、健身球、扭秧歌、腰鼓、木兰球、中老年迪斯科、舞蹈、铜鼓等班。2000年后增加威风锣鼓班。开展过程中班级有增有减，到2010年仍存8个班，学员250人。

（五）老有所为

1.关心下一代健康成长

1990年8月30日，遵照中央“全党、全社会都要关心下一代健康成长”的号召，县建立关心下一代协会。1996年2月2日更名为关心下一代工作委员会（简称“关工委”），下设办公室和宣传组织、社会工作、学校工作、政法工作、农村工作五个组。1999年后陆续在局和乡（镇）建立关工委，村（社区）为关工委小组。至2010年主要开展5项工作。

义务宣传 牵头组织、协调，配合县委宣传部、政法委、教育局、共青团、妇联等部门，利用重大节日和国内重大庆典，采取演讲、为烈士扫墓、上街宣讲、举办各类竞赛等形式，开展爱国主义、集体主义、社会主义教育和“五爱”（爱祖国、爱人民、爱劳动、爱科学、爱社会主义）教育，培育有理想、有道德、有纪律、有文化 的“四有新人”。20年累计举办大型读书、科技、法律、书画、歌舞等主题鲜明竞赛活动68次，发放图书3500册，宣传资料7280份，参与活动青年5.14万人，有38人获市表彰，其中有4人并获省表彰。

校外辅导 组织离退休老干部、老教师在全县建立家长学校10所，校外辅导组57个，从离退休干部中聘请校外辅导员97人，把握爱国主义、集体主义、社会主义教育主旋律，开展形式多样、内容丰富的辅导活动。通过学校、家庭、社会“三位一体”通力合作，全县涌现出地（市）级“三好”（思想品德好、学习好、身体好）学生158人次，县级三好生1575人次，375名学生甩掉“差生”帽子。

帮教失足青少年 通过组织帮教团，签订帮教协议，安排服刑人员回县参观或现身说法、展出等方式开展帮教工作。到2010年，利用元旦或春节等节日，由关工委牵头邀请政法委和公、检、法、司部门负责人及工、青、妇人士组成帮教团，赴劳教、劳改场所对修文籍在押人员开展帮教15次，受帮教1852人次；帮教失足青少年1215人，有786人已明显好转。

专记：帮教失足青少年初见成效

1991年5月8日，县关工委出面组织，邀请县委、县政府、人大、政协领导及政法系统各部门负责人、工、青、妇各界人士组成23人帮教团，由县委书记朱生亮带队到沙子哨劳改农场，对121名修文籍服刑人员开展帮教，给他们介绍家乡发展变化，指出他们犯罪行为给社会、家庭及亲人带来的影响，勉励他们遵守监规监纪，诚实劳动，认真接受改造，争取早日刑满回到家乡参加建设。帮教会议结束时，向服刑人员发放毛巾、口缸、牙膏、香皂等生活用品，使其感受到家乡亲人的关爱，纷纷表示一定遵守监规，老实改造，成为新人。

1995年5月14日，关工委邀请金华农场由干警带出表现好的修文籍服刑人员11名回县，在县城一中、二中和实验小学高年级共625名学生中，以他们的经历为例证，对学生进行劝导，有的服刑人员痛哭流涕地讲述由于不学法、不懂法走上盗窃、吸毒、打架斗殴致人伤残犯罪道路事实，并发誓要用劳动改造汗水洗刷自己身上毒瘤，积极改造，争取立功减刑，早日回来参加家乡建设。接着关工委又带他们参观县城建设，游览扎佐高尔夫球场，他们当即表示感谢亲人对他们关心和帮教。

培训农科人才 利用学校资源，建立农业科教培训中心，培养农村科技人才。1999年县财政投资5000元和小箐乡农工商有限责任公司投资7.1万元，在小箐中学建立培训中心，聘请农艺师、畜牧师为参加学习的历届高、初中毕业生教授科学种植和科学养殖技术。2000年财政拨款3万元建立马家桥农业中学农科教培训中心。2003年又筹资2.3万元从东北农业大学调进脱毒马铃薯5000公斤在农场镇、扎佐镇和大石乡青年农民家庭试种，由马家桥农科教培训中心专职教师上门教授种植技术和指导，成功后推广到各乡（镇）。

资助贫困学子 1997—1998年资助大中专特困生20人，发放助学金1.5万元。小箐乡苗族学生唐跃1998年8月考入西南民族学院，关工委资助1000元入学，毕业后回县报效家乡父老。

离退休干部到久长镇与贫困户座谈

2.发挥余热

老年人经过一生磨炼，积累着丰富知识和宝贵经验，为发挥其余热，县内有组织地开展4种形式活动。

参加编史修志 1985—1998年完成元朝至1990年《修文县志》编写，15名编辑中有7名为离退休人员。2003年启动县志续集及乡（镇）、县直属部门志编写，2010年已出版或完成志稿的乡（镇）和部门志书多属离退休人员所为，县志续集11名编辑中有6名为退休人员。

退休老同志参加志书编纂和审稿

参与老年人工作和关心下一代工作 自1990年8月县成立关心下一代工作委员会起，连续3届副主席中均有3名离退休干部担任，2004年3月换届置副主席10名，其中离退休老干部7名，老体协和老年大学领导成员中离退休老干部也占多数，让老干部承担工作重任。

参加公益活动 2003年起，县城组织老年人“夕阳红”卫生队，20余名离退休老干部多次上街维护公共秩序和公共卫生。

参加“三个代表”督察 2003年开展“三个代表”重要思相学习活动，10余名离退休老干部参加督察组到乡镇和县直属部门开展督察。

第四章　医疗卫生

1978年，沿袭“文化大革命”时期卫生部门的建制，有医疗机构42个。1979年拉开医疗卫生改革的序幕，到1992年，随着撤区并乡建镇的行政区划调整，原区、乡医疗机构合并组建为10个乡（镇）卫生院。1998年将管理公费医疗业务的职能从卫生局析出，分设卫生监督机构。2005年启动医疗保险制度。至2010年，全县有医疗机构234个，城乡医疗保障从建立走向逐渐完善，为全县人民铺就出一条“病有所医，医之得当”之路。

2009年在县城翠屏东路建成的县人民医院

第一节　医药改革

1978—2004年，一直沿袭原实施国家职工公费医疗制度，到2005年才开始推行医疗保险和新型农村合作医疗，保障范围从国家职工扩大到城乡居民，2010年全县参保和参合人数达26.31万人，覆盖面为86%。

一、医药体制改革

（一）多元化医疗机构并行

1978年，县、区两级医疗机构为政府事业机构，乡、村级医疗机构为集体所有，到1991年有政府医疗事业机构11所，集体医疗机构33所。1992年，乡集体医疗机构与区级医疗机构合并组建为乡（镇）卫生院，统属政府事业单位，经费由乡（镇）财政拨款，业务归县卫生局管理。1995年起，县政府松绑，允许具有职业资格的医生开办诊所，拓展多元化医疗卫生事业，以致股份制医院、个体经营医院（诊所）相继出现，到2010年除隶属贵阳市白云区的贵阳煤矿小河沟职工医院和预备役工兵团卫生队外，全县共有政府事业医疗机构13个，集体和私营医疗机构221个（含村卫生室197个），其中有14个私人诊所和龙场镇属的城南、城北村第二卫生室为营利性医疗机构，其余均为非营利性医疗机构。

（二）固定工招聘工并存

1978年沿袭计划经济体制，医疗卫生人员实行统招统配，人员试用期满即转正为固定工，其中多为大中专毕业生，少数医疗机构为开展业务需要也少量向外招聘临时工。从2005年起面向社会招聘逐年增多，到2010年，仅县人民医院和10乡（镇）卫生院对外招聘工就有221人，占核定编制总人数的44.02%。

（三）药品市场“两条腿”走路

1978年，县内药品销售、批发均属国营企业，全县统由药材公司独家经营。1985年7月《中华人民共和国药品管理法（试行）》出台，允许私人参与药品购销，致使私营药店、药房陆续开业，并由县城扩大到乡（镇）。于是，就形成国营药材公司和私营药店并行经营的“两条腿”走路的药品销售市场。到1996年始将国有公司下放给个人经营。1999年，再分离药材公司的所有权和经营权，将国营公司改为承包经营，由个人向公司交给营业场地租金。到2010年，全县共有私营药品零售企业43户、药品批发企业1户、农村零售药柜54个，其中有8家药店为贵阳市城镇职工基本医疗保险定点药店。

二、医疗制度改革

（一）公费医疗

1978年沿用原制，患者凭《就诊证》就医记账，国家行政事业单位由卫生局财会结账报销，国营企业由所在单位承担，要求按标准控制，实际是敞开报销，致医药费用只增不减，甚至出现一人公医、全家共享的问题。1985年1月，县政府加强公费医疗管理，成立公费医疗管理委员会，下设办公室（简称“公医办”）于卫生局，专司公费医疗管理。同时采取“单位承包，合同医疗，定点就医，节约奖励，超支分摊”的办法，将经济利益与享受单位、享受人员、医疗单位挂钩，实行现金看病，医院开“双处方”，一联给患者回单位报销，一联留存备查，使滥开药品行为有所收敛。

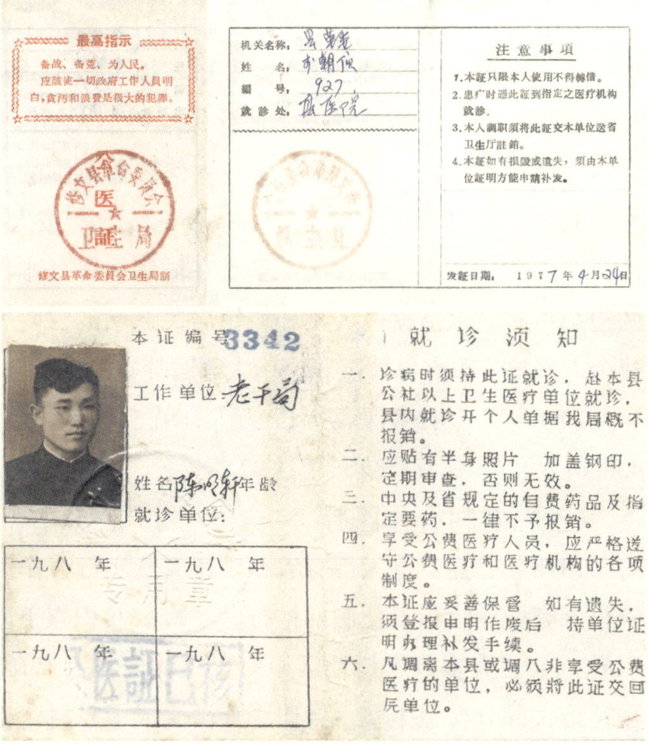

上为1978年沿用的公医证，下为20世纪80年代使用的公医证

1998年，公医办划归财政局，成立社会保障科进行管理，旨在完善定点医疗和合同医疗制度，但仍有少数自私贪财者擅钻制度空子，采取“挂床住院，全家用药”的方式进行报销，致使医疗经费连年超支。

2004年9月，县政府着手对离休干部公费医疗制度进行改革，作出4条规定：一是由县委组织部、县监察局、财政局、卫生局、物价局、审计局、离退休干部管理局各明确1名分管领导和离休干部代表2至3名，组成领导小组负责管理；二是定点就医，实行合同医疗；三是以2001年至2003年离休干部公费医疗经费年均数为基数，议标确定承包定额和定点医院进行承包，节约留用，超支不补；四是定期结算，定额报销。从改革之日起，财政按期拨付定额经费给定点医院，由定点医院统一掌握支付报销。如遇转外就医的大额医疗费，对扣除个人定额后的超支部分，由定点医院和财政按3:7比例分摊。2005年7月启动医疗保险制度，在岗干部职工（含退休）一律纳入医疗保险，离休干部继续执行公费医疗，至2010年的6年，全县离休干部公费医疗费用年均支出比2004年下降16.86%，使公费医疗经费得到有效控制。

（二）医疗保险

2005年7月，启动城镇职工基本医疗保险，规定除离休干部外，凡行政事业单位、国有企业、社会团体、民办非企业单位的在岗职工和退休职工均属保险对象，保险费由用人单位按上年职工月平均工资总额7.5%缴纳，职工个人按上年个人月平均工资总额2%缴纳，缴入资金由社会保险收付管理中心进行统筹，分别划入统筹基金账户和个人账户，统筹基金用于支付住院治疗最高限额内费用和特殊病种门诊基本费用。个人账户逐月拨给，用于门诊就诊和零售药店购药，凭统一制发的《社会保障卡》结算。为解决重病和特殊病种医疗费用，同时实行大额医疗补助，一年一保，用人单位和参保人各缴纳48元。缴则享受，不缴就不享受。资金实行调剂使用，集中支付超过基本医疗费用最高限额的费用支出。

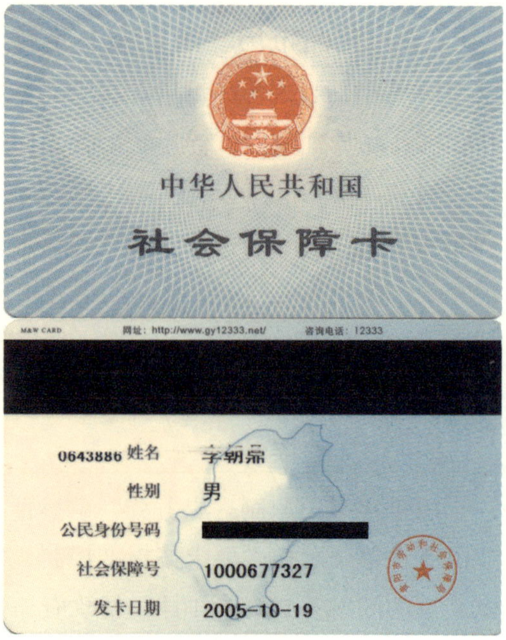

2005年7月启用的社会保障卡

2008年，城镇职工医疗保险范围扩大到灵活就业人员和城镇居民，凡县内户籍自谋职业、个体经济、非全日制灵活性或弹性工作人员均列为灵活就业人员保险对象，基本医疗保险费按上一年度全省在岗职工月平均工资为基数，年满35周岁及其以下按4%和35岁以上按5%缴纳，累计缴费年限男满30年、女满25年，实际缴费年限不少于10年不再缴纳基本医疗保险费，大额医疗费自缴。城镇居民基本医疗保险对象为县境非农业户口，但又不属城镇职工基本医疗保险覆盖范围的城镇居民，缴费以家庭或个人为单位，每人每年缴10元至150元共6个档次，中央、市、县三级政府按人补助41元至190元。也可根据自身经济承受能力和条件，与具有中小学学籍农民工子女在城镇居民基本医疗保险、新型农村合作医疗之间选择参保，但不能两边都占有。灵活就业人员和城镇居民缴纳的保险金由社会保险收付管理中心统筹，只建基金账户，不建个人账户，重点保住院和门诊大额医疗费用。

2010年，全县参保者达1.3万人，就5年6个月全县征收保险基金7504.57万元（其中大额医疗保险费453.46万元），医疗费支付率达97.39%。

（三）农村合作医疗

1978年，全县绝大部分农村生产大队实行合作医疗制度，由赤脚医生给群众看病治病。随着80年代农村家庭联产承包责任制的推行，乡村公共积累下降，管理不得力，各级卫生行政部门又未能及时加强引导，全县大多数农村地区原有以集体经济为基础的合作医疗制度遭到解体或停办，赤脚医生逐渐消失，绝大部分村卫生室（合作医疗站）成了乡村医生的私人诊所。1991年起，各行政村又建立起村卫生室为村民患者自费就诊，但不能从根本上解决农村就医看病问题，一些地方还出现了农民看病难，看不起病，甚至因病致贫现象。

2005年7月，县拉开实施新型农村合作医疗（简称“新农合”）的序幕，贵阳市选择六广镇为试点先行一步，12月试点告竣。2006年，县又被列为第二批全国新型农村合作医疗试点县，当年全县新农合入保人数达20.7万人，入保率为84.72%，其中龙场镇最高，入保人数4.38万人，入保率93.90%。新型农村合作医疗制度实行由政府组织、引导和支持，农民自愿参加，个人、集体、政府多方筹资，以大病筹集为主，兼顾小病，一年一保的农村医疗互助共济制度。资金由中央、省、市、县财政拨款补助和参合农民自缴组成，采取专户存储，封闭运行，收支两条线的方式管理。

县合医办经办人员到农村检查合作医疗工作

实行新农合之初，有的农民特别是年轻农民心存疑虑，不肯自缴资金，认为不生病不求医为什么要出钱。经过县、乡反复宣传，讲清实行新农合的目的在于人人享有基本医疗服务和促进社会公平正义；讲清采取每人以少量资金投入医疗保险帮助生病者渡过难关的共济互利方法，有利群众之间团结友爱促进社会和谐等道理，从而提高大家对实施新农合的认识，纷纷缴纳资金参与。至2010年，全县参合人数达23.9万人，参合率达到97.13%；5年半累计筹集合作医疗基金9797.56万元，其中，中央补助4135.1万元，占42.21%；省补助2821.98万元，占28.8%；市补助840.93万元，占8.58%；县补助386.36万元，占3.94%；个人自缴1613.19万元，占16.47%，医疗费支付率达到91.06%。

2005—2010年新型农村合作医疗参合与筹资统计表

表5—04—01

年度	参合（人）	参合率（%）	标准（元）						到位资金（万元）					
			合计	中央	省	市	县	个人	合计	中央	省	市	县	个人
2005	12130	73.34	30	—	—	17	3	10	32.76	—	—	20.63	—	12.13
2006	207032	84.72	45	20	7	5	3	10	828.55	311.00	144.90	103.52	62.10	207.03
2007	222724	91.13	45	20	7	5	3	10	1129.55	517.10	167.00	155.91	66.82	222.72
2008	226306	93.98	90	40	30	7	3	10	2061.69	921.00	688.08	158.41	67.89	226.31
2009	233496	96.40	100	40	30	7	3	20	2398.99	952.00	746.50	163.45	70.05	466.99
2010	239007	97.13	140	60	45	10	5	20	3346.02	1434.00	1075.50	239.01	119.50	478.01
合计									9797.56	4135.10	2821.98	840.93	386.36	1613.19

专记：六广镇新农合试点取得成功

2005年7—12月，六广镇作为贵阳市新型农村合作医疗的试点。试点工作开始，县成立以县长石洪为组长的领导小组和以纪委书记阮小燕领导的监督委员会，赓续制发《实施方案》，镇和村建立的相应组织具体抓落实。3月至4月初县卫生局组成工作组开展基线调查。5月组装宣传车进行大型宣传，发放县政府《致农村居民的公开信》2万份，主要宣传实行合作医疗，维护社会公平，有利社会和谐和解决农民看病难等的好处。宣传覆盖面100%。6月5日在深入广泛宣传发动群众的基础上召开全镇动员大会，由镇政府与村委主任签订《目标责任书》，与年终奖惩挂钩。从镇属机关抽调9人与卫生局7人分赴各村具体组织人员参合，对每人当年交10元新农合基金有困难的五保户、残疾人、现役军人的父母、退伍军人、入朝退伍战士及配偶、低保人员、孤儿、90岁以上的老人、极贫户、特困户和计划生育“三结合”户，则由县党政领导、卫生局及派驻干部、镇属部门、企业、党员帮扶，共筹集帮扶资金3.15万元，解决3150人的缴费问题。决定7月1日为新农合制度开始实施日，县、镇成立办事机构，对农合基金进行管理和经理患者就医报销。仅6个月全镇参合人数达1.21万人，参合率73.34%，贵阳市财政补助资金20.63万元，村民自缴12.13万元，组成合作医疗基金共32.76万元，累计减免5915人次，减免金额4.92万元。新农合惠及六广广大群众，无不喜笑颜开，四处奔走相告，以现身说法宣传实行合作医疗带来的好处，有的还编花灯唱词在春节联欢晚会上歌颂新型农村合作医疗制度：合作医疗进村了，病有所医花钱少，身体健康得保障，归功党的政策好。

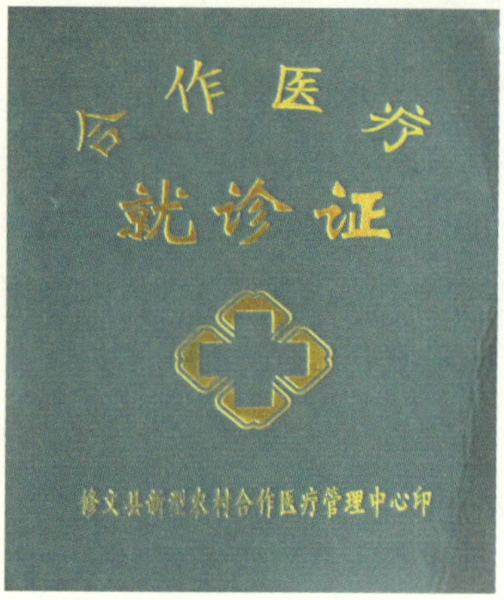

合作医疗就诊证

第二节　机构　队伍

1978年，县设医院，区设卫生院，乡设卫生所，村建合作医疗站，还有境内驻厂医院和卫生室。1979年起，随着改革开放的开展和深入，驻厂医疗机构陆续随厂迁出，民营医疗机构和红十字医院破土而出，到2010年，境内拥有医院7所，卫生院10所，疾病预防控制中心和妇幼保健站各1个，诊所14所，医务室3个，村卫生室197个，卫生队1个，从业人员776人。

一、医疗机构

（一）县直属医疗机构

县人民医院　1978年沿袭原建制，仍称县人民医院，为副科级事业单位。行政领导直属于县卫生局，业务指导属安顺地区人民医院。县医院承担医疗与护理、医学教学、医疗研究和医疗卫生人员技术培训。门诊部和住院部分置于县城健康路（今翠屏西路）和原学宫内。全院有职工60人，病床95张，分设内儿、外妇、中医、检验、放射、心电图、供应7个科（室）。1985年于环城路（今人民北路）新建2800平方米门诊大楼，加上原住院部2600平方米，业务用房共计5400平方米，职工增至110人。1993年起，先后增置科（室）和血站。2009年4月，迁于翠屏东路新建的综合楼，建筑面积1.48万平方米，其中门诊综合楼1.02万平方米，传染病区0.08万平方米，行政楼0.38万平方米。2010年增为22个行政科室，医技人员209人，其中副主任医师中有检验师、护师、药师16人，主治医师中有技师、药师、护师55人，医师中有技师、药师、护师及护士132人。是中国人民解放军第三军医大学新桥医院、贵阳市第一人民医院对口协作和帮扶医院，也是贵阳市城镇职工基本医疗保险和新型农村合作医疗定点医疗机构。

左为县人民医院1978年使用的外妇科住院部，中为1985年建于人民南路的门诊部，右为2009年启用的翠屏东路门诊部

疾病预防控制中心 1978年沿袭原卫生防疫站建制，仍称卫生防疫站，地址于东门外车站旁建房1栋，224平方米，隶属卫生局，承担疾病预防宣传、教育、控制、卫生监测等业务。1986年迁至东门河边新建房875平方米办公。1992年又于人民北路重建办公楼3176平方米，其中业务和办公用房1558平方米。2002年县编制委员会批准撤销卫生防疫站，与皮肤病防治所合并组建，称为疾病预防控制中心，属正科级事业单位。2010年设有慢病科、流病科、监督检验科和办公室，业务用房1250平方米，有职工31人，其中副主任医师3人，主治医师4人，主管检验师2人，主管护师2人，医师、技师17人。

县疾病预防控制中心大楼

妇幼保健站 1978年沿袭原建制，承担妇女、儿童系统保健业务，隶属卫生局，地址在健康路（今翠屏西路），办公用房126平方米。1980年建在龙井巷的新建办公楼落成，建筑面积854平方米，迁新址后除门诊外，还增加住院业务。2003年3月与计划生育宣传指导站合署办公，统称计划生育妇幼保健服务中心，地址于虎山路，有职工18人、归县人口与计划生育局管理，业务受计生局和卫生局监管。2005年迁阳明大道新建房办公，至2010年，体制和业务范围未变。

硝厂医院 为麻风病专科医院，地址在六桶乡黑塘沟。1978年沿袭原制，行政管理归民政局，业务接受卫生局领导。1984年8月，遵照国务院对麻风病人以社会性治病为主的指示，把5名医护人员调到新组建的皮肤病防治所，既承担硝厂医院病人的治疗，又负责院外麻风病人的社会性治疗。至2010年有职工5人，病员7人。

皮肤病防治所 1984年8月成立，为全民所有制事业单位，隶属卫生局，地址在县城北部王家湾，有职工6人，主要承担麻风病防治宣传、调查、治疗、管理、科研等工作，按照国务院指示精神对麻风病人从隔离治疗逐步转为社会性治疗。2002年撤销皮肤病防治所，其业务并入疾病防疫控制中心。

（二）乡（镇）医疗机构

1978年，4个区和1个县直属“公社”及边远的六桶公社设卫生院，属事业医疗机构；乡级公社及以下设卫生所（院）33个，属集体单位。行政关系隶属当地的区和公社，业务分别归属县卫生局和区卫生院。

1984年公社卫生所改称卫生院。1992年撤区并乡建镇，按新组建乡（镇）置10个卫生院，原区、社、乡医疗机构就地并入，属全民事业单位，诊疗科目均包括全科医疗和预防保健。2006—2010年均为新型农村合作医疗定点医疗机构。

2010年乡（镇）卫生院基本情况一览表

表5—04—02

名　称	地　址	病床（张）	职工（人）	房　屋（平方米）	救护车（辆）	业务量		业务收入（万元）
						门诊（万人次）	住院（人次）	
龙场镇卫生院	人民南路	3	39	1000	1	0.84	—	70.82
扎佐镇卫生院	大园街	57	58	3600	2	1.84	1383	335.78
久长镇卫生院	久长街	30	33	1400	1	4.27	366	258.46
六广镇卫生院	六广街	20	39	2300	1	2.36	312	78.91
谷堡乡卫生院	谷堡村	2	20	500	1	0.73	—	42.39
六屯乡卫生院	六屯街	10	13	800	1	0.92	31	50.97
小箐乡卫生院	小箐街	6	26	1227	—	1.28	120	40.58
洒坪乡卫生院	洒坪街	6	13	810	—	1.20	—	82.73
大石乡卫生院	大石街	5	13	1070	—	0.69	—	17.97
六桶乡卫生院	六桶新街	16	26	1700	1	1.81	437	110.44

（三）村级医疗机构

1978年沿袭“文化大革命”时期的合作医疗站，到1980年全县尚存171个，其中全免费52个，部分免费49个，收费70个。继后启动农村体制改革，因建于计划经济体制下的医疗机构模式僵化，资金连年短缺，致医疗站难以为继，到1990年只存47个。1991年，卫生局采取“公借私水行舟，私借公台唱戏”的办法，批准建立村卫生室122个，吸纳有一定医疗经验或初中以上学历，且热爱医疗卫生事业的年轻人，统一培训后签订《医疗卫生工作承包合同》，一次给予300元价值药品和器械，承担村内医疗、防疫、妇幼保健、计划生育和爱国卫生宣传任务。并经过考核认定三元村等26个卫生室为甲级村卫生室，城南等34个卫生室为集体办村卫生室。2003年村卫生室增到175个，其中个体办150个，集体办22个，乡与村联办3个，共有村医192人。从20世纪90年代末期起，由财政每月发给每人劳务费40元，后逐步提高到80元、100元、200元、300元。业务收入用作业务发展资金周转。2005年7月起明确村卫生室为新型农村合作医疗定点医疗机构。至2010年全县实有卫生室195个，村医205人，其中初级卫技人员5人。

（四）工矿　公安　驻军医疗机构

1978年，驻于县境的医疗机构有医院7所，卫生所1个、医务室7个。分布在龙场、扎佐、久长、谷堡4乡（镇），医务人员共450人，置病床362张，除负责本单位患者医治外，还为城乡群众提供医疗服

务。1990年后，随着企业改制推进，属县的企业医务室随厂转制停办，属驻县企业的医疗机构随厂搬迁出境，与此同时又新增有医院和医务室。1999年8月，中国人民解放军贵阳陆军预备役工兵团卫生队成立，队部设于县卫生局，职工11人全为县卫生系统医务人员兼任，局长王安全任副队长兼主治医师，下设修文、开阳、息烽、花溪4个卫生所，修文卫生所职工5人，副局长胡晓明任所长。至2010年，县境仍存驻县3所医院、3个医务室、1个卫生队，其中万江厂职工医院、扎佐林场医院、小河沟煤矿职工医院均为贵阳市城镇职工基本医疗保险定点医疗机构。

1978—2010年工矿、公安、驻军医疗机构基本情况一览表

表5—04—03

名　称	成立时间	驻　地	职工（人）	病床（张）	科室（个）	诊疗科目	变　更
三级电站医务室	1957	龙场镇干坝村	1	—	—	西医内科	20世纪90年代撤销
扎佐林场医务室（所）	1958	扎佐喻家街村	2	—	—	西医内科	2004年改建为林场医院
水电九局职工医院	1959	龙场镇平寨村	72	30	5	西医内、外、检验、B超	1985年后迁贵阳
万江厂职工医院	1966	扎佐镇新民村	20	3	—	内、外、预防保健	—
兴红厂职工医院	1967	扎佐镇兴红村	27	20	—	西医内科	2006年并入林场医院
庆文厂职工医院	1967	龙场镇城北村	13	5	—	西医内科	1993年迁白云区
华文厂职工医院	1967	谷堡乡谷堡村	12	6	—	内、外、预防保健	1993年迁小河区
烽光厂卫生所	1968	久长镇金桥村	21	12	—	西医内科	1993年迁小河区
418库医务室	1968	龙场镇小营村	2	3	2	西医内科	2003年改为龙翔医务室
011技校医务室	1968	扎佐镇大山村	12	4	4	西医内、外科	—
贵阳煤矿小河沟医院	1969	龙场镇新寨村	32	30	4	内、外、预防保健	—
三0四医院	1970	扎佐镇新民村	178	50	12	内、外、妇、儿、中医、精神、泌尿、骨伤、B超、放射、检验	1993年迁小河区
四级电站医务室	1970	谷堡乡平寨村	2	—	—	西医内科	20世纪90年代撤销
化肥厂医务室	1971	龙场镇新寨村	2	—	—	西医内科	1993年停办
耐火厂医务室	1972	龙场镇水塘村	1	—	—	西医内科	1993年停办
省林校医务室	1976	扎佐喻家街村	4	1	4	西医内科	2006年并入林场医院
105地质队医务室	1982	龙场镇小营村	1	3		西医内科	1998年迁乌当区
预备役工兵团卫生队	1999	卫生局	11	—	—	西医内、外科	—
扎佐林场医院	2004	扎佐喻家街村	100	50	10	内、外、妇、儿、中医、口腔、B超、放射、检验	—
公安看守所医务室	2009	县城看守所	2	—	—	西医内科	—

（五）红十字医疗机构

中医院 根据历届县人大代表、政协委员提议，1995年，县卫生局从县医院抽调4名医生筹建中医院，资金来源由政府投入、征拨建设用地、职工集资、吸纳社会个体投资。1996年2月，县政府批准成立县中医院，修机编〔1996〕41号文件明确为股份制管理，财务单独核算，经费差额补助纳入县卫生事业经费支出，属县级全民所有制医疗单位。6月开诊，法人吴曦，院址在县城翠屏东路，自建业务用房3080平方米，生活用房982平方米，内设中医、中医骨伤、内儿、外、妇产等19个科室，床位30张，人员编制42人。10月，修机编〔1996〕51号文件明确中医院级别与县医院同等规格。2004年5月有职工70人，其中正式工37人（内有副高级职称2人，中级职称6人，初级职称24人），外聘33人（内有高级职称1人，中级职称2人，初级职称23人）。至是年末，9年县财政累计拨付给中医院卫生事业经费203.1万元。2005年1月,中医院与县财政脱钩，财政终止拨款，31名正式职工全部转入县医院。从此改称为中西医结合医院，院长熊文欣，是年注册资金61万元，固定资产总值171万元（其中房屋建筑68万元，设备总值103万元）。2007年，转制为自主经营、自负盈亏的民营医院，法人更为荣启华，仍继续使用1995年执业许可证，国有资产部分未予验证。2010年3月，中医院租给华昇医院经营，院长李正华，报经贵阳市红十字会批准冠名红十字中医院。仍为贵阳市城镇职工基本医疗保险和新型农村合作医疗定点医疗机构，年末职工39人（其中卫技人员34人），有病床50张，当年门诊1.8万人次，住院300人次，业务收入186万元。

2010年，县城红十字会中医院正面

百信医院 2005年8月成立，为医师李权友、毛力平等6人及其他股东筹资320万元创建的股份制医院，实行董事会领导下的院长负责制，医院法人代表李权友委托毛力平任院长。于县城朝阳路租民房1200平方米，置病床25张，人员实行聘用，开设内、外、儿、妇产、急诊、口腔、中医理疗、检验、放射、B超、心电图、手术室、胃镜、麻醉、腹腔镜等15个职能科室，系集医疗、保健、预防、康复、科研为一体的综合性医院，也是贵阳市城镇职工基本医疗保险和新型农村合作医疗定点医疗机构。2007年卫生局批准为民办非企业单位，法人更为代云富。2008年1月批准冠名为红十字百信医院。2009年添租1栋5层4500平方米用房，进一步扩大业务范围。至2010年，用房建筑面积达6000平方米，其中业务用房4500平方米，有病床80张，职工136人，（含副高职称5人，中级职称8人，初级职称64人）。是年门诊10.62万人次，住院3300人次，业务收入1800万元。

2010年，县城红十字百信医院正面

（六）民营医院（诊所）

1993年，县境有个体开业行医的78人。1994年，根据国务院《医疗机构管理条例》规定，开始办理民营医疗机构审批，至2010年累计批准开业20所。

2010年民营医疗机构一览表

表5—04—04

机构名称	成立时间	职工（人）	床位（张）	驻地	诊疗科目	备注
环南诊所	1994	2	—	县城	中西医结合科	
聂德伦诊所	1998	—	—	扎佐	中医内科	
老来福中医	1999	1	—	县城	中医内科	
张德英诊所	2000	2	—	县城	西医内科	
康复诊所	2000	2	—	县城	西医内科、中医内科	
冯毅诊所	2003	2	—	久长	西医内科	
唐医师诊所	2003	5	4	县城	儿科	
爱济门诊	2003	10	5	县城	中医内科、西医内科	2008年与龙港医院合并改称华昇医院
龙港医院	2004	20	30	县城	中医内科、西医内科、妇产科	2008年与爱济门诊合并改称华昇医院
孙国栋诊所	2004	4	—	县城	中医全科	2007年合并到爱济门诊，单独核算，2010年与华昇医院承租中医院，改称红十字医院
李进口腔诊所	2005	4	—	县城	口腔科	
便民诊所	2005	2	—	六广	西医内科	
韦林诊所	2005	5	—	县城	中医针灸科	
金松诊所	2005	4	—	县城	口腔科	
张贤成诊所	2005	4	4	扎佐	西医内科、中西医结合科	
城南村第二卫生室	2007	1	—	县城	中西医结合科	
城北村第二卫生室	2007	1	—	县城	中医内科	
华昇医院	2008	20	30	县城	中医内科、西医内科、妇产科	原龙港医院、爱济门诊合并组建，2010年3月与爱济中医门诊联合承租中医院，改称红十字中医院
黄宁中西医结合诊所	2008	2	—	扎佐	中西医结合科	
华荣口腔诊所	2010	2	—	县城	口腔科	

二、医疗队伍

（一）规模

1978年，全县医疗卫生总职工数为349人，1994年增至596人。1995年起股份制医院和民营医疗机构陆续开业，医务人员逐年增加。2010年，职工人数达776人，比1978年增加1.2倍。

（二）素质

1. 文化结构

20世纪80年代的医技人员多属中专毕业生。1990年大专以上文化占15.5%，中专占56%，高中7.9%，初中以下占20.6%。1991年后大中专毕业生逐年增加，到2010年，大学本科占23.78%，大学专科占39.41%、中专占20.85%，高中及以下仅占15.96%。

2. 技术结构

1978年全县仅有专业技术人员188人，占职工总数的53.87%。1980至1981年和1987年两次进行职称考核晋升。到1990年，全县卫生系统有在职副高级职称5人、中级职称35人、初级186人。继后技术职称每年根据统一考试认定，到2010年全县有在职专业技术人员653人，占总职工人数的84.15%，其中县属卫生系统有在职副高职称12人、中级职称78人、初级157人。

（三）队伍建设

1. 职称评聘

1980—1981年进行首批专业技术职称评审，经考试、考评，有19人晋升为主治（管）医（技）师，61人晋升为医（技）师或医士。1987年第二批评审，6人晋升为副高级，36人晋升为中级。1993年县属卫生事业单位实行定岗、定员、定职聘任，对已获相应专业技术职称人员实行聘任上岗，聘期3年，期满符合条件者续聘。继后规定技术职称必须经过统一考试确定，先取得职称任职资格再由卫生行政主管部门聘任，此规定到2010年未变。

2. 教育培训

离职进修　1979—2004年，全县累计送省、地医疗单位进修学习216人，其中学习1年以上3年以下的82人（在省进修13人，在地、市进修69人），学习3个月以上1年以下的134人（在省进修42人，在地、市进修92人）。

办学授课　1979年11月，县医院受安顺地区卫生局委托，在修文、清镇等地招生。开办中专护士班1期，学员40名，1982年毕业分配到卫生部门工作。1988年县卫生局在县职业中学办中专医士班1期，学员60名，全部就业于医疗技术部门。

短期培训　1978—1984年，卫生局先后开办卫技培训班4期，中药炮制加工学习班1期，培训期1个月至1年，累计培训医务人员169人次。1995年起连续6年又对村卫生员、接生员199人进行一个月的培训，又复训188人，还安排45人到县进修。各乡（镇）卫生院采取以会代训、分片轮训方式每年培训村级卫生人员不少于12天。1997年起，遵义医学院二附院对口帮扶培训小箐乡卫生院医务人员20余次。

短期培训妇幼保健员

专题讲座　1979—1985年，县医院举办专题讲座50余次，听课者2000余人次，由贵阳医学院、遵义医学院和贵阳市传染病院的专家教授莅院主讲。1999至2004年，县医院派医护骨干到六桶乡卫生院举办学术讲座7次，进行技术帮扶。

第三节 医 疗

一、医疗设备

（一）病床

1978年，全县有病床133张。1980年妇幼保健站新置病床，县医院和各区卫生院添置病床，全县病床增至180张，1986年又增为317张，1994年达到368张。1995年后卫生事业迅猛发展，生产大队办医疗机构破土而出并日渐增多，到2010年全县病床达583张，其中县属医疗机构235张，乡（镇）卫生院140张，红十字医院130张，其他医疗机构78张。

（二）器械配置

1978年，县医院常用器械仅有显微镜、精密天平、电动和手动离心机、100毫安X光机、心电图机和外科手术器械。区卫生院只有扎佐、六广配化验和照光设备。1981年县医院增设200毫安和300毫安X光机、超声波仪、光电分析天平、病理切片机、麻醉器、光电比色器、电动离心机、电泳仪、分光光度计、万能手术台、高频电疗机、九孔无影灯等26种，到1985年县医院设备基本配齐。卫生防疫站增添冷链运转设备。各区卫生院先后配备X光机、离心机、显微镜、手术刀等11种。2000年启动妇幼卫生项目，为县、乡、村卫生机构配置骨盆测量器、方盘、紫外线灯等23种732件，价值11万元。2001年开展农村卫生人力开发项目配置设备29种1695件，价值30.49万元。2002年扎佐卫生院率先拥有纤维胃镜，2005年县医院增置县内首台螺旋CT机和CR机、电子腹腔镜。2010年，县医院设备齐全并处于领先地位，妇幼保健站产科的计划生育手术器械全部配齐，乡（镇）卫生院中的扎佐、六广卫生院器械配备比较齐全，其余8个卫生院业务器械配齐，一般疾病不出乡就能得到及时治疗。村卫生室日常使用的基本业务器械具备。

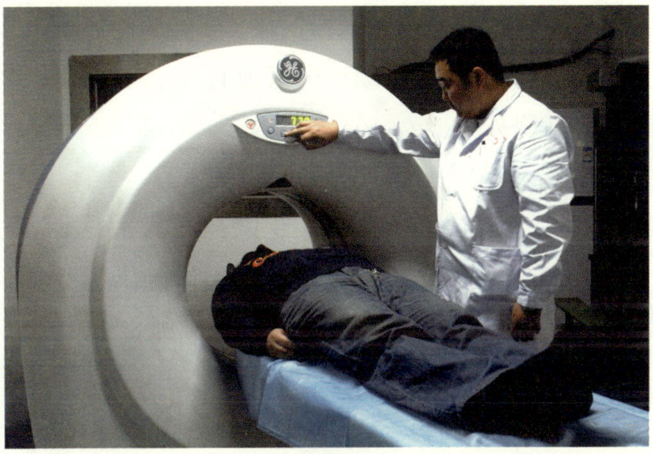

大型医疗器械

二、医疗技术

（一）中医

1978年全县有中医师16人，1981年晋升专业技术职称，其中2人晋升为主治医师，其余均为医师（士）。县医院中医科主治医师聂承先继承父亲所创医技和自己多年的临床实践，采用中医药治疗癫狂症并兼治其他疑难病症，因治愈百余人癫狂病名声远扬，县内外到中医科看病者逐年增多，1983年全科门诊2.9万人次，占全院门诊总人数的28.82%。1988年聂承先晋升为副主任医师，另有4人晋升为主治医师，到1990年全科门诊量仍保持在全院门诊人次的22%以上。主治医师张志祥1991年参加全国肝胆疾病培训后，采用中医药治疗肝胆疾病技术全县领先，对中药治疗泌尿性结石、妇科卵巢囊肿、月经不调、不孕不育效果明显；痤疮吃中药20天左右即愈。专门从事针灸治疗的韦林，经过7年进修和实践，创新出集血府逐淤汤、补阳还五汤与针灸、血注、推拿、小针刀、火针、刮痧相配合的治疗方法，不仅疗效好，而且费用低，在治疗脑血栓、颈椎腰椎骨质增生、腰椎间盘突出和周围面瘫等顽疾有独到之处。曾多次参加国际传统医学研讨、世界针灸学术研讨和香港中西医结合医学研讨等大型研讨会，其论文《透针加灸治疗周围性面瘫38例疗效观察》被译成英文在世界针灸学术研讨会获得专家认可，《穴位注射配合推拿治疗颈椎病》被县人民政府评为科技进步一等奖，《针治结合牵引治疗腰椎间盘突出症92例》被香港中西医结合医学研讨会收入《针灸治疗瘤症国际学术研讨论文汇编》。从医28年亲自诊治病人30万人次，每天接诊患者30人次以上，从未发生过医疗事故。其中上门服务的病人万余人未收取分文出诊费，因此，被群众评为"医术精、医德高的医生"。2009年获"全国优秀名中医"称号，并出席在北京人民大会堂召开的表彰大会，受到全国政协副主席陈宗兴接见并合影。小箐乡小坝村卫生室村医刘朝军以中药为主为患者治病，病人刘俊患颈椎脂肪瘤施行手术后又伴随腰部皮下脂肪瘤，服过刘朝军配方的中草药20剂痊愈。到2003年全县175个村卫生室中有近20%能开展中医业务。2010年4月县医院增加中医康复业务，采取中西医结合对慢性疾病患者康复治疗，部分微创技术在贵州省县级同行业中领先。年底，全县具有专业技术知识和实践经验的注册执业中医师52人，执业助理中医师11人，多数均开诊为患者服务。

中医科

专记：县人民医院康复治疗技术部分领先

2010年4月，县医院组建起集门诊、住院于一体的临床科室—中医康复科，设病床12张，配备有国家执业资格的医护人员18人，其中医师8人，护士10人，中级职称4人，分置治疗、牵引、针灸、电疗、推拿、微创治疗、康复功能训练、中药塌溃8个治疗室，采取中西医结合、传统康复治疗和现代康复医学相结合的方法，主要开展颈、肩、腰腿痛及骨关节病变及神经康复、肢体运动康复治疗。刚开诊一个星期床位全部住满，几次增加病床达到55张，收治各型颈椎病、腰椎间盘突（膨）出、椎管狭窄、骨关节退行性改变，股骨头坏死、脑卒中后遗症、周围神经病变等疾病，填补了县内康复医学科的空白。其规模、规范、系统康复医学在全省也属罕见，所开展的腰椎间盘减压术、神经根粘分解术、小针刀关节松解术等治疗技术在省内同级同行业中居于领先地位，100余名患者治疗后反映效果良好。至年末，全科门诊近2000人次，住院800人次，业务收入500余万元，在院全年业务收入中占15.05%，既增加经济效益，也得到患者信赖，取得较好的社会效益。

（二）西医

1. 外科

1978年能独立开展胃部大部切除、胃肠吻合、脾切除、肝破裂修补、肝脓肿穿刺引流等手术。1981

年培养两名骨科医生，开展骨脓肿、骨肿瘤切除、骨髓炎病灶清除、截肢等。1992年成功开展首例硬膜血肿清除，当年施行各种手术229例，术前术后诊断符合率达98%。1993年进行颅内血肿清除、腰椎结核病灶清除成功后，1996年又开展颅骨骨瘤摘除和痔疮开刀手术，1998年再成功开展首列开胸术。2002年和2005年引进纤维胃镜和腹腔镜等先进设备，外科手术水平明显提高，仅扎佐卫生院就施行四肢难度较大的骨科手术19例，肠癌切除2例，为金鸡村一村民切除一个8公斤重的子宫肌瘤，被《贵阳晚报》采访报道。2008年全县对白内障患者实行复明手术167例。到2010年电动多功能、腹腔镜、胃镜、冰帽、四肢骨折内固定、钉棒系统内固定、人工关节置换、肛肠脓肿一次性根治，内痔、外痔、混合痔等主要手术在县内均能施行。具有临床经验50多年的外科主治医师韩文真主持外科治疗，在治疗设备和技术力量欠缺的情况下，逐渐开展了上下腹部手术、骨折切开复位固定手术、髋关节结核和腰椎结核病灶清除植骨术、慢性骨水炎死骨摘除带蒂饥瓣填塞术以及子宫切除等，其中部分手术的开展和重危病人的抢救在全省县级医院中均处于领先地位。

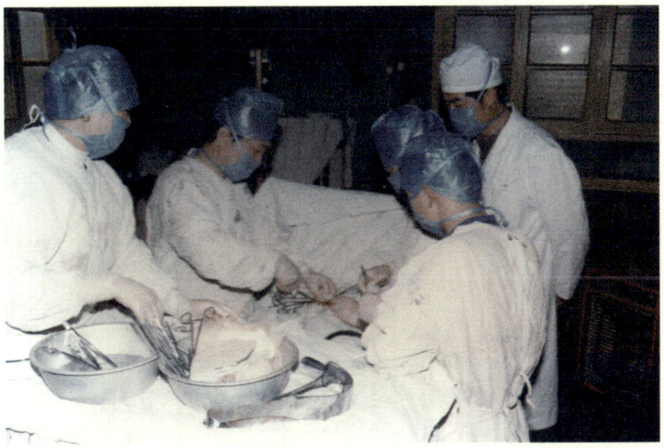

外科手术

2. 内科

1978年只能开展多种穿刺术、输血、输氧。1980年起采用相对先进的诊疗技术开展心包穿刺、骨髓穿刺、闭式引流、胃液分析、十二指肠插管引流等，收治血液系统、内分泌系统、心血管系统、精神内科疾病患者，对休克、重症感染、胃功能衰竭、中毒、乙脑惊厥和流行性出血热等危重病人抢救效果明显。临床采用双氧水治疗肺心病，小剂量胰岛素治疗糖尿病，乙脑病人把三关（降温、止惊、保持呼吸道畅通），强心剂小剂量治疗心衰，小儿中毒痢疾阿托品应用等新法均有显著疗效。1985年入院病人诊断符合率达96%。1990年首次成功抢救1例脑溢血病人。1996年县医院与贵阳市第一人民医院业务技术挂钩，联合开展“茶色素临床效果观察”课题应用。1998年增置洗胃机成功为首列病人进行救治。2001年起先后开展心脑血管疾病治疗、中西药治疗胰腺炎和胆道疾病、尿路结石、心电监护、内分泌疾病。到2010年主要针对病种有内分泌系统、心脑血管系统、呼吸系统疾病，尤其对消化系统溃疡、急慢性胃炎、慢性肝炎、上消化道出血、急慢性肠炎、发热性疾病治疗有独到之处。

3. 妇产科

1978年，仅能开展子宫全切除、剖腹产及计划生育手术，到1985年妇科病人都能在本县治疗，很少转院，入院病人诊断符合率达到99%。1997和1998年中华人民共和国卫生部、联合国儿童基金会、世界卫生组织分别授予县医院为“爱婴医院”、扎佐镇卫生院为“爱婴卫生院”后，六广、小箐、六桶乡（镇）卫生院又先后获得贵阳市级“爱婴乡镇卫生院”称号。2005年起增配大量妇科设备，对医务人员培训提高技术水平。到2008年对产科治疗评审，除县属医疗机构外，10乡（镇）卫生院中有8个能开展平产接生。到2010年能开展快速无痛人流、无痛分娩、剖宫产、全宫切除及其他妇产科手术，综合治理月经紊乱、经痛、宫颈炎、阴道炎等妇科疾病。

4. 放射科

1978年，县、区医院配有X光机，开展胃肠透、肾盂、胆囊造影、骨折及各种体位摄片。1990年始有床头X光片机。2003年起陆续新增FX200-A医用诊断X射线机、HQ-450XT洗片机、XOIC型电动诊视创、X17D型摄影床、德国螺旋CT机和DR机，到2010年除X线检查、常规各种影像学检查和常规造影检查外，还开展微创治疗、诊断各种疾病意外以及头部、胸部、腹部、全身骨骼系统检查。

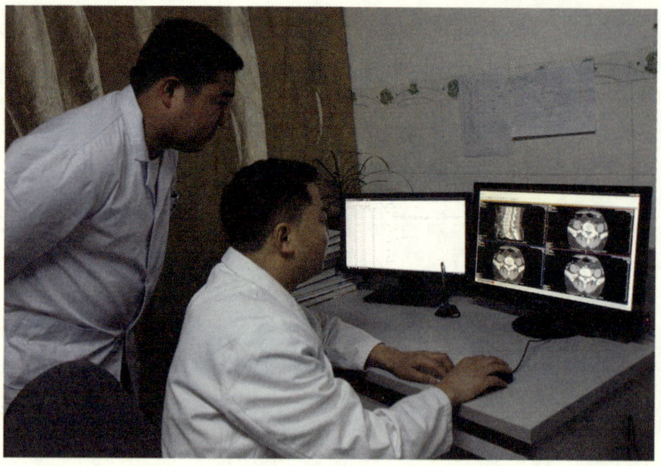
百信医院检验科室

5. 检验科

1978年，县医院只能开展肝功能、肾功能、血常规、尿妊娠、异常白细胞形态、真菌图片检查及淋球菌、霍乱弧菌、0-157大肠希菌培养及鉴定。1990年起陆续增配全自动生化分析仪、血凝机、化学分析仪等大型自动化检验仪器和检验人员。2010年检验项目有几十项，大部分检验都能当天发出检测报告，有力地配合临床治疗。

6. 功能科

1978年只能作心电图检查。1985年增置超声波诊断仪，开展心、肺、脾、肾检查及胸、腹腔积液、色块、早孕、死胎检查。1996年后陆续增配黑白及彩色B超机、智能16道脑电地型图机等先进仪器。2002年参加并完成《应用葡萄糖利尿作用对输尿管结石CDFI诊断价值》科研项目为省内县级医院首家，并在省内推广使用。到2010年开展腹部脏器及血管病变、浅表器官及组织检查，综合评价心脏各种病变，24至48小时对心脏进行监测。

7. 口腔科

1997年，县医院设立口腔科，配置先进的口腔设备和器械，职工1人。继后，口腔疾病治疗业务逐步扩大到个体医诊所，县内拥有牙科综合治疗仪、超声波牙机、牙科X光机、牙科手术专用消毒机等设备，开展牙髓治疗、牙齿美容美白、牙周综合治疗、口腔黏膜治疗、口腔颌面外科、各种复杂牙及阳生牙拔除、颌面部各科肿物手术切除、烤瓷冠及各种烤瓷冠桥、各种义齿等业务。2010年全县注册执业口腔医师8人，执业助理口腔医师1人，有的在固定医院坐诊，有的自己开业就诊。

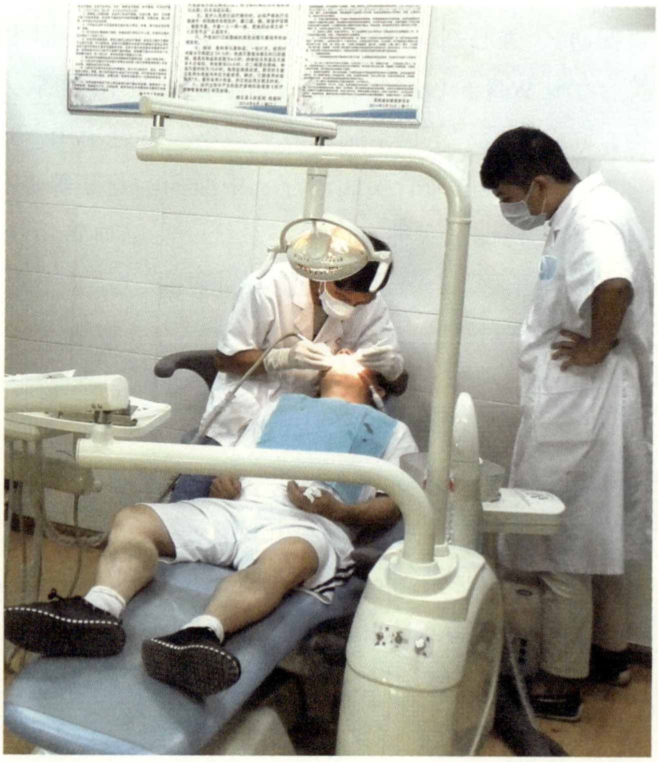
县医院口腔科

8、五官科

1991年，县医院始设五官科，配有眼科和耳、鼻、喉医师各1人及一般仪器。1996年撤科复归门诊部管理，由于医疗设备简陋，只能开展五官普通疾病诊治。2008年9月复置五官科，到2010年已拥有开放病床10张，配医师5人，护士4人，配有裂隙灯显微镜、纤维喉镜、鼻窦内窥镜、手术显微

镜、眼底镜、激光治疗仪等设备，能开展双眼皮成型术、上睑下垂、睫内外翻倒睫矫正、眼眶眼睑肿瘤切除、翼状胬肉切除+球结膜移植、抗青光眼小梁切除或虹膜周切、泪道探通术、鼻骨骨折复位、鼻中隔偏曲矫正、鼻息肉、鼻腔肿物切除和鼻窦炎等手术。

三、民间药医

县境民间中草医历史悠久，疗方较多，1978年仍传承有接骨合榫、拔火罐、烧灯火、刮痧、滚蛋、推拿等疗方，有的以赶集摆摊开诊，也有奉请出诊治疗。大石乡小坉土医罗竺轩祖传医治跌打损伤，尤以接骨合榫用药有独到之处，先后治疗患者百余人。

1991年后村卫生室建立，有的土医被招进卫生室陆续推广中草医疗方为患者治疗，到2010年，小箐乡小坝村卫生室村医刘朝军主要以中草药、针灸、推拿按摩、拔火罐为患者治病。龙场镇阳明村卫生室村医白胜军擅长小夹板接骨合榫均小有名气。

四、护理

1978年，沿袭晨护、巡视病房、“三查”（即摆药后查、处置前查、处置后查）、“七对”（即对床号、姓名、药名、剂量、浓度、时间、用法）制度，对重症病人采取床前交接班。1985年起按月计发护理人员的护士津贴，每年5月12日国际护士节都组织护理知识竞赛或专题讨论，表彰优秀护士，对从事护理工作30年以上的护理人员颁发荣誉证书，通过一系列活动加强医德教育和提高业务能力。1994年实施《中华人民共和国护士管理办法》，颁发护理人员执业证书，使护理人员准入正式步入法治化管理。2003年依照《贵州省护理文件书写规范（试行）》，全县护理文件主要有体温单、医嘱单（含临床医嘱单、长期医嘱单）、长期医嘱执行单、护理记录（含一般护理记录、重症者护理记录）、手术护理记录、入院评估表、生活护理记录单、健康教育记录单组成，2010年，护理内容及时、准确、真实、完整，静脉穿刺、药品配用、技术和服务态度均有显著提高。

五、采血供血

（一）采血

1978—1995年，公民义务献血系由上级血液机构赴县统一采集。1996年县医院组建血站开始运行，列为贵州省血液中心全血采集点，采血工作由红十字会组织。1998年1月贵阳市卫生局正式明确修文采血站只能采集本辖区范围内血源（含公民义务献血、无偿献血）。直至2003年上半年因血站未经省卫生厅批准而停业，7月省厅将龙场、扎佐、六屯、谷堡、洒坪5乡（镇）划归开阳血浆站，久长、小箐、六广、大石、六桶5乡（镇）划归息烽血浆站，2004—2010年累计组织义务献血12次1522人，献血总量38.14万毫升，从而方便临床用血和抢救危急病人用血的需求。

（二）供血

1996年4月前，医院临床及抢救危急病人用血或临时采集，或向省血液中心申请供应。5月起至2001年上半年县医院血浆站开始采集全血供县境医疗机构使用。医院血站撤销后，供血则由省血液中心提供。

六、捐献遗体器官

2005年，根据《贵阳市捐献遗体和角膜办法》，县红十字会进行广泛宣传，有在县城经商的四川籍人刘恒率先登记，自愿捐献造血干细胞挽救白血病人。2007年，文化广播电视局职工王忠频自愿登记，将遗体捐献用于医学科学研究和角膜移植。

七、医疗救助

（一）农村医疗救助

2002年前，对农村医疗困难患者多由民政部门适当补助，由卫生部门减免很少。2003年9月卫生局对在乡复员军人凭证就医免收挂号费，住院费和治疗费优惠50%，各种检查费优惠20%，药费凭单据于当年底到就诊单位减10%。2005年10月对城乡低保户在县乡医疗机构和社区卫生服务中心就医，免收挂号费和诊疗费，药品以外其他费用减10%；结核病患者免费治疗；低保对象从事个体经营免交各项卫生规费。2008年3月对城乡低保对象和县级以上政府认定的城市居民中其他特殊困难群众，可凭证在县医院和龙场镇以外的9个乡（镇）卫生院就诊，并免收普通挂号费和诊疗费，药品则按医院零售价减7.5%，其他费用（输血费和材料费除外）减50%，推行至2010年未变。

（二）降消项目救助

全称为降低孕产妇死亡率和消除新生儿破伤风基础项目，2001年开始实施，救助对象为农村住院分娩贫困孕产妇。2005年农村年人均收入低于800元孕产妇住院分娩，补助住院、生活、交通及危重抢救费，平产减40元，难产减100元。2007年增为100元和180元。至2010年，累计救助7478人，金额163.72万元。

（三）农村卫生人力开发项目救助

2004年启动，2006年结束，累计救助农村贫困家庭住院分娩孕产妇150人，贫困家庭就诊儿童54人，减免金额4.95万元。

（四）农村孕产妇住院分娩补助

2008年开始实施，至2010年累计补助农村住院分娩孕产妇6455人，金额194.34万元。

八、医疗事故处理

2002年9月1日，开始实施国务院重新颁发《医疗事故处理条例》，对构成医疗事故的必须进行赔偿，2005—2010年全县医疗机构累计补偿医疗事故或医疗纠纷25起，由相关部门或领导协调处理，对医疗机构有责任或部分责任的分别给予经济补偿；对无责任或原因不明而医患双方各持疑义的，从社会稳定和人道主义角度出发进行适当经济补偿予以安慰。6年全县累计赔付124万元，单个赔偿最低500元，最高17万元。

第四节　卫生防疫

1978—2001年，卫生防疫业务仍按原有范围开展，2002年拓宽卫生防疫业务，县防疫站改成疾病预防控制中心，通过健康教育、计划免疫接种、疾病防治等方式控制疾病的发生和蔓延。至2010年，境内麻风病、钩端螺旋体病基本消灭，地方性氟中毒得到遏制。

一、开展健康教育

1978年称卫生宣传教育，采取集会、电话会议、电视广播、出黑板报、张贴标语、图片布展、上门家访等方式宣传除害灭病讲卫生。1990年改称“健康教育”。1995年12月贵州省健康教育项目在全县铺开，次年1月县卫生局成立领导小组，3月防疫站置健教科，开展《中华人民共和国职业病防治法》《食品卫生法》《传染病防治法》和各种疾病的防治宣传。2003年建立健全健康教育网络。连续27年累计开展宣传日活动126次，举办卫生知识培训班53期5300人次，出宣传栏168期，利用宣传车到乡（镇）宣传60次，电视广播宣传53小时，法律法规宣传220次，编发卫生宣传资料18.84万份和宣传画册8.4万份。2003年抗击非典型肺炎期间，组织宣传队深入机关、厂矿、学校、社区、乡村宣传防治知识，增强群众自我保护意识，知晓率达到86.25%。久长黄磷工贸有限公司生产因黄磷中毒，卫生监督机构按照《中华人民共和国职业病防治法》规定向公司索赔6.5万元。2004年开展健康教育示范村寨活动，至2010年，龙场镇马口村等10个村和梭坡等9个组以及宾阳社区先后获得“贵阳市健康教育示范村寨”称号。

县疾病防控中心开展卫生健康教育宣传

二、免疫接种

（一）计划免疫种类

1978年有牛痘疫苗、麻疹活疫苗、脊灰疫苗、卡介苗4种。1979年增百白破。1981年因无天花传染，故停止接种牛痘疫苗。2003年增乙肝疫苗，2006年起增加流脑疫苗A、乙脑（减毒）疫苗、麻腮风疫苗、麻风疫苗、甲肝（减毒）疫苗、白破二联疫苗，到2010年增为11种。

（二）业务开展

1983年前，接种疫苗主要在冬季进行。1985年根据国际儿童基金会和世界卫生组织倡导，中国政府承诺在全国范围内实施计划免疫冷链运转。1986年省财政投资为县配置冰箱10台、速冻机2台、冷藏箱36个、冷藏包和注射器各219个，县卫生防疫站也将防疫组改置计划免疫结核病慢性病防治科，在全县范围内首次使用儿童计划免疫接种证和建立计划免疫卡，连续两年在安顺地区获计划免疫工作第一名。1988年又在城关、扎佐、久长3个区试行儿童计划免疫合同保偿制度，保偿金额每人16.5元，当年入保700人，次年全县推行，入保儿童超过80%，累计保偿收入超过10万元。1996年终止计划免疫合同保偿制度。

1992年，按照国家《1988—1995年消灭脊灰规则》，修文被列入贵州省消灭脊灰县，对县境内适龄儿童，无论有无户口、居住时间长短、以往免疫史如何，均接种脊灰疫苗。到1999年第六轮第十二次脊灰强化免疫，全县免疫覆盖率在95%以上。2000年起连续11年县内未发现脊灰病例，实现国务院总理李鹏向世界卫生组织承诺目标。2004年11月世界卫生组织彼特、中国疾病预防控制中心安志杰、省疾病预防控制中心邹志康等到县对麻疹补充免疫检查，次年县代表贵阳市接受省的审评，成绩列全省榜首。

2006年起，县疾病预防控制中心连续两年指导谷堡、小箐、六广、六桶4个乡（镇）卫生院创建计划免疫示范门诊，其他6个卫生院创建合格门诊，次年六桶卫生院通过市级验收。

县疾病防控中心利用场天开展防疫宣传

2007年起，连续3年启动中央转移支付免疫规划项目，总投资26.37万元，应种儿童建卡率和建证率均达95%以上，“五苗”全程接种率在90%以上，麻疹发病率控制在3/10万以下。

2008年贵阳市儿童预防接种信息系统建设在县试点，10乡镇完成信息录入，8月实现向国家上传数据，至2010年传输业务正常。

1986—2010年基础免疫统计表

表5—04—05

年度	卡介苗		脊灰疫苗		百白破疫苗		麻疹疫苗		乙肝疫苗		流脑疫苗		乙脑疫苗	
	应种	实种	应种	实种	应种	实种	应种	实种	应种	实种	应种	实种	应种	实种
1986	19342	17549	14123	12810	11569	11441	7628	7102	—	—	—	—	—	—
1987	7717	7308	15404	14857	15400	14775	8135	7745	—	—	—	—	—	—
1988	7326	7275	7245	7198	6978	6876	7463	7384	—	—	—	—	—	—
1989	6978	6898	6678	6579	6439	6387	7435	7386	—	—	—	—	—	—
1990	6679	6533	6198	6080	5891	5842	7255	7098	—	—	—	—	—	—
1991	7561	7413	6377	6254	8160	7948	9020	8746	—	—	—	—	—	—
1992	4517	4443	4694	4617	4583	4477	5792	5705	—	—	—	—	—	—
1993	3599	3533	3504	3453	7562	7440	3964	3908	—	—	—	—	—	—
1994	3879	3843	11379	11214	14546	14349	4062	4020	—	—	—	—	—	—
1995	3885	3819	11586	11379	11441	11099	4169	4102	—	—	—	—	—	—
1996	3531	3474	10964	10870	11593	11512	4209	4175	—	—	—	—	—	—
1997	3532	3466	10836	10667	11389	11196	4525	4437	—	—	—	—	—	—
1998	3194	3194	3520	3520	4126	4126	5973	5973	—	—	—	—	—	—
1999	3830	3796	4319	4287	4265	4239	4155	4141	—	—	—	—	—	—
2000	2993	2926	3367	3359	3237	3224	3300	3280	—	—	—	—	—	—
2001	2859	2855	3127	3127	3147	3145	2984	2984	—	—	—	—	—	—
2002	2422	2379	2292	2246	2227	2188	2566	2531	—	—	—	—	—	—
2003	2772	2687	2871	2840	2735	21657	2839	2764	1263	1238	—	—	—	—
2004	2313	2189	1977	1856	2147	2078	2108	2012	2171	2066	—	—	—	—

续表

年度	卡介苗		脊灰疫苗		百白破疫苗		麻疹疫苗		乙肝疫苗		流脑疫苗		乙脑疫苗	
	应种	实种	应种	实种	应种	实种	应种	实种	应种	实种	应种	实种	应种	实种
2005	2487	2377	2861	2739	2822	2720	2581	2478	2497	2468	—	—	—	—
2006	2294	2218	2563	2520	2512	2467	2434	2380	2218	2148	—	—	—	—
2007	2573	2565	3184	3175	3074	3064	2999	2994	2632	2627	2841	2841	2323	2314
2008	2296	2243	8875	8783	8707	8605	3984	3957	7612	7550	4403	4402	2192	2186
2009	2596	2550	3824	3764	3946	3872	4399	4188	3810	3713	3546	3494	4258	4091
2010	3512	3511	3994	3989	3706	3699	3757	3741	3895	3891	3555	3546	3971	3965

注：空白处系未开展疫苗接种

三、疾病防治

（一）健全传染病报告制度

1981年前，疫情报告制度松弛，漏报率较高。1982年起制度逐步健全，1984年区设防保组，乡配防保员，县、区、乡三级联成防疫网。1985年全县配传染病管理监督员5人，检查员59人，以区为单位进行传染病登记。统一编号使用报告卡。9月1日起国家《中华人民共和国传染病防治法》实施，规定甲、乙、丙类传染病35种逐月报告。

2004年，县疾病预防控制中心实行网络直报，10乡（镇）卫生院和县医院陆续推行。2008年4月卫生局对县城实验小学和城关二小暴发甲型肝炎疫情，要求通过疾病监测信息系统时时监测；还明确：发现霍乱，城镇不得迟于2小时和农村不得迟于6小时报告；发现伤寒、痢疾、甲肝，城镇不得迟于6小时和农村不得迟于12小时报告；如系疫情地区则实行日报和零报制度。2010年，根据全国传染病报告规定，传染病种类共39种，其中甲类2种，乙类26种、丙类11种。从此，报告统一按此规定按时报告。

（二）传染病病种防治

1. 甲类传染病防治

霍乱 1998年9月中旬，霍乱首次在龙城镇新寨村暴发流行，有腹泻病人37名，经疾控中心采集大便19份检验，有6份为阳性，饮用水源无霍乱弧菌生长，流行原因系与外地带菌者参加婚宴聚餐传播有关。当即采取措施：一是封锁疫区；二是隔离治疗病人；三是消杀疫区病菌；四是疫区人群普遍服药预防；五是搞好宣传教育，提高群众拒吃不卫生食物和饭前便后洗手自我保护能力；六是全村暂停办红白喜宴和聚众就餐。经过9天防治，使疫情得到控制，至2010年未发生病例。

2. 乙类传染病防治

白喉（俗称“长喔子”） 县境早年就有白喉病例，且死亡率较高，1979年始用百破三联菌苗对儿童普种预防，1981年起无病例报告。

百日咳 是发病较高的传染病之一，1979年使用百破三联菌苗对儿童普种基本得到控制。

麻疹（俗称“出瘀工”） 境内发病较早，有波动流行，也有暴发流行。1978年前曾用麻疹活疫苗普种3.92万人，接种率95.2%。1983年改用冻干麻苗，1985年经安顺地区卫生防疫站监测，接种质量达到部颁标准。到1990年的13年发病率从1978年前27年695.49/10万降到75.29/10万。1992年1月又在六桶乡6个村暴发流行，227人发病，卫生防疫站和乡卫生院除对患者及时治疗外，还对1886名易感人群接种，迅速控制疫情，无死亡病例。继后到2010年，19年间病情基本得到控制。

肝炎 境内常年均有发生，多采取切断饮食源、饮水源、血液传播途径控制，儿童则注射乙肝疫苗预防。1981年城关镇暴发流行乙型肝炎，当即动员隐形病毒携带者调换工作，防止传染。2003年和2007年，将乙肝疫苗及甲肝（减毒）疫苗列入计划免疫品种，每年对儿童接种。2008年4月县城实验小学和城关二小因饮用“竹源”牌桶装水，暴发甲型肝炎疫情，32个班发病66例，县卫生局立即采取措施：一是通过电视、报纸发布公告，立即停用“竹源”牌桶装水；二是确定县医院为定点治疗医院，对患者隔离治疗；三是对两所学校学生接种甲肝疫苗1836人；四是对有关环境定期消杀20.2万平方米；五是紧急编印甲肝预防知识3万份广泛宣传。至5月底，疫情得到控制，未出现各种原因引起的2代病例。据调查统计，2002—2010年发病较多，年发病最低144例，最高达389例，其中有甲、乙、丙、戊4种，甲型和乙型患者居多。

脊髓灰质炎（又称“小儿麻痹症”） 早年即有病例，1978年前采用脊灰减毒活疫苗对儿童接种预防。1992年修文被列为贵州省消灭脊髓灰质炎的县，至1998年累计开展6轮12次全国性脊灰强化免疫，实现国务院向世界卫生组织承诺2000年消灭脊灰病的目标，到2010年全县无病例。

流行性乙型脑炎 早年即有发病，1997年起每年非计划免疫接种疫苗预防，年发病控制在100例以下。2007年列入计划免疫接种，至2010年仅发生3例。

伤寒及副伤寒 境内常见传染病之一，1980年在六广、六桶、保寨3个公社暴发疫情，发病136人。1985年小箐区小坝乡胡家土村民外出带菌传入，发病28人，均以非计划免疫注射疫苗预防，致病例减少。1992年和1993年在小箐乡大兴村连续暴发，洒坪乡青山也有发生，发病111人，卫生防疫站实行以饮水为主综合治理控制疫情。2003年起年发病控制在100例以下，2010年发病仅17例。

流行性出血热 1978年前即有疫情，1982年贵州省卫生厅对县境鼠类组成、分布及携带病毒抗原情况调查，确认黑线姬鼠是此病主要宿主动物和传播源，当即采取以灭鼠为主的综合性预防，使发病率逐年下降，从2000至2010年仅发生17例。

钩端螺旋体病 1978年前发病较多，主要传染源为黑线姬鼠，发病人群大多是在田间作业的农民，经过防疫宣传和自我保护，1980年疫情有所下降。1982年老疫区疫情暴发，发病160例。1985年起，通过爱国卫生运动广泛宣传，灭鼠灭蝇，动员农民穿长筒靴下田，秋收后放干水田，加撒生石灰杀菌，每年5月对疫区15至60岁的农村劳动力接种钩端螺旋体疫苗，致发病率显著下降，1999至2010年仅发生4例。

猩红热 1978年前有发病，但未暴发流行。1993年后发病率逐渐下降，发病年份减少，发病最多年仅有7例。

流行性脑脊髓膜炎 1978年前有发病，1980年采取隔离治疗和药物预防，1981年对重点地区、重点人群接种菌苗，接种率为90.1%。继后每年开展接种，到1985年发病率从1978年前的90.37/10万降到3.17/10万。2006年纳入计划免疫病种，至2010年只发生1例。

结核病 境内发病较早，1978年前主要在3周岁以下儿童中开展卡介苗接种预防，接种只在冬季进行。1985年全国第二次结核病流行病学抽样调查，将六桶乡关寨村列为抽样点，查出患病率达0.97%。1986年县防疫站实施冷链运转，年接种率在96%以上，成功率超过80%。1987年国家将结核病纳入法定

县卫生局、疾控中心领导及员工设点宣传结核病防治知识

传染病管理。1993年世界卫生组织发布《全球结核病紧急状态宣言》。1996年将此病从丙类上升为乙类管理。1998年贵阳市随机抽样抽出城关镇新水村、久长镇清水村、谷堡乡折溪村为流调点，实查3628人，调查面为96.72%，查出患者10人，患病率283.4/10万，超过1997年的138/10万，低于贵阳市年发病率的389.3/10万。2000年全国第四次结核病抽样调查，将六广镇坪营村列为调查点，检查1021人，查出可疑病人42人，发病率4.11%。

2002年贵阳市启动含日本援助项目在内的结核病控制项目，每年拨出专款在全县10乡（镇）217个村建立报病网络进行拉网式搜索，对病例报告医师实施奖励，让患者得到减免费和规范性治疗，使治愈率达60%，症状减轻和好转率达80%。2004年再启动菲达尼斯结核病控制项目，2005至2010年实施全球基金第四轮结核病控制项目。通过项目实施，结核病得到归口管理，县疾控中心负责全县结核病诊断、治疗、管理、追踪和技术指导，至2010年免费治疗4031人，治愈率达95%以上。

狂犬病 1978年前境内即有狂犬咬人致死发生，1983年起因养狗户剧增，发病年份较多，仅1984年全县被狗咬伤的人数即有343人，当即提供狂犬疫苗注射预防。1985年县政府行文在城关镇灭狗141条，将全县发病控制在1.58/10万以内。2000至2010年发病19例。

疟疾（俗称“打摆子”） 流行历史较早，1978年疫情基本得到控制，至1998年仅发病25例。1999年至2010年无病例。

痢疾 县内发病较多，县卫生防疫站多采取加强饮水源消毒和食品业卫生监督，加上消灭传染媒介苍蝇等进行预防。1989年起县医院和驻县三O四医院在传染流行季节置肠道门诊救治。2000年起县医院、中医院和扎佐、久长卫生院肠道门诊实行“逢泻必检、逢疑必报”制度，逐个进行登记，2005至2010年每年控制在100例以下。

性病 境内发病历史较长，1978年前得到扑灭。进入20世纪80年代，人员流动增多，加上卖淫、嫖娼等社会丑恶现象沉渣泛起，致曾经绝迹的性病死灰复燃。1994年收治淋病患者2人，2002年梅毒发病2人，2003年还发现首例艾滋病感染者。2004年由中央和县财政拨款12万元，于疾控中心增建实验室和配备相应设备，开始对患者减免治疗药品费。2005年起县列入中央转移支付艾滋病防治项目县，中央、省、市、县共同投资对其监测、宣传和高危人群干预。2006年9月疾控中心美沙酮门诊开诊，每年开展治疗宣传、咨询、检测、干预、抗体筛选和治疗。在公共场所、旅店、浴室、娱乐场所发放安全套。选择入驻扎佐镇的贵航高级技工学校作为国家级青年学生艾滋病监测哨点，对800例18岁以上学生艾滋病病毒、丙型肝炎和梅毒筛查。至2010年，中央、省、市、县财政累计投入资金50万元培训卫技人员，宣传、专题讲座教育1.2万人次，发放安全套10万余只，筛查吸毒、羁押、娱乐场所、结核病等人群超过1万人，按户籍8年累计报告艾滋病毒感染者21例，发病者7例，共计28例，其中男性19例，女性9例。有320名海洛因成瘾者在美沙酮门诊接受治疗，使用美沙酮600万毫升，按美沙酮与海洛因药效折算，减少海洛因消耗1万余克，折合人民币约2500万元。

炭疽病 1978年前有发病，1991年和1992年在六广镇松江村和城关镇平地村流行，卫生防疫站对疫区易感人群接种1131人预防，仅死亡1人和牛1头、马1匹，其余年份未发现病例。

非典型肺炎 2002年11月16日，广东省佛山市发现首例非典型肺炎，且迅速蔓延，全国一致抗击。2003年2月，县卫生局拟定防治工作预案，明确县医院为定点治疗医院，设置隔离病房；县中医院、乡（镇）卫生院设立发热诊室，村卫生室负责发热登记。4月，全县从上至下开展大规模防治宣传、督察。历时5个月累计宣传咨询1370次，接受宣传30.71万人次，印发宣传资料63.65万份，专题电视广播宣传587次，出宣传栏2029期，接听电话3.3万次，处理来信来访68件，设卡检查车辆1.39万台次和人员17.99万人次，到7月中旬，全国范围疫情得到有效控制，县境无病例发生。

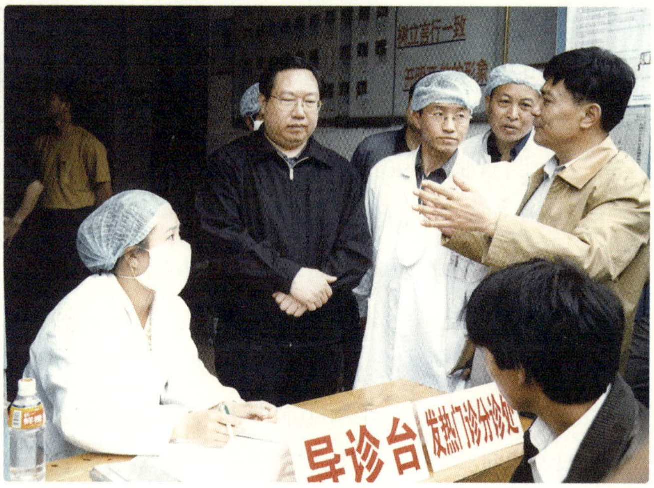

2003年5月14日贵阳市委书记王晓东（左二）副书记刘新明（右一）在扎佐卫生院检查发热门诊工作

高致病性禽流感 2004年，广西等地发现疫情后，县卫生局组建疫情控制组、诊断医疗救治组和卫生监督组进行防治。2005年配合农业部门对50户养殖场、禽肉加工户、50只以上涉禽养殖人员实施监测，至2010年全县未发生疫情。

布鲁氏菌病 2009年始发3例，均为引进奶牛带菌感染，经治愈无死亡。

3. 丙类传染病防治

麻风病 1978年前针对麻风病的发病情况，在六桶乡黑塘沟建立硝厂医院收治县内外的麻风病患者。1984年组建县皮肤病防治所对新发病人由隔离治疗转为社会防治，医师每日送药上门1次，坚持“送药到手、监服到口、吞下再走”的原则，以保疗效。到1995年，患病率从0.195‰降到0.005‰，发病村寨由94个减到3个。治疗期满每年监测一次，经体检和病菌学检查未发现复发。1997年卫生部和省、市专家莅县考察，12月12日省卫生厅明文确认修文县已基本消灭麻风病。1998年9月皮肤病防治所赵竞鸣因防治工作成绩显著，荣获全国麻风病防治先进个人。从是年起，对所有报告病例和死亡个案进行调查，并录入微机。2008年对全县累计308例既往感染者调查，仍存活87例，外迁36例，失访33例，死亡152例。至2010年连续5年未发现新病例。

县卫生局领导到六桶硝厂医院检查麻风病人生活情况

斑疹伤寒 1978年前有发病，但无暴发流行。1989年起发病率逐渐下降，发病年份减少，年发病仅在7例以下。

手足口病 2008年始发53例，2010年增到1110例，对发病4所托儿园发生聚集性疫区停课4天防治，未发生死亡。

1978—2010年主要传染病发病人数统计表

表5—04—06　　　　单位：人

年份	白喉	麻疹	流脑	流行性感冒	猩红热	百日咳	细菌性痢疾	伤寒及副伤寒	病毒性肝炎	脊髓灰质炎	疟疾	钩端螺旋体病	乙脑	斑疹伤寒	流行性出血热	肺结核	狂犬病	性病	手足口病
1978	29	135	42	1017	3	2374	431	14	51	—	1	2	33	67	1	—	—	—	—
1979	3	6	42	370	—	77	107	66	126	—	1	3	37	—	17	—	—	—	—
1980	1	21	72	1454	5	5	426	64	125	3	3	5	27	—	6	—	—	—	—
1981	—	120	13	742	2	35	6180	140	88	2	3	2	34	1	13	—	—	—	—
1982	—	497	15	2860	11	216	171	29	76	—	—	—	—	—	—	—	—	—	—
1983	—	411	3	—	26	119	656	44	83	—	3	57	24	—	52	—	—	—	—
1984	—	296	9	300	33	12	505	19	120	—	3	12	21	1	93	—	4	—	—
1985	—	799	8	96	35	29	432	152	118	—	3	1	20	—	53	—	3	—	—
1986	—	58	17	145	16	42	317	60	90	—	—	4	10	—	38	—	4	—	—
1987	—	3	18	—	39	11	351	103	90	—	—	23	10	—	29	—	3	—	—
1988	—	—	1	—	23	—	123	75	173	—	1	1	28	—	15	—	4	—	—
1989	—	1	3	—	7	4	155	75	133	—	—	—	9	—	6	—	3	—	—
1990	—	2	1	—	3	23	450	72	176	—	—	—	21	—	3	—	1	—	—
1991	—	1	—	—	11	—	386	21	83	—	—	1	7	—	20	—	3	—	—
1992	—	254	1	—	6	—	50	73	77	—	—	6	5	—	—	—	—	—	—
1993	—	45	—	—	2	—	43	52	82	2	—	47	23	—	6	—	6	—	—
1994	—	64	3	—	2	—	114	46	49	3	5	27	8	—	40	—	—	—	—
1995	—	—	—	—	—	—	185	55	60	—	—	—	—	—	2	—	—	—	—
1996	—	8	3	—	1	1	215	30	34	—	1	—	9	—	25	79	—	—	—
1997	—	35	2	—	—	5	104	28	70	—	—	12	11	—	23	84	—	4	—
1998	—	7	1	—	2	—	133	41	53	—	1	—	13	—	13	91	—	3	—
1999	—	31	1	—	1	1	165	97	150	—	—	1	4	—	15	142	—	5	—
2000	—	9	1	—	2	—	109	290	62	—	—	4	25	—	5	148	—	—	—
2001	—	3	1	—	—	—	132	80	92	—	—	—	9	—	1	134	—	—	—
2002	—	7	5	—	—	—	183	171	212	—	—	—	9	—	2	250	—	2	—
2003	—	6	—	—	—	—	212	36	145	—	—	—	4	—	1	305	—	2	—
2004	—	9	3	—	2	—	118	85	153	—	—	—	2	—	2	465	2	5	—
2005	—	—	1	—	1	—	77	56	144	—	—	—	4	—	—	438	3	17	—
2006	—	—	1	—	2	—	70	56	233	—	—	—	2	—	2	445	3	10	—

续表

年份	白喉	麻疹	流脑	流行性感冒	猩红热	百日咳	细菌性痢疾	伤寒及副伤寒	病毒性肝炎	脊髓灰质炎	疟疾	钩端螺旋体病	乙脑	斑疹伤寒	流行性出血热	肺结核	狂犬病	性病	手足口病
2007	—	3	—	—	1	—	69	43	242	—	—	—	—	—	3	461	6	14	—
2008	—	—	2	—	1	—	68	8	353	—	—	—	1	—	—	639	1	14	53
2009	—	—	1	—	2	—	51	11	389	—	—	—	1	—	1	585	1	21	474
2010	—	—	1	—	—	—	96	17	145	—	—	—	—	—	—	443	2	27	1110

四、地方性氟中毒

1984年，县卫生防疫站始对全县27个乡（镇）驻地中心小学8岁至15岁的在校学生氟中毒状况进行调查，发现患病率达98%，为贵州省重病县之一，以区划分，城关区98.3%，扎佐区97.7%，久长区98.5%，小箐区98.2%，六广区97.4%。主要原因在于居民常以原煤为生活燃料所致。1986年安顺地区卫生局下拨配套物资，在扎佐区石竹村试行改灶防氟，使用烟管排烟的封闭式炉灶。次年起实行民办公助，就地取材有计划地推行，至1988年共改灶510个。继后，随着城乡居民生活提高，生活方式改善，改煤炉为电炉，致氟污染减少，2003年氟斑牙患病率降到28.3%。2006年起利用中央财政专项资金进行健康教育干预。2007年贵州省将修文列入地氟病防治改灶项目县，连续4年中央财政专项资金投资700万元，先后在9个乡镇192个病区村改炉改灶5.13万户，超计划31.71%，受益18.49万人，项目户满意率100%，顺利通过国家级验收，获贵州省第一名。

2007年疾病防控中心向地氟病病区免费发放改炉改灶烟管

五、人口死因

2004年8月，贵阳市疾病预防控制中心开展全市疾病死亡原因调查，以修文县为调查点，调查时限为2003年，调查死因分20类26项。调查结果，前10位死因依次为：循环系统疾病、意外死亡、呼吸系统疾病、肿瘤、消化系统疾病、传染病和寄生虫病、诊断不明、泌尿系统疾病、围生期、内分泌代谢。死亡人数：10类疾病死亡422人，占总死亡人数444人的95.04%。其中男性257人，女性165人。从死亡者的结构看，随着经济迅速发展，人民生活水平提高，生活环境改善，防病意识增强，导致疾病死亡因素明显变化，与1973—1975年调查情况对照，循环系统死亡从第三位升到第一位，意外死亡、肿瘤死亡从第七位和第八位升到第二位和第四位，传染病、泌尿系统疾病、围生期、内分泌代谢患病死亡位次均有前移。2003年肺结核患病人数从2000年的148人增为305人，各型肝炎病人从62人增到145人，死亡男性多于女性，恶性肿瘤死亡从高龄向中青年转移，严重地威胁着人民身体健康。

第五节　妇幼保健

1978年沿袭原妇幼保健站建制，在搞好妇女、儿童保健的基础上于1989年增加婚前保健。2002年保留原机构并入计划生育指导站合署办公，至2010年已建立以妇幼保健站为中心的县、乡、村三级网络管理妇幼保健工作。

一、妇女保健

（一）新法接生

1978年，各医院卫生院普遍实行新法接生。妇幼保健站定期或不定期对各乡村接生员进行培训、复训，并作示范操作教授，配备接生箱及器械，按月统计督促，提高新法接生率。1985年按照“一躺三消毒”（产妇躺在产床上，产包消毒、接生员手消毒、产妇会阴消毒）的原则，不论住院接生或在家庭接生，只要按此原则就算新法接生。据统计，全县普及率达92%，但经过调查和任意抽查，实际新法接生率仅占74%。。1986年全县新法接生1441人，由于交通条件和人的保健意识差异，县城及区乡所在地附近新法接生比率较高，边远村寨计划内高于计划外。随着经济发展，人民群众健康意识提高，新法接生普遍推广，住院分娩比例上升。逐步开展产前检查、产后访视，对新生儿建卡管理和系统管理，高危孕产妇实行监管。1996年全县上报出生2734人，实施新法接生2655人，新法接生率达97.11%、产前检查率达93.74%、产后访视率猛增到92.86%。

2000年初，县卫生局与乡镇卫生院签订《妇幼工作目标责任书》，要求各乡（镇）每月召开一次接生员会议，切实制定提高新法接生率、住院分娩率的规章制度。小箐乡政府明确规定：凡领取妇幼保健卡孕产妇在乡卫生院分娩可减免20%医药费。龙场镇拟定2001年计生站和卫生院联合承诺书，规定发准生证时一次性交费城镇210元，农村190元，作为以后10次产前检查、3次产后访视和42天健康检查、平产接生包干性费用。当年全县对孕产妇2392人，活产2366人，建卡2360人，系统管理2278人，高危孕产妇346人全部监管。非住院分娩的1473人中采用新法接生的1429人，占97.01%，无新生儿破伤风病例。2008年将流动人口纳入常住人口管理范围，与常住人口同服务、同管理。2009—2010年全县新法接生率达到100%。

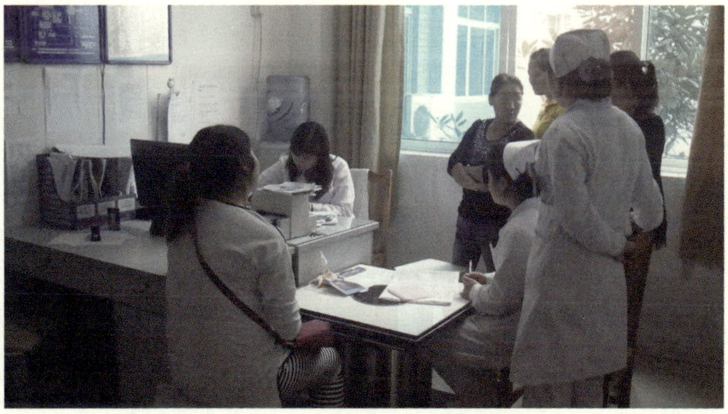

县医院妇产科门诊

（二）围产期保健

1978年至1983年对怀孕妇女围产期的检查、保健指导缺乏规范管理。1984年县妇幼保健站坚持常年门诊，对围产期妇女进行登记、检查和指导。1985年区、乡卫生院（所）配备妇保员。次年妇幼保健站增设专科门诊，对围产期妇女提供服务和孕产妇系统管理。1991年系统管理建卡110人，超地区下达指标

3人。1994年1月为降低孕产妇死亡率和婴儿死亡率，县卫生局成立围产期保健协作组，负责对全县围产期的妇女、儿童在产前、产时、产后妊娠合并症和异常分娩的诊断，每年对孕产妇和围产儿死亡逐个评审，对围产保健医院的死亡孕产妇追踪调查，定期进行死因分析和总结，判断是属可避免或属不可避免。至1996年全县上报出生2734人，产前检查率93.74%，产后访视率92.86%。

2002年4月，县政府明确妇幼保健职责是配合乡（镇）卫生院妇儿保健员完成0—6岁儿童体检、怀孕妇女围产期保健。继后，每年都对乡、村业务人员进行技术培训和技术指导，提高孕产系统的管理能力。至2005年，县以妇幼保健站为技术指导中心，10乡（镇）卫生院设预防保健办公室，村设妇幼保健员（接生员），形成三级管理网络，对保健对象基本做到情况清，底数明，对高危孕产妇进行筛查和有效管理。10月县政府又要求，为加大孕产妇和围产儿死亡监测，每年召开会议两次对围产保健医院的死亡孕产妇进行追踪调查、评审和分析，以便采取降低孕产妇死亡措施。连续6年共评审死亡孕产妇7例，其中1例属计划外怀孕，在贵阳私人诊所分娩，因产后大出血抢救不及时而死亡。

2010年，为有效干预出生人口神经管畸形缺陷，提高出生人口素质，由中央财政承担全部资金，有计划地对需生育的已婚妇女免费增补叶酸，进行有效干预。是年共发放叶酸1.39万瓶，叶酸增补2641人，围产儿中神经管缺陷有所下降。

（三）查治妇女病

1978年对妇女尿瘘和严重宫脱查治，将719例患者送贵阳医学院治疗，治疗经费由省、县卫生部门承担。1982年县妇幼保健站在六广区32个大队开展妇科病普查，查出宫脱患者227人，共上托138人。对80%的妇女患宫颈糜烂，专门研究用10味中草药制成粉剂，高温消毒后直接喷糜烂处，接受治疗者上药2—3次痊愈。

1983年县妇幼保健站和县医院进行妇科检查4337人，发现32例宫脱患者，全部进行治疗。1984年卫生局组织检查9815名妇女中查出现症病人979例，其中严重者428人，有385人进行治疗。

1986年，为方便妇女就诊，县妇幼保健站开设妇产专科门诊，县医院及各区卫生院设妇产门诊和住院病床。仅妇幼保健站年门诊达5614人次，妇查131人次，扎佐卫生院妇产门诊1800人次。继后，普查工作搁浅，仅1992年和2001年与县妇联、总工会联合在全县开展对女职工的妇科疾病普查普治，病患者多以门诊方式进行查治。

2004年，遵照贵阳市卫生局指示，对妇幼保健实行属地管理，由各居住地医院承担。10乡（镇）卫生院预防保健科，将流动人口妇幼保健纳入管理范围，由县妇幼保健站进行督导。2005年，县卫生局和人口与计划生育局会同县妇联、总工会组织普查已婚妇女妇科病，共查659人，查出疾病20余种，患病591人次，前三位疾病为乳腺小叶增生256人、宫颈炎158人、附件炎133人。

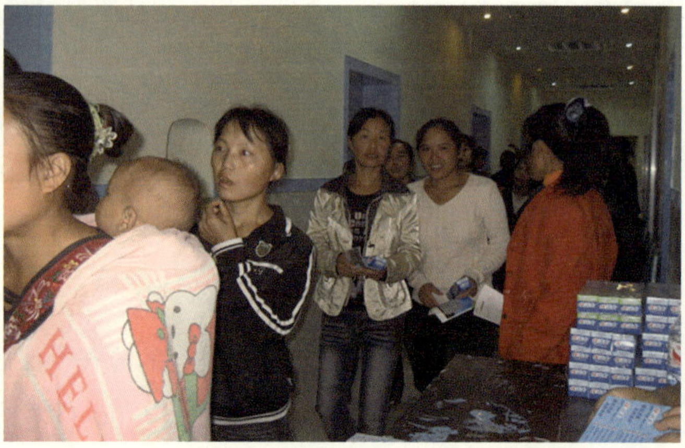

县妇幼保健站开展妇幼保健查治妇女病活动

2009年，县计划生育妇幼保健服务中心对已婚育龄妇女妇科病进行普查普治，列入创建省级计划生育优质服务先进县重要指标。5月邀请贵阳市退休医师医院专科医师与站、乡卫生院妇科医师组成普查队到乡（镇）实查1592人，查出患者563人，占35.36%，其中化验白带检出滴虫性阴道炎38例，念珠菌阴道炎32例，细菌性阴道炎36例；B超查出子宫肌瘤11例，附件包块7例，卵巢囊肿2例，附件炎21例；妇科查出Ⅱ宫颈糜烂160例，Ⅲ宫颈糜烂34例，宫颈息肉31例，纳囊26例，宫颈肥大38例；乙肝两对半查出乙肝患者75例；乳腺红外线扫描，查出乳腺增生52例。检查后，医师为患者开处方，并出具财政收费收据，由乡（镇）计生站配齐常用药品，以最低价格收费治疗，没有因药费治疗费欠交而不给治疗的问题发生。

2010年7月，为提高基层专业人员技术水平，县计划生育妇幼保健服务中心以帮带教方式，在洒坪乡卫生院开展妇科病普查普治。实查门诊1473人，患病484例，占32.86%，其中重度宫颈糜烂17例，中度宫颈糜烂59例，轻度宫颈糜烂140例，宫颈息肉162例，纳囊15例，细菌性阴道炎33例，滴虫性阴道炎10例，霉菌阴道炎10例，盆腔积液38例。检查中当场开具处方，100余人立即治病，均以低价收费。

二、儿童保健

（一）健康检查

1982年5月，由妇幼保健站承担，检查县实验幼儿园126名儿童，查出龋齿11人，心脏病2人，肠蛔虫5人立即服药驱虫。1984年“六一”节前，对县、区所在地托儿所、幼儿园、学前班688名儿童免费健康检查，为患肠蛔虫390人免费驱虫治疗。1985年，检查县、区小学及园（所）0—12岁儿童2578人，测量身高、体重、头围、胸围、上下肢长平均值，并建立儿童健康卡片。通过检查发现身高、体重等均值都较全国城市郊区儿童稍低。1986年站内开设儿保专科门诊，为各卫生院配备人体磅秤，共检查8岁以下儿童3615人，为城关小学和实验小学1240 名学生建立健康卡，至1992年全县儿童系统管理建卡3326人。

1996年，遵照卫生部《托幼园所卫生保健管理办法》，县妇幼保健站承担辖区内所有托儿所、幼儿园、学前班工作人员健康体检任务，每年进行一次健康体检。新进人员先体检，获得《身体健康合格证》方能上岗。各托幼园所、学前班，凭妇幼保健站出具健康检查证明办理入托、入园、入学手续。2001—2010年，儿童体检未开展，多作为门诊业务对来者进行健康检查。

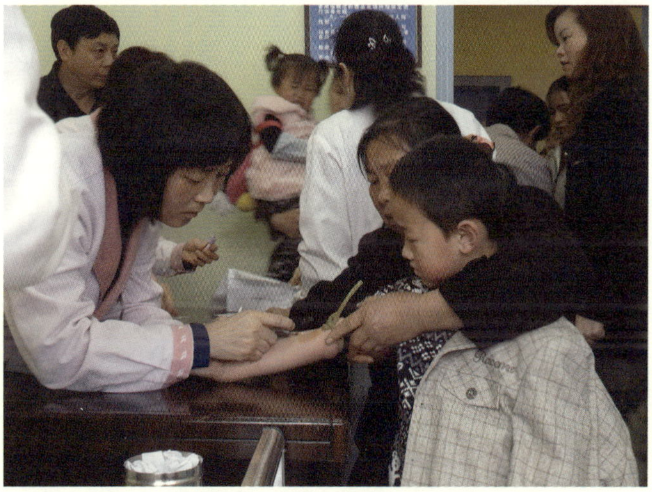

县妇幼保健站开展儿童健康体检活动

（二）预防接种

1978年，列入计划免疫（亦称“基础免疫”）有牛痘、麻疹、脊灰、卡介苗4种，每年均对儿童普查普种。属于非计划免疫的只对某些病种接种。1979年增加接种百白破。1981年牛痘疫苗停种。从1985年起，县卫生防疫站实施冷链运转，承担全部接种任务，并随着经济发展又从2003年起对非计划免疫品种逐步纳入计划免疫内。至2010年先后增加乙肝、流脑A、流脑A+C、乙脑、麻腮风、麻风、甲肝、白破二联8种，免疫制品共11种。

（三）系统保健

1984年实施系统保健，在482名独生子女中建卡登记137人，建卡率28.42%。1986年增到319人。进入20世纪90年代，订立农村“2000年人人享有卫生保健”目标，中小学开设健康教育课，增强儿童健康意识，由乡（镇）卫生院设立初级保健办公室具体实施。到2000年全县7岁以下儿童2.73万人，建卡管理2.72万人，建卡率达99.68%，顺利通过省级验收，达到农村温饱地区合格标准。2001年起，加强对7岁以下儿童保健管理和3岁以下儿童系统管理，提倡母乳喂养，对出生缺陷儿童监测和筛查。2010年全县有7岁以下儿童2.47万人，保健管理2.25万人，管理率91.34%；3岁以下儿童系统管理1.04万人，管理率城市为96.74%，农村为97.18%。

三、婚前保健

1989年在城关镇启动，县卫生局、民政局、妇联和城关镇联合成立领导小组，同时建立婚前保健检查技术鉴定小组，凡户籍在城关镇范围内的适龄婚配对象，婚姻登记前必须持个人身份证，近期照片3张，单位或街道、村委会证明，到妇幼保健站进行婚前保健检查，取得“婚前检查证明”后方可到户口所在地婚姻登记机关申请办理登记结婚。至1990年共检查238对，婚检率为82.92%。1998年11月，卫生局与民政局联合下发《关于凭婚前检查医学证明办理结婚登记的通知》，规定结婚当事人结婚前健康检查，其目的是诊断当事人是否患有禁止结婚疾病。妇幼保健站是贵阳市认证的县婚前医学检查法定机构，负责全县结婚当事人婚前保健和婚前健康检查，提出可以结婚、建议暂缓结婚、建议采取长效或永久性避孕措施后可以结婚等意见。男女双方在结婚登记时，乡（镇）民政办必须查验医学检查证明，持有法定检测机构出具婚前医学检查证明或者医学鉴定证明者，方可根据婚前健康检查医学意见进行登记，涉外婚检到贵阳市第一人民医院检查。

2001年8月，经省、市认定由县妇幼保健站和扎佐、久长、小箐、六广、六桶卫生院承担全县婚前检查工作，妇幼保健站负责全县婚前医学检查技术指导，未取得医学检查证明者不得登记结婚。2002年全县婚前检查1355对，婚检率达92%。2003年10月1日起，实施国家新的《婚姻登记条例》，婚前医学检查实行自愿婚检。由于人们对婚前检查是降低出身缺陷和预防先天疾病，提高出生人口素质的重要性认识不足，连续4年全县婚前检查率均为零，致出生缺陷发生率上升。致2006年全县出生人口2581人，有缺陷7人，缺陷率2.7%。2007年出生2676人，有缺陷17人，缺陷率6.35%。2008年5月，执行贵阳市政府决定，启动免费婚前医学检查，由乡（镇）及村计划生育专职干部和村妇保员上门摸底和宣传，当年全县婚前检查88对，体检率2.99%。2010年检查1268对，体检率增到41.46%。

第六节　爱国卫生

改革开放33年间，县政府在深入开展爱国卫生活动和“除四害”的基础上，下大力改善城市环境卫生和进行农村改水改厕以及创建卫生城市等工作，到2010年，全县改水2769处，改厕5.16万户，使城乡环境卫生得到明显改善，创建省级卫生县城和国家卫生城市取得进步。

一、开展爱国卫生活动

1978年，县有爱委会，于卫生局和5个区卫生院置爱卫办，专司开展爱国卫生运动事宜。至1988年

开展“五讲四美”（讲文明、讲礼貌、讲卫生、讲道德、讲秩序，心灵美、语言美、行为美、环境美），争创“文明卫生单位”的活动，评选出文明卫生单位97个，文明村寨180个。1989年国务院将每年4月定为爱国卫生月，更加强化群众的卫生意识，县爱卫办对51个公共卫生场所建立档案，对36户监测合格的发给卫生许可证。

1996年结合开展创建省级卫生县城，重点整治脏、乱、差，县直机关和各乡（镇）加强对公共厕所、垃圾池、垃圾处理场、下水道等公共卫生设施的管理。1998年县卫生局成立卫生执法稽查队履行卫生监督职能。1999年起以县为单位正式参加贵州省城市环境综合治理竞赛，2002—2003年，修文作为贵阳市县城组代表参赛获全省第三名。继后，每年4月7日世界爱国卫生日和爱国卫生月，均由卫生局牵头宣传食品、公共场所和饮水的卫生，讲解除四害、预防肠道传染病等知识，以增强群众的卫生习惯和防病意识。与此同时，加大整治环境卫生的力度。2010年清除户外广告3.68万条，取缔占道经营摊点864个，规范流动摊点836个，治理违规行为1312起，对其中的180起处以罚款。

2010年，县爱卫办利用场天开展爱国卫生宣传

专记：参加“黄果树”杯竞赛名列全省第三

1999年起，为增强市民文明意识和改善城市环境卫生，贵州省政府决定在全省范围内开展“黄果树”杯城市环境综合治理竞赛。修文县参加1999—2000、2002—2003年的两次竞赛，每次竞赛都由县委、县政府牵头，城建、城管、卫生、工商、环保、公安、林业、水利、国土等部门参与，县卫生局和爱卫办主要承担公共场所卫生、食品卫生和爱国卫生的宣传和治理工作，计散发食品、饮水卫生及除“四害”宣传资料4.8万份，开展除“四害”培训120人次，发放灭鼠毒饵10吨，灭蟑药笔1万盒，组织清除县城卫生死角60处，清理垃圾40吨，疏通污水沟2000米。财政拨款49.55万元（省34.55万元，县15万元），改厕9100座，消杀汛期内外环境5200平方米，培训食品从业人员4665人次，发放卫生许可证2977户，抽检餐具3344份；餐前检查152次，接待客人2.7万人。对辖区内970户食品生产经营户监督1.66万次，每户年均监督4.25次，查处违法经营户702次，分别作警告290次，责令改正168次，没收不符合卫生标准食品786公斤，价值1.57万元，暂扣封存食品42.4吨，价值5.84万元，行政罚款138次，罚款金额1.49万元。经过一系列的治理工作和竞赛活动，使城区老鼠密度由8.31%降至2.39%，蟑螂侵害率从13.71%降为2.94%。

2003年抗击非典型肺炎期间，爱卫办对县、乡、村发放预防宣传资料16万份，对进出车辆消杀1.2万台次，内外环境消杀65万平方米，开展“讲文明、讲卫生”“革陋习、树新风”活动10次，近11万人参加。通过综合治理，市民文明卫生意识得以增强，公共场所管理制度日趋健全，县城环境质量显著提高，经过评比获得“黄果树”杯竞赛第三名的优异成绩。

二、创卫工作

（一）创建省级卫生县城

1996年启动，重点开展“五不”（不说粗话、脏话，不随地吐痰，不乱扔杂物，不损坏公共设施，不违反交通规则）教育，继续治理脏、乱、差。1999年，县委、县政府把创建工作列入为民办实事的目标，当年经省政府检查组检查评估达到省级卫生县城标准，2006年通过省级复查合格。

（二）创建卫生村寨

2003年启动卫生村寨创建工作，旨在完善村寨基础设施，加强健康教育，改善农村环境卫生面貌。至2010年有龙场镇建新村、中哨村、马口村、宾阳社区，扎佐镇新庄村、大河村、长坡村，久长镇永兴村、上寨村，谷堡乡平寨村梭坡组和二组、富裕村张家堡组，六屯乡新堡村、都堡村大塘组、高峰村大寨组、全心村二洞组、西冲村下西冲组、独山村二组和三组，小箐乡杉林村、大兴村，洒坪乡小坝村，大石乡沙坝村先后荣获“贵阳市卫生村寨”称号。

2010年县卫生局与龙场镇政府联合在马口村开展创建卫生村寨活动

（三）创建国家卫生城市

2010年，中共贵阳市委、市政府作出决定在全市范围内开展“三创一办”（创建国家卫生城市、创建国家环境保护模范城市、创建国家文明城市，协助办好第九届少数民族传统体育运动会）活动。1月县成立“三创一办”领导小组，专设创建卫生城市指挥部，并设办公室于卫生局。3月印发创卫《实施方案》并展开创建工作，在中小学设健康教育课，利用新闻传媒广泛宣传，组织4050人创卫志愿者上街服务和监督，营造“我参与、我受益、我快乐”的良好创卫氛围。经过一年时间攻坚九大战役对市容环境的整治，使人民群众的卫生意识显著增强，小摊贩占道摆摊的行为得到遏制，127户公共场所和22户“五小”（小公共场所、小餐馆、小美容美发、小歌舞厅、小旅馆）行业达标率在94%以上，食品抽检合格率达99%，两年无甲、乙类传染病疫情暴发，其他指标基本或全部达标，从而顺利地通过国家级验收，为贵阳市荣获国家卫生城市的称号尽了应尽之力。

2010年创建卫生城市宣传

三、农村改水

据1979年调查，县境农村饮水有井水、泉水、龙潭水、河水、田水、沟水、自来水7类。由于环境污染或管道年久失修，部分村寨饮水量少且不卫生。1983年县政府组织66人对全县水资源进行普查，在普查的基础上于1985年开始实施人畜饮水工程，由水电局勘察设计和技术指导，财政局负责资金筹集，爱卫办组织实施。到1994年累计上级拨款32.98万元，财政投资75.24万元，群众自筹94.5万元，吸收赞助12.5万元，共计315.22万元，建成自来水107处，改井159口，受益11.36万人，占全县农村人口的47.06%。继后，结合农村四改（改水、改厕、改圈、改气）和贵阳市百村饮水工程实施，加大改水工程力度。到2000年，建成集中式改水工程313个，引水渠251条，水窖402个，受益11.3万人。2010年，国家当年投资647.38万元，进一步完善改水工程，使全县自来水厂增至2769处，水窖拥有2015个，受益23.98万人，占农业人口总数的97.94%。

四、农村改厕

1991年试点改进农村住户厕所，次年全县推行。开始由乡（镇）成立领导小组，与县政府签订目标责任书，爱卫办组织技术人员培训，并由妇女儿童工委负责监督。经费补助标准为每座三格式无害化厕所200元，卫生厕所25元，建成有顶、有墙、厕坑贮便池不渗漏、厕内清洁卫生的厕所。1996年又结合农村茅草房改造进行改厨、改厕、改圈、改沼气。到2010年，国家共投资3079.08万元，个人投资2万元，共计3081.08万元，在全县农村6.58万户中累计完成卫生改厕5.16万户，卫生厕所普及率达到75.8%，其中三格化粪池式0.65万户，三联沼气池式2.91万户，完整下水道水冲式0.04万户，其他类型1.56万户。

2001年3月，县卫生局筹资发放给龙场镇平地村改厕器材

第七节　医　药

县境地处贵州中部，大部分地区为中丘陵区，天然药源较为丰富。1997年引进药品生产企业入驻。2008年始对野生药材开展常规抚育保护，到2010年中药材已从农家种植发展到基地规模种植，引进的17户药品生产企业中有13户进行批量生产。

一、药材资源

包括天然野生药材和种植药材两部分。

（一）天然药源

1. 野生药材种类

据1985年中草药材普查统计，县境天然药材品种有1500余种，其中植物药材800余种，动物药材50余种，矿物药材8种，蕴藏量1.2万吨以上。继后由于人口增加，森林砍伐，矿产资源开采，中草药的私采私挖等因素影响，致使七叶一枝花、八爪金龙、山慈姑、大麻仁、四块瓦、白芨、石楠藤、仙桃草、朱砂莲、夜明砂、果上叶、岩白菜、鹅不食草、僵蚕、朱砂等天然药材品种逐渐减少，野生苦金盆、雪上一枝蒿、穿山甲等品种已濒临绝迹。虎、豹除扎佐野生动物园人工喂养的外，野生品种已多年不见，因此野生虎的虎骨、虎尿等药材早已灭绝。

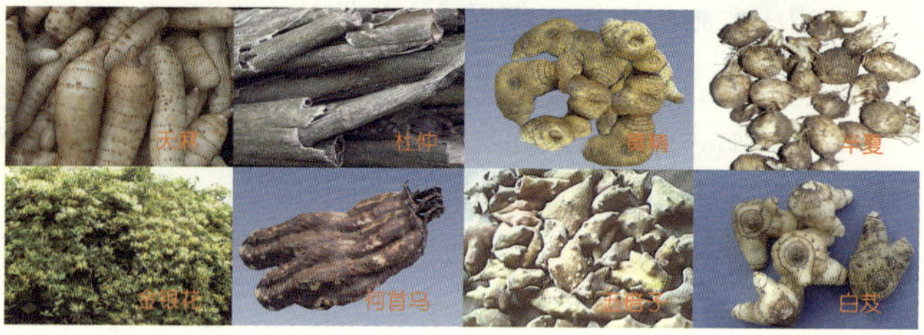

县境部分野生中药材

2. 野生药材常规抚育

2008年开始，为了保护野生药材种质资源，由贵阳市政府拨款补助，对厚朴、金银花、银杏、淫羊藿、喜树、杜仲、黄柏等主要品种实施常规抚育保护。至2010年累计拨款7.25万元，保护4.2万亩，年均亩产在120公斤以上。

（二）中药材种植

1. 农户种植

1979年县科委引进天麻种植，因难以掌握栽培技术未获成功。继后，随着农业体制改革，各乡镇农户成块种植食药两用的鱼腥草（亦称“折耳根”），尤以扎佐镇三里村四大冲折耳根在贵阳市场最有名气。杜仲、丹参、绞股蓝、山药、麦冬、三七、菊花、枸杞、天麻、金银花、党参、瓜蒌、黄柏、板蓝根、喜树等品种也陆续增种，结合植树造林种植杜仲达80余万株，2010年全县农户种植面积近3000亩，产量175吨，创产值300余万元。

2. 基地种植

1997年起，通过招商引资引进药品生产企业落地县境，所需原料药材先由外地种植，然后入境。为减少成本和保证药品质量稳定，仙灵（同济堂）药业对用量大的淫羊藿实行选种定点种植，投资1000余万元在境内建立中药材保护、种植、抚育基地。维康等药业也将外地种植基地陆续迁入县内。

2006年起，由贵阳市政府拨款补助，县农业局建立中药材生产管理站进行技术指导，按照GAP标准，采取“政府引导+基地+企业+农户”的运作模式，实行土地流转规范种植。连续5年市政府累计补助155.05万元，安泰、光正、益明源、同济堂、维康、喜儿康（中际）等药业与专门种植中药材的贵阳佳惠、花卉、卉农、合一、贵州宣和及绿金生态等公司，在全县10乡（镇）19个村建立种植基地。2005年至2010年种植半夏、厚朴、板蓝根、鱼腥草、杜仲、金银花、苦丁茶、黄柏、瓜蒌、淫羊藿、紫金莲、金荞麦、桔梗、太子参、玄参、天南星、天冬、柴胡、益母草、观音草、黄精、吴茱萸、天麻、防风、小叶黄杨、桑树、药用百合、续断共4.42万亩，产量达842.6吨，既满足药品生产企业所需原料，又增加农民的经济收入。

贵州宣和生物科技有限公司在六屯乡独山村种植的益母草

专记：药材基地成功种植紫金莲和金荞麦

紫金莲、金荞麦为扎佐医药产业园贵州安泰药业有限公司生产所需的原料药材，由公司申报，县筛选上报，贵阳市中药材办公室审核同意，确定2006年项目在小箐乡紫江村种植。之前，县农业局成立领导小组和实施小组进行协调、规划，再以项目业主方和实施单位——安泰药业签订基地建设合同，农业局负责技术培训和种植过程系列服务以及项目建设实施。安泰药业再与农户签订供种包收合同，产品按市场价格进行收购。按照CAP标准和SOP操作规程，选择土层深厚、土质疏松、排灌方便的土壤种植。紫金莲和金荞麦窝行距分别为50厘米×30厘米 、40厘米×30厘米，种植后及时中耕除草、修枝打顶、预防病虫害。连续3年贵阳市财政补助22.2万元，2006年完成规范种植紫金莲200亩，实收产品1.6万公斤，产值达32万元，示范种植成功。2007年项目扩大到杉林村，示范种植紫金莲、金荞麦200亩，种繁50亩，带动农户种植200亩，实收紫金莲1.66万公斤，金荞麦7.2万公斤，提供种苗200万株，总产值62万元。2008年，为保障药材质量、产量稳定，项目又扩至六屯乡的新埔、都堡、高峰、星中、小木5个村栽种，示范种植100亩，带动100户农户规范种植400亩，实收5.5万公斤，产值达70万元，户均增收600元。连同小箐乡紫江、杉林村种植共建基地种植紫金莲和金荞麦1100亩，产量达15.96万公斤，产值为164万元。通过规范种植实施，既促进种植业结构合理调整，增强农村科技意识，让农民增收脱贫，又推动无公害优质产品生产，保护药品生产质量，也保护了野生中药材的资源。

人工种植的紫金莲、金荞麦

二、药品生产

1997年7月，贵州绿太阳制药有限公司入驻县境扎佐，在省内独家生产膏霜制剂，开发贵州苗药。产品绿格尔系列拥有肤痔清软膏、貂胰防裂膏、日晒防痔膏及磁痔祛斑按摩乳、补天胶囊、葆肤康软膏、痔舒安软膏、绿格尔顽癣敌、绿格尔粉刺净等保健系列品种。肤痔清软膏经贵阳医学院、解放军四十四医院、北京中日友好医院、中国中医研究院等多家医院临床验证，皮肤病显效率达73.33%，痔疮显效率86.66%，妇女带下病显效率76%。产品畅销全国23个省、市及加拿大、荷兰、俄罗斯、越南和中国香港地区。2000年起县政府加大招商引资力度，先后引入安泰、仙灵（同济堂）、光正、维康、天方、长生、和仁堂、恒和、浩诚、德昌祥、杏林堂、中际（喜儿康）、科福、华德斯、华芝宝、济昇等16家药品生产企业进驻，到2010年除杏林堂、科福、华德斯、华芝宝、济昇共5家未投产外，其余12家均完成GMP改造建设，获得国家标准认证资格，累计拥有药品注册商标433个，实际生产品种136个，有40个品种列入《国家基本药物目录》，9个品种列入省增补基本药品目录。其中德昌祥药业妇科再造丸、绿太阳药业绿格尔系列产品、恒和药业枇杷止咳胶囊、同济堂药业仙灵骨葆、维康药业骨康胶

同济堂药品包装车间

囊、安泰药业妇平胶囊为省、市级名牌产品，绿太阳绿格尔系列6个保健品种获国家“星火计划”实施10周年优秀项目金奖和新产品新技术博览会金奖，同济堂仙灵骨葆胶囊获吉隆坡世界骨伤科理事会一等奖和中国骨伤科理事会特别贡献奖。

第八节 管 理

一、医政管理

（一）医疗机构管理

1978年由卫生局负责，凡具备以下条件其中之一者允许在指定地点开业：一是在本县有正式户口的中医、西医，确有一定技术水平，能独立进行一般诊疗工作，并符合未参加国家和集体医疗机构而要求开业者；二是已退职退休的中医、西医；三是中医学徒学习满5年以上，能独立应诊，国家或集体医疗机构不能安置工作的自谋职业者。1982年对其考试考核，有25名合格者获颁个体开业行医许可证。1991年为加强医疗管理，卫生局增设医政股，配医政监督员，区卫生院亦有相应配置。1992年年审核发证56个，处理医疗事故6起，责令赔偿经济损失1200元。

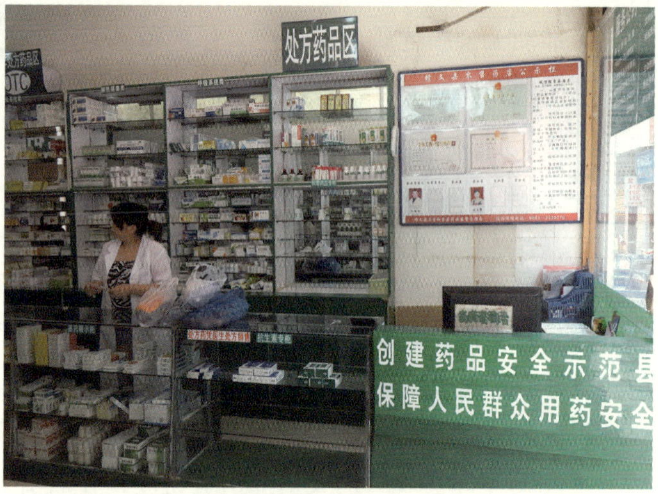

加强药品市场管理，创建药品安全示范县

1994年9月国务院出台《医疗机构管理条例》并予实施，将医疗机构和个体开业医均纳入规范化管理。1999年5月统一颁发《医疗机构执业许可证》，医政科负责医疗市场准入。2005年后村卫生室准入由卫生局业务科承担，2010年经医政科核准执业医疗机构35个，业务科核准非营利性村卫生室195个，营利性村卫生室2个，共计232个。

（二）执业注册

1994年1月实施《中华人民共和国护士管理办法》，1999年5月实施《中华人民共和国执业医师法》，对符合条件的护士、医师即办理注册手续，至此全县卫生技术人员准入正式步入法治化管理。到2010年，全县注册执业医师239人，其中口腔8人，公共卫生20人，中医52人，临床159人。同时注册护士243人。

二、药政管理

（一）药品市场管理

1985年7月，开始实施《中华人民共和国药品管理法》，卫生局设药品管理办公室专司药政管理，对经考试考核合格者重新登记，核发《药品经营许可证》。次年，规定县境医药卫生单位购药统一在县医药、药材公司采购。1988年县成立药检所，配药品监督员4人，各区配1人负责市场监督，对药品市场进行监督检查。

2002年7月，从卫生局析出药政、药检业务，由新组建的药品监督管理局（简称“药监局”）接办，广泛开展法律法规宣传，对涉药人进行法律知识培训，按期换发《药品经营许可证》。2003年起根据国家药品监督局《药品经营质量管理规范》，开展药品零售企业GSP认证和复认证，同时建立农村药品监督网和供应网。2005年1月正式聘请乡协管员20名、村信息员214名进行监督。到2010年全县有药品批发企业1户和零售药店43户，均为GSP认证企业。并有农村零售药柜54个方便群众购药。

（二）特殊药品管理

1978年，对麻醉药品、精神药品及其他专用药品等的特殊药品管理，仍沿袭原有制度，实行专人负责、专柜加锁、专用账册、专用处方、专用登记的“五专”制度。但因检查疏漏，致使一些单位未严格执行。1989年，县卫生局对“购用麻醉药品印鉴卡”进行审核，为县、区6所医疗单位重新办理建卡手术，督促建立“五专”制度并严格执行。

2002年7月，县卫生局对癌症患者因阵痛使用麻醉药品，凭二级以上医疗机构诊断证明书、户口簿和身份证，可在县以上药监局或药监与卫生行政部门认定的二级以上医疗机构办理专用卡，凭卡在具有麻醉药品使用资格的医疗机构和具有麻醉药品处方权的执业医师开具处方取药使用，各经办处均作登记备查。2005年9月卫生局正式明确县医院和扎佐、久长、六桶卫生院以及中西医结合医院、百信医院、龙港医院、扎佐林场医院、万江厂职工医院、兴红厂职工医院、贵阳煤矿（小河沟）医院为全县使用特殊药品医疗单位。至2010年，除兴红厂职工医院撤销外，其余医疗机构仍延续执行。

（三）药品执法监督

1985年7月，遵照《中华人民共和国药品管理法》规定，县卫生局与有关部门联合，依法对医疗单位和药品经销企业实行年度检查，发现过期失效、霉变、假劣、淘汰药品一律没收销毁处理。到1995年共检查销毁伪劣的药品价值2.38万元，1996年在全县范围开展药品市场检查，封存、销毁伪劣和过期失效药品74种，价值0.8万元，并取缔非法行医卖药摊23个，查处经营违禁药品摊点4个。2000年结合《药品经营许可证》年检逐户入店查看验收库存药品，对3户不达标者予以取缔。

药品执法检查

2002年7月起，药监局每年元旦、春节、“五一”、国庆等节日均开展日常检查或专项整治。对群众举报违反《中华人民共和国药品管理法》案件，经查实结案后按罚没收入财政返还金额的5%奖励举报人（最高5万元）。2002—2010年累计违规立案处理210起，罚没金额43.96万元，从而维护了药品管理法律法规的尊严。

三、行政管理

（一）职工竞聘上岗

1978—1993年，沿袭统分安置医疗职工。1994年参照企业实施《中华人民共和国公司法》，始对卫生事业单位中的电工、清洁工、驾驶员、锅炉工等技能工实行持证竞聘上岗，建立使用、升降、考核、奖罚、淘汰制度，使庞大的机关和后勤队伍得以压缩。1996年再对局机关和卫生监督机构实行“三定”（定部门职能、定岗位规范、定岗位人员）编制，裁减管理人员充实到第一线；对卫生事业单位卫技人员实行职称考聘制度，在全县卫技人员391人中聘任323人，未聘68人，从而激发了职工爱岗敬业精神。至2010年，考聘制度坚持执行。

（二）行风管理

1. 行风监督

1996年开始实行行风监督，通过思想教育、效能建设、行风评议和治理等方式进行。是年查出久长卫生院1994至1996年3月采购药品获利14.47万元，龙场镇卫生院采购药品实按92%付款获取回扣2268元。2004年1月为使效能建设制度化、经常化，县卫生局制发《局服务承诺》《医院社会承诺》《医疗卫生人员“六不准”（不准在职医务人员未经批准从事与本专业有关的第二职业；不准在医疗服务中推诿、私自转诊和无故拒诊病人，不准开大处方、滥用药、滥检查、搭车开药增加患者医疗费用负担，不准医疗科室实行收入分成和私设金库，不准将科室收入与医务人员个人报酬直接挂钩，不准非营利性机构内设营利性科室、病区、项目）》，接受社会监督。2007年聘请县政协副主席陈国邦、县政协纠风办主任彭忠镜、宾阳和栖凤两社区居民陈仁智、杨佩佩、退休医师孙国栋为行风监督员履行监督职责。2008至2010年除六广镇德政防治站在新型农村合作医疗中违规被停止定点医疗资格，10乡（镇）卫生院违规收费1.45万元和龙场镇青龙、新春、幸福村卫生室乱开处方变通用药被处罚外，未发现其他医疗机构行业作风中的违规行为。

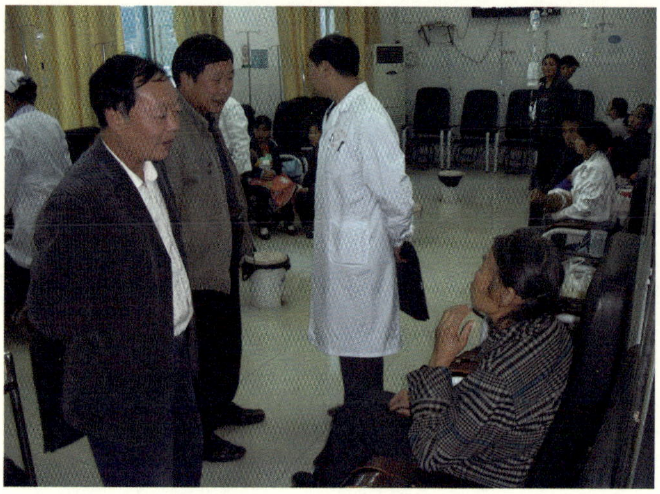

行风监督员到县人民医院检查

2. 医德医风建设

进入20世纪90年代，针对医疗部门出现的“送红包”看病的不良风气，于1992年6月在卫生系统建立思想政治工作研讨制度，不断对职工进行医德医风教育。1996年起又先后开展“树立新形象，满意在我院（站）”活动，挂牌“放心药房”“放心诊所”，让社会参加监督。2000—2003年进行“三个代表”重要思想学习教育，结合开展行风评议和效能建设，大力弘扬爱岗敬业和无私奉献的职业道德。县卫生局成立民主评议行风工作领导小组及其办公室，制定《医德医风建设实施方案》，订立政务公开和院务公开制度，制订《严禁向患者收取“红包”规定》，使职工确立“病人第一，服务第一，质量第一”观念，增强“以人为本”和“爱心、耐心、细心、责任心”的服务理念，并聘请外单位监督员进行监督。扎佐卫生院为方便急诊病人就医，5公里内免费接送病人120人次。2007年对行风建设进行“回头看”，通过实地查看和问卷调查，职工满意度达91.8%，病人满意度达88.2%。

2008年，按照省、市要求对全县399名卫生专业人员进行医德医风考评，以优秀、良好、合格、不合格4个等次建立考评档案。对县级医院和10乡（镇）卫生院进行述职述廉及民主评议方式评议，进一步增强职工的工作积极性和主动性。通过一系列的活动，使各医疗部门的医德医风均有明显好转。县医院

进行基础设施建设、医疗药品器械采购均坚持走主渠道优质优价进购，至2010年未发现过“人情药”“搭配药”进入医院。

专记：县医院抓医德医风建设见成效

县医院共有职工208人，自扩大医疗规模后，年均门诊达8万人次，住院5200人次。由于经济利益驱动，收受“红色”、拿“回扣”的腐败问题萌发，并呈蔓延之势。为杜绝不正之风，根据省、市卫生部门指示精神，坚持“谁主管、谁负责”和“管行业必须管行风”、“一岗双责”（一个岗位负责行政、业务两责）的原则，实行行业管理与行风建设相结合，医院于2009年年末和2010年年初分别成立医德医风建设和治理商业贿赂两个领导小组，3月行文明确行风建设领导小组职责是狠抓职工医德教育、健全规章制度、加强信息沟通和认真对待来信来访，把行风建设提上议事日程。4月，分别落实医德医风责任制，制定《医德医风建设条例（试行）》，规定院长、科室负责人为院、科、室第一责任人，教育职工增强“以病人为中心”的服务意识，按照医务人员行为规范认真履行职责。5月，印发《开展医德医风教育活动实施细则》，对医德行为守则进行规范。9月正式建立《奖惩制度》，对有贡献者进行奖励，违反者实行经济惩罚，并聘请县政协副主席陈国帮、宾阳社区党支部书记陈仁智、电视台记者徐麒麟、虎山社区党支部书记何兴友、工商局离休干部刘钦向为监督员履行监督职责。12月进行总结，实行行风建设一票否决，对不足之处坚决整改，使合理检查、合理治疗、合理用药、合理收费真正落到实处。经过6月和12月分别以收费、治疗、检查、服务等10个问题调查120名病人，满意度达97.2%；以班子建设、工作作风、招标采购、医务管理等10个问题调查120名职工，对管理职能部门和医院领导满意度从97.5%上升到100%，全年未发现吃回扣、收红包等行为，实现了病人、职工“双满意”，有患者反映：“不递红包看病，我们压力减轻。”有医师感悟：“不收红包开诊，我们惠及于民。”

四、财务管理

（一）事业经费管理

1978年，沿袭原有规定，卫生防疫、妇幼保健全额拨款，有业务收入的医疗机构全额管理差额补助办法。县医院按病床比例1:1.2实行人员包工资，县财政以基本工资80%拨款补助；区卫生院按人员基本工资的50%拨款补助。1992年10乡（镇）卫生院事业经费从县下划到乡级财政管理。1995年新组建中医院，属卫生医疗事业单位，实行财务独立核算，股份制经营管理。县财政只拨款补助人员经费。2004年乡（镇）卫生院事业经费又改为由县卫生局统一编制预算，再由县财政按预算拨款管理，2010年拨款补助比例实现工资总额的100%。

（二）业务收入管理

1978年，县、区医疗机构医疗收入、药品收入均为业务收入的主要资金来源，实行自收自管，按期通过会计报表向县卫生局报告。支出项目除购置大型医疗设备等大项需报经卫生局批准执行外，对医疗服务过程中发生的医疗费、药品费和其他费用由医院按规定价格计收。到2010年仍执行此制度。

五、监督管理

（一）劳动卫生与职业病监测

1982年6月，县卫生防疫站对境内厂矿普查，到1985年，31户企业中受粉尘危害者有12户，有产尘点54处，接触粉尘职工1168人，对8个单位职工体检，尘肺患病率18.6%。1993年至1994年协同县经委对工业企业有毒有害作业职工劳动卫生防护知识培训，提高自我保护能力。但因乡（镇）企业环保意识淡薄，生产环境恶浊，致有害作业点防护问题得不到解决，监测合格率仅占36%。加之企业职工又多为农民轮换工，在企业工作时间不固定，企业未进行职工健康体检，也无职业病报告。2004年改由卫生监督所接办，每年利用“4·25”职业病防治日开展《中华人民共和国职业病防治法》宣传，依法履行监督检查职能，建立企业档案，检查范围从工矿企业扩大到废品收购店、皮鞋加工店等领域，对违法者立案查处。至2010年累计建立企业档案191户，立案查处3户，罚款2.25万元。

2005—2010年职业卫生情况统计表

表5—04—07

年份	单位数（户）	接触职业危害人数（人）	培训人数（人）	健康检查		调离（人）	违规处罚	
				体检（人）	合格（人）		立案数（户）	处罚
2005	20	3200	816	816	816	—	—	—
2006	104	4569	—	1826	1826	—	—	—
2007	52	3127	2243	2026	1898	128	—	—
2008	50	2483	100	1620	1620	—	2	罚款0.25万元
2009	108	2960	—	1756	—	—	—	—
2010	109	2270	—	1224	—	—	1	罚款2万元

（二）学校卫生监督

1983年，县卫生局和防疫站对修文中学、实验小学、城关小学教室采光、噪音、学生体检监测，监测结果多数不符合要求，故以书面通知限期整改。1984年对幼儿园和小学3618名儿童体检；对27个乡（镇）8岁至15岁的7975名在校学生氟斑牙患病情况调查，建立健康卡片，到1997年止的20年，每年平均学生体检5000人次，发现视力低下和发胖者较多，高中学生高达30%，心血管疾病占1.2%，四肢发育不全占0.3%，当即采取措施由学校在体育课时适当减少高强度运动，驱虫服药年均3.1万人次。1998年执行贵州省取消中小学生体检和驱虫服药收费规定，学生体检只在修文中学高一新生和高三毕业生中进行。2003年，学校卫生监督职能移交卫生监督所接办。2005年起对学校食堂进行量化标准管理。2009年有14所学校、幼儿园食堂达到B级单位。2010年全县98所学校均建立传染病防治管理档案，配有专（兼）职人员经办。

（三）食品卫生监督

1983年7月试行首部《中华人民共和国食品卫生法》。1984年起依法对饮食服务业颁发《卫生许可证》和从业人员《健康证》，并实施监测。1987年乡（镇）和驻县厂矿配置监督员24人，至1989年全县初步形成监督网络，每年依法对饮食、食品生产单位进行检查和从业人员健康体检，要求单位必须具有《卫生许可证》和从业者《健康证》方能经营。至1997年的14年累计检查出掺杂、掺假、霉变等伪劣食品3.2万公斤，价值7.36万元，当即销毁处理，并对情节严重者罚款8600元。

1997年正式颁布实施《中华人民共和国食品卫生法》，11月县卫生局成立执法稽查队，于次年6月接办监督职责，防疫部门对其实施监测，成为贵州省首家建立卫生执法队并实行卫生监督、监测分离的

县。到2003年，连续19年累计监测餐具8919份、食肉6172份、酱油1208份、白酒1836份、糕点685份、月饼2063份、面条及其他食品2536份，合格率为96.5%，不合格部分当即销毁处理。

2004年8月在县城餐饮业推行使用消毒餐具，开展农村红白宴食品监管。2005年推行量化分级管理。2008年9月11日全国发生三鹿奶粉事件时，全县清查食品经营户3086户次，查封和扣押各种奶粉及液化奶1.36万公斤，调查3岁以下婴幼儿1.9万名，查出三鹿奶粉有害物质三聚氰胺症状者68名，5名轻型患儿住院治愈。2009至2010年检查3712户全部合格，连续13年销毁不合格食品1.21万公斤，对情节严重者罚款21.2万元。

县卫生监督局与质检局联合对食品安全检查

1997—2010年食品卫生监督管理情况统计表

表5—04—08

年度	应监督（户）	实监督			培训			健康体检			行政处罚					
		户次	合格	合格率（%）	应培训（人）	实培训（人）	培训率（%）	应体检（人）	实体检（人）	体检率（%）	户次	警告或责令改正（户次）	停业（户）	取缔户	责令销毁食品（公斤）	罚款（元）
1997	718	3256	2768	85.01	—	1112	—	1130	1112	98.41	86	27	—	1	494	500
1998	739	3174	2730	86.01	1045	1031	98.66	1045	1032	98.76	263	152	15	—	114	40
1999	841	3616	3147	87.03	1293	1277	98.76	1293	1278	98.84	238	178	5	—	66	1010
2000	890	3793	3338	88.00	1587	1568	98.80	1587	1569	98.87	229	189	11	—	132	70
2001	930	4008	3306	82.49	1649	1622	98.36	1649	1631	98.91	255	158	12	—	436	1150
2002	964	4172	3462	82.98	1685	1667	98.93	1685	1667	98.93	259	148	—	—	2737	6910
2003	977	4234	3508	82.85	1683	1665	98.93	1701	1683	98.94	321	254	—	—	730	1900
2004	989	4352	3743	86.01	1706	1675	98.18	1739	1706	98.10	325	200	—	—	2650	11950
2005	996	3984	3427	86.02	2380	2380	100.00	2432	2384	98.03	425	260	—	—	3400	41100
2006	972	4508	4409	97.80	1972	1972	100.00	2012	1972	98.01	436	303	—	—	1800	53850
2007	1074	4637	4489	96.81	1778	1778	100.00	1852	1778	96.00	108	—	—	—	—	60600
2008	1125	4752	4379	92.15	2068	2068	100.00	2099	2068	98.52	64	32	—	—	—	14100
2009	398	1620	1523	94.01	—	2461	—	2316	2298	99.22	—	—	—	—	—	1300
2010	611	1256	2264	94.77	—	2445	—	2405	2372	98.63	—	—	—	—	—	600

（四）饮水卫生监督

1983年11月始对全县水源普查，查明水源3565个，可供22.12万人饮用。同时启动农村饮水工程，到1990年共建农村饮水工程47个，受益4.6万人，水质一般为Ⅰ至Ⅲ级，适合人畜饮用。从1991年起，省、地、县采取财政投资、集资、捐款等方式筹资，在农村进行改水，修建水厂15个，受益2万余人；

在城乡和驻县厂矿所在地建水厂21个，受益4.64万人。继后每年对18个点水质监测分析，一般为Ⅰ级至Ⅱ级。1995年正式实施《中华人民共和国水资源法》，依法对自来水、自备水、自流水定期消毒和监测，对县城自来水公司供水系统每日监测一次，取样点为东、西、南、北、中近端及末梢水，累计取样1800份，不合格则派专人督促指导用余氯消毒。乡（镇）监测重点为扎佐、久长、小箐、六广居民饮用水，累计监测水样480份，水质状况时好时坏，其原因系水厂未按规定用量进行消毒。

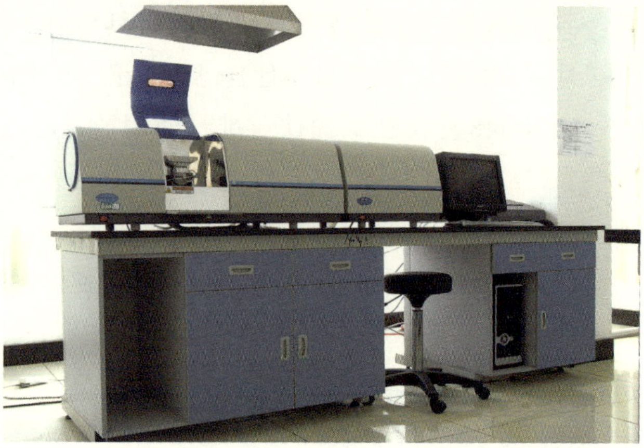

采用原子吸收仪用于饮用水检测

2003年起，监督职责从卫生防疫站改由卫生监督所承担，每年对生活饮用水单位全面监督，对从业人员全部进行体检和培训。至2010年，全县供水单位23户，从业人员53人，水质抽查达标率为96.5%；农村24户以上饮用水井252口，夏秋季消毒率达92%，消毒合格率为86.7%。由于工矿企业发展，城镇人口剧增，加之监督职能不尽到位，致水质污染和排污成为政府更进一步加大力度解决的问题。

（五）公共卫生监督

1979年县城率先成立环境卫生管理站，用手板车转运城区垃圾。1983年县卫生局与公安、文教部联合通知：影剧院内不准吸烟，不准吃带壳食物，饮食服务行业必须办理《卫生许可证》和从业人员《健康证》始准经营。

1997年县卫生局组建卫生执法稽查队，定编10人，专司面向社会公共卫生监督职责，负责卫生许可和执业许可，开展监督检查、宣传教育和投诉案件调查处理。2002年12月改为卫生监督所，每年对公共场所负责人和从业人员进行培训，不断灌输卫生知识，对六广河、桃源河漂流、珍珠岛、高尔夫度假中心等旅游景点重点检查。同时，开展创建“卫生县城”专项整治，营造干净、卫生、整洁、有序的人居环境。2009—2010年，全县范围内进行公共场所量化分级管理，将住宿业45户，美容美发88户，沐浴场所12户全部纳入，量化结果：获A级10户，B级22户，C级99户。沐浴水质监督检测结果，余氯、PH值、水温、菌落总数、总大肠菌群全部符合GB/T18204-2000标准。到2010年，6年间调离体检不合格从业人员1人，报请工商部门强行取缔1户，违规罚款处理15户（次），罚款0.58万元。

2005—2010年公共卫生情况统计表

表5—04—09

年度	从业户数		从业人员		违规处罚	
	合 计	持有效卫生许可证	合 计	持有效健康证	户数	处 罚
2005	129	129	454	454	3	罚款0.21万元
2006	94	94	353	353		
2007	147	147	332	332	4	罚款0.08万元
2008	141	141	316	301	3	罚款0.06万元，调离1人
2009	180	174	491	473	6	
2010	191	188	509	494	5	罚款0.23万元，强行取缔1户，补办2户

（六）放射卫生监督

1991年前，未开展监督业务。1992年起由卫生防疫站行使放射监督职责。1998年6月贵州省卫生厅颁发放射卫生许可证，卫生监督部门实行监管。2004年6月，改由卫生监督所负责。2005年全县11所医疗机构有200至500毫安X光机17台，每年均对从业人员体检和培训，对职业病防治、放射性同位素、放射安装安全情况进行监督检查。2010年1月，有16所医疗机构向卫生局承诺，县卫生局向贵阳市卫生局承诺，对闲置、报废医用辐射设备14台强制收储，以保人民身体健康和环境安全。至年末止的6年，对检查中发现无辐射警示标志和工作人员未进行体检等问题，当即下达《卫生监督意见书》督促整改。

（七）医疗机构监管

2003年5月前由卫生局医政科负责管理，6月改由卫生监督所履行监督职责，依法对非法行医和跨科行医、口腔器械消毒、法定传染病报病、医疗美容服务、非法采血供血、医疗废物管理和处置进行监督。2008年又对10户医疗机构和1户计划生育机构B超进行登记，严查利用B超进行胎儿性别鉴定和选择终止妊娠手术行为。至2010年，8年累计取缔非法行医192户，没收药品、器械160件和生物制品18盒全部销毁处理，罚款18.01万元。久长镇非法行医的邱天才致死人命，被依法判处有期徒刑10年。彭启祥非法行医三次移送司法机关处理。4户个体诊所漏报法定传染病被罚款1000元。并查出25户医疗机构对医疗废物的收集、运送、贮存、处理违规，其中有21户被责令整改，4户被罚款500元。

第五章　人民生活

1978年，中共十一届三中全会召开后，全县国民经济运行质量显著提升。经济的发展为提高城乡居民生活水平奠定了物质基础。至2010年，城镇居民生活已实现从温饱型到小康型的历史跨越，农村居民生活正在由温饱型向小康型迈进。

第一节　城乡居民收入

一、城镇居民收入

城镇居民家庭的收入分总收入和可支配收入，总收入是由工资性收入、经营净收入、财产性收入和转移性收入这4部分组成。衡量城镇居民收入水平最有实际意义的是可支配收入。无论是总收入或是可支配收入，城镇居民自1996年开始经济调查以来，都是连年增长的。人均可支配收入2007年跨越万元大关，2010年达1.58万元，比1996年3480元增长3.53倍，年均递增11.39%。就人均总收入的构成看，是“一升三降”。工资性收入占总收入的比重由1996年47.91%升至2010年的75.37%，其余经营净收入、财产性收入和转移性收入占总收入的比重皆有下降。

1. 工资性收入，它一直都是城镇居民收入最主要的来源，也是居民家庭总收入中增长速度最快的一个部分。1978年，全县职工人均工资为580.5元，继后进行多次工资调整，至2010年职工人均年工资上升为3.12万元，为1978年的53.71倍，年均增长13.26%，与同一时期全县生产总值（GDP）年均递增16.4%的速度基本同步。整个城镇居民年人均工资收入，1996年为1672元，2010年上升为1.22万元，增长6.3倍，年均递增15.26%。

2. 经营净收入，年度之间起伏变化较大，2001年人均838元，占人均总收入的15.16%为最高；2008年被调查户当年没有发生这项收入。1996年人均经营净收入297元，占总收入的8.5%，2010年为42元，占总收入的0.26%。

3. 财产性收入，随着金融市场的发展和城镇居民投资理财观念的增强，城镇居民通过相互借贷，参与投资，购买有价证券、股票、保险产品，银行存款所取得的利息等融资渠道，以及出租房屋所得的租金，使家庭财产性收入呈增长态势。1996年人均财产性收入74元，2010年升至177元，增长2.39倍，年均递增

6.41%。这项收入总趋势是增长，但年度之间波动较大。2010年较大财产性收入是股息与红利收入、人均59元，出租房屋收入人均29元，保险收入人均28元，它们分别占财产性收入的33.23%，16.45%和16.06%。

4、转移性收入，是城镇居民家庭仅次于工资性收入的一个重要的收入来源。由于健全养老保险制度，离退休职工养老金按时、足额发放，城镇居民最低生活保障标准不断提高，促使转移性收入增长较快。1996年人均1447元，2010年达3770元，比1996年净增2323元，年均递增7.08%。2010年转移性收入中数额较大的分别是：养老金人均3545元，占94.04%；赡养收入人均94元，占2.49%；捐赠收入人均69元，占1.28%；社会救济收入人均36元，占0.96%。

部分年份城镇居民人均总收入及其构成一览表

表5—05—01　　　　单位：元/人

指　　标	1996年	2000年	2005年	2010年	2010年为1996年的倍数	1996-2010年年均递增率（%）
家　庭　总　收　入	3490.00	5134.32	8618.50	16198.11	4.64	11.59
其中：可支配收入	3480.00	5109.72	8503.40	15755.83	4.52	11.39
占总收入比重（%）	99.71	99.52	98.66	97.27	—	—
1. 工资性收入	1671.94	2976.76	4742.30	12209.21	7.30	15.26
占家庭总收入比重（%）	47.91	57.98	55.03	75.37	—	—
2. 经营净收入	296.77	621.97	428.10	42.30	—	-12.99
占家庭总收入比重（%）	8.50	12.11	4.97	0.26	—	—
3 . 财产性收入	74.00	29.00	10.70	176.57	2.39	6.41
占家庭总收入比重（%）	2.12	0.57	0.12	1.09	—	—
4. 转移性收入	1447.29	1506.59	3437.40	3770.03	2.60	7.08
占家庭总收入比重（%）	41.47	29.34	39.88	23.28	—	—

城镇居民家庭有收入者比重提升，是收入增长的重要原因。1996—2010年期间，除个别年份有收入者占家庭总人口的比重略有波动外，总趋势是不断提升的。2010年在1996年基础上增长12.6个百分点。随着全县整个经济的健康发展，就业门路拓宽，加上政府千方百计对弱势群体、特别是无职无业的所谓“干居民”家庭进行帮扶，积极安排就业或扶持创业，消灭“零就业”家庭，从而使整个城镇居民家庭有收入的人增多，吃闲饭的人减少，这就拉动了城镇居民人均收入水平的不断提高。

部分年份有收入者人数及占被调查户人口总数的比重一览表

表5—05—02

指　标	1996年	2000年	2005年	2010年
户均年平均总人口数(人)	3.10	3.03	3.00	2.77
户均年均有收入人口(人)	1.87	1.96	2.00	2.02
有收入人口占总人口比重(%)	60.32	64.69	66.67	72.92

1996—2010年，全县城镇居民人均可支配已收入虽是高速增长的，但这一高速度是在低起点的基础上

实现的。1996年城镇居民人均可支配收入3480元，与当年全国、贵州省和贵阳市的平均水平均有一定差距。修文这项指标只分别为全国、贵州省和贵阳市的71.12%、82.64%和71.52%。至2010年，修文城镇居民人均纯收入仍赶不上全国和贵阳市的平均水平，只比贵州省的平均水平略高。但就其年均递增速度而言，1996年至2010年期间全国、贵州省和贵阳市分别为10.31%、9.04%和9.16%，而修文达11.39%，是最高的。

部分年份城镇居民人均可支配收入对照表

表5—05—03　　　　计量单位：元

年　份	全国	贵州省	贵阳市	修文县
1996年	4839	4211	4866	3480
2000年	6280	5121	6453	5110
2005年	10493	8147	9928	8503
2010年	19109	14143	16597	15756

二、农村居民收入

在1981年全县农村全面推行家庭联产承包责任制之前，较长时间处于集体统一经营时期。1978年农民从集体经济中人均分配含粮食等实物折款在内为45.97元。有63.66%的基本核算单位还处于此平均数之下。

1978年全县农民人均纯收入为141元，其中来自集体经济分配的占32.6%，来自农民家庭自营收入占67.4%。

1981年农村居民人均总收入为194元，扣除经营成本后，人均纯收入为180元。至2010年，人均总收入达6396元，比开展农村居民经济调查的1981年增长32.97倍，年均递增12.81%；人均纯收入为5152元，比1981年增长28.62倍，年均递增12.26%。农村居民直接可以支配的纯收入在不断增长的过程中，凸显了如下特点。

1. 人均纯收入的构成变化较大。1978年后，农村居民人均纯收入一直是直线上升的，没有出现过波动，但其构成情况变化却较大。1981年至1998年，纯收入是由从集体得到的收入，从经济联合体得到的收入，家庭自营收入和非借贷性收入这4部分组成。其中，家庭自营收入始终都是纯收入构成的主体，且比重呈上升态势，其余3部分都属补充性的收入，所占比重均呈现下滑。1981年，农村居民从集体得到的收入占24.31%，当年没有经济联合体的收入，非借贷性的收入占17.61%，而家庭自营收入则占58.08%。至1998年，从集体得到的收入下降至0.08%，从经济联合体得到的收入占2.34%，非借贷性收入降至5.69%，唯有家庭自营收入的比重上升至91.89%。从1999年起，农村居民纯收入的构成规范为工资性收入，家庭经营收入，财产性收入和转移性收入。农村居民经济调查的资料表明：家庭经营纯收入仍是农村居民纯收入的主要来源，只不过所占比重由1999年的77.15%降至2010年的66.55%；农村中越来越多的富余劳动力进城务工，使工资性收入所占比重一路飙升。1999年，其比重仅占2.52%，2007年高达31.85%，2010年的比重略有下降，但仍占26.38%，成为农村居民纯收入的一个重要增长点；转移性收入和财产性收入在整个纯收入中所占比重都不很大，但是农村居民纯收入来源的重要补充。随着改革的深入，农村居民收入不断增长，农户家庭资产越来越多，与其他农户、企业和政府之间的经济往来日益频繁，从2004年起，国家支持“三农”的转移性支出力度加大，农民通过各种补贴、减免、补助得到了更多的实惠，使财产性收入和转移性收入的绝对数量呈增长趋势，但占纯收入的比重却并未上升，且年度

间的波动也很大。

1999—2010年农村居民人均纯收入及构成一览表

表5—05—04

年　份	人均纯收入绝对数（元）	人均纯收入的构　成（%）				
		合　计	工资性收入	家庭经营收入	转移性收入	财产性收入
1999年	1746	100.00	2.52	77.15	18.33	2.00
2000年	1808	100.00	2.43	86.84	7.69	3.04
2001年	1906	100.00	13.32	66.37	16.53	3.78
2002年	2028	100.00	19.03	61.29	19.43	0.25
2003年	2158	100.00	19.93	71.04	8.52	0.51
2004年	2390	100.00	27.07	64.31	7.49	1.13
2005年	2702	100.00	28.83	64.21	6.48	0.48
2006年	2968	100.00	30.56	58.83	9.74	0.87
2007年	3535	100.00	31.85	58.79	5.60	3.76
2008年	4178	100.00	28.82	59.88	9.17	2.13
2009年	4620	100.00	27.01	64.44	6.86	1.69
2010年	5152	100.00	26.38	66.55	5.36	1.71

2. 传统农业在农村居民家庭经营纯收入中的比重持续下降。1981年全面实行家庭联产承包责任制后，是以家庭为单位进行经营，当年家庭经营人均实现纯收入为104.54元。其中，传统农业（农、林、牧、渔）占86%，工业占0.5%，运输和其他收入占13.5%，直至1995年，农村居民家庭经营纯收入构成仍以传统农业为主的格局并未多大变化，占82.13%，工业占2.16%，采集捕猎占0.06%，商业、饮食服务业占3.7%，运输及其他占11.95%。此后，“放开、搞活”方针的深入贯彻和农村产业结构的大力调整，农村居民家庭经营领域不断拓宽，农村产业逐步出现了以农为主，多业并举的新局面。使传统农业在家庭经营纯收入中所占比重继续下降。2010年，农村居民家庭经营实现的人均纯收入为3429元，占全年人均总纯收入5152元的66.55%。其中，传统的农、林、牧、渔业人均为2311元，其比重已降至67.39%。人均工业纯收入334元，人均建筑业纯收入232元，人均交通运输业纯收入325元，人均商业纯收入140元，其他行业人均纯收入87元，它们分别占家庭经营人均纯收入的9.74%、6.77%、9.48%、4.08%和2.54%。

3. 现金收入的比重不断上升。农村居民的收入是分现金和实物两大部分，在核算时才将实物统一折算为货币来反映。1978年集体年终决算分配，农民人均分配45.97元中，粮食等实物折款32.26元、现金13.71元，分别占70.18%和29.82%。随着农村社会化、农业生产商品化进程的加快，农村中长期以来自给，或半自给的小农经济状况得到扭转。在首先解决自身温饱问题的基础上，农民面对市场、大力发展商品生产，使农产品总量大幅增长，产品的商品率不断提高，再加上纯收入中工资性收入比重上升，转移性和财产性收入的绝对数也呈增长态势，这些都促使农村居民所实现的纯收入中，实物收入的比重逐渐下降，而现金收入的比重持续上升。2006年现金纯收入的比重突破了80%的大关，2010年增长至85.16%，实物纯收入降至14.84%，这比1978年集体分配现金收入仅占13.71%提升了71.45个百分点。单从农产品的商品率看，1978年仅有17.48%，2005年起这项指标已达60%以上。农村居民现金收入比重的提升，增强了支付能力，推动了收入增长方式和消费方式的转变。使生产、生活消费越来越多地纳入到市场经济大循环中，也在很大程度上推动了农村居民增收步伐的加快。

4. 基尼系数*处于“最佳平均状态”。2000年起，全县开始使用国际通用、反映收入分配平等程度“基尼系数”这一指标来评价小康建设进程。2000—2010年，修文这一指标均在0.3以下，处于“最佳平均状态”。按国内规定，农村居民基尼系数“温饱值”为0.2，“小康值”为0.35。2000—2010年，全县农村居民基尼系数一直处于0.25—0.29，即介于“温饱值”与“小康值”之间。

第二节　城乡居民支出

全县城镇居民1996年人均总支出3287元，2010年上升为15928元，增长3.85倍，年均递增11.93%；农村居民1981年人均总支出187.51元，2010年上升到5516元，增长28.42倍，年均递增12.37%。与城乡居民同期人均总收入年均递增速度相比，实现基本同步增长。

一、城镇居民支出

1996—2001年，家庭总支出只分消费性支出和非消费支出两大类；2002—2010年又分成消费性支出、财产性支出、转移性支出、社会保障支出和购房与建房支出五大类。1996—2001年，人均总支出除2001年在上年的基础上有下降外，总的趋势是逐年上升，其中消费性支出的绝对数保持了逐年增长的好势头，比重一直是总支出的主要构成。在温饱问题已经解决的基础上，非消费性支出的比重，除2001年在上年实际水平上有所下降外，整体是上升的，从而拉动了消费性支出在总支出中所占比重呈下降趋势。在此期间，消费性支出和非消费性支出分别以年均递增6.87%和16.17%的速度增长，后者的年递增速度高出前者9.3个百分点。

城镇居民1996—2001年人均总支出及其构成一览表

表5—05—05

指　　标	计量单位	1996年	1997年	1998年	1999年	2000年	2001年
人均总支出	元	3287.00	3720.00	4296.00	4705.00	5803.00	4983.90
1. 消费性支出	元	2730.00	3081.00	3176.00	3313.20	3517.08	3805.58
占人均总支出比重	%	83.05	82.82	73.93	70.42	60.61	76.36
2. 非消费性支出	元	557.00	639.00	1120.00	1391.80	2285.92	1178.32
占人均总支出比重	%	16.95	17.18	26.07	29.58	39.39	23.64

注* “基尼系数”：是反映收入分配平等程度的指标。实际系数均在“0”和“1”之间。系数越小，收入分配越平均，系数越大越不平均。国际公认：这一指标在0.3以下为最佳平均状态；0.3—0.4为正常状态；超过0.4为警戒状态；达到0.6则属社会动乱随时可能发生的危险状态

2002—2010年，人均总支出的绝对值是持续、稳健增长，年均递增13.86%。连贯看，从1996起至2010年，除2001年比2000年下降14.12%外，其余年份均在上年的基础上有所增长。2010年城镇居民人均总支出为1996年的4.85倍，年均递增11.93%。

（一）消费性支出

其比重一直处于60%以上，年际之间虽有上下波动，但绝对值逐年增长的态势一直未变。1996年城镇居民人均消费性支出2730元，2010年增为10926元，比1996年增长3倍，年均递增11.53%。

（二）财产性支出

2009年人均支出11元，其中非生产性贷款利息支出5.74元；2010年人均支出149元，其中非生产性贷款利息34.52元，分别占这两年人均总支出的0.09%和0.94%。

（三）转移性支出

一是绝对数量增加。2009年人均转移性支出2376元，2010年增为4185元，人均增长1809元，增幅达76.14%。二是结构呈现不规律的变化。2009年，比重最高是捐赠支出，高达59.73%，其次是其他转移性支出，为30.23%，而2010年，比重最高转为其他转移性支出，高达63.28%，再次是捐赠支出为18.67%。两项指标升降幅度大，但都是两年转移性支出最主要的构成，均占全部转移性支出的80%以上；赡养支出增长也是明显的，绝对值由2009年人均163.07%元，占转移性支出的6.83%，2010年分别升至569.43元和13.6%；缴纳所得税、购买彩票、非储蓄性保险支出，两年的变化相对较小。

捐赠支出由捐资和赠送两部分组成。捐资在城镇居民生活中实际数额较小。而人情往来的赠送支出是主要的。在相当长的时间里，社会上除婚丧酒席之外，生日酒、满月酒、搬家酒、状元酒、订婚酒、参军酒、就业酒、谢师宴等名目繁多的应酬不断蔓延，且相互攀比。此种状况使越来越多的人感到厌烦，更使低收入家庭难以应对。发出“出门吃酒玩气派，回家紧勒裤腰带”的感叹。在酒席规模上也是朝着越来越大的方向发展。有人将其概括为“二三十桌—寒酸，五六十桌—一般，八九十桌—体面，百桌以上—好汉”。大办酒席敛财之风劲刮，若干群众苦不堪言、怨声载道。

（四）社会保障支出

包括个人交纳的养老基金、住房公积金、医疗基金、失业基金及其他社会保障支出。虽年度之间人均支出绝对数不一样，但占人均总支出的比重变化不大，居于1.41%—3.24%之间，相对较稳。

（五）购房与建房支出

2002—2010年，被调查户不是每年都有发生，有这项支出发生的年份，数额波动较大，人均支出在11元至358元之间；占人均总支出的比重，2002年达4.24%，而2003年只占0.19%。

城镇居民2002—2010年人均总支出及其构成一览表

表5—05—06

指　　标	计量单位	2002年	2003年	2004年	2005年	2006年	2007年	2008年	2009年	2010年
人 均 总 支 出	元	5640	5754	6187	7877	8633	9099	9722	12473	15929
1. 消费性支出	元	4056	4664	4961	6089	6271	6945	7986	9666	10926
占人均总支出比重	%	71.91	81.06	80.18	77.30	72.64	76.33	82.14	77.50	68.59
2. 财产性支出	元	—	—	—	—	—	—	—	11	149

续表

指　　标	计量单位	2002年	2003年	2004年	2005年	2006年	2007年	2008年	2009年	2010年
占人均总支出比重	%	—	—	—	—	—	—	—	0.09	0.94
3. 转移性支出	元	1186	953	969	1675	1882	1859	1506	2376	4185
占人均总支出比重	%	21.03	16.56	15.66	21.26	21.80	20.43	15.49	19.05	26.27
4. 社会保障支出	元	159	126	142	113	122	295	230	226	371
占人均总支出比重	%	2.82	2.19	2.30	1.44	1.41	3.24	2.37	1.81	2.33
5. 购房与建房支出	元	239	11	115	—	358	—	—	194	298
占人均总支出比重	%	4.24	0.19	1.86	—	4.15	—	—	1.55	1.87

二、农村居民支出

为全面反映1981—2010年农村居民支出的具体数据及其结构变化，根据农村经济调查在不同时段指标设置不一致的实际情况，以3个阶段分别记述和列表体现。

从三个时段农村居民人均总支出的结构看，有六点变化：

一是生活消费支出的绝对数持续增长，而占总支出的比重又趋于下降。1981至2010年共30个年头，除1990年、1992年、1999年、2000年、2002年和2009年人均生活消费支出在上年的基础上有些下降之外，其余年份均是上升，整体上应视为持续增长。2010年农村居民人均消费性支出3228.82元，较1981年161.43元增长19.0倍，年均递增10.88%。在年度之间生活消费支出占总支出的比重波动较大，1981年占86.09%，1990年占66.21%，2000年占55.41%，2010年占58.54%。2010年和1981年比，下降27.55个百分点，比重下降是主流趋势。

二是家庭经营支出（1981—1998年是家庭经营支出、纳税和上交集体）的绝对数增长较大。1981年至1998年，年人均86.17元，1999—2003年，年人均525.7元，2004—2010年，年人均1057.49元。家庭经营支出占总支出的比重起伏性较大。1981—2010年平均为24.94%，除1981年占7.54%外，均在10%以上；1982年、1993年、1998年、2009年和2010年在10.01%至20%的范围内；1989年、1991年、1992年、2000年、2001年和2004年在30.01%以上外，其余18年均在20.01%至30%之间。

三是购置生产性固定资产的投入不断攀升。农村推行家庭联产承包责任制初期，由于收入水平低，实际用于购买生产性固定资产支出的比重很低，1981—1988年，仅占总支出的1.84%，其中有4年不到1%；20世纪90年代，占总支出的3.1%；2000—2010年，占总支出的4.78%。随着温饱问题逐步解决，农村居民用于购置生产性固定资产支出的比重越来越高。特别是既省力、又能极大提高工效的中、小型农机具，很受群众欢迎。就农机总动力衡量，1978年全县只有5429千瓦，至1990年增至26470千瓦，增长近4倍。2000年发展为81501千瓦，2010年又在2000年的基础上翻了一番多，达175925千瓦。农机总动力接连增长，反映出农村居民用于扩大再生产的投入加大，促使劳动生产率明显提高。

四是税费支出比例逐渐缩小。2004年农村实行税费改革，取消了农业税以及不合理的提留、摊派，使税费支出仅限于农村居民从事非农的第二、第三产业缴纳的税金及“一事一议”的筹资支出。2001年至2010年农村居民实际人年均交纳税费为18.67元，仅占总支出的0.52%。

五是财产性支出比例微薄。从2004年起，被调查的农村居民户，在核算过程中虽有财产性支出，至2010年，其占总支出的比重一直都未超过1%。

六是转移性支出（1981至2003年列入非借贷性支出）呈现上升趋势。1981年农村居民转移性支出占总支出的5.36%，2010年升为20.27%。其支出包括供给在外读书和生活的家庭成员生活费，交纳社会保险基金、交纳医疗保险、婚丧嫁娶礼金等10多个方面。其中人情往来，赠送亲友的数额：1981年人均5.26元，1985年人均39.96元，分别占转移性总支出的3.26%和12.94%。2006—2010年，人均依次是141.7元、433.9元、627.29元、723.26元和1034.99元，分别占全部转移性支出的59.41%、88.67%、94.29%、87.69%和92.56%。2006—2010年以年均递增64.4%的速度飞速增长，远远高于同期农村居民年人均纯收入平均递增14.78%的增长速度。这一现象折射出不健康的社会风气越演越烈。

1981—1998年部分年农村居民人均总支出及其构成一览表

表5—05—07

指标	计量单位	1981年	1985年	1990年	1995年	1998年
人均总支出	元	187.51	432.40	675.92	1442.32	2208.28
1. 生活消费支出	元	161.43	308.72	447.55	1004.21	1421.61
占人均总支出比重	%	86.09	71.40	66.21	69.63	64.38
2. 家庭经营支出和纳税	元	14.13	101.39	180.37	377.08	412.55
占人均总支出比重	%	7.54	23.45	26.69	26.14	18.68
3. 购买生产性固定资产支出	元	1.89	3.28	7.40	7.50	316.70
占人均总支出比重	%	1.01	0.76	1.09	0.52	14.34
4. 其他非借贷性支出	元	10.06	19.01	40.60	53.53	57.35
占人均总支出比重	%	5.36	4.39	6.01	3.71	2.60

1999—2003年农村居民人均总支出及其构成一览表

表5—05—08

指标	计量单位	1999年	2000年	2001年	2002年	2003年
人均总支出	元	1536.36	1776.00	1907.00	1739.25	2416.34
1. 生活消费支出	元	1047.16	984.00	1108.00	982.25	1298.07
占人均总支出比重	%	68.16	55.41	58.10	56.47	53.72
2. 家庭经营支出	元	412.81	571.00	621.00	432.87	591.46
占人均总支出比重	%	26.87	32.15	32.56	24.89	24.48
3. 购买生产性固定资产支出	元	19.69	4.12	36.00	132.36	265.24
占人均总支出比重	%	1.28	0.23	1.89	7.61	10.98
4. 上交集体支出	元	2.09	70.00	—	1.35	—
占人均总支出比重	%	0.14	3.94	—	0.08	—
5. 提留和摊派支出	元	6.59	8.50	7.00	4.32	—

续表

指　　标	计量单位	1999年	2000年	2001年	2002年	2003年
占人均总支出比重	%	0.43	0.48	0.37	0.25	—
6. 缴纳税金支出	元	13.60	86.46	6.20	21.20	114.35
占人均总支出比重	%	0.88	4.87	0.33	1.22	4.73
7. 其他非借贷性支出	元	34.42	51.92	128.80	164.90	147.22
占人均总支出比重	%	2.24	2.92	6.75	9.48	6.09

2004—2010年农村居民人均总支出及其构成一览表

表5—05—09

指　　标	计量单位	2004年	2005年	2006年	2007年	2008年	2009年	2010年
人均总支出	元	3152.87	3390.57	3755.90	4159.83	5167.52	5321.18	5515.46
1. 生活消费支出	元	1727.83	2102.43	2148.20	2506.94	3138.80	3077.21	3228.82
占人均总支出比重	%	54.80	62.01	57.20	60.27	60.74	57.83	58.54
2. 家庭经营支出	元	1123.06	1000.58	936.90	1056.75	1145.33	1060.75	1079.06
占人均总支出比重	%	35.62	29.51	24.94	25.40	22.17	19.94	19.57
3. 购买生产性固定资产支出	元	69.93	129.44	431.50	82.24	211.37	354.90	86.79
占人均总支出比重	%	2.22	3.82	11.49	1.98	4.09	6.67	1.57
4. 税费支出	元	17.37	—	—	23.75	3.26	0.20	0.39
占人均总支出比重	%	0.55	—	—	0.57	0.06	—	0.01
5. 财产性支出	元	20.02	0.20	0.80	0.78	3.50	3.36	2.22
占人均总支出比重	%	0.64	0.01	0.02	0.02	0.07	0.06	0.04
6. 转移性支出	元	194.66	157.92	238.50	489.37	665.26	824.76	1118.18
占人均总支出比重	%	6.17	4.65	6.35	11.76	12.87	15.50	20.27

第三节　城乡人民生活

从1978年起，经历33年的改革和建设，城乡面貌大为改观，从衣、食、住、行、用的变化，印证了城乡居民生活水平不断提高。

一、食品

（一）城镇居民

1978年，非农业人口一律按1977年11月贵州省粮食局印发的《贵州省粮食定量标准》定量按月供

应。这个“标准”划的很细。10周岁以下儿童，一、两周岁划分为一个档次，人月供口粮3.5公斤至10.5公斤。10周岁以上人群，基本上按职业划定。如区乡干部15公斤/人·月，一般干部13.5公斤/人·月，大学及中学生15至17.5公斤/人·月，县级以上居民11.5至12.5公斤/人·月，县以下居民11至12公斤/人·月。因定量供应标准普遍偏低，不能满足需要，多数家庭和机关食堂只开中、晚两餐。从1970年起，非农业人口每人每月供应0.2公斤菜油，1980年后改为每人每月供应0.25公斤。猪肉、每人每月供应0.25公斤至0.5公斤。另外，按人按月还有少量白糖和豆腐凭票供应。因修文粮食不能自给、是调入县，对非农业人口的口粮供应要视调入粮食的具体情况确定供应的品种搭配比例。多数时间大米只占一半左右，其余的为面粉、玉米、甚至是苕干。

进入20世纪80年代，逐步取消粮、油、猪肉等食品的计划供应。随着生产的发展和城镇居民收入水平的提高，城镇居民食品消费状况也跟着改善。1996年人均食品消费1408元，占整个生活消费支出2730元的51.58%。当年主要食品的人均消费量是：粮食113公斤，油脂10公斤，肉禽及制品26公斤，禽蛋5公斤，水产为1.5公斤，蔬菜90公斤，卷烟46盒，酒和饮料9公斤，奶及奶制品0.1公斤，水果及干果17公斤。除此之外，在外用餐支出，人均为83.31元。

城镇居民1996—2010年，生活消费总支出一直逐年增长，没有波动；食品消费支出总趋势虽有增长，但1999年、2002年和2003年实际消费绝对值比上年有所减少。

从2000—2010年，城镇居民食品消费支出的金额是不断增长的，其间有物价上涨因素。从食品消费的变化情况看，11年间、食品消费构成变化的特点，一是粮油类消费所占比重一直都保持在16%左右，虽年际之间有些波动但幅度很小；二是肉、禽、蛋、水产类，调味品，干、鲜瓜果，糕点、奶及奶制品占食品消费支出的比重上升；三是蔬菜类，其他食品所占比重变化不大；四是糖、烟、酒和饮料，饮食服务消费支出所占比重呈下降态势。

部分年份城镇居民人均食品消费支出及其构成一览表

表5—05—10

指　　标		计量单位	2000年	2005年	2010年	2010年较2000年数额增减幅度（%）	2000年至2010年数额年均递增（%）
食品消费总支出	数　额	元/人	1808.18	2350.80	3997.29	121.07	8.26
	所占比重	%	100.00	100.00	100.00		
1. 粮油类	数　额	元/人	306.86	391.50	671.82	118.93	8.15
	所占比重	%	16.97	16.65	16.81		
2. 肉、禽、蛋、水产类	数　额	元/人	466.66	767.80	1179.79	152.82	9.72
	所占比重	%	25.81	32.66	29.51		
3. 蔬　菜　类	数　额	元/人	190.93	266.80	326.88	71.20	5.52
	所占比重	%	10.56	11.35	8.18		
4. 调　味　品	数额	元/人	29.24	39.40	177.91	508.45	19.79
	所占比重	%	1.62	1.68	4.45		
5. 糖、烟、酒、饮料类	数　额	元/人	375.80	284.20	674.46	79.47	6.02
	所占比重	%	20.78	12.09	16.87		

续表

指标		计量单位	2000年	2005年	2010年	2010年较2000年数额增减幅度（%）	2000年至2010年数额年均递增（%）
6. 干、鲜瓜、果类	数 额	元/人	132.59	223.60	442.09	233.43	12.80
	所占比重	%	7.33	9.51	11.06		
7. 糕点、奶及奶制品	数 额	元/人	35.20	122.60	206.50	486.65	19.35
	所占比重	%	1.95	5.21	5.17		
8. 其他食品	数额	元/人	19.20	16.60	13.25	-30.99	-3.64
	所占比重	%	1.06	0.71	0.33		
9. 饮食服务	数 额	元/人	251.70	238.30	304.59	21.01	1.93
	所占比重	%	13.92	10.14	7.62		

1996—2001年，城镇居民恩格尔系数※均在50%至60%之间，单从这一指标衡量，处于温饱阶段。2002年为41.96%，处于小康阶段。2003—2010年，除2008年反弹至41.91%，应属小康阶段外，其余年份均在40%以下，即已处于富裕阶段。

（二）农村居民

改革开放前，全县农村居民主要是追求吃饱。1978年是个丰收年，社会粮食总产52970吨，人均生产粮食278.5公斤（其中：社员自营19.5公斤），人均从集体分配口粮196公斤，加自营粮食收入、农村居民实际占有粮食人均215.5公斤。除预留维持简单再生产的种子和家庭养殖的饲料用粮外，真正用于解决吃饭问题的粮食，人均每天不到0.5公斤原粮，显然不能满足生活需要。当年还由国家返销农村粮食2090吨，人均11公斤，才基本实现农户为解决吃饭问题的粮食收支平衡。因为粮食紧张，半数以上农户常年每天只吃中、晚两餐，干稀搭配、瓜菜每顿必备。油菜籽因灾减产，实现产量565吨，交售国家400吨后，农村人口人均仅0.87公斤，折合菜油0.29公斤。除约有近半农户有能力杀年猪，解决一年的肉、油问题外，多数农户只能长年吃“素”，缺少油荤。辣椒和食盐就是唯一的调味品。

1981年，农村实行家庭联产承包责任制，农村居民人均消费粮食191公斤，蔬菜191.5公斤，植物油0.95公斤，动物油1.3公斤，猪肉9.4公斤。除主食粮食已能满足基本生活需要外，主要副食品的消费也有一定数量。食品消费支出人均110.37元，其中主食48.38元，副食51.61元，其他食品5.38元，分别占食品消费支出的43.83%、51.29%和4.88%。1990年，农村居民人均消费粮食115.8公斤、蔬菜86.2公斤、植物油1.47公斤、动物油1.57公斤、猪肉7.8公斤。尽管遭旱灾使粮食比上年减产23.88%，对农村居民的食品消费有所影响，但人均食品消费还是达到119.03元，其中，主食27.31元，副食58.07元，其他食品33.65元，分别占食品消费支出的22.94%、48.79%和28.27%。2000年，农村居民食品消费水平有很大的提高，食品消费的质量也有很大改善。人均生活用粮213公斤、蔬菜151.8公斤、豆制品7.9公斤、植物油11.56公斤、动物油1.15公斤、猪肉13公斤、禽肉0.11公斤、禽蛋1.05公斤、水果3.29公斤、酒类和饮料5.55公斤。人均食品消费支出达581元，分别在1981年和1990年的基础上增长4.26倍和3.88倍。2010

※恩格尔系数：是衡量一个家庭或国家（地区）富裕程度的指标。恩格尔系数=食品支出÷生活消费总支出×100%。系数越大，说明该家庭或国家（地区）越贫穷，系数越小说明他们的生活越富足。联合国根据恩格尔系数的大小，划定了评价贫富的标准：恩格尔系数在60%以上为绝对贫困；50%—59%为温饱水平；40%—9%为小康水平；30%—39%为富裕水平；30%以下为最富裕水平。

年，农村居民食品消费以货币形式反映为896.48元，比2000年增长54.3%。其中消费谷物108.75元，薯类6.15元，豆类11.55元，食用油31.47元，蔬菜及制品41.04元，肉、禽、蛋、奶及制品223.37元，水产品及制品1.32元，烟、酒172.74元，茶叶、饮料17.44元，其他类食品133.42元。此外，还有在外就餐等食品消费服务性支出149.23元。在吃饱的基础上追求吃好，成为农村居民食品消费的显著特征。经测算，人日均蛋白质摄入量2010年为63克，超越了47克的温饱值，已比较接近75克的小康值，与城镇居民食品消费的差距正在缩小。绝大多数农村居民已和城镇居民一样，一日三餐，而且菜肴多样。由于食品的种类越来越多，特别是副食品日益丰富，主食的粮食占食品消费支出的比重明显下降。2010年只占12.86%。分别比1981年和1990年降低30.97和10.08个百分点。正如老百姓所说的“多吃油盐少吃米”。

以恩格尔系数的标准衡量，全县农村居民此指标总的是由高向低变化，全县1981—1997年的17年均在60%以上。以1998年为转折点至2010年降至50%—60%这一区间。全县农村1997年之前为贫困阶段，1998—2010年为温饱阶段。2010年恩格尔系数为50%，接近小康的标准。与同年全国和全省农村居民恩格尔系数分别为41.1%和46.3%相比，全县这一指标偏高。

二、衣着

1978年，城乡居民衣着数量少、质量差、款式单一。因此有“新三年，旧三年，缝缝补补再三年”之说。为确保困难群众的基本生活需要，政府每年都要对贫困、边远、少数民族地区缺衣少穿农户和城镇居民中的困难户以棉衣、棉被等形式进行救济。即便添置新衣，也多为机织平板布、咔叽布、灯芯绒和涤棉布，款式多为手工缝制的对襟衣和缝纫机加工的中山装。服装的色调多为藏青、铁灰、白色和黄色为主。夏秋季节，不分男女老少，脚穿塑料凉鞋比较普遍。冬春季以脚穿解放鞋居多。

（一）城镇居民

从1996年开始城镇居民的衣着消费金额基本上保持平稳增长。1996—2010年期间年均递增11.48%。在占生活消费总支出的比重上，年度之间变化不大，没有出现大起大落。由于城镇居民人均可支配收入大大高于农村居民人均纯收入，在衣着方面消费的绝对值远远高于农村居民。1996—2010年，城、乡居民用于衣着的消费均以较大幅度在增长，2010年都在1996年的基础上增4.58倍。但人均衣着消费的绝对值，城镇居民比农村居民、1996年多253.5元，2000年多359.87元，2005年多725.95元，2010年多1161.32元。城镇居民衣着消费较高的原因，主要是消费观念上发生质的变化。衣着除本来蔽体、御寒的功能之外，普遍追求的是贴身、轻便、舒适、时尚和品牌，甚至还成了追求时髦、彰显个性的一种选择。据2010年对城镇居民住户的调查，当年购买服装每件的平均单价为140.08元，鞋类每双的平均单价达135.62元。

部分年份城乡居民衣着消费情况对照表

表5—05—11

指标		计量单位	1996年	2000年	2005年	2010年
城镇居民	生活消费支出	元/人	2730.00	3517.08	6089.40	10926.18
	其中：衣着消费	元/人	316.16	426.87	819.20	1448.30
	占生活消费支出比重	%	11.58	12.14	13.45	13.26
农村居民	生活消费支出	元/人	1126.91	984.00	2102.43	2717.32
	其中：衣着消费	元/人	62.66	67.00	93.25	286.98
	占生活消费支出比重	%	5.56	6.81	4.44	10.56
城镇居民为农村居民衣着消费倍数		倍	5.05	6.37	8.78	5.05

（二）农村居民

1981年，据农经调查资料，当年农村居民人均消费棉布4.33米，化纤布0.66米，棉花0.2公斤，毛线0.05公斤，胶鞋和球鞋0.41双，皮鞋0.05双。用于衣着消费的折款25.06元，占人均生活消费总支出的15.85%。

尽管各年衣着消费占农村居民生活消费支出的比重有高有低，但1981—2010年的总趋势，其比重是下降的。2010年为10.56%，较1981年降5.29个百分点。而农村居民人均衣着消费支出的绝对数是上升的。1981—1994年，处于20元—30元之间；1995—2005年处于50元至100元之间；2006年和2007年在100元以上，200元以下；2008—2010年达200元以上；2010年为人均286.98元，在1981年人均25.06的基础上增长10.45倍，年均递增8.77%。20世纪80年代废除棉布、棉花凭票供应后，农村居民的衣着消费发生了变化，一是由原来购买布料、棉花加工制作成衣为主到直接在市场上购买成衣为主，布料和棉花的消费呈下降趋势。1981年人均消费布料6.33米，至1991年人均消费仅1.2米，1986年后，已基本无人直接购买棉花制作棉衣或加工棉絮。2006年，服装消费人均104.1元，其中直接购买成衣为91.6元，购买服装材料为12.5元，分别占87.99%和12.01%。2010年，人均服装消费支出182.99元中，直接购买成衣和购买制作服装材料的消费分别占96.66%和3.34%。二是衣着款式多样化。原来普遍穿的对襟衣、中山装已少见，取而代之的是西装、夹克衫、牛仔装和休闲服。不同季节有不同款式服装的选择。穿毛衣、羊毛衫、保暖衣已比较普遍。女性服装款式多于男性。特别是女青年，夏天穿裙子已不罕见，且随时装潮流的变化而及时更新自己的服装，色泽多样，款式新颖。衣着消费中，鞋类消费基本上已全部商品化，这部分支出，2000—2010年约占衣着消费支出的1/3，用于购买各式皮鞋、休闲鞋、胶鞋、凉鞋和布鞋。

三、居住

（一）城镇居民

城镇居民人均居住消费支出，1996—1998年在100—200元之间，1999—2001年在200—300元之间，增长较为平稳。以2002年为转折点，直至2010年人均居住消费支出均在400元以上，2010年为780.86元，而2009年达1153元为最高。1996—2001年，城镇居民居住消费占生活消费总支出的比重，平均为6.08%，2002—2010年，这一比重平均为10.42%，高出前6年4.34个百分点。

2010年第六次人口普查工作中，采取等距离抽样的方法，全县抽取7111户（其中城镇居民2280户，农村居民4831户），对他们的住房情况进行了详细的调查登记。由于抽样比重大，占全县家庭总户数80663户的8.82%（城镇居民住户占9.50%，农村居民住户占8.52%），又是等距离随机抽样，所以有很强的代表性，较全面反映了城、乡居民的住房现状。

住房面积　2000年城镇居民人均住房面积19.9平方米，2010年上升至32.65平方米，人均净增12.75平方米，增加64.07%。

建筑结构　2010年，住房属钢及钢筋混凝土结构，属混合结构，属砖木结构，属其他结构的，分别占住房总面积的10.61%、77.68%、10.09%和1.62%。

住房层数　平房住户占居民总户数的23.11%，楼房住户占76.89%，其中2—3层的占44.17%，4—6层的占27.11%，7—9层的占5.22%，10层以上的占0.39%。

住房修建时间　2010年城镇居民住房有8.11%是1980年以前修建的。1980—1989年、1990—1999年和2000至2010年修建的分别占16.32%、28.82%和46.75%。

房屋来源 城镇居民2010年居住的房屋，属购买的商品房、二手房、经济适用房和原公有房屋占23.16%，属租公、私房居住的占21.79%，属赠给、借用的占6.01%，属于自建住房的占49.04%。

住房的附属设施 2010年城镇居民全部用上了电。有90.09%的住房有室内管道自来水，有76.4%的住户有住房内厕所，有76.4%的住房有单独的室内厨房，有51.4%的住户有洗澡设施。

（二）农村居民

1981年农村居民户均住房4.53间，面积50.73平方米。其中砖木结构21.3平方米、占41.99%。不但房屋拥挤，且设施很差。有近一半的住户不通电，仍以菜油、桐油或煤油照明。除居住在县城少数农户外，都无自来水使用。无室内厕所，多为厨房与卧室同屋。

1990年，每户平均住房升为81.68平方米，人均住房16.02平方米。其中砖木结构占44.85%，钢筋混凝土结构占1.78%。此外，尚有纯木结构瓦房或草房，土墙、石墙瓦房或草房占53.37%。有二层和三层楼房的农户，占总农户的9.96%。有95.12%的村民组和90.10%的农户用上电，照明条件大为改善。

从1991年起，全县农村居民住户居住条件大改善。由于经济收入增加和人口自然增长，农村中改造旧房和新建住房成风，投入居住消费的支出也呈增长之势。这项支出，1990年为人均25.22元，2000年人均143.元，2010年达416.61元，分别占生活消费总支出的9.61%、14.53%和15.33%，比重是不断提升的。

住房面积 农村居民1981年户均50.73平方米，人均7.72平方米，1990年增至户均81.68平方米，人均16.02平方米，2010年上升为户均96.83平方米，人均31.21平方米。2010年与1981年和1990年比较，户均住房面积分别增加90.87%和18.55%，人均住房面积增加3.04倍和0.95倍。

建筑结构 2010年属钢及钢筋混凝土结构，混合结构、砖木结构和其他结构的，分别占农村居民住房面积11.55%、65.33%、17.12%和6%。

住房层数 1981年农村多是平房。1990年虽有9.96%的住户是楼房，但最高只有3层。2010年平房比重降至73.59%，拥有楼房的农村居民，其比重已升至26.41%，其中，有2至3层，4至6层和7至9层的住户，分别占农村居民总户数的25.56%、0.83%和0.02%。

住房修建时间 农村居民住房有7.51%是1980年以前修建的，1980年至1989年修建的住房占8.86%，1990—1999年修建的住房占19.52%，2000年以后修建的住房占64.11%。

住房来源 农村居民家庭居住的房屋，其来源可概括为4个方面：一是“建”，这是最主要的来源。2010年农村居民住房有94.23%是自己修建的，拥有产权；二是“购”（购买商品房，购买二手房，购买原公有房屋），住户对这类房屋也拥有产权，占总住户的1.03%；三是“租”（廉租房和租其他公、私住房），这种住户占1.61%；四是“其他”（赠给、借用），这种住户占3.13%。与租房一样，属借用的，对房屋不拥有产权。

住房的附属设施 2010年农村住户全部通电。有54.54%的住房有室内管道自来水，有47.96%的住户有室内厕所，有50.92%的住户有单独的室内厨房，有13.45%的住户有洗澡设施。

农村居民住户居住条件有很大改善，除了他们在收入增加的基础上积极将资金投入住房建设外，政府对困难群众的资金扶持也是一个重要原因。2000年12月，贵阳市委书记王晓东到谷堡乡水口村调研后，随即出台全市农村茅草房改造安排意见，要求用2到5年时间全部消除茅草房。至2004年这一工作全面完成，并在洒坪乡小坝村召开全市总结表彰会。2001—2004年实施的茅草房改造工程，市、县共投入财政资金1804.8万元，市、县部门帮扶款2377.74万元，市、县政府组织协调移民搬迁、灾民建房等项资金410.2万元，支持1.16万户农村居民，将原来居住的茅草房推倒重建，新建住房面积93.28万平方米，户均80.6平方米。继茅草房改造工程结束后，根据上级统一部署，通过财政提供一定补助的方式，对农村中的危房进行改造。2005至2010年全县实施过程中共投入中央、省、市、县财政补助资金8412.23万元，完成了原地或异地改造、重建房屋110.7万平方米，使1.3万户农村居民住户受益。

农村居民住户居住消费支出，从整体看，是仅次于食品消费的第二大支出。1981至1998年的18年，除有4年的比重占生活消费总支出的10 %以上外，其余年份均在10%以下。人均住房消费的绝对值都在100元以下。1999年后，住房消费支出占生活消费的总支出的比重，除2001年和2003年出现波动，在10%以下外，其余年份均在10%以上。其中，2004年和2009年还分别达25.93%和22.14%。人均年住房消费的绝对数，除2001年外，均在100元以上。其中，2004年、2007年、2009年和2010年，还分别达448.01元、477.08元、572.3元和416.61元。1981年至2010年，农村居民人均住房消费年均递增高达14.80%，高出同期农村居民人均生活消费总支出年均递增4.57个百分点。

与城镇居民居住消费情况相比，农村居民居住消费占生活消费总支出的比重较高，但用于居住消费的绝对数，农村居民又明显低于城镇居民，差异较大。这是因城乡居民收入差距和支付能力不一样，对住房质量，特别是装修的要求不一样导致的。支付的范围不同也是原因之一。2010年城镇居民人均承担以物业管理、门卫、垃圾清运为内容的居住服务费支出为40.3元，而农村居民就不牵涉这项开支。

部分年份城乡居民居住消费情况对照表

表5—05—12

指标		计量单位	1996年	2000年	2005年	2010年
城镇居民	生活消费支出	元/人	2730.00	3517.08	6089.40	10926.18
	其中:居住消费支出	元/人	138.95	276.04	578.80	780.86
	占生活消费支出比重	%	5.09	7.85	9.51	7.15
农村居民	生活消费支出	元/人	1126.91	984.00	2102.43	2717.32
	其中:居住消费支出	元/人	56.16	143.00	326.10	416.61
	占生活消费支出比重	%	4.98	14.53	15.51	15.33
城镇居民居住消费支出为农村居民的倍数		倍	2.47	1.93	1.77	1.87

四、家庭用品

（一）城镇居民

在家庭用品及服务方面的消费，多数年份占生活消费总支出的比重在10%以下，但人年均消费的绝对值普遍比农村居民高3至4倍。2010年城镇居民人均支出1443.29元，农村居民人均318.7元，仅为城镇居民的22.08%。城镇居民家庭，像一般的桌、椅、凳、沙发，不同款式的床、衣柜，用于取暖的铁炉或电暖炉都比较齐全。家用电器更是多种多样，如彩电、电冰箱、洗衣机、电磁炉、饮水机已经普及。代表顶端消费的家用电脑和家用汽车等商品也陆续进入普通人家。大家追求的就是方便、舒适、高效和快捷。1996年，城镇居民，特别是其中的机关干部和经商人员，使用寻呼机已比较普遍。少数人开始安装

使用固定电话。2002年，每百户城镇居民拥有固定电话83.33部。移动电话较固定电话更为方便，所以一上市后，使用者的数量快速上升。2000年，每百户城镇居民拥有移动电话3.33部，2005年增至120部，2010年再增至210部，使固定电话用户减少。每百户城镇居民由2004年的93.33部，降至2010年71部。通信消费支出，2000年人均143元，2005年和2010年分别上升至372元和628元。从1996年起至2010年，城镇居民通信消费支出年均递增18.4%。

部分年份城镇居民家庭主要耐用消费品百户拥有量一览表

表5—05—13

品　　名	计量单位	2000年	2005年	2010年
1. 洗衣机	台	90.00	106.67	106.67
2. 电冰箱	台	50.00	90.00	100.00
3. 电视机	台	100.00	110.00	126.67
其中：彩电	台	100.00	110.00	126.67
4. 家用电脑	台	—	10.00	50.00
5. 组合音响	套	—	73.33	70.00
6. 摄像机	架	—	3.33	3.33
7. 照相机	架	—	23.33	43.33
8. 高中档乐器	件	—	10.00	3.33
其中：钢琴	架	—	3.33	3.33
9. 淋浴热水器	台	—	66.67	86.67
10. 健身器材	套	—	3.33	3.33
11. 固定电话	部	—	80.00	71.00
12. 移动电话	部	3.33	120.00	210.00
13. 微波炉	台	3.33	23.33	43.33
14. 消毒碗柜	台	—	30.00	50.00

（二）农村居民

改革开放初期、农村居民的家庭设施和用品相当简陋。除了厨房的锅瓢碗盏，水缸、水桶，用于加工苞谷、小麦的石磨和必需的床、饭桌和板凳外，也就没有更多的设备和用品。冬天烤火取暖，主要是烧柴或烧煤，就地刨个火炕或砌个地炉，也用不着什么专用设备。经济条件较好的住户，开始使用木箱、衣柜和铸铁取暖煤炉。1981年，代表当时的高档消费用品，也就是“三转一响”的缝纫机、自行车、钟表和收音机。每百户分别拥有10架、3.3辆、40只和13.3台。家庭设备、用品及服务支出人均11.16元，占农村居民生活消费总支出的7.06%。

从20世纪80年代开始，收录机、电视机等家用电器进入农家，使用舒适、卫生、带烟管的铁制取暖炉的住户增多，添置碗柜、书桌、靠背椅等木制家具已成风气，用于家庭设备、用品的支出明显增加。至1985年，人均支出23.37元，较1981年的支出增加1.09倍，占整个农村居民生活消费支出的比重也提升0.71个百分点。耐用消费品的数量，除自行车和缝纫机拥有量变化不大外，每百户收音机、手表分别增加至35台和151.6只。电视机和大型家具从无到有。1985年已拥有电视机11台，大型家具28件。1990年，百户农村居民拥有自行车6.25辆，缝纫机17.5架，收音机17.4台，钟表120只，电视机37.5台，大型家具81.25件，户均拥有量的水平仍然较低。2000年每百户平均拥有自行车增至8.75辆，大型家具增至97.5件，电视机增至61.25台，其中彩电18.75台，收音机拥有数量降至11.25台。随着形势的发展，市场上日益增多的家电产品，也成了农村居民住户的选择。2010年，每百户平均拥有电视机68台，其中彩色电视机27台，洗衣机27台，电冰箱16台，热水器7台（其中太阳能热水器5台），微波炉1台，抽油烟机1台，自行车3辆，影碟机24台。耐用消费品的拥有，极大地方便生活。农村居民用于家庭用品及服务的支出，较长时间数额和占整个生活消费支出的比重不大，且增长缓慢。1981年，人均11.16元，占生活消费比重6.91%。直至2003年，人均消费不足100元。2004年突破100元大关为104.92元，接着逐年攀升。2008年人均消费208.40元。2009年和2010年分别达286.31元和318.70元，占整个生活消费支出的比重分别为9.3%和9.87%。

在家庭用品方面，现代通信工具从无到有，迅速增加。1999年开始使用呼机，随着农村有线通信网的逐渐建成，2000年有8.75%的农户安装了固定电话。2001年农村开始使用移动电话。至2010年，全部行政村通了电话，安装使用座机的农户占62.5%，平均每百户拥有移动电话166.25部。因此，通信消费支出也随之大幅增长。1998年人均支出8.92元，至2010年达159.53元，平均递增27.17%。

五、出行

（一）城镇居民

1996年，城镇居民用于交通消费支出人均57元，占生活消费总支出的2.09%。其支出主要是外出办事、走亲访友，从事经商的城镇居民到省城进货往返乘坐公共交通工具的开支。进入21世纪，县境内公路客运网络逐渐形成，县城和乡、镇集镇被称为“摩的”的客运迅速兴起，出租车（“的士”）从无到有、数量陆续增加，私人购置代步工具的人越来越多，摩托车每百户拥有量，2005年达20辆，2010年降至3.33辆。2010年有3.33%的城镇居民拥有自己的小汽车。这些因素促使城镇居民用于交通方面的消费支出迅速增长。2000年人均支出为73元，2005年升至235元，2010年达420元（2009年还高达510元）。

（二）农村居民

农村居民原来外出办事、赶场和走亲串友，多为步行，能够骑上自行车的是少数。1998年直接用于交通方面的消费支出，人均仅4.14元，占当年生活消费总支出的0.03%。进入20世纪，随着收入水平提高和人口流动性大增，农村居民在交通方面的消费支出迅猛增长。2005年含购摩托车、燃油、修理费，高达人均支出307.83元，占当年生活消费总支出的14.64%。2010年虽回落至158.36元，也仍占当年生活消费总支出的5.83%。至2010年农村居民有20.7%的住户拥有摩托车，1%的住户有生活用小汽车。“进城赶场——班车，外出吃酒—包车，独来独往—摩托车”已是普遍现象。

全县经历33年的改革开放，城、乡居民在生活消费方面一些主要、综合性指标增长速度，总体看还略高于贵州全省的平均水平，与全国平均增长速度基本同步。

1. 农民人均纯收入。全国由1978年的133.6元增至2010年的5919.01元，年均递增12.58%。同时期，贵州省由109.3元增至3471.93元，年均递增11.41%；修文县由141元增至5152元，平均递增11.90%。

2. 城镇居民人均可支配收入。由于修文是1996年才开始这项调查工作的，当年全国、全省和修文县分别是4838.9元，4210.74元和3480元。至2010年全国增至19109.4元，年均递增10.31%；全省增至14142.74元，年均递增9.04%；修文县增至15756元，年均递增11.39%。

3. 农村居民人均生活消费支出。1981年至2010年，修文县由161.43元增至3228.82元，年均递增10.88%。在同一时期，全国由201元增至4381.82元，贵州省由162.51元增至2852.48元，年均递增分别为11.21%和10.38%。

4. 城镇居民人均生活消费支出。2000年，全国、全省和修文县这一指标分别为4998元，7278.28元和3517.08元，至2010年，全国增至13471.45元，全省增至10058.29元，修文县增至10926.18元，年均递增分别为10.42%、8.92%和12%。

在城、乡居民耐用消费品方面，修文县2010年电话普及率（含移动电话）和移动电话普及率分别达101.44部/百人和75.44部/百人，高于全国86.41部/百人和63.36部/百人，全省83.9部/百人和60.38部/百人和贵阳市92.77部/百人和69.3部/百人的水平，情况相当突出。然而在家用汽车、摩托车和电脑拥有量上，数量又明显偏低。2010年，每百户城镇居民拥有家用汽车，全国为13.07辆、全省为5.96辆，贵阳市为10.82辆，修文县仅有3.33辆；农村居民每百户拥有摩托车，全国为59.02辆，全省为30.76辆，贵阳市为50辆，修文县为20.7辆；每百户居民拥有电脑，全国城镇居民为71.2台，农村居民为10.4台，贵州城镇居民百户平均拥有56.79台，贵阳市百户城镇居民平均拥有75.08台，修文县城镇居民每百户平均拥有50台。贵州省、贵阳市和修文县的农经调查资料中，没有农村居民百户平均拥有电脑的数据。2010年全国城、乡居民人均住房面积分别为31.6平方米和34.1平方米，贵州省为27.4平方米和27.3平方米，而修文县为32.65平方米和31.21平方米，略高于全省平均水平，与全国的平均数大体相当。

全县贯彻落实实施“八七扶贫攻坚计划”，经过扶贫开发和一大批扶贫项目的实施，贫困地区生产、生活的基础设施明显改善，实现了农村新型农村合作医疗的全覆盖，以农村低保为主的农村社会救助制度的全面建立，基本实现了“应保尽保”。

这些措施，使全县农村中绝对贫困人口已从1982年的7.82万人减少了至2010年的2.07万人，贫困发生率由36.00%降至7.8%，成就显著。但应看到，这部分群众现在的收入水平和生活水平都在全县的平均水平之下，生产和生活都面临更多的困难。在全面建设小康社会的进程中，还需要给他们更多的关注，进一步做好扶贫工作，使他们早日全面脱贫走上共同富裕的道路。

整体看，改革开放33年，全县城乡居民得到了巨大的实惠，促使生活水平提高，生活质量改善。他们由衷地称颂现在的生活是：住得宽敞，吃讲营养，穿跟时尚，用的高档，出行有车，幸福靠党。

专记一：龙岗居民走的小康路

地处县城北面的龙岗居民委员会，2010年居住着3279户8113人，其中户籍不在龙岗而由外地流入的常住人口2365人。改革开放前，常住龙岗的居民中，除国营和集体单位的职工外，绝大多数都是无职无业的“干居民”。职工家庭因有固定的工资收入生活较为稳定，而众多的干居民因生活没有社会保障经常陷入缺衣少食的困境。为了生计，这些干居民只得靠打零工、敲碎石、掏河沙、割马草、挑水卖等杂活去挣得微薄的收入，用来维系家庭成员的温饱。至于居住和出行那是不敢奢望的。面对经济拮据、生活贫困、为了生存起早贪黑忙于奔波的居民总是期盼早日改变贫寒的家境，过上丰衣足食的幸福生活。

随着时间的推移，社会进入现代化建设新时期，党和国家把工作重点转移到经济建设上来，实行改革开放的战略决策，带来了不断提高龙岗居民生活水平的契机，把他们引上小康建设之路。龙岗居民委员会建设小康的主要途径是拓宽就业面，使其有劳动能力的居民有业可就，劳有所酬。一是允许个体从事经营。从20世纪80年代开始就有个体工商户开业，主要是经营投资小的餐饮、修理、理发、搬运、房屋修缮和日用小百货等，但注册资金仅数百元。随着资金不断积累，经营规模也不断扩大。进入90年代，一批有胆识的居民脱颖而出，他们独立投资或聚股投资，大办企业参与市场竞争。由于经营得法，效益颇佳，有的竟成为收入“冒尖户”。到2010年，全段注册登记的个体工商户逾百户。二是外出打工。这是龙岗居民的重要选择。他们之中有的是自寻去处、自谋职业；有的是经过劳动部门组织就业培训，然后输入到沿海经济发达的地区就业。至2010年，该居民委员会出境到外地打工的居民达701人，占总人口的8.64%。三是针对家庭经济贫乏、就业又无门路的居民户由居民委员牵线搭桥，多渠道地推介就业。四是对国营企业改制后下岗的职工，政府在政策和资金上积极支持，鼓励他们再就业。就业渠道疏通后，2010年全居民委员会成年人的就业面达到73%。就业人数的增加，使居民家庭的经济收入大幅度地增长，收入来源趋于稳定。

在龙岗居民段，除有劳动能力的家庭外，尚有191户既无劳动力又无生活来源的困难家庭和无人奉养的孤寡老人家庭。此类家庭全由政府包下来，从1997年起按照城镇居民最低生活保障制度规定标准每人每月发放90元，达到“应保尽保”的要求。2010年将最低生活保障线调升为每人每月210元。

由于政策给力，方向明确，道路找准，使居民收入稳定增长。1996年全居民委员会人均可支配收入达3400元，2000年增为5050元，2005年又增为7800元。2010年跨了一大步，可支配收入增至1.5万元，比贵州省委、省政府要求年人均纯收入7000元的小康标准高出1.1倍。经济收入的增长使昔日众多的干居民富裕起来过上丰富多彩的生活，以解决温饱为主的消费性支出占人均总支出的比重由1996年的83.05%降至2010年的68.59%。相应的是财产性支出、转移性支出、社会保障支出和购房建房支出等非消费性支出的比重呈上升态势。“吃要讲营养，穿要讲时尚，住要讲宽敞，行要车来往”是构成龙岗居民现时的小康生活状貌。面对如此光景，广大居民无不发出赞叹：政策指引小康路，幸福感恩共产党。

专记二：幸福村民追逐小康梦

坐落在修文河畔的龙场镇幸福村，靠近县城。2010年村民委员会下辖8个村民组，分别居住着村民399户、1625人，有耕地805亩，其中稻田占91.3%，生产条件较好，为全县主要粮食产区。在人民公社体制下的集体经营时期，尽管村的经济在全县列为优等，被称为“排头的大雁”，但发展步伐仍然缓慢，收入仍处于低水平，有的村民生活仍感困难。群众中流行着顺口溜：“幸福名字取得好，经济就是上不了，每个劳日几毛钱，有些人总是吃不饱。”

起始于1978年的改革开放，政策松“绑”，揭开幸福村群众发展生产、增加收入、改善生活的新篇章。在党的政策指引和政府的扶持下，村党支部和村委会明确提出脱贫奔小康的奋斗目标，打破全村以农为主、单一经营的生产格局，因地制宜，奋力追逐小康梦，开创全面发展的新局面。1978年，从事传统农业的劳力高达96%。1981年实行生产责任制，在解决粮食自给问题的同时，组织部分劳力转入非农业生产，利用6个砖瓦窑烧制砖、瓦和开采铝矾土、重晶石矿，使村民增加了现金收入8万余元。1985年，乘马家桥地区乡镇企业大发展的契机，劳力向非农生产领域转移，使59%的劳力分别进入乡办、村

办及村以下的工业、建筑业和自办的运输业、商贸业、餐饮业以及其他行业。由于大批富裕劳力有其用武之地，工资性收入竟竞成为村民收入迅速增长的主要渠道，占人均年纯收入的2/3。之后，一些不安现状的年轻人，又离乡背井外出打工，很快形成一股民工潮。至2010年，全村从事非农产业的劳力占总劳力的63%。其中，外出打工的120人，占16.2%（出省82人）。使工资性收入和多种经营的纯收入在全村纯收入中的比重高达72%。农民人均纯收入上升到1.05万元，在1978年人均210元的基础上增长49倍，年均递增13%。比贵州省委、省政府要求年人均纯收入7000元的小康标准高出50%。

经济发展，收入增加，使村民的物质生活发生了天翻地覆的变化，水平有很大提高，质量有明显改善。

——吃讲营养 1978年村民面临的饮食问题，只求肚子装饱，不敢奢想吃好。当年全村粮食总产361.3吨，除完成国家征购任务73.7吨和集体扣留39.7吨后，分给群众的口粮仅247.9吨，占总产量的68.6%。全村933人，人均分得原粮265.7公斤。分配到手的口粮大部分是水稻，除去家庭养殖需用的粮食，实际用于生活安排每人每天平均不足0.5公斤贸易粮。由于副食品短缺，充饥仅靠粮食，因分得的粮食有限，以致缺粮面高达35%。有的村民除了靠国家救济、返销和借用集体储备粮之外，还不惜背上自己舍不得吃的大米，步行远至10公里外的厂矿、街道以1：2的比例换取职工和居民手中的杂粮来弥补粮食缺口。“干稀搭配瓜菜代，一日两餐度时光”竟成了多数人家无奈的选择。虽有40%的农户能宰杀年猪，但按照生猪“购五留五”政策，交售给国家一半后所剩无几。多数农户常年吃素，油荤欠缺。能够吃饱就是最大的满足。1982年，12个生产队全部实行包干到户责任制，迸发出群众的生产积极性，使当年粮食总产达406.7吨，在1978年的基础上增长17.2%，人均产粮410.4公斤。集体扣留大幅减少，完成征购任务后人均实际留粮333公斤，村民从此告别饥饿，为历史上一个重要的转折。尽管因修建贵（阳）毕（节）公路征地和集体修筑公路占地，使耕地由1978年的1074亩减至2010年的805亩，人均不足半亩，但粮食生产一直保持发展势头。2010年总产384.5吨，比1978年净增23.2吨，人均产粮236.6公斤。因免交“皇粮”和免除集体扣留，也就从整体上能保障生活的需要。要求吃好，讲究营养和健康成为新的追求。一日三餐，油荤不断。逢年过节，家家都要摆上白酒、饮料以及丰盛的菜肴让家人团聚。多数家庭过去可望而不可即的时令蔬菜、水果、鱼、肉、鸡蛋、糕点、牛奶、饮品、茶叶的消费已成寻常。每逢操办红白喜事，席面都有鸡、鸭、鱼、肉乃至海鲜烹制出的十多个菜肴招待亲友，与32年前每桌不到1斤肉的标准相比，简直是天壤之别。

——穿讲时尚 1978年前，每人每年只能买到计划供应的1.57丈棉布和4两棉花。加上人们收入水平低，市场衣着匮乏，以致出现“夏天小孩光屁股，青壮年冬天少鞋袜，大姑娘身穿补疤衣，老年人补疤摞补疤”的现象。“菜当三分粮，辣角当衣裳”是群众遮身御寒的口头禅。衣服多为手工缝制，款式以对襟衣、父母装居多，色调灰暗。男青年能够到缝纫社制作一件中山装感到时髦，女青年为能得到一件用灯芯绒制作的嫁衣感到体面。从实行生产责任制起，这种状况逐渐改变：20世纪70年代，“只图温度，不讲风度”；80年代，“衣服买现成，不进裁缝门”；90年代，“色彩多样款式新，四季服装分得清”；进入21世纪，“样式、面料翻新快，去年是新款，今年遭淘汰”。这些短语流行在村民中，生动地反映出幸福村在衣着方面变化的历程。村民家庭，一改一衣多季的状况。不同季节，备有不同样式的衣服。即使同一季节，也备有不同场合、不同款式的服装。毛料、呢绒、皮衣、皮鞋、毛线织物，也成为村民的“抢手货”。特别是女性青年服装变化更大。夏秋季节，她们穿着令人夺目。冬春服装，为顺应潮流，展现体形，正如人们调侃的那样："上穿紧身衣，脚穿长筒鞋（靴）。长裤（袜）穿在内，短裤（裙）套在外，还有耳环、戒指身上戴。"穿得舒适，穿出时尚，穿讲漂亮成为村民们的追求，多种多样的的服饰将村民们装扮得多姿多彩。

——住讲宽敞 1978年全村191户中，分别居住在茅草房里的11户，住土墙瓦面房的46户，住石墙瓦面房的96户，住高架房的38户。房屋面积小，居住拥挤。村民谢庭宽一家三代8口，4个劳力住着3间土墙茅草房，人均不足8平方米。1987年家庭经济向好，将茅草房推倒重建4间青砖瓦面平房，居住条件有所改善。继后又将瓦房推倒重建4间两楼一底、砖混结构的楼房，人均面积过50平方米，彻底解决住房紧张的问题。类似情况，还较普遍。至2010年，全村户均住房面积132.3平方米，人均32.5平方米。其中，钢筋混凝土结构的占86.5%，楼房占76.4%，最高有7层。房内都有各式装修，有的还相当豪华。为迎接阳明文化节，营造环境氛围，全村公路干道两旁，有51户由国家出资对房屋进行了立面改造。步入村境，村寨里一栋栋样式各异的民居映入眼帘，俨如稻香村里建起的一座座小城，着实可观。

——出行有车 还是实行公社体制的1978年前，村民外出办事、赶场交易、走亲串友，多靠步行。全村仅有的8辆自行车，是人们羡慕的代步工具。村境除修（文）—马（家桥）公路能通汽车外，其余全是狭窄的泥泞小道。实行家庭联产承包责任制后，人们彼此交往密切，务工、经商、办事出行的频率更高。改善道路、购置代步工具成为村民的迫切要求。在村党支部和村委会领导下，集资、投劳和协调占地，打通8个村民组往来干道，能通汽车，与修马公路相连。在政府扶持下，从2000年起大修串户路，并硬化了组与组之间的干道和串户路，使80%的农户能通小车。为方便生产、生活，村民购置代步工具的积极性高涨。1981年，全村自行车增至15辆后，具有省力、快捷优势的摩托车成了大家新的选择。1992年，村民张志友破天荒购买一辆微型面包车，自驾行驶。至2010年，全村拥有各式摩托车38辆，小车已达42辆。村民汪成长期在外承包土石方工程，耗资200余万元购买"路虎"名车一辆进出工区。早年群众向往"点灯不用油，耕田不用牛，出行坐汽车，居住小洋楼"的生活，已成现实。

——用讲高档 1978年前，村民家庭设施简陋，用品短缺。生活用水、全凭肩挑，洗衣全靠手搓，燃煤多是肩挑背磨到数公里外的煤厂搬运。即便有手板车，搬运也很艰辛，累得汗流浃背。家中洗澡更是望洋兴叹。家具只是木床、饭桌、板凳、简单的锅、碗、瓢、勺。床上只有盖的被子、睡的枕头、铺的席子。多数人家取暖就是砌地炉烧煤，有的还以柴草为燃料烤火。年轻人结婚，高档聘礼就是"三转一响"（自行车、缝纫机、手表和收音机）。女方嫁妆就是"三十二条腿"（一张双人床、一张抽屉、一个柜子、一张小桌再配上四把小靠椅），刷上红油漆，以示喜庆。随着改革开放和现代化建设的推进，延续多年的陈旧用品得以淘汰。1990年，全村农户用上自来水。由政府组织实施的农村电网改造，使村民用电更安全、更方便，并为大量的家用电器进农家创造了条件。1981年，村民尹明珍、周世惠最先将14寸黑白电视机抱回家。每当夜幕降临，邻居和外队年轻人蜂拥而至，里三层、外三层围观电视节目。继后，收录机、洗衣机、影碟机迅速增加，黑白电视机很快为彩色电视机取代，户户拥有。2000年安装使用固定电话的农户占70%。2001年始用移动电话，至2010年，成年人，包括读书的学生，80%的人都成为手机用户。与30多年前的情况相比，传统以煤或柴草为燃料，让人烟熏火燎的土灶台被推倒，全部用上了电饭锅，89%的农户用上电磁炉，部分农家还使用沼气。有60%的农户添置了电冰箱，有的还安装使用了抽油烟机。卧室内，早年使用的木架床多为"席梦思"等商品床取代。衣柜、梳妆台、写字台（或三抽桌）配在其间。多数村民客厅里彩电、沙发、茶几、饮水机、影碟机一应俱全。有的人家还配有音响。

冬天靠带烟管的铁制煤炉取暖的家庭，有的还换上了电热。2010年全村有35%的农户安装了太阳能或电热水器，62%的住宅拥有室内卫生间，家中沐浴已成现实。年轻人结婚的聘礼和嫁妆普遍配置金首饰、名表、手机、品牌服饰、冰箱、彩电、洗衣机。花车开道，车队迎亲，设宴待客。婚事新办，家人和亲友无不喜形于色。

——玩讲舒畅 改革开放前，村民日复一日地白天出工干活，晚上评工记分，生活单调，很少有属于自己安排的休闲时间。当衣食无忧、居有所住后，人们生活变得丰富多彩。电视机进家，劳作之余就是看电视、听音乐。随着生活水平提高，春节期间玩花灯，平时聚集一处下象棋、打扑克，年轻人唱唱卡拉OK、打打台球又逐渐成风。进入21世纪，在自己庭院或阳台上栽花种草、喂鱼养鸟，在河边垂钓，在家养猫喂狗，中青年妇女相约定时、定点放起歌碟翩翩起舞，有的单独或相约一起吹吹唢呐、拉拉二胡，又成了人们休闲新选择。为了健身，有的村民还购置按摩器，甚至价值数千元1把的按摩椅等器材。20世纪90年代起，随着县内阳明洞、六广河、野生动物园、桃源河魔幻漂流等景点开发或升级改造后，年轻人单独或结伴前往游玩又成为一种时尚。跨出县境，前往黄果树、龙宫、织金洞等著名景点旅游的人增多，自驾游也日渐升温。前往北京、华东五市、海南、珠海、深圳旅游的人与日俱增。特别是首都北京，更是大家向往的地方。至2010年，全村先后有80多人前往。村支书汪辉荣夫妇花了7天时间，往返登机，耗资6000多元游览北京天安门、故宫、颐和园、长城……饱尝若干名胜古迹后满意而归。更有甚者，10多个村民先后前往台湾、香港、澳门，还有6人漂洋过海，远去新加坡、马来西亚和泰国。周家寨的张志友夫妇2008年用9天时间，先游香港，再往新、马、泰三个国家，花费1.5万余元。回到家里满怀高兴地说："大开眼界，大长知识，值得！"从村民娱乐、健身和外出旅游这个侧面，折射出幸福村的群众从生存型到温饱型，再到享受型的可喜变化。

改革开放释放出红利，使幸福村旧貌换新颜，让群众得到看得见、摸得着的实惠。"改革前后两重天，今天生活尽开颜，感谢惠民政策好，继续跟党永向前"成了大家共同的心声。广大村民对提前实现党中央提出在2020年将我国全面建成小康社会的战略目标充满着信心。

第六章　方言　习俗

第一节　方　言

县境汉语方言属西南官话川黔方言黔中片区黔中方言，语音具有黔中方言的一般特点，与临近的息烽、开阳两县极为相似，与贵阳话有一定差异。与普通话相比，其特点是声母鼻边音不分，音无翘舌，韵母无后鼻音，声调平分阴阳，浊上变去，入归阳平。由于普通话的逐步推广普及、人口的迁徙流动和经济社会的发展，部分老派方言逐渐消失，而新派方言吸纳了普通话元素，尤其在语音、词汇方面变化较明显。新派方言虽有向普通话方向发展的趋势，但在声调上存在有明显差异。

一、语音

境内方言较接近普通话，仅在发声习惯和声调上有所区别，基本上适用汉语拼音注音。

（一）声母

县境方言声母有：b、p、m、f、d、t、l、ng、g、k、h、j、q、x、z、c、s、r和零声母y、w。

声母与国际音标对照表

表5—06—01

声 母	国际音标	声 母	国际音标	声 母	国际音标
b	[b]	g	[k]	z	[ts]
p	[b‘]	k	[k‘]	c	[ts‘]
m	[m]	h	[x]	s	[s]
f	[f‘]	—	—	r	[ʐ]
d	[t]	j	[tɕ]	—	—
t	[t‘]	q	[tɕ‘]	y	[j]
l	[l]	x	[ɕ]	w	[w]
ng	[ŋ]	—	—	—	—

与普通话相比，主要有以下差异：

1. 声母鼻、边音不分　舌尖中浊鼻音“n”较少，多与舌尖中浊边音“l”混用，如：“牛和流”“老和

脑”“路和怒”“兰和南”“赖和奈”均以“l”为主。但有时反过来“l”又读成“n”，如“栗”读成[ni^{55}]，有“小乌栗[xiao^{42}wu^{55} ni^{55}]”“毛栗[mao^{21} ni^{55}]”。

2. 无翘舌音 舌尖后音全部为舌尖前音，无“zh”“ch”和“sh”，“r”也按舌尖前音读。部分普通话中用“r”做声母的字在方言中则改为用“y”做声母，如：“荣、容、溶、熔和融等”字。

3. 零声母 凡是i、u、ü和i、u、ü开头的音节书写时要用y或w，如：移[yi^{55}]、五[wu^{42}]、遇[yü^{13}]等。

4. 舌根鼻辅音声母“ng” 在读以a、o、e开头的零声母字时，常在前面加舌根鼻音“ng”，如：“欧”读成[ngou^{55}]，“恩”读成[ngen^{55}]。

5. “y”变“l” 部分齐齿呼声母零声母的字读边音，如：“业[ye^{55}]读成[lie^{21}]”、“义[yì^{51}]’读成[lì^{13}]”等。

6. “h”变“f” 普通话声母是“h”、韵母为“u”的字，境内方言声母改为“f”，如虎[fu^{42}]、胡[fu^{21}]、湖[fu^{21}]等。

7. “ch”变“s” 部分普通话声母为“ch”，境内方言声母改为“s”，如撑[sen^{21}]、婵[san^{21}]、阐[san^{21}]、晨[sen^{21}]、纯[sun^{21}]等。

8. “j、q、x”变“g、k、h” 部分方言开口二等字大部分读成开口呼，普通话声母为“j、q、x”的字方言改为“g、k、h”，如豇[gang^{55}]、掐[ka^{21}]、项[hang^{13}]等。

（二）韵母

韵母共32个，四呼俱全。其中，开口呼12个，齐齿呼10个，合口呼7个，撮口呼3个。

韵母与国际音标对照表

表5—06—02

分类	开口呼		齐齿呼		合口呼		撮口呼	
	韵母	国际音标	韵母	国际音标	韵母	国际音标	韵母	国际音标
单韵母	a	[A]	i	[i]	u	[u]	ü	[y]
	o	[o]	ia	[iA]	ua	[ua]	—	—
	e	[ɛ]	ie	[iɛ]	—	—	—	—
	—	—	iu	[iu]	—	—	—	—
复韵母	ai	[ai]	—	—	uai	[uai]	—	—
	ei	[əi]	—	—	ui	[uei]	—	—
	ao	[ɑu]	iao	[iau]	—	—	—	—
	ou	[ou]	iou	[iou]	—	—	—	—
	er	[er]	—	—	—	—	—	—
鼻韵母	an	[an]	ian	[ian]	uan	[uan]	üan	[yan]
	en	[ən]	in	[in]	un	[uən]	ün	[yn]
	ang	[ɑŋ]	iang	[iɑŋ]	uang	[uɑŋ]	—	—
	ong	[oŋ]	iong	[ioŋ]	—	—	—	—

1. 方言与普通话韵母差异

（1）方言中没有韵母[uo]，普通话韵母[uo]的字在修文老方言中读[o]，如：锅[go^{55}]、果[go^{42}]、火[ho^{42}]、祸[ho^{13}]、拖[to^{55}]和裸[lo^{42}]等。

（2）部分方言中没有韵母“e”，普通话韵母“e”在修文老方言舌根声母后读“o”，在舌尖声母后读“ei”，如：哥[go^{55}]、科[ko^{55}]、喝[ho^{55}]和遮[zei^{55}]、车[cei^{55}]、奢[sei^{55}]、热[rei^{21}]。

（3）方言中有韵母“iu”，普通话则没有这个韵母，相应的字普通话韵母是“u”或“ü”，如：局[jiu^{21}]、育[yiu^{21}]、屈[qiu^{21}]、续[xiu^{21}]、俗[siu^{21}]和速[siu^{21}]等。

（4）部分方言中没有韵母“ie”“üe”，普通话“ie”“üe”韵母在修文老方言中分别读“i”、“ü”，例：叶[yi^{21}]、爹[di^{55}]、姐[ji^{42}]、月[yü^{21}]、缺[qü^{21}]和雪[xü^{21}]等。

（5）方言中没有后鼻韵“eng”，普通话“eng”韵母在老方言中读“ong”或“en”，如：绷[bong^{55}]、朋[pong^{21}]、蒙[mong^{21}]、风[fong^{55}]、彭[pen^{21}]、凳[den^{13}]和滕[ten^{21}]等。

（6）方言没有后鼻韵“ing”，普通话“ing”韵母在老方言中读前鼻韵“in”，如：平[pin^{21}]、名[min^{21}]、听[tin^{55}]、青[qin^{55}]等。

2. 方言韵母变化

由于受普通话影响，方言韵母发展逐步向普通话接近，缩小与普通话之间差异，部分已与普通话大致相同，呈现出以下几种趋势。

（1）撮口呼韵母在新方言中普遍使用，例：

例字	老方言	新方言	普通话
女	li^{42}	lü^{42}	nü^{214}
雨	yi^{42}	yü^{42}	yü^{214}
鱼	yi^{21}	yü^{21}	yü^{35}
区	qi^{55}	qü^{55}	qü^{55}
捐	jan^{55}	juan^{55}	juan^{55}
卷	jian^{42}	juan^{42}	juan^{51}
军	jin^{55}	jun^{55}	jun^{55}
云	yin^{21}	yun^{21}	yun^{35}
俊	jin^{13}	jun^{13}	jun^{51}

（2）来自古入声字的韵母“io”向“üe”“iɑo”变化，例：

例字	老方言读音	新方言读音	普通话读音
学	xio^{21}	xue^{21}	xue^{35}
觉	jio^{21}	jue^{21}	jue^{21}
确	qio^{21}	que^{21}	que^{51}
约	yo^{21}	yue^{21}	yue^{55}
药	yo^{21}	yɑo^{21}	yɑo^{51}

（3）舌尖中音声母后的“uei”向“ei”变化，例：

例字	老方言读音	新方言读音	普通话读音
累	$luei^{13}$	lei^{13}	lei^{51}
类	$luei^{13}$	lei^{13}	lei^{51}
擂	$luei^{21}$	lei^{21}	lei^{35}
雷	$luei^{21}$	lei^{21}	lei^{35}

（4）中古臻摄韵母“en”向“uen”变化，例：

例字	老方言	新方言	普通话
损	sen^{42}	sun^{42}	sun^{214}
村	cen^{55}	cun^{55}	cun^{55}
顿	den^{13}	dun^{13}	dun^{51}
屯	ten^{21}	tun^{21}	tun^{35}

（5）“iou”在舌根音声母后介音“i”丢掉，向“ou”变化，例：

例字	老方言	新方言	普通话
狗	$giou^{42}$	gou^{42}	gou^{214}
构	$giou^{13}$	gou^{13}	gou^{51}
抠	$kiou^{55}$	kou^{55}	kou^{55}
扣	$kiou^{13}$	kou^{13}	kou^{51}
呕	$ngiou^{42}$	ou^{42}	ou^{214}
欧	$ngiou^{55}$	$ngou^{55}$	ou^{55}

（6）综合性变化，例：

例字	老方言读音	新方言读音	普通话读音
批	pei^{55}	pi^{55}	pi^{55}
披	pei^{55}	pi^{55}	pi^{55}
眉	mi^{21}	mei^{21}	Mei^{35}
做	zu^{13}	zo^{13}	zuo^{51}
佛	fu^{21}	fo^{21}	fo^{35}

（三）声调

境内方言声调在调类上与普通话完全相同，均为四个调类，即阴平、阳平、上声、去声（－、/、V、\）。调型上除一声均为高平调外，其余三声调型均有差异。调值也是除第一声相同外其余三声均有不同。

方言与普通话声调对照表

表5—06—03

调类		调型		调值	
修文	普通话	修文	普通话	修文	普通话
阴平	阴平	高平	高平	55	55
阳平	阳平	低降	中升	21	35
上声	上声	中降	降升	42	214
去声	去声	低升	全降	13	51

附：调值标记

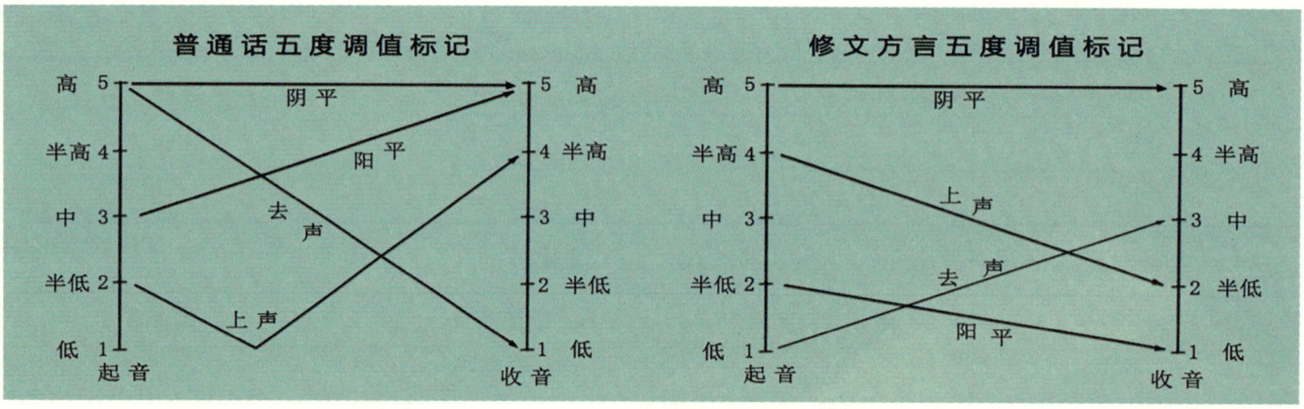

新方言发展变化逐步与普通话调类趋同，多数变化后仍读方言调值。单字声调变化主要有以下几种情况：

1. 阳平变阴平

例字	老方言	新方言	普通话
哭	ku^{21}	ku^{55}	ku^{55}
屈	qiu^{21}	qü^{55}	qü^{55}
忽	fu^{21}	fu^{55}	fu^{55}
杀	sa^{21}	sa^{55}	sa^{55}
捉	zo^{21}	zo^{55}	zuo^{55}
吸	xi^{21}	xi^{55}	xi^{55}
夹	jia^{21}	jia^{55}	jia^{55}

2. 阳平变去声

例字	老方言	新方言	普通话
牧	mu^{21}	mu^{13}	mu^{51}
木	mu^{21}	mu^{13}	mu^{51}
室	si^{21}	si^{13}	shi^{51}
业	li^{21}	yi^{13}	ye^{51}
密	mi^{21}	mi^{13}	mi^{51}

3. 去声变上声

例字	老方言	新方言	普通话
企	qi^{13}	qi^{42}	qi^{214}
导	dao^{13}	dao^{42}	dao^{214}
苟	giou^{13}	gou^{42}	gou^{214}

二、语音变异

（一）变调

1. 叠音名词由“阳平+阳平”（21+21）变为“阳平+阴平”（21+55），例：爸爸、娃娃、盆盆、坛坛、角角、芽芽、脚脚、坨坨、雀雀、皮皮、筒筒、碟碟、　篮篮、虫虫、箩箩、缺缺、索索、绳绳、瓶瓶、钵钵、盘盘、圆圆、夹夹、盒盒　叔叔、塞塞、刷刷、糊糊、头头、球球、毛毛。

2. 部分非叠音名词由“阳平+阳平”（21+21）变为“阳平+阴平”（21+55），例：头发、眉毛、舌头、额头、婆娘、杨梅、毛栗、蛤蟆、洋桃、毛虫、馄饨、疙瘩、螳螂、核桃、禾麻、茶叶、洋荷、喉咙、明年、阳郎、格螺、葡萄、木头等。

3. 表示方位的词尾“头”字由阳平变为阴平，例：

家头、外头、心头、眼头、上头、下头、锅头、碗头、水头、火头、屋头、前头、后头等。

4. 部分“儿”尾自成音节，由阳平变化阴平，例：猫儿、牛儿、猴儿、一个儿、一朵儿、低低个儿等。但有的仍不变调，读作阳平，例：幺儿、妹儿、瓜儿、猪儿和狗儿等。

5. 另有一些规律性不强的双音节词变调，前字不论什么调类，后字变为阴平，如：

高粱　花红　樱桃　牙齿　晚歇　早晨　耳朵　肚脐

（二）合音

境内方言与普通话相近，特别是新方言与普通话基本能互通，方言一字一句说清楚普通话者基本能听懂，但语速稍快极易产生合音现象，普通话者就不易听懂。合音主要分双音节合音和多音节合音。

1. 双音节合音一般是前字韵尾和后字声母很轻甚至被省略，声调由前字声调迅速过渡到后字声调，语速较快时听起来犹如一个音节，声调由后字声调决定。例：

贵阳　gui^{13}yang^{21} ——guang^{131}

不要　bu^{21}yao^{13} ——biao^{213}

今天　jin^{55}tian^{55}——jian^{555}

哪样　la^{42}yang^{13}——lang^{413}

你家　li^{42}jia^{55}——lia^{425}

人家　ren^{21}jia^{55}——renia^{215}（有的读为lia^{55}）

拿去　la^{21}qi^{13}——li^{13}

2. 多音节合音，一般是第一字和最后一字保留声韵完整，中间字声母很轻或被省略，声调由前后两字决定，最后一字声韵调较为清晰。例：

修文县　xiu^{55}wen^{21}xian^{13}——xiu^{55}en xian^{13}（老方言读为xi^{55}en xian^{13}）

出租车　cu^{55}zu^{55} ce^{55}——cu^{55}u ce^{55}

摩托车　mo^{55}to^{21}ce^{55}——mo^{55}o ce^{55}

苞谷粑　bao^{55}bu^{21}ba^{55}——bao^{55}u ba^{55}

大锅饭　da^{13}guo^{55}fan^{13}——da^{13}uo fan^{13}

烂泥山　lan^{13}li^{21}san^{55}——lan^{13}i san^{55}

马家桥　ma^{42}jia^{55}qiao^{21}——ma^{42}a qiao^{21}

各人家　go^{21} ren^{21}jia^{55} ——go^{21}en jia^{55}（老方言读为gong^{21} jia^{55}）

三、文白异读

即为书面读音与生活中的口语读音差异，一些字有文读和白读两个读音或多个读音，其差别常涉及声韵调三个方面，这在老方言中显得较突出，新方言逐步缩小其差异。

1. 声母异读例：

在　方文读“zai^{13}”，口语说“dai^{13}”（音待），如：在上班、在开会。

才　方文读“cai^{21}”，口语说“tai^{21}”（音台），如：才回家、才吃饭。

就　方文读“jiou^{13}”，口语说“dou^{13}”（音豆），如：就是不信。

凑　方文读“cou^{13}”，口语说“dou^{13}”（音豆），如：凑钱打平伙。

戳　方文读“co^{21}”，口语说“do^{21}”（音夺），如：有戳天本事。

铸　方文读“zu^{13}”，口语说“dao^{13}”（音到），如：铸铁锅。

准　方文读“zuen^{42}”，口语说“den^{42}”（音等），如：不准他休息。

他　方文读“ta^{55}”，口语说“la^{55}”（音拉），如：他们、他来了。

里　方文读“li^{42}”，口语说“yi^{42}”（音以），如：里头边（里面）。

那　方文读“la^{13}”，口语说“a^{13}”（音嗄），如：那个在那点。

间　方文读“jian^{55}”，口语说“gan^{55}”（音甘），如：房间。

陷　方文读“xian^{13}”，口语说“han^{13}”（音旱），如：陷进去。

严　方文读“lian^{21}”，口语说“ngan^{21}”（音ɑ́n），如：严丝合缝。

下　量词，方文读“xia^{13}”，口语说“ha^{13}”（音hɑ̀），如：一下、两下、三两下。

偷　方文读“tou^{55}”，口语说“lou^{55}”（音lōu），如：偷儿偷东西。

龚　方文读“gong^{55}”，口语说“jong^{55}”（音jīong），如：姓龚。

2. 韵母类异读例：

修　地名，方文读“xiu^{55}”，老方口语说“xi^{55}”（音西），如：修文。

颈　方文读“jin^{42}”，口语说“jiɑng^{42}”（音蒋），如：脖颈、吊颈。

给　方文读“gei^{42}”，口语说“gen^{55}”（音跟），如：给你说，拿给他。

茂　方文读“mao^{13}”，口语说“mong^{13}”（音孟），如：茂盛、茂密。

眉　方文读“mei^{21}”，口语说“mi^{21}”（音密），如：眉目、眉毛。

删　方文读“san^{55}”，口语说“suan^{55}”（音酸），如：删除、删改。

虱 方文读“si^{55}”，口语说“se^{21}”（音蛇），如：虱子（动物身上的寄生虫）。

陌 方文读“mo^{13}”，口语说“mei^{21}”（音梅），如：陌生、阡陌。

戒 方文读“jie^{13}”，口语说“gai^{13}”（音丐），如：猪八戒、戒烟。

明 方文读“ming^{21}”，口语说“men^{21}”（音门），主要用于时间，如：明天、明年。

四、词汇

（一）典型成语

【巴泥扯地】[ba^{55}li^{21}ce^{42}di^{13}] 逮到什么就粘连什么：糍巴太粘咯，~嘞粘得我满手都是。

【蹿天达地】[ban^{42}tian^{55}da^{21}di^{13}] 拼命挣扎：刚钓上岸来嘞鱼~嘞抓都抓不倒。

【白眉扯眼】[bei^{21}mi^{21}ce^{42}yan^{42}] 没有变化，毫无反应:说不说~的。另有近义词“白木老事”(bei^{21}mu^{21}lɑo^{42}si^{13})。

【□头沙罐】[bia^{42}tou^{21}sa^{55}guan^{13}] 一个物件形状怪异很不规则，特别是容器类物件摔扁变形后的状貌：一个铝盆被挤压得方不方、圆不圆嘞，像个~样。

【鼻涕纳聋】[bi^{21}di^{13}la^{21}long^{55}] 满脸都是鼻涕，一般形容幼儿或大哭的人：她一把鼻涕一把泪哭得~嘞哦!

【扑爬礼拜】[pu^{21} pa^{21} li^{42}bai^{13}] 扑爬即向前摔跤，礼拜即磕头。一般形容急速行走或跑：他~的追了上去。

【皮貎皮甩】[pi^{21}lɑng ^{55}pi^{21} suai^{42}] 除了皮没有多少肉：之个老母猪太瘦咯，~嘞。

【跰脚挎手】[pai^{55} jo^{21}kua^{21}sou^{42}] 脚或手残疾或受伤：你看他~嘞做起事来还扎劲得很。

【披毛搭耳】[pi^{21}mao^{21}da^{21}er^{42}] 主要指头发长了盖过耳朵又不梳理：你看他头发长得那样长咯不理发，~嘞，拿根带带来都可扎纠纠咯。

【疲塌嘴歪】[pi^{21}ta^{21}zuen^{42}wai^{55}] 同义词鼻塌嘴歪，劳累疲惫得脸都变形状：军训练习越野跑步，一个个跑得~嘞。

【马干吃尽】[ma^{42}gan^{55}ci^{21}jin^{13}] 近义词牯吃霸道、牯吃霸休：这家伙~的一点道理都不讲。

【木盐淡鲊】[mu^{21}yan^{21}dan^{13}za^{42}] 没有盐或很少有盐的菜肴：回锅肉不放盐~嘞不好吃。

【毛包垄怂】[ma^{21}bao^{55}long^{42}song^{42}] 毛发很凌乱：哪个人一点都不讲究，早上起来头不梳脸不洗，~嘞就出门。

【猫儿搞抓】[mao^{55}er^{55}ci^{55}zua^{55}] 像小猫一样好动，爱伸手惹事或抓人：你之个娃儿咋爱~，你看把人家脸都抓出血咯。

【麻打火勾】[ma^{21}da^{42}ho^{42}giu^{55}] 浑水摸鱼：他没有买电影票，~嘞就混进里面去看电影。

【肥头搭耳】[fe^{21}tou^{21}da^{21}er^{42}] 原本指头肥耳大，后形容头大体胖的人：你看哪个人长得~嘞。

【肥肉添膘】[fei^{21}ru^{21}tian^{55}biao^{55}] 好上加好：他家本来就很有钱，现在买彩票又中大奖，真是~哦。

【煳区巴锅】[fu^{21}qü^{55}ba^{55}go^{55}] 锅内食物严重烧煳：煮嘞米饭煳老火咯搞得~嘞。

【煳巴鲁处】[fu^{21}ba^{55}lu^{42}cu^{42}] 物体被烧成煳黑状：火大咯把糍粑烧得~嘞。

【糊泥棒壁】[fu^{21}li^{21}bang^{13}bi^{21}] 糨糊、泥浆等有黏性物质的特性：用浆糊洗手~嘞。

【当官降群】[dang^{55}gan^{55}xiang^{21}qin^{21}] 意为当官的人要做群众的公仆，要为群众办事：做领导要知道~

嘞道理，要不（否则）群众不会拥护你。

【倒来不去】[dao^{13}lai^{21}bu^{21}qi^{13}] 近义词“倒多不少”，进一步不够，退一步又多：这段布～嘞，做大人的裤子不够，做小娃儿嘞又多咯点。

【打屁拢怂】[da^{42}pi^{13}long^{42}song^{42}] 没有主见跟着别人起哄或行事：之个娃儿没得脑筋，一天就是～嘞跟倒别个屁股后头转。

【倒憨不痴】[dao^{13}han^{55}bu^{21}ci^{55}] 弱智、半疯半傻：你之个娃儿～嘞，尽做些孽包事。

【逗风惹祸】[dou^{55}fong^{55}rei^{42}ho^{13}] 惹是生非：这小子不学好，一天就是～嘞。

【抖栗稀颤】[tou^{42}li^{21}xi^{55}zan^{13}] 身体发抖：大冬天嘞衣服穿得单薄，冷得他～嘞。

【拖衣落食】[to^{55}yi^{55}lo^{21}si^{21}] 义为衣食无着落：一个人没得出息～嘞，简直人嫌鬼不爱！

【脱头邪板】[to^{21}tou^{21}xie^{21}ban^{42}] 幽默、跳皮：你看他～嘞跟他玩嘞人还多得很勒。

【舔口□嘴】[tian^{42}kou^{42}lia^{21}zui^{42}] 形容吃东西没吃够还要想吃：煮嘞饭只吃个半饱，吃得～嘞。

【偷闲等空】[tou^{55}xian^{21}den^{42}kong^{13}] 充分利用空闲时间：这件毛衣是她自家～打（织）出来嘞。

【老虎按猪】[lao^{42}fu^{42}an^{13}zu^{55}] 向前猛扑的动作：他冲上去一个～将坏人扑倒在地。

【老季横秋】[lao^{42}ji^{42}hun^{21}qiu^{55}] 近义词“老态龙钟”，形容年龄大、衰老：白骨精变成一个～嘞老太婆。

【泥古骚带】[li^{21}gu^{42}sao^{55}dai^{13}] 全身沾满泥土或泥浆：犁牛打耙嘞人，最后一个个都搞得～嘞。

【擂和泥汤】[lui^{21}ho^{21}li^{21}tang^{55}] 污水遍地、狼藉不堪：不会做家务嘞人把厨房头搞得～嘞。

【聊二垮三】[lia^{21}er^{13} kua^{42}san^{55}] 吊二啷当、嬉皮笑脸貌：之个娃儿～嘞，说不倒一句好话，干不倒一件正事。

【冷火秋烟】[len^{42}ho^{42}qiu^{55}yan^{55}] 非常冷清。同义词冷屁秋烟：这屋里～嘞人都没得一个。

【捞肠寡肚】[lao^{21}cang^{21}ga^{42}du^{13}] 形容腹空饥饿：没有油肉吃，饭后不久就觉得～嘞。

【搞不拢怂】[gao^{42}bu^{21}long^{42}song^{42}] 贬义词，急迫贪婪状：看到免费发纪念品，他～嘞跑去跟倒抢。

【鬼头刀把】[gui^{42}tou^{21}dao^{55}ba^{13}] 同义词稀奇古怪，形容说话做事异类：他～嘞，说不到一句人话。

【滚跟达斗】[gun^{42}gen^{55}da^{21}dou^{42}] 贬义词，形容急速行走或跑时摔倒的狼狈像：听到山下有人找他，就从山上～嘞跑咯下去。

【疙儿拱包】[gei^{21}er^{55}gong^{42}bao^{55}] 表面不光滑、不平整：那个人的脸上～嘞，就像橘子皮样。

【光脚实板】[guang^{55}jo^{21}si^{21}ban^{42}] 打赤脚，又称光脚实杆：鞋袜都是不穿～嘞。

【鼓丁爆绽】[gu^{42}din^{55}bao^{13}zan^{13}] 非常饱满：今年收成好，苞谷、谷子都长得～嘞。

【哭稀烂包】[ku^{21}xi^{55}lan^{13}bao^{55}] ①形容小儿爱哭；②形容某人委曲又没出息。近义词“哭稀烂笼”。

【瞌睡迷西】[ko^{21}sui^{13}mi^{21}xi^{55}] 睡意很浓：几天晚上没有睡好觉，走起路都是～嘞。

【旮旮角角】[ka^{55}ka^{55}go^{21}go^{21}] 原意为旮旯角落，即狭窄偏僻的地方和角落的意思：一只耗子跑进家里，哪点～都找遍咯也都找不到。

【款天磕地】[kuan^{42}tian^{55}ko^{21}di^{13}] 吹牛，侃天侃地让人生厌：你～嘞不行，要拿出点实在嘞给大家看。

【黑咕垄咚】[hei^{22} gu^{42}long^{55}dong^{42}] 形容没有光线的地方：在小土墙房中还没有窗户，把门一关～嘞啥都看不到。

【活摇活甩】[ho^{21}yao^{21}ho^{21}sai^{42}] 两物体连接处松动后似连非连的状貌：两根木棒用绳子捆在一起没有捆

紧～嘞。

【幌打糊稀】[hang^{13}da^{42}fu^{21}xi^{55}] 一时糊涂：考试嘞时候，我～嘞做错咯几道题。

【憨吃哑胀】[han^{55}ci^{21}ya^{42}zang^{13}] 不知饱足，吃饱了还要吃：之私儿～嘞，一顿吃咯四个馒头、五个包子、一碗面，好像还没得事勒。

【喝咳连天】[ho^{55}hai^{42}lian^{21}tian^{55}] 喝咳即哈欠：昨晚熬咯夜，今天白天～嘞。

【硬擿夺棒】[ngen^{13}ci^{55}do^{21}bang^{13}] 僵硬：坐久咯不活动，脚都坐得～。同义词“硬□夺杆”。

【瓮声瓮气】[ngong^{42}sen^{55}ngong^{42}qi^{13}] 鼻音或回声太重：他感冒咯说话～嘞。

【鸡呜呐叫】[ji^{55}wu^{55}la^{21}jao^{13}] 形容高声尖叫，也称鸡啦武叫、鸡呜呐喊，像鸡一样惊慌乱跑乱叫：半夜三更嘞你～搞哪样子？

【见子打子】[jian^{13}zi^{42}da^{42}zi^{42}] 见着什么做什么（褒义），形容反应快，会做事：之个娃儿～嘞，逗人喜欢。

【挤眉眨眼】[ji^{42}mi^{21}za^{47}yian^{47}] 挤眉弄眼：你们两个～嘞，搞哪样子咪嘛咒。

【挤挤喀喀】[ji^{42}ji^{42}ka^{55}ka^{55}] 形容很拥挤：房间小咯，家具多咯，家中就显得～嘞。

【假巴一二】[jia^{42}ba^{55}yi^{21}er^{13}] 好歹、好坏，一般在对方不称职时用：你～嘞还是他爹，你不管哪个管？

【七跛八跳】[qi^{21}ban^{42}ba^{21}tiao^{13}] 拼命挣扎、乱跳：用绳子拴起狗来打，打得它～嘞。

【青格啷当】[qin^{55}gei^{13}lang^{21}dang^{55}] 形容脸色疲惫、憔悴不好看：看你嘞脸色～嘞，是不是生病咯？

【气鼓肋胀】[qi^{13}gu^{42}lei^{21}zang^{13}] 腹内胀得厉害：吃饭吃多咯，胀得～嘞。

【清汤寡水】[qin^{55}tang^{55}gua^{42}sui^{42}] 缺少主要材料或油、盐做出来的稀饭或汤、菜等：米放少咯煮出来嘞稀饭～嘞。

【勤巴苦挣】[qin^{21}ba^{55}ku^{42}zen^{13}] 辛辛苦苦：解放前一家人～嘞干，还是吃不饱穿不暖。

【情顺理安】[qin^{21} suen^{13}li^{42}an^{55}] 有情有理：既有群众支持，又有领导同意，～，皆大欢喜。

【嬉儿不痴】[xi^{55}er^{55}bu^{21}xi^{55}] 不礼貌的开玩笑，嬉皮笑脸：不要跟老人家～嘞！

【稀泥烂窖】[xi^{55}li^{21}lan^{13}gao^{13}] 地面非常泥泞，深一脚浅一脚的：乡村道路没有硬化之前一下雨就～嘞。

【斜边吊垮】[xie^{21}bian^{55}diao^{13}kua^{42}] 不规整，或与主题形状不协调，近义词“歪边斜垮”：你画的这个线条没得画好，画得～嘞。

【瞎眉科多】[xia^{21}mi^{21}ko^{55}do^{55}] 指盲人或形容视力不好的人：你看他～嘞样子看得清啥子东西哦。

【旋皮达脸】[xüan^{21}pi^{21}da^{21}lian^{42}] 旋皮指皮很厚很滑，达脸及嬉皮笑脸：小叔子在他嫂子面前～嘞。

【正一捉二】[zen^{13}yi^{21}zo^{21}er^{13}] 正儿八经①言行严肃认真：我～给你说你不要给我嬉皮笑脸嘞；②正宗、真实：他～是赵家老大而不是冒充嘞。

【擿脚动手】[ci^{55}jo^{21}dong^{13}sou^{42}] 动脚动手：他有个不好嘞脾气，一说话就爱～嘞。

【钻头沕缝】[zuan^{55}tou^{21} mi^{13}fong^{13}] 刻意、专注：刚到六广，一下车就～嘞去买六广臭豆腐吃。

【装猪吃象】[zuang^{55}zu^{55}ci^{21}xiang^{13}] 装憨不说话，但心中有更大的阴谋：着冤枉咯他不说话，实际他在～。

【皱巴勒扯】[zong^{13}ba^{55}lei^{42}ce^{42}] 褶皱很多：一件衣服穿得～嘞，就像从狗屁股头拉出来嘞样。

【财大气粗】[cai^{21}da^{13}qi^{13}cu^{55}] 有钱的人口气大：之个老板真嘞是～哦，张口就说生产中死个把人有啥稀奇哦。

【惨惨场合】[can^{42}can^{42}cang^{21}ho^{21}] 惨淡或很凄凉：王小二过年一年不如一年，只能勉强维持眼前嘞之个～。

【操心劳神】[cao^{55}xin^{55}lao^{21}sen^{21}] 即费心费神：父母少不得要为一家人的生活～。

【铳头铳脑】[cong^{13}tuo^{21}cong^{13}lao^{42}] 爱出风头炫耀自己：之龟儿～嘞，尽爱搞一些虚报浮夸。

【吹牛放炮】[cui^{55}liu^{21}fang^{13}pao^{13}] 吹大牛皮：之家伙尽爱～，有几人会相信他嘛?

【长毛嘴尖】[cang^{21}mao^{21}zui^{42}jian^{55}] 形容很消瘦貌：工作既辛苦，生活又不好，几个月下来瘦得～嘞。

【搌尖夺事】[can^{42}jian^{55}do^{21}si^{13}] 多嘴多事：之个人～嘞逗人恨。

【甩哩甩当】[suai^{42}li^{55}suai^{42}dɑng^{55}] 垂吊的物体不规则的摇晃、摆动。小狗胸前吊嘞铃当，走起路来～嘞。

【瘦壳躴精】[sou^{13}kuo^{21}lang^{55}jin^{55}] 形容精瘦：～嘞人，体重一般都偏低。

【骚天湿地】[sao^{55}tian^{55}si^{21}di^{13}] 指很风骚，一般为骂人语言：一个姑娘家～嘞像个哪样子。

【手脚麻□】[sou^{42}jo^{21}ma^{21}liu^{13}] 又称手脚麻利，指手脚快而利索：她～得很，一个人做嘞事相当于两个人嘞工作量。

【生拉活扯】[sen^{55}la^{55}ho^{21}ce^{42}] 强行拖拽：刚抓住的小偷想逃走，警察～把他拖到警车上。

【日混打眉】[ri^{21}huen^{13}da^{42}mi^{21}] 混日子不做任何事：这个懒汉成天～嘞哪样事情都不做。

【日天冒牯】[ri^{21}tian^{55}mao^{13}gu^{42}] 不知天高地厚，把牛吹到天上：之个娃儿～嘞哪样事情都不怕。

【日眉牯眼】[ri^{21}mi^{21}gu^{42}yian^{42}] 像眼睛睁得大大的傻子：之个娃儿～嘞哪样事情都不晓得。

【鹞子翻身】[rao^{13}zi^{42}fan^{55}sen^{55}] 翻筋斗：孙悟空一个～要打十万八千里。

【绕天绕地】[rao^{13}tian^{55}rao^{13}di^{13}] 近义词“绕山绕水”：今天下乡，～嘞起码多走咯有十多公里路。

【软烂达稀】[ruan^{42}pa^{55}da^{21}xi^{55}] 烂软过度：糍粑水多咯做得～嘞不好吃。

【歪巴咧扯】[wai^{55}ba^{55}lie^{13}ce^{42}] 样子怪，不同常规样：之个瓜儿长得～嘞。

【歪边斜垮】[wai^{55}bian^{55}xie^{21}kua^{42}] 不正，歪歪斜斜貌：之栋房子没得修好，修得～嘞。

【窝二裹三】[wo^{55}er^{13}go^{42}san^{55}] 贬义词，几个人伙在一起不干好事：你们几个经常～嘞伙在一起是搞些哪样鬼明堂。

【歪打正着】[wai^{55}da^{42}zen^{13}zo^{21}] 不经意间做成另一件事情：一枪打出去，兔子没打着打到一只老虎，这真是～。

【挨挨擦擦】[ai^{55}ai^{55}ca^{21}ca^{21}] 有意的去挨擦别人：一个流氓在公共车上看到有几个漂亮嘞女乘客，他就挤上去～嘞耍流氓动作。

【摇尔晃荡】[yao^{21}er^{55}huang^{13}dang^{13}] 摇摇晃晃：地面不平凳张桌子～嘞。

【一锭墨黑】[yi^{21}din^{13}mei^{21}hei^{21}] 指伸手不见五指的黑暗：没有月亮的夜晚野外几乎是～。

【阴头向户】[yin^{55}tou^{21}xiang^{13}fu^{13}] 指少言寡语长于心计的人：之个人话不多～嘞。

【妖言邪法】[yao^{55}yan^{21}xie^{21}fa^{21}] 装神弄鬼、妖言惑众，后泛指用迷信的言行欺骗他人的行为：那个神婆经常尽做些～嘞事情。

【焉拜屁臭】[yian^{55}bai^{55}pi^{13}cou^{13}] 同义词焉巴屁臭，主要形容植物干焉无活力，亦可形容人疲惫、无精神：大家在太阳下晒咯一天，一个个晒得～嘞。

（二）语气词

县境方言语气词数量多，虽邻近贵阳但与贵阳方言有很多不同之处，如贵阳话中的“把”、“噢”和“噻”等在县内方言中用成“都”（dou^{55}）、“咯”、“嘛”等。有的语气词功能复杂，语气不同词义不一样，有一词多义的特点。有的语气词可按一定层次叠用，特殊语境下可多个语气词叠用，最多时可达8个语气词叠用。例如：普通话“他说这中药很苦。”用方言可说成“之个中药苦得完家嘞咯嘛哈恨！”后边“得完家嘞咯嘛哈恨”8个字全属语气词。

1. 单音节

【啊】[a^{13}] 表示惊讶：～！你把玻璃杯打烂咯。

【唉】[ai^{42}] 唉叹：～！晓得猪儿要摔死早几天我就该把它卖咯换几个钱用。

【呃】[e^{21}] 表示赞同、肯定：～！就是这样做。

【诶】[ei^{42}] 提引对方注意：两熟人相遇“～！你好！”

【嘛】[ma^{42}] 祈使语气助词，带有请求的语气：你快回家来～。有时和“咯”字叠用，组成“咯嘛”：你快点走～。

【麻】[ma^{21}] 与“嘛”相近，不同的是命令的成分占多，请求的成分减少：你快点～。

【不】[bu^{21}] 用在句末表示征求意见：上车～？

【得】[de^{21}] 语气助词：你说这件事做～做不～。

【□】[lan^{55}] （音囡）用法如“呢”：你们老板～？到哪点去咯？

【嘞】[lei^{55}] “的”字方言，用在句中作结构助词，用在句末表示确定的语气。另外还可和其他语气词叠用构成不同的词义。如“嘞咯”、“嘞嘛”、“嘞哈”、“嘞兮”、“嘞话”、“嘞恨”、“嘞呃”等。

【咯】[lo^{42}] 语气助词，用法如“了”：躲猫猫“来得～”。

【喽】[lou^{42}] 用法与“咯”相近,一般用于正在进行时：过年～！放火炮～！

【哈】 ①[ha^{55}]，表示时间：一～～。②[ha^{42}]，用在内容基本肯定疑问句末：你已经大学毕业咯～？③[ha^{13}]，量词，相当于“下”：一～、两～……

【恨】[hen^{13}] 用于复述别人或自己之前说过的话末尾：他说他不读书咯～。

【兮】[xi^{55}] 语气助词，可加重前字的分量：脏～～，哭～烂包嘞。

【说】[suo^{21}] 同“恨”相近，县中、西北用得较多：他讲他不读书咯～。

【吖】[ya^{55}] 带有号召性语气助词：走回家咯～！快来吃饭咯～！

【呀】[ya^{21}] 表示惊奇：～！你都来了？

【也】[ye^{42}] 一般用在名词后加重亲昵语气：小猪～你快吃快长大。称谓助词：妈也。

【哟】[yo^{21}] 用在句首表示突发惊讶：～！我的钱被小偷摸咯。

【呦】[you^{21}] 表示诧异：～！你哪个时候进来嘞？

2. 双音节

【算咯】[suan^{13}lo^{42}] 表示放弃：～！他这种人不要和他计较。

【是嘞】[si^{13}lei^{55}] 表示赞同：～！我家住在修文县城。

【就是】[dou^{13}si^{13}] 表示肯定：偷鸡嘞偷儿～他！

【嘞话】[lei^{55}hua^{13}] 类似“如果”，不同的是“如果”用在句首，而“嘞话”用在前半句末：你不同意

~，我们大家也就不来咯。

【要得】[yao^{13}de^{21}] 表示赞同：~！我就照你说的去做。

【喔喝】[o^{21}hou^{55}] 可惜的叹息：~！鸡蛋打破咯！

【得很】[de^{21}hen^{42}] 修饰前词并加重分量：凶~、脏~。

【该哈】[gai^{55}ha^{42}] 肯定并祈求对方同意自己的观点：这个月还没有发工资~。

【幺呃】[yao^{55} e^{21}] 长辈对晚辈的昵称，并带有语重心长之意：~！你要好好读书嘞。

【介是】[gai^{13}si^{13}] 非常是：你这人~哆嗦。

【咯嘛】[lo^{42}ma^{42}] 带有急切请求的语气：你快点出来~！

【没有】[mei^{55}you^{42}] 方言同义词“没得”，是否之意，一般放在句末：你吃饭~？

【哎呦】[ai^{42}you^{42}] 表示特别诧异：~！小祖宗！你咋过给我搞得稀王八烂嘞？

3. 多音节

【就是嘛】[dou^{13} si^{13} ma^{42}] 不可否定: ~！大家都乱拿不是要把公司拿垮。

【该是哈】[gai^{55}si^{13} ha^{42}] 表示肯定并祈求对方也赞同，一般在已求证之后单独使用：他家嘞母猪一窝下咯12个猪崽~。

【是不是】[si^{13} bu^{21}si^{13}] 与“对不对”相近，多为口头禅，一般用在推理结束后边：三加二减五等于零~？

【参你讲（说）】[can^{55}li^{42}jiang^{42}(suo^{21})] 发语词，一般用在句首：~！这样做要不得。

【来家嘞】[lai^{21} jia^{55}lei^{55}] 加重程度：今天晚上吃得饱完~。

【得完家嘞】[de^{21}wan^{21}jia^{55}lei^{55}] 意为很是、特别：中药苦~。

（三）特色新词

随着社会发展方言新词语产生逐步取代旧词语，新词语使用在城镇和青少年中较为普遍，在中老年人和农村等地较次后。

【噹】[dɑng^{21}] 脑震荡后遗症，思维不清，弱智，一般用作贬义。

【来电】[lai^{21}dian^{13}] 够刺激，带劲。

【黑山羊[hei^{21}san^{55}yang^{21}] 喻指心黑手辣，见到好处就捞的人。

【哈幺大[ha^{55}yao^{55}da^{13}]以扑克牌为工具的一种赌博方式，又称“金花”或“铺金花”。

【怪噜】[guai^{13}lu^{55}]一种扑克牌游戏方法。

【噜子】[lu^{55}zi^{42}] 头脑简单的人，多指骗子行骗的对象。

【葫芦】[fu^{55}lu^{55}] 喻指头脑呆笨，易于受骗上当的人。

【麻呜】[ma^{42}wu^{55}]酒醉神志不清状。

【马拉】[ma^{42}la^{55}] 形容快跑，多指逃避某事。常与“一个”搭配。例:喊他帮下忙，他一个~就跑了。

【绷面子】[bong^{55}mian^{13}zi^{42}] 讲排场。

【冒皮皮】[mao^{13}pi^{21}pi^{55}] 习铳、显摆。

【拿翻】[la^{21}fan^{55}] 制服，击败。

【搅统】[jiao^{42}tong^{42}] 完全、彻底制服。

【渣渣妹】[za^{55}za^{55}mei^{13}] 对文化修养差的姑娘的贬称。

【鸡婆】[ji^{55}po^{21}] 妓女。

【岩山货】[ai^{42}san^{55}ho^{13}] 乡巴佬。

【土老肥】[tu^{42}lao^{42}fei^{21}] 即土豪，没素质的暴发户。

【滑竿】[hua^{21}gan^{55}] 原指钓鱼人没有收获，后泛指生意人一笔生意都未做成。常与“挑、抬”等搭配。例：今天一个客人都不得，抬~喽。

【刷子】[sua^{21}zi^{42}] 本事，独到的技能。例：人家~硬，不得两~敢来接招不是?

【窝脚】[wo^{55}jo^{21}] 表示用脚猛踢的动量词。例：他一~脚就把门豥（zua^{21}）烂咯。

【崴货】[wai^{42}ho^{13}] 假冒伪劣商品。

【玩茶叶】[wan^{21}ca^{21}yei^{55}] 弄虚作假，欺骗别人。

【扫地出门】[sao^{42}di^{13}cu^{21}men^{21}] 赶走或解聘人。

【簸锣】[bo^{42}lo^{21}] 原指破锣，后泛指即将报废的汽车或机器等。

【背死】[bei^{13}si^{42}] 公守同盟：他俩~了的，不要想从他们那里打听到任何信息。

【唠七】[lao^{21}qi^{21}] 饶舌，夸夸其谈。

【唠七混杂】[lao^{21}qi^{21}hen^{13}za^{21}] 混乱、嘈杂的局面。

【飘】[piao^{55}] 在社会上浪荡、玩乐。

【叫雀】[jiao^{13}qio^{21}] 有本事且好表现的人。

【弹】[tan^{21}] 很出色：老板宝马车好~哦。

【弹起】[tan^{21}qi^{42}] 鼓励人的意思。与川话“雄起”相似。

【捡底】[jian^{42}di^{42}] 收拾别人的残局。

【□（音喷）杆】[pen^{55}gan^{55}] 靠山，背景。

【醒水】[xin^{42}sui^{42}] 突然明白了某事内中的奥秘，特指受骗清醒没有上当。

【捉鸡】[zuo^{21}ji^{55}] 麻将术语，常说“打捉鸡麻将”。

【吃软饭】[ci^{21}ruan^{42}fan^{13}] 男人靠女人生活。

【摩的】[mo^{55}di^{55}] 摩托车做的出租车。

【跰的】[pai^{55} di^{55}] 残疾人出租车。

【猫腻】[mao^{55}li^{13}] 不可告人的利益。

【铲铲】[cuancuan] 常用于玩笑、调侃语的否定：你晓得个~。

【做秀】[zuoxiu] 做表面工作：他这样是~给领导看的。

【脑筋闪电】[lao^{42}jin^{55}san^{42}dian^{13}] 指头脑一瞬间出点问题做错事：~把事情搞砸了。

【脑筋短路】[lao^{42}jin^{55}duan^{42}lu^{13}] 意与闪电相近。

【脑壳进水】[lao^{42}ko^{21}jin^{13}sui^{42}] 白痴。

【老鬼】[lao^{42} gui^{42}] 对老年人调侃式的称谓。

【优惠】[you^{55}hui^{13}] 商家给顾客让利，包括降低价格、提高商品质量和服务质量等。

【打折】[da^{42}zei^{42}] 一般指商品降价卖。

【回扣】[hui^{21}kou^{13}] 乙方从甲方所付款项中提取一定比例返还给甲方关键人，称为“吃回扣”。

【擩红包】[ru^{55}hong^{21}bao^{55}] 擩即塞，求人办事要给红包：不~事情就办不成。

【二气】[er^{13}qi^{13}] 憨气和铳气的合称，义为又憨又傻还要招摇显摆：这娃儿傻得巴叽嘞还要刁铳，好~哦。

第二节 民 俗

一、岁时节日

1978年，县境沿袭原有节日，主要有元旦节、春节、妇女节、劳动节、青年节、儿童节、建党节、建军节和国庆节。其中，春节休假3天，元旦节、劳动节和国庆节各休假1天，妇女节、青年节和儿童节涉及人群各休假半天或1天，建军节不休假组织有关人员召开座谈会。农历节日中的元宵节、清明节、四月八、端午节、六月六、中元节、中秋节和重阳节等在机关单位、学校、医院和厂矿基本淡出，仅在农村有部分时兴，多不敢公开活动。进入20世纪80年代，人们思想逐步放开，传统的农历节日逐渐成为生活中的主要岁时节日。从2000年开始，元旦节、春节、劳动节和国庆节被定为法定假日，除元旦节休假1天外其余3个假日休假各3天，加上调整前后两个双休日，就形成每年有3个连续7天的长假。2008年，清明节、端午节、中秋节增为国家法定节假日，各休假1天，同时“五一节”休假由3天调整为1天，每年只有有春节和国庆两个连续7天的长假。

（一）传承节日

1. 农历节日

春节 为县境城乡居民一年中最为隆重的节日，俗称过年。时间以每年农历正月初一为主，涉及前后一个半月，这段时间称之为春节期间。整个过程从上年冬至开始，特别是在农村，群众非常重视春节前的准备工作。冬至以后开始杀年猪炕腊肉。腊月初八煮黄豆祭大佛做豆豉，之后做甜酒，打糍粑、饵块粑，做新衣。腊月二十三祭灶神，并彻底打扫室内外卫生，称为“打扬尘”。腊月二十八赶校（音：较）场，购买春节所需物品。腊月最后1天（二十九或三十日），白天贴门神、春联、年画和挂灯笼；晚上称除夕，阖家团圆吃年夜饭，讲究的人家这一顿饭要吃过午夜12点钟，称“一顿饭吃要两年”；饭后晚辈祝长辈“新年快乐，恭喜发财！”长辈给晚辈发压岁钱，数额1至5元不等；之后通宵不眠，围炉谈天，称“守年老者”（守岁）。正月初一起，机关单位放假3天。初一到十五，亲朋好友相互拜年，新婚夫妇回娘家、走亲戚，民间组织耍龙灯、玩花灯、猜灯谜等活动，男女老少沉浸在一片隆重、祥和的节日气氛中，一直要持续到正月十五元宵节。有很多人认为过完元宵才算过完春节，有的机关单位要过元宵

春节贴春联

节后工作才完全步入常态，大部分农家要过元宵节后才开始准备春耕生产，相当的农民工要过元宵节后才返城务工。

1983年起，中央电视台开始举办首届春节联欢晚会后，一般除夕晚年夜饭不需要吃过午夜，多在傍晚6至7点钟开始吃年夜饭，饭后长辈发压岁钱，数额逐年成倍增长，最多的发数百上千。8点钟起全家观看春节联欢晚会节目，过年守年老者多数改为打麻将，午夜零时燃放烟花爆竹，家家华灯高照，灯火通明，以示辞旧迎新。从2000年开始，机关单位春节放假采用调休的办法，将春节3天法定假日和前后两周双休日调整到一起，共放假7天，称为“春节长假”。

元宵节 农历正月十五元宵节，又称为上元节，是春节之后第一个重要节日，是新年中第一个月圆之夜，也是春节后的第一个阖家团圆的日子，反映人们对即将结束新春佳节的眷恋。根据民俗，早晨全家在一起吃汤圆，下午准备丰盛的晚宴，阖家团圆，称作过大年，晚上为新逝亲人上坟亮灯。一些单位和社会团体还开展元宵灯展活动，人们观灯猜灯谜。民间进行耍龙灯、玩花灯等活动，结束后深夜将龙灯、花灯火化祭神，表示一年的新春佳节告结。

清明节上坟

清明节 农历二十四节气中“清明”这一天称为清明节，多在公历的4月5日前后。节期较长，一般以清明前10天和后10天都属清明节期间。是一个祭祖、扫墓的节气，在农村普遍给已逝亲人上坟挂青，有的人家给祖坟垒土、立碑，有的家族举办清明会，聚集阖族祭祖、议事。机关、学校、驻军给烈士扫墓，借以缅怀先烈，进行革命传统教育。2008年，清明节正式成为法定节假日，机关单位放假1天。2009年起，采取调休的办法调为3天，称为“小长假”。

四月八苗族跳场

四月八 农历四月初八，主要是少数民族的传统节日。苗族称之为祭祖节，届时苗族群众自动聚集到预定的地点祭祀祖先，并辅之以多彩的歌舞，称之为“跳场”。部分苗族青年还要赶赴到省城贵阳喷水池参加纪念民族英雄祝狄弄的活动。节日期间也是苗族青年相互交流和未婚青年谈婚论嫁的日子。布依族称四月八为牛王节，是纪念耕牛辛劳的节日，这天家家要吃“牛王粑”和糯米饭，并用糯米饭或糯米粑喂牛。

端午节包粽子

端午节 农历五月初五端午节，又称端阳节。是日，城乡居民普遍吃粽子；人们清晨在大门两边挂菖蒲、艾蒿，以示驱邪除魔；年轻人相约游山玩水，称作“游百病”，谓之可祛除百病；相传端午节这一天百草皆是药，有人在野外采回千里光、三角枫和陈艾等中草药熬水洗浴，治疗皮肤病和蚊虫咬伤确有奇效。2008年，端午节正式成为法定节假日，机关单位放假1天。2009年起，采取调休的办法调为放假3天。

六月六 农历六月初六是布依族祭祀祖先的隆重节日。届时布依族群众杀猪宰羊，做粑粑祭祀祖先，祈求先祖保佑子孙延续、五谷丰登、平安幸福。布依族是个喜欢唱歌的民族，每逢六月六这天，大家都从四面八方赶赴“六月六歌会”引吭高歌，一些未婚男女青年借此对歌寻偶。

六月六歌会

中元节 亦称七月半，县境多数人习惯为农历七月十三。民间相传是祖先及已故亲人亡魂回家探亲的时间。初夜，亡者的后人要为其在家门前焚烧纸钱，讲究人家要将所烧纸钱用白纸封好并按专门格式写上亡者称谓姓名（如同邮寄包裹），传说这样做是专烧给自己祖先及已故亲人亡魂的纸钱不致被其他亡魂抢走，通称为“烧包袱”。有的还要用锡箔纸折成的金银锞和纸制车、马等一并焚烧，传说是送祖先灵魂去赶阴曹丰都十五日盂兰大会，借以早升天界。

中秋节 农历八月十五日，人们习惯吃月饼过中秋节，以示亲人团聚。2008年，中秋节正式成为法定节假日，机关单位放假1天。因与国庆节放3天假相近，一般年份将两个假期合并与双休日调整共休假7天。

重阳节 农历九月初九，原本为秋收后的第一个节日，在农村要用当年产的新糯米打糍粑、做甜酒，传说“重阳所酿甜酒，终年不会发酸变味”。如遇秋高气爽天气，人们还相约结伴到郊外爬山登高望远，故又称为“九九登高节”。1988年国家将重阳节定名为“中国老年节”，重阳敬老越来越受到全社会关注。

2. 公历节日

元旦节 每年元月1日，放假1天。从2000年开始，加上调整邻近双休日，共放假3天，其活动内容有的单位是召开迎新年座谈会，总结过去安排来年工作。广大农村多不时兴过元旦节。

妇女节 每年3月8日，妇女放假半天，届时县妇联等单位要组织妇女开展活动和表彰先进。

劳动节 每年5月1日，原放假1天。届时或由县委、县政府组织表彰先进的活动，或由县总工会组织工人代表座谈会，号召广大职工再接再厉为改革开放和现代化建设建功立业。1989年，县红旗煤矿工人宋均成被评选为“全国劳动模范”，到北京出席全国“五一”表彰大会，荣获“五一劳动”奖章。2000年起至2007年假期改为法定假日3天，加上调整两个星期的双休日，共放假7天，称“五一长假”。其间，很多人选择外出旅游，时值旅游旺季，出现景区景点游客爆满。2008年法定假日又改为1天，加上调整邻近双休日，共放假3天，改称为“五一小长假”。外出旅游的人们多选择本地或就近旅游。

青年节 每年5月4日，14岁以上青年放假半天，一般情况下由共青团县委牵头组织青年开展“学雷锋，树新风”活动，还评选“先进团组织”和“优秀共青团员”予表彰。1990年开始，青年节这天有高中的学校还要组织年满18周岁的学生举行成人仪式，号召青年发扬爱国主义精神，以主人翁姿态努力创造美好的明天。

儿童节 每年6月1日，主要是小学生的节日，届时小学放假1天，由学校组织开展丰富多彩的庆祝活动。1982年起，县内的一些机关、团体和企业在这天还要向本单位职工家庭14岁以下的孩子馈赠礼物。2000年起，县妇联、团县委和关心下一代协会均分头下到各地小学和幼儿园去看望儿童，特别为外出打工家庭的留守儿童送去节日礼品，让孩子们度过最愉快的一天。

建党节 每年7月1日为中国共产党诞辰纪念日。届时，县内各级党组织均结合实际围绕主题开展各种形式的纪念活动，表彰“先进基层党组织”“优秀共产党员”和“优秀党务工作者”。每逢十年大庆，举办的纪念活动更为隆重，内容更加丰富。

建军节 每年8月1日，为中国人民解放军诞生纪念日，届时开展“拥军爱民”活动，由县委牵头慰问境内驻军部队和军、烈属，广泛宣传国防知识，增强全民国防意识。有的年份还开展军地联欢活动，以军民团结、无坚不摧的精神，在建设国防和发展经济的征程中攻坚克难，夺取更大的胜利。转业军人和复员退伍军人较多的单位还召开座谈会，号召大家继续发扬革命军人的优良作风，在各自的岗位上做好所担负的工作。

国庆节 每年10月1日为中华人民共和国华诞。原放假1天，机关单位及学校组织各种形式的庆祝活动，每年一小庆，十年一大庆。从2000年起改为法定假日3天，加上调整两个星期的双休日，共放假7天，称“十一长假”。国庆期间邻近传统节日中秋节，2008年起中秋节被列为法定节日，公休1天。有的职工在此期间利用统一调休结合个人调休将休假调整为10天以上，以便外出旅游。

（二）新兴节日

植树节 从1979年开始，每年3月12日定为植树节，在植树节前后一周期间，县林业部门组织机关、企事单位干部、职工以及学校师生上山义务植树造林，绿化环境、美化家园。

教师节 1985年开始，每年9月10日定为教师节，学校放假1天。届时，县委、县政府及教育行政部门均组织召开教师座谈会、教师大会，表彰优秀教师和先进教育工作者，倡导全社会尊师重教，发展教育。

母亲节 每年5月的第二个星期日为母亲节。2007年5月上旬，县妇女联合会发出号召，倡议母亲节这一天，子女送给母亲鲜花、蛋糕等礼物，回家看望母亲、料理家务，让母亲过一个快乐节日。此后每年，特别是大多数的青少年都以送礼物、发祝福短信等方式表达自己感谢母亲的养育之恩。

父亲节 每年6月的第三个星期日为父亲节，2007年随母亲节后兴起，其方式与母亲节大致相同。

（三）舶来节日

情人节 受西方文化影响，2000年后在县内逐渐兴起。每年2月14日这天，有的情人男女互赠礼物、互发祝福短信，相约聚会晚餐。因其属合法婚姻以外的男女关系而招致社会非议，故只流行在少部分中、青年男女中。

圣诞节 本为西方基督教节日，每年12月25日耶稣诞辰纪念日。1982年恢复宗教信仰自由政策后，主要在信奉耶稣教徒中时兴。1986年，扎佐天主教恢复活动后，其教徒主要在扎佐圣母堂举行圣诞节活动。届时县境天主教信徒齐聚教堂，凌晨举行子夜弥撒，然后读《圣经》、唱赞美诗和祷告等。2000年后，圣诞节活动逐渐扩展到县内非基督教徒中，成为一种时尚节日，但仅限于在城镇少数青年人中时兴，活动不进教堂，不读《圣经》，只是仿西方人在圣诞夜互送礼物、聚会进餐。

二、生活习俗

（一）服饰

1. 服装款式

20世纪70年代末，衣着款式主要流行中山服、四个兜的干部服和劳动布工作服，其次为青年服和夹克衫等。农村也有穿手工缝制的对襟衣和父母装的。部分赶新潮的年轻人穿西装，但为数不多。内衣以白衬衣为主，另有海魂衫、白汗衫、棉毛衫和运动衫等。下装以筒裤为主，另有少数西式短裤，亦有女式百褶裙等。冬装流行毛领短大衣，内衣有棉衣、棉裤和用毛线、纱线手工编织的衣、裤及背心。当时的大翻领服和细筒裤被视为奇装异服，人们多与所谓流氓阿非服装联系在一起。

80年代，青年服和夹克衫逐渐成为主流，西装也逐渐增多，服装款式更新加快，新增款式比较具有代表性的主要有拼接式夹克、喇叭裤、锥子裤等，其中大喇叭裤被视为奇装异服。内衣中款式新颖的棉毛衫人们习惯称其为“港衫”，机织毛衣、毛裤逐步取代手工编织的毛衣、毛裤。冬装中流行呢料大衣、滑雪衫等。80年代后期，在青少年中又流行牛仔衣和牛仔裤。

20世纪80年代老式服装

90年代以后，服装款式向多元化发展，主要流行的有休闲服、夹克衫、牛仔服等。下装有直筒裤、老板裤，西装裤、小喇叭裤和牛仔裤等。冬装有太空服、羽绒服、皮大衣、皮夹克和皮裤等。内衣有羊毛衫、羊绒衫和驼绒衫等。中小学校服流行运动衫。

2000年后，服装款式更是琳琅满目，数不胜数，各种服装在原基本款式的基础上从花色、面料和设计上都有很大突破。有根据不同花色、面料设计各种不同的装饰，有利用印染技术配上各种不同的文字和图案，还有体现自然、运动、军事、警察、休闲和潇洒等元素，有适合各个年龄段人群的各种款式：有适合青少年穿的迷彩服和运动装，有适合各种不同职业人群的工作服、校服，有男女老少皆宜的长、短袖T恤衫，有穿着舒适、暖和和美观的保暖内衣等，其中女式服装和儿童服装较为突出，女装上衣除冬装外领口设计多为“V”领，较有代表性的是蝙蝠衫，下装流行穿牛仔裤和健美裤，以体现女性的曲线美；儿童装富于变化，不仅色彩斑斓，而且突出儿童的天真烂漫及科幻、卡通形象等。

2. 材质面料

20世纪70年代末，服装的材质面料称为布料，以棉质居多，间有绦纶和毛料等，市面供不应求，国家对棉布、棉花实行定量供应，其标准为每人每年发布票1丈5尺7寸（5.23米）、棉花票3市斤（1.5公斤）。80年代，涤纶纺织品增多，布料由天然向化纤方向发展，逐步满足市场需求。1984年国家取消布票和棉花票，实行敞开供应。90年代，先后出现毛纤、麻纤、冰丝、棉麻和棉纤等各种合成纤维布料，既结实耐用，又具有天然纤维通透性好的特点，逐步取代原涤纶纺织品。2000年后，人们生态、环保意识增强，时尚天然纤维制品，纯棉、纯毛、真丝、亚麻等面料最为抢手，混纺面料次之，纯化纤不再受人欢迎。

3. 鞋袜

鞋类　20世纪70年代末，主要有解放鞋、篮球鞋、网球鞋、白边鞋和塑料凉鞋等。农村仍有人穿手

20世纪80年代流行的鞋子

工制作的布鞋、棉鞋。皮鞋在当时被视为奢侈品，其种类主要有黑皮鞋和反帮皮鞋。80年代，流行足球鞋和白边鞋，皮鞋类品种逐步增多，不再属奢侈品。面料主要有猪、牛皮革和人造革。黑皮鞋款式多样化，反帮皮鞋逐步退出历史舞台。扎佐皮鞋厂生产的皮鞋种类较多，其中“三节头皮鞋”和“毛皮鞋”较为抢手。90年代，流行旅游鞋、运动鞋、休闲鞋等，皮鞋也较普遍，大量外地生产的皮鞋进入县内市场，款式新颖多样，扎佐皮鞋不再受人们喜爱。2000年后，鞋类式样翻新，品种名目繁多。女鞋主要有高跟鞋、平跟鞋、筒靴、帆布鞋、伯妈鞋、松糕鞋、休闲鞋等；男鞋主要有正装皮鞋、休闲鞋、帆布鞋、工装鞋等。人们除讲究鞋子的材质、样式和舒适度外，还较注重品牌。这一时期较有名的鞋类品牌主要有百丽、哈森、奥卡索、奥康、骆驼、红蜻蜓、鳄鱼恤、哥雷夫、花花公子、富贵鸟、康奈、蜘蛛王和金猴等。

袜子　70年代末80年代初，较普遍的是棉纱袜，时尚一点的有尼龙袜和腈纶袜。90年代，有高弹力丝光袜和棉纤混织的合成袜，其中棉纤合成袜更受人们喜欢。2000年后，袜类品种式样繁多，人们追求健康、环保，对袜子要求透气、吸汗、无臭味，纯棉袜最受人们喜爱。这一时期较为时尚的袜子主要体现在女性方面，主要有无跟袜、中筒袜、长筒袜、腿袜、裤袜、加厚裤袜等，颜色主要有黑色和肉色两种。

4. 发型帽冠

20世纪70、80年代流行的帽子

20世纪70年代末，男式发型以短发为主，主要有平头、运动头，小分头、一风梳（又称一块瓦）和背头等，间或有个别发长齐颈者称之为“大背头”，人们将其视为二流子发型。女式发型中，较长的主要有双后辫和单后辫；中长的主要有双前辫、双刷把、侧刷把，其中双刷把中的懒刷把又称上海式较为时尚；较短的主要有齐耳型和接近于男性分头的运动头。烫发较为时尚，方法主要有热烫和化学烫两种，男式烫发用电吹风热烫，主要是在小分头和一风梳留发较长的基础上进行小波浪或大波浪造型和定型；女式烫发多用化学烫发，发型多以大波浪和小波浪为主。帽冠主要有军帽、鸭舌帽，冬季流行雷锋帽。女生头饰用品主要以发针、发夹为主。

80年代，在青年人中出现男生港式长发，“大背头”已少有人指责；女式发型以中短型为主，辫子发型逐渐减少，后扎式刷把型渐次增多。男生戴帽逐渐减少，中青年女生烫发焗油者逐渐增多。90年代，焗油染发成为一种时尚，穿戴金银首饰逐渐增多，但机关单位很少有人佩戴。

2000年后，男式发型中出现毛栗头，其型犹如山中毛栗，毛发七长八短，最时尚拉风的要数莫干西式，发脚高而短，顶发特长，有人称其为马桶盖式。境内男士除少数追求时尚发型外，多数仍喜欢传统发型。在县城传统发型理发店经常顾客爆满、应接不暇，而时尚理发店主要以焗油染发为主。这一时期女生染发成为时尚，颜色有棕、黄、红、白和蓝等，棕色较为普遍，给人以美感；其他几种颜色仅在少数青年人中流行，给人感觉特别另类。帽冠主要类型有遮阳帽、棒球帽、礼帽和毛线帽等，一般只在外出或户外活动时穿戴，老年人戴帽者居多，尤以冬天为其。

（二）饮食

1. 主食

县境居民主食大米，玉米和面粉次之。1978年，城镇人口统一按标准定量按月供应，粗细粮比例大米占60%，玉米和面粉各占20%。日均定量重体力劳动者550至880克，轻体力劳动者450至550克，区社干部500克，一般干部和中学生450克，县城居民383至416克，乡镇居民367至400克，10周岁以下儿童120至350克。城镇人口粮食供应坚持节约基本能满足消费，个别特殊情况家庭稍有欠缺，但通过申请议价粮或在自由市场购买少量也基本能解决问题。农村情况各异，城关、扎佐、久长水稻产区主食大米，小箐、六广主食玉米。口粮靠集体分配，各地每年人均120—200公斤不等，日均330至550克。由于村民大部分从事体力劳动，加上副食品短缺，劳动人口日消耗量较城镇人口大，日均消耗口粮400至600克，特别是重体力劳动者日食口粮需750—1000克以上。大部分地区主粮不够就用杂粮代替，杂粮与主粮的折算一般是薯类5折1，其余为2折1。如遇灾害年景，青黄不接时靠国家回销粮接济，接济不上就只得减少每日消费量，当时农民最大的希望就是“吃饱肚子”。1982年实行联产承包责任制后，粮食产量逐年增加，到1985年基本满足农村人口粮食需要。

1993年，取消城镇居民粮食供应制度，全面放开粮食市场，呈现购销两旺的局面。粮食供应不仅满足全县人口消费需要，而且原主食玉米的小箐、洒坪、六广、大石和六桶等地居民也逐步改为主食大米。由于副食品日渐丰富，日人均消耗口粮300—500克。生活上人们讲究不仅要吃饱而且要吃好，主食大米普遍强调其口感，对品种的选择上尤为重要，口感好的品种与口感差的品种价格相差30%—50%。

2000年后，外地各种优质大米输入县内市场，泰国香米、东北大米和省内的平坝大米争相入市。县内相当一部分原种粮的农民不种粮食改种经济价值高的农作物，连自已要吃的大米都在市场上购买。这一时期，由于副食品非常丰富，人们主食量普遍大减，人均每日消耗口粮仅200—300克。大米虽为主食，但过去不被人们看好的玉米和荞麦等杂粮又被视为能调节口味和对身体有益的食粮，加工好的玉米饭和荞麦面价格要比普通大米价格高出50%—100%以上。

2. 副食品

20世纪70年代末，县内产出的副食种类有猪肉、禽蛋、动物油、植物油、大豆制品和粉条等；外地传入在商店销售的有猪肉罐头、水果罐头、奶粉、代乳粉、海带、咸鱼等。为解决供不应求的问题，国家采取对城镇居民消费的猪肉、食用油等主要副食品实行定量供应的办法，其标准为每人每月猪肉0.5公斤、菜油0.4公斤，1980年菜油增为0.5公斤；在农村对油菜籽和生猪实行统购和派购政策，油菜籽完成统购任务后余下的部分分配给农民，生猪实行“购五留五”派购，即1头猪的1半按统一牌价交售给国家，另1半农民自己留下食用。80年代中期，各种副食产品产量增加，人们生活必需的副食品逐步实现保障供应，1985年2月取消农产品统派购政策，放开实行自由买卖。

90年代，各种副食产品产量大大增加，外地副食产品也大量销入县内，而且种类繁多，猪、羊、牛、鸡、鸭、鱼等肉类产品应有尽有，人们随时都可买到。特别是1996年县划属贵阳市管辖后，政府提出要抓好群众的“菜篮子工程”，保障社会需求，致人民生活水平得到显著提高。当时有很多人都感受到：过去要逢年过节才能吃到的东西，今天平时都能摆上餐桌。

2000年后，农副产品的生产和销售进一步改善，县内生产的蔬菜大量销往外地，外地副食产品也大量拥入县的市场，家常蔬菜、特色蔬菜、反季节蔬菜、猪牛羊肉、禽类蛋肉、生猛海鲜、珍禽野味和各种乳制产品在市场上均可买到。这一时期，人们吃讲“科学、环保”，提倡“少吃油肉多吃菜”，吃蔬菜还要选择使用农家肥生产的，禽蛋要买土生土长的，吃肉要吃低脂肪高蛋白的，故牛羊肉价格要比猪肉价格高1至2倍。农村群众与城镇居民食用副食品的差距越来越小，部分还有超过的趋势。

3. 风味食品

（1） 腊肉

每年冬至后至春节前，将猪肉用食盐腌制后再经柴火烘烤除去水分而成，使其能防腐、耐贮藏，因其多在春节前的腊月间制成，故称“腊肉”。好的腊肉肥瘦参半，肥肉亮而半透明，瘦肉红润。其味咸香，肥而不腻，风味独特。

（2）糍粑

将糯米蒸熟后由人工用木棍或木槌将其捣融制成的食品，因其新鲜时滋粘，故称为“糍粑”。其味香甜，是当地人喜爱的美食。农村居民逢年过节都要做糍粑吃，并作为招待客人的上好食品。

（3）饵块粑

用粳米做成，做法与做糍粑类似，20世纪80年代中期改用粑粑机制作。其味香而不粘，口感好，是人们喜爱的又一美食。80年代以前只在冬季腊月制作供春节期间食用，市面少有，其后逐渐发展到全年均可买到。

（4）黄粑

原料主要是玉米、糯米和大豆。玉米作用于上色，糯米作用于糍粘调节口感，大豆作用于调节甜味，关键是大豆的多少，多了黄粑不收旱，少了甜味不够。做法是先将玉米洗净磨细去皮，糯米洗净滤干，大豆磨成浆；再将3种材料拌和均匀捏成团，用玉米棒子叶包裹扎紧上甑蒸熟。蒸黄粑先用大火蒸

风味食品腊肉、糍粑、二块粑、黄粑、粽粑和泡粑

透，再用小火焖蒸8至10小时，待蒸出黄色即成。做得好的黄粑味甜滋润可口，20世纪80年代只在春节备作节日食品，之后成为商品进入市场随时均可买到。

(5) 粽粑

亦称棕子，糯米为主料。做法是先将糯米洗净滤干，再用粽粑叶（箬竹叶）将其包裹成型，再经蒸或煮熟即成。其形状有圆锥形称尖尖粽，近似方形的称为狗头粽。糯米有加火腿、腊肉、花生等佐料，其味香甜可口。粽粑是季节性食品，每年端午节前后制作食用。

(6) 泡粑

亦称发粑或发糕。用籼米、玉米和荞麦等做成，做法是先将原料磨成浆，再用适量酵母发酵后上甑蒸熟即成。蒸熟后切块的叫泡粑，用小圆形模具定型蒸熟的叫碗耳糕，用玉米叶包裹蒸熟的叫枝江苞谷粑粑，用荞麦面做的叫荞粑粑。此类食品清香酸甜，可口宜人。

(7) 霉豆腐

亦称豆腐乳。用新鲜豆腐切成4至5厘米见方的小块，任其自然发酵一星期左右，取出用白酒浸泡后包裹上一层用辣椒、花椒、山奈、八角等做成的调料，装入容器密封一星期后即成。其味香辣、回味绵长，并具有开胃、去火、调味的功能。

(8) 泡菜

用泡菜水浸泡经发酵可直接食用的蔬菜称泡菜。泡菜水又称为盐水，是用适量新鲜的花椒（或花椒叶）、冰糖、食盐和凉开水做成，有的还用红色胭脂萝卜皮一起泡，使其颜色更好看。可腌制泡菜的蔬菜有白萝卜、红萝卜、新鲜红辣椒、大蒜、蒜薹、葱头、葱果、嫩豇豆、莲花白和黄瓜等。泡菜酸碎可口，维生素丰富，具有开胃健脾功能。

(9) 糟辣角

亦称糟辣椒。用新鲜红辣椒洗净滤干，宰碎后加食盐、大蒜和生姜，再装入扑水坛中密封发酵一星期后即成。糟辣椒色泽鲜红，鲜香酸辣，风味独特，可单独成菜，亦可作凉拌菜、炒菜和下面条等的调料。深受人们喜爱，老少皆宜。

(10) 盐菜

亦称腌菜。原料以大头菜为主，大头菜块茎最佳，叶次之，另外芥菜科蔬菜和萝卜也都可做盐菜。做法是先将原材料洗净晾干，切碎后加食盐密封腌渍一星期后即成。其味咸酸可口，可凉拌，亦可煎炒和汆汤，还可与其他菜品烹调，其中盐菜肉（扣肉）和盐菜炒腊肉具有非常独特的地方风味。

(11) 酸菜

原料以芥菜科青菜为主，白菜次之。先将原材料洗净滤干，水开后将其入水焯至变色捞出，随即装入容器稍微压实，加入适量原质酸汤后盖严，置放在20℃环境下放置10至12小时即成。其味酸甜青碎，

风味食品霉豆腐、泡菜、糟辣椒、盐菜和酸菜

可凉拌、煮汤，亦可与其他菜品烹调，其中酸菜煮小豆是当地素菜中的佳品。

（12）麻糖

亦称“饴糖”，俗称“麻汤”，因用麦芽催化故又有称“麦芽糖”。用干燥、纯净、无杂质的玉米或大米、小麦等做原料。做法是先将原料粉碎除去糠皮，然后放入大锅中加水像煮稀粥似的煮熬，待完全熟透后将适量切碎的麦芽放进去使其糖化，糖化完成汤质变清后取出过滤，再将过滤下来的清水煎熬浓缩，最后得到深褐色的饴糖（俗称“秦糖”）。饴糖起锅后不断进行拉扯，使其颜色变成乳白色即成麻糖。其味香而不艳，甜而不腻，回味绵长。同时还具有消食化气的功效。

（13）甜酒

用上好的糯米作原料。先将糯米洗净，上甑蒸熟后取出散开，待温度降至23℃左右时加入适量甜酒曲拌匀，用容器盛装盖好保温，放置在25℃的环境中发酵1至2天即成。做得好的甜酒闻而清香扑鼻，视则汤质清澈透明，食之甜而浸脾，有琼浆玉液之感。

（14）洋芋粉条

用优质马铃薯淀粉为主要原料，经冲芡、和面、漏粉、煮粉、晾干等工艺制作而成。烹调时用开水将干粉条泡软，放入做好的汤菜中即可食用，其口感滑而不腻，绵而味爽，较其他材料制成的粉条更为爽口。

风味食品麻糖、甜酒和洋芋粉条

4. 风味小吃

县境地处黔中，小吃与省城贵阳类似，有不少小吃风味独特。

（1）汤臊类

主要有牛肉粉、羊肉粉、肠旺面、辣鸡面、大排面、砂锅粉、脆臊粉（面）、肉末粉和老素粉等。其中，扎佐牛肉粉味香汤鲜，修文肠旺面、辣鸡面、大排面味浓爽口，深受人们喜欢。

（2）凉吃类

主要有米豆腐、豌豆凉粉、荞凉粉、凉面、米皮、春卷（丝娃娃）、冰粉、莲子银耳汤等。

（3）油炸类

主要有油炸豆沙粑、油炸豆腐圆子、油炸豆腐干、油炸洋芋、油炸洋芋片等

（4）烙锅类

臭豆腐、煎包、韭菜烙饼、洋芋粑等。六广臭豆腐外陋内秀，闻起来臭，吃起来香气四溢，回味绵长，一经品味，常令人欲罢不能，一尝为快。

（5）烧烤类

烧糯苞谷、烤红苕、烤鸡、烤鱼、烤羊肉、烤糍粑、烧洋芋、烤豆腐果等。

5. 饮品

(1) 酒类

县境城乡一直保留有“无酒不成席”的习惯，凡遇逢年过节和喜庆均要喝酒。20世纪70年代末，酒类以本地产散装白酒为主，瓶装酒多为外地输入，主要有安酒、平坝窖酒、葡萄酒和贵阳啤酒等。80年代酒类生产政策逐步放开，县内各家酒厂大量生产白酒的同时，农村个体户也加入到白酒生产行列，县内酒厂生产的阳明大曲、三潮老窖和桂花酒一度畅销，六广酒厂生产的苞谷酒也受人青睐。这一时期，外地生产的黔春酒、鸭溪窑、董酒、习酒、金沙酒、泸州大曲和竹叶青等和国酒茅台也相继销进县内。90年代，本地酒厂因管理不善逐渐停产，白酒生产多为散装白酒，瓶装酒完全被外地酒占据市场。进入21世纪，散装白酒市场以本地生产的白酒为主，也有所谓的散装茅酒销售；瓶装酒多以黔中、黔北和川南地区生产的白酒为主。这一时期，还兴饮泡酒，即用强肾补气的中药材或维生素C含量高的水果浸泡散装白酒，其中有名的泡酒有人参枸杞酒、天麻杜仲酒，首乌生地酒、猕猴桃酒、刺梨酒、杨梅酒和拐枣酒等，这类酒既经济又实惠，口感好又养生，很受饮酒爱好者喜欢。

(2) 茶类

苦丁茶树和茶叶

茶叶为大部分家庭必备饮品，除家人自己饮用外还以茶待客。县境大部分地区盛产茶叶，茶类主要品种有绿茶、苦丁茶、老鹰茶和菊花茶等。20世纪70年代末，县内产茶除本地消费外还收购外销。当地吃茶除泡饮外还有煨茶，特别在农村比较流行。农村大部分人家都有1个专门煨茶用的砂质茶罐，容量2500毫升左右。用时先将适量茶叶放入罐中，再盛上2000毫升左右的清水，置于炉火上烧煮，待水烧开1至2分钟取下即可饮用。一般人家1天可煨1至2罐茶，可趁热饮用也可饮凉茶，客人进家首先煨新鲜茶水招待。煨茶用的茶叶一般是绿茶和苦丁茶，两种茶可单独煨也可混合煨。

80至90年代，外地的湄潭翠芽、都匀毛尖及省外的普洱茶、砣茶、铁观音、碧螺春、龙井茶等名茶相继传入县境。名茶多为茶叶爱好者喜爱，或购买作礼品馈赠亲朋好友，一般人家讲求经济实惠，习惯饮用本地绿茶和苦丁茶。

2000年后，为求时尚有的爱好饮茶者引进外地茶道技艺，购置专门的茶几、茶具，享受饮用工夫茶之乐。一般人家仍以饮用普通泡茶为主，招待客人的茶具多半由玻璃杯改为一次性杯子。原农村煨茶习惯逐渐减少，亦改成大玻璃罐泡茶。

(3) 乳品类

20世纪70年代末，境内没有乳品生产，市面仅有婴幼儿食用的全脂奶粉、炼乳和代乳粉等销售。80年代中期，贵阳产山花牛奶开始在县城销售。90年代，乌当产牛奶逐步取代山花牛奶，省外产的各种奶制品也不断进入县内市场。2003年，“好1多”牛奶生产企业入驻县境，先后在久长、扎佐、谷堡和六桶等乡（镇）建立牛奶生产基地，产品大量销往外地。与此同时，大量外地牛奶制品不断涌入县内。至2010年，境内市场销售的乳品品牌主要有好1多、山花、伊犁、蒙牛、特仑苏、津威、银鹭和娃哈哈等。

(4) 碳酸果蔬类

20世纪80年代初期，境内出现一种用红色素、碳酸水和少量酒精勾兑的饮料销售，俗称“香槟”，实为一种碳酸饮料，曾作为酒席饮料盛行一时，不几年即被可口可乐取代。80年代后期，雪碧、百事可乐、橙汁、鲜橙汁等相继出现。90年代，高橙、杏仁露、核桃露等果蔬饮料相继应市，且包装由原来的大瓶装改为小瓶装或易拉罐装。2000年开始，红牛、健力宝、王老吉、冰红茶等功能饮料相继进入县内市场。2008年，县内建起首家果汁生产企业，龙场镇的夏之行投资1000多万元创办“贵州三金圣果饮品责任有限公司”，生产猕猴桃汁产品“猕露”投入市场，产品酸甜适度，回味绵柔，并富含维生素C及人体需要的多种氨基酸和矿物质，深受消费者喜爱。至2010年，县内市面各种碳酸饮料、功能饮料和果蔬饮料品种繁多，消费者按照需要随时选购。

（三）民居

1. 城镇民居

城镇居民老式住房，多为顺街修建的一楼一底木架结构瓦房。商业区民房多为迎街面而建，一楼为店铺，有全柜型和门套柜两种铺型，柜台上装有活动铺板。地面多为石灰、泥土和石子的三合土地面，面积一般在50至100平方米左右。这种结构的房屋既可居家生活又可开铺做买卖，县内以县城居多，主要集中在中山路、民主路和阳明路等路段，健康路和南门口也有部分类式房舍。扎佐、久长、乌栗、小箐、六广和六桶等集镇也有类似民房。非商业区和背街区民房有木架板房、土墙房和石墙房，屋面大部分盖瓦少部分盖草。单位职工大部分居住砖木结构的职工宿舍。20世纪80年代修建的民房多为砖木结构，屋面为瓦房或水泥平顶房，地面多为水泥铺垫。这一时期木架板房、土墙房和石墙房基本不再修建。新修的单位职工住房多为砖混结构，每户面积40—50平方米。90年代，县城东片区开发，新修民居一般为砖混结构和框架结构，2—3层，一层均为铺面安装卷闸门或活动门，外墙贴瓷砖或水泥抹光。1992年改革单位职工住房制度，鼓励职工购买单位公有住房、集资建房和自建住房，逐步将职工住房推向市场化。21世纪初，县城东片区开发初具规模，居民自建住房多为3—6层，除一层基本为商用外，二层以上多为住宅。内部设计有客厅、饭厅、厨房、书房、储藏室、卫生间和1至3间卧室。居民重视房屋装修，地面贴地砖或铺木地板；室内墙面刮瓷粉或贴瓷砖、贴墙纸；顶上除刮瓷粉外还要吊顶塑各种造型。至2010年，住房市场化基本形成，居民多以购买商品房为主，县城内已陆续建起千禧家园、邮政花园、明河花园、翰林花园、粮贸花园和新都口岸等成熟的商品房住宅小区。

70年代的城镇民居

2. 乡村民居

乡村民房多选择在背风向阳、交通便利、地势干燥和水源有保障之地修建，特别是在公路两侧修建的民房较多。民房聚集处一般称为寨或寨子，门户多称大寨，门户少称小寨。行政村由1个大寨或多个小寨组成。老式民房主要有木架板房（亦称“高架房”）、砖墙房和土墙房，间或有少数石墙房。屋面以盖草居多，盖瓦次之。房屋户型多为“凹”形“燕窝”三开式，正中一间为“堂屋”，两侧房间称“耳间”（方言“耳干”）。燕窝正中开双扇大门进堂房，两侧开单扇门进耳间。堂屋内左右两侧又各开一门与耳间互通。无“凹”形“燕窝”的户型称为“一风梳”，多为砖、土和石墙房，开间主要有两间或3间两种。每户开1道双扇门或单扇门，部分人家另开1道后门，相邻两间之间开有1门互通。80年代新建的民房多为砖木结构平房，屋面为瓦房或水泥平顶房，地面多为水泥铺就。整幢房屋为立方体建筑，有人称其为“豆腐干式”或“火柴盒式”。90年代，农村房屋修建设计有所提高，一般为砖混结构，层高2至3层。设计采用土洋结合，古今结合，有燕窝、阳台、走廊和栏杆等。房顶虽多为平顶，但周边多砌有1米左右的女儿墙。外墙贴马赛克或各色瓷砖，女儿墙外斜面贴琉璃瓦。进入21世纪，政府大力在全县推行农村茅草房改造，资金由住户自己筹集一点、政府财政安排一点、社会捐助一点，将原茅草房改造成砖混结构住房。至2005年，全县基本消灭农村茅草房，使村民住房条件普遍改善。之后，部分已经富裕起来的农民不满足原有的住房款式，新修住房多采取别墅式样，有现代式、古今结合式和欧式等。外墙采用高级彩色涂料，室内有客厅、饭厅、厨房、麻将室、储藏室、卫生间和卧室等，并精心设计装修，建筑面积多在200平方米以上。

乡村民居

（四）家庭用具

1. 家具

传统老式家具柜类有衣柜、立柜、平柜、书柜、碗柜、床头柜等；床类有双人床、平床、花板床、四柱床和单人学生床等；桌凳类有大方桌、小方桌、圆桌、板凳、圆凳、方凳、坐箱等；架类有衣架、书架、洗脸架、碗架等。实木制作，用料多为梓木和柏杨；工艺全为榫卯结构，除达连和拉扣外忌用铁钉；式样多为方脚直腿，少有车圆、雕刻和绘画；表面涂刷生漆或油漆。家庭陪嫁女儿全套家具至少要有衣柜、平柜、碗柜、床头柜、双人床、方桌各1张和板凳4条，其余家具根据家庭情况酌情增加。家庭使用家具根据需要单独或成批制作。20世纪80年代，一批四川木工进入县境制作家具，流行川式和捷克式两种。主要有三开大立柜、独柜、平柜、书柜、落地音箱、高矮式平床、蒙板床、床头柜、梳妆台、木沙发、茶几、写字台和靠背椅等。式样讲究造型，基脚多为虎脚象腿；表面多用生漆推光漆面，有的用清漆和油漆刷面。90年代，新增家具主要有组合柜、转角柜、食品柜、电视柜、条柜、席梦思床、弹簧沙发等。21世纪初，家具制作工艺又有很大改进，多是结合房屋装修和实际需要制作。成品家具在家具商店有售，各种类型和式样不断推陈出新。用料多为人造板材，表面涂料多用聚氨酯、树脂涂料刷面。此类家具特点为工艺简单、造型美观、成本低廉，而且实用。原传统老式实木家具，虽然环保实用，但由于做工成本高，逐步被淘汰。至2010年，家具制作有改进，表面涂料由油性转向水性，还出现涂装一体化家具材料，用此种材料制作的家具，不需再涂漆，同样美观。这一时期市面有新式实木家具销售，但价格是一般家具2倍至数倍，故销售量不大。

2. 厨房器具

（1）炉具

20世纪70年代末，农村的老式炉具灶台（俗称“灶头”），是家庭生活烹调专用炉具，有专门用于冬

天取暖烤火的地火炉（又称“地炉火”），还有烹调和取暖兼用的火箱炉。城镇和厂矿居民已较普遍使用铁炉子，还有少数人家仍使用腰鼓式砂炉。80年代铁炉子向农村发展，部分使用灶台火的家庭也增加烟囱和烟管以减少室内污染。80年代后期息烽生产的回风炉传入县境，先在县城、扎佐和久长等地使用。继后县内仿制和改进生产的回风炉，其特点是干净卫生、节省燃料和热度较高。至90年代上半期，回风炉在城镇使用普遍，农村也有部分家庭购置取暖；同期在县城和扎佐等地已有家庭使用石油液化气燃气灶。90年代下半期，电器炉具开始在市面销售，有电烤箱和一些冬季取暖用的光波炉和暖风机。21世纪初，城镇液化气燃气灶使用较为普遍，原用回风炉仅为部分家庭冬季取暖。全县农村连续几年开展改灶工程，原老式灶台、地火炉和火箱炉等灶具基本淘汰，改为干净卫生的烟囱式炉灶、回风炉和液化气灶等。继后城镇炉具使用多向电器化方向发展，烹调用有微波炉、光波炉和电磁炉等，取暖用空调和各式电暖炉等。城镇炉具电器化率越来越高，广大农村也逐步改进，在一些富裕村寨和部分城乡接合部已基本达到或接近城镇水平。

（2）刀俎

20世纪70年代末，厨房刀具有菜刀（亦称薄刀）和砍刀，菜刀用于切、削食材，砍刀用于砍、剁骨头等硬物。砧板有圆形和长方形两种，材质多为皂角木做成，可存受捶、剁、砸、切各种食材。80年代初，县内流行使用的安顺菜刀以美观锋利著称。本地生产的菜刀锋利，但外观不及安顺菜刀。出现厨房辅助工具手摇绞肉机，可绞、磨肉馅、辣椒、花椒、胡椒等。90年代，市面有不锈钢菜刀销售，其身光亮美观，但不及本地菜刀锋利，多数厨师仍喜用本地铁匠定做的铁制菜刀。同期出现的厨房辅助刀具主要有刮皮器和多功能刮削器，对刮皮、拉丝较为方便。进入21世纪，四川、湖南等地菜刀相继传入县内，也曾以美观、锋利见长。多数外地菜刀除刀身光亮外仍不及本地菜刀锋利和经久耐用。这一时期，大量的塑料砧板、竹质砧板和硬木砧板涌入县内，其以轻、小、美观和实用见长，与皂角木砧板相比较为方便好用，但从环保角度远不及皂角木砧板，本地皂角木砧板在境内仍有市场。

（3）锅具

20世纪70年代末，原厨房锅具有铁锅、铝锅和砂锅等。铁锅多用铸铁铸成，分无耳和双耳两种。无耳锅有头水、二水、三水规格，功能以煮、蒸为主。直径头水锅最大在100厘米以上，三水锅较小约70厘米。双耳锅直径一般在70厘米以下，一般家庭使用较多，煎、炸、炒、煮均可。铝锅有铝铸锅和铝皮锅，口径10至40厘米，以煮、蒸为主。砂锅为黏土烧制而成，有锅、罐两大类型，口径15至40厘米，以烧、煮和炖为主。80年代，砂锅因其笨重不方便，使用家庭逐步减少。驻县内烽光厂生产的铝制高压锅普遍使用，煮饭、炖肉方便，一般人家均有。90年代，家用铁锅逐步改为单手锅，使用比双耳铁锅方便。随后厨房锅具逐步向电器化方向发展，开始使用电饭锅、电炒锅等产品。2000年后，铝制锅具逐步退出市场为不锈钢锅具所代替；铁锅种类增多，有单手炒锅、圆底锅、平底锅、不粘锅、烙锅等品种；电器锅具产品不断升级换代，主要有电饭煲、多功能压力锅、煲汤锅、热水器等。

3. 卫生器具

（1）便溺器具

20世纪70年代末，城镇居民便溺要到公共厕所，部分街道居民家庭自有简易厕所。农村为集储农家肥，每个家庭都有厕所。80年代初，县师范学校修建起带有烟囱的无臭厕所，继后有的学校、医院和单位相继仿造。90年代修建的公厕多为水冲式厕所，有的还另安装蹲便器和小便器。城镇住房制度改革后，新建住房均置有卫生间安装蹲便器或坐便器。21世纪初，全县农村连续几年开展改造厕所工程，将原来的简易厕所改造为“厕所+沼气池”的卫生厕所，使卫生条件大为改善。之后农村新建住房，大部分与城镇一样专门置卫生间安装蹲便器或坐便器。

（2）盥洗沐浴用具

20世纪70年代末，城镇居民盥洗用具一般有搪瓷脸盆、铝盆、洗脸帕、搪瓷缸和牙膏、牙刷等，街道和厂矿企业建有公共澡堂供职工洗澡。农村盥洗用具有小木盆、搪瓷洗盆、铝盆和洗脸帕等，使用牙膏、牙刷不很普遍，盥洗工具一般是大木盆或木缸，夏季有的到水库或河流中沐浴。80年代，城镇部分家庭安装淋浴器利用灶台余热将水升温洗浴，也有人家做水泥浴缸烧水沐浴。90年代新建住房，大多数人家置有卫生间安装陶瓷盥洗盆、热水淋浴器、塑料浴缸，塑料盆和不锈钢盆逐步取代搪瓷盆和铝盆。进入21世纪，盥洗沐浴用具增多，式样翻新，城镇住顶楼和农村新建住房的住家户为节约用电多安装太阳能热水器。

（3）洗涤用具

20世纪70年代末，原洗涤用具主要有木质洗衣盆（大木盆）、洗衣搓板（搓衣板）、捶衣棒、洗衣刷和鞋刷等。20世纪80年代上半期，城镇住户始用单缸电动洗衣机洗涤衣物和床上用品，下半期有的使用双缸洗衣机，既洗涤又甩干。90年代，农村洗涤也普遍使用洗衣机，塑料盆和铝盆取代原用的大木盆，搓衣板、捶衣棒也随之淘汰。

4. 家用电器

20世纪70年代末，县境城镇用电基本普及，居民使用家用电器有白炽灯、日光灯、收音机、录音机和电唱机等。农村仅有城乡接合部及厂矿附近通电，家电以白炽灯为主，功率一般15至25瓦。继后农村通电率逐年增加。80年代初，城镇有的家庭置有时尚的家电12吋黑白电视机、落地式收音机和手提录音机；中期有18吋彩色电视机、单缸洗衣机、电冰箱、电饭锅、电扇和电熨斗进家，黑白电视机开始进入农村家庭。90年代初，彩电品牌增多，较时尚的彩电是平面直角25和29吋两种；洗衣机升级为双缸洗衣机。城镇使用彩电、冰箱的家庭普遍，农村也有部分家庭使用。随后，新增家电主要有空调机、吸尘器、换气扇、热风器、电热器、热水器、电热毯、组合音响、电烤箱等。黑白电视机逐步淘汰，彩电流行35吋以上大屏幕和背投电视，冰箱升为双门无氟冰箱，洗衣机升为自动洗衣机。2000年后，新增家电有液晶电视机、摄像机、饮水机、微波炉、电磁灶等，洗衣机有全自动洗衣机和滚筒式洗衣机，电冰箱有三门电冰箱。显像管电视机逐步淘汰，代之以流行液晶电视机。农村在完成电网改造后家电使用率和普及率逐步提高，与城镇差距逐渐缩小。

（五）出行工具

20世纪70年代末，县境有公路的地方使用的交通工具主要有自行车、马车、拖拉机和汽车，农村部分地方仍有骑马出行。主干公路已开通县城至贵阳、扎佐、久长、小箐、六广和六桶的客车，除到贵阳每天有4个班次外，其余到乡（镇）每天1至2个班次。是时，农村接亲一般使用马车，有的人家能联系到1辆货车或拖拉机接亲就感到体面。机关和集体单位职工出行多是乘坐货车或拖拉机。80年代中期政策放开，县城附近农村部分赶马车的人将原马车改装成马轿车，人们称其为“马的”，专门从事县城至王官、至马家桥等地的短途客运。同时个体客运汽车在县城启运，先跑修文至贵阳，之后逐步开通到各乡（镇）的中型客车，人们称大型客车为“大巴”，称中型客车为“中巴”。同时轻骑摩托车也开始出现，其

20世纪80年代流行的永久牌自行车

型号主要有50型、100型和125型等，尤以嘉陵摩托和125型较为时髦，称“嘉陵车”或“125”。90年代初，两轮摩托和三轮摩托逐渐增多，有的将其作为短途客运工具，在县城及周边营运载客，人们称其为“摩的”，摩的出现取代了马轿车。随后，有的市民开始购置奥托、云雀等微型轿车，并在县城营运出租。进入21世纪，为安全起见，政府采取措施取消摩的营运。同时，私人购买轿车家庭逐渐增多，而且档次也逐步提高，并从城镇向农村发展。短途代步工具除普通自行车外还增加了电动自行车和电摩托。至2010年，全县已实现村村通公路、通客车，交通四通八达，大中型客车、出租车、私家车及各类轻骑车均成为人们主要出行的代步工具。

三、人生礼仪

（一）交往

1. 称谓

（1）一般称谓

20世纪70年代末，与人交往除自亲称谓外，与邻居和熟悉的人可根据关系亲疏参照家庭称谓称呼，关系密切的以男性为主按父系称谓，同辈称兄弟，对长辈称伯或叔；以女性为主的按母系称谓，同辈称姨妈姊妹或内兄内弟，对长辈称姨妈或舅舅。关系一般的在称谓前加姓氏，如张叔叔、刘伯伯、王姨妈和李大舅等。对于不熟悉的人一般不直称大爷、大娘，会被人误认为是“儿大爷”“儿大娘”对其不恭。在工作单位，有职务的在职务前加姓，如孙局长、杜主任、朱校长、罗院长等。一般人互为同志，可根据与自己年龄差异在其姓氏前加老或小，如老秦、小杨；在学校对教师普遍在称老师前加姓氏，对德高望重者省去“师”字，如“陈老”“周老”；对医生、护士普遍在医生前加姓氏，对于护士一般不直称“某护士”。与不熟悉的人交往一般互称同志，进入80年代，同志逐渐改称师傅，年纪稍大的称老师傅。对企业家、个体户多称“老板”，对服务员称“小姐”或“小师傅”。90年代，对成年女性称“姨”或“孃”，如“赵姨”“胡孃”。到了21世纪，有的将师傅改称“老板”，企业家、个体户改称老总、董事长和董事，如“郑总”“齐董事长”“马董”等。对中青年男女有的称“帅哥”“美女”，服务员中的女性忌讳称“小姐”，改称“大姐”“妹儿”或“小妹”。

（2）家庭称谓

①父辈称谓

对父亲：普遍称爸爸，部分称老爸或老者。

对继父：有称爸爸，也有称伯伯或叔叔，不称老爸或老者。

对母亲：普遍称妈或妈妈，部分称老妈，也有称妈咪的，但是少数。

对继母：有称妈或妈妈，也有称孃，姓张称张孃，姓李称李孃。

对父之兄弟：称伯或叔，堂中和族中堂伯、堂叔，除需特别解释外一般可省略“堂”“族”2字。

对父之姐妹：称姑妈，一般是按姐妹排行+姑妈，如“大姑妈”“二姑妈”；其配偶称姑爹，排行与配偶相同。

对母之兄弟：称舅，一般是按兄弟排行+舅，如“大舅”二舅；其配偶称舅妈，排行与配偶相同，也有称“嬢”，姓张称张嬢，姓李称李嬢。

对母之姐妹：称姨妈或姨，一般是按姐妹排行+姨妈或姨，如“大姨妈”“二姨妈”或“大姨”“二姨”；其配偶称姨爹，排行与配偶相同，也有称伯伯、叔叔，如“张伯伯”“李叔叔”。

对配偶之父母：理论上称老公公、老婆婆和老丈人、老丈母，实际生活中是随配偶称爸爸、妈妈。

② 祖辈称谓

对祖父：称公公或老太爷、爷爷。

对祖母：称奶奶或太太、老太太、老太。

对外祖父：称外公或公公（与称祖父为爷爷对应）。

对外祖母：称外婆或婆婆。

③ 曾祖辈称谓

对曾祖父：称老祖祖或老祖公。

对曾祖母：称老祖太。

对外曾祖父：称外老祖祖或外老祖公。

对外曾祖母：称外老祖婆。

④ 同辈称谓

夫妻间：20世纪80年代互为爱人，可直呼其姓名，或姓前加“老”字、“小”字，如老张、小李等，更为亲密者是省略姓只呼其名。90年代，出现互称老公、老婆。2000年后普遍互称老公、老婆。

兄弟姊妹间：小称大为哥哥、姐姐，多个哥姐时分别加男女排行称谓，也有称老哥、老姐；大称小为弟弟、妹妹，也有称老弟、小弟、老妹、小妹、妹妳、妹儿、幺妹等。

对兄弟姐妹的配偶：哥之妻称嫂，或加与哥相同的排行；弟之妻称兄弟媳妇，或呼其姓名；姐之夫称姐夫，或称姓+哥，姓张即张哥、姓李即李哥；妹之夫称妹夫，或称“小”+姓，姓张即小张、姓李即小李，也有直呼其姓名的。

⑤ 替代称谓

为表示对被称对象的尊重，可替代自己子女或孙辈、曾孙辈等小辈称呼对方，如北方的“他爷爷”“他奶奶”“他大舅”等，一般省去“他”字直呼称谓，如“爷爷”、“奶奶”、“大舅”等，但前提是自己要有子女才可替代、有孙辈才可替代孙辈、有曾孙才可替代曾孙称呼对方，否则会被人笑话。

2. 待客

县人历来有好客的优良传统，经济条件较差的年代，客人进家装烟沏茶是普遍习惯，接着陪客人摆谈，冷落客人是对客人的不礼貌，过后要留客人吃饭。在城镇招待一般客人是下面条或和家人一起吃随茶便饭，若是招待贵客要根据自己的条件做比平时更好吃的东西招待客人；在农村，一般客人待以随茶便饭，是贵客就要推豆花、煮腊肉和打糍粑等待客。客人在时夫妻不能吵架、打架和打骂小孩，否则会让客人感到不方便。20世纪80年代，生活条件向好，除招待来客外，亲戚、朋友间还经常相互请宴，称为联络感情。待客用好烟、好酒和好菜以示体面。90年代，招待客人除吃好、喝好外还要让客人玩好，其中的一种方式是陪客人打麻将，普通人家置办麻将必不可少，称“只有麻将才留得住客人”。进入21世纪，待客一般不太重视吃而重视玩，称之“以麻会友”，把待客的时间、精力放在陪客打麻将上，待客人饿了随便做点吃食即可。不爱好麻将的人家有客人来，若是经常往来的除用好烟、好茶、好酒和好吃的招待外，还在说话聊天时备有葵花、花生、水果等小吃，称作“混嘴的”；若是远方贵客至家，多是说话聊天在家，吃饭喝酒在宾馆饭店，玩在景区公园，有的还要到歌厅舞厅陪客人唱歌、跳舞，处处唯恐怕对客人招待不周让人说闲话。

20世纪80年代聘礼三转一响

3. 做客

县人有文雅做客的习惯，过去进门要说“恭喜发财”，出门要讲“道谢”或“打扰了”。初进门主人尚未说请坐之前不能就座，坐定后不能跷“二郎腿”和“抖脚”，接受装烟倒茶要用双手并说“谢谢”，与主人交谈要说恭维的话和赞美之词，听别人说话不能打断其话语，不要抢着说，否则会被人认为不是来做客而是来吵架的。主人请吃饭时要说“客罪”，入席饭桌上方要让给长辈、贵客或年长者就座，一般客人要主动坐左右两侧或下方。所有人未坐齐之前不能端碗先吃，主人没有发话之前不能动菜，待主人说“请”后才能动筷子。主人在请吃菜时都会说些谦虚之词，如“没有好吃的招待大家，没得哪样菜得，来来来，大家拈辣角（gó）吃。”听的人不要误认为是叫客吃辣椒，而是主人的筷子指什么菜大家就一起夹什么菜。如果没有任何人牵头说“请”，个人想吃啥就夹啥就会被视为不懂礼节。夹菜时不能在菜中挑来捡去，要哪块就夹哪块，否则会被骂为吃“猪拱食”。席上先他人吃饱放下碗筷前，要向未吃完的人逐一打招呼“慢吃”。若别人先吃饱给你打招呼，你要回一句“您要吃好哦!”。到别人家做客，若遇主人有事，自己能帮忙就帮忙，不能帮忙就赶紧离开，不要影响主人做事。若是主人无事也不能坐得太久，除非主人有意留你，否则会被人骂是“烂板凳”（赖着不走之意）。做客告别主人要说“道谢咯!”或“打扰咯！有时间请到我家去玩（做客）”等语。主人送客出门客人要请主人“留步”。这些传统礼节一直延续至今，随着社会进步，又有新的内涵。到别人家做客要讲文明礼貌，衣着要整洁、举止要文雅，不随地吐痰，不乱丢烟头、果皮等。去到房舍装修好的人家还要换上拖鞋或套上鞋套，以免弄脏地面。

（二）婚嫁

1. 谈婚

县系以汉族为主的多民族融合地区，婚俗以汉族为主，其余少数民族多逐步汉化，仅有苗族、布依族和彝族略带原族色彩。传统习俗为父母之命媒妁之言，即男方父母看中了某家女子后，请媒人到女方家向其父母提亲，得其父母同意方可建立婚约关系，再经过所谓的“三回九转”，即提亲、相亲、拿话、开庚、订婚、烧香、送期、过彩礼和接亲拜堂，其中订婚、烧香和接亲拜堂要摆酒席请客才能成婚。另是自由恋爱，即是男方追求女方，或女方追求男方，双方情意相投就确定关系。有的男方或女方看中对方后不便表白，就请双方熟悉的人向对方传话表达爱意，对方同意即确定关系。恋爱一段时间后（多则数年少则数月）选择佳期结婚。还有男女双方确定恋爱关系后，再由一方（多为男方）父母请媒人向对方父母提亲，得到同意后才能确定婚约关系，礼节过程与传统习俗大致相同，也有简化程序的。在农村多为传统习俗，自由恋爱成婚较少。在城镇、工矿、机关单位和部分少数民族自由恋爱成婚者较多。部分性格内向腼腆的青年多由亲朋好友介绍促合而成。随着社会经济发展，人们思想观念不断改变，特别是农村青年自由恋爱逐渐增多，有的在外学习或打工谈恋爱，成熟后回家办喜酒结婚。传统的“三回九转”也逐渐简化为提亲、订婚和接亲。青年人自由恋爱重视人品不重视族别，一改以往不同民族之间互不通婚的习俗，有利家庭和睦，促进了各民族团结。

2. 聘礼　陪嫁

（1）聘礼

俗称彩礼，由男方家置备。早先以物为主，多为穿戴和食肉等。彩礼多少由双方议定，一般是5至6套衣裤和两套内衣、内裤以及鞋、袜等，另加半边（约50公斤）猪肉，最多的衣裤达10套以上和猪肉1头（约100公斤），最少的仅有两套衣裤、鞋、袜等，备作日常一洗一换之用。20世纪80年代时兴除基本彩礼外还要加上“三转一响”（手表、单车、缝纫机和收音机）。过彩礼后若男方悔婚，彩礼全归女方家所有分文不退；若女方悔婚需将彩礼悉数退还，特殊情况亦可双方协商退还部分或加价退还。80年代中期，有的人家将彩礼中2至3套以上衣裤及猪肉等折成现金改为礼金，开始时千元左右，以后相互攀比，礼金数额逐渐增加。90年代，彩礼品种增加彩电、电冰箱和组合音响等，礼金增至数千上万元。进入21世纪，礼金增至数万元，最多达10万元以上。有的女方还提出要求，除礼金外还要男方家购买或自建一套新房结婚。

（2）嫁妆

主要指陪嫁的家具和床上用品。嫁妆俗称称嫁奁，有床、衣柜、平柜、橱柜、梳妆台和木箱等，陪嫁较齐全的称为“满堂嫁奁”；床上用品有被子、垫絮、床单、枕头和蚊账等，其中被子越多越体面。传统习俗是在女方家操办的烧香酒席上父母和女儿的姑妈、舅爷等自亲商议置办嫁妆之事。姑妈、舅爷等亲戚各自可根据自己的能力承诺置备至少1件家具送给待嫁的侄女，剩余部分由其父母置办。20世纪80年代中期，亲戚承诺送的家具大多折合成现金交给其父母统一置备。90年代陪嫁品增加电视机和洗衣机等家用电器。进入21世纪，有的父母将陪嫁的家具、电器等折合成现金交给其女自行购置。有的富裕家庭还陪嫁商品住房及轿车。

3. 婚庆

（1）择期

男女订婚一段时间后，开亲双方商定结婚，就由男方家请人到女方家开具女方生辰八字，称为“开庚”；拿回女方生辰八字与男方生辰八字相合择定结婚日期。择定的婚期称为“期程”，由男方家将其送到女方家，俗称“送期”；女方家接到期程后就要请自亲好友来家吃“烧香酒”，告诉大家女儿的结婚时间，并商量陪嫁事宜。择期要选择与男女双方八字相合并不犯冲的良辰吉日，要选择农历的双日，意为双喜临门或婚后夫妻不会落单。相信的人家认为期程可决定婚庆是否顺利，婚后夫妻是否和睦和家庭是否兴旺发达。20世纪70至80年代，不相信期程的年轻人多选择元旦节、三八节、劳动节、建军节和国庆节等节假日结婚。90年代，不信期程的人家也认为结婚是人生大事，“宁可信其有，不可信其无”，至少也要选择一个吉利日子举行婚礼。之后，选择节假日结婚的人家有所减少。

（2）婚礼

多定为两天，农历的单日在女方家，双日在男方家。单日男方家备好彩礼，由押礼先生带领接亲队

伍到女方家迎亲，女方家大办酒席招待男方家接亲队伍和自家的亲朋好友。次日凌晨或上午吉时，女方父母嫁女出门称为“发亲”，并请亲朋好友中的年轻女性将嫁女送至夫家称为“送亲”。到男方家后在事先择好的吉时举行男女双方拜堂。拜堂要拜天地、拜祖宗、拜父母、拜亲朋好友，原本要行跪拜之礼，后改成行鞠躬礼。拜堂结束送新婚夫妻入洞房（俗称“新房”），其后大摆婚宴庆贺。20世纪70年代末80年代初，接亲用的交通工具是马车，也有的用拖拉机、汽车和乘坐客车。这一时期复见消失多年的接亲花轿，但仅为偶然，一度时间后不复存在。县城没有像农村那么复杂，婚宴有的请在单位食堂或饭店。有的机关单位婚礼简单，仅在结婚当天请单位领导主持婚礼，请同事和亲朋好友参加并吃喜糖，主婚人宣读结婚证书，有证婚人见证即告完婚。还有的男女双方办理结婚登记后不举行婚礼，共同外出旅行，称为“旅行结婚”，旅行回来请朋友、同事和亲人吃喜糖即告成婚。当时正面宣传提倡节俭结婚，县工会、青年团和妇联等组织做了大量工作。1981年，县水泥厂3对青年人在县总工会会议室举行婚礼，开集体婚礼的先河。尽管如此，节俭结婚较难推行，大操大办、相互攀比之风日盛。80年代后期，有条件的人家联系吉普车、轿车或中巴车接亲，90年代发展到要用轿车才光彩。1999年，团县委开展“婚育新风进万家”活动，5月1日在阳明山庄举行有10对青年参加的集体婚礼，新婚夫妇还共同在园内种植一棵爱情之树以示纪念。活动的开展反映很好，但推广较难。进入21世纪，私家车日渐普及，接亲用车大多选择高档轿车。县城有婚庆公司专门从事结婚庆典服务。仪式一般在宾馆酒店举行，设置婚礼台由专业主持人主持，并请有最亲近的未婚年轻人当伴郎和伴娘，婚礼上有新婚夫妇交换戒指，证婚人和长辈代表致辞祝贺，婚礼结束后大宴宾客。在城郊和农村还有专门从事婚宴“一条龙”服务的民间组织，实行有偿服务，婚礼仪式与传统仪式大致相同。

（三）丧葬

丧事俗称“白喜事”。20世纪70年代末，民间有棺殓土葬习俗，少数民族葬俗基本与汉族同化。人离世后提倡俭葬，一般采取“吉葬三天”，即在家凭吊3日，第三天下葬安埋。是时反对做道场，但在偏远地区仍有人家悄悄为死者超度亡魂。80年代恢复宗教自由，以往的迷信习俗卷土重来。除机关单位外，一般人死亡后要请道士择期下葬，少则3天，多则5天、7天、9天、11天不等，做道场由暗地转为公开。治丧期间，死者的晚辈要戴白布孝帕，孝子除头包孝帕外腰间还要拴麻线或麻丝以示披麻戴孝；媳妇、女儿孝帕要对折缝成尖顶戴在头上和腰缠麻丝；孙辈的孝帕前额正中贴一纸质圆点，内孙为红色，外孙为绿色，曾孙辈还要贴两个。前来送礼悼念的亲朋普开见礼孝，即赠白布孝帕和寿碗。直系姻亲下祭分为猪羊祭、花祭和普祭：猪羊祭为死者的女儿家用胴猪、胴羊和祭品和祭银（现金）等祭奠；花祭为死者较亲的直系姻亲用纸扎的人、车、马、房、金童和玉女等祭奠；普祭是死者的直系姻亲要用毛毯及高档布料等做祭账和香、蜡、纸、烛和爆竹等祭奠，有的还将大面额人民币在祭账上贴成“奠”字炫耀。下葬当天起3天傍晚要送“烟火”（即火种），第一天送至坟前，第二天送至半道，第三天送至家门前不远处路边。人死后每7天要“祭七”，49天共祭7次称为“烧七”，每次除以香、烛、纸钱及酒食等祭祀外还要烧纸钱包袱，“头七”7个，以后每次递增7个，最后一次49个。进入90年代，提倡简朴治丧和火葬，在农村仍以棺殓土葬为主，丧事越办越热，档次越来越高，有的人家借机敛财。1996年，贯彻执行贵阳市殡葬改革要求，大力推行火葬，提倡厚养薄葬。1999年，县民政部门在久长镇二关坝建成火葬场投入使用。2003年加大殡葬改革力度，把殡葬工作纳入政府工作综合目标考核，并与民政、公安、国土、林业等部门和10乡（镇）签订目标责任制书，增加殡葬管理经费。为从俭治丧，民政部门和乡（镇）在村民自治活动中引导各村组织成立“红白喜事理事会”，教育群众“厚养薄葬”改变大操大办的不正之风。为节约耕地资源，各村辟出公益性墓地，将死者集中葬于公墓。农村有的地方还成立丧葬“一条龙”服务的民间组织，专门承办丧事中的筵席和丧葬礼仪，避免铺张浪费。实行殡葬改革后，全县火化率逐年提高，2005年死亡1619人全部实行火化。之后死亡实行火化已成为群众的自觉行动。至2010年，民间葬俗均已变成“火化棺殓土葬”和“火化土葬”两种，丧葬移风易俗终于实现。

（四）生日

俗称“过生日”，亦称“做生”，传统习俗较重视年长者的生日，每年长者生日家人都要集中聚会祝寿，喜逢60、70、80、90和100岁又称为“做大生”，意为祝大寿。大寿生日男女不同，习惯上称“男做九女做十”，即男做虚岁女做实岁。男性满59周岁即称“60岁大寿”，而女性“60岁大寿”必须满60周岁。凡父母只要有其中一人还健在被称“还未脱儿皮”，年纪再高也不能做大生，否则是对父母的不孝。寿主做大生其子女要筹办酒席，称为办“寿酒”。开席前鸣放鞭炮，亲友闻声莅临祝贺。有的人家借此大摆酒宴、广收寿礼，有的人家年年做生、年年摆席、年年收礼，借机敛财。长者外的其他人过生日，多是家人聚餐以示祝贺。农村人家要杀鸡、做豆腐、煮腊肉和打糍粑等供家人聚餐。小孩过生日，由父母煮1个鸡蛋给他吃即可。20世纪80年代起，世人逐渐重视给小孩过生日。城镇市民和机关职工的小孩生日要给买好吃的、好穿的和好玩的，90年代发展到买生日蛋糕。中年人过生日请最亲密的亲戚朋友聚餐一次，接受大家祝福；年轻人过生日要备生日蛋糕，要唱祝贺生日歌曲。进入21世纪，有的小孩子过生日，亲戚朋友要来祝贺并送生日礼物；父母亲过生日，子女要赠送父母亲喜欢的物品或礼金；夫妻间过生日，要买其缺少或喜爱的东西相送；情人之间过生日，多半是买鲜花相送，也有送贵重物品的；青年朋友过生日近乎“狂欢节”，要唱歌、跳舞，还要将吃剩下的蛋糕奶油相互涂脸取乐。此外，远方的亲朋好友还通过移动电话、QQ和微信等发送短信祝福生日快乐。给长者做大生要在70岁以上，也有少数50岁就开始做的。由于各种请客送礼的酒宴盛行，有的人家借长者生日大办酒宴，搜刮钱财，人们对此嗤之以鼻。

（五）喜庆

传统习俗中建房搬进新家、添人进口生小孩和企业作坊开业等属喜庆之事，亲戚朋友要上门送礼祝贺，主家即当事人要备办酒席酬客。建房搬进新家称为乔迁之喜办“搬家酒”，添人进口生小孩办“满月酒”，开业要办“开张酒”。20世纪80年代，增加参军要办“参军酒”，考取大学要办“升学酒”，进厂当工人要办“参加工作酒”，升职上任要办“上任酒”。90年代，升学酒逐步泛滥，凡是高考、中考被大、中专和技工学校录取都要办升学酒，甚至农村有的家庭孩子考取普通高中也要办酒。进入21世纪，大、中专扩大招生人数，升学率大幅提高，升学人数大量增加，每年8、9月份请吃“升学酒”极为普遍。有的人家经济不宽余，又无考取学校的子女，吃请喜庆酒宴只出不进，出于无奈就刻意制造“喜庆”，操办酒宴回收礼金。有的增修1间住房要办酒，房屋增砌一层要办酒，增配1间厨房也要办酒。办酒之风泛滥，人们叫苦不迭。一个家庭1年应对各种酒宴送礼累计数千元，多至数万元。面对不良之风蔓延，人们极为反感但又无可奈何。

四、财产继承

1. 世俗习惯

在农村显得较为突出，而且带有浓厚的重男轻女色彩。一般多子女家庭，在父母年迈逝世前就要把财产继承分割好，避免逝世后儿女们因财产分割闹矛盾。财产继承只有儿子享有，可由父母指名安排，也有由几兄弟协商处理的。父母指名安排者多向年纪最小的一个儿子倾斜，故民间有“皇帝爱长子，百姓爱幺儿”的说法。由几兄弟协商处理的家庭，多数较能处理好财产分配，方法多按兄弟数平均；少数家庭兄弟间为争夺财产相互间吵架、打架，甚至有的还闹到法院由法庭裁决。

无儿户家庭，有的在女儿中选择1个女儿入赘女婿，称“招姑爷上门”，继承父母财产，而其余嫁出去的女儿不能享有父母遗产。另有一些无儿户家庭，采取的办法是从本姓族中或外姓人家过继1个儿子来养老送终，继承全部财产。还有一些有几个儿子的家庭，如果有哪一家没有生育儿子只有女儿也不能继承遗产，其理由是“祖上的遗产不外姓”。这种现象直到21世纪初还偶有发生。

2. 新法继承

1985年10月1日起，施行《中华人民共和国继承法》，家庭财产继承开始发生变化，特别是一部分素质较高的家庭，突破过去世俗习惯增强新法观念，主张男女平等。这类家庭多见于城镇，在家庭父母财产的继承上，不分男孩女孩都一视同仁。有的父母还根据具体情况在分配财产时多向弱者倾斜。有的家庭在父母双亡后的遗产，由其子女共同继承，不分男女平均分配或协商处理。

五、迷信习俗

（一）信奉鬼神

1. 供神

以供奉香火为主，信奉人家一般在堂屋后壁正中供 “天地君亲师位”和诸大菩萨神位，下面供奉土地神和财神，正面右侧下供奉坛神。新设香火要请道士或和尚开光后才显灵验，并在逢年过节和农历初一和十五烧香祭拜，旨在保佑家人平安、消灾免难。但多数供奉香火人家认为是在供奉自家祖先，仅在逢年过节祭拜。20世纪70年代末供香火人家极少，80年代农村逐渐增多，2000年后市面纸火店有印刷并用玻璃镜框装表好的香火销售。此外，还有做生意、办企业和想发财的人家供奉财神菩萨。祈求家人平安、无灾无难的人家单独或在香火上供奉观世音菩萨。

2. 办会

亦称庙会，20世纪80年代中期恢复，之后渐有发展。办得多的是观音会和盂兰盆会，观音会于每年农历二、六、九月的十九日举办，祭祀观音菩萨；盂兰盆会在每年农历七月十五日兴办，超度信众先祖亡灵。

3. 打醮

请道士设坛做法事，祈福免灾。有祈求平安吉祥的“清醮”、祈求降雨抗旱的“雨醮”、祈求久雨转晴的“晴醮”等，20世纪80、90年代农村部分地区曾在久旱不雨时请道士打过雨醮，之后未再出现。

4. 还愿

就是通过求神保佑在菩萨面前许下的愿信，当愿望实现后履行许下的愿信称为还愿。求神保佑要达到的愿信有祈求升官、发财、生子、升学、消灾、病愈等，愿望实现后报答菩萨大愿有出资修建寺庙、给菩萨塑金身和烧高香等，一般多是许下要买多少纸钱或燃香敬献给菩萨。

5. 吃素

亦称吃斋，主要有3类人。一类是信佛吃斋，即不吃动物的肉、油和奶及其制品，认为吃了就带有杀生行为，是罪过；另一类是还愿吃斋，是祈求菩萨保佑达到愿望许下的愿信，没有礼物就用吃斋的方式报答；再一类是既不信佛又不还愿，仅是为了长寿，认为吃斋可免罪添寿。吃斋分吃常素和斋期两种，吃常素是长时间不间断地吃到寿终；吃斋期又分为“吃二、六、九”和“吃初一、十五”两种，前一种是每年吃农历的二月、六月和九月，后一种是农历每月只吃初一和十五两天即代表全月。还有的是许愿吃几年或终生。

6. 祭拜石木

民间有人把一些奇石、古树视为神灵，奇石多被尊为观音神像，古树多被尊为神树，传说可为庇佑生灵、赐福禳灾。县城北门外鸡爬坎原有一石笋略似人形，有人称其为观音菩萨神像，前来烧香许愿，相传非常灵念，致香客越来越多，后发展成为寺庙金凤寺。奇石、古树各乡镇均有，经常有信众为给家人驱灾治病前去烧香、挂红。

7. 巫师治病

有的人生病不到医院治疗，而是找巫师请神问药。有的巫师采用“烧蛋叫魂”办法治病，有的采用“香灰兑神水”给病人服用，有的采用化符驱邪“符灰兑水” 给病人咽服。对病重者巫师还要请神做法事，下到阴曹地府查病因，以便“有的放矢”。有的巫师对患者一面请神做法，另一面用草药给病人口服，称之为“神药两解”。巫师能否把病治好，只能竭尽自圆其说，多是“好言安慰，听天由命”。其中不乏庸医置病人于死地，卫生等有关部门累经制止，但未根绝。

8. 占卜算命

相信鬼神的人如遇疑难异事，就请先生占卜问事。其技法有翻斗书、测字、抽签、卜课、打卦、抹米碗、看水碗和看蛋等，或掐指推算干支，查问吉凶，祈福攘灾。算命的方法主要是立四柱八字算命法，其次为摸骨、看长相、看掌纹和翻书秤命问前程等。20世纪90年代又传入姓名笔画数算命法和姓名配五行八卦法，用以预测或判断个人的命运吉凶福祸等。

9. 赌神发咒

简称赌咒，即为发毒誓。若两人有事争执无法调解，其中有人理亏说谎，为辨明是非，两人便去菩萨面前烧香化纸，祈求神灵明断，降灾给理亏说谎者。有的当众两人面对面地赌咒发誓。还有就是在两人或多人中找出说谎者或恶人，称之为“捞油锅”。即请先生做法，将菜油倒进锅中烧热到一定温度，放入一枚铜钱，先生第一个从中捞出再放回锅中，其余人依次照做，若遇嫌疑人锅中会有异响或炸油。原理是嫌疑人心虚和受先生的话语刺激导致其手心有汗，手伸入油锅中遇热油即炸。

10. 驱鬼避邪

信鬼神者及家人生病或身体不适，采用“站筷子”“倒水饭”驱鬼。若久病不愈就要请巫师叫魂、捉鬼、送茅人、送阴棺材或放五猖找替代。再不行就要请巫师打粉火、打油火、穿“红鞋(铧)”等驱鬼除怪。为驱鬼避邪，有的人家采用画符贴门额或挂明镜于门头上，认为可吓走鬼怪避邪。端阳节很多人家门前挂菖蒲、陈艾，认为是“天师骑艾虎，手执菖蒲剑，一切妖魔鬼怪全走开”。

（二）迷信禁忌

1. 行为忌

出行忌农历丑、己、酉日出远门，这几天为“红砂日”，俗称“出门犯红砂，一去不归家”。又一种忌是“七不出门，八不归家，”否则出行不顺、不吉利。

逢“戊”日忌做耕地、挖土和除草动土的农活，称为“忌戊”，可免惊动土神，否则会遭冰雹灾害。

求神拜佛前1至3天忌吃荤菜，还要沐浴更衣，菩萨见你“虔诚”，定会赐福攘灾。

未满月的新娘和产妇忌进别家房屋内，否则会给别人家带去灾难，犯忌者要给人家道歉、挂红和放鞭炮冲喜，以此免灾。

非夫妇之间，女人忌摸男人的头，男人忌摸女人的腰，有“男人的头、女人的腰，摸到就是祸包包”之说。

人死在家门外，忌抬尸进屋，有“冷尸进房，家破人亡”之说。

忌在别家哭泣，否则会给别家带去灾难，犯忌者要给人家冲喜。

丧家所有人忌进别家门，以免触怒别家神灵降灾祸。

夫妇或成年男女忌在别人家同床睡觉，以免“野花进房，家破人亡”之灾。

忌用脚踩有字的纸和用带字的纸擦屁股，否则会被人斥为“糟蹋圣贤”，会生眼疾，一辈子读不成书当文盲。

忌在商店门处站着不进不出和坐在柜台上，以免“堵塞财路”。

做生意的人用餐忌讳用手直接端汤碗倒汤，俗称“翻汤”，生意难成。

开车的人吃鱼，不能翻动鱼身，否则会有翻车的厄运。

中元节夜间忌小儿外出，以防“七月半，鬼乱窜”鬼将小儿的魂魄摄走。

孕妇忌踩拴牛、马的绳索，否则分娩时会出现难产。

哺乳妇女忌进产妇卧室，以免把产妇的乳液带走，产妇家要找哺乳妇女的麻烦。

红白喜事客人送礼后，主人家回赠香烟，红喜赠两支，白喜赠1支。两支取“好事成双”之意，1支取“只亡1人”之意。

过年杀猪一般是选农历单日，称“杀单不杀双”。后又发展成杀猪之日的属相不能与家人属相相同，否则等于是杀自己家人。

家中摆放卧床要与房梁平行，有“顺梁顺当”之说，只有人死后尸体才与房梁垂直摆放。

未成婚的人忌吃猪蹄和带叉的萝卜，否则会“叉着媒人的嘴”，使谈婚受阻。

民间送礼忌送“钟”，犯有“送终”之嫌。

2. 语言忌

俗称“正月忌头，腊月忌尾”。正月里忌说“死、输、光”等字眼，怕给全年带来灾祸。

春节和中元节期间在家不能说“鬼”字，因已故老人是鬼，它回家探视亲人听到鬼字会不高兴，而其他的鬼魂听到后会认为是呼唤他们，纷纷拥来，会给家人带来灾难。

在煤厂上不能说“垮”“塌”“穿”等与安全有关的语言，否则会带来垮顶、塌方和挖穿水仓等厄运；煤厂上看到老鼠不能叫老鼠或耗子，更不能将其打死，因老鼠挖洞藏身，挖煤人挖洞采煤，同是挖洞的，挖煤人应叫老鼠为“师傅”，否则老鼠会报复，制造安全事故。

行船、开车和坐车的人忌说“翻”字，怕会带来翻车、翻船的厄运。

农村修猪圈忌说“拱”“不吃”“翻”等词语，怕以后喂猪不吃不长、翻圈逃跑。

忌说别人小孩身体很重，要说成“好称（音chen）手”或“好坠手”，说“重”犯了“人死体重”之嫌，主人会不高兴，以后小孩遇到事故会受责怪。

人死亡忌说“死”，一般人死亡称“过世”；未成年人死亡称“夭折”或“转去了”；老人死亡称“百年”“病故”“归天”或“老去了”，用文雅的说法称“作古”。

第三节　风　尚

一、传统美德

（一）个人品德

从小父母就要教子孙怎样做人，怎样做一个有出息的人。民间有“望子成龙，望女成凤”之说。人生下来就具有自觉向善的本能，在没有外界不良品德影响下，传统的个人优良品德会世代相传，其主要表现为：自立自强、立志做人，俗话说：“男人无志钝铁无钢，女人无志乱草无秧”；勤学上进，有一技之长，名言“少壮不努力，老大徒伤悲”；能知书达理，不恶语伤人；以助人为乐，不损人利己；拾金不昧，不占他人便宜；友善待人，态度谦恭；对人宽容大度，不小肚鸡肠；为人刚正不阿，不徇私、不屈人、安分守己，不惹是生非；诚实守信，不欺诈别人；有正义感，爱憎分明；见义勇为，不坐视不管；坚持原则，不主观臆断，不人云亦云。传统的个人美德传承和发扬，有利于社会文明进步和国家的发展壮大。

（二）家庭美德

县人大多崇尚“家和万事兴”，有的家庭还将其制作成镜框或横幅悬挂于堂中醒目之处。在家庭成员中倡导尊老爱幼，以“老有慈心小有孝心的要求增强家人的团结和睦”；夫妻间平等相处，男主外女主内，相互配合料理家务；生活勤俭持家以“穿不穷，吃不穷，不会打算一世穷”的警言计划安排全家人的衣、食、住、行；邻里间团结友爱，互相帮助，相互谦让，不争强好胜；朋友来了热情款待，宾至如归。传统的家庭美德是持家的基本准则、道德规范。履行得好的家庭称之为“家风好”，不仅有好的声誉，更有益于家庭的兴旺发达。

（三）职业道德

长期以来县人在各自行业职场中自然形成传统的职业道德，主要表现为爱岗敬业，乐于奉献；遵规守矩，自洁自律，克己奉公；实事求是，不欺上瞒下、虚报浮夸；不利用职务之便营私舞弊谋取私利等。当政者清正廉洁、勤政爱民，廉洁勤政的人多为百姓传颂；经商之人讲究社会良知，倡导公平竞争、童叟不欺，凭良心赚钱；为师者教书育人，为人师表堪为学生楷模；行医者悬壶济世，救死扶伤；其余各行业职员均以做好自己本职工作为荣，反之为耻。新时期的职业道德又赋予新的内涵，其宗旨是为人民服务。良好的职业道德与实践互相渗透，不断传承，凝聚了社会正能量，推动着社会事业的不断进步。

（四）社会公德

先辈们为维系社会公益而约定俗成且后辈能自觉践行，故有“前人兴后人跟”之说。其表现首先是爱国家、爱家乡，偶有崇洋媚外或认为家乡不及他乡而报怨者，众人皆视其为有乞丐心态。从20世纪80年代中期起，尊师重教成为社会共识，在很多学生心里老师话语分量超过父母。秉承公正是人们崇拜的偶像，有“打抱不平”“大路不平旁人铲”“一碗水端平”“秉公执法讲求公正”等行为倍受人们称赞和仿效。人们普遍提倡“勤劳致富，爱岗敬业”，否则被人视为是“混混”。人与人之间相互友好，礼貌谦让，助人为乐，不图回报。买卖之间讲究交易公平，童叟无欺。如遇危难，多数人都有扶危济困、救死

扶伤之举，“一家有难，众人齐援”。弘扬传统的社会公德，使社会和谐稳定。

二、新风尚

在弘扬传统美德的基础上，不断倡导讲文明、树新风是新时期社会发展的主流。20世纪70年代末，普遍提倡男女平等、尊老爱幼、助人为乐和热心公益事业。各级党委和政府号召开展“学习英雄模范”、“学雷锋，树新风”。1982年3月，县委，县政府贯彻执行中共中央宣传部《关于深入开展“五讲四美”活动的意见》，规定每年3月为“全民文明礼貌月”。要求各地各单位集中开展“五讲四美”（讲文明、讲礼貌、讲卫生、讲秩序、讲道德,心灵美、语言美、行为美、环境美）活动，并号召党政机关干部，企、事业单位职工和农村村民积极参与。

90年代，在青少年中特别是中、小学学生中开展“榜样在身边”活动，学习身边的道德模范和好人好事，加强对青少年道德品质教育，提高社会道德水准。凉井乡黄金村彝族共产党员张树林，率领其子张发文见义勇为与江水搏斗奋力抢救金沙县化觉乡金河村9名落水村民；洒坪中学初中一年级学生魏先志舍生忘死救助落水儿童。1998年元月，县妇联牵头开展“尊老爱幼活动月”，先后与共青团县委、县总工会和教育局等单位密切配合组织活动，全县涌现许多可歌可泣敬老爱幼事迹：有孝敬公婆、撑持起8口之家困难家庭的洒坪乡青山村妇女遗孀罗廷会；有收养疯癫智障老人和孤儿的六广镇沙坡村委会主任殷华利获贵阳市道德模范（孝老爱亲）奖和中央精神文明办公室授予“全国德孝之星”称号；有用亲情与辛勤将自己患癌妻子救回人间的国税局干部李正磊，后获贵阳市道德模范（孝老爱亲）奖，继后又获中央文明办授予“孝老爱亲中国好人”称号。

2006年，贯彻执行中共中央总书记胡锦涛关于树立社会主义荣辱观的“八荣八耻”重要论述，并将其作为当时社会价值取向和行为准则，涌现出许多爱岗敬业的典型：有甘于奉献的乡村女教师高体凤；有心为民着想、勤恳为民办事的扎佐工商所职工朱春贵；有致富不忘本、仗义疏财、带领群众共同富裕的村干部宁维华；有拾金不昧的出租车司机“好的姐”张学英，将捡到的1.92万元现金交由警察送还失主；有助人为乐献爱心的“好的哥”胡朝贵在县城义务载乘60岁以上老人和送病人去医院不收费，还有众多出租车司机每年高考期间免费接送参加高考的莘莘学子等等。

2008年“5•12”汶川地震，全县人民扶危济困、募捐救灾，共捐资64.73万元。扎佐医药园区企业无偿捐出价值35.64万元的药品。全县有15个党委、79个党支部、4904名党员交特殊党费57万元。2010年玉树地震，全县又捐款33万元。至2010年，共计全县各类捐款190.37万元，分别汇给上级组织部门和红十字会转交灾区救助灾民。

三、歪风

（一）赌博

20世纪70年代末，赌博已被严厉禁止，偶有少数不务正业的三五人在一起聚赌，赌具是用两颗玉米（胚芽面烙黑）配以碗或杯、盒，赌法猜单双，俗称“摇苞谷子”或“摇盒盒”。赌资仅限于数分或数角钱。被人发现或抓住，将被千夫所指视为另类。

80年代初，打麻将作为一种娱乐活动复出，玩法是贵州数翻麻将，翻数达不到约定翻数不能和，不带赌注。80年代后半期改为不用数翻，称为“推倒和”或“棒棒和”，兴下赌注，少则1至2角，多则1至2元。与此同时，玩扑克赌博也有出现，先是玩捉麻雀和同花顺，继后又玩“哈幺大”（又称“铺金花”），赌注一般为1至5元。进入90年代玩贵阳的“吊靠麻将”（即在“棒棒和”的基础上附加很多条件限制乱打），赌注多的提高到5至10元。90年代后半期，川麻将玩法传入，先是玩“吃豆豆”，继后又玩“吃豆豆加捉鸡”，赌注增至10到20元。进入21世纪，普遍玩“吃豆豆加捉鸡”，赌注少者1至5元，多者50至100元。与此同时，玩扑克“斗地主”也成赌博，赌注与打麻将相当。有的嫌打麻将、玩扑克输赢来得慢不够刺激，改玩“摇苞谷子”猜单双或玩骰子比大小。甚至有不法者在偏僻村庄、森林或废弃厂房开设赌场聚众赌博，赌法有“摇苞谷子”猜单双、玩骰子比大小或澳门赌法，赌注大至数千上万元。

赌博之害，胜于水火盗贼，很多家庭因参赌导致悲剧。有人因赌博输钱赔不起被迫借贷还债，甚至借高利贷参赌，常因躲避债主过着“杨伯老式生活”，严重影响家庭和睦。县城有一单位职工因打麻将赌博累教不改，不仅家庭破裂，而且每月工资除留生活费外被强制扣还债主。另有一单位职工因打麻将赌博输钱借高利贷无力偿还，最后丢弃工作悄声负债潜逃。龙场镇建新村一村民因赌博出名，先是“十赌九赢”或“逢赌必赢”，后遇“高手出千”，赌资输尽后借数百万高利贷无力偿还，丢下妻儿老小服毒自杀。

（二）大办酒席

嫁娶、丧葬人家备办酒席宴请宾客，称为“红、白喜事”，属于当地风俗无可厚非。20世纪70年代末80年代初，每家规模20桌左右，客人礼金每人1—3元，送5—10元的就是大礼。有的人家从俭操持，喜事不办酒席，只请吃喜糖或旅行结婚；丧事不收礼，只办3—5桌酬谢帮忙的亲朋。继后，随着人们生活水平提高，酒席规模和礼金也随之增大，规模30至50桌是常事，个别人家办丧事酒席上百桌。礼金增至每人10—20元，大礼50元左右。除红、白喜事外生小孩要请满月酒，搬家要请搬家酒。90年代，增加升学酒、当兵酒和祝寿酒。客人礼金增至50元左右，大礼100元以上。进入21世纪，大办酒席之风盛行，除原有的请酒外又出现小儿满100天请百日酒，买车要请买车酒，开业要请开业酒，就业上任要请上任酒，服刑满期要请冲喜酒。赠送的礼金每人100—500元，多的上千元，最多上万元。对此，县委、县政府三令五申下文禁止，然令不行禁不止，虽机关职工有所收敛，但街道、农村仍然我行我素。

（三）拉关系

20世纪70年代末流传一句顺口溜：“军属烈属抵不上人熟”，指人熟好办事，要办成事就得找熟人拉关系开后门。80年代，找熟人不一定管用，还得配以请客送礼，礼物一般是高档烟酒，所以当时世人戏称：“事要成必须‘研究、研究’”，谐音“烟酒、烟酒”。对有的工程项目施工承包，除请客送礼外，还要返还工程款的一部分给甲方关键人物，称为“回扣”。90年代，有人把请客送礼上升为一门学问，称“送礼要投其所好”，受者不喜欢分文不值办不好事情，受者喜爱价值倍增事半功倍。继后有人又认为送礼物显眼容易被人发现，逐步改成送“红包”（红纸包钞票）。进入21世纪，拉关系的方式更加微妙，认为“办事不能‘临时报佛脚’”，要把功夫下在平时交往，所以平时就有的放矢的与目标人物交朋友，在一起吃、喝、玩、乐，逢年过节送红包，有意加深印象、建立感情，一旦机会到来即可利用。于是有的政治免疫力缺乏的干部长期被这类人玩弄于股掌之中，以致触犯法律后悔莫及。拉关系者均把拉关系的费用列为攻关经费开支，加入项目成本之中，为保证自己最大限度的利益，就不惜偷工减料，加上有的质检监督人员受其恩惠监管不力，致工程质量难以保证出现严重问题。群众对此深恶痛绝，纪律监察部门将其列入腐败范畴，一经查实严加惩处。

人 物

1978年中共十一届三中全会召开拉开社会主义现代化建设的序幕后，全县广大工人、农民和知识分子登上国民经济和社会发展的舞台，为改革开放和社会主义现代化建设作出了重大贡献。其中还涌现出一批袖长善舞的精英，他们有的是优秀工人，有的是“三农”新星，有的是育人名师，有的是艺苑英华，有的是济世名医，有的是科技尖子，有的是企业名家，有的是人民公仆，有的是道德模范……为了建设社会主义新天地，有入境为官的外籍者，也有到外地作幕的本籍人，充分体现了修文“人杰地灵”的形象定位。

为了人民的利益，有的奋勇献身在战斗的岗位上，留下了可歌可泣的英雄气概。但是，也出现少数逆历史潮流而动的人物。

第一章 人物传略

本章本着“生不立传，善恶并书”的原则，为改革开放33年间在各自的岗位上做出贡献甚至为人民利益牺牲并获得良好声誉的9人立传，也为恣意妄为敢在光天化日之下危害公共安全并指使亲属采取爆炸手段杀害他人的作恶者而负面影响很大的1个人载入史册，旨在彰扬真善美，鞭笞假恶丑，使贪者廉立，怯者勇生，为社会造福。

金志林

金志林（1945—1991），民国34年（1945）8月出生在浙江省浦江县郑宅镇后芦金村一个农民家庭，1953开始发奋读书，继后从小学、初中到高中修完全部课业，1965年考入浙江大学攻读机械专业，1970年在浙大与同窗张建华一道分配至修文县农业机械厂担任技术员，从事机械图纸设计、技术指导等工作，并有《消防火栓阀体》《齿轮泵右泵体》等文面世。1971年与张建华结为伉俪，遂扎根修文。1977年10月，金志林调至县农机管理站，被评为助理工程师。1979年调任农机管理站站长。1980年加入中国共产党。1984年2月至1984年10月调任乡村工业公司经理，1984年10月至1985年12月任县委办公室副主任，1986年1月至1990年2月任主任，期间，1987年6月被选为任中共修文县第五届委员会常务委员，1990年3月任县委副书记，1991年5月因病去世。

金志林业余时间喜练书法，擅长通讯写作，兼任多家报刊编辑部业务记者，为其供稿。1982年，《贵州农机》诚聘金志林为通讯员，1983年10月，被《贵州社科通讯》聘为撰稿人，1985年11月，被《经济信息时报》聘为通讯员，记录修文发展的文章频频见诸省级报端。1985年4月至6月，金志林至中共贵州省委党校参加第三期秘书培训班。金志林不仅擅长处理公文、政策调研等，而且涉猎社科领域，参与编撰的《贵州省情》第102章“安顺地区”，1987年12月，《贵州省情》荣获贵州省科学技术进步奖二等奖。

金志林工作踏实、严谨、勤奋，待人接物特别谦和，在政务繁杂的县委上班，每天接待若干干部和群众，从不见其有厌烦情绪，对来访者的要求和期盼，均做到有交代有始终。在县委担任领导期间分管办公室，常参与起草县委重要文件，字斟句酌，对秘书科提交的文书一字不漏审改，甚至重新参与起草。

县委机关年轻同事较多，金志林格外关心他们，常在生活上和工作上予以关照，常向食堂厨师打招呼，为加班的年轻同志加餐。春节期间，放弃和家人团聚与值班人员一起吃年夜饭。

20世纪80年代，江苏镇江的一位同学联系到金志林，说镇江轻工业局有空缺职务，劝其调到江苏，时任县委书记的王向规得知后，赏识其才华和能力，婉拒调动申请，留在修文工作，金志林丢掉私心杂念，继续留在修文。

金志林在县委工作期间，将时间奉献给事业，几乎无空闲时间，其家虽在县委宿舍，但每天到办公室请示工作的人流不断，常商讨至深夜，以至无暇照顾家人。金志林夫妇一向重视对子女的教育，家育3子，由于工作繁忙，父子陪伴的时间较短，但金志林总是用一言一行影响三个儿子，要他们认真读书，从书中去寻求做事和做人的真谛，既要做好事，又要做好人。由于言传身教，三个孩子均学业有成，并服从分配到国家机关和企业部门，在自己的工作岗位上贡献智慧和力量。

1991年5月，因操劳过度，金志林病倒在办公桌前，直至生命的前一刻还在商议政务。金志林猝然离世，年仅46岁，数以千计的职工和干部前来向遗体告别，无不泪流满面，哀声此起彼伏，愿他一路走好。

马怀麟

马怀麟（1913—1995），乌栗乡（今谷堡乡）下硐村人，青少年时代先后就读于县城龙冈小学、贵阳县中和省立贵阳高级中学。在高中读书时，曾参与组织国民党贵州省党部发起的“读书竞进会”（简称“读书会”）和“青年阵地社”对抗进步学生组织。高中毕业后在国民党贵州省调查统计室工作，并任省党部社会科干事。民国27年（1938）随省党部设计委员、中统贵州特派员陈惕庐去山东，又到浙江、新疆、重庆等地任过专员和地方行政干部训练团队长等职。民国34年（1945）回贵州任力报社副社长，民国35年（1946）被选为贵州省参议会参议员。由于解放战争节节胜利，马怀麟于1949年2月16日在县境小箐发动反蒋武装暴动，任“人民自卫军乌江纵队”司令员。9月，参加地下党云南罗盘地委组建“入黔人民解放委员会”任主任委员。11月修文解放后任中国人民解放军贵阳分区基干营第一支队支队长，后任十六军侦察营营长。1951年2月转业地方后，历任贵定专署建委副主任、专署建设科科长、贵州省农业厅技术室主任、《贵州农业》编辑室主任、黔东南州农业科学研究所副所长和州农业区划办公室副主任，并任黔东南州第七届、第八届人民代表大会常务委员会委员，中国人民政治协商会议黔东南州第五届、第六届委员会常务委员。1992年3月离职休养，享受副地级待遇。

解放前，马怀麟曾辗转省内外，工作在国民党机关。解放战争开始，国民党政治腐败，经济崩溃，人民怨声四起，他对国民党失望之余，转为寄希望于共产党的胜利，便返还贵州原籍与李晓天、李思齐等办报。在报社工作期间，因《力报》报道解放战争胜利的消息被国民党将报社查封，捕杀了主编顾希钧，马怀麟当即避匿。继后转入地下活动，于民国37年（1948）3月回到家乡修文组织反蒋武装——人民自卫军乌江纵队，提出“打倒国民党，拥护共产党”的口号，集人千余和枪800支，于1949年2月16日举行武装暴动，占领了县境小箐和邻县息烽西山，旁及清镇、黔西等地。暴动震怒了国民党贵州省主席谷正伦，即令保安司令部副司令韩文焕调兵坐镇修文“进剿”，悬赏10万元缉拿马怀麟。因寡不敌众暴动失败，骨干人员中有27位惨遭杀害。有的身陷囹圄受尽酷刑。马怀麟冒着生命危险星夜急驰，奔至云南省罗盘地区找到中共地下组织。在罗盘地委领导下加入“入黔人民解放委员会”跨进贵州，继续在滇黔公路沿线开展反蒋斗争，迎来了新中国的诞生。

解放后，马怀麟较长时间在农业部门工作。他爱好农业科学并进行潜心研究，成绩斐然。20世纪60年代在凯里市舟溪镇蹲点，与群众一道摸索并实施了一套“四结合”改造望天田的新路子，受到黔东南州委表扬。70年代末至80年代初，他投身黔东南州农业自然资源调查，身先士卒，走遍州内山山水水，为查清全州资源和利用资源发展农村经济作出了积极贡献，被评为全国、全省的先进工作者。为了使家乡农民走上致富之路，马怀麟于1988年回到故里与村民共商发展大计，办起了修文县第一个联户农场——下硐猕猴桃果园场，开发非耕地5700亩，栽上从四川、陕西等省果科所引进的秦美、海洛特优质树种，3年挂果，逐渐实现规模效益，使一批批昔日温饱都难予维持的贫困农家渐渐过上了小康生活，建新房、购汽车、安电话、买彩电的果农比比皆是。在下硐猕猴桃果园场引领下，全县猕猴桃种植达6万亩。“饮水不忘挖井人”，靠发展猕猴桃逐步走向富裕的村民们无不感谢引导他们走上致富路的“马幺公”。

1995年11月17日12时，马怀麟因病与世长辞，噩耗传至乌栗，果场内外为之悲痛，在安放骨灰盒的悼唁仪式上，有场员自作挽联：

果树呜咽声声泣声声呼老马，场员悲歌字字情字字哭忠魂。

又一联：

伤时济穷敢为叛逆称野马，正谊明道但有士庶怀奇麟。

朱生亮

朱生亮（1947—2003），贵州省开阳县人，1966年7月毕业于开阳中学高中部。1968年11月至1971年2月为开阳县青禾区哨上公社知青。1971年3月至1975年2月在开阳县农机厂当工人。1975年3月至1978年9月为中共开阳县委宣传部工作员，期间，1976年6月加入中国共产党。1978年10月至1981年1月任开阳县委办公室秘书。1981年2月至1992年8月任开阳县委办公室副主任、主任。1982年9月至1987年8月任开阳县委常委、县委办公室主任，期间，1984年9月至1986年7月在中共贵州省委党校党政管理班学习。1987年9月至1990年3月任开阳县委副书记。1990年4月至1991年10月任中共修文县委副书记。1991年10月至1993年11月任修文县委书记。1993年12月至1996年12月任贵州省安顺地区行政公署副专员。1997年1月至2000年1月任中共安顺地委委员、行署常务副专员。2000年2月至2003年5月任毕节地委书记，是中共第十六次全国代表大会代表，贵州省第十届人民代表大会代表，中共贵州省第九届委员会委员。

朱生亮自幼聪明机灵，读书努力不懈，为人谦逊随和，办事勤恳务实，在35年的工作经历中，为党的事业殚精竭虑，呕心沥血，贡献了毕生精力。在开阳工作期间，他参与政务，处理事务，搞好服务，积极协助县委主要领导做了大量的艰苦细致工作，为开阳县的经济社会发展做出了突出的贡献。

到修文后，朱生亮通过调查，了解到县境有的地方还处于“马路不平，电话不灵，电灯不明”的状况，即在县委常委会上提出建设修文的思路：以交通通信为龙头，尽快改变投资环境，筑巢引凤；加快重点乡镇建设，搞活大流通，培育市场体系；积极开发旅游业，带动发展第三产业。常委分析调查论证，将这个思路定为“三部曲”进行运作，形成修文经济社会全面发展的态势，为后来的又好又快发展奠定了坚实的基础。

在抓交通建设上，朱生亮有一句话：要得富，先修路，要发达，先把桥来搭。他从县城的道路抓起，带领相关单位的干部，跑安顺，上省城，找交通部门，求有关领导，终于到位资金270万元启动人民大道的修建。开工那天，他与县长刘毓文带领机关职工在环城路洗脚塘段挥锄挖土，持锹铲泥，稀泥沾得满脸满身，周围的群众见着无不赞佩：这才是真抓实干的县委书记。施工10个月，包括粑（粑坳）修（文）、修（文）久（长）进城路段改造在内，东起阳明洞，南至王官乡，路宽10米（城内宽25米）、长近6公里横贯县城的主干道硬化通车，改变了“晴天一身灰，下雨满街泥”的交通面貌。街道两旁高楼林立，商店遍布，歌厅舞榭，彩灯夺目，呈现出修文从未有过的繁盛景象，令人耳目一新。面对崭新市街，有的说：这是修文的长安街，街名应叫“生亮路”。朱生亮说：人民的路人民修，功劳归于修文人

民，应命名“人民大道”。时间过去18年，人民大道经过风雨剥蚀，人行车驶，仍是路基坚固，路面光滑。

在修文使用旧式的手摇电话使朱生亮感到：要吸引外资引进项目，促进修文经济发展，缺少现代的通信工具怎么行？他下决心兴建程控电话，亲自到省、地邮电管理部门求援，到位资金400万元，组织邮电职工上马，购设备，搞安装，仅8个月就有自动交换机投入使用，从此结束了沿袭47年使用手摇电话的历史。程控电话开通那天，《安顺日报》以《修文有了“顺风耳”》为题作为特大喜讯报道，人们额首庆幸，连声称赞“朱生亮讲实话，办实事，见实效”。

流经县境的乌江上游六广河将修文、黔西两县隔开，世世代代群众往来单靠木船划行。朱生亮决心改变这种落后的交通运输，上贵阳，下毕节，走安顺，去黔西，恳求上级和兄弟单位应允在六广河上建设公路大桥。功夫不负有心人，终于获得贵州省交通厅关于建设六广河大桥的批复，由省、地两级出资668万元作为专项建桥资金。朱生亮喜出望外，开工那天，六广河两岸炮鸣震耳，人声鼎沸，有的说“是朱生亮‘上蹿下跳’才有这样的炮声，是朱生亮‘兴云布雨’才有这样的欢腾”。朱生亮心潮澎湃，文思涌动，当即挥毫书成楹联：六广依绿水，伴松韵，跨彩虹，东去通江达海；七峡藏奇景，听猿声，涌碧涛，西行进滇入川。对联道出了朱生亮盼望大桥早日建成造福修文和黔西人民的夙愿。居住在黔西县素朴镇勤于搜集资料编写志书的农民王观正在“好官录”上工工整整地写上“朱生亮”三个字，实实在在地记录其为修文、黔西两县人民建设六广河大桥的事迹。省交通厅的领导面对朱生亮评述道：“六广河大桥的成功修建对促进兴建贵毕高等级公路项目的立项起到了相当重要的作用，而你，应该是一名功臣。”

朱生亮在安顺行署分管财政税收工作，积极协助主要领导抓财税体制改革，采取措施完善乡镇财税体制，充分调动了乡镇开辟财源发展经济的积极性。到毕节地委主持工作，紧扣毕节试验区开发扶贫、生态建设和人口控制三大主题，围绕把毕节建成能源、绿色、畜牧、旅游四大区的奋斗目标，提出“时时抢抓发展机遇，处处改善投资环境，人人争做毕节形象”的要求，不举办大型会展，不邀请歌星舞星和笑星，而是以务实的作风，走出去的战略和抢抓机遇的意识，身体力行，不辞辛劳，亲自率队远赴山东、山西等地，成功引进山东兖矿集团、青岛红星集团和山西晋城煤业集团等大型企业，促进了毕节地区煤电资源的开发。与此同时，他还不断加强和改善党对人大和政协工作的领导，关心和支持军队建设、国防后备力量建设，亲自策划“神州大地毕节人”系列采访宣传活动，组织实施黔西北经济文化长廊建设，推动了毕节地区的物质文明建设、政治文明建设和精神文明建设协调发展。

2003年5月16日，朱生亮因病辞世，时年56岁，修文、开阳、安顺、毕节的干部和群众闻之纷纷惋惜，很多职工赶赴殡仪馆沉痛悼念，有的作赋撰联寄托哀思，有联云：

一夜寒风折劲松，
伤心堕泪唤朱公；
纵然千古留遗恨，
满目青山荡晚钟。

聂承先

聂承先（1922—2004），又名聂勋武，四川省江津县吴滩场邢家岗（今重庆市江津区吴滩镇邢家村）人，民国18年（1929）入塾念书，后又就读于当地保国民学校，民国28年（1939）小学毕业留校任教，民国31年（1942）改教从医，民国37年（1948）离家赴贵阳聂乾元药号学徒，1951年参加贵州省土改卫生工作队在毕节何官屯宣传防疫知识和培训种痘员、接生员，返筑后到中医进修班学习，1956年被分配在贵阳中医院当医生，1966年调到修文县人民医院任中医师，1968年下到六广区卫生院担负中医疹疗，1976年回到县人民医院工作，1984年起任政协修文县委员会副主席，1991年退休，1992年在修文县城开设“聂承先诊所”，2004年因肺气肿导致心衰医治无效辞世，享年82岁。

聂承先出生中医世家，父亲聂荣封为江津名医，擅长治疗癫痫病；舅父杨茂修有《温病条辨》和《中医内外妇儿及眼科论治》著作问世。聂承先涉足医药界是20岁开始的，起初随父行医济世，26岁远离父亲在筑城药店当学徒，一面拣药，一面给病人治疗，因治愈一位双目即将失明的患者而闻名遐迩。1966年，聂承先响应毛泽东“把医疗卫生工作重点放在农村去”的号召，毅然离开省城贵阳举家迁往修文，在县人民医院中医应诊，两年后下到边远的六广区卫生院任中医师，坚守8年后才返回县医院，在中医科仍任中医师。政协任职7年也未离开中医业务，期间还被县人民政府任命为中医科副主任医师。

聂承先从事中医治疗50多年，由于不断实践，医技出类拔群，不仅能治疗内、妇、儿、外等科常见病和多发病，而且对危重病和疑难杂证也能诊治，特别是以中药治疗癫痫有其独到之处，从20世纪50年代至80年代，经他治愈的癫痫病人竟达100多人，受到全省医界好评。癫痫治方虽系父传，经聂承先多年实践总结更加完善，但他从不保守，将其医术在贵州省卫生厅《红旗竞赛报》上揭示，并撰写《中医药对精神病临床分型治疗初探》录入贵州省中医学术年会资料选编。与此同时，中医药对精神病的临床治疗被列为安顺地区重点科研课题并荣获科研成果奖。

聂承先行医十分注重医德，用他的话来说：当医生要讲人道，要爱护人的生命，关怀人的幸福。数十年间，聂承先一直履行他立下的道德准则，每凡应诊患者，他都仔细询问病情，认真倾听病人口述，精准诊脉，稳慎处方。凡经聂承先诊疗过的病人都交口赞誉“聂医师的敬业精神令人敬佩”，“聂医师是我们信得过的医师”。聂承先的弟子傅兴发随其从医30多年，在其循循善诱的教诲下终于成为医药界的行家里手。提起聂承先，傅兴发总是道出真实感受：“恩师医德高尚，为人谦和，教我们学医耐心，为病人诊疗慎重，他以人民生命为重的奉献精神今天还是有很强的指导意义的。我们的时代呼唤聂承先精神，需要聂承先这样的医生。”

聂承先下一代有一子二女，长子聂坤达服务于航空航天部属华烽厂。两个女儿师承父业：长女聂坤慧工作在广东珠海，系中医主治医师；次女聂坤莲系中医执业医师，先是随父开设诊所，父亲病故后挂牌“老来福中医诊所”应诊。

李志鹏

李志鹏（1932—2004），扎佐镇人，少时在家乡念小学，后考入贵阳师范就读，民国37年（1948）入伍国民党青年远征军，民国38年（1949）年初随军徙至台湾，在军中担任二О一师六О一团机二连第一班班长。1956年退役后考取台湾省立中兴法商学院专习法律，大学毕业留校担任助教。1966年留学美国攻读海商法和国际法。1969年返台设立海事法律事务所，在基隆和台北经理律师业务，并在中兴大学和辅仁大学任课。1972年当选为“台湾立法院立法委员”，连续任职4届，并任“立法委员党部副书记长”。1985年被提名为特任大法官。1994年退休后参与社会公益事业，任台北市中央狮子会第二十五届会长。此外，李志鹏在台中后期，先后担任过“国民党黄复兴党部委员”、“立法委员党部委员”和“中央委员”、“中央考纪委员、中央评议委员”。2004年12月30日因心律不齐辞世。是日上午9时，由中国国民党主席连战担任主任的治丧委员会在台北市民权东路第一殡仪馆景厅举行公祭后，随即发引安厝于台北县万里乡天祥宝塔禅寺。

李志鹏一向勤勉好学，在中兴学院读书因经济拮据就利用课余时间进行家教挣钱交学费。在校苦读因成绩优异获奖学金和助学金，三年级即参加“考试院”高检师法官和高等法官考试，名列全校第一。继后又获得美国德州达拉斯南美以美大学奖学金。赴美学法后取得加州法学院法学博士学位。留任中兴学院助教即登讲坛讲授法学课程。任大法官司届满退休后，还专心致力于国防学和历史学的研究。

李志鹏服务于立法院10余年，以强国为重、利民为先的指导思想研究大政方针，提出“树立廉政、爱民、便民新政风”“改善劳工保险”“减轻个人负税”“革新人事制度”“尊重人权，维护审判公平”等见解，推动各项重要法案，并著书《英国契约法论》《国家·责任》和《强国富民论》公开发行。期间，因工作成绩突出，先后获得“司法院”奖章和行政奖章。在狮子会从事服务社会不遗余力，与众狮友以慈悲为怀，经常关心民众疾苦，扶孤济贫，尊老爱幼，其为民、爱民、便民的践行举措，令人赞誉。

李志鹏出生贵州，入台50多年，时时心系故里。担任台北贵州同乡会会长8年，广泛团结旅台同乡，不断通报乡情，使在台的贵州修文人罗承忠、金伯琴、罗永鸿等返里得到与亲人的团聚。为鼓励贵州青年努力向学，年年筹措经费，颁发“贵州大专优秀青年奖学金”。1993年与一批曾在修文求学的校友共同捐资购买教学设备，分别送给修文中学、扎佐中学钢琴各1台，实验小学电子琴1台，实验幼儿园手风琴1台。为促进海峡两岸文化交流，曾在台北和贵阳两地举办“海峡两岸贵州书画家联展”。1996年于贵阳举办的“中国贵州王阳明国际学术讨论会”和1989年中国贵阳第一届阳明文化节，以及2003年贵州建省590周年座谈会，李志鹏均应邀参加。

刘　熙

刘熙（1981—2004），龙场镇城北村人，家贫，少时念完小学升入修文第二中学，初中毕业后因家中经济拮据无力升入高中，便考进贵州省职业中专学校，希冀毕业后有一技之长参与劳务为父母减轻生活负担。3年修完职中课业回到家中，先后经营餐饮、修理家电、电焊机具、畜禽养殖等，继后报名参军，服役于武警广西总队玉林支队，退役后经考聘进入修文县治安巡防大队为巡防队员。

刘熙自小就生活在经济贫困的家庭，时时体贴父母，分外懂事。3年中专生涯，多靠学校助学金和课余勤工俭学——帮人卖报纸、在建房工地抬泥巴挣钱交学费完成学业，往往是饿了嚼两个馒头，渴了就找自来水龙头猛灌一通。一次，见同寝室的一位外省籍同学被小偷摸走生活费而伏在被子里失声痛哭，他即拿出自己卖报纸和抬泥巴凑来准备买饭票的50元钱递过去，使被盗的同学感动得流下热泪。由于刘熙勤俭攻读，学习努力，乐于助人，在学校加入了共产主义青年团。

中专毕业回到家里，生活的重担却落在刘熙的肩上。每天，他除了经营自己的行道外，还要回家煮饭做家务，劝解喝酒解愁的父亲，安慰体弱多病的母亲，照顾年幼上学的妹妹，但他从不叫苦叫累。街坊找他修电器、焊铁门，不论是白天晚上，也不论爬高踩险都不拒绝，报酬给多给少从不计较，邻居因此发出赞叹："这年轻人太懂事了！"

刘熙到了部队决心锻炼自己，每天从出操收操、整理内务到业务训练、警民共建，他处处走在前头。看见他的努力，老班长欣慰地说："我带过若干新兵，还是第一个见到刘熙这样刻苦训练的战士。"军营中战友生病了，他用家乡土方子为战友治病、熬姜汤，晚上烧热水为战友洗脚；冬天连队的下水道堵塞了，他跳进冰冷的脏水里进行疏通；夜晚值勤换岗，他不忍心叫醒熟睡中的战友，竟一人站岗到天亮。一次，他和战友杨家文在玉林街头，遇一伙歹徒殴打一名外地青年，刘熙大喝一声，挺身而出，吓退了歹徒，解救了这名青年。回到军营，他只字不提。两年的军旅生活，刘熙真正得到磨炼，多次获得部队嘉奖，被评为"优秀士兵"。

进入治安巡防大队，刘熙身处第一线，为了社会稳定和百姓安宁，他身着巡防制服，一直与邪恶势力进行斗争，短短半年时间，他和队友一起先后制止了47起持械斗殴事件，收缴各类管制刀具和凶器51把。2004年9月26日逢修文县城赶场，刘熙和另一巡防队员尹红江在场上执勤，见着一名扒手叫吴某的用镊子将一位买菜的男子的一叠钱夹出裤兜后正溜走，他俩立即冲上前去将扒手抓住时，扒手就挥舞着手中的长镊子反抗，刘熙和尹红江毫无惧色与之搏斗。突然间又窜出扒手的一名同伙吴某，手持折刀猛力向刘熙背部捅去，直至血染刀柄，便拔刀转身逃跑。刘熙强忍剧痛奋不顾身直追凶手，在他顽强地追击20米时，终因肺叶被刺穿失血过多倒在血泊之中。当战友们赶至现场将刘熙扶起送进修文县中医院时，他已全身被鲜血浸透说不出话来，背部被刺处和口、鼻不断涌出血水、血沫，遂停止呼吸就此牺牲，时年23岁。

9月28日，修文县公安局在县体育馆为刘熙举行追悼大会，前往悼念的群众、干部、老师、学生万余人。翌日，公安局制发修公发〔2004〕67号文件，在全局掀起向刘熙学习的活动。

2006年9月7日，经贵州省人民政府黔函〔2006〕14号文批复贵阳市人民政府，同意追认刘熙为革命烈士。

吴绍昌

吴绍昌（1921—2007），石安乡（今小箐乡）大林村人，出身农民家庭，少时入塾。修文解放初期担任本村农民协会主席，遂任乡农会主席。1953年加入中国共产党，在修文县历任区长、区委书记、县委农村工作部副部长，县人民政府副县长、县委常委、县革委副主任和县人大常委会主任等职，1984年3月退职休养，2007年4月病故。

吴绍昌作风朴实，工作勤恳。无论是在基层工作，还是到县里担任领导职务，他身着中山服，脚穿解放鞋，带上人们称的下乡“四件宝”（一把雨伞、一支手电筒、一个帆布包、一个日记本），背起背包下到乡村住进村民家，一住就是个把月，与群众同住同吃同劳动同商量，把党的政策宣传贯彻到群众中去，发动组织群众完成各项工作任务。农业合作化初期，他带工作组下至金桥乡小寨试办初级社，住在村民陶文富家，坚持把农民组织起来闹生产并不断总结建社经验指导全区工作，推动整个合作化的进程。“大跃进”期间，吴绍昌被抽到花溪参与修建阿哈水库任副指挥长，时遇农村生活极度困难，他坚守施工现场与民工共同战斗，往往是晴天一身汗，雨天一身泥。由于缺少营养，加之操劳过度，几次昏倒在工地被工人送进医院治疗，然病未痊愈又回到原地指挥施工，经过两年苦战，水库竣工才返回单位。农业学大寨运动中，他注重改土造田，大力绿化荒山，带领群众在花椰公社营造林场1000多亩，于公路两旁种植行道树千余株，如今，场里一片葱绿，路上浓荫蔽日，老百姓从林产品获得实惠后赞不绝口：“还是吴书记带领我们绿化受益，真是前人栽树后人歇凉啊！”

吴绍昌心贴群众，务实为民。他分管农业，时时不忘群众 的生产和生活。一次下到农村，正值秋收，见着五保户万富昌年迈多病，庄稼成熟收不进家，身为久长区区长的吴绍昌卷起裤管，扛着挞斗，带上两名工作人员下到齐腿深的淤泥田里，将万富昌老人1亩多地稻谷收割进家。接着，又带领群众将缺少劳力的4家困难户的水稻收进屋里。县境岩鹰山水库渠系配套完工，时遭夏旱，他感到当务之急是放水打田，于是带领干部巡回在20多公里的渠道 上，哪里堵塞就在哪里疏通，终于将库水引至历来干旱的六广、新坪、广义、广山、联丰等村，打田200多亩。村民们眼见清澈的库水流进自己的家门口，无不称赞吴绍昌“是为人民服务的好领导”。

吴绍昌干净做官，不谋私利。他是修文解放后首批发展的党员，也是当官最先的本地干部。然而为官一世，两袖清风。其妻和4个子女长期在农村从事农业劳动，他从未利用手中的权力安排一个到机关和企事业单位。家居农村，离县城10多公里，也从不用公车接送，节假日回家多是步行或乘坐班车，他牢记党的宗旨，恪守党的纪律，任何时候都没有忘记自己是一名共产党员，临终前还嘱咐大儿子为其交纳最后一个月的党费。

白进德

白进德（1923—2008），河南省濮阳县（今濮阳市）人，少时因家贫辍学，年龄稍长后帮地主家扛活。民国33年（1944）在家乡加入中国共产党，民国34年（1945）参加革命，1949年11月随军南下到修文县参与接管政权，先后担任过区民运主任、组织委员、区长、区委书记、县监委书记、组织部长、县委书记处书记、副书记、区革委主任和县人大常委会副主任等职，1984年离职休养享受地专级干部政治待遇和生活待遇。

抗日战争时期，白进德系敌后抗日根据地濮阳县八公桥村共产党的干部。民国34年（1945）3月，他参加群英会学习毛泽东《一九四五年的任务》和为改善佃雇农生活于6月参加县佃雇农集会后，回村发动群众投入减租减息运动，取得很大成效。抗战结束即任八公桥区联合会主任领导民运工作。

民国35年（1946）6月蒋介石发动全面内战开始，时为八公桥区指导员的白进德出任该区担架营的教导员，他在动员群众参加担架队时说："过去受国民党和地主压迫得我们吃不上饭，折磨得死去活来，今天随军打老蒋要不怕累，不怕苦，不怕死。"群众加入担架队后，白进德带领全体队员编入县的担架团，随军转战两个多月，在濮阳县境风雨兼程4000多里路，运弹药，送军粮，救护伤员，掩埋烈士……部队需要干什么，担架队就干什么。民国36年（1947）7月，白进德担任担架营营长，带领担架队顶着雨季运送物资的困难，全力支援解放军强渡黄河。为了不让伤员雨淋日晒，白进德经常将自己使用的草帽和衣服脱下盖在伤员身上并护送到医疗队。民国37年（1948）6月，白进德任联合组建的担架营教导员，担架队的主要任务是配合华东野战军第四纵队攻克开封。开封攻下后，白进德组织担架队员将缴获的大批武器弹药安全地运送到四纵驻地杞县小楼村。继后，因敌机轰炸黄河堤坝导致河水淹至豫东，担架队发扬不怕牺牲的精神，从战壕里救出伤员数十人。接着，又随军进至安徽亳县等新解放区，为密切党群关系和军民关系，白进德带领担架队员给群众扫地、担水、推磨、照看小孩，还下地干活，一直坚持21天后才返回濮阳。由于白进德及其带领的担架队做了许多工作，成绩突出，先后受到濮阳县委和华东军区第四纵队的多次表彰。

1949年3月，白进德作为优秀干部被选调随解放军南下开辟广大新区，告别故土，横渡长江，于4月解放江西省都昌县，负责大田区委所在地土塘镇的接管政权、借粮支前和镇压匪特暴乱等工作，8月完成各项任务后转驻上饶休整，随后向贵州进军。

白进德到修文任扎佐区民运委员会主任，时值人民政府新建，国民党残余势力妄图卷土重来，区境匪徒十分嚣张，一个号称"中国人民反共救国军西南区总司令部直属第六纵队司令"的罗铭，率匪众百余人麇集桃源，不断骚扰百姓，扬言要"攻进扎佐，占领修文"。面对严峻形势，修文县委和扎佐区委决定采取"军事打击与政治瓦解相结合"的进剿措施，先向罗铭匪部展开政治攻势。白进德自告奋勇请战，带工作员车素华壮着担子深入虎穴，下到桃源罗匪驻地，向罗铭宣传共产党和人民政府对待匪特"自首从宽，抗拒从严，立功受奖"的政策，指明走悔过自新的出路。经过整整10天的争取工作，使罗铭

带领匪副司令黄国栋等骨干分子和匪众100多人携枪99支向人民政府投械。此次不用一枪一弹促使罗铭匪部投案的军事作为受到贵州省军区通报表彰。

白进德在修文工作36年，均居领导岗位。他老老实实做人，清清白白为官，干干净净工作，深受干部群众的尊敬和爱戴，称他是“清正廉洁的领导”。

2008年7月，白进德因病去世，终年85岁。

李光明

李光明（1945—2010），沿河乡洞口（今六屯乡星中村对门前寨）人，少时念完初小即在家务农。1968年迁居久长公社石榴大队（今久长镇石榴村）仍以农耕为业。1986年加入中国共产党。从1984年起，先后建起修文县久金矿产经营部，创办开阳县金中化工厂、开阳县广门田磷矿和开阳县青龙磷矿等企业，并任过修文县磷肥厂副厂长、贵州省经济技术开发公司矿产部负责人、开阳县金中化工厂理事长，还被选为贵州省集体私人联合会理事和全国个体劳动者协会理事，是修文县第九届人民代表大会代表和政协修文县第三届委员会委员。

1984年，在党的改革开放方针指引下，李光明脱离农耕，自筹资金组建起修文县久金矿产经营部，自任经理，收购农民开采的重晶石矿销往外地。由于企业讲诚信，善经营，出现产品购销两旺，发展至1988年，销往全国的重晶石矿多至14个省、市的数十个生产建筑材料和石油支撑剂的厂家，销售总收入达600万元，为农民增加采矿收入22万元，为搬运工人增收30万元，为运输部门增收250万元，缴纳税款36万元，仅1988年就纳税12万元，日均交税333.4元。1993年，李光明又在贵阳经营餐饮，兴办“金魁五酒楼”，顾客光顾不断，生意十分火爆。1999年，又转到磷矿资源丰富的开阳县兴办磷矿企业，由于企业“蛋糕”越做越大，竟成为开阳县规模以上的重点企业并是纳税大户。从2006年起，李光明每年向国家交税翻过千万元大关，26年共纳税上亿元，吸纳农村富余劳动力就业千余人。

李光明致富不忘乡亲，热心赞助家乡的公益事业。1985年，他刚踏上致富路，为六屯小学的改建就慷慨解囊捐资1500元；1987年重建石榴村小学捐资3000元；为解决久长中学学生住校问题，出资3500元购置几十张钢丝床送给学校；金桥乡整修卫生院又捐助1000元；为维修矿山公路，又出资4000元；为解决百户村民的照明和10多亩望天水田的灌溉，他拿出2000元购置变压器。修文县磷肥厂因缺少周转资金面临倒闭，他主动以无息贷款的方式借给厂方8000元把工厂救活起来继续生产复合肥，以应烤烟生产的急需……一桩桩一件件的资助使家乡的若干困难迎刃而解，使父老乡亲深为感动，对李光明的善举赞不绝口，说他是“专做善事的善人”。

李光明致富不忘扶贫济困，老家新中村农民李光学家境贫寒买不起耕牛，常误农时影响耕种，李光明急人之困，耗资1100元购买1头水牛送给李光学，使李光学家按节令打田插秧，获得丰收。从1958年起，李光明总是给五保户李岳炎及其老伴送去资金三五百元不等，添助安度晚年。1987年，石榴村村民罗国珍因暴雨冲垮住房而被砸成重伤，李光明支付400元将伤治愈。青年农民韩志发因家境窘迫失去生活信心，甚至酗酒赌博，终日浪荡。为了不使韩志发流浪下去，李光明花了3000元为其买马两匹和马车1

辆从事运输，使其步入正道。之后，浪子回头，韩志发通过劳动建家，娶妻生子，过上了幸福生活，全家人无不感谢李光明，逢人便说“李经理给我们家的恩惠祖祖辈辈都不会忘记”。

李光明虽只读过初小，但喜好看书学习，致文化水平逐渐提升。在经办企业的同时，还参与文化活动和勤于电视新闻报道，其新闻作品多次获贵州电视台奖励，本人也多次被评为优秀通讯员。1987年，由于在全国农村农林科教电影汇报月活动中成绩突出，受到农牧渔业部、广播电影电视部、文化部、林业部、国家科委和中国科技协会表彰。1988年参加贵州省个体劳动者协会举办的演讲赛获二等奖。

李光明经商办企业名扬省内外，新闻媒体纷至沓来采访其事迹，先后在《人民日报》、中央电视台和《贵州日报》、贵州电视台报道；同时载入《中国当代企业家成长事迹录》《党的生活》《人生经纬》《人生几何》《老板传奇》和《综艺录》等书刊；还被拍成专题片《光明之路》在贵州电视台和中央电视台播放。

李光明从农耕步入兴办企业的事迹得到组织肯定和受到表彰。1986年被评为贵州省和全国的先进个体劳动者出席全国个体劳动者第一次代表大会，受到党和国家领导人邓小平、李鹏接见并合影留念。1987年，时任贵州省委书记胡锦涛到石榴村李光明家中看望，鼓励李光明保持荣誉，继续努力，并与之合影。1988年，贵州省纪委企业管理协会授予李光明优秀经理称号，同时被评为修文县优秀共产党员。1989年被评为先进个体劳动者出席贵州省第二次个体劳动者表彰大会。1990年被国家税务局和共青团中央评为个体工商守法模范纳税户，同时被邀请赴北京参加第十届亚洲运动会开幕式观礼。1991年再次出席全国个体劳动者代表大会受到国家领导人接见并合影。

李光明家富不忘教育子女艰苦守业，勤俭持家。当族人续修《李氏家谱》之际，他自立家训勉励子孙后代：出身贫寒不自卑，创业艰辛不自馁，奋力拼搏不松懈，家业富有不奢华。要将“勤、俭、信”为立身之本，以“骄、奢、逸”作终身之戒，孝悌为先，营造和谐幸福家庭。

2010年5月，李光明因病去世，终年65岁。

张福华

张福华（1956—1990），1956年12月生于宝寨乡（今六桶乡属）复兴村，1978年3月参加中国人民解放军，1979年2月加入中国共产党，在对南疆保卫战中荣立三等功，1980年6月复员，1981年6月在宝寨乡任工作员，1982年12月在宝寨乡担任武装部长，1988年3月任宝寨乡党委副书记，1989年12月任凉井乡（今六桶乡属）工作员，1990年10月因犯爆炸罪被判处死刑。

张福华任宝寨乡党委副书记期间，与在任乡长焦兴佑工作上产生矛盾，对焦不满。继后，组织上将张福华调到凉井乡当工作员，张认为是焦兴佑整他，对焦更加不满，起心杀害焦兴佑。1990年1月的一天夜里，张福华找到表哥方正祥倾诉心中的恨意说：“老表，焦兴佑把我整恼火了，你要给我报仇。”方正祥问：“咋个报法?”张说：“找点炸药、雷管把他消灭了。”方正祥说：“焦兴佑的住房在哪?”张福华告诉方：“靠我家这头这间就是焦兴佑的床铺。”杀害焦兴佑的预谋商定后，张福华就在凉井乡烟叶站建筑工地和宝寨小学施工工地以炸鱼、修房为借口，骗到手炸药3节和纸雷管2个交给方正祥。1990年6月18日夜里，方正祥拿出准备好的炸药、雷管和自存的导火绳制成炸药包，用烟头点燃导火绳后即逃离现

场，翌日凌晨2时25分钟炸药包爆炸，将焦兴佑家24厘米厚的钢筋水泥房房顶炸开1个80×70厘米的通洞，睡在房里的焦兴佑的女儿张艳梅被炸成重伤。

事发后，张福华于1990年6月26日被收审，8月8日被提请批准逮捕。经公安、司法部门听取被害人焦兴佑陈述和张福华对犯罪事实的供认，并进行刑事技术鉴定和法医鉴定，确认张福华身为国家工作人员无视国法，为泄私愤不顾他人安危而指使方正祥并提供爆炸物品和采取爆炸手段杀害他人，危害公共安全，犯罪情节特别恶劣，其行为已构成爆炸罪，是制造事端的主犯。经贵州省高级人民法院终审裁定：判处张福华死刑，剥夺政治权利终身。1990年11月，经修文县纪委常委研究决定，给予张福华开除党籍的处分。

第二章　人物简介

为了弥补“盖棺”才可“定论”的人物传记留下的缺陷，特设“人物简介”章反映改革开放33年间在县境活动中已有闪光点的人生事迹的在世人物27人。其体例主要记述在活动期间的生平事迹，不作任何结论。

周元芬

周元芬，女，清光绪二十九年（1903）4月出生于信顺里三甲（今六广镇）官庄，民国11年（1922）出嫁到二甲（今小箐乡）白果市与农民傅德全结婚成家，民国30年（1941）举家迁往龙场镇倒牌坊（今县城民主路南段）。至2010年，周元芬已达107岁高龄，用她的话来说：我是皇帝管的那个时候出生的，活到今天已经过了3个朝代，清朝8年，民国38年，新中国61年。周元芬在县内百岁以上老人中排名居首，在贵阳市27位百岁以上老人中名列第五。年逾百岁的周元芬，身板硬朗，步履稳健，思维敏捷，耳聪目明，口齿清楚。

周元芬的保健养生经验，一是劳动为本。从十五六岁起就参加农业劳动，进入中年更习惯于日出而作、日入而息的自给自足的农耕生活，迁居县城后间或兼做点油炸饮食的小本生意，80多岁还喂鸡养猪，下地干活，她感到“经常劳动就能增强消化功能，精神有了寄托，心情也开朗了”，“每天不干点活就很难过”。二是心态平和。她毋贪无求，知足常乐，满百岁时因享受待遇未予兑现，儿子傅贵林要去上访有关部门，她当即制止说：“孩子，你不要跟领导添麻烦，共产党对我家够好了，要相信党的政策，该得的政府一文也不会少。”随后，组织按享受标准每月200元给予落实。三是以人为善。她中年就学会土医，无论邻里、街坊，一旦有人牙痛、中暑、消化不良、患恐缩症等多来找她医治，她用按摩、推拿、刮痧等方法治疗，多年为患者解除病痛不计其数，但分文不取，她把这称为“善举”，做好了自己就心安理得。四是饮食平衡。步入老年，每天早餐吃两个甜酒煮鸡蛋，中餐和晚餐或1碗米饭，或1碗粉面，素晕搭配，以素为主，每餐1片肥肉、半杯白酒，多吃蔬菜，从不暴食暴饮，也不吸烟，她说“病从口入，不注意饮食调理就染病在身，调节好饮食就可以延长健康期，提高生命质量”。五是生活规律，她家居住在城郊的小街上，屋舍宽敞、空气清新，她每天天明起床，天黑就寝，睡眠充足，休息适度，饭后坚持户外散步，每周沐浴更衣1

次，保持全身整洁，冬不烤火，夏不挥扇，极少伤风感冒，偶尔患病必须在非不得已的情况下才看医生和用药。在日常生活中养成良好的卫生习惯成为周元芬延年益寿的法宝。

周元芬有1个男孩、4个女孩，女孩出嫁后由男孩傅贵林担当起赡养母亲的责任，女儿们也不断来家嘘寒问暖。全家11口四世同堂，儿孙绕膝，尊老爱幼，家庭和睦，生趣盎然。人们看见周元芬鹤发童颜的外貌和乐观豁达的精神风采，谁都不会相信她是一个百岁高龄的老人。

2009年10月，周元芬被评为健康老寿星，在贵阳市老龄工作委员会召开的“全市庆祝老年节暨居家养老工作先进单位、寿星、孝星表彰大会”上受到表彰；同时，贵州省老龄工作委员会办公室颁发给周元芬长寿证书。

郝承德

郝承德，修文县六桶乡人，民国17年（1928）出生，自幼酷爱绘画，凭着聪颖的天赋，很小的年纪就画什么像什么。1964年，郝承德进入贵阳达德学校，接触擅长画竹的老师刘复莘，他从刘复莘的教诲中立下做人的准则，只有像竹子那样具有刚正不阿的崇高品格，才能在艺术上挺直身子，有所成就。民国36（1947），郝承德考入贵州省立贵阳师范学校劳作美术科，迎来了他绘画技能快速进步期，师从贵州省著名画家张云麓、阮尔钟，吸取了新的山水画技法，并不断临摹古今著名画家黄宾虹、傅抱石、李可染等的作品，确立了自己的绘画风格和艺术语言。1949年，他考进贵阳师范学院（今贵州师范大学）艺术科，进一步钻研绘画艺术。在师院又得到了贵州省著名画家宋吟可和孟光涛的教诲。在老师的指导下，郝承德的绘画艺术产生了质的飞跃，处女作《南明河畔春来早》得到了老师的嘉奖和同学的称赞。作画同时，他经常阅读文艺理论方面的书籍，注重理论与实践的结合。离开学校后，他先后在六桶小学、扎佐小学教美术课。1953年，郝承德被调到县文化馆发挥他的专长，尽管受到“文化大革命”的冲击，他还是顶住了来自各方面的压力坚持画画，日复一日地沉浸在砚池墨海中，不懈的努力更进一步提高了他的绘画理论知识和表现技法。

中共十一届三中全会后，郝承德已年过半百，虽然历经坎坷，但他倍加珍惜自己的后半生，继续拿起画笔光明正大地从事绘画创作。群众文化工作为他提供了作画的时间和空间，他常年跋涉在山间水畔，走进苗寨侗乡，览胜云海雾都，探幽青城峨眉，涉足长江三峡，摆渡乌江水上，步履西双版纳，饱览大自然的奇峰秀水和云壑飞泉，“搜尽奇峰打草稿”，把对祖国河山的热爱绘进了五彩缤纷的画卷，形成了自己独特的带有地域特色和民族特色的艺术风格。由于执著的追求，郝承德在晚年迎来了事业的丰收季节：1992年在安顺市举办“郝承德画展”，展出作品67幅。展出期间，安顺市文艺界知名人士周青明、郑正祥、宋茨林、陈慎恪等在《安顺日报》和《安顺文艺》发表文章对展览给予高度评价。2001年作品《乌江烟雨》入选全国老年书画研究会，并在北京军事博物馆展出，获二等奖，作品入编画集。2002年北京民族文化宫举办“民族情”全国书画大展入展作品《谁人不恋侗乡情》获二等奖，并编入画集；在延安国画院举办的“走进西部”全国书画展展出作品《春染苗岭》获得一等奖并获国画院颁发的院士证，还被任命为该院院士和名誉副院长。此外，在贵州省、贵阳市、安顺地区和县内举办的书画展览中，郝承德获奖高达40余次。

2004年，集48幅作品的《郝承德画集》出版，贵州省文联主席杨长槐在《序言》中对其作品给予高度评价："他的画给人的感觉是真诚，有创意，有激情，看不出浮华虚假之意，也看不出因袭古人的痕迹以及那种贫乏无味的程式化模仿之风和循规蹈矩、生搬硬套的拘泥之气，体现出他对'无法而有法'，'我用我法'的理解以及表现黔山秀水的固有特征和深刻的内涵，以形式之美达自然之美的追求"。2006年，贵州省著名书法家陈加林题写书名的《郝承德画选》问世，18幅用红、绿、黄、黑色块纵情挥洒在山水之间，淋漓尽致地画出了故土青山苍翠、万木争荣的景象，给人一个变幻无穷、多姿多彩的山和水的世界。

鉴于郝承德的绘画出类拔萃，省、市新闻媒体不断作出报道：1995年安顺地区电视台与修文电视台合作摄制了《情系山河》专辑影片；2006年《贵州日报》以《翰墨丹青颂山河》为题撰写通讯，贵州电视台"发现贵州"栏目又摄制出《情在山水间》专辑，先后在贵州电视台和修文电视台播放。通过办展、报刊、电视等形式，让外界感受到郝承德绘画作品的最直观的电视艺术享受，也使郝承德的艺术生涯远播省内外，产生了既深远又广泛的宣传效果。

2008年郝承德已达80高龄，但他精神矍铄，仍笔耕不辍，又以最佳的作品参加2009年省、市书画知名人士戴明贤、曹新忠、黑卫平、陈加林等8人联合在安顺市举办的"回乡展"，赢得了安顺文学艺术界的赞许和社会的反响。

由于郝承德艺高资深，得到社会认可，从1981年起，他先后成为贵州省美术家协会会员、贵州省书法家协会会员，并被聘任为贵阳市老年书画研究会艺术顾问，还当选为安顺地区美术协会副主席。

郝承德虽达耄耋之龄，但仍身居画室，挥毫泼墨，奋笔疾书。他经常吟咏的晚年明志诗曰："立志不随流俗传，留心学到古人难。"有人问他："这是为什么？"他答道："趁有生之年书写我完整的人生，以体现在世的价值。"正是：寄情翰墨心犹壮，养性怡神老有为。

韩文真

韩文真，民国27年（1938）出生在石安联保文书寨（今龙场镇白莲村属文书寨），1957年毕业于贵阳医士学校，后被分配到修文县人民医院当医生。1978年加入中国共产党。1975—1981年和1984—1988年任县人民医院副院长。1981—1984年和1988—2003年任院长。其间：1979—2003年还担任县医院党支部书记，1986年晋升为外科主治医师，1993年晋升为外科副主任医师。2003年退休后留在县医院专家门诊部上班。韩文真是中国共产党修文县第四、五、六、七次代表大会代表，并被选为中共修文县委第四、五、六、七届委员。

韩文真初到县人民医院时，院里仅有简易病床15张，职工不足20人，医生只4人，医疗设备匮乏，因受设备和技术力量限制，连简单的阑尾炎手术也得转到省城的医院施行。面对现状，韩文真心情十分沉重，他只能尽最大的努力，因陋就简地进行工作。继后，多次被选派到贵阳医学院进修普外、麻醉、口腔、骨科专业，他十分珍惜"充电"的机会，如饥似渴地掌握知识，专心聆

听老师的教诲和认真进行临床实践，在指导老师的指导下做好每一例手术，诊疗好每例病人。学成归来，在他的主持下，县人民医院逐渐开展了下腹部手术、上腹部手术、骨折切开复位内固定手术、髋关节结核和腰椎结核病灶清除植骨术、慢性骨髓炎死骨摘除带蒂肌瓣填塞术以及切肢术、子宫全切除等，其中部分手术的开展和重危病人的抢救，在全省县级医院中处于领先地位。

中共十一届三中全会后，韩文真带领医院领导班子，把发展作为兴院、强院的第一要务，以提高医疗质量为重点，加强医德医风教育，促进医院健康快速发展。为使医院的医技水平得到整体提高，采取“派出去学，请进来教”的方式，分批选派医务人员到贵阳医学院、遵义医学院、贵州省人民医院以及北京、上海、杭州等地的大型医院学习；遇疑难重危病人，请上级医院专家、教授莅院会诊，指导手术，有针对性地举办学术讲座，并争取到贵阳医学院由各临床科室专家、教授、技术骨干组成医疗队到院坐诊和进行业务指导，还与贵阳市第一人民医院和贵阳市口腔医院建立长期协作医院，分批派出技术骨干到院里指导业务。采取各种方式，使医院业务技术上了一个新台阶。在韩文真担任县医疗事故鉴定、计划生育手术后遗症鉴定、伤残鉴定、职工病退鉴定和征兵体检、学生升学体检等业务把关负责人期间，从未出现过因体检责任退兵退学和鉴定判定错误。1979年，安顺地区卫生学校委托修文医院开办护士专业分校，韩文真兼任负责人并亲自兼课，3年结业参加全省会考，人人取得好成绩走上工作岗位。1996年，韩文真领导创建爱婴医院活动，通过专家评审达标，由卫生部、联合国儿童基金会和世界卫生组织授予“爱婴医院”光荣称号。

作为一院之长，韩文真坚守廉洁自律的底线，拒腐防变。从不收受红包、不接受病人宴请。医院基础设施建设、医疗药品器械采购制定的规章制度均带头执行，要求所有药品采购必须接受药事委员会的监督，坚持从主渠道优质优价购进药品，不准在办公场所外私人成交药械价购，拒绝“人情药”“搭配药”进医院。医院设备购置、房屋新建与维修实行集体讨论，公开商谈决定。他淡泊名利，临近退休，很多人劝他开私人诊所，凭其威望和技术找一笔钱过些优裕日子，但他却服从组织安排，继续留在医院，孜孜不倦地为病人诊断治疗。

韩文真既是医院管理的负责人，又是医疗领域的技术骨干。从参加工作的那一天起，他就将白求恩对工作极端负责、对同志极端热情、对技术精益求精的严格要求作为座右铭，把为病人服务视为自己的天职，对病人一视同仁，抢救伤员随喊随到，无论是检查、诊断、治疗都一丝不苟，耐心仔细。行医53年，从未离开过医疗第一线，经他亲手治疗的病人数以万计，亲自为患者做手术数千例，没有发生过一次医疗事故。1992年11月29日下午，县境修（文）六（广）公路上柿花树处发生客车翻入85米深沟的特大恶性交通事故，当即死亡23人，剩下重伤8人和轻伤1人送往县医院抢救，其中有全身多处开放性骨折的，有闭合性骨折的，有胸腹部联合损伤的，有肝脾破裂的，有重度脑外伤的……韩文真闻讯第一个赶到医院病房组织抢救，亲自上手术台施行手术，第一台手术完成接连做第二台，第二台完成又做第三台……与医护人员一道连续工作20多个小时，直到全部伤员得到妥善处理才作短暂休息。经过术后精心治疗，伤员痊愈出院，感激之情油然而生，都称“韩院长是救命恩人”。

多年的医疗实践和理论研究成就了韩文真是一位资深的专家，其医疗论著和科研成果都获得业内人士认同。撰写的10多篇论文陆续发表在省内外的医刊上。相继出席过西南四省首届骨科和全国中西医结合软组织疼痛等学术研讨会。1978年，作为协作单位领导人参与贵阳医学院组织的“呼吸四病138010人口普查”并形成报告出席贵州省科学大会获奖。1995年参与全国性“茶色素”降血压、降血脂病例观察，出席1997年中华医学会在北京举办的“茶色素”交流会和在澳门举办的“茶色素”国际交流会。2003年参与“应用葡萄糖利尿作用对输尿管结石CDH超声诊断价值”项目研究，获2003—2005年度县科学技术一等奖。

韩文真在县人民医院协助院长工作和担任院长主持工作的28年间，医院管理水平和业务技术逐年提高，收入逐年增加，医院形象也受到社会各界的好评，贵州电视台、贵阳电视台和《贵州画报》等新闻媒体多次对医院取得的成绩予以报道。韩文真本人也因为历年工作成绩突出多次被评为省、市、县的优秀党员、优秀党务工作者和先进工作者。1959年全县麻疹大流行，他被分配到麻疹病人多、病情严重的干坝村，采用中西结合方法治疗，3个多月诊治麻疹病人200余例，无一例死亡，经县、市检查评定为先进工作者出席贵州省表彰大会。2000年又因工作成绩突出出席贵州省先进工作者大会受到中共贵州省委、贵州省人民政府表彰。

李新民

李新民，1949年10月生于德政乡滥泥山（今六广镇坪营村属滥泥山），1966年修文高中毕业后因“文化大革命”停止高考辍学，1977年恢复高考考入安顺师范专科学校攻读化学专业，1979年毕业分配到修文中学当教师担任高中化学教学，1984年加入中国共产党，并任修文中学副校长兼教导主任，1985年在贵州省教育学院脱产进修获大学本科文凭，1987年返校仍任学校副校长，1996年晋升为校长主持全校工作，2009年退职休养。

李新民出生在教师家庭，父母亲都分别当过中、小学教师。由于环境的熏陶，尤其是父亲坚守三尺讲台向学生传授语文知识50多年退而不休的敬业精神对他潜移默化的影响，从小就孕育着“学而不厌，诲人不倦”的良好品格，用他的话来说：“读书就是我的嗜好，教书就是我的天职。”小学毕业上初中，初中毕业升高中，恰在高中毕业那年碰上“文化大革命”中断读书的黄金期长达11年。为了补齐读书的短板，已满28岁的李新民还是跨进大学，36岁再次踏上进修之路，从而筑牢了教书的基础。

教书就是育人，育人必先育己。这是李新民对他从事教育事业的诠释。他，为人笃实，从不去攀龙附凤拔高自己的地位，只凭自己的管理能力获得组织的信任当上一校之长；他，爱生如子，爱护学生就像爱护自己的子女一样，当的是一个循循善诱的良师；他，矢志不渝，对读初中时就热爱自然科学中的基础学科化学到上大学一直手不释卷地学习和研究物质变化的规律，成为一位深得学生爱戴的高级化学教师；他，恪尽职守，不论是站讲台，管教务，当校长，总是谨慎地搞好自己的本职工作……李新民就是这样为人师表，扎根龙岗（修文中学驻地龙岗山）30年，处处地方都成为学校师生和校外的人们做人学习的榜样。

30年间，李新民一直承担中学化学科的教学任务，任校长13年每年都承担班级学科教学工作。他教学有方，讲授内容紧密结合学生的生活实际，注重培养学生的学习兴趣；针对学生的接受程度采取差别化的授课方法，循序渐进、由浅入深地引导学生分析和归纳所学知识的规律性，让学生从中摸索到一条适合自己学习的途径。因此，学生都愿意听他的课，经他传授知识的学生成绩优良，化学科目的高考成绩经常名列邻县、市学校前茅，近百人参加省、市、县化学竞赛获奖。于是，李新民的教学能力在县内外有口皆碑，多篇教学论文在省内外的刊物上发表。1983年高考有两名学生获97分高分在全省名列前茅。1984年贵州省教材教法过关考试和教学能力考核荣获全省第一名，受到贵州省教育厅表彰，同年获修文县人民政府通报全县表彰并奖励晋升工资一级。1991年被评为全国优秀教师获国家教育委员会和人事部表彰。1996年获贵州省特级教师荣誉称号。

从主持修文中学全面工作的那天起，李新民实行一套管理学校的方法，他将学校的各项管理分工到个人，团结和带领全校领导班子成员心往一处想，劲往一处使，有序地开展工作。他始终认为，教学质量是学校的生命线，质量不佳的学校绝不是好学校。因此，在学校管理的过程中，他确立以教学为中心的指导思想，积极推进教学改革，努力探索大面积提高教学质量的途径，充分吸纳广大教职员工的合理意见，奖优罚劣，建立激励机制，有效地调动教师的教学积极性。教师的积极性迸发出来，爱岗敬业，努力钻研，积极投入教学改革，使学校的教学质量揭开新的一页。1998年，修文中学高考专科以上录取率为全省平均水平的两倍，在贵阳市所辖“一市三县”和三郊区的普通高中、完中名列第一，学校从此步入良性发展阶段，教学质量稳步上升。2002年，学校高考本科录取率为64.8%，专科上线率达92.7%，在贵阳市“一市三县”和三郊区的完全中学中排名第一。2003年至2006年，连续4年荣获贵阳市一般高中“入出口”成绩评估一等奖，2007年和2008年又分别获得二等奖和三等奖。2009年，二类本科以上上线人数达308人，创了历史新高，再次获得贵阳市一般高中“入出口”成绩评估一等奖。2010年，学校814名学生参加高考，一本上线70人，二本上线239人，高考教学质量“入出口”评估在贵阳市一般高中排名第二。若干成绩的取得，凝聚了李新民不辞辛劳办学的心血，实现了他团结全校教职工悉心管理和追求质量的初衷，也凸显出学校的办学效益，从而增强了学生、家长和社会对学校的信任感。

从教30年，桃李满天下。经李新民传道、授业、解惑撒遍大江南北的学生数以计万，他们在各自的岗位上为国家的改革和建设出力，当是李新民在教育园地辛勤耕耘结出的硕果。李新民对修文教育事业的贡献是有目共睹的。1993年，时任修文中学副校长的李新民被选为修文县第十一届人民代表大会的代表并当选为县人大常务委员会委员，赓续连选为第十二届和第十三届代表并任常务委员，3届15年的任职，是修文人民对李新民在修文教育战线上为修文教育事业上奉献青春和年华的认可。

叶　辛

叶辛，1949年10月出生于上海。1969年，叶辛作为知识青年上山下乡到久长公社永兴大队（今久长镇永兴村）砂锅寨插队落户，1975年离乡回城在修文县化肥厂当工人，1979年离开修文调进贵阳。

叶辛在砂锅寨扎根7年，加上化肥厂的时间，整整在修文生活10年半，其中7年长期居住在茅草房和土地庙里。期间，干过担粪、插秧、薅秧、割草喂牛、收苞谷、打谷子等农活，还参加过修建湘黔铁路，又在民办小学当过教师。用他自己的话来说：插队落户虽然失去了许多，但收获也很多，七年时间让我认识了生活，拉近了与农民的距离，建立起与父老乡亲的感情。叶辛一直认为：七年的知青生活是他文学创作的源泉，砂锅寨是他永志不忘的第二故乡。

1977年，叶辛取材苗寨清匪反霸而撰写的儿童文学长篇小说《高高的苗岭》发表，随即改编为电影《火娃》公映，顿时引起轰动。赓续又有《我们这一代年青人》《风凛冽》《孽债》和《蹉跎岁月》等作品问世，其中的《蹉跎岁月》和《孽债》还改编成电视连续剧在全国各地播放，并荣获全国优秀电视剧奖。至2010年，共出版著作单行本50余部，连同文集、总集、全集、选集、代表作系列总计106部，其中的短篇小说《塌方》获国际青年优秀作品一等奖，中篇小说《家教》获《十月》文学奖，长篇小说《基石》和《孽债》分别获贵州省优秀作品奖和全国优秀长篇小说奖，长篇小说《华都》获全国优秀畅销书奖。叶辛本人于1985年被评为“全国优秀文艺工作者”，荣获全国首届“五一劳动奖章”。

叶辛于青年时代就在文学界崭露头角，随着作品的不断产出，成为世人公认的著名作家。1979年进入贵州省作家协会工作，遂又担任《山花》杂志主编以及省作协副主席。1990年任《海上文坛》主编和上海市作家协会副主席。1996年任中国作家协会副主席。

2009年，叶辛已届花甲之龄，但仍笔耕不辍，以每天4000字的速度写下了他的第十部知青题材作品《客过亭》，用凝练、生动的文字去追求当年上山下乡的足迹。该书于2010年面世，深受读者尤其是当过上山下乡知青读者的青睐。

叶辛回到上海后，曾多次返回砂锅寨。当他看到生活困难的老大娘就解囊资助，看到山村面貌依旧便和村民们一起探索脱贫致富的路子。2004年，共青团贵州省委发起旨在弘扬“饮水思源，反哺故土”的中华传统美德的“春晖行动”，叶辛受其感召，于2005年偕中华企业等8家上海企业的代表赶赴砂锅寨，慷慨捐资35万元在寨里修建起全国第一所春晖学校，当地干部群众给学校命名“叶辛春晖小学”。2009年，叶辛又回到砂锅寨再次筹资扩建学校，实现他回报乡梓的心愿。贵州省春晖行动办公室和久长镇政府礼聘叶辛为“春晖使者”。

邵银芬

邵银芬，女，1952年10月出生后在清镇县（今清镇市）麦格乡龙窝村，1974年3月与修文县城关砖瓦厂工人朱开弟结婚后定居在城关镇（今龙场镇）玩易路（今民主路）朱宅，1982年12月参加工作在县爱国卫生运动委员会领属的环境卫生管理站（后分别归属过龙场镇和城乡建设局领导）当环卫工人，2006年1月退休在家赋闲。

邵银芬成家不到一年，丈夫患了间歇性的精神病不能劳动，三个孩子年幼需要抚育，养家糊口的重任就落在她一个人的身上。进到环管站时，总共6个工人要负责县城整个区域的环保卫生，邵银芬的责任区又是从县政府门口起经健家路（今翠屏西路）转环城路（今人民南路）再转县委后面长征路尽头的主城区，路长1公里多，面积1万余平方米，每天都要早出晚归，风雨无阻，把街道打扫干净后还要巡回保洁，而月工资才36元。面对家庭负担重，工作任务多，劳动报酬少的实际情况，有人发表世俗之见，说什么“干哪样不好，偏要扫大街”，又有人劝说她：“随便干什么都比扫街这个最脏、最累、最苦的工作好得多。”但单位的领导和同志们以老一代全国劳动模范掏粪工人时传祥的先进事迹感染她，用“宁愿脏一人，换来万家净”的行业精神教育她，使邵银芬对自己的工作有了清楚的认识，她说："环卫工作虽然脏累苦，但与群众身体健康息息相关，是城市中心不可少的工作，任何工作都需要人去干，只是分工不同，'七十二行，行行出状元'，时传祥当掏粪工成为劳动模范在全国群英会上受到国家主席的接见，我扫街难道就不会得到组织的认可吗！条条大道通北京，环卫工人的喜报要送到天安门。"认识端正后，她就下定决心坚守在环卫工作的岗位上，用勤劳的双手打扫干净自己的责任区，做一名优秀的"城市美容师"。

环卫工作有一定的特殊性，要求上班要早，下班要晚，尤其是清扫街道卫生必须是清晨或晚间人迹稀少的时候才便于劳作。因此，邵银芬每天总是早上5点上岗把自己的责任区打扫干净后才稍事休息，待街上行人多了又上街巡回保洁，直至傍晚天黑时下班回家。如果遇到大型活动保障和突发情况，更是不分昼夜全身心地投入其间，因而职工们对邵银芬的评价是：上岗最早，下班最晚，扫得最宽，街道最净。她就是这样日复一日，年复一年，在平凡的岗位上用扫帚和汗水扫出了一条人生道路。1996年春节来临，恰逢春节头一天赶场，邵银芬的责任区正是商品买卖最集中的路段，散场后满街垃圾狼藉，脏乱不堪，加上领导分给另外的清扫任务，以致当天难以完成责任区的保洁，只得推到春节天把家人叫在一起帮助打扫，全家4口齐出动，根本没有想到做过年夜饭，等到下午6点多钟清扫完毕去菜场买菜，不料菜贩全都收摊，一家人只得拖着疲惫的身体回到家里，将就头天剩下的白菜煮着端出来就算过年了。对此，邵银芬毫无抱怨的话，也没有提出要加班工资。

随着县城建设的发展，城区境域扩大，人口逐渐增加，垃圾数量骤增，特别是行政区划归属贵阳市管辖后，对环卫工作的要求更高，然县里保洁设备简陋，清扫工具原始，单靠手推车转运垃圾，既笨重，又费时，还不能解决当天垃圾当天运走的问题。面对这个矛盾，邵银芬忧心如焚。她总觉得，垃圾不能及时清除，不仅影响市民卫生，而且有碍观瞻，于是将家中喂养的两头肉猪赶到市场上卖得1200元，加上自己省吃俭用积蓄的800元，买了一辆二手机动三轮车让大儿子朱荣学会驾驶后，每天晚上将白天清扫的垃圾全部运往垃圾处理场，并用三轮车短运帮人运输挣得的微薄收入为车子加油，从来没有伸手向单位要过1分钱，就这样解决了长时间梗阻的垃圾运转问题，邵银芬的思想才踏实下来。

邵银芬既是环卫工，又当宣传员。她很注重环卫工人的良好形象，每天清晨洗漱之后，她就穿上橘红色的环卫服，带上保洁工具上岗。她把单位提出的"脏了我一人，干净千万家""县城是我家，保洁靠大家"，"城市不干净，我的脸无光"等创建卫生城市口号牢记心间，不论是清扫街道，还是巡回保洁，都对市民言传身教，要大家提高文明素质，自觉爱护公共卫生。遇到无视文明规约、肆行无忌的人，她总是耐心说服，谆谆告诫。一天，邵银芬在清扫大街时遇到一个边走路边丢烟头者，她当即上前制止，责成将烟头捡起丢进垃圾箱，但那人出言不逊，说什么"不关你的事"，并动手将邵银芬的头部打伤即扬长而去，旁边的群众见此情况愤愤不平，而她则认为：忍得气，心境宽，找说理，就麻烦。随即将烟头扫进垃圾箱就跑去医院，经医生检查属于轻伤，在治疗室上药并包扎完毕，她又回到责任区继续清扫街道。这件事在单位的职工中引起震撼，使大家进一步了解邵银芬，从中接受心灵的感动。

邵银芬对自己的工作恪尽职守。为转变有的青年职工怕脏、怕累、怕苦的思想，虽然年过半百，仍旧老当益壮，视"搞好环境卫生，美化城市容貌"为己任，以"工作无贵贱，行业无尊卑，宁愿一人脏，换来万人净"的职业道德观教育影响青年人安心本职工作。退休之时，反复叮嘱孩子接上母亲的班，当一名称职的环卫工人。儿子遵从母亲嘱咐，从开始驾驶三轮车换成后来的汽车，正式成为环卫车的驾驶员，每天开车行程40余公里，往返将3吨垃圾运往离县城20公里外的垃圾处理场，成为城市环境卫生守护者。

邵银芬从30岁参加工作到55岁退职休养。25年间，她一直坚守在环卫工作的岗位上，从青年到壮年，又从壮年到老年，都在用清扫街道、服务市民诠释她的人生价值取向。从而得到社会的认可和组织的赞誉。1997年10月，她获得“贵阳市城市美容师”称号并被评为市先进个人，1998年被评为贵州省先进工作者，1999年被评为修文县先进个人，2000年4月被授予“贵阳市劳动模范”称号，2002年10月，在第二届阳明文化节表现突出，被县建设局评为先进个人，2003年10月，被县建设局评为环卫战线先进工作者，2006年10月先后获“贵阳市十佳文明环卫工人”的称号、“连续从事环卫工作25周年”荣誉证书。

韩甲成

韩甲成，1953年出生于久长区石安乡山岔村（今久长镇山岔村），1969年初中毕业后跨入社会，曾从事过修筑铁路、帮人宰杀肉牛、农村合作医疗医生、承包荒山造林、饲养山羊等。1992年加入中国共产党，继后担任村党支部书记，并于2009年起任贵州瑾成农业有限公司总经理。

韩甲成家住的山岔村具有山多、地广、人稀的特点，村民全以农耕为业，作物种植单一，经济十分落后。韩甲成当上村支书后，总想找出一条致富的路子，既要自己富，又要村民们都富起来。2003年，在“三个代表”重要思想的指引下，韩甲成更是以兴村富民为己任，带头走致富之路，贷款15万元买下集体的荒山160亩栽种果树和放牧羊子，经过几年营造，树成林，羊长大，但效益不显。2009年，韩甲成外出取经，到遵义虾子镇和湄潭核桃坝参观学习规模养鸡和绿茶种植，回村后决定在自己的林地上创建以绿壳蛋鸡（乌鸡）纯天然放养为主的养殖场，生产富集微量元素、维生素和矿物质且不受色素、添加剂和环境变化影响，被卫生部批准为“保健食品”，为人们喜爱食用的绿壳鸡蛋，开辟一条带领村民致富奔小康的新路。养殖场注册取名贵州省瑾成农业开发有限公司，生产“岔沟牌”绿壳鸡蛋，韩甲成任经理。公司投资85万元兴建禽舍3500平方米，辟出牧式放养蛋鸡林地面积160多亩，从武汉黑凤种禽有限公司购进鸡苗3万只，精心呵护成为子鸡放于林地天然养殖，成蛋鸡后自进鸡舍生蛋，日均产蛋5000个，产值7500元，除去成本，纯利润3000元，经营1年，收入达100余万元。产品除在县内销售外，多销往省城贵阳。

瑾成公司创建起来后，生产经营情况良好，收益颇丰。韩甲成说：“单是公司赢利怎么行？应当以公司为抓手，把农户都带动起来共同富裕才是我们的目标。”于是，他采取“公司+农户”的方式，按照统一苗种供给、统一饲料供应、统一技术服务、统一商标销售和分建鸡舍、分户核算的“四统两分”管理模式带动农户发展绿壳蛋鸡。半年时间，全村发展蛋鸡养殖68户，占总农户的75%，存栏蛋鸡4.4万只，日均产蛋7300个由公司收购，装箱外销。农户喜欢这种运作方式，经过1年养殖，户均增收2.8万元。

蛋鸡养殖一改山岔村的贫困面貌，农民人均纯收入从原来的1800元上升到2010年的2800元。韩甲成因带领村民致富做出显著成绩被久长镇党委评为优秀党务工作者受到表彰。

陈志明

陈志明，1960年3月出生在扎佐公社扎佐管理区（今扎佐镇襄阳社区腾飞路23号），1977年高中毕业，落户六屯公社高茬村当知青。1980年在修文县电影公司扎佐电影院当放映员，1992年下岗开店修理家用电器，1994年跑运输，1995年经营汽车电路电器维修店，1996年起从事电子机械、新材料技术研究。

陈志明天资聪颖，读书好学勤问，善于独立思考，遇到问题总要寻根究底。在跑运输的过程中，碰到车出故障，他就操起工具摸索修理，实践中学会修车，于是办起了修理厂接纳汽车修理。开车，修车，他目睹了多起车祸和若干车毁人亡的惨痛事实印入他的脑际，启发了他的思维：如果有一种能提前预防或控制在行驶中的汽车刹车的应急装置代替人为控制行驶中的汽车刹车，就可避免许多交通事故的发生。从此，他步入了研究发明之路，天天开着车子在公路上转来转去，而且多在弯弯拐拐的地方行驶，见着车祸他就前去围着肇事车了解情况，还趴在车底仔细观察，又向驾驶员问个明白，甚至不惜路费专程从贵阳坐车取道都匀至广西柳州的公路一线反复考察。一年时间，走访千名驾驶员，行程数千公里，宽路窄路，平路坡路，高等级公路，低等级公路，凡是易于发生车祸的地方，他都获取了大量的数据资料。在占有充足资料的基础上，他下决心研究汽车刹车控制器，狠心将搞运输的车子卖掉，把汽车修理场典当出去，又向亲友借贷，一共凑足20万元的启动资金，用家居的院子做实验场地，卧室做实验室，一头扎进对刹车控制器的研究。知识缺乏，就到书店购置《电控技术》《汽车电工》等书籍，现学现用；不懂的地方，就求教于师；碰到难度大的问题，就请教专家。一次，去贵州工业大学找一位教授释疑解惑，但教授正在上课，他就在教室外苦等到下课，求教的实际行动感动了教授，耐心地为其讲解了遇到的难题。随着研究步步深入，需要精细制图，什么三视图、截面图、剖面图……他一窍不通，便不断向贵工大机械系的学生和老师请教，终于制出了精密的图纸。

功夫不负有心人。1997年，陈志明的科研成果出来了，第一个发明的“汽车刹车专用控制器”获得国家专利证书，经国家专利局评估，估价500万元，并将“控制器”送到澳大利亚参加“新世界、新产品、新技术世界博览会”评选，结果获得金奖。1998年，“控制器”又入选由美国爱迪生发明中心、香港科学院荣誉发明委员会和中国发明城集团公司联合举办的第二届“爱迪生世界发明博览会”，评选揭晓，获美国爱迪生特色金奖。

首次科研成功，激发起陈志明发明创造的积极性。他仍然围绕汽车做文章，瞄准“节能与环保”这个课题，试图发明一种既让汽车节约用油又利保护环境的汽车节能器。经过反复试验，失败了再研究，研究了又失败，又失败再研究，终于发明了“汽车电子脉冲节能器”，被国家专利局授给实用新型专利证书。2002年，“节能器”获日内瓦国际专利成果博览会金奖和伦敦国际专利技术博览会金奖，估价439万元公布后，被奥地利一家电子公司看中。于是，中奥双方组建合资公司，落户贵阳，陈志明任副董事长兼总工程师，专门生产电子脉冲节能器，年产达10万只，产品销往国内外，70%出口西欧，贵阳市的公交车多有此种节能器的装置。

2003年，陈志明的科研又出新招，与同行易华、黄艳萍共同研究，发明了“电子倍亚节油提升器（L

字形）”获国家专利并获香港国际专利博览会金奖；2004年发明“汽车燃料发动机电子倍压节油提升器”获国家专利。

陈志明对科研发明永不言弃，永不止步，而且逐渐拓展研究领域，从汽车部件装置到百姓家用电器，从机械产品到电子产品他都涉入。2005年研究发明了“汽车发动机自动保护器”；2006年发明“直线式汽车专用电子空调”获国家专利；2007年发明“汽车刹车冷却水故障显示及报警装置”获国家专利；2008年是成果最多年，有“全电子无压缩民用空调”和“全电子民用冰箱”“全电子冰箱柜”均获国家专利并投入应用，2009年电子降温散热器获中国专利投入应用，2010年，汽车电子空调发明专利，形成产业化应用。积十几年的科研实践经验，陈志明总结出一句话：科学研究的道路并不平坦，而成功总是属于知难而进、百折不挠的研究者。

陈志明的科技创新体现了新时期的时代精神，令世人刮目相待，也得到组织上的认可。1998年5月，陈志明被共青团贵阳市委等6家单位评为第三届“贵阳市十大杰出青年”；9月，被贵阳市总工会评为下岗职工再就业先进个人，10月，获“贵州省十大杰出青年”称号；12月，被贵阳市委、市政府授予“贵阳市国有企业下岗职工再创业明星”称号，并被编入《中华优秀人物大典》。1999年4月，被贵州省总工会授予“五一劳动奖章”。2004年2月，入选贵阳市专业技术带头人中青年科技骨干名录，2005年，被贵阳市委、市政府授予“贵阳市青年科技骨干”称号。

殷秋林

殷秋林，1961年10月出生在贵阳市乌当区狗场（今金阳新区金华镇），1963年因父母亲工作调动跟家迁住修文县城，1979年修文高中毕业被录取在贵州大学外语系攻读英美语言文学专业，1983年大学毕业后参加中国人民解放军任昆明陆军学院训练部语言教研室英语助教，后任讲师，1984年12月加入中国共产党，1992年8月考入中国人民解放军国际关系学院国际军事观察员训练班学习联合国有关组织章程和维护世界和平的业务知识，1993年2月起在南京解放军国际关系学院受训，11月被派赴联合国利比里亚观察团任国际军事观察员，1999年至今转业到昆明市公安局出入境管理处（后为出入境管理局）工作，2002年在联合国波黑（波斯尼亚和黑塞哥维那）特派团任国际警察中国警队党支部书记、队长，2005年和2009年在联合国苏丹特派团任中国警队副队长。是中国目前唯一既有国际军事维和经历又有国际警察维和经历的人。

1993年11月，殷秋林和他的战友们自北京起程，乘机远涉重洋，飞行万里，抵达内战爆发近四年的利比里亚首都蒙罗维亚，在联合国利比里亚军事观察团的领导下，参加了对利比里亚和平协议执行情况的观察和监督工作。他们作为国际军事观察员的任务是，在利内战三方的停火带设立军事观察站，将交战各方隔离开，监督各方执行停火协议的情况，调解他们之间的矛盾，监督和视察维和部队按协议收缴各派武装的武器弹药，察看难民的生活状况，与其他一些国际组织协调人道主义救援等。在这个战乱的国家，国际军事观察员们目睹了众多痛苦呻吟的难民，有严重缺乏营养的妇女，有瘦骨嶙峋的儿童，有从战火中退下来无药治疗的伤兵，还有因父母逃亡国外被遗弃而在街头流浪的孩子。此情此景，让殷秋林和他的战友们心里颇感酸楚，真切地体尝到战争给居民带来的苦难。他们及时将观察到的情况反映给上级机关，使联合国粮农组织（WFP）、联合国难民署（UNHCR）和其他一些国际救援组织及时组织救援活动。粮食虽济燃眉之急，但战争又打起来了，殷秋林和一些国际军事观察员奉命乘直升机从爱国阵线（NPFL）的首都邦嘎撤回蒙罗维亚。第二天，他们的营地就被另一派武装占领，未来得及拿走的钢盔、防弹衣、战地日记均被掠夺一空。另外一个地方的国际军事观察员队的车辆、电台还被武装分子抢走，并绑架国际军事观察员作人质，其中有一名中国军官。在联合国安理会上，中国驻联合国代表就此事件予以谴责，安理会发表公开声明施压才使被绑架的国际军事观察员队员恢复了自由。

国际维和工作就是联合国成员国派出的军事或警察代表，在安理会授权和组织下执行联合国的维持和平使命，他们既是自己国家的外交官和代表，又代表国际社会。殷秋林所在的观察员队的战友们就来自马来西亚、奥地利、乌拉圭、印度、孟加拉、约旦等不同国家的军方，大家相互关照，和睦相处。殷秋林第一次在非洲患疟疾发高烧，幸得各国同事们的悉心照料，还住进联合国任务区孟加拉部队医院治疗，并口服带来的中国抗疟药，使身体很快恢复健康。

2000年，殷秋林参加公安部举办的维和民事警察培训班选拔，并顺利地进入第八期培训班受训，结束即参加由联合国有关方面组织的甄选资格考试，考试科目有英语笔试、英语听力、英语口语、英语报告写作和汽车规定动作倒库、40公里时速“S”驾驶、急刹车以及5米、7米快速拔枪射击等，其中如有一项受挫即被淘汰出局。殷秋林一路闯关，最终以优异的成绩入选。40岁生日那天，他被任命为副队长领着9名队员从北京飞往波黑，与先期抵达的中国维和警察汇合。着落首都萨拉热窝机场，目睹机场周边和公路两旁的建筑物满布着枪炮射击后留下的弹痕和屋舍被毁后的废墟，又一次感受到战争给居民带来的创伤，深感作为维和人员使命的重大。尽管波黑内战已经结束几年了，以北约为主的多国稳定部队和联合国维和警察早已入驻波黑，然内战在民族间（塞族、穆斯林和克罗地亚族）埋下了种族间仇恨的种子，导致居民家中多藏有枪支、手榴弹等杀伤性武器，不时还传来枪声和爆炸声，对国际维和人员的威胁还来自北约部队使用贫铀弹留下的放射污染。殷秋林被分配到泽尼察市警察局做国际警察顾问，指导当地警察的执法活动，受理公民对警察的投诉，调查违反人权的案件。因第一批中国维和警察工作期满要轮换回国，经公安部外事局党委于2002年1月任命殷秋林为国际警察中国警察队党支部书记兼队长，继后，又被安排到萨拉热窝国际警察局工作。经过努力，他又考取任务区总部特别行动处人权调查官职位，专门处理波黑执法队伍中违反人权的案件。是时，西方人对中国警察当人权调查官存有偏见，作为中国人能获得人权调查官职位使许多西方人另眼相看。

2005年和2009年，殷秋林两度派到苏丹担任中国警察队副队长，工作地点位于南苏丹朱巴。他担任国际警察顾问，其任务是向当地警察官宣传国际通用警务知识，教育他们尊重人权，一定要依法履职。住在号称“世界火炉”的苏丹，旱季平时气温均在38℃—45℃之间，殷秋林的住地朱巴系南苏丹的首都是一个特大型的村庄，缺电，无自来水，更没有饭店宾馆，只能挺着用炭火烧水煮饭、洗衣。殷秋林几次感染疟疾，又经过霍乱爆发，条件的艰苦和疾病的肆虐并没有动摇过殷秋林当好维和警察的意志。有的时候还面临与死神擦肩而过的经历，幸运地躲过武装匪徒的枪林弹雨。

从1993年到2009年，殷秋林在异国他乡参加4次维和，担当起崇高而繁重的工作，一次次地圆满完成了联合国赋予的使命，体现出中国军官和中国警察的优良品质和卓越才能。当殷秋林应联合国召唤完成利比里亚的维和任务后，由联合国利比里亚军事观察团首席观察员（司令员）肯尼亚少将欧潘迪颁发证书称：殷秋林少校的良好的军人素质和实际行动履行了对联合国和平倡议的承诺，愿殷秋林对人类和平事业的爱和奉献给他带来更美好的前程。

罗廷会

罗廷会，女，彝族，1963年4月出生于黔西县铁石公社岩脚大队（今铁石苗族彝族乡岩脚村），1986年1月与洒坪公社青山大队（今洒坪乡青山村）一组的农民张利华结为夫妻，从此定居在青山。

1992年，罗廷会家中惨遭不幸：年仅28岁的丈夫张利华赴广东打工，半路遇车祸当即死亡，丢下罗廷会和6岁、4岁、2岁的3个孩子，加上长期飘泊在外的弟弟丢下的年近60的父母亲，一家6口的生活担子全落在罗廷会的肩上。面临极度困难，有人劝她："你现在才20多岁，趁年轻找个对象，既为你分忧解愁，又减轻生活负担。"还有人说："张利华走了，留下这么一大堆'破破烂烂'给你，你要为他家抚养孩子，又要服侍老人，如果找个恰当的男人嫁了，一走了之，任何人都觉得这是天经地义的事。"罗廷会没有听旁人的劝说，反而答道："孩子是我的亲生骨肉，怎么能丢下不管；老人把我们抚养长大，我们应当反哺报恩。如果当初父母遇到困难把我们丢下不管，就不会有今天的我们；如果我们不为孩子做出忠孝的榜样，今后孩子们又会怎样来对待我们呢？如果我找个对象进家，他的性情与孩子或老人合不来，不但不能很好抚养孩子、照顾老人，还会带来很多伤心。不管怎么说，我决不会抛下子女和公婆，宁愿守寡把孩子抚养好，把公婆服侍好，尽到自己的责任，我就心安理得。"人们听了她的再三陈述，见她抚育子女和奉养公婆的态度十分坚决，就不再提及改嫁的事，反而对她这种侍老抚幼的高尚品德越发钦佩。

罗廷会担上全家生活重担，就全身心投向农作物的种植，将5亩水稻和10亩苞谷的春种、夏管、秋收、冬藏都做得扎扎实实，家中的担水、养猪、喂牛、做饭、洗衣也都兼顾不误。每天下地干活，往往是出门天未亮，收工月亮上，风里来，雨里去，劳动一年下来，收获稻谷1500公斤和苞谷2500公斤，除口粮外，剩余的就背上市场换钱为孩子交书学费和开支公婆的医药费，但入不敷出，单书学费支出一年就要1200元，钱不够就去修路做小工，帮建房人家搬砖、搅拌灰浆，到餐馆洗菜、洗碗……将打工收入补助开支，就这样日复一日，年复一年，终于把3个孩子供到初中毕业，抚养成人，作为农民工远赴广东、浙江沿海一带打工，挣钱添补家用，一改多年家庭经济拮据的窘迫处境，加上政府资助进行危房改造，还搬进了砖混结构的宽敞明亮的崭新住房。

2000年，64岁的公公身染肺结核，又是骨节疏松，终日瘫痪在床，吃、喝、拉、撒、睡都要人服侍，一切都由罗廷会承担起来。除了找钱给公公治病外，每天都为公公擦拭身体和搀扶公公上厕所，但无半句怨言。2001年，婆婆脚患类风湿，行走特别困难，使罗廷会支撑的这个家雪上加霜。她将参加修路领到手的100元工资全作婆婆医病的治疗费，但两个疗程尚差20元，医生见其困难也就减收了。类风湿治愈后又出现骨质增生和高血压，再后又右膝骨折，卧床不起。她一如既往地对待困难，咬紧牙关筹集医药费，背公公婆婆到医院治疗，连揩屎擦尿都由她一个人去完成。见着罗廷会出工干活、服侍老幼和操持家务都很出色，婆婆逢人便夸："我家这个媳妇真是世上少有，她把家中一切都包揽下来，而且做得很好，全家人都满意，简直是我们张家的福气。”在洒坪乡的村村寨寨，无一人不知晓罗廷会孝敬公婆和抚育子女的高尚情操和道德实践，见着她就竖起大拇指。年逾古稀的邻居朱富奎称赞道：“像这样孝敬公婆的媳妇，我活了70多岁也只见到罗廷会一个。”

2006年10月，罗廷会被评为贵阳市第二届孝星，受贵阳市第二届“双星”评选活动组委会表彰。2010年元月，贵阳市精神文明建设指导委员会办公室和贵阳市电视台在“中天城投”杯《直播贵阳》栏目播放2009年度新闻人物——罗廷会，并颁发给“荣誉证书”。

林家华

林家华，1963年8月出生于龙场镇，1985年4月从修文县人民医院调入修文县人民法院工作，历任书记员、助理审判员、审判员、立案庭副庭长、人民法庭副庭长，1997年7月加入中国共产党，2009年10月被任命为第一人民法庭庭长，11月晋升为一级法官。

林家华在20多年的法官生涯中，恪尽职守，忠实履行人民法官为人民的司法宗旨，在追求公平正义的道路上书写出基层法官为民司法的亮丽篇章，先后承办的2000余件案件无一错案。2007年，第一人民法庭（以下简称“一法庭”）进入创建特色法庭关键期，时任立案庭副庭长的林家华被法院党组委以重任，到一法庭主持工作并推进特色法庭创建。一法庭位于县境的边远山区六广，下辖4乡1镇，人口11万，总面积500余平方公里，纵向跨度27公里。林家华到任后，深入法庭巡回审判第一线调研，了解到群众对法庭工作的建议和意见，意识到把握法庭工作的重心和落脚点。随后，结合辖区经济社会发展实际，提出以服务群众为出发点和落脚点的理念和“重调解、精审判、筑防线、创特色”的工作思路，创建“一巡（定点定时巡回与带案穿插巡回）、二访（庭前去访，调判后回访）、三调（庭前、庭审、庭后调解）、四宣（送法入校园、以案析法、定期培训人民调解员和拍摄《庭审直击》的宣传方式）”的多元巡回审判工作机制，使法庭围绕服务群众创特色注入了活力，拓展了法庭巡回审判工作的范围和内涵。2007年和2008年，一法庭建立的诉前、诉中两道纠纷化解防线成效显现，两年诉讼收案量良性回落，服判息诉率高达99%，实现了年度收案量良性减少目标，法庭工作得到了辖区党委、政府和县院领导的肯定。2008年初，六广周边出现特大凝冻灾害，气温降至-3℃。林家华坚守岗位，带领干警克服天寒路滑的困难，步履在封冻的路上，深入村寨调解纠纷80余件，指导人民调解员工作5次100人次，确保灾害期群众和谐、社会稳定。当时，法庭受理一桩离婚案件：小箐乡全兴村庙坎组的吴学平在外打工，很少回家尽丈夫和做父亲的责任，其妻孙贵菊起诉要求与吴学平离婚并提出对上高中的女儿进行抚养。在县城读书的女儿得知父母要离婚的消息后，打电话到法庭，哭着告诉林家华，她今年要参加高考，父母离婚后她求学要受到影响，要求林法官不要判决父母离婚。为了消除女孩的忧虑，使她在高考前认真学习，实现上大学的愿望，林家华立马与承办法官用麻布捆绑在鞋上，徒步在冻得发亮的山路上跌跌撞撞地赶到十多公里外的当事人家里。当找到吴学平并通知孙贵菊到指定地点时，时间已过去了6个多小时，又累又饿又冷的感觉阵阵袭来，但他俩已无心顾及，立即投入调解工作中。当林家华讲到他们的女儿打电话到法庭诉说自己的担忧时，两个人都沉默了。经调解，孙贵菊同意对女儿进行抚养，吴学平同意每月付给女儿的抚育费，双方在调解协议上签了字。当年8月，孙贵菊打电话到法庭，兴奋地告诉林家华其女儿已考上外省大学了，她正与吴学平为女儿筹措学费，感谢法官对她女儿的关心。

2008年4月的一天，六桶乡下坝村湾子组桑启林老人行动不便，其子女不给赡养费，生活陷入困境。于是他请一位学生代书一份“申告书”，并投入法庭设置的投诉箱。次日晚，林家华在审理完两起案件后赶赴该投诉箱点，查收到桑启林的“申告书”。桑启林万没有想到，劳累了一天的林家华带领干警当晚就赶到他居住的小屋，详细地询问他子女的姓名、地址及其诉讼请求，并就着简易灶炉里的火光，制作了口头起诉笔录。随后，未顾及休息，立即分赴其两个儿子的家中，连夜开展调解工作。当晚12点，桑启林的两个儿子被林家华及其带领干警的无私奉献精神感动，主动将赡养老人的口粮送至老人的小屋，并保证以后按期送交，解决了老人断粮之忧。

2009年3月4日，第一人民法庭在六桶乡宝坪村巡回接待时，收到一份看似普通其实并不普通的离婚诉状，不普通之处在于当事人原告周道兰提供的一份证据，其内容是被告查继军充满血腥、暴力的短信，扬言如果周道兰起诉与他离婚，他将以1支枪、20发子弹的“厚礼”了结他俩余生。获知此情，林家华感到问题严重，立即同六桶乡派出所民警取得联系，通过多方了解，其真情是被告查继军拥有枪支弹药属假，外出务工因交通事故致残、生活窘迫是真。但又遇结发之妻起诉离婚，顿生仇恨之心，甚至绝望。得知情况后，林家华立即召集法庭干警研讨案情，拓展问题的解决办法，当即去到查继军住处，以他的心结所在为切入点，从他的实际困难着手，明法析理，开展思想疏导工作，指出他的过激行为的危害性、违法性。经过多次驱车看望、交流谈心，使他从绝望的边缘中重新燃起对生活的希望，坦然面对困难和挫折。调解结案后，林家华又到查继军家多次回访，帮助其一步步走出感情的低谷期。2010年5月得知夫妻二人言归于好，全体干警都由衷地感到欣慰，夫妻二人也发出感叹：如果没有法庭法官的真挚关爱，我们这个支离破碎的家庭不可能破镜重圆。

2010年10月13日，林家华接待一位70多岁的老人冯绍英来访，其诉称：自己年迈多病，生活不能自理，饮食起居需要子女照料，但4个子女互相推诿，不尽赡养义务，无奈起诉到法院，请求法院责令4子女履行义务；同时，诉称次子何德林曾多次向其借款，共计6870元，何德林还用其所有的玉米喂猪，共用去1200公斤，自己多次向其催要款物未果，遂请求法院责令何德林返还财物、归还借款。林家华考虑到家庭矛盾影响了老人与子女的亲情，便带领法庭干警赶到老人及其两个儿子所居住的六广村营山组，找到老人的两个儿子，与他们进行耐心细致的交流，了解到何德林家庭困难，过春节没给老人买任何礼物，老人因此以为儿子对自己不管不顾，心存怨气。林家华认真分析案情和当事人的相关情况，决定分别去做老人及其子女的工作，对老人进行抚慰，对其子女尤其是次子进行劝导及相关法律知识的解释。经过劝解，冯绍英母子冰释前嫌，次子主动承担老人日常生活照料之责，长子每月自愿付给150元赡养费，两个子女提出的赡养协议得到了冯绍英的认可，一家人和好如初，案件得以圆满解决。

林家华就是这样一件接一件地处理这些矛盾纠纷，促使若干夫妻和睦与家庭和谐。一法庭在林家华的带领下，攻坚克难，成绩卓然。2007年和2009年，两次被省高院授予“全省优秀人民法庭”的称号。2008年，被评为“指导人民调解委员会先进集体”，受到贵阳市委、市政府的表彰，还被评为“青少年维权岗”，受到共青团贵阳市委的表彰。林家华被省高院授予“抗凝冻 保民生先进个人”，2010年又被评为贵州全省“百名优秀法官”。

刘兴林

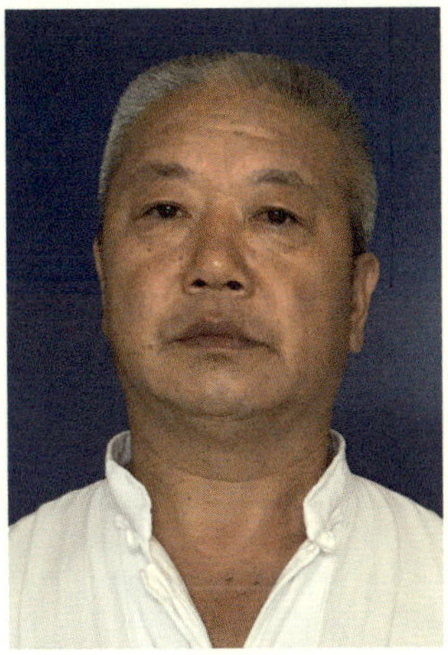

刘兴林，1963年出生于贵阳市，家住贵阳市五里冲农产品批发市场。1978年初中毕业后从事蔬菜经营，2005年起担任修文县曾艳种植开发有限公司总经理。

刘兴林从学校踏入社会就在贵阳城区经营蔬菜购销，2002年试行农商结合，投资30万元在开阳县羊场与农民签订合同，建立蔬菜生产基地，种植甜椒400亩，以订单形式收购产品直接进入市场销售，后因种植农户履行合同发错而告吹，投入的资金多数没有收回。2003年，刘兴林带着蔬菜样品，随贵阳市蔬菜公司和贵阳市农业局组织的代表团前往广州参加首届珠三角地区农业展览会。沿海客商看中黔省蔬菜，纷纷要求订货，但因需求量太大又无货源保障就不敢签订供货合同。面临的现实触动了刘兴林，他决心抓住这个商机，用多年来经营蔬菜的资金积累建立自己直接经营的蔬菜生产基地，批量产出蔬菜供给外商，进一步扩大蔬菜的经营范围。返回贵阳，刘兴林深入近郊多处考察选点，最后确定在具有耕地连片、土壤肥沃、日照充足、排灌自如、交通畅适、运输方便等优越条件的久长镇杨柳村从事产业化、规模化、标准化和无公害化的蔬菜生产。

2005年11月，由刘兴林新手营造的蔬菜生产基地初具规模，正式成立修文县曾艳种植开发有限公司，落户杨柳村，刘兴林任总经理，配有管理员8人，固定农民工82人。公司拥有种植蔬菜面积1460亩，涉及范围有久长镇属杨柳村、永兴村，芦山村和扎佳镇属泗溪村的9个村队组、660户、2289人。采取土地流转方式集中种植蔬菜，即租用农民承包的责任地，雇农民给公司务工，以市场需求为导向进行规模化的生产，做到“人无我有，人有我优，人优我特”，力求公司增效，农民增收，实现“双赢”。农民工在广袤的土地上轮优，成片种植白菜、辣椒、大葱、芹菜、甘蓝、黄瓜、西葫芦，甜玉米等。大量的鲜菜源源不断地进入市场，深受商家青睐，除供应贵阳市及其周边县、区外，还销往广州等地。在公司的带动下，周边农户种植白菜、辣椒、大葱、莴笋、莲花白等达5000余亩，多由公司收购转运外地经销。

为把公司这个“蛋糕”做大做强，刘兴林不仅倾注了若干精力，而且投入了大量财力。截至2010年，除政府扶持资金240万元外，他自筹的部分已过953万元，多用在修建办公用房和生活用房，架设输电线路，兴修机耕道，修建蓄水池，购置微耕机、潜水泵、喷雾器和运输车辆等基础设施上，也用于耕地租金和农民工工资，购买种子、肥料、农药、农膜，以及定做产品包装箱等开支。刘兴林说：“没有投入就没有产出，只要舍得投资，必定投来效益。”

经过5年营运，刘兴林办的曾艳种植开发公司效益凸显：一是农民工在公司领取耕地租金、干活工资、出售农家肥料款和享受生活补助费每人年均纯收入1.8万元，比分户种地和外出打工的收入增加20%，村民们都乐意采取土地流转收租金和给公司干活领工资的方式得到更多的实惠；二是公司的市场空间拓宽了，企业效益与日俱增；三是给农民打开一条致富路。由于公司率先迈出第一步，使商家向往刘兴林的运作模式，也使农民看到蔬菜种植的光明前景，遂由外地商家分别在久长镇的沙雁村和六屯乡的都堡村、新堡村建起100至500亩的产业化蔬菜基地，同时促使农民自发调整产业结构，原来种粮、种烟的土地多改种蔬菜。2005年久长镇蔬菜种植面积只1.03万亩，2010年发展到5万亩，蔬菜产量也由2005年的1.52万吨增为2010年的3.4万吨，农民人均纯收入从2005年的2850元上升为2010年的5597元。

刘兴林在蔬菜行业所做出的突出贡献得到政府及其有关部门的认可，他所领导的曾艳种植开发有限公司被贵州省农业经济委员会认定为无公害蔬菜生产基地，被贵阳市农业经济委员会列为重点建设项目。2006年，曾艳公司被贵阳市人民政府授予“贵阳市农业产业化重点龙头企业”称号；2007年被修文县人民政府授予“建设新农村农业产业化重点龙头企业”称号；2010年被评为“优秀非公有制企业”受到修文县人民政府表彰。继后，刘兴林当选贵州省蔬菜商会理事，贵阳市南明区蔬菜商会会长和修文县工商业联合执行委员。

梁顺堂

梁顺堂，汉族，1964年5月生，修文县久长镇人。1986年走出家门谋发展，曾任白云区绿化办苗圃绿化工程队队长兼法人代表，1999年弃职回久长镇创办顺兴苑园艺有限公司。

梁顺堂办园艺公司曾遭家人激烈反对，他千方百计说服了家人，醉心于绿化苗木和花卉的研究、栽培和市场开发。2002年，他看到贵州每年要花大量资金从省外购进花卉名品巴车夫建（俗称水红花），不信物产丰富的贵州没有品种，独自踏遍县境山山水水，终于找到一株野生水红花种苗，移植到苗圃，精心呵护，采取“多采光，少用水”的栽培技术，使水红花培植成功，并大量发展。经贵阳市林业局鉴定，该项目填补了贵州水红花品种人工繁殖的空白，仅此一项每年为公司挣得100万元以上的销售收入。

梁顺堂在发展顺兴苑园艺基地的同时，还投标承接了贵阳市第二环城生态公益林带。县境中韩合作喀斯特石质山地造林示范项目等多个标段的园林绿化建设工程，合格率达到百分之百。2004年，梁顺堂以“公司+基地+农户”的方式，带动上寨村、下堡村200多户农民搞苗木种植，使每户从此项目年平均增收2600元。他还投资18万元为上寨村修水库。至2005年，顺兴苑苗圃基地规模已达1389亩，总资产达2200万元，成为贵阳市八大育苗基地之一和市级龙头企业。其所产苗木销往武汉、重庆、内蒙古、北京等10个省、市、区，年销售近百万株。

1992年以来，梁顺堂先后担任过白云区花卉协会会员、副会长、白云区苗木协会会长、修文县第二届、第七届政协委员等社会职务。

安怀略

安怀略，1963年9月出生于贵阳市，大学学历，1984年5月加入中国共产党。

2002年，随着扎佐医药园区崛起，安怀略任落地在园区的贵州科开医药股份有限公司总经理。他确立“敬业、求是”的经营理念，立足“以人为本，以质量为生命”的经营宗旨，将公司建成以药品批发和医疗服务为主的大型医药经营企业，成为医药园区药品产、供、销不可或缺的重要纽带。

为适应药品经营“GSP”改造，安怀略壮起超群胆略，集聚巨资建成一座大型药品储备库和医疗服务综合楼以及办公用房，于2003年通过国家“GSP”论证和验收合格，使公司的竞争力显著增强，经营药品达3000多种，到2007年成为全省80多家药品生产企业和药品销售公司的贵州地区总代理商。

科开公司挺立起来了，安怀略更是信心倍增，进一步加强质量管理，推动公司一年跃上一个台阶，将仅有20名员工的小公司发展为拥有3家连锁药店、2家合股医院和1家药品销售的股份制公司。2010年，公司销售收入达到3亿多元，实现利税3000多万元，为修文创税1500多万元，成为推动贵州省医药事业发展的一支主力军。

韦　林

韦林，1964年10月出生在修文县城，1983年修文高中毕业应征入伍，在中国人民解放军00619部队当卫生战士，1987年退伍后在修文县人民医院从事中医针灸治疗，2005年在县城开办韦林中医针灸诊所。是贵州省针灸学会常务理事，中国针灸学会会员，世界中医骨伤会员，修文县工商联合会第八届、第九届执委，政协修文县第七届、第八届委员。

孜孜以求攀医峰，技不惊人死不休。这是韦林在医学医术上的执著追求。从进入县医院工作的那天起，韦林就盼望有深造的机会。1988年报名参加中华针灸进修学校函授自学，1989—1990年被派至遵义医学院附属医院针灸科进修，接着在该院临床医学外科专业成人高考专业证书班学习1年，2002年参加成人高考被录取在贵阳中医学院系统学习中西医结合理论，至2005年完成全部学科正式毕业。7年进修，韦林既系统地掌握了一套医学理论知识，又从临床实践中提高了自己的医疗技术，在不断的探索中创新出集血府逐瘀汤、补阳还五汤等与针灸、穴注、推拿、小针刀、火针、刮痧相配合的治疗方法，不仅疗效好，而且费用低，尤其是在治疗脑血栓、颈椎腰椎骨质增生、腰椎间盘突出和周围性面瘫等顽疾更有独到之处，多次应邀参加国际传统医学研讨、世界针灸学术研讨、香港中西医结合医学研讨等大型研讨会。1997年，韦林作为中国代表出席在北京国际会议中心召开的庆祝世界针灸学会联合会成立十周年暨学术研讨大会，撰写的论文《透针加灸治疗周围性面瘫38例疗效观察》被译成英文印发参会代表。1999年，论文《小针刀和推拿治疗肩周炎36例》被香港国际中西医结合学会和香港科技联合出版社选入《世界医药万果经典》。2000年又带着被译成英文的论文《针刺穴位推拿并用治疗腰椎间盘突出症32例》赴北京参加国际传统医学研讨大会。与此同时，由韦林独立组织实施的项目《穴位注射配合推拿治疗颈椎病》被修文县人民政府评为1997至1999年科技进步一等奖。2007年，经过10年实践检验的《透针加灸治疗周围性面瘫38例疗效观察》在北京召开的世界针灸学术研讨大会上获得业内人士的认可与称赞。2009年，论文《针刺结合牵引治疗腰椎间盘突出症92例》在香港中西医结合医学研讨会上被收入《针灸治疗痛症国际学术研讨论文汇编》。尽管韦林苦心孤诣，成果斐然，但他却谦虚地说："学无止境，还有不少疑难杂症急需攻克，更好地解除病人痛苦是我的天职。"

从在部队当卫生员算起，韦林的医龄已有28年。20多年间，经他诊治的病人竟达30万人次，年均1.08万人次，每天接诊患者30人次以上，从未发生过一起医疗事故。办起诊所后，虽不受规定的作息时间限制，但他坚持每天早上6点到诊所接诊，下班时间则以接诊完病人为准，有的时候中餐合并晚餐一道吃。对患者的要求，他总是尽量满足。在病房接诊的同时，还不辞辛劳出诊，为患者提供服务。截至2010年，他上门服务过的病人在万人以上，且从未收取过分文出诊费，从不接受病人的宴请和馈赠，遇到经济困难的患者则是免费服务。因此，群众对韦林的评价是：医术精，医德高。2005年，贵阳医学院职工王洋患面瘫，先在本院治疗两个月未见疗效，后转到韦林诊所由韦林亲自操刀治疗，10天痊愈，全家人感激不已。年逾古稀的晏才俊经韦林治愈后，提笔题书楹联一副挂于韦林的治疗室，联称：针灸术给病人解除病痛，慈诚心为患者谋求健康。2008年，中国针灸学会秘书长刘炜宏博士在贵州省针灸学会会长吕明庄和名誉会长贺志光教授的陪同下专程莅临韦林诊所参观，亲自看见韦林为患者主刀，深为感动，高度评价韦林的医德医术，赞扬他"天天乐助，针针见情"。贵州省针灸学会还特意赠予韦林诊所牌匾：继承祖国医学传统，发扬为人民服务精神。

韦林作为一名医务工作者，所具备高尚的医德和精湛的医疗技术得到群众认可和组织肯定。1996年，韦林被美国加利弗尼亚州世界传统医学会聘为名誉教授。2008年，韦林载入《针行天下——全球针灸风采录人物篇》。2009年获"全国优秀名中医"称号，并出席在北京人民大会堂召开的表彰大会，受到全国政协副主席陈宗兴和卫生部副部长朱庆生、国医大师路正道接见与合影。

戴宗林

戴宗林，1964年10月出生于六屯公社安新生产大队（今六屯乡安全村），1981年参加中国人民解放军，1984年12月退伍，1989年到修文从事公安工作，1989年加入中国共产党，历任基层派出所民警、副所长、县公安局刑事侦查大队副大队长、大队长，2009年任修文县公安局副局长分管刑事案件和毒品案件的侦破工作。

军人出身的戴宗林，跨入公安门槛后，一直处在除暴安民第一线，无论当警员，还是任警官，都担起刑事侦查的任务，都以军人过硬的作风和肩负重任的使命感对待刑侦工作，用他的话来说：选择了警察这个职业，就选择了奉献，就得意味着吃苦，就要承受更多的压力和挑战。戴宗林的话掷地有声。

进入21世纪，在社会转型进程加快和社会矛盾凸显的形势下，一些寻衅逞凶者置国家法纪不顾。他们奸污盗窃，谋财害命；网络黑恶势力，持械滋事骚扰；倚仗权势，称霸一方。面对严峻的现实，戴宗林认为，刑侦部门作为公安机关打击犯罪的利剑，要让这把利剑发出光芒，必须破案。于是，他提出：破案才是硬道理。2005年，为落实公安部“命案必破”的指示和南京“11·3”全国侦破命案会议精神，戴宗林配合县局拟定《侦破命案工作方案》和《侦破命案工作机制》，建立专门的侦破命案队伍，率先垂范带领全队民警发扬不怕牺牲的精神和连续战斗的作风，在第一时间内赶赴发案现场，相继破获了在修文影响较大的“黄猫湾命案”“黄顺昌故意杀人案”“六桶12·02命案”“1·13抢劫杀人案”……19起命案，使破案率升为100%。在侦破现行命案的同时，戴宗林从不放过对往年命案的侦破，又与干警一起跋山涉水，进村入户摸排线索，查遍历年未破命案嫌疑人的家庭情况和社会关系，掌握了大量的案件线索，先后获取2000年“2·6”一死一伤案件嫌疑人、“7·13”案嫌疑人、2001年“11·13”命案犯罪嫌疑人、2003年“9·12”岩洞腐尸案嫌疑人、2004年“12·28”浴室血案嫌疑人、2005年“7·17”命案嫌疑人潜逃广西、福建、四川、浙江、贵阳等地的信息，随即与侦查员商定追捕方案，深入到犯罪嫌疑人潜伏地点开展抓捕工作。经过两个多月的不懈努力，戴宗林指挥干警辗转万余公里，取得了抓获命案嫌疑人10人，破获往年命案5起的好成绩，实现了“两降一升”（发案数下降，逃犯数下降，破案率上升）的目标。与此同时，戴宗林还带领民警蹲点守候，为浙江等公安机关抓获命案嫌疑人5名，有力地支持了友邻公安部门的命案侦破工作。

经历“命案必破”的专项斗争，使戴宗林认识到：只有彻底打掉修文的黑恶势力，遏制打架斗殴和故意伤害案件的发生，才不致酿成命案。于是，他又确立“以打促防，除恶务尽”的指导思想，在省、市公安部门的领导下，在2005年参与组织侦破了“2·22”严郁华、文仁祥、杨光华等涉黑案件，2006年侦破“3·23”袁强、刘伦致死人命涉恶案，2007年侦破“8·13”徐劲松、漆初峰恶势力犯罪团伙案，2009年侦破黄明双、徐泽贵恶势力组织犯罪案。还有“谷堡专案”、“六广专案”……一批危害一方的黑恶性质犯罪组织均有戴宗林参与组织侦破。2009年2月，县委、县政府责成公安部门对龙场镇水塘村少数以身试法者多次纠集上百名不明真相的村民挡工堵路、非法拦车、设卡收费、破坏矿山生产、扰乱社会秩序的事件立案侦查。公安局党委将这起作案时间长，涉案人数多、社会影响大的恶势力犯罪案件的侦破任务落实给戴宗林。戴宗林既感到任务光荣，又觉得担子沉重，如果案件破了，既解决了困扰县委、县政府近十年的难题，又为全县的政治、经济建设踢开了绊脚石，还会转变群众对公安部门的不信任感，消除全局两百多名干警的阴影；如果案件办砸了就无法向组织上交代。思之再三，决心抛开个人得失，向局党委请战侦破水塘恶势力组织犯罪案，把案件办成铁案，办成精品案。随即抽调20名精干警力组成专案组，下设资料、调查、取证、抓捕、审讯等工作小组，提出“界定一个罪名，抓捕一批主犯，顺藤摸瓜，一网打尽”的侦破思路，并商请检察、法院两家负责批捕、公诉、审判的干警提前介入案件的侦查和监督。一切先期工作就绪，戴宗林抓住3月10日60多名水塘村民齐集省政府门口上访被龙场镇政府劝说接回的群体事件为突破口，拿准了确凿的犯罪事实，诱捕了组织上访的为首者和主要犯罪嫌疑人，接着带领参战干警夜以继日地战斗40多天，展开审讯和取证工作，终于将以黄明双、徐泽贵为首的18名恶势力团伙成员绳之以法，一举打掉了这个作恶多端、危害一方的犯罪组织，还修文一片净土，人们拍手称快，纷纷反映：像黄明双、徐泽贵这样基础厚、势力大的恶势力犯罪组织都被打垮了，确实显示出公安机关“打黑除恶”的力度和决心。

为保障人民群众安居乐业，面对抢劫、盗窃案件频发的严峻形势，县公安部门将严打“两抢一盗”（抢劫、抢夺和盗窃）提上议事日程。身为刑侦大队长的戴宗林受命于危难之际，但没有被困难吓倒，他针对治安复杂地段和案件高发区域的特点制定严打整治方案，集中优势警力，与大家共同战斗，出奇制胜。2008年，县境接连不断地发生抢劫摩托车案件：犯罪分子以打车为诱饵，将驾驶员并车辆骗至偏僻地段进行捆绑，搜其现金和物品后仓皇逃匿，一旦驾驶员反抗即遭毒打，以致人心惶惶。戴宗林下决心突破这批案件，他通过调查，对犯罪分子的作案时间、地点、手段和被害者提供情况进行分析，认定所有抢劫摩托车案件均是一伙人所为，决定进行串并案侦查，并得到贵阳市公安局相关部门配合将对象锁定，于2009年6月将犯罪嫌疑人李华、罗江波抓获。通过审讯，交代了在修文发生的4起抢劫摩托车案件均是其所为。但戴宗林并未就此满足，决心深挖犯罪，扩大战果，便组织侦查员对李华、罗江波的作案手段、活动范围进行分析，结合上网查询贵阳市同期同类案件，发现市内多起抢劫摩托车案件与李华、罗江波有关。于是，多次审讯李华和罗江波，结合反复查证，最后破获李华、罗江波在修文县、清镇市、云岩区、乌当区、白云区犯下的连绑架罪一起共27起抢劫摩托车案件，涉案总价10多万元，为法院作出对李华、罗江波判处死刑缓期二年执行的决定提供了确凿的事实依据。2010年，县境发生多起面包车被盗案件，失主受到经济损失叫苦不迭。戴宗林在刑侦大队抽调警力成立专案组，与大家一起调查和分析案情，发现被盗的多数是“五菱之光”面包车，又从发案时间和区域分析，认定盗车是同一伙人所为，于是深入排查，找准对象，蹲点守候，将犯罪嫌疑人抓获，连续审讯取证，共破获一伙在修文和贵阳市云岩区、白云区盗窃汽车案件10起，接着追赃，共为失主追回被盗面包车8辆，价值20余万元。车辆归还失主后，大家喜笑颜开，纷纷向公安局送上“为百姓除害，保一方平安”的锦旗。

戴宗林从警20多年，一直坚守在人民公安的岗位上做出了不平凡的成绩，尤其是在2007年后开展的“命案必破”“打黑除恶”和严打“两抢一盗”的专项斗争中，总是身先士卒，无私无畏，为保卫人民的生命财产和维护修文的和谐稳定挥洒着自己的汗水与心血，得到组织上的肯定并获得殊荣：2004年和2005年分别荣立二等功受到贵州省公安厅嘉奖，2000年和2007年分别荣立三等功受到贵阳市公安局奖励，2001年、2004年和2005年被省公安厅评为优秀人民警察，2004年被中共贵阳市委、市政府评为全市优秀人民警察和市公安局评为“利剑行动先进个人”，2005年被评为全国优秀人民警察受到公安部表彰，2008年被评为“十七大”安全保卫先进个人受到贵阳市公安局奖励。

徐　若

徐若，1966年3月出生在高潮公社大河生产大队（今扎佐镇大河村），2004年6月加入中国共产党，1999至2001年担任大河村第三组组长，2002至2007年任大河村村民委员会主任，2008年起任中共大河村支部委员会书记。

徐若生于农村，长在农村，从小到大，目睹父辈和众多村民终年农耕，依然过着食不果腹的贫困生活，于是痛下决心，要走出一条致富路来。1985年，他初中毕业，自费到贵州省兽医科学研究所学习兽医，一年后回到大河当起了家畜家禽的医生，由于医术过硬，加上腿勤、嘴勤、手勤，服务周到，很快得到村民们的信任，村内外都有人上门求医为牲畜治病，使徐若家1998年成为

"万元户"，走上小康路。但其他村民还是贫困。徐若感到：一家富，不算富，全村富，才算富。1999年，他当上组长，跑到挨邻的乌当区新堡村参观大面积种植艳红桃家家奔上富裕快车道的典型，联想到大河与新堡村连村，自然条件相似，他们能种，我们也能种。于是，他利用为牲畜治病的机会，不遗余力地向村民们宣传新堡村的"致富经"，并率先示范，种植艳红桃20亩。在其带动下，有31户村民跟上，种植面积达200亩。树苗栽下去了，他领着种植户到新堡学习施肥、剪枝、整形、疏花疏果和防治病虫害等技术，参观水果市场，还多次邀请贵阳市农业科学研究所的专家到大河传授果树栽培技术。由于种植和管理到位，桃树长势喜人，村民眼见为实，种植面积从组扩大到村，2000年增种700亩，2001年挂果见效益，艳红桃总产1600吨，产值160万元，人均增收1236.7元。

2002年，徐若以高票当选为村委会主任，上任后的第一件事就是改善村里的基础设施。他深信"栽下梧桐树，引得凤凰来"，只要水果有产出，就不愁果商来采购，但通往大河及其果园凹凸不平的泥巴小路是制约果品出村的瓶颈。于是东奔西跑，几次请来县、镇和农业、林业、交通等部门领导在大河现场办公，解决狭窄的土路不通车的实际问题。"精诚所至，金石为开"，莅临大河的领导们被徐若以及村民们治穷致富的决心所感动，将大河的村公路修筑列成项目，一举拨给资金10万元，加上村民投工投劳，修通了进村水泥干道7.6公里，串户路4.5公里，机耕道10公里，还修建农灌沟渠9.5公里，果园小水窖178口，沼气池142口，不仅使运输畅通，而且还满足了全村人畜饮水和果园、农作物的浇灌，为多渠道建设"立体农业"奠定了基础。徐若主持村务的2004年，带领村民种植艳红桃1500亩，板栗400亩，水晶葡萄600亩，酥李150亩，梨200亩，折耳根500亩，使90%的农户户均纯收入上万元。2006年，大河村被贵阳市委、市政府列为全市新农村建设"百村先行"示范村，被修文县委、县政府列为全县10个新农村建设示范点，村党支部和村委会根据市、县要求，作出"一年抓示范，三年见成效，五年全展开，十五年实现"的规划，以"四基"（完善基础设施、夯实基础产业、强化基础教育、健全基层组织）为抓手，完成庭院整治、房屋立面改造、排污沟疏理、垃圾池安砌和农业产业结构调整。翌年，依托邻近的桃源河魔幻漂流开发，建起以"农家乐"为主的乡村旅游业，12家餐饮正式对外营业，集吃、住、玩、购为一体，接待游客20万人次，营业收入达百万元，成为村民增收致富的又一支柱产业，人均纯收入增长300元。

2007年换届选举，徐若全票当选为村党支部书记，他组织"村两委"（党支部委员会和村民委员会）拟订三年短期发展计划，确定围绕一个目标（党支部一班人带头致富和带领群众致富），打牢五个基础（绿化河道5公里，庭院绿化150户，硬化进组公路1.5公里，完善串户路800米，建设10个30立方水窖），发展三大产业（1、3组以发展艳红桃、葡萄为主的特色田园观光农业，四、五组发展以折耳根为特色的蔬菜业，沿河发展以依托桃源河漂流和田园观光农业为主的乡村旅游业）。目标既定，狠抓落实，徐若又争取市、县、镇的支持，完成4公里的果园机耕道硬化，4.5公里的采摘便道硬化，6公里的河标道绿化，70户村民的住宅立面整治，172户庭院绿化，建成大河村球场和休闲健身场所，实现电信、电视户户通，使村民的生活水平和生活质量显著提高。2010年，全村农民人均纯收入达到5000元。徐若看见村民们的钱袋子鼓了起来，更高兴地说："父老乡亲都富裕起来就是我最大的心愿。"

大河村在徐若的带领下，新农村建设成绩斐然，大河景象欣欣向荣，村民生活蒸蒸日上。2009年，村党支部被评为贵阳市和贵州省"五好"（领导班子好，党员队伍好，工作机制好，发展业绩好，群众反映好）基层组织受到表彰，2005年和2010年，徐若分别被评为贵阳市和贵州省劳动模范，受到市人民政府和省人民政府嘉奖。

丁泽军

丁泽军，1968年9月出生于贵阳市。1986年考入贵州大学攻读法律专业，毕业后分至贵阳市人民检察院反贪污贿赂工作局工作。期间，读西南政法大学研究生班获取法律硕士学位，先后任市人民检察院助理检察员、检察员、开阳县人民检察院副检察长、贵阳市人民检察院反贪局副局长等职务。丁泽军怀着对国家法治建设的满腔热忱，对保护人民利益的无限忠诚，十几年如一日，奋斗在自己的工作岗位上，痛击贪污腐败，严惩职务犯罪，到处留下爱岗敬业的口碑。

丁泽军在市检察院反贪局工作期间，参与办理修文县人民政府副县长赵吉超和原县纪律检查委员会书记、修文县重点公路工程建设指挥部指挥长陈海龙负责贵（阳）遵（义）高等级公路扎佐联络线建设期间的职务犯罪，由于工作认真细致，恪尽职守，以法律人的执法理念身体力行地推动法治建设，全面查清了赵吉超贪污、受贿2.56万元、涉案赃款9.05万元和陈海龙贪污2.55万元、与他人共同贪污未遂5.32万元、共同挪用公款10.15万元进行营利活动的犯罪事实，为法院最终作出赵吉超犯贪污罪判处有期徒刑2年、犯受贿罪判处有期徒刑1年零6个月，决定执行有期徒刑3年；陈海龙犯贪污罪判处有期徒刑4年、犯挪用公款罪判处有期徒刑3年，决定执行有期徒刑6年的判决提供了确凿的事实依据。

2005年11月，组织决定丁泽军任修文县人民检察院党组书记和代理检察长，2006年3月在修文县第十三届人民代表大会第四次会议上全票当选为检察长。丁泽军到任后，确立案件质量是检察工作生命线的执法理念，所有案件坚持“一切从细节开始”，规范诉讼程序，强化证据意识，制订并施行《修文县人民检察院审、录分离制度》《修文县人民检察院同步录音录像管理制度》《修文县人民检察院捕、诉衔接工作机制》等案件管理机制，规范办案，文明执法，确保案件质量，无错案和涉检信访案件发生。2007年，由反渎职侵权犯罪侦查局办理的赵翔滥用职权受贿案中，赵取保候审后，多方联合证人试图翻供，庭审时观看完由检察院提供的一张时间明确、讯问规范、办案文明的全程同步录音录像光盘后，赵翔认罪服法，最终被二审法院判处有期徒刑10年。丁泽军针对各个业务部门的工作量和干警分工，与党组成员于2007年研究并制定出《修文县人民检察院绩效考核办法》《修文县人民检察干警执法业绩档案》《修文县人民检察委员议事议案规则》，建立起奖勤罚懒的激励机制，树立以能力任用，以业绩提拔，任人唯贤的用人的良好风气，增强和调动了检察干警的工作积极性。

在丁泽军任期内，修文县正处于经济发展与社会变革的非常时期，刑事案件频发，社会矛盾复杂多样，2006—2010年，县检察院共办理批准逮捕、提起公诉的刑事案件1905件3087人，不捕不诉案件113件184人。其中2009年提起公诉287件459人，为5年间办案数的最高年。5年共打击各类犯罪团伙、黑恶势力犯罪6件104人，维护了社会的稳定。六广镇广田村的李绍华、李绍雄、李绍斌、李绍友兄弟早在2003年就倚势称霸乡里，网络社会闲散人员赵兵、陈石刚、李厚贤等20余人作为骨干，组织恶势力犯罪团伙，于2005年采取利用威胁手段殴打他人，拦截车辆，垄断全镇的木材销售和运输，并指使团伙成员分别在县境六广镇、小箐乡、扎佐镇及贵阳市白云区等地盗伐国有林场、集体林场和个人所有林木，造成生态植被被破坏，严重危害社会治安和公共管理秩序，影响人民群众的正常生活。该案移送到检察院，丁泽军从“环境立市、生态立县”保驾护航的要求出发，亲自带领干警分赴各地侦查取证，查实了李绍华、李绍雄等20人聚众斗殴、敲诈勒索、寻衅滋事、盗伐林木等多项犯罪事实，为法院作出李绍华犯聚众斗殴罪判处有期徒刑7年，犯寻衅滋事罪判处有期徒刑3年，犯滥伐林木罪判处有期徒刑2年，决定执行有期徒刑11年，并处罚金5000元；李厚贤犯聚众斗殴罪判处有期徒刑5年，犯盗伐林木罪判处有期徒刑4年，并处罚金5000元，犯强奸罪判处有期徒刑1年，犯敲诈勒索罪判处有期徒刑1年，决定执行有期徒刑10年，并处罚金5000元；赵兵犯寻衅滋事罪判处有期徒刑5年，犯滥伐林木罪判处有期徒刑5年，决定执行有期徒刑9年，并处罚金1万元提供客观的事实依据。其余的17名从犯也分别受到法律制裁。将一伙黑恶势力绳之以法后，群众拍手称快，纷纷称道“人民司法为人民，丁检察长为民除害，真是人民的优秀检察官”。

面对反贪污贿赂工作，丁泽军励精图治，从规范办案入手，注重提高检察干警的办案能力和水平，使查办职务犯罪工作出现质的飞跃。从2006—2010年，共查办职务犯罪案件64件70人，年均办案12.8件，为国家挽回经济损失3000余万元。在查办贵州省茅台酒厂总经理助理、广告部副处级主任许飚受贿280万元案、上海市恒昌广告公司法人代表胡铭单位行贿1000万元案、金阳建设投资有限公司总经理徐琳受贿126万元案等一系列特大、要案的同时，还查办了驻县贵阳煤矿系列案件8件8人、农村“四改一气”工程建设中的涉农职务犯罪5件5人等窝案串案。2007年，县院在全省首次掀起查办涉农职务犯罪、教育系统基础设施建设领域职务犯罪中窝案串案的高潮，积累了工作经验，为全省检察机关移送涉农职务犯罪、教育系统基础设施建设领域职务犯罪线索共26件。2009年4月，通过对信息的调查研究、综合研判，在丁泽军的指挥下，反贪局查证了洒坪乡副乡长黄林贪污农村“四改一气”工程专项资金8.2万元、县农业局土肥站站长朱有国贪污25.95万元，接受“四改一气”沼气池工程器械供应商贿赂9.78万元，六屯乡农业服务中心副主任张健文贪污“四改一气”工程专项资金7.36万元的事实，为法院的判决提供了有力的事实证据。通过一批涉农职务犯罪案件的办理，深挖线索，一举查办了贵阳市小河区人民政府副区长陈曦受贿27万元案，打开了贵阳市检察机关查办涉农职务犯罪的新局面。

丁泽军身体力行科技强检，多方筹措资金，解决检察保障建设的资金瓶颈问题。2007年，完成了“办案用房与检察技术用房”建设并搬迁入住。新办公大楼绿化面积1300平方米，“花园式”的办公环境展现了新时期检察文化的重大发展。投入使用的办公用房和专业技术用房占地面积13亩，具备了讯问犯罪嫌疑人全程录音录像、查办职务犯罪远程监控、视频会议、网络办公、档案管理现代化、与各级检察院实现计算机专线网络联通等办公和办案等办公条件现代化功能。2009年率先在全省建成并使用驻所检察室同步录音录像系统，完善党组班子建设，形成一个团结、协作、信赖的领导核心。2010年，办案大楼2000平方米续建项目正式筹备启动；修文县院在全省首家建成“检委会会议无纸化办公系统”并投入使用。从2006到2010年，县院先后新购办案车辆11辆，将原有的陈旧交通车辆全部淘换，确保办案安全；办公设备从原来的每个科室2台电脑增为每人手提与台式各1台，为无纸化办公提供了有力的保障。

在丁泽军的带领下，修文县人民检察院2007年获得了贵州省人民检察院授予的“全省先进基层检察院”、“全省文明接待室”等荣誉称号，丁泽军本人也因工作成绩突出被贵阳市检察机关推荐为2008年北京“奥运火炬手”，被授予“2008年抗凝冻保民生先进个人”荣誉称号。

毕远会

毕远会，1968年11月出生于贵州省六枝特区，1990年重庆电力专科学校毕业后被分配至黔桂发电公司（原盘县电厂）从锅炉值班员逐级晋升为公司党支部书记和公司总经理。十几年的工作时间，把毕远会锻炼成一个好学、好钻、好交友、胸怀全局、善于企业管理的优秀人才。2008年，中共修文县委、县政府加大招商力度，实施“招大商，引巨资，开办大企业”的战略举措，吸引了毕远会选点在川黔大道旁的久长镇金桥村创办大型水泥厂，挂牌贵州金久水泥生产有限公司，毕远会任公司董事长。白手起家创办大企业，首先碰到的是建设资金问题。面对全球性的金融风波，数以亿计的巨资从哪来？毕远会沉着应对，以自己忠诚待人、踏实做事的人格魅力，取信于一个个登门造访的融资合作者，一举到位4.22亿元的启动资金，为厂房建筑和设备购置奠定了坚实的基础。资金有了眉目，又需解决征地问题，划定的833亩厂区需搬迁49户村民，毕远会配合久长镇政府将金桥村新农村建设列入全县示范点，出资9万元敦请设计部门进行建设新村的规划设计，又拿出900万元支付平场、供水、排水和通电的费用，还拨付400万元将金桥村通镇公路和人行道拓展到9米宽，并改造为水泥路面，尽力为拆迁的村民通水、通电、通路，使他们满意地搬进新居。征地和拆迁落实了，又需解决的是被征地户的就业安置问题，毕远会为解决被征地村民的后顾之忧，除如数付清征地补偿费外，对耕地被征拨完而失去生活来源的拆迁户中的有劳动能力者即优先录用进企业当农民工。

人、财、物尘埃落定，毕远会全身心地投入厂区建设。在“地方做好服务，企业加快建设”的战略思想指导下，金久公司以超前的速度推动建厂进程，仅1年多时间金久水泥厂即建成投产。通过地企共建，形成了地方为企业落户生根创造良好的外部环境，企业为地方经济发展不断输入充满活力的正能量的崭新局面。毕远会带领全厂职工沿着已铺成的道路迈步前行，期望水泥项目全部建成运营，总投资增为15亿元，年实现销售收入16亿元，创税2.3亿元，就业职工1000人。毕远会为促使修文的经济建设腾飞添砖加瓦指日可待。

谭　虎

谭虎，1972年出生于修文县城，1990年在修文一中修完高中课业即考入贵州大学攻读法律专业，1994年7月大学毕业后被分配到贵阳市人民检察院反贪污贿赂工作局工作。至2010年12月，谭虎已在市人民检察院从事职务犯罪侦察工作16年，历任院反贪局侦察处处长、副局长、局长和院党组成员。

谭虎在十多年的反贪生涯中，恪尽职守，无私无畏，忠实履行人民检察官的职责，在平凡的工作岗位上做出不平凡的业绩，先后主办、参办和指挥查办500余件贪污贿赂职务犯罪案件，无一错案，为国家挽回经济损失5亿多元。2002年，谭虎被任命为反贪局侦查处处长，他深知组织信任，重担在肩，誓将

全部身心投进反贪工作中，既挂帅，又出征，在其带领下，成功地办理了贵阳市电力系统“0·8专案”农行瑞金支行“12·3专案”和“华创专案”等在贵阳市以致贵州省都有较大影响的大案。2003年，谭虎接受查办华创证券经纪责任有限公司原上海控江路营业部经理邹军挪用公款4.5亿元的特大职务犯罪案件。由于该案系贵州省罕见的涉嫌金融、证券职务犯罪案件，涉案金额巨大，涉案人员较多，案情十分复杂，异地取证难度很大，追捕任务非常艰巨。面对困难，谭虎带领办案干警在“非典”肆虐期间，先后14次赴上海、杭州、张家港、大连等地开展追捕、追赃、取证工作，跋涉1万多公里，调取了15本卷宗的书证、物证、证人证言，并以证促审，全面查清了邹军涉嫌挪用公款4.5亿元、受贿160万元、贪污9 8万元的犯罪事实，为法院对其最终作出无期徒刑判决提供了充足的证据。赓续顺藤摸瓜，谭虎带领办案人员克服跨省、跨地区办案的重重困难，查封了19个涉案股票资金账户，冻结了涉案人员在上海招商银行、民生银行等金融部门开设的储蓄账户，查封了5处房地产，共控制了3.3亿元的动产和不动产，挽回了巨额国有资产损失，为化解因邹军滥用职权给华创公司造成的数亿元巨额债务风险奠定了坚实的基础。办案终结，得到省政府和省人民检察院的充分肯定，常务副省长王正福作的批示称：检察机关工作力度大，效果好，依法办案，掌握工作主动权，化解风险，圆满解决问题，确保省华创证券公司国有资产未受损失。

2005年，谭虎担任反贪局副局长分管侦查工作后，按照“抓系统，系统抓”的办案思路，带领反贪干警深入调研，主动出击，摸行业、部门、系统职务犯罪的规律和特点，深挖细查，先后组织、指挥了全市近百名反贪干警在国土、医疗、教育、社保系统开展调研工作，立案查办了省、市国土系统商业贿赂案件40件44人，查办了贵阳医疗系统案件64件72人，查办了省、市教育系统案件40件43人和市保障系统案件18件20人，击破了工作“瓶颈”，使贵阳市的反贪工作步入良性循环的轨道，走在全省的前列。

2008年，谭虎晋升为反贪局局长。他以反腐为己任，加大对职务犯罪大案、要案的查办力度，重点查办群众反映大的城镇建设领域职务犯罪案件。针对城镇建设领域职务犯罪多发、易发的特点，谭虎及时制订出实施方案，组织全市反贪干警深入国土、建设、交通、园林、规划等部门开展专项行动，先后查办城镇建设领域案件119件121人，名列全省城镇建设领域结案之首。其中查办高检院挂牌督办的贵阳市市长助理、金阳新区管委会主任樊中黔职务犯罪案是颇费心机的。樊中黔历任贵阳市城管局长、国土局长、建设局局长、城管委主任等要职，官阶级别高，受贿金额大，态度很顽抗，有较强的反侦察意识。该案又为社会高度关注。谭虎不畏艰难，勇挑重担，为了突破案件，他连续3个月没有在家住过一夜和吃过一餐饭，以不怕疲劳和百折不挠的精神带领专案组的50多名同志克服重重困难，一举查获樊中黔存放在5个保险柜中的现金1700余万元。接着，又组织精兵强将，掌握确凿证据，对樊中黔开展强大的法律和政策攻势，突破樊的心理防线，终于使其交代了在20年的公职时间里数百次收受74名房开商、建筑商贿赂千余万元的事实，是新中国建立后贵阳市涉案金额最大的行政长官。樊中黔的职务犯罪结案后，谭虎又发扬连续作战的作风，突破了金阳建设投资公司经理徐林受贿200万元等20余件城镇建设领域案件，成功地揪出了一个又一个的腐败分子，有力地震慑了该领域的职务犯罪。据数据显示，2005至2008年，贵阳市两级反贪部门立案侦查的564件632人职务犯罪案件中，属谭虎指挥的6大系统查办的案件达275件302人，占48.76%。市院反贪局也因查办商业贿赂案件成效显著在全国检察机关自侦工作会上作经验交流发言。

2009年，谭虎从基层院查办的一起涉农案件中敏锐地察觉到在贵阳市进行的农村“四改一气”（改厨、改厕、改圈、改造进户路和沼气池建设）工作，因市政府下拨的资金数额巨大，沼气设备完全由供应商控制，涉及全市8个市县区，其中可能存在涉农职务犯罪问题，遂选择在清镇市召开会议，明确“四改一气”的查办方向和重点，组织5家基层院开展专项工作。在不到1个月的时间里，即查办了清镇、修文、开阳、息烽、乌当等5市县区的农业部门工作人员在采购沼气设备中受贿的窝、串案18件25人，涉案金额350万元。与此同时，还发现贵州海泉沼气有限公司向贵州省的54个地州供应价值2000余万元的沼气设备时行贿235万元给相关人员。待高检院部署查办涉农职务犯罪案件时，贵阳市已立此类案件30余件。

在多年的反贪工作实践中，谭虎在积极查办案件的同时不断创新机制，构建“纵向指挥有力，横向协作密切”的贵阳市反贪工作格局。以机制建设促进案件查办，并总结出“忠诚、清廉、团结、奉献”的反贪精神，以此激励反贪干警的工作热情，有力地推动全市反贪工作平稳健康发展。从2005年起，谭虎所领导的反贪局先后1次荣立集体一等功，3次荣立集体二等功，4次荣立集体三等功，2008年获得最高人民检察院授予“全国十佳反贪局”荣誉称号，谭虎本人也荣获“全国模范检察官”的殊荣。在此之前，谭虎还先后受到各级嘉奖：1次荣立二等功，3次荣立三等功，并被授予“贵阳市优秀共产党员”“贵阳市十大杰出青年卫士”“贵州省优秀侦查能手”“贵州省人民满意的检察官”“贵州省十大杰出青年卫士”“贵州省先进工作者”等荣誉称号。

朱俊首

朱俊首，1972年出生于扎佐南街，1979年启蒙读书，1991年参军服役于中国人民解放军35221部队，1995年退伍后在修文县自来水公司工作。

朱俊首出生书香之家，祖父和父亲均擅长书法。由于自身天赋，加上书家熏陶，还是读小学的时候，他写的字就受身边的人的称道，也在学校的文艺活动中崭露头角。1985年，朱俊首刚满13岁，在母亲的全力支持下，参加了贵州省书法协会开办的书法函授班。在班里，他广泛涉猎，流连在唐楷和汉隶魏碑之间。朱俊首每天趴在3尺书桌上，练笔不辍；在部队当文书，更得到练字的环境和平台，一沓沓的旧纸报，一刀刀的宣纸，都留下他的墨迹。由于不懈努力，使朱俊首的书法出现质的飞跃。1994年，朱俊首行书作品《黄庭坚论书句》在解放军总政治部主办的“全军两用人才美术书法展”中荣获三等奖，并被列为全军16名获奖代表之一赴北京参加展览开幕式及笔会，荣获三等军功章，是获奖代表中唯一的普通士兵。正当朱俊首与获奖的代表们在笔会上挥毫泼墨的时候，却迎来了中共中央政治局常委、军委副主席刘华清。当刘华清看见朱俊首还未完成的作品即称赞说：“好呀，写得真不错。”刘华清又握着朱俊首的手鼓励道：“部队需要更多像你一样的书法家和画家来丰富基层部队的文化生活，希望继续努力，能看到你们更多更好的作品。”并当即合影留念。所在部队为朱俊首记三等功1次。

朱俊首的书法除篆书外，楷书、隶书、行书和草书兼擅，尤其长于行草。从部队退伍后，1995至2007年间，朱俊首因各种原因疏离纸笔。直到2007年重拾书艺，笔耕不辍，从2008年起，朱俊首的书法作品进入盛产期，不仅数量多，且精品迭出。连续荣获中国“梵净山杯”全国书法篆刻大赛金奖和贵州省“金海杯”第四届行草书法大赛金奖、贵州省“茫父杯”第三届书法大赛银奖、贵州省第二届楹联展铜奖、贵州省“黔冠杯”首届书法篆刻小精品三等奖，在黔南都匀举办的“全国书法篆刻展”中有朱俊首参展的一幅小草作品，好似一条在山间流淌的小溪，叮咚有声，蜿蜒有致，被参观者称为“草中君子”。2010年在贵阳美术馆举办的“中韩书法交流展”中朱俊首提供的《录王阳明过天生桥》草书，把每个笔画都写得光洁玉润，收到淋漓酣畅的艺术效果，中外嘉宾在观摩中无不交口赞誉。

由于朱俊首的书艺出类拔萃，书法作品得到社会的普遍认同，2009年起，他竟成为中国书法家协会会员，是全县唯一的国家级权威专业艺术团体会员，并先后当选为贵州省书法家协会常务理事兼草书专业委员会副主任、贵阳市书法家协会主席。

王晓刚

王晓刚，1973年10月生于安顺市（今西秀区）西街，1993年考入贵州省财经学院攻读财政专业，1996年5月考入修文县公安局交通警察大队当交通民警，2001年加入中国共产党，2009年9月起任交警大队教导员。

王晓刚一参加工作就跨进交通警察部门，且一直坚守在修文县公安局交警岗位上，担负着日常路面执勤、交通事故处理和交警内勤的担子。用他的话来说：守护交通秩序是交警的天职，个中有苦有累，但换来群众生命财产不受损失，就能从苦中得乐。

贵（阳）毕（节）高等级公路建成通车，王晓刚就被分派在贵毕路修文段执勤。他顶着严寒酷暑，不畏日晒雨淋，一干就是7年。每天，他身着佩有金色盾牌的警服，用规范、严肃的手势指挥疏导一次次车辆通过，纠正驾驶员一次次交通违章，消除一次次事故隐患，解决群众一次次求助。仅2002至2003年，他就亲手纠正各种交通违章5600多起，协助故障车辆驾驶员排除故障149次，扶老携幼960人次，解决群众求助246起。2008年1月27日夜，气温降至-7℃，大雪封山，公路凝冻，上百辆机动车被滞留在挖煤冲路段，数以千计乘客困在车厢。王晓刚闻讯后，与2名交警立即赶至贵毕公路扎佐入口处，果断地采取封路措施，并承担起长达3公里的巡逻警卫任务。他把手机号逐一告诉受困的驾驶员，以便遇险报警求助。更深夜静，严寒肆虐，他脸颊冻得通红，手脚冻僵麻木，仍来回巡逻在滞留3公里的车队之间。车子的油管堵塞了，他找来开水烫淋；乘客饿了缺少食品，他掏钱购置馒头送给充饥；发现路上凝冻没有融化的地方，他与路政人员一道挥动铁锹铲冰，抛沙撒盐防滑；为安全行驶，他督促客货车逐一套上防滑链。很多驾驶员和乘客被王晓刚细致入微的服务感动而发出肺腑之言：“公路上有这样想群众之想，帮群众之需的交警，我们就放心了。”两天过后，王晓刚抓住中午气候升温的时机，将百部车辆以及千名乘客安全带出修文境域。一次50年不遇的凝冻天气在王晓刚和他的战友们的“严防死守”下，没有发生一起重特大交通事故，没有出现一起治安刑事案件，虽然因严寒影响导致王晓刚双腿酸疼无力，他认为轻伤算不了什么，只要车好人安，心中就无限欣慰。

贵毕路开通后，由于道路设计欠合理，交通设施不齐全，导致县境下半沟大桥路段交通事故频发，仅2001年10月至2003年5月就发生事故54起，其中一般事故46起，重特大事故8起，致伤29人，死亡15人，直接经济损失187万元。面对一桩桩车毁人亡事件，王晓刚产生揪心的痛。他决心对已发生的交通事故一一加以分析，亲临事故现场进行测量、拍照，找准路段事故多发的原因，确定路段“黑点”。在此基础上，撰写出《关于在贵毕公路下半沟大桥、新田湾路段修建防撞墙的报告》《关于贵毕公路下半沟大桥道路设计存在的缺陷和采取弥补措施的报告》《关于增设贵毕公路交通标志、标线的报告》，提出了40多条整改意见和建议报送到相关部门，所提意见和建议得到省、市交警和交通部门领导的重视，制定出完善公路设施的方案，修建了下半沟、新田湾防撞墙，增设了贵毕公路修文段内10个路段的标志、标线和减速震荡带，使安全设施得以改善。自2003年4月至2004年4月，下半沟大桥发生交通事故次数、致伤人数、死亡人数同比分别减少87%、89.6%、100%。公路设施完善，交通事故减少，使王晓刚心里踏实，他从中体会到：只要交通部门、驾驶员、交警三者紧密配合就能确保旅途平安。

2003年4月，一场罕见的非典型肺炎（以下简称“非典”）突然袭扰贵州，贵阳市面临巨大的流入性“非典”病毒传染的概率。“防非”工作刻不容缓。一道道由交警、卫生防疫部门组成的公路“非典”防线——健康检疫登记点相继在各入境主干道设立，王晓刚主动请缨参加协查“非典”工作，坚守在贵毕公路扎佐站的检疫点。他在来不及配备全套防疫设备和缺乏后勤供应的情况下，仅凭一副口罩，协助医生对广东、四川等重点疫区入境的车辆和司乘人员进行体温测量和快速体检。每天，清晨6时上岗，夜晚8时回队，在高强度进行工作的14个小时里，不停地打手势，勤劝解，作记录，纠违章，还要确保运送防治“非典”药品和群众生活必需的粮、油、蔬菜车辆安全畅通。70天下来，王晓刚协助卫生防疫部门检查各种机动车2.9万辆，协助医生对17.6万过境人员进行体温测量和体格检查，发现5例可疑发热病人随即送到定点发热门诊部进一步检查，还纠正各类交通违章2202起。所辖路段没有运输“非典”防治人员和物资的车辆发生交通事故，既预防和控制“非典”病毒从扎佐入境口进入市区，又确保西南入海干道贵阳段的畅通和安全。经历一场没有硝烟的战争，王晓刚感到精疲力竭，但他又认为：身体受点折磨算不了什么，堵住“非典”病毒入市和个人意志受到磨炼才是最大的收获。

履行日常路面执勤和交通事故处理的王晓刚，还兼有交警大队的内勤工作。大队内勤涵盖的文书制作、事故档案管理、交通安全宣传、报表统计报送、交通管理凭证发放和回收全由王晓刚一人承担。他每月要制作文书20多份，容量1.2万多字；发放、收回、整理交通管理凭证3000余张；统计填报12种报表106份；还要对每个月发生的交通事故进行整理、造册登记，逐一录入计算机……若干纷繁复杂的内勤工作都担在王晓刚的肩上，往往是路面执勤后回到办公室加班完成。工作量最大的要算事故档案管理，完善一份档案要花费1个小时，每月仅用在事故档案管理上的时间就有40多个小时，40多个小时都是利用晚上休息时间，有的夜晚弄得疲惫不堪，但他从无怨言。由于作风细致严谨，工作无懈可击，需要提取的事故档案，他能在1分钟之内从数千起档案中找出来，因而王晓刚被誉为“交警大队的活档案”。

王晓刚本着全心全意为人民服务的根本宗旨，在修文县公安局交通警察的岗位上恪尽职守，贡献突出，得到组织肯定。从参加工作后的1997—2005年连续9年被修文县公安局评为先进工作者，1998至2000年和2004—2005年被评为优秀公务员，2001年被贵州省公安厅评为“全省优秀人民警察”，2002年荣立二等功获省公安厅表彰，2003年被评为“全国优秀人民警察”受国家公安部褒奖，2004年被评为修文县安全生产先进个人和贵阳市优秀共产党员，同时被中共贵阳市委、市人民政府授予“1996至2004年贵阳市公安系统优秀民警”称号，2006年被修文县委、县政府评为政法工作先进个人，被贵州省公安厅评为“大战七十天先进个人”，2007年被贵阳市公安局授予“警察之星”称号，2010年被修文县委、县政府评为涉法涉诉信访先进个人。

李根书

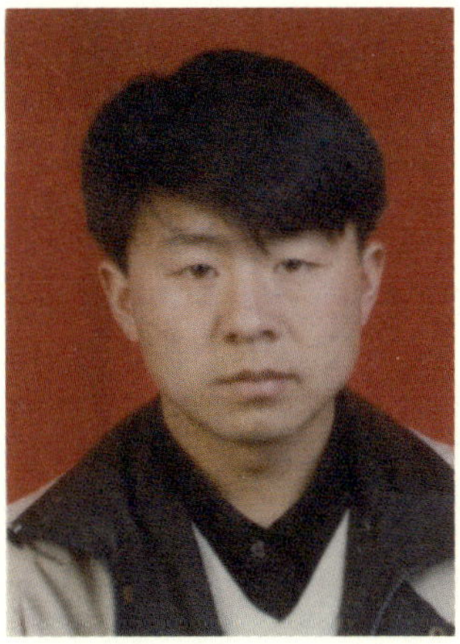

李根书，1974年1月出生于凉井公社山宝生产大队（今六桶乡山宝村）雷家湾，1992年初中毕业后到修文县农业广播学校学习农业科学知识，同时在贵阳市白云区麦架乡学习饲养家禽，1995年任六桶乡兴农养鸡场场长和养鸡协会会长。

1995年，李根书在农广校毕业，随即到居住于麦架乡的叔父李显贵家自办的养鸡场里帮助养鸡。通过实际锻炼，李根书的饲养技术进一步提高。1998年，他回到山宝村贷款5万元买下村里拍卖的98亩荒山兴办林下饲养肉鸡，挂牌“六桶乡兴农养鸡场”，自任场长，并任养鸡协会会长。办场的第一关是通路，李根书就凭自己的双手，一锤一錾地与顽石鏖战60天，终于打通了1条从山脚到山顶1000米的泥沙道路；第二关是通水，他四处寻找水源，在九岭岗上找到两股水后，接着铺设了2000米管道，将水引到养鸡场；第三关是通电，李根书以苦干、实干的精神感动供电部门，架设线路2000米，顺利地让鸡场用上了电。“三通”问题解决后，接着修起1950平方米的鸡舍，砌起180立方米的水池，栽上60亩用树叶作饲料的杨槐树，使固定资产规模达到40万元，成为六桶乡的肉鸡养殖基地。

一切筹备工作就绪，李根书采取“基地+农户+市场”的方式，吸收24名农村青年到养殖基地当工人，从务工中学习技术；并发挥鸡场的辐射功能，带动500户村民发展土鸡养殖，形成“一村一品”的农民增收致富新格局；基地帮助购进鸡苗，提供养殖技术和联系市场销售产品。李根书认为：说一千，道一万，不如做给乡亲看。他拉开饲养序幕，一举购进鸡苗1000只，白天放入林地啄食，夜间群住鸡舍，开了六桶乡规模养鸡的先河。农户眼见为实，照着基地做法放养土鸡。1998年，基地的1000只优质肉鸡出栏，农户的土鸡也进入市场，深受商家和消费者的青睐，基地、农户都获利受益，备尝甜头。继后，饲养逐年扩大规模，从1999到2010年的12年间，出栏肉鸡基地达72万只，年均6万只，获纯利润30万元，年均获纯利润30万元；农户土鸡出栏达460万只，年均30万只，获利2300万元，年均190万元。

为了向农户传授养鸡技术和帮助农户致富，李根书用于发放培训资料、防疫药品和联系销售的资金达5万多元；又购买鸡苗6000只借给3个村的100户计生贫困户，使每户年均获利7.2万元；还进行智力帮扶，联系两户计生贫困户送子女入学。

李根书营运林下养鸡致富路历尽艰辛，终于得到组织认可。2000年，李根书被评为全国计划生育协会青年志愿者和贵州省乡土拔尖人才，并获得“贵阳市劳动模范”称号；2001年，兴农养鸡场被共青团贵阳市委授予“共青团绿色示范基地”称号；2002年，兴农养鸡场被县委、县政府授予“先进民营企业”称号，山宝村被贵阳市政府命名为“无公害农产品生产基地”，李根书被选为六桶乡计生协会理事。2003年，李根书荣获“贵阳市十大杰出青年”称号；2005年，李根书被评为“贵州省劳动模范”受到表彰。2010年，李根书领取共青团中央和农业部颁发“全国农村青年创业致富带头人”的荣誉证书。

黄继虎

黄继虎，1974年12月出生于平坝县羊昌公社（今羊昌乡），1995年毕业于西安航空技术高等专科学校，随即被分配在贵阳云天航空工贸凸轮轴厂任技术员，2002年6月加入中国共产党，2003年，经过整合后的贵州龙翔能源（集团）有限公司凸轮厂入驻修文县龙场镇小营村，年仅29岁的黄继虎竟担起凸轮轴厂的重担，任技术副厂长。

黄继虎参加工作即从事新产品的开发和质量管理。是时，云天厂生产效益差，资金十分困难，职工待遇很低，但黄继虎热爱自己所学的机械加工专业，并未畏难不前，而是下决心提高云天凸轮轴的产品质量，做出品牌。在市场竞争日趋激烈的情况下，他紧紧配合各家整车厂，从市场需求出发，与车间的技术人员不断解决生产中的技术问题，使生产出来的各种型号产品，经过送样测试，在图纸设计要求和机械性能、理化性能、各项技术参数方面均达到发动机整机性能的要求。在开发试制工作中，黄继虎以工艺为突破口，大力开展技术创新，合理调整加工工艺，完善工艺参数，解决了工艺流程长、半成品热处理后变形的工艺技术问题，逐步掌握了高精度凸轮反靠补偿技术、凸轮轴相位角控制、装配变形控制等技术问题，为开发各种类型的凸轮轴组件打下了基础。2002年，黄继虎开发的豪迈50、GY6型凸轮轴组件经台湾光阳机车的严格测试，完全满足发动机的各项性能要求，所提供的产品完全达到了日本同类产品要求的品质，实现了摩托车关键零件的国产化替代了进口，台湾光阳的国内独资和合资企业的近15个品种全部由龙翔凸轮轴厂独家供应，为企业带来良好的信誉和效益。2007年开发的CF188（500CC）沙滩车凸轮轴成功地配套给春风控股集团，产品年产1万台，批量出口意大利，为企业在大排量沙滩车产品的开发上积累了经验。

2008年开发的204凸轮轴，又成功出口意大利，配套欧洲顶级摩托车制造商比亚乔，进一步奠定了“云天凸轮”的品牌。2008至2009年开发的PUA9通用机械凸轮轴，经日本川崎重工株式会社用1年时间进行发动机各项性能严格测试，其结果超过日本川崎设在美国工厂生产的同类产品。由于产品质量上乘，加之价格优势，致川崎重工关停了设在美国的工厂，将全部生产线移至江苏常州落户，PUA9凸轮轴年产10万台，生产的通用机械凸轮全部出口到美国。2009年开发新产品HS133凸轮轴，主要使用于轻型飞机，也适用于气垫船、无人直升机和消防设备动力，通过龙翔能源（集团）有限公司与金城集团航空轻型动力事业部合作，实现了企业在轻型飞机发动机关键部件的生产上零的突破，使产品进入测试阶段。

由于黄继虎的努力，为企业开拓了广阔的市场空间，使企业获得更大份额的配套数量，工厂产品从1996年的3个品种扩大到2000年的50、70、90、100、110、125、250、500CC、800C摩托车、沙滩车、通用机械等车型配套的30余种凸轮轴主件，产量从1996年的8万套年生产能力上升到2010年的42万套，产值从1996年的160万元上升到2010年的750万元，销售收入从1996年的150万元增加到2010年的720万元，向国家缴纳税金从1996年的9.3万元增为2010年的43.2万元，配套主机厂从1966年的3家扩展到2010年的10家。产品批量与南京金城，金城铃木，北京易初，常州光阳，济南轻骑，重庆隆鑫、宗申、银翔，洛阳洛嘉，浙江春风控股，黄岩本州，浙江双瑞、斯丹尼，广州天马、豪进海利，江门天钆和日本川崎重工、意大利比亚乔等骨干厂家配套，且产品直接或随主机厂配套出口欧洲、日本、东南亚、中东地区等多个国家。

由于产品质量过硬，使“云天”凸轮成为国内外知名摩托车凸轮轴品牌，并入围2004年度摩托车行业最佳零部件配套体系全明星阵容，也为多家企业开发产品替代进口，两次开发的新产品还获得贵州省新产品奖励。2009年在贵阳市科学技术委员会的领导下成立了贵阳凸轮制造研究工程技术中心，为企业的发展奠定了坚实的基础。

黄继虎多年扎根在困难企业，充分表现出他热爱所学的机械加工专业的高尚品格。由于他不计较个人得失，一心扑在专业技术和企业产品质量上，努力学习，刻苦钻研，勇于实践，不断总结，做出了不平凡的成绩，从西安航校毕业走上工作岗位的15年里，由他参加开发的凸轮轴产品达80余种型号，这些产品分别用于摩托车、汽油机、沙滩车、园林工具、计量仪器、工程机械，均取得较好的经济效益，黄继虎也逐渐锻炼成长为经验丰富的科技工作者，从2000年起不断获得殊荣。2001年，黄继虎被评为贵州省国防科技工业“九五”技术创新先进个人，受到贵州省国防科学技术工业办公室表彰；2006年，贵州省总工会颁发给黄继虎“五一劳动奖章”；2010年，黄继虎被评为贵州省劳动模范，受到省人民政府嘉奖。

肖江虹

肖江虹，1976年12月出生于花椰公社金星生产大队（今六桶乡金星村），1998年安顺师范专科学校中文系毕业后被分配到扎佐中学教书，后又被借调到县委宣传部和教育局从事通讯报道，2002年加入中国共产党，2005年考入贵州师范大学文学院本科，毕业后借用在县文学艺术联合会专事文学创作，是贵州省文学院第一届、第二届和第三届签约作家。

肖江虹出生在书香之家，自幼就受到家庭的影响和文化的熏陶，夜晚入睡之前要祖父给他讲《西游记》《三国演义》；读小学时，他就涉猎了当教师的父亲订阅的《收获》《当代》《昆仑》等文学刊物，读过若干作品后他向父亲许诺：“长大后我的文章一定要在《当代》发表。”上大学后，阅读文学作品的兴趣更浓，并且产生了文学创作的念头，甚至开始琢磨小说创作。

1997年，肖江虹将处女作小小说《脊梁》投给《修文报》，被报社编辑部看好，当即加上褒扬的按语公开发表，使他受到鼓励，从此在创作的道路上一步一步地向前迈进。2003年，短篇小说《阴谋》首次在省级文学刊物上发表，载入江苏《雨花》，使肖江虹对创作更增强信心，向着中篇进发。2007年，中篇小说《一撇一捺》在《贵州作家》发表，标志着肖江虹在创作的道路上又前进了一步。2009年，一篇以吹唢呐为题材反映现代化对乡村冲击的中篇小说《百鸟朝凤》发表在全国大型文学期刊《当代》上，随后又被全国第一流文学刊物《中篇小说选刊》《中篇小说月报》《小说选刊》《北京文学》以及《新华文摘》选载，还被中国作家协会创联部编入《2009年中篇小说精选》和小说选刊杂志社选入《2009年中国年度中篇小说》。于是，《百鸟朝凤》轰动大江南北，肖江虹也因此名扬省内外。全国著名导演吴天明意欲以《百鸟朝凤》为蓝本改编为电影剧本，便用5万元向肖江虹买下版权。2010年，中国作家协会组织开展首届“茅台杯”小说选刊年度大奖活动，要在2009年各家文学期刊已发表的1万多篇中篇和短篇小说中分别评选出10篇优秀作品列进“茅台杯”排行榜，以反映当前中、短篇小说创作的最高成就。出其不意，《百鸟朝凤》居然进入中篇小说排行榜了，肖江虹获悉后欣喜若狂，情不自禁地北上首都国际饭店参加颁奖典礼，受到全国人大常委会副委员长铁木尔·达瓦买提接见，中国作家协会主席铁凝和作协党组书记、副主席李冰亲自为肖江虹颁奖。国家领导人和中央领导的嘉奖更加促进肖江虹向高处登攀，下定决心竣稿手上的长篇作品。于是，沉下身心，住进麻风病人集中治疗的康复村，用半个多月的时间体验患者生活，回到斗室夜以继日笔耕，终于以20万字的篇幅把一个特殊群体与病魔抗争的人和事活生生地展现给读者，完成了自己最喜欢和感到最有意义的一部长篇小说《向日葵》，并通过大型文学期刊《十月》二审。从1997到2010年，肖江虹的文学创作已达12篇，其中小小说1篇，短篇小说6篇，中篇小说4篇，长篇小说1篇，总容量100万字。

肖江虹的作品多取材于农村，而且更多地关注社会的最底层。他说：“我生在农村，长在农村，总忘不了在家乡耳闻目睹过的人和事。随着时代的变迁，那些既朴素又动人的事和人几乎被人们遗忘了，能用我的笔把他们记述下来，既是对父老乡亲的一种敬爱，又能让读者回味一番逝去岁月经历过的很有意义的往事，我就感到欣慰。”这就是肖江虹坚持文学创作“源于生活，高于生活”的创作观。

经过十多年的创作实践，肖江虹认为，作品要使读者青睐，小说要做成好小说，应该具有3个条件：一要好读，这是基础，只有基础夯实了，其他功能才会发挥；二要有个性化，要摒除对传统乡土文学写作经验的依赖，对现实生活须有独特的发现；三要体现文学的哲理性，作家应有对生活的独特洞见和思考，包括作家的境界、情操、道德判断以及悲悯情怀等等都应当融进作品中去，让人读着栩栩如生的小说感到耳目一新。肖江虹发出肺腑之言：“一部作品的高低，首先取决于一个作家境界的高低，当结构、叙事、语言这些技术层面的东西都不是问题以后，作家比拼的就是境界了。”

由于肖江虹出类拔萃和他的作品赢得了读者群，也就引起社会的特别关注：2008年短篇小说《求你和我说说话》在贵州《山花》发表后就被北京大学文学院评为刊物年度最佳小说；2009年海南《天涯》推出的《肖江虹小说专辑》，除已发表过的作品外，又载入新作短篇《平行线》和《家谱》，短篇《天堂》在《山花》发表后被《小说选刊》和《新华文摘》转载，并收入中国作协编辑出版的《2010年度中国短篇小说排行榜》；2010年短篇《喊魂》在《山花》发表后被《中篇小说选刊》年末专辑选载。作品连续产出，肖江虹的影响力也随之拓展，被称为“中国70后有影响的作家”“新世纪的多产作家”，贵州省委宣传部和省文化厅举办的大型文艺演出《乌蒙颂》、大型专题报告会《道德的力量》和《新中国成立六十周年贵州大型文艺晚会》都有肖江虹参与，并主笔文学撰稿。在荣耀面前，年仅34岁的肖江虹都很低调，他说：“成绩只能说明过去，但我做得不够，我还得继续努力，站稳人民大众的立场，写出更好更多的小说献给读者，从而引起心灵的共鸣。”

唐开文

唐开文，1977年5月出生于凤冈县何坝乡，2003年在贵阳中医学院医疗系毕业，随即作为青年志愿者下至大石布依族乡卫生院支医，2004年转至六屯乡卫生院服务，2005年考为国家正式的医务工作者，2008年担任六屯乡卫生院院长。

唐开文出生中医世家，家庭连续有人行医已有4代。由于环境的熏陶，从小就立下了从医的志向。他说："经常看见垂危病人被家人抢救过来后露出患者和医生的喜悦心情，我就感到从事医务这个职业的骄傲。"一拿到大学学士文凭时，正赶上共青团中央和教育部发起"大学生志愿服务西部"的招募活动，唐开文遵照父母亲"人不可以忘本"的叮嘱，放弃了到广西壮族自治区玉林市玉林药业公司当职员年薪可以拿到8万元的机遇，却作出了到大山里去当青年志愿者支医的决定。面对选择，有同学问道："你这样做到底为了啥?"唐开文答："我说为名——没用，因为我刚走出校门，没有那种奢望；我说为利——没有，因为农村太穷。只要能把学到的知识和技术献给西部农民，我就心安理得。"于是，他带上行囊，登上服务西部的征程，下到修文县唯一的一个少数民族乡，也是县内最为贫困的一个乡——大石布依族乡，落实在乡卫生院当医生。进入卫生院，见着最好的药品就是青霉素，最好的设备只是一台200毫安X光机，但没有人会使用；4个管床医生中有两个是保送读的初级卫校，1个是跟师学技的。面临条件极差的医疗单位，唐开文没有退却，而是迎难而上。他向院长李登贵提出设置中医、针灸、推拿、妇产、化验、手术等相关临床和辅助科室的建议，被采纳后又多方奔走，终于在县民族宗教事务局争取到4万元扶贫款，添置了常用的医疗器械和中西药；同时，选派2名青年医技人员到县人民医院进修学习，增强上下之间的业务交流；又制订职工上下班签到制度、考勤制度、医疗责任制度，以此约束医务人员，规范医务秩序；还提出了降低医疗费用的建议，将原本输三四瓶生理盐水需要60元降为35元左右。经过一系列的改革，大石乡卫生院逐渐步入正轨，唐开文到大石的第二个月，业务收入从4000多元增至1万元，其中一半是唐开文完成的。经过半年拼搏，卫生院不但还清了历年所欠债务，还补足了职工的差额工资和福利待遇。每当看到大家领取报酬后又积极投入工作的表情时，唐开文又总是禁不住内心的喜悦。

大石卫生院完善科室设置后，按照分工，唐开文承担的是中医和推拿、针灸治疗，但在人力资源匮缺的农村医院，他既是中医，又是西医，既治内科，又治外科，既要坐诊，又要出诊。每天诊治的患者平均30人，最高日诊达61人。一天夜里，一个从外地来大石沙场打工叫李庆发的工人背着他自己的男孩急匆匆地闯进卫生院，使劲拽着唐开文的胳膊，边哭边说："医生，求求你，快救救我的孩子，他吃菌子中毒了。"唐开文初次碰到这种病例，如何救治心中没底，望着昏迷不醒的孩子，冒出了救人要紧、豁出去了的念头。经过两个多小时的抢救，采用洗胃、针灸、输液等疗法使奄奄一息的孩子苏醒过来，唐开文才长长地换了一口气。顿时，孩子的父亲紧紧地握住唐开文的手，感激之情油然而生。唐开文又深有体会道："实践出真知，从这个病例中，我确实学到了急救病人的方法。"又一天夜里，一位60多岁的谢芳珍婆婆从10里远的联合村赶到医院，要求唐开文为其腿伤愈后但不能动弹的老伴治疗，因为路途不熟，院长不同意出诊，但谢芳珍执意要来乡里的大学生唐开文就诊，院长只得应许。下午6点钟从医院出发，翻山越岭到了谢芳珍的家，当即给病人作了常规检查后进行静脉点滴，然后施以针灸治疗。一切手术完毕后已是深夜1点，唐开文答应以后每隔1天出诊1次遂返程，黑夜里，他在山梁上和丛林中穿梭摸爬，到达医院已是两点多钟，脚上磨起水泡痛得难受，但想到作为一名青年志愿者，其任务就是帮人之所需，解人之所难，只要能为病人减轻痛苦，自己受到一点伤痛就不在乎。经过1个月的连续诊治，谢芳珍的老伴居然能下床活动了，唐开文有一种如释重负之感，心情怡然。

唐开文在大石乡工作快1年，县卫生局又派他到六屯乡卫生院服务。离开大石的那天早晨，卫生院院子里站满了村民，手里提着鸡蛋、花生、瓜子……说是来给唐医生送行，其中就有因吃菌子中毒被抢救过来的那个男孩和他的父亲李庆发，李庆发对孩子说：“跪下，你的命是唐医师救回来的，唐医师是你的再生父母，你就喊一声爹。”孩子当即跪在唐开文的面前，眼里含着泪水喊道：“爹！”接着，院子里发出一片抽泣声，唐开文心头难忍，只得噙着泪水上车与乡亲们招手道别。唐开文从中感悟到：这是志愿精神的渗透，这是奉献精神的延续。

到六屯乡工作后，唐开文竟成为一个全科医生。出诊，简直是唐开文的家常便饭，他曾在夜间出诊遇上被农家恶狗咬破裤子，遇到过在崎岖的山路上摔坏了手电筒，出现过乘坐的车子险些坠下悬崖的惊恐……他曾在3天之内连续为4个产妇接生，只要见到新生婴儿呱呱坠地，他就忘记了劳作带来的疲惫。一天，都堡村塘坎寨64岁的老太太阮广珍住进医院，经过检查患的是脑血栓，严重到神志不清，随时都有死亡的可能。面对垂危病人，唐开文组织医护人员全力抢救，使患者暂时脱离了生命危险，但已瘫痪、失语。在医院治疗7天之后被接回家里，唐开文每天坚持去家中为病人推拿、针灸、理疗，连自己的母亲摔断肋骨都没有回家看望。经过1个多月的精心治疗，阮广珍基本恢复了健康，生活能够自理。就这样，唐开文竟成了六屯乡远近闻名的“唐医生”，只要走上六屯小街上，都会有上至90多岁的老人，下至3岁小孩向唐医师打招呼问好。当中央电视台的记者不远万里深入到六屯采访唐开文时问道：“你为老百姓做了很多实事、好事，他们会感激你吗？”唐开文答道：“一些患者和家属送的生活用品我都婉言谢绝了，留下的只是锦旗和感谢信，因为那是农民兄弟对我这个青年志愿者的鼓励和鞭策。”唐开文又说：“回过头来想我当初如果选择了药业公司，没有选择志愿服务西部，经济收入上肯定好得多，但是可能一天到晚也就是为了工资而奔波，我所学的专业根本没有机会发挥，而我做了西部志愿者，两年里挽救了至少10条人命，权衡下来，就觉得当志愿者的路走对了，我无怨无悔。”

唐开文在乡里服务两年期满，共青团中央授予贵州省唯一的“中国青年志愿服务”金奖，贵州省人民政府副省长刘鸿庥专程到六屯乡卫生院看望唐开文。为了留住唐开文，六屯乡13个行政村的村委联名写申请要求挽留他，盖了13个村的公章，很多村民摁手印送到团省委和县委、县政府、县人事劳动局；分管卫生工作的副乡长徐进还专门跑到县里和市里找指标。唐开文坚定扎根基层的决心，报考国家事业单位，以两个第一名的好成绩分别考取了六屯乡社保事务所和六屯乡卫生院，考虑再三，选择了继续在六屯乡卫生院行医，应组织安排担任六屯乡卫生院院长主持医院全面工作。在唐开文的领导下，经过全体职工的努力，2年时间，将面临倒闭的六屯乡医院建设成为一所集预防保健、临床诊疗为一体的新型综合性乡镇卫生院，被评为老百姓放心的医院。成绩面前，唐开文的话掷地有声：我是一个共产党员，是经过服务西部的志愿者锻炼后成为国家医务部门的一名职工。我既然来到这片热土，就要干出点成绩，在黔中修文留下我的足迹。倘若雁过不留声，人过不留影，则对不起组织，对不起30万修文人民，也辜

负了我的青春。

谢月红

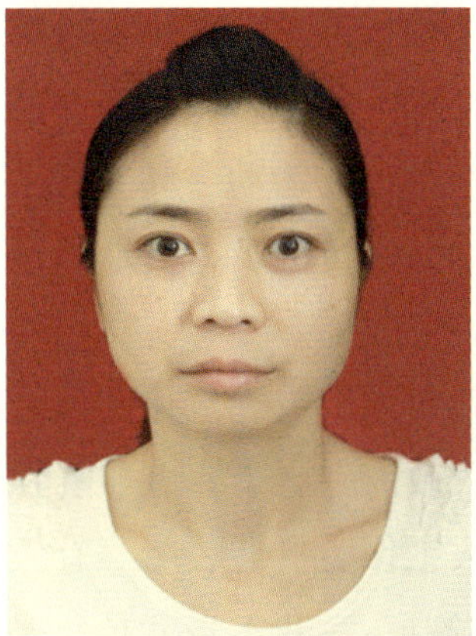

谢月红，女，1980年9月出生于六广镇六广村合群组的一个农民家庭。她还在襁褓中就患上小儿麻痹症，造成左下肢失去机能，学步时总要大人牵着，长大了只能拄着双拐行走。谢月红虽然终身致残，但意志却十分坚定，用她自己的话来说："我要读书，我要工作，我要生活，我要走出一条残而不废的自强之路，要让世人看到，残疾人照样可以为社会创造价值。"于是，她拄着拐棍，上小学，升初中，读中专，攻大学。

2000年，谢月红在安顺地区财经学校修完会计电算化课程毕业回家。面对身残和无业的现实，她决心向命运挑战，丢掉拐棍，自立献力。在市、县、镇残疾人联合会的支持和帮助下，她在贵阳骨科医院接受了两次小儿麻痹康复治疗手术，术后全靠自己的毅力挺过锥心刺骨的疼痛，终于甩开双拐站立起来独立行走，虽然跛行，但比起拄拐行走要好得多。

2002年，谢月红被贵阳市政府聘为第一批城镇低保工作员，同时又是一名残疾人工作者。2008年，县残联遵照国家"十一五"残疾人事业发展纲要的要求，为进一步加强基层残疾人组织规范化建设，便聘请谢月红为六广镇残疾人工作专职委员。2009年，在六广镇残疾人联合会第一次代表在会上，谢月红当选为镇残联副理事长。她非常珍惜这个来之不易的工作岗位。上岗伊始，就对辖区内1000名残疾人的家庭情况进行逐户调查，掌握他们的基本情况，了解他们生活中的困难，倾听他们的呼声，并一一建档立案，输入电脑，实行动态服务管理，使上千名残疾人的家庭生活状况了然于胸。与此同时，她认真学习党的方针政策、国家法律和残疾人保障法规，结合残疾人的实际困难，尽力为其办好事和办实事，使自己所在的岗位成为替党分忧、为政府解难的窗口。松江社区的一位女性聋哑人因与丈夫感情不和，身边又无亲友，不能与外界交流，对生活丧失信心。谢月红刚接触时，视谢为陌生人，不愿接近。但谢并不放弃，经常上门跟其学手语、拉家常，并买些小礼物送给小女儿，又与其丈夫沟通，消除夫妻间的矛盾，还帮助给在外地打工的父亲通电话。长时间的接触使两者建立起亲密关系，谢就帮助联系在一家美发店学徒，后当美发师，每月收入500元，从而鼓起生活的信心和勇气，便写信对谢说："我现在生活得很不错，万分感谢你，我愿意做你的妹妹。"六广村残疾人刘宽仙长期瘫痪卧床，儿子罗仕伦又是弱智，儿媳又患间歇性的精神病，家庭生活十分困难。一次，罗仕伦突被疯狗咬伤，无钱进行血清注射。谢月红积极联系社会事务办公室和县残联，为其筹措1000元的注射费用，使罗仕伦脱险。此外，又帮助刘宽仙家纳入农村最低生活保障，落实重度残疾人"阳光家园"居家托养和新型农村合作医疗补助。为改善家居环境，谢月红四处奔走协调，在镇经济发展办公室落实建房补助1万元和县残联补助建房款3200元，帮助完成危房改建，使刘宽仙一家人住进宽敞明亮的新居。松江社区城镇低保户卿光华，因骨质增生导致下肢行走困难，处境窘迫。谢月红非常同情卿的窘境，便与社区沟通，安排在街道上负责维护交通秩序，月固定收入400元，并由政府为其交纳养老保险。卿光华生活有了着落后去到谢月红的办公室连声"感谢政府，感谢谢理事长"，并主动退出城镇低保。金山村残疾人刘毕顺，双目失明成为"五保"供养户，每个季度的第三个月都要乘车10公里到谢月红的办公室，请谢帮他领取供养金，这照例是谢月红每季度不可少的“业务”，而刘毕顺从不知道帮他领钱、数钱和扶他坐车的女孩姓甚名谁，他只听到“一百元的4张，五十元的1张，你要揣好，拿这5块钱坐车回家”这句熟悉的声音……谢月红就是从这样一件件帮助残疾人解困的工作中让残疾人重新在生活中站立起来，所以她就被人们称为“谢善人”。在谢月红的努力和相关部门的支持下，全镇有100户贫困残疾人改善了住房条件，200名白内障患者实施了康复手术，100名残疾人的子女和残疾学生获得资助500次，20名精神病患者得以康复治疗，为50名行走不便的残疾人办理了残疾人证，推荐了20名残疾人体育健将和文艺爱好者参加省、市举办的运动会和文艺汇演。在“助残日”和春节期间还对残疾人进行走访慰问，开展形式多样的扶残助残宣传活动，营造出全社会关爱帮助残疾人的良好氛围。

由于谢月红爱岗敬业，任劳任怨地做好残疾人工作，从而使六广镇的基层残疾人组织规范化建设有序推进，受到省、市、县残联的表彰，2006年，谢月红被评为贵阳市委、市人民政府“‘十一五’自强不息先进个人”，继后又被评为“全国残疾人工作先进个人”，受到国务院残疾人工作委员会表彰。有人问过谢月红：“你这么努力工作，一个月只有800块钱的报酬，心理平衡吗？”谢答道：“我本身就是残疾人，最能理解残疾人的苦衷，为他们排忧解难是我的职责，我觉得这样做我的生活更充实。”

第三章　人物表

载入本章的人物，一是本志时限内担任副县级以上的领导职务者；二是修文籍人在县外行政、事业单位的副县级及其以上的干部；三是已归入县总工会档案获得荣誉证的劳动模范和先进工作者；四是已获取副高级职称的人员。

1978—2010年县委书记、副书记和常务委员一览表

表6—03—01

界　别	任次	职务	姓　名	性别	民族	籍贯	文化程度	起任年龄	任职起讫年月	备注
第三届	第十四任	县委书记	吴树贵	男	汉	吉林梨树	高中	47	1978.12—1979.8	
		县委副书记	王象文	男	汉	山东乐陵	初中	52	1978.12—1979.8	
		县委副书记	白进德	男	汉	河南濮阳	高小	54	1978.12—1979.8	
		县委副书记	谭荣先	男	汉	贵州修文	初中	44	1978.12—1979.8	
		县委常委	刘正明	男	苗	贵州修文	初中	45	1978.12—1979.8	
		县委常委	吴绍昌	男	汉	贵州修文	初中	57	1978.12—1979.8	
		县委常委	唐文开	男	汉	贵州修文	初中	48	1978.12—1979.8	
		县委常委	潘建新	女	汉	江苏常州	高中	50	1978.12—1979.8	
		县委常委	宋胜明	男	汉	贵州修文	高中	29	1978.12—1979.8	
		县委常委	朱如意	男	汉	山西灵石	初中	55	1978.12—1979.8	
		县委常委	韩保清	男	汉	河南	高小	49	1978.12—1979.8	
		县委常委	杜维顺	男	汉	山西晋城	高小	49	1978.12—1979.8	
	第十五任	县委书记	刘清德	男	汉	贵州清镇	初中	45	1979.8—1982.8	
		县委副书记	王象文	男	汉	山东乐陵	初中	54	1979.8—1980.6	
		县委副书记	白进德	男	汉	河南濮阳	高小	56	1979.8—1982.8	
		县委副书记	谭荣先	男	汉	贵州修文	初中	46	1979.8—1982.8	
		县委副书记	李培书	男	汉	四川开县	大学	41	1980.5—1982.8	
		县委常委	刘正明	男	苗	贵州修文	初中	46	1979.8—1982.8	
		县委常委	吴绍昌	男	汉	贵州修文	初中	58	1979.8—1982.8	

续表

界 别	任次	职务	姓 名	性别	民族	籍贯	文化程度	起任年龄	任职起讫年月	备注
第三届	第十五任	县委常委	唐文开	男	汉	贵州修文	初中	49	1979.8—1982.8	
		县委常委	潘建新	女	汉	江苏常州	高中	51	1979.8—1980.4	
		县委常委	宋胜明	男	汉	贵州修文	高中	30	1979.8—1979.10	
		县委常委	朱如意	男	汉	山西灵石	初中	56	1979.8—1979.10	
		县委常委	韩保清	男	汉	河南	高小	50	1979.8—1981.10	
		县委常委	杜维顺	男	汉	山西晋城	高小	50	1979.8—1982.8	
		县委常委	王光华	男	汉	贵州修文	初中	46	1981.1—1982.8	
		县委常委	蔡正昌	男	汉	江西南昌	大专	46	1981.10—1982.8	
		县委常委	王正华	男	彝	贵州修文	初中	37	1981.10—1982.8	
		县委常委	沈克植	男	汉	贵州安顺	高中	41	1982.3—1982.8	
第四届	第十六任	县委书记	刘清德	男	汉	贵州清镇	初中	48	1982.8—1985.11	
		县委副书记	王光华	男	汉	贵州修文	初中	48	1982.8—1985.11	
		县委副书记	李培书	男	汉	四川开县	大学	43	1982.8—1983.11	
		县委副书记	谭荣先	男	汉	贵州修文	初中	49	1982.8—1983.12	
		县委副书记	王向规	男	汉	湖南祁阳	大学	38	1983.12—1985.11	
		县委副书记	丁治学	男	汉	贵州关岭	大专	30	1985.10—1985.11	挂任
		县委常委	王正华	男	彝	贵州修文	初中	38	1982.8—1985.11	
		县委常委	刘正明	男	苗	贵州修文	初中	49	1982.8—1983.12	
		县委常委	沈克植	男	汉	贵州安顺	高中	41	1982.8—1983.12	
		县委常委	吴绍昌	男	汉	贵州修文	初中	61	1982.8—1983.12	
		县委常委	唐文开	男	汉	贵州修文	初中	52	1982.8—1983.12	
		县委常委	蔡正昌	男	汉	江西南昌	大专	47	1982.8—1983.12	
		县委常委	邹德全	男	汉	贵州修文	高中	39	1983.12—1985.11	
		县委常委	蔡明亮	男	回	贵州贵阳	大学	40	1983.12—1985.11	
		县委常委	刘守珍	女	汉	河南滑县	大学	38	1983.12—1985.11	
		县委常委	苏 善	男	汉	云南施甸	大专	48	1983.12—1985.11	
	第十七任	代理县委书记	王向规	男	汉	湖南祁阳	大学	40	1985.11—1986.7	
		县委书记	王向规	男	汉	湖南祁阳	大学	41	1986.7—1987.3	
		县委副书记	王光华	男	汉	贵州修文	初中	50	1985.11—1987.3	
		县委副书记	丁治学	男	汉	贵州关岭	大专	30	1985.11—1987.3	挂任
		县委副书记	曾文学	男	汉	贵州修文	初中	51	1986.3—1987.3	
		县委常委	王正华	男	彝	贵州修文	初中	41	1985.11—1987.3	

续表

界 别	任次	职务	姓 名	性别	民族	籍贯	文化程度	起任年龄	任职起讫年月	备注
第四届	第十七任	县委常委	邹德全	男	汉	贵州修文	高中	41	1985.11—1987.3	
		县委常委	蔡明亮	男	回	贵州贵阳	大学	42	1985.11—1987.3	
		县委常委	刘守珍	女	汉	河南滑县	大学	40	1985.11—1987.3	
		县委常委	苏 善	男	汉	云南施甸	大专	50	1985.11—1987.3	
	第十八任	县委书记	黄生忠	男	汉	贵州息烽	大专	43	1987.3—1987.6	
		县委副书记	王光华	男	汉	贵州修文	初中	52	1987.3—1987.6	
		县委副书记	丁治学	男	汉	贵州关岭	大专	32	1987.3—1987.6	挂任
		县委副书记	曾文学	男	汉	贵州修文	初中	52	1987.3—1987.6	
		县委常委	王正华	男	彝	贵州修文	初中	43	1987.3—1987.6	
		县委常委	邹德全	男	汉	贵州修文	高中	43	1987.3—1987.6	
		县委常委	蔡明亮	男	回	贵州贵阳	大学	44	1987.3—1987.6	
		县委常委	刘守珍	女	汉	河南滑县	大学	42	1987.3—1987.6	
		县委常委	苏 善	男	汉	云南施甸	大专	52	1987.3—1987.6	
第五届	第十九任	县委书记	黄生忠	男	汉	贵州息烽	大专	43	1987.6—1990.9	
		县委副书记	曾文学	男	汉	贵州修文	初中	52	1987.6—1990.1	
		县委副书记	丁治学	男	汉	贵州关岭	大专	32	1987.6—1988.4	挂任
		县委副书记	陈建忠	男	汉	贵州贵阳	大专	44	1988.4—1990.1	
		县委副书记	朱生亮	男	汉	贵州开阳	大专	43	1990.4—1990.9	
		县委副书记	金志林	男	汉	浙江浦江	大学	45	1990.4—1990.9	
		县委副书记	冯世南	男	汉	河南桐柏	大学	35	1990.4—1990.9	挂任
		县委副书记	刘毓文	男	汉	上海	大专	41	1990.4—1990.9	
		县委常委	王正华	男	彝	贵州修文	初中	43	1987.6—1988.6	
		县委常委	苏 善	男	汉	云南施甸	大专	52	1987.6—1990.9	
		县委常委	陈建忠	男	汉	贵州贵阳	大专	43	1987.6—1988.4	
		县委常委	邹德全	男	汉	贵州修文	高中	43	1987.6—1987.10	
		县委常委	金志林	男	汉	浙江浦江	大学	42	1987.6—1990.4	
		县委常委	彭基业	男	汉	贵州织金	高中	41	1987.6—1990.9	
		县委常委	蔡明亮	男	回	贵州贵阳	大学	44	1987.6—1990.4	
		县委常委	王光华	男	汉	贵州修文	初中	50	1987.6—1990.5	
		县委常委	李玉轩	男	汉	贵州修文	大专	37	1988.4—1990.9	
		县委常委	王占奇	男	苗	贵州修文	大专	39	1990.4—1990.9	

续表

界　别	任次	职务	姓　名	性别	民族	籍贯	文化程度	起任年龄	任职起讫年月	备注
第五届	第十九任	县委顾问	王光华	男	汉	贵州修文	初中	53	1990.5—1992.10	
第六届	第二十任	县委书记	黄生忠	男	汉	贵州息烽	大专	46	1990.9—1991.10	
		县委副书记	朱生亮	男	汉	贵州开阳	大专	43	1990.9—1991.10	
		县委副书记	刘毓文	男	汉	上海	大专	41	1990.9—1991.10	
		县委副书记	金志林	男	汉	浙江浦江	大学	45	1990.9—1991.5	
		县委副书记	冯世南	男	汉	河南桐柏	大学	35	1990.9—1991.10	挂任
		县委副书记	涂新善	男	汉	四川中江	大专	39	1991.8—1991.10	挂任
		县委常委	李玉轩	男	汉	贵州修文	大专	40	1990.9—1991.10	
		县委常委	王克勤	男	汉	贵州贵阳	中专	49	1990.9—1991.10	
		县委常委	王占奇	男	苗	贵州修文	大专	39	1990.9—1991.10	
		县委常委	苏　善	男	汉	云南施甸	大专	55	1990.9—1991.10	
		县委常委	薛占成	男	汉	贵州修文	大专	47	1990.9—1991.10	
		县委常委	彭基业	男	汉	贵州织金	高中	44	1990.9—1991.10	
		县委常委	蔡永毅	男	汉	上海	大学	41	1991.7—1991.10	挂任
	第二十一任	县委书记	朱生亮	男	汉	贵州开阳	大专	44	1991.10—1993.4	
		县委副书记	刘毓文	男	汉	上海	大专	42	1991.10—1991.12	
		县委副书记	冯世南	男	汉	河南桐柏	大学	36	1991.10—1991.12	挂任
		县委副书记	涂新善	男	汉	四川中江	大学	39	1991.10—1993.3	挂任
		县委副书记	罗筑云	男	汉	贵州贵阳	大专	44	1991.11—1993.4	
		县委副书记	陈开域	男	汉	贵州普定	中专	44	1993.3—1993.4	
		县委常委	李玉轩	男	汉	贵州修文	大专	41	1991.10—1993.4	
		县委常委	王克勤	男	汉	贵州贵阳	中专	50	1991.10—1993.4	
		县委常委	王占奇	男	苗	贵州修文	大专	40	1991.10—1993.4	
		县委常委	苏　善	男	汉	云南施甸	大专	56	1991.10—1993.4	
		县委常委	薛占成	男	汉	贵州修文	大专	48	1991.10—1993.4	
		县委常委	彭基业	男	汉	贵州织金	高中	45	1991.10—1993.4	
		县委常委	蔡永毅	男	汉	上海	大学	41	1991.10—1993.4	挂任
第七届	第二十二任	县委书记	朱生亮	男	汉	贵州开阳	大专	46	1993.4—1993.11	
		县委副书记	罗筑云	男	汉	贵州贵阳	大专	46	1993.4—1993.11	
		县委副书记	陈开域	男	汉	贵州普定	中专	44	1993.4—1993.11	
		县委常委	王正华	男	彝	贵州修文	初中	49	1993.4—1993.11	

续表

界 别	任次	职务	姓 名	性别	民族	籍贯	文化程度	起任年龄	任职起讫年月	备注
第七届	第二十二任	县委常委	李玉轩	男	汉	贵州修文	大专	43	1993.4—1993.11	
		县委常委	彭基业	男	汉	贵州织金	高中	47	1993.4—1993.11	
		县委常委	王清义	男	汉	贵州修文	高中	49	1993.4—1993.11	
		县委常委	殷建中	男	汉	湖南岳阳	大学	41	1993.4—1993.11	
		县委常委	卢永康	男	汉	贵州修文	大学	37	1993.4—1993.11	
	第二十三任	县委书记	罗筑云	男	汉	贵州贵阳	大专	46	1993.11—1996.12	
		县委副书记	陈开域	男	汉	贵州普定	中专	44	1993.11—1996.12	
		县委副书记	涂新善	男	汉	四川中江	大专	41	1993.11—1995.10	
		县委副书记	王正华	男	彝	贵州修文	初中	49	1993.11—1996.12	
		县委副书记	牛 熹	男	汉	河南	大专	47	1994.4—1996.2	挂任
		县委副书记	卢永康	男	汉	贵州修文	大学	39	1995.10—1996.12	
		县委副书记	王赤兵	男	布依	贵州罗甸	大学	37	1996.4—1996.12	挂任
		县委常委	李玉轩	男	汉	贵州修文	大专	43	1993.11—1996.12	
		县委常委	彭基业	男	汉	贵州织金	高中	47	1993.11—1996.3	
		县委常委	王清义	男	汉	贵州修文	高中	49	1993.11—1994.9	
		县委常委	殷建中	男	汉	湖南岳阳	大学	41	1993.11—1996.12	
		县委常委	卢永康	男	汉	贵州修文	大学	37	1993.11—1995.10	
		县委常委	朱丽雅	女	汉	贵州修文	大专	41	1993.11—1996.12	
		县委常委	胡晓刚	男	汉	贵州修文	大学	32	1994.9—1996.12	
		县委常委	何 松	男	汉	贵州	大学	30	1995.4—1996.12	挂任
		县委常委	熊俊华	男	汉	贵州贵阳	大学	33	1996.4—1996.12	挂任
		县委常委	李云太	男	汉	四川遂宁	高中	46	1996.11—1996.12	
	第二十四任	县委书记	黄乃铸	男	汉	贵州独山	大专	44	1996.12—1998.4	
		县委副书记	陈开域	男	汉	贵州普定	中专	47	1996.12—1998.4	
		县委副书记	王正华	男	彝	贵州修文	初中	52	1996.12—1998.4	
		县委副书记	卢永康	男	汉	贵州修文	大学	40	1996.12—1998.4	
		县委副书记	王赤兵	男	布依	贵州罗甸	大学	37	1996.12—1998.3	挂任
		县委副书记	魏明禄	男	汉	贵州息烽	大学	36	1998.2—1998.4	
		县委副书记	胡晓刚	男	汉	贵州修文	大学	36	1998.2—1998.4	
		县委常委	殷建中	男	汉	湖南岳阳	大学	44	1996.12—1998.4	
		县委常委	王清义	男	汉	贵州修文	高中	52	1996.12—1998.4	
		县委常委	李玉轩	男	汉	贵州修文	大专	46	1996.12—1998.4	
		县委常委	朱丽雅	女	汉	贵州修文	大专	44	1996.12—1998.4	
		县委常委	胡晓刚	男	汉	贵州修文	大学	34	1996.12—1998.2	

续表

界　别	任次	职务	姓　名	性别	民族	籍贯	文化程度	起任年龄	任职起讫年月	备注
第七届	第二十四任	县委常委	何　松	男	汉	贵州	大学	31	1996.12—1997.4	挂任
		县委常委	熊俊华	男	汉	贵州贵阳	大学	33	1996.12—1998.2	挂任
		县委常委	李云太	男	汉	四川遂宁	高中	46	1996.12—1998.4	
		县委常委	石光明	男	汉	贵州毕节	大学	38	1997.9—1998.4	
		县委常委	王成林	男	汉	贵州修文	大学	39	1998.2—1998.4	
		县委常委	陆秀祥	男	汉	贵州修文	大专	34	1998.2—1998.4	
第八届	第二十五任	县委书记	黄乃铸	男	汉	贵州独山	大专	46	1998.4—2003.1	
		县委副书记	魏明禄	男	汉	贵州息烽	大学	36	1998.4—2000.12	
		县委副书记	王正华	男	彝	贵州修文	初中	54	1998.4—2000.6	
		县委副书记	胡晓刚	男	汉	贵州修文	大学	36	1998.4—2003.1	
		县委副书记	王真霖	男	汉	贵州赤水	大学	36	1998.4—1999.12	挂任
		县委副书记	王成林	男	汉	贵州修文	大学	42	2000.11—2003.1	
		县委副书记	朱桂云	女	汉	山东临邑	大学	36	2002.5—2003.1	
		县委常委	殷建中	男	汉	湖南岳阳	大学	46	1998.4—2000.12	
		县委常委	李云太	男	汉	四川遂宁	高中	48	1998.4—1999.7	
		县委常委	王成林	男	汉	贵州修文	大学	40	1998.4—2000.11	
		县委常委	陆秀祥	男	汉	贵州修文	大专	34	1998.4—2003.1	
		县委常委	石光明	男	汉	贵州毕节	大学	40	1999.3—2000.10	
		县委常委	周遵富	男	汉	贵州毕节	中专	36	1999.3—2000.6	挂任
		县委常委	曾宪高	男	汉	贵州沿河	大专	43	1999.7—2003.1	
		县委常委	成华强	男	汉	四川荣县	大学	48	2000.2—2000.12	
		县委常委	刘文新	男	汉	江西萍乡	大专	33	2000.11—2002.5	
		县委常委	严贵钧	男	汉	贵州黄平	大学	38	2001.5—2003.1	
	第二十六任	县委书记	魏明禄	男	汉	贵州息烽	大学	40	2003.1—2003.3	
		县委副书记	石　洪	男	汉	贵州开阳	硕士	43	2003.1—2003.3	
		县委副书记	岳建初	男	布依	河南清丰	大学	49	2003.1—2003.3	
		县委副书记	王成林	男	汉	贵州修文	大学	45	2003.1—2003.3	
		县委副书记	朱桂云	女	汉	山东临邑	大学	37	2003.1—2003.3	
		县委副书记	胡晓刚	男	汉	贵州修文	大学	41	2003.1—2003.3	
		县委常委	严贵钧	男	汉	贵州黄平	大学	40	2003.1—2003.3	
		县委常委	魏荣华	男	汉	山东昌邑	大学	43	2003.1—2003.3	

续表

界 别	任次	职务	姓 名	性别	民族	籍贯	文化程度	起任年龄	任职起讫年月	备注
第八届	第二十六任	县委常委	张 恺	男	汉	贵州修文	大学	31	2003.1—2003.3	
		县委常委	曾宪高	男	汉	贵州沿河	大专	47	2003.1—2003.3	
第九届	第二十七任	县委书记	魏明禄	男	汉	贵州息烽	硕士	41	2003.3—2006.9	
		县委副书记	石 洪	男	汉	贵州开阳	硕士	43	2003.3—2006.9	
		县委副书记	王成林	男	汉	贵州修文	大学	45	2003.3—2006.9	
		县委副书记	岳建初	男	布依	河南清丰	大学	49	2003.3—2006.1	
		县委副书记	朱桂云	女	汉	山东临邑	大学	37	2003.3—2006.5	
		县委副书记	胡晓刚	男	汉	贵州修文	大学	41	2003.3—2003.5	
		县委副书记	付 涛	男	汉	四川泸州	大学	33	2006.1—2006.9	
		县委副书记	吴文涛	男	汉	江苏扬州	大学	49	2005.3—2006.3	挂任
		县委常委	成华强	男	汉	四川荣县	大学	51	2003.3—2006.9	
		县委常委	魏荣华	男	汉	山东昌邑	大学	43	2003.3—2006.9	
		县委常委	张 恺	男	汉	贵州修文	大学	31	2003.3—2006.9	
		县委常委	严贵钧	男	汉	贵州黄平	大学	40	2003.3—2006.9	
		县委常委	曾宪高	男	汉	贵州沿河	大专	47	2003.3—2003.5	
		县委常委	柴忠元	男	汉	贵州毕节	大学	38	2003.5—2006.9	
		县委常委	白陈新	男	汉	贵州贵阳	硕士研究生	35	2003.12—2006.9	
		县委常委	李 平	女	汉	贵州贵阳	大学	40	2003.10—2005.10	挂任
		县委常委	王诗煌	男	汉	贵州湄潭	大学	41	2006.3—2006.9	挂任
第十届	第二十八任	县委书记	魏明禄	男	汉	贵州息烽	硕士	44	2006.9—2008.7	
		县委副书记	石 洪	男	汉	贵州开阳	硕士	46	2006.9—2008.7	
		县委副书记	王成林	男	汉	贵州修文	大学	47	2006.9—2008.7	
		县委常委	白陈新	男	汉	贵州贵阳	硕士研究生	38	2006.9—2008.7	
		县委常委	刘 瑜	男	汉	贵州普安	大学	40	2006.9—2008.7	
		县委常委	阮晓燕	女	汉	贵州贵阳	大学	36	2006.9—2008.7	
		县委常委	严贵钧	男	汉	贵州黄平	研究生	43	2006.9—2007.3	
		县委常委	赵 毅	男	汉	贵州镇宁	大学	43	2006.9—2010.1	
		县委常委	柴忠元	男	汉	贵州毕节	大学	41	2006.9—2008.7	
		县委常委	魏燕飞	男	汉	贵州息烽	大学	43	2006.9—2009.3	
		县委常委	王诗煌	男	汉	贵州湄潭	大学	41	2006.9—2008.4	挂任
		县委常委	陈雄标	男	汉	广西荔浦	大学	49	2007.3—2008.7	

续表

界　别	任次	职务	姓　名	性别	民族	籍贯	文化程度	起任年龄	任职起讫年月	备注
第十届	第二十九任	县委书记	石　洪	男	汉	贵州开阳	硕士	48	2008.7—2010.12	
		县委副书记	蒋志伦	男	汉	湖南衡阳	研究生	44	2008.12—2010.12	
		县委副书记	王成林	男	汉	贵州修文	大学	50	2008.7—2010.12	
		县委副书记	向子琨	男	土家	重庆	大学	35	2010.2—2010.12	挂任
		县委常委	阮晓燕	女	汉	贵州贵阳	研究生	38	2008.7— 2010.12	
		县委常委	刘　瑜	男	汉	河南内乡	研究生	42	2008.7— 2010.12	
		县委常委	白陈新	男	汉	贵州贵阳	硕士研究生	40	2008.07—2010.9	
		县委常委	陈雄标	男	汉	广西荔浦	大学	50	2008.7— 2010.12	
		县委常委	黄文淑	女	汉	贵州镇宁	大学	45	2008.3—2010.3	挂任
		县委常委	张　恺	男	汉	贵州修文	研究生	37	2009.7—2010.12	
		县委常委	崔　红	女	汉	山东菏泽	大学	49	2009.8—2010.8	挂任
		县委常委	向　东	男	汉	重庆	大学	46	2010.2—2010.12	
		县委常委	董桂文	男	汉	河南临颍	研究生	43	2010.9—2010.12	挂任
		县委常委	柴忠元	男	汉	贵州毕节	大学	44	2008.7—2010.8	
		县委常委	李利亚	男	汉	贵州遵义	大学	41	2010.8—2010.12	

1981—2010年县人大常委会主任、副主任一览表

表6—03—02

界　别	任次	职务	姓　名	性别	民族	籍贯	文化程度	起任年龄	任职起讫年月	备注
第七届	第一任	主　任	吴绍昌	男	汉	贵州修文	初中	60	1981.1—1984.2	
		副主任	白进德	男	汉	河南濮阳	高小	58	1981.1—1984.2	
		副主任	朱如意	男	汉	山西灵石	初中	58	1981.1—1984.2	
		副主任	梁运堂	男	汉	河南濮阳	初中	66	1981.1—1984.2	
		副主任	葛恒希	男	布依	贵州修文	初中	58	1981.1—1984.2	
		副主任	刘朝文	男	汉	贵州修文	初中	56	1981.1—1984.2	
		副主任	田守国	男	汉	安徽临泉	高小	51	1982.9—1984.2	
	第二任	主　任	谭荣先	男	汉	贵州修文	初中	51	1984.3—1984.11	
		副主任	白进德	男	汉	河南濮阳	高小	58	1984.3—1984.3	
		副主任	朱如意	男	汉	山西灵石	初中	61	1984.3—1984.3	
		副主任	梁运堂	男	汉	河南濮阳	初中	69	1984.3—1984.3	
		副主任	葛恒希	男	布依	贵州修文	初中	59	1984.3—1984.3	
		副主任	刘朝文	男	汉	贵州修文	初中	59	1984.3—1984.11	

续表

界　别	任次	职务	姓　名	性别	民族	籍贯	文化程度	起任年龄	任职起讫年月	备注
第七届	第二任	副主任	田守国	男	汉	安徽临泉	高小	53	1984.9—1984.11	
		副主任	唐文开	男	汉	贵州修文	初中	54	1984.3—1984.11	
		副主任	刘正明	男	苗	贵州修文	初中	51	1984.3—1984.11	
		副主任	张德华	男	汉	贵州修文	中专	53	1984.3—1984.11	
第八届	第三任	主　任	谭荣先	男	汉	贵州修文	初中	51	1984.11—1987.8	
		副主任	唐文开	男	汉	贵州修文	初中	54	1984.11—1987.8	
		副主任	刘正明	男	苗	贵州修文	初中	51	1984.11—1987.8	
		副主任	田守国	男	汉	安徽临泉	高小	53	1984.11—1987.8	
		副主任	张德华	男	汉	贵州修文	中专	53	1984.11—1987.8	
		副主任	刘朝文	男	汉	贵州修文	初中	59	1984.11—1987.8	
第九届	第四任	主　任	谭荣先	男	汉	贵州修文	初中	54	1987.8—1990.4	
		副主任	刘守珍	女	汉	河南滑县	大学	42	1987.8—1990.04	
		副主任	唐文开	男	汉	贵州修文	初中	57	1987.8—1990.4	
		副主任	刘正明	男	苗	贵州修文	初中	54	1987.8—1990.4	
		副主任	田守国	男	汉	安徽临泉	高小	56	1987.8—1990.4	
第十届	第五任	主　任	谭荣先	男	汉	贵州修文	初中	57	1990.4—1993.4	
		副主任	刘正明	男	苗	贵州修文	初中	57	1990.4—1993.4	
		副主任	蔡明亮	男	回	贵州贵阳	大学	47	1990.4—1993.4	
		副主任	邓惠仙	女	汉	贵州普定	大专	46	1990.4—1993.4	
		副主任	何先祥	男	汉	贵州修文	中专	38	1990.04—1993.4	
第十一届	第六任	主　任	王克勤	男	汉	贵州贵阳	中专	52	1993.4—1998.3	
		副主任	邓惠仙	女	汉	贵州普定	大专	49	1993.4—1998.3	
		副主任	王占奇	男	苗	贵州修文	大专	42	1993.4—1998.3	
		副主任	王作伦	男	汉	贵州修文	大专	50	1993.4—1998.3	
		副主任	张成学	男	汉	贵州修文	中专	55	1993.4—1996.11	
第十二届	第七任	主　任	王克勤	男	汉	贵州贵阳	中专	57	1998.3—2000.6	
		代理主任	李玉轩	男	汉	贵州修文	大专	50	2000.6—2001.2	
		副主任	李玉轩	男	汉	贵州修文	大专	48	1998.3—2000.6	
		副主任	王作伦	男	汉	贵州修文	大专	55	1998.3—2001.2	
		副主任	邓惠仙	女	汉	贵州普定	大专	54	1998.3—2001.2	
		副主任	何先祥	男	汉	贵州修文	大专	46	1998.3—2001.2	

续表

界 别	任次	职务	姓 名	性别	民族	籍贯	文化程度	起任年龄	任职起讫年月	备注
第十二届	第七任	副主任	聂廷良	男	汉	贵州道真	初中	56	1998.3—2001.2	
		副主任	陈国帮	男	布依	贵州修文	大专	42	1998.3—2001.2	
	第八任	主 任	李玉轩	男	汉	贵州修文	大专	51	2001.2—2003.3	
		副主任	王作伦	男	汉	贵州修文	大专	58	2001.2—2003.3	
		副主任	邓惠仙	女	汉	贵州普定	大专	57	2001.2—2003.3	
		副主任	何先祥	男	汉	贵州修文	大专	49	2001.2—2003.3	
		副主任	聂廷良	男	汉	贵州道真	初中	59	2001.2—2003.3	
		副主任	陈国帮	男	布依	贵州修文	大专	45	2001.2—2003.3	
第十三届	第九任	主 任	李玉轩	男	汉	贵州修文	大专	53	2003.3—2006.11	
		副主任	何先祥	男	汉	贵州修文	大专	51	2003.3—2006.11	
		副主任	宋庆豪	男	汉	贵州修文	大学	49	2003.3—2006.11	
		副主任	孙庆英	女	汉	贵州修文	大学	46	2003.3—2006.11	
		副主任	罗永翔	男	苗	贵州修文	大专	46	2003.3—2006.11	
		副主任	王天镜	男	汉	贵州息烽	大学	40	2003.3—2006.11	
		副主任	汪 浩	男	汉	江西婺源	大学	41	2003.3—2005.10	
第十四届	第十任	主 任	李玉轩	男	汉	贵州修文	大专	56	2006.11—2010.12	
		副主任	何先祥	男	汉	贵州修文	大专	54	2006.11—2010.12	
		副主任	宋庆豪	男	汉	贵州修文	大学	52	2006.11—2010.12	
		副主任	孙庆英	女	汉	贵州修文	大学	49	2006.11—2010.12	
		副主任	罗永翔	男	苗	贵州修文	大专	49	2006.11—2010.12	
		副主任	王天镜	男	汉	贵州息烽	大学	43	2006.11—2010.12	

1978—2010年县人民政府（县革命委员会）县长（县革委会主任）、副县长（县革委会副主任）一览表

表6—03—03

界 别	任次	职 务	姓 名	性别	民族	籍贯	文化程度	起任年龄	任职起讫年月	备注
革委会	第十一任	主 任	吴树贵	男	汉	吉林梨树	高中	47	1978.12-1979.8	
		副主任	王象文	男	汉	山东乐陵	初中	52	1978.12—1980.9	
		副主任	白进德	男	汉	河南濮阳	高小	54	1978.12—1981.1	
		副主任	吴绍昌	男	汉	贵州修文	初中	56	1978.12—1981.1	
		副主任	刘正明	男	苗	贵州修文	初中	44	1978.12—1981.1	
		副主任	谭荣先	男	汉	贵州修文	初中	44	1978.12—1981.1	
		副主任	朱如意	男	汉	山西灵石	初中	54	1978.12—1981.1	

续表

界 别	任次	职 务	姓 名	性别	民族	籍贯	文化程度	起任年龄	任职起讫年月	备注
革委会	第十一任	副主任	许东升	男	汉	河南荥阳	初中	49	1980.5—1981.1	
第七届	第十二任	县 长	王光华	男	汉	贵州修文	初中	46	1981.1—1983.12	
		代理县长	王向规	男	汉	湖南祁阳	大学	38	1983.12—1984.11	
		副县长	谭荣先	男	汉	贵州修文	初中	48	1981.1—1984.3	
		副县长	刘正明	男	苗	贵州修文	初中	48	1981.1—1984.3	
		副县长	曾文学	男	汉	贵州修文	初中	46	1981.1—1984.11	
		副县长	熊 惠	女	汉	江西九江	中专	48	1981.1—1984.3	
		副县长	袁慎伦	女	汉	四川重庆	大学	42	1983.12—1984.11	
		副县长	王占奇	男	苗	贵州修文	大专	32	1983.12—1984.11	
第八届	第十三任	县 长	王向规	男	汉	湖南祁阳	大学	39	1984.11—1986.5	
		代理县长	曾文学	男	汉	贵州修文	初中	51	1986.5—1987.8	
		副县长	曾文学	男	汉	贵州修文	初中	49	1984.11—1986.5	
		副县长	王占奇	男	苗	贵州修文	大专	33	1984.11—1987.8	
		副县长	袁慎伦	女	汉	四川重庆	大学	43	1984.11—1987.8	
		副县长	李福盛	男	汉	吉林长春	大学	40	1985.5—1987.8	
		副县长	刘毓文	男	汉	上 海	大专	37	1986.5—1987.8	
		副县长	刘尚诚	男	汉	贵州修文	大专	42	1986.5—1987.8	
第九届	第十四任	县 长	曾文学	男	汉	贵州修文	初中	52	1987.8—1990.1	
		代理县长	刘毓文	男	汉	上 海	大专	41	1990.1—1990.4	
		副县长	刘毓文	男	汉	上 海	大专	38	1987.8—1990.1	
		副县长	林志云	男	汉	广东兴宁	大专	48	1987.8—1990.4	
		副县长	王占奇	男	苗	贵州修文	大专	36	1987.8—1990.4	
		副县长	刘尚诚	男	汉	贵州修文	大专	43	1987.8—1990.4	
		副县长	王正华	男	彝	贵州修文	初中	44	1988.6—1990.4	
第十届	第十五任	县 长	刘毓文	男	汉	上 海	大专	41	1990.4—1991.11	
		代理县长	罗筑云	男	汉	贵州贵阳	大专	44	1991.12—1992.3	
		副县长	王正华	男	彝	贵州修文	初中	46	1990.4—1992.3	
		副县长	朱丽雅	女	汉	贵州修文	大专	38	1990.4—1992.3	
		副县长	林志云	男	汉	广东兴宁	大专	51	1990.4—1992.3	
		副县长	赵吉超	男	汉	贵州修文	初中	35	1990.4—1992.3	
		副县长	甄燕驰	女	汉	山东滕县	大专	33	1990.7—1992.3	挂任

续表

界别	任次	职务	姓名	性别	民族	籍贯	文化程度	起任年龄	任职起讫年月	备注
第十届	第十六任	县长	罗筑云	男	汉	贵州贵阳	大专	45	1992.3—1993.4	
		副县长	王正华	男	彝	贵州修文	初中	48	1992.3—1993.4	
		副县长	朱丽雅	女	汉	贵州修文	大专	40	1992.3—1993.4	
		副县长	林志云	男	汉	广东兴宁	大专	53	1992.3—1993.4	
		副县长	赵吉超	男	汉	贵州修文	初中	37	1992.3—1993.4	
		副县长	甄燕驰	女	汉	山东滕县	大专	35	1992.3—1992.11	挂任
第十一届	第十七任	县长	罗筑云	男	汉	贵州贵阳	大专	46	1993.4—1993.11	
		代理县长	涂新善	男	汉	四川中江	大学	41	1993.12—1994.3	
		副县长	王正华	男	彝	贵州修文	初中	49	1993.4—1993.12	
		副县长	朱丽雅	女	汉	贵州修文	大专	41	1993.4—1994.3	
		副县长	何先祥	男	汉	贵州修文	中专	41	1993.4—1994.3	
		副县长	李德芳	男	回	贵州修文	大专	45	1993.4—1994.3	
		副县长	赵吉超	男	汉	贵州修文	初中	38	1993.4—1994.3	
		副县长	万稼实	男	汉	贵州	大学	35	1993.9—1994.3	挂任
	第十八任	县长	涂新善	男	汉	四川中江	大学	42	1994.3—1995.10	
		代理县长	陈开域	男	汉	贵州普定	中专	46	1995.10—1996.1	
		副县长	朱丽雅	女	汉	贵州修文	大专	42	1994.3—1996.1	
		副县长	何先祥	男	汉	贵州修文	中专	42	1994.3—1996.1	
		副县长	李德芳	男	回	贵州修文	大专	46	1994.3—1996.1	
		副县长	赵吉超	男	汉	贵州修文	初中	39	1994.3—1996.1	
		副县长	万稼实	男	汉	贵州	大学	36	1994.3—1994.7	挂任
		副县长	王清义	男	汉	贵州修文	高中	50	1994.9—1996.1	
		副县长	何 松	男	汉	贵州	大学	30	1995.4—1996.1	挂任
	第十九任	县长	陈开域	男	汉	贵州普定	中专	47	1996.1—1998.2	
		代理县长	魏明禄	男	汉	贵州息烽	大学	36	1998.2—1998.3	
		副县长	朱丽雅	女	汉	贵州修文	大专	44	1996.1—1998.3	
		副县长	何先祥	男	汉	贵州修文	中专	44	1996.1—1998.3	
		副县长	李德芳	男	回	贵州修文	大专	48	1996.1—1998.3	
		副县长	赵吉超	男	汉	贵州修文	初中	41	1996.1—1996.5	
		副县长	王清义	男	汉	贵州修文	高中	52	1996.1—1998.3	
		副县长	何 松	男	汉	贵州	大学	31	1996.1—1997.4	挂任

续表

界　别	任次	职　务	姓　名	性别	民族	籍贯	文化程度	起任年龄	任职起讫年月	备注
第十一届	第十九任	副县长	熊俊华	男	汉	贵州贵阳	大学	33	1996.5—1998.2	挂任
		副县长	周　毅	男	汉	贵州修文	大专	34	1996.12—1998.3	
第十二届	第二十任	县　长	魏明禄	男	汉	贵州息烽	大学	36	1998.3—2003.1	
		代理县长	石　洪	男	汉	贵州开阳	硕士	43	2003.2—2003.3	
		副县长	周　毅	男	汉	贵州修文	大专	36	1998.3—2003.3	
		副县长	宋庆豪	男	汉	贵州修文	大专	44	1998.3—2003.3	
		副县长	何汉荣	男	汉	湖　南	大专	46	1998.3—2000.2	
		副县长	王世利	男	汉	四川古蔺	大学	33	1998.3—2003.3	
		副县长	赵永祥	男	汉	贵州修文	大专	39	1998.3—2003.1	
		副县长	孙庆英	女	汉	贵州修文	中专	41	1998.3—2003.3	
		副县长	周遵富	男	汉	贵州毕节	中专	36	1999.3—2000.12	挂任
		副县长	成华强	男	汉	四川荣县	大学	48	2000.2—2000.7	
		科技副县长	李锦华	男	汉	甘肃甘谷	博士	38	2001.3—2003.3	挂任
		副县长	魏燕飞	男	汉	贵州息烽	大学	40	2003.2—2003.3	
第十三届	第二十一任	县　长	石　洪	男	汉	贵州开阳	硕士	43	2003.3—2006.11	
		常务副县长	成华强	男	汉	四川荣县	大学	51	2003.3—2006.10	
		副县长	王雄飞	男	汉	湖南慈利	大学	38	2003.3—2006.11	
		副县长	周　毅	男	汉	贵州修文	大专	41	2003.3—2006.10	
		副县长	魏燕飞	男	汉	贵州息烽	大学	40	2003.3—2006.11	
		副县长	王世利	男	汉	四川古蔺	大学	38	2003.3—2006.10	
		副县长	田茂书	女	汉	贵州贵阳	大学	36	2003.3—2006.10	
		科技副县长	李　平	女	汉	贵州贵阳	大学	40	2003.11—2005.10	挂任
		科技副县长	王诗煌	男	汉	贵州湄潭	大学	41	2006.4—2006.11	挂任
		副县长	刘　瑜	男	汉	贵州普安	大学	40	2006.10—2006.11	
		副县长	张　恺	男	汉	贵州修文	大学	34	2006.10—2006.11	
		副县长	吕念东	女	汉	重庆荣昌	硕士研究生	38	2006.10—2006.11	
		副县长	石　洋	男	汉	山东招远	大学	28	2006.10—2006.11	
		科技副县长	李锦华	男	汉	甘肃甘谷	博士	40	2003.3—2004.3	挂任
第十四届	第二十二任	县　长	石　洪	男	汉	贵州开阳	硕士	46	2006.11—2009.1	
		代理县长	蒋志伦	男	汉	湖南衡阳	研究生	45	2009.1—2009.3	
		常务副县长	魏燕飞	男	汉	贵州息烽	大学	43	2006.11—2009.3	

续表

界别	任次	职务	姓名	性别	民族	籍贯	文化程度	起任年龄	任职起讫年月	备注
第十四届	第二十二任	副县长	刘瑜	男	汉	贵州普安	大学	40	2006.11—2009.3	
		副县长	张恺	男	汉	贵州修文	大学	34	2006.11—2009.3	
		副县长	王雄飞	男	汉	湖南慈利	大学	41	2006.11—2009.3	
		副县长	吕念东	女	汉	重庆荣昌	硕士研究生	38	2006.11—2011.11	
		副县长	石洋	男	汉	山东招远	大学	28	2006.11—2009.3	
		科技副县长	王诗煌	男	汉	贵州湄潭	大学	41	2006.11—2008.4	挂任
		科技副县长	黄文淑	女	汉	贵州镇宁	大学	45	2008.4—2009.3	挂任
	第二十三任	县长	蒋志伦	男	汉	湖南衡阳	研究生	45	2009.3—2010.12	
		常务副县长	魏燕飞	男	汉	贵州息烽	大学	46	2009.3—2009.4	
		副县长	刘瑜	男	汉	贵州普安	大学	43	2009.3— 2010.12	
		副县长	王雄飞	男	汉	湖南慈利	大学	44	2009.3—2010.12	
		副县长	吕念东	女	汉	重庆荣昌	硕士研究生	41	2009.3—2010.12	
		副县长	石洋	男	汉	山东招远	大学	31	2009.3— 2010.12	
		副县长	张恺	男	汉	贵州修文	研究生	37	2009.3—2009.7	
		副县长	白陈新	男	汉	贵州贵阳	硕士	41	2009.7—2010.12	
		副县长	汤建祥	男	汉	贵州修文	大专	47	2009.7—2010.12	
		副县长	崔红	女	汉	山东菏泽	大学	49	2009.10—2010.10	挂任
		副县长	童雪涛	女	汉	安徽和县	硕士研究生	38	2010.6—2010.12	挂任
		副县长	董桂文	男	汉	河南临颍	研究生	43	2010.10—2010.12	挂任
		科技副县长	黄文淑	女	汉	贵州镇宁	大学	46	2009.3—2010.10	挂任

1983—2010年县政协主席、副主席一览表

表6—03—04

界别	任次	职务	姓名	性别	民族	籍贯	文化程度	起任年龄	任职起讫年月	备注
第一届	第一任	主席	谭荣先	男	汉	贵州修文	初中	50	1983.3—1984.3	
		副主席	徐振国	男	汉	河南杞县	初小	54	1983.3—1984.3	
		副主席	张德华	男	汉	贵州修文	中专	52	1983.3—1984.3	
		副主席	刘朝文	男	汉	贵州修文	初中	58	1983.3—1984.3	
		副主席	刘国平	男	汉	广东梅县	大学	40	1983.3—1984.3	
	第二任	主席	王光华	男	汉	贵州修文	初中	49	1984.3—1987.8	
		副主席	徐振国	男	汉	河南杞县	初小	55	1984.3—1986.2	
		副主席	刘朝文	男	汉	贵州修文	初中	59	1984.3—1984.11	

续表

界别	任次	职务	姓名	性别	民族	籍贯	文化程度	起任年龄	任职起讫年月	备注
第一届	第二任	副主席	刘国平	男	汉	广东梅县	大学	41	1984.3—1987.8	
		副主席	熊 惠	女	汉	江西九江	中专	51	1984.3—1984.7	
		副主席	李元明	男	布依	贵州修文	大专	46	1984.3—1987.8	
		副主席	童明英	女	汉	四川重庆	初中	49	1984.3—1987.8	
		副主席	聂承先	男	汉	四川江津	初中	57	1984.3—1987.8	
第二届	第三任	主 席	王光华	男	汉	贵州修文	初中	52	1987.8—1990.4	
		副主席	李元明	男	布依	贵州修文	大专	49	1987.8—1990.4	
		副主席	童明英	女	汉	四川重庆	初中	52	1987.8—1990.4	
		副主席	聂承先	男	汉	四川江津	初中	60	1987.8—1990.4	
		副主席	张德华	男	汉	贵州修文	中专	56	1987.8—1990.4	
		副主席	刘国平	男	汉	广东梅县	大学	44	1987.8—1987.11	
		副主席	虞赓禹	男	汉	云南巍山	大专	51	1987.8—1990.4	
第三届	第四任	主 席	曾文学	男	汉	贵州修文	初中	55	1990.4—1993.4	
		副主席	李元明	男	布依	贵州修文	大专	52	1990.4—1993.4	
		副主席	童明英	女	汉	四川重庆	初中	55	1990.4—1993.4	
		副主席	虞赓禹	男	汉	云南巍山	大专	54	1990.4—1993.4	
		副主席	蔡友贵	男	汉	贵州修文	大专	47	1990.4—1993.4	
第四届	第五任	主 席	林志云	男	汉	广东兴宁	大专	54	1993.4—1998.3	
		副主席	李元明	男	布依	贵州修文	大专	55	1993.4—1998.3	
		副主席	薛占成	男	汉	贵州修文	大专	50	1993.4—1998.3	
		副主席	虞赓禹	男	汉	云南巍山	大专	57	1993.4—1998.3	
		副主席	陈信梅	女	侗	贵州天柱	高中	44	1993.4—1998.3	
		副主席	孔凡修	男	汉	贵州修文	高中	52	1993.4—1998.3	
		副主席	宋庆豪	男	汉	贵州修文	大专	39	1993.4—1998.3	
第五届	第六任	主 席	王清义	男	汉	贵州修文	高中	55	1998.3—2003.3	
		副主席	薛占成	男	汉	贵州修文	大专	55	1998.3—2003.3	
		副主席	李德芳	男	回	贵州修文	大专	50	1998.3—2003.3	
		副主席	陈信梅	女	侗	贵州天柱	高中	49	1998.3—2003.3	
		副主席	孔凡修	男	汉	贵州修文	高中	57	1998.3—2003.3	
第六届	第七任	主 席	殷建中	男	汉	湖南岳阳	大学	51	2003.3—2006.11	
		副主席	陈国邦	男	布依	贵州修文	大学	47	2003.3—2006.11	
		副主席	汤建祥	男	汉	贵州修文	大专	41	2003.3—2006.11	
		副主席	陈信梅	女	侗	贵州天柱	高中	54	2003.3—2006.9	

续表

界别	任次	职务	姓名	性别	民族	籍贯	文化程度	起任年龄	任职起讫年月	备注
第六届	第七任	副主席	李德芳	男	回	贵州修文	大专	55	2003.3—2006.9	
		副主席	杨正明	男	汉	贵州修文	大学	54	2003.3—2006.9	
第七届	第八任	主　席	殷建中	男	汉	湖南岳阳	大学	54	2006.11—2010.12	
		副主席	汤建祥	男	汉	贵州修文	大专	44	2006.11—2009.7	
		副主席	陈国邦	男	布依	贵州修文	大学	50	2006.11—2010.12	
		副主席	王世利	男	汉	四川古蔺	大学	41	2006.11—2010.12	
		副主席	邓　波	男	汉	四川成都	硕士	34	2006.11—2010.12	
		副主席	胡祥碧	女	汉	贵州开阳	大学	40	2006.11—2010.12	
		副主席	林　江	男	汉	广东兴宁	大学	42	2010.3—2010.12	

1978—2010年在其他部门担任副县级及其以上领导职务者一览表

表6—03—05

职务	姓　名	性别	民族	籍贯	文化程度	起任年龄	任职起讫年月	备注
人民法院院长	王作伦	男	汉	贵州修文	大专	41	1986—1993.4	
人民法院院长	刘德利	男	汉	贵州修文	大专		1993.4—1997.12	
人民法院代理院长	刘鸿烈	男	汉	贵州贵阳	大学	45	1997.12—1998.3	
人民法院院长	刘鸿烈	男	汉	贵州贵阳	大学	46	1998.3—2000.12	
人民法院代理院长	郑炳州	男	汉	河南清丰	大学	33	2000.12—2001.2	
人民法院院长	郑炳州	男	汉	河南清丰	大学	34	2001.2—2008.3	
人民法院院长	徐　涛	男	汉	河南安阳	研究生	46	2008.3—2010.12	
人民检察院检察长	杨中华	男	汉	贵州修文	初中	52	1986—1990.4	
人民检察院检察长	聂廷良	男	汉	贵州道真	初中	48	1990.4—1997.12	
人民检察院检察长	蔺新喜	男	汉	山东临沂	大学	51	1998.3—2002.2	
人民检察院检察长	毛　鸿	男	汉	山西浮山	大学	39	2002.2—2005.12	
人民检察院检察长	丁泽军	男	汉	重庆	硕士研究生	37	2005.10—2010.12	
公安局长	董　浩	男	汉	山东茌平	大专	45	1997.12-2004.1	
公安局长	魏荣华	男	汉	山东昌邑	大学	43	2004.1—2006.10	县委常委、政法委书记
公安局长	向　东	男	汉	重庆	大学	44	2008.8—2010.12	2010年2月至12月任县委常委、政法委书记
公安局政委	罗祖文	男	汉	贵州修文	大专	48	1998.9—2001.5	
公安局政委	魏荣华	男	汉	山东昌邑	大学	41	2001.5—2003.12	
公安局政委	庹朝金	男	汉	贵州贵阳	大学	43	2003.12—2008.7	

续表

职务	姓　名	性别	民族	籍贯	文化程度	起任年龄	任职起讫年月	备注
公安局政委	杨　波	男	汉	山东菏泽	大学	39	2008.7—2010.12	
人武部部长	童代平	男	汉	贵州松桃	大学	45	2008.3—2010.12	
党校校长	胡晓刚	男	汉	贵州修文	大学	36	1998.4—2003.7	
党校校长	朱桂云	女	汉	山东临邑	大学	37	2003.7—2006.5	兼任
党校常务副校长	金　松	男	汉	浙江浦江	大学	37	2009.7—2010.12	
县工业园区建设开发办公室主任	谌　勇	男	汉	贵州修文	大学	49	2010.11—2010.12	

1978—2010年修文籍人在外地行政、事业部门担任副县级及其以上领导职务者一览表

表6—03—06

姓　名	性别	民族	文化程度	任　职　情　况				备注
				职　务	级　别	任职单位	任职起讫年月	
陈远武	男	汉	大学	第二书记	正厅级	中共安顺地委	1978.1—1983.5	
				书　记	正厅级	中共安顺地委	1983.5—1991.3	
				副主任	副部级	贵州省人大常委会	1991.3—1998.1	
刘连碧	男	汉	中专	副书记	副县(处)级	安顺地区纪委	1978.9—1987.10	
				局　长	县(处)级	安顺地区监察局	1987.10—1992.2	
				处　长	县(处)级	安顺地区政协工委	1992.2—1997.9	
刘仲瑶	男	汉	中专	副局长	副县(处)级	兴义地区农业局	1978.12—1982.5	
				副主任	副厅级	黔西南州人大常委会	1982.5—1992.5	
王丕坤	男	汉	高　中	参谋长	副县(处)级	贵州省独立师二团	1979.8—1981.6	
				部　长	县(处)级	贵州省威宁县人民武装部	1981.6—1983.9	
				参谋长　副司令员	县(处)级	贵州省毕节军分区	1983.9—1992.6	
				主　任	副厅级	贵州省乡镇企业局监察室	1992.6—1996.6	
				纪检组长	副厅级	贵州省民政厅	1996.6—2004.6	
				巡视员	正厅级	贵州省民政厅	2004.6—2005.5	
谭荣峰	男	汉	高　中	部　长	县(处)级	贵阳市云岩区人民武装部	1983.3—1985.10	
				党委书记	县(处)级	贵阳市城管大队	1985.10—1986.3	
				党委书记、主任	县(处)级	贵阳市云岩区城管委	1986.3—1987.10	
				局　长	县(处)级	贵阳市云岩区工商局	1987.10—1989.4	
				主　席	县(处)级	贵阳市云岩区总工会	1989.4—1998.10	

续表

姓名	性别	民族	文化程度	任职情况				备注
				职务	级别	任职单位	任职起讫年月	
吕维亮	男	汉	初中	副处长	副县(处)级	贵阳市人大常委会代表联络处	1983.4—1985.5	
				处长	副县(处)级	贵阳市人大常委会代表联络处	1985.5—1990.5	
				副秘书长 副主任	副县(处)级	贵阳市人大常委会代表工作委员会	1990.5—1993.5	
				副主任	副县(处)级	贵阳市人大常委会城市建设委员会	1993.12—1995.3	
				主任	县(处)级	贵阳市人大常委会城市建设委员会	1995.3—1997.12	
				主任	县(处)级	贵阳市人大常委会城市建设环保委员会	1997.12—2002.6	
李开珍	女	汉	中专	书记	副县(处)级	共青团贵州省农业科学委员会	1984.7—1987.2	
				副主席	副县(处)级	贵州省农业科学院工会	1987.2— 1990.5	
				副主席	县(处)级	贵州省农业科学院工会	1990.5—1994.12	
蔡远扬	男	汉	大学本科	主任	副县(处)级	贵阳军分区政治部	1985.5—1993.4	
				常务副书记	县(处)级	贵阳市政法委员会	1993.4—2001.9	
陈其勇	男	汉	大学本科	副所长 支部书记	副县(处)级	贵州省安顺地区农科所	1986.7—1992.2	
				副部长 副主任	副县(处)级	贵州省安顺地委农工部　农业经济委员会	1992.2—1992.9	
				局长	县(处)级	安顺地区农业局	1992.9—1997.11	
				书记	县(处)级	中共紫云苗族布依族自治县委员会	1997.11—2000.12	
				副主任	副厅级	安顺市人大常委会	2000.12—2010.12	
李朝开	男	汉	大学本科	书记	副县(处)级	贵阳市第四中学党支部	1986.12—1993.12	
				校长 书记	副县(处)级	贵阳市第十三中学学校党支部	1993.12—1998.11	
李昌伦	男	汉	大学本科	副县长	副县(处)级	关岭布依族苗族自治县人民政府	1990.5—1992.9	
				副主席	副县(处)级	安顺地区科学技术协会	1992.9—1996.6	
				主席	县(处)级	安顺地区科学技术协会	1996.6—2001.12	
				党组书记 主席	县(处)级	安顺市科学技术协会	2001.12—2007.4	

续表

姓 名	性别	民族	文化程度	任职情况				备注
				职 务	级 别	任职单位	任职起讫年月	
伍鹏程	男	汉	博士	系副主任	副县(处)级	贵州民族学院数学系	1991.6—1996.6	
				系主任	县(处)级	贵州民族学院数学系	1996.6—2000.6	
				副院长	副厅级	贵州民族学院	2000.6—2001.1	
				院 长	正厅级	贵州民族学院	2001.1—2002.1	
				校 长	正厅级	贵州师范大学	2002.1—2010.12	
李建国	男	汉	硕士研究生	副处长	副县(处)级	贵州省委宣传部理论处	1991.11—1993.5	其间：1994年2月至1996年2月挂任榕江县委副书记
				副主任	副县(处)级	贵州省委宣传部社科规划办公室	1993.5—1996.2	
				处 长	县(处)级	贵州省委宣传部理论与教育处	1996.2—2000.4	
				副部长	副厅级	贵州省委宣传部	2000.4—2008.9	
				常务副部长	正厅级	贵州省委宣传部	2008.9—2010.12	
唐文汉	男	汉	大学本科	副县长	副县(处)级	印江县人民政府	1992.3—1995.7	
胡世荣	男	汉	大学本科	督 学	副县(处)级	安顺地区行署教育督导室	1993.8—1998.4	
				主 任	副县(处)级	安顺地区行署教育督导室	1998.4—2001.3	
李阳炜	男	汉	大学本科	主 任	副县(处)级	兴义预备役师三团政治部	1997.3—1997.12	
				主 任	副县(处)级	贵州预备役师三团政治部	1997.12—2000.8	
				常务副部长	副县(处)级	四川省泸州市江阳区宣传部	2000.8—2006.8	
				常务副部长	副县(处)级	四川省泸州市江阳区统战部	2006.8—2010.12	
刘德利	男	汉	大专	院 长	副县(处)级	贵阳市白云区人民政府	1997.12—2007.7	
卢永康	男	汉	中央党校在职研究生	副部长	副县(处)级	贵阳市委宣传部	1998.4—2001.5	
				副部长 主任	副县(处)级	贵阳市委宣传部 市精神文明指导委员会办公室	2001.5—2004.4	
				局 长	县(处)级	贵阳市广播电视局	2004.4—2010.1	
				秘书长	县(处)级	政治协商会议贵阳市委员会	2010.1—2010.12	
黄亚平	男	汉	在职硕士	副主任	副县(处)级	贵阳市城管委	1998.4—2001.9	
				副局长	副县(处)级	贵阳市城管局	2001.9—2010.3	
				副局长	副县(处)级	贵阳市物价局	2010.3—2010.12	

续表

姓名	性别	民族	文化程度	任职情况				备注
				职务	级别	任职单位	任职起讫年月	
陆庆华	男	汉	硕士研究生	副局长	副县(处)级	安顺市统计局	1998.8—2002.12	
				书记	县(处)级	共青团安顺市委　党组	2002.12—2006.8	
				副书记	县(处)级	中共紫云苗族布依族自治县委员会	2006.8—2010.2	
				局长	县(处)级	安顺市政务服务局	2010.2—2010.12	
娄维高	男	汉	大学本科	副场长、副书记	副县(处)级	贵州省草种场	1998.10—2010.12	
徐钰	男	汉	在职硕士研究生	副秘书长党组成员	副县(处)级	安顺市人民政府	2001.4—2004.4	
				党组书记局长	县(处)级	安顺市林业绿化局	2009.3—2010.5	
				主任	县(处)级	贵州省能源局办公室	2010.5—2010.12	
李晓平	男	汉	硕士	副处长	副县(处)级	贵州广播电视大学教务处	2002.6—2010.2	
				书记	县(处)级	贵州广播电视大学信息系党总支	2010.2—2010.12	
蔡远明	男	汉	大学专科	副局长	副县(处)级	贵阳市交通局	2002.7—2007.8	
				副调研员	县(处)级	贵阳市交通局	2007.8—2008.4	
				调研员	县(处)级	贵阳市交通局	2008.4—2009.4	
陈良平	男	汉	在职本科	四级高级法官	副县(处)级	贵阳市中级人民法院	2002.8—2010.12	
朱丽霞	女	汉	中央党校在职研究生	副秘书长	副县(处)级	贵阳市人民政府	2002.10—2007.3	
				局长	县(处)级	贵阳市商务局	2007.3—2010.12	
陆秀祥	男	汉	中央党校在职研究生	副书记、纪委书记	副县(处)级	贵阳市经济贸易委员会	2003.1—2010.2	
				副书记、纪检组长	副县(处)级	贵阳市财政局	2010.2—2010.12	
胡晓刚	男	汉	研究生	局长	县(处)级	贵阳市粮食局	2003.2—2006.9	
				局长	县(处)级	贵阳市旅游局	2006.9—2008.11	
				局长	县(处)级	贵阳市监察局	2008.11—2010.12	
赵永祥	男	汉	大学本科	副县长	副县(处)级	息烽县人民政府	2003.2—2006.9	
李嘉宁	男	汉	中央党校在职研究生	副秘书长	副县(处)级	贵阳市委办公厅	2003.1—2010.11	
				副秘书长主任	县(处)级	贵阳市委　市委党史研究室	2010.11—2010.12	
裴晓红	男	汉	博士	副主任部长	副县(处)级	贵州省农科院党政办、武装部	2003.9—2008.7	
				党委书记	县(处)级	贵州省畜牧兽医研究所	2008.7—2010.12	

续表

姓　名	性别	民族	文化程度	任职情况				备注
				职　务	级　别	任职单位	任职起讫年月	
张林俊	男	汉	大学本科	副校长	副县(处)级	贵阳农校(科技学校)	2004.8— 2010.8	
				主　任	副县(处)级	贵阳职业技术学院旅游系	2010.8—2010.12	
唐　俊	男	汉	大学本科	副处长	副县(处)级	贵州省国家安全厅信息技术处	2005.5—2010.12	
唐　松	男	苗	在职本科	副部长　副书记	副县(处)级	贵阳市人民银行宣传群工部机关党委	2005.6—2010.12	
姜桂梅	女	汉	在职研究生	副主席	副县(处)级	贵阳市妇女联合会	2005.8—2010.12	
汪　浩	男	汉	大学本科	副调研员	副县(处)级	贵州省计划生育委员会协调督查处	2006.2—2010.10	
				副主任	副县(处)级	贵州省计划生育委员会研究室	2010.10—2010.12	
周　毅	男	汉	在职研究生	副书记　副局长	副县(处)级	贵阳市审计局	2006.9—2010.12	
邓龙江	男	汉	大学硕士	主　任	副县(处)级	贵阳市人民政府驻广州办事处	2007.3—2010.12	
黄再忠	男	汉	大学本科	组织员	副县(处)级	贵州师范大学地理与环境科学学院	2007.3—2008.10	
				副书记	副县(处)级	贵州师范大学地理与环境科学学院	2008.10—2010.12	
肖明龙	男	汉	省委党校在职研究生	副书记	副县(处)级	共青团毕节地委	2005.10 —2007.12	
				县委常委	副县(处)级	中共威宁彝族回族苗族自治县委员会	2007.12—2008.1	
				副县长	副县(处)级	威宁彝族回族苗族自治县人民政府	2008.1—2010.12	
谭　虎	男	汉	大学	局　长	副县(处)级	贵阳市人民检察反贪污贿赂局	2008.2—2010.12	
李　坤	男	汉	大学本科	副处长	副县(处)级	贵州省国家税务局征管处	2008.8—2009.5	
				副处长	副县(处)级	贵州省国家税务局纳税服务处	2009.5—2010.12	
何述烈	男	汉	中央党校在职本科	书　记	副县(处)级	贵阳市环境保护局纪委	2009.7—2010.12	
马　彪	男	汉	大学本科	副局长	副县(处)级	贵阳市粮食局	2009.10—2010.12	
刘光祥	男	汉	研究生	书　记	副县(处)级	贵阳市农业委员会纪委	2010.1—2010.12	
梅应贤	男	汉	硕士研究生	副书记	副县(处)级	贵州师范大学国际旅游文化学院党委	2010.12— 2010.12	
唐金文	男	汉	大学本科	书　记	副县(处)级	贵阳市粮食局机关党委	2010.12—2010.12	

1980—2010年荣获全国和省、市劳动模范和先进工作者称号人员一览

表6—03—07

姓名	性别	民族	所在单位	荣誉称号	表彰机关	表彰年月	备注
赵真武	男	汉	扎佐镇龙王小学	省先进工作者	贵州省委省政府	1980.3	
虞庚禹	男	汉	修文中学	省先进工作者	贵州省委省政府	1980.3	
袁廷栋	男	汉	修文三角山水泥厂	省劳动模范	贵州省委省政府	1983.12	
武克华	男	汉	修文县六屯乡都堡村	省劳动模范	贵州省委省政府	1983.12	
黄成仁	男	汉	修文县龙场镇新寨村	省劳动模范	贵州省委省政府	1983.12	
张正清	男	汉	修文县总工会	省“五一劳动奖章”	省总工会	1985.4	
袁峥	男	汉	修文县教育工会	省“五一劳动奖章”	省总工会	1988.4	
宋均成	男	汉	修文红旗煤厂	全国劳动模范	国务院	1989.9	
卢永康	男	汉	修文中学	全国优秀教师	国家教委、全国总工会、人事部	1989.9	
朱明杨	男	汉	修文中学	全国优秀教育工作者	国家教委、全国总工会、人事部	1989.9	
陈福英	女	汉	修文实验小学	全国优秀教师	国家教委、全国总工会、人事部	1989.9	
李新民	男	汉	修文中学	全国优秀教师	国家教委、全国总工会、人事部	1991	
申庆福	男	汉	修文中学	全国优秀教师	国家教委、全国总工会、人事部	1993	
张生益	男	汉	修文县三角山水泥厂	省“五一劳动奖章”	省总工会	1996.4	
陈志明	男	汉	修文县电影公司	省“五一劳动奖章”	省总工会	1999.4	
刘文新	男	汉	修文县龙场镇	市先进工作者	贵阳市委、市政府	2000.4	
罗彦华	男	汉	修文供电局六桶供电所	市先进工作者	贵阳市委、市政府	2000.4	
邵银芬	女	汉	修文县环卫站	市劳动模范	贵阳市委、市政府	2000.4	
陈德芳	男	汉	修文县龙场镇新春村	市劳动模范	贵阳市委、市政府	2000.4	
陈明忠	男	汉	修文县谷堡乡水口村	市劳动模范	贵阳市委、市政府	2000.4	
韩文真	男	汉	修文县人民医院	省先进工作者	贵州省委省政府	2000.5	
吴道明	男	汉	修文县扎佐中学	省先进工作者	贵州省委省政府	2000.5	
李朝友	男	汉	修文中学	省“五一劳动奖章”	省总工会	2003.4	
文明祥	男	汉	修文县谷堡乡平寨村	省劳动模范	贵州省委省政府	2005.4	
李根书	男	汉	修文县六桶乡山堡村	省劳动模范	贵州省委省政府	2005.4	
张元胜	男	汉	修文县谷堡乡富裕村	市劳动模范	贵阳市委、市政府	2005.4	
吴坤明	男	汉	修文县龙场镇白莲村	市劳动模范	贵阳市委、市政府	2005.4	
周明辉	女	汉	修文县六广镇烟叶站	市劳动模范	贵阳市委、市政府	2005.4	
张忠华	男	汉	兴达储运贸易有限公司	市劳动模范	贵阳市委、市政府	2005.4	
唐玉祥	男	汉	修文县政府教育督导室	市先进工作者	贵阳市委、市政府	2005.4	
付贵兴	男	汉	修文县农业局	市先进工作者	贵阳市委、市政府	2005.4	
何磊	男	汉	兴达储运贸易有限公司	省“五一劳动奖章”	省总工会	2009.4	

续表

姓　名	性别	民族	所在单位	荣誉称号	表彰机关	表彰年月	备注
黄继虎	男	汉	修文县龙翔集团	省劳动模范	贵州省委省政府	2010.4	
徐　若	男	汉	修文县扎佐镇大河村	省劳动模范	贵州省委省政府	2010.4	
何世贵	男	汉	修文县林业绿化局	全国绿化先进工作者	国家林业局	2001.4	
王树喜	男	汉	修文县六广镇大桥沟煤矿	市劳动模范	贵阳市委、市政府	2010.4	
王光忠	男	汉	金久水泥有限公司	市劳动模范	贵阳市委、市政府	2010.4	
苏贵荣	男	汉	修文县龙场镇城南村	市劳动模范	贵阳市委、市政府	2010.4	
顾永慧	女	汉	修文县国家税务局	市先进工作者	贵阳市委、市政府	2010.4	
雷云松	男	汉	修文县龙场镇阳早村	市劳动模范	贵阳市委、市政府	2010.4	
张　峰	男	汉	修文县六桶乡宝坪村	市劳动模范	贵阳市委、市政府	2010.4	
邓书连	男	汉	修文县谷堡乡红焰村	市劳动模范	贵阳市委、市政府	2010.4	
陈永梅	女	汉	修文县龙场镇城北村	市劳动模范	贵阳市委、市政府	2010.4	
杜国秀	女	汉	修文县龙场镇环卫站	市先进工作者	贵阳市委、市政府	2010.4	
沈子明	男	汉	贵州绿太阳制药有限公司	市劳动模范	贵阳市委、市政府	2010.4	

1988—2010年全县高级职称人员一览表

表6—03—08

姓　名	性别	民族	学历	工作单位（主管单位）	职称	晋职年月	备注
虞庚禹	男	白	大学专科	修文中学	中学高级教师	1988.1	
贺良知	男	汉	大学专科	修文中学	中学高级教师	1988.1	
刘楚卿	男	汉	大学专科	修文中学	中学高级教师	1988.1	
杨光泽	男	汉	大学专科	扎佐中学	中学高级教师	1988.2	
刘显光	男	汉	大学专科	修文二中	中学高级教师	1988.2	
刘永珍	女	汉	中专	县职业培训中心	中学高级教师	1988.2	
姚垂书	男	汉	大学本科	修文二中	中学高级教师	1988.2	
周忠政	男	汉	大学专科	扎佐中学	中学高级教师	1988.4	
廖昌瑜	男	汉	高中	修文中学	中学高级教师	1988.4	
杨永文	男	汉	大学本科	修文中学	中学高级教师	1988.6	
熊润梅	女	汉	大学本科	修文中学	中学高级教师	1988.6	
刘南容	男	汉	大学本科	修文中学	中学高级教师	1988.6	
刘洪祚	男	汉	大学本科	县职业培训中心	中学高级教师	1988.6	
贺立航	男	汉	大学专科	扎佐中学	中学高级教师	1988.6	
胡有恒	男	汉	大学本科	修文中学	中学高级教师	1988.6	

续表

姓　名	性别	民族	学历	工作单位(主管单位)	职称	晋职年月	备注
朱永福	男	汉	大学专科	修文二中	中学高级教师	1988.6	
冯景周	男	汉	大学本科	修文中学	中学高级教师	1988.12	
张菊定	女	汉	大学本科	修文二中	中学高级教师	1988.12	
张时荣	男	汉	大学本科	扎佐中学	中学高级教师	1988.12	
周仲才	男	汉	大学本科	县职业培训中心	中学高级教师	1988.12	
叶秀玉	女	汉	大学本科	县职业培训中心	中学高级教师	1988.12	
胡启贤	男	汉	初中	教育局教研室	小学中高级教师	1988.4	
万荣珍	女	汉	中专	实验小学	小学中高级教师	1988.6	
杜声敏	女	汉	大学专科	实验小学	小学中高级教师	1988.6	
贾福中	男	汉	大学本科	县卫生局	副主任医师	1988.8	
金宜川	女	汉	大学本科	县卫生局	副主任医师	1988.8	
黄增英	男	汉	大学本科	县委党校	高级讲师	1988.8	
周仲才	男	汉	大学本科	县委党校	高级讲师	1988.8	
潘念齐	男	侗	大学本科	县卫生局	副主任医师	1988	
聂承先	男	汉	小学	县卫生局	副主任医师	1988	
黄金湘	男	汉	大学本科	县卫生局	副主任医师	1988	
龚鸿志	男	汉	大学本科	县卫生局	副主任医师	1988	
邓宗锦	女	汉	本科	县卫生局	副主任医师	1988	
袁廷栋	男	汉	大学本科	县经委	高级工程师	1988	
王秉翰	男	汉	大学本科	县区划办	高级工程师	1988.4	
汤远声	男	汉	大学本科	县区划办	高级农艺师	1989.8	
韩文真	男	汉	中专	县卫生局	副主任医师	1993.9	
邱光健	男	汉	中专	县卫生局	副主任医师	1993.9	
赵祝元	男	汉	大学本科	教育局教研室	中学高级教师	1993.9	
杜顺庭	男	汉	大学本科	久长中学	中学高级教师	1993.9	
裴行敏	男	汉	高中	修文二中	中学高级教师	1993.9	
李新民	男	汉	大学本科	修文中学	中学高级教师	1993.9	
李惠萍	女	汉	大学本科	修文中学	中学高级教师	1993.9	
孙东升	男	汉	大学本科	修文中学	中学高级教师	1993.9	
韩永鉴	男	汉	大学本科	县职业培训中心	中学高级教师	1993.9	
王福正	男	汉	大学专科	修文二中	中学高级教师	1993.9	

续表

姓　名	性别	民族	学历	工作单位(主管单位)	职称	晋职年月	备注
李福印	男	汉	大学专科	扎佐中学	中学高级教师	1993.9	
罗国孝	男	汉	大学专科	修文中学	中学高级教师	1995.9	
刘耀辉	男	汉	大学本科	农业局	农业技术推广高级农艺师	1995.9	
杨正明	男	汉	大学专科	修文中学	中学高级教师	1996.8	
朱五义	男	汉	大学本科	修文中学	中学高级教师	1996.8	
江少恒	男	汉	大学专科	修文中学	中学高级教师	1996.8	
雷德林	男	汉	高中	文广局	主任编辑	1996.10	
裴永祥	男	汉	大学专科	修文中学	中学高级教师	1997.9	
杨　桃	女	汉	大学专科	修文中学	中学高级教师	1997.9	
陈云碧	女	汉	大学专科	修文中学	中学高级教师	1997.9	
饶忠党	男	汉	大学专科	修文中学	中学高级教师	1997.9	
蒋若一	男	汉	大学专科	修文中学	中学高级教师	1997.9	
何先伦	男	汉	大学本科	修文二中	中学高级教师	1997.9	
杨启惠	女	汉	大学专科	修文二中	中学高级教师	1997.9	
简胜荣	男	汉	大学本科	扎佐中学	中学高级教师	1997.9	
雷明扬	男	汉	大学本科	修文中学	中学高级教师	1999.1	
夏国文	男	汉	大学本科	修文中学	中学高级教师	1999.1	
崔益胜	男	汉	大学专科	县职业培训中心	中学高级教师	1999.1	
刘宏雅	女	汉	大学本科	修文中学	中学高级教师	1999.12	
罗锡祥	男	汉	大学本科	扎佐中学	中学高级教师	1999.12	
黄小曼	女	汉	大学本科	县委党校	高级讲师	1999.12	
贾明仙	女	汉	大学本科	林业局	高级工程师	1999.12	
何秀兰	女	汉	大学本科	修文二中	中学高级教师	2000.10	
吴道明	男	汉	大学本科	扎佐中学	中学高级教师	2000.10	
何先伦	男	汉	大学本科	县委党校	高级讲师	2000.12	
刘发祥	男	汉	大学本科	修文中学	中学高级教师	2001.12	
李朝友	男	汉	大学本科	修文中学	中学高级教师	2001.12	
邓德刚	男	汉	大学本科	修文二中	中学高级教师	2001.12	
杨献琴	女	汉	大学本科	修文二中	中学高级教师	2001.12	
李芳扬	男	汉	大学本科	修文中学	中学高级教师	2001.12	
邓　洪	女	汉	大学本科	修文中学	中学高级教师	2001.12	

续表

姓　名	性别	民族	学历	工作单位（主管单位）	职称	晋职年月	备注
王月华	女	汉	大学专科	卫生局	副主任药师	2001.12	
孙光贤	男	汉	大学本科	洒坪中学	中学高级教师	2002.12	
吕应发	男	汉	大学本科	修文中学	中学高级教师	2002.12	
张成孟	男	土家	大学本科	修文中学	中学高级教师	2002.12	
郭　伟	女	汉	大学本科	修文中学	中学高级教师	2002.12	
杨德俊	男	汉	中专	文体广电局	文物博物副研究馆员	2002.12	
付海燕	女	汉	大学本科	县委党校	高级讲师	2002.12	
陈田全	男	汉	大学本科	农业局	高级农艺师	2002.12	
熊文欣	男	汉	大学本科	卫生局	外科副主任医师	2002.12	
毛平力	男	汉	大学本科	卫生局	外科副主任医师	2002.12	
暨建州	男	汉	大学本科	教研室	中学高级教师	2003.12	
蔡玉霞	女	汉	大学本科	修文中学	中学高级教师	2003.12	
王河蜀	男	汉	大学本科	修文中学	中学高级教师	2003.12	
丁光平	男	汉	大学本科	扎佐中学	中学高级教师	2003.12	
余本英	女	汉	中专	卫生局	副主任医师	2003.12	
肖庆贵	男	彝	大学本科	卫生局	副主任医师	2003.12	
张传武	男	汉	大学本科	卫生局	副主任医师	2003.12	
宋庆国	男	汉	大学本科	六桶中学	中学高级教师	2003.12	
姚春丽	女	汉	大学本科	教育局教研室	中学高级教师	2004.12	
罗德敏	女	汉	大学本科	修文二中	中学高级教师	2004.12	
张立新	男	汉	大学本科	修文三中	中学高级教师	2004.12	
明长勇	男	汉	大学本科	六桶中学	中学高级教师	2004.12	
龚正刚	男	苗	大学本科	修文三中	中学高级教师	2004.12	
冉秀平	男	土家	大学本科	修文三中	中学高级教师	2005.12	
周训琼	女	汉	大学本科	修文三中	中学高级教师	2005.12	
李廷江	男	汉	大学本科	修文二中	中学高级教师	2005.12	
杨顺军	男	汉	大学本科	扎佐中学	中学高级教师	2005.12	
刘国顺	男	汉	大学本科	修文三中	中学高级教师	2005.12	
陈大吉	男	汉	大学专科	卫生局	副主任医师	2005.12	
黎洪玉	女	彝	大学本科	卫生局	副主任医师	2005.12	
陈　军	男	土家	大学本科	修文中学	中学高级教师	2006.12	

续表

姓 名	性别	民族	学历	工作单位(主管单位)	职称	晋职年月	备注
陈书敏	女	汉	大学本科	修文中学	中学高级教师	2006.12	
吕 芸	女	汉	大学本科	修文中学	中学高级教师	2006.12	
王绿芬	女	汉	大学本科	修文中学	中学高级教师	2006.12	
徐 瑶	女	汉	大学本科	修文二中	中学高级教师	2006.12	
曹成群	女	汉	大学本科	久长中学	中学高级教师	2006.12	
陈 军	男	汉	大学本科	卫生局	副主任医师	2006.12	
晏正兰	女	汉	大学本科	卫生局	副主任医师	2006.12	
李学军	男	汉	大专	贵阳云天航空工贸有限公司	高级政工师	2007.12	
邹书珍	女	汉	大学本科	修文县疾病预防控制中心	副主任医师	2007.12	
颜珊珊	女	汉	大学本科	修文县疾病预防控制中心	副主任医师	2007.12	
李学英	女	汉	大学本科	修文县医院	副主任护师	2007.12	
徐 辉	女	汉	大学专科	卫生局	副主任护师	2007.12	
许光溱	女	汉	大学本科	修文二中	中学高级教师	2008.12	
任旭云	男	土家	大学本科	修文三中	中学高级教师	2008.12	
黄书祥	男	汉	大学本科	卫生局	副主任医师	2008.12	
梁 杰	男	汉	大学本科	修文中学	中学高级教师	2009.12	
胡大明	男	汉	大学本科	修文三中	中学高级教师	2009.12	
蔡延军	男	汉	大学本科	修文中学	中学高级教师	2009.12	
程 刚	男	土家	大学本科	修文中学	中学高级教师	2009.12	
邱明权	男	汉	大学本科	扎佐中学	中学高级教师	2009.12	
袁 曜	男	汉	大学本科	修文中学	中学高级教师	2009.12	
赵传卫	女	汉	大学本科	卫生局	副主任技师	2009.12	
易太珍	女	汉	大学专科	卫生局	副主任技师	2009.12	
张 宜	女	汉	大学本科	卫生局	副主任护师	2009.12	
杨登平	男	汉	大学本科	修文中学	中学高级教师	2010.12	
刘天发	男	汉	大学本科	修文中学	中学高级教师	2010.12	
邹书云	男	汉	大学本科	修文中学	中学高级教师	2010.12	
周 敏	女	汉	大学本科	修文二中	中学高级教师	2010.12	
韩映春	女	汉	大学本科	修文二中	中学高级教师	2010.12	
张太维	女	汉	大学本科	修文三中	中学高级教师	2010.12	
彭继德	男	汉	大学本科	扎佐中学	中学高级教师	2010.12	

续表

姓　名	性别	民族	学历	工作单位(主管单位)	职称	晋职年月	备注
罗华勇	男	汉	大学本科	扎佐中学	中学高级教师	2010.12	
席　斌	男	汉	大学本科	扎佐中学	中学高级教师	2010.12	
朱　波	男	汉	大学本科	扎佐中学	中学高级教师	2010.12	
兰开碧	女	汉	大学本科	六桶中学	中学高级教师	2010.12	
李国大	男	汉	大学本科	修文县水利建设站	高级工程师	2010.12	
黄佑兰	女	汉	大学本科	修文县人民医院	副主任护师	2010.12	

第四章　人物名录

载入本章的人物系本志时限内获中级职称的人员，分年序逐年记载。1980年12月，成立县科级干部技术职称评定委员会，开始进行各系列技术干部职称考核评定工作。1983年9月，国务院决定暂停评定职称，进行整顿。1985年国务院改革职称评定工作，实行专业技术职务聘任制度。1986年，中共中央、国务院转发《关于改革职称评定、实行专业技术职务聘任制度的报告》，1987年恢复改革职称评定工作。

1980

宋正成　朱正源　聂承先　刘立身　邱光健　赵加泉

1981

叶世岑　万德山　李民枢　周登禄　周世经　华中安　陈治国　汤远声　王佑君　杨富元

1982

康贤南　唐　彦　袁廷栋　毛高富　张　翔　陆振玉　廖月清　廖尊杨　王秉翰　朱明龙　袁慎伦

1987

席德纯　林顺祥　韩文真　戴伟瑛　刘淑黔　黄时秀　金祥生　熊廷惠　陈大吉　黄兆奎　廖海琳
肖荣秀　周尚富　李显志　赵隆芳　戴益珍　朱福忠　裴永珍　邓　录　杨承章　韦　勇　潘国丰
陈树槐　张成学　邓彩林　熊兴民　赵竟鸣　张霭云　莫钟玉　刘际龙　李治烈　张志祥　孙国栋
王达莘　刘耀辉　伍翠宪　黄祖毅　张嘉生　赵秀芬　姚钧应　周孝昌　陶跃奎　肖志华　雷德麟

1988

卢永康　左兴华　石祥彬　谭超群　王启光　江少恒　冯景周　丁　渝　应锡仁　李惠萍　李新民
孙东昇　刘本均　夏国莲　夏之奎　唐盛祖　董　冰　李福印　龙卓成　高文珍　裴永祥　罗国孝
陈典林　叶毓前　叶有芬　夏文秀　杨正明　李治延　杜顺庭　高体祥　李元学　刘洪祚　雷明扬
邱富禄　裴行敏　史作经　蒋若一　韩显明　崔益胜　赵祝元　詹忠华　潘　勇　段复生　胡晓刚

徐文乐 陈杰先 陆羡敏 黄必衡 张菊定 杨启惠 陶炳能 王定瑛 李治凤 夏国文 聂 萍
李明祥 王福正 陈云碧 饶忠党 鲍灵凤 李芳扬 伍 岳 王永玲 谷昭华 张先平 雷郁森
申庆福 傅启刚 方于珍 张时荣 杨 桃 李韵民 刘国顺 严光华 汪育茂 陈应祝 黄光秀
薛占成 喻世坤 王德翔 王良友 江 熙 殷士林 卢德培 陈福英 易德玲 雷华碧 万先敏
许志璧 许明书 徐明瑶 张成智 李光珍 黄全芬 屈经武 胡映琴 熊文英 晏家瑞 王启刚
李思俊 范光志 何贵仙 李儒森 苏岳林 田 琴 熊永仙 余忠惠 徐哲懿 高泽珍 刘思珍
向素华 卢淑惠 李学良 胡家荣 叶明康 许志华 李元和 朱桂元 陈玉珍 俞文贵 唐文芬
季学珍 刘朝阳 胡成仁 王杨霞 张庆英 宋德英 包明成 张名燊 彭朝俊 谢廷超 王道则
夏怀明 戴洪奎 唐永明 陈玖美 陈仁智 杨秀文 鄢文兰 袁时达 刘承先 董登荣 刘光英
赵昭英 何德华 黄玉祥 钟代炳 周学珍 许开芬 郭玉仙 张友仙 赵 玲 张庆芬 卢秀芬
宋聚德 吴必英 文安臣 杨增裕 廖毓文 靳应芝 余济辉 路士林 陈学义 周华珍 罗依群
张德珍 耿龙珍 叶福臻 张汉珍 杨柏明 于时来 林贵芬 赵群先 邱志年 肖开训 王志航
唐泽渊 王才礼 严信立 陈文德 赵必祥 陈福秀 谭德珍 范德明 杜茂文 李继成 朱黔伦
杨发仁 李朝波 贺光荣 严忠仙 胡学钧 商伦珍 廖金梅 李永仙 姚垂丽 刘玉仙 王成艺
王光惠 余成珍 杨孝贤 刘宝珠 张继华 刘光芬 张文秀 张素芳 潘平均 疗礼荣 骆承富
晏文武 朱永斌 朱仕忠 余朝尧 罗明远 严作霖 周才学 吴学林 苟一勤 胡永兰 赵光泽
苏梅军 张乃素 金惠珍 杨德俊 张福全 杨爵贵 伍德萍 韩克英 陈典凤 陈元礼 陈信梅
吴昌芬 李鹤龄 何宣玉 肖丽忠 鲜绍兴 苏伯敏 李晓玲 刘文龙 谢凤英 吴必仙 张明英
秦正强 马尚珍 罗惠珍 朱精忠 朱代文 周兴国 黄启贵 曾祥琪 梅英珍 吕维秀 吴伦芳
李大明 王忠秀 冯广英 张思珍 魏玉伦 熊德中 黄家英 王义武 刘桂香 任洪奇 肖忠芬
杨付祥 王永芬 熊大华 刘光芬 傅明祥 饶晓丽 李元凯 苏文祥 张秀远 何高瑛 许定英
陈树明 韩永鑑 王全芬 冉秀平 曾建平 王良芬 吴祥林 兰桂芳 余 敏 杜荣庆 游来福
袁真文 杨万金 贺遵忠 刘正英 韦鼎元 刘显明 郭正彬 路仕珍 李琼芳 杨远珍 严俊明
周绍福 王友鹿 罗元喜 李再兹 张世宗 刘正刚 黄小曼 张建华 罗云珍 刘润祥 杨大全
刘玉恒 王学理 胡国忠 王耀辉 杨绍林 吴世明 王学英 陆道伦 欧启英 廖书行 田兴民
王忠俊 赵元珍 齐仕明 吕超明 吴 曦 李祖炎 吴应昌 朱五义 骆帮全 丁隆英 李德芳
葛俊声 王发仙 冯肇池 虞顺华 吴昌明 彭忠英 李清智 申家文 郑宗富 杨大明 吴有贵
欧先荣 刘昌华 郭识全 伍 瑛 杨梅珍 孔凡修 唐大秀 肖开鼎 邹德环 赵俊珍

1989

雷学敏 罗光友 范聪明 雷显富 姜明芳 叶家龙 申松柏 李如芬 游昌麟 陶永富 谌贻值
黄启璜 袁廷凯 令狐荣胜 戴良玉 朱和平

1990

唐桂林 暨建州 何先伦 胡 骥 简胜荣 王建红 陈典伦 赵昭林 何国模 朱永松 陈久怀

1993

卢德贵	骆承兰	吴天荣	王应炳	包学芝	黄筱青	童洪贵	李明祥	吕向明	王应平	苟明富
张光文	汪崇芬	王佳兰	贾开德	金应德	潘超群	蓝贵明	徐康平	蔡思荣	付汉珍	周真芳
王庭仙	王润仙	赵国英	陈泽化	刘后芳	李忠元	赵友云	李世珍	钭美菊	张帮华	周荣祥
廖胜杰	廖禄满	唐良本	王亚雄	王昌秀	蔡　玲	夏成义	贾明奇	陈顺志	马志友	周志祥
马晓林	贾佐文	孙德富	郭继芬	肖家兰	陈德庆	何发易	王正华	胡启富	王汝才	严龙贵
马仕华	李安碧	雷齐光	石玉英	黄玉洁	唐金凤	严龙英	徐永珍	孙光贤	罗锡祥	胡泽礼
陈庆秀	罗德敏	李荣川	伍鹏举	张秀月	付海燕	张兴茂	张志英	赵泽泓	王国富	李绍堃
邓　洪	张成孟	陈庆霜	韦洪波	周国刚	蔡体荣	吴亚光	罗国通	班启华	陈田全	王佳伦
鲜太珍	贾明荣	李冬梅	宁文富	张胜祥	蔡友贵	杨树凉	刘凤娇	班启刚	肖云碧	许学芬
李泽仁	魏祥贵	贾明仙	唐凤鸣	朱德林	蔡恩志	杨金培	何贵生	蔡作惠	宋　勤	王伟珍
何慧珠	罗成贵	徐　辉	胡晓明	赵家才	徐　建	余本英	蒙光忠	姚文贵	熊文欣	王明军
袁兴友	潘乐琴	孙正魁	张仕琴	陈继业	王月华	黄玉忠	杨忠平	曾基华	左定芬	王扬仙
崔惠英	江少陵	张振吉	杨德俊	任国玉	周邦跃					

1995

陈家贵	朱忠毅	张立新	朱五义	王河蜀	周训琼	陈和平	郭　伟	顾继红	刘　佐	何秀兰
罗荣德	许午青	杨献琴	李廷江	陈明英	申庆敏	吴道明	邓德刚	陈庆莲	万先梅	明长勇
肖德华	张明星	凌忠武	汪忠权	罗云珍	李继明	林梦竹	李思英	张友仙	田敏绒	李忠英
王登凤	范友仙	赵永仙	李发芬	付芝萍	邓永萍	陈泽敏	苏桂秀	李素萍	朱燕忠	文兴平
李廷熙	胡忠友	贾明刚	王敬菊	谭永玉	袁真惠	任朝夕	李兴敏	陈朝先	杨文华	唐邦松
张忠群	宋长良	韩瑞仙	肖桂林	陈光玉	张文碧	罗丛容	罗国敏	贾佐兰	王修志	陈朝富
程传远	石雪松	赵延秀	王凤英	李春秀	黄赞勇	洪保琴	李胜义	代忠尧	张道春	

1996

吕应发	刘发祥	郑德富	胡德惠	李朝友	夏之行	余志一	林成芬	张明娥	彭金芬	史述惠
段惠琴	张丽华	张启一	张秀英	朱玉兰	廖　丽	林盛德	彭润伦	刘昭明	罗乾英	朱贵刚
黄藻俊	谭晓梅	王良才	曾帮俊	孔令芬	周武琼	宋顺祥	王会荣	郑秀英	代雪里	陈书品
张传武										

1997

王路群	陈晓红	卢永琼	陆秀福	文红杠	李惠萍	郭训伸	杨安英	徐建英	蒙志萍	杨玉琼
王丽娅	黄万明	李绍玺	陈丰伦	雷仕琴	陈乾贵	周筑业	吴道颖	郑德秀	谢方珍	王学平
韦景智	罗国华	何先萍	蔡大英	王　浩	闫国民	刘建平	陈长慧	杨富荣	丁光平	李继彬
顾庆修	朱友秀	彭忠瑜	宋庆国	叶淑琴	晏正兰	李学英	廖金银	周如刚	袁真萍	王旅黔

胡蔚祥　张发琼　李昌惠　李昌兰　吴学芬　吴昌珍　宋焕玲　胡祥碧　黄亮文　刘　栩　叶国学
付海燕　林德荣　伍鹏举

1998

蔡玉霞　陈　军　瞿光荣　傅义茂　阮建国　陈晓斌　罗焕祥　姚春丽　印　江　黄　政　贾启云
李正荣　刘安邦　陈书敏　唐凤翠　王国林　朱友华　刘丽娜　梁本芳　周真芬　杨祖琼　文秀祥
吴济辉　陈以秀　李朝祥　袁明贵　刁泌鑫　王永政　费　华　袁忠秀　陈　燕　夏光琼　李应琼
刘德英　曾晓红　吴丽琼　余忠明　宋　玲　汪冬梅　包学湘　查继兰　石明群　喻志敏　陈艳碧
雷　华　李明慧　路昭琼　李仕珍　熊俊秀　陈泽群　胡蔚全　杨成菊　敖广培　陈　军　金　松
田景坤　林　葛　宋聚凤　胡启富　杜孟明　杨　琼　肖　红

1999

吕　芸　刘克黔　付　敏　许光溱　晏家平　杨显涛　凌继琴　贺　英　王阳德　张　琼　郭　明
王明富　高学华　朱黔元　李永华　李　敏　马　莲　陈冠春　刘艳芬　叶华庆　余　辉　张志英
张兴茂

2000

杨新宇　任旭云　王绿芬　韩映春　徐　瑶　彭云书　杨胜齐　杨顺军　王永祥　李　祥　曹成群
李友德　周礼祥　刘　琼　朱有君　张德智　罗　英　黎明静　任忠兰　李金娥　班　燕　胡德祥
杨　海　黄　琼　吴道琴　苏方银　周开龙　黄再仙　余显文　彭亦荣　鲍忠会　郭　翔　伍绍贤
石　萍　宁文德　罗运民　李国大　王文盛　付贵兴　冷先贵　贾明凤　颜珊珊　雷天林　朱有国
王朝兰　伍绍春　胡　蓉

2001

张兰富　严　实　周　琨　袁真慧　李开菊　蹇仕仙　任廷康　高相碧　张福凯　王伦贵　张宗芬
蒋明珍　吴　勇　李晓祥　魏忠勇　黄昌桂　罗福萍　王永秀　赵传卫　易太珍　宋庆琼　汪　翼
吴秀云　张莲芬　王朝纲　莫承杰　王家荣　李建萍　苟元华　严忠强　李权友　黄书祥　喻志峰
杨　平　刘　萍　周开涛　姚　星　李　萍　冯开惠　黎　慧　陶锦洲　张　宜　谈　菲　谢丽琴
黄佑兰

2002

刘廷斌　余顺珍　朱有刚　刘　毅　周珍利　朱兴忠　陈昌武　周　敏　叶立忠　陆礼春　聂凤鸣
胡大明　王秀德　罗章萍　刘正林　兰开碧　宋幼全　邱明权　刘建文　彭继德　汪　琼　陈　静
金仕义　虞昌亮　崔吉军　冯广源　倪家兴　蒋　英　刘占英　钟　桦　王国忠　李年福　汪丽红
刘丛惠　黄　雁　黄成义　宋庆红　罗永道　苏启英　黄以奎　宋洪仙　李元娥　李　燚　潘胜祥

陈云秀　胡　强　熊少林　邓龙涛　李桃萍　兰序宏　贺真祥　卢永琴　潘　磊　陈志芹　罗　静
邹劲松　邹书珍　彭建群　邱　艳

2003

林开基　于荷碧　倪家兰　朱　娅　谢月菊　邓德秀　夏大伦　刘忠伦　吴永霞　周星延　苏方英
李孝芬　金坤玉　何碧秀　常开学　陈荣贵　蔡延军　朱　波　林开友　韩文举　余昌龙　明成强
张云贤　赵章尧　李腾惠　杨丽文　岑之龙　赵呈斌　夏　春　晏正芳　晏华云　李湘兰　胡湘黔

2004

陆　艳　姚林玉　胡超群　陈　颖　马大勇　王成兴　胡启明　杨德俊　叶伦会　宋家祥　朱万萍
王诗鸿　陈　威　瞿明亮　兰仕军　韩幼愈　赵后贵　谌贻平　袁　曜　肖文华　杨登平　刁碧静
葛正忠　李懿菊　张仁华　周　振　严绍刚　唐　坤　罗　举　唐　英　罗华勇　程　刚　梁　杰
谌远忠　唐玉明　何志忠　何仁萍　聂坤惠　韩中奎　刘金英　王桂芬　钟毓毅　韩开华　杜孟丽
胡大颖　邓某祥　张建文　周玉平　令狐倩　秦智慧　徐明礼

2005

陈和忠　陈　斌　文崇刚　任奇政　胡荣萍　郑朝忠　唐晓华　余昌兰　张　杰　明方勇　姚兴平
王朝富　曹学清　李孝梅　吴诗燕　杨再平　朱达琴　何　叶　杨锦菊　张辉良　许应前　高体凤
刘继琼　林万秀　毛正秀　王莉萍　梁利君　刘晓敏　左定军　胡湘江　刘德秀　康礼刚　蔡仁和
许世敏　韩　红　罗群章　徐康琪　袁天明　秦瑞莲　首成珍　张　琼　屈关飞　罗　映　班玖先
周珍其　陆秀华　郑　林　付相勇　袁小燕　吕向莲　兰仕龙　杨　梅　秦晓菊　赵　菊　金　港
曹名声　林盛强　赵　华　龚春城　斯明琳　杨承广　彭　丽　张良远　席　斌　杨黔辉　何贤亮
路忠敏　邓发明　袁红霞　虞玲臻　许文洁　范先鹏　雷　芳　朱绍芳　王相平　何先江　肖仕菊
陈绍松　徐育贤　苏启尧　刘华平　陈书勇　张　艳　邵世娟　杜春香　冯明芬　田莉琴　汪雪俊
谭永元　吴　群　陈仕旭　冯　瑛　梁　珏

2006

胡光友　黄丽萍　李庭兰　李忠萍　罗　辉　王登勇　张成新　查继芹　陈书菊　付明凤　宋　娟
姚唯娅　于　钦　余晓明　朱永先　罗福英　蔡红霞　王　芳　裴兰芝　王小平　李学惠　张福菊
谢进萍　陈洪惠　袁国芳　谢安敏　汪　荣　班启林　朱永凤　杜学英　彭江涛　李登莲　朱妍契
周晓霞　姚华艳　简怀林　何　芸　杨荣凤　王韬缜　莫承莲　罗永芬　李　艳　杜向英　陈明秀
钟仕秀　张志琼　赵祖全　周开利　张明惠　姚华秀　李　玲　颜加萍　刁碧发　张晓钟　张德荣
许　丽　龙明珍　田庆菊　宗德荣　王　敏　李　梅　李晓文　蒋后勇　彭忠勋　李昌祥　熊　华
姚仕祥　曾科群　杜向珍　王　敏　李明文　李永亮　杨　艺　周　华　冉　宇　吴　军　王洪兵
宁培伦　王以巧　韦时梅　陈红宇　蔡玉梅　刘雪峰　杜明英　王　平　李　倩　梁仕英　代中易

任萍 吴伦文 敖义礓 马莱 周海波 罗翔 向学文 石勇华 颜红樱 谢勇 刁泌鑫
张勋 俞红红 罗静 李廷银 刘秀英 何晓艳 李忠敏 史瑞利 贾佐慧 汪毓平 熊大娟
路英 刘显伦 姜桂香 王学敏 刘崇芬 罗文秀 罗显珍 陈祖发 黄林 朱有嘉 李添群
杨杰 胡兴 陈飞 杨安毅 冯广亮

2007

邹丽 刘又云 杨晓艳 朱方萍 李茜 贾忠惠 邓天平 谌业新 李添秀 赵云会 刘大武
蔡碧兰 曹宽进 雷玉梅 李丽梅 李君 杨开庆 郎平 刘也静 班山莲 吴诗惠 周新寓
杨仕琴 李金铭 班正莲 张发明 冯广芬 张永春 黄芳 倪生琼 杨齐心 田仁华 吴永刚
颜加梅 杜明艳 张萍 袁吉祥 任奇友 刘卉 何先静 周剑 包飞 刘丽萍 谢箐
彭永平 李家颖 龚春雷 王福莲 罗永红 李翠兰 肖兴练 吴华艳 徐梅 李雪琼 焦明凤
唐亚新 宋庆国 陈吉 罗平 龚秀琼 谌业军 雷连贵 聂铭 龙明海 胡胜菊 罗勋荣
刘德品 刘永霜 蔡吉文 郭兴权 王贵华 周真国 周礼鸿 陈顺仙 刘文华 杜国华 伍绍贤
王文耀 王芳芬 李文峰 曾文佼 陈梅 李明珠 谌贻荣 周仕洪 颜嘉玲 袁才会 唐少芬
娄界 闵国凤 陈跃 刁艳梅 吕向敏 徐存素 韦君 汤裕淑 徐敏 刘艺 王敏
肖盛明 蒋维艳 樊高玉 朱俊忠 彭杰 熊维志 徐松 易辉明

2008

顾庆兰 代丽萍 刘书英 吴道丽 邓明静 兰序柱 邓鸿雁 徐向兰 周成余 康兴美 赵平英
朱永兰 金俊凤 王菊 杨绍英 马宁 彭飞 刘龙贵 刘佑梅 杨琴 张德菊 袁煜
杨竹 朱琼 姜礼箐 许志林 胡加菊 宋雁 李兴勇 杨家琴 刘光平 罗菊 王培菊
胡大碧 王婷 罗刚 金彦 周遵国 肖剑 彭仕荣 吕维旭 王丽萍 田实芝 熊维秀
徐微 王艳 陈凯 杨林 黄燕 陈龙 肖桂林 杨朝武 罗华章 陈会 胡德才
贺静 罗运淑 余顺文 王勇 吴桂萍 罗宇 李晓萍 李英 任燚 洪晓龙 严惠
罗永春 杨冬梅 罗洁 郭荣琼 霍江 郭元军 罗朝惠 宣莉蓉 熊永春 李庆菊 游忠琼
金艳琦

2009

廖开秀 高洪英 陈海涛 杨显仙 金艳 刘梅 叶伦碧 王怀勇 唐倩 冯芳 代传阳
冯永莲 贺明香 朱友翠 陈国杰 艾祖刚 朱习志 刘耀泽 杨荣海 李诗传 杨建 王成芬
李耀庭 朱永荣 梁伟 葛正琼 曾黔华 唐玉兰 孙国菊 李巍 祝梦琳 万春 岳晓莹
刘君 毛羽 陈海燕 王芳 贺明英 罗贵华 陈石 崔清华 安鹏飞 刘华 刘广远
刘军 王芝平 肖芳 李斌 吴晓云 吴道学 叶兴 周训禄 田毅 李志黔 罗林
孙正蓉 张坤 罗玉德 罗福芬 李春玉 母家群 杨宇希 田晓芳 王洪艳 陈明菊 严光菊
吴光琴 陈贵英 黄梅 张波 杨雷 孙成文 罗远飞 黄维 王志兰 邓德会

2010

文　艳	粟安祥	龙文英	田玉芳	谢　沙	胡　琴	桑　丽	陈继军	罗显丽	张武琼	黄　琪
向　交	胡远梅	罗世珑	蒋田心	杨树军	徐　海	任奇平	王　婧	王得君	王　澜	杨　琴
李　梅	谢福贵	陈　梅	许志海	陈菊先	王　菊	梅　霞	潘红梅	明永健	王莉莎	邓正芬
王　燕	金　一	柳　佳	宋元汶	沈卫兵	张大宇	查继勇	邓明兰	明厚进	韩　艳	袁　林
周绍昌	董用仙	何　莉	朱小荣	宋庆虹	陈忠莲	赵福春	樊增慧	刘天宇	任　华	张道品
余　波	郑传龙	李明科	舒　馨	岳　梅	叶旭刚	陈毅珍	兰序琪	杨成应	张海燕	李雪娟
朱　剑	杨尚菊	郑秀梅	付川川	林万会	廖禄君	梁大仙	朱小芳	李晓娟	王　婷	李　芳
陈云霞	曹　丽	王荣芳	王　琨	班晓林	胡茂菊	李思慧	夏珊珊	张　玲	徐德惠	何　俊
肖男英	晏华云	张永杰	杨培源	杨玉梅	孙正蓉	李　志	王绪兰	肖丽梅	贺帮琼	邓红梅
李秀梅	杜　励	陈一敏	秦志英	罗　雁	梁龙琼	冯　芳	吴　忻	付帮奎	卯　觐	李朝平
潘平西										

附　　录

一、大事记（2011—2017）

2011

1月20日　县委与贵州省扎佐林场在林场举办“安泰模式”十周年座谈会。县委副书记、县长蒋志伦说，十年来修文县与林场精诚团结，共谋发展，创建了“企业低门槛入驻，地款用税收补齐”的“安泰模式”，逐步使驻县企业上规模、有档次、有品质。县委书记石洪讲话认为，修文县和扎佐林场合作的十年，是解放思想、不断探索的十年，是相互支持、成效显著的十年，是发挥优势、共谋发展的十年。十年中，在西部大开发的背景下，通过贵州省林业厅、扎佐林场与修文县共同协作，不断探索、实践，打造出了“安泰模式”，建设出一个医药园区。在以后的合作中，要做好定位、统筹，通过机制创新，修文和林场共谋发展，铸造出新的辉煌。

26—27日　县委第十届委员会第十次全体（扩大）会议召开。会议传达贯彻中共十七届五中全会、中央经济工作会议、省委十届十次全体（扩大）会议、全省经济工作会议、贵阳市委八届十次全体（扩大）会议精神，全面总结“十一五”期间经济社会发展情况，谋划“十二五”和部署2011年的经济社会发展工作，会议还审议通过县委《关于制定修文县国民经济和社会发展第十二个五年规划的建议》。县委书记石洪作题为《抢抓机遇，振奋精神，苦干实干，推动修文在新一轮竞争中强县进位》的讲话。

2月28日　总投资71亿元的贵州轮胎股份有限公司年产1280万条高性能子午轮胎异地技改项目在扎佐镇开工建设。5月22日，时任省委书记栗战书、省长赵克志率领参加全省项目建设年现场观摩团代表莅临扎佐观摩黔轮胎项目建设情况。2013年12月，轮胎厂炼胶车间投产。2014年2月20日，在修文园区生产出首只轮胎，规格为26.5R25，标志着该公司异地技改工作取得成功，随即进入规模生产。到2015年，黔轮胎二期主体工程完成95%，公司获2015年度贵阳市市长质量奖。

3月8日　中国人民政治协商会议县第七届委员会第六次会议召开，到会委员166人。会议听取和审议政协七届常务委员会工作报告和提案办理情况报告，并作出相应决议。全体委员列席县第十四届人民代表大会第六次会议，听取和讨论会议所作的政府工作报告。

9—11日　县第十四届人民代表大会第六次会议召开，到会代表183人。会议审议通过《政府工作报告》、《修文县2010年财政预算执行情况及2011年预算报告（草案）》《修文县2010年国民经济和社会发展计划执行情况及2011年计划（草案）》《修文县国民经济和社会发展第十二个五年规划纲要》《人大常委会工作报告》《法院工作报告》《检察院工作报告》，并审查批准2011年财政预算。会议对上述报告作出相应决议。会议还依法补选王成林为县人大常委会主任。

4月5日　县政府与新加坡华德集团在腾晖酒店举行合作项目协议签约，投资20亿元建设生态环保城暨节点城市项目。

18日　由贵州光彩事业促进会、贵州省君之堂药业公司等单位投资建设的贵州迈丰生物科技公司年产3万吨有机肥料项目在谷堡乡建成，该项目的建成填补了贵州省无生物有机肥的空白。

6月10日　县委在青少年活动中心举行《中国共产党修文县历史》第一卷首发式。《中国共产党修文县历史》以23万字的容量，用翔实的资料系统回顾从民国24后（1935）中国工农红军长征经过修文至1978年中国共产党十一届三中全会召开前44年时间中国共产党在修文这片土地上不懈奋斗和艰辛探索的历程。

6月29日　10万平方米公租房项目开工建设。项目落地在龙场镇思源路和扎佐镇襄阳大道，其中龙场镇建170套，建筑面积8500平方米；扎佐镇建1830套，建筑面积9.15万平方米。10万平方米公租房建设项目系县2011年十大民生工程之一。为保障项目有序推进，县政府专门成立项目建设工作领导小组负责督促检查。

7月7日　遵照筑党办发〔2011〕11号中共贵阳市委办公厅、贵阳市人民政府办公厅《关于开展城市基层管理体制改革相关工作的意见》，对已有的居民委员会和新成立的居民委员会均不冠以“社区”称谓，规范后的居民委员会名称结构为：地址+居民委员会，据此精神，自即日起全县10个社区居委会均取消“社区”称谓。

8日　根据修党办发〔2011〕22号文件精神，成立龙岗社区服务中心，社区办公室驻县城栖凤路，其服务范围系龙场镇原下属的栖凤、虎山、宾阳、龙岗等4个居民委员会。

9月8日　县政府与贵州永盛和置业发展有限公司签约，拟投资20亿元在扎佐医药食品工业园区内建设建材家居物流中心。至2015年，永盛和商贸物流港一期市场部分及裙楼商业广场结构层完工。

10月25日　落户工业园区内的9个新建工业项目举行集中开工仪式。此次集中开工的鑫益能等9个新建项目占地1443亩，总投资19.8亿元。

10月31—11月2日　中共修文县第十一次代表大会召开，到会代表243人。县委书记石洪代表第十届县委作《立足新起点， 推动新跨越，为实现修文经济社会又好又快发展努力奋斗》的工作报告。大会选举产生新一届县委领导班子和县纪委领导班子，石洪当选为县委书记，蒋志伦、黄永辉当选为县委副书记，张君当选为县纪委书记。

12月27日　由贵州永盛和置业发展有限公司投资建设的贵州商贸物流港（扎佐建材家居物流中心）在扎佐开工建设。物流港总投资20亿元，规划占地1250亩，总建设面积140万平方米。2013年10月19日 物流港一期18万平方米商品交易展示区工程主体完工。2014年1月10日，物流港一期建设正式投入运营，首批入驻商户57户。

2012

1月5—8日 中国人民政治协商会议县第八届委员会第一次会议召开，到会委员170人。会议听取政协七届委员会常务委员会工作报告。全体委员列席县第十五届代表大会第一次会议，听取会议所作的政府工作报告、人大常务委员会工作报告和县人民法院、县人民检察院工作报告。闭幕式通过县政协八届一次会议提案审查情况报告和八届一次会议决议。会议选举产生第八届县政协领导班子，陈雄标当选为政协修文县第八届委员会主席，陈国邦、王世利、王雄飞、胡祥碧、林江、杨杏、田江涛当选为副主席，席毅龙当选为秘书长。

6—9日 县第十五届人民代表大会第一次会议召开，到会代表184名。会议听取和审议蒋志伦代表县人民政府向大会所作题为《全力以赴抓发展、奋力赶超促跨越、为实现“强县进位”目标而努力奋斗》的工作报告和王成林代表县人大常委会作的工作报告。会议还听取并审议修文县2011年国民经济和社会发展计划执行情况及2012年计划报告、修文县2011年财政预算执行情况和2012年财政预算报告、修文县人民法院工作报告、修文县人民检察院工作报告。会议选举产生第十五届县人大常委会主任、副主任、委员，选举产生新一届县人民政府县长、副县长，县人民法院院长，县人民检察院检察长以及修文县出席贵阳市第十三届人民代表大会代表。王成林当选为县第十五届人民代表大会常务委员会主任，孙庆英、罗永翔、张杰、朱永彬、刘元珍、王朝惠、文清武当选为副主任。蒋志伦当选为县人民政府县长，闫寒、汤建祥、王天镜、邓波、裴斌、王劼当选为副县长。徐涛当选为县人民法院院长。段炼当选为县人民检察院检察长。石洪、蒋志伦、王成林等28人当选为贵阳市第十三届人民代表大会代表。

2月17日 县委召开贯彻落实国发〔2012〕2号文件项目申报工作会，全县10乡（镇）及各部门主要负责人参加。会议要求各乡（镇）、各部门把深入学习文件作为当前一段时期的主要工作，深刻领会文件精神，吃透并认真把握政策，定位好自身发展。在项目申报工作中，要集中心思和精力，认真研究好全省、全市的共性项目和修文的特性项目是什么，找准突破口，使项目能争取到国家部委及省、市的支持；要突出重点，抓住贵阳市北部新区城市带建设中修文城市个性的打造，突出城市公共设施的配套建设、改造提升问题及物流配套建设，突出阳明文化园建设、新材料循环经济产业、加工制造基地、特色轻工业等重点产业的发展。县发改局要抓好衔接，积极和省、市相关部门对接，和乡（镇）、部门对接，按照贵阳市委、市政府的统一安排，申报一批质量高、有深度的项目。

是月 由县青少年活动中心创作的舞蹈《绣娃》被选为“魅力校园”第七届全国校园文艺汇演和第十二届全国校园春节联欢晚会节目，在北京参加汇演荣获文艺汇演金奖。

3月24—25日 在第七次全国实验区工作会议暨2012部委政策信息对话会上，修文被列为全国低碳国土实验区创建单位。

5月 龙场镇红旗村被国家人口和计划生育委员会和中国计划生育协会授予“全国人口和计划生育基层群众自治示范村”荣誉称号。

6月8日 县长蒋志伦代表县政府分别与贵州鑫华源房地产开发有限公司、贵州毅龙房地产开发有限公司、广西金拓置业有限公司和贵州海铭城建筑安装有限公司签订县城南片区改造项目投资协议。签约项目包括虎山路延伸段接龙麦线、栖凤大道、龙潭路、县政务服务中心、小桥河河道整治工程等，总建筑面积53.28万平方米，总投资8.28亿元，建设工期2年。

7月1日　由县委、县政府主办，县委党史研究室和县档案局承办的庆祝中国共产党成立91周年党史图片展在县体育馆广场开展。此次图片展共布置展板20块，由前言、领导关怀、历任中共修文县委书记及“文化大革命”时期党的核心领导小组组长、红军长征在修文、珍藏记忆、军大五分校、“文化大革命”印象、县城变迁、远去的工厂、岩鹰山水库建设、执政成就、结束语等12部分组成，展出珍贵图片100余张。

26日　在贵阳市十大工业园区展示开幕式暨项目推介会上，县政府分别与三一重工股份有限公司、重庆领先食品有限公司、河南济源金康达玻璃制品有限公司成功签约，引进资金6亿元。

8月16日　根据县编委办公室修机编〔2012〕109号通知建立珍珠河社区服务中心，社区办公室驻扎在珍珠河新城B区，负责管理辖区内的社会事务。

10月21日　县委、县政府召开阳明文化园规划设计暨核心景区修建性详细规划评审会。会议听取编制单位对阳明文化园规划成果的汇报，各单位部门负责人及评审团专家分别对阳明文化园建筑风格、文化的表现手法、河道景观与核心景点打造、路网铺设、公共配置等提出意见和建议，经过讨论通过评审。

12月26日　贵州省地方志协会（学会）在贵阳召开学术年会并换届选举，修文县地方志编辑部主编李祖炎继聘为协会（学会）顾问。

28日　修文县举行首届“信合杯”感动修文人物表彰大会，评选出杨昌洪、刘钦向、陈江、李元莲、刘洪祥、卯觐、包雪莉（叶鑫、杜天晶）、王波、于传文、李文军等10名“感动修文”人物和9名“感动修文”提名人物。

2013

1月22日　县委十一届第二次全体（扩大）会议召开，县委书记石洪主持会议并代表县委常委向大会作书面报告和题为《提振精神，埋头实干，为全面推进小康社会建设而奋斗》的讲话，县委副书记、县长蒋志伦总结2012年工作和部署2013年工作。会议的主要任务是：传达贯彻中共十八大、省委十一届二次全体（扩大）会议、市委九届二次全体（扩大）会议和中央经济工作会议、中央农村工作会议、全省经济工作会议精神，总结2012年全县经济社会发展情况，安排2013年经济社会发展任务，重点研究部署建设小康社会工作。全会讨论《县委、县政府关于推进生态文明城市建设加快全面建成小康社会的实施意见》、《县委常委会关于进一步加强自身建设的意见》《县委关于改进工作作风、密切联系群众的相关规定》和《县委关于进一步加强和改进新形势下党的基层组织建设的实施意见》。

2月1日　由县选送的扎佐镇中心小学乡村少年宫创作的舞蹈《山娃闹秋》在北京举行的“魅力校园”第八届全国校园文艺汇演暨第十三届全国校园春节联欢晚会活动中获文艺汇演金奖，并入选全国校园春节联欢晚会录制，在春节期间由中央电视台少儿频道播出。

3月16—18日　中国人民政治协商会议县第八届委员会第二次会议召开，到会委员152人。会上，县政协主席陈雄标代表八届常务委员会作工作报告。副主席杨杏向大会报告八届一次会议以来的提案工作情况。会议审议并同意陈雄标向大会所作的工作报告，审议并同意杨杏向大会所作的提案工作情况报告。全体委员列席县十五届人民代表大会第二次会议，听取有关报告并提出意见和建议。

17—19日　县第十五届人民代表大会第二次会议召开，到会代表179名。会议听取县长蒋志伦代表县政府向大会作的政府工作报告。县发展改革局和县财政局分别书面报告全县2012年国民经济和社会发展计划执行情况及2013年计划（草案）报告、2012年财政预算执行情况和2013年财政预算（草案）报告。县人大常委会主任王成林、县人民法院院长徐涛、县人民检察院检察长段炼分别向大会作工作报告。与会代表采取无记名投票方式补选谭永红为县人大常委会副主任。

29日 由贵州广播电视台和县委、县人民政府主办，县委宣传部、贵州广播电视台新闻综合广播承办的“浩瀚六百年 激荡新贵州”大型户外直播，首场《开天辟地贵州人》在阳明洞开播。

4月25日 根据黔府函〔2013〕79号省人民政府《关于同意贵阳市修文县六桶乡洒坪乡六屯乡撤乡设镇》的批复，同意撤销六桶乡，设置六桶镇，镇人民政府驻地盐井村；同意撤销洒坪乡，设置洒坪镇，镇人民政府驻地小坝村；同意撤销六屯乡，设置六屯镇，镇人民政府驻地都堡村。撤乡设镇后，原行政区划不变。

7月2日 县公务卡改革全面启动，10乡（镇）、县直部门主要领导和财务人员共100余人参加培训。

4日 县委、县政府出台《修文县村民委员会区划调整实施方案》，启动村民委员会调整工作。至9月22日，经县政府批准，全县村民委员会由原来的217个调整为113个，居民委会由原来的10个调整为12个。

8月23日 总投资1.6亿元，占地250亩的修文县中等职业技术学校奠基开工。新建职业学校办学规模6000人，总建筑面积13万平方米，其中，教学楼建筑面积1.8万平方米，实验及实训楼建筑面积3.2万平方米，办公楼建筑面积0.6万平方米。项目建成将进一步夯实县“9+3”教育基础。

9月4日 根据县政府《关于六桶镇村民委员会区划调整的批复》，撤销六桶、盐井2个村民委员会，改置盐井居民委员会。盐井居民委员会辖区即原六桶和盐井村民委员会所辖地域。居委会办公室使用原六桶村民委员会办公室。

22日 根据县政府《关于扎佐镇村民委员会区划调整的批复》，撤销三里和小堡2个村民委员会，改置珍珠河居民委员会。珍珠河居民委员会辖区即原三里、小堡村民委员会所辖地域。居委员会办公室设在珍珠河社区办公楼内。

11月3日 大型电影制片《不朽的时光》开机仪式在县城举行。

4日 根据修委〔2013〕66号中共修文县委《关于成立修文县珍珠河社区党委的通知》，成立中共修文县珍珠河社区委员会。

15日 高新区、白云区、修文县同城化发展框架协议在白云区签署，标志着3地将通过推进区域合作，进一步建立互利共赢、可持续发展的战略合作关系，携手合作打造全省区域合作典范。

20日 县委召开传达贯彻中共十八届三中全会精神会议。会议传达《中共中央关于全面深化改革若干重大问题的决定》和省、市相关会议精神，部署下一阶段工作。会议指出，中共十八届三中全会是在我国改革开放新的重要关头召开的一次重要会议，重点在于如何深化改革。学习好、宣传好、贯彻好、落实好十八届三中全会精神，是当前乃至今后一个时期的首要政治任务，要切实用全会精神统一思想，凝聚力量，指导实践，推动工作。

12月12日 为深入贯彻落实中共十八届三中全会关于文化强国建设的部署，弘扬中国传统文化，提升市民文化素质，增强干部群众文化自觉与自信，县委举办“重德修文”大讲堂开讲仪式暨首场讲座。2014年，以“重德修文”为总标题，延伸“道德讲堂”，开办系列讲堂讲座。囊括传统文化、阳明文化、

生态文化和道德、法制、诚信、忠义、社会主义核心价值观、“中国梦”、全面建设小康等内容，开展进机关、进社区、进学校、进乡村、进企业活动，针对不同对象分别开班。以“开微讲堂，讲大道理”为原则，小规模、多场次地开展宣讲活动。将“重德修文”做成文化品牌。全年建设乡（镇）、机关、企事业单位道德讲堂84个，开展活动516场次。举办“宣传部长上讲堂”活动宣讲12场次，参加群众达1000人次。建成学校“道德讲堂”40多所、班级“道德讲堂”600多间和乡村学校少年宫55所。

2014

1月8日　在贵州省2013年度住房保障工作考核评比中，修文县被表彰为住房保障示范县，副省长慕德贵颁发奖牌，修文县获专项奖励资金1000万元。

11日　县委第十一届委员会第三次全体（扩大）会议召开。县委委员、候补委员出席会议，县纪委委员和有关方面负责人列席会议。全会由县委常委会主持，县委书记石洪讲话。全会全面贯彻落实中共十八届三中全会、省委十一届四次全会、市委九届三次全会和中央、省、市一系列重要会议精神，听取和讨论石洪受县委常委会委托作的工作报告。县委副书记、县长蒋志伦通报2013年经济社会发展情况，并对2014年经济社会发展工作进行部署。县委副书记黄永辉作会议总结。

2月20—22日　中国人民政治协商会议县第八届委员会第三次会议召开，到会委员158人。会议听取并审议《政协第八届委员会常务委员会工作报告和八届二次会议以来提案工作情况的报告》。会议列席修文县第十五届人民代表大会第三次会议，听取并讨论《政府工作报告》和其他有关报告。

21—23日　县第十五届人民代表大会第三次会议召开，实到代表175人。会议听取并审议县人民政府工作报告、全县2013年国民经济和社会发展计划执行情况及2014年国民经济和社会发展计划报告、县2013年财政预算执行情况及2014年财政预算的报告、县人民代表大会常务委员会工作报告、县人民法院和县人民检察院工作报告。会议依法补选李继彬为县十五届人民代表大会常务委员会副主任。

3月17日　洒坪镇举行香港力扬有限公司援建洒坪小学明德教学楼和香港联合素食援建华英男生宿舍楼奠基仪式。新建洒坪小学位于小坝村，明德教学楼总建筑面积1860平方米，工程总造价340万元，由香港力扬企业有限公司捐资港币30万元，其余部分由县人民政府匹配共同修建。

18日　为加大“平安修文”和“法治修文”建设的宣传力度，县电视台开办《法治视线》专题栏目。《法治视线》栏目在修文电视台综合频道（14频道）播出，于2014年3月14日首播，每月两期，每期20分钟以上。

6月22日　2014年高考揭晓，全县参考学生1623人，文化成绩上线人数分别是：一本105人，比2013年增加18人；二本522人，比2013年增加131人。其中600分以上的5人，比上年增加4人，最高分664分。扎佐中学毕业的王定坤夺冠，他以664的高分被北京大学录取，是为1977年恢复高考38年间全县第一个考入北大的学生。

27日　白云至修文道路改扩建工程通车试运，从白云区至县城车程缩短为20分钟左右。白龙线是观山湖区向北连接白云区至修文县的主要通道，道路全长18.03公里。

7月8日　县政府引进山东济南历城第二中学与修文中学联合办学签约，3年内将组建“阳明教育集团”，修文中学新挂牌为“济南市历城二中修文实验学校”。

15—16日　县委常委班子教育实践活动专题民主生活会召开，贵阳市委副书记王保建莅会指导。会议传达贵州省委书记赵克志、贵阳市委书记陈刚关于召开县委专题民主生活会的讲话精神。王保建在会上强调：要以整风精神认真开展批评与自我批评，在坚定理想信念、整治“四风”、改善民生和加快发展上下功夫，进一步坚守信念，改进作风，推进发展，不断巩固教育实践活动成果。贵州省委第一督导组副组长宋强和贵阳市委第二督导组组长吴德屏参加会议并作点评。

8月5日　贵阳市政协组织的高新区、白云区、综保区、修文县同城化发展座谈会在修文召开，来自高新区、白云区、综保区和修文县领导共40余人汇聚一堂，围绕“三区一县”的同城化发展，为实现共赢共荣的目标献计献策。11月12日，高新区、综保区、白云区和修文县签订推进战略合作实现同城化发展的协议。协议明确将通过深化各方战略合作，在三区和修文县的龙场、扎佐、久长区域打造“一廊两带”（大数据走廊、文教旅城产业带和贸工农旅产业带），实现同城化发展。

9月6日　修文县城至金阳客车站的城际快速直达公交车（快巴）开通试车运行，始发站为修文客车站，终点站为金阳客车站。

30日　贵（阳）（节）毕公路修文收费站（改扩建原扎佐收费站）正式投入使用。项目采用收费站出口通道与入口通道错位布置的设计方案，原收费站渠化为5个入口收费通道，改建后原有剩余3个车道不设置收费岛，车辆可直接行驶至在贵（阳）毕（节）公路K39001米处新建的10个出口通道（另外预留2个收费通道空间）处出站。新投用的贵毕公路修文收费站车道由原来的3入5出增加至5入10出。

10月7日　修文中学新校区正式投入使用，校区占地面积250亩，设计办学规模为100个教学班5000个学位，建筑面积8.9万平方米，投资2.89亿元。

11月1日　作为县级公立医院综合改革关键环节之一的“药品零差率”（药品按进价销售）工作在县人民医院正式实施，此为修文县县级公立医院综合改革全面启动。

20日　县禁毒教育基地在职业教育学校开馆。该馆投入近60万元资金于2014年8月进行改造，利用职高350平方米的教室改造成县禁毒教育基地。布置10个教育展厅和1个多功能厅。

是月　上海亚洲果蔬产业秋季博览会拉开序幕，贵州修文猕香苑生态农业科技发展有限公司推展的修文猕猴桃获组委会颁发的“十大最受欢迎果品”称号。

30日　首届西南地区4城市国学经典表演赛结束，修文县选送的《教条示龙场诸生》在成都西南剧场获得一等奖。

12月24日　修文县与贵州迈达盛集团有限公司签订液化天然气项目。项目投资8亿元，日生产能力为100万立方米液化天然气和20万立方米压缩天然气，占地280余亩，可解决近200人的就业问题。

12月31日　国家质检总局发布公告，公布17个国家地理标志保护产品名单，修文猕猴桃名列其中。

2015

1月3日　位于六广河码头（阳明码头）的修文首家温泉—黔贵六广温泉开业。温泉景区占地100余亩，含室外温泉泡池区、接待中心、温泉酒店、户外游览区、码头游船区等，其中室外温泉泡池区置有泡池30余个。

17日　县委第十一届委员会第四次全体（扩大）会议召开，到会委员35人和候补委员7人。会议由县委常委会主持，县委书记石洪讲话。会议主题是贯彻落实中共十八届四中全会、中央经济工作会、中央农村工作会、贵州省委十一届五次全会、全省经济工作会和贵阳市委九届四次全会精神，听取和讨论石洪作的工作报告。县委副书记蒋志伦通报2014年全县经济工作情况并部署2015年的经济工作。县委副书记黄永辉作总结讲话。

27日　县委第十一届第六十六次常委（扩大）会议召开，传达学习贵阳市委关于修文县领导班子人事调整的决定，蒋志伦任中共修文县委书记，不再担任修文县人民政府县长职务；石洪不再担任中共修文县委书记、常委、委员职务；佘龙任中共修文县委委员、常委、副书记，并提名为修文县人民政府县长候选人，娄果任县委委员、常委、组织部长。

31日　县第十五届人大常委会第三十六次会议召开，同意接受蒋志伦辞去县人民政府县长职务，会议全票通过佘龙为县人民政府副县长并代理县长。

2月10—12日　中国人民政治协商会议县第八届委员会第四次会议召开，到会委员156名。会议听取并审议政协县第八届委员会常务委员会工作报告和八届委员会常务委员会关于八届三次会议以来提案工作情况的报告。全体委员列席县第十五届人民代表大会第四次会议，听取《政府工作报告》及其他有关报告。会议选举胡晓明为政协县八届委员会秘书长。

11—13日　县第十五届人民代表大会第四次会议召开，到会代表168名。会议听取并审议县人民政府工作报告、县2014年国民经济和社会发展计划执行情况及2015年国民经济和社会发展计划、县2014年财政预算执行情况及2015年财政预算、县人大常委会工作报告、县人民法院工作报告和县人民检察院工作报告，并对上述报告作出相应的决议。会议选举佘龙为县人民政府县长，贾兆玉为县人民检察院检察长，江之浩、刘丽萍、杨忠平为县第十五届人民代表大会常务委员会委员。

3月17日　贵阳市2015年高中教育教学工作会议公布2014年全市普通高中学校教学质量评估结果。县教育局获贵阳市2014年普通高中教学质量管理一等奖，修文中学获贵阳市2014年区（市、县）大型高中学校“入出口”成绩评估一等奖第一名，两所民办中学获一般高中学校“入出口”成绩评估一等奖。

5月25日　数博会分论坛之一“中国（贵阳）服务外包与呼叫中心发展论坛”在贵阳国际生态会议中心举行。县委常委、副县长廖勇代表修文县政府与贵州源和药业有限公司签署协议，成立修文县首个呼叫中心。

7月6日　县农产品质量安全监督检测站通过国家计量认证，领取资质认定计量认证证书。

9日　修文县举行第二届“感动修文”人物颁奖典礼，李祖炎、苏涌年、殷华忠、李政忠、颜红樱、黄仕碧、黄林、尹洪江、王仕学、毕成江等10位被评为“感动修文”人物。同时，颁奖典礼还表彰孔凡祥等7名“感动修文”人物提名奖。

22日　全县首家农特产品O2O体验店“修文供销集团电商运营中心O2O一号体验店”上线运营。体验店主营修文和贵州各类农特产品，主打修文猕猴桃系列产品。

8月1日　由贵阳大河影视文化传媒有限责任公司投资3000余万元建设的修文县“逸都国际影城”开影。影城投资3000余万元，建筑面积1450平方米。影院拥有3个2K3D立体声数字电影厅，共374个座位。9月中旬开始与全国影院同步放映电影。

27日　全省公务用车制度改革动员大会电视电话会议召开，动员部署全省推进公务用车制度改革工作，副县长廖勇及相关部门在修文分会场参加会议。贵州省公务交通补贴标准上限为：厅级每人每月

1950元，处级每人每月1200元，科级每人每月750元，科员及以下每人每月500元。修文公车改革随之启动。

31日 纪念中国人民抗日战争暨世界反法西斯战争胜利70周年座谈会在县城召开，会议举行赠书仪式，向与会者发放由胡光胤主编的《修文人与抗日战争》一书。

9月5日 县委书记蒋志伦、县长佘龙到“桃源八寨”（大河、大木、独山、葛马、金鸡、水头、西冲、长坡）调研。蒋志伦一行分别到六屯镇西冲、独山等村寨察看村寨后召开座谈会。会议要求要结合“五个定位”（打造国家AAAAA级旅游景区定位、贵州省美丽乡村建设示范点定位、国家级现代高效农业示范园区定位、全国乡村旅游样板村寨定位和全国康体休闲运动示范区定位）对接好规划设计单位，优化提升详规。按照AAAAA级景区和乡村旅游精品示范以及国家级科技农业园区的标准打造，做到每个村寨都有特色。

14日 县委书记蒋志伦到扎佐医药园区就全县医药产业发展情况进行调研。蒋志伦先后走访绿太阳制药、恒和制药、维康药业、华德斯生物制药等4家企业，了解各医药企业生产经营及建设投产情况，听取企业发展规划情况介绍。截至2015年9月，县内拥有制药企业16家，销售企业2家，在建企业3家。2015年上半年，全县医药企业实现规模以上工业总产值26.8亿元，占全县规模以上工业总产值的25.6%，实现工业增加值7.3亿元。全县医药企业累计创造就业岗位3500余个，实现就业4500余人次。

11月6日 为贯彻中共十八届五中全会精神，县委召开精准扶贫、美丽乡村建设和农村环境综合整治现场观摩推进会。会议提出未来美丽乡村要实现“一年大提升，两年大发展，三年大变样”目标。县委书记蒋志伦和县长佘龙率队查看久长镇驴坊村美丽乡村建设和农村环境综合整治情况并走进息烽县部分美丽乡村示范点考察学习。观摩村寨庭院、精品客栈、环境整治和农村电商、现代农业发展情况。考察结束后在县青少年活动中心召开推进会。会议提出做优做靓修文“一核、三带、五线”示范带（一核为桃源八寨，三带为修文至谷堡猕猴桃基地示范带、小箐至洒坪示范带，六广至大石示范带，五线为金扎城市干道、贵遵高速路、贵毕路、白龙大道、息黔高速示范线路）。

19日 第十六届中国绿色食品博览会期间，“采上果”牌修文猕猴桃获绿博会金奖。由修文猕猴桃种植企业、合作社代表参加的商展团远赴上海参加第七届亚洲果蔬产业博览会。“亚果会”组委会授予修文猕猴桃“华东地区最受欢迎的十大果蔬品牌”称号。

12月20日 由县供销集团全资企业—贵州新合电子商务有限公司投资300万元建设的中国供销·修文猕猴桃电商产业园开业。产业园是集农村电商的综合服务运营平台，建设面积1200平方米。

31日 据县统计局统计数据显示，2015年全县生产总值从上年的46.18亿元提升到140.04亿元，是2010年的3.03倍；人均5.38万元，是2010年2.9倍；财政总收入从5.4亿元提升到15亿元，是2010年的2.8倍；公共财政预算收入从2.8亿元提升到8.11亿元，是2010年的2.9倍。

2016

1月4日 县政府与浙江奥林控股集团有限公司、深圳前海福运通国际投资管理有限公司签订修文澳林电子商务商贸城建设项目及扎佐梵森迪水上主题乐园建设项目，实现新的一年招商引资“开门红”。

13日 修文县委第十一届委员会第五次全体（扩大）会议召开，出席会议的县委委员35人、候补委员7人。会议讨论通过《中共修文县委关于制定修文县国民经济和社会发展第十三个五年规划的建议》。

14日　县政府与贵阳银行签署战略合作协议，加强政银合作。

1月30日　“魅力校园”2016第十六届全国校园春节联欢晚会主会场在北京大学落幕。修文县青少年活动中心原创剧目《中华小儿郎》以第二场总分第一名的成绩进入精品专场演出。

2月19日　县委、县政府举行全县2016年首季“开门红”新建企业技改项目集中投产现场会，15家新建企业技改项目集中投产。

22日　贵州省委常委、贵阳市委书记陈刚下到小箐蔬果现代高效农业（扶贫）示范园区和岩鹰山村调研大扶贫战略行动推进情况和美丽乡村建设。

24—26日　中国人民政治协商会议县第八届委员会第五次会议召开，到会委员172名。会议听取并审议政协第八届委员会常务委员会工作报告和第八届四次会议以来提案工作情况的报告。全体委员列席县十五届人民代表大会第五次会议，听取并讨论《政府工作报告》以及其他报告。

25—27日　县第十五届人民代表大会第五次会议召开，到会代表177人。县委副书记、县长佘龙代表县人民政府作《政府工作报告》。报告回顾“十二五”时期工作和提出“十三五”时期的主要目标和任务以及2016年的工作安排。书面报告修文县国民经济和社会发展第十三个五年规划纲要（草案）、2015年国民经济和社会发展计划执行情况及2016年国民经济和社会发展计划（草案）、2015年全县财政预算执行情况及2016年财政预算(草案)并提请代表审议。

26日　中国阳明文化园楹联征集活动组委会召开一期征联作品评审结果通报会。组委会从900多件作品中评出一等奖2件、二等奖4件、三等奖8件、优秀奖40件。

3月4日　香港新源实业有限公司与修文县兴达公司共同投资建设的循环经济产业园暨中国大陆地区重晶石出口总部基地项目、毕节新民中医院和重庆联合金融集团共同投资的新民中医大健康产业城项目达成投资合作协议，随后举行签约仪式。

18日　县委、县政府领导班子2015年度考核测评会议召开，县委书记蒋志伦和县长佘龙分别代表县委班子和县政府班子作2015年述职述廉报告。

29日　省政府副省长刘远坤莅县就县供销社综合改革情况和贵农网修文县级电商运营中心、久长农资电商城、小箐蔬果现代高效休闲观光农业（扶贫）示范园等综合改革项目进行调研。

4月12日　县人民医院举行首届肾友会，庆祝肾病科血液透析室运营，填补了修文县尿毒症治疗的空白。科室拥有德国费森尤斯血液透析机6台、单泵机4台和双泵机2台。

14日　贵州省“科学理论上讲堂”活动启动仪式暨走进机关首场宣讲活动在县城举行。省委党校副校长汪建初以“王阳明的魅力”为主题，作全省“科学理论上讲堂”活动首场开讲。

29日　浙江颐高集团有限公司董事长翁南道莅县考察，与县政府签订大数据产业投资合作框架协议。

5月23日　阳明文化“九进”（机关、进农村、进企业、进学校、进社区、进部队、进景区、进家庭、进商铺）活动启动，活动邀请国务院参事室中国国学中心副主任李文亮和省文联主席、省文史馆馆长顾久到场授课。

6月12日　在青少年活动中心公开举行“修文县公务用车制度改革取消车辆”专场拍卖会，此次拍卖车辆共45辆，拍卖成交后车辆原号牌由贵阳市公安交通管理部门收回。

7月18日　贵州省首个“生产合作+供销合作+信用合作”的“三位一体”新型供销合作社在小箐乡

岩鹰山村挂牌成立。

21日　贵州省社会主义学院“黔浙阳明文化传播中心现场教学基地”授牌仪式在县举行。

8月2日　县政府召开玩易窝公园规划方案汇报会，规划单位汇报玩易窝公园“易化心源”“悟心之路”两个规划方案的设计构想，并就方案设计提出相关意见和建议。

17日　修文县委第十一届委员会第六次全体会议召开，出席全会的县委委员35人和候补委员7人。会议审议通过关于召开中共修文县第十二次代表大会的决议，表决通过乡（镇）党政正职人选提名。

是月　修文县获2016年国家级电子商务进农村综合示范县称号，是贵阳市唯一1个入选的区（市、县）。

9月2日　县委第十一届委员会第七次（全体）扩大会议召开。会议对党政领导班子五年来工作开展情况进行总结，并进行民主评议和民主测评，全额定向推荐新一届党委、人大、政府、政协领导班子成员及法院院长、检察院检察长、纪委副书记人选。

13日　县委、县政府举行项目集中签约仪式，共签约贵州体验网络商务有限公司微蒂酒柜、云计算呼叫中心BPO产业基地等6个项目，项目总投资33亿元。

25日　县城公交车运营启动，开通两条公交线路，设候车点28个，上路公交车8辆。

28日　第五届国际阳明文化节新闻发布会在贵阳召开，市委宣传部副部长、市社科联主席李云，县委书记蒋志伦分别介绍第五届国际阳明文化节活动和筹备工作情况，并回答记者提问。

10月12日　第二届猕猴桃节在谷堡乡平滩村举行，同时举行三大特色活动，分别是采果品果音乐鉴赏会、中国水果话语权高峰论坛和《印象猕猴桃.走进修文》风情歌舞表演。修文县获国家级出口猕猴桃质量安全示范区授牌。

20—21日　中共修文县第十二次代表大会召开，到会代表231人。大会听取和讨论县委县委书记蒋志伦作《关于十一届县委工作报告》和县纪委书记卢燕作《关于十一届县纪委工作报告》并作出相应的决议。大会以无记名投票的方式选举产生十二届委员会委员、县纪委委员会委员和修文县出席贵阳市第十次党代会大会代表。在县第十二届委员会第一次全体会议上，会议选举产生中国共产党修文县委新一届领导班子，蒋志伦当选为中共修文县第十二届委员会书记，佘龙、何发兵当选为副书记，王渝琪、文清武、卢燕、刘元珍、何清伦、娄果、廖勇当选为常务委员。在县第十二届纪律检查委员会召开第一次全体会议上，选举卢燕、蒋春禔、彭钟槿、邓丈冰、刘述雁、唐德贵、蒲朝阳等7人为中共修文县第十二届纪律检查委员会常务委员，卢燕任书记，蒋春禔、彭钟槿任副书记。

28日　贵阳市第七届旅游产业发展大会在县召开，大会主题为“以全域旅游理念打造世界旅游名城”。现场签约21个重点旅游项目，签约资金831.1亿元。

是月　县王阳明纪念馆新馆举行开馆仪式。该馆于2016年开建，共投入3000万元资金增建馆楼一栋，建筑面积3600平方米。馆藏国家一级文物—王阳明记功碑复制品和阳明学专著600余册。

29日　2016中国·贵阳（修文）第五届国际阳明文化节在修文揭幕。开幕式后接着举办阳明文化节主旨论坛、丙申年祭祀王阳明典礼、“我心光明—走进王阳明咏诵会”大型演出等活动。30日，文化节在颐和大酒店闭幕。

11月3日　县委、县政府召开2016中国贵阳（修文）第五届国际阳明文化节及贵阳市第七届旅游发展大会工作总结会，表彰24家先进集体和373名先进个人。

9日　根据县政府《关于久长镇久长村“村改居”的批复》，撤销久长村民委员会，改置青龙居民委员会。青龙居民委员会辖区即原久长村民委员会辖区。居委会办公室即原久长村委会办公室。

根据县政府《关于珍珠河社区服务中心红桥村和新园村“村改居”的批复》，撤销扎佐红桥村和新园村2个村民委员会，改置红桥居民委员会和新园居民委员会。红桥居民委员会和新园居民委员会辖区即原红桥村委会和新园村委员辖区。居委会办公室沿用原村委会办公室。

是月　根据县政府《关于龙场镇城南村和城北村“村改居”的批复》，撤销城南村和城北村2个村民委员会，改置成翠屏居民委员会和中山居民委员会。翠屏居民委员会和中山居民委员会辖区即原城南村委会和城北村员会辖区，居委会办公室沿用原村委办公室。至此，全县居民委员会有龙岗、栖凤、宾阳、虎山、翠屏、中山、景阳、襄阳、珍珠河、红桥、新园、万江、长久、青龙、松江、小箐、盐井等共17个，其中龙岗、栖凤、宾阳、虎山隶属龙岗社区服务中心，翠屏、中山隶属龙场镇政府，景阳、襄阳、珍珠河、红桥、新园隶属珍珠河社区服务中心，万江居委会隶属扎佐镇政府，长久、青龙居委会隶属久长镇政府，松江居委会隶属六广镇政府，小箐居委会隶属小箐乡政府，盐井居委会隶属六桶镇政府。

12月8日　修文旅游文化产业投资开发有限公司与重庆华宇园林有限公司签约。小箐乡崇恩森林公园融资项目总投资5亿元。实施项目包括小箐乡崇恩森林公园、小箐园区至茶山连路大道、小箐园区至金鸡项目美丽乡村建设。

9日　国家教育督导检查组在贵阳召开国家义务教育发展基本均衡县督导检查反馈会，修文县以95.5分排名全省第三和全市第二，达到国家规定的义务教育发展均衡县评估认定标准。

28日　县委副书记、县长佘龙主持召开县委十二届第八次常委（扩大）会议，传达学习全省经济工作会议和贵阳市委第十届第二次常委（扩大）会议精神，对全县经济工作安排部署。会议强调要强化机遇意识、自知意识和忧患意识，全面提升学习研究能力、改革创新能力和执行落实能力，打响项目建设大会战、产品提质持久战和打好增比进位保位战，奋力开创全县经济工作的新局面。

是月　县委、县政府规划将农业园区建设、美丽乡村建设、农村环境综合整治与千园之城紧密结合，建成6个省级现代高效农业示范园区。具体是谷堡果畜高效生态农业示范园区、小箐蔬果现代高效观光农业（扶贫）示范园区、久长美丽茶山休闲观光农业示范园区、洒坪山地特色农业（果蔬）示范园区、桃源河现代生态观光农业示范园区和六广现代高效农旅示范园区。6个园区规划总面积为37万亩，涉及6个乡（镇）17个行政村，辐射带动10乡（镇）113个村的发展。园区围绕“菜、畜、果、药”四大主导产业发展猕猴桃、花卉苗木、果蔬、中药材、畜禽养殖等精品产业，实施种养一体化立体循环发展。截至11月，园区总投入资金为26.82亿元，总产值达33.26亿元，实现销售收入32.05亿元，园区核心区内农村居民人均可支配收入第三季度达1.34万元，比园区外其他地区的农村居民人均可支配收入高50%以上。

是月　修文县2016年增比进位新体系综合测评得分82.21，在全省县域第一方阵22个县中排位第三。

2017

1月3—7日　中国人民政治协商会议县第九届委员会第一次会议召开，到会委员168名。会议听取并审议政协县第八届委员会常务委员会工作报告和提案工作报告。全体委员列席县十六届人民代表大会第一次会议，听取并讨论县人民政府工作报告和其他报告。选举政协修文县第九届委员会主席、副主席、秘书长、常务委员。审议通过政协修文县第九届委员会第一次会议提案审查情况报告，政协修文县第九届委员会第一次会议决议。会议举行换届选举，王世利当选为政协修文县第九届委员会主席，王雄飞、杨杏、王朝惠、姚文贵、李晓阳、甘泽志当选为副主席。

5—8日 县第十六届人民代表大会第一次会议召开，到会代表181人。县长佘龙代表县人民政府作《政府工作报告》。报告过去五年的工作回顾和今后五年的主要目标任务以及2017年的工作安排并提出坚持致良知、尽己责、全面加强政府自身建设的要求。会议还听取并审议县人大常委会工作报告和提案工作报告，审议全县国民经济和社会发展执行情况，财政预决算执行情况及其下步安排意见，听取法院、检察院工作报告。会议举行换届选举，张江华当选为县人大常委会主任，汤建祥、王天镜、胡祥碧、张杰、朱永彬、李继彬当选为副主任，佘龙当选为县长，廖勇、杨志义、谭永红、左军、唐德富、肖伦文当选为副县长，田松当选为县人民法院院长，贾兆玉当选为县人民检察院检察长。会议通过《关于修文县人民政府工作报告的决议》《关于修文县2016年国民经济和社会发展计划执行情况与2017年国民经济和社会发展计划的决议》《关于修文县2016财政预算执行情况与2017年财政预算的决议》《关于修文县第十五届人大常委会工作报告的决议》《关于修文县人民法院工作报告的决议》和《关于修文县人民检察院工作报告的决议》。

18日 县政府与北京阳光嘉瑞科技开发有限公司、贵州申御体育旅游发展有限公司、四川省宏盛源商贸有限公司和湖北省财源科技有限公司等企业对扎佐温泉养老、贵州高原水上竞技等6个项目进行签约，项目总投资14.6亿元。

19日 县委安排开展中共十八届六中全会、省委十一届八次全会和贵阳市第十次党代会精神宣讲报告会，由市委宣讲团成员张海涛主讲。县四大班子领导、县人大和县政协委室负责人、各乡（镇）和县直各部门负责人200余人聆听报告。

25日 县委常委召开2016年度“两学一做”（学党章党规、学系列讲话，做合格党员）专题民主生活会，书面通报2015年度“三严三实”（严以修身、严以用权、严以律己，谋事要实、创业要实、做人要实）专题民主生活会查摆问题整改落实情况。班子成员之间认真进行对照检查，深入查摆问题，认真开展批评与自我批评，明确整改措施和今后努力方向。市委常委、纪委书记朱江华，市纪委常委、秘书长宁康，市委组织部副部长、非公和社会组织工委书记路喜宏到会指导。

2月8日 贵阳市委副书记、市长刘文新率市直相关单位部门负责人深入到龙场镇、六屯镇和谷堡乡调研扶贫相关工作。刘文新强调要增强信心，鼓足干劲，用好三种资源（政策资源、市场资源、自身资源），在全省新一轮大扶贫战略工作中走前列、作表率。

9日 “全国社会科学普及教育基地”授牌仪式在阳明文化园举行。

10日 县委第十二届第十一次常委（扩大）会议召开，传达学习《关于深入推进农业供给侧结构性改革、加快培育农业农村发展新动能的若干意见》和贵阳市留守儿童困境儿童关爱救助保护暨“合力监护，相伴成长”专项行动推进会议精神，传达学习《关于实施中华优秀传统文化传承发展工程意见》和贵阳市委副书记、市长刘文新赴修文调研易地扶贫搬迁及扶贫开发工作讲话精神。

22日 贵阳市第四届农业嘉年华暨修文县2017一季度项目集中开工仪式在桃源八寨举行。当天“桃源八寨”农业嘉年华、金鸡产业扶贫、玩易窝路修筑工程等17个项目集中开工，总投资60.9亿元，涉及扶贫产业、基础设施、民生及社会事业项目等多个领域。

23日　县委书记蒋志伦主持召开第十二次常委（扩大）会议，传达学习《中共贵州省委、贵州省人民政府2017年脱贫攻坚春季攻势行动令》和《省委常委、市委书记陈刚在清镇市调研大扶贫攻坚工作座谈会上的讲话》精神，传达学习贵州省委办公厅转发《中央信访工作联席会议办公室关于贵州省毕节市纳雍县27名信访人在京自伤自残事件及其教训警示的通报》，书面传达贵阳市委十届七次常委会议精神，并结合全县实际对近期脱贫攻坚、信访维稳、经济工作、安全生产和招商引资等重点工作进行安排。

3月3日　以“倡导雷锋精神、弘扬阳明文化，学习先进典型，争做知行模范”为主题的志愿服务活动在县体育馆启动。

7日　贵州省委常委、贵阳市委书记陈刚率队莅县调研指导易地扶贫搬迁与产业脱贫工作。陈刚强调，要认真学习领会贯彻落实省委、省政府关于脱贫攻坚的系列决策部署精神，易地扶贫搬迁与产业脱贫是引领“高一格脱贫，快一步致富”的关键，是让群众“一步住上新房子，逐步过上好日子”的关键。

19日　澳林电子商贸城举行招商签约盛典活动。当天，澳林电子商贸城与修文县域电商服务中心签订入驻，与贵阳银行、修文县农村信用社签署战略合作协议。与此同时，现场圣象地板、雷士照明等20家主力品牌商户亦签约入驻。

24日　县委书记蒋志伦主持召开县委第十二届第十三次常委（扩大）会议，传达学习全国“两会”、全省领导干部大会及第十次、十一次市委常委会会议精神，部署近期重点工作。

4月5日　县政府在会议中心举行农商旅联动和精准扶贫示范项目签约仪式，标志着农商旅联动发展工程正式启动。

21日　根据中共贵阳市委筑干任〔2017〕111号《关于蒋志伦同志不再担任职务的通知》，并经2017年4月21日市委常委会议讨论决定，蒋志伦不在担任中共修文县委书记、常委、委员职务。

25日　县委副书记、县长佘龙主持召开县委十二届第十五次常委（扩大）会议，强调全县上下要把学习好、领会好、宣传好、贯彻好、落实好省党代会精神作为当前和今后一个时期的政治任务，迅速掀起学习贯彻热潮，知行合一，不断跨越，让省委的决策部署在修文落地落实。

27日　贵州“黔青梦工厂”在县创业小镇揭牌，是为共青团贵州省委在全省所有县份工业园区内挂牌成立的首家以“互联网+创客+乡土”“互联网+创客+健康”“互联网＋创客＋文创”为主题的创客基地。

5月11日　全省项目建设观摩组莅县观摩猕猴桃产业发展情况和了解示范引领情况。观摩组点赞修文猕猴桃产业是山地特色农业的引领者与示范区，是引领农村脱贫的新希望。参加观察组的全省各部门、各地州市和区县有关领导在观摩中听取县委副书记、县长佘龙介绍全县扶贫支柱产业修文猕猴桃发展的情况。

24日　县委、县政府举行贵州省生物医药大数据及科技成果转化服务平台项目签约仪式。按照签约协议，贵州省药品大数据平台、贵州省医药科技成果转化服务平台等项目将在县内建设运营，进一步推动全县现代医养高地暨心健康发祥地的打造。

25日　县委副书记、县长佘龙主持召开县委常委（扩大）会议，学习贯彻2017全省第一次项目建设现场观摩会、全市深化改革领导小组第二十二次会议等省市相关会议精神，审议有关议题，对脱贫攻坚、禁毒、环保、深化改革等当前重要工作进行部署。

31日　县委召开全县领导干部大会，宣布省委关于孙华忠任中共修文县委书记的决定。贵阳市委常委、市委组织部部长王华平出席会议并讲话。

6月3日 由北京国际城市发展研究院和贵州大学贵阳创新驱动发展战略研究院联合编撰的最新智库成果—《贵阳城市创新发展报告NO.2》正式发布。其中《修文篇》以修文县“十三五”如何支撑贵阳市建设创新型中心城市为研究对象，系统提出全力打造阳明心学圣地、特色农业基地、现代医养高地，奋力探索以山地为特色的新型城镇化建设新路的发展战略。

13—14日 参加2017年贵阳市“三农”工作现场观摩会的嘉宾走进修文，具体了解修文多年坚持把产业扶贫作为扶贫攻坚的主攻方向，努力推动农业“农旅对接”接二连三发展，深一层推进大扶贫战略的经验和做法。观摩组下到久长镇茶山休闲观光农业示范园区奶山羊养殖基地，现场观摩奶山羊发展模式和助农增收成效。

18日 全县开展“保护母亲河 河长大巡河”“6·18”生态日主题活动，正式启动县、乡、村三级河长制，进一步建立健全河湖管理保护体制机制，加快实施大生态战略，努力实现百姓富、生态美有机统一的良好发展态势。

26日 县委十二届第二十三次常委（扩大）会议召开，传达学习中共中央总书记习近平在深度贫困地区脱贫攻坚座谈会上的重要讲话精神和中央政治局常委、中央纪委书记王岐山在贵州检查纪检监察工作时的重要讲话精神，以及贵州省委、贵阳市委常委会议精神，并结合实际研究从严治党和经济运行等工作。

7月3日 根据黔府函〔2017〕144号《省人民政府关于同意撤销修文县谷堡乡、小箐乡设立谷堡镇、小箐镇的批复》，同意撤销谷堡乡设立谷堡镇，以原谷堡乡行政区划为谷堡镇的行政区划，谷堡镇人民政府驻折溪村。同意撤销小箐乡设立小箐镇，以原小箐乡行政区划为小箐镇的行政区划，小箐镇人民政府驻小箐村。

6日 贵阳警备区宣布修文县人武部领导班子任命称：经中共贵阳警备区党委研究决定，同意增补孙华忠为修文县人武部党委委员、第一书记，李秦林为修文县人武部党委委员、副书记，王戈为修文县人武部党委委员、纪委书记，李家亮为修文县人武部党委委员。遵照中央军委国防动员部命令，李秦林任修文县人武部部长，李利亚任修文县人武部政委。

7日 农业部党组成员、办公厅主任叶贞琴一行莅县调研“不忘初心，坚韧不拔，笃实创新，久久为功”的修文猕猴桃精神，打造修文猕猴桃产业现代农业升级版，深一层推进大扶贫战略的做法和经验。

17日 县委第十二届第二十五次常委（扩大）会议召开，传达学习全国金融工作会议精神、全省领导干部会议精神和市委常委会议精神。会议强调全县上下要坚决拥护中央决定，自觉维护以孙志刚书记为班长的省委班子权威，全力维护好全县风清气正、干事创业的良好政治生态，以安全稳定和谐的社会环境迎接党的十九大胜利召开。

27日 县委书记、县人武部党委第一书记孙华忠主持召开2017年议军会。孙华忠强调 全县上下要用心用情解决好驻县部队的实际困难，进一步强化抓经济不忘固国防、搞建设，不忘兴武装、谋发展的理念，把子弟兵的冷暖放在心上，把部队建设抓在手上，使武装工作、国防建设、经济社会发展同步推进、同步提升。

8月14日 “爱心传递热线”创始人徐坤带领30余位失独老人走进六广河温泉，开始了一场旅游疗伤之行。同时将全国首条老年人心理危机救助热线“爱心传递线”带进修文，入驻修文各乡（镇）和社区，为全县老人提供电话陪聊、心理疏导、心理危机化解等心理救助。

15日　贵旅集团党委副书记、副董事长、总经理祝胜修率集团相关负责人莅县考察旅游资源，并与县政府签订战略合作框架协议。

16日　全县2017年经济工作暨脱贫攻坚推进大会召开。会议强调要以习近平总书记系列重要讲话精神为指导，贯彻落实好贵州省第十二次党代会、贵阳市第十次党代会和全省半年经济工作会、深度贫困地区脱贫攻坚工作推进会等会议精神，围绕目标真抓实干，努力在建设公平共享创新型中心城市中作出应有的贡献。

31日　县委十二届第三十次常委（扩大）会议召开，传达学习8月29日贵州省委常委会议精神和贵阳市委常委（扩大）会议精神和贵州省脱贫攻坚秋季攻势行动暨农村“组组通”公路三年大决战启动大会精神，通报全县1至8月份经济运行情况。

9月9日　由贵州大学、贵州师范大学和贵州民族大学的30多位彝学专家、教授、考古人士组成的专家考察团走进大石布依族乡大屯村，实地考察水西安氏土司安贵荣墓遗址，并就王阳明与安贵荣的历史渊源以及2人在思想上的相互影响等学术问题进行深入交流探讨。

18日　贵阳市“组组通”公路共建项目在龙场镇放马坪村正式启动。

19日　修文县与贵州省物资集团、碧桂园公司召开座谈会，协调解决贵州凤凰谷大健康产业项目推进过程中存在的问题。项目总投资20亿元，旨在打造以温泉为核心，以休闲养生、度假疗养和高品质低密度住宅为支撑的特色化、精品化、高端化新型生态养生产品大健康产业城。

21日　新西兰植物和食品研究所专家考察团莅县考察指导修文猕猴桃产业。

23日　“阳明心学之旅”徒步活动在修文王阳明纪念馆广场正式开幕。

25日　贵阳市委外宣办副主任邓作朋主持召开贵阳市第四届农业嘉年华暨第三届猕猴桃节新闻发布会。发布会确定修文农业嘉年华将于9月28日上午在六屯镇独山村心净桃源预开园迎客，市民可免费游览，当天将举行舞狮、舞龙、威风锣鼓、现场音乐会等活动。

28日　县委、县政府召开第四届贵阳（修文）农业嘉年华暨贵阳市第三届猕猴桃节动员大会，听取工作筹备情况，研究解决最后的冲刺难题，要求举全县之力，只争朝夕，全力冲刺，打造贵阳市升级版的农业嘉年华与猕猴桃节。

30日　县委、县政府举行“铭记历史，缅怀先烈，珍爱和平，开创未来”烈士纪念日公祭活动。

10月10日　第四届贵阳农业嘉年华暨第三届猕猴桃节在六屯镇独山村隆重开幕，贵州省委常委、贵阳市委书记李再勇出席并宣布开幕。开幕式上，县委书记孙华忠致辞。中国农业大学农业规划科学研究所贵州分所、中国高原猕猴桃原生谷、以色列阿森沃亩创新农业公司现代农业科技研发中心（中国）揭牌成立。中国果品流通协会发布修文猕猴桃发展指数。

18日　县委、县政府和各乡（镇）、各部门干部集中收看中国共产党第十九次全国代表大会开幕式，听取中共中央总书记习近平向大会作题为《决胜全面建成小康社会　夺取新时代中国特色社会主义伟大胜利》的报告。

20日　白云区与修文县举行工作洽谈会议，双方就“飞地经济”合作事宜和白金大道延伸段（靛山隧道）建设事宜进行洽谈，并签署《修文县·白云区高新产业园区投资合作协议》。

24日　国家林业局驻贵阳专员办副专员喻泽龙一行莅临小箐镇岩鹰山村，调研岩鹰湖湿地公园项目推进情况。

27日 “我们的节日·重阳”暨第三届“感动修文人物”颁奖典礼在县城体育馆举行，刘元珍、陆胜军、冉树华、文建华、王庆华、王庆碧、刘发莲、陈贵碧、唐亚忠、张昌玉等10位被评为“感动修文”人物，同时，活动还表彰郑勇、陈天妃2名“感动修文”人物提名奖。

31日 县政府与西安汉唐通用机场建设有限公司就“修文县通用航空机场合作项目”举行签约仪式。西安汉唐通用机场建设有限公司将在修文出资建设机场，标准为通用航空A1级，包括停机坪、服务设施区等，项目占地500亩。

11月9日 县委、县政府举行中共十九大精神宣讲报告会，由贵州省政协原副主席、省督查组组长孙国强到会作专题辅导报告。宣讲会上,孙国强围绕中共十九大报告的内容和精神实质，从新时代、新集体、新思想、新作为、新改革、新党章、新未来7个“新”对党的十九大报告及新修订的《中国共产党章程》进行了详细的解读。

17日 县委第十二届委员会第三次全体会议召开。会议主题是：传达学习贯彻中共十九大精神，贯彻落实省委十二届二次、市委十届二次全会精神，审议通过《中共修文县委关于大生态战略修文行动实施意见（草案）》。会议要求全县各级各部门深入宣传贯彻落实党的十九大精神和习近平总书记在贵州省代表团重要讲话精神，自觉践行“创新、协调、绿色、开放、共享”发展理念，始终坚守发展和生态两条底线，围绕“三地一路”（打造阳明心学圣地、特色农业基地、现代医养高地，奋力探索一条山地特色新型城镇化道路）发展定位和“3355”（即三个目标：建成更高水平的全面小康社会，创建全国文化旅游名县，建成全省大健康医药产业示范县；三张名片：阳明文化、修文猕猴桃、桃源八寨；五大行动路径：大数据、大文化、大健康、大旅游、大民生；五美修文：产业美、文化美、生态美、环境美、精神美）发展目标，加快推进大生态战略，为贵州全省建设生态文明先行示范区和贵阳全市建成生态文明示范城市以及续写“王学圣地·秀美修文”新篇章作出应有的贡献。

22日 “温暖贵州·慈善行——大手牵小手·关注留守儿童”之“你好，阳光少年”福彩公益活动在六屯镇中心小学举行，陈明鸣等省、市、县领导共同为全省第十一个留守儿童信箱揭牌。

是月 水利部珠江水利委员会党组成员、巡视员王秋生一行莅县开展第三次全面推行河长制督导检查。

24日 国务院妇儿工委办公室儿童工作处干部曾国强带队莅县对久长镇和小箐镇儿童之家项目进行实地调研，并在座谈会上对县创建的“爱心妈妈+儿童之家”新的工作模式表示肯定。

30日 中华全国供销合作总社党组成员、理事会副主任肖仲恺一行莅县调研供销合作社综合改革工作。

12月5日 县委书记孙华忠主持召开县城三条河流生态综合治理规划专题会强调，三条河流的生态综合治理，是生态文明城市建设的需要，是广大人民群众的期盼，是经济社会发展的支撑，也是一座城市形象的必需。要求在实施过程中务必做到水与城相交、城与水相融、城因水而美、水因城而秀，真正让老百姓看得见山、望得见水、记得住乡愁。

15日 县委、县政府召开王阳明旅游文化演艺综合体项目初步方案专题汇报会，听取设计单位汇报规划编制情况，研究讨论王阳明旅游文化演艺综合体项目建设的必要性和可行性，深入分析该项目投入运营以后对宣传阳明文化以及助推修文经济社会发展方面的作用。

19日 中国核工业西南局贵州公司副总经理余光茂一行莅县寻找合作项目。

21日　以色列驻成都总领事馆商务官Aviv Doron阿维率以色列部分企业负责人莅县就设施农业水肥一体化等工作进行考察。

27日　县政府与贵阳旅文投资集团就苏格兰牧场合作事宜座谈。市旅文集团表示下一步将全力以赴支持修文，敞开合作，按照要求做好策划特色旅游项目建设，真正把苏格兰牧场做成贵阳市旅游环线上的特色小镇。

28日　县举行强制隔离戒毒所启用仪式。强制隔离戒毒所于2015年10月开工平场，2017年10月圆满竣工，历时3年建成。占地120亩，建筑面积2.5万平方米，其中行政楼6500平方米，总投资8900万元，总关押量850人。设有戒毒治疗区、拘留区、文化教育区、体育锻炼区、技能培训区、劳动就业、学员区等功能区域，预留“科学戒管、长期联动”单位办公室，配有智能化消费系统、直饮水系统、电教系统、通信系统和监控系统。

31日　据省统计局对全省27个经济强县2017年国民经济运行情况进行考评后的排位资料，修文县生产总值绝对数居全省的第13位，人均生产总产值居第9位，人均一般公共预算收入居第18位，农村居民人均可支配收入居第11位。

是月　贵阳市举行重大工业项目集中开工仪式，总投资6.3亿元的5个重点工业项目（贵州金天力药业、贵州德玛门控公司、贵州陈氏设备公司、贵州大能农通邦公司、贵州健瑞安药业）在修文分会场集中开工。

是月　渝（重庆）贵（贵阳）客专铁路上总投资1.7亿元的“修文县站”主体工程全部竣工。车站坐落在扎佐镇，是贵阳北站前往重庆经停的第一站。修文县站项目作为修文县的窗口和形象工程，将是修文区域性、交通枢纽型新型车站中心，从修文到重庆，只需2个小时的车程即可抵达。

二、2011—2017年全县国民经济和社会发展主要数据资料

公安年报人口及变化一览表

指　标	单位	2011年	2012年	2013年	2014年	2015年	2016年	2017年
总户数	户	91802	94969	97546	90693	100537	100697	101263
总人口	人	310061	305815	305546	308439	318617	321613	324743
其中:男	人	160644	159253	159661	159793	164941	167016	168147
女	人	149417	146562	145885	148646	153676	154597	156596
其中:非农业人口	人	40866	40526	40623	40809	43797	101514	106618
农业人口	人	265252	262497	262989	266269	274820	220099	218125
年平均人口	人	307989	307938	305681	306993	313528	320115	323178
迁入人口	人	2478	2613	2293	2130	2185	4006	1191
迁出人口	人	1615	2578	2147	2380	2947	4756	949
出生人口	人	3307	3960	4483	5481	11573	6496	6979
其中:男	人	1790	2200	2461	2883	5968	3440	3631
女	人	1517	1760	2022	2598	5605	3056	3348
死亡人口	人	1587	4784	1642	1748	1744	2132	2473
其中:男	人	916	2393	1012	994	1003	1202	1426
女	人	671	2391	630	754	741	930	1047
人口出生率	‰	10.74	12.86	14.67	17.9	36.9	20.3	21.5
人口死亡率	‰	5.15	15.54	5.37	5.7	5.6	6.7	7.6
人口自增率	‰	5.59	-2.86	9.3	12.2	31.3	13.6	13.9

注：2015年起，“非农业人口”为“城镇人口”，“农业人口”为“农村人口”

全县生产总值一览表

单位：万元

指　标	2011年	2012年	2013年	2014年	2015年	2016年	2017年
生产总值合计	576733	712352	887306	1197824	1400368	1655741	1874025
第一产业	87062	102680	116502	160020	195308	213451	230103
占生产总值比重(%)	15.10	14.41	13.13	13.36	13.95	12.89	12.28
第二产业	235097	317944	394228	548450	613619	785640	893086
占生产总值比重(%)	40.76	44.63	44.43	45.79	43.82	47.45	47.66
其中:工　业	181750	245632	293075	421576	458411	605683	686980
建筑业	53347	72312	101153	126874	155208	179957	206106
第三产业	254574	291728	376576	489354	591411	656650	750836
占生产总值比重(%)	44.14	40.96	42.44	40.85	42.23	39.66	40.07
1.交通运输、仓储及邮电业	57779	65548	77813	96965	130091	141501	164396
2.批发零售及贸易业	33503	39601	45467	57808	63858	68413	78569
3.住宿和餐饮业	2584	2892	3971	5689	6861	7450	10349
4.金融业	24338	28612	39317	54471	78150	96980	129527
5.房地产业	13621	13744	21612	26091	28778	29780	28033
6.其他营利性服务业	8911	11178	21722	27263	35772	42603	61039
7.非营利性服务业	113838	130153	166734	221067	247931	256517	264843

县级财政收支一览表

单位：万元

指　标	2011年	2012年	2013年	2014年	2015年	2016年	2017年
一般公共预算收 入	38682	54229	55888	70305	81071	88406	91164
其中:增值税	3588	3972	5287	7254	9663	18382	21013
营业税	9572	13911	11930	9945	9095	7913	55
一般公共财政预算支出	110409	138327	168320	200911	218639	250235	252119
其中:一般公共服务支出	20706	29239	38304	42634	37412	49159	41012
教育支出	25432	26149	32112	40265	52293	53063	13607
医疗卫生支出	10779	15216	16284	23881	28736	28567	20838
社保和就业支出	10641	12813	12319	11749	12110	13916	23667
科学技术支出	1342	1201	1597	1502	1590	4388	4427

金融一览表

单位：万元

指　标	2011年	2012年	2013年	2014年	2015年	2016年	2017年
年末存款余额	328671	412612	507060	576085	704947	982842	1267241
其中：储蓄存款	198702	253339	303800	358544	377858	462194	559276
年末贷款余额	228947	272124	328895	417422	601211	743215	1054796
其中：短期贷款	86830	129744	156203	190073	217230	243992	312996
中长期贷款	140621	140170	172692	227025	377934	463785	739836

注：“年末贷款余额”数中，含贷款单位及个人透支款在内

全部工业企业总产值（现价）一览表

单位：万元

指　标	2011年	2012年	2013年	2014年	2015年	2016年	2017年
全部工业总产值	851893	1161345	1672939	2065095	2136112	3077708	3563760
其中：县及县以下	851893	1161345	1672939	2065095	2136112	3077708	3563760
1. 500万元以上工业企业	800438	1098480	1608832	1991631	2061214	—	—
其中：国有企业	104061	119383	102029	91286	110248	—	—
集体企业	—	—	—	—	—	—	—
私营企业	170272	208470	226329	318256	379068	—	—
外资企业	166021	174131	263782	244309	144864	—	—
2. 500万元以下工业企业	51455	62865	64107	73464	74898	—	—
3. 2000万元以上 工业企业	—	—	—	—	—	2961978	3455328
其中：国有企业	—	—	—	—	—	149148	198280
集体企业	—	—	—	—	—	1943	2012
私营企业	—	—	—	—	—	481926	685402
外资企业	—	—	—	—	—	150329	131087
4. 2000万元以下工业企业	—	—	—	—	—	115730	108432

注：2016年起，“规模以上”工业企业标准为企业年主营业务收入2000万元及以上。取消原来执行企业年主营业务收入500万元及以上的标准

规模以上企业工业增加值一览表

单位：万元

指　标	2011年	2012年	2013年	2014年	2015年	2016年	2017年
工业增加值	193845	302335	384934	487583	574485	686623	885339
1.国有控股企业	24264	44901	36310	52294	59465	157415	201308

续表

指　标	2011年	2012年	2013年	2014年	2015年	2016年	2017年
2.非公有制企业	151868	164530	344553	419112	506551	518317	675873
3.高技术产业	71233	134253	140705	197882	185017	207651	183084
4.重点产业（行业）	—	—	—	—	—	560082	722404
（一）、按轻重工业分	—	—	—	—	—	—	—
轻工业	91746	160648	214810	292886	385472	450705	593357
重工业	102099	141687	170124	194697	189013	235918	291983
（二）、按登记注册类型分	—	—	—	—	—	—	—
国有企业	24264	24988	23260	16002	19955	32469	38189
集体企业	—	—	—	—	—	267	276
股份合作企业	—	—	—	—	—	—	—
联营企业	—	—	—	—	—	—	—
有限责任公司	59072	126493	193296	336649	426094	358740	523731
股份有限公司	2592	3667	5331	5625	9242	81822	100713
私营企业	51298	59551	58554	67234	69304	106400	180824
外商及港澳台投资企业	56618	87636	104493	62074	49890	106924	41530
（三）、按企业规模分	—	—	—	—	—	—	—
大型	21151	63780	36852	34332	34324	177586	134107
中型	41166	85388	34204	99562	246961	203252	314058
小微型	131527	141615	313920	353689	293200	305785	437175

规模以上工业企业主要产品产量一览表

产品名称	计量单位	2011年	2012年	2013年	2014年	2015年	2016年	2017年
原煤	吨	1448493	838644	888045	373762	604025	389901	288056
水泥	吨	2053495	2261566	2440081	2473322	2350760	1992839	1757869
耐火材料制品	吨	128443	176021	337607	495454	468582	409635	76240
生铁	吨	169158	263032	278700	277572	360154	213168	134804
粗钢	吨	—	—	—	—	70801	52621	236355
氧化铝	吨	96216	191982	35647	351995	403978	160260	165022
纸制品	吨	—	11053	46835	160865	279644	607007	691950
商品混凝土	立方米	—	39548	1337842	1339349	1946142	2186609	2125513
钢结构	吨	—	—	—	—	—	134997	169865
乳制品	吨	14226	17078	22274	25562	27579	31882	32902

续表

产品名称	计量单位	2011年	2012年	2013年	2014年	2015年	2016年	2017年
饮料酒	千升	220	387	480	1335	3970	7906	9286
中成药	吨	3960	14511	4445	7116	7361	27240	18713
橡胶轮胎外胎	条	—	—	—	—	—	3447121	4956427
碳化钙(电石)	吨	44132	57419	61649	—	—	—	—
铁合金	吨	48829	71386	112224	193825	75505	—	—
饲料	吨	37715	136354	178176	259211	264733	300284	325986
发电量	万千瓦时	110901	191228	139996	214288	227902	211279	194204
供电量	万千瓦时	89655	102308	99423	165697	194813	233937	—

农村基本情况一览表

指　标	单位	2011年	2012年	2013年	2014年	2015年	2016年	2017年
1.乡村户数	户	71285	82789	84948	88846	85250	81329	85331
2.乡村人口	人	263234	270395	269757	278246	274820	262179	273687
3.乡村从业人员数	人	168099	162884	165373	171371	173906	173802	189484
其中:男	人	89872	88177	88569	91699	92372	93665	96568
女	人	78227	74707	76797	79672	81534	80137	92916
4.从业人员按行业分	人	168099	162884	165373	171371	173906	173802	189484
①农业	人	89499	91014	84628	83832	83536	78975	96338
②工业	人	9399	11090	13425	14319	14091	15483	15202
③建 筑业	人	7212	7267	10507	11532	13507	20261	19987
④交通运输、仓储和邮政业	人	4448	5132	7023	8006	7856	8577	9524
⑤信息传输、计算机服务和软件业	人	—	—	—	2418	2342	2295	3819
⑥批发零售住宿餐饮业	人	11081	8996	11159	12425	12667	13747	6862
⑦其他行业	人	46198	38422	37328	38839	39907	34464	37752
其中:外出打工一月以上	人	39225	29527	30137	32315	37362	31054	22532
年末耕地	公顷	17467	17394	17394	17394	17394	17394	17394
其中:田	公顷	6279	6279	6279	6279	6279	6279	6217
化肥施用实物量	吨	19612	19516	20660	21144	24329	23923	23507
①氮肥	吨	6778	6698	6696	7098	8085	8218	8083
②磷 肥	吨	8264	7907	7909	7226	7157	7661	7096
③钾肥	吨	1406	1506	2130	1730	1738	1735	2022

续表

指 标	单位	2011年	2012年	2013年	2014年	2015年	2016年	2017年
④复合肥	吨	3164	3405	3925	5090	7349	6309	6306
农药使用量	吨	35	36	35	41	39	37	35
有效灌溉面积	千公顷	4.94	5.25	5.26	7．23	7.3	7.3	7.9
农用机械总动力	万千瓦	19.09	21.00	22.00	24.00	26.00	26.00	27.15

现价农业总产值·现价农业增加值一览表

单位：万元

指 标		2011年	2012年	2013年	2014年	2015年	2016年	2017年
农业总产值	合 计	144737	167826	191511	253258	293799	344758	387158
	1.农 业	101450	119214	137201	182130	192940	223703	252205
	占总产值比重(%)	70.09	71.03	71.64	71.92	65.67	64.89	65.10
	2.林 业	843	907	1284	840	499	444	469
	占总产值比重(%)	0.58	0.54	0.67	0.33	0.17	0.13	0.12
	3.牧 业	41459	46639	51872	69059	83253	101009	113652
	占总产值比重(%)	28.65	27.79	27.09	27.27	28.34	29.30	29.36
	4.渔 业	595	653	719	743	820	755	746
	占总产值比重(%)	0.41	0.39	0.37	0.29	0.28	0.22	0.19
	5.农业服务业	390	414	435	486	16287	18847	20086
	占总产值比重(%)	0.27	0.25	0.23	0.19	5.54	5.46	5.19
农业增加值	合 计	87062	102680	116502	160020	195308	226857	244183
	1.农 业	64644	72260	82362	117420	133177	154319	164397
	占总增加值比重(%)	74.25	70.37	70.69	73.38	68.19	68.02	65.14
	2.林 业	574	608	981	550	247	192	205
	占总增加值比重(%)	0.66	0.59	0.84	0.34	0.12	0.08	0.12
	3.牧 业	21269	29018	32282	41112	49036	58360	64930
	占总增加值比重(%)	24.43	28.26	27.71	25.69	25.11	25.73	29.36
	4.渔 业	286	481	544	568	645	580	571
	占总增加值比重(%)	0.33	0.47	0.47	0.36	0.33	0.26	0.19
	5.农业服务业	289	313	333	370	12203	13406	14080
	占总增加值比重(%)	0.33	0.31	0.29	0.23	6.25	5.91	5.19

主要农产品产量一览表

指　标	单位	2011年	2012年	2013年	2014年	2015年	2016年	2017年
1.粮食总产量	吨	71442	78685	80620	89891	90170	91577	72277
其中：秋粮	吨	48867	55951	56641	63020	64286	66574	56173
2.油菜籽产量	吨	7558	14088	10663	12539	13457	13581	14954
3.烤烟产量	吨	2325	2403	2757	1841	1458	1475	1251
4.蔬菜产量	万吨	31.66	36.28	39.70	42.33	45.62	53.03	56.39
5.水果产量	吨	26198	29523	32409	35611	52730	67489	91424
其中：猕猴桃	吨	6996	8120	8886	10305	34983	44000	60845
6.中草药产量	吨	—	—	—	7431	7823	1423	4800
7.茶叶产量	吨	65	156	168	345	353	357	362
8.大牲畜：年末存栏	头	39574	41989	42569	48700	44398	37517	33715
大牲畜年内出栏	头	14265	14588	15591	14938	15688	16953	22982
9.生猪、年末存栏	头	100942	120086	126598	143621	196038	191156	194758
生猪年内出栏	头	160776	166258	170127	170830	170869	145085	148474
10.家禽年内出栏	万羽	—	—	—	115.71	116.29	138.60	160.87
11.肉类总产量	吨	17599	18578	19515	19744	20100	18718	19547
12.牛奶产量	吨	—	—	—	27097	30548	25695	27803
13.禽蛋产量	吨	3233	3505	3608	3720	4097	5343	7281
14.水产品产量	吨	269	269	279	279	307	302	401

注：表中有“—”符号的，表明有产量，但无统计资料

固定资产投资一览表

单位：万元

指　标	2011年	2012年	2013年	2014年	2015年	2016年	2017年
一、全社会固定资产投资	902586	1450216	1760500	2244463	—	—	—
其中：基本建设	76501	213156	316405	507009	—	—	—
更新改造	655727	1105058	1351737	1616110	—	—	—
其他投资	37005	14327	19239	28395	—	—	—
房地产投资	65307	58246	73119	7923	—	—	—
农村私人	33254	21287	26355	51158	—	—	—
万元—50万元以下投资	29792	17542	20655	38792	—	—	—
跨地区项目投资	5000	20600	26109	51015	—	—	—
二、500万元以上项目固定资产投资	—	—	—	—	1976145	2382027	2916686

续表

指　标	2011年	2012年	2013年	2014年	2015年	2016年	2017年
1.按产业分	—	—	—	—	—	—	—
第一产业	—	—	—	—	415683	674503	587900
第二产业	—	—	—	—	709304	680328	911640
第三产业	—	—	—	—	851158	1027196	1417146
2.资金来源	—	—	—	—	1976145	2382027	2644147
①国家资金	—	—	—	—	34127	28562	8306
②贷　款	—	—	—	—	20208	226292	630538
③自筹资金	—	—	—	—	1921810	2217173	2005303
其中:企业事业自有资金	—	—	—	—	1921810	56328	70261
三、新增固定资产	—	—	—	—	1892566	2172568	2324987

注：2015年“500万元以上项目固定资产投资”栏为“50万元以上项目固定资产投资”数据

邮政·电信一览表

指　标	单位	2011年	2012年	2013年	2014年	2015年	2016年	2017年
一、邮政业务总量	万元	895	919	1200	1288	1591	1760	1953
二、邮电局所数	处	10	10	10	10	11	12	12
其中:农村局所	处	8	8	8	8	9	10	10
三、邮路总条数	条	24	24	24	24	24	24	24
四、电信业务总量	万元	13834	14906	—	19316	21900	17100	26724
五、电信电话用户	户	237765	251205	238210	303138	317386	294000	408538
其中:乡镇电话用户	户	30600	20050	—	23005	25060	33000	51638
移动电话用户	户	207165	231155	238210	280133	292326	261000	356900

社会消费品零售总额一览表

单位：万元

指　标	2011年	2012年	2013年	2014年	2015年	2016年	2017年
社会消费品零售总额	121560	142468.3	163964.3	188765.7	226803.2	257421.6	289856.7
按消费单位所在地分	—	—	—	—	—	—	—
1.城　镇	50981	59412	68373.1	78757.5	94854.4	107943.9	118841.2
其中:城区	—	17467	20101.7	23124.5	27945.7	31959.8	34939.2
2.乡　村	70579	83056.3	95591.2	110008.2	131948.8	149477.7	171015.5
按销售单位规模分	—	—	—	—	—	—	—
1.限额以上		15671.9	22713.1	40600.2	53313.1	96668.5	123282.6
2.限额以下	121560	126796.4	141251.2	148165.5	173490.1	160753.1	166574.1

教育·卫生一览表

	指 标	单位	2011年	2012年	2013年	2014年	2015年	2016年	2017年
教育	一、学校数	所	85	78	89	92	89	92	93
	1.普通中学	所	17	17	15	17	14	14	14
	2.农职中学	所	2	2	2	2	1	1	1
	3.特殊学校	所	1	1	1	1	1	1	1
	4.小　学	所	49	43	43	41	35	32	32
	5.幼儿园	所	16	15	26	31	38	44	45
	二、在校生人数	人	40313	38697	39394	41346	42819	45700	50125
	1.普通中学	人	17467	16456	13906	15471	14375	14260	13983
	2.农职中学	人	847	757	1958	495	249	227	195
	3.特殊学校	人	219	112	154	149	129	107	98
	4.小　学	人	16877	16222	15999	16962	18564	20805	23207
	5.幼儿园	人	4903	5150	7377	8269	9502	10301	12642
	三、小学适龄儿童入学率	%	99.6	—	—	—	—	—	—
	四、初中适龄少年入学率	%	106.5	—	—	—	—	—	—
卫生	五、卫生机构数	个	31	238	265	241	252	224	231
	六、卫生机构床位数	张	590	703	825	890	1016	1176	1220
	七、卫生机构工作人员	人	862	1483	1637	1651	1792	613	560
	其中:卫生技术人员	人	696	1268	985	993	1260	511	1887
	其中:执业(助理)医师	人	231	310	349	441	396	215	578

职工人数、工资总额·城乡居民人均可支配收入一览表

指 标	单位	2011年	2012年	2013年	2014年	2015年	2016年	2017年
一、年末在岗职工合计	人	16425	19402	—	—	—	—	—
1.国有单位	人	8061	8800	—	—	—	—	—
2.城镇集体单位	人	717	856	—	—	—	—	—
3.其他单位	人	7647	9746	—	—	—	—	—
二、年末在岗职工工资总额	万元	56528.7	80361.3	—	—	—	—	—
1.国有单位	万元	35963.8	45505.3	—	—	—	—	—
2.城镇集体单位	万元	3326.6	4194.8	—	—	—	—	—
3.其他单位	万元	17238.3	30661.2	—	—	—	—	—

续表

指 标	单位	2011年	2012年	2013年	2014年	2015年	2016年	2017年
三、非私营单位从业人数	人	—	—	21046	23173	23392	30405	26610
按企、事业、机关分组		—	—	—	—	—	—	—
1.企 业	人	—	—	12942	14072	14287	21589	17495
2.事 业	人	—	—	5837	6600	6404	5989	6065
3.机 关	人	—	—	2267	2501	2701	2827	3050
四、按产业分组:第一产业	人	—	—	141	182	148	148	150
第二产业	人	—	—	11025	12053	12052	19485	15031
第三产业	人	—	—	9880	10938	11192	10772	11429
五、非私营单位工资总额	万元	—	—	100549	127196	146255	199537	188291
1.企 业	万元	—	—	51226	65671	78192	125899	108849
2.事 业	万元	—	—	35651	44667	46314	49643	52487
3.机 关	万元	—	—	13672	16858	21749	23995	26955
六、城镇居民年人均可支配收入	元	18721	21720	22558	23601	26113	28586	31302
七、农村居民年人均可支配收入	元	6470	7460	8492	9807	10856	11904	13130

三、人物表和人物名录

2011—2017年县委书记、副书记和常务委员一览表

界别	任次	职务	姓名	性别	民族	籍贯	文化程度	起任年龄	任职起讫年月	备注
第十届	第二十九任	县委书记	石　洪	男	汉	贵州开阳	硕士	48	2011.1—2011.11	
		县委副书记	蒋志伦	男	汉	湖南衡阳	研究生	44	2011.1—2011.11	
		县委副书记	王成林	男	汉	贵州修文	大学	50	2011.1—2011.10	
		县委副书记	黄永辉	男	汉	贵州息烽	大学	46	2011.10—2011.11	
		县委副书记	向子琨	男	土家	重庆	大学	35	2011.1—2011.11	挂任
		县委常委	阮晓燕	女	汉	贵州贵阳	研究生	38	2011.1—2011.10	
		县委常委	刘　瑜	男	汉	河南内乡	研究生	42	2011.1—2011.10	
		县委常委	陈雄标	男	汉	广西荔浦	大学	50	2011.1—2011.10	
		县委常委	张　恺	男	汉	贵州修文	研究生	37	2011.1—2011.10	
		县委常委	向　东	男	汉	重庆	大学	46	2011.1—2011.11	
		县委常委	董桂文	男	汉	河南临颍	研究生	43	2011.1—2011.9	挂任
		县委常委	李利亚	男	汉	贵州遵义	大学	41	2011.1—2011.11	
		县委常委	谢国波	男	汉	贵州贵阳	大学	35	2011.10—2011.11	
		县委常委	黄学东	男	汉	四川自贡	大学	43	2011.4—2011.11	挂任
		县委常委	张　君	女	汉	四川资阳	研究生	38	2011.10—2011.11	
		县委常委	金　松	男	汉	浙江浦江	大学	39	2011.10—2011.11	
		县委常委	闫　寒	男	汉	辽宁抚顺	研究生	46	2011.10—2011.11	
		县委常委	吕念东	女	汉	重庆荣昌	硕士	43	2011.10—2011.11	
第十一届	第三十任	县委书记	石　洪	男	汉	贵州开阳	硕士	51	2011.11—2015.1	
		县委副书记	蒋志伦	男	汉	湖南衡阳	研究生	47	2011.11—2015.1	
		县委副书记	黄永辉	男	汉	贵州息烽	大学	46	2011.11—2015.1	
		县委副书记	向子琨	男	土家	重庆	大学	36	2011.11—2012.1	挂任
		县委常委	向　东	男	汉	重庆	大学	47	2011.11—2012.5	
		县委常委	李利亚	男	汉	贵州遵义	大学	42	2011.11—2015.1	

续表

界　别	任次	职务	姓　名	性别	民族	籍贯	文化程度	起任年龄	任职起讫年月	备注
第十一届	第三十任	县委常委	闫　寒	男	汉	辽宁抚顺	研究生	46	2011.11—2012.6	
		县委常委	吕念东	女	汉	重庆荣昌	硕士	43	2011.11—2012.9	
		县委常委	张　君	女	汉	四川资阳	研究生	38	2011.11—2014.3	
		县委常委	金　松	男	汉	浙江浦江	大学	39	2011.11—2015.1	
		县委常委	谢国波	男	汉	贵州贵阳	大学	35	2011.11—2015.1	
		县委常委	黄学东	男	汉	四川自贡	大学	43	2011.11—2012.4	挂任
		县委常委	王　健	男	布依	贵州长顺	大学	42	2012.5—2013.3	
		县委常委	廖　勇	男	土家	贵州思南	硕士	42	2012.12—2015.1	
		县委常委	倪　毅	男	汉	浙江余姚	大学	38	2012.4—2014.4	挂任
		县委常委	王光华	男	汉	四川新都	研究生	43	2013.3—2014.12	
		县委常委	刘元珍	女	汉	贵州贵阳	大学	47	2013.11—2015.1	
		县委常委	何淑平	男	汉	重庆	大学	49	2013.4—2014.3	挂任
		县委常委	黄良忠	男	汉	江西萍乡	大学	46	2014.3—2015.1	
		县委常委	马艳华	男	布依	贵州长顺	研究生	33	2014.5—2015.1	挂任
		县委常委	梁晓杰	男	汉	山东莱阳	博士	40	2014.8—2015.1	挂任
		县委常委	杨　慧	女	苗	贵州毕节	大学	41	2014.8—2015.1	挂任
	第三十一任	县委书记	蒋志伦	男	汉	湖南衡阳	研究生	51	2015.1—2016.10	
		县委副书记	佘　龙	男	汉	湖南邵东	硕士	42	2015.1—2016.10	
		县委副书记	黄永辉	男	汉	贵州息烽	大学	51	2015.1—2015.4	
		县委副书记	张江华	男	汉	河南林州	大学	50	2015.7—2016.10	
		县委副书记	马艳华	男	布依	贵州长顺	研究生	34	2015.4—2016.3	挂任
		县委副书记	何发兵	男	彝	贵州大方	大学	47	2016.9—2016.10	
		县委常委	李利亚	男	汉	贵州遵义	大学	46	2015.1—2016.10	
		县委常委	黄良忠	男	汉	江西萍乡	大学	47	2015.1—2016.9	
		县委常委	金　松	男	汉	浙江浦江	大学	43	2015.1—2016.9	
		县委常委	廖　勇	男	土家	贵州思南	硕士	45	2015.1—2016.10	
		县委常委	刘元珍	女	汉	贵州贵阳	大学	49	2015.1—2016.10	
		县委常委	娄　果	男	汉	贵州桐梓	大学	42	2015.1—2016.10	
		县委常委	何清伦	男	汉	贵州清镇	大学	51	2015.4—2016.10	
		县委常委	马艳华	男	布依	贵州长顺	研究生	34	2015.1—2015.4	挂任
		县委常委	梁晓杰	男	汉	山东莱阳	博士	41	2015.1—2015.7	挂任

续表

界　别	任次	职务	姓　名	性别	民族	籍贯	文化程度	起任年龄	任职起讫年月	备注
第十一届	第三十一任	县委常委	杨　慧	女	苗	贵州毕节	大学	42	2015.1—2015.8	挂任
		县委常委	白兴利	男	汉	山东招远	硕士	40	2015.7—2016.7	挂任
		县委常委	黄顺江	男	土家	贵州思南	大学	51	2016.1—2016.10	挂任
		县委常委	卢　燕	女	汉	贵州大方	大学	48	2016.9—2016.10	
		县委常委	王渝琪	男	汉	贵州开阳	大学	41	2016.9—2016.10	
		县委常委	王学斌	男	汉	山东潍坊	博士	35	2016.8—2016.10	挂任
第十二届	第三十二任	县委书记	蒋志伦	男	汉	湖南衡阳	研究生	52	2016.10—2017.4	
		县委副书记	佘　龙	男	汉	湖南邵东	硕士	43	2016.10—2017.5	
		县委副书记	何发兵	男	彝	贵州大方	大学	47	2016.10—2017.4	
		县委副书记	王胜利	男	汉	山东齐河	大学	42	2017.4—2017.5	
		县委常委	廖　勇	男	土家	贵州思南	硕士	46	2016.10—2017.5	
		县委常委	刘元珍	女	汉	贵州贵阳	大学	50	2016.10—2017.1	
		县委常委	娄　果	男	汉	贵州桐梓	大学	43	2016.10—2017.5	
		县委常委	何清伦	男	汉	贵州清镇	大学	52	2016.10—2017.5	
		县委常委	卢　燕	女	汉	贵州大方	大学	48	2016.10—2017.5	
		县委常委	王渝琪	男	汉	贵州开阳	大学	41	2016.10—2017.5	
		县委常委	文清武	男	汉	贵州修文	大学	42	2016.10—2017.5	
		县委常委	黄顺江	男	土家	贵州思南	大学	51	2016.10—2017.5	挂任
		县委常委	王学斌	男	汉	山东潍坊	博士	35	2016.10—2017.5	挂任
		县委常委	何　峰	男	汉	山西繁峙	大学	54	2017.1—2017.5	挂任
	第三十三任	县委书记	孙华忠	男	汉	贵州瓮安	大学	54	2017.5—2017.12	
		县委副书记	佘　龙	男	汉	湖南邵东	硕士	44	2017.5—2017.12	
		县委副书记	王胜利	男	汉	山东齐河	大学	42	2017.5—2017.12	
		县委常委	廖　勇	男	土家	贵州思南	硕士	47	2017.5—2017.12	
		县委常委	娄　果	男	汉	贵州桐梓	大学	44	2017.5—2017.12	
		县委常委	何清伦	男	汉	贵州清镇	大学	53	2017.5—2017.12	
		县委常委	卢　燕	女	汉	贵州大方	大学	49	2017.5—2017.12	
		县委常委	王渝琪	男	汉	贵州开阳	大学	42	2017.5—2017.12	
		县委常委	文清武	男	汉	贵州修文	大学	43	2017.5—2017.12	
		县委常委	黄顺江	男	土家	贵州思南	大学	52	2017.5—2017.12	挂任
		县委常委	王学斌	男	汉	山东潍坊	博士	36	2017.5—2017.8	挂任
		县委常委	何　峰	男	汉	山西繁峙	大学	54	2017.5—2017.12	挂任
		县委常委	张　勇	男	汉	山东泰安	博士	35	2017.8—2017.12	挂任

2011—2017年县人大常委会主任、副主任一览表

界别	任次	职　务	姓　名	性别	民族	籍贯	文化程度	起任年龄	任职起讫年月	备注
第十四届	第十任	主　任	李玉轩	男	汉	贵州修文	大专	56	2011.1—2011.3	
		副主任	何先祥	男	汉	贵州修文	大专	54	2011.1—2011.3	
		副主任	宋庆豪	男	汉	贵州修文	大学	52	2011.1—2011.3	
		副主任	孙庆英	女	汉	贵州修文	大学	49	2011.1—2011.3	
		副主任	罗永翔	男	苗	贵州修文	大专	49	2011.1—2011.3	
		副主任	王天镜	男	汉	贵州息烽	大学	43	2011.1—2011.3	
	第十一任	主　任	王成林	男	汉	贵州修文	大学	53	2011.3—2012.1	
		副主任	何先祥	男	汉	贵州修文	大专	59	2011.3—2012.1	
		副主任	宋庆豪	男	汉	贵州修文	大学	57	2011.3—2012.1	
		副主任	孙庆英	女	汉	贵州修文	大学	54	2011.3—2012.1	
		副主任	罗永翔	男	苗	贵州修文	大专	54	2011.3—2012.1	
		副主任	王天镜	男	汉	贵州息烽	大学	48	2011.3—2012.1	
第十五届	第十二任	主　任	王成林	男	汉	贵州修文	大学	54	2012.1—2017.1	
		副主任	孙庆英	女	汉	贵州修文	大学	55	2012.1—2017.1	
		副主任	罗永翔	男	苗	贵州修文	大专	55	2012.1—2017.1	
		副主任	张　杰	男	汉	贵州修文	大专	46	2012.1—2017.1	
		副主任	朱永彬	男	汉	贵州修文	大学	48	2012.1—2017.1	
		副主任	刘元珍	女	汉	贵州贵阳	大学	46	2012.1—2013.11	
		副主任	王朝惠	男	汉	贵州修文	大学	46	2012.1—2017.1	
		副主任	文清武	男	汉	贵州修文	大学	38	2012.1—2013.3	
		副主任	谭永红	女	汉	贵州修文	硕士	42	2013.3—2017.1	
		副主任	李继彬	男	汉	贵州修文	大学	48	2014.2—2017.1	
第十六届	第十三任	主　任	张江华	男	汉	河南林州	大学	52	2017.1—2017.12	
		副主任	汤建祥	男	汉	贵州修文	大学	55	2017.1—2017.12	
		副主任	王天镜	男	汉	贵州息烽	大学	54	2017.1—2017.12	
		副主任	胡祥碧	女	汉	贵州开阳	大学	51	2017.1—2017.12	
		副主任	张　杰	男	汉	贵州修文	大学	51	2017.1—2017.12	
		副主任	朱永彬	男	汉	贵州修文	大学	53	2017.1—2017.12	
		副主任	李继彬	男	汉	贵州修文	大学	51	2017.1—2017.12	

2011—2017年县人民政府县长、副县长一览表

界别	任次	职务	姓名	性别	民族	籍贯	文化程度	起任年龄	任职起讫年月	备注
第十四届	第二十三任	县　长	蒋志伦	男	汉	湖南衡阳	研究生	45	2011.1—2012.1	
		副县长	刘　瑜	男	汉	河南内乡	研究生	43	2011.1—2011.10	
		副县长	王雄飞	男	汉	湖南慈利	大学	44	2011.1—2012.1	
		副县长	吕念东	女	汉	重庆荣昌	硕士研究生	41	2011.1—2012.1	
		副县长	石　洋	男	汉	山东招远	大学	31	2011.1—2011.9	
		副县长	汤建祥	男	汉	贵州修文	大专	47	2011.1—2012.1	
		副县长	童雪涛	女	汉	安徽和县	硕士研究生	39	2011.1—2012.1	挂任
		副县长	董桂文	男	汉	河南临颍	研究生	43	2011.1—2011.10	挂任
		副县长	谢国波	男	汉	贵州贵阳	大学	35	2011.7—2011.10	
		副县长	黄学东	男	汉	四川自贡	大学	43	2011.6—2012.1	挂任
		副县长	闫　寒	男	汉	辽宁抚顺	硕士研究生	46	2011.10—2012.1	
		副县长	裴　斌	男	汉	四川成都	硕士	40	2011.10—2012.1	
第十五届	第二十四任	县　长	蒋志伦	男	汉	湖南衡阳	研究生	48	2012.1—2015.1	
		代理县长	佘　龙	男	汉	湖南邵东	硕士	42	2015.1—2015.2	
		副县长	闫　寒	男	汉	辽宁抚顺	硕士研究生	47	2012.1—2012.10	
		副县长	汤建祥	男	汉	贵州修文	大专	50	2012.1—2015.2	
		副县长	王天镜	男	汉	贵州息烽	大学	49	2012.1—2015.2	
		副县长	童雪涛	女	汉	安徽和县	硕士研究生	40	2012.1—2012.4	挂任
		副县长	裴　斌	男	汉	四川成都	硕士	41	2012.1—2015.2	
		副县长	邓　波	男	汉	四川成都	硕士	40	2012.1—2013.1	
		副县长	王　劼	女	布依	贵州修文	工程硕士	37	2012.1—2013.2	
		副县长	黄学东	男	汉	四川自贡	大学	44	2012.1—2012.10	挂任
		副县长	廖　勇	男	土家	贵州思南	硕士	43	2013.1—2015.2	
		副县长	文清武	男	汉	贵州修文	大学	39	2013.3—2015.2	
		副县长	何淑平	男	汉	重庆	大学	49	2013.5—2014.8	挂任
		副县长	胡祥碧	女	汉	贵州开阳	大学	47	2013.11—2015.2	
		副县长	倪　毅	男	汉	浙江余姚	大学	38	2012.4—2014.8	挂任
		副县长	马艳华	男	布依	贵州长顺	研究生	33	2014.7—2015.2	挂任
		副县长	梁晓杰	男	汉	山东莱阳	研究生博士	40	2014.8—2015.2	挂任
		副县长	杨　慧	女	苗	贵州毕节	大学	41	2014.8—2015.2	挂任
		副县长	周珊珊	女	汉	湖北当阳	研究生博士	37	2014.12—2015.2	挂任

续表

界别	任次	职　务	姓名	性别	民族	籍贯	文化程度	起任年龄	任职起讫年月	备注
第十五届	第二十五任	县 长	佘 龙	男	汉	湖南邵东	硕士	42	2015.2—2017.1	
		副县长	廖 勇	男	土家	贵州思南	硕士	45	2015.2—2017.1	
		副县长	汤建祥	男	汉	贵州修文	大专	53	2015.2—2017.1	
		副县长	文清武	男	汉	贵州修文	大学	41	2015.2—2017.1	
		副县长	胡祥碧	女	汉	贵州开阳	大学	49	2015.2—2017.1	
		副县长	裴 斌	男	汉	四川成都	硕士	44	2015.2—2016.9	
		副县长	王天镜	男	汉	贵州息烽	大学	52	2015.2—2017.1	
		副县长	马艳华	男	布依	贵州长顺	研究生	34	2015.2—2015.6	挂任
		副县长	梁晓杰	男	汉	山东莱阳	研究生博士	41	2015.2—2015.8	挂任
		副县长	杨 慧	女	苗	贵州毕节	大学	42	2015.2—2015.8	挂任
		副县长	周珊珊	女	汉	湖北当阳	研究生博士	38	2015.2—2015.10	挂任
		副县长	白 薇	女	回	广西永福	大学	46	2015.7—2016.9	挂任
		副县长	黄顺江	男	土家	贵州思南	大学	51	2016.2—2017.1	挂任
		副县长	王学斌	男	汉	山东潍坊	研究生博士	35	2016.9—2017.1	挂任
		副县长	杨志义	男	汉	贵州开阳	大学	48	2016.9—2017.1	
		副县长	臧 翊	男	汉	江苏扬州	大学	54	2016.9—2017.1	挂任
		副县长	白兴利	男	汉	山东招远	研究生	40	2015.8—2016.9	挂任
		副县长	吴心旷	男	汉	安徽庐江	硕士	34	2016.12—2017.1	挂任
第十六届	第二十六任	县 长	佘 龙	男	汉	湖南邵东	硕士	44	2017.1—2017.12	
		副县长	廖 勇	男	土家	贵州思南	硕士	47	2017.1—2017.12	
		副县长	黄顺江	男	土家	贵州思南	大学	52	2017.1—2017.12	挂任
		副县长	王学斌	男	汉	山东潍坊	研究生博士	36	2017.1—2017.9	挂任
		副县长	何 峰	男	汉	山西繁峙	大学	54	2017.4—2017.12	挂任
		副县长	张 勇	男	汉	山东泰安	研究生博士	35	2017.8—2017.12	挂任
		副县长	杨志义	男	汉	贵州开阳	大学	49	2017.1—2017.12	
		副县长	谭永红	女	汉	贵州修文	硕士	46	2017.1—2017.12	
		副县长	左 军	男	汉	贵州修文	大学	43	2017.1—2017.12	
		副县长	唐德富	男	苗	贵州修文	大学	49	2017.1—2017.12	
		副县长	肖伦文	男	汉	贵州修文	工程硕士	36	2017.1—2017.12	
		副县长	臧 翊	男	汉	江苏扬州	大学	55	2017.1—2017.4	挂任
		副县长	吴心旷	男	汉	安徽庐江	硕士	35	2017.1—2017.12	挂任
		副县长	王志良	男	汉	北京	博士	36	2017.4—2017.12	挂任
		副县长	张 弘	女	汉	辽宁新民	研究生	52	2017.5—2017.12	挂任

2011—2017年县政协主席、副主席一览表

界别	任次	职务	姓　名	性别	民族	籍贯	文化程度	起任年龄	任职起讫年月	备注
第七届	第八任	主　席	殷建中	男	汉	湖南岳阳	大学	54	2011.1—2012.1	
		副主席	陈国邦	男	布依	贵州修文	大学	50	2011.1—2012.1	
		副主席	王世利	男	汉	四川古蔺	大学	41	2011.1—2012.1	
		副主席	邓　波	男	汉	四川成都	硕士	34	2011.1—2012.1	
		副主席	胡祥碧	女	汉	贵州开阳	大学	40	2011.1—2012.1	
		副主席	林　江	男	汉	广东兴宁	大学	42	2011.1—2012.1	
第八届	第九任	主　席	陈雄标	男	汉	广西荔浦	大学	54	2012.1—2017.1	
		副主席	陈国邦	男	布依	贵州修文	大学	56	2012.1—2016.9	
		副主席	王世利	男	汉	四川古蔺	大学	47	2012.1—2017.1	
		副主席	王雄飞	男	汉	湖南慈利	大学	47	2012.1—2017.1	
		副主席	胡祥碧	女	汉	贵州开阳	大学	46	2012.1—2013.11	
		副主席	林　江	男	汉	广东兴宁	大学	45	2012.1—2014.2	
		副主席	杨　杏	女	汉	贵州瓮安	大学	46	2012.1—2017.1	
		副主席	田江涛	男	土家	贵州沿河	研究生课程进修班结业	42	2012.1—2016.9	
		副主席	姚文贵	男	汉	安徽舒城	大学	53	2014.2—2017.1	
		副主席	李晓阳	男	汉	贵州毕节	大学	49	2014.2—2017.1	
第九届	第十任	主　席	王世利	男	汉	四川古蔺	大学	52	2017.1—2017.12	
		副主席	王雄飞	男	汉	湖南慈利	大学	52	2017.1—2017.12	
		副主席	杨　杏	女	汉	贵州瓮安	大学	51	2017.1—2017.12	
		副主席	王朝惠	男	汉	贵州修文	大学	51	2017.1—2017.12	
		副主席	姚文贵	男	汉	安徽舒城	大学	56	2017.1—2017.12	
		副主席	李晓阳	男	汉	贵州毕节	大学	52	2017.1—2017.12	
		副主席	甘泽志	男	汉	贵州黔西	工程硕士	46	2017.1—2017.12	

2011—2017年其他部门担任副县级领导职务者一览表

职务	姓名	性别	民族	籍贯	文化程度	起任年龄	任职起讫年月	备注
人民法院院长	徐　涛	男	汉	河南安阳	研究生	46	2011.1—2016.12	
人民法院代理院长	田　松	男	汉	山东齐河	硕士	39	2016.12—2017.1	
人民法院院长	田　松	男	汉	山东齐河	硕士	40	2017.1—2017.12	
人民检察院检察长	丁泽军	男	汉	重庆	硕士研究生	38	2011.1—2011.10	

续表

职务	姓　名	性别	民族	籍贯	文化程度	起任年龄	任职起讫年月	备注
代理检察长	段　炼	男	苗	贵州松桃	硕士	40	2011.10—2012.2	
人民检察院检察长	段　炼	男	苗	贵州松桃	硕士	41	2012.2—2014.12	
代理检察长	贾兆玉	男	汉	河南邓州	大学	46	2014.12—2015.3	
人民检察院检察长	贾兆玉	男	汉	河南邓州	大学	47	2015.3—2017.12	
公安局局长	向　东	男	汉	重庆	大学	44	2011.1—2012.6	
公安局局长	王　健	男	布依	贵州长顺	大学	42	2012.6—2012.10	
公安局局长	周永斌	男	汉	贵州开阳	大学	43	2012.10—2017.12	
公安局政委	杨　波	男	汉	山东菏泽	大学	42	2011.1—2015.6	
公安局政委	吴敦红	男	汉	安徽怀远	大学	49	2015.11—2017.12	
党校常务副校长	金　松	男	汉	浙江浦江	大学	39	2011.1—2011.10	
党校常务副校长	李红雨	男	布依	贵州修文	大学	45	2012.7—2017.12	
经济开发区党工委副书记　管委会副主任	林　江	男	汉	广东兴宁	大学	46	2014.1—2017.12	
工业园区建设开发办公室党委委员　常务副主任	谌　勇	男	汉	贵州修文	大学	50	2011.1—2017.12	
经济开发区党工委委员管委会副主任	邓理青	女	布依	贵州清镇	研究生	42	2014.12—2017.12	
经济开发区党工委委员管委会副主任	朱启军	男	汉	贵州修文	大学	40	2015.9—2017.12	
县人武部部长	童代平	男	汉	贵州松桃	大学	45	2011.1—2011.3	
县人武部部长	罗　涛	男	汉	重庆江津	大学	39	2011.3—2013.3	
县人武部政委	李利亚	男	汉	贵州遵义	大学	47	2016.9—2017.12	
县人武部部长	李云峰	男	汉	贵州遵义	大学	37	2013.3—2016.2	
县人武部部长	李秦林	男	汉	湖南邵阳	大学	42	2017.4—2017.12	
县人民政府党组成员	王　劼	女	布依	贵州修文	工程硕士	38	2013.2—2017.12	

2011—2017年修文籍人在外地行政、事业部门担任副县级及其以上领导职务者一览表

姓　名	性别	民族	文化程度	任　职　情　况				备注
				职　务	级　别	任职单位	任职起讫年月	
李建国	男	汉	硕士研究生	常务副部长	正厅级	贵州省委宣传部	2011.1—2014.11	
伍鹏程	男	汉	博士	校　长	正厅级	贵州师范大学	2011.1—2014.12	

续表

姓名	性别	民族	文化程度	任职情况				备注
				职务	级别	任职单位	任职起讫年月	
肖明龙	男	汉	省委党校在职研究生	副县长	副县(处)级	威宁彝族回族苗族自治县人民政府	2011.1—2011.1	
				副书记	副厅级	共青团贵州省委	2011.1—2014.8	
				副州长	副厅级	贵州省黔东南州	2014.8—2017.12	
陈其勇	男	汉	大学本科	副主任	副厅级	安顺市人大常委会	2011.1—2017.12	
李昌伦	男	汉	大学本科	调研员	县(处)级	安顺市科学技术协会	2011.1—2017.12	
卢永康	男	汉	中央党校在职研究生	秘书长	县(处)级	贵阳市政治协商会议委员会	2011.1—2015.12	
胡晓刚	男	汉	研究生	局　长	县(处)级	贵阳市监察局	2011.1—2013.9	
				纪检组长 局长	县(处)级	贵州省能源局纪检组 贵阳市监察局	2013.9—2014.1	
				纪检组长	县(处)级	贵州省能源局党组成员　省纪委派驻能源局纪检组	2014.1—2015.8	
				纪检组长	县(处)级	贵州省旅游局党组成员　省纪委派驻旅游局纪检组	2015.8— 2016.6	
				纪检组长	县(处)级	贵州省旅发委党组成员　省纪委派驻旅发委纪检组	2016.6—2017.12	
朱丽霞	女	汉	中央党校在职研究生	局　长	县(处)级	贵阳市商务局	2011.1—2011.10	
				区委副书记　区长	县(处)级	贵阳市南明区委　区政府	2011.11—2014.10	
				区委书记	县(处)级	贵阳市南明区	2014.10—2017.2	
				副主任 区委书记	副厅级	贵阳市人大常委会　贵阳市南明区委	2017.2—2017.12	
李嘉宁	男	汉	中央党校在职研究生	主任 副秘书长	县(处)级	贵阳市委党史研究室 贵阳市委	2011.1—2012.2	
				副秘书长 主任	县(处)级	贵阳市委　市委政策研究室	2012.2—2015.2	
				委员 主任	县(处)级	贵阳市人大常委会 市人大常委会农业经济民族宗教委员会	2015.2—2016.7	
				副校长	县(处)级	贵阳市委党校	2016.7—2017.12	
陆庆华	男	汉	硕士研究生	局　长	县(处)级	安顺市政务服务局	2011.1— 2011.2	
				主　任	县(处)级	安顺市外事侨务办公室	2011.2—2017.12	

续表

姓　名	性别	民族	文化程度	任职情况				备注
				职　务	级　别	任职单位	任职起讫年月	
姜桂梅	女	汉	在职研究生	副主席	副县(处)级	贵阳市妇女联合会	2011.1—2015.12	
				副主席	副县(处)级	贵阳市社会科学界联合会	2015.12—2017.12	
何述烈	男	汉	中央党校在职本科	书　记	副县(处)级	贵阳市环境保护局纪委	2011.1—2012.11	
				书　记	副县(处)级	贵阳市生态文明委纪委	2012.11—2017.12	
张林俊	男	汉	大学本科	主　任	副县(处)级	贵阳职业技术学院旅游系	2011.1—2017.1	
				处　长	副县(处)级	贵阳职业技术学院科技处	2017.1—2017.12	
刘光祥	男	汉	研究生	书　记	副县(处)级	贵阳市农业委员会纪委	2011.1—2011.2	
				书　记	副县(处)级	贵阳市金阳新区纪工委	2011.2—2012.12	
				负责人	副县(处)级	贵阳市观山湖区政法委员会筹备工作组	2012.12—2013.2	
				书　记	副县(处)级	贵阳市观山湖区政法委员会	2013.2—2013.10	
				常　委	副县(处)级	贵阳市观山湖区委	2013.10—2017.2	
				主　席	县(处)级	贵阳市观山湖区政协	2017.2—2017.12	
马　彪	男	汉	大学本科	副局长	副县(处)级	贵阳市粮食局	2011.1—2014.11	
				副区长	副县(处)级	贵阳市花溪区人民政府	2014.11—2017.1	
				书　记	副县(处)级	贵阳市花溪区政法委	2017.1—2017.12	
李　坤	男	汉	大学本科	副处长	副县(处)级	贵州省国家税务局纳税服务处	2011.1—2014.12	期间：2012年3月至2014年3月在遵义市国家税务局挂任副局长
				书　记	县(处)级	贵州省税务干部学校党委	2014.12—2017.12	
邓龙江	男	汉	大学硕士	主　任	副县(处)级	贵阳市人民政府驻广州办事处	2011.1—2013.3	
				副秘书长	副县(处)级	贵阳市人民政府	2013.3—2017.4	
				副秘书长　局长　副书记　副主任	县(处)级	贵阳市委办公厅　市信访局　市群工委	2017.4—2017.12	
黄亚平	男	汉	在职硕士	副局长	副县(处)级	贵阳市物价局	2011.1—2011.11	
				副书记　副局长	副县(处)级	贵阳市水利局	2011.11—2016.5	
陆秀祥	男	汉	中央党校在职研究生	副书记、纪检组长	副县(处)级	贵阳市财政局	2011.1—2015.12	
				书记、党组副书记、纪检组长	县(处)级	贵阳市纪律检查委员会第二纪工委、贵阳市财政局	2015.12—2017.12	

续表

姓　名	性别	民族	文化程度	任　职　情　况				备注
				职　务	级　别	任职单位	任职起讫年月	
陆秀祥	男	汉	中央党校在职研究生	副书记　纪检组长	副县（处）级	贵阳市财政局	2011.1—2015.12	
				书记　党组副书记　纪检组长	县（处）级	贵阳市纪律检查委员会第二纪工委　贵阳市财政局	2015.12—2017.12	
黄再忠	男	汉	大学本科	党委副书记	副县（处）级	贵州师范大学地理与环境科学学院	2011.1—2011.10	其间：2015年9月至2017年6月副主任主持工作
				副主任	副县（处）级	贵州师范大学新校区建设办公室	2011.10—2017.6	
				处　长	县（处）级	贵州师范大学基建管理处	2017.6—2017.12	
唐　松	男	苗	在职本科	副部长　副书记	副县（处）级	贵阳市人民银行宣传群工部　机关党委	2011.1—2014.4	
				调研员　副书记	县（处）级	贵阳市人民银行宣传群工部　机关党委	2014.4—2017.12	
周　毅	男	汉	在职研究生	副书记　副局长	副县（处）级	贵阳市审计局	2011.1—2013.1	
				副书记　副主任	副县（处）级	贵阳市国有资产管理委员会	2013.1—2016.6	
				局长　书记	县（处）级	贵阳市审计局　党组	2016.6—2017.12	
汪　浩	男	汉	大学	副主任	副县（处）级	贵州省计划生育委员会研究室	2011.1—2011.12	
				副处长	副县（处）级	贵州省计划生育委员会奖励扶助处	2011.12—2013.4	
				处　长	县（处）级	贵州省计划生育委员会奖励扶助处	2013.4— 2014.4	
				副局长	县（处）级	贵州省卫生和计划生育委员会省中医药管理局	2014.4—2017.12	
谭　虎	男	汉	大学	局　长	副县（处）级	贵阳市人民检察反贪污贿赂局	2011.1—2012.6	
				副检察长	县（处）级	贵阳市人民检察	2012.6—2017.12	
徐　钰	男	汉	在职硕士研究生	主　任	县（处）级	贵州省能源局办公室	2011.1—2013.9	
娄维高	男	汉	大学本科	所　长	县（处）级	贵州省动物卫生监督所	2011.1—2017.12	

续表

姓　名	性别	民族	文化程度	任职情况				备注
				职　务	级　别	任职单位	任职起讫年月	
梅应贤	男	汉	硕士研究生	副书记	副县(处)级	贵州师范大学国际旅游文化学院党委	2011.1— 2017.6	
				副书记	副县(处)级	贵州师范大学美术学院党委	2017.6—2017.12	
唐　俊	男	汉	大学本科	副处长	副县(处)级	贵州省国家安全厅信息技术处	2011.1—2017.12	
陈良平	男	汉	在职本科	四级高级法官	副县(处)级	贵阳市中级人民法院	2011.1—2013.2	
唐金文	男	汉	大学本科	书　记	副县(处)级	贵阳市粮食局机关党委	2011.1—2017.12	
李阳炜	男	汉	大学本科	常务副部长	副县(处)级	四川省泸州市江阳区统战部	2011.1—2015.1	
				局　长	县(处)级	四川省泸州市江阳区民宗局	2015.1—2017.12	
戴宗尧	男	汉	大学	副局长	副县(处)级	贵阳市水利水电工程移民局	2013—2017.12	
刘桂均	男	汉	在职研究生	副局长	副县(处)级	贵阳市商务局	2014.11—2016.9	
				副区长	副县(处)级	贵阳市云岩区人民政府	2016.9—2017.12	
李晓平	男	汉	硕士	书　记	县(处)级	贵州广播电视大学信息系党总支	2011.1—2012.3	
				处　长	县(处)级	贵州广播电视大学人事处	2012.3—2017.12	
裴晓红	男	汉	博　士	党委书记	县(处)级	贵州省畜牧兽医研究所	2011.1—2013.4	
				党委书记	县(处)级	贵州省果树科学研究所	2013.4—2015.5	
				处　长	县(处)级	贵州省农业科学院宣传教育	2015.5—2015.12	
				委　员	县(处)级	贵州省农业科学院机关党委	2015.12—2017.12	
唐　樾	男	苗	大学本科	副市长	副县(处)级	清镇市人民政府	2011.7—2015.7	
				市委常委副市长	副县(处)级	清镇市委市人民政府	2015.7—2017.12	

续表

姓　名	性别	民族	文化程度	任职情况				备注
				职　务	级　别	任职单位	任职起讫年月	
张　恺	男	汉	中央党校在职研究生	常　委	县(处)级	贵阳市白云区委	2016.8—2016.9	
				常委　常务副区长	县(处)级	贵阳市白云区委、区人民政府	2016.9—2017.12	
陈先睦	男	汉	大学本科	总经济师	副县(处)级	贵阳市农业委员会	2012.7—2017.12	
袁　莉	女	汉	省委党校在职本科	副主席	副县(处)级	贵阳市妇女联合会	2015.1—2016.9	
				副区长	副县(处)级	贵阳市花溪区人民政府	2016.9—2017.12	
钱远清	男	汉	大学本科	主　任	副县(处)级	安顺市委党校信息工作部	2015.11—2017.12	
胡大颖	男	汉	在职硕士研究生	秘书长	副县(处)级	民建贵阳市委	2016.9—2017.12	
葛政敏	女	布依	在职硕士	秘书长	副县(处)级	农工民主党贵阳市委	2016.9—2017.12	

2011—2017年获全国和省、市劳动模范、先进工作者称号人员一览表

姓　名	性别	民族	所　在　单　位	荣誉称号	表彰机关	表彰年月	备注
徐　若	男	汉	修文县扎佐镇香巴湖村	全国劳动模范	中共中央 国务院	2015.4	
郭满辉	男	汉	金久水泥有限公司	省先进工作者	中共贵州省委 贵州省人民政府	2015.4	贵州省劳动模范
王建国	男	汉	修文县银星磨料有限公司	省先进工作者	中共贵州省委 贵州省人民政府	2015.4	贵州省劳动模范
梅应林	男	汉	贵州梅林塑业生态科技有限公司	省“五一劳动奖章”	贵州省总工会	2016.4	
令狐昌仁	男	汉	索风营发电厂	市劳动模范	中共贵阳市委 贵阳市人民政府	2016.8	
王海洋	男	白	贵阳德昌祥药业有限公司	市劳动模范	中共贵阳市委 贵阳市人民政府	2016.8	
姜安军	男	汉	贵州景诚制药有限公司	市劳动模范	中共贵阳市委 贵阳市人民政府	2016.8	
汪　杰	男	汉	修文县通源供水有限公司	市劳动模范	中共贵阳市委 贵阳市人民政府	2016.8	
彭德荣	男	汉	贵州恒和制药有限公司	市劳动模范	中共贵阳市委 贵阳市人民政府	2016.8	

续表

姓　名	性别	民族	所　在　单　位	荣　誉　称　号	表　彰　机　关	表彰年月	备　注
李政忠	男	汉	六屯镇大木村	市劳动模范	中共贵阳市委 贵阳市人民政府	2016.8	
宋佳彬	男	汉	修文县六广镇人民政府经济发展办	市先进工作者	中共贵阳市委 贵阳市人民政府	2016.8	
刘仕平	男	汉	修文县六桶中学	市先进工作者	中共贵阳市委 贵阳市人民政府	2016.8	
王文英	女	汉	修文县龙岗社区服务中心环卫站	市劳动模范	中共贵阳市委 贵阳市人民政府	2016.8	

2011-2017年全县高级职称人员一览表

姓　名	性别	民族	学历	工作单位	职称	晋职年月	备注
邵世娟	女	汉	大学本科	县人民医院	副主任医师	2011.12	
杜春香	女	汉	大学本科	县人民医院	副主任医师	2011.12	
罗　静	女	汉	大学本科	县人民医院	副主任护师	2011.12	
徐洪刚	男	土家	大学本科	修文中学	中学高级教师	2011.12	
虞玲臻	女	汉	大学本科	修文中学	中学高级教师	2011.12	
徐启义	男	汉	大学本科	修文中学	中学高级教师	2011.12	
戎承谦	男	汉	大学本科	修文中学	中学高级教师	2011.12	
周珍利	男	汉	大学本科	扎佐中学	中学高级教师	2011.12	
赵后贵	男	汉	大学本科	扎佐中学	中学高级教师	2011.12	
彭云书	男	汉	大学本科	扎佐中学	中学高级教师	2011.12	
郑德富	男	汉	大学本科	第三中学	中学高级教师	2012.12	
徐亚强	男	汉	大学专科	第三中学	中学高级教师	2012.12	
陈晓斌	男	汉	大学本科	县教育教学研究管理中心	中学高级教师	2012.12	
刘廷浩	男	汉	大学本科	扎佐中学	中学高级教师	2012.12	
刘建文	男	汉	大学专科	扎佐中学	中学高级教师	2012.12	
宋幼全	男	汉	大学本科	扎佐中学	中学高级教师	2012.12	
韦时梅	女	汉	大学本科	修文中学	中学高级教师	2012.12	
李永亮	男	汉	大学本科	修文中学	中学高级教师	2012.12	
王　平	男	汉	大学本科	修文中学	中学高级教师	2012.12	
杜明英	女	汉	大学本科	修文中学	中学高级教师	2012.12	
陈书勇	男	汉	大学本科	县人民医院	外科	2012.12	

续表

姓　名	性别	民族	学历	工作单位	职称	晋职年月	备注
路　英	女	汉	大学本科	县人民医院	中医内科医师	2012.12	
刘华平	男	汉	大学本科	县人民医院	内科医师	2012.12	
秦智慧	女	汉	大学专科	扎佐镇农业服务中心	高级农艺师	2012.12	
邓龙涛	男	汉	大学专科	县饲料草地站	高级畜牧师	2012.12	
李　萍	女	汉	大学本科	县人民医院	副主任护师	2013.12	
王文耀	女	汉	大学本科	县人民医院	副主任医师	2013.12	
岑之龙	男	布依	大学本科	县人民医院	副主任医师	2013.12	
刘显伦	男	汉	大学本科	县人民医院	副主任药师	2013.12	
王芳芬	女	汉	大学本科	县人民医院	副主任医师	2013.12	
宋洪仙	女	汉	大学本科	久长镇人口和计划生育技术服务站	副主任医师	2013.12	
晏正芳	女	汉	大学本科	县疾病预防控制中心	副主任医师	2013.12	
夏　春	女	汉	大学本科	县疾病预防控制中心	副主任技师	2013.12	
袁才会	女	汉	中专	扎佐镇卫生院	副主任护师	2013.12	
张道春	女	汉	中专	扎佐镇卫生院	副主任护师	2013.12	
喻志峰	男	汉	大学本科	扎佐镇卫生院	副主任医师	2013.12	
周尚富	男	汉	大学本科	扎佐镇卫生院	副主任医师	2013.12	
宋焕玲	女	汉	中专	扎佐镇卫生院	副主任护师	2013.12	
邱　艳	女	汉	中专	扎佐镇卫生院	副主任护师	2013.12	
宋聚凤	女	汉	中专	扎佐镇卫生院	副主任护师	2013.12	
晏华云	男	汉	中专	久长镇卫生院	副主任医师	2013.12	
罗显珍	女	汉	中专	久长镇卫生院	副主任护师	2013.12	
母家群	女	汉	中专	六广镇卫生院	副主任护师	2013.12	
黄昌平	男	汉	大学本科	贵州扬生医用器械有限公司	高级工程师	2014.1	
郑茂鑫	男	侗	大学本科	贵州扬生医用器械有限公司	高级工程师	2014.1	
聂开品	男	汉	大学本科	贵州扬生医用器械有限公司	高级工程师	2014.1	
陈　飞	女	汉	硕士研究生	中共修文县委党校	高级讲师	2014.12	
任　燚	男	土家	大学本科	修文县人民医院	副主任医师	2014.12	
杨　平	男	苗	大学专科	县疾病预防控制中心	副主任医师	2014.12	
刘　萍	女	汉	大学专科	县计划生育妇幼保健服务中心	副主任护师	2014.12	
蒙光忠	男	汉	大学专科	县疾病预防控制中心	副主任技师	2014.12	
王　浩	男	汉	大学本科	修文中学	中学高级教师	2014.12	

续表

姓　名	性别	民族	学历	工作单位	职称	晋职年月	备注
向学文	男	汉	大学本科	修文中学	中学高级教师	2014.12	
雷　芳	女	汉	大学本科	第二中学	中学高级教师	2014.12	
严绍刚	男	汉	大学本科	小箐中学	中学高级教师	2014.12	
吴　军	男	汉	大学本科	修文中学	中学高级教师	2014.12	
冉　宇	男	汉	大学本科	修文中学	中学高级教师	2014.12	
罗永红	男	苗	大学本科	修文中学	中学高级教师	2014.12	
颜红樱	女	汉	大学本科	扎佐中学	中学高级教师	2014.12	
邓国琴	女	汉	大学本科	扎佐中学	中学高级教师	2014.12	
杨黔辉	男	汉	大学本科	第二中学	中学高级教师	2014.12	
彭永平	男	汉	大学本科	修文中学	中学高级教师	2014.12	
林盛强	男	汉	大学本科	第三中学	中学高级教师	2014.12	
李翠兰	女	汉	大学本科	修文中学	中学高级教师	2014.12	
黄亚欣	女	汉	硕士	谷堡乡林业站	高级农艺师	2014.12	
陈祖发	男	汉	大学专科	扎佐镇农业综合服务中心	高级工程师	2014.12	
刘永贵	男	汉	大学专科	久长镇贵州金久水泥有限公司	高级工程师	2014.12	
李添群	女	汉	大学专科	县植保植检站	高级农艺师	2014.12	
朱有嘉	男	汉	大学专科	县中药材生产管理站	高级农艺师	2014.12	
徐存素	女	汉	大学专科	扎佐镇农业综合服务中心	高级农艺师	2014.12	
金艳琦	女	汉	大学专科	扎佐镇农业综合服务中心	高级兽医师	2014.12	
陈　军	男	汉	大学本科	县人民医院	高级主任医师	2014.12	
贾明荣	男	汉	大学本科	县种子管理站	高级农艺师	2014.12	
胡　强	男	汉	大学专科	县动物疫病预防控制中心	高级兽医师	2014.12	
叶华庆	男	汉	大学本科	县农机监理站	高级工程师	2014.12	
徐明礼	男	汉	大学专科	扎佐镇农业综合服务中心	高级兽医师	2014.12	
赵福春	女	汉	大学本科	久长中学	副高级中学教师	2015.6	
陈顺菊	女	汉	大学专科	洒坪中学	副高级中学教师	2015.6	
曾黔华	女	苗	大学本科	扎佐中学	副高级中学教师	2015.6	
孙国菊	女	汉	大学本科	小箐中学	副高级中学教师	2015.6	
陈顺仙	女	汉	大学本科	洒坪中学	副高级中学教师	2015.6	
陈忠莲	女	汉	大学专科	久长中学	副高级中学教师	2015.6	
唐　坤	男	汉	大学本科	六屯中学	副高级中学教师	2015.6	

续表

姓 名	性别	民族	学历	工作单位	职称	晋职年月	备注
金仕义	男	汉	大学本科	久长中学	副高级中学教师	2015.6	
周礼鸿	男	汉	大学本科	洒坪中学	副高级中学教师	2015.6	
王贵华	男	汉	大学本科	谷堡中学	副高级中学教师	2015.6	
肖仕菊	女	汉	大学本科	小箐中学	副高级中学教师	2015.6	
冯广源	男	汉	大学本科	扎佐中学	副高级中学教师	2015.6	
袁 林	男	汉	大学本科	扎佐中学	副高级中学教师	2015.6	
印 江	男	汉	大学本科	扎佐中学	副高级中学教师	2015.6	
葛正忠	男	布依	大学专科	扎佐中学	副高级中学教师	2015.6	
李 斌	男	布依	大学本科	六广中学	副高级中学教师	2015.6	
罗华章	男	布依	大学本科	大石布依族乡九年制义务教育学校	副高级中学教师	2015.6	
李友德	男	汉	大学本科	小箐中学	副高级中学教师	2015.6	
罗永道	男	汉	大学专科	扎佐中学	副高级中学教师	2015.6	
黄 政	男	汉	大学本科	久长中学	副高级中学教师	2015.6	
张良远	男	汉	大学本科	扎佐中学	副高级中学教师	2015.6	
杨 建	男	汉	大学专科	久长中学	副高级中学教师	2015.6	
刁泌鑫	男	汉	大学本科	久长中学	副高级中学教师	2015.6	
唐玉明	男	汉	大学本科	扎佐中学	副高级中学教师	2015.6	
李 英	女	汉	大学本科	扎佐中学	副高级中学教师	2015.6	
周 振	女	汉	大学专科	久长中学	副高级中学教师	2015.6	
胡胜菊	女	汉	大学本科	六广中学	副高级中学教师	2015.6	
刘天宇	男	汉	大学本科	久长中学	副高级中学教师	2015.6	
陈海燕	女	布依	大学本科	久长中学	副高级中学教师	2015.6	
路忠敏	女	汉	大学本科	六桶中学	副高级中学教师	2015.6	
邓发明	男	瑶	大学专科	六桶中学	副高级中学教师	2015.6	
李懿菊	女	汉	大学本科	扎佐中学	副高级中学教师	2015.6	
何贤亮	男	汉	大学本科	扎佐中学	副高级中学教师	2015.6	
崔吉军	男	汉	大学本科	六屯中学	副高级中学教师	2015.6	
陈 静	男	汉	大学专科	洒坪中学	副高级中学教师	2015.6	
刘德品	男	汉	大学专科	六桶中学	副高级中学教师	2015.6	
余昌龙	男	汉	大学本科	扎佐中学	副高级中学教师	2015.6	
刘永霜	男	汉	大学本科	六桶中学	副高级中学教师	2015.6	

续表

姓　名	性别	民族	学历	工作单位	职称	晋职年月	备注
姜　东	男	汉	大学本科	扎佐中学	副高级中学教师	2015.6	
董用仙	女	汉	大学本科	扎佐中学	副高级中学教师	2015.6	
韩幼愈	女	汉	大学本科	扎佐中学	副高级中学教师	2015.6	
张立平	男	汉	大学本科	六桶中学	副高级中学教师	2015.6	
杨承广	男	汉	大学本科	扎佐中学	副高级中学教师	2015.6	
聂　铭	男	汉	大学本科	大石布依族乡九年制义务教育学校	副高级中学教师	2015.6	
蔡吉文	男	汉	大学专科	扎佐中学	副高级中学教师	2015.6	
杨祖秀	女	汉	大学专科	谷堡乡水利站	副高级	2015.6	
韩开华	男	汉	大学本科	久长镇林业站	副高级工程师	2015.6	
肖盛明	男	汉	大学本科	谷堡乡农业综合服务中心	高级农艺师	2015.6	
朱俊忠	男	汉	大学专科	六广镇农业服务中心	高级畜牧师	2015.6	
彭　杰	男	汉	大学专科	扎佐镇农业综合服务中心	高级兽医师	2015.6	
罗　洁	女	布依	中专	大石乡人口和计划生育技术服务站	副高级专业技术职务	2015.6	
田　毅	男	汉	大学本科	县人民医院	副主任医师	2015.12	
洪晓龙	男	汉	大学本科	县人民医院	副主任医师	2015.12	
罗　林	男	汉	大学本科	县人民医院	副主任医师	2015.12	
田晓芳	女	汉	大学本科	县人民医院	副主任护师	2015.12	
杨玉梅	女	汉	大学本科	县计划生育妇幼保健服务中心	副主任医师	2015.12	
田莉琴	女	汉	大学专科	县计划生育妇幼保健服务中心	副主任医师	2015.12	
李桃萍	女	汉	大学专科	扎佐镇人口和计划生育技术服务站	副主任护师	2015.12	
李建萍	女	汉	大学专科	修文县计划生育妇幼保健服务中心	副主任护师	2015.12	
邹书珍	女	汉	大学本科	修文县疾病预防控制中心	主任医师	2015.12	
吴才友	男	苗	大学本科	修文中学	中学高级教师	2015.12	
陈　石	男	汉	大学本科	扎佐中学	中学高级教师	2015.12	
何贤亮	男	汉	大学本科	扎佐中学	中学高级教师	2015.12	
李　英	女	汉	大学本科	扎佐中学	中学高级教师	2015.12	
陈海燕	女	布依	大学本科	久长中学	中学高级教师	2015.12	
岳晓莹	女	汉	大学本科	小箐中学	中学高级教师	2015.12	
安鹏飞	男	汉	大学本科	修文中学	中学高级教师	2015.12	辞职
罗　静	女	汉	大学本科	第三中学	中学高级教师	2015.12	
姜　东	男	汉	大学本科	扎佐中学	中学高级教师	2015.12	

续表

姓　名	性别	民族	学历	工作单位	职称	晋职年月	备注
刘永霜	男	汉	本科	六桶中学	中学高级教师	2015.12	
吴道学	男	汉	本科	第二中学	中学高级教师	2015.12	
陈仕旭	男	汉	本科	水利建设站	高级工程师	2015.12	
邓德会	女	汉	大专	大石布依族乡农业综合服务中心	高级农艺师	2015.12	
苟元华	男	汉	大专	农业技术推广站	高级农艺师	2015.12	
彭　杰	男	汉	大专	扎佐镇农业综合服务中心	高级兽医师	2015.12	
陈明菊	女	苗	本科	扎佐镇卫生院	副高级	2016.1	
罗　雁	女	汉	专科	扎佐镇卫生院	副高级	2016.1	
张　波	男	汉	本科	扎佐镇卫生院	副高级	2016.1	
罗玉德	男	彝	中专	扎佐镇人口和计划生育技术服务站	副高级	2016.1	
彭建群	女	汉	中专	扎佐镇人口和计划生育技术服务站	副高级	2016.1	
吴学芬	女	汉	中专	六广镇卫生院	副高级	2016.1	
周正勇	男	汉	本科	久长镇卫生院	副高级	2016.1	
舒　健	男	汉	专科	谷堡乡乌栗中学	副高级	2016.1	
唐文平	男	汉	本科	修文县森林防火指挥部办公室	副高级工程师	2016.12	
付邦奎	男	汉	本科	修文县林业工作站	副高级工程师	2016.12	
冯广亮	男	汉	大专	扎佐镇农业综合服务中心	高级经济师	2016.12	
邓堂鑫	男	汉	大专	扎佐镇农业综合服务中心	高级农艺师	2016.12	认定
张云贤	男	汉	大专	谷堡乡农业综合服务中心	高级农艺师	2016.12	
张良荣	女	汉	专科	县人民医院	副主任护师	2016.12	
李秀梅	女	汉	本科	县人民医院	副主任护师	2016.12	
严　惠	女	汉	本科	县人民医院	副主任医师	2016.12	
王洪艳	女	汉	本科	县人民医院	副主任护师	2016.12	
王学敏	女	汉	大专	县妇幼保健院	副主任医师	2016.12	
颜嘉玲	女	汉	大专	县疾病预防控制中心	副主任护师	2016.12	
赵呈斌	男	汉	中专	久长镇水利工作站	副高级工程师	2016.12	
易辉明	男	汉	中专	扎佐镇国土资源和规划建设服务中心	高级工程师	2016.12	
朱绍芳	女	汉	大学	县教育教学研究管理中心	高级教师	2016.12	
谌贻平	男	汉	大学	修文县第一中学	高级教师	2016.12	
金　一	男	汉	大学	修文县第三中学	高级教师	2016.12	
袁红霞	女	汉	大学	县教育教学研究管理中心	高级教师	2016.12	

续表

姓　名	性别	民族	学历	工作单位	职称	晋职年月	备注
岳　梅	女	汉	大学	县第一中学	高级教师	2016.12	
罗小棋	男	布依	大学	县森林资源管理站	高级工程师	2017.12	
雷天林	男	汉	中专	龙场镇农业综合服务中心	高级农艺师	2017.12	
兰序宏	男	汉	大学	龙场镇农业综合服务中心	高级兽医师	2017.12	
唐玉兰	女	汉	大学	县第二中学	高级教师	2017.12	
李　茜	女	汉	大学	县特殊教育学校	高级教师	2017.12	
班山莲	女	布依	大学	扎佐镇中心小学	高级教师	2017.12	
肖文华	女	汉	大学	县第二中学	高级教师	2017.12	
何晓艳	女	汉	大学	县第二中学	高级教师	2017.12	
陈一敏	女	汉	大学	龙场镇卫生院	副主任护师	2017.12	
杨宇希	女	苗	大学	龙场镇卫生院	副主任护师	2017.12	
王绪兰	女	汉	大学	县疾病预防控制中心	副主任医师	2017.12	
肖丽梅	女	汉	大学	县疾病预防控制中心	副主任护师	2017.12	
罗玉兰	女	汉	大学	县妇幼保健院	副主任医师	2017.12	
冯　芳	女	汉	大学	县人民医院	副主任护师	2017.12	
杨　雷	男	汉	大学	县人民医院	副主任技师	2017.12	
陈贵英	女	布依	大学	县人民医院	副主任护师	2017.12	
严光菊	女	汉	大学	县人民医院	副主任护师	2017.12	
张凤岭	男	汉	大学	县人民医院	副主任医师	2017.12	
吕　亚	女	汉	大学	久长镇农业综合服务中心	副高级农艺师	2017.12	

2011—2017年全县中级职称人员名录

2011年

杨祖秀　刘明忠　黄友红　杨哨贵　吴　燕　张宇华　陈顺菊　林国荣　敖富晶　陈朝云　张春梅
罗　玲　晏华凤　刘廷平　敖明英　周长虹　张元品　罗永道　陈　凯　杨　洪　汤　洁　兰蕾蕾
穆春霞　尹彦敏　颜加军　刘　薇　明方莉　陈　丽　章　琴　谢金娥　王作维　高添德　冯开义
蒋德国　刘　翔　冯先鲜　刘　飞　唐红玉　窦延伟　单正操　张义霖　尹　笥　李德华　陈　春
黄发礼　雷玉军　张海铄　石仙凤　韩红梅　李克芳　马大江　雷玉会　曾庆琳　柳　琳　唐　静
姜　巧　王　成

2012年

谢昌林　戴丽霞　兰序书　陈明华　胡登举　刘发永　袁　刚　柴以菊　王科福　陈进华　吕德珍
赵婷婷　谢　燕　王以政　李先福　王桂芳　郭　强　越晓慧　童　健　蒋定超　邓　令　黄再洪
刘良均　李仕荣　岳晓群　舒　健　罗文碧　汪山华　马　莉　魏良仙　王　剑　黄　建　罗雨珊
陈德仁　曾顺喜　彭兴会　吴恒坚　陈万秀　丁动琴　席德芳　瞿祖红　罗元芬　宋安梅　顾　勇
刘　锋　蒲世仲　赵洪霞　伍文刚　蔡羽梅　黄　琛　陈红艳　蔡　敏　尹显开　陈　贵　黄　燕
李亮勇　韩玉萍　李　霞　宋　华　胡朝平　许　军　宋致惠　李庆芳　杜　敏　李贵黔　朱珍碧
卿建鹏　钟友明　王丽亚　周建华　胡荣生　郝厚禹　王付权　李清国　王佳惠　张　香　姜礼军
李和清　刘　曲　李秀英　吴小丽　陈　凤　鲜　洁　盛典智　蹇仕琼　苏　梅　段付英

2013年

张祥莲　陈荣英　杜　云　邹　容　谌业新　肖建中　罗明文　周　勇　梅录全　郑秀娟　付坤玲
申　娟　杨绍江　孔向阳　缪　宏　陈　华　秦　勇　陆再军　陈仕馨　韩　祥　苏　捷　吴　嘉
杨　芳　林　宏　王廷宽　陈　启　黄　梅　钱永锡　吴晓波　李　梅　王　梅　王晓红　柏华玉
任　艳　彭　璐　朱　森　朱有玉　黄　萍　吴　勇　李权玲　王崇禹　高　龙　杨德进　郎维鑫
刘兴波　张建兵　徐安坤　张　杰　沈　刚　熊　欢　陈明花　陈明领　郑德军　何华山　胡　蓉
周　芹　黄再桃　刘秀阳　冯　琪　杨建华　夏开祥　宋邦先　邓　恒　姚资苓　陈爱珠　刘柏玉
孔令霞　王黔霞　王　敏　朱　菲　陈　敏　周　艳　焦洪波　李贤淑　晏正平　曹学莉　陈　英
熊维忠　陆再平　袁洪俊　林　瑶　秦瑞艳　周礼文　林廷勇　赵继锋　邓彩贵　高　飞　朱海燕
许海翔　贾　涛　李　颖　陈石英　陈兴权　汪　燕　凌　丹　韦顶银　项　娟　徐国英　汪　娅
黄　坤　石正福　陆　燕　吴　丽　石　义　李德慧　罗　萍　冯开贵　袁建文　李忠敏　蒋德英
李树成　王华丽　刘　毅　邱　帼　王　艳　唐胜平　陈良清　陈顺琼　蒋　莲　李玉兰　罗天惠
陈荣翠　周真蓉　周真碧　雷连会　李　霞　张玉仙　李克凤　陈　春　李成碧　袁　敏　张　娇
袁　媛　倪　伟　雷天飞　赵剑飞　黎　燕　姚　秀　谢光萍　王晓红　刘　群　刘　静　罗　芸
罗永琴　余庆梅　游宗碧　汪　雯　班正奎　陶余琴　刘　玲　洪　俊　刘文忠　刘基勇　宋玉祥
吴维香　周礼华　吕　亚　马光云　邓堂鑫　蔡恭民　曹文祥　宁　琨　葛长琴　何光梅　严　毅
晏　菊　陶　红　何先龙　武后洪　黄正华　杨　敏　皮永红

2014年

张玲珠　王　勇　姚　雨　彭湘玲　陈旭友　余　星　陈　石　贺金玲　唐仲旭　夏丽波　吴永刚
王群英　胡学文　张　刚　蔡　君　周向珍　李　勤　梅应奎　杨忠文　王章垚　车　坤　梅　雨
罗　敏　张梦芳　伍维盾　刘兴艳　刘泽莉　熊燕梅　曾　莹　刘　丹　王雪力　黄凤丽　陈庆敏
邓　春　程秀英　张忠燕　刘玉科　熊全香　李开荣　杨　俊　谌孙文　陆恩兰　龚　娅　刘远水
高　胜　伍成红　李志波　宋　韬　龙文仙　汪辉宇　肖明康　王华菊　李生文　陈庆江　夏　婷

韩克虎	王明山	王琪洪	吕　丽	陈艳秋	朱海亮	陆荣梅	朱文婷	罗　晓	杨　晋	王华琴
熊晓娇	杨开绚	王明菊	汪艳红	夏　应	任　梅	袁　敏	陈海洪	胡　倩	刘晓涛	包仕艳
罗　琳	颜加英	陈　芳	彭德香	廖开贵	宋晓艳	童　蓉	张　滏	秦　煜	王　芳	帅中南
余　刚	韦　琼	刘　勤	胡　瑶	余春英	黄　军	吴长青	贾维珍	朱友慧	陈　梅	袁培英
陈　锈	彭　斌	柴以忠	刘　芳	陈明菊	陈　荣	吴东莉	杨正华	葛正兴	王　政	李　海
刘　颖	邓发菊	何　梅	陈　燕	袁兴刚	邵章权	王　虹	杨绍红	焦　毅	蔡禄华	蔡　鹏
王贤波	向福海	罗锡军	杨兰英	朱有为	王晓梅	徐　刚	肖淑红	李忠奎	陈　斌	杨绍祥
余　辉	雷　雨	王　静	李　妍	刘　兰	刘太金	蒋维霞	欧　俊	杨玫瑰	宋　娟	李朝敏
余　蒙	陈明琴	任　莉	黄正荣	沈兴明	杜天琴	周　艳	陈　斌	曹文慧	陈晓丽	李　燕
邓成飞	范建有	戴宗强	杨　乐	熊文彬	冯东华	王家燕	肖　芳	魏云峰	彭钲刚	罗　梅
蔡　梅	姚　瑶	杜天富	熊　方	柳元丽	胥小林	冯　梅	谭　燕	张海涛		

2015年

罗永明	王才模	李元莲	陈良芳	宋明菊	蔡　霞	刘伯毅	邵　敏	许邦静	徐顺荣	郭　兰
郑　敏	周　蕴	陈　艳	陈　云	周尚菊	李　倩	袁明娣	涂春琴	谌宏健	吕向屏	石朝艳
胡　红	蔡美蓉	李　林	杨昌明	张　萍	夏在玺	王　鑫	陈　涌	李　超	谭　静	郭友林
张　晖	刘天琴	朱沭米	王　华	姜礼雁	李举高	陈　红	兰贵丽	王明军	周先淼	杜天敏
李　勇	陈丽娟	赵　霞	晏家敏	雷　勇	冉广富	张清波	车　乾	聂升会	陶德秀	杨　萍
王　艳	秦晓敏	陈晓梅	王道静	龚　敏	孟秋香	刘星作	陈良娜	张传福	石明全	刘发明
王小满	杨　敏	罗清洪	罗　娟	陈　娴	蔡　飞	陈红因	罗　彧	王　梅	周　波	李明河
刘　蓉	杨　林	葛正锦	袁昌荣	向禄亮	韦　凤	姚　建	邓朝贵	洪国棚	李昌俊	钱冬林
郑朝平	杨开宝	谢光智	吴义香	路青蓝	贾宗玲	吴长丽	贺　敏	王曼秋	刘克书	张　丽
李治娟	王茂艳	王　燕	梁　雯	杨　媛	李明娟	赵运美	吴俊壁	袁小丽	兰贵娟	唐　燕
黄正荣	陈国燕	颜　鸣	宁培静	李成文	田　力	袁　斌	唐梅花	何亚丽	严　霞	张　慧
周汉芳	宋杼娴	高贵云	刘时菊	李远志	刘仕平	李　琴	瞿法元	周元虎	黄承勇	肖　洁
杨　帆	王紫千	李元菊	冯开荣	李建碧	王智明	毛金凤	曾凡霞	朱双水	王缓鸿	袁　琼
苏　琳	陈　瑶	代方玉	唐　平	郑海燕	杨天成	朱秋吉	李孟春	龚　丽	姚文豪	蒋鸿梅
何明国	宋诗全	雷天顺	李　江	韩克学	朱明磊	何　艳	周贵筑	李克剑	吴智凤	刘志梅
杨　斌	刘长军	瞿　琳	雷照付	陈荣平	罗洪泉	黄　彬	尚红梅	苏智华	刘文毓	韦小伟
王　凯	陈爱萍	罗明奎	王　海	王　惠	周敬昆	徐安梅	邹晓雅	郭贵禹	白远飞	龙国荣
陈德兴	李仕杰	班国榕	方正言	唐　鸿	蔡　韦	张德军	杨海兵	朱海燕	梁　兵	彭盅玮
王　松	吴维军	张玉凤	牛晋国	林选福	郑　嵩	刘东平	周海波	何治忠	王　譞	
彭永江红										

2016年

代　波 赖明刚 谢大斌 官鹏飞 明永红 杨义文 徐　琼 姜　华 周泽磊 袁小燕 罗　翔
李仕敏 葛会敏 邵　峰 和　岳 王国立 吴素芳 范妮莉 郝厚静 袁　娥 李　群 唐靖文
刘庭元 孙　艳 谌业军 梁正祥 刘高旭 刘真芳 项华军 丁贵书 罗　芸 陈永春 罗　勇
陈　云 朱咸宾 杭方洪 朱习丽 张忠荣 罗永芳 罗洪文 周　莉 吴乾辉 王家才 徐　琳
冯必才 陆再群 唐夏辉 李　静 金　果 李　春 王志兵 陈发先 倪升利 李　磊 王琪元
陶　丹 李　萍 胡　妍 郭永梅 胡向洪 张　云 唐晓娟 王　惠 李　红 秦国艳 欧国红
焦建琴 冉　梅 王守敏 邱顺碧 石京京 宋庆江 金轶群 姜小春 刘永峰 赵　雨 朱永红
邹忠文 苏秀琼 林万元 蔡　静 谭　宏 兰序培 贺文利 杜孟贵 姚　芬 喻　议 于是安
杨　筝 郑朝武 季宗奎 郭荣泉 冯　林 李　婧 张　静 任周武 田景仙 付　娟 陈明江
方学梅 王远芝 陈开艳 曹玉香 刘安元 罗灿陆 周远辉 张承源 付力琴 杨秀萍 贺　艳
虞　吉 聂　琴 廖　剑 周忠兰 叶生富 张素红 杨　菊 卿　娟 尹攀红 吴学银 刘福荣
王　君 邵明亿 聂庆祥 宋黔梅 林文菊 王　香 冉　坤 袁　莉 王　艳 谢兴院

2017年

王　雪 魏良彧 陈子界 刘林君 刘发均 况培梅 黄　玫 代金怀 王小国 陈伯祥 张　起
李秋萍 徐富兰 杜培杭 喻　进 周兴龙 刘　燕 王　彧 王叶子 李　宇 黄　华 耿华英
任珍易 邢绍明 袁念华 陈　芳 刘海艳 吴敏敏 罗勋岚 贺之雪 李明利 徐　琴 宋致兰
杨　易 李绍坤 刘　峰 李　莉 贾　媛 杨　帆 雷　曼 李明娥 唐昌金 王加立 徐国梅
陈礼强 杨燕荣 李　恒 金春平 李　刚 魏满秀 金祥银 贺文碧 周向梅 韦雪梅 王朝敏
王梅桂 李兴洪 李紫璇 张远洪 郭　恩 胡　勇 李　毅 李永英 杨毕坤 杜天菊 朱　江
董砺坚 徐　鑫 罗　裕 何　娟 周兰菊 刘　赟 徐　艳 王　倩 彭　艳 唐桂花 王　婷
彭玉萍 陈　羽 汤相芸 陈德菊 魏　丽 谭　蓓 胡　意 刘　玲 林国丽 陈亚琳 李　群
王伟菊 钟亚军 田　晶 何光江 吴思静 尹　杰 袁　平 胡　波 雷　雯 刘志红 陈吉坤
顾　燕 张　莹 余　蛟 刘青青 陈　默 陈刚芝 袁彦武 蹇德先 孟信琼 罗晓霞 潘　琦

四、人物传补遗

江务滋

江务滋，又名江德润，出生于县城江西街（今中山路）。清光绪三十三年（1907），江务滋由县保送进入贵州陆军小学堂，与进步学生席正铭、刘莘园、阎崇阶等在贵州自治学社阅读《民报》，从中受到孙中山民主革命思想的启发，在学堂内一、二、三期同学中和优级师范学校、公立中学、新军以及社会人士中发展40多位进步青年参加省城贵阳的革命活动，继后，江务滋到新军中建立哥老会组织——黄汉公，席正铭当舵头，江务滋任钱粮管事，结集新军若干将士，并联合进步学生组织起“历史研究社”，秘密宣传革命思想。

宣统三年（1911），江务滋和阎崇阶等第三期同学升学到武昌，旋又派江务滋返回陆军小学堂充任第四期学生的助教，借以掌握贵阳的两个革命阵地哥老会黄汉公和历史研究社。

10月10日，武昌起义爆发后，贵州自治学社筹备贵州光复，江务滋日夜奔走于陆军小学堂和新军之间。11月3日，由江务滋组织陆军小学堂学生和新军将士交给当场推选的临时都督杨荩诚指挥，浩浩荡荡进至贵州谘议局，监督巡抚沈瑜庆交出大印，贵州兵无血刃，宣告光复。

大汉贵州军政府成立当即表彰：发难之功以陆军小学学生和新军兵弁为最。对陆军小学学生均以正军校记名，以备下年升入贵州军官学堂肄习，江务滋还籍待命。

民国10年（1921），袁祖铭组织“定黔军”在川东，成立军务会办，由周西成主持工作，江务滋即充任周西城的“智囊”。继后，江务滋陪周西成在川中发展势力，成为一支黔军，周西成自封军长，江务滋任参谋。民国15年（1926）西成入黔主政，其部被中央编为中国国民革命军第二十五军，周西成为贵州省省长兼二十五军军长，江务滋任少将参谋。

民国18年（1929），李晓炎带领滇军犯黔，与周西成争夺黔政，周西成率部迎战于镇宁黄果树，战斗激烈，周西成和江务滋皆阵亡。李晓炎进省城贵阳主政仅18天即遭二十五军击败回滇，省政由毛光翔主持。毛光翔对黄果树阵亡将士举行哀悼会后，将江务滋遗体送入贵阳螺丝山陵园安葬。

张墨家

张墨家，又名张瑜德，西区（今谷堡乡）谷堡村滥沟人。民国24年（1935）考入广西堰塘军校受业。民国28年（1939）毕业后随中国国民革命军第七十三军赴武汉抗击日寇。民国34年（1945）部队移防西安“防共”，张墨家痛心疾首地对友人说：“我杀日本强盗手不会软，叫我去杀自家人，我怎忍心！不如解甲归田，回籍去为桑梓做点有益的事。”遂离开部队回到贵阳，在贵州省政府社会处谋到一份工作。

张墨家在贵阳与马怀麟、陈明仙、高维亚等交往密切，尤其与马怀麟情谊更深，经常在一起谈论国事，评议时局，讨论中国之命运。

张墨家爱好写作，工作之余，写有大量散文发表于报刊。成文《随军洛川行》，揭露中国广大农村在长期军阀混战和抗日战争中战祸连绵、拉兵派款、田地荒芜、生产萧条、民不聊生的生活情景；在《孔子还在活着》一文中，抨击了政府官吏不但不为民、救民，反而愚民、吃民的时弊。民国28年（1939），张墨家在一篇散文中声称“刘伯承将军智勇双全，孤军穿过黄泛区，顺利抵达国统心脏进行军事活动”，当即被贵州省政府当局斥为“为匪张目，蛊惑人心”，定张墨家为“赤化之徒”，被贵州省保安司令部逮捕入狱。

民国38年（1949）2月16日，马怀麟在小箐组织反蒋武装暴动失利。7月，由省保安司令部将张墨家和“二一六”暴动中担任前敌指挥的高维亚、担任乌江纵队保卫队长的阎永铸一起杀害于贵阳马家坡。

五、重要文件选录

国务院关于贵州省贵阳市和安顺地区部分行政区划调整的批复

国函〔1995〕69号

贵州省人民政府：

你省《关于贵阳市实行市管县体制的请示》（黔府呈〔1994〕27号）收悉。现批复如下：

同意将安顺地区的修文县、息烽县、开阳县划归贵阳市管辖，安顺地区的清镇市由省直辖。

国务院

一九九五年七月二十一日

六、首轮《修文县志》史实补正与志文勘误

社会主义新方志首轮《修文县志》出版后，县志编辑部责成成书编辑各自就所编纂的篇章进行通读，一是对记述史实再度审查，二是对志文再行校勘。与此同时，编辑部又在读者中搜集到一些反馈意见。通过自查和反馈，发现有的史实确有疏误，或错记，或错位，或缺漏；有的志文用错字，漏掉字。特此分别补正和勘误。

一、史实补正

（一）图

△政区图修文县在全省的位置图中应加“黔南州”。

△政区图久长镇内的“蛙壳堰水库”应为“蚌壳堰水库”。

△志文317页民国36年国民党组织分布情况图下横2项“直属第二区分党员21人”应为“直属第二区分部党员21人”。

△志文675页清光绪县境交通图图名“、”应为“·”。

（二）凡例

△1页11行　“民族人口”应为“人口民族”。

△1页14行　“104章，384节”应为“106章，391节”。

（三）表

△40页10行　“1330”应为“3151”。

△40页11行　“1568”应为“3820”

△40页12行　“1705”应为“4462”。

△40页13行　“1262”应为“3889”。

△40页14行　“1712”应为“4592”。

△40页15行　“4254”应为“4753”。

△40页18行　“5960”应为“8632”，“4753”应为“10045”，“7264”应为“13863”。

△184页　南区七保所属村寨中的“届坎脚”应为“庙坎脚”。

△194页　1983年县辖区、社（镇）、生产大队（居民委员会）和生产队中城关区城关镇所辖居民委员会“第一段至第二段”应为“第一段至第六段”。

△313页　清道光知县觉罗崇兴的在任时间为“清代纪年为八年，公元纪年为1828年”。

△321页倒6行　“取代县政府建制，”应删除。

△323页　表名“民国时期历任县知事县长更迭”应为“民国时期历任知县县知事县长更迭”

△323页　民国时期历任知县的罗培基、罗端荣、魏茭香的职务“县知事”应为“知县”。

△338页　第二届第八任县委领导栏应增加“副书记　刘焕然　男　汉　54　河南滑县　初中　1962・7—1965・1”。

△339页　第二界第十一任中共修文县委核心领导小组组长“王福根”应为“王福银”、“副组长　李德成　男　汉　39 河南林县　高小　1967・12—1970・10”应删除。

△340页　第二届第十二任中共修文县委核心领导小组“副组长 李德成 男 汉 43 河南林县 高小 1970・10—1971・3”应删除。

△ 341页　第四届第十六任中共修文县委副书记李培书任职年月“1982・8—1983・11”应为“1982・8—1983・5”。

△354页　解放后历任干部统计表表头右应加“单位・人”。

△374页　县人民政府副县长谢仁之的任职年月“1956・12—1958・4”应为“1952・12—1958・1”。

△375页　县革命委员会主任吴树贵的任的年月“1977・10—1978・8”应为“1977・10—1979・8”。

△386页　“政协委员会历届代表界别构成”应为“政协委员会历届委员界别构成”。

△414页　县人民武装部（兵役局）历任领导人中兵役局副局长王福银的任职年月“1953・3”应为“1958・3”。

△602页　民国37年栏河堰统计表中的“穿心堰河”应为“穿山堰河”。

△642页　1951—1990年主要地方工业企业表中“耐火厂”应为“耐火材料厂”。

△816页11行　空格内应加“822”。

△816页倒11行　空格内应加“744”。

△816页倒10行　空格内应加“847”，“1125”应为“944”。

△816页倒9行　空格内应加“944”。。

△816页倒8行　空格内应加“802”。

△816页倒7行　“1474”应为“1250”，“621”应为“421”。

△816页倒6行　“633”应为“384”。

△816页倒4行　“630”应为“293”，“769”应为“250”。

△879页　县籍科第进士表明朝中“苏国珊”应为“苏国澜”。

△888页　1990年清水小学建校时间“1921”应为“1924”。

△1161页　第十届县人大常委会主任“谭菜先”应为“谭荣先”。

△1161页　第十届人大常委会副主任王占齐的文化程度“大学”应为“大专”。

△1161页　第十一届人大常委会副主任邓惠仙的籍贯“贵州修文”应为“贵州普定”。

△1162页　县人民政府副县长万稼实的任职时间“1991・9—1939・4（挂任）”应为“1991・9—1993・4（挂任）”。

（四）志文

△3页2行　“敌博斗争”应为“敌人搏斗”。

△3页倒12行　“白色恐怖组”应为“白色恐怖，组”。

△5页倒4行　“中共中央”应为“中央”。

△55页倒2行　“县知事”应为“知县”。

△55页倒8行　“县知事”应为“知县”。

△56页2行　“是年”条应移至10行后。

△71页8行　“是月 贵州汽车总站首开贵阳经扎佐至修文客车，是为修文有固定专营客车之始”应为“6月”，并应调至该页1行。

△76页倒7行　“县委书记岳万学和副书记白进德”应为“县委第一书记岳万学和书记处书记白进德”。

△81页20行　“印发《夺权公告》”应为“发布《夺权公告》”。

△82页13行　“10日”应为“5日”。

△91页倒10行　“生产队均改为”应为“生产队分别改为”。

△93页倒6行　“11个”应为“12部”。

△97页12行　“18日至22日”应为“18日至20日”。

△97倒15、16行　“其中多属工作体会和修志理论探讨”应为“其中多属工作体会和方志理论探讨”。

△100页22行　“召开中国人民政治协商会议县第三届委员会第二次会议”应为“召开中国人民政治协商会议第三届委员会第三次会议”。

△109页17行　“3月”应删除。

△114页倒15行　“摊派”应为“乱摊派”。

△118页倒11、12行　“聂廷良拟任县人大常委会副主任”应为“聂廷良调任县委助理调研员”。

△120页倒14行前　应加“5日，全县启动延长农村土地承包”条目。

△123页倒12行和13行　“11月2日”条和“6日”条应调至19行“8日”条前。

△124页7、8行　“整治修文河小桥至北门段”应为“整治小桥河小桥经穿山堰河至修文河北门段”。

△124页10行　“健身中路”应为“健身路”。

△126页倒11、12行　“县知事”应为“知县”。

△144页19行　“打单沟”应为“美竹寨”。

△150页5行　“所提高意见”应为“所提意见”。

△150页倒3行　“1988年”应为“1983年”。

△160页倒17行　“‘四清’”应为“‘四不清’”。

△162页倒10行　“革命造反派”应为“革命派”。

△162页倒14行　“在人武部和‘支左’军代表支持下”应为“在人武部和0279部队支左军代表孟庆昌支持下”。

△162页倒15行　“‘一月风暴’”应为“‘一月革命风暴’”。

△163页倒19行　“县革命委员会”应删除。

△163页倒10行　“12月”应为“在组织知识青年上山下乡的同时，县革委”。

△163页倒15行　“与此同时”应为“12月”。

△164页倒8行　“马列主义”应为“马克思主义”。

△191页2行　“龙场”应为“独冲”，“金桥”应为“清铺”。

△191页3行　“53个乡”应为“43个乡”。

△191页4行　“独冲”应为“龙场”，“凉井”应为“龙窝”。

△216页10、11行　“1961年6月，改建为阳明公社，隶属城关区，1966年5月，改称马家桥公社”应为“1962年4月改建为马家桥公社，1963年2月改称为阳明公社，隶属城关区，1966年5月，复称马家桥公社”。

△221页10行　“1961年5月撤三元管理区，建三元公社”应为“1961年5月撤三元管理区，1963年11月建三元公社”。

△226页倒6行　“11”应为“9”。

△321页倒6行　“取代县军政府建制”应删除。

△325页16行　“征粮阶级段”应为“征粮阶段”。

△344页15行　“在国家机关、群众团体先后设立党组”应为“在国家机关先后建立党组”。

△345页14行　“但建的县乡（镇）党支部”应为“组建的是乡（镇）党支部”。

△346页7行　“会议”应为“大会”。

△347页16行　“1990年9月18日至22日在县城召开”应为“1990年9月18日至20在县城召开”。

△350页6行　“要搞马克主义”应为“要搞马克思主义”。

△358页倒1行　“·”应删除。

△364页倒9、10行　“占应出席1121人的80%”应为“占应出席121人的81%”。

△386页3行　“由75人组成。”应为“初由55人组成，后调为75人，”。

△391页倒2行　“73”应为“75”。

△400页4行　“、”应为“，”。

△404页1行　“在校生的女性”应为“在校生中的女性”。

△425页13行　“27”应为“28”。

△513页15行　“奉县”应为“奉贤县”。

△619页倒11行　“1.34万平方公里”应为“13.4平方公里”。

△638页9行　“1951年建起电力制米厂”应为“1951年，中国人民解放军军政大学第五分校在县城建起电力制米厂”。

△641页倒19行　“耐火厂”应为“耐火材料厂”。

△644页倒2行　“耐火厂”应为“耐火材料厂”。

△662页倒7页　“讨研产品质量”应为“研讨产品质量”。

△717页19行　“抛屋”应为“抛物”。

△720页6行　“御使”应为“御史”。

△823页倒3行　“三十一年（1905）”应为“三十年（1904）”。

△824页13行　“吾性自足的”应为“吾性自足”的”。

△860页倒1行　“四年秋月”应为“四年（1509）秋月”。

△861页22行23行　“对厅一间”应删除。

△864页15行　“像之来非偶也，”应为“像之来非偶也。”

△865页倒3行　“今　”应为“今年春，”。

△865页倒3行　“畯以菲材承乏兹土，”应为“畯以菲材承乏兹土。”。

△865页倒4行　“　　　　　　”应为“榛狉，先生慨然”。

△865页倒4行　“而　俗以变，　以兴”应为“而夷俗已变，女教已兴”。

△865页倒5行　“尽此　言　　　责”应为“尽此数言矣。顿念先生摘官驿丞，非有师儒之责”。

△866页1行　“无殊亲炙，”应为“无殊亲炙。”

△894页21行　“30年春。”应为“稍后”。

△1004页倒3行　“城郭，”应为“城郭、”。

△1004页倒4行　“田野、”应为“田野，”。

△1004页倒20行　“玩易时。”应为“玩易时”。

△1005页倒17行　“兼贵州巡抚”应删除。

△1007页19行　““峡”。”应为““峡”，”。

△1017页倒11行　“本章第一节《名胜·三潮水》”应为“本篇第八章第二节《名胜风光·三潮水》”。

△1019页5行　“遗载”应为“已失”。

△1021页倒16行　“见本章第一节《名胜·三潮水》”应为“见本篇第八章第二节《名胜风光·三潮水》”。

△1065页15行　“道首，1”应为“道首中的1”。

△1077页5行　“冬至”应为“‘冬至’”。

△1077页7行　“冬至”应为“‘冬至’”。

△1084页17行　“附、”应为“附：”。

二、勘误

页	行	误	正
1	3	象	像
2	倒7	揽	览
3	10	明	民
3	17	慨	概
3	倒17	4	四
4	6	作	做
4	8	2	1
51	14	使	史

51	17	板	版
52	7	珊	澜
53	1	5	2
53	11	南	贵
88	倒16	山	三
97	倒16	修	方
104	倒2	贩	败
108	倒17	娄	楼
109	10	娄	楼
110	2	吉	杏
116	6	班	斑
118	倒5	撮	摄
122	12	债	绩
128	倒5	寥	廖
133	倒19	阁	阖
161	倒10	5	8
165	倒7	资	质
166	6	注	汪
234	倒11	署	暑
236	倒11	世 世	系 系
307	6	史	使
307	11	史	使
334	倒14	委员	干事
352	倒12	那 那	哪 哪
356	倒7	谕	渝
360	14	户	人
376	倒10	5	4
380	17	局	育
383	14	0	1
425	13	7	8
510	16	4	5
548	17	上堰 卫	富裕 星
555	15	)》	》)

647	9	电	力
674	12	煜	烨
717	19	屋	物
720	6	使	史
823	倒3	惜	昔
825	8	料	科
836	19	凤	岗
857	14	。	,
861	5	只	位
861	11	鸿	洪
861	16	一	于
861	倒7	六	6
861	倒15	2	3
862	5	鸿	洪
864	倒15	夏	复
865	倒3	畸	奇
865	倒5	忆	噫!
866	3	峻	畯
879	4	25 27	26 28
894	14	麓	角
894	21	迁	始
986	3	$\underline{5\ 3}$	$\overset{\frown}{\underline{5\ 3}}$
986	4	春	晨
986	5	$\underline{\dot{3}\cdot\dot{3}}$	$\underline{\dot{3}\cdot\dot{3}}$
986	9	$\underline{2\cdot1}$	$\overset{\frown}{\underline{2\cdot1}}$
986	9	$\underline{\dot{2}\dot{1}}$ $\dot{2}\dot{3}$	$\overset{\frown}{\underline{\dot{2}\dot{1}}}$ $\overset{\frown}{\dot{2}\dot{3}}$
1002	倒9	渫	喋
1003	倒10	幅	副
1003	倒11	起	启
1003	倒15	幅	副
1004	2	现	今
1004	8	自 所	饰 面

1004	倒10	春 窍 又	青 窈 义
1004	倒15	儒	离
1005	19	三	二
1019	倒6	冥	云
1075	20	徒	徙
1123	4	令	会
1123	16	园	圆
1135	13	后	候
1149	12	67	70
1149	13	67	70
1159	倒5	梁	樑

编纂始末

恒心磨砺15年，世人终见志乘面。

《修文县志（1978—2010）》的编纂始于2003年，终于2018年，历时15个春秋。个中甘苦，难于言表，志书问世，如释重负。

鉴于起点高，任务重，操作难，唯有笨鸟缓飞，分步实施。

第一步，筹备工作领先。根据2003年3月县十三届人民代表大会第一次会议通过的《县人民政府工作报告》提出“续修《修文县志》作到机构不撤、队伍不散、经费不少、力度不减、质量不降”的要求的决议和10月县委常委会议“把《修文县志》续修列入议事日程”的决定，坚持“县委领导，政府主持”的原则，于10月以修委〔2003〕33号文印发《县委关于调整县志编纂委员会的通知》，由县委书记魏明禄任编纂委员会主任委员，县长石洪、县人大常委会主任李玉轩、县政协主席殷建忠、县委副书记王成林和副县长王世利任副主任委员，县直有关部门负责人为委员，并明确原《修文县志》主编李祖炎和副主编夏之奎继任主编和副主编，省、市方志界有关领导和史学专家为顾问。

领导机构确定后，随即进行4项工作：一是拟定《编纂方案》。《方案》明确本轮编纂的县志是新时期社会主义新方志的续本，故称“续志”或“断代志”。志书上限起于中共十一届三中全会召开的1978年，下限断至国民经济和社会发展十一五计划完成的2010年，集中记述33年间在改革开放总方针的指引下全县自然和社会变迁的史事。因为记述时段处于改革开放时期，故将志书定位为“改革开放志”。要求编纂工作必须坚持解放思想、实事求是、与时俱进的思想路线，既要继承旧志的优良传统，更要体现社会主义新方志的创新意识，力求内容和形式上都有新的突破，出版的志书要做到观点正确、体例科学、资料翔实、文字典雅、特点鲜明、图文并茂、装帧精美，要唱响改革开放的主旋律，充分地反映伟大的改革时代和多彩的修文特色，使续志贴近现实、贴近群众，立体地把修文展示给读者，力争全书质量超过首轮出版的《修文县志》，更好地发挥志书存史、教育和资政的功能。二是编写培训资料。按照理论与实际相结合和注重适用的原则编辑成书，取名《方志续修》，32开本，容量14万字，分别载入文件选编、续修基础知识、编纂方法和专题部类编写等内容，印数300册，以满足全体编辑和资料员的需求，达到人手1册。三是拟定《县志续修行文通则》。《通则》开宗明义地指出，续修县志是一项宏伟而又严肃的文化建设，强调志书必须行文规范，体例统一，并从文体文风、写作技巧、书写格式、字词标点、图照配置等作出16条规定。四是落实编务人员。由编辑部的同志分别下到各乡（镇）和县直部门与负责人对接，按照政治思想、文化素质和编辑能力等条件选定编辑和资料员，并填表上报，以备督促联系。

第二步，动员培训。2003年11月28日，县委、县政府主持召开全县编修地方志工作动员大会，正式拉开续修《修文县志》的序幕。所有乡（镇）和县直部门的负责人均出席大会。会上，县委书记、县志编纂委员会主任委员魏明禄作《总结经验，乘胜前进，努力完成我县地方志的续修任务》的动员报告。魏明禄在报告中分3个部分进行动员，从充分肯定上一轮修志的成绩转向正确认识做好续修地方志工作的重要意义，要求各级领导要把续修工作作为官职、官责尽力做成做好，接着又提出积极组织实施好全县续修工作的要求，强调把续修工作纳入各单位的目标管理，将任务层层分解，落实到单位以至个人，实行定人员、定任务、定质量、定时间、定奖惩的承编责任制，确立精品意识，实施精品战略，做出精品志书，高标准、高质量地完成全县地方志的续修任务。最后以诚恳郑重的话语作结。他说：“今天，我们正处于一个前所未有的发生着最广泛、最深刻、最激动人心的大变革时代，续修地方志适逢这样好的机遇，真是我们当领导的福气。”语重心长的短语把大家动员起来，纷纷向县委和县政府签订了目标管理责任书。全县10个乡（镇）和84个县部门分别签订编纂续志的11个，编纂通志的33个，提供资料长篇的50个，形成了编志工作的全覆盖。

紧接在动员大会后，编辑部在备好资料和落实讲课人的基础上于12月25—26日集中各单位选定的编辑和资料员共101人进行上岗前的修志业务培训，由编辑部正、副主编和具有一定修志理论功底和修志实践经验的同志上讲台讲课。讲课采取讲、听、记结合和上下互动的方法，深入浅出地从理论与实践的结合上讲清楚什么是地方志？为什么要续修方志？怎样编纂续志？使参训人员既懂得方志的基础知识，又能掌握具体的编纂方法，为进入编辑“角色”奠定基础。

第三步，搜集整理资料。培训工作结束，全体编务人员随即投入对资料的搜集。搜集的方法主要从文书档案中摘取和从当事人、知情者的口碑中采取，并辅以网络下载。经过编辑部和各单位共同努力，计获取资料1700万字。接着进行去伪存真、去粗取精的加工整理，得到可用资料1200万字，为进入县志编纂和乡（镇）志、部门志的编写打下坚实的基础。

第四步，编写志稿。志稿的编写是采取上下联动、点面结合、由低到高的方式推进的。2007年起，县志的编纂和乡（镇）志、部门志的编写全面铺开，联合行动。编辑部一手抓县志资料长篇的编排，组织25人分工按县志篇目分别进行序列汇辑；一手抓试点练兵，正、副主编分别带领8个编辑下到六广镇和村民自发组织力量编写村志的清水村，与镇、村编辑一道亲手编写镇志和村志。与此同时，还对《税务志》和《交通运输志》的编写经常指导，促其首批付印出版。《六广镇志》《清水村志》《税务志》《交通运输志》问世引起极大震动，“点燃一盏灯，照亮一大片”，既带动乡（镇）和90%的县部门先后付梓成书和成稿资料长篇，为县志的编纂提供了更加翔实的资料，又使一批编辑通过实际锻炼脱颖而出，成为志稿编纂不可多得的骨干力量。

2008年，县志编纂在资料长篇汇辑完成后展开，先组织15人撰写初稿，接着进行篇章分纂，然后按照讲政治、勤学习、敢创新、会编辑的条件遴选10人作为成书编辑进入总纂，并增加胡光胤为副主编。总纂稿出炉后，按照严体例、显主题、正观点、决去取、补遗漏、核史实、炼文词、审编排的要求对志稿进行反复精细打磨，到2015年总纂完工，志稿集述、记、志、传、图、表、录和索引为一体，全稿共6篇，39章，180节，275万字，图照1088幅。

第五步，审查验收。2016年上半年，编辑部将志稿分别检送给有关部门和领导审阅，并由编纂委员会召开审稿会议对志稿进行初审，然后由编辑部梳理对稿本的各种意见进行考证鉴别，本着实事求是、择善而从的原则进行修改，做出送审稿本。12月13日，贵阳市地方志办公室组织召开《修文县志（1978—2010）》复审会议。会议肯定志稿编纂的成功之处，并对存在的问题和不足提出修改意见。继后，编辑部按照复审会提出的意见进行认真修改，然后又将改稿送市志办审定，市志办经审定后于2016年12月28日出具正式通过复审的书面批复。接着，县志编委会将复审稿报送贵州省地方志办公室。2017年2月14日，省志办组织省、市志办领导和全省方志界的史学专家10人在修文县政府会议中心召开《修文县志（1978—2010）》终审会议。会议充分肯定志稿体现的时代特色和地方特点，并肯定志书不落窠臼、富有创意的框架设计，也指出资料缺失、载事不当、记事重复、史实有误等问题，还寄希望于经过进一步的改稿做出经得起历史检验的精品佳志。会议原则通过志稿终审。会后，编辑部又按照会议提出的修改意见，完成调整篇目、增补资料、取舍史事、核准史实、规范图照等工作，即报送省志办验收。经省志办验收合格后签发验收合格意见书，三级审稿到此告竣。

第六步，付梓印刷。2018年10月，编委会将终审稿送交方志出版社，经出版社审查通过并批给书号，随即交由深圳市新联美术印刷有限公司开机印刷。为了确保成书质量，避免出现“增一字则繁，减一字则残”的问题，编辑部组织全体成书编辑和编务人员对印稿进行初校、复校和终校，做到字斟句酌，连标点符号一个也不放过。终校签字正式印刷装订成书，10月公开发行面世。《修文县志（1978—2010）》编纂至此画上句号。

《修文县志（1978—2010）》的编纂是一项浩繁的文化工程，可喜的是众擎易举。志书的问世应归功于县委、县政府的正确领导，县人大、政协和乡（镇）、县直部门的大力支持，不畏“三苦”（条件艰苦、工作辛苦、生活清苦）的全体修志同仁的辛勤劳动，修文籍人士和社会贤达的关心爱护，县志顾问的悉心指导。历任县委书记、县长均倾注精力主持其事，魏明禄正式启动，中经石洪，至蒋志伦、佘龙、孙华忠终毕其功。省、市志办领导归然、邓忠元，总顾问史继忠，史学专家范同寿、周声浩对志稿认真审阅，并提出可行性的修改意见，不断为提高志书质量助力。在此一并谨表诚挚谢意。

编纂这部志书虽夜以继日，不敢怠工，但仍感因未尽之力导致书中的疏漏，敬请读者和专家批评指正。

修文县地方志编纂委员会
2018年10月

索 引

C

CH

D

G

I

J

L

M

N

SH

W

Z

ZH